DORLING KINDERSLEY

Illustrated
Factfinder

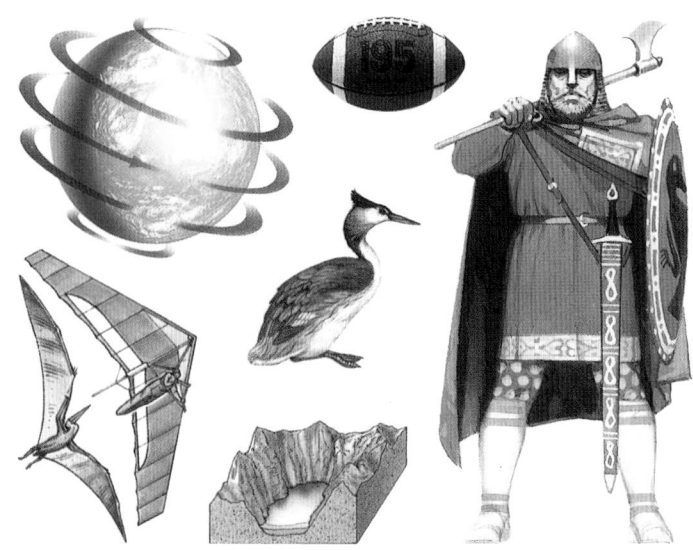

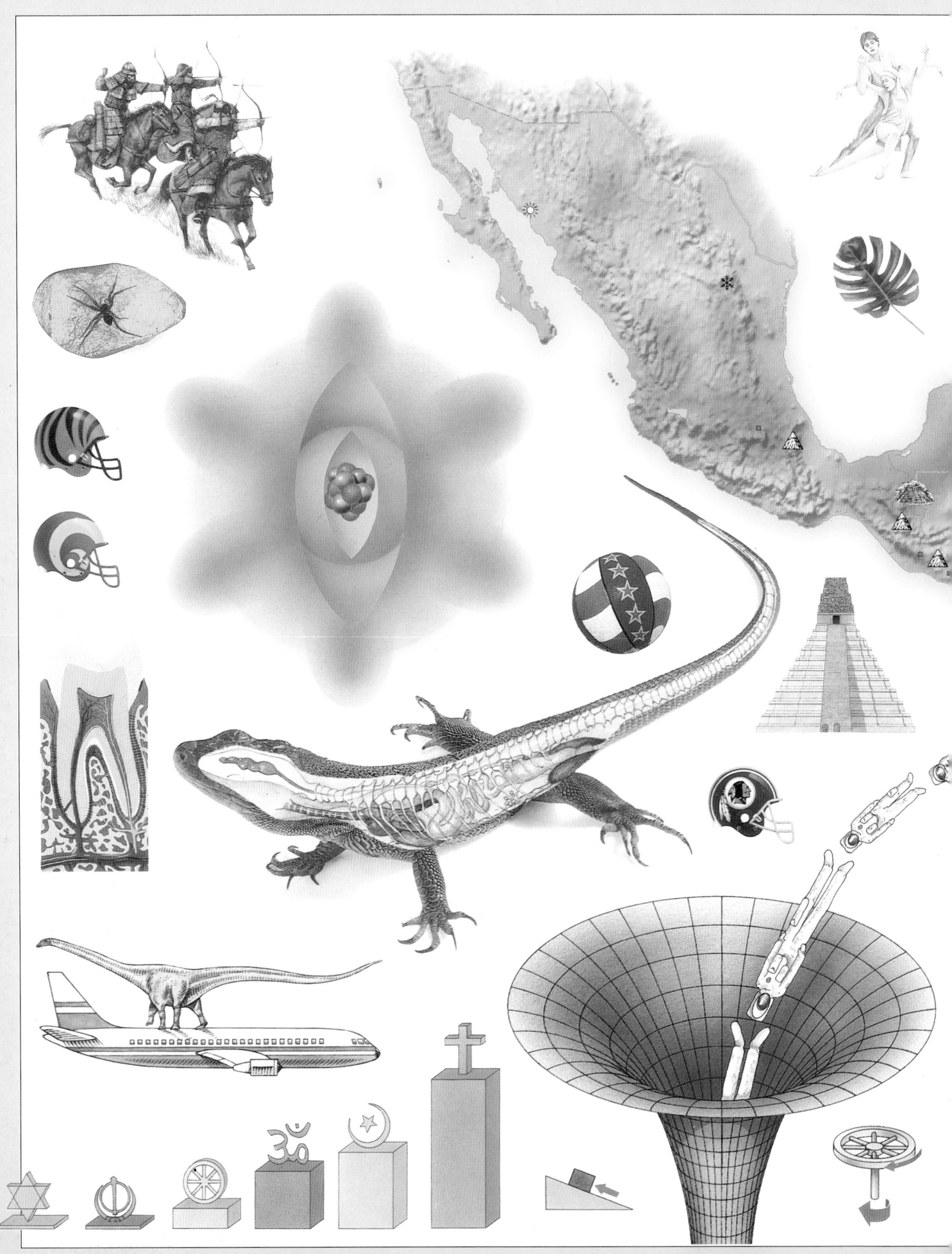

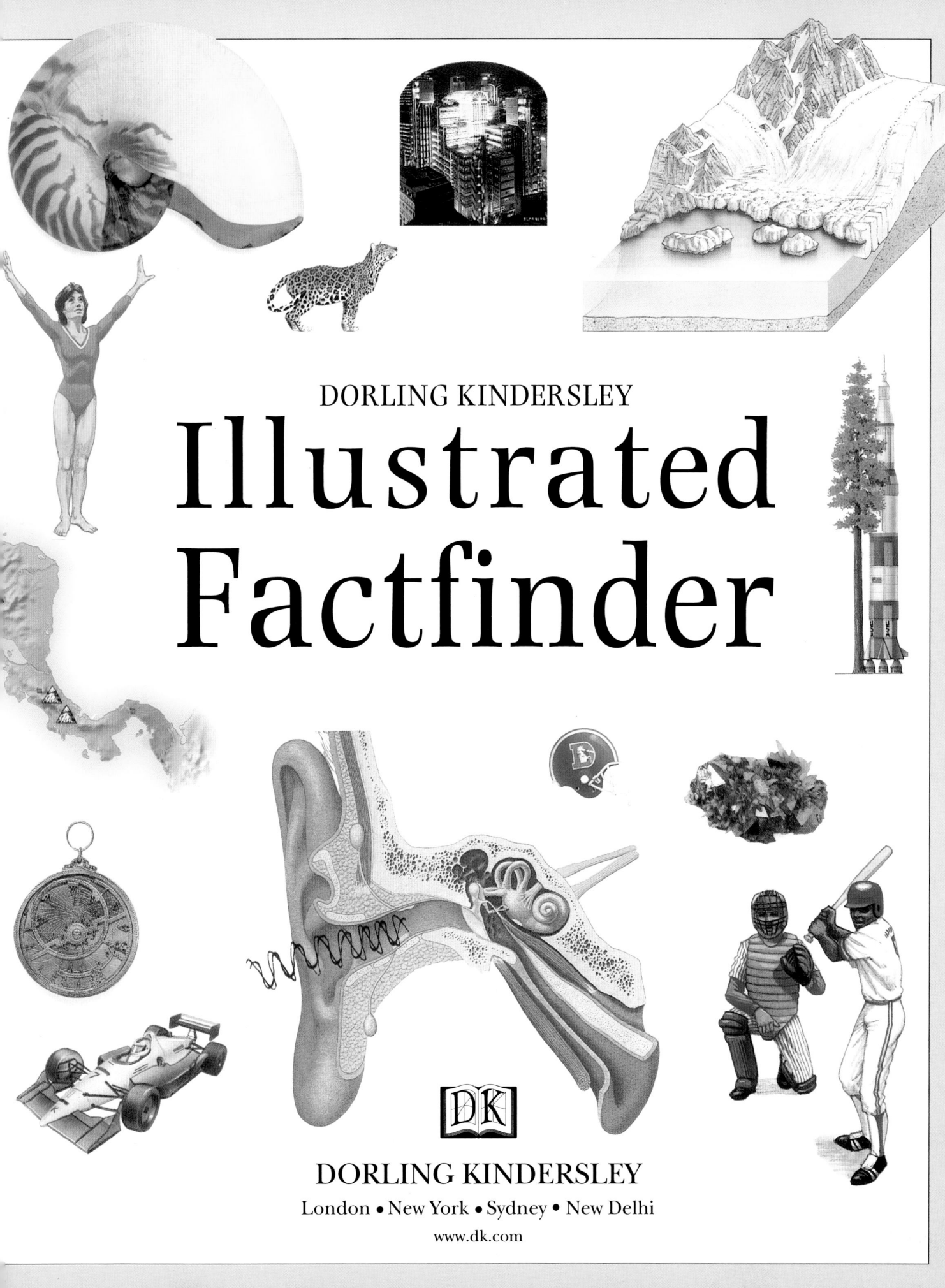

DORLING KINDERSLEY

Illustrated
Factfinder

DK

DORLING KINDERSLEY

London • New York • Sydney • New Delhi

www.dk.com

A DORLING KINDERSLEY BOOK

www.dk.com

Senior Editor Anna Kruger   **Senior Art Editor** Gillian Shaw

Section Editors

Sue Copsey, Marie Greenwood, Fran K. Jones, James Pickford

Editors

Huw Clough, Carey Denton, Deborah Murrell

Art Editors

Shirley Gwillym, Rebecca Johns, Floyd Sayers, Dominic Zwemmer

Designers

Wayne Holder, Marcus James, Joanna Pocock, Wilfrid Wood

DTP Designers

Mathew Birch, Carol Titchener, Noel Barnes

Picture Manager

Lorna Ainger

Research and Editorial Assistance

Alex Tinley, Leo Vita-Finzi, Tim Hetherington, Giles Portman, Michael Williams

Production

Catherine Semark, Samantha Larmour

Deputy Editorial Director Sophie Mitchell   **Deputy Art Director** Miranda Kennedy

Anatomical models supplied by SOMSO Modelle, Coburg, Germany

First published in Great Britain in 1999
Previously published as 'Illustrated Factopedia' in 1995 by
by Dorling Kindersley Limited
9 Henrietta Street, London WC2E 8PS

2 4 6 8 10 9 7 5 3 1

Revised edition of 'Illustrated Factopedia' © 1999
Copyright © 1999 Dorling Kindersley Limited, London

A CIP catalogue record for this book is available
from the British Library.

ISBN 0 7513 6207 7

Reproduced by Colourscan, Singapore
Printed and bound in China by L.Rex Printing Co., Ltd.

CONSULTANTS

UNIVERSE
Professor Heather Couper BSc, FRAS, Hon D. Litt
Television and radio broadcaster. Past president of the British Astronomical Association. Internationally acclaimed author.
Nigel Henbest BSc, MSc, FRAS
Internationally acclaimed writer and science broadcaster. Past consultant of the Royal Greenwich Observatory and the Science and Engineering Research Council
Doug Millard BSc, SBIS
Associate curator, Space Technology, Science Museum, London

EARTH
Maurice Crewe
Fellow, Royal Meteorological Society
Cally Hall BSc (Hons), FGA
Museum geologist, Mineralogy Department, Natural History Museum, London
Donna Rispoli BSc
Ecology and energy consultant
Bob Symes BSc, PhD
Associate keeper, Department of Mineralogy, Natural History Museum, London
Barbara Taylor BSc
Internationally acclaimed science and natural history writer

LIVING WORLD
Keith Banister BSc, PhD
Government consultant on fisheries. Broadcaster and writer
David Burnie BSc
Zoologist, biologist, and internationally acclaimed writer of science and nature books
Barry Clarke BSc, MSc, PhD
Curator of Amphibians, Natural History Museum, London
Theresa Greenaway BSc (Hons), ARCS
Botanist and natural history author
Miranda Macquitty BSc, PhD
Zoologist and best-selling natural history author
Matthew Robertson
Professional entomologist. Former Head Keeper, Invertebrate House, London Zoo

HUMAN BODY
Dr. Sarah Brewer MA, MB, BChir
General practitioner and medical author

BELIEFS, CUSTOMS, AND SOCIETY
W. Owen Cole, PhD
Lecturer and writer in religious studies
John Gray MA, BPhil
Fellow in Politics, Jesus College, University of Oxford
John Keyworth
Curator, Museum of the Bank of England
James Nicholson, BA
Financial journalist, *Guardian* newspaper
Peter Mitchell, BSc
Solicitor and legal consultant
Helen Watson PhD
Lecturer in Anthropology; Fellow St. John's College, University of Cambridge

ARTS AND THE MEDIA
Christopher Cook BA
Documentary film maker and arts presenter for BBC Radio. Film adviser, National Gallery, London
Steve Fairclough
Editor, *Amateur Photographer* magazine
Alistair Niven PhD
Literature Director, Arts Council of England
Brigid Pepin MA
Lecturer in Art History and Architecture, University of North London
T. Paul Rafferty
Managing Director, AMC Publishing, Nairobi, Kenya
Penelope Vita-Finzi PhD
Former lecturer in English Literature and Theatre, Thames Valley University, England
Rodney Wilson
Film, Video, and Broadcasting Director, Arts Council of England
Ann Wingate
Film producer, including *Howards End* and other major productions

SPORTS
Norman Barrett, MA
Sports writer and consultant
David Heidenstam
Sports writer and editor

SCIENCE
Peter Bailes BSc (Hons)
Collections information manager, Science Museum, London
Marina Benjamin BA, M.Phil, PhD
Science writer and journalist
Jack Challoner BSc, ARCS, PGCE
Formerly with the Education Unit, Science Museum, London. Science author
Eryl Davies BSc, ACGI
Science and technology writer and consultant
Carole Stott BA, FRAS
Science author. Former curator, Greenwich Royal Observatory, London, and later Head of Navigational Sciences.

TRANSPORT, COMMUNICATIONS, AND INDUSTRY
Christine Heap
Curator, National Railway Museum, York, England
Eric Kentley
Curator, National Maritime Museum, London
Bob McWilliam
Senior Curator, Civil Engineering, Science Museum, London
Andrew Nahum
Senior curator, Aeronautics, Science Museum, London
Lynda Springate, Annice Collette, Marie Tieche
Curators, National Motor Museum, Beaulieu, England

INTERNATIONAL WORLD
Dorling Kindersley Cartography in conjunction with leading cartographic consultants, embassies, and consulates

HISTORY
Brian Dooley BA
Political journalist. Former Senate aide to Edward Kennedy
Ann Kramer BA
Historian and writer
Margaret Mulvihill MA
Historian and writer
Philip Wilkinson MA
Historian and writer

HOW TO USE THIS BOOK

EACH PAGE OR DOUBLE-PAGE spread in *The Dorling Kindersley Illustrated Factopedia* is a self-contained unit, carefully designed to present the maximum number of facts about its subject in the most accessible manner. Information on each page follows a clear, logical order, beginning with the main feature and most important factual topics, then moving on to records, strange comparisons, and fascinating, collectable facts.

Main feature
Focuses on the subject and provides the most important facts.

Running head – thematic
Tells readers which thematic section they are in.

Introduction
A brief text introduction defines the subject and provides a number of key facts.

Topic headings
Easy-to-find topic headings draw the reader to sub-features within the main subject. Each page contains an average of 10 subject-related topics.

Detailed artwork
Stunning, full-colour cut-away artwork stimulates learning and provides maximum information.

Key facts
Bulleted key facts and figures give the reader the most essential facts at a glance.

Boxed types
To provide maximum information, an example of every major type of plant, animal, or object is illustrated.

Clear labels and annotation
Identify types and special features and clarify complex information.

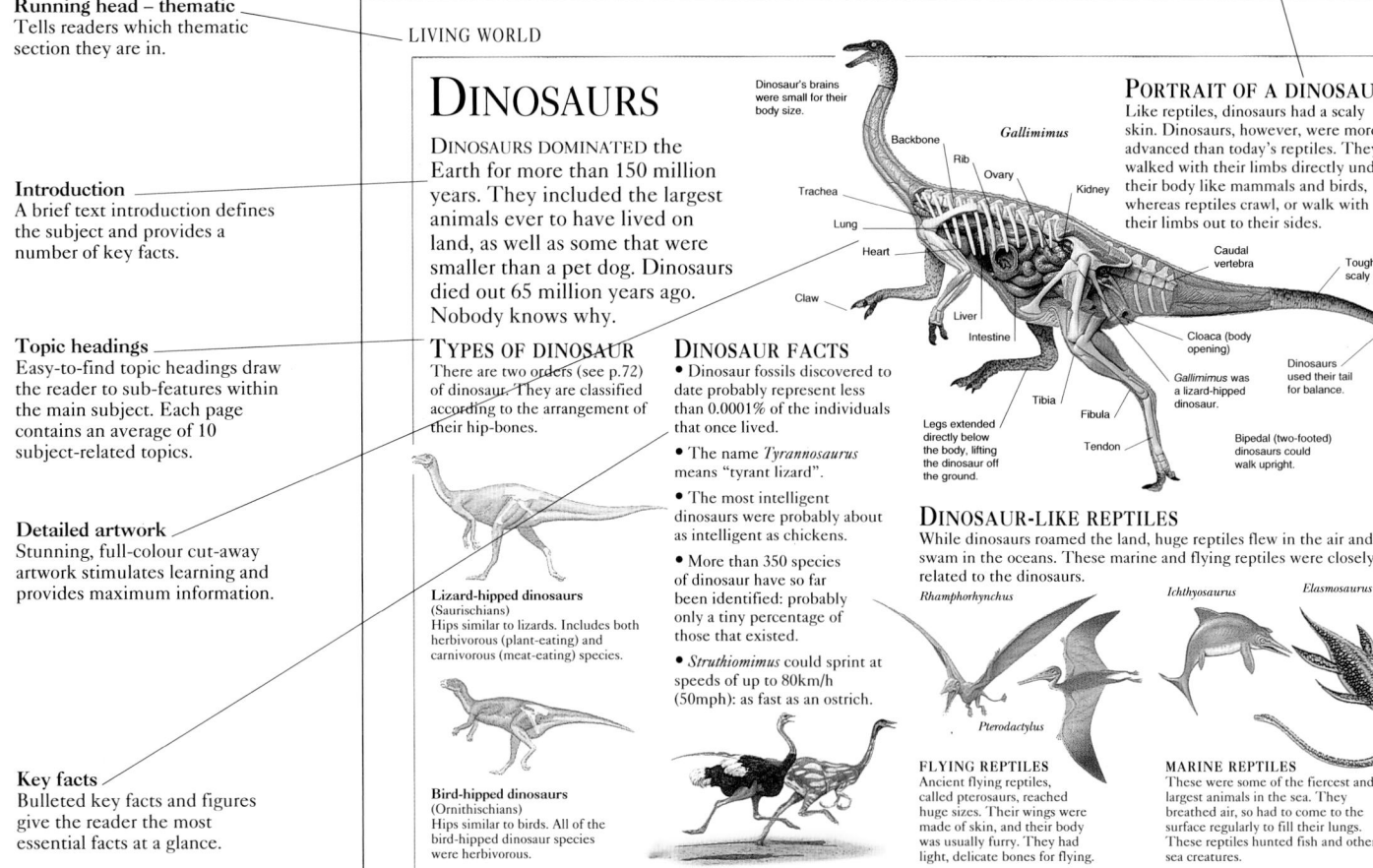

LIVING WORLD

DINOSAURS

DINOSAURS DOMINATED the Earth for more than 150 million years. They included the largest animals ever to have lived on land, as well as some that were smaller than a pet dog. Dinosaurs died out 65 million years ago. Nobody knows why.

TYPES OF DINOSAUR
There are two orders (see p.72) of dinosaur. They are classified according to the arrangement of their hip-bones.

Lizard-hipped dinosaurs
(Saurischians)
Hips similar to lizards. Includes both herbivorous (plant-eating) and carnivorous (meat-eating) species.

Bird-hipped dinosaurs
(Ornithischians)
Hips similar to birds. All of the bird-hipped dinosaur species were herbivorous.

DINOSAUR FACTS
• Dinosaur fossils discovered to date probably represent less than 0.0001% of the individuals that once lived.

• The name *Tyrannosaurus* means "tyrant lizard".

• The most intelligent dinosaurs were probably about as intelligent as chickens.

• More than 350 species of dinosaur have so far been identified: probably only a tiny percentage of those that existed.

• *Struthiomimus* could sprint at speeds of up to 80km/h (50mph): as fast as an ostrich.

Dinosaur's brains were small for their body size.

Backbone
Gallimimus
Rib
Trachea
Ovary
Kidney
Lung
Heart
Caudal vertebra
Claw
Tough, scaly skin
Liver
Cloaca (body opening)
Intestine
Gallimimus was a lizard-hipped dinosaur.
Tibia
Dinosaurs used their tail for balance.
Legs extended directly below the body, lifting the dinosaur off the ground.
Fibula
Tendon
Bipedal (two-footed) dinosaurs could walk upright.

PORTRAIT OF A DINOSAUR
Like reptiles, dinosaurs had a scaly skin. Dinosaurs, however, were more advanced than today's reptiles. They walked with their limbs directly under their body like mammals and birds, whereas reptiles crawl, or walk with their limbs out to their sides.

DINOSAUR-LIKE REPTILES
While dinosaurs roamed the land, huge reptiles flew in the air and swam in the oceans. These marine and flying reptiles were closely related to the dinosaurs.

Rhamphorhynchus
Ichthyosaurus
Elasmosaurus
Pterodactylus

FLYING REPTILES
Ancient flying reptiles, called pterosaurs, reached huge sizes. Their wings were made of skin, and their body was usually furry. They had light, delicate bones for flying.

MARINE REPTILES
These were some of the fiercest and largest animals in the sea. They breathed air, so had to come to the surface regularly to fill their lungs. These reptiles hunted fish and other sea creatures.

MAJOR DINOSAUR GROUPS
Within the two orders, dinosaurs are divided into five sub-groups. There are three sub-groups of ornithischians, and two sub-groups of saurischians.

Thyreophorans
(Ornithischians) Armoured herbivores; rows of protective studs, plates, or spikes down the back, e.g. *Stegosaurus*.

Theropods (Saurischians)
Mostly bipedal carnivores with an S-shaped neck and clawed, four-toed feet, e.g. *Tyrannosaurus*.

Marginocephalians
(Ornithischians)
Herbivores; many with bony frill at back of skull, e.g. *Styracosaurus*.

Ornithopods
(Ornithischians)
Herbivores; horny beak and bird-like feet, e.g. *Corythosaurus*.

Sauropodomorphs
(Saurischians). Herbivores; small head, long neck, bulky body, and long tail, e.g. *Saltasaurus*.

Triassic Period: 248–213mya (million years ago)	Jurassic Period: 213–144mya
Land joined in the super-continent of Pangaea (see p.40). First dinosaurs evolve and, towards the end of the period, split into two groups: lizard- and bird-hipped.	Pangaea breaks apart: Atlantic Ocean begins to form; Africa splits from South America. In late Jurassic times, huge herbivorous dinosaurs dominate life on land.

Melanorosaurus
Plateosaurus
Coelophysis
Mosasaurus
Herrerasaurus
Staurikosaurus
Technosaurus
Camptosaurus
Dryosaurus

70

MEASUREMENTS AND ABBREVIATIONS

Some words and measurements are abbreviated, or shortened, in *The Illustrated Factopedia*. The following list explains what the abbreviations stand for:

°C = degrees Celsius
°F = degrees Fahrenheit
mm = millimetre
cm = centimetre
m = metre
km = kilometre
sq km = square kilometre
km/h = kilometres per hour
in = inch

ft = foot
yd = yard
sq mile = square mile
mph = miles per hour
g = gram
kg = kilogram
oz = ounce
lb = pound
c. before a date = about

B.C. = before Christ
A.D. = Anno Domini, after the birth of Christ
b. = born
r. = reigned
d. = died
CIS = Commonwealth of Independent States (formerly Russia)

DINOSAURS

Running head – by subject
Helps guide readers to the subject they want to find out about.

DINOSAUR DISCOVERY

Pre-19th century: around the world, dinosaur fossils are believed to be various things, including dragon bones in China, and giant human bones in parts of Europe.

1800 Dinosaur footprints found in Massachusetts, USA. Their discoverer claims they were made by the raven from Noah's Ark.

1820 *Iguanodon* teeth discovered in Tilgate Forest, Sussex, England, by doctor and fossil hunter Gideon Mantell (1790–1852) and his wife. He suspects they are the remains of ancient reptiles, but his theory is dismissed as heretical (anti-religious).

1834 First glimpse of what dinosaurs looked like provided by find of a partial skeleton near Maidstone, England, known as the Maidstone *Iguanodon*.

1841 The term dinosaur, from the Greek words for "terrible" and "lizard", is coined by English anatomist Richard Owen (1804–92).

| 1800 | 1800 | 1820 | 1820 | 1830 | 1834 | 1840 | 1841 |

Timelines
Present and illustrate key historical dates, people, events, and developments for every subject.

1851 First reconstruction of dinosaurs: *Iguanodon* and *Hylaeosaurus* models are made for the Great Exhibition at Crystal Palace, London, England. Results in huge public enthusiasm for dinosaurs. Before the *Iguanodon* is completed, the sculptor holds a dinner party inside it.

Dinner party in a model dinosaur

1877 One of the greatest dinosaur collections found at Como Bluff, Wyoming, USA, by O.C. Marsh (1831–99) of Yale College.

1947 Largest number of dinosaurs ever found together: more than 100 *Coelophysis* skeletons.

1987 Evidence to support theory of warm-blooded dinosaurs found by palaeontologists Tom Rich and Patricia Vickers-Rich of the Museum of Victoria, Australia. They discover dinosaur fossils in a part of South Australia that would have been inside the Antarctic Circle when these dinosaurs lived. The mean annual temperature in this region would then have been near freezing.

Leaellynasaura lived in polar regions.

| 1850 | 1851 | 1870 | 1877 | 1940 | 1947 | 1980 | 1987 |

Topic headings
Each main topic has its own look-up heading. There are 12 separate topics on this spread.

DINOSAUR RECORDS

SMALLEST DINOSAUR was probably *Wannanosaurus*, a bipedal carnivore that measured 60cm (2ft) long. It was about the size of a chicken.

MOST PRIMITIVE KNOWN DINOSAUR is *Eoraptor*, a 228 million-year-old bipedal carnivore that was about the size of a large dog.

SMALLEST DINOSAUR BRAIN is believed to have been that of the *Stegosaurus*. It was less than 5cm (2in) long.

LARGEST DINOSAUR EGGS were probably those of *Hypselosaurus*. They measured about 30cm (12in) long and contained an estimated 3.3 litres (6 pints) of fluid: roughly the same as the fluid in 60 hens' eggs.

EARTH SHAKER

The name *Seismosaurus* means "earth-shaking lizard". This enormous plant-eating dinosaur was 40m (131ft) in length: longer than an Airbus A320.

EXTINCTION THEORIES

About 65 million years ago the dinosaurs, together with many other animal species, became extinct. Other animal groups, including turtles, frogs, birds, and mammals, survived. There are many theories for this mass-extinction: below are two of the most widely accepted.

Exciting visual comparisons
Bring facts to life and make them memorable by placing them into interesting and unusual contexts.

Records
Provide the reader with all the record-breaking features smallest, largest, fastest, slowest, earliest, and latest of every subject.

GRADUAL EXTINCTION
Gradual changes in climate and vegetation caused by continental drift (see p.40) led to the dinosaurs' slow extinction over about 50,000 years. Warm, tropical conditions were replaced by cooler, more seasonal climates, and mammals slowly replaced dinosaurs as the dominant animal group.

LARGEST CARNIVORES

Dinosaur	Estimated length	
	m	ft
Acrocanthosaurus	12	39
Tyrannosaurus	12	39
Aliwalia	11	36
Allosaurus	11	36

LARGEST HERBIVORES

Dinosaur	Estimated length	
	m	ft
Seismosaurus	40	131
Barosaurus	27	89
Diplodocus	27	89
Brachiosaurus	25	82

CATASTROPHES
The period when dinosaurs were dying out coincided with many volcanic eruptions in India. At the same time, a huge meteorite hit the Earth. Dust thrown into the atmosphere blocked out sunlight, and dinosaurs could not survive the resulting climate changes.

Data tables
Give the reader essential data in an immediately accessible form.

Detailed captions
Expand on the subject and reinforce the image.

WIDER GLIDER

The largest flying animal ever to have existed was *Quetzalcoatlus*, a flying reptile. Its wingspan measured about 12m (39ft) across: wider than the wingspan of a hang glider.

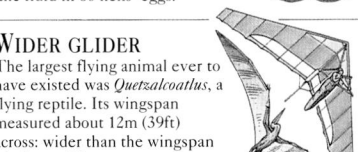

| Cretaceous Period: 144–65mya | 65mya |

Continents split further apart, eventually drifting into their present-day positions. Dinosaurs continue to flourish; those on different continents evolve separately, leading to great diversity.

Dinosaurs become extinct, together with many other animal species.

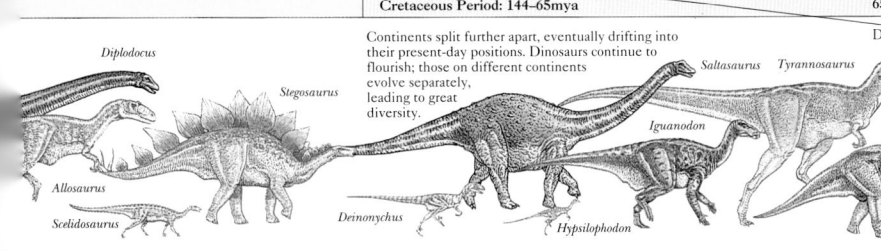

Diplodocus — *Stegosaurus* — *Saltasaurus* — *Tyrannosaurus* — *Iguanodon* — *Allosaurus* — *Scelidosaurus* — *Deinonychus* — *Hypsilophodon* — *Torosaurus*

Amazing facts
Words and pictures combine to present little-known or amazing and unusual facts.

Page size
The Dinosaurs spread is shown slightly smaller than actual size.

71

CONTENTS

Earth's tectonic plates

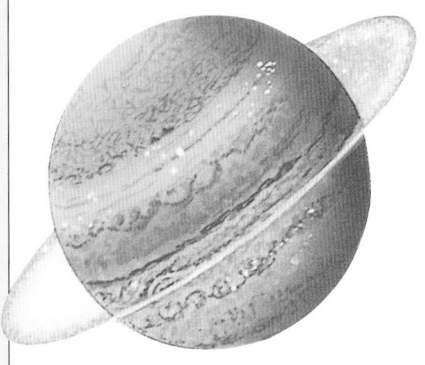

Jupiter

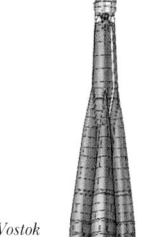

Vostok
36.4m (119.5ft)

Saturn V
110.6m (363ft)

67 LIVING WORLD

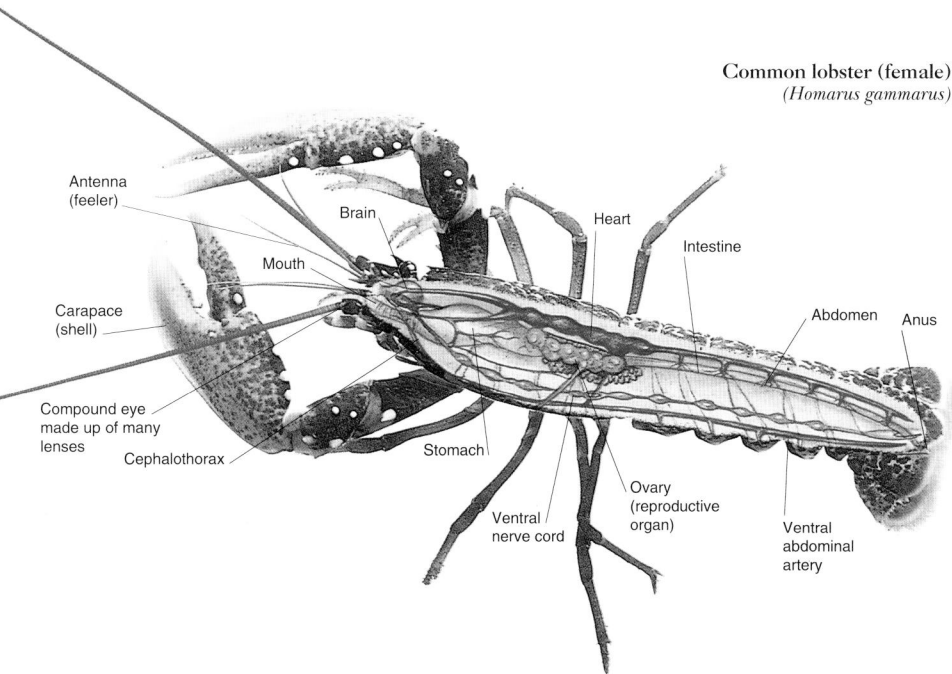

Common lobster (female)
(Homarus gammarus)

Antenna (feeler)

Brain

Heart

Intestine

Mouth

Abdomen

Anus

Carapace (shell)

Compound eye made up of many lenses

Cephalothorax

Stomach

Ventral nerve cord

Ovary (reproductive organ)

Ventral abdominal artery

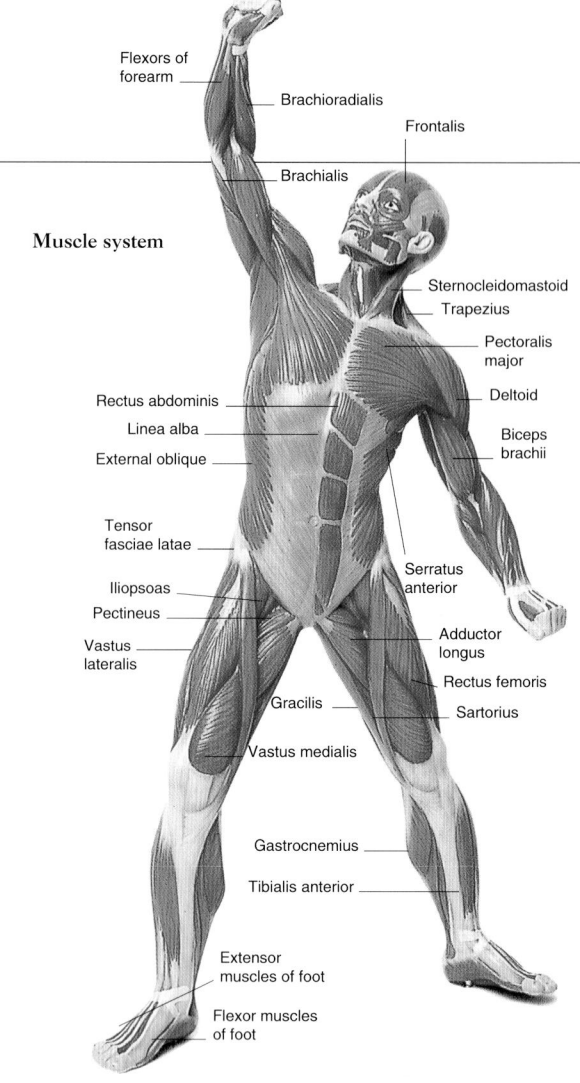

Muscle system

Flexors of
forearm
Brachioradialis
Frontalis
Brachialis
Sternocleidomastoid
Trapezius
Pectoralis
major
Rectus abdominis
Deltoid
Linea alba
External oblique
Biceps
brachii
Tensor
fasciae latae
Serratus
anterior
Iliopsoas
Pectineus
Adductor
longus
Vastus
lateralis
Rectus femoris
Gracilis
Sartorius
Vastus medialis
Gastrocnemius
Tibialis anterior
Extensor
muscles of foot
Flexor muscles
of foot

Body systems

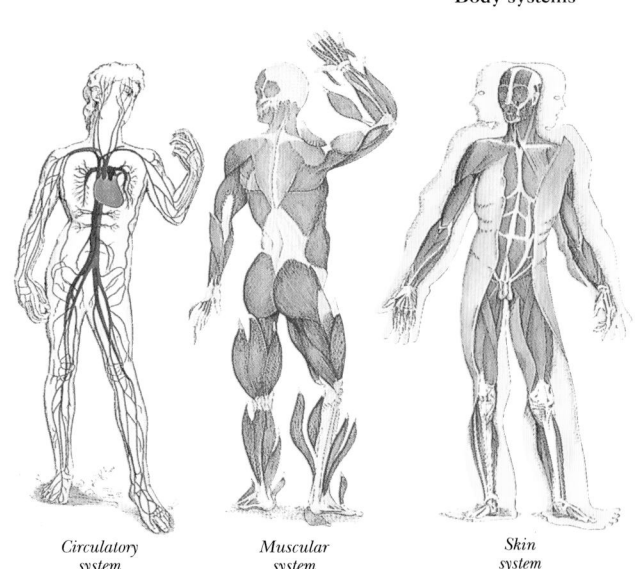

Skeletal
system

Circulatory
system

Muscular
system

Skin
system

155 ARTS AND THE MEDIA

Welsh guard   *Nun*   *Bolivian dancer*   *Arab woman*

137 BELIEFS, CUSTOMS, AND SOCIETY

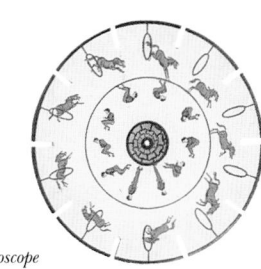

Phenakistoscope

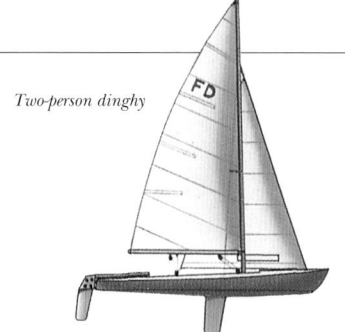

Two-person dinghy

Vaulting over

Pole vault

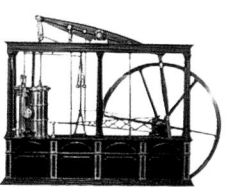
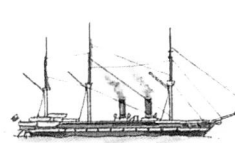

Isotopes

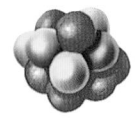

Fluorine–18 nucleus

Fluorine–19 nucleus

Nuclear-powered submarine

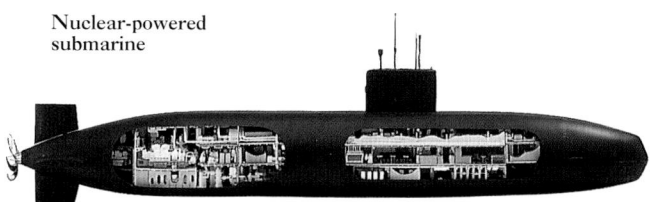

North and Central America

Japanese golfer

Traditional Arab head-dress

Bulgarians with rose petals

Decorative Islamic face-veil

West African children

South America

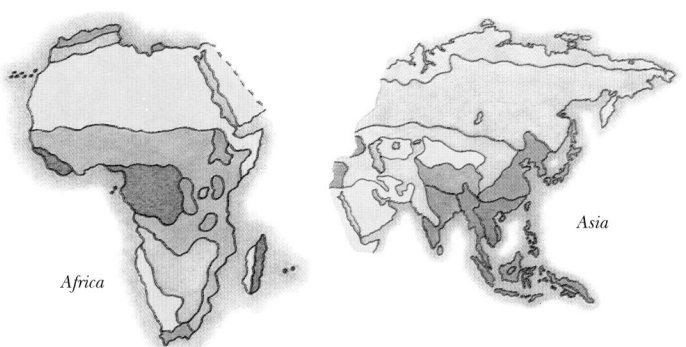

Africa

Asia

African elephants   *Giraffe*   *Mountain gorilla*

Kazakh yurts

UNIVERSE AND SPACE

Starting with the formation and scale of the known Universe, and including the latest theories about how it might end, this section provides facts and figures about every aspect of outer space. Vital statistics are given for planets, stars, the Moon, comets, meteors, and asteroids, as well as key dates in space exploration and great discoveries in astronomy.

Universe • Stars • Night Skies • Sun and Solar System
Planets • Moon • Comets, Meteors, and Asteroids • Astronomy
Space Exploration • Rockets

 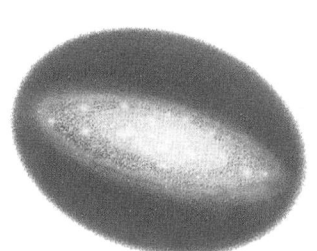 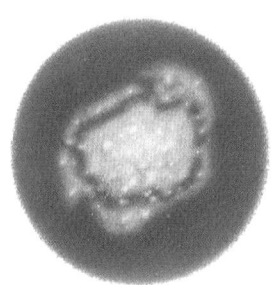

UNIVERSE

THE KNOWN UNIVERSE contains an estimated 100 billion galaxies. They are grouped in massive superclusters and separated by vast empty spaces.

EVOLUTION OF THE UNIVERSE

The Universe is thought to have exploded into existence 13 billion years ago at the Big Bang. 300,000 years later ripples of matter began to form, followed 9.2 billion years later by the first known life forms.

13 billion years ago
At the time of the Big Bang, all matter and energy is concentrated into a single, tiny point.

3 minutes later
Atomic nuclei, the centres of atoms, begin to form out of the soup of sub-atomic particles.

300,000 years after Big Bang
The first ripples of matter emerge. They form the seeds of galaxies.

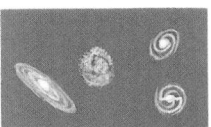

12 billion years ago
One billion years after Big Bang, the first galaxies evolve. Light from their stars begins its journey across space.

11 billion years ago
The stars of the Milky Way form from the break-up of a vast cloud of helium and hydrogen.

5 billion years ago
The Solar System is born out of a whirling cloud of gas studded with ice and rock.

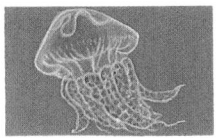

3.8 billion years ago
Life evolves on Earth, the only planet known in the Universe to support living things.

FUTURE OF THE UNIVERSE

The empty spaces of the Universe may be full of dark matter, whose nature is not yet known. If there is enough dark matter, its gravity could reverse the Universe's expansion. If not, the Universe could expand forever.

AFTER BIG BANG
The Universe could follow different courses.

Big Bang
A huge explosion creates all existing matter.

Evolution
Stars and galaxies form.

The next Universe?
After Big Crunch the Universe may end or it may be reborn in an entirely new form.

Big Crunch
All matter is contracted into a single point of infinite density.

Turning point
Dark matter begins to drag in all the galaxies.

Eternal Expansion
The most recent studies indicate that the Universe will expand forever. As stars and galaxies die, the Universe becomes a great empty void.

Expansion or Contraction?
The Universe may grow forever, or reach a maximum size.

Present day
The Universe expands.

COBE
In 1992, data from COBE, Cosmic Background Explorer satellite, found evidence for the first ripples of matter in the Universe. These ripples were the beginnings of galaxies.

FAMOUS COSMOLOGISTS

Cosmologists study the origin and structure of the Universe.

Sir Isaac Newton (1642–1727) laid the foundations of modern astronomy with his theory of Universal Gravity. He stated that it was gravity that held the planets in their orbits.

Max Planck (1858–1947) published his quantum theory concerning the nature of energy in 1900. It explained that light could take the form of waves or particles.

Albert Einstein (1879–1955) His theories of relativity explained that light was the fastest thing in the Universe, and that matter and energy were the same thing.

Edwin Hubble (1889–1953) provided the first strong evidence that the Universe was expanding. In 1924 he discovered galaxies beyond the Milky Way.

Arno Penzias (born 1933) Robert Wilson (born 1936) discovered a constant level of background radiation in the Universe, left over from the Big Bang.

Stephen Hawking (born 1942) made major discoveries about the nature of black holes and contributed greatly to our understanding of gravity.

UNIVERSE SCALE

The Universe spans more than 26 billion light-years. A light-year, the distance light travels in one year, is equal to 9,461 billion km (5,875 billion miles).

Ground level

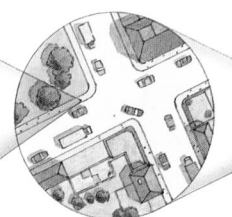

Flying at low altitude
1km (0.6 miles)

Orbiting at high altitude
1,000km (620 miles)

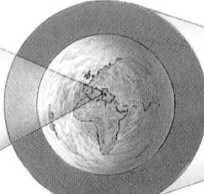

Earth from space
100,000km (62,000 miles)

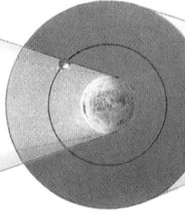

Earth and Moon
1 million km (620,000 miles)

GALAXY TYPES

Galaxies are huge families of stars held together by their own gravity. They take different forms. The Milky Way is a spiral galaxy. Other types include elliptical, barred spiral, and irregular galaxies.

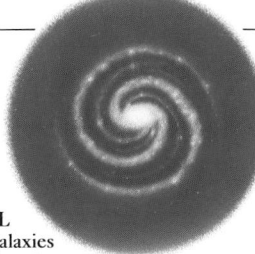
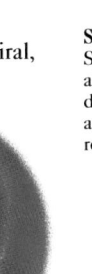

SPIRAL
Spiral galaxies are shaped like discs. They have two or more curved arms of densely packed stars that rotate around a central bulge.

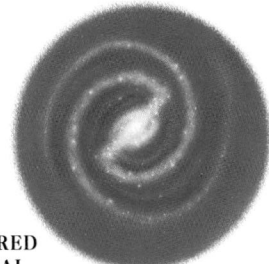

BARRED SPIRAL
Barred spiral galaxies have a rigid central bar with spiral arms beginning at the bar's ends. The central bar, made up of millions of stars, rotates.

ELLIPTICAL
All the stars in elliptical galaxies formed at the same time. Elliptical galaxies range from the smallest to the largest galaxies of all.

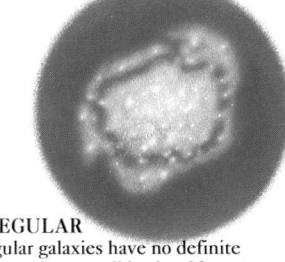

CANNIBAL
Cannibal galaxies are a type of elliptical galaxy. They are so massive and exert such a powerful gravitational pull that they swallow up smaller galaxies.

IRREGULAR
Irregular galaxies have no definite shape and are small in size. New stars continue to form inside them and they are rich in gas and dust.

MAJOR NEARBY GALAXIES

Galaxy	Type	Mass (billion solar masses)	Distance (light-years)
Andromeda (M 31)	Spiral	300	2,500,000
Milky Way galaxy	Spiral	150	0
Galaxy in Triangulum (M 33)	Spiral	10	2,500,000
Large Magellanic Cloud	Irregular	10	160,000
NGC 205	Elliptical	10	2,500,000
NGC 221	Elliptical	3	2,500,000
Small Magellanic Cloud	Irregular	2	190,000
NGC 185	Elliptical	1	2,000,000
NGC 147	Elliptical	1	1,920,000

COSMIC DUST AND THE ZONE OF AVOIDANCE

A cosmic dust grain is about one millionth of a millimetre in diameter, smaller than a particle of smoke. Clouds of these grains dim our view of the Universe by scattering the light from stars. Until the invention of radio astronomy, parts of our galaxy were hidden.

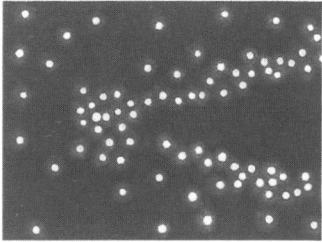

The Zone of Avoidance
Before the 1950s, astronomers were puzzled that a dark, empty zone appeared to stretch around the sky, avoided by stars and distant galaxies.

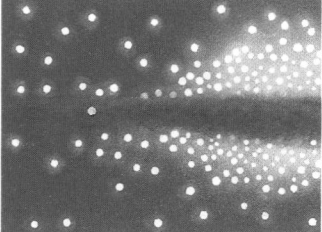

Exposing the Zone
New instruments were able to peer through the veil of dust. They revealed new stars and gas clouds at the galactic centre, and many distant galaxies.

MILKY WAY DATA

Age	About 11 billion years
Number of stars	200 billion
Diameter	100,000 light-years
Maximum thickness	20,000 light-years
Thickness at Sun	700 light-years
Distance of Sun from galactic centre	25,000 light-years
Time taken for Sun to orbit galactic centre	240 million years

GALACTIC CENTRE

This radio picture shows the centre of the Milky Way galaxy. It is a hot region of stars, possibly containing a black hole.

QUASAR FACTS

• Quasars are the violent centres of distant galaxies, brighter than the average galaxy.

• They are powered by huge black holes in their centres tearing matter apart.

• Remotest object in known Universe is quasar PC 1247 + 3406, 13.2 billion light-years away.

• In 1989, quasar PKS 0558-504 threw out as much energy in 3 minutes as the Sun throws out in 340,000 years.

• First discovered and nearest quasar is 3C–273, 2 billion light-years away. It is as bright as 200 galaxies combined.

X-ray photograph of quasar 3C-273

AMAZING JOURNEYS

A journey by jumbo jet to the nearest star, Proxima Centauri, would take 5 million years.

The flight time of a jumbo jet bound for the Sun would be 20 years.

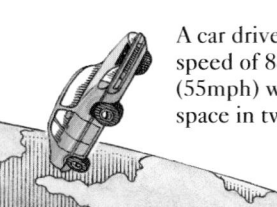

A car driven at a steady speed of 88km/h (55mph) would reach space in two hours.

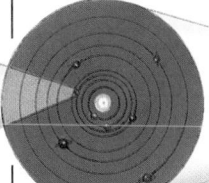

The Solar System
10 billion km
(6.2 billion miles)

Interstellar space
1,000 billion km
(620 billion miles)

Nearest stars
100 light-years

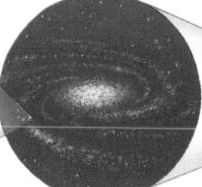

Milky Way Galaxy
100,000 light-years

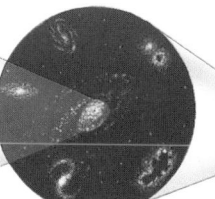

Local Group of galaxies
6 million light-years

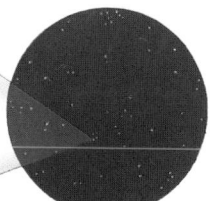

Extent of the known Universe
26 billion light-years

STARS

A STAR IS AN immense globe of fiery hydrogen gas powered by nuclear reactions at its core. Only gravity holds it together and stops it from exploding. In the first stage of its life, a star generates energy by fusing pairs of hydrogen atoms to form helium.

STAR TYPES

Most stars are part of a system composed of two or more stars. Mintaka (in Orion) consists of three stars, while Castor (in Gemini) has six. Stars form in close-knit groups from a nebula. About 60% stay in groups, held together by each other's gravity. Our Sun is unusual in being a single star.

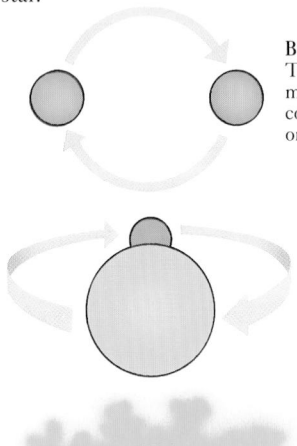

BINARY STARS
These stars of similar mass and size orbit a common centre of gravity, or central balance point.

ECLIPSING BINARY
One star in a pair regularly moves in front of the other. First we see a reduction, then a recovery in the star's light.

VARIABLE STAR
These stars vary in brightness. In some cases, explosions on the star's surface make it appear brighter than usual.

STAR RECORDS

FAINTEST KNOWN STAR
is brown star RG 0058.8-2807, with a visual brightness less than one millionth of the Sun's.

BRIGHTEST KNOWN SUPERNOVA
was SN 1006, which flared in April 1006. It was easily visible during the day.

FASTEST KNOWN PULSAR
is PSR 1937+214, which spins 642 times a second.

STAR FACTS

• Red giant diameter: up to 100 times that of Sun. Red supergiant diameter: up to 1,000 times that of Sun.

• Energy released by a supernova in one minute is equivalent to total radiated by Sun in nine billion years.

• Average galaxy has 100 billion stars – it would take 1,000 years to count them all at a rate of 3 per second.

FEATHERWEIGHT

On Earth, the average bird's feather weighs very little. On the surface of a neutron star, however, the intense gravity would cause a medium-sized feather to weigh as much as two Apollo lunar landing modules weigh on Earth.

BIRTH AND LIFE OF A MASSIVE STAR

Every star begins life as an enormous cloud of dust and gas. This cloud collapses in on itself and the star begins to shine. Death comes in two ways. A star the mass of the Sun ends its life by swelling to a red giant and puffing off its outer layers of gas, which glow for a few thousand years as a planetary nebula. A massive star ends in a supernova.

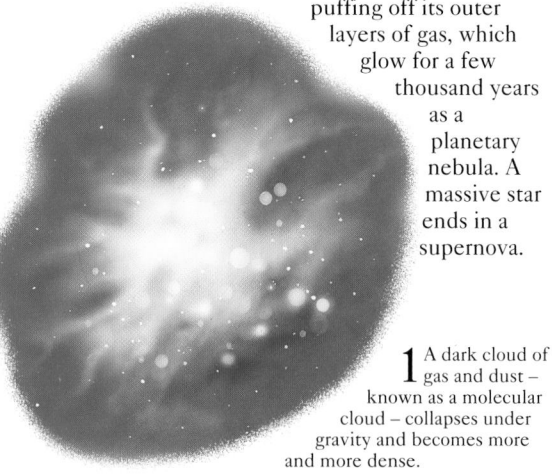

1 A dark cloud of gas and dust – known as a molecular cloud – collapses under gravity and becomes more and more dense.

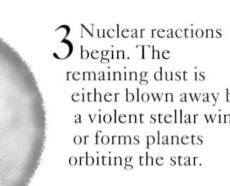

2 Parts of the cloud contract into clumps called protostars. These heat up, shrink, and become denser. Each protostar begins to spin and flattens into a disc.

3 Nuclear reactions begin. The remaining dust is either blown away by a violent stellar wind or forms planets orbiting the star.

4 On the main sequence, the star settles down into the major period of its lifespan. It shines steadily and radiates energy. Bigger and brighter stars burn hydrogen more quickly. They have shorter lifetimes.

MAIN SEQUENCE STARS

The main sequence is the central period of a star's lifetime. A star's brightness, colour, surface temperature, size, and lifespan depend on its mass. Our Sun is a yellow star, a typical star of average size and temperature.

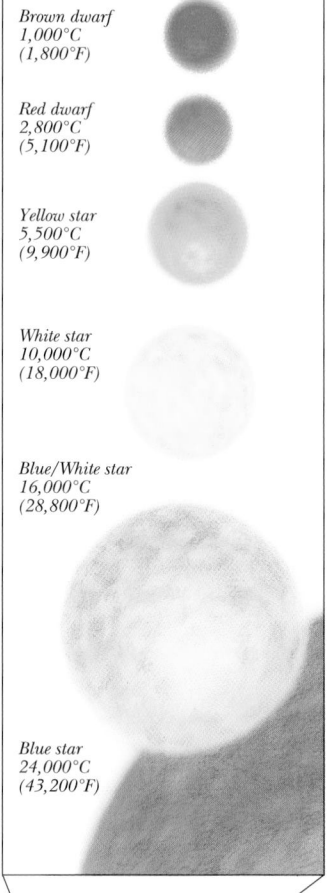

Brown dwarf 1,000°C (1,800°F)

Red dwarf 2,800°C (5,100°F)

Yellow star 5,500°C (9,900°F)

White star 10,000°C (18,000°F)

Blue/White star 16,000°C (28,800°F)

Blue star 24,000°C (43,200°F)

NEAREST STARS

Star	Star type	Distance (light years)
Sun	Yellow main sequence	0.0
Proxima Centauri	Red dwarf	4.2
Alpha Centauri A	Yellow main sequence	4.3
Alpha Centauri B	Orange main sequence	4.3
Barnard's star	Red dwarf	5.9
Wolf 359	Red dwarf	7.6
Lalande 21185	Red dwarf	8.1
Sirius A	White main sequence	8.6
Sirius B	White dwarf	8.6
UV Ceti A	Red dwarf	8.9

SUPERNOVA REMAINS

One famous supernova was seen by Chinese astronomers in 1054. Its remains, a cloud of gas and dust particles called a nebula, can now be seen as the Crab nebula. This nebula is now expanding at a speed of 1500km/sec (930 miles/sec): 130 times the top speed of the Saturn V Moon rocket.

Crab nebula

7 The core's contraction leads to a massive explosion called a supernova. The star shines as bright as a billion Suns as it blows apart. The core collapses in just one second.

6 Now a red supergiant, the swollen star swallows up its surrounding planets. Its core fuses carbon into iron, stops generating energy, and suddenly collapses under its own weight.

5 The star begins to swell when its central supply of hydrogen is exhausted. The core fuses helium into carbon. Its outer layers swell and glow red.

COLLAPSED STARS

A star's life on the main sequence ends either in a supernova explosion or a planetary nebula. Depending on its size, the remaining corpse collapses into one of three forms: white dwarf, neutron star, or black hole.

WHITE DWARF
When the planetary nebula of a typical star disperses into space, all that remains is a superdense core known as a white dwarf. Star corpses of less than 1.4 times the Sun's mass (i.e. typical star corpses) become white dwarfs.

Solid core

Gas

Radius = 6,000km (3,700 miles)

NEUTRON STAR
Neutron stars form when supernova corpses between 1.4 and 3 times the mass of our Sun collapse into the most solid state of matter possible. These neutron stars are so dense that a pinhead of their matter would weigh a million tonnes.

Solid crust

1cm (0.39in) thick atmosphere

Neutron fluid

Possible solid core

Radius = 16km (10 miles)

PULSAR
Rotating neutron stars are called pulsars. Their spin creates an intense magnetic field around them, a million million times Earth's field. Like a lighthouse, a pulsar sends out beams of radiation from hot spots on or above its surface.

Axis of rotation

Beam of radiation from pulsar can be detected as it sweeps past Earth.

Hot spot

BLACK HOLE
A black hole is a region of powerful gravity surrounding a point of infinite density called a singularity. Nothing, not even light, can escape after falling past the event horizon (the "edge" of the black hole). Supernova corpses of more than three times the Sun's mass collapse into black holes.

Through the black hole
A black hole's gravity is so strong that an astronaut falling into it would be stretched apart. Tearing matter apart in this way creates enormous heat.

A black hole's gravity distorts space into a well.

Event horizon: point of no return

BRIGHTEST STARS TO THE NAKED EYE

Star	Star type	Distance (light-years)
Sun	Yellow main sequence	0.0
Sirius A	White main sequence	8.6
Canopus	White supergiant	200
Alpha Centauri	Yellow main sequence	4.3
Arcturus	Red giant	36
Vega	White main sequence	26
Capella	Yellow giant	42
Rigel	Blue/white supergiant	910
Procyon	Yellow main sequence	11
Achernar	Blue/white main sequence	85

NIGHT SKIES

ANCIENT PEOPLES INVENTED names for different groups of stars, called constellations, to help them find their way about the skies. The stars that belong to them form patterns that have been observed and recognized over thousands of years.

CELESTIAL SPHERES

The celestial sphere is the huge, revolving, hollow ball studded with stars that encloses Earth. In fact, it is Earth that rotates and the stars are scattered about in space; but the idea of a celestial sphere allows astronomers to plot the positions of stars and follow their movements.

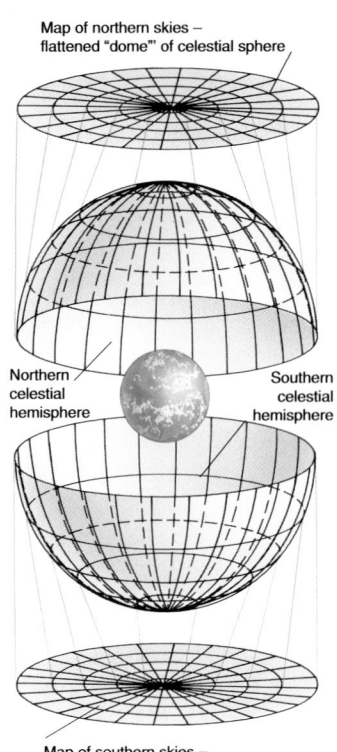

Map of northern skies – flattened "dome" of celestial sphere

Northern celestial hemisphere

Southern celestial hemisphere

Map of southern skies – flattened "bowl" of celestial sphere

OLDEST STAR MAP

The oldest example of a map of the heavens was discovered in 1987 on the ceiling of a tomb in Jiaotong University, Xian, China. It was painted in 25 B.C.

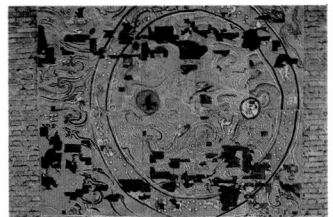

SKIES OF THE NORTHERN HEMISPHERE

The picture below shows the constellations an observer would see while standing at the North Pole and looking up into the night sky.

Pole position
In the Northern Hemisphere stars appear to revolve steadily about the star at the centre: Polaris, the Pole Star. This star lies directly along Earth's axis of rotation.

Betelgeuse: 400 times bigger than the Sun

Pisces

Cetus

Pegasus

Aries

Delphinus

Triangulum

Andromeda

Taurus

MILKY WAY

Perseus

Sagitta

Cygnus

Cassiopeia

Aquila

Cepheus

Orion

Auriga

Lyra

Polaris (North Star)

Ophiuchus

Draco

Ursa Minor

Gemini

Monoceros

Hercules

Canis Minor

Corona Borealis

Ursa Major

Cancer

Serpens Caput

Leo Minor

Hydra

Boötes

Canes Venatici

Leo

Vega: it will be the Pole Star in 14,000 A.D.. A "wobble" in the Earth's rotation makes the celestial poles slowly change position.

Virgo

Castor: in fact a family of six stars

MONTHLY STARS

Stars that lie on the other side of the Sun from Earth cannot be seen at night – night-time observers face the other way. Earth, however, revolves around the Sun once a year. So, the best time to see those stars is during the months when they lie on the opposite side of Earth from the Sun. This is why different constellations are visible at different times of the year.

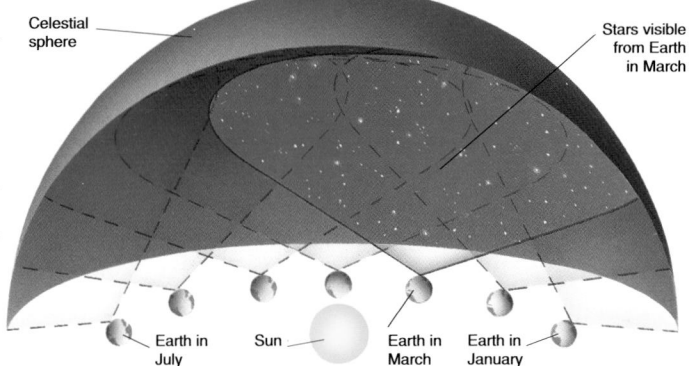

Celestial sphere

Stars visible from Earth in March

Earth in July

Sun

Earth in March

Earth in January

STARS OF THE ZODIAC

The Sun appears in front of each constellation of the zodiac on the dates shown. These astronomical dates differ from astrological ones by about one month.

Aries the ram 21 April– 21 May

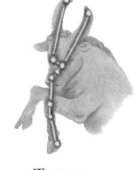

Taurus the bull 22 May– 21 June

Gemini the twins 22 June– 22 July

Cancer the crab 23 July– 23 August

Leo the lion 24 August– 22 September

Virgo the virgin 23 September– 23 October

SKIES OF THE SOUTHERN HEMISPHERE

In the South, no bright star lies along Earth's axis of rotation, so there is no Pole Star. Southern stars, however, are more spectacular.

Milky Way
The Solar System lies in the plane of the Milky Way Galaxy. So, when we look up in the sky, we see a band of bright stars, and none of the Galaxy's spiral details.

NIGHT SKY FACTS

• 2,000 years ago Sirius, the dog star, may have appeared red, and Romans used to sacrifice red dogs to it.

• Some "stars" seem to move very quickly across the night sky – these are in fact artificial satellites, reflecting the Sun's light at dawn or dusk.

• The Andromeda Galaxy is the furthest object visible to the naked eye – it lies 2.5 million light-years away.

• The ancient Chinese had constellations for every aspect of life – a celestial prison, a celestial stable, and a row of shops.

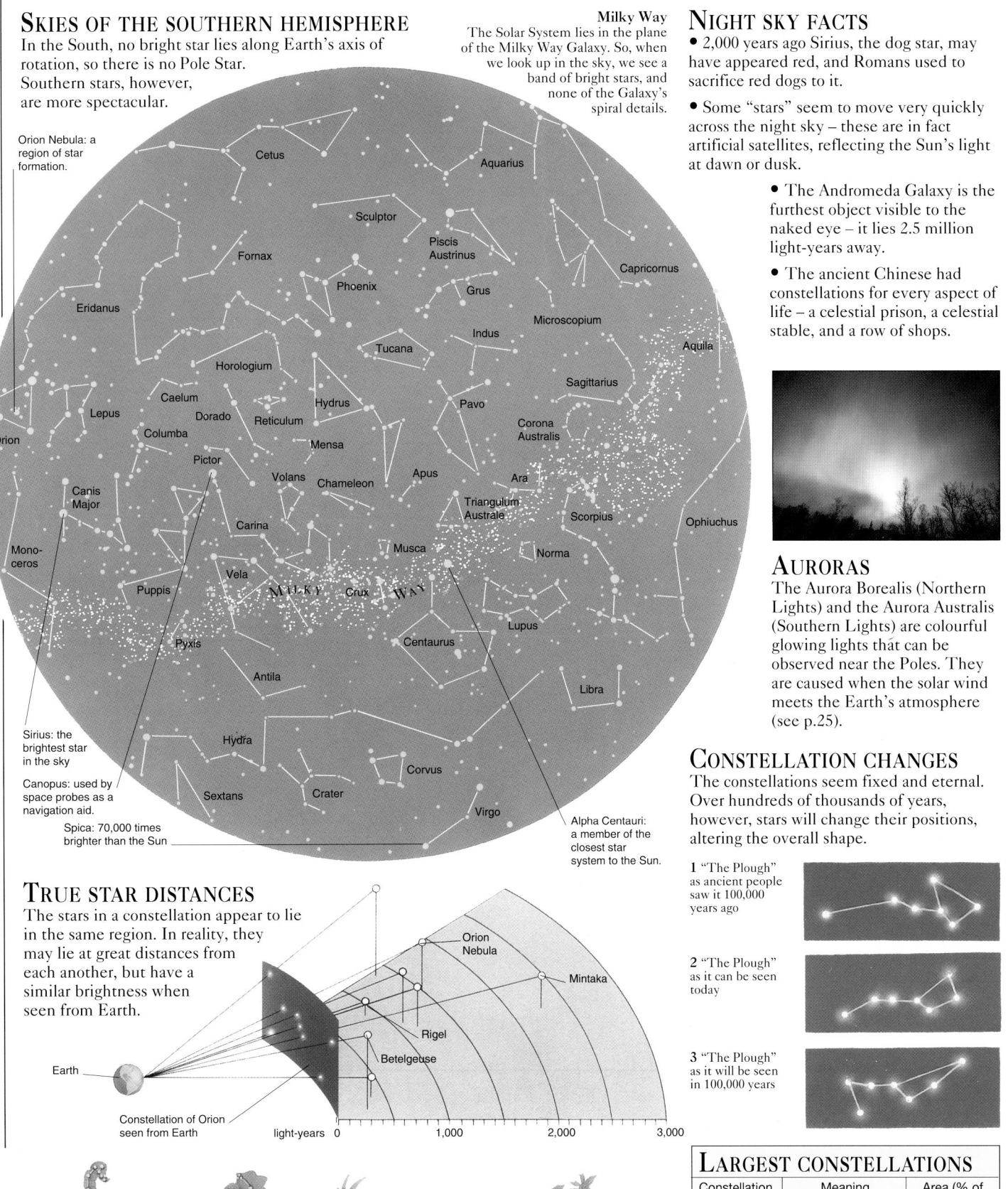

Orion Nebula: a region of star formation.

Orion

Sirius: the brightest star in the sky

Canopus: used by space probes as a navigation aid.

Spica: 70,000 times brighter than the Sun

Alpha Centauri: a member of the closest star system to the Sun.

Cetus, Aquarius, Sculptor, Piscis Austrinus, Capricornus, Fornax, Phoenix, Grus, Microscopium, Aquila, Eridanus, Indus, Sagittarius, Tucana, Pavo, Corona Australis, Horologium, Hydrus, Caelum, Mensa, Dorado, Reticulum, Lepus, Columba, Apus, Ara, Pictor, Volans, Chameleon, Triangulum Australe, Scorpius, Carina, Musca, Norma, Canis Major, Monoceros, Vela, Crux, Centaurus, Lupus, Puppis, MILKY WAY, Libra, Pyxis, Antila, Hydra, Corvus, Sextans, Crater, Virgo

AURORAS

The Aurora Borealis (Northern Lights) and the Aurora Australis (Southern Lights) are colourful glowing lights that can be observed near the Poles. They are caused when the solar wind meets the Earth's atmosphere (see p.25).

CONSTELLATION CHANGES

The constellations seem fixed and eternal. Over hundreds of thousands of years, however, stars will change their positions, altering the overall shape.

1 "The Plough" as ancient people saw it 100,000 years ago

2 "The Plough" as it can be seen today

3 "The Plough" as it will be seen in 100,000 years

TRUE STAR DISTANCES

The stars in a constellation appear to lie in the same region. In reality, they may lie at great distances from each another, but have a similar brightness when seen from Earth.

Orion Nebula
Mintaka
Rigel
Betelgeuse
Earth
Constellation of Orion seen from Earth
light-years 0   1,000   2,000   3,000

Libra
the scales
24 October–
22 November

Scorpius
the scorpion
23 November–
21 December

Sagittarius
the archer
22 December–
20 January

Capricornus
the sea-goat
21 January–
18 February

Aquarius
the water-carrier
19 February–
20 March

Pisces
the fishes
21 March–
20 April

LARGEST CONSTELLATIONS

Constellation	Meaning	Area (% of visible sky)
Hydra	The Watersnake	6.32
Virgo	The Virgin	6.28
Ursa Major	The Great Bear	6.20
Cetus	The Whale	5.97
Hercules	Hercules the Hero	5.94

SUN AND SOLAR SYSTEM

THE SUN IS THE STAR at the heart of the Solar System. Its huge gravitational pull anchors the nine planets, the asteroids, and comets in their orbits. The nuclear-reactor core at the Sun's centre radiates light and heat throughout the entire Solar System.

ANATOMY OF THE SUN

Inside the core, nuclear fusion turns hydrogen into helium, creating energy that rises out into the photosphere, and from there into space.

Convective zone
In the convective zone, rising and falling currents carry heat outwards towards the photosphere. It has a temperature of 1.5 million°C (2.7 million°F).

Radiative zone
The core's energy radiates outwards through this hydrogen layer. It has a temperature of 1.5 million–14 million°C (2.7 million–25.2 million°F).

Core
The hydrogen core works as a massive nuclear reactor. It fuses hydrogen to create helium at a temperature of 14 million°C (25.2 million°F).

Corona
The corona is a huge, thin halo of hot gas. It has a temperature of 1 million°C (1.8 million°F).

Corona seen at eclipse

Chromosphere
The chromosphere is a reddish outer layer of hydrogen that rises 1,000 km (620 miles) above the photosphere. It has a temperature of 4,000–8,000°C (7,200–14,400°F).

Photosphere
This is the surface layer of the Sun. Its white-hot hydrogen has a temperature of 5,500°C (9,900°F).

SUN DATA

Age	5 billion years
Diameter	1,392,000km (865,000 miles)
Mass (Earth = 1)	332,946
Density (water = 1)	1.41
Distance from Earth	149.6 million km (92.9 million miles)
Distance from nearest star	40,000 billion km (24,900 billion miles)
Core Temperature	14 million°C (25.2 million°F)
Surface Temperature	5,500°C (9,900°F)
Luminosity	390 billion billion megawatts
Life Expectancy	5 billion years
Speed	240 million years to orbit the galaxy

SUN FACTS

• One square metre (10.8 sq ft) of Sun's surface shines as brightly as 600,000 100-watt lightbulbs.

• Biggest observed solar prominence reached height of 700,000km (435,000 miles) in one hour in 1946.

• In one second, Sun gives out 35 million times average annual electricity supply for the entire United States.

• Solar flares can interrupt radio communications on Earth, cause magnetic storms, and confuse birds flying long distances.

• Rotation of Sun's surface varies from 25 days at equator to 35 days at poles. Radiative zone rotates regularly every 27 days.

• If Sun's cooler outer layers were peeled off, dangerous radiation from its core would destroy life on Earth.

SURFACE FEATURES OF THE SUN

SPICULES

Spicules are straight jets of gas that occur in the chromosphere. They rise as high as 10,000km (6,200 miles) at speeds of 25km/sec (16 miles/sec). After 5-10 minutes they dissolve into the surrounding corona. Spicules are thought to be caused by magnetic fields. There are 100,000 on the Sun's surface at any time.

GRANULES

The Sun's surface is made up of millions of upsurging granules. A granule is about 1,000km (620 miles) across: an area the size of France.

Granule

France

SUNSPOTS

These areas of darker, cooler gas appear in pairs at a temperature of 4,000°C (7,200°F). They occur when the heat flow from the core is blocked by the Sun's magnetic field. Sunspot activity runs in 11.5-year cycles. It will peak next in 2001.

SOLAR FLARES

These enormous and unpredictable explosions occur in the Sun's atmosphere. Solar flares can throw billions of tonnes of the Sun's material out into space. These explosions release an amount of energy equivalent to a million million times that of the first nuclear bomb.

SOLAR PROMINENCES

Solar prominences are arched plumes of flaming hydrogen gas that hang in the lower corona, supported by the force of the Sun's magnetic field. Some prominences erupt into space as great arches at speeds of 400m/sec (900 mph).

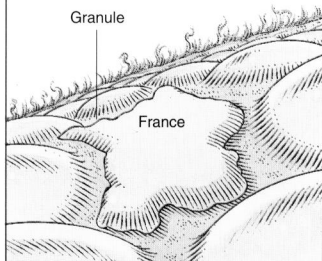

EVOLUTION OF THE SUN AND SOLAR SYSTEM

The Solar System began life 5 billion years ago as a massive cloud of gas with rocky and icy particles. When the cloud collapsed under its own gravity, the Sun formed, and the grains clumped together to form the planets.

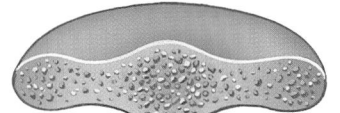

1 The Solar System begins as a spinning cloud of gas that contains particles of rock and ice, densest at the centre.

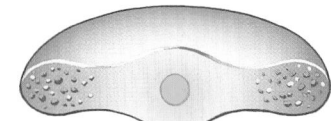

2 Gravity causes the cloud to collapse inwards. The Sun forms and begins to shine, melting ice in its inner region.

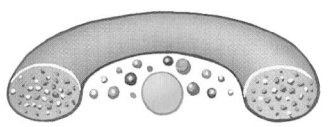

3 Rock grains nearest the Sun form planetesimals (minute planets). Further away, colder planetesimals are icy and rocky.

4 Rocky planetesimals crash into each other. Icy, rocky planetesimals grow in size as they draw in gas and dust.

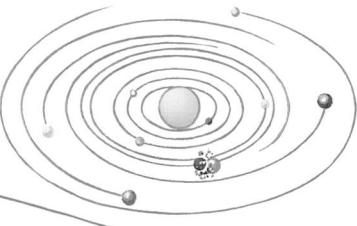

Solar System to scale: outer planets move in large orbits around the Sun.

The angle of Pluto's orbit around the Sun is steeper than that of the other planets.

Pluto

Asteroid Belts

Saturn

Uranus

Neptune

Jupiter

The inner planets are dense, rocky bodies, close to the Sun.

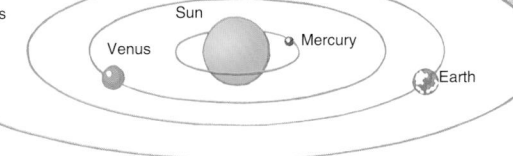

Mars

Sun

Venus

Mercury

Earth

5 Rocky inner planets form first by gathering up other planetesimals. Further out, where there is less matter, outer planets form more slowly.

AMAZING SCALES

If the Sun's diameter were the height of an average adult, then Jupiter would be the size of the head. Earth would be slightly bigger than the iris of the eyeball.

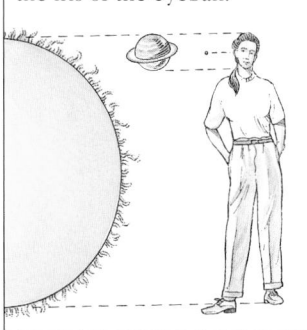

HELIOSPHERE

The Sun's magnetic field or heliosphere extends beyond the edge of the Solar System. It is generated by the gale of hot, charged particles known as the solar wind that streams in spirals off the corona. The Sun also generates a sheet of electrical current, smaller than the heliosphere.

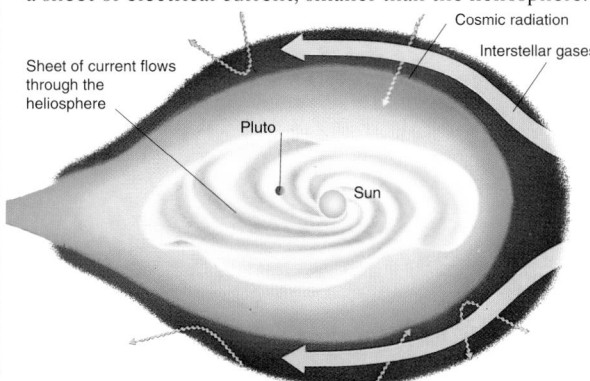

Cosmic radiation

Interstellar gases

Sheet of current flows through the heliosphere

Pluto

Sun

LARGEST BODIES IN THE SOLAR SYSTEM

Body	Maximum diameter	
	km	miles
Sun	1,392,000	865,000
Jupiter	142,984	88,846
Saturn	120,536	74,898
Uranus	51,118	31,763
Neptune	49,528	30,775
Earth	12,756	7,926
Venus	12,103	7,520
Mars	6,786	4,217
Ganymede (moon of Jupiter)	5,262	3,270
Titan (moon of Saturn)	5,150	3,200

DEATH OF THE SUN AND SOLAR SYSTEM

1 Five billion years from now, the Sun will swell to 100 times its present size, as its fuel begins to run low. Its outer layers will engulf Mercury, Venus, and possibly Earth.

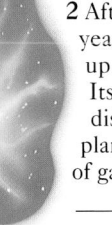

2 After a further one million years, the Sun will have used up all its available hydrogen. Its gaseous outer layers will dissolve into space as a planetary nebula, a thin cloud of gas and dust particles.

3 The remaining core will finally become a white dwarf, a superdense star about the size of Earth. It will slowly cool off and fade to a black dwarf. The outer planets of the present Solar System will still orbit this dwarf, but at a much greater distance.

PLANETS

A PLANET IS A BODY that orbits the Sun, or any other star. Our Sun has nine known planets and they can be divided into two groups: the dense, rocky inner planets, and the gassy or icy outer planets.

Sun

THE INNER PLANETS

Mercury, Venus, Earth, and Mars are known as the inner planets or terrestrials. They are made up of rocks and metals, they are smaller than the outer gas giants, and their atmospheres contain very little of the gases hydrogen and helium. Earth, as far as we know, is the only planet where there is life.

RELATIVE SIZES

Pluto is the smallest planet and also the most distant. Jupiter is bigger than all the other planets put together.

Mercury   Venus   Earth   Mars

Jupiter

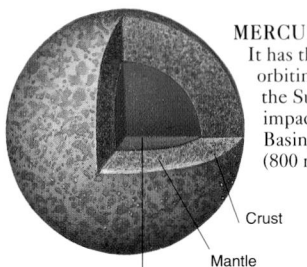

MERCURY
It has the fastest orbiting speed around the Sun. Its huge impact crater, Caloris Basin, is 1,300km (800 miles) across.

Crust
Mantle
Core

RELATIVE DISTANCES

The orbits of the four inner planets lie close to the Sun. Mercury, the nearest planet to the Sun, is 100 times closer than Pluto.

Mercury Venus Earth Mars   Jupiter   Saturn

Sun

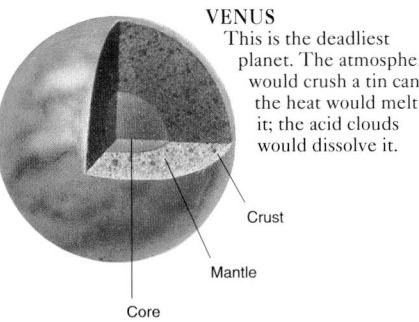

VENUS
This is the deadliest planet. The atmosphere would crush a tin can; the heat would melt it; the acid clouds would dissolve it.

Crust
Mantle
Core

INNER PLANETS

	Mercury	Venus	Earth	Mars
Distance from Sun million km (million miles)	57.9 (36.0)	108.2 (67.2)	149.6 (93.0)	227.9 (141.6)
Diameter km (miles)	4,878 (3,031)	12,103 (7,520)	12,756 (7,926)	6,786 (4,217)
Time taken to circle Sun	87.97 days	224.70 days	365.26 days	686.98 days
Orbital speed around Sun km/sec (miles/sec)	47.89 (29.76)	35.03 (21.77)	29.79 (18.51)	24.13 (14.99)
Time taken to turn on axis	58 days, 16 hours	243 days, 14 mins	23 hours, 56 mins	24 hours, 37 mins
Mass (Earth = 1)	0.055	0.81	1	0.11
Density (water = 1)	5.43	5.25	5.52	3.95
Temperature Celsius (Fahrenheit)	(on surface) -180 to +430°C (-292 to +806°F)	(on surface) 465°C (869°F)	(on surface) -70 to +55°C (-94 to +131°F)	(on surface) -120 to +25°C (-184 to +77°F)
Number of moons	-	-	1	2

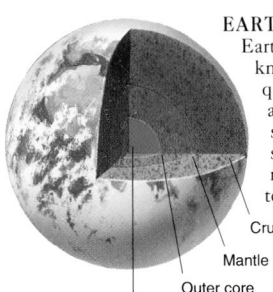

EARTH
Earth is the only planet known to have any quantity of water and oxygen, and to support life. Its surface is constantly moving due to plate tectonics (see p.40).

Crust
Mantle
Outer core
Inner core

MARS' GIANT MOUNTAIN

Olympus Mons is the biggest volcano (extinct) in the Solar System.

Olympus Mons
26km (16 miles) high

Everest
8.8km (5.5 miles) high

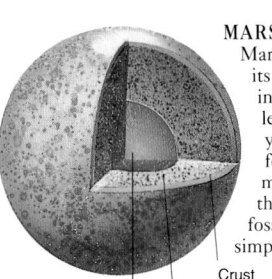

MARS
Mars is the red planet: its plains are covered in rust. Meteors that left Mars billions of years ago have been found to contain minute structures that could be the fossil remains of simple life forms.

Crust
Mantle
Core

ATMOSPHERES

Scientists have identified various gases in the atmospheres of the planets. The giant planets all contain large quantities of helium and hydrogen.

GASES FOUND IN THE ATMOSPHERE

Sodium   Hydrogen   Carbon dioxide

Helium   Nitrogen   Oxygen   Methane

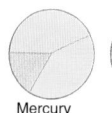 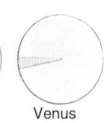 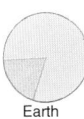  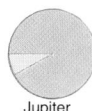    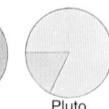

Mercury   Venus   Earth   Mars   Jupiter   Saturn   Uranus   Neptune   Pluto

THE OUTER PLANETS

Beyond the orbit of Mars lie the outer planets: Jupiter, Saturn, Uranus, Neptune, and Pluto. These planets, with the exception of Pluto, are not solid, but gigantic balls of swirling gases and liquids held together by gravity. Pluto is extremely small and made of rock and thick ice.

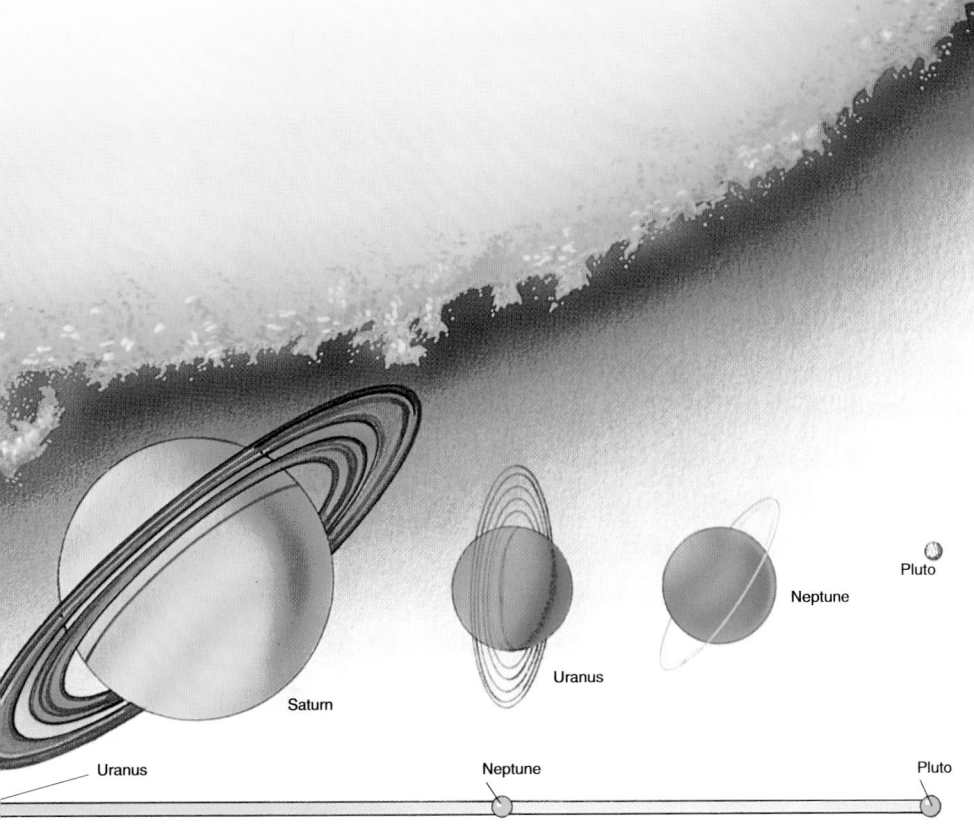

Pluto

Neptune

Saturn

Uranus

Uranus

Neptune

Pluto

JUPITER
Jupiter is the biggest and fastest spinning planet in the Solar System. It could contain 1,300 Earths.

Atmosphere

Liquid hydrogen

Metallic hydrogen

Core

SATURN
The diameter of its rings is almost the distance between Earth and the Moon. It has the lowest density. Set on a huge lake it would float.

Atmosphere

Liquid hydrogen

Metallic hydrogen

Core

URANUS
This planet has the most tilted axis and spins on its side. It has the longest-lasting seasons: each pole receives 42 years of sunlight then 42 years of darkness.

Atmosphere

Water, ammonia, methane

Core

NEPTUNE
Neptune's winds are the fastest in the Solar System at 2,000km/h (1,240mph). Its Great Dark Spot is as large as Earth.

Atmosphere

Water, ammonia, methane

Core

PLUTO
Pluto is the smallest, darkest, and coldest planet. It may just be the largest member of an outer asteroid belt called the Kuiper Belt.

Ice and frozen methane

Ice

Core

OUTER PLANETS

Jupiter	Saturn	Uranus	Neptune	Pluto
778.3 (483.6)	1,427 (886)	2,871 (1,784)	4,497 (2,794)	5,914 (3,675)
142,984 (88,846)	120,536 (74,898)	51,118 (31,763)	49,528 (30,775)	2,284 (1,419)
11.86 years	29.46 years	84.01 years	164.79 years	248.54 years
13.06 (8.12)	9.64 (5.99)	6.81 (4.23)	5.43 (3.37)	4.74 (2.95)
9 hours, 55 mins	10 hours, 40 mins	17 hours, 14 mins	16 hours, 7 mins	6 days, 9 hrs
318	95.18	14.5	17.14	0.0022
1.33	0.69	1.29	1.64	2.03
(at cloud tops) -150°C -238°F	(at cloud tops) -180°C -292°F	(at cloud tops) -210°C -346°C	(at cloud tops) -210°C -346°F	-220°C -364°F
16	18	15	8	1

PLANETARY MOON FACTS

• Saturn has the most moons of any planet in Solar System: 18. Jupiter comes second with 16.

• Europa, Jupiter's moon, has a surface of ice 97km (60 miles) thick.

• Titan, Saturn's moon, is thought to have cliffs of solid methane and rivers of liquid methane.

• Phobos, Mars' moon, is being dragged closer to Mars. In 30 million years, it will be destroyed by crashing on to the surface.

• Miranda, Uranus' moon, has canyons ten times deeper than Earth's Grand Canyon. It has an ice cliff 5.2km (3.23 miles) high.

• Callisto, Jupiter's moon, has a more cratered surface than any other body in Solar System.

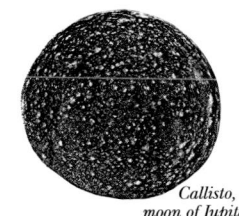

Callisto, a moon of Jupiter

MERCURY LEAP

The record women's high jump on Earth is 2.09m (6ft 10.25in). On Mercury, where gravity is weaker, the same athlete would be able to jump more than twice as high. She could leap over an elephant in one bound.

MOON

THE MOON IS EARTH'S constant companion in space. Held by our planet's gravity, it revolves around Earth in its orbit of the Sun, like a satellite. The Moon, like Earth, is 4.6 billion years old. Unlike Earth, the Moon is dead, waterless, and airless.

PHASES OF THE MOON

As the Moon orbits Earth, it receives light from the Sun, and a changing portion of its illuminated face is visible from Earth. These portions are the Moon's phases.

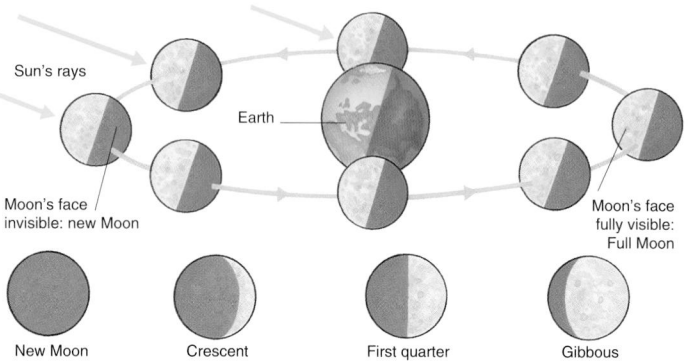

Sun's rays

Earth

Moon's face invisible: new Moon

Moon's face fully visible: Full Moon

New Moon Crescent First quarter Gibbous Full Moon Gibbous Last quarter Crescent

THEORY OF MOON'S ORIGIN

Astronomers have put forward several theories to explain the mystery of the Moon's origin. The most popular theory holds that a body the size of Mars collided with Earth in its early days. The impact threw vast amounts of matter into space, and these fragments of rock came together to form the Moon.

MOON DATA

Age	4.6 billion years
Diameter	3,476km (2,160 miles)
Mass (Earth=1)	0.012
Surface gravity (Earth=1)	0.16
Average distance from Earth	384,400km (238,000 miles)
Time taken to orbit Earth	27.3 days
Time taken to rotate on axis	27.3 days
Surface temperature	-155°C to 105°C (-247°F to 221°F)

NEAR SIDE OF THE MOON

The near side of the Moon always faces Earth and is always at least partially visible in our night sky, except at a new Moon.

Mare Frigoris

Plato: one of few craters with a dark floor of solidified lava

Mare Imbrium

Maria

The dark areas, called maria, are seas of solidified lava. They are thought to have formed billions of years ago when lava, or molten rock, seeped out from beneath the crust to fill the craters, and then solidified into darker rock.

Mare Serenitatis

Oceanus Procellarum

Mare Crisium

Mare Tranquillitatis

Copernicus: a ray crater, about 800 million years old

Mare Fecunditatis

Craters

The surface of the Moon is littered with craters formed billions of years ago by the impact of meteorites.

Mare Nectaris

Meteorite throws out smaller fragments of rock.

Ejected rocks make craters surrounding main crater.

Mare Nubium

Mare Humorum

Until recently, astronomers thought the Moon was a dry world, but in 1998 the *Lunar Prospector* satellite discovered ice hidden in deep craters at the south pole.

MOON LANDINGS

– Apollo landings (USA) – Luna landings (USSR)

Ray craters

Some craters have bright "rays" extending from their rims. The rays are fragments of rock splashed from the meteoritic impact.

Site of Apollo 17 landing: the last manned Moon mission

Site of Apollo 11 Moon landing: first people on the Moon

Highland areas

The areas between the maria are higher, rougher, and brighter than the maria.

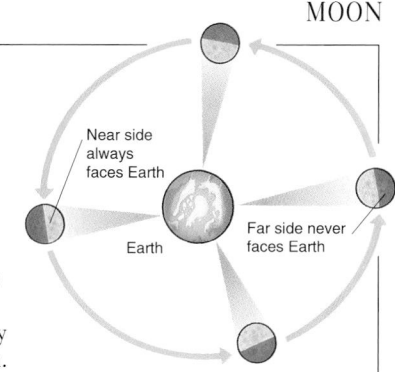

MOON AND EARTH: GRAVITY AND TIDES

The Moon is so close to Earth that it exerts a strong pull on Earth's waters. This gravitational pull produces a bulge on the side of Earth facing the Moon, and a corresponding bulge on the opposite side. So, the oceans have two daily high tides.

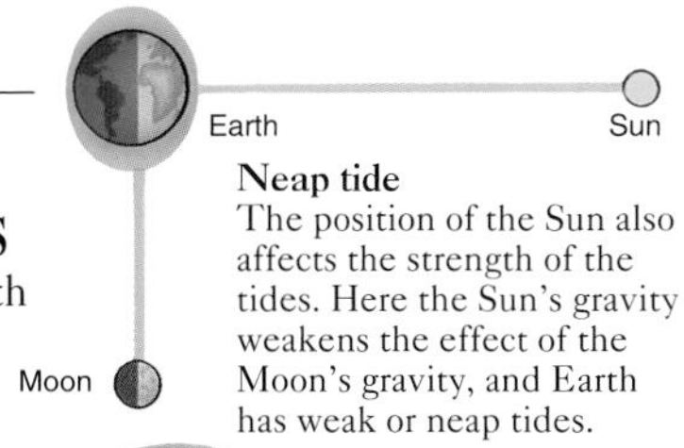

Earth   Sun

Moon

Neap tide
The position of the Sun also affects the strength of the tides. Here the Sun's gravity weakens the effect of the Moon's gravity, and Earth has weak or neap tides.

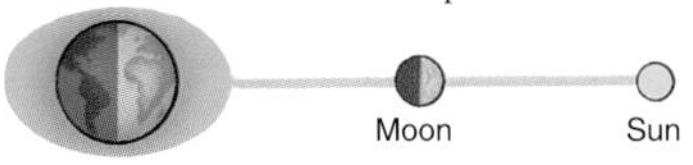

Moon   Sun

Spring tide
Here the Sun's gravity adds to the Moon's, and Earth has strong spring tides.

NEAR AND FAR SIDE

The Moon spins on its axis in exactly the same time that it takes to complete an orbit of Earth. The same side always faces us and the far side remains invisible. The Moon wobbles on its axis, and at some places on its orbit it surges forward or slows down. As a result, we can actually see 59% of its surface from Earth.

Near side always faces Earth

Earth

Far side never faces Earth

LUNAR AND SOLAR ECLIPSES

LUNAR ECLIPSE
When the Moon moves into the Earth's shadow, no sunlight is reflected off the Moon and it disappears from Earth's view. Normally the Moon passes above or below the shadow because its orbit is tilted at 5° from Earth's path.

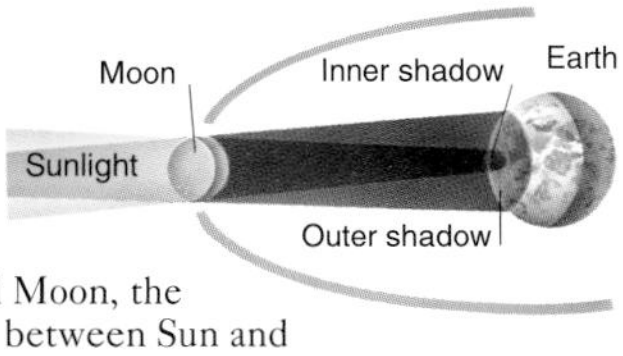

Moon

Sunlight

Earth

SOLAR ECLIPSE
By chance, the Sun and Moon appear the same size in the sky. When, at a full Moon, the Moon lines up directly between Sun and Earth, its inner shadow creates a total eclipse. People in its outer shadow see a partial eclipse.

Moon   Inner shadow   Earth

Sunlight

Outer shadow

LASTING IMPRESSION

With no air, water, or volcanic activity to erode them, the footprints and tracks left by the Moon's astronauts will remain as they are for 100 million years.

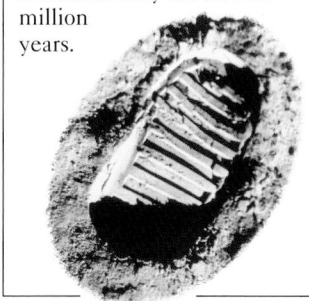

TOTAL LUNAR ECLIPSES

Date	Visible from
21 Jan 2000	Europe, Americas, Asia
16 July 2000	Pacific, Australasia, southwest Asia
9 Jan 2001	Australia, Asia, Africa, Europe
16 May 2003	Africa, Europe, Americas
8-9 Nov 2003	Asia, Africa, Europe, Americas

TOTAL SOLAR ECLIPSES

Date	Visible from
26 Feb 1998	North America, Hawaii, West Africa
11 Aug 1999	Europe, North Africa, Arabia, Greenland
21 June 2001	South Atlantic, southern Africa
4 Dec 2002	Southern Africa, southern Indian Ocean
23-24 Nov 2003	Southern Australasia, South America

FAR SIDE OF THE MOON

The far side always faces away from Earth, and is more cratered and rugged than the near side.

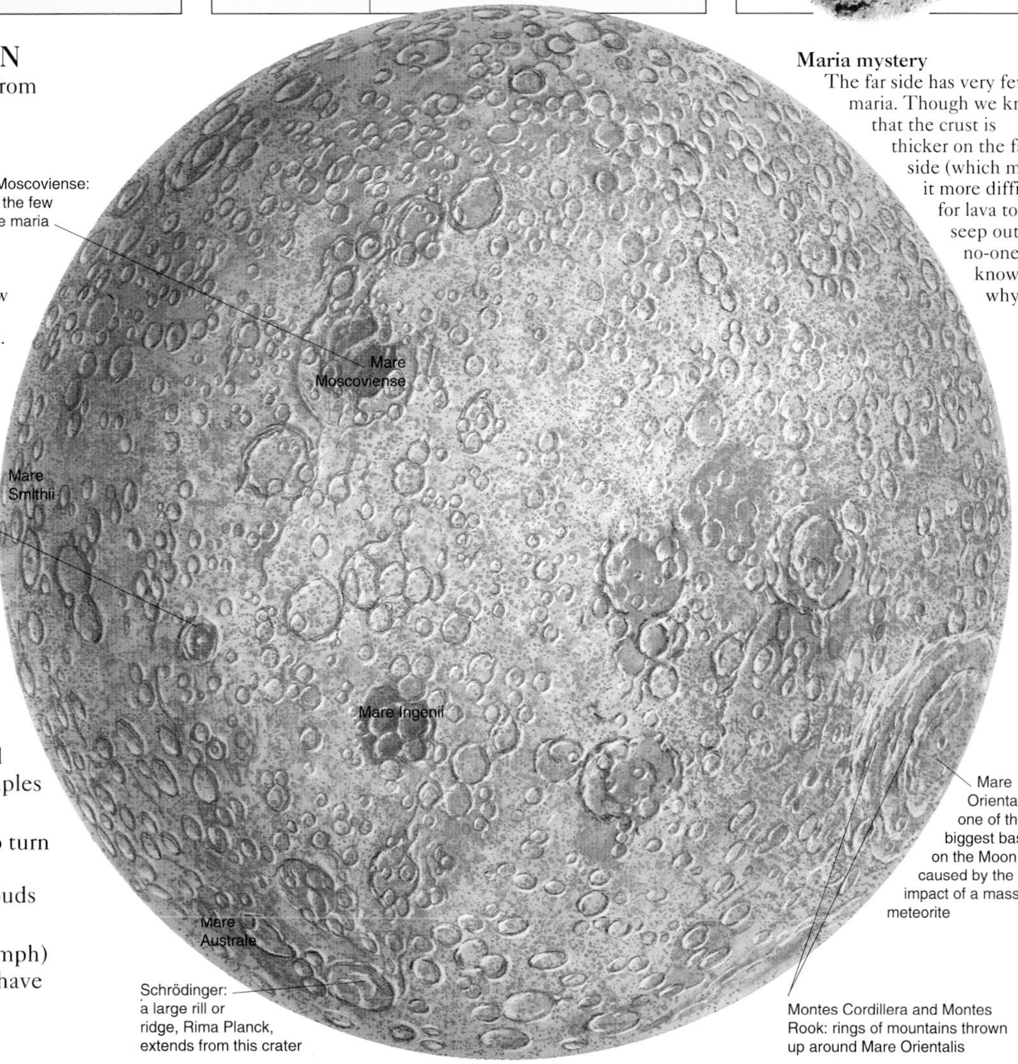

Maria mystery
The far side has very few maria. Though we know that the crust is thicker on the far side (which made it more difficult for lava to seep out), no-one knows why.

Mare Moscoviense: one of the few far side maria

Clearer view
For astronomers, who need a clear view of space, the far side would be an excellent place to build an observatory. It is totally shielded from the reflective glare and stray electrical signals of Earth, and it has no atmosphere to dim the stars' images.

Mare Moscoviense

Tsiolovsky: a crater with terraced walls and a huge central mountain structure

Mare Smithii

Mare Ingenii

MOON FACTS

- Moon's first astronauts, Americans Neil Armstrong and Buzz Aldrin, landed in 1969 in Apollo XI.
- In 1970 Russian probe Luna 16 was the first unmanned spacecraft to bring back soil samples from the surface of the Moon.
- In 1950 the Moon appeared to turn blue after a forest fire in British Columbia, Canada, threw up clouds of smoke particles.
- A mistake of only 1.6km/h (1 mph) in Apollo XI's top speed would have led to it missing the Moon by 1,600km (1,000 miles).

Mare Australe

Schrödinger: a large rill or ridge, Rima Planck, extends from this crater

Mare Orientalis: one of the biggest basins on the Moon, caused by the impact of a massive meteorite

Montes Cordillera and Montes Rook: rings of mountains thrown up around Mare Orientalis

COMETS, METEORS, AND ASTEROIDS

CHUNKS OF ROCK and metal, lumps of ice, and clouds of dust float far and wide in the Solar System. Scientists classify these wandering objects as comets, meteors, and asteroids. Rocky asteroids sometimes crash into planets or their moons, causing massive craters.

COMETS

Comets are chunks of ice and rock left over from the birth of the Solar System. Astronomers believe that these icy rocks are located in a zone called the Oort cloud, named after the Dutch astronomer Jan Oort (1900–92), that lies beyond the furthest planet in the Solar System.

Dust tail

Gas tail

Nucleus

DEFINITIONS

Comet An icy object orbiting the Sun. It produces steam when it nears the Sun and develops a tail of dust and gas.

Meteor A particle of rock that burns up in Earth's upper atmosphere, leaving a streak of light.

Asteroid A small rocky object in the Solar System. Asteroids range in size from 930km (578 miles) across down to dust particles.

Meteorite A piece of rock that has survived passage through Earth's atmosphere: thought to be a fragment of an asteroid, not of a comet.

MOST FREQUENTLY SEEN COMETS

Name	Period (years)
Encke	3.3
Grigg-Skjellerup	4.9
Honda-Mrkos-Pajdusakova	5.2
Tempel 2	5.3
Neujmin 2	5.4
Tuttle-Giacobini-Kresak	5.5
Tempel-Swift	5.7
Tempel 1	6.0
Pons-Winnecke	6.3
De Vico Swift	6.3

Jets of dust

Nucleus

Halley's comet photographed by the Schmidt telescope in 1986

HALLEY'S COMET

Every 76 years Halley's comet returns to the centre of the Solar System. In 1705, English astronomer Edmund Halley (1656–1742) correctly predicted its return in the year 1758. On the last return in 1986, the space probe Giotto penetrated to within 600km (370 miles) of the comet's nucleus.

COMET NUCLEUS

The nucleus is a chunk of rock and ice that lies at the comet's core. As the comet nears the Sun, the heat melts the ice. Gas jets spring from the Sun-facing side. Fragments of rock break off to form the dust tail.

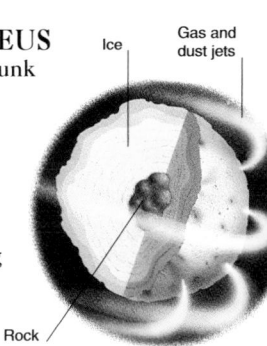

Ice

Gas and dust jets

Rock

COMET TAIL

Each comet has a dust tail and a gas tail. These are blown back by the solar wind, which forces the dust and gas away from the Sun.

Gas tail forced back by electrically charged particles of the solar wind

Dust tail follows curve of comet's path

Sun

Comet recedes from Sun, but tail always points away from Sun

SO LONG

The comet with the longest known tail was the Great Comet of 1843, which trailed for 330 million km (205 million miles). The tail could have wrapped around Earth 7,000 times. It will not return to the centre of the Solar System until 2356.

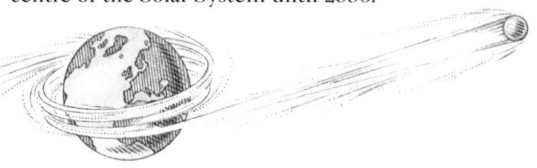

COMET RECORDS

LONGEST KNOWN PERIOD of a comet is 24 million years. This comet, Delavan's comet, was last seen in 1914.

MOST FREQUENT COMET is Encke's comet, which returns every 3.3 years.

BRIGHTEST COMET this century was the Daylight Comet of 1910. It was as bright as the planet Venus.

METEORS

Meteors, or shooting stars, are streaks of light that appear briefly in the night sky. They occur when particles of rock or dust, left by comets, burn up in Earth's atmosphere at speeds of up to 70km/sec (43 miles/sec).

METEOR SHOWER

Comets leave trails of dust and debris along their orbits around the Sun. When Earth crosses one of these trails, the dust burns up in the atmosphere and we see a meteor shower in the sky.

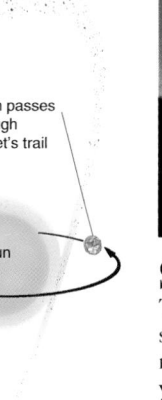

Earth passes through comet's trail

Sun

Dust trail

Comet

SHOOTING STAR

This long-exposure photograph shows a meteor from the Ursid meteor shower that occurs each year in December.

METEOR SHOWERS

Main showers (annual)	Date	Maximum number per hour
Quadrantids	3-4 Jan	50
Lyrids	22 April	10
Delta Aquarids	31 July	25
Perseids	12 Aug	50
Orionids	21 Oct	20
Taurids	8 Nov	10
Leonids	17 Nov	10
Geminids	14 Dec	50
Ursids	22 Dec	15

ASTEROIDS

Asteroids are pieces of rock smaller than planets that orbit the Sun. More than 4,000 have been found. They range in size from tiny fragments of rock to bodies hundreds of kilometres across.

Ceres
Ceres, discovered in 1801, is the biggest known asteroid with a diameter of 930km (578 miles). If Ceres were placed on Earth it would cover France.

Vesta
Vesta is smaller than Ceres, but its highly reflective surface makes it the brightest asteroid.

Psyche
Psyche is irregularly shaped, made of iron, and about 260km (160 miles) long – the size of Jamaica.

Psyche

Jamaica

ASTEROID BELTS

Most asteroids lie in the Asteroid Belts between the orbits of Mars and Jupiter. The Trojan asteroids, though, follow Jupiter's orbit in two groups. Others orbit the Sun alone.

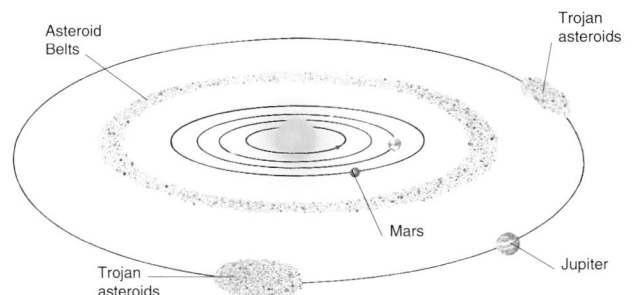

Asteroid Belts

Trojan asteroids

Mars

Jupiter

Trojan asteroids

ASTEROID FACTS

• An estimated 2,000 collisions have occurred between asteroids and Earth in the last 600 million years.

• If an asteroid of average size collided with Earth, it could destroy an entire country.

• In January 1991, an asteroid measuring about 10m (33ft) across passed between the Moon and Earth.

• In the future, asteroids could be mined for metals as resources on Earth grow scarce.

Captain James T. Kirk and Mr. Spock

• Asteroid 2309 is called Mr. Spock, after the character in the television series *Star Trek*.

• Ceres, the largest asteroid, contains a quarter of all the rock in the Asteroid Belts.

LARGEST ASTEROIDS

Name	First seen	Diameter	
		km	miles
Ceres	1801	930	578
Pallas	1802	607	377
Vesta	1807	519	322
Hygeia	1849	450	280
Euphrosyne	1854	370	230
Interamnia	1910	349	217
Davida	1903	322	200
Cybele	1861	308	191
Europa	1858	288	179
Patienta	1899	275	171

ARIZONA CRATER

On Earth, the best example of an asteroid impact crater is the Arizona Crater, USA, which is 1.2km (0.7 miles) in diameter, 180m (590ft) deep, and 50,000 years old.

Walking on the Moon
In order to prepare for their work on the surface of the Moon, the Apollo astronauts trained on the slopes of the Arizona Crater. Dressed in their spacesuits, they tested the Moon buggy and other equipment.

TUNGUSKA EVENT

In June 1908 a huge explosion occurred in the forested Tunguska region of Siberia, devastating an area of 3,900sq km (1,500sq miles). The shock wave was heard 1,000km (600 miles) away. The explosion is now thought to have been caused by an asteroid.

METEORITES

A meteorite is a piece of rock from space that escapes destruction in Earth's atmosphere, and is able to reach the ground. There are three kinds of meteorites stony, iron, and stony-iron.

Stony
Stony meteorites are the most common type. They consist mainly of the minerals olivine and pyroxene.

Iron
Iron meteorites come from small asteroids that broke up in space. They are rarer than stony meteorites.

Stony-iron
Stony iron meteorites contain both rock and metal. The picture shows bright metal enclosing the mineral olivine.

METEORITE RECORDS

OLDEST METEORITES
called carbonaceous chondrites, are 4.55 billion years old.

LARGEST METEORITE
lies at Grootfontein, Namibia. It is called Hoba, is 2.75m (9ft) long, made of iron, and weighs 59 tonnes: as much as eight elephants.

ONLY PERSON INJURED
was Mrs. A. Hodges of Alabama, USA. A 4kg (9lb) meteorite crashed through her roof in November 1954 and injured her arm.

ONLY FATAL METEORITE
killed a dog in Nakhla, Egypt in 1911.

FROM THE HAND OF GOD

The Black Stone of Mecca, housed in a shrine in Saudi Arabia, is the sacred stone of Islam. It is believed to be a meteorite that fell to Earth hundreds of years ago.

DUST COLLECTOR

Rock particles picked up from space add 10,000 tonnes to Earth's weight each year. This would be enough dust to give everyone on Earth two grams (0.07oz) per year.

ASTRONOMY

ASTRONOMY IS THE STUDY of the nature and movement of the heavenly objects in the Universe: planets, moons, comets, asteroids, stars, and galaxies.

335–323 B.C. Aristotle (384–322 B.C.), Greek physicist and philosopher, puts Earth at the centre of the Universe. This central belief dominates until the 15th century.

Aristotle's Universe

A.D. 137–145 Ptolemy (c.120–180), Greek astronomer, records the positions of 1,080 stars and divides them into 48 constellations in his book, *Almagest*. His system uses Aristotle's beliefs as its basis, and stands for 1,400 years.

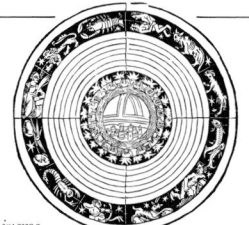
Ptolemy

| 400 B.C. | 335 | 200 B.C. | A.D. | 137 | 200 A.D. |

1543 Nicolas Copernicus (1473–1543), Polish monk, establishes the position of the Sun at the centre of the Universe in his book, *De Revolutionibus Orbium Caelestium*.

Nicolas Copernicus

1596 Tycho Brahe (1546–1601), Danish nobleman, publishes his great star catalogue, compiled from 1575 to 1595. His study fixes accurate positions for about 770 stars.

Tycho Brahe

1608 First telescope is thought to have been invented for military use by Dutch scientist Hans Lippershey (1570–1619).

1609 Elliptical motion of planets is established by German astronomer Johannes Kepler (1571–1630), overturning the theory of circular motion around the Sun.

| 1500 | 1543 | 1596 | 1600 | 1608 | 1609 |

1610 Galileo (1564–1642), Italian scientist and the first systematic user of the telescope, discovers the moons of Jupiter and identifies sunspots and craters on the Moon. He shows that Venus has phases like the Moon, adding support to the idea that the Sun is the centre of the Universe.

Galileo

17th-century telescope

1667 Isaac Newton (1642–1727), English scientist, lays down the laws of gravitation governing celestial bodies, marking the beginning of modern astronomy. In 1668 he invents and builds the first reflecting telescope.

Isaac Newton

1705 Edmund Halley (1658–1742), English astronomer, correctly predicts the return of Halley's comet in 1758.

Edmund Halley

| 1610 | 1667 | 1700 | 1705 |

1781 Uranus is discovered by German-born musician William Herschel (1738–1822). Six years later, he finds four of its moons. He discovers binary stars, catalogues thousands of clusters and nebulae, and reasons the existence of other galaxies.

William Herschel

1846 Neptune is discovered by German astronomers Johann Galle (1812–1910) and Heinrich D'Arrest (1822–1875).

1849 First star photographs are taken at Harvard Observatory, USA.

Deuterium — positron
Hydrogen
proton
neutrino
Helium-3
gamma ray
Helium-4
Fusion of hydrogen nuclei

1907 Albert Einstein (1879–1955), German-born physicist, discovers mass can turn into energy. This leads to the theory of how the Sun shines – by fusing hydrogen atoms to make helium (see p.223).

| 1781 | 1800 | 1846 | 1849 | 1900 | 1907 |

1919 Expanding Universe is suggested by American astronomer Vesto Slipher (1875–1969), who proves that most galaxies are red-shifted.

1924–30 Big Bang theory (see p.18) is independently formulated by Belgian scientist Abbé Lemaitre (1894–1966) and Russian scientist A. Friedmann (1888–1925).

Edwin Hubble

1929 Edwin Hubble (1889–1953), American astronomer, finds strong evidence for an expanding Universe.

1930 Pluto is discovered by American astronomer Clyde Tombaugh (born 1906).

1932 Radio signals from outside Earth are discovered by American engineer Karl Jansky (1905–50). His improvised aerial accidentally picks up radio waves from the Milky Way.

Karl Jansky

| 1919 | 1920 | 1924 | 1929 | 1930 | 1932 | 1950 |

1965 3K cosmic background radiation (believed to be the remains of Big Bang's radiation) is discovered by Americans Arno Penzias (born 1933) and Robert Wilson (born 1936).

1967 First pulsar (CP 1919) is identified by Belfast-born astronomer Jocelyn Bell (born 1943).

Jocelyn Bell

1986 Giotto space probe sends back the first pictures of a comet's nucleus (Halley's comet).

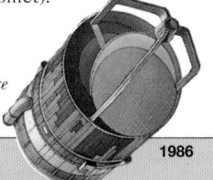
Giotto space probe (Europe)

1990 Hubble Space Telescope is launched, the first large optical telescope to be placed above Earth's atmosphere, where it has the clearest view of the Universe.

2001 Very Large Telescope – the largest telescope in the world – due to be completed.

Cosmic radiation radio antenna at New Jersey, USA.

| 1960 | 1965 | 1967 | 1970 | 1980 | 1986 | 1990 | 2001 |

DEVELOPMENT OF THE OPTICAL TELESCOPE

Early telescopes produced images that were blurred, suffered colour distortions, and showed only a small region of the sky. Better designs have produced more powerful telescopes.

REFRACTING TELESCOPE

The main glass lens focuses the starlight, while the eyepiece, a smaller lens, magnifies the image. It is called a refracting telescope because its main lens bends, or refracts, the light that enters. It can, however, introduce false colours and shows only a small region of the sky.

Refractor sees single bright galaxy.

SCHMIDT CAMERA

Estonian optical worker Bernhard Schmidt (1879–1935) made a telescope with a specially shaped lens at its front. This directs light onto a spherical mirror. The image can then be photographed on a curved plate, providing a much wider view of the sky than is usually possible.

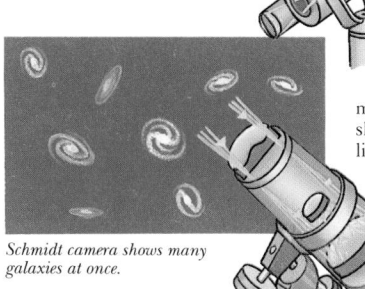

Schmidt camera shows many galaxies at once.

REFLECTING TELESCOPE

A reflecting telescope uses a curved mirror to focus light at the bottom of the tube. A second small mirror directs the light to the side of the tube or behind the main mirror. The largest and most powerful telescopes are reflectors, and they reveal the most distant objects in the Universe.

Reflector shows faint distant galaxies.

ASTRONOMY RECORDS

LOWEST OBSERVATORY

This observatory lies in the Homestake Mine, 1.5km (0.9 miles) below ground level in South Dakota, USA. It detects minute particles from space, called neutrinos, that can pass straight through the Earth. An underground tank containing a special fluid shows when a neutrino passes through.

LARGEST SINGLE RADIO DISH

(305m/1,000ft diameter) is the Arecibo radio telescope. It is built into a natural valley in the hills of Puerto Rico.

OLDEST STANDING OBSERVATORY

is the Chomsung-Dae observatory, Kyongju, South Korea. It was built in A.D. 632.

Sensitive detectors surround the tank.

Lowest observatory

ASTRONOMICAL MEASUREMENT

LIGHT-YEAR

A light-year is the distance travelled by light in one year. It is used as a measurement for vast distances and is equal to 9,461 billion km (5,879 billion miles). The light that we see today from the galaxy IC 4296 left its source 117 million years ago, when dinosaurs roamed Earth.

PARALLAX

A star appears to shift its position against the background of more distant stars if seen from opposite sides of Earth's orbit. An astronomer can thus calculate the distance of a star from Earth from the size of this parallax shift, together with the diameter of Earth's orbit.

Star's image in July

Parallax shift

Star's image in January

The smaller the shift, the further the star.

Earth in January

Sun

Earth in July

RED SHIFT

Starlight can reveal the speed at which a star moves. If the star is moving away from Earth, its light waves are stretched out, shifting its colour towards the red end of the spectrum. Astronomers measure red shifts by looking for dark lines, caused by gas in the star's atmosphere absorbing light of particular colours.

Stationary star
If the star is not moving away from or towards Earth, an observer sees the dark "absorption lines at their true wavelengths.

Retreating star
If the star is moving away from Earth, its light waves are stretched and the absorption lines are red shifted.

MAJOR WORLD OBSERVATORIES

Observatories	Height	
	metres	feet
Keck Observatory, Mauna Kea, Hawaii, USA	4,205	13,796
Hale Observatory, Palomar, California, USA	1,706	5,597
Whipple Observatory, Mt. Hopkins, USA	2,600	8,530
Kitt Peak Observatory, Arizona, USA	2,064	6,672
V.L.A., Socorro, New Mexico, USA	2,124	6,968
Anglo-Australian Telescope, Siding Spring, Australia	1,165	3,822

INSTRUMENTS OF OBSERVATION

Telescopes that observe visible light waves can study only some of the wavelengths that come from space. Telescopes that detect other wavelengths from the electromagnetic spectrum (see p.231), such as radio waves, give astronomers a fuller picture of the Universe.

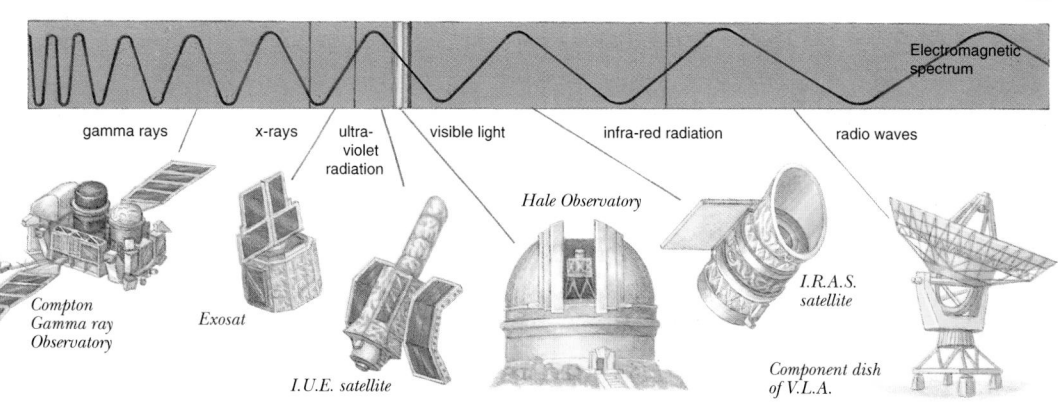

Electromagnetic spectrum

gamma rays   x-rays   ultra-violet radiation   visible light   infra-red radiation   radio waves

Compton Gamma ray Observatory

Exosat

I.U.E. satellite

Hale Observatory

I.R.A.S. satellite

Component dish of V.L.A.

SPACE EXPLORATION

IN OCTOBER 1957, THE USSR put *Sputnik 1* into orbit around the Earth; the great achievements of the Space Age had begun.

c.1200 Chinese use gunpowder rockets in battle, with handheld launching baskets.

1926 Liquid fuel rocket launched by US pioneer Robert Goddard.

1934 Liquid oxygen and alcohol rocket launched by German pioneer rocket scientist Wernher Von Braun (1912–77).

1944 German V2 rocket, designed and built by Von Braun, used against Britain in World War II.

V2 rocket

c.1200	1920	1926	1930	1934

1965 US Mars probe *Mariner 4* finds no water or life on Mars. First spacewalk by Soviet cosmonaut Leonov in *Voskhod 2*. US manned craft *Gemini 6* meets *Gemini 7* in space.

Leonov's spacewalk

1966 USSR's *Luna 9* **probe lands on Moon.** First panoramic photos of Moon surface by US *Lunar Orbiter 1*. US manned craft *Gemini 8* docks with *Agena* rocket stage.

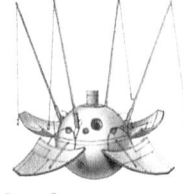

Luna 9

1968 Space observatory launched to study UV rays. Three US astronauts orbit Moon in *Apollo 8*.

1969 First people on Moon. US *Apollo 11* astronauts take rock samples.

Edwin M. Aldrin steps on to Moon's surface.

1965	1966	1968	1969

1974 Images of surface of Mercury sent by US *Mariner 10*.

1975 Images of surface of Venus sent by USSR's *Venera 9*. US and USSR craft, *Apollo 18* and *Soyuz 19*, meet in space.

Venera 9

Surface of Mars

1976 US *Viking 1* **lands on Mars.** Surface tests confirm no life on Mars. Daily weather reports sent until Spring 1983.

1977 US *Voyagers 1* **and** *2* **launched** to outer planets and beyond.

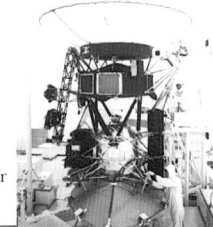

Voyager probe

Mariner 10

1974	1975	1976	1977

1982 Surface of Venus photographed in colour by USSR's *Venera 13*.

Surface of Venus

1984 Manned Manoeuvring Unit used by US astronaut Bruce McCandless to float untethered alongside shuttle *Challenger*. First retrieval and repair of a satellite, *Solar Maximum* satellite, in space. Satellite resumed observations immediately.

Bruce McCandless

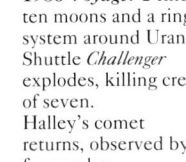

Uranus

1986 *Voyager 2* finds ten moons and a ring system around Uranus. Shuttle *Challenger* explodes, killing crew of seven. Halley's comet returns, observed by four probes.

1982	1984	1986

SPACE FACTS

- Rivalry between the two great powers after World War II, the US and USSR, resulted in the "Space Race". Each side tried to show its superiority in space and rocket technology.

- One third of the world's population watched the *Apollo 11* Moon landing on television.

- More than 300 people in total have travelled into space.

- Everything becomes weightless when spacecraft leave Earth, so untethered objects float in mid-air. Liquid and food is stored in and eaten from sealed bags.

- Some spacesuits may have as many as 15 layers of different materials to protect and insulate.

- Inside a manned spacecraft, air is constantly being removed and purified. In a space station, this process has to continue for months or years at a time.

- The building in which *Saturn V* rockets were assembled was so large that small clouds sometimes formed in its roof.

- Cosmonauts aboard *Salyut 4* were not allowed to return to Earth when their air purifying system broke down, even when mould grew up the walls.

Salyut 4

Undersuit contains pipes for cool, flowing water to protect against Sun's heat.

Suit layers of nylon, dacron and kevlar

ASTRONAUT SUIT

Spacesuits have to be tough to protect the astronaut from small meteorites. Most have internal cooling systems to absorb the Sun's heat, and a dark, mirrored visor to shield the astronaut from the Sun's glare. Spacesuits are very heavy on Earth, but are weightless when in space.

SPACE RECORDS

LONGEST TIME SPENT IN SPACE
was achieved by the Russian cosmonaut Valeri Polyakov, who spent 417 days, 17 hours on the space station *Mir* between January 1994 and March 1995.

FIRST MARRIED COUPLE IN SPACE
were Americans Mark Lee and Judy Davis, on shuttle *Endeavour* in September 1992.

1957 First artificial satellite launched, USSR's *Sputnik 1.* First living creature in space, the dog Laika, in *Sputnik 2.*

1959 Far side of Moon photographed by USSR's *Luna 3.*

Laika in Sputnik 2

1961 First man in space, Soviet cosmonaut Yuri Gagarin (1934–68) in *Vostok 1.*

1962 US *Mariner 2* approaches another planet, Venus.

Yuri Gagarin

1963 First woman in space, Soviet cosmonaut Valentina Tereshkova in *Vostok 6.*

1964 Detailed images of Moon taken by US probe *Ranger 7.*

Valentina Tereshkova

1940 1942 1950 1957 1959 1960 1961 1962 1963 1964

1970 USSR's *Venera 7* is first probe to land on another planet (Venus). Moon samples brought back by automatic probe, USSR's *Luna 16.*

Venus

1971 USSR's *Mars 3* lands on Mars. US *Mariner 9* begins orbiting Mars and sends images of its volcanoes. First orbiting space station launched, USSR's *Salyut 1.*

Mars

1972 Last manned mission to Moon (*Apollo 17*).

1973 First images of Jupiter taken by US *Pioneer 10.* First US manned space station, *Skylab.*

Jupiter

1970 1971 1972 1973

1979 US *Pioneer 11* visits Saturn, six years after launch, finding new ring and moons. *Voyagers 1* and *2* pass Jupiter, finding active volcanoes on one moon, Io, and discovering three new moons, bringing total to 16.

Sulphur volcano on Io

1980–81 *Voyager* probes pass Saturn, take first detailed images of ring systems, and find new moons, bringing total to 18.

Saturn

1981 First reusable craft launched, US space shuttle *Columbia.*

Launch of Columbia

1979 1980 1981

1988 US shuttle launches resume with *Columbia.* Soviet space shuttle, *Buran*, tested.

Voyager 2

1989 *Voyager 2* finds six new moons round Neptune, as well as Triton's nitrogen volcanoes. US COBE (Cosmic Background Explorer) satellite launched to study Big Bang's radiation.

1990 Hubble space telescope launched (with faulty mirror). US *Magellan* probe radar-maps Venus. *LDEF* (Long Duration Exposure Facility) satellite retrieved by space shuttle.

Hubble telescope

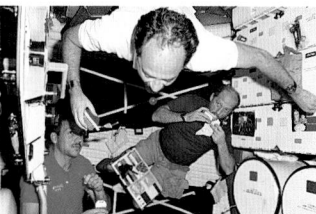

1994 Hubble space telescope mirror fault corrected by space shuttle astronauts.

1998 International Space Station construction is begun by space shuttle astronauts.

COBE satellite

1988 1989 1990 1994 1998

Air treatment system and water for cooling

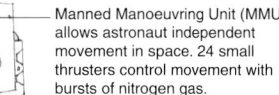

Manned Manoeuvring Unit (MMU) allows astronaut independent movement in space. 24 small thrusters control movement with bursts of nitrogen gas.

Seams and seals must be airtight to withstand the vacuum of space.

WEIGHTLESSNESS

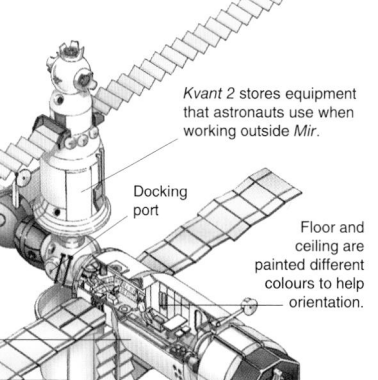

Astronauts in Mir *space station floating in weightless conditions.*

Long periods of weightlessness affect the human body in many ways: muscles weaken and waste away, so astronauts have to exercise regularly; blood and other fluids have no sense of "down", so circulation must be regularly checked; bacteria multiply at four times the normal rate; loss of balance can cause "space sickness".

Kvant 2 stores equipment that astronauts use when working outside *Mir.*

Small rockets on the side of *Mir* adjust its position to keep its orbit constant.

Docking port

Floor and ceiling are painted different colours to help orientation.

Solar panels keep *Mir* supplied with energy.

Main module for living and working, 13m (42.65ft) long

SPACE STATION

A space station enables astronauts to live and work in space for long periods. Scientific experiments in low gravity that are impossible on Earth can be carried out over months or years. Space stations are too large to put into space all at once so are assembled in pieces on separate journeys.

Kristall, a module used for experiments in materials for electronic circuits

Handrail aids astronauts when working outside.

Mir *space station*

ROCKETS

IN ORDER TO ESCAPE Earth's gravity, a rocket must reach 40,000km/h (24,900mph). Rockets burn fuel and liquid oxygen, ignited under pressure.

WHAT A BLAST!

The F1 engine of the *Saturn V* rocket (which carried the astronauts to the Moon) is the most powerful engine ever built. Each of its five nozzles is 3.81m (12.5ft) in diameter and 5.79m (19ft) high, as tall as a giraffe. At launch, each engine burns three tonnes of fuel every second.

Launch escape tower

Apollo Command Module

Apollo Service Module

Apollo Lunar Module (inside protective cover)

Third stage fuel tank (liquid oxygen and liquid hydrogen)

Single stage-3 rocket

Protective cover

Second stage fuel tanks (liquid nitrogen and liquid oxygen)

Five stage-2 engines

Protective cover for engines above

First stage fuel tank (kerosene and liquid oxygen). Burns for 2.5 minutes before being jettisoned.

Stabilizing fin

Giraffe

Saturn V – 110.64m (363ft)

SPACE MISSION FACTS

• Rockets are designed in separate stages, so that when all the fuel from a stage has been used up, that stage drops away, and the next takes over.

• The first 11 US unmanned missions to the Moon were unsuccessful: *Rangers 4* and *6* hit the Moon but failed to transmit any data. The rest missed the Moon, *Ranger 3* overshooting by 59,500km (37,000 miles).

• On 28 January 1986, the US space shuttle *Challenger* exploded 73 seconds after launch. The crew of seven was killed in the world's worst space disaster.

• A hyphen instead of a minus sign keyed into a computer caused *Mariner 1*'s launch vehicle to crash into the Atlantic in 1962.

• Each shuttle launch releases 75 tonnes of hydrogen chloride into the atmosphere, as well as tonnes of pollutant waste from the solid fuel burned during lift-off.

• The Moon's astronauts left behind them the remains of six lunar landers, three moon buggies, and more than 50 tonnes of litter.

JUNK ALERT

One great danger facing astronauts and satellites is fragments of old rockets and satellites. This crater in a space shuttle window was made by a paint fleck travelling at high speed.

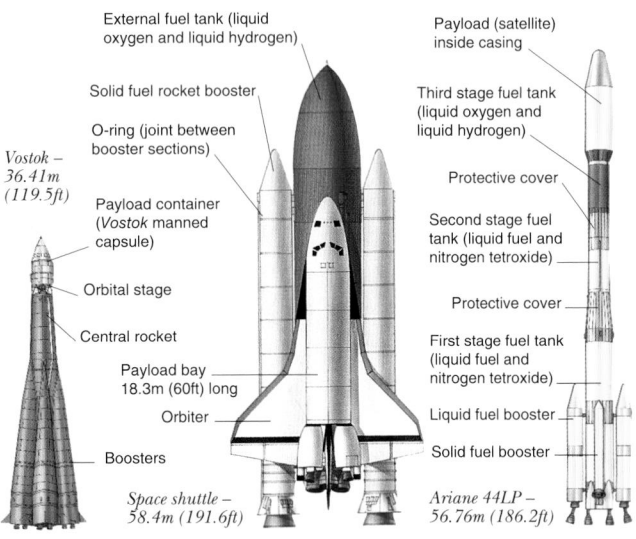

External fuel tank (liquid oxygen and liquid hydrogen)

Solid fuel rocket booster

O-ring (joint between booster sections)

Vostok – 36.41m (119.5ft)

Payload container (*Vostok* manned capsule)

Orbital stage

Central rocket

Payload bay 18.3m (60ft) long

Orbiter

Boosters

Space shuttle – 58.4m (191.6ft)

Payload (satellite) inside casing

Third stage fuel tank (liquid oxygen and liquid hydrogen)

Protective cover

Second stage fuel tank (liquid fuel and nitrogen tetroxide)

Protective cover

First stage fuel tank (liquid fuel and nitrogen tetroxide)

Liquid fuel booster

Solid fuel booster

Ariane 44LP – 56.76m (186.2ft)

Solid fuel booster rockets, designed to be used 10 times, parachute back to Earth, and are later recovered from sea.

Solid fuel rocket boosters jettisoned 2 mins 5 secs after lift-off, at an altitude of 45km (28 miles). Shuttle now travelling at 4.5 times the speed of sound (Mach 4.5).

Shuttle reaches 130km (81 miles) at Mach 15. External tank released; burns up in Earth's atmosphere.

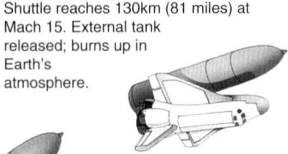

Shuttle engines put orbiter into circular orbit.

Liquid hydrogen from external fuel tank flows into orbiter engines at 3,100 litres/sec (820gal/sec).

Solid fuel (polybutadiene) burns for 2 mins. Each solid fuel rocket produces the thrust of 11 Boeing 747s at take-off.

Rupture in O-rings (joints) of left solid fuel booster caused 1986 *Challenger* shuttle explosion.

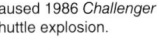

External fuel tank

Orbiter

Solid fuel rocket boosters

Main engines on orbiter take fuel from external tank. Two solid fuel boosters fire for take-off.

SATELLITE REPAIR JOB

In 1984, the shuttle *Challenger* retrieved and repaired the US *Solar Max* solar observatory while in space. One of the satellite's control systems had failed and it was falling towards Earth. The shuttle's robotic arm brought it into the cargo bay, where repairs were made. The satellite was then put back in orbit.

SPACE CENTRES

Launch site	Launches	Type of launch
Pletsetsk cosmodrome, USSR	1,056	Secret military satellites
Baikonur cosmodrome, USSR	693	Manned craft, probes, and satellites
Cape Canaveral (USAF), USA	1,045	Manned craft, probes, and satellites
Kennedy Space Center, USA	66	Apollo missions and space shuttle

FUTURE SHUTTLES

The present generation of US shuttles would be improved if they did not have to shed their huge fuel tanks at various stages after take-off. NASA are currently working on a "reusable launch vehicle" (RLV) that could travel into space and back with a single rocket stage.

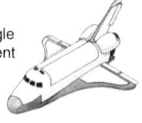

Orbiter remains in orbit for between 5 and 30 days. Mission can be carried out – new satellites put into orbit, old ones mended, experiments performed.

Cargo bay doors close. Engines rotate orbiter into re-entry position.

Orbiter manoeuvres into precise angle for re-entry. Begins 30-minute descent into atmosphere at Mach 22.4.

Parts of nose and wings reach 1,460°C (2,660°F) during re-entry. They are covered with 32,000 carbon or silica insulating tiles, each glued on by hand.

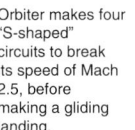
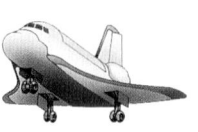

Orbiter makes four "S-shaped" circuits to break its speed of Mach 2.5, before making a gliding landing.

Orbiter lands at a speed of 345km/h (214mph). It is towed, or flown on the back of a Boeing 747 jet, to next launch site.

EARTH

From Earth's formation to the strongest earthquakes and the biggest volcanic eruptions, this section provides every essential fact and figure about our wonderful planet.

Earth • Continents • Volcanoes • Earthquakes • Rocks and Minerals
Ocean Floor • Oceans and Islands • Mountains • Valleys and Caves • Glaciation
Rivers and Lakes • Weather • Climates • Deserts • Forests • Earth's Biosphere
Earth in Danger • Saving the Earth

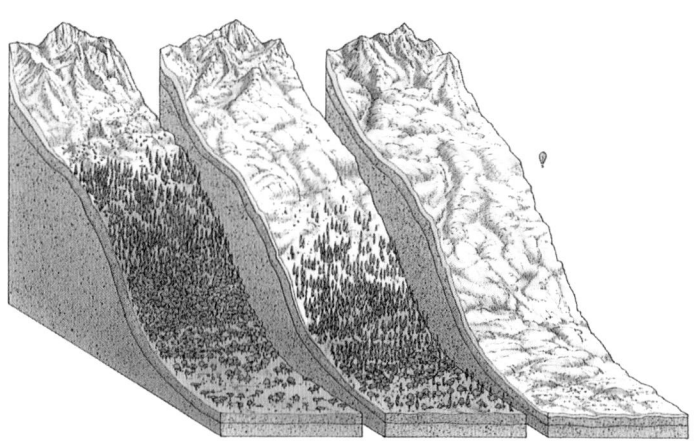

EARTH

THE EARTH IS ONE OF THE NINE planets in the Solar System. It is the fifth largest in size, and is the only planet with plentiful oxygen and water: the necessary ingredients for life.

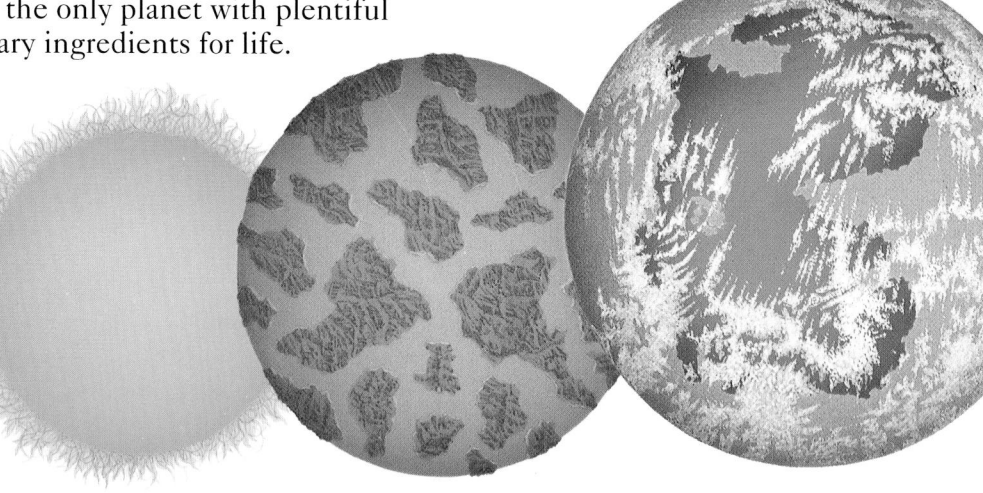

THEORY OF FORMATION

1 About 4.6 billion years ago, a dense cloud of gas and dust contracted to form the Sun. Other matter in the cloud formed solid lumps of ice and rock, and these joined together to form the planets.

2 Radioactivity in the rocks caused the new-born Earth to melt. Iron and nickel sank to form the Earth's core, while oceans of molten rock floated on the surface.

3 About 4 billion years ago, the Earth's crust began to form. At first there may have been many small platelets floating on the molten rock beneath.

4 Over millions of years the crust thickened and volcanoes erupted. Gases pouring out of volcanoes began to form the atmosphere, and water vapour condensed to fill the oceans.

ANATOMY OF THE EARTH

The Earth is made up of several layers of rock around a core of iron and nickel. The deeper the layer, the higher the temperature.

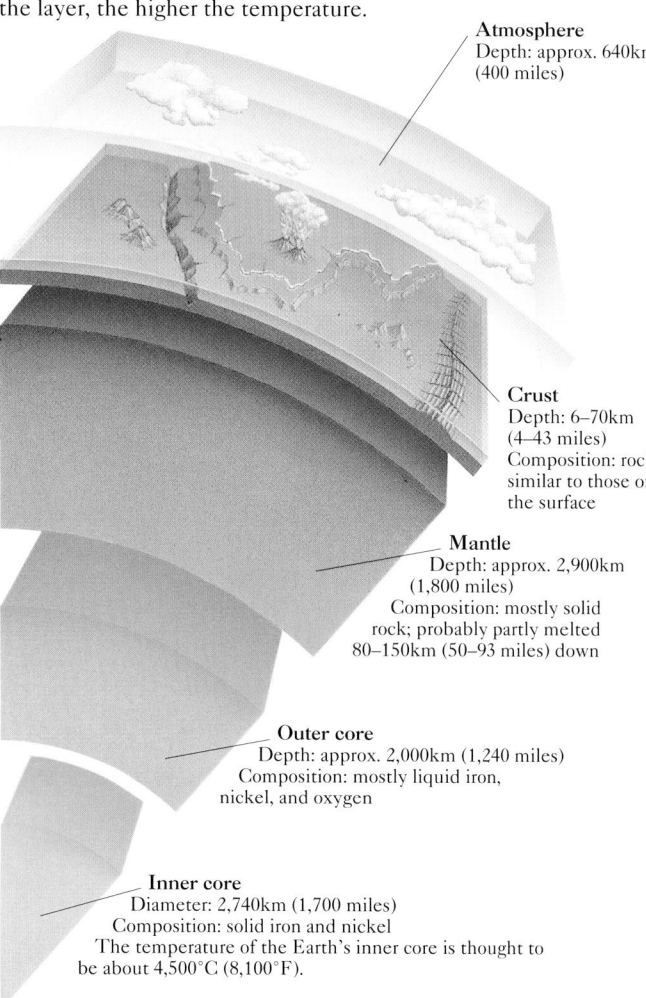

Atmosphere
Depth: approx. 640km
(400 miles)

Crust
Depth: 6–70km
(4–43 miles)
Composition: rocks
similar to those on
the surface

Mantle
Depth: approx. 2,900km
(1,800 miles)
Composition: mostly solid
rock; probably partly melted
80–150km (50–93 miles) down

Outer core
Depth: approx. 2,000km (1,240 miles)
Composition: mostly liquid iron,
nickel, and oxygen

Inner core
Diameter: 2,740km (1,700 miles)
Composition: solid iron and nickel
The temperature of the Earth's inner core is thought to
be about 4,500°C (8,100°F).

DEEPEST DRILLING INTO EARTH'S CRUST

The deepest mine in the world reaches 4.2km (2.6 miles) down into the Earth. A geological exploration has drilled more than 12km (7.5 miles) below the Earth's surface. Yet neither of these is anywhere near as deep as the bottom of the Earth's crust.

Depth (km)

8
6
4
2
Sea level
2
4
6
8
10
12
14
16
18
20
22
24
26
28
30
32
34
36
38
40

Mount Everest:
8.85km (5.5 miles)

Depth
(miles)

Sea level
2
4
6
8
10
12
14
16
18
20
22
24

A deep coal mine

Deepest mine:4.2km (2.6 miles)

Deepest
ocean drilling:
1.7km
(1.05 miles)

Deepest hole (still being drilled):
12.1km (7.4 miles)

Deepest hole projected to reach 15km (9.3 miles)

The Earth's crust is much thicker
beneath land than beneath the ocean.

CRUST

MANTLE

5 About 3.5 billion years ago most of the Earth's crust had formed, but the shapes of the continents looked very different from today. The oldest rocks on Earth date from just before this time.

6 Today the Earth is still changing. The crust has broken into huge plates (see pp.40–41) that are constantly being created and destroyed at their edges. The continents are always on the move, powered by forces deep inside the Earth .

EARTH DATA

Age	4.6 billion years
Mass	5,854 billion billion tonnes
Volume	1,083,218,915,000cu km (259,877,796,843cu miles)
Diameter at Equator	12,756km (7,926 miles)
Diameter at Poles	12,713km (7,899 miles)
Circumference at Equator	40,075km (24,901 miles)
Circumference at Poles	39,942km (24,819 miles)
Distance from the Sun	150 million km (93 million miles)
Time for one spin	23 hours, 56 minutes, 4 seconds
Time to orbit Sun	365 days, 6 hours, 9 minutes, 9.5 seconds

EARTH'S MAGNETIC FIELD

Molten iron flowing in the Earth's outer core generates electric currents. These currents create the Earth's magnetic field. This field – the magnetosphere – stretches more than 60,000km (37,000 miles) into space. Sometimes Earth's magnetic field flips: north becomes south and vice versa. No-one knows why this happens. The last pole reversal occurred about 30,000 years ago.

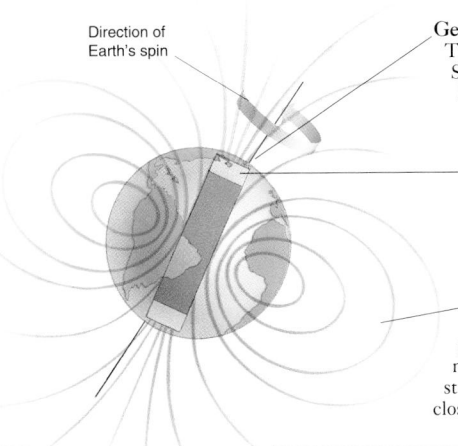

Direction of Earth's spin

Geographical poles
The geographical North and South Poles lie on the Earth's axis (the imaginary line around which the Earth spins).

Magnetic poles
The magnetic north and south poles are a short distance away from geographical north and south.

Pattern of magnetic field
These lines show the pattern of the Earth's magnetic field. The field is strongest where the lines are close together.

EARTH FACTS

• Proportion of land and sea:
Area of land: 29.2%
Area of sea: 70.8%

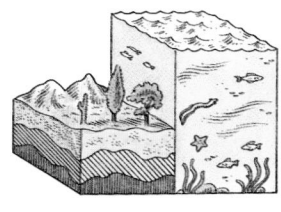

• If a car could travel non-stop around the Equator at 100km/h (62mph), it would take 16 days, 16 hrs, 45 mins. A car driving around Earth from North Pole to South Pole and back would finish 80 mins earlier, because Earth is not a perfect sphere.

• An excavator digging a hole at 1m (39ins) per min through the Earth would take 24 years to reach the other side.

JUST A PIN-PRICK

If the Earth were the size of an egg, the deepest hole ever drilled by humans would not even pierce its shell.

EARTH'S ATMOSPHERE

The atmosphere is the film of gases that surrounds the Earth. It is divided into four main layers – the troposphere, stratosphere, mesosphere, and thermosphere – and its composition is 78% nitrogen, 21% oxygen, and 1% water vapour and other gases. The atmosphere is held in place by gravity. It stops the Earth from becoming too hot or too cold, and shields the planet from the Sun's harmful ultraviolet rays.

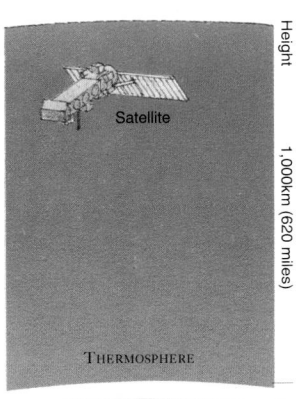

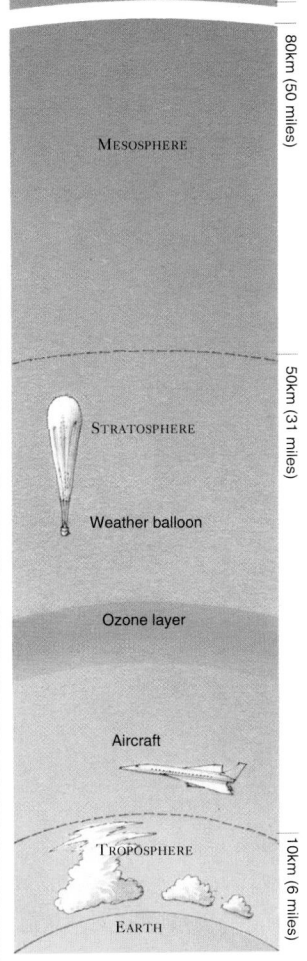

Satellite

THERMOSPHERE

MESOSPHERE

STRATOSPHERE

Weather balloon

Ozone layer

Aircraft

TROPOSPHERE

EARTH

Height

1,000km (620 miles)

80km (50 miles)

50km (31 miles)

10km (6 miles)

CONTINENTS

THE CONTINENTS ARE THE seven huge land masses that make up most of the Earth's land surface. They are always on the move, shifted around by forces deep inside the Earth. The concept of moving continents is known as continental drift.

EARTH'S TECTONIC PLATES
The Earth's crust is fragmented into vast pieces of rock, called tectonic plates. These slabs fit together like a huge jigsaw. Where the plates rise above sea level, they form continents and islands.

The Earth's crust is only 70km (43 miles) thick at its greatest depths.

CONTINENTAL DRIFT

1 Some 250 million years ago the continents were joined together in the giant super-continent of Pangaea (from the Greek word meaning "all lands"). About 200 million years ago Pangaea slowly began to break up.

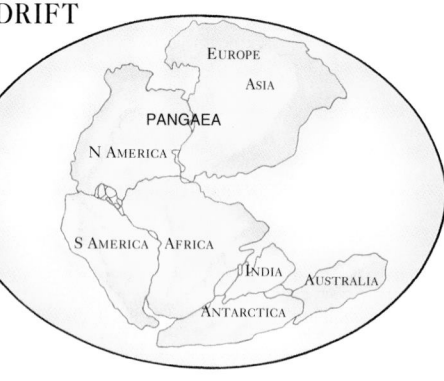

2 By 135 million years ago Pangaea had split into two main land masses, Gondwanaland and Laurasia. North America and Europe split apart, and about 120 million years ago India began to drift north towards Asia.

3 Over the next 120 million years the continents drifted into their present-day positions. The Americas moved away from Europe and Africa; India joined on to Asia; Australia and Antarctica split apart.

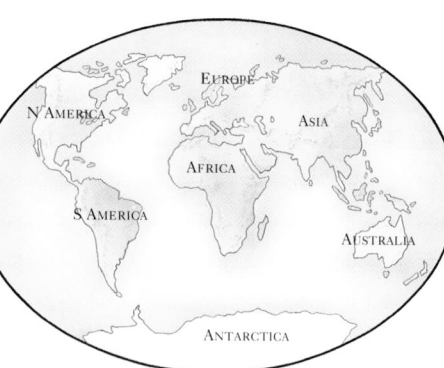

4 This is how the Earth might look 150 million years from now. Africa has split in two, and the larger section has drifted north to join Europe. Antarctica has joined Australia, and California has been crumpled against Alaska.

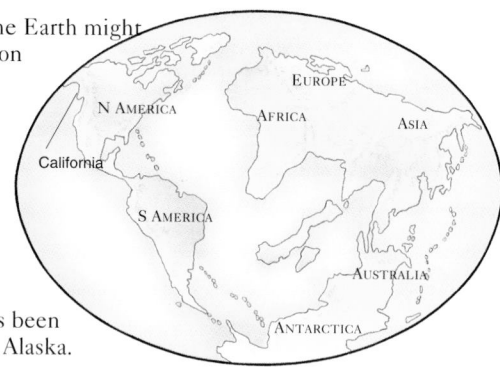

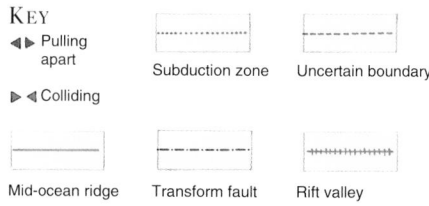

THE PLATES AND THEIR BOUNDARIES
The Earth's crust is made up of about 15 major plates. Plates that form the ocean floor are oceanic plates, and plates that form land are continental plates. Most plates are partly oceanic and partly continental. Scientists can locate the boundaries by monitoring earthquakes and volcanoes.

KEY

◀▶ Pulling apart

▶◀ Colliding

Subduction zone

Uncertain boundary

Mid-ocean ridge

Transform fault

Rift valley

SECTION THROUGH THE EARTH'S CRUST
This illustration shows a cross-section of the Earth's crust at the Equator.

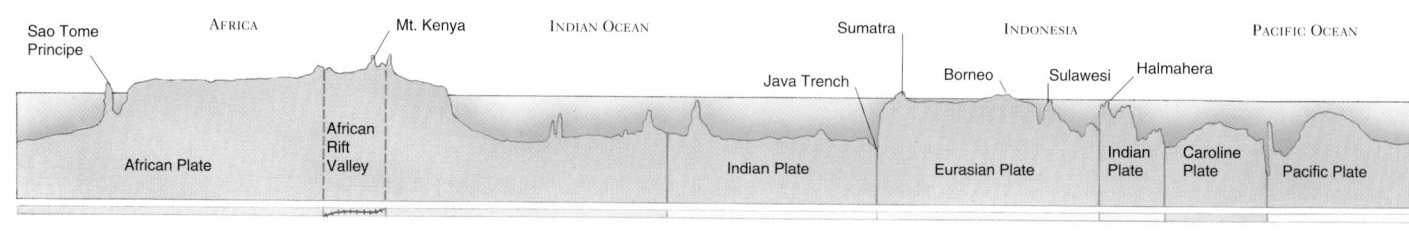

CONTINENT SIZES

Continent	Area	
	sq km	sq miles
Asia	44,485,900	17,176,090
Africa	30,269,680	11,687,180
North America	24,235,280	9,357,290
South America	17,820,770	6,880,630
Antarctica	13,209,000	5,100,020
Europe	10,530,750	4,065,940
Australasia	8,924,100	3,445,610

CONTINENT AND PLATE FACTS

• Europe and Africa would fit into Asia with room to spare.
• Europe and the Americas drift about 4cm (1.6in) further apart every year.
• The African Rift Valley grows about 1mm wider every year.
• Fossils of tropical plants are found as far north as Alaska, because North American land mass was once situated in tropics.
• Continental plates are up to 70km (43 miles) thick, but oceanic plates are only about 5km (3 miles) thick.

PROPORTION OF LAND PER CONTINENT

Asia 30%
Australasia 6%
Europe 7%
Antarctica 9%
South America 12%
North America 16%
Africa 20%

PLATE TECTONICS

Plate tectonics is the theory of how and why the Earth's plates move. At their boundaries, the plates may be colliding, pulling apart, or sliding past each other. These different types of motion build mountains, cause earthquakes and volcanoes, and create deep-sea trenches.

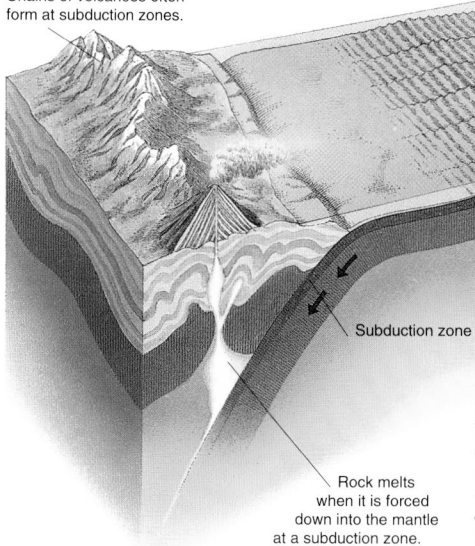

Chains of volcanoes often form at subduction zones.

Subduction zone

Mid-ocean ridge

Convergence

Transform fault

Rock melts when it is forced down into the mantle at a subduction zone.

TRANSFORM FAULT
Transform faults are boundaries where two plates are sliding past each other. Earthquakes often occur at this type of boundary, as the plates slip and judder past each other (see p.44). The San Andreas Fault in California, USA, is a transform fault.

CONVERGENCE
When two continental plates collide, the Earth's crust often buckles and folds as they push against each other, forcing up great mountain ranges. The Himalayas and the Andes were formed by colliding plates.

SUBDUCTION ZONE
When two plates collide, one plate sometimes rides over the other, forcing it down into the mantle. This type of boundary, called a subduction zone, often occurs at the edges of oceans where the thicker continental plate rides over the thinner oceanic plate. Deep ocean trenches form at these boundaries.

PULLING APART
Where two plates are pulling apart, molten rock from the mantle rises to fill the gap, creating new crust. When this type of boundary occurs beneath the sea, ridges of mountains called mid-ocean ridges form. On land, these boundaries create steep-sided rift valleys.

THEORIES OF MOVEMENT

Scientists have not yet identified exactly what makes the Earth's tectonic plates shift around, but there are several theories to explain their movements. The three main theories involve convection, gravity, and the different weights of hot and cold rock.

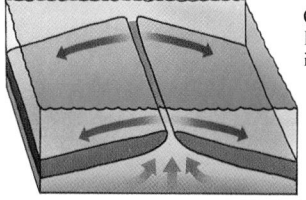

CONVECTION
Heat generated deep inside the Earth creates convection currents in the mantle. These currents slowly push the overlying plates around.

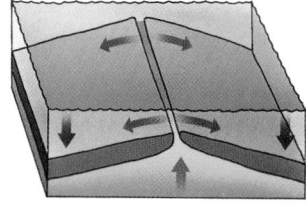

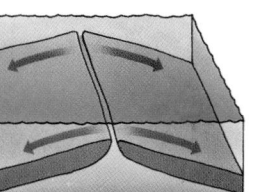

GRAVITY
The plates are about 2–3km (1–2 miles) higher at mid-ocean ridges than at ocean rims, so they could simply be sliding slowly downhill under the force of gravity.

WEIGHT OF ROCK
Hot rock rising at mid-ocean ridges cools down as it moves further away from the ridge. As it cools it becomes heavier and sinks, pulling the rest of the plate down with it.

AS FAST AS A FINGERNAIL GROWS

The tectonic plates move at different rates along their margins, and some plates move faster than others. The average rate of movement is approximately 2.5cm (1 inch) every year: about as fast as a finger-nail grows.

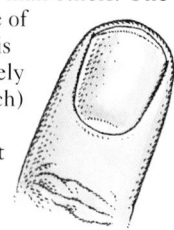

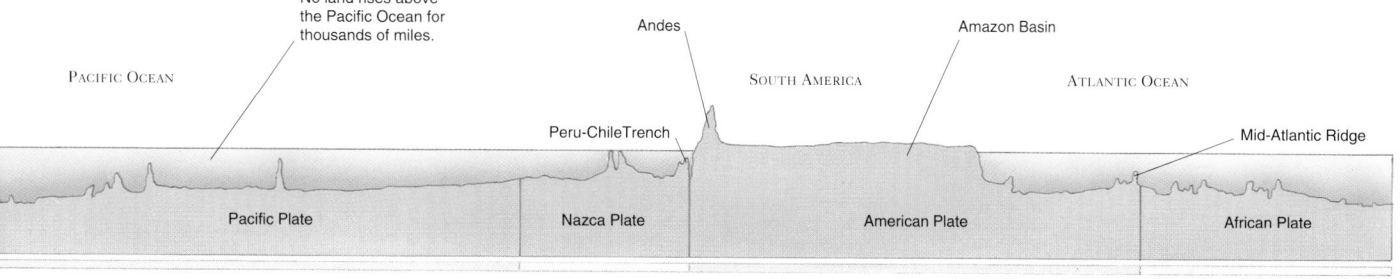

No land rises above the Pacific Ocean for thousands of miles.

Andes

Amazon Basin

PACIFIC OCEAN

SOUTH AMERICA

ATLANTIC OCEAN

Peru-ChileTrench

Mid-Atlantic Ridge

Pacific Plate

Nazca Plate

American Plate

African Plate

VOLCANOES

VOLCANOES OCCUR where magma (molten rock) from deep inside the Earth forces its way to the surface. The magma may erupt as red-hot lava, or may explode into clouds of ash and volcanic bombs. Volcanic activity also produces strange landscapes of gushing geysers, steaming lakes, and bubbling mud pools.

VOLCANIC AREAS

There are around 1,300 active volcanoes in the world, but only 20 or 30 erupt each year. Some of the major volcanoes are marked on this map. Most volcanoes are located on or close to the boundaries of the plates that make up the Earth's crust.

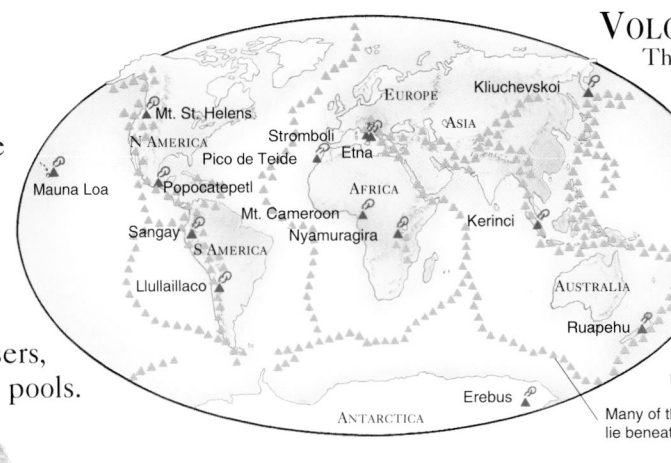

Many of the Earth's volcanoes lie beneath the oceans.

MAJOR ERUPTIONS

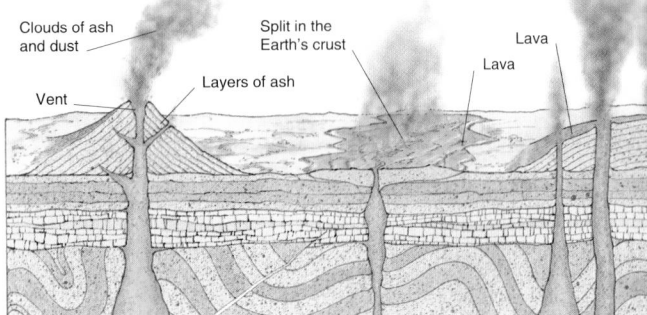

The eruption of Mount St. Helens, Washington, USA

MOUNT ST. HELENS
erupted in May 1980. The explosion was heard more than 350km (217 miles) away. Hot ash and gas rushed down the mountainside; 62 people died.

GREATEST VOLCANIC EXPLOSION
occurred when Krakatoa, Indonesia, blew up in 1883, hurling rocks 55km (34 miles) high. The explosion was heard in Australia, and generated a 40m (131ft) high seismic sea wave (see p.45); 36,000 people died.

GREATEST VOLCANIC ERUPTION
was Tambora on Sumbawa, Indonesia in 1815, which threw up more than 100cu km (24cu miles) of ash. The island was lowered by 1,250m (4,100ft); 92,000 people died.

MAJOR ACTIVE VOLCANOES

The number of volcanoes active in historic times is shown in parentheses after each region.

Name	Height		Latest eruption
	metres	feet	
Africa and Indian Ocean (14)			
Nyamuragira, Zaire	3,053	10,016	1989
Mt. Cameroon, Cameroon	4,070	13,353	1982
Antarctica (9)			
Erebus, Ross Island	3,794	12,448	1989
Asia (210)			
Kliuchevskoi, Siberia	4,850	15,912	1990
Kerinci, Indonesia	3,805	12,484	1970
SW Pacific (54)			
Ruapehu, New Zealand	2,796	9,173	1996
Europe and Middle East (20)			
Etna, Sicily, Italy	3,350	10,991	1992
Stromboli, Italy	926	3,038	1990
North America and Hawaii (56)			
Mount St. Helens, USA	2,549	8,362	1980
Mauna Loa, Hawaii	4,170	13,681	1984
Iceland and Atlantic (54)			
Pico de Teide, Canary Islands	3,713	12,181	1909
Central and South America (100)			
Sangay, Ecuador	5,230	17,159	1989
Popocatepetl, Mexico	5,465	17,930	1943
Llullaillaco, Chile	6,723	22,057	1877

ERUPTION SIZES

The amount of ash thrown out is a good indicator of the size of an eruption.

Mount Vesuvius Italy A.D. 79

Tambora Indonesia 1815

Krakatoa Indonesia 1883

Katmai Alaska 1912

Mount St. Helens Washington, USA 1980

El Chichón Mexico 1982

VOLCANO TYPES AND SHAPES

A volcano's shape depends mainly on the type of lava that comes out of it. Thick, sticky lava forms tall, steep-sided cones; thin, runny lava forms gently sloping lava shields and plateaux.

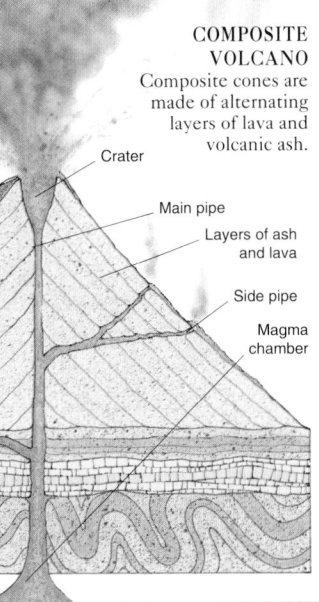

Clouds of ash and dust

Vent

Layers of ash

Split in the Earth's crust

Lava

Lava

Side vent

Lava flow

Volcanic bomb

COMPOSITE VOLCANO
Composite cones are made of alternating layers of lava and volcanic ash.

Crater

Main pipe

Layers of ash and lava

Side pipe

Magma chamber

CINDER VOLCANO
A cinder volcano is made up of layers of volcanic ash, and has a steep, conical shape. Each time the volcano erupts, another layer of ash is added.

FISSURE VOLCANO
Not all volcanoes form over a single hole. Sometimes a crack opens up in the Earth's crust, and runny lava flows out along its length, forming a plateau.

SHIELD VOLCANO
When the lava that erupts from a volcano is runny, it forms a gentle slope rather than a cone. These shield volcanoes often have many side vents.

TYPES OF LAVA

The type of lava flow that erupts from a volcano depends on several factors, such as the amount of gas it contains, and whether it is erupting on to land or into the sea. The two main types of lava flow, aa and pahoehoe, take their names from Hawaiian words.

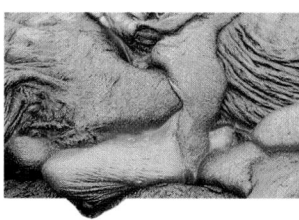

PAHOEHOE LAVA
Pahoehoe lava is runny and fast-moving. When it cools, it resembles coils of rope.

PILLOW LAVA
Lava erupting into the sea cools quickly in the water, forming pillow lava – round lumps of rock.

AA LAVA
Aa lava is thicker and stickier than pahoehoe lava. It cools to form sharp, chunky rock.

TALLEST GEYSER

In 1903, the Waimangu Geyser in New Zealand erupted to a height of about 457m (1,500ft). This is higher than the Sears Tower in Chicago, USA, which is one of the world's tallest buildings. The Waimangu Geyser has not erupted since 1904.

Sears Tower   *Waimangu Geyser*

VOLCANIC PRODUCTS

The solid products of volcanic eruptions and explosions are called pyroclasts. These include cinders, volcanic ash, and large chunks of solidified lava. Cinders and ash may blanket a huge area after an eruption.

VOLCANIC BOMB
Blobs of molten lava erupting high into the air may fall as volcanic bombs.

LAPILLI
These cinder fragments are called lapilli, from the Latin for "little stones".

PUMICE
Pumice forms from lava containing bubbles of gas. It is often so light that it can float on water.

VOLCANIC DUST
Dust thrown high into the atmosphere during an eruption may fall hundreds of kilometres away.

VOLCANIC RECORDS

LARGEST ACTIVE VOLCANO
is Mauna Loa, Hawaii, which has a diameter of 100km (62 miles).

HIGHEST ACTIVE VOLCANO
is Llullaillaco, Chile, which is 6,723m (22,057ft) high.

TALLEST ACTIVE GEYSER
is Steamboat Geyser, Wyoming, USA. It erupts to a height of 60–115m (195–380ft).

VOLCANO PHASES

Most volcanoes have three phases: an active volcano has erupted in recent historic times or is still erupting; a dormant volcano has been quiet for a long time but may erupt again; an extinct volcano has stopped erupting and is not expected to erupt again.

Castle Rock, Edinburgh, Scotland: the remains of an extinct volcano.

LARGEST VOLCANIC EXPLOSIONS

Scientists measure the size of a volcanic explosion according to the Volcanic Explosivity Index (VEI). This grades explosions on a scale of 0 (a non-explosive eruption) to 7 or 8 for the largest eruptions. There have so far been no known eruptions with a VEI of 8.

Volcano and location	Date	VEI
Crater Lake, Oregon, USA	c4895 B.C.	7
Kikai, Ryukyu Island, Japan	c4350 B.C.	7
Santorini (Thira), Greece	c1390 B.C.	6
Taupo, New Zealand	c130	7
Ilopango, El Salvador	c260	6
Oraefajokull, Iceland	1362	6
Long Island, New Guinea	c1660	6
Tambora, Indonesia	1815	7
Krakatoa, Indonesia	1883	6
Santa Maria, Guatemala	1902	6
Katmai (Novarupta), Alaska	1912	6

VOLCANOES ON OTHER PLANETS AND MOONS

Olympus Mons on Mars, which is the highest mountain in the Solar System, is an extinct volcano. The Moon also has extinct volcanoes, and there may be active volcanoes on Venus. Io, one of Jupiter's 16 moons, has active volcanoes that throw out plumes of gases up to 160km (100 miles) high.

Io's volcanoes throw out huge plumes of sulphurous gases.

VOLCANIC LANDSCAPE

Volcanic activity beneath the surface heats up water above and below the ground. This can create spectacular volcanic landscapes, called hydrothermal areas, where hot water, mud, and gases gush, bubble, and steam from vents in the ground.

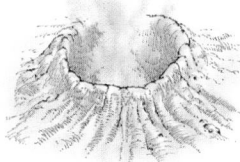

HOT SPRING
A steaming hot spring forms when underground water is heated by warm rocks. As it gets hotter, the water rises to the surface.

BUBBLING MUD POOL
A pool of hot, bubbling mud may form where hot water mixes with mineral particles. Acidic volcanic gases corrode these particles from the surrounding rocks.

FUMAROLE
A fumarole is a vent that releases jets of steam and hot, volcanic gases. These gases often give off a smell of rotten eggs, because they contain sulphur.

GEYSER
A geyser is a tall jet of water that erupts when water trapped in underground chambers is heated to boiling point by hot rocks.

SINTER TERRACE
Minerals deposited by a hot spring as it emerges on to the surface may build up into a beautiful, strangely coloured sinter terrace.

EARTHQUAKES

EARTHQUAKES ARE caused by movements of the massive plates that make up the Earth's crust. Each year scientists detect about 500,000 earthquakes and tremors (small earthquakes). Most are so small that they can hardly be felt, but about 1,000 cause damage. Severe earthquakes can reduce whole cities to rubble.

EARTHQUAKE BELTS

Most earthquakes occur on or near to the edges of the Earth's tectonic plates (see pp.40–41). The ten earthquakes with the highest known death tolls are marked on this map.

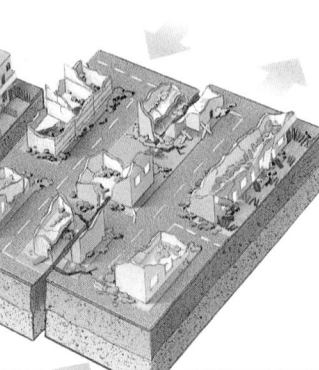

Earthquake belts usually follow the edges of the Earth's tectonic plates.

FOCUS AND EPICENTRE

The exact point at which an earthquake occurs is the focus. The point on the Earth's surface directly above the focus is the epicentre.

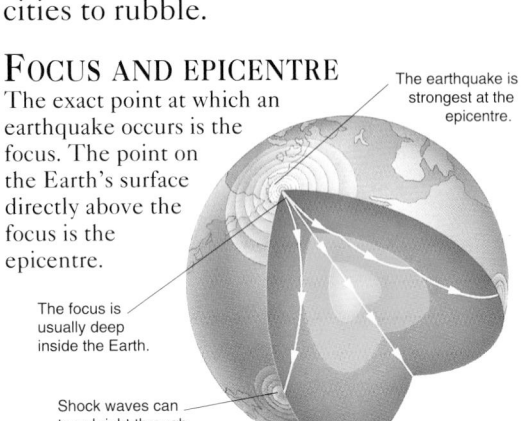

The earthquake is strongest at the epicentre.

The focus is usually deep inside the Earth.

Shock waves can travel right through the Earth to the other side.

CLOSE-UP OF AN EARTHQUAKE

Many earthquakes occur at transform faults (see pp.40–41) where the jagged edges of two moving plates may occasionally lock together. Stress builds up within the plates, until they suddenly slip, making the ground shake violently.

The plates slip and lurch past each other, causing an earthquake.

This fault line marks the boundary of two plates.

MEASURING EARTHQUAKES

The study of earthquakes is called seismology. Scientists measure and record earthquakes using seismometers. The size of an earthquake is measured either according to its magnitude (the size of the shock waves and energy it produces), or according to its effects. Magnitude is usually measured by the Richter scale; effects are graded on the Modified Mercalli Intensity scale.

THE RICHTER SCALE

The Richter scale was devised by American Charles F. Richter in the 1930s.

Charles F. Richter (1900–1985)

Magnitude	Probable effects
1	Detectable only by instruments
2–3	Can just about be felt by people
4–5	Detectable within 32km (20 miles) of the epicentre. Possible slight damage within a small area
6	Fairly destructive
7	A major earthquake
8	A very destructive earthquake

THE MODIFIED MERCALLI INTENSITY SCALE

The Mercalli scale runs from I to XII. It grades earthquakes according to their effects, such as damage to buildings. The original scale was devised by Italian Giuseppe Mercalli (1850–1914) in 1902. It was later updated to create the Modified Mercalli Intensity scale.

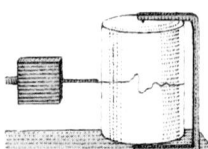

I Not felt by people, but recorded by instruments. Animals may be uneasy. Doors may swing slowly.

II May be felt by a few people indoors, particularly those on upper floors.

III Felt indoors by several as a rapid vibration. Hanging objects may swing slightly.

IV Felt indoors by many, outdoors by a few. Standing cars rock. Dishes and windows rattle.

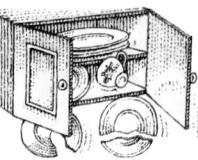

V Felt outdoors by most. Buildings tremble. Small objects are knocked over. Doors swing.

VI Felt by all: people afraid. Trees shake. Small bells ring. Dishes break. Pictures and books fall.

VII General alarm. Hard for people to stand. Chimneys crack. Plaster falls. Windows break.

VIII Difficult to drive. Considerable damage to buildings. Chimneys fall. Tree branches break.

IX General panic. Large cracks appear in the ground. Some buildings collapse.

X Water slops out of rivers. Underground pipes torn apart. Most buildings destroyed.

XI Few buildings remain standing. Bridges collapse. Railway lines buckle. Large landslides.

XII Almost all constructions destroyed. Waves seen on ground. Rivers change course.

EARTHQUAKE SIDE-EFFECTS

Earthquakes on land may flatten cities and towns, cause landslides and avalanches, and start fires. Earthquakes beneath the sea may cause giant waves called seismic sea waves or tsunamis. These can travel many kilometres across the ocean, building into a huge wall of water as they approach the coast.

FIRE
If an earthquake breaks gas mains, the slightest spark can cause huge fires.

LANDSLIDE
An earthquake may cause a huge chunk of mountainside to break away, burying all in its path.

SEISMIC SEA WAVE
A seismic sea wave can cause terrible devastation when it hits the coast.

WORST EARTHQUAKE DAMAGE ON RECORD

The most destructive earthquake happened in Kwanto, Japan in 1923. In nearby Tokyo, where many of the houses were built of wood and paper, the shaking ground overturned stoves, setting the houses on fire. A fire-storm then engulfed the city. Almost 144,000 people were killed, and 575,000 homes were destroyed.

Tokyo was devastated by the 1923 earthquake.

SAN ANDREAS FAULT

At the San Andreas Fault in California, USA, two plates are sliding past each other at a rate of about 5cm (2in) every year. Earthquakes and tremors happen frequently, and are sometimes severe. San Francisco sits on the San Andreas Fault.

San Andreas Fault, California, USA

SEISMIC SEA WAVE (TSUNAMI) RECORDS

HIGHEST SEISMIC SEA WAVE was estimated at 85m (278ft) high: almost as high as New York's Statue of Liberty. It appeared on 24 April 1971 off Ishigaki Island, Japan.

FASTEST SEISMIC SEA WAVES have been recorded travelling at approximately 900km/h (559mph): more than 300km/h (186mph) faster than the world water speed record of 556km/h (345mph), achieved by a hydroplane.

EARTHQUAKE-PROOF BUILDINGS

In earthquake-prone areas, specially designed buildings can lessen the effects of a serious earthquake. For example, a pyramidal or cone-shaped building is less likely to topple over than a building with vertical walls.

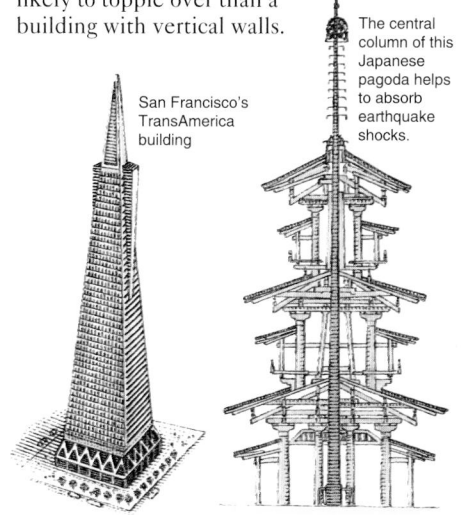

San Francisco's TransAmerica building

The central column of this Japanese pagoda helps to absorb earthquake shocks.

WORST EARTHQUAKE DEATH TOLLS

Location	Date	Estimated deaths
Shansi, China	1556	830,000
Calcutta, India	1737	300,000
Tangshan, China	1976	255,000
Aleppo, Syria	1138	230,000
Damghan, Iran	856	200,000
Gansu, China	1920	200,000
Nr. Xining, China	1927	200,000
Ardabil, Iran	893	150,000
Kwanto, Japan	1923	144,000
Messina, Italy	1908	70–100,000

STRONGEST KNOWN EARTHQUAKES

Location	Date	Magnitude Richter scale
Colombia	1906	8.9
Morioka, Japan	1933	8.9
Lisbon, Portugal	1755	8.75
Assam, India	1897	8.7

EARTHQUAKE FACTS

- Most earthquakes last less than a minute.
- Longest recorded earthquake lasted four minutes. Occurred on 27 March 1964 in Alaska, USA. It was one of the strongest known earthquakes, but killed only 115 people due to low population density.
- First instrument for recording earthquakes was the seismoscope, invented in China in A.D. 132.

- Earthquake shock waves travel through rock at approx. 25,000km/h (16,000mph): more than 20 times the speed of sound. They slow down in sand and mud.
- Some scientists believe animals can sense an earthquake's approach. Strange behaviour includes: dogs howling; chickens fleeing roosts; rats and mice leaving holes; fish thrashing about in ponds.

MOONQUAKES

Most moonquakes are caused by meteorites smashing into the Moon's surface. Moonquakes are monitored by seismometers left by American astronauts.

Seismometers on the Moon

ROCKS AND MINERALS

AT ANY POINT ON THE EARTH'S SURFACE, if you dig down far enough, you will come to rock. Rocks are the building blocks of the Earth's crust. There are many different types of rock, and they are all composed of one or more minerals.

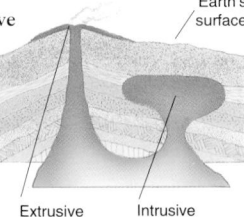

Limestone is a sedimentary rock (see below). About 75% of land is covered with sedimentary rocks.

ROCKS

The study of rocks is called geology. All types of rock fall into one of three categories: igneous, sedimentary, or metamorphic.

IGNEOUS ROCK

Igneous rock starts off deep within the Earth as magma (molten rock). The magma rises towards the surface where it may erupt from a volcano, or cool and solidify within the Earth's crust.

Basalt is an igneous rock.

Extrusive and intrusive igneous rock

Igneous rock that erupts from a volcano on to the Earth's surface is extrusive. Igneous rock that solidifies before it reaches the surface is intrusive.

Earth's surface

Extrusive igneous rock

Intrusive igneous rock

The Giant's Causeway in Northern Ireland is formed from basalt, an extrusive igneous rock.

Granite mountains in Yosemite, USA. These intrusive igneous rocks have been exposed by the erosion of overlying rocks.

SEDIMENTARY ROCK

Rocks are weathered into fragments that are carried away by water, wind, and ice. These sediments are laid down in lakes, rivers, sand dunes, and on the sea floor. Over millions of years they are compressed, forming layers of sedimentary rocks.

Sandstone is a sedimentary rock.

Ayers Rock (Uluru) in central Australia is composed of sandstone.

METAMORPHIC ROCK

Metamorphic rock is igneous or sedimentary rock that has been changed by heat and/or pressure. Heat may come from rising magma, and pressure may occur when rock is squeezed during mountain building.

Gneiss is a metamorphic rock.

This landscape in northwest Scotland is formed from gneiss.

GEOLOGICAL TIME CHART

Rocks are dated according to a geological timescale that divides the Earth's history into eras, periods, and epochs.

Era	Period	Million years ago
Cenozoic	Quaternary	
	Holocene (epoch)	0.01
	Pleistocene (epoch)	2
	Tertiary	
	Pliocene (epoch)	5
	Miocene (epoch)	25
	Oligocene (epoch)	38
	Eocene (epoch)	55
	Palaeocene (epoch)	65
Mesozoic	Cretaceous	144
	Jurassic	213
	Triassic	248
Paleozoic	Permian	286
	Carboniferous	360
	Devonian	408
	Silurian	438
	Ordovician	505
	Cambrian	590
	Precambrian (about 7 times longer than all the other periods combined)	4,600 (origin of Earth)

THE ROCK CYCLE

All rocks are constantly passing through a recycling process.

Igneous rocks are weathered away and washed into the ocean.

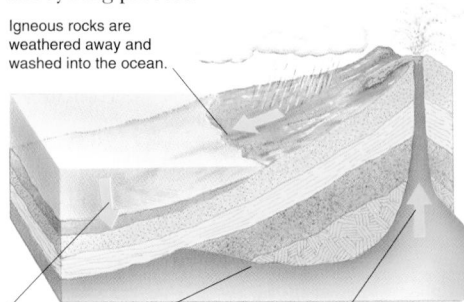

Mineral particles sink to the sea floor where they are compacted into sedimentary rock.

Heat from molten rock changes surrounding sedimentary and igneous rock into metamorphic rock.

Rock may melt and rise to the surface where it cools to form igneous rock.

MINERALS

A mineral is a natural, non-living substance. Examples include gold, silver, gypsum, quartz, and sulphur.

ROCK-FORMING MINERALS

Different combinations of minerals form different types of rock.

Granite is composed of the minerals quartz, feldspar, and mica.

Quartz

Feldspar

Mica

ORE MINERALS

Ore minerals contain metals, and about 80 types of pure metal are extracted from them.

Titanium

A light, strong metal used in aircraft manufacture.

Rutile – titanium ore

Jet airliner

Aluminium

Used in construction, and the manufacture of consumer goods, such as saucepans.

Bauxite – aluminium ore

Aluminium can

Lead

The softest common metal, used in batteries and engineering.

Galena – lead ore

Battery

Iron

Used in construction, and in the manufacture of steel.

Hematite – iron ore

Stainless steel fork

Copper

A good conductor, widely used in the electricity industry.

Chalcopyrite – copper ore

Copper pipe

Mercury

Used in scientific instruments, and in the manufacture of drugs and pesticides.

Cinnabar – mercury ore

Mercury thermometer

CRYSTALS

Crystals grow from molten minerals, or minerals that are dissolved in liquids, such as water. Of the Earth's rocks and minerals, 85% are formed from crystals.

Rock crystal – one form of quartz

Azurite forms in regions of copper deposits.

Sulphur forms bright yellow crystals.

Pyrite has a metallic lustre.

Quartz
Hardness: 7
System: hexagonal/trigonal
One of the commonest minerals. Most popular material for crystal balls.

Azurite
Hardness: 3.5
System: monoclinic
Bright blue mineral once used as a pigment (colouring).

Sulphur
Hardness: 1.5–2.5
System: orthorhombic
Forms around volcano craters. Referred to in the Bible as "brimstone".

Pyrite
Hardness: 6.5
System: cubic
Sometimes mistaken for gold, hence its popular name "fool's gold".

MINERAL HARDNESS

The hardness of a mineral is graded on a scale of 1 to 10, devised by German mineralogist Friedrich Mohs (1773–1839).

CRYSTAL SYSTEMS

The geometrical shape in which a mineral crystallizes is called its crystal system. There are six main systems.

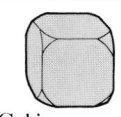 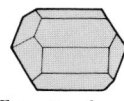 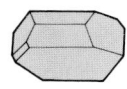 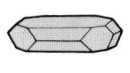 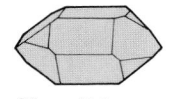 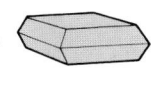

Cubic
Examples: diamond, galena, garnet

Tetragonal
Examples: zircon, rutile, vesuvianite

Hexagonal/trigonal
Examples: corundum, beryl

Orthorhombic
Examples: sulphur, olivine, topaz

Monoclinic
Examples: malachite, gypsum

Triclinic
Examples: rhodonite, kyanite, turquoise

MOHS' SCALE

1: Talc

2: Gypsum

3: Calcite

4: Fluorite

5: Apatite

6: Orthoclase

7: Quartz

8: Topaz

9: Corundum

10: Diamond

GEMSTONES

Gemstones are minerals valued for their beauty, rarity, and durability. There are about 100 types of gemstone. The most valuable include diamonds, emeralds, rubies, and sapphires.

Diamond

Ruby

Emerald

Diamond
Hardness: 10
System: cubic
Sources include: Russia, S. Africa, Australia, Brazil

Ruby
Hardness: 9
System: trigonal
Sources include: India, Thailand, Burma, Sri Lanka

Emerald
Hardness: 7–8
System: hexagonal
Sources include: Russia, USA, Zambia, Colombia

ORGANIC GEMSTONES

Organic gemstones are those that have a plant or animal origin. They include pearls, shell, jet, and amber.

Amber is the fossilized resin of trees.

BIRTHSTONES

Some gemstones are associated with different months of the year. The custom of wearing birthstones became popular in the 18th century.

January Garnet
February Amethyst
March Aquamarine
April Diamond
May Emerald
June Pearl
July Ruby
August Peridot
September Sapphire
October Opal
November Topaz
December Turquoise

GIANT GEMS

The largest diamond was the Cullinan, found in South Africa in 1905. It weighed the same as a pineapple.

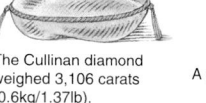

The Cullinan diamond weighed 3,106 carats (0.6kg/1.37lb).

A pineapple

The largest pearl is the Pearl of Lao-tze, found in the Philippines in 1934 in the shell of a giant clam. It weighs about the same as a four-month-old baby.

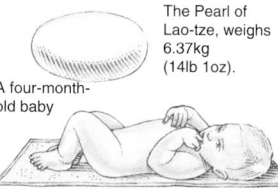

The Pearl of Lao-tze, weighs 6.37kg (14lb 1oz).

A four-month-old baby

MINERAL STRUCTURE

A mineral's hardness depends on the arrangement of its atoms. Diamond and graphite are different forms of the same element – carbon – but their hardness varies because of their different internal structures.

Diamond
Diamonds are the hardest of all minerals. Each atom is strongly bonded to four others, forming a compact, rigid structure.

Diamond ring

Arrangement of diamond atoms

Graphite
In graphite, the atoms are arranged in layers that easily slip over each other. This gives graphite its weak structure.

Graphite is used in pencil lead.

Arrangement of graphite atoms

CARATS AND BEANS

The weight of a gemstone is measured in carats: one carat = 0.2g (0.007oz). The term carat comes from the Greek word for carob seed. These seeds were once used as weights.

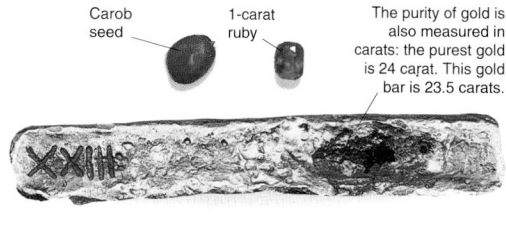

Carob seed

1-carat ruby

The purity of gold is also measured in carats: the purest gold is 24 carats. This gold bar is 23.5 carats.

ROCK AND MINERAL FACTS

• More than half the gold mined returns to Earth: it is buried in bank vaults.

• The word crystal comes from the Greek *kyros*, meaning icy cold. It was once thought that rock crystal was ice that had frozen so hard it would never thaw.

• About one in every thousand oysters and one in every three thousand mussels contains a pearl.

OCEAN FLOOR

THE OCEAN FLOOR IS the largest landscape on Earth. Beneath the oceans are mountains as high as the Himalayas, rugged mountain ranges longer than any on land, vast plains, deep canyons, and trenches plunging thousands of metres into the Earth's crust. Most of this fascinating landscape is still unexplored.

SMOKERS

Smokers are tall, chimney-like vents on the ocean floor that belch out clouds of super-heated water. They occur at volcanically active spots on mid-ocean ridges.

Heated water erupts in tall jets.

Temperature of heated water may be up to 350°C (662°F).

"Chimneys" up to 50m (164ft) high build up from minerals deposited by the hot water.

Smokers were discovered in 1977 by the American submersible "Alvin".

Heated water rises back to the surface of the ocean floor.

Clams

Tube worms

Life around smokers
Smokers support strange life forms that derive energy not from the Sun, like other life forms on Earth, but from volcanic activity.

Water seeps deep down into the sea floor where it is heated by volcanic activity.

MAJOR RIDGES AND TRENCHES

The major features of the ocean floor form at the boundaries of the plates that make up the Earth's crust (see pp.40–41). Mid-ocean ridges form where two plates are pulling apart, and trenches form at subduction zones, where one plate is plunging beneath another.

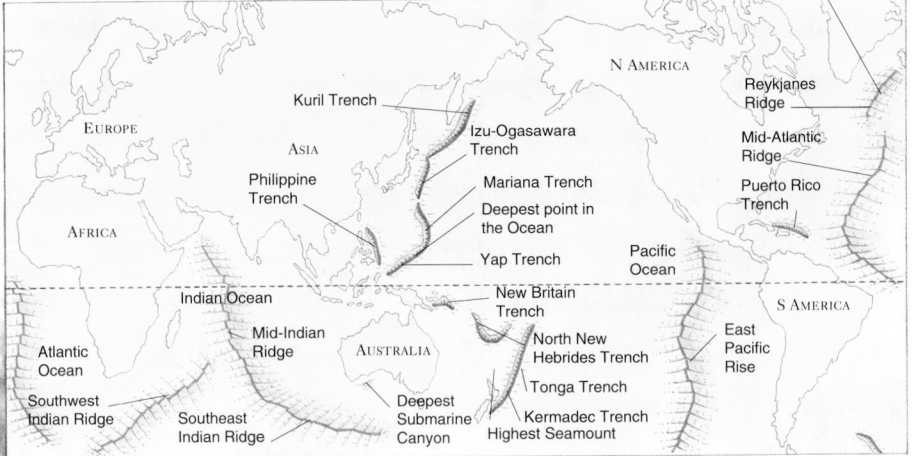

Vast undersea mountain ranges form where two tectonic plates are pulling apart.

N AMERICA
Reykjanes Ridge
Mid-Atlantic Ridge
Puerto Rico Trench

Kuril Trench
Izu-Ogasawara Trench
Mariana Trench
Deepest point in the Ocean
Yap Trench
Pacific Ocean

EUROPE
ASIA
Philippine Trench

AFRICA

Indian Ocean
New Britain Trench
S AMERICA

Mid-Indian Ridge
AUSTRALIA
North New Hebrides Trench
East Pacific Rise

Atlantic Ocean
Southwest Indian Ridge
Southeast Indian Ridge
Deepest Submarine Canyon
Tonga Trench
Kermadec Trench
Highest Seamount

DEEPEST TRENCHES
The depth of deep-sea trenches is measured from sea level.

Trench	Ocean	Depth metres	Depth feet
Mariana Trench	West Pacific	10,920	35,827
Tonga Trench	South Pacific	10,800	35,433
Philippine Trench	West Pacific	10,057	32,995
Kermadec Trench	South Pacific	10,047	32,963
Izu-Ogasawara Trench	West Pacific	9,780	32,087
Kuril Trench	West Pacific	9,550	31,332
North New Hebrides Trench	South Pacific	9,175	30,102
New Britain Trench	South Pacific	8,940	29,331
Puerto Rico Trench	West Atlantic	8,605	28,232
Yap Trench	West Pacific	8,527	27,976

FEATURES OF THE OCEAN FLOOR

The ocean floor is where the Earth's crust is created and destroyed. Volcanic activity associated with mid-ocean ridges and subduction zones (see pp.40–41) creates many ocean floor features.

SUBMARINE CANYON
A river flowing off the land into the sea may carve a deep canyon in the ocean floor.

ABYSSAL PLAIN
About 3,500–5,500m (11,480–18,040ft) below sea level is a vast plain covered with deep sediment, called the abyssal plain.

SEAMOUNT
A seamount is an underwater volcano that rises 1,000m (3,280ft) or more above the surrounding plain.

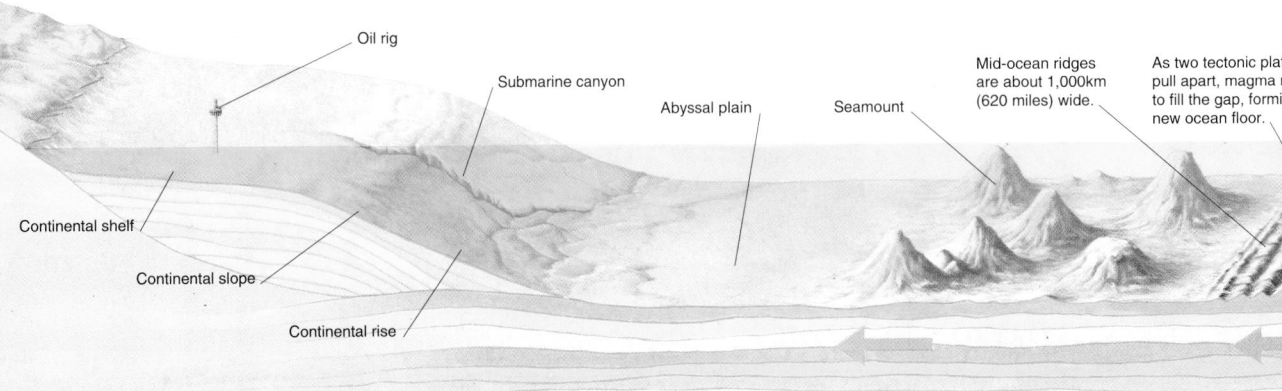

Oil rig

Submarine canyon

Abyssal plain

Seamount

Mid-ocean ridges are about 1,000km (620 miles) wide.

As two tectonic plates pull apart, magma rises to fill the gap, forming new ocean floor.

Continental shelf

Continental slope

Continental rise

CONTINENTAL SHELF
The continental shelf is the gently sloping rim of a continent.

CONTINENTAL SLOPE
The continental slope descends steeply from the continental shelf to the abyssal plain.

CONTINENTAL RISE
Below the steep continental slope, sediment may collect to form a gentler slope: the continental rise.

MID-OCEAN RIDGE
A long, undersea mountain range runs along the mid-ocean ridge, where two tectonic plates are pulling apart.

OCEAN FLOOR SEDIMENT

Close to the coast, sediment consists mainly of mud, sand, and silt washed off the land by rivers. The deep ocean floor is blanketed with ooze (the remains of dead marine plants and animals). The amount of sediment and ooze can help scientists to calculate the age of the ocean floor.

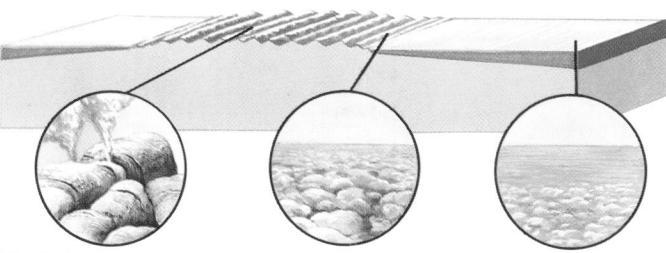

Newly formed rock
At the mid-ocean ridge, the new volcanic rock of the ocean floor is almost free of sediment.

5 million years later
The rock has moved 500km (311 miles) from the ridge. Sediment has started to gather in hollows.

10 million years later
The rock has moved 1,000km (621 miles) from the ridge. It is covered with a thick blanket of sediment.

MAPPING THE OCEAN FLOOR

Early explorations of the ocean floor were made from ships using a lead weight and line to estimate depth. Scientists today use echo-sounding techniques, and special submarines – submersibles – that can descend to the very depths of the ocean.

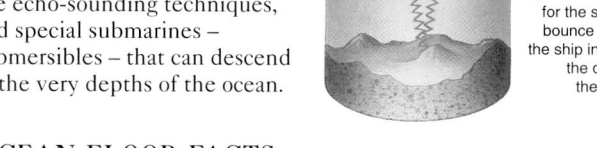

The ship sends down a signal from its transmitter.

The time taken for the signal to bounce back to the ship indicates the depth of the ocean.

OCEAN FLOOR FACTS

• A particle of ooze sinks 0.3–3m (1–10ft) per day. At this rate, it would take 25 years for the remains of a dead shrimp to sink from the ocean surface to the floor of a deep-sea trench.

• The tube worm *Alvinella pompejana* can live on smoker walls where the temperature is 105°C (221°F) – higher than any land animal can tolerate.

• The Mariana trench could hold 28 Empire State Buildings standing on top of each other.

• Oldest parts of the ocean floor are about 200 million years old. Oldest rocks on land are about 3.5 billion years old.

• At a growth rate of about 2mm (0.08in) every million years, it takes 10 million years for a manganese nodule to reach the size of a grape.

FOUND ON THE OCEAN FLOOR

Many useful products are found on or under the ocean floor. They include diamonds, oil, gas, coal, sand, and metals from manganese nodules (potato-like lumps of minerals).

DIAMONDS
These are found in shallow waters off the coasts of Africa and Indonesia.

SAND, GRAVEL, AND LIMESTONE
These are found in coastal waters.

COAL
Coal is mined beneath the sea as well as on land.

OIL AND GAS
About 20% of oil comes from the ocean floor. Natural gas is found with oil deposits.

FORMATION OF OIL AND GAS

Under certain conditions, oil and gas form from the remains of dead plants and animals that accumulate on the floor of shallow seas.

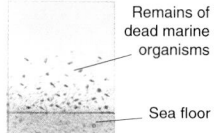

Remains of dead marine organisms

Sea floor

1 Dead plant and animal remains sink down to the floor of the continental shelf. Bacteria break the remains down into organic material.

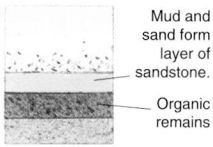

Mud and sand form layer of sandstone.

Organic remains

2 Sediments of sand and mud washed off the land by rivers form layers of sandstone, covering the organic remains.

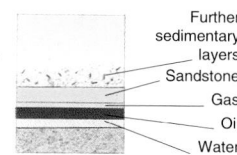

Further sedimentary layers
Sandstone
Gas
Oil
Water

3 Increased pressure from further layers of sandstone and other sedimentary rock turns the organic remains into oil and gas.

HIGHEST SEAMOUNT AND DEEPEST SUBMARINE CANYON

The highest seamount is near the Tonga Trench between Samoa and New Zealand. The deepest submarine canyon is 40km (25 miles) south of Esperance, Australia.

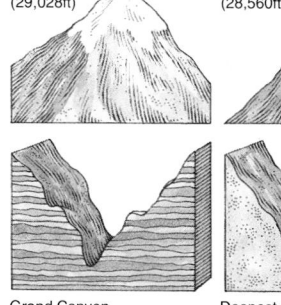

On land
Mt. Everest
8,848m (29,028ft)

Beneath the sea
Highest seamount
8,705m (28,560ft)

Grand Canyon
1,676m (5,499ft)

Deepest submarine canyon 1,800m (5,906ft)

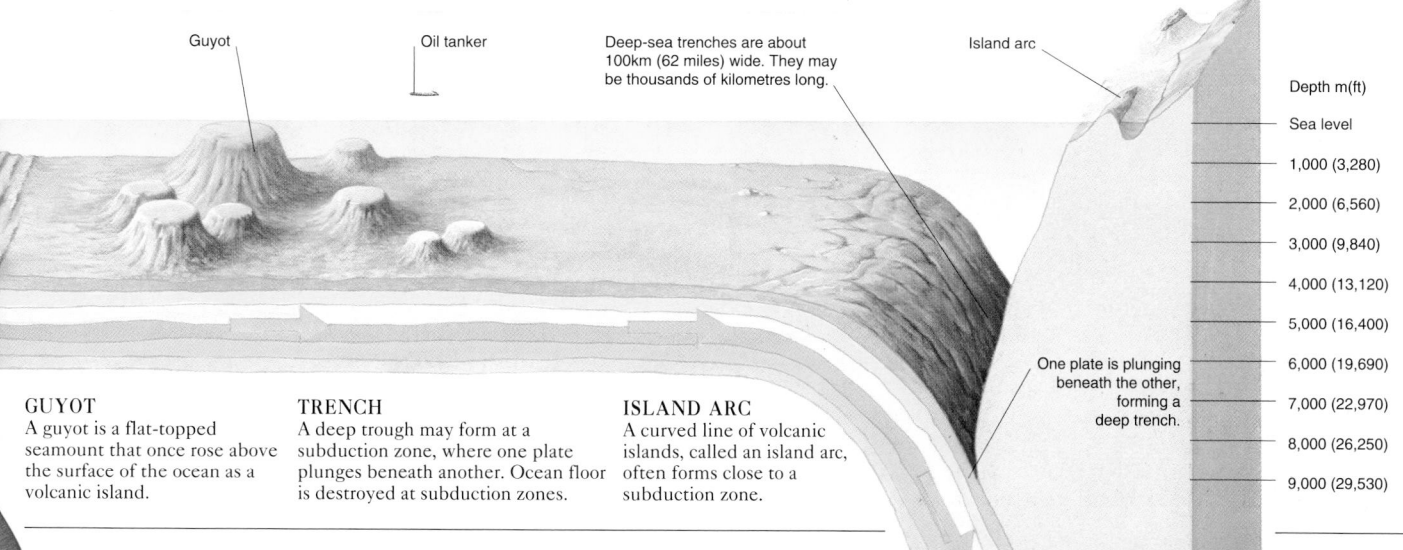

Guyot

Oil tanker

Deep-sea trenches are about 100km (62 miles) wide. They may be thousands of kilometres long.

Island arc

Depth m(ft)
Sea level
1,000 (3,280)
2,000 (6,560)
3,000 (9,840)
4,000 (13,120)
5,000 (16,400)
6,000 (19,690)
7,000 (22,970)
8,000 (26,250)
9,000 (29,530)

One plate is plunging beneath the other, forming a deep trench.

GUYOT
A guyot is a flat-topped seamount that once rose above the surface of the ocean as a volcanic island.

TRENCH
A deep trough may form at a subduction zone, where one plate plunges beneath another. Ocean floor is destroyed at subduction zones.

ISLAND ARC
A curved line of volcanic islands, called an island arc, often forms close to a subduction zone.

OCEANS AND ISLANDS

MORE THAN TWO-THIRDS of the Earth's surface lies beneath the oceans. Where the land rises above sea level it forms continents and islands. An island is a piece of land, smaller than a continent, that is surrounded by water.

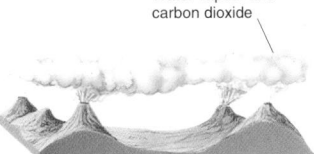

Baffin Island
Victoria Island
Ellesmere Island
Arctic Ocean
Greenland
Gulf Stream
N AMERICA
EUROPE
ASIA
Honshu
Pacific Ocean
AFRICA
Sumatra
Borneo
New Guinea
Pacific Ocean
S AMERICA
Indian Ocean
AUSTRALIA
Atlantic Ocean
Madagascar
ANTARCTICA
Great Britain

MAJOR OCEANS, ISLANDS, AND CURRENTS

This map shows the location of the world's principal oceans, islands, and ocean currents. Currents are caused by the wind, by the spin of the Earth, and by colder water sinking under warmer.

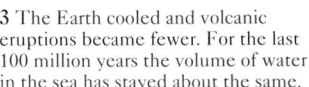

warm current   cold current

FORMATION OF THE OCEANS

The oceans began to form many millions of years ago when the Earth was still cooling and solidifying following its early molten (liquid) state. Water vapour was thrown into the atmosphere by volcanoes.

Water vapour and carbon dioxide

1 As the young Earth cooled, volcanoes erupted, throwing out a mixture of gases that formed the early atmosphere.

2 When the atmosphere was saturated with water vapour, the vapour condensed, falling as rain. Rainwater began to collect in vast hollows.

3 The Earth cooled and volcanic eruptions became fewer. For the last 100 million years the volume of water in the sea has stayed about the same.

WAVE SEQUENCE

Most waves are caused by wind blowing across the surface of the sea. The height and power of waves depends on the speed of the wind and how far it has blown.

The water in a wave appears to be moving forwards, but in fact it moves in a circle.

The base of the wave is held back by the shore. The crest of the wave moves faster, toppling over when it reaches land.

Water reaches the base of the circle in the trough of a wave.

Water reaches the top of the circle at the crest of the wave.

OCEAN DATA

Total surface area	362 million sq km (139.8 million sq miles)
Total volume	1.35 billion cu km (324 million cu miles)
Mean (average) depth	3.5km (2.2 miles)
Weight of water	1.32×10^{18} tonnes
% of Earth's water	94%
Temperature range	-1.9°C to 36°C (28°F to 97°F)
Freezing temp. of sea water	-1.9°C (28°F)
Deepest known point	10,920m (35,827ft)

FORCE OF THE WAVES

When waves break on the shore, they exert a tremendous force. The weight of the sea hitting land can create pressures of more than 25 tonnes per square metre. This is 30 times as great as the pressure exerted on land by a human foot.

OCEAN FACTS

• More than 60% of the Earth's surface is covered by water deeper than 1.6km (1 mile).

• Average depth of Pacific Ocean: 3.94km (2.4 miles); average depth of Atlantic Ocean: 3.57km (2.2 miles).

• There is more gold dissolved in seawater than there is on land. The concentration is 0.000004 parts per million.

• The Gulf Stream ocean current contains about 100 times as much water as the combined volume of all the rivers in the world.

The Pacific Ocean covers more than a third of the Earth.

WHIRLPOOLS

Whirlpools are caused by a clash of tidal flows in places where the sea floor is uneven. Currents rush towards each other, and, if they hit a rocky shelf on the sea floor, water surges upwards, turning the surface into a seething mass.

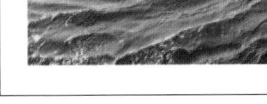

OCEAN AND SEA AREAS

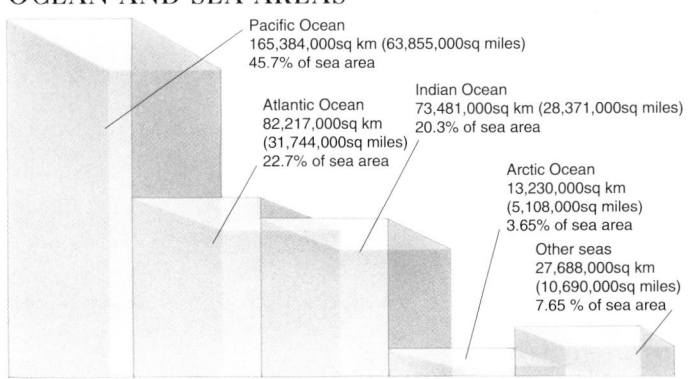

Pacific Ocean
165,384,000sq km (63,855,000sq miles)
45.7% of sea area

Indian Ocean
73,481,000sq km (28,371,000sq miles)
20.3% of sea area

Atlantic Ocean
82,217,000sq km (31,744,000sq miles)
22.7% of sea area

Arctic Ocean
13,230,000sq km (5,108,000sq miles)
3.65% of sea area

Other seas
27,688,000sq km (10,690,000sq miles)
7.65 % of sea area

OCEAN ZONES

Depth
m(ft)
0

2,000
(6,560)

6,000
(19,690)

Bathyal zone
surface – 2,000m (6,560ft)

Light disappears about
100m (330ft) down

Temperature declines
rapidly about
300m (980ft) down

Abyssal zone
2,000–6,000m
(6,560–19,690ft)

Hadal zone
below 6,000m
(19,690ft)

The temperature of
the deep ocean is
close to freezing.

Over half of
deep-sea fish species
produce their own light.

MINERALS IN THE SEA

Minerals dissolved from rocks by rivers are washed into the oceans. The most abundant are sodium and chlorine, which together form salt. The average salinity of the oceans is 33 to 38 parts salt per 1,000 parts water.

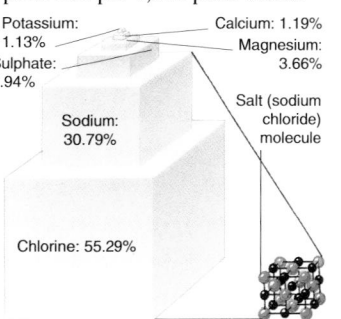

Potassium: 1.13%

Calcium: 1.19%

Magnesium: 3.66%

Sulphate: 7.94%

Salt (sodium chloride) molecule

Sodium: 30.79%

Chlorine: 55.29%

HEAPS OF SALT

The total amount of salt in the world's oceans and seas would cover Europe to a depth of 5km (3 miles).

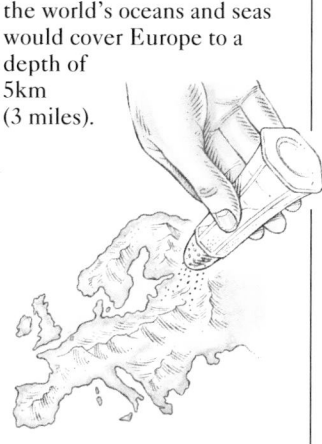

ISLANDS

Islands are found in seas, rivers, and lakes. They range in size from small mud and sand islands measuring only a few square metres, to the largest, Greenland, which measures more than 2 million square kilometres.

WORLD'S LARGEST ISLANDS

Madagascar
Indian Ocean
Area: 587,009sq km
(226,644sq miles)

Honshu
NW Pacific
Area: 227,401sq km
(87,799sq miles)

New Guinea
Western Pacific
Area: 792,493sq km
(305,981sq miles)

Baffin Island
Arctic Ocean
Area: 507,423sq km
(195,916sq miles)

Victoria Island
Arctic Ocean
Area: 217,278sq km
(83,891sq miles)

Borneo
Indian Ocean
Area: 725,416sq km
(280,083sq miles)

Great Britain
North Atlantic
Area: 218,065sq km
(84,195sq miles)

Ellesmere Island
Arctic Ocean
Area: 196,225sq km
(75,762sq miles)

Sumatra
Indian Ocean
Area: 427,325sq km
(164,990sq miles)

Greenland
Arctic Ocean
Area: 2,175,219sq km
(839,852sq miles)

TYPES OF ISLAND

There are four main types of island.

CORAL ISLAND

A coral island forms when corals (tiny marine organisms) grow up towards the surface of the ocean from an underwater platform in shallow water, such as the peak of a seamount (see p.48). The coral skeletons build up over many years until they reach the surface.

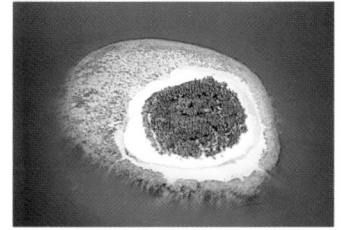

The Maldives in the Indian Ocean are coral islands.

VOLCANIC ISLAND

Volcanoes that erupt beneath the ocean may eventually grow to reach the surface, where they emerge as islands. Volcanic islands often form close to plate boundaries (see pp.40–41).

The volcanic island of Surtsey appeared south of Iceland in the Atlantic Ocean in 1963.

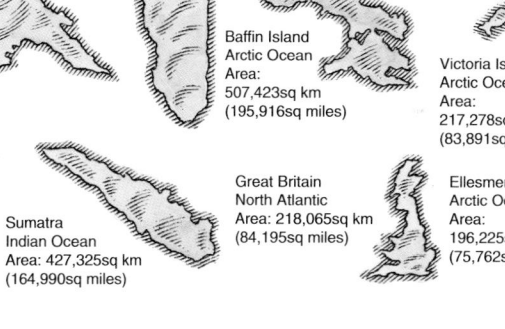

ISLAND FORMED BY A CHANGE IN SEA LEVEL

A rise in sea level, for example at the end of an ice age, may cut off an area of land from a continent, forming an island. Great Britain was formed in this way. Some pieces of land become islands at high tide.

Mont St. Michel in France becomes an island each time the tide comes in.

ISLAND ARC

An island arc is a chain of volcanic islands that usually forms close to a subduction zone (see pp.40–41). Some island arcs contain many thousands of islands. The Japanese islands were formed in this way.

Part of Indonesia, photographed from the Space Shuttle in 1983. Indonesia is the world's longest island arc.

CORAL ATOLLS

An atoll is a ring-shaped coral island with a lagoon in its centre. Atolls form when a coral reef builds up around a volcanic island, and the island subsequently sinks below sea level. As the island sinks, the coral continues to grow.

A coral reef builds up, fringing the volcanic island.

As the island starts to sink, coral continues to grow upwards.

The island has disappeared, leaving a coral atoll.

Lagoon

OCEAN AND ISLAND RECORDS

GREATEST OCEAN CURRENT is the Antarctic Circumpolar Current (also known as the West Wind Drift Current), which flows at a rate of 130,000,000cu m (4.3 billion cu ft) per second.

HIGHEST RECORDED WAVE (excluding seismic sea waves) was 34m (112ft) from trough to crest, recorded in 1933 en route from the Philippines to the USA.

REMOTEST ISLAND is Bouvet Island, about 1,700km (1,056 miles) from the nearest land (Queen Maud Land on the coast of eastern Antarctica).

LARGEST CORAL ATOLL is Kwajalein in the Marshall Islands, central Pacific Ocean. Its reef is 283km (176 miles) long, and encloses a lagoon of 2,850sq km (1,100sq miles).

MOUNTAINS

AS THE EARTH'S tectonic plates jostle and grind against each other, the crust may buckle and fold, throwing up lofty mountain ranges. Volcanoes also erupt at plate boundaries, sometimes building into high mountains.

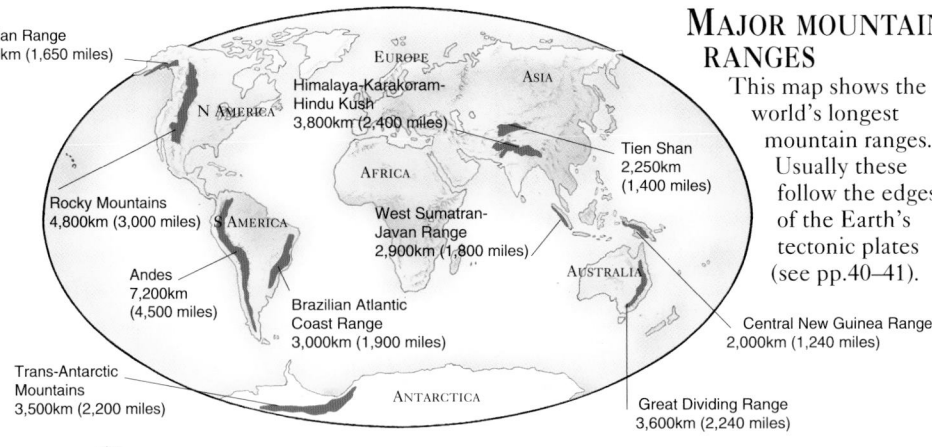

MAJOR MOUNTAIN RANGES

This map shows the world's longest mountain ranges. Usually these follow the edges of the Earth's tectonic plates (see pp.40–41).

Aleutian Range
2,650km (1,650 miles)

Himalaya-Karakoram-Hindu Kush
3,800km (2,400 miles)

Tien Shan
2,250km (1,400 miles)

Rocky Mountains
4,800km (3,000 miles)

West Sumatran-Javan Range
2,900km (1,800 miles)

Andes
7,200km (4,500 miles)

Brazilian Atlantic Coast Range
3,000km (1,900 miles)

Central New Guinea Range
2,000km (1,240 miles)

Trans-Antarctic Mountains
3,500km (2,200 miles)

Great Dividing Range
3,600km (2,240 miles)

TYPES OF MOUNTAIN

There are four main types of mountain.

FOLD MOUNTAINS

When two of the Earth's tectonic plates collide, the crust at the plate edges may crumple and fold under the strain, pushing up ranges of fold mountains.

Fold mountains form when the Earth's crust bends and buckles.

VOLCANOES

A volcano forms when magma (molten rock) from deep inside the Earth erupts on to the surface, building into a tall cone. Some of the highest mountains in the world are volcanoes.

Layers of lava build up into a mountain.

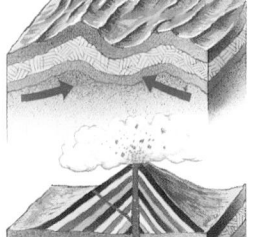

FAULT-BLOCK MOUNTAINS

Plate movements may squeeze layers of rock until they crack and snap. These cracks are faults. Mountains form when a slab or block of rock is squeezed upwards.

Fault-block mountains form where one slab or rock is thrust above another.

DOME MOUNTAINS

A large upwelling of molten rock (an igneous intrusion) beneath the Earth's surface may force up the overlying layers of rock into a huge hump. Mountains formed in this way are dome mountains.

Rising molten rock forces up overlying layers of rock into mountains.

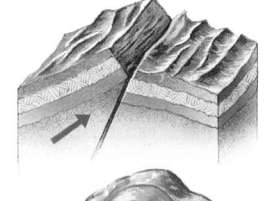

WORLD'S HIGHEST MOUNTAINS

The ten highest mountains in the world are all in the Himalayas.

Name	Location	Height	
		metres	feet
Everest	Nepal/China	8,848	29,028
K2	Kashmir/China	8,611	28,251
Kanchenjunga	Nepal/Sikkim	8,598	28,208
Lhotse	Nepal/Tibet	8,511	27,923
Makalu	Nepal/Tibet	8,480	27,821
Cho Oyu	Nepal	8,201	26,906
Dhaulagiri	Nepal	8,172	26,811
Manaslu	Nepal	8,156	26,759
Nanga Parbat	Kashmir	8,126	26,660
Annapurna	Nepal	8,078	26,503

CLOSE-UP OF A MOUNTAIN

High mountains have several zones of vegetation, due to the drop in temperature at higher altitudes.

Nothing can survive

Specially adapted alpine species

Pine forest

Broadleaf forest

Wide range of vegetation

HIGHEST MOUNTAIN PER CONTINENT

This illustration shows the comparative size of the highest mountain on each continent.

LIFE OF A MOUNTAIN

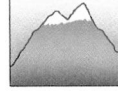

Young

YOUNG

Mountains that formed during the last few million years, or that are still growing, e.g. the Himalayas.

Mature

MATURE

Mountains several hundred million years old that have been eroded to a fraction of their former size, e.g. the Urals.

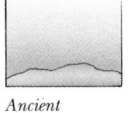

Ancient

ANCIENT

Mountains that have been eroded away until there are just a few hills on a low-lying peneplain.

The Eiffel Tower in Paris, France, is 300m (984ft) high.

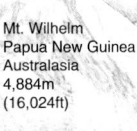

Mt. Everest
Nepal/China
Asia
8,848m
(29,028ft)

Mt. Everest was first climbed on 29 May 1953 by New Zealander Edmund Hillary (born 1919) and Sherpa Tensing Norgay (1914–86) of Nepal.

Aconcagua
Argentina
South America
6,960m
(22,834ft)

Mt. McKinley
Alaska, USA
North America
6,194m
(20,320ft)

El'brus
Russia
Europe
5,642m
(18,510ft)

Kilimanjaro
Tanzania
Africa
5,895m
(19,340ft)

Vinson Massif
Antarctica
5,140m
(16,863ft)

Mt. Wilhelm
Papua New Guinea
Australasia
4,884m
(16,024ft)

52

VALLEYS AND CAVES

THE FORCES OF EROSION are constantly attacking the land, changing its appearance. Rain flows into rivers that gash the landscape with valleys. In limestone areas, rainwater may seep into the rock, eating it away to form caves.

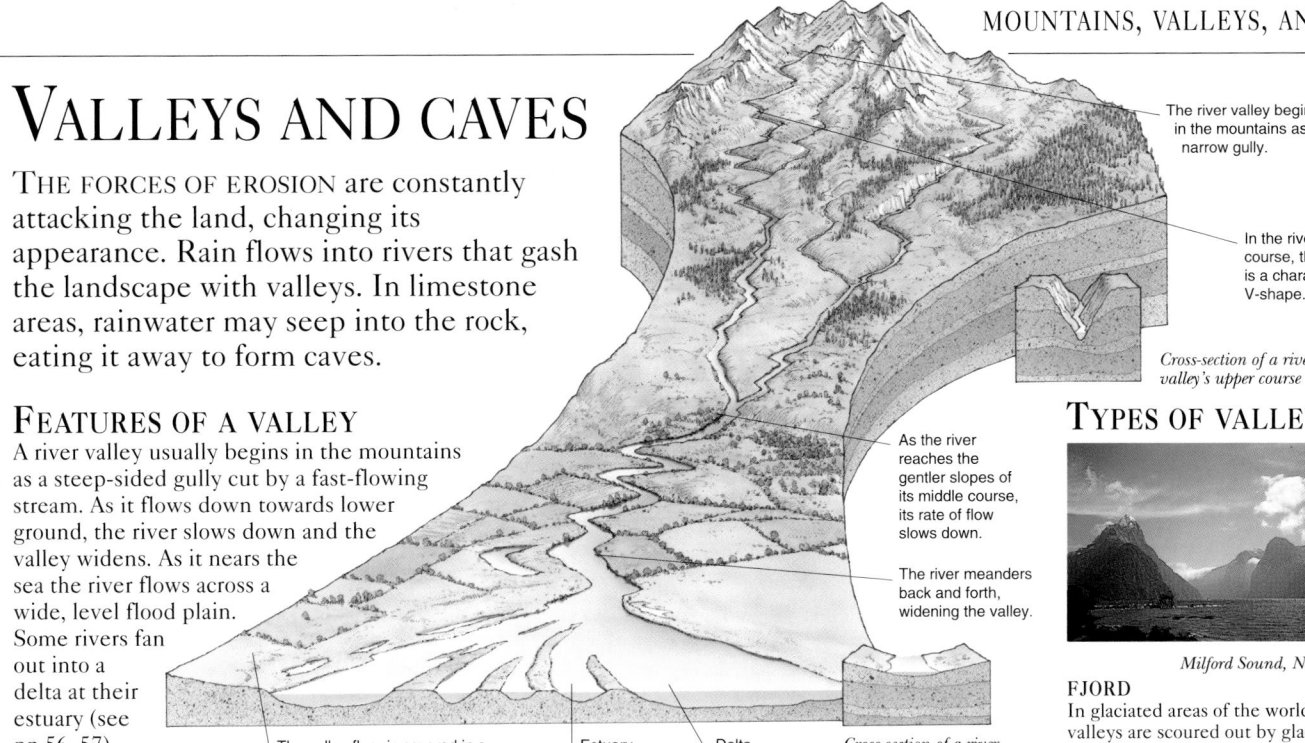

The river valley begins high in the mountains as a narrow gully.

In the river's upper course, the valley is a characteristic V-shape.

Cross-section of a river valley's upper course

FEATURES OF A VALLEY

A river valley usually begins in the mountains as a steep-sided gully cut by a fast-flowing stream. As it flows down towards lower ground, the river slows down and the valley widens. As it nears the sea the river flows across a wide, level flood plain. Some rivers fan out into a delta at their estuary (see pp.56–57).

As the river reaches the gentler slopes of its middle course, its rate of flow slows down.

The river meanders back and forth, widening the valley.

The valley floor is covered in a thick carpet of sand and mud.

Estuary (see p.56)

Delta (see p.56)

Cross-section of a river valley's lower course

CAVES

Caves are large, naturally occurring hollows in the ground, in cliffs, or in ice.

LIMESTONE CAVE
Most caves occur in limestone areas, because this type of rock is soluble (dissolves) in rainwater.

SEA CAVE
Waves crashing against cliffs erode the rocks, forming sea caves.

ICE CAVE
A stream of meltwater running beneath a glacier may carve out an ice cave.

LAVA CAVE
When the crust of a lava flow hardens, the molten lava beneath may flow out, leaving a lava cave.

CROSS-SECTION OF A LIMESTONE CAVE

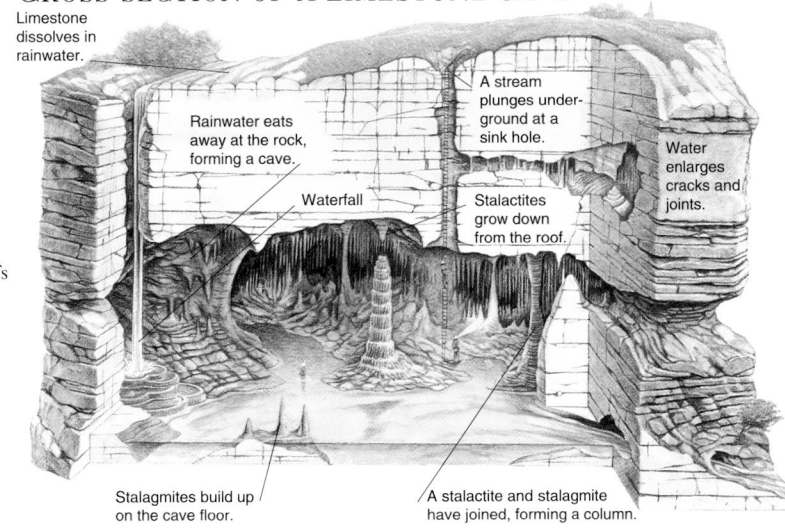

Limestone dissolves in rainwater.

Rainwater eats away at the rock, forming a cave.

Waterfall

A stream plunges underground at a sink hole.

Stalactites grow down from the roof.

Water enlarges cracks and joints.

Stalagmites build up on the cave floor.

A stalactite and stalagmite have joined, forming a column.

LIMESTONE CAVE FEATURES

Water dripping in limestone caves leaves behind tiny amounts of calcite. These mineral deposits build up to form distinctive limestone cave features. It can take from four to four thousand years for a stalactite or stalagmite to grow one inch (2.5cm).

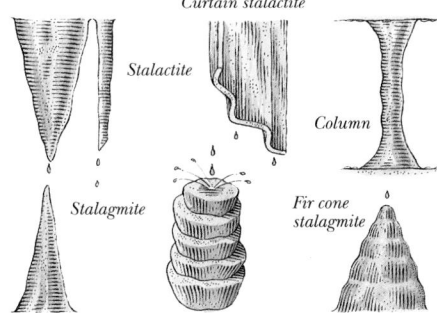

Curtain stalactite

Stalactite

Column

Stalagmite

Fir cone stalagmite

Plate stack stalagmite

VALLEY AND CAVE RECORDS

LONGEST FJORD
is Nordvest Fjord, Greenland, which extends 313km (194 miles) inland.

LARGEST GORGE
is the Grand Canyon in Arizona, USA, at 349km (217 miles) long and up to 1,676m (5,499ft) deep.

LARGEST CAVE CHAMBER
is the Sarawak Chamber in Sarawak, Malaysia, which has an area of 162,700sq m (1,751,300sq ft). The cave chamber is 700m (2,300ft) long, and has an average width of 300m (980ft). The lowest part of the roof is 70m (230ft) high.

LONGEST CAVE SYSTEM
is the Mammoth Cave system, Kentucky, USA, which is 560km (348 miles) long.

LONGEST STALACTITE
is 6.2m (20ft 4in) long. It is in the Poll an Ionana, a cave in Co. Clare, Ireland.

TALLEST STALAGMITE
is 32m (105ft) tall, in the Krásnohorska cave in the Czech Republic.

Size of tallest stalagmite compared to an adult

TYPES OF VALLEY

Milford Sound, New Zealand

FJORD
In glaciated areas of the world, deep valleys are scoured out by glaciers. When a glacier melts, for example at the end of an ice age, the sea level may rise, flooding the valley to form a fjord.

African Rift Valley

RIFT VALLEY
Rift valleys form when a long, narrow block of land sinks between two faults, at places where two tectonic plates are pulling apart (see pp.40–41).

Grand Canyon, Arizona, USA

GORGE AND CANYON
A gorge is a deep ravine with walls that are almost vertical. A canyon is a gorge, usually with water flowing through it, found in the desert. The source of its river is often outside the desert.

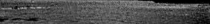

Valley of Kings, Egyptian desert

WADI
A wadi is a narrow, steep-sided desert valley that is usually dry. A wadi's characteristic shape is carved out by the flash floods that occur after torrential desert rainfall.

GLACIATION

MORE THAN A TENTH of the Earth's surface is permanently covered with ice. Ice sheets and sea ice blanket the polar areas, and ice caps and glaciers tumble down the slopes of high mountain ranges. Glaciers are found even on mountains at the Equator.

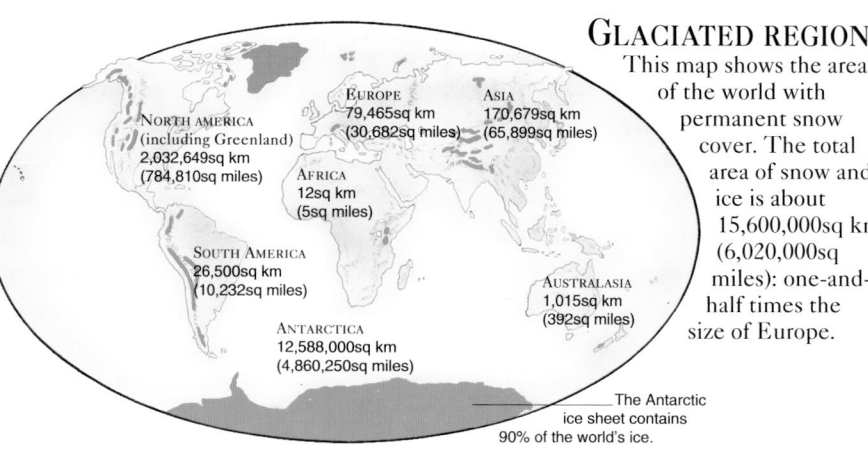

GLACIATED REGIONS

This map shows the areas of the world with permanent snow cover. The total area of snow and ice is about 15,600,000sq km (6,020,000sq miles): one-and-a-half times the size of Europe.

EUROPE
79,465sq km
(30,682sq miles)

ASIA
170,679sq km
(65,899sq miles)

NORTH AMERICA
(including Greenland)
2,032,649sq km
(784,810sq miles)

AFRICA
12sq km
(5sq miles)

SOUTH AMERICA
26,500sq km
(10,232sq miles)

AUSTRALASIA
1,015sq km
(392sq miles)

ANTARCTICA
12,588,000sq km
(4,860,250sq miles)

The Antarctic ice sheet contains 90% of the world's ice.

FORMATION OF AN ICE CAP

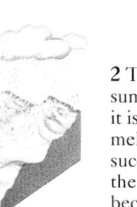

1 Heavy winter snowfall covers the land. Fresh layers compress the older snow beneath, turning it into an icy mass called firn.

2 The temperature rises in summer, but on high ground it is not warm enough to melt the ice. Over successive winters, the blanket of firn becomes thicker.

3 Eventually the firn forms an ice cap. Gravity causes it to flow down from higher ground. Tongues of ice fill the valleys, forming glaciers.

FEATURES OF A GLACIER

Glaciers usually begin high in the mountains. Most flow at a rate of up to 2m (7ft) per day, although glaciers on steeper slopes may flow much more quickly. It may take thousands of years for ice to reach the end of a slow-moving glacier.

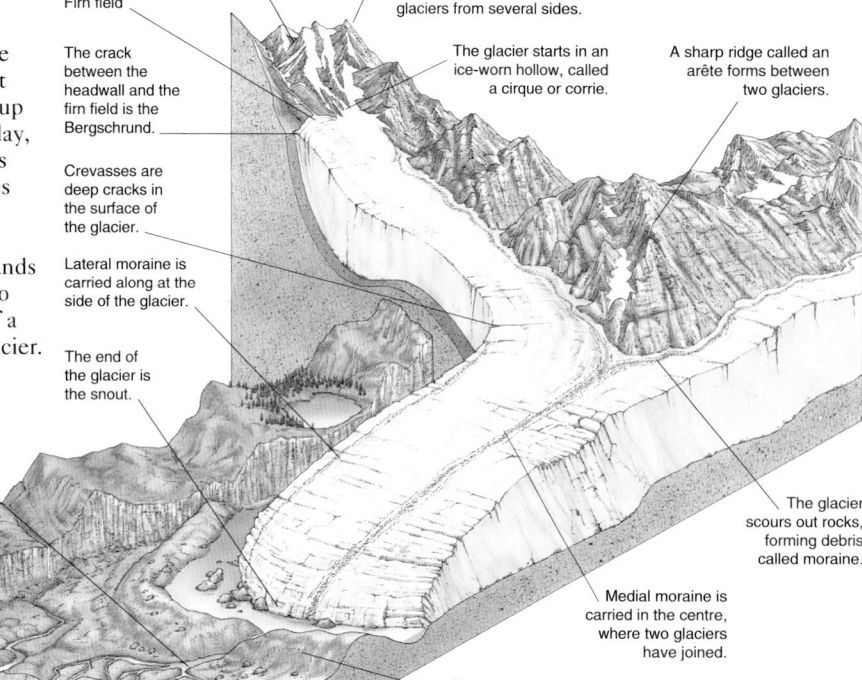

Headwall

Firn field

The crack between the headwall and the firn field is the Bergschrund.

Crevasses are deep cracks in the surface of the glacier.

Lateral moraine is carried along at the side of the glacier.

The end of the glacier is the snout.

A stream of meltwater flows out from the snout.

A pyramidal peak forms when a mountain is attacked by glaciers from several sides.

The glacier starts in an ice-worn hollow, called a cirque or corrie.

A sharp ridge called an arête forms between two glaciers.

The glacier scours out rocks, forming debris called moraine.

Medial moraine is carried in the centre, where two glaciers have joined.

Terminal moraine is dumped at the snout.

FRESHWATER RESERVOIR

More than 75% of the world's fresh water is frozen in ice sheets, ice caps, and glaciers.

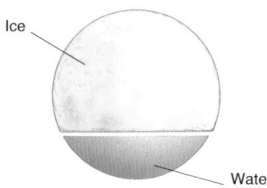

Ice

Water

PROPORTION OF ICE

About 12% of sea and 10% of land is permanently covered with ice.

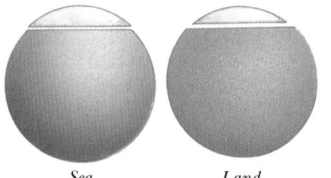

Sea   *Land*

ICE-SCULPTED LANDSCAPES

When glaciers retreat, for example at the end of an ice age, they leave behind U-shaped valleys, fjords (see p.53), and deep lakes. Piles of moraine form drumlins (small hills) and moraine ridges.

Hanging valleys open high on the sides of the main valley.

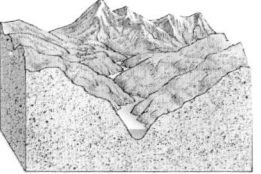

Before glaciation: a V-shaped river valley

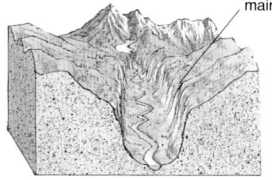

After glaciation: a U-shaped river valley

LONGEST GLACIERS

The glaciers listed below are the longest in each of the major glaciated regions of the world.

Glacier	Region	Length	
		km	miles
Lambert-Fisher Ice Passage	Antarctica	515	320
Petermanns Glacier	Greenland	200	124
Hubbard Glacier	Alaska-Yukon, N. America	128	80
Siachen Glacier	Karakoram, Asia	75	47
Skeidararjokull	Iceland	48	30
Tasman Glacier	New Zealand	29	18
Aletsch Gletscher	European Alps	24	15
Gyabrag Glacier	Himalayas	21	13

SNOWLINE

The snowline is the level that divides year-round snow from snow that melts during warmer weather. The closer an area is to the Equator, the higher the snowline.

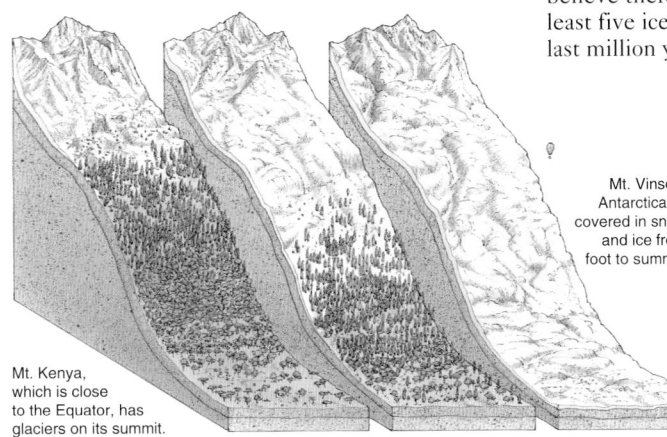

Mt. Vinson, Antarctica, is covered in snow and ice from foot to summit.

Mt. Kenya, which is close to the Equator, has glaciers on its summit.

On the Equator
the snowline lies about 4,900m (16,000ft) high.

In the European Alps
the snowline lies about 2,700m (9,000ft) high.

In polar regions
the snowline lies at sea level.

ICE AGES

Ice ages occur when the Earth's climate becomes much cooler, and the amount of ice increases. Scientists believe there have been at least five ice ages over the last million years.

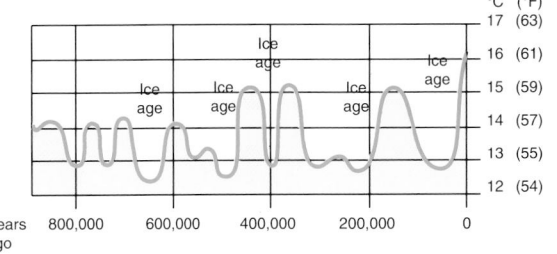

Temperature °C (°F)
17 (63)
16 (61)
15 (59)
14 (57)
13 (55)
12 (54)

Ice age
Ice age
Ice age
Ice age
Ice age

Years ago   800,000   600,000   400,000   200,000   0

MOST RECENT ICE AGE

The last ice age began about 72,000 years ago, and ended about 10,000 years ago. This map shows the areas of the world that were covered with ice. The sea level was about 150m (490ft) lower than today, because so much water was locked up in ice.

Huge ice sheets covered much of North America, Europe, and Asia.

The land where New York now stands was covered with ice.

Southern Argentina was covered by an ice sheet.

Up to 30% of the Earth's surface was glaciated.

New Zealand was covered by an ice cap.

AVALANCHES

An avalanche is a mass of snow and ice that suddenly crashes down a mountainside. It may be up to 1km (0.6 miles) across, and can move at up to 320km/h (200mph). If a town or village lies in the path of an avalanche, houses may be flattened and people killed.

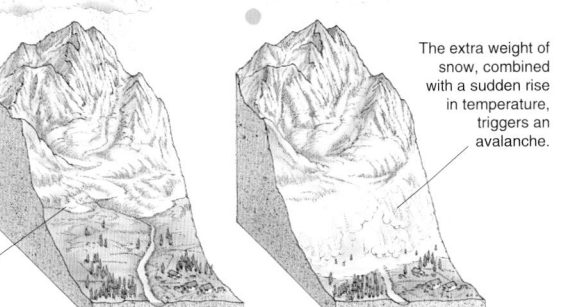

Heavy snowfall adds extra weight to the snow cover on this mountain slope.

The extra weight of snow, combined with a sudden rise in temperature, triggers an avalanche.

AVALANCHE FACTS

• An avalanche can generate winds of up to 300km/h (185mph).

• About 18,000 Austrian and Italian soldiers are thought to have been killed in a single day in 1916 by more than 100 avalanches in the Dolomites, northern Italy. Many of these avalanches were started by gunfire.

• The biggest avalanches usually occur on slopes with an angle of 30–40°.

SEA ICE

The sea freezes over when its temperature falls below -1.9°C (28°F). Sea ice is never more than about 5m (16ft) thick.

Sea ice off the western Antarctic coast

TALLEST ICEBERG

The tallest iceberg ever reported was 167m (550ft) high – taller than St. Paul's Cathedral, London. It was sighted off Greenland in 1958.

ICEBERGS

Icebergs are large chunks of ice that break off the end of ice sheets, ice caps, and glaciers, and float out to sea. The process of icebergs breaking off a body of ice is called calving.

The rising and falling tide, together with buffeting from the waves, breaks the iceberg off the end of the glacier.

Once an iceberg has broken away, its movements are controlled by ocean currents and the wind.

ICY RECORDS

FASTEST-MOVING GLACIER
is the Quarayaq, Greenland, which can flow 20–24m (65–80ft) per day.
THICKEST ICE
ever recorded is 5km (3 miles) deep, in Wilkes Land, Antarctica. This would reach over half way up Mt. Everest.

LARGEST ICEBERG
The largest iceberg ever recorded was more than 335km (208 miles) long and 97km (60 miles) wide – an area three times the size of Cyprus.
GREATEST NUMBER OF DEATHS FROM AN AVALANCHE
was 5,000 at Huaras, Peru, on 13 December 1941.

Only a small proportion of an iceberg – about 12% – is visible above the surface of the ocean. The remainder is hidden beneath the water.

ICEBERG FACTS

• About 10,000 icebergs a year break away from the glaciers of western Greenland.

• Scientists estimate that the average age of the ice in icebergs is 5,000 years.

RIVERS AND LAKES

MOST OF THE EARTH'S fresh water is frozen in ice, or is held in rocks below the surface as groundwater. Less than one per cent is contained in rivers and lakes, yet these features have a significant effect on the landscape.

MAJOR RIVERS AND LAKES

This map shows the world's major rivers and lakes. The largest lake (the Caspian Sea) covers an area almost as large as Japan, while the longest river (the Nile) could stretch from New York to Berlin.

Antarctica has no rivers or lakes: all of its fresh water is frozen.

TYPES OF RIVER

PERENNIAL RIVER
Perennial rivers flow all year round. They are usually found in temperate and tropical areas (see pp.60–61), where rain falls throughout the year.

The Nile: a perennial river

SEASONAL RIVER
Seasonal rivers only flow during wet seasons. Many Mediterranean countries have seasonal rivers that flow in the wet winter season, but are dry in summer.

Seasonal river in Crete during summer.

EPHEMERAL RIVER
Ephemeral rivers are usually dry. Many desert rivers are ephemeral, for example the Todd River in central Australia hardly ever has water in it.

The Todd River in central Australia.

RIVER RECORDS

LONGEST EUROPEAN RIVER is the Volga, Russia, which is 3,531km (2,194 miles) long.

LONGEST AUSTRALASIAN RIVER is the Murray, Australia, which is 2,589km (1,609 miles) long.

LARGEST DELTA is the Ganges and Brahmaputra delta, which covers about 75,000sq km (30,000sq miles). Sri Lanka would fit into it with room to spare.

HIGHEST WATERFALL
The Angel Falls in Venezuela have a total drop of 979m (3,212ft): almost three times as high as the Empire State Building.

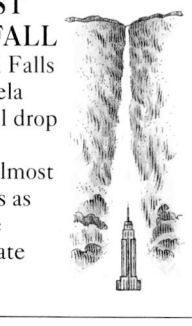

FEATURES OF A RIVER
A river is a body of water that flows downhill in a channel, usually towards the ocean. Rivers have three sections: the upper course, middle course, and lower course.

Upper course
The young, fast-flowing river rushes down a steep gradient, cutting a V-shaped gully.

The river plunges over a shelf of hard rock, forming a waterfall.

The waterfall wears away the rock and moves slowly upstream, cutting a deep gorge.

Where the river flows down a steep slope of hard rock, it forms swirling rapids.

In its upper course, the river flows over obstacles.

The river cuts further into the bank, widening the meander (loop).

A meander cut off after flooding forms an oxbow lake.

Middle course
The mature river's gradient is more gentle, and its rate of flow slower. It flows around obstacles, forming meanders.

Lower course
In its old age, with almost no gradient, the river flows sluggishly and begins to dump its sediment. It frequently floods and changes course.

The river estuary is where fresh river water meets salty sea water.

The wide, flat floodplain is submerged when the river floods.

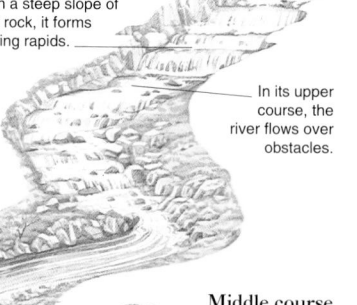

The river may block its own route with sediment, forcing it to split into separate streams. These fan out, forming a delta.

Many rivers begin in mountain ranges.

Rainfall runs off mountain slopes into the river system.

Tributary streams feed the main river.

RIVER WATER SOURCES
All rivers receive their water, either directly or indirectly, from precipitation (see pp.60–61).

OVERLAND FLOW
Rainfall runs down slopes into small streams. These tributaries eventually flow into the main river.

SPRING
Rain soaks into the ground and is absorbed into the aquifer – a layer of rock that can hold water. Where the water table (the upper surface of the groundwater) meets the ground surface, a spring may

MELTWATER
Many rivers rise (begin) in glaciated regions of the world, where they are fed by melting snow and ice.

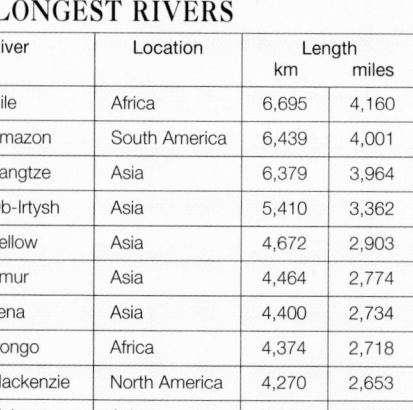

LONGEST RIVERS

River	Location	Length km	miles
Nile	Africa	6,695	4,160
Amazon	South America	6,439	4,001
Yangtze	Asia	6,379	3,964
Ob-Irtysh	Asia	5,410	3,362
Yellow	Asia	4,672	2,903
Amur	Asia	4,464	2,774
Lena	Asia	4,400	2,734
Congo	Africa	4,374	2,718
Mackenzie	North America	4,270	2,653
Mekong	Asia	4,184	2,600

TYPES OF LAKE

A lake is an inland body of water that collects in a hollow. The type of lake is determined by how it originally formed. Most lakes are fed by rivers (plus a small amount of rainfall), and most lose water into an outlet river. Some lakes, however, have no outlet and only lose water by evaporation. These lakes, such as Australia's Lake Eyre, are often salty.

EARTH MOVEMENT

When the Earth's crust is uplifted (see p.52), a body of water may be cut off from the sea, forming a lake. Similarly, when a rift valley forms (see p.53), water collects in the trough forming long, narrow lakes, e.g. Lake Nyasa, Africa.

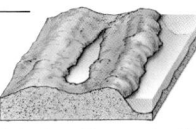
Lake formed by crustal uplift

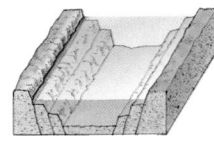
Rift valley lake

VOLCANIC ACTIVITY

Rainwater often collects in volcano craters, forming lakes such as Crater Lake in Oregon, USA. Some lakes, such as the Sea of Galilee in Israel, form when a river is dammed by a lava flow (see p.42).

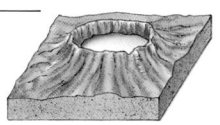
Crater lake

Lake formed by a lava dam

EROSION

Lakes fill hollows scoured out by glaciers during ice ages, e.g. the lakeland plateau of Kuopio, Finland. When desert winds erode a deflation hollow (see p.62) to below the water table, groundwater may fill the depression, forming a lake.

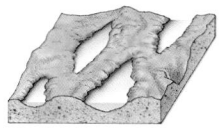
Lakes in ice-worn hollows

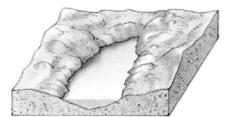
Lake in a deflation hollow

DEPOSITION

An oxbow lake forms when a meander is cut off from a river by the deposition of sediment. Deposition lakes also form when a landslide dams a river, and when sand bars and dunes cut off coastal waters from the sea.

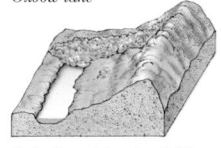
Oxbow lake

EROSION AND DEPOSITION

Glaciers carve out U-shaped valleys and corries (see p.54) that may be dammed by moraine deposited when the ice retreats. Long, narrow ribbon lakes fill the valleys, and small, circular tarns fill the corries.

Ribbon lake

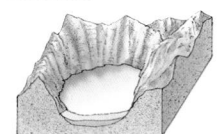
Tarn

Lake formed by a landslide

DEEPEST LAKE

Lake Baikal in Siberia has a maximum depth of 1,620m (5,315ft). Its deepest point could swallow five Eiffel Towers standing on top of each other.

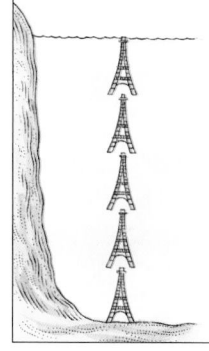

USES OF RIVERS AND LAKES

SOURCE OF FRESH WATER
Lakes and rivers supply water for factories and industry. They also provide fresh water for towns and cities.

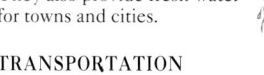

TRANSPORTATION
Lakes and rivers have been used for centuries to transport goods, animals, and people.

ELECTRICITY
Hydro-electric power is generated by dammed rivers, and by waterfalls driving turbines.

FISHING
Some of the world's larger lakes and rivers support important fishing industries.

SPORT
Sports such as sailing and wind-surfing are carried out on lakes. Canoeing and rafting are popular on rivers.

IRRIGATION
Rivers are an important source of water for irrigating crops in many arid (dry) regions.

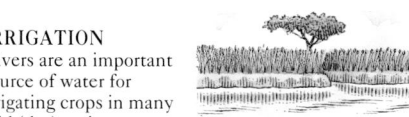

LARGEST LAKES

Lake	Location	Area sq km	sq miles
Caspian Sea	Asia	370,980	143,236
Lake Superior	North America	82,098	31,698
Lake Victoria	Africa	69,480	26,826
Lake Huron	North America	59,566	22,999
Lake Michigan	North America	57,754	22,299
Aral Sea	Asia	37,056	14,307
Lake Tanganyika	Africa	32,891	12,699
Lake Baikal	Siberia	31,498	12,161
Great Bear Lake	Canada	31,327	12,095
Lake Nyasa (Malawi)	Africa	28,877	11,149

VANISHING LAKES

Most lakes are geologically short-lived, drying up within a million years. Most are filled in by sediment dumped by rivers; others disappear when rainfall dwindles (becomes less). The remnants of lakes form swamps, marshes, and bogs.

RIVER AND LAKE FACTS

• About 180,000cu m (6.4 million cu ft) of water flows out of the Amazon into the ocean every second: it would take just over a second to fill London's St. Paul's Cathedral.

• Each year rivers dump about 20 billion tonnes of sediment in the sea, shaving the equivalent of 3.13cm (1.2in) off the land every thousand years.

• Lake Geneva will be filled in by the River Rhône within approximately 40,000 years.

LAKE RECORDS

LARGEST EUROPEAN LAKE is Lake Ladoga, Russia, which has an area of 17,702sq km (6,835sq miles).

LARGEST AUSTRALASIAN LAKE is Lake Eyre, Australia, which has an area of 9,323sq km (3,600sq miles). This salt lake is usually dry.

LARGEST SOUTH AMERICAN LAKE is Lake Titicaca in Peru and Bolivia, which has an area of 8,288sq km (3,200sq miles).

1 The river dumps its load of mud and gravel when it reaches the lake.

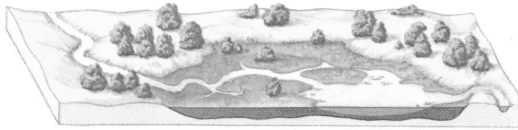
2 The sediment builds up, forming a sediment fan at one end of the lake.

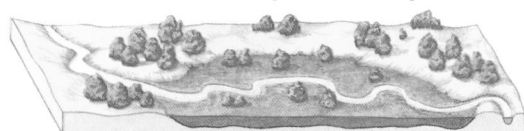
3 Further sediment extends the fan out into the lake which shrinks, forming a shallow swamp.

4 The lake is completely filled in with sediment. Plants eventually cover the old lake site.

WEATHER

EVERYTHING called weather – from sun and rain to snow and hurricanes – occurs in the bottom layer of the Earth's atmosphere. This churning layer of gas is being heated and cooled constantly by wind, water, and the Sun.

WATER CYCLE

Water moves in a never-ending cycle. The Sun's heat evaporates water from seas, lakes, and rivers. As it rises into the atmosphere, the vapour cools and condenses into clouds. Eventually the droplets fall back to Earth as rain.

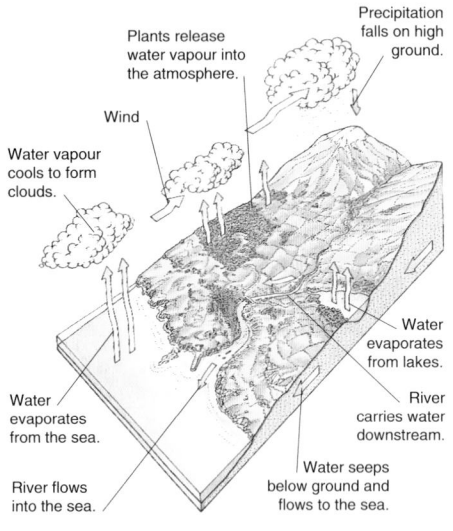

Precipitation falls on high ground.

Plants release water vapour into the atmosphere.

Wind

Water vapour cools to form clouds.

Water evaporates from lakes.

Water carries water downstream.

Water evaporates from the sea.

Water seeps below ground and flows to the sea.

River flows into the sea.

TYPES OF CLOUD

Clouds are classified according to their shape, and their height above the ground.

Cirrostratus
5,000–13,000m (16,000–40,000ft)
Semi-transparent layer; causes halo around the Sun.

Cirrocumulus
5,000–13,000m (16,000–40,000ft)
Made of icy particles; resemble fish scales. Often called "mackerel sky".

Altostratus
2,000–7,000m (6,500–23,000ft)
Thin, watery layer; forms coloured ring (corona) around Sun and Moon.

Cumulonimbus
Massive, flat-topped storm clouds that may stretch up to 15,000m (49,000ft) above the ground. Can bring heavy showers, thunderstorms, hail, or tornadoes.

Cirrus
5,000–13,000m (16,000–40,000ft)
Highest clouds; wispy.

Altocumulus
2,000–7,000m (6,500–23,000ft)
Lumpy globules of white and grey cloud.

Stratocumulus
0–2,000m (0–6,500ft)
Low sheet of grey or white, lumpy clouds.

Cumulus
0–2,000m (0–6,500ft)
Puffy clouds; grey at the bottom, brilliant white at the top.

Nimbostratus
0–2,000m (0–6,500ft)
Thick multi-layered clouds covering the sky; bring continuous rain or snow.

Stratus
0–2,000m (0–6,500ft)
Lowest clouds; hide hills in fog.

FORMATION OF CLOUDS

Clouds form when water vapour in warm air rises, cools, and condenses. The highest clouds usually consist of tiny ice crystals; lower clouds are made up mostly of water droplets.

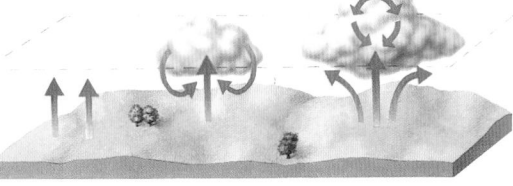

1 Warm air containing invisible water vapour rises from the ground.

2 As water vapour cools it condenses into droplets, forming a cloud.

3 Cloud goes on forming as long as warm, moist air continues to rise.

WEATHER FACTS

• The first thermometer was made in about 1600 by Italian scientist Galileo Galilei (1564–1642).

• There is enough water in the troposphere (see p.39) to flood the world to a depth of 1m (3.3ft).

• On any one day there may be 44,000 storms over the Earth.

• In 1888, 246 people died because of a hailstorm in Moredabad, India.

• Over a 30-year period in the USA, there was an average of 730 tornadoes a year, causing more than 100 deaths annually.

• During a tornado, one house can be destroyed, but another 20m (66ft) away can remain intact.

THE WORLD'S WINDS

Wind is air moving from one place to another. Winds always blow from areas of high pressure to areas of low pressure.

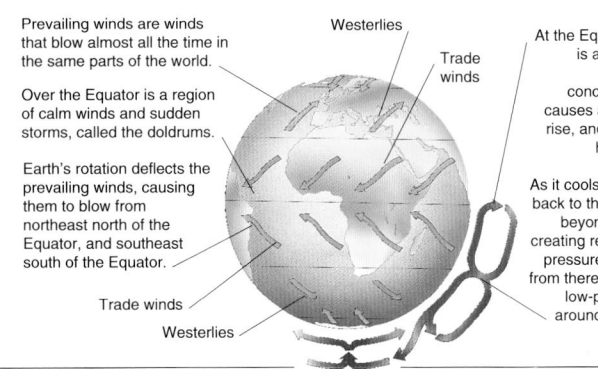

Prevailing winds are winds that blow almost all the time in the same parts of the world.

Over the Equator is a region of calm winds and sudden storms, called the doldrums.

Earth's rotation deflects the prevailing winds, causing them to blow from northeast north of the Equator, and southeast south of the Equator.

Westerlies

Trade winds

Trade winds

Westerlies

At the Equator the Sun is almost directly overhead. Its concentrated heat causes air to expand, rise, and billow out at high altitudes.

As it cools, the air sinks back to the surface just beyond the tropics, creating regions of high pressure. Winds blow from there back into the low-pressure zone around the Equator.

AIR PRESSURE

Cold air sinks, creating areas of high pressure called anticyclones, or highs. Warm air rises, creating areas of low pressure called depressions, lows, or cyclones.

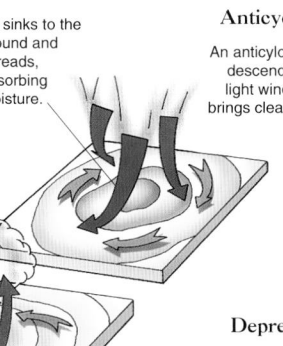

Air sinks to the ground and spreads, absorbing moisture.

Air rises, forming clouds.

In the Southern Hemisphere, air in highs and lows circulates in the opposite direction to air flows in the Northern Hemisphere.

Anticyclone

An anticyclone has descending air, light winds, and brings clear skies.

Depression

A depression often has rising air, strong winds, and may bring clouds, rain, or snow.

AIR MASSES AND FRONTS

Air masses are huge bodies of air that form over continents and oceans. They can be warm, cold, moist, or dry, depending on where they form. The boundary between two air masses is a front. As a front sweeps across the land, it usually brings a change in the weather.

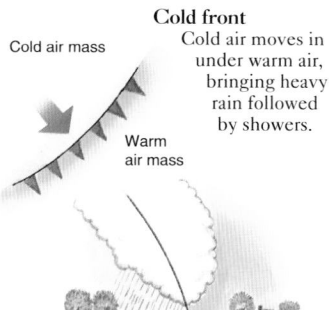

Cold front Cold air moves in under warm air, bringing heavy rain followed by showers.

Cold air mass

Warm air mass

Warm front Long spells of rain occur as warm air rises above cold air, before the front arrives on the ground.

Warm, moist air mass

Cold, moist air mass

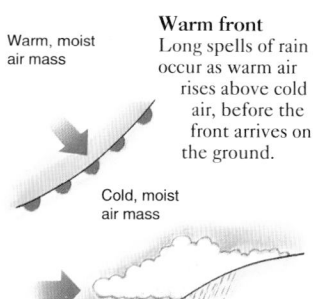

Occluded front An occluded front forms when a cold front overtakes a warm front, lifting warm air above it.

Cold air mass

Warm air mass

Cold air mass

Rain falls along the occluded front.

WEATHER WORDS

Blizzard A severe snowstorm with strong winds.

Dew Tiny drops of water that condense on cold objects near to the ground.

Fog Ground-level cloud: visibility less than 1km (0.6 miles).

Frost Ice crystals or frozen particles of moisture that form on cold surfaces.

Hail Pellets of ice that fall during storms.

Mist Thin fog: visibility 1–2km (0.6–1.25 miles).

Precipitation Rain, drizzle, hail, or snow.

Rainbow A seven-coloured arc that forms in the sky when sunlight shines through raindrops.

Squall A sudden increase in wind, accompanied by rain.

Waterspout A tornado that forms over an ocean or lake, sucking up water.

LIGHTNING

Lightning is the visible flash that occurs when electric energy is released from a cloud. It is often accompanied by thunder – a loud bang caused by rapidly expanding air.

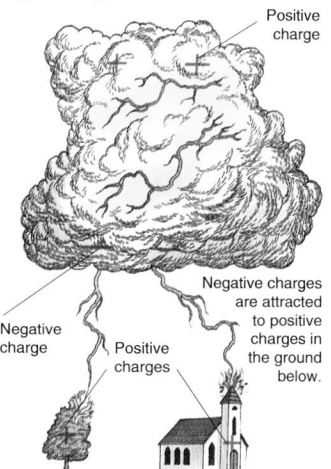

Positive charge

Negative charges are attracted to positive charges in the ground below.

Negative charge

Positive charges

TORNADO

A tornado is a violently whirling column of wind averaging 100m (300ft) across. It forms a funnel of cloud that can suck up objects lying in its path. Tornadoes last from a few minutes to two hours.

Tornadoes move at an average speed of 55km/h (35mph).

Base of tornado measures less than 1km (0.6 miles) across.

Rising air sucks up dirt, and objects as large as vehicles.

SHOCKING FACTS

• Twenty-one people died when a single bolt of lightning hit a hut near Umtali, Zimbabwe, on 23 December 1975.

• London, England, experiences an average of 4,200 lightning strikes per year.

• Every minute, there are about 6,000 flashes of lightning around the world.

• The longest lightning flashes measure up to 32km (20 miles). They occur in flat areas with very high clouds.

UNLUCKY STRIKES

US ex-park ranger Roy Sullivan was struck by lightning seven times in 35 years.

BEAUFORT SCALE

In 1805, British Admiral Francis Beaufort (1774–1857) devised a scale of 12 wind forces for use in sailing. For many years this scale has been used on land as well as at sea, although winds of force 10, 11, and 12 rarely occur over land.

0 Calm. Chimney smoke rises straight up.

1 Light air. Smoke drifts gently. Wind speed 3km/h (2mph).

2 Light breeze. Leaves rustle. Wind speed 9km/h (6mph).

3 Gentle breeze. Flags flutter. Wind speed 15km/h (9mph).

4 Moderate wind. Small branches move. Wind speed 25km/h (16mph).

5 Fresh wind. Small trees sway. Wind speed 35km/h (22mph).

6 Strong wind. Difficult to control umbrellas. Wind speed 45km/h (28mph).

7 Near-gale. Large trees sway. Wind speed 56km/h (35mph).

8 Gale. Twigs break off trees. Wind speed 68km/h (43mph).

9 Severe gale. Slates and chimney pots blow off. Wind speed 81km/h (51mph).

10 Storm. Houses damaged; trees blow down. Wind speed 94km/h (59mph).

11 Severe storm. Serious damage to buildings. Wind speed 110km/h (69mph).

12 Hurricane. Widespread damage. Wind speed 117km/h (73mph).

HURRICANE

A hurricane is a violent storm with winds spiralling inwards towards a centre of low pressure, called the eye. Some hurricanes remain over the ocean and last only a few days; others last from three to five weeks and devastate islands and coastal regions with violent winds, torrential rain, and huge waves.

Hurricanes range in size from 300km (200 miles) to 3,000km (2,000 miles) across.

Air spreads out from the top of the storm, forming a huge circle of cloud.

Many hurricanes move westwards at 19–28km/h (12–18mph).

A young storm may cross 2,000km (1,200 miles) of ocean on its way to becoming a hurricane.

Air spirals anticlockwise in the Northern Hemisphere, and clockwise in the Southern Hemisphere.

Deep cumulus clouds.

The eye may be 50km (31 miles) across, with light winds and little cloud and rain.

Winds of more than 117km/h (73mph) whirl around the eye, gusting to 360km/h (220mph).

WEATHER RECORDS

WETTEST DAY ON RECORD occurred when 1,870mm (73.63in) fell at Cilaos, Reunion Island, in March 1952.

WIND SPEED RECORD is 512km/h (318mph), recorded above a tornado in Oklahoma, USA, in 1999.

HIGHEST RECORDED TEMPERATURE is 58°C (136°F), at Azizia, Libya, in 1922. (Temperature readings are always taken in the shade.)

LOWEST RECORDED TEMPERATURE is -89°C (-128°F), at Vostok, Antarctica, in 1983.

CLIMATES

A REGION'S CLIMATE is its characteristic weather over a long period of time. The type of climate is determined by how near a region is to the Equator, and its distance from the sea.

DRY GRASSLAND
Vast expanses of dry grassland occur in the middle of some continents, where temperatures are extreme and there is not enough rainfall for forests to grow. These areas have very hot summers and very cold winters.

DESERT
Deserts are the hottest and driest climates in the world, receiving less than 250mm (10in) of rain per year. They are often found in areas of continents that are far from the sea, or in rain-shadow areas (see p.62). Only a few specially adapted plants can survive in the harsh desert climate.

TROPICAL GRASSLANDS
Tropical grasslands, such as the African savannah, occur between the equatorial forests and the hot, dry deserts. The climate is always hot, but the year is divided into a dry and a wet season. Vegetation consists of grasses that grow up to 2m (6ft) tall during the wet season, and low trees and bushes.

CLIMATIC ZONES
The world's climates run in broad zones each side of the Equator. There are many ways to classify climate: most use a combination of temperature and rainfall. A region's climate, together with the physical landscape, determines its characteristic vegetation.

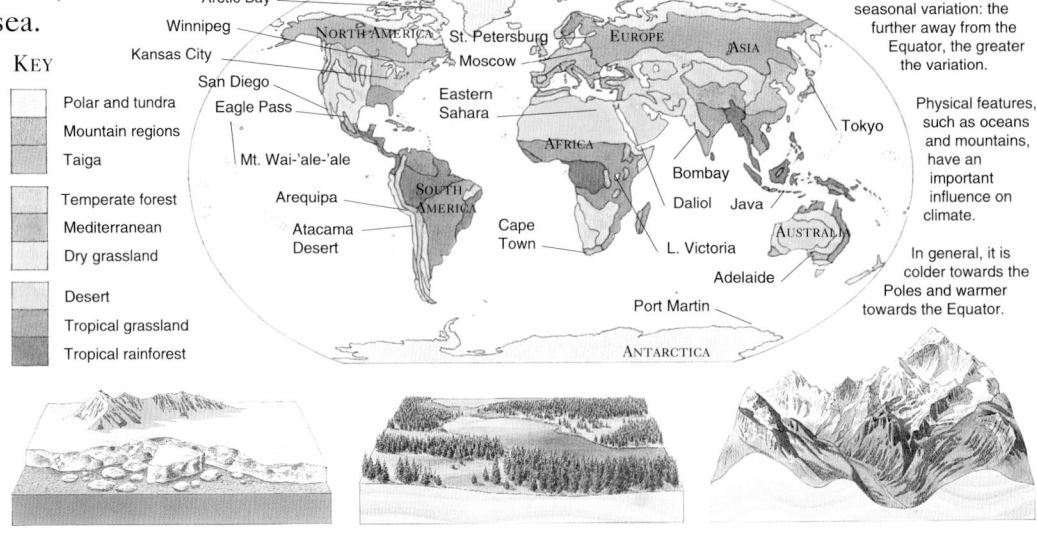

KEY
- Polar and tundra
- Mountain regions
- Taiga
- Temperate forest
- Mediterranean
- Dry grassland
- Desert
- Tropical grassland
- Tropical rainforest

Arctic Bay, Winnipeg, Kansas City, San Diego, Eagle Pass, Mt. Wai-'ale-'ale, Arequipa, Atacama Desert, NORTH AMERICA, St. Petersburg, Moscow, Eastern Sahara, SOUTH AMERICA, Cape Town, EUROPE, ASIA, AFRICA, Tokyo, Bombay, Daliol, Java, L. Victoria, Adelaide, AUSTRALIA, Port Martin, ANTARCTICA

CLIMATE MAP
This map shows the major climatic zones of the world. Also marked are places featured on the page opposite: those holding climate records; cities featured in the city climate graphs; and the locations of some of the places listed in the temperature variations table.

Most climatic regions show seasonal variation: the further away from the Equator, the greater the variation.

Physical features, such as oceans and mountains, have an important influence on climate.

In general, it is colder towards the Poles and warmer towards the Equator.

POLAR AND TUNDRA REGIONS
In Polar regions all fresh water is frozen solid, so land plants cannot grow. The sea's surface is frozen, but underneath is a rich diversity of life. The land bordering the ice caps is the tundra. The temperature in this treeless land rises above freezing only for a few months each year.

TAIGA
Taiga is a Russian word meaning "cold forest". The taiga is a huge area of coniferous forest that lies south of the tundra, stretching across northern Canada, Scandinavia, and the Russian Federation. Four to six months of the year are dark, with the temperature falling well below 0°C (32°F).

MOUNTAIN REGIONS
On mountain ranges, temperature decreases with altitude. Although mountain climates vary according to how close a region is to the Equator, most have distinct vegetation zones that change with altitude. At the highest points, temperatures are often too low for vegetation to survive.

MEDITERRANEAN
The type of climate around the Mediterranean Sea is found in several other parts of the world, including California, USA. Summers are hot and dry, and winters are cool and wet. Plants in these regions, such as olive trees, have adapted to the dry summer conditions.

TEMPERATE FOREST
Temperate climates are rarely very hot or very cold: the average temperature is usually 10°C (50°F) or more for four months of the year, and below 5°C (41°F) for at least one month. In temperate regions, many types of plant, e.g. deciduous trees (see p.78), are dormant during winter.

TROPICAL RAINFOREST
In equatorial regions the climate is hot and wet all year round. The temperature remains at about 27–28°C (80–82°F), and it rains almost every day. This climate results in the most abundant plant and animal growth in the world: equatorial forests contain 50% of all plant and animal species.

PINK PEAKS
Winds sometimes pick up dust and sand that may eventually fall as coloured rain or snow. Pink snow has fallen on the European Alps, caused by seasonal winds from the Sahara desert picking up red sand.

CLIMATE PROPORTIONS
This table shows the percentage of the Earth that has each basic climate type.

Climate	Continent %	Ocean %	Total Earth %
Polar	17	19.5	18.8
Taiga	21.3	1.7	7.3
Moist temperate	15.5	31.9	27.2
Moist tropical	19.9	42.7	36.1
Dry	26.3	4.2	10.6

MICROCLIMATES
Microclimates are small areas that have their own climate. They include cities, where the air temperature may be 6°C (11°F) higher than the surrounding area. On this special satellite photograph of Paris, the hottest areas are blue, and the coolest areas are green.

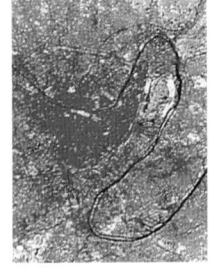

CLIMATE FACTS
- In parts of the Atacama Desert, Chile, it has not rained for 400 years.

- In India, during the summer monsoon (see opposite page), up to 75% of annual rainfall may fall in just three months.

- In the tropics, the difference between the highest annual noon temperature and the lowest, may be only 2°C (3.6°F).

SEASONS

Seasons occur because different regions of the Earth are tilted towards the Sun at various times during the year.

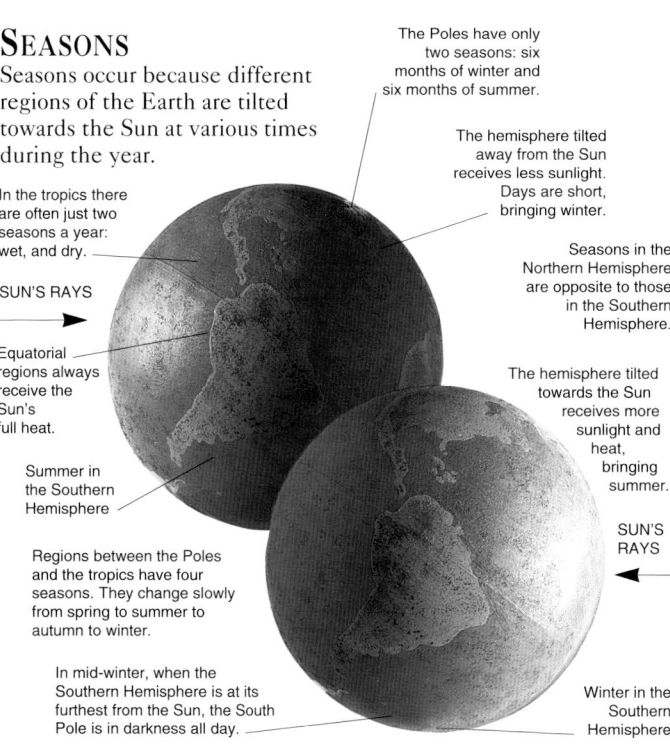

In the tropics there are often just two seasons a year: wet, and dry.

SUN'S RAYS

Equatorial regions always receive the Sun's full heat.

Summer in the Southern Hemisphere

Regions between the Poles and the tropics have four seasons. They change slowly from spring to summer to autumn to winter.

In mid-winter, when the Southern Hemisphere is at its furthest from the Sun, the South Pole is in darkness all day.

The Poles have only two seasons: six months of winter and six months of summer.

The hemisphere tilted away from the Sun receives less sunlight. Days are short, bringing winter.

Seasons in the Northern Hemisphere are opposite to those in the Southern Hemisphere.

The hemisphere tilted towards the Sun receives more sunlight and heat, bringing summer.

SUN'S RAYS

Winter in the Southern Hemisphere

MONSOONS

Monsoons are seasonal winds that affect large areas of the tropics and sub-tropics. In southern Asia, monsoons blow from southwest in summer, and northeast in winter.

Areas of the world that experience monsoons are marked in pink.

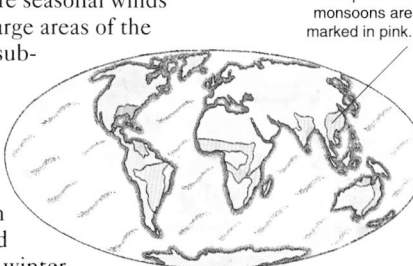

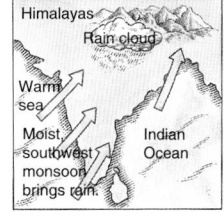

Southwest monsoon
In early summer, the hot dry lands of Asia draw in warm, moisture-laden air from the Indian Ocean.

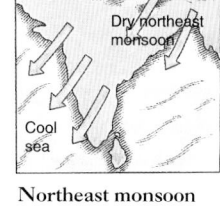

Northeast monsoon
In winter, cold dry air spreads out from central Asia, bringing chilly weather.

CLIMATE CHANGE

Factors that influence the world's climate include the atmosphere, volcanic eruptions, the oceans, the polar ice caps, and the biosphere (see p.64). The 1997/98 El Niño, a warm water current off the coast of South America, caused random and unpredictable changes in the world's weather.

Large volcanic eruptions throw dust and sulphur dioxide gas high into the atmosphere, where it forms a fine haze, blocking some of the Sun's heat.

Human activities such as deforestation, large-scale changes in land use, and the release of various chemicals into the air, can affect the world's climate.

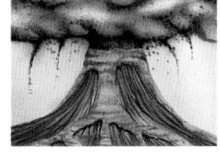

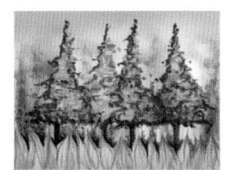

SOGGIEST SPOT

Hawaii's Mt. Wai-'ale-'ale receives an average of about 11,700mm (460.6in) of rain a year, making it the rainiest place in the world. If it did not drain away, this volume of rain would almost submerge a two-storey house.

TEMPERATURE VARIATIONS

This table illustrates how a region's temperatures depend on its closeness to the Equator. These North American locations are situated at similar longitudes; some are on the map opposite.

Location/ Maximum Temp.	Minimum Temp.
Arctic Bay 11°C (52°F)	-28°C (-50°F)
Churchill 18°C (64°F)	-24°C (-11°F)
Winnipeg 26°C (79°F)	-14°C (7°F)
Minneapolis 28°C (82°F)	-6°C (22°F)
Kansas City 33°C (92°F)	3°C (37°F)
Dallas 35°C (95°F)	13°C (56°F)
Eagle Pass 38°C (100°F)	19°C (66°F)

CLIMATE FACTS

• At the Equator, the temperature is about 25–30°C (77–86°F) every day.

• The average temperature close to the South Pole is -50°C (-122°F). This is much colder than a deep freeze, which is about -18°C (0°F).

• Tundra regions are sometimes described as cold deserts, because their climate is so dry.

CITY CLIMATES

These graphs show the average temperature and rainfall for various cities around the world. Locations are marked on the map on p.60.

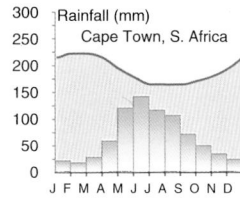

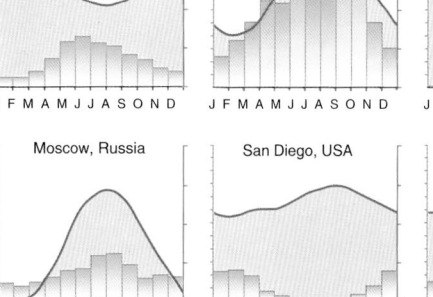

Adelaide, Australia

Tokyo, Japan

Bombay, India

Temp. (°C)
30
25
20
15
10
5
0
-5
-11

J F M A M J J A S O N D

300
250
200
150
100
50
0

Rainfall (mm)
Cape Town, S. Africa

Moscow, Russia

San Diego, USA

Arequipa, Peru

Temp. (°C)
30
25
20
15
10
5
0
-5
-11

J F M A M J J A S O N D

CLIMATE RECORDS

Most of the climate records listed below are based on annual averages.

MOST THUNDER is experienced in parts of Java, and around Africa's Lake Victoria: thunderstorms occur 200–250 days per year.

DRIEST PLACE is the Atacama Desert, Chile, with an average of only 0.51mm (0.02in) of rain per year.

SUNNIEST PLACE is the Eastern Sahara, which has sunshine for more than 90% of daylight hours.

HOTTEST PLACE is Daliol, Ethiopia, where the average temperature over a six-year period was 34.4°C (94°F).

COLDEST PLACE is Polus Nedostupnost, Antarctica, which has an annual average temperature of -57.8°C (-72°F).

WINDIEST PLACE is Port Martin, Antarctica, which had a mean wind speed of 105km/h (65mph) over a one-month period.

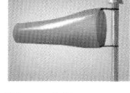

MOST RAINY DAYS are experienced by Mount Wai-'ale-'ale (altitude 1,569m/ 5,148ft) on the Hawaiian island of Kauai, which has up to 350 days of rain per year.

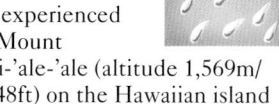

DESERTS

DESERTS ARE areas of land that receive less than 250mm (10in) of rain per year. They are barren regions of rugged hills, cliff-like canyons, and pebble or dune-covered plains. Low rainfall and high temperatures make life in the desert hard: only a few plant and animal species can survive.

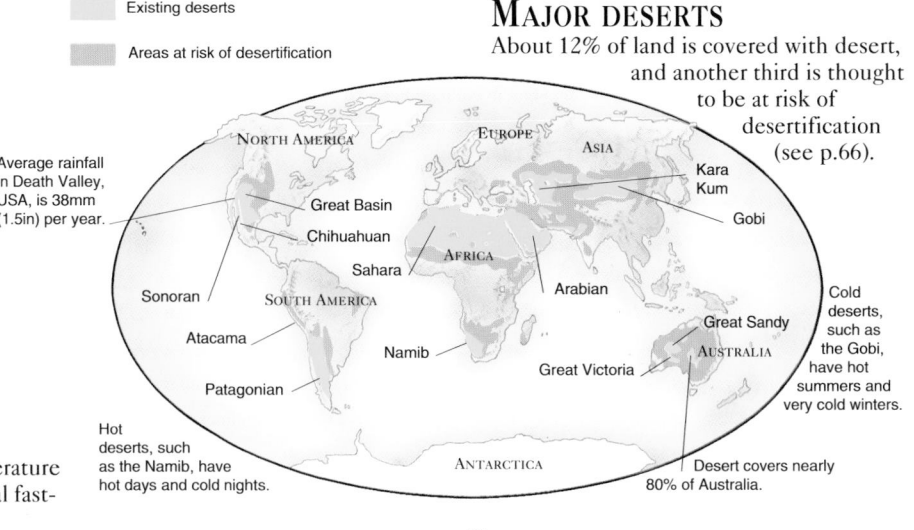

Existing deserts

Areas at risk of desertification

Average rainfall in Death Valley, USA, is 38mm (1.5in) per year.

NORTH AMERICA
EUROPE
ASIA
Kara Kum
Great Basin
Chihuahuan
Sahara
AFRICA
Gobi
Sonoran
SOUTH AMERICA
Arabian
Atacama
Namib
Great Sandy
AUSTRALIA
Patagonian
Great Victoria
ANTARCTICA

Hot deserts, such as the Namib, have hot days and cold nights.

Cold deserts, such as the Gobi, have hot summers and very cold winters.

Desert covers nearly 80% of Australia.

MAJOR DESERTS
About 12% of land is covered with desert, and another third is thought to be at risk of desertification (see p.66).

DESERT FEATURES
Weathering caused by fierce winds, huge temperature variations between day and night, and occasional fast-flowing water, forms distinctive desert features.

Mesas are steep-sided, table-like hills that form where layers of resistant rock protect softer rock beneath.

Deep canyons are usually fed by rain that falls outside the desert area.

Desert water courses, called wadis, are steep-sided with a flat floor. They are usually dry.

Buttes are isolated, flat-topped hills. They are similar to mesas, but smaller.

Mushroom-shaped pedestal rocks form where stones, blown by the wind, cut into the rock close to the ground.

Hamada (rock pavement)

Barkhans

Zeugen are parallel, flat-topped ridges with caps of hard, resistant rock perched on softer rock below.

Alluvial fans form where water flowing down wadis meets the desert plain and dumps its sediment.

Dry salt lake (playa)

Most oases form at deflation hollows where the water table (see p.56) is near the surface.

A shallow depression, called a deflation hollow, has been scooped out by the wind.

Hard sandstone

Transverse dunes

Seif dunes

SAND DUNES
Dunes develop in flat areas. They range from a few metres to 200m (660ft) high, and can be 900m (3,000ft) wide. There are several types of sand dune, including the four shown below.

BARKHANS
These crescent-shaped dunes with two horns may grow up to 30m (100ft) high. Barkhans are always moving.

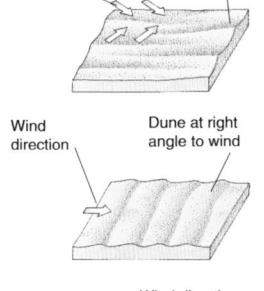

Wind direction

Crescent-shaped dune

SEIFS
Seifs are long ridges of sand that occur where there is little sand and a powerful wind. They grow up to 215m (700ft) high.

Wind direction

Parallel dunes

TRANSVERSE DUNES
These long ridges of sand are separated by deep troughs. Transverse dunes form at right angles to the wind direction.

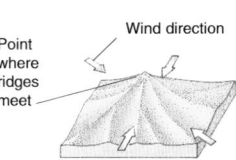

Wind direction

Dune at right angle to wind

STAR DUNES
These dunes form where several ridges of sand meet, and the wind comes from different directions.

Point where ridges meet

Wind direction

TYPES OF DESERT
CONTINENTAL DESERTS
Continental deserts, such as the Sahara (right), form because they are too far from the sea for winds to bring them much rain. Winds travel over thousands of kilometres of land before they reach these deserts, losing moisture as they do so.

RAIN-SHADOW DESERTS
Rain-shadow deserts, such as the Atacama desert in Chile (right), form next to mountain ranges. As winds rise up over the mountains, the moisture they carry falls as rain, so the winds are dry as they flow down the other side.

DEAD HOT
If a person spent a day in the Sahara with no shade, food, water, or clothes, their temperature would be about 46°C (115°F) by sunset, and they would have lost 2–3.5 litres (4–6 pints) of water. By nightfall they would be dead.

MIRAGES
Mirages are often seen in hot deserts. They occur when a layer of warm air next to the ground is trapped by cooler air above. Light bends towards the horizontal line of vision, and eventually travels upwards: the mirage is an upside-down "virtual" image.

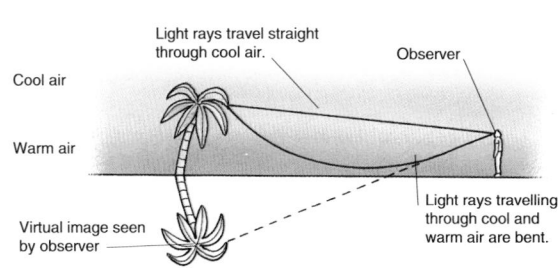

Light rays travel straight through cool air.

Observer

Cool air

Warm air

Virtual image seen by observer

Light rays travelling through cool and warm air are bent.

LARGEST DESERTS

Desert	Area	
	sq km	sq miles
Sahara	8,600,000	3,320,000
Arabian	2,330,000	900,000
Gobi	1,200,000	463,000
Patagonian	673,000	260,000
Great Victoria	647,000	250,000
Great Basin	492,000	190,000
Chihuahuan	450,000	174,000
Great Sandy	407,000	157,000
Kara Kum	350,000	135,000
Sonoran	310,000	120,000

FORESTS

A THIRD OF THE Earth's land surface is covered by forest: areas of land with dense tree cover. Forests range from the vast, cold taiga of the Northern Hemisphere, to the steamy tropical rainforest of the Amazon Basin, which contains half of all known plant and animal species.

RAINFOREST DIVERSITY

About 750 species of tree grow in a single 10-hectare patch of rainforest in Malaysia. There are only 700 species of tree in the whole of North America.

FOREST FACTS

• An area of rainforest the size of a soccer pitch disappears every second, and more than 50 species of rainforest plants and animals become extinct every day.

• A single tree in Amazonia may be home to 43 species of ant – about the same number found in the whole of the British Isles.

• Forest destruction contributes to the loss of about 50 billion tonnes of topsoil every year.

• During the monsoon (see p.61), deforested areas of Nepal may experience up to 20,000 landslides in a single day.

• One in five of all birds lives in the Amazon rainforest.

Scarlet macaw (Ara macao)

RAINFOREST REGENERATION

When large gaps occur in a forest, through natural causes or human activity, it takes at least 100 years to return to its natural state. If the soil is degraded (spoiled), the forest may be replaced by scrubby vegetation only.

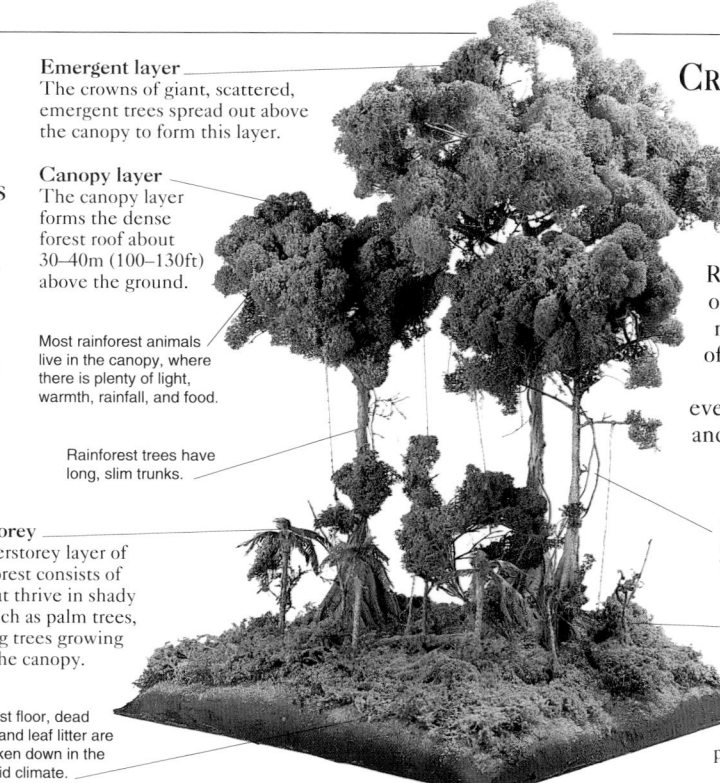

Emergent layer
The crowns of giant, scattered, emergent trees spread out above the canopy to form this layer.

Canopy layer
The canopy layer forms the dense forest roof about 30–40m (100–130ft) above the ground.

Most rainforest animals live in the canopy, where there is plenty of light, warmth, rainfall, and food.

Rainforest trees have long, slim trunks.

Understorey
The understorey layer of the rainforest consists of plants that thrive in shady places, such as palm trees, and young trees growing towards the canopy.

On the forest floor, dead organisms and leaf litter are quickly broken down in the warm, humid climate.

DESTRUCTION OF EARTH'S FORESTS

Ten thousand years ago, about half of the world's land surface was covered with trees. Today about 33% of those forests have been destroyed, and about 65% of what remains has been greatly changed. Half of the world's tropical rainforests have been felled this century.

RAINFOREST PRODUCTS

Perfumes
Rainforest plants are used in the manufacture of perfumes and incense.

Rubber
Rubber was originally used by South American Indians to make toys. Rubber tapping is now an important forest industry around the world.

Rattan
Rattan, a woody, climbing rainforest plant, is used to make furniture.

Drugs
One in four types of drug contains chemicals developed from rainforest species.

Insects
A weevil from the Cameroon forests is used to pollinate oil palms in Malaysia: a huge task that was once done by hand.

CROSS-SECTION OF A FOREST

Forests consist of several layers of vegetation. This illustration shows the layers of a rainforest. Rainforests grow in parts of the world that receive more than 200cm (80in) of rainfall per year. They consist of broadleaved evergreen trees (see p.78), and cover about 6% of the Earth's land surface.

In the understorey, lianas and other climbing plants twine around the trees.

Forest floor
The shady rainforest floor is almost bare apart from a thin blanket of leaves. Many of the plants are fungi or parasites, which do not need light to make food.

Northwest America has lost much of its forest: 60% of the Canadian part and 90% of the US part has been felled.

90% of Central America's rainforest has gone.

The Amazon rainforest originally covered an area nearly two thirds the size of the USA. An area of the size of Europe has been felled.

Trees originally covered about 95% of western and central Europe. By the late Middle Ages, only 20% of the forest was left.

Since 1950, at least 40% of the Himalayan forest has been cut down.

The Ethiopian highlands have lost 90% of their trees this century.

EUROPE
NORTH AMERICA
ASIA
AFRICA
SOUTH AMERICA
AUSTRALIA

Present-day forest cover

FOREST RECORDS

LARGEST FOREST
is the taiga (see p.60), which stretches in a wide band across the north of Europe, Asia, and North America.

LARGEST RAINFOREST
is the Amazon rainforest, which covers an area of 7 million sq km (2.7 million sq miles).

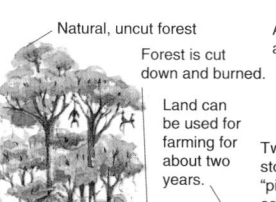

Natural, uncut forest

Forest is cut down and burned.

Land can be used for farming for about two years.

Two years after farming stopped, specialist "pioneer" species are established.

After 15 years, small primary (original) forest species appear.

After 60 years, primaries are the dominant species.

More than 100 years later, the forest has returned to its natural state.

EARTH'S BIOSPHERE

THE BIOSPHERE is the area of the Earth's surface and its immediate atmosphere that supports life. It stretches from the depths of the oceans to about 15km (9 miles) up into the atmosphere.

BIOSPHERE UNITS

Ecologists (scientists who study the relationship between living things and their environment) break down the biosphere into progressively smaller units, to make it simpler to study.

Earth
The only planet in the Universe known to support life.

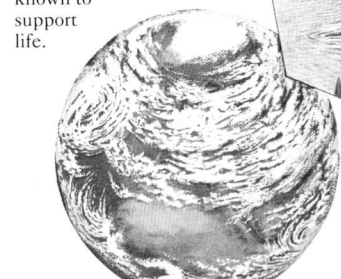

OZONE LAYER

The ozone layer encircles the Earth at a height of 15–50km (9–30 miles). Ozone is the only gas in the atmosphere that can screen out ultraviolet rays from the Sun. Without this protective layer, all life on Earth would die.

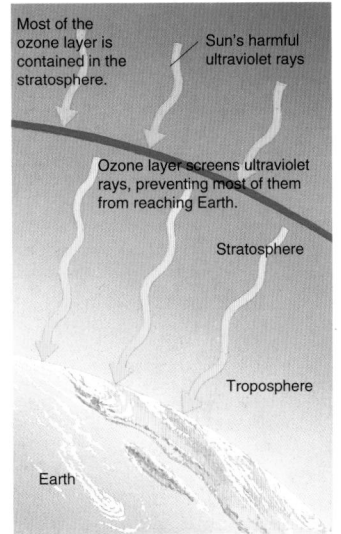

Most of the ozone layer is contained in the stratosphere.

Sun's harmful ultraviolet rays

Ozone layer screens ultraviolet rays, preventing most of them from reaching Earth.

Stratosphere

Troposphere

Earth

Niche
The position of a plant or animal within an ecosystem (see below), including how it relates to other species.

Habitat
The natural home of a plant or animal. A habitat often contains a number of niches.

Ecosystem
The combination of a plant and animal community and its non-living environment.

Biosphere
Close to the ground, this living part of Earth, includes the atmosphere. It contains many different ecosystems.

OXYGEN CYCLE

Living things take in oxygen from the air and use it to obtain energy from the food they eat. Plants and animals take in oxygen during respiration, and green plants release oxygen back into the atmosphere during photosynthesis.

Oxygen in the atmosphere

At night, plants take in oxygen and give out carbon dioxide.

In the daytime, plants take in carbon dioxide and give out oxygen during photosynthesis.

Animals breathe in oxygen and breathe out carbon dioxide.

Night

Day

BODIES OF WATER

Water circulates through the biosphere in a continuous cycle, in oceans, rivers, clouds, and as rain and snow. Living things also form part of this water cycle: the composition of almost all plants and animals, including humans, is nearly 75% water.

BIOSPHERE FACTS

• Ozone is spread so finely that, collected together, it would form a ring round the Earth no thicker than the sole of a shoe.

• Without life, the composition of the Earth's atmosphere would probably be very similar to that of the planet Mars.

• Humans are the first and only species to produce things that cannot be reabsorbed into the Earth's natural systems (non-biodegradable products). Most plastics are non-biodegradable.

• If life disappeared from Earth, nitrogen would move from the atmosphere to the oceans.

EARTH'S CYCLES

Everything in nature is constantly being recycled. Living things take in water, carbon, nitrogen, and oxygen, and use them to live and grow. When they die, they decompose (break down), and the substances they are made of are recycled back into the biosphere and used again for new life. (See p.58 for the water cycle.)

CARBON CYCLE

All living things are based on the element carbon, which originates from carbon dioxide in the Earth's atmosphere. Green plants and some bacteria take in carbon dioxide and use it to make food. When animals eat plants they take in some of this carbon. Carbon dioxide returns to the atmosphere when animals breathe out, produce waste, and finally die and decompose.

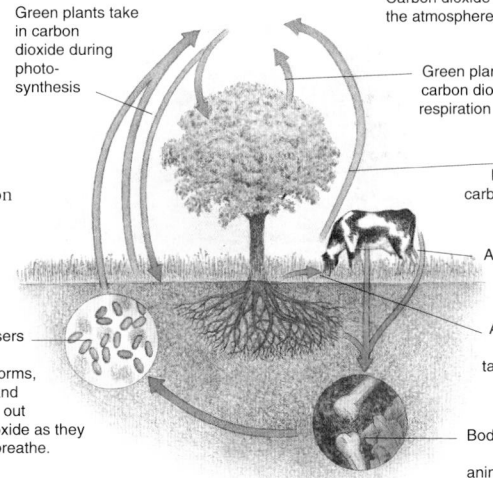

Green plants take in carbon dioxide during photosynthesis

Carbon dioxide in the atmosphere

Green plants give out carbon dioxide during respiration (see p.74).

Animals breathe out carbon dioxide.

Animal dung contains carbon.

Animals eat plants and take in some carbon.

Bodies of dead plants and animals decay.

Decomposers in the soil, such as worms, bacteria, and fungi, give out carbon dioxide as they feed and breathe.

NITROGEN CYCLE

All living things need nitrogen, but most cannot use nitrogen in the atmosphere directly: it has to be fixed (combined with other elements) by bacteria, algae, and some lichens, to form nitrates. Plants can take in nitrates, and animals obtain nitrogen by eating plants.

Nitrogen in the atmosphere

Decaying animal waste and dead organisms release nitrogen compounds into the soil.

Animals eat plants containing nitrates.

Other types of bacteria take in nitrates and release nitrogen back into the atmosphere.

Bacteria in roots and soil convert nitrogen compounds to nitrates.

GAIA THEORY

The Gaia theory was developed in 1979 by British scientist James Lovelock (born 1919) (below), and American biologist Lynn Margulis (born 1938). The basis of the theory is that the Earth acts as a single living, self-sustaining organism that can regulate and organize itself. The hypothesis was named after Gaia, the Greek goddess of the Earth.

EARTH IN DANGER

THE ACTIVITIES OF the rapidly expanding human population create environmental problems that can upset the balance of the biosphere. Pollution and the destruction of the rainforests, for example, seriously threaten the future of life on Earth.

GLOBAL WARMING

Greenhouse effect
Carbon dioxide and certain other gases in the atmosphere act like glass in a greenhouse. They let the Sun's rays through, but trap some of the heat which would otherwise be reflected back into space. This greenhouse effect has always existed.

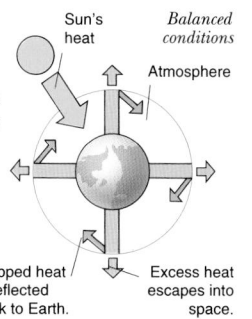

Balanced conditions
Sun's heat
Atmosphere
Trapped heat is reflected back to Earth.
Excess heat escapes into space.

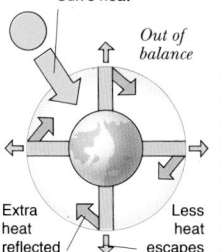

Sun's heat
Out of balance
Extra heat reflected
Less heat escapes

Raising the temperature
Burning fossil fuels (see p.272) increases the amount of carbon dioxide in the atmosphere, which traps extra heat. If we continue to release heat-trapping gases, the Earth's temperature will rise, creating many problems.

OZONE HOLES
Holes in the ozone layer occur all over the world, with particularly large ones over the poles. The main cause is the release of chemicals that destroy the ozone layer, such as chlorofluorocarbons (CFCs), into the atmosphere. The thinning of the ozone layer means that more of the Sun's ultraviolet rays can reach Earth, leading to an increase in skin cancers, and damage to crops.

ACID RAIN
Acid rain is caused mainly by sulphur and nitrogen given off by power stations, industry, and vehicle engines. When these pollutants combine with water vapour, sunlight, and oxygen in the atmosphere, they create weak sulphuric and nitric acids. This mixture falls as rain, increasing the acidity of lakes and rivers. These unfavourable conditions often cause a decline in the numbers of animals and plants.

UPSETTING THE BALANCE
The use of chemicals, such as those in pesticides and fertilizers, can interfere with Earth's natural cycles. For example, the large amount of nitrogen used in farming can lead to pollution of the water supply.

DEFORESTATION
Forests are being felled for timber, and to create land for agriculture. This reduces biodiversity (range and number of species), leads to soil erosion, upsets cycles, and contributes to global warming.

Chemicals released by factories pollute the air, rivers, lakes, and oceans.

More than a million tonnes of oil a year are deliberately discharged from tankers.

URBAN AIR POLLUTION
In many large cities, air pollution caused by vehicles and industry has become a serious problem. It causes human health problems such as eye irritation, coughs, and asthma, and damages plants and buildings.

12% of marine pollution is caused by shipping.

Litter is unsightly and unhygienic, and can harm animals that eat it.

MARINE POLLUTION
The sea has always been a dumping ground for human wastes, but in the last century the amount of pollutants being discharged into the oceans has increased dramatically. This pollution causes problems such as toxic algae, health risks to bathers, and danger to aquatic life.

Toxic algae
One of the most serious effects of marine pollution is toxic (poisonous) algae. Chemicals from sewage discharges, fertilizers, and industrial wastes nourish algae, causing a huge increase in their numbers and, consequently, the amount of poison entering the food chain (see p.108).

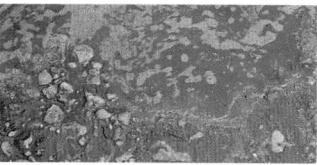

Toxic algae

POLLUTION FACTS
- Most scientists believe that global warming will cause the average world temperature to rise by 1°C (1.8°F) by the year 2030, and by 4°C (7.2°F) by the end of the 21st century.

- In January 1989, Mexico City's smog (urban pollution) was so bad that schoolchildren were given the whole month off.

- About 50 outbreaks of toxic algae occur in Japanese waters every year.

- 2,200 Swedish lakes are nearly lifeless because of acid rain, and 80% of Norway's lakes are biologically dead or threatened.

POLLUTED CITIES
The table below shows the average number of days a year that the suspended particulate matter (soot and smoke) of some of the world's most polluted cities is above the World Health Organization's recommended standard.

City	Number of days above standard
New Delhi, India	294
Beijing, China	272
Tehran, Iran	174
Bangkok, Thailand	97
Madrid, Spain	60

A FOREST A WEEK
It takes an entire forest – more than half a million trees – to supply Americans with their Sunday newspapers every week.

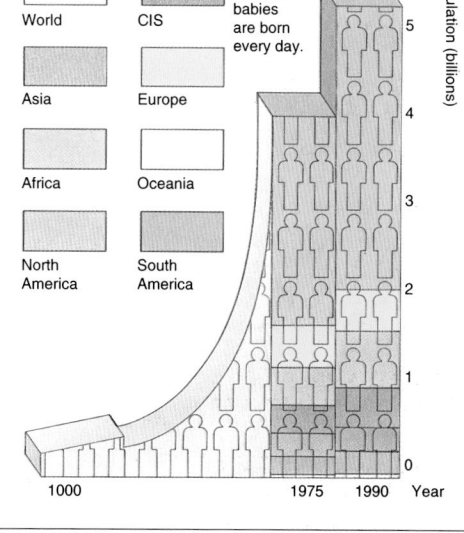

POPULATION GROWTH
Population growth creates huge pressure on the Earth's resources. This graph shows population growth over the last 1,000 years.

World
CIS
Asia
Europe
Africa
Oceania
North America
South America

About 250,000 babies are born every day.

Population (billions)

1000   1975   1990   Year

WASTING EARTH'S RESOURCES
The world's industrialized nations use a far greater proportion of the Earth's resources than the developing nations, even though their combined population is small. The richest 20% of the world's population consumes 70% of the world's energy, 75% of its metals, 85% of its wood, and 60% of its food. Many resources are unnecessarily wasted: much of what people consume ends up on rubbish tips.

SAVING THE EARTH

PEOPLE ARE beginning to accept responsibility for Earth's future. The main environmental problems have been recognized, and ways of reducing their impact are being explored. Positive steps towards the long-term survival of our planet are shown here, but there is still much work to be done.

LIMITING POPULATION GROWTH
Slowing down population growth is one of the most important factors in saving the Earth's diminishing resources. Ways include family planning, and improving standards of living. (In many countries, a large family is seen as a secure source of income.) Family planning measures introduced in Kerala, India, led to a 66% decline in the birth rate between 1983 and 1993.

PROMOTING ECOTOURISM
Tourism that benefits the environment is known as ecotourism. For example, money earned from tourism can be spent on the creation and management of national parks. A report by the US Forest Service showed that the potential earnings from forest recreational activities such as camping and canoeing are twice what could be made by selling the timber.

WAYS TO HELP THE ENVIRONMENT
• Use recycled paper and card.

• Recycle bottles, glass, cans, and waste paper.

• Avoid buying tropical hardwoods, such as mahogany.

REDUCING URBAN POLLUTION
Sharing cars, using public transport, cycling, and walking, all reduce vehicle use in urban areas. Catalytic converters can help to reduce pollution from cars. Working from home using technology such as computers ("telecommuting"), instead of travelling to an office, also reduces the number of vehicles on the roads.

HALTING DESERTIFICATION
Farming methods such as terracing (right) can reduce desertification and the loss of topsoil. In China, a "great green wall" of 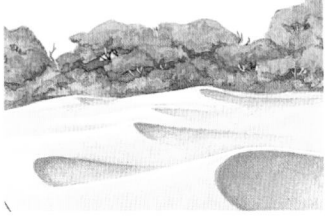 trees (the San Bei Forest Belt) has been planted to hold back the advancing desert. Somalia has begun a major anti-desertification programme that includes a ban on cutting trees for fuel.

Trees planted to hold back the desert

CONSERVING HABITATS AND SPECIES
Projects have been set up worldwide to conserve habitats and the species they contain. These include the establishment of national parks and other conservation areas – more than 5% of the world's total land area is now protected. The Convention on International Trade in Endangered Species (CITES) is an international treaty that has been signed by 122 countries. It aims to prevent trade in endangered plant and animal species, and in products such as animal skins and ivory.

The tiger is endangered.

REDUCING POLLUTION
Many countries are reducing sulphur dioxide emissions to prevent acid rain and global warming. The EC has ruled that large fossil-fuel power plants must cut emissions of sulphur dioxide by 60% by 2003. Ways of improving toxic waste treatment and disposal are also being explored. International treaties have been developed to regulate the dumping of waste at sea, and to control the discharge of other pollutants into the oceans.

• Walk, cycle, or use public transport instead of going by car whenever possible.

• Switch off lights and other appliances when not in use.

• When getting rid of an old refrigerator, make sure that its CFCs are safely removed.

Public transport   Cycling and walking   Public transport   Car sharing

USING RENEWABLE ENERGY
Fossil fuels (see p.272) will eventually run out. In the meantime, their use creates pollution and contributes to global warming. Cleaner, renewable methods of generating energy are being developed, including wind, wave, solar, and tidal power. Some countries, including Norway and Brazil, already obtain more than half their energy from renewable sources.

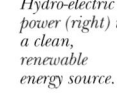
Hydro-electric power (right) is a clean, renewable energy source.

Wind turbines

Solar collectors trap sunlight to generate power.

REDUCING FIREWOOD USE
Tree cover is being lost where large amounts of wood are chopped for fire. Alternative, more efficient cooking methods are being introduced in some countries affected by this deforestation. In Kenya, where wood energy accounts for more than 75% of energy consumption, 180,000 jikos (charcoal-burning stoves) have been distributed (right).

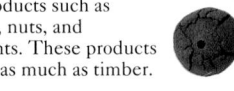

SAVING THE RAINFORESTS
Many initiatives have been introduced to try to save the remaining areas of rainforest. Debt-swap deals, in which a country protects an area of forest in return for a reduction in their foreign debt, have been negotiated. Practices that do not damage the forest, such as rubber tapping, are being encouraged, together with trade in forest products such as spices, rattan, nuts, and medicinal plants. These products may be worth as much as timber.

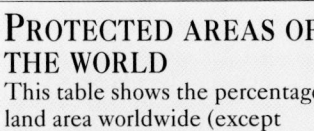
Brazil nuts

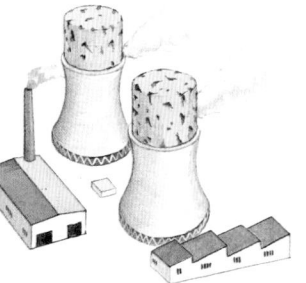
Rubber tapping

• Start a compost heap for vegetable peelings and garden waste, such as leaves and grass cuttings.

• When ordinary lightbulbs are spent, replace them with energy-efficient, compact fluorescent lightbulbs.

PROTECTED AREAS OF THE WORLD
This table shows the percentage of land area worldwide (except Antarctica) that is protected in national parks or other conservation areas. It also shows the country with the most protected land.

Area	% land protected	Country with most protected land (%)
North & Central America	10.4	Panama 17.2
Europe	7.5	Austria 19
South America	5.7	Ecuador 37.7
Oceania	5.7	New Zealand 10.5
Africa	3.9	Botswana 17.2
Asia	2.1	Bhutan 19.7

LIVING WORLD

In this fascinating survey of the natural world, all living things are classified, and every major plant and animal group is illustrated. Stunning cut-away artworks show anatomical details, and there is a wealth of factual information about attack and defence, movement, and reproduction. Tables list record breakers from the heaviest to the most deadly.

Evolution • Fossils • Dinosaurs • Classifying Living Things
Plants • Flowers • Leaves • Trees • Food Plants • Fungi and Lichens
Micro-organisms • Animals • Invertebrates • Molluscs • Insects
Arachnids • Crustaceans • Amphibians • Reptiles • Fish
Birds • Domestic Birds • Mammals • Domestic Mammals
Animal Senses and Behaviour • Migration and Homes
Food Chains and Webs • Endangered Species
Animal Records and Comparisons

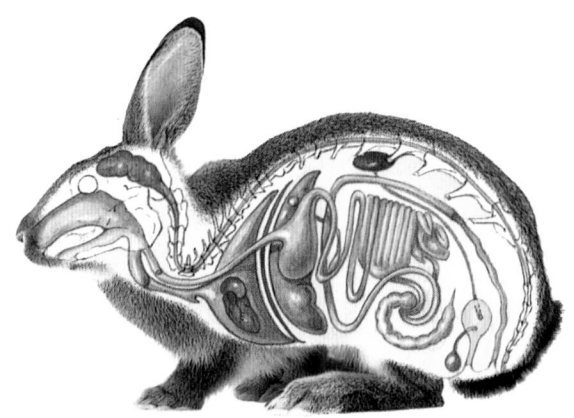

EVOLUTION

LIFE ON EARTH probably originated from chemicals dissolved in the oceans. From these simple beginnings, life has gradually developed into many different forms. All living things change as one generation succeeds another. This process is called evolution.

EVOLUTION TERMS

Variation Almost all living things vary in size, shape, colour, and strength: no two animals or plants are the same.

Adaptations These are certain features, such as colour, that may give one animal or plant a better chance of survival than another.

Inheritance Characteristics are passed on, or inherited, when living things reproduce. Most living things have a unique combination of characteristics.

Natural selection Through natural selection, inherited characteristics that help a living thing survive are passed on; those that do not gradually die out.

Competition/survival of the fittest More individuals are born than can survive. Strong, well-adapted individuals are more likely to survive than weak, poorly adapted individuals.

EVOLUTION OF THE ELEPHANT

Fossils reveal that several elephant-like species have existed and become extinct over the last 40 million years. It is likely that they were related, and that today's elephants evolved from them.

Platybelodon lived from 12 to 7 million years ago.

Trilophodon lived from 26 to 3 million years ago.

Woolly mammoth lived about 2 million years ago.

African elephant

Moenitherium lived about 38 million years ago.

ADAPTATION EXAMPLE

The 28 species of honeycreeper in the Hawaiian islands probably all evolved from one species. Each has a beak adapted for a particular way of feeding. Some are now extinct.

The iiwi's beak and tongue are adapted for sipping nectar.

The Kona grosbeak (now extinct) had a strong bill for crushing seeds.

The Kauai akialoa uses its long beak to probe for insects.

EVOLUTION FACTS

• Ninety-five per cent of all animals and plants that have ever existed on Earth have become extinct.

• Between 35 and 20 million years ago, giant rhinoceroses, such as *Paraceatherium*, roamed the Americas. This animal measured up to 8m (26ft) long and was as tall as a giraffe.

• Moas – the giant, flightless birds of New Zealand (now extinct) – show what could have happened in a world without mammals: birds would have become dominant. (New Zealand has no native mammals except for a few bats.)

• The earliest horse, *Hyracotherium*, was about the size of a modern fox terrier.

CHARLES DARWIN (1809–82)
The theory of evolution was developed by English naturalist Charles Darwin, and published in 1859 in his book *The Origin of Species*. Darwin developed his theory after studying the animals of the Galapagos Islands, which were unique, but similar to those on the South American mainland.

• Australia's largest ever marsupial (see p.102) was *Diprotodon optatum*, which was as big as a rhinoceros and weighed up to 1,500kg (3,307lb).

SLOTH GROWTH

During the Tertiary Period, South America was cut off from other landmasses, and there were few predators. Several types of mammal became gigantic, for example *Megatherium*, the giant ground sloth, grew to more than 6m (20ft) long.

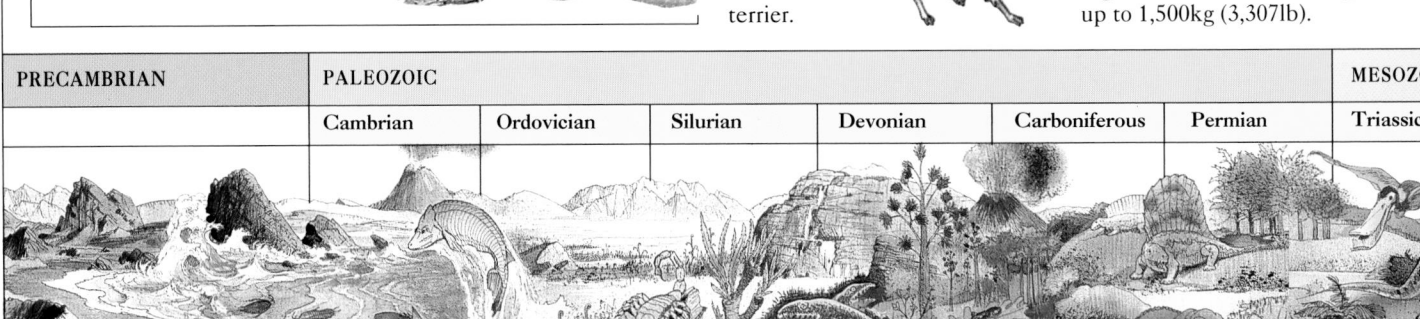

PRECAMBRIAN	PALEOZOIC						MESOZO
	Cambrian	Ordovician	Silurian	Devonian	Carboniferous	Permian	Triassic
4,600–590mya (million years ago) Earth forms and gradually cools; atmosphere has no oxygen. First bacteria appear. Blue-green algae evolve and produce oxygen-rich atmosphere. Protists (single-celled organisms) develop. Non-flowering marine plants evolve and become abundant. First animals, including worms and jellyfish, appear.	**590–505mya** Invertebrates (see p.84) become widespread in the oceans. Trilobites are common. First molluscs (see pp.86–87) evolve.	**505–438mya** First crustaceans evolve. First, fish-like vertebrates (see p.84) appear: they have no fins or jaws.	**438–408mya** First fish with jaws evolve. Coral reefs flourish in the oceans. Huge sea scorpions hunt. On land, the first small plants appear.	**408–360mya** "Age of Fish." Fish dominate life in the seas. First insects evolve. First amphibians appear on land.	**360–286mya** "The Coal Age." Warm, damp climate; huge forests lay down remains that will turn into coal. First reptiles evolve from amphibians. Insects abundant.	**286–248mya** Earth cooler. Amphibians decline; reptiles diversify. Ferns and conifers widespread. Many species vanish in greatest mass extinction known.	**248–213** Climate to warm conifers ferns for forests. First din evolve. man ev

FOSSILS

FOSSILS PROVIDE a history book of life on Earth. They are the remains of dead animals and plants that have been preserved naturally for thousands or millions of years. The study of fossils is called palaeontology.

FORMS OF FOSSILIZATION

Fossils are preserved in several different ways. Most are found in rocks, but fossils also occur in ice, tar, peat, and amber.

MINERALIZATION
This is the most common form of preservation. It occurs when the organic matter of a fossil is replaced by durable (long-lasting) minerals. Petrified wood is formed by mineralization.

Petrified wood

FREEZING
Low temperatures can preserve animal and plant remains. Well-preserved mammoths have been found in Siberian permafrost (permanently frozen ground). Flesh and skin, as well as bones, are preserved by freezing.

Fossilized mammoth

AMBER
Tree resin (sap) can trap and surround small animals such as insects and spiders. The resin, with the animal still intact inside, is fossilized, turning into amber.

Spider in amber

PEAT AND TAR
Animals and plants can be preserved in peat and tar. Human bodies more than 2,000 years old have been found in peat bogs, and animal remains up to 20,000 years old have been found in tar.

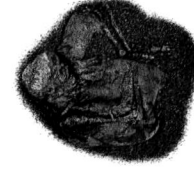
Human preserved in peat

TYPES OF FOSSIL

Any organism can be mineralized, provided it is buried by mud or sand before it rots away. Most fossils form on the sea bed, so the most common are those of sea creatures. Fossils of land animals and plants are much rarer.

Ammonites
Ammonites were marine (sea-dwelling) molluscs that became extinct about 65 million years ago. Their shells were often fossilized.

Archaeopteryx
Prehistoric flying animal believed to be the evolutionary link between reptiles and birds. Seven fossilized *Archaeopteryx* have been found.

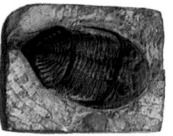

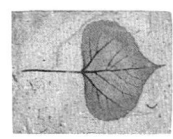

Trilobites
Marine arthropods (see p.85) distantly related to the wood louse. They died out about 286 million years ago.

Soft-bodied animals
Most fossils are the remains of bones or shells. Fossils of soft-bodied animals, such as this dragonfly, are rare.

Coprolites
These are fossilized animal droppings. Dinosaur coprolites can measure more than 60cm (2ft) long.

Plant fossils
This fossilized poplar leaf is about 25 million years old. Modern poplar leaves are almost identical: these trees have hardly changed.

FOSSIL FACTS

- Fossils are found only in sedimentary rocks (see p.46). Marine limestones, shales, and some sandstones, contain the most fossils.

- Some ammonites measured up to 2m (6.6ft) in diameter.

FORMATION OF FOSSILS

This sequence shows how the remains of sea creatures may be fossilized and brought to the land surface.

MAMMOTH MISTAKE

For centuries, fossils were associated with myths and legends. Fossilized mammoth tusks discovered in about 1600 were believed at the time to be the horns of unicorns.

1 Dead animals, such as fish, sink to the sea bed. Their remains are slowly buried by layers of sediment.

2 The lower layers of sediment turn to rock, and the animal remains are mineralized, becoming fossils.

3 Over many years the rock is folded, and the upper layers are eroded away.

4 The rock is eroded further, and the fossils are eventually exposed on the surface.

FOSSIL RECORDS

EARLIEST FOSSILS are prokaryotes (cells without nuclei) found in Western Australia, which are an estimated 3.5 billion years old.

LARGEST FOSSIL is a *Brachiosaurus* skeleton (see p.71), which is 22m (72ft) long.

		CENOZOIC							
...ssic	Cretaceous	Tertiary						Quaternary	
		Palaeocene	Eocene	Oligocene	Miocene	Pliocene	Pleistocene	Holocene

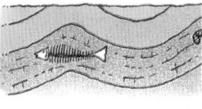
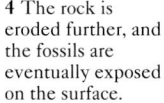

| ...144mya ...ate much ...er than ... Dinosaurs ...nate life on ... First ...n bird, ...eopteryx, ...es from ...es. | 144–65mya First flowering plants evolve. Dinosaurs flourish. Period ends with mass extinction: sweeps away many species including all dinosaurs and ammonites. | 65–55mya Climate warm and damp. Flowering plants continue to evolve and, together with insect pollinators, become widespread. | 55–38mya Mammals continue to diversify, becoming larger and more numerous. Primates (apes, monkeys, and lemurs) evolve into many forms. | 38–25mya First human-like primates appear. Many early mammals become extinct. Giant flightless hunting birds flourish. | 25–5mya Climate cools; forests begin to decrease worldwide. Hoofed mammals, such as deer, flourish. Towards the end of the epoch, the first hominids evolve. | 5–2mya Climate cold and dry. Mammals reach peak of their diversity. Many land creatures similar to today's. Bony fish dominate life in the sea. | 2m–10,000 years ago Time of ice ages. Many mammal species, including mammoths and sabre-toothed tigers, become extinct. *Homo sapiens* evolves. | 10,000 years ago – today Humans develop agriculture and technology; population expands. |

DINOSAURS

DINOSAURS DOMINATED the Earth for more than 150 million years. They included the largest animals ever to have lived on land, as well as some that were smaller than a pet dog. Dinosaurs died out 65 million years ago. Nobody knows why.

TYPES OF DINOSAUR

There are two orders (see p.72) of dinosaur. They are classified according to the arrangement of their hip-bones.

Lizard-hipped dinosaurs
(Saurischians)
Hips similar to lizards. Includes both herbivorous (plant-eating) and carnivorous (meat-eating) species.

Bird-hipped dinosaurs
(Ornithischians)
Hips similar to birds. All of the bird-hipped dinosaur species were herbivorous.

DINOSAUR FACTS

• Dinosaur fossils discovered to date probably represent less than 0.0001% of the individuals that once lived.

• The name *Tyrannosaurus* means "tyrant lizard".

• The most intelligent dinosaurs were probably about as intelligent as chickens.

• More than 350 species of dinosaur have so far been identified: probably only a tiny percentage of those that existed.

• *Struthiomimus* could sprint at speeds of up to 80km/h (50mph): as fast as an ostrich.

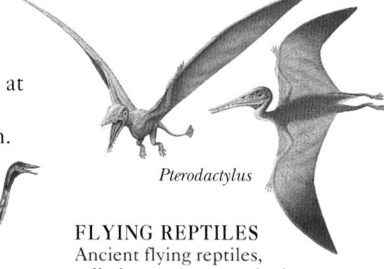

PORTRAIT OF A DINOSAUR

Like reptiles, dinosaurs had a scaly skin. Dinosaurs, however, were more advanced than today's reptiles. They walked with their limbs directly under their body like mammals and birds, whereas reptiles crawl, or walk with their limbs out to their sides.

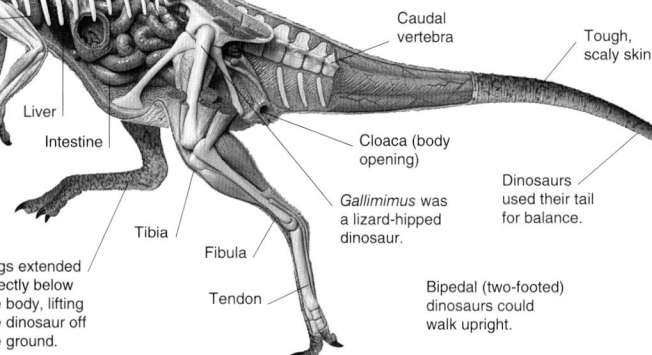

Dinosaurs' brains were small for their body size.

Gallimimus

Backbone

Rib

Trachea

Ovary

Kidney

Lung

Heart

Claw

Liver

Intestine

Caudal vertebra

Tough, scaly skin

Cloaca (body opening)

Gallimimus was a lizard-hipped dinosaur.

Dinosaurs used their tail for balance.

Tibia

Fibula

Tendon

Legs extended directly below the body, lifting the dinosaur off the ground.

Bipedal (two-footed) dinosaurs could walk upright.

DINOSAUR-LIKE REPTILES

While dinosaurs roamed the land, huge reptiles flew in the air and swam in the oceans. These marine and flying reptiles were closely related to the dinosaurs.

Rhamphorhynchus

Ichthyosaurus

Elasmosaurus

Pterodactylus

FLYING REPTILES

Ancient flying reptiles, called pterosaurs, reached huge sizes. Their wings were made of skin, and their body was usually furry. They had light, delicate bones for flying.

MARINE REPTILES

These were some of the fiercest and largest animals in the sea. They breathed air, so had to come to the surface regularly to fill their lungs. These reptiles hunted fish and other sea creatures.

MAJOR DINOSAUR GROUPS

Within the two orders, dinosaurs are divided into five sub-groups. There are three sub-groups of ornithischians, and two sub-groups of saurischians.

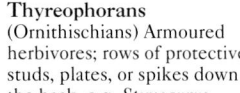

Thyreophorans
(Ornithischians) Armoured herbivores; rows of protective studs, plates, or spikes down the back, e.g. *Stegosaurus*.

Theropods (Saurischians)
Mostly bipedal carnivores with an S-shaped neck and clawed, four-toed feet, e.g. *Tyrannosaurus*.

Marginocephalians
(Ornithischians) Herbivores; many with bony frill at back of skull, e.g. *Styracosaurus*.

Ornithopods
(Ornithischians) Herbivores; horny beak and bird-like feet, e.g. *Corythosaurus*.

Sauropodomorphs
(Saurischians). Herbivores; small head, long neck, bulky body, and long tail, e.g. *Saltasaurus*.

Triassic Period: 248–213mya (million years ago)	**Jurassic Period: 213–144mya**

Land joined in the super-continent of Pangaea (see p.40). First dinosaurs evolve and, towards the end of the period, split into two groups: lizard- and bird-hipped.

Pangaea breaks apart: Atlantic Ocean begins to form; Africa splits from South America. In late Jurassic times, huge herbivorous dinosaurs dominate life on land.

Melanorosaurus

Coelophysis

Plateosaurus

Mosasaurus

Herrerasaurus

Staurikosaurus

Technosaurus

Camptosaurus

Dryosaurus

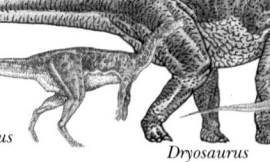

DINOSAUR DISCOVERY

Pre-19th century: around the world, dinosaur fossils are believed to be various things, including dragon bones in China, and giant human bones in parts of Europe.

1800 Dinosaur footprints found in Massachusetts, USA. Their discoverer claims they were made by the raven from Noah's Ark.

1820 *Iguanodon* teeth discovered in Tilgate Forest, Sussex, England, by doctor and fossil hunter Gideon Mantell (1790–1852) and his wife. He suspects they are the remains of ancient reptiles, but his theory is dismissed as heretical (anti-religious).

1834 First glimpse of what dinosaurs looked like provided by find of a partial skeleton near Maidstone, England, known as the Maidstone *Iguanodon*.

1841 The term dinosaur, from the Greek words for "terrible" and "lizard", is coined by English anatomist Richard Owen (1804–92).

| 1800 | 1820 | 1834 | 1841 |

1851 First reconstruction of dinosaurs: *Iguanodon* and *Hylaeosaurus* models are made for the Great Exhibition at Crystal Palace, London, England. Results in huge public enthusiasm for dinosaurs. Before the *Iguanodon* is completed, the sculptor holds a dinner party inside it.

Dinner party in a model dinosaur

1877 One of the greatest dinosaur collections found at Como Bluff, Wyoming, USA, by O.C. Marsh (1831–99) of Yale College.

1947 Largest number of dinosaurs ever found together: more than 100 *Coelophysis* skeletons.

1987 Evidence to support theory of warm-blooded dinosaurs found by palaeontologists Tom Rich and Patricia Vickers-Rich of the Museum of Victoria, Australia. They discover dinosaur fossils in a part of South Australia that would have been inside the Antarctic Circle when these dinosaurs lived. The mean annual temperature in this region would then have been near freezing.

Leaellynasaura lived in polar regions.

| 1851 | 1877 | 1947 | 1987 |

DINOSAUR RECORDS

SMALLEST DINOSAUR was probably *Wannanosaurus*, a bipedal carnivore that measured 60cm (2ft) long. It was about the size of a chicken.

MOST PRIMITIVE KNOWN DINOSAUR is *Eoraptor*, a 228 million-year-old bipedal carnivore that was about the size of a large dog.

SMALLEST DINOSAUR BRAIN is believed to have been that of the *Stegosaurus*. It was less than 5cm (2in) long.

LARGEST DINOSAUR EGGS were probably those of *Hypselosaurus*. They measured about 30cm (12in) long and contained an estimated 3.3 litres (6 pints) of fluid: roughly the same as the fluid in 60 hens' eggs.

WIDER GLIDER

The largest flying animal ever to have existed was *Quetzalcoatlus*, a flying reptile. Its wingspan measured about 12m (39ft) across: wider than the wingspan of a hang glider.

EARTH SHAKER

The name *Seismosaurus* means "earth-shaking lizard". This enormous plant-eating dinosaur was 40m (131ft) in length: longer than an Airbus A320.

LARGEST CARNIVORES

Dinosaur	Estimated length	
	m	ft
Acrocanthosaurus	12	39
Tyrannosaurus	12	39
Aliwalia	11	36
Allosaurus	11	36

LARGEST HERBIVORES

Dinosaur	Estimated length	
	m	ft
Seismosaurus	40	131
Barosaurus	27	89
Diplodocus	27	89
Brachiosaurus	25	82

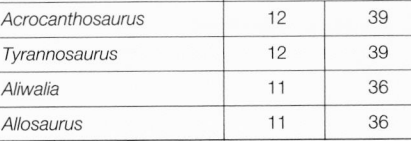

EXTINCTION THEORIES

About 65 million years ago the dinosaurs, together with many other animal species, became extinct. Other animal groups, including turtles, frogs, birds, and mammals, survived. There are many theories for this mass-extinction: below are two of the most widely accepted.

GRADUAL EXTINCTION

Gradual changes in climate and vegetation caused by continental drift (see p.40) led to the dinosaurs' slow extinction over about 50,000 years. Warm, tropical conditions were replaced by cooler, more seasonal climates, and mammals slowly replaced dinosaurs as the dominant animal group.

CATASTROPHES

The period when dinosaurs were dying out coincided with many volcanic eruptions in India. At the same time, a huge meteorite hit the Earth. Dust thrown into the atmosphere blocked out sunlight, and dinosaurs could not survive the resulting climate changes.

| Cretaceous Period: 144–65mya | 65mya |

Continents split further apart, eventually drifting into their present-day positions. Dinosaurs continue to flourish; those on different continents evolve separately, leading to great diversity.

Dinosaurs become extinct, together with many other animal species.

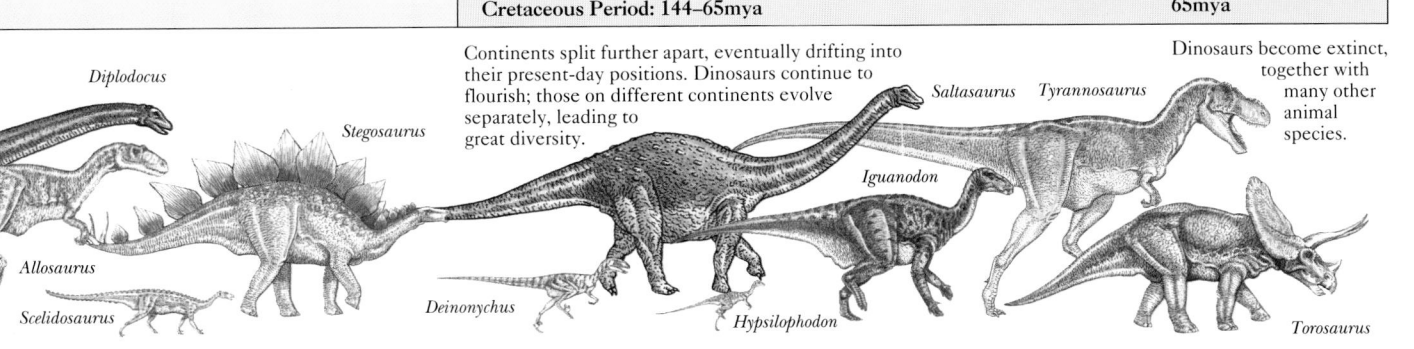

Diplodocus

Stegosaurus

Saltasaurus

Tyrannosaurus

Iguanodon

Allosaurus

Scelidosaurus

Deinonychus

Hypsilophodon

Torosaurus

CLASSIFYING LIVING THINGS

LIVING THINGS ARE classified in groups according to the features they have in common. The largest groups are the five kingdoms: animals, plants, fungi, protists, and monerans. Each kingdom is then subdivided into smaller and smaller groups.

KEY

These colours show the classification groupings used in the chart. All numbers of species are approximate. A division is the plant equivalent of a phylum.

Kingdom	Class
Phylum	Order
Sub-phylum	Division

SCIENTIFIC NAMES

Many living things have different common names around the world. To avoid confusion, every species also has a two-part scientific name which is the same worldwide. The first part of the name gives the genus; the second part the species. This system was devised by Swedish botanist Carolus Linnaeus (1707–78). Larger groups, such as orders, also have a scientific name. Throughout the *Living World* section, scientific names are given wherever possible for species and genera.

CLASSIFYING A TIGER

This illustration shows how a biologist would classify a tiger.

Kingdom Animal (Animalia) Many-celled organisms with no cell walls; cannot make their own food.

Phylum Chordate (Chordata) Animals that have a single nerve cord at some time in their life.

Class Mammal (Mammalia) Animals that suckle their young on milk and have fur or hair.

Order Carnivores (Carnivora) Land mammals specialized for hunting.

Family Cats (Felidae) Carnivores with sharp front claws that can be retracted (drawn in).

Genus Big cats *(Panthera)* The five species of big cats: lion, tiger, leopard, snow leopard, and jaguar.

Species Tiger *(Panthera tigris)*

Sponges (Porifera) 9,000 species

Sea anemones, hydras, corals, jellyfish (Cnidaria) 9,500 species

Comb jellies (Ctenophora) 90 species

Flatworms, flukes, tapeworms (Platyhelminthes) 15,000 species

Roundworms (Nematoda) 20,000 species

Horsehair worms (Nematomorpha) 250 species

Spiny-headed worms (Acanthocephala) 1,150 species

Rotifers (Rotifera) 2,000 species

Waterbears (Tardigrada) 600 species

Worms and leeches (Annelida) 18,600 species

Molluscs (Mollusca)

MONERANS (Monera)

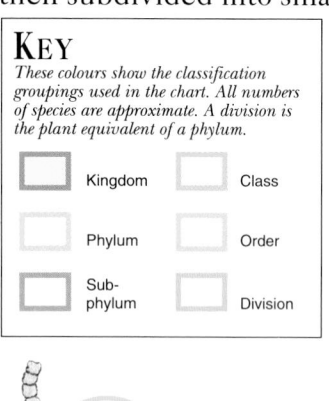

Blue-green algae (Cyanonta) 1,700 species

Bacteria (Schizonta) 4,000 species

PROTISTS (Protista)

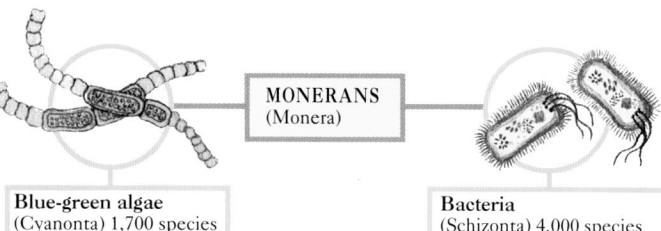

Golden algae (Chrysophyta) 650 species

Amoebas, flagellates, opalinids (Sarcomastigophora) 27,000 species

Sporozoans (Sporozoa) 5,000 species

Ciliates (Ciliophora) 8,000 species

Sea squirts (Ascidiacea) 2,500 species

Jawless fish (Agnatha) 75 species

Sharks and rays (Chondrichthyes) 800 species

Sharks, dogfish Skates, rays

Bony fish (Osteichthyes) 20,000 species

More than 20 orders including:
Eels
Herrings, anchovies
Salmon, trout
Carp
Catfish
Perch, marlins, swordfish, tunas
Flying fish

FUNGI (Fungi)

  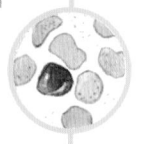 

Rusts and mildews (Oomycetes) 600 species

Moulds (Zygomycetes) 765 species

Sac fungi (Ascomycetes) 29,000 species

Club fungi (Basidiomycetes) 16,000 species

Fungi imperfecti (Deuteromycetes) 17,000 species

Slime moulds (Acrasiomycota) 6 species

PLANTS (Plantae)

Green algae (Chlorophyta) 14,000 species

Red algae (Rhodophyta) 5,000 species

Brown algae (Phaeophyta) 1,500 species

Mosses and liverworts (Bryophyta) 14,000 species

Ferns (Pteridophyta) 12,000 species

Clubmosses (Lycopodophyta) 1,000 species

Horsetails (Sphenophyta) 40 species

ANIMALS (Animalia)

Velvetworms
(Onychophora)
100 species

Lampshells
(Brachiopoda)
300 species

Moss animals
(Bryozoa) 4,000 species

c.13 other small phyla
c.2,000 species

Chitons
(Polyplacophora) 500 species

Solenogasters
(Aplacophora) 5,540 species

Deep-sea limpets
(Monoplacophora) 10 species

Tusk shells
(Scaphopoda) 350 species

Gastropods
(Gastropoda) 35,000 species

Bivalves
(Bivalvia) 8,000 species

Cephalopods
(Cephalopoda) 600 species

Arthropods
(Arthropoda)

Horseshoe crabs
(Merostomata)
4 species

Millipedes
(Diplopoda)
10,000 species

Sea spiders
(Pycnogonida)
1,000 species

Centipedes
(Chilopoda)
2,500 species

Arachnids
(Arachnida)
73,000 species

Scorpions
Tick spiders
Micro-whip scorpions
Tail-less whip scorpions
Whip scorpions
Camel spiders
Pseudoscorpions
Harvestmen
Mites and ticks
Spiders

Echinoderms
(Echinodermata)
6,000 species in 5 orders including:

Starfish
(Asteroidea)
1,500 species

Brittle stars
(Ophiuroidea)
2,000 species

Sea urchins
(Echinoidea)
950 species

Sea cucumbers
(Holothuroidea)
900 species

Crustaceans
(Crustacea) 55,400 species

Sand shrimps
(Cephalocarida)
9 species

Mystacocarideans
(Mystacocarida)
10 species

Branchiopods
(Branchiopoda)
1,000 species

Spiny sand shrimps
(Branchiura)
125 species

Mussel shrimps
(Ostracoda) 10,000 species

Barnacles
(Cirripedia) 1,220 species

Copepods
(Copepoda) 13,000 species

Crabs, lobsters, and shrimps
(Malacostraca) 30,000 species

Insects
(Insecta) 1,000,000 species

Springtails	Webspinners	Grylloblattids	Sucking lice		Stylopids
Telson-tails	Dragonflies	Earwigs	Thrips	Ants, bees, wasps	Caddisflies
Diplurans	Grasshoppers, crickets	Cockroaches	Booklice	Dobson and alderflies	Butterflies and moths
Silverfish	Stick and leaf insects	Praying mantids	Zorapterans	Snakeflies	Flies
Mayflies		Termites	Bugs	Lacewings and antlions	Fleas
Stoneflies		Biting lice	Beetles	Scorpionflies	

Chordates
(Chordata)

Amphibians
(Amphibia)
4,200 species

Frogs and toads
Newts and salamanders
Caecilians

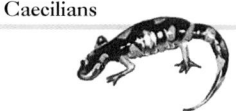

Reptiles
(Reptilia)
6,000 species

Lizards and snakes
Turtles, tortoises, and terrapins
Crocodilians
Tuatara

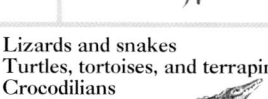

Birds
(Aves) 9,000 species

Ostrich
Rheas
Cassowaries, emu
Kiwis
Albatrosses, petrels, shearwaters, fulmars
Pelicans, gannets, cormorants, frigatebirds, darters
Penguins
Grebes
Divers or loons
Tinamous
Herons, storks, ibises, flamingos
Ducks, geese, swans
Eagles, hawks, vultures, falcons, kites, buzzards
Pheasant, partridges, grouse, turkeys

Cranes, rails, coots, bustards
Wading birds, gulls, terns, auks
Sandgrouse
Pigeons, doves
Parrots
Cuckoos, roadrunners, turacos
Owls
Nightjars, frogmouths
Swifts, hummingbirds
Trogons
Mousebirds
Kingfishers, bee-eaters, rollers, hoopoes
Woodpeckers, toucans, barbets, honeyguides, puffbirds, jacamars
Passerines

Mammals
(Mammalia) 4,600 species

Monotremes
(egg-laying mammals)
Marsupials (pouched mammals)
Insectivores
Elephant shrews
Flying lemurs
Bats
Tree shrews
Primates
Edentates (anteaters, sloths, armadillos)
Pangolins
Aardvark
Hares, rabbits, pikas
Rodents

Whales and dolphins
Carnivores
Seals, sea lions, walrus
Elephants
Hyraxes
Sea cows
Odd-toed hoofed mammals
Even-toed hoofed mammals

Monocotyledons
80,000 species

Gymnosperms
(Gymnospermae)

Conifers
(Coniferopsida) 500 species

Cycads
(Cycadopsida) 100 species

Joint pines
(Gnetopsida) 70 species

Flowering plants
(Angiospermae)

Dicotyledons
170,000 species

PLANTS

PLANTS, UNLIKE ANIMALS, can manufacture their own food. This makes them the starting point of most food chains, and almost all other living organisms depend on them for food.

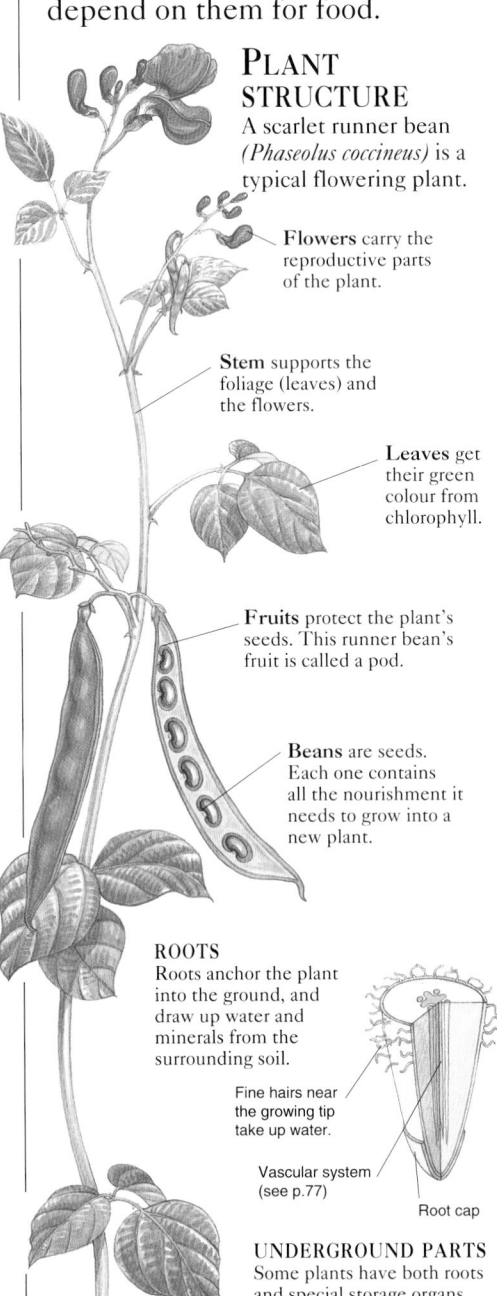

PLANT STRUCTURE

A scarlet runner bean *(Phaseolus coccineus)* is a typical flowering plant.

Flowers carry the reproductive parts of the plant.

Stem supports the foliage (leaves) and the flowers.

Leaves get their green colour from chlorophyll.

Fruits protect the plant's seeds. This runner bean's fruit is called a pod.

Beans are seeds. Each one contains all the nourishment it needs to grow into a new plant.

ROOTS

Roots anchor the plant into the ground, and draw up water and minerals from the surrounding soil.

Fine hairs near the growing tip take up water.

Vascular system (see p.77)

Root cap

UNDERGROUND PARTS

Some plants have both roots and special storage organs, such as tubers or bulbs.

Roots draw up water.

Tap root
A tap root has a large, central root and finer side-growing roots.
Carrot

Tuber
A tuber is a swollen stem or root in which the plant stores food.
Potato

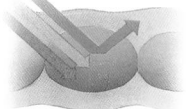

TYPES OF PLANT

NON-FLOWERING

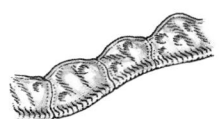  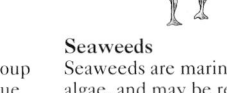  

Algae
Algae are a large group of plants with no true roots, stems, or leaves.

Seaweeds
Seaweeds are marine algae, and may be red, brown, or green.

Mosses and liverworts
Mosses and liverworts have stems and leaves, but no true roots.

Ferns
Ferns have roots, stems, and fronds, and can grow as tall as trees.

FLOWERING

Grasses
Grasses have jointed stems, narrow leaves, and seedlike fruits.

Shrubs
Shrubs are short, woody plants, with a stem that divides at ground level.

Herbs
Herbs are flowering plants that die back after producing seeds.

Trees
Most trees, such as palms (see p.78), are flowering plants.

LIFE CYCLE

SEXUAL REPRODUCTION

Many plants reproduce by ova being fertilized by pollen, whether from the same flower or plant or a different one. This is sexual reproduction.

Life cycle of a poppy

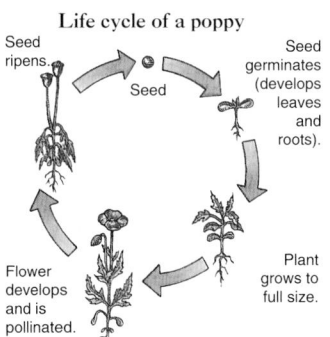

Seed ripens.

Seed

Seed germinates (develops leaves and roots).

Plant grows to full size.

Flower develops and is pollinated.

ASEXUAL REPRODUCTION

Many plants can reproduce without pollination or fertilization taking place. This is called asexual reproduction.

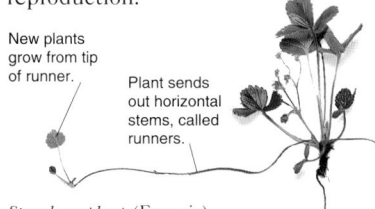

New plants grow from tip of runner.

Plant sends out horizontal stems, called runners.

Strawberry plant (Fragaria)

PHOTOSYNTHESIS

In photosynthesis, chlorophyll in the leaves uses energy from the sun to combine carbon dioxide with water. This produces food in the form of carbohydrates (sugars and starches) and oxygen.

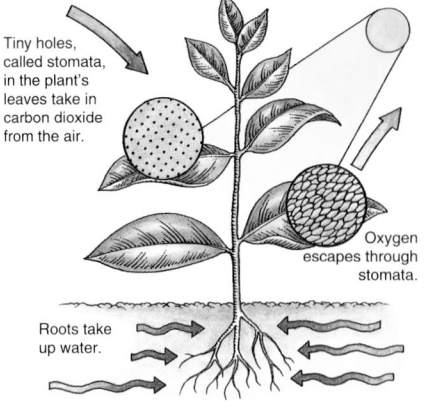

Tiny holes, called stomata, in the plant's leaves take in carbon dioxide from the air.

Oxygen escapes through stomata.

Roots take up water.

CHLOROPHYLL

Chlorophyll, a pigment, gives most leaves their green colour. It absorbs light from the sun, soaking up red and blue light, but reflecting green.

Red and blue light waves absorbed

Green light waves reflected

RESPIRATION

Plants, like humans, breathe constantly, taking up oxygen (O_2) and releasing carbon dioxide (CO_2). This process is called respiration. At twilight, plants produce equal amounts of oxygen and carbon dioxide. This is called the compensation point. Carbon dioxide is released during both day and night.

1 Daytime
Plant releases more oxygen than it uses in respiration.

2 Twilight
Compensation point. Plant produces both gases.

3 Night-time
The plant releases more carbon dioxide than it uses.

PIGMENTATION

Plants are not always green. Chlorophyll is present in most plants, but some also contain other pigments that affect their colour. These pigments may help the plant to photosynthesize in difficult conditions.

Brown seaweed (Phaeopyta)

Red seaweed (Rhodophyta)

PLANT HABITATS

Plants will grow wherever there is enough moisture, light, warmth, and nourishment in the soil. Some plants have developed particular ways of coping with extreme conditions.

Tropical
Most bromeliads (*Bromeliaceae* family) live in tropical rainforests, on tall trees where sunlight can reach their leaves.

Brackish and salt water
Mangroves (*Rhizophora*) have special pores in their roots to take in oxygen from the air.

Desert
Saguaro cactus (*Carnegia gigantea*) lacks leaves, reducing water loss. Its spines protect it from animals.

Aquatic
Water lilies (*Nymphaea*) have a waxy outer layer, so the leaves float; stomata are on the upper surface only.

Sand and shingle
Sand couch grass (*Elymus farctus*) has very long roots that can reach water below ground.

Alpine
Alpine anemone (*Pulsatilla alpina*) has white hairs on its leaves to reflect the heat of the alpine summer sun.

HORMONES

Plants, like humans, have hormones. These control whether a plant makes a leaf or a flower. They also ensure that its stem grows up towards the sun, and that its roots grow down towards underground water.

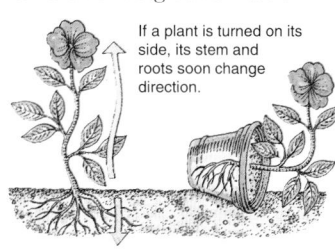

If a plant is turned on its side, its stem and roots soon change direction.

PLANT FACTS

• Air plants have no roots. They grow on tree branches in tropical and sub-tropical Americas, absorbing all the moisture they need from the air.

• Resurrection plants shrivel up in dry weather. As soon as it rains, they become green and begin to photosynthesize again.

• Ant plants have ants living in spaces, called domatia, in their stems. The ants protect the plants from attacks by other insects.

WEEDS

Daisy (Bellis perennis)

Weeds are simply plants that grow in places where they are a nuisance to people, such as gardens or crop fields. Some are as colourful and sweet-smelling as garden flowers.

PLANT GROWTH RATES

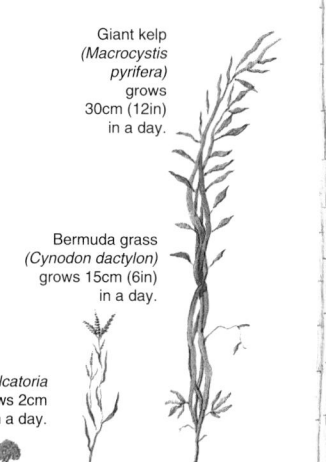

Giant bamboo (*Dendrocalamus giganteus*) grows 90cm (3ft) in a day

Giant kelp (*Macrocystis pyrifera*) grows 30cm (12in) in a day.

Bermuda grass (*Cynodon dactylon*) grows 15cm (6in) in a day.

Albizzia falcatoria grows 2cm (1in) in a day.

Eucalyptus regnans grows 1cm (0.5in) in a day.

PARASITES AND EPIPHYTES

Some plants cannot photosynthesize. Instead, they live and feed on other plants, taking their food from the stems or roots. These plants are called parasites. Epiphytes also live on other plants, but they take neither food nor water from them.

This epiphytic bromeliad (*Aechmea miniata*) grows on the bark of trees.

The plant traps water in the spaces formed by its overlapping leaf bases.

CARNIVOROUS PLANTS

Carnivorous (meat-eating) plants feed on small animals, such as insects, as well as producing their own food by photosynthesis. Insects provide minerals and other nutrients that help these plants to survive.

1 The Venus flytrap (*Dionaea muscipula*) attracts insects with its unusual leaf tips.

2 The insect touches sensory hairs, which trigger the two halves of the leaf to snap shut.

3 Comb-like teeth trap the insect, and the plant slowly digests it.

GIANT FRONDS

The Pacific giant kelp (*Macrocystis pyrifera*) has the longest fronds of any plant. Each frond can grow up to 120m (394ft), taller than the Statue of Liberty.

COMMON USES OF PLANTS

LEAVES

Panama hats, from the leaves of the jipijapa tree (*Carludovica palmata*).

Skin cream, including juice from the leaves of *Aloe vera*.

Ice cream, thickened with agar-agar from seaweeds (*Gelidium*).

SAP

FIBRE

Rubber, from the latex of the rubber tree (*Hevea brasiliensis*).

Rope, from the fibres of the hemp plant (*Cannabis sativa*).

Linen, from the fibres of the flax plant (*Linum usitatissimum*).

ENDANGERED PLANTS

Scientific name	Common name	Location
Phragmipedium exstaminodium	Chiapas slipper orchid	Mexico
Sarracenia oreophila	Green pitcher plant	USA
Marojejya darianii	Big-leaf palm	Madagascar
Euphorbia handiensis	(succulent)	Canary Islands
Kerriodoxa elegans	(palm)	Thailand
Swainsona recta	(pea)	Australia
Dicliptera dodsonii	(vine)	Ecuador
Punica protopunica	Socotran pomegranate	Socotra

FLOWERS

FLOWERS HELP ENSURE that a plant is pollinated, and protect its seeds until they are shed. Flowers are often scented, and may be brightly coloured. They consist of sepals, petals, stamens, and carpels.

INFLORESCENCES

Some plants produce a single flower on each flower stalk (pedicel). Many, though, have flowers arranged in groups on a main stalk (peduncle). This is called an inflorescence.

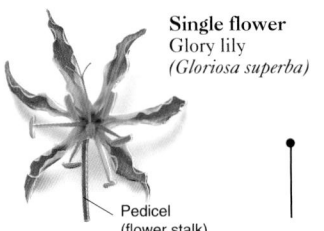

Single flower
Glory lily
(Gloriosa superba)

Pedicel
(flower stalk)

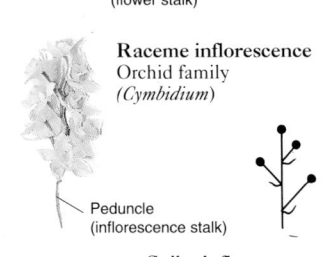

Raceme inflorescence
Orchid family
(Cymbidium)

Peduncle
(inflorescence stalk)

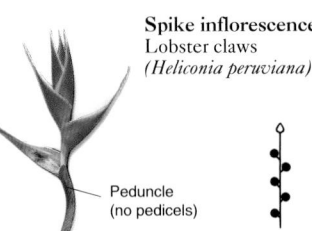

Spike inflorescence
Lobster claws
(Heliconia peruviana)

Peduncle
(no pedicels)

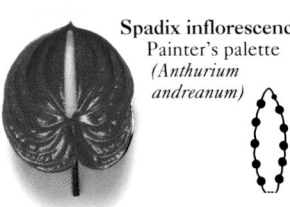

Spadix inflorescence
Painter's palette
(Anthurium andreanum)

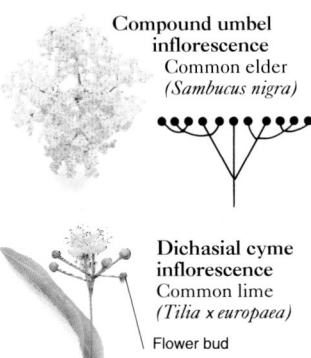

Compound umbel inflorescence
Common elder
(Sambucus nigra)

Dichasial cyme inflorescence
Common lime
(Tilia × europaea)

Flower bud

Peduncle

FLOWER STRUCTURE

Lily

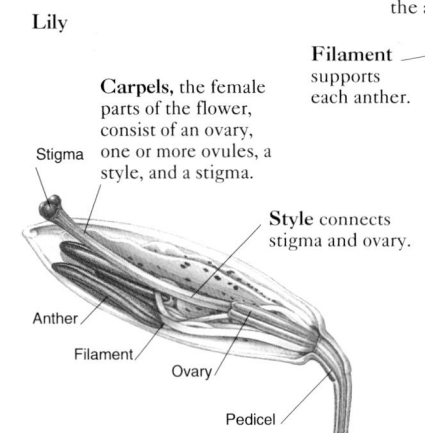

Carpels, the female parts of the flower, consist of an ovary, one or more ovules, a style, and a stigma.

Stigma

Style connects stigma and ovary.

Anther

Filament

Ovary

Pedicel

Stamens are the male parts of the flower. Each one consists of a filament and an anther.

Pollen is produced by the anthers.

Filament supports each anther.

Stigma is sticky to trap pollen.

Petals attract insects and guide them towards anthers and stigma.

Sepals protect flower while it is in bud.

Ovary contains one or more ovules with an ovum (egg cell) inside each.

POLLEN GRAIN
A pollen grain contains male gametes (reproductive cells). Once pollination has taken place, these male gametes can fertilize an ovum (female gamete).

FLOWER FACTS

• Most plants have both male and female reproductive organs in each flower. Some, such as willows *(Salix)*, have either male or female flowers.

• The largest flower, giant rafflesia *(Rafflesia arnoldii)*, grows up to 105cm (3.5ft) across and weighs up to 7kg (15.4lb).

Giant rafflesia   Hand

FLOWER EXAMPLES

Cockscomb
(Celosia argentea cristata)

Banksia
(Banksia menziesii)

Yellow calla lily
(Zantedeschia)

Cape cowslip
(Lachenalia aloides)

Urn plant
(Aechmea)

Guelder rose
(Viburnum opulus)

Hyacinth
(Hyacinthus orientalis)

Chrysanthemum
(Chrysanthemum morifolium)

Ice plant
(Sedum)

POLLINATION

Pollination is the transfer of pollen from anthers to a stigma. Many plants use insects to help spread their pollen. An insect feeding on a flower's nectar picks up pollen and carries it to the next flower.

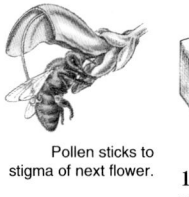
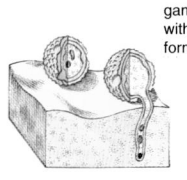
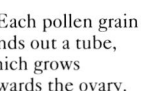

Pollen sticks to stigma of next flower.

Bee picks up pollen from anthers.

FERTILIZATION

Once a flower has been pollinated, fertilization may take place. This process produces the seed, from which a new plant will grow.

One male gamete fuses with ovum to form embryo.

One male gamete fuses with polar nuclei to form endosperm.

1 Each pollen grain sends out a tube, which grows towards the ovary.

2 Two male gametes (reproductive cells) from the pollen grain enter the ovule.

3 The embryo plant and the endosperm (food store) develop inside the seed.

LEAVES

MOST LEAVES HAVE a stalk, called a petiole, and a blade, or lamina. Chlorophyll, a pigment that the leaves use in photosynthesis (see p.74), makes them green.

VASCULAR SYSTEM
The vascular system, made up of phloem and xylem, carries nutrients around the leaf.

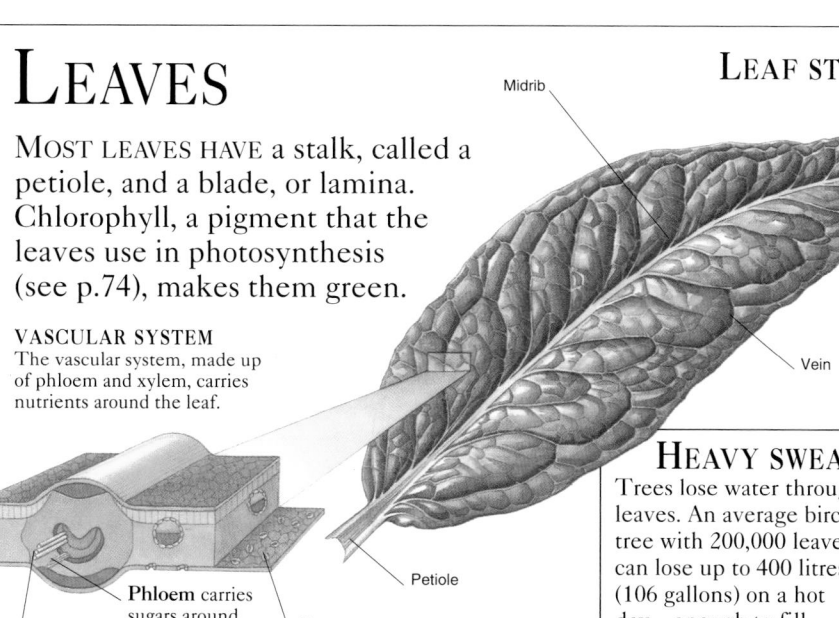

Midrib

Lamina

Vein

Phlox

Phloem carries sugars around the plant.

Xylem carries water and minerals around the plant.

Stoma (pore through which gases flow in and out)

Petiole

LEAF STRUCTURE

HEAVY SWEATER
Trees lose water through their leaves. An average birch tree with 200,000 leaves can lose up to 400 litres (106 gallons) on a hot day – enough to fill about 1,200 soft drink cans.

LEAF TEXTURES

Smooth, waxy leaves allow water to flow off, so they do not become waterlogged.

Rhododendron

Hard, spiky leaves help prevent the flower and leaf buds from being eaten by animals.

Holly

Hairy leaves trap a layer of air, so they do not burn in sunshine, or freeze in cold weather.

Tanacetum

Needle-shaped leaves offer little resistance to wind, preventing it from damaging the plant.

Cypress

LEAF EXAMPLES

Hornbeam maple (*Acer carpinifolium*)

Conifer (*Taiwania cryptomerioides*)

Castor aralia (*Kalopanax pictus*)

Asparagus (*Asparagus*)

Burr oak (*Quercus macrocarpa*)

Swiss cheese plant (*Monstera deliciosa*)

Lily family (*Lilium*)

Lungwort (*Pulmonaria officinalis*)

Robinia (*Robinia x holdtii*)

Sassafras (*Sassafras albidum*)

Blue echeveria (*Echeveria*)

Black wattle acacia (*Acacia mearnsii*)

LEAF RECORDS
LARGEST LEAVES belong to the raffia palm (*Raphia farinifera*) and the Amazonian bamboo palm (*Raphia taedigera*), growing up to 20m (64ft) long.

SMALLEST LEAVES (Flowering plants) are those of a floating duckweed (*Wolffia angusta*). Leaves grow to about 0.6mm (0.2in) long, and 0.3mm (0.1in) wide.

POISONOUS LEAVES
The leaves of many plants contain poisons. Rhubarb leaves contain high concentrations of oxalic acid, which is particularly dangerous for people suffering from rheumatism or arthritis. Jimson weed and aconite leaves can also cause sickness in humans.

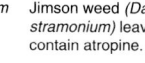

Rhubarb (*Rheum rhaponticum*) leaves contain oxalic acid.

Jimson weed (*Datura stramonium*) leaves contain atropine.

Aconite (*Aconitum napellus*) leaves contain aconitine and ephedrine.

LEAF MOULD
When dead plants and leaves decay and are broken down, they form topsoil, which contains nutrients essential for plant growth.

Plants, such as this bluebell, thrive in the fertile topsoil.

Leaf litter

1 Fallen leaves and dead plants lie on the surface. They slowly decompose, forming a layer called humus.

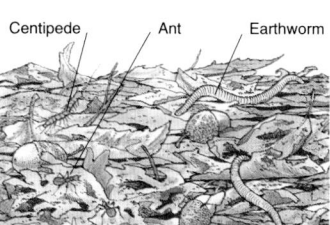

Centipede   Ant   Earthworm

2 Tiny animals, such as earthworms, eat and excrete the humus, grinding it up finely and mixing it with the soil.

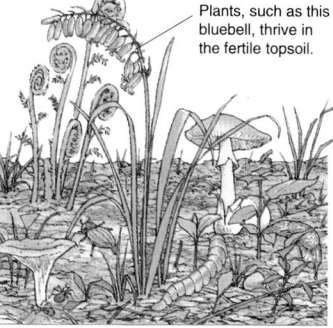

3 Valuable nutrients are released in the process, forming a rich layer of topsoil in which new plants grow.

LEAF RAFT
The leaves of the giant water lily (*Victoria amazonica*) can grow up to 2.4m (8ft) across. They can support the weight of a young child.

TREES

TREES ARE PLANTS at least six metres (20 feet) tall, with a single trunk (main stem). They are all perennial (live for many years), and most are broadleaved plants, which bear flowers.

LIFE CYCLE

Once a tree is mature, it can produce flowers, fruits, and seeds each year.

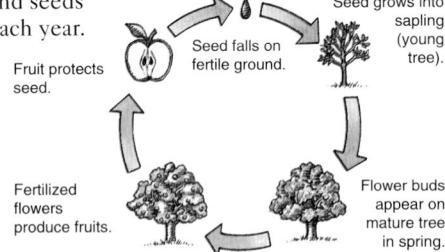

Seed falls on fertile ground.

Fruit protects seed.

Fertilized flowers produce fruits.

Seed grows into sapling (young tree).

Flower buds appear on mature tree in spring.

Buds appear in early spring. They will soon grow into flowers, called catkins.

English oak (*Quercus robur*) in **spring and autumn**

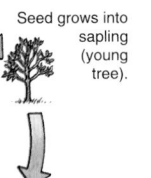

Leaves

Bark

Trunk

Roots

TREE STRUCTURE

Broadleaved trees, like most flowering plants, have a main stem, or trunk, leaves, flowers, fruits, and seeds.

Fruit of the oak tree is a nut, called an acorn. Nuts are hard, dry fruits with only one seed.

ROOTS

A tree's roots take up water from the soil. The vascular system (see p.77) transports the water around the tree.

INSIDE THE TRUNK

A tree trunk grows new layers of cells outside the old layers. Trees grow quickly in warm conditions and slowly in cold conditions, forming visible rings in the trunk. Heartwood consists of dead cells, containing chemicals such as tannins or resins, which can produce rich, deep colours.

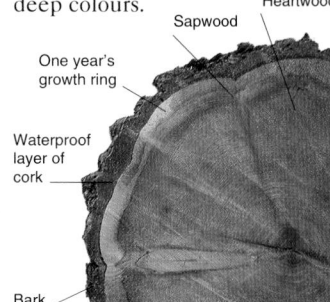

Heartwood

Sapwood

One year's growth ring

Waterproof layer of cork

Bark

HARDWOODS AND SOFTWOODS

Broadleaved trees are sometimes referred to as hardwoods, and conifers as softwoods. However, some conifers, such as Douglas fir and yew, produce harder wood than many broadleaved trees. Balsa, the softest of all, is a hardwood.

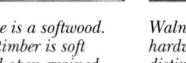
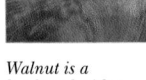

Pine is a softwood. Its timber is soft and open-grained.

Walnut is a hardwood with a distinctive colour.

TYPES OF TREE

BROADLEAVED TREES
There are many thousands of species of broadleaved trees. Most are deciduous (shed their leaves seasonally).

Most broadleaved trees, as their name suggests, have broad, flat leaves.

All the trees in this group are angiosperms (flowering plants).

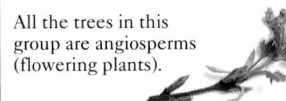

NEEDLE-LEAVED TREES
The group called needle-leaved trees includes pines, firs, and yews. There are over 500 species of needle-leaved trees, most of which are evergreen.

Many conifers have needle-shaped leaves, but some are strap-shaped, or even oval.

Most needle-leaved trees bear seeds in woody cones.

PALM TREES
The palm family contains about 2,800 species. Palms have only one growing point, called the apical bud. If this is damaged, the tree dies.

Palm trees have this name because the leaves are often shaped like a hand.

Palm trees, like broadleaved trees, are flowering plants.

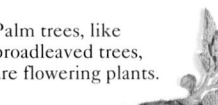

TREES AROUND THE WORLD

Trees grow wherever there is at least 20cm (7.9in) of rain each year, and a temperature of at least 10°C (50°F) in summer. These conditions are not met in the white areas on the map. No trees grow in the Arctic tundra, in Antarctica, or on very high mountain tops.

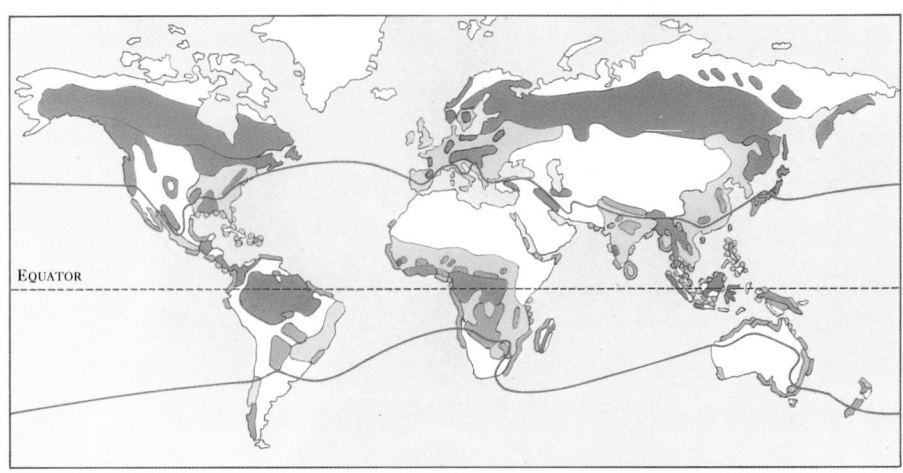

EQUATOR

MAP KEY

Boreal forest (conifers)

Tropical rainforest (broadleaved)

Mangroves

Temperate forest (mixed)

Limited forest cover

Tropical dry forest (deciduous)

Limit of palm trees

BARK

A tree's bark consists of dead cells, which protect the living cells of the sapwood. As the tree grows, the outer layer of bark splits and is replaced by a new layer. Sometimes many layers are visible at the same time.

Younger, pinkish layer shows beneath peeling outer layer.

Lenticels (cell areas) allow the tree to breathe.

The paper birch *(Betula papyrifera)* has a very pale bark.

This cherry tree *(Prunus serrula)* has a dark, glossy bark.

River birch *(Betula nigra)* has bark that peels in flaky layers.

TREE FACTS

• The Bishop pine *(Pinus muricata)* can reproduce only after a forest fire. It needs the heat of the fire to crack open its cones.

• One cubic metre (1.3 cubic yards) of dried ebony weighs 1,030kg (2,271lb). The same volume of balsa weighs only 160kg (234lb).

• Mangroves are the only trees that can grow in salty water. They have special roots that help them take in oxygen.

TRUNK ROAD

Californian redwoods *(Sequoia sempervirens)* grow up to 7.6m (25ft) across. It is sometimes easier to cut through the trunk than to remove the tree.

COMMON USES OF TREES

WOOD

   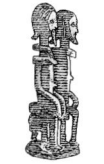

Oak *(Quercus)* for furniture.

Sycamore *(Acer pseudoplatanus)* for violins.

Poplar *(Populus)* for buildings (some countries).

Ebony *(Diospyros)* for carving work.

PULP PRODUCTS

Paper is made from the pulp of many kinds of trees. Pulp is used for paper products such as kitchen paper, tissues, and books.

FIBRE PRODUCTS

Rayon fabric is made from cellulose using wood fibres from many species of trees.

SEED PRODUCTS

Kapok stuffing is made from the hairs that cover the seeds of the kapok or silk-cotton tree *(Ceiba pentandra)*.

TREE RECORDS

TALLEST LIVING TREE is a coast redwood *(Sequoia sempervirens)* in Redwood National Park, USA. It is 111.25m (365ft) tall, about the same as an Apollo space rocket.

OLDEST KNOWN TREE, a bristlecone pine *(Pinus longaeva)* in Nevada, USA, was over 5,100 years old.

MOST DROUGHT-RESISTANT TREE, the baobab *(Adansonia digitata)* of Africa, can store up to 136,000 litres (35,900 gallons) of water in its swollen trunk.

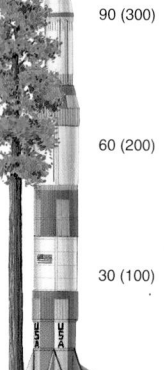

Height m(ft)
111.25 (365)

90 (300)

60 (200)

30 (100)

0

BARK

Cinnamon, from the bark of the cinnamon *(Cinnamomum zeylanicum).*

Cork, from the bark of the cork oak *(Quercus suber).*

SAP

Maple syrup from the sap of the sugar maple *(Acer saccharum).*

Chewing gum from the sap of the sapodilla tree *(Manilkara zapota).*

Turpentine from the sap of the longleaf pine *(Pinus palustris).*

Amber fossilized resin from conifer trees that are now extinct.

GROWTH RATES

Trees grow at different rates. Below and right are the heights of some trees after 15 years.

Adult human, 1.8m (6ft)

Juniper (Juniperus), 3m (10ft)

Oak (Quercus), 7.5m (25ft)

Birch (Betula), 9m (30ft)

Douglas fir (Pseudotsuga), 12.2m (40ft)

LEAF FALL

In harsh conditions, leaves do not photosynthesize properly, and water lost from them cannot be replaced if the ground is dry or frozen. So a tree withdraws the useful substances from its leaves, and then sheds them.

Deciduous forest in autumn, New England, USA

AUTUMN COLOURS

1 Chlorophyll is the first leaf pigment to break down when autumn arrives.

2 Other colour pigments, such as yellow carotenoids, now show through.

3 Carotenoids darken as they age, turning from yellow through orange to red.

4 Anthocyanins, from sugars in the leaves, give them a scarlet colour.

5 The tree deposits tannins in the leaves. These produce a dark brown colour.

6 A layer of cells, called the absission layer, forms at the base of the leaf stalk. Finally the leaf falls.

A maple leaf, as it dies, changes colour dramatically.

ENDANGERED TIMBER TREES

Scientific name	Common name	Location
Abies guatemalensis	(Fir)	North and Central America
Aniba duckei	Bois de rose	South America
Dalbergia nigra	Bahia rosewood	South America
Hopea erosa	(Dipterocarp family)	Southeast India
Rousselia erratica	(Nettle family)	Central America
Vatica soepadmoi	(Dipterocarp family)	Sumatra

FOOD PLANTS

MANY TYPES OF PLANT ARE important food sources for humans. They include fruits, vegetables, herbs, spices, and cereals.

FRUIT EXAMPLES

Fruits form an important part of the human diet. There is a huge variety of wild and cultivated fruits, some of which are shown below.

TEMPERATE

Apple
(*Malus domestica*)

Strawberry
(*Fragaria*)

Cherry
(*Prunus avium*)

TROPICAL

Papaya
(*Carica papaya*)

Durian
(*Durio zibethinus*)

Star fruit
(*Averrhoa carambola*)

NUTS

Walnut
(*Juglans regia*)

Brazil nut
(*Bertholletia excelsa*)

Hazelnut
(*Corylus avellana*)

GRAPE SCOTT!

One year's worldwide grape harvest would bury Manhattan Island, New York, to a depth of 124m (407ft).

FRUIT RECORDS

LARGEST SEED
is the "double coconut" of the coco de mer palm (*Lodoicea maldivica*), which can weigh up to 25kg (55lb).

LARGEST TREE FRUIT
comes from the jackfruit tree (*Artocarpus heterophyllus*): it can weigh up to 50kg (110lb).

FOOD PLANT ANCESTORS

The size, shape, and flavour, of many food plants have been altered by selective breeding.

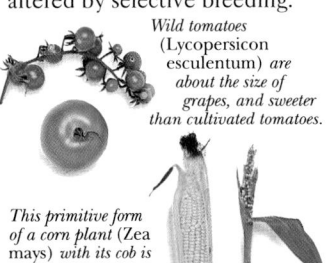

Wild tomatoes (*Lycopersicon esculentum*) *are about the size of grapes, and sweeter than cultivated tomatoes.*

This primitive form of a corn plant (Zea mays) with its cob is much smaller than a modern corn cob.

TOP FIVE FRUIT

Fruit	Annual worldwide consumption (tonnes)
Bananas (*Musa*)	40,597,200
Apples (*Malus domestica*)	34,422,144
Oranges (*Citrus sinensis*)	30,853,920
Water-melons (*Citrullus lanatus*)	19,330,912
Plantains (*Musa*)	18,130,384

FRUIT

The fruit is the part of a flower that develops to contain the seed or seeds. Fruits can be succulent or dry. Succulent fruits, such as lemons, are fleshy and brightly coloured.

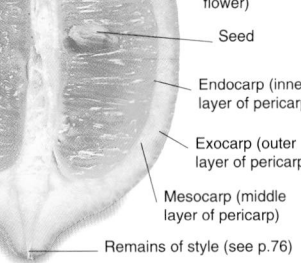

Pedicel (flower stalk)

Carpel (female parts of the flower)

Seed

Endocarp (inner layer of pericarp)

Exocarp (outer layer of pericarp)

Mesocarp (middle layer of pericarp)

Remains of style (see p.76)

Pericarp (fruit wall)

Vesicle (juice sac)

Lemon (*Citrus limon*)

NUTS

Nuts are a type of dry fruit. They have a hard wall around their seed.

Peduncle (inflorescence stalk)

Remains of stigma (see p.76)

Remains of style (see p.76)

Woody pericarp (fruit wall)

Remains of male inflorescence (see p.76)

Spiky cupule (husk around fruit)

Sweet chestnut
(*Castanea sativa*)

SEEDS

Each fruit contains one or more seeds that will germinate and grow into new plants if conditions are suitable. Some types of fruit, such as cherries and peaches, contain just one seed. Other fruits, such as strawberries and apples, contain several seeds.

Hilum (point of attachment to ovary)

Testa (seed coat)

Lemon seed

DEVELOPMENT OF A FRUIT

A plant's fruit begins to form after fertilization has taken place (see p.76).

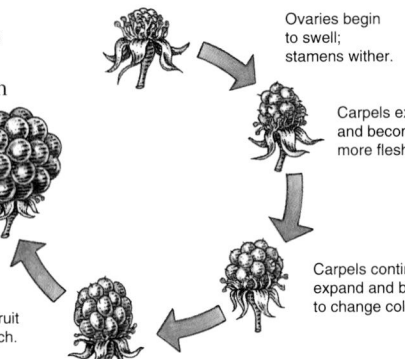

Development of a blackberry (*Rubus fruticosus*)

Ovaries begin to swell; stamens wither.

Carpels expand and become more fleshy.

Drupelets ripen fully. Fruit is ready to eat.

Carpels continue to expand and begin to change colour.

Carpels mature into drupelets: small fleshy fruit with a single seed in each.

FRUIT ORIGINS

This map shows the origins of several fruits now found worldwide.

KEY

Cherries (Egypt)

Peaches (China)

Lemons (India)

Water-melons (Africa)

Strawberries (America)

Passionfruit (Brazil)

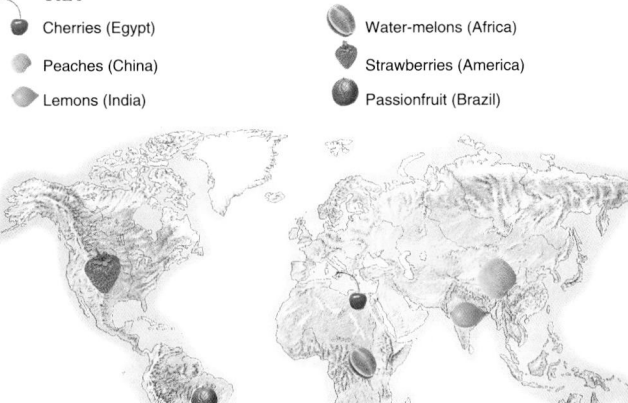

VEGETABLE EXAMPLES
Vegetables can be leaves, tubers, flowers, stalks, or shoots.

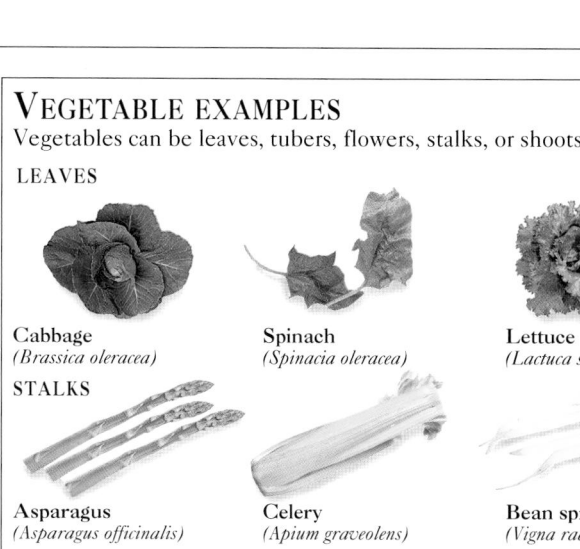

LEAVES

Cabbage
(*Brassica oleracea*)

Spinach
(*Spinacia oleracea*)

Lettuce
(*Lactuca sativa*)

STALKS

Asparagus
(*Asparagus officinalis*)

Celery
(*Apium graveolens*)

Bean sprout
(*Vigna radiata*)

FLOWERS

Globe artichoke
(*Cynara scolymus*)

Cauliflower
(*Brassica oleracea*)

Broccoli
(*Brassica oleracea*)

ROOTS

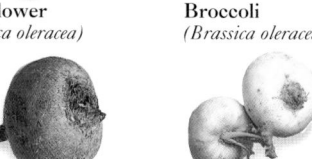

Carrot
(*Daucus carota*)

Beetroot
(*Beta vulgaris*)

Turnip
(*Brassica rapa*)

VEGETABLES
The term vegetable describes an edible plant, or part of a plant. Some fruits, such as tomatoes and aubergines, are also commonly called vegetables.

VEGETABLE RECORDS
All of the following records are held by Mr. Bernard Lavery (born 1938) of Llanharry, Wales, UK. Mr. Lavery also holds three other world records for growing large vegetables.

LARGEST CABBAGE
weighed 56.24kg (124lb).

LARGEST MARROW
(*Cucurbita pepo*) weighed 49.05kg (108.1lb).

LONGEST PARSNIP
(*Pastinaca sativa*) was 4.36m (14.3ft) long.

LONGEST CARROT
was 5.14m (16.9ft) long.

LARGEST CELERY
weighed 20.89kg (46lb).

LARGEST BRUSSELS SPROUT
weighed 8.25kg (18.2lb).

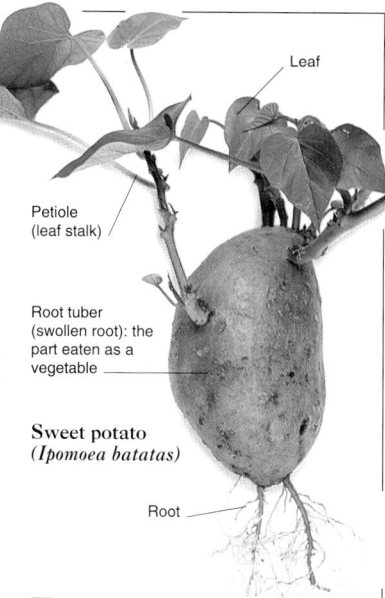

Leaf

Petiole (leaf stalk)

Root tuber (swollen root): the part eaten as a vegetable

Sweet potato
(*Ipomoea batatas*)

Root

KNOW YOUR ONIONS
Onions, chives, garlic, and leeks all belong to the lily family. Different parts of each plant are eaten as vegetables: the bulbs of onion and garlic, the stems of leeks, and the leaves of chives.

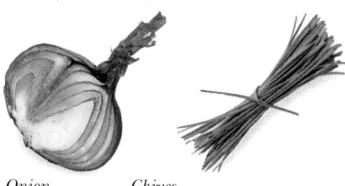

Onion
(*Allium cepa*)

Chives
(*Allium schoenoprasum*)

Garlic
(*Allium sativum*)

Leeks
(*Allium porrum*)

FRUIT AND VEGETABLE FACTS
• For 2,000 years the Chinese have considered lychees (*Litchi chinensis*) to be the finest fruits. Relays of horsemen took them to court, and in some districts, tax collectors demanded them as payment.

• Even the hottest chili pepper (*Capsicum frutescens*) derives all its heat from no more than 0.1% of the fruit.

• There are 6,000 varieties of potato in Peru.

TOP FIVE VEGETABLES

Vegetable	Annual worldwide consumption (tonnes)
Tomatoes (*Lycopersicon esculentum*)	57,525,248
Cabbages (*Brassica oleracea*)	34,418,560
Onions (*Allium cepa*)	25,943,344
Cucumbers/gherkins (*Cucumis sativus*)	15,851,327
Carrots (*Daucus carota*)	11,713,606

FRUIT EATEN AS VEGETABLES
Some foods usually regarded as vegetables are in fact fruits. Familiar examples are shown below.

Tomato
(*Lycopersicon esculentum*)

Peppers
(*Capsicum annum*)

Aubergine
(*Solanum melongena*)

Pumpkin
(*Cucurbita pepo*)

SPICE EXAMPLES
Spices are strongly flavoured plants used in cooking.

Cinnamon
(*Cinnamomum zeylandicum*)

Chili peppers
(*Capsicum frutescens*)

Cloves
(*Syzygium aromaticum*)

HERB EXAMPLES
Herbs are used to flavour food, and in medicine.

Basil
(*Ocimum basilicum*)

Coriander
(*Coriandrum sativum*)

Spearmint
(*Mentha spicata*)

FRUIT AND VEGETABLE PRODUCTS
Many products in daily use come from fruits and vegetables.

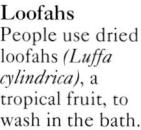

Vegetable dyes
Dyes are made from plants such as indigo (*Indigofera*) and henna (*Lawsonia inermis*).

Loofahs
People use dried loofahs (*Luffa cylindrica*), a tropical fruit, to wash in the bath.

Cooking oil
Cooking oils are extracted from several fruits and seeds, including olives (*Olea europaea*).

Chocolate
Chocolate comes from the beans of the cacao tree (*Theobroma*).

Face powder
Finely ground walnut (*Juglans regia*) shells are used to make cosmetic face powder.

Coffee
Coffee is produced from the ground beans of the *Coffea* tree.

COLOSSAL CUCUMBER
The largest cucumber ever grown weighed 9.1kg (20lb). This would have provided enough slices to make 1,137 cucumber sandwiches.

FUNGI AND LICHENS

FUNGI WERE ONCE CLASSIFIED as plants, but since about 1969 botanists have treated them as a separate kingdom. Most fungi are immobile, like plants, but cannot make their own food. Instead, they feed on living or dead plants or animals, dung, and other organic materials.

FUNGUS EXAMPLES

There are about 65,000 known species of fungus and 20,000 lichens. Many more may be discovered.

Orange peel fungus
(*Aleuria aurantia*)

Maze-gill
(*Daedalea quercina*)

Astraeus hygrometricus

Fly agaric
(*Amanita muscaria*)

Green wood-cup
(*Chlorosplenium aeruginascens*)

Clavulinopsis helvola

Scarlet hood
(*Hygrocybe coccinea*)

Chanterelle
(*Cantharellus cibarius*)

Common stinkhorn
(*Phallus impudicus*)

TYPES OF LICHEN

Lichens have a number of distinctive growth forms – some flat, others branching or bushy.

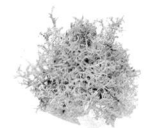  

Fruticose
(*Cladonia portentosa*)

Foliose
(*Hypogymnia physodes*)

Squamulose
(*Cladonia floerkeana*)

Gills produce and store spores

Cap

Cap curls upwards to release the spores.

Stem

Cortinarius armillatus

Hyphae form the mycelium (main body) and anchor the sporophore (fruiting body).

FUNGUS STRUCTURE

Mushrooms and toadstools are the fruiting bodies of fungi. They grow up out of the soil to spread their spores (reproductive bodies).

LICHEN STRUCTURE

Lichens consist of fungi living in association with algae (simple plants) or cyanobacteria, the only organisms apart from plants that can photosynthesize.

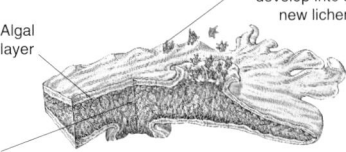
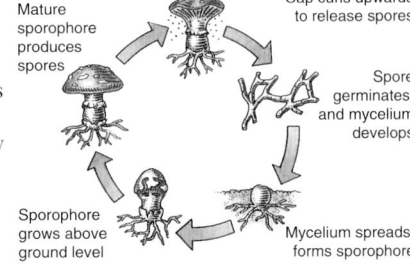

Soredium may develop into a new lichen

Algal layer

Fungal mycelium

Hypogymnia physodes

LIFE CYCLE

Fungi reproduce through spores, which are the equivalent of a plant's seeds. The fungal mycelium spreads underground until it meets another mycelium of the same species. They bond together and, given the right conditions, produce a fruiting body that generally grows above ground.

Mature sporophore produces spores

Cap curls upwards to release spores

Spore germinates, and mycelium develops

Mycelium spreads; forms sporophore

Sporophore grows above ground level

SYMBIOTIC RELATIONSHIPS

Many fungi live in close association, or symbiotic relationships, with plants and animals. The three main kinds of symbiotic relationships are parasitic, mutualistic, and saprophytic.

 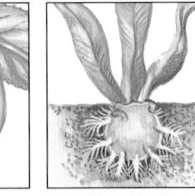 

PARASITIC
Some parasitic fungi cause galls and can even kill the plant they live on.

MUTUALISTIC
Many orchids need the presence of a fungus for their seeds to germinate.

SAPROPHYTIC
Some fungi live on dead wood, animals, and other organic matter in the soil.

FUNGUS RECORDS

LONGEST-LIVING MUSHROOM, *Ganoderma applanatum*, can live for as long as fifty years.

MOST IMPORTANT FUNGI belong to *Penicillium* genus. They are used in blue cheeses, and the antibiotic penicillin.

BIGGEST FRUITING BODY is giant puffball (*Lycoperdon gigantea*), which can measure up to 2m (6.6ft) in circumference.

TRUFFLE TREAT

Truffles (fungi that produce sporophores underground) are delicious. The White Truffle (*Tuber magnatum*) from Italy costs about £1,000 per kg.

FUNGUS AND LICHEN FACTS

• Fungus cells contain a light, strong substance called chitin. Chitin is also found in the cuticle, or outer layer, of some animals, such as insects.

• Lichen extracts produce orchil, the dye used for litmus paper, as well as the dyes once used to colour the wool in Scottish tartans.

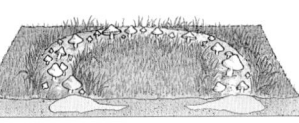

Fairy ring

• Fairy rings form when hyphae grow outwards from a central point. Mushrooms sprout at the outer edge, forming a ring.

• Lichens are very sensitive to air pollution, and several kinds are used to indicate pollution levels.

POISONOUS FUNGI

Name	Poison	Symptoms
Fly agaric (*Amanita muscaria*)	muscarine	Stomach pain, hallucinations, delirium, convulsions; rarely fatal
Death cap (*Amanita phalloides*)	amanitine, phalloidine	Nausea, liver and kidney failure, abdominal pain; can be fatal
False morel (*Gyromitra esculenta*)	gyromitrin	Stomach pain, nausea, jaundice; can be fatal

Never eat wild mushrooms unless they have been identified by an expert as edible.

MICRO-ORGANISMS

A MICRO-ORGANISM IS a life-form that is usually too small for the human eye to see. The most familiar are protists, bacteria, and viruses. Some micro-organisms are harmful, but many are vital: without them, life as we know it could not continue.

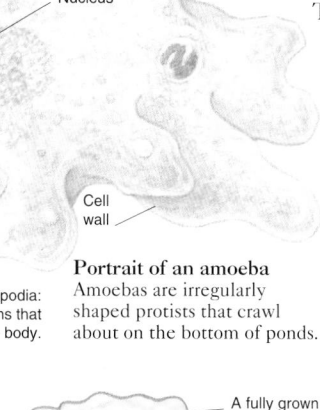

Cytoplasm

Nucleus

Food vacuole

Cell wall

Pseudopodia: extensions that flow out from the body.

Portrait of an amoeba
Amoebas are irregularly shaped protists that crawl about on the bottom of ponds.

PROTISTS

Protists are neither animals nor plants. They belong to a separate kingdom (see p.72). Protists have just one cell, which carries out all the functions necessary for them to live and reproduce. They live in watery environments, from damp soil and puddles, to lakes and oceans.

FEEDING

Many protists trap their food, which includes algae and other protists, by engulfing it with part of their jelly-like body.

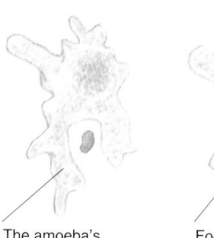

The amoeba's pseudopodia surround its prey.

Food is trapped, forming a food vacuole.

TYPES OF PROTIST

There are more than 40,000 species of protist. Two phyla are shown below.

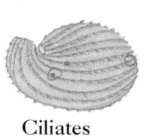
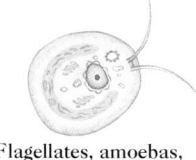

Ciliates
(Ciliophora)

Flagellates, amoebas, opalinids
(Sarcomastigophora)

REPRODUCTION

Most protists reproduce by splitting themselves in two. Each of the two halves then becomes a single cell. This process is called binary fission. Many types of bacteria also reproduce in this way.

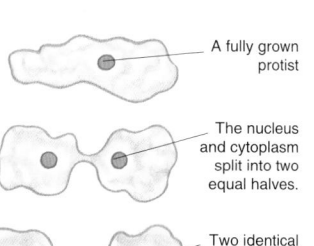

A fully grown protist

The nucleus and cytoplasm split into two equal halves.

Two identical protists result

BACTERIA

Bacteria, together with blue-green algae, belong to the Moneran kingdom. Monerans are the simplest, and probably the most ancient, forms of life on Earth. Bacteria are found everywhere, from the depths of the oceans to the upper atmosphere.

Some bacteria have flagella.

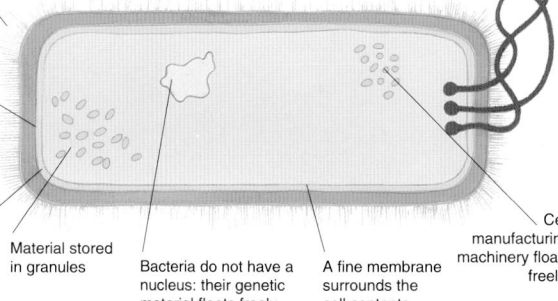

Some types of bacteria look hairy.

A rigid wall protects the bacterium.

The cell wall may be surrounded by a slimy capsule.

Material stored in granules

Bacteria do not have a nucleus: their genetic material floats freely.

A fine membrane surrounds the cell contents.

Cell manufacturing machinery floats freely.

BACTERIA SHAPES
Bacteria are often classified according to their shape, which is spherical, rod-shaped, or curved.

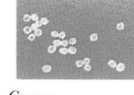
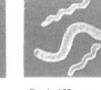

Coccus *Bacillus* *Spirillum*

VIRUSES

A virus is a tiny package of chemicals surrounded by a protein coat. There are many virus shapes, including rod-shaped, round, and many-sided. They are all so small (the largest are about 0.0003mm) that they can be seen only with an electron microscope.

Influenza virus particles seen through an electron microscope. Viruses cause many diseases, from the common cold to yellow fever.

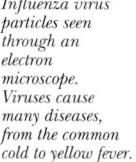

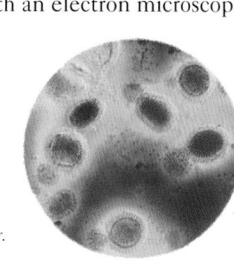

Head

DNA

Collar

Bacteriophage: a virus that invades bacteria

Tail

Tail fibres

HOW A BACTERIOPHAGE VIRUS MULTIPLIES
A virus shows no signs of life until it invades the cell of a living organism. The bacteriophage is a complex virus that reproduces by invading bacteria cells. It is replicated at a rate of 300 every half an hour.

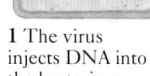
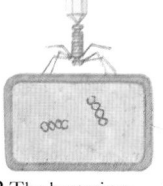

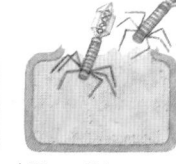

1 The virus injects DNA into the bacterium.

2 The bacterium makes copies of the virus's DNA.

3 The DNA develops into complete viruses.

4 The cell bursts open, releasing copies of the virus.

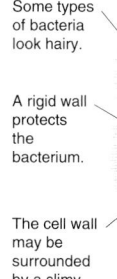
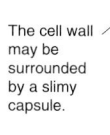

ARMPIT CITY

There are about 600 million bacteria in and on a human body. The skin of an armpit may be home to up to 800 bacteria per square millimetre (516,000 per square inch).

USEFUL BACTERIA
Bacteria are nature's most important recycling agents. They break down dead plants and animals, and return the materials to the ecosystem. Most bacteria are harmless to humans. Some are vital: without them we could not digest our food.

Bacteria are important in the production of many foods.

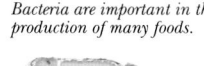

Vinegar

Cheese   *Yoghurt*

MICRO-ORGANISM FACTS

• It would take a ciliate (protist) about five minutes to swim the length of this page.
• One gram of soil may contain over 150,000 protists.

• The largest species of protist ever to have lived grew to over 20cm (7.9in) in diameter: the width of this page. It has now become extinct.

ANIMALS

MORE THAN A MILLION animal species have been discovered. They have adapted to just about every habitat: some even spend their entire life inside the body of another animal.

ANIMAL CHARACTERISTICS

Animals, unlike plants, cannot manufacture their own food, so they have to eat other organisms. They have many cells, can reproduce, and can sense and respond to their surroundings. Most animals move around at some stage in their lives.

Most animals take in food through the mouth.

Most animals have eyes.

Land-dwelling vertebrates breathe air through their nostrils.

All animals have an excretory system that gets rid of waste products.

Vertebrates have an internal bony skeleton to support the body.

Skin may be covered in scales, feathers, or fur, to protect the animal and keep it warm.

Muscles enable animals to move in search of food.

Many animals have legs to help them move efficiently.

Grey crowned crane
(Balearica regulorum)

TYPES OF ANIMAL

INVERTEBRATES

About 97% of animal species are invertebrates (have no backbone). Some of the most important phyla (see p.72) are shown here.

Sea anemones, corals, jellyfish, hydras (Cnidaria)
Ring of tentacles armed with stinging cells surrounds the mouth.

Molluscs (Mollusca)
Most have a hard shell to protect their soft body. Includes snails and slugs, squid and octopuses, clams, mussels, and scallops.

Arthropods (Arthropoda)
Jointed limbs and a tough external skeleton. Includes insects, arachnids, and crustaceans.

VERTEBRATES

Only about 3% of animal species are vertebrates (animals with a backbone). There are more than 40,000 species, in seven classes (see p.72). Three of these classes are fish.

Fish (Agnatha, Chondrichthyes, Osteichthyes). Three classes: jawless fish, sharks and rays, and bony fish.

Worms
At least ten phyla, including segmented worms (Annelida) and roundworms (Nematoda).

Starfish, sea urchins, and sea cucumbers (Echinodermata)
Marine; body usually made up of five identical parts.

Amphibians (Amphibia)
Can live both on land and in water. Includes frogs, toads, newts, and salamanders.

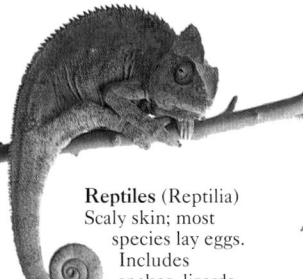

Reptiles (Reptilia)
Scaly skin; most species lay eggs. Includes snakes, lizards, crocodiles, and turtles.

Birds (Aves)
Covered with feathers. Have wings, a beak, and no teeth. Most species can fly.

Mammals (Mammalia)
Feed young on milk produced in female's body. Most have fur or hair.

ANIMAL REPRODUCTION

The main function of an animal's life is to continue its species. Some animals reproduce without mating (asexual reproduction), but most mate with a partner to produce offspring (sexual reproduction).

Asexual reproduction
Some organisms, e.g. hydras, reproduce by budding: part of the parent becomes detached and forms a new individual.

Sexual reproduction
Most animals reproduce sexually: a cell from a male (a sperm) joins with a cell from a female (an egg). This egg grows into a new individual.

ANIMAL LIFESPANS

Lifespans range from a few days for some insects, to more than 200 years for a giant clam *(Tridacna)*. Most mammals have about the same number of heartbeats in their lifetime.

Elephants and shrews have a similar number of heartbeats during their lives, but the shrew's heart beats much faster during its short life.

LARVA'S LARDER

The female tarantula wasp *(Pepsis)* paralyzes a tarantula with her sting. She then bites off its legs to make it easier to carry, puts it in a burrow, and lays an egg on it. When the larva hatches, it feeds off the still-living spider.

ANIMAL FACTS

• Only about 0.3% of animal species are mammals, and only about 0.7% are birds. Most creatures on Earth are insects or worms.

• A large locust swarm can eat 80,000 tonnes of food in a day: equivalent to the amount of food eaten by 35,000 American families in a year.

FEEDING

Some animals have specialized diets, while others eat almost anything. Animals have evolved different teeth to suit their diet.

Mongoose skull

Carnivore
Meat-eater: sharp canine teeth

Gazelle skull

Herbivore
Plant-eater: flat molars

Moonrat skull

Insectivore
Insect-eater: sharp, pointed teeth

Monkey skull

Omnivore
Meat- and plant-eater: sharp and flat teeth

ANIMAL GROUPS

A cast of hawks
A covert of coots
A bazaar of guillemots
A pride of lions
A clowder of cats
A leap of leopards
A sloth of bears
A skulk of foxes
A labour of moles
A crash of rhinoceroses
A shrewdness of apes
A pod of dolphins

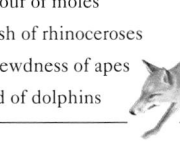

INVERTEBRATES

THE VAST MAJORITY of creatures are invertebrates – animals without a backbone. They include insects, spiders, crabs, worms, jellyfish, and corals. Many invertebrates are tiny, but others, such as the giant squid and the Japanese spider crab, can grow to be larger than humans.

TYPES OF INVERTEBRATE

There are more than a million known species of invertebrate, in about 30 phyla (see p.72). Some of the largest and most important phyla are shown below; the number of species in each is approximate.

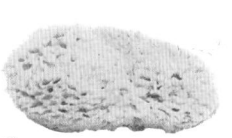

Sponges
(Porifera)
9,000 species

Sea anemones, corals, jellyfish, hydras
(Cnidaria)
9,500 species

Flatworms, flukes, and tapeworms
(Platyhelminthes)
15,000 species

Roundworms
(Nematoda)
20,000 species

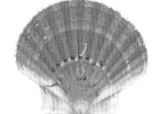

Molluscs
(Mollusca)
51,000 species

Worms and leeches
(Annelida)
18,600 species

Arthropods
(Arthropoda)
1,092,000 species

Starfish, sea urchins, and sea cucumbers
(Echinodermata)
6,000 species

PORTRAIT OF AN INVERTEBRATE

Invertebrates range from simple microscopic animals to complex, intelligent molluscs, such as octopuses. Invertebrates do not have an internal skeleton: their body shape is maintained either by a tough, external coat, called an exoskeleton, or by fluid pressing against the skin.

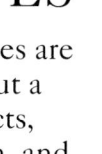

Prostomium
Mouth
Cerebral ganglion (simple brain)
Pharynx
Oesophagus
Circumoesophageal vessel (pseudoheart)
Nephridium (excretory organ)
Ventral nerve cord
Crop
Gizzard (part of stomach)
Ventral blood vessel
Spermatheca (reproductive organ)
Ovary
Gonopores (reproductive organs)
Coelom (body cavity surrounding internal organs)
Body shape maintained by fluid
Dorsal blood vessel
Intestine

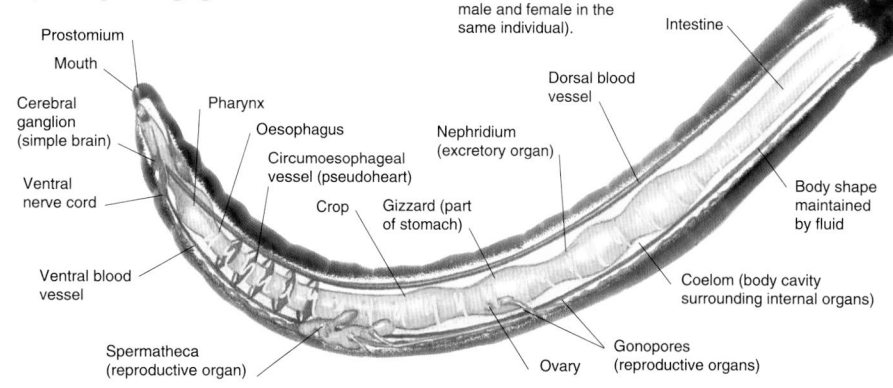

Earthworm
Dorsal surface
Clitellum (saddle)
Body is formed of many identical segments
Prostomium
Pygidium
Earthworms are hermaphroditic (both male and female in the same individual).

LIFE CYCLE

There is a huge diversity of invertebrate life cycles. Most species lay eggs, then many pass through several larval stages that may look very different to the adult stage. Other species hatch as miniature adults. Some invertebrates, such as houseflies, live for just a few weeks, but others may live for many years: the giant clam (*Tridacna*) can live to be more than 200 years old.

Life cycle of a jellyfish

Adult

Female jellyfish releases fertilized larvae which settle on the sea-bed.

Larvae grow into small polyps called scyphistoma.

At the right temperature, polyps divide into eight-armed buds called ephyrae.

Ephyrae break free and become free-swimming adults.

TAPE MEASURE

The pork tapeworm (*Taenia solium*) can grow to over 7m (23ft) long inside the human body: as long as four adult humans. It has as many as 1,500 segments, each containing 80,000 tapeworm embryos. Tapeworms can cause death if they enter the bloodstream.

WORM FACTS

• Roundworms are probably the most numerous animals on Earth. 20,000 species have been discovered, but scientists believe there are at least 500,000 species.

• Up to 500 million hookworms may be found in a single human.

ECHINODERMS

Echinoderms include starfish, sea urchins, and sea cucumbers. An echinoderm's body is divided into five parts radiating out from a central point, and it moves using tiny, water-filled tube feet. All echinoderms live in the sea.

Starfish are among the strongest animals for their size: they can prize apart the shells of bivalve molluscs, such as scallops.

ARTHROPODS

This huge phylum contains the largest variety of creatures in the animal kingdom, including insects, crustaceans, spiders, centipedes, millipedes, and horseshoe crabs. All arthropods have a tough exoskeleton, jointed limbs, and a nerve cord running the length of the body.

The tiger centipede (Scolopendra hardwickii) is the largest species of centipede. It grows to just under 30cm (12in) long.

ZOOPLANKTON

Plankton is made up of small invertebrates (zooplankton) and plants (phytoplankton) that drift along in water currents. Zooplankton includes jellyfish, and the larvae of sea creatures such as starfish and crabs.

Zooplankton

INVERTEBRATE RECORDS

LARGEST JELLYFISH is the giant North Atlantic jellyfish (*Cyanea capillata*), which grows to more than 2m (6.6ft) in diameter, and may have tentacles nearly 37m (121.4ft) long.

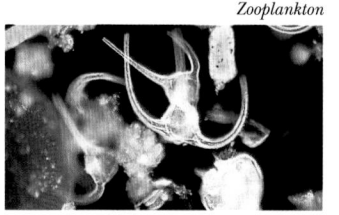

LONGEST EARTHWORM is the *Mirochaetus* earthworm from South Africa, which grows up to 6m (19.7ft) long.

MOLLUSCS

MOLLUSCS FORM the second largest group of animals on Earth. They range from tiny snails to the giant squid, which grows as long as a sperm whale. Molluscs are found all over the world. They live in oceans and seas, in fresh water, and on land.

TYPES OF MOLLUSC

There are more than 50,000 species of mollusc. They are divided into seven classes (see p.72).

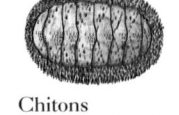
Chitons
(Polyplacophora)
coat-of-mail shells
500 species

Solenogasters
(Aplacophora)
worm-like
marine molluscs
5,540 species

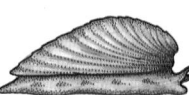
Monoplacophorans
(Monoplacophora)
deep-sea limpets
10 species

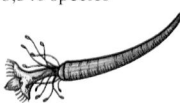
Tusk shells
(Scaphopoda)
350 species

Gastropods
(Gastropoda)
e.g. slug, snail, whelk
35,000 species

Bivalves
(Bivalvia)
two-shelled molluscs
e.g. oyster, clam
8,000 species

Cephalopods
(Cephalopoda)
squid, octopuses,
nautiluses, cuttlefish
600 species

PORTRAIT OF A MOLLUSC

A typical mollusc has a soft body divided into the head, the foot, and a hump containing the main organs. This hump is covered by a fold of skin called the mantle. The body is usually protected by a hard shell.

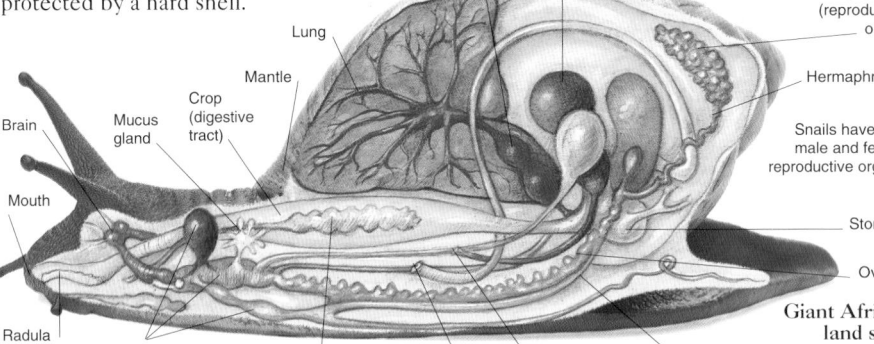

Labels: Eye, Shell, Tentacle, Collar, Foot, Heart, Kidney, Ovotestis (reproductive organ), Hermaphrodite duct, Snails have both male and female reproductive organs., Stomach, Oviduct, Lung, Mantle, Crop (digestive tract), Mucus gland, Brain, Mouth, Radula (toothed tongue), Reproductive organs, Salivary gland, Anus, Excretory gland, Sperm duct

Giant African land snail (*Achatina*)

LIFE CYCLE

Most molluscs lay eggs. Many marine (sea-dwelling) species hatch into tiny larvae. Other molluscs, such as some snails, hatch into miniature adults.

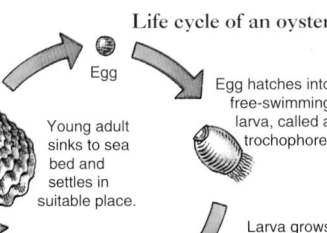

Life cycle of an oyster

Egg

Egg hatches into free-swimming larva, called a trochophore.

Larva grows larger, shell develops. This stage called a veliger larva.

Young adult sinks to sea bed and settles in suitable place.

MOLLUSC FACTS

• The giant clam (*Tridacna*) is the longest-lived animal in the world: it can live to be more than 200 years old.

• Larger species of octopus can measure up to 9m (30ft) across with their tentacles spread out.

• The mucus secreted by snails is so effective that they can crawl along the edge of a razor without cutting themselves.

• Limpets have such strong teeth on their radula that they leave scratch marks on rocks when they browse.

FEEDING

Bivalve molluscs are filter feeders, sifting tiny organisms from the water. Most other molluscs have a toothed tongue, called a radula, which they use to scratch food into their mouth.

Close-up of a snail's radula showing rows of rasping teeth

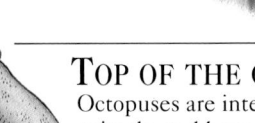

The giant clam's gills sift food from the water. The gills are also used for breathing.

MOLLUSC MOVEMENT

Some molluscs, such as mussels, anchor themselves to one place. Most molluscs, however, move around in search of food and to escape from predators.

BIVALVES

Some bivalves, e.g. scallops, suck in water then expel it rapidly by clapping their two shells together. This propels them through the water in a series of jerks.

GASTROPODS

Gastropods create a wave of muscle contractions that runs from the rear of the foot to the front. This wave slowly drags them along.

CEPHALOPODS

Cephalopods, such as squid, take in water then force it out again, pushing themselves rapidly backwards. They also have fins which they use to pull themselves forwards.

Squid can swim at speeds of up to 40km/h (25mph).

Slugs and snails secrete a slimy mucus that helps them to slide along.

This *Euglandina* snail is the fastest mollusc on land.

TOP OF THE CLASS

Octopuses are intelligent animals, and have the ability to learn. An octopus at London Zoo in England learned how to twist the lid off a jar to reach the crab inside.

Cross-section of a squid's mantle

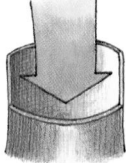

Expanded mantle cavity takes in water

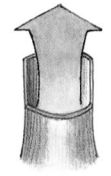

Contracted mantle cavity shoots out jet of water, propelling squid along

DEFENCE AND ATTACK

Molluscs have evolved several unique ways of protecting themselves from enemies. Many carnivorous (meat-eating) molluscs are also efficient predators.

STINGING
Some sea slugs eat jellyfish, and can swallow the stinging cells without being stung. The cells are then carried to the slug's back, where they protect it from enemies.

POISONOUS HARPOONS
Cone shells have long, barbed teeth on their radula. They thrust one of these into their prey like a harpoon, deliver a venomous sting, then pull the impaled victim back into their mouth.

SQUIRTING INK
Octopuses, squid, and cuttlefish squirt a cloud of ink at their enemy. This allows them to escape behind a dark screen. *Heteroteuthis*, a type of deep-sea squid, squirts a cloud of luminous bacteria to dazzle its enemies.

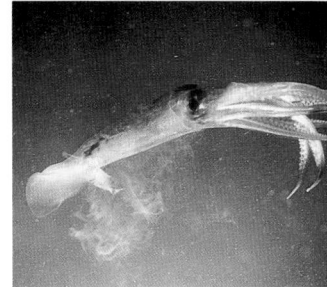

Squid squirting ink from its syphon

SAFETY IN SHELLS
Many molluscs, including gastropods and bivalves, retreat into their shell if danger threatens.

MOLLUSC FACTS

- The ink squirted by cuttlefish was the original sepia colouring used by artists.

- Several species of cone shell can kill a human with their sting.

- The Mediterranean fan mussel *(Pinna nobilis)* anchors itself to the sea bed with strong, golden-brown threads. These threads were once used to make "cloth of gold".

CHANGING COLOUR

Squid, octopuses, and cuttlefish can change colour in less than a second to blend in with their surroundings. They also change colour to indicate their mood. Male cuttlefish turn black with anger; octopuses turn white with fear, and blue with rage.

Cuttlefish with mottled brown and white colouring

The same cuttlefish has turned red. It is probably signalling to another cuttlefish.

MOLLUSC SHELLS

Mollusc shells are made of layers of calcium carbonate secreted from the mantle. They form in a huge variety of shapes, sizes, patterns, and colours.

Pacific thorny oyster

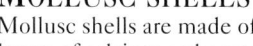

Royal cloak scallop

Nautilus: the only cephalopod with a true external shell

Rose-branch murex

Limpet

Marlinspike auger

West African margin shells

Cockle shells

HOW PEARLS FORM

Some molluscs form pearls in their shells. Oyster pearls are highly valued.

1 A tiny piece of grit or a parasite lodges in the oyster's shell, causing irritation.

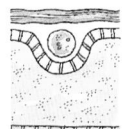

2 The oyster secretes mother-of-pearl (nacre) around the cause of irritation.

3 The pearl breaks free of the shell, removing the source of irritation.

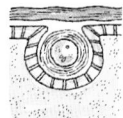

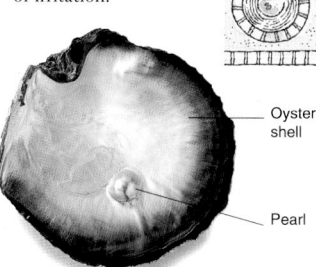

Oyster shell

Pearl

PRIZE EYES

The giant Atlantic squid has the largest eyes of any animal in the world, each with a diameter of more than 40cm (15.7in).

Cuban land snail

Elephant tusk shell

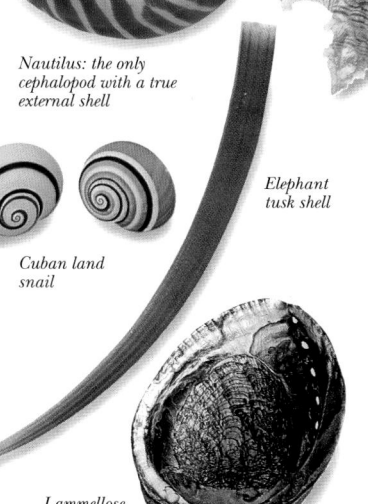

Lammellose ormer

MOLLUSC RECORDS

LARGEST MOLLUSC
and the largest invertebrate (see p.84), is the giant Atlantic squid *(Archteuthis)*, which can grow up to 20m (66ft) long.

LARGEST BIVALVE MOLLUSC
is the giant clam, which can weigh over 300kg (661lb): the equivalent of three large humans.

SMALLEST MOLLUSC
is the gastropod *Ammonicera*, which is only 1mm (0.04in) long.

LONGEST SHELL
was over 5m (16.4ft) long. It belonged to a prehistoric cephalopod.

LARGEST LAND SNAIL
is the giant African land snail, which can grow up to 39cm (15.4in) from snout to tail.

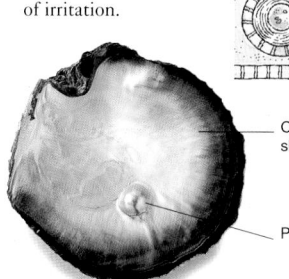

It has taken just over one minute for this *Euglandina* snail to crawl along the bottom of these two pages.

INSECTS

THERE ARE MORE species of insect than of any other group of animals on Earth. For every human, there are an estimated 200 million insects. Insects live just about everywhere, including polar lands, deserts, rainforests, and even in pools of petrol.

PORTRAIT OF AN INSECT

Insects have three distinct body regions: the head, the thorax, and the abdomen. They have six jointed legs, and a tough outer skeleton called an exoskeleton. Most insects have wings at some stage during their life.

Antenna (feeler)

Thorax (middle section of the body)

Exoskeleton

Wing

Compound eye

Abdomen (rear part of the body)

Insects have no veins: blood flows freely around the body.

Foregut

Midgut

Heart

Ovary (reproductive organ)

Brain

Mandibles (mouthparts)

Anus

Ovipositor (egg-laying tool)

Hindgut

Ventral nerve cord

Air enters through holes (spiracles) in the insect's sides and goes directly to muscles and organs.

Claw

Katydid (female)

PROPORTION OF INSECTS

Insects make up about 85% of all the animal species on Earth.

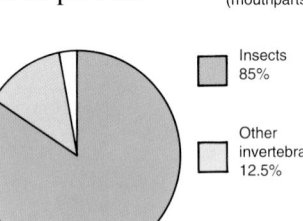

Insects 85%

Other invertebrates 12.5%

Vertebrates 2.5%

TYPES OF INSECT

There are over a million known species of insect, with perhaps 30 million still to be discovered. They are grouped into 32 orders (see p.72), including those illustrated below.

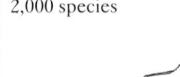

Mayflies
(Ephemeroptera)
2,000 species

Dragonflies
(Odonata)
5,000 species

Grasshoppers, crickets
(Orthoptera)
20,000 species

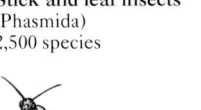

Stick and leaf insects
(Phasmida)
2,500 species

Earwigs
(Dermaptera)
1,500 species

Cockroaches
(Blattodea)
3,700 species

Praying mantids
(Mantodea)
1,800 species

Termites
(Isoptera)
2,300 species

Biting lice
(Mallophaga)
2,700 species

Bugs
(Hemiptera)
82,000 species

Beetles
(Coleoptera)
300,000 species

Ants, bees, and wasps
(Hymenoptera)
110,000 species

Butterflies and moths
(Lepidoptera)
136,800 species

Flies
(Diptera)
98,500 species

Fleas
(Siphonaptera)
1,800 species

LIFE CYCLES

The series of changes an insect goes through during its life is called its metamorphosis.

Complete metamorphosis: butterfly

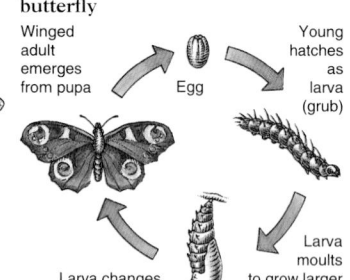

Winged adult emerges from pupa

Egg

Young hatches as larva (grub)

Larva changes into pupa

Larva moults to grow larger

Incomplete metamorphosis: grasshopper

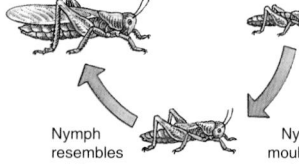

Winged adult emerges from final moult

Egg

Young hatches as wingless nymph

Nymph resembles adult

Nymph moults to grow larger

MOULTING

A young insect's tough exoskeleton cannot stretch, so the insect has to moult (shed its skin) several times in order to grow. The sequence below shows the final moult of a damselfly, as it changes from nymph to adult.

Two hours after leaving the water, the nymph has become an adult damselfly. Its old skin is left behind on the stalk.

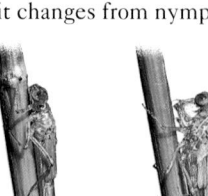

Damselfly nymphs live under water, but climb out when they are ready to become adults.

The skin has split along the back of the thorax, and the adult head has emerged.

The young adult grips the plant stem and pulls itself up and away from its old skin.

It will take a few more days for the damselfly to develop its brilliant adult colours.

INSECT FACTS

• If all the animals on Earth were weighed, ants would make up 10% of the total.

• Queen termites can lay one egg per second for more than 14 years. This gives a total of more than 440,000,000 babies from one queen.

• A bee must visit over 4,000 flowers to make one tablespoon of honey.

INSECT WINGS

Wings enable an insect to escape from predators, and to fly to new areas in search of food.

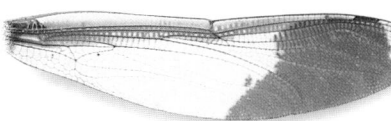
Moth wing

Dragonfly wing

Beetle forewing (elytron)

INSECT VISION

An insect's compound eyes are made up of hundreds of individual lenses.

Dragonflies have the largest eyes of any insect.

INSECT RECORDS

LOUDEST INSECTS
are cicadas, which can be heard up to 400m (1,312ft) away.

FASTEST-FLYING INSECTS
are dragonflies, which have been recorded flying at speeds of over 50km/h (31mph).

FASTEST-RUNNING INSECT
is the American cockroach (*Periplaneta americana*), which can run at speeds of almost 5km/h (3mph).

GIANT DRAGONFLY

The biggest insect ever to have lived was a prehistoric dragonfly. It had a wingspan of 75cm (29.5in): about the same as a kestrel's.

DEFENCE AND ATTACK

Insects have developed many ways of defending themselves against enemies. These include camouflage, stinging, and squirting noxious chemicals. In several cases these methods are also useful for attacking prey.

The orchid mantis *(Hymenopus coronatus)* is camouflaged as an orchid flower.

The insect curls its body, completing its leafy disguise.

CAMOUFLAGE

Many insects are so well-camouflaged that they are almost impossible for predators to spot. The green markings of this Javanese leaf insect *(Phyllium bioculatum)*, complete with holes and brown edges, make it look just like a dying leaf.

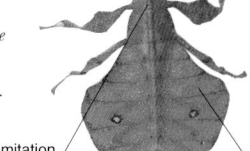
Real leaf

Imitation leaf midrib

Imitation leaf vein

When the Javanese leaf insect sits on a twig or branch, it blends in completely with its leafy surroundings.

INSECT HOMES

Bees, wasps, termites, and ants are the only insects that build permanent homes. These range from a simple hole in the ground to complex termite mounds up to 12m (39ft) high.

Common wasps (Vespula vulgaris) *build their nests from chewed-up wood fibres.*

This umbrella-shaped mound is home to the African termites Cubitermes.

Inside wasps' and bees' nests are combs of cells. A single larva develops in each cell.

HELPFUL INSECTS

BEES
Bees pollinate many types of crops, and produce honey (the first sweetener used by humans) and beeswax.

SILK MOTHS
Silk is produced from the cocoon (pupa) of the silk moth *Bombyx mori*. Each cocoon produces a thread of silk that may be over 1km (0.6 miles) long.

DUNG BEETLES
Dung beetles were introduced to Australia to eat the large amounts of dung produced by cattle.

CHEMICALS
Ants squirt stinging formic acid from their abdomen at enemies.

STINGING
Wasps and bees defend themselves by delivering a painful sting.

MIMICRY
The hover fly's colours resemble the warning stripes of wasps. This may put off predators.

INSECT SIZES

Insects range from tiny wasps smaller than a full stop, to beetles as big as a human hand. (The insects below are not shown actual size.)

SMALLEST INSECTS
are fairyfly wasps, which measure only 0.2mm long.

HEAVIEST INSECTS
are the goliath beetles *(Goliathus)*, which weigh up to 110g (3.9oz): about the same as an apple.

LONGEST INSECT
is the giant stick insect *(Pharnacia serratipes)*, which measures up to 45cm (17.7in) from leg tip to leg tip.

Giant stick insect's leg, actual size

HARMFUL INSECTS

FLEAS AND FLIES
Diseases carried by fleas and flies have caused more than half of all human deaths since the Stone Age.

BODY LICE
More than 3,800 body lice can live on one person. In unhygienic situations they can transmit disease.

KILLER BEES
An aggressive type of African honey bee *(Apis mellifera adansonii)* attacks humans without provocation. More than 300 people have been killed.

LARGEST WING-SPAN
is that of the owlet moth *(Thysania agripina)*, which measures up to 30cm (12in) across.

ARACHNIDS

SOME OF THE world's least loved animals are arachnids. They include spiders, scorpions, ticks, and mites. Most arachnids live on land. They are found all over the world in almost every habitat: there is even a species of spider that lives high on Mount Everest.

TYPES OF ARACHNID

There are more than 73,000 species of arachnid, divided into ten orders (see p.72). Six orders are illustrated below.

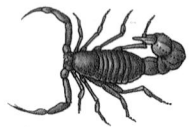

Scorpions
(Scorpiones)
2,000 species

Whip scorpions
(Uropygi)
60 species

Camel spiders
(Solifugae)
900 species

Harvestmen
(Opiliones)
4,500 species

Mites and ticks
(Acari)
30,000 species

Spiders
(Araneae)
40,000 species

SPIDER ATTACK

All spiders are carnivorous (meat-eating), feeding mainly on insects and other spiders. They are skilful hunters, and have developed ingenious ways of capturing prey. After trapping a meal, they paralyze it with venom, then wrap it in silk.

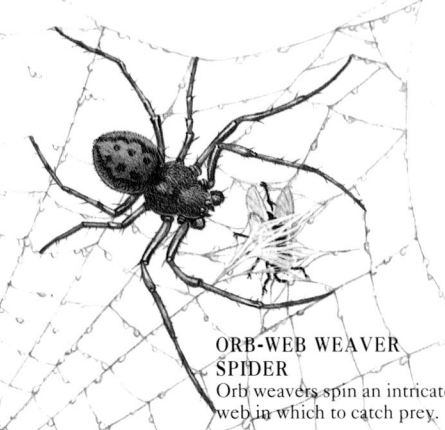

ORB-WEB WEAVER SPIDER
Orb weavers spin an intricate web in which to catch prey.

PORTRAIT OF AN ARACHNID

Arachnids have eight legs, and their body is divided into the cephalothorax (front and middle), and the abdomen (rear). They have a pair of leg-like or pincer-like pedipalps for feeling and feeding.

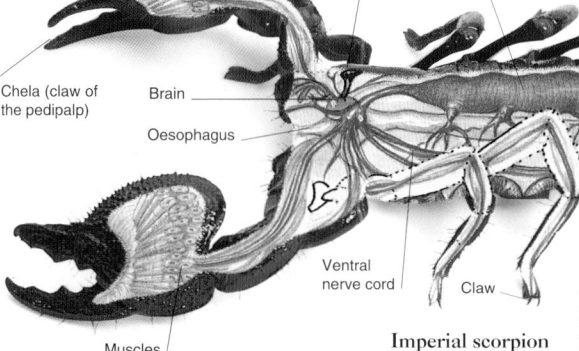

Pedipalp
Abdomen
Tail
Simple eye
Exoskeleton (outer skeleton)
Poison gland
Cephalothorax
Sting
Simple eye
Heart
Intestine
Chela (claw of the pedipalp)
Brain
Oesophagus
There are no veins: blood flows freely inside the body
Lung
Spiracle (air hole)
Ventral nerve cord
Claw
Muscles

Imperial scorpion
(*Pandinus imperator*)

LIFE CYCLE

Arachnids lay eggs that hatch into nymphs resembling adults. They moult (shed their skin) several times before they are mature. Some mites live just a few weeks; larger species of spider may live up to 30 years.

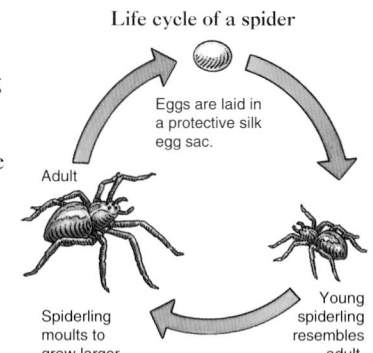

Life cycle of a spider

Eggs are laid in a protective silk egg sac.

Adult

Young spiderling resembles adult.

Spiderling moults to grow larger.

BALLOONING SPIDERS

Spiderlings can "balloon" from one area to another, travelling up to 2,000km (1,243 miles) at heights of more than 3,000m (9,843ft). They release a thread of silk from their abdomen, which is picked up by the wind.

ARACHNID RECORDS

MOST VENOMOUS SCORPION is the Israeli gold scorpion (*Leiurus quinquestriatus*).

LARGEST SPIDER WEB is spun by the tropical orb spider (*Nephila*). It measures up to 3m (10ft) across.

LARGEST ARACHNID is Leblondis' goliath bird-eating spider (*Theraphosa leblondi*): with a leg span of 28cm (11in), it can cover a dinner plate.

ARACHNID FACTS

• More people die from bee stings than from the bites and stings of all the venomous arachnids put together.

• There are more than 2 million spiders lurking in an average acre of countryside.

NET-CASTING SPIDER
The net-casting spider spins a sticky net that it holds between its front legs, ready to throw over a passing meal.

TRAPDOOR SPIDER
The trapdoor spider lives in a burrow sealed with a hinged door spun from silk. When an insect passes, it flips open the trapdoor and leaps on its prey.

JUMPING SPIDER
The jumping spider has short, strong legs, and can jump 40 times its body length. It anchors itself to the ground with a silk thread, then pounces on its prey.

BOLAS SPIDER
The bolas spider produces a scent that attracts moths, then twirls a thread of silk with a sticky blob on the end. Moths flying towards the scent are trapped on the end of the silk.

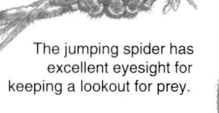

The jumping spider has excellent eyesight for keeping a lookout for prey.

CRUSTACEANS

CRUSTACEANS RANGE from tiny water fleas invisible to the human eye, to giant spider crabs with legs longer than a person. Most crustaceans are aquatic (live in water). They are found all over the world, from rivers and shorelines to the floors of the deepest oceans.

Antenna (feeler)

Antennule (feeler)

Common lobster (female)
(Homarus gammarus)

Carapace (shell)

Brain

Mouth

Compound eye made up of many lenses

Cephalothorax

Stomach

Ventral nerve cord

Ovary (reproductive organ)

Heart

Intestine

Dorsal abdominal artery

Abdomen

Anus

Ventral abdominal artery

PORTRAIT OF A CRUSTACEAN

Most crustaceans have a body divided into three parts: the head, thorax (middle), and abdomen (rear). In some species the head and thorax are joined to form the cephalothorax. Crustaceans have two pairs of antennae, and compound eyes. The body is covered by a tough coat, called the exoskeleton.

TYPES OF CRUSTACEAN

There are more than 55,000 species of crustacean. They are grouped into eight classes (see p.72), including the four illustrated below.

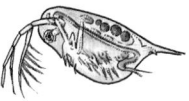

Branchiopods (Branchiopoda) e.g. fairy shrimps, water fleas 1,000 species

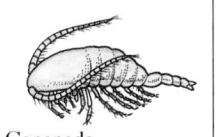

Copepods (Copepoda) tiny marine and freshwater organisms 13,000 species

Barnacles (Cirripedia) 1,220 species

Malacostracans (Malacostraca) e.g. crabs, lobsters 30,000 species

LIFE CYCLE

Most crustaceans lay their eggs in water. After hatching, many species pass through several larval stages. Crustaceans moult (shed their skin) to grow bigger.

Life cycle of a shrimp

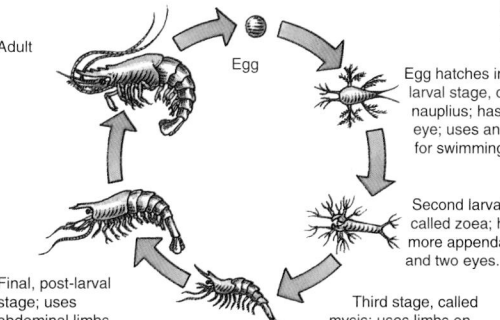

Adult

Egg

Egg hatches into first larval stage, called nauplius; has single eye; uses antennae for swimming.

Second larval stage, called zoea; has more appendages and two eyes.

Third stage, called mysis; uses limbs on thorax for swimming.

Final, post-larval stage; uses abdominal limbs for swimming.

CRUSTACEAN RECORDS

SMALLEST CRUSTACEANS are the water fleas *Alonella*, which grow only 0.25mm long.

HEAVIEST CRUSTACEAN is the North Atlantic lobster *(Homarus americanus)* which weighs up to 20kg (44lb).

LARGEST CRUSTACEAN is the Japanese spider crab *(Macrocheira kaempferi)*: its leg span can reach nearly 4m (13ft).

Japanese spider crab

CRAB DEFENCE

Most crabs have a hardened exoskeleton, called a carapace, to protect them from predators. Many crabs also use camouflage, burrowing, and running away as effective defensive tactics.

PINCER POWER
The robber crab *(Birgus latro)* defends itself with formidable pincers. These are so strong that this crab could cut its way out of a cake tin.

RUNNING SIDEWAYS
Scuttling sideways is the fastest method of escape for many crabs. It is easier for them to enter their burrow sideways because of their body shape.

BURROWING
Many crabs, such as this ghost crab *(Ocypode)*, burrow to escape predators. Their eyes may stick up above the ground, keeping a lookout for danger.

CAMOUFLAGE
Some crabs, such as this decorator crab *(Camposcia retusa)*, cover their shell with plants and sea creatures to disguise themselves on the sea bed.

CRUSTACEAN FACTS

• Copepods are probably the most numerous animals on Earth, forming much of the plankton that floats in the ocean.

• The North Atlantic lobster *(Homarus americanus)* and the robber crab *(Birgus latro)* can live for over 50 years.

• Woodlice are the only crustaceans that have successfully adapted to life on land.

• A swarm of krill (malacostracans) can cover 440sq km (170sq miles) and weigh over 2 million tonnes.

• The pancarid, a type of shrimp, is only found in a single Tunisian pool the size of a bath.

SUPERSHRIMP

The mantis shrimp can deliver a blow with the same force as a small calibre rifle. It can easily punch its way out of a fish tank.

AMPHIBIANS

MOST AMPHIBIANS CAN live both on land and in water. They need a moist environment because their skin is not waterproof and they rapidly lose body water in dry conditions. Amphibians have, nevertheless, adapted to a wide range of habitats, even deserts. They are found on every continent except Antarctica.

TYPES OF AMPHIBIAN

There are more than 4,200 species of amphibian, divided into three orders (see p.72).

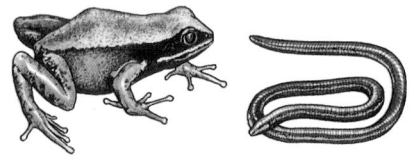

Frogs and toads (Anura) 3,700 species

Caecilians (Apoda) 170 species

Newts and salamanders (Urodela) 350 species

AMPHIBIAN FEET

Amphibians' feet are adapted for their particular way of life. Many species have webbed feet for swimming, while others' feet enable them to burrow or climb.

The palmate newt (Triturus helveticus) has webbed feet for swimming.

The tiger salamander (Ambystoma tigrinum) has flattened feet for burrowing.

The White's treefrog (Litoria caerulea) has sticky discs on its toes for gripping leaves.

The African clawed toad (Xenopus) has webbed feet for swimming, and claws for gripping slippery surfaces.

PORTRAIT OF AN AMPHIBIAN

Amphibians are vertebrates (see p.84). Their skin has no hair or scales, and is important for keeping the correct balance of water in the body. Most adult amphibians have lungs, but can also breathe through their skin.

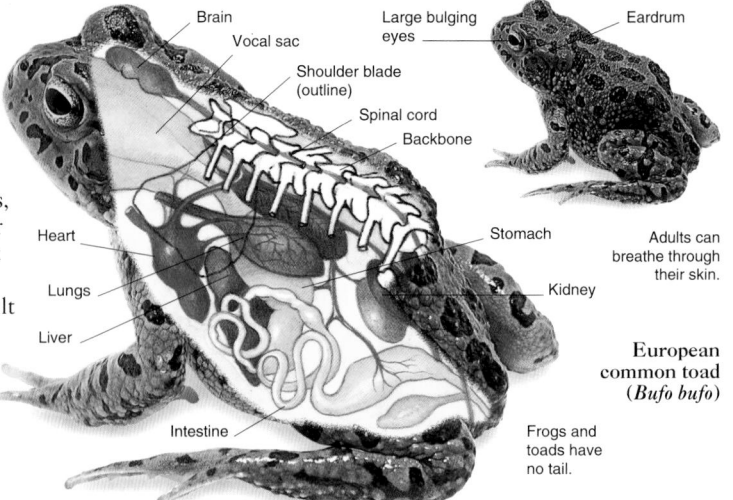

Brain
Vocal sac
Shoulder blade (outline)
Spinal cord
Backbone
Heart
Lungs
Liver
Stomach
Kidney
Intestine

Large bulging eyes
Eardrum

Adults can breathe through their skin.

European common toad (*Bufo bufo*)

Frogs and toads have no tail.

LIFE CYCLE

Most amphibians lay their eggs in water. The young pass through a series of changes, called metamorphosis, before becoming adults. Lifespans range from a brief breeding season to more than 50 years for the Japanese giant salamander (*Andrias japonicus*).

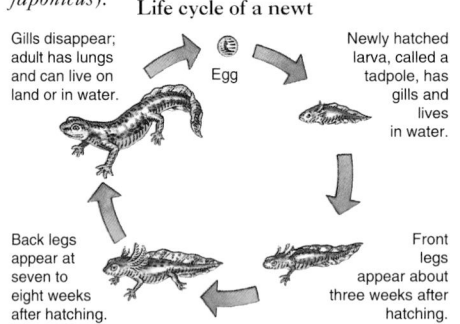

Life cycle of a newt

Gills disappear; adult has lungs and can live on land or in water.

Egg

Newly hatched larva, called a tadpole, has gills and lives in water.

Back legs appear at seven to eight weeks after hatching.

Front legs appear about three weeks after hatching.

AMPHIBIAN FACTS

• Young frogs are called froglets, and young toads are toadlets.

• Amphibian comes from the Greek words *amphi* and *bios*, meaning "double life", because amphibians can live both on land and in water.

• The smallest frog in the world, *Psyllophryne didactyla*, is smaller than a fingernail at just 10.4mm (0.41in) long.

• Poison-dart frogs are so-named because the indigenous (native) people of South America tip their arrows with their poison.

CARING FOR EGGS AND YOUNG

Many amphibians lay their eggs and then leave the young to fend for themselves. Others protect them in a variety of ways.

VOCAL SAC BROODER
The male Darwin's frog (*Rhinoderma*) swallows his tadpoles into his vocal sac for protection. When they become froglets, he spits them out one at a time.

CARRYING TO WATER
The poison-dart frog (*Dendrobates*) carries its newly hatched tadpoles on its back to a nearby pool or stream.

EGGS ON LEGS
The male midwife toad (*Alytes obstetricans*) wraps his string of eggs around his back legs and carries them until they are ready to hatch.

UNDER THE SKIN
The Surinam toad's (*Pipa pipa*) eggs are placed on the female's back. Her skin swells around them until they are almost covered. The young develop into toadlets under her skin, then hatch out of her back.

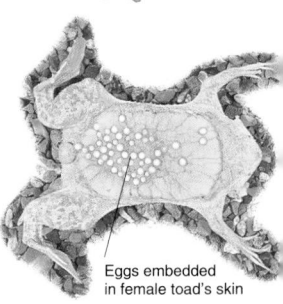

Eggs embedded in female toad's skin

LARGEST FROGS AND TOADS

Length is measured from the snout to the end of the body.

Common name	Scientific name	Size (approx) mm	in
Goliath frog	*Conraua goliath*	358	14
American bullfrog	*Pyxicephalus adspersus*	230	9
Cane toad	*Bufo marinus*	230	9
Rococo toad	*Bufo paracnemis*	230	9

BIG TADPOLE, LITTLE FROG

The South American paradoxical frog (*Pseudis paradoxa*) is larger when it is a tadpole than when it turns into an adult frog.

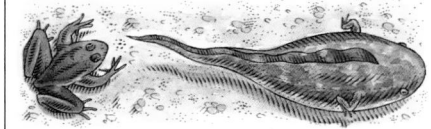

AMPHIBIAN COLOURS AND SHAPES

Amphibians have evolved a wide range of shapes and colours to suit their habitat and lifestyle. Many poisonous species are brightly coloured to warn predators to keep away, while others have colours and shapes that help them to blend in with their surroundings.

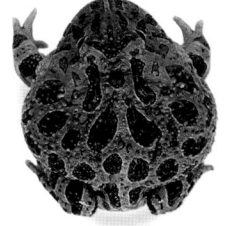
Mottled colouring helps disguise this South American horned toad (Ceratophrys).

The shape and colours of this Asian leaf frog (Megophrys nasuta) *resemble a dead leaf.*

This brightly coloured golden mantella (Mantella aurantiaca) *is a poisonous frog from Madagascar.*

This South African shovel-nosed frog (Hemisus guttatus) *uses its shovel-shaped snout for burrowing.*

The tiger salamander's (Ambystoma tigrinum) *spots are a signal to predators that it may make an unpleasant meal.*

Poison-dart frogs are the most poisonous of all amphibians. Their startling colours make them easier for enemies to spot and avoid.

The colours and shape of this Malaysian narrow-mouthed toad (Kaloula pulchra) *may fool predators into thinking it is a wet stone.*

The flattened shape of this burrowing frog (Rhinophrynus dorsalis) *helps it to slip easily through the soil.*

DEFENCE AND ATTACK

Amphibians are carnivorous (meat-eating), and many species rely on camouflage to stay hidden from prey as well as from predators. Other defensive tactics include oozing poison, looking fierce, and startling enemies.

SURPRISE
The fire-bellied toad *(Bombina bombina)* relies on its camouflage to stay hidden from enemies. But if it is attacked, the toad displays the bright warning colours on its belly, hoping that the startled predator will leave it alone.

SCARING TACTICS
If this Budgett's frog *(Lepidobatrachus asper)* is attacked, it puts on a fearsome display. It opens its mouth, screams, and makes loud grunting noises. If this performance fails to scare away the enemy, the frog may bite it.

STICKY TONGUE
Frogs have a long, sticky tongue for flicking out at prey, such as insects.

The tongue is attached to the front of the mouth.

European common frog (Rana temporaria) *attacking prey.*

LEAPING AND SWIMMING
If a frog is attacked, for example by a bird, it quickly leaps out of danger using its powerful back legs. If the frog is close to a pond or stream, it will dive into the water and swim out of the predator's reach.

LEAP FROG
The African sharp-nosed frog *(Ptychadena oxyrhynchus)* holds the frog long jump record. One individual leapt 5.35m (17.5ft) at the Calaveras County Frog Jubilee, California, in 1975.

CAMOUFLAGE
This European yellow-bellied toad *(Bombina variegata)* is almost completely hidden when it sits on a piece of bark.

Patches of green complete the toad's disguise.

Sharp rib

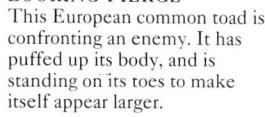

PRICKLY RIBS
The ribs of the Spanish sharp-ribbed salamander *(Pleurodeles waltl)* have needle-like tips. If a predator tries to eat it, the ribs pass through its skin giving the predator a sharp surprise.

Toad tries to make itself look bigger.

LOOKING FIERCE
This European common toad is confronting an enemy. It has puffed up its body, and is standing on its toes to make itself appear larger.

AMPHIBIAN RECORDS

LARGEST SALAMANDER
is the Japanese giant salamander, which grows up to 1.5m (5ft) long.

SMALLEST SALAMANDERS
are the Mexican lungless salamanders *(Thorius)*, which grow only 14mm (0.55in) long.

MOST POISONOUS AMPHIBIAN
is the golden-yellow poison-dart frog *(Phyllobates terribilis)*. The poison from the skin of a single frog could kill up to 20,000 mice.

MOST EGGS
are laid by the female cane toad *(Bufo marinus)*: she can produce up to 35,000 eggs in one year.

POISON
If a predator tries to eat them, many amphibians ooze a nasty tasting poison from their skin. This should make the attacker spit them out.

If attacked, the red eft, the young form of the eastern newt (Notophthalmus viridescens), *secretes poison from special glands in its skin.*

An oriental fire-bellied toad (Bombina orientalis) *swimming away from danger.*

REPTILES

REPTILES RANGE from tiny lizards to snakes up to 10m (33ft) long. They live in oceans, lakes, rivers, and on land. All reptiles have a scaly skin. They depend on their surroundings for warmth, so they are more numerous in hot countries.

PORTRAIT OF A REPTILE

Most reptiles (excluding snakes) have four legs and a tail. Their scaly skin retains water inside the body, enabling them to live in dry, barren regions.

Nostril
Mouth
Eye
Tail
Ear
Scaly skin
Brain
Spinal cord
Oesophagus
Small intestine
Vertebral column (backbone)
Trachea (windpipe)
Heart
Lung
Liver
Stomach
Kidney
Bladder
Claw
Five toes

Eyed lizard (female)
(*Lacerta lepida*)

TYPES OF REPTILE

There are nearly 6,000 species of reptile, grouped into four orders (see p.72).

Lizards and snakes
(Squamata)
5,700 species

Crocodilians
(Crocodilia)
23 species

Tuatara
(Rhynochocephalia)
2 species

Turtles, tortoises, and terrapins
(Chelonia)
200 species

LIFE CYCLE

Most reptiles lay leathery-shelled eggs, although some give birth to fully developed young. Reptiles continue to grow after reaching maturity, so older individuals may reach a huge size.

Life cycle of a gecko

Egg

Gecko reaches maturity after about 18 months.

Egg hatches into young that resembles adult.

REPTILE SHELLS

Turtles, tortoises, and terrapins have a bony shell covered with horny plates or leathery skin. The shell is for protection, and often acts as a camouflage.

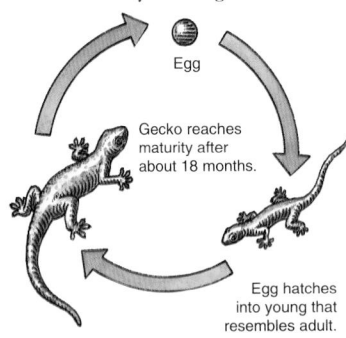

Tortoise
Tortoises usually have a strong, high-domed shell to protect the body from predators' jaws.

SLOUGHING

Snakes and lizards slough (shed) their skin from time to time, either in large flakes or in one piece. This allows them to grow, and replaces worn-out skin.

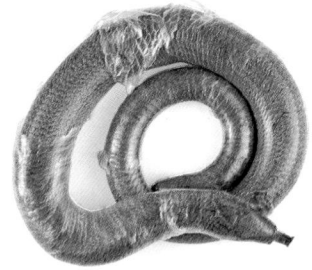

Turtle and terrapin
A turtle's shell is lighter and flatter than a tortoise's shell. The streamlined shape enables the turtle to glide through the water.

Soft-shelled turtle
These turtles have a light, flat shell for buoyancy (floating), and for hiding in the sand and mud of the riverbed.

REPTILE SKINS

The outer layer of a reptile's skin is thickened, forming waterproof scales. These scales are composed of keratin: the same substance that hoofs, hair, and fingernails are made of.

Crocodilians
Crocodilians have a tough, armour-like skin made of rough, horny scales (scutes).

Caiman skin

Snakes
Most snakes have a smooth skin. The scales overlap so that the snake can bend easily.

Snake skin

Lizards
Lizard skins range from smooth and slippery, to rough and spiky.

Gecko skin

REPTILE COLOURS

CAMOUFLAGE

Many reptiles have skin colours and patterns that enable them to blend in with their surroundings, from bright green forest lizards, to dull brown desert snakes.

WARNING COLOURS

Many venomous snakes, such as the Eastern coral snake (*Micrurus fulvius*), have bright colours to warn predators to keep away. Some harmless species have also developed these colours, to fool enemies into thinking they are dangerous.

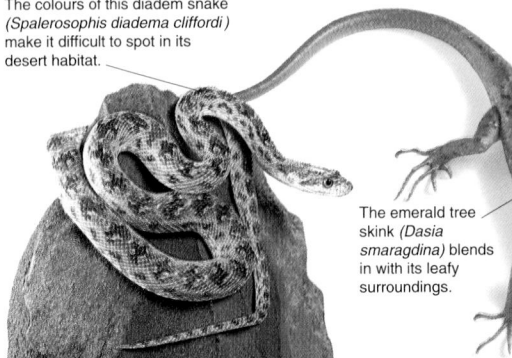

The colours of this diadem snake (*Spalerosophis diadema cliffordi*) make it difficult to spot in its desert habitat.

The emerald tree skink (*Dasia smaragdina*) blends in with its leafy surroundings.

LONGEST SNAKE

The longest and heaviest snake in the world is the anaconda (*Eunectes murinus*). The longest anaconda on record measured 10.26m (33.7ft): longer than a bus.

REPTILES ON THE ATTACK

Most reptiles are carnivorous (meat-eating). From deadly venom to sticky tongues and snapping jaws, they have evolved some of the most efficient methods of attack in the animal kingdom.

VENOM
Poisonous snakes, such as this green mamba *(Dendroaspis angusticeps)*, kill prey by biting it, and injecting venom through their fangs.

CONSTRICTION
Pythons and boas, such as this anaconda, coil their body around their prey, slowly squeezing the animal until it suffocates.

STICKY TONGUE
Chameleons have a long tongue with a sticky tip that they shoot out at prey. The chameleon's tongue is as long as its body and tail combined.

REPTILE RECORDS

LARGEST CROCODILIAN
is the saltwater crocodile *(Crocodylus porosus)*, which can grow up to 6m (20ft) long.

LARGEST LIZARD
is the Komodo dragon *(Varanus komodoensis)*, which grows up to 3m (10ft) long.

SMALLEST REPTILE
is the British Virgin Island gecko *(Sphaerodactylus parthenopion)*, with a body just 18mm (0.7in) in length.

SNAPPING BEAKS
Tortoises and turtles do not have teeth: instead, they have a sharp, horny beak. Carnivorous turtles, such as snapping turtles, have strong jaws for grabbing and chopping up a passing meal.

This alligator snapping turtle *(Macroclemys)* has a pink, worm-like tongue for luring fish into its mouth.

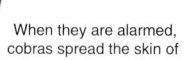

Alligators can grow up to 50 new sets of teeth in a lifetime.

TERRIBLE TEETH
Crocodiles and their relatives have formidable sharp, pointed teeth for grabbing prey and tearing off chunks of flesh.

DEFENSIVE TACTICS

Many reptiles have developed effective ways of putting off their enemies. A predator attacking a reptile may receive an unpleasant surprise.

HISSING AND SPITTING
Cobras rear up off the ground and hiss to scare off an enemy. Most cobras inject deadly venom by biting, but spitting cobras squirt jets of venom into their attacker's eyes.

When they are alarmed, cobras spread the skin of their neck into a hood.

LOOKING FIERCE
When startled, the Australian frilled lizard *(Chlamydosaurus kingi)* erects a large, ruff-like flap of loose skin on its neck. This usually scares away the attacker.

NASTY SMELLS
The stinkpot turtle *(Sternotherus odoratus)* emits a foul-smelling yellow liquid to put off attackers.

SQUIRTING BLOOD
Some horned lizards *(Phrynosoma)* squirt drops of blood from their eyes at enemies. The blood may contain irritants.

*Monocled cobra
(Naja naja kaouthia)*

REPTILE FACTS

• Some snakes push their windpipe out of their mouth to avoid being suffocated when swallowing a large animal.

• When a snake charmer's snake weaves to and fro, it is not dancing to the music, but following the snake charmer's movements.

• A chameleon's eyes can move independently. One eye can look up while the other looks down.

• Spitting cobras can squirt their venom up to 2.7m (9ft).

WALKING ON WATER
Basilisk lizards *(Basiliscus)* drop on to water and run across the surface on their back legs to escape from a predator.

"FLYING"
Some lizards, such as this flying dragon *(Draco volans)*, escape attack by leaping and gliding from tree to tree.

DEADLIEST SNAKES

Some 50,000–100,000 people die each year from snake bites. These are some of the worse culprits.

Common name and distribution	Scientific name	No. of deaths per year (approx.)
Asian cobras (Asia)	*Naja*	15,000
Saw-scaled vipers (Asia and Africa)	*Echis*	10,000
Russell's viper (Asia)	*Daboia russelii*	5,000
Kraits (Asia)	*Bungarus*	3,000
Lance-headed vipers (Central and South America)	*Bothrops*	3,000

LOSING THE TAIL
Many lizards can shed their tail if an attacker grabs hold of it; this allows them to escape. A new tail eventually grows in its place.

This lizard has recently lost part of its tail while escaping from a predator.

Two months later the tail is growing back.

After eight months the tail has almost reached its original length.

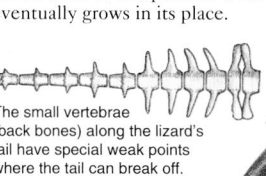

The small vertebrae (back bones) along the lizard's tail have special weak points where the tail can break off.

FISH

THERE IS NO SUCH thing as a typical fish: the three groups are as different from each other as a camel is from a crow. All fish live in water, although some species can spend time on land. Their habitats range from the cold, inky depths of the deepest oceans, to warm, sluggish, tropical rivers.

TYPES OF FISH

There are more than 20,000 species of fish, the vast majority of which are bony fish. Fish are divided into three classes (see p.72).

Jawless fish
(Agnatha)
hagfish and lampreys
75 species

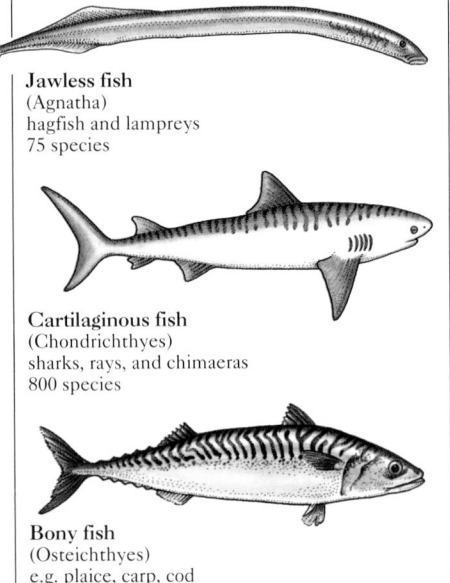

Cartilaginous fish
(Chondrichthyes)
sharks, rays, and chimaeras
800 species

Bony fish
(Osteichthyes)
e.g. plaice, carp, cod
20,000–22,000 species

FISH RECORDS

LARGEST FISH
is the whale shark (Rhincodon typus), which grows to more than 15m (50ft) long.

SMALLEST FISH
is the goby (Pandaka pygmaea), which grows just 7.6mm (0.3in) long: smaller than a housefly.

FASTEST SWIMMER
is the tunny (Thunnus), which has been recorded swimming at 71km/h (44mph).

SWIMMING

Fish swim by creating a series of S-shaped waves that travel along the body from head to tail.

PORTRAIT OF A FISH

Fish are vertebrates (see p.84). The most familiar and numerous are the bony fish, which have a skeleton made of bone, a swim bladder for buoyancy (floating), and a gill cover, called the operculum. Most fish are covered with scales.

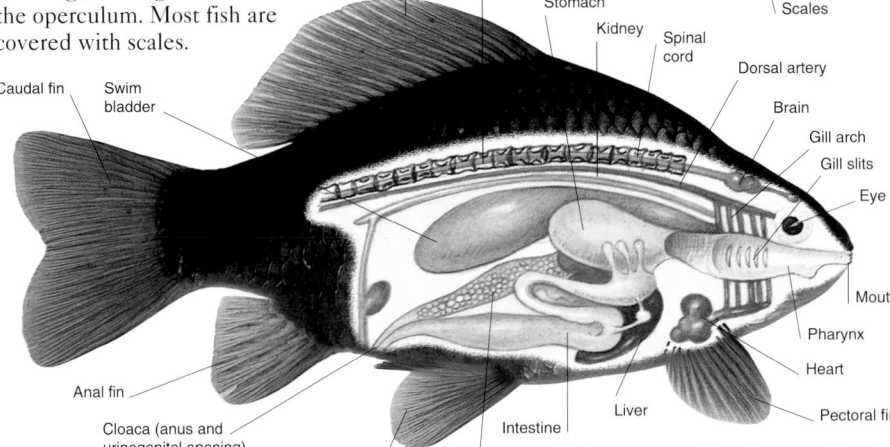

Lateral line (sense organ)
Operculum (gill cover)
Dorsal fin
Backbone
Stomach
Kidney
Spinal cord
Scales
Dorsal artery
Brain
Gill arch
Gill slits
Eye
Mouth
Pharynx
Heart
Pectoral fin
Caudal fin
Swim bladder
Anal fin
Cloaca (anus and urinogenital opening)
Pelvic fin
Ovary
Intestine
Liver

Crucian carp (female)
(Carassius carassius)

LIFE CYCLES

Most fish release eggs, although some give birth to fully formed young. Many fish produce thousands of eggs at a time, because so few survive to become adults. Lifespans range from a few months, to over 100 years for the giant sturgeon *(Huso huso)*.

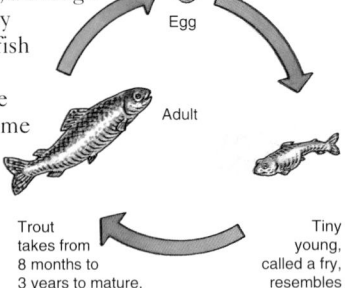

Life cycle of a trout
Egg
Adult
Trout takes from 8 months to 3 years to mature, depending on species.
Tiny young, called a fry, resembles adult trout.

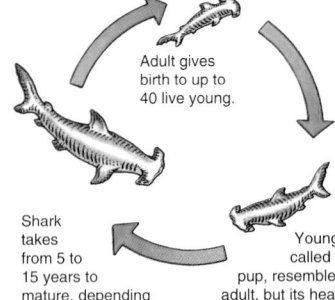

Life cycle of a hammerhead shark
Adult gives birth to up to 40 live young.
Young, called a pup, resembles adult, but its head projectiles are bent back.
Shark takes from 5 to 15 years to mature, depending on species.

HOW FISH BREATHE

Fish "breathe" using their gills. As water flows over the gills, oxygen passes through thin membranes (skins) into the blood.

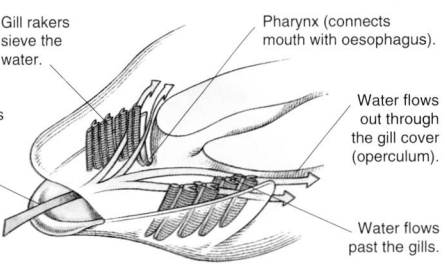

Gill rakers sieve the water.
Pharynx (connects mouth with oesophagus).
The fish takes in water through its mouth.
Water flows out through the gill cover (operculum).
Water flows past the gills.

SMALL BEGINNINGS

An adult ocean sunfish (Mola mola) is about 60 million times bigger than its young: newly hatched sunfish are about 6mm (0.25in) long, while adults measure about 3m (10ft).

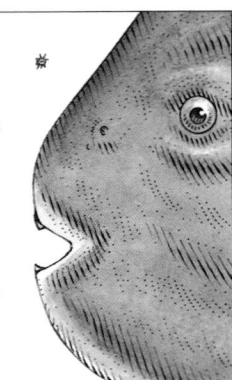

FISH MOVEMENT

Fish move in three dimensions: forwards and backwards; up and down; and left and right. They use different fins to control these movements.

ROLL
The fish uses its dorsal, pectoral, and pelvic fins to roll.

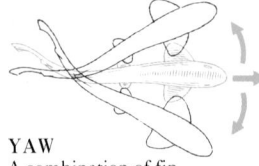

YAW
A combination of fin movements steers the fish to the left and right.

PITCH
The fish swivels its pectoral and pelvic fins to rise, stay level, and dive.

Dogfish

The S-shaped wave begins when the fish swings its head to the right.

Peak
First dorsal fin
Pelvic fin

The peak of the wave has travelled to the region of the pelvic and first dorsal fins.

Peak

The peak is now between the two dorsal fins, and the tail begins to thrust to the right.

Peak

The peak reaches the tail, and the head swings for the next wave.

CARING FOR YOUNG

Many fish do not look after their eggs and young, leaving them to fend for themselves. Others are caring parents, fiercely protecting their offspring from predators.

PROTECTIVE POUCH
The female seahorse lays her eggs into a special pouch on the male seahorse's body. The eggs grow inside the pouch, and are "born" when fully developed as young.

MOUTH BROODING
Many cichlids keep their eggs in their mouth while they develop. After hatching, the young usually stay in the mouth for safety, finally leaving it when they are mature enough.

PARENT NIBBLING
The common brown discus fish (*Symphysodon*) secretes a special nourishing substance from its skin for the young to nibble. They feed on their parents for about four weeks.

FISH SHAPES

Fish have evolved many different shapes to suit their particular way of life, from streamlined sharks shaped for fast swimming, to flatfish that lie motionless on the sea floor.

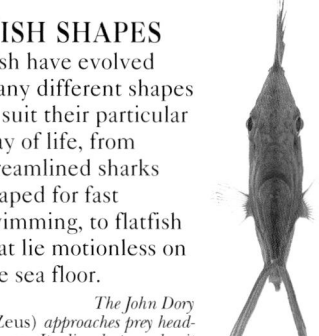

The John Dory (Zeus) approaches prey head-on. Its slim shape makes it difficult for the victim to spot.

FEEDING AND DIET

Fish feed in a variety of ways, depending on their diet. There are plant-eaters, meat-eaters, scavengers (feed on dead plants and animals), and parasites (see below).

FILTER FEEDING
Filter feeders, such as this paddlefish (*Polyodon spathula*), sift food from the water with their gill rakers.

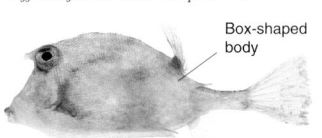

Box-shaped body

Protective bony plates beneath the cowfish's skin give it a distinctive boxy shape.

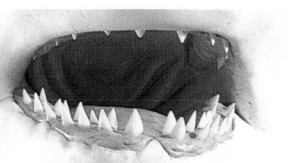

TEARING TEETH
Many fish, such as this great white shark (*Carcharodan carcharias*), have razor-sharp teeth for biting chunks out of their prey.

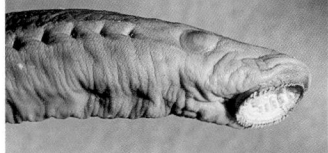

SUCKING BLOOD
The lamprey is a parasitic fish (feeds on living things). It attaches itself to prey with a sucker, rasps at the flesh with its teeth, then sucks its blood.

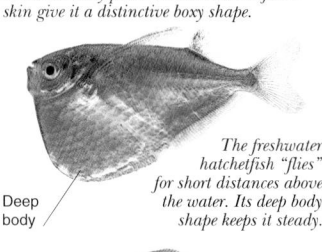

Deep body

The freshwater hatchetfish "flies" for short distances above the water. Its deep body shape keeps it steady.

DEFENSIVE TACTICS

Many fish rely on camouflage to stay hidden from predators. Several species are poisonous, while the electric eel (*Electrophorus electricus*) can deliver a 500-volt shock.

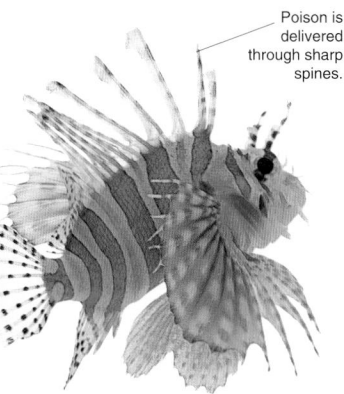

Poison is delivered through sharp spines.

POISON
More than 50 species of fish are poisonous. This lion fish (*Pterois volitans*) is one of the deadliest in the world.

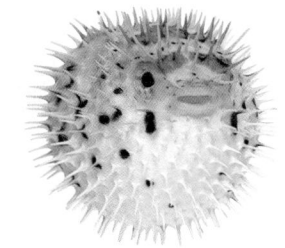

PUFFING UP
When attacked, the porcupine fish inflates its body and erects its spines in the hope that it will be too large and prickly to be eaten.

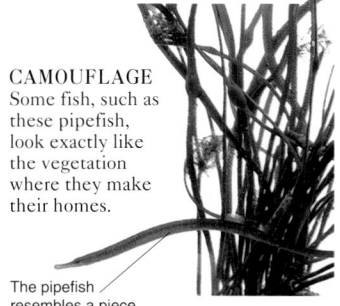

CAMOUFLAGE
Some fish, such as these pipefish, look exactly like the vegetation where they make their homes.

The pipefish resembles a piece of seaweed.

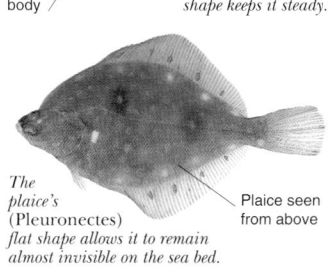

The plaice's (Pleuronectes) flat shape allows it to remain almost invisible on the sea bed.

Plaice seen from above

The long-nosed gar (Lepisosteus osseus) is a long, thin shape for quick dashes.

FISH FACTS

• The basking shark (*Cetorhinus maximus*) filters about 1,500cu m (330,000 gallons) of water per hour: enough to fill 66,000 baths.

• Needlefish are the only fish that have green bones.

• It would take 2,000 gobies (smallest fish) to equal the length of a whale shark (largest fish).

• Some sharks give birth to just one live young: the first to develop inside the mother eats all the other eggs and embryos.

• In times of drought, the African lungfish (*Protopterus*) buries itself in mud. It can survive for at least three years by digesting its own muscles.

ON THE ATTACK

Most fish rely on speed and surprise to catch prey. Some species have developed other methods of attack.

LURES
Some fish use lures to catch prey. Deep sea angler fish have a luminous organ on the end of a long, pole-like fin ray. Prey are attracted by the light, and are snapped up by the waiting fish.

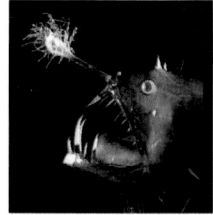

SQUIRTING
The archer fish squirts water at its prey, knocking it into the water.

FISH HABITATS

Mountain lakes and streams
Fish live at altitudes of up to 4,900m (16,000ft).

Loach: probably the highest living species

Lakes and rivers
Carp, characins, and catfish are some of the most common freshwater fish.

Upside-down catfish

Shoreline
Some species that live on the shoreline can survive for long periods out of the water.

Mudskipper

Coastal waters
In tropical coastal waters, coral reefs are home to many brightly coloured fish.

Mandarin fish

Open ocean
Many species of fish that live in the open ocean grow to a huge size.

Pacific manta ray

Caves
Several species of cave fish have no eyes: they do not need them as they spend their lives in darkness.

Blind cave characin

Deep-ocean
Food is scarce here. Many fish have large jaws to make the most of feeding opportunities.

Gulper eel

Middle ocean depths
Light disappears and fish are fewer in deeper ocean water

Oarfish

BIRDS

THERE ARE MORE than 9,000 species of bird – about two for every species of mammal. All birds have feathers, and most can fly. They range in size from tiny hummingbirds, to the ostrich, which can grow one and a half times as tall as a human. Birds are found in almost all habitats.

PORTRAIT OF A BIRD

The body of a typical bird is superbly adapted for flight. The front limbs are modified to form wings, and the body is a streamlined shape. Birds have some hollow bones to keep them light.

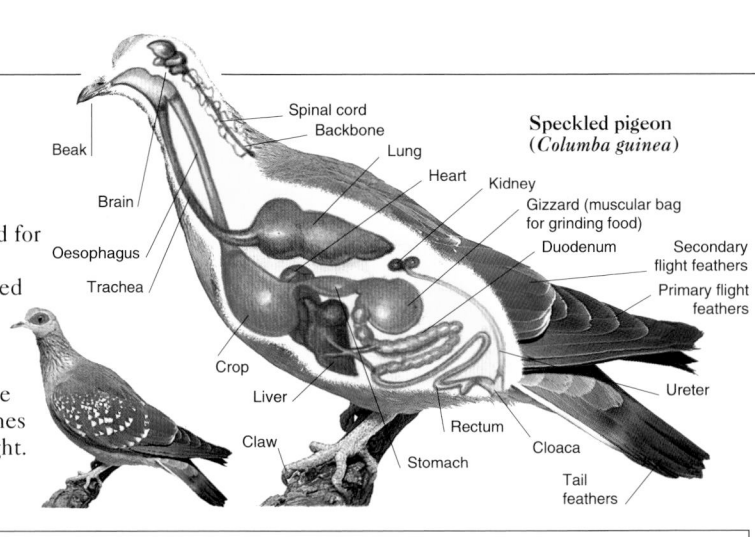

Speckled pigeon (*Columba guinea*)

Beak · Brain · Oesophagus · Trachea · Spinal cord · Backbone · Lung · Heart · Kidney · Gizzard (muscular bag for grinding food) · Duodenum · Secondary flight feathers · Primary flight feathers · Crop · Liver · Claw · Stomach · Rectum · Cloaca · Ureter · Tail feathers

TYPES OF BIRD

The 9,000 or so known species of bird are divided into 28 orders (see p.72).

Ostrich
(Struthioniformes)
1 species

Albatrosses, petrels
(Procellariiformes)
110 species

Parrots, lories, cockatoos
(Psittaciformes)
342 species

Pelicans, gannets, cormorants
(Pelecaniformes)
55 species

Rheas
(Rheiformes)
2 species

Owls
(Strigiformes)
174 species

Herons, storks, ibises
(Ciconiiformes)
117 species

Cuckoos, turacos
(Cuculiformes)
159 species

Emu, cassowaries
(Casuariiformes)
4 species

Waterfowl
(Anseriformes)
150 species

Nightjars, frogmouths
(Caprimulgiformes)
109 species

Swifts, hummingbirds
(Apodiformes)
429 species

Tinamous
(Tinamiformes)
46 species

Birds of prey
(Falconiformes)
290 species

Mousebirds
(Coliiformes)
6 species

Trogons
(Trogoniformes)
39 species

Kiwis
(Apterygiformes)
3 species

Game birds
(Galliformes)
274 species

Kingfishers, bee-eaters, hoopoes
(Coraciiformes)
204 species

Woodpeckers, toucans, barbets
(Piciformes)
381 species

Penguins
(Sphenisciformes)
18 species

Cranes, rails, bustards
(Gruiformes)
190 species

Passerines
(Passeriformes)
5,414 species

Pigeons
(Columbiformes)
300 species

Loons or divers
(Gaviiformes)
5 species

Shorebirds, gulls, terns, auks
(Charadriiformes)
337 species

Sandgrouse
(Pteroclidiformes)
16 species

Grebes
(Podicipediformes)
21 species

LIFE CYCLE

Birds lay hard-shelled eggs which one or both parents usually incubate. The hatchlings of some species are blind and helpless, and have to be looked after for many weeks. Other species are able to leave the nest just one day after hatching. Lifespans range from 5 years for some species of hummingbird, to more than 72 years for the Andean condor (*Vultur gryphus*).

HATCHING OUT

Most types of chick are ready to hatch out of their egg a few weeks after it was laid. This sequence shows a duckling chipping its way out of its shell.

1 The duckling chips a hole in the blunt end of the shell with its special eggtooth. This tooth falls off after hatching.

2 The duckling turns as it chips, cutting a circle in its shell. It takes long rests between bursts of pecking.

3 When the circle is complete, the duckling straightens its neck to push the top of the egg away.

4 After a further push with its feet and shoulders, the duckling breaks off the end of the shell.

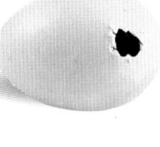
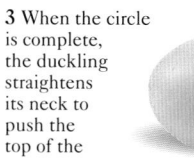

5 The duckling finally falls out of the egg. Its feathers are still wet.

6 Within two or three hours the duckling's soft, fluffy down feathers have dried. It will soon take to the water.

Life cycle of a moorhen (*Gallinula chloropus*)

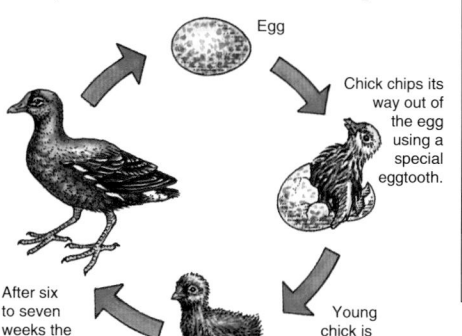
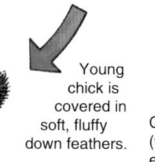

Egg

Chick chips its way out of the egg using a special eggtooth.

Young chick is covered in soft, fluffy down feathers.

After six to seven weeks the moorhen has its adult plumage and can fly.

CLOSE-UP OF A FEATHER

Feathers are strong and flexible. They are made from keratin: the same protein that hair, fingernails, and hooves contain.

Macaw feather

Tip

Outer vane (windward edge)

Downcurved edge

Inner vane (leeward edge)

Shaft of feather is hollow.

Upcurved edge

Barbs are locked tightly together to form a smooth surface.

Quill

TYPES OF FEATHER

There are four main types of feather, each with a different function.

Down feathers
These soft, fluffy feathers keep the bird warm.

Body feathers
Sleek body feathers emphasise the bird's streamlined shape.

Wing feathers
Strong wing feathers provide the surface the bird needs for flight.

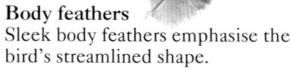

Tail feathers
The bird uses its long tail feathers for steering, balance, and braking.

POISONOUS BIRD

The only known poisonous bird is the hooded pitohui (*Pitohui dichrous*) from New Guinea. Its skin, feathers, and internal organs contain a poison similar to that secreted by poison-dart frogs (see p.93).

WING SHAPES

Birds' wings are shaped to suit their lifestyles. They may be broad or slender; long or short.

Gulls have slender, pointed wings for gliding.

Woodpeckers have broad, rounded wings for manoeuvrability.

Geese have long, broad wings to lift their heavy body and keep it airborne.

Swifts have slender, curved wings for rapid and powerful flight.

FEET SHAPES

Birds' feet come in many different shapes and sizes, to suit their various habitats and lifestyles.

The moorhen's long toes are widely spread, enabling the bird to walk across mud and floating vegetation.

*Water birds, such as Canada geese (*Branta canadensis*), have webbed feet to paddle through the water.*

Woodpeckers have two toes pointing forwards and two pointing backwards, to anchor them as they chip away at tree trunks.

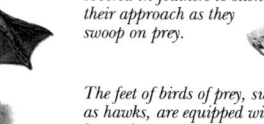

Perching birds, such as crows, have a single hind toe that enables them to hold tightly on to branches.

Owls' legs and feet are covered in feathers to silence their approach as they swoop on prey.

The feet of birds of prey, such as hawks, are equipped with long, sharp talons for gripping prey.

The wings of flightless birds, such as rheas, are useless for flight.

Penguins have paddle-shaped wings for swimming.

ATTRACTING A MATE

Birds go to great lengths to attract a mate. Usually, the males court the females: they may sing, dance, strut, or show off their colours to attract attention.

Display
Many birds display brightly coloured parts of the body to attract a female. The male raggiana bird of paradise *(Paradisaea raggiana)* may hang upside down as part of his display.

Presenting gifts
Some birds attract a female by presenting a gift. The male greater roadrunner *(Geococcyx californianus)* offers his mate a lizard, while the male sandwich tern *(Sterna sandvicensis)* (left) presents his with a fish.

Building a bower
Male bowerbirds build a bower to attract a mate. The male vogelkop gardener's *(Amblyornis inornatus)* bower is a complex shelter of twigs. The bower is only for attraction: after mating, the female builds her own nest in which to lay her eggs.

WIDEST WINGSPAN
The wandering albatross *(Diomedea exulans)* has the largest wingspan of any bird, measuring 3.6m (12ft) from wing tip to wing tip: greater than the length of a small car.

BIRDS' NESTS
Most birds build a nest in which to lay their eggs and rear their chicks. They range from simple scrapes, to intricately woven nests.

Simple nests
Some birds lay their eggs in a scrape in the ground. Others have no nest at all: guillemots (right) lay eggs on rocky ledges.

Burrows
Some birds, including puffins *(Fratercula arctica)* (right), nest inside a burrow.

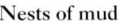

Nests of mud
Flamingos build conical pots of sand and mud to lay their eggs in.

Woven nests
Many birds weave nests of grass, leaves, or twigs. Weaver birds build elaborate grass nests (right): the long entrance stops snakes from getting inside.

Nests of sticks
The hammerkop *(Scopus umbretta)* builds a huge, roofed nest of sticks, grass, and mud. The nest measures up to 1.5m (5ft) across.

Nests of saliva
Edible-nest swiftlets *(Collocalia fuciphaga)* build their nests from saliva. These nests are used to make birds nest soup: a food delicacy in China.

HIGH FLIER
Rüppell's griffons *(Gyps rueppelli)* are the highest flying birds. They can reach heights of 11,278m (37,000ft): as high as airliners fly.

BIRD RECORDS
LARGEST BIRD is the ostrich *(Struthio camelus)*, which weighs up to 156kg (344lb), and grows up to 2.7m (8.9ft) tall.

SMALLEST BIRD is the bee hummingbird *(Mellisuga helenae)*, which weighs about 1.6g (0.056oz) and grows just 5.7cm (2.24in) long.

FASTEST SWIMMER is the gentoo penguin *(Pygoscelis papua)*, which can reach speeds of 27.4km/h (17mph).

MOST ABUNDANT BIRD is the red-billed quelea *(Quelea quelea)*, with an adult population of about 1.5 billion. There may be up to 10 million birds in a single colony.

EGGS
The type and number of eggs a bird lays depends on its lifestyle and habitat. Some species lay just one egg; others lay several. Eggs vary widely in size and shape. Many are coloured and patterned for camouflage, making them difficult for predators, such as foxes, to spot.

The eggs of the bee hummingbird (Mellisuga helenae) *are the smallest in the world, weighing only 0.25g (0.009oz).*

Ostrich (Struthio camelus) *eggs are the largest in the world, weighing up to 1.65kg (3.64lb), and measuring up to 20cm (8in) long.*

DIETS AND BEAKS
Birds eat a huge variety of food, including meat, fish, seeds, insects, and fruit. Their beaks are adapted to suit their particular diets.

Serrated beaks
Birds do not have teeth, but some, such as mergansers *(Mergus)*, have teeth-like structures on the sides of their beak. These serrations help them to catch fish.

Avocet beak
Avocets *(Recurvirostra)* have an upturned beak which they sweep from side to side to catch worms and other invertebrates in shallow estuary waters.

Fruit and nut eaters
Parrots' beaks are shaped for cracking nuts and eating fruit. The hook at the front of the beak is for tearing at fruit, and the strong base of the beak cracks open seeds.

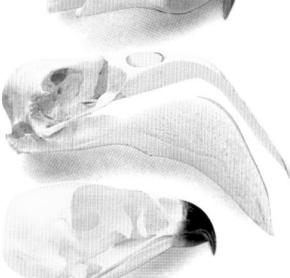

Flamingo beak
Flamingos have a "bent" beak for sifting food from water. The tongue pumps water through fringes on either side of the bill, trapping small animals and plants.

Predators
Birds of prey, such as falcons *(Falco)*, are carnivorous (meat-eating). They have a strong, hooked beak for tearing apart prey too large to be swallowed whole.

BIRD FACTS
- Hummingbirds need to eat half their body weight every day to stay alive.
- Pelican chicks can attract their parents' attention while still inside the egg: they call when they are too hot or too cold.
- Starlings are some of the best mimics in the bird world: they can mimic other birds, and even ringing telephones.
- Ostrich eggs are the largest single cells in the world.
- Once a young sooty tern *(Sterna fuscata)* takes to the wing, it may stay airborne for four years before returning to the ground to breed.
- Large birds, e.g. swans, may have more than 25,000 feathers.
- The peregrine falcon *(Falco peregrinus)* can reach speeds of 180km/h (112mph) during a stoop (dive).

FASTEST-FLYING BIRDS

Bird	Scientific name	Speed km/h	Speed mph
White-throated spine-tail swift	*Hirundapus caudacutus*	171	106
Alpine swift	*Apus melba*	160	99.4
Magnificent frigatebird	*Fregata magnificens*	159	99
Spurwing goose	*Plectropterus gambensis*	142	88
Red-breasted merganser	*Mergus serrator*	129	80

DOMESTIC BIRDS

DOMESTIC BIRDS ARE birds that are kept and bred by humans. They include chickens, ducks, and geese. Domestic birds are kept for various purposes: some are bred for their meat, eggs, or feathers; others for sports such as pigeon racing and falconry.

CHICKEN BREEDS

All chickens are descended from the red jungle fowl (*Gallus gallus*) of Southeast Asia, which is a member of the pheasant family. Chicken breeds are generally classified into American, Mediterranean, English, and Asian. Eight of the 150 breeds are illustrated here.

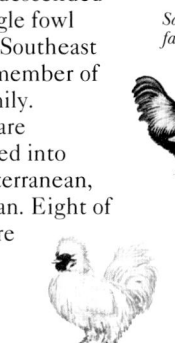
Salmon faverolle

Bantam Orpington Blue

Barred Plymouth Rock

Japanese yokohama

Silver braekel fowl

White silky

Red jungle fowl (*Gallus gallus*)

Turken

Mille fleur bantam

TURKEY FACTS

• Turkeys were first domesticated by the Aztec and Zuni Indians for food and sacrifice. They also used the feathers for decoration.

• Turkeys were first taken to Europe by the Spanish in about 1511.

• There are about 124 million domestic turkeys in the world.

CHICKEN FACTS

• Chickens were domesticated about 8,000 years ago.

• In the Middle Ages, chicken was only eaten by royalty and the aristocracy. The poor kept chickens for eggs and new chicks, and killed a hen only when it became too old to lay. Today, chicken is probably the most widely eaten meat in the world.

• Hens can lay about 250 eggs a year.

EGGSTRAORDINARY!

About 160 billion hens' eggs are laid every year in China: enough to make an omelette that would give every person in the world a piece measuring 1m (3.28ft) across.

DUCK FACT

• The Muscovy duck was first domesticated in South America by pre-Columbian Indians. The mallard (right) was domesticated in China at least 3,000 years ago.

DOMESTIC BIRD RECORDS

FASTEST EGG-LAYING CHICKEN
was a white leghorn that laid 371 eggs in 364 days.

LARGEST CHICKEN'S EGG
weighed 454g (16oz). It was laid by a white leghorn in Vineland, New Jersey, USA, in 1956.

MOST YOLKS
in a chicken's egg was nine, laid by a hen in Mount Morris, New York, USA, in 1971.

LARGEST CHICKEN PRODUCER
is the USA, which produces about 12 million tonnes of chicken meat a year.

LARGEST GOOSE EGG
weighed 680g (24oz), laid by "Speckle" in Goshen, Ohio, USA.

GOOSE FACTS

• Geese were first domesticated more than 3,000 years ago.

• Goose was considered the finest poultry for festive occasions until the turkey became more popular in the 16th and 17th centuries.

• In the Middle Ages, gooseherds in Britain would drive flocks of up to 20,000 geese to be sold at goose fairs.

TYPES OF DOMESTIC BIRD

Domestic bird	Uses	Number of breeds (approx.)	Descended from
Chicken	Meat, eggs	150	Red jungle fowl (*Gallus gallus*)
Duck	Meat, eggs, down	97	Muscovy duck (*Cairina moschata*) and wild mallard (*Anas platyrhyncos*)
Goose	Meat, eggs, down	43	Most breeds from the greylag (*Anser anser*)
Turkey	Meat	33	Common turkey (*Meleagris gallopavo*)

OTHER DOMESTIC BIRDS

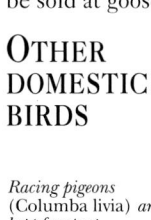
Racing pigeons (*Columba livia*) *are kept for sport.*

Racing pigeons are descended from the rock dove.

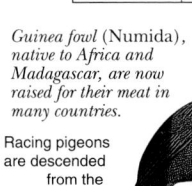
Guinea fowl (Numida), *native to Africa and Madagascar, are now raised for their meat in many countries.*

Long, tapering breast feathers

Swans are reared for their down, and as ornamental birds.

Hooked beak for tearing at prey.

Falcons are used in the sport of falconry.

Ostriches (Struthio camelus) *are reared for their meat, and their decorative feathers.*

Many types of bird are kept as pets. The budgerigar (Melopsittacus undulatus) *is particularly popular.*

The budgerigar is native to Australia.

Canaries (Serinus canaria) *are kept as pets for their beautiful song.*

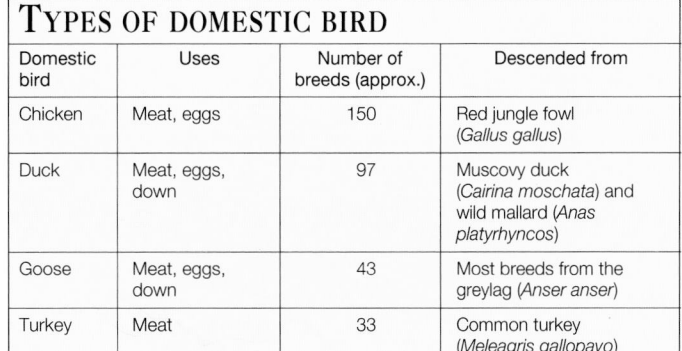

Pheasants have been introduced into Europe and North America.

Pheasants, native to Asia, are reared as game birds.

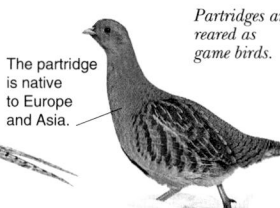
The partridge is native to Europe and Asia.

Partridges are reared as game birds.

MAMMALS

MAMMALS RANGE IN size from tiny shrews to the blue whale – the largest animal that has ever lived on Earth. Mammals are found all over the world: on land, in oceans and rivers, and even, in the case of bats, in the air.

PORTRAIT OF A MAMMAL

Mammals usually have fur or hair. Almost all species give birth to live young which they feed with milk produced in the female's body.

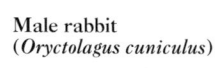
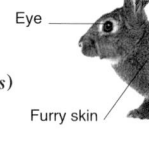

Eye

Male rabbit (*Oryctolagus cuniculus*)

Furry skin

Tail

Pinna (ear flap) directs sounds towards inner ear.

Brain

Nasal cavity

Mouth

Oesophagus

Trachea

Lung

Heart

Diaphragm

Liver

Gall bladder

Stomach

Kidney

Spinal cord

Backbone

Colon

Ureter

Bladder

Reproductive organs

Anus

ARMADILLO SHELL-TER

Some ancient mammals grew to huge sizes. The ancestors of modern armadillos measured up to 3m (10ft) long. South American Indians used their shells as roofs.

TYPES OF MAMMAL

There are more than 4,600 known species of mammal, divided into 21 orders (see p.72).

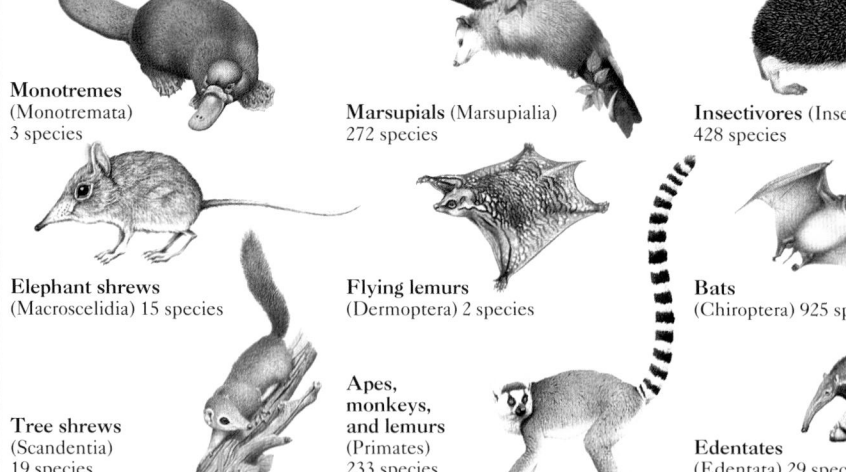

Monotremes (Monotremata) 3 species

Marsupials (Marsupialia) 272 species

Insectivores (Insectivora) 428 species

Elephant shrews (Macroscelidia) 15 species

Flying lemurs (Dermoptera) 2 species

Bats (Chiroptera) 925 species

Tree shrews (Scandentia) 19 species

Apes, monkeys, and lemurs (Primates) 233 species

Edentates (Edentata) 29 species

Pangolins (Pholidota) 7 species

Aardvark (Tubulidentata) 1 species

Hares, rabbits, pikas (Lagomorpha) 80 species

Rodents (Rodentia) 2,021 species

Whales and dolphins (Cetacea) 78 species

Carnivores (Carnivora) 237 species

Seals, sea lions, walrus (Pinnipedia) 34 species

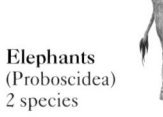

Elephants (Proboscidea) 2 species

Hyraxes (Hyracoidea) 6 species

Sea cows (Sirenia) 5 species

Odd-toed hoofed mammals (Perissodactyla) 18 species

Even-toed hoofed mammals (Artiodactyla) 220 species

MAMMAL REPRODUCTION

EGG-LAYING MAMMALS

Monotremes are the only mammals that lay eggs. Female duck-billed platypuses (*Ornithorhynchus anatinus*) (right) incubate their eggs in a nest inside their burrow; female echidnas incubate their eggs in a pouch.

MARSUPIAL MAMMALS

Marsupials, such as kangaroos, give birth when the young are at a very early stage of development. The tiny baby crawls across its mother's belly to reach the pouch, where it latches on to a teat and feeds on milk. The baby remains in the pouch for many weeks, leaving it for longer periods as it grows older.

New-born joey (baby kangaroo) in the pouch.

PLACENTAL MAMMALS

Most mammals are placental: the young grow inside the female and receive nutrients via the placenta (a connection between the mother's and baby's blood systems). At birth, the young are physically well-developed.

New-born kittens feeding on their mother's milk.

MAMMAL SKINS

Arctic fox skin

FURRY SKIN

Fur and hair enable mammals to live in almost every climate. By trapping air, a furry coat, such as the Arctic fox's *(Alopex lagopus)*, keeps out the cold, stops body heat from escaping, and protects the skin from wind, rain, and strong sunlight.

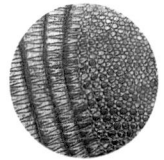

Jaguar skin

CAMOUFLAGE PATTERNS

Many mammals have skins that are coloured and patterned for camouflage. This enables them to blend in with their background, hidden from enemies and prey. A jaguar's *(Panthera onca)* spots blend in with the dappled sunlight of the forest floor where it stalks its prey.

Armadillo skin

ARMOUR PLATING

Pangolins and armadillos are covered with bony plates and scales that provide a tough, armoured coat to protect them from predators. Some, such as the three-banded armadillo *(Tolypeutes)*, can roll themselves up into a ball to defend their body completely.

Zebra skin

CONFUSING PATTERNS

A zebra's *(Equus)* stripes break up its outline, making it more difficult for predators, such as lions *(Panthera leo)*, to pick out one individual from the herd. This black and white pattern is particularly effective at night, protecting the herd from nocturnal hunters.

Dolphin skin

NAKED SKIN

Hair or fur would slow down whales and dolphins in the water, so they have lost all but a few tufts. Naked mole rats *(Heterocephalus glaber)* have also lost their hair: it is easier for them to move forwards and backwards along a tunnel with a smooth, hairless skin.

SPINY SKIN

The hairs of hedgehogs and porcupines have developed into stiff, sharp spines that form an effective defence against predators. The European hedgehog *(Erinaceus europaeus)* has up to 5,000 spines. When it senses danger, it rolls itself up into a ball.

European hedgehog skin

LONGEST GESTATION PERIODS

The gestation period is the amount of time the young take to develop inside the mother. (Humans have a gestation period of nine months.)

Mammal	Scientific name	Gestation period
African elephant	*Loxodonta africana*	22 months
Asian elephant	*Elephas maximus*	22 months
Baird's beaked whale	*Berardius bairdii*	17 months
White rhinoceros	*Ceratotherium simum*	16 months

MAMMAL HANDS AND FEET

All early mammals probably had five fingers and toes on each hand and foot. Over time, these basic digits evolved to suit different lifestyles and habitats. Humans *(Homo sapiens)* have the five fingers and toes typical of many mammals. The colours of the various parts of a human hand (right) are repeated in the illustrations that follow, to show how those parts have developed to suit different animals' lifestyles.

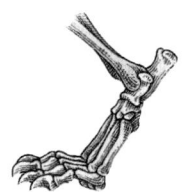

Cats walk on the tips of their toes. Each toe is armed with a sharp claw for catching prey.

Elephants have five toes on each foot, and a big fleshy pad to support their immense weight.

Tapirs' (Tapirus) front feet have four toes, while their back feet have three.

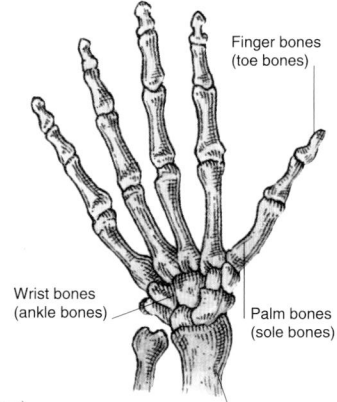

Human hand

Finger bones (toe bones)

Wrist bones (ankle bones)

Palm bones (sole bones)

Lower arm bones (lower leg bones)

Gazelles have light, dainty, two-toed feet that enable them to run very fast.

Horses (Equus) have one long, strong toe on each foot, protected by a hoof.

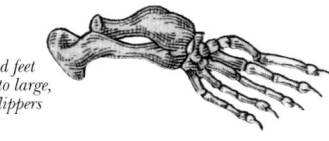

Badgers' hands and feet are adapted for digging. They are broad and strong with wide claws.

Seals' hands and feet have evolved into large, paddle-shaped flippers for swimming.

MAMMAL RECORDS

LARGEST MAMMAL

is the blue whale *(Balaenoptera musculus)*, which weighs up to 140 tonnes and grows up to 34m (111.5ft) long.

SMALLEST MAMMAL

is the Kitti's hog-nosed bat *(Craseonycteris thonglongyai)*, which weighs only 1.5g (0.05oz) and is about the size of a large bumblebee.

Kitti's hog-nosed bat and bumblebee, shown actual size.

TALLEST MAMMAL

is the giraffe *(Giraffa camelopardalis)*, which grows up to 5.9m (19.4ft) tall: more than three times the height of an adult human.

FASTEST SWIMMER

is the sei whale *(Balaenoptera borealis)*, which can swim at speeds of up to 48km/h (29.8mph).

MAMMAL FACTS

• Some types of traditional Chinese warrior armour were based on the protective overlapping scales of the pangolin's skin.

• There are only two types of poisonous mammal: the duck-billed platypus, which injects poison through a sharp spur on its ankle; and some shrews, which paralyze the earthworms they feed on with poisonous saliva.

BIG HOUSE ON THE PRAIRIE

Black-tailed prairie dog *(Cynomys ludovicianus)* colonies can cover huge areas. A colony in Texas had an area of about 62,160sq km (24,000 sq miles): twice the size of Belgium.

TUSKS, HORNS, AND ANTLERS

Some mammals have antlers, horns, or tusks, that are used mainly for fighting and establishing dominance within their social group. Antlers are shed and regrown each year; horns grow steadily throughout an animal's life. Tusks are elongated, pointed teeth.

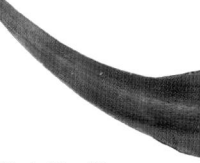
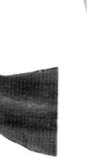

Black rhino (Diceros bicornis) horn

Elephant tusks grow about 17cm (7in) per year.

Red deer (Cervus elephus) antlers

Indian blackbuck (Antilope cervicapra) horn

MAMMAL TAILS

Most mammals have a tail. Tails have a variety of uses, including swatting flies, communication, and providing warmth.

The flying squirrel uses its flattened tail as a rudder for steering as it leaps from tree to tree. The tail also acts as an air brake.

A horse's (Equus) tail is made of many long, thick hairs. It is used mainly to keep flies and other pests away.

Some animals, for example spider monkeys (Ateles), have a prehensile tail that can grip branches like a fifth limb. This prehensile possum tail has scaly skin at the tip to give the animal a firm grip.

The fallow deer's (Dama dama) tail is dark on top and white underneath. If danger threatens, the deer holds up its tail to flash a warning to the other deer in the herd.

Elephants have wiry hair at the end of their tail. They sometimes hold each other's tails when walking along in single file.

Beavers use their flat, scaly tail as a rudder when swimming. They also slap it down on the water as a warning signal to other beavers when danger threatens.

Ring-tailed lemurs (Lemur catta) use their striped tail for signalling, and for spreading around their scent to establish dominance over other lemurs.

Foxes wrap their bushy tail around their body to keep warm. They also use their tail to signal to others in their family group.

Rats have a long, hairless, and scaly tail that they use for balance.

MAMMAL RECORDS

SHORTEST GESTATION PERIOD is that of the brindled bandicoot *(Isoodon macrourus)*. The young of this marsupial are born into the pouch after an average of just 12.5 days.

MOST TEATS are found on the common tenrec *(Tenrec ecaudatus)*, which has 29.

DEEPEST DIVER is the sperm whale *(Physeter macrocephalus)*, which can dive to depths of 1,200m (3,937ft) or more.

LONGEST LIFE-SPANS are those of the Asian elephant *(Elephas maximus)*, at up to 90 years, and humans *(Homo sapiens)*, at up to 120 years.

LARGEST ELEPHANT TUSK was 3.45m (11.3ft) long, and weighed 117kg (259lb).

LARGEST PRIMATE is the gorilla *(Gorilla gorilla)*, which weighs up to 220kg (485lb).

MAMMAL FACT

• The vampire bat *(Desmodus rotundus)* is the only mammal that lives on nothing but blood. In the 10 minutes or so it spends feeding on its victim, it can drink more than its own body weight in blood. The bat becomes so heavy that it is unable to fly for a while afterwards.

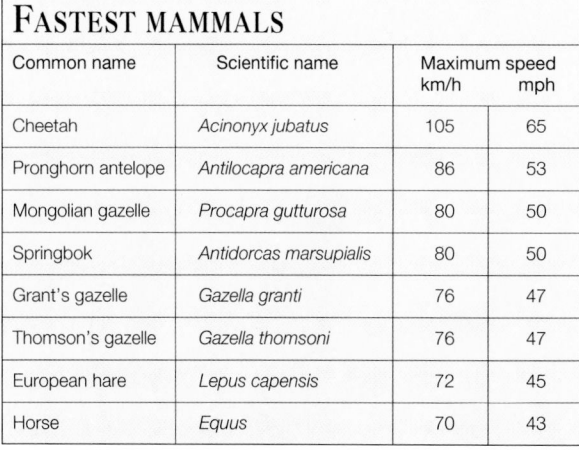

MAMMAL MOVEMENT

Most mammals walk and run on all fours. Some species have developed other ways of moving more suited to their habitat.

FLYING

Bats are the only mammals that can fly, although some, such as flying squirrels, can glide for long distances when leaping between trees.

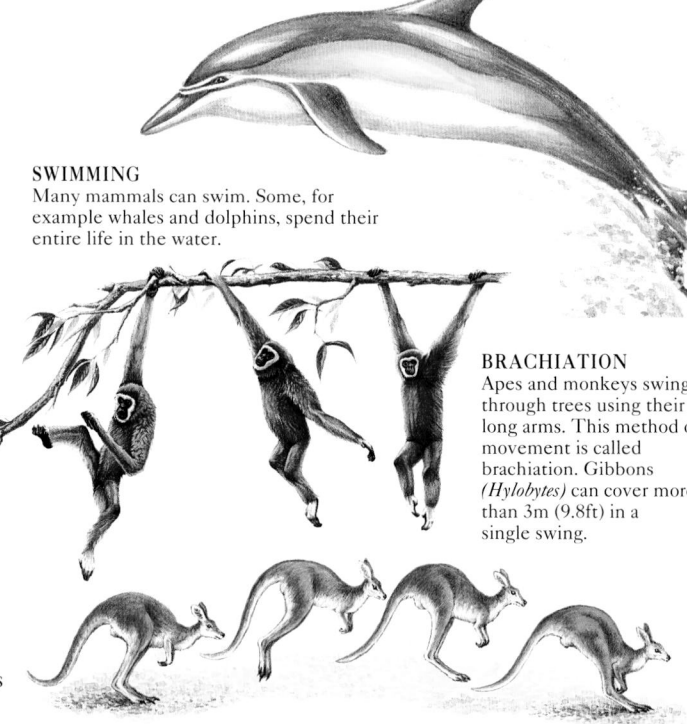

SWIMMING

Many mammals can swim. Some, for example whales and dolphins, spend their entire life in the water.

BRACHIATION

Apes and monkeys swing through trees using their long arms. This method of movement is called brachiation. Gibbons *(Hylobytes)* can cover more than 3m (9.8ft) in a single swing.

BOUNDING

Kangaroos bound along when they need to move quickly. Their tails help them to balance. Some small rodents, for example jerboas, also move around by bounding.

BURROWING

Some mammals, such as moles, spend all their time under ground. Moles have broad front paws for burrowing, and strong hind legs for bracing themselves against tunnel walls.

FASTEST MAMMALS

Common name	Scientific name	Maximum speed	
		km/h	mph
Cheetah	*Acinonyx jubatus*	105	65
Pronghorn antelope	*Antilocapra americana*	86	53
Mongolian gazelle	*Procapra gutturosa*	80	50
Springbok	*Antidorcas marsupialis*	80	50
Grant's gazelle	*Gazella granti*	76	47
Thomson's gazelle	*Gazella thomsoni*	76	47
European hare	*Lepus capensis*	72	45
Horse	*Equus*	70	43

FELINE PECKISH

A man-eating tiger *(Panthera tigris)* in Champawat district, India, was reputed to have killed 436 people. It was shot in 1907.

DOMESTIC MAMMALS

DOMESTIC MAMMALS are mammals that are kept and bred by humans. They include sheep, cattle, dogs, and cats. Many domestic mammals have been selectively bred over hundreds of years: today some breeds look and behave very differently from their wild counterparts.

DOMESTIC MAMMAL RECORDS

LARGEST DOG BREED
is the St. Bernard, which can weigh up to 77kg (170lb).

SMALLEST DOG BREED
is the chihuahua, which weighs as little as 0.45kg (1lb).

COUNTRY WITH THE MOST SHEEP
is Australia, which has about 167,781,000 individuals.

COUNTRY WITH THE MOST CATTLE
is India, which has about 197,300,000.

COUNTRY WITH THE MOST CAMELS
is Somalia, which has about 6,855,000 individuals.

SMALLEST CAT BREED
is the Singapura, which weighs as little as 1.81kg (4lb).

Chihuahua   *St. Bernard*

Singapura

Ragdoll

LARGEST CAT BREEDS
include the ragdoll : males can weigh up to 9.07kg (20lb).

TYPES OF DOMESTIC MAMMAL

Domestic mammal	Uses	Number of breeds (approx)
Sheep (*Ovis aries*)	Meat, wool	300
Llama (*Llama glama*)	Transport (pack animal), meat, wool, hides, dried dung for fuel, tallow for candles	2
Goat (*Capra*)	Milk, meat, cheese, hair, leather	300
Pig	Meat, leather	180
Cattle	Meat, milk and dairy products, leather, transport	280
Cat (*Felis catus*)	Pets, pest control	110
Dog (*Canis familiaris*)	Pets, working dogs, sports dogs	186
Buffalo	Milk, butter, transport	32
Bactrian camel (*Camelus bactrianus*)	Transport, wool, milk, hides, meat, dried dung for fuel (as for Bactrian camel)	3
Arabian camel (*Camelus dromedarius*)		4
Horse, donkey, mule (*Equus*)	Sport and leisure, transport, meat	100 (horse)

EVOLUTION OF THE DOMESTIC DOG

Dogs were the first mammals to be domesticated. They were tamed by humans about 12,000 years ago. Every breed of dog is descended from the wolf *(Canis lupus)*. This illustration shows the possible wolf ancestors of various dog breeds.

Gun dogs
Spaniels
Guard dogs
Hounds
Herding dogs
Greyhounds
Terriers
Feral dogs
Indian wolf
European wolf   *Chinese wolf*
Canis lupus
North American wolf
Oriental spaniels
European toy dogs
Oriental toy dogs
European spitz dogs
Oriental spitz dogs
Eskimo spitz dogs

CAT FACTS

• Cats were sacred to the ancient Egyptians. Many dead cats were mummified, and the Egyptians shaved off their eyebrows to mourn the loss of a cat.

• In 1951, a cat called Sugar travelled 2,414km (1,500 miles) to Oklahoma to rejoin the Woods family who had left him behind in California.

PIG FACTS

• Pigs are the most common provider of meat in China.

• In parts of Melanesia (see p.355), pigs are treated as members of the family.

• Pigs are often thought of as dirty animals, but in fact they keep themselves cleaner than most other domestic animals.

• Many Oceanic (see pp.352–53) peoples measure their wealth in terms of the number of pigs they own.

HORSES FOR COURSES

Every Thoroughbred racehorse is said to have descended from three desert stallions: the Darley Arabian, the Godolphin Barb, and the Byerly Turk. These stallions were taken to England between 1689 and 1724.

SHEEP FACTS

• The finest sheep's wool comes from the merino sheep.

• Astrakhan fur comes from the karakul sheep of central Asia.

• Parchment, an early type of writing paper, was made from untanned sheep hide.

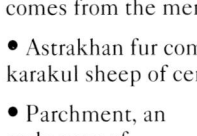
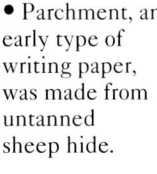

MULE FACTS

• Mules are produced by crossing a donkey *(Equus asinus)* with a female horse. Mules are surer-footed and more intelligent than horses, but cannot reproduce.

• At one time there were many different types of mules, including draft mules, farm mules, sugar mules, cotton mules, and mining mules.

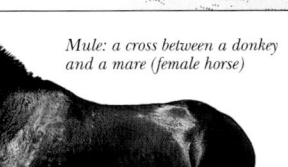

Mule: a cross between a donkey and a mare (female horse)

CATTLE FACTS

• There are about 1.21 billion cattle worldwide: more than the human population of China.

• Cattle are descended from the auroch, which once roamed across Asia and Europe. The last auroch died in 1627.

• Kenyan Masai warriors live almost entirely on blood and milk from their cattle.

ANIMAL SENSES AND BEHAVIOUR

ANIMALS HAVE EVOLVED senses and patterns of behaviour that ensure the survival of their species. Many animals have senses that are more highly developed than a human's.

COURTSHIP BEHAVIOUR

Female animals select the best available mate in order to produce strong and healthy offspring. To attract a female, male animals have evolved a fascinating range of courtship behaviour, including strutting, singing, and presenting gifts to the female.

To court a female, the peacock (Pavo cristatus) *fans out and shakes his colourful tail.*

ANIMAL SENSES

Many animals have excellent sight and hearing. Some have "sixth" senses that can detect magnetism, electricity, and even infra-red radiation.

An eagle's eyes see a magnified picture at the centre of its field of vision.

Many animals, e.g. foxes, can hear higher frequency sounds than humans.

Many mammals, e.g. dogs, have a highly developed sense of smell.

Sensitive whiskers help animals such as cats to find their way in the dark.

An invertebrate's antennae touch, taste, and smell its surroundings.

Spiders and scorpions have sensitive hairs that can detect the slightest air movements.

Fish have a lateral line: a row of sensitive pits that detect movements in the water.

Bats navigate by echolocation: they emit squeaks, and judge distances by how long the squeaks take to bounce back.

Sharks have sensors around their head that pick up electrical fields produced by prey.

Some migratory animals may navigate by sensing the Earth's magnetic field.

Pit vipers "see" an infra-red picture of their prey by detecting heat radiation given off by its body.

ATTACK AND DEFENCE BEHAVIOUR

Animals use a wide variety of attack and defence tactics. Attack strategies include stalking and pouncing; defensive tactics include stinging, and oozing poison.

The caracal (Lynx caracal) *leaps into the air to catch birds.*

Bombardier beetles (Brachinus) *spray their attackers with hot, unpleasant chemicals.*

SENSES AND BEHAVIOUR FACTS

• Net-casting spiders' eyes are 19 times more sensitive than a human's.

• The blue whale's *(Balaenoptera musculus)* call is the loudest noise made by any animal. It can travel up to 1,600km (1,000 miles).

TERRITORIAL BEHAVIOUR

Animals may fiercely defend their territory so that others cannot steal their food or harm their young. To let other animals know where their territorial boundaries lie, animals call, mark trees and bushes with scent, or leave piles of droppings.

A cheetah (Acinonyx jubatus) *marking its territory.*

• The mallee fowl's *(Leipoa ocellata)* beak acts as a thermometer. The bird incubates its eggs in a heap of rotting vegetation, checking the temperature with its beak.

• A hibernating mammal's body can be up to 32°C (90°F) below its normal temperature.

SURVIVING HEAT AND COLD

HIBERNATION

Many animals in cold climates hibernate to survive the harsh conditions and lack of food that winter brings. Their body temperature drops, their heartbeat slows down, and they go into a deep sleep, surviving on food reserves stored in the body.

AESTIVATION

Some animals aestivate to survive hot and dry periods, becoming sluggish or dormant until favourable conditions return. Many desert animals aestivate.

Dormice in cold countries hibernate for up to nine months of the year.

These snails are collecting together on grass stems ready to aestivate.

FAKE SNAKE

Some animals mimic others to defend themselves. This Costa Rican moth caterpillar fools predators into thinking it is a poisonous snake.

SOCIAL BEHAVIOUR

Animals that live in communities, such as chimpanzees *(Pan troglodytes)* and lions *(Panthera leo)*, have a social hierarchy ("pecking order"). This is reinforced in various ways.

Wolves use facial expressions to establish hierarchy, and cower in front of dominant members of the pack.

Herds of elephants are dominated by an elderly female: the matriarch. She keeps order and decides where the herd will go.

Matriarch

Herd is made up of adult females and young.

Young male

Six-year-old female

USING TOOLS

Some animals use tools to obtain food, e.g. chimpanzees poke twigs into termite mounds, and Egyptian vultures *(Neophron percnopterus)* throw stones at eggs to break them.

Sea otters (Enhydra lutris) *smash sea urchins and shellfish on a stone which they place on their stomach.*

MIGRATION AND HOMES

WHEN WINTER approaches, many animals migrate to warmer climates. Others rely on their homes to protect them from harsh conditions. Some animals live alone, while others live in pairs or in large, complex communities.

NAVIGATION

It is still a mystery how some migrating animals find their way. Most species probably use a combination of methods, including navigation by the Sun and stars, and using an inherited mental map.

Sight
Many birds can recognize physical features such as coastlines, mountain ranges, and deserts.

Using Earth's magnetic field
Some animals, e.g. monarch butterflies *(Danaus plexippus)* may navigate using a magnetic sense.

Smell
Atlantic salmon *(Salmo salar)* return to the river in which they hatched. They navigate by smell.

ANIMAL HOMES

Some animals do not build homes: they simply find a tree hole, perch on a branch, or hide under a stone for protection. Others construct intricate nests or burrows.

ANIMAL HOME NAMES

Animal	Description of home	Name of home
Squirrel	Nest of twigs	Drey
Badger	Underground chambers	Sett
Eagle	Nest of twigs	Eyrie
Rabbit	Burrow	Warren
River otter	Burrow in river bank	Holt

TYPES OF ANIMAL HOME

Nests
Many animals, including birds, mice, and ants, build nests. They use various materials such as twigs, mud, leaves, and hair.

Burrows
A burrow is a hole or tunnel dug by one or more animals. It may be a simple hole in the ground, or a complex network of tunnels and chambers, such as a rabbit warren.

Mounds
Termite colonies build complex mounds from mud. These structures have galleries, turrets, and towers, and even built-in air conditioning.

Termite mound

Pots
Potter wasps build tiny pots of mud to lay their eggs in. They build one pot for each egg.

Potter wasp's pot

Tree holes and caves
Many animals take advantage of ready-made homes, e.g. owls use tree holes, and bears often use caves.

Rabbit warren

Reed warbler's nest

KEY

Blue whale 20,000km (12,500 miles)	Monarch butterfly 5,600km (3,500 miles)
Arctic tern 40,000km (24,855 miles)	Green turtle over 2,000km (1,243 miles)
Caribou 2,250 km (1,400 miles)	Atlantic salmon over 2,000km (1,243 miles)

MIGRATION RECORDS

FURTHEST BIRD MIGRATION and the longest migration of any animal is that of the Arctic tern *(Sterna paradisaea)* (see map).

FURTHEST MAMMAL MIGRATION is undertaken by the blue whale *(Balaenoptera musculus)* (see map).

LOADS OF LEMMINGS

Norway lemmings *(Lemmus lemmus)* migrate when population explosions occur. Their huge numbers stop traffic and trains. When they reach the coast, some swim out to sea and drown, hence the tales of lemming "mass suicides".

MIGRATION

Many animals migrate to avoid the cold weather and lack of food that winter brings. Some species migrate a few kilometres from high ground to low; others travel vast distances across continents and oceans.

FURTHEST INSECT MIGRATION is undertaken by the painted lady butterfly *(Cynthia cardui)*, which flies up to 8,500km (5,282 miles) a year. (This is not marked on the map, as it does not follow a set route).

ANIMAL RELATIONSHIPS

SOLITARY ANIMALS
The giant panda *(Ailuropoda melanoleuca)* spends most of its life alone, only meeting up for mating.

PAIRS AND FAMILIES
Golden eagles *(Aquila chrysaetos)* spend their life with the same mate, raising a family each year.

LARGE GROUPS
Meerkats *(Suricata suricatta)*, a type of mongoose, live in large colonies with a complex social structure.

MUTUALISM
Some different species live together for mutual benefit: oxpeckers are picking ticks off this warthog.

COMMENSALISM
Two species may live together but only one benefits: this crab carries stinging anemones for protection.

PARASITISM
Parasites live in or on another species, causing it harm: this flea is sucking its host's blood.

ANIMAL COLONY FACT
• Australia's Great Barrier Reef is the largest structure in the world made by living things. It is more than 2,300km (1,429 miles) long, and has taken about 800 million years to build.

BEAVER DAM
Beavers dam a river, then construct their lodge on the shore, or on an island in the middle of the lake.

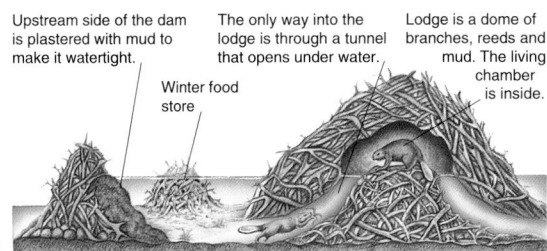

Upstream side of the dam is plastered with mud to make it watertight.

The only way into the lodge is through a tunnel that opens under water.

Lodge is a dome of branches, reeds and mud. The living chamber is inside.

Winter food store

FOOD CHAINS AND WEBS

A FOOD CHAIN shows how energy, in the form of food, passes from one living thing to another. At each chain's base is a primary producer – an organism that can make its own food. Most primary producers are plants.

FOOD CHAIN

Plant plankton is the primary producer at the bottom of this chain. When it is eaten, the plankton's energy is passed on to the next organism in the chain.

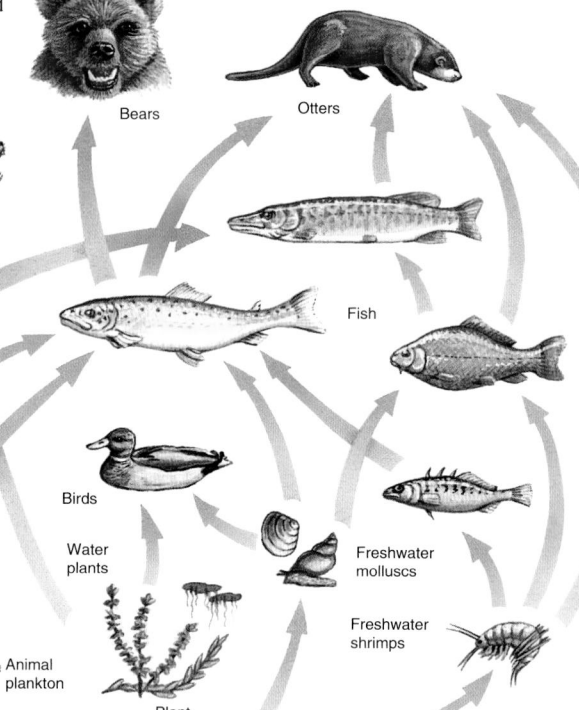

Plant plankton (microscopic water plants) use sunlight to produce energy.

Animal plankton eat plant plankton.

Insect larvae eat plankton.

Bears eat fish.

Fish eat insect larvae.

FOOD WEB

This illustration shows how the above food chain links with others to form the food web of a North American lake community. The arrows link each living thing to the organism that eats it, beginning with plankton at the bottom, and ending with carnivores (meat-eaters) at the top.

Bears

Otters

Beavers

Fish

Frogs

Beetles

Birds

Water plants

Insect larvae

Animal plankton

Plant plankton

Freshwater molluscs

Freshwater shrimps

ENERGY PYRAMID

About 90% of the energy a living thing takes in as food is used to make its body work. Only the remaining 10% is built into the body itself, and is therefore passed on to the next organism along the food chain. This means there is very little energy left towards the top of the food chain.

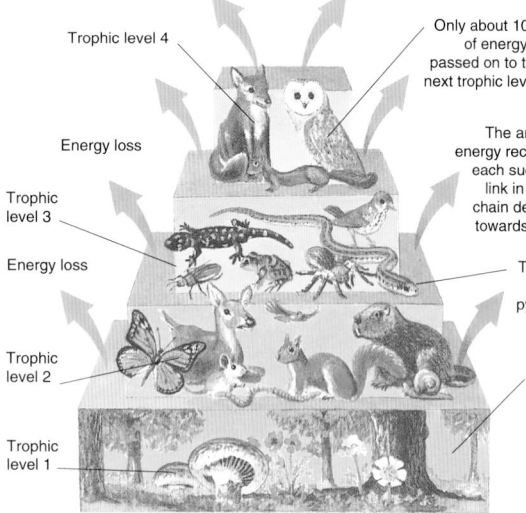

Trophic level 4

Energy loss

Trophic level 3

Energy loss

Trophic level 2

Trophic level 1

Only about 10% of energy is passed on to the next trophic level.

The amount of energy received by each successive link in the food chain decreases towards the top.

The various levels of an energy pyramid are called trophic levels.

Primary producers

PRIMARY PRODUCTIVITY

The longest food chains occur where the amount of organic matter made by primary producers (primary productivity) is high. This table shows the primary productivity of various habitats.

Habitat	Primary productivity (grams of dry plant material per sq metre per year)
Coral reef	2,500
Tropical rainforest	2,200
Temperate forest	1,250
Savannah	900
Cultivated land	650
Open sea	125
Semi-desert	90

POISONS IN THE FOOD CHAIN

Poisons, such as pesticides, are taken in by organisms at the lower end of a food chain. These poisons pass up the chain, and may eventually build into high concentrations in animals at the top of the chain. The process of poison building up in a food chain is called bioaccumulation.

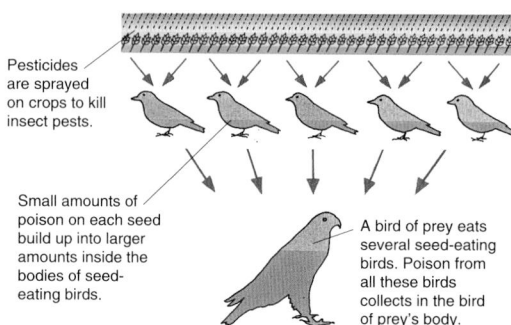

Pesticides are sprayed on crops to kill insect pests.

Small amounts of poison on each seed build up into larger amounts inside the bodies of seed-eating birds.

A bird of prey eats several seed-eating birds. Poison from all these birds collects in the bird of prey's body.

FOOD CHAIN FACTS

• The majority of food chains have three or four links.

• The only food chains that do not obtain energy from sunlight are those at deep sea vents, which derive energy from volcanic activity (see p.48).

TOXIC WHALES

Over the last 40 years, pollutants in Canada's St. Lawrence River have built up in the food chain, at the top of which is the beluga whale (*Delphinapterus leucas*). Chemicals are now so concentrated in these whales that, when they die, they are disposed of as toxic waste.

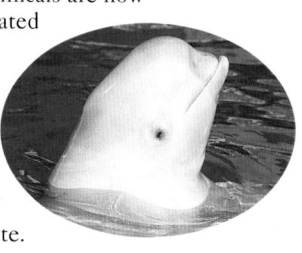

FOOD CHAIN RECORDS

SHORTEST FOOD CHAINS consist of only two organisms, for example the giant panda (*Ailuropoda melanoleuca*) and its major food source, bamboo.

Giant panda eating bamboo

LONGEST FOOD CHAINS often involve both land and water organisms, e.g. diatom (microscopic plant) to *Daphnia* (water flea), to newly hatched fish, to dragonfly larva, to adult fish, to heron.

ENDANGERED SPECIES

AN ENDANGERED SPECIES is a species that may become extinct in the near future. Throughout evolutionary history, millions of species have died out due to natural processes. Over the past 300 years, however, humans have speeded up the extinction rate more than 1,000 times: it is now estimated that one species dies out every 15 minutes.

THREATS TO WILDLIFE

Humans are responsible for almost all recent animal and plant extinctions. Threats to wildlife are caused by various human activities.

As the human population expands, more and more land is needed for planting crops, and for building settlements and roads. Natural vegetation and wildlife are destroyed.

Many animals are killed for their skins, bones, or horns. The jaguar (Panthera onca) and ocelot (Felis pardalis) are among the many species of cat that have become endangered through poaching for skins.

Pollution from industry and farming can poison wildlife. Chemical spills and acid rain (see p.65) can kill river life, and fertilizers and pesticides used in farming can upset natural systems and cycles.

When non-native animals are introduced to a country, they may have a disastrous impact on native wildlife, preying on animals and competing for food. The cane toad (Bufo marinus), introduced into Australia, has now overrun native species in some areas.

THREATENED ANIMALS

This table shows the number of threatened species in each animal group. Endangered species are monitored by the International Union for the Conservation of Nature, and recorded in their Red Data Book.

Animal group	Species at risk
Mammals	1,100
Birds	1,100
Reptiles	250
Amphibians	125
Fish	730
Insects	530
Other invertebrates	1,350

SAVING ENDANGERED SPECIES

Various measures are being used around the world in an effort to save endangered species from extinction.

Anti-poaching squads have been set up to protect animals such as rhinoceroses, elephants, and gorillas. Some countries, including Kenya, shoot poachers on sight.

The Arabian oryx (Oryx leucoryx) was hunted to extinction in the wild. After a captive-breeding programme in zoos, it was returned to its natural habitat.

DECLINING TIGER HABITAT

Tiger numbers have dropped dramatically in the last 100 years, because of the destruction of their habitat, and poaching. Tiger reserves have been established, but poaching is still a serious problem. This map shows the declining range of the tiger, and gives the estimated numbers of tigers left today.

KEY

Previous tiger range

Current, fragmented tiger range

RATES OF EXTINCTION

A species is considered to be extinct if it has not been found in the wild for 50 years. This graph illustrates the dramatic increase in the rate of extinction over the past 300 years.

The red line shows the number of species that became extinct in each year.

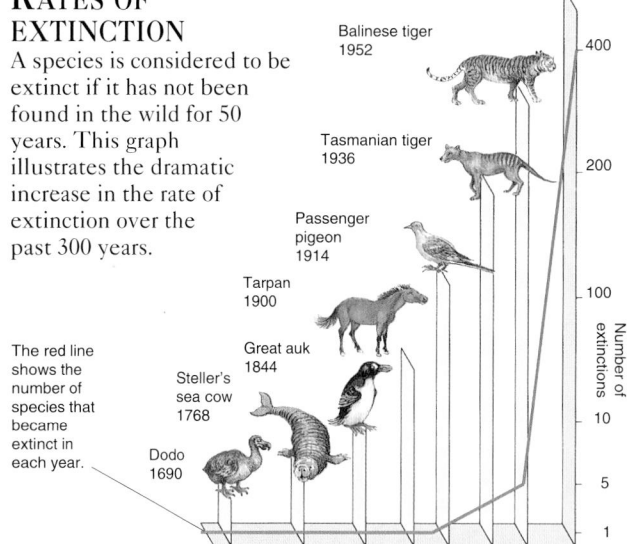

Balinese tiger 1952
Tasmanian tiger 1936
Passenger pigeon 1914
Tarpan 1900
Great auk 1844
Steller's sea cow 1768
Dodo 1690

Number of extinctions: 400, 200, 100, 10, 5, 1

Year: 1700 1750 1800 1850 1900 1925 1950

MOST ENDANGERED ANIMALS

This table lists some of the rarest animal species in the world. Some endangered species are now extinct in the wild but are being bred in captivity. They will eventually be released into the wild if conditions are safe.

Common name	Scientific name	Distribution
Tiger	*Panthera tigris*	Asia
Black rhino	*Diceros bicornis*	Africa
Giant panda	*Ailuropoda melanoleuca*	China
Mountain gorilla	*Gorilla gorilla beringei*	Africa
Kakapo	*Strigops habroptilus*	New Zealand
Hawksbill sea turtle	*Eretmochelys imbricata*	Tropical seas
Spix's macaw	*Cyanopsitta spixii*	South America
California condor	*Gymnogyps californianus*	North America
Golden lancehead snake	*Bothrops insularis*	Brazil
Chinese alligator	*Alligator sinensis*	China
Yosemite toad	*Bufo canorus*	North America
Ganges shark	*Gylphis gangeticus*	Asia

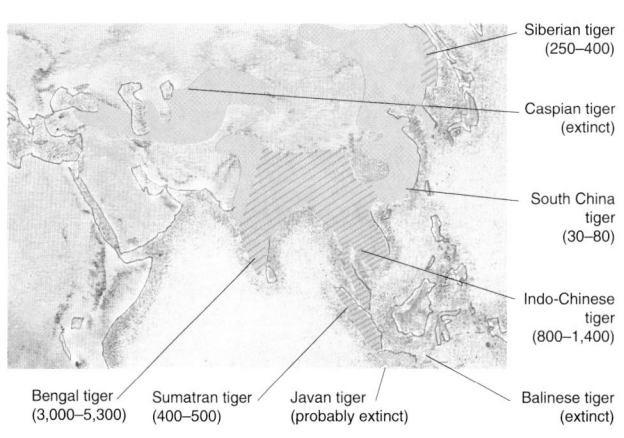

Siberian tiger (250–400)

Caspian tiger (extinct)

South China tiger (30–80)

Indo-Chinese tiger (800–1,400)

Bengal tiger (3,000–5,300)

Sumatran tiger (400–500)

Javan tiger (probably extinct)

Balinese tiger (extinct)

ANIMAL RECORDS AND COMPARISONS

THERE IS A REMARKABLE DIVERSITY within the animal kingdom, from wasps no bigger than a full stop, to crabs that grow larger than people; from tiny, deadly cone shells, to the blue whale – the gentle giant of the oceans.

LARGEST WINGSPANS

BIRD
The wandering albatross (*Diomedea exulans*) has a wingspan measuring about 3.6m (12ft) across.

BAT
Flying foxes of the *Pteropus* genus are the largest bats in the world, with wingspans up to 2m (6.6ft) across.

Wandering albatross

Flying fox (Pteropus)

LARGEST ANIMALS

Largest mollusc
Giant Atlantic squid (*Archteuthis*); 20m (66ft) long; North Atlantic Ocean

Largest insect
Goliath beetle (*Goliathus*) 110g (3.9oz) Equatorial Africa

Largest arachnid
Leblondis' goliath bird-eating spider (*Theraphosa leblondi*); leg span 28cm (11in); Brazil, Venezuela, Guyana, French Guiana

Largest crustacean
Japanese spider crab (*Macrocheira kaempferi*)
Leg span nearly 4m (13ft) Japan

Largest amphibian
Japanese giant salamander (*Andrias japonicus*) 1.5m (5ft) long Japan

Largest reptile
Saltwater crocodile (*Crocodylus porosus*); 6m (20ft) long Southeast Asia, Indonesia, Philippines, New Guinea, Australia

Largest fish
Whale shark (*Rhincodon typus*) 15m (50ft) long; Atlantic, Pacific, and Indian Oceans

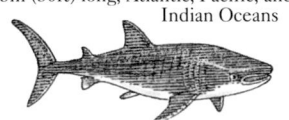

Largest bird
Ostrich (*Struthio camelus*) 2.7m (8.9ft) tall Mainly eastern and southern Africa

Largest mammal
Blue whale (*Balaenoptera musculus*) 34m (111.5ft) long; worldwide, particularly Southern Hemisphere

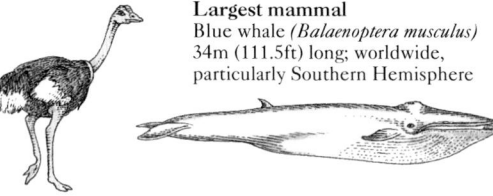

LOUDEST ANIMALS

MARINE ANIMAL
The blue whale's (*Balaenoptera musculus*) call is the loudest noise made by any animal. It registers up to 188 decibels, and can be heard by other whales up to 1,600km (1,000 miles) away.

LAND ANIMAL
The howler monkey (*Alouatta*) can be heard up to 3km (2 miles) away.

Howler monkey

INSECT
Cicadas can be heard up to 400m (1,312ft) away.

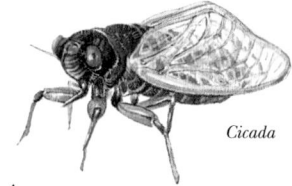

Cicada

SMALLEST ANIMALS

Smallest insect
Fairyfly wasps
0.2mm long
Worldwide

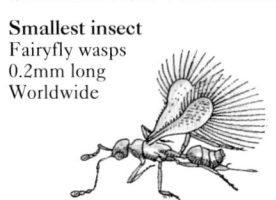

Smallest amphibian
Psyllophryne didactyla
10.4mm (0.41in) long
Brazil

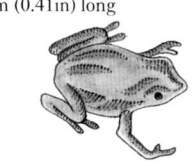

Smallest fish
Dwarf goby (*Pandaka pygmaea*)
7.6mm (0.3in) long
Philippines

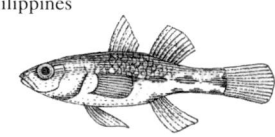

Smallest reptile
British Virgin Island gecko (*Sphaerodactylus parthenopion*)
18mm (0.7in) long
Virgin Islands

Smallest bird
Bee hummingbird (*Mellisuga helenae*)
5.7cm (2.2in) long
Cuba

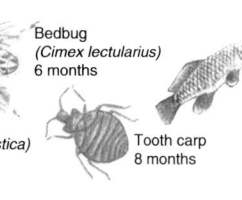

Smallest mammal
Kitti's hog-nosed bat (*Craseonycteris thonglongyai*)
3.3cm (1.3in) long
Thailand

ANIMAL REPRODUCTION FACTS

• After spending a year or more as a larva, the adult mayfly (*Ephemera danica*) has only a day in which to mate and lay eggs before it dies.

• A tapeworm may release a million eggs a day for several years. Hardly any eggs survive.

• Many fish lay millions of eggs, because so few young survive. The ocean sunfish (*Mola mola*) lays about 30 million eggs.

ANIMAL LIFESPANS

Animals live from a few days to more than 200 years. The lifespans shown here are approximate maximum ages.

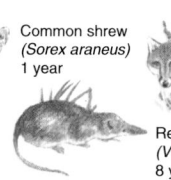
Bedbug (*Cimex lectularius*) 6 months

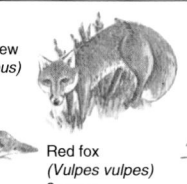
Common shrew (*Sorex araneus*) 1 year

Housefly (*Musca domestica*) 3–12 weeks

Tooth carp 8 months

Red fox (*Vulpes vulpes*) 8 years

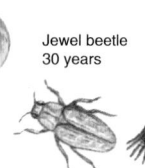
Jewel beetle 30 years

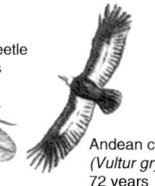
Andean condor (*Vultur gryphus*) 72 years

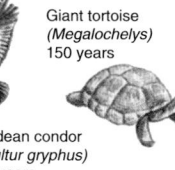
Giant tortoise (*Megalochelys*) 150 years

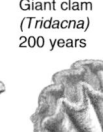
Giant clam (*Tridacna*) 200 years

1 month	3 months	6 months	9 months	1 year	5 years	10 years	50 years	100 years	150 years	200 years

POISONOUS ANIMALS

MOST POISONOUS MOLLUSCS
A sting from a blue-ringed octopus (*Hapalochlaena*) can kill a human. Three species of cone shell (*Conus*) (right) also have a deadly sting.

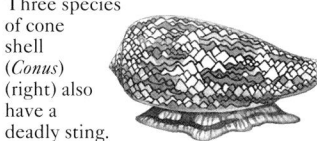

MOST POISONOUS FISH
When stepped on, the stonefish (*Synanceja*), which lurks in shallow waters in the Pacific and Indian Oceans, injects venom through spines in its dorsal fin, causing intense pain and sometimes death.

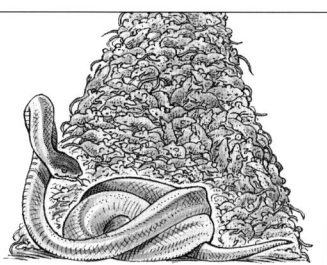

MOST POISONOUS FROG
The golden-yellow poison-dart frog (*Phyllobates terribilis*), which lives in Colombia, South America, oozes the strongest animal poison in the world from its skin. Toxin from a single frog could kill nearly 1,500 people.

MOST POISONOUS MAMMAL
The duck-billed platypus (*Ornithorhynchus anatinus*) injects venom through a spur on one of its hind legs. Its sting causes intense pain in humans. The platypus is one of only two species of poisonous mammal (see p.103).

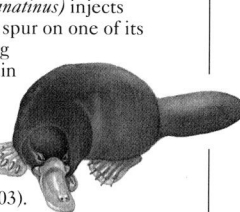

MOST POISONOUS JELLYFISH
A human stung more than six times by a chironex (*Chironex fleckeri*) can die within two to three minutes. This jellyfish occurs in huge swarms off the northern coast of Australia.

MOST POISONOUS SPIDER
The Brazilian wandering spider (*Phoneutria*), which has a leg span of 10cm (4in), has the most poisonous of all spider bites. This spider has difficulty injecting venom into humans, so it causes few deaths.

MOST POISONOUS SNAKES
Sea snakes of the genus *Hydrophis* have extremely poisonous venom. The toxin of *Hydrophis belcheri*, which lives in the Timor Sea off northwestern Australia, is about 100 times as strong as that of the taipan (see below).

MOST POISONOUS BIRD
The only bird known to be poisonous is the hooded pitohui (*Pitohui dichrous*), from New Guinea. This brightly coloured bird secretes a poison similar to that produced by poison-dart frogs, although far less toxic.

TERRIBLE TAIPAN
The taipan (*Oxyuranus*) of northeastern Australia and New Guinea is one of the most poisonous snakes in the world. The venom from just one of these snakes could kill 125,000 mice.

LARGEST INSECT HOMES
Mounds built by termites can reach up to 12m (39ft) tall: more than six times the height of an adult human.

ANIMALS OF THE DEEP

The deepest-diving bird is the emperor penguin (*Aptenodytes forsteri*), which reaches depths of up to 265m (870ft).

The deepest-diving turtle is the leatherback turtle (*Dermochelys coriacea*), which dives down to 1,200m (3,937ft).

The deepest-diving mammal is the sperm whale (*Physeter macrocephalus*), which dives down to 1,200m (3,937ft).

Rat-tails are some of the deepest-living fish in the oceans.

TALLEST ANIMALS

MAMMAL
The giraffe (*Giraffa camelopardalis*) measures up to 5.9m (19.4ft) tall.

BIRDS
The tallest bird is the ostrich. The tallest flying birds are cranes: some species, e.g. the Japanese crane (*Grus japonensis*) (above), stand nearly 2m (6.6ft) high.

HEAVIEST ANIMALS

Animal	Scientific name	Weight kg	Weight lb
Blue whale	*Balaenoptera musculus*	190,000	418,878
African elephant	*Loxodonta africanus*	5,000	11,023
Asian elephant	*Elephas maximas*	4,000	8,818
White rhinoceros	*Ceratotherium simum*	2,200	4,850
Hippopotamus	*Hippopotamus amphibius*	2,000	4,409
Giraffe	*Giraffa camelopardalis*	1,200	2,646
Saltwater crocodile	*Crocodylus porosus*	1,100	2,425
Asian gaur	*Bos frontalis*	900	1,984
Bison	*Bison*	800	1,764
Kodiak bear	*Ursus arctos middendorffi*	800	1,764
Yak	*Bos grunniens*	800	1,764

ANIMAL SPEEDS

AIR
Dragonflies 50km/h (31mph) Fastest-flying insects

Racing pigeon (*Columba livia*) 85km/h (53mph)

White-throated spine-tail swift (*Hirundapus caudacutus*) 171km/h (106mph) Fastest-flying bird

Peregrine falcon (*Falco peregrinus*) 180km/h (112mph) Fastest bird in a dive

LAND
Brown hare (*Lepus capensis*) 25km/h (16mph)

Ostrich (*Struthio camelus*) 72km/h (45mph) Fastest-running bird

Pronghorn antelope (*Antilocapra americana*) 88km/h (55mph) Fastest mammal over long distances

Cheetah (*Acinonyx jubatus*) 105km/h (65mph) Fastest mammal over short distances

SEA
Gentoo penguin (*Pygoscelis papua*) 27km/h (17mph) Fastest-swimming bird

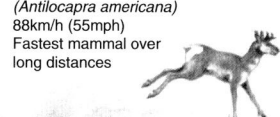

Sei whale (*Balaenoptera borealis*) 48km/h (29.8mph) Fastest-swimming mammal

Tunny (*Thunnus*) 71km/h (44mph) Fastest-swimming fish

| 0 | km/h | 10 | | 20 | | 30 | | 40 | | 50 | | 60 | | 70 | | 80 | | 90 | | 100 | | 150 | | 200 |

LEAPS AND BOUNDS

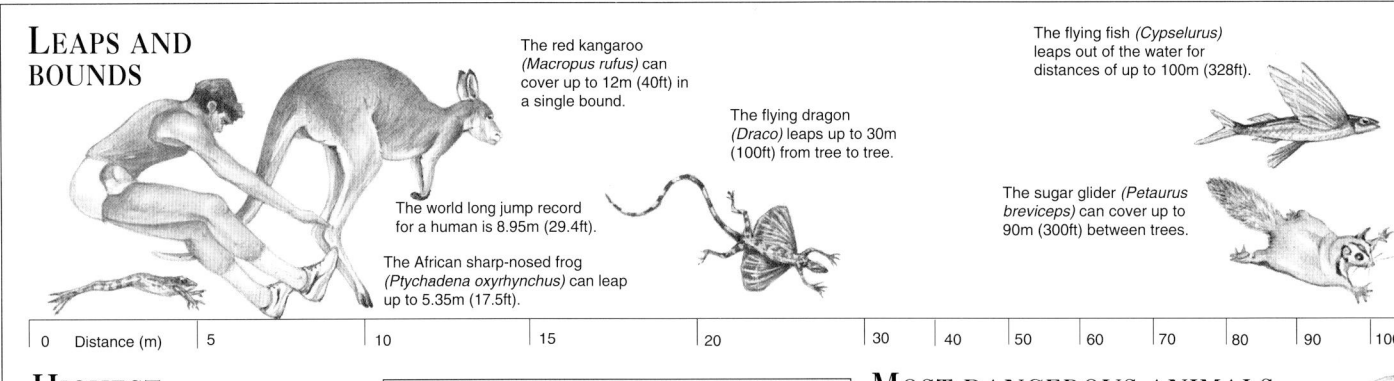

The red kangaroo (*Macropus rufus*) can cover up to 12m (40ft) in a single bound.

The flying dragon (*Draco*) leaps up to 30m (100ft) from tree to tree.

The flying fish (*Cypselurus*) leaps out of the water for distances of up to 100m (328ft).

The world long jump record for a human is 8.95m (29.4ft).

The African sharp-nosed frog (*Ptychadena oxyrhynchus*) can leap up to 5.35m (17.5ft).

The sugar glider (*Petaurus breviceps*) can cover up to 90m (300ft) between trees.

0   Distance (m)   5   10   15   20   30   40   50   60   70   80   90   100

HIGHEST LEAPERS

Fleas are the highest leapers for their body size. The common flea (*Pulex irritans*) can leap up to 19cm (7.5in) high: about 130 times its own height.

LARGEST GROUPS

CRUSTACEANS

Swarms of krill (*Euphausia superba*) have been known to cover areas of ocean measuring up to 440sq km (170sq miles). These large swarms may contain up to 80 billion individuals: about 16 times the world's human population.

BIRDS

The red-billed quelea (*Quelea quelea*) gathers in roosts of up to 10 million birds.

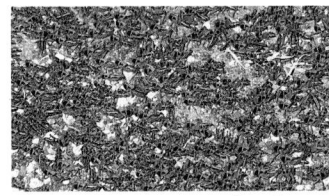

Locust swarm

INSECTS

Locusts gather in enormous numbers. In 1873, a swarm of Rocky Mountain locusts estimated to contain 10,000 billion insects crossed the USA.

BEEFY BEETLE

One of the strongest insects is the Atlas beetle (*Chalcosoma atlas*). It can lift more than 800 times its own bodyweight – equivalent to a man lifting a *Leopard 2* tank.

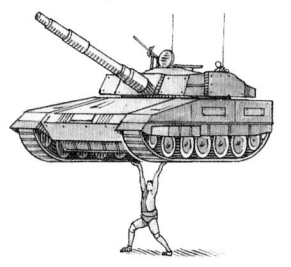

ANIMAL ENERGY REQUIREMENTS

This table compares the kilojoules (kJ, see p.134) different animal species need per day for a moderate amount of activity.

Adult animal	Scientific name	kJ required
House mouse	*Mus musculus*	45.4
European robin	*Erithacus rubecula*	89.9
Peregrine falcon	*Falco peregrinus*	277
Grey squirrel	*Sciurus carolinensis*	386
Fennec fox	*Vulpes zerda*	1,067
Domestic cat	*Felis catus*	1,554
Baboon	*Papio hamadryas*	6,762
Giant anteater	*Myrmecophaga tridactyla*	7,392
Female human	*Homo sapiens*	10,080
Male human	*Homo sapiens*	13,713
Llama	*Llama glama*	16,128
Tiger	*Panthera tigris*	33,600
Gorilla	*Gorilla gorilla*	34,020
American black bear	*Ursus americanus*	38,556
Giraffe	*Giraffa camelopardalis*	152,754
Walrus	*Odobenus rosmarus*	159,852
Male Asian elephant	*Elephas maximus*	256,872

MOST DANGEROUS ANIMALS

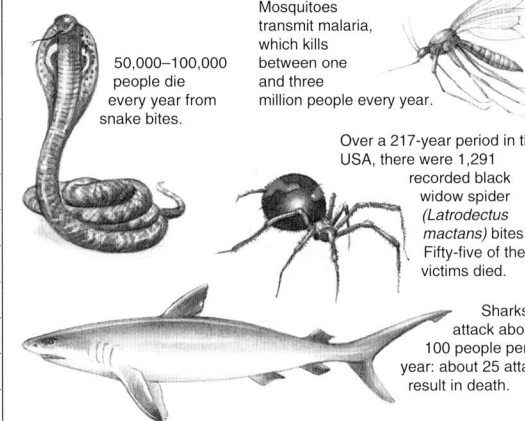

50,000–100,000 people die every year from snake bites.

Mosquitoes transmit malaria, which kills between one and three million people every year.

Over a 217-year period in the USA, there were 1,291 recorded black widow spider (*Latrodectus mactans*) bites. Fifty-five of the victims died.

Sharks attack about 100 people per year: about 25 attacks result in death.

Saltwater crocodiles (*Crocodylus porosus*) (right) and Nile crocodiles (*C. niloticus*) kill hundreds of people every year.

About one person in 200 is allergic to bee and wasp venom. In the USA, between 50 and 100 people die every year from bee and wasp stings.

In the Sunderbans region of India, 521 people were killed by tigers between 1975 and mid-1989.

GESTATION PERIODS

The gestation period is the length of time an animal takes to develop inside its mother before it is born.

Virginia opossum (Didelphis virginiana)
12 days; 8–14 young

Golden hamster (Mesocricetus auratus)
15 days; 6–8 young

House mouse (Mus musculus)
20 days; 6–8 young

Red kangaroo (Macropus rufus)
33 days
1 young

Lion (Panthera leo)
105–108 days
3–4 young

Goat (Capra)
150 days
1–2 young

Orang utan (Pongo pygmaeus)
250 days
1 young

Human (Homo sapiens)
267 days; 1 young

Cow
278 days; 1 young

Dolphin
360 days
1 young

Asian elephant (Elephas maximus)
660 days; 1 young

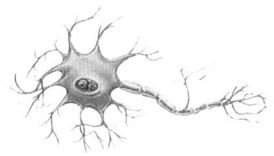

HUMAN BODY

Stunning detailed illustrations, supported by a wealth of facts and figures, show the amazing workings of the human body. Other topics include evolution, reproduction and growth, the history of medicine, traditional medicine, nutrition, and first aid.

Humankind • Human Body • The Brain • Nervous System • Eyes • Ears
Skin, Hair, and Nails • Smell, Taste, and Throat • Skeleton and Teeth • Muscles
Heart • Circulation and Blood • Respiratory System • Digestion • Urinary System
Endocrine System • Reproduction and Growth • Medicine • Nutrition
Traditional Medicine • First Aid

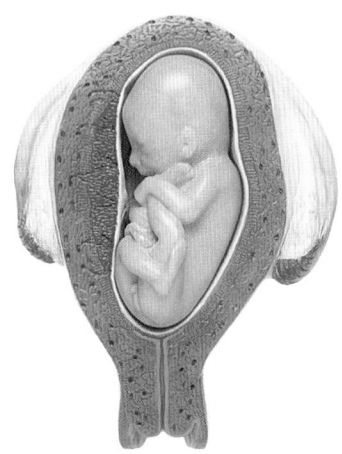

HUMANKIND

SCIENTISTS BELIEVE the first living thing on Earth was a single-celled organism that developed almost four billion years ago. From that organism, plant and animal life evolved. Finally, just five million years ago, hominids appeared.

Aegyptopithecus
30 million years ago
Ancestor of monkeys, apes, and humans

HUMAN FAMILY TREE

Sivapithecus
7–13 million years ago
Early ancestor of the orang utan

Orang utan
Differences in skull shape put them in a separate family from humans and gorillas.

Australopithecus
1.5–5 million years ago
Earliest ape people to walk upright

Chimpanzee/gorilla
Skull shape links them to human family, but they do not walk upright and brain is smaller.

Homo habilis
1.5–2 million years ago
Made tools to assist with hunter-scavenger lifestyle.

Homo sapiens sapiens
40,000 years ago
Modern humans were the first artists. Emerged in Africa and spread to all continents by 11,000 years ago.

Homo erectus
0.5–1.5 million years ago
Used fire and dwellings to survive in cooler climates.

Homo sapiens neanderthalensis
40,000–100,000 years ago
Sub-species of modern humans with overhanging brow. First burial ceremonies

BRAIN POWER

Homo habilis had a larger brain than the first ape people, but it was only half the size of a modern human brain. As the brain grew in size, people developed greater powers of reasoning and survival.

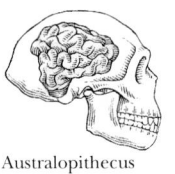
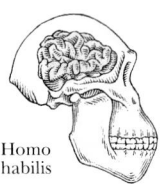
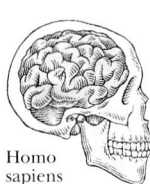

Australopithecus   Homo habilis   Homo sapiens

HUMAN FOSSILS

The structure of human remains and where they are found tell us a great deal about the growth and development of the human race.

● **Lucy**
A three million-year-old *Australopithecus* skeleton, found in Ethiopia.

● **Homo habilis skull**
Fossils and tools found in same area in East Africa.

● **Beijing man**
Homo erectus skull found. Evidence of fire in area.

● **Neanderthals**
Fossils found in Europe.

SKELETON SHAPES

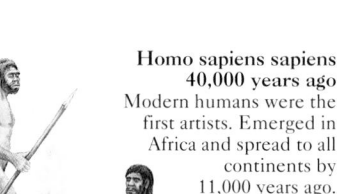

The human skeleton is designed for upright walking. Human toes point forwards, whereas a gorilla's big toe is at an angle for grasping. The *Homo sapiens* hip bone is shorter than a gorilla's for easy striding. The human head is more centrally balanced on the backbone than a gorilla's.

Gorilla foot   *Human*

Gorilla   *Human foot*

EVOLUTION FACTS

● Early humans used wisdom teeth to eat roots and berries. Today, some people do not even develop them.

● Neanderthals had a slightly bigger brain than humans today. It may have signified a stronger body, not high intelligence.

THE ICEMAN

In 1991 the oldest complete *Homo sapiens* corpse was found in a glacier in the European Alps. His internal organs, skin, and even his eyes were intact.

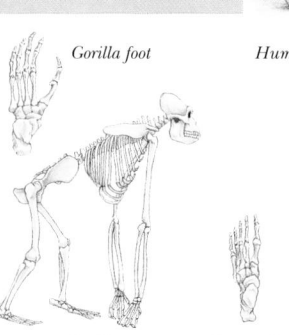

The Iceman had been frozen for 5,300 years.

HUMAN FAMILY

As humans spread across the world, they gradually evolved different features, such as dark and light hair, that were suited, for example, to a particular climate.

East Indian   *Native American*   *Australian Aboriginal*

Caucasoid   *Black African*   *Mongoloid*

EVOLUTIONARY CLOCK

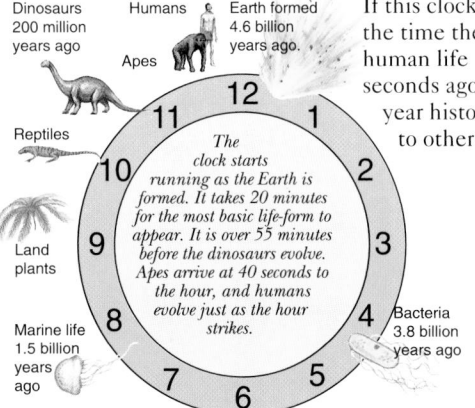

Dinosaurs 200 million years ago

Humans

Apes

Earth formed 4.6 billion years ago.

Reptiles

Land plants

Marine life 1.5 billion years ago

Bacteria 3.8 billion years ago

The clock starts running as the Earth is formed. It takes 20 minutes for the most basic life-form to appear. It is over 55 minutes before the dinosaurs evolve. Apes arrive at 40 seconds to the hour, and humans evolve just as the hour strikes.

If this clock face represents the time the Earth has existed, human life began only a few seconds ago. Our five-million-year history is short compared to other life-forms.

PILTDOWN HOAX

Remains found in Piltdown, England, were first thought to show a missing link between apes and humans. But in 1953, tests showed them to be the skull of a 14th-century man and the jaw of a 15th-century orang utan.

HUMAN BODY

EACH BODY SYSTEM is composed of organs made from different types of tissue. Tissue is made from cells all performing a similar function. There are roughly 50 billion cells in the body.

CELL GROWTH

As cells divide and multiply, children and young people grow. In later life, some cells still multiply, but this is to replace the millions of cells that die every second.

Nucleus starts to grow.

Nucleus starts to divide.

First nucleus, then cell divides in two.

Each cell may grow to size of parent cell.

THE BODY AT WORK

Each body system combines cells, tissue, and organs.

There are many millions of nerve cells in the human body.

Individual cells combine to make cell tissue, such as major nerves.

Cells, tissue, and nerves make up the brain and spinal cord: the major organs of the human nervous system.

INSIDE A CELL

Nearly all human cells are too small to see without a microscope: the average diameter is 0.02mm. Inside each there are organelles that control and run the cell.

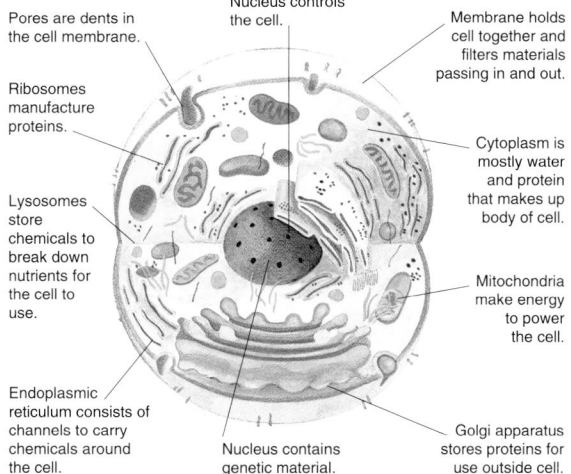

Nucleus controls the cell.

Pores are dents in the cell membrane.

Ribosomes manufacture proteins.

Lysosomes store chemicals to break down nutrients for the cell to use.

Endoplasmic reticulum consists of channels to carry chemicals around the cell.

Membrane holds cell together and filters materials passing in and out.

Cytoplasm is mostly water and protein that makes up body of cell.

Mitochondria make energy to power the cell.

Golgi apparatus stores proteins for use outside cell.

Nucleus contains genetic material.

CELL DISCOVERY

In 1838, German botanist Matthias Schleiden recognized that plants are made up of cells. In 1839, German physiologist Theodor Schwann extended this theory to animal life. Schwann cells are so-named because of his research on the nervous system.

Matthias Schleiden (1804–81)

Theodor Schwann (1810–82)

TYPES OF CELL

More than 200 cell types each perform specialized functions.

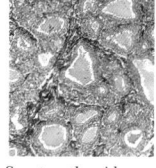
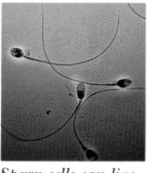
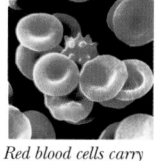

Duodenal cells use mucus to protect against stomach acid.

Secretory thyroid gland cells control the metabolism.

Sperm cells can live in the female tract for up to seven days.

Red blood cells carry oxygen and live for about 120 days.

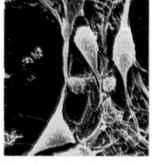

Brain cell: after 18 years we lose more than 1,000 a day.

Bone-maintaining cells develop from bone-forming cells.

CELL, CELL, CELL!

If all the cells in a human body were put end to end, they would stretch for 1,000km (620 miles): from Paris to Rome.

CELL FACTS

• Some gut cells have a life expectancy of only three days. A brain cell can last for life.

• An egg cell (ovum) is the largest human cell and can just be seen without a microscope.

• Red blood cells are the only cells without a nucleus.

• Cancer causes cells in many body systems to multiply uncontrollably, form tumours, and invade neighbouring tissue.

• All humans develop from just two cells: an ovum and a sperm.

• Neurons, the message carriers of the nervous system, are the longest cells in the human body. Some are up to 1.2m (4ft) long.

BODY SYSTEMS

The major systems shown here work together to help the body function efficiently. Each system consists of organs that carry out a similar task.

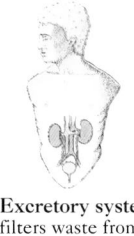

Excretory system filters waste from the blood.

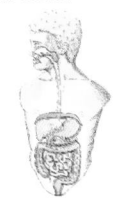

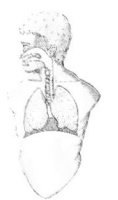

Respiratory system draws oxygen into the body and expels carbon dioxide.

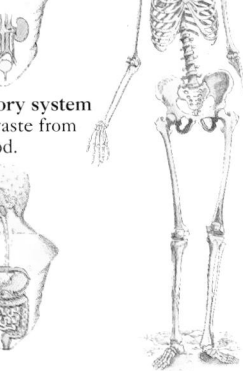

Digestive system processes food, absorbs nutrients, and expels waste.

Skeletal system is usually made up of 206 individual bones.

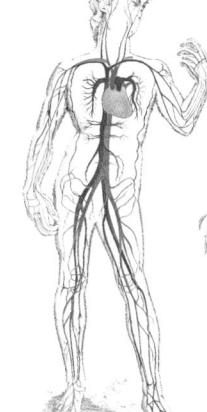

Circulatory system consists of the heart, blood, and blood vessels.

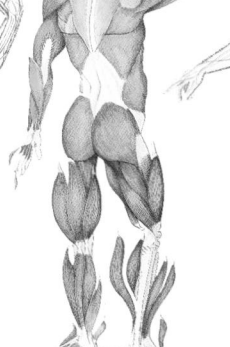

Muscular system has 650 muscles that exert pulling power on bones.

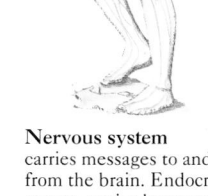

Nervous system carries messages to and from the brain. Endocrine system carries hormones.

Skin system consists of the skin, nails, and hair covering the body.

THE BRAIN

THE BRAIN IS THE major organ of the nervous system. It is the control centre of the body, responsible for thought, memory, language, and emotion. The brain is protected by the skull, which encases it, and the cerebro-spinal fluid, which cushions it.

SENSORY AREAS

Different parts of the brain carry out specialized functions. For example, the occipital lobe deals with vision, an area in the frontal lobe controls speech, and the temporal lobe receives and interprets information from the ears.

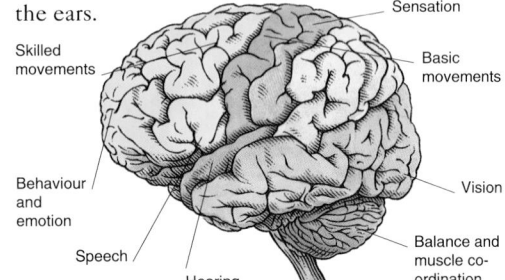

Skilled movements · Sensation · Basic movements · Behaviour and emotion · Vision · Speech · Hearing · Balance and muscle co-ordination

BRAIN FUNCTIONS

The brain stem controls digestion, breathing, and heartbeat, and the cerebellum controls muscle co-ordination. These are all involuntary activities (see p.117). Conscious functions, such as memory, learning, speech, and the conscious control of movement, take place in the cerebrum. Thoughts also occur here.

BRAIN COMPARISONS

Animals have brains of varying shapes and sizes. Some have larger brains than humans, including dolphins, elephants, and whales. An elephant's brain is four times as heavy as a human's. However, the human brain is much heavier in relation to body weight than the brain of any other animal.

Hemispheres have a cortex of nerve cells (grey matter), and inner areas of nerve fibres (white matter).

Occipitofrontalis (muscle sheet)

Skull

Fat

Skin

Frontal sinus

Nasal cavity

Hypothalamus controls part of the nervous system.

Right cerebral hemisphere

Corpus callosum

Periosteum (skull membrane)

Frontal lobe

Pituitary gland (see p.129)

Brain stem

Spinal cord

Optic nerves (see p.118)

Cerebellum

Temporal lobe

Occipital lobe

Pia mater: nourishes the brain.

Arachnoid layer: contains blood vessels and fluid.

Dura mater: toughest layer

Three layers, called meninges, cover the brain.

Parietal lobe

Left cerebral hemisphere

STRUCTURE OF THE BRAIN

The brain has three main regions: the brain stem, which merges with the spinal cord; the cerebellum; and the cerebrum, which contains the two cerebral hemispheres. The cerebrum makes up 90% of the brain.

BRAIN POWER

The brain sends and receives messages as impulses of electrical energy. The energy travels via nerve cells, called neurons, that run down the spinal cord to the rest of the body. Each neuron ends in a network of fine branches, called dendrites.

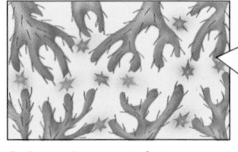

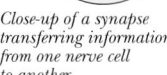

Information passes between nerve cells at the synapses: the points where the tips of dendrites from different cells meet.

Close-up of a synapse transferring information from one nerve cell to another.

CEREBRAL HEMISPHERES

The cerebrum is divided into two halves, called cerebral hemispheres. The left half is usually dominant and controls speech and thought; the right half manages artistic and imaginative activity. The corpus callosum joins the two hemispheres.

The left side of the brain is responsible for logical activities such as language and numeracy.

The right side mainly controls the imagination, and artistic activities such as music and painting.

MEMORY

Memory works in three ways: iconic memory briefly remembers things seen for a split-second; short-term memory stores things for about five minutes; and long-term memory can store things for a lifetime.

BRAIN WAVES

An electroencephalogram (EEG) records tiny electrical impulses produced by brain activity.

Alpha waves
Awake and relaxed

Beta waves
Concentrating

Delta waves
Asleep

Theta waves
Meditation and creative thought

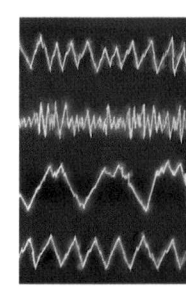

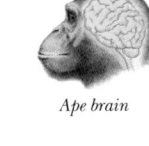

Ape brain

Human brain: the size of a cauliflower

Dolphin brain

Bird brain

Snake brain

Fish brain

MEGAMEMORY

In 1974, a man named Bhandanta Vicitsara recited 16,000 pages of Buddhist text from memory: enough to fill books equalling the height of a six-year-old.

MEMORY FACTS

• Short-term memory can hold about seven unrelated facts at any one time.

• As a person gets older, it becomes easier for them to remember past events than to remember recent events.

• The brain has to forget certain things in order to make room for new memories.

BRAIN FACTS

• A typical adult brain weighs about 1.3kg (3lb).

• About 0.85 litres (1.8 pints) of blood travel through the brain every minute.

• A human brain contains about fifteen billion cells.

• The grey matter of a brain's cortex, laid out flat, would cover an office desk.

COMMON ILLNESSES

Name	Description
Encephalitis	Inflammation of the brain; usually caused by viral infection
Meningitis	Inflammation of the meninges; usually caused by bacterial or viral infection
Alzheimer's disease	Deterioration of memory and thought processes

NERVOUS SYSTEM

THE NERVOUS SYSTEM is a huge communications network of nerves. This network allows us to feel, see, and hear the world, and to detect and respond quickly to changes inside and outside the body.

NEURONS (NERVE CELLS)

Neurons are the building blocks of the nervous system. Each consists of a cell body containing the nucleus, and a long, thread-like nerve fibre called the axon.

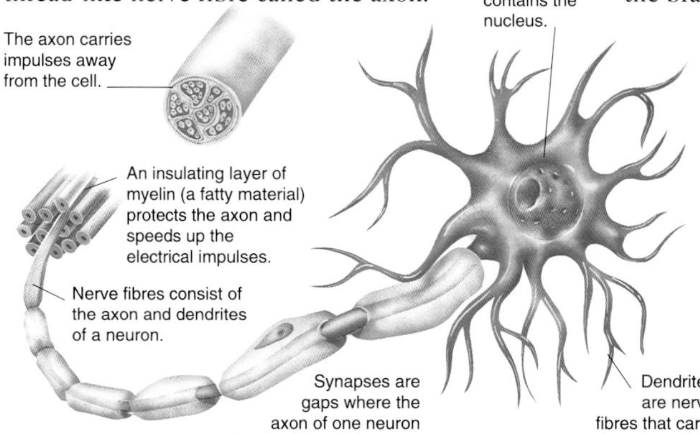

The axon carries impulses away from the cell.

An insulating layer of myelin (a fatty material) protects the axon and speeds up the electrical impulses.

Nerve fibres consist of the axon and dendrites of a neuron.

The cell body contains the nucleus.

Synapses are gaps where the axon of one neuron meets the dendrites of the next.

Dendrites are nerve fibres that carry impulses towards a cell body.

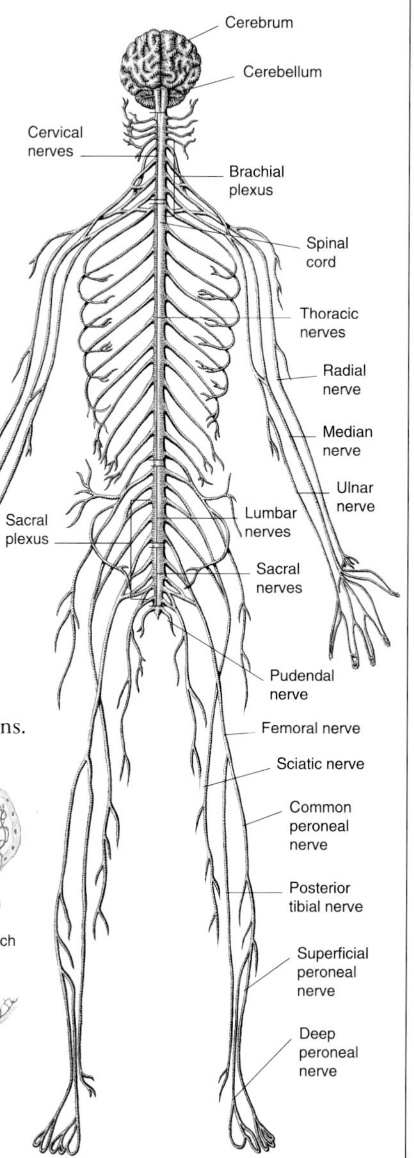

INVOLUNTARY ACTIONS

Automatic actions that the brain does not consciously decide on, such as heartbeat, are called involuntary actions. They include the actions of internal organs (autonomic actions), and reflex actions. This sequence shows how the nervous system produces an involuntary reflex action in response to touching a flame.

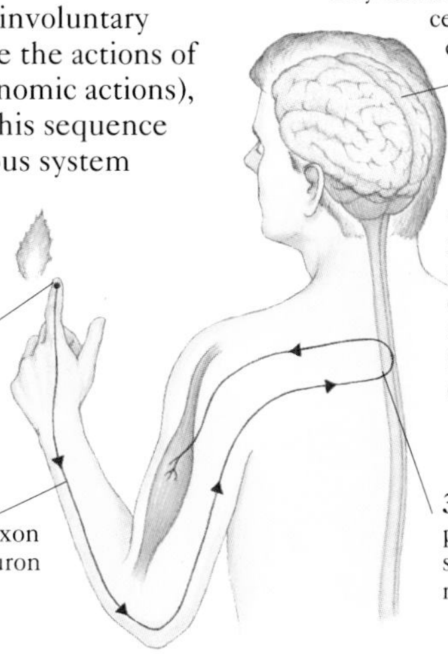

1 When the hand touches a hot object, sensory neurons produce a signal.

2 The signal passes along the neuron's axon to an association neuron in the spinal cord.

5 Signals also travel up to the brain. When they reach the cerebral cortex, the person feels pain.

4 A motor neuron makes the muscles contract, pulling the hand away from the source of pain.

3 The signal passes across a synapse to a motor neuron.

SPINAL CORD

The spinal cord is a bundle of nerves that runs down from the brain inside the backbone (see p.122). Spinal nerves branch out from the spinal cord through the gaps between the vertebrae.

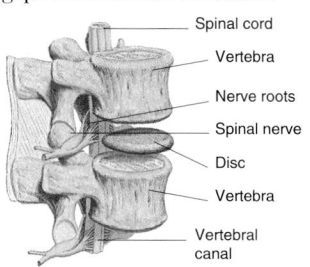

- Spinal cord
- Vertebra
- Nerve roots
- Spinal nerve
- Disc
- Vertebra
- Vertebral canal

STRUCTURE OF THE NERVOUS SYSTEM

The nervous system is made up of the central nervous system (CNS), which consists of the brain and spinal cord, and the peripheral nervous system, which consists of the nerves extending from the CNS to the rest of the body.

NERVES

There are millions of nerves and billions of nerve cells in the body. This close-up shows nerve cells in the brain.

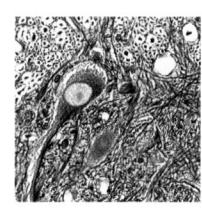

NEURON FUNCTIONS

There are three types of neuron: sensory neurons send signals triggered by sensations to the CNS; motor neurons carry signals from the CNS to muscles to make them contract; and association neurons transfer signals between other neurons.

NERVE ENDINGS

There are several types of nerve ending. Each detects a different type of feeling.

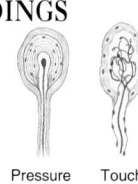
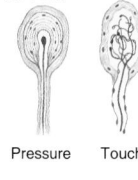

Pressure   Touch

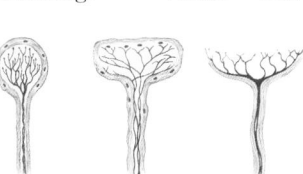
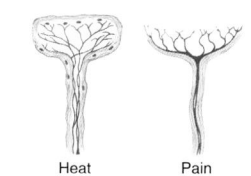

Cold   Heat   Pain

ACUPUNCTURE

This is an ancient Chinese method of treating illness by inserting fine needles into energy points on the body. These points are found along a system of channels, called meridians, that runs the length of the body, rather like the nervous system.

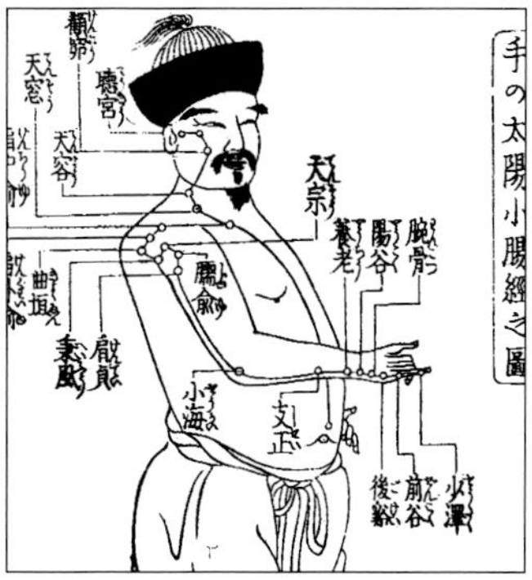

19th-century woodcut showing acupuncture points on the face, neck, shoulder, and hand.

NERVE FACTS

- Electric signals travel through some nerve fibres at more than 400km/h (248mph). Small axons conduct impulses more slowly.

- All the nerves in the body laid end to end would stretch for about 75km (47 miles).

- The tip of the index finger is one of the most sensitive parts of the body, with many thousands of sense receptors.

- The longest nerve is the sciatic nerve, stretching from base of the spine to the knee.

[Diagram of full body nervous system with labels:]
- Cerebrum
- Cerebellum
- Cervical nerves
- Brachial plexus
- Spinal cord
- Thoracic nerves
- Radial nerve
- Median nerve
- Ulnar nerve
- Lumbar nerves
- Sacral plexus
- Sacral nerves
- Pudendal nerve
- Femoral nerve
- Sciatic nerve
- Common peroneal nerve
- Posterior tibial nerve
- Superficial peroneal nerve
- Deep peroneal nerve

PHANTOM PAIN

People sometimes feel sensations in a limb they have lost. British Admiral Lord Nelson (1758–1805) had his arm cut off after it was fractured by gunshot. He felt pain in the non-existent arm for the rest of his life.

COMMON ILLNESSES

Name	Description
Neuritis	Inflammation of a nerve
Neuralgia	Pain caused by an irritated or damaged nerve
Neuroma	Benign (will not spread) tumour of nerve tissue
Multiple sclerosis	Progressive disease of the central nervous system

EYES

THE EYES ARE probably the most important of the sense organs, enabling us to see and react to the world around us. They are positioned in protective bony sockets in the skull. Eyes work in pairs to transmit images to the brain via the optic nerves.

EYE FUNCTION

Light rays enter the eye through the pupil, and are focused by the cornea and the lens to form an image on the retina. Light-sensitive cells in the retina convert the image into nerve impulses that travel along the optic nerve to the brain.

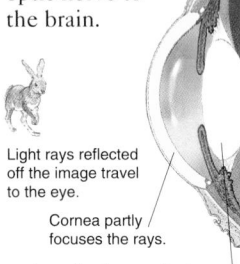

Light rays reflected off the image travel to the eye.

Cornea partly focuses the rays.

Lens fine-focuses the image.

Close-up of rods and cones

Image is reflected onto the retina.

STEREOSCOPIC VISION

Two eyes give a wide range of vision, and enable us to judge depth, distance, and speed effectively. Each eye receives a slightly different view of the same object. The brain combines the two images to give a three-dimensional interpretation of the object.

Visual region of the brain

Left eye receives this image.

Combined, three-dimensional image

Right eye receives this image.

SIGHT PROBLEMS

COLOUR BLINDNESS

Colour-blind people are unable to tell the difference between certain colours: usually red and green. The problem is normally caused by a defect in some of the retina's cone cells. True colour blindness, where people can only see shades of black and white, is very rare.

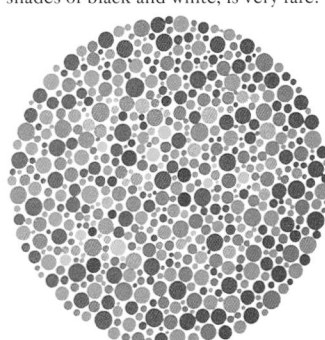

This is a test for colour blindness. If you have normal vision you can see the number 29. If you are colour blind you see the number 70.

EYE STRUCTURE

The eye is a round bag of clear, jelly-like fluid called vitreous humour, surrounded by a tough outer covering called the sclera. Each eyeball measures about 2.5cm (1in) across.

Lateral rectus muscle

Vitreous humour allows light through to retina.

Conjunctiva: thin membrane of skin; keeps eye moist

Iris: muscular body; controls pupil size

Cornea bends light.

Pupil: hole through which light enters the eye. Dilates (widens) in dim light or shrinks in bright light.

Area of optic disc (forms blind spot)

Optic nerve to brain

Retina: detects light

Retinal blood vessel

Image is upside-down, because light rays cross over behind the lens.

Image flashes along the optic nerve to the brain, where it is turned the right way up.

Aqueous humour: watery fluid; fills chamber behind cornea

Pigments in iris give eye its colour.

Lens focuses light.

Choroid: contains nourishing blood vessels.

Medial rectus muscle

Sclera forms white of the eye.

Ciliary body: muscular ring; controls shape of lens

RODS AND CONES

Millions of light-sensitive cells, called rods and cones, pick up the image. Rods see black and white, and cones see colour.

BLIND SPOT

This is a tiny, oval-shaped area on the retina where the optic nerve joins the eye. There are no rods or cones here, so this area of the retina cannot see.

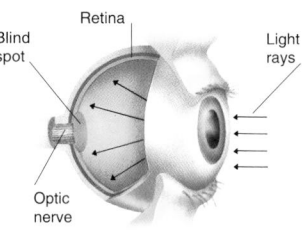

Blind spot

Retina

Light rays

Optic nerve

EYE FACTS

• Most people blink about 15 times a minute.

• About one person in thirty is colour blind. More men are affected than women.

• The best photographic film is at least 1,000 times less sensitive than the human eye.

• Male eyes are about 0.5 mm bigger than female eyes.

• Carrots help you to see in the dark: they contain vitamin A, from which the light-sensitive chemical in the rods is made.

• The body produces excess tears in times of strong emotion. No-one knows why humans cry.

MUSCLES

Each eye has six muscles to move the eyeball around. Movements are co-ordinated, so it is impossible to look in two different directions at once.

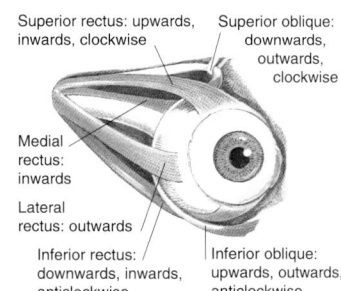

Superior rectus: upwards, inwards, clockwise

Superior oblique: downwards, outwards, clockwise

Medial rectus: inwards

Lateral rectus: outwards

Inferior rectus: downwards, inwards, anticlockwise

Inferior oblique: upwards, outwards, anticlockwise

TEARS

Tears are necessary to keep the eyes moist and clean.

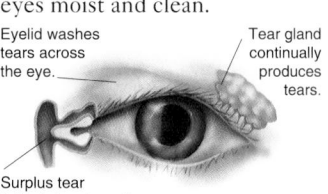

Eyelid washes tears across the eye.

Tear gland continually produces tears.

Surplus tear fluid drains down the tear ducts to the nose.

SHARP EYES

The human eye is so sensitive that it can see a lighted candle positioned 1.6km (1 mile) away in the dark.

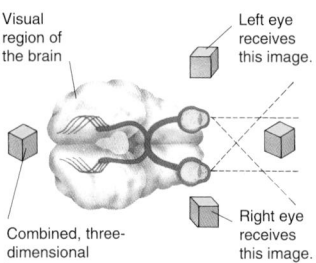

LONG- AND SHORT-SIGHTEDNESS

Short-sighted people cannot see distant objects clearly, and long-sighted people cannot see near objects clearly. These problems are caused by irregularly shaped eyeballs.

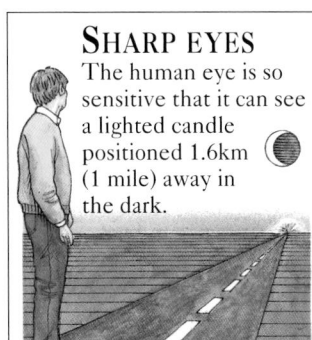
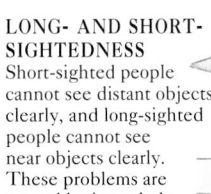
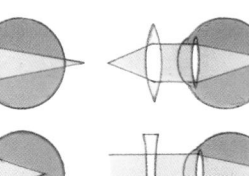
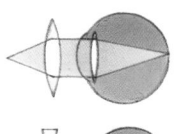

Long-sightedness: rays focused behind the retina. Convex lens corrects focus.

Short-sightedness: rays focused in front of the retina. Concave lens corrects focus.

COMMON PROBLEMS

Name	Description
Cataracts	Loss of transparency of the lens. Causes short-sightedness and distorted vision or blindness
Conjunctivitis	Inflammation of the conjunctiva. Causes redness, discomfort, and discharge
Glaucoma	Abnormally high pressure of fluid in the eye. Causes severe pain, and partial or complete loss of vision

EARS

EARS ARE THE organs of hearing and balance. Set on either side of the head, only part of each ear is visible; the rest is protected by the bones of the skull. Ears work in pairs to collect sound vibrations and turn them into signals, which are then passed to the brain, enabling us to hear.

EAR BONES

The three tiny ossicles in the middle ear are named the hammer, the anvil, and the stirrup, because of their shapes.

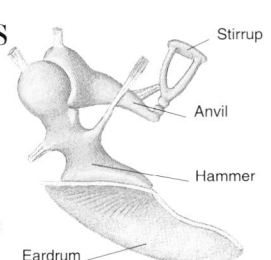

Stirrup

Anvil

Hammer

Eardrum

BALANCE

Every time the body moves, fluid, called perilymph, flows around the three semicircular canals. Tiny hair cells sense the movement and send signals to the brain to communicate the body's position. This helps the body to keep its balance.

HEARING RANGES

Animals hear different levels of sound frequency (see p.233). This diagram compares the hearing ranges of some animals.

100,000 Hz
10,000 Hz
1,000 Hz
100 Hz
10 Hz

Bat

Dolphin

Dog

Human

Ear structure diagram (centre)

Helix (outer rim)

Temporalis muscle

Skull

Pinna

Outer ear

2 Sound waves bounce off a tightly stretched membrane, called the eardrum, making it vibrate.

Hammer (malleus)

Stirrup (stapes)

Semicircular canals

Anvil (incus)

Inner ear

Cochlea

Antihelix (inner rim)

External auditory canal

Nerves to brain

Oval window under stirrup

Round window

Sound waves

1 The pinna (ear flap) directs sound waves into the ear canal.

Middle ear

Eardrum (tympanum)

Ceruminous (ear wax) glands

3 Three ear bones, called ossicles, magnify the vibrations and send them to the oval window (a membrane).

Eustachian tube: regulates air pressure

Lobule (earlobe)

4 As the oval window vibrates, liquid passes over tiny hairs in the cochlea. This produces nerve signals that pass along the auditory nerve to the brain.

Inner ear diagram

Perilymph in bony labyrinth

Nerves

Semicircular canals

Cochlea

Fluid flows over more than 20,000 fine hairs inside the cochlea.

EAR STRUCTURE

Each ear has three main parts: the outer, middle, and inner ear. The outer ear consists of the ear flap and the ear canal. The middle ear consists of the eardrum and the three ossicles. Deep within the bones of the skull is the inner ear, containing the cochlea and the three fluid-filled semicircular canals.

NOISE LEVELS

Loudness of sound is measured in decibels (dB). Sounds above 90dB cause pain to the human ear. Sounds above 130dB can damage the ear, and may cause deafness. This diagram compares some noise levels.

EAR FACTS

- Stirrup is the smallest bone in the human body, at only 3mm (0.12in) long.

- Sensation of ears "popping" is caused by the eustachian tube opening to equalize air pressure in the middle ear.

- Ear canal is about 2.5cm (1in) in length.

- Ears can detect the direction of a sound within three degrees.

- Children usually have more sensitive ears than adults.

- Ears can detect 1,500 different tones, and 350 degrees of loudness.

DIZZINESS

If you spin round and round and then stop, the fluid in the semicircular canals continues to move for a while. This confuses the brain, causing dizziness.

EAR WAX

Glands in the skin lining the ear canal produce ear wax. This wax protects the eardrum from dirt and dust, and its unpleasant smell discourages insects from entering the ear.

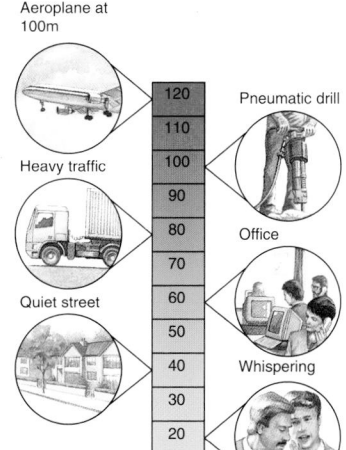

Aeroplane at 100m

Heavy traffic

Quiet street

120
110
100
90
80
70
60
50
40
30
20
Decibels

Pneumatic drill

Office

Whispering

PERFECT BALANCE

In 1973, Frenchman Henri Rochatain (b. 1926) spent 185 days on a tightrope 25m (82ft) above a supermarket in St. Etienne, France.

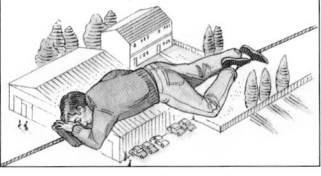

HEARING AIDS

In the past, people with hearing difficulties used large ear trumpets. Modern hearing aids are smaller and less noticeable.

Ear trumpets were held against the ear to amplify (increase) sound.

This hearing aid fits onto the frame of spectacles.

Volume control

This ear trumpet is 30cm (12in) long.

Earphone (receiver)

Modern hearing aid consisting of a microphone, amplifier, and battery; worn behind the ear.

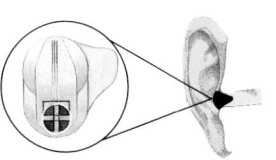

This tiny hearing aid fits inside the ear where it is almost completely hidden.

COMMON PROBLEMS

Name	Description
Deafness	Inability to hear
Tinnitus	Noises, such as ringing or buzzing, heard inside the ear
Ménière's disease	Inner ear disorder. May cause tinnitus, deafness, and vertigo (illusion of spinning)
Earache	Pain often caused by infection of the middle ear

SKIN, HAIR, AND NAILS

THE SKIN IS THE largest organ of the body. It is waterproof, bacteria-proof, and repairs itself. Hair and nails are extensions of the skin and are mainly composed of keratin, a protein that also protects the skin. The skin has nerve cells that respond to touch, heat, and pain. Hair and nails, however, lack nerve cells.

HAIR STRUCTURE

A tube of the protein keratin is pushed up from the hair follicle to form the hair shaft. Each hair is attached to a tiny muscle that allows it to move independently.

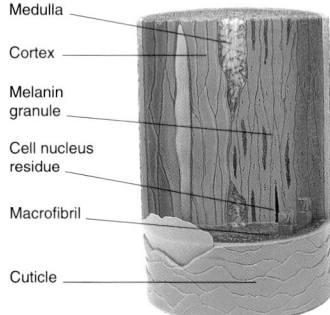

- Medulla
- Cortex
- Melanin granule
- Cell nucleus residue
- Macrofibril
- Cuticle

HAIR TYPES

The shape of the hair follicle determines whether the hair grows straight, wavy, or curly.

Curly hair grows from an oval follicle.

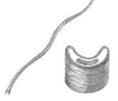

Wavy hair grows from a flat follicle.

Straight hair grows from a round follicle.

HAIR FACTS

- There are about 100,000 hairs on the head; 80 fall out every day.
- Hair grows about 2–3mm (0.08–0.1in) in a week.

RARE HAIR

These two boys have a rare medical condition known as "werewolf syndrome". Their faces are covered in hair.

Outer layers consist of dead skin cells containing a hard protein called keratin.

Movement of hairs creates the sensation of touch.

Sebaceous glands coat hair and skin in waterproof oil.

Hair follicles are surrounded by touch sensitive nerve endings.

Hair erector muscle tightens in the cold, causing hairs to stand on end and trap warmth.

Sweat gland produces sweat to cool down body temperature.

Sense receptor cells

SKIN STRUCTURE

The skin has two main layers: the outer epidermis and the inner dermis. The surface of the epidermis consists of dead skin cells. These are worn away and replaced by new skin cells from deep in the epidermis. The dermis is living and contains vital nerves, glands, hairs, and blood vessels.

Epidermis contains layers of new and dead skin cells.

Basal cell layer produces new cells which continually move towards the surface.

Blood vessels expand when body is hot. The skin flushes and heat is rapidly lost.

Beneath the skin is an insulating layer of fat.

The dermis is about four times thicker than the epidermis.

SKIN FACTS

- Protects internal organs from injury and infection.
- Sweat glands control body temperature by pushing water and salt to the surface.
- Contains thousands of nerve cells that can detect pressure, temperature, and pain.
- Contains the pigment melanin that gives the skin its colour and protects against the Sun's rays. Dark skin contains more melanin than fair skin.
- In most places skin is about 2mm (0.08in) thick.
- Freckles are due to an uneven production of melanin.
- Household dust is mostly made up of dead skin cells.

NAIL STRUCTURE

Nails are made of a tough protein called keratin. The half-moon at the base of each nail – the lunula – is covered by a flap of skin called the cuticle.

Lunula

Nail

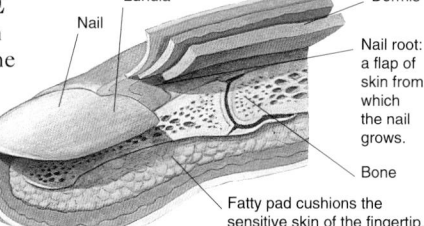

Dermis

Nail root: a flap of skin from which the nail grows.

Bone

Fatty pad cushions the sensitive skin of the fingertip.

NAIL FACTS

- Fingernails take six months to grow from the base to the tip.
- Nails grow at a rate of 0.5mm (0.02in) per week. They can grow up to 30cm (12in) long.

BLOOD CLOTTING

Red blood cells help cuts to heal quickly by binding together and forming a clot.

1 A cut in the skin triggers the release of substances to make blood cells, called platelets, sticky.

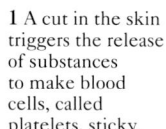

Red blood cells

2 White blood cells fight infection in the cut. Fibrin threads are made from blood-clotting factors.

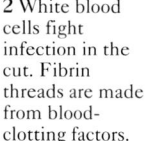

White blood cell

3 Fibrin threads contract and bind red blood cells into a clot. This hardens to a scab which protects the cut as it heals.

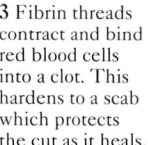

Fibrin threads stop blood flow

FINGERPRINTS

The patterns made by the ridges on your fingertips are called fingerprints. The patterns are formed months before birth, and no two fingerprint patterns are the same.

SKIN LOSS

The body sheds about 18kg (40lb) of dead skin in a lifetime: about the weight of a six- to seven-year-old child.

SKIN'S SURFACE

These magnified images show details of the skin's surface.

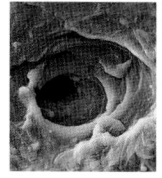

Sweat pores allow fluid to escape. This cools the skin.

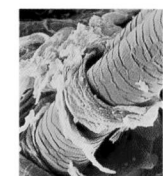

Hair grows out of pits called hair follicles.

COMMON PROBLEMS

Name	Description
Acne	Skin disorder: raised red spots that may scar
Eczema	Itchy skin inflammation: may cause blisters and scaling
Psoriasis	Skin disorder: patches of red skin often covered with silvery scales
Alopecia	Patchy loss of hair, usually on scalp

SMELL, TASTE, AND THROAT

SMELL AND TASTE are closely linked. The sensation of flavour combines messages from taste buds and smell receptors, as well as heat, texture, and sharpness. A 30 per cent change in the strength of a smell or taste is needed for the brain to register it. Humans can distinguish 2,000 to 4,000 different smells.

SENSE OF SMELL

There are specialized nerve endings at the back of the nose called smell receptors. These are sensitive to chemicals in the airstream deposited in mucus.

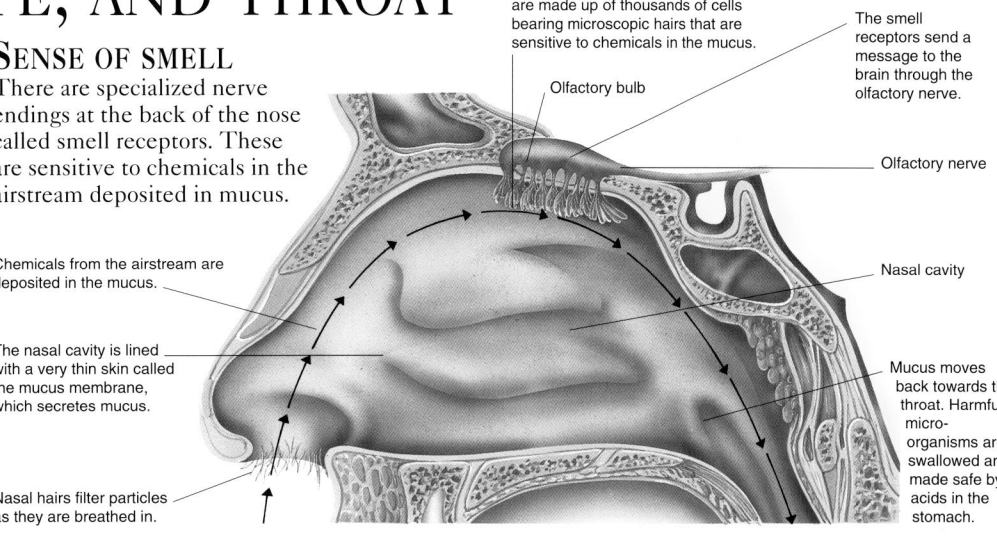

Air passes over smell receptors attached to the olfactory bulb. These are made up of thousands of cells bearing microscopic hairs that are sensitive to chemicals in the mucus.

Olfactory bulb

The smell receptors send a message to the brain through the olfactory nerve.

Olfactory nerve

Nasal cavity

Chemicals from the airstream are deposited in the mucus.

The nasal cavity is lined with a very thin skin called the mucus membrane, which secretes mucus.

Nasal hairs filter particles as they are breathed in.

Mucus moves back towards the throat. Harmful micro-organisms are swallowed and made safe by acids in the stomach.

TONGUE AND TASTE

The human tongue measures about 10cm (4in) in length, and is covered with taste buds. These microscopic nerve endings are the main organs of taste. Different areas detect different tastes. There are four basic tastes: sweet, sour, salt, and bitter.

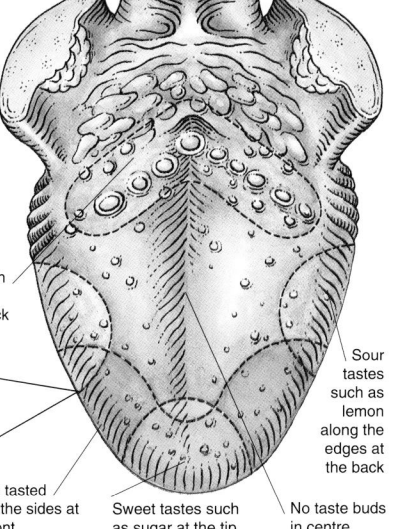

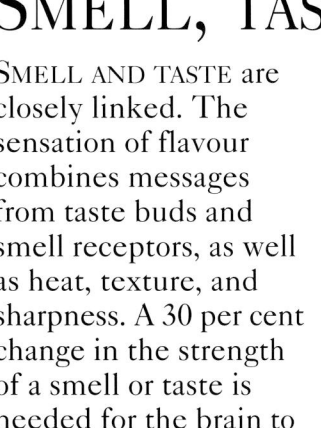

Tongue surface magnified to show sensory nerve endings.

Bitter tastes such as coffee are tasted at the back of the tongue.

Sour tastes such as lemon along the edges at the back

Salt is tasted along the sides at the front.

Sweet tastes such as sugar at the tip

No taste buds in centre

THE VOICE

Sounds are made by forcing air from the lungs up the trachea and through the vocal cords, causing them to vibrate. The tongue, throat, mouth, and lips change the sounds into words.

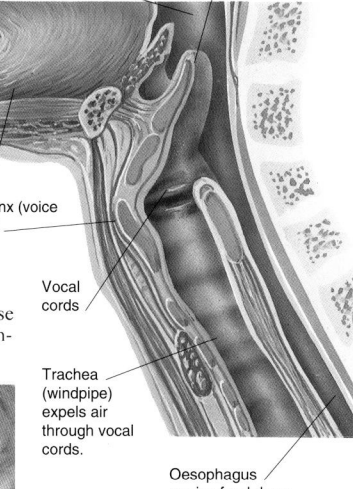

Nasal cavity and mouth passage join at the throat (pharynx).

Epiglottis flap

Tongue

Larynx (voice box)

Vocal cords

Trachea (windpipe) expels air through vocal cords.

Oesophagus carries food down to the stomach.

Relaxed chords
Vocal chords are far apart for low-pitched noise and breathing.

Active chords
Muscles bring vocal chords close together for high-pitched sound.

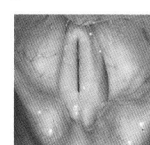

VOICE RECORDS

LOUDEST RECORDED
shout measured 119 decibels – louder than a loud rock concert.

FASTEST SPEAKERS
can say more than 300 words per minute and still be understood.

SNEEZING RECORD

An Englishwoman sneezed about 2.7 million times over 2.5 years. With each sneeze she expelled about six litres of air. During her world-record sneezing fit, she blew out enough air to fill eight hot air balloons.

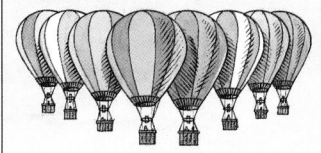

LOSS OF SMELL

Immediately after birth the efficiency of our smell receptors begins to decline. This graph shows how the sense of smell deteriorates as we age.

82%

38%

28%

Age 20   Age 60   Age 80

SMELL FACTS

• You can smell better if you sniff hard because more chemicals reach the receptors in your nose.

• The brain can become used to smells, even the most horrible ones. It simply switches off and you stop detecting them.

VOICE BOX

The vocal cords are two rubbery ligaments in the larynx.

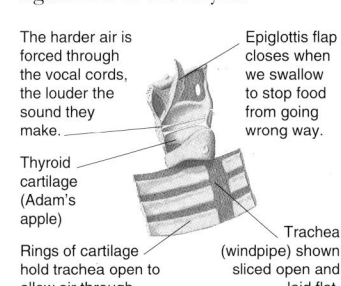

The harder air is forced through the vocal cords, the louder the sound they make.

Epiglottis flap closes when we swallow to stop food from going wrong way.

Thyroid cartilage (Adam's apple)

Rings of cartilage hold trachea open to allow air through.

Trachea (windpipe) shown sliced open and laid flat.

TASTE FACTS

• Taste buds only work when saliva dissolves chemicals in food and washes over the buds.

• Babies are born with taste buds all over their mouth. They gradually disappear, remaining only on the tongue. Adults have about 1,000 taste buds.

VOICE FACTS

• The larynx is larger in men, which is why they can produce deeper sounds.

• A boy's voice "breaks" when the larynx enlarges at puberty.

• If the larynx lining is tickled by a food particle, a reflex contraction causes coughing, which ejects the foreign body.

COMMON PROBLEMS

Name	Description
Allergic rhinitis (hay fever)	Inflammation of mucus membrane caused by allergy to pollen or dust
Common cold	Viral infection causing stuffed up, runny nose and sneezing
Laryngitis	Inflammation of the larynx caused by infection, resulting in loss of voice

SKELETON AND TEETH

THE FRAMEWORK OF bones in the human body, including the teeth, is called the skeleton, and it supports and protects delicate internal organs, such as the brain, lungs, and heart. The skeleton also provides strong, fixed points of attachment for muscles. Bones contain marrow, which generates red and white blood cells.

BONE STRUCTURE

Bones contain calcium and phosphorus, which make them hard. The strongest part of a bone is its compact outer layer. Inside longer bones, softer living tissue, called marrow, produces red and white blood cells, and stores fat.

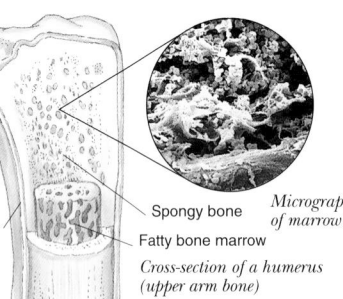

Compact bone
Spongy bone
Fatty bone marrow
Micrograph of marrow
Cross-section of a humerus (upper arm bone)

JOINTS

Where bones meet, a joint forms. In a mobile joint, the bone surface is coated with slippery cartilage and lubricated with synovial fluid. Most joints are held together by cords or bands called ligaments. Below are several types of joints.

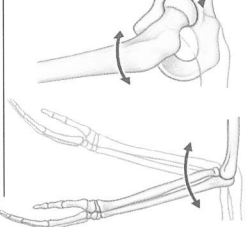

Ball-and-socket
Ball-and-socket joints (e.g. shoulder, hip) allow the most movement of any joint.

Hinge
Hinge joints (e.g. elbow, knee) allow movement in just one plane.

Fixed
Some bones lock together, allowing no movement at all (e.g. cranial joints).

Pivot
A pivot joint consists of a bony projection that pivots within a ring (e.g. skull on vertebra).

Ellipsoidal
An ellipsoidal joint (e.g. wrist) is one where an oval bone fits into an oval cavity.

A BONE TO PICK

A small piece of bone could support a nine-tonne weight. The same weight would crush a piece of cement of the same size.

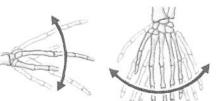

BONE RECORDS

LARGEST BONE in the body is the thigh bone (femur): average male length 46cm (18.1in)

SMALLEST BONE is the stirrup (stapes) bone in the middle ear, 2.6–3.4mm (0.1–0.13in) long.

TEETH

Teeth are covered with enamel, the hardest substance made by animals. They are connected to the jaw by strong fibres that allow slight movement when chewing or biting. Humans have two sets of teeth: the first, of 20, called "milk" teeth, starts to fall out at about age 6; the second, of 32, replaces the first and is permanent.

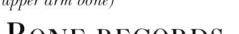

Upper jaw
Canine
Premolars
Molars
Incisors

Lower jaw
Molars
Incisors
Premolars
Canine

TOOTH TYPES

Our front 12 teeth (incisors and canines) are sharp; they grip and tear off pieces of food. Our back 20 teeth (premolars and molars) grind and crush food for later digestion. The third molars, or wisdom teeth, sometimes remain embedded beneath gum in the jawbone.

TOOTH STRUCTURE

Enamel forms the hard, non-living, surface of the tooth. The pulp contains vessels that bring blood to the tooth, enabling it to live and grow.

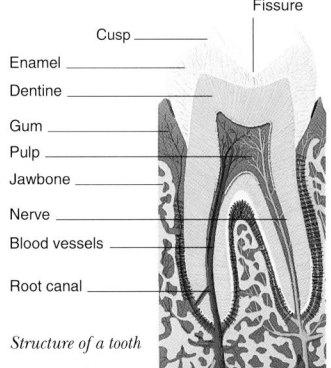

Fissure
Cusp
Enamel
Dentine
Gum
Pulp
Jawbone
Nerve
Blood vessels
Root canal

Structure of a tooth

Skeleton diagram labels

Mandible (jaw-bone)
Cranium (skull)
Clavicle
Ribs
Humerus (upper arm bone)
Vertebrae (spine)
Radius
Ulna
Carpals (wrist bones)
Sacrum
Pelvis (hip bone)
Metacarpals (finger bones)
Femur (thigh bone)
Patella
Tibia (shin-bone)
Fibula (calf-bone)
Tarsals and metatarsals (foot-bones)

Cervical
Vertebral disc
Thoracic
Lumbar
Sacrum
Coccyx

SKELETON

The average person has 206 bones. Some people have extra bones in their thumbs or big toes, called sesamoid bones. Women have shallower and wider pelvic bones than men, to help with childbirth.

BONE FACTS

- Some people have an extra (thirteenth) pair of ribs.
- A giraffe's neck contains the same number of bones as the human neck.
- The bones in a baby's head are not fused – they can overlap slightly to ease birth.
- Babies have more than 300 bones – they fuse together later.

SPINAL COLUMN

The spinal column has four curves: cervical, thoracic, lumbar, and sacral. Each bone in the spine is called a vertebra, and most are cushioned from their neighbours by a piece of cartilage called a vertebral disc. Vertebrae interlock with each other in sliding joints.

TOOTH FACTS

- Teeth decay more easily during the first 25 years of life; mature enamel is more resistant to attack.
- Some babies are born with a full set of teeth – King Louis XIV of France, for instance.
- Some adults' four back molars (wisdom teeth) never fully grow.

CARING FOR TEETH

Tooth decay can be reduced by cutting down on the sugar and starch we eat and by brushing (with a fluoride-based toothpaste) and flossing after meals.

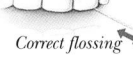
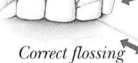

Correct brushing
Correct flossing

COMMON PROBLEMS

Name	Description
Osteoarthritis	Degeneration of cartilage or bone ends in the joints
Osteoporosis	Thinning of bone, with ageing. Bone fractures easily
Caries	Patches of decay and erosion of tooth enamel and dentine by plaque (bacteria, saliva, and food remains)
Gingivitis	Inflammation of the gums, due to infection

MUSCLES

MUSCLES CARRY OUT all the body's movements. They number more than 600, accounting for about half the body's weight. Muscles are arranged in groups of fibres that contract when triggered by nerves. Regular, vigorous exercise increases a muscle's size and improves its circulation of blood.

TYPES OF MUSCLE

Voluntary muscles (e.g. biceps) can be consciously controlled; involuntary ones do internal jobs, such as the muscles of the intestine, which move food through the digestive system.

Voluntary muscle
Voluntary (skeletal) muscle cells appear striped close up. The muscle fibres are bundled together for quick contraction.

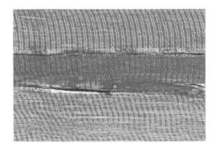

Involuntary muscle
Involuntary (smooth) muscle cells are tapered and loosely woven, and contract more slowly than other muscle types.

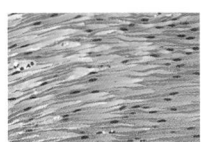

Cardiac muscle
Cardiac (heart) muscle has short, branching cells; these help spread the nerve signals that cause contraction.

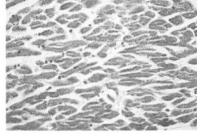

CONTRACTION

Muscle fibre contains tiny strands called myofibrils. A myofibril contains overlapping layers of two proteins: actin and myosin. When triggered by an electrical nerve signal, the actin and myosin attract each other, and their layers slide closer together. The myofibril shortens; the muscle contracts.

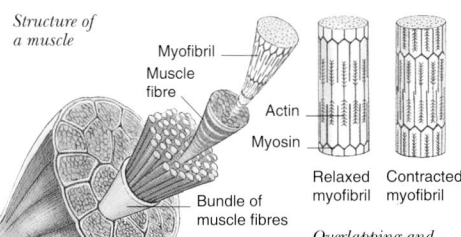

Structure of a muscle

Myofibril
Muscle fibre
Actin
Myosin
Bundle of muscle fibres
Tough membrane protects muscle.

Relaxed myofibril
Contracted myofibril

Overlapping and interlocking myosin and actin proteins

MULTI-MUSCLE MOVER

Humans have more than 600 muscles, but an average-sized caterpillar has over 2,000.

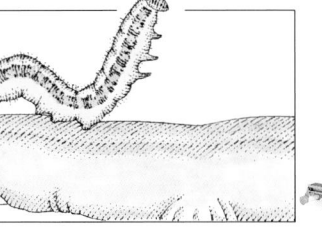

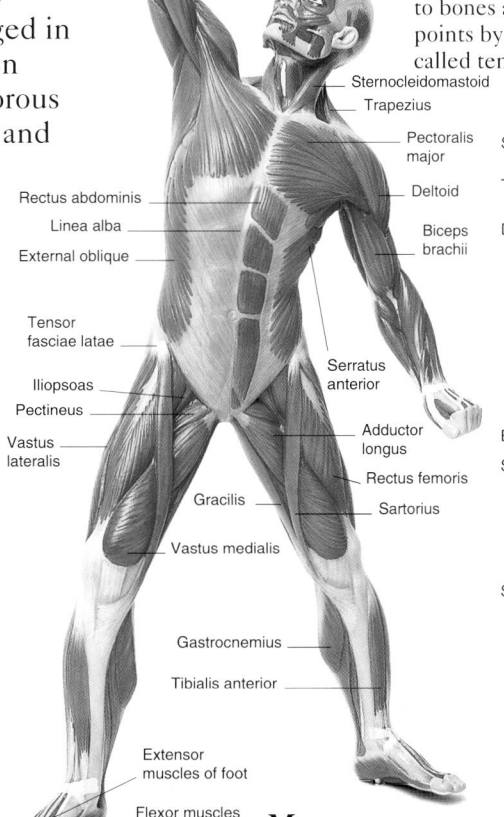

Flexors of forearm
Brachioradialis
Frontalis
Brachialis
Sternocleidomastoid
Trapezius
Pectoralis major
Rectus abdominis
Deltoid
Linea alba
Biceps brachii
External oblique
Tensor fasciae latae
Iliopsoas
Pectineus
Serratus anterior
Vastus lateralis
Adductor longus
Rectus femoris
Gracilis
Sartorius
Vastus medialis
Gastrocnemius
Tibialis anterior
Extensor muscles of foot
Flexor muscles of foot

Flexors of hand
Extensors of hand
Temporalis
Triceps brachii
Sternocleidomastoid
Teres minor
Trapezius
Teres major
Deltoid
Infraspinatus
Latissimus dorsi
Biceps femoris
Gluteus maximus
Semitendinosus
Adductor magnus
Gracilis
Gastrocnemius
Soleus
Peroneus brevis

MUSCLE SYSTEM

Muscles warm up when used, providing about four-fifths of the body's heat. Many organs, such as the heart, intestines, and bladder, have muscles. Most voluntary muscles (muscles under conscious control) are anchored to bones at two or more points by strong cords called tendons.

MUSCLE RECORDS

LONGEST MUSCLE is the sartorius, which runs from the pelvis to just below the knee.

BIGGEST MUSCLE is the gluteus maximus (buttock).

SMALLEST MUSCLE is the stapedius in the middle ear – less than 1.27mm (0.05in) long.

FASTEST MUSCLE blinks the eyelids up to five times every second.

MUSCLE ACTION

Muscles can only pull, not push. So, they often work in opposing pairs called antagonists; one muscle in the pair contracts while the other relaxes.

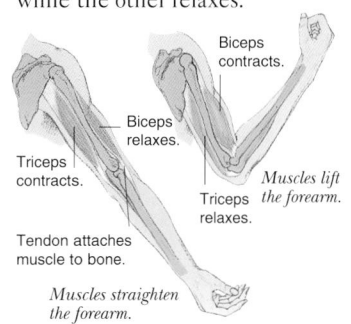

Biceps contracts.
Biceps relaxes.
Triceps contracts.
Tendon attaches muscle to bone.
Triceps relaxes.
Muscles lift the forearm.
Muscles straighten the forearm.

TYPES OF EXERCISE

Muscles normally use glucose and oxygen for day-to-day (aerobic) exercise. If glucose or oxygen are in short supply, muscles use their own energy stores. This anaerobic exercise generates lactic acid, which causes muscles to tire and ache, and makes us gasp for replacement oxygen.

Aerobic exercise
Anaerobic exercise

MUSCLE FUNCTIONS

• Move bones at joints.

• Force food through intestines.

• Blink the eyelids.

• Smile or make other facial expressions.

• Make breathing movements of chest and diaphragm.

• Contract walls of blood vessels.

MUSCLE FACTS

• Muscle cells can contract by up to one-third of their length.

• The muscles that work a gnat's wings can make them beat over 1,000 times a second.

• When we walk, we use more than 200 different muscles.

COMMON PROBLEMS

Name	Description
Cramp	Painful spasm from lactic acid build-up in muscles
Strain	Tear in muscle, causing bleeding and swelling
Tetanus	Toxin makes muscle contract continuously
Muscular dystrophy	Gradual wasting of muscle fibres, an inherited illness
Tendinitis	Inflammation of tendon, usually caused by injury

HEART

THE HEART IS a fist-sized muscular pump that carries blood around the body. It has two sides, and each side has two chambers. These chambers contract and relax about once every four-fifths of a second, ensuring that blood continually flows in the right direction.

Heart lies in middle of chest; it feels further left since left side beats stronger.

HEARTBEAT CYCLE

The heart is a special kind of muscle, a cardiac muscle, that works automatically. A heartbeat has four phases, or stages, and lasts for about four-fifths of a second.

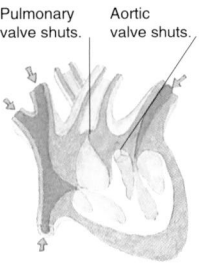

Pulmonary valve shuts.   Aortic valve shuts.

1 The left and right atria relax. Blood fills them through pulmonary veins and vena cava.

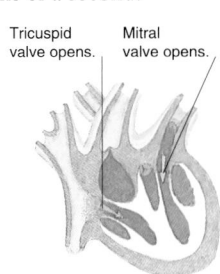

Tricuspid valve opens.   Mitral valve opens.

2 Blood passes through tricuspid and mitral valves from atria into right and left ventricles.

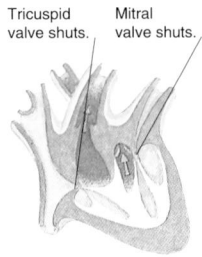

Tricuspid valve shuts.   Mitral valve shuts.

3 Ventricles contract and force blood through aortic and pulmonary valves into main arteries.

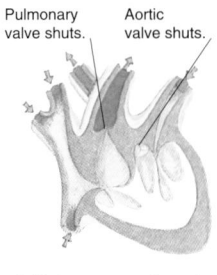

Pulmonary valve shuts.   Aortic valve shuts.

4 Pulmonary and aortic valves close as ventricles relax. Cycle restarts at phase one.

HEART STRUCTURE

The septum divides the two sides of the heart. Each side has two chambers: an atrium and a ventricle, separated by valves. The stronger left side pumps oxygenated blood from the lungs to the rest of the body; the right brings deoxygenated (used) blood back to the lungs.

Right pulmonary artery

Location of sinoatrial node

Right pulmonary vein

In this diagram, arteries are coloured red and veins are coloured blue.

Myocardium
Pericardium
Right ventricle

Superior vena cava   Aorta
Artery to head
Cardiac nerves
Right atrium
Pulmonary valve
Tricuspid valve

Cardiac nerves stimulate the heart muscle, passing electrical signals from the brain to tell the heart how fast it should beat.

Valves stop blood from going the wrong way when the heart muscle contracts.

Left pulmonary artery
Aortic valve
Left atrium
Left pulmonary vein
Mitral valve
Tendon supporting valve
Septum
Coronary vein

Coronary artery

Fat   Left ventricle   Muscular column supporting valve tendons
Aorta
Inferior vena cava

HEART FACTS

• Heart sounds are caused by the valves snapping shut, and the whoosh of blood leaving the heart.

• Bicuspid valves have two flaps; tricuspid have three.

• A heart beats more than 30 million times a year, and about 2 billion times in a lifetime.

• Our heart rate increases when we exercise, to supply our muscles with extra oxygen.

• The heart rests between beats. In an average lifetime of 70 years, the heart will be at rest for about 40 years.

HEART RECORDS

LONGEST CARDIAC ARREST lasted four hours – Norwegian fisherman Egil Refsdahl (b.1936), later revived.

FIRST HUMAN HEART TRANSPLANT was performed on 3 December 1967 by South African surgeon Christiaan Barnard, on grocer Louis Washkansky.

LONGEST-SURVIVING TRANSPLANTEE survived for 22 years, 10 months, 24 days.

HEARTBEAT PACEMAKER

The heart has a built-in pacemaker that keeps it beating rhythmically. It lies at the top of the heart, at the sinoatrial node, and sends an electrical signal around the heart just before every beat. An electrocardiograph machine can record these impulses painlessly.

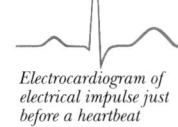

Electrocardiogram of electrical impulse just before a heartbeat

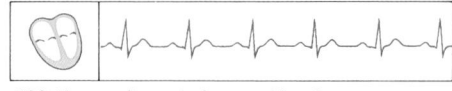

ECG (electrocardiogram) of a normal heartbeat

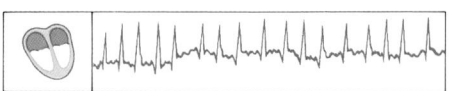

ECG of complete heart block (chambers beat independently)

BLOOD WAGON

The heart ejects about 80ml (0.14 pints) of blood with every beat. If an adult heart were connected to an 8,000-litre (1,760-gallon) container lorry, it could fill it in a single day, with blood to spare.

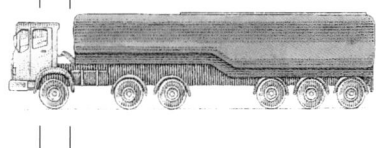

HOLE IN THE HEART

Sometimes the right and left sides of the heart connect through a hole in the septum. Holes are closed by surgery; otherwise, fresh blood from the lungs returns there directly, without going around the body.

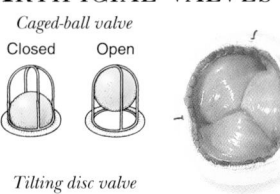

Septum
Surgical seal

Ventricular septal defect (hole in the septum)

ARTIFICIAL VALVES

Caged-ball valve
Closed   Open

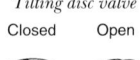

Tilting disc valve
Closed   Open

Modified pig's valve

Sometimes valves do not work properly, and blood flows the wrong way. Surgeons replace them with real valves from pigs or artificial, mechanical ones.

COMMON PROBLEMS

Name	Description
Angina	Tight heart pain caused by lack of oxygen, often from narrowed arteries
Coronary heart disease	Reduced blood supply from narrowed arteries
Cardiac arrest	Part or all of heart muscle stops beating
Endo-carditis	Infection of the heart valves, usually after rheumatic fever
Arrhythmia	Disturbance in heartbeat

CIRCULATION AND BLOOD

THE CIRCULATORY SYSTEM supplies each body cell with life-giving blood. Blood flows around the body in a continuous circuit, through a network of vessels that is thousands of kilometres long. The heart acts as a pump, keeping the entire system moving.

THE CIRCULATORY SYSTEM

Veins bring deoxygenated blood from the body to the right-hand side of the heart. The right ventricle pumps it to the lungs, where it becomes saturated with oxygen. This blood returns to the left atrium of the heart and enters the left ventricle. The ventricle then pumps it into the network of arteries, keeping the body constantly supplied with oxygen.

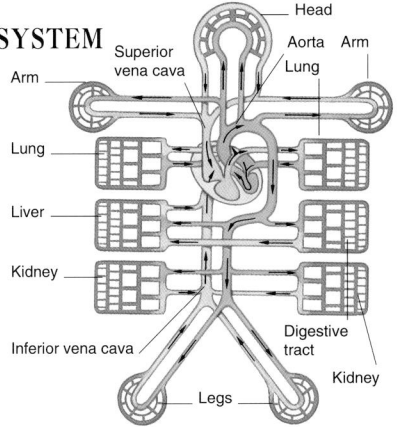

Head · Aorta · Arm · Lung · Superior vena cava · Arm · Arm · Lung · Lung · Liver · Kidney · Inferior vena cava · Digestive tract · Kidney · Legs

BLOOD

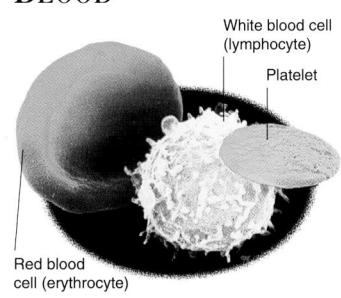

White blood cell (lymphocyte) · Platelet · Red blood cell (erythrocyte)

Blood consists of red blood cells, white blood cells, and cell fragments called platelets, floating in a fluid called plasma. Proteins, hormones, and minerals are dissolved in the plasma. Red blood cells contain haemoglobin, which stores oxygen and releases it to the body. White blood cells fight infection. Platelets help blood to clot when we cut our skin.

VESSEL RECORDS

LARGEST ARTERY
is the aorta. It has an internal diameter of 2.5cm (1in).

LARGEST VEIN
is the vena cava. It has an internal diameter of 2.5cm (1in).

LEECH LUNCH

Leeches attach themselves with suckers to animals and feed off their blood. They can drink up to ten times their own bodyweight of blood – enough to last them for nine months.

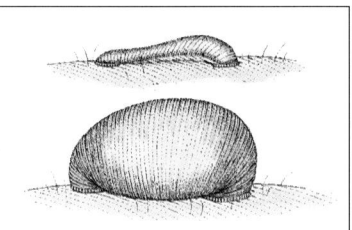

BLOOD VESSELS

Muscular-walled arteries divide into smaller arterioles, then into capillaries, which have thin walls through which oxygen can pass. Deoxygenated blood returns via venules, which join up into wider, thin-walled veins.

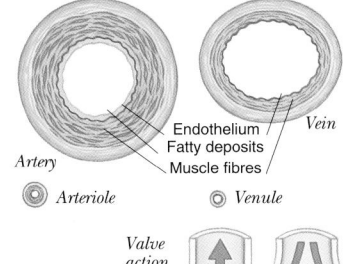

Artery · Vein · Endothelium · Fatty deposits · Muscle fibres · Arteriole · Venule

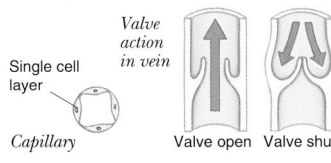

Single cell layer · Capillary · Valve action in vein · Valve open · Valve shut

BLOOD FACTS

• There are four main types, or groups, of blood: A, B, AB, and O. Blood transfusions (transfers) must use compatible groups.

• Red blood cells last about four months and make about 172,000 circuits around the body.

ARTERIES

Common carotid artery · Subclavian artery · Aortic arch · Pulmonary artery · Axillary artery · Coronary artery · Brachial artery · Gastric artery · Hepatic artery · Renal artery · Superior mesenteric artery · Inferior mesenteric artery · Ovarian artery · Palmar arch · Digital artery · Ulnar artery · Radial artery · Common iliac artery · External iliac artery · Femoral artery · Popliteal artery · Peroneal artery · Anterior tibial artery · Posterior tibial artery · Lateral plantar artery · Dorsal metatarsal artery

VEINS

Internal jugular vein · Brachiocephalic vein · Subclavian vein · Axillary vein · Superior vena cava · Pulmonary vein · Cephalic vein · Basilic vein · Hepatic portal vein · Gastroepiploic vein · Median cubital vein · Anterior median vein · Inferior vena cava · Inferior mesenteric vein · Ovarian vein · Palmar vein · Digital vein · Common iliac vein · External iliac vein · Femoral vein · Great saphenous vein · Short saphenous vein · Dorsal venous arch · Digital vein

BLOOD PRESSURE

Blood circulates under pressure. This is measured using two figures: the systole, or first figure, gives the pressure as the heart pumps blood into the system; the diastole, or second figure, gives the pressure when the heart rests between beats.

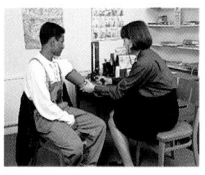

A nurse or doctor measures blood pressure.

PRESSURE CHANGES

Blood pressure is low when we sleep, and rises during exercise. Also, it may rise as we grow older. A 20-year-old might have a pressure of 110/70mm mercury; a 60-year-old of 160/90mm.

180 · 140 · 100 · 60 · Pressure · Time 8 AM 9 10 11 12 1 · Systolic · Diastolic · Exercise raises pressure · Getting up raises pressure

HIV AND AIDS

The HIV virus that causes AIDS disables the immune system. One way it achieves this is by destroying the T4-lymphocytes (white blood cells) that help "killer" lymphocytes attack invaders.

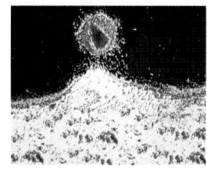

Micrograph of an HIV virus bursting from a T4-lymphocyte

COMMON PROBLEMS

Name	Description
Haemophilia	Deficiency of a blood-clotting factor
Anaemia	Haemoglobin deficiency causing lack of oxygen
Arterio-sclerosis	Thickening of artery wall due to deposits of fat
Varicose vein	Swelling, twisting, and distortion of a vein
Aneurysm	Thinning and dilation (widening) of artery wall

RESPIRATORY SYSTEM

WHEN WE BREATHE IN, we supply our bodies with oxygen from the air, and when we breathe out, we expel a waste gas, carbon dioxide. We breathe about six litres (10.56 pints) of air every minute, and adult lungs hold about three litres (5.28 pints) of air.

Location of respiratory system

RESPIRATORY SYSTEM

Air enters the body at the upper respiratory tract (nose, mouth, and trachea). The trachea splits into two bronchi (tubes), which divide into narrower bronchioles, leading to tiny, hollow, capsules called alveoli. Air is drawn in and out of this system by the action of the diaphragm muscle.

ALVEOLI

The lungs' 700 million microscopic alveoli are hollow and covered in a network of capillary arteries and veins. Their moist walls are so thin that blood passing by can release its waste carbon dioxide and take up oxygen. The capillaries then join up to form the pulmonary vein.

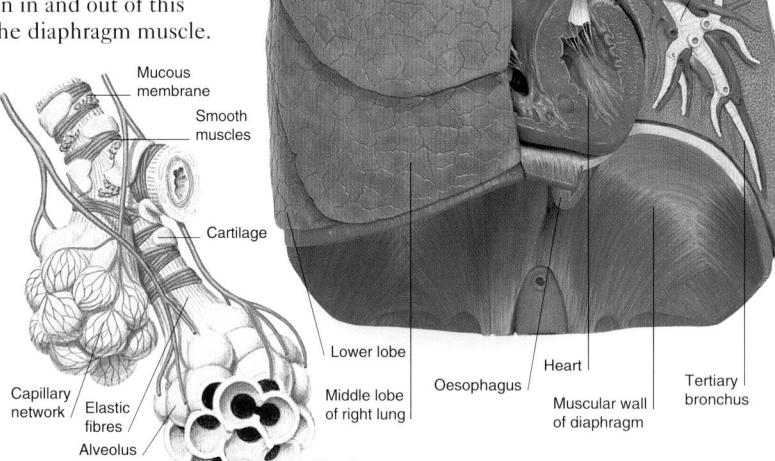

Epiglottis
Hyoid bone
Thyroid cartilage
Thyroid gland
Cricoid cartilage
Trachea
Apex of lung
Aorta
Superior vena cava
Left pulmonary artery
Upper lobe
Secondary bronchus
Mucous membrane
Smooth muscles
Cartilage
Capillary network
Elastic fibres
Alveolus
Lower lobe
Middle lobe of right lung
Oesophagus
Heart
Muscular wall of diaphragm
Tertiary bronchus

Alveoli

ACE AIRWAYS

If the inner surfaces of the lungs were laid out flat, their total area would be 180sq m (1,938sq ft). This would cover more than two-thirds of a tennis court.

BREATHING

BREATHING IN

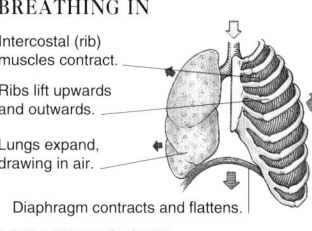

Intercostal (rib) muscles contract.
Ribs lift upwards and outwards.
Lungs expand, drawing in air.
Diaphragm contracts and flattens.

BREATHING OUT

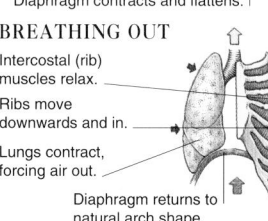

Intercostal (rib) muscles relax.
Ribs move downwards and in.
Lungs contract, forcing air out.
Diaphragm returns to natural arch shape.

The bases of our lungs rest on the diaphragm, a dome-shaped muscle. When we inhale, it pulls the bases down, and chest (intercostal) muscles expand the ribcage. Air rushes into the lungs through the trachea.

RESPIRATION FACTS

• The left lung has two lobes, or sections, and the right has three. Each lung is encased in a lubricated skin called a pleural membrane. It allows the lungs to slide easily during breathing.

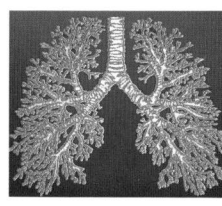

X-ray of lungs

• Rings of cartilage reinforce the trachea and bronchioles to prevent them from collapsing.

• Thousands of tiny hairs, called cilia, line the walls of the airways. They carry dust and bacteria away from the lungs. A mucous lining also catches dust.

• We can survive with just one fully working lung.

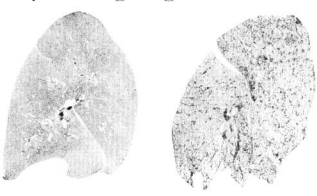

Healthy lung   *Smoker's lung*

Oxygen: 21%
Nitrogen: 75%
Carbon dioxide: 4%
Composition of inhaled air

Oxygen: 16%
Nitrogen: 75%
Carbon dioxide: 9%
Composition of exhaled air

• Nitrogen dissolves in blood plasma, but is not used in any of the body's processes.

LUNGS AND SMOKING

More than 4,000 chemicals have been identified in cigarette smoke, and many of these irritate the lungs and cause cancer. Many people die each year from the effects of smoking.

• Hiccups are caused by the rapid contraction of the diaphragm. Air is drawn in very rapidly and the vocal cords snap quickly shut, causing the noise we hear as a hiccup.

• Between the trachea and the alveoli the airways divide 23 times, making a total of 2,400km (1,491 miles) of airways.

HIC HICK

American farmer Charles Osborne (1894–1991) began hiccuping in 1922. He continued until 1990, after 68 years of constant hiccups.

COMMON PROBLEMS

Name	Description
Asthma	Causes wheezing and difficulty of breathing out
Bronchitis	Inflammation of the bronchi
Pneumonia	Inflammation of lungs caused by infection
Lung cancer	Malignant tumours of the lung
Emphysema	Damage to alveoli, causes breathlessness

SMOKING HEALTH RISK

Cigarettes per day	Lung cancer deaths per year per 100,000 males
0	10
1–14	78
15–24	127

DIGESTION

FOOD HAS TO BE broken down into small particles before the body can make use of its energy and nutrients. This process is called digestion and happens in the digestive tract, a tube 9m (29.5ft) long.

DIGESTIVE TRACT

The digestive tract runs from the mouth to the anus. Organs such as the liver, pancreas, and gall bladder connect with the tract and help it to break down and absorb food.

THE LIVER

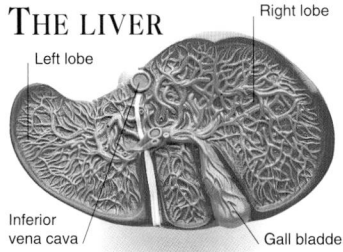

Left lobe
Right lobe
Inferior vena cava
Gall bladder

The liver receives blood from the hepatic artery and the portal (gastrointestinal) vein, and has many functions, including:
- Makes bile for digesting fat.
- Helps maintain blood sugar levels.
- Makes blood proteins.
- Helps blood to clot.
- Controls blood cell formation and destruction.
- Stores vitamins.
- Removes poisons from body.
- Stores energy.
- Makes heat.
- Destroys micro-organisms.

ABSORBING FOOD

The lining of the small intestine has millions of microscopic, finger-like projections called villi. They are packed with blood and lymph vessels and have thin walls through which nutrients from the partly digested food can easily pass.

1 MOUTH AND THROAT

Digestion begins as soon as you take a bite of food: chewing breaks down food into smaller lumps; enzymes (proteins that speed up chemical reactions) in saliva begin to break down complex carbohydrates into simpler sugars. The tongue rolls food into a bolus (lump) and pushes it to the back of the throat, where a swallowing reflex is activated. The bolus passes down the oesophagus (food pipe) towards the stomach.

Oesophagus

2 STOMACH

The lining of the stomach gives out highly acidic juices and enzymes that break down food. Acid helps the enzymes work and kills bacteria. The resulting soupy liquid is called chyme.

Stomach

3 DUODENUM

The duodenum receives bile (green, watery fluid) from the liver and juices from the pancreas. Pancreatic juice continues to break down food, but also neutralizes stomach acids so that other enzymes can act. Bile emulsifies (splits up) fats for later digestion.

Duodenum

4 ILEUM (SMALL INTESTINE)

Food is absorbed in the ileum, and some substances, such as fats, lactose, and sucrose are finally digested here. Nutrients absorbed into the blood are sent to the liver for processing. *Colon*

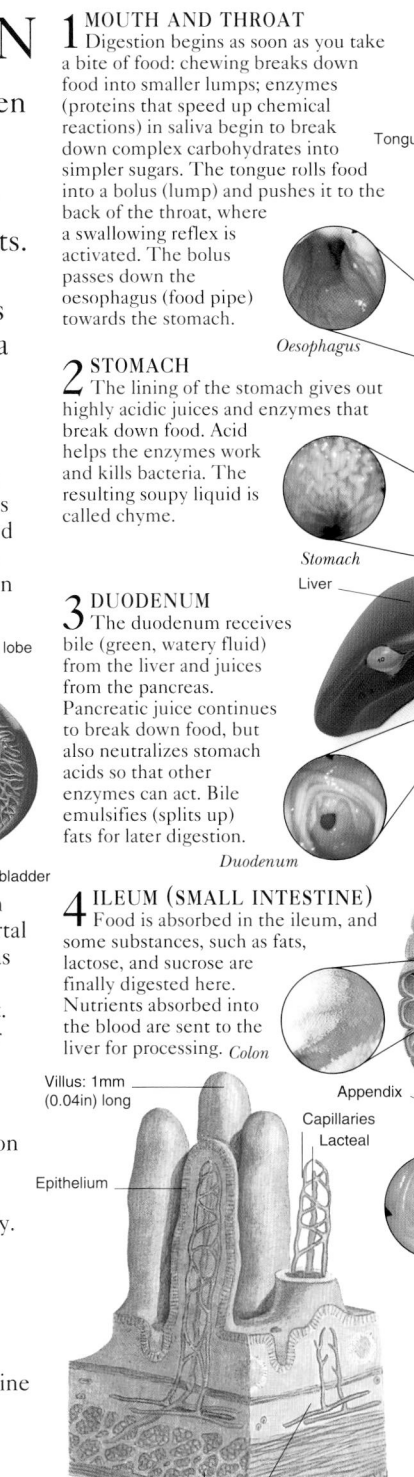

Tongue
Trachea
Maxilla (upper jaw)
Mandible (lower jaw)
Epiglottis
Oesophagus
Fold of mucous membrane
Stomach
Liver
Pancreas | Spleen
Appendix
Colon
Small intestine
Rectum
Anal sphincter muscle
Anus
Ileum

Villus: 1mm (0.04in) long
Capillaries
Lacteal
Epithelium
Muscles contract and relax to squeeze food along.
Mucosa layer contains venules, arterioles, and thin muscle sheets.

5 COLON AND RECTUM (LARGE INTESTINE)

Water and fibre from food pass into the colon, where much of the water is aborbed into the body. The large intestine does not secrete enzymes, but contains bacteria which break down the fibrous, undigested leftovers. This semi-solid waste, called faeces, then passes into the rectum, and is later expelled through the anus.

IRON AND FIBRE

Since 1966, Frenchman Michel Lolito, "Monsieur Mangetout", has eaten and digested ten bicycles, seven TVs, six chandeliers, and a Cessna light aircraft.

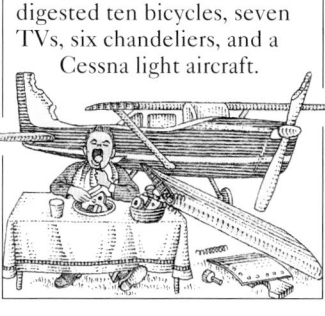

DIGESTION FACTS

- Food spends 3 to 5 hours in the stomach, and 6 to 20 hours in the large intestine.

- The stomach wall is protected by a mucus lining; otherwise, it would start to digest itself.

- When we swallow, a lid called the epiglottis covers the trachea to stop food from entering.

PERISTALSIS

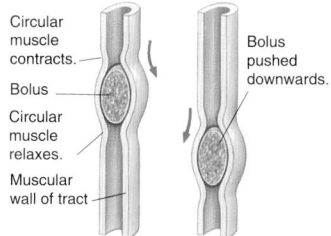

Circular muscle contracts.
Bolus
Circular muscle relaxes.
Muscular wall of tract
Bolus pushed downwards.

A muscular, wave-like movement called peristalsis pushes food through the digestive tract. The walls of the tract contain rings and lengths of muscle. These contract and relax alternately to propel food through the system.

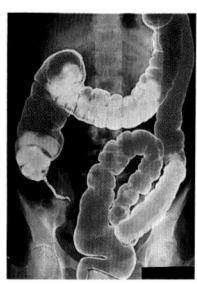

X-ray of faeces passing through the colon

KEY ENZYMES

Region	Enzymes produced	Foods acted on by enzymes
Mouth	Salivary amylase	Starch (carbohydrate)
Stomach	Pepsin and rennin	Proteins and milk protein
Duodenum	Trypsin, amylase, lipase	Proteins, peptides, starch, and fats
Ileum	Trypsin, amylase, lipase	Peptides, fats, maltose, sucrose, lactose
Colon	Bacterial enzymes	Vegetable and undigested fibre

COMMON PROBLEMS

Name	Description
Indigestion	Stomach pain, when stomach stretches with gas or acid build-up
Diarrhoea	Liquid or semi-liquid faeces caused by poisoned food or infection
Constipation	Slow bowel actions, can be caused by lack of fibre in diet
Cirrhosis	Scarring and breakdown of liver commonly caused by alcohol abuse
Hepatitis	Inflammation of liver caused by viral infection, drugs, or poisons

URINARY SYSTEM

THE KIDNEYS CONTROL the amount of water and minerals in our blood by getting rid of unwanted substances in the form of urine. Urine is expelled from the body via a muscular reservoir called the bladder. This system is known as the urinary or excretory system. The kidneys filter all the blood in the body every five minutes.

Location of urinary system

THE KIDNEYS

The two kidneys contain about 1.3 million tiny tubes, called nephrons, that cleanse the blood. As blood passes through the tubes into a network of tiny blood vessels, called the glomerulus, wastes and water are filtered out into a cup-shaped organ called a Bowman's capsule. Some of this filtrate is reabsorbed into the blood. The rest, now concentrated, travels down the ureter towards the bladder.

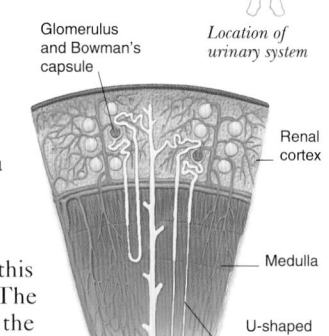

Glomerulus and Bowman's capsule

Renal cortex

Medulla

U-shaped collecting tubule

Urine-collecting tubule

Section through kidney

URINARY FACTS

• Up to about two years of age, the bladder is emptied by a reflex action. After this age, a child learns to control the bladder.

• ADH (anti-diuretic hormone), made in the pituitary gland, controls the uptake of water in the kidneys.

• We can survive with only one kidney. If one stops working the other enlarges in order to do the work for both.

KIDNEY FILTRATES

This table shows percentages of major substances in the blood serum (plasma), and how much is then filtered out by the kidneys as urine.

Compounds	Blood %	Urine %
Proteins	7–9	0
Urea	0.03	2
Uric Acid	0.005	0.05
Ammonium	0.0001	0.04
Water	90–93	95

KIDNEY STONES

Sometimes, minerals from urine solidify and block the tubes inside the kidneys, forming kidney stones. Some are smooth, like pebbles, while others, called stag-horn stones, are spiked. Passing a small stone causes intense pain. Larger stones can be broken up by ultrasound waves, or removed by surgery.

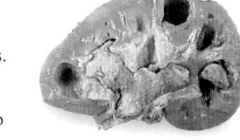

Dissected kidney with stones

1 KIDNEYS
Blood enters the kidneys and flows into the nephrons. Each nephron contains a filtering unit called a glomerulus. Water and salts pass from the blood into collecting tubules.

Suprarenal gland

Kidney

Renal artery

Renal vein

Pelvis

Testicular artery

Testicular vein

Fat

Medulla: light inner core

Cortex: dark outer region

2 URETER
The filtrate of water and salts, called urine, produced in the nephrons, leaves the kidney via a tube called the ureter.

3 BLADDER
Day and night urine trickles down the two ureters into a stretchable, muscular bag called the bladder. The adult bladder can store well over half a litre (19fl oz) of urine, until it can be released from the body at a suitable time. Urine leaves through the urethral opening in the base.

Vas deferens: carries sperm from testes.

Ureter

Inner bladder

Muscle layer

Pubic bone

Seminal vesicle

Prostate

Ampulla

Fatty pad

Ischium of pelvis

Vas deferens

Bulb of penis

Urethra

4 URETHRA
Urine leaves the body through a tube called the urethra. The male urethra is about 20cm (8in) long and stretches to the tip of the penis. The female urethra is much shorter: about 4cm (1.4in) long.

PROSTATE GLAND

This gland, found only in males, surrounds the part of the urethra nearest the bladder. It secretes a milky fluid into the urethra, which forms about 30% of the seminal fluid in which sperm are ejaculated. After the age of about 50, this gland naturally enlarges. However, sometimes it may squash the urethra and make urination difficult. Treatment usually involves removal of all or part of the gland.

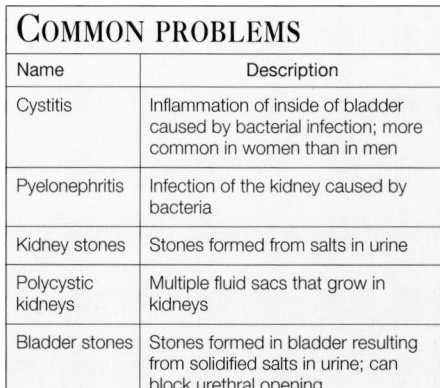

X-ray showing enlarged prostate gland

WASTE NOT

Our word "lotion" comes from the Latin word for urine, *lotium*. Romans used stale urine as a hair lotion because it prevented dandruff and killed lice. It was also used to help dye clothes.

KIDNEY DIALYSIS AND TRANSPLANT

If the kidneys fail completely, a dialysis machine can be used to filter blood. Blood passes through the machine 20 times before it is properly cleansed, and the patient must have two to three of these filtering sessions every week. More often, kidney failure is treated by transplanting a healthy organ. Drugs then prevent the body from rejecting the new kidney. Kidneys are the most commonly transplanted organ.

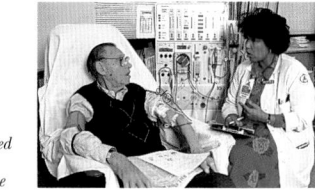

Patient connected to a kidney dialysis machine

COMMON PROBLEMS

Name	Description
Cystitis	Inflammation of inside of bladder caused by bacterial infection; more common in women than in men
Pyelonephritis	Infection of the kidney caused by bacteria
Kidney stones	Stones formed from salts in urine
Polycystic kidneys	Multiple fluid sacs that grow in kidneys
Bladder stones	Stones formed in bladder resulting from solidified salts in urine; can block urethral opening

ENDOCRINE SYSTEM

ENDOCRINE GLANDS produce chemicals that the body needs in order to grow properly and work smoothly. The chemicals that these glands (e.g. pituitary, thyroid gland) produce are called hormones and are released directly into the bloodstream. Tiny amounts can have great effects on the body's systems.

MAJOR ENDOCRINE GLANDS

Endocrine glands have no ducts or openings, but the hormones they produce enter the bloodstream as it passes through the gland. Hormones released by endocrine glands tend to have slow-acting, profound effects.

THE PITUITARY GLAND

The pituitary gland, situated in the brain, is often called the master gland; it secretes more than 10 hormones that act on other glands (e.g. thyroid, adrenals, ovaries, testes, mammary glands) to help them produce hormones of their own. Some of the functions of the pituitary gland are controlled by an area of the brain that lies just above it, called the hypothalamus. It also produces ADH (anti-diuretic hormone), which controls the level of water in the body.

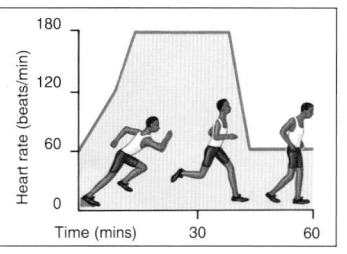

Micrograph showing cross-section of pituitary gland

The liver controls the duration of some hormones' action. When hormones pass through the liver, they are made inactive and pass, via the kidneys, into urine. (So, doctors test for pregnancy by analysing urine for hormone changes.)

Pituitary gland
Thyroid gland
Parathyroid glands
Adrenal gland
Pancreas
Ovaries

In women, the ovaries produce oestrogen and progesterone, which control the development of sexual characteristics at puberty, such as breast growth and pubic hair, and aspects of menstruation.

Testis

In men, the testes produce testosterone, a hormone that controls the development of sexual characteristics at puberty, such as pubic and body hair, and voice pitch.

FIGHT AND FLIGHT

In situations of fear, anger, or shock, adrenal glands produce adrenalin, which mobilizes the body in preparation for strong physical exertion. Levels return to normal after exercise.

Heart rate (beats/min)
180
120
60
0
Time (mins)   30   60

HORMONE IMBALANCE

One of the hormones produced by the pituitary controls our rate of growth. Too much can cause gigantism (excessive growth). Too little causes short stature.

Tallest person: 2.7m (8ft 11in) tall

Smallest person: 61cm (24 in) tall

NERVOUS ENERGY

When Mrs. Maxwell Rogers of Florida, US, found her son pinned underneath their car, fear and adrenalin gave her the strength to lift the 1.6 tonne vehicle. She cracked several vertebrae.

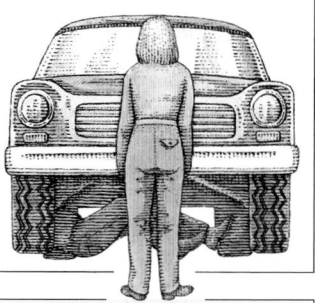

ENDOCRINE GLANDS AND THEIR HORMONES

Gland	Hormones produced	Function	Effect of deficiency	Effect of excess
Thyroid	Thyroxine, triiodothyronine	Regulate chemical activity in cells. Essential for normal physical growth and mental development in children	In children, retards growth and mental development (cretinism)	Thyrotoxicosis: over-activity, anxiety, weight loss, diarrhoea, rapid pulse
Pituitary	Growth hormone TSH Prolactin ACTH LH and FSH MSH ADH Oxytocin	Stimulates cell growth in bone, cartilage, and soft tissue Stimulates thyroid gland to secrete hormones Stimulates breast growth and milk production Stimulates adrenal glands to secrete hormones Controls functioning of sexual organs Controls skin darkening Acts on kidneys to decrease water loss Stimulates uterus contraction during birth	Short stature Slow metabolism, bloating Reduced sex drive Can cause infertility Increases water loss Prolonged labour	Gigantism Overproduction of eggs Causes fluid retention, bloating
Parathyroid	Parathyroid hormone (PTH)	Regulates blood calcium levels; important for nerves and muscle functioning	Tetany: spasm and twitching of the muscles	May cause thinning of bones (osteoporosis), or kidney stones
Adrenal	Adrenalin Cortisone Aldosterone	Mobilizes body in response to fear, anger, shock Controls metabolism, body shape Controls level of salts in body	Addison's disease: salt imbalance, low blood pressure, weakness, weight loss, intestinal upsets	Cushing's disease: obesity, moon face, high blood pressure, high blood sugar levels, hairiness
Pancreas	Insulin Glucagon	Control level of sugar in blood	Diabetes: excess sugar in blood	Rare: Coma due to reduced sugar in blood
Kidneys	Erythropoietin 1,25 dihydroxychole-calciferol Renin	Acts on bone marrow to produce red blood cells Raises amount of calcium absorbed in gut, formed from Vitamin D Helps control blood pressure	Anaemia Rickets, osteomalacia	High blood pressure
Ovaries	Oestrogen Progesterone	Stimulates breast growth and egg production, pubic and body hair, changes distribution of body fat at puberty. Thickens uterus walls after ovulation	Infertility	Levels naturally high during pregnancy: at other times, can cause blood clots
Testes	Testosterone	Stimulates sperm production, muscle and bone enlargement, deepening of voice, pubic and body hair. Small amounts present in females	In males, low sperm count and sex drive. Hair thinning	Excessive muscular development and body hair. In males, can cause painful, persistent erection (priapism)

REPRODUCTION AND GROWTH

PLANTS AND ANIMALS produce young like themselves. This creation of life is called reproduction. Humans reproduce sexually: male and female mate to produce their young. A new human life begins when a sperm cell from the father joins an egg cell from the mother. This cell divides into many cells, until it begins to look like a baby.

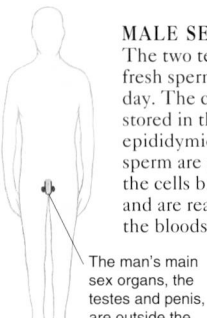

MALE SEX ORGANS
The two testes produce fresh sperm cells every day. The cells are stored in the testes and epididymides. If the sperm are not released, the cells break down and are reabsorbed into the bloodstream.

The man's main sex organs, the testes and penis, are outside the abdomen.

REPRODUCTION FACTS

● The sperm cell is about 0.05mm (0.002in) long and can be seen only with a microscope. It can swim at about 18cm (7in) per hour and takes on average two hours to reach the egg.

● The testes are kept outside the body in the scrotum, as they need to be 4°C (7°F) cooler than body temperature. If they heat up, sperm production slows down and infertility may result.

● The biggest human cell is the egg cell; it measures 0.1–0.2mm (0.004–0.008in) in diameter and is just visible to the naked eye.

Types of contraceptive

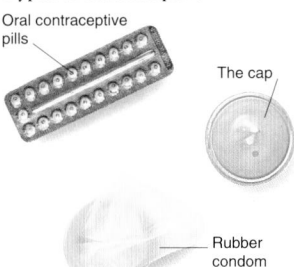

Oral contraceptive pills

The cap

Rubber condom

CONTRACEPTION
Contraceptives are used to prevent conception (pregnancy). A rubber sheath, or condom, fits over the penis to catch semen. Hormones in the oral contraceptive pill prevent eggs from being released. The cap is placed over the cervix to stop sperm from entering the uterus.

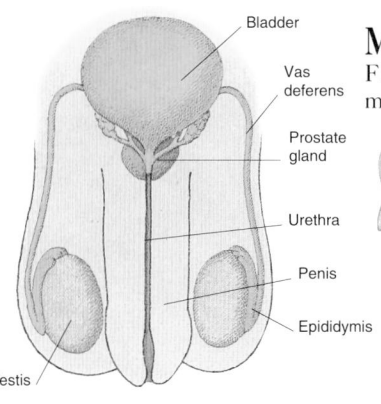

Bladder

Vas deferens

Prostate gland

Urethra

Penis

Epididymis

Testis

SEXUAL INTERCOURSE
For the egg to be fertilized by sperm, a man and woman must have sexual intercourse. The man's penis becomes erect and enters the woman's vagina. When the man climaxes, he ejaculates a fluid, semen, which contains sperm cells. The cells swim into the fallopian tube. One of these cells may reach the egg and fertilize it.

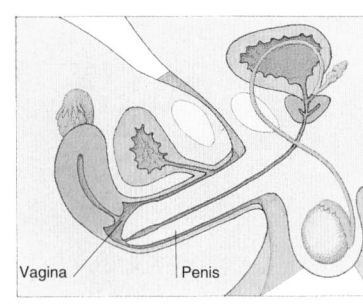

Vagina

Penis

SPERM RACE
More than 300 million sperm are ejaculated into the vagina; 50–150 sperm reach the egg in the fallopian tube, but only one may fertilize the egg.

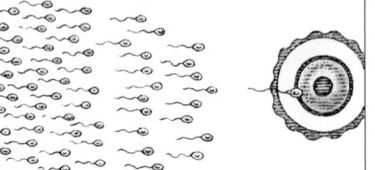

REPRODUCTION SYSTEMS

FEMALE SEX ORGANS
Eggs are stored in both ovaries. Each month, during the menstrual cycle, one egg ripens, leaves the ovary, and enters the fallopian tube. If it is then fertilized by sperm, it becomes implanted in the uterus. If it is not fertilized, it breaks up and is shed from the body (menstruation).

The woman's main sex organs, the two ovaries, are inside the abdomen.

Fallopian tube

Eggs stored in the ovary

Uterus (womb)

Ovary

The neck of the womb (cervix) opens into the vagina.

Vagina

MENSTRUAL CYCLE
From puberty (10 to 16 years of age) a woman has monthly menstrual cycles (menstruation), during which she loses blood.

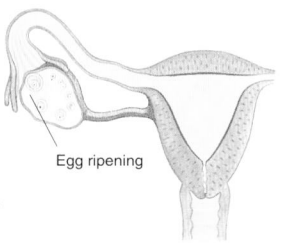

Egg ripening

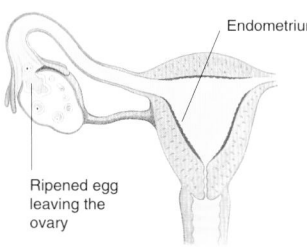

Endometrium

Ripened egg leaving the ovary

1 An egg starts to ripen in one of the ovaries. The lining of the uterus, called the endometrium, swells with blood in preparation for the egg.

2 About two weeks later, the ripe egg enters the fallopian tube. It is now ready to be fertilized.

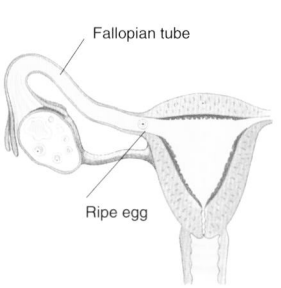

Fallopian tube

Ripe egg

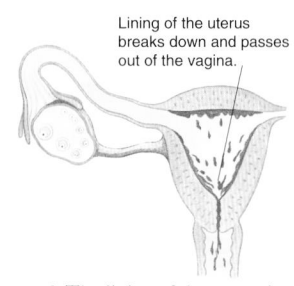

Lining of the uterus breaks down and passes out of the vagina.

3 The egg reaches the uterus. If the egg is not fertilized, it begins to break up.

4 The lining of the uterus breaks down and passes, along with the unfertilized egg, out of the vagina as menstrual blood flow.

FERTILIZATION
After sexual intercourse, sperm cells enter the uterus and travel along the fallopian tube. Only one sperm cell may break through the outer layer of the egg cell. Once the egg is fertilized, it divides into two cells, then into four, and so on.

Tadpole-shaped sperm cells are propelled by their tails.

Only one sperm cell can penetrate the outer layer of the egg.

Egg cell

IMPLANTATION
Once an egg has been fertilized, it divides into a ball of cells, called the morula, as it travels down the fallopian tube. After five days, the cells form a hollow ball, or blastocyst. About a week after fertilization, the blastocyst becomes implanted in the rich lining of the uterus.

Egg divides into two cells within 36 hours.

The egg subdivides further to form a ball of cells, called the morula.

The cells form a ball of cells, or blastocyst.

Uterus

STAGES OF GROWTH

FOUR-WEEK EMBRYO
The blastocyst quickly develops to form the placenta, umbilical cord, and the developing baby, or embryo. The embryo is protected by amniotic fluid. About now, its heart begins to beat.

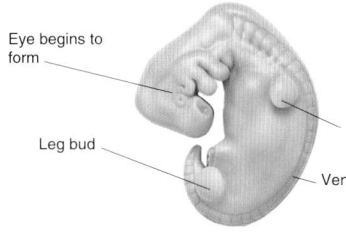

Eye begins to form

Leg bud

Arm bud

Vertebra, or backbone

EIGHT-WEEK FOETUS
The embryo is 2.5cm (1in) long and is now called a foetus. All the internal organs have developed.

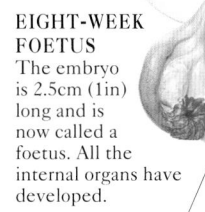

Wall of uterus

Fallopian tube

Placenta

TWELVE WEEKS
All the foetus' organs are fully formed. From this stage on, the foetus develops quickly.

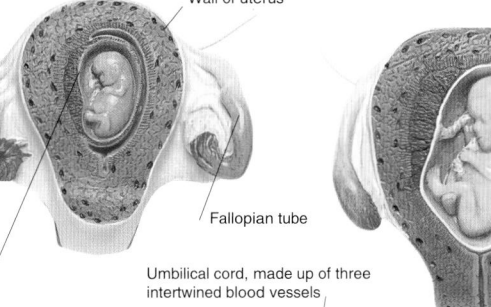

Umbilical cord, made up of three intertwined blood vessels

BABY IN WOMB
The baby receives food and oxygen from the mother's bloodstream via the placenta, a disc-shaped organ that is attached to the baby by the umbilical cord. The baby's waste products pass back into the mother's bloodstream for excretion. The baby is surrounded by amniotic fluid, which cushions it from knocks and bumps.

Psoas muscle

Chorion membrane

Amnion membrane, containing amniotic fluid

TWENTY-WEEK FOETUS
During the last six months of growth the baby develops fine details like fingernails and hair. From 16 to 20 weeks, it starts to move and kick. This is called quickening. The baby can now hear, tell light from dark, and can swallow and suck its thumb.

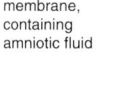

During the last few weeks of pregnancy, the baby turns round so its head is facing downwards, ready to be born.

Vagina

Placenta

CHILD DEVELOPMENT

SIX-MONTH BABY
Most babies sit propped up and can support the weight of their head. They will start to make word sounds such as "Da-Da" or "Ma-Ma". The first teeth start to show.

NINE- TO TWELVE-MONTH BABY
Most babies learn to crawl, can pull themselves upright on furniture, and stand unsupported for a second or two. By 12 months, they may have up to eight teeth and weigh three times their birth-weight.

EIGHTEEN-MONTH CHILD
Most children can walk unaided. They will know at least six words, usually many more, and can put words together to make simple phrases. They can climb stairs and make towers of bricks.

TWO- TO THREE-YEAR-OLD CHILD
Children can hold a pencil and draw. Aged three, they can talk in simple sentences and copy basic shapes.

PUBERTY FACTS
• When children reach puberty, they undergo physical and psychological changes that prepare them for sexual maturity.

• A girl's ovaries produce the hormones progesterone and oestrogen. These cause breasts to develop, hips to broaden, and pubic hair to grow. At this time menstruation begins.

• A boy's testes produce the hormone testosterone. This causes muscles to develop, hair to grow on the face and body, the voice to deepen, and sperm to be produced.

GENETICS
Egg and sperm cells each contain 23 chromosomes. When an egg and a sperm cell join, the new cell has 46 chromosomes – the same as all other types of cell in the human body. A baby's sex is determined by one chromosome, X or Y. The egg carries only X, but the sperm can carry either X or Y. If the egg is fertilized by a sperm carrying an X, the sex will be female (XX), if the sperm carries a Y, the sex will be male (XY).

Father (XY)

Mother (XX)

Girl (XX)   Boy (XY)   Girl (XX)   Boy (XY)

NEW-BORN BABY
After about 40 weeks, or 9 months, of development, the baby is ready to be born. The muscles of the uterus contract and the cervix dilates, pushing the baby out, usually head first. The baby soon takes its first breath of fresh air. The new-born baby can hear well but cannot focus its eyes properly.

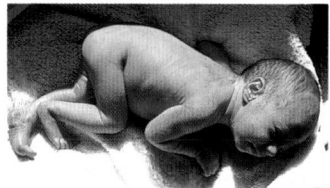

New-born baby

GROWTH FACTS
• The proportions of our bodies change as we grow. A baby's head accounts for about one quarter of its body length. By adulthood, the proportion has reduced to one eighth.

• Girls grow faster than boys during the early stages of growth. A girl is about three-quarters of her adult height by the age of 7½; a boy reaches this height by the age of 9.

• A person is about 1cm (0.4in) taller in the morning than in the evening. This is because the pads of cartilage in the spine become more compressed during the day.

COMMON PROBLEMS

Ectopic pregnancy	Foetus implanted outside the womb.
Infertility	Inability to conceive a child.
Miscarriage	Premature ending of pregnancy on or before 24 weeks.
Pre-eclampsia	High blood pressure developed during pregnancy.

MEDICINE

THROUGHOUT THE AGES, people have tried to find ways to cure illness. In early times, people believed that disease was a punishment from the gods. Today, scientists are constantly searching for new ways of treating and preventing illness.

c.10,000 B.C. Trepanning is practised in Europe and America. Holes are drilled into a person's skull to cure illness. People believed that evil spirits left through these holes.

Trepanning

2700 B.C. First named doctor is Imhotep of Egypt. He acquired a great reputation for healing. He later became known as the Egyptian god of medicine.

Imhotep

10,000 B.C.	10,000 B.C.	3000 B.C.	2700 B.C.

---

c.A.D. 130 Galen, a Greek physician, introduces the idea that a person's mood depends on the balancing of four fluids, or humours, in the body: black bile (melancholy), yellow bile (choleric), blood (sanguine), and phlegm (phlegmatic).

The four humours: choleric (with lion), sanguine (with ape), phlegmatic (with sheep), and melancholic (with hog).

1300s Leeches are used to suck blood from the body, as it was believed that too much blood was the cause of some illnesses. Blood-letting is used to treat a variety of illnesses, such as tumours, fevers, and gout.

Leech

1543 First accurate anatomical drawings of the human body are drawn by Flemish doctor, Andreas Vesalius (1514–64). Stolen corpses are used for his studies.

First anatomical drawings

c.1590 Compound microscope invented. Dutchman, Zacharias Janssen (1580–c.1638) makes lenses held in two iron tubes, one inside the other.

Early microscope

A.D. 100	A.D. 130	1300	1300	1500	1543	1590

1683 Bacteria first seen under a microscope by Antonie van Leeuwenhoek (1632–1723), a Dutch scientist.

Antonie van Leeuwenhoek

1796 Vaccination against smallpox is discovered by English doctor, Edward Jenner (1749–1823). He innoculates an eight-year-old boy with cowpox taken from a sore on the hand of a dairymaid.

Medal issued c.1800 to celebrate Edward Jenner's discovery of vaccination.

1800 Effects of electricity on muscles described by Italian physicist, Volta (1745–1827).

1805 Morphine, a painkiller, is separated from opium.

1810 Homeopathy is introduced by German physician, Samuel Hahnemann (1755–1843). This new system is based on the principle of curing like with like.

Samuel Hahnemann

1680	1683	1796	1800	1800	1805	1810

1854 Florence Nightingale (1820–1910), born in Florence, Italy, nurses soldiers during the Crimean War (1854–56) in the hospital at Scutari, Turkey. She becomes known as "the lady with the lamp". Four years later, she opens the Nightingale Training School for nurses in London, which greatly improves nursing standards.

Florence Nightingale

1860 Antiseptic, in the form of weak carbolic acid, is used to prevent infections during operations by English surgeon, Joseph Lister (1827–1912).

Joseph Lister

1864 Red Cross Society founded in Geneva, Switzerland, by Swiss businessman, Henri Dunant (1829–1910), after helping casualties at the Battle of Solferino (1859).

Henri Dunant

1850	1854	1860	1860	1864

1895 X-rays discovered by German physicist, Wilhelm Roentgen (1845–1923). He uses his wife's hand for the first pictures.

One of the first X-rays

1895 Psychoanalysis founded by Austrian doctor, Sigmund Freud (1856–1939). He treats people with mental disorders by talking to them about their dreams and childhood experiences.

Sigmund Freud

1902 Radium and polonium discovered by Polish-born Marie Curie (1867–1934) and her husband, Pierre Curie (1859–1906), of France. These elements are now used in radiotherapy to treat cancer.

Marie and Pierre Curie

1910 Four blood groups, A, B, AB, O, discovered by Austrian pathologist, Dr. Karl Landsteiner (1868–1943).

1912 Vitamins discovered by British biochemist, Sir Frederick Gowland Hopkins (1861–1947).

1920 First EI machine is developed to r electrical brain waves.

1921 First bir control clinic founded by Ma Stopes (1880– in London.

1890	1895	1900	1902	1910	1912	1920	1921

1952 Vaccine against polio produced by American scientist, Jonas Salk (1914–1995).

Jonas Salk

1953 Structure of genetic material (DNA) discovered by American biologist, James Watson (born 1928) and English biochemist, Francis Crick (born 1916).

Watson and Crick

1954 Heart–lung machine developed for use during heart surgery.

1954 First internal heart pacemaker fitted in Stockholm, Sweden.

1958 Endoscope, a telescope that looks inside the body, developed.

1967 First heart transplant, performed by South African surgeon, Christiaan Barnard (born 1922). The patient survives 18 days.

1970 Heart pacemakers in general use.

Christiaan Barnard

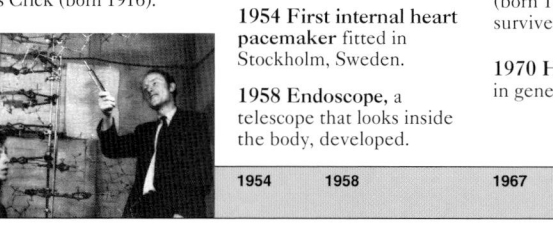

1952	1952	1953	1954	1958	1967	1970	1970

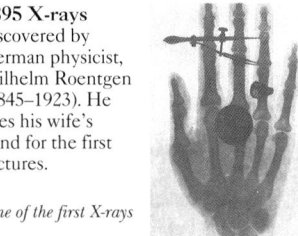

B.C. *The Canons of
cine* is written in China.
ludes an account of blood
ation.

B.C. **Surgery** practised
ia. Surgeons perform
ations, skin grafts, and
ve cataracts from eyes.

400 B.C. Greek physician, Hippocrates (c.460–377 B.C.) teaches that the first duty of a doctor is to do what is best for his patients, and makes rules for his pupils to follow. They form the basis of the Hippocratic Oath, which doctors still follow today.

Hippocrates

2 B.C. Acupuncture, puncturing the skin with needles to cure illness, is practised in China.

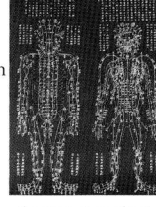

Acupuncture chart

B.C.	1000 B.C.	400 B.C.	2 B.C.

Quinine is used to
nalaria in South
ca.

First thermometer
king human
erature invented by
physician, Sanctorius
–1636).

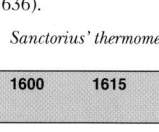

Sanctorius' thermometer

1628 First description of the circulation of the blood by Englishman William Harvey (1578–1657), physician to King James I and King Charles I of England.

William Harvey with Charles I

1600	1615	1628

First stethoscope
from a roll of paper
ench doctor, René
nec (1781–1826).

Laughing gas
us oxide) is first used
eneral anaesthetic by
e Wells (1815–48).

René Laënnec

1846 Ether used as an anaesthetic by William Morton (1819–68), an American dentist.

1847 Chloroform is used as an anaesthetic by Sir James Young Simpson (1811–70).

1849 First female medical graduate in the USA is Elizabeth Blackwell (1821–1910).

Elizabeth Blackwell

1844	1846	1847	1849

Elizabeth
ett Anderson is
oman to practise
ine in Britain.

urization invented
enchman, Louis
r (1822–95) to
eat food and kill
ia.

Louis Pasteur

1883 Bacteria that cause tuberculosis and cholera discovered by German scientist, Robert Koch (1843–1910).

1883 Cocaine used as a local anaesthetic during an eye operation.

1886 Surgical instruments are sterilized by steam. Masks, gowns, and capes are used by surgeons in operations.

Operation, 1880s

1880	1883	1886

First injection of insulin given,
year-old boy.

enicillin
red by Scottish
ologist, Sir
der Fleming
955), in a green
growing on a plate.

Alexander Fleming

1928 The Iron Lung is developed in Boston, Massachusetts, USA. It saves the life of a paralysed boy in 1932.

1950 First kidney transplant performed in Chicago, USA.

1950s Birth control pill developed for women. By the early 1960s it is widely used.

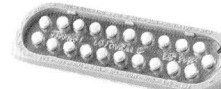

Birth control pill

1928	1950	1950

CT (computerized
raphy) scan** introduced.
es more detailed picture of
organs than an X-ray.

magnetic resonance
g) scan** uses radio waves
uce pictures of the
of the body.

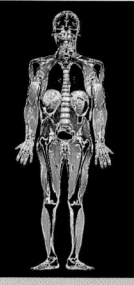

MRI scan

1976 Transistorized bionic, arm is fitted to the victim of a road accident in Australia.

1978 First test-tube baby, Louise Brown, is born in Britain.

1980s–1990s Laser surgery used in eye operations and to remove cancer cells.
Keyhole surgery is practised: operations are performed through small incisions in the body.
Gene transplants performed: defective or missing genes are replaced with artificial copies.

1976	1978	1980	1990

BRANCHES OF MEDICINE

Name	What it deals with
Cardiology	Heart and arteries
Chiropody	Feet
Dermatology	Skin
Endocrinology	Hormones
Gastroenterology	Stomach, intestines
Geriatrics	Elderly people
Gynaecology	Female reproductive organs
Haematology	Blood
Neurology	Brain and nerves
Obstetrics	Pregnancy
Oncology	Growths and tumours
Ophthalmology	Eyes
Orthopaedics	Bones, joints, muscles
Osteopathy	Manipulation of back and limbs to ease pain
Paediatrics	Children
Pathology	Body tissues and fluids
Pharmacology	Drugs
Physiotherapy	Exercise and massage of the body
Psychiatry	Mental illness
Radiology	X-rays for diagnosis
Radiotherapy	Use of X-rays to kill unwanted cells
Renal medicine	Kidneys

DRUG TYPES

Name	Use
Analgesic	Provides relief from pain, such as headache and stomach-ache.
Antacid	Counteracts acid in the stomach to relieve heartburn, indigestion, etc.
Antibiotic	Treats infections by killing bacteria in the body.
Antihistamine	Counteracts allergies such as hay fever.
Antipyretic	Reduces fevers, such as influenza.
Bronchodilator	Eases breathing in diseases such as asthma.
Decongestant	Common cold treatment; works by unblocking nasal passages.

RETURN OF THE LEECH

Leeches are being used again in modern medicine. After certain operations, they are used to restore blood circulation and to prevent the blood from clotting.

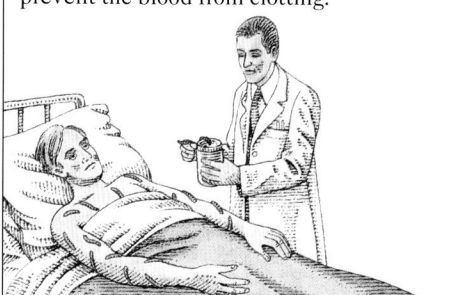

NUTRITION

A GOOD DIET is an essential part of a healthy lifestyle for children and adults. Rich in vitamins, minerals, and other nutrients, a balanced diet will assist growth and help fight against disease.

VITAL COMPONENTS OF FOOD

Nutrients are the essential elements for healthy eating and include:

Vitamins
These aid the release of energy from glucose, and assist the body's growth and repair.

Minerals
These help growth and repair processes, the release of energy from nutrients, and help form new tissues.

Fibre
The indigestible part of fruit, vegetables, bread, and cereals, fibre aids normal bowel function.

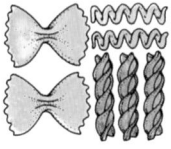

Carbohydrates
These are compounds of carbon, hydrogen, and oxygen, such as starch and sugar, that provide the body with energy.

Fats
These supply concentrated energy. They also help form chemical "messengers", such as hormones.

Protein
This is a substance the body needs for growth and repair. It is found in foods such as meat, fish, cheese, and beans.

A BALANCED DIET

The food pyramid was developed by American nutritionists at the beginning of the 1990s. It represents the proportions in which the five food groups should be eaten each day for a balanced diet.

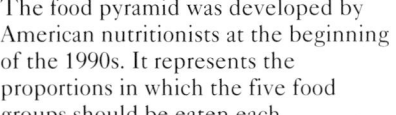
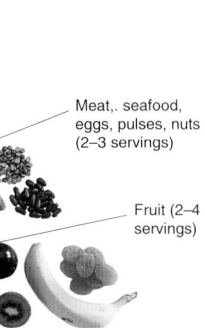
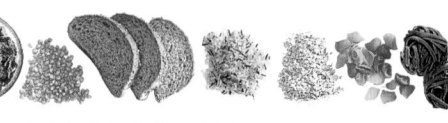

Sugars, fats, and oils (use sparingly)

Meat,. seafood, eggs, pulses, nuts (2–3 servings)

Dairy products (2–3 servings)

Vegetables (3–5 servings)

Fruit (2–4 servings)

Carbohydrates (6-11 servings)

FOOD FACTS

• Surprisingly, frozen vegetables are just as good for you as fresh vegetables.
• In India, many people are vegetarian, following the Hindu belief that all life is sacred.
• All vegetables contain some protein, but dried peas and beans have large amounts.

FOOD WORDS

Acid A substance produced by the stomach that helps digest food.
Antibodies Proteins in the blood that protect the body by fighting bacteria and viruses.
Antioxidant A substance added to foods to prevent them from oxidizing and so going stale.
Carnivore Person who eats meat.
Cholesterol A chemical found in certain foods, such as eggs, and produced in the liver from saturated fats.
Digestion The breaking down of food in the stomach so that nutrients may be absorbed into the body.
Glucose A sugar, released from the digestion of starch and sucrose, that is the body's main energy source.
Hormone Chemical "messenger" that moves in the bloodstream and controls the functions of the body.
Kilocalorie A unit used to measure the energy content of foods.
Kilojoule A unit of measurement showing energy content in food. One kilojoule equals 1,000 joules.
Metabolism The chemical processes occurring in the body that result in growth, production of energy, and elimination of waste.
Nutrient The essential dietary factors – carbohydrates, fats, proteins, vitamins, and minerals.
Saturated fat Fat that tends to increase the amount of unwanted cholesterol in the blood. Mostly found in animal fats.
Starch A polymer found in plants that is an important part of the human diet.
Unsaturated fat Fat that helps decrease unwanted types of cholesterol in the blood. Most vegetable fats are unsaturated.
Vegan Person who does not eat or use any products or byproducts from animals.
Vegetarian Person who does not eat animal products, sometimes with the exception of fish and eggs.

MAIN VITAMIN SOURCES AND REQUIREMENTS

Type of vitamin	Where found	Required for
Vitamin A	Liver, fish-liver oils, egg yolk, and yellow-orange coloured fruit and vegetables	Growth, healthy eyes and skin. Fights infection.
Vitamin B$_1$ (Thiamine)	Whole grains (wholemeal bread and pasta), brown rice, liver, beans, peas, and eggs	Healthy functioning of nervous and digestive systems.
Vitamin B$_2$ (Riboflavin)	Milk, liver, cheese, eggs, green vegetables, brewer's yeast, whole grains, and wheatgerm	Metabolism of protein, fat, and carbohydrates. Keeps tissues healthy.
Vitamin B$_3$ (Niacin)	Liver, lean meats, poultry, fish, nuts, and dried beans	Production of energy and a healthy skin.
Vitamin B$_6$ (Pyridoxine)	Liver, poultry, pork, fish, bananas, potatoes, dried beans, and most fruit and vegetables	Metabolism of protein and production of red blood cells.
Vitamin C	Citrus fruit, strawberries, and potatoes	Healthy skin, teeth, bones, and tissues, and for fighting disease.
Vitamin D	Oily fish (such as salmon), liver, eggs, cod-liver oil, and some cereals	The absorption of calcium and phosphate.
Vitamin E	Margarine, whole grain cereals, and nuts	The formation of new red blood cells. Protection of cell linings in the lungs.

BURNING KILOJOULES

The energy from food is measured in kilojoules (kJ). One kilocalorie (kcal) is equivalent to 4.2 kilojoules, and if your kilojoule intake exceeds your energy and body maintenance requirements, you will put on weight. Various physical activities (see right) help you avoid putting on weight by burning off kilojoules.

Judo
Male: 3,420kJ per hour
Female: 2,950kJ per hour

Running
Male: 3,400kJ per hour
Female: 2,900 kJ per hour

Basketball
Male: 2,430kJ per hour
Female: 2,080kJ per hour

ALTERNATIVE MEDICINE

MORE AND MORE people are now turning to traditional, or alternative, forms of medicine to improve their health or simply to stay well. Many of these therapies treat the whole person, and aim to restore the body's natural state of balance, or harmony.

This detail from the 12th-century Persian Book of Antidotes shows the growing of plants for medicinal purposes.

EARLY HEALING

For thousands of years, people have used plants and minerals to ease pain, heal wounds, and relieve the symptoms of illness. In ancient Egypt, records from about 1600 B.C. list plant remedies, such as gentian, senna, and thyme, that are still used today. Archaeologists have also found in China lists of herbs carved on oracle bones dated about the same time.

ACUPUNCTURE

Acupuncturists treat illness by inserting needles into the skin at particular points. These points lie along invisible energy channels, known as meridians, that are linked to internal organs. The needles unblock, increase, or decrease the flow of energy (called Qi) to restore balance and health.

The acupuncture points on each meridian are numbered.

ALEXANDER TECHNIQUE

This therapy aims to treat and prevent a range of disorders by improving posture. Australian actor, F. Matthias Alexander (1869–1955) developed the technique when he found that bad posture had caused him to lose his voice.

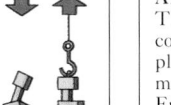

A correct posture, far right, based on the Alexander technique.

AROMATHERAPY

This form of treatment uses highly concentrated oils extracted from plants. The oils can be used in massage, added to baths, or inhaled. French chemist, Réné Gattefossé (1881-1950), who treated soldiers in the First World War, was a pioneer of modern aromatherapy.

Rose oil has a soothing effect.

AYURVEDA

The oldest system of Indian medicine is Ayurveda, from the Sanskrit word meaning "the science of life". Remedies, mainly plants, are chosen for their ability to harmonize the balance between a patient and the basic influences of life, such as diet, work, or home life.

Om – the symbol for the life force in Ayurvedic medicine.

CHINESE HERBALISM

This natural method of treatment is based on restoring the balance of Yin (female) and Yang (male) in the body's energy channels. Combinations of herbs are selected and supplied in the form of tea, powder, pills, or pastes.

In Chinese medicine, the five elements of wood, fire, earth, metal, and water are used in diagnosis.

CHIROPRACTIC

Chiropractic relieves pain by manipulating the joints, especially those of the spine. It can be used to correct disorders of the joints, muscles, and spine. American David Daniel Palmer (1845–1913) is considered the founder of modern chiropractic.

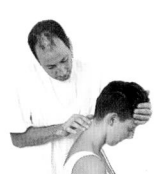

A chiropractor checks the spine.

HOMEOPATHY

Homeopathy uses a minute dose of a substance that, in large amounts, produces the same symptoms from which the patient is suffering. The aim is to stimulate the body's defences so they fight the disease. Its founder was German physician Samuel Hahnemann (1755–1843).

Samuel Hahnemann

HYDROTHERAPY

Water, in the form of hot and cold baths or sprays, is used in hydrotherapy to stimulate the body's power to heal itself. The first hydrotherapy centre in Britain was founded by a Dominican monk, Sebastian Kneipp (1821–97).

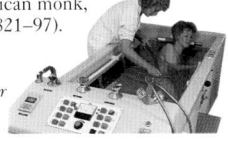

Hot and cold water sprays stimulate circulation.

OSTEOPATHY

When the body's framework is out of alignment, osteopaths can diagnose and treat disorders. They use their hands to massage and manipulate the joints to restore normal movement. Osteopathy was founded by American doctor Andrew Taylor Still (1828–1917).

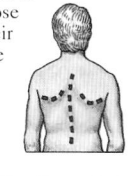

Shoulders and spine out of alignment

REFLEXOLOGY

In this form of therapy, areas on the feet, known as reflex areas, relate to certain parts of the body. By skillful massage of the relevant area, blockages in the energy channels are released allowing the affected part of the body to heal. The practice was developed in the United States by Eunice Ingham (1889–1974).

Reflex areas

SHIATSU

Shiatsu is a Japanese word meaning "finger pressure". The therapist uses pressure on hundreds of surface points along the body's meridians to rebalance the quality and quantity of energy. The system was popularized by Tokujiro Namikoshi (1905–94).

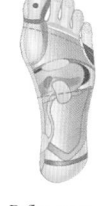

The yin-yang symbol represents harmony or balance in the body.

YOGA

This well-known Hindu system combines physical, mental, and spiritual health. The most common form is Hatha yoga, a course of exercises and postures designed to promote physical and mental well-being. Yoga has been practised in India for thousands of years.

The lotus position

Feverfew can help relieve migraines and arthritis.

Evening primrose is used for skin problems.

PLANTS IN MEDICINE

Wild flowers such as evening primrose (*Oenothera biennis*) and feverfew (*Tanacetum parthenium*) are among the most widely used medicinal herbs. Research has confirmed their power to heal.

MEDICINE FACTS

• Chinese medicine uses dried seahorse in preparations to treat kidney problems.

• In Ayurvedic medicine, the flesh from a pit viper is given to relieve muscular pain.

FIRST AID

FIRST AID IS the first assistance or treatment given to a person for any injury or sudden illness, before the arrival of an ambulance, doctor, or other qualified help. The main aim of first aid is to prevent the injury from becoming worse.

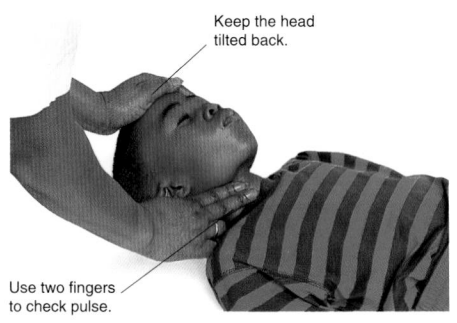

Keep the head tilted back.

Use two fingers to check pulse.

CHECK FOR A PULSE

If the heart is beating, there will be a pulse in the neck. Tilt the head back and feel for the Adam's apple with the pads of two fingers. Slide your fingers back into the gap between the windpipe and the muscle that runs beside it. Feel for ten seconds before deciding that the pulse is absent.

CALL AN AMBULANCE OR DOCTOR FOR:

• Unexplained drowsiness or loss of consciousness
• Severe bleeding
• Unexplained fits of any sort
• Difficulty in breathing
• Severe abdominal pain
• Sudden blurred vision or seeing coloured haloes around lights

FIRST-AID KIT

Every home and car should have a first-aid kit containing items needed for emergency treatment. Keep the box clean and clearly labelled, and out of reach of children. Replace items as soon as you use them.

LEARNING THE A, B, AND C

The A (Airway), B (Breathing), and C (Circulation) of any unconscious person must be established within three minutes in order to prevent permanent injury.

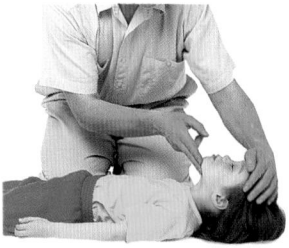

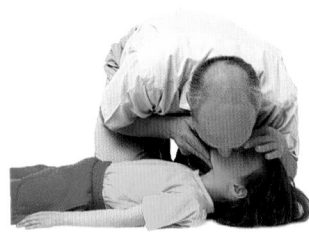

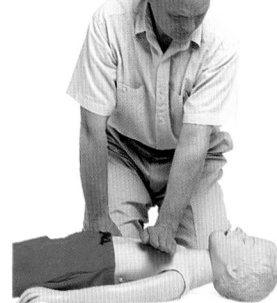

A IS FOR AIRWAY

Airway must be opened and kept open. Tilt the head of the injured person (casualty) back and lift the chin forward to open the airway.

B IS FOR BREATHING

Breathing must be established and maintained. If breathing has stopped, then start mouth-to-mouth ventilation by blowing your own expelled air into the casualty's lungs.

C IS FOR CIRCULATION

Circulation of blood must be maintained. Check the heart is beating by feeling for a pulse. If the heart has stopped "chest compressions" can be applied, together with artificial ventilation. In some countries the hand nearest the casualty's feet should be used for compressions.

RECOVERY POSITION

If an injured child is unconscious, but still breathing and has a pulse, place her or him in the recovery position.

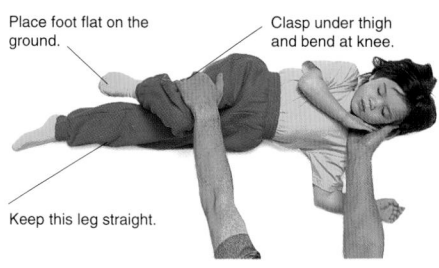

Place foot flat on the ground.

Clasp under thigh and bend at knee.

Keep this leg straight.

First, lie the child on her back and straighten her legs. Bend the arm nearest to you and lay it on the ground with the palm up. Bring the other arm across her chest and hold the palm of your hand against her cheek. Use your free hand to pull her knee up.

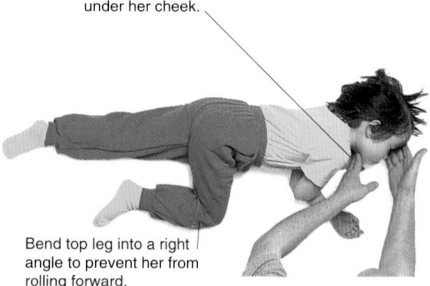

Adjust child's hand under her cheek.

Bend top leg into a right angle to prevent her from rolling forward.

Gently pull on the thigh of the bent leg, and roll the patient towards you and on to her side. Bend this same leg into a right angle to prevent her from rolling forward. Tilt her head back to make sure the airway is still open. Call an ambulance.

ADVICE NOTE

This page supplies some basic information on first aid. It does not offer complete procedures, and readers are advised to refer to a first-aid manual for full guidance.

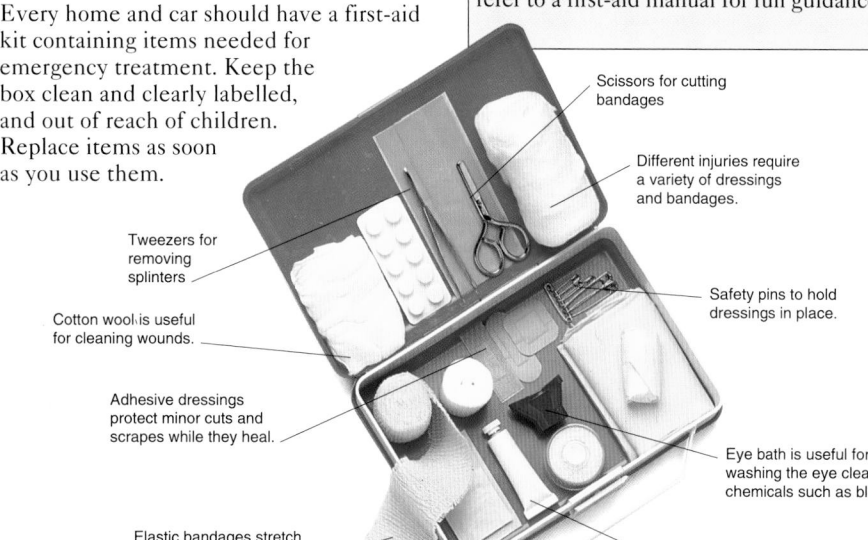

Scissors for cutting bandages

Different injuries require a variety of dressings and bandages.

Tweezers for removing splinters

Cotton wool is useful for cleaning wounds.

Adhesive dressings protect minor cuts and scrapes while they heal.

Safety pins to hold dressings in place.

Eye bath is useful for washing the eye clean of chemicals such as bleach.

Elastic bandages stretch to provide support for sprained ankles.

Antiseptic cream protects minor cuts against infection.

HOME SAFETY FACTS

Although most people think of home as the safest place, you are more likely to have an accident in the home than at work or school. To make the home a safer place:

• Do not use electrical equipment in the bathroom or near water.

• Keep saucepan handles turned inward so they do not hang over the work surface, and use the back rings of a hob first.

• Store dangerous items in a high cupboard, out of the reach of children.

• Do not put toxic substances in a familiar food or drink container.

• Run the cold water into the bath first, and keep testing the temperature as you add the hot water.

• Do not hold a hot drink when you have a baby on your lap.

• Do not put an iron on the floor to cool; put it out of reach.

BELIEFS, CUSTOMS, AND SOCIETY

Focusing on the way we live, this section provides detailed facts and figures on religion, politics, philosophy, and money around the world, as well as describing all kinds of strange customs and rituals.

Myths and Legends • Faith Systems • Other Faiths
Great Thinkers • Patterns of Family and Society • Customs and Rituals
Celebration and Decoration • Money • Politics • Law and Order

On pages 139 to 143, B.C.E. (Before the Common Era)
and C.E. (Common Era) stand for the same dates
as B.C. and A.D.

MYTHS AND LEGENDS

FROM ANCIENT TIMES people have invented stories to explain the world around them. Myths help explain events such as how the world was created and why people die, as well as natural phenomena such as the weather. Legends are closely related to myths but may be based on actual events.

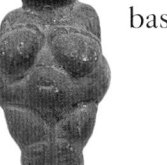

FIGURE OF VENUS
This clay figure from Austria shows the Venus of Willendorf, dated 25,000 B.C. Her full figure represents the fertility of the goddess.

AN AZTEC MYTH
Quetzalcoatl, the chief god of the Aztecs who lived in Central Mexico, took the form of a feathered serpent. He created humans and gave them knowledge, but then he sailed away on a raft of serpents. The Aztecs believed that, upon his return, their world would end.

This mask, representing the god Quetzalcoatl, is made of turquoise mosaic.

EARTH GODDESS
For thousands of years, people in different parts of the world worshipped images of the Earth Goddess, or Great Mother. As the "mother of the world," she was believed to give life to plants, animals, and humans. Because the power of fertility ensures the future of humanity, earth goddesses have always played an important role in mythology.

KING ARTHUR
A famous Arthurian legend tells how the magic sword Excalibur was given to King Arthur by the Lady of the Lake. Another version tells how he proved himself king by pulling the sword from a stone. It is thought that Arthur may have been a real king or chieftain in 5th-century Britain.

Arthur watches the sword Excalibur rise from the lake.

CREATION MYTHS
Stories that try to answer the mystery of how the world began are called creation myths.

IZANAGI AND IZANAMI
The Japanese thought the Earth was once a shapeless mass. A god and goddess, Izanagi and Izanami, stirred the mass with a long spear. Gradually the mixture thickened and dropped off the spear to form an island. The god and goddess married and had children who became the eight islands of Japan.

THE WORLD EGG
In Egyptian mythology, life began from water. The first dry land – a primeval mound – rose above the water. A large bird called the Great Cackler alighted on the land and laid the world egg, which brought the first life.

THE RAVEN
A Native American myth tells how a raven, flying over water, could find nowhere to land. He dropped pebbles to make islands and then created trees. Beasts lived in the forests and fish in the sea. When the raven had made the first man and woman out of wood and clay, the world was complete.

SACRED SITES

Mount Shasta, California, is a Native American site where the power of the Earth Spirit is strong.

Glastonbury Tor, England, is one of the reputed resting places of the Holy Grail, the cup Christ drank from at the Last Supper.

Uluru, Australia, is a special place to the Aboriginals. Paintings in rock shelters show the journeys of the ancestral beings who formed its features.

Uluru (Ayers Rock)

Cape Reinga, New Zealand, is where spirits of the dead depart for Hawaiki, far away in the mystical beginnings of Polynesia.

EGYPTIAN MYTHOLOGY
Gods in Egypt often had a human body and the head of an animal or bird to represent their power.

Name	Form
Ra (Amun-Ra)	Universal god, takes many forms
Anubis	Jackal or dog
Apis	Bull
Bastet	Cat
Hathor	Cow
Isis	Woman with a throne on her head
Khepri	Scarab
Mut	Vulture
Nut	Woman with long body, or cow
Osiris	Mummified man
Set, or Seth	Fantastic beast
Sobek	Crocodile
Tefnut	Lioness
Thoth	Ibis or baboon

MYTHICAL BEASTS
There are some frightening creatures in mythology that may have been created to represent evil. Some appear as half-human, half-animal; others take on shapes they can change at will.

DEMONS
Demons, or evil spirits, are often shown as grotesque beings who haunt cemeteries and force people to commit violent acts. They appear in various forms in the religions of the world, sometimes with cloven feet, horns, and a long tail.

MONSTERS
This figure shows a gorgon, a female monster from Greek mythology, who had snakes for hair. Medusa is the most famous of the three gorgons. After she was beheaded by the hero Perseus, her head had the power to turn anyone who looked at it into stone.

GREEK AND ROMAN MYTHOLOGY
The Greeks had 12 main gods and goddesses who cared for different aspects of their life. The Romans later adopted many Greek gods as their own, but with new names.

Greek	Roman	Role
Zeus	Jupiter	King of the gods, god of thunder
Hera	Juno	Queen of the gods, protector of women
Aphrodite	Venus	Goddess of beauty and love
Apollo	Apollo	Sun god, and god of prophecy
Ares	Mars	God of war
Artemis	Diana	Goddess of hunting, protector of animals and children
Athene	Minerva	Goddess of wisdom and war
Demeter	Ceres	Goddess of fertility, and of fruit and crops
Hephaestus	Vulcan	God of fire
Hermes	Mercury	Messenger god, god of travellers
Hestia	Vesta	Goddess of the hearth and home
Poseidon	Neptune	God of the sea

FAITH SYSTEMS

FAITH SYSTEMS ARE sets of beliefs that help to explain some of the mysteries of life and death. Most people who have a faith believe in either one god or several gods.

TOP SIX FAITHS

Faith	Number of followers
Christianity	1,833 million
Islam	971 million
Hinduism	733 million
Buddhism	315 million
Sikhism	13.5–16 million
Judaism	13–14.3 million

DIVISION OF MAJOR FAITHS BY GEOGRAPHIC AREA
Figures are given in percentages. (L.A. = Latin America. N.A. = North America)

Faith	Africa	Asia	Europe	L.A.	N.A.	Oceania	Eurasia	Total
Christianity	17.9	15.6	22.55	23.75	13.0	1.2	6.0	(100%)
Islam	28.66	65.56	1.3	0.14	0.29	0.01	4.04	(100%)
Hinduism	0.2	99.37	0.1	0.1	0.17	0.059	0.001	(100%)
Buddhism	0.01	99.42	0.08	0.17	0.18	0.01	0.13	(100%)
Sikhism	0.14	97.2	1.2	0.05	1.36	0.05	0.00	(100%)
Judaism	1.89	31.35	8.24	6.13	39.29	0.55	12.55	(100%)

WORLD PERCENTAGES
This bar chart shows the percentage distribution of the major world faiths. The figure for "Others" includes those who do not follow a faith system.

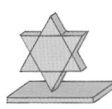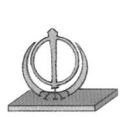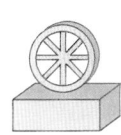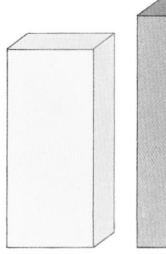

Judaism 0.3% Sikhism 0.3% Buddhism 5.7% Hinduism 13.4% Islam 17.7% Others 29.2% Christianity 33.4%

HISTORY OF RELIGIONS
B.C.E. (Before the Common Era) and C.E. (Common Era) stand for the same dates as B.C. and A.D.

JUDAISM
c.2000 B.C.E. | c.1200 B.C.E. | c.900 B.C.E. | 587 B.C.E. | C.E. 70

c.2000 B.C.E. Abraham, prophet of Judaism, Christianity, and Islam, is born in Ur, in present-day Iraq.

c.1200 B.C.E. Hebrews settle in Canaan, mainly present-day Israel, after the Exodus from Egypt.

931 B.C.E. Hebrew kingdom divides into Israel and Judah. **c.900 B.C.E. Torah**, the first five books of the Bible, is written.

587 B.C.E. Jerusalem, in present-day Israel, is captured by the Babylonians and the Jews sent into exile.

Herod's Temple

C.E. 70 Herod's Temple, Jerusalem, is destroyed by the Romans. Today, only the Western Wall remains.

ISLAM
c.2000 B.C.E. | C.E. 570 | c.C.E. 622

c.2000 B.C.E. Abraham and his son, Ishmael, build Ka'ba, an Islamic shrine, in Mecca (Makkah), in present-day Saudi Arabia.

c.C.E. 570–632 Muhammad, the last and most important Islamic prophet, is born in Mecca.

Mecca, Saudi Arabia

c.C.E. 610–632 Koran (Qur'an), the Islamic scriptures, is revealed to Muhammad by the angel Gabriel.

c.C.E. 622 Muhammad goes to Medina, in present-day Saudi Arabia. This marks the beginning of the Islamic calendar.

HINDUISM
c.1750 B.C.E. | c.1700 B.C.E. | c.1400 B.C.E. | c.800 B.C.E.

c.1750 B.C.E. Beginning of Hinduism in India is influenced by the Aryan people, who worship many gods.

c.1700 B.C.E. Hindu beliefs are revealed to the *rishis*, or holy men, and passed on by word of mouth. *The rishis*

c.1400 B.C.E. Rig Veda, the earliest and most important book of the *Vedas*, which contain Hindu beliefs, is written.

c.800 B.C.E. The Upanishads, the final books of the *Vedas*, are written. They develop the idea of Brahman, the soul of the Universe.

Brahma, the creator god, the masculine form of Brahman

BUDDHISM
c.563 B.C.E. | c.100 B.C.E. | c.C.E. 20

c.563–483 B.C.E. Siddharta Gautama, later known as Buddha, founder of Buddhism, lives in northeast India.

c.100 B.C.E. The Pali Canon, or *Tripitaka* (three baskets), the holy book of Theravada Buddhists, is written. *The Buddhist wheel of life*

c.C.E. 20–200 The Sutras (collections of sayings), the earliest holy books of Mahayana Buddhists, is written. *Shwedagon Pagoda*

c.1300 Shwedagon Pagoda, major Buddhist temple, is built in Rangoon in Burma. It is said to contain the hairs of Buddha.

CHRISTIANITY
c.4 B.C.E. | c.C.E. 40

c.4 B.C.E. Jesus Christ, founder of Christianity, is born in Bethlehem, in present-day Israel.

c.C.E. 30 Jesus is crucified on a cross. Three days later he is raised from the dead (the Resurrection). *The Crucifixion*

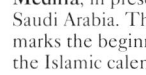

c.C.E. 40–100 New Testament of the Christian Bible is written. Christianity spreads throughout the Roman empire.

c.1506 St. Peter's Basilica, a major Christian church, is built in Rome. (Original built in c.C.E. 330.)

 *St. Peter's, Rome*

SIKHISM
c.1469 | c.1600

1469–1539 Guru Nanak, leader and founder of Sikhism, lives in the Punjab region of north India and Pakistan.

Guru Nanak and the other nine Gurus who developed Sikhism.

c.1600 Golden Temple of Amritsar, major Sikh temple, is built in the Punjab by Guru Arjan (1563–1606), the fifth Guru.

c.1604 Adi Granth, Sikh holy book, is compiled by Guru Arjan. This was later added to and called the *Guru Granth Sahib*.

A Sikh reading the Guru Granth.

CHRISTIANITY

CHRISTIANS BELIEVE THAT Jesus Christ is the Son of God. Their symbol is a cross, which stands for the cross on which Jesus was crucified.

ORIGIN
Christianity originated in about C.E. 30 in Jerusalem, in present-day Israel. Today, it is practised throughout the world.

JESUS CHRIST

Jesus was born in Bethlehem, Israel, in c.4 B.C.E. From the age of 30, he began to preach and heal the sick. A few years later he was tried and executed for having beliefs against Hebrew law.

TEN COMMANDMENTS
Christians obey these ten rules adapted from the Jewish scriptures (which Christians call the Old Testament).
1 Worship only one God.
2 Make no image of God.
3 Respect God's name.
4 Keep Sunday holy.
5 Honour your parents.
6 Do not kill.
7 Do not commit adultery.
8 Do not steal.
9 Do not tell lies.
10 Do not be envious.

KEY POINTS
• Jesus rose from the dead.

• The Holy Trinity is God as the Father, Son, and Holy Spirit.

• Jesus taught that people must love God, and love their neighbour as they love themselves.

BAPTISM
The ceremony of being dipped in water is called baptism. It is practised by Christians throughout the world, upon entering the faith. This practice dates from when Jesus was baptized by John the Baptist.

John the Baptist baptized Jesus in the River Jordan.

BIBLE
This holy book is made up of two parts, the Old and the New Testaments. The Old Testament contains the sacred writings of the Jews. The New Testament is about the life of Jesus and the growth of the early Church.

First printed Bible, 1455, by Johannes Gutenberg.

TYPES OF CHRISTIAN
- Eastern Orthodox 9.3%
- Others 10.2%
- Protestants 24.5%
- Roman Catholics 56%

ST. PETER'S BASILICA
This Roman Catholic church in the Vatican City, Rome, Italy, took more than 100 years to build. Ten architects worked on it, including Michelangelo, who designed the dome.

CHRISTIAN HOLY DAYS

Name	Event
Christmas	The birthday of Jesus Christ
Good Friday	Jesus is crucified on a cross
Easter	Jesus is resurrected from the dead
Pentecost	Coming of the Holy Spirit

CHRISTIAN WORDS
Advent Preparation for birth of Jesus.
Ascension Raising of Jesus to Heaven.
Eucharist Bread and wine taken in memory of Jesus.

Evangelist One of the four Gospel writers.
Gospel One of four accounts of Jesus' life in the New Testament.
Lent Forty days of preparation for Easter.

ISLAM

THE ISLAMIC FAITH is based on belief in one God, Allah. Followers of Islam are called Muslims. Their symbol is a star and a crescent moon.

ORIGIN
Islam originated in about C.E. 600 in Mecca *(Makkah)*, in present-day Saudi Arabia. It is now practised throughout the world.

Shahadah

MUHAMMAD
The last and greatest of the 26 Islamic prophets was Muhammad, born in Mecca in c.C.E. 570. The *shahadah* states that Muhammad is Allah's messenger.

PILLARS OF ISLAM
Muslims must obey these five rules:
1 **Shahadah** Allah is the only god, and Muhammad is his messenger.
2 **Salah** Pray five times a day.
3 **Zakah** Give aid to charity.
4 **Sawm** Fast during month of Ramadan.
5 **Hajj** Make at least one pilgrimage to Mecca in a lifetime.

KEY POINTS
• Muslims promise to obey the will of Allah.

• Islam is Allah's chosen faith for the human race.

• Muhammad is Allah's main messenger.

• The Islamic calendar has no leap years.

MECCA *(MAKKAH)*
This city in Saudi Arabia is the most sacred place in the Muslim world. It contains a cube-shaped shrine, the Ka'ba, believed to have been built by Abraham and Ishmael nearly 4,000 years ago. Every year, especially during their month of pilgrimage, Muslims flock to Mecca and gather around the Ka'ba.

KORAN *(QUR'AN)*
In this sacred book of Islam, Allah revealed to Muhammad how humankind should live on Earth. Muslims treat the book with great respect. They keep it in a clean place and wash before touching it.

TYPES OF MUSLIM
- Others 1%
- Shi'ites 16%
- Sunnis 83%

ISLAMIC FESTIVALS

Name	Event
Mawlid al-Nabi	Birthday of Muhammad
Layl'at al-Qadr	Koran revealed to Muhammad
Id al-Fitr	Celebration of end of Ramadan
Id al-Adha	End of pilgrimage to Mecca

AT PRAYER
Muslims often pray together in groups. They kneel, facing Mecca, on clean ground, or on fabric; this may be a woven carpet, straw mat, or even a handkerchief.

ISLAMIC WORDS
Ayatollah Shi'ite leader.
Hadith Stories about Muhammad.
Hafiz Muslim who has memorized the Koran.
Hajji One who has fulfilled the *Hajj*.

Jihad Striving to spread the Islamic way of life.
Shari'ah Islamic law.
Masjid Place of worship.
Mulla Scholar.

HINDUISM

MOST HINDUS BELIEVE in many gods, but in one underlying Reality, and that when a person dies the soul is reborn again in another body. Their symbol is a sacred sound, OM.

ORIGIN
Hinduism originated in India, in about 1750 B.C.E. Today it has spread throughout much of southeast Asia.

FOUNDERS
Hinduism has no single founder. Its early gods were brought by the Aryan people who invaded India. Shiva is one of the main Hindu gods.

Shiva

HINDU GODS
These are some of the most important gods:
Brahman Divine, absolute reality.
Vishnu Life-giver.
Shiva God of good and evil.
Sarasvati Goddess of truth.
Indra God of war.
Lakshmi Goddess of beauty.
Kali Goddess of death.
Krishna Hero and lover.

KEY POINTS
• People living good lives are born again in a higher life; bad lives lead to a lower life.

• Hindus aim to be free from the cycle of rebirth to become one with Brahman.

HOLY CITY
Varanasi, or Benares, in India, is one of the oldest cities in the world and the chief place of Hindu pilgrimage. Every year millions come to bathe in its sacred river, the Ganges. The waters are believed to wash away sin. People's ashes are often scattered on the river.

VEDAS
The earliest Hindu beliefs were written down as the *Vedas* in c.1400 B.C.E., which consists of hymns and chants. The *Rig Veda* is the most important book of the *Vedas*.

Rig Veda

TYPES OF HINDU
- Others 5%
- Vishnu 25%
- Vaishnavites 70%

SACRED COW
Hindus respect all animals, especially cows, as sacred beings. Most Hindus are vegetarians. The cow is a symbol of the Earth and feeding a cow is considered an act of worship.

HINDU HOLY DAYS

Name	Event
Diwali	New Year Festival of Lights
Holi	Spring Festival
Janmashtami	Birthday of Krishna
Shiva Ratri	Main festival of Shiva

HINDU WORDS
Atman Individual soul.
Avatar Appearance of Vishnu on Earth.
Guru Religious teacher.
Karma Moral law.
Mantra Sacred chant, hymn, or poem.
Moksha Release from the life cycle.
Nirvana Total peace.
Puja Worship.
Sanskrit Hindu language.
Yogi Holy man.

BUDDHISM

THE BUDDHIST FAITH is based on the teachings of the Buddha. Its symbol is an eight-spoked wheel.

ORIGIN
Buddhism originated in northern India in about 500 B.C.E. Today it has spread throughout most of southeast Asia.

BUDDHA
Siddharta Gautama was born in India c.563 B.C.E. Brought up as a prince, he left his home, aged 29, to lead a life of meditation and preaching. He was named Buddha, "the enlightened one".

FOUR TRUTHS
These holy principles are contained in the scripture, the *Dhammapada*.
1 Dukkha To live is to suffer.
2 Samudaya Desire or craving causes suffering.
3 Nirodha Freedom from desire leads to the end of suffering.
4 Magga Freedom can be found by following the Eightfold Path of Buddhism.

KEY POINTS
• Spiritual fulfilment comes from right actions and thoughts.

• Life is a sequence of birth, death, and rebirth.

GOLDEN PAGODA
The Shwedagon pagoda in Rangoon, Myanmar, is one of the earliest and most important Buddhist temples of worship. It is covered with gold and is topped by an "umbrella" of more than 4,000 diamonds.

Shwedagon pagoda

MONKS
Buddhist monks live a simple life, giving up most of their possessions. They pray, teach, meditate, and beg for their food.

Monks wear saffron-yellow robes

Begging bowl

HOLY TEXT
Extracts from the Pali Canon
The *Dhammapada* is the best-known part of the *Pali Canon*, the collected teachings of Buddha. It contains the Four Truths and the Eightfold Path: rightness of views, intention, speech, action, way of life, effort, awareness, and concentration.

TYPES OF BUDDHIST
- Other 6%
- Theravada 38%
- Mahayana 56%

BUDDHIST HOLY DAYS

Name	Event
Sakyamuni (or Wesak)	Birth of Siddharta Gautama
Bodhi Day	Buddha's enlightenment
Parinirvana	Buddha's ascent from Earth
Phagguna	Origin of life cycle

BUDDHIST WORDS
Anatta No such thing as self.
Anicca Self is impermanent.
Arahat Worthy, used to describe Buddha.
Bhikkhu Monk.
Jataka Accounts of Buddha's lives.
Nibbana State of peace.
Sangha Order of monks.
Vihaia Monastery.

SIKHISM

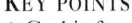

THE SIKH faith is based on the worship of one God and on the cycle of rebirth. God is the eternal Guru who inspires all religious teachers. The Sikh symbol is the Khanda, a design of weapons.

KEY POINTS
- God is found in all things.
- All humans will be reborn.
- All people are equal in the eyes of God.

FIVE K's
The Khalsa (Pure Ones) are deeply committed to Sikhism. They must wear five items:
1 **Kesh** Uncut hair, worn in a turban if a man.
2 **Kara** Steel bracelet.
3 **Kangha** Hair comb.
4 **Kirpan** Sword.
5 **Kaccha** Short trousers often worn as an undergarment.

Turban

Sword

Steel bracelet

ORIGIN
Sikhism began in the Punjab region of north India and Pakistan in about 1500 C.E. Today, it has spread to Britain and North America.

Punjab

Pakistan

India

GURU NANAK

Guru Nanak was born in the Punjab region in 1469. At the age of 30, he underwent a religious experience and founded the Sikh religion. He was succeeded by nine other Gurus.

AMRITSAR
This town in the Punjab is sacred to Sikhs. They make pilgrimages to its Golden Temple, which is situated in the middle of a lake.

Guru Granth Sahib

GURU GRANTH
The *Guru Granth Sahib* contains hymns and poems written by the Gurus, especially Guru Arjan, the fifth Guru. The book is central to Sikh ritual and is treated with great respect. Sikhs bow down before the book, which is placed under a special canopy.

MEDITATION

Sikhs believe that God is inside everybody. Guru Nanak taught the importance of meditation to strengthen a person's sense of God. Sikhs often use beads (*Mala*) during meditation.

A Sikh meditating

SIKH HOLY DAYS	
Name	Event
Baisakhi	New Year and formation of Khalsa
Diwali	Release from prison of Guru Hargobind, the sixth Guru
Guru Nanak	Birthday of the Founder

SIKH WORDS
Darbar Sahib Name for Golden Temple.
Diwan Group worship.
Gurdwara Place of worship.
Guru Name for leader, scripture, and God.

Japji Morning prayer.
Kaur Female surname.
Mool Mantra Statement of belief.
Mukti Freedom of the spirit from the cycle.
Singh Male surname.

JUDAISM

FOLLOWERS OF Judaism are called Jews. They believe in one God, who revealed the Law to his people. Their symbol is the Star of David.

RULES AND RITUALS
These are some of the traditions of Jewish life:
- Baby boys are circumcised eight days after birth.
- The Sabbath day (Saturday) is the holy day of rest.
- Pork and shellfish must not be eaten.
- A Jewish boy becomes *bar mitzvah*, an adult member of Jewish life, when he is 13.

KEY POINTS
- God created the world and all its history.
- The Jews are descendants of the Hebrew people.
- The Jews are God's chosen people, "a light to all nations".

Lebanon

Israel

Jordan

Egypt

ORIGIN
Judaism originated in about 2000 B.C.E. in Canaan, the Promised Land, mainly present-day Israel. Today, it has spread throughout the world.

ABRAHAM
Abraham, the first leader of the Hebrews, was born in Ur, in present-day Iraq, in about 2000 B.C.E. At God's command, he later settled in Canaan.

WESTERN WALL

This wall in Jerusalem, also known as the Wailing Wall, is the only remaining part of Herod's Temple, which was destroyed in C.E. 70. Today, Jews come here to pray and to tuck written prayers and requests in between the huge blocks of stone.

TENAKH
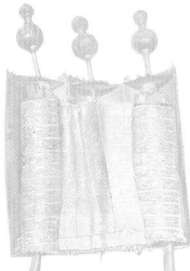
The Jewish Bible is called the *Tenakh*. It tells the history of the Jewish people. The most important part is the *Torah*, the first five books of the Bible. It contains the laws, including the Ten Commandments, that God revealed to Moses.

Tenakh scroll

TYPES OF JEW
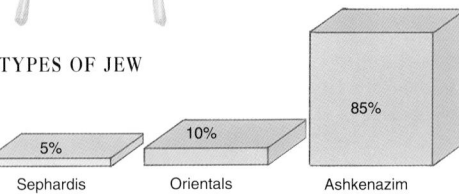
5% Sephardis
10% Orientals
85% Ashkenazim

JEWISH HOLY DAYS	
Name	Event
Hannukah	Festival of Lights
Pesach/Passover	Deliverance from slavery in Egypt
Yom Kippur	Day of Atonement

Taliith, or prayer shawl

Menorah, or branched candlestick

Yarmulke, or skull cap

The Tenakh

JEWISH WORDS
Diaspora Dispersion, or spread, of Jews.
Exodus Israelites' escape from Egypt.
Gentiles Non-Jewish people.
Kaddish Synagogue prayer.

Rabbi Teacher and leader.
Synagogue Place of worship.
Tephillin Prayer box containing words from the *Torah* worn strapped to forehead and arm.

OTHER FAITHS

THERE ARE thousands of faith systems, with millions of followers all around the world. Apart from the six major faiths already discussed, the faiths below are amongst the best-known. Each has an organized structure and established beliefs.

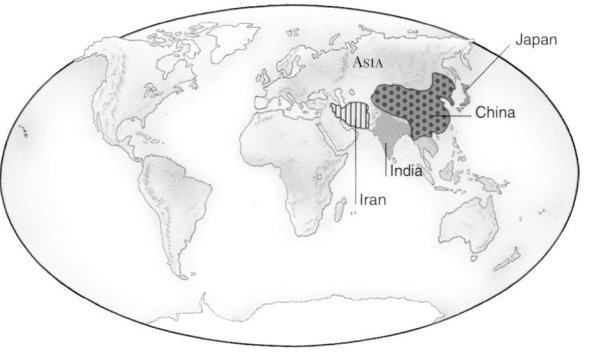

ORIGIN OF OTHER FAITHS

 Baha'ism (Iran)

 Confucianism (China)

Jainism (India)

Shintoism (Japan)

 Taoism (China)

 Zoroastrianism (Iran)

BAHA'I FAITH

The Baha'i faith is based on the worship of one God, who is at the root of all religions. The Baha'i symbol is a nine-pointed star that stands for this combination of faiths.

WORLD CENTRE
Baha'is worship in private homes and Houses of Worship. The most famous is the World Centre in Haifa, Israel, which is also the centre of administration.

FACTS

• Founded in Persia (present-day Iran) in the 19th century.

• The founder was Baha'u'llah (1817–1892).

• *Al-Kitab al-Aqdas* is the most important scripture.

• There are about 6 million followers; many of them are in India and South America.

CONFUCIANISM

Confucianism is not based on the worship of a god, but on following *The Tao* (The Way). It teaches the wisdom of living a balanced life that is in harmony with nature.

CONFUCIUS
Confucius, or K'ung Fu Tze, (551–479 B.C.E.) was the founder of Confucianism. Born in China, he worked as a government administrator, and became a respected teacher and moral philosopher. He was known for his wise sayings, such as "A good man is never alone".

FACTS

• Confucianism originated in the Shantung province of China c.6th century B.C.E.

• The *Analects* are the major scriptures.

• Confucianism is practised throughout China.

• Its main teaching is "Never do to others what you would not like them to do to you".

JAINISM

Jains do not believe in a god. Their faith is based on non-violence to all living things, or *ahimsa*. Jains believe in the cycle of rebirth. A good person is born again into a higher life.

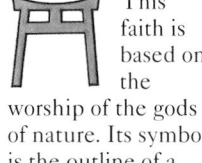

JAIN NUN
Jain nuns and monks lead a life of poverty, obedience, and chastity. They must protect all forms of life. They use a brush to sweep the ground in front of them, for fear of treading on any insects, and wear masks to prevent insects from entering their mouths.

FACTS

• Founded in India, in the 6th century B.C.E.

• The founder was Mahavira (c.540–468 B.C.E.).

• Jains worship in temples, or in shrines in the home.

• There are approximately 4 million Jains; most of them live in India.

SHINTOISM

This faith is based on the worship of the gods of nature. Its symbol is the outline of a temple gateway.

MOUNT FUJI
Shintoists love nature. Many Shinto shrines are in parks, gardens, and on mountains. Mount Fuji, in Japan, is a Shinto god. People come to pray at a shrine on its summit.

FACTS

• Shintoism started in Japan in the 8th century B.C.E.

• The *Chronicles of Japan* and the *Record of Ancient Things* contain Shinto stories.

• Shintoists worship alone, not in groups.

• One of the chief Shinto deities is Amaterasu, the Sun Goddess.

• Most followers live in Japan.

TAOISM

Taoists believe in many gods. They aim to live in harmony with nature. Their symbol, *Yin Yang*, stands for balance and harmony.

LAO TZU
Lao Tzu, the founder of Taoism, was born in about the 4th century B.C.E. His name means "Old Master". According to legend, he was born with white hair.

FACTS

• Taoism originated in China in about the 4th century B.C.E.

• The *Tao Te Ching* is the most important scripture.

• Most Taoists live in China and the Far East.

• Taoists aim to balance the calm, feminine side of the body (*Yin*), with the active, male side (*Yang*).

ZOROASTRIANISM

This faith is based on two gods: Ahura Mazda, a good spirit; and Angra Mainyu, an evil spirit. Its symbol is a winged image of Ahura.

FIRE TEMPLE
Sacred fires, symbolizing Ahura Mazda, burn continually in Zoroastrian fire temples. Priests cover their mouths when tending the sacrificial fires.

FACTS

• Founded in Persia (present-day Iran), c.1000 B.C.E.

• Zoroaster, or Zarathustra, was the major prophet.

• The scripture is the *Avesta*, which explains the struggle between good and evil.

• There are about 140,000 followers; most of them are in India and Iran.

GREAT THINKERS

FROM EARLY TIMES, philosophers have used argument and reason to try to understand the world and our place in it. They question the meaning of ideas such as reality, right and wrong, and art.

624 B.C. Thales (624–550 B.C.) is born in Miletus, Greece. He is interested in astronomy and politics, as well as philosophy. He became known as the first Western philosopher.

Thales

Pythagoras (c.580–500 B.C.), Greek philosopher, explores the importance of numbers. He discovers the mathematical relationship between sound pitch and the length of a string or pipe.

Pythagoras

650 B.C.	624 B.C.	600 B.C.	580 B.C.	500 B.C.

Aristotle (384–322 B.C.) is the last and most influential of the Greek philosophers. He stresses the importance of logic, or reasoning, in philosophy.

Aristotle tutoring Alexander the Great (356–323 B.C.).

St. Augustine (A.D. 354–430), North African philosopher, uses Plato's philosophy to express Christian ideas.

1225–74 St. Thomas Aquinas, Italian friar, aims to make Christian teaching consistent with Aristotle's philosophy.

St. Thomas Aquinas

Thomas Hobbes (1588–1679), English political philosopher, says that giving all power to the state is the only way to avoid chaos and endless war. He writes the *Leviathan* in 1651.

400 B.C.	384 B.C.	A.D. 300	A.D. 354	1200	1225	1500	1588

George Berkeley (1685–1753), Irish bishop and idealist philosopher, believes that objects, such as tables and chairs, are collections of ideas, and exist only if a person perceives (is aware of) them.

David Hume (1711–76), Scottish empiricist and sceptic, states that all knowledge is taken from ideas and experience, but denies that this knowledge can ever be proved.

David Hume

Jean-Jacques Rousseau (1712–78), French political philosopher, is against the limitations of civilized society and advises a return to nature.

Rousseau

Immanuel Kant (1724–1804), German thinker, says that we gain knowledge through both experience and understanding.

Immanuel Kant

1650	1685	1700	1711	1712	1724

John Stuart Mill (1806–73), English utilitarian, emphasizes that some pleasures are worthier than others. He writes *On Liberty* in 1859.

John Stuart Mill

Søren Kierkegaard (1813–55), Danish founder of existentialism and religious writer, claims that the only real thing is individual existence.

Karl Marx (1818–83), German revolutionary thinker, founds Communism, adapting ideas from Hegel's philosophy. He writes *Das Kapital* in 1867.

Karl Marx

William James (1842–1910), American psychologist and pragmatist, sees the truthfulness of any idea in terms of the usefulness of its results.

1800	1806	1810	1813	1818	1840	1842

Bertrand Russell (1872–1970), English thinker and political activist, tries to provide firm foundations in philosophy for mathematics.

Bertrand Russell

Martin Heidegger (1889–1976), German existentialist, writes *Being and Time* in 1927.

Ludwig Wittgenstein (1889–1951), Austrian analytic philosopher, explores the relationship between language and the world. He argues that everything that can be thought can also be said.

Ludwig Wittgenstein

Jean-Paul Sartre (1905–80), French existentialist, says there is no fixed human nature or destiny, and that people are free to choose their actions without following society's rules.

Sartre

1870	1872	1880	1889	1889	1900	1905

FAMOUS PHILOSOPHICAL SAYINGS

Philosopher	Dates	Nationality	Quotation
Protagoras	c.485-410 B.C.	Greek	*Man is the measure of all things.*
Socrates	470-399 B.C.	Greek	*The unexamined life is not worth living.*
Francis Bacon	1561-1626	English	*Knowledge is power.*
René Descartes	1596-1650	French	*I think, therefore I am.*
George Berkeley	1685-1753	Irish	*To be is to be perceived.*
David Hume	1711-76	Scottish	*Beauty in things exists in the mind which contemplates them.*
Jean-Jacques Rousseau	1712-78	French	*Man is born free, and everywhere he is in chains.*
G.W.F. Hegel	1770-1831	German	*History teaches us that people have never learned anything from history.*
John Stuart Mill	1806-73	English	*Ask yourself whether you are happy, and you cease to be so.*
Karl Marx	1818-83	German	*Philosophers have only interpreted the world, the point is to change it.*
Friedrich Nietzsche	1844-1900	German	*God is dead.*
Ludwig Wittgenstein	1889-1951	Austrian	*The limits of my language are the limits of my world.*

WARM THOUGHTS

In 1620, René Descartes thought up his most famous statement, "I think, therefore I am", as he kept warm by a stove while on military service in Bavaria, Germany.

470–399 B.C. Socrates, Greek philosopher, and Plato's teacher, uses question and answer method of inquiry. His main concern is morality (right and wrong). He is accused by the state of corrupting young people and is sentenced to death.

Socrates is forced to drink hemlock, a poison.

Plato (c.428–347 B.C.), of Athens, Greece, founds the Academy (a university) in Athens and teaches Aristotle there. He outlines his ideal city-state in *The Republic.*

Plato's Academy

470 B.C. | **470 B.C.** | **428 B.C.**

René Descartes (1596–1650), French dualist, rationalist philosopher, and mathematician, is considered the first modern philosopher. He bases all knowledge on one truth: that we cannot doubt the existence of our own thoughts.

Descartes

John Locke (1632–1704), English philosopher and political writer, founds classical British empiricism. His political writings form the foundations of modern democracy. He wrote *Two Treatises of Government* in 1690.

John Locke

1596 | **1600** | **1632**

Jeremy Bentham (1748–1832), English utilitarian, judges an action to be right by the extent to which it promotes happiness or minimizes pain.

G.W.F. Hegel (1770–1831), German idealist, says that the history of events and thoughts is a process of conflict, which will lead to an inevitable conclusion.

Hegel

Arthur Schopenhauer (1788–1860), German idealist, saw art as the only escape from a world without reason.

Schopenhauer

1740 | **1748** | **1770** | **1788**

Friedrich Wilhelm Nietzsche (1844–1900), German philosopher, argues that people are driven in life by the "will to power", and that society will evolve into a race of "supermen". He rejects Christianity, and influences the Nazi party.

Nietzsche's "Ubermenschen" ("supermen")

Edmund Husserl (1859–1938), German philosopher, develops the basic ideas of phenomenology (descriptions of human experience).

44 | **1850** | **1859**

Simone de Beauvoir (1908–86), French existentialist and founder of modern feminist philosophy.

Willard van Orme Quine (born 1908), American pragmatist, points out inconsistencies in early analytic philosophy.

Simone de Beauvoir

Michel Foucault (1926–84), French philosopher, looks at ways in which the individual is controlled by society's rules.

Jacques Derrida (born 1930), French founder of deconstructionism, which rejects the idea of any fixed truths in language and philosophy.

Michel Foucault

1906 | **1908** | **1920** | **1926** | **1930** | **1930**

PHILOSOPHY FACTS

• Pythagoras refused to eat beans, as he believed that they had souls.

• English philosopher, Francis Bacon (1561–1626), died of pneumonia, caught while stuffing a dead chicken with snow on Hampstead Heath, London, in an early attempt to preserve it by refrigeration.

• The most influential philosopher of the 20th century, Ludwig Wittgenstein, published one work in his lifetime. Parts of his *Tractatus Logico-philosophicus* were written in the trenches during World War I (1914–18), while he was on sentry duty.

• In his will, Jeremy Bentham left his body to University College, London. His corpse was preserved and dressed, and crowned with a wax head. The corpse was kept in a glass case, along with his real head, which

Jeremy Bentham

was mummified. Bentham's dressed corpse is still on display at the university.

• René Descartes was tutor to the Swedish monarch, Queen Christina (1626–89). She made him give her philosophy lessons at dawn, even though she knew his preference for lying in bed and meditating until 11 o'clock in the morning.

• Until the 18th and 19th centuries, the term "philosophy" included many branches that have since become areas of study in their own right: physics, biology, mathematics, and engineering.

PHILOSOPHY WORDS

Analytic Movement that considers philosophy to be based essentially on logic.

A priori Knowledge based on reasoning rather than experience.

Determinism Idea that all things, including "free will", are already fixed, or determined.

Dualism Belief that there are two distinct types of substance in the world: the physical and the mental.

Empiricism Belief that all knowledge is based on experience. At birth, the mind is a blank sheet, on which experience then makes its mark.

Epistemology Study of the theory of knowledge: what knowledge is, how we come to know things, how much we can hope to know, etc.

Ethics Study of moral systems, or ideas about how people ought to live and behave.

Existentialism Belief that the individual has free will, and must take responsibility for his or her actions in a world where there are no definite rights or wrongs.

Idealism Belief that the world is in some way created by the mind. Idealists do not deny that the world exists, but deny it can be separated from the mind.

Logic Series of statements that necessarily follow on from each other. Also called a chain of reasoning.

Materialism Belief that everything that exists is either matter (substance), or is dependent on matter for its existence.

Metaphysics Study of principles of nature, such as being, identity, substance, time, and space.

Objectivity Existence outside a person's mind; the opposite of subjectivity.

Pragmatism A practical view of philosophy: the truthfulness of an idea is seen in terms of the usefulness of its results.

Rationalism Belief that reason alone, without any reliance on experience, can reveal the basic truths of the Universe, and that everything can be explained by a single system.

Realism Belief, usually contrasted with idealism, that physical objects exist independently of the mind.

Relativism Belief that there are no universal standards or truths; usually a rejection of absolute rights and wrongs.

Scepticism Belief that nothing can be known for certain.

Subjectivity Existence inside a person's mind; the opposite of objectivity.

Solipsism Belief that the only reality is inside your own mind.

Utilitarianism Belief that actions are right if they result in happiness, wrong if they result in unhappiness.

PATTERNS OF FAMILY AND SOCIETY

EVERY HUMAN SOCIETY (community of people) in the world is based on the family. Types of family and marriage arrangements, however, vary from one society to the next. Organization and living habits can also be very different, according to how and where people live and work.

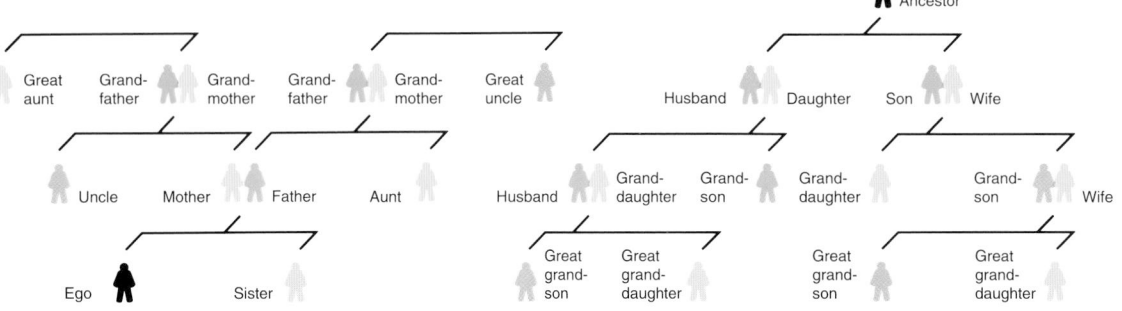
Aboriginal Rainbow Snake Dreaming

DREAMING
Aboriginal Australians believe the land and all living creatures were formed by spirit ancestors in the dawn of time called the Dreaming.

KINSHIP
Kinship is a way of describing bonds between people of the same family. A family may be defined as just parents and children, or it may include other types of relatives.

KEY

= Male = Female

Ancestor

Great aunt / Grand-father / Grand-mother / Grand-father / Grand-mother / Great uncle

Uncle / Mother / Father / Aunt

Ego / Sister

Husband / Daughter / Son / Wife

Husband / Grand-daughter / Grand-son / Grand-daughter / Grand-son / Wife

Great grand-son / Great grand-daughter / Great grand-son / Great grand-daughter

EGO-FOCUSED KINSHIP
People can use themselves as the starting point from which to construct a family tree. They trace their roots back as far as they can through both their fathers' and mothers' families. This is called ego-focused kinship.

ANCESTOR-FOCUSED KINSHIP
People can trace their roots to a known ancestor who starts off the family tree. This is called ancestor-focused kinship and is found, for example, in Scottish clans where everyone shares the same surname.

FAMILY WORDS
Ancestor An earlier member of the family.

Clan A family group descended from a common ancestor.

Dowry A wedding payment from the bride to the groom.

Lineage A line of family relations.

Marriage A legal bond between two people.

Tribe A group of people linked to an ancestor.

Western society People living in industrialized areas.

DESCENT
The system linking families to their ancestors is called descent. Inheritance of family property and titles is based on rules of descent.

Green line shows patrilineal line of descent

Orange line shows matrilineal line of descent

Duke of Westminster, a British aristocrat

PATRILINEAL DESCENT
Descent traced through the male line is called patrilineal descent. The Duke of Westminster inherited his title as the first-born son – a feature of a type of European patrilineal descent.

Trobriand Island mother and child

MATRILINEAL DESCENT
Matrilineal families trace their descent through female relatives. Many tribal societies, such as that of the Trobriand Islanders of the southwestern Pacific, are matrilineal.

HOUSEHOLDS
A household is a group of people who live together as a family. The number of people in a family household can vary widely around the world; so can the way in which members of a household organize family life and bring up their children.

Kibbutzim
In communities in Israel called kibbutzim families live and work together, helping to bring up each others' children.

Extended family
In many tribal societies several generations of the same family live together and share the responsibility for domestic duties.

Nuclear family
Anthropologists use the term nuclear family to mean a household consisting of two parents who bring up their own children.

MARRIAGE TYPES

Endogamy Marriage between members of the same family or clan.

Exogamy Marriage between members of a different family or clan.

Monogamy Marriage of one man to one wife.

Bigamy Marriage of one man to two wives or one woman to two husbands.

Polygamy Marriage of one man or one woman to several wives or several husbands at the same time.

Polyandry Marriage of one woman to several husbands at the same time.

Polygyny Marriage of one man to several wives at the same time.

Levirate Remarriage of a woman to her dead husband's brother.

Sororate Remarriage of a man to his dead wife's sister.

TAKING THE PLUNGE

On 13 September 1991, Dustin and Becca Webster of California, USA, completed their wedding by diving 21.30m (70 ft) into a swimming pool.

MARRIAGE RECORDS

LARGEST GROUP WEDDING was between 60,000 members of the Unificationist Church on 25 August 1992, in the Seoul Olympic Stadium, Korea.

MOST EXPENSIVE WEDDING was 20 million US dollars for Mohammed, son of Sheik Rashid Bin Saeed Al Maktoum, and Princess Salama, in Dubai, in May 1981.

MOST MARRIED MAN was Giovanni Vigliotto from New York, USA, who married 104 times in 15 different countries, from 1949 to 1981.

TRADITIONAL BRIDES

Brides who want a traditional wedding can choose from many different styles of outfit.

Chinese brides may wear a traditional head-dress of pierced metal strips, often silver, with a veil made from feathers and pearls.

Western brides wear a long dress and veil in white, symbolizing purity and innocence. This custom dates from the 19th century.

Japanese brides may dress in a brightly coloured traditional kimono. This contrasts with the black costumes of the brides' attendants.

Hindu brides wear a red dress and both bride and groom wear colourful garlands of flowers around their necks.

MARRIAGE AND DIVORCE STATISTICS

Country	Marriages per year		Divorces per year	
	1981	1994	1981	1994
USA	10.6	9.1	5.3	4.6
South Africa	8.2	10.7	2.0	2.5
UK	7.1	5.9	2.8	3.1
Japan	6.6	6.4	1.3	1.5
Belgium	6.5	5.1	1.6	2.2
Finland	6.3	4.9	2.0	2.7
Germany	6.2	5.4	2.0	2.0
France	5.8	4.4	1.6	1.9
Italy	5.6	5.0	0.2	0.5
Denmark	5.0	6.8	2.8	2.6
(figures given per thousand people)				

WEDDING CUSTOMS

- Ancient Romans first gave pieces of wedding cake to guests.

- Greek Orthodox couples wear wedding crowns linked by a red ribbon.

- Indian couples tie their clothes together and walk seven times around a fire.

- In Egypt the bride's father signs her wedding contract while she sits alone in a separate room.

- Japanese couples take three sips of sake (rice wine) to complete their wedding ceremony.

- Jewish couples do not eat or drink on their wedding day until the ceremony is over.

SYMBOLS

A symbol is something, such as an object, a sign, or a mark, that stands for something else. All the symbols shown below have a clear meaning.

Wedding ring A wedding ring is worn by both the bride and the groom to show their bond to each other.

The Scout Association The symbol of the Scout Association stands for this worldwide movement for boys and girls, which started in 1908.

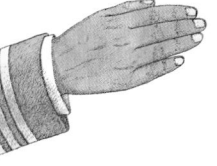

US Navy Commander Three equal lace stripes on the sleeve are worn by US Navy commanders.

Olympic rings Five coloured rings are the symbol that stands for the International Olympic Committee.

SOCIETY TYPES

Work and home life influence how people live.

City dwellers Many city dwellers live on housing estates or in blocks of flats.

Hunter-gatherers Hunters and gatherers live in small groups of several families. They move home from one place to another in search of wild animals and plants to eat.

Nomads Nomads are groups of people who have no fixed home, but who move with their animals from one grazing ground to another.

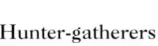

SOCIETY WORDS

Rural People who live and work in the countryside.

Urban People who live and work in towns or cities.

Suburban People who live on the edges of a large city.

Migrant People who have moved from one region to another, or one country to another.

ONE WORLD

Different societies' customs can travel all over the world via film and television. A Campa Indian boy from Peru now enjoys a game with a frisbee.

CUSTOMS AND RITUALS

THROUGHOUT THE WORLD, different societies have their own traditions for marking important events such as the birth of a child, or the harvesting of crops. These traditions are called customs and rituals, and many are based around the cycles of nature, and the mystery of life and death.

THE JAPANESE TEA CEREMONY
In Japan, drinking tea is a long-established ritual that is based on the teachings of Zen Buddhism. Tea is prepared and served in a special tea room or tea house.

BIRTH RITES
The Azande people of the Sudan gently wave newborn babies through smoke to protect them against witchcraft and to help them grow up strong and healthy.

Azande birth rites

DEATH RITES
Traditional Taoist (see p.143) funerals involve the burning of imitation money. The smoke will carry it to the dead to spend in a future life.

Taoist funeral

BIRTH AND DEATH FACTS
• Many Christian babies are baptized in holy water in a church font.

• Jewish baby boys are circumcised eight days after birth.

• Romany gypsies press a gold ring against their baby's hand to bring it wealth.

• Pregnant women in New Guinea live alone until their baby is born.

• Death rites in Melanesia last for several years, until the deceased becomes an ancestor.

• Chinese coffins are painted white to give the dead a happy future life.

GREETINGS
A greeting is a means of friendly communication. between two or more people.

Hand-shake
The gripping and shaking of hands is a formal greeting around the world.

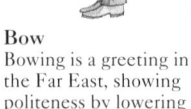

Bow
Bowing is a greeting in the Far East, showing politeness by lowering the head.

Nose rub
This Maori greeting is called a hongi. It is usually made on ceremonial occasions.

Wave
A friendly waving of the hand and arm means hello or goodbye, all around the world.

INITIATION RITES
Initiation is a rite to welcome adolescents into adulthood in many traditional societies. The White Mountain Apache from North America perform a ritual for teenage girls, called the Sunrise Dance.

1 Ground-up plants and coloured rocks are daubed over the girl's head with a brush made from plant stalks.

2 The girl kneels facing the sun, and acts out the legend of the creation of the First Woman. Finally, as a woman, she is given the powers of a goddess for four days.

GESTURES
A gesture is an action that sends a visual signal to an onlooker.

Thumbs up
Raising the thumb is a friendly gesture. It is a sign of approval or that all is going well.

V for victory
This victory gesture was made famous by Sir Winston Churchill during World War II.

Ssshh!
A finger pressed to the lips is a worldwide sign meaning "keep quiet" or "keep this a secret".

Beautiful!
This Native American gesture means beauty. It combines the signs for "good" and "looking".

CHARMS
People keep or carry certain objects to bring them good luck or to ward off evil.

Pocket-sized Buddhas are popular good-luck charms worldwide.

Horseshoe
Hanging a horseshoe over the doorway brings good luck to the household.

Cork & coin
A coin wedged into a champagne cork acts as a lucky charm.

4-leaved clover
Finding a rare four-leaved clover is said to bring good luck.

Charm bracelet
This chain holds a variety of tiny lucky charms.

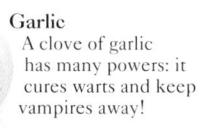

Garlic
A clove of garlic has many powers: it cures warts and keeps vampires away!

Sugar skull
This lucky sweet is eaten during the Mexican Day of the Dead Festival.

CELEBRATION AND DECORATION

CELEBRATIONS that involve the whole community mark events such as the passing of the seasons, and holy days. These events contain a mixture of customs, using music, dance, and costume.

Mexican Day of the Dead Festival

CELEBRATION FACTS

- Dragon Boat Festival of China is held to give thanks for food and water in the dry season, with races of decorated boats.

- On Thanksgiving Day in the USA and Canada, families sit down to a special meal in celebration of the harvest.

- Diwali Festival in India celebrates the harvest with decorative lights, and offerings to Lakshmi, Hindu goddess of prosperity.

- Inti Raymi is the Peruvian Festival of the Sun god, Inti, held in an Inca fortress.

- Rio de Janeiro Carnival is a mass parade of costume and dance, based on the Christian celebration of the end of Lent.

Rio de Janeiro Carnival

DRESS CODES

Wearing certain items of clothing helps to identify what a person is or does.

Mortar-board

Graduate's gown
University students wear a black gown and a hat called a mortar-board at their graduation ceremony.

Wimple

Nun's habit
Nuns wear a plain robe called a habit. Their head is covered by a hood called a wimple.

Eye-slits

Arab burka
The burka is a single length of cloth worn by Arab women. It covers the body, except for the eyes.

Devil mask

Bolivian dancer's mask
This Devil mask is worn as part of the colourful costume at the annual Diablada Festival in Bolivia.

Bearskin

Welsh Guard
Various army regiments, such as the Welsh Guards, wear ceremonial uniforms topped by hats made of bear fur.

Toque

Chef's whites
Chefs wear starched white clothing they call their whites, and a tall white cloth hat called a toque.

DANCING FOR JOY

Dancing is one of the earliest known activities of humankind. Some dances are purely for fun; others are important rituals.

A ritual tribal dance from Kenya.

The jitterbug, popular in the USA in the 1940's.

BODY DECORATION

Decorative jewellery and body scars are part of a person's appearance. Each society, however, has different ideas about what makes the body beautiful.

Forehead spot
Hindu women paint a red spot on their forehead called a *Tilak*, as a symbol of wisdom.

Earring
A ring through the ear draws attention to the eyes and adds to the beauty of the face.

Lip plug
Kaiapo men from the Brazilian Amazon wear a wooden lip plug to decorate their mouths.

MOST TATTOOS

Tom Leppard, a Scotsman, has leopard skin tattoos covering 99.2% of his body.

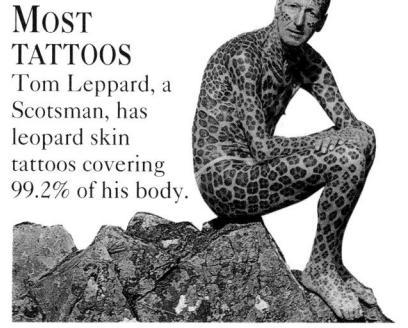

Scarification
Many African tribal people decorate their face and body with scars to add to their beauty.

Samoan tattoo
Men from the Pacific islands of Samoa are tattooed all over the body as a sign of manliness.

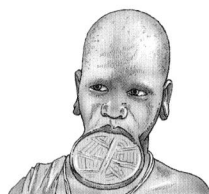

Punk jewellery
Safety pins and other unusual objects are worn as jewellery for their startling effect.

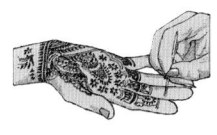

Sikh hand-painting
Sikh brides paint decorative patterns on their hands with dye from the henna plant.

COSMETIC SURGERY

The three most popular cosmetic surgery operations in the USA in 1994 were:

Women (88% of all operations)	Men (12% of all operations)
Liposuction	Nose reshaping
Eyelid surgery	Eyelid surgery
Breast augmentation	Liposuction

MONEY

MONEY COMES IN the form of cash, which consists of coins and banknotes. Anything that represents cash, such as the computer records of a bank account, a cheque, or a credit card, is also money. Today, many people prefer to pay for things with cards rather than carry around cash.

EARLY MONEY
The oldest recorded use of money was in ancient Mesopotamia (Iraq), about 4,500 years ago. Inscribed tablets describe payments made with weighed amounts of silver. Other earlier forms of money include cowrie shells, used in ancient Egypt, and feather money on Santa Cruz Island, Pacific Ocean.

THE FIRST COINS
The first known coins were made 2,700 years ago in Lydia, Turkey, from a mixture of gold and silver called electrum. They were stamped at mints to confirm their weight and value. Today, most coins are made out of cheaper metals.

BANKNOTES
Banknotes have extremely complicated designs with special security features, to make it as difficult as possible for forgers to copy them. The four main stages of making a banknote are design, papermaking, ink-mixing, and printing. When the notes are printed, three separate processes are used.

SKETCHES
An artist makes two preliminary sketches for the note: the first one shows the main features; the second shows the background details.

Position of main features

Coloured background

PAPER MONEY
Paper money – banknotes – was invented by the Chinese in the 10th century. People tired of carrying coins around and left them with merchants instead. Merchants provided vouchers (receipts) for the money and people exchanged the vouchers among themselves, rather than turn them back into cash.

BACKGROUND DESIGN
This design uses eight different coloured inks. First, these are printed on three sheets in groups of colours: blues, yellows, and reds.

Inks for each colour group are combined on a single sheet.

FINISHED NOTE
This type of specimen banknote is produced by the company, Thomas de La Rue, to show to its customers all over the world.

Sharp burins

Burnisher for smoothing

INTAGLIO ENGRAVING
The features of the note are engraved on to a steel plate by hand, using special sharp tools, called burins. The engraved area is then inked.

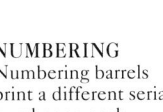

SECURITY THREAD
Banknote paper is made with a plastic thread sealed inside it. This feature is extremely difficult for forgers to copy.

NUMBERING
Numbering barrels print a different serial number on each banknote.

MONEY RECORDS
BIGGEST MINT
in the world is in Philadelphia, USA, where 15 billion coins are made each year.

FIRST CREDIT CARD
was the Diners Club card, issued in the USA in 1950. The card enabled the first 200 members to eat on credit at 27 New York restaurants.

GREATEST GOLD RESERVES
are held by the United States at Fort Knox, Kentucky. The gold bars are stored in bomb-proof vaults, surrounded by armed guards.

AMAZING MONEY
The people of Yap, a Pacific island, used large stone discs for money. The largest was about 4m (12ft) across – as big as two adults standing on each other's shoulders.

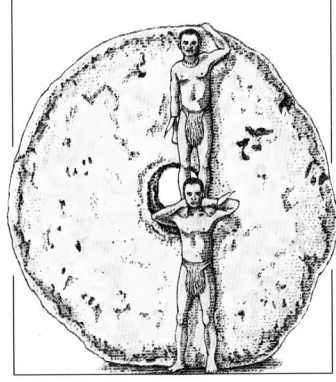

WORLD'S RICHEST PEOPLE
(excluding heads of state)

Name	Country	Business
Bill Gates	USA	Computer software
Warren Buffett	USA	Textiles
Hans Rausing	Sweden	Packaging
Yoshiaki Tsutsumi	Japan	Land, railways, leisure
Paul Sacher	Switzerland	Drug company
Tsai Wan-lin	Taiwan	Insurance

MONEY FACTS
• The ancient Greeks put a silver coin into the mouths of corpses. The purpose was to pay the ferryman, Charon, to carry their souls across the River Styx.

• Numismatists are people who collect coins. Gold coins are the oldest and most precious.

• Forgers try to make copies of notes and pass them off as genuine. Forgers are highly skilled professionals.

• "Piggy banks" have been used for saving money since the 14th century. The first pigs were pottery and had to be smashed to extract the money.

Fort Knox

BANKS

Most people find it convenient to keep their money in a bank. The bank keeps a record of how much each person takes out or puts into their account. This information is printed out in the form of a bank statement.

Automatic telling machine

STOCKS AND SHARES

People can invest in a company by buying shares (stocks) in it. If the company makes a profit, the shareholders are entitled to some of it. Share prices can rise or fall according to the company's performance. Share prices are displayed in the financial sections of newspapers.

THE STOCK MARKET

The stock market is a place where shares are bought and sold. People who want to invest in a company employ a stockbroker who buys and sells the shares for them. The activity of a stock market reflects the economic performance and prospects of a country.

Tokyo Stock Exchange

Company	Price	Weekly change + / -
Birch Interiors	69	-1
Gunzi Properties	44	-2
Kennedy Holdings PLC	46	+2
Kruger Corporation	162	+7
Shaw Associates	121	+5

Shares listing (imaginary) as shown in many newspapers

KEY STOCK EXCHANGES

Country	City	Index
Japan	Tokyo	Nikkei Average
United States	New York	Dow-Jones
United Kingdom	London	FTSE-100*
Germany	Frankfurt	DAX**

* Financial Times Stock Exchange 100

** Deutsche Aktien Index

BANKING FACTS

• Cash-dispensing machines allow people to withdraw money from their bank account 24 hours a day.

• Banks today arrange insurance, pensions, and mortgages (loans to buy houses), as well as keeping money safe.

• Cheques, written instructions to make payments, can be written on anything, even a cow.

• Banking began in the 14th century, in Lombardy, northern Italy.

FINANCIAL WORDS

Accountant A person who keeps and checks financial records for a person or business.

Credit An amount of money made available to make purchases on the basis that they will be paid for later.

Crash A very quick and very large drop in the price of shares, causing people to lose a great deal of money.

Dividend Share of a company's profits that is paid out to shareholders.

Exchange rate The amount of one country's currency needed to buy a fixed amount of another country's currency.

Merchant bank A bank that deals in finance and loans for businesses.

Share index Shows the price of selected shares being traded.

Stockbroker/Broker A member of a stock exchange who buys and sells shares.

Take-over When one company buys another.

FOREIGN CURRENCY

Every country has its own money, or currency. Some currencies hold their value longer than others because they reflect the economic strength of the country. Stable, widely traded currencies are hard currencies. Dealers buy and sell them on foreign currency markets.

THE EURO

In 1999, eleven of the countries of the European Union (EU) started to use a new, common currency – the Euro. After some years the Euro will replace the currencies of all members of the EU except those of Britain, Denmark, Sweden, and Greece.

GALLOPING INFLATION

Inflation results when prices increase and the purchasing power of money decreases. Very rapid price rises, called "hyper-inflation", took place in Germany between 1921 and 1923. At this time, money was worth so little that children used banknotes for building bricks.

German inflation, 1923

CURRENCY VALUES (1997)

Nearly every country has its own money, or currency. Usually each currency can be broken down into 100 smaller units. Currencies are worth different amounts, as you can see from the cost of an ounce (28.35g) of gold in each currency in this table.

Country	Currency	Value	Cost for an ounce of gold
Chile	Peso	100 centavos	150,916
China	Yuan	100 fen, 10 jiao	2,938
Ethiopia	Birr	100 cents	2,215
Germany	Deutschmark	100 pfennigs	570.72
India	Rupee	100 paise	12,697
Japan	Yen	100 sen	41,487
Poland	Zloty	100 groszy	1,030
South Africa	Rand	100 cents	1,646
United Kingdom	Pound	100 pence	212.34
USA	Dollar	100 cents	354.20

TODAY'S MONEY

Increasingly, plastic cards are taking the place of cash and cheques as a form of payment. Banks, credit companies, and stores issue credit, or charge, cards. These allow people to buy things and pay for them later. The latest cards, smart cards, use microchips to store information.

SMART CARDS

Money from a bank account can be transferred on to a smart card. This card can then be used to pay for many things, from goods in shops to electricity bills.

CHARGE CARDS

You can pay for something with a charge card at a store, or pay for goods over the phone. The credit company records all transactions and sends a bill each month.

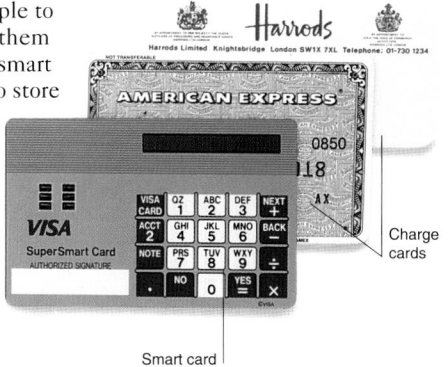

Charge cards

Smart card

POLITICS

POLITICS IS CONCERNED with the organization of society. Political parties are groups of people who agree about the way in which a country should be run and who seek to gain power in government.

POLITICAL SYSTEMS

Every political system has a central authority called a government that is responsible for organizing the duties of the state. The most common form of government in the world today is the presidential system. This system has three branches.

THE BIRTH OF DEMOCRACY

Democracy means "rule by the people". Democratic traditions of debate and voting first appeared 2,500 years ago in the ancient Greek city-state of Athens. A regular general assembly was held where every male citizen was free to speak and vote. Daily running of the city was in the hands of an elected "Council of Five Hundred". Women and slaves, however, were not allowed to vote.

Pericles, leader of Athens at the height of its power

Bill Clinton is sworn in as US President.

PRESIDENT
In a presidential system, an elected president is the head of state and chief executive. He or she proposes new laws and passes them to the legislature, which may or may not pass them, and can also refuse to pass laws proposed by the legislature. The president is Commander-in-Chief of the army and controls foreign policy.

US Congress, Washington D.C.

LEGISLATURE
The legislature is an assembly of elected representatives. Every new law must be passed by this assembly. It may propose laws itself and votes on those proposed by the president. In most presidential systems, the legislature is composed of two assemblies, or houses. In the US, the legislature is called Congress.

US Supreme Court, Washington D.C.

JUDICIARY
The judiciary is a legal body that reviews the laws passed by the legislature and ensures that they are in line with the country's written Constitution. In the US, the highest legal body is the Supreme Court. It can judge the activities of the executive and legislative branches, and reverse judicial decisions made by lower courts.

EXECUTIVE
US State Department
The president, as chief executive, is responsible for the administration of the state and for putting into practice new acts of law. He or she appoints the heads of the many administrative departments such as Defence, Trade, Education, Agriculture, and State.

PARLIAMENTARY SYSTEM
In a parliamentary system, political activity focuses on an assembly where matters are debated and laws are passed. Citizens elect members to act as their representatives. In Britain, the political party with the largest number of members elected to the House of Commons forms the government. The leader of that party becomes the Prime Minister, or chief executive. All executive power is held by the Prime Minister and his or her cabinet.

House of Commons – the political focus of Parliament and of British democracy

POLITICAL FACTS
• The word "government" comes from the latin word *gubernare*, meaning "to steer".

• In Switzerland, voting in elections is compulsory – it is regarded as every citizen's duty.

• Until the 1980s, Soviet leaders were able to rule Communist USSR as virtual dictators – with more power than US presidents.

• The terms right and left wing come from France's Assembly of the 1790s: conservatives sat on the right of the speaker's chair, and reformers sat on its left.

French Assembly, c.1865

POLITICAL RECORDS
OLDEST RECORDED LAW-MAKING BODY
is the Althing in Iceland. It was formed in about A.D. 930 and consisted of 40 local priest-chieftains. It was abolished in 1800 but then restored in 1843.

OLDEST CONSTITUTION
still in use is that of the US, which was written in 1787.

LARGEST LAW-MAKING BODY
is the National People's Congress of the People's Republic of China.

PEACEFUL PARLIAMENT
During debates in the British House of Commons, the leaders of the government and opposition stand at two swords' lengths from each other. This is a symbol of the parliamentary rule that members should never use violence to solve political problems.

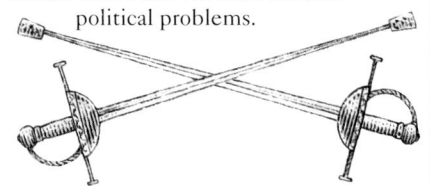

COMMUNISM
German thinker Karl Marx (1818–83) devised a new political and economic system, which he called Communism, in which all property is owned by the community and everyone shares in the country's wealth. In 1917, the USSR became the first communist state. Wealth was shared out more or less equally but, unlike Marx's ideal communist state, a single party, the Soviet Communist party, wielded total power and was able to use it unfairly.

Communist magazine, showing a worker smashing the chains of capitalism.

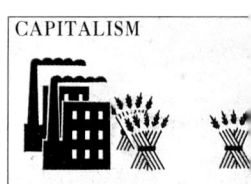

COMMUNISM
Under Communism, workers own the factories and share their profits equally.

CAPITALISM
Under capitalism, a few people own all the factories, but do not share profits with the workers.

POLITICAL ORGANIZATIONS AND PRESSURE GROUPS

Throughout the world, people and countries with shared interests form organizations to promote and defend their interests. Some, such as the United Nations, the Arab League, and the European Community, are concerned with the common interests of member states. Others, such as the environmental group Greenpeace and the human rights group Amnesty International, devote themselves to a particular cause.

Members of Greenpeace protest against plans for a nuclear power station.

VOTING

People hold elections to choose people to represent them. Each person usually casts one vote, and the candidate who receives the most votes is elected to office. This system is used in electing one representative for each constituency. An alternative system, proportional representation, allocates the seats in numbers proportional to the total number of votes given for each party.

South African citizen casts her vote in 1994 elections for president and parliament.

WOMEN'S VOTES
Women have not always shared in decisions about the way they were governed.

Country	First vote
New Zealand	1893
Australia	1902
Finland	1906
Norway	1913
Denmark	1915
Former USSR	1917
Britain	1918
USA	1920
South Africa (whites)	1930
Japan	1945

Emmeline Pankhurst, a British supporter of women's voting rights, arrested during a protest.

POLITICAL WORDS

Anarchism Movement in favour of the abolition of the state.

Cabinet Group of ministers responsible for government in a parliamentary system.

Capitalism Economic system where invested capital (accumulated wealth) and profit-making drives industry.

Coalition Temporary alliance between different parties for combined action.

Communism Political and economic system in which all property is commonly owned and each person is paid according to their needs and abilities.

Congress US legislature composed of two houses – the Senate and the House of Representatives.

Constituency Geographical area representing a body of voters.

Constitution Basic set of laws that set out the institutions through which political power is exercised.

Constitutional monarchy System of government authorized by a constitution with a monarch as the head of state.

Coup d'Etat Violent or illegal seizure of power.

Democracy System of government by whole population or its representatives.

Dictatorship Government by a ruler with unrestricted authority.

Electorate Body of people entitled to vote in an election.

Executive Branch of government that carries out laws and performs general administration.

Fascism Extreme right-wing nationalist movement.

House of Commons In Britain, the elected chamber of Parliament.

Judiciary All the nation's judges.

Legislature Assembly or group that passes laws.

Lobby Group of people seeking to influence law-makers.

Prime minister Chief executive of government in countries with a parliamentary system.

Republic State in which power is held by the people or their elected representatives.

Revolution Forcible overthrow of a government or social order.

Socialism System in which the means of production (factories, etc.) and distribution are owned by the community as a whole.

Suffrage Right to vote in a political election.

Suffragette A woman who protests for her right to vote.

Trade union Group of workers or professionals united to protect and promote their rights and interests.

Totalitarianism Dictatorial system of government that extends its control to all social institutions.

GOVERNMENT EXAMPLES AROUND THE WORLD

Power may be held by groups or individuals. Democracies may differ in structure.

Monarchies
Saudi Arabia is an absolute monarchy with no political parties.

Totalitarian regimes
China is ruled by one party, the Communist Party, and other parties are forbidden.

Facade democracies
Iran holds elections for its presidency, but candidates are chosen by those in power.

Military dictatorships
Myanmar (Burma) is ruled by a 19-member military council.

Presidential republics
France's democracy has both a president and prime minister.

KEY POLITICAL THINKERS

Thinker	Dates	Biographical details
Plato	429–347 B.C.	Greek philosopher, rejected democracy in *The Republic* and insisted that government was a science, requiring experts.
Niccolo Machiavelli	1469–1527	Italian political thinker and diplomat, wrote a book, *The Prince*, that described methods of achieving political unity.
Thomas Hobbes	1588–1679	English philosopher, argued in *Leviathan* that human nature made absolute monarchy desirable and inevitable.
Jean-Jacques Rousseau	1712–78	French philosopher. His *Social Contract* argued that people sacrifice their rights in return for protection by a head of state.
Comte de Saint-Simon	1760–1825	French social scientist, believed that society should be organized along industrial lines.
John Stuart Mill	1806–73	English philosopher and political activist, argued for truly representative democracy.
Karl Marx	1818–83	German philosopher and economist, founder of Communism. Wrote *Das Kapital*.
Emile Durkheim	1858–1917	French founder of sociology.
Max Weber	1864–1920	German economist. Described the relationship between economy and society.

FALSE STARTER

Bolivia's political system has experienced great turmoil. In the 156 years from its independence from Spain (1825) to 1981, Bolivia has had 192 changes of government. This is an average of a new government every ten months.

LAW AND ORDER

EVERY COUNTRY HAS a set of rules or laws to protect the rights of its citizens. Laws are usually enforced by government through the police and the courts. In most countries, legal systems are the result of years of development, change, and reform.

EARLY LAW
About 4,000 years ago, King Hammurabi of Babylon set out some of the first recorded codes of behaviour. He devised laws, as well as penalties, covering family, property, slaves, and wages. These laws were engraved on a stone pillar.

Hammurabi meets the god of justice.

SCALES OF JUSTICE
The Statue of Justice at the Old Bailey, London (above), holds scales to show that justice weighs opposing evidence the way a balance weighs goods. The sword represents punishment. Some countries abuse their legal powers and remove freedoms instead of upholding them.

THE FIRST COURTS
In about 450 B.C., the Romans formed a system of courts where trials were held, and judges decided if a person had broken the law. In serious cases the accused paid a lawyer, called an *advocatus*, to speak for him. Most European law is based on Roman law.

TRIAL BY JURY
Anyone accused of a serious crime has the right to a trial by a jury, usually 12 men and women, chosen at random. South Africa does not have the jury system.

The judge helps the jury on points of the law, listens to the evidence, and passes sentence if there is a guilty verdict.

Prisoner on trial (the accused)

Prosecuting lawyer

COURT PROCEDURE
A prosecuting lawyer tries to convince the jury that the accused is guilty, while a defence lawyer sets out to prove the person's innocence. After listening to evidence from various witnesses, the jury has to decide whether the prosecution has proved guilt.

Jury of 12 men and women chosen from members of the public aged over 18

Prosecution tries to prove guilt.

Defence tries to convince the jury that the prisoner is not guilty.

TYPES OF LAW
There are several branches of the law, each devised to meet the different problems of society.

CRIMINAL LAW
This branch of the law covers acts such as murder, arson, rape, and robbery. In the USA, these are broken down into first, second, third, and fourth degrees, depending on the state of mind of the accused.

CIVIL LAW
This law deals with cases in which no crime has taken place, but someone's rights have been infringed. It covers day-to-day events such as buying a house or making a will, as well as resolving disputes between companies.

RELIGIOUS LAW
This law deals with cases in which religious code determines the law. For example, Islamic Law is based on the Koran and the teachings of Muhammad and is the basis for the law in North Africa and the Middle East.

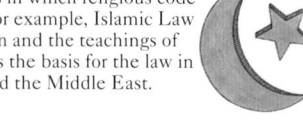

PRISON POPULATION WESTERN EUROPE (1994)

Country	Prisoners per 100,000 population
UK	92.1
Spain	91.8
Austria	87.5
Switzerland	84.9
France	83.9
Portugal	82.0
Germany	78.8
Denmark	63.0
Finland	62.6
Belgium	60.5

PRISON FACTS
• Early prisons were filthy, and people often died of a kind of typhus known as "jail fever".

• The longest prison sentence was 141,078 years, passed on a woman in Thailand, for fraud.

• The world's most secure prison was Alcatraz, on an island off the California coast. Although 24 convicts tried to break free, no one ever managed to escape.

THE DEATH PENALTY
The death penalty is still legal in 105 countries, although many of them never carry out the sentence. Offences range from murder to drug trafficking. The first country to abolish the death penalty was Austria, in 1787. From 1995 the death penalty is unconstitutional in South Africa.

LEGAL WORDS

Accused Person charged with committing a crime.
Arson Criminal damage caused by fire.

Arson

Assault Threat or attempt to physically harm a person.
Bail Money given to gain temporary release of a prisoner facing trial.
Bankruptcy Situation in which a person is unable to pay their debts.
Barrister Lawyer who practises in the higher courts.
Damages Money claimed or awarded as compensation for loss or injury.
Defence Defendant's case in a law suit.
Defendant Person prosecuted in a criminal action.
Evidence The means used for proving a disputed fact in a legal action.
Felony A crime regarded by the law as serious, usually involving violence.

English judge

Fraud Deliberate trickery to gain an advantage, often financial.
Insolvent Situation in which a company is unable to pay its debts.
Judge Official who hears and tries cases in a court of law.
Jury Group of people who give a verdict in criminal cases on the basis of evidence given in court.
Kidnap Carry off a person against their will.
Libel Words published about a person that may harm their good character.
Murder To kill a person.
Oath Formal declaration as to the truth of something.
Perjury Wilfully tell an untruth when under oath.
Probation An alternative to a prison sentence whereby an offender must report regularly to a probation officer.
Prosecution The carrying on of legal proceedings.
Rape Force a person to have sexual intercourse against their will.
Slander Words spoken about a person that may harm their good character.
Solicitor Lawyer who advises clients and instructs barristers.
Subpoena A written demand that a person appear in court.
Sue To begin legal proceedings.
Summons Call to appear before a judge or magistrate.
Theft Take another's property without their consent.

Subpoena

Trial Legal proceedings to determine issues between parties.
Verdict Decision made in a criminal case.
Warrant Written authorization allowing police to search property and make arrests.

ARTS AND THE MEDIA

All the major art forms, from architecture to music, are given detailed treatment in this section. Timelines present key developments in the arts, and tables list famous painters, composers, architects, and writers. The media pages feature the latest in modern technology, including virtual reality.

Architecture • Fine Arts • Artists and Materials • Photography
Theatre • Dance • Ballet and Modern Dance • Traditional World Dance
Music • Classical Music • Popular Music • Musical Instruments
Writing • Printing • Radio • Television • Cinema • Animation
Video • Newspapers

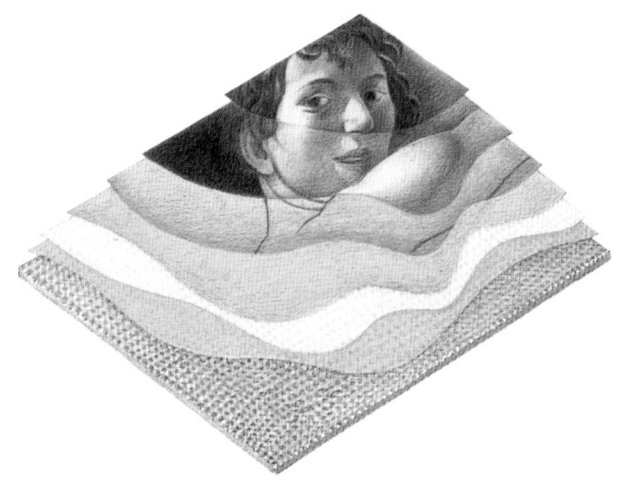

ARCHITECTURE

ARCHITECTURE IS THE art and science of designing and constructing buildings. Modern steel-and-glass structures are now a feature of cities worldwide.

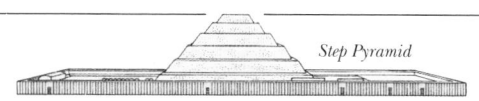

Step Pyramid

c.6500 B.C. Çatal Hüyük in Turkey, one of the first known towns, has rectangular houses built from mud bricks.

c.2650–2150 B.C. Pyramids are constructed in the lower Nile Valley, Egypt. The famous Step Pyramid at Saqqara is designed by Imhotep, a high priest and the first recorded architect.

c.2200 B.C. Stonehenge, a massive stone circle that is one of prehistoric Europe's most complex stone monuments, is erected for religious purposes.

Sto

6500 B.C.   *2600 B.C.*   *2200 B.C.*

700–400 B.C. Classical Greece. Architects of Greek temples develop three architectural "orders": Doric, Ionic, and Corinthian. Each order has its own style and proportions, based on mathematics and geometry, that are thought to be pleasing to the Greek gods.

Parthenon, Athens

Indian stupa

c.300 B.C. Buddhist stupas appear in India and Southeast Asia. These solid mounds symbolize the dome of heaven and contain sacred Buddhist relics.

c.200 B.C.–A.D. 500 Roman architectu takes over the Greek orders and Etruscan arch. The Romans develop concrete and use construct huge vaults a domes. Their public buildings include co bath houses, temple amphitheatres.

Colosseum, Rome

700 B.C.   *300 B.C.*   *200 B.C.*

607–670 Japan's temple of the Horyuji Buddhist monastery, Nara, is the world's oldest surviving wooden building.

618–782 China. Nanchan Buddhist temple, Shaanxi province, built on a holy mountain, is the earliest surviving traditional Chinese timber-framed building.

Horyuji Temple

Great Mosque, Samarra

690–850 Early Islamic mosques, palaces, and houses are designed around courtyards. Mosques have minarets (prayer towers), arcades, and vaulted porches. Surface decoration is often mosaic – patterns of glass, stone, or marble pieces.

778–850 Borobudur Buddhist temple, Indonesia, has 8 stone terraces and 72 bell-shaped stupas.

c.900–1150 Romane style of architecture develops in western Europe. Romanesque churches have massiv rubble-filled walls wit small windows. Arche semi-circular in shape stand on top of huge cylindrical columns.

Pisa Cathedral, Italy

600   *607*   *618*   *700*   *778*   *900*

c.1420 Renaissance begins in Florence, Italy. Key figures are Brunelleschi (1377–1446) and Alberti (1404–72). This study of and adaptation of classical Roman styles and building techniques soon spreads through western Europe.

The Duomo, Florence, Italy

c.1650 Baroque style in Europe re-interprets Roman and Renaissance styles. Architects are commissioned by the Catholic Church and royalty to build large-scale, grand, and very ornate churches and palaces.

Church of St. Nicholas, Prague

1750–1840 Neo-Classicism Architects rediscover the proportions and details of Roman and then Greek classical architecture. A fine example is the church of Sainte Geneviève, Paris, later renamed the "Panthéon".

Par

1400   *c.1420*   *1600*   *c.1650*   *1700*   *1750*

1900–40s American architect Frank Lloyd Wright (1867–1959) promotes "organic" architecture – buildings that blend in with nature, such as Falling Water, Pennsylvania, USA.

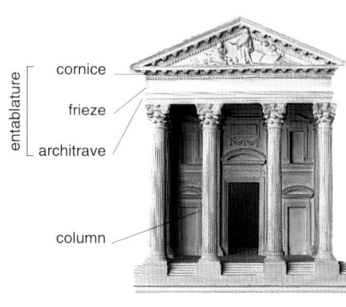

Falling Water

1919–33 Bauhaus, Germany, an influential design school led by Walter Gropius (1883–1969), teaches design based on modern industrial technologies.

Bauhaus, Dessau

1920s International Modernism. Leading Swiss-born architect, Le Corbusier (1887–1965) defines a house as "a machine for living in".

Le Corbusier

1970s High-Tech sty In the steel-and-glass buildings of Richard Rogers (born 1933) an Norman Foster (born 1935), parts of the structure and services (pipes) are left expose A typical example is t Lloyds Building, Lon

1900   *1919*   *1920*   *1970*

ORDERS

In classical Greek architecture, an order consists of an upright column supporting a horizontal entablature. A cornice, a frieze, and an architrave make up the entablature itself. The three Greek orders are Doric, Ionic, and Corinthian.

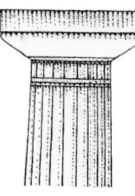

cornice
frieze
architrave
entablature
column

Doric
The Greeks used this order from about 700 B.C.

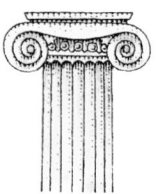

Ionic
From 600 B.C., this order appeared in western Asia.

Corinthian
This decorative order originated in Athens in 500 B.C.

Caryatids
These female statues are used as supporting columns.

Atlas (male caryatid)

Pedestal

Ziggurat, Ur

–2095 B.C.
...ians build ziggurats, ..., stepped temples of ...icks, in Mesopotamia.

c.1700–1200 B.C. Beehive tomb (*tholos*) is constructed by the Mycenean civilization on the Greek mainland.

c.1500 B.C. Minoan Palace of Knossos is rebuilt on the island of Crete, Greece. Paintings decorate the walls.

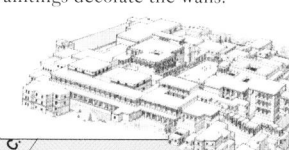

800–200 B.C. Etruscans, in modern-day Tuscany, Italy, use the arch in the construction of their buildings.

Palace of Knossos, Crete

DOMES
These curved roofs are convex (arched) in shape, and are often a feature of religious buildings worldwide.

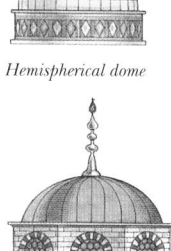
Hemispherical dome

(Timeline markers: 1700 B.C., 1500 B.C., 800 B.C.)

300–1540 Pre-Columbian ...tions build stepped pyramids ..., crowned with temples. ... the finest to survive is the ... pyramid, known as the ...aguar, built before ...0 in the ceremonial ...x at Tikal, ...nala.

Giant Jaguar

A.D. 330–1453 Byzantine architecture develops when the new Roman Imperial capital moves to Byzantium (now Istanbul). It reflects Roman and Middle Eastern styles. The largest domed church of its day, Hagia Sophia, Istanbul, is completed in 537.

Hagia Sophia

Onion dome   *Polyhedral dome*   *Saucer dome*

(Timeline markers: A.D. 300, 330)

ROOFS
Roofs are defined by the shape and structure of their supporting frames. Coverings range from tiles to reeds.

Hipped roof

c.1100–1500 Gothic style is first used for Christian churches in northern Europe. New construction methods – the pointed arch and the flying buttress – result in much taller, lighter structures.

Amiens Cathedral, France

Angkor Wat

1113–c.1150 Angkor Wat, a vast stone temple city, is built by the Khmers at their capital in Cambodia. It is crowned with lotus-bud spires and covers almost 200 hectares (495 acres).

Pavilion roof   *Turret roof*   *Gable-and-valley roof*

(Timeline markers: 1100, 1113)

–1930s Gothic ...l. Architects attempt ...ture the style of ...al buildings. They also ...reate a new style ...odern building ...ls and materials as in ...nsylvania Academy of ...ts, Philadelphia, USA.

Home Insurance Building, Chicago

19th-century Industrial Revolution results in mass-produced materials that transform construction. Plate glass is used from the 1840s, steel from 1856, and reinforced concrete from the 1860s. Following the invention of the lift, steel-framed skyscrapers are first erected in Chicago, USA.

Casa Batlló, Barcelona

1890– early 1900s Art Nouveau – "new art" – is inspired by plant forms. Buildings are very ornate.

VAULTS AND ARCHES
Vaults are arched roofs or ceilings, and there are four main types. Arches span openings and carry weight.

Barrel vault

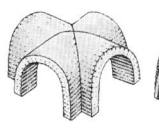 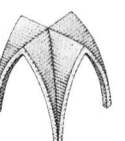 
Groin vault   *Rib vault*   *Fan vault*

(Timeline marker: 1890)

Mid-1970s Postmodernism develops, a style that refers to past styles, sometimes in a humorous way. Buildings often feature strong, bright colours, such as the Neue Staatsgalerie, Stuttgart, Germany.

Lloyds Building

Neue Staatsgalerie

1990s Sustainable architecture provides a means of maintaining an ecological balance between human needs and preservation of the environment. Architects employ technology that manages nature in their designs.

Pointed arch   *Horseshoe arch*   *Lobed arch*

(Timeline marker: 1990)

WINDOWS
A window is an opening to let in light and air. Its materials, shape, and design reflect a building's architectural style.

Casement window

...PITALS
...e top section, or head, of a ...umn is called a capital.

...yptian ...pital   *Romanesque capital*   *Korean capital*

BUTTRESSES
Made of stone or brickwork, buttresses are built against walls to strengthen them. Flying buttresses transfer the weight of the upper part of a wall to an exterior support.

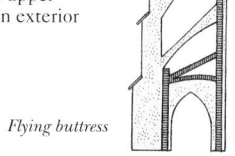
Flying buttress

Oeil-de-Boeuf (Ox-eye) window

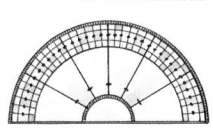
Fanlight

SEVEN WONDERS OF THE WORLD

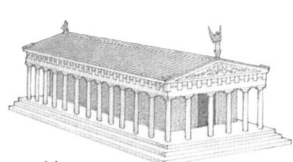

Temple of Artemis
Originally erected in about 550 B.C., this marble temple was burned down and later rebuilt. The gold statue of Artemis was destroyed, and only one of the original 127 Ionic columns remains.

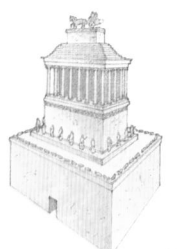 

Mausoleum at Halicarnassus
This vast marble tomb of Turkish ruler Mausolos was built in about 350 B.C. On site, only the foundations remain, but some statues are in London's British Museum.

Pharos of Alexandria
Built in about 297 B.C., this lighthouse stood on the island of Pharos, Alexandria, Egypt. At night a fire burned, reflected by bronze mirrors. Three earthquakes reduced the building to rubble.

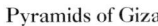

Pyramids of Giza
These pyramids were built at Giza, Egypt, between about 2575 and 2465 B.C. The Great Pyramid of Cheops is said to have taken 100,000 men 20 years to build.

Statue of Zeus, Olympia
This huge statue of the king of the gods was made from ivory and gold. The head alone measured 13m (43ft) in height.

Colossus of Rhodes
This bronze statue of the Sun god, Helios, stood more than 35m (110ft) high at the entrance to Rhodes harbour, Greece. An earthquake toppled it.

Hanging Gardens of Babylon
Nebuchadnezzar II (c.605–562 B.C.), King of Babylon, built these magnificent terraced gardens for one of his wives. Although descriptions exist, archaeologists are still looking for the site.

ARCHITECTURE FACTS

• Ancient Greeks painted the inside and outside of their temples in brilliant colours. The present whitened marble is due to weathering and bleaching by the hot sun.

• There is about 100 times more stone and brick in the Great Pyramid of Cheops than there is in the Empire State Building.

• Our ancestors' homes were dark caves. Today, in the mining community of Coober Pedy, Australia, people live in well-equipped dugouts with TVs and showers.

RECORDS

BIGGEST CASTLE
in the world is Prague Castle in the Czech Republic. Founded in about 850, the castle now covers about 8 hectares (20 acres).

TALLEST RESIDENTIAL BLOCK OF FLATS
is Lake Point Tower, Chicago, Illinois. It has 70 storeys and is 195m (639ft) high.

BIGGEST SHOPPING CENTRE
in the world is West Edmonton Mall, Alberta, Canada, which is as big as 90 American football fields.

TRADITIONAL HOMES AROUND THE WORLD

AFRICA

 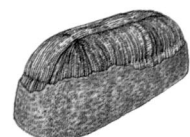 

Zulu kraal, South Africa
Kraals are traditional dome-shaped, grass-covered houses with low openings at the front.

Masai house, Kenya
The Masai people build their rounded houses from bent branches covered with cow dung.

Algerian desert village
Houses are packed tightly together, so that as little of the house as possible is exposed to the blistering heat of the sun.

Dogon village, Mali
In these West African villages, houses are built of mud-brick, and storehouse roofs are thatched.

OCEANIA

Longhouse
These communal houses are raised on wooden stilts to keep animals out.

EUROPE

  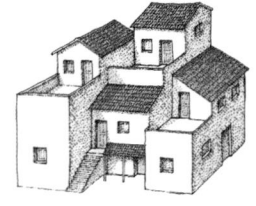

Swiss chalet
Traditional wooden chalets have sloping roofs to stop too much snow from collecting on them .

Scandinavian house
Roofs of traditionally built houses in such cold climates are turf covered to keep in the heat.

Mediterranean village house
The whitewashed stone houses of this region reflect the sun's heat, keeping the interior cool.

ASIA

Yurt
Nomads from Iran to Mongolia live in these willow-framed tents covered in felt and canvas.

Japanese house
Traditional timber-framed houses have sliding walls and doors that can be opened to the outside.

Chinese house
In China, traditional houses are arranged around a courtyard. The main part is on the north side.

AMERICAS

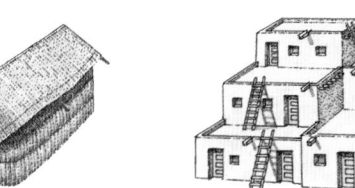 

Amyara Indian house
On Lake Titicaca, Bolivia, Amyara Indians live in houses constructed from woven reeds.

Adobe houses
In New Mexico, traditional houses are built with adobe – bricks of sun-baked mud.

New England house
The walls of these North American houses have overlapping wooden boards (clapboards).

CROSS-SECTION OF A SKYSCRAPER, HONG KONG AND SHANGHAI BANK, HONG KONG

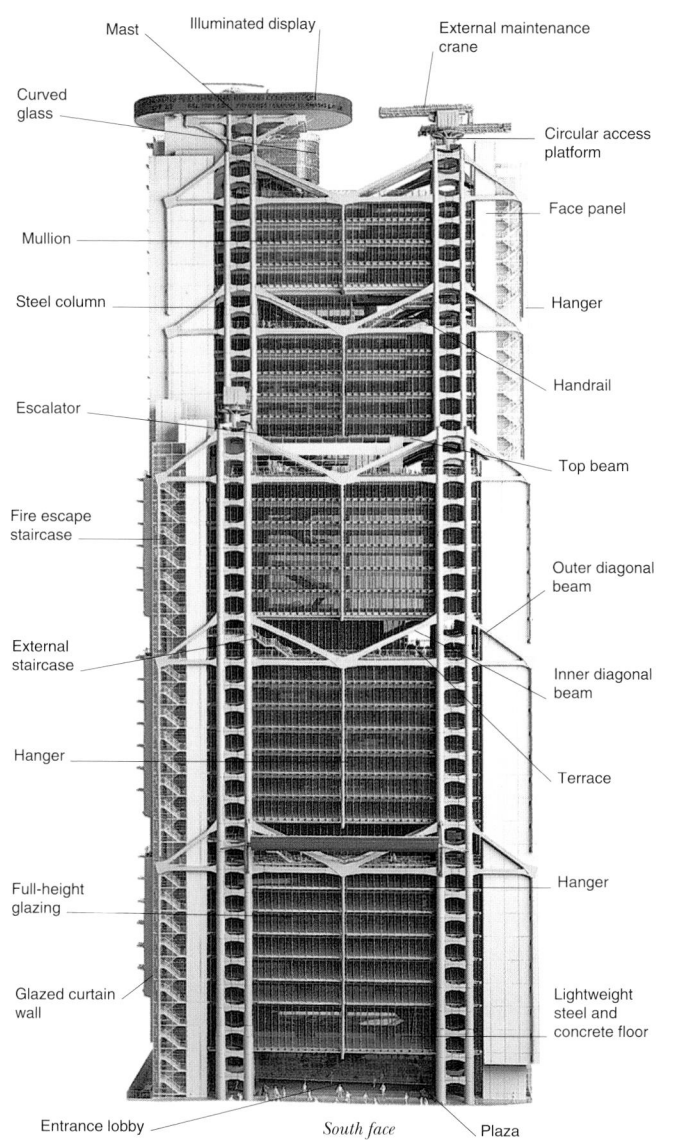

Mast
Illuminated display
External maintenance crane
Curved glass
Circular access platform
Face panel
Mullion
Hanger
Steel column
Handrail
Escalator
Top beam
Fire escape staircase
Outer diagonal beam
External staircase
Inner diagonal beam
Hanger
Terrace
Full-height glazing
Hanger
Glazed curtain wall
Lightweight steel and concrete floor
Entrance lobby
South face
Plaza

KEY ARCHITECTS

Name	Dates	Nationality	Building
Filippo Brunelleschi	1377–1446	Italian	Santa Maria del Fiore, Florence, Italy
Michelangelo Buonarroti	1475–1564	Italian	Dome of St. Peter's, Vatican City
Andrea Palladio	1508–80	Italian	Villa Rotonda, Vicenza, Italy
Inigo Jones	1573–1652	British	Banqueting House, London, England
François Mansart	1598–1666	French	Chateau de Maisons, Paris, France
Christopher Wren	1632–1723	British	St. Paul's, London, England
Jacques-Germain Soufflot	1713–80	French	The Panthéon, Paris, France
Andreyan Zakharov	1761–1811	Russian	The Admiralty, St. Petersburg, Russia
Karl Friedrich Schinkel	1781–1841	German	Altes Museum, Berlin, Germany
Antonio Gaudi	1852–1926	Spanish	La Sagrada Familia, Barcelona, Spain
Frank Lloyd Wright	1867–1959	American	Falling Water, Pennsylvania, USA
Edwin Lutyens	1869–1944	British	Viceroy's House, New Delhi, India
Adolf Loos	1870–1933	Czech	Scheu House, Vienna, Austria
Walter Gropius	1883–1969	German	Bauhaus, Dessau, Germany
Mies van der Rohe	1886–1969	German	Seagram Building, New York, USA
Erich Mendelsohn	1887–1953	German	Einstein Tower, Potsdam, Germany
Le Corbusier	1887–1965	Swiss	Notre Dame du Haut, Ronchamp, France
R. Buckminster Fuller	1895–1983	American	USA Pavilion, Expo 67, Montreal, Canada
Philip Johnson	b.1906	American	The Glass House, Connecticut, USA
Oscar Niemeyer	b.1907	Brazilian	Government Buildings, Brasilia, Brazil
Ieoh Ming Pei	b.1917	American	Louvre Pyramid, Paris, France
Richard Rogers	b.1933	British	Lloyds Building, London, England
Michael Graves	b.1934	American	Public Service Building, Oregon, USA
Norman Foster	b.1935	British	Hong Kong and Shanghai Bank, Hong Kong

ON A HIGH

When the Manhattan skyscrapers were erected, red-hot rivets were driven into holes in narrow steel beams hundreds of metres up in the air with nothing beneath. Iroquois and Mohawk Indians show no fear of heights and have put up many of these skyscrapers.

TALLEST BUILDINGS

Towers	Height m	ft
KTHI-TV Mast, North Dakota, USA	629	2,064
KSFX-TV Mast, Texas, USA	615	2,018
TV Tower, Devers, Texas, USA	607	1,991

Building and location	m	ft
1 Petronas Towers, K L, Malaysia	452	1,483
2 Sears Tower, Chicago, USA	443	1,453
3 Jin Mao Building, Shanghai, China	420	1,378
4 World Trade Center, New York, USA	417	1,368
5 Empire State Building, New York, USA	381	1,250
6 Central Plaza, Hong Kong, China	374	1,227
7 Bank of China, Hong Kong, China	368	1,207
8 T and C-T Tower, Kaoshiung, Taiwan	348	1,142
9 Amoco Building, Chicago, USA	346	1,135
10 John Hancock Center, Chicago, USA	344	1,129

Petronas Towers, Malaysia

159

FINE ARTS

EVERY CULTURE HAS its own works of art. In some cultures, artistic styles have changed significantly; others have remained more or less the same over thousands of years. Movements in Western art have been given names and dates by specialists called art historians.

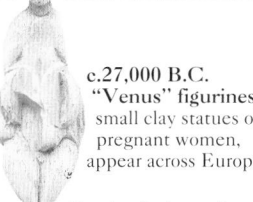

c.27,000 B.C. "Venus" figurines, small clay statues of pregnant women, appear across Europe.

Figurine, Lespugue, France

Horse, Lascaux

c.500–323 B.C. Greek Classical sculptors study the form of the human body and explore its movement, making perfect figures of gods and athletes in marble, bronze, and clay. Phidias, a famous sculptor, makes a huge statue of Athena for the Parthenon, Athens, between 445 and 432 B.C.

Bronze charioteer, Greece

323–31 B.C. Greek Hellenistic sculptors make statues that emphasize the body's gracefulness. The portrait is developed and profiles of Greek rulers appear on coins.

Detail, Trajan's column

c.100 B.C.–A.D. 400 Roman decorative art flourishes. Relief carvings (standing out from the surface), often depicting Roman military victories, adorn arches and columns.

A.D. 100–400 Gandharan sculpture, influenced by Greek art, develops in the Indus Valley region (Pakistan). Sculptures show scenes from the Buddha's life.

Gandhara Buddha teaching

1000–1200 Romanesque style in Europe is displayed in church sculpture and mural painting, and in embroideries such as the Bayeux Tapestry, showing the Norman conquest of England.

Detail, Bayeux Tapestry, 1066

1000–1600 Easter Island (Polynesia). Gigantic, half-length figures up to 10m (33ft) in height are carved from volcanic rock and erected facing the sea.

Statue, Easter Island

1368–1644 Ming Dynasty in China is famous for its glazed blue-painted porcelain bowls and vases.

1450s Printing process develops in Germany. Illustrations are first printed using carved woodblocks; images are then engraved on to copper for greater detail.

1368

1600s Dutch Golden Age painters represent scenes from everyday life, portraits and still-life subjects (such as fruit and flowers), and landscapes. Key artists are Rembrandt van Rijn (1606–69) and Jan Vermeer (1632–75).

Saskia as Flora, Rembrandt, c.1635

1600s Baroque style develops in Europe. Paintings feature energetic movement and strong contrasts of light and shadow to create dramatic effects. Michelangelo da Caravaggio (1573–1610) is one of the most influential artists.

Late 1700s to mid-1800s Romantic school of painting reflects the power of human emotions and nature. Key painters include J.M.W. Turner (1775–1851) and Caspar David Friedrich (1774–1840).

Norham Castle, Turner, 1824

1880–1905 Post-Impressionist artists Paul Cézanne (1839–1906), Vincent Van Gogh (1853–90), and Paul Gauguin (1848–1903), develop in their own different directions.

White Horse, Gauguin, 1898

1880s–90s Expressionism develops in Europe. Intense colour and free brushstrokes communicate artists' feelings. Ernst Ludwig Kirchner (1880–1938) is a key figure in Germany.

Drawing, Kirchner

1880s–90s Symbolist artists create images that portray inner feelings and suggest what may lie beneath the surface of things. Key painters include Gustave Moreau (1826–98).

1905–7 Fauves, a group of French painters that includes Henri Matisse (1869–1954), represent the world in brilliant colour harmonies.

1920s Surrealism develops from Dada and Freud's theories of psychoanalysis (see p.132). Artists such as Salvador Dali (1904–89) and Max Ernst (1891–1976) use dreams to explore their hidden feelings.

Salvador Dali, 1971

1940s Abstract Expressionism appears in New York, USA. Artists create abstract images, while experimenting with the physical properties of paint and different ways of applying it to the canvas. Jackson Pollock (1912–56) develops his paint-dripping technique as a way of expressing his feelings more directly.

Mid-1950s Pop Art develops in the USA and Britain. Artists use consumer goods and images from the media in their work. A key figure is Andy Warhol (1928–87).

Andy Warhol, 1971

Late 1950s Performa.. artists combine differe.. art forms – painting, m.. theatre, film, video – i.. their work. Key figures .. Gilbert (born 1943) and George (born 1942), an.. Joseph Beuys (1921–8..

Planted, Gilber.. George,

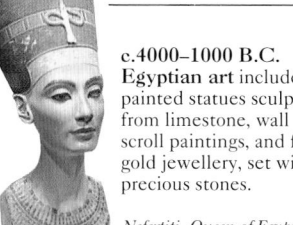

15,000 B.C. Lascaux [c]aves, France, are [de]corated with images [of] animals. Artists use [n]atural mineral colours, [ap]plying them with [fi]ngers, brushes, and by [bl]owing through hollow [re]eds.

c.4000–1000 B.C. **Egyptian art** includes painted statues sculpted from limestone, wall and scroll paintings, and fine gold jewellery, set with precious stones.

Nefertiti, Queen of Egypt

Bull-leaping, Crete

2000–1100 B.C. **Minoans** on Crete, an island near Greece, decorate the walls of their huge palaces with coloured murals.

1600–1027 **Shang Dynasty** craftsmen, China, discover how to cast in bronze and make beautiful decorated vessels for food and wine.

c.500 B.C. **Nok culture**, Nigeria, West Africa, produces lifelike terracotta figurines of humans with individual features emphasized.

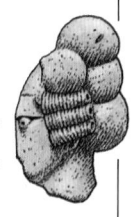

Nok terracotta head

15,000 B.C. · 5,000 B.C. · 1,500 B.C. · 500 B.C.

[A].D. 100–1000 [M]ayan carvings [co]mbine ornate [hu]man figures with [hi]eroglyphs [(]picture-writing). [C]arving is done [w]ithout metal tools.

Mayan incense burner

400–1100 **Medieval European** monks produce illuminated manuscripts, such as the Book of Kells – the four gospels copied out and illustrated by a 9th-century Irish friar.

600–1185 **Icons** (religious portraits) are developed. Painters in the Eastern Christian Church follow strict rules that govern how religious figures must be shown.

Icon, Madonna and Child

T'ang "blue and green" landscape

618–907 **T'ang Dynasty**, a golden age in Chinese art. In this period, the great tradition of Chinese landscape painting develops, and figure (people) painting continues.

A.D. 500 · 600

1400–1500 **Early Renaissance** starts in Florence, Italy, with a revival of interest in Classical sculpture and architecture. Masaccio (1401–28) is the first painter to use perspective (see p.162).

The Flood, Paolo Uccello, c.1445

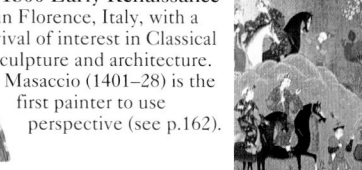

Late 1400s Islamic miniature painting flourishes in Persia (Iran). Paintings are brightly coloured and highly detailed.

15th-century miniature

The Annunciation, Leonardo da Vinci

1500s–1600s High Renaissance period in Italy, particularly Rome and Venice. Major artists are Leonardo da Vinci (1452-1519), Raphael (1483–1520), and Michelangelo (1475–1564).

1500

[1]840s **Realism** develops in [F]rance with painters such as [G]ustave Courbet (1819–77) [w]ho show ordinary people and [th]eir surroundings in a direct, [n]atural, and lifelike way.

The Winnowers, Courbet, 1855

1848 **Pre-Raphaelites** in England are inspired by painters before Raphael but develop their own style and symbols. The group includes Dante Gabriel Rossetti (1828–82) and J.E. Millais (1829–96).

1860s–90s **Impressionism** originates in France. Painters, notably Claude Monet (1840–1926) and Edouard Manet (1832–83), try to capture their impressions, in particular the light, of a fleeting moment in time. **Neo-Impressionism** develops, led by Georges Seurat (1859–91), whose work is based on dots of pure colour.

Waterlilies, Monet, 1916–19

1800 · 1848 · 1850

[1]907–1920s **Cubism** [d]evelops in Paris, [F]rance, with Pablo [P]icasso (1881–1973) [a]nd Georges Braque [(]1882–1963), who use [ge]ometric shapes to [p]ortray what they see.

[P]icasso, 1955

1910–50 **Abstract movement**, in which artists' paintings and sculptures do not directly resemble people or things in everyday life. The first abstract painting may be a work (c.1910) by Wassily Kandinsky (1866–1944).

Hornform, Kandinsky, 1924

1916 **Dada movement**, originally a protest against World War I, rejects traditional forms of art. Marcel Duchamp (1887–1968), selects and displays everyday objects, which he calls "ready-mades".

1910 · 1915 · 1916

From 1970s **Video Artists** use video and computer technology. Their installations (exhibitions) feature video projection. A key figure is Korean-born Nam Jun Paik (born 1932).

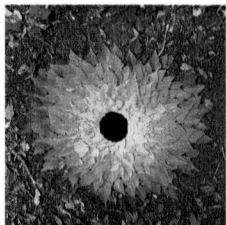

1980s **Art in Nature.** Artists such as Richard Long (born 1945) and Andy Goldsworthy (born 1956) create outdoor works of art that are in harmony with the landscape. Materials – stones, leaves, etc. – are found on-site.

Flower, Andy Goldsworthy, 1992

MOST EXPENSIVE PAINTINGS SOLD AT AUCTION

Title, artist, date sold	Price in US$
Portrait of Dr. Gachet, Van Gogh, 1990	82,500,000
Au Moulin de la Galette, Renoir, 1990	78,100,000
Self Portrait, Van Gogh, 1998	71,500,000
Still Life with Curtain, Pitcher, and Bowl of Fruit, Cezanne, 1999	60,500,000
Irises, Van Gogh, 1987	53,900,000
Les Noces de Pierette, Picasso, 1989	51,895,000
Self Portrait: Yo Picasso, Picasso, 1989	47,850,000
Au Lapin Agile, Picasso, 1989	40,700,000

Source: Sotheby's, London

1970 · 1990

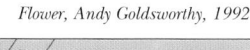

ARTISTS AND MATERIALS

ARTISTS USE PAINT to create images of the world as they see it. Originally they painted on cave walls using the most basic materials. Today, an artist can choose different materials and techniques to express his or her ideas and feelings.

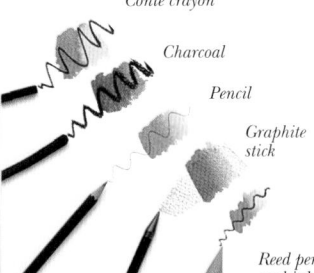

Varnish
Paint layers
Drawing layer
Imprimatura
Priming
Size
Ground

LAYERS OF A PAINTING

There are several layers to an oil painting. These can help modern historians to date a picture accurately, and also to spot whether it is a fake. This artwork, showing a section of Caravaggio's *Youth with a Ram*, reveals the layers through a typical 17th-century oil painting.

MATERIALS

Artists paint on many surfaces using a range of materials. One person may spread thick blobs of oil paint on a canvas with a knife, while another will apply delicate brushstrokes of watercolour on to a sheet of paper. Some artists paint with their fingers, or employ traditional methods such as egg tempera.

PIGMENTS

Paint is made from pigments (powdered colours). Pigments were first found in natural substances such as carbon (black), chalk (white), and red and yellow earths. The ancient Egyptians added mineral colours such as malachite (green) from copper, and ultramarine (blue) from lapis lazuli.

Malachite

Lapis lazuli

MATERIAL FACTS

• The pigment Indian yellow used to be made by boiling the urine of cows fed only on mango leaves. The urine was mixed with earth, heated, and dried.

• Brushes were once made by tying white hog bristles to a stick. The brush was then used to whitewash a wall until the bristles became supple.

• Thousands of years ago, artists in Australia mixed paint, such as red ochre or charcoal, in their mouths and spat the colour into paintings on the cave walls.

DRAWING TOOLS

Artists often make sketches (quick drawings) to record what they see, or to prepare for a finished work. Many drawings are sold as finished works of art. A variety of tools is available.

Conté crayon
Charcoal
Pencil
Graphite stick
Reed pen and ink

PAINTS
Oil paints
These are a mixture of dry pigment and an oil – usually linseed oil. They were first used by 15th-century painters, such as Jan van Eyck.

Oil paint

BRUSHES

Paintbrushes fall into two main groups, soft-hair brushes, mostly used for watercolours, and bristle brushes, used in oil painting and acrylics. Within these groups there are three main types (round, flat, and filbert) identified by the length and shape of the hairs.

Round
Flat
Filbert

Watercolour paints
These are pigments bound with gum arabic and diluted with water. They became popular with 18th-century landscape artists, such as J.M.W. Turner.

Watercolour paint

Acrylic paints
These were developed in the USA during the 1920s. Acrylic is applied with a knife, or diluted and used with a brush. Acrylic was used by Andy Warhol.

Acrylic paint

ARTIST FACTS

• Architect and artist Leon Battista Alberti (1404–72) wrote a key book about perspective in 1436. His methods enabled artists to create a geometrically controlled space on a two-dimensional surface.

• Making copies of paintings by Old Masters was considered an essential part of a young painter's training. Edouard Manet made copies of both Delacroix and Titian while working as a student.

• Pablo Picasso's famous work *Guernica* (1937) depicts scenes from the Spanish Civil War. Picasso refused to let the painting hang in Spain until the country was free. It remained in New York until 1981, when democracy was restored.

• Katsushika Hokusai (1760–1849) was a master of the Japanese ukiyo-e (pictures of the floating world) school. He made beautiful wood-block colour prints showing views of Mt. Fuji.

FAKE FACTS

• Paint can be dated by analysing its content. Cobalt blue, for example, was not produced before 1802, but is used by forgers when they need a cheap substitute for ultramarine.

• Many signed drawings and paintings, supposedly by Rembrandt, were actually done by artists of his school.

• Leonardo da Vinci's *Mona Lisa* was stolen from the Louvre in 1912. It took three years to find, during which time six forgeries turned up in the USA, each selling for a very high price.

POPULAR EUROPEAN GALLERIES (1996)

Art Gallery	Visitors
National Gallery, London	5,000,000
Louvre, Paris	4,700,000
Prado, Madrid	1,814,892
Uffizi Gallery, Florence	1,106,173
Van Gogh Museum, Amsterdam	971,479
Alte Pinakothek, Munich	335,000

SCULPTOR FACTS

• When Rodin exhibited his first major work, *The Age of Bronze* (1878), it caused a sensation. The figure was so lifelike he was accused of casting it from a living model.

• Henry Moore's work was influenced by the carvings of the Aztecs. A sculpture of their ancient rain god, Tlaloc, gave him the idea for his statues of *Reclining Women*.

LABOUR OF LOVE

Michelangelo painted the ceiling of the Sistine Chapel in Rome. The fresco covers more than 900sq m (9,688sq ft), and took four and a half years to complete.

ARTISTS' WORDS

Airbrushing Spraying on colour under pressure with an airbrush.

Alla prima A direct form of painting made in one session. Used by artists when they want to paint spontaneously.

Casting To make an object, often a sculpture, by pouring metal into a mould and letting it harden.

Chiaroscuro The treatment of light and shade in drawing and painting.

Chroma The intensity or saturation of a colour.

Collage A pictorial technique in which various materials are arranged and fixed to a backing.

Craquelure The network of small cracks that appears on a painting when, in the course of time, the pigment's varnish has become brittle.

Craquelure

Engraving The various processes of cutting a design into a plate or block of metal or wood, and the prints taken from these plates or blocks.

Etching A method of engraving in which a corrosive acid "eats" a design into a metal plate.

Ferrule The metal part of a brush which surrounds and retains the hairs.

Fresco Powdered pigments mixed in water and applied to wet lime plaster. Fresco means "fresh" in Italian.

Gesso A traditional surface for tempera and oil painting on a panel made of glue and plaster of paris.

Glaze Film of transparent colour laid over a painting once it has dried.

Gouache Similar technique to watercolour but glue is used to bind the colour together. Used since the 18th century.

Ground The surface on which colour is applied.

Gum arabic Gum from the acacia tree, which is used as a binding material in the manufacture of watercolour paints.

S'graffito

Impasto Paint put on so thickly that it stands up from the surface.

Imprimatura A thin overall film or stain of translucent colour over a white priming.

Pigment The colouring matter, usually powder, which forms the basis of all paint.

Priming The preliminary coating that is put on to the support before painting.

S'graffito A technique using a scalpel or sharp knife in which dried paint is scraped off the painted surface. Used to create texture.

Size Material such as glue or gelatine used to prepare canvas prior to priming or to reduce the absorbency of paper.

Support The material on which a painting is made, such as paper, canvas, or a wooden panel.

Tempera Usually refers to egg tempera, a pigment bound with egg white instead of glue. Most important technique for panel painting (wood) in Europe from 13th to 15th centuries before oil. Layers of paint are built up slowly.

Tone The degree of darkness or lightness of a colour.

Trompe-l'oeil A still-life painting designed to give an illusion of reality.

Varnish Protective surface over a finished painting that gives a glossy or matt appearance.

Wash A thin, transparent layer of paint.

Wash

KEY ARTISTS

Name	Dates	Nationality	Key work
Donatello	c.1386–1466	Italian	*David*
Jan van Eyck	c.1390–1441	Flemish	*Arnolfini and his Wife*
Piero della Francesca	c.1420–92	Italian	*Dream of Constantine*
Sandro Botticelli	c.1445–1510	Italian	*Birth of Venus*
Albrecht Dürer	1471–1528	German	*Melancholia*
Michelangelo Buonarroti	1475–1564	Italian	*David, The Creation of Adam*
Raphael	1483–1520	Italian	*The Sistine Madonna*
Titian	c.1487–1576	Italian	*Assumption of the Madonna*
Leonardo da Vinci	1452–1519	Italian	*Mona Lisa*
Pieter Bruegel the Elder	c.1525–69	Flemish	*A Country Wedding*
Michelangelo da Caravaggio	1573–1610	Italian	*The Supper at Emmaus*
Peter Paul Rubens	1577–1640	Flemish	*Peace and War*
Frans Hals	1580–1666	Flemish	*Laughing Cavalier*
Artemisia Gentileschi	1593–1651	Italian	*Judith and Holofernes*
Nicholas Poussin	1594–1665	French	*Et in Arcadia Ego*
Diego do Velázquez	1599–1660	Spanish	*Las Meninas*
Claude Lorrain	1600–82	French	*Landscape with Sacrifice to Apollo*
Rembrandt van Rijn	1606–69	Dutch	*The Night Watch*
Jan Vermeer	1632–75	Dutch	*Young Woman with a Water Jug*
Antoine Watteau	1684–1721	French	*Embarcation for the Isle of Cythera*
Antonio Canaletto	1697–1768	Italian	*The Stonemason's Yard*
Thomas Gainsborough	1727–88	English	*The Blue Boy*
Francisco de Goya y Lucientes	1746–1828	Spanish	*The Second of May*
Jacques-Louis David	1748–1825	French	*The Death of Marat*
Caspar David Friedrich	1774–1840	German	*Solitary Tree*
Joseph Mallord William Turner	1775–1851	English	*The Fighting Temeraire*
John Constable	1776–1837	English	*The Hay Wain*
Eugène Delacroix	1798–1863	French	*The Massacre at Chios*
Gustave Courbet	1819–77	French	*The Peasants of Flagey*
Edouard Manet	1832–83	French	*Dejeuner sur l'herbe*
Paul Cézanne	1839–1906	French	*Mont Ste. Victoire*
Auguste Rodin	1840–1917	French	*The Kiss*
Claude Monet	1840–1926	French	*The Water Lilies*
Auguste Renoir	1841–1919	French	*Le Moulin de la Galette*
Mary Cassatt	1844–1926	American	*La Loge*
Paul Gauguin	1848–1903	French	*Te Rereioa (Rest)*
Vincent van Gogh	1853–90	Dutch	*Sunflowers*
Georges Seurat	1859–91	French	*A Summer Sunday at La Grande Jatte*
Gustave Klimt	1862–1918	Austrian	*The Kiss*
Edvard Munch	1863–1944	Norwegian	*The Scream*
Henri de Toulouse-Lautrec	1864–1901	French	*Le Moulin Rouge*
Wassily Kandinsky	1866–1944	Russian	*Shrill-Peaceful Pink*
Käthe Kollwitz	1867–1945	German	*Bread*
Pierre Bonnard	1867–1947	French	*At the Table*
Henri Matisse	1869–1954	French	*La Danse*
Piet Mondrian	1872–1944	Dutch	*New York City I*
Constantin Brancusi	1876–1957	Romanian	*Endless Column*
Paul Klee	1879–1940	Swiss	*Ambassador of Autumn*
Fernand Léger	1881–1955	French	*The Outing*
Pablo Picasso	1881–1973	Spanish	*Les Demoiselles d'Avignon*
Georges Braque	1882–1963	French	*Man with a Pipe*
Marcel Duchamp	1887–1968	French	*The Large Glass*
Georgia O'Keeffe	1887–1986	American	*Lilies*
Egon Schiele	1890–1918	Austrian	*Death and the Maiden*
Max Ernst	1891–1976	German	*On the Threshold of Liberty*
Joan Miró	1893–1983	Spanish	*The Birth of the World*
René Magritte	1898–1967	Belgian	*The Use of Words*
Henry Moore	1898–1986	English	*Reclining Figure*
Alberto Giacometti	1901–66	Swiss	*The Forest*
Mark Rothko	1903–70	American	*Blue, Orange, and Red*
Barbara Hepworth	1903–75	English	*Wave*
Salvador Dali	1904–89	Spanish	*Premonition of a Civil War*
Francis Bacon	1909–92	English	*The Screaming Pope*
Jackson Pollock	1912–56	American	*Lavender Mist*
Joseph Beuys	1921–86	German	*The Pack*
Jean Tinguely	1925–91	Swiss	*Homage to New York*
Robert Rauschenberg	1925–	American	*Bed*
Andy Warhol	1928–87	American	*Marilyn Monroe*
Jasper Johns	b.1930–	American	*Three Flags*
Bridget Riley	b.1931–	English	*Late Morning*
David Hockney	b.1937–	English	*A Bigger Splash*
Gilbert and George	b.1943–, 1942–	English	*Underneath the Arches*
Anselm Kiefer	b.1945–	German	*Scorched Earth*

PHOTOGRAPHY

PHOTOGRAPHY IS a way of recording images using a lens and some light-sensitive material. Taking a good photograph depends more on the photographer's visual skills than on the equipment used.

11th century Camera obscura ("dark room") is invented in Arabia for observing solar eclipses. It later forms the basis of photography.

18th-century camera obscura includes a mirror.

1727 Johann Schulze (1687–1744), a German doctor, discovers that silver nitrate darkens when exposed to light.

1827 First photographic image is produced by Joseph Nicéphore Niepce (1765–1833). It takes eight hours of exposure time.

First photographic image

| 1100 | 1700 | 1727 | 1800 | 1827 |

1839 Daguerreotype process is developed by Frenchman Louis Daguerre (1757–1851).

Daguerreotype camera

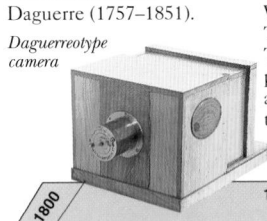

1839 Calotype process is invented by Englishman William Fox Talbot (1800–77). This negative-positive process allows photographs to be copied.

William Fox Talbot

1851 Collodion process is developed by English sculptor Frederick Archer (1813–57). His glass-plate negatives allow paper prints to be made.

Frederick Archer

1907 First practical colour photographic process is introduced by French brothers Auguste (1862–1954) and Louis (1864–1948) Lumière.

First Kodak colour film

1913 35mm film is used for the first time.

Auguste and Louis Lumière

| 1800 | 1839 | 1851 | 1900 | 1913 |

1924 The Leica I, the first 35mm camera, is launched commercially. Its frame counter runs to 36 exposures, setting the standard for later cameras.

Leica I

1935 Kodachrome film is invented, allowing colour transparencies to be both projected and reproduced.

1939 First important negative colour film is produced by Agfa.

Edwin Land

1947 First instant picture camera, invented by American Edwin Land (1909–90), is marketed by Polaroid Corporation.

1975 Using special cameras and lights, an American scientist photographs a bullet passing through an apple at one three-millionth of a second exposure.

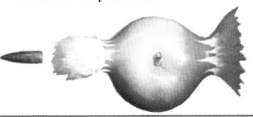

1976 First compact camera with automatic focusing is produced in Japan by Konica. It is called the Konica C35AF.

1990 First "Eye-Start" system is introduced. The camera lens automatically zooms in on the subject when you look through the viewfinder.

1990s Digital cameras are introduced. Images are stored on disks.

| 1900 | 1924 | 1935 | 1939 | 1947 | 1975 | 1976 | 1990 | 1999 |

TYPES OF CAMERA

Automatic SLR camera

Advanced compact camera

Direct vision camera

Instant camera

Panoramic camera

Manual SLR camera

6cm x 4.5cm roll-film camera

6cm x 7cm roll-film camera

Waterproof camera

Large-format camera

Basic compact camera

6cm x 6cm roll-film camera

6cm x 9cm roll-film camera

Wide-view camera

Single-use camera

PHOTOGRAPHY FACTS

• The first successful camera weighed 23kg (51lb), which is the same weight as a red-necked wallaby.

• Every day, more than two million photographs are taken around the world.

• Until about 1930, photographers made flash lights by creating small explosions with magnesium powder.

• One 35mm transparency (slide) can hold as much information as a single high-density floppy disk for a personal computer.

STIFF SHOT

The first cameras required long exposure times, so people had to stand still for long periods in order to avoid a blurred image. The photographer also attached a clamp to the subject's head and body.

PHOTOGRAPHY WORDS

Aperture The opening in the camera lens that controls the amount of light passing on to the film.

Auto-focus A system in the camera which adjusts the focus automatically.

Darkroom A lightproof room used for developing photographic film.

Electronic flash The light source on a camera that is needed for taking pictures after dark, indoors, or in dim light.

Enlargement A photographic print that is larger than the negative from which it was developed.

Motor-drive The device on a camera that enables you to take a rapid sequence of photographs.

SLR (single-lens reflex) A type of camera where the view through the viewfinder is what will actually be recorded on the film.

Transparency A positive image, in black and white or colour, that is produced on a transparent film.

Tripod A stand that supports a camera to keep it steady and avoid blurred images.

Viewfinder The device on a camera that shows what will be in the photograph.

INSIDE A CAMERA

A camera is basically a lightproof box that has a hole, or lens, at one end. An open lens allows light to enter and shine on a piece of film (light-sensitive paper) inside the camera, forming an image. The most important parts of a camera are the lens, shutter, and diaphragm.

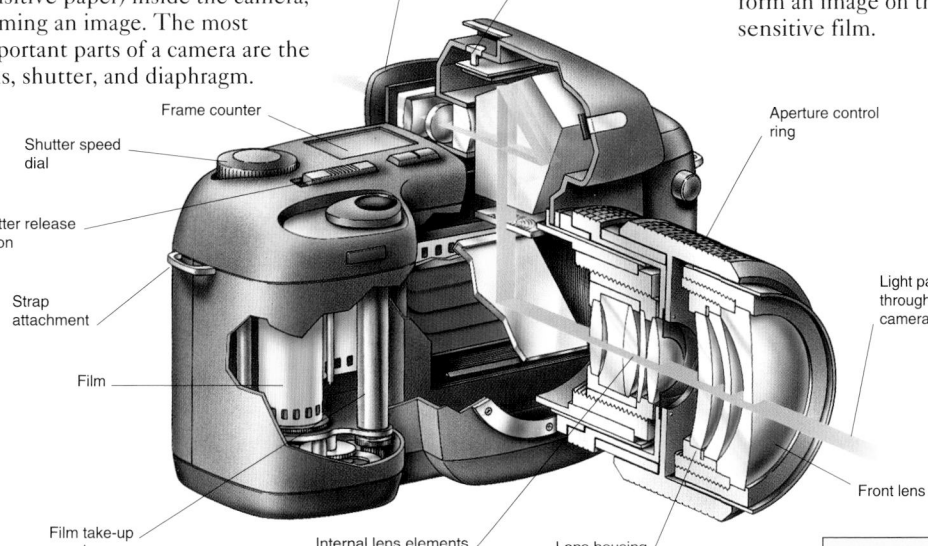

Rear viewfinder camera

Flash hot shoe

Frame counter

Shutter speed dial

Shutter release button

Strap attachment

Film

Film take-up spool

Internal lens elements

Lens housing

Aperture control ring

Light path through the camera

Front lens element

THE LIGHT PATH INSIDE THE CAMERA

This diagram shows how light is adjusted when it travels through the camera to form an image on the light-sensitive film.

Light source The light illuminating the subject is reflected through the camera lens.

Lens A piece of curved glass that reflects the light rays.

Diaphragm A device for controlling the amount of light entering the camera, made of metal plates. It forms an adjustable aperture (hole).

Shutter The shutter can be set to open and close at different speeds, which determines for how long the film is exposed to the light.

Focal plane and film The focal plane is where the light from the lens is brought into focus, coinciding with the position of the film.

TYPES OF LENSES

Lenses can be fitted on to the basic camera lens of certain types of cameras to create different effects in a photograph or to help take a better picture of difficult subjects.

Wide-angle lens allows 50% more of the subject to appear on the film than a standard lens.

Wide-angle lens

Telephoto lens is used to take close-ups of subjects from a distance and to make them appear bigger.

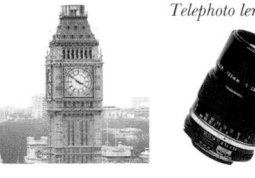

Telephoto lens

Fisheye lens is a wide-angle lens which covers up to 210° of vision.

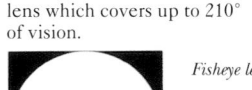

Fisheye lens

Standard lens shows the scene almost as it appears to the naked eye.

Standard lens

Super telephoto lens is a specialist lens that needs a tripod to support its weight.

Super telephoto lens

Filters are flat coloured discs that are attached to the front of a camera lens to alter or distort the subject.

Green

Purple

Orange

Red

Yellow

FILM SPEED

Film comes in various speeds, which are shown on the package as ISO (International Standards Organization) numbers. This table shows their uses for different situations and subjects.

ISO	Speed	Situations and subjects
32	Slow	Well lit, still life
200	Medium	General subjects and lighting levels
400	Moderate-fast	Dimly lit, moving subjects

FAMOUS PHOTOGRAPHERS

Julia Margaret Cameron (1815–79) British-born portrait photographer.

Robert Capa (1913–54) Hungarian-born war photographer. In 1947 Capa and Cartier-Bresson founded Magnum Studios.

Henri Cartier-Bresson (born 1908) French photographer who did much to establish photo-journalism as an art form.

Richard Avedon (born 1923) American photographer famous for portraits and fashion pictures.

DEVELOPING

A photograph is developed by fixing the image on to special photographic paper using chemicals. This process is done in the dark.

1 Each grain of silver on the film changes when it is exposed to light. The film must be processed before the image can be seen.

2 Developing and fixing chemicals imprint the image on to the film.

Equipment

3 The pictures on the film are called negatives because the light and dark areas are reversed.

Negatives

4 The negative is printed onto white paper using an enlarger.

Enlarger

5 The exposed white paper is developed and set with chemicals.

Developing tray

6 After the print has been developed, it is washed and dried.

Finished print

Colour film has three layers of light-sensitive emulsion. Each reacts to a colour – either blue, green, or red. The emulsion layers record how much of each colour there is in the image.

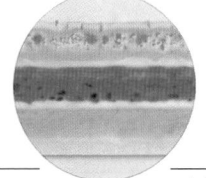

THEATRE

MODERN WESTERN THEATRE has its origins in Ancient Greece. The word itself comes from the Ancient Greek word *theatron*, meaning "place for viewing".

c. 3000 B.C. Religious ceremonies all over the world include music, dance, and elements of drama.

Egyptian hunters

c. 1000 B.C. Chinese and Indian dance-dramas develop and become more formalized in style.

Thespis' cart

534 B.C. Thespis, the first actor to step outside the chorus of singers and dancers, arrives in Athens.

c. 500 B.C. Tragedy, and soon comedy, develops in Greece.

384–322 B.C. Aristotle, Greek philosopher, explains his theories of tragedy in *The Poetics*.

Timeline: 3000 B.C. | 3000 B.C. | 1000 B.C. | 1000 B.C. | 600 B.C. | 534 B.C. | 500 B.C. | 400 B.C. | 320 B.C.

c. 200 B.C. Romans adapt Greek comedies. Plautus (c.254–184) and Terence (c.190–159) are among the most popular playwrights.

c. A.D. 1 Sanskrit theatre quickly flourishes in India.

c. A.D. 1–100 Pantomimus, a form of theatre in which actors used gesture and movement to act out tragic stories, was popular in Rome throughout the first century.

Pantomimus

c. 1200 Travelling story-tellers in Middle Eastern countries use mime to break through language barriers.

c. 1300 Indian folk theatre develops, following the decline of Sanskrit theatre. Noh theatre becomes the dominant form in Japan.

1453 The Renaissance begins in Italy, and soon spreads to the rest of Europe. Roman plays are revived, and buildings reflect the style of classical architecture.

c. 1500 Commedia dell'Arte companies from Italy travel widely in Europe, greatly influencing theatrical styles.

Harlequin

Timeline: 200 B.C. | 200 B.C. | A.D. | A.D. 1 | A.D. 1–100 | 1200 | 1200 | 1300 | 1300 | 1450 | 1453 | 1500 | 1500

1564 William Shakespeare, an English dramatist, is born.

c. 1600 Kathakali (meaning story-play) is created in India. Actors use body language and mime to tell popular Hindu epic stories.

Kathakali

1603 Okuni, a young Japanese woman, creates a new dance called **Kabuki**.

1653 Japanese authorities allow only adult males to perform Kabuki, and it begins to develop a more theatrical style.

1678 Aphra Behn (1640–1689), an English dramatist, stages *The Rover*, a Restoration comedy. Behn is the first British woman to write plays for a living. She is also a spy.

Aphra Behn

1782 Friedrich von Schiller (1759–1805), a German dramatist, stages *The Robbers*. This play is among those that inspire the German Romantic movement of the late 18th and early 19th centuries (see p.161).

Friedrich von Schiller

Timeline: 1560 | 1564 | 1600 | 1600 | 1603 | 1650 | 1653 | 1670 | 1678 | 1780 | 1782

c. 1800 Peking Opera begins in China. The performances are a mixture of mime, song, dance, dialogue, and acrobatics. In Vietnam, **Hat Boi** uses a similar theatrical style to dramatize tales of war and suffering.

Peking Opera

1877 Henrik Ibsen (1828–1906), a Norwegian dramatist, stages *The Pillars of Society*.

c. 1890 Symbolism (see p.160) begins in the German theatre.

1894 George Bernard Shaw (1856–1950), an Irish dramatist, stages *Arms and the Man*.

1894 The Olympia Theater is the first to open on Broadway, New York, USA.

1896 Alfred Jarry (1873–1907), a French dramatist, stages *Ubu Roi* in Paris. The play later influences the movement called *Theatre of the Absurd*.

Poster for Ubu Roi

c. 1910 Expressionism (see p.161) emerges in Germany. Georg Kaiser (1878–1945) and Ernst Toller (1893–1939) are popular playwrights.

Timeline: 1800 | 1800 | 1870 | 1877 | 1890 | 1890 | 1894 | 1896 | 1910 | 1910

1905 The Russian Revolution creates a need for *Agit-prop* (agitational propaganda) theatre. Actors act out political events, replacing newspapers for the many people who cannot read.

Agit-prop

1935 Antonin Artaud (1896–1948), a French dramatist, stages *Les Cenci*, the first play to represent *Theatre of Cruelty*. This style of theatre is intended to horrify the audience.

Bertolt Brecht

1949 Bertolt Brecht (1898–1956), a German dramatist, founds the Berliner Ensemble. The company stages plays in Brecht's "epic" style, always reminding the audience that it is watching a play, and not real events.

1950 Eugène Ionesco (1912–1994), a French dramatist, stages *The Bald Primadonna*, the first example of his *Theatre of the Absurd*.

1955 Tennessee Williams (1911–1983), an American dramatist, stages *Cat on a Hot Tin Roof*.

Timeline: 1900 | 1905 | 1930 | 1935 | 1940 | 1949 | 1950 | 1950 | 1955

1956 John Osborne (1929–1994), an English dramatist, stages *Look Back in Anger*. The term "kitchen sink drama" is used to describe its realistic coverage of everyday life.

Look Back in Anger

1986 Wole Soyinka (born 1934), a Nigerian dramatist, is the first black African to win the Nobel Prize for literature. He was imprisoned from 1967 to 1969 for criticizing the Nigerian government.

Wole Soyinka

1990s Musicals, especially revivals such as *Crazy for You*, are the most popular form in most commercial western theatres.

1996 Globe Theatre opens in London. It is a reconstruction of the venue in which Shakespeare's plays were originally performed.

Crazy for You

Timeline: 1950 | 1956 | 1959 | 1970 | 1980 | 1986 | 1990

A MODERN THEATRE

Many modern theatres are designed like this one, with a proscenium arch separating the real world of the audience from the pretend world of the actors. The word "proscenium" comes from the Ancient Greek *pro skene*, meaning "in front of the stage".

Upstage (furthest from the audience) actors are well lit, and draw the audience's attention. Actors are sometimes accused of "upstaging" each other.

Props (properties) are objects that the actors carry on stage. They are kept on a table in the wings.

Wings at each side of the stage provide space for scenery and costumes that will be used later.

Scenery is suspended by ropes from a grid above the stage. This area is called the "flies".

Curtain is usually lowered while stagehands change the set (scenery).

Iron, or safety curtain, separates stage and auditorium so that a fire cannot spread too quickly.

FOLLOW-SPOT OPERATOR
The follow-spot operator controls a heavy spotlight, directing the beam of light so that a moving actor is always lit. The follow-spot is usually either in the lighting box, or high up at one side of the auditorium.

Proscenium arch frames the acting area.

Dressing rooms are usually shared by members of the company.

Green room is where actors rest between scenes.

Dressing room for an actor who is taking a leading role.

Wardrobe department makes and looks after costumes.

Scenery is made and stored in the workshop.

Downstage (towards the pit) the audience's attention can easily be distracted. Actors use this area when another actor has more important lines.

Lifts like this one can make actors or scenery appear and disappear to surprise the audience. Some theatres have two or more lifts.

Orchestra pit is in front of the stage. In many theatres the pit can be covered, and the stage can be extended, or extra seating added.

Lighting operators control lighting using a board, or console. Computerized boards control every light in the theatre.

Stage manager gives "calls" to make sure that scenery moves and actors make their entrances on time.

WILLIAM SHAKESPEARE (1564–1616)
William Shakespeare was born in Stratford-upon-Avon, England, but moved to London in about 1590. There he became an actor and playwright, and a shareholder in the Globe Theatre. Today Shakespeare is the most often performed playwright in the world. He is thought to have written 37 plays, with more than 100,000 lines. The longest Shakespearean role is Hamlet, which has a total of 1,530 lines.

MOST POPULAR PLAYS 1996 (BY SCRIPT SALES)

Title	First staged	Playwright
Top Girls	1982	Caryl Churchill (born 1938)
Streetcar Named Desire	1948	Tennessee Williams (1911–83)
Our Country's Good	1988	Timberlake Wertenbaker (1951–)
The Doll's House	1879	Henrik Ibsen (1828–1906)
Educating Rita	1980	Willy Russell (born 1947)

THEATRE RECORDS

SMALLEST PROFESSIONAL THEATRE is the Piccolo in Hamburg, Germany. It can seat no more than 30 people.

LONGEST RUNNING PLAY is *The Mousetrap*, which has been running in London since 1952.

EARLIEST KNOWN STONE AMPHITHEATRE was built in Rome in about 55 B.C. It held roughly 40,000 people.

SHORTEST RECORDED PLAY, *Breath*, by Samuel Beckett, consists of 35 seconds of human cries and breaths.

THE IMAGINARY INVALID
Molière (1622–1673), France's most famous dramatist, acted and managed a theatrical company as well as writing plays. He died within hours of collapsing on stage in a production of his own play, *Le Malade Imaginaire (The Imaginary Invalid)*.

THEATRE FACTS
• Until the invention of greasepaint in the 1860s, stage make-up contained lead. Many actors died from lead poisoning.

• The title of *Macbeth* is considered unlucky in the theatre. Instead, the play is called "the Scottish play".

BUILDING THEATRES
Since the Ancient Greeks built the first theatres in the 5th century B.C. the style of theatrical buildings has altered constantly to suit the demands of the plays performed in them. In many modern theatres, the shape and size of the stage can be changed for each production.

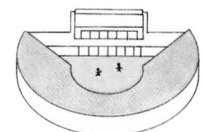

Ancient Greek theatres had seats built into the sides of a natural bowl. The centre was used for singing and dancing, and the small stage for acting.

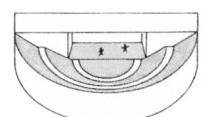

Roman theatres were built of wood or stone in a semi-circular shape. A permanent roof sheltered the actors on stage.

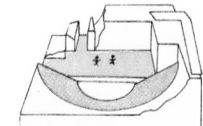

Renaissance theatres were loosely based on those of Ancient Rome, with the audience on one side only.

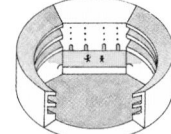

Elizabethan English theatres had several entrances and exits, used for acting out complex plots.

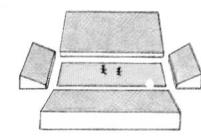

Modern stages take many forms. One is theatre-in-the-round, where the audience surrounds the stage.

JAPANESE THEATRE

The two traditional forms of Japanese theatre are *Noh* and *Kabuki*. The actors are male, and usually trained by their fathers to act a particular role. *Noh* actors wear masks, and *Kabuki* actors use make-up.

KABUKI CHARACTERS

A Noh actor

Noble male *Crab* *Wicked male*

CABARET

Cabaret may be pure entertainment, or it can contain political statements. Writers and performers often use cabaret to comment on society or challenge fixed ideas.

Au und aus, performed at the Admirals Palast, Berlin, 1926

PUPPETS AND PUPPETRY

There have been puppet shows in Europe since at least 500 B.C., and probably even earlier than this in other parts of the world.

ANIMATRONICS
The term *animatronics* is used to describe a puppet that is partly controlled by electronics. Operators control the facial movements from a distance by sending electronic signals through a cable.

SHADOW PUPPETS
Shadow puppets are one of the most versatile kinds of puppet. They are controlled by sticks joined to their arms and legs. In Indonesia shadow puppetry is called *Wayang Kulit*.

STRING PUPPETS
In some parts of the world string puppets perform complete operas or tragedies. The puppeteers move the puppets' limbs from above using strings.

FINGER PUPPETS
Finger puppets are easy to make and operate, but limited in movement. Glove puppets fit over the whole hand, and each finger moves a different part of the puppet.

The operator inside moves the puppet's body and limbs.

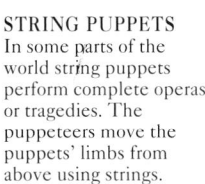

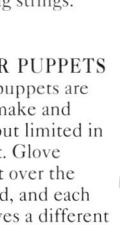

MIME

Mime, or the art of gesture and movement, has always been part of acting. But modern mime, which developed mainly in France, does not use the spoken word at all. One of the most famous mime artists is the Frenchman, Marcel Marceau (born 1923).

Tying a love knot means marriage.

COSTUMES

Costumes play an important part in any production. They can change an actor's appearance by altering shape or height, indicate the period and country in which a play is set, or completely transform an actor into an animal, an object, or a fantasy figure.

Ancient Greek actors wore masks, and often platform shoes, to make them appear god-like.

Animal costumes are usually padded and heavy, and can be difficult to move in.

Modern costumes tell us about the period as well as the character.

PUPPET FACTS
- *Wayang Kulit* plays may last a whole week, and some use as many as 200 puppets.
- Punch and Judy (British) and Petrushka (Russian) grew out of characters in *Commedia dell'Arte* (see p.166).
- It takes three puppeteers to control each of the *Bunraku* doll puppets of Japan.

LONGEST RUNNING PLAYS, UK (1999)

Play	Years
The Mousetrap	46
Cats	18
Starlight Express	15
Les Miserables	13
The Phantom of the Opera	12
Blood Brothers	11
Reduced Shakespeare	11
The Woman in Black	10
Miss Saigon	9
Buddy	9

THEATRE WORDS

Angel Someone who provides the financial backing for a production.

Apron The part of the stage in front of the proscenium arch (see p.167).

Arena A stage that is surrounded by seating for the audience.

Block To set the actors' movements around the stage.

Chorus Actors in Ancient Greek drama who sang and commented on the action.

Corpse To burst into laughter on stage.

Deus ex machina (God from the machine) a god brought in to resolve the plot in Ancient Greek drama.

Deus ex machina

Director The person who has artistic control of a production, interpreting the script and rehearsing the actors.

Dress rehearsal The last rehearsal before the opening night, with costumes, lights, and scenery.

Dry To forget one's lines.

Flats Screens painted with scenery, often on both sides, which can be moved around the stage for different effects.

Footlights Lights at the front of the stage, near the auditorium.

Fringe theatre Alternative theatre, including unconventional plays, venues, or theatrical styles.

Gallery Seats at the top rear of the auditorium. Also called "the gods".

Ham A bad actor, usually one who overacts.

House The audience.

Limelight Powerful light, like that once produced by burning lime.

Open stage A stage without a proscenium arch, with the audience seated on three sides.

Ham

Producer The person responsible for financial and practical aspects of a production. A theatrical producer is not usually involved in artistic direction.

Prompt To whisper lines to an actor who has forgotten them. A "prompt" is someone employed for this purpose.

Rake The angle of the stage. In modern theatres the rake can be altered for different productions.

Rake

Trap A trapdoor that opens into the area below the stage. Often used together with a "lift" for surprise entrances (see p.167).

Walk-on A non-speaking part.

DANCE

PEOPLE HAVE been dancing since prehistoric times. Over thousands of years, many different styles of dance have developed all over the world.

c.15,000 B.C. Stone Age rock paintings in Europe and Africa show people in dance-like ritual formation.

Tanzanian Stone Age rock painting

3000–1000 B.C. Ancient Egyptians use ritual and ceremonial dance in the worship of gods and goddesses such as Isis.

Fresco (wall painting) from Thebes, showing dancers at a banquet, 1425 B.C.

15,000 B.C. | 15,000 B.C. | 3000 B.C. | 3000 B.C.

c.1400 B.C. Bull dancing is a popular entertainment in Crete. People dance around a bull, springing on and off its back or leaping between its horns.

Bronze sculpture of boy leaping over a bull

c.1000 B.C. Chinese shamans (healers and spirit guides) use dance to bring spirits down to Earth.

c.500–400 B.C. Spartan warriors in Greece use dance as part of their training. Socrates (470–399 B.C.), Greek philosopher, states "The best dancer is also the best warrior".

Spartan warriors

c.150 B.C. Romans close all dance schools. Cicero (106–43 B.C.), Roman consul, states that no man dances unless he is insane.

c.A.D. 400 Kagura dances performed to religious chants at Shinto shrines in Japan. Dancers accompanied by drums, brass, gongs, and flutes.

Kagura dancer

c.800 Early Christians include traditional pagan dances in Christian ceremonies. Charlemagne (742–814), the Holy Roman Emperor, bans dancing, but the ban is ignored.

1400 B.C. | 1000 B.C. | 500 B.C. | 500–400 B.C. | 150 B.C. | A.D. 400 | 400 | 800 | 800

1300s Ballroom dancing emerges in the royal palaces of Europe.

1300–1500 Mass dances in Europe cause frenzy and often trances. In Italy the *tarantella* is devised to sweat the poison from a spider's bite out of the victim's body.

Medieval German peasants

1416 First European dancing manual, *On the Art of Dancing and Directing Choruses*, is published.

Late 1400s Ballo, Italian dance performance with a storyline, is the earliest form of ballet.

c.1600 Kathakali (see p.171) emerges in India.

Louis XIV in Le Ballet de la Nuit

1653 Louis XIV (1638–1715), 14-year-old French king, appears in *Le Ballet de la Nuit* (Ballet of the Night).

1681 Women are now allowed to dance in ballets, although long, bulky skirts get in the way.

1700s The waltz develops from German folk dances, and will become popular in European courts.

Waltzers in The Court Ball

1300 | 1400 | 1416 | 1600 | 1653 | 1681 | 1700

Late 1700s French ballet masters, frustrated by lack of opportunity, travel to Russia and develop the full-length story-ballet.

1830–1840s Romantic ballet develops and flourishes. The ballerina is the most important dancer in the performance.

Cancan dancer

1832 Marie Taglioni (1804–84), Italian, is the first ballerina to go *en pointe* (on points).

1870s The cancan, a high-kicking dance, becomes very fashionable in France.

Marie Taglioni

1880s–1890s Classical ballet (see p.170) reaches its peak in Russia.

1892 Loie Fuller (1862–1928), American dancer, uses fabric and lighting in her *Serpentine Dance* to create a dreamlike effect.

Loie Fuller, 1897

c.1900 American Isadora Duncan (1877–1927), the first modern dancer, develops freer forms of dance.

1909 Serge Diaghilev (1872–1929), Russian arts promoter, presents his Ballets Russes company in Paris. Dancers include Vaslav Nijinsky (1889–1950) and Anna Pavlova (1881–1931).

1700 | 1830 | 1832 | 1880 | 1892 | 1900 | 1909

1913 Nijinsky uses turned-in feet in his ballet, *The Rite of Spring*.

1920s Tap, charleston, jazz, and many other dance forms influenced by African-American dancing, are increasingly popular.

Nijinsky in Giselle

1927 Rudolf von Laban (1879–1958), Hungarian dancer and choreographer, invents a method of recording ballet movements using geometric sketches, called Labanotation.

1927 Martha Graham, (1894–1991), American modern dancer and choreographer, founds her own company.

Martha Graham

1930s Jitterbug and jive are two lively, popular jazz dances.

1933 Ted Shawn (1891–1972), American dancer, forms an all-male company to show men as dancers in their own right, not just as supports for women.

1933 Fred Astaire (1899–1987) and **Ginger Rogers** (1911–1995), American dancers, appear in the film *Flying Down to Rio*. More films follow including *The Gay Divorcée* and *Top Hat*.

Fred Astaire

1910 | 1913 | 1920 | 1927 | 1930 | 1933

1945 Latin American rumba, samba, calypso, and cha-cha-cha are added to the established ballroom dances.

1950s Rock and roll develops as a social dance, mainly for teenagers.

1952 Merce Cunningham (born 1919), American dancer and choreographer, forms his own company. He uses natural movement to create a free-flowing effect.

Rock and roll dancers, 1956

1960s Post-modern dance develops in New York. It is experimental, and often improvised.

1970s Disco dancing is popular in Europe and the USA.

1976 Twyla Tharp (born 1942), American dancer, choreographs *Push Comes to Shove*. Tharp uses elements of many other styles in her dances.

Break dancing

1980s Break dancing and body-popping are born. Dancers spin around on their backs and heads, and imitate robotic movements. These styles appear in other media, such as film.

DV8 Physical Theatre

1990s DV8 and other companies design dances for television as well as stage.

1940 | 1945 | 1950 | 1952 | 1960 | 1970 | 1976 | 1980 | 1990

BALLET AND MODERN DANCE

BALLET IS A combination of music, dance, and mime, with set steps and techniques. Modern dance developed from it as a freer, more natural form.

BALLET STYLES

The three main styles of ballet are Romantic, Classical, and modern. The style of ballet is usually reflected in the type of costume that the dancers wear.

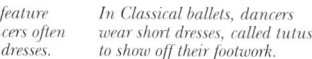
Most Romantic ballets feature spirits and magic. Dancers often wear white, calf-length dresses.

In Classical ballets, dancers wear short dresses, called tutus, to show off their footwork.

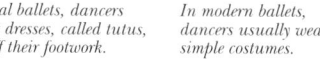
In modern ballets, dancers usually wear simple costumes.

THE FIVE POSITIONS

In ballet there are five basic positions for the arms, and five for the feet.

Positions of the arms
Second, fourth, and fifth positions have variations, e.g. in *demi-seconde*, the arms are raised half-way between first and second positions.

First position

Second position

Third position

Fourth position

Fifth position

Positions of the feet
Almost every movement danced in a ballet begins and ends with one of the five positions of the feet.

First position

Second position

Third position

Fourth position

Fifth position

MODERN DANCE

In the late 1800s, Isadora Duncan and Loie Fuller (see p.169) felt ballet movements were unnatural, and developed a new, freer style. Martha Graham and Merce Cunningham (see p.169) are the two most famous dancer-choreographers of the modern dance movement.

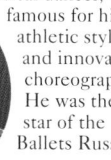

Twyla Tharp (see p.169) was a later modern dance innovator.

Isadora Duncan pioneered modern dance.

Today, new modern dance techniques are still being developed.

FAMOUS 20TH CENTURY DANCERS

Many dancers have become choreographers and teachers, passing their style and skills on to others.

Marie Rambert (1888–1982) Polish teacher and dancer, founded the Ballet Rambert (now the Rambert Dance Company).

Margot Fonteyn (1919–91) British, and **Rudolf Nureyev** (1938–93), Russian, formed the world's most famous and most popular partnership.

Vaslav Nijinsky (1890–1950) Russian Classical dancer, was famous for his athletic style and innovative choreography. He was the star of the Ballets Russes.

Arthur Mitchell (born 1934) American dancer. In 1969 he founded the Dance Theater of Harlem, the first dance company with only black dancers.

DANCE NOTATION

Like music, dance is written down using a system of symbols. There are two forms of dance notation: Benesh and Laban. The Benesh method, which is usually used for ballet, was devised by Rudolf (1916–75) and Joan Benesh (born 1920). Labanotation, named after Rudolf von Laban (see p.169), is mainly used to record modern dance.

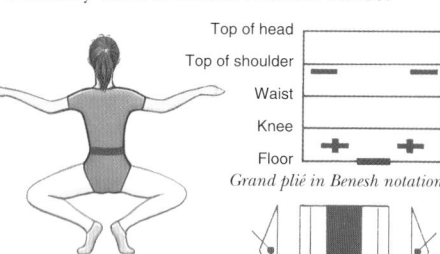

Top of head	
Top of shoulder	
Waist	
Knee	
Floor	

Grand plié in Benesh notation

This grand plié (a deep knee bend) is recorded (right) in two forms of dance notation.

Grand plié in Labanotation

BALLET RECORDS

MOST CURTAIN CALLS was 89, taken by Margot Fonteyn and Rudolf Nureyev after a performance of *Swan Lake* in Austria in 1964.

MOST EXPENSIVE COSTUME was made for the part of the Chinese conjurer in *Parade*, premièred in Paris in 1917. Designed by Pablo Picasso (see p.161), the costume fetched £28,000 at auction in 1984.

FAMOUS BALLETS

Title	Choreographer	First danced
La Sylphide	Filippo Taglioni (1777–1871), Italian	1832
Nutcracker	Lev Ivanov (1834–1901), Russian	1892
Swan Lake	Lev Ivanov and Marius Petipa (1818–1910), French	1895
Manon	Kenneth MacMillan (1929–93), British	1974

BALLET FACTS

• A ballerina who dances regularly wears out about ten pairs of *pointe* shoes each month.

• During the average length career, dancers practise for eight hours a day, six days a week: in total, about five-and-a-half years.

CHOREOGRAPHY

Choreography is the art of designing and devising the steps of a ballet or dance routine. The term comes from the ancient Greek words *khoreia* (dancing) and *graphos* (writing). Choreographers – the people who devise dance routines – work with dancers to compose a dance sequence, then record it using notation.

BALLET TERMS

Barre The bar that dancers use to help them balance during exercises

Battement A beating movement of the leg (many forms)

Corps de ballet The chorus of dancers (those not dancing solo roles)

Jeté A jump from one leg to the other

Pas de chat A jumping step

Pas de deux A dance for two people (male and female), usually the principals

Pirouette A complete 360° turn on one leg

Pas de deux

Plié A knee-bending movement

Pointe On the points or the tips of the toes (female dancers)

FEET FEAT

British dancer Wayne Sleep (born 1948) achieved six *entrechats* in 1973, crossing and uncrossing his legs six times while still in the air.

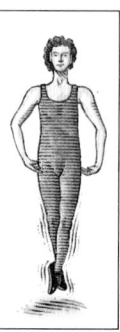

TRADITIONAL WORLD DANCE

MOST COUNTRIES OF the world have a traditional form of dance that has evolved over many years. These dances have often developed from simple religious or tribal rituals into complex dance forms with set movements.

SOUTHEAST ASIA
Classical dance is performed by highly trained artists. Dancing is slow, with complex hand movements.

POLYNESIAN DANCE
Dance plays an important role in traditional Polynesian culture. Women often swing and rotate their hips rapidly, e.g. in the Hawaiian hula.

AMERICAN DANCE
Native Americans dance at special ceremonies to win the goodwill of spirits, ancestors, and gods.

Thai classical dancer

Polynesian dancer

Native American dancer

European folk dancers

Japanese gagaku *dancer*

African tribal dancer

Indian temple dancer

EUROPEAN DANCE
Many traditional European folk dances have their roots in religious rituals. For example, dancing in a circle probably originated from circling around an object of worship.

EAST ASIA
Most East Asian dance forms part of theatrical dance drama, e.g. Chinese opera. Japanese *gagaku* and *bugaka* are the world's oldest forms of traditional court dance.

AFRICAN DANCE
Most African dance has its roots in tribal rituals. It includes Sun- and Moon-worshipping dances, weapon, fertility, and hunting dances.

INDIA
Indian classical dance developed from religious rituals in which dancers told stories about the lives of the gods. There are six styles of dance, including *kathakali* and *bharata natyam*.

TRANCE DANCES

In many cultures, people dance themselves into a trance as a way of communicating with spirits and gods. They may perform acts that would normally be dangerous, but which leave them unharmed.

Barong *dancers in Bali strike themselves with daggers while in a trance.*

DANCE PROPS

Props (items in addition to costume that a dancer may use) are important in many traditional dances.

Prop	Country	Significance
Maypole	England	The maypole is a fertility object symbolizing a tree. People dance around it, holding ribbons that represent branches.
Weapons	Worldwide	The use of weapons, e.g. swords, clubs, and shields, dates back to religious ceremonies in which the gods were asked for help in battle.
Snakes	N. America	The Hopi people use snakes in their rain dances. Snakes are believed to be brothers of the spirits that control clouds and rain.
Instruments	Worldwide	Dancers often wear or use instruments to accentuate (bring out) the rhythm of a dance, e.g. castanets in Spanish flamenco; bells worn by classical Indian dancers.

LOW-DOWN LIMBO

Caribbean limbo dancers can pass underneath bars as low as 15.25cm (6in) off the ground.

DANCE FACTS

• In North Africa, belly dancers are judged by how well they move their shoulders.

• Judges at Irish jigging contests sit under the stage to assess the speed and precision of the dancers' steps.

• The cakewalk was the first African-American dance to be taken up by white Americans. It developed from dance competitions where the prize was usually a cake.

• Between 1910 and 1920, animal dances such as the chicken scratch and the grizzly bear were popular in the USA. Not everyone approved: a woman was jailed for 50 days for doing the turkey trot, a dance that was officially denounced by the Vatican.

• Flamenco dancers can tap their heels at a rate of up to 16 taps per second.

FACE FACTS

Kathakali dancers take up to four hours to apply their make-up. They have such control over their facial muscles that they can laugh with one side of their face and cry with the other.

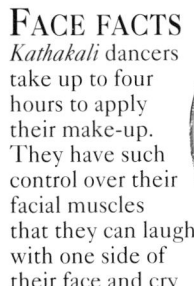

DANCE RECORDS

FASTEST TAP DANCE
was 32 taps per second by Englishman Stephen Gare (born 1967), in 1990.

LONGEST CONGA
was the Miami Super Conga in 1988, which consisted of 119,986 people.

MUSIC

FROM A PRIMITIVE war cry to the complex sound of a symphony orchestra, music has been created by every known society. Vibrations are the source of all musical sound.

MUSICAL TONE AND NOTATION

Most Western music is based on major and minor scales – traditional patterns of pitches that sound pleasing to the ear. Composers write down these pitches using notation – a code of signs and symbols that enables a musician to interpret and play a musical composition.

A key is a set of related notes. The key signature shows which key the music is in.

The tempo marking tells the musician how fast the music should go. *Allegro* means fast.

Allegro

When more than two notes are played together, the tones produced are called a chord.

A natural sign cancels the preceding sharp or flat on that particular note.

Sharps and flats are signs before a note that indicate a note should be raised by half a tone (sharp) or lowered by half a tone (flat).

A piece of music is divided into measures called bars, each with the same number of beats. The bar line shows where the measure ends.

The five horizontal lines are called the stave, or staff.

The clef, here a treble clef, shows which pitches are represented by the lines and spaces of the stave.

mf

Dynamic markings tell the player how loud or soft to play the music. *mf* stands for *mezzo-forte*, or moderately loud.

The stem and colouring of a note indicates its length. These are quavers.

The time signature shows the number of beats in a measure and which type of note gets one beat.

Rests show the musician where, and for how long, to be silent.

sf

Sforzando means that the note should be played loudly with special emphasis.

This sign, meaning *crescendo*, indicates that the music becomes gradually louder.

SCALE

Pitches are named from low to high using seven letters: A, B, C, D, E, F, and G. This series of letters is repeated as the notes continue to ascend in pitch.

Pitches lying in between stave's lines and spaces are shown using sharp (#) and flat (♭) signs.

One octave (eight notes) of the scale of C major

C D E F G A B C

C major notes on stave correspond to white keys on keyboard.

Black keys represent the notes that lie between some of the notes of the C major scale.

White key on keyboard

C D E F G A B C D E

MUSICAL WORDS

Pianissimo (*pp*) Very softly

Piano (*p*) Softly

Mezzo-piano (*mp*) Quite softly

Mezzo-forte (*mf*) Quite loudly

Forte (*f*) Loudly

Fortissimo (*ff*) Very loudly

Forte-piano (*fp*) Loud then suddenly soft

Crescendo (*cresc.*) Getting louder

Diminuendo (*dim.*) Getting softer

Dolce Sweetly

Legato Smoothly

Leggiero Lightly

Pizzicato (*pizz.*) Marking for stringed instruments meaning that the player should pluck the string

Accelerando (*accel.*) Accelerate or speed up

Ritardando (*rit.*) or rallentando Slow down

Sforzando (*sf*) Note or chord to be played loudly with special emphasis

Staccato Short, separated notes

Con brio With fire

TIME SIGNATURES

Time signature	Meaning	Examples
$\frac{2}{4}$	2 beats per measure; crotchet = 1 beat	*Twinkle, twinkle little star*; Beethoven's *Fifth Symphony*
$\frac{3}{4}$	3 beats per measure; crotchet = 1 beat	*Happy Birthday*; *God Save the Queen*
$\frac{4}{4}$	4 beats per measure; crotchet = 1 beat	*Auld Lang Syne*; *Yesterday*
$\frac{6}{8}$	2 beats per measure; 3 quavers = 1 beat	*For He's a Jolly Good Fellow Pop Goes the Weasel*

WORLD MUSIC FACTS

• Indian music uses patterns of notes called ragas. There are about 130 commonly used ragas, and each one has a special association. It can be an emotion, a time of day, or a season of the year.

• Strings on one African drum can vary the tension in the drum-head to produce different notes. Players can use it to recreate the changing tones of their language.

Nigerian "talking" drum

TEMPO MARKINGS

Largo Very slow and broad

Grave Very slow and solemn

Adagio Slow and leisurely

Andante Moderately slow

Allegretto Moderately fast

Allegro Fast and brisk

Vivace Lively and quick

Presto Very fast

Prestissimo Extremely fast

NOTE VALUES

Name	Sign	Rest
Semibreve (whole-note)	o	▬
Minim (half-note)	𝅗𝅥	▬
Crotchet (quarter-note)	♩	𝄽
Quaver (eighth-note)	♪	𝄾
Semiquaver (16th-note)	𝅘𝅥𝅯	𝄿
Demisemiquaver (32nd-note)	𝅘𝅥𝅰	𝅀

DATES IN MUSIC HISTORY

c.4000 B.C. Flutes and harps played in Egypt.

Egyptian tomb painting showing court musicians

A.D. 600 Schola Cantorum founded in Rome. This was an early music school, founded on the order of Pope Gregory the Great (c.540–604).

725 Orchestra developed in China. These orchestras included flutes, guitars, gongs, and drums.

Traditional Chinese orchestra

1480 First printed music in Europe.

Early music printed from carved woodblocks.

1553 Violin design developed into its early form in Europe.

1600s Opera begins to be developed by the *Camerata* – a group of poets and musicians – in Florence, Italy.

1709 Early pianoforte built by Italian Bartolomeo Cristofori (1655–1731).

1727 German J.S. Bach (1685–1750) composes choral work *St. Matthew Passion*.

J.S.Bach

4000 B.C.	A.D.600	725	1480	1553	1600	1709	1727

MUSICAL GROUPS

Groups range from duos, which have two performers, to symphony orchestras, which contain up to 120 (see p.174). Most classical music groups play written music. Jazz groups take a theme and invent variations on it as they play.

Duo

In a duo, one player usually plays a brass, string, or wind instrument and the other a piano. Pieces for two players are called duets.

Cello and piano duo

Trio

Trios have three players. A string trio uses a violin, viola, and cello. Piano trios are written for violin, cello, and piano.

String trio

Quartet

Jazz groups often use quartets (groups of four players). String quartets consist of two violins, a viola, and a cello.

Jazz quartet

Quintet

Quintets use five players and usually contain wind or brass instruments or instruments from different families.

Mixed quintet

Choir

A choir is a group of singers. A mixed voice choir contains men and women, who sing four parts. Most choirs sing religious music.

Small church choir

LARGER GROUPS

• Large groups of brass instrument players, called brass bands, are used in many military and civic ceremonies.

• A larger string group, often including a few wind instruments, is called a chamber orchestra. It may accompany a soloist in a piece called a concerto.

MAJOR COMPOSERS IN WESTERN MUSIC

Composer	Nationality, dates	Major work(s), date(s) composed
Renaissance (1450–1600) Guillaume Dufay	Flemish, c.1400–74	Church music and secular pieces
Josquin des Prés	Flemish, c.1445–1521	Choral church and secular music
Giovanni Palestrina	Italian, c.1525–94	Choral church and secular music
William Byrd	English, 1543–1623	Church music, string music, keyboard music, and madrigals
Baroque (1600–1750) Claudio Monteverdi	Italian, 1567–1643	*Orfeo* (1607), *Vespers* (1610)
Heinrich Schütz	German, 1585–1672	*Symphoniae Sacrae* (1650)
Jean Baptiste Lully	French, 1632–87	Operas, church compositions
Henry Purcell	English, 1659–95	*Dido and Aeneas* (1689)
Antonio Vivaldi	Italian, 1678–1741	*Four Seasons* (1725)
Jean Phillippe Rameau	French, 1683–1764	*Castor and Pollux* (1737)
Johann Sebastian Bach	German, 1685–1750	*Brandenburg Concertos* (1721), *St. Matthew Passion* (1727)
George Frederic Handel	German, 1685–1759	*The Messiah* (1741), *Music for the Royal Fireworks* (1749)
Classical (1750–1820) Joseph Haydn	Austrian, 1732–1809	*London Symphonies*: 1st set (1791–92) *London Symphonies*: 2nd set (1793–95),
Wolfgang Amadeus Mozart	Austrian, 1756–91	*Piano Concertos in C major and D minor* (1785), *The Marriage of Figaro* (1786), *Don Giovanni* (1787)
Ludwig van Beethoven	German, 1770–1827	*Symphonies No. 3* (1802), *No. 5* (1809), and *No. 9* (1823)
Romantic (1820–1900) Franz Schubert	Austrian, 1797–1828	*Piano Quintet in A* (1819), *"Unfinished" Symphony No. 8* (1822)
Hector Berlioz	French, 1803–69	*Symphonie Fantastique* (1830), *The Trojans* (1859)
Frederic Chopin	Polish, 1810–49	Piano compositions, *Preludes* (1839)
Franz Liszt	Hungarian, 1811–86	*Piano Sonata in B min* (1853), *Hungarian Rhapsodies* (1839–85)
Richard Wagner	German, 1813–83	*The Flying Dutchman* (1841), *The Ring of the Nibelung* (1848–74)
Giuseppe Verdi	Italian, 1813–1901	*Aida* (1871), *Requiem Mass* (1873), *Otello* (1887)
Johannes Brahms	German, 1833–97	*Violin Concerto in D major* (1878), *Symphony No. 4* (1884)
Peter Ilyich Tchaikovsky	Russian, 1840–93	*Piano Concerto No 1* (1874–5), *Swan Lake* (1876)
Edvard Grieg	Norwegian, 1843–1907	*Piano Concerto in A minor* (1869), *Peer Gynt* (1876)
Edward Elgar	English, 1857–1934	*Enigma Variations* (1899), *Violin Concerto* (1910)
Modern (1900 to present) Claude Debussy	French, 1862–1918	*Pelléas and Mélisande* (1892–1902), *Images* (1905-07)
Arnold Schoenberg	Austrian, 1874–1951	*First String Quartet* (1897), *Pierrot Lunaire* (1912)
Béla Bartók	Hungarian, 1881–1945	*Six String Quartets* (1939), *Concerto for Orchestra* (1944)
Igor Stravinsky	Russian, 1882–1971	*The Firebird* (1910), *The Rite of Spring* (1913)
Sergei Prokofiev	Russian, 1891–1953	*Romeo and Juliet* (1935), *Peter and the Wolf* (1936)
Lili Boulanger	French, 1893–1918	*Faust and Helène* (1913)
George Gershwin	American, 1898–1937	*Rhapsody in Blue* (1924), *Porgy and Bess* (1935)
Dmitry Shostakovich	Russian, 1906–75	*Symphonies No.5* (1937) and *No.10* (1953)
John Cage	American, 1912–92	*Music of Changes* (1951), *4' 33"* (1954)
Pierre Boulez	French, born 1925	*Le Marteau sans Maître* (1954), *Memoriales* (1975)
Karlheinz Stockhausen	German, born 1928	*Groups* (1955–57)
Philip Glass	American, born 1937	*Einstein on the Beach* (1976)

Austrian composer [Wolf]**gang A. Mozart** (1756–91) [compo]ses opera, *Don Giovanni*.

[...ng Mozart] [... the piano.]

1808 German composer Ludwig van Beethoven (1770–1827) composes Symphonies No.5 and No.6.

Ludwig van Beethoven

1874 German composer Richard Wagner (1813–83) finishes *The Ring of the Nibelung.*

c.1900 Jazz music appears in New Orleans, USA. It combines African rhythms with Western harmony.

Early jazz music

1940 Synthesizers appear, giving composer complete control over sound.

1950 Rock music appears in US.

Rock singer Chuck Berry

OFF BEAT

Jean Baptiste Lully (1632–87), court musician to Louis XIV of France, stabbed his foot with the long staff that he banged on the floor in order to keep his orchestra in time. He later died from an abscess caused by this injury.

787   1808   1874   1900   1950

CLASSICAL MUSIC

WHEN PEOPLE think of classical music, most think of orchestras and symphonies, and opera.

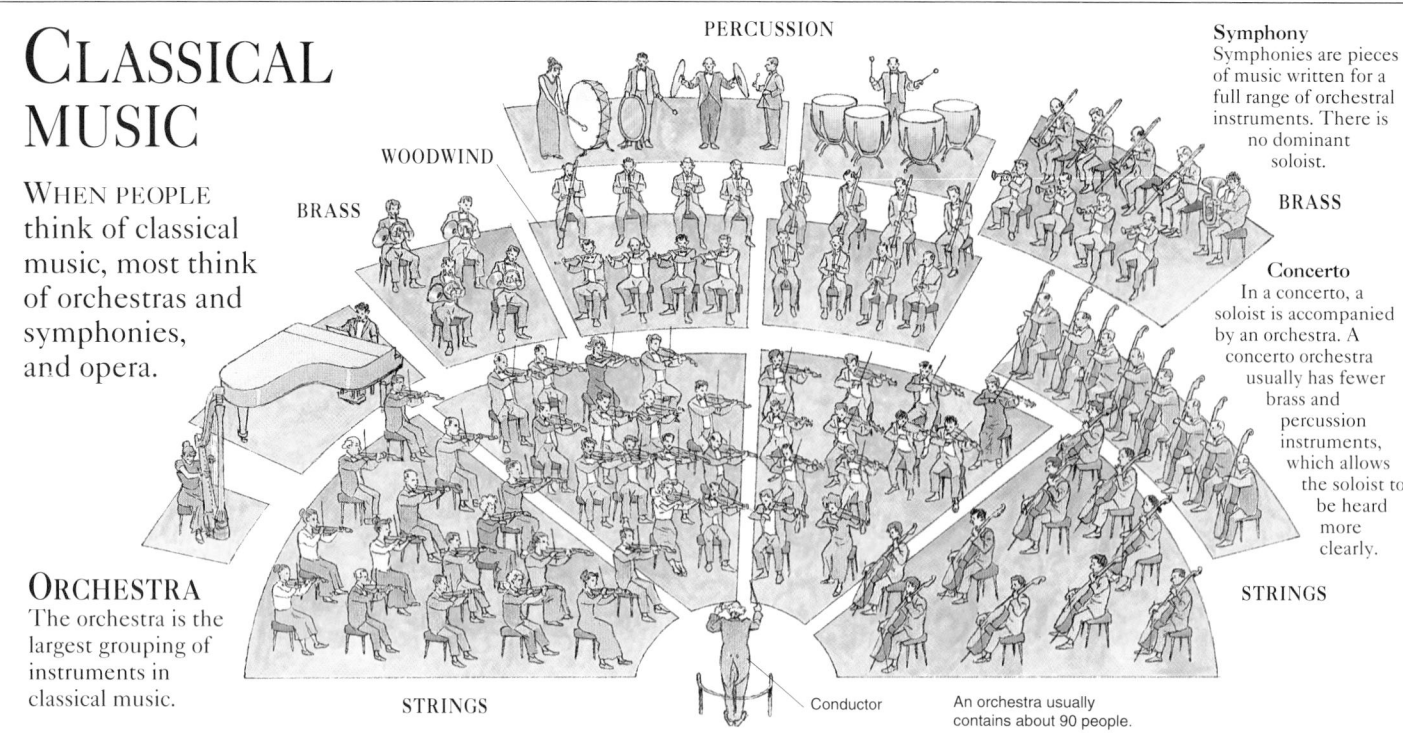

PERCUSSION

WOODWIND

BRASS

Symphony
Symphonies are pieces of music written for a full range of orchestral instruments. There is no dominant soloist.

BRASS

Concerto
In a concerto, a soloist is accompanied by an orchestra. A concerto orchestra usually has fewer brass and percussion instruments, which allows the soloist to be heard more clearly.

STRINGS

ORCHESTRA
The orchestra is the largest grouping of instruments in classical music.

STRINGS

Conductor

An orchestra usually contains about 90 people.

CONDUCTOR
A conductor directs the performance, indicating the pace of the music. He or she traces patterns through the air with a baton, according to the time signature of the piece.

Two beats in a bar

Three beats in a bar

Four beats in a bar

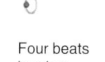
Five beats in a bar

Diagrams show traditional baton movements.

BOUNCING BACK
In *Tosca*, the heroine jumps to her death from castle battlements. In 1960, angry stagehands backstage substituted a trampoline for the usual mattress. Tosca reappeared 15 times before the curtain fell.

OPERA
Operas are musical dramas in which singers, accompanied by an orchestra, act out a story. They can be sung throughout, or sung and spoken.

Royal Opera House production, London

Madam Butterfly sings

Madam Butterfly, a moving love story, was created by Puccini in 1904. It centres on a Japanese heroine, Madam Butterfly, whose betrayal by an American sailor ends in her suicide.

US Navy Lieutenant F.B. Pinkerton sings tenor part.

Solos by major characters are called arias.

KEY OPERA SINGERS

Tito Gobbi
(1915–84), Italian operatic baritone, made his debut in Rome in 1938.

Kathleen Ferrier
(1912–53), English contralto singer, made her debut as Lucretia in Benjamin Britten's *The Rape of Lucretia* in 1946.

Luciano Pavarotti
(born 1935), Italian operatic tenor, made his international debut as Rudolfo in Puccini's *La Bohème* in 1961.

Kiri Te Kanawa
(born 1944), New Zealand operatic soprano, made her international debut in 1971, as the Countess in Mozart's *The Marriage of Figaro*.

OPERA FACTS
• There are six commonly accepted ranges of voice. From lowest to highest these are: bass, baritone, tenor, contralto, mezzo-soprano, and soprano.

• Many people believe that the quality of an opera singer's voice improves with extra body-weight. In fact, a person's weight is irrelevant: thin people may possess the finest voices.

• Many people can identify the pitch of any note that they hear, without needing to refer to an instrument. This ability is called "perfect pitch".

KEY OPERAS

Title	Composer	First performed
The Marriage of Figaro	Wolfgang Amadeus Mozart (1756–91), Austrian	1786 Vienna
The Barber of Seville	Gioacchino Rossini (1792–1868), Italian	1816 Rome
Otello	Giuseppe Verdi (1813–1901), Italian	1887 Milan, Italy
The Ring of the Nibelung	Richard Wagner (1813–83), German	1876 Bayreuth, Germany
Carmen	Georges Bizet (1838–75), French	1875 Paris
La Bohème	Giacomo Puccini (1858–1924), Italian	1896 Turin, Italy
Peter Grimes	Benjamin Britten (1913–76), British	1945 London

POPULAR MUSIC

POPULAR MUSIC

MANY DIFFERENT styles of music have evolved in the twentieth century. Here the most popular Western styles are described.

FOLK MUSIC
In the 19th century, America's southern black population, including transport workers on the railways and riverboats, as well as cotton workers, sang and listened to folk songs at work, or at the end of the day. They created a new kind of folk song in which they mixed the complex, overlapping rhythms and free melodies of West African music with the harmonies of Western music. This combination formed the foundation for music that would dominate popular tastes during the 20th century.

Album cover from a collection of early Afro-American songs

BLUES
The blues express the troubles and emotions of the performer in a simple but strict form. The performer sets three lines of poetry to 12 bars of music. The blues use a basic, set pattern of harmonies (chords), over which the performer invents variations.

Leadbelly
Leadbelly's Last Sessions

JAZZ
Jazz emerged in the early 1900s in New Orleans, USA, as a mixture of blues, religious gospel singing, and European influences. Driven by the urgent rhythms of West African music and using the melodic style of the Blues, jazz musicians improvise – they recreate the melody of a piece each time it is performed. This allows each player to express their emotions through their special version of the music. Major artists of the "jazz age" of the 1920s included American trumpeters Louis "Satchmo" Armstrong (c.1898–1971), Bix Beiderbecke (1903–31), and the orchestral composer George Gershwin (1898–1937).

Louis Armstrong
Laughing Louis

BIG BANDS AND BE-BOP
In the 1930s and early 1940s, swing, a form of jazz, was played by "big bands," under great bandleaders such as Duke Ellington (1899–1974). Later, a new style emerged, called be-bop. It was pioneered by trumpeter Dizzy Gillespie (1917–1993) and saxophonist Charlie Parker (1920–55). Be-bop led to more complex schemes of harmony. Major artists included trumpeter Miles Davis (1926–91) and saxophonist John Coltrane (1926–67).

Charlie Parker Bird Lives

COUNTRY AND WESTERN
Country and Western music takes its inspiration from the country life of the American West. Its performers, often dressed as cowboys of the old West, sing with the accent of the southern USA and are accompanied by instruments such as the banjo, fiddle, and guitar. Performers include Hank Williams (1923–1952), Johnny Cash (born 1932), and Tammy Wynette (born 1942).

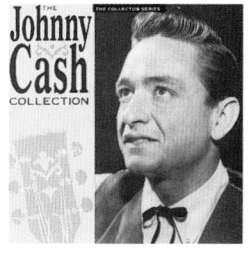
Johnny Cash
The Johnny Cash Collection

ROCK AND ROLL
Rock and roll began in the 1950s as a mix of rhythm-and-blues and country music and was played loudly on newly invented electric guitars. Although this style arose in black communities, white singer and guitarist Elvis Presley (1935–77) greatly increased its popularity.

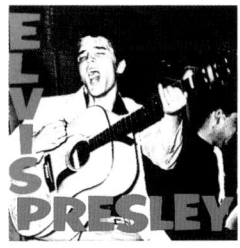
Elvis Presley Elvis Presley

ROCK
In the 1960s, rock and roll was abbreviated to "rock" music. Rock music has a heavy, driving rhythm, with eight quavers to the bar and accents on the second and fourth beats. Early rock bands included The Beatles, The Rolling Stones, Pink Floyd, The Who, and The Jimi Hendrix Experience.

The Rolling Stones
Their Satanic Majesties Request

REGGAE
West Indian reggae music was spread abroad by West Indian communities overseas. It is closely associated with the Rastafarian religion. Its most famous artist was Bob Marley (1945–81), whose music calls for an end to racism and political repression.

Bob Marley & The Wailers

DISCO
In the 1970s, new music centred around the disco movement. It was promoted by films such as *Saturday Night Fever* and by a revival of interest in 1950s music by black artists such as James Brown (born 1933). Disco artists include The Bee Gees and Donna Summer.

The Bee Gees
Saturday Night Fever

PUNK
Punk music exploded on to the scene at the close of the 1970s, led by the British groups The Sex Pistols and The Clash. It had a savage character, and appealed to young people whose dress, language, and behaviour were designed to outrage traditional tastes.

The Damned

1980s POP MUSIC
Pop music in the 1980s became lighter and more concerned with dance rhythms. Major pop artists and groups included Michael Jackson, The Pet Shop Boys, Madonna, and Duran Duran. Pop videos, in which the music was set to a piece of film, made it possible for a performer to be seen on television by millions at the same time as the release of their record.

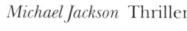
Michael Jackson Thriller

1990s POPULAR MUSIC
A specialized form of dance music, called house music, emerged in the 1980s, based on very rapid rhythms and electronic sounds. The technology for making and mixing these new sounds is now widely available to musicians and their music has since branched into the related styles of acid house, techno, trance, ambient, and jungle music.

The Orb Blue Room

BEST-SELLING SINGLES WORLDWIDE

Single	Performer/group	Copies sold (approx.)
Candle In The Wind	Elton John	35,000,000
White Christmas	Bing Crosby	30,000,000
Rock Around the Clock	Bill Haley and His Comets	17,000,000
I Want to Hold Your Hand	The Beatles	12,000,000
It's Now or Never	Elvis Presley	10,000,000
I Will Always Love You	Whitney Houston	10,000,000
Hound Dog/Don't Be Cruel	Elvis Presley	9,000,000
Diana	Paul Anka	9,000,000
Hey Jude	The Beatles	8,000,000
I'm a Believer	The Monkees	8,000,000

POP MUSIC RECORDS
MOST EXPENSIVE GUITAR was a Fender Stratocaster belonging to Jimi Hendrix (1942–70). It was sold for £180,000 (US $275,940) at Sotheby's, London, in 1990.

MOST SUCCESSFUL SONGWRITERS are Paul McCartney (born 1942), who has had 32 number one singles in the USA and 28 in the UK, and John Lennon (1940–80), with 26 number one singles in the USA and 29 in the UK.

175

MUSICAL INSTRUMENTS

MUSICAL INSTRUMENTS are designed to make vibrations that our ears and brain recognize as musical sounds. They are usually classified into percussion, stringed, woodwind, brass, and keyboard. Archaeologists excavating the sites of ancient Mesopotamian cities (see p.375) have found evidence for every basic instrument type.

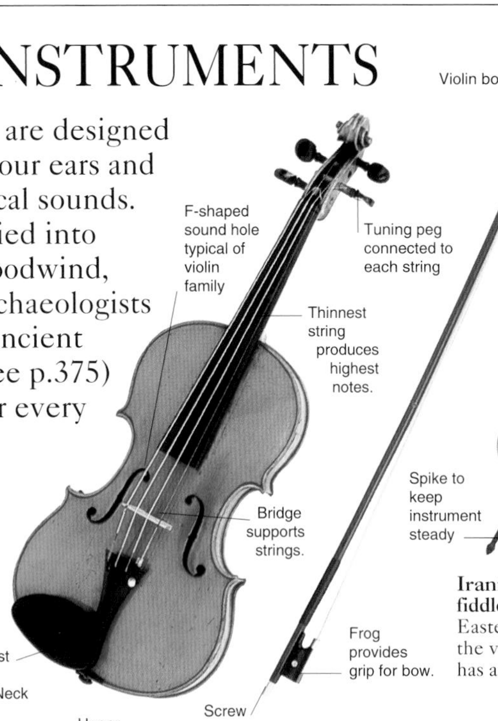

VIOLIN
The violin is the smallest stringed instrument. It also produces the highest sound. The player holds the violin between the chin and the shoulder, drawing the bow across the strings to produce a clear tone.

Violin bow

F-shaped sound hole typical of violin family

Tuning peg connected to each string

Thinnest string produces highest notes.

Bridge supports strings.

Chin-rest

Frog provides grip for bow.

Screw

Mouthpiece with reed

Neck

Upper octave key

WOODWIND INSTRUMENTS
A woodwind instrument is either a tube that the player blows across or into, or a tube that amplifies the vibrations of a thin reed at one end. Most woodwind instruments have holes running down the tube. The player covers and uncovers them to produce different notes.

Pads lined with cork and felt cover toneholes.

Key to operate pad.

Bell projects sound.

Holder allows thumb to support instrument body.

Ornate lacquer decoration

Ring for neck sling

Curved tube for deep sound

Double reed

Thumb knuckle operates these keys.

Flute blown through hole cut in side.

Opening adjusted by hand to change note.

Carved wooden dragon's head

SAXOPHONE
The saxophone, like the flute, is a woodwind instrument made of metal. It can produce a harsh, raw tone, but it also carries a smooth, lilting melody with great sensitivity. Clarinettists may easily play the saxophone since they share a common type of reed.

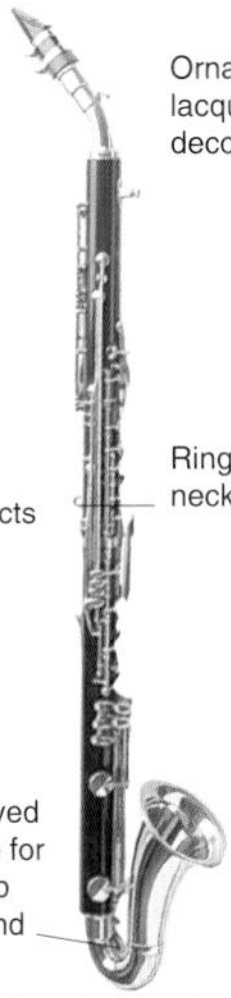

Alto clarinet produces a deeper sound than a standard clarinet.

Dragon flute or lung-ti flute, is used in Chinese ceremonies.

Oboe, an orchestral instrument, is used to tune the orchestra.

Guyanese flute with pitch controlled by hand.

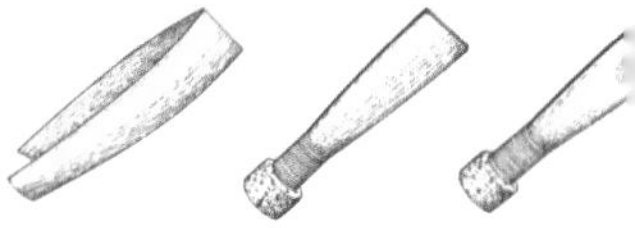

BRASS INSTRUMENTS
Brass instruments have a mouthpiece shaped like a funnel. Vibrations are produced not by the instrument itself, but by the player's lips pressed against this mouthpiece. The player alters the pitch by changing the tension in the lips, and by changing the length of tubing through which the vibrating air passes.

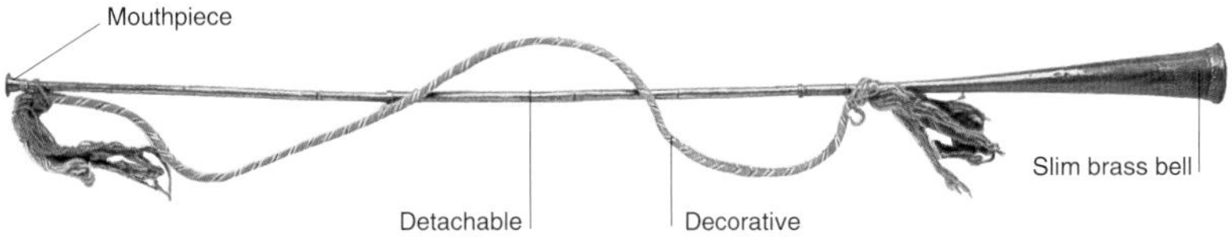

Moroccan nfir is a trumpet used in Islamic religious festivals. It is 1.5m (5ft) long and is made from brass sections that are fixed together and taken apart after use.

STRINGED INSTRUMENTS
A stringed instrument consists of a series of stretched strings connected to a hollow box that amplifies the string's vibrations. The string is set in motion by being plucked, as with a harp; by the friction of a bow, as with a violin; or by being struck, as with a piano.

Horse-hair strings

Ivory tuning peg

Carved pegbox

Triangular-shaped body

Heart-shaped sound hole

Fish-shaped body

Spike to keep instrument steady

Iranian spike fiddle, Middle-Eastern ancestor of the violin, typically has a long neck.

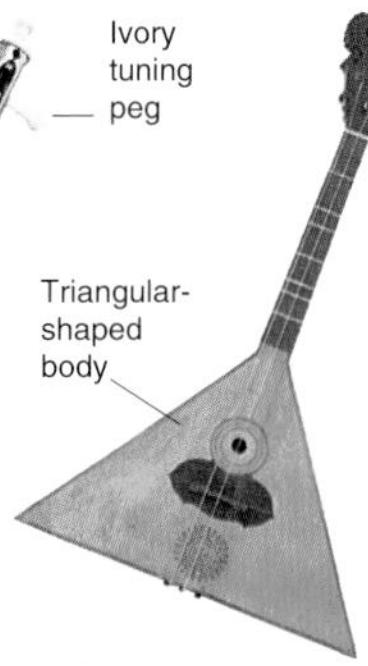

Russian balalaika uses two to four strings and may sit on the ground.

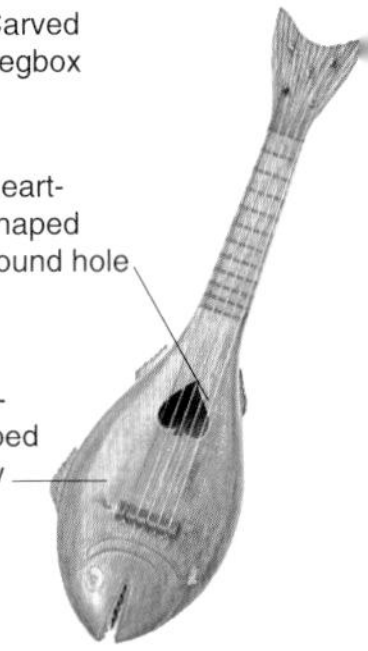

Portuguese rajao is a folk music instrument originating in Madeira, an island off North Africa.

DOUBLE REED
A double reed is made by binding the ends of a bent strip of cane and fitting them into a staple (cork tube). The bend is then sliced off.

PIED PIPERS
In 1454, French knights from the Order of the Golden Fleece held a banquet in which more than 20 musicians emerged from a giant pie to entertain the guests.

THE TRUMPET
This trumpet is a modern version of the oldest brass instrument. It has changed very little since its invention, and is the dominant instrument in many bands and orchestras.

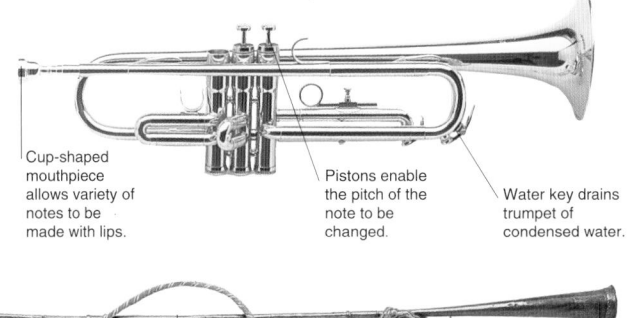

Cup-shaped mouthpiece allows variety of notes to be made with lips.

Pistons enable the pitch of the note to be changed.

Water key drains trumpet of condensed water.

Mouthpiece

Detachable brass section

Decorative carrying cord

Slim brass bell

Tenor horn is a descendant of the bugle.

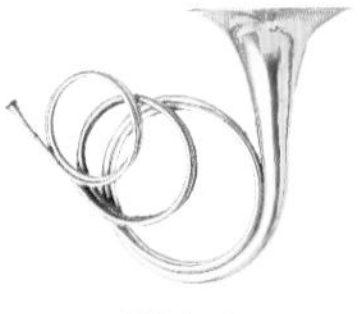

1780s horn is coiled for ease of playing

French horn has a wide flared bell.

Serpent horn has two sets of fingerholes.

PERCUSSION INSTRUMENTS

Percussion instruments are played by being struck, rubbed, or shaken; they usually provide the rhythmic beat in an instrumental group. They include snare drums, bass drums, tambourines, cymbals, gongs, castanets, maracas, tom-toms, timpani, bells, the xylophone, celesta, marimba, vibraphone, and chimes.

DRUM KIT
A drum kit consists of different types of drums and cymbals. The player uses both hands and feet to operate it.

Crash cymbal loosely fitted to allow vibrations

High-hat uses two cymbals.

Snare drum

Tom-tom drums

Ride cymbal

Key to adjust height

Floor tom-tom

Bass drum pedal

Felt-covered beater

Bass drum gives deep thud.

Egyptian darabuka is an example of the goblet drum popular in many Arab countries.

Oriental gong is struck in the centre to cause the greatest vibrations.

Nigerian gourd rattle

Chinese rattle drum

Gourd

Brazilian berimbau with resonating gourd.

Tambourine has cymbals set into frame, which sound when shaken.

KEYBOARD INSTRUMENTS

Keyboard instruments have an arrangement of levers or keys that activate the source of sound. Their popularity arose from a capacity to play melody and accompaniment at the same time. The three major keyboard instruments are the pianoforte or piano, the harpsichord, and the organ.

PIANOFORTE
The keys of a pianoforte manipulate felt-covered hammers. These strike wire strings, causing them to resonate. The player can sound many notes at once and can vary the loudness of individual notes.

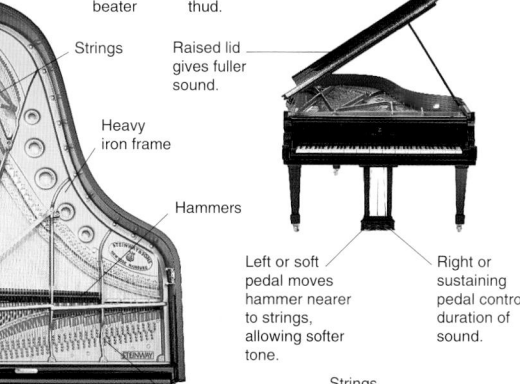

Strings

Raised lid gives fuller sound.

Heavy iron frame

Hammers

Left or soft pedal moves hammer nearer to strings, allowing softer tone.

Right or sustaining pedal controls duration of sound.

88-note keyboard

Tuning pins

Strings plucked by wooden jacks.

Wooden soundboard

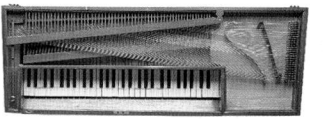

Square pianoforte made in England in 1773.

Italian spinet of 1550s used a four-octave keyboard.

MOST EXPENSIVE INSTRUMENTS

Instrument	Date made	Value $
"Mendelssohn" violin by Stradivari	1720	1,382,766
"Cholmondeley" cello by Stradivari	1698	950,460
"Bonjour" cello by Stradivari	1690	927,465
Violin by Joseph del Gesu	1743	797,160
"Marie Hall" violin by Stradivari	1709	659,190
"Schreiber" violin by Stradivari	1712	539,616
Violin by Pietro Guarneri	1715	339,560
"Ex-Kosman" violin by G. Guadagnini	c.1750	339,560
"Montagnana" violin by D. Montagnana	1741	314,265
Jimi Hendrix's *Stratocaster* guitar	1968	275,940

ELECTRONIC INSTRUMENTS

The electronic synthesizer creates sound by artificial means. It changes electric impulses into sound, and every aspect of the sound can be controlled. The synthesizer player can generate virtually any sound imaginable, from those of the natural world or of traditional instruments, to new, unique, "space-age" sounds.

Electronic keyboard can change a sound wave to produce a great variety of sounds.

Drum pad emits electric signal when struck, to produce electronic drum sound.

1950s electric guitar pioneered rock as musical form. Most bands have three guitars, a lead, rhythm, and bass.

Futuristic V-shaped wooden body

Pick-ups that convert string vibrations into electrical impulses.

Output socket

MUSIC FACTS

• Italian violinist Niccolò Paganini (1782–1840) was the most skilled violin virtuoso of the 19th century. He was the fastest violinist in the world, playing his own *Mouvement Perpetuel* in three minutes, three seconds. This translates as 12 notes per second.

• In 1846, Belgian instrument maker Adolphe Sax invented the saxophone.

• The harmonica is the world's most popular instrument. In 1965, more than 28 million were sold in the USA.

• The drum used on British explorer Sir Francis Drake's ship hangs in Buckland Abbey, England. It is believed to roll by itself when England faces danger. It was last heard in World War I (1914–18).

• In 1709, the first piano was built by Italian Bartolomeo Cristofori (1655-1731). The first iron-framed piano appeared in 1859.

WRITING

THE FIRST WRITING began as a way to keep accounts and to record details of history. Today people read books for pleasure and to learn about the world.

3000 B.C. The Egyptians invent a form of writing using picture signs called hieroglyphs. They write on scrolls made from papyrus reed.

Egyptian hieroglyphs

2000 B.C. Sumerian epic poem *Gilgamesh* is recorded on 12 clay tablets using cuneiform, a script named after the wedge-shaped pen used for writing.

600 B.C. Greek writer Aesop composes his fables, including the stories of *The Boy Who Cried Wolf*, and *The Crow and Pitcher*.

3000 B.C.	3000-2000 B.C.	2000 B.C.	2000 B.C.	1000 B.C.	600 B.C.

610–580 B.C. Female poet Sappho, from the Greek island of Lesbos, composes lyrical poetry on themes of love and jealousy.

Greek poet Sappho

500 B.C. The most famous Hindu text, the *Bhagavadgita*, is written in form of a conversation between Arjuna and Krishna.

200 B.C. Parchment (the skin of sheep or goats treated to make a smooth surface) is invented in the Greek city of Pergamum. Parchment is used in the West for 1,000 years.

A.D. 100 Plutarch writes first biography, *Parallel Lives*, which details the lives of Greek soldiers.

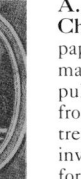
Plutarch (A.D.46–119)

A.D. 105 Chinese invent paper which they make from the pulp of fibres from mulberry trees. They keep invention a secret for 600 years.

Making paper

868 A.D. The earliest known wood-block printed book, with wood-cut illustrations, is the *Diamond Sutra*, printed in China.

610 B.C.	500–200 B.C.	A.D.100	A.D.105	A.D. 868

1007 Murasaki Shikibu (973–1014) writes *The Tale of Genji*, based on life in the Heian court of Japan. It is the world's first novel.

1048–1123 Persian poet Omar Khayyam writes the *The Rubáiyát*.

1190-1320 Writers in Iceland begin to record the oral part of their history as a story. This is known as a *saga*.

c.1450 Johann Gutenberg (c.1398–1468) invents printing by movable type. First printing is 170 bibles.

1593 William Shakespeare writes one of his first plays, *The Taming of the Shrew*.

Gutenberg bible

1605 Miguel de Cervantes (1547–1616) writes *Don Quixote*, a comic satire about the travels of an elderly Spanish knight.

1697 French author Charles Perrault writes *Tales of Mother Goose*, a collection of oral folk tales that includes *Cinderella* and *Beauty and the Beast*.

1719 Englishman Daniel Defoe (1660–1731) writes *Robinson Crusoe*. Defoe is one of the first people to write major works of literature in an "ordinary" or natural style.

ROBINSON CRUSOE
Early copy of Robinson Crusoe

1000	1007-1320	1400	1450	1593	1600	1605	1697	1700	1719

Scene with Little Nell

1800s Charles Dickens' novel, *The Old Curiosity Shop*, is published a chapter a month. Crowds at New York docks shout "is Little Nell dead?" as the ship arrives with the next instalment.

1837 First book for the blind, *A Summary of French History, Century by Century*, is printed using braille, a system of raised dots invented by Louis Braille (1809–52).

1841 American author, Edgar Allan Poe (1809–49), creates *The Murders in the Rue Morgue*, which is the first true detective story.

1847 Charlotte Brontë writes *Jane Eyre*, a love story that breaks the rules of Victorian society. She uses the false name of Currer Bell, as it is still unacceptable for women to write fiction.

Charlotte Brontë (1816–55)

1852 Harriet Beecher Stowe book, *Uncle Tom's Cabin*, draws attention to the injustice of slavery in the United States.

Scene from Uncle Tom's Cabin

1800	1800	1830	1837	1841	1847	1850

1864 Jules Verne (1828–1905) writes *Journey to the Centre of the Earth*, which is the first science fiction story.

An illustration from Journey to the Centre of the Earth

1873 First typewriter in the world is produced and sold by the American Remington Company.

Early typewriter

1901 French poet Sully Prudhomme (1839–1907) becomes first person to win Nobel Prize for literature. His work includes *The Broken Vase* and *Solitude*.

1910 First children's encyclopedia is compiled and published by Arthur Mee (1875–1943). It is called *The Children's Encyclopedia* in Great Britain.

World War I soldiers shown in action

1914–18 World War I. A group of English poets that includes Rupert Brooke, Wilfred Owen, and Siegfried Sassoon, record with great emotions the horror of life for soldiers in the war.

1860	1864	1873	1900	1901	1910	1914-18

Penguin paperbacks

1935 Penguin paperback books appear in English-speaking countries. The first title is *Ariel* by André Maurois (1885–1967) with a printing of 25,000 copies.

Anne Frank (1929–45)

1943 Anne Frank, a young Jewish girl hiding from the Nazis in occupied Holland, writes a diary that is published after her capture and death in a concentration camp.

1944 English author George Orwell writes *Animal Farm*, a satire about a group of animals who overthrow their master.

1970s Desktop publishing arrives. Word processors and computers revolutionize book printing.

Word processor

1986 The first book on CD-ROM, called *Electronic Encyclopedia*, is published in the USA by Grolier Electronic Publishing, Inc. It contains the full-text version of 20 volumes of the *Academic American Encyclopedia*.

1995 Production and marketing of CD-ROM titles increases significantly.

1930	1935	1940	1943	1944	1970s	1986	1990

LITERARY WORDS

Allegory A story with a second meaning hidden beneath its obvious meaning.

Alliteration The repetition of the same sounds (usually consonants of words or stressed syllables) e.g. "landscape-lover, lord of language" (Alfred Lord Tennyson).

Allusion An indirect reference to some event, person, place, or work of art; its nature or relevance is not explained by the writer but relies on the reader's familiarity with what is mentioned.

Autobiography An account of a person's life that is written or recorded by that person.

Biography An account of a person's life written by another.

Character A person in a story or drama, or a sketch describing some recognizable type of person.

The character Huckleberry Finn

Cliché A phrase or saying made commonplace by overuse.

Couplet A pair of rhyming verse lines.

Criticism The reasoned discussion of literary works.

Drama A story written in dialogue, or conversational, form so that it can be spoken and acted.

Elegy A poem lamenting the death of a friend or public figure, or reflecting seriously on a solemn subject.

Epic A long narrative poem celebrating, in a grand style, the great deeds of one or more legendary heroes.

Fable A short story, often about animals who behave and talk as humans, which teaches about right and wrong.

Fiction Something that is not true. A category used to describe a novel.

Genre French term for a type, species, or class of composition.

Gothic novel A story of terror and suspense, usually set in a gloomy castle or monastery.

Lyric Expressing the writer's personal feelings and thoughts. Used to describe poetry.

Metaphor A word or phrase used about a thing or an action that is not literally true, but describes it imaginatively.

A Gothic castle

Non-fiction A written work that is based on fact.

Novel An invented, or fictitious, story that usually deals with human relationships, often in a specified setting.

Onomatopoeia The use of words that seem to imitate the sounds they refer to (e.g. buzz, crackle, hiss, snap, splash).

Oral Anything that is spoken or verbal.

Plot The pattern of events in a story or a play.

Rhetoric Eloquence in public speaking or writing for the most persuasive effect.

Satire A kind of writing that makes fun of the failings of individuals, or societies, such as William Golding's *Lord of the Flies*.

Sonnet A lyric poem of 14 rhyming lines of equal length.

Tragedy A serious work representing the unhappy downfall of a central character, such as William Shakespeare's *Hamlet*.

KEY WRITERS

Name	Dates	Nationality	Key work
Homer	c.800 B.C.	Greek	*The Iliad*
Virgil	70–1 B.C.	Roman	*The Aeneid*
Dante Alighieri	1265–1321	Italian	*The Divine Comedy*
Giovanni Boccaccio	1313–75	Italian	*The Decameron*
Geoffrey Chaucer	1343–1400	English	*The Canterbury Tales*
Miguel de Cervantes	1547–1616	Spanish	*Don Quixote*
Edmund Spenser	1552–99	English	*The Faerie Queene*
John Milton	1608–74	English	*Paradise Lost*
John Bunyan	1628–88	English	*The Pilgrim's Progress*
Henry Fielding	1707–54	English	*Tom Jones*
Laurence Sterne	1713–68	Irish	*Tristram Shandy*
J. W. Von Goethe	1748–1832	German	*Faust*
William Wordsworth	1770–1850	English	*Lyrical Ballads*
Jane Austen	1775–1817	English	*Pride and Prejudice*
Mary Shelley	1797–1851	English	*Frankenstein*
Honoré de Balzac	1799–1850	French	*Old Goriot*
Victor Hugo	1802–85	French	*Les Misérables*
Charles Dickens	1812–70	English	*Oliver Twist*
Charlotte Brontë	1816–55	English	*Jane Eyre*
Emily Brontë	1818–48	English	*Wuthering Heights*
George Eliot	1819–80	English	*Middlemarch*
Herman Melville	1819–91	American	*Moby Dick*
Walt Whitman	1819–92	American	*Leaves of Grass*
Gustave Flaubert	1821–80	French	*Madame Bovary*
Feyodor Dostoyevsky	1821–81	Russian	*Crime and Punishment*
Leo Tolstoy	1828–1910	Russian	*War and Peace*
Émile Zola	1840–1902	French	*Germinal*
Thomas Hardy	1840–1928	English	*Tess of the d'Urbervilles*
Henry James	1843–1916	American	*Portrait of a Lady*
Joseph Conrad	1857–1924	British	*Heart of Darkness*
Rabindranath Tagore	1861–1941	Indian	*Gitanjali*
W. B. Yeats	1865–1939	Irish	*The Tower*
Marcel Proust	1871–1922	French	*Remembrance of Things Past*
Thomas Mann	1875–1955	German	*The Magic Mountain*
E. M. Forster	1879–1970	English	*Passage to India*
James Joyce	1882–1941	Irish	*Ulysses*
Virginia Woolf	1882–1941	English	*To the Lighthouse*
Franz Kafka	1883–1924	Czechoslovakian	*The Trial*
D. H. Lawrence	1885–1930	English	*Sons and Lovers*
Ezra Pound	1885–1972	American	*The Cantos*
T. S. Eliot	1888–1965	American	*The Waste Land*
Boris Pasternak	1890–1960	Russian	*Dr. Zhivago*
Aldous Huxley	1894–1963	English	*Brave New World*
F. Scott Fitzgerald	1896–1940	American	*The Great Gatsby*
Ernest Hemingway	1899–1961	American	*A Farewell to Arms*
Vladimir Nabokov	1899–1977	Russian	*Lolita*
Jorge Luis Borges	1899–1986	Argentinian	*Labyrinths*
John Steinbeck	1902–68	American	*The Grapes of Wrath*
George Orwell	1903–50	English	*Animal Farm*
Evelyn Waugh	1903–66	English	*Brideshead Revisited*
Pablo Neruda	1904–73	Chilean	*Great Song*
Graham Greene	1904–91	English	*The Power and the Glory*
William Golding	1911–93	English	*Lord of the Flies*
Patrick White	1912–90	Australian	*Voss*
Albert Camus	1913–60	French	*The Outsider*
Dylan Thomas	1914–53	Welsh	*Under Milk Wood*
Anthony Burgess	1917–93	English	*A Clockwork Orange*
Doris Lessing	b.1919–	English	*The Golden Notebook*
Iris Murdoch	b.1919–	English	*Bruno's Dream*
Italo Calvino	1923–85	Italian	*The Path to the Nest of Spiders*
Yukio Mishima	1925–1970	Japanese	*The Sound of Waves*
Günter Grass	b.1927–	German	*The Tin Drum*
Gabriel García Márquez	b.1928–	Colombian	*One Hundred Years of Solitude*
Toni Morrison	b.1931–	American	*Beloved*

PRINTING

BEFORE PRINTING WAS invented, information was written by hand. The introduction of printing with movable type (one block for each character or letter) meant that many copies of an original work could be made quickly and cheaply. Today, many stages of print production are done by computer.

Virtually any colour can be created from a combination of the four colours shown.

Yellow Magenta

Cyan Black

COLOUR SEPARATION

Colour illustrations are separated into four colours (magenta, cyan, yellow, and black) by an electronic scanner before printing. A laser scans the pictures four times, once for each separation. This process results in four pieces of film, one for each colour.

The illustration is placed on a revolving drum and is scanned by a laser.

Paper is fed through the press, and comes into contact with each of the colour plates in turn.

The final full-colour printed sheets appear at the far end of the press.

PRINTING PRESS

After colour separation, the details on each of the coloured films is transferred on to a plate. Each plate is treated with chemicals, then fitted to rollers on a press. The paper feeds through, and as it comes into contact with each plate, the four colours are added one by one.

TYPOGRAPHY

Typography is the design of letters and words printed on a page. Typographers create a page of print using different type styles, which when put together, make the page look appealing and easy to read. Typefaces can be divided into two main groups:

SERIF
Serif faces have little strokes (serifs) at the end of many letters. The serifs form a link between the letters, which helps bind them together as words.

A

SANS SERIF
Sans serif typefaces do not have serifs. They are harder to read than serif faces.

A

TYPESETTING
Today, this is mainly done by computer. The typeface and text width is set, and any corrections can be made on screen. A laser printer, which is connected to the computer, prints the words on to a sheet of light-sensitive film, or type film.

TYPEFACES
There are thousands of different typefaces. Some of the most common are shown on the right. A typeface comes in a range of styles (such as italics) and sizes, which are measured in points. This book is set in the Caslon typeface.

Helvetica ABCDEFGHIJKLMNOPQR STUVWXYZ

Times ABCDEFGHIJKLMNOPQ RSTUVWXYZ

Futura ABCDEFGHIJKLMNOPQRST UVWXYZ

Typeface
Caslon Roman, 30 point

Typeface
Caslon italic, 30 point

Typeface
Caslon bold, 30 point

Baskerville ABCDEFGHIJKLMNOPQRSTUVWXYZ

PRINTING WORDS

Ascender Part of a lower-case letter that is above the x-height.

Bromide Photosensitive paper on which an image is created.

ascender

Cold type Modern method of printing that produces a photographic image.

Colour correction Changing the strength of colours in an illustration before going to print.

Cropping Trimming and shaping illustrations.

flat colour

Descender Part of a lower-case letter that is below the x-height.

Em Unit of measurement.

Flat colour Area of printed colour without variations in tone.

Flop Reversal of an illustration.

Font Set of typed characters of the same style.

Format Size of a book or a page.

Gutter Margin that runs down the centre of a spread.

Hot metal Traditional method of printing in which type is cast from molten lead.

Kerning Adjusting the space between letters.

Leading Space between lines of type.

Lower case Letters that are not capitals.

Measure Length of a line of type.

Mechanical Illustrations and text drawn up for reproduction.

Orphan The start of a paragraph at the foot of the page.

Ozalid Reproduction of printed material on to chemically treated, usually blue, paper.

x-height

Phototypesetting Setting of type on film or photographic paper.

Pica Unit of type measurement equal to 12 points.

Point A measurement type equal to 0.351457mm (0.013837in).

Proof A reproduction of illustrations or text before the printing stage.

Range Lining up of type either vertically or horizontally.

descender

Reproduction Process by which artwork is reproduced, through colour separation, before printing.

Upper case Letters that are capitals.

Widow A short line.

X-height The height of a letter that does not include its ascender or descender.

PRINTING FACTS

• First printers were the Chinese, who printed scrolls and books using wooden blocks in about A.D. 770.

Chinese wooden block

• Today, there are more than 11,000 Western typefaces.

RADIO

RADIO WAVES WERE first used for communication some 30 years before television appeared. The invention of radio also made television broadcasting possible.

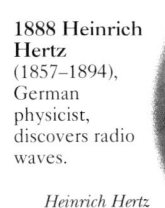

1888 Heinrich Hertz (1857–1894), German physicist, discovers radio waves.

Heinrich Hertz

1894 Guglielmo Marconi (1874–1937), Italian-born physicist, sends radio waves across a room, making a bell ring.

1901 Morse code (see p.269) is transmitted across the Atlantic by Marconi.

Guglielmo Marconi

| 1800 | 1888 | 1890 | 1894 | 1900 | 1901 |

1912 Titanic sends an emergency signal by radio after hitting an iceberg.

1920 First commercial radio station, KDKA of Pittsburgh, USA, starts broadcasting with a transmission of the presidential election results.

RMS Titanic

1927 BBC (British Broadcasting Corporation) is granted its first charter (licence).

1932 Frequency Modulation, which reduces interference, is invented by American inventor Edwin Armstrong (1890–1954).

BBC Radio microphone

1954 First transistor radio appears in the USA. Transistors replace valves.

Early transistor radio

1960 First VHF-FM stereo broadcasts, from KDKA-FM (see 1920).

1988 Radio Data System (automatic station identification and traffic news for car radios) is introduced in the UK and Sweden.

| 1910 | 1912 | 1920 | 1920 | 1927 | 1930 | 1932 | 1950 | 1954 | 1960 | 1960 | 1980 | 1988 |

RADIO FACTS

• Australian RPH radio stations broadcast only programmes for the vision impaired.

• During the five days in 1991 that Cyclone Val pounded Samoa, the island's only link with the outside world was amateur radio.

• Digital Audio Broadcasting (DAB) is a new radio system that produces CD-quality digital sound.

• The distance radio waves travel around the Earth depends partly on the number of sunspots at the time.

TOP RADIO OWNERS

Country	Radios per person
USA	2.1
Bermuda	1.4
Australia	1.3
Gibraltar	1.2
United Kingdom	1.1

RADIO FREQUENCIES

Radio waves are waves of electromagnetic energy that have varying lengths and that vibrate at varying speeds. The rate of vibration is called frequency. Radio stations use long, medium or short waves. TV satellite link-ups and microwave ovens also use radio waves.

Frequency bands are divided between radio stations so each station can broadcast on its own frequency and no clashes with other stations occur.

Radio receivers select a single radio channel and convert the waves back into sound.

Satellites provide communication between very distant locations with microwaves.

Long waves (LW) can travel almost 2,000km (1,240m). They are used for some national broadcasts.

Medium waves (MW) travel for a few hundred kms. National and local radio stations often transmit in MW.

Very high frequency waves (VHF) travel short distances.

Short waves (SW) travel thousands of kilometres. International radio stations use SW.

RADIOS OLD AND NEW

1930s This 1936 set was 41cm (16in) tall, 33cm (13in) wide, and used valves.

TODAY Radios can now be fitted inside wrist-watches.

RADIO RECORDS

LARGEST AUDIENCE is for the BBC's World Service, with at least 140 million regular listeners around the world.

LONGEST-RUNNING SHOW is *Rambling with Gambling* on WOR-NY (New York, USA), first broadcast in 1925.

LONGEST-RUNNING SOAP is *The Archers*, first broadcast by the BBC in 1950.

ALIEN ATTACK!

In 1938 American actor and director Orson Welles (1915-85) dramatised H.G. Wells' *War of the Worlds*, in which Earth is invaded by aliens. Thousands of people panicked, believing the programme to be a news bulletin.

TELEVISION

TELEVISION SETS convert radio waves into pictures and sound. A single event can be watched live by billions of people all over the world.

Paul Nipkow

1884 Nipkow disc is invented by Paul Nipkow (1860–1940), a German inventor. The spinning disc is an early alternative to the cathode ray tube.

1897 Cathode-ray tube is invented by German physicist Karl Ferdinand Braun (1850–1918). It is the forerunner of the modern TV receiver tube.

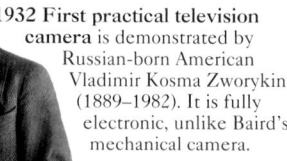

Cathode ray tube

| 1880 | 1884 | 1897 |

1926 John Logie Baird (1888–1946), a Scottish inventor, demonstrates television by showing the first recognizable pictures of a human face. He uses the Nipkow disc.

1929 Late-night transmissions of Baird's 30-line pictures are broadcast by the British Broadcasting Corporation (BBC).

1930 Sound is added to Baird's 30-line television pictures and transmitted by the BBC.

1932 First practical television camera is demonstrated by Russian-born American Vladimir Kosma Zworykin (1889–1982). It is fully electronic, unlike Baird's mechanical camera.

Baird's system

Vladimir Zworykin

| 1920 | 1926 | 1929 | 1930 | 1930 | 1931 |

1950 Colour television system is developed by the American company CBS.

1954 Eurovision formed to share transmission of programmes across Europe.

1960–61 All-transistor televisions appear for the first time in the United States.

1962 First transatlantic pictures are broadcast live from the communications satellite Telstar, launched by NASA.

Telstar satellite

1969 First Moon landing is seen by millions all over the world, filmed in colour by the Apollo XI crew.

First man on the moon

1970 Transmission direct from satellite to high-definition television (HDTV) is developed by Japan Broadcasting System (NHK).

1973 Ceefax, an information system using the spare lines on a 625-line television system, is developed in Britain.

| 1950 | 1954 | 1960 | 1961 | 1962 | 1969 | 1970 | 1973 |

1979 First regular direct broadcasting system (DBS) by satellite is launched in Canada. A dish is needed to receive broadcasts.

Satellite receiver dish

1979 Pocket television set is invented by Japanese firm Matsushita. It is no bigger than a video cassette.

Pocket TV set

1980 Cable News Network (CNN) officially begins in June. This American 24-hour television channel relies on satellites for news reporting and gives up-to-the minute news coverage in times of crisis.

1981 Camcorder revolutionises TV news gathering (see p.187).

1991 Hi-Vision, a high definition TV service, is broadcast for eight hours daily by NHK of Japan.

1999 Digital TV promises a huge increase in the number of channels.

| 1979 | 1980 | 1981 | 1986 | 1991 | 1999 |

TV SETS OLD AND NEW

TV technology has advanced rapidly over its brief history.

1930s
Early sets had small black- and- white screens but contained so much electronic equipment that they were housed in large boxes.

1960s
In the 1960s smaller, colour TVs became common. Transistors replaced valves.

TODAY
Pocket-sized TVs are now widely available. Very small sets often use liquid crystal screens.

TELEVISION RECORDS
WORLD'S LONGEST-RUNNING TV SHOW
is NBC's *Meet the Press*, first shown in the USA in 1947.

WORLD'S SMALLEST TV SET
is Seiko's TV-Wrist Watch, launched in 1982. It has a 1.2inch (30.5mm) screen.

LONGEST CONTINUOUS BROADCAST
was by GTV 9, Australia, lasting 163 hrs 18 mins, of Apollo XI's Moon mission (19-26 July 1969).

FIRST DAILY BROADCASTS
were made by the BBC, broadcasting from London, starting 10 November 1936.

TV GENERATION
Americans watch more television than any other nationality. In an average household the TV set is turned on for seven hours a day. By the time they are 65 years old, most Americans have watched more than nine years' worth of television.

POPULAR TELEVISION

SOAP OPERAS ("SOAPS")
Soaps are dramas with continuous storylines screened in regular episodes. The world's longest-running soap is *Coronation Street*, first shown on British TV in 1960. The earliest American soaps of the 1950s were sponsored by soap-powder companies.

SPORTS PROGRAMMES
One of the biggest TV audiences was about 26.5 billion for the 1990 World Cup finals.

World Cup finals, 1990

CHAT SHOWS
Chat shows are programmes where a host asks members of the audience to talk about their lives. The popularity of American chat show, *Oprah*, has made its host, Oprah Winfrey, the highest paid entertainer in the world. In 1994–5 she allegedly earned $146 million.

CHILDREN'S PROGRAMMES
Children's programmes show a wide range of material suitable for a younger audience. *Sesame Street*, first shown in the USA in 1969, is seen in 80 countries.

MAKING A DOCUMENTARY
This diagram shows one way of making a documentary. The two main players are the production company, which makes the film, and the TV station, which broadcasts it. The three main stages of the process are pre-production (organization of the shoot), production (filming) and post-production (editing).

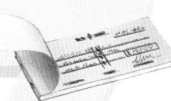

Idea is taken to the production company that will make the programme and arrange for it to be shown on TV.

Go ahead
Preliminary research into subject and possible locations (recce) is undertaken.

Treatment
This written outline is taken to a TV station.

Commissioning editor
Commissioning editor, a TV executive, receives and approves treatment .

Finance committee
Committee, which includes accountants, commissioning editor, and controller, approves project and budget.

Rushes
If shot on videotape, material can be checked instantly on playback. If film has been used, previous day's work, developed overnight, is viewed daily.

Pre-production
Equipment and crew hired, interviews set up, locations found, filming permissions obtained.

Contract
After signing, preparation and shooting of documentary can begin.

Production
Shooting begins. Crew go on location.

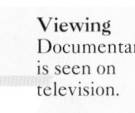

Viewing
Documentary is seen on television.

Post-production
Editor and director put the programme together in its finished version, adding sound and titles.

Delivery
Completed film is delivered to TV station.

Transmission
Programme is broadcast by TV station.

INSIDE A TELEVISION SET
The TV set's aerial picks up radio waves and converts them into electronic signals. These signals in turn are converted into pictures by the picture tube.

Electron guns fire streams of electrons (see p.226) that sweep across the inside of the screen, building up the image.

Picture tube is the most important single component of a TV set. All the air has been pumped out of the tube to allow free flow of electrons.

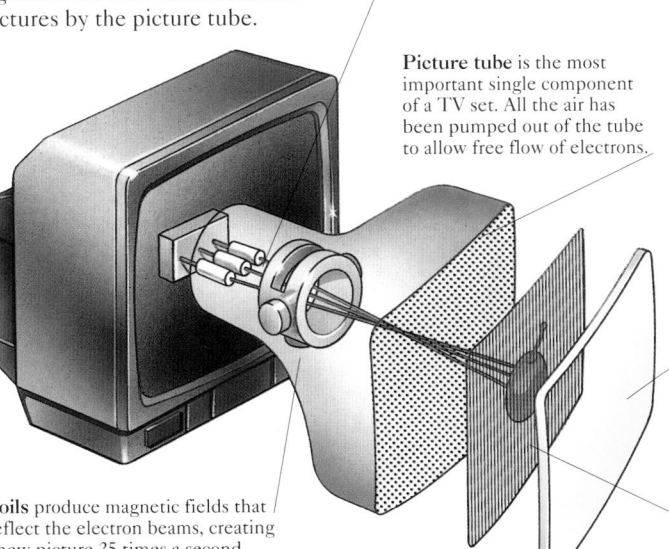

Coils produce magnetic fields that deflect the electron beams, creating a new picture 25 times a second.

Phosphor strips coat the inside of the screen. Three different types of phosphor are used: one which glows red when struck by electrons; one green; and one blue.

Shadow mask has slots which ensure that the electrons light phosphor of the correct colour.

WORLD TV VIEWING

Country	Hours per week
United States	49.35
Italy	28.93
Hong Kong	28.70
Colombia	23.80
United Kingdom	23.80
Australia	21.98
Chile	17.50
China	10.59
Malaysia	10.50
World average	19.67

TELEVISION FACTS
- By 1993 there were 746,829,000 homes with a TV set world-wide. By 2005 there will be an estimated billion.

- In 1977 hundreds of bald men invaded an English farm after a BBC April fool joke suggested that water there had hair-restoring properties.

- High-definition TV, which uses twice as many lines to build up each frame as ordinary TV, gives a much sharper picture.

- Virtual Vision Sport is a TV system in which the viewer wears a pair of special glasses. They create a colour

Virtual vision glasses

picture that appears to be 1.5m (5ft) wide floating in space about 3m (10ft) away.

CINEMA

CINEMA IS A MILLION-dollar industry that makes, sells, and shows movies worldwide. Film stars attract publicity and often become household names.

1879 Zoogyroscope (later renamed Zoopraxiscope) is developed by English photographer Eadweard Muybridge (1830-1904). It projects images of a series of photographs on to a screen, in quick succession, creating the illusion of movement.

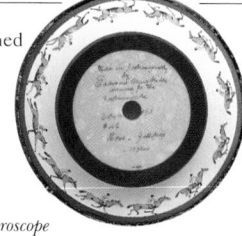
Zoogyroscope

1881 Etienne Marey (1830-1904), French photographic pioneer, invents a camera, shaped like a gun, which takes pictures on a revolving plate.

Etienne Marey

1885 Paper roll film is invented by American George Eastman (1854-1932).

1894 Kinetograph (film camera) **and Kinetoscope** (film viewer) are marketed by Americans Thomas Edison (1847-1931) and W.K.L. Dickson (1860-1933), using celluloid roll film.

Lumière projector

1895 Projection system is invented by French brothers August (1862-1954) and Louis (1864-1948) Lumière, and publicly demonstrated for the first time in Paris.

1908 Kinemacolour is invented by Englishman George Albert Smith (1864-1959) and demonstrated in London. It uses two colour filters and two reels of film.

1913 Hollywood's first feature film, *Squaw Man*, is made by American directors Jesse Lasky (1880-1958), Cecil B. de Mille (1881-1959), and Samuel Goldwyn (1879-1974).

1920s First studios in India appear, including Bombay Talkies, Ranjit Film Company, and Prabhat Film Company.

Indian film posters

Timeline: 1870 | 1879 | 1880 | 1881
1880 | 1885 | 1894 | 1890 | 1895 | 1900 | 1908 | 1913

1920s picture palace

1920s-30s Picture palaces are at the peak of their popularity, offering movie-goers magic and luxury.

1927 The first "talkie" is *The Jazz Singer*. The soundtrack to the film is recorded on a disc.

Jazz singer poster

1928 Sound is recorded on to the film itself. The first all-talking picture is *The Lights of New York*.

1929 First Oscars (Academy Awards) include Emil Jannings (best actor) and Janet Gaynor (best actress).

Oscar

1932 Technicolor process is perfected and three-colour Technicolor cameras are developed.

1937 *Becky Sharp* is the first film to be made entirely in three-strip colour.

Timeline: 1920 | 1920 | 1927 | 1928 | 1929 | 1930 | 1932 | 1937

1952 Eastman color takes over from Technicolor. A negative three-colour movie is made from which Technicolor or Eastman color prints can be taken.

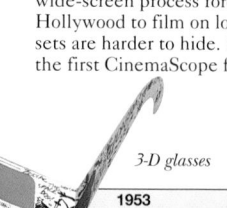
Scene from Eastman color movie, Doctor at Large

1952 *Bwana Devil* is the first 3-D film in Natural Vision (a large screen process using natural colour).

1953 CinemaScope is developed by Fox studios. This wide-screen process forces Hollywood to film on location as sets are harder to hide. *The Robe* is the first CinemaScope film.

3-D glasses

1970 Steadycam is invented. It is a camera that remains completely steady while strapped to a freely moving cameraman.

1976 OMNIMAX projection is first demonstrated. OMNIMAX films are shown on a huge dome-like screen that towers above and around the audience.

Timeline: 1950 | 1952 | 1953 | 1970 | 1970 | 1976

POPULAR FILMS

Three of the most popular types of film at the cinema are science fiction (sci-fi), action, and horror.

Arnold Schwarzenegger in Terminator 2

SCIENCE FICTION
The most expensive film ever made was the sci-fi adventure *Waterworld*. The film cost 160 million US dollars. The second most expensive film was *Terminator 2*.

ACTION
The three *Indiana Jones* films were all in the top ten most successful films of the 1980s. Each film earned at least 100 million US dollars.

HORROR
Count Dracula, the vampire, is the most frequently filmed horror character. Since his screen debut in 1931, he has appeared on film more than 160 times.

FILM FORMATS

One minute of a movie uses over 27m (90ft) of film, and a full-length feature about 2.5km (1.5 miles). The standard size used now is 35mm (standard gauge).

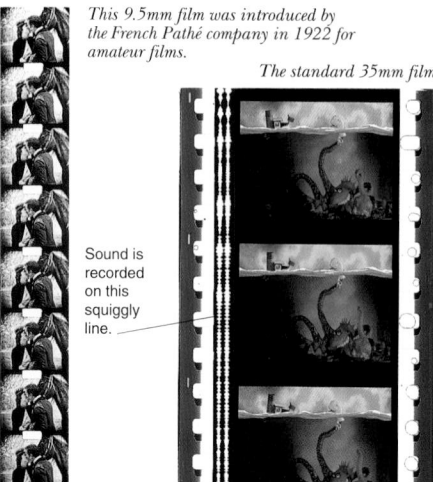
This 9.5mm film was introduced by the French Pathé company in 1922 for amateur films.

The standard 35mm film

Sound is recorded on this squiggly line.

Scene from an IMAX film

IMAX

The IMAX projection system was first demonstrated in Japan in 1970. The films are shown on giant screens with a full range of digital sound. 70mm film is used with special cameras and projectors to create very clear, vivid pictures on screen.

MOVIE MAKERS

This diagram shows many of the most important people involved in making a movie. The producer has overall financial responsibility and the director has overall creative control.

PRE-PRODUCTION
All the necessary arrangements are made to ensure that filming runs smoothly.

Producer
The producer raises money for the film and puts together the creative package: director, script, and actors. Once finance has been raised, filming begins.

Scriptwriter
Works on story to make it attractive to stars as well as to financial backers.

Production manager
Controls the budget and expenditure; oversees practicalities of the shoot such as scheduling, travel, and accommodation.

Director
Liaises with producer over script, hiring of stars, and key crew.

Finance
Once enough money has been raised, filming can begin.

Stars
Popular actors are important for the success of the film.

Casting director
Works with the director, selecting actors.

Location manager
Finds suitable locations and arranges for their use.

Production co-ordinator
Runs production office and makes sure information is circulated to crew and cast.

Production assistant
Performs a variety of tasks including liaising between office and set, and administration.

Cast
Actors for each speaking part in the script.

PRODUCTION

 Filming begins. The director is helped by experts in the various departments. Each take (uninterrupted sequence of filming) begins with the filming of a clapperboard, which is then slammed shut, making a noise on the soundtrack. This way, sound and image can be synchronized when the film is edited.

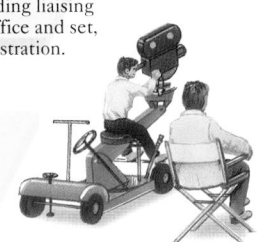

Director
The director is the creative force behind the film, controlling the action and bringing the script to life.

Director of photography
Responsible for lighting, composition, and choice of camera, lens, and film.

Production designer
Responsible for the overall design of the film, including sets and costumes.

First assitant director
Controls day-to-day filming on the set. Ensures schedule of film is on target.

Sound engineer
In charge of the sound quality of the film. Also supervises placing of microphones.

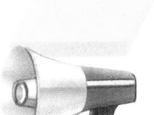 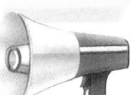

Camera operator works camera during shooting.

Focus puller adjusts focus on lens.

Clapper loader checks, cleans and loads the camera, operates the clapperboard, and sends film to the laboratory.

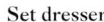

Grip lays tracks for dolly (support for camera that moves in any direction); moves dolly, as well as camera and camera equipment.

Gaffer is in charge of rigging and setting the lights.

Best boy assists the gaffer.

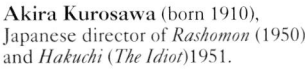

Art director draws up the designs for the sets on the film, supervises their construction, and orders the dressing of the set.

Construction manager is in charge of carpenters, painters, stagehands.

Set dresser places the many objects around the set that give it the appearance of reality.

Boom operator positions and operates the microphone known as the boom.

Second assistant director helps First assistant director and co-ordinates cast, crew, and background action.

OTHER SERVICES
Costume design and costume department (buys and maintains costumes); make-up department (applies general and special effect make-up); transport; catering; stills photography (for publicity shots).

POST-PRODUCTION
After all the film has been shot, the editor cuts up the individual film sequences and links them together. Working closely with the director, the editor then adds the sound. The finished version is sold for distribution to cinemas.

FAMOUS DIRECTORS

Fritz Lang (1890-1976), Austrian director of *Metropolis* (1926) and *Fury* (1936).

Sergei Eisenstein (1898-1948), Russian, directed *Battleship Potemkin* (1925) and *October/Ten Days That Shook the World* (1928).

Alfred Hitchcock (1899-1980), British director of *The Lady Vanishes* (1938), *Dial M for Murder* (1954), and *Psycho* (1960).

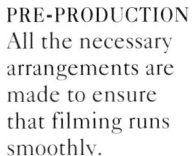

Contemporary poster advertising the film Metropolis

Akira Kurosawa (born 1910), Japanese director of *Rashomon* (1950) and *Hakuchi* (*The Idiot*)1951.

Ingmar Bergman (born 1918), Swedish director of *Smultronstallet* (*Wild Strawberries*) 1957.

Frederico Fellini (1920-1993), Italian, directed *Il Bidone* (*The Swindle*) 1955.

Satyajit Ray (1921–1992), Indian director of *The Apu Trilogy* (1955-1959).

Orson Welles (1915-1985), American who directed *Citizen Kane* (1940).

CINEMA FACTS

• Cinema screens are coated with minute plastic prisms which make the screen as bright as possible. Before their introduction, large screens were sprayed with water to improve reflection.

• First feature film was *The Story of the Kelly Gang*, made in Australia in 1906.

• Longest film ever made is *The Cure for Insomnia* (1987), directed by American J.H. Timmis. Lasts 85 hours.

MOST OSCARS WON

Name of film	Oscars
Ben Hur (1959)	11
Titanic (1998)	11
Gone with the Wind (1939)	10
West Side Story (1961)	10
Gandhi (1982)	9
The Last Emperor (1987)	9
The English Patient (1997)	9
Gigi (1958)	8
Cabaret (1972)	8
Amadeus (1984)	8

ANIMATION

ANIMATORS BRING drawings, models, or objects to life by filming them in detailed sequences. Computers are also used to create new techniques.

1832 Phenakistoscope is invented by Belgian Joseph Plateau (1801–83). Images painted in sequence on the disc seem to move when it is spun.

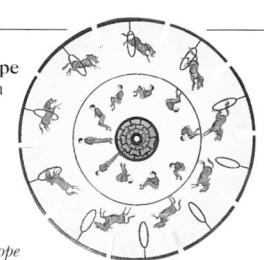

Phenakistoscope

1908 Emile Cohl (1857–1938), French animator, draws cartoons. His technique requires 16 pictures to make one second of screen time.

1914 Earl Hurd (1880–1950) and **J.R. Bray** (1879–1978), American animators, draw cartoons on clear celluloid sheets. The background does not have to be re-drawn for every frame (shot) of an animated sequence, only the moving parts.

| 1830 | 1832 | 1900 | 1908 | 1914 |

1919 Walt Disney (1901–66) meets Ub Iwerks (1901–71). These American animators refine and develop the celluloid-sheet technique. Disney Studios' Multiplane technique adds realism and depth to their cartoons.

WALT DISNEY'S
MICKEY MOUSE
in STEAMBOAT WILLIE

1928 Mickey Mouse stars in Disney's *Steamboat Willie*, the first animated cartoon with synchronized sound. Disney himself provides Mickey's voice. The cartoon causes a sensation.

Mickey Mouse

1930s Len Lye (1901–80), New Zealand animator, makes short films by drawing abstract images directly on to the film itself, thus skipping the photographic process.

Len Lye

1939 Tom and Jerry, created by Americans Bill Hanna (born 1910) and Joe Barbera (born 1911), appear in their first cartoon, *Puss Gets the Boot*. They receive the first of their seven Oscars in 1943 for *Yankee Doodle Mouse*.

| 1915 | 1919 | 1920 | 1928 | 1930 | 1939 | 1940 |

1952 Norman McLaren (1914–87), Canadian animator, photographs real people frame by frame in his short film *Neighbours*, to make them look like animated robots.

Norman McLaren

1991 *Creature Comforts*, created by Aardman Animation (UK) and featuring clay zoo animals, wins an Oscar.

A gorilla from Creature Comforts

1990s Computer graphics may be used to enhance or manipulate hand-drawn images, as in *Aladdin* (1992). Some animators save time by using them to draw the intermediate images between the key, hand-drawn positions.

Aladdin

| 1950 | 1952 | 1990 | 1991 |

ANIMATION TYPES

ANIMATION
The twin Brothers Quay, born in Philadelphia in 1947, bring strange, dead objects to life in their animated films. *Street of Crocodiles*, made in 1986, features eyeless dolls. The brothers were influenced by Czech animator, Jan Svankmajer (born 1934).

CARTOONS
Walt Disney achieved huge popularity and won a special Oscar for the first feature-length cartoon, *Snow White and the Seven Dwarfs* (1937).

ANIMATION FACTS

- First ever motion-picture cartoon film was *Humorous Phases of Funny Faces* (1906), made by American J. Stuart Blackton (1875–1941) for Vitagraph. The cartoon required 3,000 drawings.

- First animated film nominated for an Oscar for best picture was the Disney production of *Beauty and the Beast* (1991).

- Since the 1930s cartoon characters have been drawn with only three fingers instead of four. This looks just as realistic and is much quicker for the animators.

TOP BOX OFFICE HITS

Film	Production company and date
The Lion King	Disney, 1994
Aladdin	Disney, 1992
Who Framed Roger Rabbit?	Disney, 1988
Snow White and the Seven Dwarfs	Disney, 1937
Toy Story	Disney, 1995
The Santa Clause	Disney, 1994
Pocahontas	Disney, 1995
The Jungle Book	Disney, 1967

MORPHING

This computer technique is used either to transform a person or object into something different, or to create animation in a live-action film. The illustration shows part of a morphing sequence.

The points of both objects, hand and spider, are plotted on the computer. When the two sets of points coincide the transformation is complete.

The outline of the spider is just visible.

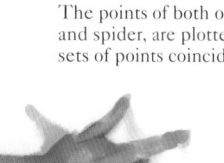

The mid-point of the morphing process.

The spider is almost complete.

VIRTUAL REALITY

Virtual reality is a three-dimensional computer-generated world. The special headset contains miniature TV screens that provide stereo vision. If you wear the headset and move around, the virtual-reality world moves with you. The data glove allows you to operate tools in the virtual world.

VIDEO

THE TERM VIDEO refers to video cassettes, video recorders, and video cameras. Many TV programmes, advertisements, and pop promos are shot on video.

1929 Phonovision is introduced by John Logie Baird (1888–1946), Scottish inventor. This video system uses 12-inch discs with pictures recorded on to them.

Phonovision disc

1956 First working video recorder, the VR1000, is introduced by Ampex corporation of California, USA.

1965 First portable video camera introduced by Japanese Company Sony. It has a bulky separate unit containing the recording equipment, and records in black and white.

```
1920    1929           1950   1956        1960    1965
```

1970 First video cassette is part of the U-Matic system, made by Sony.

Sony 1970 U-Matic video cassette

1972 First domestic video recorder is the N1500, brought out by Philips of Holland. It is the first video recorder to have its own tuner and timer.

1975 Laser Video Disc introduced by Sony/Philips.

1976 VHS system, launched by Japanese company JVC, proves more commercially successful than its rival Betamax.

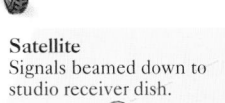
An early camcorder

1981 Camcorder is invented. It is a camera with a built-in recorder, which records on to videotape instead of film.

1990s CDTV uses pre-recorded video discs similar to music CDs, instead of video tapes.

CDTV disc

```
1970    1972  1975  1976              1980   1981    1990
```

VIDEO FACTS
- Approximately 25% of all video sales in the world are of animated films.
- Japanese companies account for over 80% of worldwide video recorder (VCR) production.

TOP VIDEO SPENDERS

Country	US $ Billions
USA	11.0
Japan	2.6
UK	1.4
Canada	1.2
France	0.7
Germany	0.7
Australia	0.7

- A basic VCR contains over 2,500 components, compared to about 360 in a colour TV set.
- Laser video discs spin approximately fifty times faster than a long-playing record. European models revolve 1,500 times a minute, and American and Japanese discs 1,800 times a minute.
- USA has the most video rental outlets in the world (55,000 in 1992). Japan is second with 11,500 stores.
- There are 230 million homes around the world with at least one VCR. The USA has the most video homes, with 65 million.

ELECTRONIC NEWS GATHERING
Electronic news gathering (ENG) teams use professional video cameras to record on to video cassettes. Unlike film, videos do not need to be processed before broadcasting.

On location abroad ENG crew films news story.

Customized van Cassette taken to van containing microwave transmitter. Pictures beamed home via nearby transmitting station.

Transmitting station Signals received from van sent on to satellite.

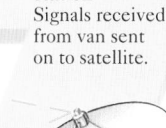

Satellite Signals beamed down to studio receiver dish.

Studio TV station can broadcast immediately or tape pictures for later use.

At home Viewer watches the news footage taken by the ENG team.

VIDEO CAMERAS
Early video cameras were carried on the shoulder and were connected by cables to separate recording equipment (called a portapak).

Portable video camera · Tripod · Video recorder

This camcorder films and records in one unit. It is small enough to be held in the palm of the hand.

VIDEO RECORDERS
The VR 1000 was 1.1m (3.7ft) high

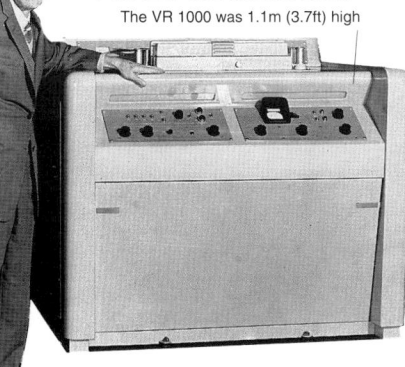

The 1956 Ampex VR1000 video recorder weighed 665kg (1,465lb), the same as a small car, and used tape which was 4 times wider than that of today's VCRs.

Modern recorders like this one are only slightly larger than the cassette inside.

VIDEO RECORDS
FASTEST VIDEOTAPE ON SALE was the wedding of HRH Prince Andrew to Sarah Ferguson on 23 July 1986. The fully edited and packaged tapes were available in Virgin Megastore, London, UK, 5 hours 41 minutes after the event.

THE FIRST POP PROMO was for *Bohemian Rhapsody* by Queen, in 1975.

BEST-SELLING VIDEO is Disney's animated feature film *The Lion King* (1994), with the voices of Whoopi Goldberg and Jeremy Irons. By July 1996 it had sold 54 million copies.

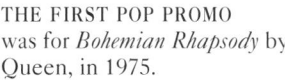

NEWSPAPERS

NEWSPAPERS KEEP everyone in touch with local, national, and world events for a small price. They give more information on a wider range of topics and more detail than TV news.

59 B.C. Romans produce the *Acta diurna* (daily acts). They report on the social and political events of the day.

Roman reading a scroll.

A.D. 618 Newsletter reporting on court affairs is circulated by civil servants in Peking, China.

1440–50 Printing by movable type is invented by Johannes Gutenberg (c.1398–1468) of Germany. This leads to more printed material being produced and a growth in readership.

Johannes Gutenberg

60 B.C.	59 B.C.	A.D. 600	618	1440

1513 Newsbooks, forerunners of newspapers, produced. One surviving copy from England, *The Trew Encountre,* dated September 1513, gives a four-page eyewitness account of the Battle of Flodden Field.

1620 One of the first papers to be printed from movable type is a Dutch newspaper, called *Corantos* (currents of news). It contains extracts from foreign journals.

Corantos

1600s–1800s In Japan, people pay a small fee for the news to be read aloud to them. It is known as *yomiuri* (sell and read). *Kawara-ban* (tile-block printing) broadsheets are also produced.

In Japan, the news is read out loud for a fee.

1645 Oldest continuously published weekly newspaper, the *Post-och inrikes tidningar,* is published in Sweden.

1500	1513	1600	1620	1645

1703 Oldest surviving daily newspaper in the world is the *Wiener Zeitung* (Viennese newspaper), Austria.

Wiener Zeitung

1704 *The Boston Newsletter,* first official newspaper in the USA, appears. It replaces newsletters that had previously been sent from London.

The Boston Newsletter

The Boston News-Letter.

1766 Sweden becomes the first country to guarantee freedom of the press.

1833 First successful penny paper, the *Sun,* appears in New York.

1842 *The Illustrated London News,* containing sketches by artists from all over the world, is established.

The Illustrated London News

1858 P. J. Reuter (1816–99), of Germany, starts a foreign news agency. It is now one of the biggest in the world.

P.J. Reuter

1700	1703	1704	1760	1766	1800	1833	1842	1858

1878 *The Hindu* is one of the first Indian newspapers to be established.

THE HINDU.

The Hindu

1903 First tabloid, the *Mirror,* is launched in Britain. The paper was half the size of other newspapers, had shortened articles, and was reasonably priced. Later, it became the *Daily Mirror.*

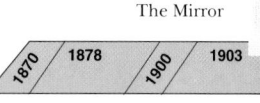

The Mirror

1910–20s American publisher, Edward Scripps (1854–1926), pioneers the collection and ownership of popular working-class newspapers. By the 1920s, there are about 6,000 newspapers in the USA.

Edward Scripps

1955 The *Village Voice* is published in New York. This paper brings a new, radical approach to news-reporting.

1970s Computers and new technology replace typesetters and printers.

1990s Many newspapers introduce web sites on the Internet.

1870	1878	1900	1903	1910	1920	1955	1970	1990

NEWSPAPER FACTS

• Sweden sells 574 newspapers for every 1,000 people: the highest sales in the world.

• First newspaper to achieve a circulation of one million was the French paper *Le Petit Journal,* in 1886.

COUNTRIES WITH THE MOST DAILY NEWSPAPERS

Country	Number
India	2,300
USA	1,586
Turkey	399
Brazil	373
Germany	355
Russia	339
Mexico	292
Pakistan	272
Argentina	190
Spain	148
Japan	124
UK	101

BEST-SELLING NEWSPAPERS IN THE WORLD

Newspaper	Country	Average daily circulation
Yomiuri Shimbun	Japan	8,700,000
Asahi Shimbun	Japan	7,400,000
People's Daily	China	6,000,000
Bild Zeitung	Germany	5,900,000
Sun	UK	4,006,979
Daily Mirror	UK	2,463,943
Daily Mail	UK	2,122,166
Wall Street Journal	USA	1,862,207
USA Today	USA	1,570,624
Daily Express	UK	1,215,509

NEWSPAPER WORDS

Broadsheet Newspaper with a large format, usually 61cm x 38cm (24in x 15in).

Circulation Number of newspapers sold each issue.

Editor Person with complete control over the contents of a newspaper.

Feature A non-news article.

Hard news Up-to-the-minute news.

Leader Article giving newspaper's own opinion.

Popular press, or tabloids. Newspapers aiming to provide lively news and entertainment for a mass readership. Also called tabloids, as they usually have a smaller format than broadsheets.

Quality press Newspapers aiming to provide serious news, information, and analysis. Also called broadsheets, as they usually have a large format.

Soft news Background news or news that is not up-to-the-minute.

Syndication Group of publishers who sell the reprint rights to articles all around the world.

Tabloid Newspaper with a smaller format, about half the size of broadsheets.

SPORTS

This factual survey covers every major sport from baseball to weightlifting, identifying Olympic sports and giving tables of Olympic events. For each sport, special clothing, and equipment are clearly illustrated, and all dimensions, weights, and distances are included. The section features rules and record breakers, glossaries to explain specialist terms, and amazing facts and comparisons.

Sports • Olympic Games • Track Events • Field Events • Weightlifting
Gymnastics • Combat Sports • Court Games • Basketball • Rugby • Football
Cricket • Baseball • Stick Games • Golf • Water Sports • Swimming
Equestrian • Winter Sports • Wheeled Sports • Target Sports

In this section the official measurements, whether
in metric or imperial, are given for each sport.

SPORTS

THE FIRST SPORTS, such as hunting and running, grew out of a need for survival. Today, people take part in sports for fitness and enjoyment.

c.3000–1500 B.C. Wrestling and boxing are practised by the early Mediterranean civilizations. **Bull sports** feature in Minoan festivals in Crete. Acrobats leap over the backs of running bulls.

Bull-leaping is practised in Crete.

c.1500 B.C. Hunting, archery, wrestling, fighting, and organized running are practised in ancient Egypt.

An Egyptian nobleman hunts for birds with a curved stick.

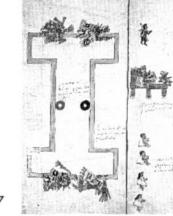

3000 B.C.	3000–1500 B.C.	1500 B.C.	1500 B.C.

c.776 B.C. First Olympic Games held at Olympia, Greece. They last one day, with sacrifices to the gods followed by a single race, a sprint of 192m (630ft), the length of the stadium. Coroebus, a cook, wins the race.

c.200 B.C. Chariot racing is popular in Rome, where the Circus Maximus arena holds 200,000 people. Gladiators fight to the death in amphitheatres such as the Colosseum, Rome.

Chariot racing, Rome

c.20 B.C. Sumo wrestling develops in Japan from Chiao-Li, a form of wrestling used by the Chinese army in training.

Sumo wrestler, Japan

c.A.D. 400 Religious ball game, *tlachtli,* is played by the Aztec Indians of Central America. Players use their elbows, knees, and hips to hit a rubber ball.

Aztec ball court

800 B.C.	776 B.C.	200 B.C.	200 B.C.	20 B.C.	20 B.C.	A.D. 400	A.D. 400

c.1100 Knights take part in jousting tournaments in England and France to practise for warfare.

Knights jousting

1200s Real tennis played by the clergy and royalty in France. **Skating** on frozen canals popular in Holland. **Bowls** played in English gardens.

Skating, Holland

1400s Calcio (kick), a form of football, is played in Florence, Italy. Each side has 27 players.

1636 Lacrosse develops from baggataway, played by the American Indian Huron tribe in present-day Ontario, Canada. The word *Crosse* describes the stick used.

Early lacrosse

1777 People surfing off the islands of Tahiti and Oahu are seen by Captain James Cook (1728–79), British explorer. Surfing was later banned by missionaries who thought it immoral.

1811 First outdoor gymnasium is opened by German teacher Friedrich Jahn (1778–1852), inventor of rings and parallel bars.

Friedrich Jahn

1200	1200	1400	1630	1636	1770	1777	1810	1811

1823 Rugby is born when William Webb Ellis, a pupil at Rugby School, England, picks up the ball and runs with it during a game of soccer.
William Webb Ellis

c.1829 Baseball, derived from the English game of rounders, is first played in the USA.

Early baseball

1839 First Grand National steeplechase is held at Aintree, England.

Jumping the Brook at the Grand National, 1839

1843 First cross-country ski race held in Tromso, Norway.

1846 Soccer rules drawn up at Cambridge University, England.

1847 Tenpin bowling is born in Connecticut, USA. Ninepins had been banned, so a pin is added.

1860 First British Open Golf Championship held at Prestwick, Scotland.

1861 First hockey club formed in London.

1865 Gloved boxing develops from bare-knuckle fighting using the Marquess of Queensberry's rules.

Bare-knuckle fighter

1820	1823	1829	1830	1840	1843	1846	1847	1860	1860	1861	1865

1866 First show jumping event is held in Paris.

1874 American football is born when teams from McGill University, Canada, and Harvard, USA, play a game that is half soccer, half rugby.

1876 Modern badminton rules are drawn up in Poona, India.

1877 First cricket Test Match held between England and Australia in Melbourne.

England cricket team, 1886

1877 First Wimbledon lawn tennis championships held in England.

Wimbledon

1882 Judo developed by Jigoro Kano (1860–1938) in Japan.

1891 Basketball invented in Massachusetts, USA, by sports instructor Dr. James Naismith, who hangs two peach baskets on a verandah for goals.

Dr. James Naismith (1861-1939)

1866	1870	1874	1876	1877	1880	1882	1890	1891

1895 Volleyball devised by William G. Morgan in Massachusetts, USA. **First motor race** held, Paris–Bordeaux–Paris.

1896 First modern Olympic Games held in Athens, inspired by Baron Pierre de Coubertin (1863-1937) of France.

1903 First Tour de France multi-stage cycle race.
1924 First Winter Olympics staged at Chamonix, France.

Canadian ice-hockey team, winners at the first Winter Olympics, 1924.

1930 Soccer's first World Cup is held in Uruguay.

1960 First Paralympics is held for handicapped people in Rome, Italy.

1972 At the Munich Olympics, Germany, Palestinian terrorists kill 11 members of the Israeli team.

1980–1990s Commercial sponsorship becomes more important in sport.

Satellites bring live international sport to worldwide TV audiences.
Regular mass marathons, with more than 15,000 entrants, are staged. Some marathons include wheelchair events. **Drugs testing** becomes a feature of major competitions.

The London marathon

1895	1896	1900	1903	1924	1930	1960	1970	1970	1972	1980	1980	1990	1999

OLYMPIC GAMES

EVERY FOUR YEARS, athletes from all over the world meet to compete in the Summer Olympic Games. About 7,000 competitors take part in more than 20 different sports.

CROWNING GLORY
In the ancient Olympic Games, winners were crowned with a sacred olive wreath.

OLYMPIC SYMBOL
The Olympic symbol is made up of five interlocking rings, standing for Europe, Asia, Africa, Australia, and America.

MEDALS
Individuals and teams compete for gold (first), silver (second), and bronze (third) medals in the modern Games.

Gold medal from the 1984 Games

OLYMPIC FLAME

This flame symbolizes the athlete's strive for perfection. A torch is carried by a series of runners from the site of the ancient Olympics in Greece to the stadium where the current Games are to be held.

SUMMER OLYMPIC VENUES

Date	Place	Country
1896	Athens	Greece
1900	Paris	France
1904	St. Louis, Missouri	USA
1908	London	Britain
1912	Stockholm	Sweden
1920	Antwerp	Belgium
1924	Paris	France
1928	Amsterdam	Netherlands
1932	Los Angeles, California	USA
1936	Berlin	Germany
1948	London	Britain
1952	Helsinki	Finland
1956	Melbourne	Australia
1960	Rome	Italy
1964	Tokyo	Japan
1968	Mexico City	Mexico
1972	Munich	Germany
1976	Montreal	Canada
1980	Moscow	USSR
1984	Los Angeles, California	USA
1988	Seoul	South Korea
1992	Barcelona	Spain
1996	Atlanta, Georgia	USA
2000	Sydney	Australia

PARALYMPIC VENUES

Date	Place	Country
1960	Rome	Italy
1964	Tokyo	Japan
1968	Tel Aviv	Israel
1972	Heidelberg	Germany
1976	Toronto	Canada
1980	Arnhem	Netherlands
1984	New York	USA
1988	Seoul	South Korea
1992	Barcelona	Spain
1996	Atlanta, Georgia	USA
2000	Sydney	Australia

PARALYMPICS
Disabled people compete in the Paralympic Games, which are held every four years. Events include cycling and judo. The Winter Paralympics have been held since 1976.

WINTER OLYMPIC VENUES

Date	Place	Country
1924	Chamonix	France
1928	St. Moritz	Switzerland
1932	Lake Placid, New York	USA
1936	Garmisch-Partenkirchen	Germany
1948	St. Moritz	Switzerland
1952	Oslo	Norway
1956	Cortina d'Ampezzo	Italy
1960	Squaw Valley, California	USA
1964	Innsbruck	Austria
1968	Grenoble	France
1972	Sapporo	Japan
1976	Innsbruck	Austria
1980	Lake Placid, New York	USA
1984	Sarajevo	Yugoslavia
1988	Calgary, Alberta	Canada
1992	Albertville	France
1994	Lillehammer	Norway
1998	Nagano	Japan

WINTER OLYMPICS
Until 1992, the Winter Games were held in the same year as the Summer Olympics. Events include skiing, figure and speed skating, and ice-hockey.

CLASSIFICATION OF SPORTS

One way of classifying the many different types of sport is to put them into three basic groups, which can then be subdivided further.

This symbol is shown next to all Olympic sports featured on the pages following.

CLASSIFICATION

RACING

 Body power

 Extension of body power

 Outside power source

OPPONENT

 Team

 Court

 Combat

ACHIEVEMENT

 Power

 Display

 Target

Examples

Running
Hurdles
Swimming

Cycling
Skiing
Rowing

Motor racing
Motorcycle racing
Yacht racing

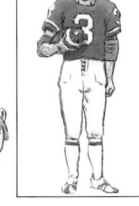
Baseball
Football
Ice-hockey

Tennis
Badminton
Squash

Boxing
Judo
Fencing

Long jump
Javelin
Weightlifting

Gymnastics
Show jumping
Figure skating

Golf
Archery
Darts

TRACK EVENTS

TRACK FACTS

- The standard track circuit, or lap, measures 400m and has 8 lanes.

- Races up to one lap in length are run in lanes.

- Races over 110m run anti-clockwise.

Competitors wear a singlet, or vest, and shorts.

SHOES
Track-racing shoes are tight-fitting, lightweight, and have a maximum of 11 spikes. Road-racing shoes do not have spikes.

Sprinting shoe

PISTOL
A starting pistol is fired into the air to signal the beginning of a race. It automatically triggers an electronic timer.

Spikes help the shoes grip the track.

STARTING BLOCKS
Starting blocks provide the runner with a firm base from which to push off. The blocks are fixed to the track just behind the starting, or scratch, line. Starting blocks are used in races up to 400m.

Adjustable foot plates

A built-in mechanism detects false starts.

STARTING POSITIONS
The 100m and 110m hurdles have a straight start. The 200m, 400m, and 800m races are staggered. Longer races start from curved lines.

Straight start

8 7 6 5 4 3 2 1

Staggered start

OLYMPIC AND WORLD CHAMPIONSHIP TRACK EVENTS

Event		Current Olympic record	
		Male (M)	Female (F)
Sprints	100m	9.84 secs	10.49 secs
	200m	19.32 secs	21.34 secs
	400m	43.49 secs	47.6 secs
Middle distance	800m	1 min 41.11 secs	1 min 53.28 secs
	1500m	3 mins 26 secs	3 mins 50.46 secs
Long distance	3,000m	–	8 mins 6.11 secs
	5,000m	12 mins 39.36 secs	14 mins 28.09 secs
	10,000m	26 mins 22.75 secs	29 mins 31.78 secs
Relays	4x100m	37.4 secs	41.37 secs
	4x400m	2 mins 54.2 secs	3 mins 15.17 secs
Hurdles	100m	–	12.21 secs
	110m	12.91 secs	–
	400m	46.78 secs	52.61 secs
Steeplechase	3,000m	7 mins 55.72 secs	–
Marathon	42.195km	2 hrs 6 mins 5 secs	2 hrs 20 mins 47 secs
Walks	10km	–	41 mins 56.23 secs
	20km	1 hr 17 mins 25.6 secs	–
	50km	3 hrs 40 mins 57.9 secs	–

TRACK
The starting lines for the track events are shown below.

International-level tracks have a synthetic surface, usually made of plastic or rubber.

1500m
3,000m and 5,000m
Back straight
3,000m steeplechase
200m
Relays, 400m, 400m hurdles
10,000m
Home straight
100m
100m hurdles
Finish line: the same for all events.
800m
110m hurdles

SPRINT

On your marks The athlete moves to the starting blocks. He presses against them with the balls of his feet. He places his hands behind the starting line.

Set The athlete raises his body forwards. He waits in this position until the starting pistol is fired.

Fire The athlete lifts his hands up. He brings his rear leg forwards while pushing his other leg against the block.

He must not move before the gun is fired, or a false start is called.

The finish
The athletes push themselves forwards at the finish. The winner is the person whose torso, or trunk, crosses the finish line first.

Chest pushed forwards

RELAY

- Each of the four team members runs one stage, or leg, of a relay.

- A baton is carried by the first runner and passed on to the next team member in a take-over zone.

- A dropped baton must be picked up by the runner who dropped it.

4 x 100M
In this relay race, an athlete stretches back his hand to take the baton from his team mate, without looking behind him.

The take-over zone measures 20m (22yd)

BATON
The baton is a smooth, hollow tube made of wood, metal, or plastic.

Baton length: 28–30cm

4 x 400M
In this relay race, an athlete will look back to receive the baton from her team mate.

HURDLES

- All races have ten hurdles in each lane.

- An athlete is not disqualified for knocking down hurdles.

- An athlete's rear leg must not trail around the outside of the hurdle.

TECHNIQUE
The athlete should clear each hurdle quickly and smoothly. In the 100m and 110m hurdles the athlete takes three strides between each hurdle.

Knee of lead leg is bent on approach.

Trail leg

The athlete stays in mid-flight for as short a time as possible, to minimize loss of speed.

He brings his trail leg forwards for the next stride.

Adjustable metal stand

Wooden bar is 1.2m wide.

Weights in the base of the stand keep the hurdle upright.

HURDLE HEIGHTS

Event	Height
100m (F)	0.838m
110m (M)	1.067m
400m (M)	0.914m
400m (F)	0.762m

MARATHON

- Marathons are run mainly on roads, but often start and finish in the stadium.

- Distances, in kilometres and miles, are shown to the runners during the race.

- Refreshments may be taken every 5km (3 miles).

Marathon race, 1988 Olympics

MARATHON ORIGIN
The marathon originated in 490 B.C. when a Greek messenger called Pheidippides ran 39km (24 miles) to report the Athenian victory over the Persians at the Battle of Marathon.

STEEPLECHASE

- At present, only men compete in the steeplechase.

- Athletes must make 28 jumps over hurdles and 7 over the water jump.

- Athletes can place their feet and hands on the hurdles when jumping over them.

WATER JUMP
The water jump is the fourth jump in each lap. The hurdle is the same height as the other hurdles, but sinks down into the ground on the far side.

Athletes clearing the water jump.

STEEPLECHASE HURDLE
These hurdles are placed on the three inside lanes of the track. They are much heavier than standard hurdles and will stand firm when struck by the athletes' feet.

Wooden bar is 3.96m wide

Hurdle height: 91.4cm

On the first lap, athletes run past the water jump.

Water jump

STEEPLECHASE TRACK
One water jump and four hurdles are placed on the three inside lanes of the track.

RACE WALKING

- A race walker must maintain unbroken contact with the ground, so his rear foot must not leave the ground until the front one has made contact.

- The leg must straighten for a moment, while the foot is on the ground.

By rotating his hips, the walker can increase the length of his stride.

Leg kept straight

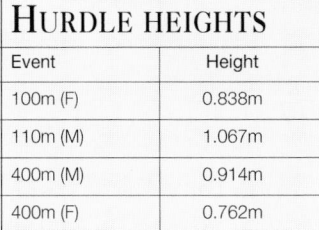

Roger Bannister

RECORD BREAKERS
FOUR-MINUTE MILE
was first broken in 1954 by Roger Bannister (born 1929), of Britain.

TEN-SECOND 100M
was first broken in 1968 by Jim Hines (born 1946), of the USA.

YOUNGEST INDIVIDUAL
world record breaker in athletics is Wang Yan (born 1971), of China. The 14-year-old girl set a women's 5,000m walk record at Jian, China, in 1986.

FIELD EVENTS

FIELD FACTS

• Field events include all the major athletic jumping and throwing sports.

• The Sydney games in 2000 will see women taking part in Olympic hammer and pole vault for the first time.

THROWING EVENTS

• Athletes must not touch any point outside the throwing area until their throw has landed.

• A white flag is shown for a correct attempt, a red flag signals a foul.

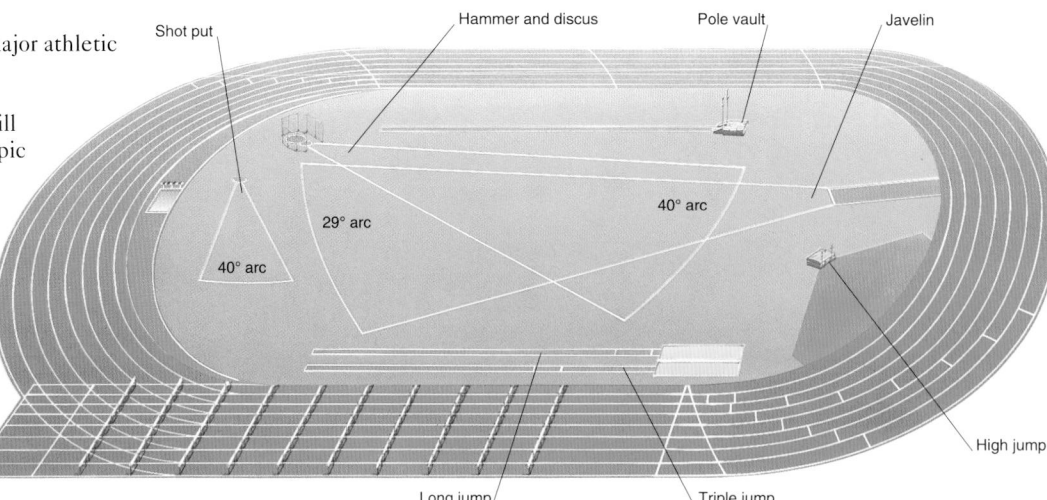

INFIELD
The positioning of the field areas varies from stadium to stadium, but, generally, events are held inside the track (the infield).

Shot put

Hammer and discus

Pole vault

Javelin

29° arc

40° arc

40° arc

High jump

Long jump

Triple jump

OLYMPIC THROWING EVENTS

Event	Weight	Current Olympic record
Javelin (F)	0.6kg	74.68m
Javelin (M)	0.8kg	89.66m
Discus (F)	1kg	72.30m
Discus (M)	2kg	69.40m
Shot put (F)	4kg	22.41m
Shot put (M)	7.26kg	22.47m
Hammer (M)	7.26kg	84.80m

JAVELIN

• The javelin is thrown from behind a curved line at the end of a run-up track, and must land within a 29° arc.

JAVELIN
The javelin looks like a spear. It has a long shaft, a cord grip, and a metal tip.

The length of the men's javelin is 260–270cm; the women's javelin measures 220–230cm.

THROWING THE JAVELIN
The athlete stretches his throwing arm behind him, to give him extra power. The javelin must land tip first, but it does not need to dig into the ground.

Sharply-pointed metal tip

Cord grip

DISCUS

• The discus is thrown from a circle and must land within a 40° arc.

• Though any holding and throwing techniques are allowed, the discus is usually held and thrown with one hand.

DISCUS
The discus has a metal rim, with a metal weight at the centre.

The width of the men's discus is 219–221mm; the width of the women's discus is 180–182mm.

THROWING THE DISCUS
The athlete stands with her back to the throwing area and turns one and a half times before releasing the discus.

The athlete usually takes one or two swings before starting to turn.

Her throwing arm is fully extended.

She turns one and a half times before release.

SHOT PUT

• The shot is thrown, or put, from a circle and must land within a 40° arc.

• Only one hand is used, and the put must not start from behind the line of the shoulders.

SHOT
The shot is a smooth metal ball. The men's shot is slightly larger than the women's.

PUTTING THE SHOT
The athlete puts the shot with a single pushing action. She must not let the hand holding the shot fall below its starting position.

She pushes the shot up and away from her.

Her body straightens on facing the throwing area.

She raises one leg and hops backwards.

The athlete nestles the shot under her chin.

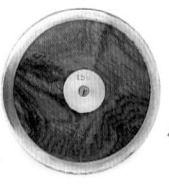

Jesse Owens

RECORD BREAKERS

SIX WORLD RECORDS, including a long jump record of 8.13m that lasted 25 years, were set in 45 minutes by Jesse Owens (1913–80) of the USA in 1935 in Michigan, USA.

OLDEST FEMALE ATHLETE ever to win an Olympic title is Lia Manoliu (born 1932) of Romania, who was 36 years old when she won the discus at the 1968 Olympics in Mexico City.

HAMMER
The hammer is a metal ball that is attached to a handle by a length of steel wire. Although the hammer weighs the same as the men's shot, the different throwing technique means that it can travel much further.

HAMMER

• The hammer is thrown from a circle surrounded by a safety cage and must land within a 40° arc.

The hammer weighs the same as the men's shot.

THROWING THE HAMMER
The athlete throws the hammer using both hands. The head of the hammer may touch the ground during the first few swings.

The athlete turns two or three times before releasing the hammer.

OLYMPIC JUMPING EVENTS

Event	Current Olympic record
High jump (M)	2.39m
High jump (F)	2.05m
Pole vault (M)	5.92m
Long jump (M)	8.90m
Long jump (F)	7.40m
Triple jump (M)	18.09m
Triple jump (F)	15.33m

The athlete jumps backwards over the bar.

He lifts his legs clear of the bar.

COMBINED EVENTS

DECATHLON
• Men compete in the Decathlon, which covers ten events.

EVENTS

First day	Second day
100m race	110m hurdles
Long jump	Discus
Shot put	Pole vault
High jump	Javelin
400m race	1500m race

HEPTATHLON
• Women compete in the Heptathlon; it covers seven events.

EVENTS

First day	Second day
100m hurdles	Long jump
High jump	Javelin
Shot put	800m race
200m race	

MODERN PENTATHLON
• Men and women compete in the Modern Pentathlon, though only men in the Olympics; it covers five events.

EVENTS

Fencing (Épée)
Freestyle swimming – 300m (M) and 200m (F)
Pistol shooting
Cross-country running – 4,000m (M) and 2,000m (F)
Riding

TRIATHLON
• Men and women compete in the Triathlon; it covers three events.

EVENTS

Course	Events		
	Swimming	Cycling	Running
Short Course	1.5km	40km	10km
Long Course	3.8km	180km	42.2km

FOSBURY FLOP
Most high-jumpers use a technique called the "Fosbury flop", in which the athlete jumps backwards over the bar.

HIGH JUMP
• The crossbar is raised for each round by a minimum of 2cm.

• The high jump has a fan-shaped run-up area.

POLE VAULT
• The crossbar is raised for each round by a minimum of 5cm.

• The pole vault has a straight run-up with a sunken box at the end.

• Poles may be of any size or material, but are usually made of fibreglass.

VAULTING OVER
The athlete must make an accurate run-up, to ensure that the pole is placed in the correct position for take-off. As he pushes off from the ground, the pole bends with the weight of his body. He levers himself over the bar, feet first.

LONG JUMP
• The athlete makes a straight run-up to a wooden take-off board which is sunk into the runway.

• Just beyond the take-off line is a soft substance that records foot faults.

• Jumps are measured to the nearest mark in the sand made by any part of the body.

TRIPLE JUMP
• This event uses the same run-up and landing area as the long jump.

• The athlete must use a hop, step, and jump action.

JUMPING EVENTS
• In all jumping events, athletes may take any length of run and may place markers to help judge their approach.

The pole vaulter tucks himself under the pole until it straightens, and then rotates to come down facing the bar.

On leaving the ground, athletes may not climb the pole (by moving the lower hand above the upper hand).

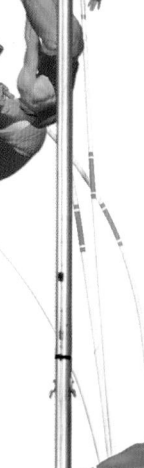

TECHNIQUE
The athlete leaves the take-off board in an upright position. She increases the distance she travels by leaning back in mid-air before landing.

The athlete throws her legs forwards as she lands.

THREE STAGES
Hop The athlete must land on the same foot that was used for take-off.

Step The athlete must land on the other foot.

Jump The athlete throws his arms and legs forwards, ready for landing.

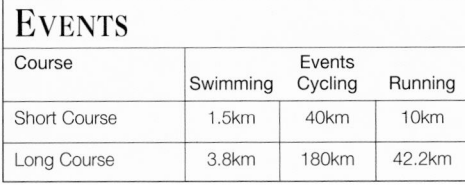

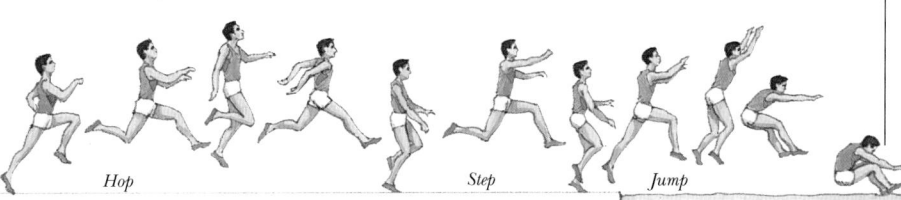

Hop   *Step*   *Jump*

WEIGHTLIFTING

- Weightlifters compete in different classes according to their body-weight.

- There are two types of lifts: the snatch, and the clean and jerk.

- Men and women compete in weightlifting, but only men take part in Olympic events.

BAR
The weightlifting bar is made progressively heavier during each round of a competition. Discs of varying weights are loaded on to the bar, with the heaviest on the inside.

Length of bar: 2m

KIT
The weightlifter must wear a one-piece costume. He may wear a T-shirt underneath if he wishes. A wide belt may be worn to support the back.

Red (25kg) Green (10kg)

The rubber- or plastic-covered discs are colour-coded according to weight.

Boots must give firm support and have a maximum height above the sole of 130mm.

DISC WEIGHTS
The cast-iron disc weights range from 0.25kg to 25kg. By adding a combination of discs, any weight can be added to the bar.

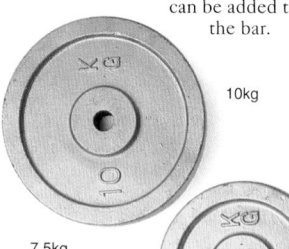
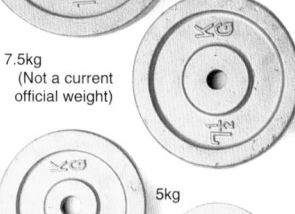
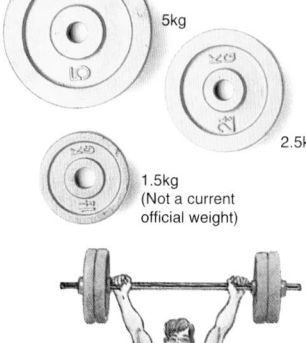
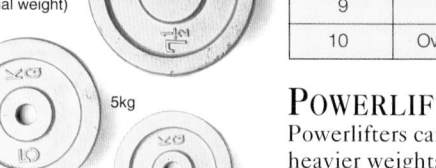

10kg

7.5kg (Not a current official weight)

5kg

2.5kg

1.5kg (Not a current official weight)

CLASSES OF WEIGHTLIFTING

Category	Weight (in kg)	
	Male	Female
1	54	46
2	59	50
3	64	54
4	70	59
5	76	64
6	83	70
7	91	76
8	99	83
9	108	Over 83
10	Over108	–

POWERLIFTING
Powerlifters can lift much heavier weights than weightlifters because they do not have to raise the bar above their heads.

TYPES OF POWERLIFTING
Squat The bar rests on a stand and the lifter squats below it. He must stand up and lift the bar across the shoulders.

Bench press The lifter lies on a bench with the bar resting on a stand above his chest. On the instruction "press", the lifter must push the bar up until both arms are straight.

Deadlift The competitor lifts the bar from the floor and rises to a standing position with the bar resting across the front of his thighs.

In the bench press, the athlete lifts the bar out of a stand.

The height of the bench is adjustable.

SNATCH
- The weightlifter must lift the bar in a single movement until the bar is above the head and the arms are fully extended.

- Once the bar is above his head, the weightlifter can take as much time as he needs to straighten his position (the recovery).

- On completing a lift, the weightlifter must hold the position until the referee signals to replace the bar.

The weightlifter uses chalk to help him grip the bar.

He may bend or split his legs during the lift.

He must not turn his wrists over until the bar is past head height.

He can take unlimited time over the recovery.

He must be completely still, and his arms and legs fully stretched, for the lift to be counted.

CLEAN AND JERK
- In the clean and jerk, the bar is lifted to the shoulders (the clean) and then to full arm's length overhead (the jerk).

- At the end of the clean, the lifter may rest the bar on the collarbones, chest, or fully bent arms, and may change his grip.

Knees may be split or bent.

As in the snatch, the lifter can take any length of time over the recovery position.

The lifter must not let the bar touch his body until it has reached his shoulders.

During the clean the lifter must not let his elbows or upper arms touch his knees or thighs.

RECORD BREAKERS
FIRST MAN TO CLEAN AND JERK more than three times his own body-weight was Stefan Topurov (born 1964), of Bulgaria, who lifted 180kg in Moscow, USSR, in 1983.

WEIGHTY MATTERS
Weightlifters can lift more than 2.5 times their own body-weight in the snatch, and more than 3 times their own body-weight in the clean and jerk. Powerlifters can lift more than 5 times their own body-weight.

Snatch

Clean and jerk

Powerlifting

GYMNASTICS

- The gymnast must combine acrobatic agility and muscle power with grace of movement.
- There are two Olympic events: artistic gymnastics, and rhythmic gymnastics, which is for women only.

ARTISTIC GYMNASTICS

- Gymnasts are awarded marks out of ten for their performances on various pieces of equipment.
- Women perform four types of exercise, men perform six.

KIT
Men wear vests and long trousers. They may wear shorts for the floor and vault exercises. Women wear leotards, and may wear gymnastic slippers or go barefoot. Handguards may be worn for the ring and bar exercises.

Gymnasts use a chalky powder to keep their hands dry while using the apparatus.

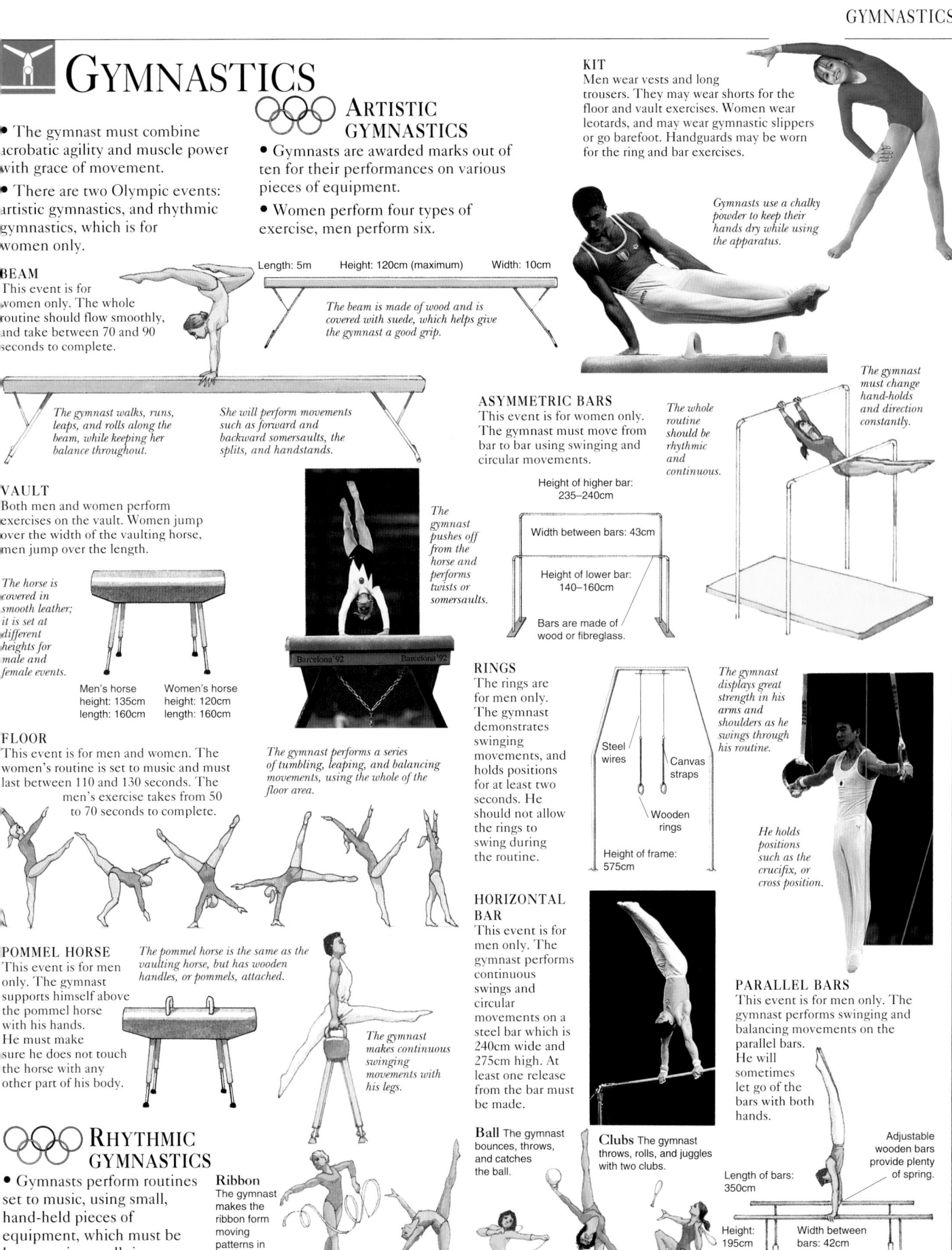

BEAM
This event is for women only. The whole routine should flow smoothly, and take between 70 and 90 seconds to complete.

Length: 5m   Height: 120cm (maximum)   Width: 10cm

The beam is made of wood and is covered with suede, which helps give the gymnast a good grip.

The gymnast walks, runs, leaps, and rolls along the beam, while keeping her balance throughout.

She will perform movements such as forward and backward somersaults, the splits, and handstands.

VAULT
Both men and women perform exercises on the vault. Women jump over the width of the vaulting horse, men jump over the length.

The horse is covered in smooth leather; it is set at different heights for male and female events.

Men's horse height: 135cm length: 160cm

Women's horse height: 120cm length: 160cm

The gymnast pushes off from the horse and performs twists or somersaults.

Barcelona '92   Barcelona '92

FLOOR
This event is for men and women. The women's routine is set to music and must last between 110 and 130 seconds. The men's exercise takes from 50 to 70 seconds to complete.

The gymnast performs a series of tumbling, leaping, and balancing movements, using the whole of the floor area.

POMMEL HORSE
This event is for men only. The gymnast supports himself above the pommel horse with his hands. He must make sure he does not touch the horse with any other part of his body.

The pommel horse is the same as the vaulting horse, but has wooden handles, or pommels, attached.

The gymnast makes continuous swinging movements with his legs.

ASYMMETRIC BARS
This event is for women only. The gymnast must move from bar to bar using swinging and circular movements.

The whole routine should be rhythmic and continuous.

Height of higher bar: 235–240cm

Width between bars: 43cm

Height of lower bar: 140–160cm

Bars are made of wood or fibreglass.

The gymnast must change hand-holds and direction constantly.

RINGS
The rings are for men only. The gymnast demonstrates swinging movements, and holds positions for at least two seconds. He should not allow the rings to swing during the routine.

Steel wires

Canvas straps

Wooden rings

Height of frame: 575cm

The gymnast displays great strength in his arms and shoulders as he swings through his routine.

He holds positions such as the crucifix, or cross position.

HORIZONTAL BAR
This event is for men only. The gymnast performs continuous swings and circular movements on a steel bar which is 240cm wide and 275cm high. At least one release from the bar must be made.

PARALLEL BARS
This event is for men only. The gymnast performs swinging and balancing movements on the parallel bars. He will sometimes let go of the bars with both hands.

Adjustable wooden bars provide plenty of spring.

Length of bars: 350cm

Height: 195cm

Width between bars: 42cm

Weighted metal frame

RHYTHMIC GYMNASTICS

- Gymnasts perform routines set to music, using small, hand-held pieces of equipment, which must be kept moving at all times.
- Balletic, rather than acrobatic, movements are performed.

Ribbon The gymnast makes the ribbon form moving patterns in the air and on the floor.

Hoop The gymnast rotates the hoop around her, and throws and catches it.

Ball The gymnast bounces, throws, and catches the ball.

Clubs The gymnast throws, rolls, and juggles with two clubs.

Rope The gymnast jumps and skips while throwing and catching the rope.

COMBAT SPORTS

- In combat sports, competitors use either striking (e.g. boxing) or holding (e.g. judo) techniques against their opponents.

- Some combat sports, such as fencing and kendo, are armed.

GRADING SYSTEM

Contestants wear different coloured belts to show their grade. Black belt is usually the highest level reached, but there are even higher grades, awarded for length of service. A red-and-white striped belt is worn by the sixth, seventh, and eighth Dan. Very few people have ever reached ninth and tenth Dan.

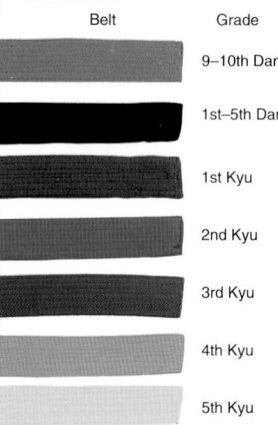

Belt	Grade
	9–10th Dan
	1st–5th Dan
	1st Kyu
	2nd Kyu
	3rd Kyu
	4th Kyu
	5th Kyu

KIT
Contestants wear loose-fitting trousers, with a jacket which is held in at the waist with a cotton belt.

 JUDO

- In judo ("the soft way"), competitors are judged on their throwing and holding techniques.

- A bout can last for up to 20 minutes.

White or off-white jacket and trousers are worn.

START
Competitors face each other at a distance of 4m and take a bow.

JUDO WORDS
Dan Leader or teacher.
Dojo Training hall.
Gake Hook or block.
Hajime Referee's call to begin.
Judo-gi Judo jacket and trousers.

Kyu Student grade.
Senshu Champion competitor.
Tsuri Lift up.
Waza-ari Half a point, awarded for a less than clean technique.

AREA
Contestants must fight within the contest area, and not step outside the danger zone.

The contest area is 9–10m x 9–10m.

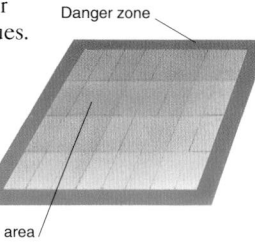

Danger zone

Contest area

BOUT
The competitors are judged on their techniques. An outright winning technique scores an ippon (one point).

An ippon is awarded for:

Lifting the opponent above shoulder height.

A forceful throw

An effective stranglehold or arm-lock.

WEIGHT TABLE

Category	Male	Female
Bantam	under 60kg	under 48kg
Feather	under 65kg	under 52kg
Light	under 71kg	under 56kg
Light-middle	under 78kg	under 61kg
Middle	under 86kg	under 66kg
Light-heavy	under 95kg	under 72kg
Heavy	over 95kg	over 72kg

OTHER MARTIAL ARTS

Karate
Contestants aim punches and kicks at their opponents.

Aikido
Flowing movements are used to throw the opponent off balance.

Ju Jitsu
As in judo, throws and holds are used in this self-defence sport.

Kendo
Contestants in armour fight with bamboo swords.

The foil

FENCING

- In fencing, two opponents compete in a bout using one of three weapons: foil, épée, or sabre.

- A bout lasts until the agreed number of hits have been made, or until the time limit has been reached, e.g. five hits within a time limit of six minutes.

PISTE
The fencing area (piste) measures 14m x 2m.

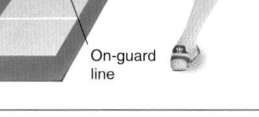

Centre line

On-guard line

KIT
Competitors must wear white clothes that give freedom of movement and maximum protection.

A mask made of steel or plastic mesh is worn to protect the head.

In events using electronic equipment, a metallic overjacket is worn, to show when a hit has been scored.

A padded glove is worn on the sword-holding hand.

FENCING BOUT
At the start, the opponents face each other, 4m apart, at the centre of the piste. The president orders *en garde*, asks the players if they are ready, then calls *allez* to start a bout.

In the attack, the fencer threatens the target with his arm outstretched.

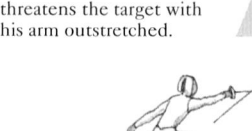

In the parry, the attacker's sword is deflected by the defender's sword.

In the riposte, the defender makes a quick return thrust after the parry.

WEAPONS AND TARGET AREAS

SABRE
The target area is the upper body and arms. The area must be struck with the point or with the blade edges.

Max weight: 500g
Blade length: 88cm

FOIL
The target area is the trunk only. The area must be struck with the point of the sword.

Max weight: 500g
Blade length: 90cm

EPEE
The target area is the whole body. The area must be struck with the point of the sword.

Max weight: 770g.
Blade length: 90cm

BOXING

- In boxing, competitors use their gloved hands to punch each other in specific areas of the body.

- Fights can be won on points, or because the opponent is counted out, retires, or is judged unfit to continue.

RING
Contests are held in a square "ring" surrounded by ropes.

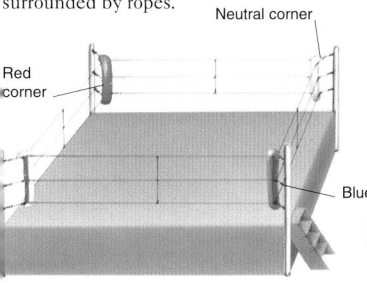

Neutral corner
Red corner
Blue corner

Maximum size: 20ft square.

BOUT
The boxer must aim for the front or sides of his opponent's trunk, and the front or sides of the head. Points are given for good hits, and, in professional boxing, for defensive moves and style.

The boxer must strike a blow using the knuckle part of the glove.

KIT
Boxers wear padded, laced-up leather gloves. Professional boxers wear shorts only, amateurs wear shorts and a vest. The shorts are loose-fitting and traditionally made of satin. The "belt" of the shorts must be clearly shown by a contrasting colour, as hitting below the belt is against the rules.

Amateur boxers wear headshields

Boxing boots are tall and lightweight; they provide support for the boxer's ankles and allow him to move quickly around the ring.

Thin sole with no heel

A gumshield is worn to protect the mouth.

Hands are bandaged underneath the gloves for extra protection.

He may aim for the side of the head.

He must not hit below the waist.

Knock-down
In a knock-down, a count of ten begins. If the fallen boxer cannot rise before the count ends, he loses the fight. If he rises, and is judged by the referee to be fit to continue, the fight goes on.

BOXING WEIGHTS

Categories	Professional lb	kg	Amateur kg
Mini flyweight/ straw weight	105	47.6	–
Light flyweight	108	49	48
Flyweight	112	50.8	51
Super flyweight	115	52.2	–
Bantamweight	118	53.5	54
Super bantamweight	122	55.3	–
Featherweight	126	57.2	57
Super featherweight	130	59	–
Lightweight	135	61.2	60
Light welterweight/ super lightweight	140	63.5	63.5
Welterweight	147	66.7	67
Super welterweight/ Light middleweight	154	70	71
Middleweight	160	72.6	75
Super middleweight	168	76.2	–
Light heavyweight	175	79.4	81
Cruiserweight	190	86.2	–
Heavyweight	over 190	over 86	91
Super heavyweight	–	–	over 91

FIGHTING FIT
The longest boxing fight on record lasted 7 hours, 19 minutes and was held in New Orleans, USA, in 1893. Andy Bowen fought Jack Burke over 110 rounds, and the match was finally declared a draw.

WRESTLING

- There are two Olympic wrestling events: freestyle and Greco-Roman.

- Points are awarded for successful moves and holds.

KIT
Wrestlers wear one-piece leotards that leave upper chest and shoulders bare. One competitor wears red, and the other blue. Wrestlers must not oil or grease their bodies.

Wrestling boots are tall and lightweight, have no heels, rings, or buckles.

FALL
The main aim in wrestling is to achieve a "fall", by forcing the opponent's shoulder blades onto the mat for one second, or for as long as it takes the referee to say to himself *tomber* (French for fall).

- In Greco-Roman contests, wrestlers must not use their legs or grip an opponent below the hips.

MAT
The contest circle, which includes the red band, is 9m in diameter.

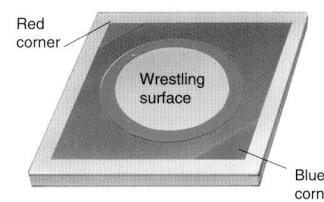

Red corner
Wrestling surface
Blue corner

WRESTLING WEIGHTS

Category	Weight limits in kg
1	48
2	52
3	57
4	62
5	68
6	74
7	82
8	90
9	100
10	130

SUMO WRESTLING

- Ritual and tradition play an important part in Sumo wrestling.

- Bouts are won by pushing an opponent out of the ring, or by making him touch the ground with any part of his body other than the soles of his feet.

- Pushes, slaps, and holds are the main techniques.

Rice is thrown up at the beginning of the bout.

A loincloth is worn wrapped around the waist and between the legs.

SUMO GRADINGS
Sumo wrestlers are graded according to skill, not weight. There are ten grades:

Jonokuchi Novice
Jonidan Qualified
Sandamne Lower junior
Makushita Leading junior
Juryo Contender
Maegashira Senior
Komusubi Second grade junior champion
Sekiwake Junior champion
Ozeki Champion
Yokozuna Grand champion

HEAVY WEIGHTS
The heaviest Sumo wrestler weighs 250kg (551lb): equal to the total average weight of four teenage boys. This is about twice the weight of the heaviest world champion boxer, and almost twice the maximum weight permitted for an Olympic wrestler.

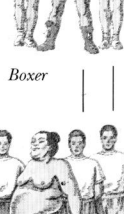

Boxer
Wrestler
Sumo wrestler

COURT GAMES

TENNIS

• The aim is to hit a ball over the net with a racket so that it lands inside the court, and cannot be returned.

• A match is divided into sets and ends when one player has won three sets (for men) or two sets (for women).

• Each set is divided into games, and a player must win at least six games, and have a two-game lead, to win a set.

• A tie-break is used if the set reaches six-all: the first player to score seven or more points, with a two-point lead, wins.

• A match lasts for a maximum of five sets for men and three sets for women.

SCORING A GAME

After scoring 4 points a player wins a game. But, if the players level at 3 points each (that is, 40-all, or *deuce*), play continues until one player has a 2-point lead.

SCORING A GAME

Points	Score
0	love
1	15
2	30
3	40

Martina Navratilova

RECORD BREAKERS

RECORD NUMBER OF WIMBLEDON SINGLES TITLES held is nine, by Martina Navratilova, USA (born in the former Czechoslovakia in 1956). MOST SINGLES CHAMPIONSHIPS won in grand slam tournaments is 24, by Margaret Court, Australia (born 1942). YOUNGEST MALE CHAMPION at Wimbledon is Boris Becker, Germany (born 1967), who won the singles title in 1985, aged 17.

KIT

Traditionally, clothing is white, though today the only professional tournament that insists on mostly white is Wimbledon, England. The kit, which is similar in all court sports, is a shirt and shorts for men, and a shirt and skirt, or a dress, for women.

Wristbands are worn for wiping the forehead and keeping palms dry.

Socks are cushioned to protect soles and heels.

SERVING

The player serves behind the baseline. He throws the ball in the air and hits it before it touches the ground. The ball must pass over the net without bouncing and touch ground in the opposing service court.

PLAYING

The player receiving the serve must let the ball bounce once before returning it. A return is still good if the ball touches the net or passes outside the net post, so long as it lands in the opposing player's half of the court.

The shoulders turn as the racket swings back.

Knees are bent.

COURT

Tennis can be played indoors and outdoors. The court surface may be grass, wood, clay, or artificial.

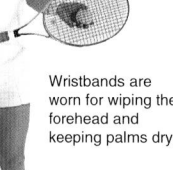

Baseline

Height of net: 3ft 6in

Doubles sideline

Left service court

Right service court

Centre line

Length of court: 78ft

Singles sideline

RACKET

Tennis racket frames are made from wood, metal, or a combination of materials.

Maximum length and width of the whole racket is 32in x 12.5in.

The maximum length and width of the strung surface is 15.5in x 11.5in.

BALL

Tennis balls are yellow or white. They weigh about 2oz.

The ball is thrown up and to the right of the leading shoulder.

The racket arm is bent back behind the neck.

Rubber-soled shoes

The racket arm is fully outstretched when hitting the ball.

The weight is thrown forwards.

In the follow through, the racket arm comes across the body.

Forehand drive

This is the most natural basic groundstroke in the game. A right-handed player plays it on his right side.

The racket is swung forwards to meet the ball.

Backhand drive

This basic stroke is less instinctive than the forehand drive. A right-handed player plays it on his left side.

In the follow through, the racket arm is fully extended.

The leading shoulder is turned away from the ball.

The ball is hit once it is to the front of the right foot.

The weight is put on to the front foot.

GRAND SLAM

Players who achieve the "grand slam" hold, all at the same time, the singles titles at these four major tournaments.

Tournament	Place	Surface
Wimbledon	London, England	Grass
United States Open	Flushing Meadow, New York, USA	Artificial material
Australian Open	Flinders Park, Melbourne, Australia	Synthetic grass
French Open	Roland Garros stadium, Paris, France	Clay

TENNIS WORDS

Ace A service beyond the reach of the receiver.
Advantage The first point scored after deuce.
Let A point that is played again.
Not up The ball has bounced twice before being hit.

Rally A long series of hits.
Seedings List showing where a player is expected to finish in a tournament.
Straight-sets Winning the match without losing a set.

BADMINTON

• In badminton, players hit a shuttlecock over a high net.

• In doubles and men's singles, the first side to score 15 points is the winner; in women's singles, it is the first player to score 11 points.

• Usually, a match is decided by the best of three games.

COURT

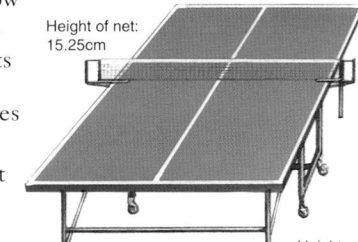

Short service line

Left service court

Right service court

Length of court: 44ft

Height of net: 5ft

Width of court: 20ft

Long service line for singles

Long service line for doubles

SHUTTLECOCK
At top-class level, the shuttlecock is made of a "skirt" of 14–16 goose feathers fixed in a cork base.

RACKET
These are usually made of metal or carbon fibre, and strung with gut.

TABLE TENNIS

• In this indoor game, the players use rackets, or bats, to hit a hollow ball across a table over a low net.

• The first side to score 21 points wins the game, but if the score reaches 20-all, the game continues until one side has a 2-point lead.

• A match is decided by the best of five games (for men), or three games (for women).

BAT
Originally, bats were made of wood only. The pimpled rubber face was added in the 1920s to allow players to give the ball spin.

Pimpled rubber

TABLE
The chipboard top is usually dark green.

Width: 1.52m

Height of net: 15.25cm

Length: 2.74m

Height: 76cm

BALL
The lightweight plastic ball is either white or yellow.

SQUASH

• Squash is played using all four walls of an enclosed court.

• The ball is hit against the front wall first and must be returned before it has bounced twice on the floor.

• A match consists of the best of five games; the winner of a game is the first to nine points.

RACKET
The head of a squash racket is smaller and rounder than that of a badminton or tennis racket.

BALL
There are four varieties of squash ball: the slower balls are used in hot conditions, and the faster balls are used in cold conditions.

Yellow dot: very slow

White dot: slow

Red dot: fast

Blue dot: very fast

JAI ALAI

• In the fast court game of Jai alai, or Pelota, players use wicker baskets, called *cestas*, in place of rackets. The court is long and narrow and has three playing walls.

The player wears a rubber glove which is sewn on to the cesta.

RACQUETBALL

In racquetball, players use a short-handled racquet and a hollow rubber ball. The ball can be hit against the ceiling, as well as all four walls of the court.

The fast game of racquetball is similar in many ways to squash.

SERVING
The player serves underarm and must hit the shuttlecock below waist level. If it is not returned, it must land within the service court diagonally opposite. Only the server can score points.

Racket is angled downwards.

Arm is bent, and the racket held behind the shoulder.

PLAYING
The receiver must return the shuttle over the net before it touches ground in the serving court. Most badminton shots are played overhead.

Racket is raised directly upwards.

The arm straightens on making contact with the shuttlecock.

Grip should be relaxed, not too tight, but not too loose.

SERVING
The ball must be thrown vertically at least 16cm from the flat palm of the hand, and the ball must not spin. At the moment of striking, the racket must be behind the end of the table. The ball must bounce on the server's side first.

The ball is hit as it begins to fall.

GRIPS
There are two main grips used in table tennis.

Handshake grip
The bat is held as though the player is shaking hands.

Penholder grip
The bat is held as though the player is holding a pen.

Out-of-court line

Length: 32ft

Cut line

Service box

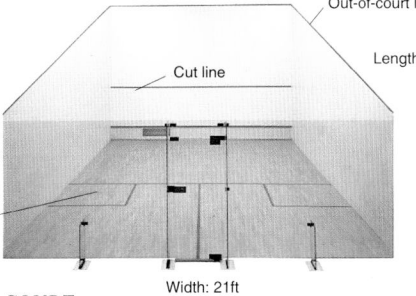

Width: 21ft

COURT
The white, concrete walls of a squash court must be completely smooth. In tournaments, courts are often made of glass and Perspex, so that spectators can watch the match from all sides of the court. In the USA, squash is played on a narrower court with a harder ball.

SERVING
The player must stand with at least one foot in the service box, throw the ball into the air, and hit it at the first attempt. The ball must hit the front wall above the cut line, but below the out-of-court line, without bouncing elsewhere first.

The server can use any kind of stroke.

TOP BALL SPEEDS

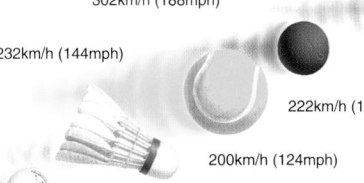

Jai alai	302km/h (188mph)
Squash	232km/h (144mph)
Tennis	222km/h (138mph)
Badminton	200km/h (124mph)
Table tennis	170km/h (106mph)

BASKETBALL

FACTS

- The aim of basketball is to throw the ball into a basket at the opponent's end of the court.

- There are ten players in each team; only five are on the court at any one time.

- Players may throw and bounce the ball, but must not carry or kick it.

- A game consists of two halves of 20 minutes each.

KIT
Players wear brightly coloured singlets and shorts. Singlets have large numbers on the front and back.

Backboard

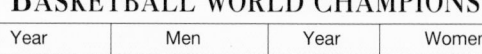

The rim of the net is 3.05m off the ground.

COURT
The dimensions given for this court are based on international rules. In the USA, the courts are slightly bigger.

Free-throw line.

Length: 28m

Three points are awarded for goals scored outside the semicircle.

Two points are awarded for goals scored inside the semicircle.

End line

Width: 15m

BALL
The ball is made of rubber encased in leather, rubber, or synthetic material.

The high, padded sides of basketball boots give firm support.

TIME RULES

Time limit	Action
3 seconds	A player may remain in the restricted area between his opponent's end line and the free-throw line.
5 seconds	A player may hold on to the ball.
10 seconds	The team with the ball must move from the back court to the front court.
30 seconds	The team with the ball must try for a goal.

BASKETBALL WORLD CHAMPIONS

Year	Men	Year	Women
1954	USA	1957	USA
1959	Brazil	1959	USSR
1963	Brazil	1964	USSR
1967	USSR	1967	USSR
1970	Yugoslavia	1971	USSR
1974	USSR	1975	USSR
1978	Yugoslavia	1979	USA
1982	USSR	1983	USSR
1986	USA	1986	USA
1990	Yugoslavia	1990	USA
1994	USA	1994	Brazil
1998	Yugoslavia	1998	USA

STARTING JUMP
At the beginning of a match, the referee throws the ball up and two opponents jump to hit it. A player may tap the ball twice after it has reached its highest point.

The player stands near the centre line, in his own half of the court.

SHOOTING
When attempting to score a goal, a player holds the ball high above his head and throws it towards the net.

MOVING WITH THE BALL
A player who has stopped while holding the ball may pivot on one foot, at the same time stepping in any direction with the other foot. A moving player may take one stride with the ball.

DRIBBLING
A player can progress with the ball by dribbling. He can take as many steps as he wishes while bouncing the ball.

VOLLEYBALL

- Volleyball is a ball game played between two teams of six players each.

- The aim of volleyball is to use any part of the body above the waist to send a ball over a net, so that the opposing team are unable to return it.

- A team may touch the ball up to three times before returning it over the net.

Length of court: 18m

Height of net: 1m

Width of court: 9m

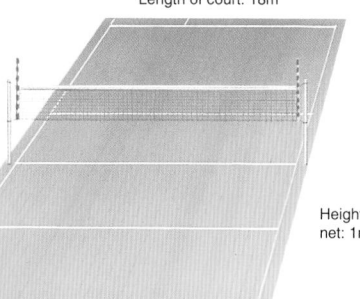

UP AND OVER
Because of the height of the net, players have to jump up high in the air to hit the ball. Players must not touch or reach over the net. The ball is smaller than a basketball or netball.

NETBALL

- The aim in netball is to throw the ball into the opponent's net.

- The game is played between two teams of seven players each.

- Each player must keep to a particular area of the court.

NETBALL POSITIONS
Players wear letters to indicate their positions, and to show which zone they should stay in.

WA — Wing attack

GS — Goal shooter

GA — Goal attack

C — Centre

WD — Wing defence

GK — Goalkeeper

GD — Goal defence

HANDBALL

- The aim is to pass or dribble the ball with the hands until a goal is scored.

- It is played between two teams of seven players each.

- Players may take three steps when holding the ball.

The player must not hold on to the ball for longer than three seconds.

RUGBY

FACTS

• The aim of rugby is to score points by placing an oval-shaped ball on or over the opponent's goal line (a try), or by kicking it over the opponent's crossbar.

• Players may carry, pass, or kick the ball, but they cannot throw the ball in front of them.

• A game consists of two halves of 40 minutes each.

• There are two types of rugby: Rugby Union (R.U.), and Rugby League (R.L.).

RUGBY UNION

• Rugby Union is the earliest and most widely played form of rugby.

• The game is traditionally played by amateurs (15 per team), but players can now also receive payment.

BALL

The oval-shaped ball is usually made of leather.

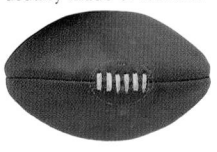

Length: 28cm

KIT

Although rugby is a tough game, players are not allowed to wear protective clothing, apart from a scrum cap made of soft leather, shin guards, and a gum shield. Sweat bands are also often worn.

BOOTS

Players may wear shoes similar to those worn by soccer players, or high-sided boots to support the ankles.

INTERNATIONAL RUGBY TEAMS

Each major international rugby team has its own symbol.

Australia

England

France

Ireland

New Zealand

Scotland

South Africa

Wales

SCORING

Type of goal	Points R.U.	R.L.	Action
Try	5	4	Placing the ball by hand on or over the goal line.
Dropped goal	3	1	Ball is dropped and kicked over the crossbar.
Penalty goal	3	2	A penalty kick awarded for a foul.
Conversion	2	2	A goal kick awarded after a try.

PITCH

The pitch usually has a grass surface, but may be made of clay or sand.

5m line
22m line
10m line
Halfway line
Length of pitch between the goal lines: 100m
The goal is 5.6m wide; the height of the crossbar is 3m.
Goal line
Dead ball line
Width of pitch: 69m
A scrum is used to restart play, usually after a foul.

PASSING THE BALL

A player can run while holding the ball, but must not pass forwards. He should, however, pass to the front of the receiving player, to enable the player to run on to the ball.

Correct throw
Foul throw

SCRUM

Players from both teams close up around the ball and link arms. The front row must be made up of three players: a "hooker" and two "props" who stand on each side of him. The ball is thrown into the scrum and the hooker will try to hook the ball to his team mates behind him.

The scrum must not break up until the ball is cleared.

LINE-OUT

A line-out is used to restart play after a ball crosses the touchline, or is "in-touch". At least two players from each team form separate lines at right angles to the touchline. The ball must be thrown straight between the two lines of players.

RUGBY LEAGUE

• This game developed from Rugby Union, and is played by professionals and amateurs.

• It is played by two teams of 13 players each.

• Rugby League, although very similar, follows slightly different rules to Rugby Union.

• One difference is that in Rugby League, players can restart the game after a tackle with the "play the ball" rule.

PLAY THE BALL RULE

A tackled player is allowed to drop the ball before kicking it in any direction, usually to a team mate behind him. This may be done for five consecutive tackles. After the sixth tackle, the team must give up possession.

Two members of the opposing team may stand directly in front of the player with the ball.

OLYMPIC RUGBY

Rugby was last staged at the Olympics in 1924, in Paris. There were three entrants: Romania, USA, and France. USA won the gold medal.

RUGBY WORDS

Backs Players who position themselves behind a scrum.

Dummy Pretending to pass the ball to another player, while keeping possession.

Dropped goal Dropping the ball and kicking it over the cross bar after it touches the ground.

Goal Combination of a try and conversion.

Knock-on The ball bouncing forward off the hand or arm of a player.

Mark Place at which a free-kick or penalty kick is given.

Maul A scrum around a player carrying the ball.

Punt Dropping the ball and kicking it before it touches the ground.

Ruck A scrum around a player who has dropped the ball.

Touch-down A player grounding the ball in his own in-goal area.

Up-and-under A ball kicked high in the air, while players run upfield to catch it.

FOOTBALL

SOCCER

- Soccer, or Association football, is a ball game played by two teams of 11 players each.

- The aim is to hit the ball into the opponent's goal, and the team that scores the most goals wins.

- Players use their feet, head, thighs, and chest to hit or control the ball; only the goalkeeper may touch the ball with his hands or arms.

- A game consists of two periods, or halves, of 45 minutes each.

FORMATIONS
Soccer is a flexible game, but most teams start with players in a particular formation. The one shown below is 4–3–3. It uses four defenders, three midfielders, and three in attack.

The 4–3–3 formation

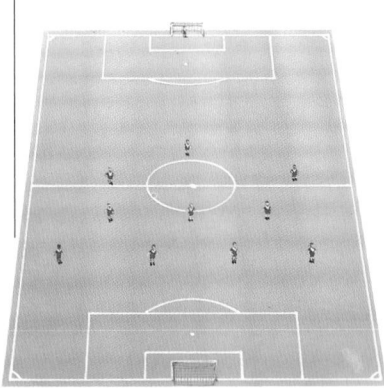

KIT
Players wear jerseys with numbers on the back. The soles of the boots may be fitted with studs or bars.

Soccer boot

Fat rubber studs for hard ground.

Aluminium for wet, slippery ground.

Nylon for soft ground.

Shin pads must be worn under socks.

Footballs used in top-class play are made of rubber encased in leather.

DRIBBLING
When dribbling, the player keeps the ball close to his feet, to prevent an opposing player taking the ball from him.

In order to get round him, the player may pretend to go one way.

He then confuses his opponent by turning to go in the opposite direction.

The player keeps close control of the ball while approaching his opponent.

PITCH

Width: 50-100yd

Centre circle

Length: 100-130yd

Penalty mark

Penalty area

Goal area

Goal line

Goalpost length: 8yd; height: 8ft

WORLD CUP COMPETITIONS

Date	Host country	Winner
1938	France	Italy
1950	Brazil	Uruguay
1954	Switzerland	West Germany
1958	Sweden	Brazil
1962	Chile	Brazil
1966	England	England
1970	Mexico	Brazil
1974	West Germany	West Germany
1978	Argentina	Argentina
1982	Spain	Italy
1986	Mexico	Argentina
1990	Italy	West Germany
1994	USA	Brazil
1998	France	France
2002	Japan/South Korea	

DEFENDING
A defender will often mark, or follow, one opponent throughout the game. Defenders must make strong tackles in order to take possession of the ball from their opponents.

GOALKEEPING
The goalkeeper can touch the ball with his hands, but only within his own penalty area. He is not allowed to pick up a back pass from a team mate.

GOAL SCORING
Any player in a team may score a goal, but the main goal-scorers are called strikers, who must be able to shoot and head the ball accurately.

Good timing is essential for a clean sliding tackle.

The defender must be careful not to foul his opponent.

He slides down in front of his opponent and wins the ball.

For a short pass, a goalkeeper will throw or roll the ball underarm.

Ideally, the ball is rolled along the ground for an accurate pass.

Opportunist sliding shot into goal.

MAJOR TEAMS
These are the basic colours worn by some of the top international teams. The flags are not part of the kits.

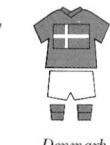

Argentina *Belgium* *Brazil* *Bulgaria* *Cameroon* *Colombia* *Denmark* *England* *France* *Germany* *Republic of Ireland*

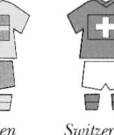

Italy *Mexico* *Netherlands* *Nigeria* *Norway* *Poland* *Spain* *Sweden* *Switzerland* *Romania* *Uruguay* *USA*

AMERICAN FOOTBALL

- American football is played by two teams of 11 players each, though frequent substitution is allowed, and up to 40 people can play for each team.

- A team earns points by making a touchdown (putting the ball behind the opposing team's goal line), or by kicking the ball between the goal posts.

- A game consists of four quarters, of 15 minutes each.

GRIDIRON
The field is commonly called the gridiron, because the lines make it look like a cooking grill. The field is marked out in yards to show how far a team has advanced.

End line

End zone

Yardline every 5 yds

Goal line

Length: 360ft

Height of crossbar: 10ft

Width of goal: 18ft 6in

Width: 160ft

KIT
There is a lot of physical contact in American football, and players wear several layers of protective clothing.

Chest protector

Shoulder pads

Groin protector

Leg pads

Tight, knee-length trousers lace up at the front.

Helmets are made of tough plastic.

Face mask

OFFENCE
The team that is in possession of the ball is the offence, or attacking team. They are allowed four attempts, or downs, at advancing with the ball by at least 10yd. If they fail to do this, their opponents gain possession of the ball.

The snap is the start of the down.

SHIRT NUMBERS
NFL players are numbered according to their positions.

Number	Position
1-19	Quarterbacks, punters, kickers
20-49	Running and defensive backs
50-59	Centres and linebackers
60-79	Defensive linemen, offensive guards, and tackles
80-89	Wide receivers and tight ends
90-99	Defensive linemen

BLOCKING
A blocker may use the upper part of his body to obstruct an opponent who does not have the ball. He may use his arms to push, but not grab hold of, him. Blocking is used by offensive and defensive players.

DEFENCE
The team that does not have the ball uses its defence players, usually the biggest men, to try to prevent the offence from advancing and scoring. A defender needs to be a good tackler. He is allowed to push, pull, or grab the person in possession of the ball, who is called the runner. If the defence manages to get hold of the ball, it is called a turnover, and possession changes to the other team.

SCORING

Score	Points	Action
Touchdown	6	Taking the ball across the opponent's goal line, or gaining possession within the opponents' end zone.
Field goal	3	Place-kicking the ball through the goal posts.
Safety	2	Tackling an opponent who is carrying the ball behind his own goal line.
Extra point (conversion)	1 or 2	A goal kick (1) or a pass into the end zone (2), after scoring a touchdown.

One point is given for scoring between the outer, or "behind" posts.

AUSTRALIAN FOOTBALL

- The game is played by two teams of 18 players. The aim is to score goals by kicking an oval-shaped ball between two tall posts.

- A player can kick, punch, and run with the ball, but he must not throw it.

- A game consists of 4 quarters, lasting 20 minutes each.

PLAYING FIELD
The game is played on an oval-shaped playing field. Six points are scored for kicking the ball between the two central "goal" posts.

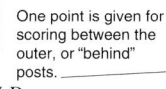
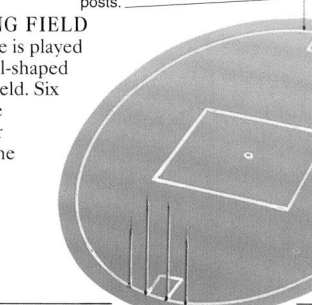
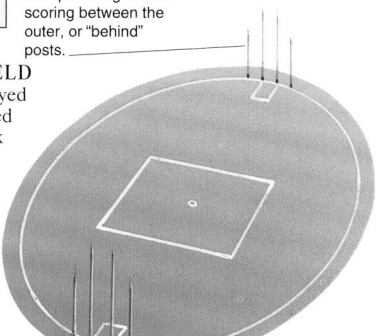

BALL
The oval-shaped ball is made of leather, and has laces and a pebbled finish to provide a good grip.

FOOTBALL LEAGUE
American football is the USA's major national sport. There are 28 teams in the National Football League (NFL), each with its own distinctive helmet design.

Atlanta Falcons

Buffalo Bills	*Chicago Bears*	*Cincinnati Bengals*

Cleveland Browns	*Dallas Cowboys*	*Denver Broncos*

Detroit Lions	*Green Bay Packers*	*Houston Oilers*

Indianapolis Colts	*Kansas City Chiefs*	*Oakland Raiders*

The Rams	*Miami Dolphins*	*Minnesota Vikings*

New England Patriots	*New Orleans Saints*	*New York Giants*

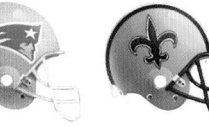

New York Jets	*Pittsburgh Steelers*	*Philadelphia Eagles*

Arizona Cardinals	*San Diego Chargers*	*San Francisco Forty-niners*

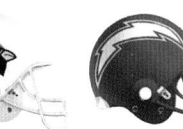

Seattle Seahawks	*Tampa Bay Buccaneers*	*Washington Redskins*

CRICKET

FACTS

• Cricket is a ball game played by two teams of 11 players each.

• The teams take it in turns to bat and field.

• During each "innings", the batting side aims to score runs between two wickets; the fielding side aims to get the batting side out.

• A match consists of one or two innings per side.

KIT
Traditionally, cricketers wear white or cream shirts, trousers, and a sweater. Coloured clothing is worn during some one-day matches.

FIELD
The playing field surrounding the pitch can be any length. Below are the major fielding positions for a right-handed batsman.

Batsmen and close fielders wear protective helmets made of metal or fibreglass.

Batting gloves give good protection, while allowing the batsman to grip and wield the bat.

Protective box

BAT
The bat is made of willow, and has a cane handle covered with rubber.

Maximum length of bat: 3ft 2in

WICKET
This has three stumps along which two bails are placed.

Bails

Width of wicket: 9in

BALL
A cricket ball is made of layers of cork and wool, covered in red leather.

Shoes have spiked or rubber soles.

Leg pads are worn by batsmen and wicketkeepers.

Wicketkeeper's gloves are heavily padded and are larger than batsmen's gloves.

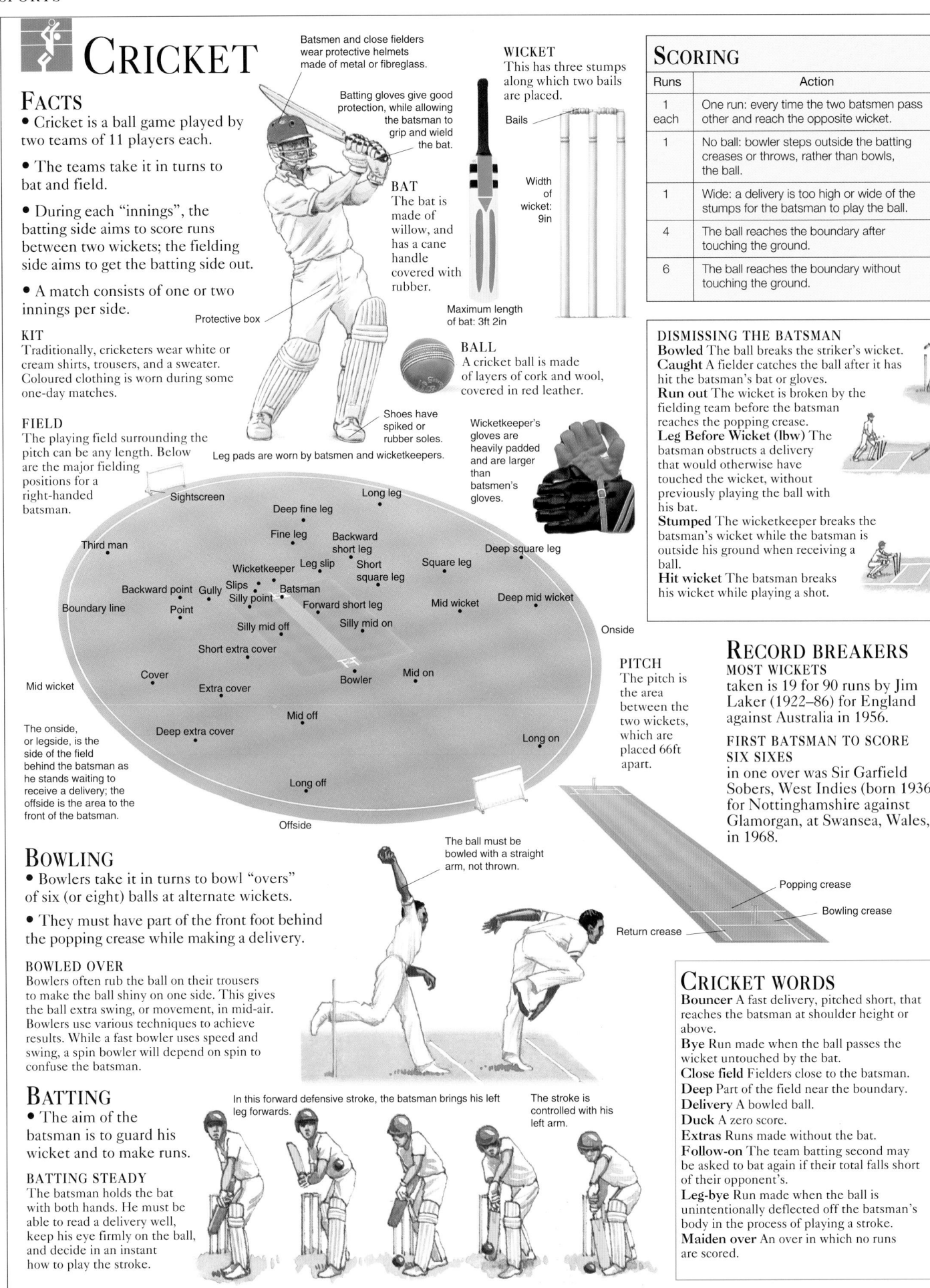

The onside, or legside, is the side of the field behind the batsman as he stands waiting to receive a delivery; the offside is the area to the front of the batsman.

Fielding positions: Sightscreen, Long leg, Deep fine leg, Fine leg, Backward short leg, Deep square leg, Third man, Wicketkeeper, Leg slip, Short square leg, Square leg, Backward point, Gully, Slips, Batsman, Short square leg, Deep square leg, Boundary line, Point, Silly point, Forward short leg, Mid wicket, Deep mid wicket, Silly mid off, Silly mid on, Onside, Short extra cover, Cover, Mid wicket, Extra cover, Bowler, Mid on, Mid off, Deep extra cover, Long on, Long off, Offside

PITCH
The pitch is the area between the two wickets, which are placed 66ft apart.

SCORING

Runs	Action
1 each	One run: every time the two batsmen pass other and reach the opposite wicket.
1	No ball: bowler steps outside the batting creases or throws, rather than bowls, the ball.
1	Wide: a delivery is too high or wide of the stumps for the batsman to play the ball.
4	The ball reaches the boundary after touching the ground.
6	The ball reaches the boundary without touching the ground.

DISMISSING THE BATSMAN
Bowled The ball breaks the striker's wicket.
Caught A fielder catches the ball after it has hit the batsman's bat or gloves.
Run out The wicket is broken by the fielding team before the batsman reaches the popping crease.
Leg Before Wicket (lbw) The batsman obstructs a delivery that would otherwise have touched the wicket, without previously playing the ball with his bat.
Stumped The wicketkeeper breaks the batsman's wicket while the batsman is outside his ground when receiving a ball.
Hit wicket The batsman breaks his wicket while playing a shot.

RECORD BREAKERS
MOST WICKETS
taken is 19 for 90 runs by Jim Laker (1922–86) for England against Australia in 1956.

FIRST BATSMAN TO SCORE SIX SIXES
in one over was Sir Garfield Sobers, West Indies (born 1936), for Nottinghamshire against Glamorgan, at Swansea, Wales, in 1968.

Popping crease
Bowling crease
Return crease

The ball must be bowled with a straight arm, not thrown.

BOWLING

• Bowlers take it in turns to bowl "overs" of six (or eight) balls at alternate wickets.

• They must have part of the front foot behind the popping crease while making a delivery.

BOWLED OVER
Bowlers often rub the ball on their trousers to make the ball shiny on one side. This gives the ball extra swing, or movement, in mid-air. Bowlers use various techniques to achieve results. While a fast bowler uses speed and swing, a spin bowler will depend on spin to confuse the batsman.

BATTING

• The aim of the batsman is to guard his wicket and to make runs.

BATTING STEADY
The batsman holds the bat with both hands. He must be able to read a delivery well, keep his eye firmly on the ball, and decide in an instant how to play the stroke.

In this forward defensive stroke, the batsman brings his left leg forwards.

The stroke is controlled with his left arm.

CRICKET WORDS
Bouncer A fast delivery, pitched short, that reaches the batsman at shoulder height or above.
Bye Run made when the ball passes the wicket untouched by the bat.
Close field Fielders close to the batsman.
Deep Part of the field near the boundary.
Delivery A bowled ball.
Duck A zero score.
Extras Runs made without the bat.
Follow-on The team batting second may be asked to bat again if their total falls short of their opponent's.
Leg-bye Run made when the ball is unintentionally deflected off the batsman's body in the process of playing a stroke.
Maiden over An over in which no runs are scored.

BASEBALL

FACTS

• Ball game played by two teams of nine players each.

• The game is similar to cricket in that teams take it in turns to bat and field.

• The aim of the batting side is to score runs around the four bases.

• A match consists of nine innings.

KIT

Players must not wear any emblems that may be mistaken for a baseball. The numbers on each shirt must be at least 6in high. The catcher wears more protective clothing than any other player.

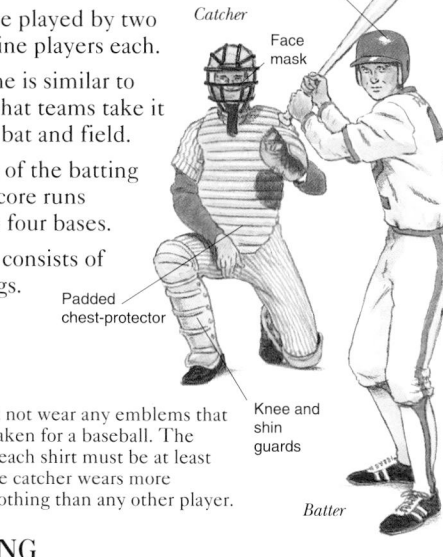

Catcher

Hard plastic helmet

Face mask

Padded chest-protector

Knee and shin guards

Batter

Maximum length: 42in

BAT
Bats are made of wood, for top-class play, or aluminium. The barrel must be smooth and well rounded.

BALL
The ball is made of cork or rubber and is covered in cowhide or horsehide.

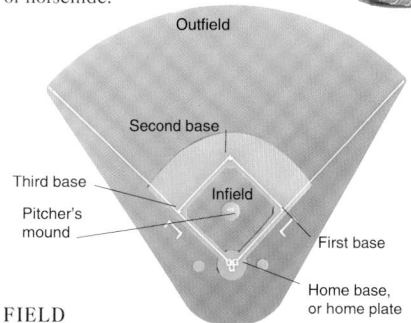

Outfield

Second base

Third base

Infield

Pitcher's mound

First base

Home base, or home plate

FIELD
The playing field is made up of an infield and outfield, known as fair territory; any other area is foul territory.

The catcher's face mask is made of thick wire and foam padding.

Each fielder wears a large leather glove.

MAJOR LEAGUES
There are two major baseball leagues in the USA. Each team has its own symbol.

AMERICAN LEAGUE

 *Baltimore Orioles*

 *Boston Red Sox*

 *California Angels*

 *Chicago White Sox*

 *Cleveland Indians*

 *Detroit Tigers*

 *Kansas City Royals*

 *Milwaukee Brewers*

 *Minnesota Twins*

 *New York Yankees*

 *Oakland Athletics*

 *Seattle Mariners*

 *Texas Rangers*

Toronto Blue Jays

NATIONAL LEAGUE

 *Atlanta Braves*

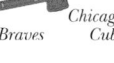 *Chicago Cubs*

 *Cincinnati Reds*

Colorado Rockies

Florida Marlins

 *Houston Astros*

 *Los Angeles Dodgers*

Montreal Expos

 *New York Mets*

 *Philadelphia Phillies*

 *Pittsburgh Pirates*

 *St. Louis Cardinals*

San Diego Padres

 *San Francisco Giants*

PITCHING

• The pitcher tries to throw the ball through the strike zone; he must not pitch the ball directly at the batter.

• He may rub the ball with his hands, but must not shine it on his clothes, or rub it on the ground.

• He may throw the ball to a base before he pitches.

Pitchers can throw the ball at speeds of more than 145km/h (90mph).

BATTING

• The batter must stay within the batter's box on receiving the ball.

• Each ball, or pitch, delivered to the batter is either a strike or a ball.

STRIKE ZONE
This is the area over home plate and between the batter's armpits and knees. If the ball falls inside this zone and the batter fails to hit it, it is a strike. A ball is called when a pitch, thrown outside the strike zone, is not struck at by the batter. After four balls, the batter may walk to first base.

The blue balls indicate a strike.

The red balls indicate a ball.

PUTTING OUT THE BATTER

Batted ball is caught before it bounces by a fielder.

Catcher catches the third strike and tags the batter or he throws the ball to first base.

Batter taps, or bunts, the ball down in front of him into foul territory; only the first two fouls count as strikes.

Batter strikes the ball three times, and is tagged before reaching first base.

RECORD BREAKERS
A PERFECT NINE INNINGS GAME (which means the pitcher allows the opposition no hits, no runs, and does not allow a player to reach first base) was first achieved by Lee Richmond (1857–1929) of the USA for Worcester against Cleveland in 1880.

MOST HOME RUNS in a season is 61 by Roger Maris (1934–85) of the USA, for the New York Yankees in 1961. This beat the record of 60 that Babe Ruth (1895–1945) of the USA set in 1927.

RUNNING

• If a runner is approaching a base that already has a runner on it, then that runner must go on to the next base (force play).

• A runner must touch base before the fielder touches him or the base with the ball.

• A runner may run to a base while the ball is being pitched to a batter (a steal).

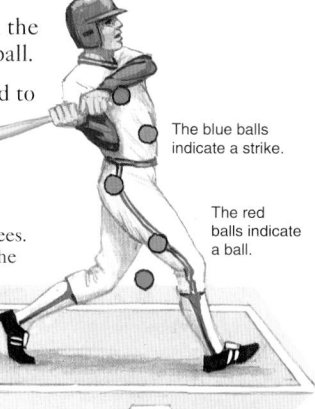

STICK GAMES

HOCKEY

- Hockey is an 11-a-side game; the aim is to shoot a ball with hooked sticks into the opposing team's goal.

- Goals may be scored only from within the striking, or shooting, circle.

- A game consists of two 35-minute halves.

STICK
Hockey sticks are steam bent, so that the grain of the wood follows the bend. This helps to strengthen the stick. The ball may be struck with the flat face of the stick only.

The stick weighs between 12oz and 28oz for men, and up to 23oz for women.

BALL
The ball is traditionally white and is made of cork and twine, with a leather casing.

BULLY
The bully is a distinctive feature of hockey. It is used to restart the game after certain stoppages. A player from each side stands over the ball. They tap the ground and each other's sticks alternately three times before attempting to play the ball.

KIT
Players wear a shirt or shorts, or skirt (women) and guards on their shins and ankles. The goalkeeper wears extra protective clothing.

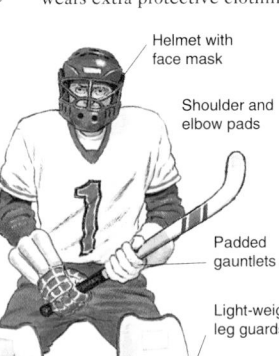

Helmet with face mask

Shoulder and elbow pads

Padded gauntlets

Light-weight leg guards

"Kickers" are worn over boots to protect the feet when kicking the hard ball.

Goalkeeper's kit

PITCH
Hockey is usually played outdoors, on grass or on artificial surfaces.

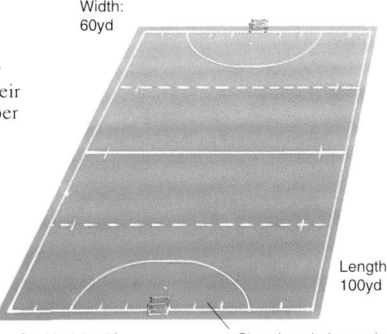

Width: 60yd

Length: 100yd

Goal height: 7ft
Goal width: 12ft

Shooting circle; goals can only be scored from inside here.

OLYMPIC HOCKEY CHAMPIONS (WOMEN)

Year	Country
1984	Netherlands
1988	Australia
1992	Spain
1996	Australia

OLYMPIC HOCKEY CHAMPIONS (MEN)

Year	Country
1920	Britain
1928	India
1932	India
1936	India
1948	India
1952	India
1956	India
1960	Pakistan
1964	India
1968	Pakistan
1972	West Germany
1976	New Zealand
1980	India
1984	Pakistan
1988	Britain
1992	Germany
1996	Netherlands

ICE-HOCKEY

- Ice-hockey is played six-a-side, with up to 14 substitutes.

- There are three periods, of 20 minutes each.

- Women's ice-hockey became an Olympic sport in 1998, at Nagano.

ICE-HOCKEY PENALTIES

Type	Minutes in "Sin Bin"
Minor	2
Major	5
Misconduct	10*
Match	Rest of game**

*Substitute may replace immediately.
**Substitute may replace after 5 minutes.

Puck is traditionally black and made from toughened rubber.
Width: 29–30m

ICE-HOCKEY STICKS
The out-fielder's stick has a shaft with an angled blade. The goalkeeper's stick is heavier and has a wider blade.

Goalkeeper's stick

Out-fielder's stick

There are four face-off circles.

Goal width: 2.53m
Goal height: 1.22m

Length: 60–61m

RINK
The rink is an iced surface surrounded by wooden boards.

LACROSSE

- Players use a net on the end of their stick (crosse) to carry and pass a ball and try to send it into the opposing team's goal.

- The men's and women's games are played under different rules. One of the main differences is that physical contact is allowed in the men's game, but not in the women's.

Women's lacrosse

OLYMPIC ICE-HOCKEY CHAMPIONS

Year	Country
1924	Canada
1928	Canada
1932	Canada
1936	Britain
1948	Canada
1952	Canada
1956	USSR
1960	USA
1964	USSR
1968	USSR
1972	USSR
1976	USSR
1980	USA
1984	USSR
1988	USSR
1992	CIS
1994	Sweden
1998	Czech Republic

LACROSSE RULES

Men's lacrosse	Women's lacrosse
10 players a-side; nine substitutes allowed.	12 players a-side; one substitute allowed.
Shoulder-to-shoulder contact and body-checking allowed.	No physical contact allowed.
Time: four 15-min periods.	Time: two 25-min periods.
Playing field usually measures 100m x 55m.	No measured boundaries.
Crosse measures: 1–1.8m.	Crosse measures: 0.9–1.1m.

HOCKEY SPEEDS
Ice-hockey is the fastest team game in the world. The puck is hit at speeds of up to 190km (118 miles) per hour. A hockey ball is hit at speeds of up to 160km (100 miles) per hour.

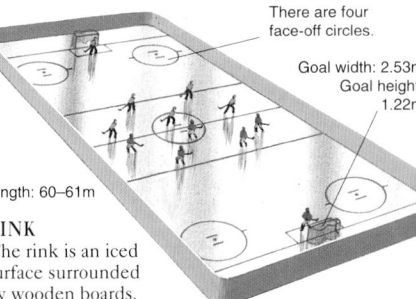

GOLF

FACTS

• A standard golf course has 18 holes of various lengths.

• There are two main types of competition: stroke play and match play.

• In stroke play, the player who completes a round in the fewest strokes wins the match; in match play the winner is the one who wins the most holes in a round.

KIT

Comfortable clothes that allow the golfer to stretch and swing with ease are ideal.

Club-head cover

Score card

Spike-studded shoes give a secure footing.

SWING TECHNIQUE

The swing is one continuous, smooth action.

The upper body turns as the arms swing up and back (the backswing).

As the club is brought down, the weight is moved from the back foot to the front foot.

Weight is fully on the left foot as the swing is followed through.

The head is kept down as the club makes contact with the ball.

The body faces the target as the club is brought past the left shoulder.

Wood

Woods are used for long shots. They are numbered 1–9. Their large heads may be made from wood, plastic, or light metal.

CLUBS

Players may not start or play a round of golf with more than 14 clubs. Most players use three or four woods, nine or ten irons, and one putter.

BAG

Beginners use a lightweight bag to carry a half set (seven clubs). Players with a full set of clubs use a trolley or have a caddy to assist them.

Bag stand

Umbrella

COURSE

A standard course consists of 18 holes, varying in length from 90–550m (100–600yd). The length determines the "par" of each hole: the average number of strokes needed to get the ball into the hole.

The teeing ground, from which the first stroke is made, is a smooth, level area.

Iron

Irons are used for a variety of shots. The steel heads are numbered 1–10. The lower numbers hit the ball furthest and lowest.

Putter

Putters are used mainly on the putting green. Unlike the other clubs, they have two striking faces. They are the lightest of the clubs.

BALL

Golf balls are covered in more than 400 dimples. They help the ball travel further and straighter through the air.

TEES

Tees are small, usually plastic, pegs on which the ball is placed for the first shot to a hole.

STRIKING DISTANCES

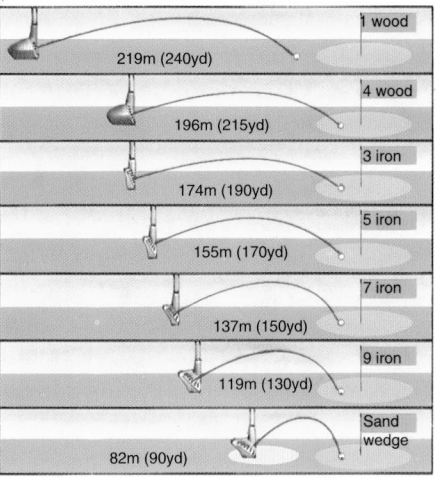

1 wood	219m (240yd)
4 wood	196m (215yd)
3 iron	174m (190yd)
5 iron	155m (170yd)
7 iron	137m (150yd)
9 iron	119m (130yd)
Sand wedge	82m (90yd)

The apron is the short grass surrounding the green.

The putting green is the smooth, grassy area that surrounds the hole.

Flagstick

Diameter of hole: 10.8cm (4.25in)

Sand bunker

Hazards may include ponds, streams, and sand bunkers.

The rough is uneven land surrounding the fairway.

The fairway is a closely mown strip of ground which stretches from tee to green, along which the players attempt to play the ball.

MAJOR GOLF TOURNAMENTS

Tournament	First held
British Open	1860
US Open	1895
US PGA	1916
US Masters	1934
Ryder Cup (male team event)	1927
Curtis Cup (female team event)	1932

LONG SHOT

In a qualifying match in Pennsylvania, USA, in the early 1900s, one entrant drove her ball into a river at the 16th hole. She set out in a boat to reach it, and finally completed the hole in 166 shots.

GOLF WORDS

Approach Shot played to the green from the fairway or rough.

Birdie A score of one stroke under par for a hole.

Bogey A score of one stroke over par for a hole.

Eagle A score of two strokes under par for a hole.

Fourball Two play against two, each player having one ball, the lower score of each pair being their score at a hole.

Foursome Two play against two, each side having one ball and taking alternate strokes at each hole.

Handicap Number of strokes a player may subtract from his or her score for a round; enables players of different abilities to compete on equal terms.

Hole A complete section, from tee to putting green; the round hole into which the ball is played.

Par The standard score for a hole or round (18 holes) on a course, based on what a top player would be expected to shoot, and allowing for two putts.

Tee The ground that marks the start of a hole; a peg on which the ball is put for the first stroke of a hole.

WATER SPORTS

ROWING

- Rowing is a racing sport for boats containing one, two, four, or eight rowers, sometimes with a cox to steer.

- In sculling, each rower uses two oars instead of one.

- Races in major championships, or regattas, take place in lanes over a distance of 2,000m.

- In head-of-the-river, or processional, races, crews start at intervals and race against the clock.

BOAT
Rowing boats used in racing vary in length depending on the event, but the basic design remains the same.

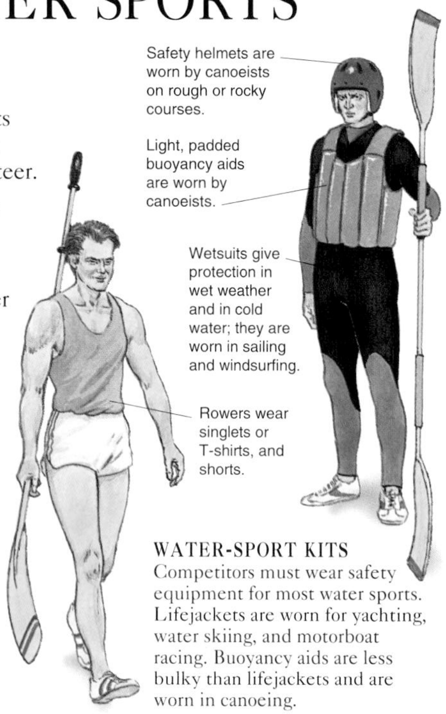

Safety helmets are worn by canoeists on rough or rocky courses.

Light, padded buoyancy aids are worn by canoeists.

Wetsuits give protection in wet weather and in cold water; they are worn in sailing and windsurfing.

Rowers wear singlets or T-shirts, and shorts.

WATER-SPORT KITS
Competitors must wear safety equipment for most water sports. Lifejackets are worn for yachting, water skiing, and motorboat racing. Buoyancy aids are less bulky than lifejackets and are worn in canoeing.

Boats are made from wood or reinforced plastic.

ROWING TECHNIQUE
The rowers lean forwards, legs are bent and arms are straight.

OLYMPIC ROWING EVENTS

Event	Approximate length of boat
Sculls	8m (26ft)
Double sculls	10m (33ft)
Quadruple sculls	13m (43ft)
Coxless pairs	10m (33ft)
Coxed pairs (men only)	11m (36ft)
Coxless fours	13m (43ft)
Coxed fours (men only)	14m (46ft)
Eights	17m (56ft)

SCULLING TECHNIQUE
The rower holds the blades just above the water.

He leans forwards and bends his knees as he pulls the oars through the water.

He straightens his legs, and then his back when the oars are at right angles to the boat.

He leans back, bent, and pulls the oars up out of the water.

Their backs straighten as they pull the blades through the water.

They lean back, arms bent, as they pull the oars out of the water.

CANOEING

- There are two main types of competition canoes: the kayak and the Canadian canoe.

- The kayak has a closed deck. The canoeist sits inside, with legs outstretched underneath the deck. The paddle has a blade at each end.

- Most Canadian canoes have an open deck. The canoeist sits or kneels, and uses a single-bladed paddle.

Kayak

Stern

Cockpit

Bow

Double-bladed paddle

Canadian canoe

Bow

Stern

Thwart

Single-bladed paddle

OLYMPIC CANOEING EVENTS

Type of boat	Length (max.)	Event	
		Male	Female
K1	5.20m	500m, 1,000m, slalom	500m, slalom
K2	6.50m	500m, 1,000m	500m
K4	11m	1,000m	500m
C1	5.20m	500m, 1,000m, slalom	—
C2	6.50m	500m, 1,000m, slalom	—

K=Kayak, C=Canadian, 1=singles, 2=twos, 4=fours

SPRINT RACING
Sprint races take place on water that is as still as possible. Kayaks race in lanes, usually over distances of 500m or 1,000m. Some courses have windbreaks to limit the effect of crosswinds.

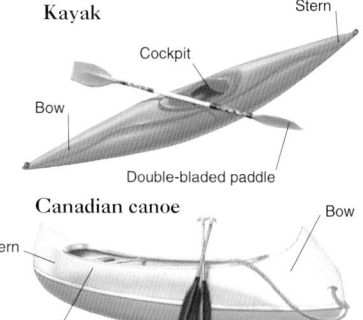
Men's K2 race

LONG-DISTANCE RACING
In 5,000m and 10,000m races, canoeists paddle round buoys at each end of the course. Canoe marathons range from 5km to 200km in length. Competitors avoid obstacles, such as locks or waterfalls, by carrying their canoes along the bank (portage).

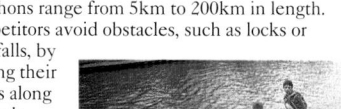
Canoe marathon

WHITE-WATER RACING
There are two types of white-water racing. In wildwater racing, canoeists are timed over a course that includes obstacles such as rocks and rapids. In slalom, canoeists negotiate several "gates".

Slalom

SAILING

YACHT TYPES

- There are two types of yacht racing: inshore and offshore.

- Inshore racing takes place off the coast on courses marked by buoys. Offshore racing takes place across the sea or ocean.

- One-design events are for boats of the same class. Handicap events are for boats of different designs.

One-person dinghy
e.g. Optimist class.
National origin: USA.

Two-person boat with trapeze e.g. 470 class.
National origin: France.

Catamaran
e.g. Tornado class.
National origin: UK.

Two-person dinghy
e.g. Flying Dutchman.
National origin: Netherlands.

Ocean-going yacht
e.g. 12m class.
National origin: Europe.

WINDSURFING

- Windsurfing, or boardsailing, is a comparatively new sport that has developed in the last 20 years.

- The sailboard is a simple craft steered by means of the sail.

- There are three main types of competition: course racing, slalom, and wave performance.

SAILBOARD

The sailboard is made up of the rig (consisting of the sail, mast, and boom) connected to the board by a universal joint. The sailor supports the rig by holding the boom.

Mast

Sail

Window

Boom

Board

Universal joint

WINDSURFING WORDS

Boom Double, or wishbone, boom used for steering, changing speed, and maintaining balance.

Daggerboard Removable fin used to stop board from slipping sideways through the water.

Freestyle Competition or exhibition in which tricks are performed.

Funboard Board designed for sailing in strong winds and performing spectacular flying jumps.

Skeg Fin that helps to keep board on course.

Uphaul Rope used to pull rig out of the water.

Boom
Daggerboard
Skeg
Funboard
Uphaul

POWERBOAT RACING

- Motorboats range from big powerboats with cabins to small inflatable dinghies fitted with outboard motors.

- The two main types of powerboat racing are inshore and offshore. There are several classes, depending on size and type of engine.

Twin-hulled powerboat

SURFING

- Surfers paddle out to sea on lightweight boards, and "ride" the waves back to shore.

- Any type of board may be used, but most competition boards have three fins on the tail (tri-fins).

KIT

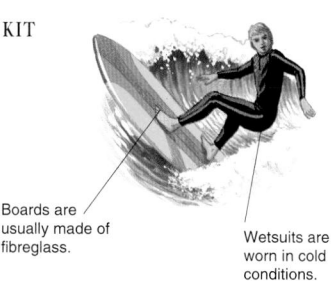

Boards are usually made of fibreglass.

Wetsuits are worn in cold conditions.

"Tube" rides are performed by riding in the hollow of the wave.

SURFING MOVES

Surfers perform a variety of moves. Judges assess surfers for style, grace, and timing, and award points, depending on the difficulty of the wave, for various aspects of the ride.

In a "turn", the surfer turns and cuts back through the wave.

WATER SPORT COMPARISONS

Water sport	First Olympics	Top speed	
		km/h	mph
Sailing	1900	69	43
Rowing	1900	21[1]	13
Powerboat racing	1908[2]	166[3]	103
Canoeing	1936	20[4]	12
Whitewater canoeing	1972	–	–
Windsurfing	1984	82	51
Water-skiing	–	230	143

(1) Average Olympic record speed for an eight over 2km. (2) Only inclusion. (3) Much higher speeds have been reached by boats specially designed for record breaking. (4) Average Olympic record speed for a K4 over 1km.

WATER-SKIING

- The water-skier is towed behind a motorboat, which needs a speed of at least 30km/h (19mph) to keep the skier upright. Competitions are divided into three sections.

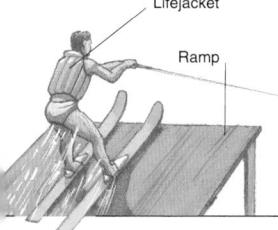

Lifejacket

Ramp

SLALOM

Skiers negotiate a series of buoys while crossing the boat's wake. There are six buoys on each run, or pass, with a "gate" at each end. Each successive pass is made with a faster boat speed to a maximum of 58km/h (36mph) for men or 55km/h (34mph) for women.

JUMPING

This is performed from a ramp and is judged on distance.

TRICKS

Points are awarded for a variety of moves, such as a backward turn, performed while being towed.

SPEEDY SKIS

The world water-skiing speed record is more than 200km/h (124mph), which is more than three times the speed of the boat. A skier will cross from side to side behind the towing motorboat, and so can travel much faster.

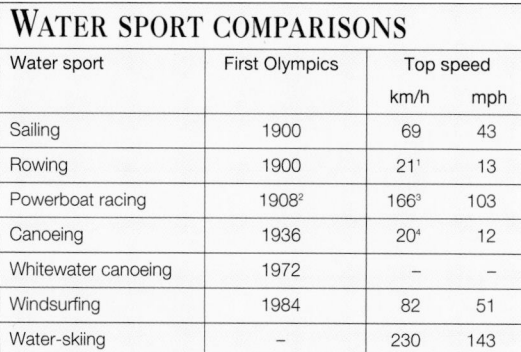

SWIMMING AND DIVING

SWIMMING

• There are four strokes in competitive swimming: freestyle (swimmers always use the front crawl), backstroke, breaststroke, and butterfly.

• Competitors dive from starting blocks in all events (except for backstroke), and race in lanes.

• They are timed to one-thousandth of a second by touching sensitive pads at the end of the race.

RACING FACTS

• Swimmers must not leave their starting blocks until the starter fires the gun or, as in relay races, until the previous swimmer in their team has touched the electronic pad.

• Rules govern the style of each stroke (except for freestyle); including the turns made at the ends of the pool.

• In the individual medley race, competitors swim each quarter with a different stroke in the following order: butterfly, backstroke, breaststroke, and freestyle.

DIVING

• Competitive diving is a sport in which contestants are awarded points by judges.

• There are two divisions of diving: springboard and highboard, or platform, diving.

KIT

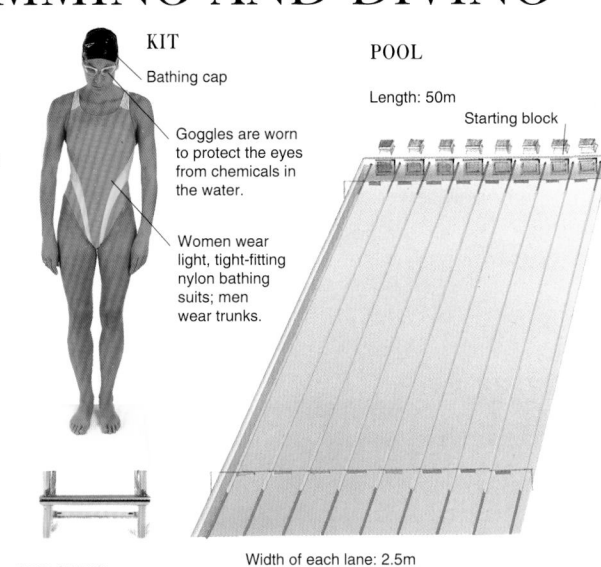

Bathing cap

Goggles are worn to protect the eyes from chemicals in the water.

Women wear light, tight-fitting nylon bathing suits; men wear trunks.

POOL

Length: 50m

Starting block

Width of each lane: 2.5m

OLYMPIC EVENTS			
Event		Men	Women
Swimming			
Freestyle	50m	√	√
	100m	√	√
	200m	√	√
	400m	√	√
	800m		√
	1500m	√	
Backstroke	100m	√	√
	200m	√	√
Breaststroke	100m	√	√
	200m	√	√
Butterfly	100m	√	√
	200m	√	√
Individual medley	200m	√	√
	400m	√	√
Freestyle relays	4x100m	√	√
	4x200m	√	
Medley relay	4x100m	√	√
Diving			
Springboard		√	√
Highboard		√	√
Synchronized swimming			
Solo			√
Duet			√
Water Polo		√	

STROKES

Front crawl
This is the fastest stroke and is used in freestyle races.

The swimmer moves his legs up and down from the hips.

His arms and legs move alternately.

He keeps his body as straight and flat as possible.

Breaststroke
This is the slowest stroke. Arms and legs stay underwater.

Her arms move together, circling from an outstretched position around and under the chin.

Her legs move together with a frog-like kick.

Backstroke
This is the only racing stroke in which the swimmers start in the water.

Her arms pull alternately in a "windmill" motion.

Her body is kept as straight as possible.

Butterfly
Like the breaststroke, this is a symmetrical stroke.

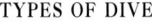

The swimmer uses a strong, double-arm pull to propel himself through the water.

He uses an up-and-down "dolphin kick" of the legs.

TYPES OF DIVE

The six types of dive are: forward, backward, twist, inward, reverse, and armstand. Within these six groups, there are many different starting positions and varieties of moves in the air, making a total of more than 100 recognized dives.

Forward dive

Forward dives may be performed from a run-up or standing position.

In the layout position, the body should not be bent at the hips or knees.

The diver must keep his feet together and his toes pointed.

He must keep his body as straight as possible when entering the water.

Backward dive

In the starting position, the diver must keep his body straight and his head up; his arms swing upwards just before leaving the platform or springboard.

Twist dive

The diver performs a twist in mid-air.

Armstand dive

Armstand dives are made from the platform only.

Inward dive

An inward dive (body facing towards board or platform) in the pike position

A forward somersault in the tuck position

SYNCHRONIZED SWIMMING

• This sport is a kind of "water ballet", in which swimmers perform artistic movements under or on the water to music.

• There are solo, pair (duet), and team (four to eight swimmers) events.

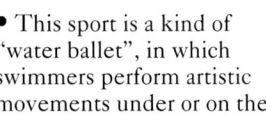

Synchronized duet

WATER POLO

• This is played 7-a-side in water. Only the goalkeeper is allowed to stand to play the ball, touch it with both hands or punch it.

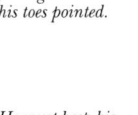

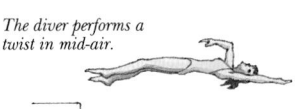
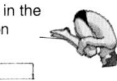

EQUESTRIAN

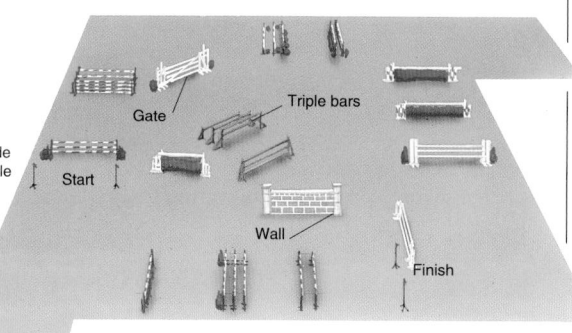

SHOW JUMPING

- Riders take their mounts around a course of obstacles such as gates, walls, fences, and a water jump.

- Penalty faults are given for errors such as a refusal, knocking off a pole, or taking longer than the specified time.

SHOW-JUMPING FAULTS

Error	Faults
Fence (or part of fence) down	4
Foot in water	4
Refusal	3
2nd refusal	6
3rd refusal	Elimination
Fall (horse or rider)	8
Exceeding time allowance	1/4 per second
Taking jumps out of sequence	Elimination

KIT
Riders must wear a hard hat or crash helmet, and formal dress for show jumping and dressage competitions.

JUMPING TECHNIQUE
When jumping, the rider should bend forwards from the hips and look up. On landing, the body must straighten up to take weight off the horse's front legs.

Flight

Take-off

Landing

Saddle

DRESSAGE

- Riders take their mounts through an official test made up of a variety of paces, movements, and figures.

- Marks are awarded for the quality of the test performance.

Walk

Canter

Trot

THREE-DAY EVENTING

- Riders take their mounts through three disciplines over three days: day one, dressage; day two, speed and endurance; day three, show jumping.

- Speed and endurance is made up of four phases (see table).

Clearing a water jump in the three-day event.

SPEED AND ENDURANCE

Phase	Distance	Details
A Roads and tracks	16-20km	Trot or slow canter
B Steeplechase	approx. 3.5-4km	9 or 10 fences
C Roads and tracks	16-20km	Trot or slow canter
D Cross-country	up to 8km	28-32 obstacles

POLO

- Polo is a game played by two teams of four players. The aim is to hit a ball between the opposition's goalposts with a long stick called a mallet.

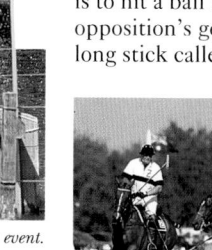

Polo

HARNESS RACING

- The horses pull their drivers round an oval track on light, two-wheeled "sulkies". Most races are 1 mile long.

Harness racing

HORSE RACING

- Flat races are for horses of 2 years old and over; most are from 5 furlongs to 1.5 miles long, with no jumps.

- Hurdle races are for 3-year-olds and over; they are from 2 to 3.25 miles long.

- Steeplechases have fences instead of hurdles. They are for 4-year-olds and over, and are from 2 to about 4.5 miles long.

MAJOR HORSE RACES

Race	Course	Distance	Type
2,000 Guineas	Newmarket, England	1 mile	Flat
1,000 Guineas (fillies)	Newmarket, England	1 mile	Flat
Derby	Epsom, England	1 mile, 4f*	Flat
Oaks (fillies)	Epsom, England	1 mile, 4f	Flat
St. Leger	Doncaster, England	1 mile, 6f, 132yd	Flat
Irish Derby	The Curragh, Ireland	1 mile, 4f	Flat
Arc de Triomphe	Longchamp, France	2,400m	Flat
Kentucky Derby	Churchill Downs, USA	1 mile, 2f	Flat
Melbourne Cup	Melbourne, Australia	3,200m	Flat
Grand National	Aintree, England	4 mile, 4f	Steeplechase
Cheltenham Gold Cup	Cheltenham, England	3 miles, 2f	Steeplechase
Champion Hurdle	Cheltenham, England	2 miles	Hurdle

*f = furlong (220yd); 8 furlongs = one mile

RECORD BREAKERS

ONLY THREE-TIME WINNER of the Grand National horse race in England is Red Rum, who won it in 1973, 1974, and 1977.

MOST WINS IN HORSE RACING is 8,833 in 40,350 races by US jockey Bill Shoemaker (born 1931) who rode his first winner in March 1949 and retired in 1990.

Winter Sports

Skiing

- There are two basic groups: alpine, which includes downhill and slalom racing, and nordic, which includes cross-country and ski jumping.

- Alpine skiing comes from the Alps; nordic skiing comes from northern Europe.

KIT
Skiers wear warm, wind- and waterproof clothing often in bright colours, so they can be seen clearly.

SKIS
Alpine skis vary in length depending on the event and the skier's own preference. Nordic skis are narrower and lighter than alpine skis.

Gloves

Alpine Skiing
RACING
There are four main types:
Downhill This is the fastest race, in which skiers follow a set route down the mountain.
Slalom A short race downhill with quick turns through a series of "gates" – 55–75 for men, 40–60 for women.
Giant slalom This has fewer, wider gates than a slalom and takes place over a longer course.
Super giant slalom This is like a downhill race with gates; it contains up to two jumps.

SKI POLES
Poles should be made of a strong, light material such as aluminium. The basket stops the pole from sinking too deep into the snow. Nordic ski poles are longer than alpine poles.

Ski pole

Goggles

BOOTS
Alpine boots are attached to the ski, but have a mechanism that allows them to come off in a fall. Nordic boots are like trainers. The heel lifts free with each stride.

Alpine boot

Basket

Giant-slalom course
The gates are wider on a giant-slalom course. Each flag is set on a pair of poles.

Open gate

Blind gate

Slalom course
A slalom gate is represented by a pair of flags that are alternately blue and red.

FREESTYLE
There are three main types:
Aerials Acrobatics performed in mid-air after taking off from a ramp, judged on style and technique.
Mogul racing Skiing down a course of large round bumps, judged on skill as well as time.
Ballet Performed to music on smooth slopes, judged on grace and skill.

Aerials

Nordic Skiing

CROSS-COUNTRY RACING
The cross-country course has no steep slopes or sharp turns, but is a test of stamina, with races ranging from 5 to 50km. Competitors start at 30-second intervals and time decides the placings.

Cross-country skier

Ski jumping
Two different ski towers, or ramps, are used from which skiers are expected to jump 70m and 90m respectively. Points are awarded for style as well as distance.

Take-off

Flight

The "table point" is at the end of the expected landing area.

Ski tower

The "norm point" is at the beginning of the expected landing area.

Landing

Inrun

Outrun area

OLYMPIC SKI AND SLED COMPETITIONS

Competition	Men	Women
Alpine ski racing		
Slalom	√	√
Giant slalom	√	√
Super giant slalom	√	√
Alpine combined (downhill and slalom)	√	√
Downhill	√	√
Freestyle		
Ballet	√	√
Moguls	√	√
Aerials	√	√
Nordic		
5km		√
10km	√	√
15km	√	√
30km	√	√
50km	√	
4 x 5km relay		√
4 x 10km relay	√	
Nordic combined		
Individual	√	
Team	√	
Ski jumping		
70m hill	√	
90m hill	√	
90m hill team	√	
Biathlon		
10km (M) / 7.5km (W)	√	√
20km (M) / 15km (W)	√	√
Relay 4 x 7.5km	√	
3 x 7.5km		√
Sled		
2-man bob	√	
4-man bob	√	
Single luge	√	√
Double luge	√	
Toboggan*	√	

*Held only on Cresta Run at St. Moritz, Switzerland (1928 and 1948).

OTHER NORDIC COMPETITIONS
Ski marathons Long-distance (40–150km) cross-country events with mass starts, also called "citizen racing".
Nordic combined Two-day event with ski jumping (70m hill) on the first day and cross-country (15km) on the second.
Relays Races between teams of four.
Biathlon Combination of cross-country skiing and rifle shooting. The skier carries his weapon on his back and stops regularly to shoot at targets, incurring time penalties for missing.

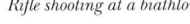

Rifle shooting at a biathlon

Car Skiing
To find the best position for skiing in special high speed events on smooth slopes, a skier practises on top of a fast-moving car.

SLED RACING

LUGE TOBOGGANING
A luge is a one- or two-person toboggan with no steering or brakes. It is ridden face-up in a sitting or lying position.

BOBSLEIGH RACING
Bobsleighs, for two or four men, have metal runners, steering, and brakes.

SKELETON TOBOGGANING
Competitors ride face-down on an open toboggan. There is only one major competition, the Cresta Run at St. Moritz, Switzerland.

SPEED SKATING

- Competitors race in pairs against the clock around an oval two-lane track, 400m in length.

- Competitors switch lanes each lap in a change-over zone.

- In short-track speed skating, a maximum of six competitors race around a 110-metre oval track. The first to finish is the winner.

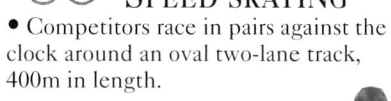

Competitors wear body-hugging suits to cut down air resistance.

Speed skates have a thin aluminium blade attached to a lightweight boot.

TRACK

Length of track: 400m

Width of lane: 4–5m

FIGURE SKATING

- Competitors perform routines to music containing compulsory movements and moves they choose themselves.

- A maximum of nine judges give marks for technical merit and artistic impression; 6.0 is the perfect score.

Top female skaters wear short fitted skirts or dresses.

KIT
Top male skaters often wear all-in-one bodysuits made of stretch material.

Figure skating usually takes place on adapted ice-hockey rinks.

RINK
Maximum length: 60m
Maximum width: 30m

FIGURE SKATE
A figure skate has a steel blade about 3mm wide. The bottom of the blade is concave to make two edges. Figures are skated on one or other of these edges.

Toe-rake helps in spinning and in certain jumps.

CURLING

- In curling, two four-a-side teams slide curling stones across the ice, aiming to get them as close as possible to the centre (tee) of a target area (house).

- Team-mates with brooms sweep the ice in front of the stones to change their speed and direction.

Curling

RECORD BREAKER
THREE CONSECUTIVE OLYMPIC GOLD MEDALS (1928–36) and ten consecutive world championships (1927–36) were won by Sonja Henie, a Norwegian figure skater. She then turned professional and made several Hollywood films featuring her grace and skills on ice.

SINGLES
Solo competitions, for men and women, have two parts: a short programme with compulsory moves and a long programme (freestyle).

Lutz jump

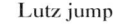

The skater increases her speed before attempting the jump.

She makes one turn, or two for a double lutz, in the air before landing.

The skater lifts one leg behind him, and holds it parallel to the ice.

Camel spin

PAIRS
Pair competitions are made up of two parts: a short programme and a free-skating programme.

A skating pair perform a high lift.

ICE DANCE
Ice-dance competitions have three parts: compulsory dances, original set pattern dance, and free dance. Couples choose their own music and movements in the free dance. During their routine, they must not separate more than five times, or for longer than five seconds. Lifts must not be made above shoulder-height.

Expressiveness is important in ice dancing.

OLYMPIC SKATING EVENTS

	Men	Women
Figure skating	√	√
Pairs	Together	
Ice dancing	Together	
Speed skating		
500m	√	√
1,000m	√	√
1500m	√	√
3,000m		√
5,000m	√	√
10,000m	√	
Short-track		
500m	√	√
1,000m	√	√
3,000m		√
5,000m	√	

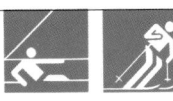

WHEELED SPORTS

MOTOR RACING

- Competitions are held for different types of car on a variety of tracks. Races are held around circuits, on roads, and on grass and dirt tracks.

FORMULA 1

- Grand Prix races take place on circuits.

- Drivers and car-makers aim to win points for the world championships.

RACE CIRCUIT

A Grand Prix circuit has corners and straights to test the drivers' car-handling skills. Above is a plan of the Suzuka circuit in Japan.

Straight

Spoon curve

S-curve

Start/Finish

GRAND PRIX CIRCUITS

Grand Prix	Circuit	Length (km)	Laps
Argentina	Buenos Aires	4.26	72
Austria	A1-Ring	4.32	71
Australia	Adelaide	3.78	81
Belgium	Spa-Francorchamps	6.94	44
Brazil	Interlagos	4.32	71
Canada	Gilles Villeneuve	4.43	69
France	Magny-Cours	4.25	72
Germany	Hockenheim	6.81	45
Great Britain	Silverstone	5.23	59
Hungary	Hungaroring	3.97	77
Italy	Monza	5.80	53
Japan	Suzuka	5.86	53
Luxembourg	Nürburgring	4.57	67
Monaco	Monte Carlo	3.33	78
San Marino	Imola (Italy)	5.04	61
Spain	Catalunya	4.75	65

FLAG SIGNALS

Flags are held out during the race. Each colour has its own meaning.

Chequered: end of race

Yellow: danger

Red and yellow stripes: oil on course

White: service car on track

Black: car must stop in pits

Red: all cars must stop

KIT

Motor-racing drivers wear a crash helmet and a thick, fire-resistant suit for protection in case of an accident.

Crash helmet

Face shield

Driving gloves

Heavy-duty racing suit

Driving shoes

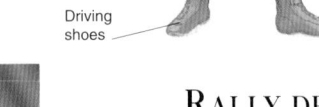

Smooth tyres called slicks for use in dry weather.

Body shell

Detachable steering wheel

Aerofoil pushes the car down on the track.

Roll-over bar

FORMULA 1 RACING CAR

These streamlined cars are made of lightweight materials to make them go as fast as possible.

INDYCAR RACING

- Most races take place in the USA, mainly on oval circuits.

- The annual championships are decided on points. The cars are similar to Formula One cars.

Turns bank at 9°

INDY 500

The most famous Indycar circuit is the Indianapolis, which is 4km long. The Indy 500 race is held over 200 laps of the circuit.

Pits area

Start/Finish

KARTING

- The simplest karts have a 100cc engine and no gearbox. The most powerful karts are like small racing cars and can reach speeds of 240 km/h (150 mph).

RALLY DRIVING

- In rally driving, strengthened saloon cars race against the clock, rather than each other. The route is divided into sections called "stages", with time-control points between them. Points are lost for exceeding time.

Rally cars are faster and stronger than ordinary cars.

DRAG RACING

- Races are held along straight 400m (¼ mile) tracks called drag strips.

- Cars race in pairs. They reach speeds of 485km/h (300mph), and need parachutes to slow down.

DRAGSTER

A dragster has a lightweight body, with big wheels that give good grip at the back, and smaller, lighter front wheels. The fastest dragsters are called top-fuellers.

Aerofoil

Powerful, supercharged engine

Rear slicks

Lightweight front wheels

RECENT FORMULA 1 WORLD CHAMPION DRIVERS

Year	Driver	Country of origin
1988	Ayrton Senna	Brazil
1989	Alain Prost	France
1990	Ayrton Senna	Brazil
1991	Ayrton Senna	Brazil
1992	Nigel Mansell	UK
1993	Alain Prost	France
1994	Michael Schumacher	Germany
1995	Michael Schumacher	Germany
1996	Damon Hill	UK
1997	Jacques Villeneuve	Canada
1998	Mika Hakkinen	Finland

RECORD BREAKERS

MOST FORMULA 1 WORLD DRIVERS' CHAMPIONSHIP WINS is five by Juan Manuel Fangio (1911–1995) of Argentina.

CLOSEST FINISH TO A WORLD CHAMPIONSHIP GRAND PRIX RACE is 0.014 seconds, when Ayrton Senna (1960-94) of Brazil, beat Nigel Mansell (born 1953) of UK.

LONGEST ANNUALLY HELD RALLY RACE is the Safari Rally, Kenya. The race has covered up to 6234km (3874 miles).

MOTORCYCLE SPORT

- There are a variety of competitions for different types of bike. They take place on circuits or cross-country tracks.

MOTORCYCLE RACING

- Grand Prix races take place on circuits.
- There are different classes for bikes of different engine sizes, and a class for sidecars.

RACING MOTORBIKE

The bikes are powerful machines designed for speed.

Streamlined plastic body

Light aluminium frame

CYCLE SPORTS

- Races range from track sprints held over 1,000m (1,094yd) to multi-stage road races lasting several weeks.
- The bicycles differ according to the type of race.

WORLD CHAMPIONSHIP MOTORCYCLE CLASSES

Motorcycle	Racing	Motocross
500cc	√	√
250cc	√	√
125cc	√	√
80cc	√	
Sidecar	√	√

RACING SIDECAR

A racing sidecar is a bike and sidecar moulded together to make one piece. The driver and passenger work together as a team. The passenger leans over behind the driver to help with cornering. The passenger platform may be attached to either side of the bike.

Racing sidecar

ROAD RACING

- Races are run on courses set along ordinary roads.
- In stage races, such as the Tour de France, each stage is a race in itself, and the overall winner is the one with the lowest aggregate time.

KIT

Bicycle riders wear long close-fitting shorts to prevent thighs chafing against the saddle, and a top that allows the body to breathe and soaks up sweat.

A helmet is compulsory.

TRACK RACING

- Races take place on hard tracks including tightly banked wooden indoor tracks and almost flat asphalt outdoor tracks. Some races are held on closed circuits (roads that have been closed to the public).

MOTOCROSS

- Motocross, also known as scrambling, is the "cross-country" branch of motorcycle racing.
- Races take place on tracks that include muddy slopes, grass, and bumps.

MOTOCROSS BIKE

These bikes are adapted to cope with rough ground.

Swinging arm allows vertical movement of wheel.

Mudguard

Chunky-tread tyres for gripping loose surfaces

OTHER MOTORCYCLE SPORT

Speedway Riders race over four laps of a dirt track. The bikes have no brakes or gearbox so riders slow down by sliding their machines through turns.

Trials Riders negotiate a natural course with obstacles such as boulders, fast-flowing water, loose rocks, and deep mud, and lose points for putting a foot down or stopping.

TYPES OF TRACK RACING

Points race Points are scored on each lap for crossing the line first, with double points on the last lap.

Sprint Riders spend most of the race jockeying for position before making a final dash for the line.

Individual pursuit Two riders start on opposite sides of the track, and the race is decided on time, or if one rider catches the other.

Team pursuit Similar to individual pursuit, but there are two teams of four riders. Only the times of the first three riders in each team are counted.

Italian pursuit For teams of up to five riders. The leading cyclist in each team drops out after each lap. The finishing time of the last rider of each team decides the race.

Devil-take-the-hindmost Last rider over the line at the end of each lap is eliminated.

Time trial Competitors ride on their own over a set distance from a standing start, and the rider with the fastest time wins.

OLYMPIC CYCLING EVENTS

	Men	Women
Track:		
Sprint	√	√
Time trial	√	
Pursuit	√	√
Team pursuit	√	
Points race	√	
Road:		
Individual	√	√

ROAD-RACING BICYCLE

The best bicycles are made of carbon tubing to save weight and are designed to be as streamlined as possible yet reliable and stable.

TOUR DE FRANCE

This famous race covers 3,400km in 24 one-day stages. Each year the route changes. The tour can even leave France and stretch over the border into neighbouring countries.

Tour de France route (1990)

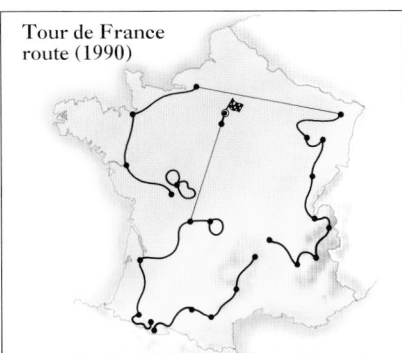

Colour codes
Colour-coded jerseys help spectators identify leading riders in the Tour de France.

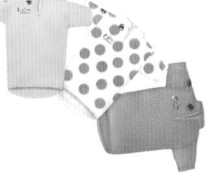

Yellow top is worn by the rider with the lowest overall time after each stage and by the ultimate winner of the Tour.

Polka-dot top is worn by the rider with most points from the climbing stages.

Green top worn by the rider with most points from sprints.

OFF-ROAD RACING

- Cyclocross takes place on cross-country courses, and competitors may carry their bikes across obstacles.
- Mountain-bike racing includes several different styles, including trials and cross-country racing.

A cyclist carrying his bike across a river during a cyclocross race.

TARGET SPORTS

BOWLS

- Individuals or teams roll bowls, called woods, along a flat, smooth green, aiming at a target ball, or jack.

- A point is scored for each bowl that is nearer to the jack than any opponent's wood.

WOOD

Woods can be made of wood, rubber, or a composition material.

They are weighted, or biased, on one side so they curve when rolled.

Jack

ARCHERY

- Competitors use a bow to fire a certain number of arrows at targets set at different distances.

- The closer to the centre of the target an arrow lands, the higher the score.

BOW AND ARROWS

The bow is usually made of fibreglass. The arrow shafts are made of aluminium or carbon.

DARTS

- Opponents take it in turns to throw three darts at a board from a distance of 2.4m.

- Each player usually starts with a score of 501 and must reduce it to the exact score of zero by finishing with a double or an inner bull.

DARTBOARD

The board is divided into different scoring sections, indicated by the numbers on the outer ring. Certain areas count double or treble.

Bull

Dart   Treble ring   Double ring

SNOOKER

- Players score points by "potting" balls. A cue is used to hit a cue ball against a red or coloured ball, causing it to fall into a pocket.

TABLE

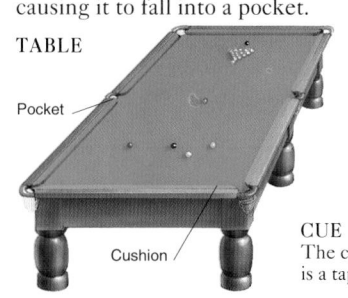

Pocket

Cushion

BOULES

- In boules, which is similar to bowls, metal balls are thrown at a small wooden target ball.

- The game can be played on any bare stretch of land, but is usually played on sandy ground.

Boule

TENPIN BOWLING

- This is an indoor sport in which players roll a ball down an alley, aiming to knock down the pins.

- Points are scored for each pin knocked down. Bonuses are given for knocking down all ten pins in one go (a strike) or two goes (a spare).

BOWLING TECHNIQUES

In boules, the boule is lobbed.

In bowls, the wood must be rolled along the ground.

PINS
The pins are made from maple wood covered with plastic.

LANE
The pins are arranged in a triangular pattern at one end of the lane, which is made of plastic or wood.

TENPIN BALL
The bowling ball has three holes for the thumb and two middle fingers.

Ball made of hard rubber or plastic

TARGET
There are five coloured rings, each with an inner and an outer part. Scores range from one point for the outer white, to ten points for the inner gold.

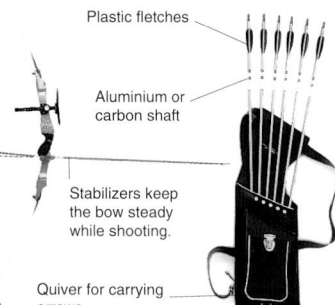

Plastic fletches

Aluminium or carbon shaft

Stabilizers keep the bow steady while shooting.

Quiver for carrying arrows

Straw butt

Bull's-eye

Paper target face

OLYMPIC ARCHERY QUALIFYING DISTANCES		
	Men	Women
30m	√	√
50m	√	√
60m		√
70m	√	√
90m	√	

SHOOTING

- Rifles, pistols, and shotguns are used in shooting sports. The size of the target varies with the weapon and distance.

- Pistol shooting includes rapid-fire pistol shooting, in which 5 targets are exposed for only 4–8 seconds, and free pistol shooting in which competitors fire at a fixed target.

- Shotgun is firing with a double-barrelled gun at saucer-shaped targets released randomly from a spring-catapult.

RIFLE SHOOTING POSITIONS

Standing

Kneeling

Prone

OLYMPIC SHOOTING EVENTS		
	Men	Women
Free pistol	√	
Rapid-fire pistol	√	
Air pistol	√	√
Sport pistol		√
Free rifle – prone	√	
– 3 positions	√	
Air rifle	√	√
Running target	√	
Standard rifle		√
Shotgun – Skeet	√	
– Trap	√	
– Double trap	√	√

POOL

- One player tries to pot balls 1–7 (or colours) and then the black 8-ball to win, while the other player pots balls 9–15 (or stripes) and then black.

Black ball (7 points)

Fifteen red balls (1 point each)

Pink ball (6 points)

Blue ball (5 points)

Green ball (3 points)

Cue ball

Brown ball (4 points)

Yellow ball (2 points)

Chalk is rubbed on the tip of the cue to improve contact with the cue ball.

Seven colours

One black

Seven stripes

A pool table is smaller than a snooker table.

One white cue ball

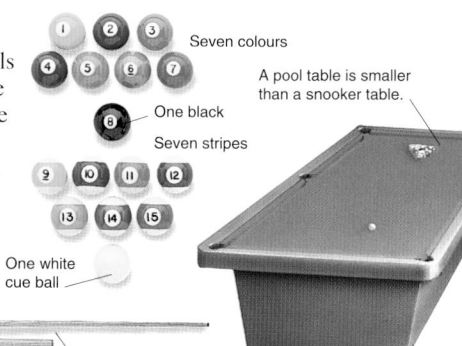

CUE
The cue, used in both snooker and pool, is a tapered stick with a leather tip.

Two-piece cue

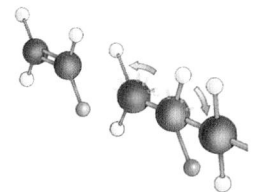

SCIENCE AND TECHNOLOGY

From the atom to the latest in information technology, this
section offers a wealth of scientific facts and figures.

Matter • Atoms • Periodic Table • Energy
Forces and Machines • Electricity and Magnetism • Light and Colour
Sound • Electronics • Computers • Mathematics • Weights and Measures
Time • Engines • Space and Time • Natural Science
Physical Science • Weapons

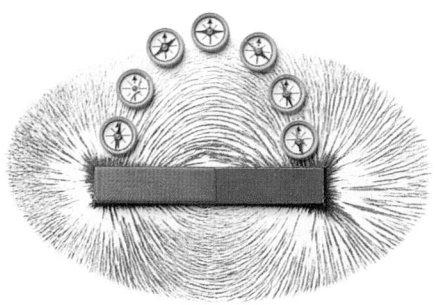

MATTER

EVERYTHING IS MADE up of matter. It can be a solid, such as wood or iron, a liquid, such as water or oil, or a gas, such as air. Heat or pressure can change matter from one state into another.

Lead: solid

Glass: transparent solid

Terrarium, containing many types of matter

Droplets of water condensed from vapour

STATES OF MATTER

Matter exists in three basic forms, called states, depending on how their atoms and molecules (see p.222) are arranged.

GAS

A gas is a substance that does not have a fixed volume but fills all the space it occupies. Gas particles are not bound together and move fast and freely in all directions.

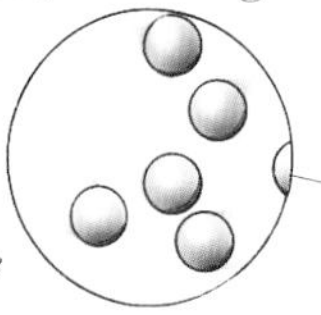

Gas particles, free to move around

LIQUID

A liquid has a fixed volume but can change shape to fit the space it occupies. Its particles are in contact with each other but can move around with some freedom.

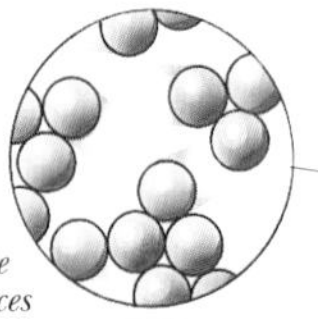

Liquid particles, able to move short distances

SOLID

A solid is a substance with a definite size and shape. A solid's particles are tightly linked by strong bonds, making a firm structure.

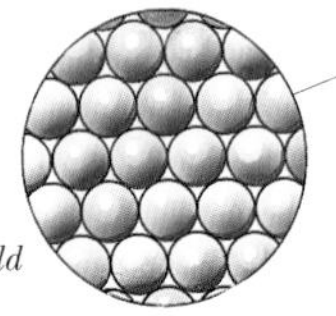

Solid particles, held in a rigid pattern

THREE IN ONE

Water is one substance we often find in its different states.

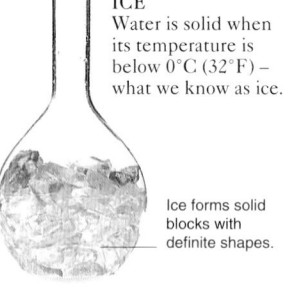

ICE
Water is solid when its temperature is below 0°C (32°F) – what we know as ice.

Ice forms solid blocks with definite shapes.

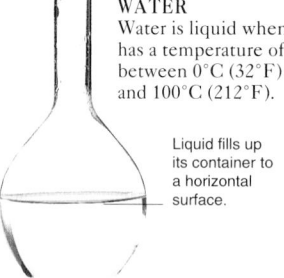

WATER
Water is liquid when it has a temperature of between 0°C (32°F) and 100°C (212°F).

Liquid fills up its container to a horizontal surface.

STEAM
Water turns to steam, a gas, when it has a temperature of more than 100°C (212°F).

Liquid turns to gas.

CHANGING STATES

Evaporation and condensation
Particles can free themselves from the body of a liquid (evaporation). Above the boiling point, all of the liquid becomes gas. When the gas cools, it becomes a liquid (condenses) again.

Freezing and melting
A liquid becomes a solid (freezes) below a temperature called its freezing point. It becomes a liquid again (melts) if the temperature rises above the freezing point.

Sublimation
Some substances, such as carbon dioxide, will change from a solid to a gas when heated, without becoming liquid in between. This is sublimation. The reverse process, from a gas to a solid, is also called sublimation.

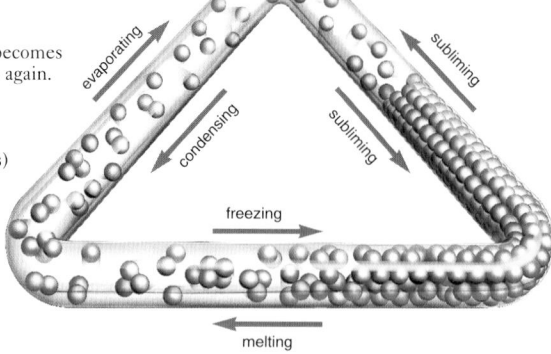

Changes of state

evaporating

condensing

subliming

subliming

freezing

melting

TYPES OF MIXTURE

There are two main types of mixture: colloids and solutions. In a solution, two or more substances are broken down into individual atoms or molecules. A colloid is a mixture of larger particles of one substance, distributed in another.

Emulsion
Paint is an emulsion of oil particles dispersed in another liquid, water.

Gel
Hair gel is composed of particles of oil suspended in a solid.

Foam
Shaving foam is composed of bubbles of gas suspended in liquid.

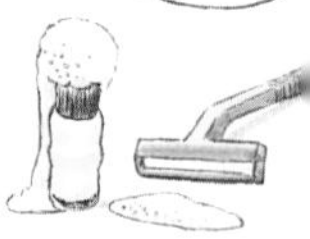

Mist
Steam from a kettle is a mist of liquid particles suspended in a gas.

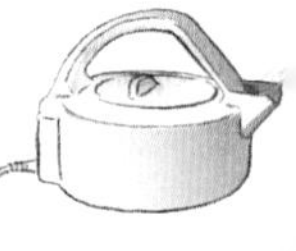

Smoke
A bonfire gives off a cloud of smoke composed of solid matter suspended in air.

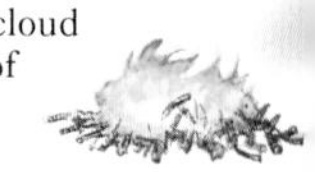

Solution
A solvent, such as water, makes a solution by dissolving another substance, the solute.

WEB FEAT
Some of the threads in a spider's web are stronger than a steel wire of the same width.

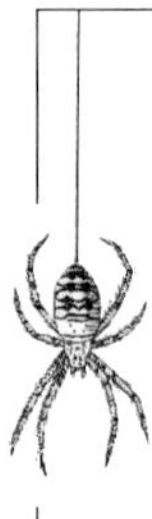

LIQUID GLASS
Over long periods of time, glass behaves like a liquid. Ancient Roman glassware has been found slightly flattened.

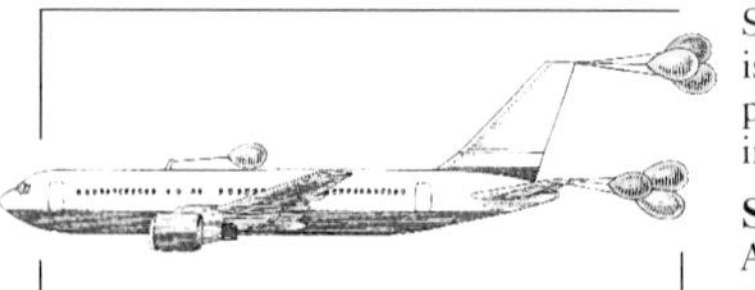

AIR SPEED
Each of the billions of air molecules that fill a balloon travels at the average speed of a jet plane.

COMPOUNDS

Elements that exist on their own are rare in the natural world. Most substances are made up of two or more elements bonded together by chemical reaction to form a compound. When iron and sulphur are heated together, a chemical reaction bonds their atoms into a solid structure.

MIXTURE

Iron filings and sulphur

Iron filings and sulphur can be mixed up together, but their atoms will not be chemically bound unless a chemical reaction takes place.

COMPOUND

A new substance, iron sulphide

When iron and sulphur are heated together, their atoms bind to form a new compound of iron sulphide. It is a completely new substance.

PHYSICAL PROPERTIES

There is a wide variety of matter, with a range of different properties. These properties help to identify the substance, and also determine to what use it can be put.

Viscosity
Viscous matter is liquid that does not flow easily. Friction between molecules makes a liquid viscous. Honey is highly viscous, whereas water is not.

Ductility and malleability
Ductile matter can be drawn out into a wire. Malleable matter can be moulded or beaten into other shapes.

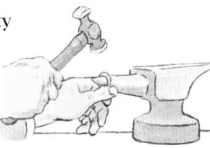

Elasticity
Elastic matter can be stretched or squeezed and returns to its original size and shape.

Density
Two objects of the same size may not have the same mass, so they will not weigh the same. The denser of the two will weigh more, because it has more matter packed into the same space.

Dense tip

Conductivity
Matter that transfers heat and electricity is conductive. Many solids have a close-knit molecular structure that causes them to be cold to the touch, because it conducts heat away quickly.

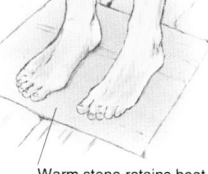

Warm stone retains heat.

ANTIMATTER

For every type of particle that exists, such as the electron (see p.222), there is a corresponding antiparticle. Just as matter consists of particles, antimatter consists of antiparticles. If matter and antimatter are brought together, they will violently destroy each other, to become energy.

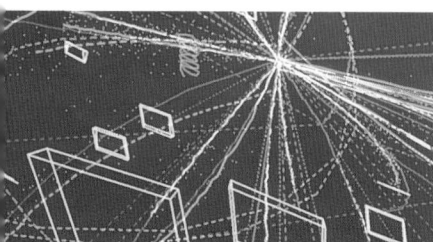

False-colour image of subatomic particles

COMBUSTION (BURNING)

A substance burns when it reacts with oxygen, releasing heat. A candle is made from carbon and hydrogen. These elements burn to form carbon dioxide and water.

Candle flame
A candle flame contains tiny particles of carbon. As they burn, they become so hot that they glow bright yellow.

Burning food
Food dissolved in your blood "burns" as it reacts with oxygen. The heat released provides you with the energy you need to live.

PLASTIC

Most synthetic plastics are made from chemicals in oil in a chemical process called polymerization. To make PVC, small molecules of chloroethene polymerize to form a long chain, or polymer.

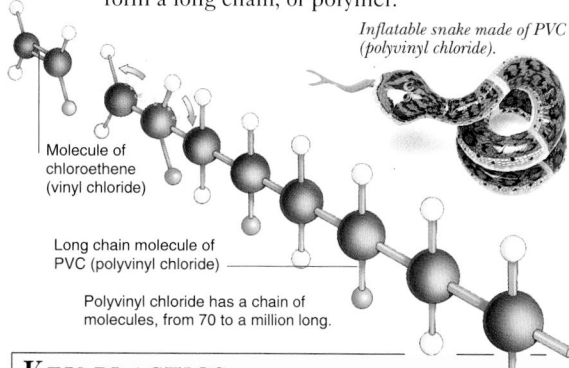

Inflatable snake made of PVC (polyvinyl chloride).

Molecule of chloroethene (vinyl chloride)

Long chain molecule of PVC (polyvinyl chloride)

Polyvinyl chloride has a chain of molecules, from 70 to a million long.

KEY PLASTICS

Name	Uses
Polystyrene	Packaging, cups, bowls, ceiling tiles
Polyester	Artificial fibres, fibreglass
Polythene	Carrier bags, bottles, food wrapping
Nylon	Artificial fibres, carpets, fishing nets
PVC (Polyvinyl chloride)	Raincoats, garden hoses, guttering
Polyurethane	Plastic packaging foam, adhesives
Polymethyl methacrylate (perspex)	Substitute for glass

DEGRADABILITY

In time, most matter will degrade naturally, breaking down into simpler substances. Non-degradable pollution will remain in rivers, seas, and the atmosphere.

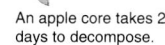

An apple core takes 20 days to decompose.

Plastic can take more than 100 years to decompose.

Glass takes more than 4,000 years to decompose.

SAVOURY SEA

1cu metre (220 gallons) of typical sea water contains 23cu cm (1.4cu inches) of salt (sodium chloride). Sea water also contains other dissolved salts.

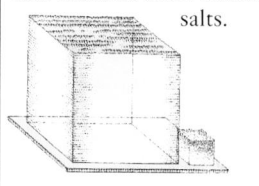

ACIDS AND ALKALIS

Acids are substances that dissolve in water to form sharp-tasting solutions. Alkalis dissolve in water to form soapy solutions. Both acids and alkalis can be corrosive. The strength of an acid or alkali is measured by its pH.

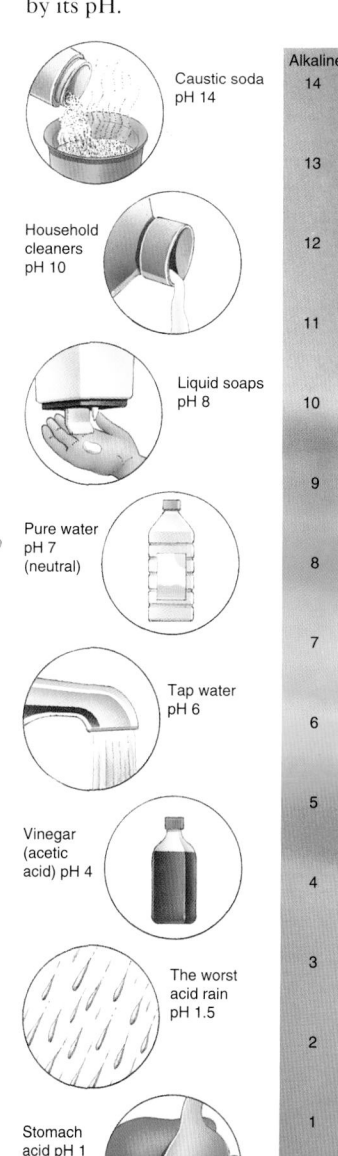

Caustic soda pH 14

Household cleaners pH 10

Liquid soaps pH 8

Pure water pH 7 (neutral)

Tap water pH 6

Vinegar (acetic acid) pH 4

The worst acid rain pH 1.5

Stomach acid pH 1

Alkaline
14
13
12
11
10
9
8
7
6
5
4
3
2
1
0
Acidic

ATOMS

EVERYTHING AROUND YOU is made up of tiny particles called atoms. Different atoms make up different kinds of matter.

ELEMENTS

Elements are substances made up of one kind of atom only. One element is fluorine.

INSIDE THE FLUORINE ATOM

If a fluorine atom could be cut open, it might look like this.

The illustration below distorts the real sizes of the atomic components – the nucleus is very large compared to electrons, and electrons orbit at a great distance from the nucleus.

Nucleus
The central core of the atom is called the nucleus. It consists of protons and neutrons. The nucleus makes up 99.9% of an atom's mass, but only a tiny part of its volume.

Inner electron orbital

Electrons
Electrons are negatively charged particles. They surround the nucleus in regions called orbitals.

Ions
When an atom loses or gains an electron, it becomes an ion. If it loses an electron, it becomes positively charged and is called a cation. If it gains an electron, it becomes negatively charged and is called an anion.

Neutrons
Neutrons are particles in a nucleus. They have no electric charge. They cling to the protons and to each other, keeping the nucleus together.

Protons
Protons are particles in a nucleus that carry a positive electric charge. The number of protons in an atom is called its atomic number. Fluorine has nine.

ATOM FACTS

- Quarks are named after a word that appears in the novel *Finnegan's Wake* by Irish writer James Joyce (1882–1941).

- Some atomic isotopes are highly dangerous – if stored in large enough quantities, a nuclear reaction can occur.

- In 1995 physicists cooled several hundred atoms to a few billionths of a degree above absolute zero (-273°C), the lowest possible temperature. The atoms all became one super atom, known as a Bose-Einstein condensate.

ISOTOPES

Some atoms of the same element may have different numbers of neutrons. These different kinds of atoms are called isotopes. These two nuclei are from isotopes of fluorine. Fluorine–19 has 10 neutrons, while fluorine–18 has 9 neutrons.

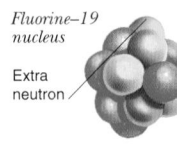

Fluorine–19 nucleus

Extra neutron

Fluorine–18 nucleus

INTO THE ATOM

What would happen if you could tear this book in half, and then in half again and again – until you broke it down into the tiniest particles possible?

The book becomes...

scraps of paper, which become...

wood pulp fibres, which become...

molecules of cellulose, which become...

atoms of the different substances that made up the molecules, which can be divided into...

protons, neutrons and electrons. Protons and neutrons are each made up of...

quarks.

MOLECULES

There are only about 100 kinds of atom, but there are millions of different compounds. Most compounds are made of particular combinations of atoms joined together, called molecules.

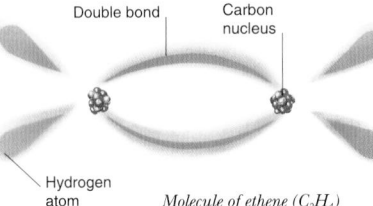

Double bond

Carbon nucleus

Hydrogen atom

Molecule of ethene (C₂H₄)

Quarks
Protons and neutrons are made up of even smaller particles, called quarks. There are two main types of quark. Up quarks have a positive charge. Down quarks have a negative one. Neutrons have one Up and two Down quarks. Protons have two Up and one Down.

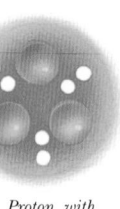

Proton, with two Up quarks and one Down

FORCES OF ATTRACTION

If an atom's nucleus were the size of a sports stadium, some of its electrons would revolve at the distance of a low-orbiting satellite.

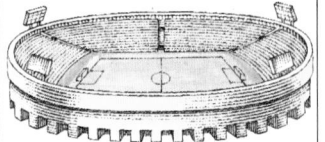

ATOMIC BONDING

Atoms join to form molecules. They do this by bonding (sticking together). There are two main types of bonding: ionic and covalent. In each case, the electrons form the bond.

IONIC BOND

In an ionic bond, atoms lose or gain electrons to form ions of opposite charge. These opposite charges attract each other, and bond the two ions together.

Fluorine atom

Electron

Lithium atom loses electron to become a positive ion, or cation.

Fluorine atom gains electron to become a negative ion, or anion.

Ions attract each other to form a molecule of lithium fluoride.

Molecule of lithium fluoride

COVALENT BOND

A covalent bond occurs where electrons are shared between atoms. This sharing keeps the atoms together. One or two, or occasionally three, nuclei are attracted to the same electrons at once. Water and nitrogen gas are substances with covalent bonds.

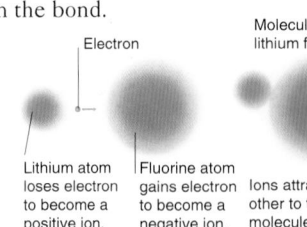

Hydrogen atom

Fluorine atom

Shared electron

Both fluorine and hydrogen atoms need one electron to become stable.

Atoms form a covalent bond, becoming stable as they do so.

RADIOACTIVITY

Large nuclei can be unstable, and they can decay. When they do, charged particles are lost from them. This process is called radioactivity. Most elements have unstable forms, called radioisotopes. Some occur naturally, others are made in nuclear reactors. The most radioactive substances have the highest number of particles in their nuclei. Uranium has 238.

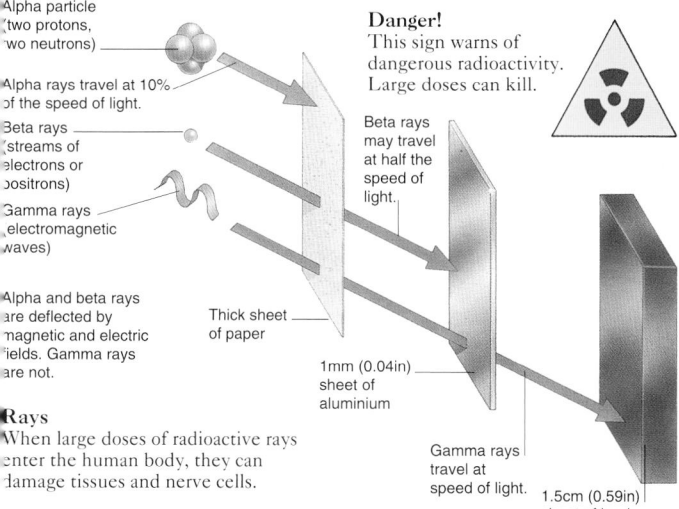

Alpha particle (two protons, two neutrons)

Alpha rays travel at 10% of the speed of light.

Beta rays (streams of electrons or positrons)

Gamma rays (electromagnetic waves)

Alpha and beta rays are deflected by magnetic and electric fields. Gamma rays are not.

Danger!
This sign warns of dangerous radioactivity. Large doses can kill.

Beta rays may travel at half the speed of light.

Thick sheet of paper

1mm (0.04in) sheet of aluminium

Gamma rays travel at speed of light.

1.5cm (0.59in) sheet of lead

Rays
When large doses of radioactive rays enter the human body, they can damage tissues and nerve cells.

RADIATION FACTS

- Levels of radiation can be measured with a device called a Geiger counter. A probe filled with gas at low pressure triggers an electric pulse, heard as a click, when radiation is near.

- About 200 million gamma rays pass through the body every hour from soil and buildings.

- All-out nuclear war would force people to live underground for months, and possibly years.

- Exposure to gamma rays can kill bacteria in food. This process, called irradiation, keeps the food fresh for longer, but many people are afraid of its possible long-term health risks.

NUCLEAR REACTIONS

There are two kinds of nuclear reaction – fission and fusion. Both are a release of the "binding energy" that keeps the nucleus of an atom together. Atoms are called "stable" if they have a lot of binding energy, "unstable" if they have little.

NUCLEAR FISSION
If a neutron hits the nucleus of the unstable element uranium–235, the nucleus splits into two lighter nuclei. More neutrons shoot off to bombard other nuclei in a chain reaction. Energy is released. In nuclear power stations, this energy is used to generate electricity.

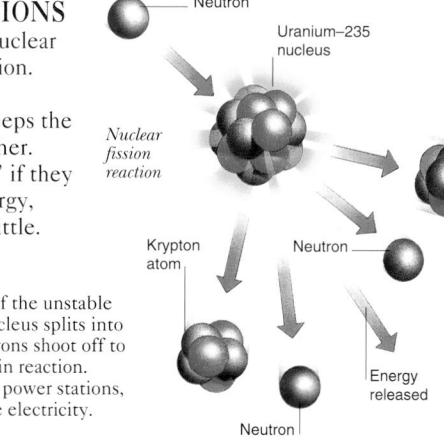

Neutron

Uranium–235 nucleus

Nuclear fission reaction

Krypton atom

Neutron

Neutron

Helium nucleus

Barium atom

Energy released

Energy released

SUBATOMIC PARTICLES

Many types of particle other than electrons, protons, and neutrons are known to exist, and are generally referred to as subatomic particles. More and more particles are being discovered, through the use of particle accelerators, and physicists face the task of making sense of them all. One of the greatest puzzles concerns neutrinos – particles produced during nuclear reactions in the Sun. Neutrinos are elusive particles, and strange experiments are performed to detect them and measure their mass.

USES OF RADIATION

ALPHA RADIATION
Alpha rays are charged particles of two protons and two neutrons. Nuclear batteries, which give off harmless alpha rays, power heart pacemakers, because they last much longer than normal ones.

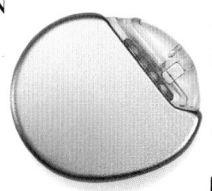

Alpha rays from the radio-isotope plutonium power heart pacemakers.

Heart pacemaker

BETA RADIATION
During radioactive decay, a neutron can change into a proton, and vice versa. Streams of electrons or positrons are given off in this process – these are beta rays. The isotope carbon–14, found in all living things, produces beta radiation as it decays. Scientists can date once-living things by seeing how much carbon–14 has decayed. This is called carbon dating.

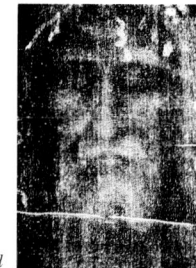

Once thought to be the 2,000-year-old death shroud of Jesus Christ, the cloth was carbon dated and found to be only 600 years old.

The Turin shroud

GAMMA RADIATION
Gamma radiation, an electromagnetic wave, travels at the speed of light, but with much more energy. These waves, like light or radio waves, are given off when a nucleus has too much energy. Not often found on their own, they are given off with alpha and beta particles.

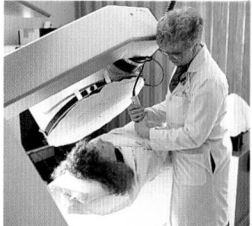

Person undergoes radiotherapy (cancer treatment)

Cobalt–60 produces gamma radiation. Here, it is being used to kill cancerous body cells. It can also be used to sterilize medical instruments.

KEY HALF-LIVES
The half-life of an element is the time it takes for half its atoms to decay into other materials. A strongly radioactive substance has a short half-life – it decays quickly.

Isotope	Half-life	Type of decay	Use
Radium–221	30 sec	Alpha and gamma	Cancer therapy
Iron (Fe–59)	45 days	Beta and gamma	Testing car parts
Carbon–14	5570 yrs	Beta and gamma	Carbon dating
Uranium–238	500 million yrs	Alpha and gamma	Nuclear energy

Hydrogen isotope deuterium

Nuclear fusion reaction

Hydrogen nuclei fuse

Hydrogen isotope tritium

Neutron released

NUCLEAR FUSION
When the nuclei of lighter elements are forced together they combine and form a new, heavier nucleus, releasing energy. In the Sun, hydrogen atoms fuse together to make helium, and produce the Sun's heat. Scientists hope to find a safe way of creating fusion on Earth.

MARIE CURIE
French scientist Marie Curie (1867–1934) pioneered the study of radiation. A flask that she used in her experiments turned blue after constant exposure to radioactive ores.

COLD ENERGY
In 1989, Stanley Pons and Martin Fleischmann claimed to have succeeded in making fusion reactions at room temperature. This claim has since been shown to be false.

PERIODIC TABLE

THE ELEMENTS THAT MAKE UP all of the matter around us can be arranged into a table. The table is arranged in vertical columns, called groups, and in horizontal rows, called periods. The complete table includes elements that do not occur naturally, but have been made artificially.

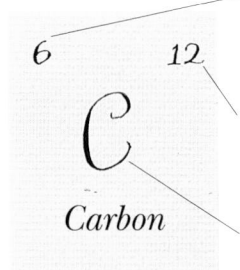

Carbon–12 nucleus

6 12

C

Carbon

Atomic number
The number of protons in the nucleus defines what element a particular atom is. This is the atomic number.

Atomic mass
Carbon occurs with 6, 7, 8, and 9 neutrons in its nucleus, in addition to its 6 protons, giving it a mass of between 12 and 15.

Chemical symbol
Each element has a symbol; it is used for identification in chemical equations.

Proton – total number is atomic number

Neutron – with protons, makes atomic mass

TABLE PATTERNS
We can tell a lot about an element from its position on the periodic table. Elements situated in the same area behave in the same way.

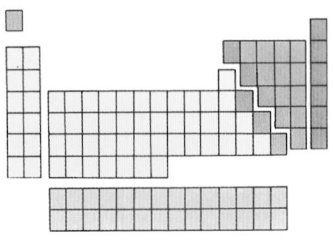

Metals
Metals are mostly solids, and are all good conductors of heat and electricity.

Non-metals
Non-metals are not good conductors of heat or electricity, and can be solid, liquid, or gas.

Metalloids
Metalloids, also called semi-metals, are non-metals that behave like metals in some ways, or in some conditions.

Noble gases
Noble gases are also called inert gases because they are not reactive. They are all gas at room temperature.

Lanthanides and actinides
These elements are separated out from the table to give it a regular shape.

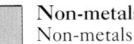

GROUPS AND PERIODS

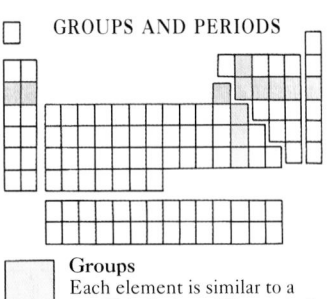

Groups
Each element is similar to a handful of others. The periodic table is arranged so that similar elements are put together in vertical columns, or groups.

Periods
Elements are arranged into horizontal rows, or periods. The electron arrangement around the nucleus (see p.222) determines the period's length.

1 1		
H		Elements on handwritten cards were known in Mendeleyev's time.
Hydrogen		

3 7	**4 9**
Li	*Be*
Lithium	*Beryllium*

11 23	**12 24**
Na	*Mg*
Sodium	*Magnesium*

19 39	**20 40**
K	*Ca*
Potassium	*Calcium*

37 85	**38 88**
Rb	*Sr*
Rubidium	*Strontium*

55 133	**56 137**
Cs	*Ba*
Caesium	*Barium*

87 223	**88 226**
Fr	Ra
Francium	*Radium*

PERIODIC PIONEER
The first person to arrange the elements into the shape of a table was Russian chemist, Dmitri Mendeleyev (1834–1907). In 1869, he made cards for each element, and laid them out according to the property of each element. The cards formed the periodic table.

SODIUM
There are about 18,000,000,000,000 tonnes of this element in the world's oceans; most of it is in a solution of sodium chloride.

RUBIDIUM
Rubidium is typical of elements in its group. It reacts violently with water or even air, catching fire immediately. Its salts give a red flame when heated.

21 45	**22 48**	**23 51**	**24 52**	**25 55**	**26 56**	**27**
Sc	*Ti*	*V*	*Cr*	*Mn*	*Fe*	*Co*
Scandium	*Titanium*	*Vanadium*	*Chromium*	*Manganese*	*Iron*	*Cobalt*

39 89	**40 91**	**41 93**	**42 96**	**43 97**	**44 101**	**45**
Y	*Zr*	*Nb*	*Mo*	Tc	*Ru*	*Rh*
Yttrium	*Zirconium*	*Niobium*	*Molybdenum*	*Technetium*	*Ruthenium*	*Rhodium*

57 139	**72 180**	**73 181**	**74 184**	**75 187**	**76 190**	**77 19**
La	Hf	*Ta*	*W*	Re	*Os*	*Ir*
Lanthanum	*Hafnium*	*Tantalum*	*Tungsten*	*Rhenium*	*Osmium*	*Iridium*

89 227	**104 260**	**105 262**	**106 263**	**107 262**	**108 265**	**109 26**
Ac	Db	Jl	Rf	Bh	Hn	Mt
Actinium	*Dubnium*	*Joliotum*	*Rutherfordium*	*Bohrium*	*Hahnium*	*Meitnerium*

CAESIUM
The nucleus of this element can be made to vibrate at an extremely reliable rate – 9,192,631,770 times every second. Caesium is used in atomic clocks, which are accurate to one second in thousands of years.

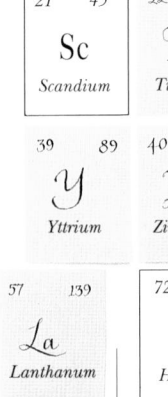

Lanthanides

58 140	**59 141**	**60 142**	**61 145**	**62 152**	**63 153**	**64**
Ce	Pr	Nd	Pm	Sm	Eu	Gd
Cerium	*Praseodymium*	*Neodymium*	*Promethium*	*Samarium*	*Europium*	*Gadolinium*

Actinides

90 232	**91 231**	**92 238**	**93 237**	**94 244**	**95 243**	**96 2**
Th	Pa	*U*	Np	Pu	Am	Cm
Thorium	*Protactinium*	*Uranium*	*Neptunium*	*Plutonium*	*Americium*	*Curium*

URANIUM
There are two main types, or isotopes, of uranium. Uranium–238 (with 92 protons and 146 neutrons) accounts for 99% of all uranium. The isotope that is useful in nuclear reactors, uranium–235 (with 92 protons and 143 neutrons), accounts for only about 1%.

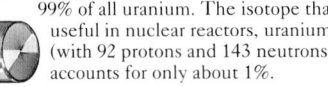

TUNGSTEN
Tungsten has the highest boiling point of all the elements. It boils at a temperature of 6,200°C (11,190°F), which makes it useful for filaments in electric light bulbs. These temperatures would melt most of the other elements.

ABUNDANT ELEMENTS

The most abundant elements in the Earth's crust (by mass), in elemental or compound form

Element	Abundance (%)
Oxygen	49
Silicon	26
Aluminium	7
Iron	4
Calcium	3

FLUORINE

Fluorine is very reactive – a typical property of the elements in its group. It is often added to water supplies and to toothpaste in the form of fluoride ions (fluorine atoms with an extra electron).

MERCURY

Used in thermometers, mercury is the only metal that is liquid at room temperature. It is very poisonous, and affects mental health. The phrase "mad as a hatter" arose because hatters, who used mercury, often went mad.

ELEMENT RECORDS

RAREST METAL
is Rhodium. Just 3 tonnes are produced each year, compared with 1,500 tonnes of gold.

MOST COMMON ELEMENT
in the Universe is hydrogen; the next is helium.

NITROGEN

Nitrogen accounts for over 75% of the Earth's atmosphere and is essential to plants and animals. It is an ingredient in fertilizers, and plants need it to help them grow.

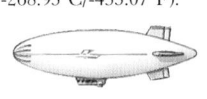

ELEMENT FACTS

• In 1994, elements 104–109 were renamed by an international commission. Disputes over who had discovered them first had led to a temporary system of naming by their atomic number.

HELIUM
The lowest possible temperature is 0K (-273.16°C/-459.69°F). Helium has the lowest boiling point of any element: 4.23K (-268.93°C/-453.07°F).

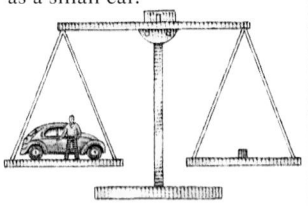

• The element dysprosium is named after the Greek word *dysprositos*, which means "difficult to obtain".

• Helium was discovered by analyzing light from the Sun. Its name comes from *helios*, the Greek word for Sun.

HEAVY METAL

The densest element is osmium; a cube 33x33x33cm (13x13x13in) weighs as much as a small car.

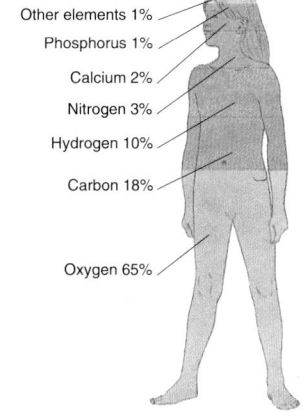

BODY ELEMENTS

Many elements are essential to the human body. Minute amounts of certain elements, called trace elements, are important for health.

Other elements 1%
Phosphorus 1%
Calcium 2%
Nitrogen 3%
Hydrogen 10%
Carbon 18%
Oxygen 65%

Element tiles

2 · 4 He Helium

| 5 · 11 B Boron | 6 · 12 C Carbon | 7 · 14 N Nitrogen | 8 · 16 O Oxygen | 9 · 19 F Fluorine | 10 · 20 Ne Neon |

| 13 · 27 Al Aluminium | 14 · 28 Si Silicon | 15 · 31 P Phosphorus | 16 · 32 S Sulphur | 17 · 35.5 Cl Chlorine | 18 · 40 Ar Argon |

| 28 · 59 Ni Nickel | 29 · 63.5 Cu Copper | 30 · 65 Zn Zinc | 31 · 69 Ga Gallium | 32 · 74 Ge Germanium | 33 · 75 As Arsenic | 34 · 79 Se Selenium | 35 · 80 Br Bromine | 36 · 84 Kr Krypton |

| 46 · 106 Pd Palladium | 47 · 108 Ag Silver | 48 · 112 Cd Cadmium | 49 · 115 In Indium | 50 · 119 Sn Tin | 51 · 122 Sb Antimony | 52 · 128 Te Tellurium | 53 · 127 I Iodine | 54 · 132 Xe Xenon |

| 78 · 195 Pt Platinum | 79 · 197 Au Gold | 80 · 201 Hg Mercury | 81 · 204 Tl Thallium | 82 · 207 Pb Lead | 83 · 209 Bi Bismuth | 84 · 209 Po Polonium | 85 · 210 At Astatine | 86 · 222 Rn Radon |

PLUTONIUM

If the artificial element plutonium–239 is not produced and stored in quantities of less than 300g (0.66lb), a spontaneous nuclear reaction begins, and dangerous amounts of energy are released.

SILICON

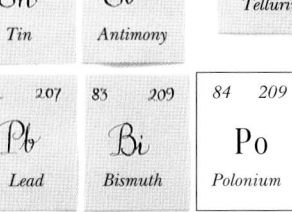

Pure silicon, a semiconductor, is used in electronic devices to provide a base for minute integrated circuits.

Lanthanide/actinide tiles

| 65 · 159 Tb Terbium | 66 · 164 Dy Dysprosium | 67 · 165 Ho Holmium | 68 · 167 Er Erbium | 69 · 169 Tm Thulium | 70 · 174 Yb Ytterbium | 71 · 175 Lu Lutetium |

| 97 · 247 Bk Berkelium | 98 · 251 Cf Californium | 99 · 254 Es Einsteinium | 100 · 257 Fm Fermium | 101 · 258 Md Mendelevium | 102 · 255 No Nobelium | 103 · 256 Lr Lawrencium |

TECHNETIUM

This element does not occur naturally, and was the first of many elements to be made artificially, in nuclear reactions. It is used to some extent in medical diagnosis.

IODINE

Once prepared from seaweed, iodine is essential to the human diet. It turns into a violet vapour when heated.

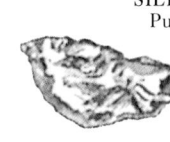

HEAVY ELEMENTS

Uranium (atomic number 92) is the element with the heaviest atoms that exist naturally on Earth. Since 1940 several heavier – transuranium – elements have been produced in laboratories.

Element	Atomic number	Year produced
Neptunium	93	1940
Curium	96	1944
Californium	98	1950
Fermium	100	1952
Nobelium	102	1958
Lawrencium	103	1961
Element 107	107	1976
Element 108	108	1984
Element 109	109	1985
Element 110	110	1994
Element 111	111	1994
Element 112	112	1996

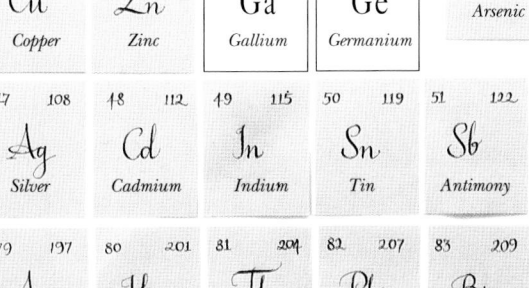

ENERGY

ENERGY AND FORCES constantly change the world. Energy takes many forms – the only visible one is light energy – and people have built many types of machine to convert and control all its forms.

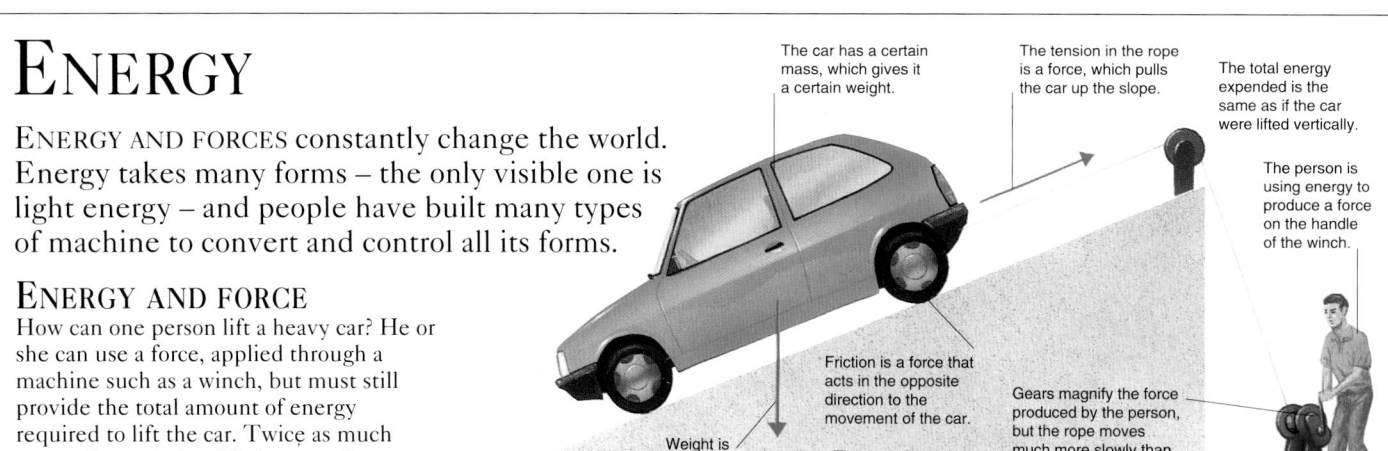

The car has a certain mass, which gives it a certain weight.

The tension in the rope is a force, which pulls the car up the slope.

The total energy expended is the same as if the car were lifted vertically.

The person is using energy to produce a force on the handle of the winch.

Friction is a force that acts in the opposite direction to the movement of the car.

Gears magnify the force produced by the person, but the rope moves much more slowly than the winch handle.

Weight is a force.

The ramp is a machine.

ENERGY AND FORCE
How can one person lift a heavy car? He or she can use a force, applied through a machine such as a winch, but must still provide the total amount of energy required to lift the car. Twice as much energy is needed to lift the car twice as high, or if the car is twice as heavy.

ENERGY CONVERSION
Energy can be neither destroyed, nor can it be created from nothing. Whenever anything happens, one form of energy is simply changed into another.

TEMPERATURE SCALE
Temperature is measured in degrees of Fahrenheit or Celsius, but also in kelvins (K).

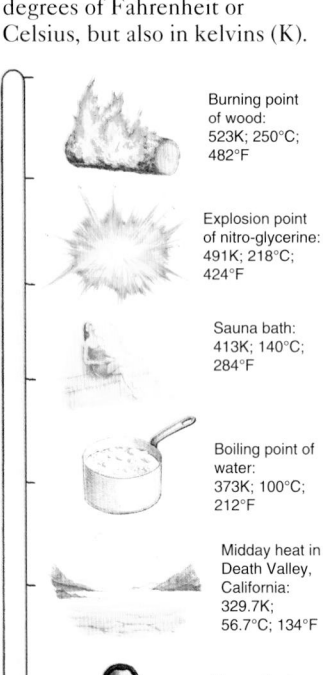

Burning point of wood: 523K; 250°C; 482°F

Explosion point of nitro-glycerine: 491K; 218°C; 424°F

Sauna bath: 413K; 140°C; 284°F

Boiling point of water: 373K; 100°C; 212°F

Midday heat in Death Valley, California: 329.7K; 56.7°C; 134°F

Human body temperature: 310K; 37°C; 98.6°F

Body temperature of spiny anteater: 295K; 22°C; 71.6°F

Freezing point of pure water: 273K; 0°C; 32°F

Freezing point of mercury: 234K; -39°C; -38°F

Absolute zero: 0K; -273°C; -459°F

ENERGY CONVERSION IN A CAR JOURNEY

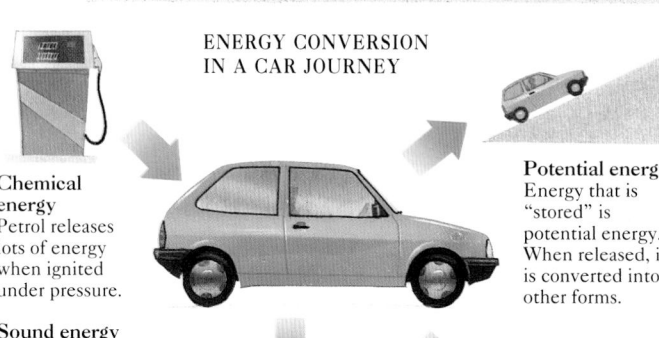

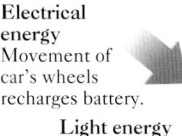

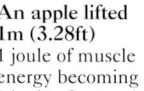

Chemical energy
Petrol releases lots of energy when ignited under pressure.

Sound energy
Radio and loudspeakers convert electrical energy into sound.

Kinetic energy
Any moving object possesses kinetic energy. The faster it moves and the greater its mass, the greater its kinetic energy.

Electrical energy
Movement of car's wheels recharges battery.

Light energy
Car headlights are powered by battery.

Potential energy
Energy that is "stored" is potential energy. When released, it is converted into other forms.

Heat energy
Movement of engine parts generates heat.

Heat energy (brakes)
When brakes are applied, friction between car tyres and ground generates heat.

ENERGY MEASURE
All forms of energy – potential, kinetic, sound, chemical, light, heat, etc. – can be measured in units called joules.

Energy of a thunderstorm
About 1,000 million million joules of heat and potential (stored) energy.

Energy released by a lightning strike
100 million joules of electrical energy becoming 100 million joules of heat energy.

An apple lifted 1m (3.28ft)
1 joule of muscle energy becoming 1 joule of potential (stored) energy.

1 second of a 100-watt light bulb
100 joules of electrical energy becoming 15 joules of light energy and 85 joules of heat energy.

1 second of Itaipu Dam, Brazil
Potential energy becoming 12.6 million joules of electrical energy.

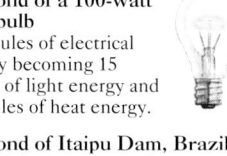

EVER READY
The amount of atomic energy in a kilogram of radioactive uranium–235 would keep a 100-watt light bulb alight for 27,400 years.

TEMPERATURE
The particles that make up all matter, such as atoms, are constantly in motion, vibrating to and fro or speeding through space. The temperature of matter is the average energy of its particles. Matter with more energy can raise the temperature of other matter around it.

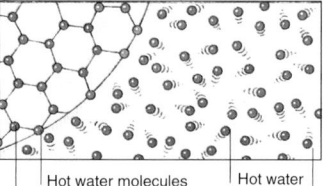

Hot water molecules transfer kinetic energy to ice molecules – ice melts.

Ice molecules have low energy.

Hot water molecules have more energy.

Hot water

ENERGY UNITS
Other energy units can be converted into joules

Unit	Joule equivalent
Joule (J)	
Watts (W)	1J per second
Horsepower (Hp)	2,600,000 J
Calories (Kcal)	4,184 J
Kilowatt hour (kWh)	3,600,000 J

FORCES

A FORCE IS a push or a pull. A force can start an object moving, slow it down, or change its direction. Forces can also change the shape of an object.

GRAVITY

One of the most familiar forces is a force of attraction between objects, called gravity. Gravity keeps us on the Earth and gives us weight. Anything with mass exerts gravity, and the size of this force depends on the masses of the objects and the distance between them. It becomes weaker as bodies move further apart or lose mass.

Moon gravity
The Moon exerts less gravitational force than Earth because it has less mass.

Earth gravity
Earth's large mass makes things on its surface weigh six times more than on the Moon.

ADDING FORCES TOGETHER

If more than one force acts on an object, the overall effect will be the same as one force acting in one direction. This force is called the resultant.

BOW AND ARROW
The force of an arrow fired from a bow is the resultant of the two forces that act along the upper and lower halves of the bowstring.

TUG OF WAR
In a tug of war, the resultant force is almost zero, because the two forces on the rope act in exactly opposite directions.

Opposing forces

TURNING FORCES

Forces can turn objects. The greater the force, and the greater its distance from the turning point, the greater the turning force.

TURNING NUTS
The spanner is useful for turning a nut because its long handle means that you can apply a force far away from the nut. This produces a stronger turning force (moment).

NEWTON'S LAWS OF MOTION

In 1687, English mathematician Isaac Newton (1642–1725) identified three laws that describe the motion of objects under the influence of forces.

NEWTON'S FIRST LAW

An object will not change its motion unless a force acts upon it.

A frog will stay still unless a force makes it move. If the frog was drifting along at a constant speed, it would continue to do so until a force stopped it, slowed it down, or made it speed up.

NEWTON'S SECOND LAW

A change in an object's motion depends upon the force acting on it, and on the mass of the object.

The frog needs twice as much force to change its motion twice as much.

NEWTON'S THIRD LAW

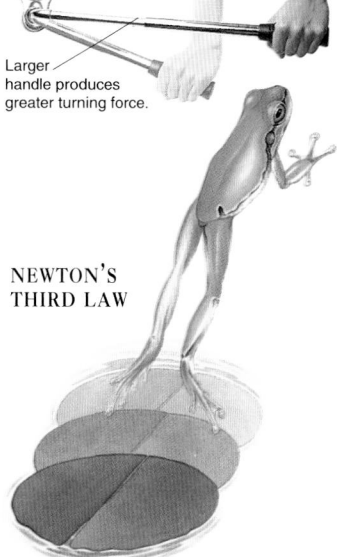

For every force there is an equal force acting in the other direction.

Forces come in pairs. The frog and the lilypad push against each other.

CIRCULAR MOTION

A moving object will travel in a straight line, unless a force changes its direction.

Hammer thrower
To make a hammer go in a circle, an athlete must supply a force, called centripetal force, that constantly pulls it around in a circle. As soon as the athlete lets go, the hammer flies off in a straight line.

Athlete uses centripetal force to throw hammer.

PRESSURE

Pressure is a measure of how "concentrated" a force is. A force applied over a small area exerts more pressure than the same force applied over a large area.

PRESSURE AND AREA
If a watering can and trowel are pushed into sand with about the same force, the trowel sinks further into the sand. This is because the force is exerted over a smaller area – the trowel's thin blade.

Larger handle produces greater turning force.

FORCES WORDS

Acceleration Rate of change of velocity.

Centre of gravity The point on an object at which it balances.

Equilibrium State produced when forces acting on an object balance, so that there is no resultant.

Momentum Mass of an object multiplied by its velocity.

Newton Unit of force. One newton (1N) causes a mass of one kilogram to move with an acceleration of one metre (3.28ft) per second per second.

Resultant Force produced by combining two or more forces.

Velocity Speed and direction of an object.

BRAIN POWER

The ancient Greek scientist Archimedes was said to have constructed a pulley mechanism that enabled a ship that had run aground to be dragged into open water by just one man.

MACHINES

A machine is a device that can change the size and direction of a force. With a block and tackle, for example, a person can lift a very heavy load. This is because the arrangement of ropes in the block and tackle means that the person needs to pull a long length of rope to lift the load a small distance.

PULLEY
Effort is magnified by the rope and the wheels in order to lift the load.

WEDGE
The slope allows less effort to lift the load than by picking it up vertically.

SCREW
Effort is magnified by the thread, acting as a long slope wrapped around the screw.

WHEEL AND AXLE
Effort applied to the wheel is magnified by the axle, turning it with greater force.

Fulcrum

LEVER
Effort applied at one end of a bar is magnified by the fulcrum to lift the load at the other end.

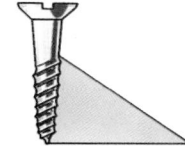

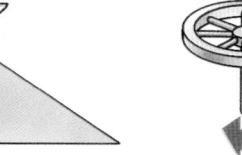
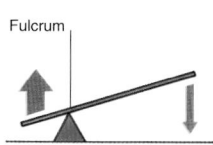

ELECTRICITY AND MAGNETISM

PUT A PIN CLOSE to a magnet, and it will cling to the magnet. Rub a balloon on a sweater and the balloon will cling to a wall. These things happen because invisible forces are at work – electricity and magnetism. These forces are important, as they hold almost everything together.

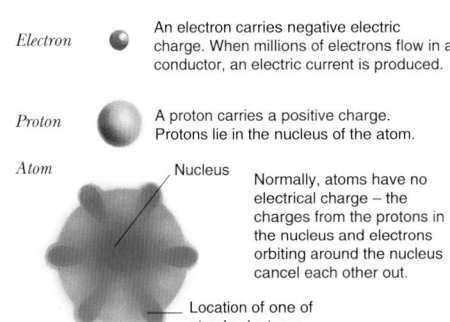

Electron — An electron carries negative electric charge. When millions of electrons flow in a conductor, an electric current is produced.

Proton — A proton carries a positive charge. Protons lie in the nucleus of the atom.

Atom — Nucleus — Normally, atoms have no electrical charge – the charges from the protons in the nucleus and electrons orbiting around the nucleus cancel each other out.

Location of one of atom's electrons

CURRENT ELECTRICITY

The unit of charge is the coulomb. One coulomb is equal to the charge of 6 million million million electrons. An electric current is a flow of electrons. A current of one ampere (see below) means that a charge of one coulomb is flowing per second.

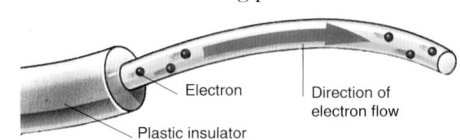

Electron — Direction of electron flow — Plastic insulator

STATIC ELECTRICITY

When you rub a balloon on a jumper, some electrons get separated from their atoms. This creates an electrical charge. Charges of the same type repel (push each other away). Opposite charges attract. The balloon gains a negative charge. This gives the wall a positive charge, and the balloon clings to it.

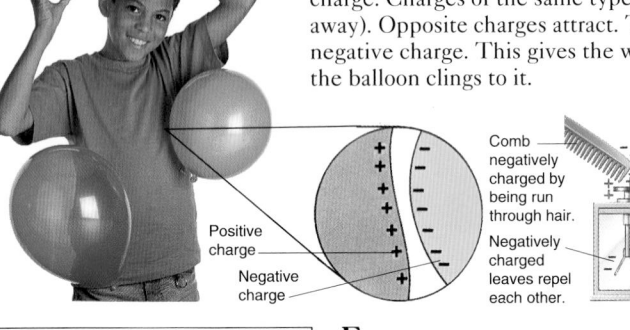

Comb negatively charged by being run through hair.

Negatively charged leaves repel each other.

Positive charge

Negative charge

ELECTROSCOPE

An electroscope is an instrument for detecting electric charge. It has two pieces of gold leaf fixed to a brass rod. The leaves separate when an electric charge is brought near to the rod.

ELECTRICITY WORDS

Ampere The unit of current. If a wire carries one ampere (1A), one coulomb (1C) of charge is flowing along the wire each second.

Volt The unit of voltage or electromotive force. This is a measure of how much energy charges have. One volt (1V) means that each coulomb (1C) has one joule (1J) of energy.

Ohm The unit of resistance. If a wire has a one ohm (1Ω) resistance, a voltage of one volt will produce a current of one ampere.

Watt The unit used to measure power. An electric current of one ampere (1A) at one volt (1V) will have a power of one watt (1W).

SHOCKING CURE

The bite of the South American Bushmaster snake can be treated by a series of short electric shocks at about 20,000–25,000V. In remote areas, car or outboard motors are sometimes used to deliver the voltage.

ELECTRIC FACTS

• The word "electricity" comes from the Greek word for amber, *elektron*. The ancient Greeks noticed that when amber was rubbed with a cloth, small objects would cling to it.

• A television on "standby" uses one-third as much electrical power as a television that is switched on.

• The body's nerves carry electric currents to and from the brain at speeds of up to 400km/h (249mph).

Small, positively charged particles move to top of cloud.

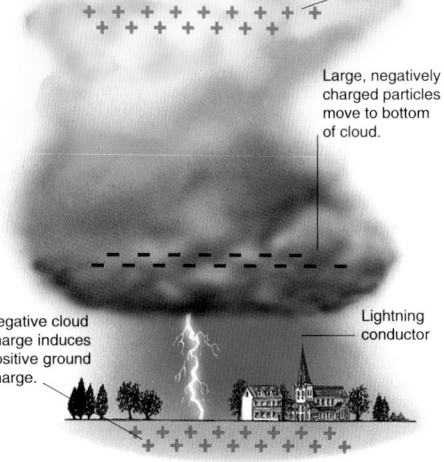

Large, negatively charged particles move to bottom of cloud.

Negative cloud charge induces positive ground charge.

Lightning conductor

LIGHTNING

Lightning is a tremendous spark of electricity, caused by a build-up of electric charge in clouds. The spark passes between clouds, or from the cloud to the ground. Many buildings are fitted with lightning conductors, which reduce the risk of lightning striking by draining electric charge away from clouds.

BATTERY

Inside a battery, chemical reactions separate electrons from atoms of the chemicals present. These electrons move around a circuit from the negative to the positive terminal.

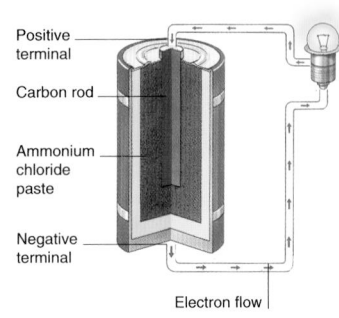

Positive terminal

Carbon rod

Ammonium chloride paste

Negative terminal

Electron flow

SERIES AND PARALLEL CIRCUITS

Two bulbs one after the other in a circuit are said to be "in series". Each bulb only gets half the energy (voltage), so they shine dimly. In parallel, the bulbs would shine more brightly, since each bulb gets the full voltage – but the current will be doubled.

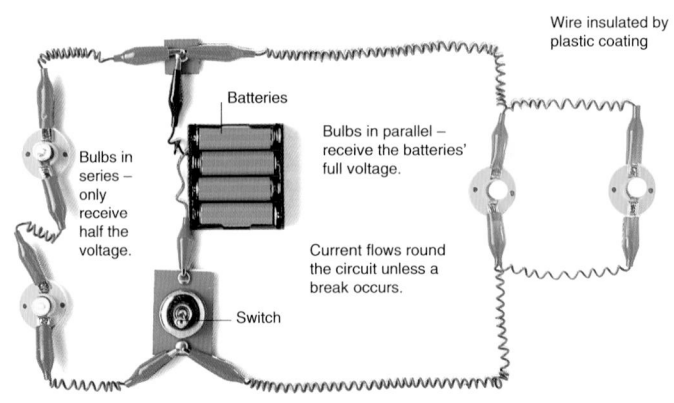

Wire insulated by plastic coating

Batteries

Bulbs in series – only receive half the voltage.

Bulbs in parallel – receive the batteries' full voltage.

Current flows round the circuit unless a break occurs.

Switch

RESISTANCE

The resistance of a material is a measure of how easily electric current will flow through it. Resistance depends upon the material, its width and its length.

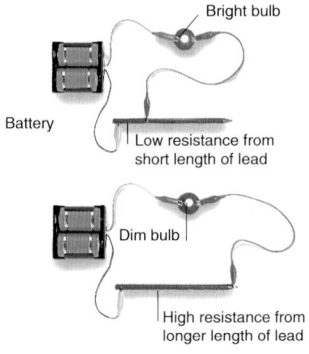

Bright bulb

Battery

Low resistance from short length of lead

Dim bulb

High resistance from longer length of lead

MAGNETISM

Certain materials exert invisible forces, similar to electric forces. A magnet will attract objects made of iron, and a few other metals. Also magnets will attract or repel other magnets. Every magnet has two ends, called poles, where the forces it exerts are strongest. One is called the north pole and the other is called the south pole.

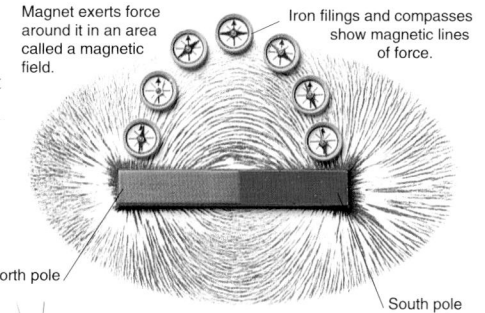

Magnet exerts force around it in an area called a magnetic field.

Iron filings and compasses show magnetic lines of force.

North pole

Lines of force loop around magnet and splay out from poles.

South pole

Unlike poles attract
If unlike poles – one north and one south – are placed together, they attract each other.

Fields of attracting magnets

Like poles repel
If like poles – both north or both south – are put together they repel each other.

Fields of repelling magnets

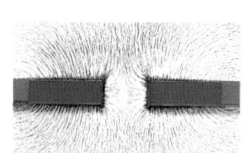

Iron filings show distortion of normal lines of force when two magnets meet.

Magnet
When a magnet attracts objects, the objects become magnetized and can attract other objects.

LODESTONE

Lodestone is a magnetic rock of iron oxide that occurs naturally. In ancient times people used lodestones as compasses and later to make magnetic compass needles.

Metal objects, such as pins, are attracted to the lodestone.

Each steel ball acts as a magnet.

DOMAINS

Magnetic objects contain small regions, between 0.1 and 1mm across, called domains. Each domain has two poles, and most of a magnet's domains lie in the same direction. If the domains are made to point in different directions the magnet will lose its magnetism.

Domain poles not in line

Poles line up.

Magnets also demagnetized by heating

Domains are jumbled up In unmagnetized iron or steel.

Domains may be aligned by stroking with another magnet.

Striking with a hammer jumbles up domains, demagnetizing the bar.

ELECTROMAGNETISM

Magnetic forces are not only produced by magnets. Magnetism is also produced by an electric current flowing through a wire. This magnetism can be made stronger by wrapping the wire around an iron core, such as a nail.

Insulated copper wire wrapped around iron nail

Wire connected to a battery

Metal objects are attracted to electromagnet.

Magnetic field

North pole

South pole

Flow of current

ELECTRIC MAGNET

The magnetism produced by an electric current is exactly the same as magnetism produced by a magnet – it has a magnetic field, and a north and south pole. It can be switched on and off, however, with the electric current.

EARTH MAGNET

The Earth's metallic core is a giant magnet, which lines up near to the true North Pole and South Pole, moving slightly every year. A compass contains a magnetized needle, which always points towards the magnetic north and south poles, enabling navigators to find their way.

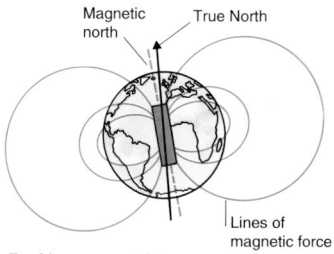

Magnetic north

True North

Lines of magnetic force

Earth's magnetic field

BARKING MAD

Scottish physicist James Clerk Maxwell, who first explained the relationship between electricity and magnetism, used to talk through his theories with his dog, often at noisy parties.

MAGNETISM FACTS

• A wire carrying an electric current straight into this page would have a magnetic field going clockwise around it.

• Keepers are pieces of iron that help a magnet keep its power.

• Near the North and South Poles, the Earth's magnetic field traps charged particles emitted by the Sun. These particles react with the Earth's field to produce layers of coloured lights in the night sky, called Northern Lights or aurora borealis in the North, and Southern Lights or aurora australis in the south.

MAGNETIC FIELDS

Field	Strength in tesla (unit of field measurement)
Weakest measured field	0.000000000008T
Earth's field	0.00003T
Powerful magnet	1T
Highest field on record	30.1T

ELECTRIC MOTOR

An electric motor contains magnets and coils of wire. When current passes through the coil, it produces magnetism, which makes the coil turn in the magnetic field of the magnets.

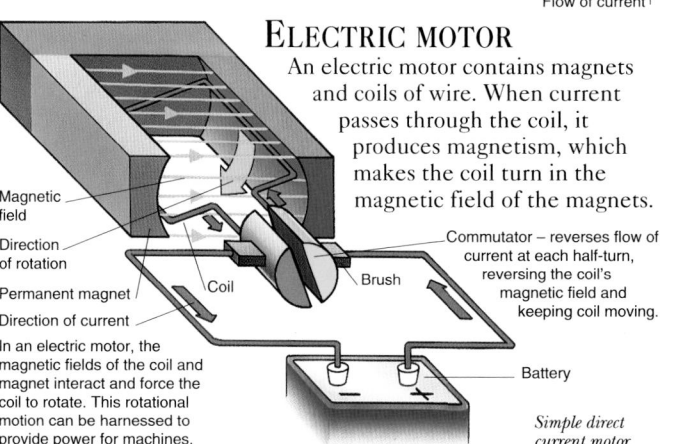

Magnetic field

Direction of rotation

Permanent magnet

Direction of current

In an electric motor, the magnetic fields of the coil and magnet interact and force the coil to rotate. This rotational motion can be harnessed to provide power for machines.

Coil

Brush

Commutator – reverses flow of current at each half-turn, reversing the coil's magnetic field and keeping coil moving.

Battery

Simple direct current motor

GENERATOR

A generator is like a motor in reverse. Turning the coil inside the magnet's field produces an electric current. Power stations use huge generators to produce electricity for homes, schools, and factories.

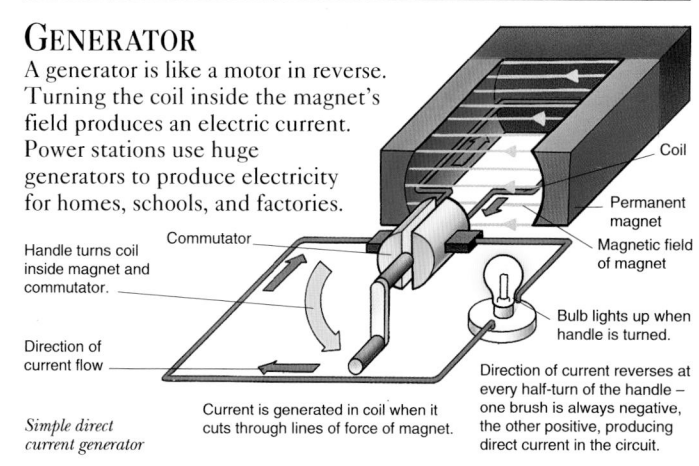

Coil

Permanent magnet

Magnetic field of magnet

Bulb lights up when handle is turned.

Commutator

Handle turns coil inside magnet and commutator.

Direction of current flow

Simple direct current generator

Current is generated in coil when it cuts through lines of force of magnet.

Direction of current reverses at every half-turn of the handle – one brush is always negative, the other positive, producing direct current in the circuit.

LIGHT AND COLOUR

WITHOUT LIGHT, WE would not be able to see. Nature provides our most important light source – the Sun – and its light, either directly, or by bouncing off our surroundings, enters our eyes and enables us to recognize our world.

LIGHT LAWS

Law of reflection
The angle at which light hits a mirror is equal to the angle that light leaves the mirror.

Incident light ray (ray approaching mirror) | Reflected light ray

Law of refraction
Light changes speed when it passes from one material to another. The more it slows down, the more it bends.

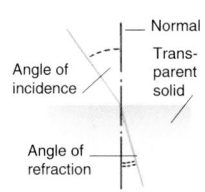

Angle of incidence | Normal | Transparent solid

Angle of refraction

Ray of light passes from less dense medium (air) a more dense one (glass)

LIGHT ACTION
Light travels in straight lines at 300 million m/sec (980 million ft/sec). It creates shadows, bounces or reflects off smooth surfaces, and bends when it passes through different transparent materials.

LIGHT SPEED
Knowing the speed of light, astronomers have measured the distance to the Moon very accurately, by bouncing a laser beam off a mirror left there by astronauts, and timing its return journey.

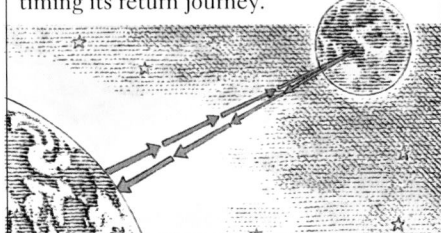

BRIGHTNESS
Light is given off by many different light sources, such as candles and light bulbs. Some light sources are brighter than others, and will provide better illumination.

Brightness in candela
The luminous intensity (brightness) of a light source is measured in candela (cd). One candela is approximately equal to the brightness of a candle.

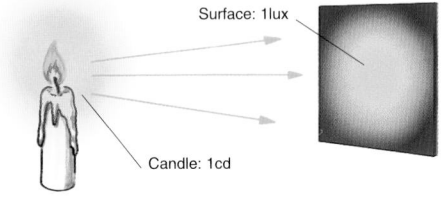

Surface: 1lux

Candle: 1cd

Illumination in lux
Light from a source illuminates a surface placed in its path. This illumination is measured in lux (lx). From a distance of 1m (3.28ft) away, a source of light intensity one candela (1cd) will illuminate a 1sq m (10.8sq ft) surface with an illumination of 1lux.

EYE SEE
When comparing areas of different colour, in good light and using both eyes, the human eye can distinguish surfaces of 10 million different colours. No machine yet invented can distinguish as many colours.

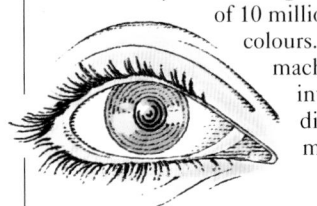

REFLECTION
When light bounces off a surface, we say it is reflected. Few things we see give off their own light – we see them only because of reflection. Flat and shiny surfaces, such as mirrors, reflect light evenly to form an image, or picture.

Surface reflection
Most surfaces are not flat, even if they seem to be. When light reflects from an irregular surface, the reflected rays return at many different angles.

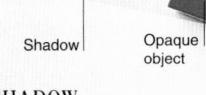

Shadow | Opaque object

SHADOW
Light travels through transparent substances, such as water or glass, in straight lines. Non-transparent (opaque) materials, such as wood or metal, do not allow light to pass through them. They cause a shadow to be cast on the opposite side from the light source.

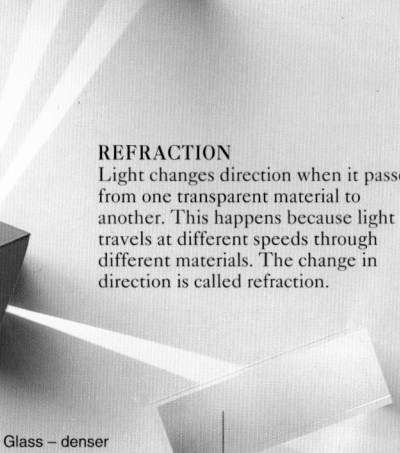

Mirror – flat and shiny surface

Image appears "behind" mirror.

REFRACTION
Light changes direction when it passes from one transparent material to another. This happens because light travels at different speeds through different materials. The change in direction is called refraction.

Glass – denser substance than air

Angle of light ray changes.

Emerging light ray is parallel to original ray but shifted to left.

LENSES
Lenses are specially shaped pieces of glass, or other transparent substances, that focus or disperse light evenly.

Convex lens
A block of glass that curves outwards is called a convex lens. Its shape focuses light on a point. It is used in cameras, magnifying glasses, and microscopes.

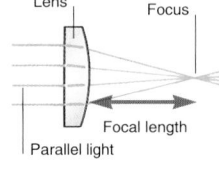

Lens | Focus

Focal length

Parallel light

Concave lens
A block of glass that curves inwards is called a concave lens. Its shape causes light to diverge (spread out). It is used in wide-angle and telephoto lenses.

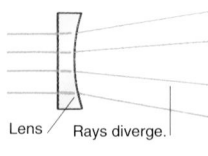

Lens | Rays diverge.

MIRROR
If the light falls on a completely smooth surface, all the rays are reflected regularly, at the same angle. An image forms, and the object looks as if it is behind the mirror.

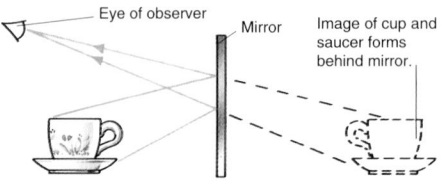

Eye of observer | Mirror | Image of cup and saucer forms behind mirror.

HOW LIGHT IS MADE
There are two ways of making light – incandescence and luminescence. Incandescence happens when something gets very hot. Luminescence happens in four major ways.

Incandescence
In a light bulb, the fine filament heats up and gives out incandescent light. Other forms of incandescent light are candle flames, or the red glow from an electric element.

Phosphorescence
Phophorescent paint makes the numbers on clock faces glow in the dark. The paint stores energy when light falls on it. The energy is slowly released, as light, so the paint can be seen at night.

Fluorescence
Fluorescent chemicals in some washing powders make clothes look brighter in sunlight. Ultraviolet light energy is briefly stored, then released as visible light.

Bioluminescence
Some animals, such as the firefly, produce chemicals that release light energy when combined in their bodies.

Triboluminescence
Some substances, such as sugar, give out light when suddenly broken apart or crushed.

ELECTROMAGNETIC SPECTRUM

Light is part of a range of radiation called the electromagnetic spectrum. Different parts of the spectrum have different energy – from low-energy radio waves to high-energy gamma rays. Wavelengths can be as short as one nanometre (nm – one thousand millionth of a metre).

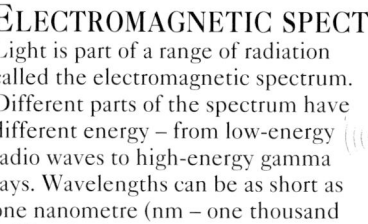

Television waves – about 1m (3.28ft)

Infrared – about 1mm

Ultraviolet – 100nm

X-rays – 1nm

Radio waves – up to 1km (0.62 miles)

Microwaves – about 1cm (0.37in)

Visible light – 400–700nm

Wavelength of electromagnetic wave (number given after type of light)

SKY COLOUR

Tiny particles in the sky scatter sunlight in all directions as it penetrates the Earth's atmosphere. They scatter blue light better than red, yellow, and green.

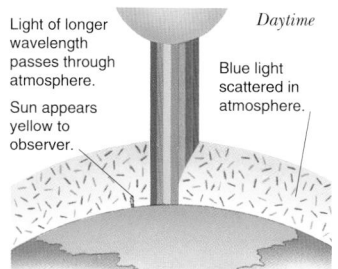

Daytime

Light of longer wavelength passes through atmosphere.

Blue light scattered in atmosphere.

Sun appears yellow to observer.

BLUE SKIES

During the day, the blue parts of sunlight are scattered in all directions, making the sky look blue. The rest of the light gets through, to give the Sun a yellow appearance.

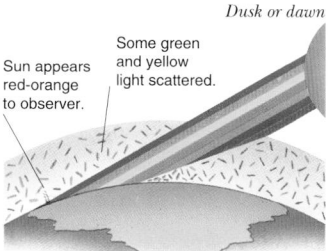

Dusk or dawn

Some green and yellow light scattered.

Sun appears red-orange to observer.

SUNSET RED

In the evening, sunlight passes through a longer distance in the atmosphere. This means that some green and yellow light also gets scattered. Only orange and red light gets through, so the Sun looks orange-red.

MIRAGES

Light is refracted as it passes through layers of air at different temperatures. This can make objects seem nearer than they are and can make hot air layers look like water. When hot air lies above cool air, objects far away, such as ships, can seem to loom upside down. This occurs because light rays travelling from cool to hot air bend down and form an inverted image.

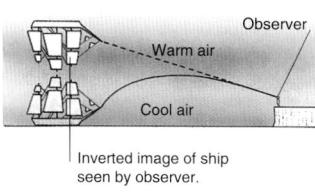

Observer

Warm air

Cool air

Inverted image of ship seen by observer.

VISIBLE SPECTRUM

Ordinary white light is made up of a range of colours. When white light passes through a prism, a triangular transparent block, the prism splits up its various wavelengths and all the colours can be seen separately. This range of colours is called the spectrum.

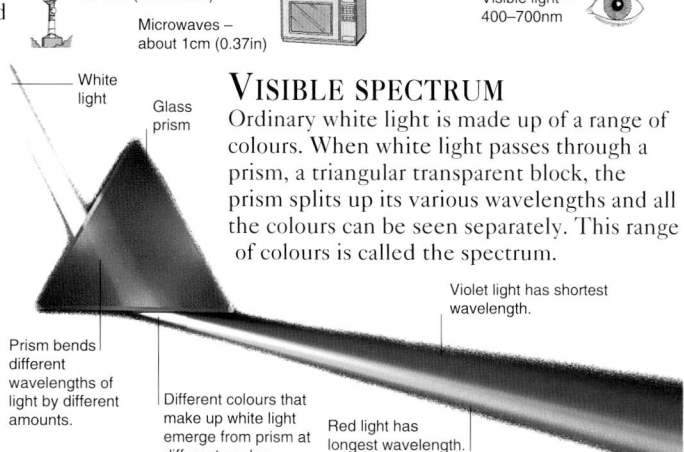

White light

Glass prism

Prism bends different wavelengths of light by different amounts.

Different colours that make up white light emerge from prism at different angles.

Violet light has shortest wavelength.

Red light has longest wavelength.

RAINBOW

When white sunlight falls on rain, the colours are split up and reflected inside the droplets, just as they are in a prism. The colours form a rainbow.

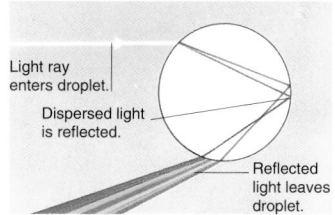

Light ray enters droplet.

Dispersed light is reflected.

Reflected light leaves droplet.

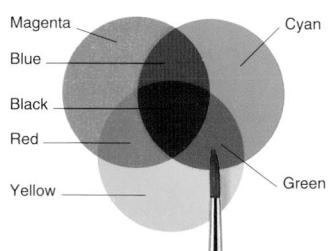

Rainbow

Red seen at 42° to the horizontal.

Observer

Violet seen at 40° to the horizontal.

MIXING COLOURS

Magenta

Blue

Black

Red

Yellow

Cyan

Green

PIGMENTS

Any colour of paint, ink, or dye can be formed from the three "secondary" colours of magenta, cyan, and yellow. Together they produce black.

INTERFERENCE

When light strikes a bubble, it is reflected off both the inside and outside surfaces. The two rays combine in a process called interference and create beautiful colours on the thin surface.

Colours vary with thickness of bubble.

Colours on bubble surface

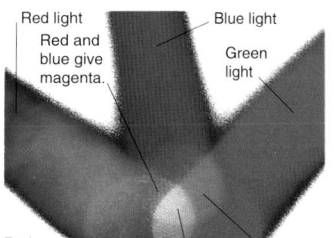

Red light

Blue light

Red and blue give magenta

Green light

Red and green give yellow.

White light

Blue and green give cyan.

LIGHT

Beams of light of the "primary" colours of red, green, and blue, can be mixed to form any other colour. When all the primaries are mixed, we get white light.

LIGHT AND ATMOSPHERE

Not every wavelength of light from space reaches the ground. Some infrared waves (1,100–2,300nm) are absorbed by carbon dioxide, water vapour, and ozone. "Hard" ultraviolet waves (about 220nm) are filtered out by ozone.

Effects of atmosphere on wavelengths of light

COLOUR WAVELENGTHS

Colour	Wavelength (Nanometres)
Violet	370–440
Blue	440–500
Green	500–575
Yellow	575–580
Orange	580–610
Red	610–720

LASERS

When certain materials are given enough energy, their atoms begin to give off light. Inside a laser, mirrors reflect this light back and forth until it is intense enough to escape at one end. Laser light is special because it is light of just one wavelength, and its waves are all aligned with each other. This means it can be very powerful and precise.

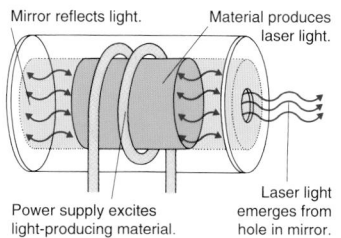

Mirror reflects light.

Material produces laser light.

Power supply excites light-producing material.

Laser light emerges from hole in mirror.

LIGHT FACTS

• Electromagnetic radiation can be thought of as waves. The higher the energy, the shorter the wavelength.

• Bees' eyes can detect ultraviolet light. A flower looks bright to a bee because the petals reflect a lot of ultraviolet.

• The word laser stands for Light Amplification by Stimulated Emission of Radiation.

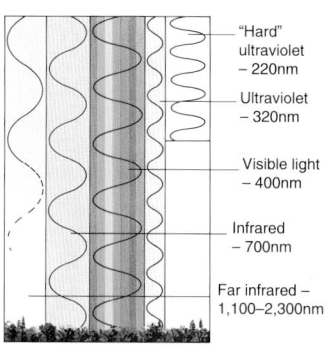

"Hard" ultraviolet – 220nm

Ultraviolet – 320nm

Visible light – 400nm

Infrared – 700nm

Far infrared – 1,100–2,300nm

SOUND

SOUND IS PRODUCED by objects vibrating. This vibration first pushes the air forwards, compressing (squashing) it, then pulls it back, causing it to expand. These contractions and expansions travel through the air as vibrations, called sound waves.

THE DECIBEL SCALE

The loudness of sound is measured in decibels (db). A 10-db sound increase corresponds to a ten*fold* increase in loudness.

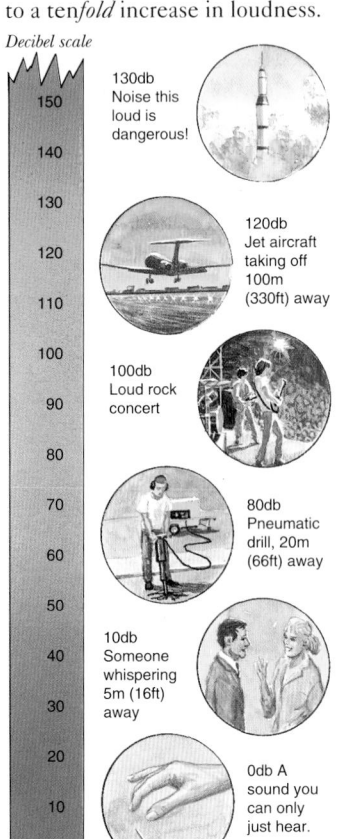

Decibel scale

150 — 130db Noise this loud is dangerous!

140

130

120 — 120db Jet aircraft taking off 100m (330ft) away

110

100

90 — 100db Loud rock concert

80

70

60 — 80db Pneumatic drill, 20m (66ft) away

50

40 — 10db Someone whispering 5m (16ft) away

30

20

10 — 0db A sound you can only just hear.

0

SOUND WAVE

When people shout, they use the vocal cords in their throat to make a sound. Vocal cords vibrate as air passes through them.

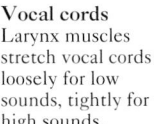
Tough, elastic strips covered with membrane

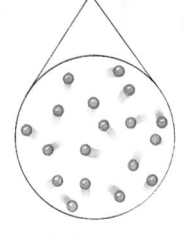

Vocal cords
Larynx muscles stretch vocal cords loosely for low sounds, tightly for high sounds.

Rarefaction
When air expands, the molecules are spread out. This is called rarefaction. The air exerts less pressure than normal.

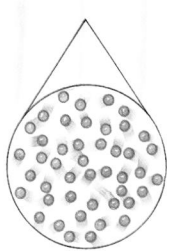

Compression
When air is compressed, all its molecules are pushed together. The air exerts more pressure than normal.

SOUND FACTS

• Sometimes, a sound and its echo are so close together they seem to be one long sound. This is called reverberation.

• You can hear the sound of a horse's hooves a long time before it arrives, by putting your ear to the ground. Sound waves travel much faster through the ground than through air.

• Sound travels quickly, but light travels much more quickly. You can work out how far away a storm is from the time between the lightning flash and the thunder. Sound travels at about 334m/s (1,096ft/sec). So a storm is about 1km (0.62 miles) away for every three seconds.

SOUND SPEEDS
Sound travels at different speeds through different materials.

Material	Speed	
	m/sec	ft/sec
Rubber	54	177
Air at 0°C	334	1,096
Air at 100°C	366	1,201
Water	1,284	4,213
Mercury	1,452	4,764
Wood (Oak)	3,850	12,631
Iron	5,000	16,404
Glass	5,000	16,404

ECHOES

An echo is heard when a sound wave bounces off a hard surface. The length of time between the original sound and the echo depends on how far the sound travels before it bounces back. The further it travels, the longer it is before the echo is heard. Most sounds we hear arrive at our ears as a mixture of direct waves and echoes bouncing off surrounding surfaces.

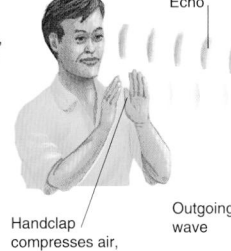

Listener hears one sound only, because sound wave travels quickly from hands to wall and back.

Echo

Handclap compresses air, creating sound wave.

Outgoing wave

Wall acts as barrier to sound wave. Distant barriers, such as cliffs or hills, will create separate echo, heard slightly later.

ULTRASOUND

Ultrasound is sound at a frequency too high for humans to hear. Some animals can hear ultrasounds by echolocation and some make ultrasounds. Bats use ultrasound to catch their food. Depending on their frequency, the sounds they make bounce off flying insects, which the bat can locate and catch.

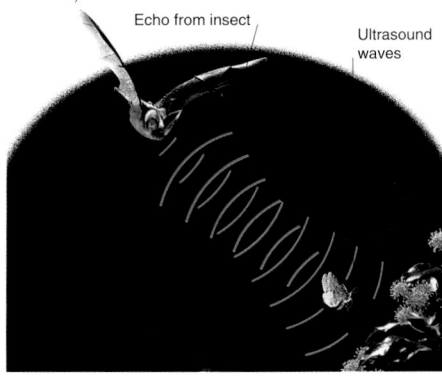
Echo from insect

Ultrasound waves

SOUND MAN

One of the most important contributors to our understanding of how we hear sounds was Georg von Békésy. In his research into hearing, he examined the ears of a dead zoo elephant that he had rescued from a glue factory.

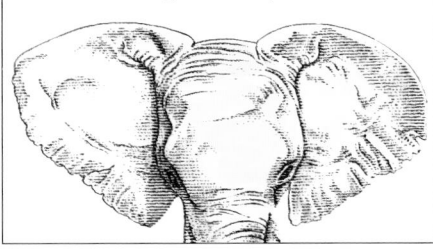

SONIC BOOM

A sonic boom happens when the source of a sound, such as a jet aircraft, travels faster than the sound it produces (at about 1,200km/h, or 745mph). At such times, many wave fronts reach the ears of people standing directly below at the same time, making a very loud noise like a huge clap of thunder.

Subsonic flight

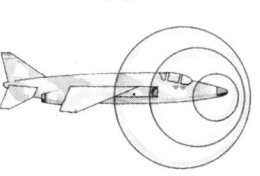

When flying below speed of sound, jet aircraft compresses air in front of it. Near to speed of sound, a wall or barrier of compressed air forms.

Supersonic flight

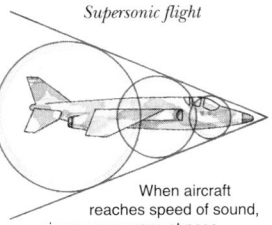

When aircraft reaches speed of sound, air pressure wave at nose produces massive shock wave. This causes sonic boom.

FREQUENCY

Frequency is the number of sound waves per second. The higher the number, the higher the pitch of the sound. Frequency is measured in hertz (Hz).

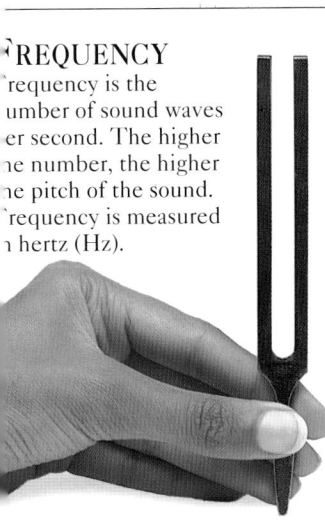

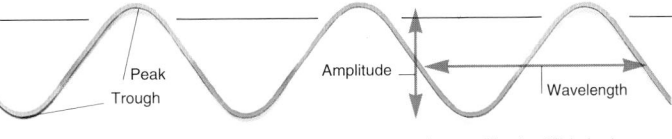

Peak
Trough
Amplitude
Wavelength

Sound wave The loudness of a sound depends on its amplitude. This is the difference between the point in a sound wave where the air is exerting the least pressure, and the point where it exerts the most.

Soft sound
There is not much difference between the low-pressure area of the sound wave and the high-pressure area.

Loud sound
As a sound gets louder, there is a greater difference between areas of high and low pressure.

Low sound
Low-pitched sounds have low frequency – fewer waves per second.

High sound
The sound waves are closer together – there are more of them per second.

SHATTERED

If a sound makes an object vibrate at its natural frequency, the vibrations will build to a greater and greater amplitude. This effect is called resonance, and it can even make an object break.

DOPPLER EFFECT

A police car's siren becomes more high-pitched as it approaches, and less high-pitched as it moves away. This is called the Doppler effect, and is caused by sound waves being pushed together in front of a moving source of sound, and spaced out behind it.

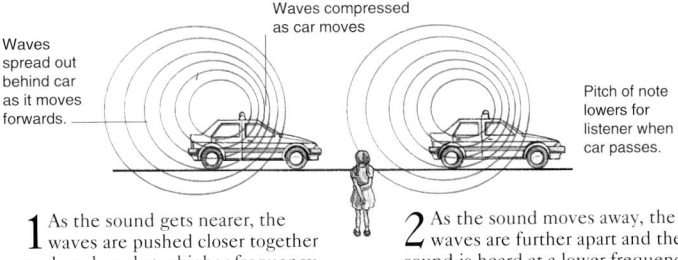

Waves compressed as car moves

Waves spread out behind car as it moves forwards.

Pitch of note lowers for listener when car passes.

1 As the sound gets nearer, the waves are pushed closer together and are heard at a higher frequency.

2 As the sound moves away, the waves are further apart and the sound is heard at a lower frequency.

KEY FREQUENCY RANGES

Various animals and machines make or detect sounds over different ranges of frequency. The human voice creates sound over a relatively narrow range of frequencies.

Bat
Hears: 1,000–120,000Hz
Makes: 10,000–120,000Hz

Human
Hears: 20–20,000Hz
Makes: 85–1,100Hz

Ultrasound scanner
Makes and receives:
3,500,000–
7,500,000Hz

SONAR ECHO

SONAR (Sound Navigation and Ranging) is a way of using echoes from ultrasound to detect the presence of objects. The echoes are used to form a picture on a screen.

Pictures from sound
Waves of ultrasound can be directed into the human body – to an unborn child, for example. The ultrasound echoes off the unborn child, then the ultrasound equipment picks up the echo and turns it into electrical impulses. These form a picture of the baby on a screen.

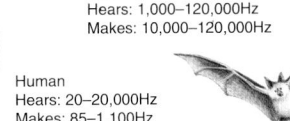

Frequency scale
Infrasound

Audible sounds

Ultrasounds

Elephant
Hears: 1–20,000Hz
Makes: 12Hz–unknown

Nuclear explosion:
as low as 0.01Hz

Dog
Hears: 15–50,000Hz
Makes: 450–1,080Hz

Porpoise
Hears: 150–150,000Hz
Makes: 7,000–120,000Hz

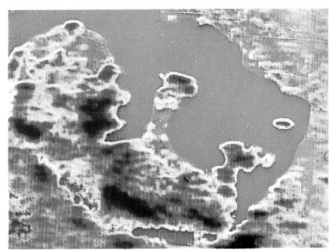

Ultrasound scan of foetus in womb

MUSIC

Musical instruments may make the same notes (sounds of different pitch) but they sound different because each one has its own quality. Although the main frequency is the same for each, they also produce overtones of other frequencies. These vary for each instrument.

Ranges
Some instruments produce a greater range of frequency than others.

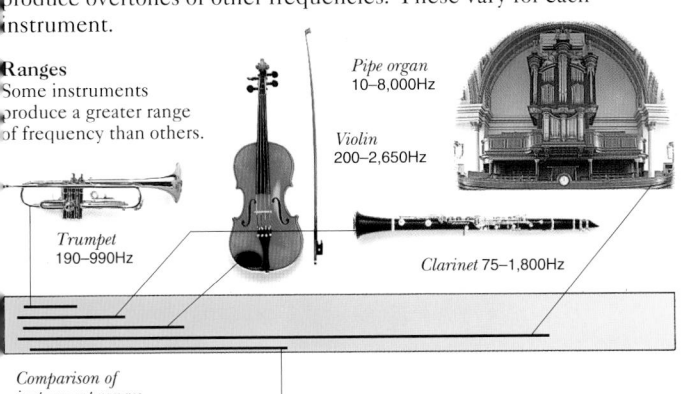

Pipe organ
10–8,000Hz

Violin
200–2,650Hz

Trumpet
190–990Hz

Clarinet 75–1,800Hz

Comparison of instrument ranges

Piano
30–4,100Hz

RECORDING SOUND

There are several different ways of recording sound. All recorders work by turning the sound into some sort of electrical signal, which can be turned back into a sound later.

Vinyl records
These record signals appear as a wavy groove. They make the stylus vibrate, which in turn creates electrical signals that can be turned into sound.

Cassette tapes
Sounds are recorded as signals on a magnetic tape. A pattern of strong or weak magnetic signals forms on the tape. This can be played back, making electrical signals later used to make a sound.

Compact discs
Sounds are recorded in the CD's surface as tiny pits, which pass under a laser beam. Reflections from the beam are turned into electrical signals and used to make sound.

Vinyl record

Cassette tape

Compact disc

Record player's stylus fits into spiral groove.

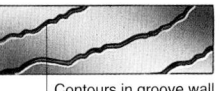

Contours in groove wall record loudness and frequency of sound.

Magnetic alignment of particles on tape records sound.

Track is thinner than a hair and several kilometres long.

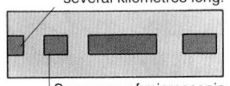

Sequence of microscopic pits records sound.

ELECTRONICS

ELECTRONICS, WHICH IS concerned with the movement and control of electrons, plays a crucial role in the efficient operation of modern technology.

1879 Cathode rays observed by English physicist William Crookes (1832–1919), using a specially designed vacuum tube. He finds that the rays, which he calls cathode rays, are deflected by magnetic fields.

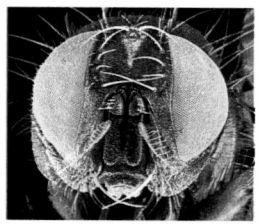

Crookes tube

1880 American inventor Thomas Edison (1847–1931) observes tiny currents flowing from a lamp filament. This becomes known as the Edison effect.

1882 Edison effect investigated by Englishman John Ambrose Fleming (1849–1945).

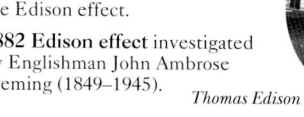

Thomas Edison

| 1850 | 1879 | | | 1880 | 1882 |

1906 Use of crystals as radio wave detectors discovered independently by Americans H.H.C. Dunwoody and G.W. Pickard.

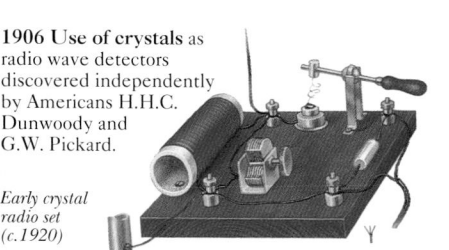

Early crystal radio set (c.1920)

1917 First crystal grown by artificial means by German J. Czochralski (1885–1953).

1918/19 Switching circuits devised by British scientists W.H. Eccles and F.W. Jordan.

1931 Electron microscope invented by German scientists Ernst Ruska (1906–88) and Max Knoll (1897–1969).

1940 Electronic computers (using va developed. These first computers are as buildings.

1943 Printed circuit boards perfecte Austrian-born Paul Eisler (1907–92).

1947 Transistor invented by Americ William Shockley (1910–89), John Bar (1908–91), and Walter Brattain (1902–

Image from modern electron microscope

| 1917 | 1918 | 1931 | 1940 | 1943 | 1947 |

TRANSISTOR

The transistor, the most important component in electronics, replaced the valve (below). It can turn a current on and off, and it can alter its strength. If enough transistors are connected together, their particular state at any time (on or off) can be used by computers to store and manipulate numbers, words, and pictures.

Audion valve of 1907, invented by Lee de Forest

Plate (anode)

Grid gives off weak signal.

Filament (cathode) gives off electrons.

VALVE

Valves control the strength and direction of a current. A red-hot filament (cathode) in a vacuum tube gives off streams of electrons. These are attracted towards a positively charged plate (anode), but a grid placed in the flow's path and given its own current will copy any variations in its current on to the larger current.

MINIATURIZED TRANSISTOR

A transistor can permit or prevent a current from flowing using a small charge.

1 A small, positive electric charge is given to a layer of conductive polysilicon that is embedded in non-conductive silicon dioxide.

2 The positive charge in the polysilicon attracts electrons from the base layer of P-type silicon (see below).

3 The flow of electrons towards the polysilicon makes current flow from the N-type silicon point, called the source, to another, the drain.

4 When current flows between source and drain in this way, the transistor is switched on. If the polysilicon is negatively charged, current stops, and the transistor switches off.

Semiconductors

Silicon is used for microchips because it is a semiconductor – it varies in conductivity. Different types of silicon – N-type and P-type – placed side-by-side, allow current flow to be directed. This property directs current in miniature transistors.

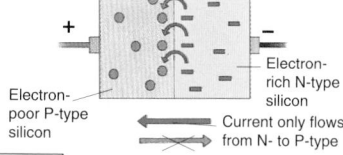

+

−

Electron-poor P-type silicon

Electron-rich N-type silicon

Current only flows from N- to P-type

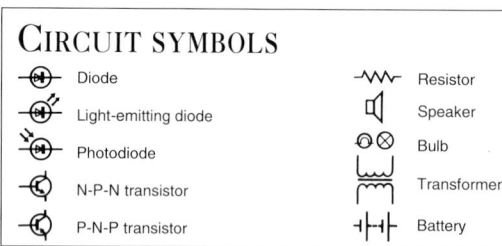

Aluminium lead

Polysilicon

Non-conductive silicon dioxide

Aluminium lead

Aluminium lead

Polysilicon

Source

Drain

N-type silicon −

N-type silicon

P-type silicon

CIRCUIT SYMBOLS

- Diode
- Light-emitting diode
- Photodiode
- N-P-N transistor
- P-N-P transistor

- Resistor
- Speaker
- Bulb
- Transformer
- Battery

CHIP RESULT

A single microchip produced in 1994 contained 9 million transistors. A similar number of transistors in 1950 would cover an area larger than eight football fields.

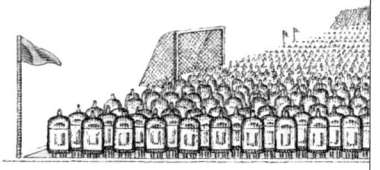

MAKING A MICROCHIP

Thousands of tiny transistors (above) and other components can be put on one tiny slice of silicon to make a complete electronic circuit – an integrated circuit, or microchip. Most electronic devices contain one or more of these silicon chips.

Design

The first stage in making a microchip is to plan and map the thousands of transistors and other components that the chip needs to perform its tasks. Modern chips are so complicated that most of this work is done by computers, not people.

Photography and checking

Once the circuit has been planned, computers check the proposed chip for possible design weaknesses. Microchips contain layers of different materials, and transparent, enlarged plans are used to check that each layer fits precisely with all the others.

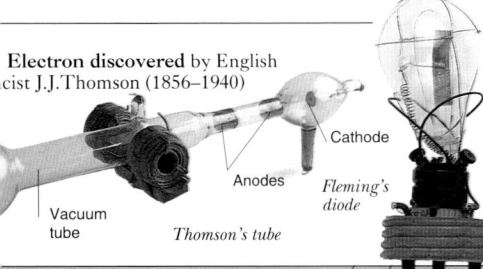

Electron discovered by English [physi]cist J.J.Thomson (1856–1940)

Vacuum tube

Thomson's tube

Anodes

Cathode

Fleming's diode

1904 Diode valve produced by John Ambrose Fleming. It is the first practical electronic device and conducts current in one direction only.

1906 Triode invented by American inventor Lee de Forest (1873–1961). His valve can amplify (make stronger) weak electric signals and becomes crucial to the development of electronics.

Lee de Forest

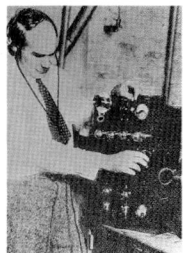

1907 Electric charge of electron measured by American physicist Robert Millikan (1868–1953).

1912 Electronic circuits using valves devised. This leads to broadcasting and radio communication.

| 1897 | 1900 | 1904 | 1906 | 1907 | 1912 |

First integrated [circu]it, made from single [piec]e of semiconductor [mate]rial, produced by [Ame]rican Jack Kilby [(b.1]923).

[19]60 [inte]grated circuit [prod]uction begins.

Modern circuit board with components

Shockley, Bardeen, and Brattain, at Bell Laboratories, US

1971 First microprocessor developed by the Intel Corporation.

1973 Home video recorders (VCR) produced.

1983 First mobile telephone network introduced in Chicago, USA.

1987 Transatlantic optical fibre telephone cable laid, enlarging capacity of communications network.

1997 MMX processor chip introduced for multimedia computers.

1998 Iridium telephone network begins operation, using satellites in low orbits to offer global coverage for mobile telephones.

Fibre-optic installation

| 1958 | 1959 | 1971 | 1973 | 1983 | 1987 | 1997 | 1998 |

[E]VERYDAY ELECTRONICS

Modern car control systems

Automatic camera

Washing machine

Medical scanner

Mobile telephone

Radar system

Factory robot

Electronic shaver

LIQUID CRYSTAL DISPLAYS

Liquid crystals have a regular structure. Controlled currents force their molecules to allow or prevent the passage of light. Liquid crystal displays can display colour images as well as black and white. They are used mainly for portable electronic items, such as computers and hand-held games.

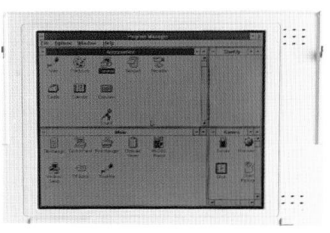

ELECTRONICS WORDS

Analogue signal Electrical copy of sound, vision, or other form of information.

Cathode Negative electrode in a valve or tube.

Digital signal Electrical stream of information in the form of on or off pulses.

Diode Permits electric current in circuit to travel in one direction only.

LED Light-emitting diode.

Microprocessor Integrated circuit that can decode instructions and manipulate information.

Resistor Controls amount of current flowing in a circuit.

Semiconductor Substance that conducts slightly; it can be combined with other substances to control conductivity.

Solid-state Using the electronic properties of solids, especially semiconductors, to act as valves.

Transistor Miniature electronic device that can amplify electric current and turn it on or off.

[E]LECTRONICS [R]ECORDS

[D]ENSEST MICROCHIP (1996) [i]s a thumbnail-sized [m]icroprocessor which contains [1]25 million transistors.

[L]ARGEST VALVES [a]re about 2m (6.6ft) long and [h]andle about 10 million watts. [T]hey are used in military radars [a]nd particle accelerators.

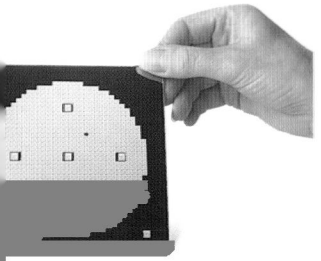

[S]ilicon slice [S]ilicon metal, which is cheap and [s]trong, needs to be highly refined [b]efore it can be used in chips. A pure [e]nough piece, sliced and polished into [t]hin wafers, is treated in a chemical [p]rocess that etches the grid of [c]omponents and tracks onto its surface.

ELECTRONICS FACTS

• Microchips are the size of a fingernail, and yet a drawing showing all their workings in detail would be bigger than a detailed map of a major city.

Chemical and heat treatment
The potential microchip is now heated to a high temperature at which the chemicals that will form its several layers can fix on to the etched silicon surface. The delicacy of this process requires extreme cleanliness. All workers wear gowns and gloves.

• Fibre-optic cables, made of hair-fine glass, transmit information in the form of pulses of light. They are able to carry much more data than traditional copper cables.

• Filmmakers use electronics to generate astonishing special effects in their films. Animation, once produced by hand, can now be done by computers.

Electronics in special effects – scene from Disney film Tron

Integrated circuit (chip)

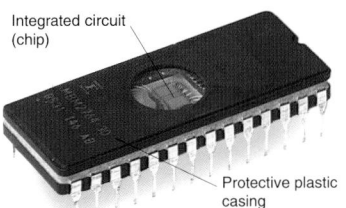

Protective plastic casing

Chip with connections
When the silicon slice has been fully treated, it is placed on a plastic base and connected to metal leads that expand and connect to other parts of a circuit. These conductive leads send out the chip's signals and receive signals from other components.

Pocket calculators – covered and uncovered

Liquid crystal display

Microchip

Uncovered keyboard

Product
The pocket calculator (above) uses just one integrated circuit, but most modern appliances contain several. Other types of electronic items, such as liquid crystal displays, may be included in a final product.

COMPUTERS

COMPUTERS ARE AUTOMATIC electronic devices that can perform complex tasks by breaking them down into many simple calculations and doing them extremely quickly. Their ability to store, manipulate, and communicate information has had a massive impact on our lives.

1945 First electronic general-purpose calculator, ENIAC (Electronic Numerical Integrator and Calculator), built in US. Using valves, it weighs 30 tonnes, consumes 150kW, and averages 5,000 operations per second. The US Army uses it to calculate artillery aiming tables.

ENIAC

1964 BASIC (Beginners All-Purpose Symbolic Instruction Code) programming language is created by professors at Dartmouth College, USA. BASIC later becomes popular among users of personal computers.

1965 First commercially successful minicomputer, DEC PDP–8, is produced in USA. It sits on a desk-top.

1971 First microprocessor chip, the Intel 4004, produced in USA. It performs 60,000 operations per second.

1975 Microsoft founded by American businessmen Bill Gates (born 1955) and Paul Allen (born 1953). They develop DOS, which later becomes the dominant operating system for computers.

1976 Cray–1 supercomputer built. Word processor for personal computers, *Electric Pencil,* developed. **Apple** computer company formed.

1977 Mass-produced personal computer, Commodore PET (Personal Electronic Transactor), appears.

Early Commodore personal computer

1979 Applica software for personal computers, Visicalc, appea A spreadsheet program, it sell 100,000 copies its first year.

Timeline: 1940 — 1945 — 1960 — 1964 — 1965 — 1971 — 1975 — 1976 — 1977 — 1979

ANATOMY OF A COMPUTER

Every computer has four basic parts, or units: an input unit, such as a keyboard, that feeds information into the computer; a central processing unit (CPU) that performs the computer's tasks; an output unit, such as a monitor, that displays the results; a memory unit for storing information and instructions.

Input and output devices
These allow the computer to communicate with people and other computers. The keyboard and mouse are input devices. The monitor and printer are output devices.

Microprocessor
The microprocessor is the central control unit. It carries out a program's instructions and controls the information flowing around the computer on the Bus and the input and output devices.

Bus
The Bus links the microprocessor, memory, and input and output devices.

RAM (Random-Access Memory)
RAM is used to store programs that are being run. When a computer is switched off the information in the RAM is lost.

ROM (Read-Only Memory)
When you switch on a computer, a program that is permanently stored in the ROM checks the computer and makes it ready for use. The ROM's program cannot be changed.

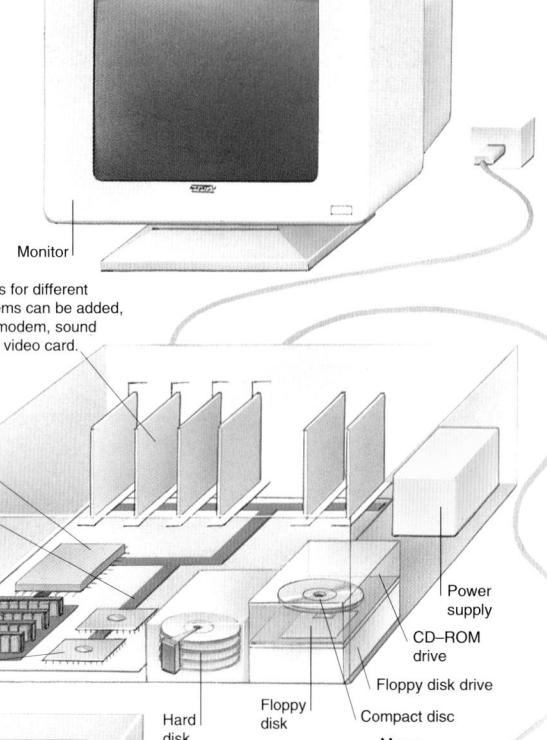

Monitor

Cards for different systems can be added, e.g. modem, sound card, video card.

Power supply

CD–ROM drive

Floppy disk drive

Compact disc

Hard disk

Floppy disk

Mouse pad

Mouse

Keyboard

COMPUTER WORDS

Applications software Software use for specific tasks, e.g. word processor databases.

Bit Binary digit (a 1 or a 0).

Bug Error in a program.

Byte Piece of information. One byte contains eight bits.

Database Set of data on computer accessible in various ways.

Hardware Machinery and components of the computer.

Internet Worldwide network of computer networks.

Megabyte One million bytes.

Modem Device that allows compute to exchange information using the telephone network.

Operating system The program tha enables the computer to perform general operations.

Software The variety of programs used by a computer.

CD–ROM drive
Compact discs, read using lasers, store more data than floppy disks.

Hard disk
The hard disk stores data when the computer is switched off. It is usually used to store larger amounts of data than the RAM

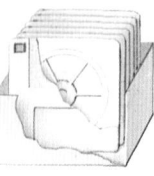

Floppy disks
These can be used to transfer data between computers

GENERATIONS OF COMPUTER

Generation	Dates	Characteristic
1st	1944–59	Use valves (vacuum tubes)
2nd	1959–64	Use transistors
3rd	1964–75	Large Scale Integrated Circuits (LSI)
4th	1975–	Very Large Scale Integrated Circuits (VLSI)
5th	Under development	"Artificial Intelligence"-based computers

MODERN COMPUTERS

• In 1996 the first ever computer that can carry out one trillion calculations per second was unveiled.

• Digital versatile disc, or digital video disc, (DVD) was released in 1996. It began to replace CD-ROMs and may soon become standard on personal computers.

• In 1997 a computer called Deep Blue 2 beat the reigning world chess champion, Garry Kasparov.

7 Transistor,
ntial storage device
omputers, invented
merican engineers
am Shockley
0–89), John Bardeen
8–91), and Walter
ain (1902–87).

1948 First stored-program computer, Manchester Mark 1, built in UK. Using valves, it can perform about 500 operations per second and has the first RAM (see opposite). It fills a room the size of a small office.

Visible portion of Manchester Mark 1 computer

1951 Early computer game, *Nim,* played by Ferranti Nimrod Computer at the Festival of Britain.

1957 FORTRAN (Formula Translator) programming language invented at IBM.

1958 Integrated circuit (microchip) produced by American engineer Jack Kilby (born 1923). His circuit is made on a single piece of semiconductor.

Jack Kilby

1947 **1948** **1950** **1951** **1957** **1958**

First portable computer, orne 1, produced. At the size and ht of a sewing machine, however, it is h less convenient than current able computers.

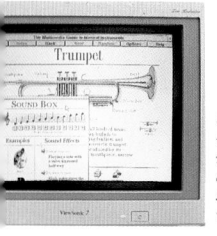

Osborne 1 portable computer

1981 IBM launches IBM PC on the personal computer market. IBM makes the first massive sales in the personal computer market.

1984 Apple Macintosh computer (or Apple Mac) becomes first successful personal computer with a mouse (see opposite) and easy-to-use Graphical User Interface (GUI).

Microsoft Windows title screen

1985 Microsoft launches Windows for the PC. Windows is a Graphical User Interface similar to the Apple Mac's, making personal computers much easier to use.

1990 IBM Pentium PC produced. It holds up to 4,000 megabytes of RAM and can perform up to 112 million instructions per second. The microprocessor chip at the heart of the computer measures 16mm by 17mm and contains 3.1 million transistors. It is designed using a system called VLSI (Very Large Scale Integration).

1981 **1984** **1985** **1990**

OMPUTER FACTS

ll the data that computers use is inary code: a signal of electrical ses that is either on (1) or off Words, numbers, and pictures be expressed as sequences of ary code.

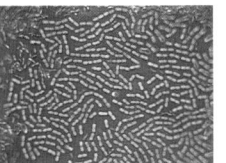

Computer viruses may multiply in a computer's memory like bacteria.

• Computer viruses are programs that destroy stored information. A virus may enter the computer's memory and copy itself so many times that it uses up all the memory, or it may make the computer destroy all the data in its memory.

• Computers can communicate with each other over a telephone line, using a machine called a modem.

• Computer performance increased by a factor of about a million between 1950 and 1990.

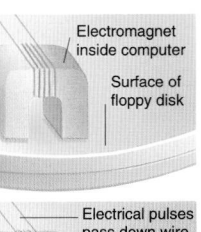

CD-ROM is useful for reference books and can use sound and moving images.

D–ROM is a form of compact player modified for computers. s for CD–ROM can store 450 es as much data as can be held a floppy disk.

PROGRAMS

A program is the set of instructions that a computer needs to carry out a particular task, such as word processing. Instructions may be written in "machine code", or other computer languages, such as BASIC or FORTRAN.

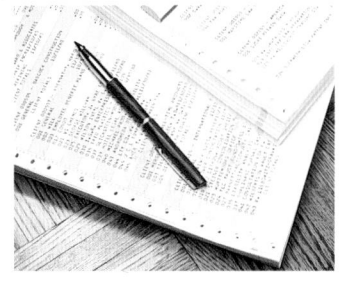

A computer's program may be printed out.

SUPERCOMPUTERS

Computers designed to operate at the highest possible speeds are called supercomputers. By performing several processes at once and by being cooled – which causes their components to conduct electricity more efficiently – they can calculate at a very fast rate.

Cray X–MP/48 supercomputer, used in study of particle physics at CERN, Switzerland.

OW A FLOPPY DISK WORKS

mputer users can store data on floppy disks transfer it to other computers.

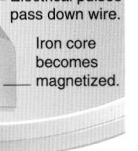

Electromagnet inside computer

Surface of floppy disk

Electrical pulses pass down wire.

Iron core becomes magnetized.

Band pair represents one bit.

1 The surface of a floppy disk is coated with iron particles. Small bands of these particles can be made to line up in one direction or another by an electromagnet inside the computer.

2 Current is passed down a coil, magnetizing an iron core and forcing the iron particles to line up. If current is reversed, the particles line up in the other direction.

3 One pair of particle bands makes up a bit of data. If the bands in the pair lie in the same direction, they represent the binary number 0. If not, the pair represents 1.

IMAGES ON SCREEN

A computer screen consists of a grid of small picture cells called pixels. Each pixel has a horizontal and vertical position code and a colour code. The computer's microprocessor generates the picture as a series of these codes, lighting up each pixel in a certain colour.

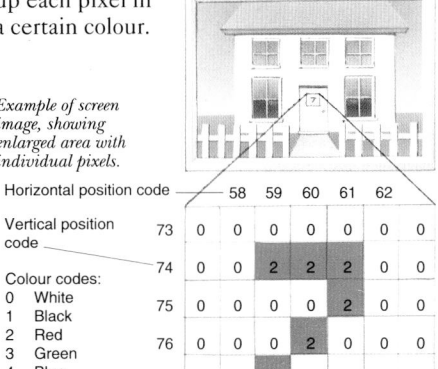

Example of screen image, showing enlarged area with individual pixels.

Horizontal position code →		58	59	60	61	62		
Vertical position code →	73	0	0	0	0	0	0	0
	74	0	0	2	2	2	0	0
	75	0	0	0	0	2	0	0
	76	0	0	0	2	0	0	0
	77	0	0	2	0	0	0	0
	78	0	0	0	0	0	0	0

Colour codes:
0 White
1 Black
2 Red
3 Green
4 Blue
5 Cyan
6 Yellow
7 Magenta

COMPUTER-AIDED DESIGN

Computers allow engineers to test new designs without having to build prototype models. They can also be used to help model complex systems, such as weather systems.

Computer model of airflow over aeroplane

BRAIN DRAIN

The first all-purpose computer, ENIAC, required so much electricity to process information that the lights in a nearby town dimmed each time it was used.

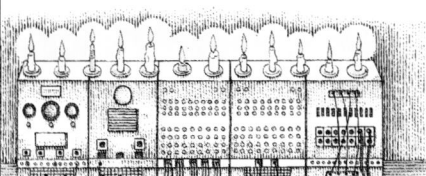

MATHEMATICS

MATHEMATICS IS THE study of numbers and shapes. It is a vital tool, not only for scientists and engineers, but for everyone. Algebra is the branch of mathematics that uses abstract symbols in place of numbers, while geometry deals with shapes and lines.

MATHS TOOLS

Set squares and compasses enable us to draw shapes precisely, such as circles and squares. Electronic tools, such as the calculator, save time.

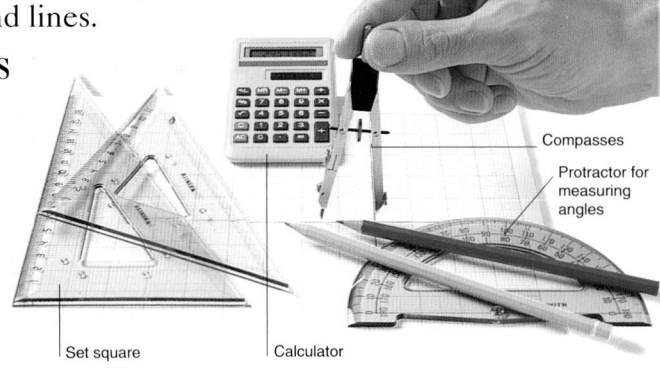

Compasses

Protractor for measuring angles

Set square

Calculator

ONE TO TEN: SYMBOL SYSTEMS

Different civilizations have used different symbols for numbers, and some do not include a zero symbol.

Number	Babylonian	Roman	Mayan	Arabic
Zero				0
One		I		1
Two		II		2
Three		III		3
Four		IV		4
Five		V		5
Six		VI		6
Seven		VII		7
Eight		VIII		8
Nine		IX		9
Ten		X		10

NEGATIVE NUMBERS

Sometimes it is useful to use numbers less than zero – negative numbers. For example, if the temperature on a winter's day falls below zero, it is referred to as a negative number, such as -3.

-5 -4 -3 -2 -1 0 1 2 3 4 5

Number line

9-dot matrix, 3-by-3 square

SQUARE NUMBERS

When a number is multiplied by itself, it is said to be squared. This is usually written as the number, with a small 2 next to and above it. So, three squared is $3^2 = 3 \times 3 = 9$.

BINARY SYSTEM

We use a number system based on the number ten, but a number system can be based on any number. Computers use binary numbers, based on the number two. Binary uses only two digits: 0 and 1.

Base 10 number	Binary number
1	1
2	10
3	11
4	100
5	101
6	110
7	111

PRIME NUMBERS

Prime numbers are those that can be divided only by themselves and 1, e.g. 17. 12 is not a prime, since it can be divided by 2, 3, 4, and 6, as well as by itself and 1.

2	3	5	7
11	13	17	19
23	29	31	37
41	43	47	53
59	61	67	71
73	79	83	89
97	101	103	107
109	113	127	131

FRACTIONS

When a cake is halved, each piece is equivalent to the whole divided by two. This is written $^1/_2$, the line meaning "divided by". So, $^3/_4$ (three-quarters) means three divided by four.

PERCENTAGES

It is sometimes useful to write fractions as percentages. Per cent means "for each hundred". Written as a percentage, $^1/_2$ becomes 50%, since half of 100 is 50.

DECIMALS

Numbers less than one can be written as decimals. A decimal point is used. The number after the decimal point represents a number of tenths. So, one-half is written as 0.5 ($^5/_{10}$).

STYLE TABLE

Fractions	Decimals	Percentages
$^1/_2$	0.5	50%
$^1/_4$	0.25	25%
$^1/_{10}$	0.1	10%
$^1/_{100}$	0.01	1%

MATHEMATICAL SYMBOLS

Symbol	Meaning	Symbol	Meaning	Symbol	Meaning
+	Add (plus)	=	Equal to	√	Square root of
−	Subtract (minus)	≠	Not equal to	%	Per cent
×	Multiply (times)	<	Less than	≤	Less than or equal to
÷	Divided by	>	Greater than	≥	Greater than or equal to

CHAOS THEORY

The intricate pattern (below) was created using a simple mathematical equation. These equations are a product of a recent field of mathematics called chaos theory.

Fractal (computer-generated image)

SCIENTIFIC NOTATION

Very large or small numbers are often written using a system called scientific notation.

Number	Number between 1 and 10	Power of ten	Scientific notation
10	1	10	1×10
150	1.5	$10^2 (= 100)$	1.5×10^2
274,000,000	2.74	$10^8 (= 100,000,000)$	2.74×10^8
0.0023	2.3	$10^{-3} (= 0.001)$	2.3×10^{-3}

DEAD RIGHT

At 20 years of age, Pierre Galois wrote his most important mathematical ideas in a letter to a friend, the night before he was killed in a duel. His results are still used today.

GEOMETRY

Geometry is the study of lines, angles, solid shapes, and surfaces.

PLANE FIGURES

Any two-dimensional (flat) shape, such as a circle, is a plane figure. A polygon is a plane figure with three or more straight sides.

Area

The area of a shape or surface is a measure of the size of the surface. For example, the area of a football pitch is greater than the area of a tennis court.

SOLIDS

Solids are not flat, but three-dimensional (they take up space). A polyhedron is a solid that has plane (flat) faces.

Volume

The volume of a solid is the amount of space it takes up. For example, a football has a greater volume than that of a golf ball.

Square *Polygon with four equal sides, all meeting at right angles*
Area = length^2

Circle *Curve on which all points are equidistant from the centre*
Area = π x radius^2

Equilateral triangle *Has three equal sides*
Area (of any triangle) = ½ x base x height

Isoceles triangle *Triangle with two equal sides*
Area = ½ x base x height

Quadrilateral *Polygon with four sides*

Rhombus *Quadrilateral with sides of equal length*
Area = 2x (a x b)

Rectangle *Quadrilateral with opposite sides of equal length that meet at right angles*
Area = base x height

Parallelogram *Quadrilateral with opposite sides that are parallel and of equal length*
Area = a x b

Trapezium *Quadrilateral with only two sides parallel*
Area = ½ x sum of parallel sides x distance between them

Pentagon *Polygon with five sides*

Hexagon *Polygon with six sides*

Octagon *Polygon with eight sides*

Tetrahedron *Polyhedron with four triangles as faces*

Cube *Six squares of equal sides as faces*
Volume = length^3

Octahedron *Polyhedron with eight faces*

Square pyramid *Pentahedron with one square face and four triangular faces*

Triangular prism *Solid figure with two triangular ends*
Volume = area of triangular ends x distance between them

Rectangular block
Volume = length x breadth x height

Apex

Sphere *Globe-shaped figure with every point on its surface equidistant from its centre*
Volume = ⁴/₃ x π x radius^3
Surface area = 4 x π x radius^2

Hemisphere *Half-sphere*

Spheroid *Egg-shaped figure*

Cone *Circular base, narrowing to a point, or apex*
Volume = ⅓ x π x radius^2 x height

Cylinder *Two circular faces, connected by a tube*
Surface area = π x diameter x length
Volume = π x radius^2 x length

CIRCLE TERMS

Arc Part of curve.

Circumference Distance around edge of circle.

Chord Straight line joining any two points on circumference.

Diameter Line from one side of circle to other, passing through centre.

Pi (π) Ratio of circumference to diameter (approx. 3.14159, same for all circles).

Radius Distance from centre of circle to edge.

Sector Slice of circle between two radii.

Segment Part of circle between chord and edge.

PYTHAGORAS' THEOREM

For any right-angled triangle, the squares of the two sides adjacent to the right angle (B and C, below) add up to the square of the longest side, or hypotenuse (A).

$$A^2 = B^2 + C^2$$

B A

Right angle

C

ANGLE

An angle is a measure of the space between two lines, formed when one line is rotated (turned). The hands of a clock form an angle between each other as they turn. Angles are measured in degrees (°), or radians.

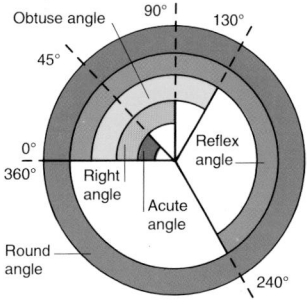

Obtuse angle   90°   130°
45°
Reflex angle
0°
360°   Right angle
Acute angle
Round angle
240°

TRIGONOMETRY

Trigonometry is the study of the relationships between the sides and angles of triangles.

TRIGONOMETRIC RATIOS

Three simple relationships, or ratios, are commonly used in trigonometry: sine (sin), cosine (cos), and tangent (tan). The sine of an angle in a right-angled triangle is given by dividing the length of the side opposite the angle by the length of the hypotenuse.

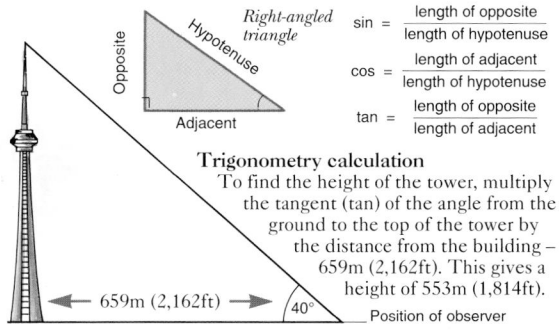

Right-angled triangle

Opposite   Hypotenuse
Adjacent

$$\sin = \frac{\text{length of opposite}}{\text{length of hypotenuse}}$$

$$\cos = \frac{\text{length of adjacent}}{\text{length of hypotenuse}}$$

$$\tan = \frac{\text{length of opposite}}{\text{length of adjacent}}$$

Trigonometry calculation
To find the height of the tower, multiply the tangent (tan) of the angle from the ground to the top of the tower by the distance from the building – 659m (2,162ft). This gives a height of 553m (1,814ft).

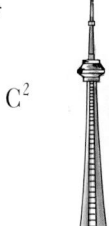

← 659m (2,162ft) →   40°
Position of observer

KEY MATHEMATICIANS

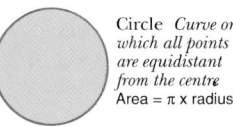

Euclid (c.300 B.C.), Greek mathematician, whose geometric proofs in *The Elements* were taught in schools for 2,000 years. He studied irrational numbers (numbers, such as √2, that cannot be written as fractions or decimals).

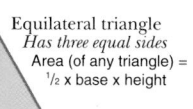

Gottfried Wilhelm Leibniz (1646–1716), German mathematician and philosopher, independently invented the theory of calculus, at the same time as Isaac Newton. He built a mechanical multiplying machine.

Karl Friedrich Gauss (1777–1855), German mathematician and astronomer. He wrote first major book on number theory, which included a theory of complex numbers. He contributed to many areas.

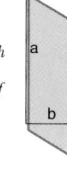

Baron Augustin-Louis Cauchy (1789–1857), French mathematician, modernized the calculus, contributed to an area of mathematics called group theory. He is said to have more theorems named after him than any other mathematician.

MATHS FACTS

• Perfect numbers are those that are equal to the sum of their factors (a number that divides equally into another number). The first perfect number is six, since 1 + 2 + 3 = 6.

• The theorem that Greek mathematician Pythagoras discovered and that bears his name was known by Babylonian and Egyptian mathematicians hundreds of years earlier.

• The Maya in South America were the first people to invent a symbol for the number zero.

• There is an infinite number of prime numbers.

• The mathematical term "algorithm" is derived from the name of the 9th-century Arabic mathematician al-Khwarizmi. The term "algebra" comes from the title of his book.

WEIGHTS AND MEASURES

THERE ARE TWO MAJOR systems of measurement. The metric system, based on the number ten, is the most common and is used by scientists worldwide. Certain countries, such as the USA, use the older imperial system. You can convert between systems using conversion tables (right).

ANCIENT MEASURES

MAYAN NUMBER KNOTS
The ancient Maya of Central America used an arrangement of knotted strings, called a quipu, to record numerical information. The type and position of knot and the length and colour of string were all significant.

ASSYRIAN WEIGHTS
The first standard system of weights arose when traders needed to measure quantities of goods. Assyrian weights (right) were made for King Shalmaneser III.

Mayan quipu

Assyrian ingot weights

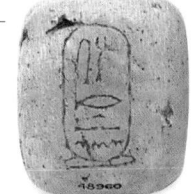
5 kite

4 deben

2 kite

1 kite

EGYPTIAN WEIGHTS
Ancient Egyptians used a weight called a deben, made of copper. The value of the standard deben was later increased, and divided into ten "kite".

INDUS VALLEY WEIGHTS
The people of Mohenjo-Daro, a city of the Indus valley civilization (c. 2500 B.C.) used cubic weights made of a stone called chert. The largest of these weights could not be lifted by one person alone.

Indus valley chert weights

THE SEVEN BASE SI UNITS

SI (Système Internationale d'Unités) is the standard system of units for scientists throughout the world. There are seven base units, from which the other units are derived (shown below).

Quantity	Unit	Symbol
Mass	Kilogram	kg
Length	Metre	m
Time	Second	s
Electric current	Ampere	A
Temperature	Kelvin	K
Luminous intensity	Candela	cd
Amount of substance	Mole	mole

MEASUREMENT FACTS
• The metric system was first adopted in France in 1791. King Louis XVI approved it the day before he attempted to flee the revolution that was unfolding.

• China was the first country to use a decimal system. Wooden rulers divided into units of ten that date back to the 6th century B.C. have been found.

• Units used today in the imperial system have evolved over centuries, mainly by custom. The origins of some of these units can be found in the earliest civilizations of the Near and Middle East. The metric system commonly used today – the SI system – was devised by scientists and adopted in a single period by many nations.

STANDARDS
To ensure that everyone means the same thing when stating measurements, several units have very precisely defined standards. A few are defined below.

THE STANDARD SECOND
One second is defined as "the duration of 9,192,631,770 periods of the radiation corresponding to the transition between the two hyperfine levels of the ground state of the caesium–133 atom."

Caesium clock

THE STANDARD KILOGRAM
A kilogram of the metal platinum was made as a worldwide standard for the kilogram. It is kept under carefully controlled conditions at the International Bureau of Weights and Measures at Sèvres, France.

Standard kilogram

THE STANDARD METRE
One metre is defined as "the length equal to 1,650,763.73 wavelengths, in a vacuum, of the radiation corresponding to the transition between the levels $2p_{10}$ and $5d_5$ of the krypton–86 atom."

Krypton gas

DERIVED UNITS
This table shows a selection of the derived units in the SI (Système Internationale d'Unités).

Quantity	Unit	Symbol
Frequency	Hertz	Hz
Energy	Joule	J
Force	Newton	N
Power	Watt	W
Pressure	Pascal	Pa
Electric charge	Coulomb	C
Electrical resistance	Ohm	Ω
Electric potential difference	Volt	V
Radiation activity	Becquerel	Bq

MUSICAL MEASURE
In ancient China, a vessel that was used to measure out grain or wine was known to contain the correct volume of goods if it made the right sound when struck.

NUMBER TERMS: GREAT AND SMALL
Prefixes inserted before a unit signify multiples or fractions of that unit.

Prefix	Symbol	Meaning	Prefix	Symbol	Meaning
tera	T	One million million	deci	d	One-tenth
giga	G	One thousand million	centi	c	One-hundredth
mega	M	One million	milli	m	One-thousandth
kilo	k	One thousand	micro	μ	One-millionth
hecto	h	One hundred	nano	n	One-thousand millionth

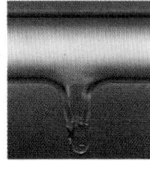

LENGTH

1 inch (in)	
1 foot (ft)	12 in
1 yard (yd)	3 ft
1 mile	1,760 yd
1 millimetre (mm)	
1 centimetre (cm)	10 mm
1 metre (m)	100 cm
1 kilometre (km)	1,000 m

AREA

1 square inch (in^2)	
1 sq foot (ft^2)	144 in^2
1 sq yard (yd^2)	9 ft^2
1 acre	4,840 yd^2
1 sq mile	640 acres
1 sq millimetre (mm^2)	
1 sq centimetre (cm^2)	100 mm^2
1 sq metre (m^2)	10,000 cm^2
1 hectare (ha)	10,000 m^2
1 sq kilometre (km^2)	1,000,000 m^2

VOLUME

1 cubic inch (in^3)	
1 cubic foot (ft^3)	1,728 in^3
1 cubic yard (yd^3)	27 ft^3
1 fluid ounce (fl oz)	
1 pint (pt)	20 fl oz
1 gallon (gal)	8 pt
1 cubic mm (mm^3)	
1 cubic cm (cm^3)	1,000 mm^3
1 cubic metre (m^3)	1,000,000 cm^3
1 litre (l)	1,000 cm^3

MASS AND WEIGHT

1 ounce (oz)	
1 pound (lb)	16 oz
1 stone	14 lb
1 hundredweight (cwt)	8 stones
1 ton	20 cwt
1 gram (g)	
1 kilogram (kg)	1,000 g
1 tonne (t)	1,000 kg

BODY MEASURE

Ancient civilizations used proportions of the body as units of measurement because of their convenience. Since the unit varied slightly according to the size of the person making the measurement, a master unit, or standard was often made.

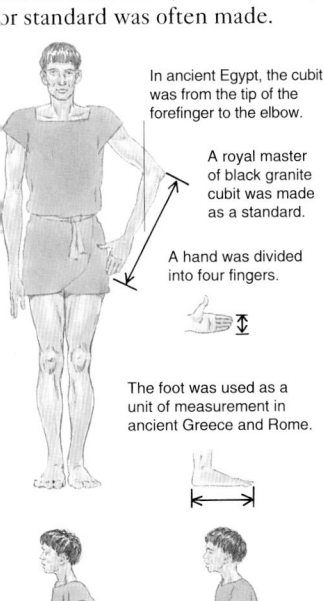

In ancient Egypt, the cubit was from the tip of the forefinger to the elbow.

A royal master of black granite cubit was made as a standard.

A hand was divided into four fingers.

The foot was used as a unit of measurement in ancient Greece and Rome.

Two steps = one pace

The mile originated in Rome – it consisted of 1,000 paces, each of which was two steps.

LENGTH CONVERSION

To convert:	Into:	Multiply by:
Inches	Centimetres	2.54
Feet	Metres	0.3048
Yards	Metres	0.9144
Miles	Kilometres	1.6093
Centimetres	Inches	0.3937
Metres	Feet	3.2808
Metres	Yards	1.0936
Kilometres	Miles	0.6214

VOLUME CONVERSION

To convert:	Into:	Multiply by:
Cubic inches	Cubic centimetres (millilitres)	16.3871
Cubic feet	Litres	28.3169
Cubic yards	Cubic metres	0.7646
Fluid ounces	Cubic centimetres (millilitres)	28.4131
Pints	Litres	0.5683
Gallons	Litres	4.5461
Cubic centimetres (millilitres)	Cubic inches	0.0610
	Fluid ounces	0.0352
Litres	Cubic feet	0.0353
Cubic metres	Cubic yards	1.3080
Cubic centimetres (millilitres)	Fluid ounces	0.0352
Litres	Pints	1.7598
	Gallons	0.2200

AREA CONVERSION

To convert:	Into:	Multiply by:
Sq inches	Sq centimetres	6.4516
Sq feet	Sq metres	0.0929
Sq yards	Sq metres	0.8361
Acres	Hectares	0.4047
Sq miles	Sq kilometres	2.5900
Sq centimetres	Sq inches	0.155
Sq metres	Sq feet	10.7639
Sq metres	Sq yards	1.1960
Hectares	Acres	2.4711
Sq kilometres	Sq miles	0.3861

MASS AND WEIGHT CONVERSIONS

To convert:	Into:	Multiply by:
Ounces	Grams	28.3495
Pounds	Kilograms	0.4536
Stones	Kilograms	6.3503
Hundredweights	Kilograms	50.802
Tons	Tonnes	1.0161
Grams	Ounces	0.0352
Kilograms	Pounds	2.2046
	Stones	0.1575
	Hundredweights	0.0197
Tonnes	Tons	0.9842

TEMPERATURE CONVERSION

To convert Fahrenheit (°F) into centigrade (°C), use the following formula:
$$°C = (°F - 32) ÷ 1.8$$

To convert centigrade (°C) into Fahrenheit (°F), use the following formula:
$$°F = (°C × 1.8) + 32$$

SPEED CONVERSION

To convert:	Into:	Multiply by:
Miles per hour	Kilometres per hour	1.6093
	Metres per second	0.4470
Kilometres per hour	Miles per hour	0.6214
Metres per second	Miles per hour	2.2370
Feet per second	Miles per hour	0.6818

MEASURING MARATHON

An acre was originally defined as the area of land that a pair of oxen could plough in one day.

TIME

TIME IS THE INTERVAL between one instant and another. People measure time by recording the movements of the Earth travelling in space: one Earth spin is a day and one orbit of the Earth around the Sun is a year. People keep time with mechanical timekeepers such as clocks and watches.

NATURAL TIME

DAYS AND YEARS

The Earth orbits the Sun in one year. At the same time, the Earth spins on its own axis. It completes one spin in a single day and 365 ¼ spins in a year. The quarter day is impractical, so after four years they are added together, and every fourth year has 366 days, a leap year.

Day

The Earth completes one spin on its axis in one day.

Year

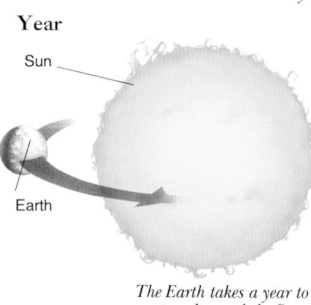

The Earth takes a year to travel round the Sun.

STANDARD TIME

The time measured at Greenwich, London, is the standard time for the whole world. For every 15 degrees of longitude east or west of Greenwich, the time is one hour ahead of or behind Greenwich time.

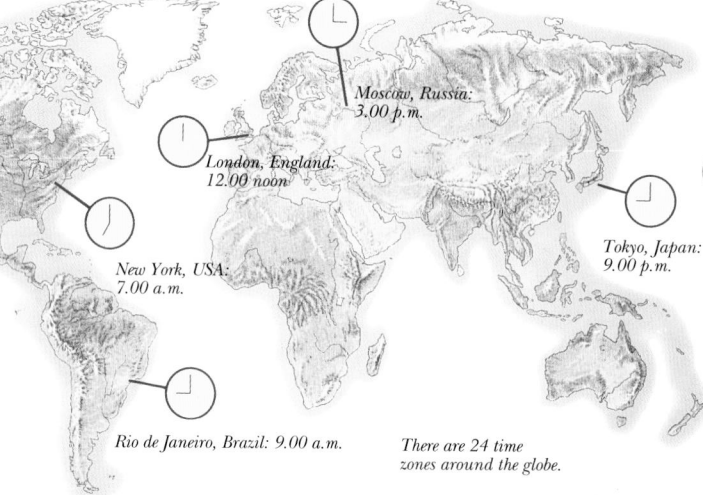

Moscow, Russia: 3.00 p.m.

London, England: 12.00 noon

New York, USA: 7.00 a.m.

Tokyo, Japan: 9.00 p.m.

Rio de Janeiro, Brazil: 9.00 a.m.

There are 24 time zones around the globe.

MONTH

While the Earth orbits the Sun, the Moon orbits the Earth. The phases of the moon add up to 29.5 days. This cycle is the lunar month and is the basis of our present-day months.

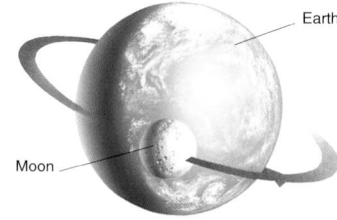

Earth

Moon

TIME FACTS

• The Earth is slowing down: a few million years from now leap years will not be needed.

• The Sumerians of Mesopotamia (present-day Iraq) first divided hours into 60 minutes, and minutes into 60 seconds in about 3000 B.C. They used 60, because it was easily divisible by 2, 3, and 4.

TIME WORDS

a.m. Before noon (ante meridiem)

Equinox The two times in a year when the Sun crosses the Equator and day and night are of equal length.

Local time The time at points that

are on the same meridian.

Meridian Line of longitude

p.m. After noon (post meridiem)

Solstice The two times in the year when the Sun is farthest from the Equator. These are the shortest and the longest days.

HISTORY OF TIMEKEEPING

People originally measured time by the position of the Sun in the sky. Later, they began to rely on machines for timekeeping, with mechanical motions that were repeated over and over again. Today, people use clocks and watches that can measure time in fractions of a second.

c.2200 B.C. Stonehenge stone circles, England, may have been used by Neolithic people to tell the time. The position of the circles allows the Sun to shine through or rise above certain stones.

Stonehenge

2200 B.C.

c.1500 B.C. Sundials are used by the Egyptians. A shadow cast by the Sun's rays indicates the time on a marked surface.

Position of the stars is used by the peoples of Babylon, Egypt, and China to tell the time.

1500 B.C.

1500 B.C.

Su

1335 First mechanical clock is erected in Milan, Italy. The turret, or tower, clock has no face, but simply strikes the hours. Turret clocks are later built throughout Europe.

1364 First known domestic clocks made by Giovanni Dondi (1318–89) of Italy. These early clocks are small versions of turret clocks, with the addition of an hour hand.

1386 Oldest mechanical clock still working is built at Salisbury Cathedral, England.

The clock in Salisbury Cathedral is driven by a revolving drum.

1510 First portable clocks made by Peter Henlein (1479–1542), a German locksmith. These small clocks are driven by a spring. The open face has an hour hand only.

Early portable clock

1330 1335 1360 1364 1380 1386 1500 1510

c.1730 Cuckoo clocks first introduced in the Black Forest, Germany.

1754 Lever escapement combined with the balance spring, gives an accuracy to within ten seconds a day.

Cuckoo clock

1759 An accurate marine timekeeper, Harrison 4, is introduced by Englishman John Harrison (1693-1776). It can withstand the changing movement and temperatures on board ship and has less than one minute of error after five months at sea.

1880 Greenwich time, time measured at the Royal Observatory, Greenwich, becomes standard time in Britain. Four years later it becomes standard time for the whole world.

c.1900 First wristwatches introduced. At first only women wear them, until World War I (1914–18), when they become popular with me in the trenches.

Early electric clock

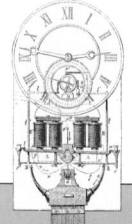

1730 1730 1754 1759 1800 1880 1900 1900

GREGORIAN CALENDAR

Most Western countries use the Gregorian calendar, which is based on the time it takes for the Earth to circle the Sun. At first, the Romans began their year in March, which is why September to December are named after the Latin numbers seven to ten. Later, in about 150 B.C., January became the first month of the year.

NAMES OF THE MONTHS

January Janus, god of gateways

February Februa, festival of purification

March Mars, god of war

April Aperire, to open

May Maia, goddess of fertility

June Juno, goddess of the Moon

July Julius Caesar

August Augustus, the first Roman emperor

September Septem, seven
October Octo, eight
November Novem, nine
December Decem, ten

LONGEST YEAR

The longest year ever was 46 B.C., which lasted for 455 days. Lengthened by 90 days to bring it in line with the solar year, it became known as the Year of Confusion.

HEBREW AND MUSLIM CALENDARS

These are based on the Moon's cycle.

Hebrew months	Muslim months	Gregorian date
Tishri	Muharram	Sept. to Oct.
Heshvan	Safar	Oct. to Nov.
Kislev	Rabi I	Nov. to Dec.
Tevet	Rabi II	Dec. to Jan.
Shevat	Jumada I	Jan. to Feb.
Adar	Jumada II	Feb. to Mar.
Nisan	Rajab	Mar. to Apr.
Iyar	Sha'ban	Apr. to May
Sivan	Ramadan	May to June
Tammuz	Shawwal	June to July
Av	Dhu al-Qa'dah	July to Aug.
Elul	Dhu al-Hijjah	Aug. to Sept.

ANCIENT CHINESE CALENDAR

This calendar, based on the Sun and the Moon, is no longer used in China, but is still in use in some Asian countries. It is divided into 24 seasons.

Season	Meaning	Gregorian date
Li Chun	Spring begins	5 Feb. to 19 Feb.
Yu Shui	Rain water	19 Feb. to 5 Mar.
Jing Zhe	Excited insects	5 Mar. to 20 Mar.
Chun Fen	Vernal equinox	20 Mar. to 5 Apr.
Qing Ming	Clear and bright	5 Apr. to 20 Apr.
Gu Yu	Grain rains	20 Apr. to 5 May
Li Xia	Summer begins	5 May to 21 May
Xiao Man	Grain fills	21 May to 5 June
Mang Zhong	Grain in ear	5 June to 21 June
Xia Zhi	Summer solstice	21 June to 7 July
Xiao Shu	Slight heat	7 July to 23 July
Da Shu	Great heat	23 July to 7 Aug.
Li Qiu	Autumn begins	7 Aug. to 23 Aug.
Chu Shu	Limit of heat	23 Aug. to 7 Sept.
Bai Lu	White dew	7 Sept. to 23 Sept.
Qui Fen	Autumn equinox	23 Sept. to 8 Oct.
Han Lu	Cold dew	8 Oct. to 23 Oct.
Shuang Jiang	Frost descends	23 Oct. to 7 Nov.
Li Dong	Winter begins	7 Nov. to 22 Nov.
Xiao Xue	Little snow	22 Nov. to 7 Dec.
Da Xue	Heavy snow	7 Dec. to 22 Dec.
Dong Zhi	Winter solstice	22 Dec. to 6 Jan.
Xiao Han	Little cold	6 Jan. to 21 Jan.
Da Han	Severe cold	21 Jan. to 5 Feb.

1400 B.C. Water clocks used by the Egyptians. A bowl with a hole in the bottom is filled with water. The passing of time is shown by a drop in the level of water, which lines up with one of the marks carved into the bowl. *Water clock*

c.A.D. 890 Clock candles are used by the English king, Alfred the Great (849–899). When a candle, which has hours marked down its length, has burnt down to a mark, it indicates that an hour has passed by.

1100s Hourglasses used in navigation, by physicians to time a pulse, and by teachers and preachers to time lessons and sermons. Sand drains from the top glass bulb to the bottom. Some glasses measure 15 or 30 minutes as well as up to one or two hours.

1300s Monasteries use simple machinery that sounds bells at regular intervals to call worshippers to prayer. A person called a clock jack rings the bells. *Hourglass*

| 1400 B.C. | A.D. 500 | A.D. 890 | 1100 | 1100 | 1300 | 1300 |

1582 Regularity of pendulum's swing shown by Italian scientist, Galileo (1564–1642). *Galileo's design for a pendulum*

1657 First pendulum clock is made by Dutch astronomer, Christiaan Huygens (1629–95). The pendulum controls the rotation of the wheels of the clock.

1670 Long, or seconds, pendulum is introduced by William Clement (c.1638–1704), an English clockmaker.

1675 Spiral balance spring, giving clocks an accuracy to within two minutes a day, is invented by Huygens. *Huygens' balance spring*

c.1690s Astronomers at the Royal Observatory, Greenwich, London, measure the stars to determine time.

Royal Observatory

| 1582 | 1650 | 1657 | 1670 | 1670 | 1675 | 1690 | 1690 |

1939 First quartz crystal clock is installed at Greenwich. The crystals' vibrations are controlled, counted, recorded, and used to establish precise time. *Early wrist-watch*

1948 First atomic clock developed in the USA. It works by counting the natural vibrations of caesium atoms, which vibrate 9,192,631,770 times per second. Time for the whole world is now established by using 80 atomic clocks from 24 countries.

1970 Atomic clock is accurate to one second in 30,000 years.

1970s–1990s Digital watches are popular. A microchip changes the numbers every second, so that the time kept is very precise. *Early atomic clock*

1990s Global positioning system (GPS) employs geostationary satellites, each with three atomic clocks.

1997 Caesium fountain atomic clock tells time to an accuracy of one second in 3 million years.

| 1930 | 1939 | 1940 | 1948 | 1970 | 1970 | 1990 | 1997 | 2000 |

ENGINES

AN ENGINE TURNS different forms of energy into motion, or kinetic energy. In the last two centuries, engine efficiency has substantially improved.

50 B.C. Chinese engineers build water wheels that use the energy of moving water.

A.D. c.600 Early windmills appear, converting wind energy into mechanical motion.

1712 Practical steam engine using piston and cylinder built by English inventor Thomas Newcomen (1663–1729).

1769 Steam carriage built by French military engineer Nicolas-Joseph Cugnot (1725–1804).

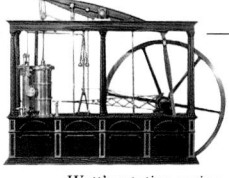

Watt's rotative engine

1783 Steam-powered paddleboat, *Pyroscaphe,* sailed up Saône River, France, by French engineer Jouffroy d'Abbans (1751–1832).

1782 Rotative steam engine built by Scottish engineer James Watt (1736–1819). Watt's engine is much more efficient and practical than Newcomen's engine.

| 50 B.C. | A.D. 1 | 600 | 1700 | 1712 | 1769 | 1782 | 1783 |

1892 German Rudolf Diesel (1858–1913) invents engine (later named diesel engine) with fuel that ignites on compression. When later built, the engine is more efficient than existing internal combustion engines.

1897 Ship powered by new steam turbine launched by British engineer Charles Parsons (1854–1931), revolutionizing marine engineering. His ship, *Turbinia,* unexpectedly appears at a British naval review and, at 34.5 knots, easily outruns the launch sent to stop it.

Queen (1904), fitted with marine turbine

1903 Powered flight by American brothers, Orville (1871–1948) and Wilbur (1867–1912) Wright, using internal combustion engine.

First sustained powered flight of Kitty Hawk

1907 Supercharger used on a car by American engineer Lee S. Chadwick.

1926 Liquid-fuel rocket launched by American Robert Goddard (1882–1945).

Robert Goddard

| 1892 | 1897 | 1900 | 1903 | 1907 | 1926 |

INTERNAL COMBUSTION ENGINE

The internal combustion engine, developed in the 19th century, has several advantages over earlier types of engine: it does not require stoking, like a steam engine; it is portable, unlike windmills or water wheels; and its fuel is highly efficient.

FOUR-STROKE ENGINE CYCLE

1 Inlet valve opens. Piston slides down cylinder, sucking in a mixture of fuel and air, called the charge.

Induction stroke

2 Inlet valve snaps shut and piston rises, squeezing charge into small space, under pressure.

Compression stroke

3 Spark ignites compressed charge. Expanding gases force piston down cylinder. Piston spins crankshaft.

Power stroke

4 Exhaust valve opens. Hot gases escape, pushed out by rising piston. Cycle restarts.

Exhaust stroke

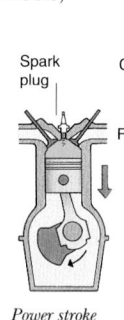
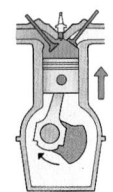

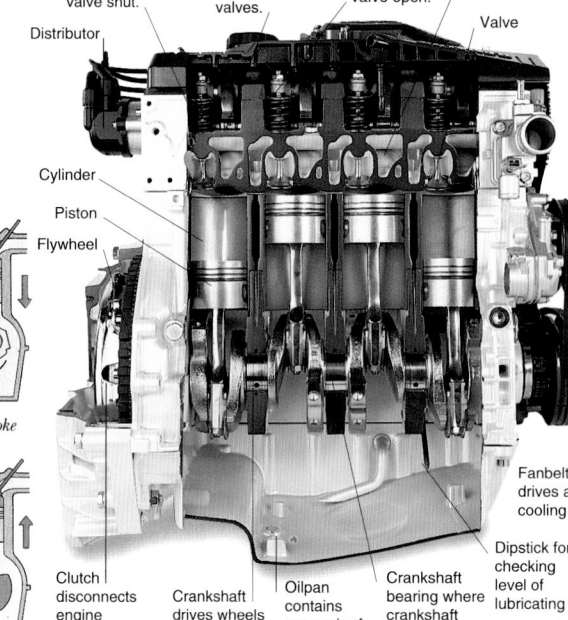

Spring snaps valve shut.

Camshaft controls opening and closing of valves.

Rocker arm pushes valve open.

Channels for cooling water

Distributor

Valve

Spark plug

Cylinder

Piston

Flywheel

Clutch disconnects engine while driver changes gear.

Crankshaft drives wheels via gearbox and clutch.

Oilpan contains reservoir of oil for lubricating engine parts.

Crankshaft bearing where crankshaft runs through engine block

Dipstick for checking level of lubricating oil

Fanbelt drives a cooling fan.

ENGINE WORDS

Carburettor Device that mixes fuel and air before its combustion in the cylinder.

Catalytic converter Device fitted to exhaust that converts pollutant gases into harmless products.

Crankshaft Shaft that turns the up and down movement of the pistons into rotary (spinning) movement.

Distributor Device that sends a spark to each cylinder at the right moment to ignite fuel.

Flywheel Heavy wheel attached to the crankshaft to smooth out the power from individual cylinders.

Horsepower Measure of the power of an engine; one horsepower is equal to 746 watts.

Internal combustion engine Engine in which fuel is burned (combusted) inside the cylinder of the engine, e.g., petrol engine.

Throttle Flap controlling flow of air and fuel through carburettor.

r.p.m. Revolutions (of the crankshaft) per minute.

TYPES OF ENGINE

The first engines harnessed natural forces to produce motive force. In the 20th century, several new types appeared.

WINDMILL
The force of the wind across the sails produces a stronger driving force at the central shaft.

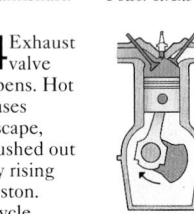

STEAM ENGINE
Water, heated by a furnace, produces steam. Expanding steam drives a piston back and forth.

PETROL ENGINE
Hot gases from an ignited petrol and air mixture push a piston down a cylinder, moving a crankshaft.

TURBO JET
Jet engines, used mainly in planes, draw in, compress, and throw out air at high speeds.

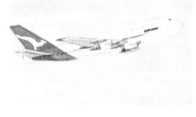

LINEAR ENGINE
Magnetic fields lift the train from the track, and shifting fields then propel it along the track.

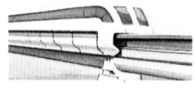

ROCKET
Rocket fuel burns in a combustion chamber and the resultant hot gases drive the rocket forwards.

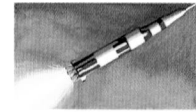

ION MOTOR
Ionized molecules (see p.222) are made to rush out by an electrical process in the motor.

STEAM ENGINE

Water in a boiler is heated by a coal fire and turns to steam. The expanding steam, fed into a cylinder, moves a piston back and forth, and the piston turns the train's wheels via a connecting rod and crank. Ships were also powered by steam engines.

Steam engines are external combustion engines, since their fuel is burned outside the cylinder.

Furnace

Steam is fed into the cylinder under high pressure.

Cylinder

Water turns to steam in the boiler.

Piston

0 First engine to use
a pressure steam built
English engineer Richard
Trithick (1771–1833).

2 Steam-powered
hip built by French
neer Henri Giffard
5–82).

1859 Internal combustion
engine built by Belgian-
French inventor Etienne
Lenoir (1822–1900).

1877 Four-stroke internal
combustion engine built
by German Nikolaus Otto
(1832–91).

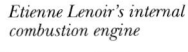
*Etienne Lenoir's internal
combustion engine*

1883 High-speed internal
combustion engine built
by German Gottlieb W.
Daimler (1834–1900).

1884 Steam turbine
generator for electricity
is built by English
engineer Charles
Parsons (1854–1931).

1885 Motorbike engine
built by Daimler.
**Three-wheeled
automobile**, built by
German Karl Benz
(1844–1929), is
the first petrol
driven motor
vehicle.

| 1800 | 1852 | 1859 | 1877 | | 1883 | 1884 | 1885 |

7 First
king jet
ne built by
ish engineer
k Whittle
7–1996).

1939 First plane with
a jet engine, Heinkel
He178, built and
flown by
German
engineer
Hans von
Ohain.

1962 First
nuclear-
powered ship,
USS Savannah,
begins sea
trials.

1970 Bypass ("turbofan") jet
engine used, now the most
common type of jet engine; *Boeing
747* "Jumbo Jet" goes into service.

1979 Catalytic converter
developed by British firm,
Ricardo Consulting
Engineers, to remove
harmful gases from
exhaust fumes.

1990s
Alternative fuel
research begins.
Possibilities
include hydrogen
fuel cells and
liquid nitrogen.

1999 Aerospike
rocket engine
successfully
tested.

*Frank Whittle (right)
with early jet engine*

USS Savannah

| 1937 | 1939 | 1960 | 1962 | 1970 | 1979 | 1990 | 1999 |

T ENGINE

et engine sucks in and compresses air using
blades. When this air is ignited with
osene, the hot gases produced thrust the
gine forwards. Before leaving the exhaust
zzle, these gases pass over and drive turbines
t are connected to the initial compressor
des. In a turbofan jet engine, air flows
und the engine, cooling and quietening it.

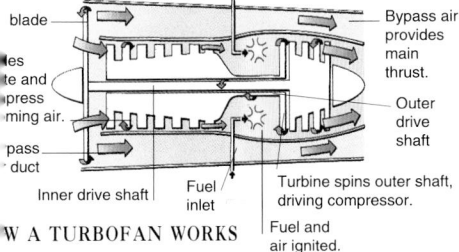

blade

les
te and
press
ming air.

pass
duct

Inner drive shaft

Fuel
inlet

Bypass air
provides
main
thrust.

Outer
drive
shaft

Turbine spins outer shaft,
driving compressor.

Fuel and
air ignited.

W A TURBOFAN WORKS

OCKET ENGINE

ckets, the simplest and
st powerful type of
ine, are powered by
id or liquid fuel. The
l burns in a combustion
mber with
open
l, and the
aping hot
es thrust
rocket
wards.

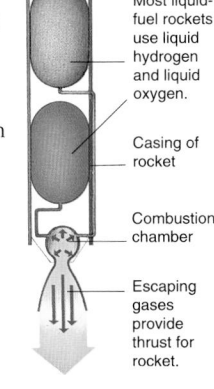

aturn V *rocket*
t take-off

Most liquid-
fuel rockets
use liquid
hydrogen
and liquid
oxygen.

Casing of
rocket

Combustion
chamber

Escaping
gases
provide
thrust for
rocket.

NGINE EFFICIENCY

n engine with 100% efficiency converts all
fuel's energy into useful work.

gine Type		Efficiency
eam		7%
ernal combustion	Petrol	25–35%
	Diesel	30–40%
wer station (oil or coal-burning)		35%
dro-electric plant		80%

Inlet cone
(rotates)

Low-pressure
fan

Oil tank

High-pressure
compressor

Fuel
nozzle

Combustion
chamber

High-pressure turbine

Exhaust cone

Fan
duct

Fuel
shut-off
valve
cable

Low-
pressure
turbine

Electronic
engine control unit

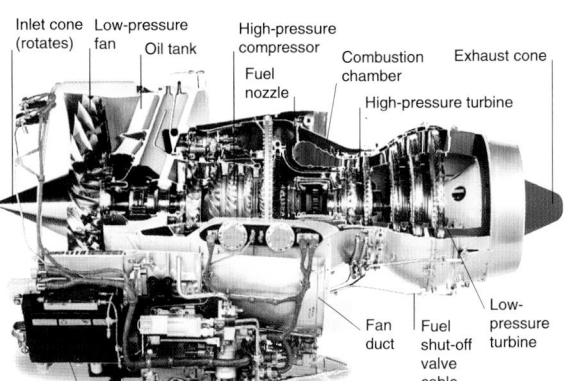

MODERN TURBOFAN JET ENGINE – CANADA PW 305
Most jet aircraft, including passenger airliners, use turbofan engines.
Their main thrust comes from the air that bypasses the engine
itself. Fuel and fan adjustments are controlled electronically.

HOT ROD

The temperature
inside the cylinders of
an internal combustion
engine can reach
1,700°C (3,100°F) – as
hot as molten lava.

EXTRA POWER

There are several ways of getting more power from an engine.

SUPERCHARGERS AND TURBOCHARGERS
Petrol and diesel engines can be fitted with pumps
that force the fuel and air mixture
into the cylinders. This
increases the strength of the
explosion on the power
stroke. Two types of pump
are used – supercharger and
turbocharger.

*Supercharged 1935
Auburn Speedster*

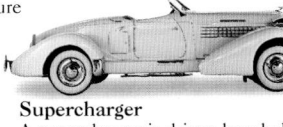

Supercharger
A supercharger is driven by a belt
or gears from the engine itself.

AFTERBURNERS
Afterburners inject extra fuel into the hot jet exhaust,
giving the engine extra thrust, almost like a rocket.
Jet aircraft such as Concorde use afterburners for
take-off, or for sudden, fast manoeuvres. They use
much more fuel and are extremely loud.

Afterburners on a jet-fighter aircraft

LINEAR ENGINE

A linear engine uses powerful
magnetism to lift a train off its
track and propel it forwards.
These trains are called maglev
(magnetic levitation) trains,
because they glide along just
above their tracks.

Maglev train, Birmingham airport, UK

ENGINE RECORDS

SMALLEST INTERNAL
COMBUSTION ENGINE
is the 0.1cc model aircraft.

LARGEST INTERNAL
COMBUSTION ENGINES
are Sulzer ship engines,
providing up to 60,000
horsepower, at 100 r.p.m.

Turbocharger

Inlet
duct

Inlet rotor
squeezes
extra fuel
and air in
cylinder.

Turbocharger
Turbochargers are more
common today; they are driven directly
by the engine's exhaust gases.

SPACE AND TIME

THE UNIVERSE IN WHICH we live is vast, and it has existed for a very long time. Everything we see or do takes place in space and time. Objects in space have physical dimensions and mass. Time runs from the past into the future, never the other way around.

TIME SLOWED DOWN

The Theory of Relativity (below) describes how space and time are related. It shows that, since the speed of light is always the same, time may speed up or slow down, and space may stretch or shrink.

Two rockets fly past Earth at a speed close to that of light. To the astronauts aboard, a flash of light sent from one to the other seems to travel in a straight line between them. To an observer on Earth, the flash follows a diagonal line. Since light travels at a constant speed, its crossing time for those on Earth must be longer than for those on board. Time passes at different rates for different observers.

JET SET

Relativity states that clocks run faster in weaker gravity. In 1975, this was proved using two atomic clocks. One, carried in a plane at high altitude, ran faster.

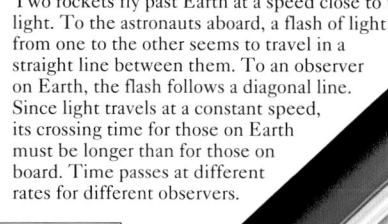

To observers on Earth, a light flash between rockets appears to follow a long path, and take a longer time to cross space.

To astronauts on rocket, same light flash follows shorter route straight between rockets, taking a short time to cross.

Rockets travel at speed close to speed of light.

TIME AND SPACE FACTS

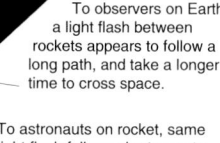

- The smallest unit of time that scientists believe we can measure is called the "Planck time". One second contains 600,000,000,000 000,000,000,000,000,000,000 000,000,000 Planck times.

- Gravity has an effect on the passage of time. Time runs more quickly at the top of a mountain, where gravity is weaker, than at sea level.

Time, like length, can be divided only a finite number of times.

- In a famous experiment during a solar eclipse in 1919, it was shown that light from a distant star was "bent". The strong gravity of the Sun has a tiny effect on time and space nearby, not normally visible.

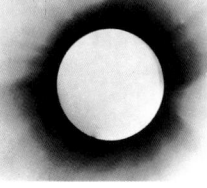

Solar eclipse of 1919 showed bending of light – the first evidence in support of Einstein's Theory of Relativity.

TIME PERIODS

Time is usually measured in seconds, or hours and minutes.

Time period		Example
0.000 000 000 001	second	A gas molecule to spin around once
0.000 000 001	second	The time it takes light to travel 30cm in air
0.000 001	second	The duration of a flash of lightning
0.001	second	The time it takes sound to travel 30cm in air
0.1	second	Olympic sprinter to run 1m
1	second	Quartz in a watch to vibrate 32,768 times
1 000	seconds	Time for a snail to move 10m
1 000 000	seconds	11.5 days
1 000 000 000	seconds	Time for Saturn to orbit the Sun once
1 000 000 000 000	seconds	Age of the earliest cave paintings

RELATIVITY

In 1905, German scientist Albert Einstein (1879–1955) published the *Special Theory of Relativity*. It shocked the scientific world because it showed that time and space are not fixed things. His *General Theory of Relativity* (1915) later suggested that space is distorted by matter. In this theory, space and time co-exist as spacetime. Spacetime can be visualized as a rubber sheet, which stretches as objects are placed upon it. Objects with mass deform real spacetime in a similar way. The larger the mass, the more spacetime deforms.

Albert Einstein

DISTANCES: SMALL AND GREAT

The range of distances in the Universe is vast. The table below gives a scale of distances in metres.

Distance		Example
0.000 000 000 000 001	m	The diameter of an atomic nucleus
0.000 000 000 001	m	The wavelength of high energy X-rays
0.000 000 001	m	The diameter of an oil molecule
0.000 001	m	The diameter of a single-celled organism
0.001	m	The wavelength of microwave radiation
0.1	m	The diameter of a croquet ball
1	m	Height of a child
1 000	m	One kilometre
1 000 000	m	The width of Egypt
1 000 000 000	m	The diameter of the Sun
1 000 000 000 000	m	The distance from Saturn to the Sun
1 000 000 000 000 000	m	1/40 the distance to the nearest star

NATURAL SCIENCE

THE STUDY of the origins and processes of life is called natural science. Scientific discoveries have helped us to understand and influence these processes.

c.350–340 B.C. Greek thinker Aristotle (384–322B.C.) attempts system of animal classification, distinguishing between animals with blood and animals without.

Aristotle

1543 Science of anatomy developed by Flemish doctor Andreas Vesalius (1514–64). His accurate illustrations of dissected bodies appear in *The Fabric of the Human Body* (1543).

Andreas Vesalius

| 400 B.C. | 350 | A.D. 1 | 1500 | 1543 |

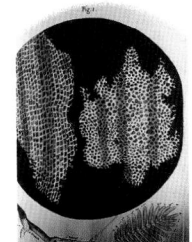

1665 English scientist Robert Hooke (1635–1703) publishes *Micrographia*, showing detailed microscopic drawings. He introduced the term "cell" to biology and helped improve the design of the compound microscope.

Drawing of magnified slice of cork

1677 Protozoa discovered by Dutch scientist Antonie van Leeuwenhoek (1632–1723), using a simple microscope. He later becomes first person to observe bacteria.

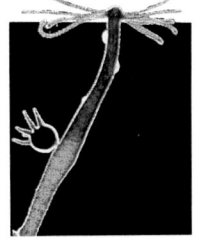

1701 Asexual reproduction first observed by Antonie van Leeuwenhoek, while watching hydra under a microscope (see p.83).

Hydra

1735 System of classification of living organisms invented by Swedish botanist Carolus Linnaeus (1707–78). His binomial (two-part) system identifies each species and shows its relation to others.

Carolus Linnaeus

| 1600 | 1665 | 1677 | 1700 | 1701 | 1735 |

1749 French naturalist Georges-Louis Buffon (1707–88) suggests that some species of plants or animals give rise to others.

1771 Connection between muscle movements and electrical impulses discovered by Italian anatomist Luigi Galvani (1737–98), while experimenting on the leg muscles of a dissected frog.

Galvani demonstrates nerve impulses.

Diagram of typical cell

1779 Process of photosynthesis discovered by Dutch-born scientist Jan Ingenhousz (1730–99).

1805 Term "biology" coined by Jean-Baptiste Lamarck (1744–1829) and Gottfried Treviranus (1776–1837). Science of anthropology founded by German Johann Blumenbach (1750–1840).

1812 Science of palaeontology (fossil studies) developed by pioneer French zoologist Georges Cuvier (1769–1832). He showed the connection between patterns of rock layers and patterns of fossil remains.

Fossil jawbone of a palaeotherium

| 1749 | 1771 | 1779 | 1800 | 1805 | 1812 |

1839 Cell theory founded by German scientists Theodor Schwann (1810–82) and Matthias Schleiden (1804–81), which holds that all living things are made from cells. Also observed that single egg-cells grow into organisms.

1855 Theory of homeostasis proposed by French physiologist Claude Bernard (1813–78), describing how organs interact to maintain steady internal conditions.

1856 French chemist Louis Pasteur (1822–95) disproves long-held idea that living organisms could grow from non-living matter (spontaneous generation).

Louis Pasteur

1859 Charles Darwin (1809–82) publishes *Origin of Species,* which explains his principle of natural selection and theory of evolution (see p.68).

Cartoon of Charles Darwin, mocking idea that humans are descended from apes

| 1839 | 1855 | 1856 | 1859 |

1860s Science of heredity (how characteristics are inherited) pioneered by Austrian monk and botanist Gregor Mendel (1822–84), after long experimentation on pea plants.

Gregor Mendel

1889 Important role of acids in food digestion discovered by German researchers. **Russian scientist Ivan Pavlov** (1849–1936) shows that reflex actions can be conditioned (learned), and are not just inbuilt. His proof involves teaching dogs to salivate at the ring of a bell.

1937 Chemistry of respiration, the way that food is converted into energy in cells, discovered by German-born biochemist Hans Krebs (1900–81). The series of chemical reactions that he identifies is central to nearly all metabolic reactions (reactions in living organisms).

Spiral of DNA

1953 Double-helix structure of DNA, the substance responsible for heredity, discovered by American and British biologists James Watson (born 1928) and Francis Crick (born 1916).

| 1860 | 1889 | 1900 | 1937 | 1953 |

1963 Mechanism by which nerves convey messages explained by Australian John Eccles (born 1903) and British doctors Andrew Huxley (born 1917) and Alan Hodgkin (born 1914).

Eccles receives Nobel prize

1974 Oldest and most complete skeleton of early upright-walking hominid discovered by American anthropologists in Ethiopia. This hominid, *Lucy,* is estimated to be 3–3.5 million years old.

Bone fragments from Lucy

1979 "Gaia" theory proposed by British scientist James Lovelock (born 1919). He suggests that the Earth is a living, self-regulating organism.

1984 Genetic fingerprinting developed by British scientist Alec Jeffreys.

James Lovelock

1990 Human genome project begins in several countries. It aims to map the position of all the genetic material in human chromosomes. This will enable scientists to eradicate inherited diseases.

1996 Dolly the sheep is born, a clone of a single cell from an adult sheep – the first time this is achieved in a mammal.

| 1963 | 1974 | 1979 | 1984 | 1990 | 1996 |

PHYSICAL SCIENCE

EVEN BEFORE THE TERM science was coined, people devised experiments to test their ideas about the physical universe.

Democritus

c.400 B.C. Greek thinker Democritus (c.460–361 B.C.) teaches that matter consists of small, hard, indivisible particles, called atoms.

c.260 B.C. Flotation principle discovered by Greek scientist Archimedes (c.287–212 B.C.). He also studied principles of levers and invented many machines.

Archimedes realizes that the volume of his body is equal to the volume of water spilled from full bath.

400 B.C. — **260** — **200 B.C.**

1643 Air pressure discovered and measured by Italian scientist and pupil of Galileo, Evangelista Torricelli (1608–47). He measures it using mercury barometer, his invention.

Mercury barometer

1687 Laws of motion and law of gravitation formulated by English mathematician Isaac Newton (1642–1727) in *Principia Mathematica*. Also discovers that white light is made up of a spectrum of colours.

Isaac Newton

1701 French scientist Joseph Sauveur (1653–1716) studies relationship between sound waves and vibrations and suggests term "acoustics" for the science of sound.

1706 Friction machine to generate electrical sparks made by English scientist Francis Hauksbee (1666–1713).

1712 Successful steam engine, with piston and cylinder, built by English engineer Thomas Newcomen (1663–1729).

Newcomen's engine, used for draining mines.

1643 — **1687** — **1700** — **1701** — **1706** — **1712**

1800 Infrared waves discovered by Anglo-German astronomer William Herschel (1738–1822). Infrared is an invisible form of electromagnetic wave (see p.231). Herschel discovered Uranus and hundreds of stars and nebulae.

William Herschel

Dalton's atomic models

1803 Atomic theory of matter proposed by Englishman John Dalton (1766–1844), introducing modern ideas about elements and compounds made of atoms and molecules.

1807–8 Potassium, sodium, magnesium, barium, calcium, and strontium discovered by British chemist Humphry Davy (1778–1829).

Davy performs a public experiment.

1811 Avoga[...] Law formula[...] by Italian phys[...] Amedeo Avoga[...] (1776–1856). [...] law states that [...] same volume [...] any gas contai[...] the same num[...] of molecules.

1800 — **1803** — **1807** — **1811**

1843 Relationship between heat, power, and work investigated and formulated by English scientist James Joule (1818–89).

Joule's machine for measuring energy conversion

1846 Laws of thermodynamics developed by British physicist William Thomson (1824–1907), later Lord Kelvin. In 1862 he uses them to estimate Earth's age.

1865 Relationship between electricity and magnetism formulated by Scottish physicist James Clerk Maxwell (1831–79).

1869 Periodic Table devised by Russian schoolteacher Dmitri Mendeleyev (1834–1907). It classifies elements into family groups by atomic weight.

James Clerk Maxwell

1876 Telephone invented by Scottish-[...] speech therapist and inventor Alexander Graham Bell (1847–1922). His device use[...] thin diaphragm to convert the vibrations [...] the human voice into electrical signals, t[...] reconverts them into sound waves.

Alexa[...] Graha[...] Bell's telepho[...]

1840 — **1843** — **1846** — **1865** — **18[...]**

1900 Quantum theory proposed by German physicist Max Planck (1858–1947), stating that energy consists of small units, called "quanta". This leads to theory that light acts as both a wave and particles.

Albert Einstein

1905 *Special Theory of Relativity* published by German physicist Albert Einstein (1879–1955). Together with *General Theory* (1915), it revolutionizes the foundations of physics.

1909 First stable plastic, "Bakelite", developed by American chemist Leo Henrick Baekeland (1863–1944). This helped to found plastics industry.

Telephone receiver made of early plastic

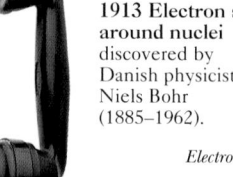

1911 Atomic nucleus discovered by New Zeal[...] born physicist Ernest Rutherford (1871–1937).

1913 Electron shells around nuclei discovered by Danish physicist Niels Bohr (1885–1962).

Electron shells

1900 — **1905** — **1909** — **1911** — **1913**

1938 Nuclear fission, splitting of nuclei to release energy, discovered by German physicists Otto Hahn (1879–1968) and Fritz Strassmann (1902–80).

Uranium fission reaction

1939 Nature of the chemical bond between atoms and molecules explained by American chemist Linus Pauling (1901–94).

1942 First nuclear reactor built by Italian physicist Enrico Fermi (1901–54).

Fermi's reactor, built in a squash court at Chicago University

1945 Heating effect of microwaves discovered by American engineer Percy Le Baron Spencer (1894–1970), when a sweet melts in his pocket during experiments with microwaves.

1946 Carbon dating invented by American scientist Willard Frank Libby (1908-80).

1960 First laser built by American physicist Theodore Maiman (born 1927), based on work of American physicist Gordon Gould in 1957.

Replica of early transistor

1938 — **1939** — **1942** — **1945** — **1946** — **1947** — **1960**

. 1100s Compass
d by Italian and
nese navigators.
y independently
over that a free or
ting magnetic
dle always
cates north.

**1600 English doctor
William Gilbert**
(1544–1603), in his
book *De Magnete*, claims
that the core of the
Earth is a great magnet
with poles at its north
and south points.

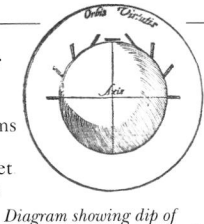

*Diagram showing dip of
compass at different latitudes.*

**1620s Modern
scientific method**
developed by
English philosopher
Francis Bacon
(1561–1626). He
advocates experiment
as the best basis for
knowledge.

1638 Science of mechanics founded
by Italian scientist Galileo Galilei
(1564–1642) in *Dialogue Concerning Two
New Sciences*. He investigated how force
causes acceleration and discovered the
properties of the pendulum.

*Apparatus to demonstrate Galileo's
work on the paths of projectiles
(objects thrown up and along)*

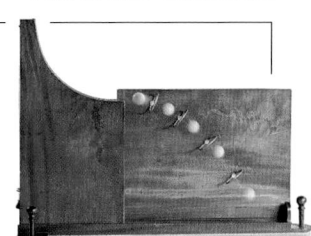

1000 1100 1600 1620 1638

---

5 Carbon dioxide
overed by Scottish
mist Joseph Black
28–99), who calls it
ed air".

**5 First efficient steam
ine built** by Scottish
ineer James Watt
36–1819).

1766 Hydrogen
discovered by
English chemist
Henry Cavendish
(1731–1810),
who calls the gas
"inflammable air".

Henry Cavendish

1779 Oxygen named by
French chemist Antoine
Lavoisier (1743–94), who
demonstrates its role in
combustion. Also shows air
to be a mixture of gases, and
that water is a compound of
oxygen and hydrogen.

*Antoine Lavoisier with wife
and co-worker Marie-Anne*

1799 Battery
invented by Italian
chemist Alessandro
Volta (1745–1827),
using different
metals separated by
salt solutions.

— Cell

*Voltaic pile or battery
(collection of cells)*

1755 1765 1766 1779 1799

0s German chemists focus on carbon
he basis of the organic chemistry of
ng things. Carbon takes many forms,
n coal to diamonds.

**1831 English scientist Michael
Faraday** (1791–1867)
uses magnetism to
make electricity, a process
called electromagnetic
induction. American
Joseph Henry (1797–1878)
makes same discovery
independently.

*Faraday's
induction ring*

1836 Catalysts
discovered by
Swedish scientist
Jöns Berzelius
(1779–1848).
Catalysts speed up
certain chemical
reactions without
themselves being
used in the reactions.

**1839 Practical photographic
processes invented** independently
by Englishman William Fox Talbot
(1800–77) and Frenchman Louis
Daguerre (1789–1851).

*Daguerreotype
image on
copper plate*

1831 1836 1839

**1888 Existence of radio
waves demonstrated** by
German physicist Heinrich
Hertz (1857–94).
Induction motor invented
by Croatian-born physicist
Nikolai Tesla (1856–1943).

Heinrich Hertz

Marconi

1894 Radio communication
invented by 20-year-old Italian
Guglielmo Marconi (1874–1937).

1895 X-rays discovered by German
physicist Wilhelm Roentgen
(1845–1925).

1896 Effects of radioactivity
discovered by French physicist
Antoine-Henri Becquerel (1852–1908).

1897 Electron discovered by British
physicist Joseph John Thompson
(1856–1940).

**1898 Elements radium and
polonium isolated** by Polish-born
chemist Marie Curie (1867–1934) and
Pierre Curie (1859–1906). She calls the
powerful
emissions of
radiation
"radioactivity".

*Marie and
Pierre Curie*

1876 1888 1894 1895 1896 1897 1898

---

15 X-ray crystallography, a way of
ding out the structure of crystals,
ented by British father and
physicists, William H.
gg (1862–1942) and
wrence Bragg
90–1971).

*Mineral with
rystalline
tomic
structure*

**1919 New Zealand-born
physicist Ernest
Rutherford** (1871–1937)
changes one element
into another. He
converts nitrogen nuclei
into oxygen nuclei.

Ernest Rutherford

1931 Neutron (particle in nucleus)
discovered by British physicist
James Chadwick (1891–1974).

**1932 First subatomic particle
accelerator built** by British
physicists J. Cockcroft (1897–1967)
and Ernest Walton (1903–1995).
Positron, a particle of antimatter,
discovered by American physicist
Carl David Anderson (1905–1991).

**1935 Nylon
developed** by
American
chemist Wallace
H. Carothers
(1896–1937).

*First particle
accelerator, built
at Manchester
University, UK*

1915 1919 1920 1931 1932 1935

---

64 Existence of quarks, the constituent parts of
utrons and protons, proposed by Murray Gell-Mann,
erican physicist (born 1929).

80s Chaos theory developed by American
thematicians, based on the unpredictability of nature.
aos theory is used to
to predict
mplex systems.

*tomic nucleus,
howing quarks*

1986 Superconductors,
substances with
extremely low resistance
to electricity, are
developed.

*Fractal: computer-
generated pattern derived
from chaos theory*

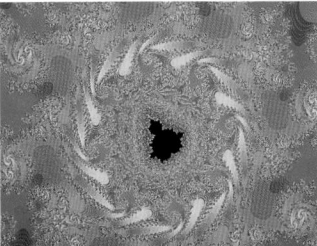

1990s "Theory of everything" is
worked on by physicists as a means
of explaining the origin of matter,
energy, and forces.

1990s Scanning probe microscopes,
first invented in the 1980s, give
chemists their first glimpses of actual
atoms, linked together to form surfaces
of materials.

1997 "Atom laser", giving a beam of
individual atoms, is built by American
scientists. It may be used to build tiny
structures.

1964 1980 1986 1990 1997

WEAPONS

WEAPONS ARE TOOLS for attacking people and animals. Technology has made weapons increasingly efficient in their ability to wound and kill.

Flint handaxe

c.100,000 B.C. Neanderthal people use sharpened wooden spear point and simple stone axe.

c.2800–2000 B.C. Composite bow, first effective military bow, developed in Middle East. Made of strips of wood, animal horn, and sinew, glued together.

Egyptian battle chariot

c.2000–1500 B.C. Two-wheeled fighting chariot introduced. Provides fast and stable platform for archers and spearmen.

c.1000 B.C. Iron sword developed in southern and central Europe. Far superior to weapons made from bronze, iron is hard and sharp.

| 100,000 B.C. | 2800 | 2000 B.C. | 1000 | *Viking sword, c.1000* |

---

200 B.C.–A.D. 400 Siege weapons used by Roman soldiers to batter down walls of enemies.

Ballista (giant crossbow)

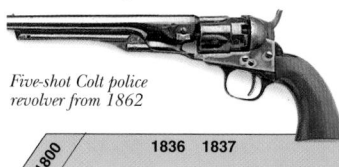

Bolt

1100 Mace becomes a common weapon of war. It can smash human bones protected by plate armour or chain mail.
Crossbow developed and used for 400 years, a powerful weapon that can be used with little training.

Bronze mace on modern haft

1340–1400 Cannons introduced into warfare. Powered by gunpowder, they fire small stone balls or large crossbow-type arrows. Large cannon, called bombards, lay open castles to attack.

Replica of small early cannon   Muzzle

1500 Arquebus developed, a hand-held firearm capable of being operated by a single infantryman.

1550 Naval warfare revolutionized as ships are fitted with cannons.

1680 Flintlock musket is dominant weapon for infantry soldiers for next 140 years. A piece of flint ignites gunpowder in musket's barrel.

| A.D. 1 | 1000 | 1100 | 1340 | 1500 | 1550 | 1680 |

1836 First effective revolver developed by American gunsmith Samuel Colt (1814–62). Revolvers can fire several shots in a row before they need reloading.

Five-shot Colt police revolver from 1862

1837 Bolt-action, breech-loading rifle developed by Prussian gunsmith J. N. Dreyse (1787–1867), with increased accuracy and firing rate. Soon all armies are armed with this type of rifle. It remains in use today.

1890s Belt-fed machine guns introduced. Allows two people to fire at great speed. Fires 600 bullets per minute, over 1km (0.62 miles).

RAF No.1 Squadron of 1918

1915 Aircraft first used as weapons when armed with machine guns.

1916 First tank used in war during Battle of the Somme. Although slow and unreliable, the lumbering British tanks cause panic among German troops.

Early British tank

| 1800 | 1836 1837 | 1890 | 1900 | 1915 1916 |

1940s Submarines, with torpedoes, become a decisive weapon of war. German U-boats almost defeat Allies in Battle of the Atlantic (1939–44).

German U-boat submarine

1945 Dropping of atomic bomb on Japan changes nature of warfare. Now a single bomb can destroy a whole city.

1950s Missiles become effective weapons delivery system. Inter-Continental Ballistic Missiles (ICBMs) carry nuclear warheads thousands of kilometres; smaller missiles are used to knock out fighter aircraft and tanks.

1960s Assault rifle introduced in large numbers. It provides infantrymen with a light weapon capable of full automatic fire.

US M16A1 assault rifle fitted with 40mm grenade launcher

1980s Attack helicopter, armed with laser-guided missiles and machine guns, proves highly effective in battle. It becomes a key element in rapid reaction forces.

Tiger anti-tank attack helicopter

| 1940 | 1945 | 1950 | 1960 | 1980 |

AUTOMATIC PISTOL

A pistol is loaded with cartridges, each containing a lead bullet and a casing packed with explosive. When the trigger is pulled, the hammer forces the firing pin into the back of the cartridge, igniting the explosive. The force of this explosion drives the bullet down the barrel and it leaves the pistol at high speed.

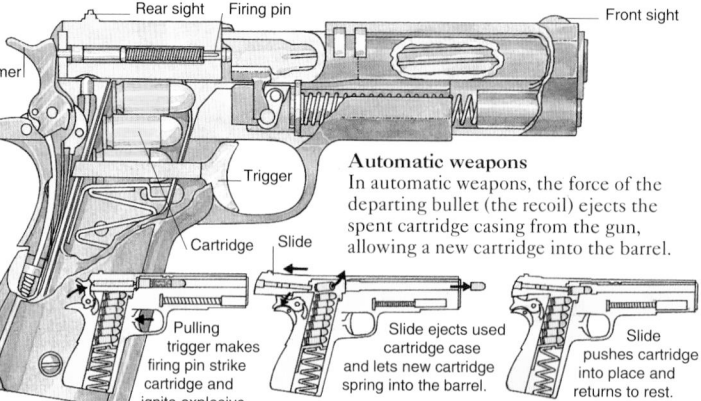

Rear sight   Firing pin   Front sight
Hammer
Trigger
Cartridge   Slide

Automatic weapons
In automatic weapons, the force of the departing bullet (the recoil) ejects the spent cartridge casing from the gun, allowing a new cartridge into the barrel.

Pulling trigger makes firing pin strike cartridge and ignite explosive.

Slide ejects used cartridge case and lets new cartridge spring into the barrel.

Slide pushes cartridge into place and returns to rest.

WEAPONS FACTS

• Powered by their own nuclear reactors, nuclear submarines can remain underwater for months on end, and can fire nuclear missiles over thousands of kilometres without being detected. They are the deadliest of modern weapons systems.

• "Smart" weapons allow a warhead to be guided directly on to its target. Some "smart" missiles have television cameras in their nose, while others use radar or infrared homing to reach their targets.

Tomahawk Cruise missile, with 454kg (1,000lb) warhead, locates and destroys target below in pre-programmed attack.

READY... AIM...

In 1830, a musket could fire a maximum of four bullets every minute. A modern M61 cannon will fire up to 100 bullets every second.

• In the 19th century, the development of rifled barrels (with spiral grooves running inside the barrel) made guns much more accurate. They made the bullet spin in flight, allowing it to travel further and straighter.

TRANSPORT, COMMUNICATIONS, AND INDUSTRY

Factual coverage of every major transport group and major world industries, plus global communications, including alphabets and major languages.

Cars • Bicycles • Motorcyles • Trains • Boats • Warships and Submarines
Aircraft • Airline Insignia • Communications • Language • Alphabets and Scripts
Energy • Major Industries • Roads • Construction

CARS

THE FIRST mass-produced car, the Oldsmobile, appeared less than a hundred years ago. Since then, car ownership around the world has grown dramatically: there will probably be a billion cars on the road by the year 2025.

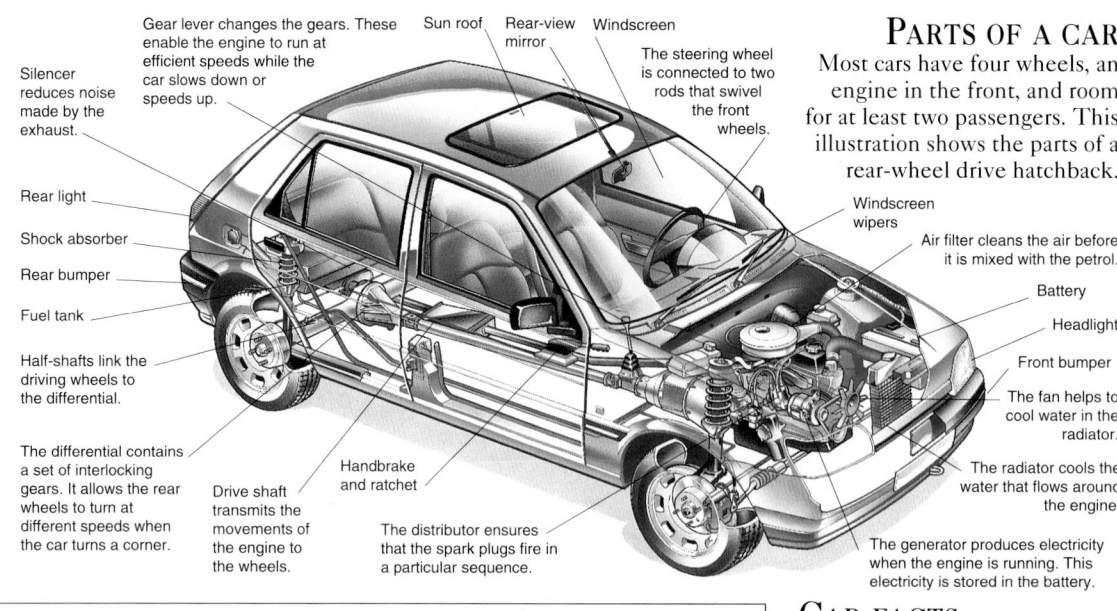

Gear lever changes the gears. These enable the engine to run at efficient speeds while the car slows down or speeds up.

Silencer reduces noise made by the exhaust.

Rear light

Shock absorber

Rear bumper

Fuel tank

Half-shafts link the driving wheels to the differential.

The differential contains a set of interlocking gears. It allows the rear wheels to turn at different speeds when the car turns a corner.

Drive shaft transmits the movements of the engine to the wheels.

Handbrake and ratchet

The distributor ensures that the spark plugs fire in a particular sequence.

Sun roof

Rear-view mirror

Windscreen

The steering wheel is connected to two rods that swivel the front wheels.

PARTS OF A CAR

Most cars have four wheels, an engine in the front, and room for at least two passengers. This illustration shows the parts of a rear-wheel drive hatchback.

Windscreen wipers

Air filter cleans the air before it is mixed with the petrol.

Battery

Headlight

Front bumper

The fan helps to cool water in the radiator.

The radiator cools the water that flows around the engine

The generator produces electricity when the engine is running. This electricity is stored in the battery.

TYPES OF CAR

Veteran car
Veteran cars are the oldest surviving cars. They were built between 1896 and 1903.

Vintage car
Vintage cars are those that were built between 1904 and 1930.

Classic car
Classic cars are outstanding examples of design and engineering.

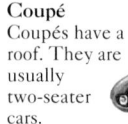

Saloon (sedan)
Saloon cars can usually carry four passengers, and have a boot for luggage.

Estate (station wagon)
Estate cars are similar to saloons, with a large loading space at the rear.

Hatchback
Hatchbacks have a rear door that lifts upwards for easy access to the loading space.

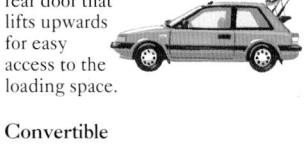

Convertible
These are open-topped cars. The roof folds back, or can be lifted off.

Coupé
Coupés have a sloping roof. They are usually two-seater cars.

Limousine
These extended cars are designed for comfort and luxury. Some have a television and cocktail cabinet.

Sports car
Sports cars display a high performance and good road handling. Most have two seats.

Racing car
Racing cars are purpose-built for racing on a track. There are several types (see p.255).

Tourer
Tourers were designed for touring, with room for several passengers and plenty of luggage.

Custom car
Custom cars are adapted by their owners to their personal preferences.

Off-road car
Off-road cars are designed for driving on rough terrain. They have four-wheel drive.

Gull-wing car
These cars have upswinging doors that, when open, resemble the wings of a seagull.

CAR FACTS
• After WWII, British motor manufacturers turned down the chance to make the German Beetle on the grounds that it was too ugly and would not sell. It has since become the best-selling car of all time, with more than 20 million produced.

Volkswagen Beetle

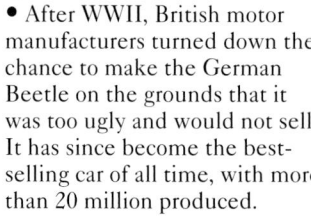

• This "motorized orange" was manufactured during the 1970s by a firm that sold fruit. It had a Mini engine with a specially built chassis and fibreglass skin.

• The most widely travelled car is the Moon Buggy, which the US astronauts drove on the Moon in 1971/72. It also has one of the lowest recorded mileages, at only 29km (18 miles).

HISTORY OF CARS

1886 Gottlieb Daimler (1834–1900, German) fixes an engine to a horse-drawn carriage.

1891 Frenchmen René Panhard (1841–1908) and Emile Levassor (1844–97) produce a car that establishes the classic layout.

1901 First mass-produced car, the Oldsmobile, is produced by Ransom Eli Olds (1864–1950, American).

Oldsmobile

1906 Charles Rolls (1877–1910, British) and Henry Royce (see opposite page) introduce their 40/50 horsepower Rolls-Royce car series, which includes the *Silver Ghost*.

1910 First car to be assembled on a moving production line was the Model T, created by Henry Ford (see opposite page).

Model T

1913 Mass-production begins in Britain. William Morris's opposite page) M Oxford.

Morr Oxfo

1880	1886	1890	1891	1900	1901	1906	1910	1910	1913

FASTEST LUXURY SALOON CARS

Car	Top speed	
	km/h	mph
Lotus Carlton	282	175
Maserati Quattroporte	264	164
Mercedes S600	256	159
BMW M5	254	158
Audi A8 4.2 Quattro	249	155
BMW 7501	249	155
BMW 540i	249	155
Jaguar XJ12	249	155
Lexus LS400	249	155
Mercedes S500	249	155

TOP CAR-OWNING COUNTRIES

Country	Total cars registered
USA	141,251,695
Japan	30,776,243
Germany	29,190,322
Italy	23,500,000
France	22,370,000
UK	20,923,423
CIS	15,874,700
Canada	11,900,000
Brazil	11,760,459
Spain	10,787,424

CAR FACTS

• The luxurious interior of a 1927 Rolls-Royce Phantom 1 was upholstered in Aubusson silk tapestry.

• William Morris hated the popular Morris Minor, which was built for 31 years. He called it the "poached egg".

WORLD'S TOP CAR MANUFACTURERS

Company	Total annual car production
General Motors	5,662,843
Ford Motor Company	4,234,583
Toyota	3,093,692
Volkswagen	2,748,152
Peugeot-Citroën	2,227,528
Nissan	2,016,626
Fiat	1,790,631
Renault	1,767,516

FAMOUS MOTOR MEN

Henry Royce (1863–1933, British) was the engineering partner of Rolls-Royce. He once said: "There is no such thing as good enough".

Henry Ford (1863–1947) a talented American mechanic, revolutionized the motor industry by introducing assembly-line production.

Herbert Austin (1866–1941) set up his own company in Britain after working for the car builders Wolseley.

Frederick Lanchester (1868–1946) designed cars in Britain from 1896. His key inventions included a semi-automatic gearbox.

William Morris (1877–1963) produced the "Bullnose" Morris, and played an important role in the British motor industry.

Ettore Bugatti (1882–1947) was an Italian engineer who built the Classic type 35 racing car, as well as beautiful touring models.

Kiichiro Toyoda (1895–1952) founded Toyota cars in Japan. His dream was to see as many cars on the streets of Japan as on those of America.

Alexander Issigonis (1904–88) was a Turkish car designer who went to the UK in 1922. He designed the Morris Minor and the Mini.

HELPING HAND

Before indicators were invented, drivers used hand signals. This false hand clipped on to the car door. It mimicked each signal.

TOP CAR-PRODUCING COUNTRIES

Country	Total annual production
Japan	9,052,406
USA	6,823,097
Germany	4,563,673
France	3,409,017
Italy	1,971,969

CAR RECORDS

WORLD LAND SPEED RECORD is 1,227km/h (763mph), achieved in October 1997 by Briton Andy Green driving the jet car *Thrust SSC*. The record is 208km/h (130mph) faster than the previous record set in *Thrust II*.

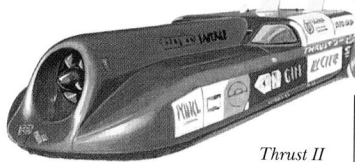

Thrust II

LONGEST PRODUCTION CAR was the Bugatti Royale (below) with a length of more than 6.7m (22ft). The first was produced in 1927, but only six were made.

MOST ECONOMICAL PRODUCTION CAR is the Daihatsu Charade Diesel Turbo (below), which can achieve 28km/l (79.1mpg) at a steady 90km/h (56mph).

HIGHEST PRICE PAID FOR A CAR THROUGH PRIVATE SALE was over $15 million for a 1962 Ferrari 250 GTO (below) in 1989. The vendor had bought the car for $7,665 in 1971.

...enchman André ... (1878–1935) ...es front-wheel ...ction avant). This ...nent bankrupts ...who dies a year

1935 World's first parking meter is installed, in Oklahoma, USA.
1936 Austrian Dr. Ferdinand Porsche (1875–1951) is instructed by Hitler (see p.404) to make a "people's car", and develops the Beetle.

1949 The Citroën 2CV, the people's car of France, is launched.

1958 The Austin Mini is launched. It can seat four people despite its small size.

1979 The catalytic converter is introduced. It reduces pollution from car exhausts.
1988 Fastest speed by a solar-powered vehicle is achieved by the General Motors *Sunraycer* (see p.254), which reaches 78.4km/h (48.71mph).

1990s New safety features, such as air bags, are developed. Other safety options are researched; the experimental *Venus* has two cameras to help the driver see the road in bad conditions.

1930s Citroën *Beetle* *Citroën 2CV* *Austin Mini* *Venus*

| 1934 | 1935 | 1936 | 1940 | 1949 | 1950 | 1958 | 1970 | 1979 | 1980 | 1988 | 1990 |

MARQUES AND MAKES

Motor manufacturers each have a badge, called a marque, to identify their vehicles. Some well-known marques are shown below.

MOTORING WORDS

Air bag A safety device that fills with air on impact to protect the driver in a collision.

Anti-lock braking system (ABS) A system that prevents skidding by detecting if a wheel is about to lock during braking.

Brake horsepower (BHP) The power of an engine calculated in terms of the force needed to stop it.

Catalytic converter A filter that absorbs many exhaust pollutants.

Fuel-injection (FI) The direct introduction of fuel under pressure into the engine.

Ignition The mechanism that starts a car's engine.

Power steering A steering system that reduces the effort needed to park and manoeuvre at low speeds.

Roll-bar An overhead bar that strengthens the car, protecting passengers if the vehicle overturns.

Spoiler An extension that improves a car's road-holding at high speeds.

Supercharger A mechanism that supplies air or fuel to the engine at above-normal pressure to increase efficiency.

Turbocharger A supercharger driven by a turbine powered by the engine's exhaust gases.

CAR FACTS

• André Citroën (see p.253) used many attention-grabbing forms of publicity. He once hired the Eiffel Tower in Paris, and had his name picked out in lights down the side. More than 250,000 light bulbs were used.

• The car that reached a production of one million in the shortest time was the Volkswagen Golf. Introduced in 1974, it passed the million mark in 31 months.

MANY IN A MINI

Since the Austin Mini was first produced (see p.253), records have been set and broken for how many people can squeeze inside one. The record currently stands at 24.

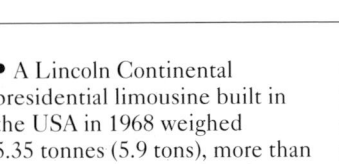

• A Lincoln Continental presidential limousine built in the USA in 1968 weighed 5.35 tonnes (5.9 tons), more than half of which was protective armour plating.

• In the early days of motoring, Italians drove on the right-hand side of the road in the country, and on the left in towns. One of the last towns to end this practice was Milan, in 1926.

• From 1865 to 1896, British law stated that every car on the road had to have a person running along in front of it waving a red flag.

AMAZING CARS

Car designers have produced some unusual models over the years. Some have been built purely to break records, others as experiments in car design.

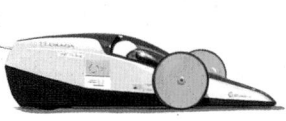

Honda's *Genius E* holds the record for lowest petrol consumption. It achieved 2,279km/l (6,409mpg).

The *Peel* is one of the smallest cars ever built, at only 1.34m (4.4ft) long. It has no reverse gear.

The *Sunraycer* runs on solar energy. It has special panels that convert sunlight into electrical energy.

A limousine built in the USA had 26 wheels and was more than 30m (98ft) long. It had a swimming pool and a helicopter landing pad.

MOST EXPENSIVE CARS SOLD AT AUCTION

Make	Car	Price US$
Any car	1962 Ferrari 250 Gran Turismo Berlinetta Competition GTO	8,853,690
Bugatti	1931 Bugatti Type 41 Royale Sports Coupé	7,665,000
Rolls Royce	1907 Rolls-Royce Silver Ghost 40/50hp tourer	2,386,706
Mercedes-Benz	1936 Mercedes-Benz 500 K Special Roadster	2,222,850

DASHBOARD AND CONTROLS

Pedals to control the car's acceleration, clutch, and brakes are situated on the car floor. Instruments to indicate speed, fuel levels, temperature, and so on are usually found on the dashboard.

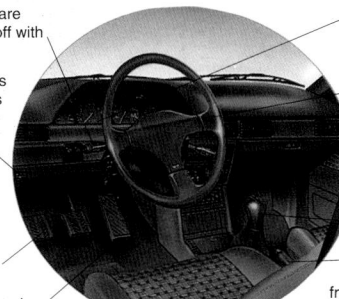

Indicator lights are flicked on and off with this lever.

The driver slows down and stops the car with the brake pedal.

The driver pushes down the clutch pedal when changing gear.

Accelerator controls the car's speed.

Speedometer indicates the car's speed.

Steering wheel

Small items are stored in the glove box

Gear lever

Handbrake stops the car from moving when it is parked.

RACING CARS

RACING CARS ARE designed to compete on a race track. They range from simple stock cars to high-technology Formula 1 racing cars, which can achieve speeds of more than 300km/h (190mph).

MOTOR RACING FACTS

• Ferrari are the only motor racing team to have competed in the Formula 1 world championship every year since it started in 1950.

• The youngest world champion racing driver was Brazilian Emerson Fittipaldi (born 1946), who won his first world championship in 1972, at the age of 25 years and 9 months.

Emerson Fittipaldi

• The oldest world champion racing driver was Argentinian Juan Manuel Fangio (1911–1995). When Fangio won his last world championship race in 1957, he was 46 years and 41 days old.

TYPES OF RACING CAR

Formula 1
These are the fastest racing cars. They compete in races called Grand Prix.

Formula 2
These are the second most powerful class of racing car after Formula 1.

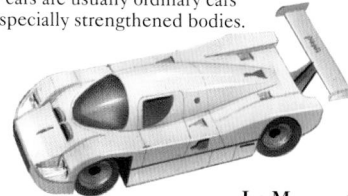

Formula 3
These racing cars have engines of up to 2,000cc.

Rally cars
Rally cars are usually ordinary cars with specially strengthened bodies.

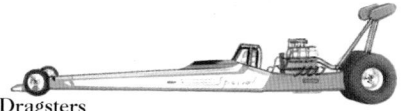

Indycars
Indycars are similar to Formula 1 cars, but are larger. They are named after the Indianapolis 500, the most famous race in which they compete.

Le Mans
These racing cars are specially adapted sports cars that race at the 24-hour Le Mans circuit in France.

US stock cars
These are simple cars that are raced around oval dirt tracks.

Dragsters
Dragsters race a short distance along a straight track, at speeds of more than 485km/h (300mph).

WINNING FORMULA

It takes 150 Renault-Sport staff to produce one of their Formula 1 engines, including 35 mechanics and 25 engineers.

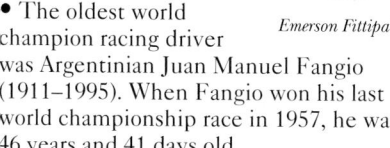

RACING RECORDS

FASTEST PIT STOP
(break in a race for refuelling or servicing) was four seconds, made by American Robert William "Bobby" Unser (born 1934) in the 1976 Indianapolis 500.

COUNTRY WITH MOST FORMULA 1 DRIVERS
from 1950 to 1993 was Great Britain, which had 131 drivers (21% of total drivers).

WORST CRASH
in a motor race occurred at Le Mans in 1955: 83 spectators were killed and more than 100 were injured when a car somersaulted over the safety barrier, burst into flames, and disintegrated. The driver also died.

LONGEST RALLY
was from Covent Garden, London, UK, to the Sydney Opera House, Australia: a distance of 31,107km (19,329 miles).

HISTORY OF MOTOR RACING

1895 First motor race to include petrol-engine vehicles takes place, from Paris, France, to Bordeaux and back. The first car past the finishing line averages 24km/h (15mph) for the race.

1906 First Grand Prix in Le Mans, France, is won by Austro-Hungarian Ferencz Szisz (1873–1970).

Ferencz Szisz

1907 First track constructed for motor car racing opens: the Brooklands Motor Course, UK.

1911 First Indianapolis 500 race takes place in Indianapolis, USA.

1929 Bentley cars take first, second, third, and fourth places at Le Mans.

| 1895 | 1900 | 1906 | 1907 | 1910 | 1911 | 1920 | 1929 |

1950 First international Formula 1 race, the Pau Grand Prix, is held in France. It is won by Juan Manuel Fangio (see above). Formula 1 cars are cigar-shaped with front-mounted engines. The driver sits in an upright position.

1951 Fangio wins the first of five World Drivers' Championships.
1958 First rear-mounted engines appear in Formula 1 cars.

Cooper 45, 1958

1960s Formula 1 drivers wear helmets and fireproof overalls, and sit in a more reclined position.

1968 Aerofoil wings are introduced by Ferrari and Brabham to produce downforce (holds the car flat on the track).

1988 Raised noses are introduced on Formula 1 cars. They improve air flow past the chassis.

1993 Use of electronic aids is outlawed.

| 1950 | 1950 | 1951 | 1958 | 1960 | 1968 | 1970 | 1980 | 1990 | 1993 |

BICYCLES

BICYCLES ARE RIDDEN by millions of people around the world. They range from simple models with no gears, to sophisticated, multi-geared mountain bicycles and racers. Bicycles are the most energy-efficient of all forms of transport.

PARTS OF A BICYCLE

The basic design of all bicycles (bikes) is the same. They are made up of a frame, wheels, transmission (cogs, chains, and gears), brakes, stem, handlebars, and saddle. This photograph shows the parts of a racing bike.

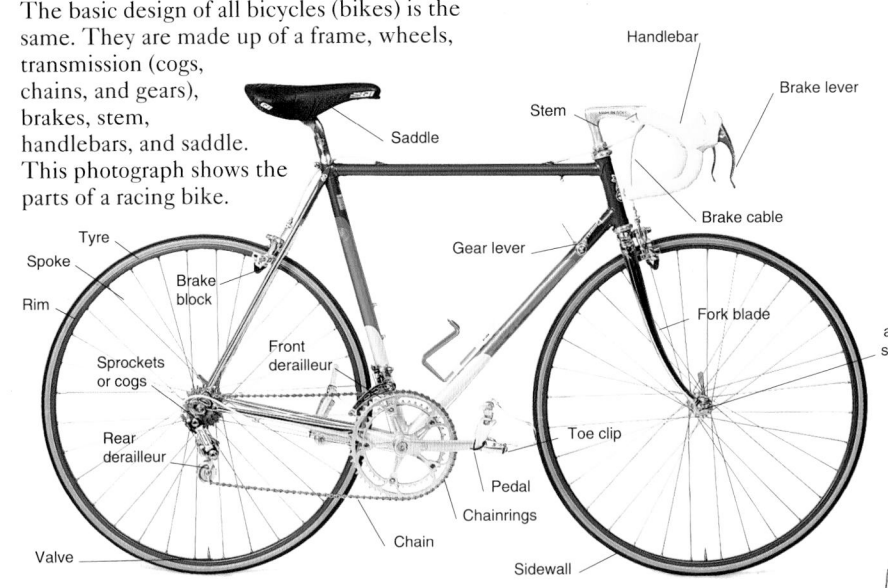

Handlebar
Brake lever
Stem
Saddle
Brake cable
Gear lever
Fork blade
Hub axle or spindle
Tyre
Spoke
Rim
Brake block
Front derailleur
Sprockets or cogs
Rear derailleur
Toe clip
Pedal
Chainrings
Chain
Valve
Sidewall

TYPES OF BICYCLE

Racing bicycle
Racing bicycles are fast, lightweight, and multi-geared, with drop handlebars.

Mountain bicycle
These bicycles are built for off-road cycling. They have thick tyres, a lightweight frame, and a wide range of gears.

BMX (Bicycle Motocross)
The BMX bike is designed for rough-terrain cycling, and is often used for acrobatics and tricks.

Tandem
Tandems are bicycles for two riders, with two saddles, two handlebars, and two wheels.

Bicycle rickshaw
Rickshaws are bicycles adapted to carry two passengers behind or in front, in a wheeled chair.

BICYCLE OWNERSHIP AROUND THE WORLD

This table shows the number of bicycles owned in various different countries.

Country	Bicycles (millions)
China	300
USA	103
Japan	60
India	45
Mexico	12
Netherlands	11
Australia	6.8
South Korea	6
Argentina	4.5
Egypt	1.5
Tanzania	0.5

GEAR SYSTEMS

Many bicycles have gear systems that enable the cyclist to travel quickly or slowly while pedalling at a comfortable rate. By moving the gear lever, the cyclist lifts the chain from one cog to another.

A small cog turns the wheel quickly, producing extra force for climbing uphill.

A large cog turns the wheel slowly, allowing the bicycle to travel fast downhill, or on flat ground.

BICYCLE RECORDS

LONGEST BICYCLE
is 22.24m (72.96ft) long. Built in 1988, it was ridden by four riders for a distance of 246m (807ft).

LARGEST BICYCLE
(front-wheel diameter) is the *Frankencycle*, with a diameter of 3.05m (10ft).

BICYCLE FACTS

• There are 800 million bicycles in the world: they outnumber cars two to one.

• The Belgian army added elbow rests to the bicycles ridden by their regimental bands, so that they could play their instruments whilst cycling.

HISTORY OF BICYCLES

1790 The *célérifère*, a wooden, hobby horse-like machine, is built by a Frenchman, the Compte de Sivrac.

1813 The *Draisienne* is built by Carl Von Drais (1785–1851, German). It has a steerable front wheel and a saddle.

1839 First bicycle with pedals to turn the rear wheel is built. It is nicknamed the "Boneshaker".

| 1790 | 1790 | 1800 | 1813 | 1830 | 1839 |

PEDAL POWER

The fastest speed on a bicycle was 245.08km/h (152.3mph), achieved by American John Howard in 1985. He was helped by the slipstreaming effect of the leading vehicle.

1861 First bicycle with pedals on the front wheel is built. The saddle is mounted on a spring for comfort, and there is a braking system for the front wheel.

c.1870 The Penny Farthing, named after two British coins, is developed. It proves unsafe.

1879 First commercial bicycle, the Bicyclette, is patented.

1959 First new bicycle design for 50 years – the Moulton – is produced.

1970s BMX bikes are launched. They appeal particularly to children.

1990s Human-powered vehicles (HPVs), such as this *Windcheetah SL*, are developed. They can reach greater speeds than ordinary bicycles.

1990s Lightweight composite materials, such as carbon fibre, and new aerodynamic shapes revolutionize bicycle design.

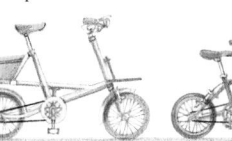

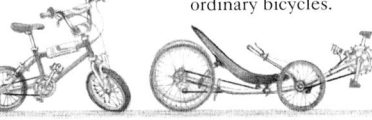
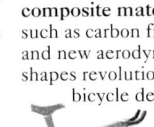

| 1860 | 1861 | 1870 | 1879 | 1950 | 1959 | 1990 |

MOTORCYCLES

THE BASIC DESIGN of a motorcycle consists of a bicycle powered by an engine. Motorcycles range from small-engined mopeds, to racing motorcycles that can reach speeds of more than 500km/h (311mph).

PARTS OF A MOTORCYCLE

The largest to the smallest machines are all built in a similar way, with a piston engine and telescopic forks. Motorcycle engine sizes range from 50cc (cubic centimetres) to more than 1,000cc. This Yamaha motorcycle has a 1,002cc engine.

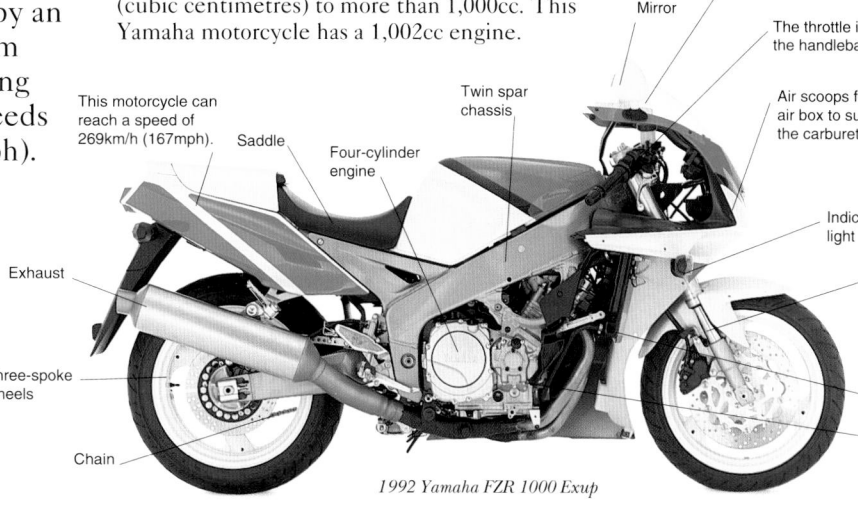

Windscreen

Mirror

The throttle is on the handlebars.

Twin spar chassis

Air scoops feed the air box to supply the carburettors.

This motorcycle can reach a speed of 269km/h (167mph).

Saddle

Four-cylinder engine

Indicator light

Exhaust

This motorcycle has upside-down telescopic forks; the lower section of the fork slides into the upper.

Three-spoke wheels

Radiator

Chain

The fairing (front enclosure) has been removed to show the engine.

1992 Yamaha FZR 1000 Exup

TYPES OF MOTORCYCLE

Motorcycle rickshaw
These three-wheeled taxis are adapted motorcycles.

Trail bike
Lightweight trail motorcycles are designed for rough terrain.

Custom motorcycle
These motorcycles are adapted by their owners to individual specifications.

Moped
Mopeds are 50cc motorcycles restricted by law to 48km/h (30mph).

Scooter
Scooters are small-wheeled motorcycles.

Combination
Combination or outfit motorcycles are those with a sidecar attached.

MOTORCYCLE RECORDS

LONGEST JUMP FROM A RAMP
was 76.5m (251ft), by American Doug Danger on a 991 Honda CR 500.

LONGEST WHEELIE (travelling non-stop on the rear wheel) was 331km (205.7 miles), by Yasuyuki Kudoh of Japan.

LARGEST MOTORCYCLE PYRAMID consisted of 45 riders of the Indian Army motorcycle display team. They rode eight motorcycles a distance of 800m (2,625ft).

LONGEST STREET-LEGAL MOTORCYCLE was 4.57m (15ft) long, built by American Gregg Reid.

SMALLEST MOTORCYCLE had a wheelbase of 10.79cm (4.25in), a seat height of 9.5cm (3.75in), a front wheel diameter of 1.9cm (0.75in), and a back wheel diameter of 2.41cm (0.95in). It was ridden over a distance of 1m (3.3ft).

Smallest motorcycle

FASTEST PRODUCTION MOTORCYCLES
(Motorcycles built for general sale)

Motorcycle	Speed	
	km/h	mph
Bimota YB11	289.6	180
Honda Blackbird	281.6	175
Kawasaki ZZR1100	273.6	170
Yamaha Thunder Ace	268.7	167

MOST EXPENSIVE PRODUCTION MOTORCYCLES

Motorcycle	Price US$
Bimota Tesi 1D ES	35,259
Bimota Tesi 1D SR	33,343
Bimota YB10 Furano	32,193

HISTORY OF MOTORCYCLES

1818 First idea for a motorcycle, a steam-driven *Velocipedraisiavaporianna,* appears in a cartoon in Paris, France.

1884 Britain's first motorcycle, the *Petrolcycle,* is patented. It is not built until 1888.

1885 Germans Wilhelm Maybach (1846–1929) and Gottlieb Daimler (1834–1900) build a motorcycle with a wooden frame and wheels, powered by Daimler's four-stroke internal combustion engine. Daimler's son rides 10km (6 miles) before the saddle catches fire.

MOTORCYCLE MADNESS

The most people to ride one motorcycle was 47, in 1995. The riders were members of the Army Corps of Brasília, Brazil, on a 1200cc Harley Davidson.

| 1818 | 1818 | 1884 | 1885 |

1892 First commercially produced motorcycle is launched.

1901 One of the first practical motorcycles, the new Werner, is produced.

1904 Harley Davidson begin motorcycle production with their *Silent Grey Fellow.*

1907 First TT (Tourist Trophy) race is held in the Isle of Man, UK.

1910 Sidecars become popular.

1959 Triumph introduce their most famous motorcycle, the high performance Bonneville.

1972 First superbike produced by Honda.

1978 New motorcycle speed record set by Donald Vesco (born 1939), who reaches 512km/h (318mph) (below).

1990s The R1100, with computerized engine management, is launched by German company BMW.

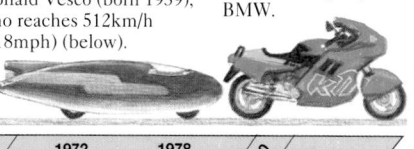

| 1890 | 1892 | 1900 | 1901 | 1904 | 1907 | 1910 | 1950 | 1959 | 1970 | 1972 | 1978 | 1990 |

TRAINS

A TRAIN IS A SERIES of vehicles pushed or pulled along a track (a railway) by a locomotive. Trains are an efficient method of transport: they use less fuel than cars and lorries.

TYPES OF TRAIN

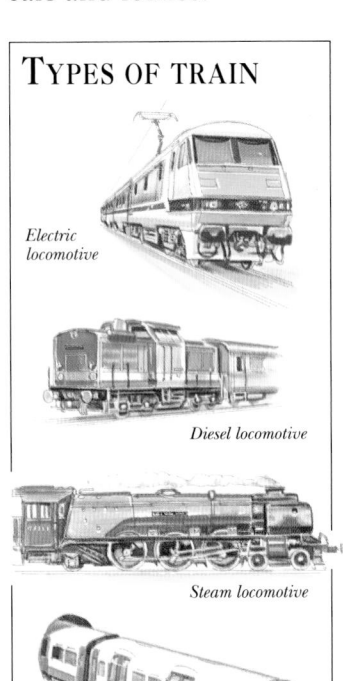

Electric locomotive

Diesel locomotive

Steam locomotive

Underground train

Funicular train

Monorail

Tilting train

PARTS OF A TRAIN

This illustration shows the *Train à Grande Vitesse* (TGV) – the French high-speed train. It runs on specially built tracks with gentle grades and curves. The TGV was introduced in 1983.

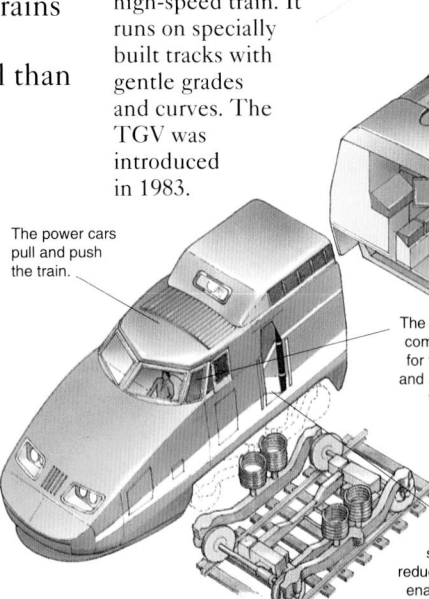

The pantograph picks up an electric current from overhead cables.

Air-conditioned carriages

An air-powered suspension system and large shock absorbers enable the train to run smoothly.

Trains run on "trucks", which have four or more wheels. The trucks swivel to enable the train to go around curves.

The wheels under the power cars and the leading carriage are driven by electric motors.

The power cars pull and push the train.

The driver's cab has a computer that checks for faults on the train, and a radio that keeps the driver in touch with the signalling centre and other trains.

The TGV's streamlined shape reduces air resistance, enabling it to travel at high speeds.

TRAIN FACTS

• Steam trains are still used in several countries, including Zimbabwe, India, and China.

• The first toilets on trains appeared in the 1850s, in the USA and Europe.

RAILS AND SWITCHES

Rails are usually welded into one continuous track as they are laid, allowing trains to run smoothly. Switches, or points, are intersections in the rails that move trains on to a new section of track.

When a switch takes place, one rail of the track on to which the train will pass slides up against the far rail of the track on which it has been travelling.

A small gap opens in the near rail of the old track, and the train moves on to the new track.

The track rests on beams of wood or concrete called ties or sleepers.

BRING YOUR OWN CARRIAGE

On some of the earliest trains, passengers' own carriages were attached to wagons pulled behind the locomotive. Passengers sat in them during the journey.

RAILWAY GAUGES

The gauge of a railway is the distance between the two running rails. Railways are laid to different gauges in different parts of the world. This table shows some of the countries that have the various gauges.

Gauge		Countries
metric	imperial	
1,676mm	5ft 6in	Argentina, Chile, India, Pakistan, Portugal, Spain
1,600mm	5ft 3in	Brazil, Ireland, South Australia, Victoria (Australia)
1,520mm	5ft	Finland, former USSR
1,435mm	4ft 8.5in	Canada, China, France, Germany, Great Britain, Italy, New South Wales (Australia), Scandinavia (except Finland), USA
1,067mm	3ft 6in	Japan, Queensland, Tasmania, Western Australia (Australia), South Africa, Zimbabwe
1m	3ft 3in	Argentina, Brazil, Burma, Chile, East Africa, Thailand

HISTORY OF TRAINS

Pre-19th century
Wagons are pulled along tracks by horses and humans.

Stones being hauled along a track

1804 First successful steam railway locomotive built by Richard Trevithick (1771–1833, English) for the Pen-y-darren ironworks in South Wales, UK.

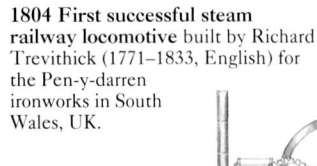

1829 *Rocket* **built by Robert Stephenson** (see opposite page). It is the first locomotive to incorporate modern features.

1830 First public steam railway for goods and passengers, the Liverpool and Manchester railway, UK, opens.

1881 World's first public electric railway opens, in Germany.

1890 World's first electric underground railway, the City and South London Line, UK opens (below).

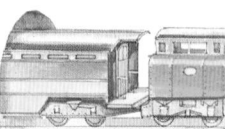

| B.C. | 1800 | 1804 | 1829 | 1830 | 1881 | 1890 |

TRAIN RECORDS

MOST POWERFUL SINGLE-UNIT DIESEL-ELECTRIC LOCOMOTIVES
are 6,600 horsepower, owned by the US Union Pacific Railroad.

LONGEST AND HEAVIEST FREIGHT TRAIN
was a 660-car iron ore train that stretched for 7.3km (4.5 miles) and weighed 69,393 tonnes. It ran on the Shishen and Saldanha railroad, South Africa.

Grand Central Terminal, New York

LARGEST STATION
is the Grand Central Terminal in New York, USA, which has 44 platforms.

HIGHEST STATION
is at Condor, Bolivia. It is situated at an altitude of 4,787m (15,705ft).

OLDEST SURVIVING STATION
is Liverpool Road, Manchester, UK, which opened in 1830. It is now part of the Museum of Science and Industry.

MAJOR PASSENGER RAILWAY USERS
This table shows the countries with the highest passenger railway usage.

Country	Distance travelled (in billions)	
	km	miles
Russia	410.7	255.2
Japan	390	242
Germany	65.9	40.9
France	64.3	40.0
Italy	44.4	27.6
UK	33.2	20.6

FAMOUS TRAINS

ROCKET
This early steam engine was designed by English engineers Robert Stephenson (1803–59) and Henry Booth in 1829. It reached 47km/h (29mph), and heralded the age of the passenger train.

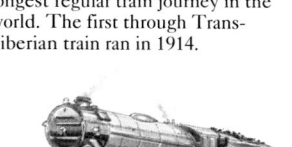

THE GENERAL
This train was built for the Western and Atlantic Railroad in 1855. It was typical of the steam engines that opened up the American West, with a cowcatcher on the front, and a large funnel for catching sparks.

ORIENT EXPRESS
The luxurious *Orient Express* was introduced in 1883. It ran between London, Paris, Vienna, Budapest, and Constantinople (Istanbul). So many secret agents used this train that it became known as the "Spies Express".

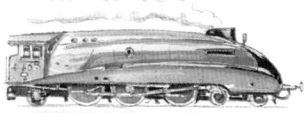

TWENTIETH CENTURY LTD
This luxury train was run by the New York Central and Hudson River Railroad. It ran between New York and Chicago from 1902 to 1967, and had a rear observation car and on-board barber shop.

TRAIN FACTS
• A high-speed diesel railcar introduced in Germany in 1933 ran at speeds of 161km/h (100mph) between Berlin and Hamburg. It was widely known as the *Flying Hamburger*.

TRANS-SIBERIAN EXPRESS
This service runs from Moscow to Vladivostock, taking almost eight days to cover 9,297km (5,777 miles) – the longest regular train journey in the world. The first through Trans-Siberian train ran in 1914.

FLYING SCOTSMAN
Flying Scotsman – London and North Eastern Railway locomotive No. 4472 – was built in 1923. It hauled express passenger trains between London, England, and Edinburgh, Scotland, until 1963.

HIAWATHA
Hiawatha was a steam-powered train built to provide a high-speed passenger service in the USA. It began in 1935, and travelled between Chicago and Minneapolis-St. Paul, taking just five hours and five minutes.

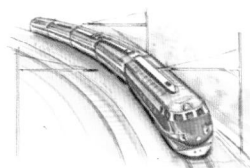

MALLARD
This steam locomotive – London and North Eastern Railway locomotive No. 4468 – holds the world speed record for steam traction. In 1938 it reached a speed of 203km/h (126mph), pulling a seven-coach train.

Steam locomotive works, Newcastle, UK, 1864

BLUE TRAIN
The *Blue Train* is probably the most luxurious train in the world: it has been described as "a five-star hotel on wheels". Introduced in 1939, it runs between the South African cities of Pretoria and Cape Town.

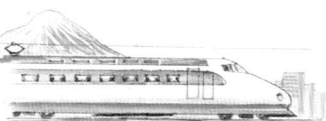

"BIG BOYS"
These locomotives were built from 1941 to 1944 by the American Locomotive Company, for the Union Pacific Railroad. They were among the largest conventional steam locomotives ever built.

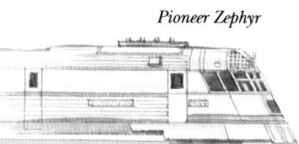

ETR450 TILTING TRAIN
This Italian train was introduced in 1988. It runs fast passenger services on routes between Rome and other cities in Italy. It can tilt at an angle of up to 10°, and has a maximum speed of 250km/h (155mph).

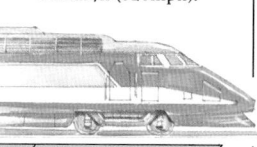

BULLET TRAIN
This is the nickname of Japan's high-speed train, which began running between Tokyo and Osaka in 1965. The Bullet Train's aerodynamic shape enables it to travel at speeds of up to 210km/h (130mph).

• Between 1804 and 1968, more than 130,000 steam locomotives were built in Britain.

• The first railway to serve meals on a train was the US Baltimore and Ohio Railroad, in 1853.

1895 Electric traction is introduced in the USA, on a 6km (3.7 mile) stretch of track in Baltimore.

1913 First diesel-powered railcar, built in Sweden, enters service.

1923 Flying Scotsman (see above) enters service.

1934 Pioneer Zephyr, a streamlined diesel-electric train, is introduced in the USA. It sets the long-distance non-stop speed record.

1968 Last scheduled passenger steam train runs on British Railways: the 21.15 Preston to Liverpool.

1987 World speed record for diesel traction is set by British Railways' High-Speed Train, which achieves 283.9km/h (176.4mph).

1990 World speed record for an electric locomotive is set by the French TGV. It achieves a speed of 515km/h (320mph).

Flying Scotsman

Pioneer Zephyr

British Rail High-Speed Train

| 1900 | 1913 | 1920 | 1923 | 1930 | 1934 | 1960 | 1968 | 1980 | 1987 | 1990 |

BOATS

FROM HUGE OIL tankers to simple dugout canoes, boats play a vital role in the transport of people and goods. For many centuries, much of the world's trade has depended on shipping.

SAILS

Sails catch the wind to provide power for boats.

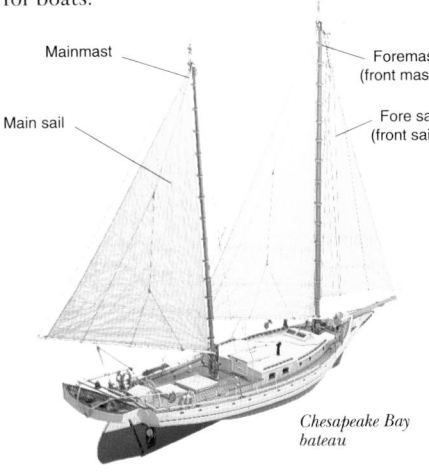

Mainmast

Main sail

Foremast (front mast)

Fore sail (front sail)

Chesapeake Bay bateau

PARTS OF A BOAT

Sailing has its own language, with special terms to describe many of the features found on boats. This racing yacht shows most of the parts of a modern boat.

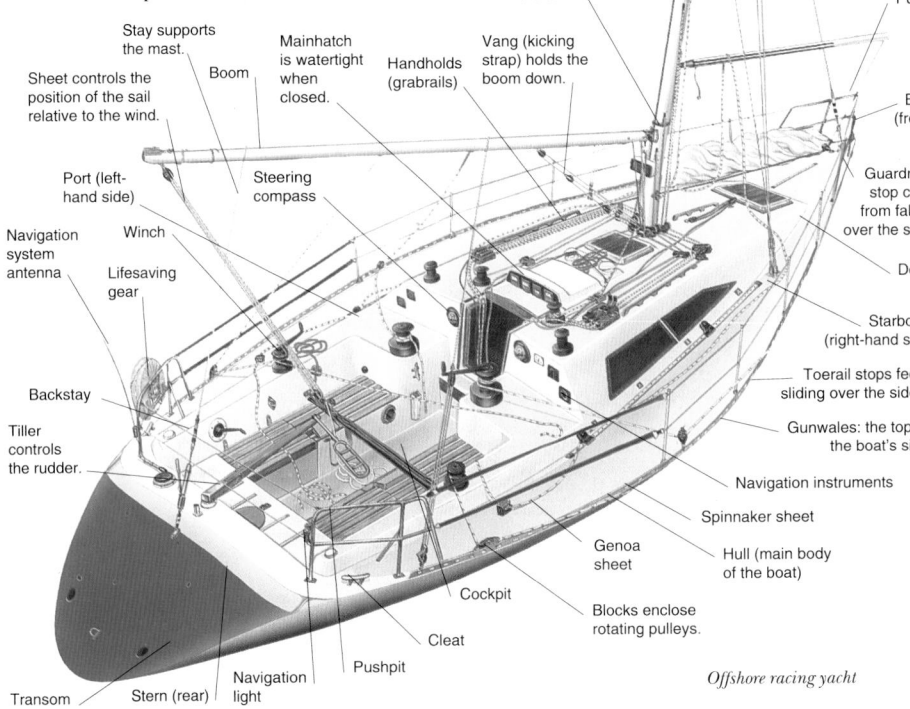

Mast

Shrouds support the mast.

Forestay

Halyards hoist (raise) or lower the sails.

Pulpit

Vang (kicking strap) holds the boom down.

Bow (front)

Handholds (grabrails)

Mainhatch is watertight when closed.

Guardrails stop crew from falling over the side.

Boom

Deck

Stay supports the mast.

Starboard (right-hand side)

Sheet controls the position of the sail relative to the wind.

Steering compass

Toerail stops feet sliding over the side.

Port (left-hand side)

Winch

Gunwales: the tops of the boat's sides

Navigation system antenna

Lifesaving gear

Navigation instruments

Backstay

Spinnaker sheet

Tiller controls the rudder.

Genoa sheet

Hull (main body of the boat)

Cockpit

Blocks enclose rotating pulleys.

Cleat

Pushpit

Navigation light

Offshore racing yacht

Transom

Stern (rear)

TYPES OF SHIP AND BOAT

Boats can be divided into various categories according to their function: passenger, cargo, sport, service, fishing, or military (see p.262).

PASSENGER/CARGO

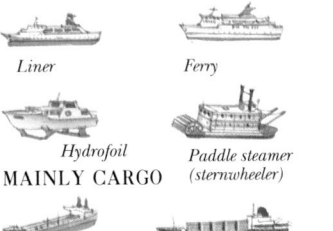

Liner

Ferry

Hovercraft

Hydrofoil

Paddle steamer (sternwheeler)

Pacific Island canoe

MAINLY CARGO

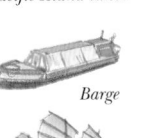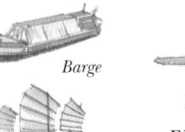

Oil tanker

Container ship

Barge

Dhow

Clipper

Junk

Sampan

Tramp steamer

Heavy lift

SERVICE

Police patrol boat

Dredger

Lifeboat

Weather ship

Lightship

Tug

Icebreaker

Submersible

SPORT AND LEISURE

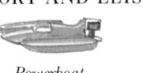

Powerboat

Motor cruiser

Steam river launch

Jet ski

Racing four

Rowing boat

Kayak

Punt

FISHING

Stern trawler

Seiner netter

Factory ship

Titicaca reed boat

Grand Banks dory

Coracle

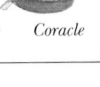

HISTORY OF BOATS

c.3500 B.C. Early **Egyptian boats** are made from bundles of reeds.

Egyptian reed sailing boat

c.2450 B.C. Egyptians develop ocean-going planked boats, powered by about 30 rowers.

c.500–c.323 B.C. The age of the trireme: ancient Greek warships powered by oars, with a bronze ram at the bow for piercing enemy ships.

Greek trireme

489 B.C. Battle of Salamis: Greeks defeat the much larger Persian forces in a major sea battle.

A.D. 400–1200 Viking longships dominate north European waters.

Viking longship

1000 Vikings land in North America.

c.1240 Centreline rudder introduced in Europe.

Centreline rudder

1492 Italian expl
Christopher Col
(1451–1506) land
the Caribbean.

Santa Maria

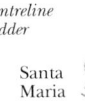

3500 B.C.	2500 B.C.	500 B.C.	489	A.D.	400	1000	1200	1240	1400	1492

SAILING WORDS

Aft At or near the stern.

Beating Sailing into the wind; wind coming from the bow.

Forward At or towards the bow.

Gangplank Portable bridge for boarding or leaving the boat.

Gybing Turning the stern of a boat through the wind.

Heave-to To slow or stop a boat using the sails and rudder.

Knot Unit of speed used by ships and aircraft: one knot = one nautical mph.

Log The record of a ship's voyage.

Nautical mile Unit of length used in sailing: one nautical mile = 1,852m (6,076ft). (One land mile = 1,609m/5,279ft.)

Reaching Sailing across the wind; wind coming from the beam (side).

Running Sailing with the wind coming from astern.

Tacking Turning the bow of a boat through the wind.

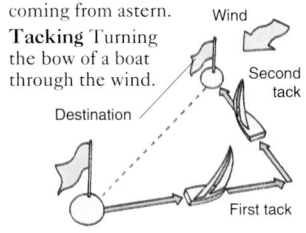

SHIP RECORDS

LARGEST SAILING SHIP was the *France*, which measured 127.7m (418.8ft) long.

LARGEST CONTAINER SHIPS are owned by American President Lines. Five of their ships are 275m (902ft) long. These ships are too large for the Panama Canal, and are known as *Post-Panamax* ships.

Queen Elizabeth

LARGEST PASSENGER LINER is the *France/Norway*, which is 1,035ft (315.5m) long. The *Queen Elizabeth*, launched in 1938, was 314m (1,031ft) long.

FAMOUS SHIPS

SANTA MARIA
This was the flagship of Italian explorer Christopher Columbus (1451–1506) on his voyage of discovery to the West Indies in 1492. *Santa Maria* was wrecked, and Columbus continued on the *Nina*.

BOUNTY
In 1788, a famous mutiny took place on the *Bounty*. Lieutenant Fletcher Christian (1764–c.1790) led a revolt against commanding officer William Bligh (1754–1817) after the ship had collected breadfruit from Tahiti.

MAYFLOWER
This square-rigged sailing ship took 100 Puritans from Southampton, England, in 1620, to form the first permanent European colony in New England, USA. Plymouth, Massachussets now stands on the site.

CUTTY SARK
This was the most famous of the clippers. By the time the *Cutty Sark* was launched in 1869, the Suez Canal was open and steamships could travel east economically. The era of the sailing ship was drawing to an end.

ENDEAVOUR
Captain James Cook (1728–79) undertook his first scientific and exploratory voyage in this ship, in 1768. During this three-year voyage, Cook mapped 8,000km (5,000 miles) of coastline.

KON TIKI
Norwegian Thor Heyerdahl (born 1914) built the raft *Kon Tiki* in 1947 to prove that the Polynesian islands could have been populated from South America. He sailed 6,115km (3,800 miles) from Peru to Raroia.

VIKING VERY LONG SHIP
The world's largest ship is the Norwegian oil tanker *Jahre Viking*, which is 458m (1,503ft) long. It takes five minutes to walk from one end to the other.

SHIPWRECKS AND DISASTERS

Ship	Date	Shipwreck/disaster
Armada	1588	Spanish fleet of 130 ships sent to invade England. After losing the battle, the surviving ships fled north around Scotland and Ireland where many were wrecked by storms. Only 60 ships returned to Spain; about 15,000 sailors died.
Marie Celeste	1872	Found abandoned and empty, with no trace of the ten people originally on board.
Titanic	1912	Struck an iceberg and sank, with the loss of about 1,500 lives.
Lusitania	1915	Torpedoed with the loss of 1,198 lives.
Wilhelm Gustloff	1945	Torpedoed with the loss of more than 7,000 lives.
Dona Paz	1963	Collided with motor tanker *Vector*: 4,386 people died.
Queen Elizabeth	1972	Burned and sank in Hong Kong harbour whilst being refitted.
Amoco Cadiz	1978	Spilled 223,000 tonnes of oil, with drastic environmental consequences.

SHIP FACTS
• Japanese companies own 3,041 large- and medium-sized ships (those with more than 1,000 gross tonnes); Greek companies own 2,773, and US companies own 1,654.

• A large oil tanker carries about 132,925,040 litres (29,240,000 gallons) of petrol: this is enough to enable a car to drive around the Earth nearly 47,000 times.

• About 92% of the world's trading goods are carried by ships.

SUPERSTORER
Large container ships can carry about 2,700 containers. Stacked, they would stand almost twice as high as Mt. Everest.

-22 First **mnavigation** **world by** **guese** **er** **nand** **lan** **-1521).**

c.1700 Introduction of the steering wheel.

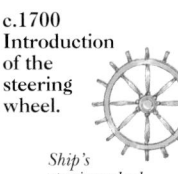

Ship's steering wheel

1838 First crossing of the Atlantic entirely under steam, by *Sirius*.

Sirius

1850–59 Heyday of the clipper: fast sailing ship that transports tea from China to Europe and North America.

Clipper

1968–69 First non-stop solo circumnavigation of the world from west to east, by English yachtsman Robin Knox-Johnston (born 1939), in *Suhaili*.

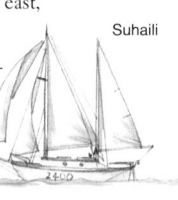

Suhaili

1994 Englishman Mike Golding (born 1960) breaks east-west, single-handed, non-stop round-the-world record, in *Group 4* (sloop). Voyage takes 161 days, 16 hours, 32 minutes.

| 1519 | 1700 | 1800 | 1838 | 1850 | 1900 | 1968 | 1994 |

WARSHIPS AND SUBMARINES

THERE ARE MANY types of fighting vessel, from light, speedy frigates, to massive aircraft carriers and nuclear-powered submarines. A country or state's fighting force of ships and submarines is called its navy.

TYPES OF WARSHIP
The main function of a warship is to defend its country, sea-lanes, and shipping from enemy attack.

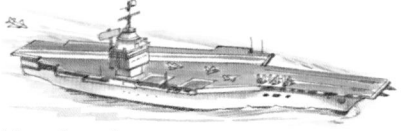

Aircraft carrier
The aircraft carrier is the largest of all warships. It acts as a floating airfield for up to 100 aircraft, and may have a crew of more than 2,000, plus a flying crew of more than 1,000.

Cruiser
The cruiser's speed and endurance are considered more important than its protection (self-defence) and weapons. Cruiser functions vary from navy to navy.

Battleship
Before aircraft carriers were built, the battleship was the most heavily armed and armoured ship. There are now very few battleships remaining in service.

Destroyer
The destroyer was originally intended to defend fleets against attack from torpedo boats. Today's destroyers are armed with guided missiles.

Frigate
The frigate was developed during World War II to escort convoys and protect them from submarines. Today's frigates perform a variety of functions.

Minesweeper
Minesweepers have special equipment for locating and destroying mines. They are usually small craft of 400–800 tonnes (440–880 tons).

PARTS OF A WARSHIP
Modern warships are armed with guns and guided missiles for attack and defence. Most are also equipped with advanced electronic equipment for detecting targets.

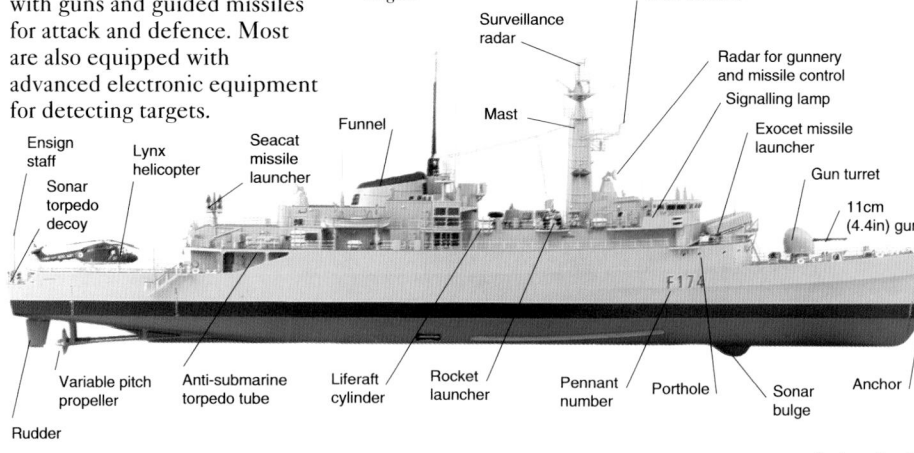

Frigate

SUBMARINES
There are two main types of military submarine: patrol submarines, which seek and destroy ships, and missile-carrying submarines. Today's nuclear missile-carrying submarines are the most powerful weapons carriers of all time.

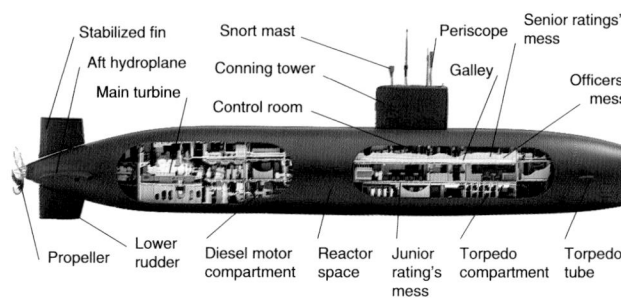

Nuclear-powered submarine

WARSHIP AND SUBMARINE RECORDS
LARGEST SUBMARINE is the Russian Typhoon class, which measures about 170m (558ft) long.

Russian Typhoon class submarine

FASTEST SUBMARINE is the Russian *Alpha*, which can probably exceed 42 knots (see p.261) when submerged.
WARSHIP WITH THE LARGEST NUMBER OF HEAVY GUNS was the battleship *Agincourt*, built in 1914, which had fourteen 30.5cm (12in) guns.

WARSHIP HARDSHIP
During the late 18th century, only about 9% of deaths on British Royal Navy warships were due to enemy action. About 50% were caused by disease, 31% by accidents, and about 10% by fires and wrecks.

FAMOUS FIGHTING SHIPS

VICTORY
The *Victory*, built in 1765, was British Admiral Lord Nelson's (1758–1805) flagship. It had 100 guns and a crew of 850.

BISMARCK
This German WWII battleship, launched in 1939 and sunk in May 1941, had eight 38cm (15in) guns.

WARRIOR
The *Warrior*, built in 1860, was the first iron battleship. This British ship was protected by a 114mm (4.5in) iron belt.

YAMATO
This Japanese battleship, launched in 1940, was the largest battleship of all time. It was sunk in 1945.

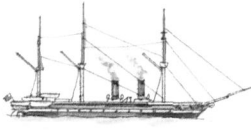

MONITOR
In 1862, during the American Civil War, the US *Monitor* took part in the first battle between ironclad warships.

ESSEX
The US aircraft carrier *Essex*, launched in 1942, could carry 91 aircraft and achieve a speed of 32 knots.

DREADNOUGHT
This British ship, built in 1906, was the first modern battleship. It was armed with heavy guns and protected by thick steel.

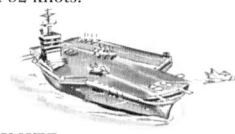

NIMITZ
The US nuclear-powered aircraft carrier *Nimitz* was completed in 1975. It carries 90 aircraft.

AIRCRAFT

THE TERM AIRCRAFT refers to all flying machines, including aeroplanes, helicopters, and hot-air balloons. Aircraft range from simple hang-gliders to the enormous Boeing 747, which can carry more than 550 people.

The fin stops the back of the plane swinging from side to side.

The elevators control the plane's ascent and descent.

Piper Cherokee

Wings are covered with thin aluminium sheeting.

Fuselage

Pilot's seat

The rudder steers the plane.

Strong metal cables run from the pilot's control stick and rudder pedals to the control surfaces.

Ailerons control the plane's balance and, together with the rudder, steer the plane.

Flap

Fuel tanks in the wings and wing tips hold up to 320 litres (70 gallons) of fuel.

Engine

Spinner

Propeller

Nose landing gear

Wings are made from spars. These are long, strong rods that stretch from the fuselage to the wing tip.

Undercarriage (main landing gear)

PARTS OF AN AIRCRAFT

This small, propellered light aircraft shows the features of a typical aeroplane. Its main structures are the fuselage, wings, tailplane, and fin, which together are called the airframe.

TYPES OF AEROPLANE

Aeroplanes (planes) are powered, heavier-than-air aircraft with fixed wings. There are many different types of aeroplane; their uses include transport, warfare, and sport.

Jet aircraft
Jet aircraft are powered by jet engines (see p.247). Most civil airliners (large passenger aircraft) and military planes have jet engines.

Propellered plane
Propellered planes are cheaper to run than jet aircraft, and can take off easily from short runways. Many airlines use turboprop aircraft for regional air services. The propellers of these planes are driven by gas turbines.

Biplane
Biplanes have two sets of wings, one above the other, braced with wires. Early planes were built in this style because two wings were stronger than one long, single wing. Today's biplanes are strong enough to withstand aerobatic displays.

Light aircraft
Light aircraft are powered by piston engines similar to those found in cars. These small aeroplanes are used mainly for leisure and short business trips.

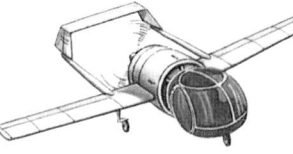

Observation plane
Observation planes are used by police, rescue services, and armies. They are usually standard light aircraft, although the *Edgeley Optica* (above) is a purpose-built model.

Supersonic plane
Supersonic planes are jet aircraft that can fly faster than the speed of sound (see p.236). Their shape is different from that of conventional aeroplanes, because air flows in a different way at such high speeds.

Seaplane
Seaplanes can take off from and land on water. They are used mainly in remote areas with few airfields, such as northern Canada and Alaska, where the country is undeveloped and there are many lakes.

FLIGHT DECK

The flight deck contains the controls and data-display instruments. Today's flight decks, such as this 1980s airliner cockpit, have CRTs (cathode-ray tubes). These display computerized information on screens that can be changed at the touch of a button.

Primary flight display CRT: includes artificial horizon, altimeter, and airspeed indicator.

Landing and taxi light switches

Warning lights

Second CRT displays navigational information, and functions as a simple compass, radar screen, or map display.

Engine throttles

Navigation computer equipment

Independent weather radar

Wing flap control

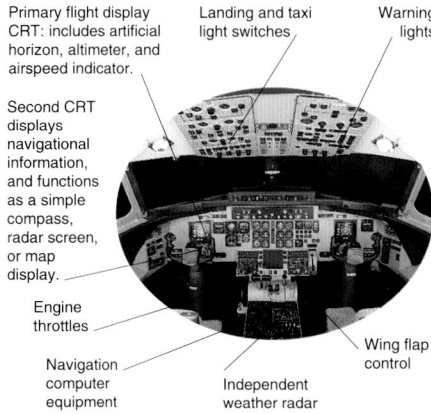

FLYING A PLANE

Aeroplanes have three main controls: the throttle, which controls the speed; the rudder pedals, and the control column.

Rolling
To roll, the pilot moves the control column to the left or right, raising the ailerons on one wing and lowering them on the other.

The plane rolls when the ailerons are raised and lowered.

Control column

Aileron

Elevator

Pitching
To pitch the plane up or down, the pilot pushes or pulls the control column, raising or lowering the elevator flaps on the tail wing.

Yawing
To make the plane yaw (swerve) to the left or right, the pilot swivels the rudder bar with the feet. This turns the upright rudder on the tail.

Rudder pedals steer the plane to the left and right.

Rudder

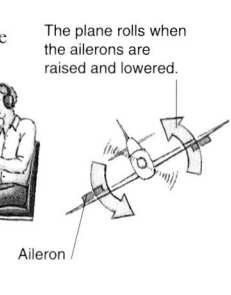

The control column tilts the aircraft to either side (rolling), and up and down (pitching).

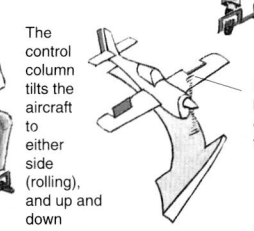

Plane banks in order to turn.

Banking
Aeroplanes have to bank in order to turn. The pilot uses the control column and the rudder pedals together, so that the aircraft rolls and yaws at the same time.

HISTORY OF FLIGHT

For centuries, people tried to fly. They made elaborate wings, launching themselves from high places, often with fatal results. Only in the last 100 years have humans learned to fly, advancing from simple machines to jet aeroplanes.

Daedalus

c.2000 B.C. According to legend, Daedalus, a craftsman working on the labyrinth for King Minos of Crete, makes wings for himself and his son to escape the island.

1010 Oliver of Malmesbury (c.980–1066), a Benedictine monk, attaches wings to his arms and jumps from a tower. He travels for a short distance, but breaks his legs.

1486–1500 Italian artist Leonardo da Vinci (1452–1519) sketches designs for flapping wing craft (ornithopters), as well as parachutes and helicopters.

| 2000 B.C. | A.D. | 1000 | 1010 | 1400 | 1486 |

1853 Sir George Cayley builds a full-size glider which, it is claimed, carries his coachman across a small valley.

1891–96 The world's first aviator, German Otto Lilienthal (1848–96), invents a practical hang-glider and becomes the first person to make repeated controlled flights.

Otto Lilienthal, 1896

1896 American scientist Samuel Langley (1834–1906) builds a tandem-winged, steam-powered model, the *Aerodrome*.

Samuel Langley flew 1km (0.6 miles) in the Aerodrome.

1903 The world's first powered aeroplane flight is made by the Wright brothers, Orville (1871–1948) and Wilbur (1867–1912), who fly 2⁶⁰ (853ft) at Kitty Hawk, eastern

| 1853 | 1891 | 1896 | 1900 | 1903 |

1919 First non-stop flight across the Atlantic is made by British aviators John Alcock (1892–1919) and Arthur Whitten-Brown (1886–1948), in a Vickers Vimy with Rolls-Royce engines. It takes 16 hours.
Alcock and Brown

1920s Vast airships fly people across the Atlantic in ocean-liner style.

1924 Hugo Junkers (1859–1935, German) produces a pioneering all-metal three-engined monoplane airliner.

All-metal Junkers airliner

1927 First solo flight across the Atlantic is made by American Charles Lindbergh (1902–74) in a Ryan monoplane, *Spirit of St. Louis*.

Spirit of St. Louis

1928 First flight the mid-Pacific by Australian Cha Kingsford Smith (1897–1935).

1928 World's fir modern airport at Croydon, near London, UK.

| 1919 | 1920 | 1924 | 1927 | 1928 |

1937 First experimental jet engine is designed by British engineer Frank Whittle (1907–1996) (above right).

1939 First jet-propelled flight is made by a Heinkel He178, powered by an engine designed by German Hans von Ohain (born 1911).

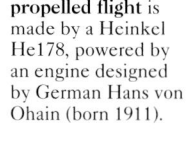
Heinkel He178

1940 Battle of Britain: the victory of the British Royal Air Force over the German Luftwaffe ensures Britain is not invaded.

1941 Frank Whittle's jet engine is used in the Gloster E28/39.

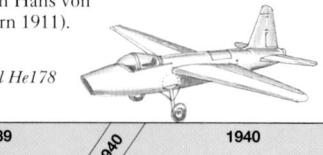
Gloster E28/39

1947 The Bell X-1 experimental rocket plane, piloted by American Chuck Yeager (born 1923), breaks the sound barrier.

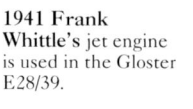
Bell X-1

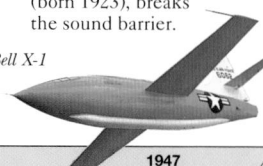

1952 The world's first jetl the De Havilland Comet, co into service, halving interna flight times. Two years later withdrawn following crashes to metal fatigue.

| 1939 | 1940 | 1940 | 1941 | 1947 | 1950 | 1952 |

OTHER AIRCRAFT TYPES

HOT-AIR BALLOON
Hot-air balloons are used mainly for recreation. Modern hot-air balloons use propane burners carried above the balloon's basket to heat up the air.

AIRSHIP
Modern airships are filled with helium or hot air. Their long, thin shape keeps them stable. Airships can be steered, and many have swivelling propellers to assist with take-off and landing. Airships are sometimes used for advertising, with messages displayed on their sides.

GLIDER
Gliders are unpowered planes with a wide wingspan measuring up to 25m (82ft). They use currents of hot, rising air (thermals) to stay aloft, and are controlled with a rudder, elevators, and ailerons (see p.263).

HANG-GLIDER
Hang-gliders are made of material stretched across a simple frame, forming wings. The pilot hangs beneath the wings in a harness or body-bag, and steers by shifting his or her weight from side to side. Hang-gliders are not powered: the pilot relies on thermals for lift.

MICROLIGHT
A microlight is basically a powered hang-glider. It has a small engine and an open fibreglass car, called a trike, that can hold a crew of two. The trike is suspended on a strong frame, and the pilot steers by shifting his or her weight against the frame. Microlights can reach speeds of up to 160km/h (100mph).

HELICOPTER
Helicopters are powered, lifted, and steered by rotating blades. They take off vertically, fly slowly and hover, and move in any direction. This manoeuvrability makes them ideal for functions such as crop-spraying, traffic surveillance, and rescue.

Montgolfier brothers' balloon

rench brothers and Etienne lfier (1740–1810; 9) launch a balloon rsailles, France, ockerel, a sheep, ck on board. A few ater they fly a new carrying two men.

1804 British baronet Sir George Cayley (1773–1857) invents the practical aeroplane: he builds a model glider that provides the basis for later aircraft design.

Aerial Steam Carriage design

1844 First design for a complete mechanically powered aeroplane: William Henson (1812–88, British) designs the *Aerial Steam Carriage* and makes a 6m (20ft) model version.

1852 First airship is built and flown by Henri Giffard (1825–82, French). It is a cigar-shaped balloon powered by a steam engine.

Henri Giffard's airship

| 1783 | 1800 | 1804 | 1844 | 1850 | 1852 |

---

907 First helicopter flight is made by French mechanic Paul Cornu (1881–1944). He lifts off the ground for 20 seconds.

Paul Cornu's helicopter

1909 First flight across the English Channel is made by Louis Blériot (1872–1936, French), who flies from France to England in a monoplane.

Blériot's monoplane, the Blériot Type XI

1909 Baroness de Laroche (?–1919) is the first woman to make a solo flight.

Baroness de Laroche

1914–18 WWI: first use of aircraft in war. The aeroplane becomes a weapon; there is a huge increase in speed, range, and strength.

WWI German biplanes

| 1907 | 1909 | 1909 |

---

ritish aviator Amy Mollison hnson) (1903–41) flies solo agland to Australia in *Gypsy Moth*.

1932 American aviator Amelia Earhart (1898–1937) is the first woman to fly solo across the Atlantic.

1933 World's first modern airliner, the Boeing 247, is launched.

Boeing 247

Macchi M72

1934 Italian Macchi M72 floatplane sets the world speed record at 708km/h (440mph).

1936 First practical helicopter, the Focke Achgelis FW-61, flies.

Focke Achgelis FW-61

1937 The airship *Hindenburg* **is destroyed** in an accident, killing 35 people.

| 1932 | 1933 | 1934 | 1936 | 1937 |

---

he Hawker P1127 e first hovering trials t thrust. It is the essor of the Harrier, the OL (vertical take-off d landing) aircraft to enter service.

Hawker P1127

1965 The Lockheed SR71 Blackbird spy plane sets a new world speed record of 3,331km/h (2,070mph).

Blackbird

1970 The first wide-bodied jet, the Boeing 747 "Jumbo Jet", comes into service. It carries up to 550 passengers, and makes international jet travel commonplace.

Boeing 747

Concorde

1976 The Anglo-French supersonic airliner Concorde goes into service, reaching speeds of 2,494km/h (1,550mph).

Right: Gossamer Albatross, designed by American Paul Macready (born 1925)

1979 First human-powered aircraft, the *Gossamer Albatross,* crosses the English Channel.

1986 First non-stop round-the-world flight, by Americans J. Yeager (born 1936) and D. Rutan (born 1952), in *Rutan Voyager*.

| 1960 | 1965 | 1970 | 1970 | 1976 |

AIRCRAFT FACTS

● One of first airline services was provided by German Zeppelin airships. They carried a total of 35,000 passengers between Lake Constance, Berlin, and other cities.

● The world's first electrically powered aircraft, the MB–E1, flew in 1973, in Germany.

WINGED THING

In the 1890s, Horatio Phillips (1845–1926, British) built a plane with 20 sets of wings. It looked like a venetian blind.

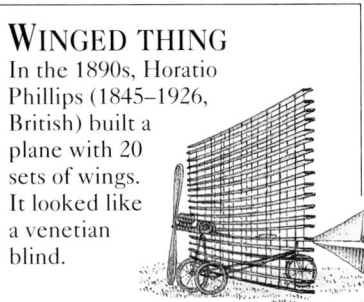

AIRCRAFT RECORDS

LARGEST AIRCRAFT WINGSPAN is that of the Hughes H4 Hercules flying boat *Spruce Goose*, which measures 97.51m (319.9ft) across.

Hughes H4 Hercules flying boat Spruce Goose

SMALLEST BIPLANE is *Bumble Bee Two*, which is just 2.64m (8.7ft) long, and weighs 179.6kg (396lb).

HEAVIEST AIRCRAFT is the Antonov An-225 Mriya (*Dream*), which weighs 600 tonnes.

WORST AIR DISASTERS

Year	Incident	Number of people killed
1977	Two Boeing 747s (KLM and Pan Am) collided on the runway at Tenerife, Canary Islands.	583
1985	A Japan Airlines Boeing 747 crashed en route from Tokyo to Osaka.	520
1996	A Saudi Arabian Boeing 747 collided above India with a Kazakh Airways Ilyushin 76.	350
1974	A Turkish Airlines DC-10 crashed at Ermenonville, France, immediately after take-off from Paris.	346
1985	An Air India Boeing 747 exploded in mid-air off the Irish coast, en route from Vancouver to Delhi.	329

LARGEST AIRLINER is the Boeing 747-400, which has a wingspan of 64.4m (211ft). It can carry up to 567 passengers.

TYPES OF WARPLANE

Fighter
Fighter planes are designed to win air superiority so that other, slower aircraft, such as bombers and observers, can operate over battle zones. Fighters also attack enemy bombers.

Bomber
Bombers can carry a wide range of weapons and bombs, including nuclear weapons, and special bombs for destroying runways.

Transport aircraft
Modern armies rely on transport planes and helicopters to move troops and equipment rapidly into battle zones.

Helicopter gunship
Helicopter gunships are heavily armed helicopters, with rapid-fire machine guns that fire from the turret. They were widely used by US forces in Vietnam (see p.409).

Aerial reconnaissance plane
Army commanders rely on airborne observers to report on the movements of enemy forces. Observation planes are a prime target for enemy fighters, so pilotless, remote-controlled aircraft (RPVs) are often used.

VTOL aircraft
VTOL (vertical take-off and landing) aircraft use the immense power of the jet engine to rise vertically, or after a short run. VTOL craft do not need a long runway, and can therefore be hidden near the battlefront.

PARTS OF A FIGHTER
Modern fighter planes are equipped with sophisticated electronic instruments for detecting and attacking enemy aircraft and ground targets. This fighter can fly at more than 2,980km/h (1,852mph), at a height of 18,288m (60,000ft).

Two turbofan (jet) engines

F-15E Eagle

This fighter carries a crew of two: the pilot, and the weapon systems operator.

The crew can escape from ejector seats if the aircraft is in danger of crashing.

The large, transparent canopy gives the crew a good range of vision.

An infrared heat-sensitive camera enables the crew to fly in the dark.

Radar antennae detect other aircraft.

Terrain-following radar enables the plane to fly at high speeds close to the ground.

The rotary cannon can fire more than 6,000 rounds of ammunition per minute.

Four air-to-air missiles for shooting down enemy aircraft.

The plane's fuselage is made of composite plastic materials and light metal alloys.

AIRCREW
Aircrew consists of flying crew, who fly in the planes, and ground crew. Armourers ensure that the planes are adequately equipped with ammunition and bombs.

The pilot flies the aircraft. He or she carries flight plans in knee pads.

Women flying crew do not usually fly aircraft in battles.

Aircraft engineers check the planes after every flight.

The ground crew carry out maintenance and repair of the aircraft.

FAMOUS WAR PLANES

FOKKER TRIPLANE
German WWI flying ace Manfred von Richthofen (1892–1918), the "Red Baron", flew many aircraft. The best-known was the Fokker Triplane.

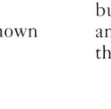

SPITFIRE
The Spitfire was the fastest and most effective British fighter plane of WWII. It had a Rolls-Royce Merlin engine, and could reach a speed of 684km/h (425mph).

FOCKE-WULF FW 190A
Brought into operation in 1941, the powerful FW 190A became one of the German Luftwaffe's principal fighter aircraft during World War II.

FLYING FORTRESS
These heavily armed US WWII bombers were designed for daylight raids. Fortresses were meant to fly in formation and protect each other, but this strategy failed. They were only safe when escorted by fighters.

AVRO LANCASTER
This was the main British bomber used by the RAF during WWII. It flew mainly at night to avoid detection by enemy fighters.

TORNADO
The Tornado is NATO's (see p.406) most powerful fighting plane. It is built in two forms: one carries bombs and guided weapons for ground attack; the other attacks enemy fighters.

VULCAN
The Vulcan was the main British nuclear attack aircraft in the 1950s and 1960s. Although it was not supersonic, its large delta wing allowed it to fly higher than Soviet fighters.

MIG 25
The Russian MIG 25 is one of the fastest aircraft in service, reaching speeds of Mach 2.8 (see p.236). It was developed to counter the threat of American supersonic nuclear bombers.

NORTHROP B-2
"STEALTH" BOMBER
This US bomber is designed to absorb or deflect enemy radar, so that it can remain undetected when approaching its targets. It is made of composite plastics.

 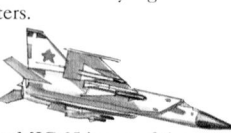

MIRAGE
This plane is used by air forces around the world. Different models are used as fighters, fighter-bombers, and for reconnaissance.

KING OF THE ACES
During WWII, German Major Erich Hartmann (1922–93) shot down 352 planes, making him the war's top air ace.

AIR FORCE RECORDS
LARGEST AIR FORCE
ever was the US Army Air Corps (now the US Air Force), which in 1944 numbered 79,908 aircraft and 2,411,294 personnel.

HEAVIEST BOMBER
is the Boeing B-52H Stratofortress (below). It has a max. take-off weight of 221,353kg (488,000lb), and can carry 12 SRAM thermo-nuclear short-range missiles or 24 340kg (750lb) bombs under its wings, and 8 SRAMS or 84 227kg (500lb) bombs in the fuselage.

TOP WOMAN ACE
was Junior Lieutenant Lydia Litvak (1921–43) of the USSR, who shot down 12 planes between 1941 and 1943.

TOP JET ACE
was Captain Joseph McConnell Jr. (1922–54), of the US Air Force, who shot down 16 planes in the Korean War.

AIRLINE INSIGNIA

MOST COUNTRIES OF
the world have a
national airline. Each
airline has its own
distinctive insignia
(emblem) and colours,
which make its aircraft
easy to identify. A
selection of airline
insignia is shown here.

Aer Lingus
Irish airline

AEROLINEAS ARGENTINAS

AIR ALGERIE

AIR FRANCE

Air Namibia

air new zealand

AIRLANKA

AUSTRIAN AIRLINES

Avianca
The Airline of Colombia

Bahamasair

BALKAN
BULGARIAN AIRLINES

BRITISH AIRWAYS

WE ARE THE CARIBBEAN

CAMEROON AIRLINES

Canadian
Canadian Airlines International

CROATIA AIRLINES

CYPRUS AIRWAYS

EgyptAir

EL AL
Israel airlines

ETHIOPIAN AIRLINES

FINNAIR

Garuda Indonesia

GHANA AIRWAYS

GULFAIR

IBERIA
Spanish airline

ICELANDAIR

İstanbul Airlines
Ihre türkischen Ferienflieger

JAL
Japan Airlines

JERSEY EUROPEAN

Kenya Airways
The Pride of Africa

KLM
KLM Royal Dutch Airlines

KOREAN AIR

Lauda-air
Independent airline

POLISH AIRLINES
LOT

Lufthansa
German airlines

LUXAIR
Luxembourg airlines

malaysia
AIRLINES

MEA
Middle East Airlines

NIGERIA AIRWAYS LIMITED

NORTHWEST AIRLINES
American airline

OLYMPIC AIRWAYS

Greek airlines

Philippine Airlines

PIA
Pakistan International Airlines

QANTAS
Australian airlines

sabena
Belgian airlines

SAS
Scandinavian Airlines System

saudia
SAUDI ARABIAN AIRLINES

SINGAPORE AIRLINES

SAA
SOUTH AFRICAN AIRWAYS

swissair

Thai
Thai Airways International Limited

TURKISH AIRLINES

UZBEKISTAN
airways

VARIG
Brazilian Airlines

virgin atlantic

COMMUNICATIONS

DEVELOPMENTS IN COMMUNICATION systems
have changed people's lives. Today, a person can
make instant contact, whether by phone or fax,
with someone on the other side of the world.
People can travel to distant countries in a matter
of hours. Advances in computer technology have
transformed many workplaces.

TELECOMMUNICATIONS

Telecommunications covers
communication by telephone, fax,
television, and radio. All these
forms of communication need a
transmitter to send out the
information, something to carry
the signal, and a receiver to
convert the signal back into an
understandable message.

FIBRE OPTICS

Today, most international calls are
routed through fibre optic cables,
which lie on the sea bed. A telephone
call is carried as a pulse of light along
a cable that is made up of a few fine
strands of pure glass, called
optical fibres.

Fibre optic cable

POSTAL COMMUNICATIONS

One of the earliest, cheapest, and
most reliable forms of communication
is the postal service. Letters and
parcels can be sent by air from one
part of the world to another in a
matter of days.

POSTAL STAGES

1 Letters and small packages
are dropped in a letter box.

2 They are collected by postal
workers and taken to the local
sorting office.

3 Letters and packages are
sorted and put in a sack with
others going to the same area.

4 They are transported by road,
rail, or air to their
destination.

5 The mail is taken to a main sorting
office and is sorted into
districts.

6 It is taken to a local
sorting office.

7 The letters are sorted by street.

8 They are then delivered by
foot, bicycle, or van.

POSTAL SORTING

Most letter sorting
in post offices is
done by machine.
An operator
reads the
address on a
letter and
punches a
keyboard that
prints a code of dots or
bars. Other sorting
machines "read" the
codes and sort the letters
further.

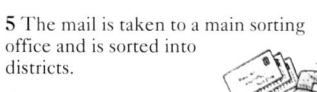

Letter sorting

FIBRE OPTIC SUBMARINE SYSTEMS
This map shows the fibre optic routes existing today; many more are in the
process of being built.

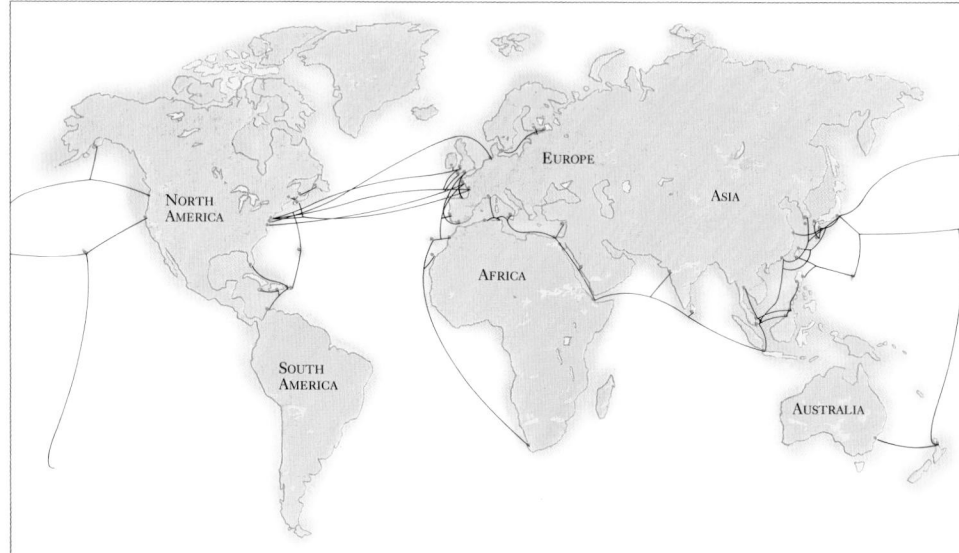

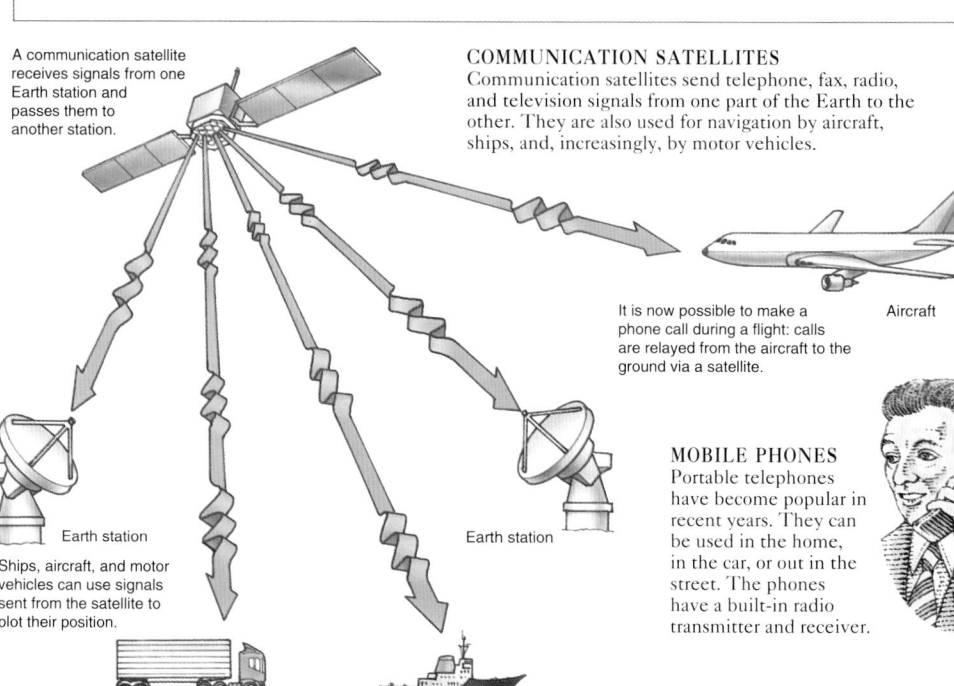

A communication satellite
receives signals from one
Earth station and
passes them to
another station.

Earth station

Ships, aircraft, and motor
vehicles can use signals
sent from the satellite to
plot their position.

Truck

Ship

Earth station

COMMUNICATION SATELLITES

Communication satellites send telephone, fax, radio,
and television signals from one part of the Earth to the
other. They are also used for navigation by aircraft,
ships, and, increasingly, by motor vehicles.

Aircraft

It is now possible to make a
phone call during a flight: calls
are relayed from the aircraft to the
ground via a satellite.

MOBILE PHONES

Portable telephones
have become popular in
recent years. They can
be used in the home,
in the car, or out in the
street. The phones
have a built-in radio
transmitter and receiver.

MORSE CODE

The earliest form of telecommunication was the
electric telegraph. An electric current was sent
along a wire in long and short bursts, known as
Morse code.

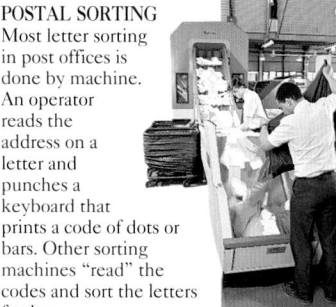

AIR TRAVEL

There are hundreds of airline companies operating throughout the world, offering safe, affordable travel to billions of people.

AIR TRAVEL FACTS

Chicago International Airport in the USA is the busiest airport in the world. Aircraft take off or land about every [ ] seconds.

London's Heathrow Airport handles the most international flights in the world.

AIR TRAFFIC CONTROL

Aeroplanes carry a device, called a transponder, which sends out a signal when it receives a pulse of radio energy from the secondary scanner. This signal tells air traffic control the aircraft's identity, height, and speed.

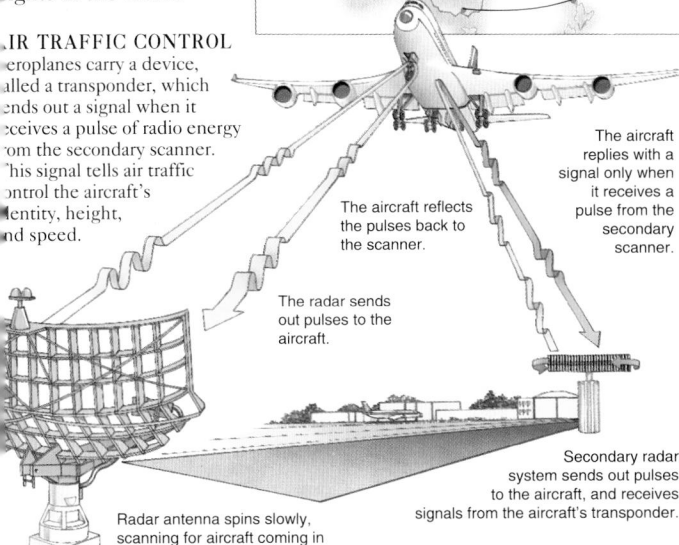

A MAJOR AIRLINE'S WORLD ROUTES

The aircraft reflects the pulses back to the scanner.

The aircraft replies with a signal only when it receives a pulse from the secondary scanner.

The radar sends out pulses to the aircraft.

Secondary radar system sends out pulses to the aircraft, and receives signals from the aircraft's transponder.

Radar antenna spins slowly, scanning for aircraft coming in different directions.

BUSINESS COMMUNICATIONS

The development of communications technology in the workplace has changed the way many people do their work. Because of the speed of communication possible with the use of fax machines, electronic mail, and telephone systems, it is likely that in the future more people will be able to work from home.

VIDEO CONFERENCE

Instead of spending time and money travelling to meetings, people can now communicate with each other by going to video conference centres. People speak through microphones and are able to see each other on screens. Although not yet widespread, video conferences are expected to become more common in the future.

At video conference centres, people can see each other on screen.

Computer screen

Keyboard

FAX MACHINE

Text and illustrations can be sent through a facsimile (fax) machine. Whatever is written or drawn on the page is transmitted in the same way as a telephone message.

Fax machine

COMMUNICATION WORDS

Cable television Television programmes delivered by a metal or fibre optic cable.

CD-ROM Compact Disc Read-Only Memory: a laser disc used to store computer data. The data cannot be removed, and new data cannot be recorded.

Database Information stored on a computer.

Navigation Finding a route between two places.

Network A system of interconnected pieces of equipment that communicate with each other.

Satellite An object held in orbit around a planet.

COMPUTERS

Information can be collected, stored, processed, and transmitted very quickly on computer.

INTERNET

The world's largest computer network is called the Internet. It enables all types of computer to share services and communicate directly.

INTERNET SERVICES

Some of the services available on Internet include:
Electronic mail (E-mail) This allows messages to be sent from one computer to another.
CU SeeMe This enables up to eight people to see and hear each other on their computer screens.
Usernet A collection of electronic bulletin boards (called Newsgroups) set up by subject matter. It is used for news and information.

COMMUNICATION FACTS

• A post office sorting machine can sort about 36,000 letters an hour.

• A pair of optical fibres can hold up to 61,440 telephone conversations at any one time.

• First country to introduce car navigation systems was Japan, in 1990.

• More than 4,000,000,000 messages are sent by E-mail in North America each year.

SEMAPHORE

Semaphore flag signals were used for signalling between ships until the early 1900s and by the army. It remains a quick method of visual signalling, and is still used for passing messages between ships sailing close to each other.

LANGUAGE

LANGUAGE is a system of sounds and signs that people use to express their thoughts and communicate with others. There are thousands of languages throughout the world.

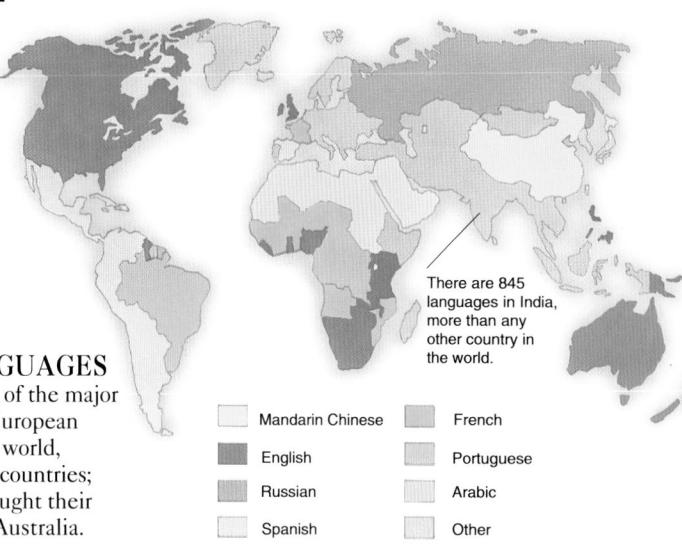

There are 845 languages in India, more than any other country in the world.

COMMON WORLD LANGUAGES

This map shows the distribution of the major world languages. It shows how European nations, when they explored the world, brought their languages to other countries; for example, English settlers brought their language to North America and Australia.

Legend:
- Mandarin Chinese
- English
- Russian
- Spanish
- French
- Portuguese
- Arabic
- Other

MOST COMMON LANGUAGES

Language	Number of speakers
Chinese (Mandarin)	1,093 million
English	450 million
Hindi	367 million
Spanish	352 million
Russian	204 million
Arabic	202 million
Bengali	187 million
Portuguese	175 million
Malay-Indonesian	145 million
Japanese	126 million

HOW TO SAY "YES" AND "NO" IN DIFFERENT LANGUAGES AROUND THE WORLD

Words in brackets are a guide to pronunciation.

Language	Yes	No	Language	Yes	No	Language	Yes	No
Arabic	نَعَم (Na'am)	لا (La'a)	German	Ja	Nein	Polish	Tak	Nie
Bengali	হাঁ (Haa)	না (Naa)	Greek	Ne	Óhee	Portuguese	Sim	Não
Bulgarian	Da	He	Hebrew	כֵּן (Ken)	לא (Lo)	Punjabi	ਹਾਂ (Haan)	ਨਹੀਂ (Nahi)
Chinese (Cantonese)	係 (Hai)	唔係 (M hai)	Hindi	हां (Haan)	नहीं (Nahi)	Romanian	Da	Nu
Chinese (Mandarin)	是 (Shi)	不是 (Bu shi)	Hungarian	Igen	Nem	Russian	Да (Dah)	Нет (Nyet)
Czech	Ano	Ne	Icelandic	Já	Nei	Serbo-Croat	Da	Ne
Danish	Ja	Nej	Indonesian	Ja	Tidak	Slovak	Áno	Nie
Dutch	Ja	Nee	Italian	Sì	No	Spanish	Si	No
English	Yes	No	Japanese	はい (Hai)	いいえ (Lie)	Swedish	Ja	Nej
Finnish	Kyllä	Ei	Korean	네 (Ne)	아니오 (A-ni-yo)	Thai	ค่ะ (Kha [female])	ไม่ค่ะ (Mai kha [female])
Flemish	Ja	Nee	Malay	Ya	Tidak	Thai	ครับ (Khrap [male])	ไม่ครับ (Mai khrap [male])
French	Oui	Non	Norwegian	Ja	Nei	Turkish	Evet	Hayir

SIGN LANGUAGE

People who cannot hear or speak can communicate through sign language. Signs may stand for whole words as well as individual letters. There are many different sign language systems. The example shown is used in Britain.

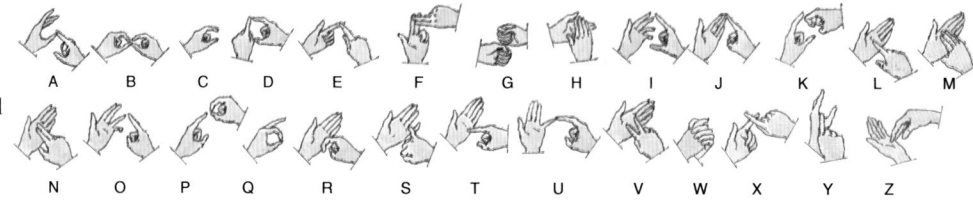

A B C D E F G H I J K L M
N O P Q R S T U V W X Y Z

SCRIPTS

SCRIPTS ARE SETS of symbols that we use
to write things down. One script can be used
to form different languages, for example, the
Roman alphabet is used in many European
languages, such as English and French.

PICTOGRAMS

The first scripts were
pictograms. Pictures were drawn
of an object or idea. These
pictures were gradually
simplified, to make them
quicker and easier to write.

CUNEIFORM

The first successful pictogram script
was cuneiform, which means
"wedge-shaped". It was invented by
the Sumerians of Mesopotamia
(present-day Iraq) in about 3000 B.C.
The script was written on damp clay
with a wedge-shaped stylus. After a
while, the pictograms were written
sideways and developed into simple,
stylized symbols.

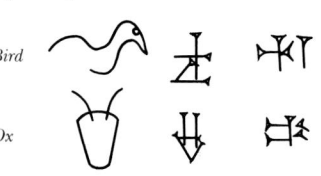

Bird

Ox

PRESENT-DAY SCRIPTS

CYRILLIC (RUSSIAN)

А Б В Г Д Е Ж З И Й К Л М Н О П Р С
Т У Ф Х Ц Ч Ш Щ Ъ Ы Ь Ѣ Э Ю Я Ѳ V

DEVANAGARI (HINDI)

There are about 200 Indian scripts in use today.
The most widely known is Devanagari.

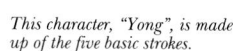

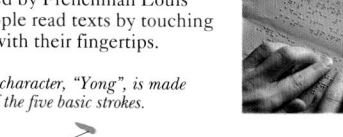
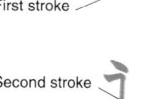
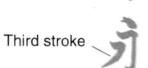

BRAILLE

People who are blind or have poor eyesight can read
by using Braille, invented by Frenchman Louis
Braille (1809–1852). People read texts by touching
a raised pattern of dots with their fingertips.

CHINESE

The Chinese use
more than 50,000
signs, but only a
few thousand are
commonly used.
A character is
made up of a
combination of
up to 26 different
strokes, which
must be made in
particular order.

*This character, "Yong", is made
up of the five basic strokes.*

First stroke

Second stroke

Third stroke

Fourth stroke

Fifth stroke

Braille

HIEROGLYPHS

The ancient Egyptians had a system
of picture writing called hieroglyphs,
meaning "sacred carvings". They were
carved and painted on temple walls
and tombs.

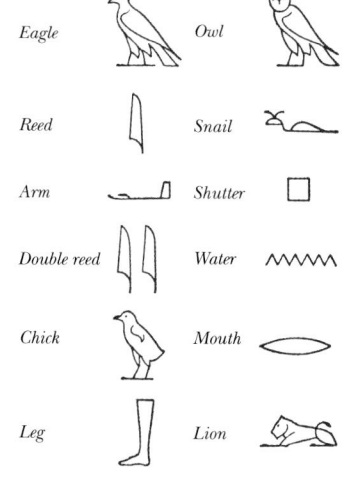

Eagle *Owl*

Reed *Snail*

Arm *Shutter*

Double reed *Water*

Chick *Mouth*

Leg *Lion*

The Cyrillic alphabet is named after St. Cyril,
who spread the Christian faith to the Slavonic
peoples in A.D. 800.

JAPANESE

The Japanese adapted Chinese characters so that they could
write down their spoken language, which in fact belongs to a
different family from Chinese. Japanese, like Chinese, is
written and read in vertical columns from right to left.

Japanese book

ALPHABETS

The letters of an alphabet are signs that
represent sounds. This way of writing
was quicker and easier to remember than
pictogram writing.

DEVELOPMENT OF ALPHABETS

The Phoenicians developed the first
alphabet around 1600 B.C. The Greek
alphabet was adapted by the Etruscans in
about 700 B.C. The Romans based their
alphabet on the Etruscans'. The modern
Hebrew alphabet has changed little from
the original biblical Hebrew, and has
similarities to the Phoenician alphabet.

GREEK WORDS

The ancient Greeks based their own
alphabet on the Phoenician one. To
begin with, they wrote
in almost any
direction, even
in a spiral.

*Greek
inscription*

Phoenician	Modern Hebrew	Early Greek	Classical Greek	Etruscan	Classical Roman	Modern Roman
						A
						B
						C
						D
						E
						F
						G
						H
						I
						J
						K
						L
						M
						N
						O
						P
						Q
						R
						S
						T
						U
						V
						W
						X
						Y
						Z

SCRIPT FACTS

• The oldest letter still in use is "O", which
has not changed its shape since it was part of
the Phoenician alphabet in about 1600 B.C.

• Children in Japan are taught 881
characters in their first six years at school.

• The longest alphabet is Cambodian
(Khmer), with 74 letters.

ENERGY RESOURCES

INDUSTRY, TRANSPORT, and homes require energy to power everything from furnaces to televisions. Much of this energy is produced by burning fossil fuels, such as oil. Renewable energy sources, such as wind and solar power, are also playing an increasing role in energy generation.

FOSSIL FUELS
Oil, coal, and natural gas are called fossil fuels because they are made of the remains of long-dead plants and animals. When burned they release energy, which is used to generate power. Fossil fuels are non-renewable energy sources, because they will eventually run out.

COAL
About 20% of the world's energy is generated from coal, and its use is increasing.

OIL AND NATURAL GAS
About 60% of the world's energy comes from oil and natural gas. Oil is the main fuel used in transportation, and both oil and gas are burned to produce heat.

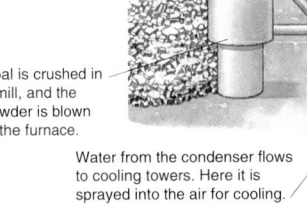

Some heat escapes through the chimney.

Cooling tower

Coal is crushed in a mill, and the powder is blown to the furnace.

Water from the condenser flows to cooling towers. Here it is sprayed into the air for cooling.

GENERATING ELECTRICITY
This illustration shows a coal-fired power station. Coal is burned in a furnace to heat water and produce steam. The steam drives a turbine attached to an electricity generator, which sends electricity down a network of cables called a grid.

Steam turns the turbines.

Electricity generator

Transformer changes the voltage before it is supplied to homes and factories

Furnace   Condenser

MAJOR OIL PRODUCERS

Country	Million tonnes per year
CIS	570
USA	417.6
Saudi Arabia	327.1
Iran	155.3
Mexico	145.3
China	139
Venezuela	119.4

FOSSIL FUELS IN RESERVE
In 1960, it was estimated that existing underground fossil fuels would last for about 40 years. By 1990, more reserves had been found, but the rate at which they were being used had increased. In 1990, the reserves were still estimated to last about 40 years.

41 billion tonnes of known reserves

1.1 billion tonnes used in 1960

142 billion tonnes of known reserves

3 billion tonnes used in 1990

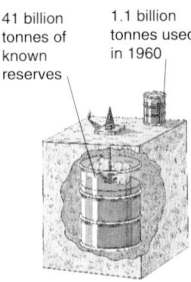

1960 fossil fuel consumption

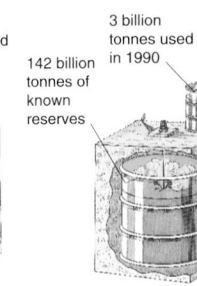

1990 fossil fuel consumption

RENEWABLE ENERGY SOURCES
Renewable energy sources are those that will not run out in the foreseeable future. Most "renewables" are cleaner and less harmful to the environment than fossil fuels.

WIND POWER
Wind turbines generate electricity at "wind farms", such as the one at Altmont Pass, California, USA (right). During the 1980s more than 20,000 wind turbines were erected worldwide. Scientists estimate that by 2030, wind power could provide more than 10% of the world's electricity.

SOLAR POWER
The Sun is a non-polluting source of renewable energy. Solar energy is converted into electricity in photovoltaic (solar) cells, which are used to power various devices, including calculators, space satellites, and telephone links in remote areas. The Sun's heat is also used to heat water in many hot countries.

TIDAL POWER
Tidal power is generated at barrages (barriers) built across estuaries. As the tide rises or falls, water is kept at high or low tide level inside the barrage. When the water level differs by about 3m (10ft) water flows through huge turbines.

HYDROELECTRIC POWER
Hydroelectric power is generated at dams and waterfalls. Falling water drives turbines, which in turn drive electricity generators. About 7% of the world's energy is provided by hydroelectricity.

GEOTHERMAL ENERGY
Geothermal energy is generated by heat energy in the Earth's crust. At present, most geothermal energy is generated in volcanically active regions, such as Iceland and New Zealand. Approximately 20 countries use geothermal energy for heating, or for generating electricity.

WAVE POWER
Wave power is still being researched and developed. Several experimental generators have been built. Some are sited on the seashore. Others are designed for the deep sea, where the energy content per metre of wave can be equivalent to the power source for 50 single-bar electric fires.

BIOMASS ENERGY
Biomass energy is derived from organic matter, such as wood and agricultural waste. Biomass power plants are being built in many countries. They produce little air pollution and do not usually contribute to global warming.

ENERGY FACTS
• Watching colour television accounts for 20% of the average British person's energy consumption.

• Worldwide, lighting accounts for about 17% of electricity use.

• The average person in the UK uses 10 times more energy each year than the average person in India.

MAJOR WOOD USERS
Many developing countries depend on wood for fuel and energy production.

Country	Wood as % of total energy consumption
Mali	97
Rwanda	96
Tanzania	94
Burkina	94
Ethiopia	93
Central African Republic	91
Somalia	90

NUCLEAR ENERGY

Nuclear energy is generated by the breakdown of uranium and plutonium atoms. There are about 350 nuclear power stations around the world, and they supply more than 5% of the world's electricity. Nuclear power stations do not emit polluting gases or contribute to global warming, but accidents and the disposal of fuel rods pose serious risks.

The core is surrounded by a thick concrete shield that absorbs radiation.

Heated fluid is used to produce steam.

Cooling tower

The steam is piped to turbines linked to electricity generators.

Pellet of uranium or uranium dioxide

Fuel rods are made of several pellets.

The fuel rods are embedded in a material that slows down the neutrons (see pp.226–227), called a moderator.

There are about 90,000 fuel rods in the nuclear reactor core.

Fluid circulates through the core to carry away heat produced by nuclear fission.

NUCLEAR ENERGY RISKS

Nuclear waste remains dangerously radioactive for thousands of years, and has to be buried deep underground or at sea. Accidents at nuclear power plants, such as the Chernobyl disaster in Ukraine in 1986, can expose hundreds of thousands of people to radiation and contaminate millions of square kilometres of land.

MAJOR NUCLEAR POWER USERS

Country	% of total electricity generated by nuclear power
Lithuania	85.59
France	76.14
Belgium	55.52
Sweden	46.61
Bulgaria	46.43
Slovakia	44.14
Hungary	42.30
Switzerland	39.92
Slovenia	39.46
Ukraine	37.83

MAJOR ENERGY CONSUMERS

This table includes commercially traded fuels (oil, coal, gas, etc.) only. Fuels such as wood and animal waste are excluded, as figures are unreliable.

Country	Consumption as % of world total
USA	24.6
CIS	16.8
China	8.4
Japan	5.4
Germany	4.3
Central Europe	4.2
Canada	3
France	2.6

ENERGY CONSUMPTION OF VARIOUS HOUSEHOLD PRODUCTS IN THE USA

Household product	% of homes with product	Typical energy consumption (kilowatts per year)
Freezer (frost-free)	34.5	1,820
Refrigerator	84.6	1,591
Aquarium/terrarium	15	200–1,000
Colour television	98	75–1,000
Electric stove or oven	61.5	650
Personal computer	23.3	25–400
Dishwasher	45.2	165
Iron	40	20–150
Clock	100	17-50
Video recorder	98	10–70

RENEWABLE ENERGY FACTS

• The amount of sunshine that falls on roads in the USA in one year contains twice as much energy as all the coal and oil used worldwide in a year.

• Owing to better energy efficiency standards, new houses in Sweden use at least three times less energy to keep their houses warm in winter than the average British home.

Energy-efficient Swedish village

• Tokyo, Japan, has more than 1.5 million solar collectors for domestic water heating.

• About 90% of Israel's domestic hot water is supplied by solar heating.

GREAT LENGTHS

The world's largest wind turbines have blades up to 50m (164ft) long. One hundred people could stand side by side on a single blade.

ALTERNATIVE VEHICLE ENERGY

Oil will eventually run out, and in the meantime vehicle exhaust fumes are polluting the atmosphere. It is therefore important that clean, renewable energy sources are developed. Those being researched include compressed natural gas, electricity, hydrogen, ethanol (grain alcohol), and methanol (wood alcohol).

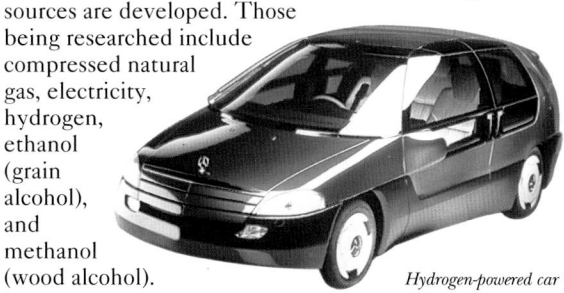

Hydrogen-powered car

OIL FACTS

• About 500,000 different materials can be made from crude oil. The products on the right are all made from materials derived from crude oil. They include wax, plastics, fertilizers, and detergents.

• One day's world oil supply took 110,000 years to fossilize.

• More than 500 oil wells are drilled every week in the USA.

• If all the barrels of oil produced worldwide in one day were laid end to end, they would stretch twice around the Equator.

HOW THE WORLD OBTAINS ITS ENERGY

This diagram shows the percentage of each energy source currently used worldwide.

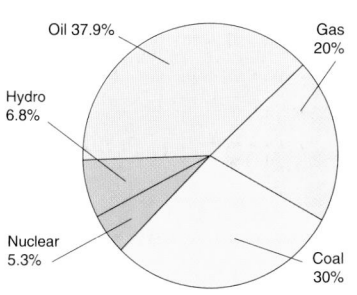

Oil 37.9%
Gas 20%
Hydro 6.8%
Nuclear 5.3%
Coal 30%

INDUSTRY

INDUSTRY IS AN organized economic activity. It deals with the extraction and use of raw materials, with manufacturing and construction, and with putting the products of these activities to profitable use.

CLASSIFICATION OF INDUSTRIES

There are three basic types of industry.

PRIMARY

These industries are concerned with the extraction of basic raw materials. Examples include agriculture, forestry, fishing, and mining.

Forestry industry

SECONDARY

These industries convert raw materials into other products. They can be further divided into heavy industry, e.g. shipbuilding, and light industry, e.g. textiles and clothing.

Clothing industry

TERTIARY

Tertiary (third order) industries offer a service rather than a product, e.g. banking and tourism. Today, this type of industry is expanding.

Cashier at work in a building society.

MAJOR INDUSTRIAL PRODUCERS

All total figures given are in millions, except where indicated. Where a country has a large share of the market, producer and figure are given in parentheses.

Industry	Top producers	Total (in millions)	World total (in millions)
Transport Cars, buses, and trucks	Europe Asia North America	15 (Germany: 4.5) 14 (Japan: 9.7) 12	45
Commercial aircraft	North America Europe	2203* 814*	3,207*
Ships	Asia Europe	814 (Japan: 535)* 546*	1,452*
Bicycles	Asia Europe	59 (China: 36) 10	84
Communications TV and radio	Asia Europe	172 (China: 42) 32	253
Telephones	Asia North America	66 18.7	107
Electronic components	Japan North America	78,000 480	81,000
Fuel Coal	Asia North America Europe	1,421 tonnes (China:1,100) 873 tonnes 525 tonnes	3,453 tonnes
Crude oil	Asia North America	1,094 tonnes (Saudi Arabia: 404) 597 tonnes	2,971 tonnes
Construction and engineering Cement	Asia Europe	588 tonnes (China: 244) 232 tonnes	1,148 tonnes
Pig-iron for steel-making	Asia Europe	216 tonnes 123 tonnes	526 tonnes
Timber	Asia North America	1,074 cubic metres 717 cubic metres	3,450 cubic metres

* Figures for commercial aircraft and ships are not in millions.

DISTRIBUTION OF MAJOR INDUSTRIES

Cars, buses, and trucks

Commercial aircraft

Ships

Bicycles

TV and radio sets

Telephones

Transistors and semiconductors

Coal

Crude oil

Cement

Pig-iron for steel-making

Timber

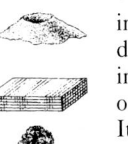

INDUSTRY FACTS

• Japan, which lacks most of the important industrial minerals, depends heavily on imports, importing about 95% of its iron ore, tin, copper, zinc, and lead. It is the world's largest importer of coal, natural gas, and oil.

• Mexico produces one-fifth of the world's silver.

• British Columbia produces about one-quarter of the marketable timber in North America. It also supplies the world with chopsticks.

• Wind power from approximately 1,100 windmills in Denmark supplies 3% of its energy needs.

• Gold provides between 20% and 30% of South Africa's export earnings.

OIL INDUSTRY

Oil is found under the sea bed or in places that were once covered by sea. Complex technology is used to drill deep wells and extract oil from the sea bed. Despite concerns about pollution and oil wells running dry, there is no sign of any fall in the demand for oil for fuel and for making chemicals.

TYPES OF OIL RIG

Shallow water
A jack-up rig is used. Its legs extend to the sea bed.

Deep water
A tension-leg rig is used. It floats, but is chained to the sea bed.

Very deep water
Ships are used. The oil drill comes out through a hole in the hull.

COAL INDUSTRY

Coal is valuable as an industrial fuel and for making chemicals. It is formed from the remains of decaying plant life, which solidified into coal over millions of years.

TYPES OF COAL MINE

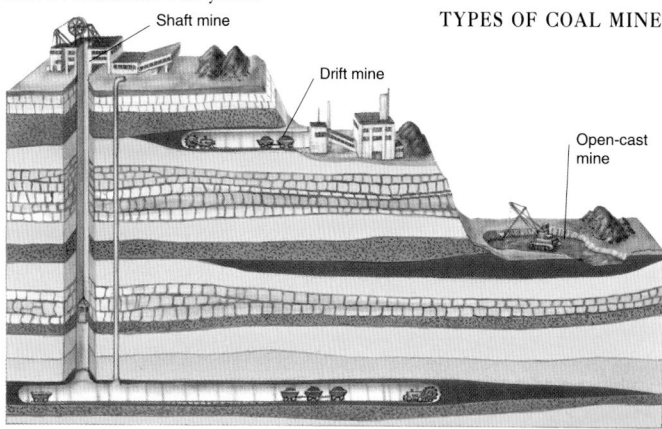

Shaft mine

Drift mine

Open-cast mine

Shaft mine
Miners tunnel vertically when coal is deep under the ground.

Drift mine
Miners tunnel horizontally if a coal seam emerges near the surface of the ground.

Open-cast mine
If the coal is near the surface, the covering layers of ground are stripped away to reveal the coal.

FOOD INDUSTRY

The food industry processes much of our food so that it is safe to eat, looks appealing, and will remain fresh for a longer period of time. Food can be processed in many different ways.

MILK INTO CHEESE

There are many types of cheese, but most of them share the same basic stages of production.

A tanker will transport milk to the dairy.

The milk is pasteurized to destroy bacteria.

Another type of bacteria is added to the milk to produce lactic acid. The acid thickens the milk and turns it sour.

The milk is warmed, and rennet, which comes from a calf's stomach, is added. This makes the milk lumpy.

The watery part of the milk (the whey) is drained away and made into food for farm animals, leaving solid lumps, called curds.

Salt is added to the curds, which are pressed to get rid of any remaining whey. The curds are shaped into moulds. They are left in a cool place to ripen into cheese.

WAYS OF PROCESSING FOOD

Canning

Foods are boiled, put in cans, then heated to kill any remaining bacteria. The cans are then sealed to prevent air from bringing oxygen and bacteria to the food.

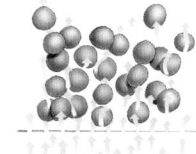

Cans on an assembly line

Freeze-drying
Food is frozen, and the water is removed. This kills all the bacteria, which cannot live without water.

Astronauts in space use freeze-dried food.

Pasteurizing

Liquids such as milk are heated to 70°C (160°F) for 15 seconds and then cooled quickly. This preserves the flavour while killing the bacteria.

Freezing

In fluidized freezing, small food items, such as peas, pass over very cold air (-34°C/-29°F) on a conveyer belt. The food freezes in minutes.

The cold air makes the peas rise.

ADDITIVES

Additives are natural or synthetic chemicals that are added to food to prevent it from going bad too quickly, and to make food look appetizing.

Beta carotene, a natural colouring from carrots, may be added to orange juice to strengthen colour.

Synthetic chemicals are added to cola to improve flavour.

Colourings and flavourings

Natural colour pigments may break up, so artificial or natural colourings are used as a replacement. Synthetic flavourings, which copy natural flavourings, may also be used.

Emulsifiers ensure fat and water remain combined. They are used in such foods as yoghurt.

The synthetic chemical – butylated hydroxytoluene (BHT) – stops the fat in corn chips from decaying.

In biscuits, bases such as sodium and ammonium hydrogen carbonate improve flavour and prevent changes in acidity and colour.

The preservative sodium nitrite is added to salami and hot dogs.

In bread rolls, a natural chemical such as vitamin C stops oxygen reacting with the fat in bread.

PAPER INDUSTRY

Paper is made in large factories called paper mills. Wood is ground down, mixed with water, and turned into wood pulp. The pulp is then pressed and rolled by machine into a layer of paper.

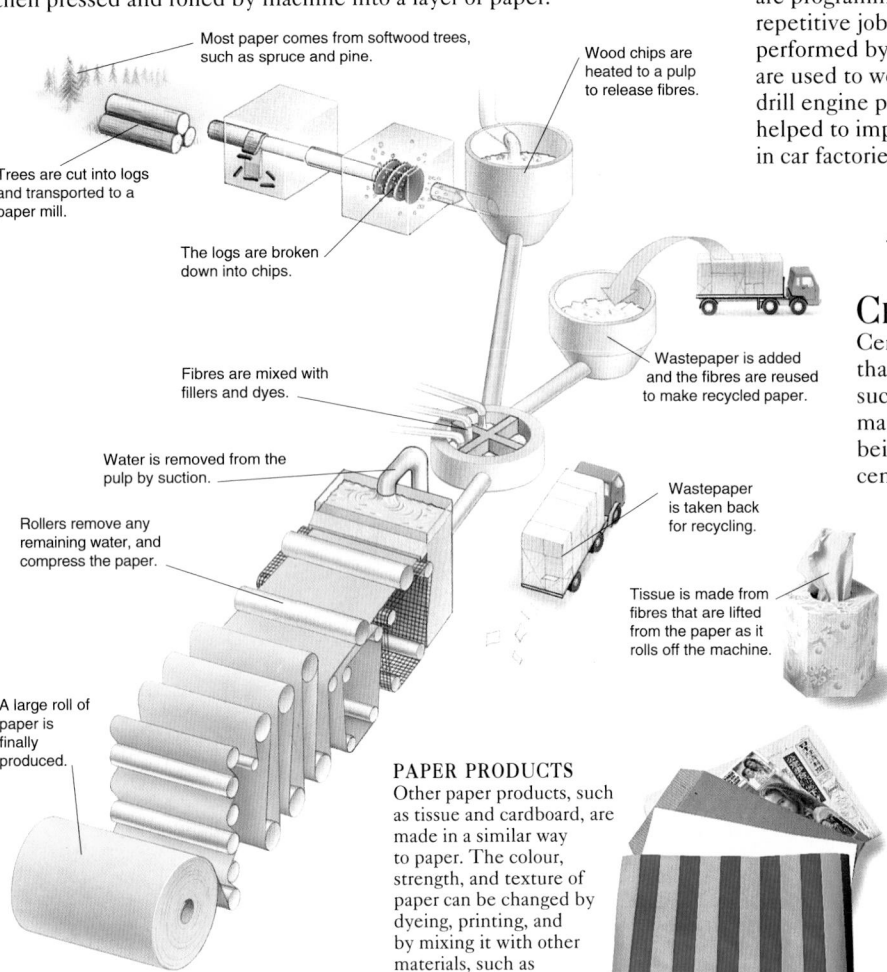

Most paper comes from softwood trees, such as spruce and pine.

Trees are cut into logs and transported to a paper mill.

The logs are broken down into chips.

Wood chips are heated to a pulp to release fibres.

Fibres are mixed with fillers and dyes.

Wastepaper is added and the fibres are reused to make recycled paper.

Water is removed from the pulp by suction.

Rollers remove any remaining water, and compress the paper.

Wastepaper is taken back for recycling.

Tissue is made from fibres that are lifted from the paper as it rolls off the machine.

A large roll of paper is finally produced.

PAPER PRODUCTS

Other paper products, such as tissue and cardboard, are made in a similar way to paper. The colour, strength, and texture of paper can be changed by dyeing, printing, and by mixing it with other materials, such as wax or plastic.

MOTOR INDUSTRY

In the motor industry, computer-controlled robots are programmed to carry out repetitive jobs previously performed by people. Robots are used to weld, paint, or drill engine parts. This has helped to improve efficiency in car factories.

Motor cars being spray-painted by robots.

CERAMIC INDUSTRY

Ceramics may be divided into two groups: materials that are moulded into shape before being heated, such as pottery and bricks, and materials that are shaped after being treated by heat, such as cement.

Building bricks

Ceramic head made from cement mixture.

POTTERY INDUSTRY

Pottery clay is a mixture of two clays: kaolin (china clay), which gives clay its smooth texture, and ball clay, which adds strength. The moist clay is moulded, then placed in a kiln and heated until it hardens.

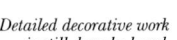

Detailed decorative work is still done by hand.

ELECTRICITY FACTS

- The amount of electricity a country produces is closely related to its industrial activity.
- Electricity production is measured in units, or kilowatt-hours. One unit is equivalent to leaving a hundred-watt light bulb on for ten hours.
- A typical household uses 6,000 units in a year.
- The world production of electricity is more than 12 trillion units.
- About 60% of production is used in industry, commerce, transport, and for public lighting.

MAJOR ELECTRICITY PRODUCERS

Producer	Units produced
North America	3.774 trillion
Asia (mostly Japan and the Pacific Coast)	2.7 trillion
Europe	2.0 trillion

GLASS INDUSTRY

Glass has many advantages. It is easily shaped, it is rust-proof, it is cheap to make, and it can be recycled.

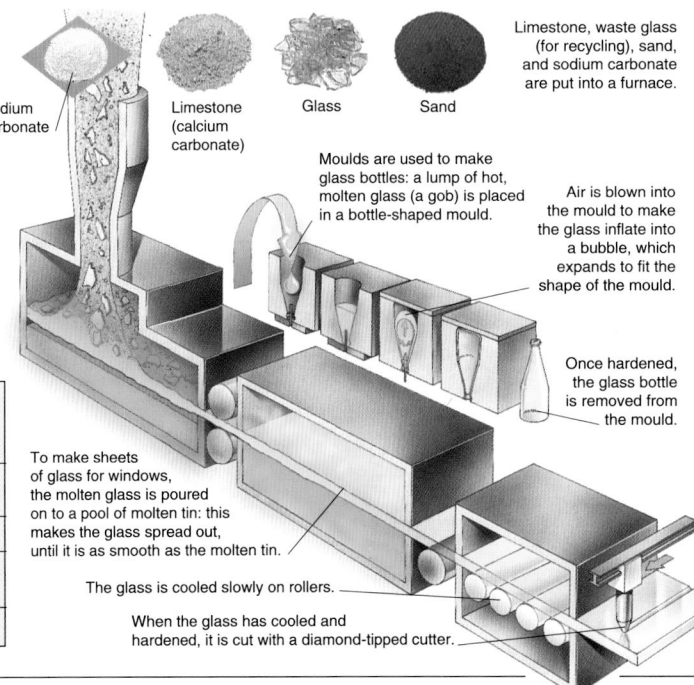

Sodium carbonate

Limestone (calcium carbonate)

Glass

Sand

Limestone, waste glass (for recycling), sand, and sodium carbonate are put into a furnace.

Moulds are used to make glass bottles: a lump of hot, molten glass (a gob) is placed in a bottle-shaped mould.

Air is blown into the mould to make the glass inflate into a bubble, which expands to fit the shape of the mould.

Once hardened, the glass bottle is removed from the mould.

To make sheets of glass for windows, the molten glass is poured on to a pool of molten tin: this makes the glass spread out, until it is as smooth as the molten tin.

The glass is cooled slowly on rollers.

When the glass has cooled and hardened, it is cut with a diamond-tipped cutter.

INDUSTRIAL WORDS

Automation Repetitive work carried out by machines that need little human control.

Component One part of a finished product.

Consumerism Economic system based on the continued increase of goods produced to satisfy increased human need.

Depression A period of low output in trade and industry.

Economy The administration of a country's trade, industry, and money supply.

GNP Gross National Product. The total value of a country's industrial production.

Mass production Manufacture of goods repeating the same processes on a large scale.

Nationalize To make an industry operate under state control.

Production line The assembling, in several stages, of a product by the workforce.

Robotics Use of computer-controlled machines that carry out jobs previously done by humans.

Staple industry A country's most important industry.

ROADS

THE FIRST MAJOR road builders were the Romans, who built roads for their armies and messengers. Today, networks of roads and motorways cover most countries, linking cities, towns, and country areas. Increasing numbers of cars, buses, coaches, and trucks use the roads to transport people and goods.

ANCIENT ROADS

The Romans created a system of roads to serve their empire in Europe from about 400 B.C. to A.D. 400. The straight, wide roads were made up of several layers. Many of these roads are still in use today.

COUNTRIES WITH THE BUSIEST ROADS

Country	Distance travelled by a vehicle per km of road	
	x 1,000km	x 1,000 miles
Portugal	1,716	1,066
UK	1,140	708
Italy	1,138	707
Netherlands	896	557
Germany	866	538
Spain	687	427
Switzerland	628	390
Finland	513	319
USA	510	317
Sweden	435	270

COUNTRIES WITH MOST ROADS

Country	x 1,000km of road	x 1,000 miles of road
USA	6,328	3,932
Russia	1,588	987
Japan	1,120	696
France	811	504
Germany	549	341
UK	380	236

MODERN ROADS

Today's roads are built to withstand heavy traffic. First, the ground is levelled and trenches are dug. Drains are laid to carry water away. The road is composed of several layers of crushed stone and soil, with a top layer of concrete or asphalt and stone chips.

Ditch for drainage of water

Crushed stone

Large paving stones

Slabs of stone in cement

Sand

Tarmac, cement, or concrete

Sand, gravel, or stone

COUNTRIES WITH DENSEST ROAD NETWORK

Country	km (per 1,000 sq km of land)	miles
Belgium	4,205	2,613
Japan	3,002	1,865
Netherlands	2,478	1,540
Luxembourg	1,970	1,224
Germany	1,900	1,181
Switzerland	1,722	1,070
Denmark	1,643	1,021
UK	1,553	965

ROAD NETWORK

Different types of road have different functions. Motorways and dual carriageways link towns and cities. Smaller roads intersect towns and cities to connect neighbourhoods and homes. In most countries people drive on the right-hand side of the road. In some countries, such as Australia, Britain, and Japan, people drive on the left-hand side.

COUNTRIES WITH MOST MOTORWAYS

Country	x 1,000km of motorway	x 1,000 miles of motorway
USA	84.9	52.8
Germany	10.8	6.7
France	7.6	4.7
Italy	6.8	4.2
Japan	4.9	3.0
UK	3.2	2.0

MOTORWAY

A wide road, usually consisting of three lanes in each direction, a motorway is specially designed for fast-moving traffic travelling long distances.

BYPASS

This type of road carries traffic around the edges of cities, avoiding city centres.

ROUNDABOUT

A roundabout allows traffic to change direction without crossing other lines of traffic.

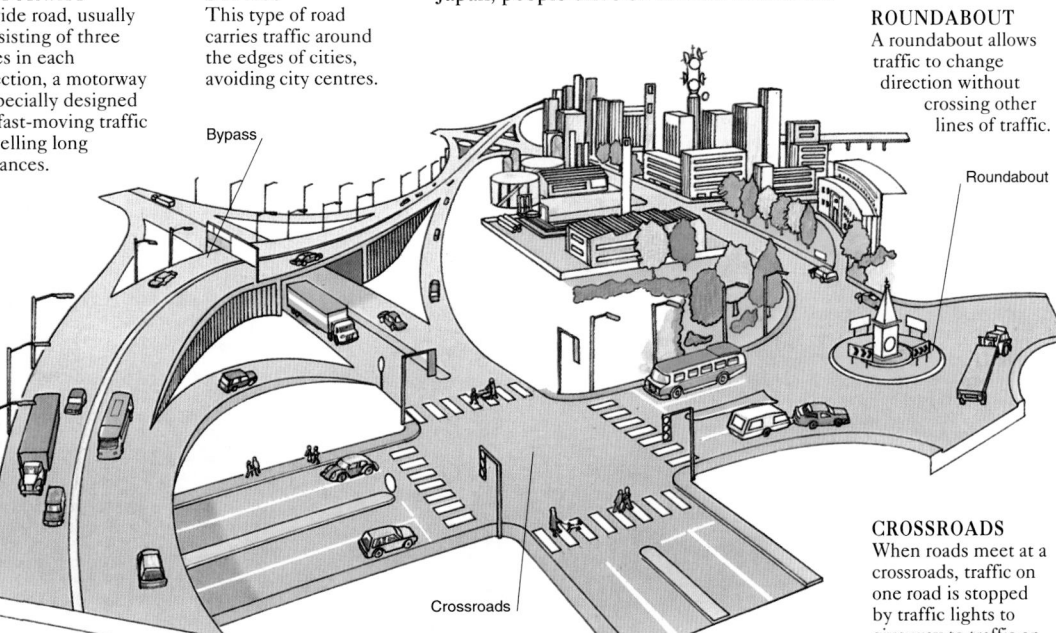

Bypass

Roundabout

Crossroads

CROSSROADS

When roads meet at a crossroads, traffic on one road is stopped by traffic lights to give way to traffic on the other road.

ROAD RECORDS

EARLIEST LONG DISTANCE road was the Persian Royal Road, which was 2,857km (1,775 miles) long. It ran from Susa in the Middle East to Smyrna, present-day Izmir in Turkey.

LONGEST ROAD is the Pan-American Highway. It runs from Alaska, USA, to Brasilia, Brazil, and is more than 24,140km (15,000 miles) in length.

HIGHEST ROAD lies between Tibet and Xinjiang, China. In places it is 5,633m (18,480ft) above sea level.

LOWEST ROAD is by the Dead Sea in Israel. It lies 393m (1,290ft) below sea level.

CONSTRUCTION

FROM EARLY TIMES, people have built all kinds of structures: tunnels and bridges to cross natural barriers; canals for transporting goods and for irrigation. Today, engineers are constantly improving construction methods and materials to produce canals that link oceans, and skyscrapers that are more than a hundred storeys high.

BRIDGES

The first bridges were made by placing tree trunks across rivers, and laying flat stones on rocks in the middle of streams. Today, bridges made of concrete and steel span lakes, rivers, deep valleys, roads, and railway lines.

Early clapper bridge, England

TYPES OF BRIDGE

Suspension
The deck, or roadway, is suspended from long steel cables attached to tall towers standing near each end of the bridge. The cables are made of thousands of steel wires bound tightly together.

Arch
This type of bridge is supported by an arch, propped up by abutments. The deck is usually straight, and does not follow the curve of the arch. It is sometimes built below, as well as above, the arch.

Bascule
This is a type of drawbridge. Its two sections can be raised at an angle to allow ships to pass through.

Beam
Most bridges with a short span are beam bridges. Each end of the bridge rests on the ground or on piers.

Swing
This type of bridge can be swung to one side to allow ships to pass through.

Suspension bridge

Arch bridge

Cantilever bridge

Cable-stayed bridge

Bascule bridge

Beam bridge

Cantilever
This is a type of beam bridge. Each half of the bridge balances on a supporting pier that is embedded in the river.

Cable-stayed
The deck is supported by steel cables connected to towers. Early cable-stayed bridges had pairs of towers, but today, single towers are also built in the centre of the deck. Its style is midway between a beam bridge and a suspension bridge. It requires fewer piers than a beam bridge, and does not need the heavy anchorages of a suspension bridge.

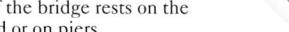

This swing bridge, in the foreground of the picture, is in Newcastle-upon-Tyne, England.

Pontoon
This type of bridge floats on the water. The deck rests on hollow concrete blocks, called pontoons, which lie on the water. Each pontoon is anchored to concrete blocks which are buried in the bed of the lake.

Pontoon bridge, Istanbul, Turkey

BRIDGES HOLDING WORLD RECORD FOR LONGEST MAIN SPAN

Bridge	Country	Date built	Type	Length m	Length ft
Ponte D'Augusto	Italy	220 B.C.	stone arch	30	98
Martorell	Spain	218 B.C.	stone arch	37	121
Chaochow	China	A.D. 617	stone arch	37	121
Bern	Switzerland	1204	stone arch	46	151
Scaligero	Italy	1356	stone arch	49	161
Trezzo over R. Adda (destroyed in 1416)	Italy	1377	stone arch	72	236
Schaffhausen	Switzerland	1755	wooden arch	59	193
Reichenau	Switzerland	1758	wooden arch	73	239
Union Bridge	Scotland	1820	suspension	137	449
Menai Straits	Wales	1826	suspension	177	581
Fribourg	Switzerland	1834	suspension	265	869
Cincinnati	USA	1867	suspension	323	1,060
Brooklyn	USA	1883	suspension	487	1,598
Forth Rail	Scotland	1889	cantilever	521	1,709
Quebec	Canada	1917	cantilever	549	1,801
Ambassador	Canada/USA	1929	suspension	565	1,854
George Washington	USA	1931	suspension	1,067	3,501
Golden Gate	USA	1937	suspension	1,280	4,199
Verrazano Narrows	USA	1964	suspension	1,298	4,258
Humber	England	1981	suspension	1,410	4,626
Great Belt East	Denmark	1997	suspension	1,624	5,328
Akashi Kaikyo	Japan	1998	suspension	1,990	6,529

SUSPENSION BRIDGES WITH LONGEST MAIN SPAN

Bridge	Country	Date built	Length m	Length ft
Akashi Kaikyo, Hyogo	Japan	1998	1,990	6,529
Great Belt East	Denmark	1997	1,624	5,328
Humber	England	1981	1,410	4,626
Tsing Ma	Hong Kong	1997	1,377	4,518
Verrazano Narrows	USA	1964	1,298	4,258
Golden Gate	USA	1937	1,280	4,199
Höga Kusten	Sweden	2000*	1,210	3,970
Mackinac Straits	USA	1957	1,158	3,799
Minami Bisan Seto	Japan	1988	1,100	3,609
Bosphorus 2	Turkey	1988	1,090	3,576
Bosphorus 1	Turkey	1973	1,074	3,524
George Washington	USA	1931	1,067	3,501
Kurushima 3, Ehime	Japan	1999	1,030	3,379
Kurushima 2, Ehime	Japan	1999	1,020	3,346
April 25	Portugal	1966	1,013	3,323
Forth Road	Scotland	1964	1,006	3,300
Kita Bisan Seto, Kagawa	Japan	1988	990	3,248
Severn	England	1966	988	3,241
Shimotsui	Japan	1988	940	3,084
Ohnaruto	Japan	1985	876	2,874

* Planned completion date

BRIDGE FACTS

• The first bridge made of iron was built in 1779 in Shropshire, England.

Ironbridge, England

• The longest bridge in the world is the Second Lake Pontchartrain Causeway, in Louisiana, USA. Each of its concrete spans measures 17m (56ft). The total length of the bridge is nearly 38km (24 miles). Land cannot be seen from its centre.

• The Tay Bridge in Scotland had been standing for just over two years when it collapsed during a stormy night in 1879. A train was crossing the wrought-iron bridge at the time, and 75 people were killed.

BRIDGE WORDS

Pier

Abutment End support for an arch.
Aqueduct Water-carrying bridge.
Box girder Hollow girder, or beam, built in the shape of a box for strength.

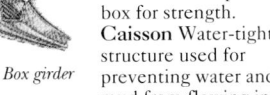

Box girder

Caisson Water-tight structure used for preventing water and mud from flowing into foundation excavations.
Clapper A type of bridge made of large slabs of stone placed over boulders.

Clapper bridge

Cofferdam Temporary dam used to keep out water while people work on a riverbed.
Creep Gradual change in shape of certain materials while under pressure.
Formwork Structure built to form, or shape, concrete on a bridge and to hold it while it hardens.
Hangers The wires or bars that connect the cables to the deck in a suspension bridge.
Lift bridge A bridge with a deck that rises in the air, like a lift.
Pier A support for the middle spans of a beam or arch bridge. The foundation of the tower on a suspension or cantilever bridge.
Reinforced concrete Concrete that contains steel rods, bars, wires, or mesh.
Viaduct A bridge carrying a road or railway.
Wrought iron Iron that is hammered into shape.

Lift bridge

CANALS

Canals are man-made waterways. Most canals are used by boats to transport cargo and people, others are used to take water to dry land, or drain water from marshy ground. Some canals, such as the Suez Canal in the Middle East and the Panama Canal in Central America, link seas and oceans.

HOW A LOCK WORKS

A canal lock is used to change the water level. A lock is a section of canal, large enough to take one or more boats, that has large, water-tight gates at each end. By opening and closing paddles, or valves, in one pair of gates, water is allowed to run into or out of the lock, and so raise or lower the water level to the same height as that in the next section of canal.

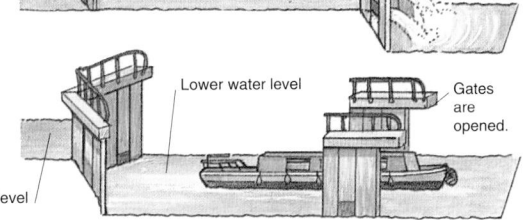

The narrowboat passes through the open gate into the lock.

Open gates

Upper water level

Closed gates

Lower water level

The paddles, or valves, in the lower gates are opened to let water out and the narrowboat is carried down with the dropping water level.

Gates are now closed.

The narrowboat is fully inside the lock.

Paddles are opened, and water rushes out.

The lower gates can now be opened for the boat to pass through.

Lower water level

Gates are opened.

Upper water level

DAMS

People need a constant supply of water to live. Efficient collection and storage of water is essential, especially in countries where there is little rainfall. Dams are built either to divert or store water.

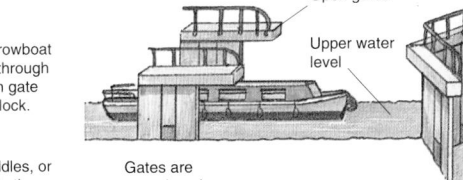

DAM RECORDS

OLDEST KNOWN DAM in the world is the Sadd el-Kafara in Egypt. It was built out of earth and rock in about 3000 B.C.

LARGEST DAM in the world is the Syncrude Tailings dam in Canada, at 540,000,000 cu m (706,000,000cu ft).

LONGEST SEA DAM in the world is the Afsluitdijk in the Netherlands. Built in two sections, its total length is 62.5km (38.8 miles).

Canal	Location	Date built	Length km	Length miles
Suez	Links the Red Sea with the Mediterranean Sea	1869	174	108
Kiel	Links the North Sea with the Baltic Sea, Germany	1895	99	61
Panama	Links the Atlantic Ocean and the Caribbean Sea with the Pacific Ocean	1914	81	50
Manchester	England	1894	57	35

LONGEST SHIP CANALS

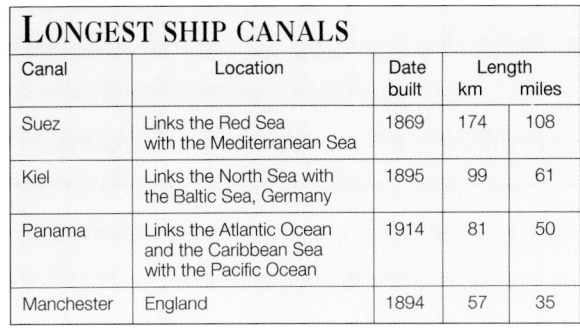

CANAL FACTS

• The Chinese were the first people to build canal locks along the Great Canal of China, which ran from Peking to Hangzhou. The canal was built during the 1200s and is still used today.

• Leonardo da Vinci (1452–1519), Italian artist and engineer, designed locks for the Languedoc Canal, France, which was completed in 1681. It linked the Mediterranean Sea with the Atlantic Ocean.

• The largest lock in the world is the Berendrecht lock in Antwerp, Belgium. It is 500m (1,640ft) long and 68m (223ft) wide. It has four sliding lock gates.

• The Netherlands has more than 8,000km (4,971 miles) of canals.

TYPES OF DAM

Arch dam
This has a curved shape, with the inside of the curve facing downstream.

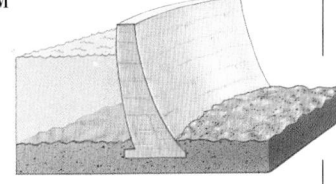

Arch dam

Buttress dam
This has a series of props, or buttresses, which are on the side of the dam facing downstream.

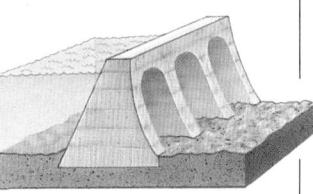

Buttress dam

Embankment dam
This is made of a huge pile of soil or rocks. Like the massive dam, the embankment dam relies on its sheer bulk to hold back water.

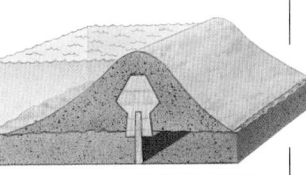

Embankment dam

Massive dam
This is built of concrete and relies on its size and weight to withstand the pressure of a huge amount of stored water.

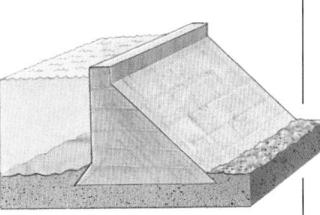

Massive dam

TALLEST DAMS

Dam	Location	Date built	Height m	Height ft
Rogun	Tajikistan	1989	325	1066
Nourek	Tajikistan	1979	317	1040
Grande Dixence	Switzerland	1962	285	935
Inguri	Georgia, USA	1979	271	889
Vaiont	Italy	1961	265	869
Mica	British Columbia, Canada	1973	244	800

TUNNELS

Tunnels have a variety of uses. Many are built for transport purposes: to pass through or under obstacles such as mountains, rivers, and busy roads. They are also used to carry sewage, water from reservoirs, power and communication cables, and in mining.

TYPES OF TUNNEL
Road tunnels
These are built to allow traffic to pass through mountains, under rivers and busy crossroads.

Pedestrian tunnel

Pedestrian tunnels
These allow people to cross busy streets safely.

Train tunnels
There are underground train systems in many of the major cities of the world. They offer a fast form of transport, and save valuable space above ground.

Train tunnel

Road tunnel

Water tunnel

Water tunnels
These are built just underneath the surface. Some carry fresh water, others carry sewage.

HOW A TUNNEL IS BUILT
Tunnelling shields are used to drive a tunnel through soft ground. As the shield moves forwards, the front cutting edge bores through rock and earth. Tunnel lining, fitted behind the shield, prevents the walls and roof of the tunnel from collapsing. In hard ground, huge drilling machines, called moles, are often used.

SKYSCRAPERS
From early times, people have built tall buildings. The Romans built blocks of flats 15 storeys high. Today, advances in construction methods have resulted in many high-rise buildings, such as the Sears Tower, USA, which is 110 storeys high.

A tunnelling shield breaking through earth

BUILDING A SKYSCRAPER
A skyscraper has an inner frame made of steel or concrete. The frame holds the floors and walls (often made of glass) together. The building is supported by a foundation – usually a pit containing reinforced concrete.

LONGEST ROAD TUNNELS

Tunnel	Country	Date built	Length km	miles
St. Gotthard	Switzerland	1980	16.3	10.1
Arlberg	Austria	1978	13.97	8.69
Frejus	France/Italy	1978	12.7	7.9
Mont Blanc	France/Italy	1965	11.6	7.2
Gudvangen	Norway	1992	11.40	7.08

TUNNEL FACTS
• The Channel Tunnel, which links England and France, was completed in 1994. Trains carry people, cars, and goods through the tunnel. It is 51.8km (32.2 miles) long.

• The longest water tunnel in the world is the Delaware Aqueduct, built in 1944. It is 168.9km (104.9 miles) long, more than twice the length of the second longest, the Orange-Fish in South Africa.

• The fastest rate of tunnel-driving in soft ground, using a tunnelling shield, is 501m (1,644ft) in five days, on the London Ring Main Tunnel in 1992.

LONGEST RAILWAY TUNNELS

Tunnel	Country	Date built	Length km	miles
AlpTransit Link	Switzerland	2007*	57	35.4
Seikan	Japan	1985	53.9	33.5
Channel	France/England	1994	51.8	32.2
Northern line	England	1939	27.8	17.3
Daishimizu	Japan	1982	22.2	13.8
Simplon 2	Switzerland/Italy	1922	19.8	12.3
Simplon 1	Switzerland/Italy	1906	19.8	12.3
Shin Kanmon	Japan	1973	18.7	11.6
Apennines	Italy	1931	18.6	11.5
Rokko	Japan	1971	16.2	10
Henderson	USA	1975	15.8	9.8
Haruna	Japan	1982	15.4	9.6
St. Gotthard	Switzerland	1882	15	9.3
Nakayama	Japan	1982	14.8	9.2
Lötschberg	Switzerland	1913	14.5	9

* Planned completion date

TALLEST TOWERS

Tower	Location	Date built	Height m	ft
KTHI-TV Mast	North Dakota, USA	1963	629	2,064
KSLA-TV Mast	Louisiana, USA	1982	579	1,900
CN Tower	Toronto, Canada	1975	555	1,821
Ostankino TV Tower	Moscow, Russia	1967	537	1,762
WTVM & WRBL TV Mast	Georgia, USA	1962	533	1,749
WBIR TV Mast	Tennessee, USA	1963	533	1,749
KFVS TV Mast	Cape Girardeau, USA	1960	511	1,676

Liquid concrete is pumped to the upper levels of the skyscraper.

Concrete is mixed in a revolving drum to stop it from setting.

TALLEST OFFICE BLOCKS

Office block	Location	Date built	Height m	ft
Shanghai World Finance Centre	Shanghai, China	2001*	460	1,509
Chongqing Tower	Chongqing, China	2000*	457	1,499
Petronas Tower	Kuala Lumpur, Malaysia	1996	452	1,483
Sears Tower	Chicago, USA	1974	443	1,453
Jin Mao Building	Shanghai, China	1997	420	1,378
Tour Sans Fin	Paris, France	2000*	419	1,375
World Trade Center	New York, USA	1973	417	1,368
Empire State Building	New York, USA	1931	381	1,250
T & C Tower	Kao-hsiung, Taiwan	1997	348	1,142

INTERNATIONAL WORLD

In this section, the latest computer-generated maps show all the countries of the world in amazing detail. Data boxes provide up-to-date statistics, and lifestyle facts, prepared in association with embassies worldwide, give authoritative information about how people live today.

The Physical World • The Political World • How To Use The Map Pages
All the Countries and Continents of the World • Flags • Mapping
Raw Materials • Farming and Fisheries • Population
Living Standards • Debt and Wealth

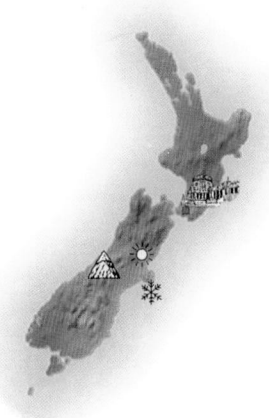

THE PHYSICAL WORLD

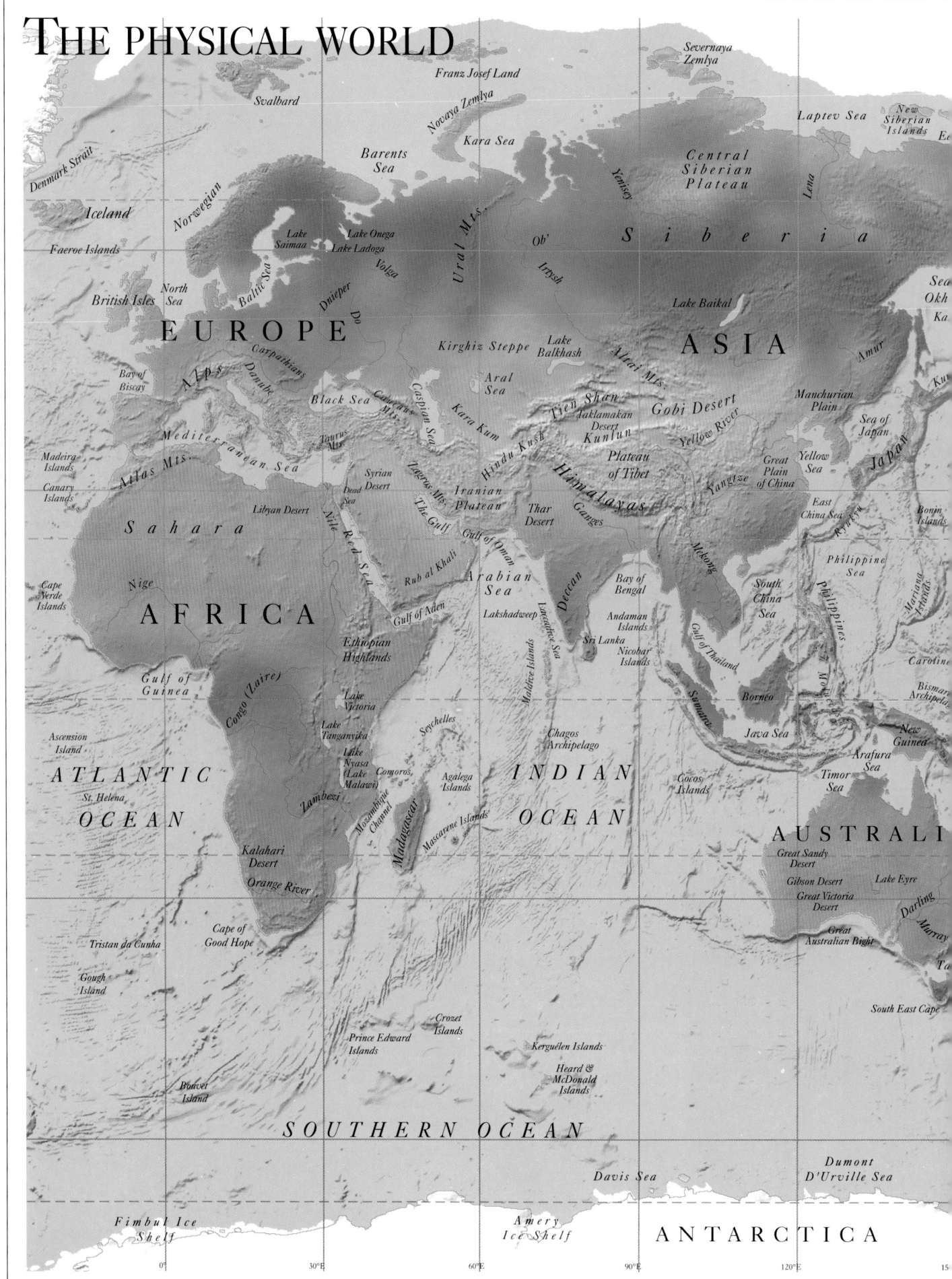

Severnaya Zemlya

Franz Josef Land

Svalbard

Novaya Zemlya

Kara Sea

Laptev Sea

New Siberian Islands

Ee

Central Siberian Plateau

Denmark Strait

Sea Okh

Ka

Norwegian

Iceland

Barents Sea

Lena

Faeroe Islands

Lake Saimaa

Lake Onega

Lake Ladoga

Ural Mts.

Ob'

S i b e r i a

Lake Baikal

British Isles

North Sea

Baltic Sea

Volga

Dnieper

Do

Irtysh

Amur

EUROPE

Kirghiz Steppe

Lake Balkhash

ASIA

Carpathians

Aral Sea

Altai Mts.

Manchurian Plain

Sea of Japan

Ku

Bay of Biscay

Alps

Danube

Black Sea

Caucasus Mts.

Caspian Sea

Kara Kum

Tien Shan

Taklamakan Desert

Gobi Desert

Kunlun

Yellow River

Great Plain of China

Yellow Sea

Japan

Mediterranean Sea

Taurus Mts.

Zagros Mts.

Hindu Kush

Plateau of Tibet

Himalayas

Yangtze

East China Sea

Bonin Islands

Madeira Islands

Atlas Mts.

Syrian Desert

Dead Sea

Iranian Plateau

Ganges

Thar Desert

Ryukyu

Canary Islands

The Gulf

Gulf of Oman

Mekong

Philippine Sea

Sahara

Libyan Desert

Nile

Red Sea

Rub al Khali

Arabian Sea

Deccan

Bay of Bengal

South China Sea

Mariana Islands

Cape Verde Islands

Nige

AFRICA

Gulf of Aden

Lakshadweep

Andaman Islands

Philippines

Mo

Caroline

Gulf of Guinea

Ethiopian Highlands

Laccadive Sea

Sri Lanka

Nicobar Islands

Gulf of Thailand

Bismarck Archipelago

Ascension Island

Congo (Zaire)

Lake Victoria

Maldive Islands

Seychelles

Chagos Archipelago

INDIAN

Borneo

New Guinea

Lake Tanganyika

Java Sea

ATLANTIC

Lake Nyasa (Lake Malawi)

Comoros

Agalega Islands

OCEAN

Cocos Islands

Arafura Sea

St. Helena

Zambezi

Timor Sea

OCEAN

Madagascar

Mozambique Channel

Mascarene Islands

AUSTRALI

Kalahari Desert

Great Sandy Desert

Gibson Desert

Lake Eyre

Orange River

Great Victoria Desert

Darling

Cape of Good Hope

Great Australian Bight

Murray

Tristan da Cunha

Ta

Gough Island

South East Cape

Crozet Islands

Prince Edward Islands

Kerguélen Islands

Bouvet Island

Heard & McDonald Islands

SOUTHERN OCEAN

Davis Sea

Dumont D'Urville Sea

Fimbul Ice Shelf

Amery Ice Shelf

ANTARCTICA

0°   30°E   60°E   90°E   120°E   15

ARCTIC OCEAN

Chukchi
Sea

Beaufort
Sea

Queen Elizabeth Islands

Baffin
Bay

Greenland

Greenland Sea

Arctic Circle

60°N

Bering
Strait

Yukon

Mackenzie

Great Bear
Lake

Great Slave
Lake

Hudson
Bay

Labrador
Sea

Davis Strait

Bering
Sea

Gulf of
Alaska

Coast Mountains

Rocky Mountains

Newfoundland

Aleutian Islands

Coast Ranges

Missouri

N O R T H
A M E R I C A

Great Lakes

A T L A N T I C

Azores

Sonoran
Desert

Rio Grande

Sierra Madre

Mississippi

Appalachian

O C E A N

30°N

Midway Islands

Hawaiian Islands

Gulf of
Mexico

Bermuda
Islands

Bahamas

Tropic of Cancer

P A C I F I C

O C E A N

C E N T R A L
A M E R I C A

Greater Antilles

Leeward
Islands

Windward Islands

Caribbean Sea

Galápagos
Islands

Llanos

Amazon

Equator 0°

Phoenix Islands

Line Islands

Amazonia

S O U T H

Marquesas Islands

Samoa

Society Islands

Tahiti

Tuamotu

A M E R I C A

São Francisco

Lake Titicaca

Andes

Plateau of
Mato Grosso

Tropic of Capricorn

Fiji

Cook Islands

Tubuai
Islands

Pitcairn Islands

Sala y Gómez

Easter Island

Atacama Desert

Paraná

Pampas

30°S

New
Zealand

Chatham Islands

Juan Fernández
Islands

Patagonia

A T L A N T I C

Bounty Islands

Antipodes
Islands

Falkland
Islands

O C E A N

Cape Horn

Scotia Sea

South
Sandwich
Islands

Ross Sea

Drake Passage

South Orkney
Islands

60°S

South Shetland
Islands

Antarctic Circle

Bellingshausen
Sea

Amundsen Sea

A N T A R C T I C A

Weddell Sea

180°

150°W

120°W

90°W

60°W

30°W

THE POLITICAL WORLD

THE COUNTRIES OF the world, which number 192, are spread over seven continents and vary greatly in size. The Russian Federation, for example, is almost 39 million times bigger than the Vatican City.

INTERNATIONAL TIME ZONES

The world is made up of 24 different time zones, as shown on the map below. In each zone, the clocks are set to a different time of day. Time zones ensure that noon in each country is fixed at about midday, and that midnight falls in the middle of the night.

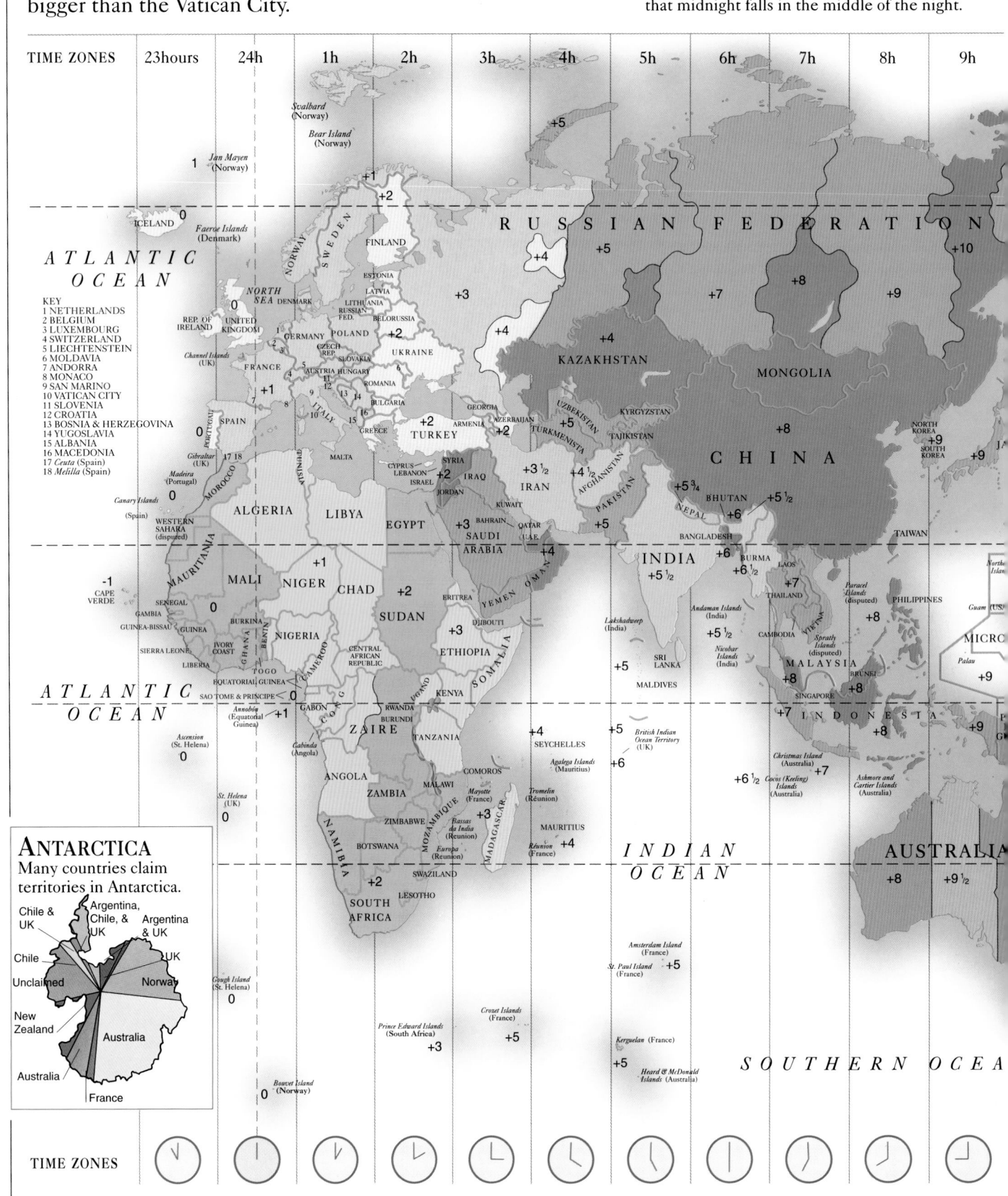

| TIME ZONES | 23hours | 24h | 1h | 2h | 3h | 4h | 5h | 6h | 7h | 8h | 9h |

KEY
1 NETHERLANDS
2 BELGIUM
3 LUXEMBOURG
4 SWITZERLAND
5 LIECHTENSTEIN
6 MOLDAVIA
7 ANDORRA
8 MONACO
9 SAN MARINO
10 VATICAN CITY
11 SLOVENIA
12 CROATIA
13 BOSNIA & HERZEGOVINA
14 YUGOSLAVIA
15 ALBANIA
16 MACEDONIA
17 *Ceuta* (Spain)
18 *Melilla* (Spain)

ANTARCTICA
Many countries claim territories in Antarctica.

Chile & UK
Argentina, Chile, & UK
Argentina & UK
Chile
UK
Unclaimed
Norway
New Zealand
Australia
Australia
France

| TIME ZONES | | | | | | | | | | | |

RECORDS

CONTINENT WITH MOST COUNTRIES
is Africa with 54 countries.

ONLY CONTINENT THAT IS ALSO
A COUNTRY is Australia.

LARGEST ISLAND
is Greenland, at 2,175,219sq km (839,852sq miles).

LARGEST COUNTRY
is the Russian Federation, with an area of
17,075,400sq km (6,592,846sq miles).

SMALLEST COUNTRY
is the Vatican City with an area of just
0.44sq km (0.17sq miles).

INTERNATIONAL
DATE LINE
When you cross this imaginary
line from east to west, the date
changes. The western side is a day
ahead of the eastern side.

KEY
20 *Cayman Is.* (UK)
21 *Navassa Island* (USA)
22 *Virgin Is.* (USA)
23 ST. KITTS & NEVIS
24 *Montserrat* (UK)
25 *Martinique* (France)
26 ST. VINCENT & THE GRENADINES
27 *Netherlands Antilles* (Netherlands)
28 *Aruba* (Netherlands)

HOW TO USE THE MAP PAGES

THE MAPS IN International World are organized into sections, based on continents. There is a section for North America, South America, Europe, Africa, Asia, and Australasia. At the start of each section there is a map showing the whole continent, followed by maps of the countries in that continent. This page explains the information and symbols that appear on and around these country maps.

LOCATOR MAPS
The red area on the globe shows the location of the countries on the page, or spre in relation to the continent.

LANGUAGE
This spells out a traditional greeting in the main language of the country.

DATA BOXES
Every country in this section has a box with important statistics about that country. Some of the main countries contain more detailed information than others.

Flag
The national flag for each country or territory is shown at the top of the data box.

Area
The figure shown is the total area of the country, and includes all inland water (e.g. lakes, reservoirs, and rivers).

Government
The type of government ruling the country at time of going to press is described. Some governments, however, are fairly unstable and may change at short notice.

Independence
This is the date when a country broke free from the control of another power and became independent. The date when a republic was formed, or a state was declared, may also be given.

Currency
The paper or metal money used as the system of exchange, and in current use in that country, is named.

Population
This figure is the number of people registered in the most recent census as living in the country. Most countries round up their estimated population to the nearest thousand. Migration and famine will affect these figures.

Density
The average number of people occupying each square kilometre or square mile of the country is given. The figure is based on land area only and not on the total area.

Official Language
This language, or languages, is used by the government, and is not necessarily the most widely spoken language.

Major Religions
The percentage breakdown of religions currently practised by the population is shown. A religious symbol, such as this cross for Christianity, appears when a religion is followed by 75% or more of the population.

ICELAND
ICELAND, EUROPE'S second largest island, has the lowest population density in Europe. The remote interior can be reached only by special vehicle, pony, or small plane.

Area 103,000sq km (39,770sq miles)
Government Constitutional republic
Independence 1944, from British and US control during World War II
Currency Icelandic króna
Population 300,000
Density 3 per sq km (8 per sq mile)
Official Language Icelandic
Major Religions Evangelical Lutheran Church of Iceland 96%, other Protestant and Roman Catholic 3%, non-religious 1%

WEATHER FACTS
30°C (86°F)   860mm (33.9in)   -36°C (-32.8°F)
10.6°C (51.8°F)   0.2°C (32.4°F)

LAND PROFILE

LIFESTYLE FACTS
• The Althing, the Icelandic parliament, has been in existence since the 13th century and is one of the oldest surviving assemblies in the world.

• Iceland has the most solfataras (volcanic vents) and hot springs in the world. Many of its towns are heated by underground hot water.

• Iceland produces more than a third of the world's cod-liver oil, and is the biggest consumer of it.

LANGUAGE
A traditional greeting in Icelandic is *gódan daginn*.

HOT SPRINGS
Deildartunguhver hot springs blow out 250 litres (55 gallons) of hot water every second. Over a 24-hour period, they produce enough water to fill 105,600 baths.

DENMARK
DENMARK, WHICH IS divided into numerous islands, has a 4,500-mile (7,300km) coastline. It was the first Scandinavian country to belong to the European Community (EC).

Area 43,069sq km (16,629sq miles)
Government Constitutional monarchy
State founded c. 950
Territories Faeroe Islands, Greenland
Currency Danish krone
Population 5,200,000
Density 123 per sq km (319 per sq mile)
Official Language Danish
Major Religions Evangelical Lutheran Church 91%, Roman Catholic 2%, other and non-religious 7%

WEATHER FACTS
35°C (95°F)   704mm (27.7in)   -24°C (-11.2°F)
16.3°C (61.3°F)   1.3°C (34.3°F)

LAND PROFILE
Almost two-thirds of the land is farmed.

LANGUAGE
A traditional greeting in Danish is *goddag*.

LIFESTYLE FACTS
• Lego was created by a Danish carpenter in the 1930s. Legoland Park is a miniature, working village created from 35 million plastic bricks.

• Denmark has one of the lowest private ownerships of cars in Europe. Cyclists are encouraged with special lanes, and Copenhagen was the first city to create a pedestrian street.

• Denmark has over twice as many pigs as humans, and Danish bacon is a successful export product. Danish farmers produce three times more food than is needed to feed the population.

LITTLE MERMAID
Situated by Copenhagen harbour, this statue of the mermaid from Hans C. Andersen's fairy tale was sculpted in 1913 by Edvard Eriksen (1876–1959). Her head has had to be replaced several times.

NORWAY
NORWAY IS A LAND of beauti fjords (valleys flooded by ris levels after the last ice age): longest is Sogne Fjord, at 2 kilometres (126 miles).

Area 323,900sq km (125,060sq miles)
Government Constitutional m
Independence from Swede
Territories Svalbard archipelag Mayen Island
Currency Norwegian kröne
Population 4,300,000
Density 14 per sq km (36 per
Official Language Nynorsk (n Norwegian) and Bokmaal (older
Major Religions Evangelica Lutheran and other Protestant 8 other Christian 12%

WEATHER FACTS
34°C (93°F)   730mm (28.7in)   -3.5°C (

LAND PROFILE

WEATHER FACTS

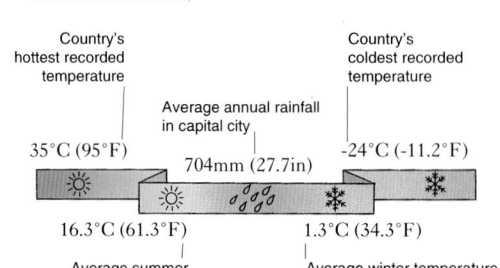

Country's hottest recorded temperature

Average annual rainfall in capital city

Country's coldest recorded temperature

35°C (95°F)   704mm (27.7in)   -24°C (-11.2°F)

16.3°C (61.3°F)   1.3°C (34.3°F)

Average summer temperature in capital city

Average winter temperature in capital city

LANDMARK
This is the country's most recognizable building or statue, and has been chosen by the embassy or consulate of th featured country. The map show location of the landmark, with an illustration similar to the photogra

286

LAND PROFILE

This artwork shows how the land in a country divides into areas such as forest or desert, how much is built on (urban), and how much is available for farming (agriculture). Barren land indicates areas such as the bare rocks of mountain tops, or salt flats.

KEY

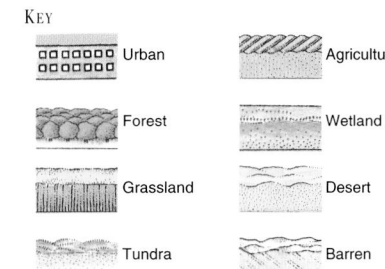

- Urban
- Forest
- Grassland
- Tundra
- Agriculture
- Wetland
- Desert
- Barren

KEY TO MAPS

The maps in this section have been created to give an accurate representation of the landscape.

COLOURS

The different physical features and climate zones are listed below.

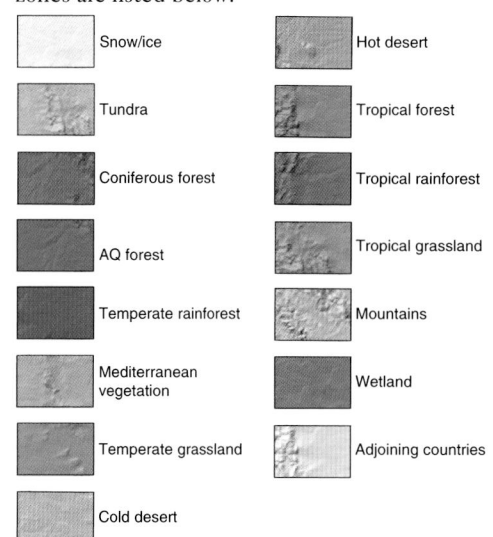

- Snow/ice
- Tundra
- Coniferous forest
- AQ forest
- Temperate rainforest
- Mediterranean vegetation
- Temperate grassland
- Cold desert
- Hot desert
- Tropical forest
- Tropical rainforest
- Tropical grassland
- Mountains
- Wetland
- Adjoining countries

SYMBOLS

The symbols below appear on the map to represent places and physical features.

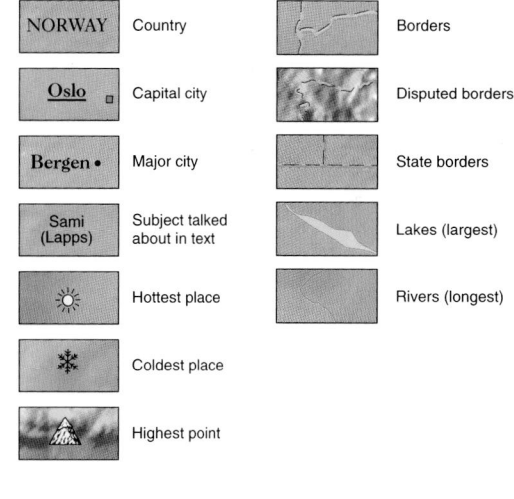

- NORWAY — Country
- Oslo — Capital city
- Bergen • — Major city
- Sami (Lapps) — Subject talked about in text
- ☀ Hottest place
- ❄ Coldest place
- Highest point
- Borders
- Disputed borders
- State borders
- Lakes (largest)
- Rivers (longest)

SWEDEN

...IRDS OF the land in Sweden ...ed by forests, and there are ... lakes. Timber products, ...g paper, account for nearly ... of all Swedish exports.

Area 449,960sq km (173,730sq miles)
...ment Constitutional monarchy
...stablished 1523
...rency Swedish krona
...lation 8,800,000
...y 20 per sq km (50 per sq mile)
Language Swedish
r Religions Evangelical
...Church of Sweden 94%,
...Catholic 2%, other 4%

...RIZES
...Nobel (1833–96) was a Swedish
...nd inventor of dynamite. He
...fund for the Nobel prizes,
...each year for sciences, literature,
...e, to those who have given the
...enefit to humankind.

LANGUAGE
A traditional greeting in Norwegian is *go dag*.

100 kroner

...KOLLEN
...mp at Holmenkollen, outside
...e oldest in existence. The first
...competition was held in
...the event continues
...l every March.

...E FACTS
...merfest, the world's
...herly town, the sun
...midnight for just over
...hs in the summer.

...y's annual contribution of its
...ncome (1.17%) towards foreign aid
...hest proportion in the world.

...gians read more newspapers than
...se in the world, and buy more
...ooks than any other non-English-
...country.

LANGUAGE
A traditional greeting in Swedish is *god dag.*

100 kroner

LAND PROFILE
The land is mainly forested or used for farming.

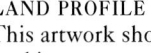

- 2.5
- 4.5
- 5.5
- 2.5
- 75

LIFESTYLE FACTS
- Each year 12,000 cross-country skiers take part in a race from Salen to Mora in central Sweden. The course is 90km (56 miles) long.
- In 1910, Sweden was the first European country to establish national parks. Animals that can be found in the parks include lynx, bear, and moose.
- Stockholm's waterways are so pure that people can safely swim and fish in them.

WEATHER FACTS
35°C (95°F)   622mm (24.5in)   -38°C (-36.4°F)
16.5°C (61.7°F)   -2°C (28.4°F)

CITY HALL
Stockholm's fine City Hall, called the Stadshus, was built between 1911 and 1923. Its Golden Hall has 19 million gilded tiles.

B A R E N T S   N
Hammerfest
Sami (Lapps)
Lofoten Islands
Katnekaisa 2,111m (6,926ft)
Padelanta National Park
Arctic Circle
Piteå
Trondheim
Galdhøpiggen 2,469m (8,103ft)
Femund
Sogne Fjord Lillehammer
Bergen Mjøsa
Holmenkollen Glama
Oslo
Drammen Mora
Stavanger Uppsala
Vänern Stockholm
Örebro Stadshus
Norrköping
Linköping
Gothenburg Vättern Gotland
Ålborg Öland
DENMARK Ytding Skovhøj 179m (587ft)
Legoland Læsø
Fanø
Copenhagen Malmö
Odense Little Mermaid
GERMANY
NORTH SEA
SKAGERRAK
Gulf of Bothnia
Baltic Sea

THE SAMI
The Sami (Lapps) have inhabited the arctic regions of Norway and Sweden since ancient times. Today, there are about 60,000 and 70% speak the Sami language. About 70,000 reindeer live in Sami territories, and the main occupation of the people is reindeer breeding. The woven clothes worn by the Sami are practical and beautiful.

- More than 50% of Norwegian families have a weekend home in the mountains or by the sea. These second homes are made of wood, and some have turf-covered roofs.

HIGHEST WATERFALLS

Name	Height	
	m	ft
Utigord	800	2,625
Mongefossen	774	2,540
Ostre Mardola Foss	657	2,154
Tyssetrengane	646	2,120
Kjelfossen	561	1,841

0   500km
0   300 mile

...STYLE FACTS
...e facts give details
...t food, sports, industry,
...ents that are unique to
...country. They have been
...en from information
...d by the country itself
...ealistically reflect life in
...country.

SCALE
This shows how distance on the map relates to kilometres and miles, and can be used to see how big a country is. Not all maps are drawn to the same scale.

COMPASS POINT
This fixes the direction of North (N), and gives the position of the country in relation to North.

TABLES
These provide easy-to-follow information about the top features of a country. They may list the highest waterfalls, as shown here, or the most cars manufactured, or chief exports.

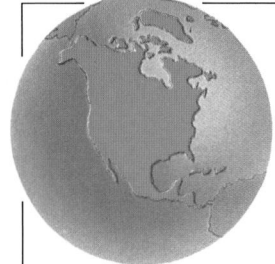

NORTH AND CENTRAL AMERICA

CANADA AND THE United States of America cover most of the continent of North America. To the south lie Mexico and the seven small countries of Central America. The western side of the continent is dominated by the Rocky Mountains, which run from Canada to Mexico.

Area 24,238,000sq km (9,358,340sq miles)
Countries 24
Largest Canada
Smallest Grenada
Population 431,352,677
Density 20 per sq km (52 per sq mile)
Major Languages English, Spanish, French, Amerindian and Inuit languages, Nahuatl (Aztec)

■ **Highest point** Mount McKinley, Alaska, 6,194m (20,320ft)
■ **Lowest point** Death Valley, California 86m (282ft) below sea level
☀ **Highest temperature** 57°C (135°F) Death Valley, California
❄ **Lowest temperature** -66°C (-87°F) Northice, Greenland

COUNTRIES, TERRITORIES, AND CAPITALS

Name	Capital	Name	Capital
Antigua and Barbuda	St. John's	Guatemala	Guatemala City
Bahamas	Nassau	Haiti	Port-au-Prince
Barbados	Bridgetown	Honduras	Tegucigalpa
Belize	Belmopan	Jamaica	Kingston
Canada	Ottawa	Mexico	Mexico City
Costa Rica	San José	Nicaragua	Managua
Cuba	Havana	Panama	Panama City
Dominica	Roseau	St. Kitts and Nevis	Basseterre
Dominican Republic	Santo Domingo	St. Lucia	Castries
El Salvador	San Salvador	St. Vincent and the Grenadines	Kingstown
Greenland	Godthåb	Trinidad and Tobago	Port of Spain
Grenada	St. George's	USA	Washington, D.C.

TIME ZONES

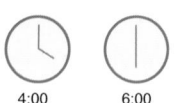

4:00 Vancouver | 6:00 Mexico City | 9:00 Godthåb | 12:00 Greenwich

TOP CITY POPULATIONS

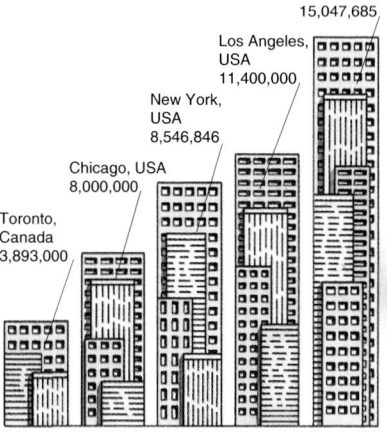
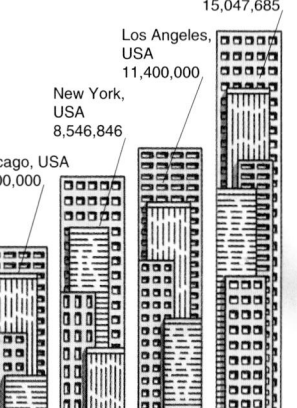

Mexico City, Mexico 15,047,685
Los Angeles, USA 11,400,000
New York, USA 8,546,846
Chicago, USA 8,000,000
Toronto, Canada 3,893,000

CLIMATE ZONES

KEY
Polar and tundra
Mountain regions
Taiga
Temperate forest
Dry grassland
Hot desert
Tropical grassland
Rainforest

RUSSIAN FEDERATION
Bering Strait
AL
Mount Mc 6 (20,
Bering Sea
Aleutian Islands

CONTINENT FACTS
- British Columbia produces 25% of the timber sold in North America. It also supplies the world with chopsticks.
- Grenada is the only country in the Western world where spices such as nutmeg, cinnamon, and cloves grow in abundance.

- Surfing as a competitive spo began on the island of Oahu in Hawaii. Surfing waves can rea about 8m (26ft) high.

Midway Islands (USA)
Hawaiian Islan
PACIFIC OCEA

GRAND CANYON
The Grand Canyon was gouged out of rock by the Colorado River. The canyon is 349km (217 miles) long, up to 30km (19 miles) wide, and 1.6km (1 mile) deep. At its deepest point it cuts through rock 2,000 million years old.

AGE BREAKDOWN

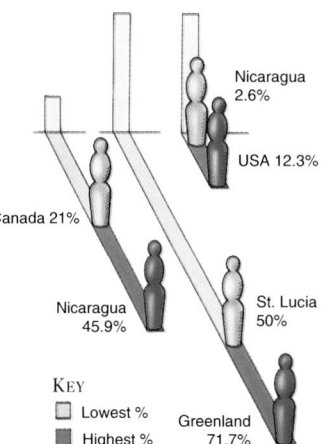

| Under 15 years | 15 to 65 years | Over 65 years |

Nicaragua 2.6%
USA 12.3%
Canada 21%
Nicaragua 45.9%
St. Lucia 50%
Greenland 71.7%

KEY
☐ Lowest %
■ Highest %

FEWEST DOCTORS

Haiti	1 to 7,040 people
St. Vincent	1 to 3,760 people
Honduras	1 to 2,330 people
El Salvador	1 to 2,312 people
St. Kitts and Nevis	1 to 2,180 people

LONGEST LIFESPAN

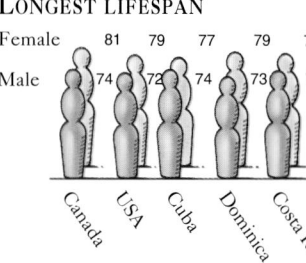

| | Female | 81 | 79 | 77 | 79 | 7 |
| | Male | 74 | 72 | 74 | 73 | |

Canada | USA | Cuba | Dominica | Costa

LONGEST ROADS (see map on pages 292-3)

Trans-Canada Highway: St. John's, Newfoundland to Victoria, B.C. 7,821km (4,860 miles)

US 20: Boston, Massachusetts to Newport, Oregon 5,415km (3,365 miles)

US 6: Provincetown, Massachusetts to Bishop, California 5,229km (3,249 miles)

US 30: Atlantic City, N.J. to Astoria, Oregon 5,019km (3,119 miles)

CROSS-SECTION ACROSS CONTINENT

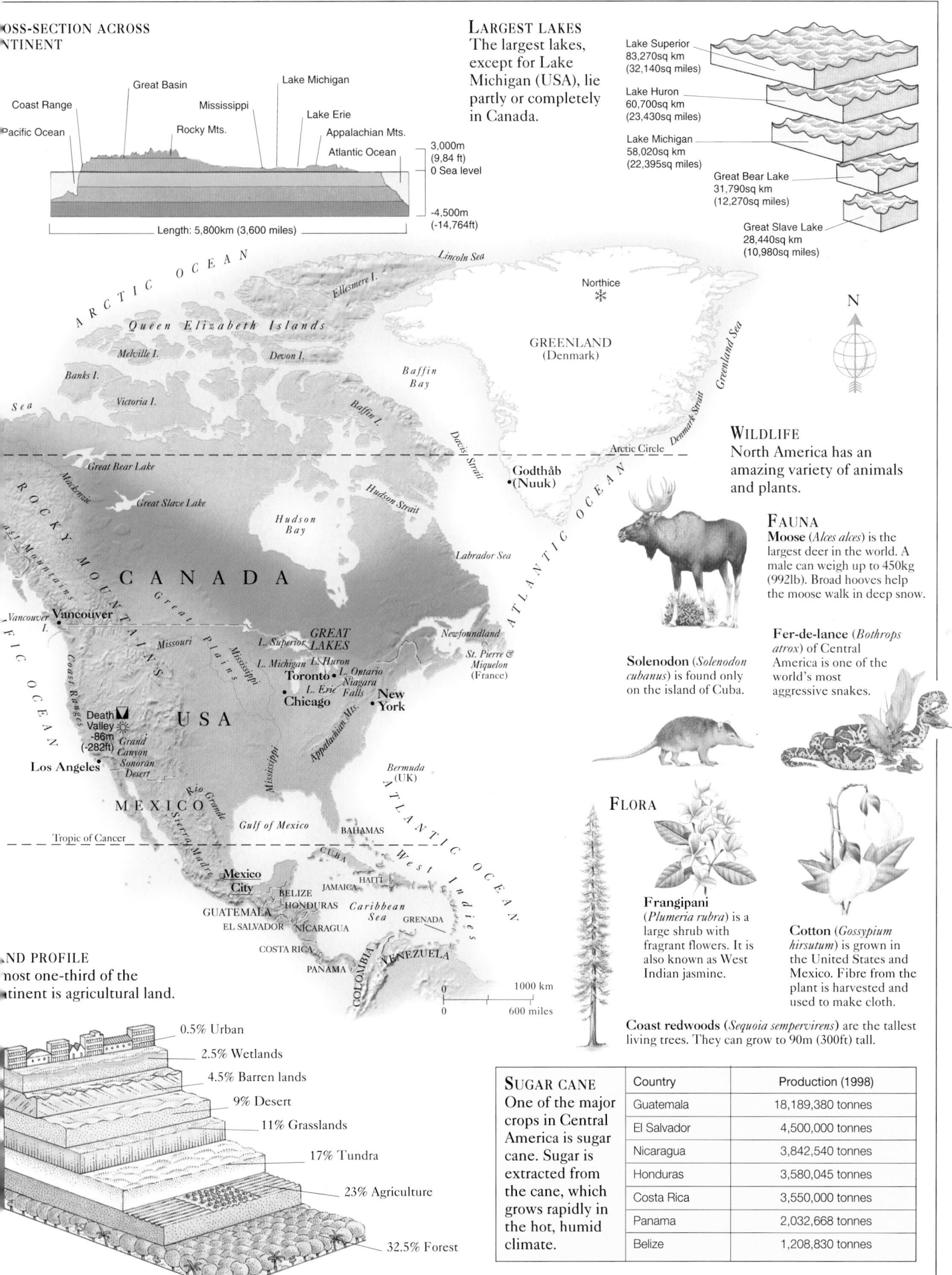

Coast Range
Great Basin
Mississippi
Lake Michigan
Lake Erie
Rocky Mts.
Appalachian Mts.
Pacific Ocean
Atlantic Ocean

3,000m (9,84 ft)
0 Sea level
-4,500m (-14,764ft)

Length: 5,800km (3,600 miles)

LARGEST LAKES
The largest lakes, except for Lake Michigan (USA), lie partly or completely in Canada.

Lake Superior 83,270sq km (32,140sq miles)

Lake Huron 60,700sq km (23,430sq miles)

Lake Michigan 58,020sq km (22,395sq miles)

Great Bear Lake 31,790sq km (12,270sq miles)

Great Slave Lake 28,440sq km (10,980sq miles)

WILDLIFE
North America has an amazing variety of animals and plants.

FAUNA
Moose (*Alces alces*) is the largest deer in the world. A male can weigh up to 450kg (992lb). Broad hooves help the moose walk in deep snow.

Fer-de-lance (*Bothrops atrox*) of Central America is one of the world's most aggressive snakes.

Solenodon (*Solenodon cubanus*) is found only on the island of Cuba.

FLORA
Frangipani (*Plumeria rubra*) is a large shrub with fragrant flowers. It is also known as West Indian jasmine.

Cotton (*Gossypium hirsutum*) is grown in the United States and Mexico. Fibre from the plant is harvested and used to make cloth.

Coast redwoods (*Sequoia sempervirens*) are the tallest living trees. They can grow to 90m (300ft) tall.

LAND PROFILE
almost one-third of the continent is agricultural land.

0.5% Urban
2.5% Wetlands
4.5% Barren lands
9% Desert
11% Grasslands
17% Tundra
23% Agriculture
32.5% Forest

SUGAR CANE
One of the major crops in Central America is sugar cane. Sugar is extracted from the cane, which grows rapidly in the hot, humid climate.

Country	Production (1998)
Guatemala	18,189,380 tonnes
El Salvador	4,500,000 tonnes
Nicaragua	3,842,540 tonnes
Honduras	3,580,045 tonnes
Costa Rica	3,550,000 tonnes
Panama	2,032,668 tonnes
Belize	1,208,830 tonnes

CANADA

CANADA IS THE second largest country in the world. Across the centre of the country lie the Prairies, a flat plain used for growing wheat and grazing cattle. Most Canadians live around the Great Lakes and the St. Lawrence River.

Area 9,976,140sq km (3,851,788sq miles)
Government Federal democracy, with British sovereign as constitutional monarch
🔑 **Independence** 1931, from Britain
🔗 **Currency** Canadian dollar
👤 **Population** 29,500,000
Density 3 per sq km (8 per sq mile)
Official Languages English, French
✝ **Major Religions** Roman Catholic 46%, Protestant 30%, other 24%

LIFESTYLE FACTS

• Canada is such a vast country that it takes 3 days and 3 nights to travel by train from Toronto to Vancouver – a distance of 4,467 km (2,776 miles).

• Dinosaur Provincial Park, on the banks of the Red Deer River in Alberta, is one of the greatest sites for dinosaur remains in the world. The *Albertosaurus* is one of the large dinosaurs that once roamed around this area.

• Canada produces 75% of the world's maple syrup. Each March, sap is collected from sugar maple trees and boiled down into syrup. A maple leaf is the symbol of Canada.

• Some places in Canada are freezing cold for months on end. A family can flood their garden and use it as an ice-hockey rink.

CANADIAN PEOPLE

Many people have settled in Canada. The largest ethnic groups, after the British and French, are Italian and German.

Languages spoken	% of population
English	66.3
French	23.2
Italian	5.9
German	1.1
Chinese	0.4
Other	3.1

WEATHER FACTS

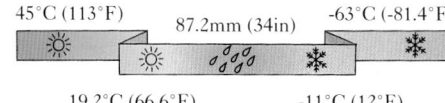

45°C (113°F)   87.2mm (34in)   -63°C (-81.4°F)
19.2°C (66.6°F)   -11°C (12°F)

LAND PROFILE

More than half the land in Canada is covered by forest.

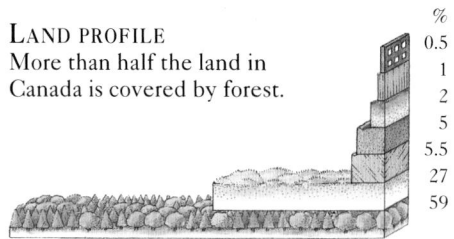

%
0.5
1
2
5
5.5
27
59

WOOD AND PAPER EXPORTS (1992)

Canada is the world's largest exporter of forest products. These include timber for building as well as wood pulp for paper.

Destination	Amount (in tonnes)
United States	9,508,754
Europe	4,877,883
Asia	1,728,895
South America	657,159
Central America	211,608

10 Canadian dollars

THE CN TOWER

The Canadian National (CN) Tower in Toronto is the tallest free-standing structure in Canada at 555m (1,821ft) high. It was built as a TV transmitter and was completed in 1975.

TORONTO SKYDOME

• SkyDome is the world's first stadium with a moving roof. Seating is on four levels and can hold 50,000 people.

• The field is covered with 106 rolls of Astroturf, joined together with 12.8km (8 miles) of zip fasteners.

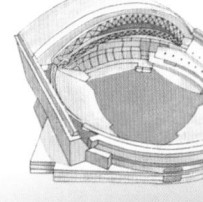

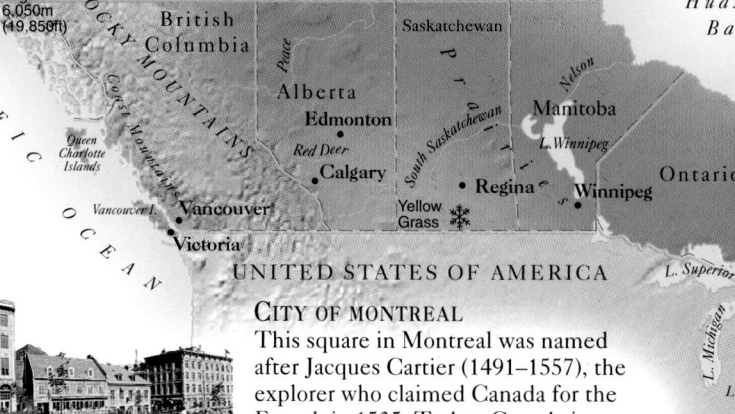

CITY OF MONTREAL

This square in Montreal was named after Jacques Cartier (1491–1557), the explorer who claimed Canada for the French in 1535. Today, Canada is a bilingual country and two-thirds of the people in Montreal still speak French.

GREENLAND

THE WORLD'S LARGEST island,
Greenland is part of Denmark.
Almost all of Greenland lies within
the Arctic Circle. Most of the island is
permanently covered with ice
and is uninhabited.

Area 2,175,600sq km
(840,004sq miles)
Government Constitutional monarchy,
as part of kingdom of Denmark
Currency Danish krone
Population 55,732
Density 0.16 per sq km (0.4 per sq mile)
Official Language Greenlandic, Danish
Major Religions Evangelical
Lutheran 99%, Roman Catholic 1%

LIFESTYLE FACTS

• Greenland's 55,000-plus inhabitants live in
the capital, Godthåb, 16 small towns, and 66
other settlements. There are no roads or rail
links between areas so travel is by air or sea.

• In winter the skidoo, a kind
of motorcycle on skis, is used
to move across the snow.

• More than 85% of
Greenland is a massive ice sheet
with an average thickness of 1,524m
(5,000ft). Icebreaker ships are used to keep
the sea channels open.

• Only low-growing plants with shallow
roots, such as the Arctic rhododendron,
Arctic poppy, saxifrage, and bilberry, can
survive the harsh climate.

*Arctic rhododendron
(Rhododendron
lapponicum)*

*Arctic poppy
(Papaver
lapponicum)*

*Saxifrage
(Saxifraga sp.)*

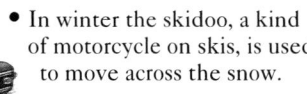
*This fishing community
lies near Cape Farvel on
the southernmost tip of
Greenland.*

ALONG THE COAST

Greenland has more than 39,315km (24,430
miles) of jagged coastline. Most people live
along the coast and work in the fishing
industry. In the south, the Gulf Stream
current helps keep the sea free of ice.

FISH EXPORTS

Greenland's fishing rights cover
more than 2,000,000sq km
(772,204,000sq miles) of sea. Shrimp
accounts for 80% of the country's exports.
Cod, salmon, haddock, and other fish make
up the remaining 20%.

WILDLIFE

Conditions
within the Arctic
Circle are harsh,
but the animals
that live there are
well adapted to
the ice and snow.

Caribou *(Rangifer
tarandus)* has broad
hooves to walk in snow.

Hooded seal *(Cystophora
cristata)* lives in the seas
around the polar ice cap.

Walrus *(Odobenus
rosmarus)* has long tusks
which it uses to haul
itself up on to the ice.

Polar bear *(Thalarctos
maritimus)* feeds on seals
which it catches through
holes in the ice.

Arctic fox *(Alopex
lagopus)* has fur that
changes from brown to
pure white in winter.

INUIT ART

Kenojuak, a famous Inuit
painter, is shown with her
work. Inuit art also
includes fine carvings
in ivory and bone.

Lincoln Sea

Wandel Sea

GREENLAND
(Denmark)

Greenland
Sea

Davis Strait

Disko I.

• Ilulissat

Gunnbjørn Fjeld
3,702m (12,146ft)

Denmark Strait

• Sisimrut

Arctic Circle

• Godthåb
(Nuuk)

ATLANTIC OCEAN

Cape Farvel

Labrador
Sea

Newfoundland

• St. John's

St. Pierre &
Miquelon
(France)

N

0   700 km

0   400 miles

INUIT FACTS

• Large areas of Canada and Greenland are still
inhabited by the original settlers of these lands.
They are called the Inuit, which means "people."

• Inuit build temporary
snowhouses (correctly
called *illuviga*) when
they go hunting. Igloo is
their word for any other
kind of house.

• The main food source for the Inuit is the
animals they hunt. Hunting is vital to their
survival and provides food and clothing. Inuit
hunt caribou, seal, walrus, and fish.

• Some words we use, such as kayak and
anorak, are taken from the Inuit language.

*Inuit child
from Hudson
Bay, Canada*

THE NUNAVUT AGREEMENT

This agreement took effect in 1999. It is
the largest land claim in Canadian history.
Its terms include:

• The Inuit receive title to 350,000sq km
(135,136sq miles) of land in 1999.

• They also have 36,257sq km (13,999sq
miles) of underground mineral rights.

• The Inuit are granted $1.15 billion by
Canada in compensation to be paid over
14 years (this sum based on value with
interest by end of 14-year period).

UNITED STATES OF AMERICA

THE UNITED STATES of America (USA) is made up of 50 states plus the District of Columbia. Two of the states, Alaska and Hawaii, are separate from the others. The USA is the world's wealthiest country with vast areas of rich farmland and supplies of coal, oil, and minerals.

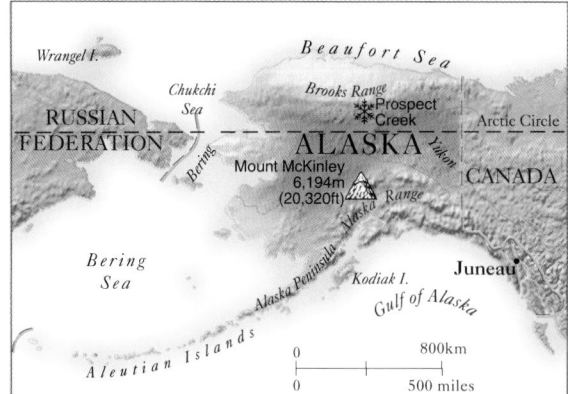

10 US dollars

Area 9,372,610sq km (3,618,783sq miles)
Government Federal democracy
Independence 1776, from Britain
Territories Northern Mariana Islands, Puerto Rico, American Samoa, Guam, United States Virgin Islands, Johnston Atoll, Line Islands, Midway Islands, Wake Island, Baker and Howland Islands, Jarvis Island, Kingman Reef, Navassa Island, Palmyra Atoll
Currency United States dollar
Population 263,300,000
Density 29 per sq km (75 per sq mile)
Official Language English
✝ Major Religions Protestant 56%, Roman Catholic 28%, Jewish 2%, other 14%

WEATHER FACTS

57°C (135°F)   976mm (38.4in)   -62°C (-79.6°F)

24°C (75.2°F)   2.2°C (36°F)

LAND PROFILE
More than one-third of the country is covered in forest.

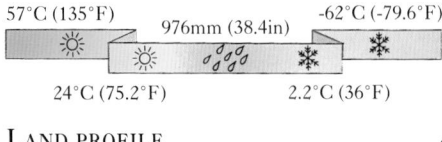

%
0.5
2.5
3.5
5
9.5
12
29.5
37.5

MAJOR AREAS OF WILD LANDS (1994)
Large areas of wild land have been set aside as parks and nature reserves.

State	% of state	Key animal
Alaska	15.03	Moose
Idaho	6.98	Cougar
Washington	5.91	Grizzly bear
California	5.81	Mountain lion
Wyoming	4.91	American buffalo
Florida	3.78	Manatee

LIFESTYLE FACTS
• Alaska was bought from Russia in 1867 for 2 cents an acre. Today the state is rich in oil and other natural resources.

• Inland storms called tornadoes, or twisters, suck up dust as they swirl across the landscape.

• The average American eats 50kg (110lb) of meat each year; more than twice as much as the average European.

• The USA is the major producer of household waste. Every day, the average person produces about 1.8kg (4lb) of rubbish.

• There is one television for every 1.2 people living in the United States.

HOLLYWOOD
Hollywood is the film capital of America. The fine weather and varied landscape attracted film directors from the East Coast to a small town called Hollywood in about 1910.

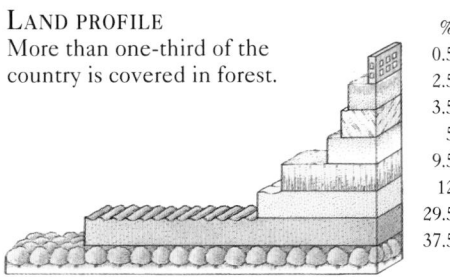

THE FIRST AMERICANS
The first people to live in North America arrived from Asia more than 20,000 years ago. This Native American, Chief Looking Horse (above), is a member of the Sioux from a reservation at Wounded Knee in South Dakota.

NATIVE AMERICAN FACTS
• Today 544 tribes of about 1.5 million Native Americans live on reservations which they govern themselves.

• The Navajo of Arizona, New Mexico, and Utah is the biggest tribe. People still practise traditional pottery and weaving: Navajo rugs are woven into geometric patterns, and are coloured with natural dyes.

HAWAIIAN ISLANDS
Hawaii is a group of 20 volcanic islands in the Pacific Ocean. One of the largest active volcanoes in the world, Mauna Loa, is located on the main island of Hawaii. It last erupted in 1984. Two types of lava, *aa* and *pahoehoe*, get their names from Hawaiian words.

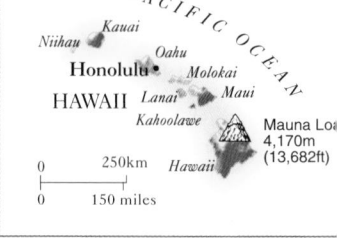

WHEATFIELDS OF NEBRASKA
The United States is the largest exporter of wheat and produces more than half the world's maize. This supply of food is grown on the open plains, or prairies, which stretch across the Midwest.

WASHINGTON, DISTRICT OF COLUMBIA
Washington is the capital city of the USA. It is home to the Capitol Building, which is the centre of government and houses the Senate and the House of Representatives.

BASEBALL
Baseball is America's national sport. The first game between two organized teams was played in New Jersey in 1846.

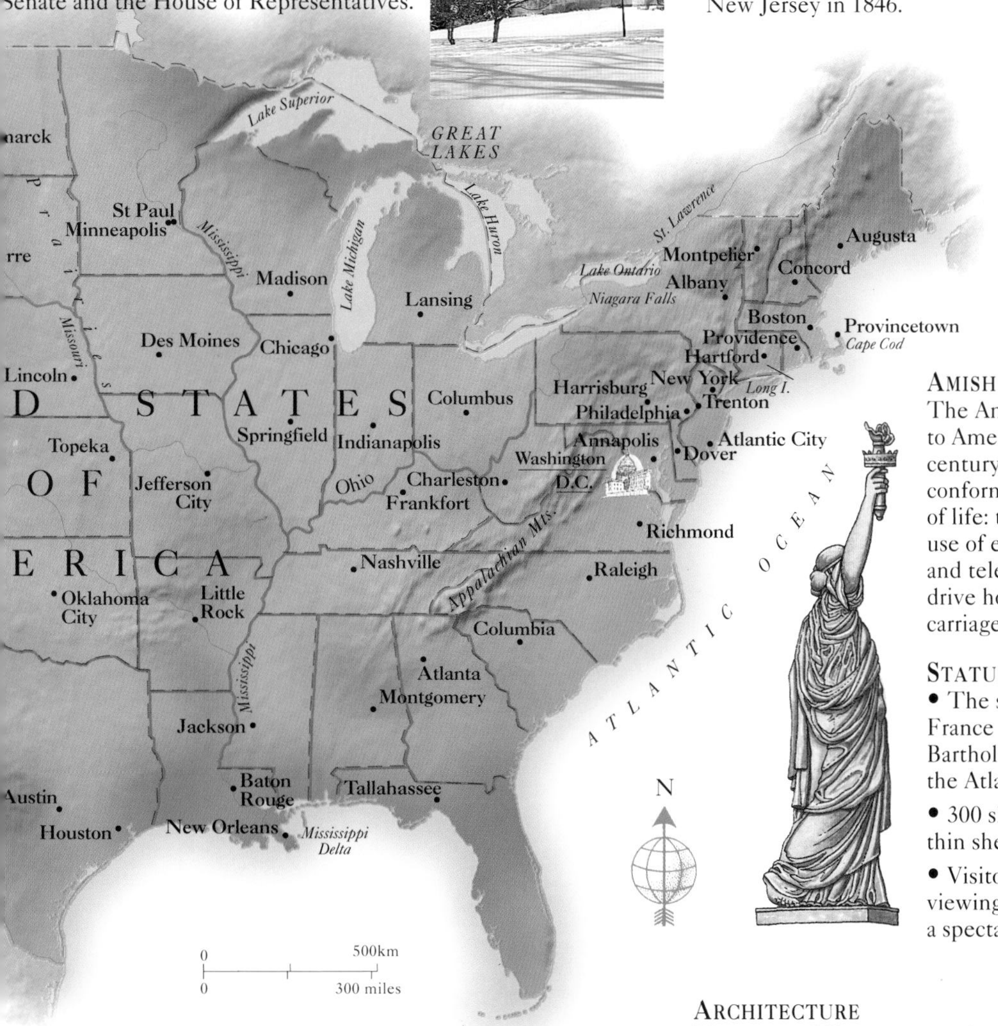

THE CAR INDUSTRY
The USA has more cars on the road than any other country (see page 277 for longest roads). It also has the highest ratio of cars, with 570 for every 1,000 persons.

BEST-SELLING CARS (1998)

Model	Number sold
Toyota Camry	429,575
Honda Accord	401,071
Ford Taurus	371,074
Honda Civic	334,562
Ford Escort	291,936
Chevrolet Cavalier	256,099
Toyota Corolla	250,501
Saturn	231,703
Chevrolet Malibu	223,703
Pontiac Grand Am	180,428

AMISH
The Amish are a Protestant group who came to America from Switzerland in the 18th century. Members do not conform to modern ways of life: they reject the use of electric lights and telephones, and drive horses and carriages rather than cars.

STATUE OF LIBERTY, NEW YORK
• The statue was given to the USA by France in 1884. It was designed by Auguste Bartholdi (1834–1904) and shipped across the Atlantic, packed in 210 crates.

• 300 sheets of copper were beaten into a thin sheet to act as the lady's "skin".

• Visitors can climb 171 steps up to the viewing gallery in the head of the statue for a spectacular view of the New York skyline.

Map labels: Lake Superior, GREAT LAKES, Lake Michigan, Lake Huron, St. Lawrence, Lake Ontario, Niagara Falls, St Paul, Minneapolis, Bismarck, Pierre, Madison, Lansing, Des Moines, Chicago, Lincoln, Columbus, Montpelier, Albany, Concord, Augusta, Boston, Providence, Hartford, Provincetown, Cape Cod, New York, Long I., Trenton, Harrisburg, Philadelphia, Annapolis, Atlantic City, Dover, Topeka, Springfield, Indianapolis, Washington D.C., Jefferson City, Ohio, Charleston, Frankfort, Richmond, Oklahoma City, Little Rock, Nashville, Raleigh, Columbia, Atlanta, Montgomery, Jackson, Austin, Houston, Baton Rouge, New Orleans, Tallahassee, Mississippi Delta, Mississippi, Missouri, Appalachian Mts., ATLANTIC OCEAN, UNITED STATES OF AMERICA

0   500km
0   300 miles

N

EVERGLADES FACTS
• Southern Florida has a vast area of cypress swamp called the Everglades. It is home to many rare animals and plants.

• The green tree frog has sticky suction pads on its toes that help it to grip the slippery branches.

Tree frog

• The American alligator grows up to 3.6m (12ft) long and may live for 50 years. It propels itself through the water with its tail.

MISSISSIPPI RIVER
The Mississippi is one of the world's busiest waterways. Ships can travel for nearly 2,900km (1,802 miles) from Minneapolis to New Orleans. The first steamboat appeared on the Mississippi in 1811.

ARCHITECTURE
The many different styles of American architecture reflect the diverse climate and conditions of the USA.

Clapboard
Houses in the eastern states are often built of overlapping wooden boards, known as clapboard, to keep out rain.

Plantation homes
People who grew rich on the profits of the plantations in the 19th century built grand mansions in European styles.

Art deco style
William van Alen (1882–1954) designed the Chrysler building in the 1920s.

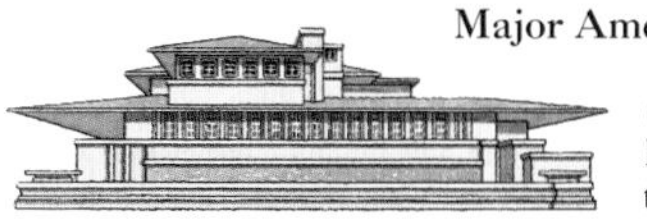

Major American architect
Frank Lloyd Wright (1867–1959) designed houses that blend with the landscape.

UNITED STATES OF AMERICA: STATES OF THE UNION

THE UNITED STATES of America originally consisted of 13 colonies on the East Coast, all of them ruled by Britain until independence in 1776. Today there are 50 states, ruled by the federal government in Washington, D.C., each with its own set of laws. For example, the age for holding a driving licence varies, as does the number of states that uphold the death sentence for murder.

The bald eagle is the national symbol of the USA.

ALABAMA

Area 133,916sq km (51,705sq miles)
Capital Montgomery
Population 4,252,938
Entry into Union 14 December, 1819
✱ **State flower** Camellia

ALASKA

Area 1,530,690sq km (591,000sq miles)
Capital Juneau
Population 603,617
Entry into Union 3 January, 1959
✱ **State flower** Forget-me-not

ARIZONA

Area 295,260sq km (114,000sq miles)
Capital Phoenix
Population 4,217,940
Entry into Union 14 February, 1912
✱ **State flower** Saguaro blossom

ARKANSAS

Area 137,754sq km (53,187sq miles)
Capital Little Rock
Population 2,483,769
Entry into Union 15 June, 1836
✱ **State flower** Apple blossom

Stretch limo

CALIFORNIA

Area 411,049sq km (158,707sq miles)
Capital Sacramento
Population 31,589,153
Entry into Union 9 September, 1850
✱ **State flower** California poppy

COLORADO

Area 269,596sq km (104,091sq miles)
Capital Denver
Population 3,746,585
Entry into Union 1 August, 1876
✱ **State flower** Columbine

CONNECTICUT

Area 12,997sq km (5,018sq miles)
Capital Hartford
Population 3,274,662
Entry into Union 9 January, 1788
✱ **State flower** Mountain laurel

DELAWARE

Area 5,297sq km (2,045sq miles)
Capital Dover
Population 717,917
Entry into Union 7 December, 1787
✱ **State flower** Peach blossom

FLORIDA

Area 151,940sq km (58,664sq miles)
Capital Tallahassee
Population 14,165,570
Entry into Union 3 March, 1845
✱ **State flower** Orange blossom

Baseball game

GEORGIA

Area 152,577sq km (58,910sq miles)
Capital Atlanta
Population 7,200,882
Entry into Union 2 January, 1788
✱ **State flower** Cherokee rose

Surfer

HAWAII

Area 16,760sq km (6,471sq miles)
Capital Honolulu
Population 1,186,815
Entry into Union 21 August, 1959
✱ **State flower** Yellow hibiscus

IDAHO

Area 231,971sq km (89,564sq miles)
Capital Boise
Population 1,163,261
Entry into Union 3 July, 1890
✱ **State flower** Mock orange

ILLINOIS

Area 145,933sq km (56,345sq miles)
Capital Springfield
Population 11,829,940
Entry into Union 3 December, 1818
✱ **State flower** Native violet

Appaloosa horse

INDIANA

Area 93,719sq km (36,185sq miles)
Capital Indianapolis
Population 5,803,471
Entry into Union 11 December, 1816
✱ **State flower** Peony

IOWA

Area 145,752sq km (56,275sq miles)
Capital Des Moines
Population 2,841,764
Entry into Union 28 December, 1846
✱ **State flower** Wild rose

KANSAS

Area 213,097sq km (82,277sq miles)
Capital Topeka
Population 2,565,328
Entry into Union 29 January, 1861
✱ **State flower** Native sunflower

Cowboy hat

KENTUCKY

Area 104,662sq km (40,410sq miles)
Capital Frankfort
Population 3,860,219
Entry into Union 1 June, 1792
✱ **State flower** Golden rod

LOUISIANA

Area 123,678sq km (47,752sq miles)
Capital Baton Rouge
Population 4,342,334
Entry into Union 30 April, 1812
✱ **State flower** Southern magnolia

MAINE

Blueberries

Area 86,156sq km (33,265sq miles)
Capital Augusta
Population 1,241,382
Entry into Union 15 March, 1820
✱ **State flower** White pine cone

MARYLAND

Area 27,091sq km (10,460sq miles)
Capital Annapolis
Population 5,042,438
Entry into Union 28 April, 1788
✱ **State flower** Black-eyed susan

MASSACHUSETTS

Area 21,456sq km (8,284sq miles)
Capital Boston
Population 6,073,550
Entry into Union 6 February, 1788
✱ **State flower** Mayflower

MICHIGAN

Area 151,585sq km (58,527sq miles)
Capital Lansing
Population 9,549,353
Entry into Union 26 January, 1837
✱ **State flower** Apple blossom

THE WHITE HOUSE

The White House in Washington, D.C., is the official residence of the president and his family. The 3-storey, 100-room mansion was designed by Irish-born architect James Hoban (1762–1831) and completed in 1800. The building is made of grey sandstone painted white, which is how it got its name.

American beaver

MINNESOTA

Area 218,601sq km (84,402sq miles)
Capital St. Paul
Population 4,609,548
Entry into Union 11 May, 1858
✱ **State flower** Showy lady's slipper

Dixieland jazz band

MISSISSIPPI

Area 123,515sq km (47,689sq miles)
Capital Jackson
Population 2,697,243
Entry into Union 10 December, 1817
✱ **State flower** Magnolia

MISSOURI
Area 180,515sq km
(69,697sq miles)
Capital Jefferson City
Population 5,323,523
Entry into Union 10 August, 1821
❀ **State flower** Hawthorn

MONTANA
Area 380,849sq km
(147,046sq miles)
Capital Helena
Population 870,281
Entry into Union 8 November, 1889
❀ **State flower** Bitterroot

American football

NEBRASKA
Area 200,349sq km
(77,355sq miles)
Capital Lincoln
Population 1,637,112
Entry into Union 1 March, 1867
❀ **State flower** Golden rod

NEVADA
Area 286,353sq km
(110,561sq miles)
Capital Carson City
Population 1,530,108
Entry into Union 31 October, 1864
❀ **State flower** Sagebrush

NEW HAMPSHIRE
Area 24,033sq km
(9,279sq miles)
Capital Concord
Population 1,148,253
Entry into Union 21 June, 1788
❀ **State flower** Lilac

Yellow taxicab

NEW JERSEY
Area 20,168sq km
(7,787sq miles)
Capital Trenton
Population 7,945,298
Entry into Union 18 December, 1787
❀ **State flower** Purple violet

Roadrunner

NEW MEXICO
Area 314,926sq km
(121,593sq miles)
Capital Sante Fe
Population 1,685,401
Entry into Union 6 January, 1912
❀ **State flower** Yucca

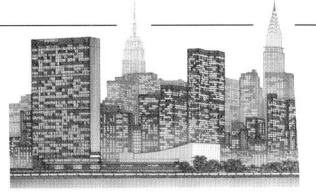
New York skyline

NEW YORK
Area 127,190sq km
(49,108sq miles)
Capital Albany
Population 18,136,081
Entry into Union 26 July, 1788
❀ **State flower** Rose

NORTH CAROLINA
Area 136,490sq km
(52,699sq miles)
Capital Raleigh
Population 7,195,138
Entry into Union 21 November, 1789
❀ **State flower** Flowering dogwood

NORTH DAKOTA
Area 183,118sq km
(70,702sq miles)
Capital Bismarck
Population 641,367
Entry into Union 2 November, 1889
❀ **State flower** Wild prairie rose

OHIO
Area 107,045sq km
(41,330sq miles)
Capital Columbus
Population 11,150,506
Entry into Union 1 March, 1803
❀ **State flower** Scarlet carnation

OKLAHOMA
Area 181,090sq km
(69,919sq miles)
Capital Oklahoma City
Population 3,277,687
Entry into Union 16 November, 1907
❀ **State flower** Mistletoe

OREGON
Area 251,419sq km
(97,073sq miles)
Capital Salem
Population 3,140,585
Entry into Union 14 February, 1859
❀ **State flower** Oregon grape

PENNSYLVANIA
Area 117,348sq km
(45,308sq miles)
Capital Harrisburg
Population 12,071,842
Entry into Union 12 December, 1787
❀ **State flower** Mountain laurel

RHODE ISLAND
Area 3,139sq km
(1,212sq miles)
Capital Providence
Population 989,794
Entry into Union 29 May, 1790
❀ **State flower** Violet

Chopper bike

SOUTH CAROLINA
Area 199,730sq km
(77,116sq miles)
Capital Columbia
Population 3,673,287
Entry into Union 23 May, 1788
❀ **State flower** Yellow jessamine

*Mount Rushmore
National Monument*

SOUTH DAKOTA
Area 199,730sq km
(77,116sq miles)
Capital Pierre
Population 729,034
Entry into Union 2 November, 1889
❀ **State flower** Pasqueflower

TENNESSEE
Area 109,152sq km
(42,144sq miles)
Capital Nashville
Population 5,256,051
Entry into Union 1 June, 1796
❀ **State flower** Iris

Cowboys roping cattle

TEXAS
Area 691,030sq km
(266,807sq miles)
Capital Austin
Population 18,723,991
Entry into Union 29 December, 1845
❀ **State flower** Bluebonnet

UTAH
Area 219,888sq km
(84,899sq miles)
Capital Salt Lake City
Population 1,951,408
Entry into Union 4 January, 1896
❀ **State flower** Sego lily

Halloween lantern

VERMONT
Area 24,900sq km
(9,614sq miles)
Capital Montpelier
Population 584,771
Entry into Union 4 March, 1791
❀ **State flower** Red clover

VIRGINIA
Area 105,586sq km
(40,767sq miles)
Capital Richmond
Population 6,618,358
Entry into Union 25 June, 1788
❀ **State flower** Flowering dogwood

WASHINGTON
Area 176,480sq km
(68,139sq miles)
Capital Olympia
Population 5,430,940
Entry into Union 11 November, 1889
❀ **State flower** Coast rhododendron

WEST VIRGINIA
Area 62,761sq km
(24,232sq miles)
Capital Charleston
Population 1,828,140
Entry into Union 20 June, 1863
❀ **State flower** Rhododendron

WISCONSIN
Area 145,436sq km
(56,153sq miles)
Capital Madison
Population 5,122,871
Entry into Union 29 May, 1848
❀ **State flower** Wood violet

WYOMING
Area 253,325sq km
(97,809sq miles)
Capital Cheyenne
Population 480,184
Entry into Union 10 July, 1890
❀ **State flower** Indian paintbrush

STATE FACTS

• Only about 800 grizzly bears are left in the USA; many of them roam wild in the mountain forests of Idaho and Wyoming.

• Georgia grows nearly half the USA's total crop of peanuts. Half the crop is used for making peanut butter, the rest for edible oil and animal feed.

• Rhode Island is the smallest state. It gave its name to a chicken, the Rhode Island Red, first bred in 1857.

• There are more engineers and scientists in New Jersey than in any other state.

• The Stock Exchange on Wall Street, New York, is the largest in the world, handling more than 100 million shares a day.

• Silicon Valley, south of San Francisco, has one of the world's largest concentrations of high-technology industry.

• One-third of the world's cherry crop is grown along the shores of Lake Michigan.

• The USA's top tourist destinations include Disney World in Florida, with more than 20 million visitors a year.

MEXICO

THIS IS A land of contrasts with snow-capped mountains, a high central plateau, and tropical rainforests. It is the world's leading producer of silver. The capital, Mexico City, is the largest city in the world. Southern Mexico is often affected by earthquakes.

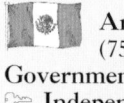 **Area** 1,958,200sq km (756,061sq miles)
Government Multiparty republic
Independence 1821, from Spain
Currency Mexican new peso
Population 93,700,000
Density 49 per sq km (127 per sq mile)
Official Language Spanish
✝ **Major Religions** Roman Catholic 89%, Protestant 6%, other 5%

WEATHER FACTS

47°C (117°F)   929mm (36in)   -4°C (25°F)

22.8°C (73°F)   17.8°C (64°F)

LAND PROFILE

More than one-third of Mexico is desert.

%
0.5
0.5
15.5
20.5
26
37

LIFESTYLE FACTS

• There are more Spanish speakers in Mexico than in any other country.

• Bee-keeping is an important activity, especially in the south. Mexico is one of the world's main exporters of natural honey.

• Mexicans eat a variety of spicy foods using chillies. Pancakes, called *tortillas*, are made from maize flour and filled with meat, vegetables, and cheese.

• Many familiar garden plants, such as poinsettias, marigolds, and dahlias, originated in Mexico.

• Mexico has more than 9,650km (6,000 miles) of coastline, and fishing for shrimp is an important industry. Natural bath sponges are harvested in the Gulf of Mexico.

FEAST DAY

Day of the Dead (November 1) is a feast day when food and drink are offered to dead relatives. Bakers sell sweets in the shapes of skulls and coffins.

DESERT FACTS

• The largest of all cacti is the giant saguaro from the Sonoran Desert. It can grow to 18m (60ft) high.

• The tiny elf owl hides from the heat of the day in the cool branches of the saguaro.

Elf owl

10 Mexican pesos

LANGUAGE

A traditional greeting in Spanish is *buenos días*.

JAGUAR

The jaguar (*Panthera onca*) lives in the jungles of Central America. Its spotted coat acts as a camouflage.

SILVER

Mexico is rich in minerals and supplies one-fifth of the world's silver. Some of the silver is made into jewellery; it is also used as a coating for photographic film.

Silver jewellery

ACAPULCO BEACH

Tourism is a vital part of Mexico's economy. The busy resort of Acapulco, on the Pacific Coast, has more than 1,900,000 visitors every year.

GUATEMALA

HIGH MOUNTAINS AND volcanoes, tropical forests, and lakes cover Guatemala. More than half the population are Maya Indians.

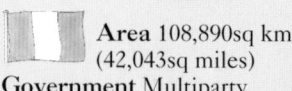 **Area** 108,890sq km (42,043sq miles)
Government Multiparty republic
Independence 1821, from Spain
Currency Quetzal
Population 10,600,000
Density 98 per sq km (255 per sq mile)
Official Language Spanish
✝ **Major Religions** Roman Catholic 65%, Protestant 33%, other 2%

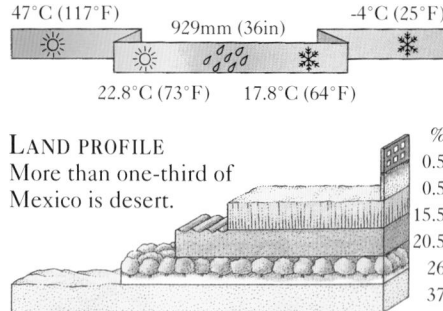

NATIONAL BIRD

The quetzal bird (*Pharomachrus mocinno*) is found in Guatemala. The male has long tail feathers to help him attract a mate.

WEAVING

Traditional textiles from Guatemala are made in more than 325 variations of style and colour. Every Maya village has its unique style of dress made from handwoven textiles.

EL SALVADOR

A LINE OF volcanoes dominates El Salvador. The layers of volcanic ash and lava make fertile soil for growing coffee.

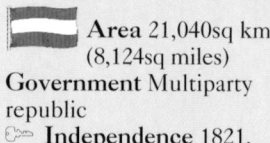 **Area** 21,040sq km (8,124sq miles)
Government Multiparty republic
Independence 1821, from Spain
Currency Salvadorean colon
Population 5,800,000
Density 280 per sq km (726 per sq mile)
Official Language Spanish
✝ **Major Religions** Roman Catholic 75%, other 25%

HONDURAS

MOST PEOPLE WORK on small farms growing rice, beans, and maize for themselves. Cattle are raised for beef exports.

 **Area** 112,090sq km (43,278sq miles)
Government Multiparty republic
Independence 1821, from Spain
Currency Lempira
Population 5,700,000
Density 51 per sq km (133 per sq mile)
Official Language Spanish
✝ **Major Religions** Roman Catholic 97%, other 3%

UNITED STATES OF AMERICA

Sonoran
Desert

adalupe I.

Río Grande

 Guaymas

Baja California

Gulf of California

Torreón

Monterrey

Sierra Madre Oriental

MEXICO

Sierra Madre Occidental

PACIFIC

500km

300 miles

Marías
Islands

Guadalajara

León

Tula

L. Chapala

Mexico City Tenochtitlán

Puebla

Citlatépetl
5,700m
(18,702 ft)

Sierra Madre del Sur

Acapulco

Gulf of
Tehuantepec

OCEAN

Gulf of
Mexico

Yucatán
Peninsula

Cerros

BELIZE
Belmopan

Tikal

Victoria Peak
1,122m (3,681ft)

Palenque

Tajumulco
4,220m (13,845ft)

GUATEMALA

L. Izabal

HONDURAS
Copán

Guatemala City

Santa Ana
2,385m (7,825ft)

San Salvador

EL
SALVADOR

Tegucigalpa

Pico Mogotón
2,107m (6,618ft)

NICARAGUA

Managua

L. Nicaragua

San
Juan

COSTA RICA San José

Chirripó Grande
3,819m (12,530ft)

Volcán Barú
3,475m (11,401ft)

Mosquito Coast

Coco

Caribbean

Sea

Panama
Canal

Panama City

Chagres

PANAMA

Gulf of
Panamá

COLOMBIA

N

PEOPLE OF BELIZE
More than half the population of Belize are Creole. All Creoles are of African descent and speak the English-Creole dialect.

BELIZE

BELIZE IS A land of tropical jungles, mountains, and swamps. The climate is ideal for growing citrus fruits, as well as sugar cane.

Area 22,960sq km (8,865sq miles)
Government Parliamentary democracy
☞ **Independence** 1981, from Britain
🪙 **Currency** Belizean dollar
🛉 **Population** 200,000
Density 9 per sq km (23 per sq mile)
Official Language English
✝ **Major Religions** Christian 87%, other 13%

PALENQUE, CITY OF THE MAYA
For many years, Mexico was home to a series of native American peoples. One of the most important groups, the Maya, built the city of Palenque in about 500 A.D.

ANCIENT SITES IN CENTRAL AMERICA

Site	Culture	Country
Tula	Toltec	Mexico
Tenochtitlán	Aztec	Mexico
Copán	Maya	Honduras
Tikal	Maya	Guatemala
Cerros	Maya	Belize

LAKE NICARAGUA
Lake Nicaragua is the only freshwater lake to contain ocean animals such as the bullshark. The lake was once part of an ocean bay which was cut off by volcanic activity.

CACAO PLANT FACTS
• Central America is a major exporter of cacao, from which cocoa and chocolate are made.

• The cacao tree is a tropical plant. It sprouts long, thin pods, called cherelles, which grow to about 25cm (10in) long.

• Each pod contains 30 to 40 beans. In the 16th century, cacao beans were considered so valuable the Aztecs used them as money.

PANAMA

PANAMA FORMS A land link between the North and South American continents. The country is cut through by the Panama Canal, which links the Caribbean Sea with the Pacific Ocean.

Area 77,080sq km (29,761sq miles)
Government Multiparty republic
☞ **Independence** 1903, from Colombia
🪙 **Currency** Balboa
🛉 **Population** 2,600,000
Density 34 per sq km (88 per sq mile)
Official Language Spanish
✝ **Major Religions** Roman Catholic 93%, other 7%

NICARAGUA

THE LARGEST COUNTRY in Central America after Mexico, Nicaragua has large forests and a swampy Caribbean shore, called the Mosquito Coast.

Area 130,000sq km (50,193sq miles)
Government Multiparty republic
☞ **Independence** 1821, from Spain
🪙 **Currency** Cordoba
🛉 **Population** 4,400,000
Density 37 per sq km (96 per sq mile)
Official Language Spanish
✝ **Major Religions** Roman Catholic 95%, other 5%

COSTA RICA

ONE-THIRD OF Costa Rica, which means "rich coast", is covered with forests that include mahogany and tropical cedar trees.

Area 51,100sq km (19,730sq miles)
Government Multiparty republic
☞ **Independence** 1821, from Spain
🪙 **Currency** Costa Rican colon
🛉 **Population** 3,400,000
Density 67 per sq km (174 per sq mile)
Official Language Spanish
✝ **Major Religions** Roman Catholic 95%, other 5%

PANAMA CANAL FACTS
• The canal opened in 1914 and cut the sailing distance from New York to San Francisco by 13,000km (8,000 miles).

• More than 153 million cubic metres (200 million cubic yards) of rubble were removed to make room for the 80-km (50-mile) canal.

THE CARIBBEAN

THESE ISLANDS, ALSO known as the West Indies, form a 3,200-km (2,000-mile) chain stretching from the coast of Florida almost to Venezuela. Tourists flock to the beautiful beaches: 1.5 million people each year to the Bahamas alone.

CUBA

CUBA IS THE only communist state in the Western Hemisphere, and Fidel Castro has been its leader since January 1959. World-famous Cuban cigars are a major export.

Area 110,860sq km (42,803sq miles)
Government Socialist republic
Independence 1898, from Spain. US troops withdrew in 1902
Currency Cuban peso
Population 10,800,000
Density 97 per sq km (251 per sq mile)
Official Language Spanish
Major Religions Roman Catholic 85%, other 15%

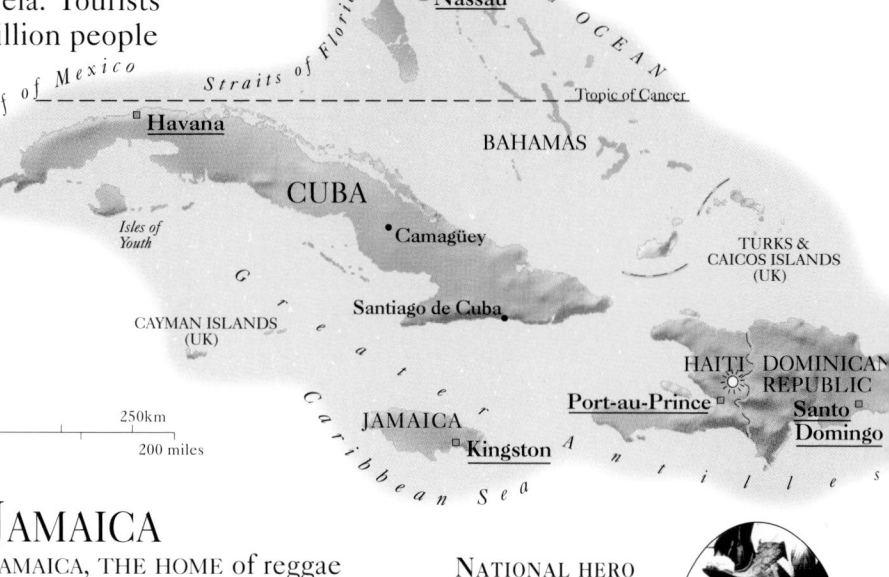

ATLANTIC OCEAN
☐ **Nassau**
Gulf of Mexico
Straits of Florida
Tropic of Cancer
☐ **Havana**
BAHAMAS
CUBA
Isles of Youth
• Camagüey
TURKS & CAICOS ISLANDS (UK)
CAYMAN ISLANDS (UK)
Santiago de Cuba•
Greater
HAITI DOMINICAN REPUBLIC
Port-au-Prince
Santo Domingo
JAMAICA
Kingston
Caribbean Sea
Antilles

| 0 | 250km |
| 0 | 200 miles |

THE SMALLEST BIRD

Cuba is the home of the world's smallest bird. The Bee Hummingbird, known in Cuba as the *zunzuncito*, is just 6cm (2.4in) long: roughly the same size as a Red Admiral butterfly.

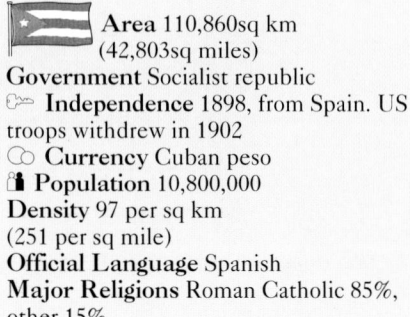

Bee Hummingbird

Red Admiral

JAMAICA

JAMAICA, THE HOME of reggae music, is the third largest of the Caribbean islands. Most of its income is derived from mining bauxite, the chief source of aluminium, and the tourist industry.

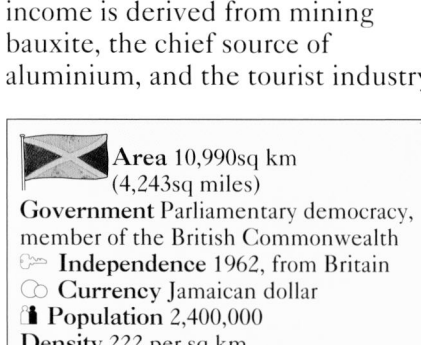

Area 10,990sq km (4,243sq miles)
Government Parliamentary democracy, member of the British Commonwealth
Independence 1962, from Britain
Currency Jamaican dollar
Population 2,400,000
Density 222 per sq km (577 per sq mile)
Official Language English
Major Religions Christian 60%, other 40%

NATIONAL HERO

Marcus Garvey (1887-1940) is one of Jamaica's national heroes. He founded the Universal Negro Improvement Association in 1914.

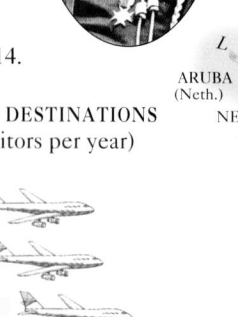

ARUBA (Neth.)

NETH. AN

MAJOR TOURIST DESTINATIONS

(Figures show visitors per year)

Cayman Islands 381,188

Barbados 447,083

US Virgin Islands 562,062

Jamaica 1,056,000

Bahamas 1,368,038

BAHAMAS

THE BAHAMAS are made up of more than 700 islands and cays (small islands). Only about 30 of these are inhabited.

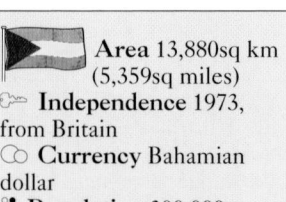

Area 13,880sq km (5,359sq miles)
Independence 1973, from Britain
Currency Bahamian dollar
Population 300,000
Official Language English

HAITI

THE PEOPLE of this mountainous country are French-speaking, and many practise the folk religion called voodoo.

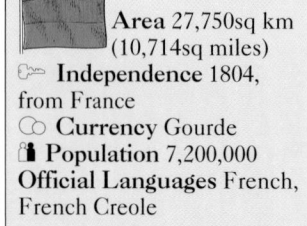

Area 27,750sq km (10,714sq miles)
Independence 1804, from France
Currency Gourde
Population 7,200,000
Official Languages French, French Creole

DOMINICA

THE IMPERIAL parrot, shown on the Dominican flag, is found only in the dense tropical forests of the northern mountains.

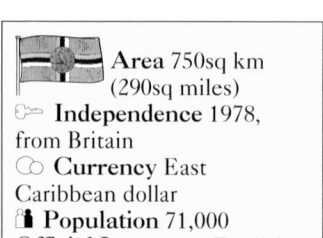

Area 750sq km (290sq miles)
Independence 1978, from Britain
Currency East Caribbean dollar
Population 71,000
Official Language English

ST. LUCIA

THE PITONS, twin volcanic peaks that rise about 800m (2,600ft) above the lush forests, are St. Lucia's best-known landmarks.

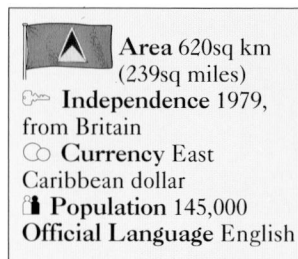

Area 620sq km (239sq miles)
Independence 1979, from Britain
Currency East Caribbean dollar
Population 145,000
Official Language English

BEST-KNOWN CARIBBEAN FRUIT

Guava
The guava is a pear-shaped fruit with cream or pink flesh.

Pawpaw
The flesh of the pawpaw is orange, like an apricot's.

Mango
The juicy mango is green, red, or orange-pink in colour.

Leeward Islands
BRITISH VIRGIN ISLANDS (UK)
ANGUILLA (UK)
an
VIRGIN ISLANDS (USA)
ANTIGUA & BARBUDA
ST. KITTS & NEVIS
MONTSERRAT (UK)
GUADELOUPE (France)
DOMINICA
MARTINIQUE (France)
ST. LUCIA
BARBADOS
ST. VINCENT & THE GRENADINES
GRENADA
TRINIDAD & TOBAGO
Port of Spain
Caribbean Sea
Windward Islands
Spanish Antilles
ATLANTIC OCEAN

N

REGIONAL WEATHER

Records

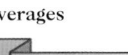

5°C (41°F)
38°C (100.4°F)

Averages

27°C (80.6°F)   1,529mm (60in)   24.5°C (76°F)

DOMINICAN REPUBLIC

THE DOMINICAN REPUBLIC is called *Quisqueya* in native Arawak Indian. It is the second largest country in the Caribbean.

Area 48,730sq km (18,815sq miles)
Independence 1865, from Spain
Currency Dominican Republic peso
Population 7,800,000
Official Language Spanish

CARIBBEAN MUSIC AND DANCE FACTS

• The biggest and most famous carnival in the Caribbean takes place in Trinidad and Tobago every year. People spend months creating the costumes.

• Calypso music originated in Trinidad, although it is popular throughout the Caribbean. Steel bands are musicians who play calypso and their drums, called pans, are made out of oil drums. The rhythms of calypso music show a strong African influence.

• Reggae music emerged in Jamaica in the 1970s and developed from earlier Jamaican musical styles. Reggae has achieved worldwide popularity through the songs of musicians such as Bob Marley.

• Bob Marley (1945–81) was the most famous Jamaican reggae singer, who had hit records around the world in the 1970s. He believed in world peace and equality among people, and his songs were a powerful means of spreading this message.

ANTIGUA AND BARBUDA

SUGAR WAS once the main export from these islands. Today tourism is more important and Barbuda is also an animal reserve.

Area 440sq km (170sq miles)
Independence 1981, from Britain
Currency East Caribbean dollar
Population 65,000
Official Language English

BARBADOS

TOURISM IS the leading industry in Barbados, employing almost 40% of the workforce. Sugar is an important export, and a traditional local dish is the famous flying fish.

Area 430sq km (166sq miles)
Independence 1966, from Britain
Currency Barbados dollar
Population 300,000
Official Language English

GRENADA

ON GRENADA, the "spice island", nutmeg, cloves, cinnamon, and saffron grow abundantly. Cacao is also an important export.

Area 340sq km (131sq miles)
Independence 1974, from Britain
Currency East Caribbean dollar
Population 92,000
Official Language English

GREATEST WEST INDIES BATSMEN (1994)

Cricketer	Tests	Runs
I.V.A. Richards	121	8,540
G.S. Sobers	93	8,032
C.G. Greenidge	108	7,558
C.H. Lloyd	110	7,515
D.L. Haynes	103	7,487

ST. KITTS AND NEVIS

ST. CHRISTOPHER is commonly known as St. Kitts. It is separated from its sister island, Nevis, by a 3-km-wide (2 mile) sea channel.

Area 360sq km (140sq miles)
Independence 1983, from Britain
Currency East Caribbean dollar
Population 44,000
Official Language English

ST. VINCENT AND THE GRENADINES

ST. VINCENT, the largest of the islands of this nation, has black volcanic beaches. The Grenadines group consists of 32 smaller islands.

Area 340sq km (131sq miles)
Independence 1979, from Britain
Currency East Caribbean dollar
Population 111,000
Official Language English

TRINIDAD AND TOBAGO

TRINIDAD, the larger of these two islands, is rich in oil and natural gas. Tobago has fine beaches and an 18-hole championship golf course.

Area 5,130sq km (1,980sq miles)
Independence 1962, from Britain
Currency Trinidad & Tobago dollar
Population 1,300,000
Official Language English

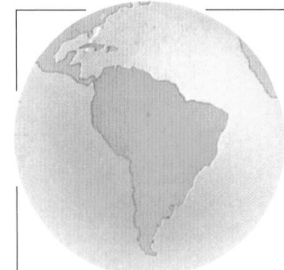

SOUTH AMERICA

THE CONTINENT OF South America is dominated by the Andes, the world's longest mountain chain, passing through seven countries. Brazil is the largest country, occupying almost half of the continent.

Area 17,716,530sq km (6,840,388sq miles)
Countries 12
Largest Brazil 8,511,970sq km (3,286,489sq miles)
Smallest Surinam 163,270sq km (63,039sq miles)
Population 305,074,803
Density 17 per sq km (44 per sq mile)
Major Languages Spanish, Portuguese, Quechua, Guarani, Aymara
▲ **Highest point** Mount Aconcagua 6,959m (22,831ft)
▼ **Lowest point** Valdés Peninsula 40m (131ft) below sea level
☼ **Highest temperature** 49°C (120°F) Rivadavia, Argentina
❄ **Lowest temperature** -33°C (-27°F) Sarmiento, Argentina

CLIMATE ZONES
KEY

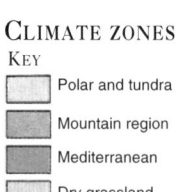

- Polar and tundra
- Mountain region
- Mediterranean
- Dry grassland
- Hot desert
- Rainforest
- Tropical grassland

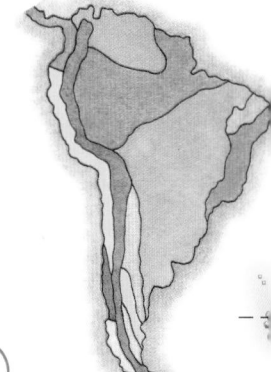

TIME ZONES

| 7:00 Lima | 8:00 Caracas | 9:00 Buenos Aires | 12:00 Greenwich |

FEWEST DOCTORS

Guyana	1 to 6,200 people
Chile	1 to 2,150 people
Surinam	1 to 1,800 people
Uruguay	1 to 1,500 people

CONTINENT FACTS
- At 4,000m (13,000ft) above sea level, Lake Titicaca is the world's highest lake. It lies across the borders of Peru and Bolivia.
- The continent of South America experiences extremes of weather. In parts of Colombia, more than 11,700mm (460in) of rain falls per year, while the Atacama Desert, Chile, is the world's driest place.
- Both the tomato and the potato originated in South America. Andean farmers grow potatoes at altitudes of more than 2,000m (6,550ft).

COUNTRIES AND CAPITALS

Name	Capital
Argentina	Buenos Aires
Bolivia	La Paz
Brazil	Brasilia
Chile	Santiago
Colombia	Santa Fe de Bogotá
Ecuador	Quito
Guyana	Georgetown
Paraguay	Asunción
Peru	Lima
Surinam	Paramaribo
Uruguay	Montevideo
Venezuela	Caracas

AGE BREAKDOWN

Under 15 years / 15 to 65 years / Over 65 years

3.4% Paraguay
11.4% Uruguay
25.8% Uruguay
42.5% Bolivia
54.1% Bolivia
63.6% Chile

KEY
- Lowest %
- Highest %

LONGEST LIFESPAN

Female	77	76	75	73	72
Male	70	68	68	67	66

Uruguay, Chile, Argentina, Venezuela, Colombia

NATIVE PEOPLE
The homes of the Quechua Indians of Ecuador and Peru are some of the highest settlements in the world. These Andean peoples have adapted physically to the low-oxygen atmosphere.

Quechua children outside their school

TOP CITY POPULATIONS
(Metropolitan Area)

Santiago Chile 5,170,293
Lima Peru 5,706,127
Rio de Janeiro Brazil 10,192,097
Buenos Aires Argentina 11,255,618
São Paulo Brazil 16,583,234

RAINFOREST AREA
The Amazonian rainforest is 12.8 times bigger than France.

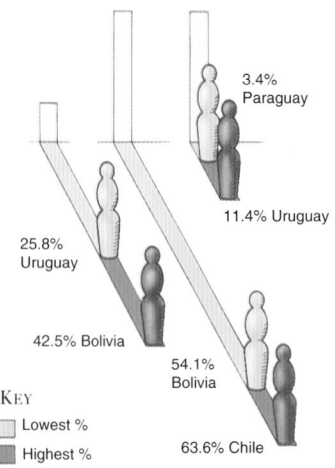

Amazon area 7 million sq km (2.7 million sq miles)

France area 545,630sq km (210,669sq miles)

HIGHEST WATERFALLS

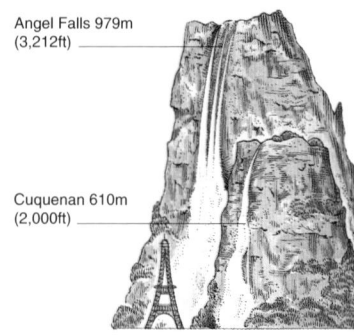

Angel Falls 979m (3,212ft)

Cuquenan 610m (2,000ft)

WORLD'S LONGEST MOUNTAIN RANGES

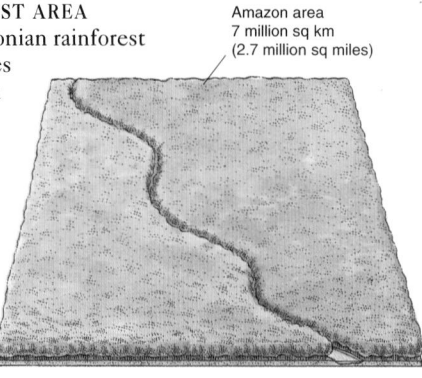

Mt. Aconcagua
Andes 7,200km (4,500 miles)

Mt. McKinley
Rocky Mountains, USA 4,800km (3,600 miles)

Map labels

Caribbean Sea
Caracas
Margarita I.
ATLANTIC
VENEZUELA
Georgetown
Lake Maracaibo
Paramaribo
Angel Falls
GUYANA
Bogotá
Llanos
Orinoco
SURINAM
FRENCH GUIANA (France)
COLOMBIA
Guiana Highlands
Cayenne
Caquetá
OCEAN
Quito
Equator
JADOR
Río Negro
Rocas I. (Brazil)
Marañón
Amazon
Fernando de Noronha I. (Brazil)
A m a z o n i a
Madeira
S e l v a s
BRAZIL
Tocantins
São Francisco
PERU
Lima
BOLIVIA
Plateau of Mato Grosso
Brasilia
Lake Titicaca
La Paz
Brazilian Highlands
Altiplano
L. Poopó
Salar de Uyuni
Paraguay
Paraná
Rio de Janeiro
PARAGUAY
São Paulo
Tropic of Capricorn
Rivadavia
Gran Chaco
Asunción
San Ambrosio I. (Chile)
Paraná
Pampas
Aconcagua 6,960m (22,836ft)
URUGUAY
Santiago
Buenos Aires
Montevideo
Plate
ARGENTINA
ATLANTIC OCEAN
CHILE
ANDES
Patagonia
Valdés Peninsula -40m (-131ft)
Los Chonos Archipelago
Sarmiento
Gulf of San Jorge
Lake Buenos Aires
Falkland Islands (UK)
Lake Argentino
Bahía Grande
Strait of Magellan
Tierra del Fuego
Cape Horn

0 — 500km
0 — 300 miles

COFFEE TREE

Coffee is the fruit of the coffee tree, an evergreen that reaches a height of 2–3m (6.6–9.9ft). After or at the same time as flowering, the branches bear green "cherries" that ripen to red. The cherries split open to reveal two seeds – the coffee beans – which are then washed, dried, and roasted.

TOP COFFEE EXPORTERS (1997)

Country	Bags	Tonnes
Brazil	14,484,300	869,058
Colombia	10,294,116	617,647
Peru	1,468,217	88,093
Ecuador	658,450	39,507

WILDLIFE

Rainforests and mountains are home to a huge variety of animals and plants.

FAUNA

Giant armadillo (*Priodontes giganteus*) has the biggest claws of any living animal.

Toco toucan (*Ramphastos toco*) has the largest bill of all the toucans.

Llama (*Llama glama*) is most important for transport in the Andes.

FLORA

Opuntia (*Cactaceae*) bear pear-shaped fruits known as prickly pears.

Puya (*Puya raimondii*) is the world's tallest herb and has 8,000 flowers.

Monkey puzzle (*Araucaria araucana*), the Chile Pine, is native to the Andes.

CROSS-SECTION

4,500m (14,764ft)
0 Sea level
-6,000m (-19,686ft)
Pacific Ocean
Andes
Amazon Basin
Guiana Highlands
Atlantic Ocean
Peru-Chile trench
Length: 4,400km (2,700 miles)

LAND PROFILE

Urban 0.5%
Wetlands 1%
Barren land 4%
Desert 4%
Forest 66.5%
Agriculture 5%
Grassland 19%

N

COLOMBIA

COLOMBIA IS FAMOUS for producing high-quality coffee – its major cash crop. Some of the finest emeralds are mined here and account for 90 per cent of world output.

Area 1,038,910sq km (439,733sq miles)
Government Multiparty republic
Independence 1819, from Spain
Territories San Andres, Providencia, San Bernardo, Islas del Rosario, Isla Fuerte and Gorgona, Gorgonilla, and Malpelo
Currency Colombian peso
Population 35,100,000
Density 34 per sq km (88 per sq mile)
Official Language Spanish
✝ Major Religions Roman Catholic 95%, other 5%

ECUADOR

ECUADOR'S NAME COMES from its position on the Equator. It is a country of very varied landscape, from low coastal regions to high Andean peaks and dense jungle.

Area 283,560sq km (109,480sq miles)
Government Multiparty republic
Independence 1830, from Spain
Currency Sucre
Population 11,500,000
Density 42 per sq km (109 per sq mile)
Official Language Spanish
✝ Major Religions Roman Catholic 95%, other 5%

LAND PROFILE
More than 90% of Ecuador is forested or used for farming.

%
.5
5
41.5
53

GALAPAGOS ISLANDS
The Galapagos islands lie 970km (603 miles) off the coast of Ecuador. Many of the animals there are not found anywhere else. British scientist Charles Darwin (1809–82) made important discoveries there concerning his theory of natural selection (see p.68).

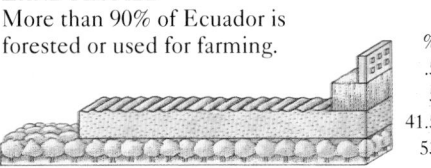
Galapagos tortoise

WEATHER FACTS

49°C (120°F)   444mm (17.4in)   -10°C (14°F)
23°C (73°F)   6°C (42°F)

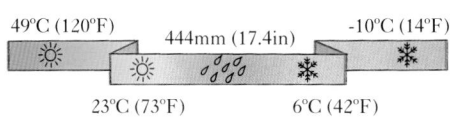

LAND PROFILE
Almost half of Colombia is covered with dense forest.

%
0.5
1
1
16
33
48.5

LIFESTYLE FACTS
• Many great writers have come from Colombia, including world-famous novelist Gabriel García Márquez (born 1928), who won the Nobel Prize for literature in 1982.

• Colombia is one of the world's biggest exporters of quality coffee.

• Colombians are great music lovers. The *tiple*, a small guitar, is the national instrument.

• Ninety-six per cent of Colombians live on less than half the land area. Almost all live in the west of the country.

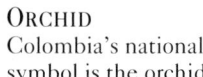
10,000 pesos

ORCHID
Colombia's national symbol is the orchid.

THE WALLED CITY
Cartagena, in northern Colombia became famous in the 16th century. Spanish ships stopped off there to collect South American gold

THE ANDES
The Andes mountain range stretches from the top to the bottom of South America. It runs through seven countries

VENEZUELA

VENEZUELA IS THE world's third greatest oil producer. Oil provides 0 per cent of export earnings and as made Venezuela one of the ichest countries in South America.

 Area 912,050sq km (352,143sq miles)
Government Presidential republic
Independence 1821, from Spain
Currency Bolivar
Population 21,800,000
Density 25 per sq km (65 per sq mile)
Official Language Spanish
Major Religions Roman Catholic 96%, Protestant 2%, other 2%

WEATHER FACTS

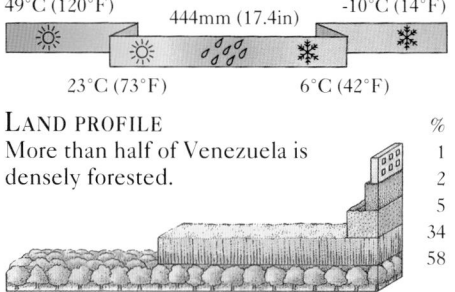

49°C (120°F)   444mm (17.4in)   -10°C (14°F)
23°C (73°F)   6°C (42°F)

LAND PROFILE

More than half of Venezuela is densely forested.

%
1
2
5
34
58

ANGEL FALLS

The Angel Falls, in southeastern Venezuela, is the highest waterfall in the world, with a drop of 979m (3,212ft) The falls are named after American pilot Jimmy Angel (died 1956), who found them in 1935.

BOLIVIA

BOLIVIA IS A mountainous country with no coastline. Farmers make up half of its population; many of them are very poor, and grow just enough food for their families to live on.

Area 1,098,580sq km (424,160sq miles)
Government Multiparty republic
Independence 1825, from Spain
Currency Boliviano
Population 7,400,000
Density 7 per sq km (18 per sq mile)
Official Languages Spanish, Quechua, and Aymara
Major Religions Roman Catholic 95%, other 5%

LAND PROFILE

Two-thirds of Peru is jungle.

%
0.5
7
13
13
66.5

PERU

PERU CONTAINS many spectacular uins. They were built during the ime of the Inca empire (see p.389), which was destroyed by Spanish nvaders in the 16th century.

Area 1,285,220sq km (496,223sq miles)
Government Multiparty republic
Independence 1824, from Spain
Currency Nuevo sol
Population 23,800,000
Density 19 per sq km (49 per sq mile)
Official Languages Spanish and Quechua
Major Religions Roman Catholic 95%, other 5%

WEATHER FACTS

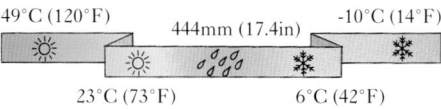

49°C (120°F)   444mm (17.4in)   -10°C (14°F)
23°C (73°F)   6°C (42°F)

NAZCA LINES

Huge animal figures and strange shapes were cut into the ground in southern Peru thousands of years ago. The whole design can be seen only from the air.

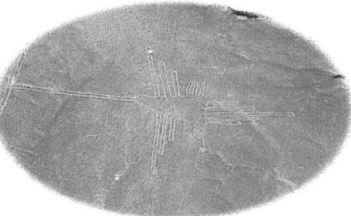

Nazca hummingbird figure

HIGHEST TRACK

The highest section of railway track in the world, in Peru, lies at an altitude of 4,782m (15,688ft). The track passes through a tunnel on the Morochocha branch of Peruvian State Railways.

Andean condor

ANDEAN CONDOR

The Andean condor is the heaviest bird of prey in the world, with a wingspan of more than 3m (10ft). It lives in the highest parts of the Andes mountains and feeds on dead animals.

Highest railway in the world

GUYANA

A FERTILE COASTAL strip of land just 6km (10 miles) wide is where 0 per cent of the population lives. Much of the rest of Guyana is overed with dense rainforest.

 **Area** 214,970sq km (83,000sq miles)
Independence 1966, from Britian
Currency Guyana dollar
Population 800,000
Official Language English

SURINAM

SURINAM'S CLIMATE is humid and tropical. Its rich wildlife includes jaguars, pumas, and ocelots, plus a variety of reptiles such as iguanas, rattlesnakes and boa constrictors.

 Area 163,270sq km (63,039sq miles)
Independence 1975, from Netherlands
Currency Surinam guilder
Population 400,000
Official Language Dutch

FRENCH GUIANA

FRENCH GUIANA IS the only European colony in South America. It is a part of France, and sends two members to the French National Assembly (parliament).

 Area 90,000sq km (34,750sq miles)
Currency French franc
Population 118,000
Official Language French

ARGENTINA

CENTRAL ARGENTINA is covered with lush grasslands called the *pampas*, where crops are grown and cattle and sheep are reared. This area produces three-quarters of Argentina's income.

Area 2,766,890sq km (1,068,296sq miles)
Government Multiparty republic
Independence 1816, from Spain
Currency Argentinian peso
Population 34,600,000
Density 13 per sq km (34 per sq mile)
Official Language Spanish
✝ **Major Religions** Roman Catholic 90%, Jewish 2%, others 8%

WEATHER FACTS

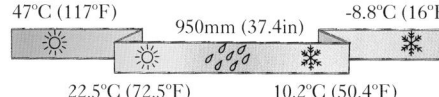

47°C (117°F)   950mm (37.4in)   -8.8°C (16°F)

22.5°C (72.5°F)   10.2°C (50.4°F)

LIFESTYLE FACTS

• Soccer is the national sport. Argentina hosted and won the World Cup in 1978, then won again in Mexico City in 1986.

• The Argentinian daily drink is a tea called *maté*. It is made from a tree used since ancient times by native South Americans.

• *Gauchos*, cowboys who work on the huge Argentinian cattle ranches, are folklore heroes. They also created dances which feature fast, complex footwork.

PATAGONIA

The region of Patagonia in southern Argentina is home to unique wildlife such as the pudu, the smallest known deer.

Pudu

THE CEIBO FLOWER

The ceibo is Argentina's national flower.

PALACIO DEL CONGRESO

The Argentinian government meets in the magnificent *Palacio del Congreso* (Congress building) in the *centro* (city centre) area of the capital, Buenos Aires.

WELSH TEAS

Welsh immigrants settled in Patagonia more than 100 years ago. Their descendants still follow Welsh traditions, such as eating porridge for breakfast, drinking tea, and singing Welsh songs.

CHILE

CHILE RETURNED to being a democracy in 1989: elections were held for the first time in nearly 20 years.

Area 756,950sq km (292,258sq miles)
Government Multiparty republic
Independence 1818, from Spain
Currency Chilean peso
Population 14,300,000
Density 19 per sq km (49 per sq mile)
Official Language Spanish
✝ **Major Religions** Roman Catholic 89%, Protestant 11%

WEATHER FACTS

37°C (98.6F°)   361mm (14.2in)   -12°C (11°

20°C (68°F)   9.3°C (48.7°F)

LIFESTYLE FACTS

• Soccer is the sport with the largest following in Chile. Skiing is popular in winter; the world speed ski record of 171km/h (106mph) was set there.

• More copper is produced in Chile than any other country in the world.

• Chileans are very well educated: 94% of the population can read and write.

• Chile is famous for its fine wines. Chilean grapes are also used to make *pisco*, a spirit.

PARAGUAY

NINETY PER CENT of Paraguayans are *Mestizo* – a mixture of native Guarani Indian and Spanish blood. Half of the working population is employed in agriculture.

Area 406,750sq km (157,046sq miles)
Independence 1811, from Spain
Currency Guarani
Population 5,000,000
Official Language Spanish

URUGUAY

ALMOST HALF of Uruguay's population lives in the capital city, Montevideo. Much of the city's electricity is provided by hydroelectric dams.

Area 174,810sq km (67,494sq miles)
Independence 1825, from Spain
Currency Uruguayan peso
Population 3,200,000
Official Language Spanish

PERU
BOLIVIA
Gran Chaco
Pilcomayo
Paraguay
PARAGUAY
Asunción
Lake Ypoá
San Miguel de Tucumán
Santiago del Estero
Ojos del Salado 6,880 m (22,573 ft)
Salado
Paraná
Córdoba
Aconcagua 6,960m (22,836ft)
Rosario
Mendoza
Negro
Lake Mirim
Santiago
URUGUAY
Buenos Aires
La Plata
Plate
Montevideo
Victorica
Congress Hall
Concepción
Colorado
Pampas
Chiloé Island
ATLANTIC OCEAN
Patagonia
PACIFIC OCEAN
Lake General Carrera
Baker
Lake Argentino
Punta Arenas
Tierra del Fuego
Cape Horn
CHILE
ARGENTINA
ANDES
BRAZIL
PACIFIC OCEAN

N

0   500km
0   300 miles

BRAZIL

BRAZIL OCCUPIES NEARLY half the continent of South America and is the fifth largest country in the world. The country supplies 85 per cent of the world's orange juice and is the largest producer of coffee. Around 70 per cent of the population is aged under 30.

Area 8,511,970sq km (3,286,472sq miles)
Government Multiparty republic
Independence 1822, from Portugal
Currency Real, formerly cruzeiro
Population 161,800,000
Density 19 per sq km (49 per sq mile)
Official Language Portuguese
Major Religions Roman Catholic 90%, others 10%

WEATHER FACTS

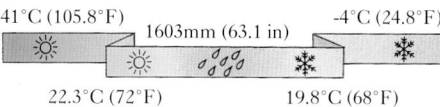

41°C (105.8°F)   1603mm (63.1 in)   -4°C (24.8°F)

22.3°C (72°F)   19.8°C (68°F)

LAND PROFILE
Tropical rainforests cover almost 60% of Brazil.

%
0.3
0.5
10
29.7
59.5

LIFESTYLE FACTS
• More than 1.5 million of Rio de Janeiro's 5 million plus population live in shanty towns known as *favelas*.

• Football is Brazil's favourite sport, and the country has more than 20,000 soccer teams. The brilliant Brazilian player, Pelé, is known throughout the world.

• Brasilia, the capital city since 1960, was built on the Central Plains to help develop inland areas of Brazil. The modern cathedral is the city's main landmark.

1,000 cruzeiros

LANGUAGE
A traditional greeting in Portuguese is *bom dia*.

BRAZILIAN INSTANT COFFEE EXPORTS (1997)	
Destination	Tonnes
Eastern Europe	29,240
North America	8,771
Far East	7,196
South America	1,372

AMAZON RAINFOREST FACTS
• The Amazon Basin lies across the Equator. This hot, wet, region contains the world's largest tropical rainforest, which is 12 times the size of France.

• The Amazon River and its tributaries make up 20% of the world's supply of fresh water. This powerful river delivers an average of 773 billion litres (170 billion gallons) of water per hour into the Atlantic Ocean.

MAJOR RAINFOREST PEOPLES	
Name of tribe and territory	Estimated population
Tikuna	25,000
Yanomami	7,500
Guajajara	7,000
Xavante	5,000
Sateré Maué	4,700

The Yanomami live in vine and leaf-thatched homes in the forests of northern Brazil and southern Venezuela.

RAINFOREST WILDLIFE FACTS
• The rainforest is home to 250 varieties of mammals, 1,800 species of birds, and more than 10,000 species of trees.

• The humming-bird beats its wings 55 times per second – 200 times per second during courtship flights. It can also hover in one place, or even fly backwards.

• The two-toed sloth is the world's slowest animal. It takes 6.5 hours to cover just 1.6km (1 mile). The sloth also spends 21.5 hours asleep each day.

• The anaconda is the world's heaviest snake, and can weigh up to 230kg (507lb).

CHRIST THE REDEEMER
The statue of Christ the Redeemer overlooks Rio de Janeiro from Mount Corcovado. It was designed by French sculptor Paul Landowsky, and was completed in 1931.

RIO CARNIVAL
The carnival in Rio de Janeiro is the biggest in the world and takes place every year before Lent. The highlight of the carnival is the parade of the Samba schools.

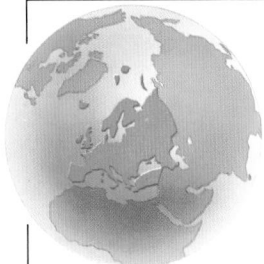

EUROPE

EUROPE IS THE second smallest continent and has a varied landscape and climate. Southern Europe is mostly hilly or mountainous and generally warm and dry. The north is wetter and cooler with flat plains and thick forests. Europe includes the western third of the Russian Federation.

Area 23,947,919sq km (9,246,339sq miles)
Countries 48
Largest Russian Federation 17,075,400sq km (6,592,846sq miles): European Russia 3,955,818sq km (1,527,349sq miles)
Smallest Vatican City 0.44sq km (0.17sq miles)
Population 750,582,660
Density 31 per sq km (80 per sq mile)

Major Languages Russian, German, Turkish, Italian, English
▲ **Highest point** Mount El'brus, Russian Federation 5,642m (18,510 ft)
▼ **Lowest point** Caspian Sea 28m (92ft) below sea level
☀ **Highest temperature** 50°C (122°F), Seville, Spain
❄ **Lowest temperature** -55°C (-67°F), Ust 'Shchugor, Russian Federation

TIME ZONES

| 12.00 Greenwich | 13.00 Berlin | 14.00 Athens | 15.00 Moscow |

LONGEST RIVERS

Volga 3,530km (2,194 miles)
Danube 2,858km (1,776 miles)
Ural 2,534km (1,575 miles)
Dnieper 2,285km (1,420 miles)
Don 1,969km (1,224 miles)

CLIMATE ZONES
KEY
- Temperate forest
- Mediterranean
- Dry grassland
- Polar and tundra
- Taiga
- Mountain regions

MOST POPULAR CITIES

The cities of Europe are popular with tourists from all over the world. The most visited cities in 1993 were, in order, London, Paris, Rome, Vienna, and Madrid

TOP CITY POPULATIONS

St. Petersburg, Russian Federation 4,446,000
Istanbul, Turkey 6,748,000
London, UK 6,803,100
Paris, France 9,318,000
Moscow Federati 8,717,0(

COUNTRIES, TERRITORIES, AND CAPITALS

Name	Capital
Albania	Tirana
Andorra	Andorra la Vella
Armenia	Yerevan
Austria	Vienna
Azerbaijan	Baku
Belgium	Brussels
Belorussia	Minsk
Bosnia & Herzegovina	Sarajevo
Bulgaria	Sofia
Croatia	Zagreb
Cyprus	Nicosia
Czech Republic	Prague
Denmark	Copenhagen
Estonia	Tallinn
Finland	Helsinki
France	Paris
Georgia	Tbilisi
Germany	Berlin
Greece	Athens
Hungary	Budapest
Iceland	Reykjavik
Ireland, Republic of	Dublin
Italy	Rome
Latvia	Riga

Name	Capital
Liechtenstein	Vaduz
Lithuania	Vilnius
Luxembourg	Luxembourg
Macedonia	Skopje
Malta	Valetta
Moldavia	Kishinev or Chisinau
Monaco	Monaco
Netherlands	Amsterdam
Norway	Oslo
Poland	Warsaw
Portugal	Lisbon
Romania	Bucharest
Russian Federation	Moscow
San Marino	San Marino
Slovakia	Bratislava
Slovenia	Ljubljana
Spain	Madrid
Sweden	Stockholm
Switzerland	Berne
Turkey	Ankara
Ukraine	Kiev
United Kingdom	London
Vatican City	Vatican City
Yugoslavia	Belgrade

AGE BREAKDOWN

Under 15 years | 15 to 65 years | Over 65 years

Turkey 4.3%
Monaco 22.6%
Monaco 11.9%
Turkey 34.8%
Turkey 60.9%
Andorra 72.2%

KEY
- Lowest %
- Highest %

FEWEST DOCTORS

Ukraine	1 to 1,260 people
Cyprus	1 to 1,100 people
Ireland	1 to 630 people
Switzerland	1 to 630 people
Bosnia/Herz.	1 to 600 people

LONGEST LIFESPAN

Female | 81 | 81 | 81 | 80 |
Male | 74 | 75 | 74 | 75 |

Switzerland | Sweden | Italy | Iceland | Norw

CONTINENT FACTS

- Most of the world's amber is found along the Baltic coast of Lithuania. Amber, the fossilized sap of ancient trees, is a precious stone. It is used in the treatment of arthritis.

- The French are the world's greatest snail eaters. They eat about 25,000 tonnes each year. Snails, *Helix pomatia* and *Helix aspersa*, are gathered from the wild.

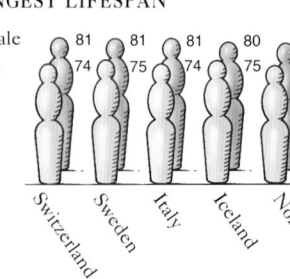

- Germany is Europe's leading producer of chemicals; they are used in industry to make paint, cosmetics, and medicines.

- The Vatican City is the only place in the world where Latin is the official language.

- The St. Gotthard tunnel in Switzerland is the world's longest road tunnel. It is 16.3 km (10.1 miles) long.

- The largest cotton mill in Europe is in Estonia. Cotton is grown in the Baltic States.

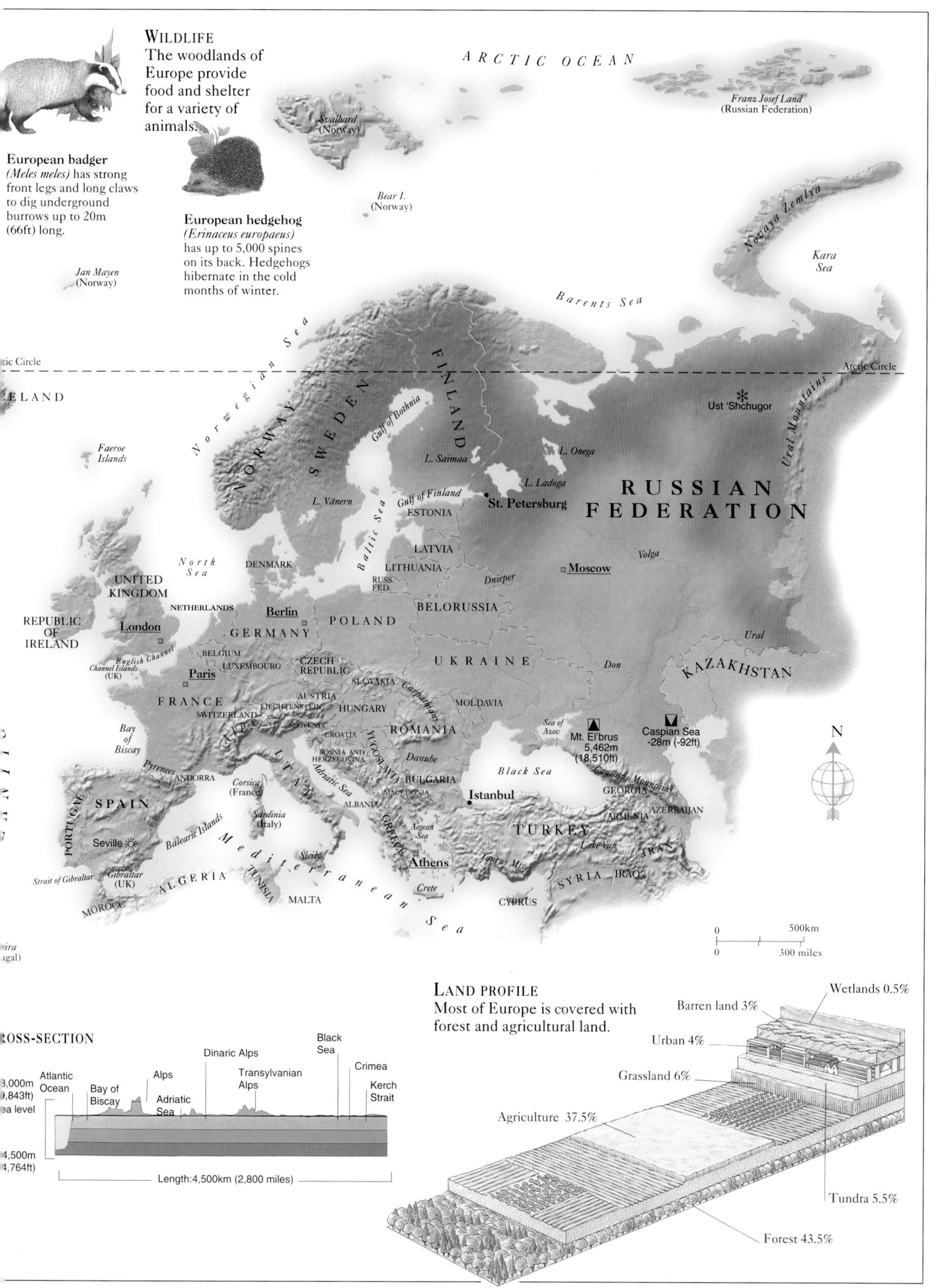

WILDLIFE
The woodlands of Europe provide food and shelter for a variety of animals.

European badger
(*Meles meles*) has strong front legs and long claws to dig underground burrows up to 20m (66ft) long.

European hedgehog
(*Erinaceus europaeus*) has up to 5,000 spines on its back. Hedgehogs hibernate in the cold months of winter.

LAND PROFILE
Most of Europe is covered with forest and agricultural land.

Wetlands 0.5%
Barren land 3%
Urban 4%
Grassland 6%
Agriculture 37.5%
Tundra 5.5%
Forest 43.5%

CROSS-SECTION

Atlantic Ocean
Bay of Biscay
Alps
Adriatic Sea
Dinaric Alps
Transylvanian Alps
Black Sea
Crimea
Kerch Strait

3,000m (9,843ft)
Sea level
4,500m (4,764ft)

Length:4,500km (2,800 miles)

ICELAND

ICELAND, EUROPE'S second largest island, has the lowest population density in Europe. The remote interior can be reached only by special vehicle, pony, or small plane.

Area 103,000sq km (39,770sq miles)
Government Constitutional republic
Independence 1944, from British and US control during World War II
Currency Icelandic króna
Population 300,000
Density 3 per sq km (8 per sq mile)
Official Language Icelandic
✝ **Major Religions** Evangelical Lutheran Church of Iceland 96%, other Protestant and Roman Catholic 3%, non-religious 1%

WEATHER FACTS

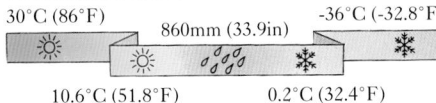
30°C (86°F)　　860mm (33.9in)　　-36°C (-32.8°F)
10.6°C (51.8°F)　　0.2°C (32.4°F)

LAND PROFILE

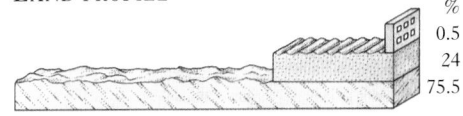
%
0.5
24
75.5

LIFESTYLE FACTS

• The Althing, the Icelandic parliament, has been in existence since the 13th century and is one of the oldest surviving assemblies in the world.

• Iceland has the most solfataras (volcanic vents) and hot springs in the world. Many of its towns are heated by underground hot water.

• Iceland produces more than a third of the world's cod-liver oil, and is the biggest consumer of it.

HOT SPRINGS

Deildartunguhver hot springs blow out 250 litres (55 gallons) of hot water every second. Over a 24-hour period, they produce enough water to fill 105,600 baths.

100 krónur

LANGUAGE

A traditional greeting in Icelandic is *gódan daginn*.

- - Arctic Circle - -
Siglufjördur
Akureyri
I C E L A N D
Deildartunguhver
Reykjavik
Hafnarfjördhur　Kópavogur
Thingvallavatn
Vatnajöknull
Hvannadalshnúkur 2,119m (6,954ft)
Te

N

0　500km
0　300 miles

DENMARK

DENMARK, WHICH IS divided into numerous islands, has a 4,500-mile (7,300km) coastline. It was the first Scandinavian country to belong to the European Community (EC).

Area 43,069sq km (16,629sq miles)
Government Constitutional monarchy
State founded c. 950
Territories Faeroe Islands, Greenland
Currency Danish krone
Population 5,200,000
Density 123 per sq km (319 per sq mile)
Official Language Danish
✝ **Major Religions** Evangelical Lutheran Church 91%, Roman Catholic 2%, other and non-religious 7%

WEATHER FACTS

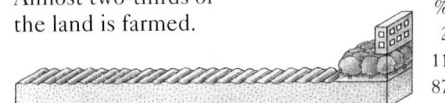
35°C (95°F)　　704mm (27.7in)　　-24°C (-11.2°F)
16.3°C (61.3°F)　　1.3°C (34.3°F)

LAND PROFILE

Almost two-thirds of the land is farmed.
%
2
11
87

LANGUAGE

A traditional greeting in Danish is *goddag*.

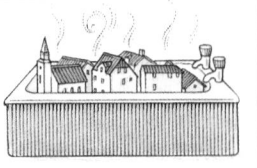
100 kroner

LIFESTYLE FACTS

• Lego was created by a Danish carpenter in the 1930s. Legoland Park is a miniature, working village created from 35 million plastic bricks.

• Denmark has one of the lowest private ownerships of cars in Europe. Cyclists are encouraged with special lanes, and Copenhagen was the first city to create a pedestrian street.

• Denmark has over twice as many pigs as humans, and Danish bacon is a successful export product. Danish farmers produce three times more food than is needed to feed the population.

LITTLE MERMAID

Situated by Copenhagen harbour, this statue of the mermaid from Hans C. Andersen's fairy tale was sculpted in 1913 by Edvard Eriksen (1876–1959). Her head has had to be replaced several times.

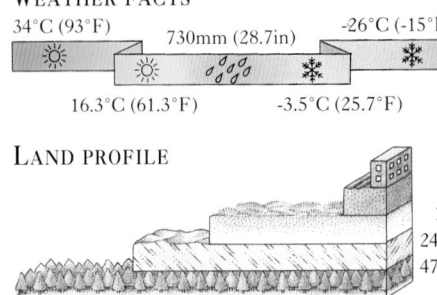

NORWAY

NORWAY IS A LAND of beautiful fjords (valleys flooded by rising sea levels after the last ice age): the longest is Sogne Fjord, at 203 kilometres (126 miles).

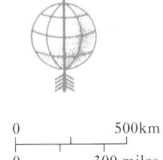
Area 323,900sq km (125,060sq miles)
Government Constitutional monarchy
Independence from Sweden, 1905
Territories Svalbard archipelago, Jan Mayen Island
Currency Norwegian krone
Population 4,300,000
Density 14 per sq km (36 per sq mile)
Official Language Nynorsk (new Norwegian) and Bokmaal (older)
✝ **Major Religions** Evangelical Lutheran and other Protestant 88%, other Christian 12%

WEATHER FACTS

34°C (93°F)　　730mm (28.7in)　　-26°C (-15°F)
16.3°C (61.3°F)　　-3.5°C (25.7°F)

LAND PROFILE

%
24.
47.

SWEDEN

TWO-THIRDS OF the land in Sweden is covered by forests, and there are 100,000 lakes. Timber products, including paper, account for nearly one-fifth of all Swedish exports.

Area 449,960sq km (173,730sq miles)
Government Constitutional monarchy
State established 1523
Currency Swedish krona
Population 8,800,000
Density 20 per sq km (50 per sq mile)
Official Language Swedish
Major Religions Evangelical Lutheran Church of Sweden 94%, Roman Catholic 2%, other 4%

NOBEL PRIZES
Alfred B. Nobel (1833–96) was a Swedish scientist and inventor of dynamite. He created a fund for the Nobel prizes, awarded each year for sciences, literature, and peace, to those who have given the greatest benefit to humankind.

LANGUAGE
A traditional greeting in Norwegian is *go dag*.

100 kroner

HOLMENKOLLEN
The ski-jump at Holmenkollen, outside Oslo, is the oldest in existence. The first ski-jump competition was held in 1892, and the event continues to be held every March.

LIFESTYLE FACTS
• In Hammerfest, the world's most northerly town, the sun shines at midnight for just over two months in the summer.

• Norway's annual contribution of its national income (1.17%) towards foreign aid is the highest proportion in the world.

• Norwegians read more newspapers than anyone else in the world, and buy more English books than any other non-English-speaking country.

100 kronor

LANGUAGE
A traditional greeting in Swedish is *god dag*.

LAND PROFILE
The land is mainly forested or used for farming.

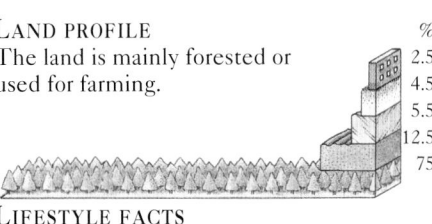

%
2.5
4.5
5.5
12.5
75

LIFESTYLE FACTS
• Each year 12,000 cross-country skiers take part in a race from Salen to Mora in central Sweden. The course is 90km (56 miles) long.

• In 1910, Sweden was the first European country to establish national parks. Animals that can be found in the parks include lynx, bear, and moose.

• Stockholm's waterways are so pure that people can safely swim and fish in them.

• More than 50% of Norwegian families have a weekend home in the mountains or by the sea. These second homes are made of wood, and some have turf-covered roofs.

WEATHER FACTS
35°C (95°F) 622mm (24.5in) -38°C (-36.4°F)

16.5°C (61.7°F) -2°C (28.4°F)

CITY HALL
Stockholm's fine City Hall, called the Stadshus, was built between 1911 and 1923. Its Golden Hall has 19 million gilded tiles.

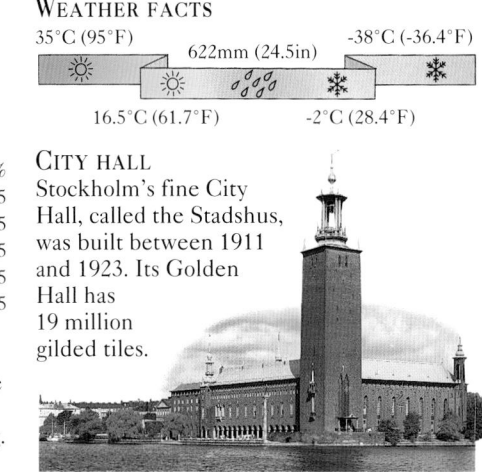

THE SAMI
The Sami (Lapps) have inhabited the arctic regions of Norway and Sweden since ancient times. Today, there are about 60,000 and 70% speak the Sami language. About 70,000 reindeer live in Sami territories, and the main occupation of the people is reindeer breeding. The woven clothes worn by the Sami are practical and beautiful.

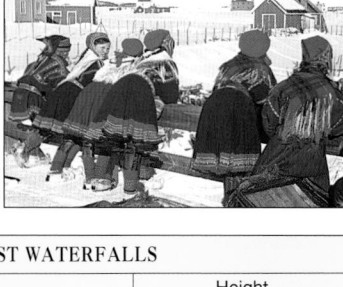

HIGHEST WATERFALLS

Name	Height	
	m	ft
Utigord	800	2,625
Mongefossen	774	2,540
Ostre Mardola Foss	657	2,154
Tyssetrengane	646	2,120
Kjellfossen	561	1,841

UNITED KINGDOM

THE UNITED KINGDOM, also known as Britain, is made up of England, Wales, Scotland, and Northern Ireland. London, the capital, has a population of almost 7 million, and is the political and financial centre.

Area 244,880sq km
(94,550sq miles)
Government Constitutional monarchy
Unification 1707, between England/Wales and Scotland; 1801, between Britain and Ireland
Territories Anguilla, Bermuda, British Antarctic Territory, British India Ocean Territory, British Virgin Islands, Cayman Islands, Falkland Islands, Gibraltar, Montserrat, Pitcairn Islands, St. Helena and dependencies, South Georgia and the South Sandwich Islands, Turks and Caicos Islands
Currency Pound sterling
Population 58,300,000
Density 241 per sq km (625 per sq mile)
Official Language English
Major Religions Protestant 52%, Roman Catholic 9%, Muslim 3%, other 36%

WEATHER FACTS

34°C (93°F)   593mm (23in)   -17°C (2°F)

14.6°C (58.3°F)   6.5°C (43.7°F)

LAND PROFILE

Almost three-quarters of the land is farmed.

	%
	4
	11
	14
	71

LIFESTYLE FACTS

• There are more than 25,000 different names for the public houses (pubs) where people in Britain meet to talk and drink. The most popular name is *The Red Lion*.

• The Eistedfodd is a Welsh arts festival held every August. The festival dates back to 1176 when competitions were held for poet-musicians. The winner was awarded a "chair", or position, in the royal court.

HOUSES OF PARLIAMENT

This palace is the headquarters of the British Government. Its famous clock tower has a great bell called Big Ben.

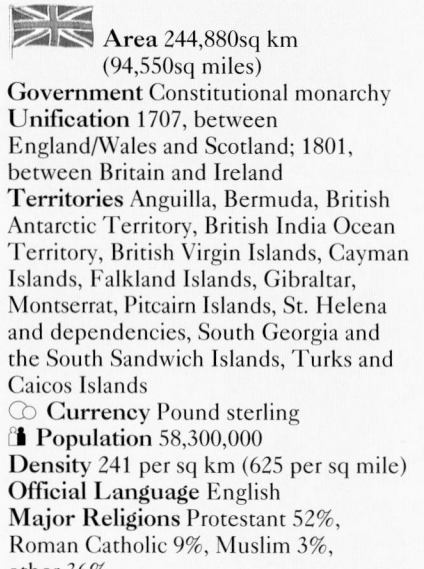

SCOTTISH TARTAN

Members of a Scottish clan have their own tartan. This cloth, often worn as a kilt, is woven with a criss-cross pattern. There are more than 2,000 varieties of tartan.

LANGUAGE

A traditional greeting in English is hello.

0   150km
0   100 miles

Shetland Is.
Orkney Is.
Outer Hebrides
Lewis
North Uist
Skye
South Uist
North West Highlands
Moray Firth
Ben Nevis 1,343m (4,406ft)
SCOTLAND
Islay
Glasgow • Edinburgh
Southern Uplands
• Newcastle upon Tyne
NORTHERN IRELAND
Belfast
Donegal Bay
Lough Neagh
REPUBLIC OF IRELAND
Mullingar
Trinity College
Dublin
Dun Laoghaire
Galway
Shannon
Limerick
Carantuohill 1,041m (3,416ft)
Cork
Waterford
St. George's Channel
Cardigan Bay
Irish Sea
Isle of Man
Anglesey
Liverpool • Manchester
Wicklow Mts.
Cambrian Mts.
Severn
Birmingham
WALES
Brecon Beacons
Cardiff
Bristol Channel
UNITED KINGDOM
North Sea
ENGLAND
Thames
The Wash
London
Houses of Parliament
Stonehenge
Isle of Wight
Plymouth
English Channel
Isles of Scilly
ATLANTIC OCEAN
N

£10 *10 pounds sterling*

SYMBOLS

England, rose; Wales, daffodil; Scotland, thistle; and Ireland, shamrock

STONEHENGE

This prehistoric stone circle in southern England was completed in about 1600 B.C.

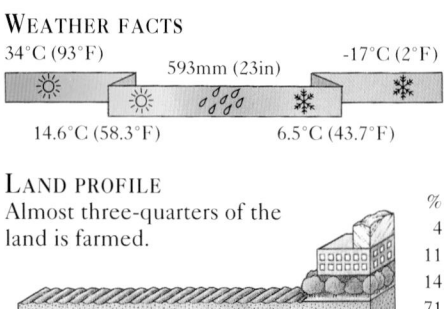

REPUBLIC OF IRELAND

IRELAND IS A mainly rural country. It has a wet and mild climate with rich grass for dairy farming. Tourists come to fish in the rivers and lakes.

Area 70,280sq km
(27,135sq miles)
Government Multiparty republic
Independence 1921, Irish Free State granted 26 counties
Currency Punt
Population 3,600,000
Density 52 per sq km (135 per sq mile)
Official Language Irish
Major Religions Roman Catholic 93%, Anglican 5%, other 2%

Guernsey
Channel Islands
Jersey
(U.K.)

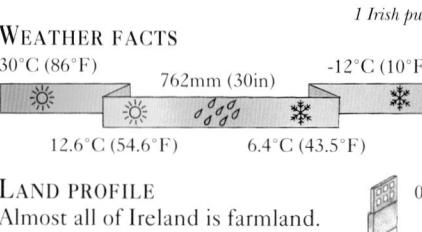

1 Irish punt

WEATHER FACTS

30°C (86°F)   762mm (30in)   -12°C (10°F)

12.6°C (54.6°F)   6.4°C (43.5°F)

LAND PROFILE

Almost all of Ireland is farmland.

	%
	0.5
	3.
	14.
	80.

BOOK OF KELLS

This page is from the *Book of Kells*, the four gospels set down by a 8th-century Irish monk. It is displayed in the Trinity College Library, Dublin, where a page is turned each day.

SPAIN

SPAIN IS THE SECOND largest country in Europe, and one of the most mountainous. Madrid, the capital, is Europe's highest city. Spain's warm climate and fine beaches attract 50 million visitors a year.

Area 504,780sq km (194,900sq miles)
Government Constitutional monarchy
Independence 1469, reunification of Spain against Moorish invaders
Territories Canary Islands, Balearic Islands, Ceuta, Melilla, Islas Chafarinas; Peñón de Vélez de la Gomera; Peñón de Alhucemas
Currency Peseta
Population 39,600,000
Density 79 per sq km (205 per sq mile)
Official Language Castilian Spanish
Major Religions Roman Catholic 99%, other 1%

ALHAMBRA PALACE
This beautiful palace of the Moorish (Muslim) rulers of 14th-century Spain sits high above the city of Granada. Also a fortress with huge towers, Alhambra means "red castle".

PORTUGAL

IN THE 15TH CENTURY Portugal was a great seafaring nation with many famous explorers. Today, Portuguese is the seventh most spoken language in the world.

LANGUAGE
A traditional greeting in Portuguese is *bom dia*.

Area 92,390sq km (35,670sq miles)
Government Multiparty republic
Independence 1910, Republic declared
Territories Azores, Madeiras, Macao
Currency Escudo
Population 9,800,000
Density 107 per sq km (277 per sq mile)
Official Languages Portuguese
Major Religions Roman Catholic 97%, Protestant 1%, other 2%

WEATHER FACTS
49°C (120°F)   444mm (17.4in)   -20°C (-6°F)

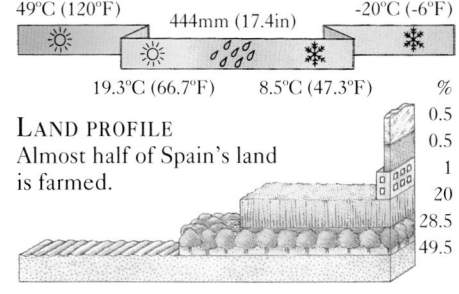

19.3°C (66.7°F)   8.5°C (47.3°F)

%
0.5
0.5
1
20
28.5
49.5

LAND PROFILE
Almost half of Spain's land is farmed.

LIFESTYLE FACTS
• Spain is the world's third largest wine producer. Famous Spanish wines include sherry, first produced in the town of Jerez.

• During the "running of the bulls" in Pamplona, men test their courage by running in front of a herd of bulls.

LANGUAGE
A traditional greeting in Castilian Spanish is *buenos días*.

FLOWER
The red carnation is the Spanish national flower.

AMAZING OLIVES
Spain is the world's top producer of olives and olive products. In one year, enough olives are grown to supply every person in the world with 70 each.

The cockerel is Portugal's national symbol.

WEATHER FACTS
49°C (120°F)   708mm (27.8in)   -12°C (10°F)

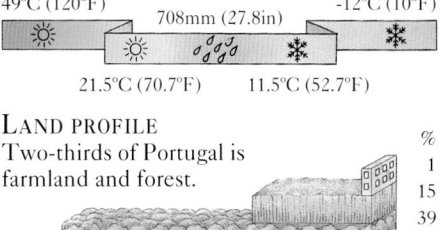

21.5°C (70.7°F)   11.5°C (52.7°F)

LAND PROFILE
Two-thirds of Portugal is farmland and forest.

%
1
15
39
45

CORK FACTS
• Cork is made from the bark of the cork oak tree.

• Portugal supplies more than half the world's cork.

• The main product made from cork is the bottle stopper.

Map labels
Bay of Biscay
La Coruña Gijón
Cantabrian Mountains Bilbao
Pamplona
FRANCE
ANDORRA
Andorra La Vella
Pyrenees
Vigo
Ebro
Bragança
Oporto Valladolid Duero Zaragoza
Barcelona
Hospitalet
Douro
S P A I N
Estrela 1993m (5539 ft)
Coimbra
Sierra Gredos
Madrid
Serrania de Cuenca
Tagus Cuenca
Alcántara Reservoir
Valencia
Balearic Islands Minorce
Majorca
Palma
Lisbon
Guadiana
Ibiza
Sierra Morena Alicante
Murcia
Córdoba Guadalquivir
Alhambra Palace
Seville
MEDITERRANEAN SEA
Granada Mulhacén 3478 m (11,411 ft)
Málaga
Jérez
0   100   200 km
0   125 miles
GIBRALTAR (UK)
ATLANTIC OCEAN
PORTUGAL
Tagus

ANDORRA

ANDORRA IS TUCKED away in the high valleys of the Pyrenees and its perpetual snow attracts many skiers. It is the fourth smallest independent state in Europe.

Area 468sq km (181sq miles)
Government Co-principality (France and Spain)
Independence 1278, established as a state
Currencies French franc and Spanish peseta
Population 64,000
Density 138 per sq km (357 per sq mile)
Official language Catalan

NETHERLANDS

THE DUTCH PEOPLE made their fortunes from the sea in the 17th century with a worldwide trading network. Today, Rotterdam is the world's largest and busiest port.

Area 37,330sq km (14,410sq miles)
Government Constitutional monarchy
Kingdom established 1830
Territories Aruba, Netherlands Antilles
Currency Guilder
Population 15,500,000
Density 457 per sq km (1,188 per sq mile)
Official Language Dutch
Major Religions Roman Catholic 36%, Protestant 27%, other 37%

DUTCH WATER FACTS

● Without protective dunes and dykes, half the land area of the Netherlands would be flooded by the sea twice a day.

● Almost 20% of the Netherlands is made up of inland water. Windmills once pumped out water; now, the pumps are electric.

BELGIUM

BELGIUM COMBINES two cultures: the French-speaking Walloons and the Dutch-speaking Flemings. Brussels, the capital, is host to the Commission of the European Union (EU).

Area 33,100sq km (12,780sq miles)
Currency Belgian franc
Government Constitutional monarchy
Independence 1830, from the Netherlands
Population 10,100,000
Density 308 per sq km (798 per sq mile)
Official Languages French, Dutch, and German
✝ Major Religions Roman Catholic 75%, other 25%

ATOMIUM

Erected in 1958 in Brussels, this space-age structure, called the Atomium, represents an iron crystal. It houses a permanent scientific exhibition on the history of medicine.

LAND PROFILE
The Netherlands is intensively farmed.

%
3.5
12
84.5

LIFESTYLE FACTS

● There are 14 million bicycles between 15 million people in the Netherlands. This is the highest proportion in the world.

● If the canals freeze over, the Dutch take part in a *tocht*, a long skating tour. Official tour routes between villages are announced on TV and radio.

● More Dutch cheese is exported than any other cheese in the world. Half of all milk produced is made into cheese.

FLOWER POWER
The Netherlands is the world's largest exporter of flowers and bulbs. In spring, fields packed with brightly coloured tulips attract thousands of visitors.

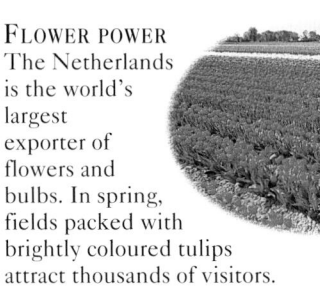

0   75km
0   40 miles

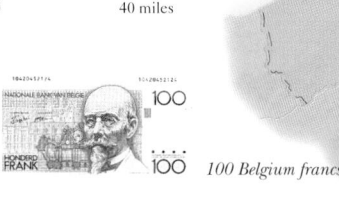
100 Belgium francs

WEATHER FACTS
37°C (98.6°F)   -18°C (0°F)
825mm (32in)

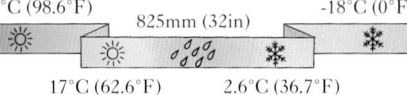

17°C (62.6°F)   2.6°C (36.7°F)

LAND PROFILE

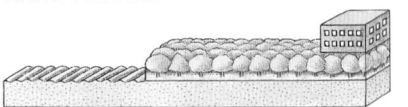

%
7
35
58

LIFESTYLE FACTS

● Belgium is the third biggest producer of chocolates in the world.

● Belgians spend more on food and drink than their European neighbours. Brussels has 25 restaurants holding a prized Michelin rosette – more than twice as many as London, which is eight times bigger.

● Bruges is the centre of European lacemaking; women have made exquisite lace here for centuries.

● Belgium has the world's densest railway system: there are 8,408km (5,224 miles) of tracks.

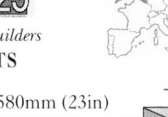
25 guilders

WEATHER FACTS
37°C (98.6°F)   -25°C (-13°F)
580mm (23in)

16.5°C (61.7°F)   2.3°C (36.1°F)

LUXEMBOURG

LUXEMBOURG IS A Grand Duchy, with a Grand Duke as Head of State. Luxembourg City is a major international banking centre.

Area 2,586sq km (998sq miles)
Currency Luxembourg franc, Belgian franc
Government Constitutional monarchy
Independence 1839, from the Netherlands
Population 400,000
Density 155 per sq km (403 per sq mile)
Official Language Luxembourgish
✝ Major Religions Roman Catholic 97%, other 3%

FRANCE

FRANCE IS THE LARGEST of the fifteen countries in the European Union (EU), and its leading agricultural power. Ninety per cent of the land is farmed, and one in five French people lives and works in the countryside.

Area 551,500sq km (219,930sq miles)
Government Multiparty republic
Independence 1789
Territories Corsica, French Guiana, Guadeloupe, Martinique, Reunion, Mayotte, St. Pierre & Miquelon, Bassas da India, Clipperton Island, Europa Island, French Polynesia, French Southern and Antarctic Lands, Juan de Nova Island, New Caledonia, Glorioso Islands, Tromelin Island, Wallis, Futuna
Currency Franc
Population 58,000,000
Density 105 per sq km (272 per sq mile)
Official Language French
Major Religions Roman Catholic 90%, other 10%

EIFFEL TOWER
A.G. Eiffel (1832–1923) designed this famous tower. It is 300m (984ft) high and was built for the Paris World Exposition of 1889.

WEATHER FACTS

39°C (102°F) 444mm (17.4in) -17°C (1°F)
23°C (73°F) 6°C (42°F)

LAND PROFILE
The majority of land is farmed and there are extensive forests.

%
1
3
36
60

LIFESTYLE FACTS
• France is the world's second biggest producer of cheese and curd. There is a different cheese for every single day of the year.

• Cycle races are a top spectator sport in France. The Tour de France is the world's longest cycle race. It covers 3,720km (2,312 miles) and takes three weeks. The first race was held in 1913.

FASTEST TRAIN
France holds the record for the fastest train, the TGV. It reached 515.3km/h (320.1mph) in 1990. The fastest recorded journey is between Paris and Mâcon, covered at an average speed of 217km/h (135mph).

100 French francs

LANGUAGE
A traditional greeting in French is *bonjour*.

PARIS, CITY OF CULTURE
Paris is a very successful mix of different architectural styles, from world-famous historic monuments to ultra-modern glass-and-steel structures.

The *Grand Louvre* museum, France's second most visited monument, houses the world-famous *Mona Lisa*. The glass pyramid over the entrance was built in 1989.

The *Centre Georges Pompidou*, which contains France's National Museum of Modern Art, is the most visited public building in the country. The centre was opened in 1977.

BEST CELLAR
France, along with Italy, is the world's leading wine producer. In 1997, wine production totalled 7,400,000,000 bottles: enough for a bottle taller than the Statue of Liberty.

MONACO

THE TINY COUNTRY of Monaco, which has an orchestra larger than its army, is the most densely populated country in Europe.

Area 1.95sq km (0.75sq mile)
Government Constitutional monarchy
Independence 1861, state established
Currency French franc
Population 31,000
Density 15,897 per sq km (41,332 per sq mile)
Official Language French
Major Religions Roman Catholic 95%, other 5%

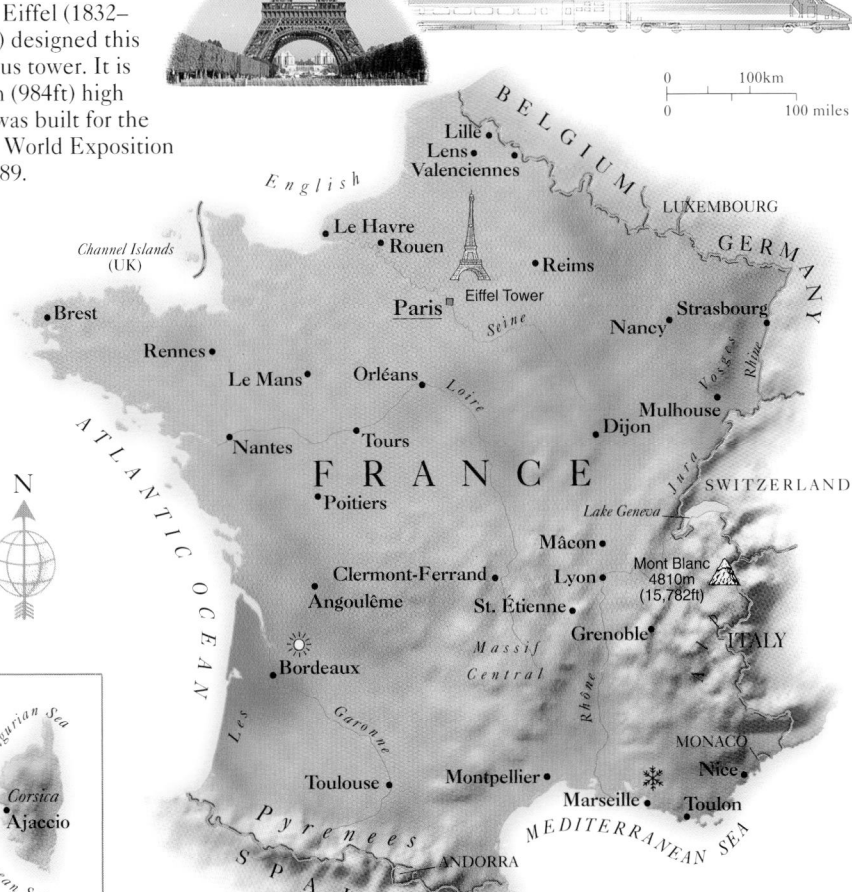

BELGIUM
English
Channel Islands (UK)
LUXEMBOURG
GERMANY
Lille
Lens
Valenciennes
Le Havre
Rouen
Reims
Brest
Paris
Eiffel Tower
Strasbourg
Nancy
Seine
Rennes
Le Mans
Orléans
Loire
Nantes
Tours
FRANCE
Poitiers
Dijon
Mulhouse
SWITZERLAND
Lake Geneva
Mâcon
Mont Blanc 4810m (15,782ft)
Clermont-Ferrand
Lyon
Angoulême
St. Étienne
Grenoble
ITALY
Bordeaux
Massif Central
Rhône
MONACO
Nice
Toulouse
Montpellier
Marseille
Toulon
MEDITERRANEAN SEA
Pyrenees
SPAIN
ANDORRA
ATLANTIC OCEAN
N
Ligurian Sea
Corsica
Ajaccio
Mediterranean Sea
0 100km
0 100 miles

GERMANY

THE FEDERAL REPUBLIC of Germany holds a key position in Central Europe. A divided country for 41 years, reunification with the German Democratic Republic took place on 3 October 1990.

Area 356,910sq km
(137,800sq miles)
Government Multiparty republic
Reunification 3 October 1990
◎ **Currency** Mark
Population 81,600,000
Density 233 per sq km
(604 per sq mile)
Official Language German
Major Religions Protestant 45%, Roman Catholic 37%, other 18%

WEATHER FACTS

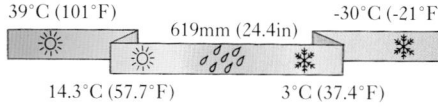
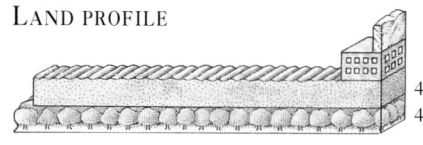

39°C (101°F)   619mm (24.4in)   -30°C (-21°F)
14.3°C (57.7°F)   3°C (37.4°F)

LAND PROFILE

%
0.5
5.5
45.5
48.5

BRANDENBURG GATE
From 1961, this last town gateway was blocked, separating East Berlin from West Berlin. On 22 December 1989, the gate was re-opened.

10 Deutschmark

LANGUAGE
A traditional greeting in German is *Guten Tag*.

LIFESTYLE FACTS
• West Germany's football team won the World Cup championship three times: Berne in 1954, Munich in 1974, and Rome in 1990.

• 40 million Germans travel abroad for their holidays every year: this represent 51% of the population.

• The Federal Republic is the third largest producer of cars in the world, after Japan and the United States. In 1991, 4.6 million cars were produced, and 2.2 million of these were exported.

• Wurst (sausage) is a traditional and popular German food. There are about 1,500 varieties.

FAIRS AND FESTIVALS

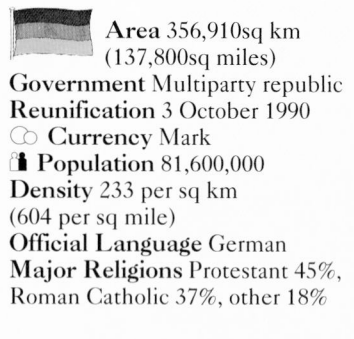

• Frankfurt Book Fair, held every October, attracts publishers and booksellers from all over the world. In 1996, there were 274,000 visitors and 6,819 exhibitors.

FAIRYTALE CASTLE
Neuschwanstein Castle, one of the most fantastic, fairytale castles in the world, was dreamed up by King Ludwig II of Bavaria (1845–86). Sadly, Ludwig, who had a two-storey room built for his gold and ivory throne, died before the castle was completed.

• Since 1810, Europe's best-known beer festival has been held at Munich. In 1993, visitors drank 4.8 million litres of beer.

• Each spring, the world's biggest trade fair is held in Hanover. Exhibitors from 50 countries display the latest industrial technology.

• Cologne carnival is a five-day festival held seven weeks before Easter. The most important day is Rose Monday, when chocolates and gifts are thrown to the crowd from carnival processions.

BAYREUTH
Each year, the Bavarian city of Bayreuth hosts a festival in honour of the famous composer Richard Wagner (1813–83). His operas are staged in the purpose-built *Festspielhaus* (Festival Theatre).

Wagner's Opera
Lohengrin

TOP GERMAN CAR MANUFACTURERS (1997)

Manufacturer	Number of cars produced
Volkswagen	1,188,601
Opel	1,040,298
Ford	754,140
Mercedes-Benz	696,445
BMW	599,493
Audi	557,777

DENMARK

NORTH SEA
North Frisian Is.
East Frisian Is.

BALTIC SEA

NETHERLANDS

Hamburg
Bremen
Oderhaff
Elbe
Oder

Hanover
Berlin
Brandenburg Gate

GERMANY

Harz Mts.
Brocken 1,142m (3,747ft)
Leipzig

BELGIUM
LUX.
Duisburg
Essen • Dortmund
Düsseldorf

Thuringian Forest

Ore Mts.

Cologne
Bonn
Wasser Kuppe 950m (3,117ft)
Grosser Beerberg 982m (3,222ft)

CZECH. REP.

Frankfurt
Bayreuth

Main

Nuremberg

Franconian Jura
Bohemian Forest

FRANCE
Rhine
Black Forest
Stuttgart
Danube
Swabian Jura

Munich
AUSTRIA

Freiburg im Breisgau
Lake Constance
Neuschwanstein
Rhine

Bavarian Alps
Zugspitze 2,963m (9,271ft)

SWITZERLAND

N

0   150km
0   100 miles

SWITZERLAND

JUST ONE-QUARTER of Switzerland is habitable: the remaining land consists of mountains, forests, and ice. Every minute, 20 to 30 square metres of Swiss land are built on.

Area 41,290sq km (15,940sq miles)
Government Federal republic
Independence 1648, from the Holy Roman Empire
Currency Swiss franc
Population 7,200,000
Density 181 per sq km (469 per sq mile)
Official Languages German, French, Italian
Major Religions Roman Catholic 48%, Protestant 44%, other 8%

JET D'EAU
The water from the jet d'eau, the famous fountain situated in the centre of Geneva's harbour, gushes 140 metres (460ft) in the air.

Jet d'eau

WEATHER FACTS
38°C (100°F)   444mm (17.5in)   -30°C (-23°F)
23°C (73.4°F)   6°C (42.8°F)

LAND PROFILE
%
2
21
34.5
42.5

LIFESTYLE FACTS
• The Swiss are famous bankers, and their banks attract money from investors all over the world. There is a bank for every 1,600 Swiss people.

• Watches are Switzerland's best-known export. The watchmaking centre in Neuchâtel developed both the quartz watch and the atomic clock.

• The surplus of home-produced milk led to two important Swiss inventions, baby food and condensed milk. Other Swiss milk products are cheese and fine chocolate.

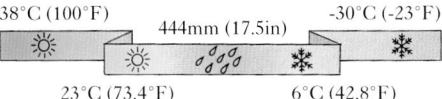
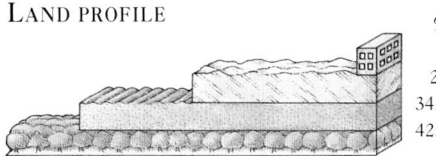
50 Swiss francs

LANGUAGE
A traditional greeting in French is *Bonjour*; in German *Guten Tag*; in Italian *Buongiorno*.

TOP CHOCOLATE EATERS		
Country	Amount per person kg	lb
Switzerland	10.18	22.45
Norway	10.12	22.31
Belgium	10.06	22.18

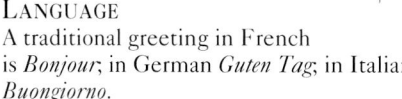

N

0   100km
0   60 miles

TOP SKI RESORTS
Swiss   Austria

LANDMARK
St. Stephan's Cathedral, more than 600 years old, is one of Vienna's most famous buildings.

AUSTRIA

AUSTRIA'S FINE CITIES and beautiful, mountainous landscape – 40 per cent of the land lies at an altitude of more than 1,000 metres – attract about 18 million visitors a year.

Area 83,850sq km (32,375sq miles)
Government Multiparty republic
Independence 1918, Republic declared
Currency Schilling
Population 8,000,000
Density 97 per sq km (251 per sq mile)
Official Language German
Major Religions Roman Catholic 85%, Evangelical 6%, other 9%

100 Austrian schillings

LANGUAGE
A traditional greeting in German is *Guten Tag*.

WEATHER FACTS
38°C (100.4°F)   640mm (25.2in)   -27°C (-16.6°F)
19.3°C (66.7°F)   0°C (32°F)

LAND PROFILE
Almost two-thirds of the land is farmed.
%
1
4
30
65

LIFESTYLE FACTS
• Many great composers were Austrian; they include Mozart (1756–91), Haydn (1732–1809), Schubert (1797–1828), and Johann Strauss (1825–99), who composed the famous Viennese waltz, *The Blue Danube*.

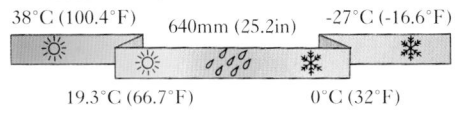

• Skiing is Austria's national sport. The first ski school was set up at St. Anton am Arlberg, and Austrian Annemarie Moser-Proll (b. 1953) is a celebrated woman skier.

LIECHTENSTEIN

THIS TINY COUNTRY is ruled by a prince. Liechtenstein is famous for its royal art collection and its postage stamps. One of the principal exports is false teeth.

Area 160sq km (62sq miles)
Government Constitutional monarchy
Independence 1866, from the German Confederation
Currency Swiss franc
Population 30,630
Density 191 per sq km (495 per sq mile)
Official Language German

ITALY

THIS IMPORTANT INDUSTRIAL nation has most of its factories as well as rich farmland concentrated in the north. The south is mountainous and farmers grow olives, and grapes for making wine. Italy includes the large islands of Sicily and Sardinia.

Area 301,270sq km (116,320sq miles)
Government Multiparty republic
Republic Declared in 1948
Currency Lira
Population 57,200,000
Density 195 per sq km (505 per sq mile)
Official Language Italian
✝ **Major Religions** Roman Catholic 99%, other 1%

WEATHER FACTS

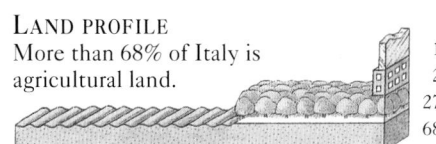

42°C (107.6°F)   744mm (29in)   -11°C (13°F)
19°C (66.2°F)   12.3°C (54.1°F)

LAND PROFILE

More than 68% of Italy is agricultural land.

%
1.5
2.5
27.5
68.5

LIFESTYLE FACTS

• The Palio of Siena is a twice yearly bareback horse race round the city's main square. The palio is the silk banner awarded to the winner.

• The most popular resort is Venice, with more than 7.5 million tourists a year. The city has 118 islands, 177 canals, and 400 bridges.

VATICAN CITY

• The Vatican City in Rome is the world's smallest independent state. It is the world centre for the Roman Catholic religion and its ruler is the pope.

• There has been a pope for more than 1,900 years – since the time of St. Peter, who was the first pope.

• St. Peter's is the largest and most important cathedral in the Christian world, first built by the Roman Emperor Constantine in about A.D.330.

TOWER OF PISA

The leaning tower of Pisa is made of white marble and was built between 1174 and 1350. It is 54m (177ft) tall and leans at an angle of 11.3 degrees from the vertical.

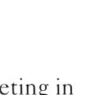

1,000 lira

LANGUAGE

A traditional greeting in Italian is *buongiorno*.

MAJOR TOURIST ATTRACTIONS	
Location	People
Excavations, Pompeii	1,296,633
Uffizi Gallery, Florence	1,020,972
Franciscan Abbey, Cassino	956,200
Pantheon, Rome	857,585
Galleria dell'Accademia, Florence	687,428
The Forum, Rome	651,183

FOOD FACTS

• There are more than 600 different types of pasta.

• More than 4 million tonnes of tomatoes are grown in Italy every year. Many are used to make sauces for pasta dishes.

• Genuine mozzarella cheese is made from the milk of the water buffalo. It is made fresh daily in many parts of Italy.

SAN MARINO

THE TINY REPUBLIC of San Marino is located in the mountains of central Italy. Tourism accounts for 60 per cent of the country's income.

Area 61sq km (24sq miles)
Independence 1631, recognition as a city state
Currency Italian lira
Population 24,000
Official Language Italian

MALTA

MALTA IS AN island country in the Mediterranean. The climate is warm but there are no rivers and little rain to provide water for crops.

Area 320sq km (124sq miles)
Independence 1964, from Britain
Currency Maltese lira
Population 400,000
Official Languages English, Maltese

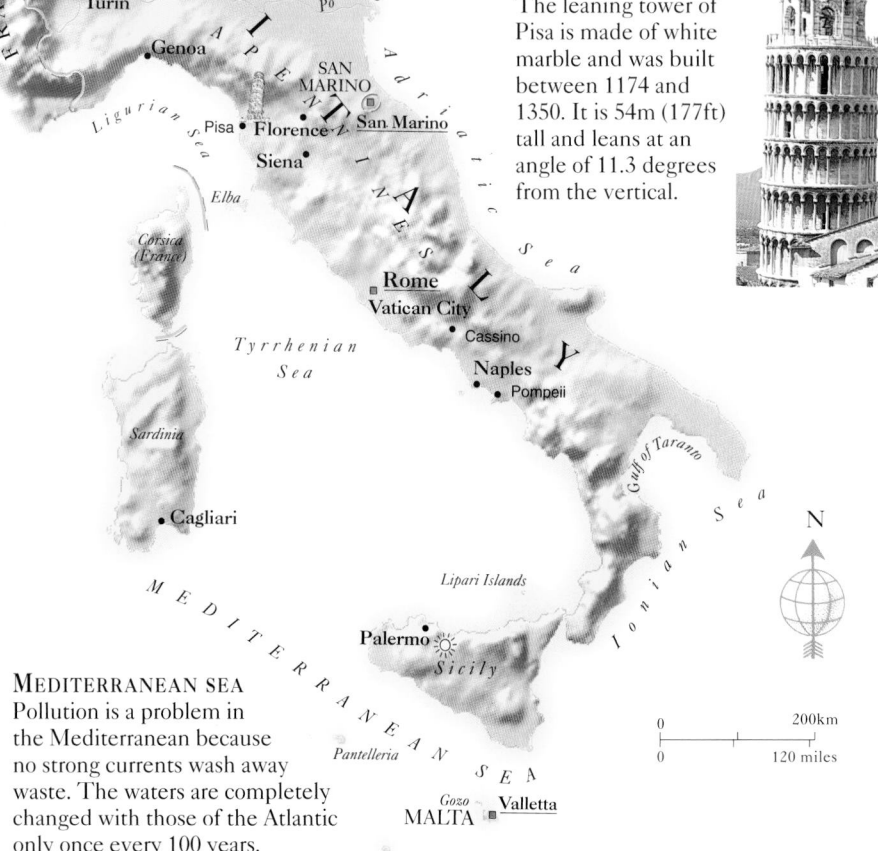

AUSTRIA
SWITZERLAND
SLOVENIA
ALPS
Dolomites
Mont Blanc 4,807m (15,771ft)
Milan
Lake Garda
Venice
Gulf of Venice
Turin
Po
FRANCE
Genoa
Ligurian Sea
SAN MARINO
Pisa
Florence
San Marino
Siena
Adriatic Sea
Elba
Corsica (France)
APENNINES
ITALY
Rome
Vatican City
Tyrrhenian Sea
Cassino
Naples
Pompeii
Sardinia
Gulf of Taranto
Cagliari
Ionian Sea
N
Lipari Islands
MEDITERRANEAN
Palermo
Sicily
Pantelleria
SEA
Gozo   Valletta
MALTA
Pelagie Islands

0   200km
0   120 miles

MEDITERRANEAN SEA

Pollution is a problem in the Mediterranean because no strong currents wash away waste. The waters are completely changed with those of the Atlantic only once every 100 years.

FINLAND

A COUNTRY WITH 187,888 lakes, Finland also has vast forests of pine and spruce. Timber, used to make paper and furniture, provides most of the wealth of the country. Finland also includes part of Lapland.

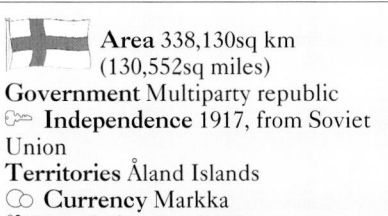

Area 338,130sq km (130,552sq miles)
Government Multiparty republic
Independence 1917, from Soviet Union
Territories Åland Islands
Currency Markka
Population 5,100,000
Density 17 per sq km (44 per sq mile)
Official Languages Finnish, Swedish
Major Religions Lutheran 89%, Finnish Orthodox 1%, other 10%

LIFESTYLE FACTS

• Finnish women were the first in Europe to get the vote, in 1906.

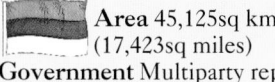

• The world's longest cross-country ski race is held in March each year. Skiers race from Kuusamo on the Russian border to Tornio on the Swedish border, across southern Lapland.

• Savonlinna Opera Festival is the most successful cultural event in Finland. It was founded in 1912 by opera singer Aino Ackte and is held in the courtyard of the medieval Olavinlinna Castle.

ESTONIA

MUCH OF ESTONIA is flat countryside with fields and forests, marshes and lakes. The main industries include engineering and textiles.

Area 45,125sq km (17,423sq miles)
Government Multiparty republic
Independence 1991, from Soviet Union
Currency Kroon
Population 1,600,000
Density 37 per sq km (86 per sq mile)
Official Language Estonian
Major Religions No figures available. Most people Evangelical Lutheran, also Russian Orthodox

HELPING HANDS

In 1989, the Estonians formed a chain across their land, and into Latvia and Lithuania. The 644-km (400-mile) link symbolized their bid for freedom from the Soviet Union.

WEATHER FACTS

33°C (91.4°F)   688mm (27in)   -41°C (-43°F)

20.3°C (68.5°F)   -2.6°C (27.3°F)

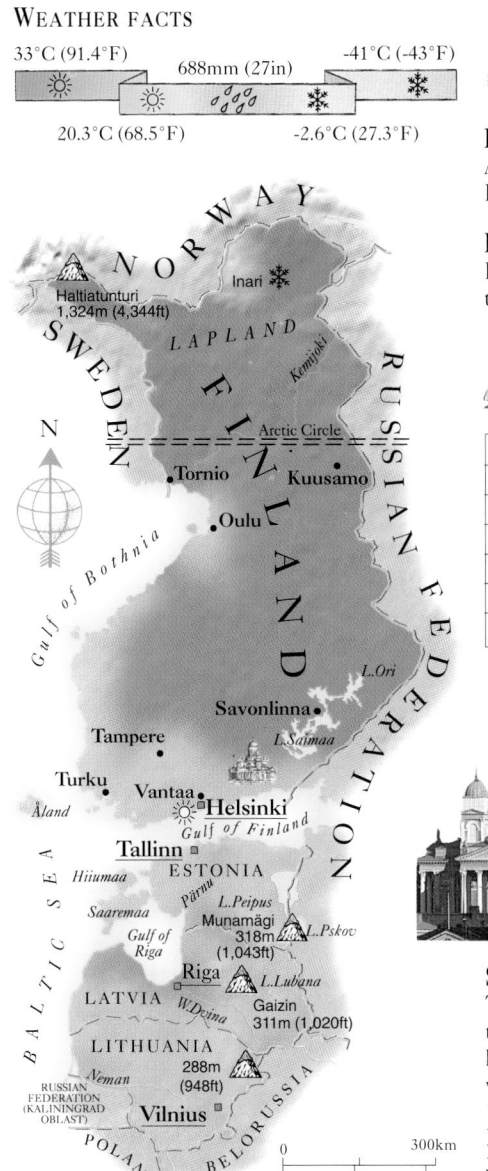

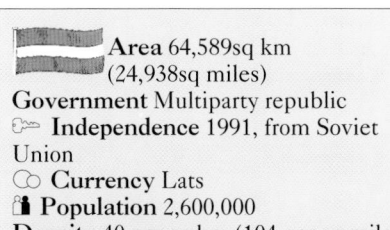

LATVIA

A MIXTURE OF forested hills and plains, Latvia is often called Amberland because so much amber can be found on its Baltic shore.

Area 64,589sq km (24,938sq miles)
Government Multiparty republic
Independence 1991, from Soviet Union
Currency Lats
Population 2,600,000
Density 40 per sq km (104 per sq mile)
Official Language Latvian
Major Religions No figures available. Predominantly Lutheran, also Roman Catholic and Russian Orthodox

100 markka

LANGUAGE

A traditional greeting in Finnish is *hyvää päivää*.

LAND PROFILE

Forests cover 80% of the total area of Finland.

%
0.25
0.5
1.5
7.5
10.25
80

FINNISH TIMBER EXPORTS (1997)	
Europe	78%
Asia	10%
North America	5%
Africa	3%
South America	2%
Oceania	2%

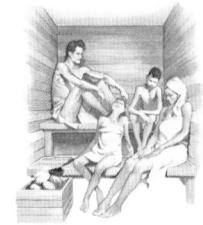

HELSINKI CATHEDRAL

This fine cathedral was designed in the 19th century by architect Carl Engel. It was laid out in its present form of a Greek cross with a central tower.

SAUNA BOX

The sauna is a national tradition and Finns have at least one a week. There are about 1.4 million saunas in Finland: one for every 3.5 people.

LITHUANIA

MOST OF LITHUANIA is a low-lying plain with many small lakes formed by glaciers. Winter temperatures can fall below freezing for four months.

Area 65,200sq km (25,174sq miles)
Government Multiparty republic
Independence 1991, from Soviet Union
Currency Litas
Population 3,700,000
Density 57 per sq km (148 per sq mile)
Official Language Lithuanian
Major Religions No figures available. Predominantly Roman Catholic, also Evangelical Lutheran and Reformist

POLAND

POLAND IS AN industrial country rich in coal and copper. It has large textile, iron, steel, and shipbuilding industries. Much of the landscape is flat and about one third of the people work on the land.

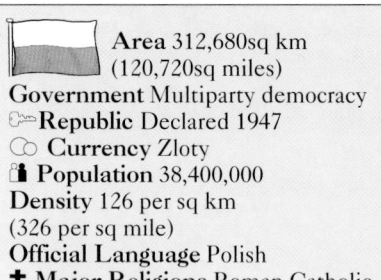

Area 312,680sq km (120,720sq miles)
Government Multiparty democracy
Republic Declared 1947
Currency Zloty
Population 38,400,000
Density 126 per sq km (326 per sq mile)
Official Language Polish
✝ **Major Religions** Roman Catholic 95%, other 5%

CZECH REPUBLIC

THE HOMELAND OF the Czechs was originally called Bohemia. Much of the country is flat farmland. Prague, the capital, has many churches with gilded roofs which gave the city the name *zlata Praha*, or golden Prague.

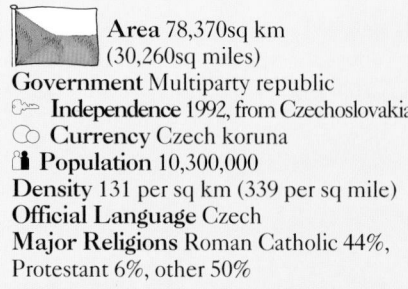

Area 78,370sq km (30,260sq miles)
Government Multiparty republic
Independence 1992, from Czechoslovakia
Currency Czech koruna
Population 10,300,000
Density 131 per sq km (339 per sq mile)
Official Language Czech
Major Religions Roman Catholic 44%, Protestant 6%, other 50%

SLOVAKIA

FORMERLY PART OF the kingdom of Hungary, Slovakia is a hilly country of thick forests dominated by the Carpathian Mountains. Bratislava, on the Danube, is the capital city and main export point.

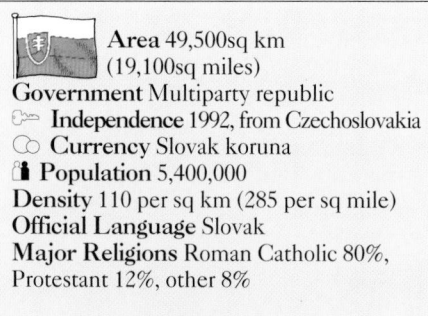

Area 49,500sq km (19,100sq miles)
Government Multiparty republic
Independence 1992, from Czechoslovakia
Currency Slovak koruna
Population 5,400,000
Density 110 per sq km (285 per sq mile)
Official Language Slovak
Major Religions Roman Catholic 80%, Protestant 12%, other 8%

WEATHER FACTS

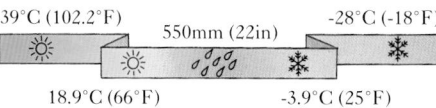

39°C (102.2°F)   550mm (22in)   -28°C (-18°F)

18.9°C (66°F)   -3.9°C (25°F)

LAND PROFILE

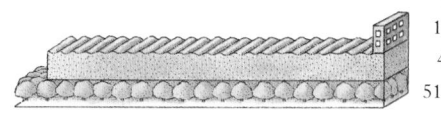

%
1.5
47
51.5

LIFESTYLE FACTS

• Poland has Europe's oldest operating salt mine at Wieliczka, near Kraków. The layers of salt go down to 327m (1,073ft).

• Education is compulsory between the ages of 7 and 18, and 98 per cent of Poles can read and write.

• Open-air museums, known as *skansens*, exhibit a selection of typical, old wooden buildings such as barns, churches, and windmills.

PRAGUE'S CLOCK

The astronomical clock in the Old Town Hall, Prague, was installed in 1410. The clock's interlocking circles show phases of the Sun and Moon. It has run non-stop since 1572.

100,000 zloty

LANGUAGE

A traditional greeting in Polish is *dzien dóbry*.

WAWEL CASTLE

Wawel Castle is built on a rocky embankment of the Vistula River in the old capital of Kraków. Many Polish kings are buried in the castle's underground crypts.

TRADITIONAL POLISH FOOD

Poland can be extremely cold, so many dishes are planned to be warm and filling.
Krupnik A thick soup made with barley or buckwheat. Also the name of a strong drink.
Pierozki Dumplings filled with meat, mushrooms, cooked cabbage or cheese.
Bigos A meat stew using wild boar, hare, or venison and *wiejska*, a Polish sausage.

Polish dumplings

UKRAINE

MUCH OF THE Ukraine consists of vast flat plains called steppes. Chief crops include winter wheat, maize, barley, sugar beet, and potatoes.

Area 603,700sq km (233,090sq miles)
Government Multiparty republic
Independence 1991, from USSR
Currency Karbovanets (temporary)
Population 51,400,000
Density 85 per sq km (220 per sq mile)
Official Language Ukrainian
Major Religions No figures available

UKRAINE CROPS (1998)
In thousand tonnes)

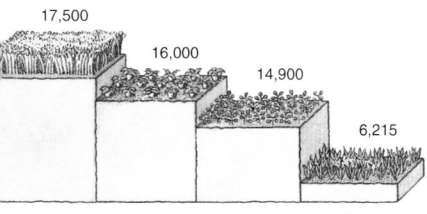

| 17,500 | 16,000 | 14,900 | 6,215 |
| Potatoes | Sugar beet | Wheat | Vegetables |

BISON
The Bialowieza Forest is the largest ancient forest in Europe. It is home to the last 500 or so remaining European bison. The bison is the biggest European mammal and can measure 2m (6.6ft).

Hand-carved wooden cross from Romania

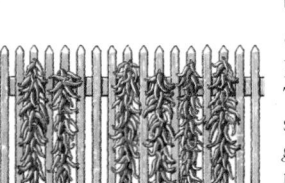

BELORUSSIA

AGRICULTURE IS THE main occupation in Belorussia, despite poor soil. The capital city, Minsk, produces agricultural machinery.

Area 207,600sq km (80,154sq miles)
Government Multiparty republic
Independence 1991, from USSR
Currency Belorussian rouble
Population 10,199,709
Density 50 per sq km (129 per sq mile)
Official Language Belorussian
Major Religions Russian Orthodox 60%, Roman Catholic 8%, other 32%

ROMANIA

FORESTS COVER ABOUT a quarter of Romania and timber is an important product. The River Danube is used for transport and as a source of hydroelectric power.

Area 237,500sq km (91,700sq miles)
Government Multiparty republic
Independence 1881, from Ottoman Empire
Currency Leu
Population 22,800,000
Density 99 per sq km (257 per sq mile)
Official Language Romanian
Major Religions Romanian Orthodox 70%, Roman Catholic 6%, Catholic Eastern Rite 3%, Protestant 6%, other 15%

FACTS ABOUT ROMANIA AND HUNGARY
• There are about 410,000 gypsies (or Romanies) in Romania. The gypsies are thought to have arrived from India (via the Middle East) in about the 5th century A.D.

• Transylvania, which means "beyond the forest", is an area of Romania where music and folk art remain untouched. This wayside cross shows the skill of the woodcarver.

• Sunflowers are grown in Hungary for the oil which is extracted from their seeds. The stems of sunflowers turn so that the flowers can always face towards the sun.

• Peppers are cultivated in Hungary and ground into the spice, paprika. The rose paprika of Hungary has a special sweet flavour and is used in stews such as *gulyas*, or goulash. Paprika is made from the pods of the pepper *Capsicum annuum*.

MOLDAVIA

WARM SUMMERS AND mild winters make Moldavia ideal for growing fruit, especially grapes. Moldavian people are Romanian in origin.

Area 33,700sq km (13,000sq miles)
Government Multiparty republic
Independence 1991, from USSR
Currency Moldavian leu
Population 4,400,000
Density 131 per sq km (339 per sq mile)
Official Language Romanian
Major Religions Romanian Orthodox 98%, other 2%

HUNGARY

HUNGARY HAS FERTILE soil and farmers grow wheat, sugar beet, and tobacco. The capital, Budapest, was originally Buda and Pest, two towns on either side of the River Danube.

Area 93,030sq km (35,919sq miles)
Government Multiparty republic
Independence 1918, after collapse of Austro-Hungarian monarchy
Currency Forint
Population 10,100,000
Density 109 per sq km (282 per sq mile)
Official Language Hungarian
Major Religions Roman Catholic 68%, Protestant 25%, other 7%

The Gellert Baths in Budapest

• Hungary is famous for its medicinal waters, and Budapest has at least 120 hot springs. Every day, about 70 million litres (15.4 million gallons) of water well up to the surface, allowing thousands of people to enjoy the healing baths.

• The River Danube rises in the Alps of Germany and flows through eight countries on its journey to the Black Sea. The Danube is also called the Donau, Danuj, Duna, Dunav, Dunarea, and Dunay.

BULGARIA

BULGARIA HAS HIGH mountains and more than 600 natural springs. Grapes grow abundantly on the fertile plains, making Bulgaria the world's fourth largest wine exporter.

Area 110,910sq km (42,822sq miles)
Government Multiparty republic
Republic declared 1946
Currency Lev
Population 8,800,000
Density 80 per sq km (207 per sq mile)
Official Language Bulgarian
Major Religions Bulgarian Orthodox (Christian) 85%, Muslim 13%, Jewish 1%, other 1%

LANDMARK
St. Alexander Nevsky Cathedral, Sofia, completed in 1912, was built in honour of the Russian soldiers who died in the 1877–78 Russo–Turkish War.

GREECE

MORE THAN 1,400 islands surround Greece's heavily indented coastline; only 154 are inhabited. Greece has the second largest fleet of merchant ships in the world.

Area 131,990sq km (50,961sq miles)
Government Multiparty republic
Independence 1829, from Ottoman Empire
Currency Drachma
Population 10,500,000
Density 80 per sq km (207 per sq mile)
Official Language Greek
Major Religions Greek Orthodox (Christian) 98%, Muslim 1%, other 1%

LAND PROFILE
Even though 80% of Greece is mountainous, almost two-thirds of the land is used for farming and grazing.

5,000 drachmas

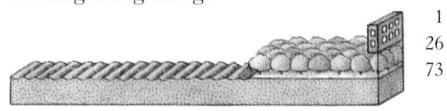

%
1
26
73

WEATHER FACTS
40.6°C (104°F)   635mm (25in)   -25°C (-13°F)
20°C (69°F)   -2.2°C (28°F)

LIFESTYLE FACTS
• Rose oil is one of the most precious ingredients of perfume. Bulgaria is the major supplier of rose oil and has the world's largest rose gardens at Kazanluk.

• Bulgarians nod their heads when they mean "no" and shake them when they mean "yes".

• In Gabrovo, Bulgaria, there is a national museum devoted entirely to humour called The House of Humour and Satire.

OLIVE
The national symbol of Greece is the olive branch.

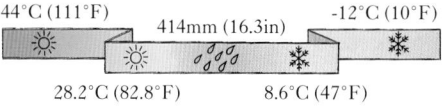

LANGUAGE
A traditional greeting in Greek is *kalimera*. καΛημερα

WEATHER FACTS
44°C (111°F)   414mm (16.3in)   -12°C (10°F)
28.2°C (82.8°F)   8.6°C (47°F)

GREEK MUSIC
One of the most important instruments in traditional Greek music is the bouzouki, which has metal strings. Traditional music is played at religious festivals and special occasions such as weddings.

LANGUAGE
A traditional greeting in Bulgarian is *dobró útro*.

LAND PROFILE
Bulgaria has extensive forests, and the land is mainly used for farming.

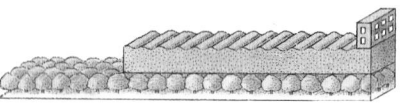

9
3
5

LION
The lion is the national symbol of Bulgaria and is depicted on its coat of arms.

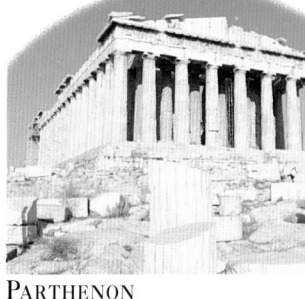

PARTHENON
The Parthenon is a world-famous classical Greek temple dedicated to the goddess of Athens, Athena. It sits on a hill in Athens called the Acropolis, and was constructed between 447 and 432 B.C.

TURKEY

TURKEY LIES IN both Europe and Asia. The two continents are separated by the Bosphorus, site of the beautiful city of Istanbul, and one of the world's busiest waterways.

Area 779,450sq km (300,950sq miles)
Government Multiparty republic
Republic declared 1923
Currency Turkish lira
Population 61,000,000
Density 80 per sq km (207 per sq mile)
Official Language Turkish
Major Religions Muslim 99%, Orthodox Christian, Roman Catholic, Protestant, Jewish 1%

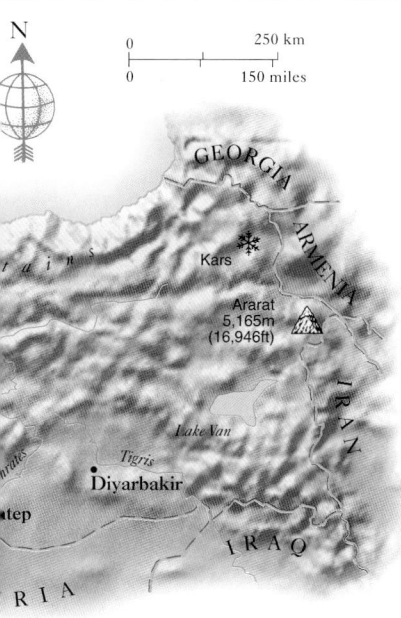

N

0 — 250 km
0 — 150 miles

GEORGIA
ARMENIA
Kars
Ararat
5,165m
(16,946ft)
IRAN
Lake Van
Tigris
Diyarbakir
IRAQ
tep
RIA

LIFESTYLE FACTS
- Greece, with its many mountains, has the greatest number of hill-farms in Europe. Goats are ideally suited to the terrain.

- In summer the flat roofs of houses on Greek islands are used for drying fruit and, in winter, for collecting rainwater.

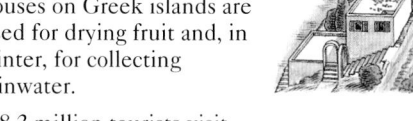

- 8.2 million tourists visit Greece every year, drawn there by its ancient sites and sunny beaches.

TOP GREEK TOURIST RESORTS (1997)

Resort	Visitor-nights
Crete	10,619,000
Rhodes	8,238,000
Athens	3,438,000
Corfu	2,819,000

Source: Greek National Tourism Office

WEATHER FACTS

43°C (109°F)   367mm (14.4in)   -36°C (-33°F)

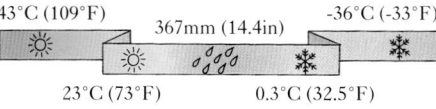

23°C (73°F)   0.3°C (32.5°F)

LAND PROFILE

Land use in Turkey is predominantly agricultural.

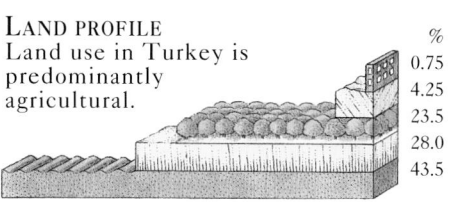

%
0.75
4.25
23.5
28.0
43.5

LIFESTYLE FACTS

- Grapes, one of the world's oldest crops, were first grown in Anatolia. From here they spread to other parts of the world.

- Turkey's national sport is wrestling. *Kirkpinar*, the feast of wrestling, has been held each spring for 626 years.

PAMUKKALE

Pamukkale, meaning "cotton castle", is a brilliant-white hillside of cascading thermal pools fringed with stalactites. People have bathed in the warm, healing waters since Roman times.

LANGUAGE

A traditional greeting in Turkish is *iyi günler*.

TURKISH CARPETS

Turkey produces about 44 million sq m (474 million sq ft) of carpets each year. There are about 400 types of carpet, produced in centres such as Hereke, Malatya, Konya, and Kayseri.

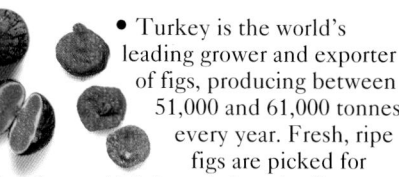

- Turkey is the world's leading grower and exporter of figs, producing between 51,000 and 61,000 tonnes every year. Fresh, ripe figs are picked for eating from mid-July, or left to dry first on the tree branches, and then for a further two to four days in the hot sun.

TULIP

Turkey's national symbol is the tulip.

ALBANIA

MOST ALBANIANS live in remote mountain villages in this tiny, mountainous country. Albania's main crops are wheat, barley, tobacco, potatoes, and fruit.

Area 28,750sq km (11,100sq miles)
Government Multiparty republic
Independence 1912, from Turkey
Currency Lek
Population 3,400,000
Density 124 per sq km (321 per sq mile)
Official Language Albanian
Major Religions Muslim 70%, Greek Orthodox 20%, Roman Catholic 10%

LIFESTYLE FACTS

- Since World War II, Albania has had the fastest-growing population in Europe. Good health care services for mother and child receive the highest priority from the government.

- More than half of the Albanian people earn their living from farming.

- In 1992, there were only about 6,000 telephones in the whole of Albania – one for every 550 people.

CYPRUS

CYPRUS IS THE LARGEST island in the eastern Mediterranean. It has both Greek and Turkish communities and, since 1974, the island has been split into two parts.

Area 9,251sq km (3,572sq miles)
Government Multiparty republic
Independence 1960, from Britain
Currency Cyprus pound/Turkish lira
Population 700,000
Density 77 per sq km (197 per sq mile)
Official Languages Greek and Turkish
Major Religions Greek Orthodox (Christian) 77%, Muslim 18%, other 5%

LIFESTYLE FACTS

- The ancient monuments of Cyprus are so important that some have been added to the UNESCO World Cultural Heritage list.

- Clothing, footwear, potatoes, grapes, and citrus fruit are Cyprus' main exports.

- The moufflon *(Ovis musimon)*, a reddish-brown wild sheep, is native to Cyprus. It is the smallest wild sheep, reaching a height of just 74cm (29in).

SLOVENIA

SLOVENIA IS AN industrialized country with supplies of iron and steel. It is also a major producer of mercury, which is used in thermometers.

Area 20,250sq km (7,820sq miles)
Government Multiparty democracy
Currency Tolar
Population 1,900,000
Density 94 per sq km (244 per sq mile)
Official Language Slovene
Major Religions Roman Catholic 96%, other 4%

CROATIA

PART OF CROATIA runs along the coast of the Adriatic Sea, and was once a popular tourist destination. Supplies of limestone around Split help support the concrete industry.

Area 56,540sq km (21,830sq miles)
Government Multiparty democracy
Currency Kuna
Population 4,500,000
Density 80 per sq km (207 per sq mile)
Official Language Croatian
† Major Religions Roman Catholic 77%, Orthodox 11%, Muslim 1%, other 11%

LANGUAGE
A traditional greeting in Serbo-Croat is *dobró utro*.

REGIONAL LIFESTYLE FACTS

- The Dalmatian dog is named after the coastal region of Dalmatia in Croatia, which was its first known home.
- Walnuts grow well in the warm summers and well-drained soils of Yugoslavia.
- Dubrovnik, a city on Croatia's Adriatic coast, is famous for its traditional costumes of white dresses, embroidered blouses, and waistcoats.
- The picturesque city of Ljubljana is surrounded by mountains. Dominated by a medieval fortress, the city has an opera house, an art gallery, and a museum.

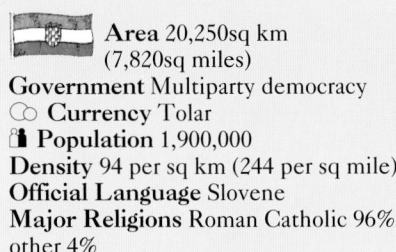

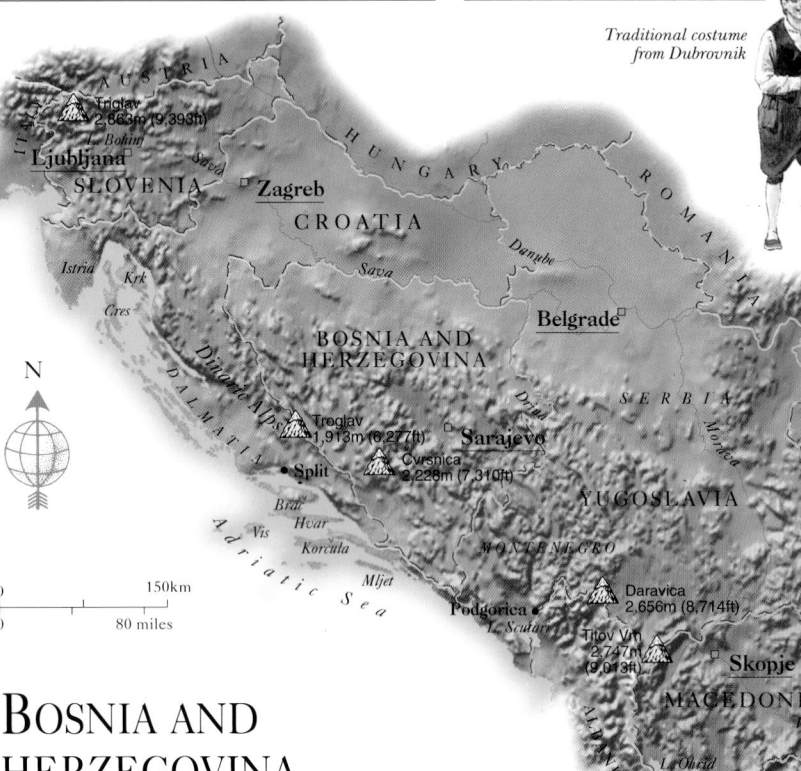

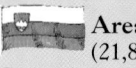
Traditional costume from Dubrovnik

YUGOSLAVIA

MADE UP OF the republics of Serbia and Montenegro, Yugoslavia is mountainous in the south, while the north is flat farmland. The capital, Belgrade, lies on the River Danube.

Area 102,173sq km (39,449sq miles)
Government Presidential republic
Currency Dinar
Population 10,580,892
Density 104 per sq km (269 per sq mile)
Official Language Serbian
Major Religions Christian 65%, Muslim 19%, other 16%

MACEDONIA

ONCE PART OF YUGOSLAVIA, Macedonia is a mountainous region. Farmers grow wheat, millet, and barley in the upland valleys. Tobacco is the main crop grown for export.

Area 25,715sq km (9,929sq miles)
Government Parliamentary republic
Currency Denar
Population 1,900,000
Density 74 per sq km (192 per sq mile)
Official Language Macedonian
Major Religions Christian 64.5%, Muslim 21%, other 14.5%

BOSNIA AND HERZEGOVINA

MINING FOR MINERALS, such as iron, copper, and silver, is an important part of the country's economy. Farmers grow olives, pomegranates, figs, rice, and tobacco.

Area 51,130sq km (19,741sq miles)
Government Parliamentary republic
Currency Bosnian dinar
Population 3,500,000
Density 68 per sq km (176 per sq mile)
Official Language Serbo-Croat
Major Religions Muslim 40%, Orthodox Catholic 31%, other 29%

CIVIL WAR
In 1990, Yugoslavia began to break up into independent countries. Serbia resisted this process, and in 1991 fighting broke out in Slovenia, Croatia, and Bosnia and Herzegovina. In 1995 the Dayton agreement separated the country into a Serb republic and a federation of Muslims and Croats.

The war-torn city of Sarajevo

GEORGIA

MOST OF GEORGIA is mountainous. The Black Sea coast is popular with tourists. The country has a humid climate that is ideal for growing tea and citrus fruits.

Area 69,700sq km (26,911sq miles)
Government Republic
Independence 1991, from Soviet Union
Currency Coupons
Population 5,500,000
Official Language Georgian
Major Religions Georgian Orthodox 70%, Russian Orthodox 10%, other 20%

N

0 — 150km
0 — 80 miles

LIFESTYLE FACTS

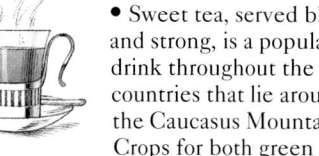

- Vines thrive on the warm, sunny hills of eastern Georgia, where wine and brandy are produced.
- Visitors are attracted to Georgia's health spas, waterfalls, and natural caves.

THE BLACK SEA
Tourism is a major part of the Georgian economy. Many resorts and spas, with beaches and forests, attract tourists to the coast of the Black Sea.

The Black Sea resort of Bat'umi

- Sweet tea, served black and strong, is a popular drink throughout the countries that lie around the Caucasus Mountains. Crops for both green and black teas are grown on large plantations in Georgia.

LANGUAGE
A traditional greeting in Georgian is *garmardzobat*.

TEXTILES
Georgia is famous for its silk and textiles. Brightly patterned cloth is woven with gold and silver thread. The cloth is often worn as a headscarf.

ARMENIA

ARMENIA IS A mainly mountainous country, and most people live in the foothills or around the Ararat Plain. Crops include orchard fruits such as peaches, apricots, and cherries.

Area 29,000sq km (11,505sq miles)
Government Multiparty republic
Independence 1991, from Soviet Union
Currency Dram
Population 3,600,000
Official Language Armenian
Major Religions Armenian Apostolic 90%, other 10%

LIFESTYLE FACTS

- Armenia grows rare plants used in perfumery and medicine, including geranium, rose, peppermint, cinchona bark, and basma.
- Lake Sevan is a major recreation area and offers windsurfing, sailing, swimming, and water skiing.

MAIN AGRICULTURAL PRODUCTS (1998)

Product	Amount (thousand tonnes)
Vegetables	452
Potatoes	425
Fruit	295
Wheat	165
Grapes	150
Meat	42

AZERBAIJAN

OIL AND NATURAL gas are the most important products in Azerbaijan and Baku, the capital, is the major industrial centre. Fruit, walnuts, and hazelnuts are valuable export crops.

Area 86,600sq km (33,436sq miles)
Government Multiparty republic
Independence 1991, from Soviet Union
Currency Manat
Population 7,600,000
Official Language Azerbaijani
Major Religions Muslim 83%, Armenian Apostolic and Russian Orthodox 17%

LIFESTYLE FACTS

- In the warm climate around Länkäran, farmers grow oranges, lemons, and figs.
- Light industry in Azerbaijan includes cotton and woollen goods, footwear, traditional household items, and souvenirs.

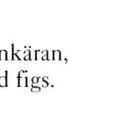

WILDLIFE FACTS

- The mountains and forests of Azerbaijan are home to a variety of wildlife, including wild boar, brown bears, European bison, chamois, and leopards, although the leopard is now very rare.

Chamois

- The mild winters attract many birds to the coast of the Caspian Sea. A reservation provides a seasonal resting place for flamingoes, swans, pelicans, herons, and buzzards.

Pelican

- Musical tradition is strong in Azerbaijan. The music of the *ashugs*, who improvise songs to their own accompaniment on a stringed instrument called a *kobuz*, is extremely popular.
- Almost 90% of Azerbaijan's electricity is produced at hydroelectric power stations throughout the country.

Map labels

RUSSIAN FEDERATION
Caucasus Mountains
Shkara 5,202m (17,068ft)
Bazar-Dyuzi 4,480m (14,699ft)
Black Sea
GEORGIA
Tbilisi
Bat'umi
Kura
L. Paravani
L. Adzhinour
Caspian Sea
Baku
TURKEY
Aragats 4,090m (13,419ft)
L. Sevan
AZERBAIJAN
Razdan
Yerevan
ARMENIA
Ararat Plain
Kura
AZERBAIJAN
Naxçivan
Aras
Länkäran
IRAN

RUSSIAN FEDERATION

THE LARGEST COUNTRY in the world, the Russian Federation stretches across two continents – Europe and Asia – that are separated by the Ural Mountains. Most people live in the western third of the country.

Area 17,075,400sq km (6,592,800sq miles)
Government Presidential republic
Independence 1991, from the former Soviet Union
Currency Rouble
Population 147,021,869
Density 9 per sq km (23 per sq mile)
Official Language Russian
Major Religions Russian Orthodox 80%, others (including Jewish and Muslim) 20%

WEATHER FACTS

39°C (102°F)   575mm (22.6in)   -68°C (-90°F)

18.9°C (66°F)   -9°C (16°F)

LAND PROFILE
Half the land in the Russian Federation is covered in forest.

%
0.5
2
6
10
13
18.5
50

ST. BASIL'S CATHEDRAL
The 16th-century St. Basil's Cathedral in Moscow is a magnificent example of old Russian architecture. It is situated within the Kremlin, the original fortress at the historic heart of the city. The cathedral was completed in 1560 and has nine great domes. It is now open as a museum.

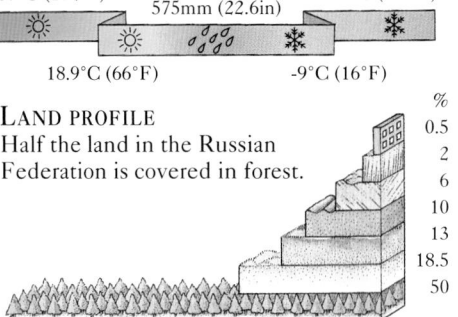

St. Basil's was built on the orders of Tsar Ivan IV the Terrible in gratitude for his military victories.

LANGUAGE
A traditional greeting in Russian is *zdravstvuyitye.*
Здравствуйте

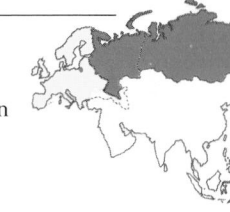

NATIONAL ANIMAL
The brown bear *(Ursus arctos)* is the national symbol of Russia. In folklore it is linked with kindness and wisdom. Bears eat fruits, berries, and bulbs that they dig up with their claws.

(map labels: Barents Sea; Arctic Circle; NORWAY; FINLAND; ESTONIA; LATVIA; LITHUANIA; RUSSIAN FED.; BELORUSSIA; UKRAINE; St. Petersburg; Moscow; Nizhniy Novgorod; Chelyabi; KAZA; Astrakhan; Black Sea; Caspian Sea; Caucasus Mountains; R U S)

0   600km
0   300 miles

LIFESTYLE FACTS
• Ballet is a popular form of entertainment in Russia. The dance company that became the Bolshoi Ballet was founded in 1773. It is famous for classical ballets such as *Swan Lake*.

• From October to March, Moscow receives an average of 15 minutes sunshine a day. Snow can lie on the ground for up to five months every year.

• Russians love to eat ice-cream, which can be bought from places marked *morozhenoe*.

ST. PETERSBURG
St. Petersburg, formerly called Leningrad, is a major industrial centre. The centre of the city is the Nevsky Prospekt, a street lined with shops, cafés, and theatres.

PASTIMES
• One of the most famous circuses in the world is in Russia. The acrobats of the New Moscow Circus are highly skilled.

• Chess is a popular game, and many people practise in Gorky Park, Moscow.

TOLSTOY
Leo Tolstoy (1828–1910) is one of the world's greatest novelists. His most famous book, *War and Peace*, is set in Russia during the Napoleonic Wars. It examines the feelings of the Russians as the French invade their country in 1812.

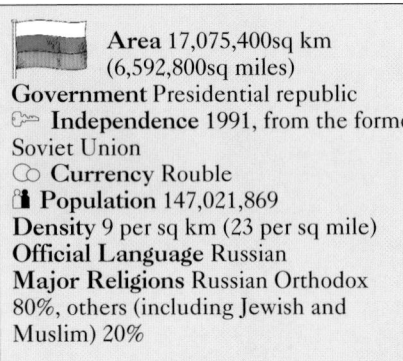

FAMOUS RUSSIAN WRITERS

Name	Date	Key work
Alexander Pushkin	1799–1837	*Eugene Onegin*
Fyodor Dostoyevsky	1821–81	*Crime and Punishment*
Boris Pasternak	1890–1960	*Dr. Zhivago*
Vladimir Nabokov	1899–1977	*Lolita*
Alexander Solzhenitsyn	b.1918–	*The Gulag Archipelago*

• The former Soviet Union had more than half of all cinemas in the world, selling an average of 80 million tickets a week. Sergei Eisenstein, a famous Russian film maker from the 1920s, made *Battleship Potemkin*.

• Reading is popular in Russia. Men spend one-eighth of their free time reading a book or newspaper. Women spend one-sixth of their free time reading.

POPULAR RUSSIAN FOOD
Russians have a fattening diet that include potatoes, fats, and sugar. Their food energy intake is 70% higher than the USA's.

Borscht This pinkish-red soup is made from beetroot, and can be eaten hot or cold It is often served with sour cream.

Blinis These pancakes are made using buckwheat, filled with meat or cheese, and then browned.

Charlotte Russe This special pudding wa created for Russian royalty. It is made in a mould lined with sponge, and filled with both ice-cream and whipped cream.

A plate of blinis served with red caviar.

SIBERIA FACTS
• The region of Siberia covers 12.5 million sq km (4.8 million sq miles) of the eastern, or Asiatic, part of Russia. Its name comes from the word "sibi" which means "sleeping land".

• In the north lies the tundra, where the ground is frozen for much of the year. This is known as permafrost.

• The snowy owl (*Nyctea scandiaca*) glides over the tundra hunting for small mammals.

• South of the tundra, vast expanses of conifer trees make up the largest forest in the world. The cones of the larch, fir, and spruce trees provide food for animals during the long winter.

• The Chukchi people live on the Kamchatka peninsula and survive by hunting, herding reindeer, and fishing. The Siberian husky dog was first raised by the Chukchi, who used the dogs as companions and to pull their sleds.

...RIAN WEALTH
...eath its icy surface, western ...ria has vast reserves of coal, ...and oil. The area provides ...for the industries of western ...sia, and gas is piped to western ...ope.

GOLD AND DIAMONDS
During the 1840s, prospectors found gold in the area around the River Lena, in northern Siberia. Today the area has four major gold fields as well as 800 diamond mines.

Heavy-duty machinery digs for minerals in northern Siberia.

...AL MOUNTAIN FACTS
...he Ural Mountains ...tch for 2,100km (1,300 ...s) from the Kara Sea in ...north to Kazakhstan in ...south.

...nly 40–200km (25–125 ...s) wide, the mountains ...Russia open to attack in ...arly history.

RUSSIAN ICONS
Beautiful icons, religious images painted on wood, adorn Russian churches and homes. For many years Christians were persecuted in the old Soviet Union.

This icon shows the Madonna and Child.

TIME DIFFERENCE
The Russian Federation covers 10 time zones. This means that when it is morning in the west, it is already early evening in the east.

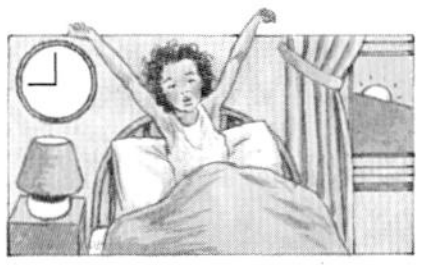

Time to get up in St. Petersburg

At school in Irkutsk

Getting ready for bed in Anadyr'

TRANS-SIBERIAN EXPRESS
The longest railway line in the world crosses the Russian Federation. Started in 1881, the railway was vital for the mining and transport of Siberia's minerals. The journey from Moscow to Vladivostock takes about 165 hours.

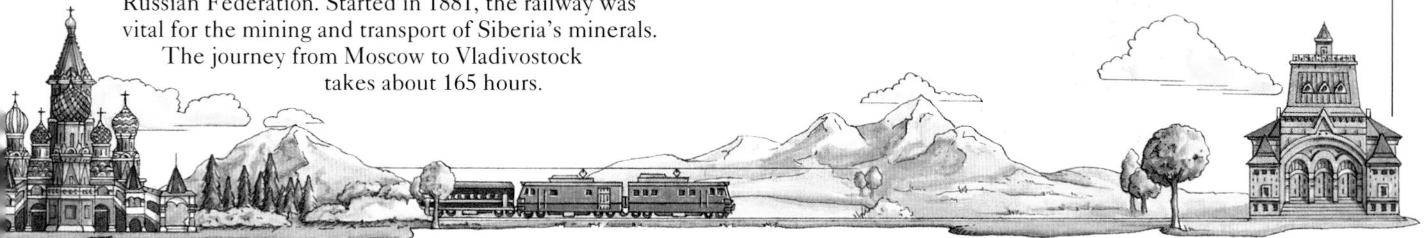

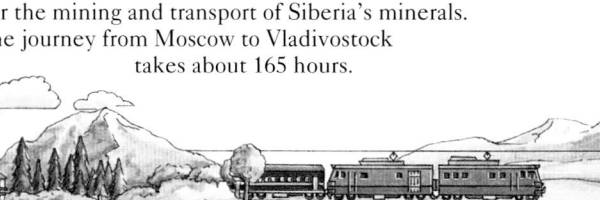

Moscow	3,219km (2,000 miles)	Novosibirsk	1,609km (1,000 miles)	Irkutsk	1,448km (900 miles)	Chita	3,621km (2,250 miles)	Vladivostok

Map labels
ARCTIC OCEAN
Severnaya Zemlya
...Sea
Laptev Sea
New Siberian Islands
East Siberian Sea
Bear Islands
Wrangel I.
Chukchi Sea
Bering Strait
Central Siberian Plateau
Lena
Verkhoyansk
Arctic Circle
Anadyr'
Siberia
FEDERATION
Kamchatka
Bering Sea
Sea of Okhotsk
Klyuchevskaya Sopka 4,750m (15,585ft)
Commander Islands
Novosibirsk
L. Baikal
Irkutsk
Chita
Sakhalin I.
N
MONGOLIA
CHINA
Kurile Islands
Vladivostok
Sea of Japan
PACIFIC OCEAN

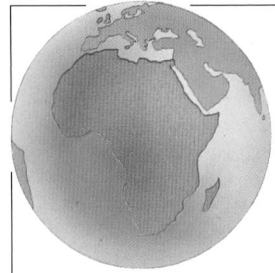

AFRICA

AFRICA IS THE second largest and warmest of the continents. It is also the only continent through which the Equator and both Tropics pass. Landscape and vegetation include rainforest, grassy savannah, and hot desert.

Area 30,131,536sq km (11,633,846sq miles)
Countries 54
Largest Sudan 2,505,810sq km (967,498sq miles)
Smallest Seychelles 280sq km (108sq miles)
Population 678,428,967
Density 21 per sq km (54 per sq mile)
Major Languages Arabic, Swahili, Hausa, Somali, Amharic

■ **Highest point** Kilimanjaro, Tanzania 5,895m (19,341ft)
◩ **Lowest point** Lake Assal, Djibouti 156m (512ft) below sea level
☀ **Highest temperature** 58°C (136°F) Al' Aziziyah, Libya
❄ **Lowest temperature** -24°C (-11°F) Ilfrane, Morocco

CLIMATE ZONES

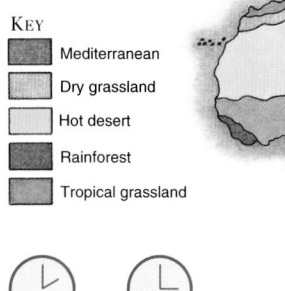

KEY
- Mediterranean
- Dry grassland
- Hot desert
- Rainforest
- Tropical grassland

TIME ZONES

12:00 Greenwich — 13:00 Libreville — 14:00 Cairo — 15:00 Addis Ababa

CONTINENT FACTS

- The world's largest desert is the African Sahara, with an area of 8,600,000sq km (3,320,000sq miles). It is bigger than all of Australia.
- Half of all Africans are under 15, making Africa the continent with the world's highest percentage of young people. Only 3 out of 100 can expect to live to be 65 years of age.
- Western Sahara, with just one person per sq km (2.6 per sq mile), is the world's least densely populated country.
- The earliest evidence of humans – the oldest known human footprints – were found in the Olduvai Gorge, Tanzania.
- Africa has more countries than any other continent: 54 in total.

COUNTRIES, TERRITORIES, AND CAPITALS

Name	Capital	Name	Capital
Algeria	Algiers	Madagascar	Antananarivo
Angola	Luanda	Malawi	Lilongwe
Benin	Porto-Novo	Mali	Bamako
Botswana	Gaborone	Mauritania	Nouakchott
Burkina	Ouagadougou	Mauritius	Port Louis
Burundi	Bujumbura	Morocco	Rabat
Cameroon	Yaoundé	Mozambique	Maputo
Cape Verde	Praia	Namibia	Windhoek
Central African Republic	Bangui	Niger	Niamey
Chad	N'Djamena	Nigeria	Abuja
Comoros	Moroni	Rwanda	Kigali
Congo	Brazzaville	Sao Tome and Principe	São Tomé
Djibouti	Djibouti	Senegal	Dakar
Egypt	Cairo	Seychelles	Victoria
Equatorial Guinea	Malabo	Sierra Leone	Freetown
Eritrea	Asmara	Somalia	Mogadishu
Ethiopia	Addis Ababa	South Africa	Pretoria
Gabon	Libreville	Sudan	Khartoum
Gambia	Banjul	Swaziland	Mbabane
Ghana	Accra	Tanzania	Dodoma
Guinea	Conakry	Togo	Lomé
Guinea-Bissau	Bissau	Tunisia	Tunis
Ivory Coast	Yamoussoukro	Uganda	Kampala
Kenya	Nairobi	Western Sahara	Laâyoune
Lesotho	Maseru	Zaire	Kinshasa
Liberia	Monrovia	Zambia	Lusaka
Libya	Tripoli	Zimbabwe	Harare

AGE BREAKDOWN

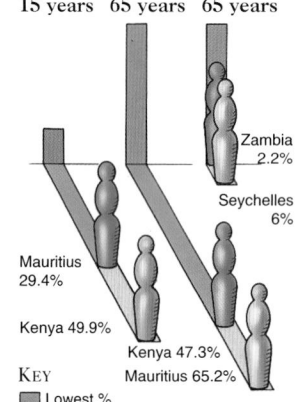

Under 15 years, 15 to 65 years, Over 65 years

Mauritius 29.4%, Kenya 49.9%, Kenya 47.3%, Mauritius 65.2%, Zambia 2.2%, Seychelles 6%

KEY
- Lowest %
- Highest %

FEWEST DOCTORS

Rwanda	1 to 72,990 people
Burkina	1 to 57,320 people
Botswana	1 to 51,590 people
Guinea	1 to 46,000 people
Malawi	1 to 45,740 people

LONGEST LIFESPAN

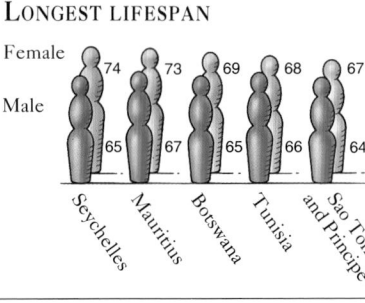

Female 74, 73, 69, 68, 67
Male 65, 67, 65, 66, 64
Seychelles, Mauritius, Botswana, Tunisia, Sao Tome and Principe

GREAT RIFT VALLEY

This valley, the longest crack in the Earth's crust, stretches for 8,700km (5,400 miles). In East Africa, the sides of the valley are 1,250m (4,100ft) high.

LONGEST RIVERS

Zambesi 2,735km (1,700 miles)
Niger 4,167km (2,589 miles)
Congo (Zaire) 4,373km (2,717
Nile 6,695km (4,160 miles)
Cairo

TOP CITY POPULATIONS

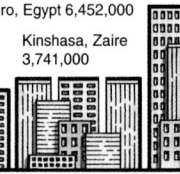

Abidjan, Ivory Coast 1,929,079
Casablanca, Morocco 3,200,000
Alexandria, Egypt 3,328,000
Cairo, Egypt 6,452,000
Kinshasa, Zaire 3,741,000

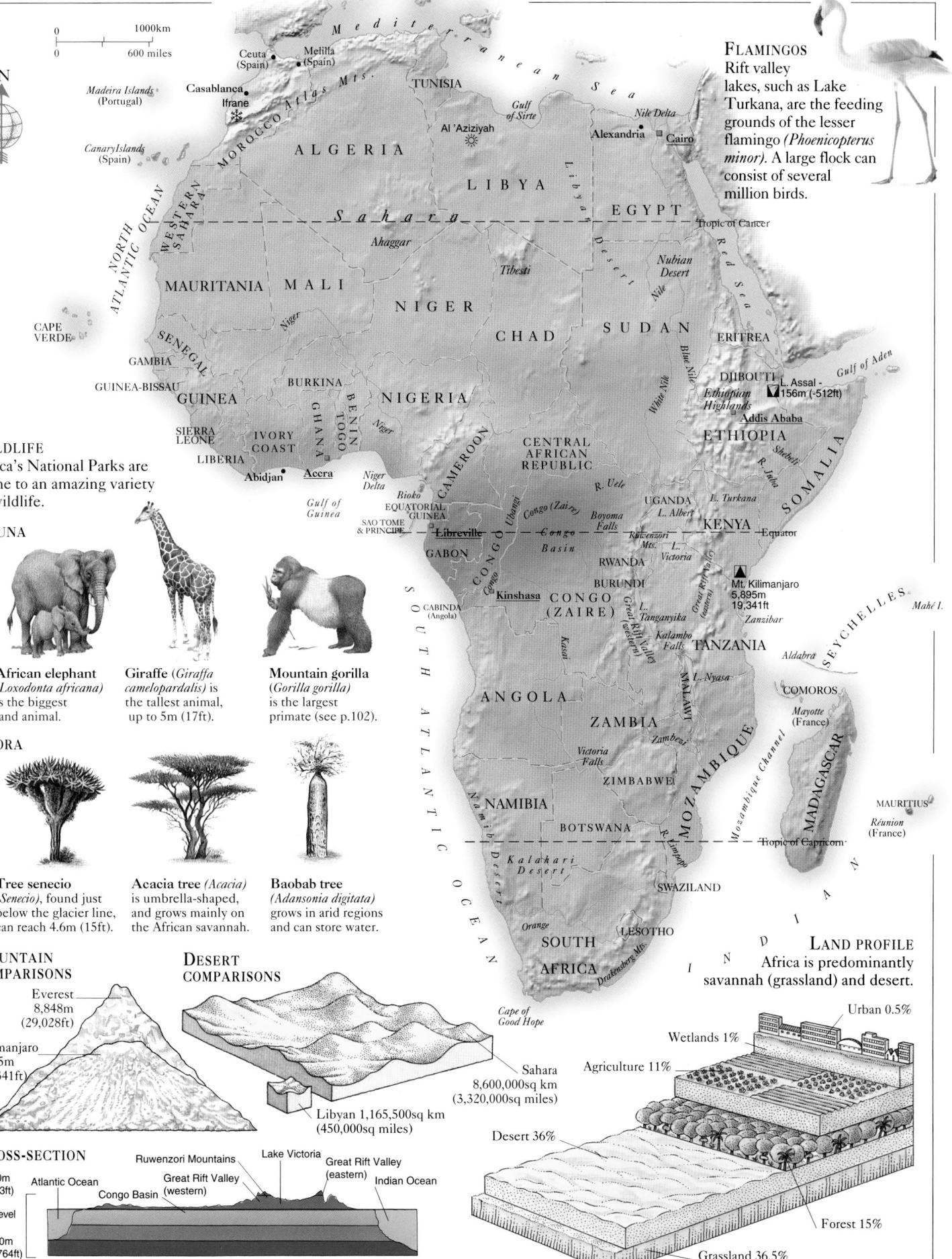

0 1000km
0 600 miles

N

FLAMINGOS
Rift valley lakes, such as Lake Turkana, are the feeding grounds of the lesser flamingo *(Phoenicopterus minor)*. A large flock can consist of several million birds.

...DLIFE
...ca's National Parks are ...ne to an amazing variety ...ildlife.

...UNA

African elephant
(Loxodonta africana)
...s the biggest
...and animal.

Giraffe *(Giraffa camelopardalis)* is the tallest animal, up to 5m (17ft).

Mountain gorilla
(Gorilla gorilla)
is the largest
primate (see p.102).

...ORA

Tree senecio
(Senecio), found just ...below the glacier line, ...can reach 4.6m (15ft).

Acacia tree *(Acacia)* is umbrella-shaped, and grows mainly on the African savannah.

Baobab tree
(Adansonia digitata)
grows in arid regions
and can store water.

...UNTAIN ...MPARISONS

Everest
8,848m
(29,028ft)

...manjaro
...5m
...341ft)

DESERT COMPARISONS

Sahara
8,600,000sq km
(3,320,000sq miles)

Libyan 1,165,500sq km
(450,000sq miles)

...OSS-SECTION

...0m
...3ft)
Atlantic Ocean
Congo Basin
...evel
...0m
...764ft)

Ruwenzori Mountains
Great Rift Valley (western)
Lake Victoria
Great Rift Valley (eastern)
Indian Ocean

Length: 4,500km (2,800 miles)

LAND PROFILE
Africa is predominantly savannah (grassland) and desert.

Urban 0.5%
Wetlands 1%
Agriculture 11%
Desert 36%
Forest 15%
Grassland 36.5%

Map labels:

Mediterranean Sea
Madeira Islands (Portugal)
Canary Islands (Spain)
Ceuta (Spain)
Melilla (Spain)
Casablanca
Ifrane
Atlas Mts.
MOROCCO
WESTERN SAHARA
TUNISIA
Gulf of Sirte
Al 'Aziziyah
ALGERIA
LIBYA
EGYPT
Nile Delta
Alexandria
Cairo
Tropic of Cancer
Sahara
Ahaggar
Tibesti
Libyan Desert
Nubian Desert
Nile
Red Sea
Gulf of Aden
CAPE VERDE
MAURITANIA
MALI
NIGER
CHAD
SUDAN
ERITREA
Niger
SENEGAL
GAMBIA
GUINEA-BISSAU
GUINEA
BURKINA
SIERRA LEONE
LIBERIA
IVORY COAST
GHANA
TOGO
BENIN
NIGERIA
Abidjan
Accra
Niger Delta
Gulf of Guinea
Bioko
EQUATORIAL GUINEA
SAO TOME & PRINCIPE
Libreville
GABON
CAMEROON
CENTRAL AFRICAN REPUBLIC
Blue Nile
White Nile
DJIBOUTI
L. Assal -156m (-512ft)
Ethiopian Highlands
Addis Ababa
ETHIOPIA
SOMALIA
R. Shebeli
R. Jubba
R. Uele
Ubangi
Congo (Zaire)
Boyoma Falls
Congo Basin
UGANDA
L. Albert
L. Turkana
KENYA
Equator
Ruwenzori Mts.
L. Victoria
RWANDA
BURUNDI
Kinshasa
CABINDA (Angola)
CONGO (ZAIRE)
Kasai
Congo
L. Tanganyika
Kalambo Falls
Great Rift Valley (western)
Great Rift Valley (eastern)
Mt. Kilimanjaro 5,895m 19,341ft
Zanzibar
TANZANIA
SEYCHELLES
Mahé I.
Aldabra
L. Nyasa
MALAWI
COMOROS
Mayotte (France)
ANGOLA
ZAMBIA
Zambesi
Victoria Falls
ZIMBABWE
MOZAMBIQUE
MADAGASCAR
MAURITIUS
Réunion (France)
Mozambique Channel
NAMIBIA
BOTSWANA
Kalahari Desert
Namib Desert
Limpopo
Orange
SWAZILAND
LESOTHO
SOUTH AFRICA
Drakensberg Mts.
Cape of Good Hope
NORTH ATLANTIC OCEAN
SOUTH ATLANTIC OCEAN
INDIAN OCEAN

EGYPT

MOST OF EGYPT is barren desert, with 99 per cent of the population living by the River Nile. Farmers, called *fellahin*, grow cotton, wheat, rice, and vegetables. The Great Pyramid at Giza is one of the seven wonders of the ancient world.

Area 1,001,450sq km (386,662sq miles)
Government Presidential republic
Independence 1936, from Britain
Currency Egyptian pound
Population 62,900,000
Density 63 per sq km (163 per sq mile)
Official Language Arabic
Major Religions Muslim 94%, other 6%

WEATHER FACTS

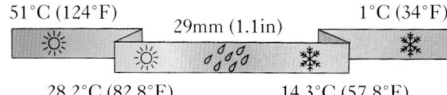

51°C (124°F)   29mm (1.1in)   1°C (34°F)
28.2°C (82.8°F)   14.3°C (57.8°F)

LAND PROFILE
Only 4.5 per cent of the land in Egypt can be cultivated.

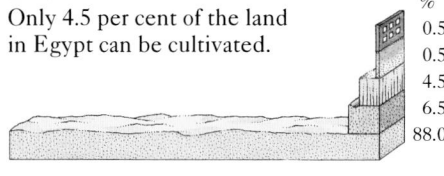

%
0.5
0.5
4.5
6.5
88.0

LIFESTYLE FACTS
• Overpopulation is a problem in Egypt. The estimated birth rate is one baby born every 24 seconds.

• Egypt is the world's top producer of dates, and the fourth largest producer of water-melons.

• Tolls from the Suez Canal, completed in 1869, now bring the Egyptian government more than US $500 million each year.

One Egyptian pound

LANGUAGE
A traditional greeting in Arabic is *ahlan wasahlan.* أهلا و سهلا

GREAT PYRAMIDS
The pyramids at Giza were built in about 2600 B.C. to house the mummified bodies of Egyptian kings, or pharaohs. The largest pyramid contains more than 2 million stone blocks and took 100,000 men more than 20 years to build.

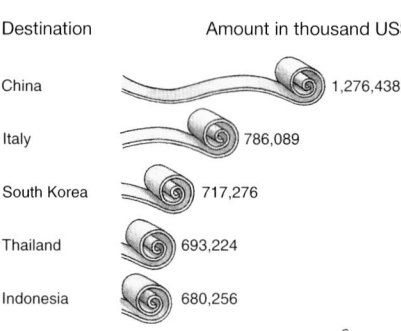

MAJOR COTTON IMPORTERS FROM ALL SOURCES (1996)

Destination		Amount in thousand US$
China		1,276,438
Italy		786,089
South Korea		717,276
Thailand		693,224
Indonesia		680,256

SUDAN

SUDAN IS THE largest country in Africa and includes the swampy Sudd region. Sudan exports gum arabic, used in watercolour painting.

Area 2,505,815sq km (967,493sq miles)
Independence 1956, from Anglo-Egyptian agreement
Currency Sudanese dinar
Population 28,100,000
Official Language Arabic
Major Religions Muslim 70%, Christian 5%, traditional beliefs 20%, other 5%

ETHIOPIA

FOUR OUT OF five Ethiopians work on the land, with coffee as the main cash crop. The Blue Nile flows from Lake Tana in the north.

Area 1,221,900sq km (471,778sq miles)
Foundation More than 2,000 years; never colonized
Currency Birr
Population 51,300,000
Official Language Amharic
Major Religions Muslim 40%, Ethiopian Orthodox 40%, traditional beliefs 15%, other 5%

LOCUST ATTACK
Massive swarms of locusts sometimes sweep across the African continent, destroying huge areas of crops in just minutes. Large swarms can weigh up to 50,000 tonnes.

SOMALIA

SOMALIA'S ECONOMY is based on rearing animals for use or profit. Bananas, a major export, are grown on riverside plantations.

Area 637,660sq km (246,200sq miles)
Independence 1960, formation of Somali Republic
Currency Somali shilling
Population 9,300,000
Official Languages Arabic, Somali
Major Religions Muslim 99%, other 1%

WATER FACTS
• Two billion people in the world lack access to safe water.

• A family of six needs about 91 litres (20 gallons) of water a day for basic needs, such as drinking and keeping clean.

• In Ethiopia 39.5 million people have no access to a safe supply of water. In Sudan the figure is 14.7 million, in Somalia, 4.8 million.

• In the Sudan it takes at least 2 hours, or a journey of 8km (5 miles), every day to fetch water. The work is usually done by women and children.

DJIBOUTI

DJIBOUTI IS AN important trading port for Ethiopia and occupies a prime site between the Indian Ocean and the Red Sea.

Area 23,200sq km (8,958sq miles)
Independence 1977, from France
Currency Djibouti franc
Population 500,000
Official Language Arabic, French
Major Religions Muslim 94%, other 6%

ERITREA

ERITREA IS A hot country with very little rainfall and locust plagues that make farming difficult. Many people live as nomads.

Area 93,679sq km (36,170sq miles)
Independence 1993, from Ethiopia
Currency Birr
Population 3,500,000
Official Language Amharic
Major Religions No figures available. People of the mountains are Christians; lowland Eritreans are Muslim

TANZANIA

THE MAIN EXPORT crops of Tanzania include sisal, which is used to make rope. Most of the world's cloves grow on the islands of Zanzibar.

Area 945,090sq km (364,900sq miles)
Independence 1961, from Britain
Currency Tanzanian shilling
Population 29,700,000
Official Language English, Swahili
Major Religions Traditional beliefs 42%, Christian 27%, Muslim 31%

N

KENYA

KENYA LIES ON the Equator. It consists of dry grasslands, which are home to wildlife such as elephants, lions, and zebras. Most people live in the highlands of the southwest, where there is enough rain to grow crops and graze cattle and sheep.

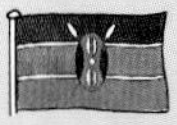

Area 580,370sq km (224,081sq miles)
Government Presidential republic
Independence 1963, from Britain
Currency Kenya shilling
Population 28,300,000
Density 50 per sq km (130 per sq mile)
Official Language Swahili
Major Religions Christian 66%, Traditional beliefs 26%, other 8%

WEATHER FACTS

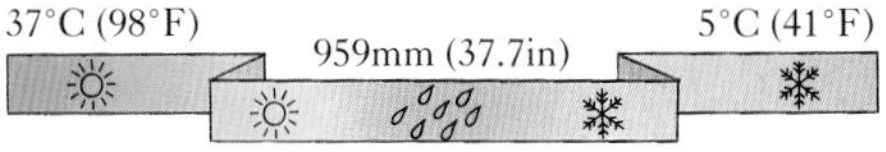

37°C (98°F)   959mm (37.7in)   5°C (41°F)

18.6°C (65.6°F)   16.5°C (61.7°F)

LIFESTYLE FACTS

• Kenya has the world's youngest population with about 50% of the people under 15 years of age.

• There are two rainy seasons in Kenya. The "long" rains are between March and May and "short" rains between October and November.

• Kenya produces 80% of the world's pyrethrum. The flowers of this type of chrysanthemum are dried and used for making insecticide.

LAND PROFILE
Almost two-thirds of Kenya is covered in grassland.

%
0.5
2.6
8.6
10.7
14.9
62.7

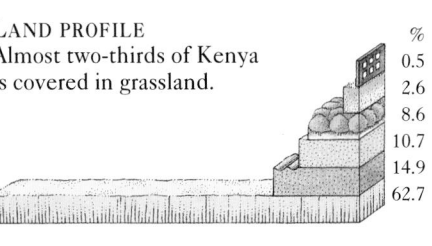

Masai warriors

MASAI FACTS
• The Masai are a tribe of nomadic herders who live on the borders of Kenya and Tanzania.

• They survive on the meat, blood, and milk of their herds.

• Between the ages of 14 and 30, the young men live in the bush learning the skills that will make them great warriors.

UGANDA

ONE-FIFTH OF Uganda consists of large lakes and swamps. Most farmers grow their own food, such as sweet potatoes, maize, and beans, although coffee is grown for export.

Area 235,880sq km (91,073sq miles)
Independence 1962, from Britain
Currency New Uganda shilling
Population 21,300,000
Official Languages English, Swahili
Major Religions Christian 66%, Traditional beliefs 18%, Muslim 16%

MAJOR NATIONAL PARKS AND GAME RESERVES

Name	Size	Key animal
Selous Tanzania, Tanzania	45,000sq km (17,375sq miles)	
Tsavo National Park, Kenya	20,812sq km (8,035sq miles)	
Serengeti National Park, Tanzania	14,76 sq km (5,700sq miles)	
Ruaha National Park, Tanzania	12,950sq km (5,000sq miles)	
Ngorongoro Conservation Area, Tanzania	8,292sq km (3,201sq miles)	

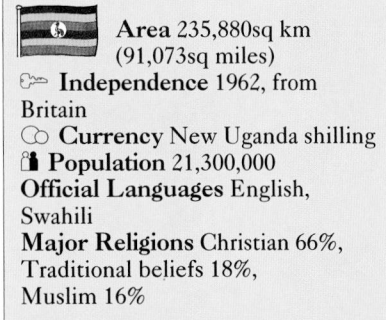

Map labels:
Mediterranean Sea
LIBYA
Alexandria
El Mahalla el Kubra
Tanta
Port Said
Giza
Cairo
Pyramids
Sinai
Mt. Katherina 2,637m (8,652ft)
Red Sea
EGYPT
Nile
Aswan
Tropic of Cancer
Libyan Desert
L. Nasser (L. Malawi)
Nubian Desert
Port Sudan
Nile
SUDAN
Engershatu 2,575m (8,449ft)
ERITREA
Asmara
Khartoum
Ras Dashen 4,620m (15,158ft)
El Obeid
Blue Nile
Gonder
L. Tana
Moussa Ali 2,020m (6,628ft)
DJIBOUTI
Gulf of Aden
Djibouti
Dire Dawa
Shimbiris 2,408m (7,900ft)
Nuba Mts.
White Nile
Addis Ababa
Ethiopian Highlands
Horn of Africa
Sudd
ETHIOPIA
Shebeli
SOMALIA
CENTRAL AFRICAN REPUBLIC
Kinyeti 3,187m (10,457ft)
L. Turkana
Chalbi Desert
Mogadishu
UGANDA
Margherita Peak 5,110m (16,762ft)
Victoria Nile
KENYA
Kampala
Kirinyaga 5,200m (17,601ft)
Equator
Kisumu
INDIAN OCEAN
RWANDA
L. Victoria
Great Rift Valley
Nairobi
Tana
Kagera
BURUNDI
Kilimanjaro 5,895m (19,341ft)
L. Tanganyika
ZAIRE
Masai Steppe
Pemba I.
Dodoma
Zanzibar
Mafia I.
TANZANIA
Rufiji
Great Rift Valley
Western Rift Valley
ZAMBIA
MALAWI
L. Nyasa
MOZAMBIQUE

700km
400 miles

MOROCCO

MOROCCO HAS MILD winters and hot, dry summers. On the fertile coastal plains farmers grow fruits and vegetables that are canned for export. Most people are Berbers, the name given to them by their Arab conquerors in the 7th century.

Area 698,670sq km (269,757sq miles)
Government Constitutional monarchy
Independence 1956, from France
Currency Moroccan dirham
Population 27,000,000
Density 60 per sq km (155 per sq mile)
Official Language Arabic
Major Religions Sunni Muslim 99%, Christian, Jewish and other 1%

WEATHER FACTS

49°C (120°F)   -3°C (27°F)
503mm (20in)
22.2°C (72°F)   13°C (55.4°F)

LAND PROFILE

Almost 40% of Morocco is grassland.

%
0.2
2.3
11.1
23.0
24.5
38.9

FLOWER FACTS

• In Morocco, roses, gladioli, carnations, irises, and marigolds are grown for export. In 1991, production reached 2,500 tonnes.

• Saffron, used to flavour rice, is produced in the eastern region of Morocco. Saffron comes from the crocus flower, and it takes about 400,000 stamens to make 1kg (2.2lb).

CAPE VERDE

THE VOLCANIC Cape Verde islands are divided into the Windward and Leeward groups. Most of the people are Creole, and the main crops include bananas and sugar-cane.

Area 4,030sq km (1,556sq miles)
Independence 1975, from Portugal
Currency Cape Verde escudo
Population 400,000
Official Language Portuguese
Major Religions Roman Catholic 98%, Protestant and other 2%

LIFESTYLE FACTS

• A covered market, called a souk, is where Moroccan traders sell spices, fruits, and textiles.

• Skilled craftworkers make beautiful pictures using wood from lemon, cedar, and sandalwood trees.

• The Moroccan leather industry produces shoes, bags, and clothes. Tanning, the process of turning animal skins into leather, is also an important industry.

FANTASIA

Every year in Morocco there is an event called the Fantasia. Two groups of horsemen in traditional dress charge the length of the arena, firing rifles. The spectacle dates back to the ancient warfare tactics of Berber horsemen.

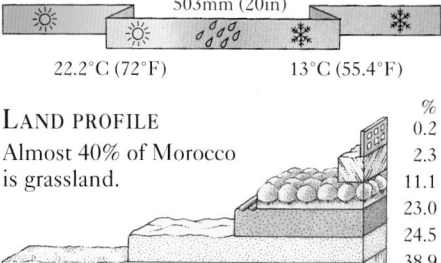

WESTERN SAHARA

WESTERN SAHARA IS the emptiest country in the world with just one person per sq km (2.6 per sq mile). Few crops are grown, but farmers raise goats and sheep.

Area 252,120sq km (97,344sq miles)
Independence 1976, from Spain;currently occupied by Morocco
Currency Moroccan dirham
Population 200,000
Official Language None; most people speak different Arabic dialects
Major Religion Muslim 100%

MALI

ONLY ABOUT 2 per cent of Mali is arable land. Cotton and groundnuts are the main crops. The Malinke and Songhai tribes have a reputation for fine music and dancing.

Area 1,240,190sq km (478,837sq miles)
Independence 1960, from France
Currency CFA franc
Population 10,800,000
Official Language French
Major Religions Muslim 80%, Christian and other 2%, traditional beliefs 18%

LANGUAGE

A traditional greeting in Arabic is *ahlan wasahlan*.

أَهْلاً وَسَهْلاً

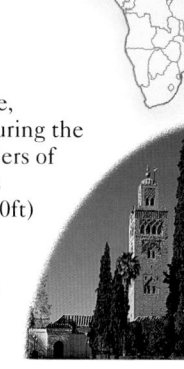

MARRAKESH MOSQUE

The Koutoubia Mosque, Marrakesh, was built during the 11th century on the orders of Yacoub El Mansour. Its minaret stands 70m (230ft) tall. It is known as the booksellers' mosque because traders used to gather outside to sell their books.

MAJOR EXPORTS (1996–97)	
Product	Value in US$
Canned fish	180,624,000
Tomatoes	90,894,000
Green beans	893,000
Apricots	59,000
Olives	58,000

MAURITANIA

MAURITANIA IS HOT and dry, and sand dunes cover half the country. Antelopes, lions, and elephants live in the southern grasslands. Fish from the Atlantic are exported.

Area 1,025,520sq km (395,955sq miles)
Independence 1960, from France
Currency Ouguiya
Population 2,200,000
Official Language Arabic
Major Religions Sunni Muslim 99%, other 1%

NIGER

NORTHERN NIGER is almost empty and most people live in the south. One-sixth of the population still lives as nomads. Niger is one of the world's top producers of uranium.

Area 1,267,000 sq km (489,188sq miles)
Independence 1960, from France
Currency CFA franc
Population 9,200,000
Official Language French
Major Religions Muslim 85%, traditional beliefs 14%, Christian 1%

ALGERIA

MORE THAN 80 per cent of Algeria lies within the Sahara desert. The discovery of oil and natural gas in the desert has made these the country's main exports.

Area 2,381,740sq km (919,590sq miles)
Independence 1962, from France
Currency Algerian dinar
Population 27,900,000
Official Language Arabic
Major Religions Sunni Muslim 99%, Christian, Jewish and other 1%

SAHARA FACTS

• The Sahara (the word means desert) is the world's largest desert and covers 8,600,000 sq km (3,320,000sq miles): almost as large as the United States of America.

• The dromedary camel is adapted to life in the desert. It can travel 160km (100 miles) a day for eight days without drinking any water.

• Despite its popular image, only about 20% of the Sahara is continuous sand. The sand often forms into pyramid-shaped dunes which can be up to 230m (750ft) tall.

DESERT TRIBES

The Tuareg, who are of Berber origin, are nomadic tribes who live on the edge of the Sahara. Long scarves protect them from the heat and dust.

ROCK ART

This rock painting from Tassili N'Ajjer, dated about 6000 B.C., shows nomadic herders. Until about 4500 B.C., the Sahara was not a desert. There was enough rain to support animals, such as gazelles and buffaloes.

PIPED WATER

Beneath the Sahara there are vast underground supplies of water. The Libyans have built a series of pipelines to carry water to the coastal areas for increased crop production.

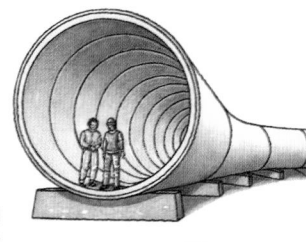

TUNISIA

GENERALLY TUNISIA HAS poor soil and relies on tourism for most of its income. Esparto grass, which grows on the plains, is used to make quality paper.

Area 163,610sq km (63,170sq miles)
Independence 1956, from France
Currency Tunisian dinar
Population 8,900,000
Official Language Arabic
Major Religions Muslim 99%, Christian, Jewish, and other 1%

FALCONRY

In Tunisia, falcons are used to hunt quail, hare, and partridge during the summer.

LIBYA

LIBYA IS ONE of the world's leading producers of oil. Although the country is mainly desert, citrus fruits, figs, and dates are grown in the southern oases.

Area 1,759,540sq km (679,358sq miles)
Independence 1951, from Italy
Currency Libyan dinar
Population 5,400,000
Official Language Arabic
Major Religions Sunni Muslim 97%, other 3%

CHAD

CHAD HAS A landscape of desert, grassland, and tropical forests. Most crops, including cotton, are grown in the south. Sodium bicarbonate (natron) is mined near Lake Chad.

Area 1,284,000sq km (495,752sq miles)
Independence 1960, from France
Currency CFA franc
Population 6,400,000
Official Languages Arabic, French
Major Religions Muslim 44%, Christian 33%, traditional beliefs 23%

Map labels

MEDITERRANEAN SEA
Strait of Gibraltar
Melilla (Spain)
Ceuta (Spain)
Rabat
Koutoubia Mosque (Marrakesh)
Algiers
Tunis
Chambi 1,544m (5,066ft)
Chott Melrhir
Chott El Jerid
Tripoli
Gulf of Sirte
ATLAS MOUNTAINS
MOROCCO
Oum er Rbia
Chelif
Medjerda
TUNISIA
Libyan Desert
EGYPT
ALGERIA
LIBYA
SAHARA
Tassili N'Ajjer
Laâyoune
WESTERN SAHARA
Kediet Ijill 915m (3,002ft)
Tahat 2,918m (9,574ft)
Ahaggar
Plateau du Manguéni
Bette 2,286m (7,500ft)
Tibesti
Emi Koussi 3,415m (11,205ft)
MAURITANIA
Nouakchott
L. Rkiz
MALI
Tropic of Cancer
Tropic du Tafassasset
Talak Aïr
Bagzane 2,022m (6,634ft)
NIGER
CHAD
L.Faguibine
L.Chad
N'Djamena
SUDAN
CAPE VERDE
São Tiago Praia
ATLANTIC OCEAN
Senegal
SENEGAL
Niger
Bamako
765m (2,510ft)
BURKINA
Niamey
SAHEL
NIGERIA
Chari
GUINEA
IVORY COAST
CAMEROON
CENTRAL AFRICAN REPUBLIC

N
0 75km
0 40 miles

NIGERIA

NIGERIA IS AFRICA'S most heavily populated country, and two-thirds of the people live in farming villages. The most valuable crops are cacao, palm products, and rubber, with oil as the main export.

Area 923,770sq km (356,669sq miles)
Government Multiparty republic
Independence 1960, from Britain
Currency Naira
Population 111,700,000
Density 123 per sq km (319 per sq mile)
Official Language English

SENEGAL

IN THIS FLAT country, peanuts (groundnuts) are grown to make oil for export. The capital, Dakar, is West Africa's most important port.

Area 196,720sq km (75,950sq miles)
Independence 1960, from France; republic declared
Currency CFA franc
Population 8,300,000
Official Language French

THE GAMBIA

GAMBIA IS AFRICA'S smallest country, and stretches for 320km (200 miles) on either side of the River Gambia. The main cash crop is peanuts.

Area 11,300sq km (4,363sq miles)
Independence 1965, from Britain; 1970, republic declared.
Currency Dalasi
Population 1,100,000
Official Language English

GUINEA-BISSAU

THE COAST HAS a monsoon climate with heavy rainfall between May and October. Water birds include pelicans and flamingos.

Area 36,120sq km (13,940sq miles)
Independence 1974, from Portugal
Currency Guinea peso
Population 1,100,000
Official Language Portuguese

LAND PROFILE
More than half of Nigeria is grassland.

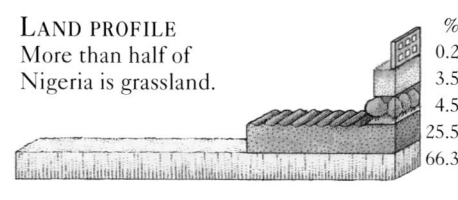

%
0.2
3.5
4.5
25.5
66.3

LIFESTYLE FACTS
• Nigeria spends a lot of money on education. The country has 33 universities with more than 243,000 students.

• All twins in Nigeria, boys and girls, are given the same names. The firstborn is called Taiwo, the second is Kehinde.

• The main ethnic groups in Nigeria are the Hausa (north), the Ibo (east), and the Yoruba (south and west).

10 naira

A traditional greeting in the Hausa language is *ina-kwna.*

MARKETS
This scene in Benin City shows a woman buying chillis for the hot sauce used in cooking. She wears a length of patterned cloth, called a *pagne*, around her waist.

PEANUT FACTS
• Peanuts (or groundnuts) are a major crop in West Africa. Despite the name, it is not a true nut.

• The pod, or peanut, has the unusual habit of ripening underground.

• There are about 300 by-products of peanuts, including flour, soap, and plastics.

GUINEA

GUINEA IS THE world's second biggest producer of the mineral bauxite. Iron ore, gold, and diamonds are also mined here.

Area 245,860sq km (94,926sq miles)
Independence 1958, from France
Currency Guinean franc
Population 6,700,000
Official Language French

SIERRA LEONE

PORTUGUESE EXPLORERS in the 15th century named this country, which means "lion mountain". Diamonds and bauxite are the main exports.

Area 71,740sq km (27,699sq miles)
Independence 1961, from Britain
Currency Leone
Population 4,500,000
Official Language English

LANGUAGE RHYTHMS
The Ashanti language of West Africa is a tonal language, and a special drum can be played to reproduce the tonal pattern of a word. Drum language, which has its own vocabulary, can be used to send messages from one village to another.

TALKING DRUMS
The *kalungu*, or talking drum, is held together with thongs that link the two skins. When the "waist" is squeezed, the sound can be changed.

animal skin

"waist"

leather thongs

LIBERIA
LIBERIA WAS FOUNDED as a home for freed slaves from the USA. High-quality iron ore has replaced rubber as the country's most valuable product.

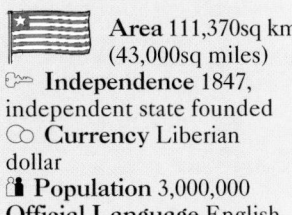

Area 111,370sq km (43,000sq miles)
Independence 1847, independent state founded
Currency Liberian dollar
Population 3,000,000
Official Language English

IVORY COAST
THERE ARE 66 different tribes living in the Ivory Coast. One tribe, the Dan, carve beautiful masks for use in their traditional ceremonies.

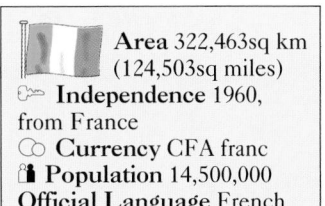

Area 322,463sq km (124,503sq miles)
Independence 1960, from France
Currency CFA franc
Population 14,500,000
Official Language French

BURKINA
BURKINA IS AN inland country on the southern edge of the Sahara Desert. Infertile soils mean that less than 10 per cent of the land can be farmed.

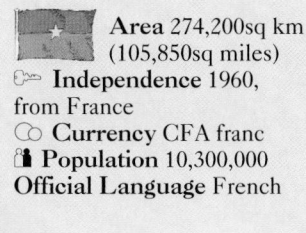

Area 274,200sq km (105,850sq miles)
Independence 1960, from France
Currency CFA franc
Population 10,300,000
Official Language French

NIGERIA WEATHER FACTS

46°C (114°F)   1838mm (72in)   6°C (43°F)

27.6°C (81.7°F)   26°C (78.8°F)

ANCIENT KINGDOM OF BENIN
The kingdom of Benin, founded in the forests of what is now Nigeria, rose to power during the 14th century. Its skilled craftworkers made spectacular bronze heads and figures.

WEST AFRICAN RELIGIONS
Percentages of population

	Muslim	Christian	Traditional
Benin	15	18	67
Burkina	35	10	55
Gambia	90	9	1
Ghana	12	43	45
Guinea	95	1.5	3.5
Guinea-Bissau	38	8	54
Ivory Coast	23	12	65
Liberia	14	68	18
Nigeria	50	40	10
Senegal	90	5	5
Sierra Leone	30	10	60
Togo	15	35	50

(Map: N I G E R, CHAD, NIGERIA, L. Chad, Komadugu Yobe, Kano, Niger, Abuja, Dimlang 2,042m (6,700ft), CAMEROON, Benin City, Niger Delta, Bight of Benin, Lagos, Porto-Novo, Lomé, TOGO, BENIN, 641m (2,103ft), Atakora Mts, Oti, Ouémé, Mono, Agou 986m (3,235ft), gadougou, NA)

GHANA
GHANA WAS THE first African country to win its independence. Ghana exports more cacao than any other country in the world.

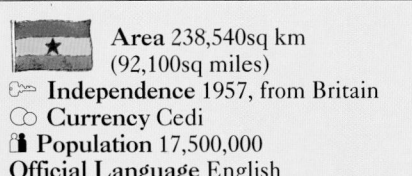

Area 238,540sq km (92,100sq miles)
Independence 1957, from Britain
Currency Cedi
Population 17,500,000
Official Language English

TOGO
THE POPULATION OF Togo has about 30 ethnic groups, many from other parts of West Africa. Nearly half the people are under 15 years of age.

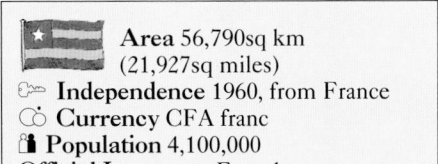

Area 56,790sq km (21,927sq miles)
Independence 1960, from France
Currency CFA franc
Population 4,100,000
Official Language French

BENIN
BENIN HAS A coastline fringed with saltwater lakes. Lake villages and old palaces make Benin popular with tourists.

Area 112,620sq km (43,480sq miles)
Independence 1960, from France
Currency CFA franc
Population 5,400,000
Official Language French

GABON

GABON LIES ACROSS the Equator and is hot and rainy. About 75 per cent of the country is rainforest. Gabon is the world's fourth largest producer of manganese.

Area 267,670sq km (103,347sq miles)
Independence 1960, from France
Currency CFA franc
Population 1,300,000
Official Language French
Major Religions Roman Catholic and other Christians 96%, Muslim 2%, other 2%

TRADITIONAL BELIEFS

• Many Africans follow religious systems that existed before the introduction of the major faiths, such as Islam and Christianity.

• Many of these traditions suggest that natural objects, such as mountains and rivers, have a spirit. Spirits can be good or evil.

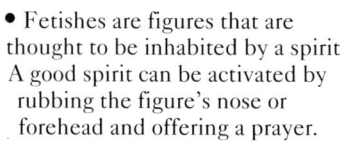

• Fetishes are figures that are thought to be inhabited by a spirit. A good spirit can be activated by rubbing the figure's nose or forehead and offering a prayer.

EQUATORIAL GUINEA

THIS COUNTRY IS made up of Rio Muni, on the mainland, and the island of Bioko. Most people belong to the Fang, a group who are known for their storytelling and music.

Area 28,050sq km (108,30sq miles)
Independence 1968, from Spain
Currency CFA franc
Population 400,000
Official Language Spanish
Major Religions Roman Catholic 89%, other 11%

TURTLE BEACH
In January and February each year, thousands of turtles come to the south shore of the island of Bioko, to lay their eggs. Only one in every 100 will survive.

Green turtle

CAMEROON

TROPICAL RAINFORESTS COVER much of the Republic of Cameroon. The country's main export is cacao, which is used to make cocoa and chocolate.

Area 475,440sq km (183,570sq miles)
Independence 1960, from France
Currency CFA franc
Population 12,500,000
Official Languages English, French
Major Religions Traditional beliefs 51%, Christian 33%, Muslim 16%

LIVING IN THE RAINFOREST

• Large areas of Central Africa are covered in rainforest. The forest is warm and damp and home to wildlife such as chimpanzees, leopards, and a wealth of birdlife.

• In the rainforests, there are groups of people commonly known as pygmies (a name they dislike). They survive by hunting animals and gathering wild plants, nuts, and honey.

• Forest homes are made from a framework of poles tied together and thatched with large leaves. The people do not plant crops so have no need to cut down their forest retreat.

• The main forest people are the Twa, the BaKa, and the Mbuti, who live in an area that covers parts of Gabon, Congo, Central African Republic, Cameroon, and Zaire.

SAO TOME AND PRINCIPE

THESE VOLCANIC ISLANDS lie in the Gulf of Guinea. About 40 per cent of the land is planted with cacao trees. Most people live in São Tomé.

Area 964sq km (372sq miles)
Independence 1975, from Portugal
Currency Dobra
Population 125,000
Official Language Portuguese
Major Religions Roman Catholic 90%, other Christian 10%

YAOUNDÉ
Yaoundé is the capital city and business centre of Cameroon. It also has many schools and research institutes.

CENTRAL AFRICAN REPUBLIC

TIMBER, COFFEE, and cotton are the main exports here. Along the rivers, used for access to the sea, there are hippopotamuses and crocodiles.

Area 622,980sq km (240,530sq miles)
Independence 1960, from France
Currency CFA franc
Population 3,300,000
Official Languages French, Sango
Major Religions Christian 50%, traditional beliefs 27%, Muslim 15%, other 8%

CONGO

ALMOST TWO-THIRDS of the Congo is covered with tropical rainforests. The coast and swamps contain coconut palms and mangrove forest.

Area 342,000sq km (132,040sq miles)
Independence 1960, from France
Currency CFA franc
Population 2,600,000
Official Language French
Major Religions Roman Catholic 50%, traditional beliefs 48%, other 2%

ANGOLA

THE MAIN PRODUCTS of Angola are oil and diamonds. The long coastline also provides good fishing for sardines and mackerel.

Area 1,246,700sq km (481,551sq miles)
Independence 1975, from Portugal
Currency New kwanza
Population 11,100,000
Official Language Portuguese
Major Religions Christian 64%, traditional beliefs 34%, other 2%

N

0 ____ 75 km
0 ____ 40 miles

CHAD

SUDAN

NIGERIA

CENTRAL
AFRICAN
REPUBLIC

Mt.Toussoro
1,330m (4,364ft)

Katto

Bangui

Bomu

Uele

CAMEROON
Cameroon Mountain
4,095m (13,436ft)

Sanaga

Malabo

Bioko

Yaoundé

Ubangi

Congo (Zaire)

Margherita Peak
5,110m (16,766ft)

Aruwimi

UGANDA

Gulf of Guinea

EQUATORIAL
GUINEA

Rio
Muni

SAO TOME &
PRINCIPE
São Tomé

Mont Tembo
1,200m (3,937ft)

Ogooué

Libreville

CONGO

L. Onangué

GABON

Equator

Karisimbi
4,507m (14,787ft)

L. Kivu

Kigali
RWANDA
Bujumbura
BURUNDI

Monts de la Lékéti
1,040m (3,412ft)

Brazzaville

Kinshasa

CABINDA
(Angola)

Cabinda

DEMOCRATIC
REPUBLIC OF
CONGO (ZAIRE)

Lomami

Mitumba Mts

TANZANIA

MALAWI

Luanda

Cuanza

ATLANTIC OCEAN

Serra do Môco
2,620m (8,596ft)

ANGOLA

2,067m
(6,782ft)

ZAMBIA

Lusaka

Mucharka Mts

MOZAMBIQUE

Zambezi

L. Kariba

Victoria
Falls

NAMIBIA

ZIMBABWE

BOTSWANA

FISHING METHODS
...coasts of Angola are
...ed with fishing villages.
...e fish are caught by
...g conical traps that
...g from specially built
...folding.

REGIONAL LIFESTYLE FACTS

• Sao Tome has the highest literacy rate
in Central Africa (63%) and the
third highest life expectancy in
all of Africa.

• The wooden masks of Central
Africa inspired the Spanish
painter Picasso (see p.163).

Mask from Congo (Zaire)

CONGO (ZAIRE)

THIS COUNTRY IS the world's largest
producer of industrial diamonds.
Minerals, mainly copper, make up
80 per cent of total exports.

Area 2,345,410sq km
(905,563sq miles)
Independence 1960, from Belgium
Currency Zaire
Population 43,900,000
Official Language French
Major Religions Christian 70%,
Traditional beliefs 20%, Muslim 10%

• A vegetarian dish from the Central African
Republic is made with spinach or greens
mixed with peanut butter to make a thick
stew. It is served with rice or cornmeal.

• Makossa, the music of Cameroon,
is popular all over Africa.
Musicians use a thumb piano
(sanza), flute, and
percussion.

Thumb piano

• In parts of Zambia, areas of dense
forest are burned to clear the land for
farming. The ash acts as a fertilizer.

VICTORIA FALLS
Victoria Falls lies on
the border of Zambia
and Zimbabwe.
Water falls 108m
(354ft), and has twice
the drop of Niagara
Falls. The spray can
be seen from 65km
(40 miles) away.

RWANDA

RWANDA IS ONE of Africa's most
densely populated countries. Main
exports include coffee, tungsten,
tea, and pyrethrum.

R
Area 26,340sq km
(10,170sq miles)
Independence 1962, from Belgium
Currency Rwanda franc
Population 8,000,000
Official Languages Kinyarwanda,
French
Major Religions Christian 74%,
traditional beliefs 25%, other 1%

GORILLAS OF RWANDA
One of the last remaining sanctuaries of the
mountain gorilla is in
Rwanda. The largest
of all primates,
gorillas live in
female
groups with
one male.

BURUNDI

A TINY, DENSELY populated country,
Burundi is only 265 km (165 miles)
wide. Nickel, copper, and cobalt are
mined in the southeast.

Area 27,830sq km
(10,745sq miles)
Independence 1962, from Belgium
Currency Burundi franc
Population 6,400,000
Official Languages French, Kirundi
Major Religions Christian 68%,
traditional beliefs 32%

ZAMBIA

ZAMBIA IS A large, land-locked
country. The economy relies on road
and rail transport through the port
of Dar-es-Salaam in Tanzania.

Area 740,720sq km
(285,992sq miles)
Independence 1964, from Britain
Currency Zambian kwacha
Population 9,500,000
Official Language English
Major Religions Christian 63%,
traditional beliefs 35%, other 2%

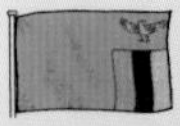

SOUTH AFRICA

MOST OF South Africa lies on a plateau, or tableland, about 900 metres (2,953 feet) above sea level. Land is used for grazing and wool is an important export. Minerals, such as gold, platinum, diamonds, and coal, provide most of the wealth.

Area 1,221,040sq km (471,443sq miles)
Government Multiparty democracy
Foundation 1910, declaration of Union of South Africa
Territories Transkei, Bophuthatswana, Ciskei, and Venda
Currency Rand
Population 41,500,000
Density 34 per sq km (88 per sq mile)
Official Languages Afrikaans, English
Major Religions Christian 64%, Hindu and Muslim 2%, other 34%

CENTRE OF GOVERNMENT

The Parliament Building in Cape Town was used for the first time in 1885. The building provided chambers for the two Houses of the Cape Parliament, as  well as a large library. Nelson Mandela took up his post here as the first black president of South Africa in May 1994.

MAJOR SOUTH AFRICAN LANGUAGES

Language	Number of speakers
Zulu	8,343,590
Xhosa	6,646,568
Afrikaans	5,702,535
Tswana	3,482,657
North Sotho	3,530,616
English	3,414,900

NAMIBIA

THIS HOT DRY country includes the barren Namib Desert and part of the Kalahari. Namibia's main exports are diamonds and minerals.

Area 824,290sq km (318,260sq miles)
Independence 1990, from South Africa
Currency Namibian dollar
Population 1,500,000
Official Language English
Major Religions Christian 90%, traditional beliefs 10%

WEATHER FACTS

42°C (107°F)   784mm (31in)   -9°C (16°F)

21.5°C (70.7°F)   13.9°C (57°F)

LAND PROFILE

In South Africa 27% of the land is used for agriculture.

%
0.5
10
12.5
27
50

LIFESTYLE FACTS

- In April 1994, the first-ever free elections were held. These followed years of apartheid, which denied black South Africans any voting power.
- Every year Zulus celebrate Shaka Day. Between 1818 and 1828, a great warrior called Shaka created the Zulu nation from many black clans in South Africa.
- South Africa has the fourth largest Indian community in the world.
- South Africa has the world's deepest gold mine. It is 4,200m (13,780 ft) deep.

SWAZILAND

THIS SMALL COUNTRY lies within South Africa. It is well-watered from four rivers which provide irrigation for citrus fruits and sugar-cane.

Area 17,360sq km (6,703sq miles)
Independence 1968, from Britain
Currency Lilangeni
Population 900,000
Official Languages English, Swazi
Major Religions Christian 60%, traditional beliefs 40%

SAVANNAH FACTS

- The springbok, a small antelope, lives on the grasslands. If alarmed, it can leap 3.5m (11.5ft) in the air with its back arched. This is called "pronking".
- The trees in the African savannah include several species of acacia. The sweet-thorn acacia sends tap roots down 65m (213ft) to seek out water.
- The oldest surviving inhabitants of southern Africa are the San (Bushmen). These people now live in the semi-desert regions of Botswana and Namibia.

10 rand

LANGUAGE

A traditional greeting in Zulu is *kunjani*.

NATIONAL BIRD

The blue crane is the national bird, and lives in protected areas throughout South Africa.

PRECIOUS MINERALS

South Africa is the world's leading supplier of gold and platinum. The country produces 40% of the world's gold, and 72% of its platinum.

MAJOR PLATINUM MARKETS (1992)

Destination	Amount in grams/ounces
Japan	52,731,000g (1,860,000oz)
Western Europe	23,814,000g (840,000oz)
North America	20,270,250g (715,000oz)
Other	10,914,750g (385,000oz)

LESOTHO

LESOTHO IS AN independent kingdom within South Africa. The mountain slopes provide good pasture for cattle and sheep.

Area 30,350sq km (11,718sq miles)
Independence 1966, from Britain
Currency Loti
Population 2,100,000
Official Languages English, Sotho
Major Religions Christian 93%, traditional beliefs 7%

BOTSWANA

THE KALAHARI, A semi-desert with grass and thorn bushes, covers much of Botswana. Most of its income comes from mining diamonds.

Area 581,730sq km (224,600sq miles)
Independence 1966, from Britain
Currency Pula
Population 1,500,000
Official Language English
Major Religions Traditional beliefs 50%, Christian 50%

ZIMBABWE

MOST PEOPLE IN the land-locked country of Zimbabwe belong to the Shona or Ndebele tribes. Main cash crops are tobacco, cotton, and sugar.

Area 390,580sq km (150,800sq miles)
Independence 1980, from Britain
Currency Zimbabwe dollar
Population 11,300,000
Official Language English
Major Religions Syncretic (part Christian, part traditional beliefs) 50%, Christian 26%, traditional beliefs 24%

CAPITAL OF ZIMBABWE
Harare, named after the African chief Neharawe, is the capital of Zimbabwe. It is a modern city with wide, tree-lined streets.

NDEBELE HOMES
Ndebele women decorate their homes with bright geometric patterns.

COMOROS

THE THREE MAIN islands of Comoros lie between mainland Africa and Madagascar. More than half of its food has to be imported.

Area 2,230sq km (861sq miles)
Independence 1975, from France
Currency CFA franc
Population 600,000
Official Languages Arabic, French
Major Religions Muslim 86%, Roman Catholic 14%

MADAGASCAR

THE MAIN EXPORTS of Madagascar are coffee, cloves, and vanilla. The fourth largest island in the world, Madagascar has a varied climate and a wide range of wildlife.

Area 587,040sq km (226,600sq miles)
Independence 1960, from France
Currency Malagasy franc
Population 14,800,000
Official Languages French, Malagasy
Major Religions Traditional beliefs 52%, Christian 41%, Muslim 7%

MADAGASCAR WILDLIFE FACTS
• Many unique animals evolved on Madagascar, which is isolated from mainland Africa.
• Two-thirds of the world's chameleons live on the island. These animals can change colour when threatened.
• Madagascar is also home to the Indri, the largest of the world's lemurs.

PEOPLE OF MADAGASCAR
The fertility rate of women here is one of the highest in the world. More than two-fifths of the population is under 15 years of age.

MOZAMBIQUE

MOZAMBIQUE IS ONE of the poorest countries in the world. Most farms are state owned and exports include coconuts, cotton, tea, and sugar.

Area 801,590sq km (309,493sq miles)
Independence 1975, from Portugal
Currency Metical
Population 16,000,000
Official Language Portuguese
Major Religions Traditional beliefs 60%, Christian 30%, Muslim 10%

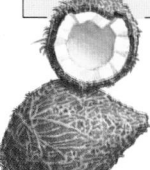

COCONUT
Copra, the dried flesh of the coconut, is used to make soap, shampoo, and margarine.

MALAWI

THIS NARROW COUNTRY is only 160km (100 miles) wide. Tobacco has recently overtaken tea as Malawi's major cash crop.

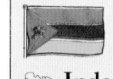
Area 118,840sq km (45,745sq miles)
Independence 1964, from Britain
Currency Malawi kwacha
Population 11,100,000
Official Language English
Major Religions Christian 66%, traditional beliefs 18%, other 16%

Map labels

TANZANIA
MALAWI
L. Nyasa (L. Malawi)
Lilongwe
Mt Mulanje 3,000m (9,843ft)
ZAMBIA
ANGOLA
Etosha Pan
NAMIBIA
Brandberg 2,606m (8,550ft)
Tsodilo Hills 1,375m (4,511ft)
Okavango Delta
Makgadikgadi Pans
Windhoek
BOTSWANA
KALAHARI DESERT
Gaborone
Harare
L. Kariba
Inyangani 2,592m (8,504ft)
ZIMBABWE
Monte Binga 2,436m (7,993ft)
Zambezi
MOZAMBIQUE
Mozambique Channel
Moroni
COMOROS
Mayotte I. (France)
Massif du Tsaratanana 2,876m (9,436ft)
MADAGASCAR
Betsiboka
Antananarivo
Tropic of Capricorn
Limpopo
Komati
Pretoria
Johannesburg
Vereeniging
Maputo
Mbabane
SWAZILAND
Lake Saint Lucia
Vaal
Orange
Fish
Bloemfontein
Maseru
LESOTHO
Giant's Castle 3,312m (10,868ft)
Durban
SOUTH AFRICA
KAROO
DRAKENSBERG
Parliament Building
Cape Town
Cape of Good Hope
Port Elizabeth
ATLANTIC OCEAN
INDIAN OCEAN
N
0 75km
0 40 miles

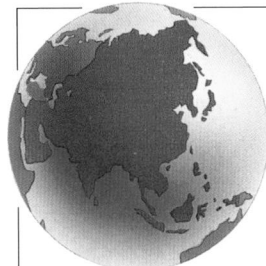

ASIA

ASIA IS THE world's largest continent and includes hot, dry deserts, icy tundra, and tropical rainforests. Asia also has the largest population of any continent with sixty per cent of the world's people.

Area 44,680,718sq km (17,251,315sq miles)
Countries 44
Largest Russian Federation 17,075,400sq km (6,592,846sq miles)
Smallest Maldives 300sq km (116 sq miles)
🏙 **Population** 3,184,078,671
Density 73per sq km (189per sq mile)
Major Languages Chinese, Hindi, Japanese, Bengali, Punjabi

🔺 **Highest point** Mount Everest, Nepal/China 8,848m (29,029ft)
🔻 **Lowest point** Dead Sea, Israel/Jordan 400m (1,312ft) below sea level
☀ **Highest temperature** 54°C (129°F), Tirat Tsvi, Israel
❄ **Lowest temperature** -68°C (-90°F) Verkhoyansk and Oimekon, Russian Federation

CLIMATE ZONES

KEY

- Mountain regions
- Polar and tundra
- Taiga
- Dry grassland
- Mediterranean
- Temperate forest
- Rainforest
- Tropical grassland
- Hot desert

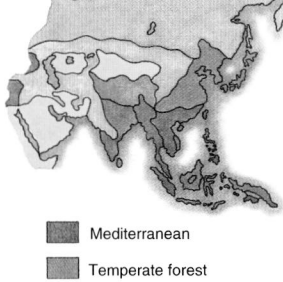

TIME ZONES

12:00 Greenwich | 15:30 Tehran | 17:30 New Delhi | 21:00 Tokyo

TOP CITY POPULATIONS

Tokyo, Japan 7,968,000
Delhi, India 8,419,084
Shanghai, China 8,760,000
Calcutta, India 11,021,000
Bombay, India 12,596,000

COUNTRIES, TERRITORIES AND CAPITALS

Name	Capital	Name	Capital
Afghanistan	Kabul	Mongolia	Ulan Bator
Bahrain	Al Manama	Nepal	Kathmandu
Bangladesh	Dhaka	North Korea	Pyongyang
Bhutan	Thimphu	Oman	Muscat
Brunei	Bandar Seri Begawan	Pakistan	Islamabad
Burma	Rangoon	Philippines	Manila
Cambodia	Phnom Penh	Qatar	Doha
China	Beijing	Russian Federation	Moscow
India	New Delhi	Saudi Arabia	Riyadh
Indonesia	Jakarta	Singapore	Singapore
Iran	Tehran	South Korea	Seoul
Iraq	Baghdad	Sri Lanka	Colombo
Israel	Jerusalem	Syria	Damascus
Japan	Tokyo	Taiwan	Taipei
Jordan	Amman	Tajikistan	Dushanbe
Kazakhstan	Astana (Akmola)	Thailand	Bangkok
Kuwait	Kuwait	Turkmenistan	Ashkhabad
Kyrgyzstan	Bishkek	United Arab Emirates	Abu Dhabi
Laos	Vientiane	Uzbekistan	Tashkent
Lebanon	Beirut	Vietnam	Hanoi
Malaysia	Kuala Lumpur	Yemen	Sana
Maldives	Male		

AGE BREAKDOWN

Under 15 years | 15 to 65 years | Over 65 years

Hong Kong 21%
Qatar 1%
Israel 8.9%
Yemen 49%
Yemen 48%
Qatar 71%

KEY
- Lowest %
- Highest %

FEWEST DOCTORS

Cambodia	1 to 25,000 people
Maldives	1 to 20,300 people
Nepal	1 to 16,830 people
Bhutan	1 to 13,110 people
Indonesia	1 to 7,050 people

LONGEST LIFESPAN

Female 82 78 77 77 76
Male 76 76 74 74 71 72

Japan Israel Brunei Singapore Kuwait

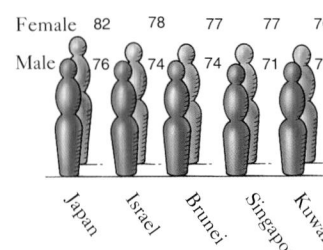

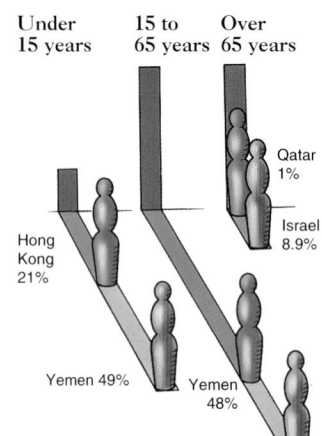

GROWING RICE
Ninety per cent of the world's rice is grown in Asia. Rice, along with wheat and maize, supplies the basic food needs for more than half the population of the world.

ASIA FACTS

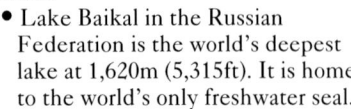

Baikal seal

- Lake Baikal in the Russian Federation is the world's deepest lake at 1,620m (5,315ft). It is home to the world's only freshwater seal.

- The world's top five tea growers are all in Asia – India, China, Sri Lanka, Japan, and the Russian Federation.

- All the world's major religions originated in Asia. They include Christianity, Islam, Judaism, Hinduism, Buddhism, and Sikhism.

- The highest city in the world is Lhasa, in Tibet, which lies at 3,650m (11,975ft) above sea level.

TALLEST MOUNTAINS

K2 (Mount Godwin Austen), Kashmir/China, 8,611m (28,251ft)

Lhotse, Tibet/Nepal 8,516m (27,940ft)

Mount Everest, Nepal/China, 8,848m (29,030ft)

Kangchenjunga, India/Nepal, 8,586m (28,169ft)

Makalu, Tibet/Ne 8,463m (27,766ft)

CROSS-SECTION (NORTH AND SOUTH)

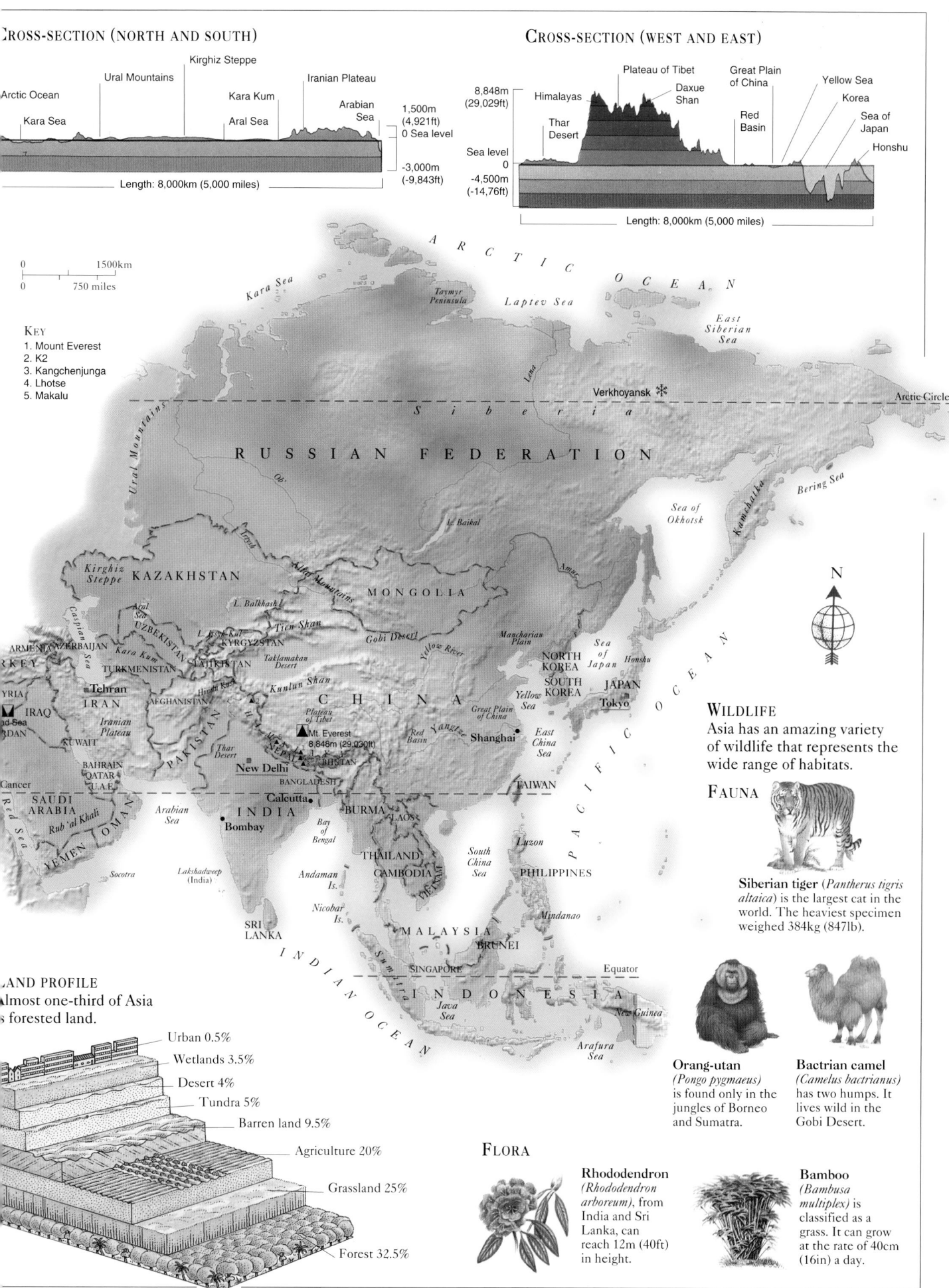

Kirghiz Steppe

Ural Mountains

Iranian Plateau

Arctic Ocean

Kara Kum

Arabian Sea

Kara Sea

Aral Sea

1,500m (4,921ft)

0 Sea level

-3,000m (-9,843ft)

Length: 8,000km (5,000 miles)

CROSS-SECTION (WEST AND EAST)

Plateau of Tibet

Great Plain of China

Himalayas

Daxue Shan

Yellow Sea

8,848m (29,029ft)

Korea

Thar Desert

Red Basin

Sea of Japan

Sea level 0

Honshu

-4,500m (-14,76ft)

Length: 8,000km (5,000 miles)

0   1500km
0   750 miles

KEY
1. Mount Everest
2. K2
3. Kangchenjunga
4. Lhotse
5. Makalu

A R C T I C   O C E A N

Kara Sea

Taymyr Peninsula

Laptev Sea

East Siberian Sea

Lena

S i b e r i a

Verkhoyansk ✳

Arctic Circle

R U S S I A N   F E D E R A T I O N

Ural Mountains

Ob

L. Baikal

Sea of Okhotsk

Kamchatka

Bering Sea

Kirghiz Steppe

KAZAKHSTAN

Irtysh

Altai Mountains

M O N G O L I A

Amur

Aral Sea

L. Balkhash

Gobi Desert

Manchurian Plain

Sea of Japan

N

Caspian Sea

UZBEKISTAN

L. Issyk Kul

Tien Shan

Yellow River

NORTH KOREA

Honshu

ARMENIA AZERBAIJAN

Kara Kum

KYRGYZSTAN

Taklamakan Desert

SOUTH KOREA

JAPAN

RKEY

TURKMENISTAN

TAJIKISTAN

Kunlun Shan

C H I N A

Tokyo

YRIA

Tehran

Hindu Kush

Plateau of Tibet

Yellow Sea

ad Sea

I R A N

AFGHANISTAN

Mt. Everest 8,848m (29,030ft)

Great Plain of China

East China Sea

RDAN

Iranian Plateau

Yangtze

Shanghai

KUWAIT

PAKISTAN

Thar Desert

NEPAL

Red Basin

P A C I F I C

Cancer

BAHRAIN QATAR U.A.E.

New Delhi

BHUTAN

TAIWAN

SAUDI ARABIA

BANGLADESH

O C E A N

Red Sea

Arabian Sea

Calcutta

Rub 'al Khali

I N D I A

BURMA

OMAN

Bombay

Bay of Bengal

LAOS

South China Sea

Luzon

YEMEN

Socotra

Lakshadweep (India)

THAILAND

CAMBODIA

PHILIPPINES

Andaman Is.

VIETNAM

Mindanao

Nicobar Is.

SRI LANKA

M A L A Y S I A

BRUNEI

I N D I A N

SINGAPORE

Equator

Sumatra

I N D O N E S I A

O C E A N

Java Sea

New Guinea

Arafura Sea

WILDLIFE
Asia has an amazing variety of wildlife that represents the wide range of habitats.

FAUNA

Siberian tiger (*Pantherus tigris altaica*) is the largest cat in the world. The heaviest specimen weighed 384kg (847lb).

Orang-utan (*Pongo pygmaeus*) is found only in the jungles of Borneo and Sumatra.

Bactrian camel (*Camelus bactrianus*) has two humps. It lives wild in the Gobi Desert.

FLORA

Rhododendron (*Rhododendron arboreum*), from India and Sri Lanka, can reach 12m (40ft) in height.

Bamboo (*Bambusa multiplex*) is classified as a grass. It can grow at the rate of 40cm (16in) a day.

LAND PROFILE
Almost one-third of Asia is forested land.

Urban 0.5%

Wetlands 3.5%

Desert 4%

Tundra 5%

Barren land 9.5%

Agriculture 20%

Grassland 25%

Forest 32.5%

ISRAEL

ABOUT FOUR-FIFTHS of Israelis are Jewish, and many Jews all over the world consider the State of Israel their homeland. The average age in Israel is very young: 25.6 years.

Area 20,700sq km (7,992sq miles)
Government Multiparty republic
Independence 1948, from Britain
Territories Disputes over land with Jordan and Syria
Currency New shekel
Population 5,600,000
Density 251 per sq km (650 per sq mile)
Official Languages Hebrew and Arabic
✡ **Major Religions** Jewish 83%, Muslim 13%, Christian 2%

LAND PROFILE
Almost half of Israel is desert.

%
1.5
5.0
20.5
29.5
43.5

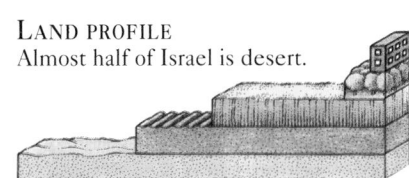

50 New shekels

LIFESTYLE FACTS
• Israel produces 95% of its own food, including delicious oranges, bananas, and avocados.

WESTERN WALL
Also called the Wailing Wall, this is a most sacred Jewish place of prayer and pilgrimage. It is all that remains of the Second Temple of Solomon, built about 200 B.C.

• 3% of Israelis live on 270 *kibbutzim*. These are communities, often farms, where families live together and share decision-making, work, and property.

DEAD SEA
This inland sea lies 400m (1,300ft) below sea level, and is the lowest point on Earth. Its water is the saltiest known, and this allows people to float easily.

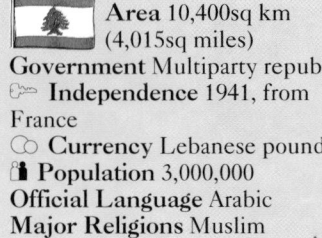

LEBANON

UNTIL THE outbreak of civil war in 1975, Lebanon was the trading and financial centre of the Middle East. Its fertile inland plain yields fruits, vegetables, grains, and tobacco.

Area 10,400sq km (4,015sq miles)
Government Multiparty republic
Independence 1941, from France
Currency Lebanese pound
Population 3,000,000
Official Language Arabic
Major Religions Muslim 57%, Christian 43%

SYRIA

THIS LAND OF rocky deserts and ancient cities has been called the cradle of civilization: the world's first alphabet was found in Ugarit.

Area 185,180sq km (71,500sq miles)
Government Single party republic
Independence 1946, from France
Currency Syrian pound
Population 14,700,000
Official Language Arabic
Major Religions Sunni Muslim 74%, Alawite, Druze, and other Muslim sects 16%, Christian 10%

DAMASCUS
The capital of Syria, Damascus is the world's most ancient inhabited city. It is famous for its souqs (markets).

PALMYRA
Palmyra (city of palms) now lies in ruins. It was once a major stopping place for travelling merchants taking the shortest route to the Mediterranean.

REGIONAL WEATHER FACTS
Records

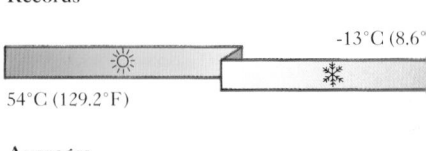

-13°C (8.6°
54°C (129.2°F)

Averages

484mm (19.1in)
24.3°C (75.7°F)   -10°C (14°

JORDAN

THE ARABIAN desert covers almost two-thirds of Jordan. Nomadic bedouin herders were the first desert-dwellers; now their numbers are dwindling.

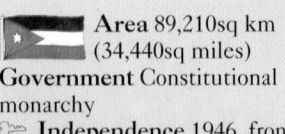

Area 89,210sq km (34,440sq miles)
Government Constitutional monarchy
Independence 1946, from Britain
Currency Jordanian dinar
Population 5,400,000
Official Language Arabic
Major Religions Muslim 95%, Christian 5%

PETRA
This beautiful, rose-red city was carved from solid rock more than 2,000 years ago.

Map labels
TURKEY
Aleppo
Jabal 'Abd al 'Aziz
Lake Asad
Jabbul Salt Marsh
Euphrates
Tigris
Orontes
SYRIA
IRAQ
Homs
Palmyra
Tripoli
Qornet es Saouda 3,087m (10,132ft)
Beirut
LEBANON
Litani
Damascus
Syrian Desert
Mt. Hermon 2,814m (9,236ft)
Har Meron 1,208m (3,965ft)
Haifa
Tirat Tsvi
Petah Tiqwa
Tel Aviv-Jaffa
Holon
West Bank
Jordan
Amman
Jerusalem
Western Wall
Gaza Strip
Dead Sea
Ardh es Suwwan
ISRAEL
JORDAN
SAUDI
EGYPT
Negev
Petra
Ma'an
Eilat
Gulf of Aqaba
Jabal Ram 1,754m (5,757ft)
MEDITERRANEAN SEA

N

0   150km
0   100 miles

IRAQ

IRAQ'S STATE religion is Islam, and its followers are called Muslims. From 1980 to 1988, Iraq was at war with Iran.

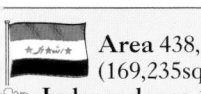

Area 438,320sq km (169,235sq miles)
Independence 1932, from Britain
Currency Iraqi dinar
Population 20,400,000

SAUDI ARABIA

THIS KINGDOM is the world's leading producer and exporter of oil, and holds 25 per cent of world oil reserves.

Area 2,149,690sq km (829,995sq miles)
Independence and Unification 1932
Currency Saudi riyal
Population 17,900,000

ARABIC

Arabic is the religious language of Muslims all over the world, whether they are Arabs or not.

LANGUAGE

A traditional greeting in Arabic is *ahlan wasahlan*.
أهلاً وسهلاً

ARAB HOUSES

Most Arabs are of the Muslim faith, which says that women must cover themselves from everyone except their families. Muslim houses have a screened balcony that shields women from the outside, and also keeps the house cool.

KUWAIT

IRAQ INVADED oil-rich Kuwait in 1990. The Iraqis were driven out seven months later during the Gulf War.

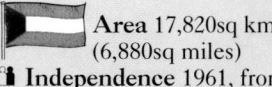

Area 17,820sq km (6,880sq miles)
Independence 1961, from Britain
Currency Kuwaiti dinar
Population 1,500,000

BAHRAIN

BAHRAIN IS MADE up of 33 islands in the west of the Arabian Gulf. It was the first Arab nation to strike oil, in 1932.

Area 680sq km (263sq miles)
Independence 1971, from Britain
Currency Bahrain dinar
Population 600,000

ARAB HEADDRESS
Headcloths are worn by both men and women to protect them from the sun. Arab women often wear a veil or mask.

Chequered headcloth, or smagh — *White headcloth, or ghoutra* — *Headcloth, or misfa, worn with a veil* — *Misfa worn with a mask*

MAJOR OIL PRODUCERS	Country	Barrels per day (1998)
The countries in the table are members of OPEC (Organization of Petroleum Exporting Countries), which was formed in 1960.	Saudi Arabia	8,248,000
	Iran	3,586,000
	United Arab Emirates	2,261,000
	Kuwait	2,074,000
	Data supplied by OPEC bulletin	

YEMEN

NORTH AND South Yemen were united in 1990 to form the Republic of Yemen. Oil finds are small compared to wealthy neighbouring countries.

Area 527,970sq km (203,849sq miles)
Unification 1990
Currency Northern riyal and southern dinar
Population 14,500,000

OMAN

SINCE 1970, when Sultan Qaboos took power, Oman's oil wealth has been used to develop industry, education, and health care.

Area 212,460sq km (82,030sq miles)
Independence 1951, from Britain
Currency Omani rial
Population 2,200,000

QATAR

UP TO 70 per cent of Qatar's people were attracted there by jobs in the oil industry. Qatar has one of the lowest death rates in the world.

Area 11,000sq km (4,247sq miles)
Independence 1971, from Britain
Currency Qatar riyal
Population 600,000

UNITED ARAB EMIRATES

THE UAE HAS some of the richest oil deposits in the world. Money from oil is used to turn the desert into farmland.

Area 83,600sq km (32,278sq miles)
Independence 1971, from Britain
Currency UAE dirham
Population 1,900,000

Mosul
Baghdad
Basra
KUWAIT
Kuwait City
An Nafud
Manama
BAHRAIN
OMAN
QATAR
Doha
Dubai
Abu Dhabi
U.A.E.
Muscat
Jabal ash Sham 3018m (9,902ft)
Riyadh
Medina
Jeddah
Mecca
SAUDI ARABIA
Rub al Khali
Jabal Abhā 3133m (10,279ft)
OMAN
Wal al Masila
Jabal an Nabi Shu'ayb 3760m (12,337ft)
Sana
YEMEN
Aden
Gulf of Aden
Gulf of Oman
Arabian Sea
The Gulf
Red Sea
Asir
Al-Hijaz
Syrian Desert
IRAQ
SYRIA
IRAN
JORDAN
TURKEY
Euphrates
Tigris

N

500km
400 miles

IRAN

IRAN, ORIGINALLY CALLED Persia, is a flat, mainly barren land surrounded by mountains. The only fertile areas are near the Caspian Sea and the mountain foothills. The country has large reserves of oil, natural gas, and minerals.

 Area 1,648,000sq km (636,293sq miles)
Government Islamic republic
Independence 1925, from Britain
Currency Iranian rial
Population 67,300,000
Density 41 per sq km (106 per sq mile)
Official Language Farsi (Persian)
Major Religions Shi'ite Muslim 95%, Sunni Muslim 4%, Baha'i, Christian, Jewish, Zoroastrian 1%

ARCHITECTURE

The Imam Mosque is in the traditional Islamic architectural style. The mosque, built in 1020, is decorated with fine tile work.

Imam Mosque, Isfahan

The modern Shayad Monument was built to commemorate King Cyrus' birth, 2,500 years ago. He united the Persian Empire.

Shayad Monument, Tehran

WEATHER FACTS

51°C (123.8°F)   246mm (9.7in)   -21°C (-5°F)

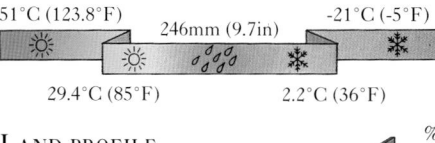

29.4°C (85°F)   2.2°C (36°F)

LAND PROFILE

Only 6.5% of Iran is agricultural land.

%
0.5
0.5
6.5
11.5
22
59

LIFESTYLE FACTS

• All Iranian men have to join the armed forces at the age of 16. The only reasons for exemption are poor health or the death of a brother in military service since 1979.

• Wrestling and horse-racing are traditional sports, although rugby and volleyball are the most popular modern games.

• Iran is the world's second largest oil producer. Oil accounts for 80% of revenue and 95% of foreign exchange earnings.

• Most towns get their water supply from a series of long irrigation tunnels, called *qanat*, which bring water from the mountains.

MUSLIM FACTS

• Muslims believe that the greatest and last of the prophets was Muhammad, who was born in Arabia in A.D. 570. Islam is the name that the prophet Muhammad gave to the religion of the Muslims.

• All women in Iran, even tourists, must cover their bodies. Only hands, feet, and face may show. Records are kept of anyone breaking this law.

Iranian woman in traditional headcloth

LANGUAGE

A traditional greeting in Farsi is *salam*.

سلام

MAJOR OIL MARKETS	
Importer	Thousand barrels per day
Western Europe	1,195
Asia and Far East	938
Eastern Europe	185
Latin America	125
Africa	45
Middle East	30

PERSIAN CARPETS

Hand-woven carpets are Iran's second largest export. Persian carpets have different patterns according to their region of origin. These include Isfahan, Kashan, Kerman, Qom, Shiraz, and Tabriz.

• After Muhammad's death, there was a dispute among his followers about who should lead the Muslims. The Sunnis followed the Caliphs while the Shi'ites decided to follow Muhammad's cousin, Ali.

• Under Islam it is possible for a ma[n] to have four wives, but he must treat them all equally.

• The Koran is the Holy Book of the Muslims. It is the basis for Muslim law on all important aspects of life, and is treated with great respect.

TURKMENISTAN

TURKMENISTAN IS AN extremely dry land, with large supplies of natural gas beneath the Kara Kum desert. In irrigated areas, farmers grow cotton, wheat, grapes, and melons.

 Area 488,100sq km (188,455sq miles)
Government Single party republic
Independence 1991, from Soviet Union
Currency Manat
Population 4,100,000
Density 8 per sq km (21 per sq mile)
Official Language Turkmen
Major Religions Muslim 85%, Eastern Orthodox 10%, other 5%

AFGHANISTAN

THIS AGRICULTURAL COUNTRY is divided by the Hindu Kush Mountains, where many people still live as nomads. In villages, farmers raise sheep to export the lambskins.

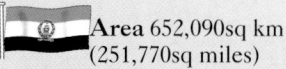 **Area** 652,090sq km (251,770sq miles)
Government Mujahideen coalition
Independence 1919, from Britain
Currency Afghani
Population 20,100,000
Density 31 per sq km (80 per sq mile)
Official Languages Dari (Persian) and Pashtu
Major Religions Sunni Muslim 84%, Shi'ite Muslim 15%, Hindu, Jewish, Sikh 1%

TAJIKISTAN

THE PAMIR MOUNTAINS of Tajikista[n] have one of the world's longest mountain glaciers – 72 km (45 miles) long. In the valleys, farmers grow fruit, rice, and cotton.

 Area 143,100sq km (55,251sq miles)
Government Single party republic
Independence 1991, from Soviet Union
Currency Rouble
Population 6,100,000
Density 43 per sq km (111 per sq mile)
Official Language Tajik
Major Religions Sunni Muslim 85%, Shi'ite Muslim 5%, other 10%

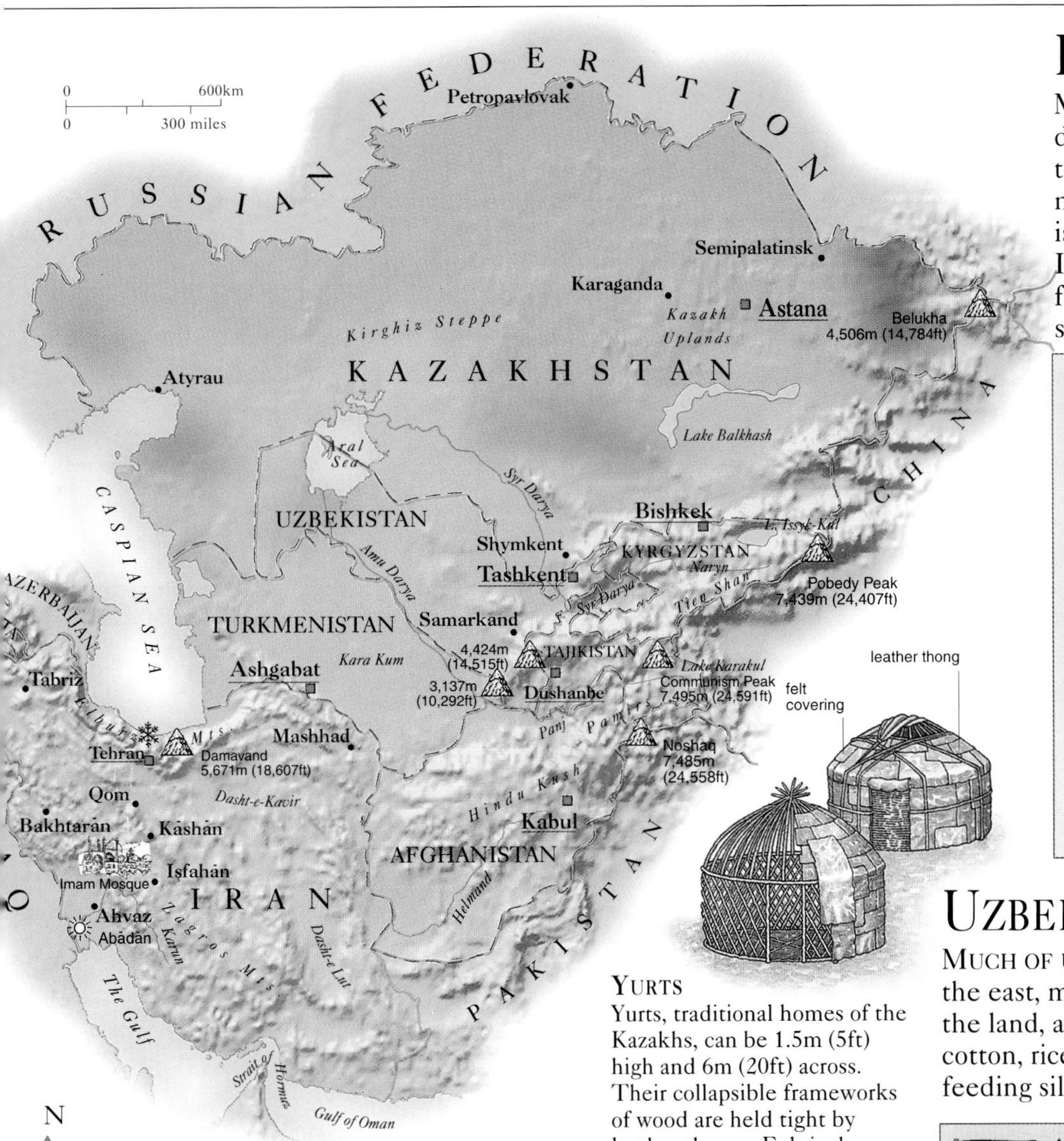

Map labels:

RUSSIAN FEDERATION

0 — 600km
0 — 300 miles

Petropavlovsk

Semipalatinsk

Karaganda

Kirghiz Steppe

Kazakh Uplands

Astana

Belukha
4,506m (14,784ft)

KAZAKHSTAN

Atyrau

Aral Sea

Lake Balkhash

C H I N A

UZBEKISTAN

Bishkek

Shymkent

Syr Darya

KYRGYZSTAN

Tashkent

Naryn

Amu Darya

Tz Issyk-Kul

CASPIAN SEA

AZERBAIJAN

TURKMENISTAN

Samarkand

Syr Darya

Tien Shan

Pobedy Peak
7,439m (24,407ft)

Tabriz

Ashgabat

Kara Kum

4,424m (14,515ft)

TAJIKISTAN

3,137m (10,292ft)

Dushanbe

Lake Karakul
Communism Peak
7,495m (24,591ft)

felt covering

leather thong

Tehran

Damavand
5,671m (18,607ft)

Mashhad

Panj

Pamir

Noshaq
7,485m (24,558ft)

Qom

Dasht-e-Kavir

Hindu Kush

Kabul

AFGHANISTAN

Bakhtaran

Kashan

Imam Mosque

Isfahan

I R A N

Zagros Mts

Ahvaz

Abadan

Helmand

Dasht-i-Lut

The Gulf

P A K I S T A N

Strait of Hormuz

Gulf of Oman

N

KAZAKHSTAN

MOST OF KAZAKHSTAN is a dry plain, with mountains to the southeast. The main crop is wheat which is grown in the north. Industries include mining for copper, lead, gold, and silver.

Area 2,717,300sq km (1,049,150sq miles)
Government Multiparty republic
Independence 1991, from Soviet Union
Currency Tenge
Population 17,100,000
Density 6 per sq km (16 per sq mile)
Official Language Kazakh
Major Religions Muslim 47%, other (mostly Russian Orthodox and Lutheran) 53%

YURTS
Yurts, traditional homes of the Kazakhs, can be 1.5m (5ft) high and 6m (20ft) across. Their collapsible frameworks of wood are held tight by leather thongs. Felt is then stretched over the frame and lashed into position.

UZBEKISTAN

MUCH OF UZBEKISTAN is desert. In the east, mountain streams irrigate the land, and farmers can grow cotton, rice, and mulberry trees for feeding silkworms.

Area 439,733sq km (172,742sq miles)
Government Single party republic
Independence 1991, from Soviet Union
Currency Sum
Population 22,800,000
Density 51 per sq km (132 per sq mile)
Official Language Uzbek
Major Religions Muslim 88%, Orthodox Christian 12%

KYRGYZSTAN

MANY OF THE Kyrgyz people are nomads who tend their flocks on the slopes of the Tien Shan Mountains. In Bishkek, there are factories for processing leather and soap.

Area 198,500sq km (76,640sq miles)
Government Multiparty republic
Independence 1991, from Soviet Union.
Currency Som
Population 4,700,000
Density 24 per sq km (62 per sq mile)
Official Language Kyrgyz
Major Religion Muslim 65%, other 35%

CASPIAN SEA
• The Caspian Sea is the largest inland lake in the world and covers an area of 371,000 sq km (143,205 sq miles).

• Sturgeon, a kind of fish, are found in the Caspian Sea. They can grow up to 7m (23ft) long, and their eggs, called caviar, are an expensive delicacy. Caviar is a major export from Iran.

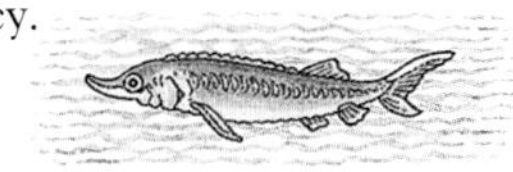

• Salmon, bream, mullet, carp, catfish, and perch are also caught for export.

MAKING SILK
Silk is produced by the white moth caterpillar, or silkworm. After caterpillars have spun a silken cocoon, they are put into boiling water. The silk is removed and spun into threads.

mulberry leaves

silkworm

INDIA

INDIA HAS THE world's second largest population, and a wide variety of peoples, religions, and languages. The mountainous north contrasts with the low-lying south.

Area 3,287,590sq km (1,269,338sq miles)
Government Multiparty republic
Independence 1947, from Britain
Currency Indian rupee
Population 935,700,000
Density 315 per sq km (816 per sq mile)
Official Languages Hindi, English, Bengali, Punjabi, Gujarati; 19 languages recognized constitutionally
Major Religions Hindu 83%, Muslim 11%, Christian 2%, Sikh 2%, Buddhist 1%, Jain 0.5%, Parsee and Jewish 0.43%, other 0.07%

WEATHER FACTS

46°C (114.8°F) 642mm (25.3in) -14°C (6.8°F)
31.6°C (88.9°F) 14°C (57.2°F)

LAND PROFILE

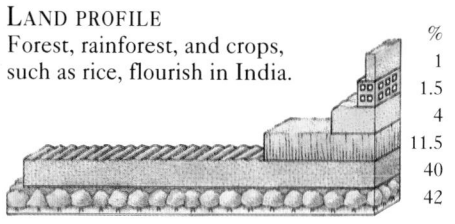

Forest, rainforest, and crops, such as rice, flourish in India.

%
1
1.5
4
11.5
40
42

LIFESTYLE FACTS

• Each Indian region has its own unique range of dishes. There are at least a hundred different ways of preparing curry sauces, and up to 30 spices to choose from.

• Kabaddi is an ancient sport, popular all over India. Two teams (women or men) play on a pitch, raiding each other's territory, while chanting.

100 Indian rupees

LANGUAGE

A traditional greeting in Hindi is *namaskar.* नमस्कार

Traditional seven-stringed sitar

• In classical Indian music, rhythms are very complicated, and the ability to sing is very highly regarded. The tabla (twin drums) and stringed instruments, such as the tambura and sitar, accompany the voice.

• India produces more films than any other country in the world: more than 800 every year. Bombay is the centre of the Indian film industry.

NATIONAL SYMBOL

India's national symbol is the Royal Bengal tiger, which is a protected species.

TAJ MAHAL

The Taj Mahal, situated just outside Agra, was built by Mughal emperor Shah Jahan (1592–1666) as a tomb and monument to his favourite wife, Mumtaz Mahal. Her body lies beneath it. The Taj Mahal took 22 years to build and is one of the most visited buildings in the world.

INDIAN TEA PRODUCTION, (1996)

Area	Tonnes
Assam, Bengal, Bihar, and Tripura	565,422
Punjab, Uttar Pradesh, and Himachal Pradesh	2,551
South India	185,949
Total	753,922

Source: International Tea Committee

TEXTILES

Textiles and clothing together make up India's second biggest export sector, after gems and jewellery. Textiles and clothes are produced in factories, but many people still work at home to produce beautiful, and often ancient, designs.

Map labels: AFGHANISTAN, PAKISTAN, IRAN, Peshawar, Islamabad, Rawalpindi, Gujranwala, Lahore, Faisalabad, Srinagar, K2 8,611m (28,251ft), Controlled by China, claimed by India, Nanda Devi 7,817m (25,646ft), HIMALAYA, Siwalik Range, Sulaiman Range, Indus, Multan, Jacobadad, Minar-e-Pakistan, New Delhi, Thar Desert, Jaipur, Agra, Lucknow, Kathmandu, NEPAL, Pashupatinath, Mt. Everest 8,848m (29,029ft), Kula Kangri 7,554m (24,783ft), Thimphu, BHUTAN, Cherrapunji, Karachi, Hyderabad, Taj Mahal, Kanpur, Ghaghra, Patna, Ganges, Jamuna, Brahmaputra, Dhaka, BANGLADESH, Calcutta, Tropic of Cancer, Ahmadabad, Vindhya Range, Narmada, Surat, Satpura Range, Nagpur, INDIA, Bombay, Pune, Godavari, Chilika Lake, Hyderabad, Arabian Sea, Western Ghats, Eastern Ghats, Bay of Bengal, Bangalore, Madras, INDIAN OCEAN

N

0 500km
0 300 miles

RAINFALL

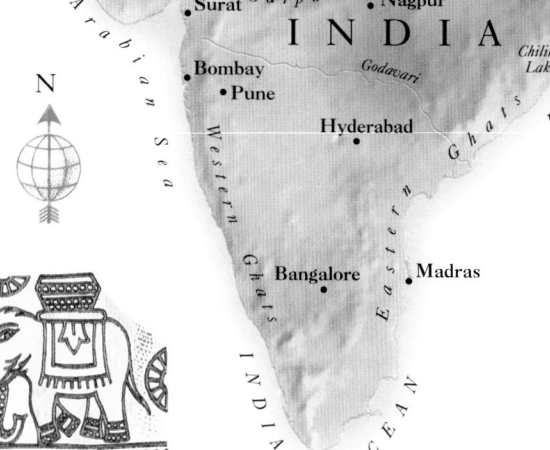

The rainiest town in the world is Cherrapunji, northeastern India, with an average 11,437mm (450in) of rainfall per year. This amount of rain would almost cover six adults standing on each other's shoulders.

PAKISTAN

IN 1988, BENAZIR BHUTTO became the only woman to lead a Muslim country when she was first elected prime minister of Pakistan.

Area 796,100sq km (307,374sq miles)
Government Federal parliamentary democracy
Independence 1947, from Britain
Currency Pakistani rupee
Population 140,500,000
Density 182 per sq km (472 per sq mile)
Official Language Urdu
Major Religions Muslim 97%, Hindu 2%, Christian 1%

WEATHER FACTS

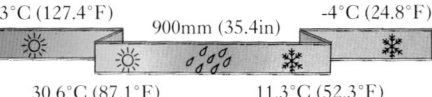

53°C (127.4°F)   900mm (35.4in)   -4°C (24.8°F)

30.6°C (87.1°F)   11.3°C (52.3°F)

LAND PROFILE

Pakistan is mostly covered in grassland and desert.

%
1
1.5
4
11.5
40
42

LIFESTYLE FACTS

• Pakistan's population, with one of the world's highest growth rates, is set to reach 150 million by the 21st century. Half the population is less than 15 years old.

• Pakistan has one of the world's best cricket teams. They won the cricket world cup in 1992 under captain Imran Khan.

100 Pakistani rupees

MINAR-E

The Minar-e-Pakistan is a fine tower in Lahore. It was built on a historic spot in 1940 to commemorate Pakistan Day.

• Pakistan's male squash players are the best in the world. Jahangir Khan (b.1963) remained unbeaten for 5 years, 7 months, and one day: an all-time world record.

LANGUAGE

A traditional greeting in Urdu is *assalm-u-alaikum.* اسلام علیکم

NEPAL

NEPAL IS A mountainous country, lying mostly in the Himalayas. About 250,000 people visit each year, mainly for mountain trekking.

LIFESTYLE FACTS

• In Nepal the traditional greeting is to press the palms together in a prayer-like gesture.

• The Nepalese celebrate 50 religious festivals each year, involving 120 days of celebrations. They are so frequent that they often overlap.

LANGUAGE

A traditional greeting in Nepali is *namaste.*

HINDU STATE

Nepal is the world's only Hindu state. Its many superb temples include gold-roofed Pashupatinath, the holiest of all the Nepalese temples dedicated to the god Shiva. Non-Hindus are not allowed to enter the temple.

Area 140,800sq km (54,363sq miles)
Government Constitutional monarchy
State established 1869
Currency Nepalese rupee
Population 21,100,000
Density 151 per sq km (391 per sq miles)
Official Language Nepali
Major Religions Hindu 90%, Buddhist 5.3%, Muslim 2.7%, Christian 0.21%, other 1.79%

BHUTAN

BHUTAN IS A Buddhist state, ruled by a king who allows only 2,250 tourists per year. Nine out of ten Bhutanese are farmers and herders.

Area 47,000sq km (18,147sq miles)
Government Constitutional monarchy
Independence 1949, from Britain
Currency Ngultrum
Population 1,600,000
Density 34 per sq km (88 per sq mile)
Official Language Dzongkha
Major Religions Mahayana Buddhist 70%, Hindu 24%, other 6%

VEGETATION

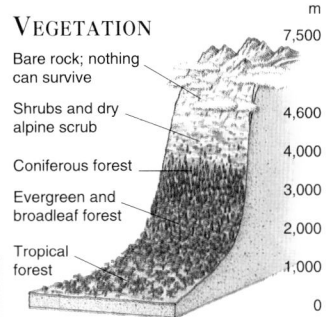

Bare rock; nothing can survive

Shrubs and dry alpine scrub

Coniferous forest

Evergreen and broadleaf forest

Tropical forest

m
7,500
4,600
4,000
3,000
2,000
1,000
0

LIFESTYLE FACTS

• Bhutanese food is hot and spicy. The national dish is *emadatsi*, made of chilli peppers in cheese sauce.

• Rare blue sheep and snow leopards live on high ground.

• Archery is the Bhutanese national sport. Competitors may distract each other by jumping in front of the targets.

BANGLADESH

BANGLADESH IS A low, flat land, and hundreds of square kilometres are flooded every year. It is the world's most densely populated country.

Area 143,998sq km (55,598sq miles)
Government Multiparty republic
Independence 1971, from Pakistan
Currency Taka
Population 120,400,000
Density 899 per sq km (2,330 per sq miles)
Official Language Bengali
Major Religions Muslim 83%, Hindu 16%, Buddhist and Christian 1%

FLOOD PLAIN

Bangladesh, located on a low-lying delta, is flooded by monsoon rainfall from June to the end of September.

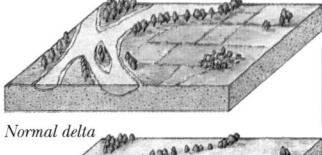

Normal delta

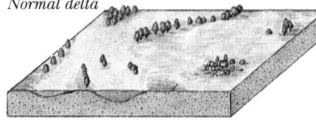

Flooded delta

LIFESTYLE FACTS

• Bangladesh's economy is based mainly on agriculture; the main export is jute, a plant used like cotton.

• Rivers form a huge transport network: there are about 8,370 kilometres of waterways in Bangladesh.

SRI LANKA

FORMERLY CALLED CEYLON, Sri Lanka is an island country off the southeast coast of India. It has a warm, tropical climate with two monsoon seasons each year. Tea and rubber plantations cover much of the land. Gemstones and spices are important exports.

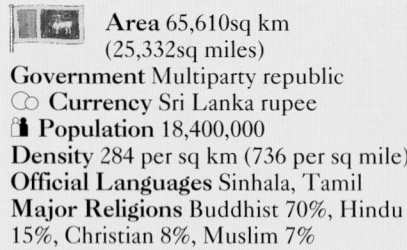

Area 65,610sq km (25,332sq miles)
Government Multiparty republic
Currency Sri Lanka rupee
Population 18,400,000
Density 284 per sq km (736 per sq mile)
Official Languages Sinhala, Tamil
Major Religions Buddhist 70%, Hindu 15%, Christian 8%, Muslim 7%

LIFESTYLE FACTS

• Most Sri Lankans make their own curry powder by grinding a mixture of local spices and herbs with a mortar and pestle.

• Every summer there is a festival when elephants in beautiful embroidered cloth parade through the city of Kandy.

• Sri Lanka has 242 species of butterfly. During March and April, the seasonal migration is a spectacular sight.

TEA GROWING
Sri Lanka is one of the world's top tea growers. Each year, more than 182 million kg (400 million lb) of tea are exported worldwide. Expert tasters will check the quality and value before making a purchase.

WEATHER FACTS

40°C (104°F)   -3°C (27°F)
2,527mm (99.5in)
27.2°C (81°F)   26.7°C (80°F)

LANGUAGE
A traditional greeting in Sinhalese is *aubowan*.

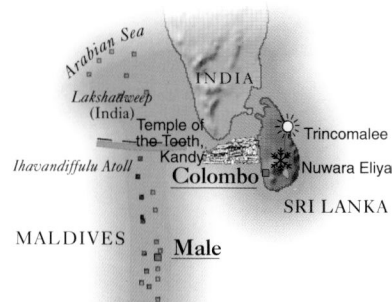

NATIONAL LANDMARK
The city of Kandy is home to the 16th-century Buddhist Temple of the Tooth *(Dalada Maligawa)*. This is where a sacred tooth, said to be one of Buddha's, is kept in a special casket.

INDIAN ELEPHANT
The Indian elephant *(Elephas maximus)* is similar to its African relative, but it has smaller ears and four nails on each back foot instead of three.

Arabian Sea
INDIA
Lakshadweep (India)
Temple of the Tooth
Trincomalee
Kandy
Ihavandiffulu Atoll
Colombo
Nuwara Eliya
SRI LANKA
MALDIVES
Male
Equator
Fua Mulaku I.
Addu Atoll
I N D I A N
BRITISH INDIAN OCEAN TERRITORY (UK)
Chagos Archipelago
Diego Garcia
N
SEYCHELLES
Victoria
Amirante Is.
Mahé
Aldabra Is.
Farquhar Is.
Agalega Is. (Mauritius)
O C E A N
COMOROS
Mayotte (France)
Cargados Carajos Shoals (Mauritius)
Tromelin (Réunion)
MADAGASCAR
Port Louis
Rodrigues I. (Mauritius)
Réunion (France)
MAURITIUS

0   1000km
0   500 miles

ISLAND PARADISE
The island of Mauritius is a popular tourist destination. Almost 50% of the visitors are European, most of them from France.

MALDIVES

THE HOT, TROPICAL climate of the Maldives means that most islands are covered with lush vegetation. Tourist resorts on the island of Male help to boost the economy.

Area 300sq km (116sq miles)
Government Republic
Currency Rufiyaa
Population 300,000
Official Language Dhivehi (Maldivian)
Major Religions Sunni Muslim 100%

SEYCHELLES

MAHÉ IS THE largest of the 115 islands that form the Seychelles. Tourism is the most important industry, along with exports of fish, copra, and cinnamon.

Area 280sq km (108sq miles)
Government Multiparty republic
Currency Seychelles rupee
Population 73,000
Official Language Seselwa (French Creole)
✝ Major Religions Roman Catholic 90%, other 10%

MAURITIUS

MAURITIUS LIES ABOUT 2,000 km (1,200 miles) off the coast of Africa. The most important crops are sugar cane, tea, and aloe – a medicinal and cosmetic plant.

Area 1,860sq km (718sq miles)
Government Multiparty republic
Currency Mauritian rupee
Population 1,100,000
Official Language English
Major Religions Hindu 52%, Roman Catholic 26%, Muslim 17%, other 5%

THAILAND

THAILAND IS THE world's leading exporter of rice, and paddy fields cover much of the land. Most Thais are Buddhists and the country has more than 30,000 Buddhist temples.

 Area 513,120sq km (198,116sq miles)
Government Constitutional monarchy
Unification 1782, Thailand never colonized
Currency Baht
Population 58,800,000
Density 115 per sq km (298 per sq mile)
Official Language Thai
Major Religions Buddhist 95%, Muslim 3.8%, Christian 0.5%, Hindu 0.1%, other 0.6%

BURMA

THE NORTH OF Burma is flat and farmers grow peanuts, millet, and cotton. Teak forests cover the south. The timber is hauled to rivers by elephants, and floated to sawmills.

 Area 676,550sq km (261,200sq miles)
Government Military regime
Independence 1948, from Britain
Currency Kyat
Population 46,500,000
Density 71 per sq km (184 per sq mile)
Official Language Burmese
Major Religions Buddhist 89%, Muslim 4%, other 7%

REGIONAL WEATHER FACTS

1744mm (68.7in)
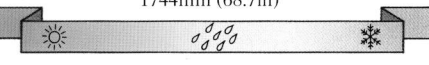
27°C (80.6°F)   25.4°C (77.7°F)

MONSOON
Most of Southeast Asia is affected by the monsoon winds, which bring heavy rainfall every year from May to October. Monsoon comes from the Arabic word meaning "season". Although the rains are vital for crops, such as rice, they can also cause disastrous floods.

LIFESTYLE FACTS
• Burma's rubies are considered the finest in the world. In the East, a ruby is thought to protect the wearer from harm.

• All young men in Thailand are expected to become monks for at least three months of their lives and reject all material wealth.

ANGKOR WAT
The magnificent temple city of Angkor Wat in Cambodia was built by the Khmers in the 12th century A.D.

LANGUAGE
A traditional greeting in Thai is *sawatdee*. สวัสดี

THAI BOXING
Thai boxers use their feet, knees, elbows and fists to fight.

(Map labels: Hkakabo Razi 5,881m (19,296ft), L. Indawgyi, Mandalay, Fan Si Pan 3,143m (10,312ft), Hanoi, Gulf of Tongking, BANGLADESH, Chin Hills, Irrawaddy, Kachin Range, CHINA, Salween, Mekong, Luang Prabang Range, BURMA, Bia 2,820m (9,252ft), Inthanon 2,595m (8,514ft), LAOS, Bay of Bengal, Rangoon, Mae Nam Ping, Vientiane, VIETNAM, Gulf of Martaban, Andaman Sea, THAILAND, Bangkok, Angkor Wat, Batdambang, Tonle Sap, CAMBODIA, Gulf of Thailand, Aoral 1,813m (5,834ft), Phnom Penh, SOUTH CHINA SEA, Ho Chi Minh City, Isthmus of Kra, Samui I., Phuket I., Luang Lagoon, Songkhla, MALAYSIA, N)

0   500km
0   300 miles

CAMBODIA

MOST PEOPLE IN Cambodia are descendants of the Khmers who arrived in Southeast Asia in about 2000 B.C. Today, farmers grow rice, bananas, coconuts, and cotton.

 Area 181,040sq km (69,000sq miles)
Government Parliamentary democracy
Independence 1953, from France
Currency Riel
Population 10,300,000
Density 58 per sq km (150 per sq mile)
Official Language Khmer
Major Religions Buddhist 88%, Muslim 20%, other 10%

LAOS

LAOS HAS MANY mountains and forests, and most people live in the Mekong River valley. Only about 4 per cent of the land is suitable for agriculture. Tin is mined for export.

 Area 236,800sq km (91,429sq miles)
Government Single party republic
Independence 1949, from France. 1954 independent state established
Currency Kip
Population 4,900,000
Density 21 per sq km (54 per sq mile)
Official Language Laotian
Major Religions Buddhist 85%, Christian 2%, other 13%

VIETNAM

VIETNAM IS A WARM, monsoon land with heavy rainfall and thick forests. Many forests were destroyed during the Vietnam War. Rice, maize, and sweet potatoes are the main crops.

Area 329,560sq km (127,243sq miles)
Government Communist state
Unification 1976, proclamation of Socialist Republic of Vietnam
Currency New dong
Population 74,500,000
Density 229 per sq km (593 per sq mile)
Official Language Vietnamese
Major Religions Buddhist 55%, Christian 7%, other 38%

CHINA

THE THIRD LARGEST country in the world, China contains almost a quarter of the world's people. The landscape varies enormously. In the north there are dry deserts, while the south is warm and humid. Rice grows well in the warm, moist soil.

 Area 9,396,960sq km (3,628,166sq miles)
Government Single party republic
Unification 221 B.C., separate states united under First Emperor
Currency Yuan
Population 1.2 billion
Density 131 per sq km (340 per sq mile)
Official Language Mandarin Chinese
Major Religions Confucianist 20%, Buddhist 6%, Taoist 2%, other 72%

WEATHER FACTS

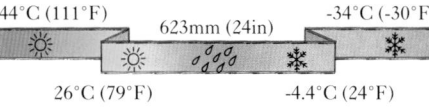

44°C (111°F)   -34°C (-30°F)
          623mm (24in)
26°C (79°F)   -4.4°C (24°F)

GREAT WALL OF CHINA
The Great Wall of China is the longest man-made structure in the world. In 214 B.C. the First Emperor ordered one huge wall over 2,350km (1,460 miles) long to guard the northern frontier.

MONGOLIA

THE CLIMATE IN Mongolia is severe and it is one of the least populated countries in the world. Most people were nomadic herders but land is now organized into state farms.

 **Area** 1,565,000sq km (604,247sq miles)
Government Constitutional monarchy
Republic Mongolian People's Republic declared, 1924
Currency Tughrik
Population 2,400,000
Density 2 per sq km (5 per sq mile)
Official Language Khalka Mongol
Major Religions Limited religious practice due to former communist regime. Principal religion is Tibetan Buddhist, with 4% Muslim

LAND PROFILE
Most Chinese live in just 15% of the total land area.

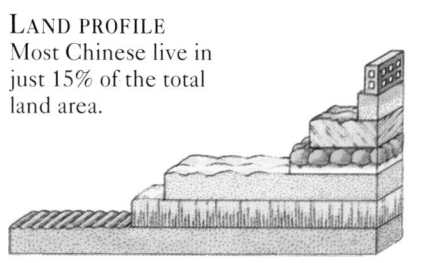

%
1.5
2
6.5
9
21
24
36

LIFESTYLE FACTS
• The population in China increases by about 17 million people a year. To try to limit the expansion, one-child families are given priority for housing and medical care.

• One in five Chinese live in large cities, the rest live in the countryside. Most people travel by bicycle and there are 17,500,000 made in China every year.

REGIONAL CHINESE FOOD
• Peking (now Beijing) dishes often include duck and sweet and sour sauces.

• Food from the region of Sichuan is usually spicy, with garlic, chillies, and ginger.

• Cantonese cooking often features shellfish and other seafoods.

 • Shanghainese dishes can include steamed dumplings, as well as bird's nest soup made from the nests of cave swiftlets in southeast China.

TIBET FACTS
• Tibet lies in the highlands of southwest China at an average height of 4,500m (14,800ft). This is higher than most European mountains.

• Prayer flags are a Tibetan tradition symbolizing the Buddhist faith. Before the Chinese occupation, they flew from every home as a symbol of good luck.

Tibetan prayer flags

MONGOLIAN LIFESTYLE FACTS
• One third of Mongolia is covered by the vast Gobi Desert. Gobi is the Mongolian word for "waterless place".

 • Mongols are expert horsemen. The Three Games of Men festival takes place every July and includes a 32-km (20-mile) horse race for children aged seven to twelve, wrestling, and archery.

• Mongolia has resources of coal, oil, and gold. The main coal mines are found near the capital city of Ulan Bator.

10 yuan

LANGUAGE
A traditional greeting in Mandarin is *nin hao*. 你好

IMPERIAL PALACE, BEIJING
The Imperial Palace in Beijing was built for the Emperor Zhu Di during the Ming Dynasty (1368–1644). The palace complex contains nearly 1,000 buildings. Only the emperor's family and people doing business were allowed into the central palace, which became known as the Forbidden City.

MAIN CHINESE OCCUPATIONS (1992)

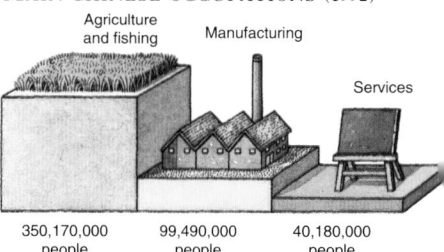

Agriculture and fishing   Manufacturing   Services

350,170,000 people   99,490,000 people   40,180,000 people

• The Dalai Lama is the head of the Tibetan Buddhists. He went into exile in India after Tibet was invaded by China in 1950. Dalai Lama is a Mongolian word meaning "great ocean".

• Tibetans consider it bad luck if it snows during a marriage procession. But it is good luck to meet a funeral procession or a passer-by carrying a pitcher of water.

• Because of the cool, dry air of Tibet, grain can be stored for up to 60 years.

MACAO

THIS SMALL TERRITORY lies on the south coast of China. Textiles, incense, and fireworks are Macao's major exports.

 Area 20sq km (8sq miles)
Government Under Chinese administration
Currency Pataca
Population 355,693
Official Languages Cantonese, Portuguese

SOUTH KOREA

FORESTS COVER 70 per cent of the land in South Korea. The country's chief crops are rice and tobacco, and fishing is an important industry.

Area 99,020sq km (38,232sq miles)
Government Multiparty republice
Republic Republic of Korea declared, 1948
Currency South Korean won
Population 45,000,000
Density 456 per sq km (1,182 per sq mile)
Official Language Korean
Major Religions Mahayana Buddhist 47%, Protestant 38%, Roman Catholic 11%, Confucian 3%, other 1%

NORTH KOREA

NORTH KOREA IS a mountainous country and most people live on coastal plains in the east. Minerals such as copper and zinc are mined.

Area 120,540sq km (46,540sq miles)
Government Single party republic
Republic Democratic People's Republic of Korea founded in 1948
Currency North Korean won
Population 23,900,000
Density 198 per sq km (515 per sq mile)
Official Language Korean
Major Religions Organized religion not encouraged by the state

NORTH AND SOUTH KOREA FACTS

• Korean ginseng is a plant that is highly valued for its ability to improve memory and restore energy. The plant takes about seven years to mature.

• For centuries women divers, called *haenyo*, have collected seaweed and sea cucumbers from the coast off Cheju Island. A *haenyo* can dive to 18m (60ft) and hold her breath for four minutes.

• The remains of the oldest observatory in the world are in eastern South Korea. It was built in about A.D. 643.

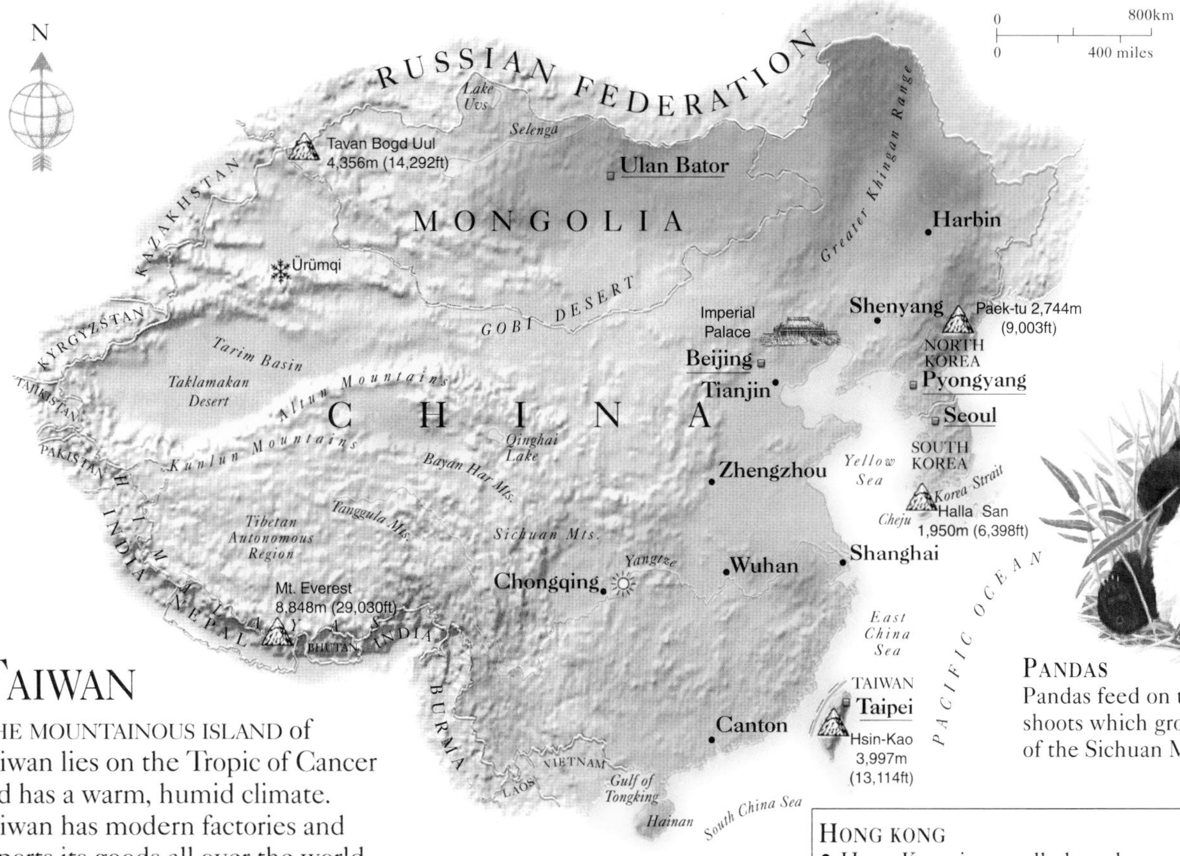

PANDAS

Pandas feed on the bamboo shoots which grow in the forests of the Sichuan Mountains.

TAIWAN

THE MOUNTAINOUS ISLAND of Taiwan lies on the Tropic of Cancer and has a warm, humid climate. Taiwan has modern factories and exports its goods all over the world.

Area 36,179sq km (13,969sq miles)
Government Multiparty republic
State founded In 1949
Currency New Taiwan dollar
Population 20,900,000
Density 645 per sq km (1,670 per sq mile)
Official Language Mandarin Chinese
Major Religions Buddhist-Confucian-Taoist 93%, Christian, Muslim, other 7%

TAIWAN'S TOP EXPORTS (1996)

Product	US$ m
Data-processing machines	16,253
Electronic components	8,146
Textiles	4,823
Plastics	4,780
Transmission apparatus	2,772
Electric motors & generators	1,852
Sports equipment	1,516

HONG KONG

• Hong Kong is a small, densely populated area with 5,859 people per sq km (15,175 per sq mile).

• Hong Kong is a major financial centre and attracts investors from around the world.

• In 1842, Britain took control of Hong Kong under the Treaty of Nanjing. In 1898, Britain agreed to rent the island and part of the mainland for 99 years. On 1 July 1997, it was handed back to China.

JAPAN

JAPAN IS MADE up of a chain of about 3,900 volcanic islands. The four main islands are Hokkaido, Honshu, Shikoku, and Kyushu. Tokyo, the capital, is one of the most densely populated cities in the world.

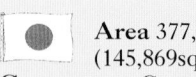

Area 377,800sq km (145,869sq miles)
Government Constitutional monarchy
Independence Restored, 1952, after World War II occupation
Territories Ogasawara Islands
Currency Yen
Population 125,100,000
Density 322 per sq km (834 per sq mile)
Official Language Japanese
Major Religions Shinto and Buddhist 76%, Buddhist 16%, other 8%

HORIYUJI TEMPLE

Buddhism was introduced into Japan in A.D. 538. The Horyuji Temple in Nara, first built in 607, is the world's oldest wooden building.

WEATHER FACTS

38°C (100.4°F)   1460mm (57.5in)   -24°C (-11.2°F)

23.8°C (74.8°F)   4.3°C (39.7°F)

LANGUAGE

A traditional greeting in Japanese is *konnichiwa*. こんにちは

Sea of Okhotsk
Kurile Islands
Iturup
Kunashir
Shikotan
Hokkaido
Ishikari Mts.
• Sapporo
Tsugaru Strait
Ou Mountains
Akita
Sado
Sea of Japan
Shinano Honshu
Oki Is.
Mt. Fuji 3,776m (12,385ft)
L. Biwa
Imperial Palace
Tokyo
• Yokohama
• Nagoya
Chugoku Mts.
Kobe• •Osaka
Nara
JAPAN
N
Tsushima
Shikoku
Kyushu
PACIFIC OCEAN
0   250km
0   150 miles
East China Sea
Osumi Is.
Amami Is.
Ryukyu Islands
Okinawa

PHEASANT

The pheasant often appears in Japanese folklore and is the national bird.

1,000 Japanese yen

BLOSSOM

Cherry blossom is the national flower of Japan and is celebrated with festivals in spring.

LIFESTYLE FACTS

• A Japanese employee works longer hours (2,100 hours per year) than a worker in the United States (1,900 hours), or in Germany or France (1,600 hours).

• Japan has more golf courses per sq km than any other country. Due to lack of suitable space, there are multi-storey driving ranges.

• The Ainu, the aboriginal people of Japan, have their own culture, language, and religion. They live on Hokkaido island.

• In Japan, traditional flower arranging is called *ikebana*. The display is based on three main lines that symbolize heaven, earth, and humankind.

IMPERIAL PALACE

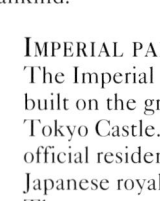

The Imperial Palace was built on the grounds of Tokyo Castle. It is the official residence of the Japanese royal family. The present emperor, Akihito, is a direct descendant of the legendary first emperor Jimmu (660-585 B.C.).

FOOD FROM THE SEA

• Japan is the world's greatest fishing nation in terms of volume of catch. Almost 10 million tonnes of fish are caught each year.

• Fish is the major source of protein and each person in Japan eats an average of 30kg (66lb) of fish a year.

• Life expectancy in Japan is the highest in the world: 81.8 years for women and 75.9 years for men.

MOUNT FUJI FACTS

• Mount Fuji is one of Japan's 60 active volcanoes. It has not erupted since 1707.

• Mount Fuji is sacred to the Japanese, and in summer people climb to the shrine on the summit.

SUMO WRESTLERS

Sumo wrestlers may weigh up to 280kg (617lb). To maintain this colossal weight, a wrestler eats a daily stew of seafood, meat, vegetables, and tofu, called *chanko-nabe*.

TOP ELECTRONIC EXPORTS (1996)
(Value in US $1,000's)

Export	Value
TV cameras	4,078,154
Video recorders	2,826,193
Televisions	2,031,576
Tape recorders	1,904,653
Radios	1,518,825

LAND PROFILE

Most of Japan is mountainous. Only 15% is suitable for farming.

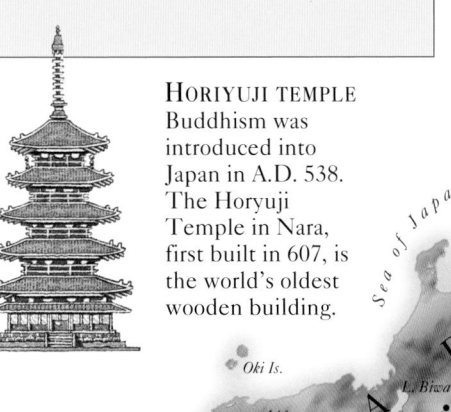

%
4
5.5
90.5

INDONESIA

INDONESIA IS THE world's biggest island chain. It has more than 17,000 islands and covers three time zones. The weather is hot, wet, and humid. Rice is the most important food crop.

Area 1,904,570sq km (735,555sq miles)
Government Multiparty republic
Independence 1949, declared Republic of the United States of Indonesia
Currency Rupiah
Population 197,600,000
Density 109 per sq km (282 per sq mile)
Official Language Bahasa Indonesia
Major Religions Muslim 87%, Christian 10%, Hindu 2%, Buddhist 1%

REGIONAL WEATHER FACTS

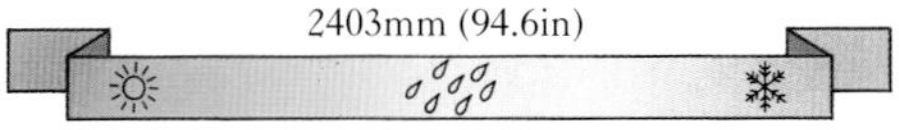

2403mm (94.6in)

26.8°C (80.2°F)　　　26.7°C (80.1°F)

REGIONAL FACTS

- In Malaysia, workers collect latex from rubber trees. They make a diagonal cut in the tree and then collect the white latex, or rubber, that oozes from the cut.

- Java produces the world's finest batik: traditional cloth decorated using wax and dyes.

- Indonesia is the largest Islamic country in the world.

LANGUAGE

A traditional greeting in Bahasa is *selamat pagi*.

PHILIPPINES

THE PHILIPPINES IS a collection of more than 7,000 islands. Rainfall can be heavy, and typhoons sweep through the northern islands.

Area 300,000sq km (115,830sq miles)
Government Multiparty republic
Independence 1946, from United States
Currency Philippine peso
Population 67,600,000
Density 227 per sq km (588 per sq mile)
Official Languages Filipino, English
Major Religions Roman Catholic 83%, Protestant 9%, Muslim 5%, Buddhist and other 3%

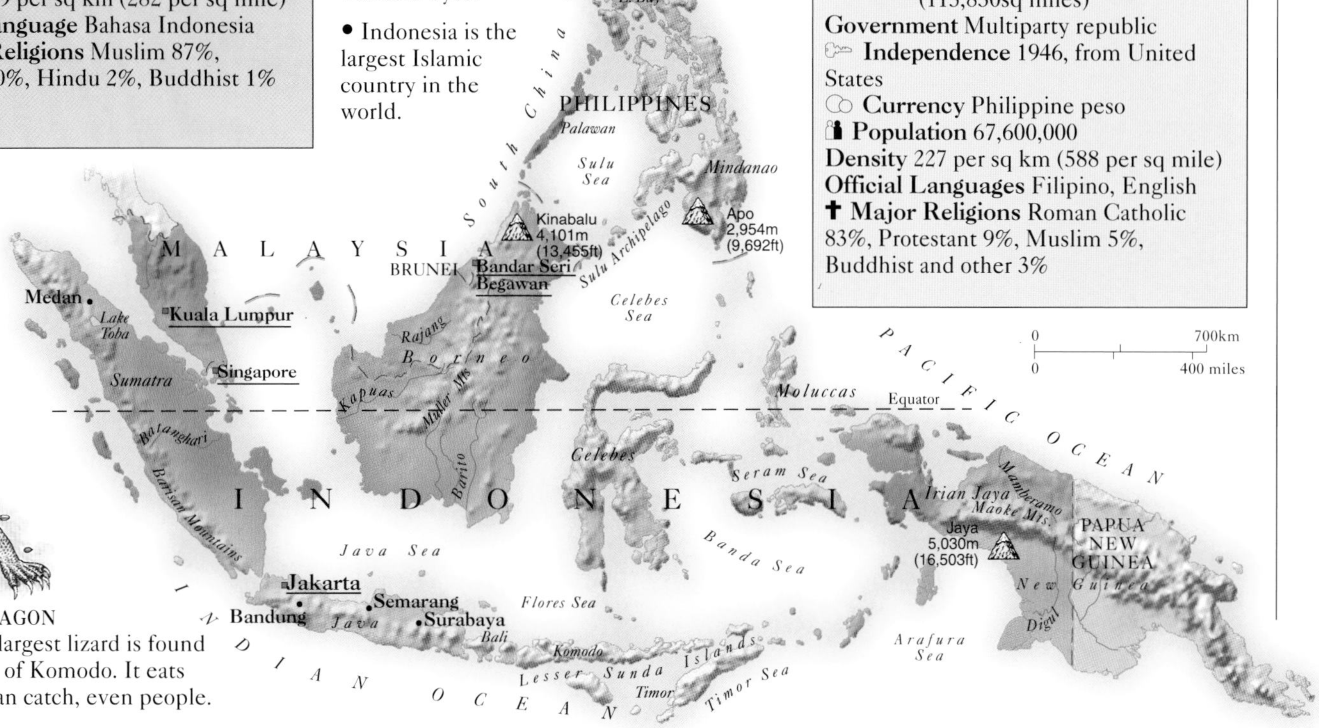

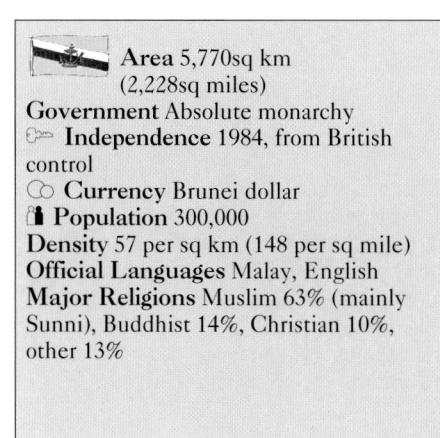

KOMODO DRAGON
The world's largest lizard is found on the island of Komodo. It eats anything it can catch, even people.

MALAYSIA

THE COUNTRY OF Malaysia covers the Malay Peninsula and northern Borneo. Malaysia is the world's leading producer of natural rubber.

Area 329,750sq km (127,317sq miles)
Government Federal constitutional monarchy
Independence 1957, from Britain
Currency Ringgit
Population 20,100,000
Density 61 per sq km (158 per sq mile)
Official Languages Bahasa Malaysia, English
Major Religions Muslim 53%, Buddhist 19%, Chinese faiths 11.6%, Christian 7%, Hindu 6.9%, traditional beliefs 2%, Sikh and other 0.5%

SINGAPORE

SINGAPORE IS A small and successful country. Most people work in industries making electrical goods, clothes, and transport items.

Area 620.5sq km (239sq miles)
Government Multiparty democracy
Independence 1965, breaks away from Malaysia
Currency Singapore dollar
Population 2,800,000
Density 4,590 per sq km (11,894 per sq mile)
Official Languages Bahasa Malaysia, English, Mandarin, Tamil
Major Religions Buddhist 30%, Christian 20%, Muslim 17%, other 33%

BRUNEI

BRUNEI IS A tiny, but extremely rich, country on the island of Borneo. The wealth comes from local oil, and the people of Brunei pay no taxes.

Area 5,770sq km (2,228sq miles)
Government Absolute monarchy
Independence 1984, from British control
Currency Brunei dollar
Population 300,000
Density 57 per sq km (148 per sq mile)
Official Languages Malay, English
Major Religions Muslim 63% (mainly Sunni), Buddhist 14%, Christian 10%, other 13%

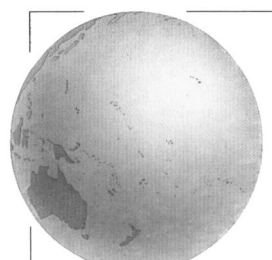

AUSTRALASIA AND OCEANIA

THIS AREA COVERS the continent of Australia, as well as New Zealand and numerous island groups in the Pacific Ocean. Climate zones vary greatly across the region, and include the wet, tropical conditions of the Pacific Islands as well as the hot, dry deserts of central Australia.

Area 8,508,238sq km (3,285,048sq miles)
Countries 13
Largest Australia 7,686,850sq km (2,967,908sq miles)
Smallest Nauru 21sq km (8sq miles)
▓ **Population** 26,370,088
Density 3 per sq km (8 per sq mile)
Major Languages English, Italian (Australia), Fijian (Fiji), Hindi (Fiji), Greek (Australia)

▲ **Highest point** Mt. Wilhelm, Papua New Guinea 4,509 m (14,794 ft)
▼ **Lowest point** Lake Eyre, Australia -16m (-52ft)
☀ **Highest temperature** 53°C (128°F), Bourke, Australia
❄ **Lowest temperature** -22°C (-8°F), Canberra, Australia

CLIMATE ZONES

KEY

▓	Mountains
▓	Hot desert
▓	Dry grassland
▓	Mediterranean
▓	Temperate forest
▓	Tropical grassland
▓	Rainforest

COUNTRIES, TERRITORIES, AND CAPITALS

Name	Capital
Australia	Canberra
Fiji	Suva
Kiribati	Bairiki
Marshall Islands	Majuro
Micronesia (Federated States of)	Palikir
Nauru	No capital
New Zealand	Wellington
Palau	Oreor
Papua New Guinea	Port Moresby
Samoa	Apia
Solomon Islands	Honiara
Tonga	Nuku'alofa
Tuvalu	Fongafale
Vanuatu	Vila

TIME ZONES

Greenwich 12:00   Perth 20:00   Sydney 22:00   Majuro 24:00 (midnight)

INTERNATIONAL DATE LINE

The Date Line is an imaginary north–south line that runs through the Pacific Ocean. The date is different east and west of the line (east is a day behind).

TOP CITY POPULATIONS

 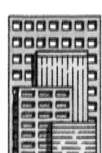 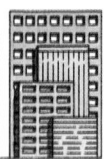

Adelaide, Australia 1,080,000   Perth, Australia 1,262,000   Brisbane, Australia 1,488,000   Melbourne, Australia 3,217,000   Sydney, Australia 3,770,000

MILFORD SOUND

Milford Sound in New Zealand is a spectacular fjord that was created when the sea flooded a glaciated valley.

CONTINENT FACTS

• In Australia, the Royal Flying Doctor Service provides emergency medical treatment for people who live vast distances from the nearest source of medical help.

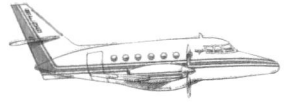

• New Zealand's North Island is a volcanic region, with three active volcanoes, hot springs, geysers, and boiling mud pools.

• There are about 25,000 islands in the Pacific Ocean, but only a few thousand are inhabited. The islands stretch across an area that is larger than the entire continent of Asia.

LARGEST DESERTS

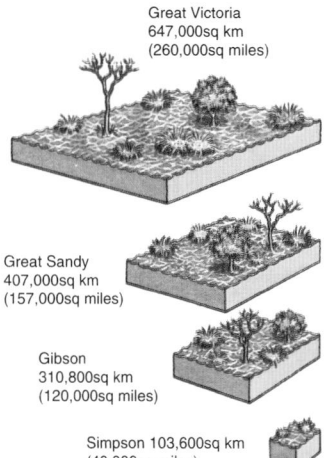

Great Victoria 647,000sq km (260,000sq miles)

Great Sandy 407,000sq km (157,000sq miles)

Gibson 310,800sq km (120,000sq miles)

Simpson 103,600sq km (40,000sq miles)

AGE BREAKDOWN

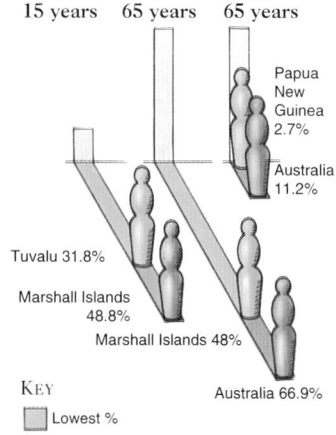

Under 15 years   15 to 65 years   Over 65 years

Papua New Guinea 2.7%
Australia 11.2%
Tuvalu 31.8%
Marshall Islands 48.8%
Marshall Islands 48%
Australia 66.9%

KEY
□ Lowest %
■ Highest %

FEWEST DOCTORS

Papua New Guinea	1 to 12,870 people
Solomon Islands	1 to 10,000 people
Vanuatu	1 to 5,500 people
Marshall Islands	1 to 4,000 people
Tuvalu	1 to 2,500 people

LONGEST LIFESPAN

Female   80   79   68   69
Male   73   73   65   64

Australia   New Zealand   Tuvalu   Nauru

Map labels

Equator
INDO
Arafura Sea
Timor Sea
Darwin
Kimberley Plateau
INDIAN OCEAN
Hamersley Range
Great Sandy Desert
Macdonell R
Gibson Desert
AUSTRA
Simpson Desert
Great Victoria Desert
Lake -15m
Perth
Great Australian Bight

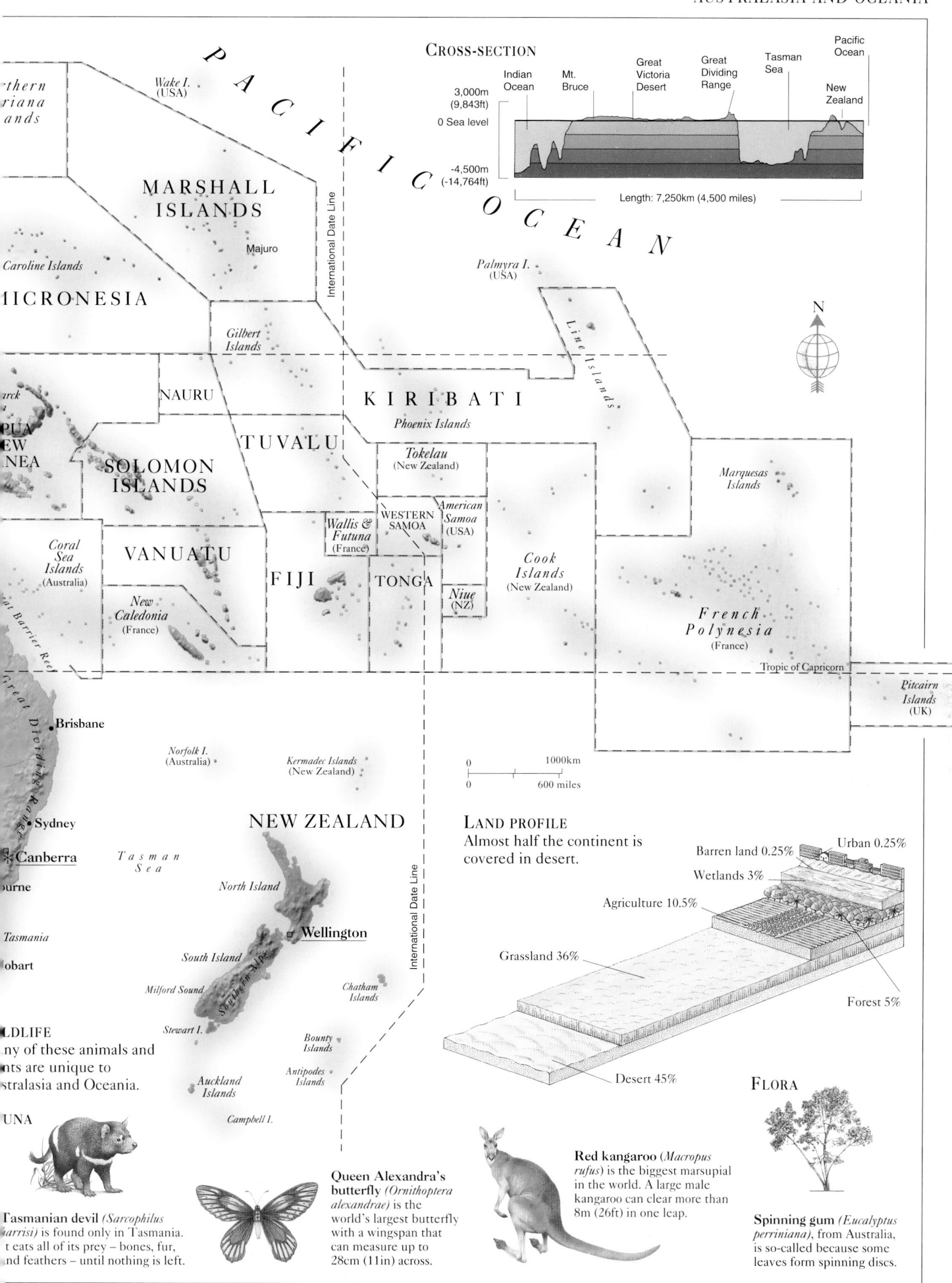

PACIFIC OCEAN

Wake I.
(USA)

MARSHALL
ISLANDS

Caroline Islands

Majuro

MICRONESIA

International Date Line

Palmyra I.
(USA)

Line Islands

NAURU

KIRIBATI

ark

PUA
EW
NEA

SOLOMON
ISLANDS

TUVALU

Phoenix Islands

Tokelau
(New Zealand)

Marquesas
Islands

Coral
Sea
Islands
(Australia)

VANUATU

Wallis &
Futuna
(France)

WESTERN
SAMOA

American
Samoa
(USA)

Cook
Islands
(New Zealand)

French
Polynesia
(France)

New
Caledonia
(France)

FIJI

TONGA

Niue
(NZ)

Barrier Reef

Tropic of Capricorn

Pitcairn
Islands
(UK)

Brisbane

Great Dividing Range

Sydney

Canberra

Norfolk I.
(Australia)

Kermadec Islands
(New Zealand)

0   1000km
0   600 miles

ourne

Tasman
Sea

NEW ZEALAND

North Island

International Date Line

LAND PROFILE
Almost half the continent is
covered in desert.

Tasmania

Wellington

Urban 0.25%

Barren land 0.25%

obart

South Island

Wetlands 3%

Milford Sound

Southern Alps

Chatham
Islands

Agriculture 10.5%

Grassland 36%

Stewart I.

Bounty
Islands

Forest 5%

LDLIFE
ny of these animals and
nts are unique to
stralasia and Oceania.

Auckland
Islands

Antipodes
Islands

Desert 45%

FLORA

Campbell I.

UNA

Queen Alexandra's
butterfly *(Ornithoptera*
alexandrae) is the
world's largest butterfly
with a wingspan that
can measure up to
28cm (11in) across.

Red kangaroo *(Macropus*
rufus) is the biggest marsupial
in the world. A large male
kangaroo can clear more than
8m (26ft) in one leap.

Spinning gum *(Eucalyptus*
perriniana), from Australia,
is so-called because some
leaves form spinning discs.

Tasmanian devil *(Sarcophilus*
arrisi) is found only in Tasmania.
t eats all of its prey – bones, fur,
nd feathers – until nothing is left.

CROSS-SECTION

Indian
Ocean

Mt.
Bruce

Great
Victoria
Desert

Great
Dividing
Range

Tasman
Sea

Pacific
Ocean

New
Zealand

3,000m
(9,843ft)
0 Sea level

-4,500m
(-14,764ft)

Length: 7,250km (4,500 miles)

N

NEW ZEALAND

TWO MAIN ISLANDS and a number of smaller islands make up New Zealand. Its rich pastureland makes it one of the world's main producers of meat, dairy products, and wool. New Zealand is in an earthquake zone, and tremors are felt every year.

Area 268,860sq km (103,730sq miles)
Government Unitarian parliamentary democracy, with British sovereign as constitutional monarch
Independence 1947, from Britain
Territories Cook Islands, Niue, Tokelau
Currency New Zealand dollar
Population 3,600,000
Density 13 per sq km (34 per sq mile)
Official Languages English, Maori
✝ **Major Religions** Protestant 62%, Roman Catholic 18%, other 20%

BEEHIVE BUILDING

This circular building, in the capital city of Wellington, is one of three parliament buildings. It was designed by British architect Sir Basil Spence (1907–76) and was opened in 1977.

SHEEP FARMING

The mild climate of New Zealand provides permanent pasture for the country's 52.6 million sheep. About 340,000 tonnes of wool are shorn a year, most of it used to supply high-class knitting yarns for export.

MAORI FACTS

• New Zealand's first settlers were the Maori – Polynesians who arrived in about A.D. 950. They called the country Aotearoa, which means "the land of the long white cloud."

• At the time of the 1991 census, the Maori population of New Zealand stood at 434,847, with 89% living on North Island. Almost one-third of Maoris are under 10 years of age.

• *Maoritanga* is the word for Maori culture, and traditional Maori art is preserved through woodcarving and stone sculpture.

WEATHER FACTS

35°C (95°F)   1,205mm (47.4in)   -6°C (21.2°F)
16.3°C (61.3°F)   9.5°C (49.1°F)

LIFESTYLE FACTS

• Sport is important to the people of New Zealand. The most popular sports for people over 15 years of age are swimming, diving, waterpolo, cycling, snooker and pool, tennis, and aerobics.

• In 1893, New Zealand became the first country where women could vote in national elections.

• Orchards produce a wide range of fruits ranging from apples to tamarillos, avocadoes, and kiwi fruit.

kiwi fruit

• Hiking is a popular pastime in New Zealand, where 13% of the land is turned over to National Parks.

NEW ZEALAND

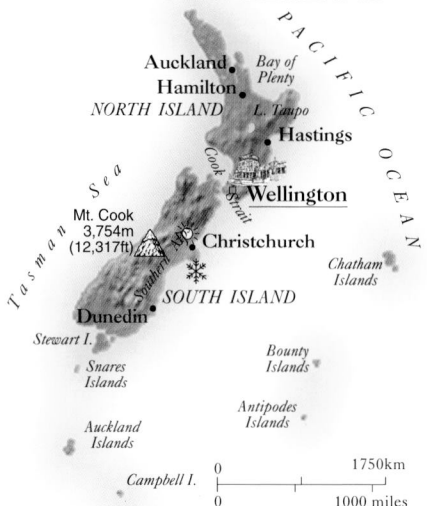

PACIFIC OCEAN
Auckland
Hamilton
Bay of Plenty
NORTH ISLAND
L. Taupo
Hastings
Tasman Sea
Cook Strait
Wellington
Mt. Cook 3,754m (12,317ft)
Christchurch
Chatham Islands
SOUTH ISLAND
Dunedin
Stewart I.
Snares Islands
Bounty Islands
Auckland Islands
Antipodes Islands
Campbell I.

0   1750km
0   1000 miles

PAPUA NEW GUINEA

PAPUA NEW GUINEA occupies the eastern half of a large island. The land is mountainous, and there are deposits of gold, oil, and copper.

Area 462,840sq km (178,700sq miles)
Government Parliamentary democracy
Independence 1975, from Australian administration
Currency Kina
Population 5,000,000
Density 13 per sq km (34 per sq mile)
Official Language English

LAND PROFILE

More than two-thirds of the land is used for grazing.

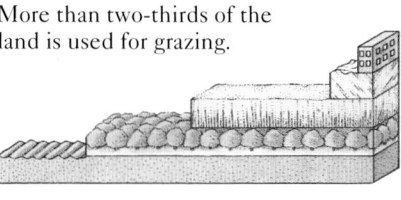
10 New Zealand dollars

MICRONESIA

MORE THAN 600 islands and islets make up the Federated States of Micronesia. Plants include black pepper, which is grown for export.

Area 2,900sq km (1,120sq miles)
Independence 1986, from United States administration
Currency United States dollar
Population 107,000
Density 152 per sq km (394 per sq mile)
Official Language English

NAURU

THE SMALL ISLAND of Nauru is surrounded by a coral reef. The country has very little agriculture because of the infertile soil.

Area 21sq km (8sq miles)
Independence 1968, from UN supervision
Currency Australian dollar
Population 10,000
Density 476 per sq km (1,233 per sq mile)
Official Language Nauruan

SOLOMON ISLANDS

MOST OF THE eight main islands in this group are thickly forested and have a hot, wet climate. Islanders catch tuna for export.

Area 28,900sq km (11,158sq miles)
Independence 1978, from Britain
Currency Solomon Islands dollar
Population 400,000
Density 11 per sq km (28 per sq mile)
Official Language English

MARSHALL ISLANDS

THE MARSHALL ISLANDS consist of two parallel chains of coral atolls. Farming and fishing, as well as raising pigs are the main activities.

Area 181sq km (70sq miles)
Independence 1986, from UN supervision
Currency United States dollar
Population 48,000
Density 265 per sq km (686 per sq mile)
Official Language English

SAMOA

THE PEOPLE OF Samoa are mainly Polynesians, descendants of the Maori. Frequent typhoons cause widespread damage to the islands.

Area 2,840sq km (1,096sq miles)
Independence 1962, from UN supervision
Currency Tala
Population 169,000
Density 60 per sq km (155 per sq mile)
Official Languages English, Samoan

KIRIBATI

THE ISLANDS OF Kiribati have poor soil, so people rely on fishing. They use leaves from the pandanus tree to thatch their traditional homes.

Area 710sq km (274sq miles)
Republic Declared 1979
Currency Australian dollar
Population 66,000
Density 93 per sq km (241 per sq mile)
Official Language English

KIRIBATI CANOE
Fishing from canoes is traditional for the Pacific Ocean islanders. This fisherman from Kiribati has an outrigger, or float, on his canoe to help balance in rough seas.

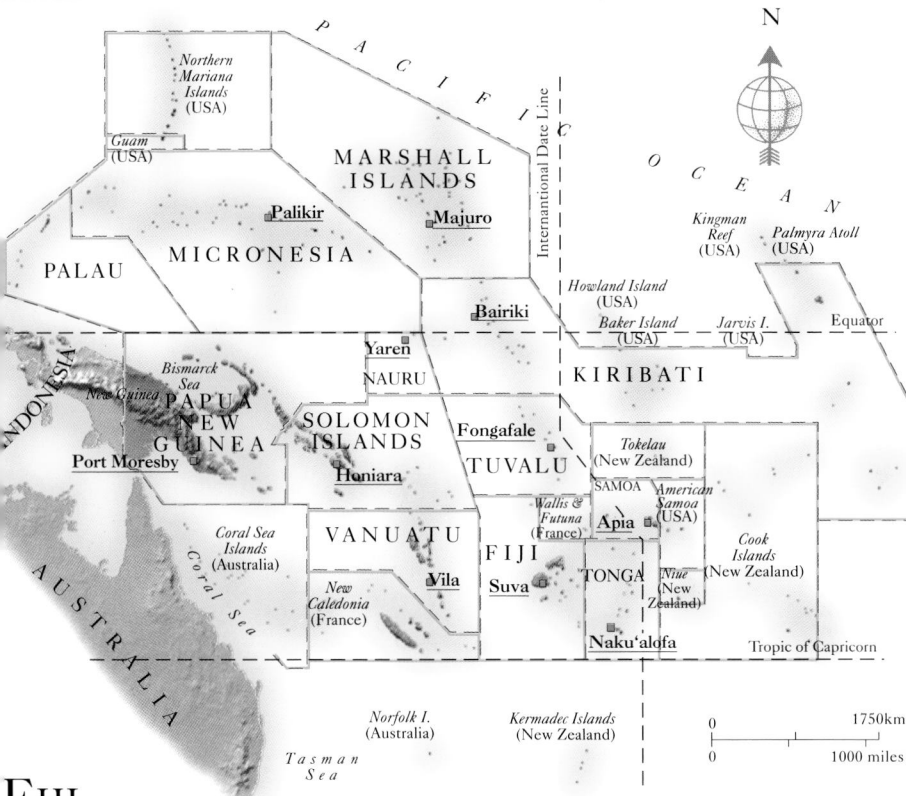

TUVALU

TUVALU, FORMERLY the Ellice Islands, is made up of nine small coral atolls. Sales of postage stamps is an important source of income.

Area 26sq km (10sq miles)
Independence 1978, from Britain
Currency Australian dollar and Tuvaluan dollar
Population 9,000
Density 346 per sq km (896 per sq mile)
Official Language English

FIJI

MADE UP OF 322 islands, more than half of Fiji's land area is covered with forests. Coconuts are grown on plantations around the coasts.

Area 18,270sq km (7,054sq miles)
Independence 1970, from Britain
Currency Fiji dollar
Population 800,000
Density 44 per sq km (114 per sq mile)
Official Language English

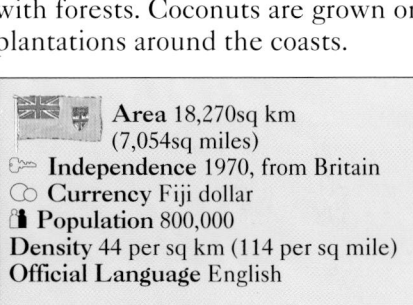

SUGAR CANE
Sugar is the main cash crop in Fiji. Women cut the cane using machetes.

VANUATU

THE VANUATU ISLANDS form a chain about 800km (497 miles) long. Bananas, oranges, and pineapples are grown in the fertile volcanic soil.

Area 12,190sq km (4,707sq miles)
Independence 1980, from France and Britain
Currency Vatu
Population 163,000
Density 13 per sq km (34 per sq mile)
Official Languages Bislama, English, French

TONGA

THERE ARE 169 islands in Tonga, some made of coral and some that are volcanic. Tonga is the last remaining Polynesian kingdom.

Area 750sq km (290sq miles)
Independence 1970, from Britain
Currency Pa'anga
Population 94,000
Density 131 per sq km (339 per sq mile)
Official Languages English, Tongan

AUSTRALIA

AUSTRALIA IS ONE of the oldest landmasses and is the flattest of the continents. Much of the country is hot and dry and farmers graze sheep and cattle, growing crops in places where irrigation is possible. Most people live in cooler coastal cities.

Area 7,686,850sq km (2,967,908sq miles)
Government Parliamentary democracy with British monarch as head of state
Independence 1901, Commonwealth of Australia created
Territories Australian Antarctic Territory, Christmas Island, Cocos (Keeling) Islands, Norfolk Island, Heard and McDonald Islands, Ashmore and Cartier Islands, Coral Sea Islands.
Currency Australian dollar
Population 18,758,000
Density 2 per sq km (5 per sq mile)
Official Language English
Major Religions Protestant 60%, Roman Catholic 26%, other 14%

WEATHER FACTS

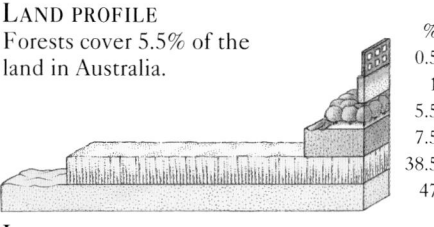

52°C (126°F)   629mm (24.8in)   -22°C (-7.6°F)

20.2°C (68.4°F)   6.7°C (44.1°F)

LAND PROFILE

Forests cover 5.5% of the land in Australia.

%
0.5
1
5.5
7.5
38.5
47

LIFESTYLE FACTS

• Voting is compulsory in Australia. Failure to vote is punishable by a fine.

• Australia is the world's leading producer of wool (30%). There are about 7 sheep for every person in Australia.

• Melbourne, the state capital of Victoria, has the fifth largest Greek population of any city in the world.

20 Australian dollars

GREAT BARRIER REEF

This reef, the largest structure built by living creatures, stretches for 2,000km (1,243 miles) off the Queensland coast. There are more than 400 types of coral and 1,500 species of fish.

AUSTRALIAN FLOWER

The national flower is the golden wattle.

An Aboriginal rock painting that shows a Dreamtime ancestor.

THE FIRST AUSTRALIANS

The Aboriginals were the first people to live in Australia about 50,000 years ago. They hold deep spiritual links with the land, believing it and all living things were created by their ancestor beings at the beginning of time.

N

MINING AND MINERALS

Australia is a major source of minerals. It is the world's largest exporter of coal, and has the world's most productive diamond mine near Lake Argyle in Western Australia.

MAJOR MINERAL EXPORTS (1996)

Mineral	Value in thousand US$
Coal	6,123,550
Gold	4,101,202
Iron ore	2,278,644
Aluminium ores	1,994,489
Zinc ores	348,540

AUSTRALIAN MARSUPIAL FACTS

• Marsupials are animals that carry and suckle their young in a pouch in front of their body.

• The koala feeds on the leaves of eucalyptus trees found in Eastern Australia.

• The grey kangaroo has powerful hind legs and can jump at least 8m (26ft).

• The striped possum eats ants, bees, and termites in the rainforests of Queensland.

Koala

ISLAND STATE

Tasmania is the smallest of the Australian states. The south-west of the island is a natural wilderness and has been made a World Heritage Site.

MOST POPULAR SPORTS (1998)

Australians are keen on sport and will host the Olympic Games in the year 2000.

Sport	Club members
Swimming	1,628,800
Fitness	1,379,200
Golf	1,116,200
Tennis	937,800
Fishing	641,500
Cycling	626,000
Tenpin bowling	438,000

Arafura Sea
Timor Sea
Torres Strait
•Darwin
Gulf of Carpentaria
Coral Sea
Lake Argyle
INDIAN OCEAN
PACIFIC OCEAN
Great Sandy Desert
Northern Territory
Queensland
Great Barrier Reef
Great Dividing Range
Tropic of Capricorn
A U S T R A L I A
Western Australia
Gibson Desert
Uluru (Ayers Rock)
Simpson Desert
Brisbane •
Great Victoria Desert
L. Eyre
South Australia
Bourke
New South Wales
Sydney Opera House
•Perth
Great Australian Bight
Australian Capital Territory
Sydney
Adelaide •
Canberra
Victoria
Kosciuszko 2,228m (7,310ft)
Melbourne •
Murray
Bass Strait
Tasman Sea
Tasmania
•Hobart

0   750km
0   450 miles

SYDNEY OPERA HOUSE

Sydney Opera House, designed by Danish architect Jörn Utzon (born 1918), was completed in 1973. The shell-shaped roofs are covered with more than one million Swedish ceramic tiles.

ANTARCTICA

ANTARCTICA IS THE coldest, windiest place on Earth. The harsh conditions mean there are no permanent inhabitants, only visiting scientists working in research stations. The land is rich in oil and minerals, but mining is prohibited under the laws of the Antarctic Treaty.

WEATHER FACTS

15°C (59°F)   303mm (12in)   -89°C (-128.2°F)

Area 14,200,000sq km (5,500,000sq miles)
Government None
Currency Not applicable
Population Staff of scientific stations – in winter about 1,000 people, in summer about 4,000
Density Not applicable
Official Language Not applicable
Major Religions Not applicable

THE ANTARCTIC TREATY

Antarctica is owned by no-one. In 1959, a group of nations agreed to set the land aside for peaceful uses only, and suspended the issue of territorial rights. The Antarctic Treaty was originally signed by Argentina, Australia, Belgium, Chile, France, Japan, New Zealand, Norway, South Africa, Russia, the UK, and USA. Since 1959, a further 28 countries have joined the Treaty.

LIFESTYLE FACTS

Between 2,000 and 3,000 tourists a year admire the dramatic beauty of the landscape from the comfort of their cruise ships.

- Scientists in Antarctica carry out many experiments, such as studying the effect of the Antarctic ice sheet on the world's weather patterns, or observing the behaviour of marine life.

- Polar clothing is designed to keep the body warm, especially fingers and toes. Goggles help to protect eyes from the glare of the ice.

PROTECTING THE LAND

In 1987, British scientists discovered a hole in the ozone layer above Antarctica. The Greenpeace environmental organization would like Antarctica to be a World Park to protect the land for the future.

Greenpeace boat patrols the icy seas.

Map labels

Scotia Sea · South Orkney Islands (UK) · South Shetland Islands (UK) · Palmer Archipelago · Drake Passage · Antarctic Circle · Antarctic Peninsula · Alexander I. · Bellingshausen Sea · Peter I I. (Norway) · Thurston I. · Amundsen Sea · Carney I. · Siple I. · PACIFIC OCEAN · Scott I. · Balleny Islands · Siple · Vinson Massif 5,140m(16,864ft) · Ellsworth Mts. · West Antarctica · Ross Ice Shelf · Roosevelt I. · Ross Sea · Vanda · ATLANTIC OCEAN · Fimbul Ice Shelf · Riiser-Larsen Ice Shelf · Lyddan I. · Weddell Sea · Berkner Island · Ronne Ice Shelf · Transantarctic Mountains · ANTARCTICA · East Antarctica · South Pole · Vostok · Amery Ice Shelf · West Ice Shelf · Davis Sea · Shackleton Ice Shelf · Mill I. · Casey · Dumont d'Urville Sea · INDIAN OCEAN · Antarctic Circle · N

0   750km
0   400 miles

CROSS-SECTION OF ANTARCTICA

Most of Antarctica is covered by a huge sheet of ice up to 2km (1.2 miles) thick.

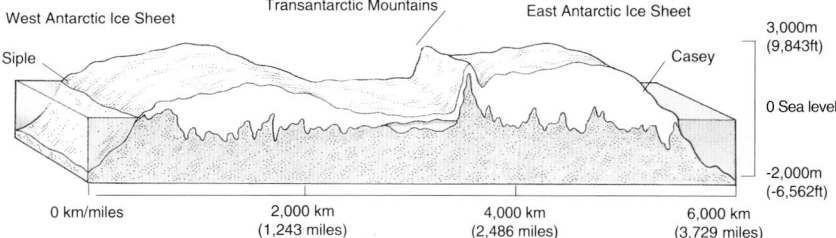

West Antarctic Ice Sheet · Transantarctic Mountains · East Antarctic Ice Sheet · Siple · Casey · 3,000m (9,843ft) · 0 Sea level · -2,000m (-6,562ft)

0 km/miles · 2,000 km (1,243 miles) · 4,000 km (2,486 miles) · 6,000 km (3,729 miles)

ROSS ICE SHELF

Antarctica has the world's largest floating body of ice, the Ross Ice Shelf (shown left), which is as large as France. At some points the ice reaches 60m (197ft) high. Its flat surface provides the best approach to the interior.

SOUTH POLE

At the beginning of this century, many nations tried to reach the South Pole. On 14 December, 1911, Norwegian Roald Amundsen became the first person to reach the South Pole.

WILDLIFE

Antarctica is too cold for any land animals except the smallest insects. But the sea is rich in food, and many sea birds and sea mammals live on and around the nearby islands.

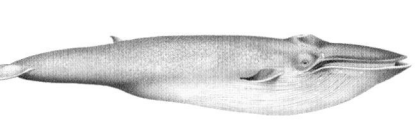

Blue whale *(Balaenoptera musculus)* is the largest animal ever to have lived, and can be up to 30m (98ft) long. It spends summers in Antarctic waters.

Emperor penguin *(Aptenodytes forsteri)* is the world's largest penguin, and can grow up to 1.2m (4ft) tall. The female lays one egg, which the male carries on his feet until the egg hatches.

FLAGS

THESE NATIONAL FLAGS represent the 198 main countries and territories of the world. The designs usually reflect the country's culture or religion.

NORTH AND CENTRAL AMERICA
Blue appears in many flags here.

 *Canada*

 *Greenland*

 *USA*

 *Mexico*

Nicaragua

Panama

El Salvador

Costa Rica

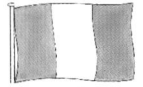 *Guatemala*

 *Honduras*

Belize

Cuba

Haiti

Jamaica

Trinidad & Tobago

Dominican Republic

Barbados

Bahamas

Antigua & Barbuda

Dominica

Grenada

St. Christopher & Nevis

St. Lucia

St. Vincent & The Grenadines

SOUTH AMERICA
The three-striped flag, or tricolour, is often used here.

Colombia

Peru

Venezuela

Bolivia

Ecuador

Guyana

 *Surinam*

 *Brazil*

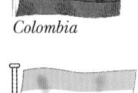 *Argentina*

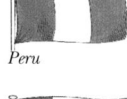 *Chile*

 *Uruguay*

 *Paraguay*

EUROPE
Many of the European flags use a variation of the cross.

Sweden

Denmark

Norway

Iceland

United Kingdom

Scotland

 *England*

Wales

Northern Ireland

Republic of Ireland

Spain

Portugal

Andorra

Netherlands

Belgium

Luxembourg

France

Monaco

Germany

Austria

Switzerland

Liechtenstein

Italy

Vatican City

Malta

San Marino

Finland

Lithuania

Latvia

Estonia

Ukraine

Poland

Czech Republic

Hungary

Romania

Moldavia

Belorussia

Slovakia

Turkey

Greece

Bulgaria

Albania

Cyprus

Yugoslavia

Croatia

Bosnia and Herzegovina

 *Slovenia*

Macedonia

Armenia

Azerbaijan

Georgia

Russian Federation

AFRICA
Many African flags include the colours green, yellow, and red.

Egypt

Ethiopia

Kenya

Tanzania

 *Uganda*

 *Somalia*

 *Sudan*

Eritrea

Djibouti

Algeria

FLAG FACTS
• Vexillology is the word for the study of flags. The name comes from the Latin *vexillum*, a banner carried by Roman soldiers.
• Throughout the world, a white flag is flown to indicate a truce.
• At sea, lowering the ship's flag, or ensign, is a sign of surrender.
• The continent of Antarctica has no flags. The land belongs to no-one and can be used only for peaceful research.

AFRICA
(Flags of Africa continued)

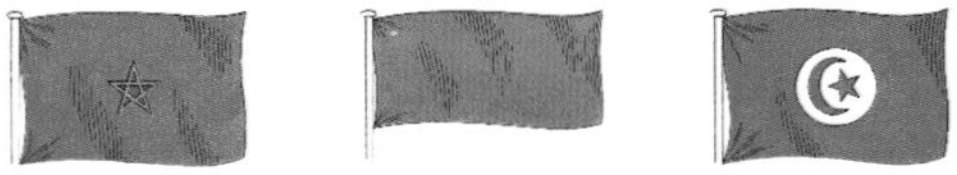
Morocco *Libya* *Tunisia*

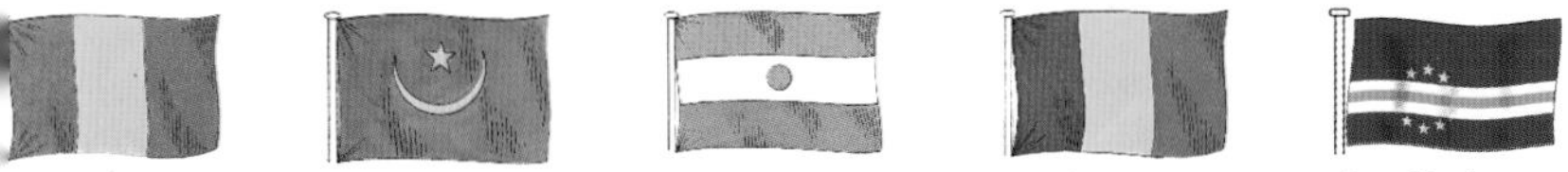
Mali *Mauritania* *Niger* *Chad* *Cape Verde*

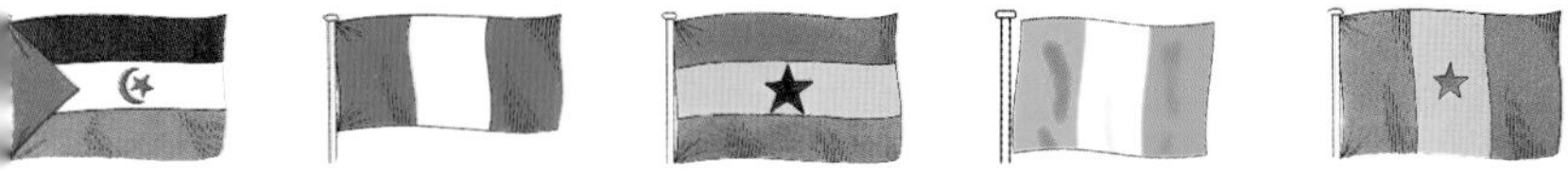
Western Sahara *Nigeria* *Ghana* *Ivory Coast* *Senegal*

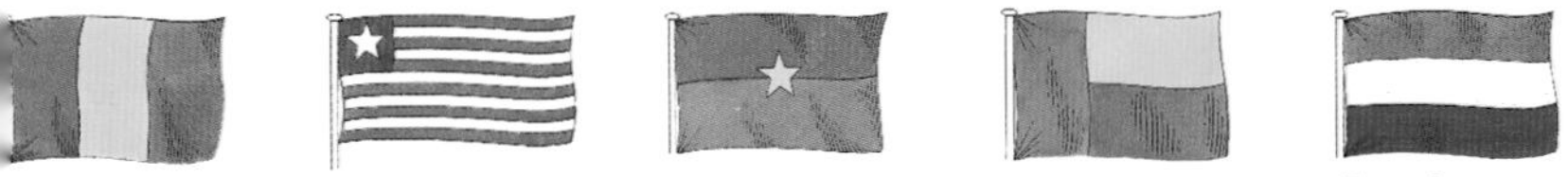
Guinea *Liberia* *Burkina* *Benin* *Sierra Leone*

INTERPRETING THE FLAG

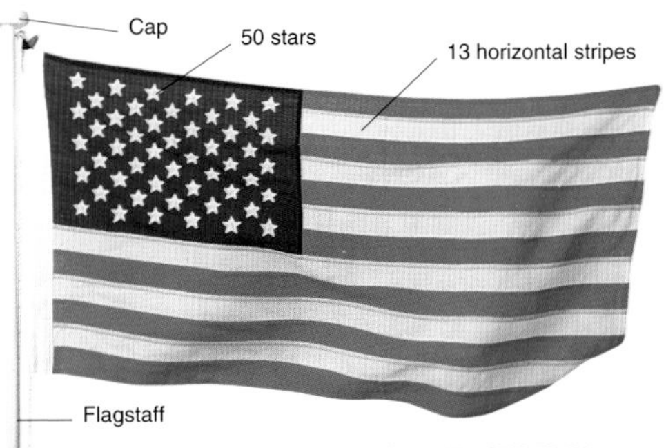

THE STARS AND STRIPES
The American flag has 50 stars – one for each of today's states. The horizontal stripes represent the country's original 13 states.

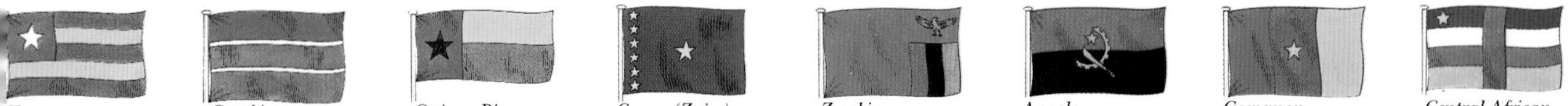
Togo *Gambia* *Guinea-Bissau* *Congo (Zaire)* *Zambia* *Angola* *Cameroon* *Central African Republic*

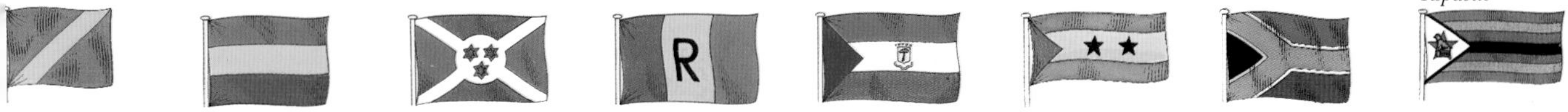
Congo *Gabon* *Burundi* *Rwanda* *Equatorial Guinea* *Sao Tome & Principe* *South Africa* *Zimbabwe*

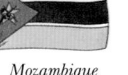

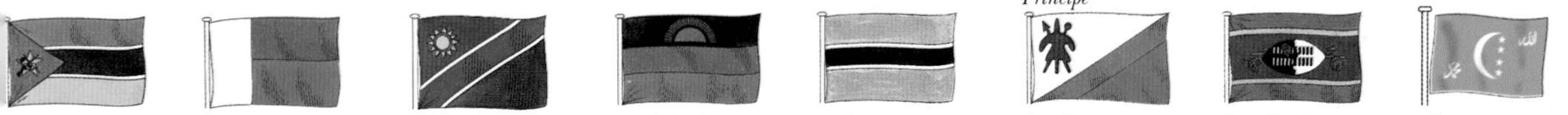
Mozambique *Madagascar* *Namibia* *Malawi* *Botswana* *Lesotho* *Swaziland* *Comoros*

ASIA
Symbols of the Sun and the crescent of Islam can be seen.

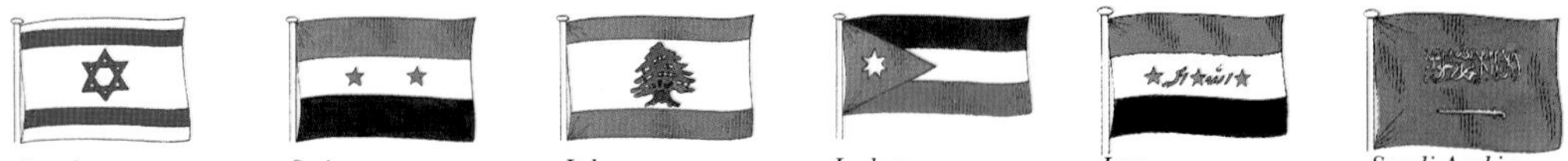
Israel *Syria* *Lebanon* *Jordan* *Iraq* *Saudi Arabia*

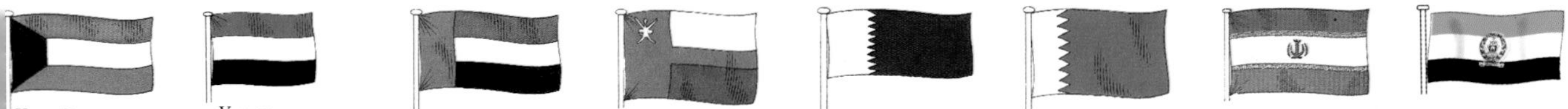
Kuwait *Yemen* *United Arab Emirates* *Oman* *Qatar* *Bahrain* *Iran* *Afghanistan*

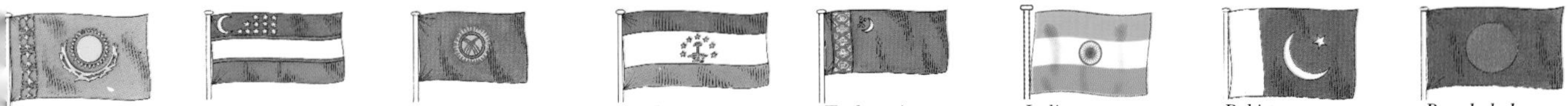
Kazakhstan *Uzbekistan* *Kyrgyzstan* *Tajikistan* *Turkmenistan* *India* *Pakistan* *Bangladesh*

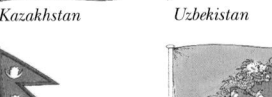

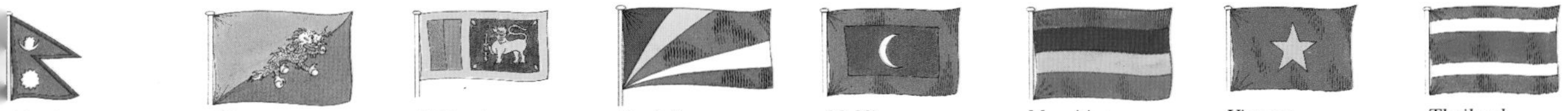
Nepal *Bhutan* *Sri Lanka* *Seychelles* *Maldives* *Mauritius* *Vietnam* *Thailand*

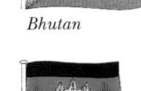

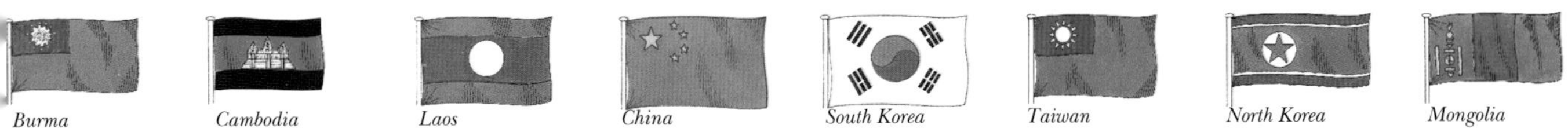
Burma *Cambodia* *Laos* *China* *South Korea* *Taiwan* *North Korea* *Mongolia*

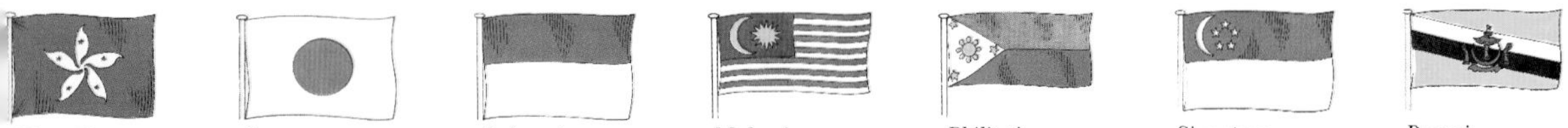
Hong Kong *Japan* *Indonesia* *Malaysia* *Philippines* *Singapore* *Brunei*

AUSTRALASIA AND OCEANIA
Navigational stars are often used.

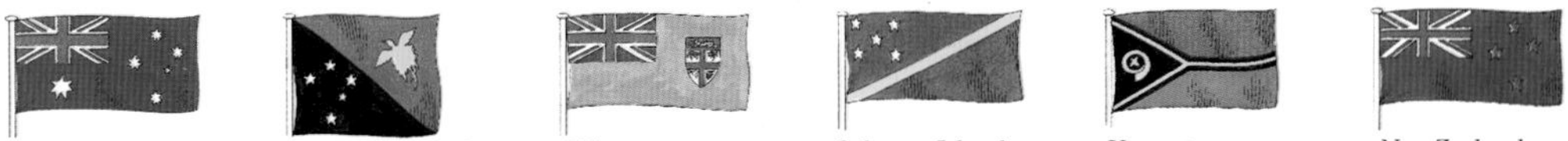
Australia *Papua New Guinea* *Fiji* *Solomon Islands* *Vanuatu* *New Zealand*

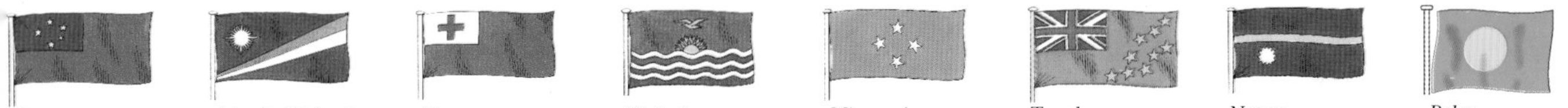
Samoa *Marshall Islands* *Tonga* *Kiribati* *Micronesia* *Tuvalu* *Nauru* *Palau*

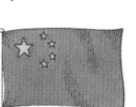

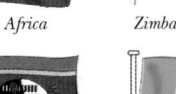

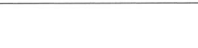

MAPPING

TODAY, MOST PLACES in the world have been visited and mapped; and photographs taken from space have given us an accurate picture of the Earth's surface. Over the years, mapmakers, known as cartographers, have created maps for different purposes. People can use an atlas to find a particular place, or a smaller-scale map to drive or walk from one place to another.

EARLY MAPPING

Before the world was mapped out as it is today, people understood only the world that they knew. This clay tablet shows the earliest map of the world, which was made in Babylon (now Iraq) in about 1000 B.C. The outer circle is marked as the ocean with the known world depicted in the centre.

READING A MAP

A map is like an aerial photograph of the landscape and is designed to show a detailed part of the Earth's surface. To make good use of a map you must know how to "read" it.

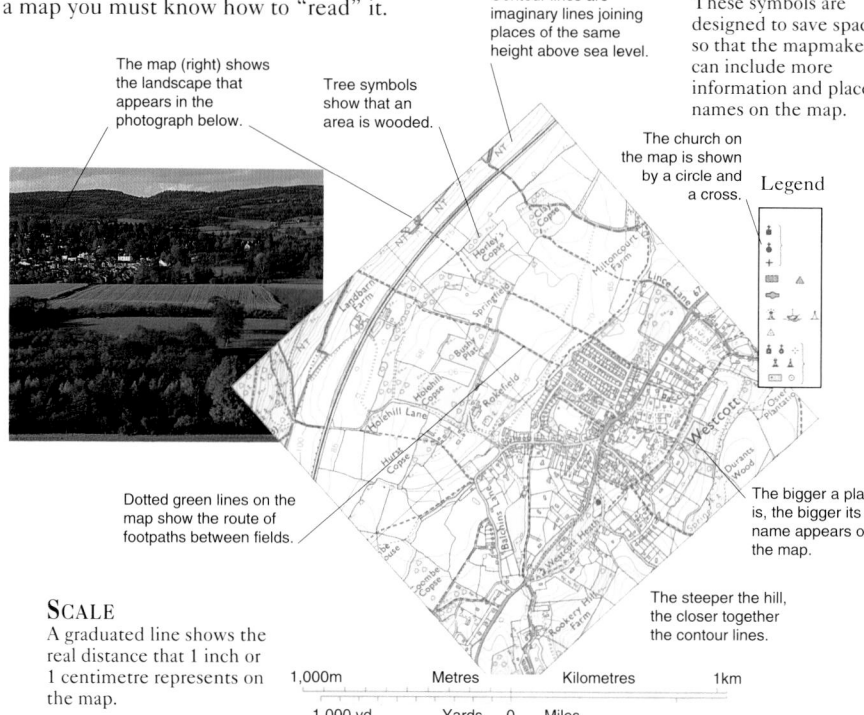

The map (right) shows the landscape that appears in the photograph below.

Tree symbols show that an area is wooded.

Contour lines are imaginary lines joining places of the same height above sea level.

The church on the map is shown by a circle and a cross.

LEGEND
Modern maps have a panel called a legend, or key, explaining what the symbols mean. These symbols are designed to save space so that the mapmakers can include more information and place names on the map.

Legend

The bigger a place is, the bigger its name appears on the map.

The steeper the hill, the closer together the contour lines.

Dotted green lines on the map show the route of footpaths between fields.

SCALE
A graduated line shows the real distance that 1 inch or 1 centimetre represents on the map.

1,000m   Metres   Kilometres   1km
1,000 yd   Yards   0   Miles

USING A COMPASS

A compass is an instrument used to find directions. The Earth's magnetism pulls the magnetised compass needle so that it points north. However, it points to magnetic north, which is not true north. Markers within the compass also show south, west, east, and the angles in between.

North
Northwest   Northeast
West   East
Southwest   Southeast
South

LONGITUDE AND LATITUDE

Lines of longitude are vertical lines that run through the Poles, while lines of latitude are horizontal lines that run parallel to the Equator. These imaginary lines on the Earth's surface help map readers to locate places on a map.

North Pole 90°   Greenwich meridian
60°   Tropic of Cancer
30°   60°   30°
0°   0°
Equator
30°   30°
Tropic of Capricorn   60°   60°
90°
South Pole

Lines of latitude run parallel to the Equator.

Lines of longitude run north to south between the Poles.

PROJECTIONS

To show the Earth on a flat sheet of paper, mapmakers use a projection. Imagine a glass globe with a light at its centre. This light projects shadows on to a sheet of paper, which forms the basis of the map.

CONICAL
In this projection, the imaginary sheet of paper forms a cone, touching the Earth along a particular line of latitude. This system shows the least distortion to areas.

Conical projection

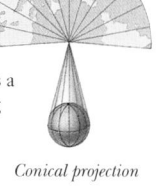

CYLINDRICAL
The paper is rolled around the Earth, touching it at the Equator. This shows north at the top, but the areas are distorted.

Cylindrical projection

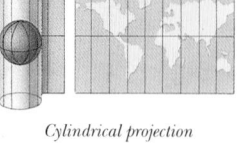

ZENITHAL
The paper touches the globe at one point. If this point is the Pole, then the lines of longitude show their correct angles.

Zenithal projection

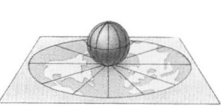

MERCATOR
Gerard Kremer (1512–94) was a Flemish geographer who found a way to show the globe on a flat map. He was called Mercator, or merchant, because he made maps for ocean-going traders.

WORLD MAPS
Mercator's world map was made in 1569. His projection shows the correct shapes of the continents but distorts their areas. Arno Peters' projection, made in 1977, distorts the shapes of countries but shows their true size.

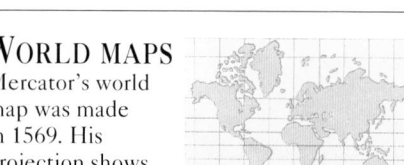

Mercator's projection

Peters' projection

MAP FACTS
• Amerigo Vespucci (1454–1512) made maps of the New World based on the reports of his sea captains. His maps were referred to as Amerigo's land, or America.

• In 1884, when Britain was a great sea power, Greenwich was chosen as the place from which all measurements of longitude were to be made.

SATELLITE MAPS
With space technology, we can now compile maps from satellite photographs. This view of the Earth from space was made using thousands of separate images.

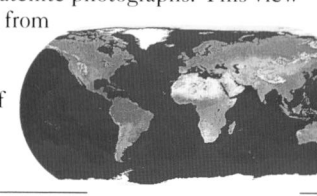

RAW MATERIALS

NATURAL SUBSTANCES THAT are extracted from the ground, from water, or from the air are called raw materials. These substances can be changed by chemical processes into many different types of material that can be put to everyday use.

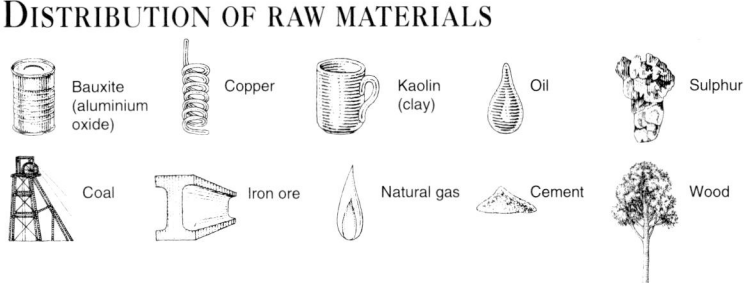

Bauxite (aluminium oxide)   Copper   Kaolin (clay)   Oil   Sulphur

Coal   Iron ore   Natural gas   Cement   Wood

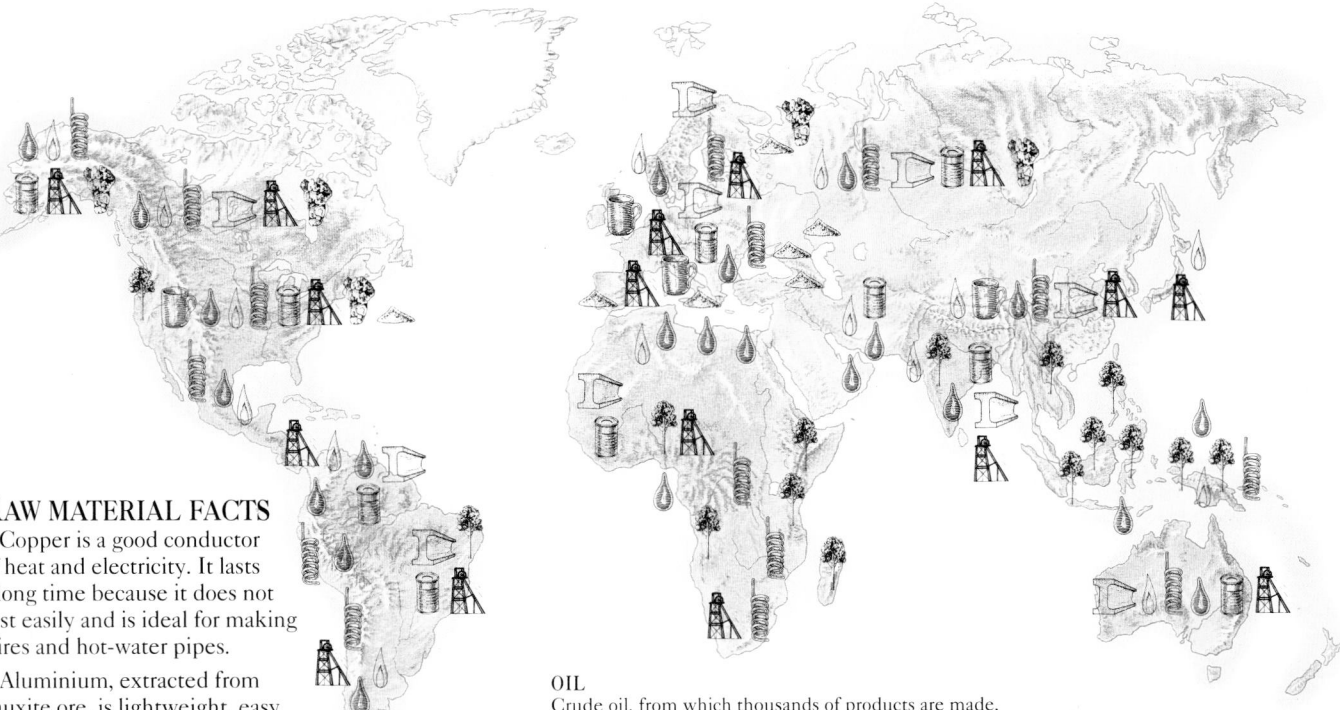

RAW MATERIAL FACTS

• Copper is a good conductor of heat and electricity. It lasts a long time because it does not rust easily and is ideal for making wires and hot-water pipes.

• Aluminium, extracted from bauxite ore, is lightweight, easy to work and shape, yet durable. It is ideal for making bicycle frames, aircraft, and motor-vehicle parts.

OIL

Crude oil, from which thousands of products are made, is found under the ground or sea. The oil is separated into various parts by a process called fractional distillation: it is heated to form different gases, then each gas condenses back into a liquid at a different temperature.

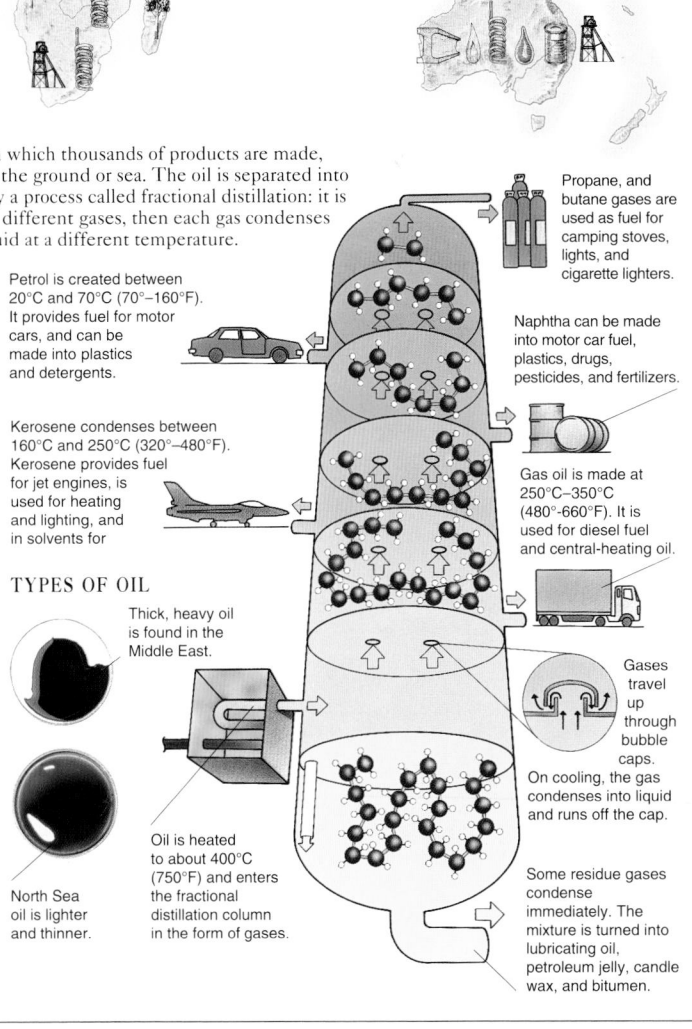

Petrol is created between 20°C and 70°C (70°–160°F). It provides fuel for motor cars, and can be made into plastics and detergents.

Kerosene condenses between 160°C and 250°C (320°–480°F). Kerosene provides fuel for jet engines, is used for heating and lighting, and in solvents for

TYPES OF OIL

Thick, heavy oil is found in the Middle East.

North Sea oil is lighter and thinner.

Oil is heated to about 400°C (750°F) and enters the fractional distillation column in the form of gases.

Propane, and butane gases are used as fuel for camping stoves, lights, and cigarette lighters.

Naphtha can be made into motor car fuel, plastics, drugs, pesticides, and fertilizers.

Gas oil is made at 250°C–350°C (480°-660°F). It is used for diesel fuel and central-heating oil.

Gases travel up through bubble caps. On cooling, the gas condenses into liquid and runs off the cap.

Some residue gases condense immediately. The mixture is turned into lubricating oil, petroleum jelly, candle wax, and bitumen.

LEADING PRODUCERS OF RAW MATERIALS

Material	Top producers	Total* (in millions)	World total* (in millions)
Bauxite (aluminium oxide)	Australia	37.4	
	Guinea	16.5	1,064
Coal	China	1,054	
	USA	889	5,882
Copper	Chile	1.6	
	USA	1.5	9.2
Natural Gas	CIS	796,000m³	
	USA	488,749m³	2,100,000 m³
Iron ore	CIS	241	
	China	165	984
Kaolin (clay)	CIS	2.0	
	Republic of Korea	1.3	23.1
Oil	CIS	607	
	USA	373	
	Saudi Arabia	257	2,987
Salt	USA	35.5	
	China	28.3	189
Sulphur	USA	11.6	
	China	7.4	60.3
Wood	USA	1,109m³	
	CIS	862m³	7,147m³

*All figures in tonnes apart from m³ = cubic metres.

FARMING AND FISHERIES

In 9000 B.C., people in the Middle East began to grow crops. They were the first farmers. Since then, people have tried many different ways of producing crops, rearing animals, and catching fish. Today, farming and fishing are major international industries.

MAJOR WORLD CROPS AND LIVESTOC

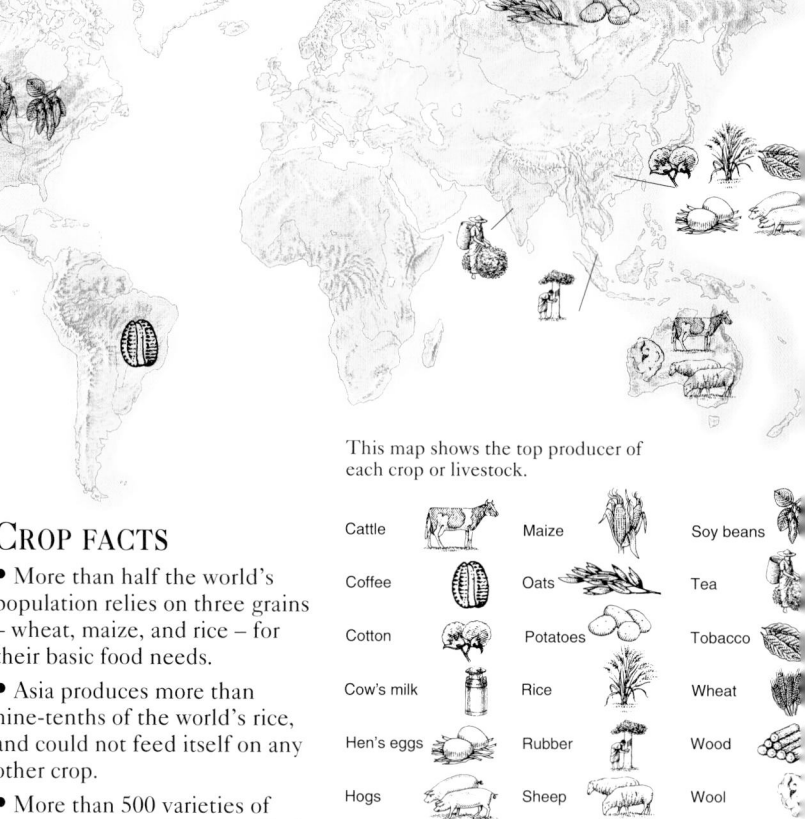

This map shows the top producer of each crop or livestock.

Cattle	Maize	Soy beans
Coffee	Oats	Tea
Cotton	Potatoes	Tobacco
Cow's milk	Rice	Wheat
Hen's eggs	Rubber	Wood
Hogs	Sheep	Wool

TOP AGRICULTURAL PRODUCERS

Product	Top Producer	Second	Third
Cattle	Australia	Brazil	USA
Coffee	Brazil	Colombia	Indonesia
Cotton	China	USA	Former USSR
Cow's milk	USA	Germany	Russia
Hen's eggs	China	USA	Russia
Hogs	China	USA	Russia
Maize	USA	China	Brazil
Oats	Former USSR	USA	Canada
Potatoes	Russia	Poland	China
Rice	China	India	Indonesia
Rubber	Malaysia	Indonesia	Thailand
Sheep	Australia	China	New Zealand
Soy beans	USA	Brazil	China
Tea	India	China	Sri Lanka
Tobacco	China	USA	India
Wheat	China	Former USSR	USA
Wood	USA	Russia	China
Wool	Australia	Former USSR	New Zealand

CROP FACTS

• More than half the world's population relies on three grains – wheat, maize, and rice – for their basic food needs.

• Asia produces more than nine-tenths of the world's rice, and could not feed itself on any other crop.

• More than 500 varieties of grape are grown along the Black Sea coast in Georgia.

• Eighty-five per cent of the world's orange juice is supplied by Brazil.

• Malaysia's rubber trees are descended from about 11 seedlings, sent to Malaysia from Kew Gardens, England, in 1877.

SHEEP JAM

In New Zealand, sheep outnumber people by 20 to 1, and have right of way on the roads.

SELECTING AND CULTIVATING CROPS

Only the strongest plants are selected and cultivated. This has caused the size, shape, and flavour of many crops to change over the years.

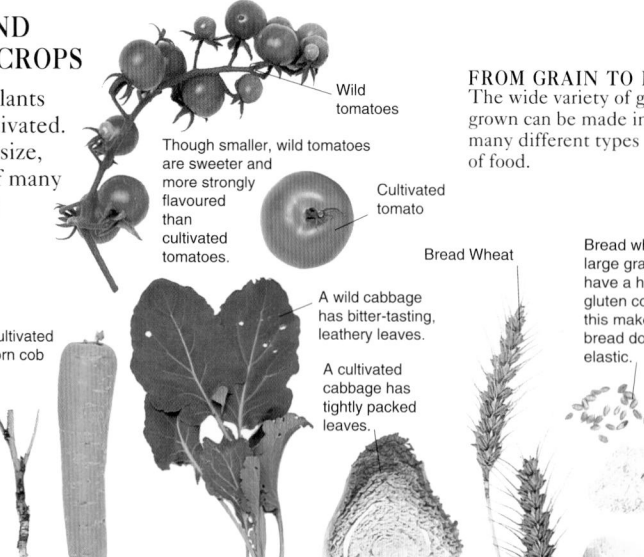

Wild tomatoes

Though smaller, wild tomatoes are sweeter and more strongly flavoured than cultivated tomatoes.

Cultivated tomato

Cultivated corn cob

Wild carrot

Cultivated carrot

Early corn cob

A wild cabbage has bitter-tasting, leathery leaves.

A cultivated cabbage has tightly packed leaves.

Bread Wheat

Bread wheat's large grains have a high gluten content – this makes bread dough elastic.

FROM GRAIN TO FOOD
The wide variety of grain grown can be made into many different types of food.

Wholewheat flour

White bread, from bleached flour

Brown bread, from unbleached flour

Long grain rice

Rice plant

Durum wheat has a low gluten content, and is used to make pasta and biscuits.

Types of pasta
Pasta comes in a variety of shapes and sizes.

Ruotedi carro, or "cartwheel"

Spaghe

FARMING PROCESSES

SUBSISTENCE FARMING

When farmers grow enough food to support themselves and their families, but leave little or nothing to be sold, this is known as subsistence farming. Subsistence farming is more common in developing countries, such as Kenya, Africa.

Subsistence farming in Sudan

INTENSIVE FARMING

In this type of farming, production of crops and livestock is maximized by the use of machinery and chemicals. Up to ten people can be fed from land that once fed one person.

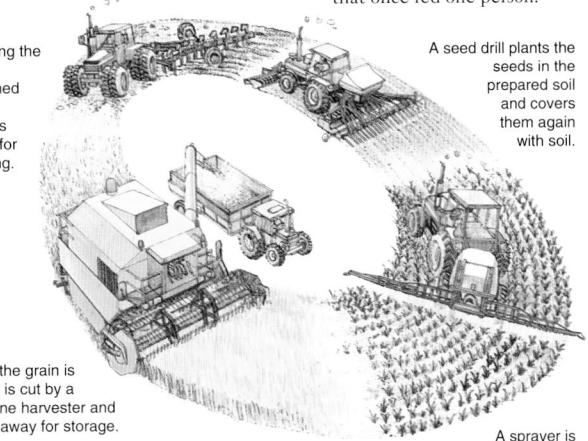

In spring the soil is ploughed into furrows ready for planting.

Once the grain is ripe, it is cut by a combine harvester and taken away for storage.

A seed drill plants the seeds in the prepared soil and covers them again with soil.

A sprayer is used to spray crops with pesticides to kill any insects that may harm the young plants.

Battery hens

One disadvantage of intensive farming is that it can lead to animals being treated in an unnatural way. Egg-laying hens are often kept in cages in buildings called batteries where they do not have enough space to flap their wings or turn around. Because of concern for animal welfare and a preference for naturally grown food, more people are returning to natural, or organic, farming methods.

Battery hens, Texas, USA

FISHING INDUSTRY

Most fish are caught in the seas near the coast, above the continental shelf. Different fishing methods are used, largely depending on whether the fish swim near the surface of the sea (pelagic fish) or on or near the sea bed (demersal fish).

WAYS OF CATCHING FISH

Deep-water trawling
Cone-shaped nets, about 30m (100ft) wide, are pulled along the sea bed by a trawler. Used to catch demersal fish, such as cod.

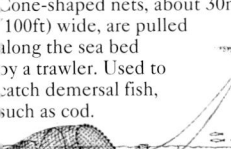

Mid-water trawling
Trawling nets are towed by either one or two trawlers. Used to catch pelagic fish, such as herring.

Trawler

Drift nets
Long nets, up to 95km (60 miles) in length, are left to drift in the water and used to catch pelagic fish.

Drift nets are attached to a boat.

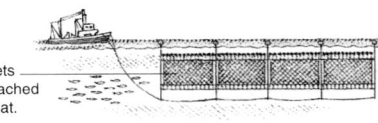

Purse-seining
Pelagic fish are surrounded by a huge net and the net lines are drawn together, like purse strings, until the fish are completely enclosed in the net.

Lining
Long lines with baited hooks are laid, either on the sea bed, to catch demersal fish, or near the surface, to catch tuna and mackerel.

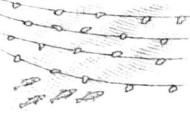

Baskets or netting pots
These are used to catch shellfish, such as crabs and lobsters. The openings are designed so the fish can easily swim inside but find it difficult to get out.

FISHING GROUNDS
The continental shelf (shown in blue on the map) is the land surrounding each continent, covered by shallow sea water. It is rich in nutrients, and is an excellent feeding ground for fish.

FISHING FACTS

• At least 25% of the world's diet of animal protein is derived from fish and other seafood.

• Japan catches about 10 million tonnes of fish each year, more than any other country in the world.

• Fish and fish products account for about 70% of Iceland's export earnings. They consume more cod-liver oil than any other nation, and produce more than one third of the world's supply.

• In Vietnam, bomb craters remaining after the Indochinese conflicts (1946–75) have since been turned into pools for farming fish.

WORLD DISTRIBUTION OF FISH CATCHES

Area	Catch in million metric tonnes (1989–91)
Pacific Ocean	48.32
Atlantic Ocean	20.17
Indian Ocean	5.93
Mediterranean and Black Sea	1.29
Antarctic	0.40
World total	76.11

FISH PRODUCTS

Meal and oil 29.7%

Fresh 23.8%

Frozen 21.1%

Cured 13.4%

Canned 12%

FISH FARMING
Some types of fish, such as trout and carp, are kept on fish farms. Enclosures are built on lakes, ponds, or estuaries. Most fish farming occurs in fresh water, but in some countries, such as Japan, fish farms have been built along sheltered coastal waters.

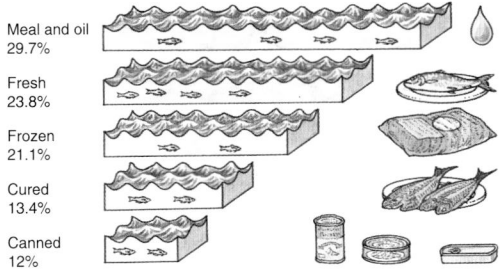

Salmon farm, Norway

AGRICULTURAL WORDS

Agroforestry System of growing trees and crops together.
Biotechnology To scientifically change plants and animals for the benefit of humans.
Cash crops Crops grown for trade.
Hydroponics Growing plants without soil using water and nutrients.

Irrigation To water dried-up land by using water channels, pipes, or sprinklers.
Nomadic Moving from place to place to find new grazing land, food, and water.
Rainforest A forest that grows in hot, tropical areas that have high rainfall.
Subsoil Layer of soil underneath topsoil.
Topsoil The uppermost, fertile layer of soil.

POPULATION

THE TOTAL POPULATION of the world now stands at 5.6 billion. Some continents are experiencing a population explosion, others are beginning to stabilize their growth. Many people think that an increasing population is the greatest problem facing the world.

WORLD POPULATION

Europe:
750,582,660
13.9% of world
population

North/Central America:
431,352,677.
8% of world
population

South America:
305,074,803
5.6% of world
population

Oceania:
26,370,088
0.5% of world
population

Asia:
3,184,078,671
59.3% of world
population

Africa:
678,428,967
12.7% of world
population

MOST POPULATED COUNTRIES

Country	Total population (in millions)
China	1,200.0
India	935.7
United States	263.3
Indonesia	197.6
Brazil	161.8
Russia	149.9
Pakistan	140.5
Japan	125.1
Bangladesh	120.4
Nigeria	111.7
Mexico	93.7
Germany	81.6
Vietnam	74.5
Philippines	67.6

Source: Population Concern

FERTILITY RATES

The fertility rate corresponds to the average number of children born to a woman in her lifetime. Even if every couple had only two children starting tomorrow, the world's population would still grow to at least 8 billion.

8.5 Rwanda
7.6 Malawi
6.4 Saudi Arabia
5.1 Nicaragua
4.5 Cambodia
3.9 India
2.2 China
1.5 Germany

POPULATION GROWTH RATES

This table shows the current rate of population increase and the time it will take each region to double in size.

Region	Increase (annual %)	Doubling Time (years)
Africa	2.9	24
Latin America	2.0	35
Asia	1.7	41
Oceania	1.2	57
North America	0.7	98
Europe	0.1	1,025

Source: Population Concern

GROWTH FACT

• About 97% of global population growth between now and 2050 is projected to occur in Africa, Asia, and Latin America – the countries least able to absorb such increases.

POPULATION MOMENTUM

Three people are born every second, nearly 11,000 every hour, and more than 255,000 every day.

POPULATION FACTS

• One-third of the world's people are under the age of 15.

• By 2025, the total number of people aged 60 and over will be about 1.2 billion (14% of the world's population). The majority of them, almost 71%, will be living in the developed countries.

• 75% of the world's population cannot be expected to reach their sixtieth birthday.

AGEING POPULATION

Ageing populations occur in more developed countries. Here, people choose not to have many children because infant mortality is low and the cost of living high. Advanced medicines help to increase life expectancy and enable the existing population to live longer.

YOUNG POPULATION

People in developing countries have more children. Health care is poor, many babies die at birth, and people do not have long lives. In such countries, numbers of young people have increased dramatically: in Africa almost half the population is under the age of 15.

LEAST DENSELY POPULATED COUNTRIES

Country	Population per sq km	per sq mile
Western Sahara	1	2.6
Mongolia	1	2.6
Namibia	2	5.2
Australia	2	5.2

URBANIZATION

Modern technology has enabled more people to live in a smaller space. Today, nearly 50% of the world's population, about 2.6 billion people, live in cities. Of these urban dwellers, half live in cities of more than 500,000 people.

Sprawling suburbs of Mexico City

WORLD URBAN GROWTH

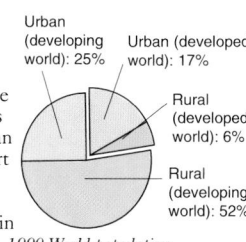

Key
2000
1990
1970
1950

London
New York
Mexico City
São Paulo
Cairo
Tehran
Bombay
Tokyo
Shanghai
Bangkok

This map shows major world city populations in millions from 1950 projected to 2000.

POPULATION MANAGEMENT

The education of women is now recognized as the most important factor in population control. Programmes that give women choice in matters of family planning and contraception (see p.130) are becoming more widespread.

Urban and rural population predictions
These diagrams show the proportion of the world's population living in urban and rural areas. The chart for 2025 forecasts the majority of the developing world living in urban areas.

Urban (developing world): 25%
Urban (developed world): 17%
Rural (developed world): 6%
Rural (developing world): 52%
1990 World population

Urban (developing world): 46%
Urban (developed world): 13%
Rural (developed world): 4%
Rural (developing world): 37%
2025 World population

THE CAIRO CONFERENCE

In 1994, the Cairo Conference on world population agreed on a twenty-year programme that laid emphasis on giving women greater power in matters of family planning. The UN claims that if this programme succeeds, world population will rise to 7.27 billion by 2015. If it fails, the population will reach 7.92 billion people by 2015, and 12.5 billion by 2050.

Delegates at the Cairo Conference

FAMILY PLANNING FACTS

- Less than 2% of government spending in the developing world, and less than 2% of all international aid, is currently devoted to family planning programmes.

- Financial incentives are used in China to promote a policy of one child per family.

SHIFTING POPULATIONS

Refugees are people who have fled their country in fear; today they number 20 million. People become refugees for many reasons such as war, politics, and religious and racial discrimination. Some refugees, like the Vietnamese boat people, have undertaken difficult and dangerous journeys to safety.

WORLD'S LARGEST CITIES

City (metropolitan area)	Total Population (millions)
Tokyo, Japan	27.242
Mexico City, Mexico	16.908
São Paulo, Brazil	16.792
New York, USA	16.390
Bombay, India	15.725
Shanghai, China	13.659
Los Angeles, USA	12.576
Calcutta, India	12.118
Buenos Aires, Argentina	11.931
Seoul, South Korea	11.768

Source: UN "Urban Agglomerations"

THE REFUGEE POPULATION

Country of origin	Number of refugees (millions)
Afghanistan	4.0
Rwanda	3.0
Palestine	2.8
Former Yugoslavia	1.3
Burundi	0.8
Mozambique	0.7
Liberia	0.7
Angola	0.5
Sri Lanka	0.5
Sudan	0.4
Azerbaijan	0.3

Source: The Refugee Council

YEAR ZERO

When the Khmer Rouge took power in Cambodia in 1976, they said that cities were corrupt places. They hoped to begin a new era by forcing people to abandon them.

MASS MIGRATIONS

Throughout history, people have chosen to leave their homelands or have abandoned them against their will.

- From 1600 to 1810, ten million Africans were taken as slaves to the Americas to work on plantations.

- Expansion in North America came via mass immigration: from 1860 to 1910, the population rose from 31 to 92 million.

SPACE POPULATIONS

Scientists explore ways to enable people to live on other planets. An experiment in Texas to create an artificial atmosphere was called Biosphere II. Although it failed, there is still hope that one day people may live in artificial atmospheres on the Moon.

LIVING STANDARDS

HIGH STANDARDS IN health, nutrition, and education are considered fundamental to the well-being of a nation. Generally, if a country is wealthy, its population will enjoy a high standard of living. If it is poor, people may not get enough to eat and may also lack social services such as hospitals and schools. Poverty also exists in developed countries, where a high standard of living for a few people can mean that others struggle to afford necessities.

World Health Organization

CHILD MORTALITY RATES
This table shows how many children under 5 die each year per 1,000 children.

Country	Infant deaths
Niger	320
Angola	292
Mozambique	287
Afghanistan	257
Sierra Leone	249
Finland	7
Singapore	7
Sweden	7
Japan	6

Source: UNICEF (1992)

BIRTH AND DEATH RATES

Region	Births (millions per year)	Deaths (millions per year)
Asia	84.8	27.1
Africa	29.4	9.1
South America	12.7	3.3
Europe	8.7	8.0
North America	4.6	2.6
Oceania	0.6	0.2

LIFE EXPECTANCY
The graph below shows the average age to which men and women are expected to live.

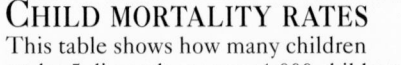

41 42 45 49 68 71 55 56 74 80 72 79

Women
Men

Afghanistan Burkina China India Australia USA

DISEASE
In tropical countries, infections are spread by organisms that carry disease from person to person. Developing countries also tend to suffer from diseases carried by contaminated food and water. In these countries, children are most at risk: life expectancy is low and disease cripples many. Diseases linked with industrialization and wealth, such as cancer and heart disease, have brought new health problems to developed countries.

DISEASE FACTS
- Measles, diarrhoea, and pneumonia kill an estimated 7 million children a year.
- Tetanus kills 600,000 babies each year even though immunization exists.
- Every year polio cripples 140,000 children.
- Following WWI, a global influenza epidemic killed nearly 22 million people between 1918 and 1920.

SAFE WATER
UNICEF (United Nations Children's Fund) defines safe water as "20 litres per person per day, at a source within one kilometre from the user's dwelling". Most diseases are spread through water contaminated by waste. Dehydration also causes many deaths. WHO aims to provide as many people as possible with clean water and proper sanitation.

WATER FACTS
- 22% of Mozambique's population has safe water.
- Two-thirds of the world's families do not have running water in their homes.
- If clean, safe water was made available for the world's population, 80% of sickness and disease would be prevented.
- Almost 2 billion people, most of them in the developing world, do not have access to the minimum level of safe drinking water.

SALAAM BOMBAY
Every year, an estimated 13 million children die, the equivalent of the entire population of Bombay, India.

HEALTH AND SICKNESS
The World Health Organization (WHO) defines "health" as a state of physical, mental, and social well-being. The absence of adequate food and sanitation causes much sickness around the world. The availability of doctors and hospitals also contributes to maintaining a nation's health.

Malaria has killed more than any other disease in recorded history. It kills at least 2 million people every year, most of them children in Africa, and infects 10 million with the disease. Mosquitoes carry the malarial protozoa, which is becoming increasingly resistant to western medicines.

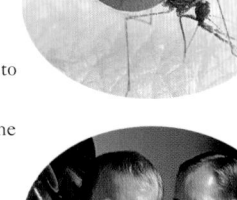

AIDS stands for Acquired Immune Deficiency Syndrome. In 1990, it was believed that more than 80% of the estimated 8.8 million people infected with HIV (see p.125) live in developing countries. More than 1.8 million people will have died as a result of AIDS by the year 2000.

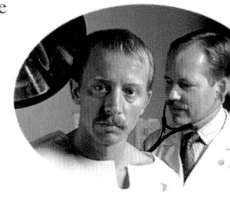

- Infectious diseases account for 25% of all deaths in the developing world, compared with just 1.4% of total deaths in the developed world.

Children collecting water in Africa

DOCTORS PER POPULATION
The graph below shows how many people there are per doctor in each country.

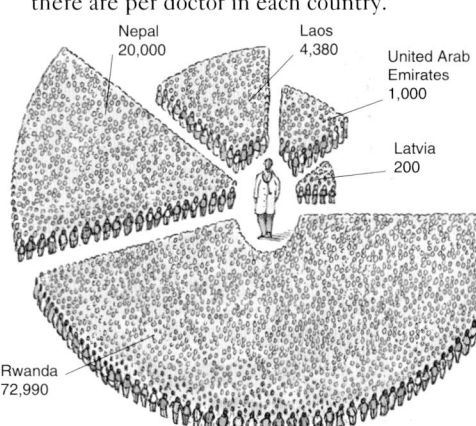

Nepal 20,000
Laos 4,380
United Arab Emirates 1,000
Latvia 200
Rwanda 72,990

FOOD AND NUTRITION

Food production has been increased to deal with the growing world population. Nutrition is not just a matter of good food; immunization, safe water supply, and a basic education would all reduce child malnutrition. Millions of people, most of them in the developing world, still suffer from malnutrition.

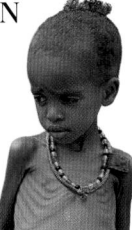

Undernourished child

FOOD PRODUCTION

The Food and Agriculture Organization (FAO) was set up in 1945, as part of the United Nations. It aims to reduce malnutrition, to improve efficiency in food production and distribution, and to improve life in rural areas.

Food and Agriculture Organization

EDUCATION

Education remains the single most important factor in creating a better world. Educating women has been shown to improve health care, reduce infant mortality, and lead to greater control over population growth.

Family planning in Africa

EDUCATION FACTS

• In 1993, almost 130 million children, two-thirds of them girls, were denied primary education.

• About one billion adults cannot read or write.

NORTH–SOUTH DIVIDE

Economic differences between developed and developing countries are also seen as a physical divide. The developed countries mainly occupy the northern part of the planet and the developing countries the south. This is known as the "North–South divide".

ECONOMIC FACTS

• A person from a developed nation consumes 20 to 30 times more of the world's resources than a person from the developing world.

• The average Ghanaian spends $5 a year in the shops compared to $9,000 for the average Japanese.

FOOD SUPPLY

The "Dietary energy supply" (DES) is the amount of food available per person per day, and is measured in calories. The table below compares the DES in some developed and developing countries.

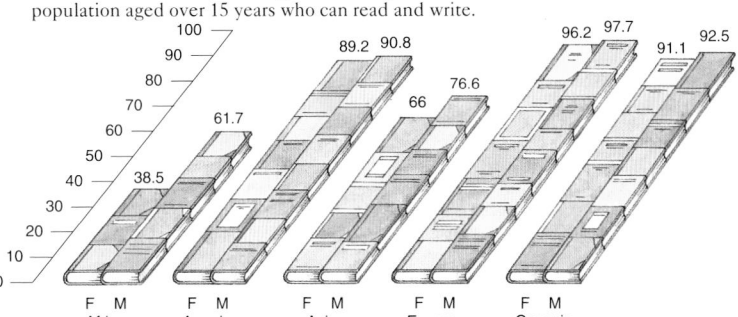

Ireland — 3,837
Greece — 3,816
USA — 3,732
Denmark — 3,664
Chad — 1,989
Mozambique — 1,680

ADULT LITERACY RATES

This table shows the percentage of each region's male and female population aged over 15 years who can read and write.

Africa: F 38.5, M 61.7
America: F 89.2, M 90.8
Asia: F 66, M 76.6
Europe: F 96.2, M 97.7
Oceania: F 91.1, M 92.5

HIGHEST SPENDERS ON EDUCATION

This table shows % of income (GNP) spent on education.

Country	% of GNP
Liechtenstein	11.8
Surinam	9.7
Libya	9.6
Algeria	9.1
Seychelles	9.1

LOWEST SPENDERS ON EDUCATION

This table shows % of income (GNP) spent on education.

Country	% of GNP
Somalia	0.4
Indonesia	0.9
Congo (Zaire)	0.9
Paraguay	1.0
Laos	1.2

THE HUMAN INDEX

Many people now consider GNP (see p.368) to be an unreliable reflection of a nation's development. The United Nations publishes "The Human Development Index", which is an alternative way of measuring the well-being and economic progress of a nation. Different indicators of living standards are recorded (e.g. education, life expectancy, nutrition, access to water), to help to establish an accurate world ranking for development. This index also recognizes poor living standards in the developed world.

NUTRITION FACTS

• About one-third of the developing world's children are underweight.

• 80% of the food for home consumption in Africa is grown by women.

SCHOOL'S OUT

Almost 80 million children in developing countries do not attend primary school.

BEST PUPIL/ TEACHER RATIO

Country	Pupils per teacher
San Marino	6
Sweden	6
Austria	11
Qatar	11

WORST PUPIL/ TEACHER RATIO

Country	Pupils per teacher
Central African Republic	90
Equatorial Guinea	68
Chad	67
Burundi	67

HIGHEST LIVING STANDARDS

Country	Rank	Assessment
Japan	1	High income and savings by individuals
Canada	2	Among the highest figures of GNP per person
Norway	3	High standards of health and social services
Switzerland	4	High income per person

Source: United Nations (1993)

LOWEST LIVING STANDARDS

Country	Rank	Assessment
Guinea	173	Just 32% of population has access to safe water
Sierra Leone	172	Daily calorie supply is only 79% of requirements
Afghanistan	171	Average life expectancy is about 40 years
Burkina	170	69% of population have access to safe water

Source: United Nations (1993)

DEBT AND WEALTH

LEVELS OF PROSPERITY around the world differ from country to country. Although the wealth of a nation is not simply a matter of money, what a country has or owes can indicate its prosperity.

WEALTH AND TRADE
A country's wealth depends on factors of production such as natural resources, capital, and labour. Some countries are rich in large amounts of mineral deposits like coal, oil, gold, and copper. Others may have a large amount of capital in the form of money from business, or a highly skilled workforce. These resources are traded within a country, as well as on the world market.

Out of sight, out of mind: a South American shanty town situated on the fringe of the c[...]

IMPORTS AND EXPORTS
Imports are what one country buys from another; exports are what it sells to another. By trading internationally, a country can sell what it produces to pay for things it is unable to produce itself. When a country does not produce enough wealth, it must borrow money from another country to pay for its imports.

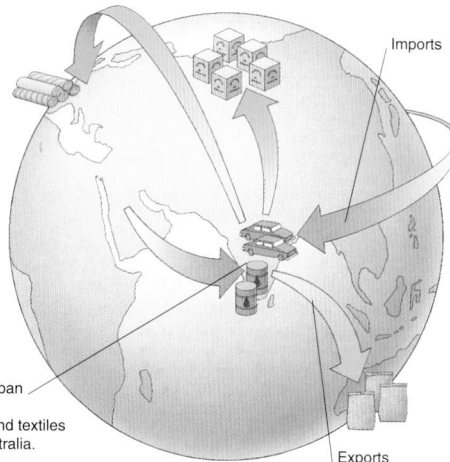

Imports

India imports cars from Japan and oil from the Arabian peninsula. It exports tea and textiles to Europe, and rice to Australia.

Exports

THE UNEQUAL WORLD
The world has experienced an exceptional growth in wealth since the 1950s with technology making the means of production more efficient. Many countries, particularly those situated in the southern hemisphere of the planet, have not benefited from this growth and are known as "developing" countries. The resulting inequality is known as the "North–South" divide.

THE DEBT CRISIS
Some developing countries borrow money for development from banking organizations like the World Bank. These institutions charge interest on the money borrowed. The longer a country takes to pay back the loan, the more interest they are charged. Some countries have to use much of the money they earn from trade to repay this interest, instead of using it for development. Developed countries have been criticized for controlling developing countries through debt.

IMF AND WORLD BANK
The International Monetary Fund (IMF) and World Bank were set up after World War II to help Europe redevelop. When developing countries became independent they also turned to these banks for aid.

International Monetary Fund

The World Bank

Economic inequalities
Economic alliances between developed countries have widened th[...] gap between rich and poor nations.

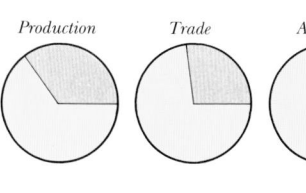

Production   *Trade*   *A[...]*

Rest of the world | 24 richest countries

Chart of debt in comparison with GNP

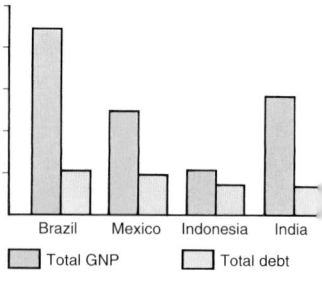

Brazil   Mexico   Indonesia   India

Total GNP | Total debt

NOT-SO-GOLDEN HANDSHAKE
Ten countries are home to three-quarters of the world's poor, and yet they receive only 26% of total global aid.

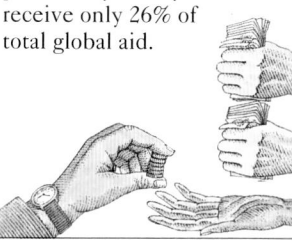

RICHEST AND POOREST
Economists judge a nation's wealth by looking at its Gross National Product, or GNP (the income generated per year). GNP per capita shows the average income of each person. Although useful, many believe that this does not reflect the true prosperity of a country.

Country	GNP per capita (US$)	Country	GNP per capita (US$)
Switzerland	37,930	Rwanda	80
Japan	34,630	Mozambique	90
Denmark	27,970	Ethiopia	100
Norway	26,390	Eritrea	100
USA	25,880	Somalia	120
Germany	25,580	Tanzania	140
Austria	24,630	Burundi	160
Sweden	23,530	Sierra Leone	160
France	23,420	Malawi	170

OIL WEALTH
Producers of particular goods have formed alliances to protect their mutual economic interests. OPEC, the Organization of Petroleum Exporting Countries, was set up to represent the interests of petroleum-exporting, developing countries. The price of oil has a greater effect on the international economy than any other product.

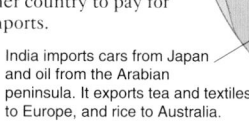

Representatives at an OPEC conference

OIL CRISIS
In 1973, OPEC restricted the amount of oil it was exporting, which in turn increased the price of oil around the world. This affected the wealth of many countries, especially the USA with its high consumption of oil by industry. To save petrol, the American authorities had to introduce a 50km/h (30mph) speed limit.

Cars queuing for petrol during the oil crisis.

TOP AID DONORS

Aid supplier	Aid as % of GNP (1994)
Norway	1.05
Denmark	1.03
Sweden	0.96
Netherlands	0.76
France	0.64
Canada	0.43

Source: UNICEF "The Progress of Nations"

HISTORY

Spanning the period from 40,000 B.C. to the present day, this extensive and absorbing section includes all the key dates and events in world history. Comparative timelines provide a global overview of events in each continent at any given time, and detailed tables list key personalities for every historical era.

Early Toolmakers and Artists • Early Farmers and Towns • Egypt and Mesopotamia
Expanding Empires and Mediterranean Trade • Ancient Greece and the Rise of Rome
Imperial Rome and Christianity • Islam and the Vikings • Mongols and Crusaders
Marco Polo and the Black Death • Renaissance and the Americas
Religious Conflict and Akbar • Manchu China, Supreme Rulers, and Slavery
Enlightenment, Revolution, and Napoleon • Europe in Turmoil and the British Empire
American Civil War and the Scramble for Africa • World War I and the Russian Revolution
Interwar Years and Communists in China • World War II • Cold War and the Middle East
African Independence • Middle East and the End of the Cold War • Great Civilizations
Rulers and Leaders • Presidents and Prime Ministers • Explorers • Battles and Wars
Revolutions and Rights • Archaeology and History

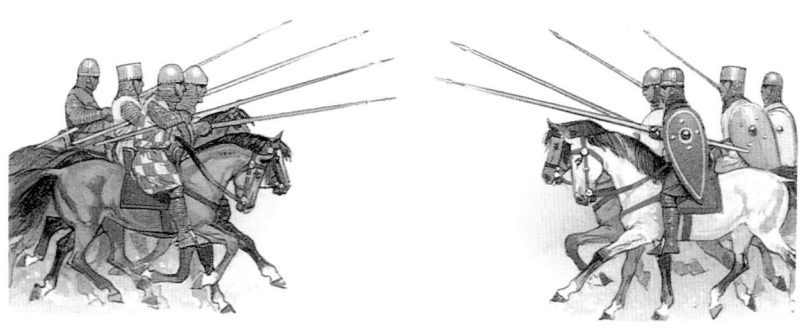

40,000 B.C.

AFRICA		30,000 Disappearance of the Neanderthals

ASIA **40,000** Cro-Magnon humans
living at Skhül and Kafzel (Israel)

27,000–19,000 Female statu
made at various sites, includi
locations in Russia

EUROPE **40,000** Neanderthals active in France at
La Chapelle-Aux-Saints, La Ferassie, and La Quina.
Cro-Magnons start to spread to Europe

35,000 Start of Upper Paleolithic Period
(flaked stone tools, bone and horn implements)

30,000 Probable date of earliest figurative art i
(Dordogne). Disappearance of Neanderthals
27,000–19,000 Female statu
at various sites in France and

AMERICAS **35,000** First humans arrive
in North America from Asia

OCEANIA **40,000** Probable arrival of
Aboriginals in Australia

THE FIRST TOOLMAKERS

In this period our human ancestors *(Homo sapiens sapiens)* became the dominant species on Earth. These early humans made great advances in toolmaking, and examples of their tools survive today. With great skill, they shaped stone and other materials, such as bone and wood, to produce a useful toolkit.

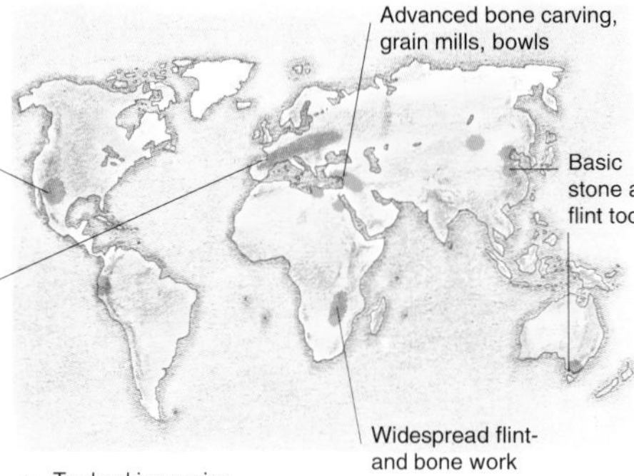

Area of skilfully flaked flint points. Use of nets and snares

Advanced bone carving, grain mills, bowls

Advanced flintwork, spear throwers, lamps and palettes for cave painting

Basic stone and flint tools

Widespread flint- and bone work

● Toolmaking region

REGIONS OF TOOLMAKING INDUSTRIES

Where early humans found such raw materials as stone, flint, bone, antler, shell, wood, and ivory, the started up toolmaking industries. Examples of tools have been found in continental and southern Europ in southern Africa, Mesopotamia, and the Americas

Felled trees allow greater use of timber for homes and tools.

Binding a wooden haft to a stone axehead allowed user to swing it with great force.

The sickle's long edge could be used to reap corn.

Axe-head
Split shaft

Pin

Toolmaker fits flints into shaft.

Handaxe used to skin animal.

Flint flakes from handaxe kept to make other tools.

Point and double edge allow many uses.

Toolmaker uses burin to carve antler.

Antler

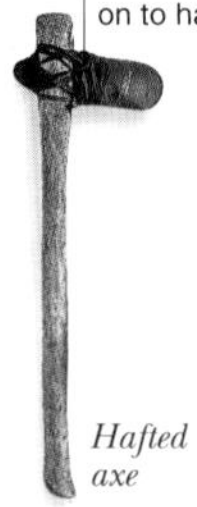

Flint axe-head fitted on to haft

When a f piece became blunt it c be replace easily.

1 FLINT HANDAXE

The most commonly found tool of early humans is the flint handaxe. Toolmakers used such techniques as pressure flaking, which controls the size of the chip, to give the stone a fine point and a sharp, straight, double edge.

Flint handaxe

2 STONE BURIN

After the handaxe, toolmakers developed the burin. This smaller, thinner stone tool was used to carve materials other than stone, such as antler and bone. Toolmakers made fine items including needles, fish hooks, and spear throwers.

Burin

3 COMBINING MATERIALS

The next advances came when toolmakers found they could combi different materials.

Small, sharp pieces of flint

Split b
s

Hafted axe

KEY INNOVATIONS

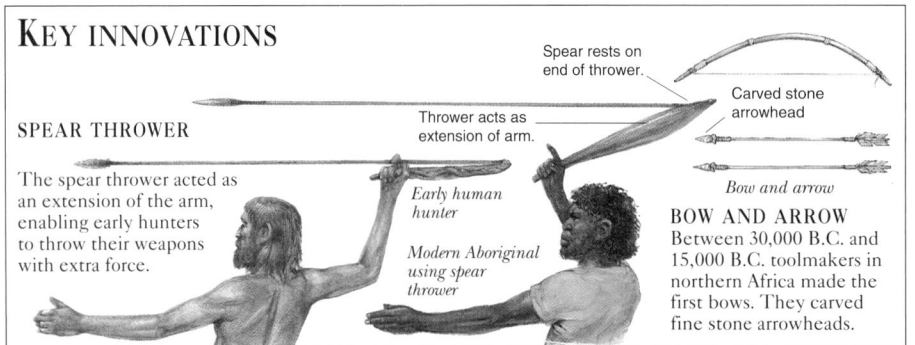

Spear rests on end of thrower.

Thrower acts as extension of arm.

Carved stone arrowhead

SPEAR THROWER

The spear thrower acted as an extension of the arm, enabling early hunters to throw their weapons with extra force.

Early human hunter

Modern Aboriginal using spear thrower

Bow and arrow

BOW AND ARROW

Between 30,000 B.C. and 15,000 B.C. toolmakers in northern Africa made the first bows. They carved fine stone arrowheads.

ANCIENT TECHNOLOGY

Item	Function	Location of find
	Comb	Mesopotamia
	Needle	Eastern Mediterranean
	Harpoon	Continental Europe
	Fish hook	Continental Europe
	Beads	Eastern Mediterranean

.C.   10,000 B.C.

15,000 Last rainy period in northern Africa

16,000 Coldest point   **12,500** Rise of Magdalenian toolmakers
in glaciation   (bone and antler harpoons, fishing spears)

14,000–11,000 El-Kebareh   **11,000** Rise of Natufian culture.
culture (Israel), with free-
standing round huts   **10,500** Earliest pottery:
                                   Fukui cave, Japan

15,000 Cave paintings,   **12,500** Rise of Magdalenian toolmakers
Lascaux, France   (bone and antler harpoons, fishing spears)

15,000–10,000 Magdalenian culture,   **11,000** Cave paintings,
high point of mural and portable art   Altimira, Spain

ave dwellers present in Brazil   **15,000** Cave art begins in
                                   Brazil (shelter of Toca do
                                   Boqueirao de Pedra Furada)

4,000 Earliest known cremation, Lake   **16,000** Cave art,
Mungo, New South Wales, Australia   north coast of Australia

THE FIRST ARTISTS

Creating art is an activity that marks out humans from other animals. Early artists used the walls of caves to paint animals and images, but they rarely painted people, and never landscapes. They did, though, carve small statues of people.

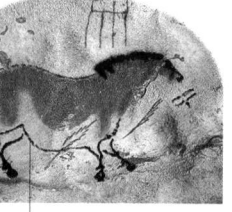

Brown powder sprayed on

LASCAUX ART
This painted horse of about 15,000 B.C. was found in the Lascaux caves, France. The feathered dots may have been magical hunting symbols.

ARTISTS' METHODS
Early artists used natural materials for different coloured paints. They painted with brushes of hair or sticks, or pads made from moss or animal skin. They drew lines with sharp stones.

Charcoal, for black

Clay, for brown

Green clay, for green

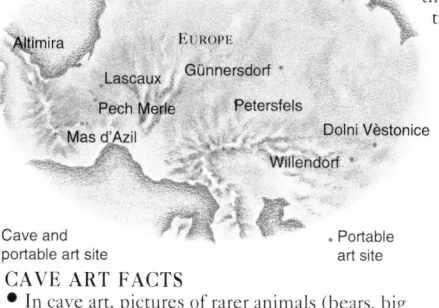

Cave and portable art site   *Portable art site*

CAVE ART FACTS
● In cave art, pictures of rarer animals (bears, big cats, rhinoceroses) often appear in more remote parts of the cave; common ones (aurochs, deer, mammoths) often appear at the entrance.

● The Lascaux paintings have suffered more in the last 50 years from human perspiration, body heat, and micro-organisms than in the 15,000-year period during which they lay undisturbed.

● Artists may have applied some colours by blowing paint through hollow reeds on to the cave wall.

LOCATIONS OF ANCIENT ART
The best-preserved paintings are on the walls of caves in France and Spain that remained undiscovered until this century. Objects carved in wood, stone, or bone are known as portable art objects.

"VENUS" FIGURINES
Several small female statues, called "Venus" figurines, have been found across Europe, and may represent goddesses; their large size may symbolize pregnancy (for fertility worship) or obesity (for abundant food).

A CAVE DISCOVERED
In 1940 Marcel Ravidat led three friends to a hole he had spied while walking his dog at Lascaux, France. He dropped down through the hole into a cave. By matchlight he saw beautiful paintings, made thousands of years earlier.

ICE-AGE LIFE

For at least the last two million years the world's climate has regularly swung between cold and warm periods. When cold struck, landscapes, rivers, lakes, and vegetation changed greatly. Humans had to adapt to the new environment to survive.

Ice-Age hunters trap a mammoth

ICE-AGE HUNTERS
Ice-Age people used many parts of the animals that they hunted: they made warm clothes from their fur and skin, and some used mammoth bones to support the animal-skin walls of their huts.

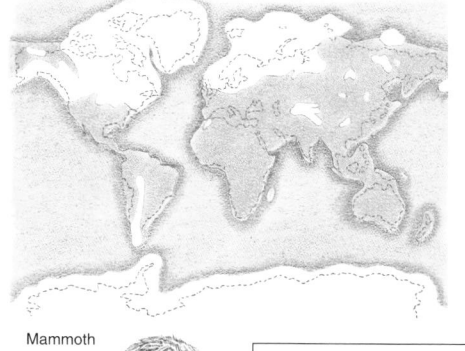

Mammoth bone hut

Harpoon

ICE-AGE SPREAD
At the peak of the last Ice Age, ice sheets covered huge areas of the world, and sea levels dropped. Emerging land formed bridges between continents separated today.

Ice-Age coast
Present-day coast
Ice sheet c.18,000 B.C.

TROPICAL THAMES
The world experienced warm periods as well as ice ages. Bones found underneath Trafalgar Square, London, prove that hippopotamuses swam in the River Thames during one of these warmer spells.

NATUFIAN CULTURE
In 11,000 B.C. the Natufians of Palestine became probably the first people to abandon a hunter-based, nomadic lifestyle and settle down. They began to live permanently in caves, or in circular huts.

Grain store   Huts of mud, reed, and timber

Natufians gathered wild grain and stored it in huts.   House

Wild grain made coarse bread that wore down Natufians' teeth.

Headdress of shell beads

Burial customs
Natufians often buried their dead with personal items: necklaces and bracelets of bone or beads.

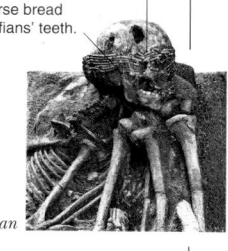

Natufian woman

10,000 B.C.

AFRICA	**10,000** Hunting camps established in Sahara region after Ice Age ends	**8500** First rock paintings, Sahara region	**8000** Pottery made in Sahara region

ASIA	**10,000** Ice cap retreats	**9000–8000** Cereals (wheat and barley) grown in Jordan and Syria. Pottery made at Mureybet, Syria. Domestication of goats and sheep in Iran and Jordan	**8000** Jericho, the first town, appears. Ice Age ends in Far East **7500** Domestication of pigs, Crimea

EUROPE	**10,000** Ice cap retreats **8300** Retreat of glaciers

AMERICAS		**9000** First people reach southern tip of South America	**8500** Cultivation of wild grasses and beans, Peru **8000** Semi-permanent settlements, North America 

OCEANIA

THE FIRST FARMERS

In 8000 B.C., people in the Middle East cultivated crops for the first time. They grew mainly varieties of wheat and barley. The new strains of wheat they developed slowly spread around the Mediterranean, then further afield.

EARLY CROPS

Wild species of wheat were not ideal as food crops because their seed heads would shatter when ripe. Farmers solved this by hybridization (combining different wheat strains) to create new types of wheat.

Wild and hybridized species of grain

Wild einkorn   Einkorn   Wild emmer   Emmer

Wheat
Early cereal grain used for

Barley
Milled for bread, also used for beer

Lentil
Pulse, dried or eaten fresh

Yam
Large tuber, high in starch

Millet
Asian cereal high in protein

Rice
High-protein cereal

Maize
Grows in cobs (heads)

Tapioca
From root of manioc plant

THE SPREAD OF AGRICULTURE

In western Asia and Europe knowledge of farming spread from the central area of Syria, Palestine, Iran, Iraq, and Turkey. Farmers in Southeast Asia developed their crops independently, while in the Americas farmers appeared later, in about 7000 B.C.

DOMESTICATED ANIMALS

When they began to grow crops, farmers also domesticated wild animals. Domestication often changed a species' appearance.

Wild Animal   Domesticated Animal

Asiatic moufflon   Sheep
Near East 8000 B.C.

Wild Animal   Domesticated Animal

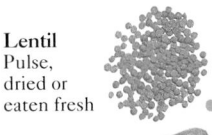
Wolf   Dog
Near East 11,000 B.C.

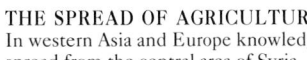

Wild boar   Pig
Near East 7500 B.C.

Bezoar goat   Goat
Near East 8900 B.C.

Aurochs   Cow
Near East 7000 B.C.

DOLMENS

Chûn Quoit, Cornwall, U

Dolmens are the first great stone monuments of Europe and date from about 4500 B.C. They are the remains of ancient chamber tombs, and consist of a large, flat, stone, supported by upright stones. Their existence shows a great knowledge of engineering.

EARLY BREADMAKING

Early humans collected the seed heads of wild wheats and ground them using a stone quern (hand mill). After separating the husks from the coarse flour, they mixed the flour with water and baked unleavened (unrisen) bread.

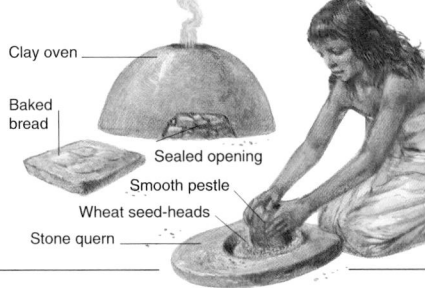

Clay oven

Baked bread

Sealed opening

Smooth pestle

Wheat seed-heads

Stone quern

GREEN SAHARA

The Sahara Desert was once a fertile region with organized communities. 8,000-year-old paintings on cliff walls at Tassili-n-Ajjer, Libya, show many species of animal, hunters, a woman pounding flour, wedding ceremonies, and a family with a pet dog.

CROPS FOR TEXTILES

By 5000 B.C. the Egyptians were growing flax to make linen fabric. They harvested the flax at different times to produce various linen goods: young green stems were used for fine cloth and the tougher fibres of ripe flax could be made into ropes or mats.

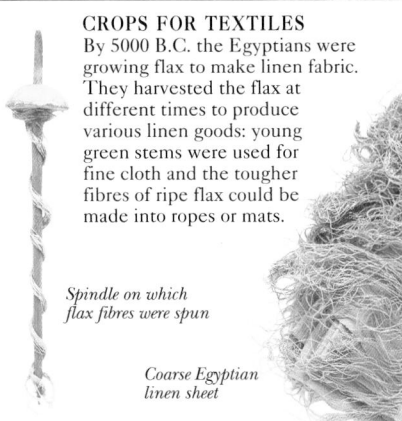

Spindle on which flax fibres were spun

Coarse Egyptian linen sheet

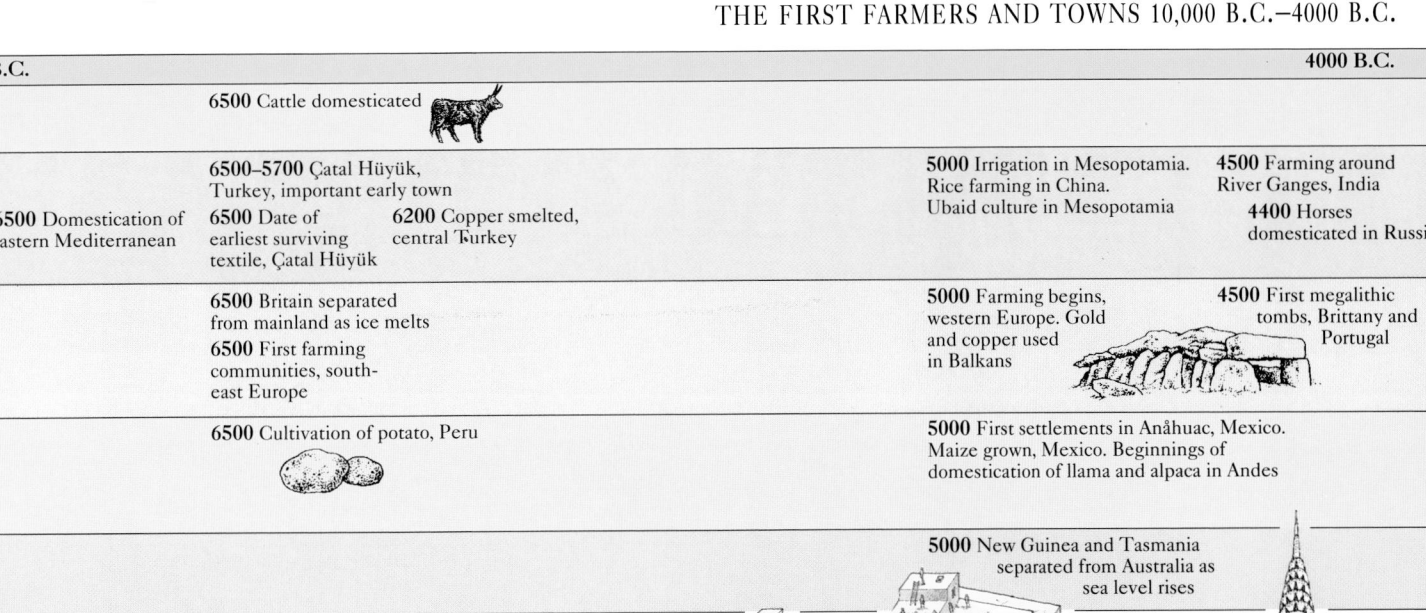

6500 Cattle domesticated

6500–5700 Çatal Hüyük, Turkey, important early town

6500 Domestication of eastern Mediterranean

6500 Date of earliest surviving textile, Çatal Hüyük

6200 Copper smelted, central Turkey

5000 Irrigation in Mesopotamia. Rice farming in China. Ubaid culture in Mesopotamia

4500 Farming around River Ganges, India
4400 Horses domesticated in Russia

6500 Britain separated from mainland as ice melts

6500 First farming communities, south-east Europe

5000 Farming begins, western Europe. Gold and copper used in Balkans

4500 First megalithic tombs, Brittany and Portugal

6500 Cultivation of potato, Peru

5000 First settlements in Anâhuac, Mexico. Maize grown, Mexico. Beginnings of domestication of llama and alpaca in Andes

5000 New Guinea and Tasmania separated from Australia as sea level rises

THE FIRST TOWNS

Towns and trade began to develop at the same time as agriculture and in the same parts of the world. The first townspeople were craft workers, priests, and traders. They depended on nearby farmers for food and on areas further afield for trade.

Reconstruction of Çatal Hüyük

Sometimes a courtyard was used as a rubbish dump by surrounding houses.

Mud-brick walls

Ladder

Entrance through rooftop

Timber and reed support roofs

Lack of streets made town easy to defend.

JERICHO

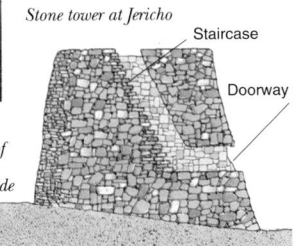

Jericho in the Near East was probably the first town, built in about 8000 B.C. It had a strong stone wall, a tower and defensive ditch, and a large and well-organized population.

SMALL WORLD
In 10,000 B.C. the entire population of the world was about 12 million. This is two-thirds of the current population of New York State.

Staircase

Doorway

Cross-section of Jericho Tower, 10m (32ft) wide

Ditch

ÇATAL HÜYÜK
Çatal Hüyük is the site of a well-preserved town in Turkey from 6500 B.C. Its mud-brick houses had shared walls; there were no streets. Its people went about by climbing over the rooftops.

TRADERS
Goods from distant lands were found in the ruins of Çatal Hüyük: obsidian (volcanic glass), cowrie shells from the Mediterranean, and turquoise from Sinai.

EVIDENCE OF RELIGION

Human skulls
Jericho's dead were sometimes buried beneath the floors of the houses with their skulls (though not the jaw) removed and decorated.

Cowrie shells   Plaster

Turkish obsidian

Turquoise

Cowrie shells

Shrine paintings
Some rooms in Çatal Hüyük were decorated with religious images. Here vultures with human legs (perhaps priests in costume) attack a headless figure.

KEY EARLY TOWNS

Town	Area	Date	Industry/Craft
Jericho	Eastern Mediterranean	8000 B.C.	Pottery
Çatal Hüyük	Turkey	7000 B.C.	Obsidian toolmaking
Jarmo	Iraq	c.7000 B.C.	Textile weaving
Khirokitia	Cyprus	c.6000 B.C.	Stone and wood articles

TOWN FACTS
• Early towns were sited in places with reliable springs; with mountains nearby where wild crops could grow; and with enough rainfall for the crops.

• In Çatal Hüyük, the average man lived to the age of 34, the average woman to the age of 30.

• Excavations at Jarmo revealed eleven towns, each one built on top of the other at different times.

Early clay stamps

• From about 6000 B.C. town dwellers in the Middle East began using clay stamps to mark their personal property. Traders may also have used them to mark their goods.

FIRST POTTERY
The earliest pottery is more than 12,000 years old and comes from Japan. People from Africa and the Near East discovered it about 3,000 years later.

Pinching method

Potter hollows out solid lump of clay.

Potter coils single stretched piece of clay.

Coiling method

Decorated pot from Nasunahara, Japan: one of the earliest-known pottery vessels

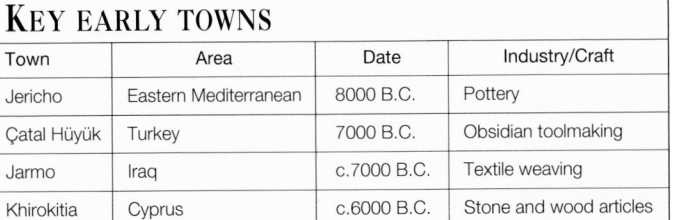

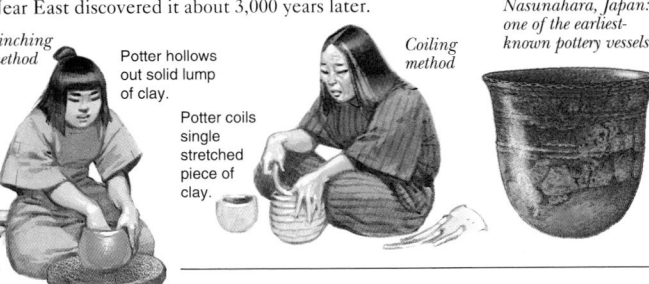

FIRST METALWORKERS
In 7000–6000 B.C. people discovered that certain rocks, called ores, would release pure metal when heated. The metal could then be beaten into shape to make useful objects, or be melted and poured directly into moulds.

Copper spearhead

Furnace at c.1200°C (c.2200°F)

Molten metal is poured into mould.

Bag bellows

Clay nozzle

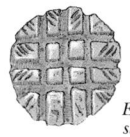

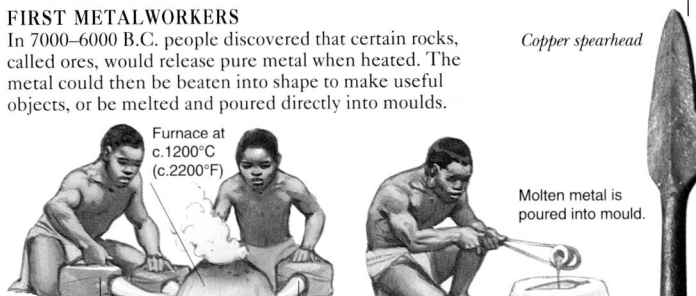

4000 B.C.

AFRICA
3750 First bronze alloy (also used by Sumerians)
3500 First sailing vessels, Egypt

3000 Development of hieroglyphic writing
2590 Building of Pyramid of Khuf
3100 Menes the Fighter unites Upper and Lower Egypt
2686 Beginning of Egyptian Old Kingdom
2646 Pyramid of Zoser at

ASIA
4000 Beginning of bronze casting, Middle East
3500 Earliest Chinese city, Liang-ch'eng chen. Mesopotamians invent wheel and plough
3250 Earliest pictographic writing, Mesopotamia
3000 Development of Sumerian cities
2850 Legendary Golden Age in China
2750 Gilgamesh, legendary king of

EUROPE

3200 Beginnings of early Cycladic civilization in Aegean islands
3000 Spread of copper use
2900 Danubian culture, central Europe

AMERICAS
3200 Maize farmed in South America
3000 First pottery in Americas

OCEANIA
3000 Probable introduction of dogs in Australia

ANCIENT EGYPT

In about 3500 B.C. Egyptians established one of the world's longest-lasting civilizations along the fertile banks of the Nile. Ruled by pharaohs (kings) and serviced by a large priesthood, Egyptians were famous for their stone building skills, their hieroglyphic writing, and their elaborate cult of the dead.

PYRAMID BUILDERS

Egyptians had a ready supply of stone, a good transport system on the Nile, and a large labour force. This enabled them to become the first people to build in stone on a large scale. The details of their building methods, however, have been lost.

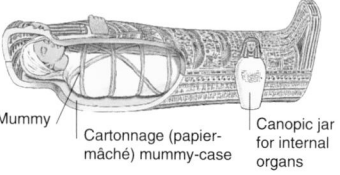

Mummy
Cartonnage (papier-mâché) mummy-case
Canopic jar for internal organs

BURIAL FACTS

• Any important Egyptian was carefully mummified after death. Internal organs were placed in jars, and the body preserved with natron (salts) and wrapped in linen bandages.

• Egyptians placed mummies in a series of decorated cases, often painted with a portrait of the dead person. The nest of cases was then placed in a stone coffin, called a sarcophagus.

Saqqara Earliest pyramid (stepped) and first known stone building

Dahshur Bent pyramid of King Snefru, about 100m (330ft) high

Giza Khufu's tomb and world's largest stone structure

• City
Ancient coastline
• Heliopolis
• Memphis
• Thebes

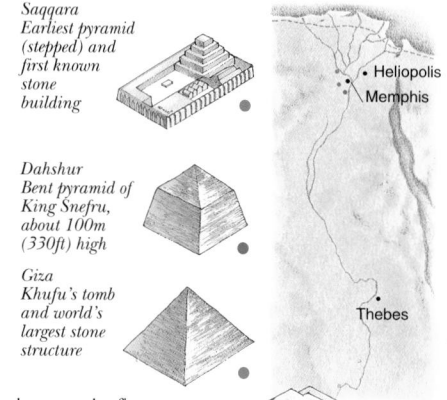

Slave team

Probable method of pyramid construction

Temporary ramp
Stones dragged up on rollers

HIEROGLYPHIC WRITING

Egyptians used hieroglyphs for temple inscriptions and religious texts. A hieroglyph can stand for an object, an idea, or a sound. Scribes and priests, who alone understood hieroglyphs, grew more powerful when their writing skills were needed for administration.

Tutankhamun's cartouche (name inscription)

LANDMARKS IN STONE

From the Nile delta as far south as modern-day Sudan, Egyptians built pyramid tombs in various styles, and temples to their gods. Many of these monuments are still standing.

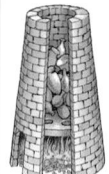
Abu Simbel Temple of Rameses II, cut into solid rock face

Sphinx Khafre's guard, 73m (240ft) long

KEY INNOVATIONS

SAIL

Egyptians constructed sailing ships from about 3500 B.C. Ships were first built from the Nile's reeds, and later from foreign timber.

POTTERY KILN

Kilns, invented in both Egypt and Mesopotamia, produced better-quality pots.

KEY PHARAOHS

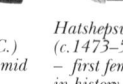

Zoser (c.2700 B.C.) – first pyramid builder.

Hatshepsut (c.1473–58 B.C.) – first female ruler in history.

Thutmose III (1479–25 B.C.) expanded empire's territories.

Akhenaton (1370–52 B.C.) started a new religion.

Tutankhamun (1353–35 B.C.), a boy-king, revived old gods.

Rameses II (1290–24 B.C.) – last great military pharaoh.

STONEHENGE

Stonehenge is a circle of stones on Salisbury Plain, England. Construction began in about 2200 B.C. Some of the huge stones had to be transported more than 216km (134 miles), from Wales. On the summer solstice, the sun rises directly over the axis of the monument.

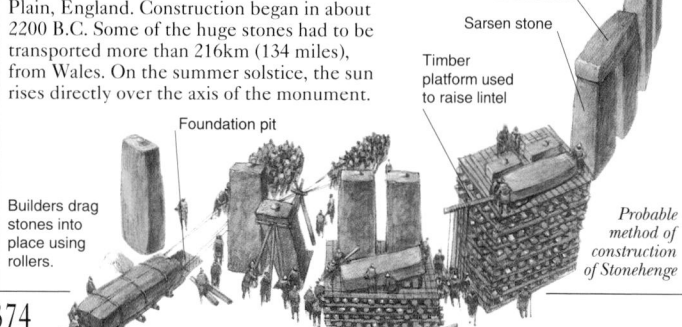

Lintel stone
Sarsen stone
Timber platform used to raise lintel
Foundation pit
Builders drag stones into place using rollers.
Probable method of construction of Stonehenge

INDUS VALLEY CIVILIZATION

In 1921 archaeologists discovered remains of a unknown civilization from about 2500 B.C. Based in the Indian cities of Harappa and Mohenjo-Daro, its people lived in mud-brick houses and had baths, vast granaries, and drainage systems. Their writing appears on seals, but it has never been deciphered.

Mohenjo-Daro sculpture (c.2100 B.C.), probably of a priest or divine king

Great Bath, Mohenjo-Daro

Ritual baths

The size of the Great Bath at Mohenjo-Daro and the footbath at its entrance suggest that it was used for purifying rituals, perhaps by priests.

...nings of desiccation /) of Sahara region

2133 Beginning of Egyptian Middle Kingdom

2150 End of Egyptian Old Kingdom

1786 End of Egyptian Middle Kingdom

1652 War between Egypt and Hyksos people from Asia

1550 Beginning of Egyptian New Kingdom

...nings of Indus civilization. ...esticated, Central Asia

2371 Semites under Sargon of Akkad begin to occupy entire plain of Shinar – greatest Mesopotamian empire established

2000 Hittites begin invasions of Anatolia

1900 Decline of Indus civilization

1800 Beginnings of Assyrian empire

1792 Birth of Hammurabi, founder of Babylonian empire

1500 Chinese ideographic script in use

...est barrow burials in Britain. ...s of Dolmen period of ...an Neolithic age

2200 Building of Stonehenge starts. End of Scandinavian Dolmen period

1600 Beginnings of Mycenean civilization, Greece

1500 Linear B script in use on Crete

...est large settlements in ..., with temple mounds

2000 Beginnings of Minoan civilization, Crete

2000 First metalworking, Peru. Inuits reach northern Greenland

2000 Beginnings of settlement of Melanesia, South Pacific

MESOPOTAMIA

The fertile region of Mesopotamia, between the rivers Tigris and Euphrates, nurtured some of the world's most influential civilizations. This area saw the invention of writing, the birth of mathematics, and great experiments in irrigation.

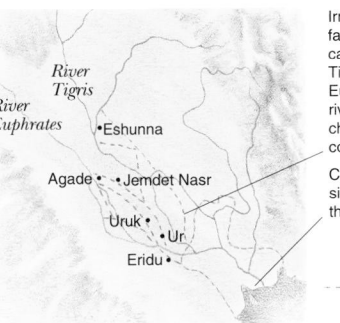

Irrigation for farming often caused the Tigris and Euphrates rivers to change course.

Centuries of silt extended the coastline.

Ancient river

Ancient coastline

MESOPOTAMIAN CITY-STATES

Mesopotamia lies in modern-day Iraq. Different ...ities dominated the region at different times: Agade ...n about 2300 B.C.; Ur from 2112 B.C. to 2095 B.C.; ...abylon after 1750 B.C. At other times the cities ...hared power over the region.

ONE FOR THE ROAD

Kings and their servants were often found in the same grave. In the Royal Graves at Ur small cups lay near the skeletons of the king's servants, which may have contained poison.

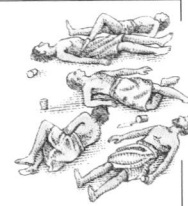

MESOPOTAMIAN INNOVATIONS

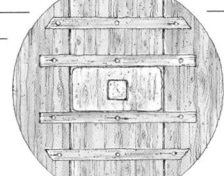

WHEEL
Mesopotamians invented the wheel between 3500 and 3250 B.C. Their wheels were strong and solid, but heavy.

PLOUGH
The plough appeared c.3500 B.C. Pulled by oxen, it made the job of sowing seeds much quicker and easier.

WRITING
Picture-writing appeared c.3000 B.C. The pictures grew more abstract, becoming cuneiform script.

EPIC
The Epic of Gilgamesh, the first epic story to be written down (c.2000 B.C.), tells of godlike Gilgamesh of Uruk.

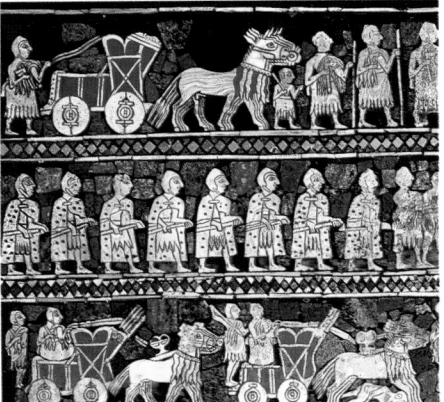

THE STANDARD OF UR
A famous inlaid box (c.2600 B.C.), called the Standard of Ur, was found in the grave pits at Ur. It shows kings, priests, musicians, soldiers, wheeled chariots, farmers, fishermen, and many animals. No-one knows what it was used for.

BABYLON'S HEYDAY
Under King Hammurabi (c.1792–50 B.C.) the city of Babylon became a centre of law, mathematics, medicine, and literature. The king had his legal code, the first known, carved on a famous granite stela (pillar).

ZIGGURAT
Mesopotamians built great mud-brick temples, called ziggurats, to their sun and moon gods. The huge size of many of these ziggurats suggests that religion was very important in Mesopotamian society.

Ziggurat at Ur – about 45m

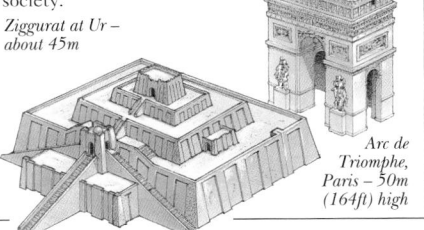

Arc de Triomphe, Paris – 50m (164ft) high

MINOAN CULTURE

...Minoans were Mediterranean ...raders. Their civilization ...asted from 2000 B.C. to ...400 B.C. and was centred ...round huge palaces, the ...argest of which was the ...alace of Minos (after the ...egendary King Minos) in ...nossos, Crete. Sea trade ...nade Minoans very wealthy.

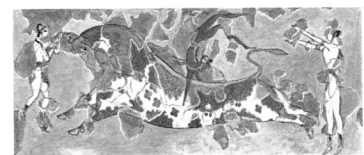

MINOAN WALL-PAINTINGS
The walls of Minoan palaces were decorated with colourful murals. One famous painting shows a religious ceremony in which young athletes somersault over the horns of a bull.

MINOAN FACTS
• Minoan women wore colourful, topless dresses, sometimes with layered skirts.

• Minoans developed a script, later named Linear B. British architect Michael Ventris deciphered it in 1952. An earlier Minoan script, Linear A, remains undeciphered.

• Palaces not only served as royal residences, but also as stores for farm produce, as craft workshops, and as depots for sea trade.

BIG URNERS
Archaeologists found enormous clay jars called *pithoi* at Knossos, some over 5ft (1.5m) tall. Minoans used the jars to store their trade goods: grain, wine, and olive oil.

1500 B.C.

AFRICA

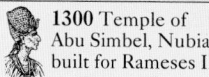
1300 Temple of Abu Simbel, Nubia, built for Rameses II

1218 First invasion of Egypt by Sea Peoples

1182 Second invasion of Egypt by Sea Peoples

ASIA **1500** People from Thrace, Balkans, move to Asia Minor, leading to establishment of Phrygia. Composition of hymns of Rig Veda

1400 Chinese capital moved to Anyang, present-day S. Korea. Extensive use of iron in Asia Minor and India

1200 Hittite Empire collapses. Jews settle in Palestine

1100 Phoenicians begin out from eastern Mediter

1027 (overth dynast

EUROPE **1500** Beginning of Bronze Age in Scandinavia

1450 End of Minoan civilization, Crete

1200 Decline of Mycenaean culture, Greece

AMERICAS

1300 Beginning of Olmec civilization in Mexico

OCEANIA

1200 First settlers from Indonesia and Philippines arrive in Fiji and spread throughout Polynesia

---

EXPANDING EMPIRES

After the first civilizations were established in the Middle East, their peoples began to expand their territories and build large empires. These warlike peoples used their military might to conquer weaker groups and extracted tax, tribute, or trading advantages from their victims.

HITTITE EMPIRE

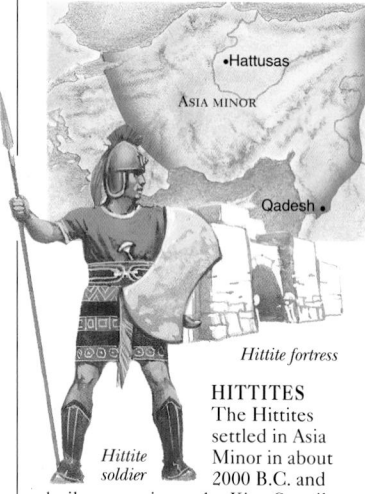

Hittite fortress

Hittite soldier

HITTITES
The Hittites settled in Asia Minor in about 2000 B.C. and built an empire under King Suppiluliuma (c.1386–48 B.C.) In 1294 B.C. Hittites fought Egyptians at Qadesh in a great battle for control of Palestine. Egypt claimed victory, but withdrew.

Hittite culture

10,000 cuneiform tablets, found at the Hittite capital of Hattusas, tell us most of what we know of their later history. Few Hittite artefacts survive.

ASSYRIAN EMPIRE

NEW KINGDOM EGYPT

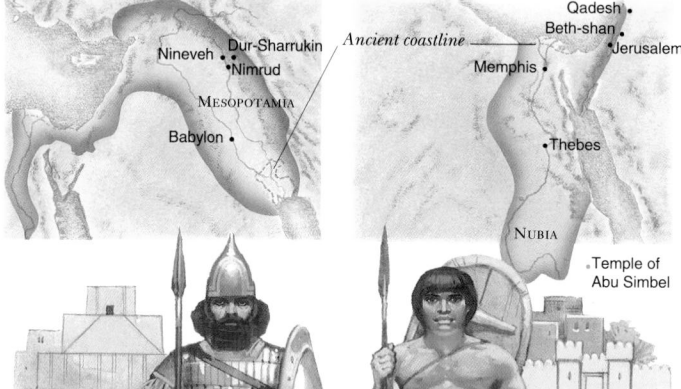

Ancient coastline

Buhen fortress, Egypt

ASSYRIANS
Tiglath-Pileser I (1114–1076 B.C.) ruled the Assyrian empire at its height. Assyrians were known for their cruelty, and used fear and threats to plunder their neighbours.

Egyptian soldier

Assyrian soldier

EGYPTIANS
The New Kingdom, established in Egypt in 1550 B.C., covered Palestine (including Canaan), Syria, and the southern Nile (Nubia). It was the greatest Egyptian empire of all time.

Royal hunter
Beautiful reliefs decorated Assyrian palace walls. King Ashurbanipal I kills a lion (right).

Ivory decorations
Assyrians demanded payment from their defeated enemies. The Phoenician ivory carving (left) is from Nimrud.

Amarna letters
The Amarna letters record some of Egypt's diplomatic dealings. A rival king wrote to ask Pharaoh Amenophis IV for his continued friendship (right).

Hebrews
When Egypt invaded Canaan, many inhabitants (Hebrews) hid in the hills of Judea.

EMPIRE TIMESCALE

Empire	Dates
Hittite	c.1400–1200 B.C.
Assyrian	1500–612 B.C.
New Kingdom Egypt	1550–1050 B.C.
Neo-Babylonian (Chaldean)	626–539 B.C.

NEO-BABYLONIAN EMPIRE

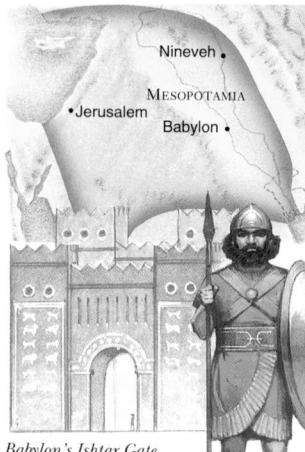

Babylon's Ishtar Gate

Chaldean soldier

CHALDEANS
Nebuchadnezzar II rebuilt the city of Babylon in 605 B.C. He created its famous Hanging Gardens for his homesick Persian wife.

Cylinder seals

Chaldeans marked their property using inscribed cylinders. They rolled them over wet clay or soft wax.

KEY INNOVATIONS

HITTITE CHARIOTS

Hittites were the first systematic users of chariots to break through enemy infantry.

ASSYRIAN FLOAT
Assyrian soldiers used inflatable animal skins to help them swim across fast rivers.

EGYPTIAN MATHS
The Rhind Papyrus, from about 1600 B.C., shows that Egyptians were advanced mathematicians, skilled in geometry and arithmetic.

STARGAZERS
Chaldeans were the first people to make long-term astronomical records, which they wrote on wax-covered boards.

600 B.C.

900 Foundation of kingdom of Kush in Nubia

814 Phoenicians found their colony at Carthage

600 Phoenicians sail around Africa

...gdom of Israel g David

800 Aryans from present-day Iran expand into southern India

771 Chou state collapses in China

721–05 Assyrian Empire at its greatest extent

660 Jimmu, legendary first Japanese emperor

650 Chinese begin to use iron

612 Decline of Assyrian power after Medes and Scythians destroy Nineveh

604 Nebuchadnezzar II is ruler of Babylonian Empire

...uscans ...taly

776 First recorded Olympic Games, Greece

753 Traditional date of foundation of Rome

750 Greek city-states establish settlements around Mediterranean

700 Beginning of Halstatt culture (Iron Age) in central and western Europe

650 Earliest surviving Latin inscriptions

621 First written laws of Athens (Laws of Dracon)

900 Height of Chavin civilization in Andes

800 Zapotec civilization of Central America produces first writing in Americas

...t of Polynesian Islands settled

OLMECS
The Olmecs were one of the earliest civilizations of Central America (1300–400 B.C.). They lived between the Gulf of Mexico and the Pacific Ocean, and traded with present-day Mexico and Costa Rica. Some of their colossal carved stone heads are still standing.

...salt head of an Olmec king

...AVIN
...avin was one of the ...rliest civilizations of South ...merica (c.900 B.C.). Based ...the Andes (Peru), its ...ople were farmers, and ...ilt a canal that ran for ...m (5.6 miles), partly ...derground.

Chavin carving of warrior with severed enemy head

ETRUSCANS
Etruscans lived in northern Italy from about 1000 B.C. in loosely connected city-states. Etruscan farmers supplied the Greek markets, and their craftsmen produced high-quality bronzes, pottery, and wall paintings. The Romans later destroyed their race and language.

...uscan tomb fresco ...ll painting) showing ...sician and dancer.

TRAVELLERS AND TRADERS
The Mycenaeans were sea-going Greeks who built a Mediterranean empire based on a mixture of war and trade. They were followed by the more peaceful Phoenicians from northern Palestine, who set up trading bases along the Mediterranean coast.

MYCENAEAN RICHES
Amazing gold items have been found at Mycenaean sites, such as the death mask of a Mycenaean king (left).

Gold Mycenaean death mask

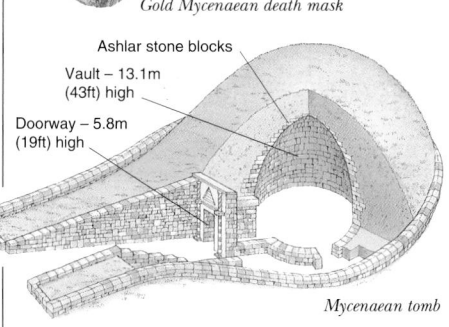

Ashlar stone blocks

Vault – 13.1m (43ft) high

Doorway – 5.8m (19ft) high

Mycenaean tomb

MYCENAEAN MONUMENTS
Mycenaeans built great stone tombs for their kings. The Treasury of Atreus (above) was built in about 1250 B.C. of ashlar stone, and was covered by an artificial mound of earth.

PHOENICIAN TRADERS
Phoenician sailors built colonies throughout the Mediterranean, trading in glassware and their famous purple cloth dyed with an extract from the murex shell. Their ships' timber came from the forests of the Phoenician homeland in northern Palestine.

Mycenae
Panormus
Byblos
Sidon
Tyre
Gades
Leptis Minor
Carthage
Hippo Regius
Knossos
Leptis Magna

Mycenaean empire
• Mycenaean city
· Phoenician city

MYCENAEANS AND PHOENICIANS
Mycenaeans dominated southern Greece from about 1600 B.C. to 1200 B.C. In about 1000 B.C. the Phoenicians began colonizing the coast from their homeland cities of Tyre, Sidon, and Byblos in present-day Lebanon.

Phoenician sailors trade cloth and glass for ivory at an Egyptian port.

Phoenician merchant
Egyptian merchant
Coloured glass jars
Egyptian ivory

...ANG CHINA
...ngs of the Shang ...nasty ruled China ...m about 1600 B.C. ...il 1027 B.C. Shang ...ople produced: ...azing bronzework, ...ts with harnesses, ...ting, and had a ...hly developed ...an culture. They ...d cowrie shells for ...ney, and traded far ...d wide in beautiful ...e carvings.

Fang Ding (four-legged food vessel)

Wine vessel

WHAT'S COOKING?
Shang people made predictions by engraving questions about the future on cattle bones, then interpreting the cracks that appeared after they had heated up the bones.

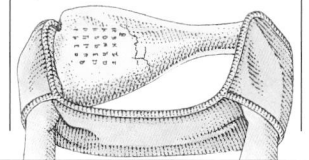

KEY PEOPLE

Name	Dates	Biographical details
Rameses II	r.1279–13 B.C.	Great military pharaoh, fought Hittites at Qadesh
David	d.962 B.C.	Israelite king, unified Israel with Jerusalem as capital
Homer	c.800 B.C.	Blind Greek epic poet, author of *Iliad* and *Odyssey*
Romulus	c.700 B.C.	Legendary founder of Rome (with brother Remus)
Nebuchadnezzar	630–562 B.C.	Chaldean king, captured Jerusalem, rebuilt Babylon
Ashurbanipal	d.627 B.C.	Last great Assyrian king, founded first catalogued library of ancient Middle East at Nineveh
Sappho	c.600 B.C.	Greek lyric poetess from island of Lesbos

600 B.C.

AFRICA **600** Building of temple of the Sun at Meroë, Sudan

500 Iron Age in sub-Saharan Africa. Beginning of Nok culture in northern Nigeria

304 Eg independ under P

ASIA **560** *Tao Te Ching* appears, Taoist philosophical work by Lao-Tze

550 Cyrus II of Persia defeats Medes and founds Persian Empire

539 Persians conquer Neo-Babylonian Empire

521 Height of the Persian Empire under Darius I

500 Caste system established in India

479 Death of Confucius (b.551)

486 Death of Buddha

403 Start of "Warring States" period in China

334–26 Alexander the Great (b.356) Asia Minor, Persia, and parts of India

323 Death of Alexander the Great and division of his em

322 Chandragupta founds Mauryan Empire in India

EUROPE **510** Foundation of Roman Republic

505 Establishment of democracy in Athens

490 Greeks defeat Persians at Battle of Marathon

478 Confederacy of Delos (Athenian League) founded

480 Greeks defeat Persians at Battle of Salamis

450 La Tène (Iron Age) culture in central and western Europe

431–04 Peloponnesian Wars: Sparta defeats Athens

338 Macedonians gain control of Greece at Battle of Chaeronea

AMERICAS **400** Decline of Olmec civilization

OCEANIA **500** Trading contacts established in South Pacific islands

ANCIENT GREECE

In the fifth century B.C., Greek civilization produced arts, philosophy, and political ideas that have had a deep and lasting effect on later societies, especially in the West. Early in the century, Greece united to defeat Persia; later rivalries led to a long internal war that weakened and finally destroyed Greek dominance in the Mediterranean.

ATHENS

Athens was the most important city of ancient Greece. With a long coastline for shipping trade, and with rich silver mines, the city-state of Athens grew wealthy. Its leaders, notably Pericles, built great temples and state buildings on the Acropolis, the city's old fortress. The Parthenon was the largest of all.

The Parthenon: the marble temple of goddess Athena, built by Pericles in 447–432 B.C. It contained a 12m (40ft) gold and ivory statue of Athena.

The Propylaea: grand entrance to the Acropolis

Temple of Athena Nike

Sanctuary of Asclepius: medical and religious centre dedicated to the god of healing

Theatre of Dionysus: festival performances twice a year with prizes for best writer, play, producer, and actor

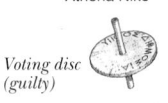

Voting disc (guilty)

Voting disc (not guilty)

BIRTH OF DEMOCRACY

Athenians were the first people to have the chance to vote on how their city or state was run. Male citizens met in the agora (market-place) to discuss politics as well as to do business, but women and slaves were not allowed to vote.

KEY PEOPLE OF ANCIENT GREECE

Name	Dates	Biographical details
Peisistratus	c.580–527	Tyrant of ancient Athens, encouraged trade and arts
Themistocles	c.524–460	Athenian politician and soldier, defeated Xerxes at Salamis, saving Greece from Persian domination
Pericles	c.495–429	Athenian leader, empire builder; developed democracy; made Athens cultural focus of Greece
Thucydides	c.465–403	Athenian historian, recorded Peloponnesian Wars

ANCIENT GREECE

The Greek world consisted of many city-states (independent cities with surrounding territory). In the later fifth century B.C., two city-states, Athens and Sparta, grew more powerful, and began to compete for dominance of the Mediterranean.

Delphi • Athens • Corinth • Sparta

ANCIENT GREECE FACTS

● Greek artists were the first to use an understanding of human anatomy to make their art more realistic. They sculpted in marble, bronze, and clay, and painted beautiful scenes on their pottery and walls.

● Sparta was ruled by a small military aristocracy (the Spartiates). Spartan men began military training a the age of seven, but weaker boys were abandoned at birth.

Spartan runner

● A united Greek force defeated invading Persians on the plains at Marathon in 490 B.C., and at the sea battle of Salamis in 480 B.C. This later victory led to Athenian dominance.

● Sparta defeated Athens in the Peloponnesian Wars (431–404 B.C.), and ruled Greece until 371 B.C.

ALEXANDER

In just eight years Alexander the Great (356–323 B.C.) built the largest empire the world had ever seen. He helped spread Greek, or Hellenistic, culture all over Asia, but his early death, at the age of 33, left his empire leaderless and divided.

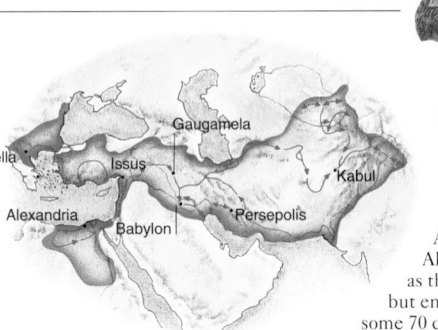

Pella, Issus, Gaugamela, Kabul, Alexandria, Babylon, Persepolis

→ Alexander's route

▨ Alexander's empire

ALEXANDER'S CONQUESTS

Alexander led his forces to victory from Greece as far as the Indus valley. He took with him not only soldiers, but engineers, artists, and philosophers. He founded some 70 cities, notably Alexandria in Egypt.

Alexander at Issus

BATTLE OF ISSUS

Outnumbered six to one, Alexander defeated the Persian Emperor, Darius, at Issus in 333 B.C.

BRIDE BRIBE

After conquering Darius, Alexander encouraged the Hellenistic and Persian cultures to mix. He offered money to the first 10,000 Macedonian soldiers who wished to marry Persian women.

Foundation of library [Alexandria], Egypt

149–6 Rome destroys Carthage in Third Punic War, founding province of Africa

100 Camel introduced into Sahara region

30 Egypt becomes Roman province on death of Mark Antony (b.82) and Cleopatra (b.69)

262 Mauryan Emperor Asoka converts to Buddhism

221 Ch'in Shih huang-ti (c.259–210), the first emperor, unites China

185 Bactrians from present-day Afghanistan conquer northwest India

112 "Silk Road" opens up, giving West some access to China

64 Roman general Pompey (106–28) conquers Syria

240 Beginning of Parthian dynasty in northern Persia

207 Chinese unity disintegrates

202 China reunited under Han dynasty

53 Parthia halts Roman eastward expansion

[R]ome gains control of central Italy

264–41 First Punic War (Rome versus Carthage): Rome wins control of Sicily

218–01 Second Punic War: Roman general Scipio defeats Hannibal

49 Julius Caesar invades Gaul

46 Julius Caesar reforms calendar

45 Julius Caesar becomes sole ruler of Rome after civil war

44 Julius Caesar murdered

31 Battle of Actium gives Octavian (later Emperor Augustus) power over Rome

27 Roman Empire replaces Republic

[...] of North American mound-building cultures. [...] of Early Maya Period, Central America

200 Height of Nazca civilization, Peru, South America

100 Anasazi, Hohokam, and Mogollon peoples begin farming in southwestern North America. Okvik hunters settle in northern Alaska

Patricians   *Soldier and slave*   *Plebeians*

THE RISE OF ROME

[Fr]om a shepherds' village in central Italy, [R]ome grew to be the focus of an empire that [co]ntrolled most of western Europe. Its rise to [po]wer was based on discipline, virtue, and [mi]litary prowess, but it took [ce]nturies of warfare for Romans [to] secure their empire. They [ex]ported Rome's lifestyle and [te]chnology to all their provinces.

201 B.C.
44 B.C.
A.D.14
A.D.117

[R]OME'S EXPANSION AND EMPIRE

[Ro]me secured the Mediterranean only after three long [wa]rs, the Punic Wars, in which it defeated the sea-based [em]pire of Carthage. Julius Caesar later conquered Gaul.

Londinium
Trier
GAUL
Byzantium
Rome
Antioch
Carthage
Alexandria

ROMAN SOCIETY

Roman society was divided into several levels: patricians (aristocrats), plebeians (citizens), subjects (in the provinces), and slaves. Women were expected to be mothers, but rich females had some freedom.

KEY INNOVATIONS

HEATED BATHS

Roman baths were heated by external fires, stoked by slaves. The fire's hot air circulated underneath a raised floor and heated the water above.

AQUEDUCTS

Roman engineers built great aqueducts. Water in this one at Nîmes dropped only 17m (56ft) over 50km (31 miles).

Nîmes aqueduct

THE ROMAN ARMY

Legate (general)

Centurion

Aquilifer (standard bearer)

Trumpeter

Auxiliary

[A]rmy structure and command

[Th]e Roman army was divided into [abo]ut 28 legions of about 5,000 infantry [sol]diers each; a legion contained 10 [coh]orts; a cohort contained 6 centuries [of] 80 men each. Officers called [cen]turions commanded each century, [an]d wore crests on their helmets so [tha]t they could easily be seen in battle.

Foreign legions

When their empire began to expand, Romans had to recruit soldiers, called auxiliaries, from the countries they had conquered. After 25 years auxiliaries could become Roman citizens.

Boulders placed here.

Military technology

The Roman catapult, or *ballista*, could launch boulders or arrows over an enemy's defences. Covered siege towers and battering rams protected soldiers inside.

Protected battering ram

Frame built to withstand high tension.

Twisted cord

Soldiers collect ammunition.

Testudo

Siege tower

Roman tactics

Soldiers advancing under attack would form a *testudo* (tortoise), a formation of upheld shields that protected them from arrows, missiles, or burning oil.

[MA]URYAN EMPIRE

[Ma]uryan emperor Asoka conquered [and] unified India. In 262 B.C. he [beca]me a Buddhist and set up [thou]sands of stupas (monuments) to Buddha around the empire. Each is said to contain a part of Buddha's body.

Buddhist stupa at Sanchi, India, c.150 B.C.

CH'IN DYNASTY OF CHINA

In 221 B.C. China was unified under its first emperor, Ch'in Shih huang-ti (c.259–210 B.C.). He centralized the government, standardized money, weights and measures, and built grand monuments in his own honour.

The Great Wall: a 3,000km- (1,900mile-) long defence against northern Huns

Terracotta army

Ch'in Shih huang-ti built himself a great underground tomb.

Tomb had 7,000 statues of fully armed warriors, some with horses.

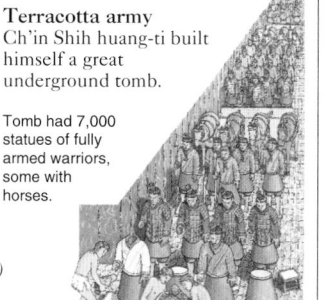

ADENA AND HOPEWELL

From 700 B.C. to A.D. 400 the Adena, and later the Hopewell, farming societies flourished in North America. They built huge, mysterious, earth mounds, and filled their graves with beautifully carved objects.

Serpent mound, Ohio: 1,310ft (400m) uncoiled

A.D. 1

AFRICA	**50** Kingdom of Axum (Ethiopia) begins to expand	**150** Berbers and Mandingos start to dominate Sudan area	**250** Axum controls trade in Red Sea

ASIA **9** Han dynasty overthrown in China   **70** Romans seize Jerusalem and destroy Jewish temple
25 Han dynasty restored   **105** Paper first used in China
30 Jesus Christ crucified in Jerusalem   **132** Jewish revolt against Rome, leading to dispersal of Jews
46–57 St. Paul's missionary journeys
60 Beginning of Kushan Empire in India

200 Completion of Mishnah (Jewish law). Composition of Ramayana, Mahabharata (Indian epics), and Bhagavad Gita (Hindu scripture)
220 Han dynasty ends; China divided into three
224 Sassanian dynasty founded in Persia   **245** China and Funan (Southeast Asian state)

EUROPE **43** Romans invade Great Britain   **79** Eruption of Vesuvius, southern Italy   **117** Roman Empire reaches its maximum extent

238 Goths begin to encroach on Roman Empire   **293** Diocl reorg Rom

AMERICAS **1** Beginning of Moche civilization in northern Peru

OCEANIA **1–100** Hindu-Buddhists from Southeast Asia colonize Sumatra and Java

---

IMPERIAL ROME

The Roman Republic was shaken by a series of civil wars that began in 49 B.C. In 27 B.C., the general and adopted son of Julius Caesar, Octavian, defeated his rival Mark Antony and, as Augustus, became the first emperor. His reforms brought peace and prosperity to the Empire and created a power structure that lasted until the last emperor, Romulus Augustulus, was deposed in A.D. 476.

AUGUSTUS

Though he preserved many of the Republic's old institutions, Augustus (previously Octavian) had overall power; he even encouraged a cult of Augustus, in which he was worshipped as a god. He passed his title and powers on to his son Tiberius in A.D. 14.

Emperor Augustus

IMPERIAL TRIUMPH

Emperors used military triumphs to reinforce their power. They paraded defeated enemies through Rome to the cheers of onlookers.

ROMAN CHARIOT RACES

Rome's *Circus Maximus* was a great stadium in which chariot races were held. Races were often dangerous and the teams (reds, blues, greens, whites) inspired fans throughout the empire.

KEY PEOPLE OF ANCIENT ROME

Name	Dates	Biographical details
Julius Caesar	100–44 B.C.	Conquered Gaul, won civil war, dictator of Rome (46–44), murdered 44 B.C.
Augustus	63 B.C.–A.D.19	Julius Caesar's adopted son, defeated Mark Antony to become first emperor
Trajan	A.D. 53–117	Popular emperor, extended Empire eastward, began vast building programm
Hadrian	A.D. 76–138	Emperor, secured boundaries of Empire, built Hadrian's Wall as defence
Diocletian	A.D. 245–316	Emperor, restored order after near anarchy. Last persecutor of Christians

DECLINE OF THE ROMAN EMPIRE
Reliance on army
The emperor Septimius Severus ended a civil war in A.D. 193, but his reliance on the army to restore order showed that no future emperor could enjoy total power: he would need the support of the army.

Collaboration with barbarians
In the third century A.D., hostile barbarians from northern Europe stepped up pressure on the Empire's borders. Rome increasingly relied on local forces in their provinces and many locals rose to important government positions. Later, these leaders took more power into their own hands.

Shifting centre
In the fourth and fifth centuries A.D., the Empire gradually fragmented; there were capitals at different times at Ravenna, Milan, Trier, Sirmium, and Constantinople.

Visigoth

DIVISION OF EMPIRE
In A.D. 293, Emperor Diocletian changed the structure of the empire. He divided it into two parts (east and west), each with an emperor and a deputy. He ruled the east, and gave the west to Maximian. He called the new system a tetrarchy, and it helped him deal with the growing problem of civil unrest.

The four tetrarchs

PAVING THE WAY
By the early 4th century A.D., Romans had built a road network of 85,000km (52,800 miles). It took six days to go from Londinium (London) to Rome. In the 1800s the journey took just as long.

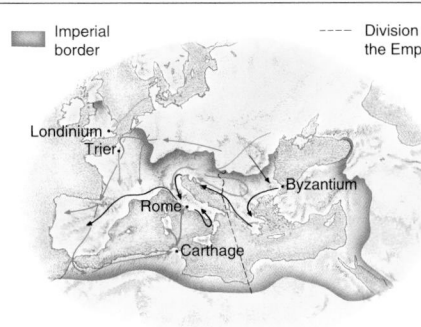

Imperial border	- - - - Division the Emp

Londinium · Trier · · Byzantium · Rome · · Carthage

→ Visigoths   → Vandals   → Burgundia
→ Ostrogoths   → Franks   → Angles

ROME UNDER SIEGE
Rome devoted much of its resources to defending i long borders. From the 4th century A.D., economic problems forced a weakening in defence. Visigoths under Alaric captured and sacked Rome in A.D. 41 and Attila the Hun invaded Gaul in A.D. 451.

325 Axum destroys
kingdom of Meroë

400 Christianity adopted in Axum
439 Vandals establish kingdom in northern Africa

533 Emperor Justinian wins
back northern Africa for Rome

vasion of Huns
splits up China

480 End of
Gupta Empire

520 Rise of mathematics in India;
decimal number system invented

320 Chandragupta I founds
Gupta Empire in northern India

531 Height of Sassanian Empire

550 Buddhism introduced into Japan

589 China reunified
under Sui dynasty

13 Toleration of Christians in Roman
mpire as result of Edict of Milan

410 Visigoths invade Italy and Spain, sack Rome
450 Angles, Jutes, and Saxons settle in Great Britain

552 Emperor Justinian restores
Italy to Roman control

330 Emperor Constantine moves capital
of Roman Empire to Constantinople

476 Last western
Roman emperor,
Romulus Augustulus,
overthrown

486 Clovis establishes Frankish kingdom
in present-day northern France, Belgium,
and parts of western Germany

568 Lombards take
over northern Italy

370 Huns appear in Europe

493 Ostrogoths take over in Italy

590 Pope Gregory the Great
(c.540–604) expands papal power

civilized states in Mexico
ban, Teotihuacán)

600 Height of Mayan
civilization, central America

n Polynesia settled

THE COMING OF CHRISTIANITY

Christianity began as a minor sect in a remote corner of the Roman Empire. A series of events brought it wider fame, until Emperor Constantine was himself converted. In A.D. 391, Emperor Theodosius I made it Rome's official religion and banned all other religions.

Mainly Christian
by A.D. 600

Christian centre

Cantauri
Turones
Augusta Treverorum
Arelate
Toletum
Roma
Byzantium
Artashat
Ephesus
Edessa
Antioch
Damascus
Jerusalem
Carthage
Alexandria

JESUS OF NAZARETH

n about A.D. 30, the Jewish eacher Jesus of Nazareth, who was seen by the Roman nd Jewish authorities as a evolutionary, was crucified. His apostles, or followers, pread his message.

SPREAD OF CHRISTIANITY

After Jesus' death, his apostles took his message abroad. Christianity spread rapidly within the Roman Empire. The centres of Antioch and Edessa carried it eastward into Persia. Later it reached China and India.

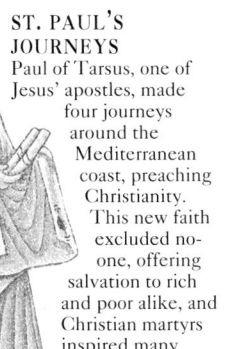

ST. PAUL'S JOURNEYS

Paul of Tarsus, one of Jesus' apostles, made four journeys around the Mediterranean coast, preaching Christianity. This new faith excluded no-one, offering salvation to rich and poor alike, and Christian martyrs inspired many people to convert.

St. Paul, in a mosaic from St. Peter's, Rome

EARLY CHRISTIANITY FACTS

Christian fish symbol

Captive lion

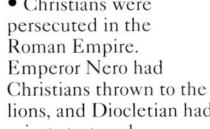

Fragment of Gospel text

- The fish was an early Christian symbol. In Greek, the letters of the word for fish stand for, "Jesus Christ, God's Son, Saviour."

- Christians were persecuted in the Roman Empire. Emperor Nero had Christians thrown to the lions, and Diocletian had priests tortured.

- Key books of the New Testament – the gospels of disciples Matthew, Mark, and Luke – were written in A.D. 65–70.

CONSTANTINE

In A.D. 313 Emperor Constantine became a Christian and gave Christians freedom to worship with the Edict of Milan. The Church could then flourish.

SASSANIAN EMPIRE

The Sassanian Empire lasted from A.D. 224 to 641 and was centred around the city of Ctesiphon (Baghdad). At its height under King Khosrow (A.D. 531–79), it stretched from the River Indus to the Euphrates. Sassanians were great architects and followed the Zoroastrian religion (see p.143).

Ramparts form perfect circle 2km (1.2 miles) in diameter

Circular city at Firuzabad

MAYAN CIVILIZATION

The Mayan civilization of Central America flourished between A.D. 300 and 900. Mayans built great pyramidal temples; they also developed writing and advanced mathematics. Mayan astronomers had calculated the exact length of the solar year and lunar month and could predict eclipses. They played a form of basketball that was half religious ceremony, half sport. Anyone who scored had the right to demand the property of any spectator they managed to catch.

Players could only use hips, elbows, and ankles to control the ball.

ROME AND JUDAISM

rom A.D. 66 to 70, ws in Palestine, led by portant priests and arisees, revolted inst Roman rule. mperor Vespasian, h his son Titus, ntally suppressed the olt. A second Jewish ellion of A.D. 132 to 5 was put down by mperor Hadrian.

Capture of Jerusalem

In A.D. 70, Titus captured Jerusalem, plundering and destroying its great Jewish temple. The resulting diaspora (dispersal) of Jews carried Judaism as far as Spain and Africa.

Sacking of the temple of Jerusalem

Masada

In A.D. 73 the last Jewish stronghold, at Masada on the shores of the Dead Sea, fell to the Romans. When the Romans broke into the fortress, they found that all 960 Jews inside had killed themselves rather than be captured.

Remains of siege ramp

Fortress at Masada

AXUM

In the 4th century A.D., Axum in northeastern Africa overthrew the rule of the city of Meroë and became an important power. Its exports of African ivory and sea trade brought great wealth. Axumites built great granite towers, or stelas, as monuments to their civilization. The tallest surviving stela stands at 23m (75.5ft) high – as high as 16 people standing on each other's shoulders.

Great Stela at Axum

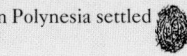

600

AFRICA

c.700 Kingdom of Ghana prospers on trans-Saharan trade. Bantu Africans cross the River Limpopo, taking iron-working technology to the south

ASIA

618 China reunified by T'ang dynasty

637 Muslims conquer Jerusalem

647 Central Asian Hun tribes invade India, causing decline of Gupta Empire

786 Harun-al-Rashid becomes caliph of Baghdad

802 Khmers fou in Cambodia and

622 Year One of Islamic calendar, the year of Muhammad's flight from Mecca to Medina

642 Islam replaces Zoroastrianism as major religion in Persia

674 Islam reaches modern Pakistan

751 Muslims defeat Mongols at Samarkand

794 Kyoto, ancient capital of Japan, is established

814 Arabs Indian num

EUROPE

711 Moors invade Spain

732 Muslims defeated at Tours by Frankish leader Charles Martel (c.688–741), halting Islam's advance in Europe

800 Charlemagne, the Franks, is crow first Holy Roman

AMERICAS

OCEANIA

RISE AND SPREAD OF ISLAM

In 610, an Arab merchant called Muhammad (c.570–632) founded a new religion: Islam. His teachings were an inspiration to the Arab peoples, and by 750, Muslims (the followers of Islam) had gained control of a massive area stretching from Spain to Afghanistan. The Muslim advance spread trade, culture, and science, as well as Islam.

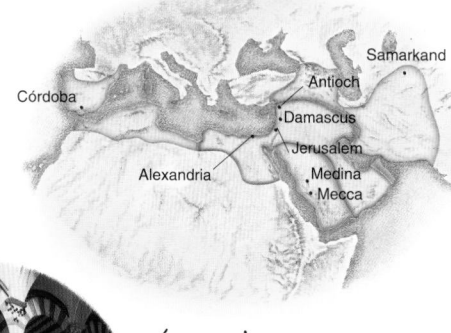

	622–32
	632–44
	644–750
	750–850

EXPANSION OF ISLAM
Muhammad died in 632, but his teachings spread rapidly after his death. By 850, Muslims had made Islam the most important civilization after China.

Great Mosque at Córdoba

CÓRDOBA'S GREAT MOSQUE
Arab colonists built the Great Mosque at Córdoba, southern Spain, between 784 and 990. One of the largest and most complex Islamic mosques, it has 850 marble columns supporting arches on two levels.

EL CID
Rodrigo Diaz de Vivar (c.1043–99) was the real name of "El Cid", a Spanish knight and outlaw who fought against Muslim colonists. His greatest achievement was the capture of the Spanish city of Valencia in 1094, which made him a national hero.

El Cid

Muslim at prayer

Prayer rug

MUHAMMAD'S JOURNEY
Muhammad's religious ideas were initially unpopular. In 622, established merchants forced him to flee Mecca for Medina, but in 630, Muhammad returned to the city in triumph. Since then, Muslims at prayer have always faced Mecca.

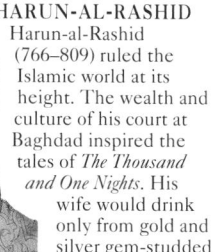

HARUN-AL-RASHID
Harun-al-Rashid (766–809) ruled the Islamic world at its height. The wealth and culture of his court at Baghdad inspired the tales of *The Thousand and One Nights*. His wife would drink only from gold and silver gem-studded vessels.

Harun-al-Rashid

ARAB TECHNOLOGY

PAPER
Following the capture of Chinese papermakers in 751, Arabs spread their craft throughout the Islamic world.

WINDMILL
Arab colonists brought windmill technology to Spain from Persia in the 10th century.

OPTICS
Arabic scholar Alhazen (c.965–1039) wrote the first accurate account of vision. He gave us the term "lens".

CHARLEMAGNE
King Charlemagne of the Franks (742–814) conquered most of the Christian lands of western Europe and founded the Holy Roman Empire in 800. He encouraged learning with a new, clear, script called Carolingian miniscule.

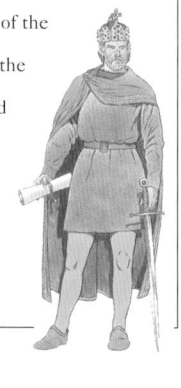

KEY PEOPLE

Name	Dates	Biographical details
Muhammad	c.570–632	Arab merchant and religious teacher, founder of Islam
Rabiah-al-Adawiyah	712–801	Female Arab mystic and religious teacher
Charlemagne	742–814	King of the Franks (people of northwestern Europe), conquered Western Europe, spread Christianity
Harun-al-Rashid	766–809	Caliph of Baghdad, ruled Islamic world at its height
Leif Eriksson	c.1000	Viking explorer, reached North American coast in 1000
William of Normandy	c.1028–87	Duke of Normandy, conquered England in 1066
El Cid	c.1043–99	Spanish knight and outlaw, fought Muslims in Spain

POPE SYLVESTER
Pope Sylvester II (940–1003) introduced Arabic numerals (0–9) and the astrolabe (an aid to navigation) to Europe from Muslim Spain.

Astrolabe

900			1100

900 Hausa kingdom of Daura founded in northern Nigeria

920 Ghana's Golden Age begins

980 Arab traders settle on East African coast

1054 Ghana conquered by Muslim Almoravid dynasty

---

888 Chola dynasty of Tamil kings replaces the Pallavas in southern India and Sri Lanka

935–41 Civil war in Japan

960 Sung Dynasty takes over China

---

861 The Vikings discover Iceland

Kenneth MacAlpine (d. 858) ...ts the Picts and unites Scotland

911 The Viking Rollo is granted Normandy

930 Cordoba becomes seat of Arab learning in Spain

966 Poles converted to Christianity

982 Erik the Red settles in Greenland

997 Stephen I (977–1038) becomes first King of Hungary

1000 Leif Eriksson, son of Erik the Red, sails down North American coast. He names it "Vinland"

1066 William of Normandy invades England

1096 First Crusade begins

---

900 Mixtec civilization begins in Mexico

980 Toltecs set up capital at Tula (Mexico)

1000 Chimu civilization of Peru founded

---

950 Polynesian navigator Kupe discovers New Zealand, and first Maori settlers arrive

---

TRADERS AND RAIDERS

Late in the eighth century people from present-day Denmark, Norway, and Sweden, called Vikings, began to leave their overcrowded homelands in search of treasure to plunder or new land to settle. Their golden age of trade, exploration, and colonization lasted until 1100.

Viking homeland
Settlement
--- Sea route
— River route

Novgorod
York
Dublin
Birka
L'Anse aux Meadows
Byzantium (Istanbul)
Baghdad

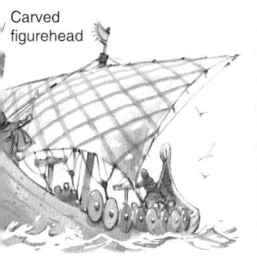

Carved figurehead

VIKING LONGSHIPS
The key to Viking success was their skill in building and sailing ships. Their longships were the fastest ships of the time; they had both sail and oar, and their flat bottoms enabled them to navigate both seas and inland rivers.

ROUTES OF VIKING TRAVEL
Vikings were great traders. They dealt in many goods, exchanging slaves, fur, wood, honey, walrus tusks, whale oil, feathers, and down for silver, silk, spices, and wine.

Viking trading post

Viking traders carried their goods in knorrs – small, stable ships.

VIKING TRADING POSTS
Many great cities such as York, England, and Dublin, Ireland, started as places where Vikings met with locals to exchange goods.

Novgorod

VIKING FACTS
• Viking graffiti can still be seen in a gallery of Istanbul's great mosque, Hagia Sophia.

• Vikings reached the Americas in 1000, 500 years before Christopher Columbus.

• After a battle, Viking women would feed those with belly wounds a strong-smelling soup of onions and herbs. If, later, they smelled this mix at the wound, they knew that the intestine had been pierced and that the victim would soon die.

VIKING SUPERMEN
The Emperor of Byzantium was so impressed by the courage, strength, and size of the Viking warriors he had seen that he recruited them for his personal bodyguard. It was called the Varangian guard.

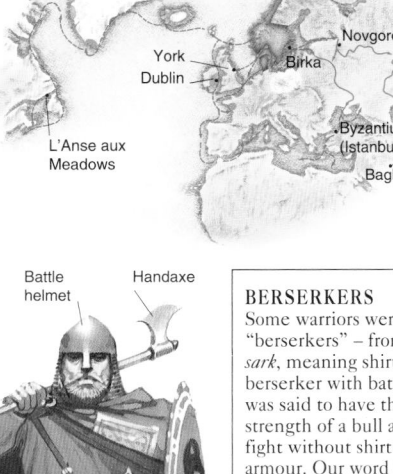

Battle helmet
Handaxe

Broadsword

Varangian guard

BERSERKERS
Some warriors were called "berserkers" – from *bare sark*, meaning shirtless. A berserker with battle-fever was said to have the strength of a bull and would fight without shirt or armour. Our word "berserk" comes from the name for these Viking madmen.

ROLLO OF NORMANDY
In 911, Rollo, a Norseman chief, was granted land in northern France by the King of France, in return for his promise to defend it. William the Conqueror was Rollo's descendant.

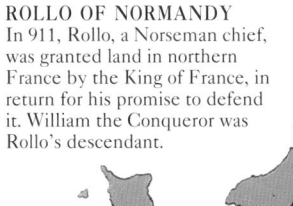

Rollo of Normandy   NORMANDY

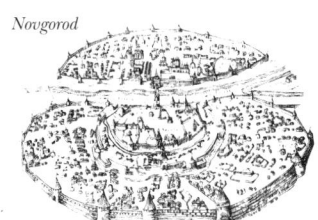

BIRTH OF RUSSIA
According to the 12th-century Russian Chronicle, Novgorod Slavs invited Vikings to rule over them. Vikings were also called "Rus", so when they took over the area it was called the Land of Rus, and later, Russia.

KING WENCESLAS
Wenceslas (907–29) was the first ruler of Bohemia, central Europe. He became a Christian and helped spread Christianity in Bohemia. Murdered outside his church by his own brother, Wenceslas was later made the patron saint of Hungary, Poland, and Bohemia.

KEY INVENTIONS

GUNPOWDER
In 1044, Chinese chemist Wu Ching Tsao Yao published the first known recipe for gunpowder. The explosive mix was first used for fireworks.

FIRST PRINTED BOOKS
The Diamond Sutra, dated 868, is the world's oldest printed book. It is a Buddhist scripture printed from blocks of wood on to sheets of paper and joined into a scroll.

FIRST NOVEL
In 1007, a Japanese noblewoman called Murasaki Shikibu wrote the first novel. Over 600,000 words long, *The Tale of Genji* tells of a prince's quest for true love and wisdom.

1100

AFRICA	**c.1100** First Iron Age settlement in Zimbabwe 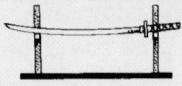	**1169** Saladin (1137– becomes ruler of E
ASIA	**1104** Crusaders capture Acre	**1156** Civil war between rival clans in Japan leads to domination by samurai warlords
EUROPE	**1115** French philosopher Peter Abelard (1079–1142) begins teaching in Paris. St. Bernard (1090–1153) founds important monastery at Clairvaux **1119** Bologna University, one of Europe's oldest, founded in Italy	**1143** Alfonso Henriques (c.1109–85) becomes first King of Portugal	**1170** Murder c Thomas Becke (1118–70), Arch of Canterbury,
AMERICAS		**1151** Fall of the Toltec Empire in Mexico
OCEANIA	**1100s** Giant statues first erected on Easter Island, South Pacific	

MONGOL EXPANSION

In the late 1100s, Temujin, a young chieftain of central Asia, united a group of tribes to form a powerful Mongol army. In 1211, the Mongols invaded China, then swept through Asia. Temujin was later proclaimed as Genghis Khan, which means "Universal Ruler".

GENGHIS KHAN

Genghis Khan was born just as his father had killed a rival chief named Temujin. As a baby he was given the name Temujin because it was believed that the courage of a defeated enemy magically entered the newborn.

Genghis Khan

- - - - - Genghis' campaigns
───── Successors' campaigns

Area under direct Mongol control

Area under loose Mongol control

Karakorum · Peking
Novgorod
Bolgar
Legnica
New Sarai · Kashgar
Gran
Tiflis
Baghdad
Jerusalem
Canton

ROUTES OF MONGOL CONQUEST

At its height, the greatest land empire in the history of the world spanned almost all of Asia, from Korea in the east to Poland in the west, and from the Arctic south to Persia.

SORROW AND SLAUGHTER

In 1227, Genghis Khan grew ill and died while on campaign in China. When his men brought his body back to Mongolia for burial, they killed every living creature that crossed the path of the homebound procession. At his funeral forty jewelled slave girls and forty horses were slaughtered in his honour.

POWDERED MILK

Mongols would mix sun-dried mare's milk with water in the morning, and place it in their saddlebags. By the evening the shaken mix had formed an edible porridge.

Strengthened leather armour

Mongol cavalrymen

MONGOL CAVALRY

Mongol cavalrymen had immense advantages over their enemies. They could ride up to 120km (75 miles) a day with just one stop for food and water, and hit targets at full gallop.

MONGOL FACTS

- Mongol archers had whistling arrows for signalling, armour-piercing arrows, and even arrows tipped with grenades.

- From the age of three, Mongol children were regularly strapped onto their ponies to help them learn to ride.

Whistling arrowheads

MONGOL HOME LIFE

Mongols were nomads and lived in moveable tents, or yurts, made of animal skins or textiles stretched over a wooden frame. The women kept herds of livestock and tribes competed with each other for the best grazing lands.

- One of Genghis Khan's tactics was t set fire to live animals, such as elephants and horses, and send them rushing at the enemy's battle lines.

- Genghis lived in simple Mongol style even at the height of his power.

- Mongols were the first to use gunpowder as a military weapon.

A SPORTING CONTEST TO THE DEATH

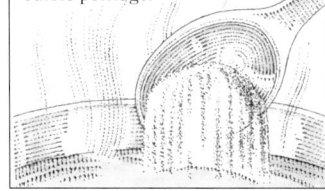

In 1180, one of the greatest medieval tournaments was staged at Lagny-sur-Marne, France. More than 3,000 armed and mounted knights jousted for sport and honour, "with no holds barred".

KEY PEOPLE

Name	Dates	Biographical details
Genghis Khan	1162–1227	Mongolian warrior, conqueror, and Emperor of China, Iran, Iraq, and Central Asia
Saladin	1137–93	Sultan of Egypt and Muslim hero of Third Crusad famed for his chivalry and courage
Richard I	1157–99	Popular English king and English hero of Third Crusade, also called "Richard The Lionheart"
St. Francis of Assisi	1181–1226	Founder of Franciscan order and leader of Church reform
Sun Diata	d.1255	Founder of Mali Empire, West Africa, established unity and brought prosperity to empire

1244 Egyptians retake Jerusalem

1190 Lalibela becomes Emperor of Ethiopia

1235 Sun Diata (d.1255) founds empire of Mali, West Africa

7 Saladin captures alem from Crusaders

1191 Zen Buddhism first introduced to Japan

1206 Genghis Khan (1162–1227) founds Mongol Empire. Islam takes root in new Kingdom of Delhi, India, founded by Aibak, a former slave

1229 Sixth Crusaders recapture Jerusalem

1237 Mongol army begins to conquer Russia

1232 Explosive rockets used in war between Chinese and conquering Mongols

ork begins on on Bridge, ridge, and aning Tower"

1204 Fourth Crusaders sack and loot Constantinople. King John of England (1167–1216) loses French lands

1209 St. Francis (1181–1226) founds Franciscan order

1215 St. Dominic (1170–1221) founds Dominican Order. King John of England seals Magna Carta

1240s German towns begin regional trades, later forming powerful and protective trading alliance, the Hanseatic League

c.1200 Cuzco, Peru, becomes an Inca centre. First maize farmers settle along banks of Mississippi

N BUDDHISM

1191, Zen Buddhism was introduced Japan by a monk named Eisai 41–1215). Zen Buddhism stressed rsonal instruction by a master (rather an the study of scriptures) as the path self-knowledge.

MAGNA CARTA

In 1215, King John of England was forced to seal the Magna Carta, or Great Charter. It gave political rights to his most powerful subjects and made the king subject to law.

Royal seal

THIRTEENTH-CENTURY BUILDINGS

Chartres Cathedral, the finest example of French Gothic architecture, took 31 years to build in the mid-13th century. At the same time, the Mayans of Central America began building the massive temples of their new capital at Mayapan, in modern-day Mexico.

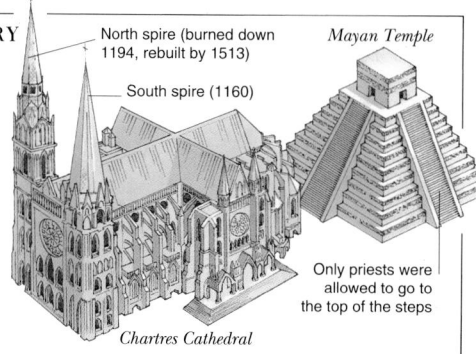

North spire (burned down 1194, rebuilt by 1513)

South spire (1160)

Mayan Temple

Only priests were allowed to go to the top of the steps

Chartres Cathedral

HE CRUSADES

y 1095 the Saracens (Muslims) had ained control of the holy lands in the Middle East. European Christians, urged n by Pope Urban II, organized armed xpeditions, or crusades, to recapture the nds. The First Crusade was a riumph. Others were less successful, nd the last ended in 1291.

— 1st Crusade
---- 2nd Crusade
→ 3rd Crusade

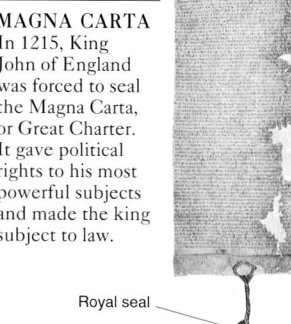

Paris, Bruges, Vienna, Genoa, Toulouse, Marseilles, Rome, Constantinople, Damascus, Acre, Jerusalem

CRUSADE ROUTES

The first two crusader armies assembled at meeting points in Europe, and fought their way overland across Asia Minor. Later, European control of the Mediterranean allowed crusaders to take a sea route to the Holy Land.

Conical helmet

Nasal (nose-guard)

Shield

CHILDREN'S CRUSADE

In 1212, thousands of unarmed children believing in the power of innocence set off from Europe for the Holy Land. Most died on the way, or were sold as slaves in Africa.

Helmet
Surcoat
Haubert (chain-mail shirt)

CRUSADER

Crusaders took their name from the cross (Latin *crux*) that was sewn on to their clothing. Crusader knights wore suits of armour and vowed to follow strict codes of chivalry.

Chausses (chain-mail leggings)

Typical Crusader of the order of Knights Templar

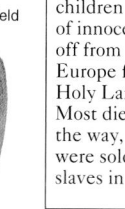

Saracen warrior

Scimitar

SARACEN WARRIOR

The term Saracen was used to describe any Arab, Turk, or other follower of Islam. They used a shield of Persian design and a long, curved sword called a scimitar.

OME OF THE ROCK

he magnificent Dome of the Rock osque in Jerusalem was built by an rab caliph between 685 and 691 on a wish temple site. When the crusaders ntrolled Jerusalem, however, they rned it into a Christian church.

Shield of the order of Knights Hospitaller

Shield of the order of Teutonic Knights

KRAK DES CHEVALIERS

Begun in 1142, and now in modern-day Syria, this is the most impressive crusader fortress. Its storerooms could provide hundreds of people with food for five years.

MAJOR CRUSADES

Crusade	Dates	Result
First Crusade	1096–99	Crusaders take Antioch, then Jerusalem in July 1099
Second Crusade	1147–49	Incompetence leads to Crusader defeat in Anatolia
Third Crusade	1189–92	Crusaders win coast from Tyre to Jaffa but Jerusalem remains uncaptured
Fourth Crusade	1202–04	Crusaders loot Constantinople
Children's Crusade	1212	Thousands of innocent children march to death and slavery in North Africa
5th–8th	1218–91	Partial and short–lived Crusader victories

1250

AFRICA	**1250** Mamelukes, rebel slave-soldiers, become rulers of Egypt		**1300** Foundation of Benin kingdom in Nigeria	**1324** Mansa Musa (d.1332), emperor of Mali, makes pilgrimage to Mecca	**1348** Plag devastates

ASIA	**1250** A Japanese monk, Nicherin (1222–82), proclaims *Lotus Sutra* the supreme Buddhist scripture	**1260** Mamelukes halt Mongol advance at Battle of Ain Jalut in Palestine	**1281** The *Kamikaze* (Divine Wind) drives Mongol invaders from Japan	**1291** Saracens capture Acre, ending the Crusades

c.1294 Persians convert to Islam | **1340** Hindu empire of Vijayanagar in India becomes centre of resistance to Islam  |

EUROPE	**1273** Rudolf Habsburg (1218–91) becomes ruler of Germany, founding the powerful Habsburg dynasty	**1309** Pope moves to Avignon, leading to great rift in Western Church (1378)	**1346** Battle of Cré Hundred Years W England and Fran

1347 Plague (Death) reaches |

AMERICAS	**c.1250** Mayans restore empire and build new capital at Mayapan. Incas expand their capital at Chan-chan in northern Peru	**c.1300** Incas begin major expansion through Andes	**1325** Aztecs found their capital at Tenochtitlán (now Mexico City)

OCEANIA	**c.1250** Religious assembly platforms built throughout Polynesian Islands

MARCO POLO'S EPIC JOURNEY

In 1271, brothers Niccolo and Maffeo Polo, merchants of Venice, Italy, took Niccolo's 16-year-old son Marco on their second trading journey to the East. Marco had many amazing experiences in the depths of China, and when he returned to Europe 24 years later, he was able to give the first detailed account of daily life in the East.

POLO'S FOOTSTEPS

On their second journey the Polos travelled the ancient Silk Route of central Asia, which, before the Mongol Empire, could only be used by Arab traders. They took three-and-a-half years to reach the palace of the Mongol emperor, including a year's rest for Marco to recover from illness

Venice
Constantinople
Shangtu · Peking
Kashgar · Nanking
Cheng-tu · Foochow
HIMALAYAS · Yunnan
Acre
Pagan
Jerusalem
Polo's journey (1271–95)

VENICE

In the 13th century, Venice was the busiest port in the world. Venetian traders supplied Europe's markets with the precious products of the East: silk, spices, and porcelain.

Polos leave Venice

PASTA AND ICE-CREAM

The Chinese invented two of modern Italy's most famous dishes: pasta and ice-cream. Italian merchants returning from the East brought back the recipes.

The court of Kublai Khan

KUBLAI KHAN

Mongol Emperor Kublai Khan, was eager to learn about European society and he welcomed the Polos at his palace in Shangtu, China.

HUMAN KITE-RIDERS

Marco Polo told terrifying tales of wickerwork kites. These hoisted live prisoners into the sky, both to test the wind and to bring good luck before ships sailed. Few of the prisoners survived.

POLO TELLS HIS STORY

In 1298, Marco Polo was locked up in Genoa, Italy. There he dictated the story of his journey to a fellow prisoner called Rustichello. The tale amazed Europeans and was translated into several languages.

POLO'S TRUE STORIES

• Polo described Eastern springs that gushed oil. Europeans had doubts, but Polo had not lied: he had seen the Baku oilfields in modern-day Azerbaijan.

• Polo spoke of rocks that could be ground up and spun into a fireproof cloth: they were asbestos rocks, well known in China, but unheard-of in 13th-century Europe.

• The Chinese were the first people to use paper money as currency. Venetian merchants, who still used gold and silver coins as currency, could not believe this.

Early Chinese paper mone

KAMIKAZE – DIVINE WIND OF JAPAN

In 1281, the Mongols attacked Japan by sea, hoping to enlarge their vast empire. A timely typhoon destroyed their fleet and put to flight those Mongols already on land. The Japanese named this typhoon the "Divine Wind" or *Kamikaze*.

The Mongol fleet breaks up on Japan's coast

KEY INNOVATIONS

SPECTACLES
By the early 14th century, reading glasses with curved lenses were being made in a Venice factory.

ACCOUNTANCY
From the 1340s, European merchants began using double-entry book-keeping to record their business.

JOAN OF ARC

In 1431, Joan of Arc (1412–31) was tried by her English enemies and burned as a witch. Inspired by divine visions, the young French shepherdess had led the armies of King Charles VII to a great victory that proved to be the turning point of the Hundred Years War. Since that time she has been honoured as a saint.

Moroccan scholar
...ttuta (1304–68)
...his great journey
...Sahara to Mali

c.1400 Kingdom of Zimbabwe
thrives on gold trade

1432 Portuguese explorers
reach the Azores

...pahit Empire
...Java

1368 Tai Tsu (1328–98),
founder of Ming dynasty,
drives Mongols from China

1398 Mongol leader Tamerlane
(1336–1405) sacks Delhi

1404–33 Chinese navigator
Cheng Ho (1371–1435)
explores India and East Africa

1405 Death of Tamerlane
and fall of Mongol Empire

1411 Ahmad Shah founds
Ahmadabad, important
commercial city in India

1448 Major reforms
in Thailand under
King Traillok
(1431–88)

1358 The *Jacquerie*:
French peasants
revolt against raised
taxes. Rebel peasants
defeated and killed

1380 Russians halt Tatar
Mongols at Battle of Kulikovo

1381 Peasants' Revolt in England
led by Wat Tyler and John Ball

1389 Ottoman Turks crush Serbs
and neighbours at Battle of Kosovo

1429 Siege of Orléans
lifted by French soldier-
saint Joan of Arc's forces

...hapitzin becomes Aztec ruler,
...Aztec power

1400 Viracocha (d.1438): first Inca overlord to
establish permanent rule over conquered tribes

1438 Inca overlord Pachacuti (d.1471)
greatly enlarges Inca Empire

...is create rock
...Zealand

...NSA MUSA

...e African empire of Mansa Musa (d.1332)
...famed for its size and wealth. Stopping in
...ypt during a pilgrimage to Mecca, Mansa Musa,
...80 camels laden with gold, spent so much that
...es rose dramatically all over Egypt. On his return
...had a great mosque
...lt at
...mbuktu.

*Mansa
Musa*

Gold
nugget

*...at Mosque
...imbuktu*

KEY PEOPLE

Name	Date	Biographical details
Kublai Khan	1215–94	Mongol Emperor of China, patronized the arts
Marco Polo	c.1254–1324	Venetian merchant-explorer, reached court of Kublai Khan and served as his envoy
Ibn Battuta	1304–68	Moroccan explorer of Africa, India, Russia, China
Mansa Musa	d.1332	Wealthy Emperor of Mali, conquered Songhai empire
Tamerlane	1336–1405	Mongol conqueror of modern-day Iraq and Iran
Joan of Arc	1412–31	French soldier-saint, heroine of Hundred Years War
Pachacuti	d.1471	Inca overlord, started great expansion of Empire

...HE BLACK DEATH

...n 1347, a horrific disease hit Europe: the
...lack Death. A combination of bubonic
...nd pneumonic plague, it caused one of the
...orst disasters in human
...istory, wiping out a quarter
...f the European population
...n just four
...ears.

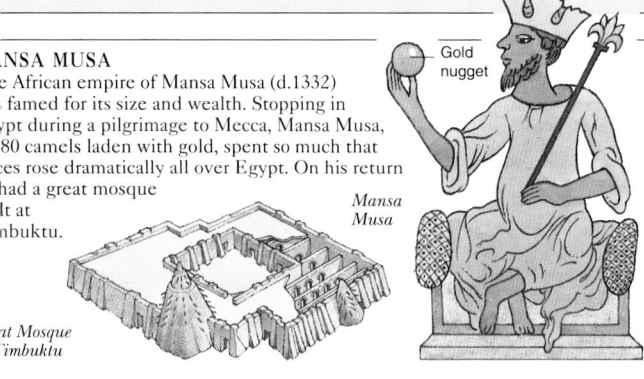

Warsaw
FLANDERS
London
Paris
Marseilles

c.1353
c.1351
1350
1349
POLAND
Prague
Milan
Genoa

*Black Death
Timetable*

Autumn 1348

Summer 1348

Extent by 1347

THE JOURNEY OF DEATH
Genoese traders brought the Black Death to Sicily in
1347. It took hold of the ports of Pisa, Genoa, and
Marseilles, then swept into France and Spain. A few
areas escaped: Milan, Flanders, and parts of Poland.

...OW THE PLAGUE SPREAD
...leas on animals, such as rats, carried and transmitted
...e Black Death. Humans caught the disease either
...om fleabites or from other infected people. Even
...hen all ships were quarantined for 40 days, rats
...ving on board could simply swim ashore.

BLACK DEATH FACTS
• The term "bubonic plague" comes from the
buboes, or dark swellings, that appear in the
armpits and groin of an infected person.

• At the height of the Black Death, the Rhône
river in France was consecrated
as a graveyard; many
hundreds of victims
were thrown into it.

• Milan, Italy,
survived the first
plague because the
Bishop ordered the
first three houses that it
struck to be walled up. The
dead, sick, and healthy were all trapped inside.

Condemned homes

• In 1348 the Black Death killed the great
Italian historian Giovanni Villani (b.1275). His
writings end in mid-sentence, with, "And this
plague lasted until....."

...HOT UNDER THE COLLAR
On doctors' orders, Pope
Clement VI spent the hot
summer of 1348
sitting between two
fires that were
kept permanently
stoked. Although
he didn't know
it, the heat
probably kept
the fleas at bay,
and he survived.

SCALE OF DEATH
The Black Death
claimed an enormous
25 million lives in
Europe alone: at least a
quarter of its population.
This is more than three
times the number of
soldiers killed in
World War I.

25m

8m

Black
Death

World
War I

= 2 million
dead

FLAGELLANTS
Many believed that the
plague was God's
punishment for their
sins. Some, called
Flagellants, would whip
themselves until they
bled, hoping for salvation.

PEASANTS' REVOLTS
Survivors of the plague,
which had greatly
reduced Europe's
workforce, demanded
higher pay and better
conditions. French
peasants revolted in 1358;
English peasants in 1381.
Both revolts were crushed
and their leaders killed.

Rebel leader Wat Tyler is murdered.

1450

AFRICA
1464 Sonni Ali (d.1492) becomes ruler of Songhai in West Africa

1482 Portuguese begin settling on Gold Coast, West Africa

1488 Portuguese navigator Bartolomeu Diaz (1450–1500) rounds Cape of Good Hope, South Africa, opening the sea route from Europe to Asia

ASIA

1467 Onin War, lasting over 100 years, begins in Japan. Leads to end of feudal system and rise of large territories

1497–98 Portuguese navigator Va Gama (1460–1524) reaches India

EUROPE
1450 Florence, Milan, and Naples form alliance

1450s German craftsman Johannes Gutenberg (c.1398–1468) produces first printed books in Europe

1453 Constantinople falls, ending Byzantine empire

1463 Turkey and Venice fight for control of Mediterranean until 1479

1478 Ivan III (1440–1505) begins to unify Russia

1479 Marriage of Ferdinand of Aragon and Isabella of Castille unites Spain. Lorenzo de Medici (1449–92) becomes unofficial ruler of Florence

1492 Conquest of Granada ends Moorish Spain and results in expulsion of Jews

1494 Under Treaty of Tordesillas, Sp Portugal agree to divide unexplored w

AMERICAS
1492 Italian explorer Christopher Colum (1451–1506) discovers the Caribbean

1497 Italian explorer John Cabot (c.1450–c.1498) discovers Newfo

OCEANIA

FALL OF BYZANTIUM
In 1453, Constantinople, capital of the centuries-old Byzantine Empire, fell to the Ottoman sultan Muhammad II. He had dragged 70 ships overland to avoid a huge iron chain protecting the waterway into the city.

PRINCE DRACULA (THE IMPALER)
The cruelties of the sadistic Romanian prince Vlad Dracul or "Vlad the Impaler" inspired the Dracula legend. He reigned for less than ten years, yet caused at least 50,000 deaths. After his own violent death in 1476, his severed head was impaled on a stake for public display.

FERDINAND AND ISABELLA
In 1479, Ferdinand of Aragon ar Isabella of Castille married an formed a larger, Christian Spanish kingdom. In 1492, their forces captured Granada, the last Muslim outpo in Spain. The new rulers were intolera of other religions: 165,000 Jews were to to convert to Christianity or leave Spain.

THE RENAISSANCE
15th-century Europe experienced a great cultural movement called the Renaissance (meaning "rebirth"). It began in the prosperous cities of Italy and was inspired by the rediscovery of ancient Greek and Roman ideas on art, literature, and science.

RENAISSANCE FLORENCE
At the height of its power, Florence was run by the Medici family, the greatest financier in Europe. They were educated in the classics and supported new artists and their ideas. Michelangelo's first commissions came from Lorenzo de Medici, and it was Medici money that attracted Leonardo da Vinci to the city.

RENAISSANCE INNOVATIONS

COAL MINING
In the 1520s, the first coal mines were opened in Newcastle, England, and Liège, Belgium.

FLIGHT DESIGNS
Leonardo da Vinci made detailed designs for a flying machine, a parachute, and a helicopter.

PRINTING PRESS
German printer Johannes Gutenberg (d.1468) made the first European moveable-type printing press in Mainz, Germany.

LUCREZIA BORGIA
Lucrezia Borgia (1480–1519) was the daughter of Rodrigo Borgia (Pope Alexander VI). She was famed for her charity and great learning – she wrote poetry in three languages. Exhausted by eleven pregnancies, she died in childbirth.

ENIGMATIC SMILE
Leonardo da Vinci's greatest painting, the *Mona Lisa*, was sold to Francis I of France. He kept it in his bathroom.

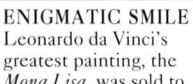
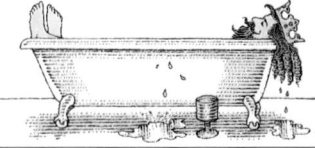

MICHELANGELO
By studying Greek and Roman art, Renaissance artists learned how to draw "in perspective" – to show depth on a flat canvas – and how to depict the proportions of the body. Michelangelo's huge statue of the biblical hero David, completed in Florence in 1504, is the most famous example of classical Renaissance sculpture.

David – height 5.49m (18ft)

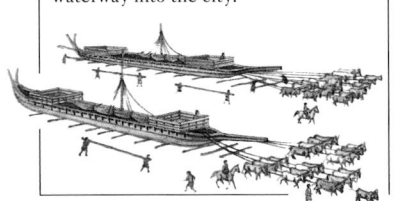

RENAISSANCE FIGURES

Name	Dates	Biographical details
Lorenzo de Medici	1449–92	Florentine patron of the arts, poet, classical scholar, banker, ruler of Florence
Leonardo da Vinci	1452–1519	Italian artist, sculptor, architect, engineer, inventor, anatomist
Desiderius Erasmus	1466–1536	Influential Dutch Renaissance thinker and priest, critical of the church
Niccolo Machiavelli	1469–1527	Florentine statesman, author of political masterpiece *The Prince*
Albrecht Dürer	1471–1528	German artist of the Northern Renaissance; painter and printmaker
Michelangelo	1475–1564	Italian painter, sculptor, and architect; painted ceiling of Sistine Chapel, Vatican
Andreas Vesalius	1514–64	Anatomist and physician; wrote first complete description of the human body

1517 Egypt conquered by Ottomans

...tus in southern ...e with Europeans. ...es develop in ...a

...avid dynasty ...Persia

1517 Syria conquered by Ottomans

1520–21 Portuguese traders reach China
1526 Babur becomes first Mogul Emperor of India

1542 Portuguese traders reach Japan

1546 Burma united under King Tabin Shweti

Leonardo da ...452–1519)
Mona Lisa

1512 Italian artist Michelangelo (1475–1564) completes ceiling of Sistine Chapel

1517 German monk Martin Luther (1483–1546) sets off the Reformation

1529 Ottoman Turks besiege Vienna

1520 Suleiman I (1494–1566) begins greatest reign of Ottoman empire

1533 Ivan the Terrible comes to the throne in Russia

1541 French Protestant reformer Jean Calvin (1509–64) sets up Puritan state in Geneva

1545 Council of Trent starts Catholic Counter-Reformation

...Italian Amerigo Vespucci ...2) explores coast of ...rican slaves ...he ...ies

1519 Portuguese explorer Ferdinand Magellan (1480–1521) sails across Pacific Ocean. Spaniard Hernán Cortés (1485–1547) overthrows Aztec empire

1532 Spaniard Francisco Pizarro (1475–1541) brings down Inca empire, South America

1534 French explorer Jacques Cartier (1491–1557) sails St. Lawrence River, Canada

1526 Portuguese landings in Polynesia

1550 Maoris settle on South Island, New Zealand

Battle of Mohács

...LEIMAN THE MAGNIFICENT
...leiman I, "The Magnificent" (1494–1566), was the ...atest of the Ottoman (Turkish) sultans. He ...ormed the educational and legal systems, and built ...at mosques, bridges, fortresses, and aqueducts. At ...Battle of Mohács in 1526, his huge victory over ...ngary marked the height of the Ottoman empire.

MAORI MIGRATION
Around 1550, Maoris sailed from North Island, New Zealand, in large double canoes to settle South Island. Overcrowding on North Island had led to violent competition for new lands.

BABUR I OF INDIA
Babur (1483–1530), a descendant of Genghis Khan, was the first Mogul Emperor of India and made Delhi his capital in 1526. He was a brilliant military leader, but was also fascinated by art and poetry.

LUTHER'S THESES
In 1517 a German monk called Martin Luther (1483–1546) nailed a list of complaints, his "95 Theses", to the door of his church at Wittenberg. He criticized the Catholic Church for its increasing corruption and called for reform. This sparked off a movement called the Reformation, and led to the formation of the Protestant churches (churches of protest).

...ZTECS AND INCAS
...dvanced civilizations were ...stablished in the Americas long before ...he Europeans arrived: the Aztec capital ...as bigger than any city in Europe. ...stronomy, mathematics, and the arts ...ourished, and great temples were raised in honour of their gods.

TWO GREAT EMPIRES
The Aztecs controlled an empire of 500 towns and 15 million people in modern-day Mexico. The Inca Empire stretched hundreds of miles down the Pacific coast.

Aztec empire

Inca empire

COUNTER-REFORMATION
In 1545 Catholic leaders met at the Council of Trent in northern Italy to settle the main principles of Catholicism and to organize a campaign against the spread of the Reformation. This movement was called the Counter-Reformation.

Council of Trent

...avoured ...ubjects
Montezuma
Nobles
Steps
War Council
Wise men

Montezuma's court and ceremonial chamber

Sacrificial ceremony

CALENDAR SYSTEM
Aztecs had a sophisticated calendar system that enabled them to date events centuries-apart with great accuracy.

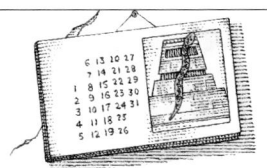

...ONTEZUMA, AZTEC KING
...ontezuma II (1466–1520) was ...lected king in 1503. In 1520 he was ...urdered by the Spanish conqueror ...ernan Cortés (1485–1547).

...ZTEC AND INCA FACTS
• Before Europeans arrived, ...either Aztecs nor Incas had ...een horses. Incas used runners, ...rained from birth, to deliver ...fficial messages.

• The Aztec punishment for ...hieves was for them to repay ...wice what they had stolen.

• The Aztecs' lucky number ...was 13.

• Aztecs feared that the world ...might end every 52 years, and ...hrew away all their possessions ...n preparation.

HUMAN SACRIFICE
Both Aztecs and Incas believed their angry gods were only soothed by blood sacrifice. In the early 1500s, Aztec priests were tearing the hearts from an estimated 20,000 people every year.

FALL OF THE INCAS
In 1532, the Spaniard Francisco Pizarro (1475–1541) marched into Peru with just 200 soldiers and kidnapped the Inca Emperor Atahualpa (1502–33). Pizarro asked for a ransom of a room full of gold, then murdered Atahualpa. The leaderless empire crumbled.

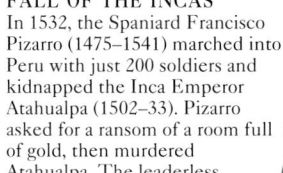

FIELD OF THE CLOTH OF GOLD
In 1520 the French King Francis I, met the English King Henry VIII, at a lavish ceremony in France to sign a peace treaty. The field was named after the fabulous cloth of their royal tents.

Timeline 1550

	1550				

AFRICA

1591 Moroccans and Euro[pean]
mercenaries destroy Songh[ai]

ASIA

1566 Death of
Suleiman I:
Ottoman empire at
greatest extent

1577 Akbar the Great (1542–1605)
completes unification of northern India

1590 Shah Abbas of Persia (15[ ])
makes peace with Ottoman T[urks]

1592 Japan invades Ko[rea;]
commander Hideyoshi

EUROPE

1555 Peace of Augsburg
permits each German ruler to
decide religion of subjects

1564 Death of
Michelangelo.
Shakespeare
born

1571 Battle of Lepanto: Christian European
alliance defeats Ottoman Turkish fleet

1572 St. Bartholomew's Day
Massacre of Protestants in France

1588 England defeats
Spanish Armada

1582 Gregorian calendar reform
introduced in Catholic countries

1598 Edict of [Nantes]
ends civil war [in France]
giving Catholic[s and]
Huguenots eq[ual rights]

AMERICAS

1567 Portuguese establish
Rio de Janeiro, Brazil

1579 Francis Drake (c.1540-96)
establishes British claim to west
coast of North America

OCEANIA

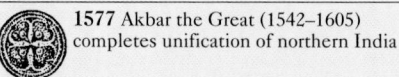

1567 Spanish explorer Mendaña (1541–95)
becomes first European to reach Solomon Islands

1595 Mendaña lands on [Marquesas]
Islands, central South Pac[ific]

RELIGION DIVIDES EUROPE

Luther's protests led to the formation of Protestant churches and split Christians in Europe into violent rival groups. War often broke out as each country struggled with the new religious alliances.

Battle of Lepanto

BATTLE OF LEPANTO
In 1571 an alliance of European sea powers led by the Pope defeated the Ottoman fleet at the Battle of Lepanto, Greece. The battle ended Turkish threats to Europe by sea, and allowed Catholics to turn to their struggles with European Protestants.

DIVINE DICTATION
St. Mary-Magdalen dei Pazzi (1566–1607) was famed for the length of her religious trances, during which she was thought to speak sacred truths. Six secretaries would record her words for hours, and sometimes days, at a time.

ELIZABETH I OF ENGLAND

The Protestant Elizabeth I ruled England from 1558 to 1603 and showed tolerance towards other religions. She never married and so avoided sharing her power with a foreign king.

The Spanish had 130 ships.
The English had less than 100.

Battle of the Spanish Armada

SPANISH ARMADA
In August 1588 the English fleet defeated Philip's massive invasion fleet, the Spanish Armada. The victory was a triumph for Protestantism.

PHILIP OF SPAIN

Philip II of Spain was the most powerful Catholic monarch in Europe. When Queen Elizabeth I executed the Catholic Mary Queen of Scots, he organized a fleet (the Spanish Armada) to invade England and restore Catholic rule. It set sail in July 1588.

RETRACTABLE BLADE
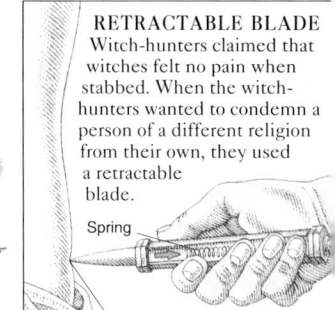
Witch-hunters claimed that witches felt no pain when stabbed. When the witch-hunters wanted to condemn a person of a different religion from their own, they used a retractable blade.

Spring

Blade does not pierce skin

LANDMARKS OF A RELIGIOUS AGE

St. Bartholomew's Day Massacre

Catherine de Medici with Huguenots

St. Bartholomew's Day Massacre
On 24 August 1572, the Catholic queen regent of France, Catherine de Medici, secretly ordered the massacre of thousands of French Protestants (Huguenots). This St. Bartholomew's Day Massacre was meant to destroy the Huguenots; instead it re-opened hostilities between Huguenots and Catholics.

Edict of Nantes (1598)
In 1593, the Protestant Henry of Navarre became a Catholic in order to be confirmed as Henry IV of France. His law, the Edict of Nantes, ended France's religious wars by allowing Protestants to worship.

Gunpowder Plot
In 1605, a Catholic plot to murder James I of England was discovered. Guy Fawkes was planning to light gunpowder in the cellars of Parliament while James was giving an address; he was caught and executed after torture. The discovery of the Gunpowder Plot led to greater persecution of English Catholics.

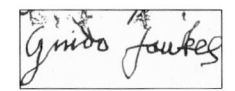

Guy Fawkes' signature before his torture

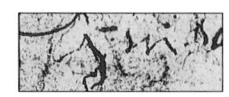

Guy Fawkes' signature after his torture

Jesuit missionaries
Spanish nobleman Ignatius de Loyola founded the Society of Jesus, or the Jesuits, as the missionaries of the Catholic Counter-Reformation. From 1550, Jesuits were in action all over Europe, and soon they began converting the peoples of the Americas to Christianity. Wherever traders went, Jesuits followed.

Persecuted Puritans
Rival groups of Protestants sometimes persecuted each other. In 1620, a group of Puritans called the Pilgrim Fathers set sail from Plymouth, England, to North America in search of religious freedom.

The Mayflower

l major European powers
trading posts on African coast

1620s Queen Nzinga of Mbundu
defeats the Portuguese

ginning of Tokugawa period in Japan.
ast India Company founded

2 Dutch East India Company founded

1604 Russians settle in Siberia

1605 Failure of Gunpowder Plot
and arrest of Guy Fawkes

1610 Assassination of French
King Henry IV (b.1553)

1613 Michael Romanov (r.1613–45)
becomes first Russian Romanov tsar

1618 Beginning of
Thirty Years War

1631 Sacking of
Magdeburg, Germany:
worst atrocity of
Thirty Years War

1607 John Smith (1580–1631) founds
colony of Virginia at Jamestown

1608 Quebec founded

1609 Henry Hudson (c.1565–1611)
sails up Hudson river

1620 Mayflower
sets sail for
North America

1625 French begin
to settle West Indies

1626 Dutch found New
Amsterdam (now New York)

1630 Dutch East India
Company seizes part of
Brazil for its sugar and silver

1629 Massachusetts colony founded

1606 Portuguese navigator De Quiros arrives at Tahiti, and Spanish
navigator Luis Vaez de Torres sails between Australia and New Guinea

AKBAR THE GREAT
The Mogul Emperor Akbar (1542–1605) gave
his expanding empire a superb structure of
government. Although he was a Muslim, he
also won the support of non-Muslims by
his tolerance of other religions. He even
tried to start a new religion – Din Illahl –
and supported many Hindu practices.

HINDU MARRIAGES
In 1562 and 1570, Akbar married
Hindu Rajput princesses, despite
his Islamic beliefs. The marriages
demonstrated his respect for his
Hindu subjects.

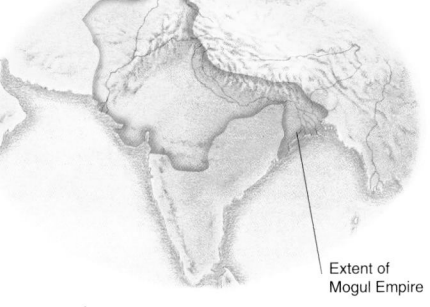

*Extent of
Mogul Empire*

AKBAR'S MOGUL EMPIRE
At his death Akbar's empire stretched from
Afghanistan in the north, to Bengal in the east,
and Gujarat in the west.

*Muslim Emperor Akbar
with his Hindu bride*

AKBAR'S FAVOURITE
Akbar, a keen hunter, trained
cheetahs to catch and kill his prey.
His favourite once jumped a
ravine to kill a blackbuck deer.
From then it was carried into the
hunt on a cushioned litter.

*Festivities at
the birth of
Akbar's son*

AKBAR'S ART
The arts blossomed
under Akbar. A
series of beautiful
paintings, called *The
Annals of Akbar*, were
prepared in the late
1590s and show
scenes from his life.

INABAT-KHANA
In 1575, Akbar built
the Inabat-Khana
(house of worship) in
which Muslims of
many traditions,
Zoroastrians, Hindu
pandits, and yogis
came to discuss their
religious beliefs.

*Akbar in religious
discussion*

TOKUGAWA JAPAN
In 1603 Ieyasu (1543–1616) of the
Tokugawa clan became *shogun* (ruler) of
Japan after defeating his rivals at the Battle
of Sekigahara (1600). He placed the
government in Edo (now Tokyo) and
forced his remaining rivals to move there.

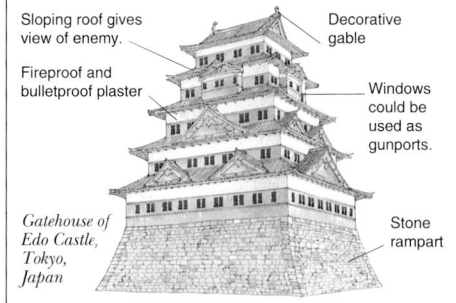

Sloping roof gives
view of enemy.

Decorative
gable

Fireproof and
bulletproof plaster

Windows
could be
used as
gunports.

*Gatehouse of
Edo Castle,
Tokyo,
Japan*

Stone
rampart

DISTRACTING HIS RIVALS
From 1604 to 1614, Ieyasu forced his rival *daimyo*
(samurai warlords) to build and enlarge a castle at
Edo. By the time he died he had built
the world's biggest castle.

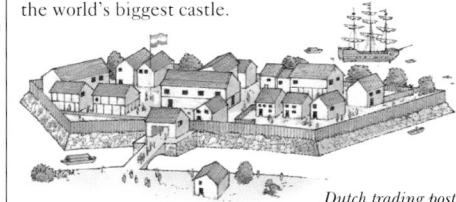

Dutch trading post

JAPAN IN ISOLATION
In 1636, the Tokugawa regime prevented all Japanese
from travelling abroad, and in 1641 expelled all
foreigners. A Dutch trading post in Nagasaki Bay was
the only contact with the outside world until 1854.

KEY PEOPLE

ame	Dates	Biographical details
natius de Loyola	1491–1556	Spanish ex-soldier and priest, founded Society of Jesus (Jesuits) in 1534
hilip II	1527–98	King of Spain and Portugal, champion of the Catholic Counter-Reformation
zabeth I	1533–1603	Queen of England during period of naval supremacy, artistic excellence, and international trade
kbar	1542–1605	Mogul emperor, famous for religious tolerance and support of the arts
okugawa Ieyasu	1543–1616	Shogun (ruler) of Japan, ended wars, unified country, banned Christianity
enry IV	1553–1610	King of France, converted to Catholicism from Protestantism to re-unify France
illiam Shakespeare	1564–1616	English dramatist and poet; plays include Hamlet and King Lear

KEY INNOVATIONS

PENCILS
Pencils were first produced
in England in 1565.

MERCATOR'S MAP
In 1569, Flemish
geographer Gerhard
Mercator (1512–94)
published a map on his
new projection, which
is still in use today.

1640

| AFRICA | | **1652** Dutch found Cape colony in southern Africa | **1663** Death of Queen Nzinga of Mbundu | **1670s** French settle in Senegal | 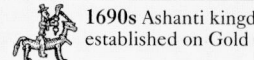 **1690s** Ashanti kingdo established on Gold C |

ASIA
1644 Manchu dynasty replaces Ming dynasty in China
 1657 Edo (Tokyo) is destroyed by a great fire
1661 English East India Company acquires Bombay
1662 K'ang Hsi begins reign in China
1669 Mogul Emperor Aurangzeb prohibits Hinduism
1683 K'ang Hsi conquers Formosa (Taiwan)
1688 Genroku Period, rise merchant class in Japan (u

EUROPE
1642 Civil War in England
1643 Louis XIV begins reign
1648 End of the Thirty Years War
1649 Charles I of England executed. Commonwealth set up under Oliver Cromwell
1660 English monarchy restored
1661 Bank of Sweden issues first European bank notes
1672 Third Anglo-Dutch trade war begins
1677 Ottomans at war with Russia
1682 Peter the Great begins reign
1683 Siege of Vienna by Ottoman forces fails
1688 England's "Glorious Revolution"
1690 Battle of the E Protestant William defeats Catholic Jan

AMERICAS
1642 French explorer De Maisonneuve founds Ville-Marie (now Montreal)
1664 England seizes New Amsterdam (now New York) from Dutch
1670 Colony of South Carolina founded. English Hudson's Bay Company founded
1675 War between colonists and Native Americans devastates New England
1683 William Penn signs treaty with Native Americans
1680 French explorer Robert Cavalier de la Salle claims Mississippi valley for France
1692 S witch t New E

OCEANIA
1642 Dutch explorer Abel Tasman becomes first European to reach Van Diemen's Land (Tasmania)
1680 The dodo becomes extinct

MANCHU CHINA

In 1644, the Manchus invaded China at the request of an unhappy Ming (Chinese) general. After the conquest, however, the Manchu leader Fu-lin (r.1638–61) made himself emperor. The *Ch'ing*, or Pure, dynasty that he founded ruled China for more than 250 years.

Under Manchu control by:
- 1644
- 1660
- 1760

MANCHURIAN EMPIRE
Manchuria lies in the northeastern region of modern-day China.

MING MANDARINS
Mandarins were the top officials of Ming China and were famed for their organizing skills. When the Manchus conquered China the mandarins were left to carry on with their work.

Manchus forced the Chinese to braid their hair, as they did, into a queue, or pigtail, as a sign of inferiority.

Manchu lord with Ming Chinese

Art of Manchu period

ART AND LEARNING
The second Emperor K'ang Hsi (1654–1722), like Fu-lin, saw the value of Ming culture. He requested scholars to write a Ming history, as well as dictionaries, encyclopedias, and technical works.

SUPREME RULERS

Kings and queens held massive political power in seventeenth-century Europe. Louis XIV of France (1638–1715), the most powerful of all, made decisions without regard to parliament or leading aristocrats.

THE AGE OF LOUIS XIV
• Louis ruled France for 62 years – during this time it became the most powerful country in Europe.

• Louis forced the nobles to live at his Versailles palace so that he could watch them closely.

• Louis' keen support of the arts earned him the nickname "The Sun King", after Apollo, Greek god of the arts.

Hall of Mirrors at Versailles

• In 1685, Louis abolished a law called the Edict of Nantes, which had protected the rights of French Protestants (Huguenots). Many went to England, where their businesses and crafts were successful.

CHARLES I
In 1649, the unpopular Charles I (1600–49) was beheaded by his English subjects, an event that shocked Europe. Parliament limited his successors' powers.

Execution of Charles I

A boyar (Russian noble)

Peter the Great forces the old-fashioned boyars, or nobles, to shave their beards in modern European style.

King Louis XIV of France in classical costume

SUICIDAL CHEF
In 1676, Le Grand Vatel, the famous chef to the Prince de Condé, committed suicide because a meal he had prepared for Louis XIV did not meet with the king's full approval.

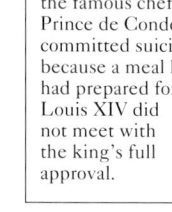

PETER THE GREAT
In 1682, Peter the Great (1672–1725) became Tsar of Russia. He was a leader of great energy and re-organized the army, founded the navy, and built a new capital at St. Petersburg.

KEY PEOPLE

Name	Dates	Biographical details
Nzinga of Mbundu	1582–1663	Queen of Mbundu, West Africa, fought Portuguese slave traders, offered shel to runaway slaves from neighbouring states
Oliver Cromwell	1599–1658	Victorious commander of English Parliamentary forces in civil war of 1642–48, Lord Protector (ruler) of England, 1653–58
Charles I	1600–49	British king executed after losing civil war against Parliamentary armies
Louis XIV	1638–1715	Absolute ruler during period when France led in politics, arts, and culture
Fu-lin	r.1638–61	First Manchu Emperor of China, increased number of Chinese in government
Peter the Great	1672–1725	Tsar of Russia, imported Western Europe's ideas and technology

French win Asiento (monopoly on ...ng of Africans to Spanish colonies)

1712 Rise of Futa Jalon kingdom in West Africa

1713 King Philip V of Spain grants Asiento to England

1707 Death of Aurangzeb leads to fall of Mogul Empire and opportunities for European traders

1708 Jesuit map-makers plot accurate maps of China

1727 Border fixed between China and Russia

1739 Nadir Shah captures Delhi with a Persian army, defeating the Moguls

1740s Anglo-French rivalry in India until 1760s

...les II of Spain dies ...ench heir: starts War of ...uccession (1701–13)

1707 England and Scotland united

1709 English ironmaster Abraham Darby produces coke, and uses it to smelt (extract metal from) iron ore, starting Industrial Revolution

1748 Marie Theresa becomes Empress of Austria

...703 Hungary revolts against Austria. ...ter the Great founds St. Petersburg

1709 Russia conquers Swedish Baltic provinces

1746 Culloden: last infantry battle in Britain ends Scottish revolt

1709 Mass emigration of Germans to America begins

1710 South Sea Company increases British trade with South America

1720–22 Spain occupies Texas. English South Sea and French Mississippi Companies collapse

1733 Molasses Act: England forbids trade between American and West Indian colonies. Colony of Georgia founded

1739 Slave uprising in South Carolina

1722 Dutch navigator Roggeveen reaches Samoa and Easter Island

THE SLAVE TRADE

When Europeans settled in the Americas, they transported Africans to work as slaves on the cotton, sugar, and tobacco plantations and in the silver mines. Slaves were forced to travel in horrific conditions, and were often worked to death once they had arrived.

Queen Nzinga seated on her attendant's back meets with the Portuguese at Luanda.

QUEEN NZINGA
Queen Nzinga of Mbundu, West Africa, opposed European slave traders. Her army was swelled by runaway slaves who had fled to her lands.

KING AGAJA
King Agaja (1673–1740) of Dahomey raided and enslaved his weaker neighbours. European and Arab traders bought his captives as slaves.

Sugar, cotton, and rum

English-owned and French-owned slaves

Arab-owned slaves

Portuguese-owned slaves

THE TRIANGULAR SLAVE ROUTE
Slave ships took a triangular route. They sailed from Europe to Africa to get slaves, over to the Americas to exchange slaves for sugar, cotton, and rum, then returned to Europe to sell those goods.

TRADER PORTS PROSPER
Atlantic ports such as Bristol, England, and Bordeaux, France, grew rich due to their strategic position between Europe, Africa, and the West Indies.

Bristol docks

Branding mark burned into skin.

MARKETS FOR PEOPLE
Once slaves reached the Caribbean, South America, or the colonies of North America, they were sold to the highest bidder. If different traders had used the same ship they had their own slaves branded with hot irons to identify them after the journey.

European slave traders assemble their captured slaves for sale.

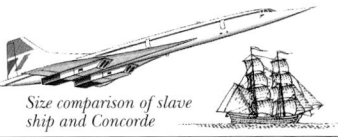

Slaves packed in as tightly as possible.

Plan of slave ship owned by Brookes of Liverpool, England

THE MIDDLE PASSAGE
The slave ship shown was designed to carry more than 400 people on the journey from Africa to America, called the Middle Passage. The supersonic jet *Concorde* would require three trips to transport 400 people over the Atlantic, yet *Concorde* is three times this ship's length.

Size comparison of slave ship and Concorde

SLAVE TRADE FACTS
• Between 1500 and 1800, European ships transported about 12 million people from their homes in Africa to the colonies of the Americas – two million more than the entire population of 15th-century North America.

• By 1800, the total African slave population of South America was just 1.2 million; most slaves died of overwork within a few years of arriving.

• The slave trade was more profitable than the trade in ebony, ivory, or gold.

• The Portuguese called their slave ships *tumbeiros*, meaning coffins, because they lost more than 30% of their human cargo during the voyage.

• In 1781, the captain of the *Zong* threw 132 slaves overboard to collect the insurance.

...OFFEE AND CROISSANTS
...1683, the Ottomans ended ...eir siege of Vienna, ...stria, and gave up their ...vasion of Europe. ...ennese survivors tasted ...ange beans found in the ...tomans' camp: coffee ...ans. Viennese ...kers made crescent-...aped pastries called ...issants to celebrate ...e end of the siege.

KEY INNOVATIONS

18th-century orrery shows planetary motion

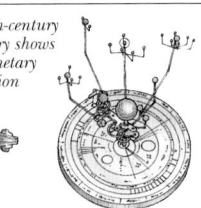

STRADIVARIUS' VIOLIN
Italian craftsman Antonio Stradivarius (c.1644–1737) perfected the art of violin-making. The secret of his varnish has never been discovered.

NEWTON'S LAWS
English scientist Isaac Newton (1642–1727) first formulated the laws of gravity in his book *Principia* (1687).

IRON SMELTING
In 1709, Englishman Abraham Darby (c.1678–1717) made the first industrial iron by smelting pig iron with coke, not charcoal.

1750

AFRICA

1768 Ali Bey becomes
ruler of independent Egypt

ASIA 1750 China conquers Tibet | 1757 Battle of Plassey: British conquer Bengal | 1761 Battle of Panipat: Marathas defeated by Afghans

EUROPE

1755 Earthquake at Lisbon, Portugal
1756–63 Seven Years War between Britain and France

1762 Catherine the Great begins reign over Russia

1769 Richard Arkwright builds first cotton factory

1757 First English canal built

1772 First Partition of Poland between Prussia, Russia, and Austria

1771 Russia conquers Crimea

1789 Storming of th French Revolution

1781 Joseph II abolishes serfdom (a form of peasant slavery) in Austrian Empire

AMERICAS

1759 English forces defeat French on Plains of Abraham, Quebec

1763 Pontiac (1720–69) leads Native American uprising against British in North America

1773 Boston Tea Party: protest against British tea tax

1775–83 American War of Independence

1776 US Declaration of Independence signed

1780 Tupac Amara leads Incas of Peru in revolt against Spain

1787–9 US Constitutio Bill of Rights written a

OCEANIA

1768–71 Captain Cook's first voyage on *Endeavour*

1788 British colony of South Wales, Australia

THE ENLIGHTENMENT

Followers of the 18th-century movement called the Enlightenment believed that reason and science could help to free people from rigid governments and religious intolerance. Enlightenment ideas about justice, equality, and freedom for all inspired the American and French revolutions.

THE ENCYCLOPEDIA

French philosophers Denis Diderot and Jean Le Rond d'Alembert collected and published the ideas of the Enlightenment in the multi-volume *L'Encyclopédie* between 1751 and 1786. It included contributions by thinkers such as Voltaire and Rousseau.

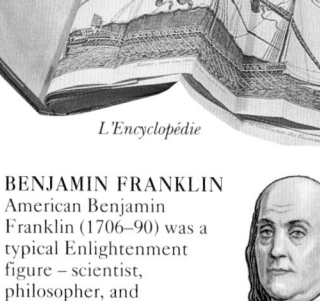
L'Encyclopédie

VOLTAIRE

The French thinker Voltaire (1694–1778) was a key figure in the Enlightenment. His witty writings criticized religious intolerance and backward governments and rulers.

Marble sculpture of Voltaire

BENJAMIN FRANKLIN

American Benjamin Franklin (1706–90) was a typical Enlightenment figure – scientist, philosopher, and statesman. In 1776, he went to France to raise support for the American struggle against British rule.

Benjamin Franklin

CAPTAIN COOK

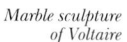
Ship's cloth Lobster

English navigator James Cook (1728–79) explored the South Pacific. He sensibly kept his ships clean and well ventilated; he gave his crews fresh vegetables and lime juice which saved them from scurvy.

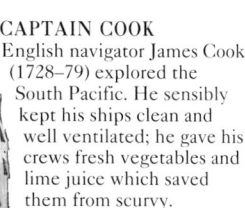
Cook trades with Islanders

COWPOX FOR SMALLPOX

Catherine the Great of Russia, who used to write to Voltaire, set an example to her fearful subjects when she had herself and her heir vaccinated by cowpox against smallpox.

REVOLUTION AND UNREST

Washington crosses the Delaware Rive before battle.

American War of Independence 1775–83

Americans disliked paying taxes to a government in which they had no representation. Led by George Washington, they had won independence by 1783.

French Revolution, 1789

In return for funding the bankrupt Louis XVI, the French lords, clergy, and commons demanded more power. On 14 July 1789, their supporters in Paris stormed the Bastille prison, an ancient symbol of royal authority, and launched the French Revolution

Reign of Terror

In 1792, France chose a new form of government: a republic. Louis XVI was executed in January 1793, and from mid-1793 to July 1794 anti-republicans were executed, often without trial. The period was called "The Terror".

Guillotine

Execution of Louis XVI

Toussaint L'Ouverture

In 1791, slaves in the French colony of Sainte Domingue (Haiti) rose up to fight for their freedom. Their leader Toussaint L'Ouverture (1743–1803) was himself a former slave. In spite of his successes he was captured by Napoleon and died a prisoner in France.

KEY PEOPLE

Name	Dates	Biographical details
Voltaire	1694–1778	Key French intellectual of the Enlightenment, wrote novel, *Candide* (1759)
Benjamin Franklin	1706–90	American author, publisher, inventor, scientist, and diplomat, helped frame the US Declaration of Independence, inspired French revolutionaries
Jean–Jacques Rousseau	1712–78	French philosopher and political writer, inspired leaders of revolution
Catherine the Great	1729–96	Empress of Russia, brought Russia fully into Western European cultural life
George Washington	1732–99	American commander-in-chief (1775–83) and first US President (1789–97)
Napoleon Bonaparte	1769–1821	French general, later emperor, established the principles of the French Revolution in law and government and spread them by military conquest

EUROPE COLONIZES OCEANIA

In 1788, the first 750 European settlers in Australia set up camp on the shores of Sydney Harbour. They were convicts who had been shipped from the overcrowded prisons of repressive, 18th-century Britain.

Convicts disembark at Sydney Cove.

1830

1804 British win control of Cape of Good Hope

1822 Liberia founded for freed slaves

1824–7 First Ashanti War between Britain and the Ashanti of the Gold Coast (Ghana)

794 Qaja Dynasty of Persia egins; rules until 1925

1819 Singapore founded by Stamford Raffles (1721–1826)

1824 Britain and Burma at war

Louis XVI executed. d Partition of Poland

1796 Napoleon's Italian campaigns. Jenner introduces smallpox vaccine

1804 Napoleon becomes Emperor of the French

1805 Battle of Trafalgar   **1815** Battle of Waterloo

1821–9 Greek War of Independence from Ottoman Turkey

New French government, irectory, set up

1801 Union of Great Britain and Ireland

1814 Congress of Vienna restores European monarchies

1825 First passenger railway opened in England

Constitutional Act creates Upper Canada (Ontario) ower Canada (Quebec). Revolution in Haiti y former slave Toussaint L'Ouverture (1743–1803) York (now Toronto) founded

1810 Buenos Aires gains independence

1811 Paraguay and Venezuela gain independence

1812–14 US and Britain at war: Washington DC burned

1818 Chile gains independence

1819 US purchases Florida from Spain

1821 Mexico gains independence

1822 Brazil gains independence

1823 Monroe Doctrine: US declares Americas free from European intervention

1806 First white women arrive in New Zealand

1817 First European emigrants settle Australian grasslands

1825 Van Diemen's Land becomes separate colony

EY INNOVATIONS

PINNING JENNY
1764, English weaver mes Hargreaves invented s "Spinning Jenny". It abled one worker to spin veral threads at once.

Spinning Jenny

OTTON MILLS
In 1769, English businessman Richard Arkwright (1732–92) set up the first cotton "mill" or factory.

FIRST TRAINS
In 1829, English engineer George Stephenson built one of the first steam locomotives, *The Rocket*.

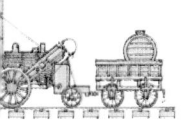

OT AIR BALLOON
he first manned flight took place in 83 in a hot air balloon made and flown the French Montgolfier brothers. ney sailed over Paris for 25 minutes.

LACK HOLE OF CALCUTTA
he Black Hole of Calcutta was a ffocatingly small cell in hich a local Indian official ld 64 British prisoners in 56. The British publicized e resulting deaths of 43 of e prisoners in its campaign r total control of India.

Cell measured 5.5m (18ft) by 4.5m (14ft 10in)

ritish prisoners in Calcutta

CHAKA: ZULU WARLORD
The great Zulu warlord Chaka (d.1828) owed his success to a brilliantly organized and highly trained army. For greater speed, his warriors went into battle barefoot. They were not allowed to marry until the age of 40, when they could leave the army.

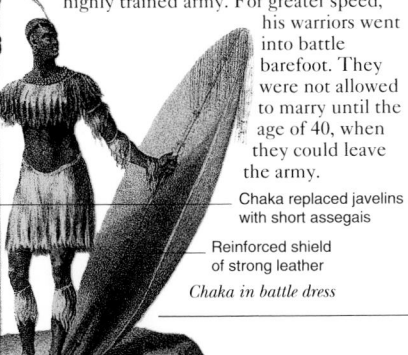

Chaka replaced javelins with short assegais

Reinforced shield of strong leather

Chaka in battle dress

NAPOLEON'S IMPACT
By 1812, the brilliant French general Napoleon Bonaparte (1769–1821) had conquered almost all of Europe. He gave himself great power, but also made the French government and army more efficient and open.

Napoleon crowned himself Emperor of the French in 1804.

x Major battle
—— French border
—— Campaign route
☐ French empire

NAPOLEON'S CAMPAIGNS
Napoleon's greatest campaigns were fought in Italy in 1796 and in Austria, Prussia, and the Rhine in 1806–7. His Russian campaign of 1812 was a disaster and he was defeated for good at Waterloo, Belgium, in 1815.

JOSEPHINE
Josephine de Beauharnais (1763–1814), Napoleon's first wife, had political connections that were very useful to him in his early career.

NAPOLEON FACTS
• On 5 October 1795, Napoleon saved the post-revolutionary government when he ordered his artillery to shoot down royalist rebels in Paris.

• Many ancient monuments, including the Sphinx, were excavated on Napoleon's Egyptian campaigns.

• Napoleon owed the success of his own career to talent. So, he made promotion in his army depend on ability, rather than on birth and money.

• In 1812, Napoleon fought his way to Moscow with 450,000 men. Russians burned the city and he was forced to return to France. 440,000 of his men died of cold and hunger.

SIMON BOLIVAR
While Napoleon was conquering Spain, the Spanish colonies of South America, led by Simon Bolivar and José de San Martin, rose up in rebellion. By 1825, they had all gained full independence.

EROICA SYMPHONY
German composer Ludwig van Beethoven (1770–1827) dedicated his Third Symphony to Napoleon, whom he saw as a champion of democracy. After Napoleon made himself Emperor of the French, Beethoven crossed out the dedication on his manuscript copy.

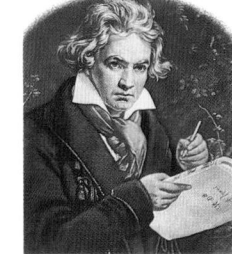

Ludwig van Beethoven

Simon Bolivar

DEADLY DECOR
Napoleon was finally exiled to the Atlantic island of St. Helena. Mould in the green dye (arsenic oxide) of his bedroom wallpaper is now thought to have contributed to his slow death.

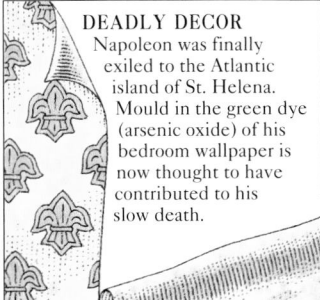

1830

AFRICA	**1830** French invade Algeria. British and Boers (Dutch South Africans) clash in South Africa	**1836** Start of Great Trek of the Boer farmers to establish independent Transvaal	**1839** British capture Aden **1838** Boers defeat Zulus at the Battle of Blood River	**1843** Nata British col

ASIA	**1839–42** China seizes opium imports from India, starting First Opium War	**1842** Treaty of opens Chinese British trade an Hong Kong to

EUROPE	**1830** July Revolution overthrows King Charles X of France. Belgium declares independence from Netherlands	**1832** First Reform Act extends voting rights in Britain	**1837** Queen Victoria begins reign	**1840** Penny postage introduced in Britain

AMERICAS	**1832** Samuel Morse (1791–1872) invents electric telegraph	**1836** Texas wins independence from Mexico and becomes a republic	**1839** American Charles Goodyear (1800–60) vulcanizes rubber, making it stable at both high and low temperatures	**1842** First general ana by America C. W. Long

OCEANIA	**1840** New Zealand: Treaty of Waitangi. Last convict-settlers arrive in Australia

EUROPE IN TURMOIL

In 1848, demands for democracy and national independence shook Europe's towns and cities. Industrial growth had made many people rich; now they wanted their fair share of political power. They rose up with students and workers and called for equality and democracy.

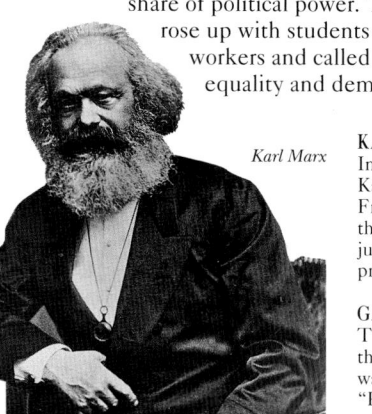

Karl Marx

KARL MARX
In 1848 German thinkers Karl Marx (1818–83) and Friedrich Engels (1820–95) published the *Communist Manifesto*. It described a just society, without classes of people or private property: a communist society.

GARIBALDI AND RISORGIMENTO
The Italian revolts of 1848–9 failed, but the 1860 *Risorgimento* (Reawakening) was a triumph. Patriot and leader of the "Redshirts", Giuseppe Garibaldi used guerilla war tactics in the struggle for Italian unification. He captured Sicily and southern Italy to form a new Italian state.

Garibaldi

MONARCHIES IN CRISIS
The last king of France
In 1848, the unpopular King Louis Philippe of France abdicated. Louis Napoleon became president of the new republic; monarchy was over in France.

Frankfurt parliament
In 1848, Germans in Frankfurt set up their first national parliament. Though it soon failed, this parliament fuelled hopes of a unified German nation.

Boy emperor
In 1848, 18-year-old Franz Joseph became emperor of the troubled Habsburg realms of central Europe. His uncle, Ferdinand I, had abdicated in the Vienna revolution.

Emperor Franz Joseph

FLASHPOINTS OF REVOLUTION
In the first four months of 1848, Europe was rocked by almost 50 separate revolutions in France, Prussia, Austria, and almost all the minor German and Italian states.

Berlin
Frankfurt
Prague
Vienna
Paris
Budapest
Milan
Venice
Rome
Palermo

▼ Centre of revolution

CONCENTRATION OF POWER
In no European nation of 1830 did voters exceed more than 5% of the population. This meant only one in twenty had a say in their government.

CHOLERA
Cholera, caused by drinking contaminated water, spread easily in the overcrowded cities of industrial Europe. Public panic about the disease encouraged revolution.

FAMINE AND EMIGRATION
In the 1840s, sometimes called "The Hungry Forties", famine struck much of Europe – it killed more than one million people in Ireland alone. As a result many Europeans emigrated, chiefly to the Americas.

KEY INNOVATIONS

FARADAY'S COIL
English scientist Michael Faraday's copper coil (see p.229) demonstrated the connection between electricity and magnetism.

PHOTOGRAPHY
In 1839, French artist and physicist Louis Jacques Daguerre developed his superior photographic process, the Daguerreotype.

POSTAGE STAMPS
Postage stamps were first issued in Britain in 1840, and in the US in 1847. The first stamp was the "penny black".

RAIL NETWORK
By 1847, steam-powered trains served all parts of Britain. The rest of the world soon built rail networks.

THE LURE OF GOLD
American carpenter John Marshall discovered flake of gold on land in California in 1848. Despite his efforts to keep the discovery secret, the news soon broke out and people rushed from Europe and from the eastern US in the hope of finding their fortunes. A similar gold rush occurred in New South Wales, Australia, in 1851.

Gold nugget

1847 Bantus defeated by British in southern Africa

1854 Independent Orange Free State and Transvaal set up, South Africa

1855 Livingstone discovers Victoria Falls, sparking off European exploration of the African interior

British and Sikhs
h defeat leads
rule over their
the Punjab

1848 Nasir ad-Din begins reign as Shah (ruler) of Persia

1850–64 Taiping revolt in China

1852–53 Second war between England and Burma

1853–54 US forces Japan to open up to Western trade

1856 Persia's seizure of Herat, Afghanistan, leads to war with Britain, until 1857

1857 Britain governs India directly after "Indian Mutiny"

1858 Treaty of Tientsin forces China to trade with West

Failure of
p in Ireland
vere famine

1848 Year of Revolution in Europe

1849 Collapse of revolutionary movements

1851 Great Exhibition held in London

1852 Louis Napoleon Bonaparte becomes Napoleon III

1853–56 Crimean War between Russia, Britain and France

1856 Bessemer invents industrial steel-making process

1858 *S.S. Great Eastern*, largest ship of its time, launched

1859–61 War of Italian unification

as and Florida
S states
6 US and Mexico
ar over Texas

1848 California Gold Rush helps open up west US. First US women's rights convention in New York State

1850 California becomes a US state

1851 I. S. Singer makes first pedal-powered sewing machine

1853 Completion of railroad from New York to Chicago

1850 Australian Colonies Act enables New South Wales, Tasmania, and South Australia to have virtual self-government

1851 Australian Gold Rush begins

THE BRITISH EMPIRE

etween 1830 and 1860, Western powers
orced isolated countries to open their ports
o Western goods: Turkey, Egypt, Persia,
China, then Japan. The British, with the
trongest navy and the most advanced
ndustries in the world, took control of these
ch eastern markets by
iplomacy or force, and
uilt a vast trading empire.

QUEEN VICTORIA
Queen Victoria
(.1837–1901) had the
ongest reign of any British
monarch. She presided over
he peak of the British
ndustrial Revolution and
ver the development of an
normous colonial empire.

British empire	Under British influence

THE BRITISH EMPIRE
In 1860, the British had either direct control or great influence over territories throughout the world. Important groups of islands gave them control of the major sea routes and trading advantages.

Chinese opium smokers

THE FIRST OPIUM WAR
Opium grown in India was bought by the British and sold in China for silks, spices, and tea. In 1839 Britain crushed a Manchu attempt to stop the drug trade at Canton. They forced the Chinese to grant trade and land rights to Western powers.

TREATY OF WAITANGI
In 1840 Britain and the Maori leaders of North Island, New Zealand, made an agreement which gave Britain formal possession in return for recognizing ancient Maori land rights.

Ceremonial dress of Maori leader

British and Maoris at Waitangi

LADY WITH THE LAMP
In 1854, Florence Nightingale (1820–1910) pioneered modern nursing by organizing the care of British soldiers during the Crimean War. Every night she walked 6km (4 miles) on her ward rounds.

GREAT EXHIBITION FACTS

Visitors at the Great Exhibition

• In 1851, London hosted the first international exhibition. The Great Exhibition showed 14,000 objects in celebration of the industrial age.

• Victoria's adored husband Prince Albert (1819–61) made the exhibition his pet project and much of its success was due to him. He died of typhoid, caused, ironically, by inferior, old-fashioned sanitation.

• The exhibition was housed in a glass and cast iron building called the Crystal Palace. It was built in five months in Hyde Park and covered 7.7 hectares.

INDIAN UPRISING
The "Indian Mutiny" of 1857 began when Indian soldiers refused to bite open cartridges greased with animal fats, forbidden to Hindus and Muslims. The rebellion became a massive protest against British rule.

US OPENS JAPAN TO TRADE
In 1853, Commodore Perry of the US Navy steamed into Tokyo Bay to demand that Japan open its ports to trade. His "black ships" forced the Japanese to give in.

KEY PEOPLE

Name	Dates	Biographical details
Michael Faraday	1791–1867	English scientist, discovered relationship between electricity and magnetism
Samuel Morse	1791–1872	American inventor of electric telegraph and developer of Morse code (1838)
Giuseppe Garibaldi	1807–82	Italian leader of Risorgimento "Redshirts", refused honours for service
David Livingstone	1813–73	Scottish missionary and explorer, influenced Western attitudes towards Africa
Karl Marx	1818–83	Philosopher and economist, wrote The Communist Manifesto and Das Kapital
Victoria	1819–1901	Queen of Great Britain and Ireland, Empress of India from 1876, revived popularity of monarchy in Britain over her long and stable reign
Florence Nightingale	1820–1910	English nurse, pioneered nursing as a profession during Crimean War (1853–6)

1860

AFRICA	**1860s** Britain, France, Belgium, Germany, and Portugal begin to explore and colonize inner Africa	**1869** Suez Canal opens	**1879** Zulu War: British defeat Cetewayo at Ulundi in South A

ASIA	**1861** Empress Tze Hsi begins 47-year rule of China	**1870s** Japan industrializes	**1872** Samurai's feudal control of Japan ends. Compulsory education introduced

EUROPE	**1864** International Red Cross founded by Swiss Henri Dunant. Otto von Bismarck leads Prussia to victory against Denmark	**1866** Dynamite invented by Swedish chemist Alfred Nobel. Prussia, led by Bismarck, defeats Austria	**1870s** Most Western European countries industrialize **1871** Bismarck invades and defeats France. Britain legalizes trade unions	**1876** French build refrigerated cargo ship

AMERICAS	**1861** US Civil War begins **1862** Billy Barker strikes gold in Williams Creek, British Columbia	**1865** Union wins Civil War. Lincoln assassinated **1867** Mexicans force French withdrawal from Mexico. British North America Act brings Dominion of Canada into being, with Sir John A. Macdonald as first prime minister. US buys Alaska from Russia **1869** First transcontinental railroad completed across US	**1876** Sioux and Cheyenne tribes defeat Custer at the Battle of Little Bighorn **1877–1911** Rule of Porfirio Diaz in **1879** Chile defeats Peru and B in war over nitrates (ends 1883) Electric light bulb invented

OCEANIA	**1860–70** Maori Wars in New Zealand: Maoris fight white settlers		**1876** New Zealand–Australia telegraph cable laid

AMERICAN CIVIL WAR

In 1861, deep divisions between northern and southern American states plunged the country into open warfare. The agricultural South, with its workforce of black slaves, feared the industrial North's economic power and resented its efforts to ban the spread of slavery. In 1865, the North won, but more than 600,000 had died in the fight.

NORTH AGAINST SOUTH
The 11 southern states of the Confederacy made Richmond, Virginia, their capital, while the 23 Union states were based at Washington. In 1861, the Confederates won the first major battle of the war at Bull Run, Virginia, and almost overran Washington. But the great Union victory at Gettysburg (1863) foreshadowed the end of Confederate resistance.

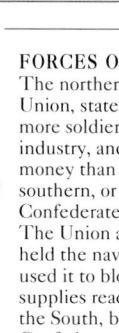

Union general   *Confederate general*

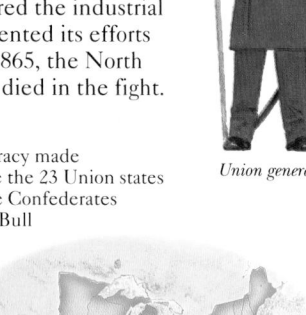

Union states
Slave states remaining in the Union
Confederate states

Washington
Richmond

CIVIL WAR FACTS
• More than 200,000 black soldiers fought for the Union.

• Twice as many men died of disease as died in battle.

• The 1860 election of anti-slavery president Abraham Lincoln was the immediate cause of war. His leadership brought victory to the Union and an end to slavery, but he was shot dead at a theatre by a Confederate just five days after their surrender.

FORCES OF WAR
The northern, or Union, states had more soldiers, industry, and money than the southern, or Confederate, states. The Union also held the navy, and used it to block supplies reaching the South, but the Confederacy had excellent generals.

WHITE ELEPHANTS
The King of Siam, Southeast Asia, offered Abraham Lincoln the use of a troop of his war elephants in the fight to preserve the Union. The President declined the offer.

LEVI'S JEANS
In the 1860s, American tailor Levi Strauss made the first pair of denim jeans. The tough cotton fabric, woven only in Nîmes, France, was ideal for miners of the Gold Rush. Later, workers, railwaymen, farmers, and cowboys began wearing jeans.

WOMEN VOTERS
In 1893, New Zealand became the first country to give women the right to vote in national elections. Almost a quarter of the female population had signed petitions demanding votes.

BOXER REBELS
In the late 19th century, economic and natural disasters weakened China's government. Western powers there grew stronger until, in 1899, an officially supported peasant rebellion, the Boxer Rebellion, tried to rid China of all foreigners. It was soon crushed by Western forces.

KEY BATTLES

Battle	Date	Victor	Details
Bull Run	July 1861	Confederacy	5,000 dead
Antietam	Sep 1862	Union	21,000 dead in one day
Gettysburg	July 1863	Union	40,000 dead

Otto von Bismarck

BISMARCK
Otto von Bismarck (1815–98) was the chief minister of Prussia, Germany. He led Prussia to victory against Denmark (1864), Austria (1866), and France (1871). He then founded a German Empire with Prussian King William I (1797–1888) as emperor.

GERMANY FACTS
• Before 1867, Germany consisted of more than 38 states. After 1871, Bismarck proclaimed all Germany an empire.

• After political unification, Germany rapidly built up its industries and armies. By 1914, the German army was twice the size of France's, and 12 times the size of Britain's.

• Bismarck was known as the "Iron Chancellor". In reality, he was prone to nervous attacks.

KEY PEOPLE

Name	Dates	Biographical details
Abraham Lincoln	1809–65	US President, preserved Union in US Civil War, emancipated slaves. Shot dead while at theatre
Otto von Bismarck	1815–98	Founder and first Chancellor of German Empire
Susan B. Anthony	1820–1906	Crusader for US women's right to vote
Harriet Tubman	1821–1913	Escaped US slave, helped 300 slaves flee to No
Alfred Nobel	1833–96	Swedish chemist, invented dynamite in 1866
Karl Benz	1844–1929	German engineer, built first practical car
Sigmund Freud	1856–1939	Austrian doctor, founder of psychoanalysis

1900

First Anglo-Boer War
1882 British begin rule in Egypt

1886 Gold discovered in South Africa

1895–96 Italy and Ethiopia at war: Ethiopia wins
1899 Second Boer War

...ain and France
...Burma and Vietnam

1885 Indian National
Congress Party formed

1899 Boxer Rebellion
of Chinese peasants

1884 Berlin conference decides
colonial divisions in Africa.
First deep underground railway
built in London
1885 Karl Benz builds first car driven
by internal combustion engine

1888 Scottish surgeon John
Dunlop (1840–1921) patents
pneumatic (air-filled) tyre
1889 English chemist Frederick
Abel invents cordite (explosive)

1896 Modern Olympic
Games introduced in Greece

1897 Greece and Turkey at war

1882 Thomas Edison designs
first hydroelectric power station
1884 First skyscraper built in Chicago

1889 Pedro II abdicates and
Brazil declared a republic
1890 Battle of Wounded Knee: last
massacre of Native Americans in US.
First moving picture (film) shows
appear in New York

1895 Cuban revolt against Spanish rule
1896 Gold struck in Klondike, Canada
1898 US wins Spanish-American
War and takes over the
Philippines. Cuba obtains
independence from Spain

1884 Volcano erupts on island of Krakatau
1885 Britain and Germany divide up New Guinea

1893 Women granted the vote in New Zealand. New Zealand
Prime Minister Richard Seddon introduces advanced social reforms

---

...NDUSTRY AND INNOVATION

The later 19th century saw a dramatic ...rowth in technology and industry. Factories ...ultiplied and cities expanded, aided by ...mproved transport, ...uch as railways, and ...ew inventions.

...OCIALISM
...any people who worked ...n the new factories lived ...n bad conditions. They ...egan to demand rights ...hrough trade unions and ...ocialist organizations.

INDUSTRY FACTS
• With industrial growth came an explosion in the size and population of cities. Germany in 1871 consisted mainly of small towns. By 1914 it had 30 cities of more than 100,000 people.

• After 1870, new industries – the chemical and electrical industries – joined the older coal, iron, and textile industries as a result of scientific discoveries.

KEY INNOVATIONS

SKYSCRAPERS
The large-scale production of steel made it possible for architects to construct buildings around steel "skeletons". The first skyscraper, the Chicago Home Insurance Building, was built in 1884.

CAR
In 1885, German engineer Karl Benz built the first car driven by an internal combustion engine. He fitted the engine on to a two-seat tricycle and patented the invention in 1886.

LIGHT BULB
Englishman Joseph Swan and American Thomas Edison invented light bulbs in the late 1870s.

TELEPHONE
Scottish-born speech therapist Alexander Graham Bell invented the telephone in 1876.

...CRAMBLE FOR AFRICA

...efore 1870, European interest in ...frica was confined to coastal ...owns that were important ...or sea trade. In the 1870s ...uropean armies ...ollowed missionaries ...nd explorers into the ...nterior, and by 1914 ...early all Africa had ...een colonized.

...ARVING UP AFRICA
...rance and Britain held the ...reatest proportion of African ...erritories. Germany, Italy, ...ortugal, and Belgium also held ...erritories. Most of today's borders come ...rom the lines drawn by Europeans at an ...884 conference in Berlin. No native ...fricans were invited to attend.

...ICE TO DIAMONDS
Cecil Rhodes, the empire-builder of British South Africa, began his career selling ice to diamond-mine workers. He later gained control of 90% of the world's production of diamonds.

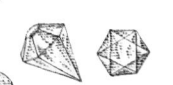

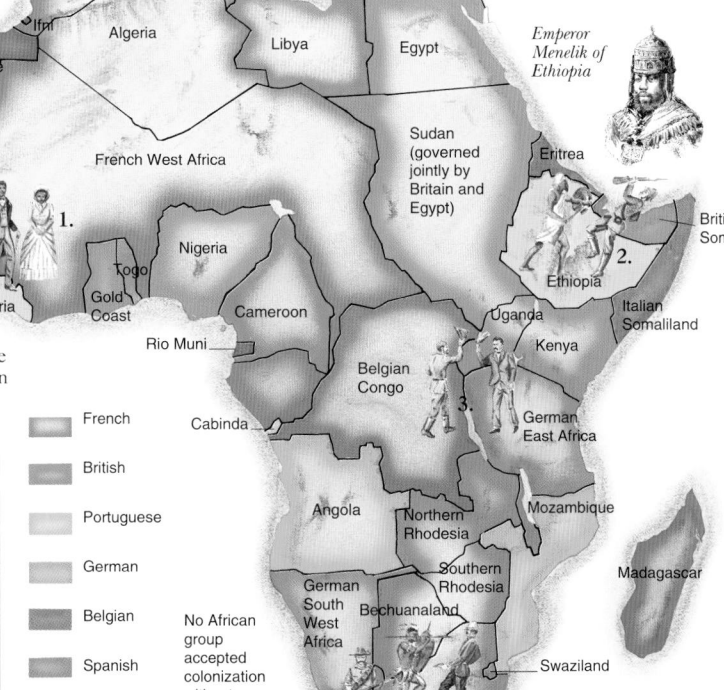

The British wanted to unite their southern and northern territories in Africa; the French, their western and eastern lands.

Emperor Menelik of Ethiopia

Key (map legend):
- French
- British
- Portuguese
- German
- Belgian
- Spanish
- Italian
- Independent

No African group accepted colonization without resistance.

1. Independent Liberia
Liberia was the first African country to become independent, in 1847. It was founded by freed American slaves.

2. Menelik's victory
Though Europeans had guns, African resistance to the European advance was often fierce. In 1896, Emperor Menelik of Ethiopia defeated the Italians at a famous battle at Adowa and secured Ethiopia's independence.

Stanley's hat

Livingstone's hat

3. Intrepid explorers
From 1850, several Europeans, including Richard Burton, Henry Speke, Mary Kingsley, David Livingstone, and Henry Stanley, explored Central Africa.

4. Fight for South Africa
In South Africa, Africans had to fight both British and Boers (white Dutch settlers). Zulus, led by King Cetewayo, held out, but were finally defeated by Britain in 1879.

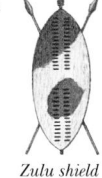

Zulu shield

5. The Boers
In 1899, a major war broke out between the British and the Boers. By 1902, Britain had defeated the Boers, who were mostly farmers. Within ten years, though, Britain gave Boers the power to rule South Africa.

1900

AFRICA	**1902** Ovimbundu people of Angola revolt against Portuguese rule **1905** Maji Maji rebellion in Tanzania against German rule leaves 75,000 dead.
ASIA	**1901** Peace of Peking ends Boxer Rebellion in China **1905** Japan wins Russo-Japanese War **1907** British company discovers oil in Persia **1909** Chin Tibet
EUROPE	**1900** German navy law calls for increases in sea power. Britain responds with similar increases; arms race begins **1903** Women's Union formed in Britain by suffragette Emmeline Pankhurst. First Tour de France cycle race **1905** October Manifesto: Tsar of Russia forced to grant democratic rights. Einstein formulates his Special Theory of Relativity **1908** First steel and glas AEG turbine factory, Be **1904** Entente Cordiale (friendly understanding) between Britain and France
AMERICAS	**1900** Coca Cola first produced **1902** British and German fleets seize Venezuelan navy. Plastic invented in USA **1906** US forces occupy Cuba. Earthquake in San Francisco, USA **1909** US e Robert Pea (1856–1920 to have rea North Pole **1901** Theodore Roosevelt becomes youngest-ever US president after assassination of President McKinley **1903** US bicyclemakers Orville and Wilbur Wright build first aeroplane and make first successful powered flight **1907** First comic strips appear in USA
OCEANIA	**1901** Commonwealth of Australia proclaimed. New Zealand takes over Cook Islands **1907** New Zealand becomes a dominion Federal basic wage set in Australia

WORLD WAR I

In the early 1900s, Europe was kept at peace by a complex system of alliances. When the heir to the Austro-Hungarian Empire, Archduke Ferdinand, was shot dead in 1914, the system collapsed, and war broke out. A combination of new weapons with old tactics resulted in war on a huge scale and a vast death toll: more than 20 million dead.

WAR ON TWO FRONTS
World War I involved so many countries that it became known as the Great War. Although it was fought mainly in Europe, other nations, notably Japan and the USA, were also involved. In western Europe, French and Commonwealth forces fought Germans around Belgium and France.

Soldiers lived, slept, ate, fought, and often died in trenches. Heavy guns would pound an enemy's trenches before an attack.

British trench

WORLD WAR I FACTS

• World War I was the first to make use of entire adult populations. Men were conscripted (called up) into the armed forces, and women worked in armaments factories and on farms. It changed the way wars were fought forever.

• Poison gas, in this case chlorine, was first used in war by Germans at the Battle of Ypres (1915).

• Governments concealed the extent of the slaughter from the public by publishing false statistics.

• The Germans surrendered at 11.00 a.m. on the 11th of November 1918. On every anniversary of this day the war dead are remembered in religious services around the world.

KEY BATTLES

Battle	Date	Outcome
Tannenberg	Aug 1914	Germans halt Russian advance
The Marne	Sep 1914	Last mobile action of western war; Germans pushed back to trench front
Passchendaele	July 1917	British defeated in sea of mud
Cambrai	Nov 1917	First successes with British tanks

Allied powers   Front lines
Central powers   ---- 1914
Neutral states   ----- 1915   —— 1918

TRENCH WARFARE
Much fighting took place between lines of trenches dug by soldiers. When one army charged at another, many died, since both sides had machine guns. The area between trenches, called No Man's Land, was often a muddy wasteland covered in dead bodies and craters. Conditions were terrible and disease was rife.

SINKING OF THE LUSITANIA
On 7 May 1915, the British passenger liner *Lusitania* was sunk by a German submarine. It went down with 1,198 civilians, including 198 Americans. The attack hastened US entry into the war.

Victims from the Lusitania

KEY INNOVATIONS

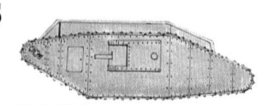

MACHINE GUN
Machine guns turned the western front from a mobile war into a static, trench war. A few could kill thousands.

TANKS
The first practical tank, *Big Willie*, was built by the British in 1916. Tanks proved slow but effective.

BATTLE OF THE SOMME
More people – 1,265,000 – died in the Battle of the Somme in 1916 than in any other World War I battle. Artillery gunfire from the battle could be heard in England.

Somme death toll

650,000 German
420,000 British
195,000 French

German trench

FIRST WARPLANES
Aircraft were first used to spy on enemy trenches, but later were fitted with bombs and machine guns. The most successful fighter pilots, such as the German Baron von Richthofen who was credited with shooting down 80 enemy planes, were called aces.

n of
a formed

1911 Lamogi people of Uganda rebel against British rule
1912 African National Congress formed in South Africa to fight for black people's rights

1917 Rebellion against French rule in Chad forces 3-year French withdrawal

takes

1911 Chinese revolution overthrows Manchu dynasty
1912 British arrest Mohandas Gandhi (1869–1948)

1915 Mohandas Gandhi becomes leader of Indian National Congress Party

1917 China joins Allies

y's
ars

1911 Norwegian explorer Roald Amundsen (1872–1928) reaches South Pole
1912 Sinking of *Titanic*
1912–13 Balkan Wars: Greece, Serbia, Bulgaria, Montenegro against Turkey

1914 World War I begins
1915 British liner *Lusitania* sunk by German torpedo. Bulgaria joins Central Powers (Germany, Austro-Hungary). Italy joins Allies (Britain, France, Russia, Serbia)

1916 Irish revolt against British rule
1917 Russian Revolution: Communists take over from Tsar. Russia leaves World War I and civil war breaks out. Greece joins Allies
1918 World War I ends

1911 Mexican dictator Diaz overthrown in revolution
1912–33 US troops occupy Nicaragua

1914 Panama Canal opens
1915–16 US troops put down disorders in Haiti and Dominican Republic

1917 US enters World War I

1914 Australia and New Zealand join Allies in World War I

Aurora

Winter Palace, St. Petersburg

The Bolsheviks had supporters in the Navy. During the October Revolution, the cruiser *Aurora* steamed upriver towards St. Petersburg. It fired blanks over the roof of the Winter Palace during the siege of the temporary government.

RUSSIAN REVOLUTION

In the early 20th century, rapid industrialization threatened the rule of the tyrannical Tsar Nicholas II, when workers began to demand their rights. In 1917, Vladimir Lenin, leader of the Bolshevik Party, led a revolution that overthrew tzarist rule. In its place he set up the world's first Communist regime and pulled Russia out of World War I.

RUSSIAN REVOLUTION FACTS
In March 1917, food and fuel were in short supply in the cities. Angry citizens in St. Petersburg began strikes and riots. Troops ordered to break up the riots joined the rioters instead. The Tsar abdicated, and a temporary government was set up.

In November 1917, the war was going badly for Russia and the temporary government had failed to ease the food and fuel shortages. The Bolsheviks were able to seize power after besieging the government in the Winter Palace in St. Petersburg.

In July 1918, Tsar Nicholas II and his family were shot by the Bolsheviks.

The "October Revolution" actually happened in November, because at that time Russians used a different calendar from the rest of the world. Lenin brought it into line in 1918.

Lenin's Communists were called the Red Army, and were led by Trotsky.

• Lenin gave land from old estates to the peasants, gave workers the power to run their factories, and confiscated the property of the Church. He faced armed opposition from "White" Russians, who wanted the Tsar restored. A civil war began, ending in 1921 with the Red Army triumphant.

REVOLUTION EXPRESS
Until April 1917, Lenin had been in exile in Switzerland. When Russian communists gained permission for him to return, the German government agreed, on condition that he remain on a sealed train until his destination.

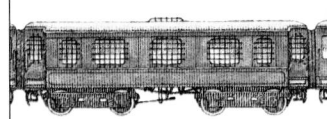

KEY PEOPLE OF THE REVOLUTION

Tsar Nicholas II
(1868–1918) became unpopular after his 1905 promises of democracy proved empty. When he became personally involved in the war, he also took the blame for the army's successive defeats.

Leon Trotsky (1879–1940) was a brilliant writer and speaker, and the most popular leader after Lenin. He created the Red Army, led it to victory in the Civil War, and defeated a Polish invasion.

Vladimir Lenin
(1870–1924) formed the Social Democratic Party in 1898, which had to meet in secret, as the tsarist government immediately banned it. When the time came, Lenin's followers, the Bolsheviks, were ready.

Josef Stalin
(1879–1953) was a key administrator in the Bolshevik party. When Lenin died in 1924, Stalin struggled with Trotsky for power. Stalin succeeded and ruled the country until 1953.

RUSSO–JAPANESE WAR 1904–05

In 1904, Japan, hoping to capture Manchuria, launched a surprise attack on Russian forces there. Japan won a series of victories ending in 1905 with the total destruction of the Russian fleet. It was the first time in modern history that an Asian power had defeated a European power.
Battle of Liao-Yang, 1904

SINKING OF THE TITANIC

At midnight on April 15, 1912, the *Titanic*, the world's largest ocean liner, struck an iceberg on its maiden voyage. It sank with the loss of 1,513 lives.

IRELAND AND THE EASTER RISING
In 1912, Britain agreed to give Ireland home rule, but when World War I began, the plan was postponed. In 1916, those Irish who wanted independence organized armies, took control of Dublin, and declared a republic. Britain put down this "Easter Rising", but it led to greater support for a republic.

Dublin barricades

1919

AFRICA
1922 Egypt wins conditional independence from Britain
1923 Ethiopia joins League of Nations

ASIA **1919** Amritsar Massacre: 379 people die when British fire on peaceful Indian protest

1923 Earthquake in Tokyo. Ottoman Empire ends

EUROPE **1919** Paris Peace Conference. First international daily air service between London and Paris

1921 Heavy German reparations announced

1922 Mussolini (1883–1945) forms Italian government

1924 Lenin (born 1870) dies. Stalin (1879–1953) succeeds as leader of Russia

1926 General strike in Britain

1920 Red Army wins Russian Civil War. Poland takes advantage of Russian turmoil and attacks Russia, claiming much new territory

1923 Ireland wins partial independence from Britain

AMERICAS **1920** Manufacture and sale of alcohol banned in USA. Women granted vote in USA

1924 US military planes make first airborne trip around the world

1927 *The Jazz Singer,* first film with speaki singing, is released

OCEANIA **1919** Australia acquires former German colonies in the Pacific

1923 Ross area of Antarctica becomes New Zealand dependency

1927 Canberra beco capital of Australia

AFTERMATH OF WAR
After World War I, various plans were laid to make sure such a war could never happen again. Germany was blamed and severely punished, while the Allies drew together and formed a pact to protect themselves from further attacks. The victors thought they had secured lasting peace.

PARIS PEACE CONFERENCE
In 1919, the victors organized a conference at which Germany lost much of its territory, including its African colonies. It was forced to disarm and make huge reparations (compensation). Many felt that the Allies had treated Germany harshly and unfairly.

The signing of the peace treaty between the Allies and Germany in the Hall of Mirrors at Versailles in 1919

THE WORLD BETWEEN THE WARS
• The victors joined together to form the League of Nations and promised to seek peaceful solutions to problems. Defeated countries were not allowed to join and the USA preferred to stay out of world affairs.

• Hitler's economic policies eased Germany's crisis, and few stood against his 1934 seizure of power.

• In the late 1920s Stalin forced Russia to industrialize very quickly; millions died of starvation. Later he enforced his rule by intimidating and murdering millions of Soviet citizens.

Soviet (Russian) worker

Finland
Norway
Sweden
Estonia
Denmark
Latvia
Russia
Lithuania
East Prussia
Germany
Poland
Czechoslovakia
Austria
Hungary
Switzerland
Yugoslavia
Romania
Italy
Bulgaria
Albania
Turkey
Greece

| German Empire 1914 | | Austro-Hungarian Empire 1914 |
| Russian Empire 1914 | | Post-war borders |

THE POST-WAR SETTLEMENT
The defeat of Germany, the destruction of the Austro-Hungarian Empire, and the Bolshevik Revolution, completely changed the map of Europe. Several states, such as Poland, and the Baltic and Yugoslavian states, gained independence.

REPARATIONS
The reparations the Allies forced on the Germans gave their economy no chance to recover, and they had to borrow again to keep paying. In 1923, it took a whole wheelbarrow of German marks to buy a loaf of bread.

Amount borrowed: 33 million marks

Reparation payments: 36.1 million marks

1918–1931

THE GREAT DEPRESSION
In October 1929, share dealers in New Yo having pushed share prices above their re value, panicked, and sold 13 million share in one day. This event, called the Wall Street Crash, was a major cause of the worldwide economic crisis that followed. Millions of people lost jobs, businesses, savings, and homes.

THE DUST BOWL
Drought struck the midwestern and western USA at the time of the Crash, and the soil of the farmlands was blown away in strong winds. Their land now a desert, many farmers lost everything and went west. The region was called the Dust Bowl.

Homeless victims of the Great Depression

GREAT DEPRESSION FACTS

• By 1933 the USA had 14 millio unemployed. Franklin D. Roosev elected president in 1932, devise his "New Deal" policy to create j and ease the depression.

• German factory production leve halved between 1929 and 1932. Germans blamed their system of government, a view that the Nazi later used to take absolute power.

• Britain's Labour government fa to deal with the depression. In 19 the National government, made u from every party, took over, but it was largely conservative.

• Japan's rice and textile markets suffered greatly and the military widespread economic misery to s power from the elected rulers.

A FISTFUL OF WOOD
In 1932, a shortage of ready cash led the authorities of Tenino, Washington, USA, to issue "notes" made of wood. There were notes worth $10, $5, $1, 50¢, and 25¢.

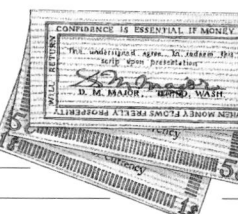

KEY PEOPLE

Name	Dates	Biographical details
Mohandas Gandhi	1869–1948	Crusader for Indian independence, founder of modern Indian state
Adolf Hitler	1889–1945	*Führer* (leader) of the German Nazi Party, dictator from August 1934
Francisco Franco	1892–1975	Spanish general and dictator 1939–75
Haile Selassie	1892–1975	Progressive Emperor of Ethiopia
Al Capone	1899–1947	Notorious gangster in Chicago, USA
Jesse Owens	1913–80	Black US Olympic athlete, challenged Hitler's belief in white superiority

GANGSTERS
The sale of alcohol was banned in the USA in 1920. An illegal trade in alcohol immediately sprang up in major cities, backed by gangs of criminals. Gang leaders, such as Al "Scarface" Capone, grew very powerful. Capone was eventually jailed in 1930, for tax evasion.

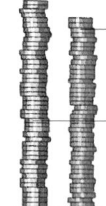

Al Capone (centre)

1930 Ras (Prince) Tafari crowned as Haile Selassie I in Ethiopia	**1931** South Africa gains independence from Britain	**1934** Lagos Youth Movement formed, demanding self-government for Nigeria **1935** Italy invades Ethiopia

1930s Gandhi leads non-violent opposition to British rule in India

1934–35 Long March in China

1936 Japan signs alliance with Germany

1937 Japan and China at war. Japan occupies much of Chinese coast

...cillin discovered

1931 Spain becomes a republic. "National" Government formed in Britain

1933 Adolf Hitler, (1889–1945), *führer* (leader) of Nazi Party, becomes German Chancellor

1936 Germany hosts Olympic Games in Berlin

1936–39 Spanish Civil War between Republicans and Nationalists: Nationalist victory

1937 Jet engine invented in Britain

1938 Hitler takes over Czechoslovakia

...Wall Street Crash: ...of shares on American ...exchange fall rapidly

1931 British Parliament gives Canada independence

1933 Franklin D. Roosevelt becomes US President. Ban on sale and manufacture of alcohol lifted

1931 First solo flight between Australia and New Zealand. Airmail service from Australia to Britain introduced

1937 Royal New Zealand Air Force formed

REVOLUTION IN CHINA

...etween the wars, Communism rose to be ...e major force in China. From 1927, ...Communists led by Mao Tse-tung tried to ...verthrow Chiang Kai-shek's corrupt ...Nationalist government in a bloody civil ...ar. In 1937, Japan took advantage of ...China's domestic turmoil by invading the ...orth, further damaging Chiang's power. ...Mao and Communism triumphed in 1949.

KEY LEADERS

Chiang Kai-shek
(1887–1975), although at first allied with the Communists who helped him take power in 1925, broke with them soon after. His rule was harsh and corrupt, and the fortunes he amassed while his people starved made him unpopular.

Mao Tse-tung
(1893–1976) drew support from peasants, but early in the Civil War was outfought by Chiang's armies. On the Long March, he became leader of the party and wrote the *Red Book*, which described life under Communism.

...HINA FACTS
- ...Mao Tse-tung was born a peasant ...d educated himself. He became ...volved in peasant affairs in 1921.

- ...In April 1927, Chiang Kai-shek had ...veral hundred Communists and ...nion organizers shot in Shanghai. The ...nsuing chaos in the Communist Party ...nabled him to seize power.

- ...In 1929, Mao established a strong ...ommunist base in Kiangsi. ...ommunist troops from all over China ...ed there after Chiang Kai-shek broke ...s alliance with the Communists.

- ...Mao was forced to leave behind his ...vo children on the Long March. He ...ever located them after the war.

TURMOIL IN THE EAST
Chiang Kai-shek's forces, called the Kuomintang (Nationalists), drove the Communists into the southern hills of Jiangxi. Although the Kuomintang ruled most of China, Communists held many remote, agricultural areas.

- *O*   Area of early Communist rule
- →   Route of the Long March
- Under Japanese rule by 1938
- Under Communist rule by 1945
- Communist base

During the 10,000-km Long March, more than three-quarters of the original 100,000 died of cold, hunger, or from attacks by Chiang's forces or local warlords.

THE LONG MARCH
In October 1934, 100,000 Communists, mainly peasants, marched for a year across swamps, mountains, and large rivers, to escape Chiang Kai-shek's armies. Survivors set up a base at Yenan, in a deep gorge where they lived in cliff caves.

HEN HORNS
Hens in crates on boats on the crowded Shanghai River acted as horns, warning other craft at night.

THE RISE OF JAPAN
- In the late 1930s, Japan's military seized power and were keen to show Japan's strength in war and empire-building. They invaded China in 1937 and occupied much territory.

- Japan withdrew after defeat in World War II, but its occupation had weakened Chiang's armies and helped bring Mao to power.

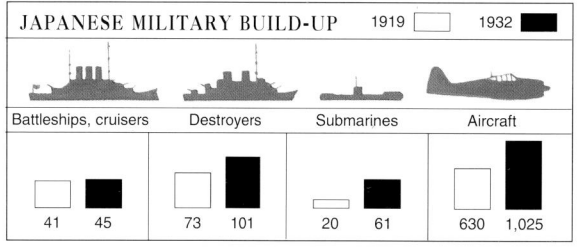

JAPANESE MILITARY BUILD-UP	1919 ☐	1932 ■	
Battleships, cruisers	Destroyers	Submarines	Aircraft
41 45	73 101	20 61	630 1,025

	1939	1940	1941
AFRICA		**1940** British Navy sinks French fleet at Oran to prevent its capture by Germany	**1941** Allied troops overrun Italy's African colonies. German forces, led by Erwin Rommel, arrive in Libya to help Italy
ASIA		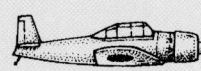	**1941** Japan takes over French colonies in Southeast Asia and attacks US Navy at Pearl Harbor **1941–42** Japan captures Hong Kong, Philippines, Malaya, Singapore, Burma, and Indonesia
EUROPE	**1939** Germany invades Poland; Britain and France declare war on Germany	**1940** Germany occupies Denmark, Norway, France, Belgium, and the Netherlands. Italy joins war to help Germany. Winston Churchill becomes Prime Minister of Britain. Battle of Britain: British air force fights off German air attack, preventing German invasion of Britain	**1941** Germans in eastern Europe take over Hungary, Bulgaria, Greece, and parts of Yugoslavia and Russia
AMERICAS		**1940** Xerox copying machine invented. Antibiotics (e.g. penicillin) developed	**1941** US Navy attacked by Japanese planes at Pearl Harbor in Hawaii. USA joins Allies in war against Germany and Japan
OCEANIA	**1939** Australia and New Zealand join Allied forces	**1940s** Australia prepares for Japanese invasion, which never comes	

WORLD WAR II

Militaristic and nationalistic governments rose to power in Germany, Italy, and Japan, as a result of the Great Depression of the 1930s and the Versailles Treaty of World War I. All were intent on expanding their power and territory. Global war broke out with Germany's invasion of Poland in 1939, eventually costing over 50 million lives.

LEADERS OF THE AXIS POWERS

Adolf Hitler (1889–1945) founded the Nazi Party in the 1920s. He seized power in 1933, and quickly destroyed all opposition. His dreams of empire ended with the failure of his Russian invasion. At the war's end he shot himself.

Benito Mussolini (1883–1945) founded the Fascist movement in Italy in 1919. In 1922, he gained power, and ruled as a dictator. He took Italy into the war in 1940 on the Axis side and, after their defeat, was captured and executed by Italian rebels in April 1945.

Emperor Hirohito (1901–89), though seen as a god in Japan, had little power. Japanese pilots thought it an honour to die for the Emperor. They went on *kamikaze* missions in which they flew into Allied ships in planes packed with explosives.

WORLD WAR II FACTS
• Germany brutally put down any resistance to its rule. Those suspected of opposing German occupation were often tortured or killed by the feared Nazi police, the Gestapo. In occupied countries many joined secret resistance groups.

• In August 1939, the USSR signed a pact with Germany, called the Nazi–Soviet pact, which carved up Poland and the Baltic states between the two. In June 1941, Germany's invasion of Russia, called "Operation Barbarossa", broke the pact.

• The Nazis passed laws to discriminate against Jews. During the war they built camps around Europe, called concentration camps, where they killed six million Jews, along with Slavs, Gypsies, homosexuals, and political prisoners.

Belsen concentration camp

German soldier

Italian soldier

Japanese soldier

The 1940 "Blitz" of London was the first long, large-scale bombing campaign from the air.

Leningrad
Moscow
London
Berlin
Paris
Stalingrad
Rome

■ Maximum extent of Axis empire (1942)
■ Allied states
■ Neutral states
→ British and US advances (1943–5)
→ Russian advances (1943–5)

THE OCCUPATION OF EUROPE
By 1942, Germany had conquered most of Europe and a great area of Russia. Its *blitzkrieg* (lightning campaign) tactics devastated the Allies and it was not until 1943, with US entry into the war and the Allies' huge rearmament programmes, that the tide turned against Germany. In June 1944, the Allies landed in Normandy, France. Russia matched their successes, and by May 1945 the war in Europe was over.

BOMBING AND THE BLITZ
World War II marked the first use of large-scale bombing raids, or blitzes, to try to destroy civilian morale and industrial efficiency. In 1945, a single British raid on the German city of Dresden killed more people than either of the atomic bombs dropped on Japan.

KEY GENERALS

Name	Dates	Biographical details
D. MacArthur	1880–1964	US general, recaptured much of South Pacific from Japanese, received Japanese surrender aboard USS *Missouri*
B. L. Montgomery	1887–1976	British general, defeated Rommel, led Allied invasion of France
Erwin Rommel	1891–1944	German tank commander, won huge victories in North Africa
G. K. Zhukov	1896–1974	Red Army (Russian) commander, recaptured Russian lands; his troops were first to enter Berlin at end of war

Allied troops land in Morocco and force mel's troops to retreat from El Alamein

US Navy defeats Japan in Coral Sea ew Guinea and at Midway Island

1943–44 Series of island-hopping victories by USA pushes Japanese back

1944 Japan attacks India but is defeated at Kohima

1945 USA drops first atomic bombs on Japanese cities of Hiroshima and Nagasaki. Emperor Hirohito authorizes Japanese surrender

1943 Allies invade Italy
1943–44 Germans driven out of Russia

1944 Allies invade France and drive back Germans

1945 German forces surrender

Enrico Fermi builds first nuclear r, USA. Mexico and Brazil join Allies

1943 Argentine Revolution brings Juan Perón to power as virtual dictator

1945 US tests first atomic bomb in New Mexico

Japanese bomb Darwin, Australia, vade New Guinea and part of Papua

1944 Japanese prisoners of war in Australia stage mass breakout

1945 Australia recovers New Guinea and Papua territory from Japan

LEADERS OF THE ALLIED POWERS

Josef Stalin
(1879–1953) was taken by surprise when Germany invaded. Hitler's troops came very close to Moscow, but were pushed back by cold, hunger, and the bravery of Soviet troops: millions of them died on the eastern front.

Winston Churchill
(1874–1965), a veteran of World War I, had warned against the rise of Hitler and Nazism during the 1930s. Britain turned to him for leadership in the war, and his many rousing speeches on the radio inspired the Allies to victory.

Franklin D. Roosevelt
(1882–1945), US President, urged America into the war despite its initial reluctance. He supported the Allies with large amounts of arms and food. He died just before the Allied victory.

KEY INNOVATIONS
RADAR
Britain developed the first radar powerful enough to detect approaching enemy aircraft. It gave Britain a huge advantage in the air.

NYLON
In 1942, nylon was first produced in the USA. It was first used for hosiery and parachutes.

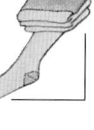

Russian soldier   *British soldier*   *American soldier*

WORLD WAR II IN ASIA AND THE PACIFIC
In December 1941, Japan made a surprise attack on the USA Navy at Pearl Harbor, Hawaii, sinking or damaging 18 ships, and destroying 200 aircraft. The USA immediately declared war, but within six months Japan had conquered the USA, British, and Dutch colonies in the Indian and Pacific Oceans. Japan could not, however, defend such a vast empire and by 1943 the USA had begun a series of bitterly fought, island-hopping, victories.

Maximum extent of Japanese occupation, August 1942

US, British, Commonwealth advances (1943–5)

Soviet advances (1943–5)

Nagasaki · Tokyo
Hiroshima
· Hong Kong
· Singapore

WORLD WAR II LIFESTYLE FACTS
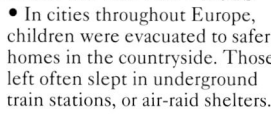
• In cities throughout Europe, children were evacuated to safer homes in the countryside. Those left often slept in underground train stations, or air-raid shelters.

• At night, the smallest amount of light was visible from the air, so cities introduced blackouts to make it hard for enemy pilots to find targets. Curtains had to be closed and the use of car headlights minimized.

• Some foods, such as meat, eggs, and sweets, were scarce during the war, so families had "ration books" showing their weekly allowance.

• The army floated huge balloons over London. Enemy planes had to avoid the steel cables that tied them to the ground, and so could not get close to their targets.

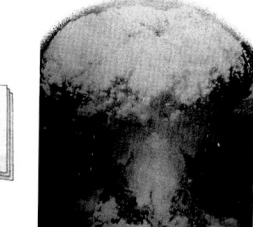

THE ATOMIC BOMB
On 6 August 1945, US President Harry Truman ordered an atomic bomb to be dropped on Hiroshima, Japan. It instantly killed about 80,000 people. A second was dropped on Nagasaki three days later and led to Japan's surrender. The war was over, but people were still dying from radiation sickness decades later.

Mushroom cloud following bombing of Nagasaki

KEY BATTLES

Battle	Date	Victor
Crossing of the Meuse	1940	Germany pierces French "Maginot Line" defences
Battle of Britain	1941	Britain's air defence prevents German seaborne invasion
Midway	1942	US cripples Japanese Navy
El Alamein	1942	British push back Rommel
Normandy (D-Day)	1944	Largest seaborne attack ever: Allies force German retreat

THE HUMAN COST OF WORLD WAR II
Estimates of total deaths in World War II vary between 40 and 60 million, because the mass dispersal of armies and huge migrations at the war's end made it impossible to compile statistics. More civilians died than soldiers, largely from famine, disease, air raids, and executions by occupying forces. Poland lost 20% of its pre-war population.

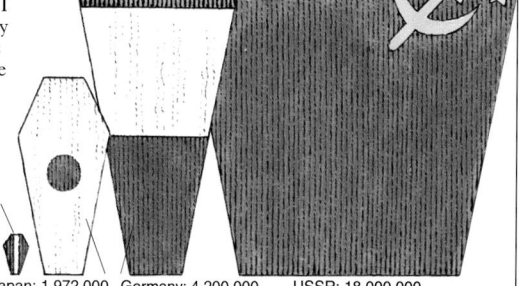

Italy: 395,000
Britain: 357,000
USA: 298,000
Japan: 1,972,000   Germany: 4,200,000   USSR: 18,000,000

1946			
AFRICA		**1948** National Party under leadership of D.F. Malan came into power in South Africa	**1950** Group Areas Act, South Africa orders segregation of races (apartheid) **1951** Libyan independence from Italy sanctioned by UN
ASIA	**1947** India wins independence from Great Britain amid riots that kill half a million	**1948** Gandhi assassinated in India; Nehru takes over. State of Israel created **1949** Mao Tse-tung proclaims new Communist Republic of China. Vietnam, with aid from China, fights French rule	**1950** China occupies Tibet. Korean War begins between North Korea (supported by China) and South Korea (supported by UN); ends 1953
EUROPE	**$** **1947** Marshall Plan offers US aid to European countries to help rebuild their economies after World War II	**1948** Berlin Airlift overcomes USSR's blockade of West Berlin. Communist coup in Czechoslovakia	**1949** Germany split into East and West. NATO formed **1952** Greece and Turkey join NATO
AMERICAS		**1948** Harry Truman (1884–1972) wins US Presidential election	**1950** US Senator Joseph McCarthy begins anti-Communist "witch-hunts"
OCEANIA	**1947** South Pacific Commission formed to discuss economic and health issues of South Pacific islands		**1951** Australia, New Zealand, and USA sign ANZUS Pact defence alliance

THE COLD WAR

After World War II, Europe was split by an "iron curtain" dividing USSR-backed East from US-backed West. This rivalry was known as the Cold War, with each side distrusting the other and expecting an attack at any time. The USA and the USSR began stockpiling nuclear weapons, and the arms race was born. In 1945, there were only three nuclear weapons in the world; in 1962, there were 2,000. Later, each side had enough to destroy the world many times over.

THE TWO GERMANIES

Germany was carved up by its conquerors at the end of World War II. The USA, France, and Great Britain controlled the West and the USSR controlled the East. The old capital, Berlin, was in East Germany, but was also divided between the two sides, by a wall erected in August 1961.

The Berlin Wall

NATO FACTS

• The North Atlantic Treaty Organization, NATO, was founded in 1949 by the Western countries to protect themselves against attack from the USSR and its allies.

• The USA provided over $25 billion of military aid in NATO's first 20 years, a third of its total funds.

• By 1959, the USA had more than 1,400 military bases, including 275 bases for nuclear bombers, in 31 countries around the world.

• The first hydrogen bomb, tested in 1952, was as powerful as the total of all bombs dropped on Germany and Japan during World War II, including the atomic bombs dropped on Hiroshima and Nagasaki.

• Between 1950 and 1954, Senator Joe McCarthy led a "witch-hunt" to identify Communist sympathizers in the USA. In some areas of society people were encouraged to betray friends and colleagues. Many were wrongly accused and lost their jobs; some were imprisoned.

USSR and aligned Communist countries

NATO countries and allies

THE WEST

In response to the growing threat of Communism in the East, the countries of Western Europe formed a military alliance with North America. The USA, via the Marshall Plan, funded these countries to help them rebuild their economies after World War II.

THE EAST

Immediately after World War II, Stalin closed the borders of Eastern Europe and placed the countries bordering Russia under the control of the USSR. Opponents of Communism were imprisoned and more than a million were killed.

WARSAW PACT FACTS

• The Warsaw Pact was founded in 1955. It allowed Soviet troops to be stationed in any Communist Eastern European country.

• Between 1949 and 1958, three million people escaped from East to West Berlin. In 1961, East Germany erected the Berlin Wall to close off access between the two sectors.

• The USSR's inter-continental ballistic missiles (ICBMs), first developed in 1957, had a range of 11,300km (7,000 miles).

HUNGARIAN UPRISING

In 1956, many Hungarians rebelled against Soviet domination and communist rule of their country, and Hungary tried to leave the Warsaw Pact. However, tanks and troops from the USSR quickly ended their revolt and killed the leaders.

Hungarian rebel

THE THIRD WAY

The USA and the USSR encouraged many countries to take sides in the Cold War. Some, like India, Egypt, and Yugoslavia chose the "Third Way" and stayed out of the conflict.

Nasser (Egypt), Nehru (India), and Tito (Yugoslavia)

AERIAL ASSISTANCE

In 1948, the USSR blockaded Berlin, forcing the West to deliver supplies by air. For five months, planes landed at Tempelhof airport, Berlin, every four minutes. There was only one accident.

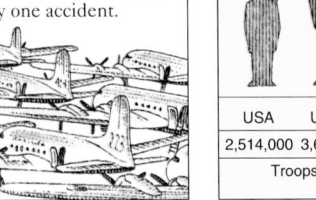

ARMS COMPARISON, 1960

 USA  USSR

USA	USSR	USA	USSR	USA	USSR	USA	USSR
2,514,000	3,623,000	450	190	18	35	32	—
Troops		Long-range missile bombers		Land-based missiles		Submarines	

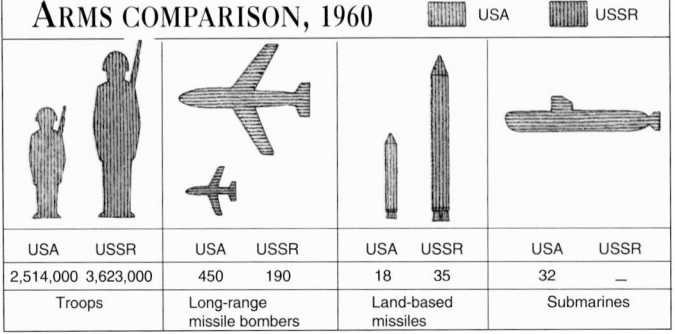

...tary coup in Egypt ends
and establishes a republic

1954 Algerian National Liberation
Front formed to fight French rule

...und Hillary and Sherpa Tenzing Norgay climb Everest
1954 French defeated at Dien Bien Phu,
north Vietnam. Vietnam divided into
communist North and US-backed South

1955 ANC pressure group in South
Africa adopts anti-racist Freedom Charter

1956 Suez Crisis: French and
British troops forced to withdraw

1956 Sinai Campaign: Israel
captures Sinai peninsula from
Arab forces in eight days

1958 Military revolt in Iraq removes King Faisal II; republic formed
1959 Tibetan uprising crushed
by Chinese; Dalai Lama flees

1955 Warsaw Pact defence treaty signed by
Communist nations. West Germany joins
NATO; East Germany joins Warsaw Pact

1957 European Common Market formed.
USSR launches Sputnik I, the world's first satellite

1956 Soviet troops put down anti-Communist uprising in Hungary

...k between smoking and
...r first established in USA

1954 US Supreme Court prohibits
racial separation in schools

1955 Military coup in Argentina overthrows
President Juan Perón (1895–1974)

1958 First atomic-powered submarine, USS *Nautilus*,
makes first undersea crossing of North Pole

1959 Revolution in Cuba; Communist guerrilla
Fidel Castro overthrows dictator Batista

1956 Olympics held in Melbourne, Australia.
British nuclear testing in Maralinga, Australia

1959 Antarctic Treaty
preserves area for research

THE MIDDLE EAST

During the 1930s and 1940s, many Jews fled from Hitler's persecution to their ancient homeland in British-controlled Palestine. They claimed the territory as their own and set up the state of Israel. In 1948, Britain gave control of the area to the United Nations, and decades of conflict between Arabs and Israelis began.

NASSER

Egyptian leader Gamal A. Nasser (1918–70) planned to unite the Arab countries against Israel. In 1956, he took over the important Suez Canal Company, owned by Britain and France, and became even more popular.

Arab woman during failed Anglo-French attempt to recapture Suez Canal

ALGERIAN WAR

Civil war broke out in Algeria in 1954, with Ahmed Ben Bella's National Liberation Front (FLN) seeking Algerian independence from France. A guerrilla war between the FLN and colonists ended in a French withdrawal in 1962.

French soldiers check Algerian identity papers

MIDDLE EAST MAP

The Middle East was governed by Great Britain and France between the two World Wars. In 1917, Britain had promised to create a Jewish homeland, and in 1948, Palestine was divided between Jordan and the new Jewish settlers. Israel was created in place of Palestine.

THE UNITED NATIONS

The United Nations (UN) was established in 1945, in the hope that international disputes could be solved without war and to foster friendly relations between nations. Its offices opened in New York.

UN peacekeeper

WELL OILED

Oil was first discovered in the Middle East in 1908, but major production did not begin until the 1940s. In 1945, 101,156 barrels of oil were produced. By 1959, the figure had risen to 1,055,986 barrels.

ARAB-ISRAELI CONFLICT

War of Independence, 1948

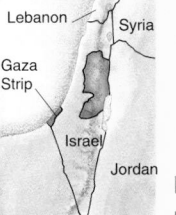

When Israel became independent in 1948, the surrounding Arab countries immediately invaded. After 15 months' fighting, Jordan controlled much of the West Bank of the River Jordan.

☐ Under Jordanian rule
☐ Under Egyptian rule

Sinai Campaign, 1956

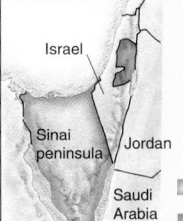

Owing to increased Arab trade blockades, Israel invaded the Sinai peninsula in October 1956 and captured the entire area in eight days. Following a UN peace-keeping mission, Israel withdrew.

☐ Area captured (1956) and returned (1957) by Israel
☐ Under Jordanian rule

THE DALAI LAMA

Tibet's spiritual leader, the Dalai Lama, was forced to flee the country with 100,000 followers in 1959 after an unsuccessful Tibetan revolt against Chinese occupation. He has lived in exile ever since, travelling the world and gaining support for the Tibetan cause. He won the Nobel Peace Prize in 1989 for this work.

KEY PEOPLE

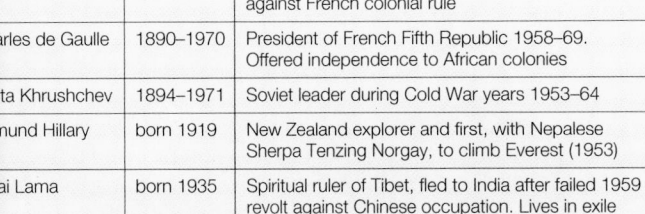

...me	Dates	Biographical details
...Chi Minh	1890–1969	Leader of North Vietnam, 1945–69. Led fight against French colonial rule
...arles de Gaulle	1890–1970	President of French Fifth Republic 1958–69. Offered independence to African colonies
...ita Khrushchev	1894–1971	Soviet leader during Cold War years 1953–64
...mund Hillary	born 1919	New Zealand explorer and first, with Nepalese Sherpa Tenzing Norgay, to climb Everest (1953)
...ai Lama	born 1935	Spiritual ruler of Tibet, fled to India after failed 1959 revolt against Chinese occupation. Lives in exile

KEY INNOVATIONS

HEART PACEMAKER

In 1951, the first heart pacemaker was invented. It used electric shocks to stabilize the heartbeat.

Heart pacemaker

NON-STICK FRYING PAN

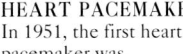

The first non-stick frying pan, lined with a low-friction plastic, appeared in 1956.

SATELLITE

In 1957, the USSR launched Sputnik 1, the world's first space satellite. It stayed in orbit until early 1958, when it burned up in Earth's atmosphere.

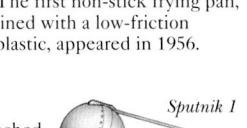

Sputnik 1

1960

AFRICA **1960** 17 African colonies gain independence. Peaceful demonstration at Sharpeville against white rule in South Africa; 69 protestors killed and ANC banned

1961 Patrice Lumumba, first Prime Minister of Congo, assassinated

1962 UN imposes sanctions on South Africa in protest at apartheid

1964 ANC leader Nelson Mandela jailed in South Africa

1965 White-ruled Rhodesia declares independence from Britain

ASIA **1963** Diem, leader of South Vietnam, assassinated in military coup

1964–65 War between Indonesia and Malaysia

1965 USA starts bombing North Vietnam

1966 Cultural Rev begins in China; R Guard formed

EUROPE **1961** Berlin Wall built. Russian cosmonaut Yuri Gagarin is first man in space

1963 Russian Valentina Tereshkova is first woman in space

1964 Fighting between Greeks and Turks in Cyprus

AMERICAS **1961** John F. Kennedy (1917–63) becomes youngest elected US President

1962 Cuban Missile Crisis

1963 President Kennedy assassinated

1965 Civil rights leader Malcolm X assassinated. Riots in Chicago and Los Angeles

OCEANIA **1965** Ferdinand E. Marcos (1917–89) elected President of the Philippines

AFRICAN INDEPENDENCE

Weakened by World War II, France and Britain found it hard to maintain their overseas colonies. During the 1950s and 1960s, many African countries gained independence. These new states faced great financial problems and were dependent on aid donated by richer countries. Many also suffered civil wars as military leaders seized control.

NELSON MANDELA
The African National Congress (ANC), a black political party, was banned in South Africa in 1960. In 1964, its leader, Nelson Mandela, was imprisoned for life. In 1990 he was released and in 1994 he became president of South Africa.

Ian Smith

RHODESIA
In 1965, the white government of Rhodesia, led by Ian Smith, declared independence from Britain. After a long guerrilla war, the black majority finally won power in 1980, and Rhodesia was renamed Zimbabwe.

TRUNK ROAD
In 1971, an East German woman wa smuggled from East to West by her French fiancé. She spent a 70-minu train journey hidden inside two adjacent suitcases. Her fiancé had removed two of the side panels befo the train's inspectors arrived.

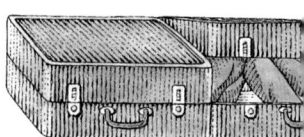

AFRICAN INDEPENDENCE TABLE

	Country	Independence	Biographical details
	Ghana	1957, from Great Britain	First leader, Kwame Nkrumah (1909–72), became one of Africa's most powerful politicians, but corruption led to his defeat in 1966
	Congo	1960, from France	First president Fulbert Youlou was forced to resign in 1963. Congo then had a Marxist government until elections were held in 1992.
	Senegal	1960, from France	Able leader and distinguished poet, Léopold Senghor (b.1906), ruled for two decades following independence
	Nigeria	1960, from Great Britain	Military coups have left the army in control of the country for 25 of the 34 years since independence
	Mauritania	1960, from France	Mokhtar Ould Daddah (b.1924), first Mauritanian lawyer, led the country from independence until the military overthrew him in 1978
	Uganda	1962, from Great Britain	Following independence, the government changed seven times, four of them resulting in violence, and there were two civil wars
	Kenya	1963, from Great Britain	Jomo Kenyatta (c.1894–1978), who had fought against British rule in the 1950s, became the country's first leader
	Mozambique	1975, from Portugal	Independence leader, Samora Machel (1933–86), set out to provide education and health care for all, despite his country's debts
	Angola	1975, from Portugal	Independence led to a civil war that has continued for more than 20 years

KEY INNOVATIONS

LASER
In 1960, American physicist T.H. Maiman made the first laser, using a synthetic ruby crystal. Laser are used in industry and medicine.

CONCORDE
In 1969, the first supersonic airliner, *Concorde*, crossed the Atlantic in thre hours, flying at 1,600km/h (1,000mp

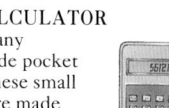

POCKET CALCULATOR
From 1972, many companies made pocket calculators. These small computers were made possible by the production of tiny electronic circuits, called silicon chips.

KEY PEOPLE

Name	Dates	Biographical details
Antonio Salazar	1889–1970	Dictator of Portugal, 1932–68. Kept Portugal's African colonies while other countries decolonized
Kwame Nkrumah	1909–72	Independence leader and first President of Ghana
Richard Nixon	1913–94	US President 1969–74. Began bombing of Cambodia. Resigned over Watergate scandal
Yuri Gagarin	1934–68	Russian cosmonaut. First man in space, aboard spacecraft Vostok 1. Orbited Earth in 89 minutes
The Beatles	1960s	British pop group; most influential of the period. Hits include *She Loves You* and *Let It Be*

CASTRO AND CUBA
In 1962, the Cuban dictator Fidel Castro (born 1926) allowed the USSR to build missile bases in Cuba, which threatened the USA. President Kennedy ordered the USA Navy to blockade Cuba and the Russians agreed to withdraw.

Fidel Castro

MOON LANDING
In July 1969, 600 million television viewers saw US astronaut Neil Armstrong become the first person to set foot on the moon. He and two other astronauts arrived there after a four-day journey aboard the spacecraft Apollo 11.

Neil Armstrong

War in Nigeria. Biafra region ...ay from Nigerian Federation. ...ian Barnard completes first ...splant in South Africa

1970 Biafra defeated by Federal Nigerian Government in a civil war

1975 Portugal grants independence to its African colonies

Day War between Israelis and Arabs
1968 US troops kill hundreds of unarmed civilians in Vietnamese village of My Lai

1971 Indian troops defeat West Pakistan in Kashmir. Newly independent East Pakistan becomes Bangladesh
1970 USA bombs Cambodia

1973 October War: Arab states attack Israel. Arab states restrict oil supplies and start world economic crisis
1972 Ceylon becomes republic, as Sri Lanka

tary coup in Greece
1968 Riots in Paris by students and workers. Anti-communist uprising in Prague

1969 Britain sends troops to Northern Ireland
1971 Women granted the right to vote in Switzerland

1973 Britain, Ireland and Denmark join the Common Market

1975 Spanish dictator Franco dies; Juan Carlos becomes king

1968 Civil rights leader Martin Luther King, Jr. assassinated in Memphis
1969 American Neil Armstrong the first person on the moon

1973 Military coup in Chile removes Marxist President Salvador Allende
1974 US President Richard Nixon resigns over Watergate scandal

w Zealand vote extended to 20- Aboriginals become Australian nd gain full voting rights

1973 Sydney Opera House opens

1975 Papua New Guinea becomes independent

SOCIAL REVOLUTION

During the 1960s and 1970s, people all over the world began to demand greater rights. Some protested against sexual and racial discrimination, and against war. Others used the new freedom to express themselves through music, cinema, and literature. During this period people questioned many old traditions and chose different lifestyles.

MUSIC

Popular music became a way of criticizing war. In 1969, 400,000 people attended a concert near Woodstock, New York, to hear singers such as Joan Baez and Jimi Hendrix. Meanwhile, the Beatles and the Rolling Stones (left) were selling millions of records a year.

CIVIL RIGHTS

Following independence movements in Africa, many black Americans sought more rights. Leaders, such as Martin Luther King, Jr. and Malcolm X, staged protests demanding equality.

CIVIL RIGHTS FACTS

- Until the Civil Rights Act (1964), shops, cinemas, and libraries could be divided into separate areas for blacks and whites.

- In August 1965, civil unrest led to five days of rioting on the streets of Los Angeles. 35 people were killed, $175 million of damage was caused, and 14,000 National Guardsmen were called in to control rioters and looters.

HIPPIES

Hippies felt that the West was dominated by big business, so they "dropped out" of society. Some lived in communes and grew their own food. They were also associated with the use of narcotics (drugs).

VIETNAM WAR

In 1965, the USA, with Australia and New Zealand, sent troops to help South Vietnam fight the communist North. By 1973, terrible casualties led all allied troops to withdraw and Vietnam became a communist country.

CIVILIAN SUFFERING

Intensive bombing left hundreds of thousands of civilians dead or injured and countless others as homeless refugees.

WOMEN'S MOVEMENT

Women all over the world began to demand equality with men and more recognition. The contraceptive pill and legalized abortion gave many women much greater freedom.

ANTI-GOVERNMENT PROTESTS

Protests against governments broke out in countries on both sides in the Cold War. In 1968, students rioted in Paris and took over the universities. In the same year, Soviet troops invaded Prague to crush the reforms of Czech leader Alexander Dubcek, which they feared would weaken the Warsaw Pact. In the USA, huge demonstrations against involvement in the Vietnam War took place across the country.

VIETNAM WAR FACTS

- Money: the USA spent $150 billion on the war.

- Deaths: two million Vietnamese and 58,000 allied soldiers and nurses died in Vietnam.

- Trees: chemicals such as Agent Orange destroyed large parts of Vietnam's jungle; much is still deforested today.

EY ASSASSINATIONS

ohn F. Kennedy
917–63) became the ...ungest elected US President in 1961. He was shot in a motorcade in Dallas, Texas. Controversy surrounds his death.

Malcolm X (1925–65) was a militant Muslim black rights leader. After hostility with a rival Muslim group, he was shot at a rally in Harlem, New York.

Martin Luther King, Jr. (1929–68), a black Baptist minister, was a brilliant speaker for the Civil Rights Movement. He was shot in Memphis, Tennessee.

Robert Kennedy (1925–68), US Attorney General, Senator, and John Kennedy's brother, was shot while campaigning for the US Presidential nomination.

THE CULTURAL REVOLUTION IN CHINA

In China, Mao Tse-tung began his own social revolution. From 1966 to 1977, he brought industry and agriculture under state control. He closed schools and colleges and forced teachers and students to work on the land. Any opposition was brutally put down by the Red Guards, or Communist Party police.

Children recite phrases from the Red Book during the Cultural Revolution.

	1976			
AFRICA	**1976** Riots in black townships across South Africa	**1979** Ugandan leader Idi Amin (born 1925) ousted by Tanzanian-backed rebels	**1980** Robert Mugabe (born 1924) becomes first leader of an independent Zimbabwe	**1983** Famine in Ethiopia
ASIA	**1976** North and South Vietnam reunited after 22 years of separation	**1978** UN intervenes in Lebanon. Vietnam invades Cambodia	**1979** Russian intervention in Afghanistan (until 1988). Camp David peace treaty between Egypt and Israel. Iranian Revolution. US hostage crisis (until 1981) **1980–88** Iran-Iraq War	**1984** Sikh extremists force Golden Temple at Amritsar in bloody siege. Prime Mini Indira Gandhi (born 1917) l assassinated by her Sikh bo
EUROPE		**1979** Margaret Thatcher (born 1925) becomes Britain's first woman prime minister SOLIDARNOŚĆ	**1980** President Tito (born 1892) of Yugoslavia dies. Lech Walesa leads Solidarity trade union **1981** 11 Irish republicans die on hunger strike	**1984** French and US scient independently identify AID
AMERICAS	**1977** Jimmy Carter (born 1924) becomes US President	**1979** Marxist (Communist) Sandinistas take power in Nicaragua	**1981** Ronald Reagan (born 1911) becomes US President	**1982** Falklands War: Argentine forces driven fro British-held islands after brief occupation. Canada creates constitution independent of UK passes Canada Act with Charter of Rights and F
OCEANIA		**1978** Solomon Islands, Tuvalu, and Dominica become independent nations		**1984** New Zealand declares itself a nuclear-free zone

THE MIDDLE EAST

During the 1970s and 1980s, violent conflict continued to break out in the Middle East. The main causes of war and unrest were religious differences and territorial disputes. Oil brought great wealth to the region.

Iranian supporters of the Ayatollah Khomeini

Oil fields in Libya

PLO members

OIL
In 1973, Arab states raised their oil prices, causing economic disaster in many countries that depended on their oil. In 1990, Saddam Hussein, the Iraqi leader, invaded oil-rich Kuwait. He was expelled by a United Nations coalition force.

IRANIAN REVOLUTION
In 1979, a revolution overthrew the Shah (King) of Iran and brought the Ayatollah Khomeini to power. The Ayatollah, a fundamentalist (strict) Muslim, was hostile to the West. When the Shah entered the USA, Iranian students stormed the US embassy in Tehran and held 53 Americans hostage for more than a year.

PLO AND ISRAEL
The Palestine Liberation Organization (PLO) represents Palestinians living in exile or under Israeli rule. It was responsible for bombings, hijackings, and attacks on Israelis. In 1993, the PLO and Israel agreed to make peace. A year later, PLO leader Yasir Arafat returned from exile in Tunis and Palestinians in the Gaza Strip became self-governing.

KEY MIDDLE-EAST LEADERS

Anwar Sadat (1918–81), president of Egypt from 1970, unsuccessfully invaded Israeli-held territory in 1973. He signed first major Arab peace treaty with Israel and was assassinated by Muslim fundamentalists.

Saddam Hussein (born 1937), president of Iraq since coup in 1968, put down opposition using secret police, warred with Iran (1980–88), and unsuccessfully invaded Kuwait in 1990.

Muammar Gaddafi (born 1942), leader of Libya since coup in 1969, made Libya strictly Muslim, nationalized the oil industry, promoted Arab unity, and funded terrorist groups worldwide.

Ayatollah Khomeini (1900–89), political and religious leader of Iran after revolution of 1979, declared Iran a strictly Islamic republic.

Yasir Arafat (born 1929), leader of Palestinians-in-exile and chairman of PLO from 1968, eventually secured Palestinian independence from Israel in the Gaza Strip in 1993.

KEY CONFLICTS OF THE MIDDLE EAST

Region/conflict	Year	Details
Mecca, Saudi Arabia	1979	Muslim extremists seize Grand Mosque. Saudis recapture it after bloody battle
Iran–Iraq War	1980–88	War begins when Iraqi forces attack the world's largest oil refinery at Abadan, Iran. Iraq gains minimal territory. More than a million lives are lost
Lebanon	1982	Israel invades Lebanon, destroys PLO power base, and forces PLO to evacuate
West Bank, Gaza Strip (see p.340)	1987–8	Intifada (Palestinian uprising) leads to rioting and unrest in Israeli-held territories. Severely suppressed by Israeli military: 300 killed, thousands wounded
Gulf War	1990–91	Iraq invades oil-rich Kuwait. US-led UN forces expel Sadam Hussein's troops

KEY INNOVATIONS

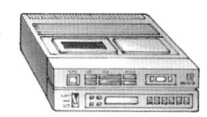

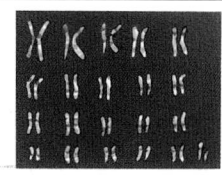

TEST-TUBE BABY
In 1978, the first human conceived outside the mother's body – an English girl called Louise Brown – was born.

VIDEO RECORDER
In 1975, the first home videotape system – the *Betamax* system – was launched by the Japanese company, Sony.

PERSONAL COMPUTER
In 1981, the American company IBM produced the first desktop computer, the IBM-PC.

GENOME PROJECT
Since 1991, scientists have been trying to map all the genetic material in human chromosomes – the human genome.

RISE OF ASIAN ECONOMIES
Since the 1960s, the economies of many East Asian countries have expanded and prospered. With stabl governments, advanced factories, and plentiful, cheap labour, living standards have risen dramatically in Japan, Hong Kong, Singapore, South Korea, and Taiwan. From 1997, economic turmoil has made this process falter.

Japanese executives at a business training camp

1990 Namibia gains independence. Three-year civil war begins in Liberia

1991 Government rule in Somalia collapses

1992 UN troops led by USA enter Somalia

1993 Eritrea gains independence from Ethiopia

1994 ANC wins South Africa's first free elections. Civil war in Rwanda

...ident Marcos (1917–89) ...hilippines. Corazon Aquino ...) becomes president

1987 Palestinian *Intifada* (uprising) erupts

1989 Chinese security forces kill pro-democracy protestors in Beijing's Tiananmen Square. Martial law imposed in Lhasa, Tibet, after anti-Chinese protests

1990 Iraq invades Kuwait

1991 Gulf War. Iraq driven from Kuwait. Indonesian forces kill pro-independence protestors in Dili, East Timor

1992 Muslim-Hindu riots spread across India

1994 PLO gains autonomy in Gaza Strip

1995 Israel's Prime Minister, Yitzhak Rabin, is assassinated

1989 Communist governments overthrown in Romania, Hungary, East Germany, and Czechoslovakia

1991 Break-up of Soviet Union

1992 Civil war begins in former Yugoslavia

1996 A peace agreement is signed in Northern Ireland

...ngate" scandal: US ...Reagan admits to ...s deals with Iran

1989 USA invades Panama. George Bush (born 1924) becomes US President

1993 Bill Clinton (born 1946) becomes US President

1997 Bill Clinton starts second term of office

1999 Inuit people are given control of Nunavut, a huge territory in Northern Canada

1991 Paul Keating (born 1944) becomes Prime Minister of Australia

1996 John Howard becomes Prime Minister of Australia

THE COLD WAR ENDS

Communist leader Mikhail Gorbachev launched a new era of freedom in the USSR. The failure of his economic plans made him and his party unpopular, and in 1991 democrat Boris Yeltsin gained power in the country's first free elections.

GLASNOST AND PERESTROIKA

When Mikhail Gorbachev came to power he pressed for economic reforms. His policy of *glasnost* (openness) revealed how weak the Soviet Union had become, but his *perestroika* (remodelling) policy failed to solve his country's problems.

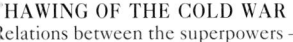

Queues for food in Soviet Russia

THAWING OF THE COLD WAR

Relations between the superpowers – the USA and USSR – improved greatly after Gorbachev came to power. In 1987, Gorbachev and US President Ronald Reagan agreed to reduce the number of nuclear weapons in their countries.

Gorbachev and Reagan meet.

Anti-communists remove statue of Felix Dzerzhinsky, founder of USSR's secret service.

AUGUST COUP

In August 1991, a powerful group of Communists who wished to halt the progress of reform took Gorbachev prisoner and, with the support of the army, seized power. The radical reformer Boris Yeltsin and the people of Moscow gathered in defiance around the Russian Parliament building, and the coup soon failed. A few days later, Yeltsin and Gorbachev banned the Communist party. Communist rule in the Soviet Union was over.

SOVIET SPLIT

The USSR was home to more than 140 different national groups. When Communism weakened, many of these called for, and were given, self-rule. On 21 December 1991, the Soviet Union ceased to exist.

THE FALL OF COMMUNISM

Glasnost encouraged open demands for independence from republics and allies of the USSR. When economic hardship caused unrest in some of these states, Gorbachev was unwilling to intervene using force. In December 1989, the Berlin Wall came down. Within two years, people in the USSR's allied states had toppled their Communist leaders.

Yeltsin outside Russian Parliament during 1991 coup.

GLOBAL AWARENESS

Today, aided by campaigning environmental groups, people have become more aware of the terrible damage inflicted on the Earth by industrial pollution, overuse of natural resources, overpopulation, and widespread deforestation.

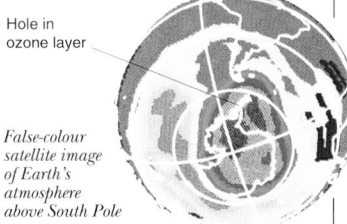

Hole in ozone layer

False-colour satellite image of Earth's atmosphere above South Pole

ENVIRONMENTAL FACTS

• In 1987, 33 countries agreed to phase out the use of CFCs, the industrial gases responsible for damage to the ozone layer.

• In 1984, the leakage of poisonous gas from an American-owned pesticide company caused the death of more than 2,500 people in Bhopal, India.

• In 1986, the world's worst nuclear accident occurred at Chernobyl, Ukraine. Clouds of radiation spread over Europe and beyond.

• In 1992, the Earth Summit in Rio de Janeiro, Brazil, brought together representatives from more than 170 countries to discuss global environmental issues.

...RICAN FAMINE

...the 1970s and 1980s, famine and ...r hit Africa. Ethiopia, the Sudan, ...gola, and people living along the ...uthern Sahara suffered most, and ...llions died. Western aid has helped, but has not cured, these countries' problems.

Live Aid benefit concert for African famine

KEY PEOPLE

Name	Dates	Biographical details
Nelson Mandela	born 1918	Leader of ANC, jailed for 26 years, elected president in South Africa's first free elections (1994)
Margaret Thatcher	born 1925	Britain's first woman prime minister, developed a rigid (strict) style of politics called Thatcherism
Mikhail Gorbachev	born 1931	Reformist Soviet leader, initiated nuclear disarmament and presided over end of Cold War
Boris Yeltsin	born 1931	First elected president of Russian Federation
Lech Walesa	born 1943	Polish trade union leader, led anti-communist Solidarity movement. President 1990–1995

WAR IN FORMER YUGOSLAVIA

From 1991 Yugoslavia started disintegrating: national and religious divisions led to bloody fighting. In 1995 Bosnia settled down to an uneasy peace, but in 1999 war broke out between NATO countries and Serbia.

Woman in Sarajevo mourns child, shot by sniper.

GREAT CIVILIZATIONS

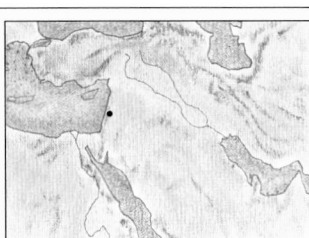

7000–1580 B.C.
Jericho
Region Jordan
Major cities Jericho
Features of civilization First true urban settlement; fortifications (including ramps); plastered skulls

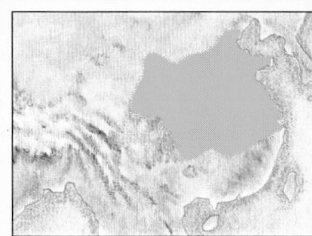

1600–1027 B.C.
Shang China
Region China
Major cities Zhengzhou, Anyang
Features of civilization Ideographic script; development of bronze casting; bone oracles

c.3400 B.C.
Sumerian
Region Lower Mesopotamia
Major cities Ur, Eridu, Lagash, Uruk
Features of civilization Early cities; advances in architecture (ziggurats), and sculpture; invention of writing (cuneiform); legal codes; money economy; division of labour

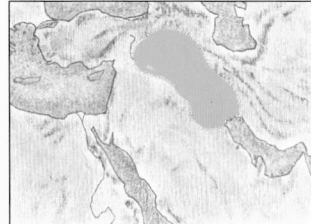

c.1500–1300 B.C.
Mycenean
Region Mainland southern Greece, Crete
Major cities Mycenae, Tiryns, Pylos
Features of civilization Architecture (fortified cities, megaron houses, and tholos tombs); ivory-, gold-, and bronzework; linear B script

3050–322 B.C.
Egyptian
Region Nile Valley
Major cities Saqqara, Giza, Luxor, Thebes
Features of civilization Stone building; hieroglyphic writing (also demotic and hieratic writing); funerary art; sailing boats; agriculture

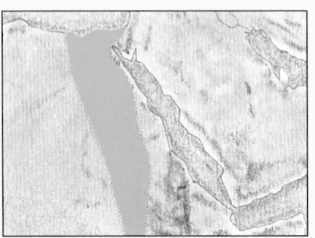

1027–256 B.C.
Chou China
Region China (for some time divided into eastern and western sections)
Major cities Loyang
Features of civilization Jadework and cast ironworking; composite bow; Confucianism, Taoism

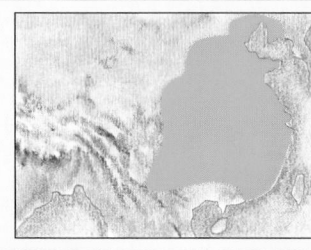

c.2500–1400 B.C.
Minoan
Region Crete
Major cities Knossos, Mallia, Phaistos
Features of civilization Palace architecture and interior decoration; linear scripts; decorated pottery; bronze- and goldwork

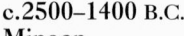 

c.1000–574 B.C.
Phoenician
Region Coastal plane of Lebanon and Syria; then trading posts or colonies around Mediterranean
Major cities Tyre, Sidon, Byblos, Carthage
Features of civilization Ships and trading; purple dye from murex shells; alphabet

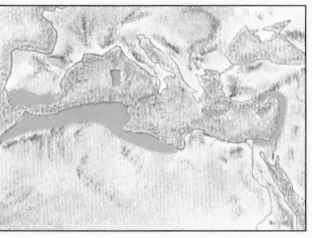

c.2600–2000 B.C.
Indus
Region Indus Valley, Pakistan
Major cities Mohenjo-Daro, Harappa
Features of civilization Town planning (grid plans and drains, granaries); seal stones with indecipherable script; copper-bronze technology; standardized weights and measures

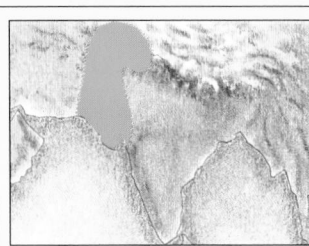

1000–600 B.C.
Olmec
Region Mexico
Major cities San Lorenzo, Tenochtitlán
Features of civilization Stone carvings (masks); jade carvings

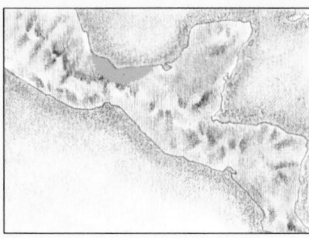

c.1750–1200 B.C.
Hittite
Region Anatolia (Turkey), and outposts in northern Syria
Major cities Boghazköy
Features of civilization Fortifications; iron smelting; use of chariot in warfare

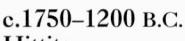 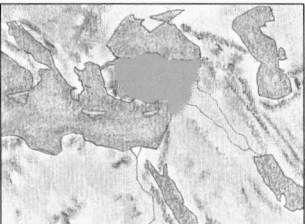

c.1000–200 B.C.
Chavin
Region Peru, Andes
Major cities Chavin de Huantár
Features of civilization Pottery; metalwork; sculpture (human and jaguar heads)

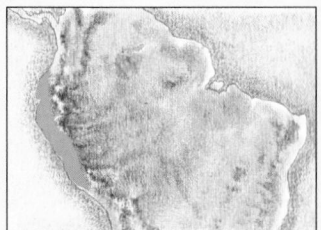

c.1792–c.1595 B.C.
Babylonian
Later Neo-Babylonian, 626–539 B.C.
Region Mesopotamia
Major cities Babylon
Features of civilization Fortifications (Ishtar Gate and great fortified city walls); astronomy and mathematics; law-making; famous for "Hanging Gardens"

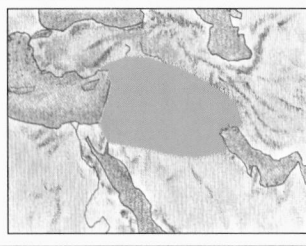

c.900–100 B.C.
Etruscan
Region Northern Italy
Major cities Populonia, Tarquinia, Caere (modern Tuscany)
Features of civilization Bronzeworking; sculpture

  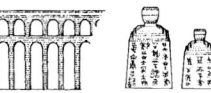  

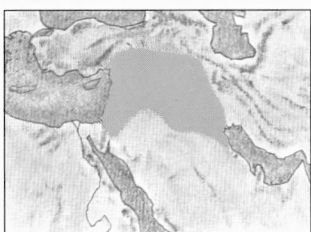

883–612 B.C. (at height)
Assyrian
Region Mesopotamia, Iran, Turkey, Syria
Major cities Assur, Nineveh, Nimrud, Khorsabad
Features of civilization Palace and temple complexes; sculpture, especially carved reliefs; military conquests

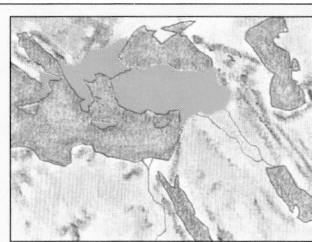

A.D. 330–1453
Byzantine
Region Eastern Roman Empire
Major cities Constantinople
Features of civilization Mosaic art and wall paintings; jewellery and metalwork; fortifications; legal codes; philosophy; history; literature

750 B.C.–A.D. 350
Meroë
Region Sudan (Nubia)
Major cities Meroë
Features of civilization Ironworking; trade in gold, ivory, and raw materials; temple architecture

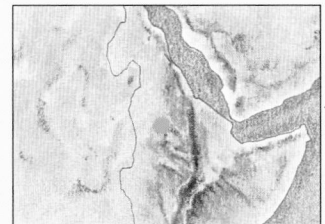

A.D. 600–794
Nara
Region Japan
Major cities Nara
Features of civilization Buddhist culture including pagoda-type temples

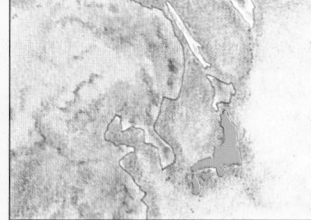

c.800–300 B.C.
Classical Greek
Region Greece, Aegean Sea
Major cities Athens, Sparta, Delphi
Features of civilization Classical architecture; flourishing of literature (drama, poetry, philosophy, history); pottery (vase painting), and sculpture; politics (democracy)

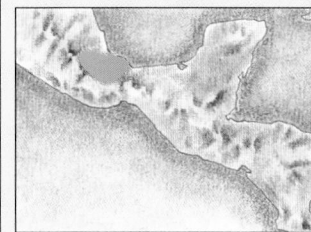

A.D. 900–1168
Toltec
Region Central Mexico
Major cities Tula, Chichen Itza
Features of civilization Continuation of Maya culture; use of metals

509 B.C.–A.D. 410
Roman
Region Mediterranean, Middle East, Italy, Spain, France, Britain
Major cities Rome
Features of civilization Building and civil engineering using vaults, arches, concrete (temples, walls, roads, aqueducts, ampitheatres); military organization and technology

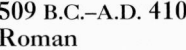

A.D. c. 900–1400
Khmer
Region Cambodia
Major cities Angkor
Features of civilization Temple architecture; relief sculpture; agricultural irrigation programme

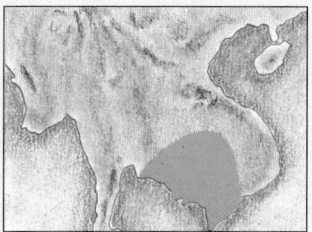

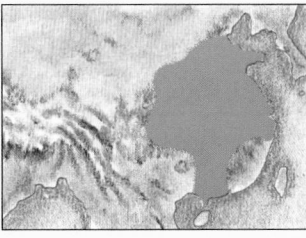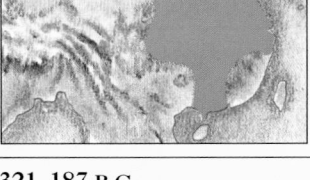

221–206 B.C.
Ch'in China
Region China
Major cities Hsienyang, Loyang, Chiuyuan, Lingling
Features of civilization Great Wall; imperial tombs; standardization of script, weights and measures, and currency; unification of China

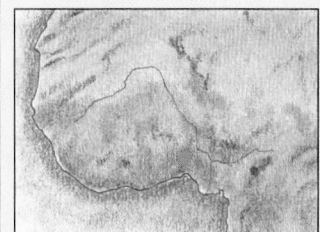

A.D. 1100–1350
Ife
Region Southwest Nigeria
Major cities Ife
Features of civilization Sculpture (human heads) in terracotta, or cast in copper or brass

321–187 B.C.
Mauryan
Region India
Major cities Pataliputra (Patoa), Sanchi
Features of civilization Adoption of Buddhism, stupas; road network; unification of India

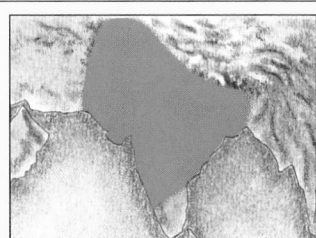

A.D. 1200–1572
Inca
Region Peru
Major cities Cuzco, Machu Picchu
Features of civilization Stone building: roads, palaces, fortifications, and temples; quipus (form of writing using knots); textiles

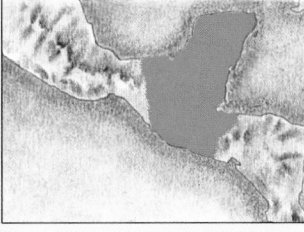

A.D. 300–900
Maya (Classic)
Region Mexico, Guatemala
Major cities Tikal, Copan, Chichen Itza
Features of civilization Pictorial writing; astronomy, mathematics, and calendar system; stone temples on stepped pyramids; decorative art

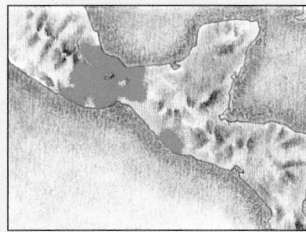

A.D. 1345–1521
Aztec
Region Mexico
Major cities Tenochtitlán
Features of civilization Jewellery and featherwork; codex-form books; military organization; religious architecture

RULERS AND LEADERS

EGYPTIAN PERIODS AND DYNASTIES

Period	Dynasty	Dates	Main pharaohs
Early dynastic	1-2	c.3100–c.2686 B.C.	Narmer (Menes)
Old Kingdom	3-6	c.2686–c.2160 B.C.	Zoser
			Khufu
First Intermediate Period	7-10	c.2160–c.2130 B.C.	
Middle Kingdom	11-12	c.2130–c.1786 B.C.	Mentuhotep II
Second Intermediate Period	13-17	c.1786–c.1550 B.C.	Hyksos rule
New Kingdom	18-20	c.1550–c.1050 B.C.	Amenhotep I
			Queen Hatshepsut
			Thutmose III
			Akhenaton
			Tutankhamun
			Rameses II
Third Intermediate Period	21-25	c.1085–667 B.C.	Nubian rule
Late Period	26-31	c.664–333 B.C.	Darius III
Foreign rulers		333–30 B.C.	Alexander the Great
			Ptolemy I Soter
			Queen Cleopatra VII

(Note: Hatshepsut and Cleopatra strictly queen regents)

ANCIENT EMPIRES FACTS

• Under the Roman Emperor Augustus, the Empire, arts, and literature flourished, and the era was called the Golden Age. Augustus came to be regarded as a god, and from then on all successful emperors were worshipped as gods after their deaths.

• The Roman Emperor Caligula was thought to have had his father, mother, and two elder brothers murdered in order to become emperor. Nero had his mother and his first wife murdered. Both Emperors were so hated that their reigns were erased from the official Roman records.

• China got its name in the 3rd century B.C. It comes from the ruling name of the first emperor, Ch'in Shih huang-ti (221–202 B.C.).

• When the daughter of the T'ang dynasty Emperor Yizong fell ill, twenty leading doctors were called to the capital to cure her. All failed, and all were beheaded.

• Egyptian Emperor Rameses II (c.1250–1213 B.C.) was a captain in the army and had his own harem by the time he was ten years old. By the end of his reign, at the age of 90, he had fathered 111 sons and 67 daughters.

KEY ROMAN RULERS

ROMAN REPUBLIC

Ruler	Reign
Lucius Cornelius Sulla	82–78 B.C.
Pompey, Crassus, Caesar (First Triumvirate)	60–53 B.C.
Pompey	52–47 B.C.
Julius Caesar	46–44 B.C.
Mark Antony, Octavian, Lepidus (Second Triumvirate)	43–31 B.C.

ROMAN EMPIRE

Emperor	Reign
Augustus (Octavian)	27 B.C.–A.D. 14
Tiberius	14–37
Caligula	37–41
Claudius	41–54
Nero	54–68
Vespasian	69–79
Titus	79–81
Domitian	81–96
Trajan	98–117
Hadrian	117–138
Antoninus Pius	138–161
Marcus Aurelius	161–180
Commodus	180–192
Septimius Severus	193–211
Alexander Severus	222–235
Valerian	253–259
Diocletian (in the east)	284–305
Maximian (in the west)	286–305
Constantine the Great	311–337
Valentinian I (west)	364–375
Valens (east)	364–378
Theodosius the Great (east; and, after 394, west)	379–395
Honorius (west)	395–423
Theodosius II (east)	408–450
Valentinian III (west)	425–455
Zeno (east)	474–491
Romulus Augustulus (west)	475–476

CHINESE DYNASTIES AND REPUBLICS

Dynasty	Dates	Main rulers
Hsia	c.2200–c.1600 B.C.	
Shang	c.1600–c.1027 B.C.	Wu-ting
Chou	c.1027–c.256 B.C.	Wen-wang
Qin (Ch'in)	221–206 B.C.	Ch'in Shih huang-ti
Early Han	206 B.C.–A.D. 9	Wu-ti
Hsin	A.D. 9–25	Wang Mang
Later Han	25–220	Kuang-wuti
Three Kingdoms	220–265	
Western Chin	265–317	Liu Yüan
Eastern Chin	317–420	
Southern	420–589	Wu-ti
Sui	581–618	Wen-ti
T'ang	618–690	T'ai-tsung
Chou	690–705	Wu-hou
T'ang	705–907	Hsüan-tsung
Northern Five, Southern Ten	907–960	
Song (Sung)	960–1279	T'ai-tsu
Yuan (Mongol)	1279–1368	Kublai Khan
Ming	1368–1644	Ch'eng Tsu
Qing (Manchu)	1644–1911	Ch'ien-lung
Republic (Nationalist)	1911–1949	Sun Yat-sen, Chiang Kai-shek
People's Republic (Communist)	1949–	Mao Tse-tung, Deng Xiaoping

Emperor Wu-ti

JAPANESE PERIODS

Periods	Dates
Yamato	250–710
Nara	710–794
Heian	794–1192
Kamakura	1192–1333
Muromachi	1333–1573
Momoyama	1573–1603
Edo	1603–1867
Meiji	1867–1912
Taisho	1912–1926
Showa	1926–1989
Heisei	1989–

• Few Japanese emperors have wielded true power. Aristocrats and, later, military dictatorship, or shogunates, ruled in the emperor's name. The last shoguns were the Tokugawa clan, a clan that held power throughout the Edo Period.

• The Japanese people saw their emperors as gods. After Japan's defeat in World War II, Emperor Hirohito (Showa) renounced his divinity.

KEY HOLY ROMAN EMPERORS

Emperor	Reign
Charlemagne	800–814
Otto I, the Great	936–973
Henry IV	1056–1106
Frederick I, Barbarossa	1152–90
Frederick II	1212–50
Rudolf I	1273–92
Adolf of Nassau	1292–98
Albrecht I, King of Germany	1298–1308
Albrecht II	1437–39
Frederick III	1440–93
Maximilian I	1493–1519
Charles V (Charles I of Spain)	1519–56
Ferdinand I	1556–64
Maximilian II	1564–76
Rudolf II	1576–1612
Matthias	1612–19
Ferdinand II	1619–37
Ferdinand III	1637–57
Leopold I	1658–1705
Joseph I	1705–11
Charles VI	1711–40
(War of Austrian Succession	1740–48)
Charles VII of Bavaria	1742–45
Francis I of Lorraine	1745–65
Joseph II	1765–90
Leopold II	1790–92
Francis II	1792–1806
(Last Holy Roman Emperor)	

• From 1437 to 1806, all the Holy Roman Emperors came from the Habsburg dynasty.

RUSSIAN RULERS

Tsars and Tsarinas	Reign
Ivan III, the Great	1462–1505
Basil III	1505–33
Ivan IV, the Terrible	1533–84
Fyodor I	1584–98
Boris Godunov	1598–1605
Fyodor II	1605
Demetrius	1605–06
Basil (IV) Shuiski	1606–10
Interregnum	1610–13
Michael Romanov	1613–45
Alexis	1645–76
Fyodor III	1676–82
Ivan V and	
Peter the Great	1682–89
Peter I	1689–1725
Catherine I	1725–27
Peter II	1727–30
Anna	1730–40
Ivan VI	1740–41
Elizabeth	1741–1762
Peter III	1762
Catherine II, the Great	1762–96
Paul I	1796–1801
Alexander I	1801–25
Nicholas I	1825–55
Alexander II	1855–81
Alexander III	1881–94
Nicholas II	1894–1917

KEY POPES

Pope	Reign
St. Peter	c.42–67
St. Clement I	c.88–97
St. Stephen I	254–257
St. Leo I, the Great	440–461
St. Gregory I, the Great	590–604
St. Leo IX	1049–54
St. Gregory VII	1073–85
Urban II	1088–99
Innocent III	1198–1216
Alexander VI	1492–1503
Paul III	1534–49
Gregory XIII	1572–85
Pius IX	1846–78
John XXIII	1958–63
John Paul II	1978–

POPE FACTS

• The pope is the chief bishop of the Roman Catholic Church. He is considered the successor to St. Peter, the first pope.

• New popes are elected by the College of Cardinals in the Vatican, Rome, at a secret meeting. The Cardinals may not leave the Vatican until a new pope has been chosen.

• There have been more than 30 antipopes, rivals to the officially elected popes.

• Pope John XXI served for 9 months, but was killed in 1277 when a ceiling collapsed on him.

• The shortest-serving pope was Urban VII, who reigned for just 12 days in 1590.

• The longest-serving pope, Pius IX, had 31 years in office and died at the age of 85.

FRENCH RULERS

Name	Reign	Name	Reign
Carolingians		Charles VII	1422–61
Louis IV	936–954	Louis XI	1461–83
Lothair	954–986	Charles VIII	1483–98
Louis V	986–987	Louis XII	1498–1515
Capets		Francis I	1515–47
Hugh Capet	987–996	Henry II	1547–59
Robert II, the Pious	996–1031	Francis II	1559–60
Henry I	1031–60	Charles IX	1560–74
Philip I	1060–1108	Henry III	1574–89
Louis VI	1108–37	**Bourbon**	
Louis VII	1137–80	Henry IV, of Navarre	1589–1610
Philip II	1180–1223	Louis XIII	1610–43
Louis VIII	1223–26	Louis XIV	1643–1715
Louis IX	1226–70	Louis XV	1715–74
Philip III	1270–85	Louis XVI	1774–93
Philip IV	1285–1314		
Louis X	1314–16	**First Republic and Empire**	
Philip V	1316–22	Napoleon Bonaparte	1799–1814
Charles IV	1322–28	(After 1804, as Emperor Napoleon I)	
Valois		**Restoration of monarchy**	
Philip VI	1328–50	Louis XVIII	1814–24
John II	1350–64	Charles X	1824–30
Charles V	1364–80	Louis Philippe	1830–48
Charles VI	1380–1422	**Second to Fifth Republics**	1848–

Francis I

SPANISH RULERS

Name	Reign	Name	Reign
Ferdinand II of Aragon	1479–1516	Ferdinand VII	1808
and Isabella I of Castille	1474–1504	(Joseph Bonaparte	1808–13)
Habsburgs		Ferdinand VII (2nd time)	1814–33
Charles I	1516–56	Isabella II	1833–68
Philip II	1556–98	Amadeus of Savoy	1870–73
Philip III	1598–1621	**First Republic**	1873–74
Philip IV	1621–65		
Charles II	1665–1700	**Bourbons (restored)**	
Bourbons		Alfonso XII	1874–85
Philip V (abdicated)	1700–24	Maria Cristina (Regent)	1885–86
Louis I	1724	Alfonso XIII	1886–1931
Philip V (restored)	1724–46	**Second Republic**	1931–39
Ferdinand VI	1746–59	Francisco Franco (Dictator)	1939–75
Charles III	1759–88	**Bourbons (restored)**	
Charles IV	1788–1808	Juan Carlos I	1975–

KINGS AND QUEENS OF GREAT BRITAIN

ENGLAND

Monarch	Reign
Saxons	
Egbert	827–839
Ethelwulf	839–858
Ethelbald	858–860
Ethelbert	860–865
Ethelred I	865–871
Alfred the Great	871–899
Edward the Elder	899–924
Athelstan	924–939
Edmund	939–946
Edred	946–955
Edwy	955–959
Edgar	959–975
Edward the Martyr	975–978
Ethelred II, the Unready	978–1016
Edmund Ironside	1016
Danes	
Canute	1016–35
Harold I Harefoot	1035–40
Hardicanute	1040–42
Saxons	
Edward the Confessor	1042–66
Harold II	1066
Normans	
William I, the Conqueror	1066–87
William II	1087–1100
Henry I	1100–35
Stephen	1135–54
Plantagenets	
Henry II	1154–89
Richard I	1189–99
John	1199–1216
Henry III	1216–72
Edward I	1272–1307
Edward II	1307–27
Edward III	1327–77
Richard II	1377–99
Lancaster	
Henry IV	1399–1413
Henry V	1413–22
Henry VI	1422–61

Alfred the Great

Monarch	Reign
York	
Edward IV	1461–83
Edward V	1483
Richard III	1483–85
Tudors	
Henry VII	1485–1509
Henry VIII	1509–47
Edward VI	1547–53
Mary I	1553–58
Elizabeth I	1558–1603

BRITAIN

Monarch	Reign
Stuarts	
James I, VI of Scotland	1603–25
Charles I	1625–49
Commonwealth	1649–60
Stuarts (restoration)	
Charles II	1660–85
James II	1685–88
William III, jointly with	1689–1702
Mary II	1689–94
Anne	1702–14
House of Hanover	
George I	1714–27
George II	1727–60
George III	1760–1820
George IV	1820–30
William IV	1830–37
Victoria	1837–1901
House of Saxe-Coburg	
Edward VII	1901–10
House of Windsor	
George V	1910–36
Edward VIII	1936
George VI	1936–52
Elizabeth II	1952–

Henry VIII

Elizabeth II

SCOTLAND

Monarch	Reign
Malcolm II	1005–34
Duncan I	1034–40
Macbeth	1040–57
Malcolm III Canmore	1058–93
Donald Bane	1093–94
Duncan II	1094
Donald Bane (restored)	1094–97
Edgar	1097–1107
Alexander I	1107–24
David I	1124–53
Malcolm IV	1153–65
William the Lion	1165–1214
Alexander II	1214–49
Alexander III	1249–86
Margaret of Norway	1286–90
Interregnum	1290–92
John Balliol	1292–96
Interregnum	1296–1306
Robert I, the Bruce	1306–29
David II	1329–71
Stuarts	
Robert II	1371–90
Robert III	1390–1406
James I	1406–37
James II	1437–60
James III	1460–88
James IV	1488–1513
James V	1513–42
Mary, Queen of Scots	1542–67
James VI, I of England	1567–1625

Mary, Queen of Scots

SAFE RAVEN

Legend has it that when ravens leave the Tower of London, the throne of England will fall. So, a family of ravens is kept at the tower with their wings clipped.

PRESIDENTS OF THE UNITED STATES

President	Term of office	President	Term of office	President	Term of office
George Washington	1789–97	Abraham Lincoln	1861–65	Herbert C. Hoover	1929–33
John Adams	1797–1801	Andrew Johnson	1865–69	Franklin D. Roosevelt	1933–45
Thomas Jefferson	1801–09	Ulysses S. Grant	1869–77	Harry S. Truman	1945–53
James Madison	1809–17	Rutherford B. Hayes	1877–81	Dwight D. Eisenhower	1953–61
James Monroe	1817–25	James A. Garfield	Mar–Sept 1881	John F. Kennedy	1961–63
John Quincy Adams	1825–29	Chester A. Arthur	1881–85	Lyndon B. Johnson	1963–69
Andrew Jackson	1829–37	Grover S. Cleveland	1885–89	Richard M. Nixon	1969–74
Martin van Buren	1837–41	Benjamin Harrison	1889–93	Gerald R. Ford	1974–77
William H. Harrison	Mar–April 1841	Grover S. Cleveland	1893–97	James E. Carter	1977–81
John Tyler	1841–45	William McKinley	1897–1901	Ronald W. Reagan	1981–89
James K. Polk	1845–49	Theodore Roosevelt	1901–09	George Bush	1989–93
Zachary Taylor	1849–50	William H. Taft	1909–13	William J. Clinton	1993–
Millard Fillmore	1850–53	Woodrow Wilson	1913–21		
Franklin Pierce	1853–57	Warren G. Harding	1921–23		
James Buchanan	1857–61	Calvin Coolidge	1923–29		

F. D. Roosevelt

BRITISH PRIME MINISTERS

Prime Minister	Term of office
Sir Robert Walpole	1721–42
Earl of Wilmington	1742–43
Henry Pelham	1743–54
Duke of Newcastle	1754–56
Duke of Devonshire	1756–57
Duke of Newcastle	1757–62
Earl of Bute	1762–63
George Grenville	1763–65
Marquess of Rockingham	1765–66
Earl of Chatham (Pitt the Elder)	1766–67
Duke of Grafton	1767–70
Lord North	1770–82
Marquess of Rockingham	1782
Earl of Shelburne	1782–1783
Duke of Portland	1783
William Pitt, the Younger	1783–1801
Henry Addington	1801–04
William Pitt	1804–06
Lord Grenville	1806–07
Duke of Portland	1807–09
Spencer Perceval	1809–12
Earl of Liverpool	1812–27
George Canning	1827
Viscount Goderich	1827–28
Duke of Wellington	1828–30
Earl Grey	1830–34
Viscount Melbourne	1834
Sir Robert Peel	1834–35
Viscount Melbourne	1835–41
Sir Robert Peel	1841–46
Lord John Russell	1846–52
Earl of Derby	1852
Earl of Aberdeen	1852–55
Viscount Palmerston	1855–58
Earl of Derby	1858–59
Viscount Palmerston	1859–65

Robert Walpole

Pitt the Younger

Prime Minister	Term of office
Earl Russell	1865–66
Earl of Derby	1866–68
Benjamin Disraeli	1868
William Gladstone	1868–74
Benjamin Disraeli	1874–80
William Gladstone	1880–85
Marquess of Salisbury	1885–86
William Gladstone	1886
Marquess of Salisbury	1886–92
William Gladstone	1892–94
Earl of Rosebery	1894–95
Marquess of Salisbury	1895–1902
Arthur Balfour	1902–05
Sir Henry Campbell-Bannerman	1905–08
Herbert Asquith	1908–16
David Lloyd-George	1916–22
Andrew Bonar Law	1922–23
Stanley Baldwin	1923–24
James Ramsay-MacDonald	1924
Stanley Baldwin	1924–29
James Ramsay-MacDonald	1929–35
Stanley Baldwin	1935–37
Neville Chamberlain	1937–40
Winston Churchill	1940–45
Clement Attlee	1945–51
Sir Winston Churchill	1951–55
Sir Anthony Eden	1955–57
Harold Macmillan	1957–63
Sir Alec Douglas-Home	1963–64
Harold Wilson	1964–70
Edward Heath	1970–74
Harold Wilson	1974–76
James Callaghan	1976–79
Margaret Thatcher	1979–90
John Major	1990–97
Tony Blair	1997–

Winston Churchill

AUSTRALIAN PRIME MINISTERS

Prime Minister	Term of office
Edmund Barton	1901–03
Alfred Deakin	1903–04
John C. Watson	1904
George Houston Reid	1904–05
Alfred Deakin	1905–08
Andrew Fisher	1908–09
Alfred Deakin	1909–10
Andrew Fisher	1910–13
Joseph Cook	1913–14
Andrew Fisher	1914–15
William M. Hughes	1915–23
Stanley M. Bruce	1923–29
James H. Scullin	1929–32
Joseph A. Lyons	1932–39
Robert Gordon Menzies	1939–41
Arthur William Fadden	1941
John Curtin	1941–45
Joseph Benedict Chifley	1945–49
Robert Gordon Menzies	1949–66
Harold Edward Holt	1966–67
John Grey Gorton	1968–71
William McMahon	1971–72
Edward Gough Whitlam	1972–75
John Malcolm Fraser	1975–83
Robert James Hawke	1983–91
Paul Keating	1991–96
John Howard	1996–

Stanley M. Bruce

BRITISH GOVERNORS AT THE CAPE, 1806-1910

Prime Minister	Term of office
Sir David Baird (acting)	1806–07
Count Caledon	1807–11
Sir John Francis Cradock	1811–14
Lord Charles H. Somerset	1814–26
Sir Rufane S. Donkin (acting)	1820–21
Sir Richard Bourke (acting)	1826–28
Sir Galbraith L. Cole	1828–33
Sir Benjamin D'Urban	1834–38
Sir George T. Napier	1838–44
Sir Peregrine Maitland	1844–47
Sir Harry Smith	1847–52
Sir George Cathcart	1852–54
Sir George Grey	1854–61
Sir Philip Wodehouse	1862–70
Sir Henry Barkly	1870–77
Sir Henry B. E. Frere	1877–80
Sir Hercules G. Robinson	1881–89
Lord Henry B. Loch	1889–95
Sir Hercules G. Robinson	1895–97
Lord Alfred Milner	1897–01
Sir W. F. Hely-Hutchinson	1901–10

RUSSIAN LEADERS

General secretaries	Term of office
Vladimir Illich Lenin	1917–22
Josef Stalin	1922–53
Nikita Khrushchev	1953–64
Leonid Brezhnev	1964–82
Yuri Andropov	1982–84
Konstantin Chernenko	1984–85
Mikhail Gorbachev	1985–92
Russian presidents	
Boris Yeltsin	1992–

INDIAN PRIME MINISTERS

Prime Minister	Term of office
Jawaharlal Nehru	1947–64
Lal Bahadur Shastri	1964–66
Indira Gandhi	1966–77
Morarji Desai	1977–79
Indira Gandhi	1980–84
Rajiv Gandhi	1984–89
V.P. Singh	1989–90
Chandra Shekhar	1990–91
P.V. Narasima Rao	1991–96
H.D. Deve Gowda	1996-

Indira Gandhi

WORLD LEADER FACTS

• In 1803, Thomas Jefferson wanted to buy part of the French colony of Louisiana for the US and was prepared to pay up to $10 million. France, however, threatened by war in Europe, agreed to sell much more land. Jefferson was able to double the size of the US for just $15 million.

• William Pitt the Younger, prime minister of Britain at the end of the 18th century, took office at the very young age of 24.

• In 1809, George Canning, Britain's foreign minister, who later became prime minister, fought a duel with Lord Castlereagh, the war minister. Canning was wounded in the leg, and both Ministers resigned afterwards.

• The White House, the US president's official home, is built from sandstone that is naturally grey. Only after it was burned in a major fire in 1814 was it painted white to hide the smoke stains.

READY TEDDY GO

Teddy bears get their name from US President Theodore "Teddy" Roosevelt, who, when on a hunting trip in Mississippi, refused to shoot a bear cub.

EXPLORERS

PEOPLE HAVE ALWAYS WANTED to travel to distant regions that are unknown to them, for various reasons. Trade, conquest, and settlement were common motives in the past; scientific research or sheer adventure often inspire today's explorers. Some explorers, such as the Polynesians who sailed across the Pacific Ocean, are little known to us, as they left no written records of their journeys.

NORTHERN PASSAGES
NORTH-WEST PASSAGE (NWP)

1497 John Cabot, Italian, backed by British merchants, reached Newfoundland in Canada in search of NWP. He believed he had found Asia. A second voyage in 1498 ended in mystery, as Cabot was never seen again.

Cabot's men could scoop up cod from the Grand Banks.

1576 Martin Frobisher, British, reached Baffin Island in search of NWP. Found Frobisher Bay.

1610–11 Henry Hudson, British, backed by Dutch, reached Hudson Bay in search of NWP. Abandoned to die after his crew mutinied.

1845–47 John Franklin, British, died west of King William Island in search of NWP. Ship stuck in ice.

NORTH-EAST PASSAGE (NEP)

1596–98 Willem Barents, Dutch, reached Kara Sea in search of NEP.

1878–79 Nils Nordenskjold, Norwegian, first explorer to complete the NEP. Also a scientific expedition.

NORTH ATLANTIC OCEAN AND NORTH AMERICA

c.330 B.C. Pytheas, Greek, sailed into North Atlantic, around Britain and "Thule" (Iceland or Norway).

800–1100 Viking travellers (Leif Eriksson, Erik the Red) crossed North Atlantic, starting settlements in Newfoundland and Greenland; they discovered "Vinland" (modern USA).

1527–28 Pánfilo de Narváez, Spanish, reached Florida, USA.

1534–42 Jacques Cartier, French, sailed through the Gulf of St. Lawrence into the St. Lawrence River, in Canada. Huron Indian villages that he found became Quebec and Montreal.

1615–16 Samuel de Champlain, French, founder of French Canada, helped establish the fur trade.

NORTH AND CENTRAL AMERICA

1492–93 Christopher Columbus, Italian, backed by the Spanish, sailed the Atlantic to the West Indies and, on later voyages, the coasts of Central and South America. Columbus died believing that he had been the first European to find a westerly route to Asia, not the first European in Central America.

1519–21 Hernán Cortés, Spanish, captured Mexico for Spain. He conquered the massive Aztec empire of Mexico with the help of thousands of local rebels.

1528–36 Álvar Núñez Cabeza de Vaca, Spanish, travelled to Florida with Spanish *conquistador* (conqueror) Pánfilo de Narváez. Starvation, disease, and hostility killed most of the company. De Vaca was saved by Yaqui tribesmen and journeyed into Mexico.

1678–80 Robert Cavelier de la Salle, French, explored the Great Lakes and sailed down the Mississippi River to the Gulf of Mexico. In 1687, his expedition to find the Mississippi delta from the sea ended in failure and his death.

BURNING BOATS

When Cortés decided to invade the Aztec empire with a force of just 508 soldiers and 100 sailors, he burned his ships, so that his men would see victory or death.

1804–06 Meriwether Lewis and William Clark, Americans, were sent by US President Thomas Jefferson to search for a route to the Pacific Ocean from St. Louis. Their journeys took them along the Missouri, Yellowstone, and Columbia rivers by canoe, meeting with local peoples on the way.

SOUTH AMERICA

1531–33 Francisco Pizarro, Spanish, conquered Inca empire.

1735–44 Charles de la Condamine, French, explored River Amazon and northwest coast of South America.

1799–1804 Alexander von Humboldt, German naturalist, explored northwest South America.

1831–35 Charles Darwin, British, explored South America and Galapagos Islands.

Map labels: Greenland, Baffin Island, Frobisher Bay, Hudson Bay, ATLANTIC OCEAN, NORTH AMERICA, Great Lakes, Newfoundland, St. Lawrence River, Mississippi River, West Indies, CENTRAL AMERICA, River Niger, River Amazon, SOUTH AMERICA

CIRCUMNAVIGATIONS

1519–22 Ferdinand Magellan, Portuguese, set off to circumnavigate the globe. Just one of his 5 ships and 18 of his 260-man crew survived. In 1521, Magellan himself was killed by locals in the Philippines. Sebastián de Elcano took command.

1577–80 Francis Drake, English, circumnavigated the globe in the *Golden Hind*, plundering Spanish ships and lands on the way.

Ferdinand Magellan

SOUTH POLE

1839 James Clark Ross, British, explored Antarctic coast and ice sheet in his ships *Erebus* and *Terror*.

1910–12 Roald Amundsen, Norwegian, was first to reach South Pole. He used sleds pulled by dogs.

1910–13 Robert Falcon Scott, British, was just beaten to Pole by Amundsen. He used both ponies and dogs, but difficult conditions killed all the animals. The four-man team died on the return journey.

Antarctic region

Amundsen's team

NORTH POLE

1871 Charles Hall, American, made three expeditions, came close to North Pole. Died three weeks after third and last expedition.

1893–96 Fridtjof Nansen, Norwegian, attempted [an]d failed to reach North Pole by ship [an]d sled. Nansen was picked up by a [Bri]tish ship on Franz Joseph Land.

[1]908–09 Robert Peary, American, [aft]er last of eight expeditions, [cla]imed to have reached Pole; there is [stil]l doubt about his claim.

Nansen's ship Fram *was designed to move with ice floes, without being crushed*

EURASIA

138–116 B.C. Chang Ch'ien, Chinese, travelled westwards across Asia to Samarkand and beyond, to find allies for emperor Wu-Ti.

Chang Ch'ien at the court of Wu-Ti

A.D. 399–414 Fa Hsien, Chinese, travelled across Asia on the Silk Road to Khotan, then down into India, before crossing the sea to Sri Lanka. He was a Buddhist monk, and wanted to learn more about the origins and texts of Buddhism.

629–649 Hsüan Tsang, Chinese, followed Fa Hsien's route to India, and travelled extensively there.

800–1100 Viking travellers and traders sailed along Dnieper and Volga Rivers, and reached Constantinople and Baghdad.

1260–71 Polo brothers Niccolo and Maffeo, and Niccolo's son Marco, from Venice, travelled across Asia to China. Marco stayed for 20 years, working for Kublai Khan.

1541–52 Francis Xavier, Spanish Jesuit, sailed to Japan. First European to visit Japan.

1602–07 Bento de Goes, Portuguese, joined Jesuits in India and went from Agra across Asia as far as Suchow.

1661–64 John Grueber and Albert d'Orville, German and Belgian, were the first Europeans to reach Lhasa, Tibet, from China.

1725–29 and 1734–41 Vitus Bering, Danish, appointed by Tzar of Russia, crossed Asia by land before going out to find out whether Russia and America were joined.

KARA SEA

River Volga

EURASIA

CHINA

INDIA

PACIFIC OCEAN

River Congo

INDIAN OCEAN

Zambezi River

Cape Cross

AUSTRALIA

Darling River

Cape of Good Hope

AUSTRALIA

1828–30 and 1844–45 Charles Sturt, British, mapped Murray and Darling Rivers, then explored central Australia.

1840–41 Edward Eyre, British, found land route along south coast from Adelaide to Albany.

1860–61 Robert Burke, William Wills, Irish and English, make south–north journey across Australia from Melbourne.

1861–62 John Stuart, Scottish, crossed Australia from Adelaide to Darwin (south to north).

Burke and Wills, who died on their return journey to Melbourne

PACIFIC

1567–1607 Mendaña, Quirós, Torres, Spanish, made various voyages across Pacific from South America past Pacific islands and, on one journey, as far as Manila.

1642–43 Abel Janszoon Tasman, Dutch, sailed from Mauritius to Tasmania, New Zealand, Fiji, New Guinea, Java.

1766–69 Louis Bougainville, French, sailed from Falklands, across Pacific to Great Barrier Reef, then to New Guinea and Java.

1768–79 James Cook, British, made three voyages around Pacific, visiting New Zealand and Australia. Extensive mapping of southern Pacific and its islands.

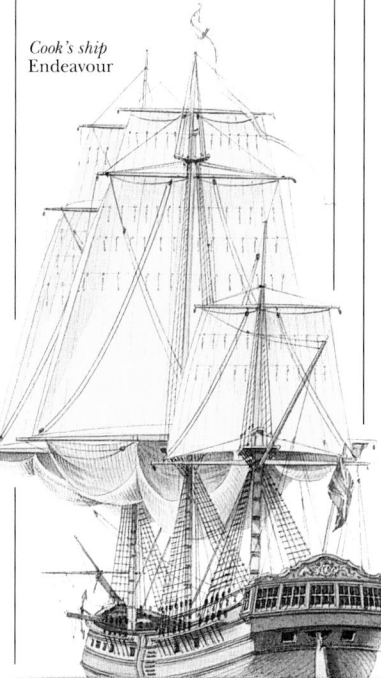

Cook's ship Endeavour

[A]FRICA

[1]500 B.C. Queen Hatshepsut, [Eg]yptian, sent explorers to the land of [Pu]nt (possibly East Africa).

[?]500 B.C. Hanno, Phoenician, sailed [fro]m Carthage, down the West African [co]ast, and up the River Senegal, looking [for] sites for Phoenician colonies.

[13]24–53 Ibn Battuta, from Tangier, [No]rth Africa, travelled through Sahara to [M]ali and Timbuktu, also travelled [ext]ensively in Middle East and Arabia.

[17]95–97, 1805–06 Mungo Park, [Sc]ottish, reached River Niger in West [Af]rica, later followed it upstream.

[18]27–28 René Caillié, French, [tra]velled from West Africa across Sahara [to] Tangier. First European in Timbuktu.

Livingstone on the Zambezi River, Africa

1841–73 David Livingstone, Scottish, four expeditions, crossed southern Africa and travelled south to Cape Town and Port Elizabeth.

1844–45, 1850–55 Heinrich Barth, German, travelled across Sahara and in West Africa.

1857–63 Richard Burton and John Hanning Speke, British, made three expeditions to Africa.

1871–89 Henry Morton Stanley, American, made three expeditions, across Africa and up River Congo.

SOUTH ATLANTIC OCEAN AND AFRICA

1485–86 Diogo Cão, Portuguese, first of the professional explorers, sailed down the West African coast as far as Cape Cross.

1487–88 Bartolemeu Días, Portuguese, sailed down the West African coast, past the southernmost point, the Cape of Good Hope. He then entered the Indian Ocean, before turning back.

1497–98 Vasco da Gama, Portuguese, sailed down the West African coast, around the Cape of Good Hope, up the East African coast and across the Indian Ocean to Calicut, India. He was the first European to reach India by sea.

BATTLES AND WARS

MAJOR WARS

B.C. **c.3100**	First recorded war in history, between Upper and Lower Egypt. Pharaoh Narmer (Menes) unified Egypt.
c.1600–600	Continual warring between the three great powers of the Middle East: Egypt, Babylon, and Assyria.
c.1200 **Trojan War**	Legendary war between Greeks and Trojans, described in Homer's *Iliad*. However, legend was probably based on a real war between Greeks and people of Troy.
490–479 **Persian Wars**	Fought between Persia and anti-Persian alliance of Sparta and Athens. Persia ultimately defeated.
431–404 **Peloponnesian War**	Fought between Athens and Sparta, two long-standing rivals. Sparta was the land power, Athens the sea power. Sparta was victorious.
264–146 **Punic Wars**	Prolonged struggle between Rome and Carthage. Ended in Rome's victory and total destruction of Carthage.
A.D. **c.1096–1291** **Crusades**	Series of warring pilgrimages undertaken by European Christians to recapture Jerusalem from Turkish Muslims. In 1099, Crusaders captured Jerusalem but in 1187 Saladin recaptured the city. In 1291, the Crusaders were finally thrown out.
c.1337–1453 **Hundred Years War**	Irregular succession of wars between France and England. Ended in victory for France.
1455–85 **Wars of the Roses**	English war between Houses of Lancaster and York. House of Lancaster was victorious.
1618–48 **Thirty Years War**	Complex European war fought mainly on German soil. Began as a struggle of German Protestants against Habsburgs, Catholics, and the Holy Roman Empire. War gradually involved most European powers, and ended with Protestant victory.
1642–49 **English Civil War**	Fought between Parliament (Roundheads) and Royalists (Cavaliers). Parliament victorious. War ended with execution of King Charles I. Monarchy later restored.
1700–21 **Great Northern War**	Fought between Russia and Sweden. Sweden defeated.
1701–13 **War of the Spanish Succession**	Struggle between France and Austria over who was to rule Spain. France defeated.
1756–63 **Seven Years War**	Fought between Austria, France, Russia, and Sweden on one side; Britain, Hanover, and Prussia on the other. Britain and the German states victorious.
1775–83 **American Revolution**	Fought between British-ruled American colonies and Britain. Colonies gained independence and formed United States of America.
1792–1815 **Napoleonic Wars**	Fought between France and an alliance between Austria, Britain, Russia, Prussia, and Sweden. France defeated.
1812–14 **War of 1812**	Fought between United States and Britain. USA victorious.
1821–29 **Greek War of Independence**	Greece fought for and gained independence from Turkey.
1839–42 **First Opium War**	Trade war between Britain and China. China forced to open trade ports to Western countries.
1846–48 **Mexican-American War**	Fought between USA and Mexico. Mexico was defeated.
1853–56 **Crimean War**	Britain, France, Sardinia, and Turkey fought against Russia, and won.
1861–65 **American Civil War**	Fought between Union (northern states) and Confederacy (southern states). Union victorious. First war to be photographed extensively.
1866 **Austro-Prussian War**	Fought between Austria and Prussia. Austria defeated.
1870–71 **Franco-Prussian War**	Prussia and other German states fought France, and won.
1894–95 **Chinese-Japanese War**	Fought between China and Japan. Japan victorious.
1898–99 **Spanish-American War**	Fought between USA and Spain. USA victorious.
1899–1902 **Second Boer War**	Britain and Commonwealth countries fought Boers and won control of South Africa.
1904–05 **Russo-Japanese War**	Fought between Russia and Japan. Japan victorious.
1914–18 **World War I (The Great War)**	Fought between Germany, Austria-Hungary, and Turkey on one side; British Commonwealth, Belgium, France, Italy, Russia, and USA on the other. Germany defeated.
1918–21 **Russian Civil War**	Fought between Reds (Bolsheviks) and anti-Communists, known as Whites. Bolsheviks victorious.
1931–1933 **Chinese-Japanese War**	Fought between Japan and China. Japan victorious.
1936–39 **Spanish Civil War**	Anarchist uprising that became a struggle between Nationalists (Fascists) and Republicans. Nationalists won.
1937–45 **Chinese-Japanese War**	Fought between China and Japan. China victorious.
1939–45 **World War II**	Global conflict involving every major world power. Fought between Axis powers of Nazi Germany, Italy, and Japan on one side; Allied powers of British Commonwealth, USSR, USA, on the other. Germany and the Axis powers defeated. USA and USSR become global "superpowers".

1950–53 Korean War	Fought between North Korea (aided by China) and South Korea (aided by USA and allies). Ceasefire negotiated.	1971 Pakistan Civil War	Fought between Bangladesh (east Pakistan) and west Pakistan. Bangladesh victorious.
1965–75 Vietnam War	Fought between North (Communist) Vietnam and South Vietnam (aided by USA and allies). USA withdrew in 1973. In 1975, North Vietnam won the war.	1973 October War	Arabs and Israelis fought. United Nations (UN) called a ceasefire.
1967 Six-Day War	Fought between Israel and Arab forces led by Egypt. Israel won.	1980–88 Iran-Iraq War	Iran and Iraq fought. Ceasefire was negotiated.
1967–70 Nigerian Civil War	Fought between Biafra and Federal Government. Biafra was defeated.	1991 Gulf War	Iraq fought UN forces, headed by USA. Iraq defeated and Kuwait liberated.
1968– Northern Ireland	Prolonged conflict between Protestants and Catholics. Peace agreement was signed on Good Friday 1998.	1991– Civil War, former Yugoslavia	Prolonged ethnic, territorial, and religious conflict involving Serbs, Croats, Bosnians, and Albanians. In 1999 NATO intervened against the Serbs.

MAJOR BATTLES

B.C. 490 Marathon (Greece)	10,000 Athenians and allies defeated 50,000 Persian troops. After battle, Pheidippides, a runner, ran to Athens to report victory. Exhausted, he delivered message and died. The modern marathon is named after his achievement.	732 Tours (France)	The Franks, led by Charles Martel, defeated Muslim invaders from Spain, securing Western European independence.
480 Salamis (Greece)	Combined Greek fleet, led by Athenian Themistocles and Spartan Eurybiades, defeated larger invading Persian fleet under King Xerxes. Secured Greek independence in the Mediterranean.	1260 Ain Jalut (Palestine)	Muslim general Kutuz defeated combined Mongol and Christian mounted forces. First major victory against massive Mongol empire, also ended Crusaders' hopes of recovering Holy Land.
415–413 Siege of Syracuse (Sicily)	40,000-strong Athenian force massacred in failed invasion of Syracuse. Ended Athenian military supremacy over Greek world.	1066 Hastings (Britain)	Norman (French) soldiers, led by William the Conqueror, crossed English Channel and defeated Saxon forces, led by Harold II. Norman conquest brought England into realm of Western Europe and created a unified, centralized state.
405 Aegispotamoi (Turkey)	Spartan fleet under Lysander defeated last Athenian fleet, ending Peloponnesian War.	1415 Agincourt (France)	10,000 English under Henry V defeated 30,000 French, and recaptured Normandy. Demonstrated superiority of English longbowmen over French knights.
331 Gaugamela (Persia)	Alexander the Great's supreme victory. He defeated Persian King Darius and opened up the East to Greek ideas and culture.	1429 Siege of Orléans (France)	English siege of Orléans lifted by French forces. England's hopes of total conquest of France destroyed by Joan of Arc, who revived French unity and courage. Decisive moment of Hundred Years War.
202 Zama (Tunisia)	Roman force under Scipio ended Punic Wars against Carthage with a massive victory over Hannibal. End of 400-year-old Carthaginian empire.	1453 Siege of Constantinople (Turkey)	Ottoman Turks, led by Sultan Mehmed II, besieged and captured Constantinople (Istanbul). Marked end of the Byzantine Empire.
31 Actium (Greece)	Octavian (later Augustus) defeated Mark Antony and Cleopatra at sea, ending decades of civil war. Marked end of Roman Republic and beginning of Imperial Rome.	1521 Siege of Tenochtitlán (Mexico)	Landing with a small force, Spanish explorer Hernán Cortés won allies from enemies of Aztecs, and attacked Aztec capital, Tenochtitlán. Siege ended in total defeat of Aztecs, who had the greatest empire in Americas. Started European colonization.
A.D. 378 Adrianople (Turkey)	Goths (Germanic tribes) inflicted a crippling defeat on Roman army, sending panic throughout Roman Empire. Emperor Valens was killed in the battle, and Roman tactics shown to be outdated.	1571 Lepanto (Greece)	Christian fleet of more than 200 galleys, led by Don John of Austria, defeated Turkish fleet of more than 200 galleys, led by Ali Pasha. More than 30,000 men drowned in one afternoon. Last major naval battle to use oar-powered galleys.
636 Yarmuk (Israel)	Arab leader Khalid ibn-al Walid, with 25,000 men, defeated and killed 50,000-strong Byzantine force in a desert sandstorm. Brought Jerusalem under Arab control, and opened the way to Arab expansion in Egypt, North Africa, and Spain.	1588 Spanish Armada (Britain)	Spanish fleet of 130 ships, led by Duke of Medina Sidonia, defeated by 97 English ships and heavy storms. 86 Spanish ships survived. Major blow to Counter-Reformation.
718 Siege of Constantinople (Turkey)	Leo the Isaurian, Emperor of Byzantium, defeated Saracen Arabs using "greek fire", an inflammable substance that ignited on contact with water. Halted Arab advance into Western Europe.		

1645 **Naseby (Britain)**	14,000 British Parliamentary troops, under Fairfax, defeated 10,000 Royalist troops under Prince Rupert. Spelled the end of Charles I's power and beginning of Republican rule.	**1876** **Little Bighorn** **(United States)**	About 3,000 Sioux and Cheyenne warriors, led by Sitting Bull and Crazy Horse, destroyed part of the 7th US Cavalry, led by Colonel George Custer. The only survivor from Custer's force was a horse.
1704 **Blenheim** **(Germany)**	British-Austrian army, under Duke of Marlborough, defeated a French-Bavarian force, under Marshal Tallard. Ended Stuart claims to throne of England, and prevented French domination in Europe.	**1905** **Tsushima (West of Japan)**	Japanese fleet under Admiral Togo destroyed Russian fleet, under Rozhdestvenski. Decisive battle of Russo-Japanese War.
1709 **Poltava (Ukraine)**	Russian Tsar, Peter the Great, defeated Sweden for control of Baltic Sea. Ended 80 years of Swedish military domination and began Russian empire's expansion.	**1914** **The Marne (France)**	Strategic victory for French and British Commonwealth forces that halted the German advance. Last mobile battle in the west in World War I. Long trench battles followed.
1757 **Plassey (India)**	Robert Clive's 3,200-strong British force defeated 50,000-strong Bengali army to install a puppet nawab (king) and to seize power for British East India Company. First step on road to British domination of India.	**1916** **The Somme (France)**	The Somme was the bloodiest battle of World War I, taking 1,265,000 lives. British Commonwealth and French forces captured just 320sq km (125sq miles) of ground.
1759 **Quebec (Canada)**	British general James Wolfe defeated French forces under the Marquis de Montcalm in a night attack on the Plains of Abraham outside Quebec. Gave Britain control of Canada. Both generals died in battle.	**1917** **Passchendaele (Belgium)**	5-month battle of trench warfare. British Commonwealth gained 8km (5 miles) and lost more than 400,000 men. 57,000 were killed in just a few hours on 1 July 1917.
1777 **Saratoga (United States)**	Decisive American victory in American Revolution. British troops, led by Burgoyne, surrendered to Americans.	**1940** **Britain**	German air force of 2,500 planes launched attack on Britain. Smaller Royal Air Force defeated them and prevented planned seaborne invasion.
1781 **Yorktown (United States)**	General Cornwallis, with 8,000 British troops, was hemmed in, and surrendered to a larger American force under George Washington. End of American Revolution.	**1942** **Midway (Pacific)**	Japanese attempt to capture Midway Island defeated by US Navy. First naval battle in which opposing ships never saw each other. Marked the new dominance of the aircraft carrier.
1805 **Trafalgar (South of Spain)**	Nelson destroyed French-Spanish fleet south of Cadiz, Spain, and with it Napoleon's plans to invade England.	**1942** **El Alamein (Egypt)**	Allied forces, led by General Montgomery (British), drove German Afrika Korps, under Erwin Rommel, out of Egypt, deep into Libya. Britain's greatest victory of WWII.
1805 **Austerlitz (Czech Republic)**	65,000 French troops, led by Napoleon Bonaparte, defeated 83,000 Austrian and Russian forces. Napoleon's greatest victory.	**1942–43** **Stalingrad (Russia)**	German forces surrendered to Soviet Russians after long siege of Stalingrad (Volgograd). One of the bloodiest battles in history: more than 600,000 Soviet soldiers killed and more than 1 million dead in total.
1815 **Waterloo (Belgium)**	Napoleon was defeated by combined British, Dutch, Belgian, and Prussian forces. This finally ended Napoleonic Wars.	**1944** **Normandy (France)** **D-Day**	Allied forces, led by General Eisenhower (American), invaded German-occupied northern France. Largest-ever seaborne attack: 38 convoys of 745 ships, with more than 4,000 landing craft, 156,000 men, and 300 minesweepers.
1854 **Balaclava (Crimea)**	British defeat of a Russian attack in the Crimean War. Famous for charge of Lord Cardigan's Light Brigade, which only one-third of his men survived.		
1863 **Gettysburg (United States)**	Decisive battle of American Civil War. Federal forces under George Meade defeated Confederates under Robert E. Lee. Heavy losses on both sides: approximately 40,000 Union and Confederate troops killed.	**1954** **Dien Bien Phu (Vietnam)**	Vietnamese defeated French forces, ending French control of Vietnam. Led to establishment of North and South Vietnam: one Communist, the other US-aided.
1870 **Sedan (France)**	Prussia, led by Moltke, inflicted crushing defeat on France. This ended Second Empire and forced abdication of Emperor Napoleon III.	**1991** **Operation Desert Storm** **(Iraq)**	Airborne attack on Iraq by United Nations Coalition forces. Broke Iraqi resistance, liberated Kuwait, and led to swift end of Gulf War.

WAR FACTS

• The Geneva Convention of 1949 separates civilians from the military in four major ways: the military wear clothes that show they are soldiers, openly carry weapons, are under the control of a commander, and obey the laws and customs of war.

• Germ warfare's use was first recorded in the 14th century. Tartars, besieging a Crimean city, catapulted plague-infected corpses over the walls, spreading disease among the inhabitants.

• War in this century has killed more than 100 million people; 20 million since 1945.

• In 1905, Russia's Baltic fleet took seven months to reach its enemy, Japan. Japanese Navy destroyed it in 36 hours.

• In World War I, about 19 million died: 95% soldiers, 5% civilians. In World War II, more than 50 million died: 50% soldiers, 50% civilians.

WAR RECORDS

MOST WARLIKE LEADER was Sargon of Akkad (c.2370 B.C.), who waged 34 wars in 55 years.

SHORTEST WAR lasted just 38 minutes, between Britain and Zanzibar (East Africa) in 1896.

REVOLUTIONS AND RIGHTS

FRENCH REVOLUTION

1788 France bankrupt
King Louis XVI, nobles, and Church hold power. Louis summons Estates-General (ancient parliament) to raise extra taxes.

1789 Meeting of Estates-General at Versailles, 5 May. Third Estate (middle-class representatives) demands democratic reforms.

National Assembly set up by Third Estate rebels to rule France, 10 June. Louis sends troops to Versailles.

Storming of the Bastille (royal fortress and hated symbol of tyranny) by people of Paris, 14 July. Revolution spreads around France. Peasants burn chateaux and manors.

Declaration of the Rights of Man adopted by Assembly, 27 August.

1790 Nobility abolished.

1791 Royal family flee Paris, but are captured, June.

1792 Revolutionary War begins, as Austria and Prussia attack France. Monarchy abolished; France declared a republic.

1793 Louis XVI executed (Jan. 21).

Jacobins (extreme revolutionary group) take power in July.

Reign of Terror, from September 1793 to July 1794. 300,000 people arrested and about 17,000 guillotined.

1795 The Directory (a five-man executive body) takes power.

1799 Napoleon Bonaparte overthrows Directory and takes power.

KEY PEOPLE

Name	Dates	Biographical details
Louis XVI	1754–93	King of France, opposed to reform. Tried for treason and guillotined
Georges Danton	1759–94	Jacobin leader and Minister of Justice. Voted for execution of King but opposed Reign of Terror. Arrested and guillotined
Maximilien Robespierre	1758–94	Lawyer and Jacobin revolutionary. Head of Committee of Public Safety. Key figure in Reign of Terror. Arrested and guillotined
Olympes de Gouges	1748–94	Revolutionary. Wrote *Declaration of the Rights of Women and Citizens*. Arrested and guillotined

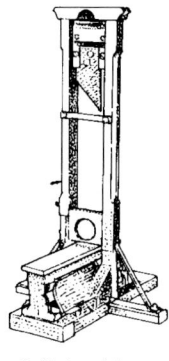

Guillotine of the French Revolution, invented as a humane method of execution.

RUSSIAN REVOLUTION

1917 Petrograd bread riots (8 March). Army joins with workers. Soviets (councils) of soldiers, peasants, and workers set up all over Russia.

Tsar abdicates (15 March). Moderate provisional (temporary) government set up. Power struggles begin between government and soviets, and between Mensheviks (moderates) and Bolsheviks (Communists).

Lenin returns to Russia (April). His "April Theses" declare independence of Bolsheviks, and call for revolution.

Bolsheviks take over Petrograd, led by Trotsky (7–8 November).

Bolsheviks seize control of Moscow and European Russia. Lenin passes law giving land to peasants. Creates Cheka (secret police force) to enforce party's decisions. Abolishes ranks in society and army. Nationalizes all factories and banks. Takes schools from Church and gives to state (November–December).

1918 Russia leaves World War I after Treaty of Brest-Litovsk between Russia and Germany, 3 March.

Tsar and royal family executed, in Yekaterinburg (now Sverdlovsk), July.

KEY PEOPLE

Name	Dates	Biographical details
Nicholas II	1868–1918	Last Tsar of Russia, overthrown in revolution
Vladimir Illich Lenin	1870–1924	Founder of Bolshevik Party and leader of revolution. Ruled Soviet Union 1917–24
Leon Trotsky	1879–1940	Bolshevik and head of Red Army. Organized revolution with Lenin; murdered by Stalin
Josef Stalin	1879–1953	Succeeded Lenin. Forced intense industrialization and collectivization of land

1918–21 Civil War between Reds (Bolsheviks) and Whites (anti-Bolsheviks) results in Red victory. More than 20 million die.

1918–22 Socialist reforms

1922 Soviet Union established, the world's first Communist state.

CHINESE REVOLUTION

1921 Chinese Communist Party holds first meeting in Shanghai.

1926 Northern Expedition Communists and Nationalists unite against tyrannical warlords.

1927 Nationalist leader Chiang Kai-shek executes hundreds of Communists in lightning coup, April.

Chinese Communist Party cap

1934–35 Long March. Communists retreat 8,000km (5,000 miles) to escape Nationalist forces. Mao Tse-tung emerges as Communist Party leader.

1945 Civil war erupts between Communists and Nationalists after Japanese surrender in World War II.

1946 Communists wage successful guerilla war against Nationalists.

1947 People's Liberation Army organized by Communist leader and military genius, Lin Bao. Mao Tse-tung establishes Communist capital at Shih-chia-chuang (November). Peasant uprisings throughout China.

KEY PEOPLE

Name	Dates	Biographical details
Chiang Kai-shek	1887–1975	Chinese general. President of Chinese Republic and head of Kuomintang (Nationalist party). Fled to Taiwan following Communist victory
Mao Tse-tung	1893–1976	Chinese Communist leader and first chairman of the People's Republic
Lin Bao	1907–71	Founder and leader of People's Liberation Army

1949 Communists capture Peking (Beijing). Nationalist resistance collapses. Chiang Kai-shek flees to Taiwan and sets up Nationalist Government.

Mao Tse-tung proclaims People's Republic of China, (1 October), in Peking (Beijing), with himself as leader. People's Liberation Army control entire Chinese mainland.

BLACK RIGHTS

1600–1810 Ten million Africans are taken to the Americas as slaves.

1823–33 Anti-slavery society set up in Britain to end slavery in colonies.

1909 W.E.B. Du Bois (1889–1963) helps found National Association for the Advancement of Coloured People to end racial inequality in the USA.

1912 African National Congress (ANC) founded in South Africa to secure racial equality and black representation in parliament.

1914 Marcus Garvey (1887–1940) founds Universal Negro Improvement Association in Harlem, New York.

1925 A. Philip Randolph (1889–1979) organizes and leads the first successful black trade union.

1950–59 Apartheid laws set up in South Africa. These discriminate against blacks, "coloureds" and Asians.

1954 US Supreme Court rules that segregated education (by colour) is "inherently unequal".

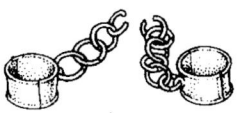

1955 Martin Luther King, Jr. (1929–68) organizes campaign to desegregate bus service in Montgomery, Alabama. This becomes a mass protest across southern USA.

1960 Sharpeville Massacre. 69 die and 200 injured in protest against South Africa's racist "Pass Laws".

1964 Nelson Mandela (born 1918), leader of military wing of ANC, jailed for life in South Africa.

1965–68 US Congress outlaws discrimination. Martin Luther King assassinated.

1990 F.W. De Klerk, president of South Africa, lifts ban on ANC and releases Nelson Mandela.

1994 First all-party elections in South Africa. ANC wins 62% of vote; Nelson Mandela becomes president.

ARCHAEOLOGY AND HISTORY

ARCHAEOLOGISTS HELP US to understand the past by digging up ancient sites and studying what they find there. In the past, they often looked only for treasure. Today, archaeologists use science to piece together a full picture of an ancient society.

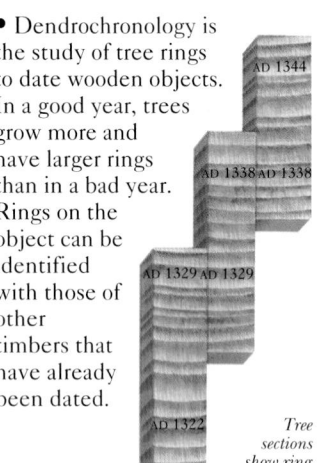

At every stage of an excavation, archaeologists take photographs, make drawings, and write detailed notes on everything they find, and where they find it.

The site's finds are later processed. This includes recording, labelling, bagging, examining, drawing, conserving, and documenting.

EXCAVATION

When archaeologists discover a site that they wish to investigate, they organize an excavation, or "dig". They work in teams, and each person has a different skill, such as surveying, excavation, drawing, or photography. Most archaeologists today work on "rescue" digs, where construction work, such as city centre redevelopment, threatens to disturb or destroy ancient remains.

ANALYSIS METHODS

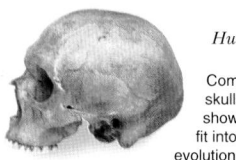

Human skull

Comparisons of skulls can also show where they fit into an evolutionary pattern.

• Looking at bone finds can tell scientists about the diet and health of ancient peoples, as well as their burial customs.

• Analysis of materials such as seeds, pollen, and animal remains builds up a picture of the ancient environment. It can show which crops were grown for food, and how people lived.

• Dendrochronology is the study of tree rings to date wooden objects. In a good year, trees grow more and have larger rings than in a bad year. Rings on the object can be identified with those of other timbers that have already been dated.

AD 1344
AD 1338 AD 1338
AD 1329 AD 1329
AD 1322

Tree sections show ring matches.

• Many sites have had different inhabitants at different times. Archaeologists dig a vertical cross-section through the earth of a site. This reveals the "layers" of time, the most recent occurring at the top.

• Radio-carbon dating is a very accurate scientific method of dating. All living things contain some radioactive carbon (C-14). After a living thing dies, this C-14 decays (its atoms break down) at a known rate. If the amount of C-14 in an organic find (wood, antler, etc.) is known, its age can be estimated.

DETECTION METHODS

• Using geophysics, we can show what lies underground without excavating. One technique, called resistivity, uses two electrical probes driven into the ground at different places. The resistance of the ground to the current can indicate underground remains.

• X-rays can reveal details of objects that are too brittle to be handled, or encrusted with rock.

AERIAL PHOTOGRAPHY

Sun at noon

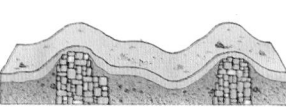

During the daytime, the slight bumps made by buried remains cannot be seen clearly.

Sun at dawn or dusk
Shadows form

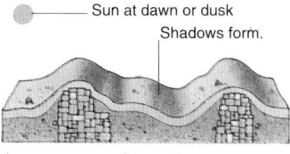

At sunset or dawn, bumps cast shadows easily seen from the air.

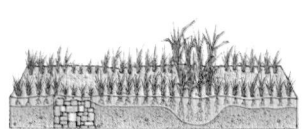

Crop growth can be affected by old earthworks or stoneworks, and this can be seen easily from the air.

PHASES OF HISTORY

Phase		Historian	Characteristics
Ancient Near Eastern:		Egyptian/Mesopotamian chroniclers	Recorded and praised the deeds of kings and emperors with little concern for accuracy
Classical:	Greece	Herodotus (c.484–c.425 B.C.)	His histories tell of famous military and political activities
		Thucydides (455–400 B.C.)	Closely examined military events of his time and their political consequences
	Rome	Livy (c.60 B.C.–A.D. 17)	Interested in historical figures and morality. He tried to be unbiased
		Tacitus (c.A.D. 56–120)	Wrote vivid, detailed accounts with some accuracy
Medieval:	Europe	Orosius (c.417)	First Christian historian. Promoted Christian world view over Paganism
		Bede (c.672–735)	"The Father of English History", who carefully researched the reliability of his sources
		Villehardouin (c.1150–c.1213)	His histories included eyewitness accounts of military activity
		Froissart (c.1333–1401)	His closely researched accounts emphasized the lives and battles of knights
	Muslim World	Al-Tabari (c.923)	Produced a religious history of the conflicts and customs of Muslims
		Ibn Khaldun (1332–1406)	Wrote political, economic, and social history
Renaissance:		Biondo (1392–1463)	Used many accurate sources in his chronological history of Italy
		Guicciardini (1483–1540)	Described historical events in a clear and methodical manner
Enlightenment:	18th Century	Gibbon (1737–94)	His writings examined the movement and patterns of historical events
	19th Century	Ranke (1795–1886)	Attempted to understand the past through scientific research methods
	20th Century	Febvre (1878–1956) Braudel (1902–85)	They broadened the subject matter by emphasizing social and economic matters, as well as describing military, political, and geographical affairs

WORLD ATLAS

This section is arranged into continental sections, starting
with the Americas and moving eastwards.

North and Central America • South America • Africa
Europe • North and West Asia • South and East Asia
Australasia and Oceania

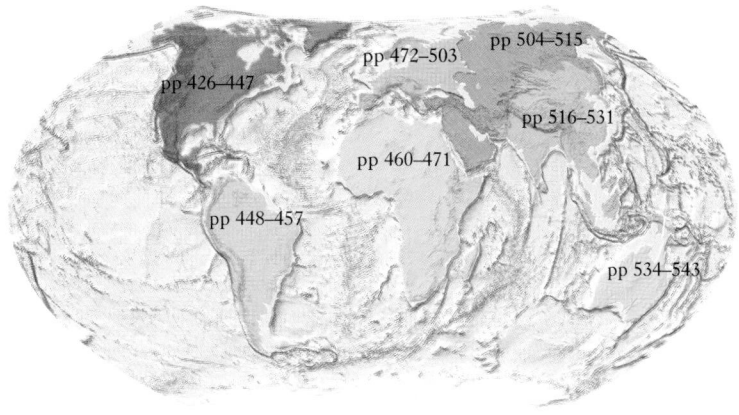

pp 426–447
pp 448–457
pp 460–471
pp 472–503
pp 504–515
pp 516–531
pp 534–543

NORTH AND CENTRAL AMERICA

POPULATION

Less than
50,000
○

50,000 –
100,000
◌

100,000 –
500,000
◉

Over
500,000
▣

EUROPE

Barents
Sea

Mohns Ridge

SVALBARD
(to Norway)

JAN MAYEN
(to Norway)

473

Denmark Strait

Iceland

Reykjanes
Basin

Greenland
Sea

Kong
Frederik VIII
Land

Kong
Christian X
Land

GREENLAND
(to Denmark)

Kong
Christian IX
Land

Kong Frederik VI Kyst

NUUK

North Atlantic Mid-Ocean Canyon

Newfoundland

St John's

Nansen Basin

Nansen Cordillera

North
Pole

Lomonosov Ridge

Makarov
Basin

Alpha Cordillera

Wandel
Sea

Kap Morris Jesup

Lincoln
Sea

Ellesmere
Island

Queen Elizabeth
Islands

Baffin
Bay

Davis Strait

Labrador
Sea

Labrador
Basin

Smallwood
Reservoir

Labrador

Mountains

504

ARCTIC

OCEAN

Mendeleyev Ridge

Chukchi
Plateau

Canada
Basin

Beaufort
Sea

Banks
Island

Victoria
Island

Prince
of Wales
Island

Lancaster Sound

Gulf of Boothia

Foxe
Basin

Southampton
Island

Hudson

Bay

Belcher
Islands

Hudson Strait

Péninsule
d'Ungava

Ungava
Bay

James Bay

Laptev
Sea

East
Siberian
Sea

Wrangel Island

Chukchi
Sea

Limit of winter pack ice

Great Bear
Lake

Great Slave Lake

Lake Athabasca

Reindeer Lake

Lake Winnipeg

C A N A D A

Saskatoon

Regina

ASIA

505

Bering Strait

Bering
Sea

Saint Lawrence
Island

Norton
Sound

Yukon

Alaska
(part of US)

Brooks Range

Mount McKinley
6194m

Alaska Range

Anchorage

Arctic Circle

Mackenzie

Mackenzie
Mountains

Mount Logan
5959m

R o c k y
Mountains

Athabasca

Calgary

Edmonton

Coast Mountains

Vancouver

G

Aleutian Basin

Nunivak Island

Bristol
Bay

Aleutian Range

Kodiak Island

Aleutian Trench

Gulf of
Alaska

Juneau

Alexander
Archipelago

Queen Charlotte
Islands

Vancouver
Island

Victoria

Seattle

Cascadia
Basin

Mount Rainier
4392m

M

Snake

Eugene

Aleutian Islands

545

PACIFIC

OCEAN

426

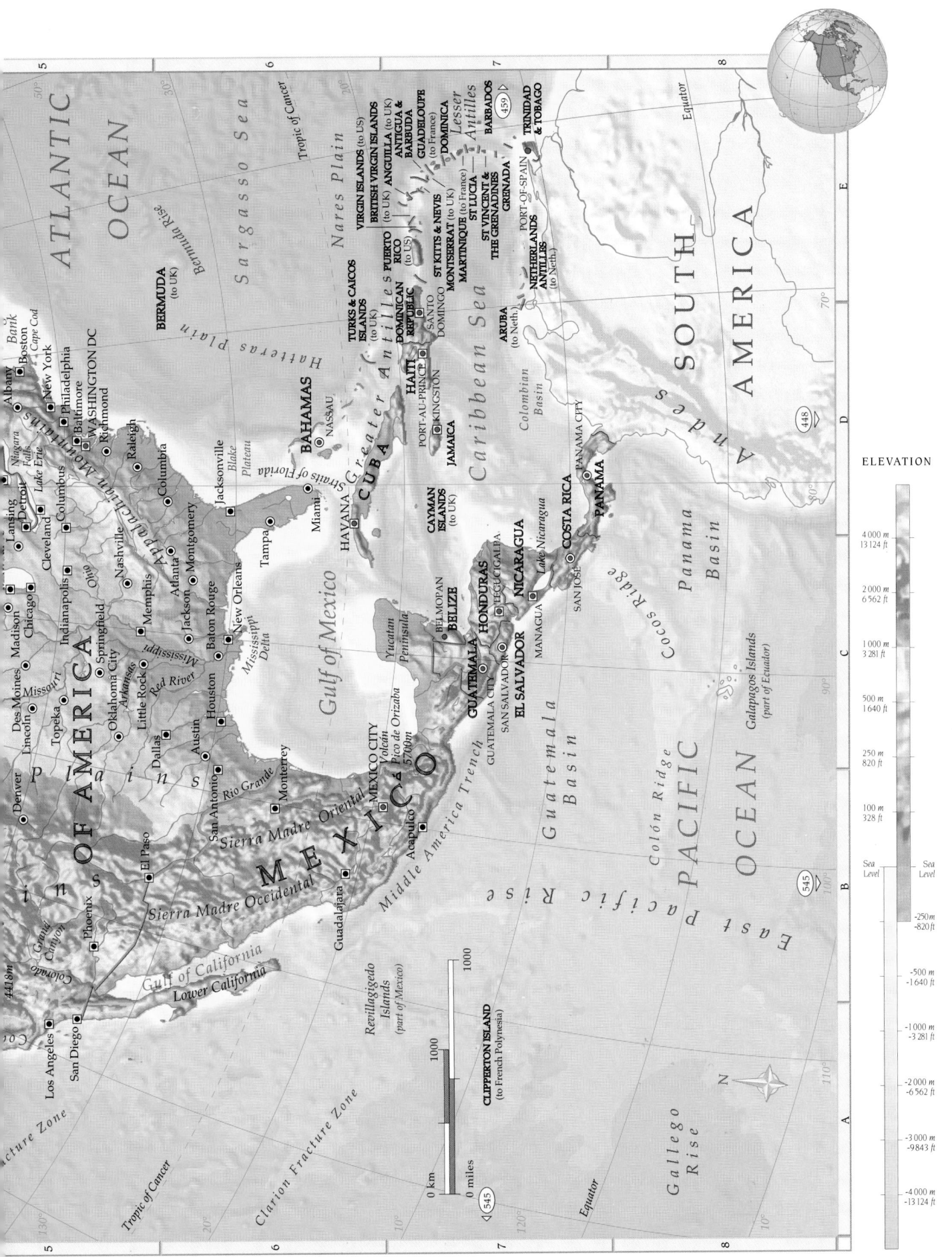

ELEVATION

4 000 m	13 124 ft
2 000 m	6 562 ft
1 000 m	3 281 ft
500 m	1 640 ft
250 m	820 ft
100 m	328 ft
Sea Level	Sea Level
-250 m	-820 ft
-500 m	-1 640 ft
-1 000 m	-3 281 ft
-2 000 m	-6 562 ft
-3 000 m	-9 843 ft
-4 000 m	-13 124 ft

RUSSIAN FEDERATION

Poluostrov Kamchatka

507

Arctic Circle

Ostrov Vrangelya

A R C T

Chukchi Sea

Wevok
Point Lay
Barrow
Kivalina

Colville River

Prud
Umiat

Brooks Range

Near Islands

Attu Island

Bering Sea

544

Gambell
Wales
Deering

Saint Lawrence Island

Norton Sound

Alakanuk

Grayling
Yukon River
Kokrines

Fort Yukon

Rat Islands

Amchitka Island

Nunivak Island

Kwigillingok

A L A S K A
(part of US)

Fairbanks

Pribilof Islands

Platinum

Kuskokwim Mts

McKinley Park

Aleutian Islands

Andreanof Islands

Atka

Bristol Bay

Iliamna Lake

Alaska Range

△ *Mount McKinley 6194m*

Susitna

YUK

Umnak Island
Unalaska Island

Dutch Harbor

Anchorage ◉

Hope
Valdez
Cordova

Gulkana
Chitina

TERRI

Unimak Island

Belkofski

Alaska Peninsula

Kodiak

Katalla

Mount Logan △ 5959m

Shumagin Islands

Kodiak Island

Whitehors

Yakutat

Gulf of Alaska

Haines
Gustavus

At

Juneau
Kake

Alexander Archipelago

Port Alexander

Ketchikan

Prince Rupert

Kitima

Queen Charlotte Islands

Ocean Fal

P A C I F I C

O C E A N

Queen Charlotte Sound

Wa

Port Hardy
Campbell

Vancouver Island

N

535

535

POPULATION

Less than 50,000 ○

50,000 – 100,000 ○

100,000 – 500,000 ◉

Over 500,000 ▣

0 km   400

0 miles   400

ELEVATION

4 000 m
13 124 ft

2 000 m
6 562 ft

1 000 m
3 281 ft

500 m
1 640 ft

250 m
820 ft

100 m
328 ft

Sea
Level

Sea
Level

−250 m
−820 ft

−500 m
−1 640 ft

−1 000 m
−3 281 ft

−2 000 m
−6 562 ft

−3 000 m
−9 843 ft

−4 000 m
−13 124 ft

Eastern Canada

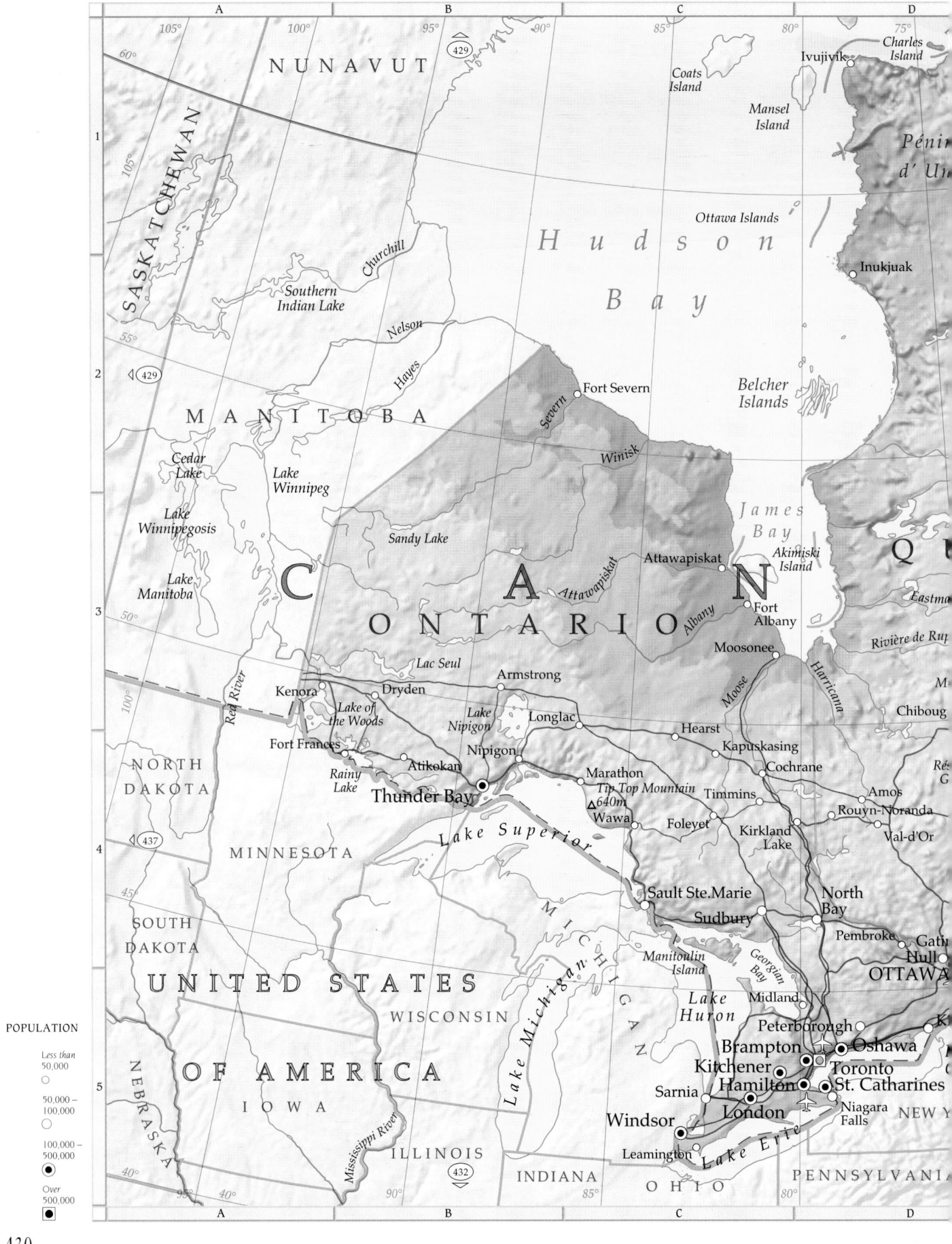

NUNAVUT

SASKATCHEWAN

Churchill

Southern Indian Lake

Nelson

Hayes

MANITOBA

Cedar Lake

Lake Winnipeg

Lake Winnipegosis

Lake Manitoba

Sandy Lake

C A N

O N T A R I O

Lac Seul

Kenora

Dryden

Armstrong

Lake of the Woods

Lake Nipigon

Longlac

Hearst

Kapuskasing

Cochrane

Fort Frances

Atikokan

Nipigon

Marathon

Tip Top Mountain
△640m

Timmins

Amos

Rouyn-Noranda

Val-d'Or

Rainy Lake

Thunder Bay

Wawa

Foleyet

Kirkland Lake

NORTH DAKOTA

Red River

MINNESOTA

Lake Superior

Sault Ste.Marie

Sudbury

North Bay

Pembroke

Gati

Hull

OTTAWA

SOUTH DAKOTA

M I C H I G A N

Manitoulin Island

Georgian Bay

Lake Huron

Midland

Peterborough

UNITED STATES

WISCONSIN

Lake Michigan

Brampton

Kitchener

Hamilton

Sarnia

London

Oshawa

Toronto

St. Catharines

K

OF AMERICA

IOWA

Windsor

Leamington

Niagara Falls

NEW Y

NEBRASKA

Mississippi River

ILLINOIS

INDIANA

OHIO

PENNSYLVANIA

HUDSON

Bay

Coats Island

Mansel Island

Ivujivik

Charles Island

Péni d'U

Ottawa Islands

Inukjuak

Belcher Islands

Fort Severn

Severn

Winisk

James Bay

Akimiski Island

Attawapiskat

Attawapiskat

Albany

Fort Albany

Moosonee

Moose

Harricana

Chibou

Rivière de Rup

Eastma

Qu

Lake Erie

Lake Huron

POPULATION

Less than 50,000
○

50,000 –
100,000
○

100,000 –
500,000
◉

Over 500,000
●

E 65° 60° F 55° G 60° 50° 45° H

⌒
474

L a b r a d o r   S e a

1

Resolution
Island

Button Islands

Akpatok
Island

ngava
Bay

55°
40°

458

2

Rivière à la Baleine

Nain

Hopedale
Makkovik

Cape Harrison

Cartwright

Caniapiscau

Schefferville

Smallwood
Reservoir

Lake Melville

50°

NEWFOUNDLAND

Churchill

r de
cau

St.Anthony

ELEVATION

C

D

A

Strait of Belle Isle

4 000 m
13 124 ft

2 000 m
6 562 ft

éservoir
ouagan

Havre-St-Pierre

Laurentian Mountains

Sept-Îles

Île d'Anticosti

Corner Brook

Gander

Grand Falls

Newfoundland

St.Johns

1 000 m
3 281 ft

500 m
1 640 ft

3

Baie-Comeau

St.Lawrence

Gaspé

Gulf of
St. Lawrence

Channel-Port
aux Basques

Cape Race

45°

250 m
820 ft

Matane
Péninsule de
Gaspé

Chicoutimi

Rimouski

Îles de la
Madeleine

Cabot Strait

100 m
328 ft

Rivière-du-Loup

Edmundston

**PRINCE
EDWARD
ISLAND**

Glace Bay

**ST PIERRE
& MIQUELON**
(French territorial
collectivity)

Sea
Level

Sea
Level

Charlesbourg

**NEW
BRUNSWICK**

Charlottetown

Sydney

Cape Breton
Island

4

Québec

Moncton

Amherst

-250 m
-820 ft

St-Georges

Oromocto

New Glasgow

458

50°

rés

mondville

Fredericton

Truro

NOVA SCOTIA

-500 m
-1 640 ft

MAINE

Saint John

Dartmouth

Sable Island

herbrooke

Halifax

Bay of Fundy

Liverpool

-1 000 m
-3 281 ft

Yarmouth

40°

-2 000 m
-6 562 ft

NEW
MPSHIRE

A T L A N T I C

5

-3 000 m
-9 843 ft

HUSETTS

Cape Cod

N

O C E A N

0 km   400

458

0 miles   400

65°
70°

40°

60°

55°

-4 000 m
-13 124 ft

RHODE ISLAND

LICUT

E F G H

NORTHEAST USA

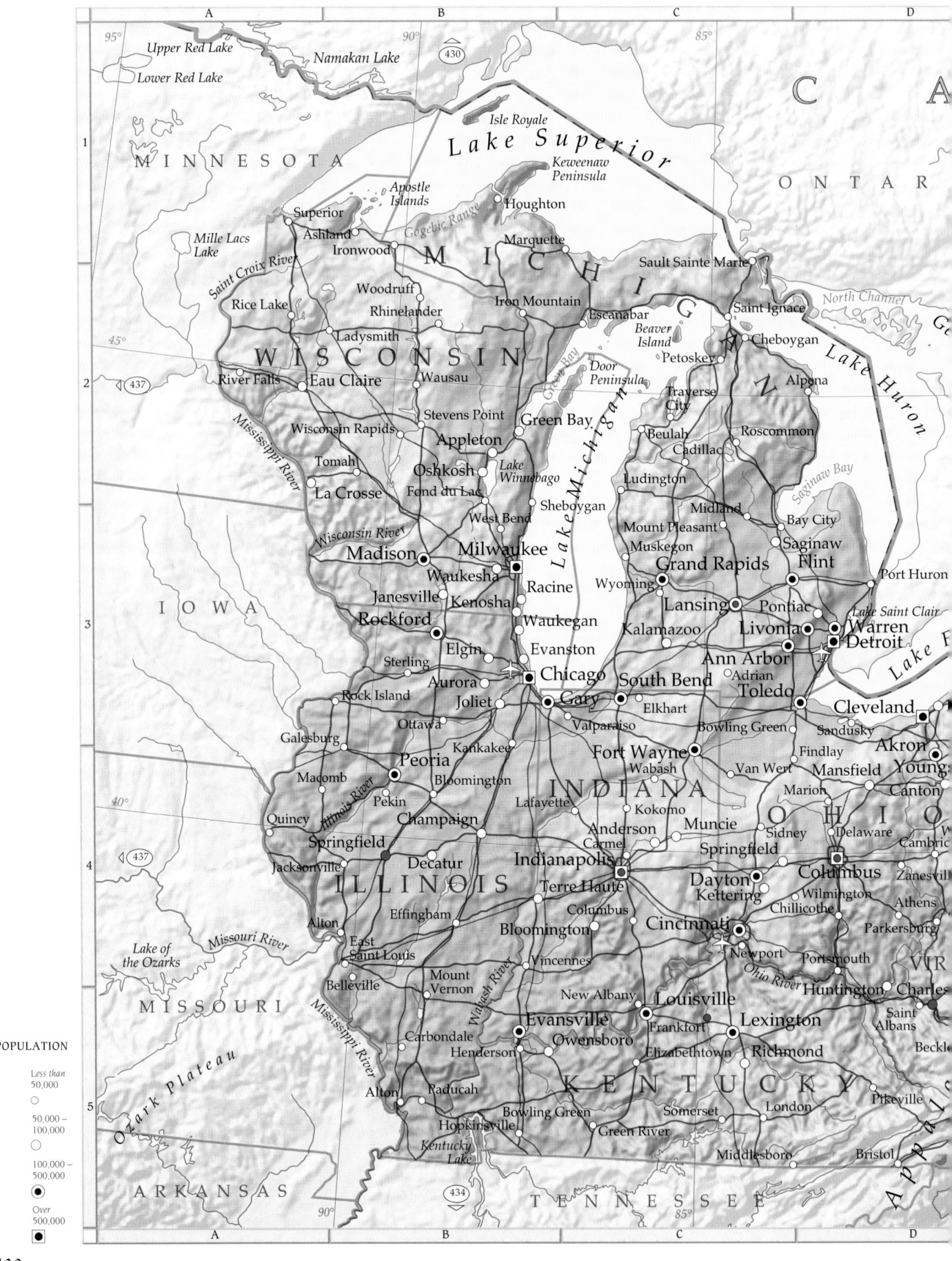

MINNESOTA

Upper Red Lake
Lower Red Lake
Namakan Lake

Isle Royale
Lake Superior
Keweenaw Peninsula

Apostle Islands
Superior
Ashland
Ironwood
Houghton
Marquette

Mille Lacs Lake
Saint Croix River
Woodruff
Iron Mountain
Sault Sainte Marie
North Channel

Rice Lake
Rhinelander
Escanaba
Saint Ignace

WISCONSIN
Ladysmith
Beaver Island
Cheboygan
Lake Huron

MICHIGAN
Petoskey
Alpena

River Falls
Eau Claire
Wausau
Traverse City
Roscommon

Wisconsin Rapids
Stevens Point
Green Bay
Beulah
Cadillac

Tomah
Appleton
Door Peninsula
Ludington

La Crosse
Oshkosh
Lake Winnebago
Midland
Bay City

Fond du Lac
Sheboygan
Mount Pleasant
Saginaw Bay

West Bend
Muskegon
Saginaw
Flint

Wisconsin River
Madison
Milwaukee
Grand Rapids
Port Huron

Waukesha
Racine
Wyoming
Lansing
Pontiac
Lake Saint Clair

Janesville
Kenosha
Kalamazoo
Livonia
Warren
Detroit

Rockford
Waukegan
Ann Arbor
Lake Erie

Elgin
Evanston
South Bend
Adrian
Toledo

Sterling
Chicago
Gary
Elkhart
Cleveland

Aurora
Joliet
Valparaiso
Bowling Green
Sandusky
Akron

Rock Island
Ottawa
Fort Wayne
Findlay
Youngstown

Galesburg
Kankakee
Wabash
Van Wert
Mansfield
Canton

Peoria
Bloomington
INDIANA
Marion

Macomb
Lafayette
Kokomo
Sidney
Delaware
Cambridge

Quincy
Champaign
Anderson
Muncie
OHIO

Pekin
Carmel
Springfield
Columbus
Zanesville

Springfield
Decatur
Indianapolis
Dayton
Kettering

Jacksonville
ILLINOIS
Terre Haute
Wilmington
Athens

Alton
Effingham
Columbus
Chillicothe
Parkersburg

East Saint Louis
Bloomington
Cincinnati
Portsmouth

Missouri River
Vincennes
Newport
Huntington
Charleston

Belleville
Mount Vernon
Wabash River
New Albany
Louisville
Lexington
Saint Albans

MISSOURI
Carbondale
Evansville
Frankfort
Beckley

Henderson
Owensboro
Elizabethtown
Richmond

Lake of the Ozarks
Ohio River

Alton
Paducah
KENTUCKY
London
Pikeville

Ozark Plateau
Hopkinsville
Bowling Green
Somerset

ARKANSAS
Kentucky Lake
Green River
Middlesboro
Bristol

TENNESSEE

ONTARIO
CANADA

IOWA

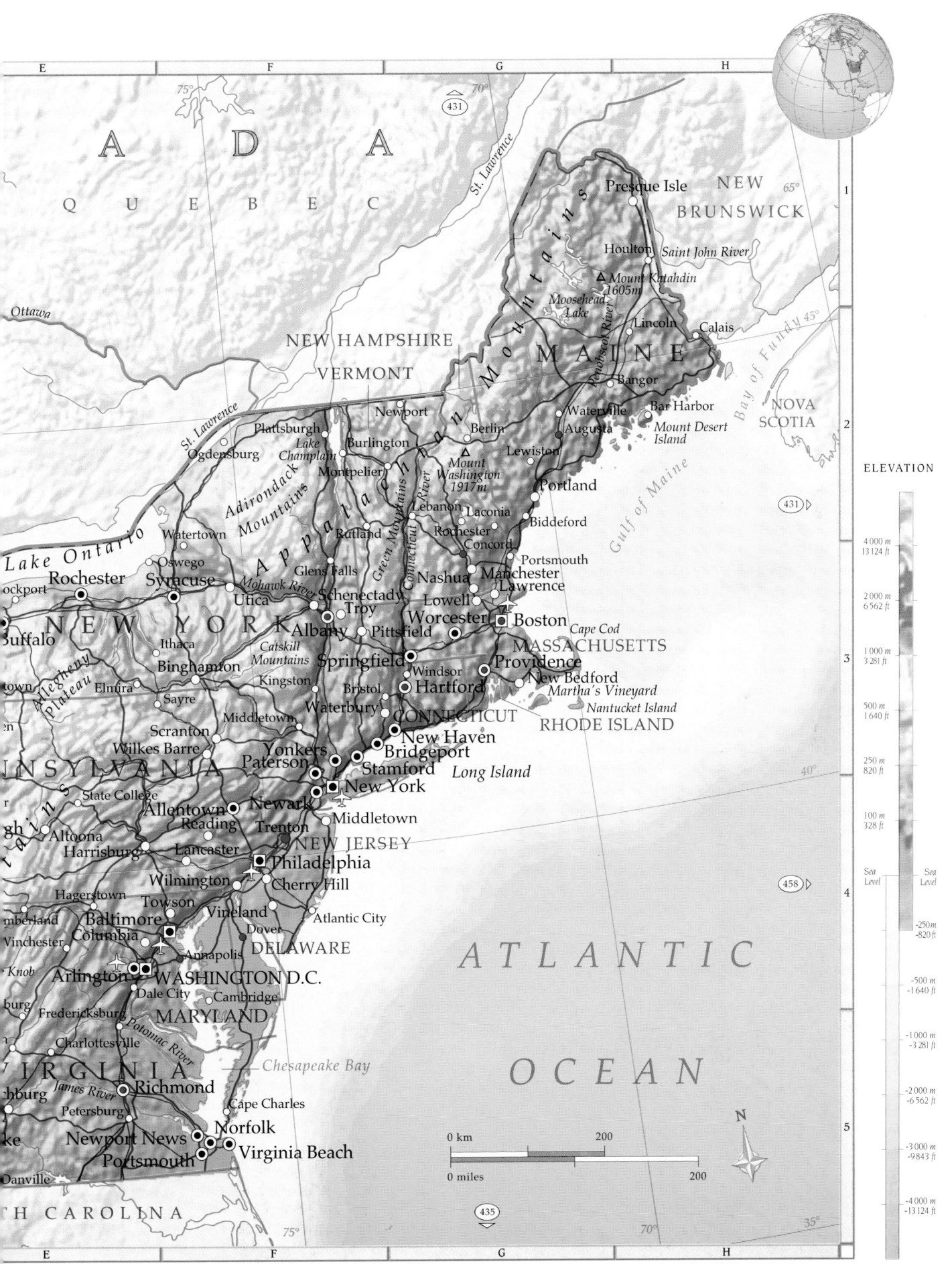

E   F   G   H

75°   *70°*   431   *65°*   1

C   A   D   A   NEW
BRUNSWICK

QUEBEC

Presque Isle

St. Lawrence

Houlton   *Saint John River*

△ *Mount Katahdin*
     1605m

Lincoln   Calais

Ottawa   *Moosehead
Lake*

M A I N E

Bay of Fundy *45°*

Bangor

NOVA
SCOTIA

NEW HAMPSHIRE

VERMONT   Waterville   Bar Harbor

Newport   Berlin   Augusta   *Mount Desert
Island*

Plattsburgh   Burlington   Lewiston   *Gulf of Maine*   2

St. Lawrence   Ogdensburg   *Lake
Champlain*   Montpelier   *Mount
Washington
1917m*   Portland

431 ▷

*Adirondack
Mountains*   Rutland   Lebanon   Laconia   Biddeford

Watertown   Rochester

Glens Falls   Concord   Portsmouth

Oswego   *Mohawk River*   Schenectady   Nashua   Manchester

Lake Ontario   Rochester   Syracuse   Utica   Troy   Lowell   Lawrence

ockport   N E W   Y O R K   Albany   Pittsfield   Worcester   Boston   *Cape Cod*   3

Buffalo   Ithaca   *Catskill
Mountains*   Springfield   Providence

*Allegheny
Plateau*   Binghamton   Kingston   Windsor   M A S S A C H U S E T T S

town   Elmira   Sayre   Bristol   Hartford   New Bedford

en   Waterbury   *Martha's Vineyard*

Middletown   C O N N E C T I C U T   *Nantucket Island*

Scranton   New Haven   RHODE ISLAND

Wilkes Barre   Yonkers   Bridgeport

PENNSYLVANIA   Paterson   Stamford   *Long Island*   *40°*

           New York

State College   Allentown   Newark

ginia   Altoona   Reading   Middletown

     Harrisburg   Lancaster   Trenton

untains   NEW JERSEY

Hagerstown   Wilmington   Philadelphia

      Towson   Cherry Hill

mberland   Baltimore   Vineland   Atlantic City   4

inchester   Columbia   Dover

      Annapolis   DELAWARE

Knob   Arlington   WASHINGTON D.C.   A T L A N T I C

burg   Dale City   Cambridge

Fredericksburg   MARYLAND

      Charlottesville   *Potomac River*   O C E A N

VIRGINIA   *Chesapeake Bay*

hburg   *James River*   Richmond

Petersburg

      Cape Charles

ke   Norfolk

Newport News   Virginia Beach   5

Danville   Portsmouth

0 km   200   N

0 miles   200

TH CAROLINA

75°   435   *70°*   *35°*

E   F   G   H

ELEVATION

4 000 m	13 124 ft
2 000 m	6 562 ft
1 000 m	3 281 ft
500 m	1 640 ft
250 m	820 ft
100 m	328 ft
Sea Level	Sea Level
-250 m	-820 ft
-500 m	-1 640 ft
-1 000 m	-3 281 ft
-2 000 m	-6 562 ft
-3 000 m	-9 843 ft
-4 000 m	-13 124 ft

SOUTHEAST USA

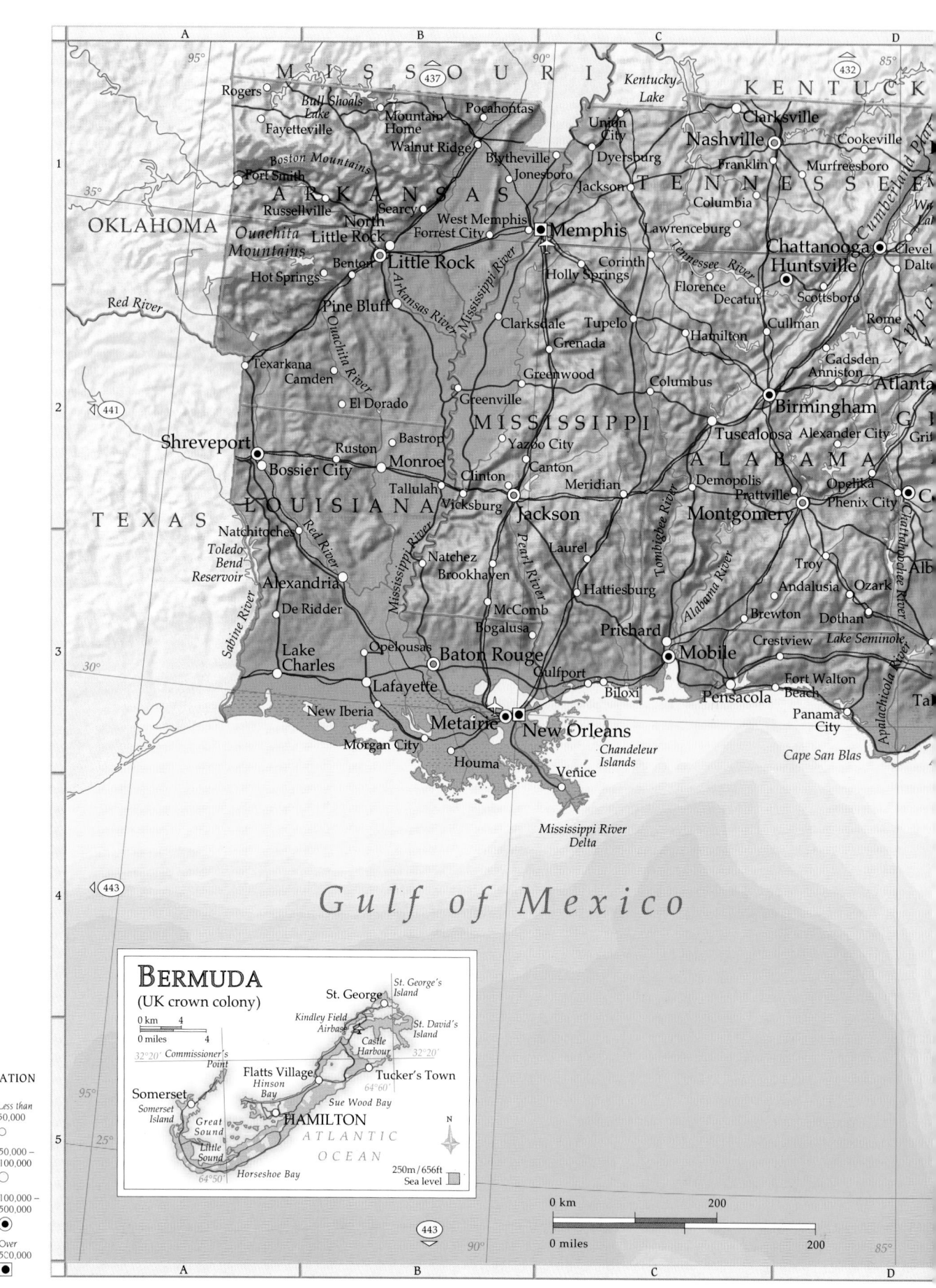

MISSOURI

Rogers
Bull Shoals
Lake
Fayetteville
Mountain
Home
Pocahontas
Walnut Ridge
Boston Mountains
Blytheville
Jonesboro
Fort Smith

OKLAHOMA

35°

ARKANSAS

Russellville
Searcy
West Memphis
Jackson
Ouachita
Mountains
North
Little Rock
Forrest City
Memphis
Little Rock
Benton
Little Rock
Holly Springs
Clarksdale
Corinth
Hot Springs
Pine Bluff
Ouachita River
Greenwood
Grenada
Tupelo

Red River

Texarkana
Camden
El Dorado
Greenville
Columbus

30°

Shreveport
Bossier City
Ruston
Monroe
Bastrop
Yazoo City
Canton
MISSISSIPPI
Clinton
Tallulah
Vicksburg
Jackson
Meridian

TEXAS

LOUISIANA

Natchitoches
Toledo
Bend
Reservoir
Natchez
Brookhaven
Laurel
Alexandria
De Ridder
McComb
Hattiesburg
Bogalusa
Prichard
Lake
Charles
Opelousas
Baton Rouge
Gulfport
Mobile
Lafayette
Metairie
Biloxi
Pensacola
New Iberia
New Orleans
Morgan City
Chandeleur
Islands
Houma
Venice
Cape San Blas

Mississippi River
Delta

TENNESSEE

Kentucky
Lake
Union
City
Dyersburg
Clarksville
Nashville
Cookeville
Franklin
Murfreesboro
Columbia
Lawrenceburg
Florence
Decatur
Chattanooga
Huntsville
Scottsboro
Cullman
Rome
Hamilton
Gadsden
Anniston
Atlanta

ALABAMA

Birmingham
Tuscaloosa
Alexander City
Demopolis
Prattville
Opelika
Montgomery
Phenix City
Troy
Andalusia
Ozark
Brewton
Dothan
Crestview
Lake Seminole
Fort Walton
Beach
Panama
City

Gulf of Mexico

BERMUDA
(UK crown colony)

0 km   4
0 miles   4

32°20'   Commissioner's
Point

Somerset
Somerset
Island
Great
Sound
Little
Sound

St. George's
Island
St. George
Kindley Field
Airbase
St. David's
Island
Castle
Harbour
32°20'
Flatts Village
Hinson
Bay
Tucker's Town
64°60'
Sue Wood Bay

HAMILTON

ATLANTIC
OCEAN

64°50'   Horseshoe Bay

250m/656ft
Sea level

POPULATION

Less than
50,000
○

50,000 –
100,000
○

100,000 –
500,000
◉

Over
500,000
◾

0 km   200

0 miles   200

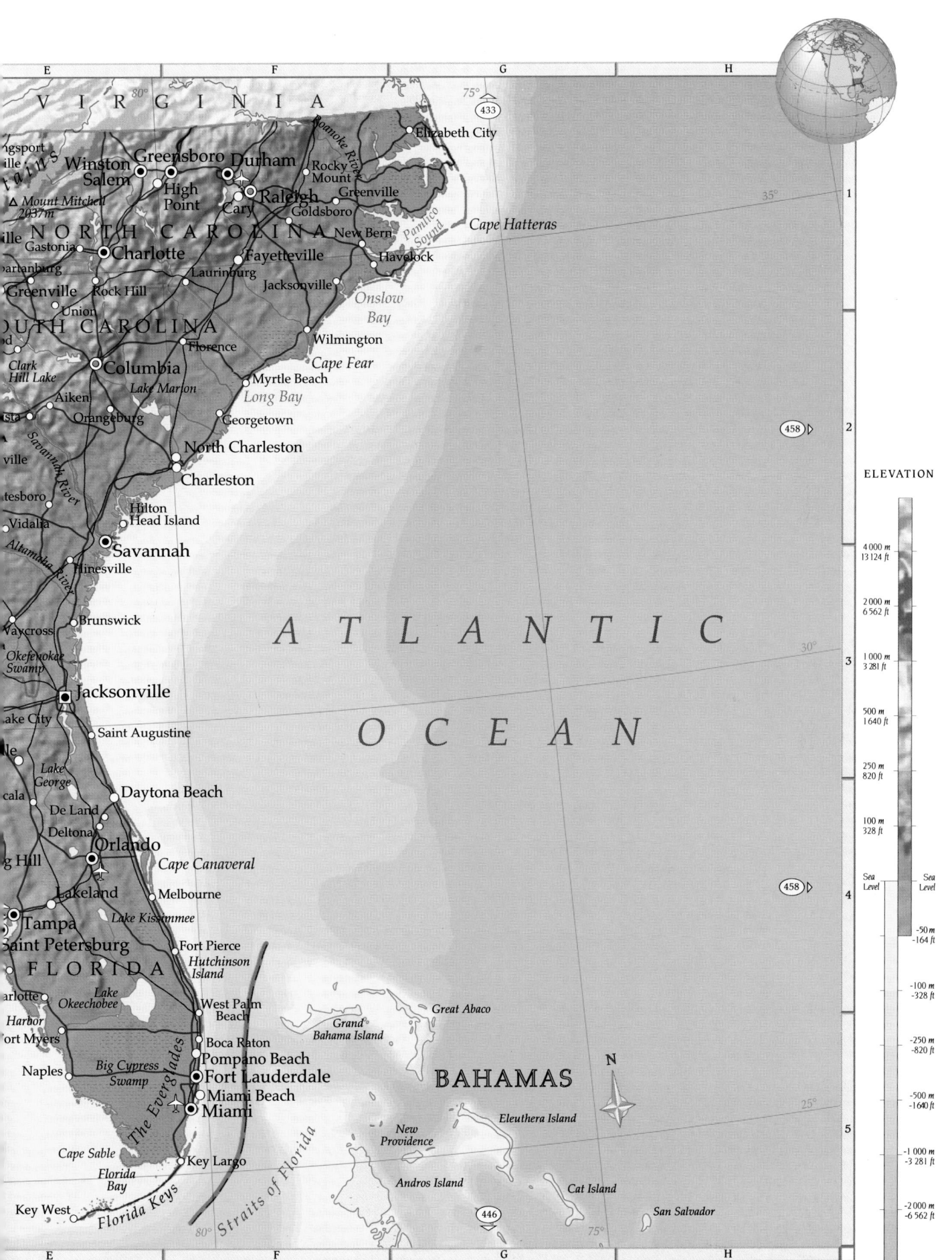

E   F   G   H

80°

VIRGINIA

gsport
ille
ws

75°

433

Elizabeth City

Winston
Salem

Greensboro Durham

High
Point

△ *Mount Mitchell*
2037m

Rocky
Mount

Greenville

Cary Raleigh

Goldsboro

Roanoke River

NORTH CAROLINA

New Bern

*Pamlico
Sound*

Cape Hatteras

35° 1

ile
Gastonia

Charlotte

Fayetteville

Havelock

Greenville Rock Hill

Laurinburg

Jacksonville

*Onslow
Bay*

Union

UTH CAROLINA

Wilmington

*Clark
Hill Lake*

Florence

Columbia

Lake Marion

Cape Fear

Myrtle Beach

Long Bay

2 458

Aiken

Orangeburg

Georgetown

sta

North Charleston

ville

Charleston

Savannah River

Hilton
Head Island

tesboro

Savannah

Vidalia

Hinesville

Altamaha River

Waycross

Brunswick

*Okefenokee
Swamp*

A T L A N T I C

30° 3

Jacksonville

ake City

O C E A N

le

Saint Augustine

*Lake
George*

cala

Daytona Beach

De Land

Deltona

g Hill

Orlando

Lakeland

Cape Canaveral

Melbourne

4 458

Tampa

Lake Kissimmee

aint Petersburg

FLORIDA

Fort Pierce

arlotte

*Lake
Okeechobee*

*Hutchinson
Island*

Harbor

ort Myers

West Palm
Beach

Great Abaco

Naples

*Big Cypress
Swamp*

Boca Raton

*Grand
Bahama Island*

Pompano Beach

Fort Lauderdale

The Everglades

Miami Beach

BAHAMAS

N

Miami

Eleuthera Island

Cape Sable

25° 5

Key Largo

*New
Providence*

*Florida
Bay*

Key West

Florida Keys

80° *Straits of Florida*

Andros Island

75°

Cat Island

San Salvador

446

E   F   G   H

ELEVATION

4 000 m	13 124 ft
2 000 m	6 562 ft
1 000 m	3 281 ft
500 m	1 640 ft
250 m	820 ft
100 m	328 ft
Sea Level	Sea Level
-50 m	-164 ft
-100 m	-328 ft
-250 m	-820 ft
-500 m	-1 640 ft
-1 000 m	-3 281 ft
-2 000 m	-6 562 ft

CENTRAL USA

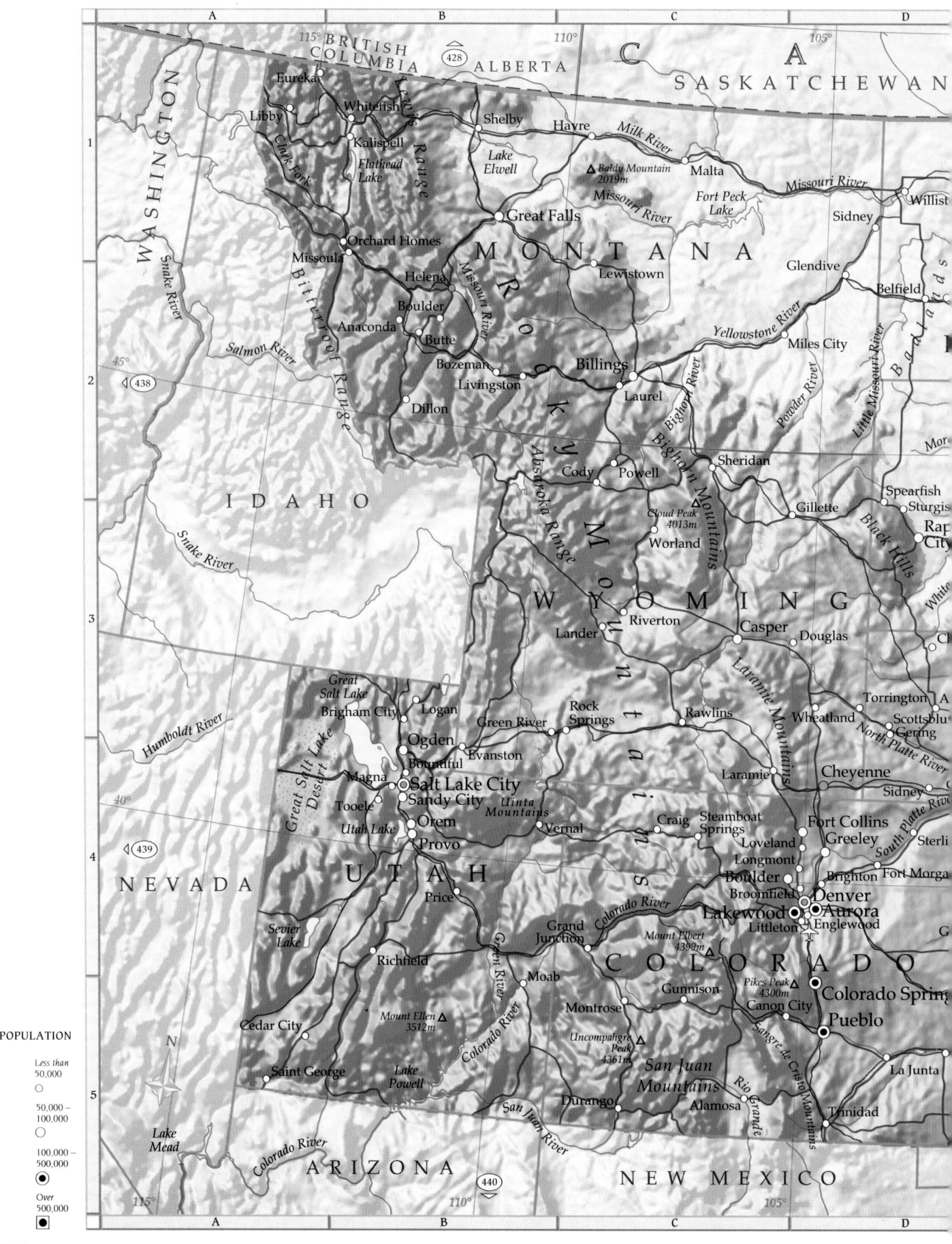

A   N   A   D   A

SASKATCHEWAN

BRITISH COLUMBIA

ALBERTA

428

Eureka

Libby

Whitefish

Shelby

Havre

Milk River

Malta

Missouri River

Willist

Kalispell

Flathead Lake

Lake Elwell

△ Baldy Mountain 2019m

Fort Peck Lake

Sidney

Louis Range

Clark Fork

Great Falls

M   O   N   T   A   N   A

Missouri River

Glendive

Belfield

Orchard Homes

Missoula

Helena

Lewistown

Yellowstone River

Miles City

Bitterroot Range

Boulder

Anaconda

Missouri River

Butte

Billings

Laurel

Powder River

Little Missouri River

Mor

Bozeman

Livingston

Dillon

Snake River

Salmon River

438

Absaroka Range

Bighorn River

Sheridan

Spearfish

Sturgis

Cody

Powell

Bighorn Mountains

Gillette

Black Hills

Rap City

I   D   A   H   O

Cloud Peak 4013m

Worland

White

Snake River

R   o   c   k   y

W   Y   O   M   I   N   G

Lander

Riverton

Casper

Douglas

Ch

Torrington

Scottsblu

Gering

Humboldt River

Great Salt Lake

Logan

Brigham City

Green River

Rock Springs

Rawlins

Laramie Mountains

Wheatland

North Platte River

Ogden

Evanston

Cheyenne

Great Salt Lake Desert

Bountiful

Magna

Salt Lake City

Sandy City

Uinta Mountains

Vernal

Craig

Steamboat Springs

Loveland

Fort Collins

Greeley

Sidney

Sterli

M   o   u   n   t   a   i   n   s

South Platte Rive

Tooele

Orem

Longmont

N   E   V   A   D   A

Utah Lake

Provo

Boulder

Brighton

Fort Morga

U   T   A   H

Price

Broomfield

Denver

Lakewood

Aurora

Littleton

Englewood

Sevier Lake

Grand Junction

Colorado River

Mount Elbert 4399m △

Richfield

Moab

C   O   L   O   R   A   D   O

Pikes Peak 4300m △

Colorado Spring

Gunnison

Canon City

Montrose

Cedar City

Green River

Mount Ellen △ 3512m

Uncompahgre Peak 4361m △

Pueblo

Colorado River

San Juan Mountains

Rio Grande

Sangre de Cristo Mountains

La Junta

Saint George

Lake Powell

San Juan River

Durango

Alamosa

Trinidad

Lake Mead

Colorado River

A   R   I   Z   O   N   A

440

N   E   W   M   E   X   I   C   O

WASHINGTON

438

439

N

POPULATION

Less than 50,000 ○

50,000 – 100,000 ○

100,000 – 500,000 ◉

Over 500,000 ◼

436

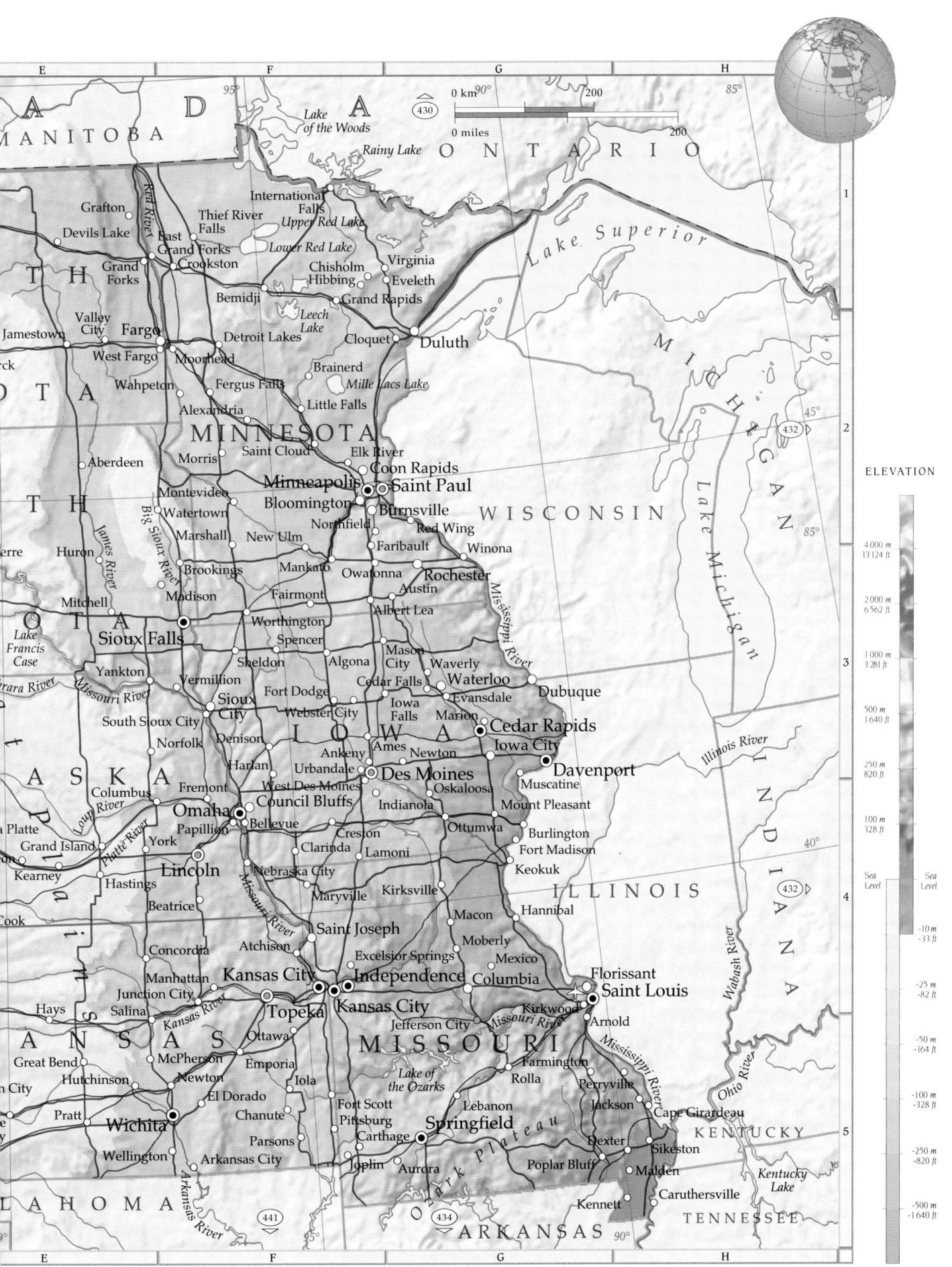

E   F   G   H

C A N A D A

MANITOBA

Lake of the Woods

Rainy Lake

O N T A R I O

430

0 km   90°   200

0 miles   200

85°

1

Grafton

Devils Lake

Red River

Thief River Falls

International Falls

Upper Red Lake

Lower Red Lake

Lake Superior

East Grand Forks

Crookston

Grand Forks

Chisholm
Hibbing

Virginia
Eveleth

Bemidji

Grand Rapids

Leech Lake

M I C H I G A N

Valley City

Jamestown

Fargo

West Fargo

Moorhead

Detroit Lakes

Cloquet   Duluth

45°

432

2

Wahpeton

Fergus Falls

Brainerd

Mille Lacs Lake

Lake Michigan

Aberdeen

Alexandria

M I N N E S O T A

Little Falls

Saint Cloud   Elk River

Morris

Coon Rapids

W I S C O N S I N

85°

ELEVATION

Montevideo

Minneapolis   Saint Paul

Watertown

Bloomington   Burnsville

James River

Marshall

New Ulm

Northfield

Red Wing

4 000 m
13 124 ft

Huron

Brookings

Mankato

Owatonna

Faribault

Winona

2 000 m
6 562 ft

Big Sioux River

Madison

Fairmont

Albert Lea

Austin

Rochester

Mississippi River

Mitchell

Worthington

Spencer

Algona

Mason City

Waverly

1 000 m
3 281 ft

Lake Francis Case

Sioux Falls

Sheldon

Cedar Falls

Waterloo

Dubuque

500 m
1 640 ft

Yankton

Vermillion

Fort Dodge

Iowa Falls

Evansdale

Niobrara River

Missouri River

Sioux City

Webster City

Ames

Marion

Cedar Rapids

Iowa City

3

South Sioux City

I O W A

Newton

Davenport

250 m
820 ft

N E B R A S K A

Norfolk

Denison

Harlan

Ankeny
Urbandale

Des Moines

Muscatine

I N D I A N A

Columbus

Loup River

Fremont

West Des Moines

Oskaloosa

Mount Pleasant

Illinois River

100 m
328 ft

Platte River

Omaha

Council Bluffs

Indianola

Ottumwa

Burlington

Grand Island

Papillion

Bellevue

Creston

Fort Madison

York

Clarinda

Lamoni

Keokuk

40°

432

Sea Level

Platte

Lincoln

Nebraska City

Kirksville

I L L I N O I S

Kearney

Hastings

Maryville

Macon

Hannibal

4

-10 m
-33 ft

Cook

Beatrice

Saint Joseph

Moberly

Wabash River

-25 m
-82 ft

Concordia

Atchison

Excelsior Springs

Mexico

Florissant

Manhattan

Kansas City

Independence

Columbia

Saint Louis

Hays

Junction City

Kansas City

Kirkwood

Arnold

-50 m
-164 ft

Salina

Topeka

Kansas River

Jefferson City

Missouri River

K A N S A S

Ottawa

M I S S O U R I

Mississippi River

Farmington

Perryville

-100 m
-328 ft

Great Bend

McPherson

Emporia

Rolla

Jackson

Cape Girardeau

Ohio River

K E N T U C K Y

Hutchinson

Newton

Iola

Lake of the Ozarks

Lebanon

5

Pratt

El Dorado

Chanute

Fort Scott

Pittsburg

Springfield

Dexter

Sikeston

-250 m
-820 ft

Wichita

Parsons

Carthage

Ozark Plateau

Poplar Bluff

Malden

Wellington

Arkansas City

Joplin

Aurora

Kennett

Caruthersville

T E N N E S S E E

Arkansas River

O K L A H O M A

441

434

A R K A N S A S

90°

-500 m
-1 640 ft

Kentucky Lake

E   F   G   H

WEST USA

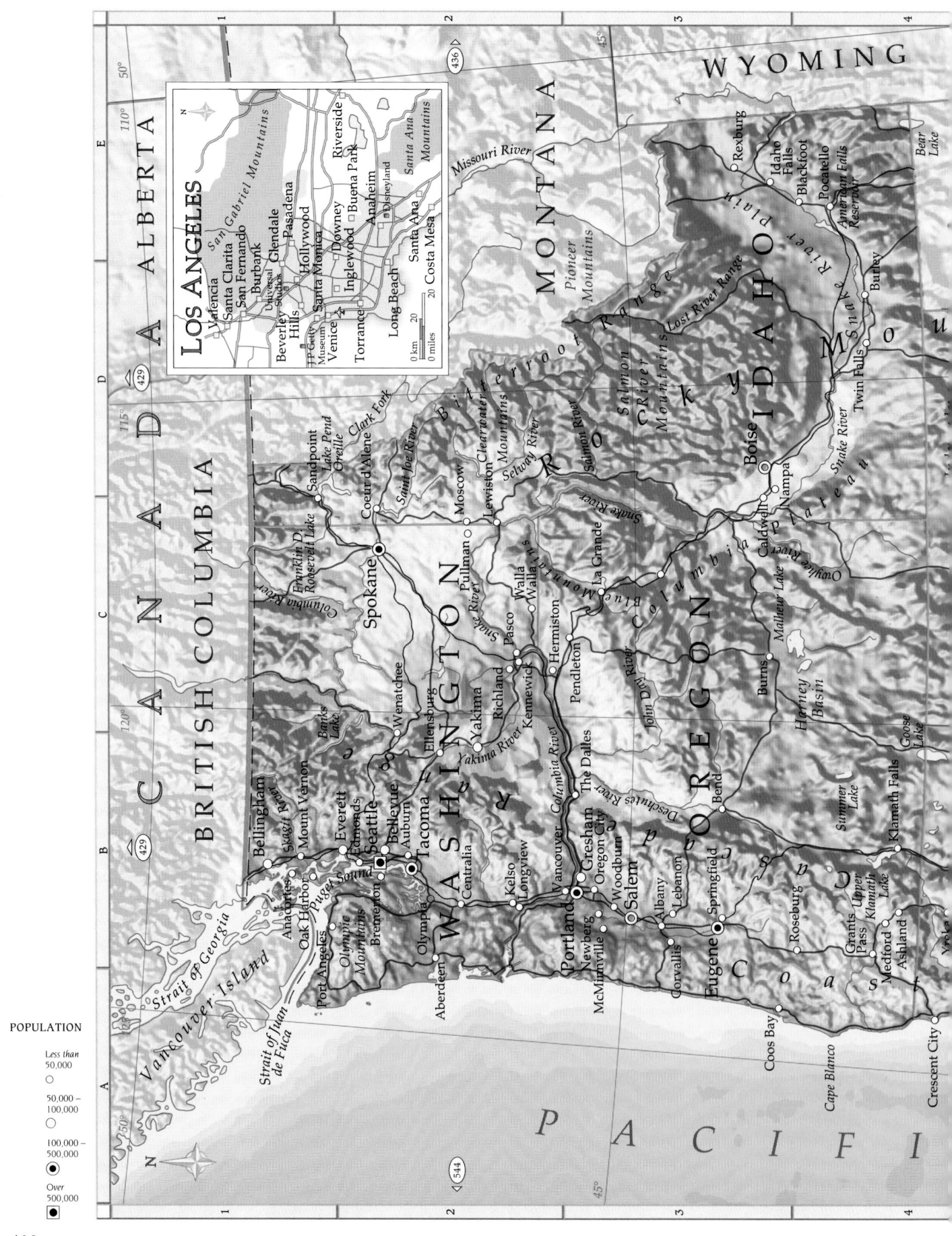

WYOMING

MONTANA

IDAHO

OREGON

WASHINGTON

CANADA

BRITISH COLUMBIA

ALBERTA

LOS ANGELES

N

Valencia
Santa Clarita
San Fernando
Burbank
Beverley
Hills
J Getty
Museum
Venice
Torrance

Santa Gabriel Mountains
Glendale
Pasadena
Universal
Studios
Hollywood
Santa Monica
Inglewood

Riverside

Downey
Buena Park
Anaheim
Disneyland

Santa Ana
Mountains

Santa Ana
Costa Mesa

Long Beach

0 km   20
0 miles   20

Missouri River

Pioneer
Mountains

Bitterroot

Salmon River
Mountains

Rexburg
Idaho
Falls
Blackfoot
Pocatello
American Falls
Reservoir

Bear
Lake

Burley

Snake River Plain

Twin Falls

Salmon River

Boise
Nampa

Caldwell

Payette River
Owyhee River

Snake River
Malheur Lake

Burns

Harney
Basin

Goose
Lake

Sandpoint
Lake Pend
Oreille
Coeur d'Alene
Clark Fork

Saint Joe River

Moscow
Pullman
Lewiston
Clearwater
Selway River

Walla
Walla

La Grande

Blue Mountains

Columbia River

John Day River

Deschutes River

Summer
Lake

Klamath Falls

Upper
Klamath
Lake

Franklin D.
Roosevelt Lake

Columbia River

Spokane

Banks
Lake

Wenatchee

Ellensburg

Yakima

Yakima River

Snake River

Pasco
Richland
Kennewick

Hermiston

Pendleton

The Dalles

Bend

Roseburg

Grants
Pass

Medford
Ashland

Yreka

Bellingham
Skagit River
Mount Vernon
Everett
Edmonds
Seattle
Bellevue
Auburn
Tacoma

Anacortes
Oak Harbor
Puget Sound
Bremerton
Olympia

Port Angeles
Olympic
Mountains

Strait of Juan
de Fuca

Strait of Georgia

Vancouver Island

Aberdeen

Centralia

Kelso
Longview

Vancouver
Gresham
Oregon City
Portland
Newberg
McMinnville
Woodburn
Salem
Albany
Lebanon
Corvallis
Eugene
Springfield

Coos Bay

Cape Blanco

Crescent City

Cascade

Coast

PACIFI

429

429

436

544

50°

110°

115°

120°

45°

45°

50°

E

D

C

B

A

1

2

3

4

Rocky Mountains

Columbia
Plateau

Lost River Range

POPULATION

Less than
50,000
○

50,000 –
100,000
○

100,000 –
500,000
◉

Over
500,000
◼

N

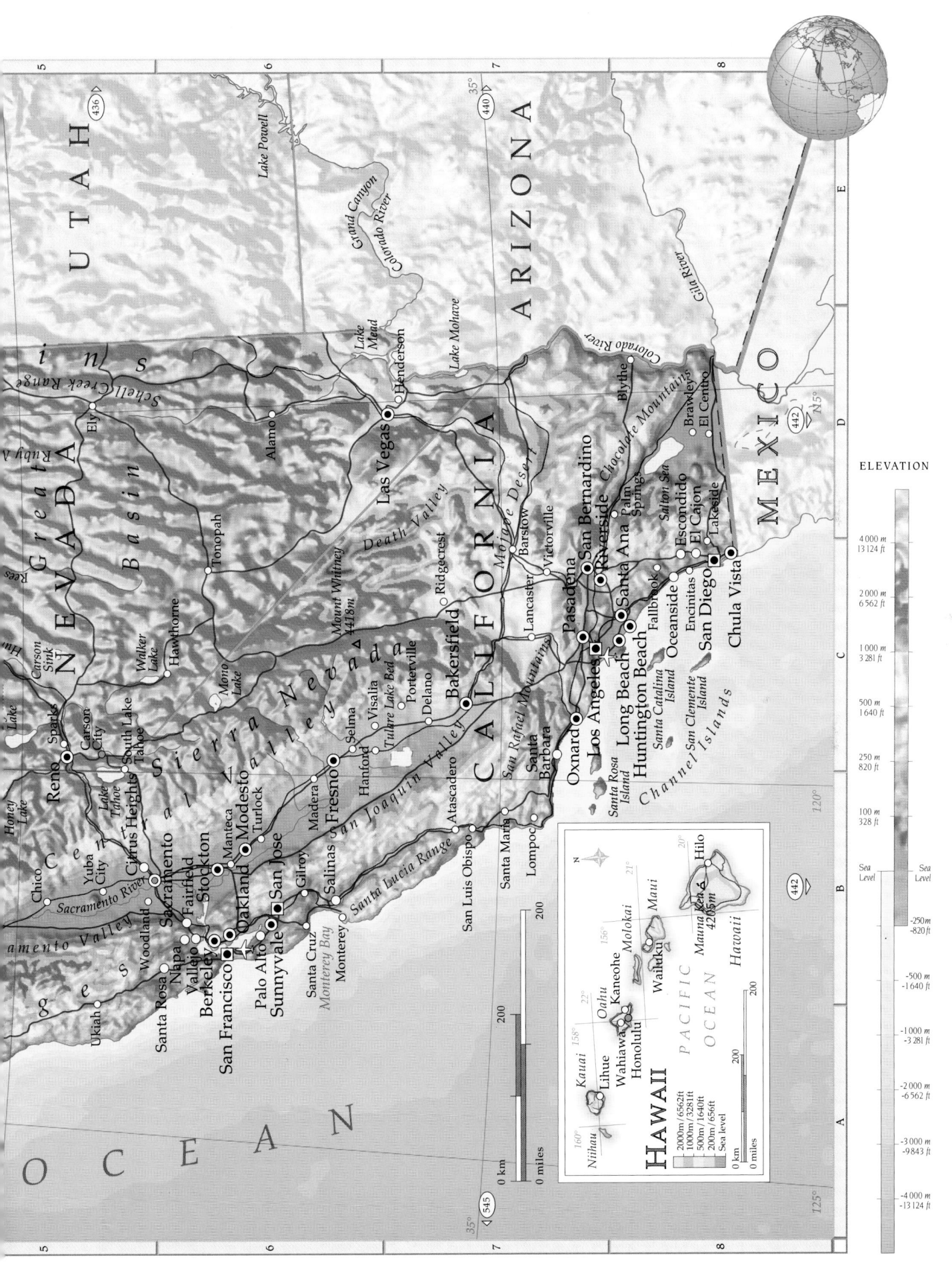

5

UTAH

436

Lake Powell

Grand Canyon

Colorado River

ARIZONA

35°

440

E

Gila River

MEXICO

N 5°

442

D

ins

Schell Creek Range

s

Ely

Lake Mead

Lake Mohave

Henderson

Las Vegas

Colorado River

Blythe

Chocolate Mountains

Brawley

El Centro

Lakeside

Ruby *Lake*

Rees

NEVADA

Great Basin

Alamo

Death Valley

Mojave Desert

Barstow

Victorville

San Bernardino

Riverside

Salton Sea

Escondido

El Cajon

San Diego

Chula Vista

Tonopah

Hawthorne

Mount Whitney 4418m

Ridgecrest

Bakersfield

Lancaster

CALIFORNIA

Pasadena

Santa Ana

Palm Springs

Fallbrook

Oceanside

Encinitas

Carson Sink

Sierra Nevada

Walker Lake

Mono Lake

Porterville

Delano

Visalia

Tulare Lake Bed

San Rafael Mountains

Los Angeles

Long Beach

Huntington Beach

Santa Catalina Island

San Clemente Island

Reno

Sparks

Carson City

South Lake Tahoe

Selma

Hanford

Fresno

San Joaquin Valley

Oxnard

Santa Barbara

Santa Rosa Island

Channel Islands

Lake

Honey Lake

Lake Tahoe

Madera

Atascadero

Santa Maria

Lompoc

San Luis Obispo

Chico

Yuba City

Woodland

Citrus Heights

Sacramento

Stockton

Manteca

Modesto

Turlock

Gilroy

Salinas

Santa Lucia Range

Santa Cruz

Monterey Bay

Monterey

Sacramento River

Napa

Fairfield

Vallejo

Berkeley

Oakland

San Francisco

Palo Alto

Sunnyvale

San Jose

Ukiah

Santa Rosa

Sacramento Valley

Central Valley

Ranges

P A C I F I C

O C E A N

200

200

0 km

0 miles

545

35°

125°

120°

B

C

A

HAWAII

N

Kauai

Lihue

Niihau

Oahu

Wahiawa

Kaneohe

Honolulu

Molokai

Maui

Wailuku

Hawaii

Hilo

Mauna Kea 4205m

PACIFIC

OCEAN

20°

21°

22°

156°

158°

160°

2000m / 6562ft
1000m / 3281ft
500m / 1640ft
200m / 656ft
Sea level

0 km

0 miles

200

200

442

ELEVATION

4 000 m	13 124 ft
2 000 m	6 562 ft
1 000 m	3 281 ft
500 m	1 640 ft
250 m	820 ft
100 m	328 ft
Sea Level	Sea Level
-250 m	-820 ft
-500 m	-1 640 ft
-1 000 m	-3 281 ft
-2 000 m	-6 562 ft
-3 000 m	-9 843 ft
-4 000 m	-13 124 ft

6

7

8

SOUTHWEST USA

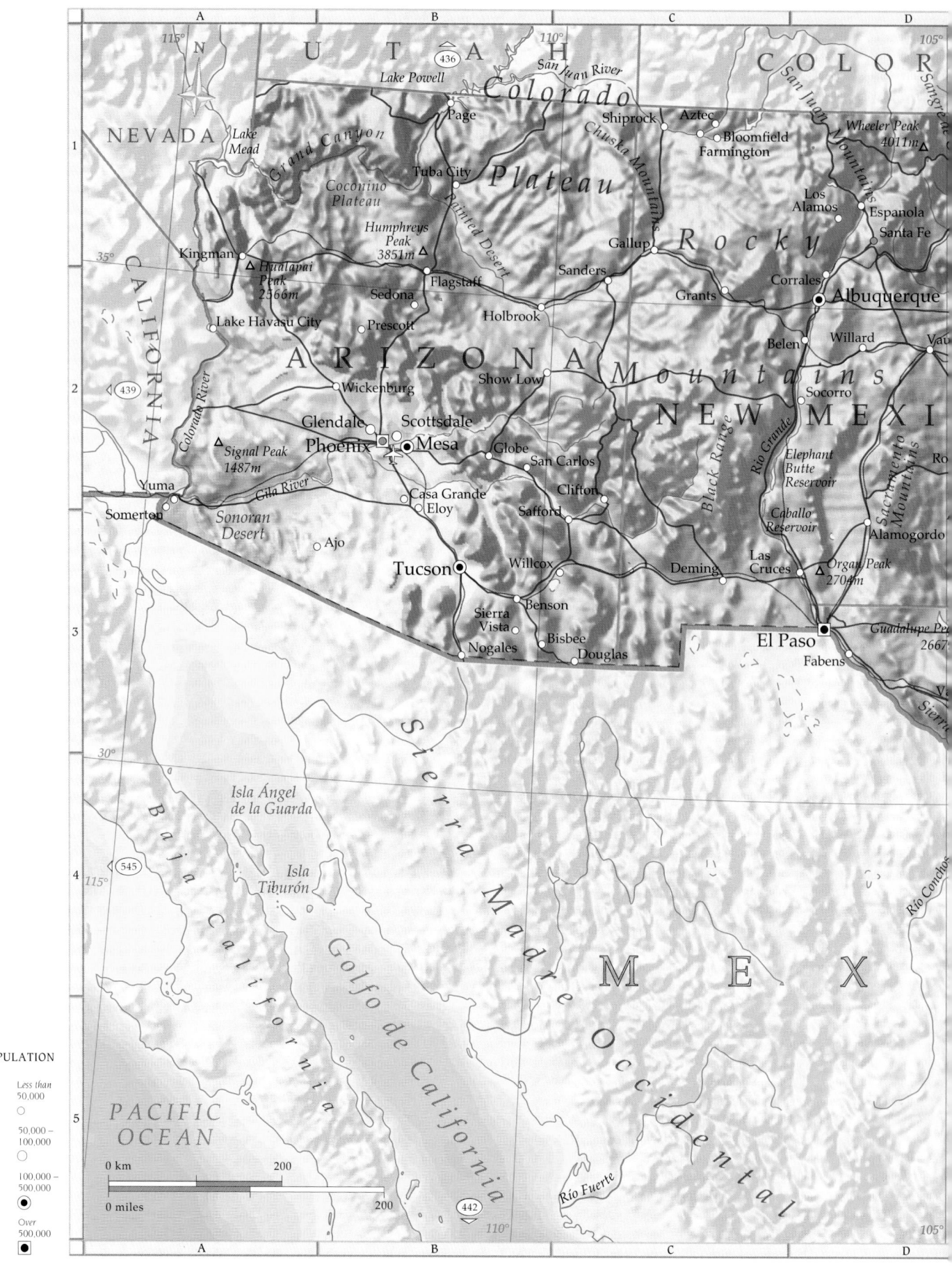

POPULATION

Less than
50,000
○

50,000 –
100,000
○

100,000 –
500,000
◉

Over
500,000
◉

0 km   200

0 miles   200

440

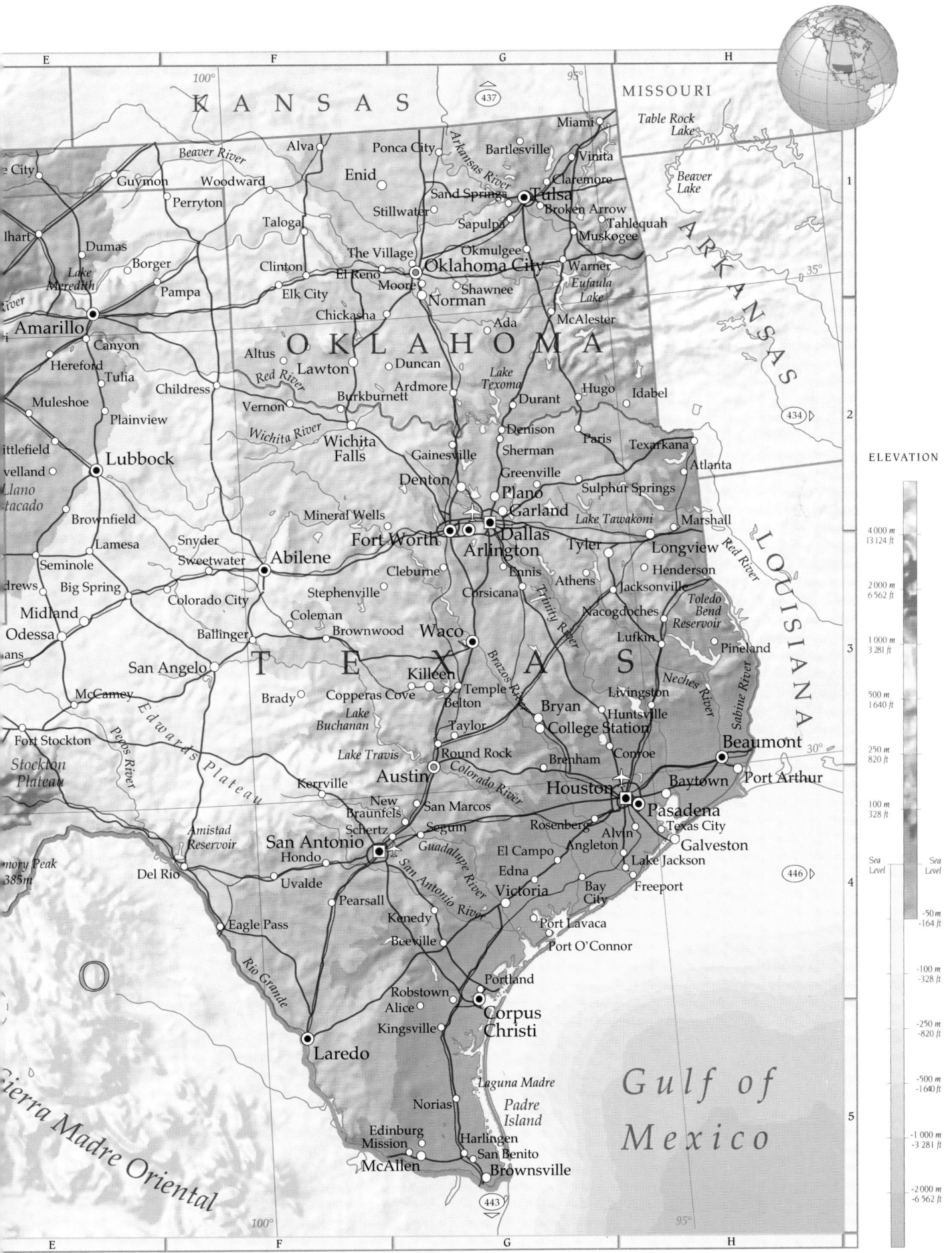

KANSAS

100°

95°

437

MISSOURI

E

F

G

H

Beaver River

Guymon
Woodward
Perryton

e City
lhart
Dumas
Borger
Pampa

Alva
Ponca City
Enid
Taloga
Stillwater

Arkansas River

Bartlesville
Miami
Vinita
Claremore
Sand Springs Tulsa
Sapulpa Broken Arrow
Tahlequah
Muskogee

Table Rock Lake

Beaver Lake

1

Lake Meredith
Amarillo

The Village
Clinton
El Reno
Elk City
Chickasha

Okmulgee
Oklahoma City
Moore
Norman
Shawnee

Warner
Eufaula Lake
McAlester

35°

Canyon
Hereford
Tulia
Muleshoe
Plainview

Childress

Altus
Lawton
Duncan
Ardmore

OKLAHOMA

Ada

Lake Texoma

Hugo
Durant

Idabel

ittlefield
velland
Lubbock

Red River

Vernon
Burkburnett

Wichita Falls

Wichita River

Gainesville

Sherman
Denison

Paris

Texarkana
Atlanta

LOUISIANA

2

Brownfield
Lamesa
Seminole
drews
Big Spring

Snyder
Sweetwater

Abilene

Denton

Greenville

Sulphur Springs

Llano stacado

Plano
Garland
Fort Worth Dallas
Arlington
Cleburne

Tyler

Lake Tawakoni

Marshall

Longview

Red River

Midland
Odessa
ans

Colorado City

Stephenville
Coleman

Ennis
Corsicana

Athens
Jacksonville

Henderson

Nacogdoches

ELEVATION

4 000 m
13 124 ft

San Angelo

Ballinger
Brownwood
Waco

T E X

Brazos River

Lufkin

Toledo Bend Reservoir

Pineland

2 000 m
6 562 ft

3

McCamey

Brady
Copperas Cove
Killeen
Temple
Belton
Taylor

Lake Buchanan

Trinity River

A S

Bryan
College Station

Livingston
Huntsville

Neches River

Sabine River

1 000 m
3 281 ft

500 m
1 640 ft

Fort Stockton

Edwards Plateau

Pecos River

Kerrville

Lake Travis

Round Rock
Austin

Colorado River

Brenham

Conroe

Beaumont

30°

250 m
820 ft

Stockton Plateau

nory Peak 385m

Del Rio

Amistad Reservoir

New Braunfels
Schertz
San Antonio
Hondo

San Marcos
Seguin

Guadalupe River

Houston

Rosenberg

Alvin
Angleton

Pasadena
Baytown
Port Arthur

Texas City
Galveston

100 m
328 ft

Sea Level

Sea Level

4

Uvalde
Pearsall

San Antonio River

Kenedy
Beeville

El Campo
Edna
Victoria

Bay City

Lake Jackson
Freeport

Port Lavaca
Port O'Connor

446

-50 m
-164 ft

Eagle Pass

Rio Grande

Robstown
Alice
Kingsville

Portland
Corpus Christi

-100 m
-328 ft

-250 m
-820 ft

Laredo

Norias

Laguna Madre

Padre Island

Gulf of Mexico

-500 m
-1 640 ft

5

Sierra Madre Oriental

Edinburg
Mission
McAllen

Harlingen
San Benito
Brownsville

95°

-1 000 m
-3 281 ft

-2 000 m
-6 562 ft

100°

443

443

E

F

G

H

MEXICO

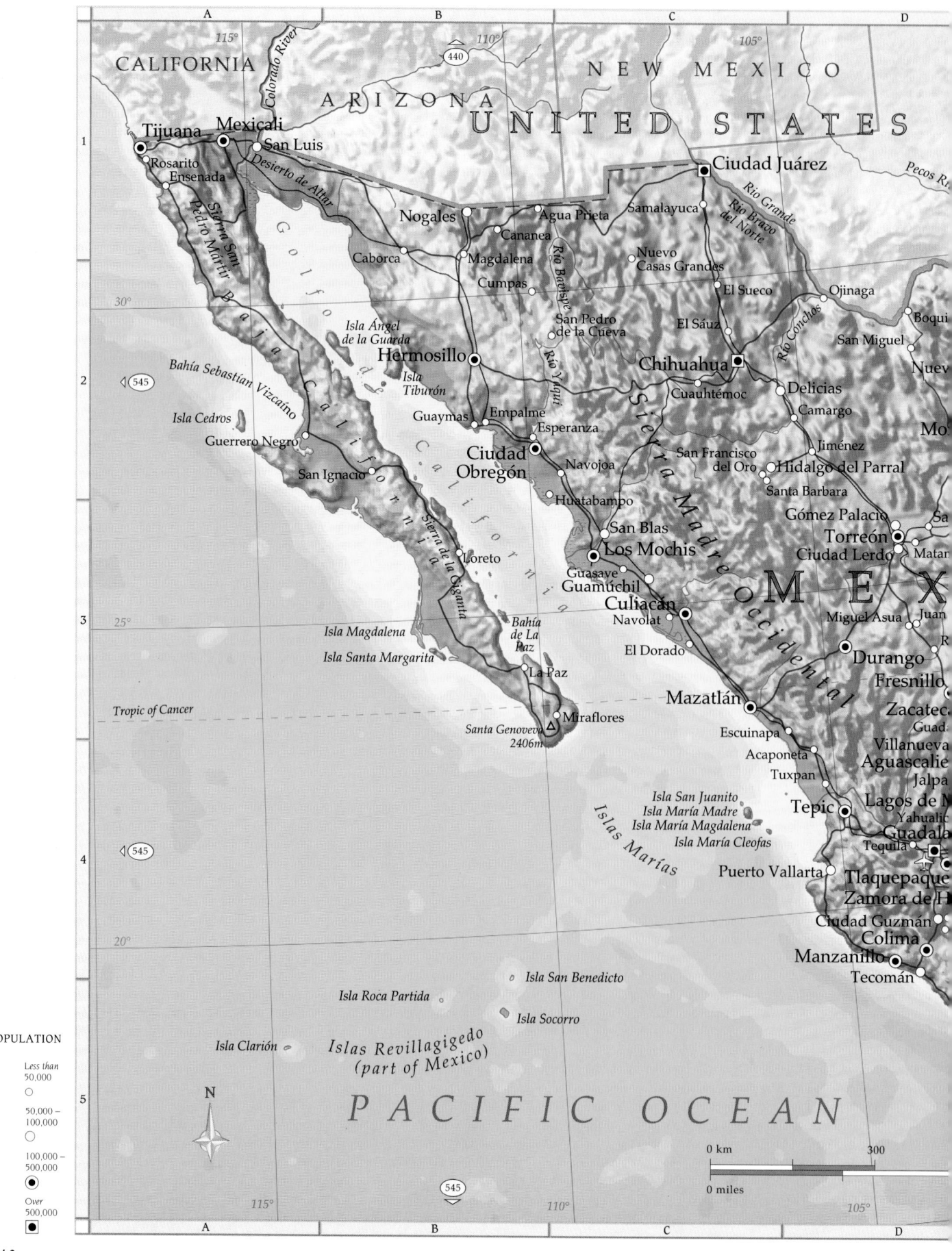

CALIFORNIA

ARIZONA

NEW MEXICO

UNITED STATES

Colorado River

440

115°

110°

105°

Tijuana
Mexicali
San Luis
Rosarito
Ensenada

Ciudad Juárez

Pecos R.

Río Grande
Río Bravo
del Norte

Nogales
Agua Prieta
Samalayuca

Cananea
Caborca
Magdalena
Cumpas

Río Bavispe

Nuevo
Casas Grandes

El Sueco
Ojinaga

Boqui

San Pedro
de la Cueva

El Sáuz
San Miguel

Desierto de Altar

Sierra San Pedro Mártir

Bahía Sebastián Vizcaíno

Isla Ángel de la Guarda

Hermosillo

Chihuahua

Nuev

Isla Tiburón

Cuauhtémoc
Delicias
Camargo

Mo

Golfo de California

Guaymas
Empalme
Esperanza

Jiménez

Isla Cedros

Guerrero Negro

San Ignacio

Ciudad
Obregón

Navojoa

San Francisco
del Oro

Hidalgo del Parral
Santa Barbara

Huatabampo

Gómez Palacio

Sierra de la Giganta

Sierra Madre Occidental

San Blas
Los Mochis

Torreón
Ciudad Lerdo
Matan

Loreto

Guasave
Guamúchil

M E X
Culiacán

Baja California

Navolat

Miguel Asua
Juan

Isla Magdalena

Bahía de La Paz

El Dorado

Durango
R

Isla Santa Margarita

La Paz

Fresnillo

Tropic of Cancer

Mazatlán

Zacatec

Santa Genoveva
2406m

Miraflores

Escuinapa

Guad.

Acaponeta

Villanueva
Aguascalie

Tuxpan

Jalpa

Isla San Juanito
Isla María Madre
Isla María Magdalena
Isla María Cleofas

Lagos de

Tepic

Yahualic
Guadala

Islas Marías

Tequila
Puerto Vallarta

Tlaquepaque
Zamora de I

Ciudad Guzmán
Colima

Manzanillo

Isla San Benedicto

Tecomán

Isla Roca Partida

Isla Socorro

POPULATION

Less than
50,000
○

50,000 –
100,000
○

100,000 –
500,000
◉

Over
500,000
◼

Isla Clarión

Islas Revillagigedo
(part of Mexico)

P A C I F I C   O C E A N

N

0 km   300

0 miles

115°

110°

105°

A   B   C   D

442

CENTRAL AMERICA

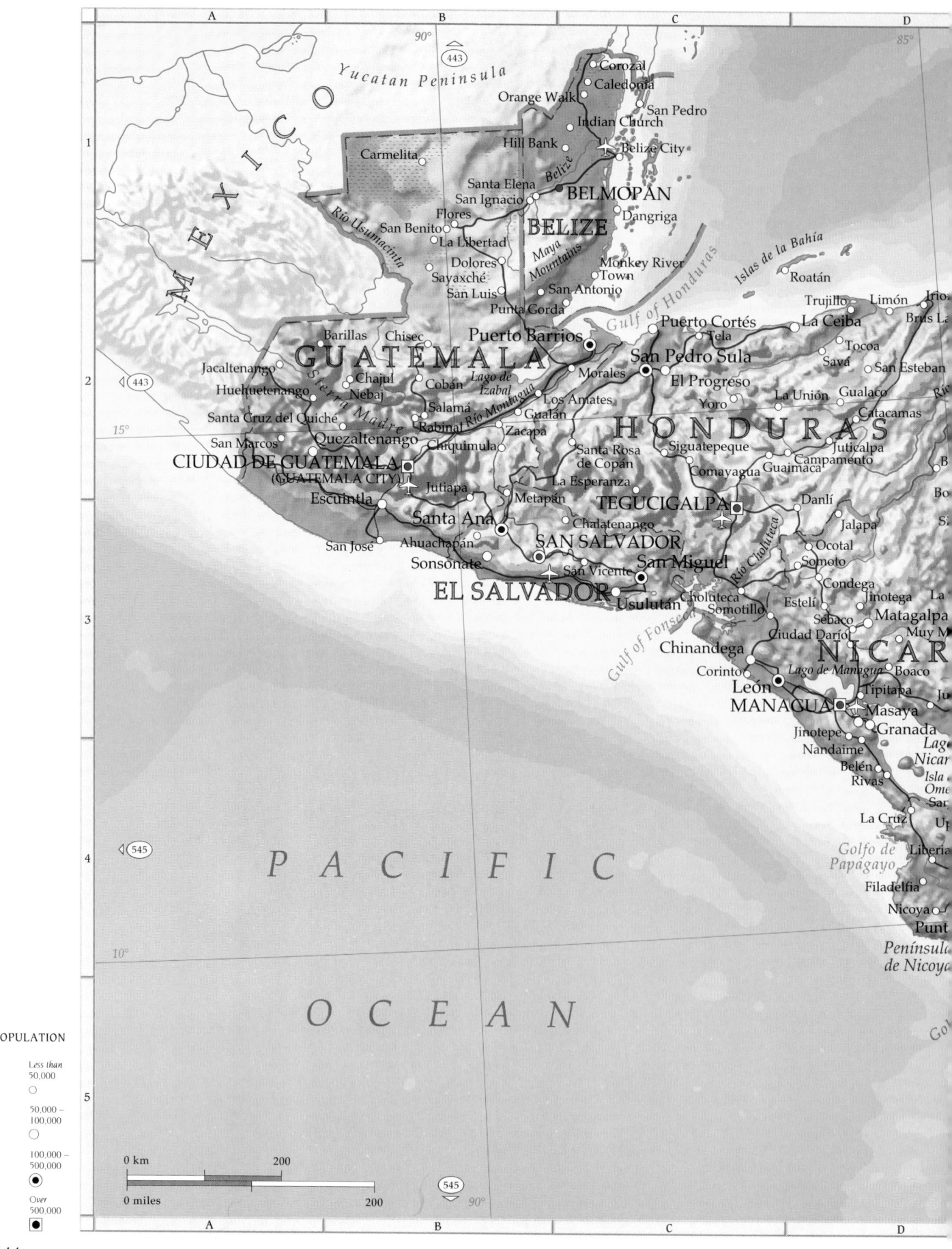

MEXICO

Yucatan Peninsula

443

Corozal
Caledonia
Orange Walk
San Pedro
Indian Church
Hill Bank
Belize City
Carmelita
Santa Elena
San Ignacio
Flores
Belize
BELMOPAN
San Benito
BELIZE
Dangriga
La Libertad
Dolores
Maya
Monkey River
Sayaxché
Mountains
Town
San Luis
San Antonio
Punta Gorda
Islas de la Bahía
Roatán
Gulf of Honduras
Puerto Cortés
Trujillo
Limón
Irio
Barillas
Chisec
Puerto Barrios
Tela
La Ceiba
Brus La
Jacaltenango
GUATEMALA
Morales
San Pedro Sula
Tocoa
Chajul
Lago de
San Esteban
Huehuetenango
Nebaj
Cobán
Izabal
Savá
El Progreso
Salamá
Río Montagua
Los Amates
La Unión
Gualaco
Santa Cruz del Quiché
Rabinal
Gualán
Yoro
Catacamas
Sierra Madre
Zacapa
HONDURAS
Rio
San Marcos
Quezaltenango
Chiquimula
Juticalpa
Santa Rosa
Siguatepeque
CIUDAD DE GUATEMALA
de Copán
Campamento
(GUATEMALA CITY)
Jutiapa
Comayagua Guaimaca
B
Escuintla
Metapán
La Esperanza
TEGUCIGALPA
Danlí
San José
Santa Ana
Chalatenango
Jalapa
 Si
Ahuachapán
SAN SALVADOR
Ocotal
Sonsonate
San Miguel
Somoto
EL SALVADOR
San Vicente
Condega
Usulután
Choluteca
Estelí
Jinotega
La
Río Choluteca
Somotillo
Sebaco
Matagalpa
Gulf of Fonseca
Chinandega
Ciudad Darío
NICAR
Muy M
Corinto
Lago de Managua
Boaco
León
Tipitapa
Ju
MANAGUA
Masaya
Jinotepe
Granada
Nandaime
Lag
Belén
Nicar
Rivas
Isla
Ome
Sar
La Cruz
U
Golfo de
Liberia
Papagayo
Filadelfia
Nicoya
Punt
Península
de Nicoya

PACIFIC

OCEAN

Go

POPULATION

Less than
50,000
○

50,000 –
100,000
○

100,000 –
500,000
◉

Over
500,000
◼

0 km   200

0 miles   200

545

90°

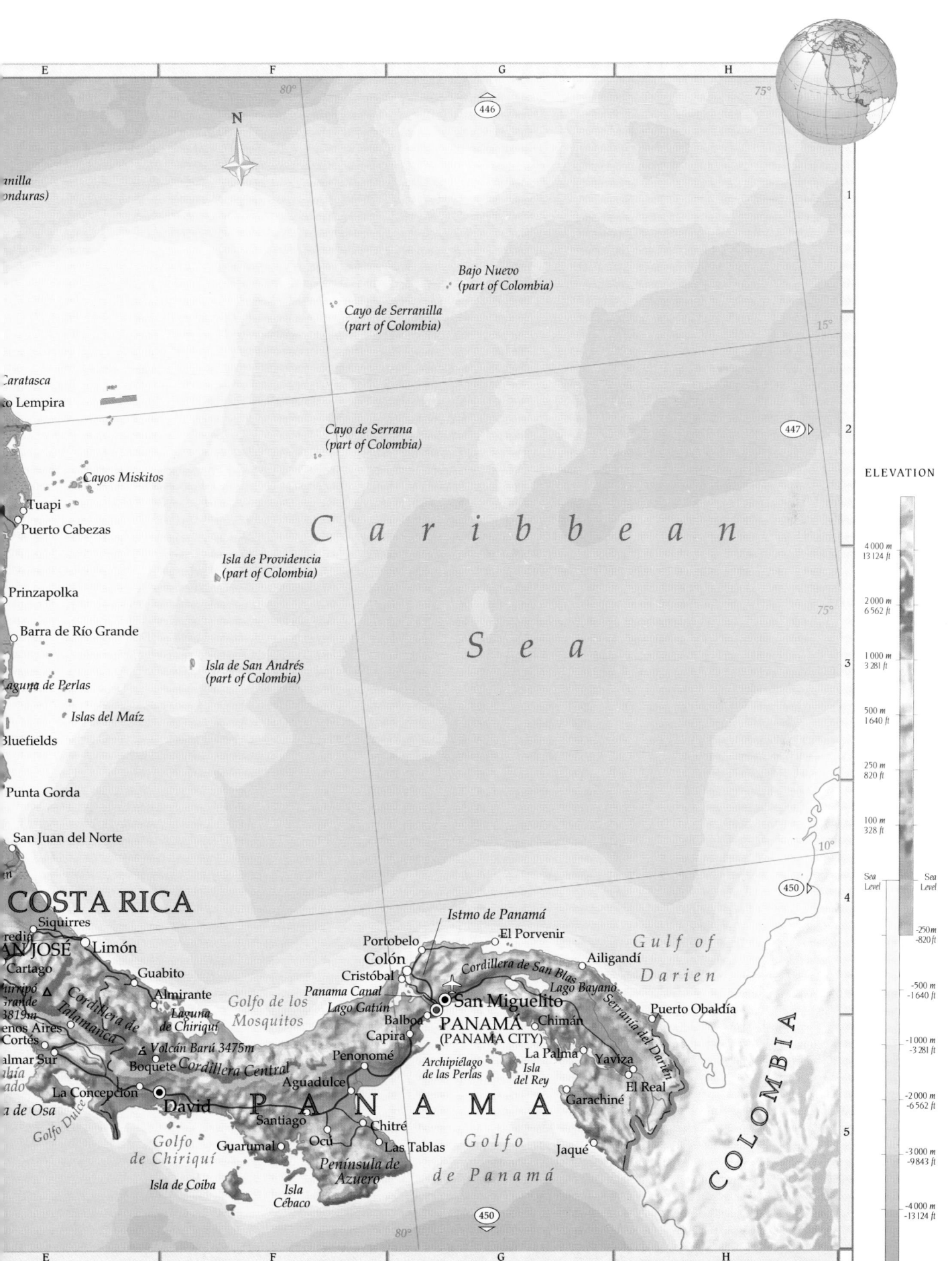

E   F   G   H

80°

446

75°

1

Bajo Nuevo
(part of Colombia)

Cayo de Serranilla
(part of Colombia)

15°

Cayo de Serrana
(part of Colombia)

447

2

Cayos Miskitos

Tuapi
Puerto Cabezas

C a r i b b e a n

Isla de Providencia
(part of Colombia)

75°

Prinzapolka

S e a

Barra de Río Grande

1 000 m
3 281 ft

3

Isla de San Andrés
(part of Colombia)

Laguna de Perlas

500 m
1 640 ft

Islas del Maíz

Bluefields

250 m
820 ft

Punta Gorda

100 m
328 ft

San Juan del Norte

10°

Sea
Level

450

4

COSTA RICA

Siquirres

Istmo de Panamá

El Porvenir

Gulf

Portobelo

-250 m
-820 ft

AN JOSÉ   Limón

Colón

Ailigandí

of

Cartago

Cristóbal

Cordillera de San Blas

Darien

Guabito

Panama Canal

Lago Bayano

urripó
Grande
3819m

Cordillera de Talamanca

Almirante

Golfo de los
Mosquitos

Lago Gatún

San Miguelito

-500 m
-1 640 ft

enos Aires

Laguna
de Chiriquí

Balboa

PANAMÁ

Chimán

Puerto Obaldía

Cortés

Volcán Barú 3475m

Capira

(PANAMA CITY)

-1 000 m
-3 281 ft

almar Sur

Boquete *Cordillera Central*

Penonomé

La Palma

Yaviza

a de Osa

Archipiélago

ado

de las Perlas

Isla

El Real

-2 000 m
-6 562 ft

La Concepción

Aguadulce

del Rey

Garachiné

Golfo Dulce

David P A N A M A

Santiago

COLOMBIA

Chitré

Guarumal   Ocú

Golfo

-3 000 m
-9 843 ft

Golfo
de Chiriquí

Las Tablas

de Panamá

Jaqué

Isla de Coiba

Península de
Azuero

Isla
Cébaco

-4 000 m
-13 124 ft

80°

450

5

E   F   G   H

ELEVATION

4 000 m
13 124 ft

2 000 m
6 562 ft

Sea
Level

THE CARIBBEAN

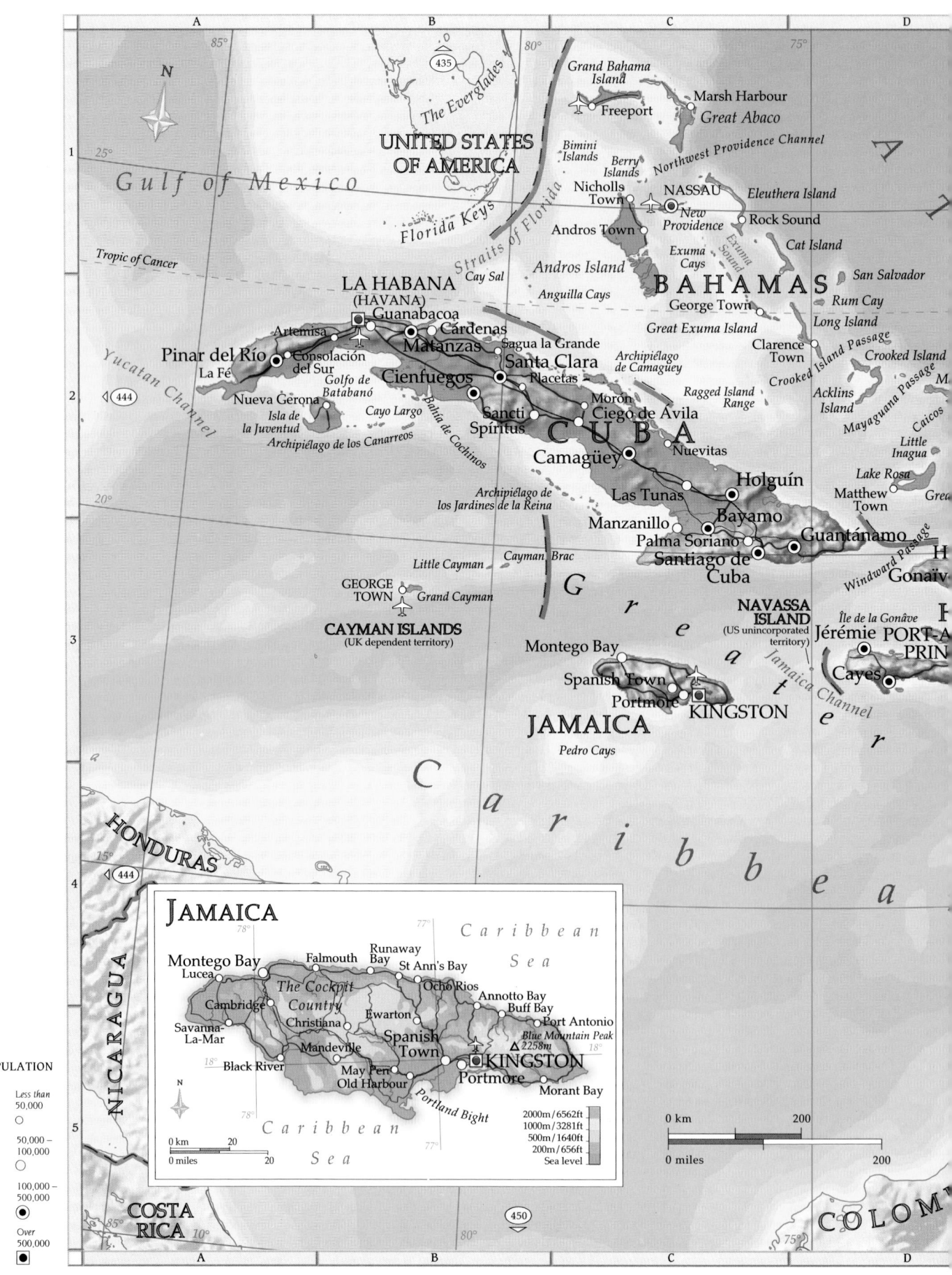

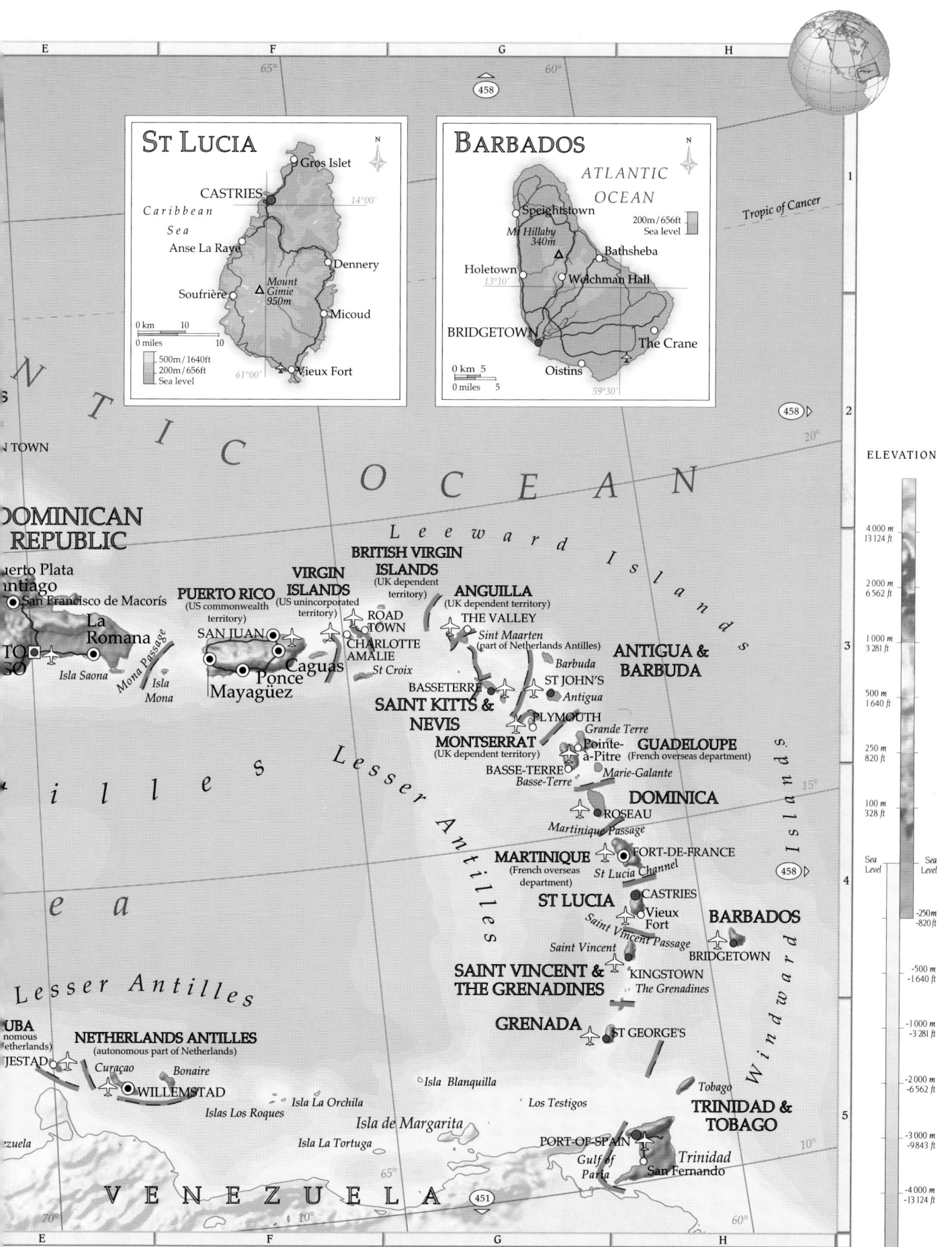

ST LUCIA

N

Gros Islet

CASTRIES

Caribbean Sea

14°00'

Anse La Raye

Dennery

Soufrière

△ *Mount Gimie 950m*

Micoud

0 km 10
0 miles

61°00'

61°00'

Vieux Fort

500m / 1640ft
200m / 656ft
Sea level

BARBADOS

N

ATLANTIC OCEAN

Speightstown

Mt Hillaby 340m

Bathsheba

Holetown

13°10'

△

Welchman Hall

BRIDGETOWN

The Crane

0 km 5
0 miles 5

Oistins

59°30'

200m / 656ft
Sea level

458

458

Tropic of Cancer

20°

458

ELEVATION

4 000 m
13 124 ft

2 000 m
6 562 ft

1 000 m
3 281 ft

500 m
1 640 ft

250 m
820 ft

100 m
328 ft

Sea Level

Sea Level

-250 m
-820 ft

-500 m
-1 640 ft

-1 000 m
-3 281 ft

-2 000 m
-6 562 ft

-3 000 m
-9 843 ft

-4 000 m
-13 124 ft

A T L A N T I C   O C E A N

N TOWN

DOMINICAN REPUBLIC

uerto Plata

ntiago

San Francisco de Macorís

La Romana

TO
O

Isla Saona

Isla Mona

Mona Passage

PUERTO RICO
(US commonwealth territory)

SAN JUAN

Caguas

Ponce

Mayagüez

VIRGIN ISLANDS
(US unincorporated territory)

CHARLOTTE AMALIE

St Croix

ROAD TOWN

BRITISH VIRGIN ISLANDS
(UK dependent territory)

L e e w a r d   I s l a n d s

ANGUILLA
(UK dependent territory)

THE VALLEY

Sint Maarten
(part of Netherlands Antilles)

Barbuda

ANTIGUA & BARBUDA

Antigua

ST JOHN'S

BASSETERRE

SAINT KITTS & NEVIS

PLYMOUTH

MONTSERRAT
(UK dependent territory)

Grande Terre

Pointe-à-Pitre

GUADELOUPE
(French overseas department)

BASSE-TERRE

Basse-Terre

Marie-Galante

DOMINICA

ROSEAU

Martinique Passage

MARTINIQUE
(French overseas department)

FORT-DE-FRANCE

St Lucia Channel

ST LUCIA

CASTRIES

Vieux Fort

458

Saint Vincent Passage

Saint Vincent

BARBADOS

BRIDGETOWN

SAINT VINCENT & THE GRENADINES

KINGSTOWN

The Grenadines

Lesser Antilles

GRENADA

ST GEORGE'S

W i n d w a r d   I s l a n d s

Tobago

TRINIDAD & TOBAGO

UBA
nomous
etherlands)

JESTAD

L e s s e r   A n t i l l e s

NETHERLANDS ANTILLES
(autonomous part of Netherlands)

Curaçao

Bonaire

WILLEMSTAD

Islas Los Roques

Isla La Orchila

Isla Blanquilla

Los Testigos

Isla de Margarita

Isla La Tortuga

PORT-OF-SPAIN

Gulf of Paria

Trinidad

San Fernando

ezuela

V E N E Z U E L A

451

A n t i l l e s

L e s s e r   A n t i l l e s

e a

15°

10°

10°

70°

65°

60°

SOUTH AMERICA

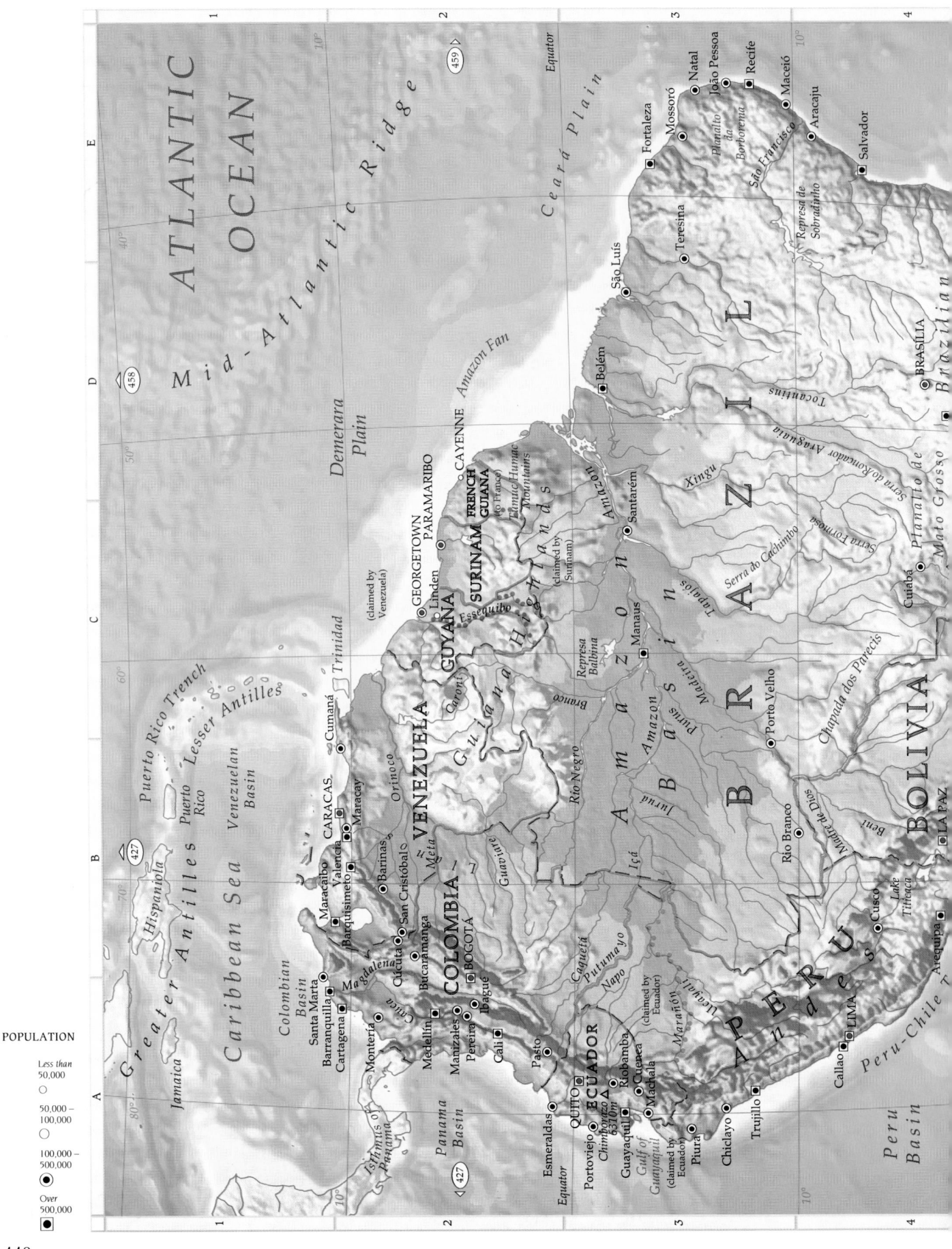

ATLANTIC OCEAN

Mid-Atlantic Ridge

Demerara Plain

Amazon Fan

Ceará Plain

Represa de Sobradinho

Natal
João Pessoa
Recife
Maceió
Aracaju
Salvador
Planalto da Borborema
São Francisco
Mossoró
Fortaleza
Teresina
São Luís
Belém
BRASÍLIA
B R A Z I L
Brazilian
Tocantins
Xingu
Santarém
Amazon
Serra do Cachimbo
Serra Formosa
Serra do Roncador
Araguaia
Tapajós
Planalto de Mato Grosso
Chapada dos Parecis
Cuiabá
CAYENNE
FRENCH GUIANA
(to France)
SURINAM
PARAMARIBO
GEORGETOWN
Linden
GUYANA
Essequibo
(claimed by Surinam)
Tumuc-Humac Mountains
Guiana Highlands
Manaus
Represa Balbína
Branco
Madeira
Purus
Amazon
Porto Velho
Rio Branco
BOLIVIA
LA PAZ
Lake Titicaca
Madre de Dios
Beni
A m a z o n B a s i n
Rio Negro
Juruá
Içá
Caroni
(claimed by Venezuela)
Trinidad
Cumaná
VENEZUELA
CARACAS
Maracay
Valencia
Barquisimeto
Maracaibo
Barinas
San Cristóbal
Cúcuta
Bucaramanga
Orinoco
Meta
Guaviare
Vaupés
COLOMBIA
BOGOTÁ
Ibagué
Medellín
Manizales
Pereira
Cali
Pasto
Magdalena
Cauca
Montería
Cartagena
Santa Marta
Barranquilla
Caquetá
Putumayo
Napo
Marañón
Ucayali
(claimed by Ecuador)
P E R U
A n d e s
Cusco
Arequipa
Callao
LIMA
Peru-Chile Trench
Chiclayo
Trujillo
Piura
ECUADOR
QUITO
Chimborazo 6310m △
Riobamba
Cuenca
Machala
Guayaquil
Gulf of Guayaquil
Portoviejo
Esmeraldas
Equator
(claimed by Ecuador)
Panama Basin
Isthmus of Panama
Colombian Basin
Caribbean Sea
Greater Antilles
Jamaica
Hispaniola
Puerto Rico
Lesser Antilles
Puerto Rico Trench
Venezuelan Basin
Peru Basin

Equator

458

459

427

427

POPULATION

Less than 50,000 ○

50,000 – 100,000 ○

100,000 – 500,000 ◉

Over 500,000 ◼

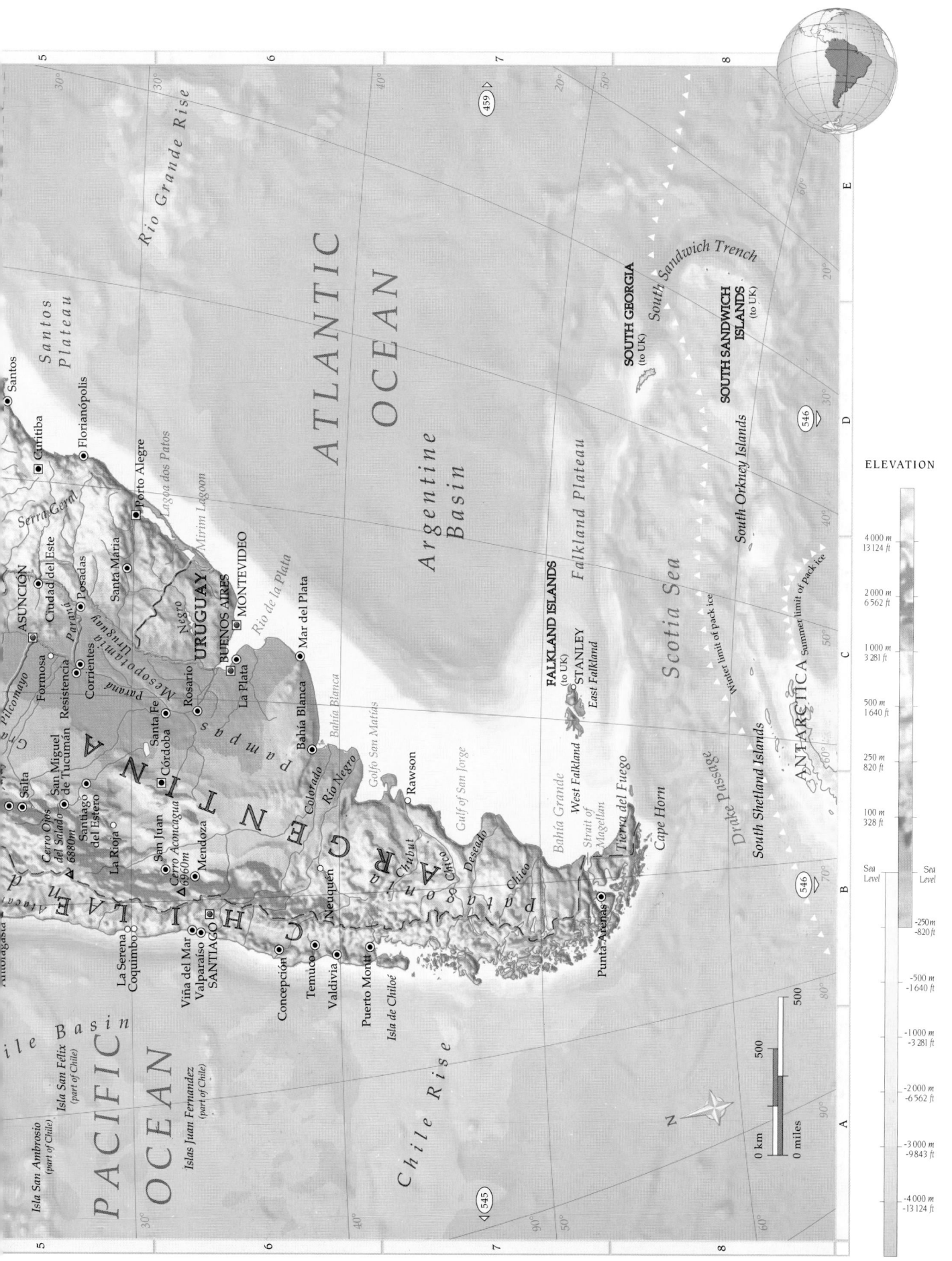

ATLANTIC

OCEAN

Rio Grande Rise

Santos Plateau

Santos

Curitiba

Florianópolis

Porto Alegre

Serra Geral

Laguna dos Patos

Mirim Lagoon

Santa Maria

Argentine

Basin

ASUNCIÓN

Ciudad del Este

Posadas

Formosa

Resistencia

Corrientes

Santa Fe

Córdoba

Santiago del Estero

San Miguel de Tucumán

Salta

Cerro Ojos del Salado 6880m

La Rioja

San Juan

Cerro Aconcagua 6960m

Mendoza

Pilcomayo

Paraná

Paraguay

Mesopotamia

Gran Chaco

URUGUAY

BUENOS AIRES

MONTEVIDEO

La Plata

Negro

Río de la Plata

Mar del Plata

Bahía Blanca

Bahía Blanca

Pampas

Colorado

Río Negro

Neuquén

Rawson

Chubut

Chico

Chico

Deseado

Golfo San Matías

Gulf of San Jorge

Bahía Grande

Strait of Magellan

Tierra del Fuego

Cape Horn

Punta Arenas

Drake Passage

Patagonia

ARGENTINA

Concepción

Temuco

Valdivia

Puerto Montt

Isla de Chiloé

La Serena

Coquimbo

Viña del Mar

Valparaíso

SANTIAGO

CHILE

Altiplano

Antofagasta

Isla San Ambrosio (part of Chile)

Isla San Félix (part of Chile)

Islas Juan Fernández (part of Chile)

Chile Basin

PACIFIC

OCEAN

Chile Rise

FALKLAND ISLANDS (to UK)

STANLEY

East Falkland

West Falkland

Falkland Plateau

SOUTH GEORGIA (to UK)

South Sandwich Trench

SOUTH SANDWICH ISLANDS (to UK)

South Orkney Islands

Scotia Sea

South Shetland Islands

ANTARCTICA

Winter limit of pack ice

Summer limit of pack ice

459

546

546

545

N

ELEVATION

4 000 m 13 124 ft	
2 000 m 6 562 ft	
1 000 m 3 281 ft	
500 m 1 640 ft	
250 m 820 ft	
100 m 328 ft	
Sea Level	Sea Level
-250 m -820 ft	
-500 m -1 640 ft	
-1 000 m -3 281 ft	
-2 000 m -6 562 ft	
-3 000 m -9 843 ft	
-4 000 m -13 124 ft	

0 km 500

0 miles 500

449

Northern South America

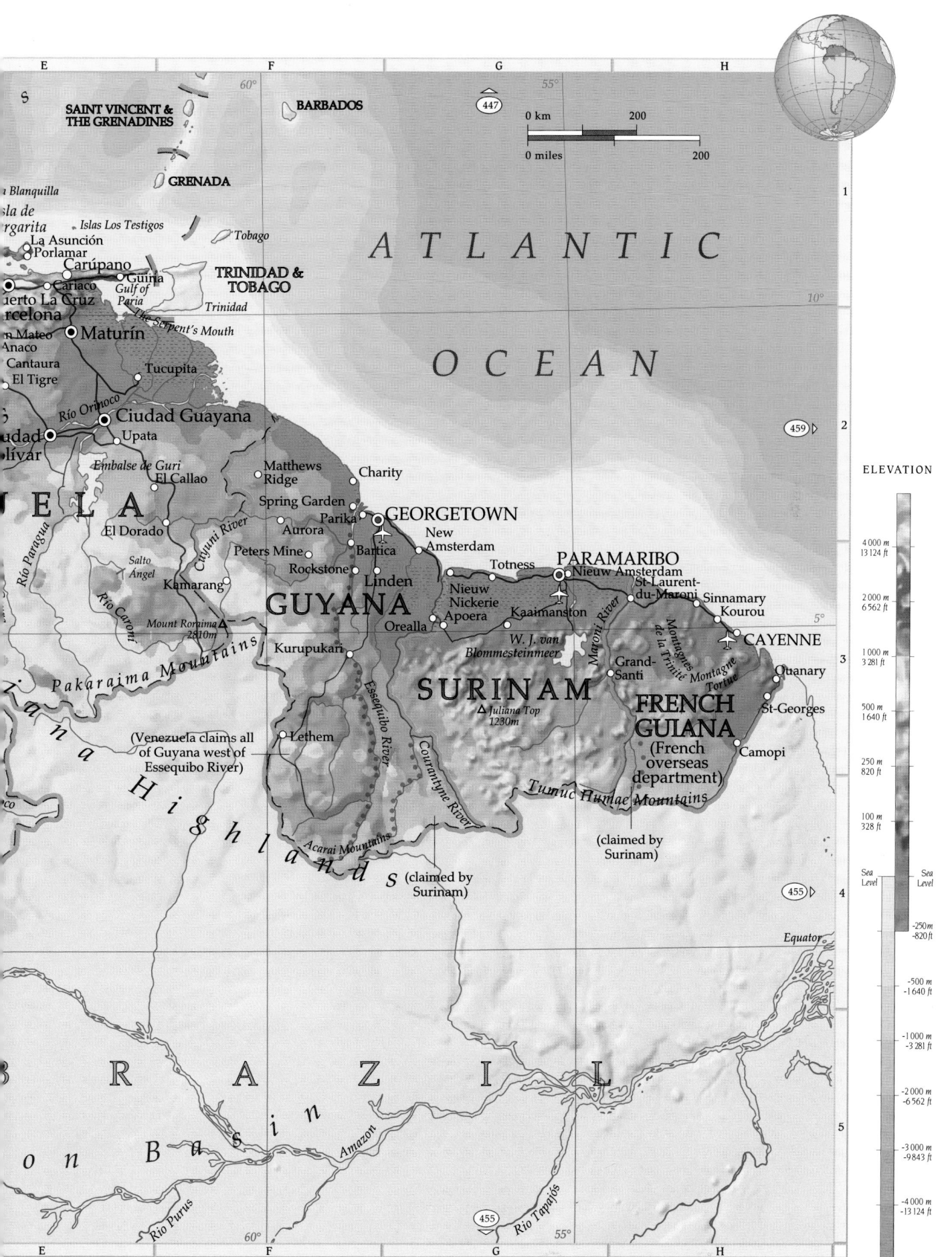

WESTERN SOUTH AMERICA

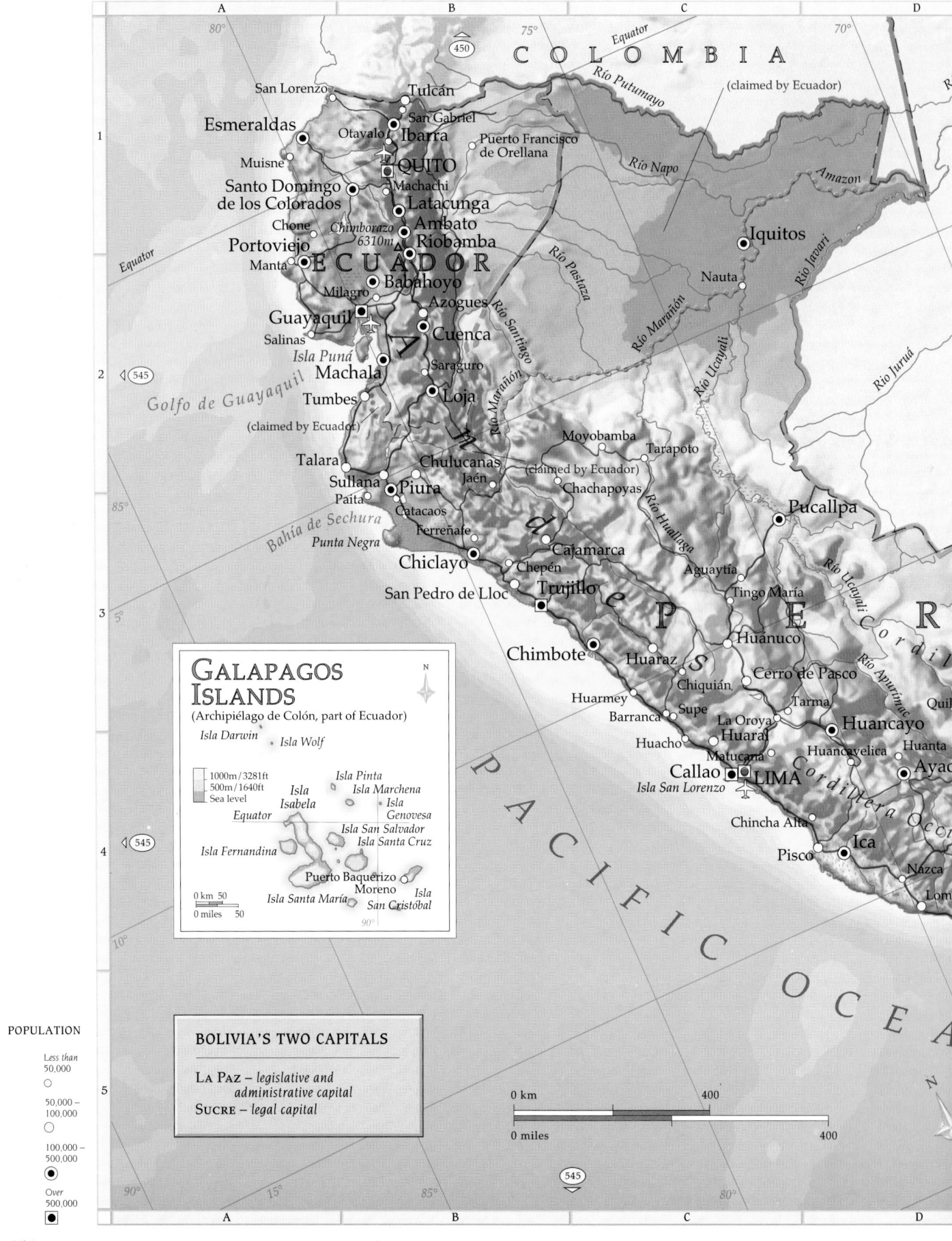

COLOMBIA

San Lorenzo
Tulcán
San Gabriel
Esmeraldas
Otavalo Ibarra
Muisne
QUITO
Santo Domingo
de los Colorados
Machachi
Latacunga
Chone
Chimborazo
6310m
Ambato
Riobamba
Portoviejo
ECUADOR
Manta
Babahoyo
Milagro
Azogues
Guayaquil
Cuenca
Salinas
Saraguro
Isla Puná
Machala
Tumbes
Loja
Golfo de Guayaquil
(claimed by Ecuador)

Talara
Chulucanas
Sullana
Piura
Paita
Jaén
Catacaos
Bahía de Sechura
Ferreñafe
Punta Negra
Chiclayo
Chepén
San Pedro de Lloc
Trujillo

Chimbote
Huaraz

Río Putumayo
Equator
(claimed by Ecuador)

Río Napo
Amazon
Iquitos
Río Pastaza
Nauta
Río Santiago
Río Marañón
Río Javari
Río Ucayali
Río Juruá

Moyobamba
Tarapoto
(claimed by Ecuador)
Chachapoyas
Río Huallaga
Cajamarca
Pucallpa
Aguaytía

Tingo María
P
E
Río Ucayali
Huánuco
Cerro de Pasco
Chiquián
Tarma
Cordil
Huarmey
Supe
Barranca
La Oroya
Huancayo
Huanta
Huacho
Huaral
Huancavelica
Quil
Cordillera Occi
Matucana
Callao
LIMA
Ayac
Isla San Lorenzo
Chincha Alta
Ica
Pisco
Nazca
Río Apurímac

PACIFIC OCEAN

GALAPAGOS ISLANDS
(Archipiélago de Colón, part of Ecuador)

N

Isla Darwin
Isla Wolf

	1000m / 3281ft
	500m / 1640ft
	Sea level

Isla Pinta
Isla
Isabela
Isla Marchena
Isla
Genovesa
Equator
Isla Fernandina
Isla San Salvador
Isla Santa Cruz
Puerto Baquerizo
Moreno
Isla Santa María
Isla
San Cristóbal

0 km 50
0 miles 50

90°

BOLIVIA'S TWO CAPITALS

LA PAZ – *legislative and administrative capital*
SUCRE – *legal capital*

0 km 400
0 miles 400

545

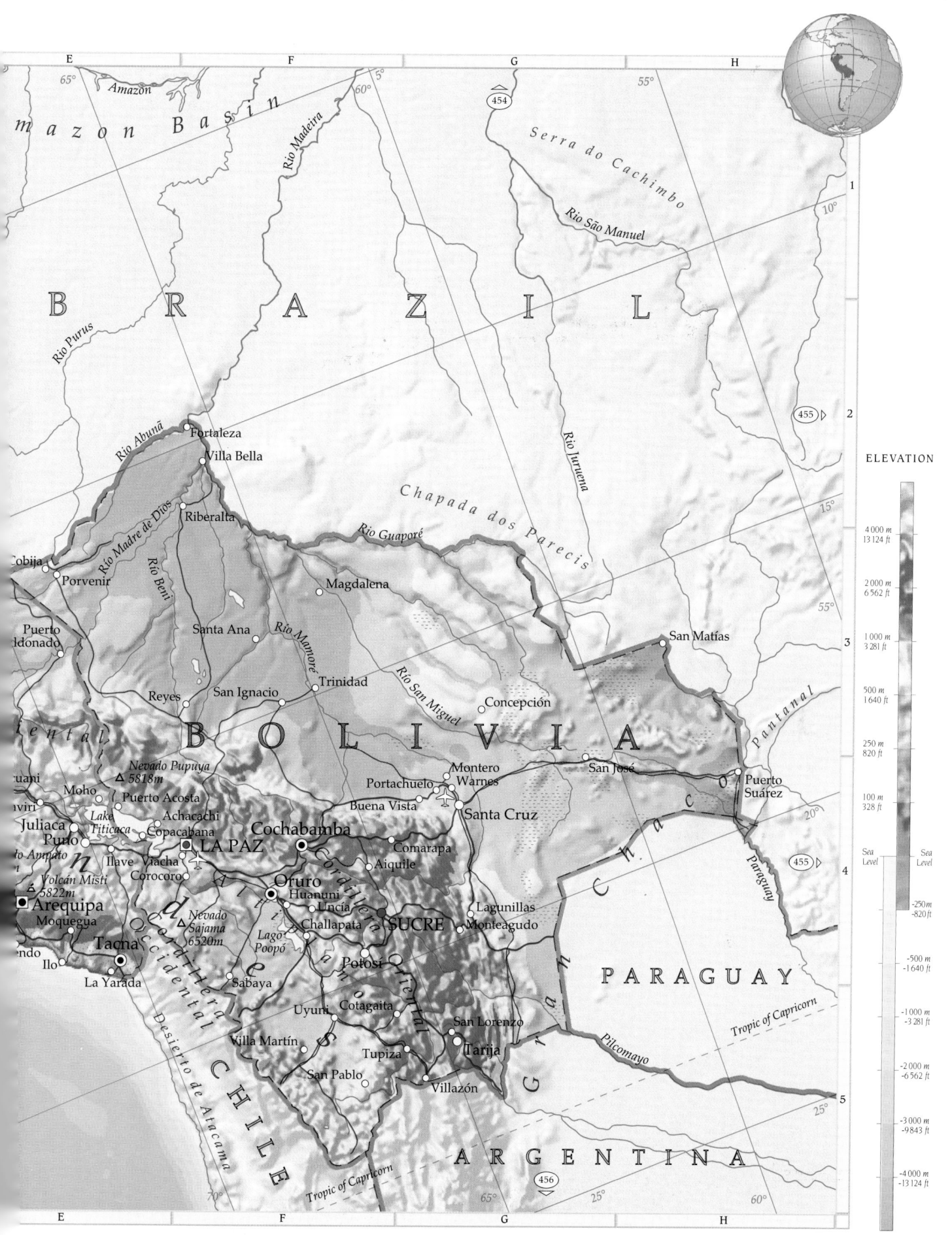

E · 65° · Amazon

F · 60° · 5°

G · 55°

H

454

Amazon Basin

Rio Madeira

Serra do Cachimbo

Rio São Manuel

1 · 10°

B R A Z I L

Rio Purus

455

2

Rio Abunā

Fortaleza

Villa Bella

Chapada dos Parecis

Rio Iruena

Rio Madre de Dios

Riberalta

Rio Guaporé

15°

Cobija

Porvenir

Rio Beni

Magdalena

San Matías

55°

3

Puerto
Maldonado

Santa Ana

Rio Mamoré

Reyes

San Ignacio

Trinidad

Rio San Miguel

Concepción

B O L I V I A

San José

Puerto
Suárez

Pantanal

uani

Nevado Pupuya
△ 5818m

Moho

Puerto Acosta

Achacachi

Montero
Warnes

Portachuelo

San José

iviri

Juliaca

Lake
Titicaca

Copacabana

Cochabamba

Buena Vista

Santa Cruz

20°

Puno

Ilave

Viacha

LA PAZ

Comarapa

455

4

o Ampato

Corocoro

Aiquile

Chaco

Paraguay

Volcán Misti
△ 5822m

Oruro

Huanuni

Arequipa

Uncía

Lagunillas

Moquegua

Nevado
Sajama
△ 6520m

Challapata

SUCRE

Monteagudo

ndo

Tacna

Lago
Poopó

Potosí

P A R A G U A Y

Ilo

Sabaya

La Yarada

Uyuni

Cotagaita

Tropic of Capricorn

Villa Martín

San Lorenzo

Pilcomayo

Tupiza

Tarija

San Pablo

Villazón

25°

5

Desierto de Atacama

C H I L E

Cordillera Occidental

Cordillera Oriental

Gran Chaco

A R G E N T I N A

Tropic of Capricorn

70°

65°

456

25°

60°

E

F

G

H

BRAZIL

POPULATION

Less than
50,000
○

50,000 –
100,000
○

100,000 –
500,000
◉

Over
500,000
◉

454

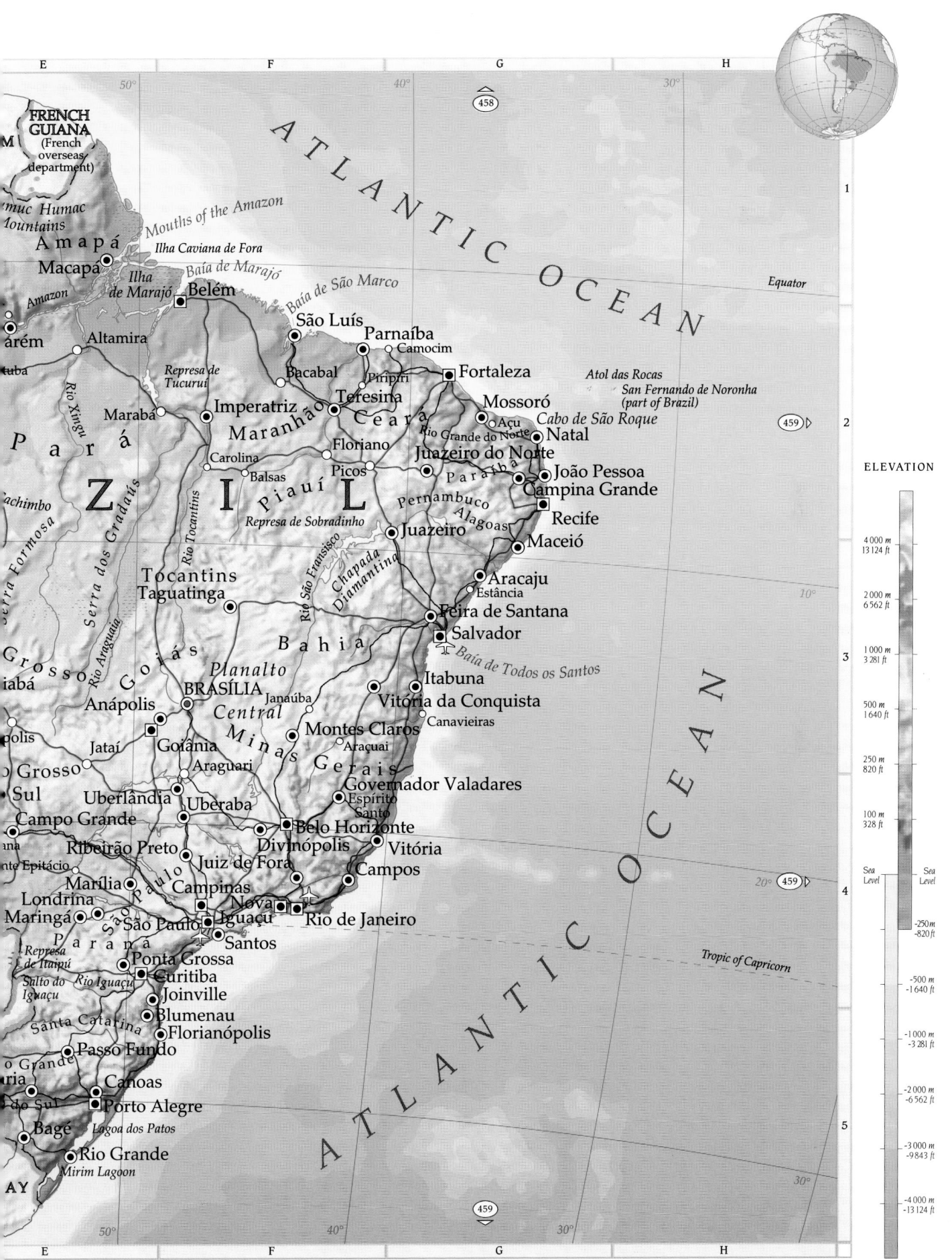

E   F   G   H

50°   40°   30°

458

FRENCH GUIANA
(French overseas department)

muc Humac Mountains

Mouths of the Amazon

A T L A N T I C   O C E A N

Amapá

Ilha Caviana de Fora

Macapa

Baía de Marajó

Ilha de Marajó

Belém

São Luís

Baía de São Marco

Parnaíba

Equator

1

Amazon

árém

Altamira

Represa de Tucuruí

Bacabal

Camocim

Piripirí

Fortaleza

Atol das Rocas

San Fernando de Noronha (part of Brazil)

459

tuba

Imperatriz

Teresina

Mossoró

Maranhão

Ceará

Açu

Rio Grande do Norte

Natal

Cabo de São Roque

2

P a r á

Marabá

Floriano

Juazeiro do Norte

Paraíba

João Pessoa

Z

I

L

Carolina

Picos

Campina Grande

achimbo

Balsas

Piauí

Pernambuco

Recife

Serra Formosa

Represa de Sobradinho

Alagoas

Juazeiro

Maceió

Rio Xingu

Serra dos Gradaús

Rio Tocantins

Chapada Diamantina

Aracaju

Estância

ELEVATION

Tocantins

Taguatinga

Rio São Francisco

Feira de Santana

10°

4 000 m
13 124 ft

3

Grosso

Rio Araguaia

Goiás

Planalto

B a h i a

Salvador

Baía de Todos os Santos

2 000 m
6 562 ft

iabá

Anápolis

BRASÍLIA

Central

Janaúba

Itabuna

Vitória da Conquista

Canavieiras

1 000 m
3 281 ft

polis

Jataí

Goiânia

M i n a s

Montes Claros

Araçuai

500 m
1 640 ft

Grosso

Araguari

G e r a i s

Governador Valadares

250 m
820 ft

Sul

Uberlândia

Uberaba

Espírito Santo

100 m
328 ft

Campo Grande

Belo Horizonte

na

Ribeirão Preto

Divinópolis

Vitória

Sea Level

Sea Level

nte Epitácio

Juiz de Fora

Campos

20°

459

4

Marília

Campinas

Londrina

Nova

-250 m
-820 ft

Maringá

São Paulo

Iguaçu

Rio de Janeiro

Paraná

Santos

Tropic of Capricorn

P a r a n á

Represa de Itaipú

Ponta Grossa

-500 m
-1 640 ft

ulto do Iguaçu

Rio Iguaçu

Curitiba

Joinville

-1 000 m
-3 281 ft

Santa Catarina

Blumenau

Florianópolis

A T L A N T I C   O C E A N

-2 000 m
-6 562 ft

Passo Fundo

ria

Canoas

-3 000 m
-9 843 ft

o Grande

do Sul

Porto Alegre

30°

5

Bagé

Lagoa dos Patos

-4 000 m
-13 124 ft

AY

Rio Grande

Mirim Lagoon

459

E   F   G   H

50°   40°   30°

SOUTHERN SOUTH AMERICA

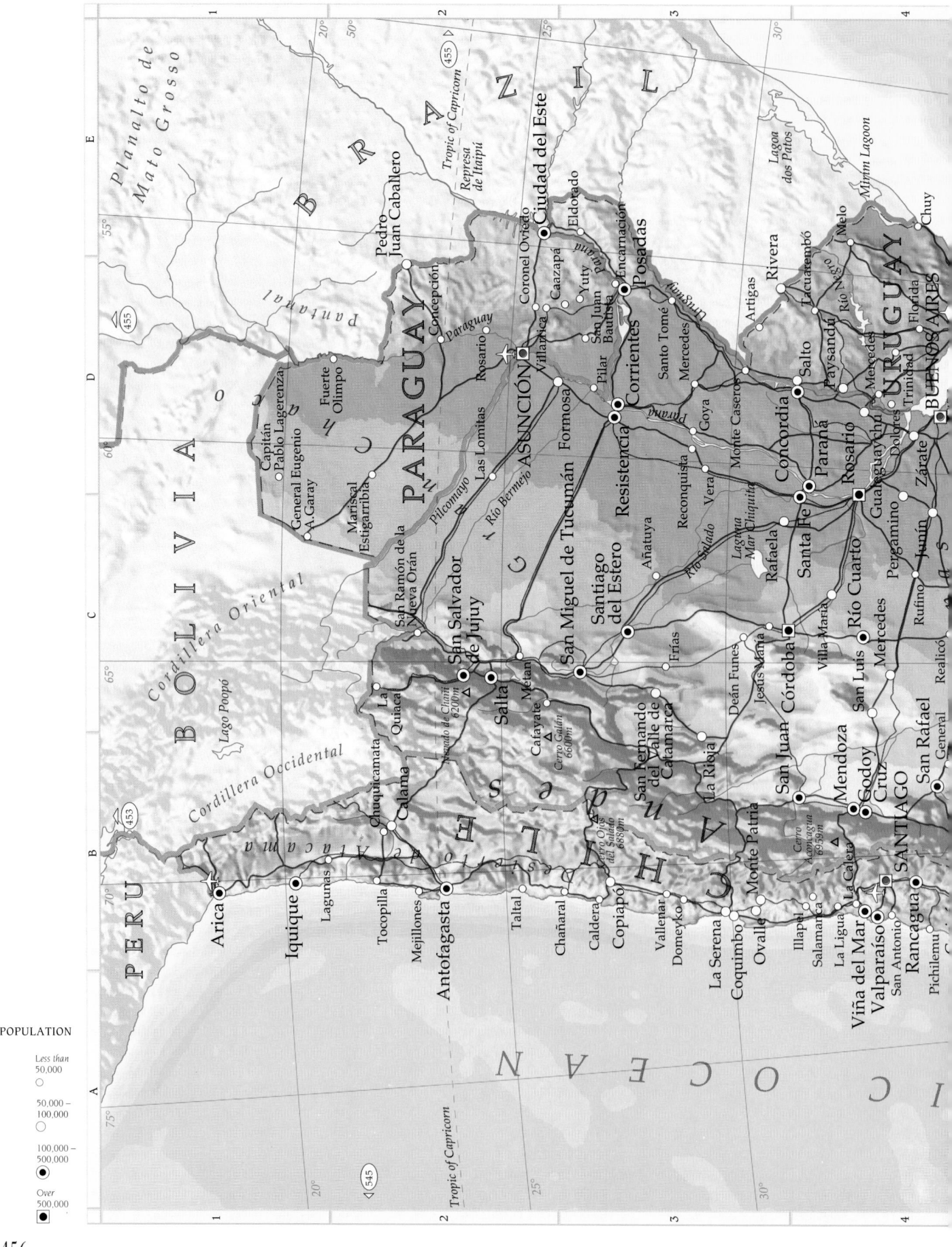

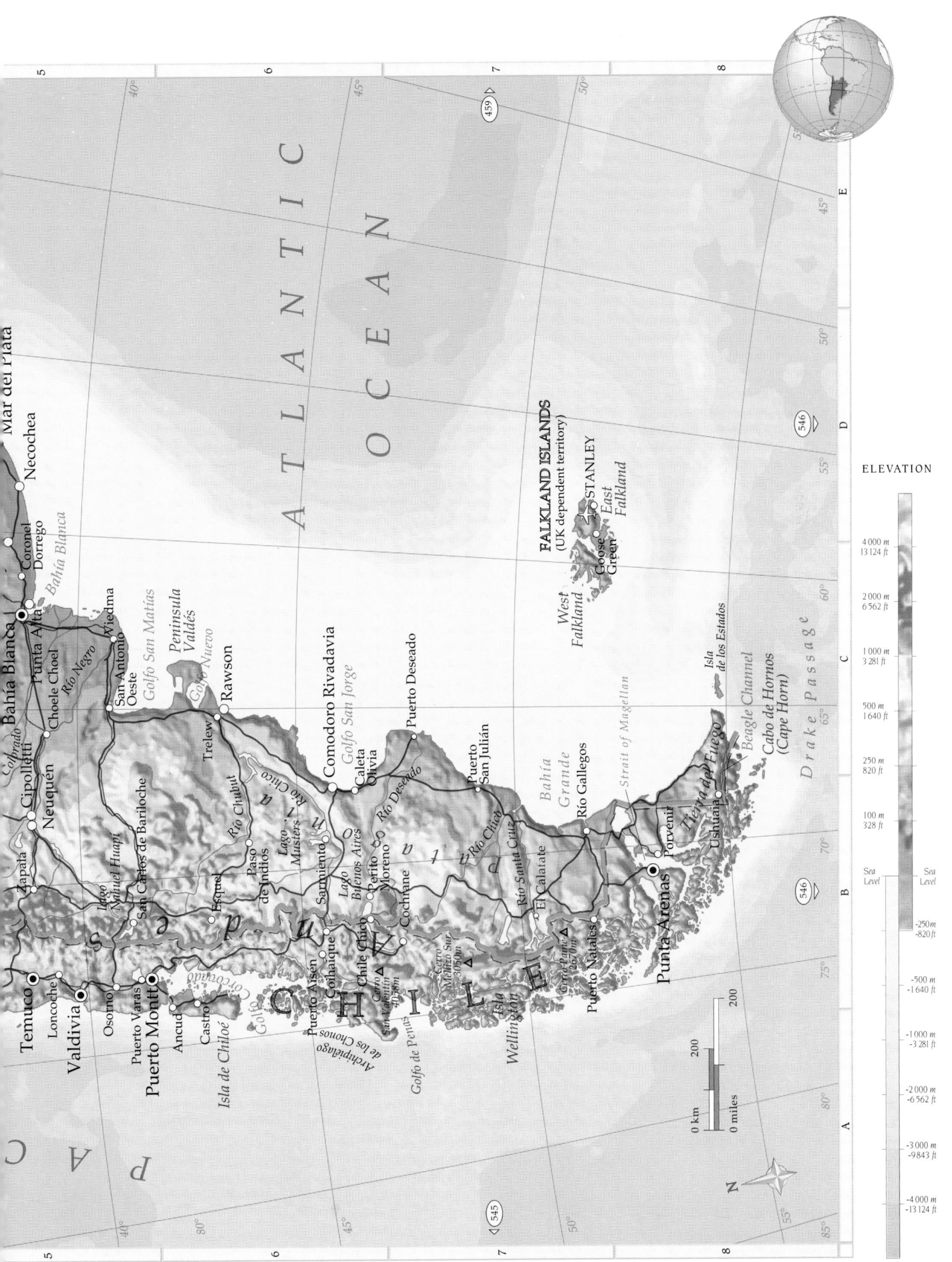

ATLANTIC

OCEAN

PACIFIC

Mar del Plata
Necochea
Coronel
Dorrego
Bahía Blanca
Bahía Blanca
Punta Alta
Cipolletti
Neuquén
Zapala
Viedma
San Antonio
Oeste
Choele Choel
Río Negro
Golfo San Matías
Península
Valdés
Golfo Nuevo
Rawson
Trelew
Río Chubut
Paso
de Indios
Río Chico
Lago
Musters
Comodoro Rivadavia
Golfo San Jorge
Caleta
Olivia
Río Deseado
Puerto Deseado
Puerto
San Julián
Bahía
Grande
Río Santa Cruz
Río Gallegos
Río Chico
Strait of Magellan

Temuco
Loncoche
Valdivia
Osorno
Puerto Varas
Puerto Montt
Ancud
Castro
Isla de Chiloé
Lago
Llanquihue
San Carlos de Bariloche
Esquel
Sarmiento
Lago
Buenos Aires
Perito
Moreno
Chile Chico
Cochrane
Coyhaique
Puerto Aisén
Golfo
Corcovado
Archipiélago
de los Chonos
Golfo de Penas
Isla
Wellington
Cerro
San Valentín
4058 m
Cerro
Chico
Cerro
Melimoyu
3050 m
Cerro
Murallón
2681 m
El Calafate
Puerto Natales
Punta Arenas
Porvenir
Tierra del Fuego
Ushuaia
Isla
de los Estados
Beagle Channel
Cabo de Hornos
(Cape Horn)

CHILE

ARGENTINA

FALKLAND ISLANDS
(UK dependent territory)
STANLEY
East
Falkland
Goose
Green
West
Falkland

Drake Passage

459

546

546

545

N

0 km   200
0 miles   200

ELEVATION

4000 m
13124 ft

2000 m
6562 ft

1000 m
3281 ft

500 m
1640 ft

250 m
820 ft

100 m
328 ft

Sea
Level

Sea
Level

-250 m
-820 ft

-500 m
-1640 ft

-1000 m
-3281 ft

-2000 m
-6562 ft

-3000 m
-9843 ft

-4000 m
-13124 ft

THE ATLANTIC OCEAN

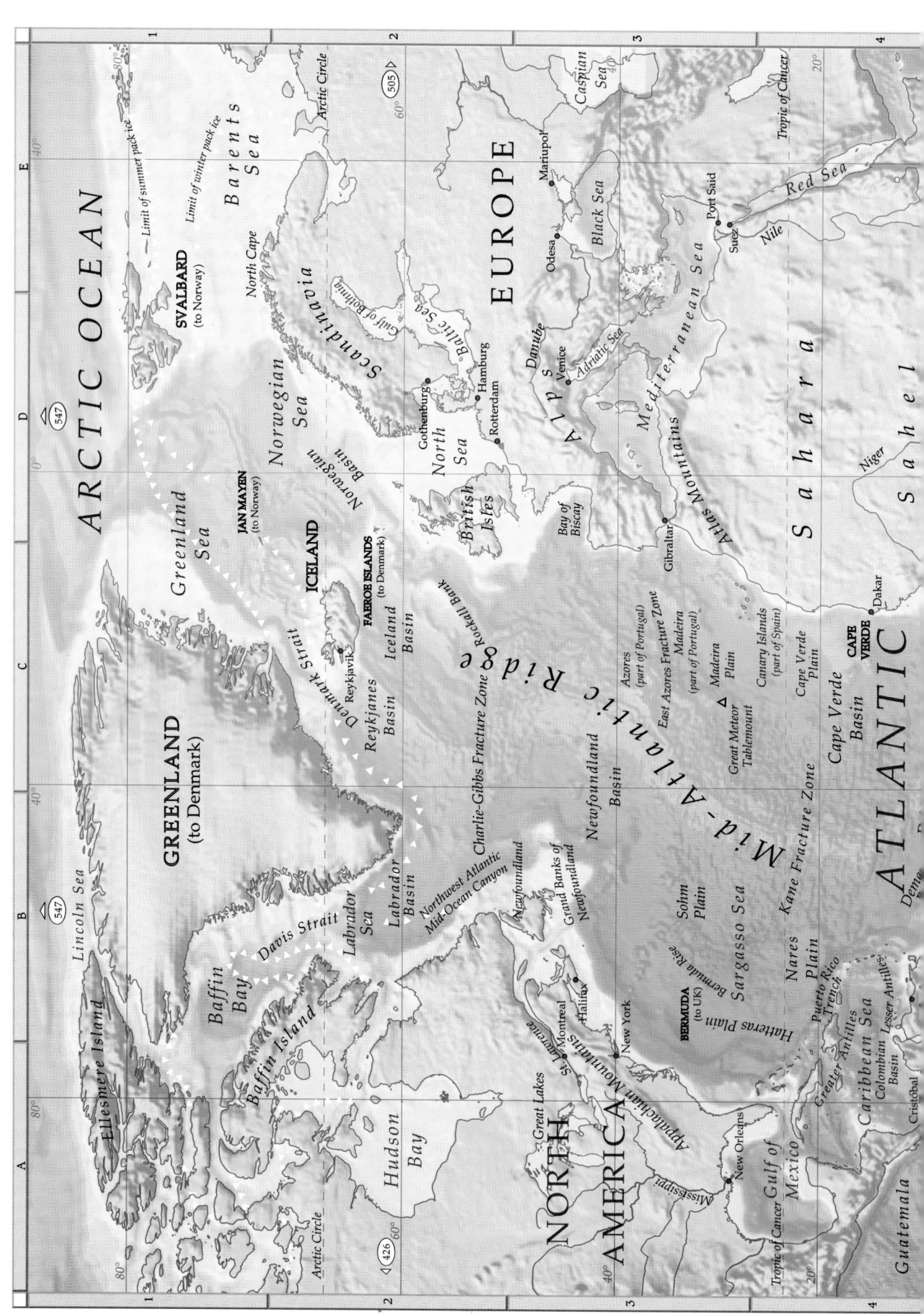

ARCTIC OCEAN

EUROPE

NORTH AMERICA

ATLANTIC

Limit of summer pack ice
Limit of winter pack ice

Arctic Circle

SVALBARD (to Norway)

Barents Sea

North Cape

Scandinavia

Norwegian Sea

Gulf of Bothnia

Baltic Sea

Danube

Mariupol'

Black Sea

Caspian Sea

Port Said

Red Sea

Suez

Nile

Gothenburg

Hamburg

North Sea

Odesa

Alps

Venice

Adriatic Sea

Mediterranean Sea

Rotterdam

Sahara

Saherl

Niger

Dakar

CAPE VERDE

ATLANTIC

GREENLAND (to Denmark)

Greenland Sea

JAN MAYEN (to Norway)

ICELAND

Reykjavik

Denmark Strait

Reykjanes Basin

Iceland Basin

FAEROE ISLANDS (to Denmark)

Rockall Bank

British Isles

Bay of Biscay

Gibraltar

Atlas Mountains

Azores (part of Portugal)

East Azores Fracture Zone

Madeira (part of Portugal)

Great Meteor Tablemount

Madeira Plain

Canary Islands (part of Spain)

Cape Verde Plain

Cape Verde Basin

Mid-Atlantic Ridge

Charlie-Gibbs Fracture Zone

Newfoundland Basin

Kane Fracture Zone

Lincoln Sea

Ellesmere Island

Davis Strait

Labrador Sea

Baffin Bay

Baffin Island

Labrador Basin

Northwest Atlantic Mid-Ocean Canyon

Newfoundland

Grand Banks of Newfoundland

Sohm Plain

Bermuda Rise

Nares Plain

Puerto Rico Trench

Demer

Hudson Bay

Great Lakes

St. Lawrence

Montreal

Halifax

New York

BERMUDA (to UK)

Hatteras Plain

Sargasso Sea

Greater Antilles

Caribbean Sea

Lesser Antilles

Colombian Basin

Cristóbal

Appalachian Mountains

New Orleans

Gulf of Mexico

Mississippi

Tropic of Cancer

Guatemala

Arctic Circle

Tropic of Cancer

547

547

505

426

458

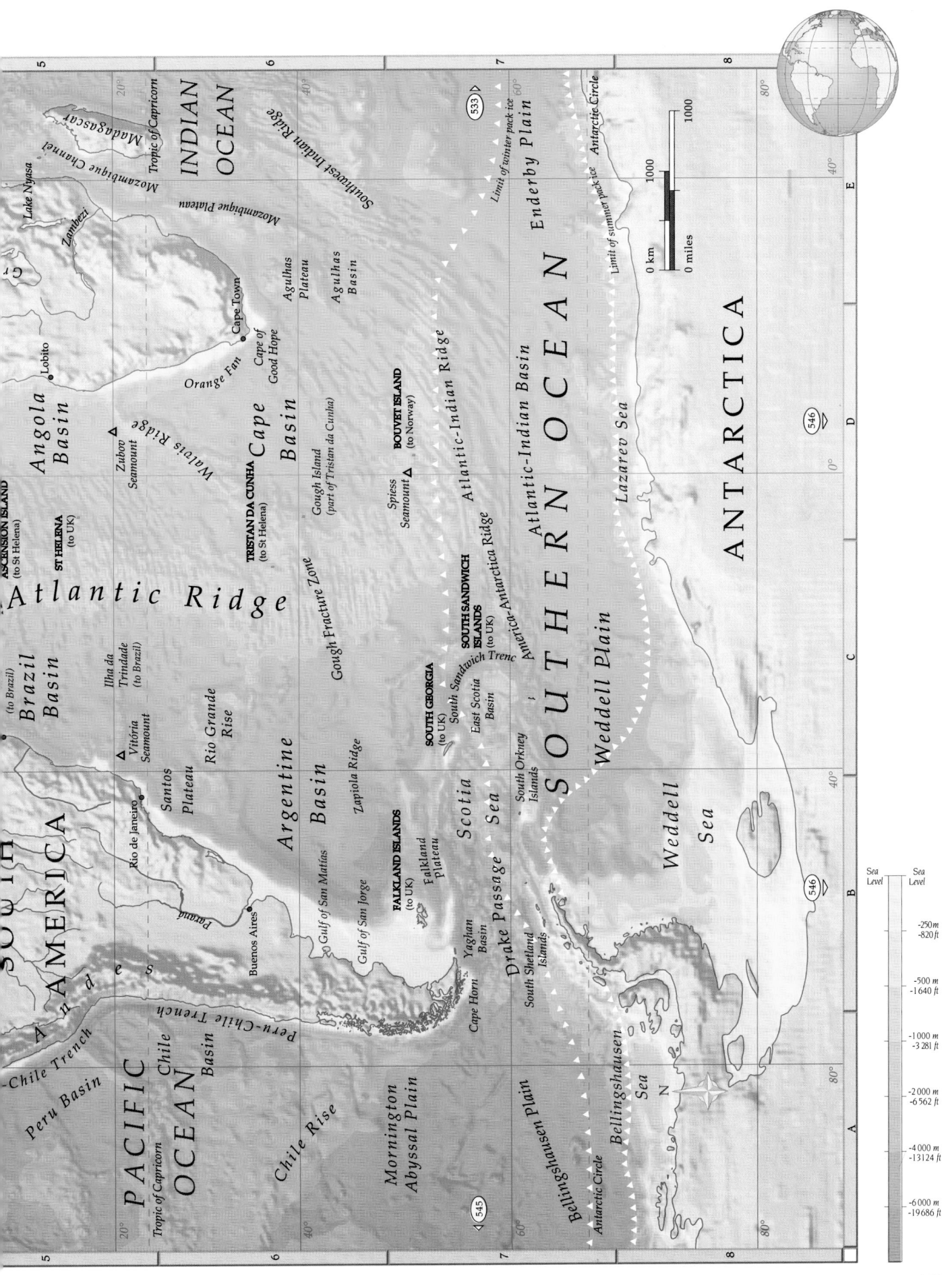

INDIAN OCEAN

Tropic of Capricorn

Madagascar

Mozambique Channel

Lake Nyasa

Zambezi

Mozambique Plateau

Southwest Indian Ridge

Limit of winter pack ice

Antarctic Circle

533

Enderby Plain

Limit of summer pack ice

1000

1000

0 km

1000

0 miles

Agulhas Plateau

Agulhas Basin

Cape Town

Cape of Good Hope

Orange Fan

Lobito

Angola Basin

Zubov Seamount

Walvis Ridge

Cape Basin

Gough Island (part of Tristan da Cunha)

BOUVET ISLAND (to Norway)

Atlantic–Indian Ridge

Atlantic–Indian Basin

Lazarev Sea

546

ANTARCTICA

ASCENSION ISLAND (to St Helena)

ST HELENA (to UK)

TRISTAN DA CUNHA (to St Helena)

Spiess Seamount

Atlantic Ridge

Gough Fracture Zone

SOUTH SANDWICH ISLANDS (to UK)

America–Antarctica Ridge

Weddell Plain

S O U T H E R N   O C E A N

Brazil Basin

Ilha da Trindade (to Brazil)

Vitória Seamount

Rio Grande Rise

Argentine Basin

Zapiola Ridge

SOUTH GEORGIA (to UK)

South Sandwich Trenc

East Scotia Basin

South Orkney Islands

Weddell Sea

SOUTH AMERICA

Rio de Janeiro

Santos Plateau

Paraná

Buenos Aires

Gulf of San Matías

Gulf of San Jorge

FALKLAND ISLANDS (to UK)

Falkland Plateau

Scotia Sea

Drake Passage

Yaghan Basin

Cape Horn

South Shetland Islands

Weddell Sea

Bellingshausen Sea

N

Andes

Peru–Chile Trench

Chile Trench

Chile Basin

Mornington Abyssal Plain

Bellingshausen Plain

Antarctic Circle

Bellingshausen Plain

PACIFIC OCEAN

Peru Basin

Chile Rise

Tropic of Capricorn

545

Sea Level

Sea Level

-250 m
-820 ft

-500 m
-1 640 ft

-1 000 m
-3 281 ft

-2 000 m
-6 562 ft

-4 000 m
-13 124 ft

-6 000 m
-19 686 ft

AFRICA

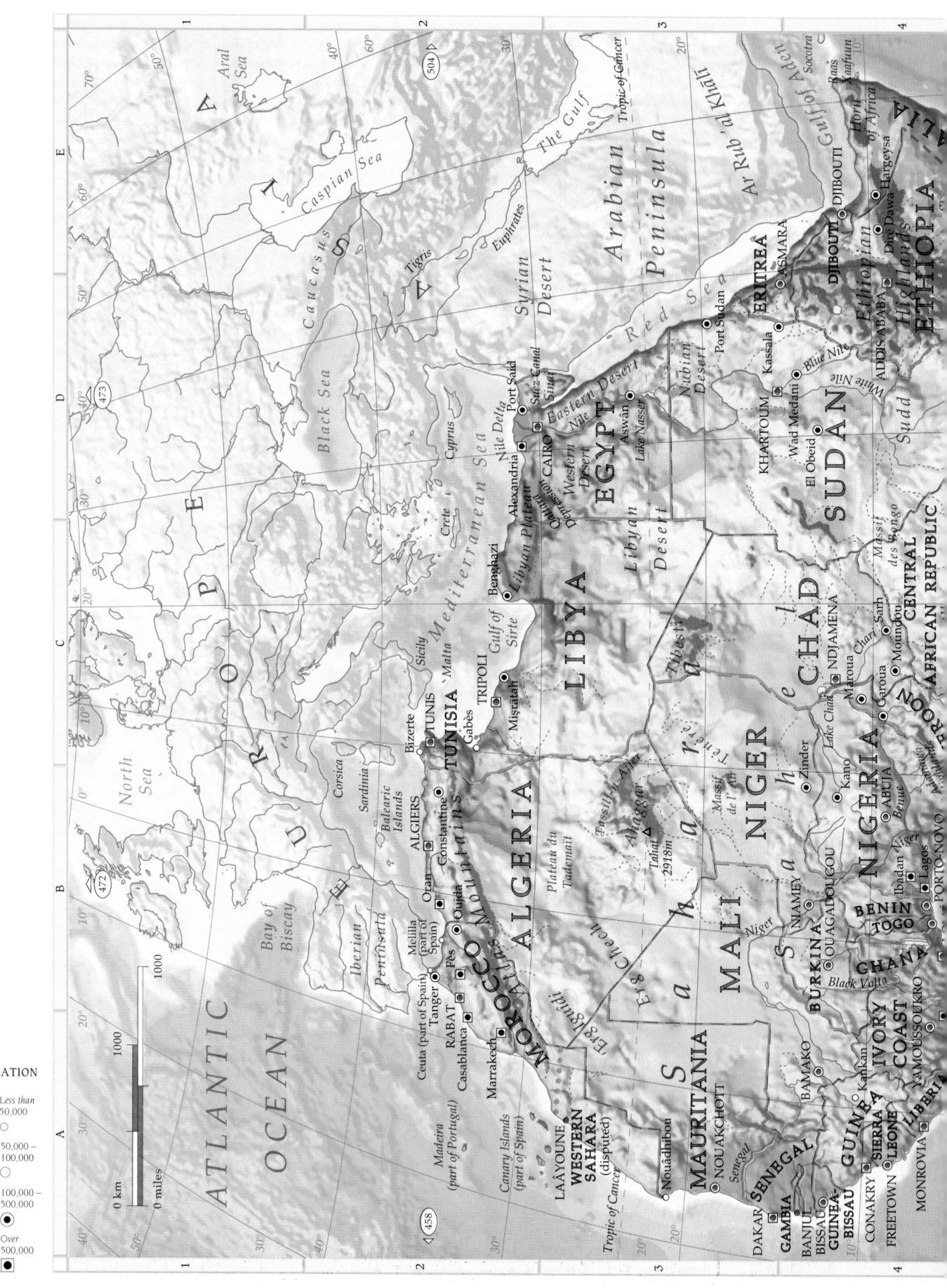

POPULATION

Less than
50,000
○

50,000 –
100,000
○

100,000 –
500,000
◉

Over
500,000
◉

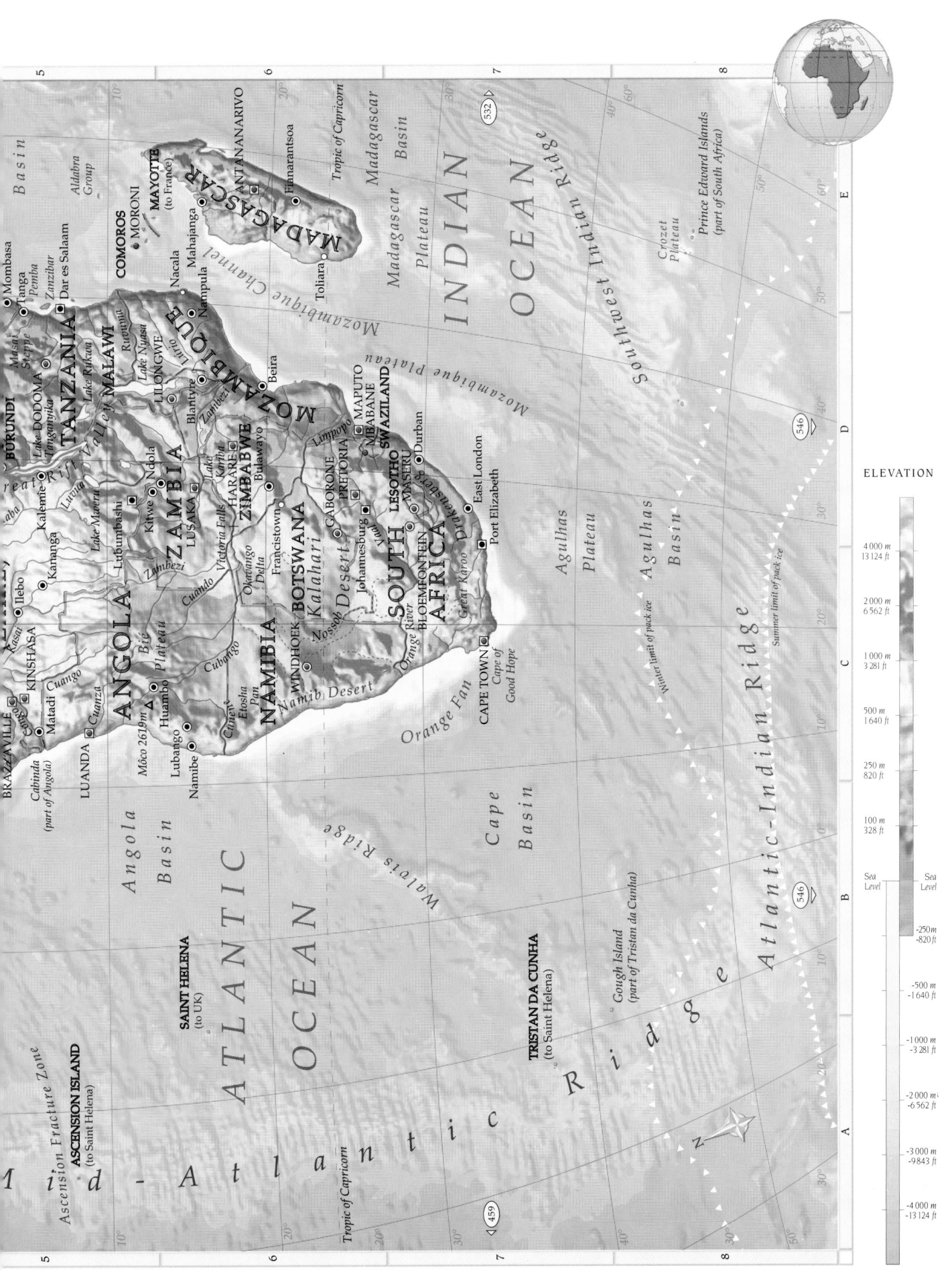

ELEVATION

4 000 m	
13 124 ft	
2 000 m	
6 562 ft	
1 000 m	
3 281 ft	
500 m	
1 640 ft	
250 m	
820 ft	
100 m	
328 ft	
Sea Level	Sea Level
-250 m	
-820 ft	
-500 m	
-1 640 ft	
-1 000 m	
-3 281 ft	
-2 000 m	
-6 562 ft	
-3 000 m	
-9 843 ft	
-4 000 m	
-13 124 ft	

NORTHWEST AFRICA

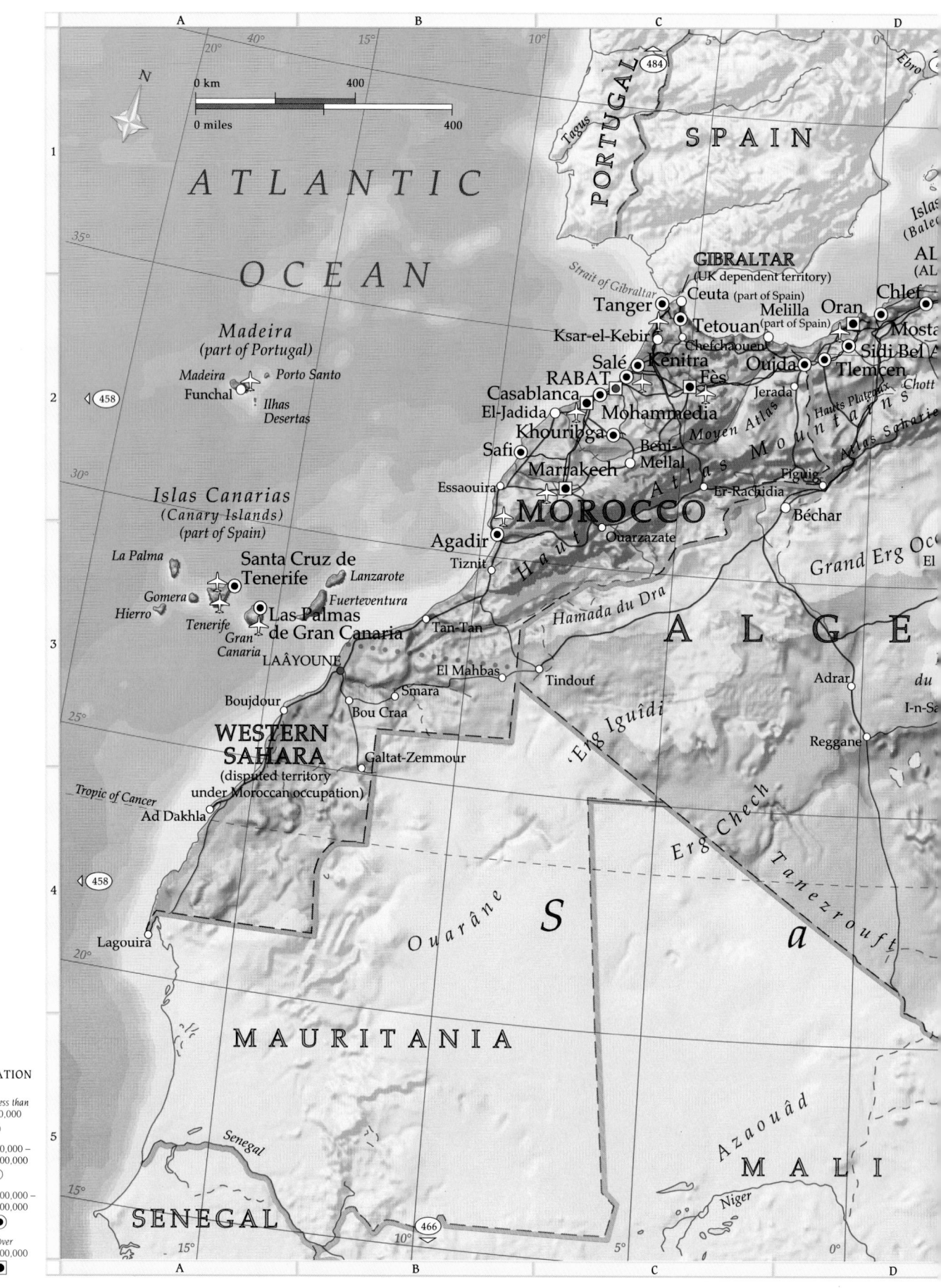

ATLANTIC OCEAN

Madeira
(part of Portugal)

Madeira • *Porto Santo*
Funchal • *Ilhas*
Desertas

◁ 458 ▷

Islas Canarias
(Canary Islands)
(part of Spain)

La Palma
Santa Cruz de
Tenerife • *Lanzarote*
Gomera • *Fuerteventura*
Hierro *Tenerife* Las Palmas
Gran de Gran Canaria
Canaria
LAÂYOUNE

Boujdour

WESTERN
SAHARA
(disputed territory
under Moroccan occupation)
Galtat-Zemmour

Tropic of Cancer
Ad Dakhla

◁ 458 ▷

Lagouira

MAURITANIA

SENEGAL
Senegal
466 ▽

SPAIN
Tagus

PORTUGAL
484

GIBRALTAR
(UK dependent territory)
Tanger Ceuta (part of Spain)
Melilla Oran Chlef
Ksar-el-Kebir Tetouan (part of Spain) Mosta
Chefchaouen Sidi-Bel
Salé Kenitra Ouijda Tlemcen
RABAT Fès Jerada *Chott*
Casablanca *S*
El-Jadida Mohammedia *Hauts Plateaux*
Khouribga *Moyen Atlas*
Safi Béni *Atlas Saharié*
Marrakeech Mellal Figuig
Essaouira *A t l a s   M o u n t a i n s*
Er-Rachidia
MOROCCO Béchar
Agadir Ouarzazate
Tiznit *Grand Erg Occ*
El
Hamada du Dra
H a u Tan-Tan
Smara Tindouf Adrar *du*
Bou Craa El Mahbas *I-n-Sa*
Erg Iguîdi **ALGE**
Reggane
Erg Chech
Ouarâne **S** *Tanezrouft*
a
Azaouâd
Niger **MALI**

Islas
(Bale
AL
(AL

Strait of Gibraltar
Islas
Ebro

POPULATION

Less than
50,000
○

50,000 –
100,000
○

100,000 –
500,000
◉

Over
500,000
◼

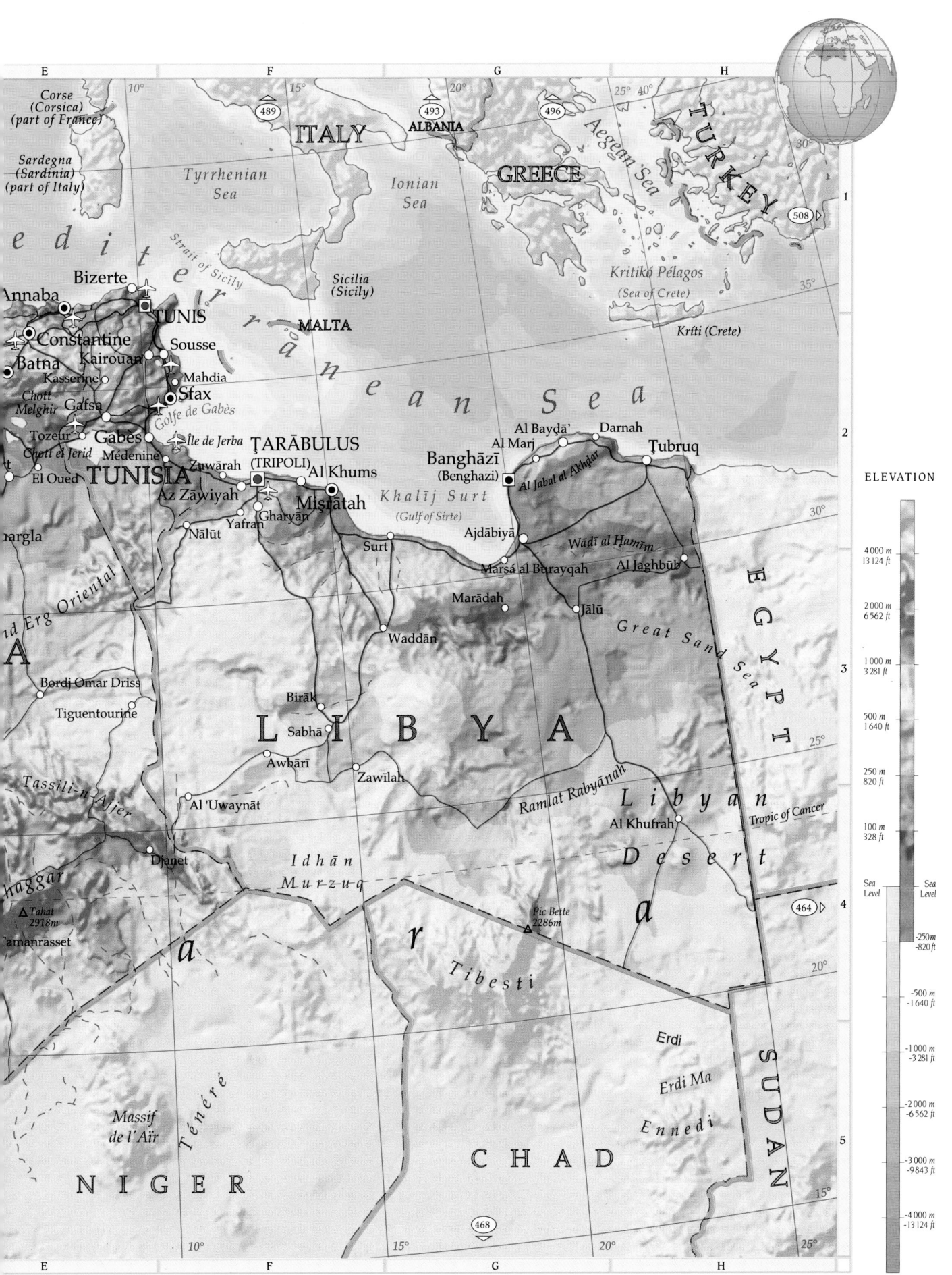

Corse
(Corsica)
(part of France)

Sardegna
(Sardinia)
(part of Italy)

ITALY

ALBANIA

GREECE

TURKEY

Tyrrhenian
Sea

Ionian
Sea

Aegean Sea

489

493

496

508

Bizerte

e d i t e r r a

Annaba

TUNIS

Constantine

Batna

Kasserine

Chott
Melghir

Gafsa

Sousse

Kairouan

Mahdia

Sfax

Golfe de Gabès

Tozeur

Gabes

Île de Jerba

Médenine

TUNISIA

El Oued

Zuwārah

Az Zāwiyah

Gharyān

Nālūt

Yafran

Kritikó Pélagos
(Sea of Crete)

Kríti (Crete)

MALTA

Sicilia
(Sicily)

Strait of Sicily

M e d i t e r r a n e a n   S e a

ȚARĀBULUS
(TRIPOLI)

Al Khums

Mişrātah

Surt

Al Baydā'

Al Marj

Banghāzī
(Benghazi)

Darnah

Ţubruq

Al Jabal al Akhḍar

Khalīj Surt
(Gulf of Sirte)

Ajdābiyā

Marsá al Burayqah

Wādī al Ḥamīm

Al Jaghbūb

EGYPT

argla

nd Erg Oriental

A

Bordj Omar Driss

Tiguentourine

Chott el Jerid

L   I   B   Y   A

Marādah

Waddān

Jālū

Great Sand Sea

Birāk

Sabhā

Awbārī

Zawīlah

Al 'Uwaynāt

Tassili-n-Ajjer

Ramlat Rabyānah

Al Khufrah

L i b y a n

D e s e r t

Tropic of Cancer

464

Djanet

haggar

Tahat
2918m

amanrasset

I d h ā n

M u r z u q

a

r

Pic Bette
2286m

Tibesti

Erdi

Erdi Ma

a

Ennedi

SUDAN

Massif
de l'Aïr

Ténéré

CHAD

N   I   G   E   R

468

ELEVATION

| 4 000 m / 13 124 ft |
| 2 000 m / 6 562 ft |
| 1 000 m / 3 281 ft |
| 500 m / 1 640 ft |
| 250 m / 820 ft |
| 100 m / 328 ft |
| Sea Level / Sea Level |
| -250 m / -820 ft |
| -500 m / -1 640 ft |
| -1 000 m / -3 281 ft |
| -2 000 m / -6 562 ft |
| -3 000 m / -9 843 ft |
| -4 000 m / -13 124 ft |

NORTHEAST AFRICA

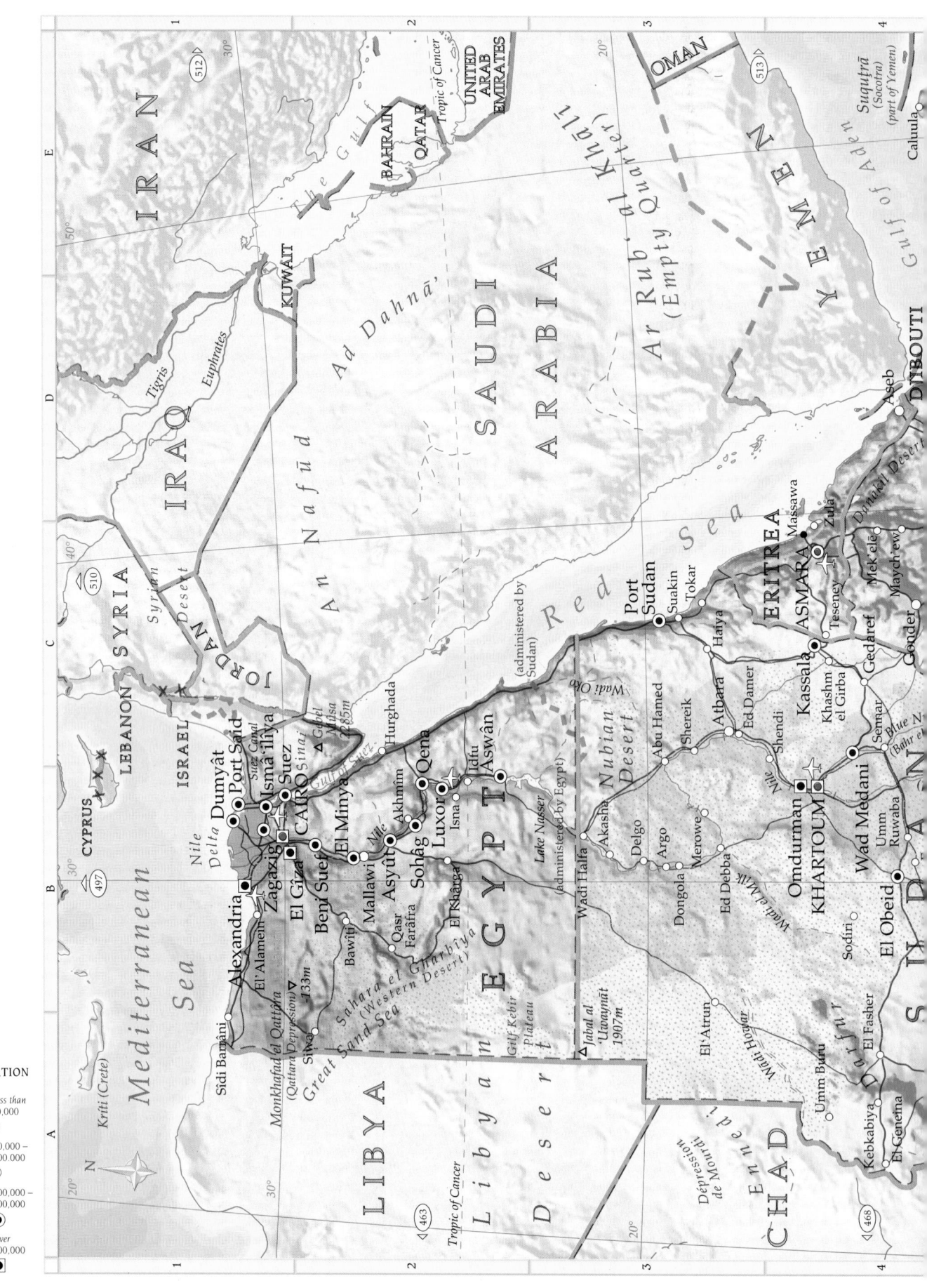

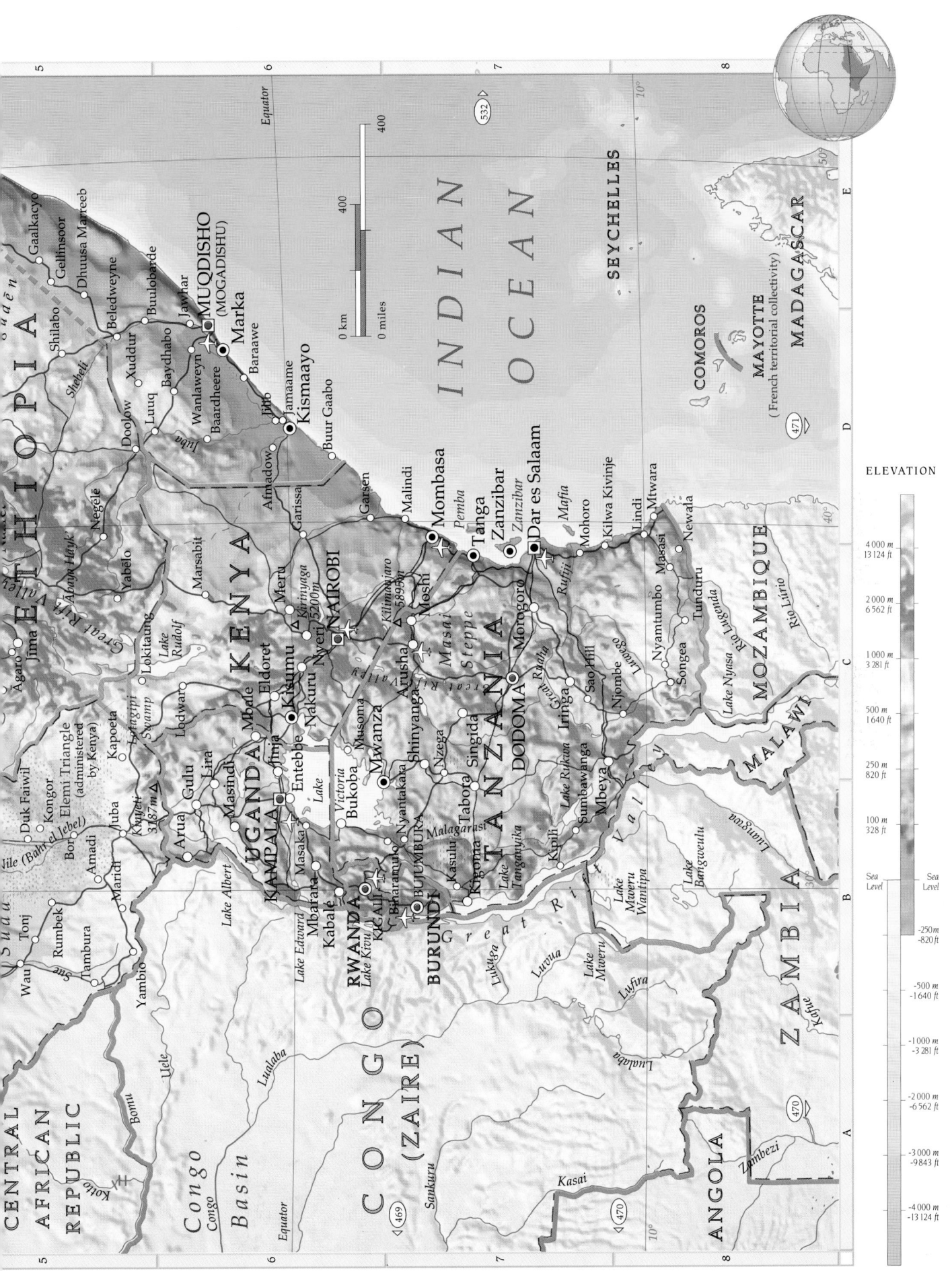

ELEVATION

4 000 m
13 124 ft

2 000 m
6 562 ft

1 000 m
3 281 ft

500 m
1 640 ft

250 m
820 ft

100 m
328 ft

Sea
Level

Sea
Level

-250 m
-820 ft

-500 m
-1 640 ft

-1 000 m
-3 281 ft

-2 000 m
-6 562 ft

-3 000 m
-9 843 ft

-4 000 m
-13 124 ft

WEST AFRICA

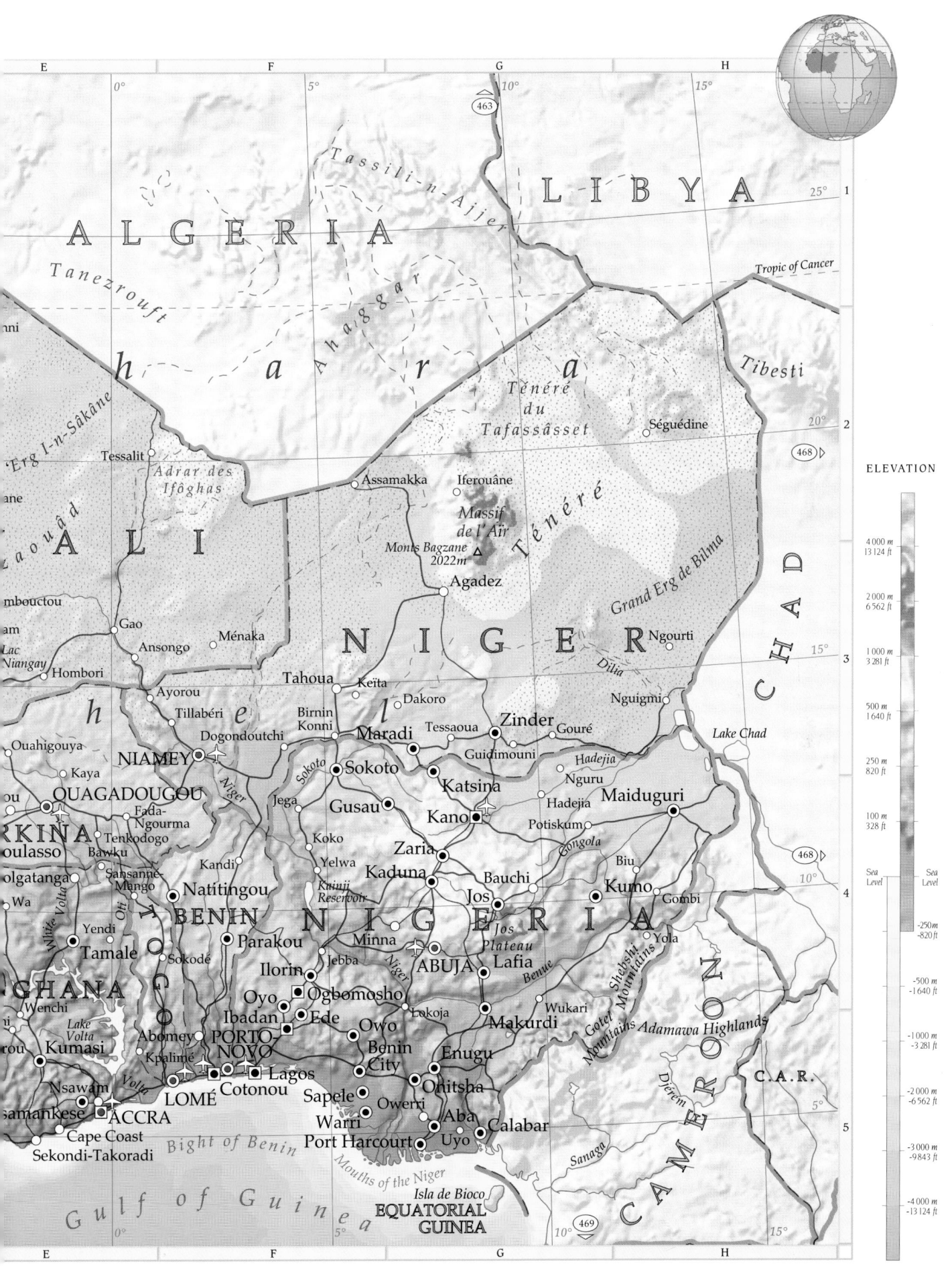

ELEVATION

4 000 m
13 124 ft

2 000 m
6 562 ft

1 000 m
3 281 ft

500 m
1 640 ft

250 m
820 ft

100 m
328 ft

Sea
Level

Sea
Level

-250 m
-820 ft

-500 m
-1 640 ft

-1 000 m
-3 281 ft

-2 000 m
-6 562 ft

-3 000 m
-9843 ft

-4 000 m
-13 124 ft

CENTRAL AFRICA

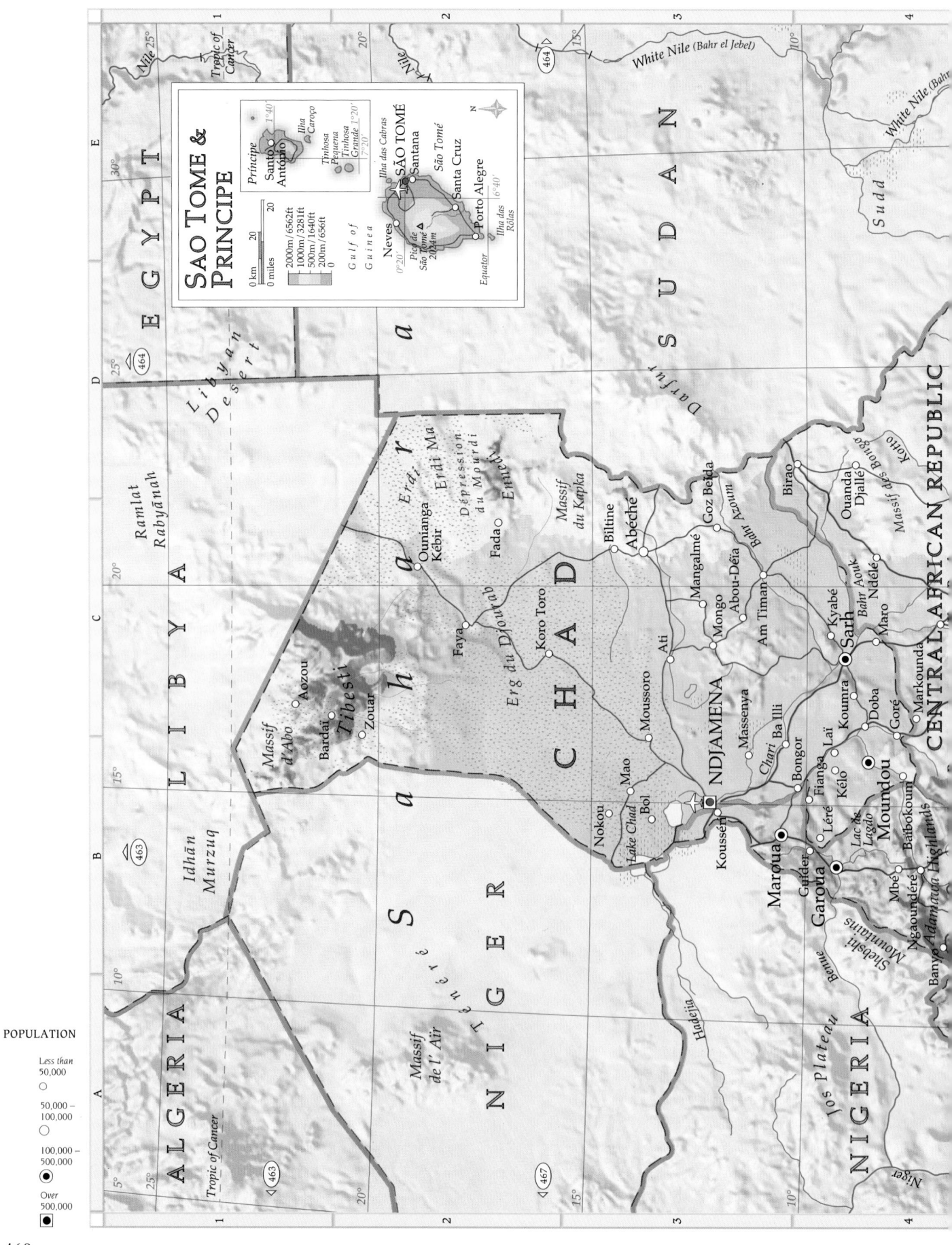

SÃO TOMÉ & PRÍNCIPE

Príncipe
Santo António
Ilha Caroço
Tinhosa Pequena
Tinhosa Grande
Ilha das Cabras
SÃO TOMÉ
Santana
São Tomé
Santa Cruz
Neves
Pico de São Tomé 2024m
Porto Alegre
Ilha das Rôlas
Gulf of Guinea
Equator

0 km   20
0 miles   20
2000m / 6562ft
1000m / 3281ft
500m / 1640ft
200m / 656ft

Tropic of Cancer

Nile

White Nile (Bahr el Jebel)
White Nile (Bahr

E G Y P T

L I B Y A

Libyan Desert

Ramlat Rabyānah

Idhān Murzuq

S U D A N

Sudd

Darfur

S a h a r a

Ennedi
Erdi Ma
Erdi
Dépression du Mourdi
Ouniangá Kébir
Fada
Massif du Kapka
Biltine
Abéché
Mangalmé
Goz Beïda
Birao
Ouanda Djallé
Ndélé
Koto
Massif des Bongo

Faya
Koro Toro
Erg du Djourab

C H A D

Ati
Mongo
Abou-Déïa
Am Timan
Kyabé
Sarh
Maro
Markounda

Massif d'Abo
Aozou
Bardaï
Tibesti
Zouar

Mao
Moussoro
Massenya
Chari Ba Illi
Koumra
Doba
Goré
Gore

Nokou
Lake Chad
Bol
NDJAMENA
Bongor
Lai
Fianga
Kélo
Léré

CENTRAL AFRICAN REPUBLIC

N I G E R

Massif de l'Aïr

Ténéré

Koussèri
Maroua
Guider
Garoua
Mbé
Baïbokoum
Lac de Léré
Lago
Moundou

Shebshi Mountains
Benue
Ngaoundéré
Banyo Adamaua Highlands

N I G E R I A

Jos Plateau

Hadejia

Niger

Tropic of Cancer

POPULATION

Less than 50,000

50,000 – 100,000

100,000 – 500,000

Over 500,000

468

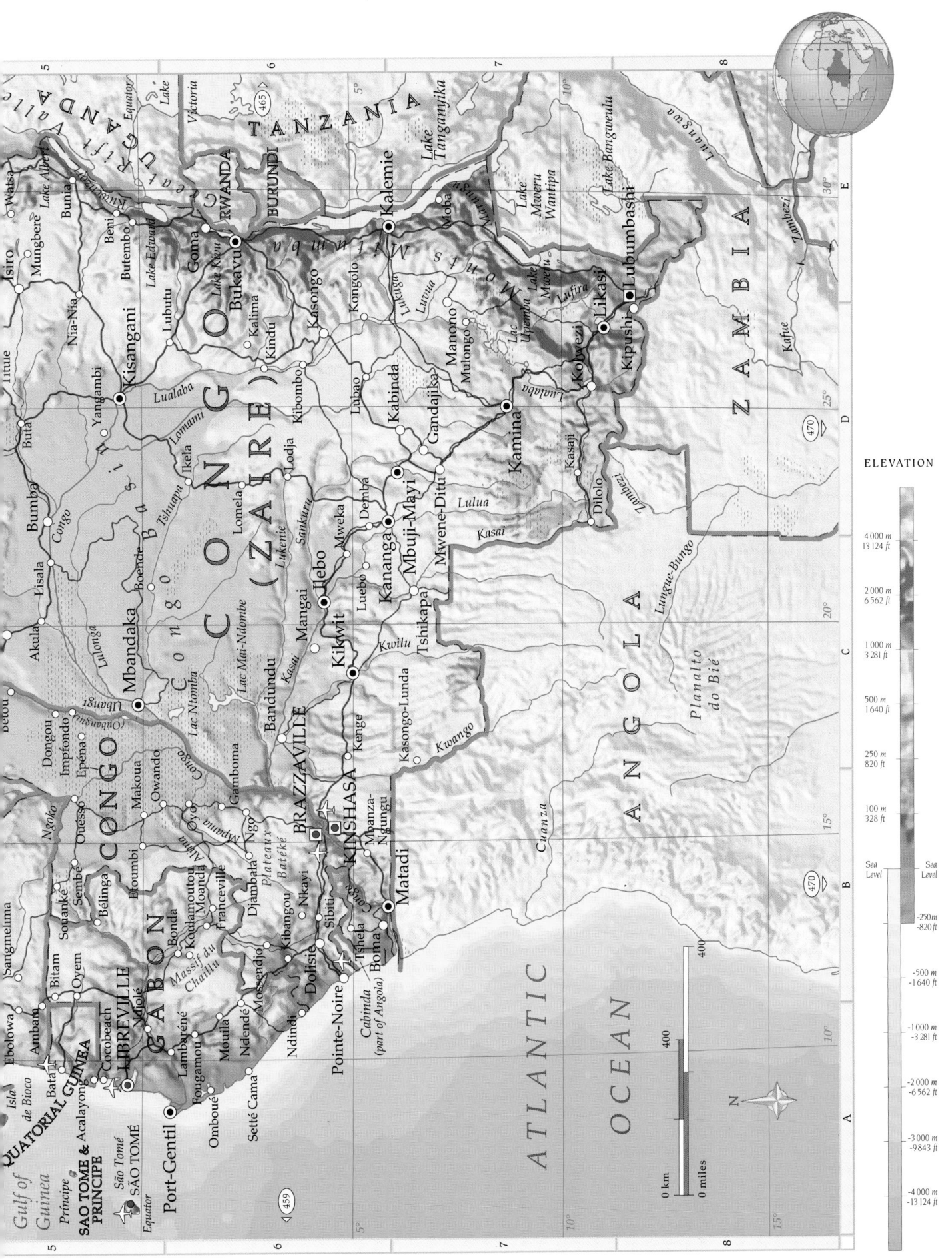

ELEVATION

4 000 m
13 124 ft

2 000 m
6 562 ft

1 000 m
3 281 ft

500 m
1 640 ft

250 m
820 ft

100 m
328 ft

Sea Level

Sea Level

−250 m
−820 ft

−500 m
−1 640 ft

−1 000 m
−3 281 ft

−2 000 m
−6 562 ft

−3 000 m
−9 843 ft

−4 000 m
−13 124 ft

SOUTHERN AFRICA

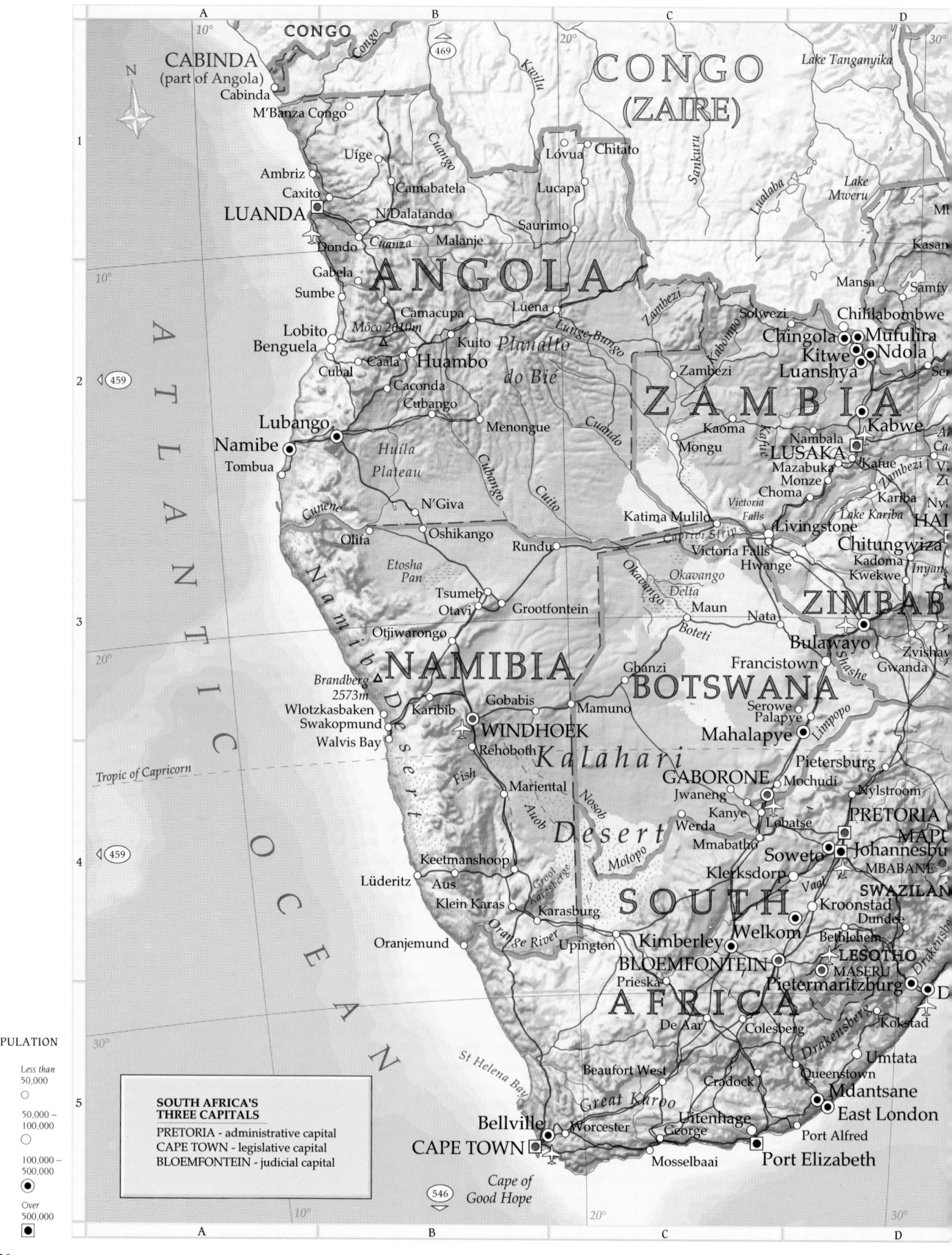

CONGO

CABINDA
(part of Angola)
Cabinda
M'Banza Congo

CONGO
(ZAIRE)

Lake Tanganyika

Uíge
Ambriz
Caxito
LUANDA
Dondo

Camabatela
N'Dalatando
Malanje

Lovua Chitato
Lucapa
Saurimo

Lake
Mweru

ANGOLA

Gabela
Sumbe
Lobito
Benguela
Cubal

Camacupa
Môco 2610m
Kuito
Caála Huambo
Caconda
Cubango

Luena

Planalto
do Bie

Luanda-Bango

Zambezi

Mansa Samfy

Solwezi Chililabombwe
Chingola Mufulira
Kitwe Ndola
Zambezi Luanshya

Kasan

Lubango
Namibe
Tombua

Huíla
Plateau

Menongue

Cuando

Cuito

Katima Mulilo

ZAMBIA
Kaoma
Mongu

Nambala
LUSAKA
Mazabuka
Monze
Choma

Kabwe

Kafue

Kariba

Kabwe

N'Giva
Olifa
Oshikango
Rundu

Etosha
Pan

Victoria
Falls

Capirivi Strip

Livingstone
Victoria Falls
Hwange

Chitungwiza
Kadoma
Kwekwe

Inyan

Tsumeb
Otavi
Grootfontein

Okavango
Delta

Okavango

Maun

Nata

Boteti

ZIMBAB

Bulawayo

Otjiwarongo

Brandberg
2573m

NAMIBIA

Ghanzi

BOTSWANA

Francistown
Gwanda

Zvishav

Shashe

Wlotzkasbaken
Swakopmund
Walvis Bay

Karibib
Rehoboth

Gobabis

Mamuno

Serowe
Palapye

Mahalapye

Limpopo

Pietersburg

WINDHOEK

Kalahari

Fish

Mariental

Nosob

GABORONE
Jwaneng
Kanye
Werda
Mmabatho

Mochudi

Nylstroom

PRETORIA

Tropic of Capricorn

Auob

Desert

Molopo

Lobatse

MAPU

Keetmanshoop

Groot

Karasberge

Karasburg

SOUTH

Klerksdorp

Soweto Johannesbu
MBABANE
SWAZILAN

Lüderitz
Aus
Klein Karas

Oranjemund

Orange River

Upington

Kimberley

BLOEMFONTEIN

Prieska

Kroonstad
Welkom

Dundee

Bethlehem
LESOTHO
MASERU
Pietermaritzburg

Drakensberg

AFRICA

De Aar

Colesberg

Kokstad

Umtata

St Helena Bay

Beaufort West

Cradock

Queenstown
Mdantsane
East London

Great Karoo

Bellville
Worcester

CAPE TOWN

George

Uitenhage
Mosselbaai

Port Alfred
Port Elizabeth

Cape of
Good Hope

ATLANTIC OCEAN

Namib Desert

POPULATION

Less than
50,000
○

50,000 –
100,000
○

100,000 –
500,000
◉

Over
500,000
◉

SOUTH AFRICA'S
THREE CAPITALS
PRETORIA - administrative capital
CAPE TOWN - legislative capital
BLOEMFONTEIN - judicial capital

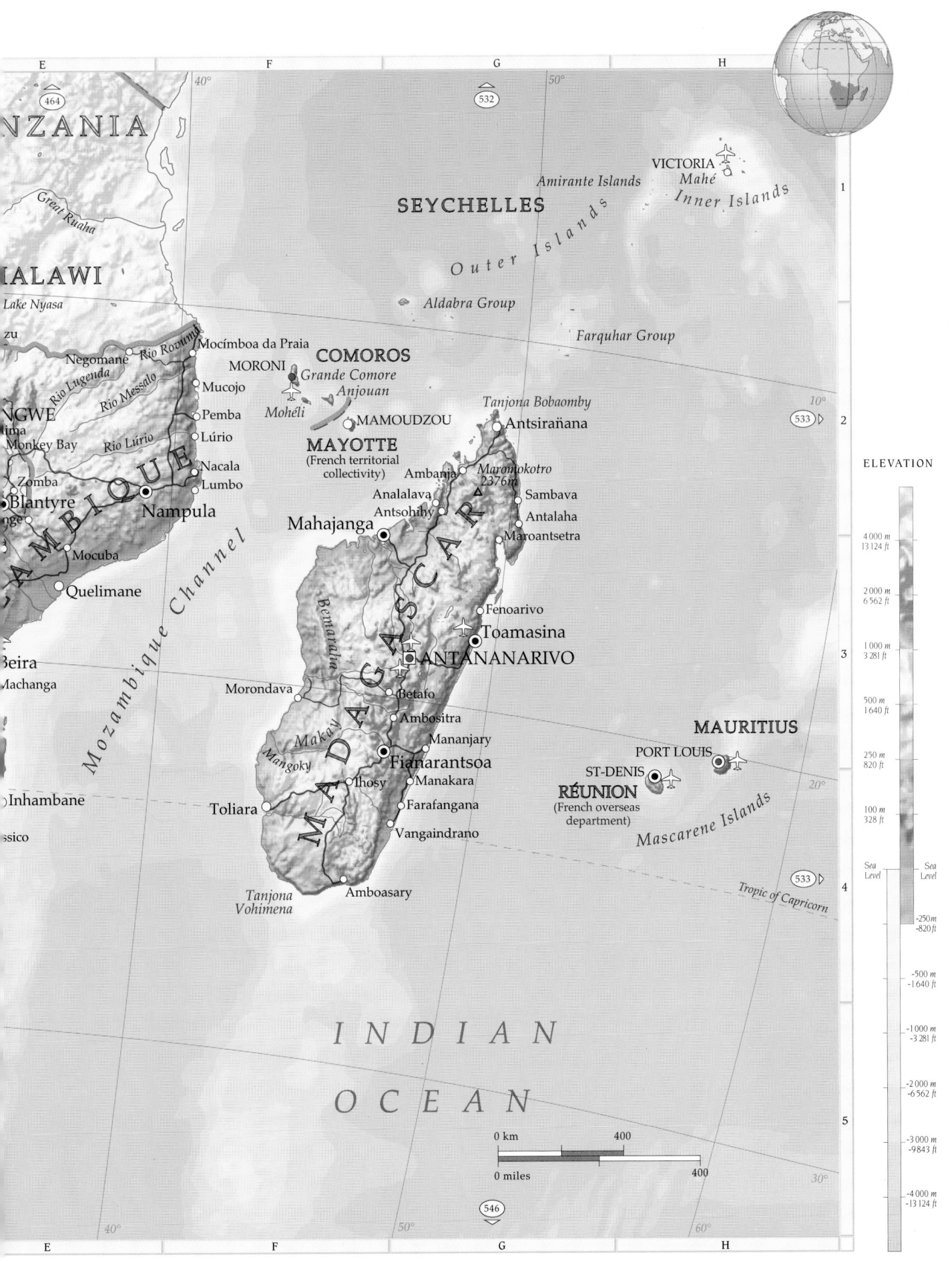

SEYCHELLES

Amirante Islands

VICTORIA
Mahé
Inner Islands

Outer Islands

Aldabra Group

Farquhar Group

NZANIA

464

MALAWI

Lake Nyasa

zu

Great Ruaha

Negomane
Rio Rovuma
Mocímboa da Praia
MORONI
COMOROS
Grande Comore
Anjouan

Tanjona Bobaomby

NGWE
Mucojo
Rio Lugenda
Rio Messalo
Mohéli
MAMOUDZOU
Antsirañana

ima
Pemba
MAYOTTE
(French territorial
collectivity)
Ambanja
Maromokotro 2376m

Monkey Bay
Rio Lúrio
Lúrio
Analalava
Sambava

Zomba
Nacala
Antsohihy
Antalaha

Blantyre
Lumbo
Mahajanga
Maroantsetra

ge
Nampula

ZAMBIQUE

Mocuba

Quelimane

Mozambique Channel

Bemaraha

Fenoarivo

eira

Toamasina

Machanga
ANTANANARIVO

Morondava
MADAGASCAR
Betafo

Ambositra

Makay
Mananjary

Mangoky
Fianarantsoa

MAURITIUS

PORT LOUIS

Inhambane
Ihosy
Manakara
ST-DENIS

Toliara
Farafangana
RÉUNION
(French overseas
department)

ssico
Vangaindrano

Mascarene Islands

Tanjona Vohimena
Amboasary

Tropic of Capricorn

I N D I A N

O C E A N

532

533

533

546

| 0 km | | 400 | |
| 0 miles | | 400 | |

ELEVATION

4 000 m	13 124 ft
2 000 m	6 562 ft
1 000 m	3 281 ft
500 m	1 640 ft
250 m	820 ft
100 m	328 ft
Sea Level	Sea Level
-250 m	-820 ft
-500 m	-1 640 ft
-1 000 m	-3 281 ft
-2 000 m	-6 562 ft
-3 000 m	-9 843 ft
-4 000 m	-13 124 ft

EUROPE

REYKJANES Basin

547

Reykjanes Ridge

REYKJAVÍK

ICELAND

Vatnajökull

Limit of winter pack ice

Arctic Circle

Norwegian Basin

Charlie-Gibbs Fracture Zone

Iceland Basin

Faeroe-Iceland Ridge

Norwegian Sea

458

Hatton Ridge

FAEROE ISLANDS
(to Denmark)

Faeroe-Shetland Trough

Trondheim

Mid-Atlantic Ridge

Rockall Bank

Shetland Islands

Shetland Islands

Rockall Trough

Outer Hebrides

Orkney Islands

Bergen

N

British Isles

Stavanger

OSLO

Porcupine Plain

Glasgow

Ireland

Edinburgh

North Sea

Gothenburg

ATLANTIC

Belfast

UNITED

Ålborg

OCEAN

REPUBLIC
OF
IRELAND

DUBLIN
ISLE OF MAN
(to UK)

KINGDOM

Jylland

DENMARK

Liverpool

Manchester

Britain

Odense

Celtic Sea

Birmingham

Hamburg

Celtic Shelf

Cardiff

LONDON

NETHERLANDS

AMSTERDAM

Hannover

BERLIN

English Channel

THE HAGUE

Rotterdam

Elbe

Biscay Plain

Channel Islands
(to UK)

le Havre

BELGIUM

BRUSSELS

Bonn

GERMANY

Azores-Biscay Rise

Charcot Seamounts

Rennes

Seine

Liège

LUXEMBOURG

Frankfurt
am Main

PARIS

LUXEMBOURG

Rhine

Nantes

Orleans

Strasbourg

Stuttgart

Iberian Plain

Loire

FRANCE

Zürich

Munich

A Coruña

Bay of Biscay

Bordeaux

BERN

SWITZERLAND

LIECH.

VII

Galicia Bank

Bilbao

Lyon

Massif Central

Mont Blanc
4807m

Innsbruck

AUST

458

Porto

Duero

Garonne

Rhône

Milan

Venice

SLOVEN

Tagus Plain

PORTUGAL

Iberian

Zaragoza

Pyrenees

Toulouse

Turin

Po

Trieste

Cordillera Cantábrica

Ebro

Nice

Bologna

Apennines

Adri

Tagus

MADRID

ANDORRA

Marseille

MONACO

SAN MARINO

LISBON

SPAIN

Peninsula

Barcelona

Corsica

ITALY

VATICAN CITY

Horseshoe Seamounts

Guadalquivir

Valencia

Sardinia

ROME

Madeira
(part of Portugal)

Seville

Palma

Balearic Islands

Algerian Basin

Naples

Strait of Gibraltar

Málaga

Cagliari

Tyrrhenian Sea

Cosenza

GIBRALTAR
(to UK)

Ceuta
(part of Spain)

Mediterra

Palermo

POPULATION

Melilla
(part of Spain)

Sicily

Ca

*Less than
50,000*
○

Canary Islands
(part of Spain)

N

Atlas Mountains

AFRICA

MALTA
VALLETTA

*50,000 –
100,000*
○

*100,000 –
500,000*
◉

460

*Over
500,000*
◼

Barents Sea

North Cape
Ostrov Kolguyev

Arctic Circle

Ob'

Irtysh

Murmansk
Kola
Peninsula

White
Sea

Archangel

R U S S I A N

Perm'

F I N L A N D

Lake Onega

F E D E R A T I O N

Tampere

Lake Ladoga

Vologda

Turku HELSINKI

Saint Petersburg

Kazan'

Ufa

OLM TALLINN

Yaroslavl'

Nizhniy
Novgorod

ESTONIA

MOSCOW

Ul'yanovsk

Orenburg

LATVIA

Samara

Ural

RĪGA

THUANIA
GRAD
s-Fed. Kaunas

Vitsyebsk

Central
Russian
Upland

Aral Sea

VILNIUS

Syr Darya

MINSK

Babruysk

Homyel'

Voronezh

Volga Uplands

Ural

Amu Darya

BELORUSSIA

RSAW

Pripet
Marshes

Brest

Don

Dnieper Lowlands

Kharkiv

Volgograd

KIEV

Dnieper

Astrakhan'

L'viv

Dnipropetrovs'k

Dniester

UKRAINE

Donets'k

Chernivtsi

Rostov-na-Donu

MOLDAVIA

CHIŞINĂU

Stavropol'

Sea of
Azov

Cluj-Napoca

Odesa

Crimea

Caspian Sea

ROMANIA

Braşov

Simferopol'

Caucasus

El'brus 5642m

RADE

BUCHAREST

Constanţa

Black Sea

Danube

BULGARIA

Varna

Balkan Mountains

Burgas

OPJE

SOFIA

RD.

Aegean
Sea

Anatolia

Zagros Mountains

GREECE

ATHENS

Piraeus

onnese

Irákleio

Cyprus

Tigris

Euphrates

Crete

0 km   500

0 miles   500

THE NORTH ATLANTIC

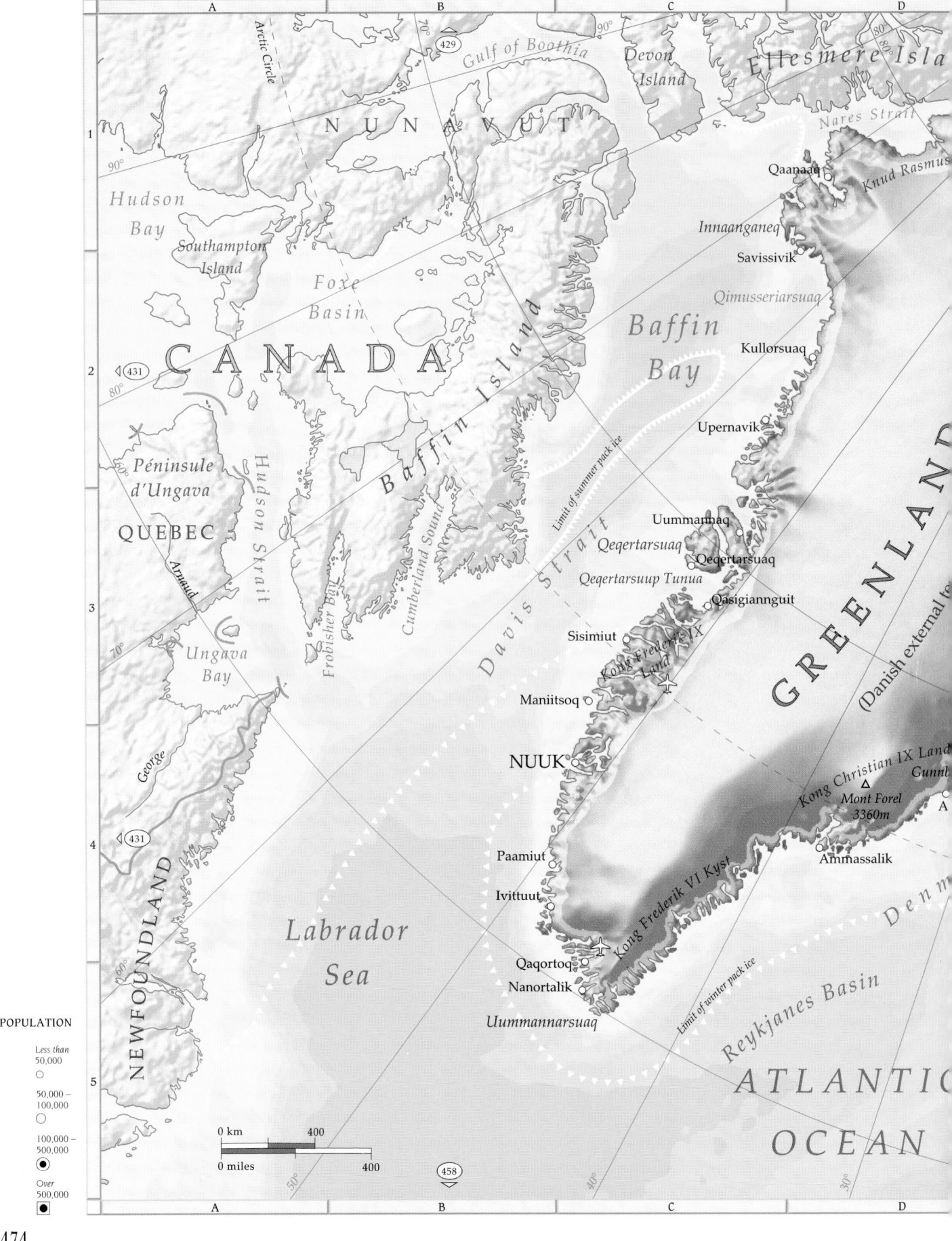

A
B
C
D

Arctic Circle

70°
90°

429

Gulf of Boothia

Devon
Island

Ellesmere Isla

Nares Strait

N U N A V U T

90°

Knud Rasmus

Qaanaaq

80°

1

Hudson
Bay

Southampton
Island

Foxe
Basin

Innaanganeq

Savissivik

Qimusseriarsuaq

C A N A D A

431

Baffin
Bay

Kullorsuaq

80°

2

Baffin Island

Upernavik

Péninsule
d'Ungava

Hudson Strait

Davis Strait

Uummannaq

QUEBEC

Limit of summer pack ice

Qeqertarsuaq

Qeqertarsuaq

Cumberland Sound

Qeqertarsuup Tunua

Qasigiannguit

Arnaud

Sisimiut

Kong Frederik IX
Land

GREENLAND

70°

3

Frobisher Bay

Ungava
Bay

Maniitsoq

(Danish external te

Kong Christian IX Land

George

NUUK

Gunnb

Mont Forel
3360m

A

431

Paamiut

Kong Frederik VI Kyst

Ammassalik

4

Ivittuut

Denm

60°

Labrador
Sea

Limit of winter pack ice

Qaqortoq

Nanortalik

NEWFOUNDLAND

Reykjanes Basin

Uummannarsuaq

POPULATION

Less than
50,000
○

50,000 –
100,000
○

100,000 –
500,000
◉

Over
500,000
◉

ATLANTIC

OCEAN

50°

0 km   400

0 miles   400

458

40°

30°

A
B
C
D

ARCTIC

OCEAN

Kap Morris Jesup

Wandel
Sea

Independence Fjord

Nord

SVALBARD
(Norwegian dependency)

Kvitøya

Nordaustlandet

Kong Karls Land

Spitsbergen

Barentsøya

Edgeøya

LONGYEARBYEN

Barentsberg

Greenland
Sea

Storfjorden

Limit of winter pack ice

Zemlya
Frantsa-Iosifa

Novaya
Zemlya

Barents
Sea

Daneborg

Kong Oscar Fjord

Ittoqqortoormiit

Kangikajik

JAN MAYEN
(Norwegian dependency)

Bjørnøya
(part of Norway)

Nordkapp
(North Cape)

FINLAND

Arctic Circle

Mohns Ridge

Norwegian

Sea

Norwegian Basin

Vestfjorden

SWEDEN

ICELAND

Siglufjördhur

Raufarhöfn

Húsavík

Akureyri

Seydhisfjördhur

Neskaupstadhur

EYKJAVÍK

Belfoss

Vatnajökull

Djúpivogur

Hvannadalshnúkur
2119m

Vestmannaeyjar

FAEROE ISLANDS
(Danish external territory)

TÓRSHAVN

Shetland
Islands
(part of UK)

Gulf
of
Bothnia

N O R W A Y

N

ELEVATION

4 000 m
13 124 ft

2 000 m
6 562 ft

1 000 m
3 281 ft

500 m
1 640 ft

250 m
820 ft

100 m
328 ft

Sea
Level

Sea
Level

-250 m
-820 ft

-500 m
-1 640 ft

-1 000 m
-3 281 ft

-2 000 m
-6 562 ft

-3 000 m
-9 843 ft

-4 000 m
-13 124 ft

SCANDINAVIA AND FINLAND

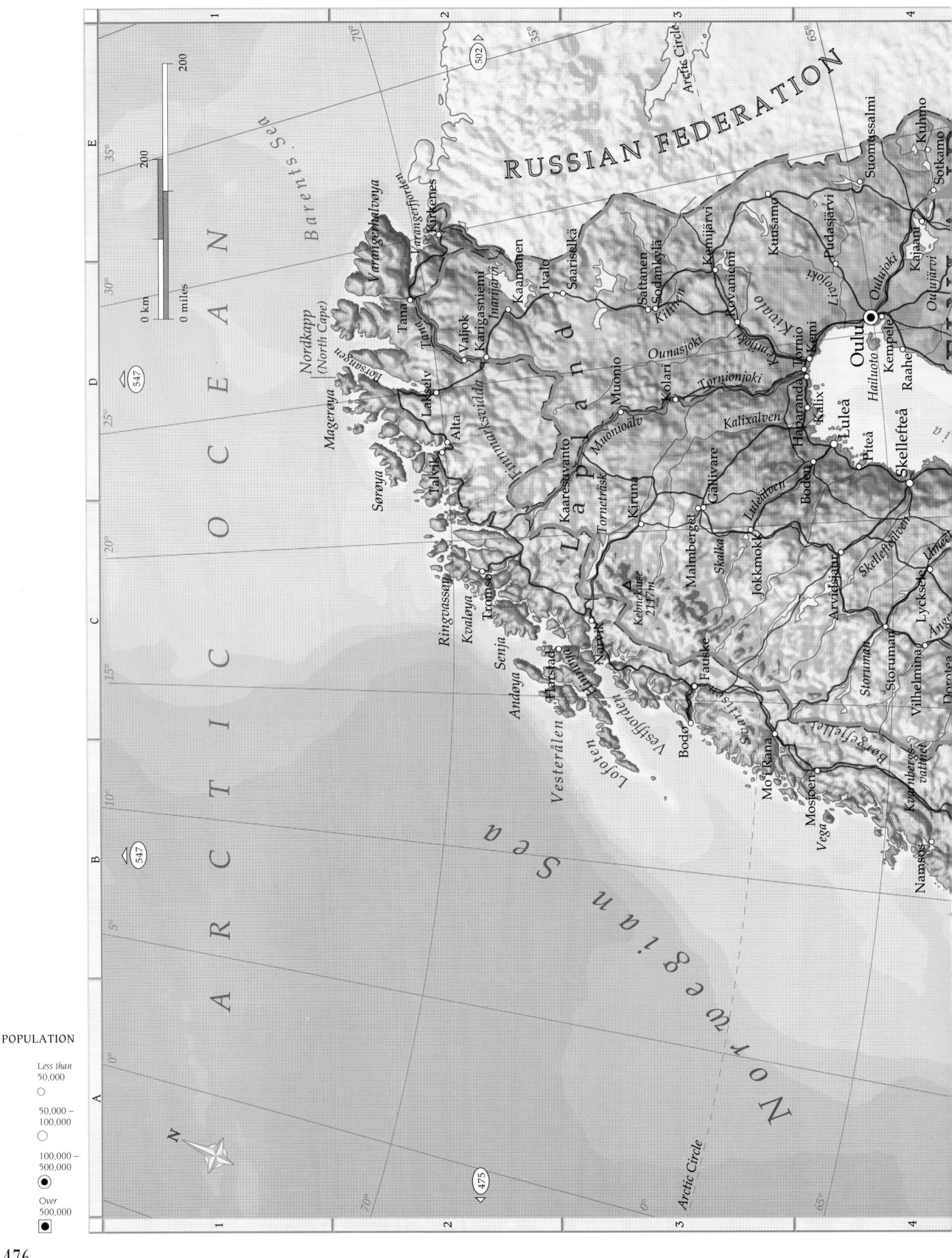

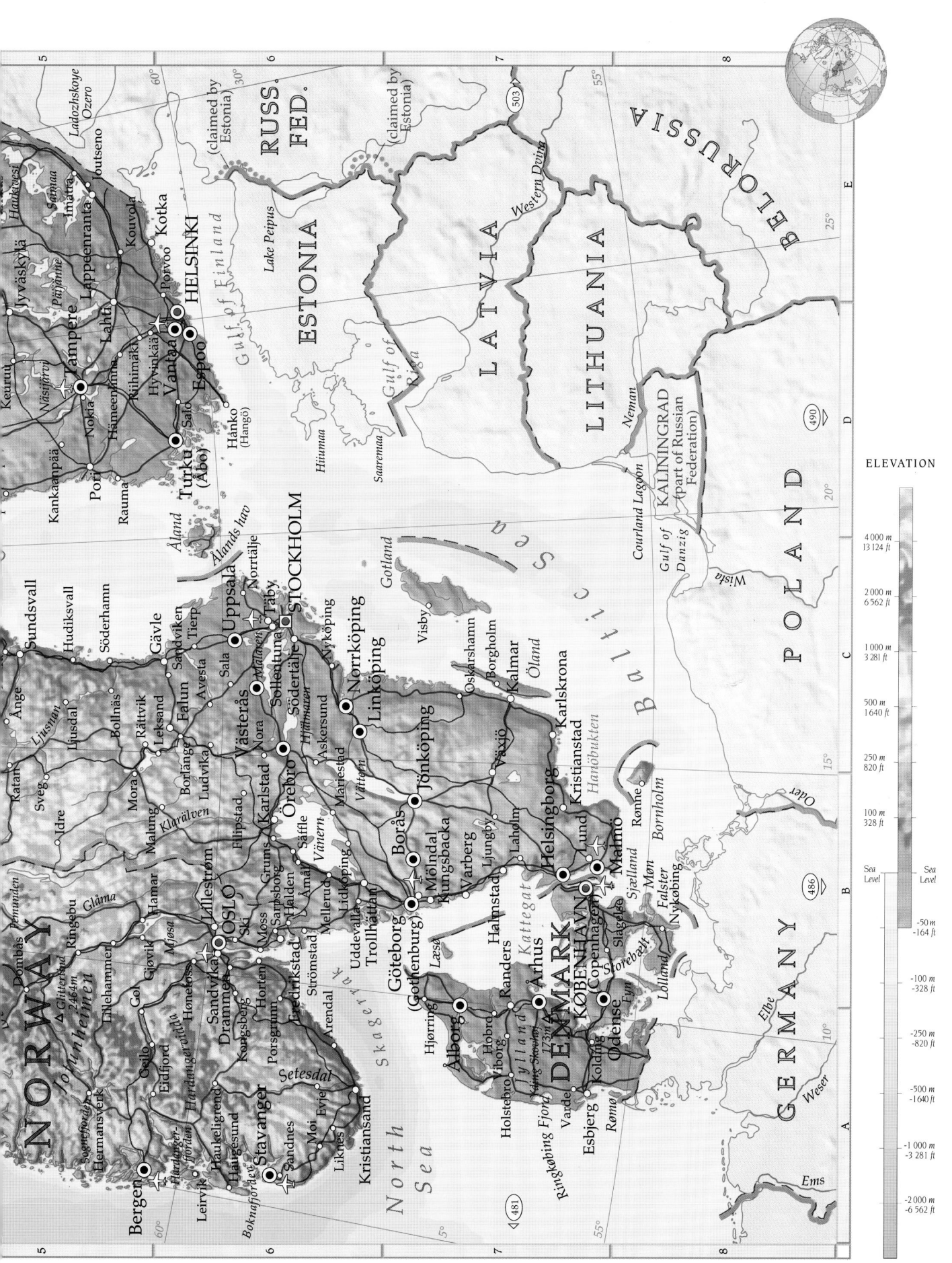

THE LOW COUNTRIES

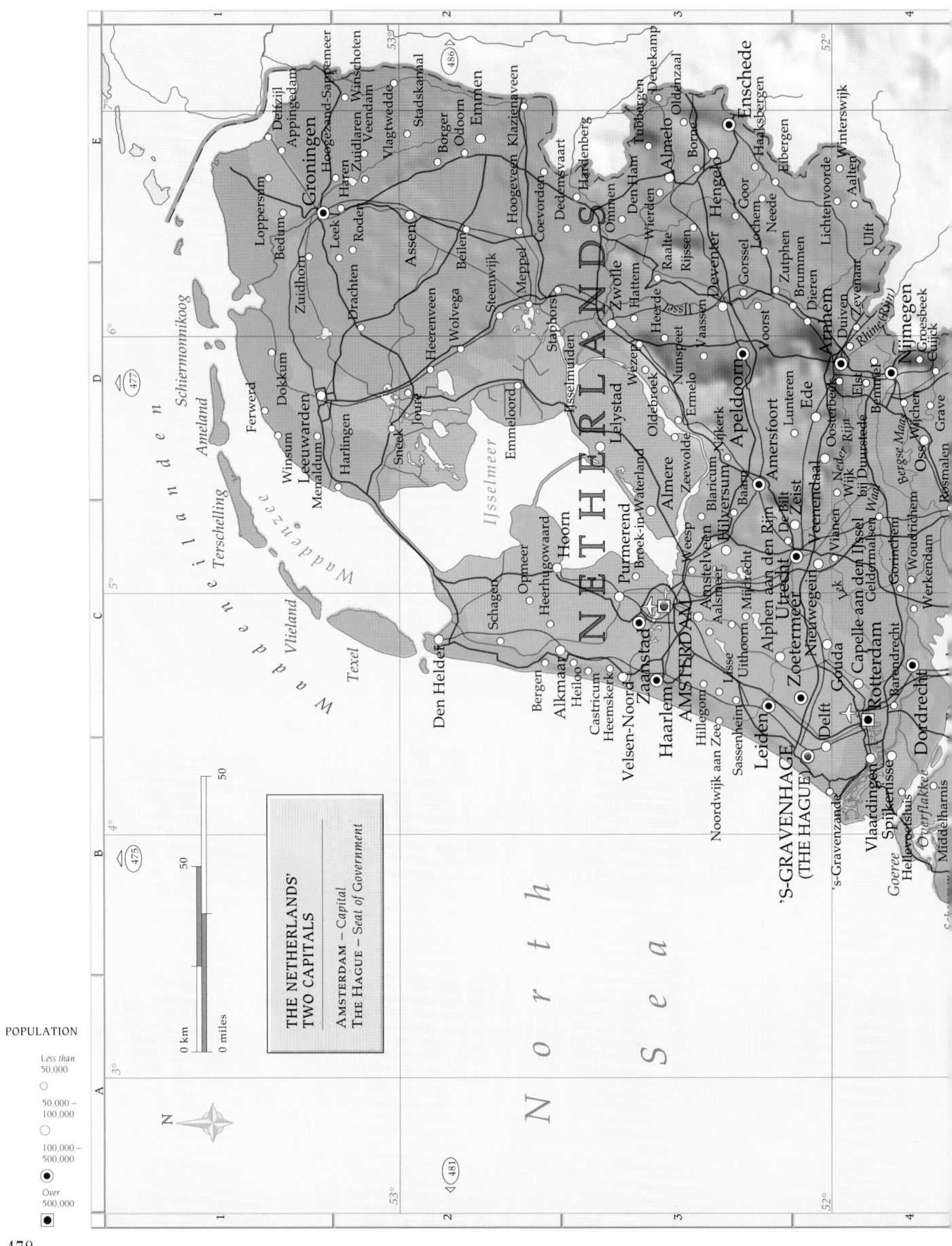

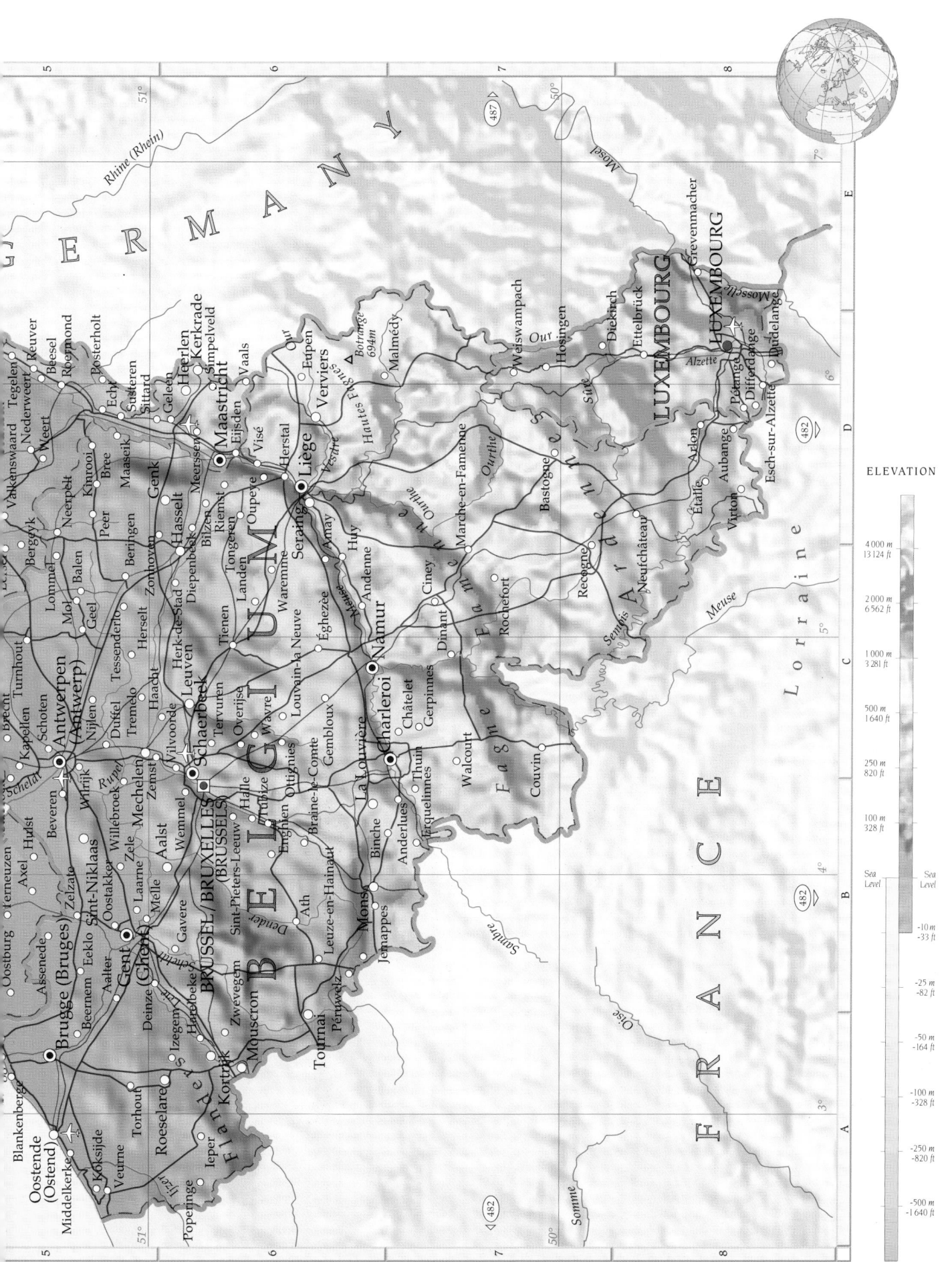

THE BRITISH ISLES

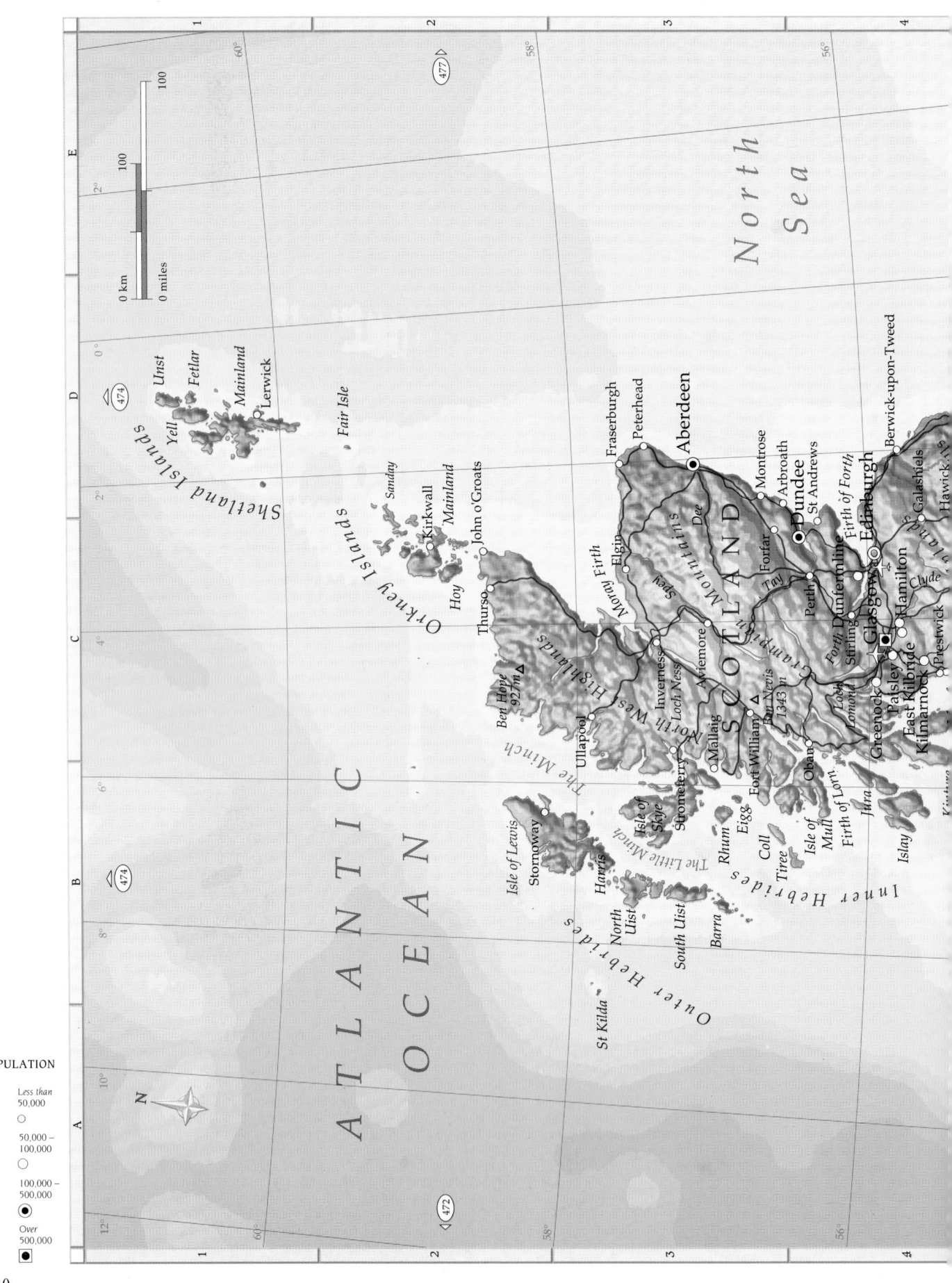

North Sea

Atlantic Ocean

SCOTLAND

Shetland Islands
Unst
Yell
Fetlar
Mainland
Lerwick
Fair Isle

Orkney Islands
Sanday
Kirkwall
Mainland
Hoy
John o'Groats

Thurso
B017

Ben Hope
922m △
North West Highlands
Ullapool
The Minch
Isle of Lewis
Stornoway
Harris
The Little Minch
Isle of Skye
Stromeferry
Mallaig
Rhum
Eigg
Coll
Tiree
Isle of Mull
Firth of Lorn
Jura
Islay

Outer Hebrides
North Uist
South Uist
Barra
St Kilda

Inner Hebrides

Fraserburgh
Peterhead
Aberdeen
Elgin
Moray Firth
Dee
Grampian Mountains
Spey
Inverness
Loch Ness
Aviemore
Ben Nevis
1343 m △
Fort William
Oban
Loch Lomond

Montrose
Arbroath
Dundee
St Andrews
Firth of Forth
Forfar
Tay
Perth
Dunfermline
Forth
Stirling
Glasgow
Paisley
Greenock
East Kilbride
Hamilton
Clyde
Kilmarnock
Prestwick
Kintyre

Edinburgh
Berwick-upon-Tweed
Galashiels
Hawick
Uplands
Southern

477
474
474
472

100
100
0 km
0 miles

N

POPULATION

Less than
50,000
○

50,000 –
100,000
○

100,000 –
500,000
◉

Over
500,000
◼

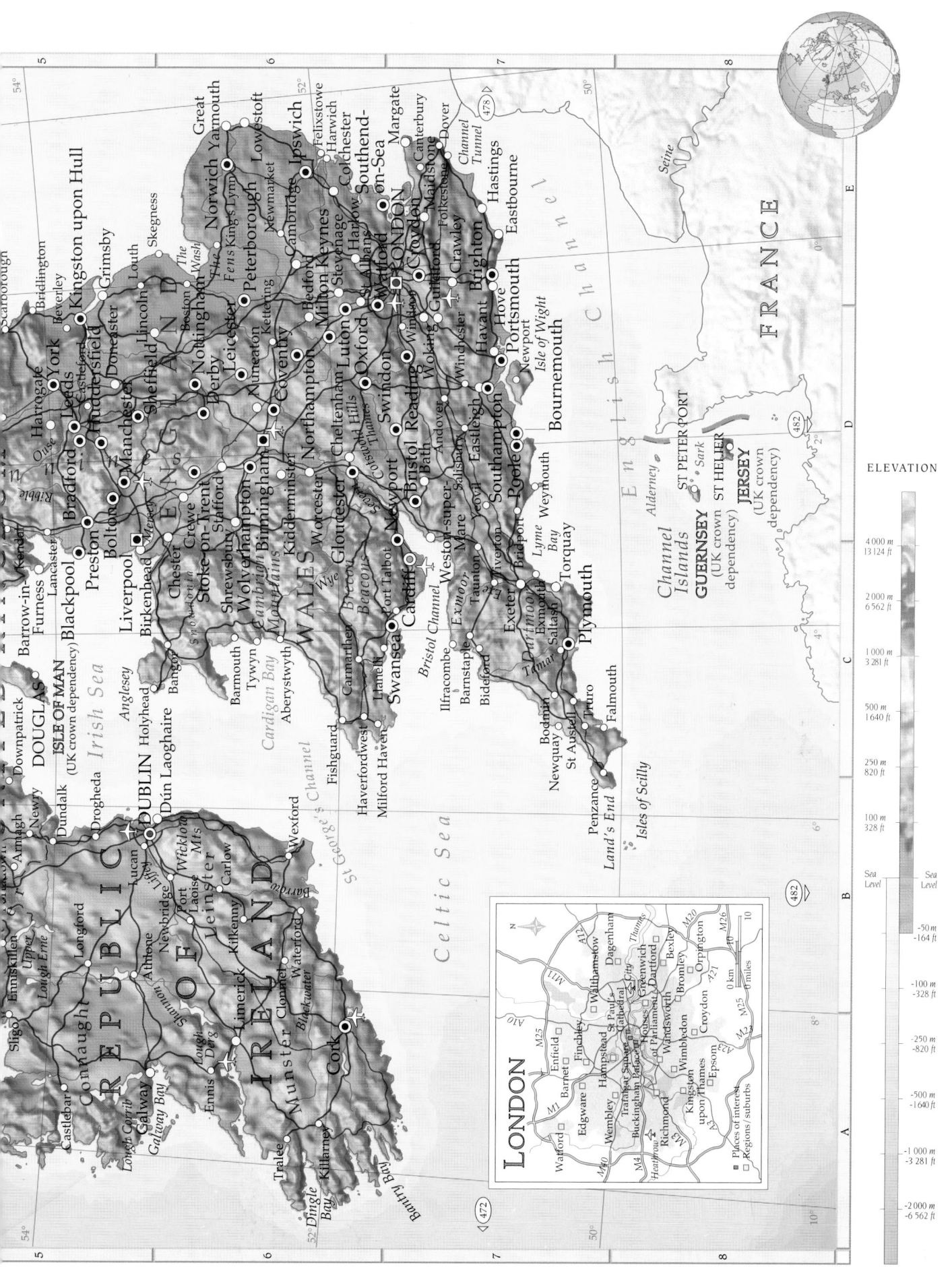

FRANCE, ANDORRA AND MONACO

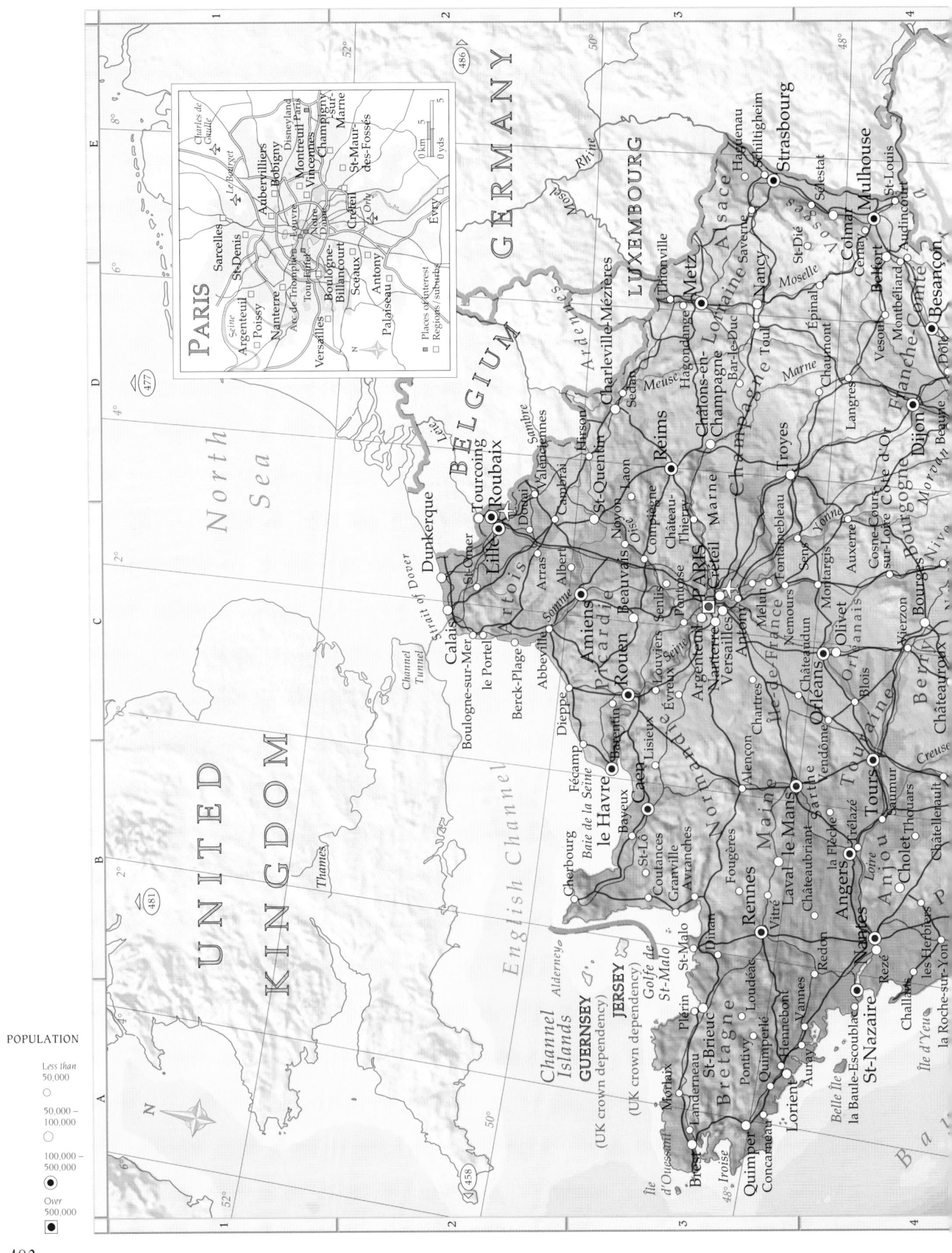

GERMANY

LUXEMBOURG

BELGIUM

UNITED KINGDOM

North Sea

Strait of Dover

Channel Tunnel

English Channel

Channel Islands
GUERNSEY
(UK crown dependency)

JERSEY
(UK crown dependency)

Dunkerque
Calais
Boulogne-sur-Mer
le Portel
Berck-Plage
Abbeville
Dieppe
Fécamp
le Havre
Cherbourg
Baie de la Seine
Bayeux
St-Lô
Coutances
Granville
Avranches
St-Malo
Dinan
St-Brieuc
Morlaix
Landerneau
Brest
Quimper
Concarneau
Lorient
Quimperlé
Hennebont
Auray
Vannes
Redon
Nantes
Rezé
Challans
Île d'Yeu
la Roche-sur-Yon
la Baule-Escoublac
St-Nazaire

St-Omer
Lille
Roubaix
Tourcoing
Douai
Arras
Amiens
Rouen
Beauvais
Louviers
Évreux
Barentin
Lisieux
Caen
Alençon
Fougères
Rennes
Vitré
Laval
Châteaubriant
Angers
Cholet
les Herbiers
Thouars
Saumur
la Flèche
le Mans

Valenciennes
Cambrai
St-Quentin
Noyon
Laon
Oise
Compiègne
Château-Thierry
Senlis
Pontoise
PARIS
Argenteuil
Nanterre
Créteil
Versailles
Antony
Melun
Nemours
Montargis
Chartres
Châteaudun
Vendôme
Orléans
Blois
Tours
Châtellerault
Châteauroux

Hirson
Charleville-Mézières
Sedan
Reims
Châlons-en-Champagne
Troyes
Sens
Auxerre
Cosne-Cours-sur-Loire
Bourges
Vierzon

Thionville
Metz
Hagondange
Toul
Bar-le-Duc
Chaumont
Langres
Dijon
Beaune
Morvan

Hagenau
Schiltigheim
Strasbourg
Sélestat
Colmar
Cernay
Mulhouse
St-Louis
Audincourt
Belfort
Montbéliard
Vesoul
Dôle
Besançon
Saverne
Nancy
St-Dié
Épinal

Seine
Marne
Meuse
Meuse
Moselle
Rhine
Lys
Escaut
Sambre
Somme
Yonne
Loire
Loire
Creuse
Sarthe
Marne
Moselle

Picardie
Artois
Normandie
Bretagne
Maine
Anjou
Île-de-France
Touraine
Berry
Champagne
Lorraine
Alsace
Vosges
Bourgogne
Côte d'Or
Franche-Comté
Ardennes

Île d'Ouessant
Île de Groix
Belle Île
Golfe de St-Malo
Alderney
Plérin
Pontivy
Loudéac

48°
50°
52°
8°
6°
4°
2°
2°

PARIS

Sarcelles
St-Denis
Aubervilliers
Bobigny
Montreuil
Paris
Vincennes
Champigny-sur-Marne
St-Maur-des-Fossés
Argenteuil
Poissy
Nanterre
Arc de Triomphe
Tour Eiffel
Louvre
Notre-Dame
Boulogne-Billancourt
Sceaux
Antony
Versailles
Palaiseau
Évry
Créteil
Orly
Disneyland
Le Bourget
Charles de Gaulle
Seine

N

■ Places of interest
▨ Regions/suburbs

0 km   5
0 yds   5

POPULATION

○   Less than 50,000

○   50,000 – 100,000

◉   100,000 – 500,000

◼   Over 500,000

N

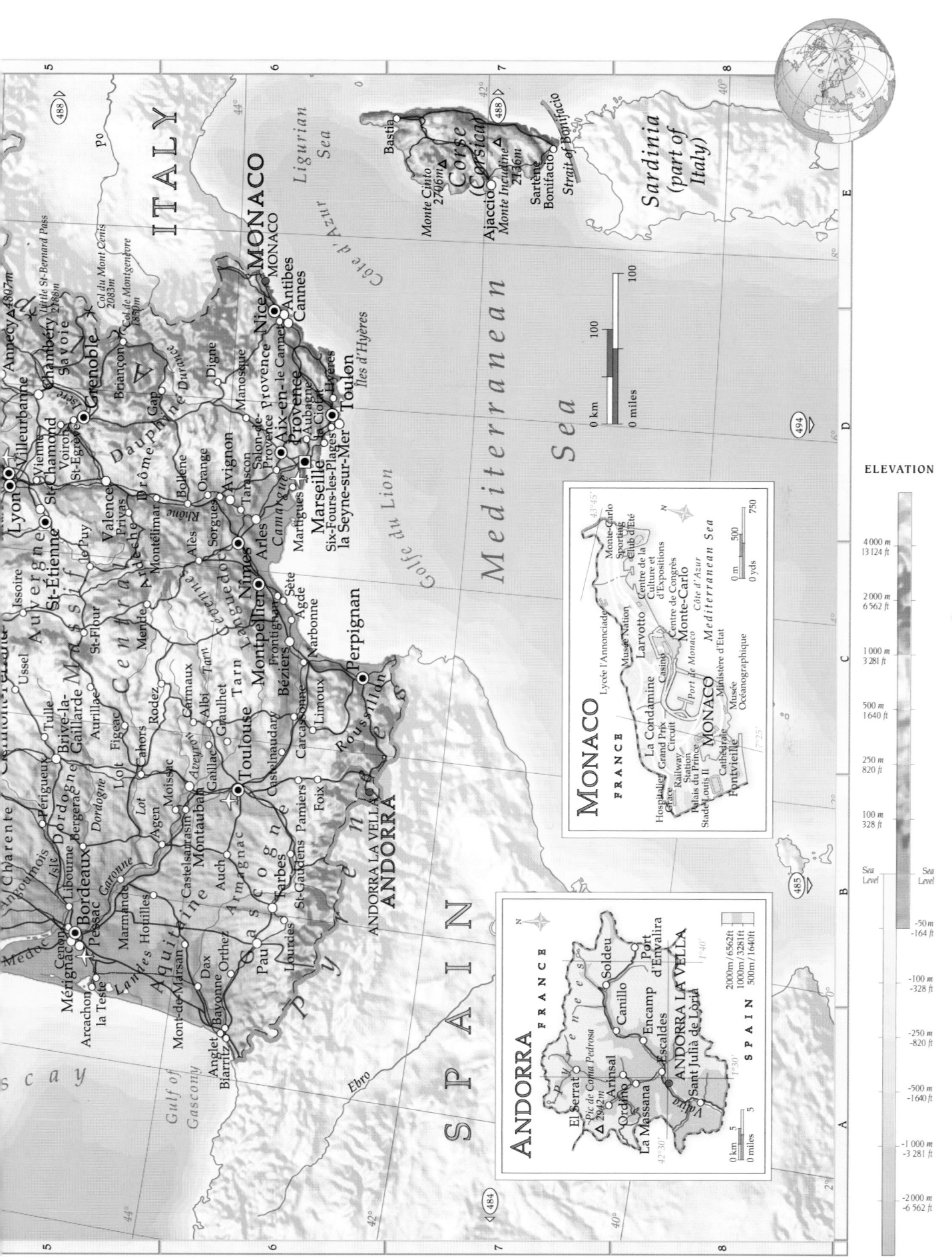

ITALY

Po

MONACO
MONACO

Ligurian
Sea

Côte d'Azur

Bastia

*Corse
(Corsica)*
(to France)

Monte Cinto
2706m △
Ajaccio
△ Monte Incudine
2136m
Sartène
Bonifacio
Strait of Bonifacio

*Sardinia
(part of
Italy)*

Little St-Bernard Pass
2188m
Col du Mont Cenis
Col de Montgenèvre
1850m
Annecy △ 4807m
Chambéry
Savoie
Grenoble
Briançon
Villeurbanne
Vienne
Lyon
Voiron
St-Egrève
St-Chamond
St-Étienne
Le Puy

Dauphiné

Digne

Valence
Privas
Montélimar
Gap

Manosque

Provence
Aix-en-le-Cannet
Nice
Antibes
Cannes

MONACO

Aubagne
la Ciotat
Toulon
Hyères
Îles d'Hyères

*Mediterranean

Sea*

Orange
Bollène
Avignon
Tarascon
Sorgues
Salon-de-Provence
Arles
Martigues
Marseille
Six-Fours-les-Plages
la Seyne-sur-Mer

Golfe du Lion

0 km   100

0 miles   100

Auvergne
Issoire

Central Massif

Ussel
Tulle
Brive-la-Gaillarde
Périgueux

St-Flour
Aurillac

Rodez

Mende

Alès
Nîmes
Sète
Agde

Montpellier
Béziers
Narbonne

Languedoc

Perpignan

Roussillon

Bordeaux
Pessac
Cenon
Mérignac
Médoc
Arcachon
la Teste

Libourne
Bergerac

Agen
Moissac

Montauban
Toulouse
Castelsarrasin
Gaillac
Albi
Figeac
Cahors

Castelnaudary
Carcassonne
Limoux

Pamiers
Foix

ANDORRA LA VELLA
ANDORRA

Gascogne

Marmande
Landes
Hostilles
Dax
Mont-de-Marsan
Orthez
Pau
Lourdes
Tarbes
St-Gaudens

Bayonne
Anglet
Biarritz

Aquitaine

Gulf of
Gascony

Pyrenees

SPAIN

Ebro

Bay of *Biscay*

MONACO

FRANCE

Monte-Carlo
Sporting
Club d'Été
Larvotto
Musée National
Centre de la
Culture et
d'Expositions
Casino
Centre de Congrès
Monte-Carlo
La Condamine
Port de Monaco
Côte d'Azur

Mediterranean Sea

Hospital
Grand Prix
Circuit
Railway
Station
Palais du Prince
Stade Louis II
Cathédrale
Fontvieille
Ministère d'Etat
Musée
Océanographique

MONACO

0 m   500
0 yds   750

ANDORRA

FRANCE

El Serrat
Pic de Coma Pedrosa
△ 2942m
Arinsal
Ordino
La Massana

Soldeu
Canillo
Port
d'Envalira
Encamp
Escaldes
ANDORRA LA VELLA
Sant Julià de Lòria

SPAIN

Valira

2000m/6562ft
1000m/3281ft
500m/1640ft

0 km   5
0 miles 5

ELEVATION

4 000 m	13 124 ft
2 000 m	6 562 ft
1 000 m	3 281 ft
500 m	1 640 ft
250 m	820 ft
100 m	328 ft
Sea Level	Sea Level
-50 m	-164 ft
-100 m	-328 ft
-250 m	-820 ft
-500 m	-1 640 ft
-1 000 m	-3 281 ft
-2 000 m	-6 562 ft

SPAIN AND PORTUGAL

458

ATLANTIC OCEAN

PORTUGAL

A Coruña · Ferrol · Betanzos · Laracha · Vilalba · Vilaboa · Luarca · Avilés · Gijón · Santa · Costa Ve

Santa Comba · Outes · Muros · Santiago · Lalín · Chantada · Monforte · Ponferrada · León · Reinosa · Cant

Ribeira · Pontevedra · Carballiño · Ourense · Astorga · Benavente · Palencia

Vigo · Ponteareas · Xinzo de Limia · Castilla-León

Viana do Castelo · Ponte da Barca · Bragança · Embalse de Ricobayo · Valladolid

Póvoa de Varzim · Vila do Conde · Braga · Guimarães · Chaves · Zamora · Toro · Duero

Matosinhos · Porto (Oporto) · Vila Nova de Gaia · Vila Real · Medina del Campo · Salamanca

Ovar · Douro · Lamego · São João da Madeira · Embalse de Almendra

Albergaria-a-Velha · Aveiro · Viseu · Ciudad-Rodrigo · Ávila · Seg

Ílhavo · Alto da Torre 1993m · Guarda · Béjar · Sistema Cent · MAD

Coimbra · Serra da Estrela · Covilhã · Plasencia · Sierra de Gredos · Ge

Figueira da Foz · Coria · Talavera de la Reina · Toled

Leiria · Castelo Branco · Tagus · Embalse de Alcántara · Cáceres · Embalse de Valdecañas

Caldas da Rainha · Tomar · Entroncamento · Trujillo · Herrera del Duque

Peniche · Abrantes · Portalegre · Extremadura · Mérida · Villanueva de la Serena

Torres Vedras · Santarém · Coruche · Estremoz · Elvas · Don Benito · Ciudad R

Sintra · Cascais · LISBOA (LISBON) · Badajoz · Castuera · Puertollan

Almada · Barreiro · Évora · Serra d'Ossa · Almendralejo · Villafranca de los Barros

Setúbal · Alcácer do Sal · Guadiana · Zafra · Pozoblanco · La

Baía de Setúbal · Jerez de los Caballeros · Azuaga · Sierra Morena

Sines · Beja · Córdoba · Bujalance · Montoro

Ourique · Cortegana · Nerva · Guadalquivir · Palma del Río · Marto · Andalu

Valverde del Camino · La Algaba · Carmona · Ecija · Lucena · Osuna

Algarve · Ayamonte · Lepe · Sevilla (Seville) · Dos Hermanas · Gr · Arch

Portimão · Faro · Isla Cristina · Huelva · Las Cabezas de San Juan · Antequera

Lagos · Tavira · Olhão · Golfo de Cádiz · Lebrija · Olvera · Ronda · Alora · Mā · Co

Cabo de São Vicente · Sanlúcar de Barrameda · Ubrique · Costa

El Puerto de Santa María · Jerez de la Frontera · Fuengir · Marbella · Estepona

Cádiz · San Fernando · Vejer de la Frontera

Barbate de Franco · GIBRALTAR (UK dependent territ)

Algeciras · Ceuta (part of Spain)

Costa de la Luz · Strait of Gibraltar

MOROCCO

462

AZORES (part of Portugal)

Corvo
Flores · São Jorge · Graciosa · Terceira
Faial · Pico · São Miguel
Ponta Delgada
Santa Maria

0 km 100
0 miles 100

200m/656ft
Sea level

POPULATION

○ Less than 50,000

○ 50,000 – 100,000

◉ 100,000 – 500,000

● Over 500,000

FRANCE

Bermeo
Zarautz
Eibar
Bergara
Vasco
-Gasteiz
iranda
Ebro
ño
Arnedo
a Rioja
Tudela
Tarazona
Soria
Medinaceli
alajara
Henares
de Ardoz
ma
I N
Daroca
Alcañiz
ncón
Cuenca
lla-La Mancha
Mota del Cuervo
o de Criptana
Socuéllamos
elloso
La Roda
es
a
Albacete
Almansa
anueva de los Infantes
Hellín
as de Segura
Moratalla
carrillo
orla
Huéscar
os
Baza
ix
rja
Almería

Donostia-San Sebastián
Irún
Tolosa
Pamplona
Estella
Jaca
Monte Perdido 3348m
La Seo d'Urgel
Calahorra
Ejea de los Caballeros
Huesca
Barbastro
Monzón
Balaguer
Zaragoza
Lleida (Lérida)
Cervera
Fraga
Tàrrega
Vilafranca del Penedès
Valls
Reus
Sitges
El Vendrell
Tarragona
Tortosa
Amposta
Sant Carles de la Ràpita
Vinaròs
Calatayud
Aragón
Teruel
Javalambre 2020m
Onda
Castelló de la Plana
Burriana
Vall d' Uxó
Burjassot
Sagunto
Torrente
Valencia
Catarroja
Sueca
Algemesí
Cullera
Xàtiva
Gandía
Oliva
Denia
Alcoy
Ontinyent
Villena
Benidorm
Jumilla
Elda
Villajoyosa
Monóvar
San Juan de Alicante
Elche
Alicante
Cieza
Callosa de Segura
Mula
Orihuela
Murcia
Totana
La Unión
Lorca
Cartagena
Aguilas
Mojácar
Segura
Júcar

ANDORRA
Figueres
Ripoll
Banyoles
Berga
Girona
Manlleu
Cataluña
Vic
Palafrugell
Palamós
Sabadell
Blanes
Terrassa
Arenys de Mar
Mataró
Barcelona
L'Hospitalet de Llobregat
Costa Brava

Golfe du Lion

Pyrenees

Navarra

Ebro

País Valenciano

Costa del Azahar

Golfo de Valencia

Costa Blanca

Mediterranean Sea

ALGERIA

Ciutadella de Menorca
Menorca (Minorca)
Mahón
Pollença
Sa Pobla
Palma
Manacor
Llucmajor
Felanitx
Mallorca (Majorca)
Cabrera

Eivissa (Ibiza)
Eivissa
Formentera

Islas Baleares
(Balearic Islands)

482

488

489

463

GIBRALTAR (to UK)

N
5° 21'
SPAIN
Gibraltar Airport
North Mole
Gibraltar Harbour
Bay of Gibraltar
Catalan Bay
The Rock
Catalan Bay
36° 8'
Rosia
Summit 426m
Sandy Bay
Rosia Bay
Buena Vista
Little Bay
Europa Point
Strait of Gibraltar

200m / 656ft
Sea level
0 km   1
0 mile   1

ELEVATION

4 000 m 13 124 ft	
2 000 m 6 562 ft	
1 000 m 3 281 ft	
500 m 1 640 ft	
250 m 820 ft	
100 m 328 ft	
Sea Level	Sea Level
-250 m -820 ft	
-500 m -1 640 ft	
-1 000 m -3 281 ft	
-2 000 m -6 562 ft	
-3 000 m -9 843 ft	
-4 000 m -13 124 ft	

100

100

GERMANY AND THE ALPINE STATES

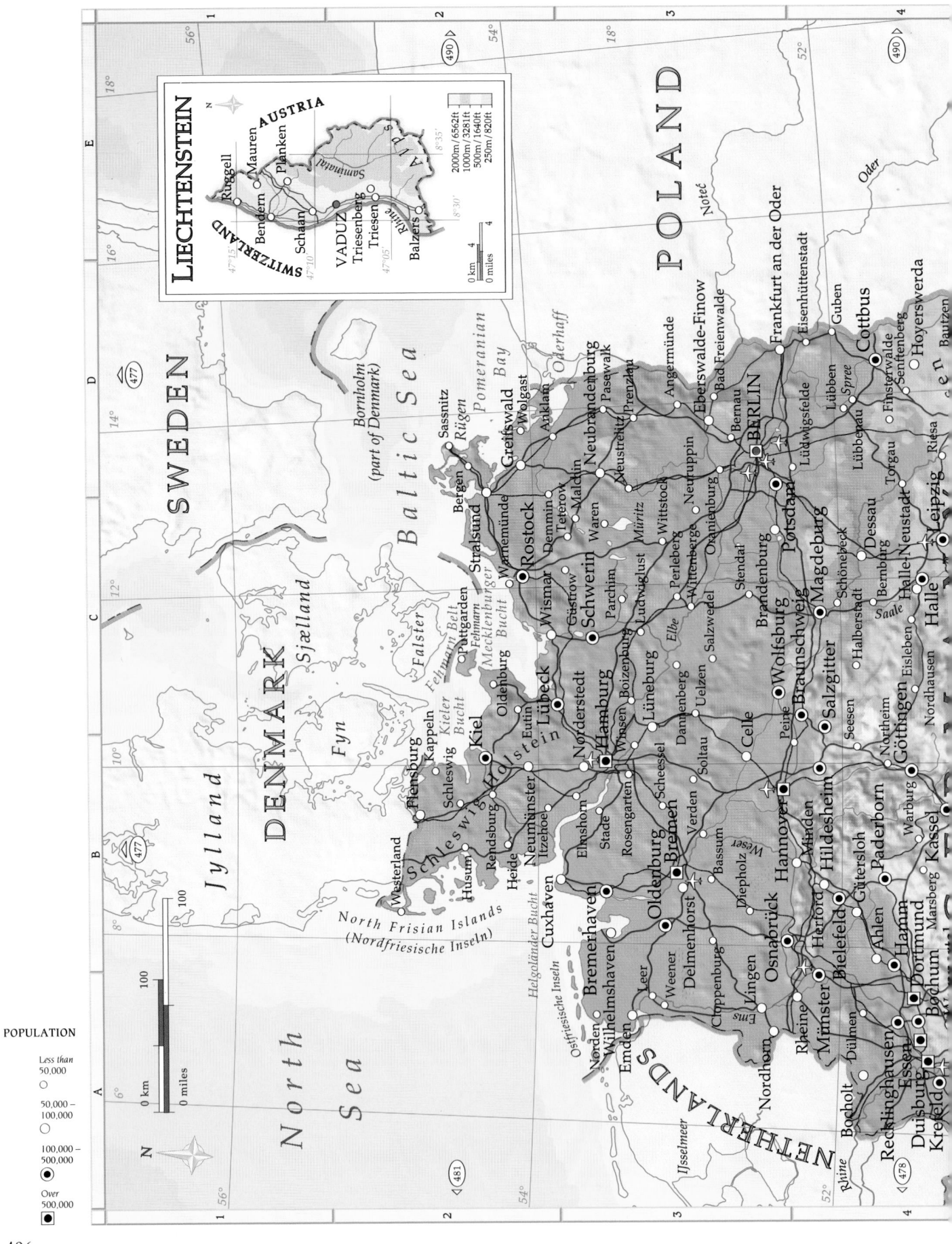

POPULATION

Less than
50,000
○

50,000 –
100,000
○

100,000 –
500,000
◉

Over
500,000
◼

LIECHTENSTEIN

SWITZERLAND

AUSTRIA

Ruggell
Mauren
Planken
Bendern
Schaan
VADUZ
Triesenberg
Triesen
Balzers

Saminatal

Rhine

Alps

2000m/6562ft
1000m/3281ft
500m/1640ft
250m/820ft

0 km   4
0 miles   4

POLAND

Oder

Noteć

Frankfurt an der Oder
Eisenhüttenstadt
Guben
Cottbus
Hoyerswerda
Senftenberg
Bautzen
Riesa

BERLIN
Eberswalde-Finow
Bad Freienwalde
Angermünde
Bernau
Ludwigsfelde
Lübben
Lübbenau
Finsterwalde
Torgau

Spree

Leipzig

SWEDEN

DENMARK

Bornholm
(part of Denmark)

Baltic Sea

Pomeranian Bay

Oderhaff

Sassnitz
Rügen
Bergen
Stralsund
Greifswald
Wolgast
Anklam
Pasewalk
Prenzlau
Neubrandenburg
Neustrelitz

Warnemünde
Rostock
Demmin
Teterow
Waren
Müritz
Neuruppin
Oranienburg
Wittstock

Wismar
Güstrow
Schwerin
Parchim
Perleberg
Wittenberge
Potsdam
Magdeburg
Brandenburg
Stendal
Schönebeck
Dessau
Bernburg
Halle-Neustadt
Halle
Eisleben
Nordhausen

Ludwigslust
Salzwedel
Elbe
Saale

Jylland

Sjælland

Fyn

Falster

Fehmarn Belt
Puttgarden
Fehmarn
Mecklenburger Bucht
Oldenburg Bucht

Flensburg
Kappeln
Kieler Bucht
Schleswig
Kiel
Eutin
Lübeck
Norderstedt
Hamburg
Wolfsburg
Braunschweig
Salzgitter
Seesen
Göttingen
Northeim
Warburg
Kassel
Marsberg

Schleswig-Holstein

Boizenburg
Lüneburg
Lüchow
Dannenberg
Uelzen
Celle
Peine
Hannover
Hildesheim
Minden
Halberstadt

Neumünster
Rendsburg
Itzehoe
Wilster
Scheessel
Soltau
Verden

Husum
Heide
Westerland

North Frisian Islands
(Nordfriesische Inseln)

Helgoländer Bucht

North Sea

Ostfriesische Inseln

Helgoländer Bucht

Cuxhaven
Bremerhaven
Wilhelmshaven
Norden
Emden
Leer
Weener
Cloppenburg
Vechta
Delmenhorst
Oldenburg
Bremen
Bassum
Diepholz
Osnabrück
Herford
Bielefeld
Gütersloh
Paderborn
Ahlen
Hamm

Ems

Weser

Stade
Elmshorn
Rosengarten

Nordhorn
Rheine
Münster
Dülmen
Bocholt
Recklinghausen
Duisburg
Essen
Krefeld
Bochum
Dortmund

Lingen
Ijsselmeer
Rhine

NETHERLANDS

N

0 km
0 miles

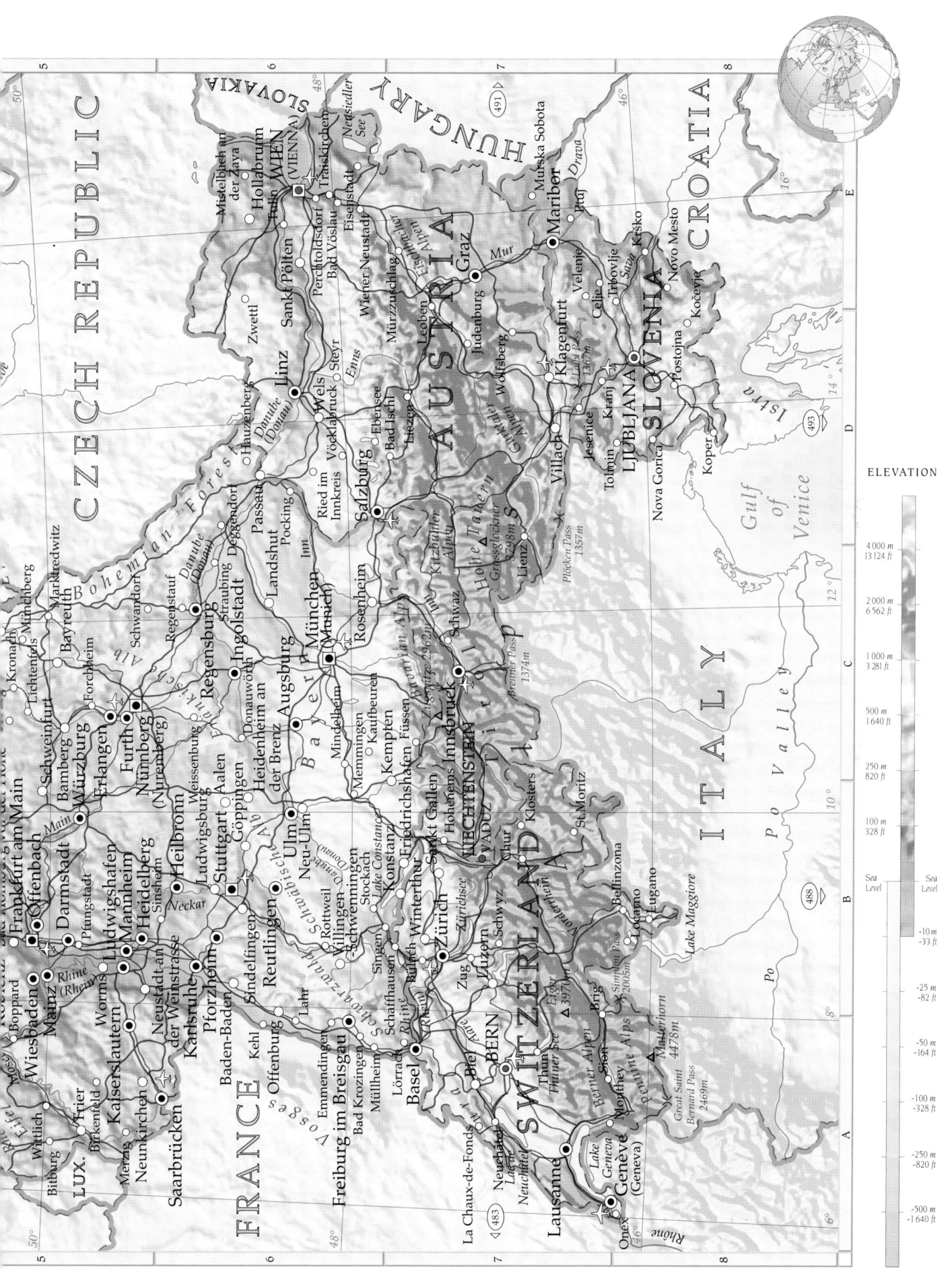

SLOVAKIA

HUNGARY

CROATIA

CZECH REPUBLIC

Mistelbach an
der Zaya
Hollabrunn
Traiskirchen
WIEN
(VIENNA)
Neusiedler
See
Murska Sobota
Krško
Maribor
Ptuj
Drava
Stockerau
Korneuburg
Eisenstadt
Wiener Neustadt
Novo Mesto
Kočevje
Postojna
Sankt Pölten
Perchtoldsdorf
Bad Vöslau
Mürzzuschlag
Velenje
Celje
Trbovlje
Krško
Graz
Leoben
Judenburg
Klagenfurt
Kranj
LJUBLJANA
SLOVENIA
Nova Gorica
Koper

Zwettl

Linz
Danube
(Donau)
Wels
Vöcklabruck
Steyr
Enns
Bad Ischl
Ebensee
Liezen
Niedere Tauern
Wolfsberg
Villach
Jesenice
Tolmin
Loibl Pass
1367m

Gulf of
Venice

Istra

Hauzenberg

AUSTRIA

Salzburg
Ried im
Innkreis
Pocking
Passau
Deggendorf

Danube
(Donau)

Bohemian Forest

Marktredwitz
Münchberg
Bayreuth
Kronach
Lichtenfels
Bamberg
Schwandorf
Regenstauf
Regensburg
Straubing
Landshut
Inn
Rosenheim
Bayerischer Alpen
Hohe Tauern
Grossglockner
3798m
Kitzbühler
Alpen
Lienz
Plöcken Pass
1357m

ITALY

Po Valley

Schweinfurt
Würzburg
Erlangen
Fürth
Nürnberg
(Nuremberg)
Forchheim
Ingolstadt
Donauwörth
Augsburg
Heidenheim an
der Brenz
München
(Munich)
Mindelheim
Kaufbeuren
Kempten
Füssen
Garmisch
Zugspitze 2962m
Innsbruck
Schwaz
Brenner Pass
1374m
Tirol

Weissenburg
Aalen
Göppingen
Stuttgart
Ludwigsburg
Heilbronn
Sinsheim
Neckar
Ludwigshafen
Mannheim
Heidelberg
Darmstadt
Offenbach
Frankfurt am Main
Main
Wiesbaden
Mainz
Rhine
(Rhein)
Worms

Schwäbisch Alb
Ulm
Neu-Ulm
Memmingen
Schwäbische Alb
Donau
(Danube)
Rottweil
Villingen-
Schwenningen
Singen
Konstanz
Lake Constance
Friedrichshafen
Sankt Gallen
Hohenems
LIECHTENSTEIN
VADUZ
Chur
Klosters
St Moritz

Reutlingen
Sindelfingen
Pforzheim
Karlsruhe
Baden-Baden
Kehl
Offenburg
Lahr
Emmendingen
Bad Krozingen
Freiburg im Breisgau
Müllheim
Lörrach
Basel
Schaffhausen
Bülach
Winterthur
Zürich
Zürichsee
Schwyz
Luzern
Zug
Belfinzona
Lugano
Lake Maggiore
Lago
Locarno

Schwarzwald
Neustadt an
der Weinstrasse
Kaiserslautern
Neunkirchen
Saarbrücken
FRANCE
Vosges
Trier
Birkenfeld
Merzag
Bitburg
Wittlich
Boppard
LUX.
Eifel
Mosel
Rhine
(Rhein)

SWITZERLAND
BERN
Biel
Aare
Thun
Thuner See
Eiger
3970m
Brig
Simplon Pass
2005m
Matterhorn
4478m
Berner Alpen
Sion
Morthey
Pennine Alps
Great Saint
Bernard Pass
2469m
Säntis
2469m

La Chaux-de-Fonds
Neuchâtel
Lac de
Neuchâtel
Lausanne
Lake
Geneva
Genève
(Geneva)
Onex
Rhône

487

ITALY

SAN MARINO

500m / 1640ft
200m / 656ft
100m / 328ft

Gualdicciolo
Borgo Maggiore
SAN MARINO
ITALY
Chiesanuova

Dogana
Serravalle
Fiorina
Falungo
Monte Titano
739m
Murata
Faetano
Montegiardino
ITALY

0 km 2
0 miles 2

POPULATION

Less than
50,000
○

50,000 –
100,000
○

100,000 –
500,000
◉

Over
500,000
■

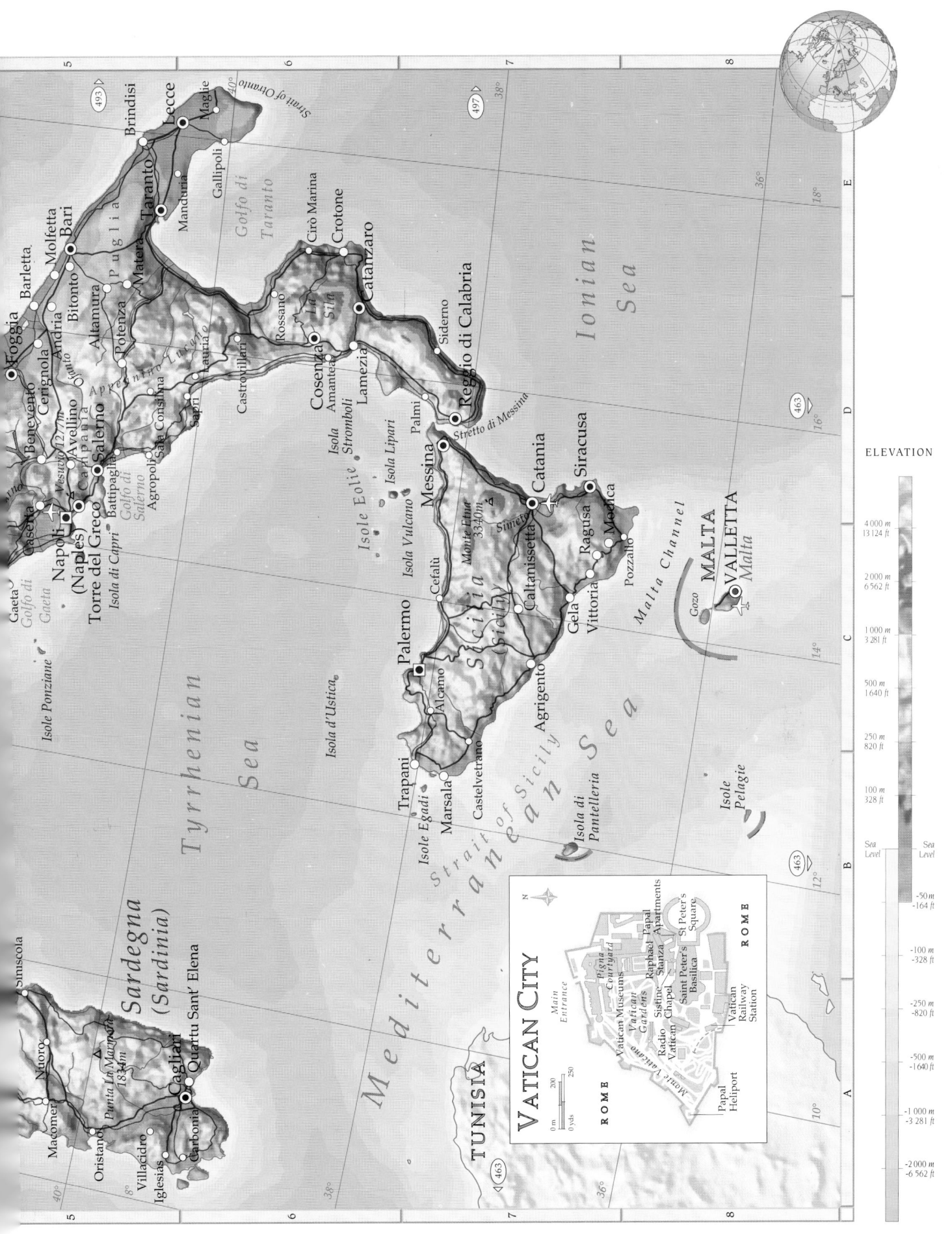

ELEVATION

4 000 m	13 124 ft
2 000 m	6 562 ft
1 000 m	3 281 ft
500 m	1 640 ft
250 m	820 ft
100 m	328 ft
Sea Level	Sea Level
-50 m	-164 ft
-100 m	-328 ft
-250 m	-820 ft
-500 m	-1 640 ft
-1 000 m	-3 281 ft
-2 000 m	-6 562 ft

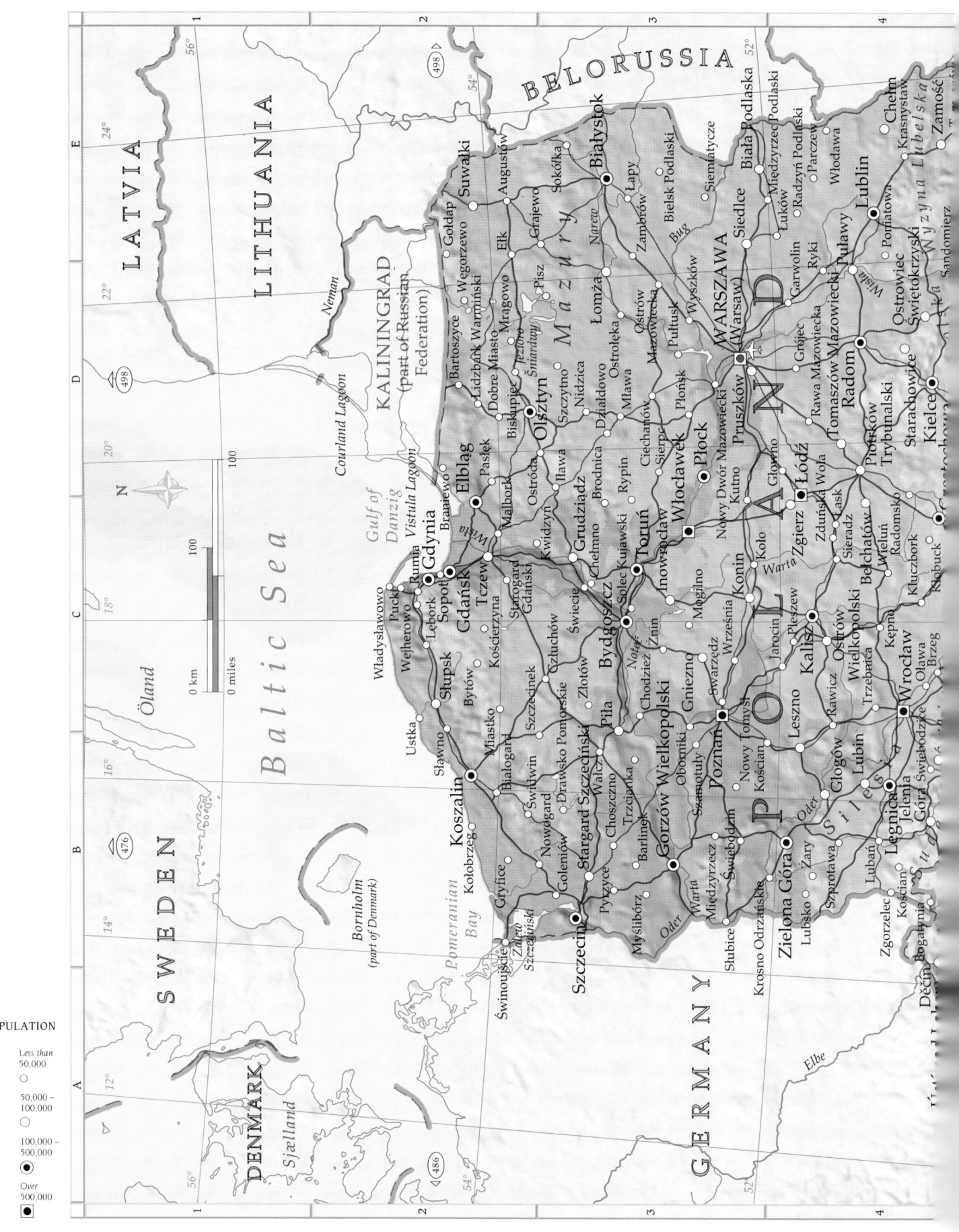

POPULATION

Less than
50,000
○

50,000 –
100,000
○

100,000 –
500,000
◉

Over
500,000
◉

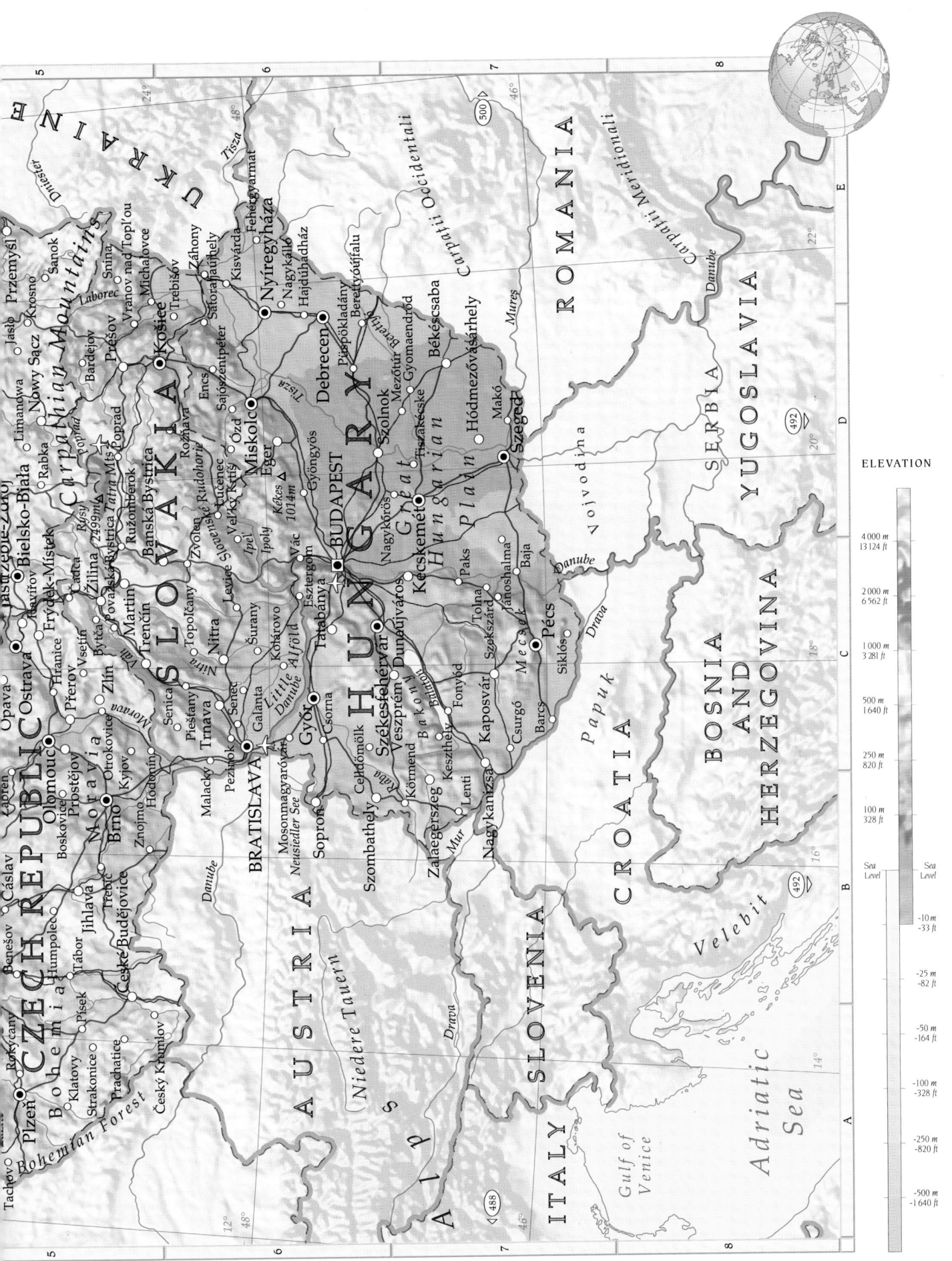

ELEVATION

4 000 m
13 124 ft

2 000 m
6 562 ft

1 000 m
3 281 ft

500 m
1 640 ft

250 m
820 ft

100 m
328 ft

Sea
Level

Sea
Level

-10 m
-33 ft

-25 m
-82 ft

-50 m
-164 ft

-100 m
-328 ft

-250 m
-820 ft

-500 m
-1 640 ft

WESTERN BALKANS

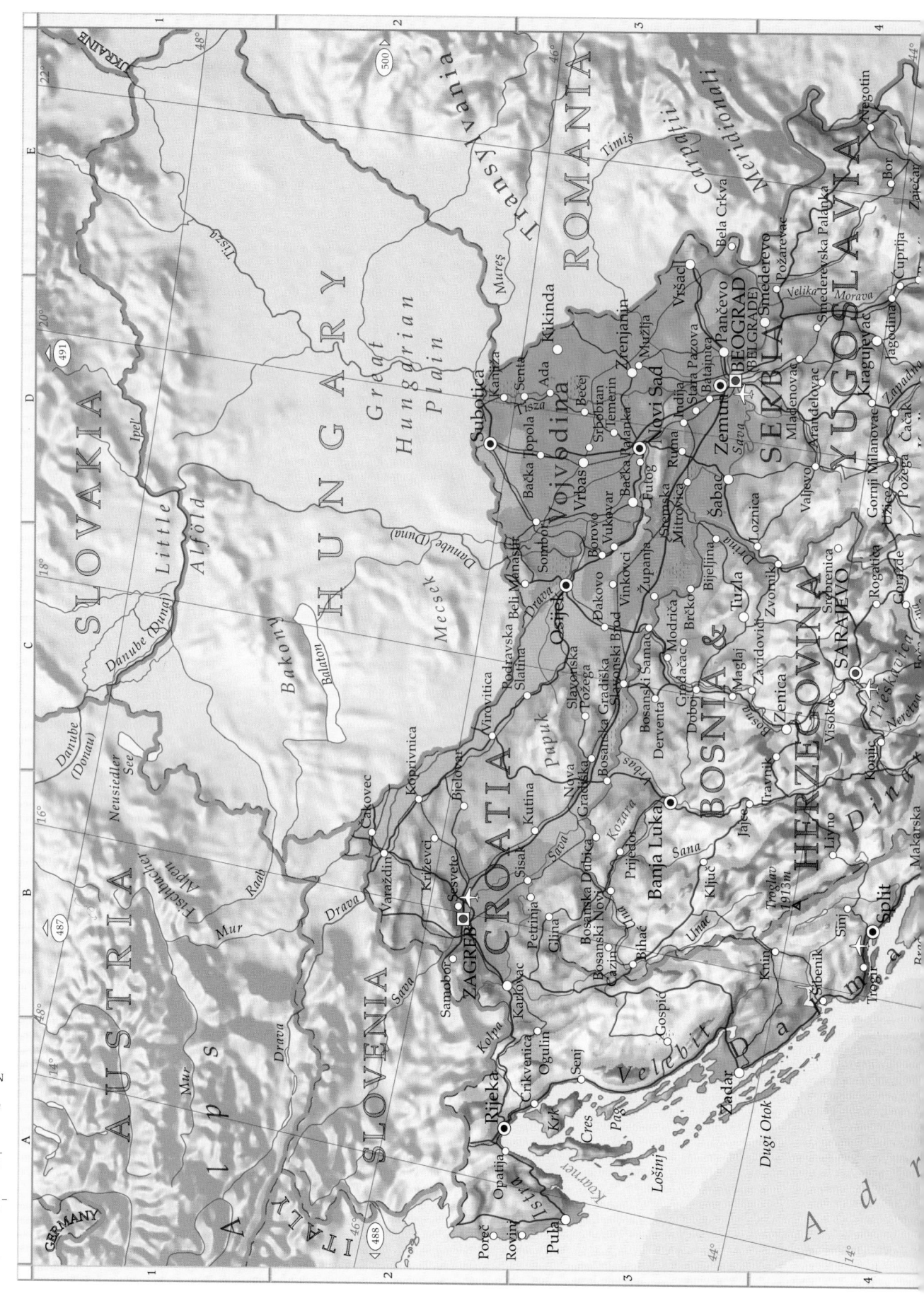

1   2   3   4

48°

22°

500

46°

Timiş

ROMANIA

Carpaţii Meridionali

20°

E

18°

D

SLOVAKIA

HUNGARY

Tisza

Great
Hungarian
Plain

Mureş

Transylvania

Negotin

Bor

Zaječar

SERBIA

YUGOSLAVIA

Bela Crkva

Vršac

Kikinda

Pančevo

Požarevac

Smederevo

Smederevska Palanka

BEOGRAD
(BELGRADE)

Zemun

Velika Morava

Jagodina

Ćuprija

Subotica

Kanjiža

Senta

Ada

Srbobran

Bečej

Temerin

Zrenjanin

Mužlja

Vojvodina

Bačka Topola

Bačka Palanka

Novi Sad

Ruma

Stara Pazova

Indija

Batajnica

Mladenovac

Arandelovac

Valjevo

Gornji Milanovac

Kragujevac

Požega

Čačak

Užice

Zapadna

C

Ipeľ

Little
Alföld

Bakony

Mecsek

Danube (Duna)

Danube (Duna)

Balaton

Sombor

Beli Manastir

Vrbas

Borovo

Vukovar

Šumska Mitrovica

Sava

Šabac

Loznica

Drina

Bijeljina

Tuzla

Zvornik

Srebrenica

Rogatica

Goražde

491

Neusiedler See

Danube (Donau)

Slavonska
Požega

Podravska Slatina

Virovitica

Osijek

Đakovo

Vinkovci

Županja

Bosanski Šamac

Brčko

Modriča

Gradačac

Doboj

Maglaj

Zavidovići

Zenica

Visoko

SARAJEVO

Treskavica

16°

B

Fischbacher
Alpen

Raab

Mur

Drava

Koprivnica

Bjelovar

Papuk

Nova Gradiška

Bosanska Gradiška

Slavonski Brod

Derventa

Kozara

Banja Luka

Sana

Jajce

Travnik

Bosna

Vareš

Konjic

Neretva

487

Čakovec

Varaždin

Sesvete

ZAGREB

Križevci

Kutina

Sisak

CROATIA

Bosanska Dubica

Bosanski Novi

Prijedor

Una

Ključ

Troglav
1913m

Livno

BOSNIA &

HERZEGOVINA

Dinara

AUSTRIA

14°

Mur

Drava

Sava

Samobor

Petrinja

Karlovac

Glina

Cazin

Bihać

Unac

Knin

Sinj

Dinara

Makarska

Split

Solin

A

SLOVENIA

Kolpa

Rijeka

Crikvenica

Senj

Ogulin

Gospić

Velebit

Zadar

Šibenik

Trogir

Dalmacija

48°

ITALY

Opatija

Poreč

Rovinj

Pula

Istra

488

Krk

Cres

Pag

Lošinj

Kvarner

Dugi Otok

Adr

44°

Adria

46°

44°

14°

GERMANY

POPULATION

Less than
50,000
○

50,000 –
100,000
○

100,000 –
500,000
◉

Over
500,000
◼

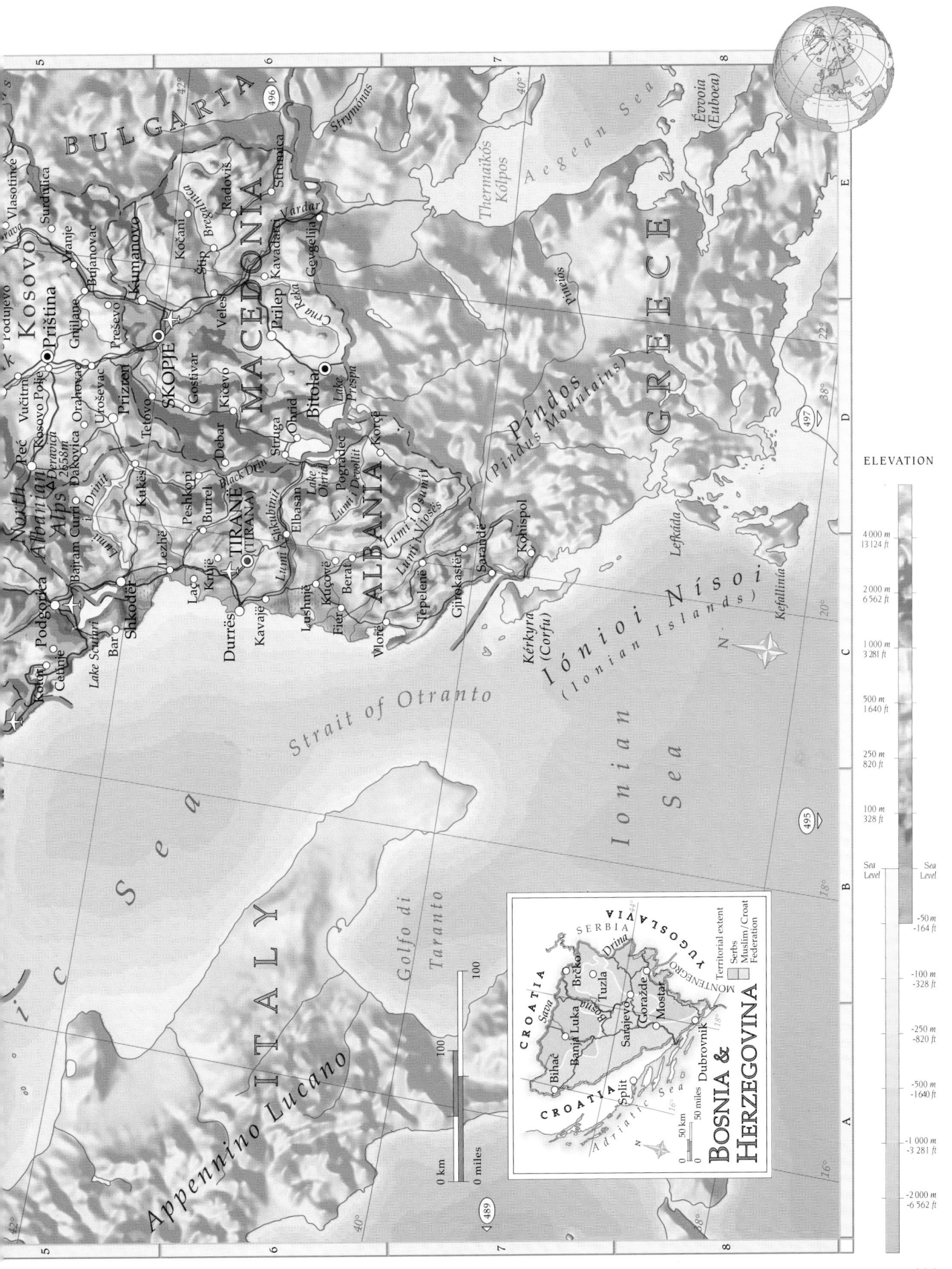

THE MEDITERRANEAN

ATLANTIC OCEAN

Bay of Biscay

5°

N

Quimper

482

St-Nazaire
Île d'Yeu
Nantes
Tours
Loire

FRANCE

Seine

Dijon
Zürich
LIECH.
VADUZ

487

10°

GERMA

Île de Ré
Île d'Oléron

Limoges
Clermont-Ferrand

Lyon
Lake Geneva
BERN
SWITZ.
Mont Blanc
4807 m

Milano
(Milan)

45°

Bordeaux
Dordogne
Garonne

Massif Central

Rhône

Torino
(Turin)

Po

Bologna

A Coruña
Santander

Toulouse
Montpellier
Nîmes
MONACO

Nice
Marseille
Côte d'Azur

Genova
(Genoa)
Golfo di Genova

Pisa

Bilbao
Cordillera Cantábrica
Sistema Ibérico
Ebro
Pyrenees
ANDORRA
Perpignan
Golfe du Lion

Ligurian Sea

Corse
(Corsica)

Isola d'Elba
ROMA
(ROME)

Vigo

458

Duero
Valladolid
Zaragoza
Barcelona
Costa Brava

Ajaccio

VATICAN CITY

Porto

Tarragona

Isola Asinara

40°

Sistema Central
Tagus
MADRID
SPAIN
Castelló de la Plana
Mallorca
(Majorca)
Menorca
(Minorca)
Sardegna
(Sardinia)
Sassari

PORTUGAL

LISBOA
(LISBON)

Valencia
Golfo de Valencia
Palma
Eivissa
(Ibiza)
Formentera
Islas Baleares
(Balearic Islands)

Cagliari

Tyrrh

Sierra Morena
Guadalquivir
Alicante
Costa Blanca

M   e   d   i   t

Sic
(Sic

Sevilla
(Seville)
Sistemas Béticos
Murcia
Cartagena

Cap Bougaroun
Golfe de Tunis
Cap

Golfo de Cádiz
Cádiz
Málaga
Almería
Costa del Sol
ALGER
(ALGIERS)
Tizi Ouzou
Annaba
TUNIS

Golfe de Hamman

35°

Strait of Gibraltar
GIBRALTAR (to UK)
Ceuta (part of Spain)
Tangier
Tétouan
Melilla
(part of Spain)
Tlemcen
Oran
Mostaganem
Atlas Tellien
Sétif
Constantine
Massif de l'Aurès
Chott el Hodna
Sousse

Sfax
Îles Ker

RABAT
Fès
Oujda
Chott ech Chergui
Haut Plateaux
Chott Melghir
Chott el Jerid
Golfe de Gabès
Gabès
Île

Casablanca
MOROCCO
Moyen Atlas
Haut Atlas
Atlas Mountains
ALGERIA
TUNISIA
TAR

458

Safi

MALTA

Mediterranean Sea

14°30'

36°

N

Victoria
Nadur
Comino
(Kemmuna)
Gozo
Mġarr

Mellieħa
St Julian's
Sliema
Mosta
VALLETTA
Ħamrun
Paola
Malta
Rabat
Birżebbuġa

250m/820ft
100m/328ft
Sea Level

0 km   10
0 miles   10

CYPRUS

Mediterranean Sea

Agialoúsa
(Yenierenköy)
TURKISH REPUBLIC
NORTHERN CYPRU
(recognized only by Turk

Lápithos
(Lapta)
Kerýneia
(Girne)

Kólpos Ammóchostos
(Gazimağusa Körfezi)

Mórfou
(Güzelyurt)
Kythréa
(Değirmenlik)
Ammóchostos
(Gazimağusa/
Famagusta)

Pólis
NICOSIA
Dekeleia

35°

Tróodos
Lárnaka

Páfos
Sovereign
Base Area
(to UK)
Sovereign
Base Area
(to UK)

N

Akrotírion
Lemesós
(Limassol)

33°
34°

1000m/3281ft
500m/1640ft
250m/820ft
Sea Level

0 km   25
0 miles   25

POPULATION

Less than
50,000

50,000 –
100,000

100,000 –
500,000

Over
500,000

S

462

a

0°

h

5°

a

10°

r

SLOVAKIA
491
500
501
UKRAINE

Danube
BUDAPEST
Satu Mare
Tisza
Carpathian Mountains
Bâlti
Kakhovs'ka Vodoskhovyshche

HUNGARY
Great Hungarian Plain
Târgu Mures
MOLD.
Dniester
Berdyans'k
1

ZAGREB
ROMANIA
CHIŞINĂU
Odesa
Dnieper
Sea of Azov

CROATIA
Novi Sad
Carpaţii Meridonali
Galaţi
Kerch
Kryms'kyy Pivostrov
RUSS. FED.

BOSNIA & HERZ.
Sava
BEOGRAD (BELGRADE)
BUCUREŞTI (BUCHAREST)
Danube
Constanţa
Sevastopol'
Novorossiysk

SARAJEVO
BULGARIA
Black Sea

YUGOSLAVIA
Pristina
Balkan Mountains
Varna
2

SOFIYA (SOFIA)
Burgas

TIRANË (TIRANA)
SKOPJE
MACED.
Rhodope Mountains
İstanbul Boğazi (Bosporus)
Küre Dağlari
509

Bari
ALBANIA
Edirne
İstanbul
Zonguldak
Samsun
Ordu

1277m
Lecce
Pindus Mts
Thessaloníki (Salonica)
Marmara Denizi
Bursa
ANKARA
Kizil Irmak

Strait of Otranto
Golfo di Taranto
Kérkyra (Corfu)
Límnos
Balikesir
TURKEY
Kayseri

Ionian Sea
GREECE
Aegean Sea
Lárisa
İzmir
Tuz Gölü
3

Catanzaro
Kefallinía
ATHÍNA (ATHENS)
Chíos
Sámos
Toros Dağlari
Gaziantep

Etna
Zákynthos
Kykládes (Cyclades)
Dodekánisos (Dodecanese)
Antalya
Adana
Halab (Aleppo)
Euphrates

Kýthira
Mirtóo Pelagos
Ródos (Rhodes)
Antalya Körfezi
İskenderun Körfezi
SYRIA

Kritikó Pélagos (Sea of Crete)
Kárpathos
NICOSIA
Lárnaka

Irákleio
Kríti (Crete)
CYPRUS
Lemesós (Limassol)
LEBANON
BEYROUTH (BEIRUT)

Darnah
DIMASHQ (DAMASCUS)
4

Banghāzī (Benghazi)
Hefa

Khalīj Surt (Gulf of Sirte)
Ţubruq
ISRAEL
'AMMAN
511

Surt
Libyan Plateau
Alexandria
Nile Delta
Port Said
Tel Aviv-Yafo
JERUSALEM
Gaza
Dead Sea

Ajdābiyā
Suez Canal
CAIRO
JORDAN

Waddān
Great Sand Sea
Munkhafad al Qattāra (Qattara Depression)
El Giza
Suez
Elat
Al 'Aqabah

LIBYA
Nile
Sinai
SAUDI ARABIA
5

Libyan Desert
EGYPT
Sahara el Sharqiya (Eastern Desert)
Gulf of Suez
Red Sea

463
464

ELEVATION
4 000 m / 13 124 ft
2 000 m / 6 562 ft
1 000 m / 3 281 ft
500 m / 1 640 ft
250 m / 820 ft
100 m / 328 ft
Sea Level
-250m / -820 ft
-500 m / -1 640 ft
-1 000 m / -3 281 ft
-2 000 m / -6 562 ft
-3 000 m / -9 843 ft
-4 000 m / -13 124 ft

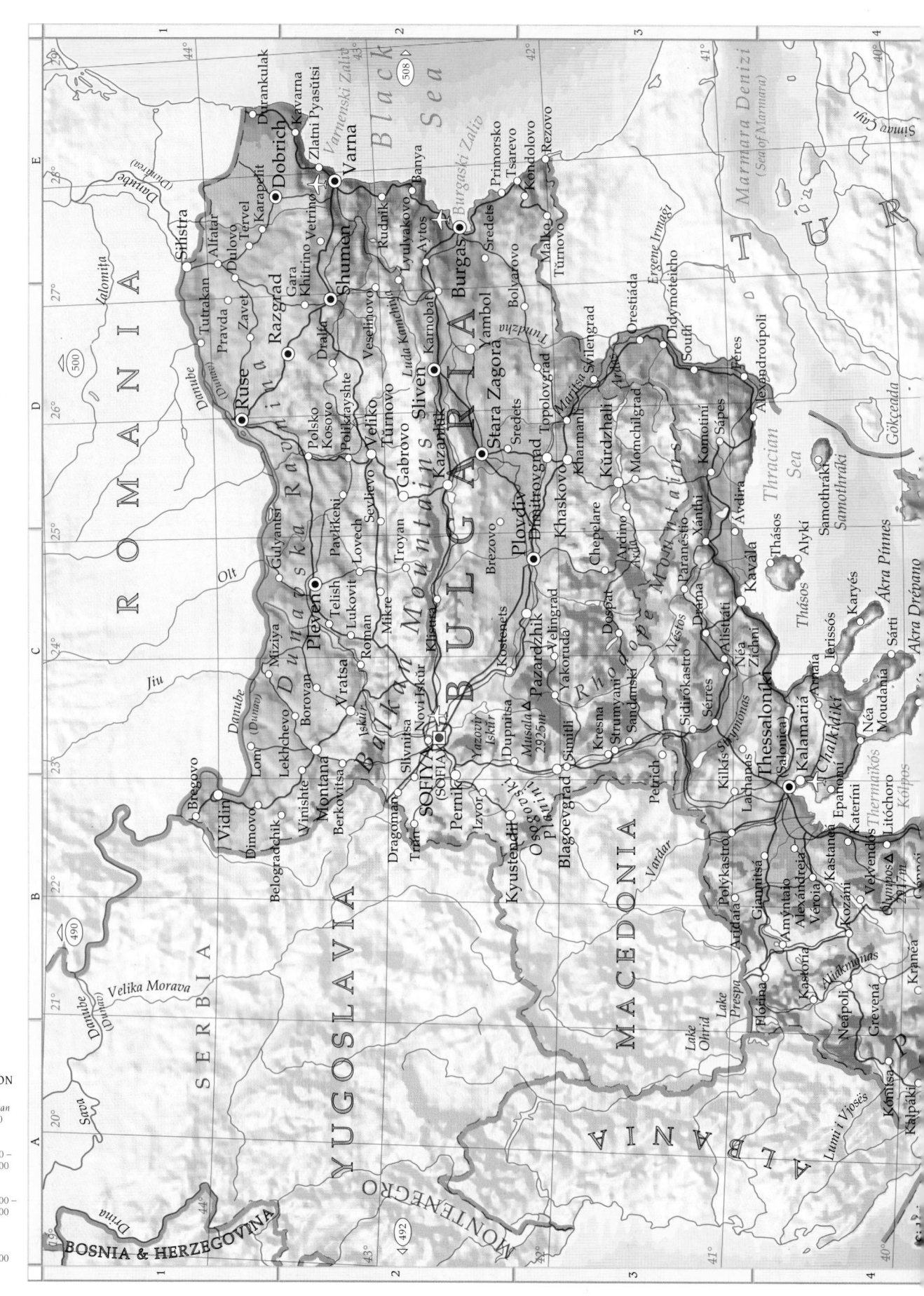

BULGARIA AND GREECE

POPULATION

Less than
50,000
○

50,000 –
100,000
○

100,000 –
500,000
◉

Over
500,000
◉

496

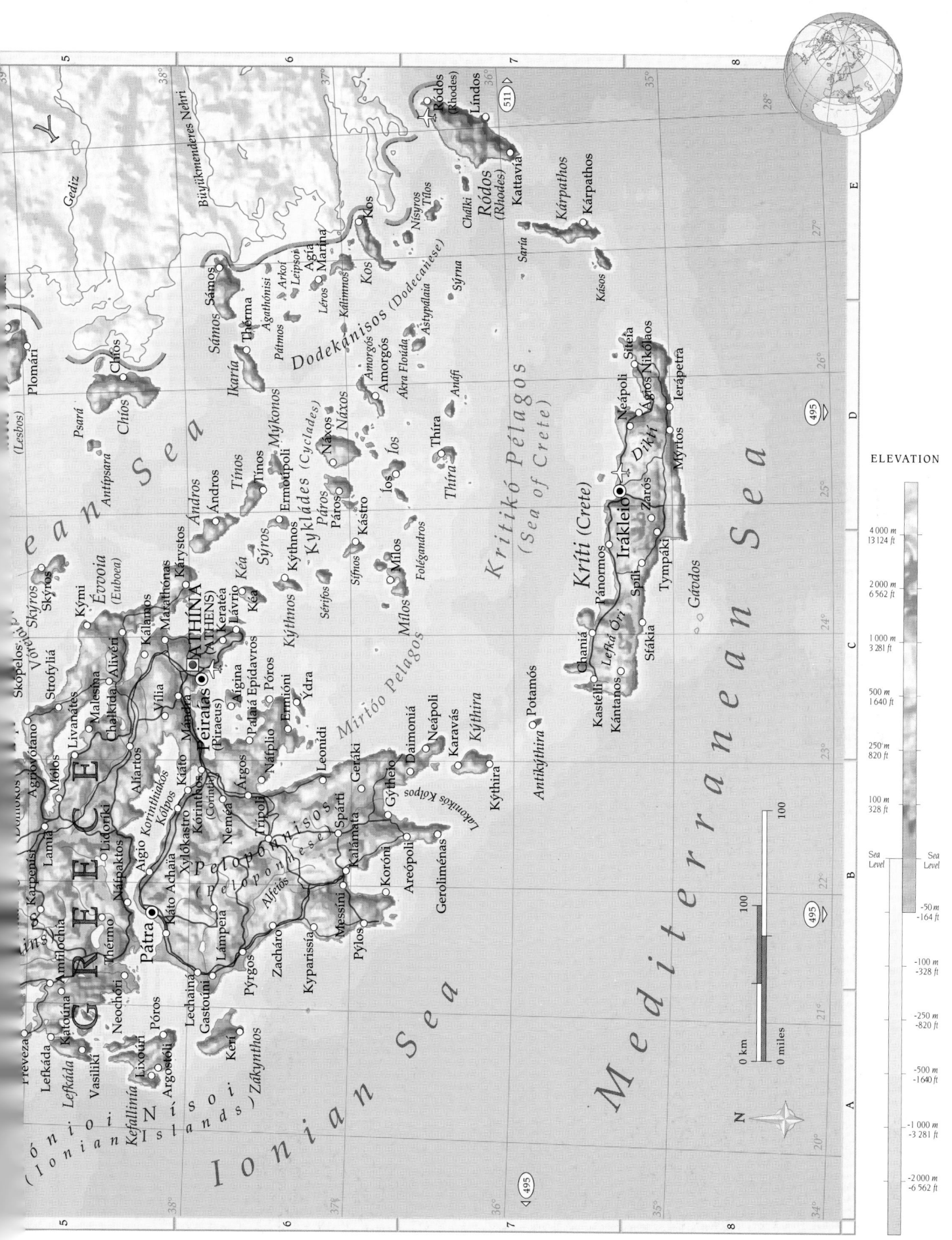

ELEVATION

4 000 m
13 124 ft

2 000 m
6 562 ft

1 000 m
3 281 ft

500 m
1 640 ft

250 m
820 ft

100 m
328 ft

Sea Level	Sea Level

-50 m
-164 ft

-100 m
-328 ft

-250 m
-820 ft

-500 m
-1 640 ft

-1 000 m
-3 281 ft

-2 000 m
-6 562 ft

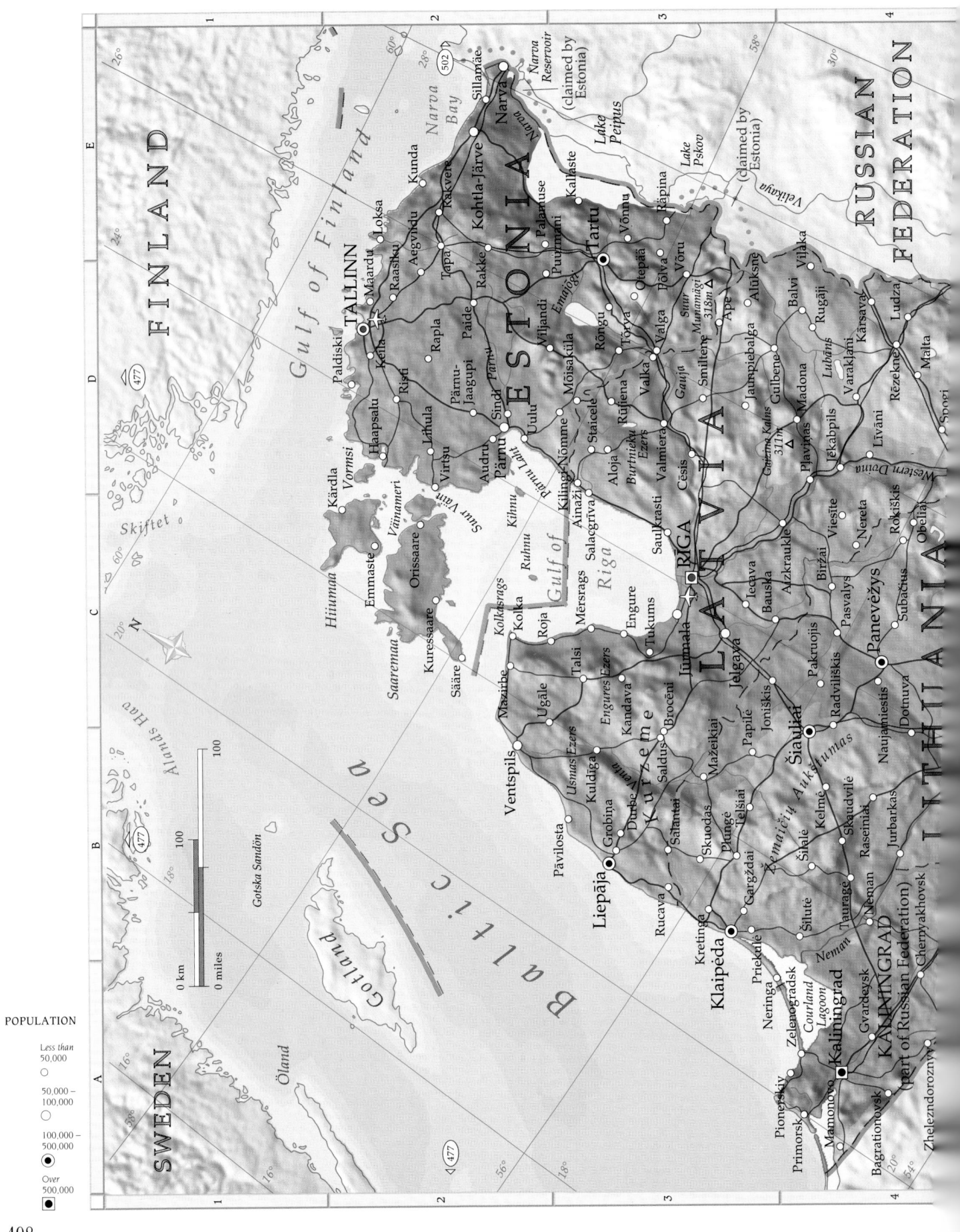

POPULATION

Less than
50,000
○

50,000 –
100,000
○

100,000 –
500,000
◉

Over
500,000
▣

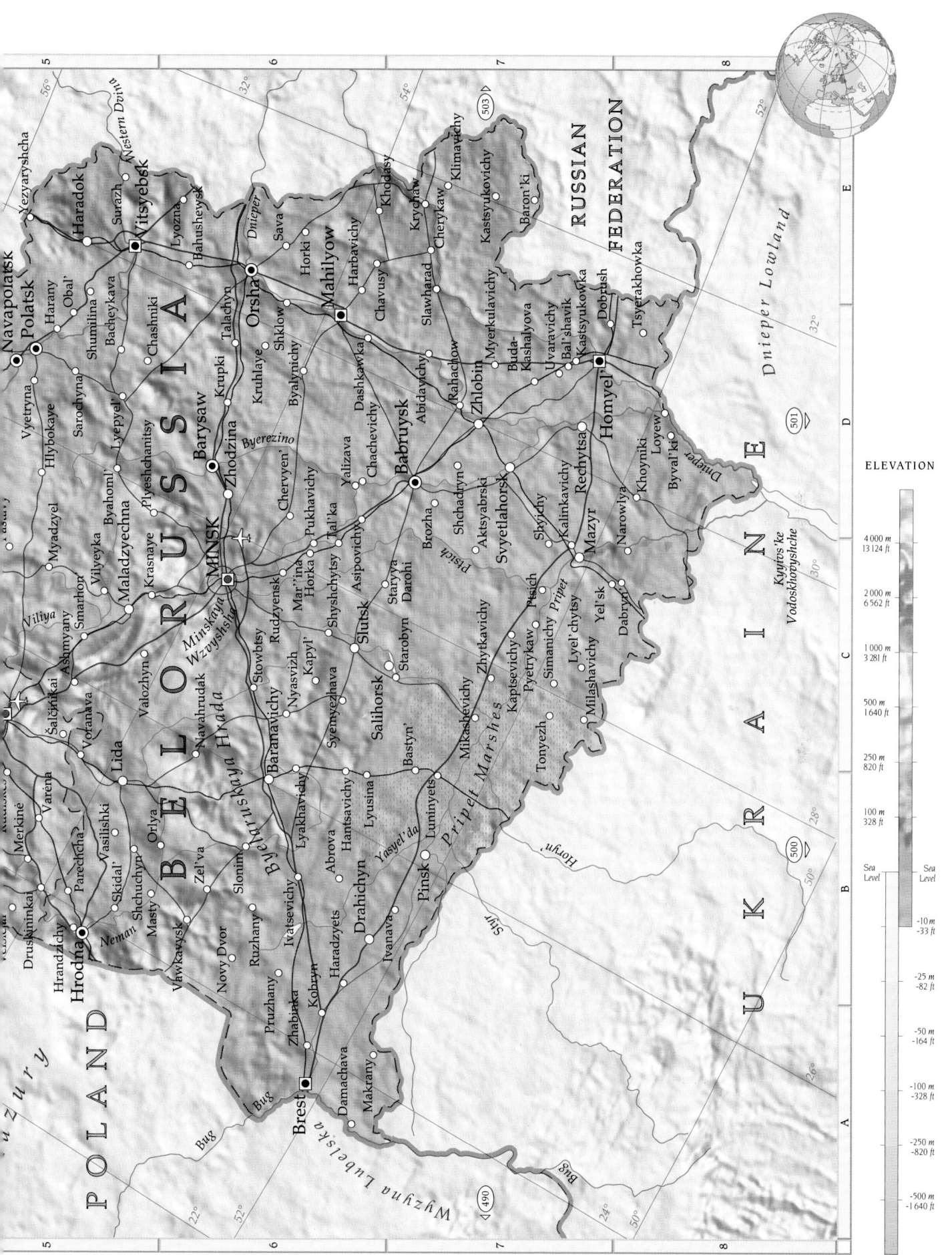

POLAND

U K R A I N E

B E L O R U S S I A

Navapolatsk
Polatsk
Vyetryna
Vyezyarshcha
Yezyaryshcha
Haradok
Surazh
Vitsyebsk
Lyozna
Bahushevysk
Sava
Western Dvina

Harany
Obal'
Shumilina
Badheykava
Chashniki
Talachyn
Orsha
Shklow
Horki
Dnieper
Khodasy
Cherykaw
Klimavichy
Kastsyukovichy
Baron'ki
Kryzhaw
Mahilyow
Harbavichy
Chavusy
Slawharad
Tsyerakhowka

Hlybokaye
Myadzyel
Sarodyna
Lyepyel'
Plyeshchanitsy
Barysaw
Krupki
Kruhlaye
Byalynichy
Dashkawka
Rahachow
Dobrush
Buda-Kashalyova
Uvaravichy
Bal'shavik
Kastsyukowka
Homyel'

Vyetryna
Byahoml'
Zhodzina
Byerezino
Chervyen'
Chachevichy
Abidavichy
Zhlobin
Babruysk
Loyew
Byval'ki

Vilyeyka
Krasnaye
MINSK
Mar''ina Horka
Pukhavichy
Tal'ka
Brozha
Shchadryn
Aktsyabrski
Svyetlahorsk
Khoyniki
Narowlya
Mazyr

Smarhon'
Ashmyany
Valozhyn
Rudzyensk
Shyshchytsy
Asipovichy
Staryya Darohi
Zhytkavichy
Pesich
Kalinkavichy
Rechytsa
Dnieper

Vyerena
Viliya
Salčininkai
Varanava
Stowbtsy
Slutsk
Starobyn
Kaptsevichy
Pyetrykaw
Simanichy Pripet
Lyel'chytsy
Yel'sk
Dabryn'

Merkine
Lida
Nyasvizh
Kapyl'
Salihorsk
Bastyn'
Mikashevichy
Tonyezh
Milashavichy
Horyn'

Druskininkai
Skidal'
Shchuchyn
Baranavichy
Syemyezhava
Lyusina
Luninyets
Pinsk
Yasyel'da

Hrandzichy
Hrodna
Neman
Masty
Zel'va
Slonim
Navahrudak Hrada
Lyakhavichy
Abrova
Hantsavichy
Drahichyn
Ivanava
Shir

Parechcha
Vasilishki
Orlya
Byelaruskaya
Pruzhany
Ivatsevichy
Haradzyets
Kobryn

Vawkavysk
Novy Dvor
Ruzhany
Zhabinka
Brest
Damachava
Makrany
Bug
Bug

Wyżyna Lubelska

Minskaya Wzvyshsha

Pripet Marshes

Pisch

Dnieper Lowland

Kyytvs'ke Vodoskhovyshche

POPULATION

Less than
50,000
○

50,000 –
100,000
○

100,000 –
500,000
◉

Over
500,000
◉

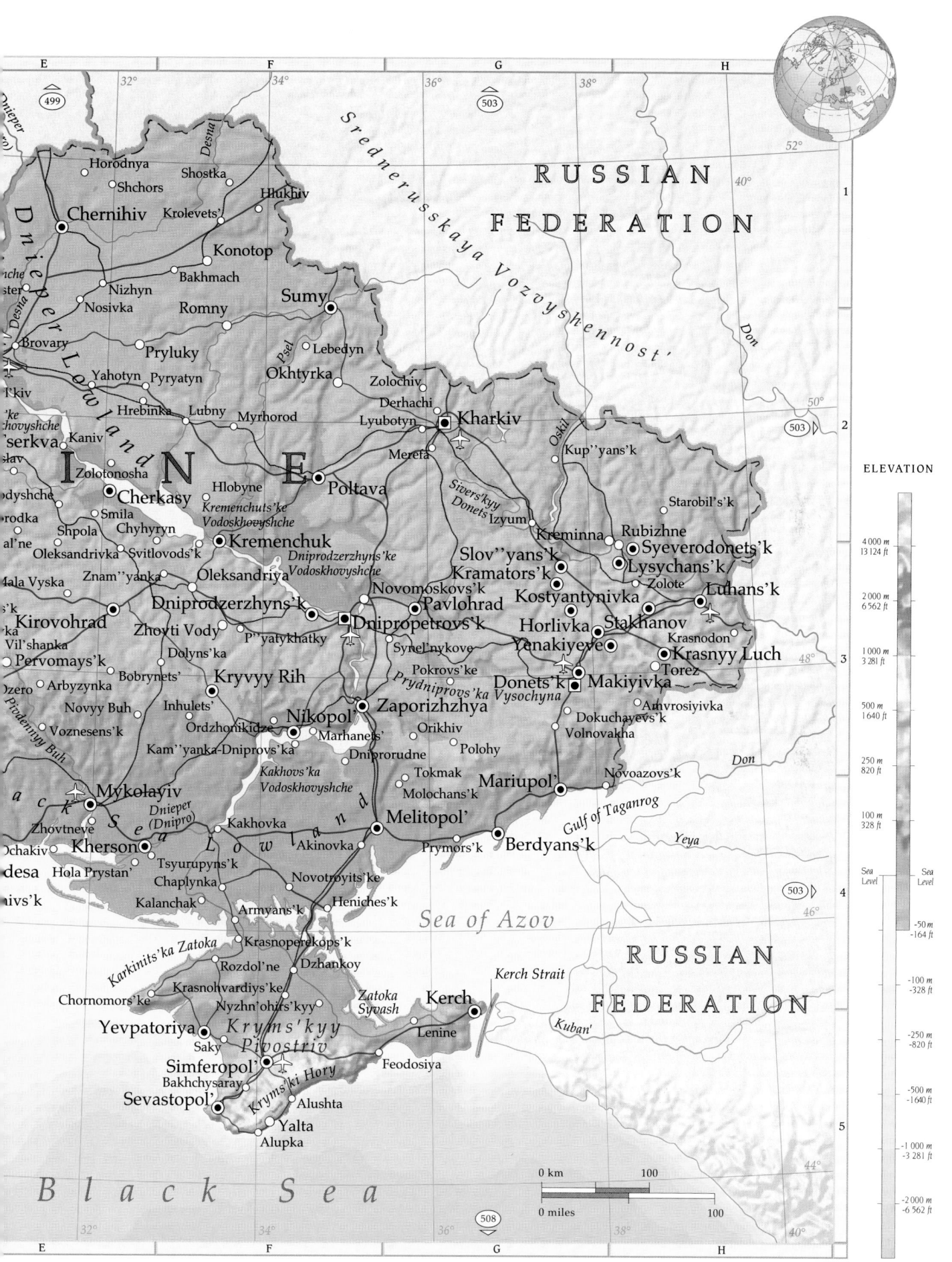

E   32°   F   34°   36°   G   38°   H

499

503

52°

40°

RUSSIAN

FEDERATION

Srednerusskaya Vozvyshennost'

Desna

Horodnya

Shchors

Shostka

Hlukhiv

Chernihiv

Krolevets'

Konotop

Don

Dnieper Lowland

Nizhyn

Bakhmach

Nosivka

Romny

Sumy

Brovary

Pryluky

Psel

Lebedyn

Yahotyn

Pyryatyn

Okhtyrka

Zolochiv

't'kiv

Hrebinka

Lubny

Myrhorod

Derhachi

50°

'ke

hovyshche

Kaniv

Lyubotyn

Kharkiv

503

2

'serkva

Zolotonosha

Merefa

Oskil

Kup''yans'k

I N E

odyshche

Sivers'kyy

Donets

Starobil's'k

rodka

Cherkasy

Hlobyne

Poltava

Izyum

Kreminna

Rubizhne

Smila

Kremenchuts'ke

Chyhyryn

Vodoskhovyshche

Kremenchuk

Slov''yans'k

Syeverodonets'k

al'ne

Shpola

Lysychans'k

Oleksandrivka

Svitlovods'k

Oleksandriya

Dniprodzerzhyns'ke

Kramators'k

Zolote

Mala Vyska

Znam''yanka

Vodoskhovyshche

Novomoskovs'k

Kostyantynivka

Luhans'k

Dniprodzerzhyns'k

Pavlohrad

Horlivka

Stakhanov

Kirovohrad

Zhovti Vody

Dnipropetrovs'k

Krasnodon

Vil'shanka

P''yatykhatky

Yenakiyeve

Pervomays'k

Dolyns'ka

Synel'nykove

Krasnyy Luch

'ka

Bobrynets'

Kryvyy Rih

Pokrovs'ke

Torez

Dzero

Arbyzynka

Prydniprovs'ka

Donets'k

Makiyivka

48°

Vysochyna

Novyy Buh

Inhulets'

Nikopol'

Zaporizhzhya

Ahvrosiyivka

Pivdennyy Buh

Voznesens'k

Ordzhonikidze

Marhanets'

Orikhiv

Dokuchayevs'k

Kam''yanka-Dniprovs'ka

Polohy

Volnovakha

Kakhovs'ka

Dniprorudne

Vodoskhovyshche

Tokmak

Don

Mykolayiv

Dnieper

Molochans'k

Novoazovs'k

(Dnipro)

Mariupol'

Zhovtneve

Kakhovka

L o w l a n d

Melitopol'

Gulf of Taganrog

a c k

Kherson

Akinovka

Prymors'k

Yeya

S e

Hola Prystan'

 Tsyurupyns'k

Berdyans'k

Ochakiv

a

Chaplynka

Novotroyits'ke

desa

Kalanchak

Heniches'k

Sea of Azov

503

4

niv's'k

Armyans'k

RUSSIAN

46°

Karkinits'ka Zatoka

Krasnoperekops'k

Rozdol'ne

Dzhankoy

Kerch Strait

FEDERATION

Chornomors'ke

Krasnohvardiys'ke

Zatoka

Syvash

Kerch

Nyzhn'ohirs'kyy

Yevpatoriya

Kryms'kyy

Lenine

Kuban'

Saky

Pivostriv

Simferopol'

Feodosiya

Bakhchysaray

Krymski Hory

Sevastopol'

Alushta

Yalta

Alupka

5

B l a c k   S e a

44°

0 km   100

0 miles   100

508

32°   34°   36°   38°   40°

E   F   G   H

ELEVATION

4 000 m	13 124 ft
2 000 m	6 562 ft
1 000 m	3 281 ft
500 m	1 640 ft
250 m	820 ft
100 m	328 ft
Sea Level	Sea Level
-50 m	-164 ft
-100 m	-328 ft
-250 m	-820 ft
-500 m	-1 640 ft
-1 000 m	-3 281 ft
-2 000 m	-6 562 ft

EUROPEAN RUSSIA

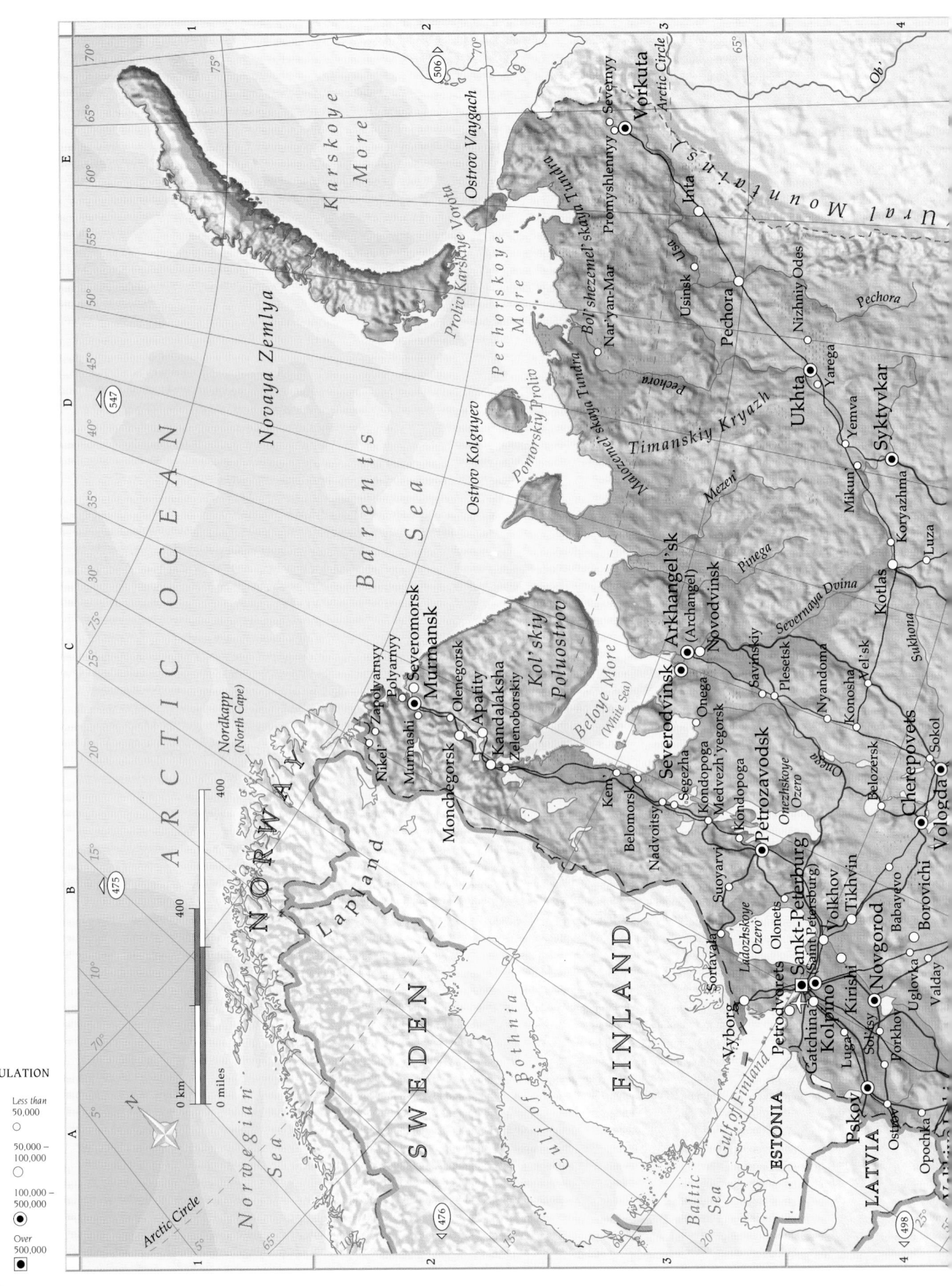

POPULATION

Less than
50,000

50,000 –
100,000

100,000 –
500,000

Over
500,000

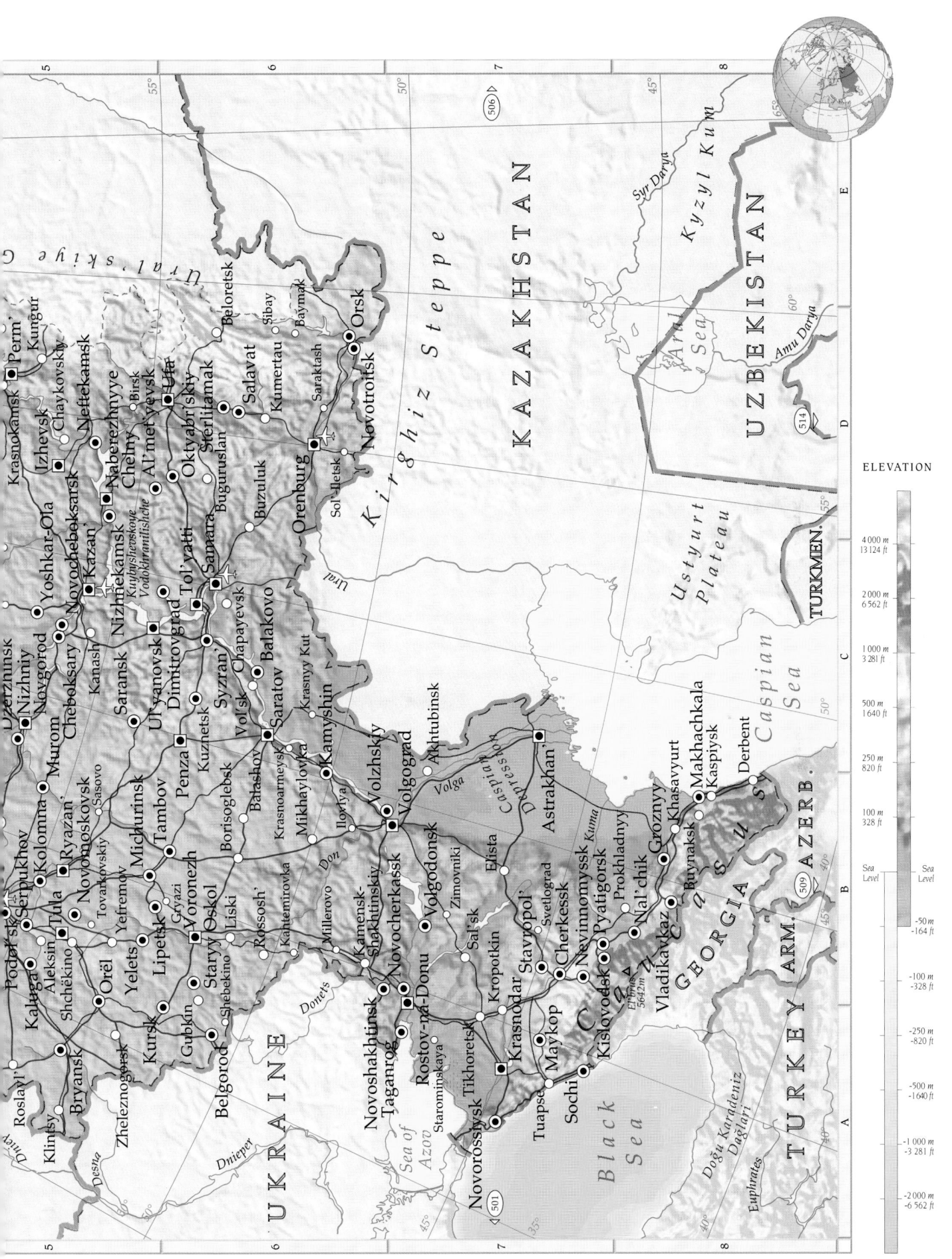

NORTH AND WEST ASIA

Franz Josef Land

ARCTI

Severnay.

Ostrov Komsomolets

Ostrov Oktyabr'skoy Revolyutsii
Ostrov Bol'shevik

Norwegian
Sea   North Cape

Barents
Sea

Summer limit of pack ice

Winter limit of pack ice

Novaya Zemlya

East Novaya Zemlya Trench

Kara Sea

Poluostrov Ta

North Sib

Gulf of Ob

Arctic Circle

Murmansk

Kola
Peninsula

Ostrov
Kolguyev

Poluostrov
Yamal

Noril'sk

Centr
Siber
Plate

Kureyka

Lower Tunguska

White Sea

Archangel

R   U   S   S   I   A   N

West Siberian
Plain

Yenisey

Stony Tunguska

Gulf of Bothnia

Lake
Onega

Northern
Dvina

Ob'

Angara

Lake Ladoga

Saint Petersburg

Vologda

Perm'

Yekaterinburg

Irtysh

Ob'

Chulym

Tomsk

Yaroslavl'

Nizhniy
Novgorod

Irtysh

Novosibirsk

Krasnoyarsk

MOSCOW

Kazan'

Chelyabinsk

Ishim

Omsk

Novokuznetsk

Baltic Sea

Kaliningrad

Central
Russian
Upland

Ul'yanovsk

Volga

Ufa

Samara

Ural

Orenburg

ASTANA

Sayanskiy Khrebet

KALININGRAD
(part of Russ. Fed.)

Voronezh

Saratov

Volga

Ural'sk

Karaganda

A

Semipalatinsk

S

E   U   R   O   P   E

Rostov-na-Donu

Don

Volgograd

Astrakhan'

Stavropol'

Caspian Sea

Aral'sk

Kirghiz
Steppe

Kazakh Uplands

Altai Mountains

KAZAKHSTAN

Aral
Sea

Syr Darya

Lake
Balkhash

Ozero
Zaysan

Danube

Black Sea

El'brus
5642m

Caucasus

Aktau

Ustyurt
Plateau

Kyzyl
Kum

Kzyl-Orda

Zhambyl

Ili

Almaty
(Alma-Ata)

Istanbul

Küre Dağları

GEORGIA

T'BILISI

Dashkhovuz

Amu Darya

UZBEKISTAN

BISHKEK

Tien Shan

Anatolia

ANKARA

ARMENIA

AZERB.

BAKU

Kara Kum

TURKMENISTAN

TASHKENT

KYRGYZSTAN

YEREVAN

TURKEY

Lake
Van

Tabriz

ASHGABAT

DUSHANBE

TAJIKISTAN

Adana

Gaziantep

Mosul

TEHRAN

Hindu Kush

Kunlun Mountains

Aleppo

Qom

KABUL

Jalalabad

Tripoli

SYRIA

IRAQ

Isfahan

Iranian
Plateau

AFGHANISTAN

Herat

Khyber Pass

BEIRUT

DAMASCUS

BAGHDAD

Tigris

Zagros

LEBANON

Syrian
Desert

Euphrates

Basra

ISRAEL

AMMAN

Iranian
Plateau

IRAN

Himalayas

JERUSALEM

JORDAN

KUWAIT

Zahedan

Ganges

An Nafud

KUWAIT

Shiraz

Bandar-e 'Abbas

Thar Desert

MANAMA

Dubai

Gulf of Oman

BAHRAIN

The Gulf

DOHA

U.A.E.

MUSCAT

Indus Fan

RIYADH

QATAR

ABU
DHABI

Sur

Tropic of Cancer

SAUDI ARABIA

Arabian
Peninsula

Murray Ridge

Ganges Fan

Nile

At Ta'if

OMAN

Bay of
Bengal

AFRICA

Red Sea

Ar Rub' al Khali

Arabian
Sea

SANA

YEMEN

Socotra
(part of Yemen)

Ta'izz

Aden

Gulf of Aden

POPULATION

Less than
50,000
○

50,000 –
100,000
○

100,000 –
500,000
◉

Over
500,000
◉

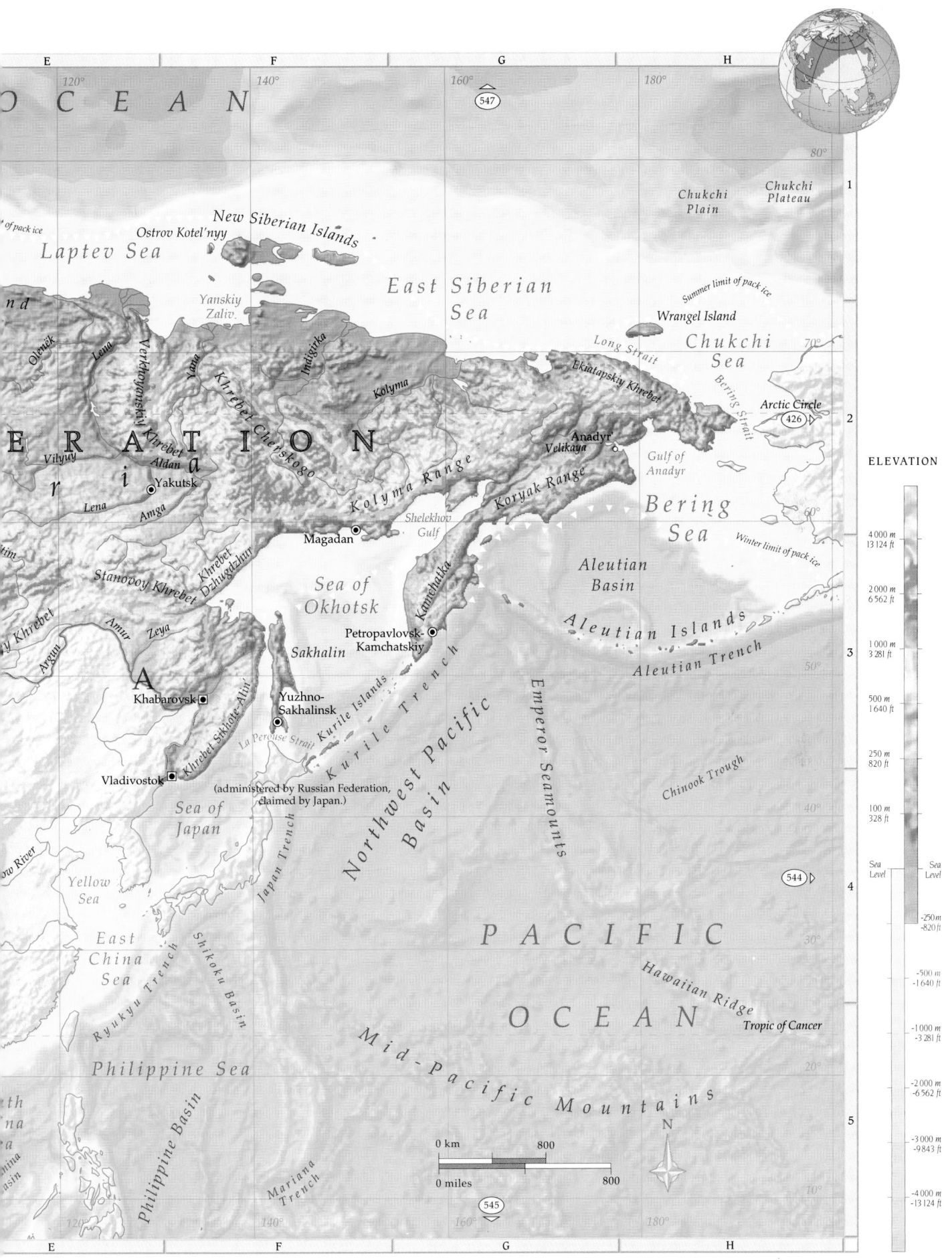

OCEAN

120°

140°

160°

547

180°

80°

1

of pack ice

New Siberian Islands

Chukchi
Plain

Chukchi
Plateau

Laptev Sea

Ostrov Kotel'nyy

East Siberian
Sea

Yanskiy
Zaliv

Wrangel Island

Summer limit of pack ice

nd

Olenek

Lena

Verkhoyanskiy Khrebet

Indigirka

Long Strait

Chukchi
Sea

70°

Ekiatapskiy Khrebet

Bering Strait

Arctic Circle

426

2

Yana

Khrebet Cherskogo

Kolyma

ERATION

Anadyr

Velikaya

Gulf of
Anadyr

Vilyuy

Aldan

r

i

a

Kolyma Range

Koryak Range

Bering
Sea

Yakutsk

Lena

Amga

Shelekhov
Gulf

Kamchatka

Winter limit of pack ice

4 000 m
13 124 ft

Magadan

Aleutian
Basin

Khrebet
Dzhugdzhur

Sea of
Okhotsk

2 000 m
6 562 ft

Stanovoy Khrebet

Aleutian Islands

1 000 m
3 281 ft

y Khrebet

Amur

Zeya

Petropavlovsk-
Kamchatskiy

Aleutian Trench

50°

3

Argun

Sakhalin

Kurile Trench

Khabarovsk

Yuzhno-
Sakhalinsk

Khrebet Sikhote-Alin

Kurile Islands

Northwest Pacific

Emperor Seamounts

Chinook Trough

40°

500 m
1 640 ft

250 m
820 ft

100 m
328 ft

Vladivostok

La Perouse Strait

Japan Trench

Basin

544

Sea level

Sea level

4

Sea of
Japan

PACIFIC

30°

-250 m
-820 ft

ow River

Yellow
Sea

East
China
Sea

Ryukyu Trench

Shikoku Basin

Hawaiian Ridge

OCEAN

Tropic of Cancer

-500 m
-1 640 ft

Philippine Sea

Mid-Pacific Mountains

20°

-1 000 m
-3 281 ft

5

-2 000 m
-6 562 ft

th
na
a

Philippine Basin

0 km   800

0 miles   800

N

-3 000 m
-9 843 ft

Mariana
Trench

545

10°

-4 000 m
-13 124 ft

120°

140°

160°

180°

E   F   G   H

ELEVATION

(administered by Russian Federation,
claimed by Japan.)

RUSSIA AND KAZAKHSTAN

NETH.

NORWAY

DENMARK

SWEDEN

GERMANY

Gulf of Bothnia

FINLAND

SVALBARD
(Norwegian dependency)

475

Arctic Circle

60°   70°   10°   80°   20°

Zemlya
Iosi

Barents
Sea

Nordkapp
(North Cape)

ARCT

KALININGRAD
(part of Russ. Fed.)

Baltic Sea

Gulf of Finland

Murmansk

Kol'skiy
Poluostrov

Novaya Zemlya

Ostrov B

Di

Kaliningrad
POLAND

Kandalaksha

500

LITH.   LAT.   EST.

Sankt-Peterburg

BELORUSSIA

Pskov
Novgorod

Ladozhskoye
Ozero

Petrozavodsk

Onezhskoye
Ozero

Beloye More

Severnaya Dvina

Severodvinsk
Arkhangel'sk

Ostrov
Kolguyev

Karskoye More

Nar'yan-Mar

Poluostrov Yamal

Smolensk

Cherepovets

Obskaya Guba

Nor

MOSKVA
(MOSCOW)

Tver'

Vologda

Vel'sk

Pechora

Ukhta

Vorkuta

Salekhard

Ob'

Igar

MOLDAVIA

Bryansk

Yaroslavl'

Kineshma

Kotlas

Syktyvkar

Ob'

Nadym

Nyagan'

Zapadno-

UKRAINE

Tula

Ryazan'

Vladimir

Nizhniy Novgorod

Kirov

Solikamsk

Serov

Khanty-Mansiysk

Sibirskaya

Belgorod

Voronezh

Tambov

Penza

Kazan'

Glazov

Perm'

Ravnina

Nizhnevartovs

Sea of Azov

Mikhaylovka

Ul'yanovsk

Izhevsk

Naberezhnyye
Chelny

Yekaterinburg

Surgut

RUSSIA

Rostov-na-
Donu

Saratov

Tol'yatti

Samara

Chelny

Ufa

Tyumen'

Tobol'sk

Chulym

Krasnodar

Balakovo

Volgograd

Sterlitamak

Ural'sk

Orenburg

Chelyabinsk

Ishim

Sochi

Stavropol'

El'brus
5642m

Astrakhan'

Ural

Magnitogorsk

Orsk

Petropavlovsk

Irtysh

Ob'

Nal'chik

Caucasus

Vladikavkaz

Aktyubinsk

Alga

Rudnyy

Kustanay

Omsk

Tomsk

Grozny

Atyrau

Tobol

Ishim

GEORGIA

Makhachkala

Emba

Kokshetau

Novosibirsk

Krasnc

ARM.

512

Fort-Shevchenko

Chelkar

Atbasar

Shchuchinsk

Astana

Kemer

AZERBAIJAN

Aktau

Novyy Uzen'

KAZAKHSTAN

ASTANA

Pavlodar

Barnaul

Novokuznetsk

Caspian Sea

Ustyurt
Plateau

Aral
Sea

Aral'sk

Novokazalinsk

Temirtau

Saran'

Karaganda

Semipalatinsk

Leninogorsk

Syr Darya

Dzhusaly

Zhezkazgan

Kazakhskiy
Melkosopochnik

Charsk

Zyryanovsk

Gora Belukh
4506m

TURKMENISTAN

Kzyl-Orda

Ust'-Kamenogorsk

Ayaguz

UZBEKISTAN

Kyzyl Kum

Balkhash

Ozero
Zaysan

Altai Mountain

Amu Darya

Turkestan

Kentau

Shymkent

Karatau

Shu

Ozero
Balkhash

Taldykorgan

Tekeli

Arys'

Zhambyl

Kirghiz Range

Almaty
(Alma-Ata)

IRAN

TAJIKISTAN

KYRGYZSTAN

Tien Shan

CHINA

AFGHANISTAN

514

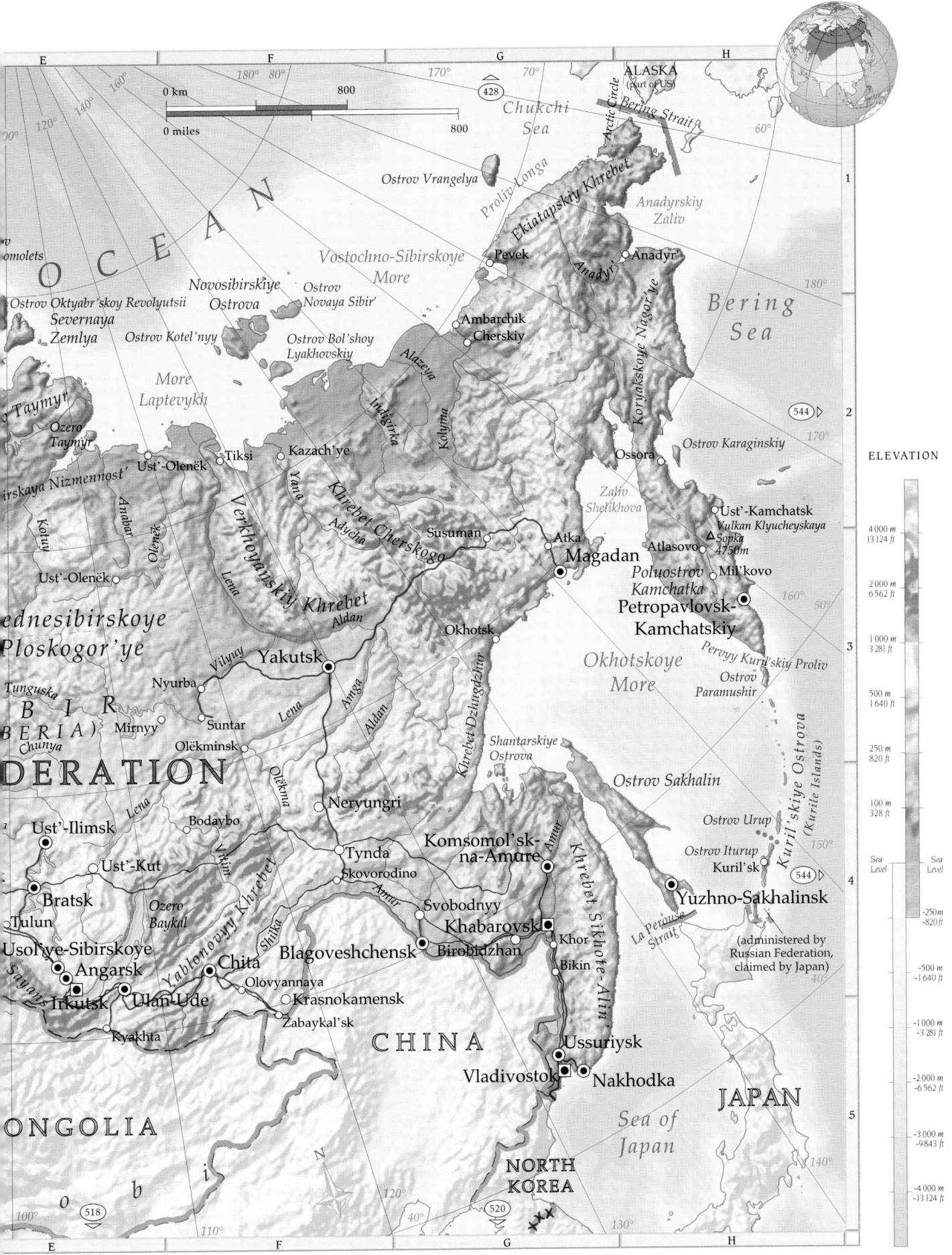

 O C E A N

~omolets

Chukchi
Sea

ALASKA
(part of US)

428

Arctic Circle

Bering Strait

Ostrov Vrangelya

Vostochno-Sibirskoye
More

Proliv Longa

Ekiatapskiy Khrebet

Pevek

Anadyrskiy
Zaliv

Bering
Sea

Anadyr

Anadyr'

Novosibirskiye
Ostrova

Ostrov
Novaya Sibir'

Ambarchik
Cherskiy

Koryakskoye Nagor'ye

544

Ostrov Oktyabr'skoy Revolyutsii

Ostrov Bol'shoy
Lyakhovskiy

Alazeya

Severnaya
Zemlya

Ostrov Kotel'nyy

Indigirka

Kolyma

Ossora

Ostrov Karaginskiy

~v Taymyr

More
Laptevykh

Tiksi

Kazach'ye

Khrebet Cherskogo

Yana

Zaliv
Shelikhova

Ust'-Kamchatsk

Vulkan Klyucheyskaya
△ Sopka
4750m

~irskaya Nizmennost'

Ust'-Olenëk

Ozero
Taymyr

Anabar

Olenëk

Adycha

Susuman

Atka

Atlasovo

Mil'kovo

Magadan

Poluostrov
Kamchatka

~v Taymyr

Kotuy

Verkhoyanskiy Khrebet

Aldan

Okhotsk

Petropavlovsk-
Kamchatskiy

Ust'-Olenëk

Lena

Khrebet Dzhugdzhur

Okhotskoye
More

Pervyy Kuril'skiy Proliv

~ednesibirskoye
Ploskogor'ye

Vilyuy

Yakutsk

Amga

Ostrov
Paramushir

Nyurba

Lena

Aldan

Shantarskiye
Ostrova

Tunguska

Mirnyy

Suntar

Ostrov Sakhalin

~B I R

~B E R I A)

Chunya

Olëkminsk

Ostrov Urup

~DERATION

Lena

Olëkma

Neryungri

Ostrov Iturup

Kuril'sk

544

Ust'-Ilimsk

Bodaybo

Vitim

Tynda

Komsomol'sk-
na-Amure

Amur

Khrebet Sikhote-Alin'

Ust'-Kut

Skovorodino

Yuzhno-Sakhalinsk

Bratsk

Yablonovyy Khrebet

Amur

Svobodnyy

La Perouse Strait

~Tulun

Ozero
Baykal

Shilka

Khabarovsk

Khor

(administered by
Russian Federation,
claimed by Japan)

Usol'ye-Sibirskoye

Blagoveshchensk

Birobidzhan

Bikin

Angarsk

Chita

~Sayans

Irkutsk

Ulan-Ude

Olovyannaya

Krasnokamensk

CHINA

Ussuriysk

~ONGOLIA

Kyakhta

Zabaykal'sk

Vladivostok

Nakhodka

JAPAN

o   b   i

N

Sea of
Japan

NORTH
KOREA

518

520

✕✕✕

ELEVATION

4 000 m
13 124 ft

2 000 m
6 562 ft

1 000 m
3 281 ft

500 m
1 640 ft

250 m
820 ft

100 m
328 ft

Sea
Level

Sea
Level

-250m
-820 ft

-500 m
-1 640 ft

-1 000 m
-3 281 ft

-2 000 m
-6 562 ft

-3 000 m
-9 843 ft

-4 000 m
-13 124 ft

TURKEY AND THE CAUCASUS

ROMANIA

UKRAINE

Krynm's'kyy Pivostriv

Lacul Razim

Lacul Sinoie

BULGARIA

B l a c k   S e a

Varnenski Zaliv

Burgaski Zaliv

Maritsa

Kırklareli

Edirne

İnebolu   Sinop

Cide   Gerze

Küre Dağları   Bafra

Zonguldak   Bartın   Samsun

Ergene Nehri   Çorlu   Devrek   Karabük   Kastamonu

Tekirdağ   İstanbul   Kargı

                        İzmit   Adapazarı   Çerkeş   Merzifon

Çanakkale   *Marmara Denizi* Yalova   Bolu   Gerede   Çorum

              (Sea of Marmara) *İznik Gölü*   Çankırı   *Kızıl Irmak*   *Canik Dağları*

Bandırma   Bursa   Kalecik   Tokat

              Simav Çayı   Bilecik   Eskişehir   ANKARA   Alaca

Balıkesir   Bozüyük   Kırıkkale   Sorgun   Yıldıze

Edremit   Kütahya   T   U   R   *Hirfanlı Barajı*   Şarkışla

Ayvalık   Polatlı   Kulu   Boğazlıyan

Lésvos   Akhisar   Simav   *Tuz Gölü*   Bünyan

              Manisa   Gediz   Uşak   Afyon   Cihanbeyli   İncesu

Chios Menemen *Gediz Nehri*   Akşehir   Aksaray   Nevşehir   Kayseri   Gürür

İzmir   Alaşehir   A n a t o l i a   Göksun

        Ödemiş   Nazilli   Dinar   Konya   Niğde   Kahraman

Sámos Aydın   Denizli *Beyşehir Gölü*   Ga

        Söke *Büyükmenderes Nehri* Burdur Isparta   Ereğli

              Milas   Tavas *Burdur Gölü*   *Suğla Gölü*   Karaman   *Toros Dağları*   Tarsus   Ceyhan   Osmani

        Bodrum   Muğla   Mut   Mersin   Adana   Kilis

              Marmaris   Dalaman   Antalya   Manavgat   T o r o s   D a ğ l a r ı İskenderun   Kırıkha

Dodecánese   Fethiye   Alanya   Antakya

              Kaş   Finike *Antalya Körfezi*   Silifke

Ródos (Rhodes)   Anamur

Kárpathos

                                              TURKISH REPUBLIC OF
                                              NORTHERN CYPRUS
CYPRUS   (recognised only by Turkey)

M e d i t e r r a n e a n   *Orantes*

S e a   LEBANON

0 km   200

0 miles   200

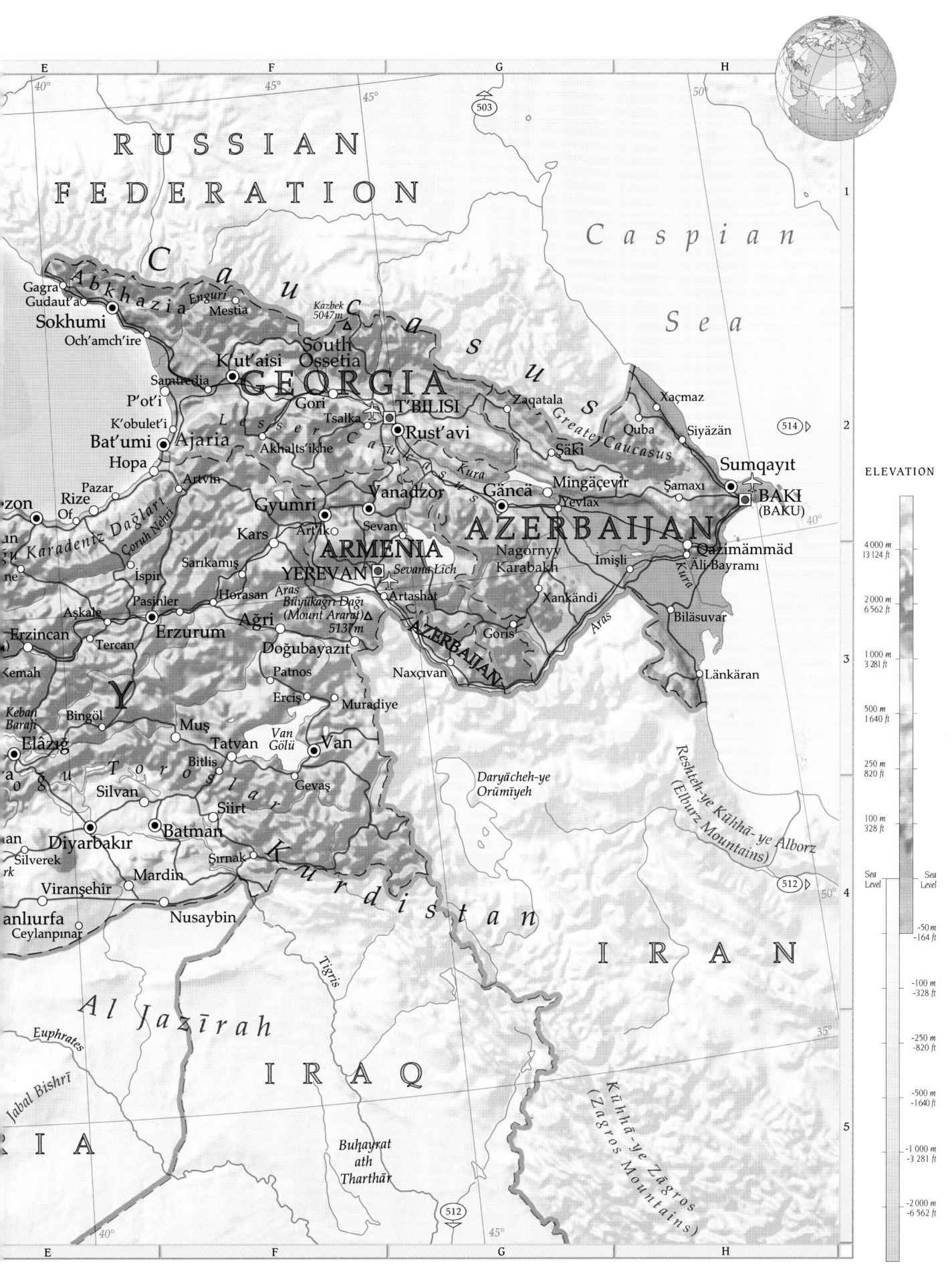

RUSSIAN

FEDERATION

Caspian

Sea

C a u c a s u s

Gagra
Gudaut'a
Sokhumi
Och'amch'ire

A b k h a z i a
Enguri
Mestia

Kazbek
5047m △

K'ut'aisi
South
Ossetia
Samtredia
GEORGIA
Gori
Tsalka
T'BILISI
Rust'avi
Zaqatala
Xaçmaz
Quba
Siyäzän
514

P'ot'i
K'obulet'i
Bat'umi
Hopa
Ajaria
L e s s e r
Akhalts'ikhe
C a u c
Säki
Greater Caucasus
Şamaxı
Sumqayıt
BAKI
(BAKU)

zon
Rize
Pazar
Of
Artvin
Gyumri
Vanadzor
Gäncä
Mingäçevir
Yevlax
Qazimämmäd
Äli Bayramı

Karadeniz Dağları
Çoruh Nehri
İspir
Kars
Arт̇ik
Sevan
ARMENIA
YEREVAN
Sevana Lich
Nagornyy
Karabakh
İmişli
Xankändi
Bilˉasuvar

un
ne
Aşkale
Sarıkamış
Pasinler
Horasan
Aras
Büyükağrı Dağı
(Mount Ararat) △
5137m
Artashat
AZERBAIJAN
Goris
Aras

Erzincan
Tercan
Erzurum
Ağrı
Doğubayazıt
Patnos
Naxçıvan
Länkäran

Kemah
Bingöl
Y
Elâzığ
Keban
Baraji
Muş
Tatvan
Erciş
Van
Gölü
Muradiye
Van
Daryācheh-ye
Orūmīyeh

Reşteh-ye Kūhhā- ye Alborz
(Elburz Mountains)
512

IRAN

Silvan
Bitlis
Siirt
Gevaş
T o r o s

Diyarbakır
Batman
Şırnak
K u r d i s t a n

an
Silverek
rk
Viranşehir
Mardin
Nusaybin
anlıurfa
Ceylanpınar

A l   J a z ī r a h
Euphrates
IRAQ
Tigris

RIA
Jabal Bishrī

Buhayrat
ath
Tharthār
512

Kūhhā-ye Zagros
(Zagros Mountains)

ELEVATION

4 000 m
13 124 ft

2 000 m
6 562 ft

1 000 m
3 281 ft

500 m
1 640 ft

250 m
820 ft

100 m
328 ft

Sea
Level

Sea
Level

-50 m
-164 ft

-100 m
-328 ft

-250 m
-820 ft

-500 m
-1 640 ft

-1 000 m
-3 281 ft

-2 000 m
-6 562 ft

THE NEAR EAST

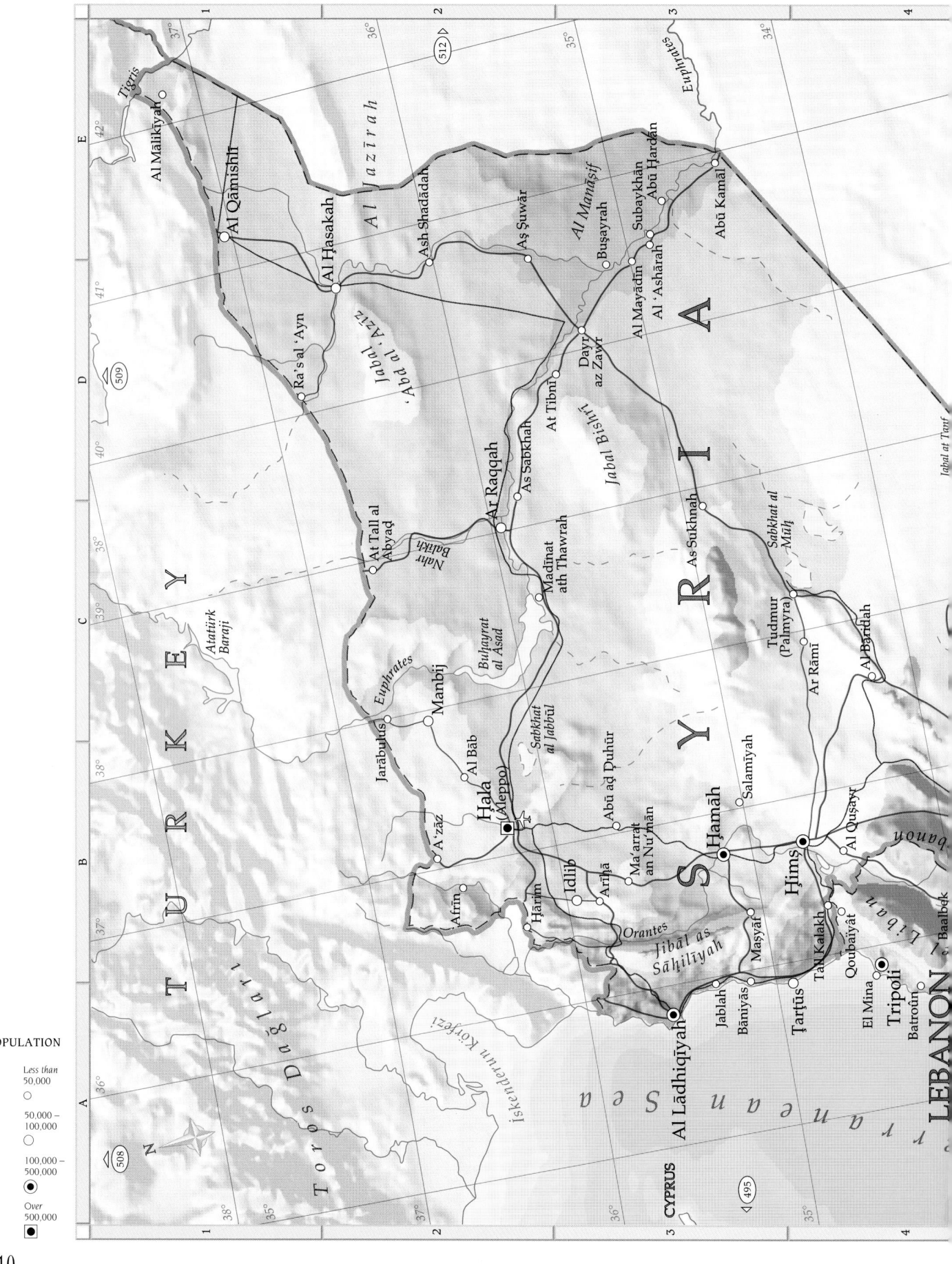

POPULATION

Less than
50,000
○

50,000 –
100,000
○

100,000 –
500,000
◉

Over
500,000
◼

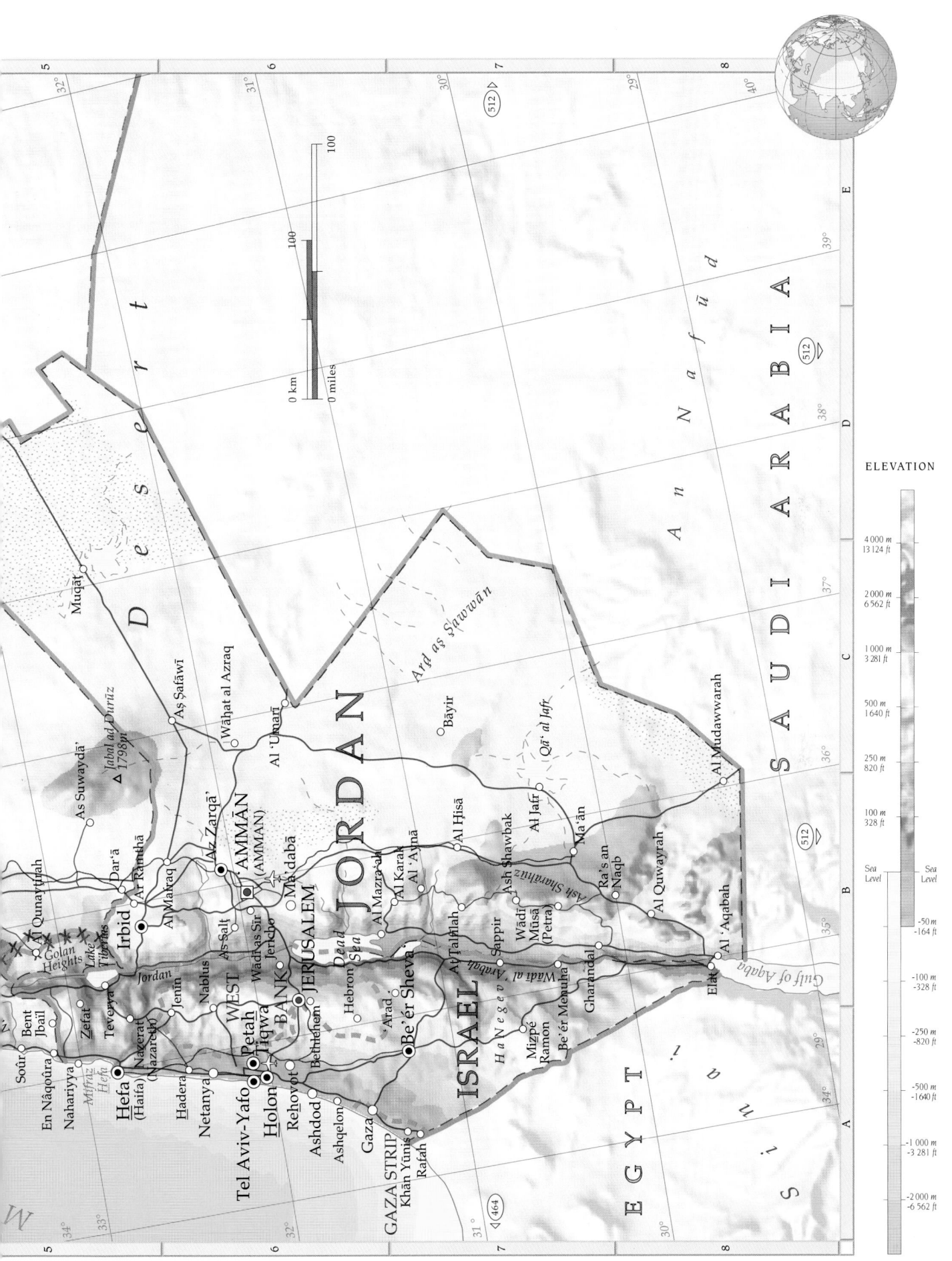

ELEVATION

4 000 m	13 124 ft
2 000 m	6 562 ft
1 000 m	3 281 ft
500 m	1 640 ft
250 m	820 ft
100 m	328 ft
Sea Level	Sea Level
-50 m	-164 ft
-100 m	-328 ft
-250 m	-820 ft
-500 m	-1 640 ft
-1 000 m	-3 281 ft
-2 000 m	-6 562 ft

100

100

0 km

0 miles

512 ▷

512 ▽

512 ▽

464 ◁

S A U D I   A R A B I A

A n   N a f ū d

Ard aṣ Ṣawwān

A n

J O R D A N

I S R A E L

E G Y P T

D e s e r t

Golan Heights

WEST BANK

GAZA STRIP

Gulf of Aqaba

Dead Sea

Lake Tiberias

Jordan

Wādī al ‘Arabah

HaNegev

Ash Sharāh

Al Mudawwarah

Al Jafr

Qa‘ al Jafr

Bāyir

Ma‘ān

Al Ḥisā

Al ‘Aynā

Al Karak

Al Mazra‘ah

Ma‘dabā

(AMMAN)
AMMĀN

Az Zarqā’

Al ‘Umarī

Wāḥat al Azraq

Aṣ Ṣafāwī

Al Mafraq

Ar Ramthā

As Suwaydā’

△ Jabal ad Durūz 1798m

Muqaṭ

Dar‘ā

Irbid

Qunayṭrah

Bent Jbail

En Nâqoûra

Nahariyya

Zefat

Nazerat (Nazareth)

Teverya

Jenin

Nablus

As Salt

Jericho

Wādī as Sir

JERUSALEM

Bethlehem

Hebron

Arad

Be’ér Sheva‘

At Tafīlah

Sappir

Wādī Mūsā (Petra)

Ash Shawbak

Ra’s an Naqb

Al Quwayrah

Al ‘Aqabah

Elat

Gharandal

Be’ér Menuḥa

Mizpé Ramon

Ashqelon

Ashdod

Rehovot

Holon

Petaḥ Tiqwa

Tel Aviv-Yafo

Hefa (Haifa)

Miffaẓ Hefa

Hadera

Netanya

Khân Yûnis

Rafaḥ

Gaza

Soûr

THE MIDDLE EAST

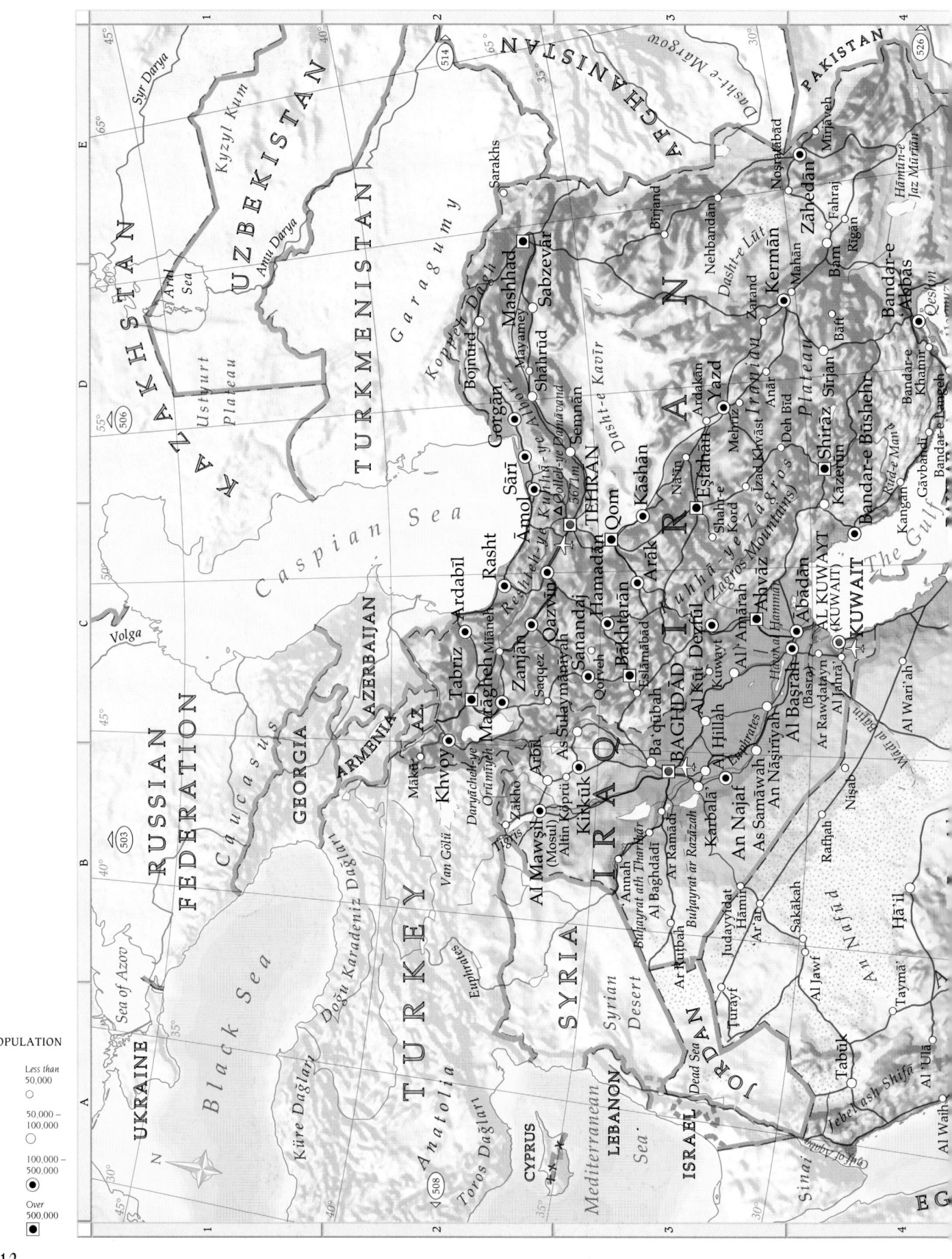

POPULATION

Less than
50,000
○

50,000 –
100,000
○

100,000 –
500,000
◉

Over
500,000
◉

UKRAINE

RUSSIAN FEDERATION

KAZAKHSTAN

UZBEKISTAN

TURKMENISTAN

GEORGIA

ARMENIA

AZERBAIJAN

AZ

TURKEY

SYRIA

LEBANON

CYPRUS

ISRAEL

JORDAN

IRAQ

I R A N

KUWAIT

AFGHANISTAN

PAKISTAN

EG

Syr Darya

Kyzyl Kum

Amu Darya

Aral Sea

Ustyurt Plateau

Caspian Sea

Garagumy

Koppeh Dāgh

Volga

Black Sea

Sea of Azov

Caucasus

Doğu Karadeniz Dağları

Küre Dağları

Anatolia

Toros Dağları

Van Gölü

Euphrates

Tigris

Mediterranean Sea

Dead Sea

Syrian Desert

An Nafūd

Jebel ash Shifā'

Gulf of Aqaba

Sinai

Dasht-e Margow

Dasht-e Lūt

Dasht-e Kavīr

Iranian Plateau

Zāgros (Zāgros Mountains)

Rūd-e Mand

Qaʿen

The Gulf

Wādi al Bāţin

Mashhad

Sabzevār

Shāhrūd

Mayamey

Semnān

Bojnūrd

Gorgān

Sārī

Āmol

Rasht

Ardabīl

Tabrīz

Marāgheh

Mīāneh

Zanjān

Qazvīn

Qollel-ye Damāvand 5671 m

Reẕvānshahr

TEHRAN

Qom

Kashān

Nāʾīn

Eşfahān

Shahr-e Kord

Ardakān

Yazd

Mehrīz

Anār

Deh Bid

Shīrāz

Sīrjān

Kāzerūn

Bandar-e Būshehr

Kangān

Gāvbandī

Bandar-e Kangān

Bandar-e Lengeh

Bandar-e Khamīr

Bandar-e ʿAbbās

Qeshm

Baft

Bam

Kermān

Zarand

Māhān

Rīgān

Fahraj

Hāmūn-e Jaz Mūrīān

Zāhedān

Mīrjāveh

Nosratābād

Nehbandān

Bīrjand

Sarakhs

Saqqez

Sanandaj

Qorveh

Hamadān

Islāmābād

Bākhtarān

Arāk

Khvoy

Mākū

Orūmīyeh

Daryācheh-ye Orūmīyeh

Zākho

Al Mawşil (Mosul)

Arbīl

Kirkūk

Altin Köprü

As Sulaymānīyah

Annah

Ḥadīthah

Buḥayrat ath Tharthār

Al Baghdādī

Ar Ramādī

Baʿqūbah

BAGHDAD

Al Kūt

Al Hillah

Buḥayrat ar Razāzah

Karbalāʾ

An Najaf

As Samāwah

An Nāşirīyah

Ar Kubah

Judayyidat Ḥāmir

Arʿar

Sakākah

Rafḥah

Nişāb

Hāʾil

Al Wari'ah

Al Jawf

Taymāʾ

Tabūk

Turayf

Al ʿUlā

Al Waih

Dezfūl

Shūsh

Al ʿAmārah

Ahvāz

Ḥawr al Ḥammār

Abādān

Al Başrah (Basra)

Al Jahrā

Ar Rawdatayn

AL KUWAYT (KUWAIT)

Kuwayt

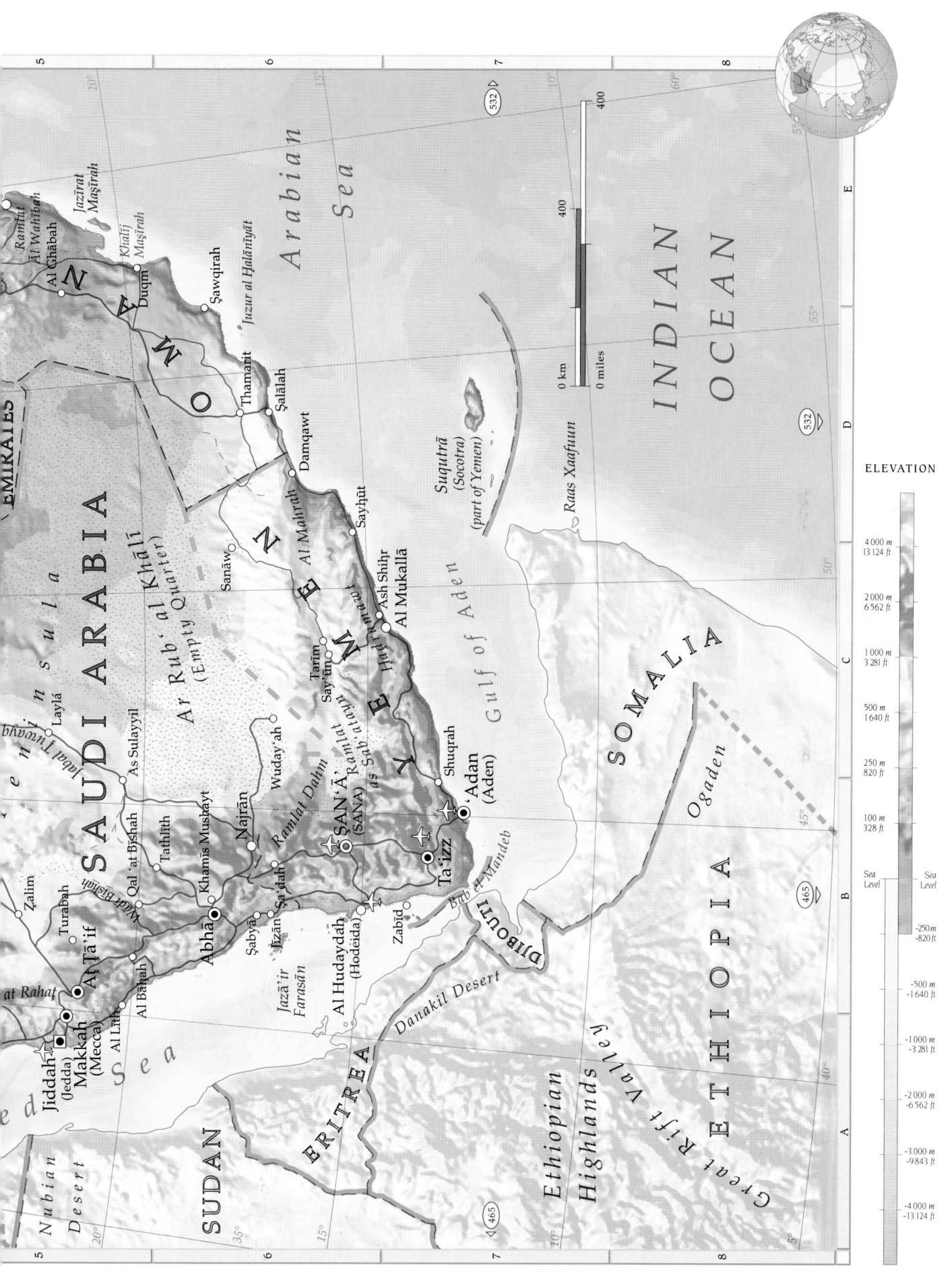

INDIAN

OCEAN

Arabian

Sea

Red Sea

ELEVATION

4 000 m	13 124 ft
2 000 m	6 562 ft
1 000 m	3 281 ft
500 m	1 640 ft
250 m	820 ft
100 m	328 ft
Sea Level	Sea Level
-250 m	-820 ft
-500 m	-1 640 ft
-1 000 m	-3 281 ft
-2 000 m	-6 562 ft
-3 000 m	-9 843 ft
-4 000 m	-13 124 ft

EMIRATES

SAUDI ARABIA

Arabian Peninsula

Ar Rub' al Khālī
(Empty Quarter)

O M A N

Y E M E N

Jabal Tuwayq

Najd

Ramlat Dahm

Ramlat as Sab'atayn

Hadramawt

Al Mahrah

Gulf of Aden

Suquṭrā
(Socotra)
(part of Yemen)

Raas Xaafuun

SOMALIA

Ogaden

DJIBOUTI

ERITREA

ETHIOPIA

Ethiopian Highlands

Great Rift Valley

Danakil Desert

SUDAN

Nubian Desert

Bāb el Mandeb

Ramītt
Al Wahībah
Al Ghābah
Jazīrat Maṣīrah
Khalīj Maṣīrah
Al Khābah
Duqm
Ṣawqirah
Thamarīt
Ṣalālah
Damqawt
Sayḥūt
Ash Shiḥr
Al Mukallā
Sanāw
Tarīm
Say'ūn
Shuqrah
'Adan (Aden)
SAN'Ā' (SANA)
Ta'izz
Zabīd
Al Hudaydah (Hodeida)
Jazā'ir Farasān
Jīzān
Ṣabyā
Sa'dah
Khamīs Mushayṭ
Najrān
Abhā
Tathlīth
Qal 'at Bīshah
Wādī Bīshah
Al Bāḥah
Al Līth
Turabah
Aṭ Ṭā'if
Zalim
at Raḥaṭ
Jiddah (Jedda)
Makkah (Mecca)
Wuday'ah
As Sulayyil
Laylā

0 km   400

0 miles   400

532

465

513

CENTRAL ASIA

GEORGIA

*Caspian
Sea*

AZERBAIJAN

*Ustyurt
Plateau*

*Aral
Sea*

o w l a n

Mŭynoq

Chimboy

Takhtakŭpir

Kёneurgench

Takhiatosh

Nukus

K y z

Gubadag

Uch

Il'yaly

Urganch

UZB

Dashkhovuz

Türtkŭl

Khiwa

Gaz-Achak

Lebap

Zar

T u r a n

Plato Kaplangky

Peski Uchtagan

Darvaza

*Zaunguzskiye
Garagumy*

Amu Darya

Turkmenbashi

*Krasnovodskiy
Zaliv*

Cheleken

Nebitdag

Gazandzhyk

TURKMENISTAN

G

Buk

*Turkmenskiy
Zaliv*

Gyzylarbat

Kara-Kala

Kopetdag Gershi

Bakharden

G a r a g u m y

Seydi

Deynau

Chardzhev

Geok-Tepe

Byuzmeyin

*Gora Chapan
2889m*

ASHGABAT

Say

Garagu

Tedzhen

Mary

Bayramaly

Kaakhka

Murgab

Murgab

Vozvyshe

Serakhs

Karal

Reshteh-ye Kŭhhā-ye Alborz

Bālā Morghāb

Gushgy

Towraghoudī

Daryā-y

Selseleh-ye Safid Ki

Ghūriān

Herāt

AFGHA

K ŭ h h ā - y e   Z ā g r o s

Shīndand

I R A N

Iranian

Farāh

Farāh Rŭd

Delārā

Dasht-e Khāsh

Plateau

*Hāmūn-e
Şāberī*

Lashkar Gāh

Chakhānsūr

Zaranj

Dasht-e Mārgow

K

Deh Shū

Daryā-ye Helmand

Chāgai H

0 km   200

0 miles   200

514

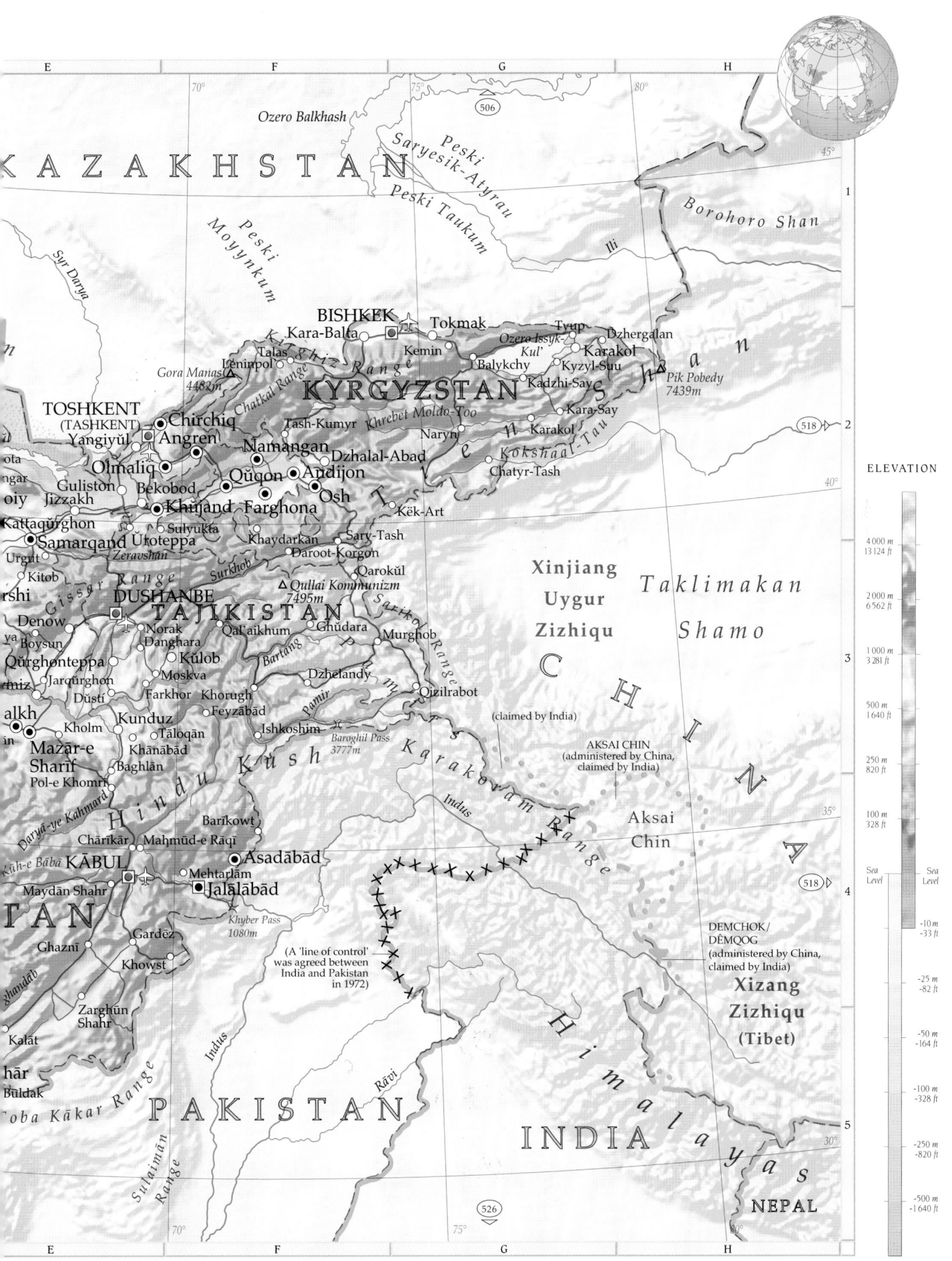

KAZAKHSTAN

Ozero Balkhash

Peski *Moyynkum*

Saryesik-Atyrau

Peski *Peski Taukum*

506

Ili

Borohoro Shan

BISHKEK
Kara-Balta • Tokmak
Kemin ○ Tyup ○ Dzhergalan
Talas ○ *Ozero Issyk-* Karakol
Leninpol ○ *Kul'* Kyzyl-Suu
Kadzhi-Say ○ Balykchy
△ *Gora Manasi*
4482m

Kirghiz Range

Chatkal Range

KYRGYZSTAN

Khrebet Moldo-Too ○ Kara-Say
Tash-Kumyr ○ Naryn ○ Karakol
Pik Pobedy
7439m

Kokshaal-Tau

Dzhalal-Abad
Andijon
Namangan ○ Osh
Qŭqon ● Chatyr-Tash
Farghona ○ Kék-Art

TOSHKENT
(TASHKENT)
Chirchiq
Yangiyŭl ● Angren
Olmaliq ○ Bekobod
Guliston ○ Khŭjand
Jizzakh
Kattaqŭrghon ○ Sulyukta ○ Uroteppa
Samarqand ○ Khaydarkan ○ Sary-Tash
Urgut *Zeravshan* Daroot-Korgon
Kitob
△ *Qullai Kommunizm*
7495m

Xinjiang
Uygur
Zizhiqu

Taklimakan
Shamo

DUSHANBE
TAJIKISTAN
Norak ○ Qal'aikhum ○ Ghŭdara
Danghara ○ Murghob
Kŭlob ○ Dzhelandy
Moskva *Bartang*
Farkhor ○ Khorugh ○ Qizilrabot
Feyzābād ○ Ishkoshim

Gissar Range

Surkhob

Sarikol Range

Pamir

C H I N A

Denow
Boysun
Qŭrghonteppa
Jarqŭrghon ○ Dŭsti

Kunduz ○ Tāloqān
Kholm ○ Khānābād
Baghlān
Pol-e Khomrī

Hindu Kush

Baroghil Pass
3777m

(claimed by India)

AKSAI CHIN
(administered by China,
claimed by India)

Mazār-e
Sharīf

Darya-ye Kahmard

Karakoram Range

Indus

Aksai
Chin

518

Chārīkār ○ Mahmūd-e Rāqi
Barīkowt
Asadābād
Mehtarlām
KĀBUL ○ Jalālābād
Maydān Shahr

Kŭh-e Bābā

Khyber Pass
1080m

(A 'line of control'
was agreed between
India and Pakistan
in 1972)

DEMCHOK/
DÊMQOG
(administered by China,
claimed by India)

Xizang
Zizhiqu
(Tibet)

Ghaznī
Gardēz
Khowst

Zarghūn
Shahr

Kalāt

Indus

Rāvi

Himalayas

-hāndāb
Buldak

Toba Kākar Range

PAKISTAN

Sulaimān Range

INDIA

526

NEPAL

ELEVATION

4 000 m	13 124 ft
2 000 m	6 562 ft
1 000 m	3 281 ft
500 m	1 640 ft
250 m	820 ft
100 m	328 ft
Sea Level	Sea Level
-10 m	-33 ft
-25 m	-82 ft
-50 m	-164 ft
-100 m	-328 ft
-250 m	-820 ft
-500 m	-1 640 ft

SOUTH AND EAST ASIA

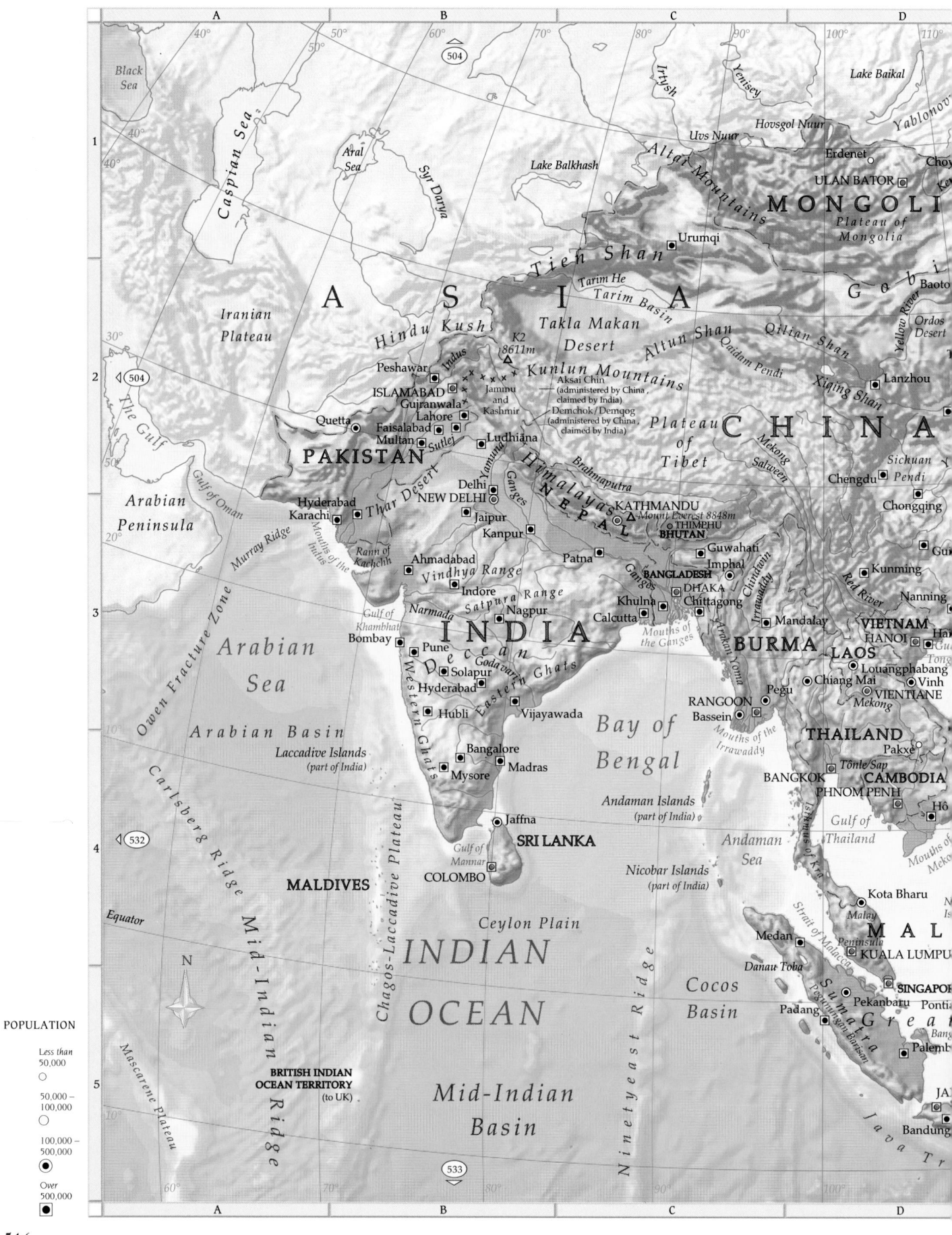

POPULATION

Less than
50,000
○

50,000 –
100,000
○

100,000 –
500,000
◉

Over
500,000
◼

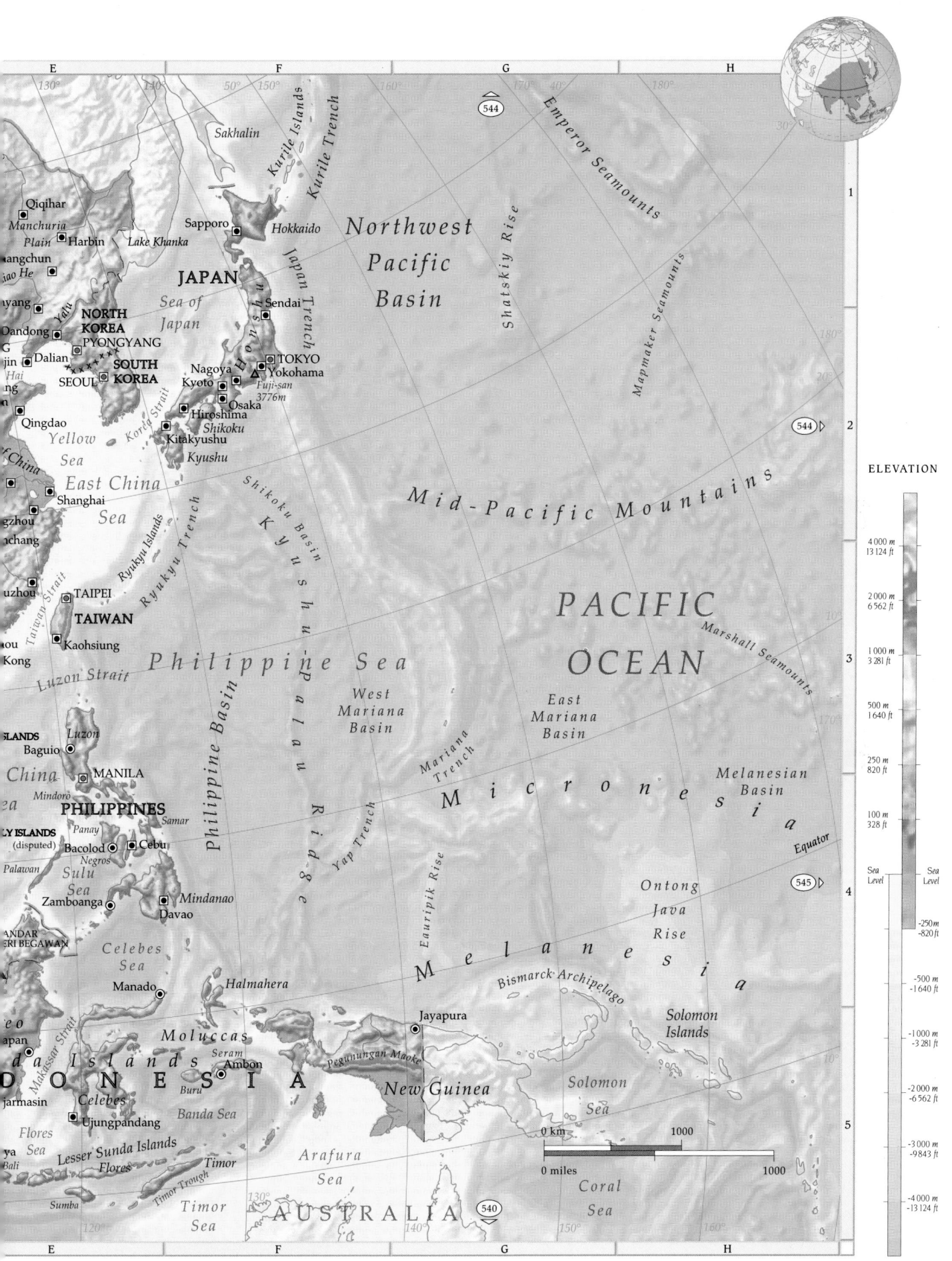

Qiqihar
Manchuria
Plain
Harbin
Lake Khanka
angchun
iao He
yang
NORTH
KOREA
Dandong
PYONGYANG
G
Dalian
ng
SOUTH
Qingdao
SEOUL
KOREA

Sakhalin

Kurile Islands
Kurile Trench

Sapporo
Hokkaido

JAPAN

Sea of
Japan

Sendai

Honshu

Japan Trench

TOKYO
Nagoya
Yokohama
Kyoto
Fuji-san
3776m
Osaka
Hiroshima
Shikoku
Kitakyushu
Kyushu

Northwest
Pacific
Basin

Shatskiy Rise

Emperor Seamounts

Mapmaker Seamounts

544

544

1

180°

2

ELEVATION

Yellow
Sea

Korea Strait

East China
Shanghai
Sea

gzhou
nchang

uzhou

Mid-Pacific Mountains

Shikoku Basin

Kyushu

Ryukyu Islands

Ryukyu Trench

Taiwan Strait

TAIPEI

TAIWAN

Kaohsiung

Hong Kong

Luzon Strait

Philippine Sea

Philippine Basin

Kyushu-Palau Ridge

West
Mariana
Basin

East
Mariana
Basin

Mariana
Trench

PACIFIC
OCEAN

Marshall Seamounts

Melanesian
Basin

4 000 m
13 124 ft

2 000 m
6 562 ft

1 000 m
3 281 ft

500 m
1 640 ft

250 m
820 ft

100 m
328 ft

Sea
Level

Sea
Level

10°

ISLANDS
Luzon
Baguio

China

Mindoro

PHILIPPINES
Panay

LY ISLANDS
(disputed)
Bacolod
Cebu
Palawan
Negros
Samar

Sulu
Sea
Zamboanga
Mindanao
Davao

Celebes
Sea

Manado

eo
apan

da Islands

DONESIA
jarmasin

Flores
ya
Sea

Sumba

Makassar Strait

Moluccas
Seram
Ambon
Buru

Celebes

Ujungpandang

Banda Sea

Lesser Sunda Islands
Flores
Timor

Halmahera

Pegunungan Maoke

New Guinea

Arafura
Sea

Timor
Sea

Micronesia

Euripik Rise

Yap Trench

Melanesia

Bismarck Archipelago

Jayapura

Solomon
Sea

Solomon
Islands

Ontong
Java
Rise

Equator

545

4

–250m
–820 ft

–500 m
–1 640 ft

–1 000 m
–3 281 ft

–2 000 m
–6 562 ft

–3 000 m
–9 843 ft

–4 000 m
–13 124 ft

5

0 km   1000

0 miles   1000

Coral
Sea

AUSTRALIA

540

WESTERN CHINA AND MONGOLIA

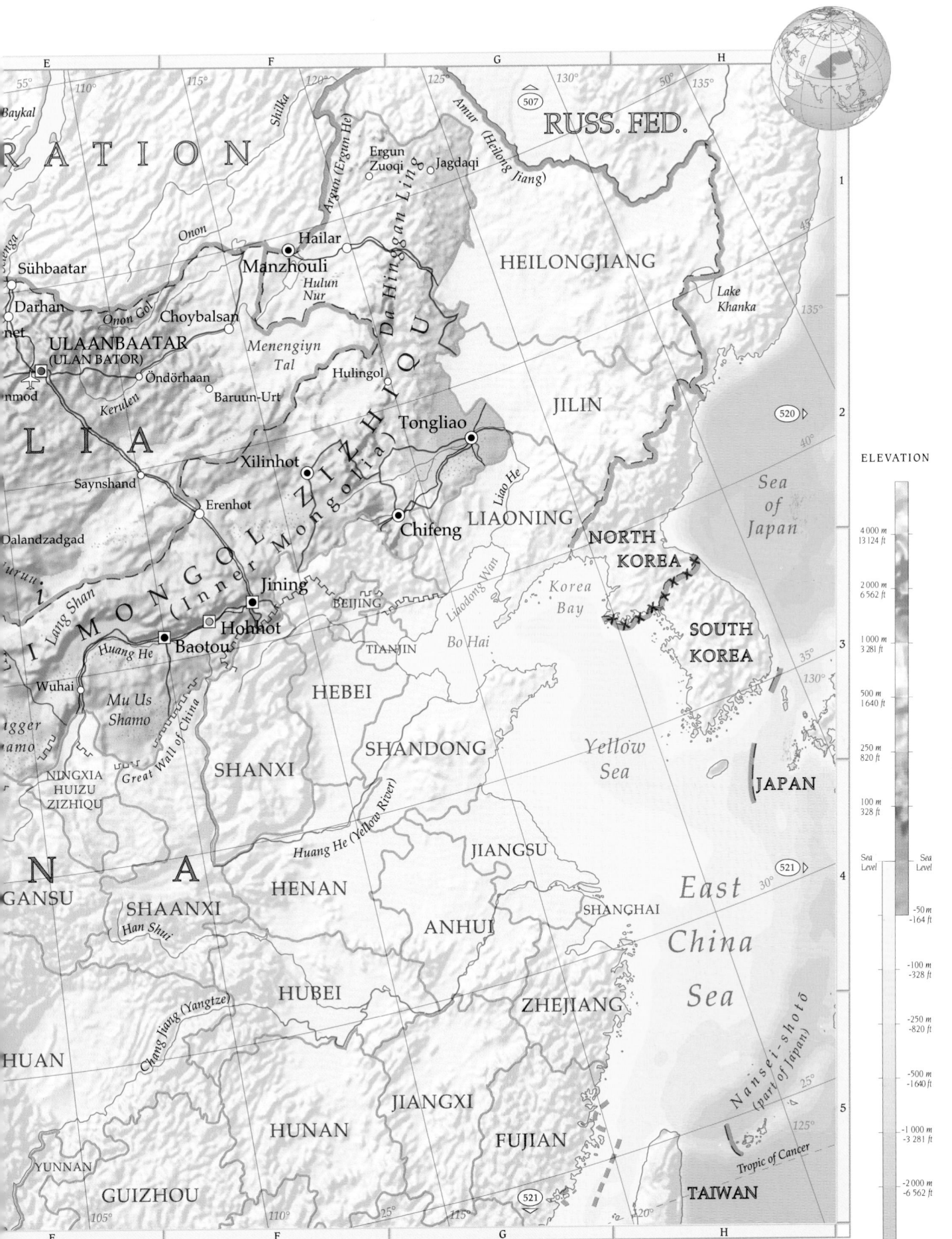

RUSS. FED.

Baykal

R A T I O N

Shitka

Amur (Heilong Jiang)

Ergun
Zuoqi   Jagdaqi

HEILONGJIANG

Lake
Khanka

Onon

Hailar

Manzhouli

Argun (Ergun He)

*Hulun
Nur*

Sühbaatar

Darhan

net

ULAANBAATAR
(ULAN BATOR)

Onon Gol

Choybalsan

*Menengiyn
Tal*

Da Hinggan Ling

JILIN

Öndörhaan

Kerulen

Baruun-Urt

Hulingol

nmod

L I A

iguruu

Saynshand

Dalandzadgad

N E I   M O N G O L   Z I Z H I Q U
(Inner Mongolia)

Xilinhot

Tongliao

Liao He

Erenhot

Chifeng

LIAONING

NORTH
KOREA

Sea
of
Japan

Gang Shan

Jining

Hohhot

Lihodong Wan

BEIJING

Korea
Bay

SOUTH
KOREA

Wuhai

Huang He

Baotou

*Mu Us
Shamo*

TIANJIN

Bo Hai

Great Wall of China

HEBEI

gger

amo

NINGXIA
HUIZU
ZIZHIQU

SHANXI

SHANDONG

*Yellow
Sea*

JAPAN

N   A

HUAN

GANSU

SHAANXI

HENAN

Han Shui

Huang He (Yellow River)

JIANGSU

East

SHANGHAI

ANHUI

China

HUBEI

Chang Jiang (Yangtze)

ZHEJIANG

Sea

*Nansei-shotō
(part of Japan)*

HUAN

JIANGXI

HUNAN

FUJIAN

Tropic of Cancer

YUNNAN

GUIZHOU

TAIWAN

ELEVATION

4 000 m
13 124 ft

2 000 m
6 562 ft

1 000 m
3 281 ft

500 m
1 640 ft

250 m
820 ft

100 m
328 ft

Sea
Level

Sea
Level

-50 m
-164 ft

-100 m
-328 ft

-250 m
-820 ft

-500 m
-1 640 ft

-1 000 m
-3 281 ft

-2 000 m
-6 562 ft

EASTERN CHINA AND KOREA

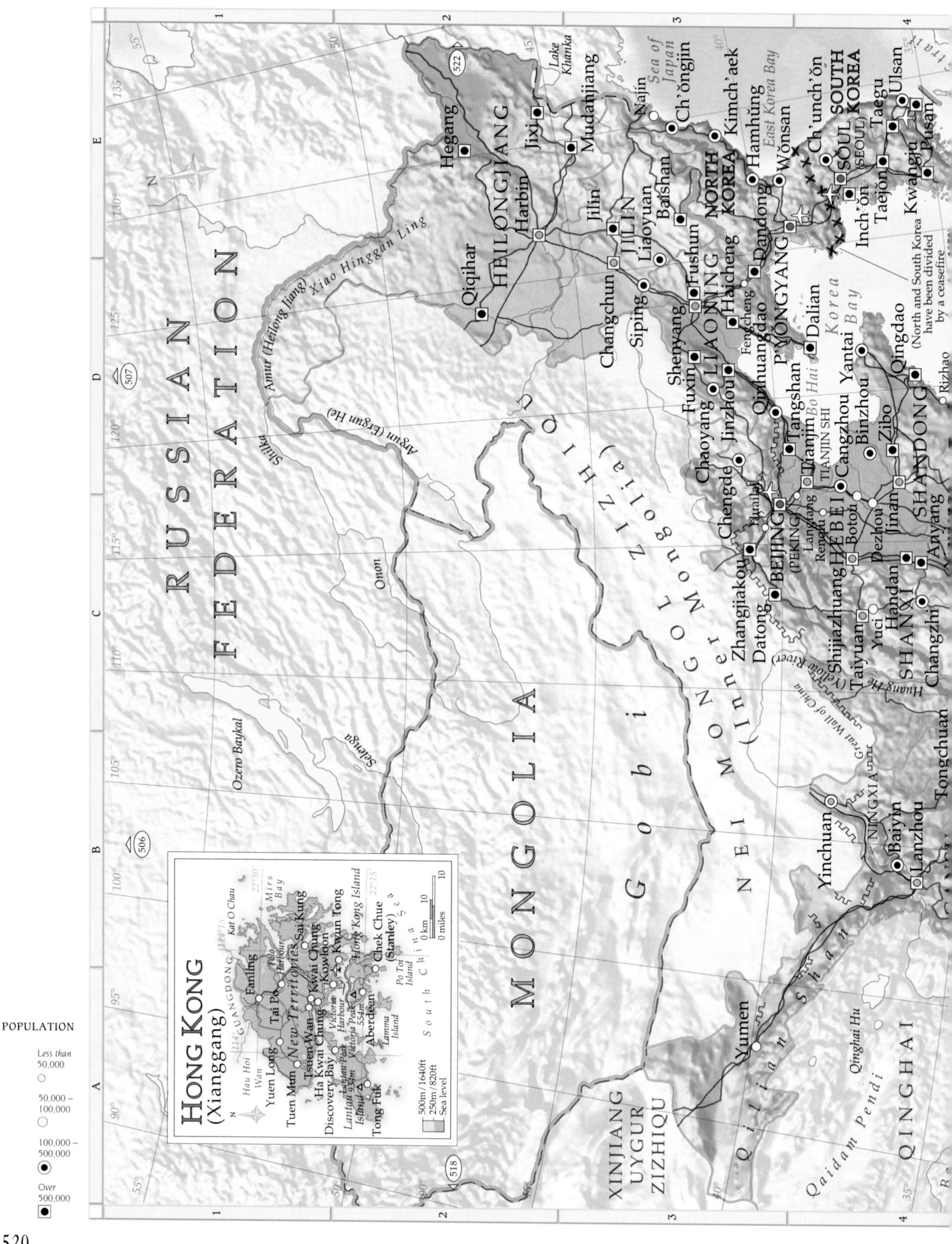

RUSSIAN FEDERATION

MONGOLIA

NEI MONGOL (Inner Mongolia)

Gobi

Ozero Baykal

Selenga

Onon

Xiao Hinggan Ling

Amur (Heilong Jiang)

Argun (Ergun He)

Shilka

HEILONGJIANG

Hegang

Jixi

Mudanjiang

Lake Khanka

Sea of Japan

Qiqihar

Harbin

Changchun

Jilin

JILIN

Siping

Liaoyuan

Baishan

Fushun

Shenyang

Fuxin

LIAONING

Jinzhou

Haicheng

Dandong

Fengcheng

Chaoyang

Chengde

Huailai

Zhangjiakou

Datong

BEIJING (PEKING)

Langfang

Tangshan

Tianjin (TIANJIN SHI)

Bo Hai

Qinhuangdao

HEBEI

Renqiu

Botou

Dezhou

SHANXI

Taiyuan

Yuci

Handan

Changzhi

Shijiazhuang

Anyang

SHANDONG

Jinan

Zibo

Binzhou

Cangzhou

Yantai

Qingzhou

Qingdao

Rizhao

NINGXIA

Yinchuan

Baiyin

Lanzhou

Changzhou

Tongchuan

QINGHAI

Qinghai Hu

Qaidam Pendi

Qilian Shan

Yumen

XINJIANG UYGUR ZIZHIQU

Great Wall of China

Huang He (Yellow River)

Najin

Ch'ŏngjin

Kimch'aek

Hamhŭng

Wŏnsan

East Korea Bay

NORTH KOREA

PYONGYANG

Dalian

Korea Bay

Korea Strait

Ch'unch'ŏn

SŎUL (SEOUL)

SOUTH KOREA

Inch'ŏn

Taejŏn

Kwangju

Taegu

Ulsan

Pusan

(North and South Korea
have been divided
by a ceasefire)

East China Sea

HONG KONG (Xianggang)

Hau Hoi Wan

GUANGDONG

Kat O Chau

Mirs Bay

Sai Kung

Fanling

Tolo Harbour

Yuen Long

Tai Po

New Territories

Kwai Chung

Tuen Mun

Tsuen Wan

Ha Kwai Chung

Kowloon

Kwun Tong

Discovery Bay

Lantau Island 934m

Victoria Harbour

Victoria Peak 554m

Aberdeen

Chek Chue (Stanley)

Hong Kong Island

Po Toi Island

Lamma Island

Tong Fuk

South China Sea

500m/1640ft
250m/820ft
Sea level

10

0 km   10

0 miles 10

POPULATION

Less than
50,000

50,000 –
100,000

100,000 –
500,000

Over
500,000

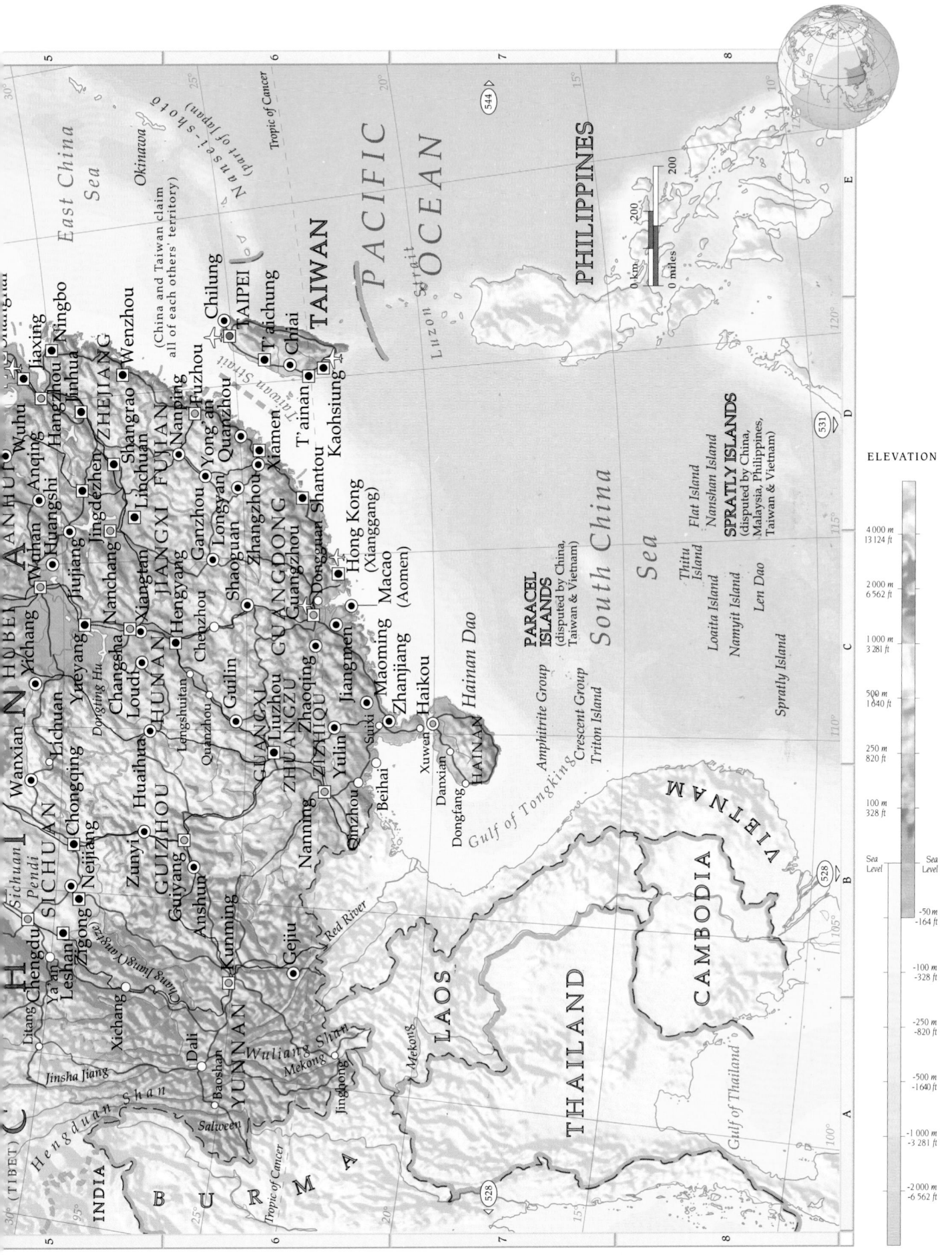

PACIFIC

OCEAN

East China
Sea

Okinawa

(China and Taiwan claim
all of each others' territory)

Nansei-shotō
(Ryukyu)

Tropic of Cancer

PHILIPPINES

Luzon Strait

0 km 200
0 miles 200

544

531

ELEVATION

TAIWAN

Chilung
TAIPEI
T'aichung
T'aichai
T'ainan
Kaohsiung

Taiwan Strait

Shanghai
Jiaxing
Ningbo
Wuhu
Hangzhou
Wenzhou
Anqing
ZHEJIANG
Jinhua
Huangshi
Shangrao
Jingdezhen
Lichuan
Fuzhou
Nanping
FUJIAN
Quanzhou
Yong'an
Xiamen
Quanzhou
Shantou

South China

Sea

SPRATLY ISLANDS
(disputed by China,
Malaysia, Philippines,
Taiwan & Vietnam)

Thitu
Island
Flat Island
Nanshan Island

Loaita Island
Namyit Island
Len Dao

Spratly Island

4 000 m
13 124 ft

2 000 m
6 562 ft

1 000 m
3 281 ft

ANHUI
Wuhan
HUBEI
Yichang
Huaihua
Jiujiang
Nanchang
Xiangtan
JIANGXI
Ganzhou
Longyan
Zhangzhou
GUANGDONG
Shaoguan
Guangzhou
Hong Kong
(Xianggang)
Macao
(Aomen)

PARACEL
ISLANDS
(disputed by China,
Taiwan & Vietnam)

500 m
1640 ft

250 m
820 ft

CHINA
Wanxian
Lichuan
SICHUAN
Chongqing
Neijiang
Zigong
Zunyi
GUIZHOU
Guiyang
Anshun
Kunming
Gejiu
YUNNAN

Changsha
HUNAN
Loudi
Hengyang
Chenzhou
Quanzhou
Guilin
GUANGXI
Liuzhou
ZHUANGZU
Nanning
Yulin
Qinzhou
Beihai

Jiangmen
Maoming
Zhanjiang
Zhaoqing
Suixi
Haikou
Xuwen
Danxian
Dongfang
HAINAN
Hainan Dao

Amphitrite Group
Crescent Group
Triton Island

100 m
328 ft

Sea
Level

Sea
Level

-50 m
-164 ft

Sichuan
Pendi
Chengdu
Litang
Ya'an
Leshan
Xichang
Baoshan
Dali
Jindong
Wuliang Shan
Mekong

Red River
Jinsha Jiang
Salween

Hengduan Shan

(TIBET)
INDIA

BURMA

Tropic of Cancer

LAOS

Mekong

THAILAND

Gulf of Tongking

Gulf of Thailand

VIETNAM

CAMBODIA

528

528

-100 m
-328 ft

-250 m
-820 ft

-500 m
-1640 ft

-1 000 m
-3 281 ft

-2 000 m
-6 562 ft

JAPAN

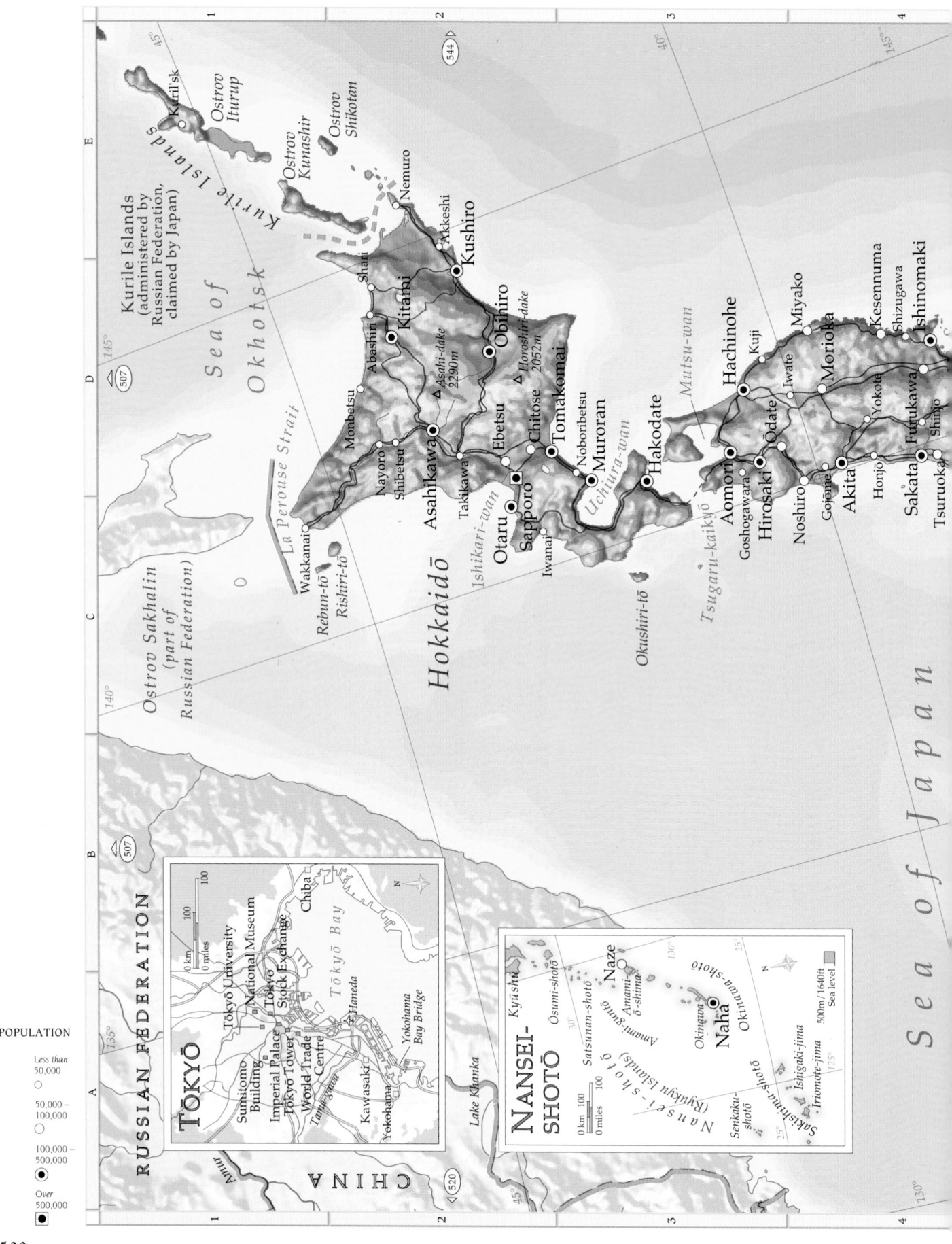

Kuril'sk

Ostrov Iturup

Ostrov Kunashir

Ostrov Shikotan

Kurile Islands (administered by Russian Federation, claimed by Japan)

Sea of Okhotsk

Nemuro

Akkeshi

Kushiro

Shari

Abashiri

Kitami

Obihiro

Horoshiri-dake 2052m

Mombetsu

△ *Asahi-dake 2290m*

Tomakomai

Noboribetsu

Muroran

Nayoro

Shibetsu

Ebetsu

Chitose

Takikawa

Asahikawa

Uchiura-wan

Hakodate

Mutsu-wan

Hachinohe

Kuji

Iwate

Miyako

Shizugawa

Kesennuma

Ishinomaki

Morioka

Odate

Yokote

Futukawa

Shinjō

Wakkanai

Rebun-tō

Rishiri-tō

Otaru

Sapporo

Iwanai

Hokkaidō

Ishikari-wan

Aomori

Goshogawara

Hirosaki

Noshiro

Gojōme

Akita

Honjō

Sakata

Tsuruoka

Oshima-tō

Oshushiri-tō

Tsugaru-kaikyō

La Perouse Strait

Ostrov Sakhalin (part of Russian Federation)

Sea of Japan

RUSSIAN FEDERATION

Amur

Lake Khanka

CHINA

TŌKYŌ

Chiba

Tōkyō Bay

Tokyo University

National Museum

Tōkyō

Stock Exchange

Sumitomo Building

Imperial Palace

Tōkyō Tower

World Trade Centre

Haneda

Yokohama

Bay Bridge

Tama-gawa

Kawasaki

Yokohama

0 km 100

0 miles

N

NANSEI-SHOTŌ

Kyūshū

Naze

Amami

ō-shima

Satsunan-shotō

Ōsumi-shotō

Amami-guntō

Naha

Okinawa

Okinawa-shotō

Nansei-shotō (Ryukyu Islands)

Ishigaki-jima

Iriomote-jima

Sakishima-shotō

Senkaku-shotō

500m/1640ft

Sea level

N

0 km 100

0 miles

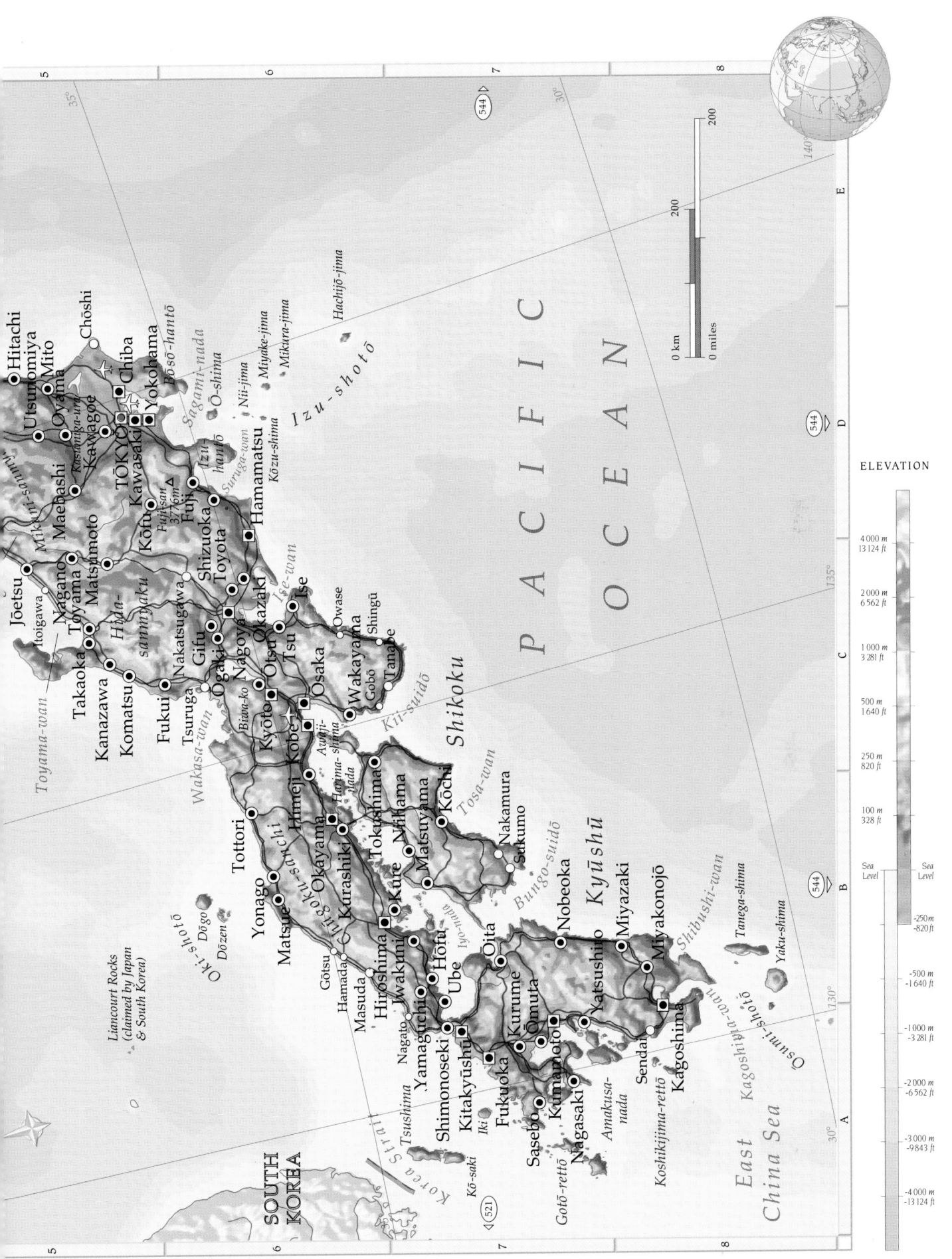

PACIFIC

OCEAN

Izu-shotō

Hitachi
Utsunomiya
Mito
Oyama
Chōshi
Chiba
Yokohama
Bōsō-hantō
Kawagoe
TOKYO
Kawasaki
Kasumiga-ura
Kōfu
Izu-hantō
Fuji
Fujisan 3776m △
Shizuoka
Hamamatsu
Toyota
Sagami-nada
Suruga-wan
Maebashi
Matsumoto
Nagano
Toyama
Matsumoto
Jōetsu
Itoigawa
Takaoka
Kanazawa
Komatsu
Fukui
Tsuruga
Gifu
Ogaki
Nagoya
Okazaki
Hida-sanmyaku
Nakatsugawa
Otsu
Tsu
Ise
Ise-wan
Owase
Shingū
Wakayama
Tanabe
Gobō
Kyōto
Kōbe
Ōsaka
Biwa-ko
Awaji-shima
Harima-nada
Himeji
Okayama
Kurashiki
Kure
Tokushima
Mihama
Matsuyama
Kōchi
Shikoku
Tosa-wan
Nakamura
Sukumo
Kii-suidō
Tottori
Yonago
Matsue
Chūgoku-sanchi
Gōtsu
Hamada
Masuda
Hiroshima
Iwakuni
Hōfu
Ube
Ōita
Yamaguchi
Shimonoseki
Kitakyūshū
Fukuoka
Sasebo
Nagasaki
Kumamoto
Ōmuta
Kurume
Yatsushiro
Sendai
Kagoshima
Miyakonojō
Miyazaki
Nobeoka
Kyūshū
Bungo-suidō
Iyo-nada
Suō-nada
Shibushi-wan
Tanega-shima
Yaku-shima
Kagoshima-wan
Ōsumi-shotō
Koshikijima-rettō
Amakusa-nada
Gotō-rettō
Kō-saki
Iki
Tsushima
Nagato
Korea Strait
Kō-saki
SOUTH
KOREA
*Liancourt Rocks
(claimed by Japan
& South Korea)*
Oki-shotō
Dōgo
Dōzen
Toyama-wan
Wakasa-wan
Mikuni-sanmyaku

544
544
544
521

E
D
C
B
A

5
6
7
8

35°
30°
30°
140°
135°
130°

East
China Sea

ELEVATION

4 000 m	13 124 ft
2 000 m	6 562 ft
1 000 m	3 281 ft
500 m	1 640 ft
250 m	820 ft
100 m	328 ft
Sea Level	Sea Level
-250 m	-820 ft
-500 m	-1 640 ft
-1 000 m	-3 281 ft
-2 000 m	-6 562 ft
-3 000 m	-9 843 ft
-4 000 m	-13 124 ft

200
200
0 km
0 miles

SOUTH INDIA AND SRI LANKA

Kalyān
Bombay (Mumbai)
Pune · Ahmadnagar
Bārāmati · Nizāmābād
Nānded
Andhra Pradesh
Karīmnagar
Jagdalp
INDIA
Solāpur
Sāngli
Kolhāpur
Gulbarga · Hyderābād
Secunderābād
Vizianagaran
Visākha
Rājahm
Kāki

Belgaum
Panaji (Goa)
Hubli
Deccan
Karnātaka
Rāichūr
Kurnool
Krishna
Vijayawāda
Machilīpat

Gadag
Nandyāl
Chīrala
Ongole
Kāvali

Tungabhadra Reservoir
Dāvangere
Tādpatri
Anantapur
Nellore

Shimoga
Bhadrāvati
Cuddapah

Udupi
Tumkūr

Mangalore
Bangalore
Vellore
Madras

Kāsaragod
Mandya
Krishnagiri
Tiruppattūr
Kānchīpuram

Cannanore
Mysore
Salem
Pondicherry

Calicut
Erode
Neyveli

Coimbatore
Tamil Nādu
Trichūr
Tiruchchirāppalli
Ernākulam
Dindigul
Cochin
Madurai
Palk Strait
Alleppey
Rājapālaiyām
Jaffna
Quilon
Mannar
SRI LAN
Tuticorin
Vavuniya
Trincomalee
Trivandrum
Nāgercoil
Puttalam
Anuradhapura

Gulf of Mannar
Batticale
Matale
Negombo
Kandy
COLOMBO
Sri Jayawardanap
Kalutara
Ratnapura
Galle
Matara

Arabian Sea

Amīndivi Islands
Malabār Coast
Lakshadweep
(Laccadive Islands)
(part of India)
Kavaratti Island
Kalpeni Island
Nine Degree Channel
Minicoy Island
Eight Degree Channel

Ihavandippolhu Atoll

MALDIVES

Faadhippolhu Atoll
Horsburgh Atoll
Ari Atoll
Male' Atoll
MALE'
Felidhu Atoll
Mulaku Atoll
Kolhumadulu Atoll
Hadhdhunmathi Atoll
North Huvadhu Atoll
South Huvadhu Atoll

Equator

Gan
Addu Atoll

INDIAN

Coromandel Coast

Godāvari

Western Ghats

Eastern Ghats

POPULATION

Less than
50,000
○

50,000 –
100,000
○

100,000 –
500,000
◉

Over
500,000
◉

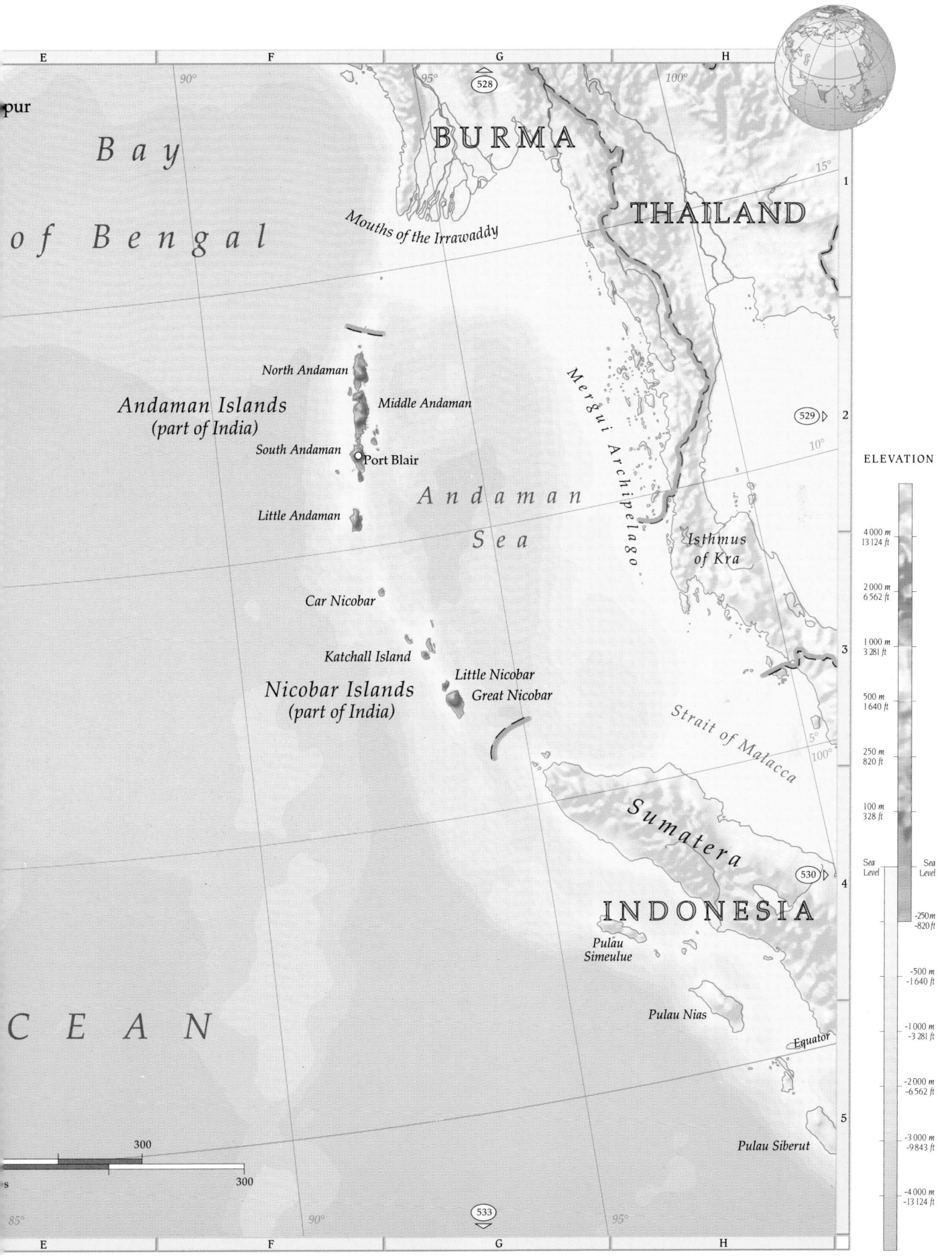

90°

95°

528

100°

15°

1

pur

Bay

of Bengal

BURMA

THAILAND

Mouths of the Irrawaddy

North Andaman

*Andaman Islands
(part of India)*

Middle Andaman

South Andaman

Port Blair

Merguí Archipelago

529

2

10°

Little Andaman

A n d a m a n

S e a

Car Nicobar

Katchall Island

*Nicobar Islands
(part of India)*

Little Nicobar

Great Nicobar

*Isthmus
of Kra*

ELEVATION

4 000 m
13 124 ft

2 000 m
6 562 ft

1 000 m
3 281 ft

3

500 m
1 640 ft

Strait of Malacca

5°

100°

250 m
820 ft

100 m
328 ft

S u m a t e r a

530

4

Sea
Level

Sea
Level

INDONESIA

-250 m
-820 ft

*Pulau
Simeulue*

-500 m
-1 640 ft

C E A N

Pulau Nias

Equator

-1 000 m
-3 281 ft

-2 000 m
-6 562 ft

5

-3 000 m
-9 843 ft

300

Pulau Siberut

300

-4 000 m
-13 124 ft

85°

90°

533

95°

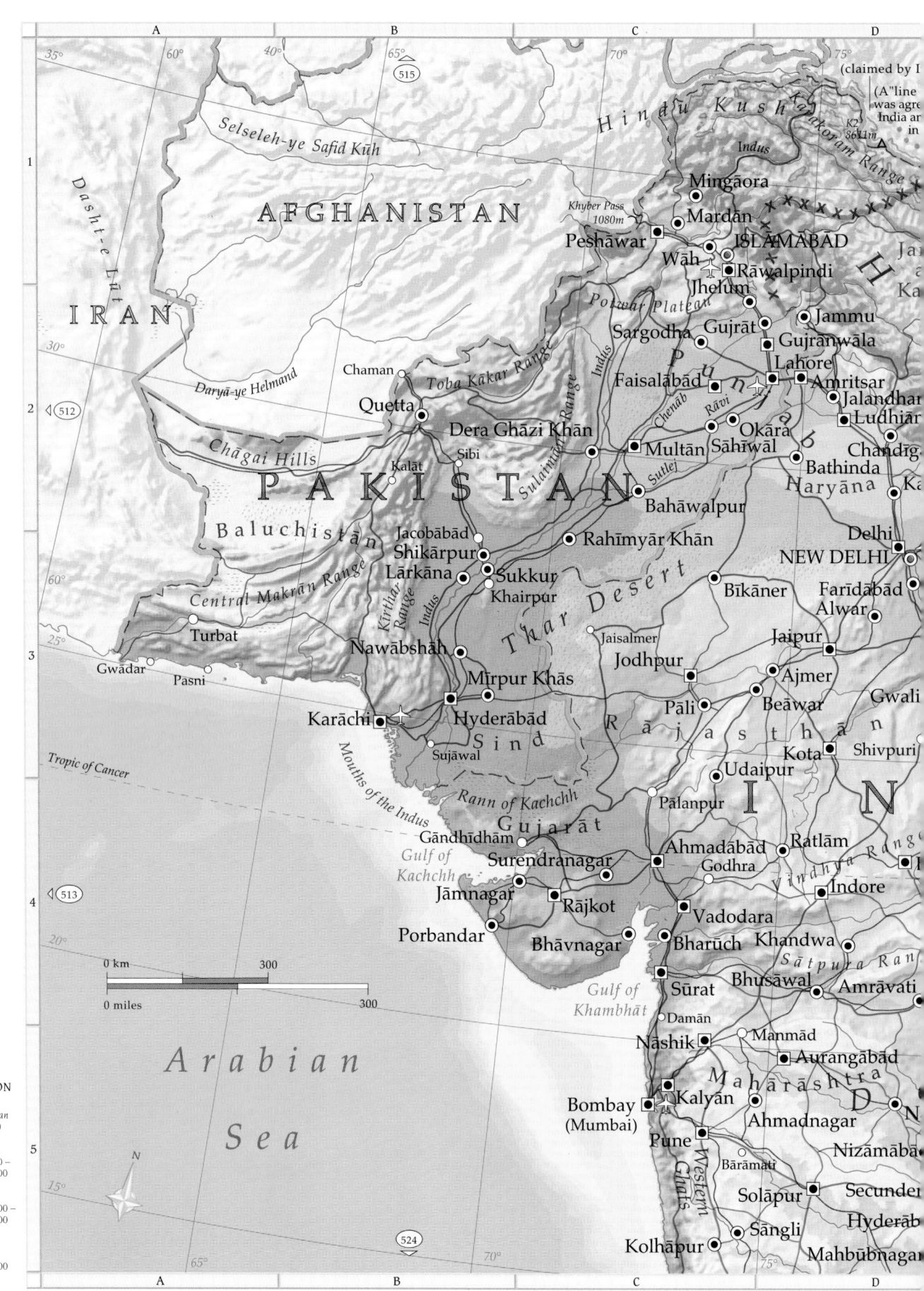

POPULATION

Less than
50,000
○

50,000 –
100,000
○

100,000 –
500,000
◉

Over
500,000
■

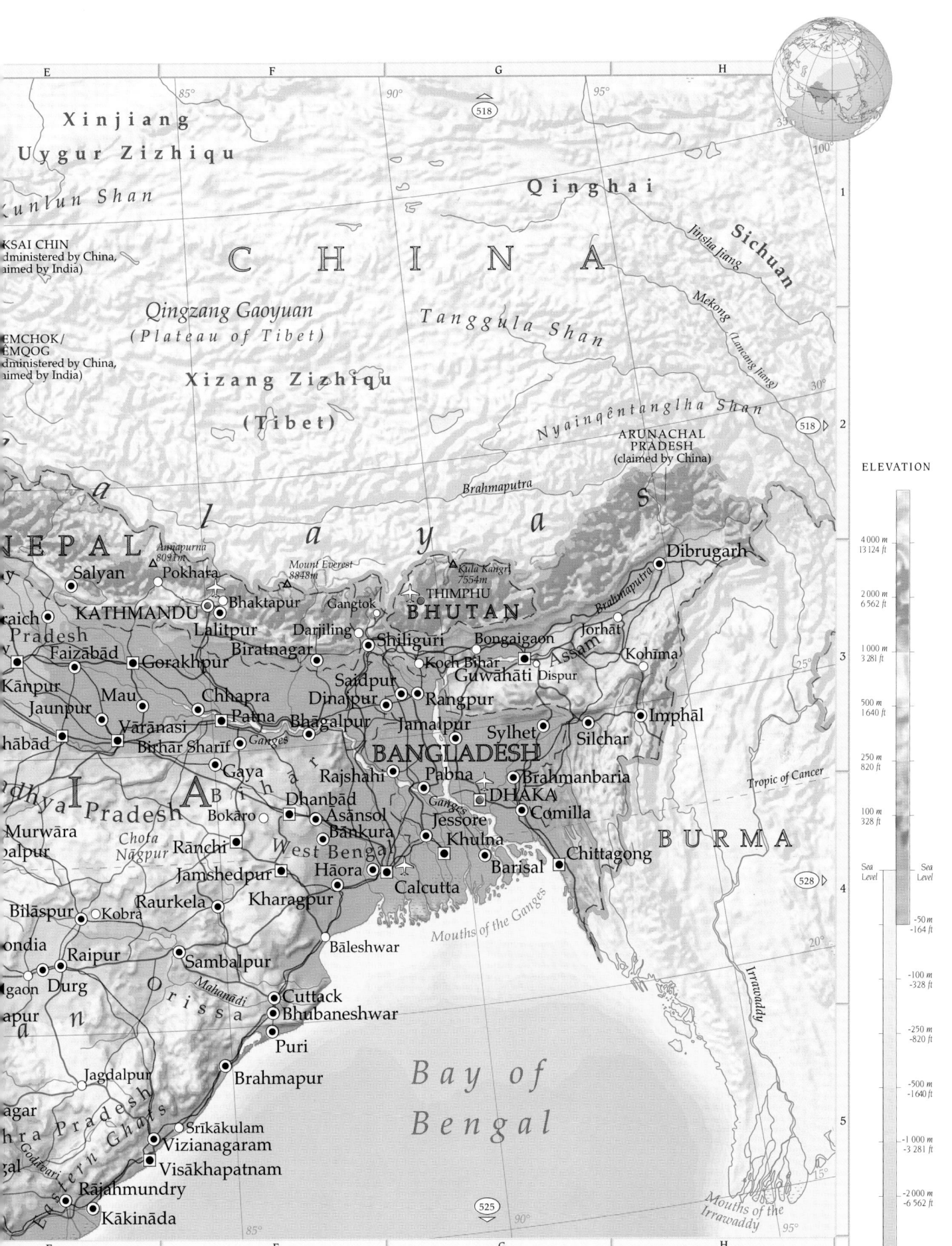

Xinjiang
Uygur Zizhiqu

Kunlun Shan

AKSAI CHIN
(administered by China,
claimed by India)

EMCHOK/
EMQOG
(administered by China,
claimed by India)

C H I N A

Qinghai

Sichuan

Jinsha Jiang

Mekong (Lancang Jiang)

Qingzang Gaoyuan
(Plateau of Tibet)

Tanggula Shan

Xizang Zizhiqu

(Tibet)

Nyainqêntanglha Shan

ARUNACHAL
PRADESH
(claimed by China)

Brahmaputra

NEPAL

Annapurna
8091m

Mount Everest
8848m

Kula Kangri
7554m

H   i   m   a   l   a   y   a   s

Dibrugarh

Brahmaputra

Salyan
Pokhara

KATHMANDU
Bhaktapur

Lalitpur

raich

Pradesh

Faizābād
Gorakhpur

Kānpur
Mau

Jaunpur
Varānasi

Birhar Sharīf

hābād

Darjiling

Gangtok

THIMPHU

BHUTAN

Biratnagar

Chhapra
Patna
Bhagalpur

Shiliguri

Koch Bihar

Saidpur
Dinajpur

Bongaigaon

Jorhat

Assam

Kohīma

Guwāhāti
Dispur

Rangpur

Jamalpur

Sylhet

Silchar

Imphāl

Ganges

BANGLADESH

Gaya

Rajshahi

Pabna

Brahmanbaria

Murwāra
lpur

Madhya
Pradesh

Bihar

Dhanbād
Bokāro

Ranchī

Bhāgalpur

Asānsol
Bankura

DHAKA

Comilla

Jessore

Ganges

Tropic of Cancer

B U R M A

Chota
Nāgpur

Jamshedpur

West Bengal

Khulna

Chittagong

Raurkela

Kharagpur

Hāora

Barisal

Calcutta

Bilāspur
Kobra

Raurkela

Bāleshwar

ondia

Raipur

Sambalpur

Mouths of the Ganges

Irrawaddy

gaon Durg

Orissa

Mahānadi

Cuttack

apur

a

n

Bhubaneshwar

Puri

Bay of

Jagdalpur

Brahmapur

Bengal

agar

Pradesh

Eastern Ghats

Srīkākulam

Vizianagaram

Visākhapatnam

Godāvari

Rājahmundry

Kākināda

Mouths of the
Irrawaddy

MAINLAND SOUTHEAST ASIA

POPULATION

Less than
50,000
○

50,000 –
100,000
○

100,000 –
500,000
◉

Over
500,000
◼

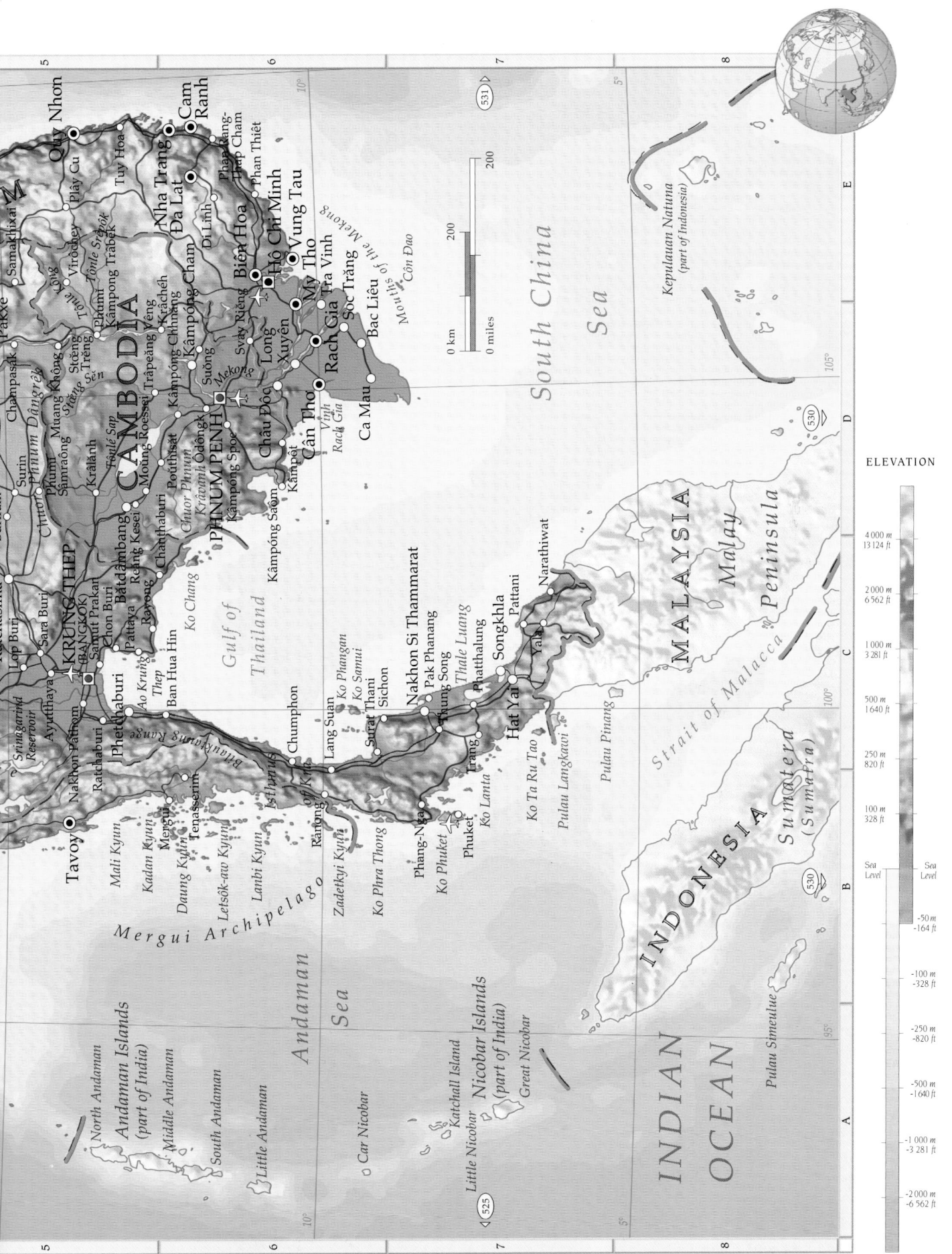

Quy Nhon
Play Cu
Samakhixai
Nha Trang
Cam Ranh
Tuy Hoa
Đà Lạt
Phan Rang-
Thap Cham
Phan Thiết
Virôchey
Tônle Sẽpôk
Di Linh
Pakxe
Champasak
Stœng Trêng
Plumm Dângrêk
Phtum
Kâmpóng Trabêk
Stœng Trêng
Kâmpóng Cham
Biên Hoa
Ho Chi Minh
Vung Tau
Surin
Muang Khong
Krâchéh
Kâmpóng Chhnang
Svay Riêng
My Tho
Tra Vinh
Chttorng
Phumm Samrong
Stœng Sèn
Trâpeáng Vèng
Suông
Long Xuyên
Rach Gia
Sóc Trăng
Bạc Liêu
Lop Buri
Sara Buri
Moung Roessei
Trâpeáng Vèng
Châu Đôc
Cần Thơ
Ca Mau
Côn Đảo

CAMBODIA

Battdâmbâng
Poŭthĭsăt
Reăng Kesei
Chuor Phnum
Krâvanh
PHNUM PENH
Kâmpóng Spoe

South China

Sea

Kepulauan Natuna
(part of Indonesia)

KRUNG THEP
(BANGKOK)
Samŭt Prakan
Chon Buri
Pattaya
Rayong
Ko Chang

Gulf
of
Thailand

Kâmpónt
Kâmpóng Saôm

Ayutthaya
Nakhon Pathom
Ratchaburi
Phetchaburi

Ban Hua Hin
Ao Krung
Thep

MALAYSIA

Malay
Peninsula

Sriangarind
Reservoir

Bilauktaung Range

Chumphon

Ko Phangan
Ko Samui

Nakhon Si Thammarat

Pak Phanang

Thung Song

Thale Luang

Songkhla
Pattani
Narathiwat

Strait of Malacca

Lang Suan

Surat Thani
Sichon

Phatthalung

Yala
Hat Yai
Trang

Pulau Pinang

Tavoy

Mali Kyun

Kadan Kyun

Mergui
Tenasserim

Daung Kyun

Letsok-aw Kyun

Lanbi Kyun

Ranong
Ko Kut

Isthmus of Kra

Phang-Nga
Ko Phra Thong
Ko Phuket
Phuket

Ko Lanta
Ko Ta Ru Tao
Ko Lanta

Pulau Langkawi

INDONESIA

Sumatera
(Sumatra)

Andaman

Sea

Mergui Archipelago

Zadetkyi Kyun

North Andaman

Andaman Islands
(part of India)

Middle Andaman

South Andaman

Little Andaman

Car Nicobar

Katchall Island

Little Nicobar

Nicobar Islands
(part of India)

Great Nicobar

Pulau Simeulue

INDIAN

OCEAN

ELEVATION

4 000 m
13 124 ft

2 000 m
6 562 ft

1 000 m
3 281 ft

500 m
1 640 ft

250 m
820 ft

100 m
328 ft

Sea
Level

Sea
Level

-50 m
-164 ft

-100 m
-328 ft

-250 m
-820 ft

-500 m
-1 640 ft

-1 000 m
-3 281 ft

-2 000 m
-6 562 ft

MARITIME SOUTHEAST ASIA

BURMA

100° 529

Gulf of Tongking

110°

Hainan Dao (part of China)

PARACEL ISLANDS
(disputed by China, Taiwan and Vietnam)

South Chi

Sea

L A O S   V I E T N A M

THAILAND

Mekong

CAMBODIA

Mouths of the Mekong

SPRATLY ISLANDS
(disputed by China, Malaysia, Philippines, Taiwan and Vietnam)

SINGAPORE

0 km 10
0 miles 10

MALAYSIA

Johore Strait

Causeway

Pulau Ubin

Pulau Tekong

Lim Chu Kang

Hougang

Choa Chu Kang

Bukit Panjang New Town

Changi

Bukit Timah 176m

1°20′

Jurong Industrial Estate

Queenstown

City

Bedok New Town

Telok Blangah

Sentosa

104°

Selat Pandan

Pulau Sudong

103°50′

Pulau Pawai

103°40′

Strait of Singapore

N

Urban areas
Open areas
Nature reserves

Andaman Sea

525

Gulf of Thailand

10°

Nicobar Islands (part of India)

Isthmus of Kra

Bal

Gunung

Bandaaceh Sigli

George Town

Kota Bharu

Kota Kinabalu

BANDAR SERI BEGAWAN

Butterworth

Kuala Terengganu

Langsa

Pulau Pinang

Taiping

Dungun

BRUNEI

Miri

Meulaboh

Ipoh

Cukai

Medan

Pulau Simeulue

Tebingtinggi

Klang

Kuantan

Kepulauan Natuna

Bintulu

Batang Rajang

Pematangsiantar

KUALA LUMPUR

Seremban

Sibu

Sarawak

Sri Aman

Sungai

Kepulauan Banyak

Danau Toba

Melaka

Muar

M A L A Y S I A

Kuching

Sibolga

Keluang

Selat Serasan

Pegunungan Muller

Pulau Nias

Batu Pahat

Johor Bahru

SINGAPORE

Singkawang

Sidas

B o r n e o

Equator

Pekanbaru

Singkawang

Solok

Rengat

Kepulauan Lingga

Pontianak

Sungai Kapuas

Samarin

Padang

Pulau Siberut

Batang Hari

Jambi

Kalimantan

Balikpap

Kepulauan Mentawai

Sungaipenuh

Pangkalpinang

Bangka

Sampit

Sungai Barito

Am

Kara

525

Palembang

Lahat

Pulau Belitung

I N D

Banjarma

Bengkulu

Kotabumi

Pul La

0 km 400
0 miles 400

Sumatera (Sumatra)

Bandarlampung

Serang

Cirebon

Tegal

Pekalongan

Semarang

Kudus

J a v a   S e a

Pulau Madura

JAKARTA

Bogor

Selat Sunda

Sukabumi

Bandung

Surabaya

Probolinggo

Jember

Malang

De

POPULATION

Less than 50,000

50,000 – 100,000

100,000 – 500,000

Over 500,000

Tasikmalaya

Cilacap

Magelang

Yogyakarta

Surakarta

Kediri

Madiun

Bali

Pul

Lom

Jawa (Java)

I N D I A N

O C E A N

10°

100° 533 110°

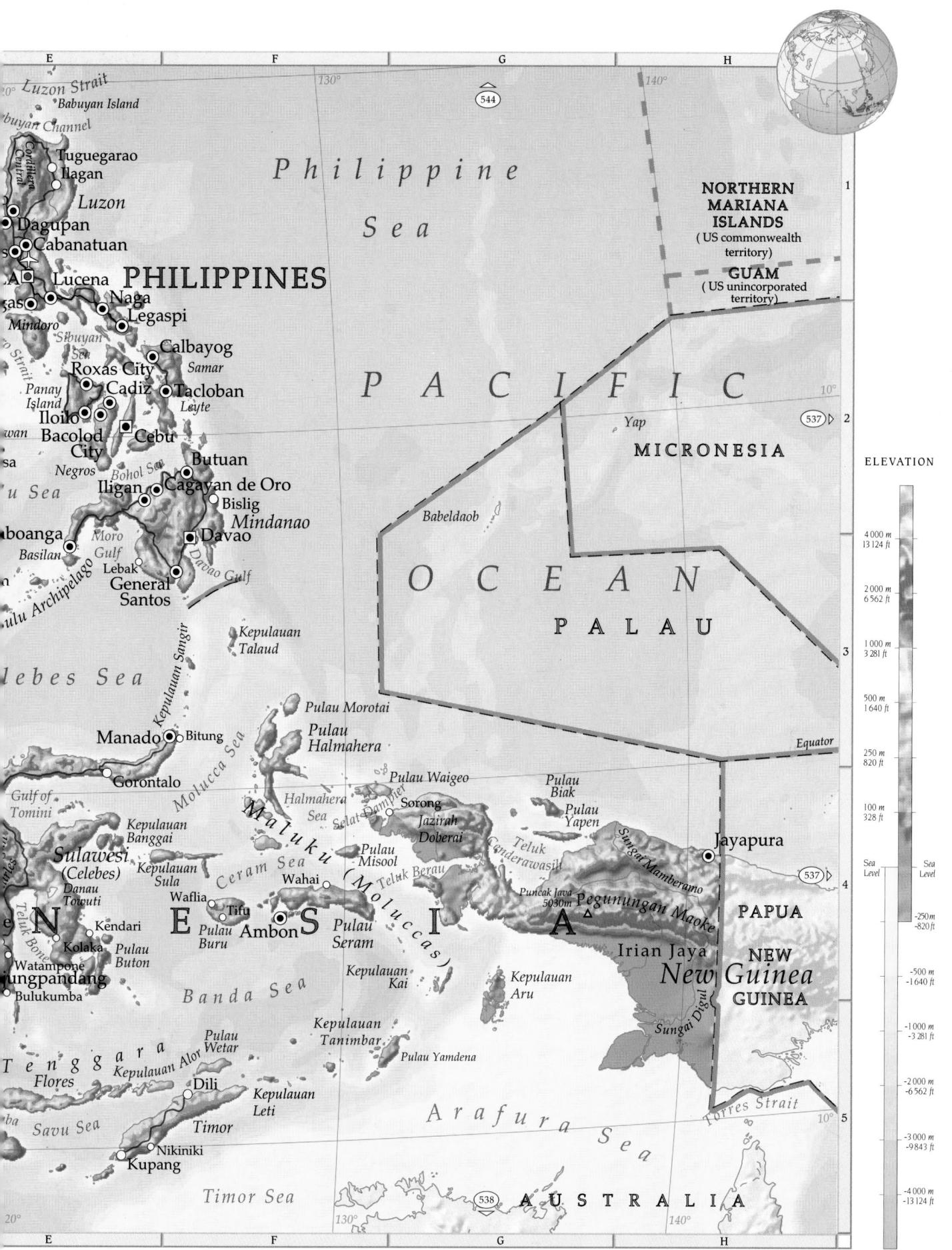

Luzon Strait
20° Babuyan Island
buyan Channel

Cordillera
Central
Tuguegarao
Ilagan
Luzon

Dagupan
Cabanatuan

Lucena
PHILIPPINES

Naga
Legaspi

Mindoro

Sibuyan
Sea

Calbayog

Roxas City
Cadiz
Samar
Tacloban
Panay
Island
Leyte
Iloilo

Bacolod
City
Cebu

Negros
Butuan

Bohol Sea
Iligan
Cagayan de Oro
boanga
Bislig
Basilan
Moro
Gulf
Mindanao
Davao

Lebak
Davao Gulf

ulu Archipelago
General
Santos

Philippine

Sea

PACIFIC

O C E A N

Kepulauan
Talaud

Celebes Sea

Kepulauan Sangir

Manado
Bitung

Gorontalo

Gulf of
Tomini

Molucca Sea

Kepulauan
Banggai
Sulawesi
(Celebes)
Kepulauan
Sula
N
Kendari

Kolaka
Pulau
Buton
Watampone
ungpandang
Bulukumba

Pulau Morotai

Pulau
Halmahera

Halmahera
Sea

Maluku (Moluccas)

Waflia
Tifu
Pulau
Buru
S
Ambon
Ceram Sea
Pulau
Seram
Wahai

Banda Sea

Kepulauan
Kai

Kepulauan
Tanimbar

Pulau Yamdena

T e n g g a r a
Flores
Kepulauan Alor
Pulau
Wetar

Dili
Kepulauan
Leti

Savu Sea
Timor

ba
Nikiniki
Kupang

Timor Sea

NORTHERN
MARIANA
ISLANDS
(US commonwealth
territory)

GUAM
(US unincorporated
territory)

Yap

MICRONESIA

Babeldaob

P A L A U

Equator

Pulau Waigeo
Sorong
Jazirah
Doberai
Pulau
Biak
Pulau
Yapen

Pulau
Misool
Teluk Berau
Selat Dampier
Teluk
Cenderawasih

Puncak Jaya
5030m
Pegunungan Maoke
Sungai Mamberamo
Jayapura

A
Irian Jaya
New
Sungai Digul

Torres Strait

Arafura Sea

A U S T R A L I A

PAPUA

NEW
GUINEA
Guinea

ELEVATION

4 000 m
13 124 ft

2 000 m
6 562 ft

1 000 m
3 281 ft

500 m
1 640 ft

250 m
820 ft

100 m
328 ft

Sea
Level

Sea
Level

-250 m
-820 ft

-500 m
-1 640 ft

-1 000 m
-3 281 ft

-2 000 m
-6 562 ft

-3 000 m
-9 843 ft

-4 000 m
-13 124 ft

THE INDIAN OCEAN

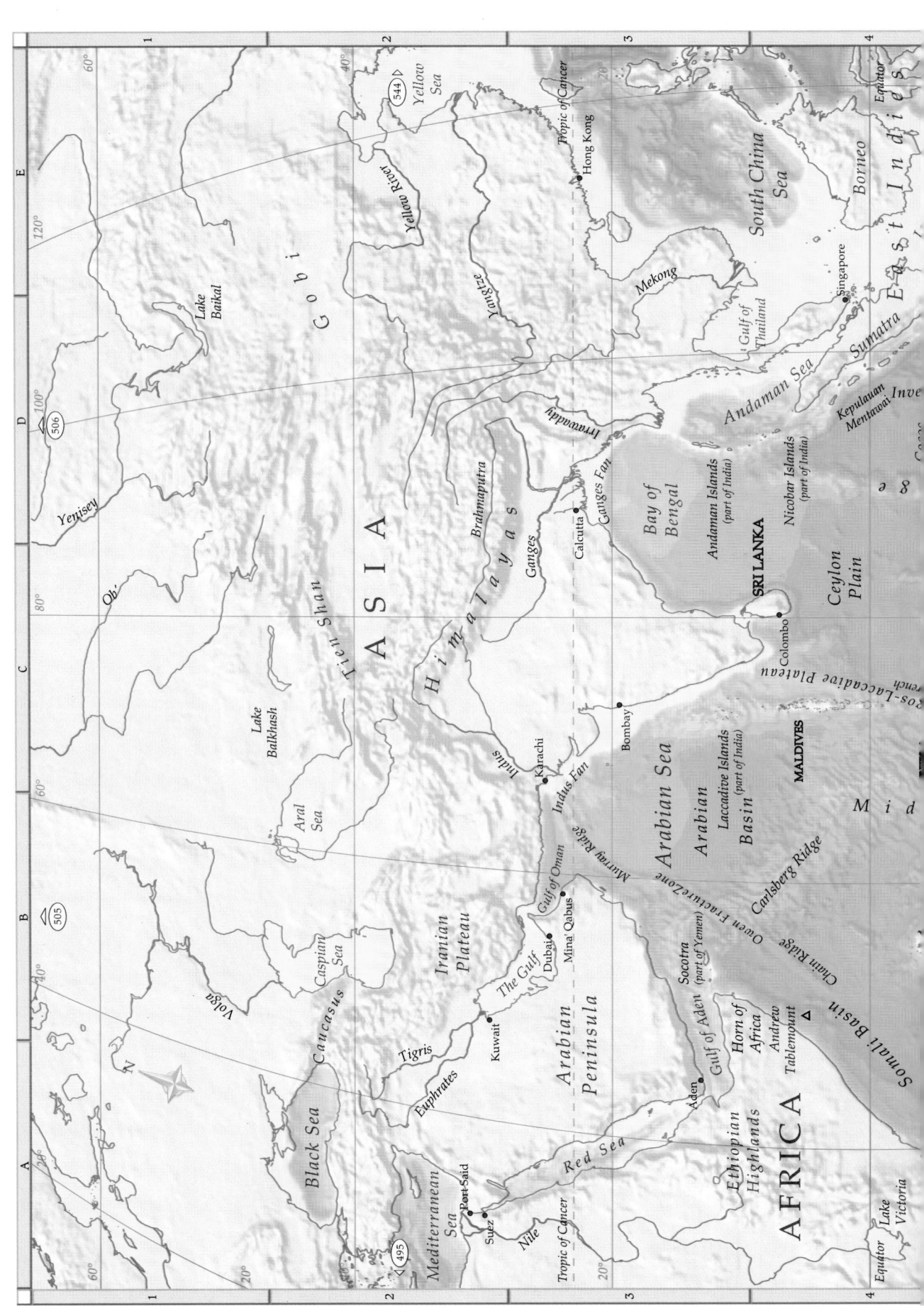

60°

120°

100°

80°

60°

40°

20°

40°

20°

ASIA

Gobi

Lake Baikal

Yenisey

Ob'

Tien Shan

Lake Balkhash

Aral Sea

Caspian Sea

Volga

Caucasus

Black Sea

Mediterranean Sea

Port Said

Suez

Nile

Tigris

Euphrates

Kuwait

Iranian Plateau

Arabian Peninsula

The Gulf

Dubai

Mina Qabus

Gulf of Oman

Red Sea

Aden

Gulf of Aden

Horn of Africa

Socotra (part of Yemen)

Andrew Tablemount

Ethiopian Highlands

AFRICA

Equator

Lake Victoria

Somali Basin

Owen Fracture Zone

Chain Ridge

Carlsberg Ridge

Murray Ridge

Arabian Basin

Arabian Sea

Indus Fan

Karachi

Indus

Himalayas

Ganges

Brahmaputra

Irrawaddy

Ganges Fan

Calcutta

Bay of Bengal

Bombay

Laccadive Islands (part of India)

MALDIVES

Chagos-Laccadive Plateau

Ceylon Plain

Colombo

SRI LANKA

Andaman Islands (part of India)

Nicobar Islands (part of India)

Andaman Sea

Kepulauan Mentawai Inve

Sumatra

Gulf of Thailand

Singapore

Mekong

Yangtze

Yellow River

Yellow Sea

Hong Kong

Tropic of Cancer

South China Sea

Borneo

East Indies

Equator

M i d

505

506

544

495

Tropic of Cancer

A B C D E

1 2 3 4

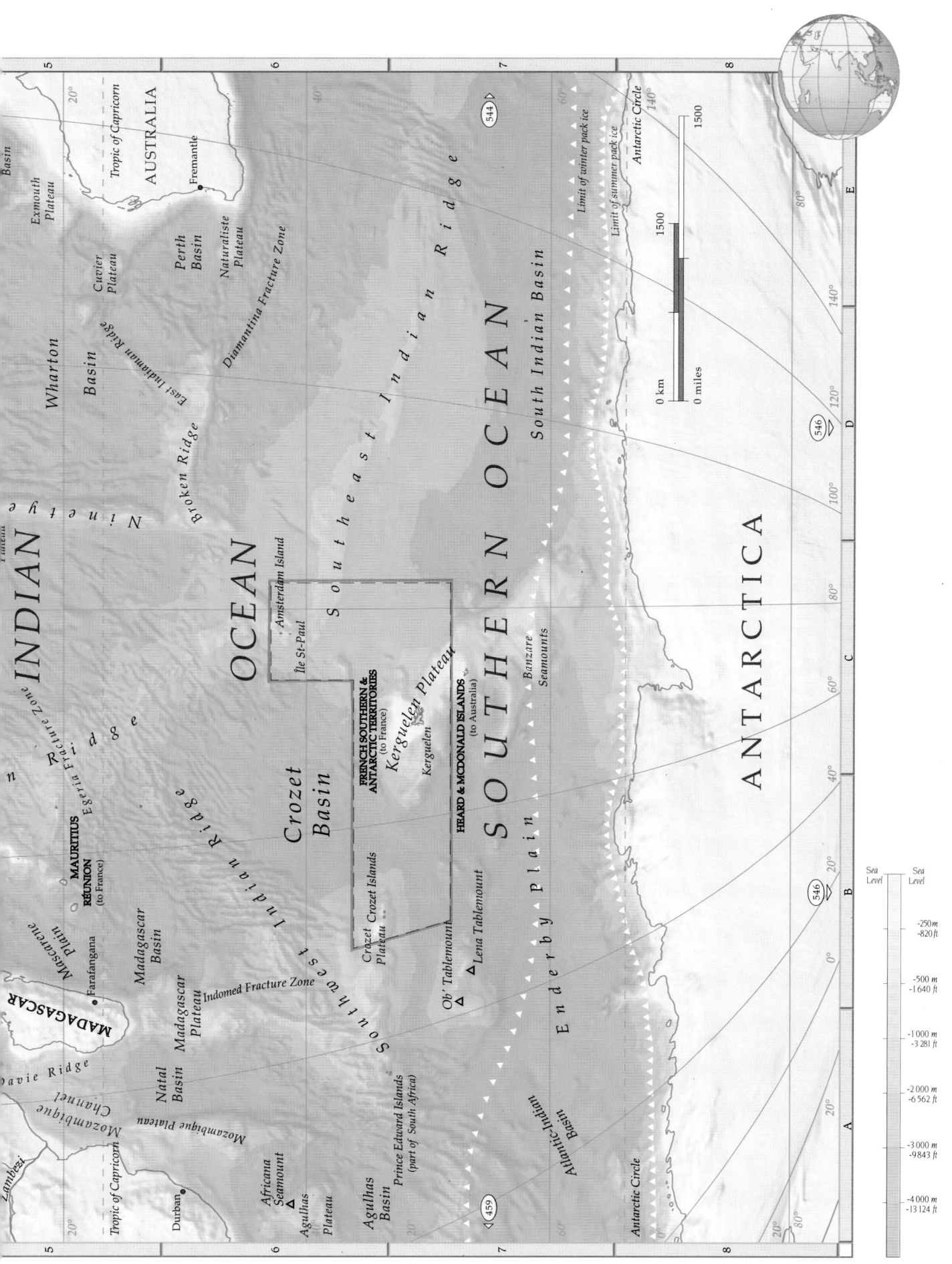

Basin

Exmouth
Plateau

Cuvier
Plateau

Perth
Basin

Naturaliste
Plateau

Tropic of Capricorn

AUSTRALIA

Fremantle

Wharton

Basin

East Indiaman Ridge

Diamantina Fracture Zone

Broken Ridge

S o u t h e a s t   I n d i a n   R i d g e

544

Antarctic Circle

Limit of winter pack ice

Limit of summer pack ice

1500

1500

0 km

0 miles

1500

South Indian Basin

S O U T H E R N   O C E A N

546

Ninetye

Plateau

Egeria Fracture Zone

R i d g e

I N D I A N

O C E A N

Amsterdam Island

Île St-Paul

FRENCH SOUTHERN &
ANTARCTIC TERRITORIES
(to France)

Kerguelen Plateau

Kerguelen

HEARD & MCDONALD ISLANDS
(to Australia)

Banzare
Seamounts

A N T A R C T I C A

60°

C

546

Crozet
Basin

S o u t h w e s t   I n d i a n   R i d g e

Indomed Fracture Zone

Crozet   Crozet Islands
Plateau

Ob' Tablemount

Lena Tablemount

E n d e r b y   P l a i n

40°

20°

B

MAURITIUS
RÉUNION
(to France)

Madagascar
Basin

Madagascar
Plateau

Farafangana

MADAGASCAR

Natal
Basin

Mozambique Plateau

Prince Edward Islands
(part of South Africa)

Atlantic-Indian
Basin

459

Davie Ridge

Mozambique
Channel

Zambezi

Tropic of Capricorn

Durban

Africana
Seamount

Agulhas
Plateau

Agulhas
Basin

Antarctic Circle

Mascarene
Plain

Antarctic Circle

Sea
Level

Sea
Level

-250 m
-820 ft

-500 m
-1640 ft

-1000 m
-3281 ft

-2000 m
-6562 ft

-3000 m
-9843 ft

-4000 m
-13124 ft

AUSTRALASIA AND OCEANIA

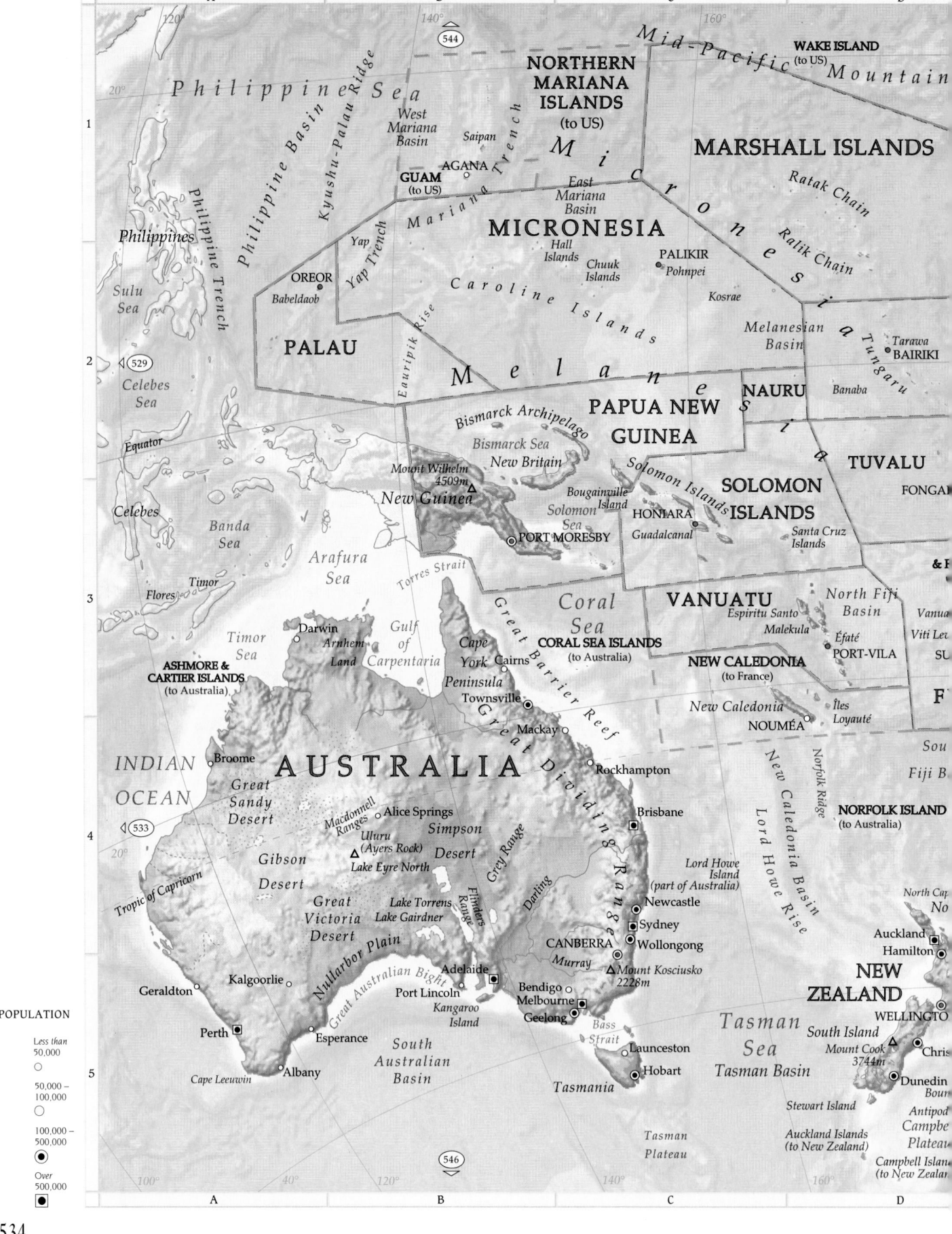

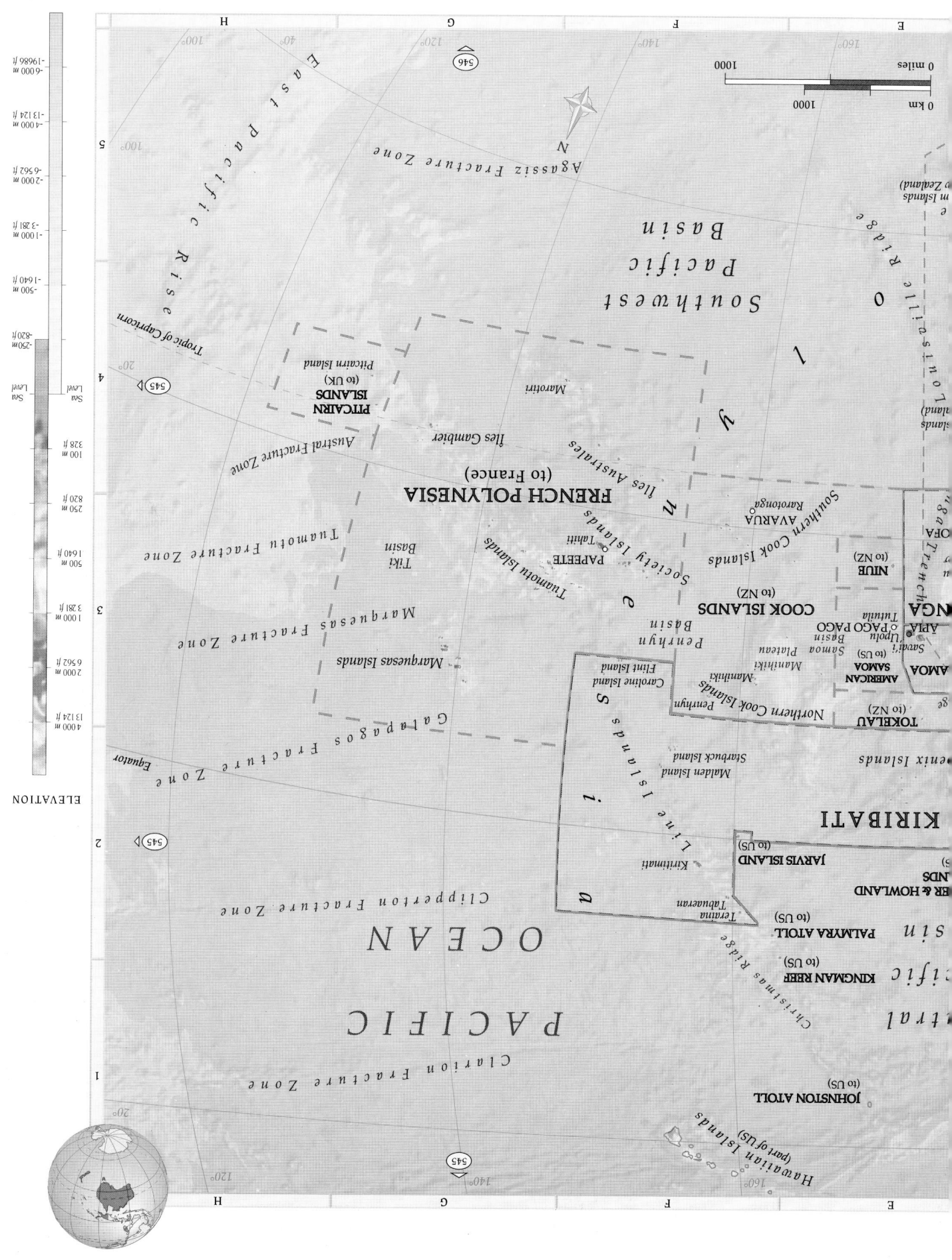

POPULATION

Over 500,000

100,000 – 500,000

50,000 – 100,000

Less than 50,000

THE SOUTHWEST PACIFIC

AUSTRALIA

Macdonnell Ranges

Tropic of Capricorn

NORTHERN TERRITORY

QUEENSLAND

Barkly Tableland

Arnhem Land

Groote Eylandt

Gulf of Carpentaria

Cape York Peninsula

Great Dividing Range

Great Barrier Reef

0 miles 750

0 km 750

NEW CALEDONIA
(French overseas territory)

New Caledonia

NOUMÉA

Îles Loyauté

Lifou Maré

Ouvéa

Tanna Anatom

Erromango

PORT-VILA

Efaté

VANUATU

Epi

Ambrym

Malakula

Pentecost

Maéwo

Espiritu Santo

Banks Islands

CORAL SEA ISLANDS
(Australian external territory)

Coral Sea

SOLOMON ISLANDS

Rennell

Santa Cruz Islands

San Cristobal

Guadalcanal

HONIARA

Malaita

Santa Isabel

New Georgia Islands

Choiseul

Bougainville Island

Solomon Sea

Solomon Islands

PORT MORESBY

Louisiade Archipelago

D'Entrecasteaux Islands

Gulf of Papua

Owen Stanley Range

PAPUA NEW GUINEA

Lae

Mount Wilhelm 4509m

Madang

Central Range

New Guinea

New Britain

Bismarck Sea

New Ireland

Bismarck Archipelago

St. Matthias Group

Admiralty Islands

INDONESIA

Equator

NAURU

Banaba

M   e   l   a   n   e   s   i   a

PALAU

OREOR

Babeldaob

Yap

Caroline Islands

Chuuk Islands

PALIKIR

Pohnpei

Kosrae

MICRONESIA

M   i   c   r   o   n   e   s   i   a

GUAM
(US unincorporated territory)

AGAÑA

Rota

NORTHERN MARIANA ISLANDS
(US commonwealth territory)

Tinian

Saipan

MARSHALL ISLANDS

Bikini Atoll

Enewetak Atoll

Rongelap Atoll

Ujelang Atoll

Ailinglapalap Atoll

Namu Atoll

Kwajalein Atoll

Jaluit Atoll

Mili Atoll

Maloelap Atoll

Wotje

Ratak Chain

Ralik Chain

Ailuk Atoll

Mili

Arafura Sea

Torres Strait

531

538

541

544

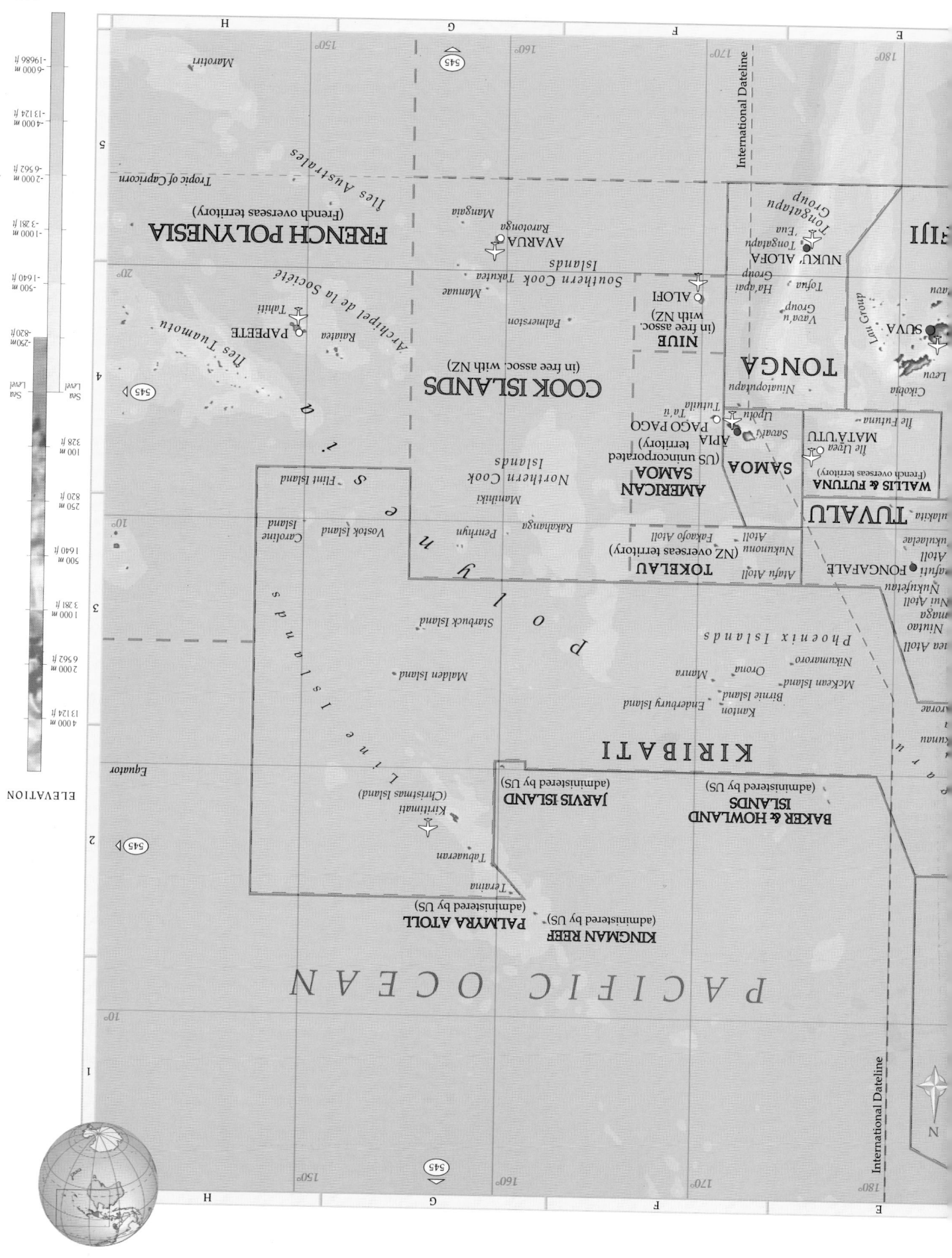

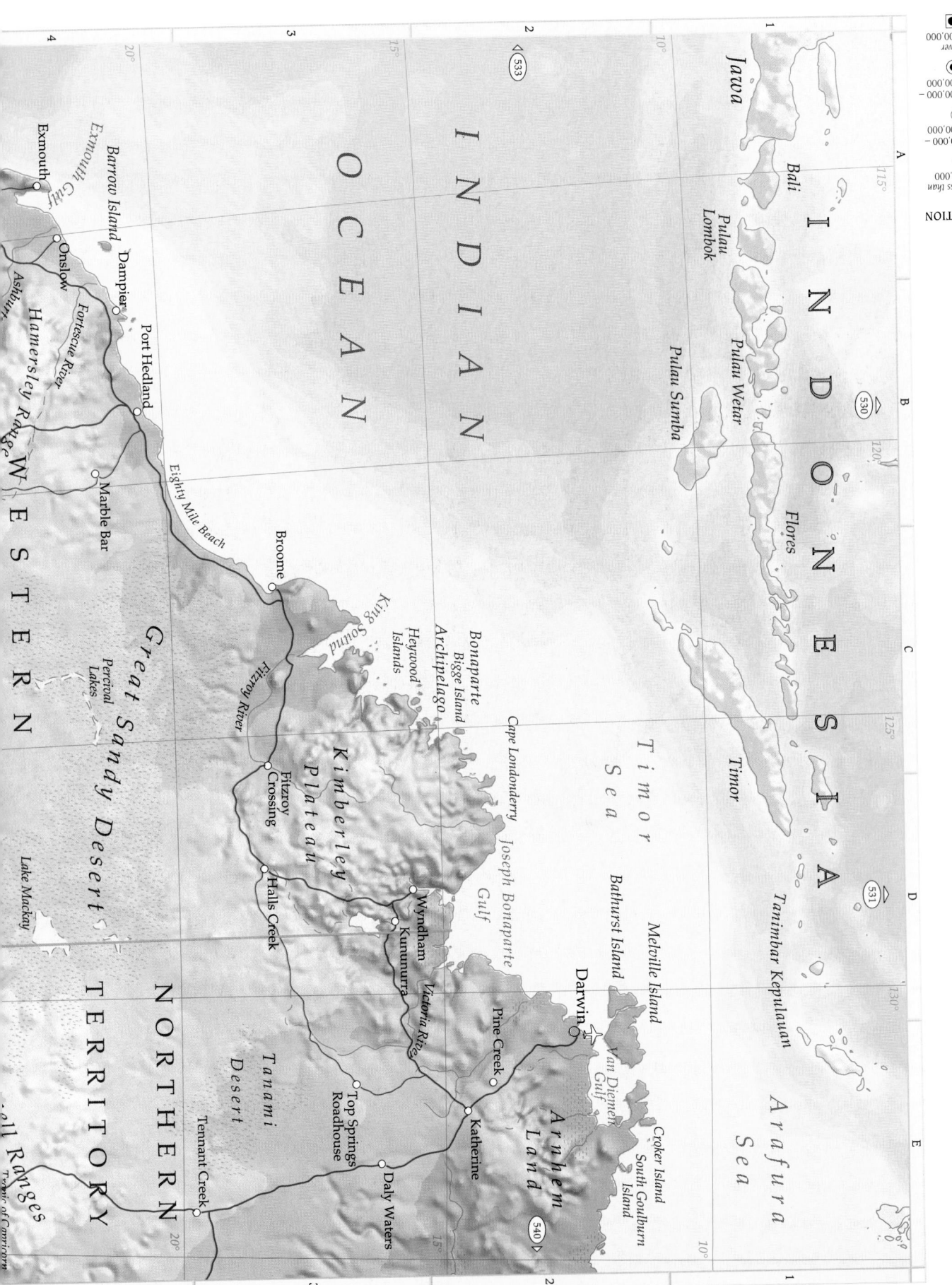

POPULATION

■ Over 500,000

◉ 100,000 – 500,000

○ 50,000 – 100,000

○ Less than 50,000

Jawa

Bali

Pulau
Lombok

Pulau Wetar

Pulau Sumba

Flores

Timor

Tanimbar Kepulauan

INDONESIA

I N D I A N

O C E A N

Timor Sea

Arafura Sea

Van Diemen
Gulf

Croker Island

South Goulburn
Island

Melville Island

Bathurst Island

Darwin

Arnhem Land

Pine Creek

Katherine

Cape Londonderry

Joseph Bonaparte
Gulf

Bonaparte
Archipelago

Bigge Island

Heywood
Islands

King Sound

Kimberley
Plateau

Fitzroy River

Wyndham

Kununurra

Victoria River

Top Springs
Roadhouse

Daly Waters

Tennant Creek

Tanami
Desert

NORTHERN
TERRITORY

Halls Creek

Fitzroy
Crossing

Broome

Eighty Mile Beach

Great Sandy Desert

Percival
Lakes

Lake Mackay

WESTERN

Marble Bar

Port Hedland

Dampier

Onslow

Barrow Island

Exmouth

Exmouth Gulf

Hamersley Range

Fortescue River

Ashburn

ell Ranges

Tropic of Capricorn

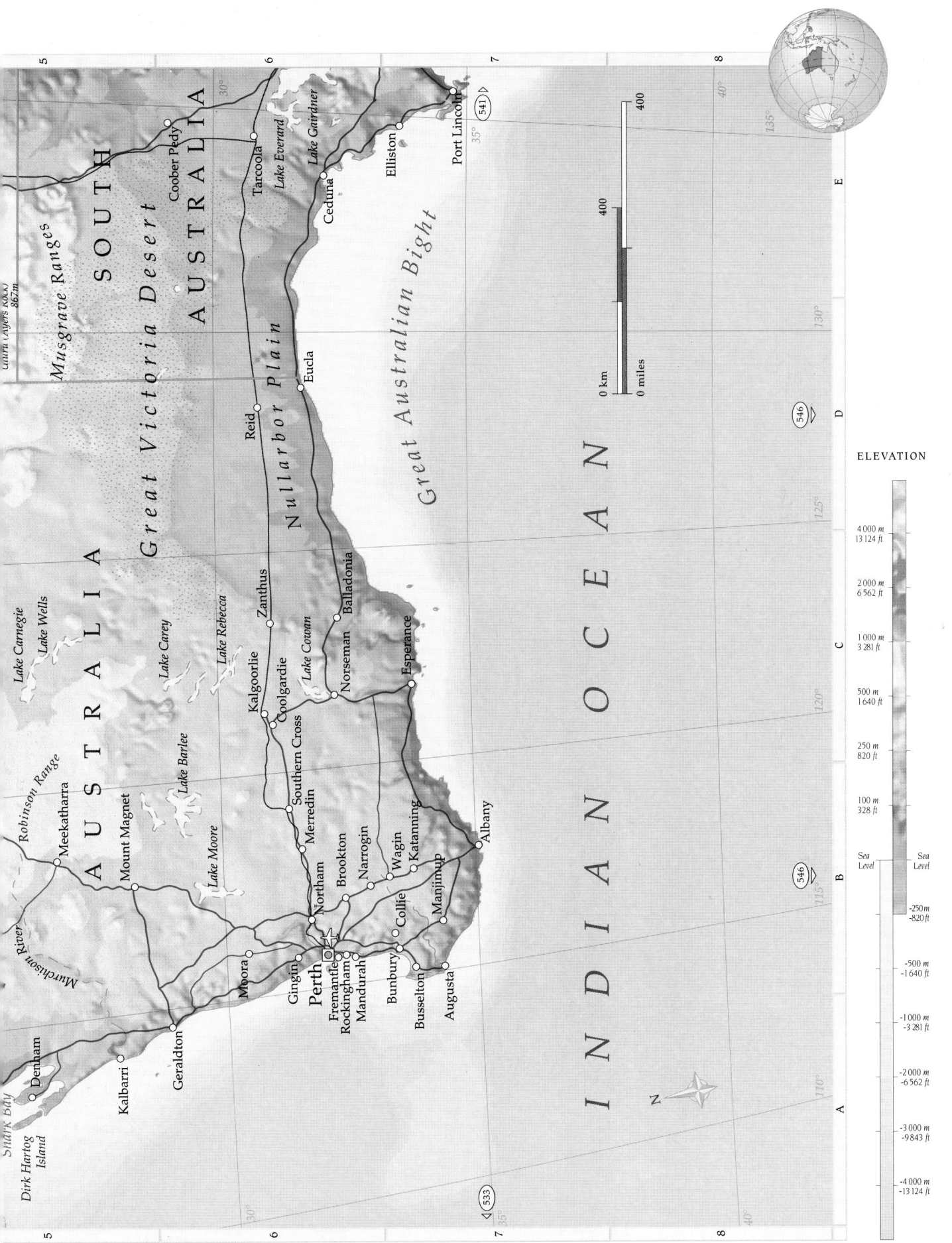

SOUTH AUSTRALIA

Great Victoria Desert

Musgrave Ranges

Uluru (Ayers Rock)
867m

Coober Pedy

Tarcoola

Lake Everard

Lake Gairdner

Ceduna

Elliston

Port Lincoln

Nullarbor Plain

Great Australian Bight

Reid

Eucla

INDIAN OCEAN

Zanthus

Balladonia

Lake Rebecca

Lake Cowan

Norseman

Esperance

Lake Carey

Kalgoorlie

Coolgardie

Lake Barlee

Southern Cross

Merredin

Lake Carnegie

Lake Wells

AUSTRALIA

Robinson Range

Meekatharra

Mount Magnet

Lake Moore

Northam

Brookton

Narrogin

Wagin

Katanning

Albany

Manjimup

Collie

Murchison River

Moora

Gingin

Perth

Fremantle
Rockingham
Mandurah

Bunbury

Busselton

Augusta

Denham

Shark Bay

Dirk Hartog Island

Kalbarri

Geraldton

N

ELEVATION

4 000 m	13 124 ft
2 000 m	6 562 ft
1 000 m	3 281 ft
500 m	1 640 ft
250 m	820 ft
100 m	328 ft
Sea Level	Sea Level
-250 m	-820 ft
-500 m	-1 640 ft
-1 000 m	-3 281 ft
-2 000 m	-6 562 ft
-3 000 m	-9 843 ft
-4 000 m	-13 124 ft

400

400

0 km

0 miles

541

546

546

533

Eastern Australia

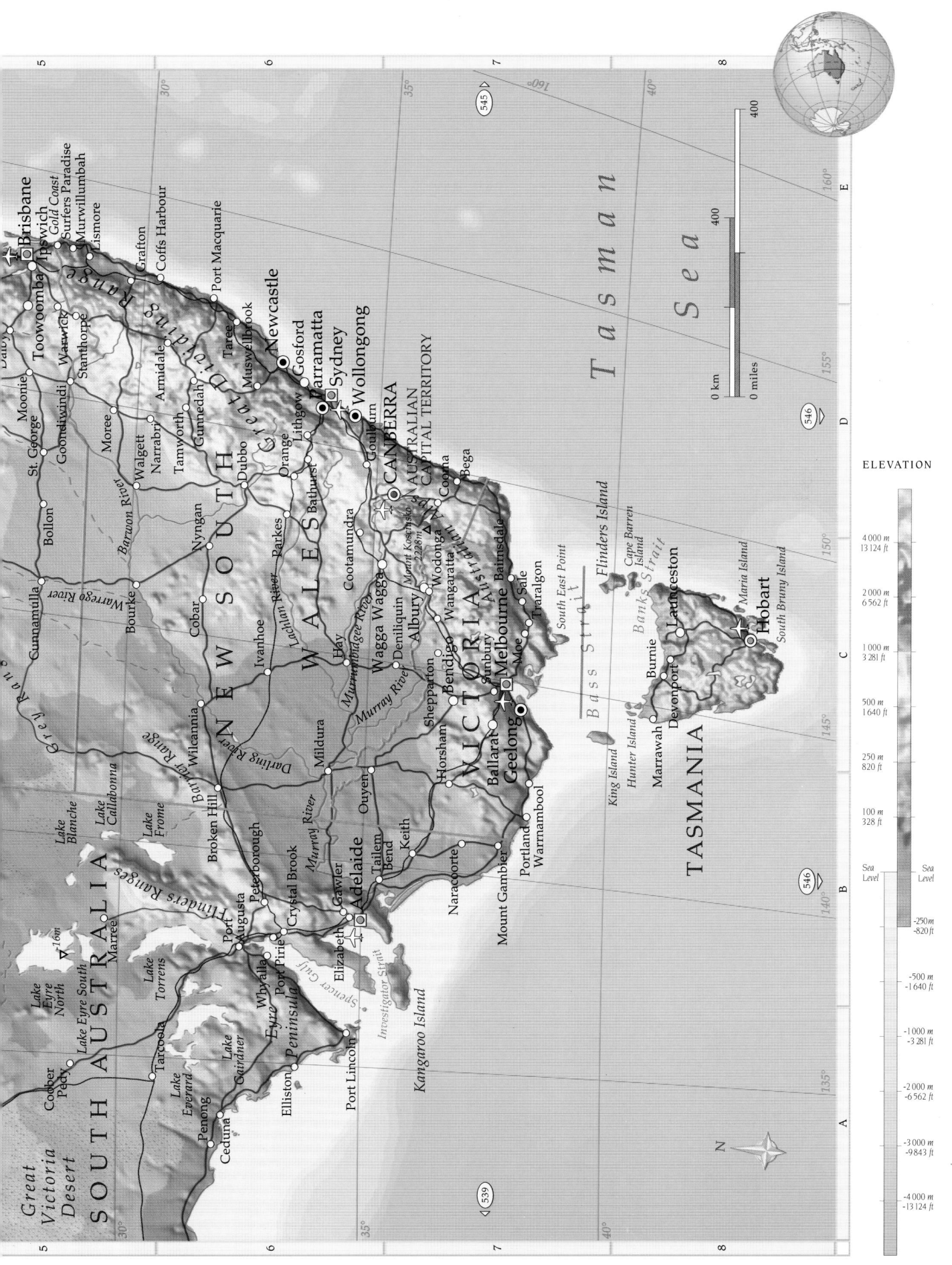

ELEVATION

4 000 m	13 124 ft
2 000 m	6 562 ft
1 000 m	3 281 ft
500 m	1 640 ft
250 m	820 ft
100 m	328 ft
Sea Level	Sea Level
-250 m	-820 ft
-500 m	-1 640 ft
-1 000 m	-3 281 ft
-2 000 m	-6 562 ft
-3 000 m	-9 843 ft
-4 000 m	-13 124 ft

NEW ZEALAND

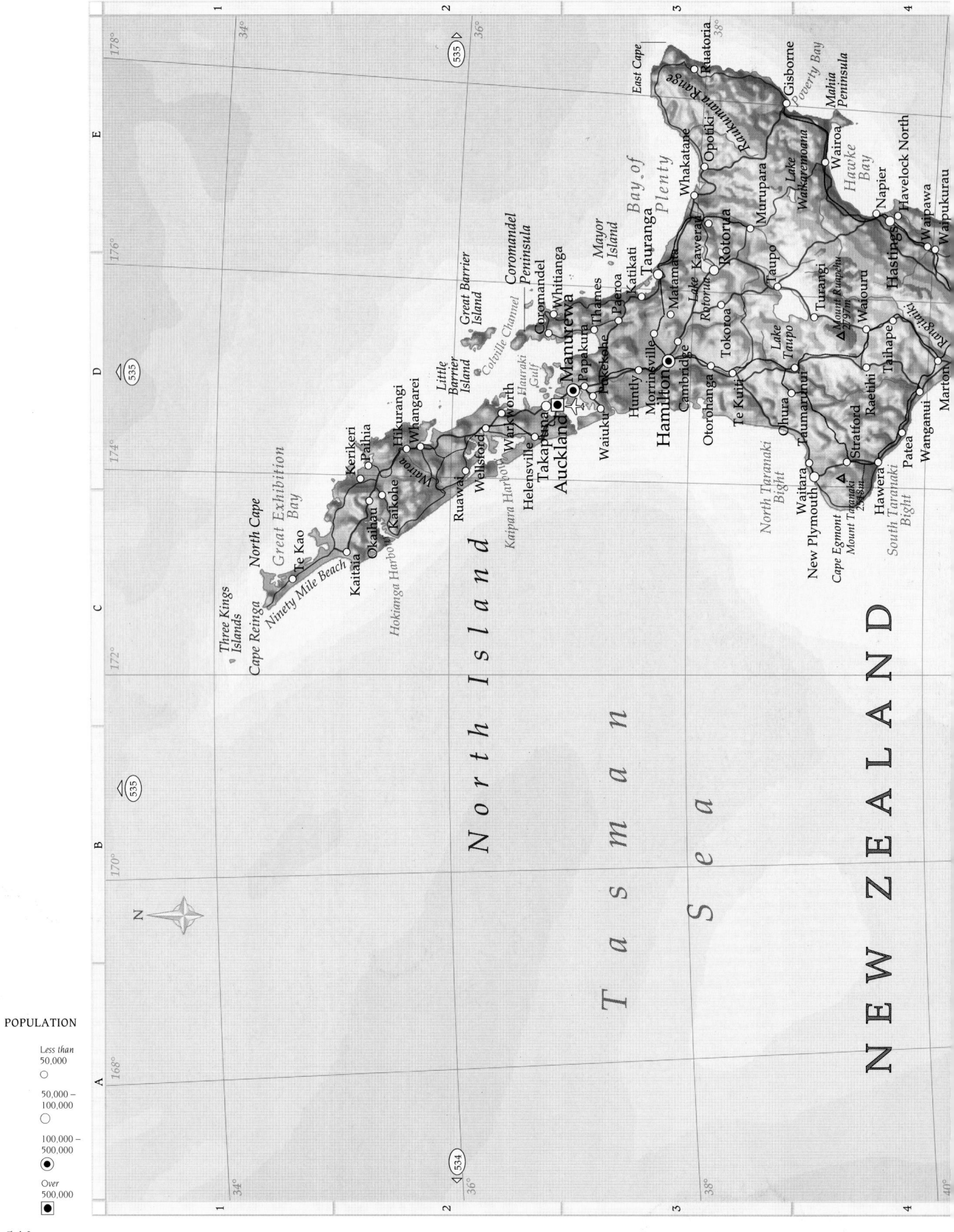

POPULATION

Less than
50,000
○

50,000 –
100,000
○

100,000 –
500,000
◉

Over
500,000
◼

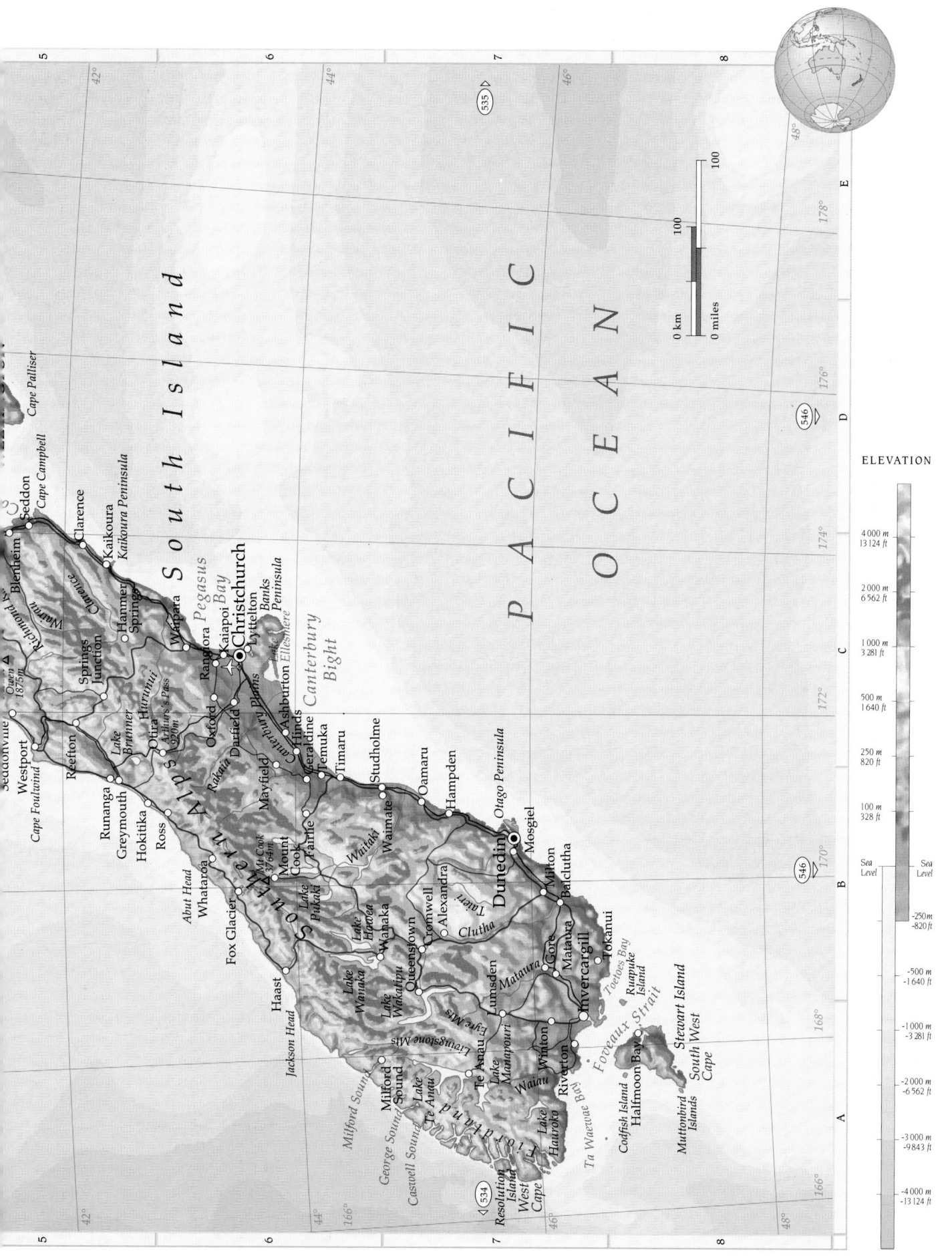

ELEVATION

4 000 m
13 124 ft

2 000 m
6 562 ft

1 000 m
3 281 ft

500 m
1 640 ft

250 m
820 ft

100 m
328 ft

Sea
Level

Sea
Level

-250 m
-820 ft

-500 m
-1 640 ft

-1 000 m
-3 281 ft

-2 000 m
-6 562 ft

-3 000 m
-9 843 ft

-4 000 m
-13 124 ft

PACIFIC OCEAN

South Island

NEW ZEALAND

Cape Palliser
Cape Campbell
Seddon
Clarence
Kaikoura
Kaikoura Peninsula
Blenheim
Waimea
Richmond Range
Wairau
Awatere
Hanmer Springs
Waipara
Pegasus Bay
Kaiapoi
Christchurch
Lyttelton
Banks Peninsula
Lake Ellesmere
Rangiora
Springs Junction
Hurunui
Otira
Arthur's Pass
920 m
Oxford
Darfield
Rakaia
Canterbury Plains
Ashburton
Hinds
Geraldine
Temuka
Timaru
Studholme
Canterbury Bight
Reefton
Lake Brunner
Mayfield
Rangitata
Fairlie
Waitaki
Waimate
Oamaru
Hampden
Westport
Cape Foulwind
Runanga
Greymouth
Hokitika
Ross
Abut Head
Whataroa
Fox Glacier
Mt Cook
3 764 m
Mount Cook
Lake Pukaki
Lake Hawea
Wanaka
Cromwell
Alexandra
Taieri
Clutha
Otago Peninsula
Mosgiel
Dunedin
Milton
Balclutha
Haast
Jackson Head
Lake Wanaka
Lake Wakatipu
Queenstown
Eyre Mts
Lumsden
Mataura
Gore
Mataura
Tokanui
Toetoes Bay
Milford Sound
George Sound
Caswell Sound
Milford Sound
Lake Te Anau
Te Anau
Te Anau
Lake Manapouri
Waiau
Winton
Riverton
Invercargill
Foveaux Strait
Ruapuke Island
Stewart Island
Codfish Island
Halfmoon Bay
Muttonbird Islands
South West Cape
Livingstone Mts
Lake Hauroka
Te Waewae Bay
Resolution Island
West Cape

534

546

546

535

Southern Alps

543

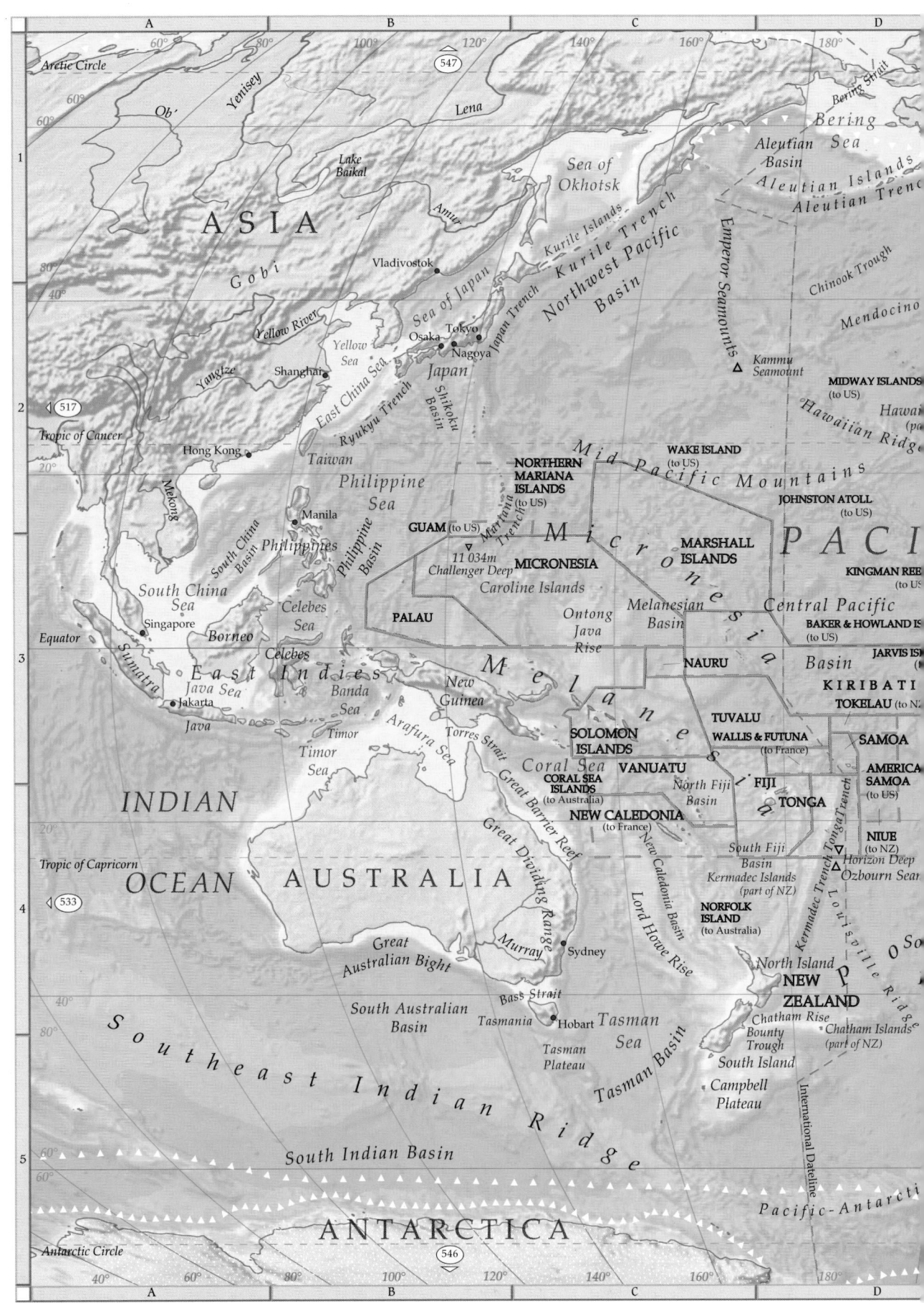

ASIA

Arctic Circle

Ob'

Yenisey

Lena

547

Lake Baikal

Amur

Sea of Okhotsk

Gobi

Vladivostok

Kurile Islands

Kurile Trench

Bering Strait

Bering Sea

Aleutian Basin

Aleutian Islands

Aleutian Trench

Chinook Trough

Mendocino

Emperor Seamounts

Yellow River

Yellow Sea

Osaka Tokyo

Nagoya

Japan

Sea of Japan

Japan Trench

Northwest Pacific Basin

Kammu Seamount

MIDWAY ISLANDS (to US)

Shanghai

517

Tropic of Cancer

Yangtze

Shikoku Basin

Ryukyu Trench

East China Sea

Hawaii (pa

Hawaiian Ridge

Hong Kong

Taiwan

20°

Philippine Sea

Mid Pacific Mountains

WAKE ISLAND (to US)

NORTHERN MARIANA ISLANDS (to US)

JOHNSTON ATOLL (to US)

Mekong

Manila

Philippines

South China Basin

GUAM (to US)

11 034m Challenger Deep

MICRONESIA

Caroline Islands

Mariana Trench

Micronesia

PACI

MARSHALL ISLANDS

KINGMAN REE (to US

South China Sea

Philippine Basin

PALAU

Ontong Java Rise

Melanesian Basin

Central Pacific

BAKER & HOWLAND IS (to US)

Singapore

Borneo

Celebes Sea

NAURU

Melanesia

Basin

JARVIS ISL (

Equator

East Indies

Celebes

New Guinea

KIRIBATI

TOKELAU (to N

Java Sea

Jakarta

Banda Sea

TUVALU

Java

Timor

Torres Strait

Arafura Sea

SOLOMON ISLANDS

WALLIS & FUTUNA (to France)

SAMOA

Timor Sea

Great Barrier Reef

Coral Sea

CORAL SEA ISLANDS (to Australia)

VANUATU

North Fiji Basin

FIJI

TONGA

AMERICA SAMOA (to US)

INDIAN

NEW CALEDONIA (to France)

New Caledonia Basin

Tonga Trench

Kermadec Trench

NIUE (to NZ)

Horizon Deep

Ozbourn Sea

20°

Tropic of Capricorn

533

OCEAN

AUSTRALIA

Great Dividing Range

Lord Howe Rise

South Fiji Basin

Kermadec Islands (part of NZ)

NORFOLK ISLAND (to Australia)

Louisville Ridge

P

So

Great Australian Bight

Murray

Sydney

North Island

NEW ZEALAND

40°

South Australian Basin

Bass Strait

Tasmania

Hobart

Tasman Sea

Chatham Rise

Bounty Trough

Chatham Islands (part of NZ)

South Island

Tasman Plateau

Tasman Basin

Campbell Plateau

Southeast Indian Ridge

International Dateline

South Indian Basin

Pacific-Antarc

ANTARCTICA

546

Antarctic Circle

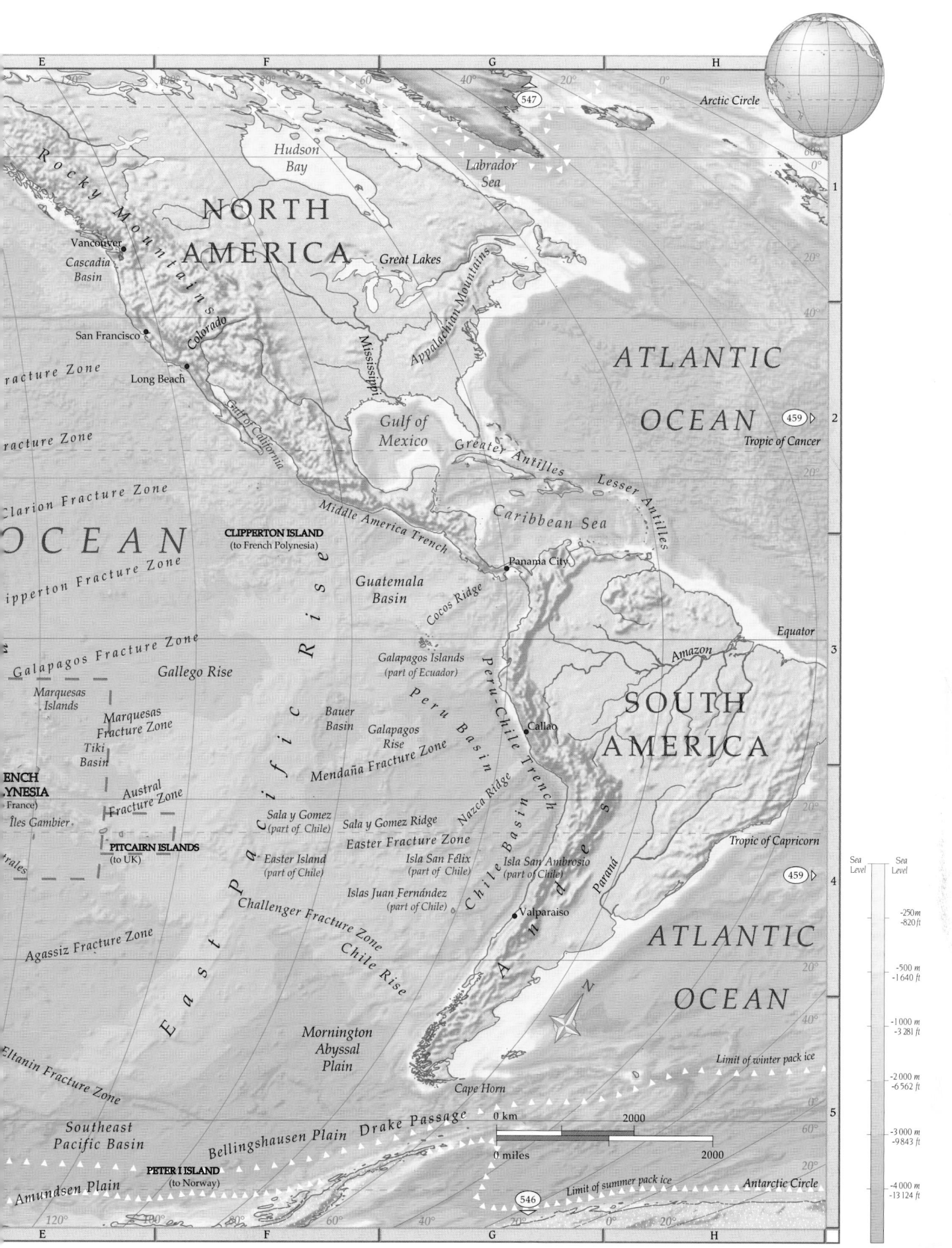

E   F   G   H

Arctic Circle

Rocky Mountains

Hudson
Bay

Labrador
Sea

547

NORTH
AMERICA

Vancouver

*Cascadia
Basin*

Great Lakes

San Francisco

Colorado

Long Beach

Fracture Zone

Gulf of California

racture Zone

Mississippi

Appalachian Mountains

ATLANTIC

OCEAN

459

Tropic of Cancer

Gulf of
Mexico

Greater Antilles

Clarion Fracture Zone

OCEAN

Middle America Trench

CLIPPERTON ISLAND
(to French Polynesia)

Caribbean Sea

Lesser Antilles

lipperton Fracture Zone

Guatemala
Basin

Panama City

Cocos Ridge

Galapagos Fracture Zone

Gallego Rise

Galapagos Islands
(part of Ecuador)

East Pacific Rise

Equator

Amazon

3

*Marquesas
Islands*

*Marquesas
Fracture Zone*

Bauer
Basin

Galapagos
Rise

Peru Basin

SOUTH
AMERICA

*Tiki
Basin*

Mendaña Fracture Zone

Callao

Nazca Ridge

ENCH
YNESIA
(France)

Austral
Fracture Zone

Sala y Gomez
(part of Chile)

Sala y Gomez Ridge

Peru–Chile Trench

Îles Gambier

Easter Fracture Zone

Chile Basin

Tropic of Capricorn

PITCAIRN ISLANDS
(to UK)

Easter Island
(part of Chile)

Isla San Félix
(part of Chile)

Isla San Ambrosio
(part of Chile)

459

Islas Juan Fernández
(part of Chile)

Andes

Valparaiso

Challenger Fracture Zone

ATLANTIC

Agassiz Fracture Zone

Chile Rise

Paraná

OCEAN

East Pacific Rise

N

Sea
Level

Sea
Level

Mornington
Abyssal
Plain

Eltanin Fracture Zone

Limit of winter pack ice

-250 m
-820 ft

Cape Horn

0 km   2000

5

-500 m
-1640 ft

Southeast
Pacific Basin

Bellingshausen Plain   Drake Passage

0 miles   2000

-1000 m
-3281 ft

PETER I ISLAND
(to Norway)

-2000 m
-6562 ft

Amundsen Plain

Limit of summer pack ice

Antarctic Circle

-3000 m
-9843 ft

546

-4000 m
-13124 ft

E   F   G   H

ANTARCTICA

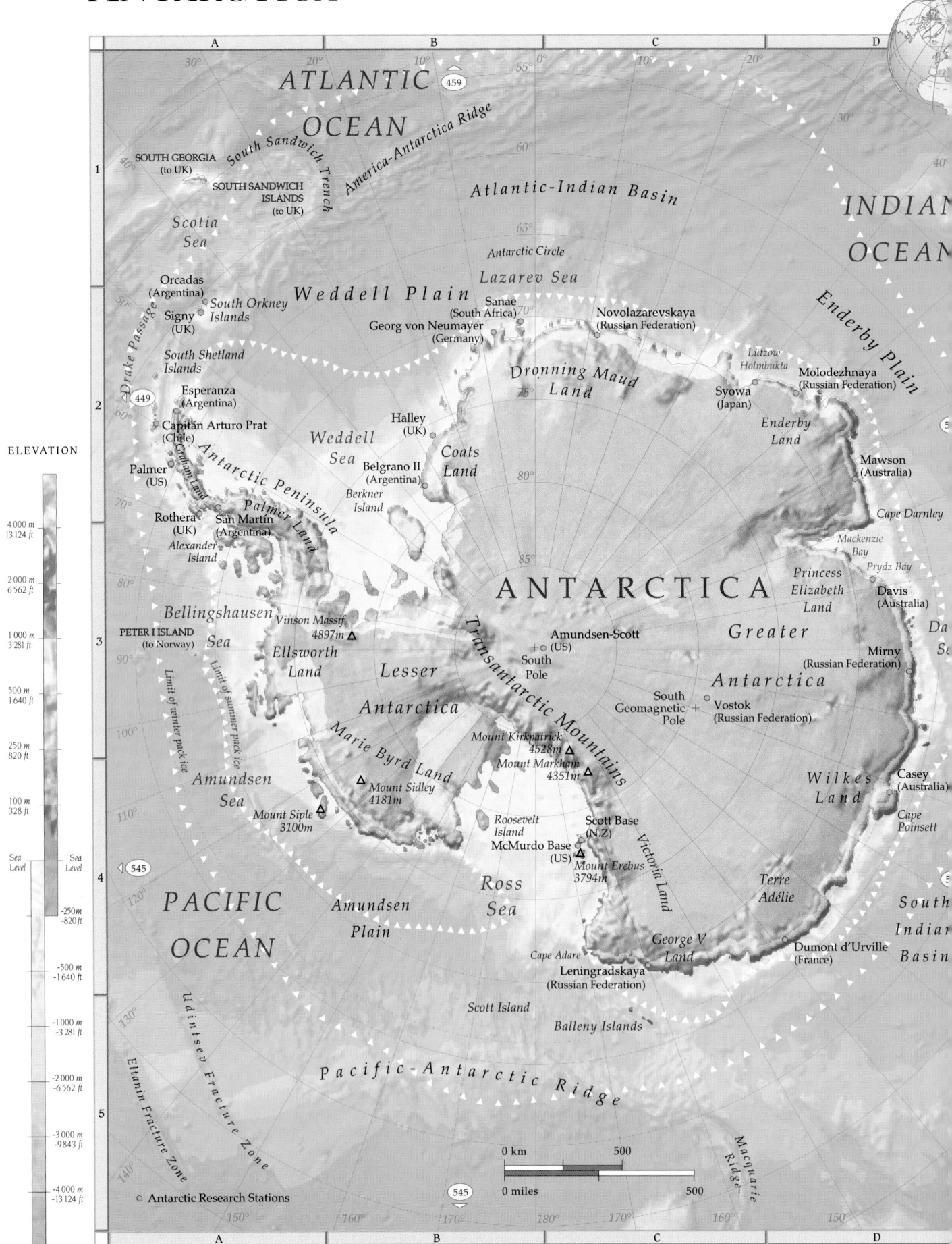

ATLANTIC

OCEAN

459

South Sandwich Trench

America-Antarctica Ridge

SOUTH GEORGIA
(to UK)

SOUTH SANDWICH
ISLANDS
(to UK)

*Scotia
Sea*

INDIAN

OCEAN

Atlantic-Indian Basin

Antarctic Circle

Lazarev Sea

Orcadas
(Argentina)

*South Orkney
Islands*

Signy
(UK)

Drake Passage

*South Shetland
Islands*

Esperanza
(Argentina)

449

Weddell Plain

Sanae
(South Africa)

Georg von Neumayer
(Germany)

Novolazarevskaya
(Russian Federation)

*Dronning Maud
Land*

*Lützow
Holmbukta*

Molodezhnaya
(Russian Federation)

Syowa
(Japan)

Enderby Plain

*Enderby
Land*

*Weddell
Sea*

Halley
(UK)

*Coats
Land*

Mawson
(Australia)

Cape Darnley

Capitán Arturo Prat
(Chile)

Palmer
(US)

Graham Land

Antarctic Peninsula

Belgrano II
(Argentina)

*Berkner
Island*

*Mackenzie
Bay*

Prydz Bay

Rothera
(UK)

San Martín
(Argentina)

*Palmer
Land*

*Princess
Elizabeth
Land*

Davis
(Australia)

*Alexander
Island*

ANTARCTICA

Greater

Da

Bellingshausen

Vinson Massif
4897m △

Transantarctic Mountains

Amundsen-Scott
(US)

South
Pole

Mirny
(Russian Federation)

PETER I ISLAND
(to Norway)

Sea

*Ellsworth
Land*

Lesser

Antarctica

South
Geomagnetic
Pole

Vostok
(Russian Federation)

Limit of winter pack ice

Limit of summer pack ice

Antarctica

Marie Byrd Land

Mount Kirkpatrick
4528m △

Mount Markham
4351m △

*Wilkes
Land*

Casey
(Australia)

*Amundsen
Sea*

Mount Sidley
4181m △

*Roosevelt
Island*

Scott Base
(N.Z)

McMurdo Base
(US)

Mount Erebus
3794m △

Victoria Land

*Cape
Poinsett*

Mount Siple
3100m △

*Terre
Adélie*

PACIFIC

OCEAN

545

*Amundsen
Plain*

*Ross
Sea*

Cape Adare

George V
Land

Dumont d'Urville
(France)

South

Indian

Basin

Leningradskaya
(Russian Federation)

Scott Island

Balleny Islands

Pacific-Antarctic Ridge

Udintsev Fracture Zone

Eltanin Fracture Zone

*Macquarie
Ridge*

ELEVATION

	4 000 m / 13 124 ft
	2 000 m / 6 562 ft
1 000 m / 3 281 ft	
500 m / 1 640 ft	
250 m / 820 ft	
100 m / 328 ft	
Sea Level	Sea Level
	-250 m / -820 ft
	-500 m / -1 640 ft
	-1 000 m / -3 281 ft
	-2 000 m / -6 562 ft
	-3 000 m / -9 843 ft
	-4 000 m / -13 124 ft

○ Antarctic Research Stations

0 km   500

0 miles   500

545

ΛRCTIC OCEAN

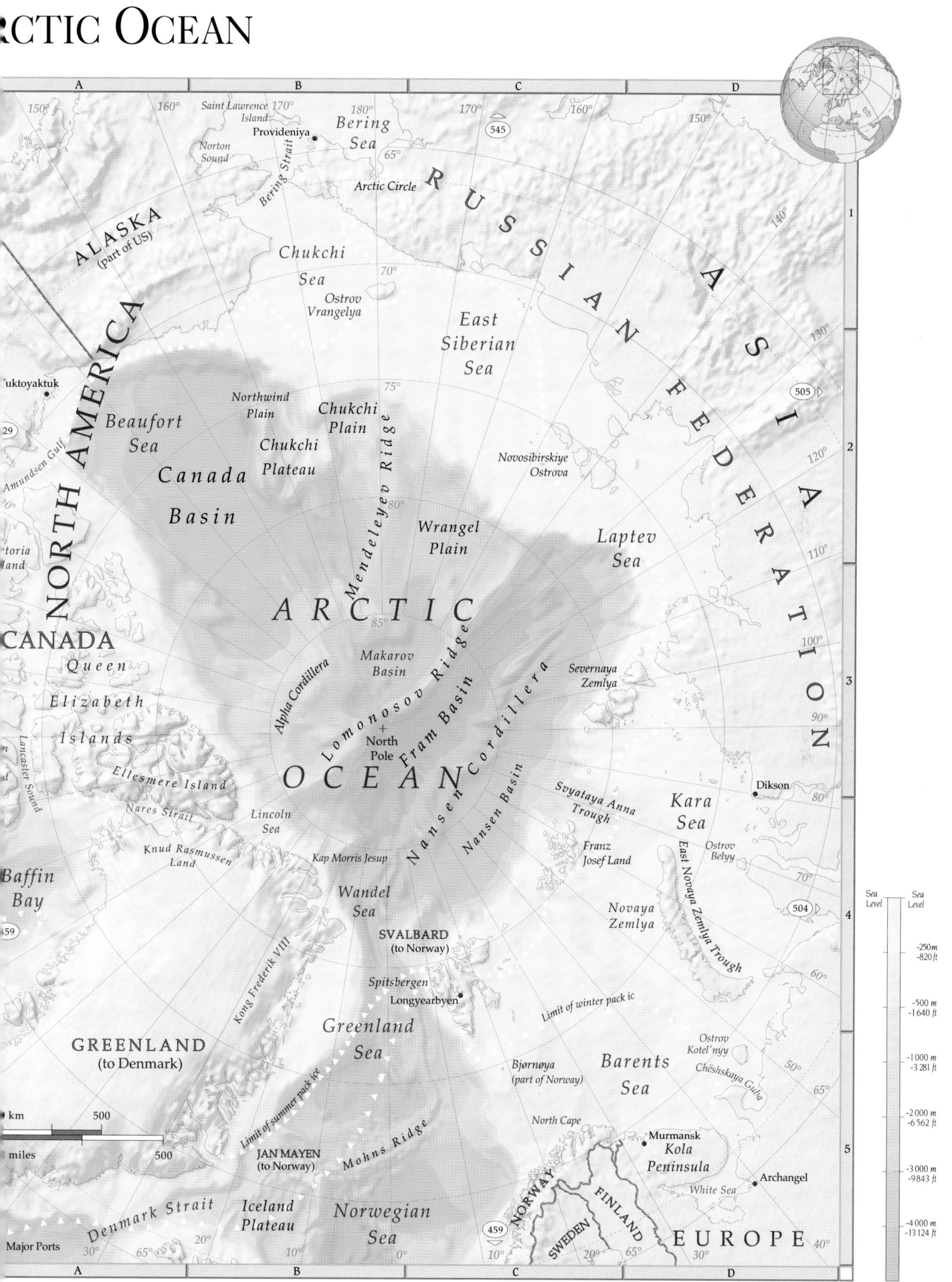

Aachen - Alès

Glossary of Abbreviations

This Glossary provides a comprehensive guide to the abbreviations used in the World Atlas pages, and in the Index.

A **abbrev** abbreviation
Afr. Afrikaans
Alb. Albanian
Amh. Amharic
anc. ancient
Ar. Arabic
Arm. Armenian
Az. Azerbaijani

B **Basq.** Basque
Bel. Belorussian
Ben. Bengali
Bibl. Biblical
Bret. Breton
Bul. Bulgarian
Bur. Burmese

C **Cam.** Cambodian
Cant. Cantonese
Cast. Castilian
Cat. Catalan
Chin. Chinese
Cro. Croat
Cz. Czech

D **Dan.** Danish
Dut. Dutch

E **Eng.** English
Est. Estonian
est. estimated

F **Faer.** Faeroese
Fij. Fijian
Fin. Finnish
Flem. Flemish
Fr. French
Fris. Frisian

G **Geor.** Georgian
Ger. German
Gk. Greek
Guj. Gujarati

H **Haw.** Hawaiian
Heb. Hebrew
Hind. Hindi
hist. historical
Hung. Hungarian

I **Icel.** Icelandic
Ind. Indonesian
Inuit Inuit
Ir. Irish
It. Italian

J **Jap.** Japanese

K **Kaz.** Kazakh
Kir. Kirghiz
Kor. Korean
Kurd. Kurdish

L **Lao.** Laotian
Lapp. Lappis
Lat. Latin
Latv. Latvian
Lith. Lithanian
Lus. Lusatian

M **Mac.** Macedonian
Mal. Malay
Malg. Malagasy
Malt. Maltese
Mong. Mongolia

N **Nepali.** Nepali
Nor. Norwegian

O **off.** offically

P **Pash.** Pashtu
Per. Persian
Pol. Polish
Port. Portuguese
prev. previously

R **Rmsch.** Romansch
Roman. Romanian
Rus. Russian

S **SCr.** Serbian & Croatian
Serb. Serbian
Slvk. Slovak
Slvn. Slovene
Som. Somali
Sp. Spanish
Swa. Swahili
Swe. Swedish

T **Taj.** Tajik
Th. Thai
Tib. Tibetan
Turk. Turkish
Turkm. Turkmenistan

U **Uigh.** Uighur
Ukr. Ukrainian
Uzb. Uzbek

V **var.** variant
Vtn. Vietnamese

W **Wel.** Welsh

X **Xh.** Xhosa

Y **Yugo.** Yugoslavia

Atlas Index

A

Aachen *486 A4 Dut.* Aken, *Fr.* Aix-la-Chapelle; *anc.* Aquae Grani, Aquisgranum. Nordrhein-Westfalen, W Germany
Aaiún *see* Laâyoune
Aalborg *see* Ålborg
Aalen *487 B6* Baden-Württemberg, S Germany
Aalsmeer *478 C3* Noord-Holland, C Netherlands
Aalst *479 B6 Fr.* Alost. Oost-Vlaanderen, C Belgium
Aalten *478 E4* Gelderland, E Netherlands
Aalter *479 B5* Oost-Vlaanderen, NW Belgium
Äänekoski *477 D5* Keski-Suomi, C Finland
Aar *see* Aare
Aare *487 A7 var.* Aar. *river* W Switzerland
Aarhus *see* Århus
Aat *see* Ath
Aba *467 G5* Abia, S Nigeria
Aba *469 E5* Haut-Zaïre, NE Congo (Zaire)
Abā as Su'ūd *see* Najrān
Abaco Island *see* Great Abaco
Ābādān *512 C4* Khūzestān, SW Iran
Abai *see* Blue Nile
Abakan *506 D4* Respublika Khakasiya, S Russian Federation
Abancay *452 D4* Apurímac, SE Peru
Abariringa *see* Kanton
Abashiri *522 D2 var.* Abasiri. Hokkaidō, NE Japan
Abasiri *see* Abashiri
Ābaya Hāyk' *465 C5 Eng.* Lake Margherita, *It.* Abbaia. *lake* SW Ethiopia
Ābay Wenz *see* Blue Nile
Abbeville *482 C2 anc.* Abbatis Villa. Somme, N France
'Abd al 'Azīz, Jabal *510 D2 mountain range* NE Syria
Abéché *468 C3 var.* Abécher, Abeshr. Ouaddaï, SE Chad
Abécher *see* Abéché
Abela *see* Ávila
Abemama *536 D2 var.* Apamama; *prev.* Roger Simpson Island. *atoll* Tungaru, W Kiribati
Abengourou *467 E5* E Ivory Coast
Aberdeen *480 D3 anc.* Devana. NE Scotland, UK
Aberdeen *437 E2* South Dakota, N USA
Aberdeen *438 B2* Washington, NW USA
Abergwaun *see* Fishguard
Abertawe *see* Swansea
Aberystwyth *481 C6* W Wales, UK
Abeshr *see* Abéché
Abhā *512 B6* 'Asīr, SW Saudi Arabia
Abidavichy *499 D7 Rus.* Obidovichi. Mahilyowskaya Voblasts', E Belorussia
Abidjan *467 E5* S Ivory Coast
Abilene *441 F3* Texas, SW USA
Abingdon *see* Pinta, Isla
Abkhazia *509 E1 autonomous republic* NW Georgia
Åbo *477 D6* Turku-Pori, SW Finland
Aboisso *467 E5* SE Ivory Coast
Abo, Massif d' *468 B1 mountain range* NW Chad
Abomey *467 F5* S Benin
Abou-Déïa *468 C3* Salamat, SE Chad
Abrantes *484 B3 var.* Abrántes. Santarém, C Portugal
Abrolhos Bank *448 E4 undersea feature* W Atlantic Ocean
Abrova *499 B6 Rus.* Obrovo. Brestskaya Voblasts', SW Belorussia
Abrud *500 B4 Ger.* Gross-Schlatten, *Hung.* Abrudbánya. Alba, SW Romania
Abruzzese, Appennino *488 C4 mountain range* C Italy
Absaroka Range *436 B2 mountain range* Montana/Wyoming, NW USA
Abū aḍ Ḍuhūr *510 B3 Fr.* Aboudouhour. Idlib, NW Syria
Abu Dhabi *504 see* Abū Ẓaby
Abu Hamed *464 C3* River Nile, N Sudan
Abū Ḩardān *510 E3 var.* Hajîne. Dayr az Zawr, E Syria
Abuja *467 G4 country capital* (Nigeria) Federal Capital District, C Nigeria
Abū Kamāl *510 E3 Fr.* Abou Kémal. Dayr az Zawr, E Syria
Abula *see* Ávila
Abunã, Rio *454 C2 var.* Río Abuná. *river* Bolivia/Brazil
Abut Head *543 B6 headland* South Island, NZ
Ābuyē Mēda *464 D4 mountain* C Ethiopia
Abū Ẓabī *see* Abū Ẓaby
Abū Ẓaby *513 C5 var.* Abū Ẓabī, *Eng.* Abu Dhabi. *country capital* (UAE) Abū Ẓaby, C UAE
Abyla *see* Ávila
Acalayong *469 A5* SW Equatorial Guinea
Acaponeta *442 D4* Nayarit, C Mexico
Acapulco *443 E5 var.* Acapulco de Juárez. Guerrero, S Mexico
Acapulco de Juárez *see* Acapulco
Acarai Mountains *451 F4 Sp.* Serra Acaraí. *mountain range* Brazil/Guyana
Acarigua *450 D2* Portuguesa, N Venezuela
Accra *467 E5 country capital* (Ghana) SE Ghana
Achacachi *453 E4* La Paz, W Bolivia
Acklins Island *446 C2 island* SE Bahamas
Aconcagua, Cerro *456 B4 mountain* W Argentina
Açores *see* Azores
A Coruña *484 B1 Cast.* La Coruña, *Eng.* Corunna; *anc.* Caronium. Galicia, NW Spain
Acre *454 C2 off.* Estado do Acre. *state* W Brazil
Açu *455 G2 var.* Assu. Rio Grande do Norte, E Brazil
Acuña *442 D2 var.* Villa Acuña. Coahuila de Zaragoza, NE Mexico
Ada *441 G2* Oklahoma, C USA
Ada *492 D3* Serbia, N Yugoslavia
Adalia, Gulf of *see* Antalya Körfezi
Adama *see* Nazrēt
Adamawa Highlands *468 B4 plateau* NW Cameroon
'Adan *513 B7 Eng.* Aden. SW Yemen
Adana *508 D4 var.* Seyhan. Adana, S Turkey
Adapazarı *508 B2 prev.* Ada Bazar. Sakarya, NW Turkey
Adare, Cape *546 B4 headland* Antarctica
Ad Dahnā' *512 C4 desert* E Saudi Arabia
Ad Dakhla *462 A4 var.* Dakhla. SW Western Sahara
Ad Dalanj *see* Dilling
Ad Damar *see* Ed Damer
Ad Damazīn *see* Ed Damazin
Ad Dāmir *see* Ed Damer
Ad Dammān *512 C4 var.* Dammām. Ash Sharqīyah, NE Saudi Arabia
Ad Dāmūr *see* Damoûr
Ad Dawḩah *512 C4 Eng.* Doha. *country capital* (Qatar) C Qatar
Aḍ Ḍiffah *see* Libyan Plateau
Addis Ababa *460 see* Ādīs Ābeba
Addu Atoll *524 A5 atoll* S Maldives
Adelaide *541 B6 state capital* South Australia
Aden *504 see* 'Adan
Aden, Gulf of *513 C7 gulf* SW Arabian Sea
Adige *488 C2 Ger.* Etsch. *river* N Italy
Adirondack Mountains *433 F2 mountain range* New York, NE USA
Ādīs Ābeba *465 C5 Eng.* Addis Ababa. *country capital* (Ethiopia) C Ethiopia
Adıyaman *509 E4* Adıyaman, SE Turkey
Adjud *500 C4* Vrancea, E Romania
Admiralty Islands *536 B3 island group* N PNG
Adra *485 E5* Andalucía, S Spain
Adrar *462 D3* C Algeria
Adrar des Iforas *see* Ifôghas, Adrar des
Adrian *432 C3* Michigan, N USA
Adriatic Sea *495 E2 Alb.* Deti Adriatik, *It.* Mare Adriatico, *SCr.* Jadransko More, *Slvn.* Jadransko Morje. *sea* N Mediterranean Sea
Adycha *507 F2 river* NE Russian Federation
Aegean Sea *497 C5 Gk.* Aigaíon Pélagos, Aigaío Pélagos, *Turk.* Ege Denizi. *sea* NE Mediterranean Sea
Aegviidu *498 D2 Ger.* Charlottenhof. Harjumaa, NW Estonia
Aelana *see* Al 'Aqabah
Aelok *see* Ailuk Atoll
Aelōnlaplap *see* Ailinglaplap Atoll
Aeolian Islands *see* Eolie, Isole
Afar Depression *see* Danakil Desert
Afghanistan *514 C4 off.* Islamic State of Afghanistan, *Per.* Dowlat-e Eslāmī-ye Afghānestān; *prev.* Republic of Afghanistan. *country* C Asia
Afmadow *465 D6* Jubbada Hoose, S Somalia
Africa *460 continent*
Africa, Horn of *460 E4 physical region* Ethiopia/Somalia
Africana Seamount *533 A6 undersea feature* SW Indian Ocean
'Afrīn *510 B2* Ḩalab, N Syria
Afyon *508 B3 prev.* Afyonkarahisar. Afyon, W Turkey
Agadez *467 G3 prev.* Agadès. Agadez, C Niger
Agadir *462 B3* SW Morocco
Agana *536 B1 var.* Agaña. *dependent territory capital* (Guam) NW Guam
Āgaro *465 C5* W Ethiopia
Agassiz Fracture Zone *535 G5 tectonic feature* S Pacific Ocean
Agathónisi *497 D6 island* Dodekánisos, Greece, Aegean Sea
Agde *483 C6 anc.* Agatha. Hérault, S France
Agedabia *see* Ajdābiyā
Agen *483 B5 anc.* Aginnum. Lot-et-Garonne, SW France
Aghri Dagh *see* Büyükağrı Dağı
Agiá *496 B4 var.* Ayiá. Thessalía, C Greece
Agialoúsa *494 D4 var.* Yenierenköy. NE Cyprus
Agía Marína *497 E6* Léros, Dodekánisos, Greece, Aegean Sea
Ágios Nikólaos *497 D8 var.* Áyios Nikólaos. Kríti, Greece, E Mediterranean Sea
Āgra *526 D3* Uttar Pradesh, N India
Ağrı *509 F3 var.* Karaköse; *prev.* Karakılısse. Ağrı, NE Turkey
Agri Dagi *see* Büyükağrı Dağı
Agrigento *489 C7 Gk.* Akragas; *prev.* Girgenti. Sicilia, Italy, C Mediterranean Sea
Agriovótano *497 C5* Évvoia, C Greece
Agropoli *489 D5* Campania, S Italy
Aguachica *450 B2* Cesar, N Colombia
Aguadulce *445 F5* Coclé, S Panama
Agua Prieta *442 B1* Sonora, NW Mexico
Aguascalientes *442 D4* Aguascalientes, C Mexico
Aguaytía *452 C3* Ucayali, C Peru
Aguilas *485 E4* Murcia, SE Spain
Aguililla *442 D4* Michoacán de Ocampo, SW Mexico
Agulhas Basin *461 D8 undersea feature* SW Indian Ocean
Agulhas Plateau *459 D6 undersea feature* SW Indian Ocean
Ahaggar *467 F2 high plateau region* SE Algeria
Ahlen *486 B4* Nordrhein-Westfalen, W Germany
Ahmadābād *526 C4 var.* Ahmedabad. Gujarāt, W India
Ahmadnagar *526 C5 var.* Ahmednagar. Mahārāshtra, W India
Ahmedabad *see* Ahmadābād
Ahmednagar *see* Ahmadnagar
Ahuachapán *444 B3* Ahuachapán, W El Salvador
Ahvāz *512 C3 var.* Ahwāz; *prev.* Nāsiri. Khūzestān, SW Iran
Ahvenanmaa *see* Åland
Ahwāz *see* Ahvāz
Aïdin *see* Aydın
Aígina *497 C6 var.* Aíyina, Egina. Aígina, C Greece
Aígio *497 B5 var.* Egio; *prev.* Aíyion. Dytikí Ellás, S Greece
Aiken *435 E2* South Carolina, SE USA
Ailigandí *445 G4* San Blas, NE Panama
Ailinglaplap Atoll *536 D2 var.* Aelōnlaplap. *atoll* Ralik Chain, S Marshall Islands
Ailuk Atoll *536 D1 var.* Aelok. *atoll* Ratak Chain, NE Marshall Islands
Ainaži *498 D3 Est.* Heinaste, *Ger.* Hainasch. Limbaži, N Latvia
'Aïn Ben Tili *466 D1* Tiris Zemmour, N Mauritania
Aintab *see* Gaziantep
Aïoun el Atrous *see* 'Ayoûn el 'Atroûs
Aïoun el Atroûss *see* 'Ayoûn el 'Atroûs
Aiquile *453 F4* Cochabamba, C Bolivia
Aïr *see* Aïr, Massif de l'
Air du Azbine *see* Aïr, Massif de l'
Aïr, Massif de l' *467 G2 var.* Aïr, Air du Azbine, Asben. *mountain range* NC Niger
Aiud *500 B4 Ger.* Strassburg, *Hung.* Nagyenyed; *prev.* Engeten. Alba, SW Romania
Aix *see* Aix-en-Provence
Aix-en-Provence *483 D6 var.* Aix; *anc.* Aquae Sextiae. Bouches-du-Rhône, SE France
Aíyina *see* Aígina
Aíyion *see* Aígio
Aizkraukle *498 C4* Aizkraukle, S Latvia
Ajaccio *483 E7* Corse, France, C Mediterranean Sea
Ajaria *509 F2 autonomous republic* SW Georgia
Aj Bogd Uul *518 D2 mountain* SW Mongolia
Ajdābiyā *463 G2 var.* Agedabia, Ajdābiyah. NE Libya
Ajdābiyah *see* Ajdābiyā
Ajjinena *see* El Geneina
Ajmer *526 D3 var.* Ajmere. Rājasthān, N India
Ajmere *see* Ajmer
Ajo *440 A3* Arizona, SW USA
Akaba *see* Al 'Aqabah
Akamagaseki *see* Shimonoseki
Akasha *464 B3* Northern, N Sudan
Akchâr *466 C2 desert* W Mauritania
Akhalts'ikhe *509 F2* SW Georgia
Akhisar *508 A3* Manisa, W Turkey
Akhmîm *464 B2 anc.* Panopolis. C Egypt
Akhtubinsk *503 C7* Astrakhanskaya Oblast', SW Russian Federation
Akimiski Island *430 C3 island* Nunavut, C Canada
Akinovka *501 F4* Zaporiz'ka Oblast', S Ukraine
Akita *522 D4* Akita, Honshū, C Japan
Akjoujt *466 C2 prev.* Fort-Repoux. Inchiri, W Mauritania
Akkeshi *522 E2* Hokkaidō, NE Japan
Aklavik *428 D3* Northwest Territories, NW Canada
Akmola *see* Astana
Akpatok Island *431 E1 island* Nunavut, E Canada
Akra Dhrepanon *see* Drépano, Ákra
Akra Kanestron *see* Palioúri, Ákra
Akron *432 D4* Ohio, N USA
Akrotiri *see* Akrotírion
Akrotírion *494 C5 var.* Akrotiri. *UK air base* S Cyprus
Aksai Chin *516 B2 Chin.* Aksayqin. *disputed region* China/India
Aksaray *508 C4* Aksaray, C Turkey
Akşehir *508 B4* Konya, W Turkey
Aktau *506 A4 Kaz.* Aqtaū; *prev.* Shevchenko. Mangistau, W Kazakhstan
Aktsyabrski *499 C7 Rus.* Oktyabr'skiy; *prev.* Karpilovka. Homyel'skaya Voblasts', SE Belorussia
Aktyubinsk *506 B4 Kaz.* Aqtöbe. Aktyubinsk, NW Kazakhstan
Akula *469 C5* Equateur, NW Congo (Zaire)
Akureyri *475 E4* Nordhurland Eystra, N Iceland
Akyab *see* Sittwe
Alabama *443 G1 off.* State of Alabama; also known as Camellia State, Heart of Dixie, The Cotton State, Yellowhammer State. *state* S USA
Alabama River *434 C3 river* Alabama, S USA
Alaca *508 C3* Çorum, N Turkey
Alagoas *455 G2 off.* Estado de Alagoas. *state* E Brazil
Alajuela *445 E4* Alajuela, C Costa Rica
Alakanuk *428 C2* Alaska, USA
Al 'Alamayn *see* El 'Alamein
Al 'Amārah *512 C3 var.* Amara. E Iraq
Alamo *439 D6* Nevada, W USA
Alamogordo *440 D3* New Mexico, SW USA
Alamosa *436 C5* Colorado, C USA
Åland *477 C6 var.* Aland Islands, *Fin.* Ahvenanmaa. *island group* SW Finland
Aland Islands *see* Åland
Aland Sea *see* Ålands Hav
Ålands Hav *477 C6 var.* Aland Sea. *strait* Baltic Sea/Gulf of Bothnia
Alanya *508 C4* Antalya, S Turkey
Alappuzha *see* Alleppey
Al 'Aqabah *511 B8 var.* Akaba, Aqaba, 'Aqaba; *anc.* Aelana, Elath. Ma'ān, SW Jordan
Alaşehir *508 A4* Manisa, W Turkey
Al 'Ashārah *510 E3 var.* Ashara. Dayr az Zawr, E Syria
Alaska *428 C3 off.* State of … also known as Land of the Midnight Sun, The Last F… Seward's Folly; *prev.* Russi… America. *state* NW USA
Alaska, Gulf of *428 C4 var* … de Alasca. *gulf* Canada/U…
Alaska Peninsula *428 C3* … Alaska, USA
Alaska Range *426 B2 mou… range* Alaska, USA
Al-Asnam *see* Chlef
Al Awaynāt *see* Al 'Uwayn…
Al 'Aynā *511 B7* Al Karak, W Jordan
Alazeya *507 G2 river* NE R… Federation
Al Bāb *510 B2* Ḩalab, N Sy…
Albacete *485 E3* Castilla-L… Mancha, C Spain
Al Baghdādī *512 B3 var.* K… al Baghdādī. SW Iraq
Al Bāha *see* Al Bāḩah
Al Bāḩah *513 B5 var.* Al Bā… Al Bāḩah, SW Saudi Arab…
Al Baḩr al Mayyit *see* Dea…
Alba Iulia *500 B4 Ger.* Wei… *Hung.* Gyulafehérvár; *pre…* Bălgrad, Karlsburg, Károl… Fehérvár. Alba, W Romar…
Albania *493 C7 off.* Republ… Albania, *Alb.* Republika e… Shqipërisë, Shqipëria; *pre…* People's Socialist Republi… Albania. *country* SE Euro…
Albany *430 C3 river* Ontar… S Canada
Albany *433 F3 state capital* … York, NE USA
Albany *434 D3* Georgia, SE…
Albany *438 B3* Oregon, NW…
Albany *539 B7* Western Au…
Al Bāridah *510 C4 var.* Bā… Ḩimş, C Syria
Al Başrah *512 C3 Eng.* Bas… Busra, Bussora. SE Iraq
Al Batrūn *see* Batroûn
Al Bayḍā' *463 G2 var.* Beid… NE Libya
Albemarle Island *see* Isab…
Albemarle Sound *435 G1* … W Atlantic Ocean
Albergaria-a-Velha *484 B…* N Portugal
Albert *482 C3* Somme, N F…
Alberta *429 E4 province* SW…
Albert Edward Nyanza *se…* Edward, Lake
Albert, Lake *465 B6 var.* A… Nyanza, Lac Mobutu Ses… *lake* Uganda/Congo (Zair…
Albert Lea *437 F3* Minnes… N USA
Albert Nyanza *see* Albert, …
Albi *483 C6 anc.* Albiga. Ta… S France
Ålborg *472 D3 var.* Aalbor… Ålborg-Nørresundby; *an…* Alburgum. Nordjylland, N Denmark
Ålborg-Nørresundby *see* …
Alborz, Reshteh-ye Kūh… *C2 Eng.* Elburz Mountain… *mountain range* N Iran
Albuquerque *440 D2* New… SW USA
Al Burayqah *see* Marsá al …
Alburgum *see* Ålborg
Albury *541 C7* New South… SE Australia
Alcácer do Sal *484 B4* Setu… W Portugal
Alcalá de Henares *485 E3* … Alkal'a; *anc.* Complutum… C Spain
Alcamo *489 C7* Sicilia, Ital… C Mediterranean Sea
Alcañiz *485 F2* Aragón, N…
Alcántara, Embalse de *48…* *reservoir* W Spain
Alcaudete *484 D4* Andalu… S Spain
Alcázar *see* Ksar-el-Kebir
Alcoi *see* Alcoy
Alcoy *485 F4 var.* Alcoi. Pa… Valenciano, E Spain
Aldabra Group *471 G2 isl…* SW Seychelles
Aldan *507 F3 river* NE Rus… Federation
al Dar al Baida *see* Rabat
Alderney *482 A2 island* Ch… Islands
Aleg *466 C3* Brakna, SW M…
Aleksandropol' *see* Gyum…
Aleksin *503 B5* Tul'skaya … W Russian Federation
Aleksinac *492 E4* Serbia, SE Yugoslavia
Alençon *482 B3* Orne, N F…
Alenquer *455 E2* Pará, NE…
Aleppo *504 see* Ḩalab
Alert *429 F1* Ellesmere Isla… Nunavut, N Canada
Alès *483 C6 prev.* Alais. Ga… S France

Aleşd – Antayla Körfezi

500 B3 *Hung.* Élesd. Bihor, omania
ndria 488 B2 *Fr.* Alexandrie. onte, N Italy
d 477 A5 Møre og Romsdal, way
an Basin 505 G3 *undersea* e Bering Sea
an Islands 428 A3 *island* Alaska, USA
an Range 426 A2 *mountain* Alaska, USA
an Trench 505 H3 *undersea* e S Bering Sea
der Archipelago 428 D4 l *group* Alaska, USA
der City 434 D2 Alabama, A
der Island 546 A3 *island* ctica
dra 543 B7 Otago, South l, NZ
dreia 496 B4 *var.* ndria. Kentrikí Makedonía, eece
dria 464 B1 *Ar.* kandarīyah. N Egypt
dria *see* Alexándreia
ndria 434 B3 Louisiana, A
ndria 437 F2 Minnesota, A
ndria 500 C5 Teleorman, nania
droúpoli 496 D3 *var.* ndroúpolis, *Turk.* Dedeagaç, agach. Anatolikí Makedonía hráki, NE Greece
droúpolis *see* ndroúpoli
hir *see* El Fasher
r 496 E1 Razgradska Oblast, ulgaria
s 497 B6 *prev.* Alfiós, *anc.* eius, Alpheus. *river* S Greece
see Great Hungarian Plain
06 B4 *Kaz.* Algha. ubinsk, NW Kazakhstan
e 484 B4 *cultural region* tugal
ras 484 C5 Andalucía, pain
esí 485 F3 País Valenciano, ain
nain *see* El Geneina
463 E1 *var.* Algiers, El Djazaïr, zair. *country capital* (Algeria) geria
a 462 C3 *off.* Democratic and lar Republic of Algeria. *try* N Africa
an Basin 472 C5 *var.* Balearic *undersea feature* editerranean Sea
ıbah 513 E5 *var.* Ghaba. nan
ro 489 A5 Sardegna, Italy, editerranean Sea
ırdaqah *see* Hurghada
s *see* Alger
ea *see* El Goléa
a 437 F3 Iowa, C USA
ār al Gharbī 513 D5 *ntain range* N Oman
sakah 510 D2 *var.* Al Hasijah, aseke, *Fr.* Hassetché. asakah, NE Syria
sijah *see* Al Ḥasakah
lah 512 B3 *var.* Hilla. C Iraq
sā 511 B7 Aṭ Ṭafilah, rdan
daydah 513 B6 *Eng.* Hodeida. emen
fūf 512 C4 *var.* Hofuf. Ash qīyah, NE Saudi Arabia
monas 496 B4 *prev.* kmon, *anc.* Haliacmon. *river* eece
os 497 C5 Stereá Ellás, eece
nte 485 F4 *Cat.* Alacant; *Lat.* ntum. País Valenciano, pain
441 G5 Texas, SW USA
Springs 540 A4 Northern tory, C Australia
see Alykí
469 B6 *river* C Congo
ao 468 C4 Basse-Kotto, ntral African Republic
ippa 432 D4 Pennsylvania, USA
āti 496 C3 Kentrikí edonía, NE Greece
ri 497 C5 *var.* Alivérion. ia, C Greece
ion *see* Alivéri
al Akhḍar 463 G2 *ntain range* NE Libya
al ash Sharqī *see* Anti- non
r 511 B7 Ma'ān, S Jordan
hbūb 463 H3 NE Libya
rā' 512 C4 *var.* Al Jahrah, . C Kuwait
rah *see* Al Jahrā'

Al Jawf 512 B4 *var.* Jauf. Al Jawf, NW Saudi Arabia
Al Jazair *see* Alger
Al Jazīrah 510 E2 *physical region* Iraq/Syria
Al Jīzah *see* El Gîza
Al Junaynah *see* El Geneina
Al Karak 511 B7 *var.* El Kerak, Karak, Kerak; *anc.* Kir Moab, Kir of Moab. Al Karak, W Jordan
Al-Kasr al-Kebir *see* Ksar-el-Kebir
Al Khalīl *see* Hebron
Al Khārijah *see* El Khârga
Al Khufrah 463 H4 SE Libya
Al Khums 463 F2 *var.* Homs, Khoms, Khums. NW Libya
Alkmaar 478 C2 Noord-Holland, NW Netherlands
Al Kūt 512 C3 *var.* Kūt al 'Amārah, Kut al Imara. E Iraq
Al-Kuwait *see* Al Kuwayt
Al Kuwayt 512 C4 *var.* Al-Kuwait, *Eng.* Kuwait, Kuwait City; *prev.* Qurein. *country capital* (Kuwait) E Kuwait
Al Lādhiqīyah 510 A3 *Eng.* Latakia, *Fr.* Lattaquié; *anc.* Laodicea, Laodicea ad Mare. Al Lādhiqīyah, W Syria
Allahābād 527 E3 Uttar Pradesh, N India
Allanmyo 528 B4 Magwe, C Burma
Allegheny Plateau 433 E3 *mountain range* New York/Pennsylvania, NE USA
Allentown 433 F4 Pennsylvania, NE USA
Alleppey 524 C3 *var.* Alappuzha; *prev.* Alleppi. Kerala, SW India
Alleppi *see* Alleppey
Alliance 436 D3 Nebraska, C USA
Al Līth 513 B5 Makkah, SW Saudi Arabia
Alma-Ata 504 *see* Almaty
Almada 484 B4 Setúbal, W Portugal
Al Madīnah 513 A5 *Eng.* Medina. Al Madīnah, W Saudi Arabia
Al Mafraq 511 B6 *var.* Mafraq. Al Mafraq, N Jordan
Al Mahdīyah *see* Mahdia
Al Mahrah 513 C6 *mountain range* E Yemen
Al Majma'ah 512 B4 Ar Riyāḍ, C Saudi Arabia
Al Mālikīyah 510 E1 Al Ḥasakah, NE Syria
Al Manāmah 512 C4 *Eng.* Manama. *country capital* (Bahrain) N Bahrain
Al Manāṣif 510 E3 *mountain range* E Syria
Almansa 485 F4 Castilla-La Mancha, C Spain
Al Marj 463 G2 *var.* Barka, *It.* Barce. NE Libya
Almaty 506 C5 *var.* Alma-Ata. Almaty, SE Kazakhstan
Al Mawṣil 512 B2 *Eng.* Mosul. N Iraq
Al Mayādīn 510 D3 *var.* Mayadin, *Fr.* Meyadine. Dayr az Zawr, E Syria
Al Mazra' *see* Al Mazra'ah
Al Mazra'ah 511 B6 *var.* Al Mazra', Mazra'a. Al Karak, W Jordan
Almelo 478 E3 Overijssel, E Netherlands
Almendra, Embalse de 484 C2 *reservoir* Castilla-León, NW Spain
Almendralejo 484 C4 Extremadura, W Spain
Almere 478 C3 *var.* Almere-stad. Flevoland, C Netherlands
Almere-stad *see* Almere
Almería 485 E5 *Ar.* Al-Mariyya; *anc.* Unci, *Lat.* Portus Magnus. Andalucía, S Spain
Al'met'yevsk 503 D5 Respublika Tatarstan, W Russian Federation
Al Mīnā' *see* El Mina
Al Minyā *see* El Minya
Almirante 445 E4 Bocas del Toro, NW Panama
Al Mudawwarah 511 B8 Ma'ān, SW Jordan
Al Mukallā 513 C6 *var.* Mukalla. SE Yemen
Al Obayyid *see* El Obeid
Alofi 537 F4 *dependent territory capital* (Niue) W Niue
Aloja 498 D3 Limbaži, N Latvia
Alónnisos 497 C5 *island* Vóreioi Sporádes, Greece, Aegean Sea
Álora 484 D5 Andalucía, S Spain
Alor, Kepulauan 531 E5 *island group* E Indonesia
Al Oued *see* El Oued
Alpen *see* Alps
Alpena 432 D2 Michigan, N USA
Alpes *see* Alps
Alpha Cordillera 548 B3 *var.* Alpha Ridge. *undersea feature* Arctic Ocean
Alpha Ridge *see* Alpha Cordillera
Alphen *see* Alphen aan den Rijn

Alphen aan den Rijn 478 C3 *var.* Alphen. Zuid-Holland, C Netherlands
Alpi *see* Alps
Alpine 441 E4 Texas, SW USA
Alpi Transilvaniei *see* Carpaţii Meridionali
Alps 494 C1 *Fr.* Alpes, *Ger.* Alpen, *It.* Alpi. *mountain range* C Europe
Al Qaḍārif *see* Gedaref
Al Qāmishlī 510 E1 *var.* Kamishli, Qamishly. Al Ḥasakah, NE Syria
Al Qaṣrayn *see* Kasserine
Al Qayrawān *see* Kairouan
Al-Qsar *see* Ksar-el-Kebir
Al Qubayyāt *see* Qoubaïyât
Al Qunayṭirah 511 B5 *var.* El Kuneitra, El Quneitra, Kuneitra, Qunaytra. Al Qunayṭirah, SW Syria
Al Quṣayr 510 B4 *var.* El Quseir, Quṣayr, *Fr.* Kousseir. Ḥimṣ, W Syria
Al Quwayrah 511 B8 *var.* El Quweira. Ma'ān, SW Jordan
Alsace 482 E3 *cultural region* NE France
Alsdorf 486 A4 Nordrhein-Westfalen, W Germany
Alt *see* Olt
Alta 476 D2 *Fin.* Alattio. Finnmark, N Norway
Altai *see* Altai Mountains
Altai Mountains 518 C2 *var.* Altai, *Chin.* Altay Shan, *Rus.* Altay. *mountain range* Asia/Europe
Altamaha River 435 E3 *river* Georgia, SE USA
Altamira 455 E2 Pará, NE Brazil
Altamura 489 E5 *anc.* Lupatia. Puglia, SE Italy
Altar, Desierto de 442 A1 *var.* Sonoran Desert. *desert* Mexico/USA *see also* Sonoran Desert
Altay 518 C2 *Chin.* A-le-t'ai, *Mong.* Sharasume; *prev.* Ch'eng-hua, Chenghwa. Xinjiang Uygur Zizhiqu, NW China
Altay *see* Altai Mountains
Altay 518 D2 Govĭ-Altay, W Mongolia
Altay Shan *see* Altai Mountains
Altin Köprü 512 B3 *var.* Altun Kupri. N Iraq
Altiplano 453 F4 *physical region* W South America
Alton 432 B5 Illinois, N USA
Alton 432 B4 Missouri, C USA
Altoona 433 E4 Pennsylvania, NE USA
Alto Paraná *see* Paraná
Altun Kupri *see* Altin Köprü
Altun Shan 518 C3 *var.* Altyn Tagh. *mountain range* NW China
Altus 441 F2 Oklahoma, C USA
Altyn Tagh *see* Altun Shan
Al Ubayyiḍ *see* El Obeid
Alūksne 498 D3 *Ger.* Marienburg. Alūksne, NE Latvia
Al 'Ulā 512 A4 Al Madīnah, NW Saudi Arabia
Al 'Umarī 511 C6 'Ammān, E Jordan
Alupka 501 F5 Respublika Krym, S Ukraine
Alushta 501 F5 Respublika Krym, S Ukraine
Al 'Uwaynāt 463 F4 *var.* Al Awaynāt. SW Libya
Alva 441 F1 Oklahoma, C USA
Alvarado 443 F4 Veracruz-Llave, E Mexico
Alvin 441 H4 Texas, SW USA
Al Wajh 512 A4 Tabūk, NW Saudi Arabia
Alwar 526 D3 Rājasthān, N India
Al Wari'ah 512 C4 Ash Sharqīyah, N Saudi Arabia
Alykí 496 C4 *var.* Aliki. Thásos, N Greece
Alytus 499 B5 *Pol.* Olita. Alytus, S Lithuania
Alzette 479 D8 *river* S Luxembourg
Amadeus, Lake 539 D5 *seasonal lake* Northern Territory, C Australia
Amadi 465 B5 Western Equatoria, SW Sudan
Amadjuak Lake 429 G3 *lake* Baffin Island, Nunavut, N Canada
Amakusa-nada 523 A7 *gulf* Kyūshū, SW Japan
Åmål 477 B6 Älvsborg, S Sweden
Amami-guntō 522 A3 *island group* SW Japan
Amami-Ō-shima 522 A3 *island* S Japan
Amantea 489 D6 Calabria, SW Italy
Amapá 455 E1 Amapá, NE Brazil
Amara *see* Al 'Amārah
Amarapura 528 B3 Mandalay, C Burma
Amarillo 441 E2 Texas, SW USA
Amay 479 C6 Liège, E Belgium

Amazon 455 E1 *Sp.* Amazonas. *river* Brazil/Peru
Amazon Basin 454 D2 *basin* N South America
Amazon, Mouths of the 455 F1 *delta* NE Brazil
Ambam 469 B5 Sud, S Cameroon
Ambanja 471 G2 Antsiranana, N Madagascar
Ambarchik 507 G2 Respublika Sakha (Yakutiya), NE Russian Federation
Ambato 452 B1 Tungurahua, C Ecuador
Ambérieu-en-Bugey 483 D5 Ain, E France
Amboasary 471 F4 Toliara, S Madagascar
Ambon 531 F4 *prev.* Amboina, Amboyna. Pulau Ambon, E Indonesia
Ambositra 471 G3 Fianarantsoa, SE Madagascar
Ambrim *see* Ambrym
Ambriz 470 A1 Bengo, NW Angola
Ambrym 536 D4 *var.* Ambrim. *island* C Vanuatu
Amchitka Island 428 A2 *island* Aleutian Islands, Alaska, USA
Amdo 518 C5 Xizang Zizhiqu, W China
Ameland 478 D1 *Fris.* It Amelân. *island* Waddeneilanden, N Netherlands
America-Antarctica Ridge 459 C7 *undersea feature* S Atlantic Ocean
American Falls Reservoir 438 E4 *reservoir* Idaho, NW USA
American Samoa 537 E4 *US unincorporated territory* W Polynesia
Amersfoort 478 D3 Utrecht, C Netherlands
Ames 437 F3 Iowa, C USA
Amfilochía 497 A5 *var.* Amfilokhía. Dytikí Ellás, C Greece
Amfilokhía *see* Amfilochía
Amga 507 F3 *river* NE Russian Federation
Amherst 431 F4 Nova Scotia, SE Canada
Amida *see* Diyarbakır
Amiens 482 C3 *anc.* Ambianum, Samarobriva. Somme, N France
Amíndaion *see* Amýntaio
Amindeo *see* Amýntaio
Amīndīvi Islands 524 A2 *island group* Lakshadweep, India, N Indian Ocean
Amirante Islands 471 G1 *var.* Amirantes Group. *island group* C Seychelles
Amirantes Group *see* Amirante Islands
Amistad Reservoir 441 F4 *var.* Presa de la Amistad. *reservoir* Mexico/USA
'Ammān 511 B6 *var.* Amman; *anc.* Philadelphia, *Bibl.* Rabbah Ammon, Rabbath Ammon. *country capital* (Jordan) 'Ammān, NW Jordan
Amman 504 *see* 'Ammān
Ammassalik 474 D4 *var.* Angmagssalik. S Greenland
Ammóchostos 494 D5 *var.* Famagusta, Gazimağusa. E Cyprus
Āmol 512 D2 *var.* Amul. Māzandarān, N Iran
Amorgós 497 D6 *island* Kykládes, Greece, Aegean Sea
Amorgós 497 D6 Amorgós, Kykládes, Greece, Aegean Sea
Amos 430 D4 Québec, SE Canada
Amourj 466 D3 Hodh ech Chargui, SE Mauritania
Amoy *see* Xiamen
Ampato, Nevado 453 E4 *mountain* S Peru
Amposta 485 F2 Cataluña, NE Spain
Amrāvati 526 D4 *prev.* Amraoti. Mahārāshtra, C India
Amritsar 526 D2 Punjab, N India
Amstelveen 478 C3 Noord-Holland, C Netherlands
Amsterdam 478 C3 *country capital* (Netherlands) Noord-Holland, C Netherlands
Amsterdam Island 533 C6 *island* NE French Southern and Antarctic Territories
Am Timan 468 C3 Salamat, SE Chad
Amu Darya 514 D2 *Rus.* Amudar'ya, *Taj.* Dar"yoi Amu, *Turkm.* Amyderya, *Uzb.* Amudaryo; *anc.* Oxus. *river* C Asia
Amu-Dar'ya 515 E3 Lebapskiy Velayat, NE Turkmenistan
Amul *see* Āmol
Amund Ringnes Island 429 F2 *island* Northwest Territories, N Canada
Amundsen Basin *see* Fram Basin
Amundsen Gulf 429 E2 *gulf* Northwest Territories, N Canada

Amundsen Plain 546 A4 *undersea feature* S Pacific Ocean
Amundsen-Scott 546 B3 *US research station* Antarctica
Amundsen Sea 546 A4 *sea* S Pacific Ocean
Amuntai 530 D4 *prev.* Amoentai. Borneo, C Indonesia
Amur 507 G4 *Chin.* Heilong Jiang. *river* China/Russian Federation
Amvrosiyivka 501 H3 *Rus.* Amvrosiyevka. Donets'ka Oblast', SE Ukraine
Amýntaio 496 B4 *var.* Amindeo; *prev.* Amíndaion. Dytikí Makedonía, N Greece
Anabar 507 E2 *river* NE Russian Federation
An Abhainn Mhór *see* Blackwater
Anaco 451 E2 Anzoátegui, NE Venezuela
Anaconda 436 B2 Montana, NW USA
Anacortes 438 B1 Washington, NW USA
Anadolu Dağları *see* Doğu Karadeniz Dağları
Anadyr' 507 G1 *river* NE Russian Federation
Anadyr' 507 H1 Chukotskiy Avtonomnyy Okrug, NE Russian Federation
Anadyr, Gulf of 505 *see* Anadyrskiy Zaliv
Anadyrskiy Zaliv 507 H1 *Eng.* Gulf of Anadyr. *gulf* NE Russian Federation
Anáfi 497 D7 *anc.* Anaphe. *island* Kykládes, Greece, Aegean Sea
'Ānah *see* 'Annah
Anaheim 438 E2 California, W USA
Anaiza *see* 'Unayzah
Analalava 471 G2 Mahajanga, NW Madagascar
Anamur 508 C5 İçel, S Turkey
Anantapur 524 C2 Andhra Pradesh, S India
Anápolis 455 F3 Goiás, C Brazil
Anār 512 D3 Kermān, C Iran
Anatolia 508 C4 *plateau* C Turkey
Anatom 536 D5 *var.* Aneityum; *prev.* Kéamu. *island* S Vanuatu
Añatuya 456 C3 Santiago del Estero, N Argentina
An Bhearú *see* Barrow
Anchorage 428 C3 Alaska, USA
Ancona 488 C3 Marche, C Italy
Ancud 457 B6 *prev.* San Carlos de Ancud. Los Lagos, S Chile
Åndalsnes 477 A5 Møre og Romsdal, S Norway
Andalucía 484 D4 *cultural region* S Spain
Andalusia 434 C3 Alabama, S USA
Andaman Islands 516 B4 *island group* India, NE Indian Ocean
Andaman Sea 516 C4 *sea* NE Indian Ocean
Andenne 479 C6 Namur, SE Belgium
Anderlues 479 B7 Hainaut, S Belgium
Anderson 432 C4 Indiana, N USA
Andes 456 B3 *mountain range* W South America
Andhra Pradesh 527 E5 *state* E India
Andijon 515 F2 *Rus.* Andizhan. Andijon Wiloyati, E Uzbekistan
Andikíthira *see* Antikýthira
Andipaxi *see* Antípaxoi
Andípsara *see* Antípsara
Ándissa *see* Ántissa
Andkhvoy 514 D3 Fāryāb, N Afghanistan
Andorra 483 A7 *off.* Principality of Andorra, *Cat.* Valls d'Andorra, *Fr.* Vallée d'Andorre. *country* SW Europe
Andorra *see* Andorra la Vella
Andorra la Vella 483 A8 *var.* Andorra, *Fr.* Andorre la Vielle, *Sp.* Andorra la Vieja. *country capital* (Andorra) C Andorra
Andorra la Vieja *see* Andorra la Vella
Andorre la Vielle *see* Andorra la Vella
Andover 481 D7 S England, UK
Andøya 476 C2 *island* C Norway
Andreanof Islands 428 A3 *island group* Aleutian Islands, Alaska, USA
Andrews 441 E3 Texas, SW USA
Andrew Tablemount 532 A4 *var.* Gora Andryu. *undersea feature* W Indian Ocean
Andria 489 D5 Puglia, SE Italy
An Droichead Nua *see* Newbridge
Ándros 497 C6 *island* Kykládes, Greece, Aegean Sea
Ándros 497 D6 Ándros, Kykládes, Greece, Aegean Sea
Andros Island 446 B2 *island* NW Bahamas

Andros Town 446 C1 Andros Island, NW Bahamas
Aneityum *see* Anatom
Ānewetak *see* Enewetak Atoll
Angara 507 E4 *river* C Russian Federation
Angarsk 507 E4 Irkutskaya Oblast', S Russian Federation
Ånge 477 C5 Västernorrland, C Sweden
Ángel de la Guarda, Isla 442 B2 *island* NW Mexico
Angeles 531 E1 *off.* Angeles City. Luzon, N Philippines
Angel Falls *see* Ángel, Salto
Ángel, Salto 451 E3 *Eng.* Angel Falls. *waterfall* E Venezuela
Ångermanälven 476 C4 *river* N Sweden
Angermünde 486 D3 Brandenburg, NE Germany
Angers 482 B4 *anc.* Juliomagus. Maine-et-Loire, NW France
Anglesey 481 C5 *island* NW Wales, UK
Anglet 483 A6 Pyrénées-Atlantiques, SW France
Angleton 441 H4 Texas, SW USA
Angmagssalik *see* Ammassalik
Ang Nam Ngum 528 C4 *lake* C Laos
Angola 470 B2 *off.* Republic of Angola; *prev.* People's Republic of Angola, Portuguese West Africa. *country* SW Africa
Angola Basin 461 B5 *undersea feature* E Atlantic Ocean
Angostura, Presa de la 443 G5 *reservoir* SE Mexico
Angoulême 483 B5 *anc.* Iculisma. Charente, W France
Angoumois 483 B5 *cultural region* W France
Angren 515 F2 Toshkent Wiloyati, E Uzbekistan
Anguilla 447 G3 *UK dependent territory* E West Indies
Anguilla Cays 446 B2 *islets* SW Bahamas
Anhui 520 C5 *var.* Anhui Sheng, Anhwei, Wan. Admin. region *province* E China
Anhui Sheng *see* Anhui
Anhwei *see* Anhui
Anina 500 A4 *Ger.* Steierdorf, *Hung.* Stájerlakanina; *prev.* Ştaierdorf-Anina, Steierdorf-Anina, Steyerlak-Anina. Caraş-Severin, SW Romania
Anjou 482 B4 *cultural region* NW France
Anjouan 471 F2 *var.* Nzwani, Johanna Island. *island* SE Comoros
Ankara 508 C3 *prev.* Angora, *anc.* Ancyra. *country capital* (Turkey) Ankara, C Turkey
Ankeny 437 F3 Iowa, C USA
Anklam 486 D2 Mecklenburg-Vorpommern, NE Germany
Anykščiai 498 C4 Anykščiai, E Lithuania
An Longfort *see* Longford
An Mhuir Cheilteach *see* Celtic Sea
Annaba 463 E1 *prev.* Bône. NE Algeria
An Nafūd 512 B4 *desert* NW Saudi Arabia
'Annah 512 B3 *var.* 'Ānah. NW Iraq
An Najaf 512 B3 *var.* Najaf. S Iraq
Annamitique, Chaîne 528 D4 *mountain range* C Laos
Annapolis 433 F4 *state capital* Maryland, NE USA
Annapurna 527 E3 *mountain* C Nepal
An Nāqūrah *see* En Nâqoûra
Ann Arbor 432 C3 Michigan, N USA
An Nāṣirīyah 512 C3 *var.* Nasiriya. SE Iraq
Annecy 483 D5 *anc.* Anneciacum. Haute-Savoie, E France
An Nīl al Azraq *see* Blue Nile
Anniston 434 D2 Alabama, S USA
Annotto Bay 446 B4 C Jamaica
An Ómaigh *see* Omagh
Anqing 520 D5 Anhui, E China
Anse La Raye 447 F1 NW Saint Lucia
Anshun 520 B6 Guizhou, S China
Ansongo 467 E3 Gao, E Mali
An Srath Bán *see* Strabane
Antakya 508 D4 *anc.* Antioch, Antiochia. Hatay, S Turkey
Antalaha 471 G2 Antsirañana, NE Madagascar
Antalya 508 B4 *prev.* Adalia, *anc.* Attaleia, *Bibl.* Attalia. Antalya, SW Turkey
Antalya, Gulf of *see* Antalya Körfezi
Antalya Körfezi 508 B4 *var.* Gulf of Adalia, *Eng.* Gulf of Antalya. *gulf* SW Turkey

Antananarivo – Auxerre

Antananarivo *471 G3 prev.* Tananarive. *country capital* (Madagascar) Antananarivo, C Madagascar
Antarctica *546 B3 continent*
Antarctic Peninsula *546 A2 peninsula* Antarctica
Antep *see* Gaziantep
Antequera *484 D5 anc.* Anticaria, Antiquaria. Andalucía, S Spain
Antequera *see* Oaxaca
Antibes *483 D6 anc.* Antipolis. Alpes-Maritimes, SE France
Anticosti, Île d' *431 F3 Eng.* Anticosti Island. *island* Québec, E Canada
Antigua *447 G3 island* S Antigua and Barbuda, Leeward Islands
Antigua and Barbuda *447 G3 country* E West Indies
Antikýthira *497 B7 var.* Andikíthira. *island* S Greece
Anti-Lebanon *510 B4 var.* Jebel esh Sharqi, *Ar.* Al Jabal ash Sharqī, *Fr.* Anti-Liban. *mountain range* Lebanon/Syria
Anti-Liban *see* Anti-Lebanon
Antípaxoi *497 A5 var.* Andipaxi. *island* Iónioi Nísoi, Greece, C Mediterranean Sea
Antipodes Islands *534 D5 island group* S NZ
Antípsara *497 D5 var.* Andípsara. *island* E Greece
Ántissa *497 D5 var.* Ándissa. Lésvos, E Greece
An tIúr *see* Newry
Antofagasta *456 B2* Antofagasta, N Chile
Antony *482 E2* Hauts-de-Seine, N France
Antserana *see* Antsirañana
An tSionainn *see* Shannon
Antsirañana *471 G2 var.* Antserana; *prev.* Antsirane, Diégo-Suarez. Antsirañana, N Madagascar
Antsirane *see* Antsirañana
Antsohihy *471 G2* Mahajanga, NW Madagascar
An-tung *see* Dandong
Antwerp *see* Antwerpen
Antwerpen *479 C5 Eng.* Antwerp, *Fr.* Anvers. Antwerpen, N Belgium
Anuradhapura *524 D3* North Central Province, C Sri Lanka
Anyang *520 C4* Henan, C China
A'nyêmaqên Shan *518 D4 mountain range* C China
Anzio *489 C5* Lazio, C Italy
Aomori *522 D3* Aomori, Honshū, C Japan
Aóos *see* Vjosës, Lumi i
Aosta *488 A1 anc.* Augusta Praetoria. Valle d'Aosta, NW Italy
Ao Thai *see* Thailand, Gulf of
Aoukâr *466 D3 var.* Aouker. *plateau* C Mauritania
Aouk, Bahr *468 C4 river* Central African Republic/Chad
Aouker *see* Aoukâr
Aozou *468 C1* Borkou-Ennedi-Tibesti, N Chad
Apalachee Bay *434 D3 bay* Florida, SE USA
Apalachicola River *434 D3 river* Florida, SE USA
Apamama *see* Abemama
Apaporis, Río *450 C4 river* Brazil/Colombia
Apatity *502 C2* Murmanskaya Oblast', NW Russian Federation
Ape *498 D3* Alūksne, NE Latvia
Apeldoorn *478 D3* Gelderland, E Netherlands
Apennines *see* Appennino
Āpia *537 F4 country capital* (Samoa) Upolu, SE Samoa
Apoera *451 G3* Sipaliwini, NW Surinam
Apostle Islands *432 B1 island group* Wisconsin, N USA
Appalachian Mountains *427 D5 mountain range* E USA
Appennino *488 E2 Eng.* Apennines. *mountain range* Italy/San Marino
Appingedam *478 E1* Groningen, NE Netherlands
Appleton *432 B2* Wisconsin, N USA
Apure, Río *450 C2 river* W Venezuela
Apurímac, Río *452 D3 river* S Peru
Apuseni, Munții *500 A4 mountain range* W Romania
Aputiteeq *474 D4 var.* Aputitêq. C Greenland
Aputitêq *see* Aputiteeq
'Aqaba *see* Al 'Aqabah
'Aqaba, Gulf of *512 A4 var.* Gulf of Elat, *Ar.* Khalīj al 'Aqabah; *anc.* Sinus Aelaniticus. *gulf* NE Red Sea
Āqchah *515 E3 var.* Āqcheh. Jowzjān, N Afghanistan
Āqcheh *see* Āqchah
Aquae Augustae *see* Dax
Aquae Sextiae *see* Aix-en-Provence
Aquae Tarbelicae *see* Dax
Aquidauana *455 E4* Mato Grosso do Sul, S Brazil
Aquila *see* L'Aquila
Aquila degli Abruzzi *see* L'Aquila
Aquitaine *483 B6 cultural region* SW France
'Arabah, Wādī al *511 B7 Heb.* Ha'Arava. *dry watercourse* Israel/Jordan
Arabian Basin *516 A4 undersea feature* N Arabian Sea
Arabian Desert *see* Eastern Desert
Arabian Peninsula *513 B5 peninsula* SW Asia
Arabian Sea *516 A3 sea* NW Indian Ocean
Aracaju *455 G3 state capital* Sergipe, E Brazil
Araçuai *455 F3* Minas Gerais, SE Brazil
Arad *500 A4* Arad, W Romania
'Arad *511 B7* Southern, S Israel
Arafura Sea *534 A3 Ind.* Laut Arafuru. *sea* W Pacific Ocean
Aragón *485 E2 cultural region* E Spain
Araguaia, Río *455 E3 var.* Araguaya. *river* C Brazil
Araguari *455 F3* Minas Gerais, SE Brazil
Araguaya *see* Araguaia, Río
Arāk *512 C3 prev.* Sultānābād. Markazī, W Iran
Arakan Yoma *528 A3 mountain range* W Burma
Aral Sea *514 C1 Kaz.* Aral Tengizi, *Rus.* Aral'skoye More, *Uzb.* Orol Dengizi. *inland sea* Kazakhstan/Uzbekistan
Aral'sk *506 B4 Kaz.* Aral. Kzyl-Orda, SW Kazakhstan
Aranda de Duero *484 D2* Castilla-León, N Spain
Aranđelovac *492 D4 prev.* Arandjelovac. Serbia, C Yugoslavia
Aranjuez *484 D3 anc.* Ara Jovis. Madrid, C Spain
Araouane *467 E2* Tombouctou, N Mali
'Ar'ar *512 B3* Al Ḩudūd ash Shamālīyah, NW Saudi Arabia
Aras *509 G3 Arm.* Arak's, *Az.* Araz Nehri, *Per.* Rūd-e Aras, *Rus.* Araks; *prev.* Araxes. *river* SW Asia
Arauca *450 C2* Arauca, NE Colombia
Arauca, Río *450 C2 river* Colombia/Venezuela
Arbela *see* Arbīl
Arbīl *512 B2 var.* Erbil, Irbil, *Kurd.* Hawlēr; *anc.* Arbela. N Iraq
Arbroath *480 D3 anc.* Aberbrothock. E Scotland, UK
Arbyzynka *501 E3 Rus.* Arbuzinka. Mykolayivs'ka Oblast', S Ukraine
Arcachon *483 B5* Gironde, SW France
Arcata *438 A4* California, W USA
Archangel *548 see* Arkhangel'sk
Archangel Bay *see* Chëshskaya Guba
Archidona *484 D5* Andalucía, S Spain
Archipel des Australes *see* Australes, Îles
Archipel des Tuamotu *see* Tuamotu, Îles
Archipel de Tahiti *see* Société, Archipel de la
Arco *488 C2* Trentino-Alto Adige, N Italy
Arctic-Mid Oceanic Ridge *see* Nansen Cordillera
Arctic Ocean *548 B3 ocean*
Arda *496 C3 var.* Ardhas, *Gk.* Árdas. *river* Bulgaria/Greece *see also* Ardas
Arda *see* Ardas
Ardabīl *512 C2 var.* Ardebil. Ardabīl, NW Iran
Ardakān *512 D3* Yazd, C Iran
Ardas *496 D3 var.* Ardhas, *Bul.* Arda. *river* Bulgaria/Greece *see also* Arda
Ardas *see* Arda
Arḑ aş Şawwān *511 C7 var.* Ardh es Suwwān. *plain* S Jordan
Ardebil *see* Ardabīl
Ardèche *483 C5 cultural region* E France
Ardennes *479 C8 plateau* W Europe
Ardhas *see* Ardas
Ardh es Suwwān *see* Arḑ aş Şawwān
Ardino *496 D3* Khaskovska Oblast, S Bulgaria
Ard Mhacha *see* Armagh
Ardmore *441 G2* Oklahoma, C USA
Arelas *see* Arles
Arelate *see* Arles
Arendal *477 A6* Aust-Agder, S Norway
Arenys de Mar *485 G2* Cataluña, NE Spain
Areópoli *497 B7 prev.* Areópolis. Pelopónnisos, S Greece
Arequipa *453 E4* Arequipa, SE Peru
Arezzo *488 C3 anc.* Arretium. Toscana, C Italy
Argalastí *497 C5* Thessalía, C Greece
Argenteuil *482 D1* Val-d'Oise, N France
Argentina *457 B5 off.* Republic of Argentina. *country* S South America
Argentina Basin *see* Argentine Basin
Argentine Basin *449 C7 var.* Argentina Basin. *undersea feature* SW Atlantic Ocean
Argentine Rise *see* Falkland Plateau
Arghandāb, Daryā-ye *515 E5 river* SE Afghanistan
Argirocastro *see* Gjirokastër
Argo *464 B3* Northern, N Sudan
Argo Fracture Zone *533 C5 tectonic feature* C Indian Ocean
Árgos *497 B6* Pelopónnisos, S Greece
Argostóli *497 A5 var.* Argostólion. Kefallinía, Iónioi Nísoi, Greece, C Mediterranean Sea
Argostólion *see* Argostóli
Argun *517 E1 Chin.* Ergun He, *Rus.* Argun'. *river* China/Russian Federation
Argyrokastron *see* Gjirokastër
Århus *477 B7 var.* Aarhus. Århus, C Denmark
Aria *see* Herāt
Ari Atoll *524 A4 atoll* C Maldives
Arica *456 B1 hist.* San Marcos de Arica. Tarapacá, N Chile
Aridaía *496 B3 var.* Aridea, Aridhaía. Dytikí Makedonía, N Greece
Aridea *see* Aridaía
Aridhaía *see* Aridaía
Arīḩā *510 B3 var.* Arīhā. Idlib, W Syria
Arinsal *483 A7* NW Andorra
Arizona *440 A2 off.* State of Arizona; also known as Copper State, Grand Canyon State. Admin. region *state* SW USA
Arkansas *434 A1 off.* State of Arkansas; also known as The Land of Opportunity. *state* S USA
Arkansas City *437 F5* Kansas, C USA
Arkansas River *441 G1 river* C USA
Arkhangel'sk *506 B2 Eng.* Archangel. Arkhangel'skaya Oblast', NW Russian Federation
Arkoí *497 E6 island* Dodekánisos, Greece, Aegean Sea
Arles *483 D6 var.* Arles-sur-Rhône; *anc.* Arelas, Arelate. Bouches-du-Rhône, SE France
Arles-sur-Rhône *see* Arles
Arlington *441 G2* Texas, SW USA
Arlington *433 E4* Virginia, NE USA
Arlon *479 D8 Dut.* Aarlen, *Ger.* Arel; *Lat.* Orolaunum. Luxembourg, SE Belgium
Armagh *481 B5 Ir.* Ard Mhacha. S Northern Ireland, UK
Armagnac *483 B6 cultural region* S France
Armenia *509 F3 off.* Republic of Armenia, *var.* Ajastan, *Arm.* Hayastani Hanrapetut'yun; *prev.* Armenian Soviet Socialist Republic. *country* SW Asia
Armenia *450 B3* Quindío, W Colombia
Armidale *541 D6* New South Wales, SE Australia
Armstrong *430 B3* Ontario, S Canada
Armyans'k *501 F4 Rus.* Armyansk. Respublika Krym, S Ukraine
Arnaía *496 C4 var.* Arnea. Kentrikí Makedonía, N Greece
Arnaud *474 A3 river* Québec, E Canada
Arnea *see* Arnaía
Arnedo *485 E2* La Rioja, N Spain
Arnhem *478 D4* Gelderland, SE Netherlands
Arnhem Land *540 A2 physical region* Northern Territory, N Australia
Arno *488 B3 river* C Italy
Arnold *437 G4* Missouri, C USA
Arorae *537 E3 atoll* Tungaru, W Kiribati
Arquipélago da Madeira *see* Madeira
Arquipélago dos Açores *see* Azores
Ar Rahad *see* Er Rahad
Ar Ramādī *512 B3 var.* Ramadi, Rumadiya. SW Iraq
Ar Rāmī *510 C4* Ḩimş, C Syria
Ar Ramthā *511 B5 var.* Ramtha. Irbid, N Jordan
Arran, Isle of *480 C4 island* SW Scotland, UK
Ar Raqqah *510 C2 var.* Rakka; *anc.* Nicephorium. Ar Raqqah, N Syria
Arras *482 C2 anc.* Nemetocenna. Pas-de-Calais, N France
Ar Rawḑatayn *512 C4 var.* Raudhatain. N Kuwait
Arriaga *443 G5* Chiapas, SE Mexico
Ar Riyāḑ *513 C5 Eng.* Riyadh. *country capital* (Saudi Arabia) Ar Riyāḑ, C Saudi Arabia
Ar Rub 'al Khālī *513 C6 Eng.* Empty Quarter, Great Sandy Desert. *desert* SW Asia
Ar Rustāq *513 E5 var.* Rostak, Rustaq. N Oman
Ar Ruţbah *512 B3 var.* Rutba. SW Iraq
Árta *497 A5 anc.* Ambracia. Ípeiros, W Greece
Artashat *509 F3* S Armenia
Artemisa *446 B2* La Habana, W Cuba
Artesia *440 D3* New Mexico, SW USA
Arthur's Pass *543 C6 pass* South Island, NZ
Artigas *456 D3 prev.* San Eugenio, San Eugenio del Cuareim. Artigas, N Uruguay
Art'ik *509 F2* W Armenia
Artois *482 C2 cultural region* N France
Artsyz *500 D4 Rus.* Artsiz. Odes'ka Oblast', SW Ukraine
Artvin *509 F2* Artvin, NE Turkey
Arua *465 B6* NW Uganda
Aruângua *see* Luangwa
Aruba *450 C1 var.* Oruba. *Dutch autonomous region* S West Indies
Aru, Kepulauan *531 G4 Eng.* Aru Islands; *prev.* Aroe Islands. *island group* E Indonesia
Arunāchal Pradesh *527 G3 cultural region* NE India
Arusha *465 C7* Arusha, N Tanzania
Arviat *429 G4 prev.* Eskimo Point. Nunavut, C Canada
Arvidsjaur *476 C4* Norrbotten, N Sweden
Arys' *506 B5 Kaz.* Arys. Yuzhnyy Kazakhstan, S Kazakhstan
Asadābād *515 F4 var.* Asadābād; *prev.* Chaghasarāy. Kunar, E Afghanistan
Asad, Buḩayrat al *510 C2 Eng.* Lake Assad. *lake* N Syria
Asahi-dake *522 D2 mountain* Hokkaidō, N Japan
Asahikawa *522 D2* Hokkaidō, N Japan
Asamankese *467 E5* SE Ghana
Āsānsol *527 F4* West Bengal, NE India
Asben *see* Aïr, Massif de l'
Ascension Fracture Zone *461 A5 tectonic feature* C Atlantic Ocean
Ascension Island *459 A5 dependency of St. Helena* C Atlantic Ocean
Ascoli Piceno *488 C4 anc.* Asculum Picenum. Marche, C Italy
Aseb *464 D4 var.* Assab, *Amh.* Āseb. SE Eritrea
Ashara *see* Al 'Ashārah
Ashburton *543 C6* Canterbury, South Island, NZ
Ashburton River *538 A4 river* Western Australia
Ashdod *511 A6 anc.* Azotos, *Lat.* Azotus. Central, W Israel
Asheville *435 E1* North Carolina, SE USA
Ashgabat *514 C3 prev.* Ashkhabad, Poltoratsk. *country capital* (Turkmenistan) Akhalskiy Velayat, C Turkmenistan
Ashkelon *see* Ashqelon
Ashland *438 B4* Oregon, NW USA
Ashland *432 B1* Wisconsin, N USA
Ashmore and Cartier Islands *534 A3 Australian external territory* E Indian Ocean
Ashmyany *499 C5 Rus.* Oshmyany. Hrodzyenskaya Voblasts', W Belorussia
Ashqelon *511 A6 var.* Ashkelon. Southern, C Israel
Ash Shadādah *510 D2 var.* Ash Shaddādah, Jisr ash Shadadi, Shaddādī, Shedadi, Tell Shedadi. Al Ḩasakah, NE Syria
Ash Shaddādah *see* Ash Shadādah
Ash Shām *see* Dimashq
Ash Sharāh *511 B7 var.* Esh Sharā. *mountain range* W Jordan
Ash Shāriqah *512 D4 Eng.* Sharjah. Ash Shāriqah, NE UAE
Ash Shawbak *511 B7* Ma'ān, W Jordan
Ash Shiḩr *513 C6* SE Yemen
Asia *385 C2 continent*
Asinara, Isola *488 A4 island* W Italy
Asipovichy *499 D6 Rus.* Osipovichi. Mahilyowskaya Voblasts', C Belorussia
Aşkale *509 E3* Erzurum, NE Turkey
Askersund *477 C6* Örebro, C Sweden
Asmara *464 C4 Amh.* Āsmera. *country capital* (Eritrea) C Eritrea
Assab *see* Aseb
As Sabkhah *510 D2 var.* Sabkha. Ar Raqqah, NE Syria
Aş Şafāwī *511 C6* Al Mafraq, N Jordan
Aş Şaḩrā' al Gharbīyah *see* Sahara el Gharbîya
Aş Şaḩrā' al Lībīyah *see* Libyan Desert
Aş Şaḩrā' ash Sharqīyah *see* Eastern Desert
As Salamīyah *see* Salamīyah
As Salţ *511 B6 var.* Salt. Al Balqā', NW Jordan
Assamaka *see* Assamakka
Assamakka *467 F2 var.* Assamaka. Agadez, NW Niger
As Samāwah *512 B3 var.* Samawa. S Iraq
Assen *478 E2* Drenthe, NE Netherlands
Assenede *479 B5* Oost-Vlaanderen, NW Belgium
Assiout *see* Asyût
Assiut *see* Asyût
Assouan *see* Aswân
Assu *see* Açu
Assuan *see* Aswân
As Sukhnah *510 C3 var.* Sukhne, *Fr.* Soukhné. Ḩimş, C Syria
As Sulaymānīyah *512 C3 var.* Sulaimaniya, *Kurd.* Slēmānī. NE Iraq
As Sulayyil *513 B5* Ar Riyāḑ, S Saudi Arabia
Aş Şuwār *510 D2 var.* Şuwār. Dayr az Zawr, E Syria
As Suwaydā' *511 B5 var.* El Suweida, Es Suweida, Suweida, *Fr.* Soueida. As Suwaydā', SW Syria
Astacus *see* İzmit
Astana *506 C4 prev.* Akmola, Akmolinsk, Tselinograd, Aqmola. *country capital* (Kazakhstan). Akmola, N Kazakhstan
Astarabad *see* Gorgān
Asterābād *see* Gorgān
Asti *488 A2 anc.* Asta Colonia, Asta Pompeia, Hasta Colonia, Hasta Pompeia. Piemonte, NW Italy
Astipálaia *see* Astypálaia
Astorga *484 C1 anc.* Asturica Augusta. Castilla-León, N Spain
Astrabad *see* Gorgān
Astrakhan' *503 C7* Astrakhanskaya Oblast', SW Russian Federation
Asturias *484 C1 cultural region* NW Spain
Astypálaia *497 D7 var.* Astipálaia, *It.* Stampalia. *island* Kykládes, Greece, Aegean Sea
Asunción *456 D2 country capital* (Paraguay) Central, S Paraguay
Aswân *464 B2 var.* Assouan, Assuan; *anc.* Syene. SE Egypt
Asyût *464 B2 var.* Assiout, Assiut, Siut; *anc.* Lycopolis. C Egypt
Atacama Desert *see* Atacama, Desierto de
Atacama, Desierto de *456 B2 Eng.* Atacama Desert. *desert* N Chile
Atafu Atoll *537 E3 island* NW Tokelau
Aţâr *466 C2* Adrar, W Mauritania
Atas Bogd *518 D3 mountain* SW Mongolia
Atascadero *439 B7* California, W USA
Atatürk Barajı *509 E4 reservoir* S Turkey
Atbara *464 C3 var.* 'Aţbārah. River Nile, NE Sudan
'Aţbārah *see* Atbara
Atbasar *506 C4* Akmola, N Kazakhstan
Atchison *437 F4* Kansas, C USA
Ath *479 B6 var.* Aat. Hainaut, SW Belgium
Athabasca *429 E5 var.* Athabaska. *river* Alberta, SW Canada
Athabasca *429 E5* Alberta, SW Canada
Athabasca, Lake *429 F4 lake* Alberta/Saskatchewan, SW Canada
Athabaska *see* Athabasca
Athens *see* Athína
Athens *435 E2* Georgia, SE USA
Athens *432 D4* Ohio, N USA
Athens *441 G3* Texas, SW USA
Atherton *540 D3* Queensland, NE Australia
Athína *497 C6 Eng.* Athens; *prev.* Athínai, *anc.* Athenae. *country capital* (Greece) Attikí, C Greece
Athlone *481 B5 Ir.* Baile Átha Luain. C Ireland
Ath Thawrah *see* Madīnat ath Thawrah
Ati *468 C3* Batha, C Chad
Atikokan *430 B4* Ontario, S Canada
Atka *428 A3* Atka Island, Alas USA
Atka *507 G3* Magadanskaya (E Russian Federation
Atlanta *434 D2 state capital* G SE USA
Atlanta *441 H2* Texas, SW US
Atlantic City *433 F4* New Jers NE USA
Atlantic-Indian Basin *459 D undersea feature* SW Indian
Atlantic-Indian Ridge *461 b undersea feature* SW Indian
Atlantic Ocean *458 B4 ocean*
Atlas Mountains *462 C2 mou range* NW Africa
Atlasovo *507 H3* Kamchatska Oblast', E Russian Federatio
Atlas Saharien *462 D2 var.* Sa Atlas. *mountain range* Algeria/Morocco
Atlas Tellien *494 C3 Eng.* Tell *mountain range* N Algeria
Atlin *428 D4* British Columbi W Canada
Aţ Ţafīlah *511 B7 var.* Et Tafil Tafila. Aţ Ţafīlah, W Jordan
Aţ Ţā'if *513 B5* Makkah, W S Arabia
At Tall al Abyaḑ *510 C2 var.* al Abyaḑ, Tell Abyad, *Fr.* Tell Abiad. Ar Raqqah, N Syria
Aţ Ţanf *510 D4* Ḩimş, S Syria
Attapu *see* Samakhixai
Attawapiskat *430 C3 river* Or S Canada
Attawapiskat *430 C3* Ontario C Canada
At Tibnī *510 D2 var.* Tibnī. Da Zawr, NE Syria
Attopeu *see* Samakhixai
Attu Island *428 A2 island* Ale Islands, Alaska, USA
Atyrau *506 B4 prev.* Gur'yev. Atyrau, W Kazakhstan
Aubagne *483 D6 anc.* Albania Bouches-du-Rhône, SE Fran
Aubange *479 D8* Luxembourg SE Belgium
Aubervilliers *482 E1* Seine-S Denis, N France
Auburn *438 B2* Washington, NW USA
Auch *483 B6 Lat.* Augusta Auscorum, Elimberrum. Ge S France
Auckland *542 D2* Auckland, N Island, NZ
Auckland Islands *534 C5 isla group* S NZ
Audincourt *482 E4* Doubs, E France
Audru *498 D2 Ger.* Audern. Pärnumaa, SW Estonia
Augathella *541 D5* Queenslar E Australia
Augsburg *487 C6 Fr.* Augsbou *anc.* Augusta Vindelicorum. Bayern, S Germany
Augusta *433 G2 state capital* M NE USA
Augusta *435 E2* Georgia, SE U
Augusta *539 A7* Western Aust
Augustów *490 E2 Rus.* Avgust Suwałki, NE Poland
Auob *470 B4 var.* Oup. *river* Namibia/South Africa
Aurangābād *526 D5* Mahārās C India
Auray *482 A3* Morbihan, NW France
Aurès, Massif de l' *494 C4 mountain range* NE Algeria
Aurillac *483 C5* Cantal, C Fra
Aurora *436 D4* Colorado, C U
Aurora *432 B3* Illinois, N USA
Aurora *437 G5* Missouri, C US
Aurora *451 F2* NW Guyana
Aus *470 B4* Karas, SW Namibi
Ausa *see* Vic
Austin *441 G3 state capital* Tex S USA
Austin *437 G3* Minnesota, N
Australes, Îles *535 F4 var.* Arc des Australes, Îles Tubuai, Tu Islands, *Eng.* Austral Islands. *group* SW French Polynesia
Austral Fracture Zone *535 H tectonic feature* S Pacific Ocea
Australia *534 A4 off.* Commonwealth of Australia. *country*
Australian Alps *541 C7 moun range* SE Australia
Australian Capital Territory *D7 prev.* Federal Capital Terr *territory* SE Australia
Austral Islands *see* Australes,
Austria *487 D7 off.* Republic o Austria, *Ger.* Österreich. *cour* C Europe
Auvergne *483 C5 cultural regio* C France
Auxerre *482 C4 anc.* Autesiod Autissiodorum. Yonne, C Fra

Avarua – Bartica

a 537 G5 dependent territory
al (Cook Islands) Rarotonga,
ok Islands
a 496 C3 Anatolikí Makedonía
hráki, NE Greece
484 B2 anc. Talabriga.
o, W Portugal
ee Ávila
o 489 D5 anc. Abellinum.
oania, S Italy
477 C6 Kopparberg,
eden
on 483 C6 river S France
ano 488 C4 Abruzzi, C Italy
ore 480 C3 N Scotland, UK
on 483 D6 anc. Avenio.
use, SE France
ee Ávila
484 D3 var. Avila; anc. Abela,
a, Abyla, Avela. Castilla-León,
ain
484 C1 Asturias, NW Spain
ches 482 B3 Manche,
ance
shima 523 C6 island
apan
465 D5 var. Hawash. river
iopia
i 463 F3 SW Libya
Dax
79 B5 Zeeland,
Netherlands
eiberg Island 429 E1 var.
Heiburg. island Nunavut,
nada
eiburg see Axel Heiberg
d
cho 452 D4 Ayacucho, S Peru
z 506 C5 Kaz. Ayaköz; prev.
opol. Semipalatinsk,
zakhstan
onte 484 C4 Andalucía,
ain
i 453 E4 Puno, S Peru
kŭl 515 E2 Rus. Ozero
rkul'. lake C Uzbekistan
508 A4 var. Aïdin; anc.
es. Aydın, SW Turkey
Rock see Uluru
rwady see Irrawaddy
e Agiá
Evstratios see Efstrátios,
s
Nikólaos see Ágios Nikólaos
u 467 E3 Tillabéri, W Niger
n el 'Atroûs 466 D3 var.
n el Atrous, Aïoun el Atroûss.
n el Gharbi, SE Mauritania
80 C4 W Scotland, UK
496 E2 Burgaska Oblast,
lgaria
haya 529 C5 var. Phra Nakhon
utthaya. Phra Nakhon Si
thaya, C Thailand
k 508 A3 Balıkesir, W Turkey
r, Costa del 485 F3 coastal
n E Spain
ad 467 E3 desert C Mali
510 B2 Ḥalab, NW Syria
aijan 509 G2 off. Azerbaijani
iblic, Az. Azărbaycan,
baycan Respublikasï; prev.
baijan SSR. country SE Asia
abad see Patna
ues 452 B2 Cañar, S Ecuador
s 484 A4 var. Açores, Ilhas dos
es, Port. Arquipélago dos
es. island group Portugal,
Atlantic Ocean
s-Biscay Rise 472 A3
rsea feature E Atlantic Ocean
m, Bahr 468 C3 seasonal river
had
Sea of 495 H1 Rus. Azovskoye
e, Ukr. Azovs'ke More. sea
Black Sea
, Wāḥat al 511 C6 oasis
rdan
440 C1 New Mexico, SW USA
ga 484 C4 Extremadura,
pain
ro, Península de 445 F5
nsula S Panama
457 D5 Buenos Aires,
gentina
Côte d' 360 E6 Coastal region
rance
qāziq see Zagazig
rqā' 511 B6 var. Zarqa. Az
ā', NW Jordan
wiyah 463 F2 var. Zawia.
Libya
lfī 512 B4 Ar Riyāḍ, N Saudi
bia
nia see Isernia

2 D3 prev. Mba. Viti Levu,
iji
ek 510 B4 var. Ba'labakk; anc.
opolis. E Lebanon
Daingin see Dingle Bay
heere 465 D6 var. Bardere, It.
era. Gedo, SW Somalia
-Hertog 479 C5 Antwerpen,
lgium

Baarn 478 C3 Utrecht, C Netherlands
Babadag 500 D5 Tulcea, SE Romania
Babahoyo 452 B2 prev. Bodegas. Los Ríos, C Ecuador
Bābā, Kūh-e 515 E4 mountain range C Afghanistan
Babayevo 502 B4 Vologodskaya Oblast', NW Russian Federation
Babeldaob 536 A1 var. Babeldaop, Babelthuap. island N Palau
Babeldaop see Babeldaob
Bab el Mandeb 513 B7 strait Gulf of Aden/Red Sea
Babelthuap see Babeldaob
Bá Bheanntraí see Bantry Bay
Babruysk 499 D7 Rus. Bobruysk. Mahilyowskaya Voblasts', E Belorussia
Babuyan Channel 531 E1 channel N Philippines
Babuyan Island 531 E1 island N Philippines
Bacabal 455 F2 Maranhão, E Brazil
Bacău 500 C4 Hung. Bákó. Bacău, NE Romania
Băc Giang 528 D3 Ha Băc, N Vietnam
Bacheykava 499 D5 Rus. Bocheykovo. Vitsyebskaya Voblasts', N Belorussia
Back 429 F3 river Nunavut, N Canada
Bačka Palanka 492 D3 prev. Palanka. Serbia, NW Yugoslavia
Bačka Topola 492 D3 Hung. Topolya; prev. Hung. Bácstopolya. Serbia, N Yugoslavia
Bac Liêu 529 D6 var. Vinh Loi. Minh Hai, S Vietnam
Bacolod 517 E4 off. Bacolod City. Negros, C Philippines
Bacolod City see Bacolod
Bácsszenttamás see Srbobran
Badajoz 484 C4 anc. Pax Augusta. Extremadura, W Spain
Baden-Baden 487 B6 anc. Aurelia Aquensis. Baden-Württemberg, SW Germany
Bad Freienwalde 486 D3 Brandenburg, NE Germany
Bad Hersfeld 486 B4 Hessen, C Germany
Bad Homburg see Bad Homburg vor der Höhe
Bad Homburg vor der Höhe 487 B5 var. Bad Homburg. Hessen, W Germany
Bá Dhún na nGall see Donegal Bay
Bad Ischl 487 D7 Oberösterreich, N Austria
Bad Krozingen 487 A6 Baden-Württemberg, SW Germany
Badlands 436 D2 physical region North Dakota, N USA
Badu Island 540 C1 island Queensland, NE Australia
Bad Vöslau 487 E6 Niederösterreich, NE Austria
Baetic Cordillera see Béticos, Sistemas
Baetic Mountains see Béticos, Sistemas
Bafatá 466 C4 C Guinea-Bissau
Baffin Bay 429 G2 bay Canada/Greenland
Baffin Island 429 G2 island Nunavut, NE Canada
Bafing 466 C3 headstream W Africa
Bafoussam 468 A4 Ouest, W Cameroon
Bafra 508 D2 Samsun, N Turkey
Bāft 512 D4 Kermān, S Iran
Bagaces 444 D4 Guanacaste, NW Costa Rica
Bagdad see Baghdād
Bagé 455 E5 Rio Grande do Sul, S Brazil
Baghdād 512 B3 var. Bagdad, Eng. Baghdad. country capital (Iraq) C Iraq
Baghlān 515 E3 Baghlān, NE Afghanistan
Bago see Pegu
Bagoé 466 D4 river Ivory Coast/Mali
Bagrationovsk 498 A4 Ger. Preussisch Eylau. Kaliningradskaya Oblast', W Russian Federation
Bagrax Hu see Bosten Hu
Baguio 531 E1 off. Baguio City. Luzon, N Philippines
Bagzane, Monts 467 F3 mountain N Niger
Bahama Islands see Bahamas
Bahamas 446 C2 off. Commonwealth of the Bahamas. country N West Indies
Bahamas 427 D6 var. Bahama Islands. island group N West Indies
Bahāwalpur 526 C2 Punjab, E Pakistan
Bahía 455 F3 off. Estado da Bahia. state E Brazil
Bahía Blanca 457 C5 Buenos Aires, E Argentina
Bahía, Islas de la 444 C1 Eng. Bay Islands. island group N Honduras
Bahir Dar 464 C4 var. Bahr Dar, Bahrdar Giyorgis. NW Ethiopia
Bahraich 527 E3 Uttar Pradesh, N India
Bahrain 512 C4 off. State of Bahrain, Dawlat al Bahrayn, Ar. Al Baḥrayn; prev. Bahrein, anc. Tylos or Tyros. country SW Asia
Baḥr al Milḥ see Razāzah, Buḥayrat ar
Baḥrat Lūt see Dead Sea
Bahrat Tabariya see Tiberias, Lake
Bahr Dar see Bahir Dar
Bahrdar Giyorgis see Bahir Dar
Bahr el Azraq see Blue Nile
Bahr el Jebel see White Nile
Bahret Lut see Dead Sea
Bahr Tabariya, Sea of see Tiberias, Lake
Bahushewsk 499 E6 Rus. Bogushëvsk. Vitsyebskaya Voblasts', NE Belorussia
Baia Mare 500 B3 Ger. Frauenbach, Hung. Nagybánya; prev. Neustadt. Maramureş, NW Romania
Baia Sprie 500 B3 Ger. Mittelstadt, Hung. Felsőbánya. Maramureş, NW Romania
Baïbokoum 468 B4 Logone-Oriental, SW Chad
Baidoa see Baydhabo
Baie-Comeau 431 E3 Québec, SE Canada
Baikal, Lake 544 see Baykal, Ozero
Baile Átha Luain see Athlone
Bailén 484 D4 Andalucía, S Spain
Baile na Mainistreach see Newtownabbey
Băileşti 500 B5 Dolj, SW Romania
Ba Illi 468 B3 Chari-Baguirmi, SW Chad
Bainbridge 434 D3 Georgia, SE USA
Bā'ir see Bāyir
Baireuth see Bayreuth
Bairiki 536 D2 country capital (Kiribati) Tarawa, NW Kiribati
Bairnsdale 541 C7 Victoria, SE Australia
Baishan 521 E3 prev. Hunjiang. Jilin, NE China
Baiyin 520 B4 Gansu, C China
Baja 491 C7 Bács-Kiskun, S Hungary
Baja California 440 A4 Eng. Lower California. peninsula NW Mexico
Baja California 442 B2 state NW Mexico
Bajo Boquete see Boquete
Bajram Curri 493 D5 Kukës, N Albania
Bakala 468 C4 Ouaka, C Central African Republic
Bakan see Shimonoseki
Baker and Howland Islands 537 E2 US unincorporated territory W Polynesia
Baker Lake 429 F3 Nunavut, N Canada
Bakersfield 439 C7 California, W USA
Bakharden 514 C3 Turkm. Bäherden; prev. Bakherden. Akhalskiy Velayat, C Turkmenistan
Bakhchysaray 501 F5 Rus. Bakhchisaray. Respublika Krym, S Ukraine
Bakhmach 501 F1 Chernihivs'ka Oblast', N Ukraine
Bākhtarān 512 C3 prev. Kermānshāh, Qahremānshahr. Kermānshāhān, W Iran
Bakı 509 H2 Eng. Baku. country capital (Azerbaijan) E Azerbaijan
Bakony 491 C7 Eng. Bakony Mountains, Ger. Bakonywald. mountain range W Hungary
Baku 504 see Bakı
Balabac Island 521 C8 island W Philippines
Balabac Strait 530 D2 var. Selat Balabac. strait Malaysia/Philippines
Ba'labakk see Baalbek
Balaguer 485 F2 Cataluña, NE Spain
Balakovo 503 C6 Saratovskaya Oblast', W Russian Federation
Bālā Morghāb 514 D4 Laghmān, NW Afghanistan
Balashov 503 B6 Saratovskaya Oblast', W Russian Federation
Balaton 491 C7 var. Lake Balaton, Ger. Plattensee. lake W Hungary
Balaton, Lake see Balaton
Balbina, Represa 454 D1 reservoir NW Brazil
Balboa 445 G4 Panamá, C Panama
Balcarce 457 D5 Buenos Aires, E Argentina
Balclutha 543 B7 Otago, South Island, NZ
Baldy Mountain 436 C1 mountain Montana, NW USA
Bâle see Basel
Baleares, Islas 485 G3 Eng. Balearic Islands. island group Spain, W Mediterranean Sea
Balearic Islands see Baleares, Islas
Balearic Plain see Algerian Basin
Baleine, Rivière à la 431 E2 river Québec, E Canada
Balen 479 C5 Antwerpen, N Belgium
Bāleshwar 527 F4 prev. Balasore. Orissa, E India
Bali 530 D5 island C Indonesia
Balıkesir 508 A3 Balıkesir, W Turkey
Balīkh, Nahr 510 C2 river N Syria
Balikpapan 530 D4 Borneo, C Indonesia
Balkan Mountains 496 C2 Bul./SCr. Stara Planina. mountain range Bulgaria/Yugoslavia
Balkh 515 E3 anc. Bactra. Balkh, N Afghanistan
Balkhash 506 C5 Kaz. Balqash. Zhezkazgan, SE Kazakhstan
Balkhash, Lake 516 see Balkhash, Ozero
Balkhash, Ozero 506 C5 Eng. Lake Balkhash, Kaz. Balqash. lake SE Kazakhstan
Balladonia 539 C6 Western Australia
Ballarat 541 C7 Victoria, SE Australia
Balleny Islands 546 B5 island group Antarctica
Ballinger 441 F3 Texas, SW USA
Balochistān see Baluchistān
Balş 500 B5 Olt, S Romania
Balsas 455 F2 Maranhão, E Brazil
Balsas, Río 443 E5 var. Río Mexcala. river S Mexico
Bal'shavik 499 D7 Rus. Bol'shevik. Homyel'skaya Voblasts', SE Belorussia
Balta 500 D3 Odes'ka Oblast', SW Ukraine
Bălţi 500 D3 Rus. Bel'tsy. N Moldavia
Baltic Sea 477 C7 Ger. Ostee, Rus. Baltiskoye More. sea N Europe
Baltimore 433 F4 Maryland, NE USA
Baluchistān 526 B3 var. Balochistān, Beluchistan. Admin. region province SW Pakistan
Balvi 498 D4 Balvi, NE Latvia
Balykchy 515 G2 Kir. Ysyk-Köl; prev. Issyk-Kul', Rybach'ye. Issyk-Kul'skaya Oblast', NE Kyrgyzstan
Balzers 486 E2 S Liechtenstein
Bam 512 E4 Kermān, SE Iran
Bamako 466 D4 country capital (Mali) Capital District, SW Mali
Bambari 468 C4 Ouaka, C Central African Republic
Bamberg 487 C5 Bayern, SE Germany
Bamenda 468 A4 Nord-Ouest, W Cameroon
Banaba 536 D2 var. Ocean Island. island Tungaru, W Kiribati
Bandaaceh 530 A3 var. Banda Atjeh; prev. Koetaradja, Kutaradja, Kutaraja. Sumatera, W Indonesia
Banda Atjeh see Bandaaceh
Bandama 466 D5 var. Bandama Fleuve. river S Ivory Coast
Bandama Fleuve see Bandama
Bandar 'Abbās see Bandar-e 'Abbās
Bandarbeyla 465 E5 var. Bender Beila, Bender Beyla. Bari, NE Somalia
Bandar-e 'Abbās 512 D4 var. Bandar 'Abbās; prev. Gombroon. Hormozgān, S Iran
Bandar-e Būshehr 512 C4 var. Būshehr, Eng. Bushire. Būshehr, S Iran
Bandar-e Khamīr 512 D4 Hormozgān, S Iran
Bandar-e Langeh 512 D4 var. Bandar-e Lengeh, Lingeh. Hormozgān, S Iran
Bandar-e Lengeh see Bandar-e Langeh
Bandar Kassim see Boosaaso
Bandarlampung 530 C4 prev. Tanjungkarang, Teloekbetoeng, Telukbetung. Sumatera, W Indonesia
Bandar Maharani see Muar
Bandar Masulipatnam see Machilīpatnam
Bandar Seri Begawan 530 D3 prev. Brunei Town. country capital (Brunei) N Brunei
Bandar Sri Aman see Sri Aman
Banda Sea 531 F5 var. Laut Banda. sea E Indonesia
Bandırma 508 A3 var. Penderma. Balıkesir, NW Turkey
Bandundu 469 C6 prev. Banningville. Bandundu, W Congo (Zaire)
Bandung 530 C5 prev. Bandoeng. Jawa, C Indonesia
Bangalore 524 C2 Karnātaka, S India
Bangassou 468 D4 Mbomou, SE Central African Republic
Banggai, Kepulauan 531 E4 island group C Indonesia
Banghāzī 463 G2 Eng. Bengazi, Benghazi, It. Bengasi. NE Libya
Bangka, Pulau 530 C4 island W Indonesia
Bangkok 516 see Krung Thep
Bangkok, Bight of see Krung Thep, Ao
Bangladesh 527 G3 off. People's Republic of Bangladesh; prev. East Pakistan. country S Asia
Bangor 481 B5 Ir. Beannchar. E Northern Ireland, UK
Bangor 433 G2 Maine, NE USA
Bangor 481 C6 NW Wales, UK
Bangui 469 B5 country capital (Central African Republic) Ombella-Mpoko, SW Central African Republic
Bangweulu, Lake 465 B8 var. Lake Bengweulu. lake N Zambia
Ban Hat Yai see Hat Yai
Ban Hin Heup 528 C4 Viangchan, C Laos
Ban Houayxay see Houayxay
Ban Houei Sai see Houayxay
Ban Hua Hin 529 C6 var. Hua Hin. Prachuap Khiri Khan, SW Thailand
Bani 466 D3 river S Mali
Banias see Bāniyās
Banī Suwayf see Beni Suef
Bāniyās 510 B3 var. Banias, Baniyas, Paneas. Ṭarṭūs, W Syria
Baniyas see Bāniyās
Banja Luka 492 B3 NW Bosnia and Herzegovina
Banjarmasin 530 D4 prev. Bandjarmasin. Borneo, C Indonesia
Banjul 466 B3 prev. Bathurst. country capital (Gambia) W Gambia
Banks Island 429 E2 island Banks Island, Northwest Territories, NW Canada
Banks Islands 536 D4 Fr. Îles Banks. island group N Vanuatu
Banks Lake 438 B1 reservoir Washington, NW USA
Banks Peninsula 543 C6 peninsula South Island, NZ
Banks Strait 541 C8 strait SW Tasman Sea
Bānkura 527 F4 West Bengal, NE India
Ban Mak Khaeng see Udon Thani
Banmo see Bhamo
Bañolas see Banyoles
Ban Pak Phanang see Pak Phanang
Ban Sichon see Sichon
Banská Bystrica 491 C6 Ger. Neusohl, Hung. Besztercebánya. Stredné Slovensko, C Slovakia
Bantry Bay 481 A7 Ir. Bá Bheanntraí. bay SW Ireland
Banya 496 E2 Burgaska Oblast, E Bulgaria
Banyak, Kepulauan 530 A3 prev. Kepulauan Banjak. island group NW Indonesia
Banyo 468 B4 Adamaoua, NW Cameroon
Banyoles 485 G2 var. Bañolas. Cataluña, NE Spain
Banzare Seamounts 533 C7 undersea feature S Indian Ocean
Baoji 520 B4 var. Pao-chi, Paoki. Shaanxi, C China
Baoro 468 B4 Nana-Mambéré, W Central African Republic
Baoshan 520 A6 var. Pao-shan. Yunnan, SW China
Baotou 519 F3 var. Pao-t'ou, Paotow. Nei Mongol Zizhiqu, N China
Ba'qūbah 512 B3 var. Qubba. C Iraq
Baquerizo Moreno see Puerto Baquerizo Moreno
Bar 493 C5 It. Antivari. Montenegro, SW Yugoslavia
Baraawe 465 D6 It. Brava. Shabeellaha Hoose, S Somalia
Baraji, Hirfanli 508 C3 lake C Turkey
Bārāmati 526 C5 Mahārāshtra, W India
Baranavichy 499 B6 Pol. Baranowicze, Rus. Baranovichi. Brestskaya Voblasts', SW Belorussia
Barbados 447 G1 country SE West Indies
Barbastro 485 F2 Aragón, NE Spain
Barbate de Franco 484 C5 Andalucía, S Spain
Barbuda 447 G3 island N Antigua and Barbuda
Barcaldine 540 C4 Queensland, E Australia
Barce see Al Marj
Barcelona 485 G2 anc. Barcino, Barcinona. Cataluña, E Spain
Barcelona 451 E2 Anzoátegui, NE Venezuela
Barcoo see Cooper Creek
Barcs 491 C7 Somogy, SW Hungary
Bardaï 468 C1 Borkou-Ennedi-Tibesti, N Chad
Bardejov 491 D5 Ger. Bartfeld, Hung. Bártfa. Východné Slovensko, NE Slovakia
Bardera see Baardheere
Bardere see Baardheere
Bareilly 527 E3 var. Bareli. Uttar Pradesh, N India
Bareli see Bareilly
Barendrecht 478 C4 Zuid-Holland, SW Netherlands
Barentin 482 C3 Seine-Maritime, N France
Barentsberg 475 G2 Spitsbergen, W Svalbard
Barentsøya 475 G2 island E Svalbard
Barents Sea 502 C2 Nor. Barents Havet, Rus. Barentsevo More. sea Arctic Ocean
Barents Trough 473 E1 undersea feature SW Barents Sea
Bar Harbor 433 H2 Mount Desert Island, Maine, NE USA
Bari 489 E5 var. Bari delle Puglie; anc. Barium. Puglia, SE Italy
Bāridah see Al Bāridah
Bari delle Puglie see Bari
Barikot see Barīkowṭ
Barīkowṭ 515 F4 var. Barikot. Kunar, NE Afghanistan
Barillas 444 A2 var. Santa Cruz Barillas. Huehuetenango, NW Guatemala
Barinas 450 C2 Barinas, W Venezuela
Barisal 527 G4 Khulna, S Bangladesh
Barisan, Pegunungan 530 B4 mountain range Sumatera, W Indonesia
Barito, Sungai 530 D4 river Borneo, C Indonesia
Barium see Bari
Barka see Al Marj
Barkly Tableland 540 B3 plateau Northern Territory/Queensland, N Australia
Bârlad 500 D4 prev. Bîrlad. Vaslui, E Romania
Barlavento, Ilhas de 466 A2 var. Windward Islands. island group N Cape Verde
Bar-le-Duc 482 D3 var. Bar-sur-Ornain. Meuse, NE France
Barlee, Lake 539 B6 lake Western Australia
Barlee Range 538 A4 mountain range Western Australia
Barletta 489 D5 anc. Barduli. Puglia, SE Italy
Barlinek 490 B3 Ger. Berlinchen. Gorzów, W Poland
Barmouth 481 C6 NW Wales, UK
Barnaul 506 D4 Altayskiy Kray, C Russian Federation
Barnet 481 A7 SE England, UK
Barnstaple 481 C7 SW England, UK
Baroghil Pass 515 F3 var. Kowtal-e Barowghil. pass Afghanistan/Pakistan
Baron'ki 499 E7 Rus. Boron'ki. Mahilyowskaya Voblasts', E Belorussia
Barquisimeto 450 C2 Lara, NW Venezuela
Barra 480 B3 island NW Scotland, UK
Barra de Río Grande 445 E3 Región Autónoma Atlántico Sur, E Nicaragua
Barragem de Sobradinho see Sobradinho, Represa de
Barranca 452 C3 Lima, W Peru
Barrancabermeja 450 B2 Santander, N Colombia
Barranquilla 450 B1 Atlántico, N Colombia
Barreiro 484 B4 Setúbal, W Portugal
Barrier Range 541 C6 hill range New South Wales, SE Australia
Barrow 481 B6 Ir. An Bhearú. river SE Ireland
Barrow 428 D2 Alaska, USA
Barrow-in-Furness 481 C5 NW England, UK
Barrow Island 538 A4 island Western Australia
Barstow 439 C7 California, W USA
Bar-sur-Ornain see Bar-le-Duc
Bartang 515 F3 river SE Tajikistan
Bartica 451 F3 N Guyana

Bartın – Bishrī, Jabal

Bartın *508 C2* Zonguldak, N Turkey
Bartlesville *441 G1* Oklahoma, C USA
Bartoszyce *490 D2 Ger.* Bartenstein. Olsztyn, N Poland
Baruun-Urt *519 F2* Sühbaatar, E Mongolia
Barú, Volcán *445 E5 var.* Volcán de Chiriquí. *volcano* W Panama
Barwon River *541 D5 river* New South Wales, SE Australia
Barysaw *499 D6 Rus.* Borisov. Minskaya Voblasts', NE Belorussia
Basarabeasca *500 D4 Rus.* Bessarabka. SE Moldavia
Basel *487 A7 Eng.* Basle, *Fr.* Bâle. Basel-Stadt, NW Switzerland
Basilan *531 E3 island* SW Philippines
Basle *see* Basel
Basra *504 see* Al Başrah
Bassano del Grappa *488 C2* Veneto, NE Italy
Bassein *528 A4 var.* Pathein. Irrawaddy, SW Burma
Basse-Terre *447 G4 dependent territory capital* (Guadeloupe) Basse Terre, SW Guadeloupe
Basse Terre *447 G4 island* W Guadeloupe
Basseterre *447 G3 country capital* (Saint Kitts and Nevis) Saint Kitts, Saint Kitts and Nevis
Bassikounou *466 D3* Hodh ech Chargui, SE Mauritania
Bass Strait *541 C7 strait* SE Australia
Bassum *486 B3* Niedersachsen, NW Germany
Bastia *483 E7* Corse, France, C Mediterranean Sea
Bastogne *479 D7* Luxembourg, SE Belgium
Bastrop *434 B2* Louisiana, S USA
Bastyn' *499 B7 Rus.* Bostyn'. Brestskaya Voblasts', SW Belorussia
Basuo *see* Dongfang
Bata *469 A5* NW Equatorial Guinea
Batabanó, Golfo de *446 A2 gulf* W Cuba
Batajnica *492 D3* Serbia, N Yugoslavia
Batangas *531 E2 off.* Batangas City. Luzon, N Philippines
Bătdâmbâng *529 C5 prev.* Battambang. Bătdâmbâng, NW Cambodia
Batéké, Plateaux *469 B6 plateau* S Congo
Bath *481 D7 hist.* Akermanceaster, *anc.* Aquae Calidae, Aquae Solis. SW England, UK
Bathinda *526 D2* Punjab, NW India
Bathsheba *447 G1* E Barbados
Bathurst *431 F4* New Brunswick, SE Canada
Bathurst *541 D6* New South Wales, SE Australia
Bathurst Island *538 D2 island* Northern Territory, N Australia
Bathurst Island *429 F2 island* Parry Islands, Nunavut, N Canada
Bāţin, Wādī al *512 C4 dry watercourse* SW Asia
Batman *509 E4 var.* İluh. Batman, SE Turkey
Batna *463 E2* NE Algeria
Baton Rouge *434 B3 state capital* Louisiana, S USA
Batroûn *510 A4 var.* Al Batrūn. N Lebanon
Batticaloa *524 D3* Eastern Province, E Sri Lanka
Battipaglia *489 D5* Campania, S Italy
Bat'umi *509 F2* W Georgia
Batu Pahat *530 B3 prev.* Bandar Penggaram. Johor, Peninsular Malaysia
Bauchi *467 G4* Bauchi, NE Nigeria
Bauer Basin *545 F3 undersea feature* E Pacific Ocean
Bauska *498 C3 Ger.* Bauske. Bauska, S Latvia
Bautzen *486 D4 Lus.* Budyšin. Sachsen, E Germany
Bavarian Alps *487 C7 Ger.* Bayrische Alpen. *mountain range* Austria/Germany
Bavispe, Río *442 C2 river* NW Mexico
Bawîţi *464 B2* N Egypt
Bawku *467 E4* N Ghana
Bayamo *446 C3* Granma, E Cuba
Bayan Har Shan *518 D4 var.* Bayan Khar. *mountain range* C China
Bayanhongor *518 D2* Bayanhongor, C Mongolia
Bayan Khar *see* Bayan Har Shan
Bayano, Lago *445 G4 lake* E Panama
Bay City *432 C3* Michigan, N USA
Bay City *441 G4* Texas, SW USA
Baydhabo *465 D6 var.* Baydhowa, Isha Baydhabo, *It.* Baidoa. Bay, SW Somalia
Baydhowa *see* Baydhabo
Bayern *487 C6 cultural region* SE Germany
Bayeux *482 B3 anc.* Augustodurum. Calvados, N France
Bāyir *511 C7 var.* Bā'ir. Ma'ān, S Jordan
Baykal, Ozero *507 E4 Eng.* Lake Baikal. *lake* S Russian Federation
Baymak *503 D6* Respublika Bashkortostan, W Russian Federation
Bayonne *483 A6 anc.* Lapurdum. Pyrénées-Atlantiques, SW France
Bayramaly *514 D3 prev.* Bayram-Ali. Maryyskiy Velayat, S Turkmenistan
Bayreuth *487 C5 var.* Baireuth. Bayern, SE Germany
Bayrūt *see* Beyrouth
Baytown *441 H4* Texas, SW USA
Baza *485 E4* Andalucía, S Spain
Beagle Channel *457 C8 channel* Argentina/Chile
Béal Feirste *see* Belfast
Beannchar *see* Bangor
Bear Lake *438 E4 lake* Idaho/Utah, NW USA
Beas de Segura *485 E4* Andalucía, S Spain
Beata, Isla *447 E3 island* SW Dominican Republic
Beatrice *437 F4* Nebraska, C USA
Beaufort Sea *428 D2 sea* Arctic Ocean
Beaufort West *470 C5 Afr.* Beaufort-Wes. Western Cape, SW South Africa
Beaumont *441 H3* Texas, SW USA
Beaune *482 D4* Côte d'Or, C France
Beauvais *482 C3 anc.* Bellovacum, Caesaromagus. Oise, N France
Beaver Island *432 C2 island* Michigan, N USA
Beaver Lake *441 H1 reservoir* Arkansas, C USA
Beaver River *441 F1 river* Oklahoma, C USA
Beāwar *526 C3* Rājasthān, N India
Bečej *492 D3 Ger.* Altbetsche, *Hung.* Óbecse, Rácz-Becse; *prev.* Magyar-Becse, Stari Bečej. Serbia, N Yugoslavia
Béchar *462 D2 prev.* Colomb-Béchar. W Algeria
Beckley *432 D5* West Virginia, NE USA
Bedford *481 D6* E England, UK
Bedum *478 E1* Groningen, NE Netherlands
Be'ér Menuḥa *511 B7* Southern, S Israel
Beernem *479 A5* West-Vlaanderen, NW Belgium
Beersheba *see* Be'ér Sheva'
Be'ér Sheva' *511 A7 var.* Beersheba, *Ar.* Bir es Saba. Southern, S Israel
Beesel *479 D5* Limburg, SE Netherlands
Beeville *441 G4* Texas, SW USA
Bega *541 D7* New South Wales, SE Australia
Beida *see* Al Bayḍā'
Beihai *520 B6* Guangxi Zhuangzu Zizhiqu, S China
Beijing *520 C3 var.* Pei-ching, *Eng.* Peking; *prev.* Pei-p'ing. *country/municipality capital* (China) Beijing Shi, E China
Beilen *478 E2* Drenthe, NE Netherlands
Beira *471 E3* Sofala, C Mozambique
Beirut *504 see* Beyrouth
Beiuş *500 B3 Hung.* Belényes. Bihor, NW Romania
Beja *484 B4 anc.* Pax Julia. Beja, SE Portugal
Béjar *484 C3* Castilla-León, N Spain
Bejraburi *see* Phetchaburi
Békéscsaba *491 D7 Rom.* Bichiş-Ciaba. Békés, SE Hungary
Bekobod *515 E2 Rus.* Bekabad; *prev.* Begovat. Toshkent Wiloyati, E Uzbekistan
Bela Crkva *492 E3 Ger.* Weisskirchen, *Hung.* Fehértemplom. Serbia, W Yugoslavia
Belau *see* Palau
Belchatow *see* Bełchatów
Bełchatów *490 C4 var.* Belchatow. Piotrków, C Poland
Belcher Islands *430 C2 Fr.* Îles Belcher. *island group* Nunavut, SE Canada
Beledweyne *465 D5 var.* Belet Huen, *It.* Belet Uen. Hiiraan, C Somalia
Belém *455 F1 var.* Pará. *state capital* Pará, N Brazil
Belen *440 D2* New Mexico, SW USA
Belén *444 D4* Rivas, SW Nicaragua
Belet Huen *see* Beledweyne
Belet Uen *see* Beledweyne
Belfast *481 B5 Ir.* Béal Feirste. *admin capital* E Northern Ireland, UK
Belfield *436 D2* North Dakota, N USA
Belfort *482 E4* Territoire-de-Belfort, E France
Belgaum *524 B1* Karnātaka, W India
Belgium *479 B6 off.* Kingdom of Belgium, *Dut.* België, *Fr.* Belgique. *country* NW Europe
Belgorod *503 A6* Belgorodskaya Oblast', W Russian Federation
Belgrade *see* Beograd
Belgrano II *546 A2 Argentinian research station* Antarctica
Belice *see* Belize City
Beligrad *see* Berat
Beli Manastir *492 C3 Hung.* Pélmonostor; *prev.* Monostor. Osijek-Baranja, NE Croatia
Bélinga *469 B5* Ogooué-Ivindo, NE Gabon
Belitung, Pulau *530 C4 island* W Indonesia
Belize *444 B1 Sp.* Belice; *prev.* British Honduras, Colony of Belize. *country* Central America
Belize *444 B1 river* Belize/Guatemala
Belize *see* Belize City
Belize City *444 C1 var.* Belize, *Sp.* Belice. Belize, NE Belize
Belkofski *428 B3* Alaska, USA
Belle Île *482 A4 island* NW France
Belle Isle, Strait of *431 G3 strait* Newfoundland, E Canada
Belleville *432 B4* Illinois, N USA
Bellevue *437 F4* Iowa, C USA
Bellevue *438 B2* Washington, NW USA
Bellingham *438 B1* Washington, NW USA
Belling Hausen Mulde *see* Southeast Pacific Basin
Bellingshausen Abyssal Plain *see* Bellingshausen Plain
Bellingshausen Plain *545 F5 var.* Bellingshausen Abyssal Plain. *undersea feature* SE Pacific Ocean
Bellingshausen Sea *546 A3 sea* Antarctica
Bellinzona *487 B8 Ger.* Bellenz. Ticino, S Switzerland
Bello *450 B2* Antioquia, W Colombia
Bellville *470 B5* Western Cape, SW South Africa
Belmopan *444 C1 country capital* (Belize) Cayo, C Belize
Belogradchik *496 B1* Oblast Montana, NW Bulgaria
Belo Horizonte *455 F4 prev.* Bello Horizonte. *state capital* Minas Gerais, SE Brazil
Belomorsk *502 B3* Respublika Kareliya, NW Russian Federation
Beloretsk *503 D6* Respublika Bashkortostan, W Russian Federation
Belorussia *499 B6 off.* Republic of Belarus, *var.* Belarus, *Latv.* Baltkrievija; *prev.* Belorussian SSR, *Rus.* Belorusskaya SSR. *country* E Europe
Beloye More *502 C3 Eng.* White Sea. *sea* NW Russian Federation
Belozersk *502 B4* Vologodskaya Oblast', NW Russian Federation
Belton *441 G3* Texas, SW USA
Beluchistan *see* Baluchistān
Belukha, Gora *506 D5 mountain* Kazakhstan/Russian Federation
Belyy, Ostrov *506 D2 island* N Russian Federation
Bemaraha *471 F3 var.* Plateau du Bemaraha. *mountain range* W Madagascar
Bemidji *437 F1* Minnesota, N USA
Bemmel *478 D4* Gelderland, SE Netherlands
Benaco *see* Garda, Lago di
Benavente *484 D2* Castilla-León, N Spain
Bend *438 B3* Oregon, NW USA
Bender Beila *see* Bandarbeyla
Bender Beyla *see* Bandarbeyla
Bender Cassim *see* Boosaaso
Bendern *486 E1* NW Liechtenstein
Bender Qaasim *see* Boosaaso
Bendigo *541 C7* Victoria, SE Australia
Benešov *491 B5 Ger.* Beneschau. Střední Čechy, W Czech Republic
Benevento *489 D5 anc.* Beneventum, Malventum. Campania, S Italy
Bengal, Bay of *516 C4 bay* N Indian Ocean
Bengbu *520 D5 var.* Peng-pu. Anhui, E China
Benghazi *see* Banghāzī
Bengkulu *530 B4 prev.* Bengkoeloe, Benkoelen, Benkulen. Sumatera, W Indonesia
Benguela *470 A2 var.* Benguella. Benguela, W Angola
Benguella *see* Benguela
Bengweulu, Lake *see* Bangweulu, Lake
Ben Hope *480 B2 mountain* N Scotland, UK
Beni *448 B4 var.* El Beni. *Admin. region department* N Bolivia
Beni *469 E5* Nord Kivu, NE Congo (Zaire)
Benidorm *485 F4* País Valenciano, SE Spain
Beni-Mellal *462 C2* C Morocco
Benin *467 F4 off.* Republic of Benin; *prev.* Dahomey. *country* W Africa
Benin, Bight of *467 F5 gulf* W Africa
Benin City *467 F5* Edo, SW Nigeria
Beni, Río *453 E3 river* N Bolivia
Beni Suef *464 B2 var.* Banī Suwayf. N Egypt
Ben Nevis *480 C3 mountain* N Scotland, UK
Benson *440 B3* Arizona, SW USA
Bent Jbaïl *511 A5 var.* Bint Jubayl. S Lebanon
Benton *434 B1* Arkansas, C USA
Benue *468 B4 Fr.* Bénoué. *river* Cameroon/Nigeria
Benue *467 G4 state* SE Nigeria
Beograd *492 D3 Eng.* Belgrade, *Ger.* Belgrad; *anc.* Singidunum. *country capital* (Yugoslavia) Serbia, N Yugoslavia
Berane *493 D5 prev.* Ivangrad. Montenegro, SW Yugoslavia
Berat *493 C6 var.* Berati, *SCr.* Beligrad. Berat, C Albania
Berati *see* Berat
Berau, Teluk *531 G4 var.* MacCluer Gulf. *bay* Irian Jaya, E Indonesia
Berbera *464 D4* Woqooyi Galbeed, NW Somalia
Berbérati *469 B5* Mambéré-Kadéï, SW Central African Republic
Berck-Plage *482 C2* Pas-de-Calais, N France
Berdyans'k *501 G4 Rus.* Berdyansk; *prev.* Osipenko. Zaporiz'ka Oblast', SE Ukraine
Berdychiv *500 D2 Rus.* Berdichev. Zhytomyrs'ka Oblast', N Ukraine
Berehove *500 B3 Cz.* Berehovo, *Hung.* Beregszász, *Rus.* Beregovo. Zakarpats'ka Oblast', W Ukraine
Berettyó *491 D7 Rom.* Barcău; *prev.* Berătău, Beretău. *river* Hungary/Romania
Berettyóújfalu *491 D6* Hajdú-Bihar, E Hungary
Berezhany *500 C2 Pol.* Brzeżany. Ternopil's'ka Oblast', W Ukraine
Berezniki *503 D5* Permskaya Oblast', NW Russian Federation
Berga *485 G2* Cataluña, NE Spain
Bergamo *488 B2 anc.* Bergomum. Lombardia, N Italy
Bergara *485 E1* País Vasco, N Spain
Bergen *477 A5* Hordaland, S Norway
Bergen *486 D2* Mecklenburg-Vorpommern, NE Germany
Bergen *478 C2* Noord-Holland, NW Netherlands
Bergerac *483 B5* Dordogne, SW France
Bergeyk *479 C5* Noord-Brabant, S Netherlands
Bergse Maas *478 D4 river* S Netherlands
Beringen *479 C5* Limburg, NE Belgium
Bering Sea *428 A2 sea* N Pacific Ocean
Bering Strait *428 C2 Rus.* Beringov Proliv. *strait* Bering Sea/Chukchi Sea
Berja *485 E5* Andalucía, S Spain
Berkeley *439 B6* California, W USA
Berkner Island *546 A2 island* Antarctica
Berkovitsa *496 C2* Oblast Montana, NW Bulgaria
Berlin *486 D3 country capital* (Germany) Berlin, NE Germany
Berlin *433 G2* New Hampshire, NE USA
Bermejo, Río *456 C2 river* N Argentina
Bermeo *485 E1* País Vasco, N Spain
Bermuda *427 D6 var.* Bermuda Islands, Bermudas; *prev.* Somers Islands. *UK crown colony* NW Atlantic Ocean
Bermuda Islands *see* Bermuda
Bermuda Rise *427 E6 undersea feature* C Sargasso Sea
Bermudas *see* Bermuda
Bern *487 A7 Fr.* Berne. *country capital* (Switzerland) Bern, W Switzerland
Bernau *486 D3* Brandenburg, NE Germany
Bernburg *486 C4* Sachsen-Anhalt, C Germany
Berne *see* Bern
Berner Alpen *487 A7 var.* Berner Oberland, *Eng.* Bernese Oberland. *mountain range* SW Switzerland
Berner Oberland *see* Berner Alpen
Bernese Oberland *see* Berner Alpen
Bernier Island *539 A5 island* Western Australia
Berry *482 C4 cultural region* C France
Berry Islands *446 C1 island group* N Bahamas
Bertoua *469 B5* Est, E Cameroon
Beru *537 E2 var.* Peru. *atoll* Tungaru, W Kiribati
Berwick-upon-Tweed *480 D4* N England, UK
Berytus *see* Beyrouth
Besançon *482 D4 anc.* Besontium, Vesontio. Doubs, E France
Beskra *see* Biskra
Betafo *471 G3* Antananarivo, C Madagascar
Betanzos *484 B1* Galicia, NW Spain
Bethlehem *511 B6 Ar.* Bayt Laḥm, *Heb.* Bet Leḥem. C West Bank
Bethlehem *470 D4* Free State, C South Africa
Béticos, Sistemas *484 D4 var.* Sistema Penibético, *Eng.* Baetic Cordillera, Baetic Mountains. *mountain range* S Spain
Bétou *469 C5* La Likouala, N Congo
Bette, Picco *see* Bette, Pic
Bette, Pic *463 G4 var.* Bikkū Bīttī, *It.* Picco Bette. *mountain* S Libya
Bette, Picco *see* Bette, Pic
Beulah *432 C2* Michigan, N USA
Beveren *479 B5* Oost-Vlaanderen, N Belgium
Beverley *481 D5* E England, UK
Bexley *481 B8* SE England, UK
Beyla *466 D4* Guinée-Forestière, SE Guinea
Beyrouth *510 A4 var.* Bayrūt, *Eng.* Beirut; *anc.* Berytus. *country capital* (Lebanon) W Lebanon
Beyşehir *508 B4* Konya, SW Turkey
Beyşehir Gölü *508 B4 lake* C Turkey
Béziers *483 C6 anc.* Baeterrae, Baeterrae Septimanorum, Julia Beterrae. Hérault, S France
Bhadrāvati *524 C2* Karnātaka, SW India
Bhāgalpur *527 F3* Bihār, NE India
Bhaktapur *527 F3* Central, C Nepal
Bhamo *528 B2 var.* Banmo. Kachin State, N Burma
Bharūch *526 C4* Gujarāt, W India
Bhāvnagar *526 C4 prev.* Bhaunagar. Gujarāt, W India
Bhopāl *526 D4* Madhya Pradesh, C India
Bhubaneshwar *527 F5 prev.* Bhubaneswar, Bhuvaneshwar. Orissa, E India
Bhuket *see* Phuket
Bhusāwal *526 D4 prev.* Bhusaval. Mahārāshtra, C India
Bhutan *527 G3 off.* Kingdom of Bhutan, *var.* Druk-yul. *country* S Asia
Biak, Pulau *531 G4 island* E Indonesia
Biała Podlaska *490 E3* Biała Podlaska, E Poland
Białogard *490 B2 Ger.* Belgard. Koszalin, NW Poland
Białystok *490 E3 Rus.* Belostok, Bielostok. Białystok, E Poland
Biarritz *483 A6* Pyrénées-Atlantiques, SW France
Bicaz *500 C3 Hung.* Békás. Neamţ, NE Romania
Biddeford *433 G2* Maine, NE USA
Bideford *481 C7* SW England, UK
Biel *487 A7 Fr.* Bienne. Bern, W Switzerland
Bielefeld *486 B4* Nordrhein-Westfalen, NW Germany
Bielsko-Biała *491 C5 Ger.* Bielitz, Bielitz-Biala. Bielsko-Biała, S Poland
Bielsk Podlaski *490 E3* Białystok, E Poland
Bien Bien *see* Điện Biên
Biên Hoa *529 E6* Đông Nai, S Vietnam
Bienville, Lac *430 D2 lake* Québec, C Canada
Bié, Planalto do *470 B2 var.* Bié Plateau. *plateau* C Angola
Bié Plateau *see* Bié, Planalto do
Big Cypress Swamp *435 E5 wetland* Florida, SE USA
Bigge Island *538 C2 island* Western Australia
Bighorn Mountains *436 C2 mountain range* Wyoming, C USA
Bighorn River *436 C2 river* Montana/Wyoming, NW US
Bignona *466 B3* SW Senegal
Big Sioux River *437 E2 river* Iowa/South Dakota, N USA
Big Spring *441 E3* Texas, SW
Bihać *492 B3* NW Bosnia and Herzegovina
Bihār *527 F4 prev.* Behar. Adm region *state* N India
Biharamulo *465 B7* Kagera, NW Tanzania
Bihosava *499 D5 Rus.* Bigoso Vitsyebskaya Voblasts', NW Belorussia
Bijeljina *492 C3* NE Bosnia ar Herzegovina
Bijelo Polje *493 D5* Monteneg SW Yugoslavia
Bīkāner *526 C3* Rājasthān, NW India
Bikin *507 G4* Khabarovskiy K SE Russian Federation
Bikini Atoll *536 C1 var.* Pikin *atoll* Ralik Chain, NW Marsh Islands
Bīkkū Bīttī *see* Bette, Pic
Bilāspur *527 E4* Madhya Prad C India
Biläsuvar *509 H3 Rus.* Bilyasu *prev.* Pushkino. SE Azerbaija
Bila Tserkva *501 E2 Rus.* Bela Tserkov'. Kyyivs'ka Oblast', N Ukraine
Bilauktaung Range *529 C6 v* Thanintari Taungdan. *moun range* Burma/Thailand
Bilbao *485 E1 Basq.* Bilbo. Pa Vasco, N Spain
Bilecik *508 B3* Bilecik, NW Tu
Billings *436 C2* Montana, NW
Bilma, Grand Erg de *467 H3* NE Niger
Biloela *540 D4* Queensland, E Australia
Biloxi *434 C3* Mississippi, S U
Biltine *468 C3* Biltine, E Chad
Bilwi *see* Puerto Cabezas
Bilzen *479 D6* Limburg, NE Belgium
Bimini Islands *446 C1 island* W Bahamas
Binche *479 B7* Hainaut, S Belg
Bindloe Island *see* Marchena,
Binghamton *433 F3* New Yor NE USA
Bingöl *509 E3* Bingöl, E Turke
Bint Jubayl *see* Bent Jbaïl
Bintulu *530 D3* Sarawak, East Malaysia
Binzhou *520 D4* Shandong, E
Bío Bío, Río *457 B5 river* C Cl
Bioco, Isla de *469 A5 var.* Bio *Eng.* Fernando Po, *Sp.* Fernan Póo; *prev.* Macías Nguema B *island* NW Equatorial Guine
Bioko *see* Bioco, Isla de
Birāk *463 F3 var.* Brak. C Liby
Birao *468 D3* Vakaga, NE Cen African Republic
Biratnagar *527 F3* Eastern, SE Nepal
Bir es Saba *see* Be'ér Sheva'
Birhār Sharīf *527 F3* Bihar, N
Bīrjand *512 E3* Khorāsān, E I
Birkenfeld *487 A5* Rheinland SW Germany
Birkenhead *481 C5* NW Engl UK
Birmingham *434 C2* Alabam S USA
Birmingham *481 C6* C Engla UK
Bir Moghrein *see* Bîr Mogreïn
Bîr Mogreïn *466 C1 var.* Bir Moghrein; *prev.* Fort-Trinqu Tiris Zemmour, N Mauritan
Birnie Island *537 E3 atoll* Pho Islands, C Kiribati
Birni-Nkonni *see* Birnin Kon
Birnin Konni *467 F3 var.* Birr Nkonni. Tahoua, SW Niger
Birobidzhan *507 G4* Yevreysk Avtonomnaya Oblast', SE Ru Federation
Birsk *503 D5* Respublika Bashkortostan, W Russian Federation
Biržai *498 C4 Ger.* Birsen. Birž NE Lithuania
Birżebbuġa *494 B5* SE Malta
Bisbee *440 B3* Arizona, SW U
Biscay, Bay of *472 B4 Sp.* Golf Vizcaya, *Port.* Baía de Biscaia France/Spain
Biscay Plain *472 B3 undersea feature* SE Bay of Biscay
Bīshah, Wādī *513 B5 dry watercourse* C Saudi Arabia
Bishkek *515 G2 var.* Pishpek; Frunze. *country capital* (Kyrgyzstan) Chuyskaya Ob N Kyrgyzstan
Bishop's Lynn *see* King's Lynn
Bishrī, Jabal *510 D3 mountain range* E Syria

Biskara – Brunswick

a *see* Biskra
a *463 E2 var.* Beskra, Biskara.
Algeria
piec *490 D2 Ger.*
hofsburg. Olsztyn, N Poland
531 F2 Mindanao,
ilippines
rck *437 E2 state capital* North
ota, N USA
rck Archipelago *536 B3*
d group NE PNG
rck Sea *536 B3 sea* W Pacific
an
lok *see* Phitsanulok
i *466 B4 country capital*
nea-Bissau) W Guinea-Bissau
ta *500 B3 Ger.* Bistritz, *Hung.*
terce; *prev.* Nösen. Bistrița-
ăud, N Romania
469 B5 Woleu-Ntem,
abon
rg *487 A5* Rheinland-Pfalz,
Germany
509 F3 Bitlis, SE Turkey
493 D6 Turk. Monastir; *prev.*
j. S FYR Macedonia
o *489 D5 anc.* Butuntum.
ia, SE Italy
root Range *438 D2 mountain*
e Idaho/Montana, NW USA
g *531 F3 prev.* Bitoeng.
wesi, C Indonesia
57 H4 Borno, E Nigeria
ko *523 C6 lake* Honshū,
Japan
e *463 E1 Ar.* Banzart, *Eng.*
rta. N Tunisia
var *492 B2 Hung.* Belovár.
ovar-Bilogora, N Croatia
øya *475 F3 Eng.* Bear Island.
d N Norway
all *540 C4* Queensland,
stralia
Drin *493 D6 Alb.* Lumi i
it të Zi, *SCr.* Crni Drim. *river*
nia/FYR Macedonia
foot *438 E4* Idaho, NW USA
Forest *see* Schwarzwald
Hills *436 D3 mountain range*
h Dakota/Wyoming, N USA
pool *481 C5* NW England,

Range *440 C2 mountain*
e New Mexico, SW USA
River *528 C3 Chin.* Babian
g, Lixian Jiang, *Fr.* Rivière
e, *Vtn.* Sông Đa. *river*
na/Vietnam
River *446 A5* W Jamaica
Rock Desert *439 C5 desert*
ada, W USA
Sand Desert *see* Garagumy
Sea *508 B1 var.* Euxine Sea,
Cherno More, *Rom.* Marea
gră, *Rus.* Chernoye More, *Turk.*
deniz, *Ukr.* Chorne More. *sea*
/Europe
Sea Lowland *501 E4 Ukr.*
hornomors'ka Nyzovyna.
ession SE Europe
Volta *467 E4 var.* Borongo,
houn, Moun Hou, *Fr.* Volta
e. *river* W Africa
water *481 A6 Ir.* An Abhainn
r. *river* S Ireland
evgrad *496 C3 prev.* Gorna
umaya. Sofiyska Oblast,
ulgaria
veshchensk *507 G4*
urskaya Oblast', SE Russian
eration
Plateau *427 D6 var.* Blake
ace. *undersea feature*
tlantic Ocean
Terrace *see* Blake Plateau
a, Bahía *457 C5 bay*
gentina
a, Costa *485 F4 physical*
n SE Spain
he, Lake *541 B5 lake* South
ralia
, Mont *483 D5 It.* Monte
co. *mountain* France/Italy
o, Cape *438 A4 headland*
gon, NW USA
s *485 G2* Cataluña, NE Spain
enberge *479 A5* West-
anderen, NW Belgium
kenheim *487 A5* Nordrhein-
tfalen, W Germany
quilla, Isla *451 E1 var.* La
quilla. *island* N Venezuela
yre *471 E2 var.* Blantyre-
be. Southern, S Malawi
yre-Limbe *see* Blantyre
cum *478 C3* Noord-Holland,
etherlands
eim *543 C5* Marlborough,
h Island, NZ
462 D2 var. El Boulaida,
oulaïda. N Algeria
nfontein *470 C4 var.*
gaung. *country capital* (South
ca-judicial capital) Free State,
uth Africa
482 C4 anc. Blesae. Loir-et-
, C France

Bloomfield *440 C1* New Mexico, SW USA
Bloomington *432 B4* Illinois, N USA
Bloomington *432 C4* Indiana, N USA
Bloomington *437 F2* Minnesota, N USA
Bloomsbury *540 D3* Queensland, NE Australia
Bluefield *432 D5* West Virginia, NE USA
Bluefields *445 E3* Región Autónoma Atlántico Sur, SE Nicaragua
Blue Mountain Peak *446 B5 mountain* E Jamaica
Blue Mountains *438 C3 mountain range* Oregon/Washington, NW USA
Blue Nile *460 D4 var.* Abai, Bahr el Azraq, *Amh.* Ābay Wenz, *Ar.* An Nīl al Azraq. *river* Ethiopia/Sudan
Blue Nile *464 C4 state* E Sudan
Blumenau *455 E5* Santa Catarina, S Brazil
Blythe *439 D8* California, W USA
Blytheville *434 C1* Arkansas, C USA
Bo *466 C4* S Sierra Leone
Boaco *444 D3* Boaco, S Nicaragua
Boa Vista *466 A3 island* Ilhas de Barlavento, E Cape Verde
Boa Vista *454 D1 state capital* Roraima, NW Brazil
Bobaomby, Tanjona *471 G2 Fr.* Cap d'Ambre. *headland* N Madagascar
Bobigny *482 E1* Seine-St-Denis, N France
Bobo-Dioulasso *466 D4* SW Burkina
Bobrynets' *501 E3 Rus.* Bobrinets. Kirovohrads'ka Oblast', C Ukraine
Boca Raton *435 F5* Florida, SE USA
Bocay *444 D2* Jinotega, N Nicaragua
Bocche del Po *see* Po, Foci del
Bocholt *486 A4* Nordrhein-Westfalen, W Germany
Bochum *486 A4* Nordrhein-Westfalen, W Germany
Bocșa *500 A4 Ger.* Bokschen, *Hung.* Boksánbánya. Caraș-Severin, SW Romania
Bodaybo *507 F4* Irkutskaya Oblast', E Russian Federation
Boden *476 D4* Norrbotten, N Sweden
Bodmin *481 C7* SW England, UK
Bodø *476 C3* Nordland, C Norway
Bodrum *508 A4* Muğla, SW Turkey
Boende *469 C5* Equateur, C Congo (Zaire)
Boetoeng *see* Buton, Pulau
Bogale *528 B4* Irrawaddy, SW Burma
Bogalusa *434 B3* Louisiana, S USA
Bogatynia *490 B4 Ger.* Reichenau. Jelenia Góra, SW Poland
Boğazlıyan *508 D3* Yozgat, C Turkey
Bogor *530 C5 Dut.* Buitenzorg. Jawa, C Indonesia
Bogotá *450 B3 prev.* Santa Fe, Santa Fe de Bogotá. *country capital* (Colombia) Cundinamarca, C Colombia
Bo Hai *520 D4 var.* Gulf of Chihli. *gulf* NE China
Bohemia *491 A5 Cz.* Čechy, *Ger.* Böhmen. *cultural and historical region* W Czech Republic
Bohemian Forest *487 C5 Cz.* Ceský Les, Šumava, *Ger.* Böhmerwald. *mountain range* C Europe
Böhmisch-Krumau *see* Český Krumlov
Bohol Sea *531 E2 var.* Mindanao Sea. *sea* S Philippines
Bohoro Shan *518 B2 mountain range* NW China
Bohuslav *501 E2 Rus.* Boguslav. Kyyivs'ka Oblast', N Ukraine
Boise *438 D3 var.* Boise City. *state capital* Idaho, NW USA
Boise City *see* Boise
Boise City *441 E1* Oklahoma, C USA
Boizenburg *486 C3* Mecklenburg-Vorpommern, N Germany
Bojador *see* Boujdour
Bojnūrd *512 D2 var.* Bujnurd. Khorāsān, N Iran
Bokāro *527 F4* Bihār, N India
Boké *466 C4* Guinée-Maritime, W Guinea
Bokhara *see* Bukhoro
Boknafjorden *477 A6 fjord* S Norway
Bol *468 B3* Lac, W Chad
Bolgatanga *467 E4* N Ghana
Bolhrad *500 D4 Rus.* Bolgrad. Odes'ka Oblast', SW Ukraine
Bolívar, Pico *450 C2 mountain* W Venezuela

Bolivia *453 F3 off.* Republic of Bolivia. *country* W South America
Bollene *483 D6* Vaucluse, SE France
Bollnäs *477 C5* Gävleborg, C Sweden
Bollon *541 D5* Queensland, C Australia
Bologna *488 C3* Emilia-Romagna, N Italy
Bol'shevik, Ostrov *507 E2 island* Severnaya Zemlya, N Russian Federation
Bol'shezemel'skaya Tundra *502 E3 physical region* NW Russian Federation
Bol'shoy Lyakhovskiy, Ostrov *507 F2 island* NE Russian Federation
Bolton *481 D5 prev.* Bolton-le-Moors. NW England, UK
Bolu *508 B3* Bolu, NW Turkey
Bolungarvík *475 E4* Vestfirdhir, NW Iceland
Bolyarovo *496 D3 prev.* Pashkeni. Burgaska Oblast, SE Bulgaria
Bolzano *488 C1 Ger.* Bozen; *anc.* Bauzanum. Trentino-Alto Adige, N Italy
Boma *469 B6* Bas-Zaïre, W Congo (Zaire)
Bombay *526 C5 Guj.* Mumbai. Mahārāshtra, W India
Bomu *468 D4 var.* Mbomou, Mbomu, M'Bomu. *river* Central African Republic/Congo (Zaire)
Bonaire *447 F5 island* E Netherlands Antilles
Bonanza *444 D2* Región Autónoma Atlántico Norte, NE Nicaragua
Bonaparte Archipelago *538 C2 island group* Western Australia
Bon, Cap *494 D3 headland* N Tunisia
Bonda *469 B6* Ogooué-Lolo, C Gabon
Bondoukou *467 E4* E Ivory Coast
Bone *see* Watampone
Bone, Teluk *531 E4 bay* Sulawesi, C Indonesia
Bongaigaon *527 G3* Assam, NE India
Bongo, Massif des *468 D4 var.* Chaîne des Mongos. *mountain range* NE Central African Republic
Bongor *468 B3* Mayo-Kébbi, SW Chad
Bonifacio *483 E7* Corse, France, C Mediterranean Sea
Bonifacio, Strait of *488 A4 Fr.* Bouches de Bonifacio, *It.* Bocche de Bonifacio. *strait* C Mediterranean Sea
Bonn *487 A5* Nordrhein-Westfalen, W Germany
Bononia *see* Boulogne-sur-Mer
Boosaaso *464 E4 var.* Bandar Kassim, Bender Qaasim, Bosaso, *It.* Bender Cassim. Bari, N Somalia
Boothia, Gulf of *429 F2 gulf* Nunavut, NE Canada
Boothia Peninsula *429 F2 prev.* Boothia Felix. *peninsula* Nunavut, NE Canada
Boppard *487 A5* Rheinland-Pfalz, W Germany
Boquete *445 E5 var.* Bajo Boquete. Chiriquí, W Panama
Boquillas *442 D2 var.* Boquillas del Carmen. Coahuila de Zaragoza, NE Mexico
Boquillas del Carmen *see* Boquillas
Bor *465 B5* Jonglei, S Sudan
Bor *492 E4* Serbia, E Yugoslavia
Borås *477 B7* Älvsborg, S Sweden
Borborema, Planalto da *448 E3 plateau* NE Brazil
Bordeaux *483 B5 anc.* Burdigala. Gironde, SW France
Bordj Omar Driss *463 E3* E Algeria
Børgefjellet *476 C4 mountain range* C Norway
Borger *478 E2* Drenthe, NE Netherlands
Borger *441 E1* Texas, SW USA
Borgholm *477 C7* Kalmar, S Sweden
Borgo Maggiore *488 E1* NW San Marino
Borisoglebsk *503 B6* Voronezhskaya Oblast', W Russian Federation
Borlänge *477 C6* Kopparberg, C Sweden
Borne *478 E3* Overijssel, E Netherlands
Borneo *530 C4 island* Brunei/Indonesia/Malaysia
Bornholm *477 B8 island* E Denmark
Borohoro Shan *515 H1 mountain range* NW China
Borongo *see* Black Volta
Borovan *496 C2* Oblast Montana, NW Bulgaria
Borovichi *502 B4* Novgorodskaya Oblast', W Russian Federation

Borovo *492 C3* Vukovar-Srijem, NE Croatia
Borșa *500 C3 Hung.* Borsa. Maramureș, N Romania
Boryslav *500 B2 Pol.* Borysław, *Rus.* Borislav. L'vivs'ka Oblast', NW Ukraine
Bosanska Dubica *492 B3* NW Bosnia and Herzegovina
Bosanska Gradiška *492 B3* N Bosnia and Herzegovina
Bosanski Novi *492 B3* NW Bosnia and Herzegovina
Bosanski Šamac *492 C3* N Bosnia and Herzegovina
Bosaso *see* Boosaaso
Boskovice *491 B5 Ger.* Boskowitz. Jižní Morava, SE Czech Republic
Bosna *492 C4 river* N Bosnia and Herzegovina
Bosnia and Herzegovina *492 B3 off.* Republic of Bosnia and Herzegovina. *country* SE Europe
Bōsō-hantō *523 D6 peninsula* Honshū, S Japan
Bosphorus *see* İstanbul Boğazı
Bosporus *see* İstanbul Boğazı
Bosporus Cimmerius *see* Kerch Strait
Bosporus Thracius *see* İstanbul Boğazı
Bossangoa *468 C4* Ouham, C Central African Republic
Bossembélé *468 C4* Ombella-Mpoko, C Central African Republic
Bossier City *434 A2* Louisiana, S USA
Bosten Hu *518 C3 var.* Bagrax Hu. *lake* NW China
Boston *481 E6 prev.* St.Botolph's Town. E England, UK
Boston *433 G3 state capital* Massachusetts, NE USA
Boston Mountains *434 B1 mountain range* Arkansas, C USA
Botany *540 E2* New South Wales, SE Australia
Botany Bay *540 E2 inlet* New South Wales, SE Australia
Boteti *470 C3 var.* Botletle. *river* N Botswana
Bothnia, Gulf of *477 D5 Fin.* Pohjanlahti, *Swe.* Bottniska Viken. *gulf* N Baltic Sea
Botletle *see* Boteti
Botoșani *500 C3 Hung.* Botosány. Botoșani, NE Romania
Botou *520 C4 prev.* Bozhen. Hebei, E China
Botrange *479 D6 mountain* E Belgium
Botswana *470 C3 off.* Republic of Botswana. *country* S Africa
Bouar *468 B4* Nana-Mambéré, W Central African Republic
Bou Craa *462 B3 var.* Bu Craa. NW Western Sahara
Bougainville Island *534 B3 island* NE PNG
Bougaroun, Cap *494 C3 headland* NE Algeria
Bougouni *466 D4* Sikasso, SW Mali
Boujdour *462 A3 var.* Bojador. W Western Sahara
Boulder *436 C4* Colorado, C USA
Boulder *436 B2* Montana, NW USA
Boulogne *see* Boulogne-sur-Mer
Boulogne-Billancourt *482 D1 prev.* Boulogne-sur-Seine. Hauts-de-Seine, N France
Boulogne-sur-Mer *482 C2 var.* Boulogne; *anc.* Bononia, Gesoriacum, Gessoriacum. Pas-de-Calais, N France
Boûmdeïd *466 C3 var.* Boumdeït. Assaba, S Mauritania
Boumdeït *see* Boûmdeïd
Boundiali *466 D4* N Ivory Coast
Bountiful *436 B4* Utah, W USA
Bounty Basin *see* Bounty Trough
Bounty Islands *534 D5 island group* S NZ
Bounty Trough *544 C5 var.* Bounty Basin. *undersea feature* S Pacific Ocean
Bourbonnais *482 C4* Illinois, N USA
Bourg *see* Bourg-en-Bresse
Bourgas *see* Burgas
Bourge-en-Bresse *see* Bourg-en-Bresse
Bourg-en-Bresse *483 D5 var.* Bourg, Bourge-en-Bresse. Ain, E France
Bourges *482 C4 anc.* Avaricum. Cher, C France
Bourgogne *482 C4 Eng.* Burgundy. *cultural region* E France
Bourke *541 C5* New South Wales, SE Australia
Bournemouth *481 D7* S England, UK
Boutilimit *466 C3* Trarza, SW Mauritania

Bouvet Island *459 D7 Norwegian dependency* S Atlantic Ocean
Bowen *540 D3* Queensland, NE Australia
Bowling Green *432 B5* Kentucky, S USA
Bowling Green *432 C3* Ohio, N USA
Boxmeer *478 D4* Noord-Brabant, SE Netherlands
Boyarka *501 E2* Kyyivs'ka Oblast', N Ukraine
Boysun *515 E3 Rus.* Baysun. Surkhondaryo Wiloyati, S Uzbekistan
Bozeman *436 B2* Montana, NW USA
Bozüyük *508 B3* Bilecik, NW Turkey
Brač *492 B4 var.* Brach, *It.* Brazza; *anc.* Brattia. *island* S Croatia
Brach *see* Brač
Bradford *481 D5* N England, UK
Brady *441 F3* Texas, SW USA
Braga *484 B2 anc.* Bracara Augusta. Braga, NW Portugal
Bragança *484 C2 Eng.* Braganza; *anc.* Julio Briga. Bragança, NE Portugal
Brahmanbaria *527 G4* Chittagong, E Bangladesh
Brahmapur *527 F5* Orissa, E India
Brahmaputra *527 H3 var.* Padma, Tsangpo, *Ben.* Jamuna, *Chin.* Yarlung Zangbo Jiang, *Ind.* Bramaputra, Dihang, Siang. *river* S Asia
Brăila *500 D4* Brăila, E Romania
Braine-le-Comte *479 B6* Hainaut, SW Belgium
Brainerd *437 F2* Minnesota, N USA
Brak *see* Birāk
Bramaputra *see* Brahmaputra
Brampton *430 D5* Ontario, S Canada
Branco, Rio *448 C3 river* N Brazil
Brandberg *470 A3 mountain* NW Namibia
Brandenburg *486 C3 var.* Brandenburg an der Havel. Brandenburg, NE Germany
Brandenburg an der Havel *see* Brandenburg
Brandon *429 F5* Manitoba, S Canada
Braniewo *490 D2 Ger.* Braunsberg. Elbląg, N Poland
Brasília *455 F3 country capital* (Brazil) Distrito Federal, C Brazil
Brașov *500 C4 Ger.* Kronstadt, *Hung.* Brassó; *prev.* Orașul Stalin. Brașov, C Romania
Bratislava *491 C6 Ger.* Pressburg, *Hung.* Pozsony. *country capital* (Slovakia) Západné Slovensko, SW Slovakia
Bratsk *507 E4* Irkutskaya Oblast', C Russian Federation
Brattia *see* Brač
Braunschweig *486 C4 Eng./Fr.* Brunswick. Niedersachsen, N Germany
Brava, Costa *485 H2 coastal region* NE Spain
Bravo del Norte *see* Grande, Rio
Bravo del Norte, Río *see* Bravo, Río
Bravo del Norte, Río *see* Bravo, Río
Bravo del Norte, Río *see* Grande, Rio
Bravo, Río *442 C1 var.* Río Bravo del Norte, Rio Grande. *river* Mexico/USA
Bravo, Río *see* Grande, Rio
Brawley *439 D8* California, W USA
Brazil *454 C2 off.* Federative Republic of Brazil, *Port.* República Federativa do Brasil, *Sp.* Brasil; *prev.* United States of Brazil. *country* South America
Brazil Basin *459 C5 var.* Brazilian Basin, Brazil'skaya Kotlovina. *undersea feature* W Atlantic Ocean
Brazilian Basin *see* Brazil Basin
Brazilian Highlands *see* Central, Planalto
Brazil'skaya Kotlovina *see* Brazil Basin
Brazos River *441 G3 river* Texas, SW USA
Brazza *see* Brač
Brazzaville *469 B6 country capital* (Congo) Capital District, S Congo
Brčko *492 C3* NE Bosnia and Herzegovina
Brecht *479 C5* Antwerpen, N Belgium
Brecon Beacons *481 C6 mountain range* S Wales, UK
Breda *478 C4* Noord-Brabant, S Netherlands
Bree *479 D5* Limburg, NE Belgium
Bregalnica *493 E6 river* E FYR Macedonia
Bregovo *496 B1* Oblast Montana, NW Bulgaria
Bremen *486 B3 Fr.* Brême. Bremen, NW Germany

Bremerhaven *486 B3* Bremen, NW Germany
Bremerton *438 B2* Washington, NW USA
Brenham *441 G3* Texas, SW USA
Brenner Pass *488 C1 var.* Brenner Sattel, *Fr.* Col du Brenner, *Ger.* Brennerpass, *It.* Passo del Brennero. *pass* Austria/Italy
Brennerpass *see* Brenner Pass
Brenner Sattel *see* Brenner Pass
Brescia *488 B2 anc.* Brixia. Lombardia, N Italy
Bressanone *488 C1 Ger.* Brixen. Trentino-Alto Adige, N Italy
Brest *499 A6 Pol.* Brześć nad Bugiem, *Rus.* Brest-Litovsk; *prev.* Brześć Litewski. Brestskaya Voblasts', SW Belorussia
Brest *482 A3* Finistère, NW France
Bretagne *482 A3 Eng.* Brittany; *Lat.* Britannia Minor. *cultural region* NW France
Brewton *434 C3* Alabama, S USA
Brezovo *496 D2 prev.* Abrashlare. Plovdivska Oblast, C Bulgaria
Bria *468 D4* Haute-Kotto, C Central African Republic
Briançon *483 D5 anc.* Brigantio. Hautes-Alpes, SE France
Bridgeport *433 F3* Connecticut, NE USA
Bridgetown *447 G2 country capital* (Barbados) SW Barbados
Bridlington *481 D5* E England, UK
Bridport *481 D7* S England, UK
Brig *487 A7 Fr.* Brigue, *It.* Briga. Valais, SW Switzerland
Brigham City *436 B3* Utah, W USA
Brighton *436 D4* Colorado, C USA
Brighton *481 E7* SE England, UK
Brindisi *489 E5 anc.* Brundisium, Brundusium. Puglia, SE Italy
Brisbane *541 E5 state capital* Queensland, E Australia
Bristol *481 D7 anc.* Bricgstow. SW England, UK
Bristol *433 F3* Connecticut, NE USA
Bristol *432 D5* Virginia, NE USA
Bristol Bay *428 B3 bay* Alaska, USA
Bristol Channel *481 C7 inlet* England/Wales, UK
Britain *472 C3 var.* Great Britain. *island* UK
British Columbia *428 D4 Fr.* Colombie-Britannique. *province* SW Canada
British Indian Ocean Territory *533 B5 UK dependent territory* C Indian Ocean
British Isles *481 island group* NW Europe
British Virgin Islands *447 F3 var.* Virgin Islands. *UK dependent territory* E West Indies
Brive-la-Gaillarde *483 C5 prev.* Brive, *anc.* Briva Curretia. Corrèze, C France
Brno *491 B5 Ger.* Brünn. Jižní Morava, SE Czech Republic
Broceni *498 B3* Saldus, SW Latvia
Brodeur Peninsula *429 F2 peninsula* Baffin Island, Northwest Territories, NE Canada
Brodnica *490 C3 Ger.* Buddenbrock. Toruń, N Poland
Broek-in-Waterland *478 C3* Noord-Holland, C Netherlands
Broken Arrow *441 G1* Oklahoma, C USA
Broken Bay *540 E1 bay* New South Wales, SE Australia
Broken Hill *541 B6* New South Wales, SE Australia
Broken Ridge *533 D6 undersea feature* S Indian Ocean
Bromley *481 B8* SE England, UK
Brookhaven *434 B3* Mississippi, S USA
Brookings *437 F3* South Dakota, N USA
Brooks Range *428 D2 mountain range* Alaska, USA
Brookton *539 B6* Western Australia
Broome *538 B3* Western Australia
Broomfield *436 D4* Colorado, C USA
Broucsella *see* Brussel
Brovary *501 E2* Kyyivs'ka Oblast', N Ukraine
Brownfield *441 E2* Texas, SW USA
Brownville *441 G5* Texas, SW USA
Brownwood *441 F3* Texas, SW USA
Brozha *499 D7* Mahilyowskaya Voblasts', E Belorussia
Brugge *479 A5 Fr.* Bruges. West-Vlaanderen, NW Belgium
Brummen *478 D3* Gelderland, E Netherlands
Brunei *530 D3 off.* Sultanate of Brunei, *Mal.* Negara Brunei Darussalam. *country* SE Asia
Brunner, Lake *543 C5 lake* South Island, NZ
Brunswick *435 E3* Georgia, SE USA

Brusa – Carson Sink

Brusa see Bursa
Brus Laguna 444 D2 Gracias a Dios, E Honduras
Brussa see Bursa
Brussel 479 var. Brussels, Fr. Bruxelles, Ger. Brüssel; anc. Broucsella. country capital (Belgium) Brussels, C Belgium see also Bruxelles
Brüssel see Brussel
Brussels see Brussel
Bruxelles see Brussels
Bryan 441 G3 Texas, SW USA
Bryansk 503 A5 Bryanskaya Oblast', W Russian Federation
Brzeg 490 C4 Ger. Brieg; anc. Civitas Altae Ripae. Opole, SW Poland
Bucaramanga 450 B2 Santander, N Colombia
Buchanan 466 C5 prev. Grand Bassa. SW Liberia
Buchanan, Lake 441 F3 reservoir Texas, SW USA
Bucharest see București
Bu Craa see Bou Craa
București 500 C5 Eng. Bucharest, Ger. Bukarest; prev. Altenburg, anc. Cetatea Damboviţei. country capital (Romania) București, S Romania
Buda-Kashalyova 499 D7 Rus. Buda-Koshelëvo. Homyel'skaya Voblasts', SE Belorussia
Budapest 491 C6 off. Budapest Főváros, SCr. Budimpešta. country capital (Hungary) Pest, N Hungary
Budaun 526 D3 Uttar Pradesh, N India
Buena Park 438 E2 California, W USA
Buenaventura 450 A3 Valle del Cauca, W Colombia
Buena Vista 485 H5 S Gibraltar
Buena Vista 453 G4 Santa Cruz, C Bolivia
Buenos Aires 456 D4 hist. Santa Maria del Buen Aire. country capital (Argentina) Buenos Aires, E Argentina
Buenos Aires 445 E5 Puntarenas, SE Costa Rica
Buenos Aires, Lago 457 B6 var. Lago General Carrera. lake Argentina/Chile
Buffalo 433 E3 New York, NE USA
Buffalo Narrows 429 F4 Saskatchewan, C Canada
Buff Bay 446 B5 E Jamaica
Buftea 500 C5 București, S Romania
Bug 473 E3 Bel. Zakhodni Buh, Eng. Western Bug, Rus. Zapadnyy Bug, Ukr. Zakhidnyy Buh. river E Europe
Buga 450 B3 Valle del Cauca, W Colombia
Bughotu see Santa Isabel
Buguruslan 503 D6 Orenburgskaya Oblast', W Russian Federation
Buḩayrat Nāşir see Nasser, Lake
Buḩeirat Nâşir see Nasser, Lake
Bujalance 484 D4 Andalucía, S Spain
Bujanovac 493 E5 Serbia, SE Yugoslavia
Bujnurd see Bojnūrd
Bujumbura 465 B7 prev. Usumbura. country capital (Burundi) W Burundi
Bukavu 469 E6 prev. Costermansville. Sud Kivu, E Congo (Zaire)
Bukhara see Bukhoro
Bukhoro 514 D2 var. Bokhara, Rus. Bukhara. Bukhoro Wiloyati, C Uzbekistan
Bukoba 465 B6 Kagera, NW Tanzania
Bülach 487 B7 Zürich, NW Switzerland
Bulawayo 470 D3 var. Buluwayo. Matabeleland North, SW Zimbabwe
Buldur see Burdur
Bulgan 519 E2 Bulgan, N Mongolia
Bulgaria 496 C2 off. Republic of Bulgaria, Bul. Bŭlgariya; prev. People's Republic of Bulgaria. country SE Europe
Bull Shoals Lake 434 B1 reservoir Arkansas/Missouri, C USA
Bulukumba 531 E4 prev. Boeloekoemba. Sulawesi, C Indonesia
Buluwayo see Bulawayo
Bumba 469 D5 Equateur, N Congo (Zaire)
Bunbury 539 A7 Western Australia
Bundaberg 540 E4 Queensland, E Australia
Bungo-suidō 523 B7 strait SW Japan
Bunia 469 E5 Haut-Zaïre, NE Congo (Zaire)
Bünyan 508 D3 Kayseri, C Turkey
Buraida see Buraydah
Buraydah 512 B4 var. Buraida. Al Qaşīm, N Saudi Arabia
Burdur 508 B4 var. Buldur. Burdur, SW Turkey
Burdur Gölü 508 B4 salt lake SW Turkey
Burē 464 C4 W Ethiopia
Burgas 496 E2 var. Bourgas. Burgaska Oblast, E Bulgaria
Burgaski Zaliv 496 E2 gulf E Bulgaria
Burgos 484 D2 Castilla-León, N Spain
Burhan Budai Shan 518 D4 mountain range C China
Buri Ram see Buriram
Buriram 529 D5 var. Buri Ram, Puriramya. Buri Ram, E Thailand
Burjassot 485 F3 País Valenciano, E Spain
Burkburnett 441 F2 Texas, SW USA
Burketown 540 B3 Queensland, NE Australia
Burkina 467 E4 off. Burkina Faso; prev. Upper Volta. country W Africa
Burley 438 D4 Idaho, NW USA
Burlington 437 G4 Iowa, C USA
Burlington 433 F2 Vermont, NE USA
Burma 528 A3 off. Union of Myanmar, var. Myanmar. country SE Asia
Burnie 541 C8 Tasmania, SE Australia
Burns 438 C3 Oregon, NW USA
Burnside 429 F3 river Nunavut, NW Canada
Burnsville 437 F2 Minnesota, N USA
Burrel 493 D6 var. Burreli. Dibër, C Albania
Burreli see Burrel
Burriana 485 F3 País Valenciano, E Spain
Bursa 508 B3 var. Brussa; prev. Brusa, anc. Prusa. Bursa, NW Turkey
Burtnieks see Burtnieku Ezers
Burtnieku Ezers 498 C3 var. Burtnieks. lake N Latvia
Burundi 465 B7 off. Republic of Burundi; prev. Kingdom of Burundi, Urundi. country C Africa
Buru, Pulau 531 F4 prev. Boeroe. island E Indonesia
Buşayrah 510 D3 Dayr az Zawr, E Syria
Būshehr see Bandar-e Būshehr
Bushire see Bandar-e Būshehr
Busselton 539 A7 Western Australia
Buta 469 D5 Haut-Zaïre, N Congo (Zaire)
Butembo 469 E5 Nord Kivu, NE Congo (Zaire)
Butler 433 E4 Pennsylvania, NE USA
Buton, Pulau 531 E4 var. Pulau Butung; prev. Boetoeng. island C Indonesia
Butte 436 B2 Montana, NW USA
Butterworth 530 B3 Pinang, Peninsular Malaysia
Button Islands 431 E1 island group Nunavut, NE Canada
Butuan 531 F2 off. Butuan City. Mindanao, S Philippines
Buulobarde 465 D5 var. Buulo Berde. Hiiraan, C Somalia Africa
Buulo Berde see Buulobarde
Buur Gaabo 465 D6 Jubbada Hoose, S Somalia
Buynaksk 503 B8 Respublika Dagestan, SW Russian Federation
Büyükağrı Dağı 509 F3 var. Aghri Dagh, Agri Dagi, Koh I Noh, Masis, Eng. Great Ararat, Mount Ararat. mountain E Turkey
Büyükmenderes Nehri 508 A4 river SW Turkey
Buzău 500 C4 Buzău, SE Romania
Buzuluk 503 D6 Orenburgskaya Oblast', W Russian Federation
Byahoml' 499 D5 Rus. Begoml'. Vitsyebskaya Voblasts', N Belorussia
Byalynichy 499 D6 Rus. Belynichi. Mahilyowskaya Voblasts', E Belorussia
Bydgoszcz 490 C3 Ger. Bromberg. Bydgoszcz, W Poland
Byelaruskaya Hrada 499 B6 Rus. Belorusskaya Gryada. ridge N Belorussia
Byerezino 499 D6 Rus. Berezina. river C Belorussia
Byron Island see Nikunau
Bytča 491 C5 Stredné Slovensko, NW Slovakia
Bytów 490 C2 Ger. Bütow. Słupsk, NW Poland
Byuzmeyin 514 C3 Turkm. Büzmeyin; prev. Bezmein. Akhalskiy Velayat, C Turkmenistan
Byval'ki 499 D8 Homyel'skaya Voblasts', SE Belorussia
Byzantium see İstanbul

C

Caála 470 B2 var. Kaala, Robert Williams, Port. Vila Robert Williams. Huambo, C Angola
Caazapá 456 D3 Caazapá, S Paraguay
Caballo Reservoir 440 C3 reservoir New Mexico, SW USA
Cabañaquinta 484 D1 Asturias, N Spain
Cabanatuan 531 E1 off. Cabanatuan City. Luzon, N Philippines
Cabimas 450 C1 Zulia, NW Venezuela
Cabinda 470 A1 var. Kabinda. Cabinda, NW Angola
Cabinda 470 A1 var. Kabinda. Admin. region province NW Angola
Cabora Bassa, Lake see Cahora Bassa, Albufeira de
Caborca 442 B1 Sonora, NW Mexico
Cabot Strait 431 G4 strait E Canada
Cabras, Ilha das 468 E2 island S Sao Tome and Principe
Cabrera 485 G3 anc. Capraria. island Islas Baleares, Spain, W Mediterranean Sea
Cáceres 484 C3 Ar. Qazris. Extremadura, W Spain
Cachimbo, Serra do 455 E2 mountain range C Brazil
Caconda 470 B2 Huíla, C Angola
Čadca 491 C5 Hung. Csaca. Stredné Slovensko, N Slovakia
Cadillac 432 C2 Michigan, N USA
Cadiz 531 E2 off. Cadiz City. Negros, C Philippines
Cádiz 484 C5 anc. Gades, Gadier, Gadir, Gadire. Andalucía, SW Spain
Cádiz, Golfo de 484 B5 Eng. Gulf of Cadiz. gulf Portugal/Spain
Cadiz, Gulf of see Cádiz, Golfo de
Caen 482 B3 Calvados, N France
Caene see Qena
Caenepolis see Qena
Caerdydd see Cardiff
Caer Gybi see Holyhead
Caesarea Mazaca see Kayseri
Cafayate 456 C2 Salta, N Argentina
Cagayan de Oro 531 E2 off. Cagayan de Oro City. Mindanao, S Philippines
Cagliari 489 A6 anc. Caralis. Sardegna, Italy, C Mediterranean Sea
Caguas 447 F3 E Puerto Rico
Cahora Bassa, Albufeira de 470 D2 var. Lake Cabora Bassa. reservoir NW Mozambique
Cahors 483 C5 anc. Cadurcum. Lot, S France
Cahul 500 D4 Rus. Kagul. S Moldavia
Caicos Passage 446 D2 strait Bahamas/Turks and Caicos Islands
Caiffa see Ḩefa
Cailungo 488 E1 N San Marino
Caiphas see Ḩefa
Cairns 540 D3 Queensland, NE Australia
Cairo 464 B2 Ar. Al Qāhirah, var. El Qâhira. country capital (Egypt) N Egypt
Caisleán an Bharraigh see Castlebar
Cajamarca 452 B3 prev. Caxamarca. Cajamarca, NW Peru
Čakovec 492 B2 Ger. Csakathurn, Hung. Csáktornya; prev. Ger. Tschakathurn. Međimurje, N Croatia
Calabar 467 G5 Cross River, S Nigeria
Calabozo 450 D2 Guárico, C Venezuela
Calafat 500 B5 Dolj, SW Romania
Calafate see El Calafate
Calahorra 485 E2 La Rioja, N Spain
Calais 433 H2 Maine, NE USA
Calais 482 C2 Pas-de-Calais, N France
Calama 456 B2 Antofagasta, N Chile
Calamianes see Calamian Group
Calamian Group 521 C7 var. Calamianes. island group W Philippines
Călăras see Călărași
Călărași 500 D3 var. Călăras, Rus. Kalarash. C Moldavia
Călărași 500 C5 Călărași, SE Romania
Calatayud 485 E2 Aragón, NE Spain
Calbayog 531 E2 off. Calbayog City. Samar, C Philippines
Calcutta 527 G4 West Bengal, NE India
Caldas da Rainha 484 B3 Leiria, W Portugal
Caldera 456 B3 Atacama, N Chile
Caldwell 438 C3 Idaho, NW USA
Caledonia 444 C1 Corozal, N Belize
Caleta see Catalan Bay
Caleta Olivia 457 B6 Santa Cruz, SE Argentina
Calgary 429 E5 Alberta, SW Canada
Cali 450 B3 Valle del Cauca, W Colombia
Calicut 524 C2 var. Kozhikode. Kerala, SW India
California 439 B7 off. State of California; also known as El Dorado, The Golden State. state W USA
California, Golfo de 442 B2 Eng. Gulf of California; prev. Sea of Cortez. gulf W Mexico
California, Gulf of 545 see California, Golfo de
Călimănești 500 B4 Vâlcea, SW Romania
Callabonna, Lake 541 B5 lake South Australia
Callao 452 C4 Callao, W Peru
Callosa de Segura 485 F4 País Valenciano, E Spain
Calmar see Kalmar
Caloundra 541 E5 Queensland, E Australia
Caltanissetta 489 C7 Sicilia, Italy, C Mediterranean Sea
Caluula 464 E4 Bari, NE Somalia
Camabatela 470 B1 Cuanza Norte, NW Angola
Camacupa 470 B2 var. General Machado, Port. Vila General Machado. Bié, C Angola
Camagüey 446 C2 prev. Puerto Príncipe. Camagüey, C Cuba
Camagüey, Archipiélago de 446 C2 island group C Cuba
Camaná 453 E4 Arequipa, SW Peru
Camargo 442 D2 Chihuahua, N Mexico
Camargue 483 D6 physical region SE France
Ca Mau 529 D6 prev. Quan Long. Minh Hai, S Vietnam
Cambodia 529 D5 off. Kingdom of Cambodia, var. Democratic Kampuchea, Roat Kampuchea, Cam. Kampuchea; prev. People's Democratic Republic of Kampuchea. country SE Asia
Cambrai 482 C2 Flem. Kambryk; prev. Cambray, anc. Cameracum. Nord, N France
Cambrian Mountains 481 C6 mountain range C Wales, UK
Cambridge 481 E6 Lat. Cantabrigia. E England, UK
Cambridge 433 F4 Maryland, NE USA
Cambridge 432 D4 Ohio, NE USA
Cambridge 446 A4 W Jamaica
Cambridge 542 D3 Waikato, North Island, NZ
Cambridge Bay 429 F3 district capital Victoria Island, Nunavut, NW Canada
Camden 434 B2 Arkansas, C USA
Cameroon 468 A4 off. Republic of Cameroon, Fr. Cameroun. country W Africa
Camocim 455 F2 Ceará, E Brazil
Camopi 451 H3 E French Guiana
Campamento 444 C2 Olancho, C Honduras
Campania 489 D5 cultural region SE Italy
Campbell, Cape 543 D5 headland South Island, NZ
Campbell Island 534 D5 island S NZ
Campbell Plateau 534 D5 undersea feature SW Pacific Ocean
Campbell River 428 D5 Vancouver Island, British Columbia, SW Canada
Campeche 443 G4 Campeche, SE Mexico
Campeche, Bahía de 443 F4 Eng. Bay of Campeche. bay E Mexico
Cẩm Pha 528 E3 Quang Ninh, N Vietnam
Câmpina 500 C4 prev. Cîmpina. Prahova, SE Romania
Campina Grande 455 G2 Paraíba, E Brazil
Campinas 455 F4 São Paulo, S Brazil
Campobasso 489 D5 Molise, C Italy
Campo Criptana see Campo de Criptana
Campo de Criptana 485 E3 var. Campo Criptana. Castilla-La Mancha, C Spain
Campo dos Goitacazes see Campos
Campo Grande 455 E4 state capital Mato Grosso do Sul, SW Brazil
Campos 455 F4 var. Campo dos Goitacazes. Rio de Janeiro, SE Brazil
Câmpulung 500 B4 prev. Câmpulung-Mușcel, Cîmpulung. Argeș, S Romania
Campus Stellae see Santiago
Cam Ranh 529 E6 Khanh Hoa, S Vietnam
Canada 426 B4 country N North America
Canada Basin 426 C2 undersea feature Arctic Ocean
Canadian River 441 E2 river SW USA
Çanakkale 508 A3 var. Dardanelli; prev. Chanak, Kale Sultanie. Çanakkale, W Turkey
Çanakkale Boğazı 508 A2 Eng. Dardanelles. strait NW Turkey
Cananea 442 B1 Sonora, NW Mexico
Canarias, Islas 462 A2 Eng. Canary Islands. island group Spain, NE Atlantic Ocean
Canarreos, Archipiélago de los 446 B2 island group W Cuba
Canary Islands see Canarias, Islas
Cañas 444 D4 Guanacaste, NW Costa Rica
Canaveral, Cape 435 E4 headland Florida, SE USA
Canavieiras 455 G3 Bahia, E Brazil
Canberra 534 C4 country capital (Australia) Australian Capital Territory, SE Australia
Cancún 443 H3 Quintana Roo, SE Mexico
Candia see Irákleio
Canea see Chaniá
Cangzhou 520 D4 Hebei, E China
Caniapiscau 431 E2 river Québec, E Canada
Caniapiscau, Réservoir de 430 D3 reservoir Québec, C Canada
Canik Dağları 508 D2 mountain range N Turkey
Canillo 483 A7 C Andorra
Çankırı 508 C3 var. Chankiri; anc. Gangra, Germanicopolis. Çankın, N Turkey
Cannanore 524 B2 var. Kananur, Kannur. Kerala, SW India
Cannes 483 D6 Alpes-Maritimes, SE France
Canoas 455 E5 Rio Grande do Sul, S Brazil
Canon City 436 C5 Colorado, C USA
Cantabria 484 D1 cultural region N Spain
Cantábrica, Cordillera 484 C1 mountain range N Spain
Cantaura 451 E2 Anzoátegui, NE Venezuela
Canterbury 481 E7 hist. Cantwaraburh, anc. Durovernum, Lat. Cantuaria. SE England, UK
Canterbury Bight 543 C6 bight South Island, NZ
Canterbury Plains 543 C6 plain South Island, NZ
Cần Thơ 529 D6 Cần Thơ, S Vietnam
Canton see Guangzhou
Canton 434 B2 Mississippi, S USA
Canton 432 D4 Ohio, N USA
Canton Island see Kanton
Canyon 441 E2 Texas, SW USA
Cao Bằng 528 D3 var. Caobang. Cao Bằng, N Vietnam
Caobang see Cao Bằng
Cape Barren Island 541 C8 island Furneaux Group, Tasmania, SE Australia
Cape Basin 461 B7 undersea feature S Atlantic Ocean
Cape Breton Island 431 G4 Fr. Île du Cap-Breton. island Nova Scotia, SE Canada
Cape Charles 433 F5 Virginia, NE USA
Cape Coast 467 E5 prev. Cape Coast Castle. S Ghana
Cape Farewell see Uummannarsuaq
Cape Girardeau 437 H5 Missouri, C USA
Cape Horn 545 see Hornos, Cabo de
Capelle aan den IJssel 478 C4 Zuid-Holland, SW Netherlands
Cape Palmas see Harper
Cape Town 470 B5 var. Ekapa, Afr. Kaapstad, Kapstad. country capital (South Africa-legislative capital) Western Cape, SW South Africa
Cape Verde 466 A2 off. Republic of Cape Verde, Port. Cabo Verde, Ilhas do Cabo Verde. country E Atlantic Ocean
Cape Verde Basin 458 C4 undersea feature E Atlantic Ocean
Cape Verde Plain 458 C4 undersea feature E Atlantic Ocean
Cape York Peninsula 540 C2 peninsula Queensland, N Australia
Cap-Haïtien 446 D3 var. Le Cap. N Haiti
Capira 445 G5 Panamá, C Panama
Capitán Arturo Prat 546 A2 Chilean research station Sout[h] Shetland Islands, Antarctica
Capitán Pablo Lagerenza 45[…] var. Mayor Pablo Lagerenza. Chaco, N Paraguay
Capri, Isola di 489 C5 island […]
Caprivi Strip 470 C3 Ger. Caprivizipfel; prev. Caprivi Concession. cultural region NE Namibia
Caquetá 448 B3 off. Departam[ento] del Caquetá. province S Colo[mbia]
Caquetá, Río 450 C5 var. Rio Japurá, Yapurá. river Brazil/Colombia see also Japu[rá,] Rio
CAR see Central African Repu[blic]
Caracal 500 B5 Olt, S Romani[a]
Caracaraí 454 D1 Rondônia, W Brazil
Caracas 450 D1 country capita[l] (Venezuela) Distrito Federal N Venezuela
Caratasca, Laguna de 445 E2 lagoon NE Honduras
Carballiño 484 C1 Galicia, NW Spain
Carbondale 432 B5 Illinois, N[…]
Carbonia 489 A6 var. Carbon[ia] Centro. Sardegna, Italy, C Mediterranean Sea
Carbonia Centro see Carbon[ia]
Carcassonne 483 C6 anc. Car[…] Aude, S France
Cárdenas 446 B2 Matanzas, W Cuba
Cardiff 481 C7 Wel. Caerdydd admin capital S Wales, UK
Cardigan Bay 481 C6 bay W […] UK
Carei 500 B3 Ger. Gross-Karol[…] Karol, Hung. Nagykároly; pre[v.] Careii-Mari. Satu Mare, NW Romania
Carey, Lake 539 B6 lake Weste[rn] Australia
Cariaco 451 E1 Sucre, NE Venezuela
Caribbean Sea 446 C4 sea W Atlantic Ocean
Carlisle 480 C4 anc. Caer Luel[…] Luguvallium, Luguvallum. NW England, UK
Carlow 481 B6 Ir. Ceatharlach SE Ireland
Carlsbad 440 D3 New Mexico SW USA
Carlsberg Ridge 532 B4 unde[rsea] feature S Arabian Sea
Carlsruhe see Karlsruhe
Carmana see Kermān
Carmarthen 481 C6 SW Wale[s]
Carmaux 483 C6 Tarn, S Fran[ce]
Carmel 432 C4 Indiana, N US[A]
Carmelita 444 B1 Petén, N Guatemala
Carmen 443 G4 var. Ciudad d[el] Carmen. Campeche, SE Mex[ico]
Carmona 484 C4 Andalucía, S Spain
Carnaro see Kvarner
Carnavon 539 A5 Western Au[stralia]
Carnegie, Lake 539 B5 salt la[ke] Western Australia
Car Nicobar 525 F3 island Ni[cobar] Islands, India, NE Indian Oc[ean]
Caroço, Ilha 468 E1 island N […] Tome and Principe
Carolina 455 F2 Maranhão, E […]
Caroline Island 537 H3 prev. Thornton Island. atoll Line Is[lands,] E Kiribati
Caroline Islands 536 C2 islan[d] group C Micronesia
Caroní, Río 451 E3 river E Venezuela
Caronium see A Coruña
Carora 450 C1 Lara, N Venezu[ela]
Carpathian Mountains 473 […] Carpathians, Cz./Pol. Karpat[y,] Karpaten. mountain range E Europe
Carpathians see Carpathian Mountains
Carpaţii Meridionali 500 B4 […] Alpi Transilvaniei, Carpaţii S[…] Eng. South Carpathians, Transylvanian Alps, Ger. Südkarpaten, Transsylvanisc[he] Alpen, Hung. Déli-Kárpátok, Erdélyi-Havasok. mountain r[ange] C Romania
Carpaţii Occidentali 491 E7 […] Western Carpathians. mount[ain] range W Romania
Carpaţii Sudici see Carpaţii Meridionali
Carpentaria, Gulf of 540 B2 g[ulf] N Australia
Carpi 488 C2 Emilia-Romagn[a,] N Italy
Carrara 488 B3 Toscana, C Ita[ly]
Carson City 439 C5 state capi[tal] Nevada, W USA
Carson Sink 439 C5 salt flat Nevada, W USA

Cartagena – Chimoio

ena 485 F4 anc. Carthago . Murcia, SE Spain
ena 450 B1 var. Cartagena de des. Bolívar, NW Colombia
ena de los Indes see gena
o 445 E4 Cartago, C Costa
ge 437 F5 Missouri, C USA
right 431 F2 Newfoundland, nada
ano 451 E1 Sucre, enezuela
nersville 437 H5 Missouri, A
35 F1 North Carolina, SA
anca 462 C2 Ar. Dar-el- ı. NW Morocco
rande 440 B2 Arizona, JSA
de Range 438 B3 mountain Oregon/Washington, USA
dia Basin 426 A4 undersea re NE Pacific Ocean
s 484 B4 Lisboa, C Portugal
a 489 D5 Campania, S Italy
546 D4 Australian research n Antarctica
483 C8 New South Wales, istralia
491 B5 Ger. Tschaslau. ní Čechy, C Czech Republic
r 436 C3 Wyoming, C USA
n Depression 503 B7 Kaz. ıy Mangy Oypaty, Rus. spiyskaya Nizmennost'. ssion Kazakhstan/Russian ration
n Sea 506 A4 Az. Xäzär zi, Kaz. Kaspiy Tengizi, Per. -e Khazar, Daryā-ye Khazar, Kaspiyskoye More. inland sea Europe
see Kasai
noni see Kastamonu
gio 488 B2 Lombardia, ly
ó de la Plana 485 F3 var. llón. País Valenciano, E Spain
lón see Castelló de la Plana
naudary 483 C6 Aude, nce
o Branco 484 C3 Castelo co, C Portugal
sarrasin 483 B6 Tarn-et- nne, S France
vetrano 489 C7 Sicilia, Italy, editerranean Sea
a-La Mancha 485 E3 cultural n NE Spain
a-León 484 C2 cultural n NW Spain
bar 481 A5 Ir. Caisleán an raigh. W Ireland
ford 481 D5 N England, UK
Harbour 434 B5 inlet uda, NW Atlantic Ocean
cum 478 C3 Noord-Holland, etherlands
es 447 F1 country capital t Lucia) N Saint Lucia
457 B6 Los Lagos, W Chile
villari 489 D6 Calabria, taly
era 484 D4 Extremadura, pain
ll Sound 543 A7 sound South d, NZ
amas 444 D2 Olancho, nduras
os 452 B3 Piura, NW Peru
n Bay 485 H4 var. Caleta. bay oraltar
ña 485 G2 cultural region ain
arca see San Fernando del de Catamarca
ia 489 D7 Sicilia, Italy, editerranean Sea
zaro 489 D6 Calabria, taly
roja 485 F3 País Valenciano, ain
land 446 C1 island hamas
ll Mountains 433 F3 ntain range New York, JSA
, Río 450 B2 river olombia
sia 450 B2 Antioquia, Colombia
sus 473 G4 Rus. Kavkaz. ntain range Georgia/Russian ration
, Río 451 E3 river nezuela
a 466 D5 var. Cavally, Cavally ve. river Ivory Coast/Liberia
y see Cavalla
y Fleuve see Cavalla
na de Fora, Ilha 455 E1 var. Caviana. island N Brazil
470 B1 Bengo, NW Angola

Cayenne 451 H3 dependent territory capital (French Guiana) NE French Guiana
Cayes 446 D3 var. Les Cayes. SW Haiti
Cayman Brac 446 B3 island E Cayman Islands
Cayman Islands 446 B3 UK dependent territory W West Indies
Cay Sal 446 B2 islet SW Bahamas
Cazin 492 B3 NW Bosnia and Herzegovina
Cazorla 485 E4 Andalucía, S Spain
Ceadâr-Lunga see Ciadîr-Lunga
Ceará 455 F2 off. Estado do Ceará. state C Brazil
Ceara Abyssal Plain see Ceará Plain
Ceará Plain 448 E3 var. Ceara Abyssal Plain. undersea feature W Atlantic Ocean
Ceatharlach see Carlow
Cébaco, Isla 445 F5 island SW Panama
Cebu 531 E2 off. Cebu City. Cebu, C Philippines
Cecina 488 B3 Toscana, C Italy
Cedar City 436 A5 Utah, W USA
Cedar Falls 437 G3 Iowa, C USA
Cedar Lake 430 A2 lake Manitoba, C Canada
Cedar Rapids 437 G3 Iowa, C USA
Cedros, Isla 442 A2 island W Mexico
Ceduna 541 A6 South Australia
Cefalù 489 C7 anc. Cephaloedium. Sicilia, Italy, C Mediterranean Sea
Celebes 544 see Sulawesi
Celebes Sea 531 E3 Ind. Laut Sulawesi. sea Indonesia/Philippines
Celje 487 E7 Ger. Cilli. C Slovenia
Celldömölk 491 C6 Vas, W Hungary
Celle 486 B3 var. Zelle. Niedersachsen, N Germany
Celtic Sea 481 B7 Ir. An Mhuir Cheilteach. sea SW British Isles
Celtic Shelf 472 B3 undersea feature E Atlantic Ocean
Cenderawasih, Teluk 531 G4 var. Teluk Cendrawasih. bay NW Irian Jaya
Cendrawasih, Teluk see Cenderawasih, Teluk
Cenon 483 B5 Gironde, SW France
Central African Republic 468 C4 var. République Centrafricaine, abbrev. CAR; prev. Ubangi-Shari, Oubangui-Chari, Territoire de l'Oubangui-Chari. country C Africa
Central, Cordillera 447 E3 mountain range C Dominican Republic
Central, Cordillera 445 F5 mountain range C Panama
Central, Cordillera 531 E1 mountain range Luzon, N Philippines
Central, Cordillera 450 B3 mountain range W Colombia
Central Group see Inner Islands
Centralia 438 B2 Washington, NW USA
Central Indian Ridge see Mid-Indian Ridge
Central Makrān Range 526 A3 mountain range W Pakistan
Central Pacific Basin 534 D1 undersea feature C Pacific Ocean
Central, Planalto 455 F3 var. Brazilian Highlands. mountain range E Brazil
Central Range 536 B3 mountain range NW PNG
Central Russian Upland 504 see Srednerusskaya Vozvyshennost'
Central Siberian Plateau 504 see Srednesibirskoye Ploskogor'ye
Central Siberian Uplands see Srednesibirskoye Ploskogor'ye
Central, Sistema 484 D3 mountain range C Spain
Central Valley 439 B6 valley California, W USA
Ceram see Seram, Pulau
Ceram Sea 531 F4 Ind. Laut Seram. sea E Indonesia
Cerasus see Giresun
Cereté 450 B2 Córdoba, NW Colombia
Cerignola 489 D5 Puglia, SE Italy
Cerigo see Kýthira
Çerkeş 508 C2 Çankırı, N Turkey
Cernay 482 E4 Haut-Rhin, NE France
Cerro Chirripó see Chirripó Grande, Cerro
Cerro de Mulhacén see Mulhacén
Cerro de Pasco 452 C3 Pasco, C Peru
Cervera 485 F2 Cataluña, NE Spain
Cesena 488 C3 anc. Caesena. Emilia-Romagna, N Italy

Cēsis 498 D3 Ger. Wenden. Cēsis, C Latvia
České Budějovice 491 B5 Ger. Budweis. Jižní Čechy, SW Czech Republic
Český Krumlov 491 A5 var. Böhmisch-Krumau, Ger. Krummau. Jižní Čechy, SW Czech Republic
Cetinje 493 C5 It. Cettigne. Montenegro, SW Yugoslavia
Ceuta 462 C2 enclave Spain, N Africa
Cévennes 483 C6 mountain range S France
Ceyhan 508 D4 Adana, S Turkey
Ceylanpınar 509 E4 Şanlıurfa, SE Turkey
Ceylon Plain 516 B4 undersea feature N Indian Ocean
Ceyre to the Caribs see Marie-Galante
Chachapoyas 452 B2 Amazonas, NW Peru
Chachevichy 499 D6 Rus. Chechevichi. Mahilyowskaya Voblasts', E Belorussia
Chaco see Gran Chaco
Chad 468 C3 off. Republic of Chad, Fr. Tchad. country C Africa
Chad, Lake 468 B3 Fr. Lac Tchad. lake C Africa
Chadron 436 D3 Nebraska, C USA
Chadyr-Lunga see Ciadîr-Lunga
Chāgai Hills 526 A2 var. Chāh Gay. mountain range Afghanistan/Pakistan
Chaghasarāy see Asadābād
Chagos-Laccadive Plateau 516 B4 undersea feature N Indian Ocean
Chagos Trench 533 C5 undersea feature N Indian Ocean
Chāh Gay see Chāgai Hills
Chaillu, Massif du 469 B6 mountain range C Gabon
Chaîne des Dangrek see Dângrêk, Chuŏr Phnum
Chaîne des Mitumba see Mitumba, Monts
Chaîne des Mongos see Bongo, Massif des
Chain Ridge 532 B4 undersea feature W Indian Ocean
Chajul 444 B2 Quiché, W Guatemala
Chakhānsūr 514 D5 Nīmrūz, SW Afghanistan
Chala 452 D4 Arequipa, SW Peru
Chalatenango 444 C3 Chalatenango, N El Salvador
Chalcidice see Chalkidikí
Chalcis see Chalkída
Chálki 497 E7 island Dodekánisos, Greece, Aegean Sea
Chalkída 497 C5 var. Halkida; prev. Khalkís, anc. Chalcis. Evvoia, E Greece
Chalkidikí 496 C4 var. Khalkidhikí; anc. Chalcidice. peninsula NE Greece
Challans 482 B4 Vendée, NW France
Challapata 453 F4 Oruro, SW Bolivia
Challenger Deep 544 B3 undersea feature W Pacific Ocean
Challenger Fracture Zone 545 F4 tectonic feature SE Pacific Ocean
Châlons-en-Champagne 482 D3 prev. Châlons-sur-Marne, hist. Arcae Remorum, anc. Carolopois. Marne, NE France
Chalon-sur-Saône 482 D4 anc. Cabillonum. Saône-et-Loire, C France
Cha Mai see Thung Song
Chaman 526 B2 Baluchistān, SW Pakistan
Chambéry 483 D5 anc. Camberia. Savoie, E France
Champagne 482 D3 Yukon Territory, W Canada
Champaign 432 B4 Illinois, N USA
Champasak 529 D5 Champasak, S Laos
Champlain, Lake 433 F2 lake Canada/USA
Champotón 443 G4 Campeche, SE Mexico
Chanak see Çanakkale
Chañaral 456 B3 Atacama, N Chile
Chanchiang see Zhanjiang
Chandeleur Islands 434 C3 island group Louisiana, S USA
Chandigarh 526 D2 Punjab, N India
Chandrapur 527 E5 Mahārāshtra, C India
Changan see Xi'an
Changane 471 E3 river S Mozambique
Changchun 520 D3 var. Ch'angch'un, Ch'ang-ch'un; prev. Hsinking. Jilin, NE China
Ch'angch'un see Changchun

Chang Jiang 520 B5 var. Yangtze Kiang, Eng. Yangtze. river C China
Changkiakow see Zhangjiakou
Chang, Ko 529 C6 island S Thailand
Changsha 520 C5 var. Ch'angsha, Ch'ang-sha. Hunan, S China
Ch'angsha see Changsha
Changzhi 520 C4 Shanxi, C China
Chaniá 497 C7 var. Hania, Khaniá, Eng. Canea; anc. Cydonia. Kríti, Greece, E Mediterranean Sea
Chañi, Nevado de 456 B2 mountain NW Argentina
Chankiri see Çankırı
Channel Islands 481 C8 Fr. Îles Normandes. island group S English Channel
Channel Islands 439 B8 island group California, W USA
Channel-Port aux Basques 431 G4 Newfoundland, SE Canada
Channel, The see English Channel
Channel Tunnel 482 C2 tunnel France/UK
Chantabun see Chanthaburi
Chantaburi see Chanthaburi
Chantada 484 C1 Galicia, NW Spain
Chanthaburi 529 C6 var. Chantabun, Chantaburi. Chantaburi, S Thailand
Chanute 437 F5 Kansas, C USA
Chaouèn see Chefchaouen
Chaoyang 520 D3 Liaoning, NE China
Chapala, Lago de 442 D4 lake C Mexico
Chapan, Gora 514 B3 mountain C Turkmenistan
Chapayevsk 503 C6 Samarskaya Oblast', W Russian Federation
Chaplynka 501 F4 Khersons'ka Oblast', S Ukraine
Charcot Seamounts 472 B3 undersea feature E Atlantic Ocean
Chardzhev 514 D3 prev. Chardzhou, Chardzhui, Leninsk-Turkmenski, Turkm. Chärjew. Lebapskiy Velayat, E Turkmenistan
Charente 483 B5 cultural region W France
Charente 483 B5 river W France
Chari 468 B3 var. Shari. river Central African Republic/Chad
Chārīkār 515 E4 Parwān, NE Afghanistan
Charity 451 F2 NW Guyana
Charkhlik see Ruoqiang
Charkhliq see Ruoqiang
Charleroi 479 C7 Hainaut, S Belgium
Charlesbourg 431 E4 Québec, SE Canada
Charles de Gaulle 482 E1 international airport (Paris) Seine-et-Marne, N France
Charles Island 430 D1 island Nunavut, NE Canada
Charles Island see Santa María, Isla
Charleston 432 D5 state capital West Virginia, NE USA
Charleston 435 F2 South Carolina, SE USA
Charleville 541 D5 Queensland, E Australia
Charleville-Mézières 482 D3 Ardennes, N France
Charlie-Gibbs Fracture Zone 458 B2 tectonic feature N Atlantic Ocean
Charlotte 435 E1 North Carolina, SE USA
Charlotte Amalie 447 F3 prev. Saint Thomas. dependent territory capital (Virgin Islands (US)) Saint Thomas, N Virgin Islands (US)
Charlotte Harbor 435 E5 inlet Florida, SE USA
Charlottesville 433 E5 Virginia, NE USA
Charlottetown 431 F4 Prince Edward Island, Prince Edward Island, SE Canada
Charsk 506 D5 Semipalatinsk, E Kazakhstan
Charters Towers 540 D3 Queensland, NE Australia
Chartres 482 C3 anc. Autricum, Civitas Carnutum. Eure-et-Loir, C France
Charus Nuur 518 C2 lake NW Mongolia
Chashniki 499 D5 Rus. Chashniki. Vitsyebskaya Voblasts', N Belorussia
Châteaubriant 482 B4 Loire-Atlantique, NW France
Châteaudun 482 C3 Eure-et-Loir, C France
Châteauroux 482 C4 prev. Indreville. Indre, C France
Château-Thierry 482 C3 Aisne, N France
Châtelet 479 C7 Hainaut, S Belgium
Châtelherault see Châtellerault

Châtellerault 482 B4 var. Châtelherault. Vienne, W France
Chatham Island see San Cristóbal, Isla
Chatham Island Rise see Chatham Rise
Chatham Islands 535 E5 island group NZ, SW Pacific Ocean
Chatham Rise 534 D5 var. Chatham Island Rise. undersea feature S Pacific Ocean
Chatkal Range 515 F2 Rus. Chatkal'skiy Khrebet. mountain range Kyrgyzstan/Uzbekistan
Chattahoochee River 434 D3 river SE USA
Chattanooga 434 D1 Tennessee, S USA
Chatyr-Tash 515 G2 Narynskaya Oblast', C Kyrgyzstan
Châu Đôc 529 D6 var. Chauphu, Chau Phu. An Giang, S Vietnam
Chauk 528 A3 Magwe, W Burma
Chaumont 482 D4 prev. Chaumont-en-Bassigny. Haute-Marne, N France
Chau Phu see Châu Đôc
Chaves 484 C2 anc. Aquae Flaviae. Vila Real, N Portugal
Chávez, Isla see Santa Cruz, Isla
Chavusy 499 E6 Rus. Chausy. Mahilyowskaya Voblasts', E Belorussia
Chaykovskiy 503 D5 Permskaya Oblast', NW Russian Federation
Cheb 491 A5 Ger. Eger. Západní Čechy, W Czech Republic
Cheboksary 503 C5 Chuvashskaya Respublika, W Russian Federation
Cheboygan 432 C2 Michigan, N USA
Chechaouèn see Chefchaouen
Chech, Erg 466 D1 desert Algeria/Mali
Che-chiang see Zhejiang
Cheduba Island 528 A4 island W Burma
Chefchaouen 462 C2 var. Chaouèn, Chechaouèn, Sp. Xauen. N Morocco
Chefoo see Yantai
Cheju-do 521 E4 Jap. Saishū; prev. Quelpart. island S South Korea
Cheju Strait 521 E4 strait S South Korea
Chekiang see Zhejiang
Cheleken 514 B2 Balkanskiy Velayat, W Turkmenistan
Chelkar 506 B4 Aktyubinsk, W Kazakhstan
Chełm 490 E4 Rus. Kholm. Chełm, SE Poland
Chełmno 490 C3 Ger. Culm, Kulm. Toruń, N Poland
Cheltenham 481 D6 C England, UK
Chelyabinsk 506 C3 Chelyabinskaya Oblast', C Russian Federation
Chemnitz 486 D4 prev. Karl-Marx-Stadt. Sachsen, E Germany
Chenāb 526 C2 river India/Pakistan
Chengchiatun see Liaoyuan
Ch'eng-chou see Zhengzhou
Chengchow see Zhengzhou
Chengde 520 D3 var. Jehol. Hebei, E China
Chengdu 520 B5 var. Chengtu, Ch'eng-tu. Sichuan, C China
Chenghsien see Zhengzhou
Ch'eng-tu see Chengdu
Chennai see Madras
Chen Xian see Chenzhou
Chen Xiang see Chenzhou
Chenzhou 520 C6 var. Chenxian, Chen Xian, Chen Xiang. Hunan, S China
Chepelare 496 C3 Plovdivska Oblast, S Bulgaria
Chepén 452 B3 La Libertad, C Peru
Cher 482 C4 river C France
Cherbourg 482 B3 anc. Carusbur. Manche, N France
Cherepovets 502 B4 Vologodskaya Oblast', NW Russian Federation
Chergui, Chott ech 462 D2 salt lake NW Algeria
Cherkasy 501 E2 Rus. Cherkassy. Cherkas'ka Oblast', C Ukraine
Cherkessk 503 B7 Karachayevo-Cherkesskaya Respublika, SW Russian Federation
Chernihiv 501 E1 Rus. Chernigov. Chernihivs'ka Oblast', NE Ukraine
Chernivtsi 500 C3 Ger. Czernowitz, Rom. Cernăuţi, Rus. Chernovtsy. Chernivets'ka Oblast', W Ukraine
Cherno More see Black Sea
Chernoye More see Black Sea
Chernyakhovsk 498 A4 Ger. Insterburg. Kaliningradskaya Oblast', W Russian Federation
Cherry Hill 433 F4 New Jersey, NE USA
Cherski Range see Cherskogo, Khrebet

Cherskiy 507 G2 Respublika Sakha (Yakutiya), NE Russian Federation
Cherskogo, Khrebet 507 F2 var. Cherski Range. mountain range NE Russian Federation
Chervonohrad 500 C2 Rus. Chervonograd. L'vivs'ka Oblast', NW Ukraine
Chervyen' 499 D6 Rus. Cherven'. Minskaya Voblasts', C Belorussia
Cherykaw 499 E7 Rus. Cherikov. Mahilyowskaya Voblasts', E Belorussia
Chesapeake Bay 433 F5 inlet NE USA
Chesha Bay see Chëshskaya Guba
Chëshskaya Guba 548 D5 var. Archangel Bay, Chesha Bay, Dvina Bay. bay NW Russian Federation
Chester 481 C6 Wel. Caerleon; hist. Legaceaster, Lat. Deva, Devana Castra. C England, UK
Chetumal 443 H4 var. Payo Obispo. Quintana Roo, SE Mexico
Cheviot Hills 480 D4 hill range England/Scotland, UK
Cheyenne 436 D4 state capital Wyoming, C USA
Cheyenne River 436 D3 river South Dakota/Wyoming, N USA
Chhapra 527 F3 prev. Chapra. Bihār, N India
Chiai 520 D6 var. Chia-i, Chiayi, Kiayi, Jiayi, Jap. Kagi. C Taiwan
Chia-i see Chiai
Chiang-hsi see Jiangxi
Chiang Mai 528 B4 var. Chiangmai, Chiengmai, Kiangmai. Chiang Mai, NW Thailand
Chiangmai see Chiang Mai
Chiang Rai 528 C3 var. Chianpai, Chienrai, Muang Chiang Rai. Chiang Rai, NW Thailand
Chiang-su see Jiangsu
Chian-ning see Nanjing
Chianpai see Chiang Rai
Chianti 488 C3 cultural region C Italy
Chiapa see Chiapa de Cerzo
Chiapa de Cerzo 443 G5 var. Chiapa. Chiapas, SE Mexico
Chiayi see Chiai
Chiba 522 B1 var. Tiba. Chiba, Honshū, S Japan
Chibougamau 430 D3 Québec, SE Canada
Chicago 432 B3 Illinois, N USA
Ch'i-ch'i-ha-erh see Qiqihar
Chickasha 441 G2 Oklahoma, C USA
Chiclayo 452 B3 Lambayeque, NW Peru
Chico 439 B5 California, W USA
Chico, Río 457 B6 river S Argentina
Chico, Río 457 B7 river SE Argentina
Chicoutimi 431 E4 Québec, SE Canada
Chiengmai see Chiang Mai
Chienrai see Chiang Rai
Chiesanuova 488 D2 SW San Marino
Chieti 488 D4 var. Teate. Abruzzi, C Italy
Chifeng 519 G2 var. Ulanhad. Nei Mongol Zizhiqu, N China
Chih-fu see Yantai
Chihli see Hebei
Chihli, Gulf of see Bo Hai
Chihuahua 442 C2 Chihuahua, NW Mexico
Childress 441 F2 Texas, SW USA
Chile 456 B3 off. Republic of Chile. country SW South America
Chile Basin 449 A5 undersea feature E Pacific Ocean
Chile Chico 457 B6 Aisén, W Chile
Chile Rise 449 A7 undersea feature SE Pacific Ocean
Chililabombwe 470 D2 Copperbelt, C Zambia
Chi-lin see Jilin
Chillán 457 B5 Bío Bío, C Chile
Chillicothe 432 D4 Ohio, N USA
Chiloé, Isla de 457 A6 var. Isla Grande de Chiloé. island W Chile
Chilpancingo 443 E5 var. Chilpancingo de los Bravos. Guerrero, S Mexico
Chilpancingo de los Bravos see Chilpancingo
Chilung 520 D6 var. Keelung, Jap. Kirun, Kirun'; prev. Sp. Santissima Trinidad. N Taiwan
Chimán 445 G5 Panamá, E Panama
Chimborazo 452 A1 volcano C Ecuador
Chimbote 452 C3 Ancash, W Peru
Chimboy 514 D1 Rus. Chimbay. Qoraqalpoghiston Respublikasi, NW Uzbekistan
Chimoio 471 E3 Manica, C Mozambique

China – Corinth, Gulf of

China *516 C2 off.* People's Republic of China, *Chin.* Chung-hua Jen-min Kung-ho-kuo, Zhonghua Renmin Gongheguo; *prev.* Chinese Empire. *country* E Asia
Chi-nan *see* Jinan
Chinandega *444 C3* Chinandega, NW Nicaragua
Chincha Alta *452 D4* Ica, SW Peru
Chin-chiang *see* Quanzhou
Chin-chou *see* Jinzhou
Chinchow *see* Jinzhou
Chindwin *528 B2 river* N Burma
Ch'ing Hai *see* Qinghai Hu
Chingola *470 D2* Copperbelt, C Zambia
Ching-Tao *see* Qingdao
Chinguetti *466 C2 var.* Chinguetti. Adrar, C Mauritania
Chin Hills *528 A3 mountain range* W Burma
Chinhsien *see* Jinzhou
Chinnereth *see* Tiberias, Lake
Chinook Trough *505 H4 undersea feature* N Pacific Ocean
Chioggia *488 C2 anc.* Fossa Claudia. Veneto, NE Italy
Chíos *497 D5 var.* Hios, Khíos, *It.* Scio, *Turk.* Sakiz-Adasi. Chíos, E Greece
Chíos *497 D5 var.* Khíos. *island* E Greece
Chipata *470 D2 prev.* Fort Jameson. Eastern, E Zambia
Chiquián *452 C3* Ancash, W Peru
Chiquimula *444 B2* Chiquimula, SE Guatemala
Chīrāla *524 D1* Andhra Pradesh, E India
Chirchiq *515 E2 Rus.* Chirchik. Toshkent Wiloyati, E Uzbekistan
Chiriquí, Golfo de *445 E5 Eng.* Chiriqui Gulf. *gulf* SW Panama
Chiriquí, Laguna de *445 E5 lagoon* NW Panama
Chirripó Grande, Cerro *444 D4 var.* Cerro Chirripó. *mountain* SE Costa Rica
Chisec *444 B2* Alta Verapaz, C Guatemala
Chisholm *437 F1* Minnesota, N USA
Chisimaio *see* Kismaayo
Chisimayu *see* Kismaayo
Chişinău *500 D4 Rus.* Kishinev. *country capital* (Moldavia) C Moldavia
Chita *507 F4* Chitinskaya Oblast', S Russian Federation
Chitato *470 C1* Lunda Norte, NE Angola
Chitina *428 D3* Alaska, USA
Chitose *522 D2 var.* Titose. Hokkaidō, NE Japan
Chitré *445 F5* Herrera, S Panama
Chittagong *527 G4 Ben.* Chāttagām. Chittagong, SE Bangladesh
Chitungwiza *470 D3 prev.* Chitangwiza. Mashonaland East, NE Zimbabwe
Chlef *462 D2 var.* Ech Cheliff, Ech Chleff; *prev.* Al-Asnam, El Asnam, Orléansville. NW Algeria
Chocolate Mountains *439 D8 mountain range* California, W USA
Chodzież *490 C3* Piła, NW Poland
Choele Choel *457 C5* Río Negro, C Argentina
Choiseul *536 C3 var.* Lauru. *island* NW Solomon Islands
Ch'ok'ē *464 C4 var.* Choke Mountains. *mountain range* NW Ethiopia
Choke Mountains *see* Ch'ok'ē
Cholet *482 B4* Maine-et-Loire, NW France
Choluteca *444 C3* Choluteca, S Honduras
Choluteca, Río *444 C3 river* SW Honduras
Choma *470 D2* Southern, S Zambia
Chomutov *490 A4 Ger.* Komotau. Severní Čechy, NW Czech Republic
Chona *505 E2 river* C Russian Federation
Chon Buri *529 C5 prev.* Bang Pla Soi. Chon Buri, S Thailand
Chone *452 A1* Manabí, W Ecuador
Ch'ŏngjin *521 E3* NE North Korea
Chongqing *520 B5 var.* Ch'ung-ching, Ch'ung-ch'ing, Chungking, Pahsien, Tchongking, Yuzhou. Sichuan, C China
Chonnacht *see* Connaught
Chonos, Archipiélago de los *457 A6 island group* S Chile
Chorne More *see* Black Sea
Chornomors'ke *501 E4 Rus.* Chernomorskoye. Respublika Krym, S Ukraine
Chortkiv *500 C2 Rus.* Chortkov. Ternopil's'ka Oblast', W Ukraine
Chorum *see* Çorum
Chorzów *491 C5 Ger.* Königshütte; *prev.* Królewska Huta. Katowice, S Poland
Chōshi *523 D5 var.* Työsi. Chiba, Honshū, S Japan
Choszczno *490 B3 Ger.* Arnswalde. Gorzów, W Poland
Chota Nāgpur *527 E4 plateau* N India
Chott el-Hodna *see* Hodna, Chott El
Chott Melrhir *see* Melghir, Chott
Choûm *466 C2* Adrar, C Mauritania
Choybalsan *519 F2* Dornod, E Mongolia
Christchurch *543 C6* Canterbury, South Island, NZ
Christiana *446 B5* C Jamaica
Christiansand *see* Kristiansand
Christianshåb *see* Qasigiannguit
Christiansund *see* Kristiansund
Christmas Island *533 D5 Australian external territory* E Indian Ocean
Christmas Ridge *535 E1 undersea feature* C Pacific Ocean
Chuan *see* Sichuan
Ch'uan-chou *see* Quanzhou
Chubut *449 B7 off.* Provincia de Chubut. Admin. region *province* S Argentina
Chubut, Río *457 B6 river* SE Argentina
Ch'u-chiang *see* Shaoguan
Chūgoku-sanchi *523 B6 mountain range* Honshū, SW Japan
Chuí *see* Chuy
Chukai *see* Cukai
Chukchi Plain *548 B2 undersea feature* Arctic Ocean
Chukchi Plateau *426 C2 undersea feature* Arctic Ocean
Chukchi Sea *426 B2 Rus.* Chukotskoye More. *sea* Arctic Ocean
Chula Vista *439 C8* California, W USA
Chulucanas *452 B2* Piura, NW Peru
Chulym *506 D4 river* C Russian Federation
Chumphon *529 C6 var.* Jumporn. Chumphon, SW Thailand
Ch'unch'ŏn *521 E4 Jap.* Shunsen. N South Korea
Ch'ung-ching *see* Chongqing
Chungking *see* Chongqing
Chunya *507 E3 river* C Russian Federation
Chuquicamata *456 B2* Antofagasta, N Chile
Chur *487 B7 Fr.* Coire, *It.* Coira, *Rmsch.* Cuera, Quera; *anc.* Curia Rhaetorum. Graubünden, E Switzerland
Churchill *430 B2 river* Manitoba/Saskatchewan, C Canada
Churchill *431 F2 river* Newfoundland, E Canada
Churchill *429 G4* Manitoba, C Canada
Chuska Mountains *440 C1 mountain range* Arizona/New Mexico, SW USA
Chusovoy *503 D5* Permskaya Oblast', NW Russian Federation
Chuuk Islands *536 B2 var.* Hogoley Islands; *prev.* Truk Islands. *island group* Caroline Islands, C Micronesia
Chuy *456 E4 var.* Chuí. Rocha, E Uruguay
Chyhyryn *501 E2 Rus.* Chigirin. Cherkas'ka Oblast', N Ukraine
Ciadîr-Lunga *500 D4 var.* Ceadâr-Lunga, *Rus.* Chadyr-Lunga. S Moldavia
Cide *508 C2* Kastamonu, N Turkey
Ciechanów *490 D3 prev.* Zichenau. Ciechanów, C Poland
Ciego de Ávila *446 C2* Ciego de Ávila, C Cuba
Ciénaga *450 B1* Magdalena, N Colombia
Cienfuegos *446 B2* Cienfuegos, C Cuba
Cieza *485 E4* Murcia, SE Spain
Cihanbeyli *508 C3* Konya, C Turkey
Cikobia *537 E4 prev.* Thikombia. *island* N Fiji
Cilacap *530 C5 prev.* Tjilatjap. Jawa, C Indonesia
Cill Airne *see* Killarney
Cill Chainnigh *see* Kilkenny
Cill Mhantáin *see* Wicklow
Cincinnati *432 C4* Ohio, N USA
Ciney *479 C7* Namur, SE Belgium
Cinto, Monte *483 E7 mountain* Corse, France, C Mediterranean Sea
Cipolletti *457 B5* Río Negro, C Argentina
Cirebon *530 C4 prev.* Tjirebon. Jawa, S Indonesia
Cirò Marina *489 E6* Calabria, S Italy
Cisnădie *500 B4 Ger.* Heltau, *Hung.* Nagydisznód. Sibiu, SW Romania
Citlaltépetl *see* Orizaba, Volcán Pico de
Citrus Heights *439 B5* California, W USA
Ciudad Bolívar *451 E2 prev.* Angostura. Bolívar, E Venezuela
Ciudad Cortés *see* Cortés
Ciudad Darío *444 D3 var.* Dario. Matagalpa, W Nicaragua
Ciudad de Dolores Hidalgo *see* Dolores Hidalgo
Ciudad de Guatemala *444 B2 Eng.* Guatemala City; *prev.* Santiago de los Caballeros. *country capital* (Guatemala) Guatemala, C Guatemala
Ciudad del Carmen *see* Carmen
Ciudad del Este *456 E2 prev.* Cuidad Presidente Stroessner, Presidente Stroessner, Puerto Presidente Stroessner. Alto Paraná, SE Paraguay
Ciudad Delicias *see* Delicias
Ciudad de México *see* México
Ciudad de Panamá *see* Panamá
Ciudad Guayana *451 E2 prev.* San Tomé de Guayana, Santo Tomé de Guayana. Bolívar, NE Venezuela
Ciudad Guzmán *442 D4* Jalisco, SW Mexico
Ciudad Hidalgo *443 G5* Chiapas, SE Mexico
Ciudad Juárez *442 C1* Chihuahua, N Mexico
Ciudad Lerdo *442 D3* Durango, C Mexico
Ciudad Madero *443 E3 var.* Villa Cecilia. Tamaulipas, C Mexico
Ciudad Mante *443 E3* Tamaulipas, C Mexico
Ciudad Miguel Alemán *443 E2* Tamaulipas, C Mexico
Ciudad Obregón *442 B2* Sonora, NW Mexico
Ciudad Ojeda *450 C1* Zulia, NW Venezuela
Ciudad Porfirio Díaz *see* Piedras Negras
Ciudad Quesada *see* Quesada
Ciudad Real *484 D3* Castilla-La Mancha, C Spain
Ciudad-Rodrigo *484 C3* Castilla-León, N Spain
Ciudad Valles *443 E3* San Luis Potosí, C Mexico
Ciudad Victoria *443 E3* Tamaulipas, C Mexico
Ciutadella *see* Ciutadella de Menorca
Ciutadella de Menorca *485 H3 var.* Ciutadella. Menorca, Spain, W Mediterranean Sea
Civitanova Marche *488 D3* Marche, C Italy
Civitavecchia *488 C4 anc.* Centum Cellae, Trajani Portus. Lazio, C Italy
Claremore *441 G1* Oklahoma, C USA
Clarence *543 C5 river* South Island, NZ
Clarence *543 C5* Canterbury, South Island, NZ
Clarence Town *446 D2* Long Island, C Bahamas
Clarinda *437 F4* Iowa, C USA
Clarion Fracture Zone *545 E2 tectonic feature* NE Pacific Ocean
Clarión, Isla *442 A5 island* W Mexico
Clark Fork *436 A1 river* Idaho/Montana, NW USA
Clark Hill Lake *435 E2 var.* J.Storm Thurmond Reservoir. *reservoir* Georgia/South Carolina, SE USA
Clarksburg *432 D4* West Virginia, NE USA
Clarksdale *434 B2* Mississippi, S USA
Clarksville *434 C1* Tennessee, S USA
Clayton *441 E1* New Mexico, SW USA
Clearwater *435 E4* Florida, SE USA
Clearwater Mountains *438 D2 mountain range* Idaho, NW USA
Cleburne *441 G3* Texas, SW USA
Clermont *540 D4* Queensland, E Australia
Clermont-Ferrand *483 C5* Puy-de-Dôme, C France
Cleveland *432 D3* Ohio, N USA
Cleveland *434 D1* Tennessee, S USA
Clifton *440 C2* Arizona, SW USA
Clinton *434 B2* Mississippi, S USA
Clinton *441 F1* Oklahoma, C USA
Clipperton Fracture Zone *545 E3 tectonic feature* E Pacific Ocean
Clipperton Island *427 A7 French dependency of French Polynesia* E Pacific Ocean
Cloncurry *540 B3* Queensland, C Australia
Clonmel *481 B6 Ir.* Cluain Meala. S Ireland
Cloppenburg *486 B3* Niedersachsen, NW Germany
Cloquet *437 G2* Minnesota, N USA
Cloud Peak *436 C3 mountain* Wyoming, C USA
Clovis *441 E2* New Mexico, SW USA
Cluain Meala *see* Clonmel
Cluj-Napoca *500 B3 Ger.* Klausenburg, *Hung.* Kolozsvár; *prev.* Cluj. Cluj, NW Romania
Clutha *543 B7 river* South Island, NZ
Clyde *480 C4 river* W Scotland, UK
Coari *454 D2* Amazonas, N Brazil
Coast Mountains *428 D4 Fr.* Chaîne Côtière. *mountain range* Canada/USA
Coast Ranges *438 A4 mountain range* W USA
Coats Island *429 G3 island* Nunavut, NE Canada
Coats Land *546 B2 physical region* Antarctica
Coatzacoalcos *443 G4 var.* Quetzalcoalco; *prev.* Puerto México. Veracruz-Llave, E Mexico
Cobán *444 B2* Alta Verapaz, C Guatemala
Cobar *541 C6* New South Wales, SE Australia
Cobija *453 E3* Pando, NW Bolivia
Coburg *487 C5* Bayern, SE Germany
Coca *see* Puerto Francisco de Orellana
Cochabamba *453 F4 hist.* Oropeza. Cochabamba, C Bolivia
Cochin *524 C3 var.* Kochi. Kerala, SW India
Cochinos, Bahía de *446 B2 Eng.* Bay of Pigs. *bay* SE Cuba
Cochrane *457 B7* Aisén, S Chile
Cochrane *430 C4* Ontario, S Canada
Cocibolca *see* Nicaragua, Lago de
Cockburn Town *447 E2 var.* Grand *Turk. dependent territory capital* (Turks and Caicos Islands) Grand Turk Island, SE Turks and Caicos Islands
Cockpit Country, The *446 A4 physical region* W Jamaica
Cocobeach *469 A5* Estuaire, NW Gabon
Coconino Plateau *440 B1 plain* Arizona, SW USA
Coco, Río *445 E2 var.* Río Wanki, Segoviao Wangkí. *river* Honduras/Nicaragua
Cocos Basin *516 C5 undersea feature* E Indian Ocean
Cocos Island Ridge *see* Cocos Ridge
Cocos Islands *533 D5 island group* E Indian Ocean
Cocos Ridge *427 C8 var.* Cocos Island Ridge. *undersea feature* E Pacific Ocean
Cod, Cape *433 G3 headland* Massachusetts, NE USA
Codfish Island *543 A8 island* SW NZ
Codlea *500 C4 Ger.* Zeiden, *Hung.* Feketehalom. Braşov, C Romania
Cody *436 C2* Wyoming, C USA
Coeur d'Alene *438 C2* Idaho, NW USA
Coevorden *478 E2* Drenthe, NE Netherlands
Coffs Harbour *541 E6* New South Wales, SE Australia
Cognac *483 B5 anc.* Compniacum. Charente, W France
Coiba, Isla de *445 E5 island* SW Panama
Coihaique *457 B6 var.* Coyhaique. Aisén, S Chile
Coimbatore *524 C3* Tamil Nādu, S India
Coimbra *484 B3 anc.* Conimbria, Conimbriga. Coimbra, W Portugal
Coín *484 D5* Andalucía, S Spain
Coirib, Loch *see* Corrib, Lough
Colby *437 E4* Kansas, C USA
Colchester *481 E6 hist.* Colneceaste, *anc.* Camulodunum. E England, UK
Col du Brenner *see* Brenner Pass
Coleman *441 F3* Texas, SW USA
Coleraine *480 B4 Ir.* Cúil Raithin. N Northern Ireland, UK
Colesberg *470 C5* Northern Cape, C South Africa
Colima *442 D4* Colima, S Mexico
Coll *480 B3 island* W Scotland, UK
College Station *441 G3* Texas, SW USA
Collie *539 A7* Western Australia
Colmar *482 E4 Ger.* Kolmar. Haut-Rhin, NE France
Cöln *see* Köln
Cologne *see* Köln
Colombia *450 B3 off.* Republic of Colombia. *country* N South America
Colombian Basin *448 A1 undersea feature* SW Caribbean Sea
Colombo *524 C4 country capital* (Sri Lanka) Western Province, W Sri Lanka
Colón *445 G4 prev.* Aspinwall. Colón, C Panama
Colonia Agrippina *see* Köln
Colón Ridge *427 B8 undersea feature* E Pacific Ocean
Colorado *436 C4 off.* State of Colorado; also known as Centennial State, Silver State. *state* C USA
Colorado City *441 F3* Texas, SW USA
Colorado Plateau *440 B1 plateau* W USA
Colorado, Río *457 C5 river* E Argentina
Colorado, Río *see* Colorado River
Colorado River *427 B5 var.* Río Colorado. *river* Mexico/USA
Colorado River *441 G4 river* Texas, SW USA
Colorado Springs *436 D5* Colorado, C USA
Columbia *438 B3 river* Canada/USA
Columbia *435 E2 state capital* South Carolina, SE USA
Columbia *433 E4* Maryland, NE USA
Columbia *437 G4* Missouri, C USA
Columbia *434 C1* Tennessee, S USA
Columbia Plateau *438 C3 plateau* Idaho/Oregon, NW USA
Columbus *432 D4 state capital* Ohio, N USA
Columbus *434 D2* Georgia, SE USA
Columbus *432 C4* Indiana, N USA
Columbus *434 C2* Mississippi, S USA
Columbus *437 F4* Nebraska, C USA
Colville Channel *542 D2 channel* North Island, NZ
Colville River *428 D2 river* Alaska, USA
Comacchio *488 C3 var.* Commachio; *anc.* Comactium. Emilia-Romagna, N Italy
Comactium *see* Comacchio
Comalcalco *443 G4* Tabasco, SE Mexico
Coma Pedrosa, Pic de *483 A7 mountain* NW Andorra
Comarapa *453 F4* Santa Cruz, C Bolivia
Comayagua *444 C2* Comayagua, W Honduras
Comer See *see* Como, Lago di
Comilla *527 G4 Ben.* Kumillā. Chittagong, E Bangladesh
Comino *494 A5 Malt.* Kemmuna. *island* C Malta
Comitán *443 G5 var.* Comitán de Domínguez. Chiapas, SE Mexico
Comitán de Domínguez *see* Comitán
Commachio *see* Comacchio
Commissioner's Point *434 A5 headland* W Bermuda
Communism Peak *see* Kommunizm, Qullai
Como *488 B2 anc.* Comum. Lombardia, N Italy
Comodoro Rivadavia *457 B6* Chubut, SE Argentina
Como, Lago di *488 B2 var.* Lario, *Eng.* Lake Como, *Ger.* Comer See. *lake* N Italy
Como, Lake *see* Como, Lago di
Comoros *471 F2 off.* Federal Islamic Republic of the Comoros, *Fr.* République Fédérale Islamique des Comores. *country* W Indian Ocean
Compiègne *482 C3* Oise, N France
Compostella *see* Santiago
Comrat *500 D4 Rus.* Komrat. S Moldavia
Conakry *466 C4 country capital* (Guinea) Conakry, SW Guinea
Concarneau *482 A3* Finistère, NW France
Concepción *456 D2 var.* Villa Concepción. Concepción, C Paraguay
Concepción *see* La Concepción
Concepción *457 B5* Bío Bío, C Chile
Concepción *453 G3* Santa Cruz, E Bolivia
Concepción de la Vega *see* La Vega
Conchos, Río *442 D2 river* C Mexico
Conchos, Río *440 D4 river* NW Mexico
Concord *433 G3 state capital* New Hampshire, NE USA
Concordia *456 D4* Entre Ríos, E Argentina
Concordia *437 E4* Kansas, C USA
Côn Đao *529 E7 var.* Con Son. *island* S Vietnam
Condate *see* Cosne-Cours-sur-Loire
Condega *444 D3* Estelí, NW Nicaragua
Congo *469 D5 off.* Republic … Congo, *Fr.* Moyen-Congo; … Middle Congo. *country* C A…
Congo *469 C6 off.* Republic … *prev.* Belgian Congo, Cong… (Kinshasa). *country* C Afri…
Congo *469 C6 var.* Kongo, *Fr…* *river* C Africa
Congo Basin *469 C6 draina…* W Congo (Zaire)
Connacht *see* Connaught
Connaught *481 A5 var.* Con… *Ir.* Chonnacht, Cúige. *cultu…* *region* W Ireland
Connecticut *433 F3 off.* Stat… Connecticut; also known a… Law State, Constitution Sta… Land of Steady Habits, Nut… State. *state* NE USA
Connecticut *433 G3 river* Canada/USA
Conroe *441 G3* Texas, SW U…
Consolación del Sur *446 A…* del Río, W Cuba
Con Son *see* Côn Đao
Constance *see* Konstanz
Constance, Lake *487 B7 Ge…* Bodensee. *lake* C Europe
Constanţa *500 D5 var.* Küst… *Eng.* Constanza, *Ger.* Konst… *Turk.* Küstence. Constanţa, SE Romania
Constantia *see* Konstanz
Constantine *463 E2 var.* Qa… *Ar.* Qoussantîna. NE Algeri…
Constantinople *see* İstanbul
Constanz *see* Konstanz
Constanza *see* Constanţa
Coober Pedy *541 A5* South Australia
Cookeville *434 D1* Tenness… S USA
Cook Islands *537 F4 territor…* *free association with NZ* S P… Ocean
Cook, Mount *543 B6 prev.* A… Aorangi. *mountain* South I… NZ
Cook Strait *543 D5 var.* Rau… *strait* NZ
Cooktown *540 D2* Queensla… NE Australia
Coolgardie *539 B6* Western Australia
Cooma *541 D7* New South V… SE Australia
Coon Rapids *437 F2* Minne… N USA
Cooper Creek *540 C4 var.* B… Cooper's Creek. *seasonal ri…* Queensland/South Australi…
Cooper's Creek *see* Cooper…
Coos Bay *438 A3* Oregon, N…
Cootamundra *541 D6* New … Wales, SE Australia
Copacabana *453 E4* La Paz, W Bolivia
Copenhagen *see* København
Copiapó *456 B3* Atacama, N…
Copperas Cove *441 G3* Texa… SW USA
Coppermine *429 E3 var.* Qurlurtuuq. Nunavut, NW Canada
Coquimbo *456 B3* Coquimb… N Chile
Corabia *500 B5* Olt, S Roma…
Coral Harbour *429 G3* Southampton Island, North… Territories, NE Canada
Coral Sea *534 B3 sea* SW Pa… Ocean
Coral Sea Islands *536 B4 Australian external territory* SW Pacific Ocean
Corantijn Rivier *see* Courar… River
Corcaigh *see* Cork
Corcovado, Golfo *457 B6 g…* S Chile
Cordele *434 D3* Georgia, SE…
Cordillera Ibérica *see* Ibéric… Sistema
Cordoba *see* Córdoba
Córdoba *484 D4 var.* Cordol… Cordova; *anc.* Corduba. Andalucía, SW Spain
Córdoba *456 C3* Córdoba, C Argentina
Córdoba *443 F4* Veracruz-L… E Mexico
Cordova *see* Córdoba
Cordova *428 C3* Alaska, US…
Corduba *see* Córdoba
Corentyne River *see* Courar… River
Corfu *see* Kérkyra
Coria *484 C3* Extremadura, W Spain
Corinth *see* Kórinthos
Corinth *434 C1* Mississippi, …
Corinth, Gulf of *see* Korinth… Kólpos

Corinthiacus Sinus – Desna

thiacus Sinus *see*
nthiakós Kólpos
to *444 C3* Chinandega,
Nicaragua
481 A6 Ir. Corcaigh. S Ireland
508 A2 Tekirdağ, NW Turkey
er Brook *431 G3*
foundland, E Canada
Islands *see* Maíz, Islas del
wallis Island *429 F2 island*
thwest Territories, N Canada
450 C1 prev. Santa Ana de
). Falcón, NW Venezuela
coro *453 F4* La Paz, W Bolivia
mandel *542 D2* Waikato,
th Island, NZ
mandel Coast *524 D2 coast*
dia
mandel Peninsula *542 D2*
nsula North Island, NZ
nado, Bahía de *444 D5 bay*
sta Rica
nel Dorrego *457 C5* Buenos
s, E Argentina
nel Oviedo *456 D2* Caaguazú,
araguay
zal *444 C1* Corozal, N Belize
us Christi *441 G4* Texas,
USA
ales *440 D2* New Mexico,
USA
b, Lough *481 A5 Ir.* Loch
rib. *lake* W Ireland
entes *456 D3* Corrientes,
Argentina
za *see* Korçë
483 E7 Eng. Corsica. *island*
nce, C Mediterranean Sea
ca *see* Corse
cana *441 G3* Texas, SW USA
gana *484 C4* Andalucía,
ain
s *445 E5 var.* Ciudad Cortés.
tarenas, SE Costa Rica
na d'Ampezzo *488 C1*
eto, NE Italy
che *484 B3* Santarém,
ortugal
h Nehri *509 E3 Geor.*
orokhi, *Rus.* Chorokh. *river*
rgia/Turkey
m *508 D3 var.* Chorum.
um, N Turkey
nna *see* A Coruña
allis *438 B3* Oregon, NW USA
o *485 A5 var.* Ilha do Corvo.
nd Azores, Portugal,
Atlantic Ocean
nza *489 D6 anc.* Consentia.
abria, SW Italy
e-Cours-sur-Loire *482 C4*
Cosne-sur-Loire; *anc.*
date. Nièvre, C France
e-sur-Loire *see* Cosne-Cours-
Loire
a Mesa *438 D2* California,
USA
a Rica *445 E4 off.* Republic of
ta Rica. *country* Central
erica
gaita *453 F5* Potosí, S Bolivia
d'Or *482 D4 cultural region*
rance
nou *467 F5 var.* Kotonu.
enin
one *see* Crotone
wold Hills *481 D6 var.*
swolds. *hill range* S England,

wolds *see* Cotswold Hills
ous *486 D4 prev.* Kottbus.
ndenburg, E Germany
ncil Bluffs *437 F4* Iowa, C USA
antyne River *451 G4 var.*
antijn Rivier, Corentyne River.
r Guyana/Surinam
land Lagoon *498 A4 Ger.*
risches Haff, *Rus.* Kurskiy Zaliv.
oon Lithuania/Russian
eration
ances *482 B3 anc.* Constantia.
nche, N France
in *479 C7* Namur, S Belgium
ntry *481 D6 anc.* Couentrey.
ngland, UK
hã *484 C3* Castelo Branco,
ortugal
an, Lake *539 B6 lake* Western
stralia
n Hole *see* Roatán
n Hole *see* Roatán
aique *see* Coihaique
mel, Isla *443 H3 island*
Mexico
ock *470 C5* Eastern Cape,
outh Africa
g *436 C4* Colorado, C USA
ova *500 B5* Dolj, SW Romania
brook *429 E5* British
umbia, SW Canada
e *see* The Crane
ley *481 E7* SE England, UK
nona *488 B2* Lombardia,
aly
492 A3 It. Cherso; *anc.* Crexa.
nd W Croatia

Crescent City *438 A4* California,
W USA
Crescent Group *520 C7 island group* C Paracel Islands
Creston *437 F4* Iowa, C USA
Crestview *434 D3* Florida, SE USA
Crete *see* Kríti
Créteil *482 E2* Val-de-Marne,
N France
Crete, Sea of *see* Kritikó Pélagos
Creuse *482 B4 river* C France
Crewe *481 D6* C England, UK
Crikvenica *492 A3 It.* Cirquenizza; *prev.* Cirkvenica, Crjkvenica.
Primorje-Gorski Kotar,
NW Croatia
Crimea *473 F4 var.* Krym, *Eng.* Crimea, Crimean Oblast; *prev. Rus.* Krymskaya ASSR,
Krymskaya Oblast'. Admin. region *province* SE Ukraine
Crimean Oblast *see* Crimea
Cristóbal *445 G4* Colón, C Panama
Cristóbal Colón, Pico *450 B1 mountain* N Colombia
Cristuru Secuiesc *500 C4 prev.* Cristur, Cristuru Săcuiesc, Sitaş Cristuru, *Ger.* Kreutz, *Hung.* Székelykeresztúr, Szitás-Keresztúr.
Harghita, C Romania
Crna Reka *493 D6 river* S FYR
Macedonia
Croatia *492 B3 off.* Republic of Croatia, *Ger.* Kroatien, *SCr.* Hrvatska. *country* SE Europe
Crocodile *see* Limpopo
Croia *see* Krujë
Croker Island *538 E2 island* Northern Territory, N Australia
Cromwell *543 B7* Otago, South Island, NZ
Crooked Island *446 D2 island* SE Bahamas
Crooked Island Passage *446 D2 channel* SE Bahamas
Crookston *437 F1* Minnesota,
N USA
Croton *see* Crotone
Crotona *see* Crotone
Crotone *489 E6 var.* Cotrone; *anc.* Croton, Crotona. Calabria,
SW Italy
Croydon *481 A8* SE England, UK
Crozet Basin *533 B6 undersea feature* S Indian Ocean
Crozet Islands *533 B7 island group* French Southern and Antarctic Territories
Crozet Plateau *533 B7 var.* Crozet Plateaus. *undersea feature* SW Indian Ocean
Crozet Plateaus *see* Crozet Plateau
Crystal Brook *541 B6* South Australia
Csorna *491 C6* Győr-Moson-Sopron, NW Hungary
Csurgó *491 C7* Somogy,
SW Hungary
Cuando *470 C2 var.* Kwando. *river* S Africa
Cuango *470 B1 var.* Kwango. *river* Angola/Congo (Zaire) *see also* Kwango
Cuan na Gaillimhe *see* Galway Bay
Cuanza *470 B1 var.* Kwanza. *river* C Angola
Cuauhtémoc *442 C2* Chihuahua,
N Mexico
Cuautla *443 E4* Morelos, S Mexico
Cuba *446 B2 off.* Republic of Cuba. *country* W West Indies
Cubal *470 B2* Benguela, W Angola
Cubango *470 B2 var.* Kavango, Kavengo, Kubango, Okavango, Okavanggo. *river* S Africa *see also* Okavango
Cubango *470 B2 var.* Kuvango, *Port.* Vila Artur de Paiva, Vila da Ponte. Huíla, SW Angola
Cúcuta *450 C2 var.* San José de Cúcuta. Norte de Santander,
N Colombia
Cuddapah *524 C2* Andhra Pradesh, S India
Cuenca *485 E3 anc.* Conca. Castilla-La Mancha, C Spain
Cuenca *452 B2* Azuay, S Ecuador
Cuernavaca *443 E4* Morelos,
S Mexico
Cuiabá *455 E3 prev.* Cuyabá. *state capital* Mato Grosso, SW Brazil
Cúige *see* Connaught
Cúige Laighean *see* Leinster
Cúige Mumhan *see* Munster
Cuijck *478 D4* Noord-Brabant,
SE Netherlands
Cúil Raithin *see* Coleraine
Cuito *470 B2 var.* Kwito. *river* SE Angola
Cukai *530 B3 var.* Chukai, Kemaman. Terengganu, Peninsular Malaysia
Culiacán *442 C3 var.* Culiacán Rosales, Culiacán-Rosales. Sinaloa, C Mexico
Culiacán-Rosales *see* Culiacán

Cullera *485 F3* País Valenciano,
E Spain
Cullman *434 C2* Alabama, S USA
Culpepper Island *see* Darwin, Isla
Cumaná *451 E1* Sucre,
NE Venezuela
Cumbal, Nevada de *450 A4 mountain* SW Colombia
Cumberland *433 E4* Maryland,
NE USA
Cumberland Plateau *434 D1 plateau* E USA
Cumberland Sound *429 H3 inlet* Baffin Island, Nunavut,
NE Canada
Cumpas *442 B2* Sonora,
NW Mexico
Cunene *461 C6 var.* Kunene. *river* Angola/Namibia *see also* Kunene
Cunene *470 A3 province* S Angola
Cuneo *488 A2 Fr.* Coni. Piemonte, NW Italy
Cunnamulla *541 C5* Queensland,
E Australia
Ćuprija *492 E4* Serbia, E Yugoslavia
Curaçao *447 E5 island* Netherlands Antilles
Curicó *456 B4* Maule, C Chile
Curitiba *455 E4 prev.* Curytiba. *state capital* Paraná, S Brazil
Curtea de Argeş *500 C4 var.* Curtea-de-Arges. Argeş,
S Romania
Curtea-de-Arges *see* Curtea de Argeş
Curtici *500 A4 Ger.* Kurtitsch, *Hung.* Kürtös. Arad, W Romania
Curtis Island *540 E4 island* Queensland, SE Australia
Cusco *453 E4 var.* Cuzco. Cusco,
C Peru
Cusset *483 C5* Allier, C France
Cutch, Gulf of *see* Kachchh, Gulf of
Cuttack *527 F4* Orissa, E India
Cuvier Plateau *533 E6 undersea feature* E Indian Ocean
Cuxhaven *486 B2* Niedersachsen, NW Germany
Cuyuni, Río *see* Cuyuni River
Cuyuni River *451 F3 var.* Río Cuyuni. *river* Guyana/Venezuela
Cuzco *see* Cusco
Cyclades *see* Kykládes
Cydonia *see* Chaniá
Cymru *see* Wales
Cyprus *494 C4 off.* Republic of Cyprus, *Gk.* Kypros, *Turk.* Kıbrıs, Kıbrıs Cumhuriyeti. *country* E Mediterranean Sea
Cythera *see* Kýthira
Cythnos *see* Kýthnos
Czech Republic *491 A5 Cz.* Česká Republika. *country* C Europe
Częstochowa *490 C4 Ger.* Czenstochau, Tschenstochau, *Rus.* Chenstokhov. Częstochowa,
S Poland
Człuchów *490 C3 Ger.* Schlochau. Słupsk, NW Poland

D

Dabajuro *450 C1* Falcón,
NW Venezuela
Dabeiba *450 B2* Antioquia,
NW Colombia
Dąbrowa Tarnowska *491 D5* Tarnów, SE Poland
Dabryn' *499 C8 Rus.* Dobryn'. Homyel'skaya Voblasts',
SE Belorussia
Dagana *466 B3* N Senegal
Dagda *498 D4* Krāslava, SE Latvia
Dagenham *481 B8* SE England, UK
Dağliq Qarabağ *see* Nagornyy Karabakh
Dagupan *531 E1 off.* Dagupan City. Luzon, N Philippines
Da Hinggan Ling *519 G1 Eng.* Great Khingan Range. *mountain range* NE China
Dahm, Ramlat *513 B6 desert* NW Yemen
Daimiel *484 D3* Castilla-La Mancha, C Spain
Daimoniá *497 B7* Pelopónnisos,
S Greece
Dairen *see* Dalian
Dakar *466 B3 country capital* (Senegal) W Senegal
Dakhla *see* Ad Dakhla
Dakoro *467 G3* Maradi, S Niger
Đakovica *493 D5 var.* Djakovica, *Alb.* Gjakovë. Serbia, S Yugoslavia
Đakovo *492 C3 var.* Djakovo, *Hung.* Diakovár. Osijek-Baranja,
E Croatia
Dalai *see* Hulun Nur
Dalain Hob *see* Ejin Qi
Dalaman *508 A4* Muğla, SW Turkey
Dalandzadgad *519 E3* Ömnögovĭ,
S Mongolia
Đa Lat *529 E6* Lâm Đông,
S Vietnam
Dalby *541 D5* Queensland,
E Australia
Dale City *433 E4* Virginia, NE USA

Dalhart *441 E1* Texas, SW USA
Dali *520 A6 var.* Xiaguan. Yunnan, SW China
Dalian *520 D4 var.* Dairen, Dalien, Lüda, Ta-lien, *Rus.* Dalny. Liaoning, NE China
Dalien *see* Dalian
Dallas *441 G2* Texas, SW USA
Dalmacija *492 B4 Eng.* Dalmatia, *Ger.* Dalmatien, *It.* Dalmazia. *cultural region* S Croatia
Dalny *see* Dalian
Dalton *434 D1* Georgia, SE USA
Daly Waters *540 A2* Northern Territory, N Australia
Damachava *499 A6 var.* Damachova, *Pol.* Domaczewo, *Rus.* Domachëvo. Brestskaya Voblasts', SW Belorussia
Damachova *see* Damachava
Damān *526 C4* Damān and Diu,
W India
Damara *468 C4* Ombella-Mpoko,
S Central African Republic
Damas *see* Dimashq
Damasco *see* Dimashq
Damascus *504 see* Dimashq
Damāvand, Qolleh-ye *512 D3 mountain* N Iran
Dammām *see* Ad Dammān
Damoûr *511 A5 var.* Ad Dāmūr.
W Lebanon
Dampier *538 A4* Western Australia
Dampier, Selat *531 F4 strait* Irian Jaya, E Indonesia
Damqawt *513 D6 var.* Damqut.
E Yemen
Damqut *see* Damqawt
Damxung *518 C5* Xizang Zizhiqu, W China
Danakil Desert *464 D4 var.* Afar Depression, Danakil Plain. *desert* E Africa
Danakil Plain *see* Danakil Desert
Danané *466 D5* W Ivory Coast
Đă Nẵng *529 E5 prev.* Tourane. Quang Nam-Đa Nẵng, C Vietnam
Danborg *see* Daneborg
Dandong *520 D3 var.* Tan-tung; *prev.* An-tung. Liaoning, NE China
Daneborg *475 E3 var.* Danborg.
N Greenland
Dänew *see* Deynau
Dangerous Archipelago *see* Tuamotu, Îles
Danghara *515 E3 Rus.* Dangara. SW Tajikistan
Danghe Nanshan *518 D3 mountain range* W China
Dangla *see* Tanggula Shan
Dângrêk, Chuŏr Phnum *529 D5 var.* Phanom Dang Raek, Phanom Dong Rak, *Fr.* Chaîne des Dangrek. *mountain range* Cambodia/Thailand
Dangriga *444 C1 prev.* Stann Creek. Stann Creek, E Belize
Danish West Indies *see* Virgin Islands (US)
Danlí *444 D2* El Paraíso,
S Honduras
Danmarksstraedet *see* Denmark Strait
Dannenberg *486 C3* Niedersachsen, N Germany
Dannevirke *542 D4* Manawatu-Wanganui, North Island, NZ
Danube *473 E4 Bul.* Dunav, *Cz.* Dunaj, *Ger.* Donau, *Hung.* Duna, *Rom.* Dunărea. *river* C Europe
Danville *433 E5* Virginia, NE USA
Dan Xian *see* Danxian
Danxian *520 C7 var.* Dan Xian, Nada. Hainan, S China
Danziger Bucht *see* Danzig, Gulf of
Danzig, Gulf of *490 C2 var.* Gulf of Gdańsk, *Ger.* Danziger Bucht, *Pol.* Zakota Gdańska, *Rus.* Gdan'skaya Bukhta. *gulf* N Poland
Daqm *see* Duqm
Dar'ā *511 B5 var.* Der'a, *Fr.* Déraa. Dar'ā, SW Syria
Darabani *500 C3* Botoşani,
NW Romania
Daraut-Kurgan *see* Daroot-Korgon
Dardanelli *see* Çanakkale
Dar es Salaam *465 C7* Dar es Salaam, E Tanzania
Darfield *543 C6* Canterbury, South Island, NZ
Darfur *464 A4 var.* Darfur Massif. *cultural region* W Sudan
Darfur Massif *see* Darfur
Darhan *519 E2* Selenge, N Mongolia
Darien, Gulf of *450 A2 Sp.* Golfo del Darién. *gulf* S Caribbean Sea
Darién, Serranía del *445 H5 mountain range* Colombia/Panama
Dario *see* Ciudad Darío
Darjeeling *see* Darjiling
Darjiling *527 F3 prev.* Darjeeling. West Bengal, NE India
Darling River *541 C6 river* New South Wales, SE Australia
Darlington *481 D5* N England, UK

Darmstadt *487 B5* Hessen,
SW Germany
Darnah *463 G2 var.* Dérna.
NE Libya
Darnley, Cape *546 D2 headland* Antarctica
Daroca *485 E2* Aragón, NE Spain
Daroot-Korgon *515 F3 var.* Daraut-Kurgan. Oshskaya Oblast', SW Kyrgyzstan
Dartford *481 B8* SE England, UK
Dartmoor *481 C7 moorland* SW England, UK
Dartmouth *431 F4* Nova Scotia, SE Canada
Darvaza *514 C2 Turkm.* Derweze. Akhalskiy Velayat,
C Turkmenistan
Darwin *538 D2 prev.* Palmerston, Port Darwin. *territory capital* Northern Territory, N Australia
Darwin, Isla *452 A4 var.* Culpepper Island. *island* W Ecuador
Daryācheh-ye Hāmūn *see* Şāberī, Hāmūn-e
Daryācheh-ye Sīstān *see* Şāberī, Hāmūn-e
Daryā-ye Morghāb *see* Murgab
Daryā-ye Pāmīr *see* Pamir
Daryoi Pomir *see* Pamir
Dashkawka *499 D6 Rus.* Dashkovka. Mahilyowskaya Voblasts', E Belorussia
Dashkhovuz *514 C2 Turkm.* Dashhowuz; *prev.* Tashauz. Dashkhovuzskiy Velayat,
N Turkmenistan
Datong *520 C3 var.* Tatung, Ta-t'ung. Shanxi, C China
Daugavpils *498 D4 Ger.* Dünaburg; *prev.* Rus. Dvinsk. *municipality* Daugvapils, SE Latvia
Daung Kyun *529 B6 island* S Burma
Dauphiné *483 D5 cultural region* E France
Dāvangere *524 C2* Karnātaka,
W India
Davao *531 F3 off.* Davao City. Mindanao, S Philippines
Davao Gulf *531 F3 gulf* Mindanao, S Philippines
Davenport *437 G3* Iowa, C USA
David *445 E5* Chiriquí, W Panama
Davie Ridge *533 A5 undersea feature* W Indian Ocean
Davis *546 D3 Australian research station* Antarctica
Davis Sea *546 D3 sea* Antarctica
Davis Strait *474 B3 strait* Baffin Bay/Labrador Sea
Dawei *see* Tavoy
Dax *483 B6 var.* Ax; *anc.* Aquae Augustae, Aquae Tarbelicae. Landes, SW France
Dayr az Zawr *510 D3 var.* Deir ez Zor. Dayr az Zawr, E Syria
Dayton *432 C4* Ohio, N USA
Daytona Beach *435 E4* Florida,
SE USA
De Aar *470 C5* Northern Cape,
C South Africa
Dead Sea *511 B6 var.* Bahret Lut, Lacus Asphaltites, *Ar.* Al Baḩr al Mayyit, Baḩrat Lūt, *Heb.* Yam HaMelaḥ. *salt lake* Israel/Jordan
Dealnu *see* Tana
Deán Funes *456 C3* Córdoba,
C Argentina
Death Valley *439 C7 valley* California, W USA
Debar *493 D6 Ger.* Dibra, *Turk.* Debre. W FYR Macedonia
De Bildt *see* De Bilt
De Bilt *478 C3 var.* De Bildt. Utrecht, C Netherlands
Debrecen *491 D6 Ger.* Debreczin, *Rom.* Debreţin; *prev.* Debreczen. Hajdú-Bihar, E Hungary
Decatur *434 C1* Alabama, S USA
Decatur *432 B4* Illinois, N USA
Deccan *526 D5 Hind.* Dakshin. *plateau* C India
Děčín *490 B4 Ger.* Tetschen. Severní Čechy, NW Czech Republic
Dedeagaç *see* Alexandroúpoli
Dedeagach *see* Alexandroúpoli
Dedemsvaart *478 E3* Overijssel,
E Netherlands
Dee *480 C3 river* NE Scotland, UK
Deering *428 C2* Alaska, USA
Deggendorf *487 D6* Bayern,
SE Germany
Değirmenlik *494 C5* N Cyprus
Deh Bīd *512 D3* Fārs, C Iran
Dehli *see* Delhi
Deh Shū *514 D5 var.* Deshu. Helmand, S Afghanistan
Deinze *479 B5* Oost-Vlaanderen,
NW Belgium
Deir ez Zor *see* Dayr az Zawr
Deirgeirt, Loch *see* Derg, Lough
Dej *500 B3 Hung.* Dés; *prev.* Deés. Cluj, NW Romania
Dékoa *468 C4* Kémo, C Central African Republic
De Land *435 E4* Florida, SE USA

Delano *439 C7* California, W USA
Delārām *514 D5* Farāh,
SW Afghanistan
Delaware *433 F4 off.* State of Delaware; also known as Blue Hen State, Diamond State, First State. *state* NE USA
Delaware *432 D4* Ohio, N USA
Delft *478 B4* Zuid-Holland,
W Netherlands
Delfzijl *478 E1* Groningen,
NE Netherlands
Delgo *464 B3* Northern, N Sudan
Delhi *526 D3 var.* Dehli, *Hind.* Dilli; *hist.* Shahjahanabad. Delhi,
N India
Delicias *442 D2 var.* Ciudad Delicias. Chihuahua, N Mexico
Déli-Kárpátok *see* Carpaţii Meridionali
Delmenhorst *486 B3* Niedersachsen, NW Germany
Del Rio *441 F4* Texas, SW USA
Deltona *435 E4* Florida, SE USA
Demba *469 D6* Kasai Occidental,
C Congo (Zaire)
Dembia *468 D4* Mbomou,
SE Central African Republic
Demchok *516 var.* Dêmqog. *disputed region* China/India *see also* Dêmqog
Demchok *518 A4 var.* Dêmqog. China/India *see also* Dêmqog
Demerara Plain *448 C2 undersea feature* W Atlantic Ocean
Deming *440 C3* New Mexico,
SW USA
Demmin *486 C2* Mecklenburg-Vorpommern, NE Germany
Demopolis *434 C2* Alabama, S USA
Dêmqog *515 var.* Demchok. *disputed region* China/India *see also* Demchok
Denali *see* McKinley, Mount
Dender *479 B6 Fr.* Dendre. *river* W Belgium
Denekamp *478 E3* Overijssel,
E Netherlands
Den Haag *see* 's-Gravenhage
Den Ham *478 E3* Overijssel,
E Netherlands
Denham *539 A5* Western Australia
Den Helder *478 C2* Noord-Holland, NW Netherlands
Denia *485 F4* País Valenciano,
E Spain
Deniliquin *541 C7* New South Wales, SE Australia
Denison *437 F3* Iowa, C USA
Denison *441 G2* Texas, SW USA
Denizli *508 B4* Denizli, SW Turkey
Denmark *477 A7 off.* Kingdom of Denmark, *Dan.* Danmark; *anc.* Hafnia. *country* N Europe
Denmark Strait *474 D4 var.* Danmarksstraedet. *strait* Greenland/Iceland
Dennery *447 F1* E Saint Lucia
Denow *515 E3 Rus.* Denau. Surkhondaryo Wiloyati,
S Uzbekistan
Denpasar *530 D5 prev.* Paloe. Bali, C Indonesia
Denton *441 G2* Texas, SW USA
D'Entrecasteaux Islands *536 B3 island group* SE PNG
Denver *436 D4 state capital* Colorado, C USA
Der'a *see* Dar'ā
Déraa *see* Dar'ā
Dera Ghāzi Khān *526 C2 var.* Dera Ghāzikhān. Punjab, C Pakistan
Dera Ghāzikhān *see* Dera Ghāzi Khān
Đeravica *493 D5 mountain* S Yugoslavia
Derbent *503 B8* Respublika Dagestan, SW Russian Federation
Derby *481 D6* C England, UK
Derelí *see* Gónnoi
Derg, Lough *481 A6 Ir.* Loch Deirgeirt. *lake* W Ireland
Derhachi *501 G2 Rus.* Dergachi. Kharkivs'ka Oblast', E Ukraine
De Ridder *434 A3* Louisiana, S USA
Dérna *see* Darnah
Derry *see* Londonderry
Derventa *492 B3* N Bosnia and Herzegovina
Deschutes River *438 B3 river* Oregon, NW USA
Desē *464 C4 var.* Desse, *It.* Dessie. N Ethiopia
Deseado, Río *457 B7 river* S Argentina
Desertas, Ilhas *462 A2 island group* Madeira, Portugal, NE Atlantic Ocean
Deshu *see* Deh Shū
Desierto de Altar *see* Sonoran Desert
Des Moines *437 F3 state capital* Iowa, C USA
Desna *501 E2 river* Russian Federation/Ukraine

Dessau – Ed Damazin

Dessau 486 C4 Sachsen-Anhalt, E Germany
Desse see Desē
Dessie see Desē
Detroit 432 D3 Michigan, N USA
Detroit Lakes 437 F2 Minnesota, N USA
Deurne 479 D5 Noord-Brabant, SE Netherlands
Deva 500 B4 Ger. Diemrich, Hung. Déva. Hunedoara, W Romania
Đevđelija see Gevgelija
Deventer 478 D3 Overijssel, E Netherlands
Devils Lake 437 E1 North Dakota, N USA
Devoll see Devollit, Lumi i
Devollit, Lumi i 493 D6 var. Devoll. river SE Albania
Devon Island 429 F2 prev. North Devon Island. island Parry Islands, Nunavut, NE Canada
Devonport 541 C8 Tasmania, SE Australia
Devrek 508 C2 Zonguldak, N Turkey
Dexter 437 H5 Missouri, C USA
Deynau 514 D3 var. Dyanev, Turkm. Dänew. Lebapskiy Velayat, NE Turkmenistan
Dezfūl 512 C3 var. Dizful. Khūzestān, SW Iran
Dezhou 520 D4 Shandong, E China
Dhaka 527 G4 prev. Dacca. country capital (Bangladesh) Dhaka, C Bangladesh
Dhanbād 527 F4 Bihār, NE India
Dhekélia 494 C5 Eng. Dhekelia. Gk. Dekéleia. UK air base SE Cyprus
Dhidhimótikhon see Didymóteicho
Dhíkti Ori see Díkti
Dhodhekánisos see Dodekánisos
Dhomokós see Domokós
Dhráma see Dráma
Dhuusa Marreeb 465 E5 var. Dusa Marreb, It. Dusa Mareb. Galguduud, C Somalia
Diakovár see Đakovo
Diamantina, Chapada 455 F3 mountain range E Brazil
Diamantina Fracture Zone 533 E6 tectonic feature E Indian Ocean
Diarbekr see Diyarbakır
Dibrugarh 527 H3 Assam, NE India
Dickinson 436 D2 North Dakota, N USA
Didimotiho see Didymóteicho
Didymóteicho 496 D3 var. Dhidhimótikhon, Didimotiho. Anatolikí Makedonía kai Thráki, NE Greece
Diégo-Suarez see Antsirañana
Diekirch 479 D7 Diekirch, C Luxembourg
Điên Biên 528 D3 var. Bien Bien, Dien Bien Phu. Lai Châu, N Vietnam
Dien Bien Phu see Điên Biên
Diepenbeek 479 D6 Limburg, NE Belgium
Diepholz 486 B3 Niedersachsen, NW Germany
Dieppe 482 C2 Seine-Maritime, N France
Dieren 478 D4 Gelderland, E Netherlands
Differdange 479 D8 Luxembourg, SW Luxembourg
Digne 483 D6 var. Digne-les-Bains. Alpes-de-Haute-Provence, SE France
Digne-les-Bains see Digne
Digoin 482 C4 Saône-et-Loire, C France
Digul, Sungai 531 H5 prev. Digoel. river Irian Jaya, E Indonesia
Dihang see Brahmaputra
Dijon 482 D4 anc. Dibio. Côte d'Or, C France
Dikhil 464 D4 SW Djibouti
Dikson 506 D2 Taymyrskiy (Dolgano-Nenetskiy) Avtonomnyy Okrug, N Russian Federation
Díkti 497 D8 var. Dhíkti Ori. mountain range Kríti, Greece, E Mediterranean Sea
Dili 531 F5 var. Dilli, Dilly. Timor, C Indonesia
Dilia 467 G3 var. Dillia. river SE Niger
Di Linh 529 E6 Lâm Đông, S Vietnam
Dilli see Delhi
Dilli see Dili
Dillia see Dilia
Dilling 464 B4 var. Ad Dalanj. Southern Kordofan, C Sudan
Dillon 436 B2 Montana, NW USA
Dilly see Dili
Dilolo 469 D7 Ngounié, S Gabon
Dimashq 511 B5 var. Ash Shām, Esh Sham, Eng. Damascus, Fr. Damas, It. Damasco. country capital (Syria) Dimashq, SW Syria
Dimitrovgrad 496 D3 Khaskovska Oblast, S Bulgaria
Dimitrovgrad 503 C6 Ul'yanovskaya Oblast', W Russian Federation
Dimovo 496 B1 Oblast Montana, NW Bulgaria
Dinajpur 527 F3 Rajshahi, NW Bangladesh
Dinan 482 B3 Côtes d'Armor, NW France
Dinant 479 C7 Namur, S Belgium
Dinar 508 B4 Afyon, SW Turkey
Dinara see Dinaric Alps
Dinaric Alps 492 C4 var. Dinara. mountain range Bosnia and Herzegovina/Croatia
Dindigul 524 C3 Tamil Nādu, SE India
Dingle Bay 481 A6 Ir. Bá an Daingin. bay SW Ireland
Dinguiraye 466 C4 Haute-Guinée, N Guinea
Diourbel 466 B3 W Senegal
Dirē Dawa 465 D5 E Ethiopia
Dirk Hartog Island 539 A5 island Western Australia
Disappointment, Lake 538 C4 salt lake Western Australia
Dispur 527 G3 Assam, NE India
Divinópolis 455 F4 Minas Gerais, SE Brazil
Divo 466 D5 S Ivory Coast
Diyarbakır 509 E4 var. Diarbekr; anc. Amida. Diyarbakır, SE Turkey
Dizful see Dezfūl
Djajapura see Jayapura
Djakovica see Đakovica
Djakovo see Đakovo
Djambala 469 B6 Plateaux, C Congo
Djambi see Jambi
Djanet 463 E4 prev. Fort Charlet. SE Algeria
Djéblé see Jablah
Djelfa 462 D2 var. El Djelfa. N Algeria
Djéma 468 D4 Haut-Mbomou, E Central African Republic
Djérablous see Jarābulus
Djerba see Jerba, Île de
Djérem 468 B4 river C Cameroon
Djevdjelija see Gevgelija
Djibouti 464 D4 off. Republic of Djibouti, var. Jibuti; prev. French Somaliland, French Territory of the Afars and Issas, Fr. Côte Française des Somalis, Territoire Français des Afars et des Issas. country E Africa
Djibouti 464 D4 var. Jibuti. country capital (Djibouti) E Djibouti
Djourab, Erg du 468 C2 dunes N Chad
Djúpivogur 475 E5 Austurland, SE Iceland
Dnieper 473 F4 Bel. Dnyapro, Rus. Dnepr, Ukr. Dnipro. river E Europe
Dnieper Lowland 501 E2 Bel. Prydnyaprowskaya Nizina, Ukr. Prydniprovs'ka Nyzovyna. lowlands Belorussia/Ukraine
Dniester 473 E4 Rom. Nistru, Rus. Dnestr, Ukr. Dnister; anc. Tyras. river Moldavia/Ukraine
Dnipro see Dnieper
Dniprodzerzhyns'k 501 F3 Rus. Dneprodzerzhinsk; prev. Kamenskoye. Dnipropetrovs'ka Oblast', E Ukraine
Dniprodzerzhyns'ke Vodoskhovyshche 501 F3 Rus. Dneprodzerzhinskoye Vodokhranilishche. reservoir C Ukraine
Dnipropetrovs'k 501 F3 Rus. Dnepropetrovsk; prev. Yekaterinoslav. Dnipropetrovs'ka Oblast', E Ukraine
Dniprorudne 501 F3 Rus. Dneprorudnoye. Zaporiz'ka Oblast', SE Ukraine
Doba 468 C4 Logone-Oriental, S Chad
Döbeln 486 D4 Sachsen, E Germany
Doberai, Jazirah 531 G4 Dut. Vogelkop. peninsula Irian Jaya, E Indonesia
Doboj 492 C3 N Bosnia and Herzegovina
Dobre Miasto 490 D2 Ger. Guttstadt. Olsztyn, N Poland
Dobrich 496 E1 Rom. Bazargic; prev. Tolbukhin. Varnenska Oblast, NE Bulgaria
Dobrush 499 D7 Homyel'skaya Voblasts', SE Belorussia
Dodecánese see Dodekánisos
Dodekánisos 497 D6 var. Nóties Sporádes, Eng. Dodecanese; prev. Dhodhekánisos. island group SE Greece
Dodge City 437 E5 Kansas, C USA
Dodoma 461 D5 country capital (Tanzania) Dodoma, C Tanzania
Dodoma 465 C7 region C Tanzania
Dogana 488 E1 NE San Marino
Dōgo 523 B6 island Oki-shotō, SW Japan
Dogondoutchi 467 F3 Dosso, SW Niger
Doğubayazıt 509 F3 Ağrı, E Turkey
Doğu Karadeniz Dağları 509 E3 var. Anadolu Dağları. mountain range NE Turkey
Doha 504 see Ad Dawḥah
Doire see Londonderry
Dokkum 478 D1 Friesland, N Netherlands
Dokuchayevs'k 501 G3 var. Dokuchayevsk. Donets'ka Oblast', SE Ukraine
Dokuchayevsk see Dokuchayevs'k
Doldrums Fracture Zone 458 C4 tectonic feature W Atlantic Ocean
Dôle 482 D4 Jura, E France
Dolisie 469 B6 prev. Loubomo. Le Niari, S Congo
Dolomites see Dolomitiche, Alpi
Dolomiti see Dolomitiche, Alpi
Dolomitiche, Alpi 488 C1 var. Dolomiti, Eng. Dolomites. mountain range NE Italy
Dolores 456 D4 Buenos Aires, E Argentina
Dolores 444 B1 Petén, N Guatemala
Dolores 456 D4 Soriano, SW Uruguay
Dolores Hidalgo 443 E4 var. Ciudad de Dolores Hidalgo. Guanajuato, C Mexico
Dolyna 500 B2 Rus. Dolina. Ivano-Frankivs'ka Oblast', W Ukraine
Dolyns'ka 501 F3 Rus. Dolinskaya. Kirovohrads'ka Oblast', S Ukraine
Domachëvo see Damachava
Domaczewo see Damachava
Dombås 477 B5 Oppland, S Norway
Domel Island see Letsôk-aw Kyun
Domeyko 456 B3 Atacama, N Chile
Dominica 447 H4 off. Commonwealth of Dominica. country E West Indies
Dominica Channel see Martinique Passage
Dominican Republic 447 E2 country C West Indies
Domokós 497 B5 var. Dhomokós. Stereá Ellás, C Greece
Don 503 B6 var. Duna, Tanais. river SW Russian Federation
Donau see Danube
Donauwörth 487 C6 Bayern, S Germany
Don Benito 484 C3 Extremadura, W Spain
Doncaster 481 D5 anc. Danum. N England, UK
Dondo 470 B1 Cuanza Norte, NW Angola
Donegal 481 B5 Ir. Dún na nGall. NW Ireland
Donegal Bay 481 A5 Ir. Bá Dhún na nGall. bay NW Ireland
Donets 501 G2 river Russian Federation/Ukraine
Donets'k 501 G3 Rus. Donetsk; prev. Stalino. Donets'ka Oblast', E Ukraine
Dongfang 520 B7 var. Basuo. Hainan, S China
Dongguan 520 C6 Guangdong, S China
Đông Ha 528 E4 Quang Tri, C Vietnam
Đông Hơi 528 D4 Quang Binh, C Vietnam
Dongliao see Liaoyuan
Dongola 464 B3 var. Donqola, Dunqulah. Northern, N Sudan
Dongou 469 C5 La Likouala, NE Congo
Dongting Hu 520 C5 var. Tung-t'ing Hu. lake S China
Donostia-San Sebastián 485 E1 País Vasco, N Spain
Donqola see Dongola
Doolow 465 D5 SE Ethiopia
Doornik see Tournai
Door Peninsula 432 C2 peninsula Wisconsin, N USA
Dooxo Nugaaleed 465 E5 var. Nogal Valley. valley E Somalia
Dordogne 483 B5 cultural region SW France
Dordogne 483 B5 river W France
Dordrecht 478 C4 var. Dordt, Dort. Zuid-Holland, SW Netherlands
Dordt see Dordrecht
Dorohoi 500 C3 Botoşani, NE Romania
Dorotea 476 C4 Västerbotten, N Sweden
Dorre Island 539 A5 island Western Australia
Dort see Dordrecht
Dortmund 486 A4 Nordrhein-Westfalen, W Germany
Dos Hermanas 484 C4 Andalucía, S Spain
Dospad Dagh see Rhodope Mountains
Dospat 496 C3 Plovdivska Oblast, SW Bulgaria
Dothan 434 D3 Alabama, S USA
Dotnuva 498 B4 Kėdainiai, C Lithuania
Douai 482 C2 prev. Douay, anc. Duacum. Nord, N France
Douala 469 A5 var. Duala. Littoral, W Cameroon
Douglas 481 C5 dependent territory capital (Isle of Man) E Isle of Man
Douglas 440 C3 Arizona, SW USA
Douglas 436 D3 Wyoming, C USA
Douro 484 B2 Sp. Duero. river Portugal/Spain see also Duero
Dover 481 E7 Fr. Douvres; Lat. Dubris Portus. SE England, UK
Dover 433 F4 state capital Delaware, NE USA
Dover, Strait of 482 C2 var. Straits of Dover, Fr. Pas de Calais. strait England, UK/France
Dover, Straits of see Dover, Strait of
Dovrefjell 477 B5 plateau S Norway
Downpatrick 481 B5 Ir. Dún Pádraig. SE Northern Ireland, UK
Dōzen 523 B6 island Oki-shotō, SW Japan
Drač see Durrës
Drachten 478 D2 Friesland, N Netherlands
Drăgăşani 500 B5 Vâlcea, SW Romania
Dragoman 496 B2 Sofiyska Oblast, W Bulgaria
Dra, Hamada du 462 C3 var. Hammada du Drâa, Haut Plateau du Dra. plateau W Algeria
Drahichyn 499 B6 Pol. Drohiczyn Poleski, Rus. Drogichin. Brestskaya Voblasts', SW Belorussia
Drakensberg 470 D5 mountain range Lesotho/South Africa
Drake Passage 449 B8 passage Atlantic Ocean/Pacific Ocean
Dralfa 496 D2 Razgradska Oblast, N Bulgaria
Dráma 496 C3 var. Dhráma. Anatolikí Makedonía kai Thráki, NE Greece
Drammen 477 B6 Buskerud, S Norway
Drau see Drava
Drava 492 C3 var. Drau, Eng. Drave, Hung. Dráva. river C Europe see also Drau
Dráva see Drava
Drave see Drava
Drawsko Pomorskie 490 B3 Ger. Dramburg. Koszalin, NW Poland
Drépano, Ákra 496 C4 var. Akra Dhrepanon. headland N Greece
Dresden 486 D4 Sachsen, E Germany
Drin see Drinit, Lumi i
Drina 492 C3 river Bosnia and Herzegovina/Yugoslavia
Drinit, Lumi i 493 D5 var. Drin. river NW Albania
Drobeta-Turnu Severin 500 B5 prev. Turnu Severin. Mehedinţi, SW Romania
Drogheda 481 B5 Ir. Droichead Átha. NE Ireland
Drohobych 500 B2 Pol. Drohobycz, Rus. Drogobych. L'vivs'ka Oblast', NW Ukraine
Droichead Átha see Drogheda
Drôme 483 D5 cultural region SE France
Dronning Maud Land 546 B2 physical region Antarctica
Drummondville 431 E4 Québec, SE Canada
Druskininkai 499 B5 Pol. Druskienniki. Druskininkai, S Lithuania
Dryden 430 B3 Ontario, C Canada
Drysa 499 D5 Rus. Drissa. river N Belorussia
Duala see Douala
Dubai 504 see Dubayy
Dubăsari 500 D3 Rus. Dubossary. NE Moldavia
Dubawnt 429 F4 river Nunavut, NW Canada
Dubayy 512 D4 Eng. Dubai. Dubayy, NE UAE
Dubbo 541 D6 New South Wales, SE Australia
Dublin 481 B5 Ir. Baile Átha Cliath; anc. Eblana. country capital (Ireland), E Ireland
Dublin 435 E2 Georgia, SE USA
Dubno 500 C2 Rivnens'ka Oblast', NW Ukraine
Dubrovnik 493 B5 It. Ragusa. Dubrovnik-Neretva, SE Croatia
Dubuque 437 G3 Iowa, C USA
Dudelange 479 D8 var. Forge du Sud, Ger. Dudelingen. Luxembourg, S Luxembourg
Dudelingen see Dudelange
Duero 484 D2 Port. Douro. river Portugal/Spain see also Douro
Duesseldorf see Düsseldorf
Duffel 479 C5 Antwerpen, C Belgium
Dugi Otok 492 A4 var. Isola Grossa, It. Isola Lunga. island W Croatia
Duisburg 486 A4 prev. Duisburg-Hamborn. Nordrhein-Westfalen, W Germany
Duiven 478 D4 Gelderland, E Netherlands
Duk Faiwil 465 B5 Jonglei, SE Sudan
Dulan 518 D4 var. Qagan Us. Qinghai, C China
Dulce, Golfo 445 E5 gulf S Costa Rica
Dülmen 486 A4 Nordrhein-Westfalen, W Germany
Dulovo 496 E1 Razgradska Oblast, NE Bulgaria
Duluth 437 G2 Minnesota, N USA
Dūmā 511 B5 Fr. Douma. Dimashq, SW Syria
Dumas 441 E1 Texas, SW USA
Dumfries 480 C4 S Scotland, UK
Dumont d'Urville 546 C4 French research station Antarctica
Dumyât 464 B1 Eng. Damietta. N Egypt
Duna see Danube
Duna see Don
Dunaj see Danube
Dunaújváros 491 C7 prev. Dunapentele, Sztálinváros. Fejér, C Hungary
Dunav see Danube
Dunavska Ravnina 496 C2 Eng. Danubian Plain. plain N Bulgaria
Duncan 441 G2 Oklahoma, C USA
Dundalk 481 B5 Ir. Dún Dealgan. NE Ireland
Dún Dealgan see Dundalk
Dundee 480 C4 E Scotland, UK
Dundee 470 D4 KwaZulu/Natal, E South Africa
Dunedin 543 B7 Otago, South Island, NZ
Dunfermline 480 C4 C Scotland, UK
Dungu 469 E5 Haut-Zaïre, NE Congo (Zaire)
Dungun 530 B3 var. Kuala Dungun. Terengganu, Peninsular Malaysia
Dunkerque 482 C2 Eng. Dunkirk, Flem. Duinekerke; prev. Dunquerque. Nord, N France
Dún Laoghaire 481 B6 Eng. Dunleary; prev. Kingstown. E Ireland
Dún na nGall see Donegal
Dún Pádraig see Downpatrick
Dunqulah see Dongola
Dunărea see Danube
Dupnitsa 496 C2 prev. Marek, Stanke Dimitrov. Sofiyska Oblast, W Bulgaria
Duqm 513 E5 var. Daqm. E Oman
Durance 483 D6 river SE France
Durango 442 D3 var. Victoria de Durango. Durango, W Mexico
Durango 436 C5 Colorado, C USA
Durankulak 496 E1 Rom. Răcari; prev. Blatnitsa, Duranulac. Varnenska Oblast, NE Bulgaria
Durant 441 G2 Oklahoma, C USA
Durazzo see Durrës
Durban 470 D4 var. Port Natal. KwaZulu/Natal, E South Africa
Durbe 498 B3 Ger. Durben. Liepāja, W Latvia
Durg 527 E4 prev. Drug. Madhya Pradesh, C India
Durham 481 D5 hist. Dunholme. N England, UK
Durham 435 F1 North Carolina, SE USA
Durostorum see Silistra
Durrës 493 C6 var. Durrësi, Dursi, It. Durazzo, SCr. Drač, Turk. Draç. Durrës, W Albania
Durrësi see Durrës
Dursi see Durrës
Durūz, Jabal ad 511 C5 mountain SW Syria
D'Urville Island 542 C4 island C NZ
Dusa Mareb see Dhuusa Marreeb
Dusa Marreb see Dhuusa Marreeb
Dushanbe 515 E3 var. Dyushambe; prev. Stalinabad, Taj. Stalinobod. country capital (Tajikistan) W Tajikistan
Düsseldorf 486 A4 var. Duesseldorf. Nordrhein-Westfalen, W Germany
Dūsti 515 E3 Rus. Dusti. SW Tajikistan
Dutch Harbor 428 B3 Unalaska Island, Alaska, USA
Dutch New Guinea see Irian Jaya
Duzdab see Zāhedān
Dvina 504 see Severnaya Dvina
Dvina Bay see Chëshskaya Guba
Dyanev see Deynau
Dyersburg 434 C1 Tennessee, S USA
Dyushambe see Dushanbe
Dza Chu see Mekong
Dzerzhinsk 503 C5 Nizhegorodskaya Oblast', W Russian Federation
Dzhalal-Abad 515 F2 Kir. Ja Abad. Dzhalal-Abadskaya (W Kyrgyzstan
Dzhankoy 501 F4 Respublik Krym, S Ukraine
Dzhelandy 515 F3 SE Tajikis
Dzhergalan 515 G2 Kir. Jyrg Issyk-Kul'skaya Oblast', NE Kyrgyzstan
Dzhugdzhur, Khrebet 507 mountain range E Russian Federation
Dzhusaly 506 B4 Kaz. Zhols Kzyl-Orda, SW Kazakhstan
Działdowo 490 D3 Ciechanó C Poland
Dzuunmod 519 E2 Töv, C Mongolia

E

Eagle Pass 441 F4 Texas, SW
East Açores Fracture Zone East Azores Fracture Zone
East Antarctica see Greater Antarctica
East Australian Basin see Ta Basin
East Azores Fracture Zone var. East Açores Fracture Z tectonic feature E Atlantic O
Eastbourne 481 E7 SE Engla
East Cape 542 E3 headland N Island, NZ
East China Sea 517 E2 Chin. Hai. sea W Pacific Ocean
Easter Fracture Zone 545 G tectonic feature E Pacific Oc
Easter Island 545 F4 var. Ra island E Pacific Ocean
Eastern Desert 460 D3 var. Ṣaḥrā' ash Sharqīyah, Eng. Desert, Eastern Desert. dese E Egypt
Eastern Ghats 516 B3 mount range SE India
Eastern Sayans 507 E4 Mong Dzüün Soyonï Nuruu, Rus. Vostochnyy Sayan. mountai Mongolia/Russian Federati
East Falkland 457 D8 var. So island E Falkland Islands
East Grand Forks 437 E1 Minnesota, N USA
East Indiaman Ridge 533 D undersea feature E Indian O
East Indies 544 A3 island gro SE Asia
East Kilbride 480 C4 S Scotla UK
East Korea Bay 521 E3 bay E Korea
Eastleigh 481 D7 S England,
East London 470 D5 Afr. Oos Londen; prev. Emonti, Port Eastern Cape, S South Afric
Eastmain 430 D3 river Québe C Canada
East Mariana Basin 534 B1 undersea feature W Pacific C
East Novaya Zemlya Trench C1 var. Novaya Zemlya Tren undersea feature W Kara Sea
East Pacific Rise 545 F4 unde feature E Pacific Ocean
East Saint Louis 432 B4 Illin N USA
East Scotia Basin 459 C7 un feature SE Scotia Sea
East Sea see Japan, Sea of
East Siberian Sea 548 see Vostochno-Sibirskoye More
Eau Claire 432 A2 Wisconsin N USA
Eauripik Rise 534 B2 unders feature W Pacific Ocean
Ebensee 487 D6 Oberösterrei N Austria
Eberswalde-Finow 486 D3 Brandenburg, E Germany
Ebetsu 522 D2 var. Ebetu. Hokkaidō, NE Japan
Ebetu see Ebetsu
Ebolowa 469 A5 Sud, S Came
Ebon Atoll 536 D2 var. Epoo Ralik Chain, S Marshall Islar
Ebro 485 E2 river NE Spain
Ebusus see Eivissa
Ech Cheliff see Chlef
Ech Chleff see Chlef
Echo Bay 429 E3 Northwest Territories, NW Canada
Echt 479 D5 Limburg, SE Netherlands
Ecija 484 D4 anc. Astigi. Anda SW Spain
Ecuador 452 B1 off. Republic Ecuador. country NW South America
Ed Da'ein 464 A4 Southern D W Sudan
Ed Damazin 464 C4 var. Ad Damazīn. Blue Nile, E Sudan

Ed Damer – Falster

ner 464 C3 var. Ad Damar,
āmir. River Nile, NE Sudan
ɔba 464 B3 Northern,
lan
8 D4 Gelderland,
herlands
7 F5 Osun, SW Nigeria
59 A5 Littoral, SW Cameroon
Murzuq see Murzuq, Idhān
e Idfu
ya 475 G2 island S Svalbard
re 481 A7 SE England, UK
ırg 441 G5 Texas, SW USA
ırgh 480 C4 admin capital
land, UK
508 A2 Eng. Adrianople; anc.
nopolis, Hadrianopolis.
e, NW Turkey
ıds 438 B2 Washington,
JSA
ıton 429 E5 Alberta,
anada
ıdston 431 E4 New
swick, SE Canada
41 G4 Texas, SW USA
488 B1 Lombardia, N Italy
it 508 A3 Balıkesir,
Turkey
d, Lake 469 E5 var. Albert
rd Nyanza, Edward Nyanza,
di Amin, Lake Rutanzige. lake
da/Zaire
d Nyanza see Edward, Lake
ds Plateau 441 F3 plain
, SW USA
479 B5 var. Eekloo. Oost-
aderen, NW Belgium
see Eeklo
479 C5 Noord-Brabant,
herlands
36 D4 Fr. Vaté; prev.
wich Island. island C Vanuatu
ham 432 B4 Illinois, N USA
Sud 500 D5 Constanța,
mania
ios, Ágios 496 D4 var. Ayios
atios. island E Greece
Isole 489 B7 island group
y
91 D6 Ger. Erlau. Heves,
Hungary
Fracture Zone 533 C5
ic feature W Indian Ocean
ee 479 C6 Namur, C Belgium
see Aígina
e Aígio
ıt see Taranaki, Mount
ıt, Cape 542 C4 headland
Island, NZ
ee Johannesburg
464 B2 off. Arab Republic of
t, Ar. Jumhūrīyah Mişr
abīyah; prev. United Arab
blic, anc. Aegyptus. country
frica
485 E1 País Vasco, N Spain
en 478 E3 Gelderland,
herlands
rd 477 A5 Hordaland,
rway
erg see Suur Munamägi
87 A5 plateau W Germany
487 B7 mountain
itzerland
80 B3 island W Scotland, UK
Degree Channel 524 B3
nel India/Maldives
Mile Beach 538 B4 beach
ern Australia
n 479 D6 Limburg,
etherlands
ee Elat
oven 479 D5 Noord-Brabant,
herlands
ee Ipel'
ee Ipoly
üttenstadt 486 D4
denburg, E Germany
tadt 487 E6 Burgenland,
stria
en 486 C4 Sachsen-Anhalt,
rmany
485 G3 var. Iviza, Cast.
; anc. Ebusus. island Islas
ares, Spain, W Mediterranean
485 G3 var. Iviza, Cast.
; anc. Ebusus. Eivissa, Spain,
Mediterranean Sea
e los Caballeros 485 E2
ón, NE Spain
i 518 D3 var. Dalain Hob. Nei
gol Zizhiqu, N China
see Cape Town
pskiy Khrebet 507 G1
ntain range NE Russian
ration
ımein 464 B1 var.
lamayn. N Egypt
am see Chlef
1 B8 var. Eilat, Elath.
hern, S Israel
Gulf of see Aqaba, Gulf of
see Al 'Aqabah
see Elat

El'Atrun 464 B3 Northern Darfur, NW Sudan
Elâzığ 509 E3 var. Elâziz. Elâzığ, E Turkey
Elâziz see Elâzığ
Elba, Isola d' 488 B4 island Archipelago Toscano, C Italy
Elbasan 493 D6 var. Elbasani. Elbasan, C Albania
Elbasani see Elbasan
Elbe 472 D3 Cz. Labe. river Czech Republic/Germany
El Beni see Beni
Elbert, Mount 436 C4 mountain Colorado, C USA
Elbing see Elbląg
Elbląg 490 C2 var. Elblag, Ger. Elbing. Elbląg, N Poland
El Boulaida see Blida
El'brus 503 A8 var. Gora El'brus. mountain SW Russian Federation
El Burgo de Osma 485 E2 Castilla-León, C Spain
El Cajon 439 C8 California, W USA
El Calafate 457 B7 var. Calafate. Santa Cruz, S Argentina
El Callao 451 E2 Bolívar, E Venezuela
El Campo 441 G4 Texas, SW USA
El Carmen de Bolívar 450 B2 Bolívar, NW Colombia
El Centro 439 D8 California, W USA
Elche 485 F4 var. Elx-Elche; anc. Ilici, Lat. Illicis. País Valenciano, E Spain
Elda 485 F4 País Valenciano, E Spain
El Djazaïr see Alger
El Djelfa see Djelfa
El Dorado 434 B2 Arkansas, C USA
El Dorado 451 F2 Bolívar, E Venezuela
El Dorado 437 F5 Kansas, C USA
El Dorado 442 C3 Sinaloa, C Mexico
Eldorado 456 E3 Misiones, NE Argentina
Eldoret 465 C6 Rift Valley, W Kenya
Elektrostal' 503 B5 Moskovskaya Oblast', W Russian Federation
Elemi Triangle 465 B5 disputed region Kenya/Sudan
Elephant Butte Reservoir 440 C2 reservoir New Mexico, SW USA
Eleuthera Island 446 C1 island N Bahamas
El Fasher 464 A4 var. Al Fāshir. Northern Darfur, W Sudan
El Ferrol see Ferrol
El Ferrol del Caudillo see Ferrol
El Gedaref see Gedaref
El Geneina 464 A4 var. Ajjinena, Al-Genain, Al Junaynah. Western Darfur, W Sudan
Elgin 432 B3 Illinois, N USA
Elgin 480 C3 NE Scotland, UK
El Gîza 464 B1 var. Al Jīzah, Gîza, Gizeh. N Egypt
El Goléa 462 D3 var. Al Golea. C Algeria
El Hank 466 D1 cliff N Mauritania
El Haseke see Al Ḩasakah
Elista 503 B7 Respublika Kalmykiya, SW Russian Federation
Elizabeth 541 B6 South Australia
Elizabeth City 435 G1 North Carolina, SE USA
Elizabethtown 432 C5 Kentucky, S USA
El-Jadida 462 C2 prev. Mazagan. W Morocco
Ełk 490 E2 Ger. Lyck. Suwałki, NE Poland
Elk City 441 F1 Oklahoma, C USA
El Kerak see Al Karak
El Khalil see Hebron
El Khârga 464 B2 var. Al Khārijah. C Egypt
Elkhart 432 C3 Indiana, N USA
El Khartûm see Khartoum
Elk River 437 F2 Minnesota, N USA
El Kuneitra see Al Qunayţirah
Ellef Ringnes Island 429 E1 island Nunavut, N Canada
Ellen, Mount 436 B5 mountain Utah, W USA
Ellensburg 438 B2 Washington, NW USA
Ellesmere Island 429 F1 island Queen Elizabeth Islands, Nunavut, N Canada
Ellesmere, Lake 543 C6 lake South Island, NZ
Elliston 541 A6 South Australia
Ellsworth Land 546 A3 physical region Antarctica
El Mahbas 462 B3 var. Mahbés. SW Western Sahara
El Mina 510 B4 var. Al Mīnā'. N Lebanon
El Minya 464 B2 var. Al Minyā, Minya. C Egypt
Elmira 433 E3 New York, NE USA
El Mreyyé 466 D2 desert E Mauritania
Elmshorn 486 B3 Schleswig-Holstein, N Germany
El Muglad 464 B4 Western Kordofan, C Sudan
El Obeid 464 B4 var. Al Obayyid, Al Ubayyiḑ. Northern Kordofan, C Sudan
El Ouâdi see El Oued
El Oued 463 E2 var. Al Oued, El Ouâdi, El Wad. NE Algeria
Eloy 440 B2 Arizona, SW USA
El Paso 440 D3 Texas, SW USA
El Porvenir 445 G4 San Blas, N Panama
El Progreso 444 C2 Yoro, NW Honduras
El Puerto de Santa María 484 C5 Andalucía, S Spain
El Quneitra see Al Qunayţirah
El Quseir see Al Quşayr
El Quweira see Al Quwayrah
El Rama 445 E3 Región Autónoma Atlántico Sur, SE Nicaragua
El Real 445 H5 var. El Real de Santa María. Darién, SE Panama
El Real de Santa María see El Real
El Reno 441 F1 Oklahoma, C USA
El Salvador 444 B3 off. Republica de El Salvador. country Central America
El Sáuz 442 C2 Chihuahua, N Mexico
El Serrat 483 A7 N Andorra
Elst 478 D4 Gelderland, E Netherlands
El Sueco 442 C2 Chihuahua, N Mexico
El Suweida see As Suwaydā'
Eltanin Fracture Zone 545 E5 tectonic feature SE Pacific Ocean
El Tigre 451 E2 Anzoátegui, NE Venezuela
Elvas 484 C4 Portalegre, C Portugal
El Vendrell 485 G2 Cataluña, NE Spain
El Vigía 450 C2 Mérida, NW Venezuela
El Wad see El Oued
Elwell, Lake 436 B1 reservoir Montana, NW USA
Elx-Elche see Elche
Ely 439 D5 Nevada, W USA
El Yopal see Yopal
Emajõgi 498 D3 Ger. Embach. river SE Estonia
Emba 506 B4 Kaz. Embi. Aktyubinsk, W Kazakhstan
Emden 486 A3 Niedersachsen, NW Germany
Emerald 540 D4 Queensland, E Australia
Emerald Isle see Montserrat
Emesa see Ḩimş
Emmaste 498 C2 Hiiumaa, W Estonia
Emmeloord 478 D2 Flevoland, N Netherlands
Emmen 478 E2 Drenthe, NE Netherlands
Emmendingen 487 A6 Baden-Württemberg, SW Germany
Emory Peak 441 E4 mountain Texas, SW USA
Empalme 442 B2 Sonora, NW Mexico
Emperor Seamounts 505 G3 undersea feature NW Pacific Ocean
Emporia 437 F5 Kansas, C USA
Empty Quarter see Ar Rub 'al Khālī
Ems 486 A3 Dut. Eems. river NW Germany
Encamp 483 A8 C Andorra
Encarnación 456 D3 Itapúa, S Paraguay
Encinitas 439 C8 California, W USA
Encs 491 D6 Borsod-Abaúj-Zemplén, NE Hungary
Endeavour Strait 540 C1 strait Queensland, NE Australia
Enderbury Island 537 F3 atoll Phoenix Islands, C Kiribati
Enderby Land 546 C2 physical region Antarctica
Enderby Plain 546 D2 undersea feature S Indian Ocean
Enewetak Atoll 536 C1 var. Ānewetak, Eniwetok. atoll Ralik Chain, W Marshall Islands
Enfield 481 A7 SE England, UK
Engannim see Jenīn
Enghien 479 B6 Dut. Edingen. Hainaut, SW Belgium
England 481 D5 Lat. Anglia. national region UK
Englewood 436 D4 Colorado, C USA
English Channel 481 D8 var. The Channel, Fr. la Manche. channel NW Europe
Engure 498 C3 Tukums, W Latvia
Engures Ezers 498 B3 lake NW Latvia
Enguri 509 F1 Rus. Inguri. river NW Georgia
Enid 441 F1 Oklahoma, C USA
Enikale Strait see Kerch Strait
Eniwetok see Enewetak Atoll
En Nâqoûra 511 A5 var. An Nāqūrah. SW Lebanon
Ennedi 468 D2 plateau E Chad
Ennis 481 A6 Ir. Inis. W Ireland
Ennis 441 G3 Texas, SW USA
Enniskillen 481 B5 var. Inniskilling, Ir. Inis Ceithleann. SW Northern Ireland, UK
Enns 487 D6 river C Austria
Enschede 478 E3 Overijssel, E Netherlands
Ensenada 442 A1 Baja California, NW Mexico
Entebbe 465 B6 S Uganda
Entroncamento 484 B3 Santarém, C Portugal
Enugu 467 G5 Enugu, S Nigeria
Eolie, Isole 489 C6 var. Isole Lipari, Eng. Aeolian Islands, Lipari Islands. island group S Italy
Epanomí 496 B4 Kentrikí Makedonía, N Greece
Epéna 469 B5 La Likouala, NE Congo
Eperies see Prešov
Eperjes see Prešov
Épi 536 D4 island C Vanuatu
Épinal 482 D4 Vosges, NE France
Epiphania see Ḩamāh
Epitoli see Pretoria
Epoon see Ebon Atoll
Epsom 481 A8 SE England, UK
Equatorial Guinea 469 A5 off. Republic of Equatorial Guinea. country C Africa
Erautini see Johannesburg
Erbil see Arbil
Erciş 509 F3 Van, E Turkey
Erdélyi-Havasok see Carpaţii Meridionali
Erdenet 519 E2 Bulgan, N Mongolia
Erdi 468 C2 plateau NE Chad
Erdi Ma 468 D2 desert NE Chad
Erebus, Mount 546 B4 mountain Ross Island, Antarctica
Ereğli 508 C4 Konya, S Turkey
Erenhot 519 F2 var. Erlian. Nei Mongol Zizhiqu, NE China
Erevan see Yerevan
Erfurt 486 C4 Thüringen, C Germany
Ergene Irmağı 508 A2 var. Ergene Irmaği. river NW Turkey
Erg Iguid see Iguîdi, 'Erg
Ergun He see Argun
Ergun Zuoqi 519 F1 Nei Mongol Zizhiqu, N China
Erie 432 D3 Pennsylvania, NE USA
Erie, Lake 432 D3 Fr. Lac Érié. lake Canada/USA
Eritrea 464 C4 off. State of Eritrea, Tig. Ērtra. country E Africa
Erivan see Yerevan
Erlangen 487 C5 Bayern, S Germany
Erlian see Erenhot
Ermelo 478 D3 Gelderland, C Netherlands
Ermióni 497 C6 Pelopónnisos, S Greece
Ermoúpoli 497 D6 var. Hermoupolis; prev. Ermoúpolis. Sýros, Kykládes, Greece, Aegean Sea
Ermoúpolis see Ermoúpoli
Ernākulam 524 C3 Kerala, SW India
Erode 524 C2 Tamil Nādu, SE India
Erquelinnes 479 B7 Hainaut, S Belgium
Er-Rachidia 462 C2 var. Ksar al Soule. E Morocco
Er Rahad 464 B4 var. Ar Rahad. Northern Kordofan, C Sudan
Erromango 536 D4 island S Vanuatu
Ertis see Irtysh
Erzgebirge 487 C5 Cz. Krušné Hory, Eng. Ore Mountains. mountain range Czech Republic/Germany see also Krušné Hory
Erzincan 509 E3 var. Erzinjan. Erzincan, E Turkey
Erzinjan see Erzincan
Erzurum 509 E3 prev. Erzerum. Erzurum, NE Turkey
Esbjerg 477 A7 Ribe, W Denmark
Escaldes 483 A8 C Andorra
Escanaba 432 C2 Michigan, N USA
Esch-sur-Alzette 479 D8 Luxembourg, S Luxembourg
Escondido 439 C8 California, W USA
Escuinapa 442 D3 var. Escuinapa de Hidalgo. Sinaloa, C Mexico
Escuinapa de Hidalgo see Escuinapa
Escuintla 443 G5 Chiapas, SE Mexico
Escuintla 444 B2 Escuintla, S Guatemala
Eşfahān 512 C3 Eng. Isfahan; anc. Aspadana. Eşfahān, C Iran
Esh Sham see Dimashq
Esh Sharā see Ash Sharāh
Eskişehir 508 B3 var. Eskishehr. Eskişehir, W Turkey
Eskishehr see Eskişehir
Eslāmābād 512 C3 var. Eslāmābād-e Gharb; prev. Harunabad, Shāhābād. Kermānshāhān, W Iran
Eslāmābād-e Gharb see Eslāmābād
Esmeraldas 452 A1 Esmeraldas, N Ecuador
Esna see Isna
Espanola 440 D1 New Mexico, SW USA
Esperance 539 B7 Western Australia
Esperanza 546 A2 Argentinian research station Antarctica
Esperanza 442 B2 Sonora, NW Mexico
Espinal 450 B3 Tolima, C Colombia
Espinhaço, Serra do 448 D4 mountain range SE Brazil
Espírito Santo 455 F4 off. Estado do Espírito Santo. state E Brazil
Espiritu Santo 536 C4 var. Santo. island W Vanuatu
Espoo 477 D6 Swe. Esbo. Uusimaa, S Finland
Esquel 457 B6 Chubut, SW Argentina
Essaouira 462 B2 prev. Mogador. W Morocco
Es Semara see Smara
Essen 486 A4 var. Essen an der Ruhr. Nordrhein-Westfalen, W Germany
Essen 479 C5 Antwerpen, N Belgium
Essen an der Ruhr see Essen
Essequibo River 451 F3 river C Guyana
Es Suweida see As Suwaydā'
Estacado, Llano 441 E2 plain New Mexico/Texas, SW USA
Estados, Isla de los 457 C8 prev. Eng. Staten Island. island S Argentina
Estância 455 G3 Sergipe, E Brazil
Estelí 444 D3 Estelí, NW Nicaragua
Estella 485 E1 Navarra, N Spain
Estepona 484 D5 Andalucía, S Spain
Estevan 429 F5 Saskatchewan, S Canada
Estonia 498 D2 off. Republic of Estonia, Est. Eesti Vabariik, Ger. Estland, Latv. Igaunija; prev. Estonian SSR, Rus. Estonskaya SSR. country NE Europe
Estrela, Serra da 484 C3 mountain range C Portugal
Estremoz 484 C4 Évora, S Portugal
Esztergom 491 C6 Ger. Gran; anc. Strigonium. Komárom-Esztergom, N Hungary
Étalle 479 D8 Luxembourg, SE Belgium
Etāwah 526 D3 Uttar Pradesh, N India
Ethiopia 465 C5 off. Federal Democratic Republic of Ethiopia; prev. Abyssinia, People's Democratic Republic of Ethiopia. country E Africa
Ethiopian Highlands 465 C5 var. Ethiopian Plateau. plateau N Ethiopia
Ethiopian Plateau see Ethiopian Highlands
Etna, Monte 489 C7 Eng. Mount Etna. volcano Sicilia, Italy, C Mediterranean Sea
Etna, Mount see Etna, Monte
Etosha Pan 470 B3 salt lake N Namibia
Etoumbi 469 B5 Cuvette, NW Congo
Et Tafila see Aţ Ţafilah
Ettelbrück 479 D8 Diekirch, C Luxembourg
'Eua 537 E5 prev. Middleburg Island. island Tongatapu Group, SE Tonga
Euboea see Évvoia
Eucla 539 D6 Western Australia
Euclid 432 D3 Ohio, N USA
Eufaula Lake 441 G1 var. Eufaula Reservoir. reservoir Oklahoma, C USA
Eufaula Reservoir see Eufaula Lake
Eugene 438 B3 Oregon, NW USA
Eupen 479 D6 Liège, E Belgium
Euphrates 504 B4 Ar. Al Furāt, Turk. Firat Nehri. river SW Asia
Eureka 439 A5 California, W USA
Eureka 436 A1 Montana, NW USA
Europa Point 485 H5 headland S Gibraltar
Europe 426 E1 continent
Eutin 486 C2 Schleswig-Holstein, N Germany
Euxine Sea see Black Sea
Evansdale 437 G3 Iowa, C USA
Evanston 432 B3 Illinois, N USA
Evanston 436 B4 Wyoming, C USA
Evansville 432 B5 Indiana, N USA
Eveleth 437 G1 Minnesota, N USA
Everard, Lake 541 A6 salt lake South Australia
Everest, Mount 518 B5 Chin. Qomolangma Feng, Nep. Sagarmatha. mountain China/Nepal
Everett 438 B2 Washington, NW USA
Everglades, The 435 F5 wetland Florida, SE USA
Evje 477 A6 Aust-Agder, S Norway
Évora 484 B4 anc. Ebora, Lat. Liberalitas Julia. Évora, C Portugal
Évreux 482 C3 anc. Civitas Eburovicum. Eure, N France
Évros see Maritsa
Évry 482 E2 Essonne, N France
Évvoia 493 E8 Lat. Euboea. island C Greece
Ewarton 446 B5 C Jamaica
Excelsior Springs 437 F4 Missouri, C USA
Exe 481 C7 river SW England, UK
Exeter 481 C7 anc. Isca Damnoniorum. SW England, UK
Exmoor 481 C7 moorland SW England, UK
Exmouth 481 C7 SW England, UK
Exmouth 538 A4 Western Australia
Exmouth Gulf 538 A4 gulf Western Australia
Exmouth Plateau 533 E5 undersea feature E Indian Ocean
Extremadura 484 C3 cultural and historical region W Spain
Exuma Cays 446 C1 islets C Bahamas
Exuma Sound 446 C1 sound C Bahamas
Eyre Mountains 543 A7 mountain range South Island, NZ
Eyre North, Lake 541 A5 salt lake South Australia
Eyre Peninsula 541 A6 peninsula South Australia
Eyre South, Lake 541 A5 salt lake South Australia

F

Faadhippolhu Atoll 524 B4 var. Fadiffolu, Lhaviyani Atoll. atoll N Maldives
Fabens 440 D3 Texas, SW USA
Fada 468 C2 Borkou-Ennedi-Tibesti, E Chad
Fada-Ngourma 467 E4 E Burkina
Fadiffolu see Faadhippolhu Atoll
Faenza 488 C3 anc. Faventia. Emilia-Romagna, N Italy
Faeroe-Iceland Ridge 472 C1 undersea feature NW Norwegian Sea
Faeroe-Shetland Trough 472 C2 undersea feature NE Atlantic Ocean
Faeroes Islands 475 E5 Dan. Færøerne, Faer. Føroyar. Danish external territory N Atlantic Ocean
Faetano 488 E2 E San Marino
Făgăraş 500 C4 Ger. Fogarasch, Hung. Fogaras. Braşov, C Romania
Fagibina, Lake see Faguibine, Lac
Fagne 479 C7 hill range S Belgium
Faguibine, Lac 467 E3 var. Lake Fagibina. lake NW Mali
Fahlun see Falun
Fahraj 512 E4 Kermān, SE Iran
Faial 484 A5 var. Ilha do Faial. island Azores, Portugal, NE Atlantic Ocean
Fairbanks 428 D3 Alaska, USA
Fairfield 439 B6 California, W USA
Fair Isle 480 D2 island NE Scotland, UK
Fairlie 543 B6 Canterbury, South Island, NZ
Fairmont 437 F3 Minnesota, N USA
Faisalābād 526 C2 prev. Lyallpur. Punjab, NE Pakistan
Faizābād see Feyzābād
Faizābād 527 E3 Uttar Pradesh, N India
Fakaofo Atoll 537 F3 island SE Tokelau
Falam 528 A3 Chin State, W Burma
Falconara Marittima 488 C3 Marche, C Italy
Falkland Islands 457 D7 var. Falklands, Islas Malvinas. UK dependent territory SW Atlantic Ocean
Falkland Plateau 449 D7 var. Argentine Rise. undersea feature SW Atlantic Ocean
Falklands see Falkland Islands
Fallbrook 439 C8 California, W USA
Falmouth 481 C7 SW England, UK
Falmouth 446 A4 W Jamaica
Falster 477 B8 island SE Denmark

Garagumskiy Kanal – Great Meteor Seamount

umskiy Kanal 514 D3 var. Kum Canal, Karakumskiy l, Turkm. Garagum Kanaly. C Turkmenistan
umy 514 C3 var. Qara Qum, Black Sand Desert, Kara , Turkm. Garagum; prev. Peski kumy. desert C Turkmenistan
Khitrino 496 D2 Varnenska st, NE Bulgaria
, Lago di 488 C2 var. Benaco, Lake Garda, Ger. Gardasee. NE Italy
, Lake see Garda, Lago di
see see Garda, Lago di
n City 437 E5 Kansas, C USA
yz see Gardēz
z 515 E4 var. Gardeyz, iaz. Paktiā, E Afghanistan
dai 498 B3 Gargždai, thuania
sa 465 D6 Coast, E Kenya
nd 441 G2 Texas, SW USA
an, Loch see Wexford
see Garoowe
ne 483 B5 anc. Garumna. S France
we 465 E5 var. Garoe. Nugaal, malia
a 468 B4 var. Garua. Nord, meroon
gala see Kara-Kala
Lake 429 F3 lake Nunavut, nada
n 465 D6 Coast, S Kenya
see Garoua
lin 490 D4 Siedlce, E Poland
ncun see Gar
432 B3 Indiana, N USA
n 450 B4 Huila, S Colombia
gne 483 B6 Eng. Gascony. ral region S France
ny, Gulf of 483 A6 var. Golfe ascogne. gulf France/Spain
yne River 539 A5 river ern Australia
431 F3 Québec, SE Canada
, Péninsule de 431 E4 var. nsule de la Gaspésie. peninsula ec, SE Canada
nia 435 E1 North Carolina, SA
ini 497 B6 Dytikí Ellás, ece
na 502 B4 Leningradskaya st', NW Russian Federation
eau 430 D4 Québec, anada
, Lago 445 F4 reservoir ama
498 D3 Ger. Aa. river nia/Latvia
ng see Johannesburg
ndi 512 D4 Hormozgān, n
s 497 C8 island SE Greece
e 479 B6 Oost-Vlaanderen, Belgium
477 C6 var. Gäfle; prev. Gefle. borg, C Sweden
r 541 B6 South Australia
527 F3 Bihār, N India
ah 541 E5 Queensland, stralia
11 A6 Ar. Ghazzah, Heb. . NE Gaza Strip
chak 514 D2 Turkm. Gazojak. pskiy Velayat, urkmenistan
dzhyk 514 B2 Turkm. njyk; prev. Kazandzhik. anskiy Velayat, urkmenistan
Strip 511 A7 Ar. Qiţā' zah. disputed region SW Asia
ntep see Gaziantep
ntep 508 D4 var. Gazi Antep; Aintab, Antep. Gaziantep, key
ağusa see Ammóchostos
ağusa Körfezi see Kólpos nóchostos
514 D2 Bukhoro Wiloyati, bekistan
ga 466 D5 var. Gbarnga. eria
ga see Gbanga
k 490 C2 Fr. Dantzig, Ger. ig. Gdańsk, N Poland
skaya Bukhta see Danzig, of
k, Gulf of see Danzig, Gulf of
a 490 C2 Ger. Gdingen. sk, N Poland
ef 464 C4 var. Al Qaḑārif, daref. Gedaref, E Sudan
508 B3 Kütahya, W Turkey
Nehri 508 A3 river W Turkey
79 C5 var. Gheel. Antwerpen, lgium
ng 541 C7 Victoria, ustralia
u see Golmud
ee Gävle
477 A5 Buskerud, S Norway

Gejiu 520 B6 var. Kochiu. Yunnan, S China
Gëkdepe see Geok-Tepe
Gela 489 C7 prev. Terranova di Sicilia. Sicilia, Italy, C Mediterranean Sea
Geldermalsen 478 C4 Gelderland, C Netherlands
Geleen 479 D6 Limburg, SE Netherlands
Gelinsoor see Gellinsoor
Gellinsoor 465 E5 var. Gelinsoor. Mudug, NE Somalia
Gembloux 479 C6 Namur, Belgium
Gemena 469 C5 Equateur, NW Congo (Zaire)
Gemona del Friuli 488 D2 Friuli-Venezia Giulia, NE Italy
Genck see Genk
General Alvear 456 B4 Mendoza, W Argentina
General Eugenio A.Garay 456 C1 Guairá, S Paraguay
General Machado see Camacupa
General Santos 531 F3 off. General Santos City. Mindanao, S Philippines
Geneva see Genève
Geneva, Lake 487 A7 Fr. Lac de Genève, Lac Léman, le Léman, Ger. Genfer See. lake France/Switzerland
Genève 487 A7 Eng. Geneva, Ger. Genf, It. Ginevra. Genève, SW Switzerland
Genf see Genève
Genk 479 D6 var. Genck. Limburg, NE Belgium
Gennep 478 D4 Limburg, SE Netherlands
Genoa see Genova
Genova 494 D1 Eng. Genoa, Fr. Gênes; anc. Genua. Liguria, NW Italy
Genova, Golfo di 488 A3 Eng. Gulf of Genoa. gulf NW Italy
Genovesa, Isla 452 B4 var. Tower Island. island Galapagos Islands, Ecuador, E Pacific Ocean
Gent 479 B5 Eng. Ghent, Fr. Gand. Oost-Vlaanderen, NW Belgium
Geok-Tepe 514 C3 var. Gëkdepe, Turkm. Gökdepe. Akhalskiy Velayat, C Turkmenistan
George 474 A4 river Newfoundland/Québec, E Canada
George 470 C5 Western Cape, S South Africa
George, Lake 435 E3 lake Florida, SE USA
Georges Bank 427 D5 undersea feature W Atlantic Ocean
George Sound 543 A7 sound South Island, NZ
Georges River 540 D2 river New South Wales, SE Australia
George Town 446 B3 var. Georgetown. dependent territory capital (Cayman Islands) Grand Cayman, SW Cayman Islands
George Town 530 B3 var. Penang, Pinang. Pinang, Peninsular Malaysia
George Town 446 C2 Great Exuma Island, C Bahamas
Georgetown 451 F2 country capital (Guyana) N Guyana
Georgetown 435 F2 South Carolina, SE USA
George V Land 546 C4 physical region Antarctica
Georgia 509 F2 off. Republic of Georgia, Geor. Sak'art'velo, Rus. Gruzinskaya SSR, Gruziya; prev. Georgian SSR. country SW Asia
Georgia 434 D2 off. State of Georgia; also known as Empire State of the South, Peach State. state SE USA
Georgian Bay 432 D2 lake bay Ontario, S Canada
Georgia, Strait of 438 A1 strait British Columbia, W Canada
Georg von Neumayer 546 A2 German research station Antarctica
Gera 486 C4 Thüringen, E Germany
Geráki 497 B6 Pelopónnisos, S Greece
Geraldine 543 B6 Canterbury, South Island, NZ
Geraldton 539 A6 Western Australia
Geral, Serra 449 D5 mountain range S Brazil
Gerede 508 C2 Bolu, N Turkey
Gereshk 514 D5 Helmand, SW Afghanistan
Gering 436 D3 Nebraska, C USA
Germanicopolis see Çankiri
Germany 486 B4 off. Federal Republic of Germany, Ger. Bundesrepublik Deutschland, Deutschland. country N Europe
Geroliménas 497 B7 Pelopónnisos, S Greece
Gerona see Girona

Gerpinnes 479 C7 Hainaut, S Belgium
Gerunda see Girona
Gerze 508 D2 Sinop, N Turkey
Gesoriacum see Boulogne-sur-Mer
Gessoriacum see Boulogne-sur-Mer
Getafe 484 D3 Madrid, C Spain
Gevaş 509 F3 Van, SE Turkey
Gevgeli see Gevgelija
Gevgelija 493 E6 var. Đevđelija, Djevdjelija, Turk. Gevgeli. SE FYR Macedonia
Ghaba see Al Ghābah
Ghana 467 E5 off. Republic of Ghana. country W Africa
Ghanzi 470 C3 var. Khanzi. Ghanzi, W Botswana
Gharandal 511 B7 Ma'ān, SW Jordan
Ghardaïa 462 D2 N Algeria
Gharvān see Gharyān
Gharyān 463 F2 var. Gharvān. NW Libya
Ghaznī 515 E4 var. Ghazni. Ghaznī, E Afghanistan
Ghazni see Ghaznī
Gheel see Geel
Gheorgheni 500 C4 prev. Gheorghieni, Sînt-Miclăuş, Ger. Niklasmarkt, Hung. Gyergyószentmiklós. Harghita, C Romania
Ghijduwon 514 D2 Rus. Gizhduvan. Bukhoro Wiloyati, C Uzbekistan
Ghŭdara 515 F3 var. Gudara, Rus. Kudara. SE Tajikistan
Ghurdaqah see Hurghada
Ghūrīān 514 D4 Herāt, W Afghanistan
Giannitsá 496 B4 var. Yiannitsá. Kentrikí Makedonía, N Greece
Gibraltar 485 G4 UK dependent territory SW Europe
Gibraltar, Bay of 485 G5 bay Gibraltar/Spain
Gibraltar, Strait of 484 C5 Fr. Détroit de Gibraltar, Sp. Estrecho de Gibraltar. strait Atlantic Ocean/Mediterranean Sea
Gibson Desert 539 B5 desert Western Australia
Giedraičiai 499 C5 Molėtai, E Lithuania
Giessen 487 B5 Hessen, W Germany
Gifu 523 C6 var. Gihu. Gifu, Honshū, SW Japan
Giganta, Sierra de la 442 B3 mountain range W Mexico
Gihu see Gifu
Gijón 484 D1 Asturias, NW Spain
Gilani see Gnjilane
Gila River 440 A2 river Arizona, SW USA
Gilbert River 540 C3 river Queensland, NE Australia
Gilf Kebir Plateau 464 A2 Ar. Haḑabat al Jilf al Kabīr. plateau SW Egypt
Gillette 436 D3 Wyoming, C USA
Gilroy 439 B6 California, W USA
Gimie, Mount 447 F1 mountain C Saint Lucia
Gimma see Jīma
Ginevra see Genève
Gingin 539 A6 Western Australia
Giohar see Jawhar
Girardot 450 B3 Cundinamarca, C Colombia
Giresun 509 E2 var. Kerasunt; anc. Cerasus, Pharnacia. Giresun, NE Turkey
Girin see Jilin
Girne see Kerýneia
Girona 485 G2 var. Gerona; anc. Gerunda. Cataluña, NE Spain
Gisborne 542 E3 Gisborne, North Island, NZ
Gissar Range 515 E3 Rus. Gissarskiy Khrebet. mountain range Tajikistan/Uzbekistan
Githio see Gýtheio
Giulianova 488 D4 Abruzzi, C Italy
Giumri see Gyumri
Giurgiu 500 C5 Giurgiu, S Romania
Gīza see El Gîza
Gizeh see El Gîza
Gjakovë see Đakovica
Gjilan see Gnjilane
Gjinokastër see Gjirokastër
Gjirokastër 493 C7 var. Gjirokastra; prev. Gjinokastër, Gk. Argyrokastron, It. Argirocastro. Gjirokastër, S Albania
Gjirokastra see Gjirokastër
Gjoa Haven 429 F3 King William Island, Nunavut, NW Canada
Gjøvik 477 B5 Oppland, S Norway
Glace Bay 431 G4 Cape Breton Island, Nova Scotia, SE Canada
Gladstone 540 E4 Queensland, E Australia
Glåma 477 B5 river SE Norway
Glasgow 480 C4 S Scotland, UK

Glavn'a Morava see Velika Morava
Glazov 503 D5 Udmurtskaya Respublika, NW Russian Federation
Glendale 440 B2 Arizona, SW USA
Glendive 436 D2 Montana, NW USA
Glens Falls 433 F3 New York, NE USA
Glina 492 B3 Sisak-Moslavina, NE Croatia
Glittertind 477 A5 mountain S Norway
Gliwice 491 C5 Ger. Gleiwitz. Katowice, S Poland
Globe 440 B2 Arizona, SW USA
Głogów 490 B4 Ger. Glogau, Glogow. Legnica, W Poland
Gloucester 481 D6 hist. Caer Glou, Lat. Glevum. C England, UK
Głowno 490 D4 Łódź, C Poland
Gniezno 490 C3 Ger. Gnesen. Poznań, C Poland
Gnjilane 493 D5 var. Gilani, Alb. Gjilan. Serbia, S Yugoslavia
Goa see Panaji
Gobabis 470 B3 Omaheke, E Namibia
Gobi 518 D3 desert China/Mongolia
Gobō 523 C6 Wakayama, Honshū, SW Japan
Godāvari 516 B3 var. Godavari. river C India
Godhavn see Qeqertarsuaq
Godhra 526 C4 Gujarāt, W India
Godoy Cruz 456 B4 Mendoza, W Argentina
Godthaab see Nuuk
Godthåb see Nuuk
Goeree 478 B4 island SW Netherlands
Goes 479 B5 Zeeland, SW Netherlands
Goettingen see Göttingen
Gogebic Range 432 B1 hill range Michigan/Wisconsin, N USA
Goiânia 455 E3 prev. Goyania. state capital Goiás, C Brazil
Goiás 455 E3 Goiás, C Brazil
Gojōme 522 D4 Akita, Honshū, NW Japan
Gökçeada 496 D4 var. Imroz Adası, Gk. Imbros. island NW Turkey
Gökdepe see Geok-Tepe
Göksun 508 D4 Kahramanmaraş, C Turkey
Gol 477 A5 Buskerud, S Norway
Golan Heights 511 B5 Ar. Al Jawlān, Heb. HaGolan. mountain range SW Syria
Gołdap 490 E2 Ger. Goldap. Suwałki, NE Poland
Gold Coast 541 E5 cultural region Queensland, E Australia
Golden Bay 542 C4 bay South Island, NZ
Goldsboro 435 F1 North Carolina, SE USA
Goleniów 490 B3 Ger. Gollnow. Szczecin, NW Poland
Golfe de Gascogne see Gascony, Gulf of
Golfo de Alasca see Alaska, Gulf of
Golfo de Paria see Paria, Gulf of
Golmo see Golmud
Golmud 518 D4 var. Ge'e'mu, Golmo, Chin. Ko-erh-mu. Qinghai, C China
Goma 469 E6 Nord Kivu, NE Congo (Zaire)
Gombi 467 H4 Adamawa, E Nigeria
Gombroon see Bandar-e 'Abbās
Gomera 462 A3 island Islas Canarias, Spain, NE Atlantic Ocean
Gómez Palacio 442 D3 Durango, C Mexico
Gonaïves 446 D3 var. Les Gonaïves. N Haiti
Gonâve, Île de la 446 D3 island C Haiti
Gondar see Gonder
Gonder 464 C4 var. Gondar. NW Ethiopia
Gondia 527 E4 Mahārāshtra, C India
Gonggar 518 C5 Xizang Zizhiqu, W China
Gongola 467 G4 river E Nigeria
Gonni see Gónnoi
Gónnoi 496 B4 var. Gonni, Gónnos; prev. Dereli. Thessalía, C Greece
Gónnos see Gónnoi
Good Hope see Fort Good Hope
Good Hope, Cape of 470 B5 Afr. Kaap de Goede Hoop, Kaap die Goeie Hoop. headland SW South Africa
Goodland 436 D4 Kansas, C USA
Goondiwindi 541 D5 Queensland, E Australia
Goor 478 E3 Overijssel, E Netherlands
Goose Green 457 D7 East Falkland, Falkland Islands

Goose Lake 438 B4 var. Lago dos Gansos. lake California/Oregon, W USA
Göppingen 487 B6 Baden-Württemberg, SW Germany
Gora Andryu see Andrew Tablemount
Gora El'brus see El'brus
Gorakhpur 527 E3 Uttar Pradesh, N India
Goražde 492 C4 SE Bosnia and Herzegovina
Gordiaz see Gardēz
Gore 543 B7 Southland, South Island, NZ
Gorē 465 C5 W Ethiopia
Goré 468 C4 Logone-Oriental, S Chad
Gorgān 512 D2 var. Astarabad, Astrabad, Gurgan; prev. Asterābad, anc. Hyrcania. Māzandarān, N Iran
Gori 509 F2 C Georgia
Gorinchem 478 C4 var. Gorkum. Zuid-Holland, C Netherlands
Goris 509 G3 SE Armenia
Gorkum see Gorinchem
Görlitz 486 D4 Sachsen, E Germany
Gornji Milanovac 492 C4 Serbia, C Yugoslavia
Gorontalo 531 E4 Sulawesi, C Indonesia
Gorontalo, Teluk see Tomini, Gulf of
Gorssel 478 D3 Gelderland, E Netherlands
Gory Putorana see Putorana, Plato
Gorzów Wielkopolski 490 B3 Ger. Landsberg, Landsberg an der Warthe. Gorzów, W Poland
Gosford 541 D6 New South Wales, SE Australia
Goshogawara 522 D3 var. Gosyogawara. Aomori, Honshū, C Japan
Gospić 492 A3 Lika-Senj, C Croatia
Gostivar 493 D6 W FYR Macedonia
Gosyogawara see Goshogawara
Göteborg 477 B7 Eng. Gothenburg. Göteborg och Bohus, S Sweden
Gotel Mountains 467 G5 mountain range E Nigeria
Gotha 486 C4 Thüringen, C Germany
Gothenburg see Göteborg
Gothenburg 472 D3 Nebraska, C USA
Gotland 477 C7 island SE Sweden
Gotō-rettō 523 A7 island group SW Japan
Gotska Sandön 498 B1 island SE Sweden
Gōtsu 523 B6 var. Gôtu. Shimane, Honshū, SW Japan
Göttingen 486 B4 var. Goettingen. Niedersachsen, C Germany
Gôtu see Gōtsu
Gouda 478 C4 Zuid-Holland, C Netherlands
Gough Fracture Zone 459 C6 tectonic feature S Atlantic Ocean
Gough Island 461 B8 island Tristan da Cunha, S Atlantic Ocean
Gouin, Réservoir 430 D4 reservoir Québec, SE Canada
Goulburn 541 D6 New South Wales, SE Australia
Goundam 467 E3 Tombouctou, NW Mali
Gouré 467 G3 Zinder, SE Niger
Governador Valadares 455 F4 Minas Gerais, SE Brazil
Govĭ Altayn Nuruu 519 E3 mountain range S Mongolia
Goya 456 D3 Corrientes, NE Argentina
Goz Beïda 468 C3 Ouaddaï, SE Chad
Gozo 489 C8 Malt. Ghawdex. island N Malta
Graciosa 484 A5 var. Ilha Graciosa. island Azores, Portugal, NE Atlantic Ocean
Gradačac 492 C3 N Bosnia and Herzegovina
Gradaús, Serra dos 455 E3 mountain range C Brazil
Grafton 541 E5 New South Wales, SE Australia
Grafton 437 E1 North Dakota, N USA
Graham Land 546 A2 physical region Antarctica
Grajewo 490 E3 Łomża, NE Poland
Grampian Mountains 480 C3 mountain range C Scotland, UK
Granada 485 D5 Andalucía, S Spain
Granada 444 D3 Granada, SW Nicaragua
Gran Canaria 462 A3 var. Grand Canary. island Islas Canarias, Spain, NE Atlantic Ocean
Gran Chaco 456 D2 var. Chaco. lowland plain South America
Grand see Cockburn Town

Grand Bahama Island 446 B1 island N Bahamas
Grand Banks of Newfoundland 426 E4 undersea feature NW Atlantic Ocean
Grand Canary see Gran Canaria
Grand Canyon 440 A1 canyon Arizona, SW USA
Grand Cayman 446 B3 island SW Cayman Islands
Grande, Bahía 457 B7 bay S Argentina
Grande Comore 471 F2 var. Njazidja, Great Comoro. island NW Comoros
Grande de Chiloé, Isla see Chiloé, Isla de
Grande Prairie 429 E4 Alberta, W Canada
Grand Erg Occidental 462 D3 desert W Algeria
Grand Erg Oriental 463 E3 desert Algeria/Tunisia
Grande, Rio 427 B6 var. Río Bravo, Sp. Río Bravo del Norte, Bravo del Norte. river Mexico/USA
Grande, Rio 441 F4 river Texas, SW USA
Grande, Rio see Bravo, Río
Grande, Río 443 E2 river S Mexico
Grande Terre 447 G3 island E West Indies
Grand Falls 431 G3 Newfoundland, SE Canada
Grand Forks 437 E1 North Dakota, N USA
Grand Island 437 E4 Nebraska, C USA
Grand Junction 436 C4 Colorado, C USA
Grand Rapids 432 C3 Michigan, N USA
Grand Rapids 437 F1 Minnesota, N USA
Grand-Santi 451 G3 W French Guiana
Gran Lago see Nicaragua, Lago de
Gran Malvina see West Falkland
Gran Paradiso 488 A2 Fr. Grand Paradis. mountain NW Italy
Gran Santiago see Santiago
Grants 440 C2 New Mexico, SW USA
Grants Pass 438 B4 Oregon, NW USA
Granville 482 B3 Manche, N France
Graulhet 483 C6 Tarn, S France
Grave 478 D4 Noord-Brabant, SE Netherlands
Grayling 428 C2 Alaska, USA
Graz 487 E7 prev. Gratz. Steiermark, SE Austria
Great Abaco 446 C1 var. Abaco Island. island N Bahamas
Great Alfold see Great Hungarian Plain
Great Ararat see Büyükağrı Dağı
Great Australian Bight 539 D7 bight S Australia
Great Barrier Island 542 D2 island N NZ
Great Barrier Reef 540 D2 reef Queensland, NE Australia
Great Basin 439 C5 basin W USA
Great Bear Lake 429 E3 Fr. Grand Lac de l'Ours. lake Northwest Territories, NW Canada
Great Belt see Storebælt
Great Bend 437 E5 Kansas, C USA
Great Bermuda see Bermuda
Great Britain see Britain
Great Comoro see Grande Comore
Great Dividing Range 540 D4 mountain range NE Australia
Greater Antarctica 546 C3 var. East Antarctica. physical region Antarctica
Greater Antilles 446 D3 island group West Indies
Greater Caucasus 509 G2 Az. Bas Qafqaz Silsiläsi, Geor. Kavkasioni, Rus. Bol'shoy Kavkaz. mountain range Asia/Europe
Greater Sunda Islands 516 D5 var. Sunda Islands. island group Indonesia
Great Exhibition Bay 542 C1 inlet North Island, NZ
Great Exuma Island 446 C2 island C Bahamas
Great Falls 436 B1 Montana, NW USA
Great Hungarian Plain 491 C7 var. Great Alfold, Plain of Hungary, Hung. Alföld. plain SE Europe
Great Inagua 446 D2 var. Inagua Islands. island S Bahamas
Great Indian Desert see Thar Desert
Great Karroo see Great Karoo
Great Lakes 427 C5 lakes Ontario, Canada/USA
Great Meteor Seamount see Great Meteor Tablemount

Ibarra – Jarqŭrghon

Ibarra *452 B1 var.* San Miguel de Ibarra. Imbabura, N Ecuador

Iberian Mountains *see* Ibérico, Sistema

Iberian Peninsula *472 B4 physical region* Portugal/Spain

Iberian Plain *472 B4 undersea feature* E Atlantic Ocean

Ibérico, Sistema *485 E2 var.* Cordillera Ibérica, *Eng.* Iberian Mountains. *mountain range* NE Spain

Ibiza *see* Eivissa

Ibo *see* Sassandra

Ica *452 D4* Ica, SW Peru

Içá *see* Putumayo, Río

Icaria *see* Ikaría

Içá, Rio *454 C2 var.* Río Putumayo. *river* NW South America *see also* Putumayo, Río

Iceland *475 E4 off.* Republic of Iceland, *Dan.* Island, *Icel.* Ísland. *country* N Atlantic Ocean

Iceland Basin *472 B1 undersea feature* N Atlantic Ocean

Icelandic Plateau *see* Iceland Plateau

Iceland Plateau *548 B5 var.* Icelandic Plateau. *undersea feature* S Greenland Sea

Iconium *see* Konya

Idabel *441 H2* Oklahoma, C USA

Idaho *438 D3 off.* State of Idaho; also known as Gem of the Mountains, Gem State. *state* NW USA

Idaho Falls *438 E3* Idaho, NW USA

Idensalmi *see* Iisalmi

Idfu *464 B2 var.* Edfu. SE Egypt

Ídhra *see* Ýdra

Idi Amin, Lac *see* Edward, Lake

Idini *466 B2* Trarza, W Mauritania

Idlib *510 B3* Idlib, NW Syria

Idre *477 B5* Kopparberg, C Sweden

Iecava *498 C3* Bauska, S Latvia

Ieper *479 A6 Fr.* Ypres. West-Vlaanderen, W Belgium

Ierápetra *497 D8* Kríti, Greece, E Mediterranean Sea

Ierisós *see* Ierissós

Ierissós *496 C4 var.* Ierisós. Kentrikí Makedonía, N Greece

Iferouâne *467 G2* Agadez, N Niger

Ifôghas, Adrar des *467 E2 var.* Adrar des Iforas. *mountain range* NE Mali

Igarka *506 D3* Krasnoyarskiy Kray, N Russian Federation

Iglesias *489 A5* Sardegna, Italy, C Mediterranean Sea

Igloolik *429 G2* Nunavut, N Canada

Igoumenítsa *496 A4* Ípeiros, W Greece

Iguaçu, Rio *455 E4 Sp.* Río Iguazú. *river* Argentina/Brazil *see also* Iguazú, Río

Iguaçu, Salto do *455 E4 Sp.* Cataratas del Iguazú; *prev.* Victoria Falls. *waterfall* Argentina/Brazil *see also* Iguazú, Cataratas del

Iguala *443 E4 var.* Iguala de la Independencia. Guerrero, S Mexico

Iguala de la Independencia *see* Iguala

Iguîdi, 'Erg *462 C3 var.* Erg Iguid. *desert* Algeria/Mauritania

Ihavandiffulu Atoll *see* Ihavandippolhu Atoll

Ihavandippolhu Atoll *524 A3 var.* Ihavandiffulu Atoll. *atoll* N Maldives

Ihosy *471 F4* Fianarantsoa, S Madagascar

Iisalmi *476 E4 var.* Idensalmi. Kuopio, C Finland

IJssel *478 D3 var.* Yssel. *river* Netherlands/Germany

IJsselmeer *478 C2 prev.* Zuider Zee. *lake* N Netherlands

IJsselmuiden *478 D3* Overijssel, E Netherlands

Ijzer *479 A6 river* W Belgium

Ikaría *497 D6 var.* Kariot, Nicaria, Nikaria; *anc.* Icaria. *island* Dodekánisos, Greece, Aegean Sea

Ikela *469 D6* Equateur, C Congo (Zaire)

Iki *523 A7 island* SW Japan

Ilagan *531 E1* Luzon, N Philippines

Ilave *453 E4* Puno, S Peru

Iława *490 D3 Ger.* Deutsch-Eylau. Olsztyn, N Poland

Ilebo *469 C6 prev.* Port-Francqui. Kasai Occidental, W Congo (Zaire)

Île-de-France *482 C3 cultural region* N France

Îles de la Société *see* Société, Archipel de la

Îles Tubuai *see* Australes, Îles

Ilfracombe *481 C7* SW England, UK

Ilha Caviana *see* Caviana de Fora, Ilha

Ilha de Madeira *see* Madeira

Ilha do Corvo *see* Corvo

Ilha do Faial *see* Faial

Ilha do Pico *see* Pico

Ilha do Porto Santo *see* Porto Santo

Ilha Graciosa *see* Graciosa

Ilhas dos Açores *see* Azores

Ilha Terceira *see* Terceira

Ílhavo *484 B2* Aveiro, N Portugal

Ili *504 C3 Kaz.* Ile, *Rus.* Reka Ili. *river* China/Kazakhstan

Iliamna Lake *428 C3 lake* Alaska, USA

Ilici *see* Elche

Iligan *531 E2 off.* Iligan City. Mindanao, S Philippines

Illapel *456 B4* Coquimbo, C Chile

Illichivs'k *501 E4 Rus.* Il'ichevsk. Odes'ka Oblast', SW Ukraine

Illicis *see* Elche

Illinois *432 A4 off.* State of Illinois; also known as Prairie State, Sucker State. *state* C USA

Illinois River *432 B4 river* Illinois, N USA

Ilo *453 E4* Moquegua, SW Peru

Iloilo *531 E2 off.* Iloilo City. Panay Island, C Philippines

Ilorin *467 F4* Kwara, W Nigeria

Îlots de Bass *see* Marotiri

Ilovlya *503 B6* Volgogradskaya Oblast', SW Russian Federation

Iluh *see* Batman

Il'yaly *514 C2 var.* Yylanly. Dashkhovuzskiy Velayat, N Turkmenistan

Imatra *477 E5* Kymi, SE Finland

Imbros *see* Gökçeada

İmişli *509 H3 Rus.* Imishli. C Azerbaijan

Imola *488 C3* Emilia-Romagna, N Italy

Imperatriz *455 F2* Maranhão, NE Brazil

Imperia *488 A3* Liguria, NW Italy

Impfondo *469 C5* La Likouala, NE Congo

Imphāl *527 H3* Manipur, NE India

Imroz Adası *see* Gökçeada

Inagua Islands *see* Great Inagua

Inagua Islands *see* Little Inagua

Inarijärvi *476 D2 Lapp.* Aanaarjävri, *Swe.* Enareträsk. *lake* N Finland

Inawashiro-ko *523 D5 var.* Inawasiro Ko. *lake* Honshū, C Japan

Inawasiro Ko *see* Inawashiro-ko

İncesu *508 D3* Kayseri, C Turkey

Inch'ŏn *521 E4 off.* Inch'ŏn-gwangyŏksi, *Jap.* Jinsen; *prev.* Chemulpo. NW South Korea

Incudine, Monte *483 E7 mountain* Corse, France, C Mediterranean Sea

Indefatigable Island *see* Santa Cruz, Isla

Independence *437 F4* Missouri, C USA

Independence Fjord *475 E1 fjord* N Greenland

Independence Mountains *438 C4 mountain range* Nevada, W USA

India *516 B3 off.* Republic of India, *var.* Indian Union, Union of India, *Hind.* Bhārat. *country* S Asia

Indiana *432 B4 off.* State of Indiana; also known as The Hoosier State. *state* N USA

Indianapolis *432 C4 state capital* Indiana, N USA

Indian Church *444 C1* Orange Walk, N Belize

Indian Desert *see* Thar Desert

Indianola *437 F4* Iowa, C USA

Indigirka *507 F2 river* NE Russian Federation

Inđija *492 D3 Hung.* India; *prev.* Indjija. Serbia, N Yugoslavia

Indomed Fracture Zone *533 B6 tectonic feature* SW Indian Ocean

Indonesia *530 B4 off.* Republic of Indonesia, *Ind.* Republik Indonesia; *prev.* Dutch East Indies, Netherlands East Indies, United States of Indonesia. *country* SE Asia

Indore *526 D4* Madhya Pradesh, C India

Indus *526 C2 Chin.* Yindu He; *prev.* Yin-tu Ho. *river* S Asia

Indus Cone *see* Indus Fan

Indus Fan *504 C5 var.* Indus Cone. *undersea feature* N Arabian Sea

Indus, Mouths of the *526 B4 delta* S Pakistan

İnebolu *508 C2* Kastamonu, N Turkey

Ineu *500 A4 Hung.* Borosjenő; *prev.* Ināu. Arad, W Romania

Infiernillo, Presa del *443 E4 reservoir* S Mexico

Inglewood *438 D2* California, W USA

Ingolstadt *487 C6* Bayern, S Germany

Inhambane *471 E4* Inhambane, SE Mozambique

Inhulets' *501 F3 Rus.* Ingulets. Dnipropetrovs'ka Oblast', E Ukraine

I-ning *see* Yining

Inis *see* Ennis

Inis Ceithleann *see* Enniskillen

Inn *487 C6 river* C Europe

Innaanganeq *474 C1 var.* Kap York. *headland* NW Greenland

Inner Hebrides *480 B4 island group* W Scotland, UK

Inner Islands *471 H1 var.* Central Group. *island group* NE Seychelles

Inner Mongolia *519 F3 var.* Nei Mongol, *Eng.* Inner Mongolia, Inner Mongolian Autonomous Region; *prev.* Nei Monggol Zizhiqu. Admin. region *autonomous region* N China

Inner Mongolian Autonomous Region *see* Inner Mongolia

Innisfail *540 D3* Queensland, NE Australia

Inniskilling *see* Enniskillen

Innsbruch *see* Innsbruck

Innsbruck *487 C7 var.* Innsbruch. Tirol, W Austria

Inoucdjouac *see* Inukjuak

Inowrocław *490 C3 Ger.* Hohensalza; *prev.* Inowrazlaw. Bydgoszcz, C Poland

I-n-Salah *462 D3 var.* In Salah. C Algeria

In Salah *see* I-n-Salah

Insula *see* Lille

Inta *502 E3* Respublika Komi, NW Russian Federation

International Falls *437 F1* Minnesota, N USA

Inukjuak *430 D2 var.* Inoucdjouac; *prev.* Port Harrison. Quebec, NE Canada

Inuuvik *see* Inuvik

Inuvik *428 D3 var.* Inuuvik. Northwest Territories, NW Canada

Invercargill *543 A7* Southland, South Island, NZ

Inverness *480 C3* N Scotland, UK

Investigator Ridge *533 D5 undersea feature* E Indian Ocean

Investigator Strait *541 B7 strait* South Australia

Inyangani *470 D3 mountain* NE Zimbabwe

Ioánnina *496 A4 var.* Janina, Yannina. Ípeiros, W Greece

Iola *437 F5* Kansas, C USA

Ionia Basin *see* Ionian Basin

Ionian Basin *472 D5 var.* Ionia Basin. *undersea feature* Ionian Sea, C Mediterranean Sea

Ionian Islands *see* Iónioi Nísoi

Ionian Sea *495 E3 Gk.* Iónio Pélagos, *It.* Mar Ionio. *sea* C Mediterranean Sea

Iónioi Nísoi *497 A5 Eng.* Ionian Islands. *island group* W Greece

Íos *497 D6 var.* Nio. *island* Kykládes, Greece, Aegean Sea

Íos *497 D6* Íos, Kykládes, Greece, Aegean Sea

Iowa *437 F3 off.* State of Iowa; also known as The Hawkeye State. *state* C USA

Iowa City *437 G3* Iowa, C USA

Iowa Falls *437 G3* Iowa, C USA

Ipel' *491 C6 var.* Ipoly, *Ger.* Eipel. *river* Hungary/Slovakia

Ipiales *450 A4* Nariño, SW Colombia

Ipoh *530 B3* Perak, Peninsular Malaysia

Ipoly *491 C6 var.* Ipel', *Ger.* Eipel. *river* Hungary/Slovakia

Ippy *468 C4* Ouaka, C Central African Republic

Ipswich *481 E6 hist.* Gipeswic. E England, UK

Ipswich *541 E5* Queensland, E Australia

Iqaluit *429 H3 prev.* Frobisher Bay. *Territory capital* Baffin Island, Nunavut, NE Canada

Iquique *456 B1* Tarapacá, N Chile

Iquitos *452 C1* Loreto, N Peru

Irákleio *497 D7 var.* Herakleion, *Eng.* Candia; *prev.* Iráklion. Kríti, Greece, E Mediterranean Sea

Iráklion *see* Irákleio

Iran *512 C3 off.* Islamic Republic of Iran; *prev.* Persia. *country* SW Asia

Iranian Plateau *512 D3 var.* Plateau of Iran. *plateau* N Iran

Iran, Plateau of *see* Iranian Plateau

Irapuato *443 E4* Guanajuato, C Mexico

Iraq *512 B3 off.* Republic of Iraq, *Ar.* 'Irāq. *country* SW Asia

Irbid *511 B5* Irbid, N Jordan

Irbīl *see* Arbīl

Ireland *472 C3 Lat.* Hibernia. *island* Ireland/UK

Ireland, Republic of *481 A5 off.* Republic of Ireland, *var.* Ireland, *Ir.* Éire. *country* NW Europe

Irian Barat *see* Irian Jaya

Irian Jaya *531 H4 var.* Irian Barat, West Irian, West New Guinea; *prev.* Dutch New Guinea, Netherlands New Guinea. Admin. region *province* E Indonesia

Iringa *465 C7* Iringa, C Tanzania

Iriomote-jima *522 A4 island* Sakishima-shotō, SW Japan

Iriona *444 D2* Colón, NE Honduras

Irish Sea *481 C5 Ir.* Muir Éireann. *sea* C British Isles

Irkutsk *507 E4* Irkutskaya Oblast', S Russian Federation

Irminger Basin *see* Reykjanes Basin

Iroise *482 A3 sea* NW France

Iron Mountain *432 B2* Michigan, N USA

Ironwood *432 B1* Michigan, N USA

Irrawaddy *528 B2 var.* Ayeyarwady. *river* W Burma

Irrawaddy, Mouths of the *529 A5 delta* SW Burma

Irtish *see* Irtysh

Irtysh *506 C4 var.* Irtish, *Kaz.* Ertis. *river* C Asia

Irún *485 E1* País Vasco, N Spain

Isabela, Isla *452 A4 var.* Albemarle Island. *island* Galapagos Islands, Ecuador, E Pacific Ocean

Isaccea *500 D4* Tulcea, E Romania

Isachsen *429 F1* Ellef Ringnes Island, Northwest Territories, N Canada

Ísafjördhur *475 E4* Vestfirdhir, NW Iceland

Isbarta *see* İsparta

Ise *523 C6* Mie, Honshū, SW Japan

Isère *483 D5 river* E France

Isernia *489 D5 var.* Æsernia. Molise, C Italy

Ise-wan *523 C6 bay* S Japan

Isha Baydhabo *see* Baydhabo

Ishigaki-jima *522 A4 var.* Isigaki Zima. *island* Sakishima-shotō, SW Japan

Ishikari-wan *522 C2 bay* Hokkaidō, NE Japan

Ishim *506 C4 Kaz.* Esil. *river* Kazakhstan/Russian Federation

Ishim *506 C4* Tyumenskaya Oblast', C Russian Federation

Ishinomaki *522 D4 var.* Isinomaki. Miyagi, Honshū, C Japan

Ishkoshim *515 F3 Rus.* Ishkashim. S Tajikistan

Isigaki Zima *see* Ishigaki-jima

Isinomaki *see* Ishinomaki

Isiro *469 E5* Haut-Zaïre, NE Congo (Zaire)

Iskăr *see* Iskŭr

İskenderun *508 D4 Eng.* Alexandretta. Hatay, S Turkey

İskenderun Körfezi *510 A2 Eng.* Gulf of Alexandretta. *gulf* S Turkey

Iskŭr *496 C2 var.* Iskăr. *river* NW Bulgaria

Iskŭr, Yazovir *496 B2 prev.* Yazovir Stalin. *reservoir* W Bulgaria

Isla Cristina *484 C4* Andalucía, S Spain

Islāmābād *526 C1 country capital* (Pakistan) Federal Capital Territory Islāmābād, NE Pakistan

I-n-Sâkâne, 'Erg *467 E2 desert* N Mali

Islas de los Galápagos *see* Galapagos Islands

Islas Malvinas *see* Falkland Islands

Islay *480 B4 island* SW Scotland, UK

Isle *483 B5 river* W France

Isle of Man *481 B5 UK crown dependency* NW Europe

Ismailia *see* Ismâ'ilîya

Ismâ'ilîya *464 B1 var.* Ismailia. N Egypt

Ismid *see* İzmit

Isna *464 B2 var.* Esna. SE Egypt

Isoka *470 D1* Northern, NE Zambia

Isola Grossa *see* Dugi Otok

Isola Lunga *see* Dugi Otok

Isole Lipari *see* Eolie, Isole

İsparta *508 B4 var.* Isbarta. Isparta, SW Turkey

İspir *509 E3* Erzurum, NE Turkey

Israel *511 A7 off.* State of Israel, *var.* Medinat Israel, *Heb.* Yisrael, Yisra'el. *country* SW Asia

Issiq Köl *see* Issyk-Kul', Ozero

Issoire *483 C5* Puy-de-Dôme, C France

Issyk-Kul', Ozero *515 G2 var.* Issiq Köl, *Kir.* Ysyk-Köl. *lake* E Kyrgyzstan

İstanbul *508 B2 Bul.* Tsarigrad, *Eng.* Istanbul; *prev.* Constantinople, *anc.* Byzantium. İstanbul, NW Turkey

İstanbul Boğazı *508 B2 var.* Bosporus Thracius, *Eng.* Bosphorus, Bosporus, *Turk.* Karadeniz Boğazı. *strait* NW Turkey

Istra *492 A3 Eng.* Istria, *Ger.* Istrien. *cultural region* NW Croatia

Istra *488 D2 Eng.* Istria. *peninsula* NW Croatia

Itabuna *455 G3* Bahia, E Brazil

Itagüí *450 B3* Antioquia, W Colombia

Itaipú, Represa de *455 E4 reservoir* Brazil/Paraguay

Itaituba *455 E2* Pará, NE Brazil

Italy *488 C3 off.* The Italian Republic, *It.* Italia, Republica Italiana. *country* S Europe

Italy *472 D4* Texas, SW USA

Iténez, Río *see* Guaporé, Rio

Ithaca *433 E3* New York, NE USA

Itoigawa *523 C5* Niigata, Honshū, C Japan

Itseqqortoormiit *see* Ittoqqortoormiit

Ittoqqortoormiit *475 E3 var.* Itseqqortoormiit, *Dan.* Scoresbysund, *Eng.* Scoresby Sound. C Greenland

Iturup, Ostrov *507 E2 island* Kuril'skiye Ostrova, SE Russian Federation

Itzehoe *486 B2* Schleswig-Holstein, N Germany

Ivalo *476 D2 Lapp.* Avveel, Avvil. Lappi, N Finland

Ivanava *499 B7 Pol.* Janów, Janów Poleski, *Rus.* Ivanovo. Brestskaya Voblasts', SW Belorussia

Ivanhoe *541 C6* New South Wales, SE Australia

Ivano-Frankivs'k *500 C2 Ger.* Stanislau, *Pol.* Stanisławów, *Rus.* Ivano-Frankovsk; *prev.* Stanislav. Ivano-Frankivs'ka Oblast', W Ukraine

Ivanovo *503 B5* Ivanovskaya Oblast', W Russian Federation

Ivatsevichy *499 B6 Pol.* Iwacewicze, *Rus.* Ivantsevichi, Ivatsevichi. Brestskaya Voblasts', SW Belorussia

Ivigtut *see* Ivittuut

Ivittuut *474 B4 var.* Ivigtut. S Greenland

Iviza *see* Eivissa

Ivory Coast *466 D4 off.* Republic of the Ivory Coast, *Fr.* Côte d'Ivoire, République de la Côte d'Ivoire. *country* W Africa

Ivujivik *430 D1* Quebec, NE Canada

Iwaki *523 D5* Fukushima, Honshū, N Japan

Iwakuni *523 B7* Yamaguchi, Honshū, SW Japan

Iwanai *522 C2* Hokkaidō, NE Japan

Iwate *522 D3* Iwate, Honshū, N Japan

Ixtapa *443 E5* Guerrero, S Mexico

Ixtepec *443 F5* Oaxaca, SE Mexico

Iyo-nada *523 B7 sea* S Japan

Izabal, Lago de *444 B2 prev.* Golfo Dulce. *lake* E Guatemala

Īzad Khvāst *512 D3* Fārs, C Iran

Izegem *479 A6 prev.* Iseghem. West-Vlaanderen, W Belgium

Izhevsk *503 D5 prev.* Ustinov. Udmurtskaya Respublika, NW Russian Federation

Izmayil *500 D4 Rus.* Izmail. Odes'ka Oblast', SW Ukraine

İzmir *508 A3 prev.* Smyrna. İzmir, W Turkey

İzmit *508 B2 var.* Ismid; *anc.* Astacus. Kocaeli, NW Turkey

İznik Gölü *508 B3 lake* NW Turkey

Izu-hantō *523 D6 peninsula* Honshū, S Japan

Izu Shichito *see* Izu-shotō

Izu-shotō *523 D6 var.* Izu Shichito. *island group* S Japan

Izvor *496 B2* Sofiyska Oblast, W Bulgaria

Izyaslav *500 C2* Khmel'nyts'ka Oblast', W Ukraine

Izyum *501 G2* Kharkivs'ka Oblast', E Ukraine

J

Jabal ash Shifā *512 A4 desert* NW Saudi Arabia

Jabalpur *527 E4 prev.* Jubbulpore. Madhya Pradesh, C India

Jabbūl, Sabkhat al *510 B2 salt flat* NW Syria

Jablah *510 A3 var.* Jeble, *Fr.* Djéblé. Al Lādhiqīyah, W Syria

Jaca *485 F1* Aragón, NE Spain

Jacaltenango *444 A2* Huehuetenango, W Guatemala

Jackson *434 B2 state capital* Mississippi, S USA

Jackson *437 H5* Missouri, C USA

Jackson *434 C1* Tennessee, S USA

Jackson Head *543 A6 headland* South Island, NZ

Jacksonville *435 E3* Florida, SE USA

Jacksonville *432 B4* Illinois, N

Jacksonville *435 F1* North Ca SE USA

Jacksonville *441 G3* Texas, SW USA

Jacmel *446 D3 var.* Jaquemel.

Jacobābād *526 B3* Sind, SE Pa

Jaén *484 D4* Andalucía, SW Sp

Jaén *452 B2* Cajamarca, N Per

Jaffna *524 D3* Northern Provi N Sri Lanka

Jagannath *see* Puri

Jagdalpur *527 E5* Madhya Pra C India

Jagdaqi *519 G1* Nei Mongol Zizhiqu, N China

Jagodina *492 D4 prev.* Svetoza Serbia, C Yugoslavia

Jahra *see* Al Jahrā'

Jaipur *526 D3 prev.* Jeypore. Rājasthān, N India

Jaisalmer *526 C3* Rājasthān, NW India

Jajce *492 B3* W Bosnia and Herzegovina

Jakarta *530 C5 prev.* Djakarta Batavia. *country capital* (Indonesia) Jawa, C Indones

Jakobstad *476 D4 Fin.* Pietars Vaasa, W Finland

Jalālābād *515 F4 var.* Jalalabac Jelalabad. Nangarhār, E Afghanistan

Jalandhar *526 D2 prev.* Jullun Punjab, N India

Jalapa *see* Xalapa

Jalapa *444 D3* Nueva Segovia, NW Nicaragua

Jalapa Enríquez *see* Xalapa

Jalpa *442 D4* Zacatecas, C Me

Jālū *463 G3 var.* Jūlā. NE Liby

Jaluit Atoll *536 D2 var.* Jālwōj Ralik Chain, S Marshall Islar

Jālwōj *see* Jaluit Atoll

Jamaame *465 D6 It.* Giamame Margherita. Jubbada Hoose, S Somalia

Jamaica *446 A4 country* W W Indies

Jamaica *448 A1 island* W Wes Indies

Jamaica Channel *446 D3 cha* Haiti/Jamaica

Jamālpur *527 F3* Bihār, NE Ir

Jambi *530 B4 var.* Telanaipura Djambi. Sumatera, W Indon

James Bay *430 C3 bay* Ontario/Quebec, E Canada

James River *437 E2 river* Nor Dakota/South Dakota, N US

James River *433 E5 river* Virg NE USA

Jamestown *433 E3* New York, NE USA

Jamestown *437 E2* North Dal N USA

Jammu *526 D2 prev.* Jummoo Jammu and Kashmir, NW Ir

Jammu and Kashmīr *526 D disputed region* India/Pakista

Jāmnagar *526 C4 prev.* Navan Gujarāt, W India

Jamshedpur *527 F4* Bihār, N

Jamuna *see* Brahmaputra

Janaúba *455 F3* Minas Gerais SE Brazil

Janesville *432 B3* Wisconsin, N USA

Janīn *see* Jenīn

Janina *see* Ioánnina

Jan Mayen *475 F4 Norwegian dependency* N Atlantic Ocea

Jánoshalma *491 C7 SCr.* Jank Bács-Kiskun, S Hungary

Japan *522 C4 var.* Nippon, *Jap* Nihon. *country* E Asia

Japan, Sea of *522 A4 var.* Eas *Rus.* Yapanskoye More. *sea* NW Pacific Ocean

Japan Trench *517 F1 underse feature* NW Pacific Ocean

Japiim *454 C2 var.* Máncio Li Acre, W Brazil

Japurá, Rio *454 C2 var.* Río Caquetá, Yapurá. *river* Brazil/Colombia *see also* Cac Río

Jaqué *445 G5* Darién, SE Pana

Jaquemel *see* Jacmel

Jarablos *see* Jarābulus

Jarābulus *510 C2 var.* Jarablos Jerablus, *Fr.* Djérablous. Ḥal N Syria

Jardines de la Reina, Archipiélago de los *446 B2 group* C Cuba

Jarocin *490 C4* Kalisz, C Pola

Jarosław *491 E5 Ger.* Jaroslau Yaroslav. Przemyśl, SE Polan

Jarqŭrghon *515 E3 Rus.* Dzharkurgan. Surkhondary Wiloyati, S Uzbekistan

Jarvis Island – Karaman

Island *537 G2 US* *corporated territory* C Pacific n
91 D5 Krosno, SE Poland
bie-Zdrój *491 C5* Katowice, and
55 E3 Goiás, C Brazil
see Xátiva
e Al Jawf
ebalga *498 D3* Gulbene, atvia
ur *527 E3* Uttar Pradesh, dia
4 A3 prev. Djawa. *island* donesia
mbre *485 E3 mountain* ain
Rio *454 C2 var.* Yavarí. *river* l/Peru
a *530 D4 Ind.* Laut Jawa. *sea* donesia
rench *516 D5 var.* Sunda h. *undersea feature* E Indian n
465 D6 var. Jowhar, *It.* ar. Shabeellaha Dhexe, nalia
uncak *531 G4 prev.* Puntjak ensz, Puntjak Sukarno. *tain* Irian Jaya, E Indonesia
ra *531 H4 var.* Djajapura, Hollandia; *prev.* Kotabaru, rnapura. Irian Jaya, donesia
Bin Ghalfān *see* Ḥalāniyāt, al
Jarbah *see* Jerba, Île de
n-ye Qeshm *see* Qeshm
irīān, Hāmūn-e *512 E4 lake* an
467 F4 Kwara, W Nigeria
sh Sharqi *see* Anti-Lebanon
Jweinat *see* 'Uwaynāt, Jabal al
ee Jablah
jów *490 D4 Ger.* Endersdorf. e, S Poland
on City *437 G5 state capital* ouri, C USA
57 F4 Kebbi, NW Nigeria
ee Chengde
ils *498 D4 Ger.* Jakobstadt. pils, S Latvia
ad *see* Jalālābād
Góra *490 B4 Ger.* chberg, Hirschberg im engebirge, Hirschberg in engebirge, Hirschberg in sien. Jelenia Góra, SW Poland
a *498 C3 Ger.* Mitau. Jelgava, via
pes *479 B6* Hainaut, gium
r *530 D5 prev.* Djember. Jawa, donesia
36 C4 Thüringen, C Germany
511 A6 var. Janīn, Jinīn; *anc.* nnim. N West Bank
us *see* Jarābulus
462 D2 NE Morocco
Île de *463 F2 var.* Djerba, at Jarbah. *island* E Tunisia
ie *446 D3* SW Haiti
ee Jeréz de la Frontera
le la Frontera *484 C5 var.* ; *prev.* Xeres. Andalucía, Spain
le los Caballeros *484 C4* emadura, W Spain
o *511 B6 Ar.* Arīḥā, *Heb.* o. E West Bank
Chott el *463 E2 var.* Shaṭṭ īd. *salt lake* SW Tunisia
481 D8 UK dependent *ory* NW Europe
lem *495 H4 Ar.* Al Quds, ds ash Sharīf, *Heb.* halayim; *anc.* Hierosolyma. *ry capital* (Israel) Jerusalem, srael
lem *504 A4* Admin. region *ct* E Israel
ce *487 D7 Ger.* Assling. Slovenia
e *527 G4* Khulna, angladesh
María *456 C3* Córdoba, gentina
526 D3 Uttar Pradesh, dia
n *526 C2* Punjab, NE Pakistan
Hebei
lin
nen *520 C6* Guangdong, na
u *520 D4 var.* Chiang-su, su Sheng, Kiangsu, Su. in. region *province* E China
u Sheng *see* Jiangsu
i *520 C6 var.* Chiang-hsi, Jiangxi Sheng, Kiangsi. in. region *province* S China
i Sheng *see* Jiangxi
g *520 D5* Zhejiang, SE China
e Chiai
see Djibouti

Jiddah *513 A5 Eng.* Jedda. Makkah, W Saudi Arabia
Jih-k'a-tse *see* Xigazê
Jihlava *491 B5 Ger.* Iglau, *Pol.* Igława. Jižní Morava, S Czech Republic
Jilib *465 D6 It.* Gelib. Jubbada Dhexe, S Somalia
Jilin *520 D3 var.* Chi-lin, Girin, Ji, Jilin Sheng, Kirin. Admin. region *province* NE China
Jilin *521 E3 var.* Chi-lin, Girin, Kirin; *prev.* Yungki, Yunki. Jilin, NE China
Jilin Sheng *see* Jilin
Jīma *465 C5 var.* Jimma, *It.* Gimma. SW Ethiopia
Jimbolia *500 A4 Ger.* Hatzfeld, *Hung.* Zsombolya. Timiș, W Romania
Jiménez *442 D2* Chihuahua, N Mexico
Jimma *see* Jīma
Jimsar *518 C3* Xinjiang Uygur Zizhiqu, NW China
Jin *see* Shanxi
Jin *see* Tianjin Shi
Jinan *520 C4 var.* Chinan, Chi-nan, Tsinan. Shandong, E China
Jingdezhen *520 C5* Jiangxi, S China
Jinghong *520 A6 var.* Yunjinghong. Yunnan, SW China
Jinhua *520 D5* Zhejiang, SE China
Jinīn *see* Jenin
Jining *519 F3* Shandong, E China
Jinja *465 C6* S Uganda
Jinotega *444 D3* Jinotega, NW Nicaragua
Jinotepe *444 D3* Carazo, SW Nicaragua
Jinsha Jiang *520 A5 river* SW China
Jinzhou *520 D3 var.* Chin-chou, Chinchow; *prev.* Chinhsien. Liaoning, NE China
Jisr ash Shadadi *see* Ash Shadādah
Jiu *500 B5 Ger.* Schil, Schyl, *Hung.* Zsil, Zsily. *river* S Romania
Jiujiang *520 C5* Jiangxi, S China
Jixi *521 E2* Heilongjiang, NE China
Jīzān *513 B6 var.* Qīzān. Jīzān, SW Saudi Arabia
Jizzakh *515 E2 Rus.* Dzhizak. Jizzakh Wiloyati, C Uzbekistan
João Pessoa *455 G2 prev.* Paraíba. *state capital* Paraíba, E Brazil
Jo'burg *see* Johannesburg
Jo-ch'iang *see* Ruoqiang
Jodhpur *526 C3* Rājasthān, NW India
Joensuu *477 E5* Pohjois-Karjala, SE Finland
Jōetsu *523 C5 var.* Zyôetu. Niigata, Honshū, C Japan
Johanna Island *see* Anjouan
Johannesburg *470 D4 var.* Egoli, Erautini, Gauteng, *abbrev.* Jo'burg. Gauteng, NE South Africa
John Day River *438 C3 river* Oregon, NW USA
John o'Groats *480 C2* N Scotland, UK
Johnston Atoll *535 E1 US unincorporated territory* C Pacific Ocean
Johor Baharu *see* Johor Bahru
Johor Bahru *530 B3 var.* Johor Baharu, Johore Bahru. Johor, Peninsular Malaysia
Johore Bahru *see* Johor Bahru
Johore Strait *530 A1 Mal.* Selat Johor. *strait* Malaysia/Singapore
Joinvile *see* Joinville
Joinville *455 E4 var.* Joinvile. Santa Catarina, S Brazil
Jokkmokk *476 C3* Norrbotten, N Sweden
Joliet *432 B3* Illinois, N USA
Jonava *498 B4 Ger.* Janow, *Pol.* Janów. Jonava, C Lithuania
Jonesboro *434 B1* Arkansas, C USA
Joniškis *498 C3 Ger.* Janischken. Joniškis, N Lithuania
Jönköping *477 B7* Jönköping, S Sweden
Jonquière *431 E4* Quebec, SE Canada
Joplin *437 F5* Missouri, C USA
Jordan *511 B5 Ar.* Urdunn, *Heb.* HaYarden. *river* SW Asia
Jordan *511 B6 off.* Hashemite Kingdom of Jordan, *Ar.* Al Mamlakah al Urdunīyah al Hāshimīyah, Al Urdunn; *prev.* Transjordan. *country* SW Asia
Jorhāt *527 H3* Assam, NE India
Jos *467 G4* Plateau, C Nigeria
Joseph Bonaparte Gulf *538 D2 gulf* N Australia
Jos Plateau *467 G4 plateau* C Nigeria
Jotunheimen *477 A5 mountain range* S Norway
Joûnié *510 A4 var.* Juniyah. W Lebanon
Joure *478 D2 Fris.* De Jouwer. Friesland, N Netherlands

Joutseno *477 E5* Kymi, SE Finland
Jowhar *see* Jawhar
JStorm Thurmond Reservoir *see* Clark Hill Lake
Juan Aldama *442 D3* Zacatecas, C Mexico
Juan de Fuca, Strait of *438 A1 strait* Canada/USA
Juan Fernández, Islas *449 A6 Eng.* Juan Fernandez Islands. *island group* W Chile
Juazeiro *455 G2 prev.* Joazeiro. Bahia, E Brazil
Juazeiro do Norte *455 G2* Ceará, E Brazil
Juba *465 D6 Amh.* Genalē Wenz, *It.* Guiba, *Som.* Ganaane, Webi Jubba. *river* Ethiopia/Somalia
Juba *465 B5 var.* Jūbā. Bahr el Gabel, S Sudan
Júcar *485 E3 var.* Jucar. *river* C Spain
Juchitán *443 F5 var.* Juchitán de Zaragosa. Oaxaca, SE Mexico
Juchitán de Zaragosa *see* Juchitán
Judayyidat Hāmir *512 B3* S Iraq
Judenburg *487 D7* Steiermark, C Austria
Juigalpa *444 D3* Chontales, S Nicaragua
Juiz de Fora *455 F4* Minas Gerais, SE Brazil
Jujuy *see* San Salvador de Jujuy
Jūlā *see* Jālū
Juliaca *453 E4* Puno, SE Peru
Juliana Top *451 G3 mountain* C Surinam
Jumilla *485 E4* Murcia, SE Spain
Jumporn *see* Chumphon
Junction City *437 F4* Kansas, C USA
Juneau *428 D4 state capital* Alaska, USA
Junín *456 C4* Buenos Aires, E Argentina
Junīyah *see* Joûnié
Junkseylon *see* Phuket
Jur *465 B5 river* C Sudan
Jura *480 B4 island* SW Scotland, UK
Jura *487 A7 canton* NW Switzerland
Jura *482 D4 department* E France
Jurbarkas *498 B4 Ger.* Georgenburg, Jurburg. Jurbarkas, W Lithuania
Jūrmala *498 C3* Rīga, C Latvia
Juruá, Rio *454 C2 var.* Río Yuruá. *river* Brazil/Peru
Juruena, Rio *454 D3 river* W Brazil
Jutiapa *444 B2* Jutiapa, S Guatemala
Juticalpa *444 D2* Olancho, C Honduras
Juventud, Isla de la *446 A2 var.* Isla de Pinos, *Eng.* Isle of Youth; *prev.* The Isle of the Pines. *island* W Cuba
Južna Morava *493 E5 Ger.* Südliche Morava. *river* SE Yugoslavia
Juzur Qarqannah *see* Kerkenah, Îles de
Jwaneng *470 C4* Southern, SE Botswana
Jylland *477 A7 Eng.* Jutland. *peninsula* W Denmark
Jyväskylä *477 D5* Keski-Suomi, C Finland

K

K2 *518 A4 Chin.* Qogir Feng, *Eng.* Mount Godwin Austen. *mountain* China/Pakistan
Kaafu Atoll *see* Male' Atoll
Kaaimanston *451 G3* Sipaliwini, N Surinam
Kaakhka *514 C3 var.* Kaka. Akhalskiy Velayat, S Turkmenistan
Kaala *see* Caála
Kaamanen *476 D2 Lapp.* Gámas. Lappi, N Finland
Kaapstad *see* Cape Town
Kaaresuvanto *476 C3 Lapp.* Gárassavon. Lappi, N Finland
Kabale *465 B6* SW Uganda
Kabinda *see* Cabinda
Kabinda *469 D7* Kasai Oriental, SE Congo (Zaire)
Kābol *see* Kābul
Kabompo *470 C2 river* W Zambia
Kābul *515 E4 var.* Kabul, *Per.* Kābol. *country capital* (Afghanistan) Kābul, E Afghanistan
Kabul *see* Kābul
Kabwe *470 D2* Central, C Zambia
Kachchh, Gulf of *526 B4 var.* Gulf of Cutch, Gulf of Kutch. *gulf* W India
Kachchh, Rann of *526 B4 var.* Rann of Kachh, Rann of Kutch. *salt marsh* India/Pakistan
Kachh, Rann of *see* Kachchh, Rann of
Kadan Kyun *529 B5 prev.* King Island. *island* Mergui Archipelago, S Burma
Kadavu *537 E4 prev.* Kandavu. *island* S Fiji
Kadoma *470 D3 prev.* Gatooma. Mashonaland West, C Zimbabwe

Kadugli *464 B4* Southern Kordofan, S Sudan
Kaduna *467 G4* Kaduna, C Nigeria
Kadzhi-Say *515 G2 Kir.* Kajisay. Issyk-Kul'skaya Oblast', NE Kyrgyzstan
Kaédi *466 C3* Gorgol, S Mauritania
Kaffa *see* Feodosiya
Kafue *470 C2 river* C Zambia
Kafue *470 D2* Lusaka, SE Zambia
Kaga Bandoro *468 C4 prev.* Fort-Crampel. Nana-Grébizi, C Central African Republic
Kâgheṭ *466 D1 var.* Karet. *physical region* N Mauritania
Kagi *see* Chiai
Kagoshima *523 B8 var.* Kagosima. Kagoshima, Kyūshū, SW Japan
Kagoshima-wan *523 A8 bay* SW Japan
Kagosima *see* Kagoshima
Kahmard, Daryā-ye *515 E4 prev.* Darya-i-Surkhab. *river* NE Afghanistan
Kahraman Maraş *see* Kahramanmaraş
Kahramanmaraş *508 D4 var.* Kahraman Maraş, Maraş, Marash. Kahramanmaraş, S Turkey
Kaiapoi *543 C6* Canterbury, South Island, NZ
Kaifeng *520 C4* Henan, C China
Kai, Kepulauan *531 F4 prev.* Kei Islands. *island group* Maluku, SE Indonesia
Kaikohe *542 C2* Northland, North Island, NZ
Kaikoura *543 C5* Canterbury, South Island, NZ
Kaikoura Peninsula *543 C5 peninsula* South Island, NZ
Kainji Lake *see* Kainji Reservoir
Kainji Reservoir *467 F4 var.* Kainji Lake. *reservoir* W Nigeria
Kaipara Harbour *542 C2 harbour* North Island, NZ
Kairouan *463 E2 var.* Al Qayrawān. E Tunisia
Kaisaria *see* Kayseri
Kaiserslautern *487 A5* Rheinland-Pfalz, SW Germany
Kaišiadorys *499 B5* Kaišiadorys, S Lithuania
Kaitaia *542 C2* Northland, North Island, NZ
Kajaani *476 E4 Swe.* Kajana. Oulu, C Finland
Kaka *see* Kaakhka
Kake *428 D4* Kupreanof Island, Alaska, USA
Kakhovka *501 F4* Khersons'ka Oblast', S Ukraine
Kakhovs'ka Vodoskhovyshche *501 F4 Rus.* Kakhovskoye Vodokhranilishche. *reservoir* SE Ukraine
Kākināda *524 D1 prev.* Cocanada. Andhra Pradesh, E India
Kaktovik *428 D2* Alaska, USA
Kalahari Desert *470 B4 desert* Southern Africa
Kalamariá *496 B4* Kentrikí Makedonía, N Greece
Kalámata *497 B6 prev.* Kalámai. Pelopónnisos, S Greece
Kalamazoo *432 C3* Michigan, N USA
Kalambaka *see* Kalampáka
Kálamos *497 C5* Attikí, C Greece
Kalampáka *496 B4 var.* Kalambaka. Thessalía, C Greece
Kalanchak *501 F4* Khersons'ka Oblast', S Ukraine
Kalarash *see* Călărași
Kalasin *528 D4 var.* Muang Kalasin. Kalasin, E Thailand
Kalāt *515 E5 Per.* Qalāt. Zābul, S Afghanistan
Kalāt *526 B2 var.* Kelat, Khelat. Baluchistān, SW Pakistan
Kalbarri *539 A5* Western Australia
Kalecik *508 C3* Ankara, N Turkey
Kalemie *469 E6 prev.* Albertville. Shaba, SE Congo (Zaire)
Kale Sultanie *see* Çanakkale
Kalgan *see* Zhangjiakou
Kalgoorlie *539 B6* Western Australia
Kalima *469 D6* Maniema, E Congo (Zaire)
Kalimantan *530 D4 Eng.* Indonesian Borneo. *geopolitical region* Borneo, C Indonesia
Kálimnos *see* Kálymnos
Kaliningrad *see* Kaliningradskaya Oblast'
Kaliningrad *498 A4* Kaliningradskaya Oblast', W Russian Federation
Kaliningradskaya Oblast' *498 B4 var.* Kaliningrad. Admin. region *province and enclave* W Russian Federation
Kalinkavichy *499 C7 Rus.* Kalinkovichi. Homyel'skaya Voblasts', SE Belorussia

Kalispell *436 B1* Montana, NW USA
Kalisz *490 C4 Ger.* Kalisch, *Rus.* Kalish; *anc.* Calisia. Kalisz, C Poland
Kalix *476 D4* Norrbotten, N Sweden
Kalixälven *476 D3 river* N Sweden
Kallaste *498 E3 Ger.* Krasnogor. Tartumaa, SE Estonia
Kallavesi *477 E5 lake* SE Finland
Kalloní *497 D5* Lésvos, E Greece
Kalmar *477 C7 var.* Calmar. Kalmar, S Sweden
Kalmthout *479 C5* Antwerpen, N Belgium
Kalpáki *496 A4* Ípeiros, W Greece
Kalpeni Island *524 B3 island* Lakshadweep, India, N Indian Ocean
Kaluga *503 B5* Kaluzhskaya Oblast', W Russian Federation
Kalush *500 C2 Pol.* Kałusz. Ivano-Frankivs'ka Oblast', W Ukraine
Kalutara *524 D4* Western Province, SW Sri Lanka
Kalvarija *499 B5 Pol.* Kalwaria. Marijampolė, S Lithuania
Kalyān *526 C5* Mahārāshtra, W India
Kálymnos *497 D6 var.* Kálimnos. *island* Dodekánisos, Greece, Aegean Sea
Kama *502 D4 river* NW Russian Federation
Kamarang *451 F3* W Guyana
Kamchatka *505 see* Kamchatka, Poluostrov
Kamchatka, Poluostrov *507 G3 Eng.* Kamchatka. *peninsula* E Russian Federation
Kamensk-Shakhtinskiy *503 B6* Rostovskaya Oblast', SW Russian Federation
Kamina *469 D7* Shaba, S Congo (Zaire)
Kamishli *see* Al Qāmishlī
Kamloops *429 E5* British Columbia, SW Canada
Kammu Seamount *544 C2 undersea feature* N Pacific Ocean
Kampala *465 B6 country capital* (Uganda) S Uganda
Kâmpóng Cham *529 D6 prev.* Kompong Cham. Kâmpóng Cham, C Cambodia
Kâmpóng Chhnăng *529 D6 prev.* Kompong. Kâmpóng Chhnăng, C Cambodia
Kâmpóng Saôm *529 D6 prev.* Kompong Som, Sihanoukville. Kâmpóng Saôm, SW Cambodia
Kâmpóng Spoe *529 D6 prev.* Kompong Speu. Kâmpóng Spœ, S Cambodia
Kâmpôt *529 D6* Kâmpôt, SW Cambodia
Kam"yanets'-Podil's'kyy *500 C3 Rus.* Kamenets-Podol'skiy. Khmel'nyts'ka Oblast', W Ukraine
Kam"yanka-Dniprovs'ka *501 F3 Rus.* Kamenka Dneprovskaya. Zaporiz'ka Oblast', SE Ukraine
Kamyshin *503 B6* Volgogradskaya Oblast', SW Russian Federation
Kanaky *see* New Caledonia
Kananga *469 D6 prev.* Luluabourg. Kasai Occidental, S Congo (Zaire)
Kananur *see* Cannanore
Kanara *see* Karnātaka
Kanash *503 C5* Chuvashskaya Respublika, W Russian Federation
Kanazawa *523 C5* Ishikawa, Honshū, SW Japan
Kanbe *528 B4* Yangon, SW Burma
Kānchīpuram *524 C2 prev.* Conjeeveram. Tamil Nādu, SE India
Kandahār *515 E5 Per.* Qandahār. Kandahār, S Afghanistan
Kandalakša *see* Kandalaksha
Kandalaksha *502 B2 var.* Kandalakša, *Fin.* Kantalahti. Murmanskaya Oblast', NW Russian Federation
Kandangan *530 D4* Borneo, C Indonesia
Kandava *498 C3 Ger.* Kandau. Tukums, W Latvia
Kandi *467 F4* N Benin
Kandy *524 D3* Central Province, C Sri Lanka
Kane Fracture Zone *458 B4 tectonic feature* NW Atlantic Ocean
Kaneohe *439 A8 Haw.* Kāne'ohe. Oahu, Hawaii, USA, C Pacific Ocean
Kangān *512 D4* Būshehr, S Iran
Kangaroo Island *541 A7 island* South Australia
Kangertittivaq *475 E4 Dan.* Scoresby Sund. *fjord* E Greenland
Kangikajik *475 E4 var.* Kap Brewster. *headland* E Greenland
Kaniv *501 E2 Rus.* Kanëv. Cherkas'ka Oblast', C Ukraine

Kanivs'ke Vodoskhovyshche *501 E2 Rus.* Kanevskoye Vodokhranilishche. *reservoir* C Ukraine
Kanjiža *492 D2 Ger.* Altkanischa, *Hung.* Magyarkanizsa, Ókanizsa; *prev.* Stara Kanjiža. Serbia, N Yugoslavia
Kankaanpää *477 D5* Turku-Pori, SW Finland
Kankakee *432 B3* Illinois, N USA
Kankan *466 D4* Haute-Guinée, E Guinea
Kannur *see* Cannanore
Kano *467 G4* Kano, N Nigeria
Kānpur *527 E3 Eng.* Cawnpore. Uttar Pradesh, N India
Kansas *441 F1 off.* State of Kansas; also known as Jayhawker State, Sunflower State. *state* C USA
Kansas *437 F5* Kansas, C USA
Kansas City *437 F4* Kansas, C USA
Kansas City *437 F4* Missouri, C USA
Kansas River *437 F5 river* Kansas, C USA
Kansk *507 E4* Krasnoyarskiy Kray, S Russian Federation
Kansu *see* Gansu
Kantalahti *see* Kandalaksha
Kántanos *497 C7* Kríti, Greece, E Mediterranean Sea
Kantemirovka *503 B6* Voronezhskaya Oblast', W Russian Federation
Kanton *537 F3 var.* Abariringa, Canton Island; *prev.* Mary Island. *atoll* Phoenix Islands, C Kiribati
Kanye *470 C4* Southern, SE Botswana
Kaohsiung *520 D6 var.* Gaoxiong, *Jap.* Takao, Takow. S Taiwan
Kaolack *466 B3 var.* Kaolak. W Senegal
Kaolak *see* Kaolack
Kaolan *see* Lanzhou
Kaoma *470 C2* Western, W Zambia
Kap Brewster *see* Kangikajik
Kapelle *479 B5* Zeeland, SW Netherlands
Kapellen *479 C5* Antwerpen, N Belgium
Kap Farvel *see* Uummannarsuaq
Kapka, Massif du *468 C2 mountain range* E Chad
Kaplangky, Plato *514 C2 ridge* Turkmenistan/Uzbekistan
Kapoeta *465 C5* Eastern Equatoria, SE Sudan
Kaposvár *491 C7* Somogy, SW Hungary
Kappeln *486 B2* Schleswig-Holstein, N Germany
Kapstad *see* Cape Town
Kaptsevichy *499 C7 Rus.* Koptsevichi. Homyel'skaya Voblasts', SE Belorussia
Kapuas, Sungai *530 C4 prev.* Kapoeas. *river* Borneo, C Indonesia
Kapuskasing *430 C4* Ontario, S Canada
Kapyl' *499 C6 Rus.* Kopyl'. Minskaya Voblasts', C Belorussia
Kap York *see* Innaanganeq
Kara-Balta *515 F2* Chuyskaya Oblast', N Kyrgyzstan
Karabil', Vozvyshennost' *514 D3 mountain range* S Turkmenistan
Karabük *508 C2* Zonguldak, N Turkey
Karāchi *526 B3* Sind, SE Pakistan
Karadeniz *see* Black Sea
Karadeniz Boğazı *see* İstanbul Boğazı
Karaferiye *see* Véroia
Karaganda *506 C4 Kaz.* Qaraghandy. Karaganda, C Kazakhstan
Karaginskiy, Ostrov *507 H2 island* E Russian Federation
Karak *see* Al Karak
Kara-Kala *514 C3 var.* Garrygala. Balkanskiy Velayat, W Turkmenistan
Karakax *see* Moyu
Karakılısse *see* Ağrı
Karakol *515 G2 prev.* Przheval'sk. Issyk-Kul'skaya Oblast', NE Kyrgyzstan
Karakol *515 G2 var.* Karakolka. Issyk-Kul'skaya Oblast', NE Kyrgyzstan
Karakolka *see* Karakol
Karakoram Range *526 D1 mountain range* C Asia
Karaköse *see* Ağrı
Kara Kum *504 see* Garagumy
Kara Kum Canal *see* Garagumskiy Kanal
Karakumskiy Kanal *see* Garagumskiy Kanal
Karamai *see* Karamay
Karaman *508 C4* Karaman, S Turkey

Karamay – Kirkūk

Karamay 518 B2 var. Karamai, Kelamayi, prev. Chin. K'o-la-ma-i. Xinjiang Uygur Zizhiqu, NW China
Karamea Bight 543 B5 gulf South Island, NZ
Karapelit 496 E1 Rom. Stejarul. Varnenska Oblast, NE Bulgaria
Kara-Say 515 G2 Issyk-Kul'skaya Oblast', NE Kyrgyzstan
Karasburg 470 B4 Karas, S Namibia
Kara Sea 548 see Karskoye More
Karatau 506 C5 Kaz. Qarataū. Zhambyl, S Kazakhstan
Karavás 497 B7 Kýthira, S Greece
Karbalā' 512 B3 var. Kerbala, Kerbela. S Iraq
Kardhítsa see Kardítsa
Kardítsa 497 B5 var. Kardhítsa. Thessalía, C Greece
Kärdla 498 C2 Ger. Kertel. Hiiumaa, W Estonia
Karet see Kâgheṭ
Kargı 508 C2 Çorum, N Turkey
Kargilik see Yecheng
Kariba 470 D2 Mashonaland West, N Zimbabwe
Kariba, Lake 470 D3 reservoir Zambia/Zimbabwe
Karibib 470 B3 Erongo, C Namibia
Karies see Karyés
Karigasniemi 476 D2 Lapp. Garegegasnjárga. Lappi, N Finland
Karimata, Selat 530 C4 strait W Indonesia
Karīmnagar 526 D5 Andhra Pradesh, C India
Karin 464 D4 Woqooyi Galbeed, N Somalia
Kariot see Ikaría
Káristos see Kárystos
Karkinits'ka Zatoka 501 E4 Rus. Karkinitskiy Zaliv. gulf S Ukraine
Karkūk see Kirkūk
Karlovac 492 B3 Ger. Karlstadt, Hung. Károlyváros. Karlovac, C Croatia
Karlovy Vary 491 A5 Ger. Karlsbad; prev. Eng. Carlsbad. Západní Čechy, W Czech Republic
Karlskrona 477 C7 Blekinge, S Sweden
Karlsruhe 487 B6 var. Carlsruhe. Baden-Württemberg, SW Germany
Karlstad 477 B6 Värmland, C Sweden
Karnāl 526 D2 Haryāna, N India
Karnātaka 524 C1 var. Kanara; prev. Maisur, Mysore. Admin. region state W India
Karnobat 496 D2 Burgaska Oblast, E Bulgaria
Karnul see Kurnool
Karpaten see Carpathian Mountains
Kárpathos 497 E7 It. Scarpanto; anc. Carpathos, Carpathus. island SE Greece
Kárpathos 497 E7 Kárpathos, SE Greece
Karpaty see Carpathian Mountains
Karpenísi 497 B5 prev. Karpenísion. Stereá Ellás, C Greece
Kars 509 F2 var. Qars. Kars, NE Turkey
Kārsava 498 D4 Ger. Karsau; prev. Rus. Korsovka. Ludza, E Latvia
Karskiye Vorota, Proliv 502 E2 Eng. Kara Strait. strait N Russian Federation
Karskoye More 506 D2 Eng. Kara Sea. sea Arctic Ocean
Karyés 496 C4 var. Karies. Ágion Óros, N Greece
Kárystos 497 C6 var. Káristos. Évvoia, C Greece
Kasai 469 C6 var. Cassai, Kassai. river Angola/Congo (Zaire)
Kasaji 469 D7 Shaba, S Congo (Zaire)
Kasama 470 D1 Northern, N Zambia
Kāsaragod 524 B2 Kerala, SW India
Kāshān 512 C3 Eşfahān, C Iran
Kashi 518 A3 Chin. Kaxgar, K'o-shih, Uigh. Kashgar. Xinjiang Uygur Zizhiqu, NW China
Kasongo 469 D6 Maniema, E Congo (Zaire)
Kasongo-Lunda 469 C7 Bandundu, SW Congo (Zaire)
Kásos 497 D7 island S Greece
Kaspiysk 503 B8 Respublika Dagestan, SW Russian Federation
Kassai see Kasai
Kassala 464 C4 Kassala, E Sudan
Kassel 486 B4 prev. Cassel. Hessen, C Germany
Kasserine 463 E2 var. Al Qaşrayn. W Tunisia
Kastamonu 508 C2 var. Castamoni, Kastamuni. Kastamonu, N Turkey
Kastamuni see Kastamonu
Kastaneá 496 B4 Kentrikí Makedonía, N Greece
Kastélli 497 C7 Kríti, Greece, E Mediterranean Sea
Kastoría 496 B4 Dytikí Makedonía, N Greece
Kástro 497 C6 Sífnos, Kykládes, Greece, Aegean Sea
Kastsyukovichy 499 E7 Rus. Kostyukovichi. Mahilyowskaya Voblasts', E Belorussia
Kastsyukowka 499 D7 Rus. Kostyukovka. Homyel'skaya Voblasts', SE Belorussia
Kasulu 465 B7 Kigoma, W Tanzania
Kasumiga-ura 523 D5 lake Honshū, S Japan
Katahdin, Mount 433 G1 mountain Maine, NE USA
Katalla 428 C3 Alaska, USA
Katana see Qaṭanā
Katanning 539 B7 Western Australia
Katawaz see Zarghūn Shahr
Katchall Island 525 F3 island Nicobar Islands, India, NE Indian Ocean
Kateríni 496 B4 Kentrikí Makedonía, N Greece
Katha 528 B2 Sagaing, N Burma
Katherine 540 A2 Northern Territory, N Australia
Kathmandu 516 C3 prev. Kantipur. country capital (Nepal) Central, C Nepal
Katikati 542 D3 Bay of Plenty, North Island, NZ
Katima Mulilo 470 C3 Caprivi, NE Namibia
Katiola 466 D4 C Ivory Coast
Káto Achaïa 497 B5 var. Kato Ahaia, Káto Akhaía. Dytikí Ellás, S Greece
Kato Ahaia see Káto Achaïa
Káto Akhaía see Káto Achaïa
Katoúna 497 A5 Dytikí Ellás, C Greece
Katowice 491 C5 Ger. Kattowitz. Katowice, S Poland
Katsina 467 G3 Katsina, N Nigeria
Kattaqŭrghon 515 E2 Rus. Kattakurgan. Samarqand Wiloyati, C Uzbekistan
Kattavía 497 E7 Ródos, Dodekánisos, Greece, Aegean Sea
Kattegat 477 B7 Dan. Kattegatt. strait N Europe
Kauai 439 A7 Haw. Kaua'i. island Hawaiian Islands, Hawaii, USA, C Pacific Ocean
Kaufbeuren 487 C6 Bayern, S Germany
Kaunas 498 B4 Ger. Kauen, Pol. Kowno; prev. Rus. Kovno. Kaunas, C Lithuania
Kavadarci 493 E6 Turk. Kavadar. C FYR Macedonia
Kavajë 493 C6 It. Cavaia, Kavaja. Tiranë, W Albania
Kavála 496 C3 prev. Kaválla. Anatolikí Makedonía kai Thráki, NE Greece
Kāvali 524 D2 Andhra Pradesh, E India
Kavango see Cubango
Kavaratti Island 524 A3 island Lakshadweep, India, N Indian Ocean
Kavarna 496 E2 Varnenska Oblast, NE Bulgaria
Kavengo see Cubango
Kavīr, Dasht-e 512 D3 var. Great Salt Desert. salt pan N Iran
Kavīr-e Lūt see Lūt, Dasht-e
Kawagoe 523 D5 Saitama, Honshū, S Japan
Kawasaki 522 A2 Kanagawa, Honshū, S Japan
Kawerau 542 E3 Bay of Plenty, North Island, NZ
Kaya 467 E3 C Burkina
Kayan 528 B4 Yangon, SW Burma
Kayan, Sungai 530 D3 prev. Kajan. river Borneo, C Indonesia
Kayes 466 C3 Kayes, W Mali
Kayseri 508 D3 var. Kaisaria; anc. Caesarea Mazaca, Mazaca. Kayseri, C Turkey
Kazach'ye 507 F2 Respublika Sakha (Yakutiya), NE Russian Federation
Kazakhskiy Melkosopochnik 506 C4 Eng. Kazakh Uplands, Kirghiz Steppe, Kaz. Saryarqa. uplands C Kazakhstan
Kazakhstan 506 B4 off. Republic of Kazakhstan, var. Kazakstan, Kaz. Qazaqstan, Qazaqstan Respublikasy; prev. Kazakh Soviet Socialist Republic, Rus. Kazakhskaya SSR. country C Asia
Kazakh Uplands 504 see Kazakhskiy Melkosopochnik
Kazan' 503 C5 Respublika Tatarstan, W Russian Federation
Kazanlŭk 496 D2 prev. Kazanlik. Khaskovska Oblast, C Bulgaria
Kazbegi see Kazbek
Kazbek 509 F1 var. Kazbegi, Geor. Mqinvartsveri. mountain N Georgia
Kāzerūn 512 D4 Fārs, S Iran
Kazvin see Qazvīn
Kéa 497 C6 prev. Kéos, anc. Ceos. island Kykládes, Greece, Aegean Sea
Kéa 497 C6 Kéa, Kykládes, Greece, Aegean Sea
Kea, Mauna 439 B8 mountain Hawaii, USA, C Pacific Ocean
Kéamu see Anatom
Kearney 437 E4 Nebraska, C USA
Keban Barajı 509 E3 reservoir C Turkey
Kebkabiya 464 A4 Northern Darfur, W Sudan
Kebnekaise 476 C3 mountain N Sweden
Kecskemét 491 D7 Bács-Kiskun, C Hungary
Kediri 530 D5 Jawa, C Indonesia
Keelung see Chilung
Keetmanshoop 470 B4 Karas, S Namibia
Kefallinía 497 A5 var. Kefallonía. island Iónioi Nísoi, Greece, C Mediterranean Sea
Kefallonía see Kefallinía
Kefe see Feodosiya
Kehl 487 A6 Baden-Württemberg, SW Germany
Keila 498 D2 Ger. Kegel. Harjumaa, NW Estonia
Keïta 467 F3 Tahoua, C Niger
Keitele 476 D4 lake C Finland
Keith 541 B7 South Australia
Këk-Art 515 G2 prev. Alaykel', Alay-Kuu. Oshskaya Oblast', SW Kyrgyzstan
Kékes 491 C6 mountain N Hungary
Kelamayi see Karamay
Kelang see Klang
Kelat see Kalāt
Kelifskiy Uzboy 514 D3 salt marsh E Turkmenistan
Kelkit Çayı 509 E3 river N Turkey
Kelmė 498 B4 Kelmė, C Lithuania
Kélo 468 B4 Tandjilé, SW Chad
Kelowna 429 E5 British Columbia, SW Canada
Kelso 438 B2 Washington, NW USA
Keluang 530 B3 var. Kluang. Johor, Peninsular Malaysia
Kem' 502 B3 Respublika Kareliya, NW Russian Federation
Kemah 509 E3 Erzincan, E Turkey
Kemaman see Cukai
Kemerovo 506 D4 prev. Shcheglovsk. Kemerovskaya Oblast', C Russian Federation
Kemi 476 D4 Lappi, NW Finland
Kemijärvi 476 D3 Swe. Kemiträsk. Lappi, N Finland
Kemijoki 476 D3 river NW Finland
Kemin 515 G2 prev. Bystrovka. Chuyskaya Oblast', N Kyrgyzstan
Kempele 476 D4 Oulu, C Finland
Kempten 487 B7 Bayern, S Germany
Kendal 481 D5 NW England, UK
Kendari 531 E4 Sulawesi, C Indonesia
Kenedy 441 G4 Texas, SW USA
Kenema 466 C4 SE Sierra Leone
Këneurgench 514 C2 Turkm. Köneürgench; prev. Kunya-Urgench. Dashkhovuzskiy Velayat, N Turkmenistan
Kenge 469 C6 Bandundu, SW Congo (Zaire)
Keng Tung 528 C3 var. Kentung. Shan State, E Burma
Kénitra 462 C2 prev. Port-Lyautey. NW Morocco
Kennett 437 H5 Missouri, C USA
Kennewick 438 C2 Washington, NW USA
Kenora 430 A3 Ontario, S Canada
Kenosha 432 B3 Wisconsin, N USA
Kentau 506 B5 Yuzhnyy Kazakhstan, S Kazakhstan
Kentucky 432 C5 off. Commonwealth of Kentucky; also known as The Bluegrass State. state C USA
Kentucky Lake 432 B5 reservoir Kentucky/Tennessee, S USA
Kentung see Keng Tung
Kenya 465 C6 off. Republic of Kenya. country E Africa
Keokuk 437 G4 Iowa, C USA
Kępno 490 C4 Kalisz, C Poland
Keppel Island see Niuatoputapu
Kepulauan Sangihe see Sangir, Kepulauan
Kerak see Al Karak
Kerala 524 C2 state S India
Kerasunt see Giresun
Keratea see Keratéa
Keratéa 497 C6 var. Keratea. Attikí, C Greece
Kerbala see Karbalā'
Kerbela see Karbalā'
Kerch 501 G5 Rus. Kerch'. Respublika Krym, SE Ukraine
Kerchens'ka Protska see Kerch Strait
Kerchenskiy Proliv see Kerch Strait
Kerch Strait 501 G4 var. Bosporus Cimmerius, Enikale Strait, Rus. Kerchenskiy Proliv, Ukr. Kerchens'ka Protska. strait Black Sea/Sea of Azov
Kerguelen 533 C7 island C French Southern and Antarctic Territories
Kerguelen Plateau 533 C7 undersea feature S Indian Ocean
Kerí 497 A6 Zákynthos, Iónioi Nísoi, Greece, C Mediterranean Sea
Kerikeri 542 D2 Northland, North Island, NZ
Kerkenah, Îles de 494 D4 var. Kerkenna Islands, Ar. Juzur Qarqannah. island group E Tunisia
Kerkenna Islands see Kerkenah, Îles de
Kerki 514 D3 Lebapskiy Velayat, E Turkmenistan
Kérkira see Kérkyra
Kerkrade 479 D6 Limburg, SE Netherlands
Kerkuk see Kirkūk
Kérkyra 496 A4 var. Kérkira, Eng. Corfu. island Iónioi Nísoi, Greece, C Mediterranean Sea
Kermadec Islands 544 C4 island group NZ, SW Pacific Ocean
Kermadec Trench 535 E4 undersea feature SW Pacific Ocean
Kermān 512 D3 var. Kirman; anc. Carmana. Kermān, C Iran
Kerrville 441 F4 Texas, SW USA
Kerulen 519 E2 Chin. Herlen He, Mong. Herlen Gol. river China/Mongolia
Kerýneia 494 C5 var. Girne, Kyrenia. N Cyprus
Kesennuma 522 D4 Miyagi, Honshū, C Japan
Keszthely 491 C7 Zala, SW Hungary
Ketchikan 428 D4 Revillagigedo Island, Alaska, USA
Kettering 481 D6 C England, UK
Kettering 432 C4 Ohio, N USA
Keuruu 477 D5 Keski-Suomi, C Finland
Keweenaw Peninsula 432 B1 peninsula Michigan, N USA
Key Largo 435 F5 Key Largo, Florida, SE USA
Key West 435 E5 Florida Keys, Florida, SE USA
Khabarovsk 507 G4 Khabarovskiy Kray, SE Russian Federation
Khairpur 526 B3 Sind, SE Pakistan
Khalīj al 'Aqabah see Aqaba, Gulf of
Khalīj al 'Arabī see Gulf, The
Khalīj-e Fars see Gulf, The
Khalkidhikí see Chalkidikí
Khalkís see Chalkída
Khambhāt, Gulf of 526 C4 Eng. Gulf of Cambay. gulf W India
Khamīs Mushayt 513 B6 var. Hamīs Musait. 'Asīr, SW Saudi Arabia
Khānābād 515 E3 Kunduz, NE Afghanistan
Khān al Baghdādī see Al Baghdādī
Khandwa 526 D4 Madhya Pradesh, C India
Khanh see Soc Trăng
Khaniá see Chaniá
Khanka, Lake 521 E2 var. Hsing-k'ai Hu, Lake Hanka, Chin. Xingkai Hu, Rus. Ozero Khanka. lake China/Russian Federation
Khanthabouli 528 D4 prev. Savannakhét. Savannakhét, S Laos
Khanty-Mansiysk 506 C3 prev. Ostyako-Voguls'k. Khanty-Mansiyskiy Avtonomnyy Okrug, C Russian Federation
Khān Yūnis 511 A7 var. Khān Yūnus. S Gaza Strip
Khān Yūnus see Khān Yūnis
Khanzi see Ghanzi
Kharagpur 527 F4 West Bengal, NE India
Kharbin see Harbin
Kharkiv 501 G2 Rus. Khar'kov. Kharkivs'ka Oblast', NE Ukraine
Kharmanli 496 D3 Khaskovska Oblast, S Bulgaria
Khartoum 464 B4 var. El Khartûm, Khartum. country capital (Sudan) Khartoum, C Sudan
Khartum see Khartoum
Khasavyurt 503 B8 Respublika Dagestan, SW Russian Federation
Khāsh, Dasht-e 514 D5 Eng. Khash Desert. desert SW Afghanistan
Khashim Al Qirba see Khashm el Girba
Khashm al Qirbah see Khashm el Girba
Khashm el Girba 464 C4 var. Khashim Al Qirba, Khashm al Qirbah. Kassala, E Sudan
Khaskovo 496 D3 Khaskovska Oblast, S Bulgaria
Khaydarkan 515 F2 var. Khaydarken. Oshskaya Oblast', SW Kyrgyzstan
Khaydarken see Khaydarkan
Khelat see Kalāt
Kherson 501 E4 Khersons'ka Oblast', S Ukraine
Kheta 507 E2 river N Russian Federation
Khíos see Chíos
Khiwa 514 D2 Rus. Khiva. Khorazm Wiloyati, W Uzbekistan
Khmel'nyts'kyy 500 C2 Rus. Khmel'nitskiy; prev. Proskurov. Khmel'nyts'ka Oblast', W Ukraine
Khodasy 499 E6 Rus. Khodosy. Mahilyowskaya Voblasts', E Belorussia
Khodoriv 500 C2 Pol. Chodorów, Rus. Khodorov. L'vivs'ka Oblast', NW Ukraine
Khodzhent see Khŭjand
Khoi see Khvoy
Khojend see Khŭjand
Khokand see Qŭqon
Kholm 515 E3 var. Tashqurghan, Pash. Khulm. Balkh, N Afghanistan
Khoms see Al Khums
Khong Sedone see Muang Khôngxédôn
Khon Kaen 528 D4 var. Muang Khon Kaen. Khon Kaen, E Thailand
Khor 507 G4 Khabarovskiy Kray, SE Russian Federation
Khorat see Nakhon Ratchasima
Khorugh 515 F3 Rus. Khorog. S Tajikistan
Khotan see Hotan
Khouribga 462 B2 C Morocco
Khovd see Hovd
Khowst 515 F4 Paktīā, E Afghanistan
Khoy see Khvoy
Khoyniki 499 D8 Rus. Khoyniki. Homyel'skaya Voblasts', SE Belorussia
Khrebet Kolymskiy see Kolyma Range
Khrebet Kopetdag see Koppeh Dāgh
Khrebet Lomonsova see Lomonosov Ridge
Khudzhand see Khŭjand
Khŭjand 515 E2 var. Khodzhent, Khojend, Rus. Khudzhand; prev. Leninabad, Taj. Leninobod. N Tajikistan
Khulm see Kholm
Khulna 527 G4 Khulna, SW Bangladesh
Khums see Al Khums
Khust 500 B3 Cz. Chust, Husté, Hung. Huszt. Zakarpats'ka Oblast', W Ukraine
Khvoy 512 C2 var. Khoi, Khoy. Āzarbāyjān-e Bākhtarī, NW Iran
Khyber Pass 526 C1 var. Kowtal-e Khaybar. pass Afghanistan/Pakistan
Kiangmai see Chiang Mai
Kiang-ning see Nanjing
Kiangsi see Jiangxi
Kiangsu see Jiangsu
Kiáto 497 B6 prev. Kiáton. Pelopónnisos, S Greece
Kiayi see Chiai
Kibangou 469 B6 Le Niari, SW Congo
Kibombo 469 D6 Maniema, E Congo (Zaire)
Kičevo 493 D6 SW FYR Macedonia
Kidderminster 481 D6 C England, UK
Kiel 486 B2 Schleswig-Holstein, N Germany
Kielce 490 D4 Rus. Keltsy. Kielce, SE Poland
Kieler Bucht 486 B2 bay N Germany
Kiev see Kyyiv
Kiffa 466 C3 Assaba, S Mauritania
Kigali 465 B6 country capital (Rwanda) C Rwanda
Kigoma 465 B7 Kigoma, W Tanzania
Kihnu 498 C2 var. Kihnu Saar, Ger. Kühnö. island SW Estonia
Kihnu Saar see Kihnu
Kii-suidō 523 C7 strait S Japan
Kikinda 492 D3 Ger. Grosskikinda, Hung. Nagykikinda; prev. Velika Kikinda. Serbia, N Yugoslavia
Kikládhes see Kykládes
Kikwit 469 C6 Bandundu, W Congo (Zaire)
Kilien Mountains see Qilian Shan
Kilimane see Quelimane
Kilimanjaro 465 C7 var. Uhuru Peak. mountain NE Tanzania
Kilimanjaro 461 E5 region E Tanzania
Kilingi-Nõmme 498 D3 Ger. Kurkund. Pärnumaa, SW Es
Kilis 508 D4 Gaziantep, S Tur
Kiliya 500 D4 Rom. Chilia-N Odes'ka Oblast', SW Ukrain
Kilkenny 481 B6 Ir. Cill Chair S Ireland
Kilkís 496 B3 Kentrikí Maked N Greece
Killarney 481 A6 Ir. Cill Airn SW Ireland
Killeen 441 G3 Texas, SW US
Kilmain see Quelimane
Kilmarnock 480 C4 W Scotla UK
Kilwa see Kilwa Kivinje
Kilwa Kivinje 465 C7 var. Kil Lindi, SE Tanzania
Kimberley 470 C4 Northern C South Africa
Kimberley Plateau 538 C3 pl Western Australia
Kimch'aek 521 E3 prev. Sŏng E North Korea
Kinabalu, Gunung 530 D3 mountain East Malaysia
Kindersley 429 F5 Saskatchev S Canada
Kindia 466 C4 Guinée-Mariti SW Guinea
Kindley Field 434 A4 air base E Bermuda
Kindu 469 D6 prev. Kindu-Po Empain. Maniema, C Congo (Zaire)
Kineshma 503 C5 Ivanovskay Oblast', W Russian Federati
King Island 541 B8 island Tasmania, SE Australia
Kingman 440 A1 Arizona, SV
Kingman Reef 537 E2 US ter C Pacific Ocean
Kingsford Smith 540 E2 international airport (Sydney South Wales, SE Australia
King's Lynn 481 E6 var. Bish Lynn, Kings Lynn, Lynn, Ly Regis. E England, UK
King Sound 538 B3 sound W Australia
Kingsport 435 E1 Tennessee,
Kingston 446 B5 country cap (Jamaica) E Jamaica
Kingston 433 F3 New York, NE USA
Kingston 430 D5 Ontario, SE Canada
Kingston upon Hull 481 D5 Hull. E England, UK
Kingston upon Thames 481 SE England, UK
Kingstown 447 H4 country c (Saint Vincent and the Grenadines) Saint Vincent, Vincent and the Grenadines
Kingsville 441 G5 Texas, SW
King William Island 429 F3 Nunavut, N Canada Arctic
Kinrooi 479 D5 Limburg, NE Belgium
Kinshasa 469 B6 prev. Léopol country capital (Congo (Zai Kinshasa, W Congo (Zaire)
Kintyre 480 B4 peninsula W Scotland, UK
Kinyeti 465 B5 mountain S Su
Kiparissía see Kyparissía
Kipili 465 B7 Rukwa, W Tanz
Kipushi 469 D8 Shaba, SE Co (Zaire)
Kirdzhali see Kŭrdzhali
Kirghiz Range 515 F2 Rus. Kirgizskiy Khrebet; prev. Alexander Range. mountain Kazakhstan/Kyrgyzstan
Kirghiz Steppe 504 see Kazal Melkosopochnik
Kiriath-Arba see Hebron
Kiribati 537 F2 off. Republic Kiribati. country C Pacific O
Kırıkhan 508 D4 Hatay, S Tu
Kırıkkale 508 C3 Kırıkkale, C Turkey
Kirin see Jilin
Kirinyaga 465 C6 prev. Mour Kenya. volcano C Kenya
Kirishi 502 B4 var. Kirisi. Leningradskaya Oblast', NW Russian Federation
Kirisi see Kirishi
Kiritimati 537 G2 prev. Chris Island. atoll Line Islands, E
Kirkenes 476 E2 var. Kirkkor Finnmark, N Norway
Kirkkoniemi see Kirkenes
Kirkland Lake 430 D4 Ontar S Canada
Kırklareli 508 A2 prev. Kirk-Kilise. Kırklareli, NW Turkey
Kirkpatrick, Mount 546 B3 mountain Antarctica
Kirksville 437 G4 Missouri,
Kirkūk 512 B3 var. Karkūk, K N Iraq

all 480 C2 NE Scotland, UK
ood 437 G4 Missouri, C USA
n see Kermān
ab see Al Karak
503 C5 prev. Vyatka. skaya Oblast', NW Russian ation
-Chepetsk 503 D5 skaya Oblast', NW Russian ation
hrad 501 E3 Rus. ograd; prev. Kirovo, vetgrad, Zinov'yevsk. ohrads'ka Oblast', C Ukraine
r Range 526 B3 mountain S Pakistan
see Chilung
a 476 C3 Norrbotten, eden
gani 469 D5 prev. Stanleyville. -Zaïre, NE Congo (Zaire)
odsk 503 B7 Stavropol'skiy SW Russian Federation
ayo 465 D6 var. Chisimayu, ayu, It. Chisimaio. Jubbada e, S Somalia
yu see Kismaayo
ougou 466 C4 Guinée-stière, S Guinea
mee, Lake 435 E4 lake da, SE USA
u 465 C6 prev. Port Florence. za, W Kenya
da 491 E6 Ger. Kleinwardein. olcs-Szatmár-Bereg, ngary
56 D3 Kayes, W Mali
ūshū 523 A7 var. yûsyû. Fukuoka, Kyūshū, apan
ûsyû see Kitakyūshū
i 522 D2 Hokkaidō, NE Japan
ner 430 C5 Ontario, nada
a see Kýthira
os see Kýthnos
at 428 D4 British Columbia, Canada
n 476 D3 river N Finland
515 E3 Rus. Kitab. qadaryo Wiloyati, bekistan
470 D2 var. Kitwe-Nkana. perbelt, C Zambia
-Nkana see Kitwe
ihler Alpen 487 C7 mountain W Austria
na 428 C2 Alaska, USA
476 D3 ridge C Finland
si 500 C1 Pol. Kiwerce, Rus. tsy. Volyns'ka Oblast', Ukraine
Lake 469 E6 Fr. Lac Kivu. lake nda/Congo (Zaire)
rmak 508 C3 river C Turkey
Kum see Kyzyl Kum
o 491 A5 Střední Čechy, Czech Republic
nfurt 487 D7 Slvn. Celovec. ten, S Austria
da 498 B3 Ger. Memel. pėda, NW Lithuania
ath Falls 438 B4 Oregon, USA
ath Mountains 438 A4 ntain range California/Oregon, SA
530 B3 var. Kelang; prev. Port tenham. Selangor, Peninsular aysia
ven 477 B6 river way/Sweden
vy 491 A5 Ger. Klattau. dní Čechy, SW Czech ublic
naveen 478 E2 Drenthe, Netherlands
Karas 470 B4 Karas, mibia
úra 497 A5 Ípeiros, W Greece
sdorp 470 D4 North-West, outh Africa
vichy 499 E7 Rus. novichi. Mahilyowskaya asts', E Belorussia
y 503 A5 Bryanskaya Oblast', ussian Federation
a 496 C2 Plovdivska Oblast, lgaria
492 B3 NW Bosnia and zegovina
ck 490 C4 Częstochowa, land
ers 487 B7 Graubünden, witzerland
g see Keluang
bork 490 C4 Ger. Kreuzburg, uzburg in Oberschlesien. le, SW Poland
hevskaya Sopka, Vulkan H3 volcano E Russian eration
492 B4 Zadar-Knin, S Croatia
evac 492 E4 Serbia, goslavia
Knokke-Heist 479 A5 West-Vlaanderen, NW Belgium
Knoxville 434 D1 Tennessee, S USA
Knud Rasmussen Land 474 D1 physical region N Greenland
Kōbe 523 C6 Hyōgo, Honshū, SW Japan
København 477 B7 Eng. Copenhagen; anc. Hafnia. country capital (Denmark) Sjælland, København, E Denmark
Kobenni 466 D3 Hodh el Gharbi, S Mauritania
Koblenz 487 A5 prev. Coblenz, Fr. Coblence, anc. Confluentes. Rheinland-Pfalz, W Germany
Kobra 527 E4 Madhya Pradesh, C India
Kobryn 499 A6 Pol. Kobryn, Rus. Kobrin. Brestskaya Voblasts', SW Belorussia
K'obulet'i 509 F2 W Georgia
Kočani 493 E6 NE FYR Macedonia
Kočevje 487 D8 Ger. Gottschee. S Slovenia
Koch Bihār 527 G3 West Bengal, NE India
Kōchi 523 B7 var. Kôti. Kōchi, Shikoku, SW Japan
Kochi see Cochin
Kochiu see Gejiu
Kodiak 428 C3 Kodiak Island, Alaska, USA
Kodiak Island 428 C3 island Alaska, USA
Koeln see Köln
Ko-erh-mu see Golmud
Koetai see Mahakam, Sungai
Koetaradja see Bandaaceh
Kōfu 523 D5 var. Kôhu. Yamanashi, Honshū, S Japan
Kogarah 540 E2 New South Wales, SE Australia
Kogon 514 D2 Rus. Kagan. Bukhoro Wiloyati, C Uzbekistan
Kohīma 527 H3 Nāgāland, E India
Koh I Noh see Büyükağrı Dağı
Kohtla-Järve 498 E2 Ida-Virumaa, NE Estonia
Kôhu see Kōfu
Kokand see Qŭqon
Kokkola 476 D4 Swe. Karleby; prev. Swe. Gamlakarleby. Vaasa, W Finland
Koko see Qinghai Hu
Koko 467 F4 Kebbi, W Nigeria
Kokomo 432 C4 Indiana, N USA
Koko Nor see Qinghai
Kokrines 428 C2 Alaska, USA
Kokshaal-Tau 515 G2 Rus. Khrebet Kakshaal-Too. mountain range China/Kyrgyzstan
Kokshetau 506 C4 Kaz. Kökshetaū; prev. Kokchetav. Kokshetau, N Kazakhstan
Koksijde 479 A5 West-Vlaanderen, W Belgium
Koksoak 430 D2 river Quebec, E Canada
Kokstad 470 D5 KwaZulu/Natal, E South Africa
Kola see Kol'skiy Poluostrov
Kolaka 531 E4 Sulawesi, C Indonesia
Kolam see Quilon
K'o-la-ma-i see Karamay
Kola Peninsula 548 see Kol'skiy Poluostrov
Kolari 476 D3 Lappi, NW Finland
Kolárovo 491 C6 Ger. Gutta; prev. Guta, Hung. Gúta. Západné Slovensko, SW Slovakia
Kolda 466 C3 S Senegal
Kolding 477 A7 Vejle, C Denmark
Kölen 473 E1 Nor. Kjølen. mountain range Norway/Sweden
Kolguyev, Ostrov 502 C2 island NW Russian Federation
Kolhāpur 524 B1 Mahārāshtra, SW India
Kolhumadulu Atoll 524 A5 var. Kolumadulu Atoll, Thaa Atoll. atoll S Maldives
Kolín 491 B5 Ger. Kolin. Střední Čechy, C Czech Republic
Kolka 498 C2 Talsi, NW Latvia
Kolkasrags 498 C2 prev. Eng. Cape Domesnes. headland NW Latvia
Kollam see Quilon
Köln 486 A4 var. Koeln, Eng./Fr. Cologne; prev. Cöln, anc. Colonia Agrippina, Oppidum Ubiorum. Nordrhein-Westfalen, W Germany
Koło 490 C3 Konin, C Poland
Kołobrzeg 490 B2 Ger. Kolberg. Koszalin, NW Poland
Kolokani 466 D3 Koulikoro, W Mali
Kolomna 503 B5 Moskovskaya Oblast', W Russian Federation
Kolomyya 500 C3 Ger. Kolomea. Ivano-Frankivs'ka Oblast', W Ukraine
Kolpa 492 A2 Ger. Kulpa, SCr. Kupa. river Croatia/Slovenia
Kolpino 502 B4 Leningradskaya Oblast', NW Russian Federation
Kólpos Ammóchostos 494 C5 var. Famagusta Bay. bay E Cyprus
Kol'skiy Poluostrov 502 C2 Eng. Kola Peninsula. peninsula NW Russian Federation
Kolumadulu Atoll see Kolhumadulu Atoll
Kolwezi 469 D7 Shaba, S Congo (Zaire)
Kolyma 507 G2 river NE Russian Federation
Kolyma Range 505 G2 var. Khrebet Kolymskiy, Eng. Kolyma Range. mountain range E Russian Federation
Komatsu 523 C5 var. Komatu. Ishikawa, Honshū, SW Japan
Komatu see Komatsu
Kommunizma Pik see Kommunizm, Qullai
Kommunizm, Qullai 515 F3 var. Qullai Garmo, Eng. Communism Peak, Rus. Kommunizma Pik; prev. Stalin Peak. mountain E Tajikistan
Komoé 467 E4 var. Komoé Fleuve. river E Ivory Coast
Komoé Fleuve see Komoé
Komotiní 496 D3 var. Gümüljina, Turk. Gümülcine. Anatolikí Makedonía kai Thráki, NE Greece
Komsomolets, Ostrov 507 E1 island Severnaya Zemlya, N Russian Federation
Komsomol'sk-na-Amure 507 G4 Khabarovskiy Kray, SE Russian Federation
Kondolovo 496 E3 Burgaska Oblast, SE Bulgaria
Kondopoga 502 B3 Respublika Kareliya, NW Russian Federation
Kondoz see Kunduz
Kondūz see Kunduz
Kong Christian IX Land 474 D4 Eng. King Christian IX Land. physical region SE Greenland
Kong Frederik IX Land 474 C3 Eng. King Frederik IX Land. physical region SW Greenland
Kong Frederik VIII Land 475 E2 Eng. King Frederik VIII Land. physical region NE Greenland
Kong Frederik VI Kyst 474 C4 Eng. King Frederik VI Coast. physical region SE Greenland
Kong Karls Land 475 G2 Eng. King Charles Islands. island group SE Svalbard
Kongo see Congo
Kongolo 469 D6 Shaba, E Congo (Zaire)
Kongor 465 B5 Jonglei, SE Sudan
Kong Oscar Fjord 475 E3 fjord E Greenland
Kongsberg 477 B6 Buskerud, S Norway
Kông, Tônle 529 E5 Lao. Xê Kong. river Cambodia/Laos
Konia see Konya
Konieh see Konya
Konin 490 C3 Ger. Kuhnau. Konin, C Poland
Konispol 493 C7 var. Konispoli. Vlorë, S Albania
Konispoli see Konispol
Kónitsa 496 A4 Ípeiros, W Greece
Konjic 492 C4 S Bosnia and Herzegovina
Konosha 502 C4 Arkhangel'skaya Oblast', NW Russian Federation
Konotop 501 F1 Sums'ka Oblast', NE Ukraine
Konstanz 487 B7 var. Constanz, Eng. Constance; hist. Kostnitz, anc. Constantia. Baden-Württemberg, S Germany
Konstanza see Constanța
Konya 508 C4 var. Konieh; prev. Konia, anc. Iconium. Konya, C Turkey
Kopaonik 493 D5 mountain range S Yugoslavia
Koper 487 D8 It. Capodistria; prev. Kopar. SW Slovenia
Kopetdag Gershi 514 C3 mountain range Iran/Turkmenistan
Koppeh Dāgh 512 D2 var. Khrebet Kopetdag. mountain range Iran/Turkmenistan
Koprivnica 492 B2 Ger. Kopreinitz, Hung. Kaproncza. Koprivnica-Križevci, N Croatia
Korat see Nakhon Ratchasima
Korat Plateau 528 D4 plateau E Thailand
Korça see Korçë
Korçë 493 D6 var. Korça, Gk. Korytsa, It. Corriza; prev. Koritsa. Korçë, SE Albania
Korčula 492 B4 It. Curzola; anc. Corcyra Nigra. island S Croatia
Korea Bay 519 G3 bay China/North Korea
Korea Strait 523 A7 Jap. Chōsen-kaikyō, Kor. Taehan-haehyŏp. channel Japan/South Korea
Korhogo 466 D4 N Ivory Coast
Korinthiakós Kólpos 497 B5 Eng. Gulf of Corinth; anc. Corinthiacus Sinus. gulf C Greece
Kórinthos 497 B6 Eng. Corinth; anc. Corinthus. Pelopónnisos, S Greece
Koritsa see Korçë
Kōriyama 523 D5 Fukushima, Honshū, C Japan
Korla 518 C3 Chin. K'u-erh-lo. Xinjiang Uygur Zizhiqu, NW China
Körmend 491 B7 Vas, W Hungary
Koróni 497 B6 Pelopónnisos, S Greece
Koror see Oreor
Korosten' 500 D1 Zhytomyrs'ka Oblast', NW Ukraine
Koro Toro 468 C2 Borkou-Ennedi-Tibesti, N Chad
Kortrijk 479 A6 Fr. Courtrai. West-Vlaanderen, W Belgium
Koryak Range 505 see Koryakskoye Nagor'ye
Koryakskiy Khrebet see Koryakskoye Nagor'ye
Koryakskoye Nagor'ye 507 H2 var. Koryakskiy Khrebet, Eng. Koryak Range. mountain range NE Russian Federation
Koryazhma 502 C4 Arkhangel'skaya Oblast', NW Russian Federation
Korytsa see Korçë
Kos 497 E6 It. Coo; anc. Cos. island Dodekánisos, Greece, Aegean Sea
Kos 497 E6 Kos, Dodekánisos, Greece, Aegean Sea
Kō-saki 523 A7 headland Nagasaki, Tsushima, SW Japan
Kościan 490 B4 Ger. Kosten. Leszno, W Poland
Koscian see Lubań
Kościerzyna 490 C2 Gdańsk, NW Poland
Kosciusko, Mount 541 C7 mountain New South Wales, SE Australia
Koshikijima-rettō 523 A8 var. Kosikizima Rettô. island group SW Japan
Košice 491 D6 Ger. Kaschau, Hung. Kassa. Východné Slovensko, E Slovakia
Kosikizima Rettô see Koshikijima-rettō
Koson 515 E3 Rus. Kasan. Qashqadaryo Wiloyati, S Uzbekistan
Kosovo 493 D5 prev. Autonomous Province of Kosovo and Metohija. cultural region S Yugoslavia
Kosovo Polje 493 D5 Serbia, S Yugoslavia
Kosovska Mitrovica 493 D5 Alb. Mitrovicë; prev. Mitrovica, Titova Mitrovica. Serbia, S Yugoslavia
Kosrae 536 C2 prev. Kusaie. island Caroline Islands, E Micronesia
Kossou, Lac de 466 D5 lake C Ivory Coast
Kosten see Lubań
Kostenets 496 C2 prev. Georgi Dimitrov. Sofiyska Oblast, W Bulgaria
Kostnitz see Konstanz
Kostroma 502 B4 Kostromskaya Oblast', NW Russian Federation
Kostyantynivka 501 G3 Rus. Konstantinovka. Donets'ka Oblast', SE Ukraine
Koszalin 490 B2 Ger. Köslin. Koszalin, NW Poland
Kota 526 D3 prev. Kotah. Rājasthān, N India
Kota Baharu see Kota Bharu
Kota Bahru see Kota Bharu
Kotabaru see Jayapura
Kota Bharu 530 B3 var. Kota Baharu, Kota Bahru. Kelantan, Peninsular Malaysia
Kotabumi 530 B4 prev. Kotaboemi. Sumatera, W Indonesia
Kota Kinabalu 530 D3 prev. Jesselton. Sabah, East Malaysia
Kotel'nyy, Ostrov 507 E2 island Novosibirskiye Ostrova, N Russian Federation
Kôti see Kōchi
Kotka 477 E5 Kymi, S Finland
Kotlas 502 C4 Arkhangel'skaya Oblast', NW Russian Federation
Kotonu see Cotonou
Kotor 493 C5 It. Cattaro. Montenegro, SW Yugoslavia
Kotovs'k 500 D3 Rus. Kotovsk. Odes'ka Oblast', SW Ukraine
Kotovsk see Hînceşti
Kotte see Sri Jayawardanapura
Kotto 468 D4 river Central African Republic/Congo (Zaire)
Kotuy 507 E2 river N Russian Federation
Koudougou 467 E4 C Burkina
Koulamoutou 469 B6 Ogooué-Lolo, C Gabon
Koulikoro 466 D3 Koulikoro, SW Mali
Koumra 468 C4 Moyen-Chari, S Chad
Kourou 451 H3 N French Guiana
Kousseir see Al Quşayr
Kousséri 468 B3 prev. Fort-Foureau. Extrême-Nord, NE Cameroon
Koutiala 466 D4 Sikasso, S Mali
Kouvola 477 E5 Kymi, S Finland
Kovel' 500 C1 Pol. Kowel. Volyns'ka Oblast', NW Ukraine
Kowloon 520 A2 Chin. Jiulong. Hong Kong, S China
Kowtal-e Barowghīl see Baroghil Pass
Kowtal-e Khaybar see Khyber Pass
Kozáni 496 B4 Dytikí Makedonía, N Greece
Kozara 492 B3 mountain range NW Bosnia and Herzegovina
Kozhikode see Calicut
Kōzu-shima 523 D6 island E Japan
Kozyatyn 500 D2 Rus. Kazatin. Vinnyts'ka Oblast', C Ukraine
Kpalimé 467 E5 var. Palimé. SW Togo
Krâchéh 529 D6 prev. Kratie. Krâchéh, E Cambodia
Kragujevac 492 D4 Serbia, C Yugoslavia
Kra, Isthmus of 529 B6 isthmus Malaysia/Thailand
Kraków 491 D5 Eng. Cracow, Ger. Krakau; anc. Cracovia. Kraków, S Poland
Krâlânh 529 D5 Siĕmréab, NW Cambodia
Kraljevo 492 D4 prev. Rankovićevo. Serbia, C Yugoslavia
Kramators'k 501 G3 Rus. Kramatorsk. Donets'ka Oblast', SE Ukraine
Kramfors 477 C5 Västernorrland, C Sweden
Kranéa 496 B4 Dytikí Makedonía, N Greece
Kranj 487 D7 Ger. Krainburg. NW Slovenia
Krāslava 498 D4 Krāslava, SE Latvia
Krasnaye 499 C5 Rus. Krasnoye. Minskaya Voblasts', C Belorussia
Krasnoarmeysk 503 C6 Saratovskaya Oblast', W Russian Federation
Krasnodar 503 A7 prev. Ekaterinodar, Yekaterinodar. Krasnodarskiy Kray, SW Russian Federation
Krasnodon 501 H3 Luhans'ka Oblast', E Ukraine
Krasnohvardiys'ke 501 F4 Rus. Krasnogvardeyskoye. Respublika Krym, S Ukraine
Krasnokamensk 507 F4 Chitinskaya Oblast', S Russian Federation
Krasnokamsk 503 D5 Permskaya Oblast', W Russian Federation
Krasnoperekops'k 501 F4 Rus. Krasnoperekopsk. Respublika Krym, S Ukraine
Krasnovodskiy Zaliv 514 A2 Turkm. Krasnowodsk Aylagy. lake gulf W Turkmenistan
Krasnoyarsk 506 D4 Krasnoyarskiy Kray, S Russian Federation
Krasnystaw 490 E4 Rus. Krasnostav. Chełm, SE Poland
Krasnyy Kut 503 C6 Saratovskaya Oblast', W Russian Federation
Krasnyy Luch 501 H3 prev. Krindachevka. Luhans'ka Oblast', E Ukraine
Krâvanh, Chuŏr Phnum 529 C6 Eng. Cardamom Mountains, Fr. Chaîne des Cardamomes. mountain range W Cambodia
Krefeld 486 A4 Nordrhein-Westfalen, W Germany
Kremenchuk 501 F2 Rus. Kremenchug. Poltavs'ka Oblast', NE Ukraine
Kremenchuts'ke Vodoskhovyshche 501 F2 Eng. Kremenchuk Reservoir, Rus. Kremenchugskoye Vodokhranilishche. reservoir C Ukraine
Kremenets' 500 C2 Pol. Krzemieniec, Rus. Kremenets. Ternopil's'ka Oblast', W Ukraine
Kreminna 501 G2 Rus. Kremennaya. Luhans'ka Oblast', E Ukraine
Kresena see Kresna
Kresna 496 C3 var. Kresena. Sofiyska Oblast, SW Bulgaria
Kretikon Delagos see Kritikó Pélagos
Kretinga 498 B3 Ger. Krottingen. Kretinga, NW Lithuania
Krishna 524 C1 prev. Kistna. river C India
Krishnagiri 524 C2 Tamil Nādu, SE India
Kristiansand 477 A6 var. Christiansand. Vest-Agder, S Norway
Kristianstad 477 B7 Kristianstad, S Sweden
Kristiansund 476 A4 var. Christiansund. Møre og Romsdal, S Norway
Kríti 497 C7 Eng. Crete. island Greece, Aegean Sea
Kritikó Pélagos 497 D7 var. Kretikon Delagos, Eng. Sea of Crete; anc. Mare Creticum. sea Greece, Aegean Sea
Križevci 492 B2 Ger. Kreuz, Hung. Kőrös. Varaždin, NE Croatia
Krk 492 A3 It. Veglia; anc. Curieta. island NW Croatia
Krolevets' 501 F1 Rus. Krolevets. Sums'ka Oblast', NE Ukraine
Kronach 487 C5 Bayern, E Germany
Kroonstad 470 D4 Free State, C South Africa
Kropotkin 503 A7 Krasnodarskiy Kray, SW Russian Federation
Krosno 491 D5 Ger. Krossen. Krosno, SE Poland
Krosno Odrzańskie 490 B3 Ger. Crossen, Kreisstadt. Zielona Góra, W Poland
Krško 487 E8 Ger. Gurkfeld; prev. Videm-Krško. E Slovenia
Kruhlaye 499 D6 Rus. Kruglоye. Mahilyowskaya Voblasts', E Belorussia
Kruja see Krujë
Krujë 493 C6 var. Kruja, It. Croia. Durrës, C Albania
Krummau see Český Krumlov
Krung Thep 529 C5 var. Krung Thep Mahanakhon, Eng. Bangkok. country capital (Thailand) Bangkok, C Thailand
Krung Thep, Ao 529 C5 var. Bight of Bangkok. bay S Thailand
Krung Thep Mahanakhon see Krung Thep
Krupki 499 D6 Rus. Krupki. Minskaya Voblasts', C Belorussia
Krychaw 499 E7 Rus. Krichëv. Mahilyowskaya Voblasts', E Belorussia
Krym see Crimea
Krymskaya Oblast' see Crimea
Kryms'ki Hory 501 F5 mountain range S Ukraine
Kryms'kyy Pivostriv 501 F5 peninsula S Ukraine
Kryve Ozero 501 E3 Odes'ka Oblast', SW Ukraine
Kryvyy Rih 501 F3 Rus. Krivoy Rog. Dnipropetrovs'ka Oblast', SE Ukraine
Ksar al Kabir see Ksar-el-Kebir
Ksar al Soule see Er-Rachidia
Ksar-el-Kebir 462 C2 var. Alcázar, Ksar al Kabir, Ksar-el-Kébir, Ar. Al-Kasr al-Kebir, Al-Qsar al-Kbir, Sp. Alcazarquivir. NW Morocco
Ksar-el-Kébir see Ksar-el-Kebir
Kuala Dungun see Dungun
Kuala Lumpur 530 B3 country capital (Malaysia) Kuala Lumpur, Peninsular Malaysia
Kuala Terengganu 530 B3 var. Kuala Trengganu. Terengganu, Peninsular Malaysia
Kuala Trengganu see Kuala Terengganu
Kualatungkal 530 B4 Sumatera, W Indonesia
Kuang-chou see Guangzhou
Kuang-hsi see Guangxi Zhuangzu Zizhiqu
Kuang-tung see Guangdong
Kuang-yuan see Guangyuan
Kuantan 530 B3 Pahang, Peninsular Malaysia
Kuban' 501 G5 var. Hypanis. river SW Russian Federation
Kubango see Cubango
Kuching 530 C3 prev. Sarawak. Sarawak, East Malaysia
Kūchnay Darweyshān 514 D5 Helmand, S Afghanistan
Kuçova see Kuçovë
Kuçovë 493 C6 var. Kuçova; prev. Qyteti Stalin. Berat, C Albania
Kudara see Ghūdara
Kudus 530 C5 prev. Koedoes. Jawa, C Indonesia
Kuei-chou see Guizhou
Kuei-lin see Guilin
Kuei-Yang see Guiyang
Kueyang see Guiyang
Kuhmo 476 E4 Oulu, E Finland
Kūhnō see Kihnu
Kuibyshev see Kuybyshevskoye Vodokhranilishche
Kuito 470 B2 Port. Silva Porto. Bié, C Angola
Kuji 522 D3 var. Kuzi. Iwate, Honshū, C Japan
Kukës 493 D5 var. Kukësi. Kukës, NE Albania

Lowell – Malyn

Lowell 433 G3 Massachusetts, NE USA
Lower California see Baja California
Lower Hutt 543 D5 Wellington, North Island, NZ
Lower Lough Erne 481 A5 *lake* SW Northern Ireland, UK
Lower Red Lake 437 F1 *lake* Minnesota, N USA
Lower Tunguska 504 see Nizhnyaya Tunguska
Lowestoft 481 E6 E England, UK
Lo-yang see Luoyang
Loyauté, Îles 536 D5 *island group* S New Caledonia
Loyew 499 D8 *Rus.* Loyev. Homyel'skaya Voblasts', SE Belorussia
Loznica 492 C3 Serbia, W Yugoslavia
Lu see Shandong
Lualaba 469 D6 *Fr.* Loualaba. *river* SE Congo (Zaire)
Luanda 470 A1 *var.* Loanda, *Port.* São Paulo de Loanda. *country capital* (Angola) Luanda, NW Angola
Luang Prabang see Louangphabang
Luang, Thale 529 C7 *lagoon* S Thailand
Luangua, Rio see Luangwa
Luangwa 465 B8 *var.* Aruângua, Rio Luangua. *river* Mozambique/Zambia
Luanshya 470 D2 Copperbelt, C Zambia
Luarca 484 C1 Asturias, N Spain
Lubaczów 491 E5 *var.* Lúbaczów. Przemyśl, SE Poland
Lubań 490 B4 *var.* Koscian, *Ger.* Kosten. Jelenia Góra, SW Poland
Lubānas Ezers see Lubāns
Lubango 470 B2 *Port.* Sá da Bandeira. Huíla, SW Angola
Lubāns 498 D4 *var.* Lubānas Ezers. *lake* E Latvia
Lubao 469 D6 Kasai Oriental, C Congo (Zaire)
Lübben 486 D4 Brandenburg, E Germany
Lübbenau 486 D4 Brandenburg, E Germany
Lubbock 441 E2 Texas, SW USA
Lübeck 486 C2 Schleswig-Holstein, N Germany
Lubelska, Wyżyna 490 E4 *plateau* SE Poland
Lubin 490 B4 *Ger.* Lüben. Legnica, W Poland
Lublin 490 E4 *Rus.* Lyublin. Lublin, E Poland
Lubliniec 490 C4 Częstochowa, S Poland
Lubny 501 F2 Poltavs'ka Oblast', NE Ukraine
Lubsko 490 B4 *Ger.* Sommerfeld. Zielona Góra, W Poland
Lubumbashi 469 E8 *prev.* Élisabethville. Shaba, SE Congo (Zaire)
Lubutu 469 D6 Maniema, E Congo (Zaire)
Lucan 481 B5 *Ir.* Leamhcán. E Ireland
Lucano, Appennino 489 D5 *Eng.* Lucanian Mountains. *mountain range* S Italy
Lucapa 470 C1 *var.* Lukapa. Lunda Norte, NE Angola
Lucca 488 B3 *anc.* Luca. Toscana, C Italy
Lucea 446 A4 W Jamaica
Lucena 531 E1 *off.* Lucena City. Luzon, N Philippines
Lucena 484 D4 Andalucía, S Spain
Lučenec 491 D6 *Ger.* Losontz, *Hung.* Losonc. Stredné Slovensko, S Slovakia
Luchow see Hefei
Lucknow 527 E3 *var.* Lakhnau. Uttar Pradesh, N India
Lüda see Dalian
Luda Kamchiya 496 D2 *river* E Bulgaria
Lüderitz 470 B4 *prev.* Angra Pequena. Karas, SW Namibia
Ludhiāna 526 D2 Punjab, N India
Ludington 432 C2 Michigan, N USA
Luduș 500 B4 *Ger.* Ludasch, *Hung.* Marosludas. Mureș, C Romania
Ludvika 477 C6 Kopparberg, C Sweden
Ludwiglust 486 C3 Mecklenburg-Vorpommern, N Germany
Ludwigsburg 487 B6 Baden-Württemberg, SW Germany
Lüdwigsfelde 486 D3 Brandenburg, NE Germany
Ludwigshafen 487 B5 *var.* Ludwigshafen am Rhein. Rheinland-Pfalz, W Germany
Ludwigshafen am Rhein see Ludwigshafen
Ludza 498 D4 *Ger.* Ludsan. Ludza, E Latvia
Luebo 469 C6 Kasai Occidental, SW Congo (Zaire)
Luena 470 C2 *var.* Lwena, *Port.* Luso. Moxico, E Angola
Lufira 469 E7 *river* SE Congo (Zaire)
Lufkin 441 H3 Texas, SW USA
Luga 502 A4 Leningradskaya Oblast', NW Russian Federation
Lugano 487 B8 *Ger.* Lauis. Ticino, S Switzerland
Lugenda, Rio 471 E2 *river* N Mozambique
Lugo 484 C1 *anc.* Lugus Augusti. Galicia, NW Spain
Lugoj 500 A4 *Ger.* Lugosch, *Hung.* Lugos. Timiș, W Romania
Luhans'k 501 H3 *Rus.* Lugansk; *prev.* Voroshilovgrad. Luhans'ka Oblast', E Ukraine
Luimneach see Limerick
Lukapa see Lucapa
Lukenie 469 C6 *river* C Congo (Zaire)
Lukovit 496 C2 Loveshka Oblast, NW Bulgaria
Łuków 490 E4 *Ger.* Bogendorf. Siedlce, E Poland
Lukuga 469 D7 *river* SE Congo (Zaire)
Luleå 476 D4 Norrbotten, N Sweden
Luleälven 476 C3 *river* N Sweden
Lulonga 469 C5 *river* NW Congo (Zaire)
Lulua 469 D7 *river* S Congo (Zaire)
Lumbo 471 F2 Nampula, NE Mozambique
Lumsden 543 A7 Southland, South Island, NZ
Lund 477 B7 Malmöhus, S Sweden
Lüneburg 486 C3 Niedersachsen, N Germany
Lungkiang see Qiqihar
Lungué-Bungo 470 C2 *var.* Lungwebungu. *river* Angola/Zambia see also Lungwebungu
Lungwebungu see Lungué-Bungo
Luninyets 499 B7 *Pol.* Łuniniec, *Rus.* Luninets. Brestskaya Voblasts', SW Belorussia
Lunteren 478 D4 Gelderland, C Netherlands
Luong Nam Tha see Louangnamtha
Luoyang 520 C4 *var.* Honan, Lo-yang. Henan, C China
Lúrio 471 F2 Nampula, NE Mozambique
Lúrio, Rio 471 E2 *river* NE Mozambique
Lusaka 470 D2 *country capital* (Zambia) Lusaka, SE Zambia
Lushnja see Lushnjë
Lushnjë 493 C6 *var.* Lushnja. Fier, C Albania
Luso see Luena
Lūt, Dasht-e 512 D3 *var.* Kavīr-e Lūt. *desert* E Iran
Luton 481 D6 SE England, UK
Łutselk'e 429 F4 *prev.* Snowdrift. Northwest Territories, W Canada
Luts'k 500 C1 *Pol.* Łuck, *Rus.* Lutsk. Volyns'ka Oblast', NW Ukraine
Lutzow-Holm Bay see Lützow Holmbukta
Lützow Holmbukta 546 C2 *var.* Lutzow-Holm Bay. *bay* Antarctica
Luuq 465 D6 *It.* Lugh Ganana. Gedo, SW Somalia
Luvua 469 D7 *river* SE Congo (Zaire)
Luwego 465 C8 *river* S Tanzania
Luxembourg 479 D8 *off.* Grand Duchy of Luxembourg, *var.* Lëtzebuerg, Luxemburg. *country* NW Europe
Luxembourg 479 D8 *country capital* (Luxembourg) Luxembourg, S Luxembourg
Luxor 464 B2 *Ar.* Al Uqșur. E Egypt
Luza 502 C4 Kirovskaya Oblast', NW Russian Federation
Luz, Costa de la 484 C5 *coastal region* SW Spain
Luzern 487 B7 *Fr.* Lucerne, *It.* Lucerna. Luzern, C Switzerland
Luzon 531 E1 *island* N Philippines
Luzon Strait 517 E3 *strait* Philippines/Taiwan
L'viv 500 B2 *Ger.* Lemberg, *Pol.* Lwów, *Rus.* L'vov. L'vivs'ka Oblast', W Ukraine
Lwena see Luena
Lyakhavichy 499 B6 *Rus.* Lyakhovichi. Brestskaya Voblasts', SW Belorussia
Lycksele 476 C4 Västerbotten, N Sweden
Lycopolis see Asyūt
Lyel'chytsy 499 C7 *Rus.* Lel'chitsy. Homyel'skaya Voblasts', SE Belorussia
Lyepyel' 499 D5 *Rus.* Lepel'. Vitsyebskaya Voblasts', N Belorussia
Lyme Bay 481 C7 *bay* S England, UK
Lynchburg 433 E5 Virginia, NE USA
Lynn Regis see King's Lynn
Lyon 483 D5 *Eng.* Lyons; *anc.* Lugdunum. Rhône, E France
Lyozna 499 E6 *Rus.* Liozno. Vitsyebskaya Voblasts', NE Belorussia
Lypovets' 500 D2 *Rus.* Lipovets. Vinnyts'ka Oblast', C Ukraine
Lysychans'k 501 H3 *Rus.* Lisichansk. Luhans'ka Oblast', E Ukraine
Lyttelton 543 C6 Canterbury, South Island, NZ
Lyubotyn 501 G2 *Rus.* Lyubotin. Kharkivs'ka Oblast', E Ukraine
Lyulyakovo 496 E2 *prev.* Keremitlik. Burgaska Oblast, E Bulgaria
Lyusina 499 B6 *Rus.* Lyusino. Brestskaya Voblasts', SW Belorussia

M

Ma'ān 511 B7 Ma'ān, SW Jordan
Maardu 498 D2 *Ger.* Maart. Harjumaa, NW Estonia
Ma'aret-en-Nu'man see Ma'arrat an Nu'mān
Ma'arrat an Nu'mān 510 B3 *var.* Ma'aret-en-Nu'man, *Fr.* Maarret enn Naamâne. Idlib, NW Syria
Maarret enn Naamâne see Ma'arrat an Nu'mān
Maaseik 479 D5 *prev.* Maeseyck. Limburg, NE Belgium
Maastricht 479 D6 *var.* Maestricht; *anc.* Traietum ad Mosam, Traiectum Tungorum. Limburg, SE Netherlands
Macao 520 C6 *Chin.* Aomen, *Port.* Macau. *former Portugese territory* E Asia
Macapá 455 E1 *state capital* Amapá, N Brazil
Macassar see Ujungpandang
MacCluer Gulf see Berau, Teluk
Macdonnell Ranges 538 D4 *mountain range* Northern Territory, C Australia
Macedonia, FYR 493 D6 *off.* the Former Yugoslav Republic of Macedonia, *var.* Macedonia, *Mac.* Makedonija, *abbrev.* FYR Macedonia, FYROM. *country* SE Europe
Maceió 455 G3 *state capital* Alagoas, E Brazil
Machachi 452 B1 Pichincha, C Ecuador
Machala 452 B2 El Oro, SW Ecuador
Machanga 471 E3 Sofala, E Mozambique
Machilīpatnam 524 D1 *var.* Bandar Masulipatnam. Andhra Pradesh, E India
Machiques 450 C2 Zulia, NW Venezuela
Macías Nguema Biyogo see Bioco, Isla de
Măcin 500 D5 Tulcea, SE Romania
Macizo de las Guayanas see Guiana Highlands
Mackay 540 D4 Queensland, NE Australia
Mackay, Lake 538 C4 *salt lake* Northern Territory/Western Australia
Mackenzie 429 E3 *river* Northwest Territories, NW Canada
Mackenzie Bay 546 D3 *bay* Antarctica
Mackenzie Mountains 428 D3 *mountain range* Northwest Territories, NW Canada
Macleod, Lake 538 A4 *lake* Western Australia
Macomb 432 A4 Illinois, N USA
Macomer 489 A5 Sardegna, Italy, C Mediterranean Sea
Macon 433 D6 Georgia, SE USA
Macon 437 G4 Missouri, C USA
Mâcon 483 D5 *anc.* Matisco, Matisco Ædourum. Saône-et-Loire, C France
Macquarie Ridge 546 C5 *undersea feature* SW Pacific Ocean
Macuspana 443 G4 Tabasco, SE Mexico
Ma'dabā 511 B6 *var.* Mādabā, Madeba; *anc.* Medeba. 'Ammān, NW Jordan
Madagascar 471 F3 *off.* Democratic Republic of Madagascar, *Malg.* Madagasikara; *prev.* Malagasy Republic. *country* W Indian Ocean
Madagascar 471 F3 *island* W Indian Ocean
Madagascar Basin 461 E7 *undersea feature* W Indian Ocean
Madagascar Plateau 461 E7 *var.* Madagascar Ridge, Madagascar Rise, *Rus.* Madagaskarskiy Khrebet. *undersea feature* W Indian Ocean
Madagascar Ridge see Madagascar Plateau
Madagascar Rise see Madagascar Plateau
Madagaskarskiy Khrebet see Madagascar Plateau
Madang 536 B3 Madang, N PNG
Madanīyīn see Médenine
Made 478 C4 Noord-Brabant, S Netherlands
Madeba see Ma'dabā
Madeira 462 A2 *var.* Ilha de Madeira. *island* Portugal, NE Atlantic Ocean
Madeira 462 A2 *var.* Madeira, *Port.* Arquipélago da Madeira. *island group* Portugal, NE Atlantic Ocean
Madeira Plain 458 C3 *undersea feature* E Atlantic Ocean
Madeira, Rio 454 D2 *Sp.* Río Madera. *river* Bolivia/Brazil see also Madera, Río
Madeleine, Îles de la 431 F4 *Eng.* Magdalen Islands. *island group* Québec, E Canada
Madera 439 B6 California, W USA
Madhya Pradesh 527 E4 *prev.* Central Provinces and Berar. Admin. region *state* C India
Madīnat ath Thawrah 510 C2 *var.* Ath Thawrah. Ar Raqqah, N Syria Asia
Madison 432 B3 *state capital* Wisconsin, N USA
Madison 437 F3 South Dakota, N USA
Madiun 530 D5 *prev.* Madioen. Jawa, C Indonesia
Madona 498 D4 *Ger.* Modohn. Madona, E Latvia
Madras see Tamil Nādu
Madras 524 D2 *var.* Chennai. Tamil Nādu, S India
Madre de Dios 448 B4 *off.* Departamento de Madre de Dios. *department* E Peru
Madre de Dios, Río 453 E3 *river* Bolivia/Peru
Madre del Sur, Sierra 443 E5 *mountain range* S Mexico
Madre, Laguna 443 F3 *lagoon* NE Mexico
Madre, Laguna 441 G5 *lake* Texas, SW USA
Madre Occidental, Sierra 442 C3 *var.* Western Sierra Madre. *mountain range* C Mexico
Madre Oriental, Sierra 443 E3 *var.* Eastern Sierra Madre. *mountain range* C Mexico
Madrid 484 D3 *country capital* (Spain) Madrid, C Spain
Madurai 524 C3 *prev.* Madura, Mathurai. Tamil Nādu, S India
Madura, Pulau 530 D5 *prev.* Madoera. *island* C Indonesia
Maebashi 523 D5 *var.* Maebasi, Mayebashi. Gunma, Honshū, S Japan
Maebasi see Maebashi
Mae Nam Khong see Mekong
Mae Nam Nan 528 C4 *river* NW Thailand
Mae Nam Yom 528 C4 *river* W Thailand
Maestricht see Maastricht
Maewo 536 D4 *prev.* Aurora. *island* C Vanuatu
Mafia 465 D7 *island* E Tanzania
Mafraq see Al Mafraq
Magadan 507 G3 Magadanskaya Oblast', E Russian Federation
Magangué 450 B2 Bolívar, N Colombia
Magdalena 448 A2 *off.* Departamento del Magdalena. *province* N Colombia
Magdalena 453 F3 Beni, N Bolivia
Magdalena 442 B1 Sonora, NW Mexico
Magdalena, Isla 442 B3 *island* W Mexico
Magdalena, Río 450 B2 *river* C Colombia
Magdeburg 486 C4 Sachsen-Anhalt, C Germany
Magelang 530 C5 Jawa, C Indonesia
Magellan, Strait of 457 B8 *Sp.* Estrecho de Magallanes. *strait* Argentina/Chile
Magerøy see Magerøya
Magerøya 476 D1 *var.* Magerøy. *island* N Norway
Maggiore, Lake 488 B1 *It.* Lago Maggiore. *lake* Italy/Switzerland
Maglaj 492 C3 N Bosnia and Herzegovina
Maglie 489 E6 Puglia, SE Italy
Magna 436 B4 Utah, W USA
Magnesia see Manisa
Magnitogorsk 506 B4 Chelyabinskaya Oblast', C Russian Federation
Magta' Lahjar 466 C3 *var.* Magta Lahjar, Magta' Lahjar, Magtá Lahjar. Brakna, SW Mauritania
Magway see Magwe
Magwe 528 A3 *var.* Magway. Magwe, W Burma
Mahajanga 471 F2 *var.* Majunga. Mahajanga, NW Madagascar
Mahakam, Sungai 530 D4 *var.* Koetai, Kutai. *river* Borneo, C Indonesia
Mahalapye 470 D3 *var.* Mahalatswe. Central, SE Botswana
Mahalatswe see Mahalapye
Mahān 512 D3 Kermān, E Iran
Mahanādi 527 F4 *river* E India
Mahārāshtra 526 D5 *state* W India
Mahbés see El Mahbas
Mahbūbnagar 526 D5 Andhra Pradesh, C India
Mahdia 463 F2 *var.* Al Mahdīyah, Mehdia. NE Tunisia
Mahé 471 H1 *island* Inner Islands, NE Seychelles
Mahia Peninsula 542 E4 *peninsula* North Island, NZ
Mahilyow 499 D6 *Rus.* Mogilëv. Mahilyowskaya Voblasts', E Belorussia
Mahmūd-e 'Erāqī see Maḩmūd-e Rāqī
Maḩmūd-e Rāqī 515 E4 *var.* Mahmūd-e 'Erāqī. Kāpīsā, NE Afghanistan
Mahón 485 H3 *Cat.* Maó, *Eng.* Port Mahon; *anc.* Portus Magonis. Menorca, Spain, W Mediterranean Sea
Maicao 450 C1 La Guajira, N Colombia
Mai Ceu see Maych'ew
Mai Chio see Maych'ew
Maidstone 481 E7 SE England, UK
Maiduguri 467 H4 Borno, NE Nigeria
Maimāna see Meymaneh
Main 487 B5 *river* C Germany
Mai-Ndombe, Lac 469 C6 *prev.* Lac Léopold II. *lake* W Congo (Zaire)
Maine 433 G2 *off.* State of Maine; also known as Lumber State, Pine Tree State. *state* NE USA
Maine 482 B3 *cultural region* NW France
Maine, Gulf of 433 H2 *gulf* NE USA
Main Island see Bermuda
Mainland 480 C2 *island* Orkney, N Scotland, UK
Mainland 480 D1 *island* Shetland, NE Scotland, UK
Mainz 487 B5 *Fr.* Mayence. Rheinland-Pfalz, SW Germany
Maio 466 A3 *var.* Mayo. *island* Ilhas de Sotavento, SE Cape Verde
Maisur see Karnātaka
Maisur see Mysore
Maizhokunggar 518 C5 Xizang Zizhiqu, W China
Maíz, Islas del 445 E3 *var.* Corn Islands. *island group* SE Nicaragua
Mājro see Majuro Atoll
Majunga see Mahajanga
Majuro Atoll 536 D2 *var.* Mājro. *atoll* Ratak Chain, SE Marshall Islands
Makale see Mek'elē
Makarov Basin 548 B3 *undersea feature* Arctic Ocean
Makarska 492 B4 *It.* Macarsca. Split-Dalmacija, SE Croatia
Makasar see Ujungpandang
Makassar see Ujungpandang
Makassar Strait 530 D4 *Ind.* Selat Makasar. *strait* C Indonesia
Makay 471 F3 *var.* Massif du Makay. *mountain range* SW Madagascar
Makeni 466 C4 C Sierra Leone
Makhachkala 506 A4 *prev.* Petrovsk-Port. Respublika Dagestan, SW Russian Federation
Makin 536 D2 *prev.* Pitt Island. *atoll* Tungaru, W Kiribati
Makira see San Cristobal
Makiyivka 501 G3 *Rus.* Makeyevka; *prev.* Dmitriyevsk. Donets'ka Oblast', E Ukraine
Makkah 513 A5 *Eng.* Mecca. Makkah, W Saudi Arabia
Makkovik 431 F2 Newfoundland, NE Canada
Makó 491 D7 *Rom.* Macău. Csongrád, SE Hungary
Makoua 469 B5 Cuvette, C Congo
Makran Coast 512 E4 *coastal region* SE Iran
Makrany 499 A6 *Rus.* Mokrany. Brestskaya Voblasts', SW Belorussia
Mākū 512 B2 Āzarbāyjān-e Bākhtarī, NW Iran
Makurdi 467 G4 Benue, C Nigeria
Mala see Malaita
Malabār Coast 524 B3 *coast* SW India
Malabo 469 A5 *prev.* Santa Isab… *country capital* (Equatorial Guinea) Isla de Bioco, NW Equatorial Guinea
Malacca see Melaka
Malacca, Strait of 530 B3 *Ind.* Malaka. *strait* Indonesia/Mala…
Malacky 491 C6 *Hung.* Malack… Západné Slovensko, W Slovak…
Maladzyechna 499 C5 *Pol.* Molodeczno, *Rus.* Molodechn… Minskaya Voblasts', C Beloru…
Málaga 484 D5 *anc.* Malaca. Andalucía, S Spain
Malagarasi River 465 B7 *river* W Tanzania
Malaita 536 C3 *var.* Mala. *islan…* N Solomon Islands
Malakal 465 B5 Upper Nile, S Sudan
Malakula see Malekula
Malang 530 D5 Jawa, C Indone…
Malange see Malanje
Malanje 470 B1 *var.* Malange. Malanje, NW Angola
Mälaren 477 C6 *lake* C Sweden
Malatya 509 E4 *anc.* Melitene. Malatya, SE Turkey
Mala Vyska 501 E3 *Rus.* Malay… Viska. Kirovohrads'ka Oblast… S Ukraine
Malawi 471 E1 *off.* Republic of Malaŵi; *prev.* Nyasaland, Nyasaland Protectorate. *coun…* S Africa
Malawi, Lake see Nyasa, Lake
Malay Peninsula 516 D4 *penin…* Malaysia/Thailand
Malaysia 530 B3 *var.* Federatio… Malaysia; *prev.* the separate territories of Federation of M… Sarawak and Sabah (North Borneo) and Singapore. *coun…* SE Asia
Malaysia, Federation of see Malaysia
Malbork 490 C2 *Ger.* Marienbu… Marienburg in Westpreussen. Elbląg, N Poland
Malchin 486 C3 Mecklenburg-Vorpommern, N Germany
Malden 437 H5 Missouri, C U…
Malden Island 537 G3 *prev.* Independence Island. *atoll* E Kiribati
Maldives 524 A4 *off.* Maldivian Divehi, Republic of Maldives. *country* N Indian Ocean
Male' 524 B4 Male' Atoll, C Maldives
Male' Atoll 524 B4 *var.* Kaafu A… *atoll* C Maldives
Malekula 536 D4 *var.* Malakul… *prev.* Mallicolo. *island* W Van…
Malesína 497 C5 Stereá Ellás, E Greece
Malheur Lake 438 C3 *lake* Ore… NW USA
Mali 467 E3 *off.* Republic of M… République du Mali; *prev.* Fre… Sudan, Sudanese Republic. *co…* W Africa
Malik, Wadi al see Milk, Wadi…
Mali Kyun 529 B5 *var.* Tavoy Is… *island* Mergui Archipelago, S Burma
Malindi 465 D7 Coast, SE Ken…
Malko Tŭrnovo 496 E3 Burgas… Oblast, SE Bulgaria
Mallaig 480 B3 N Scotland, UK
Mallawi 464 B2 C Egypt
Mallicolo see Malekula
Mallorca 485 G3 *Eng.* Majorca… Baleares Major. *island* Islas Baleares, Spain, W Mediterra… Sea
Malmberget 476 C3 Norrbotte… N Sweden
Malmédy 479 D6 Liège, E Belg…
Malmö 477 B7 Malmöhus, S Sweden
Maloelap see Maloelap Atoll
Maloelap Atoll 536 D1 *var.* Maloelap. *atoll* E Marshall Isl…
Małopolska 490 D4 *plateau* S Poland
Malozemel'skaya Tundra 502… *physical region* NW Russian Federation
Malta 489 C8 *off.* Republic of M… *country* C Mediterranean Sea
Malta 489 C8 *island* Malta, C Mediterranean Sea
Malta 436 C1 Montana, NW U…
Malta 498 D4 Rēzekne, SE Latv…
Malta Channel 489 C8 *It.* Cana… Malta. *strait* Italy/Malta
Maluku 531 F4 *Dut.* Molukken… Moluccas; *prev.* Spice Islands. *island group* E Indonesia
Malung 477 B6 Kopparberg, C Sweden
Malyn 500 D2 *Rus.* Malin. Zhytomyrs'ka Oblast', N Ukr…

Mamberamo, Sungai – Melanesian Basin

ıberamo, Sungai 531 H4 *river*
ı Jaya, E Indonesia
ıij *see* Manbij
onovo 498 A4 *Ger.*
igenbeil. Kaliningradskaya
ast', W Russian Federation
oré, Rio 453 F3 *river*
via/Brazil
ou 466 C4 Moyenne-Guinée,
uinea
oudzou 471 F2 *dependent*
itory capital (Mayotte)
layotte
uno 470 C3 Ghanzi,
3otswana
acor 485 G3 Mallorca, Spain,
Mediterranean Sea
ado 531 F3 *prev.* Menado.
awesi, C Indonesia
agua 444 D3 *country capital*
caragua) Managua,
Nicaragua
agua, Lago de 444 C3 *var.*
otlán. *lake* W Nicaragua
akara 471 G4 Fianarantsoa,
Madagascar
ama 504 *see* Al Manāmah
anjary 471 G3 Fianarantsoa,
Madagascar
apouri, Lake 543 A7 *lake*
th Island, NZ
ar *see* Mannar
as, Gora 515 E2 *mountain*
gyzstan/Uzbekistan
aus 454 D2 *prev.* Manáos. *state*
ital Amazonas, NW Brazil
avgat 508 B4 Antalya,
Turkey
bij 510 C2 *var.* Mambij, *Fr.*
nbidj. Ḩalab, N Syria
chester 481 D5 *Lat.*
ncunium. NW England, UK
chester 433 G3 New
npshire, NE USA
-chou-li *see* Manzhouli
churia 517 E1 *cultural region*
China
cio Lima *see* Japiim
d *see* Mand, Rūd-e
dalay 528 B3 Mandalay,
urma
dan 437 E2 North Dakota,
JSA
deville 446 B5 C Jamaica
dra 497 C6 Attikí, C Greece
d, Rūd-e 512 D4 *var.* Mand.
r S Iran
durah 539 A6 Western
stralia
duria 489 E5 Puglia, SE Italy
dya 524 C2 Karnātaka, C India
fredonia 489 D5 Puglia,
Italy
gai 469 C6 Bandundu,
Congo (Zaire)
gaia 537 G5 *island group*
ook Islands
galia 500 D5 *anc.* Callatis.
nstanța, SE Romania
galmé 468 C3 Guéra, SE Chad
galore 524 B2 Karnātaka,
India
gaung *see* Bloemfontein
go *see* Sansanné-Mango
goky 471 F3 *river*
Madagascar
hattan 437 F4 Kansas, C USA
icouagan, Réservoir 430 D3
Québec, E Canada
ihiki 537 G4 *atoll* N Cook
ands
ihiki Plateau 535 E3 *undersea*
ture C Pacific Ocean
iitsoq 474 C3 *var.* Manîtsoq,
n. Sukkertoppen. S Greenland
ila 531 E1 *off.* City of Manila.
ntry capital (Philippines)
zon, N Philippines
isa 508 A3 *var.* Manissa; *prev.*
uhan, *anc.* Magnesia. Manisa,
Turkey
issa *see* Manisa
itoba 429 F5 *province* S Canada
itoba, Lake 429 F5 *lake*
anitoba, S Canada
itoulin Island 430 C4 *island*
tario, S Canada
îtsoq *see* Maniitsoq
izales 450 B3 Caldas,
Colombia
jimup 539 A7 Western
stralia
kato 437 F3 Minnesota, N USA
lleu 485 G2 Cataluña, NE Spain
ly 540 E1 New South Wales,
Australia
mād 526 C5 Mahārāshtra,
India
nar 524 C3 *var.* Manar.
rthern Province, NW Sri Lanka
nar, Gulf of 524 C3 *gulf*
ia/Sri Lanka
nheim 487 B5 Baden-
rttemberg, SW Germany
ono 469 E7 Shabo, SE Congo
ire)

Manosque 483 D6 Alpes-de-Haute-Provence, SE France
Manra 537 F3 *prev.* Sydney Island. *atoll* Phoenix Islands, C Kiribati
Mansa 470 D2 *prev.* Fort Rosebery. Luapula, N Zambia
Mansel Island 429 G3 *island* Northwest Territories, NE Canada
Mansfield 432 D4 Ohio, N USA
Manta 452 A2 Manabí, W Ecuador
Manteca 439 B6 California, W USA
Mantova 488 B2 *Eng.* Mantua, *Fr.* Mantoue. Lombardia, NW Italy
Manuae 537 G4 *island* S Cook Islands
Manukau *see* Manurewa
Manurewa 542 D3 *var.* Manukau. Auckland, North Island, NZ
Manzanares 485 E3 Castilla-La Mancha, C Spain
Manzanillo 442 D4 Colima, SW Mexico
Manzanillo 446 C3 Granma, E Cuba
Manzhouli 519 F1 *var.* Man-chou-li. Nei Mongol Zizhiqu, N China
Mao 468 B3 Kanem, W Chad
Maoke, Pegunungan 531 H4 *Dut.* Sneeuw-gebergte, *Eng.* Snow Mountains. *mountain range* Irian Jaya, E Indonesia
Maoming 520 C6 Guangdong, S China
Mapmaker Seamounts 517 H2 *undersea feature* N Pacific Ocean
Maputo 470 D4 *prev.* Lourenço Marques. *country capital* (Mozambique) Maputo, S Mozambique
Marabá 455 F2 Pará, NE Brazil
Maracaibo 450 C1 Zulia, NW Venezuela
Maracaibo, Lago de 450 C2 *var.* Lake Maracaibo. *inlet* NW Venezuela
Maracaibo, Lake *see* Maracaibo, Lago de
Maracay 450 D2 Aragua, N Venezuela
Marada *see* Marādah
Marādah 463 G3 *var.* Marada. N Libya
Maradi 467 G3 Maradi, S Niger
Maragha *see* Marāgheh
Marāgheh 512 C2 *var.* Maragha. Āzarbāyjān-e Khāvarī, NW Iran
Marajó, Baía de 455 F1 *bay* N Brazil
Marajó, Ilha de 455 E1 *island* N Brazil
Marakesh *see* Marrakech
Maramba *see* Livingstone
Maranhão 455 F2 *off.* Estado do Maranhão. *state* E Brazil
Marañón, Río 452 B2 *river* N Peru
Maraş *see* Kahramanmaraş
Marash *see* Kahramanmaraş
Marathon 430 C4 Ontario, S Canada
Marathónas 497 C5 *prev.* Marathón. Attikí, C Greece
Marbella 484 D5 Andalucía, S Spain
Marble Bar 538 B4 Western Australia
Marburg an der Lahn 486 B4 *hist.* Marburg. Hessen, W Germany
March *see* Morava
Marche 483 C5 *cultural region* C France
Marche 488 C3 *cultural region* E Italy
Marche-en-Famenne 479 C7 Luxembourg, SE Belgium
Marchena, Isla 452 B4 *var.* Bindloe Island. *island* Galapagos Islands, Ecuador, E Pacific Ocean
Mar Chiquita, Laguna 456 C3 *lake* C Argentina
Marcounda *see* Markounda
Mardān 526 C1 North-West Frontier Province, N Pakistan
Mar del Plata 457 D5 Buenos Aires, E Argentina
Mardin 509 E4 Mardin, SE Turkey
Maré 536 D5 *island* Îles Loyauté, E New Caledonia
Marea Neagră *see* Black Sea
Mare Creticum *see* Kritikó Pélagos
Mareeba 540 D3 Queensland, NE Australia
Margarita, Isla de 451 E1 *island* N Venezuela
Margate 481 E7 *prev.* Mergate. SE England, UK
Marghita 500 B3 *Hung.* Margitta. Bihor, NW Romania
Marhanets' 501 F3 *Rus.* Marganets. Dnipropetrovs'ka Oblast', E Ukraine
María Cleofas, Isla 442 C4 *island* C Mexico
Maria Island 541 C8 *island* Tasmania, SE Australia
María Madre, Isla 442 C4 *island* C Mexico
María Magdalena, Isla 442 C4 *island* C Mexico
Mariana Trench 517 G4 *undersea feature* W Pacific Ocean
Mariánské Lázně 491 A5 *Ger.* Marienbad. Západní Čechy, W Czech Republic
Marías, Islas 442 C4 *island group* C Mexico
Maribor 487 E7 *Ger.* Marburg. NE Slovenia
Marica *see* Maritsa
Maridi 465 B5 Western Equatoria, SW Sudan
Marie Byrd Land 546 A3 *physical region* Antarctica
Marie-Galante 447 G4 *var.* Ceyre to the Caribs. *island* SE Guadeloupe
Mariental 470 B4 Hardap, SW Namibia
Mariestad 477 B6 Skaraborg, S Sweden
Marietta 434 D2 Georgia, SE USA
Marijampolė 498 B4 *prev.* Kapsukas. Marijampolė, S Lithuania
Marília 455 E4 São Paulo, S Brazil
Marín 484 B1 Galicia, NW Spain
Mar"ina Horka 499 C6 *Rus.* Mar'ina Gorka. Minskaya Voblasts', C Belorussia
Maringá 455 E4 Paraná, S Brazil
Marion 437 G3 Iowa, C USA
Marion 432 D4 Ohio, N USA
Marion, Lake 435 E2 *reservoir* South Carolina, SE USA
Mariscal Estigarribia 456 D2 Boquerón, NW Paraguay
Maritsa 496 D3 *var.* Marica, *Gk.* Évros, *Turk.* Meriç; *anc.* Hebrus. *river* SW Europe *see also* Évros/Meriç
Maritzburg *see* Pietermaritzburg
Mariupol' 501 G4 *prev.* Zhdanov. Donets'ka Oblast', SE Ukraine
Marka 465 D6 *var.* Merca. Shabeellaha Hoose, S Somalia
Markham, Mount 546 B4 *mountain* Antarctica
Markounda 468 C4 *var.* Marcounda. Ouham, NW Central African Republic
Marktredwitz 487 C5 Bayern, E Germany
Marmande 483 B5 *anc.* Marmanda. Lot-et-Garonne, SW France
Marmara Denizi 508 A2 *Eng.* Sea of Marmara. *sea* NW Turkey
Marmara, Sea of *see* Marmara Denizi
Marmaris 508 A4 Muğla, SW Turkey
Marne 482 C3 *cultural region* N France
Marne 482 D3 *river* N France
Maro 468 C4 Moyen-Chari, S Chad
Maroantsetra 471 G2 Toamasina, NE Madagascar
Maromokotro 471 G2 *mountain* N Madagascar
Maroni River 451 G3 *Dut.* Marowijne. *river* French Guiana/Surinam
Maros *see* Mureş
Marosch *see* Mureş
Marotiri 535 F4 *var.* Îlots de Bass, Morotiri. *island group* Îles Australes, SW French Polynesia
Maroua 468 B3 Extrême-Nord, N Cameroon
Marquesas Fracture Zone 545 E3 *tectonic feature* E Pacific Ocean
Marquesas Islands 545 E3 *island group* N French Polynesia
Marquette 432 B1 Michigan, N USA
Marrakech 462 C2 *var.* Marakesh, *Eng.* Marrakesh; *prev.* Morocco. W Morocco
Marrakesh *see* Marrakech
Marrawah 541 C8 Tasmania, SE Australia
Marree 541 B5 South Australia
Marsá al Burayqah 463 G3 *var.* Al Burayqah. N Libya
Marsabit 465 C6 Eastern, N Kenya
Marsala 489 B7 *anc.* Lilybaeum. Sicilia, Italy, C Mediterranean Sea
Marsberg 486 B4 Nordrhein-Westfalen, W Germany
Marseille 483 D6 *Eng.* Marseilles; *anc.* Massilia. Bouches-du-Rhône, SE France
Marshall 437 F2 Minnesota, N USA
Marshall 441 H2 Texas, SW USA
Marshall Islands 536 C1 *off.* Republic of the Marshall Islands. *country* W Pacific Ocean
Marshall Seamounts 517 H3 *undersea feature* SW Pacific Ocean
Marsh Harbour 446 C1 Great Abaco, W Bahamas
Martaban 528 B4 *var.* Moktama. Mon State, S Burma
Martha's Vineyard 433 G3 *island* Massachusetts, NE USA
Martigues 483 D6 Bouches-du-Rhône, SE France
Martin 491 C5 *Ger.* Sankt Martin, *Hung.* Turócszentmárton; *prev.* Turčianský Svätý Martin. Stredné Slovensko, NW Slovakia
Martinique 447 G4 *French overseas department* E West Indies
Martinique Channel *see* Martinique Passage
Martinique Passage 447 G4 *var.* Dominica Channel, Martinique Channel. *channel* Dominica/Martinique
Marton 542 D4 Manawatu-Wanganui, North Island, NZ
Martos 484 D4 Andalucía, S Spain
Marungu 469 E7 *mountain range* SE Congo (Zaire)
Mary 514 D3 *prev.* Merv. Maryyskiy Velayat, S Turkmenistan
Maryborough *see* Portlaoise
Maryborough 540 D4 Queensland, E Australia
Mary Island *see* Kanton
Maryland 433 E5 *off.* State of Maryland; also known as America in Miniature, Cockade State, Free State, Old Line State. *state* NE USA
Maryland 434 D1 Tennessee, S USA
Maryville 437 F4 Missouri, C USA
Masai Steppe 465 C7 *grassland* NW Tanzania
Masaka 465 B6 SW Uganda
Masallı 509 H3 *Rus.* Masally. S Azerbaijan
Masasi 465 C8 Mtwara, SE Tanzania
Masawa *see* Massawa
Masaya 444 D3 Masaya, W Nicaragua
Mascarene Basin 533 B5 *undersea feature* W Indian Ocean
Mascarene Islands 471 H4 *island group* W Indian Ocean
Mascarene Plain 533 B5 *undersea feature* W Indian Ocean
Mascarene Plateau 533 B5 *undersea feature* W Indian Ocean
Maseru 470 D4 *country capital* (Lesotho) W Lesotho
Mashhad 512 E2 *var.* Meshed. Khorāsān, NE Iran
Masindi 465 B6 W Uganda
Masīra *see* Maşīrah, Jazīrat
Masira, Gulf of *see* Maşīrah, Khalīj
Maşīrah, Jazīrat 513 E5 *var.* Masīra. *island* E Oman
Maşīrah, Khalīj 513 E5 *var.* Gulf of Masira. *bay* E Oman
Masis *see* Büyükağrı Dağı
Maskat *see* Masqaţ
Mason City 437 F3 Iowa, C USA
Masqaţ 513 E5 *var.* Maskat, *Eng.* Muscat. *country capital* (Oman) NE Oman
Massa 488 B3 Toscana, C Italy
Massachusetts 433 G3 *off.* Commonwealth of Massachusetts; also known as Bay State, Old Bay State, Old Colony State. *state* NE USA
Massawa 464 C4 *var.* Masawa, *Amh.* Mits'iwa. E Eritrea
Massenya 468 B3 Chari-Baguirmi, SW Chad
Massif Central 483 C5 *plateau* C France
Massif du Makay *see* Makay
Massoukou *see* Franceville
Masterton 543 D5 Wellington, North Island, NZ
Masty 499 B5 *Rus.* Mosty. Hrodzyenskaya Voblasts', W Belorussia
Masuda 523 B6 Shimane, Honshū, SW Japan
Masuku *see* Franceville
Masvingo 470 D3 *prev.* Fort Victoria, Nyanda, Victoria. Masvingo, SE Zimbabwe
Maşyāf 510 B3 *Fr.* Misiaf. Ḩamāh, C Syria
Matadi 469 B6 Bas-Zaïre, W Congo (Zaire)
Matagalpa 444 D3 Matagalpa, C Nicaragua
Matale 524 D3 Central Province, C Sri Lanka
Matam 466 C3 NE Senegal
Matamata 542 D3 Waikato, North Island, NZ
Matamoros 442 D3 Coahuila de Zaragoza, NE Mexico
Matamoros 443 E2 Tamaulipas, C Mexico
Matane 431 E4 Québec, SE Canada
Matanzas 446 B2 Matanzas, NW Cuba
Matara 524 D4 Southern Province, S Sri Lanka
Mataram 530 D5 Pulau Lombok, C Indonesia
Mataró 485 G2 *anc.* Illuro. Cataluña, E Spain
Mataura 543 B7 *river* South Island, NZ
Mataura 543 B7 Southland, South Island, NZ
Mata Uta *see* Matā'utu
Matā'utu 537 E4 *var.* Mata Uta. *dependent territory capital* (Wallis and Futuna) Île Uvea, Wallis and Futuna
Matera 489 E5 Basilicata, S Italy
Matías Romero 443 F5 Oaxaca, SE Mexico
Mato Grosso 455 E4 *prev.* Vila Bela da Santissima Trindade. Mato Grosso, W Brazil
Mato Grosso do Sul 455 E4 *off.* Estado de Mato Grosso do Sul. *state* S Brazil
Mato Grosso, Planalto de 448 C4 *plateau* C Brazil
Matosinhos 484 B2 *prev.* Matozinhos. Porto, NW Portugal
Matsue 523 B6 *var.* Matsuye, Matue. Shimane, Honshū, SW Japan
Matsumoto 523 C5 *var.* Matumoto. Nagano, Honshū, S Japan
Matsuyama 523 B7 *var.* Matuyama. Ehime, Shikoku, SW Japan
Matsuye *see* Matsue
Matterhorn 487 A8 *It.* Monte Cervino. *mountain* Italy/Switzerland *see also* Cervino, Monte
Matthews Ridge 451 F2 N Guyana
Matthew Town 446 D2 Great Inagua, S Bahamas
Matucana 452 C4 Lima, W Peru
Matue *see* Matsue
Matumoto *see* Matsumoto
Maturín 451 E2 Monagas, NE Venezuela
Matuyama *see* Matsuyama
Mau 527 E3 *var.* Maunāth Bhanjan. Uttar Pradesh, N India
Maui 439 B8 *island* Hawaii, USA, C Pacific Ocean
Maulmain *see* Moulmein
Maun 470 C3 Ngamiland, C Botswana
Maunāth Bhanjan *see* Mau
Mauren 486 E1 NE Liechtenstein
Mauritania 466 C2 *off.* Islamic Republic of Mauritania, *Ar.* Mūrītānīyah. *country* W Africa
Mauritius 471 H3 *off.* Republic of Mauritius, *Fr.* Maurice. *country* W Indian Ocean
Mauritius 533 B5 *island* W Indian Ocean
Mawlamyine *see* Moulmein
Mawson 546 D2 *Australian research station* Antarctica
Maya 444 B1 *river* E Russian Federation
Mayadin *see* Al Mayādīn
Mayaguana 446 D2 *island* SE Bahamas
Mayaguana Passage 446 D2 *passage* SE Bahamas
Mayagüez 447 F3 W Puerto Rico
Mayamey 512 D2 Semnān, N Iran
Maya Mountains 444 B2 *Sp.* Montañas Mayas. *mountain range* Belize/Guatemala
Maych'ew 464 C4 *var.* Mai Chio, *It.* Mai Ceu. N Ethiopia
Maydān Shahr 515 E4 Wardag, E Afghanistan
Mayebashi *see* Maebashi
Mayfield 543 B6 Canterbury, South Island, NZ
Maykop 503 A7 Respublika Adygeya, SW Russian Federation
Maymana *see* Meymaneh
Maymyo 528 B3 Mandalay, C Burma
Mayo *see* Maio
Mayor Island 542 D3 *island* NE NZ
Mayor Pablo Lagerenza *see* Capitán Pablo Lagerenza
Mayotte 471 F2 *French territorial collectivity* E Africa
May Pen 446 B5 C Jamaica
Mazabuka 470 D2 Southern, S Zambia
Mazaca *see* Kayseri
Mazār-e Sharīf 515 E3 *var.* Mazār-i Sharif. Balkh, N Afghanistan
Mazār-i Sharif *see* Mazār-e Sharīf
Mazatlán 442 C3 Sinaloa, C Mexico
Mažeikiai 498 B3 Mažeikiai, NW Lithuania
Mazirbe 498 C2 Talsi, NW Latvia
Mazra'a *see* Al Mazra'ah
Mazury 490 D3 *physical region* NE Poland
Mazyr 499 C7 *Rus.* Mozyr'. Homyel'skaya Voblasts', SE Belorussia
Mbabane 470 D4 *country capital* (Swaziland) NW Swaziland
Mbacké *see* Mbaké
M'Baiki *see* Mbaïki
Mbaïki 469 C5 *var.* M'Baiki. Lobaye, SW Central African Republic
Mbaké 466 B3 *var.* Mbacké. W Senegal
Mbala 470 D1 *prev.* Abercorn. Northern, NE Zambia
Mbale 465 C6 E Uganda
Mbandaka 469 C5 *prev.* Coquilhatville. Equateur, NW Congo (Zaire)
M'Banza Congo 470 B1 *var.* Mbanza Congo; *prev.* São Salvador, São Salvador do Congo. Zaire, NW Angola
Mbanza-Ngungu 469 B6 Bas-Zaïre, W Congo (Zaire)
Mbarara 465 B6 SW Uganda
Mbé 468 B4 Nord, N Cameroon
Mbeya 465 C7 Mbeya, SW Tanzania
Mbomou *see* Bomu
M'Bomu *see* Bomu
Mbour 466 B3 W Senegal
Mbuji-Mayi 469 D7 *prev.* Bakwanga. Kasai Oriental, S Congo (Zaire)
McAlester 441 G2 Oklahoma, C USA
McAllen 441 G5 Texas, SW USA
McCamey 441 E3 Texas, SW USA
McClintock Channel 429 F2 *channel* Nunavut, N Canada
McComb 434 B3 Mississippi, S USA
McCook 437 E4 Nebraska, C USA
McKean Island 537 E3 *island* Phoenix Islands, C Kiribati
McKinley, Mount 428 C3 *var.* Denali. *mountain* Alaska, USA
McKinley Park 428 C3 Alaska, USA
McMinnville 438 B3 Oregon, NW USA
McMurdo Base 546 B4 *US research station* Antarctica
McPherson *see* Fort McPherson
McPherson 437 E5 Kansas, C USA
Mdantsane 470 D5 Eastern Cape, SE South Africa
Mead, Lake 439 D6 *reservoir* Arizona/Nevada, W USA
Mecca *see* Makkah
Mechelen 479 C5 *Eng.* Mechlin, *Fr.* Malines. Antwerpen, C Belgium
Mecklenburger Bucht 486 C2 *bay* N Germany
Mecsek 491 C7 *mountain range* SW Hungary
Medan 530 B3 Sumatera, E Indonesia
Medeba *see* Ma'dabā
Medellín 450 B3 Antioquia, NW Colombia
Médenine 463 F2 *var.* Madanīyīn. SE Tunisia
Medford 438 B4 Oregon, NW USA
Medgidia 500 D5 Constanța, SE Romania
Mediaş 500 B4 *Ger.* Mediasch, *Hung.* Medgyes. Sibiu, C Romania
Medicine Hat 429 F5 Alberta, SW Canada
Medinaceli 485 E2 Castilla-León, N Spain
Medina del Campo 484 D2 Castilla-León, N Spain
Mediterranean Sea 494 D3 *Fr.* Mer Méditerranée. *sea* Africa/Asia/Europe
Médoc 483 B5 *cultural region* SW France
Medvezh'yegorsk 502 B3 Respublika Kareliya, NW Russian Federation
Meekatharra 539 B5 Western Australia
Meemu Atoll *see* Mulaku Atoll
Meerssen 479 D6 *var.* Mersen. Limburg, SE Netherlands
Meerut 526 D2 Uttar Pradesh, N India
Mehdia *see* Mahdia
Meheso *see* Mī'ēso
Me Hka *see* Nmai Hka
Mehrīz 512 D3 Yazd, C Iran
Mehtar Lām *see* Mehtarlām
Mehtarlām 515 F4 *var.* Mehtar Lām, Meterlam, Methariam, Metharlam. Laghmān, E Afghanistan
Meiktila 528 B3 Mandalay, C Burma
Mejillones 456 B2 Antofagasta, N Chile
Mek'elē 464 C4 *var.* Makale. N Ethiopia
Mékhé 466 B3 NW Senegal
Mekong 516 D3 *var.* Lan-ts'ang Chiang, *Cam.* Mékôngk, *Chin.* Lancang Jiang, *Lao.* Mènam Khong, *Th.* Mae Nam Khong, *Tib.* Dza Chu, *Vtn.* Sông Tiên Giang. *river* SE Asia
Mékôngk *see* Mekong
Mekong, Mouths of the 529 E6 *delta* S Vietnam
Melaka 530 B3 *var.* Malacca. Melaka, Peninsular Malaysia
Melanesia 536 D3 *island group* W Pacific Ocean
Melanesian Basin 534 C2 *undersea feature* W Pacific Ocean

Montegiardino – Nandyāl

egiardino 488 E2 SE San
no
ego Bay 446 A4 var. Mobay.
maica
limar 483 D5 anc. Acunum
io, Montilium Adhemari.
ne, E France
emorelos 443 E3 Nuevo León,
Mexico
enegro 493 C5 Serb. Crna
a. Admin. region republic
Yugoslavia
e Patria 456 B3 Coquimbo,
ile
erey see Monterrey
erey 439 B6 California,
SA
erey Bay 439 A6 bay
ornia, W USA
ería 450 B2 Córdoba,
Colombia
ero 453 G4 Santa Cruz,
olivia
errey 443 E3 var. Monterey.
vo León, NE Mexico
es Claros 455 F3 Minas
is, SE Brazil
evideo 456 D4 country capital
guay) Montevideo, S Uruguay
evideo 437 F2 Minnesota,
SA
genèvre, Col de 483 D5 pass
ce/Italy
gomery 434 D2 state capital
ama, S USA
ney 487 A7 Valais,
Switzerland
luçon 482 C4 Allier, C France
oro 484 D4 Andalucía, S Spain
pelier 433 G2 state capital
ont, NE USA
pellier 483 C6 Hérault,
nce
réal 431 E4 Eng. Montreal.
bec, SE Canada
rose 436 C5 Colorado, C USA
rose 480 D3 E Scotland, UK
serrat 447 G3 var. Emerald
UK dependent territory E West
es
wa 528 B3 Sagaing, C Burma
a 488 B2 Lombardia, N Italy
a 470 D2 Southern, S Zambia
ón 485 F2 Aragón, NE Spain
ie 541 D5 Queensland,
stralia
a 539 A6 Western Australia
e 441 G1 Oklahoma, C USA
e, Lake 539 B6 lake Western
ralia
head 437 F2 Minnesota,
SA
e 430 C3 river Ontario,
nada
ehead Lake 433 G1 lake
e, NE USA
onee 430 C3 Ontario,
anada
467 E3 Mopti, C Mali
egua 453 E4 Moquegua,
eru
477 C5 Kopparberg, C Sweden
es 444 C2 Izabal, E Guatemala
nt Bay 446 B5 E Jamaica
alla 485 E4 Murcia, SE Spain
va 491 C5 var. March. river
rope see also March
va see Velika Morava
via 491 B5 Iowa, C USA
Firth 480 C3 inlet
otland, UK
a see Pelopónnisos
au River 436 D2 river South
ota, N USA
e 541 D5 New South Wales,
ustralia
ia 443 E4 Michoacán de
mpo, S Mexico
a, Sierra 484 C4 mountain
e S Spain
ni 500 C5 Dâmbovița,
mania
ou 494 C5 W Cyprus
an City 434 B3 Louisiana,
A
hāb, Daryā-ye 514 D4 var.
gap Deryasy, Rus. Murgab.
Afghanistan/Turkmenistan
oka 522 D4 Iwate, Honshū,
pan
ix 482 A3 Finistère,
France
ington Abyssal Plain 459 A7
rsea feature SE Pacific Ocean
ington Island 540 B2 island
esley Islands, Queensland,
stralia
cco 462 B3 off. Kingdom of
occo, Ar. Al Mamlakah.
try N Africa
cco see Marrakech
goro 465 C7 Morogoro,
nzania
Gulf 531 E3 gulf S Philippines
n 446 C2 Ciego de Ávila,
ba

Mörön 518 D2 Hövsgöl, N Mongolia
Morondava 471 F3 Toliara, W Madagascar
Moroni 471 F2 country capital (Comoros) Grande Comore, NW Comoros
Morotai, Pulau 531 F3 island Maluku, E Indonesia
Morotiri see Marotiri
Morrinsville 542 D3 Waikato, North Island, NZ
Morris 437 F2 Minnesota, N USA
Morris Jesup, Kap 475 E1 headland N Greenland
Morro de Môco see Môco
Morvan 482 D4 physical region C France
Moscow 504 see Moskva
Moscow 438 C2 Idaho, NW USA
Mosel 487 A5 Fr. Moselle. river W Europe see also Moselle
Moselle 479 E8 Ger. Mosel. river W Europe see also Mosel
Moselle 482 D3 department NE France
Mosgiel 543 B7 Otago, South Island, NZ
Moshi 465 C7 Kilimanjaro, NE Tanzania
Mosjøen 476 B4 Nordland, C Norway
Moskva 503 B5 Eng. Moscow. country capital (Russian Federation) Gorod Moskva, W Russian Federation
Moskva 515 E3 Rus. Moskovskiy; prev. Chubek. SW Tajikistan
Mosonmagyaróvár 491 C6 Ger. Wieselburg-Ungarisch-Altenburg; prev. Moson and Magyaróvár, Ger. Wieselburg and Ungarisch-Altenburg. Győr-Moson-Sopron, NW Hungary
Mosquito Coast 445 E3 var. Miskito Coast. coastal region E Nicaragua
Mosquitos, Golfo de los 445 F4 Eng. Mosquito Gulf. gulf N Panama
Moss 477 B6 Østfold, S Norway
Mosselbaai 470 C5 var. Mosselbai, Eng. Mossel Bay. Western Cape, SW South Africa
Mossendjo 469 B6 Le Niari, SW Congo
Mossoró 455 G2 Rio Grande do Norte, NE Brazil
Most 490 A4 Ger. Brüx. Severní Čechy, NW Czech Republic
Mosta 494 B5 var. Musta. C Malta
Mostaganem 462 D2 var. Mestghanem. NW Algeria
Mostar 492 C4 S Bosnia and Herzegovina
Mosul 504 see Al Mawṣil
Mota del Cuervo 485 E3 Castilla-La Mancha, C Spain
Motagua, Río 444 B2 river Guatemala/Honduras
Motril 484 D5 Andalucía, S Spain
Motru 500 B4 Gorj, SW Romania
Motueka 543 C5 Tasman, South Island, NZ
Motul 443 H3 var. Motul de Felipe Carrillo Puerto. Yucatán, SE Mexico
Motul de Felipe Carrillo Puerto see Motul
Mouanda see Moanda
Mouhoun see Black Volta
Mouila 469 A6 Ngounié, C Gabon
Mould Bay 429 E2 Prince Patrick Island, Northwest Territories, N Canada
Moulins 482 C4 Allier, C France
Moulmein 528 B4 var. Maulmain, Mawlamyine. Mon State, S Burma
Moundou 468 B4 Logone-Occidental, SW Chad
Moŭng Roessei 529 D5 Bătdâmbâng, W Cambodia
Moun Hou see Black Volta
Mountain Home 434 B1 Arkansas, C USA
Mount Ara see Büyükağrı Dağı
Mount Cook 543 B6 Canterbury, South Island, NZ
Mount Desert Island 433 H2 island Maine, NE USA
Mount Fuji see Fuji-san
Mount Gambier 541 B7 South Australia
Mount Isa 540 B3 Queensland, C Australia
Mount Magnet 539 B5 Western Australia
Mount Pleasant 437 G4 Iowa, C USA
Mount Pleasant 432 C3 Michigan, N USA
Mount Vernon 432 B5 Illinois, N USA
Mount Vernon 438 B1 Washington, NW USA

Mourdi, Dépression du 468 C2 desert lowland Chad/Sudan
Mouscron 479 A6 Dut. Moeskroen. Hainaut, W Belgium
Mouse River see Souris River
Moussoro 468 B3 Kanem, W Chad
Moyen Atlas 462 C2 Eng. Middle Atlas. mountain range N Morocco
Moyobamba 452 B2 San Martín, NW Peru
Moyu 518 B3 var. Karakax. Xinjiang Uygur Zizhiqu, NW China
Moyynkum, Peski 515 F1 Kaz. Moyynqum. desert S Kazakhstan
Mozambique 471 E3 off. Republic of Mozambique; prev. People's Republic of Mozambique, Portuguese East Africa. country S Africa
Mozambique Basin see Natal Basin
Mozambique Channel 471 E3 Fr. Canal de Mozambique, Mal. Lakandranon' i Mozambika. strait W Indian Ocean
Mozambique Plateau 461 D7 var. Mozambique Rise. undersea feature SW Indian Ocean
Mozambique Rise see Mozambique Plateau
Mpama 469 B6 river C Congo
Mpika 470 D2 Northern, NE Zambia
Mqinvartsveri see Kazbek
Mragowo 490 D2 Ger. Sensburg. Olsztyn, NE Poland
Mtwara 465 D8 Mtwara, SE Tanzania
Mualo see Messalo, Rio
Muang Chiang Rai see Chiang Rai
Muang Kalasin see Kalasin
Muang Không 529 D5 Champasak, S Laos
Muang Khôngxédôn 529 D5 var. Khong Sedone. Salavan, S Laos
Muang Khon Kaen see Khon Kaen
Muang Lampang see Lampang
Muang Loei see Loei
Muang Lom Sak see Lom Sak
Muang Nakhon Sawan see Nakhon Sawan
Muang Namo 528 C3 Oudômxai, N Laos
Muang Nan see Nan
Muang Phalan 528 D4 var. Muang Phalane. Savannakhét, S Laos
Muang Phalane see Muang Phalan
Muang Phayao see Phayao
Muang Phitsanulok see Phitsanulok
Muang Phrae see Phrae
Muang Roi Et see Roi Et
Muang Sakon Nakhon see Sakon Nakhon
Muang Samut Prakan see Samut Prakan
Muang Sing 528 C3 Louang Namtha, N Laos
Muang Ubon see Ubon Ratchathani
Muar 530 B3 var. Bandar Maharani. Johor, Peninsular Malaysia
Mucojo 471 F2 Cabo Delgado, N Mozambique
Mudanjiang 521 E3 var. Mu-tan-chiang. Heilongjiang, NE China
Mudon 529 B5 Mon State, S Burma
Muenchen see Munich
Muenster see Münster
Mufulira 470 D2 Copperbelt, C Zambia
Mughla see Muğla
Muğla 508 A4 var. Mughla. Muğla, SW Turkey
Mūḩ, Sabkhat al 510 C3 lake C Syria
Muir Éireann see Irish Sea
Muisne 452 A1 Esmeraldas, NW Ecuador
Mukacheve 500 B3 Hung. Munkács, Rus. Mukachevo. Zakarpats'ka Oblast', W Ukraine
Mukalla see Al Mukallā
Mula 485 E4 Murcia, SE Spain
Mulaku Atoll 524 B4 var. Meemu Atoll. atoll C Maldives
Muleshoe 441 E2 Texas, SW USA
Mulhacén 485 E5 var. Cerro de Mulhacén. mountain S Spain
Mulhouse 482 E4 Ger. Mülhausen. Haut-Rhin, NE France
Muller, Pegunungan 530 D4 Dut. Müller-gerbergte. mountain range Borneo, C Indonesia
Müllheim 487 A6 Baden-Württemberg, SW Germany
Mull, Isle of 480 B4 island W Scotland, UK
Mulongo 469 D7 Shaba, SE Congo (Zaire)
Multān 526 C2 Punjab, E Pakistan
Mumbai see Bombay
Munamägi see Suur Munamägi
Münchberg 487 C5 Bayern, E Germany
Muncie 432 C4 Indiana, N USA
Mungbere 469 E5 Haut-Zaïre, NE Congo (Zaire)

Mu Nggava see Rennell
Munich 472 D4 var. Muenchen, Bayern, SE Germany
Munkhafaḍ al Qaṭṭārah see Qaṭṭâra, Monkhafad el
Munster 481 A6 Ir. Cúige Mumhan. cultural region S Ireland
Münster 486 A4 var. Muenster, Münster in Westfalen. Nordrhein-Westfalen, W Germany
Münster in Westfalen see Münster
Muong Xiang Ngeun 528 C4 var. Xieng Ngeun. Louangphabang, N Laos
Muonio 476 D3 Lappi, N Finland
Muonioälv 476 D3 river Finland/Sweden
Muqāṭ 511 C5 Al Mafraq, E Jordan
Muqdisho 465 D6 Eng. Mogadishu, It. Mogadiscio. country capital (Somalia) Banaadir, S Somalia
Mur 487 E7 SCr. Mura. river C Europe
Muradiye 509 F3 Van, E Turkey
Murapara see Murupara
Murata 488 E2 S San Marino
Murchison River 539 A5 river Western Australia
Murcia 485 E4 cultural region SE Spain
Murcia 485 F4 Murcia, SE Spain
Mureș 500 A4 var. Maros, Mureșul, Ger. Marosch, Mieresch. river Hungary/Romania see also Maros
Mureșul see Mureș
Murfreesboro 434 D1 Tennessee, S USA
Murgab 514 D3 prev. Murgap. Maryyskiy Velayat, S Turkmenistan
Murgab 514 D3 var. Murghab, Pash. Daryā-ye Morghāb, Turkm. Murgap Deryasy. river Afghanistan/Turkmenistan
Murgab see Morghāb, Daryā-ye
Murgap Deryasy see Murgab
Murghab see Murgab
Murghob 515 F3 Rus. Murgab. SE Tajikistan
Murgon 541 E5 Queensland, E Australia
Müritz 486 C3 var. Müritzee. lake NE Germany
Müritzee see Müritz
Murmansk 502 C2 Murmanskaya Oblast', NW Russian Federation
Murmashi 502 C2 Murmanskaya Oblast', NW Russian Federation
Murom 503 B5 Vladimirskaya Oblast', W Russian Federation
Muroran 522 D3 Hokkaidō, NE Japan
Muros 484 B1 Galicia, NW Spain
Murray Fracture Zone 545 E2 tectonic feature NE Pacific Ocean
Murray Range see Murray Ridge
Murray Ridge 504 C5 var. Murray Range. undersea feature N Arabian Sea
Murray River 541 B6 river SE Australia
Murrumbidgee River 541 C6 river New South Wales, SE Australia
Murska Sobota 487 E7 Ger. Olsnitz. NE Slovenia
Murupara 542 E3 var. Murapara. Bay of Plenty, North Island, NZ
Murviedro see Sagunto
Murwāra 527 E4 Madhya Pradesh, N India
Murwillumbah 541 E5 New South Wales, SE Australia
Murzuq, Idhān 463 F4 var. Edeyin Murzuq. desert SW Libya
Mürzzuschlag 487 E7 Steiermark, E Austria
Muş 509 F3 var. Mush. Muş, E Turkey
Mûsa, Gebel 464 C2 mountain NE Egypt
Musala 496 B3 mountain W Bulgaria
Muscat 504 see Masqaṭ
Muscatine 437 G3 Iowa, C USA
Musgrave Ranges 539 D5 mountain range South Australia
Mush see Muş
Muskegon 432 C3 Michigan, N USA
Muskogee 441 G1 Oklahoma, C USA
Musoma 465 C6 Mara, N Tanzania
Musta see Mosta
Musters, Lago 457 B6 lake S Argentina
Muswellbrook 541 D6 New South Wales, SE Australia
Mut 508 C4 İçel, S Turkey
Mu-tan-chiang see Mudanjiang
Mutare 470 D3 var. Mutari; prev. Umtali. Manicaland, E Zimbabwe
Mutari see Mutare
Mutsu-wan 522 D3 bay N Japan
Muttonbird Islands 543 A8 island group SW NZ

Mu Us Shamo 519 E3 var. Ordos Desert. desert N China
Muy Muy 444 D3 Matagalpa, C Nicaragua
Mŭynoq 514 C1 Rus. Muynak. Qoraqalpoghiston Respublikasi, NW Uzbekistan
Mužlja 492 D3 Hung. Felsőmuzslya; prev. Gornja Mužlja. Serbia, N Yugoslavia
Mwali see Mohéli
Mwanza 465 B6 Mwanza, NW Tanzania
Mweka 469 C6 Kasai Occidental, C Congo (Zaire)
Mwene-Ditu 469 D7 Kasai Oriental, S Congo (Zaire)
Mweru, Lake 469 D7 var. Lac Moero. lake Congo (Zaire)/Zambia
Mweru Wantipa, Lake 469 E7 lake N Zambia
Myadzyel 499 C5 Pol. Miadzioł Nowy, Rus. Myadel'. Minskaya Voblasts', N Belorussia
Myanaung 528 B4 Irrawaddy, SW Burma
Myaungmya 528 A4 Irrawaddy, SW Burma
Myerkulavichy 499 D7 Rus. Merkulovichi. Homyel'skaya Voblasts', SE Belorussia
Myingyan 528 B3 Mandalay, C Burma
Myitkyina 528 B2 Kachin State, N Burma
Mykolayiv 501 E4 Rus. Nikolayev. Mykolayivs'ka Oblast', S Ukraine
Mýkonos 497 D6 var. Míkonos. island Kykládes, Greece, Aegean Sea
Myrhorod 501 F2 Rus. Mirgorod. Poltavs'ka Oblast', NE Ukraine
Mýrina 496 D4 var. Mírina. Límnos, SE Greece
Myrtle Beach 435 F2 South Carolina, SE USA
Mýrtos 497 D8 Kríti, Greece, E Mediterranean Sea
Myślibórz 490 B3 Gorzów, W Poland
Mysore 524 C2 var. Maisur. Karnātaka, W India
Mysore see Karnātaka
My Tho 529 D6 var. Mi Tho. Tiên Giang, S Vietnam
Mytilene see Mytilíni
Mytilíni 497 D5 var. Mitilíni; anc. Mytilene. Lésvos, E Greece
Mzuzu 471 E2 Northern, N Malawi

N

Naberezhnyye Chelny 503 D5 prev. Brezhnev. Respublika Tatarstan, W Russian Federation
Nablus 511 A6 var. Nābulus, Heb. Shekhem; anc. Neapolis, Bibl. Shechem. N West Bank
Nābulus see Nablus
Nacala 471 F2 Nampula, NE Mozambique
Nacogdoches 441 H3 Texas, SW USA
Nada see Danxian
Nadi 537 E4 prev. Nandi. Viti Levu, W Fiji
Nadur 494 A5 Gozo, N Malta
Nadvirna 500 C3 Pol. Nadwórna, Rus. Nadvornaya. Ivano-Frankivs'ka Oblast', W Ukraine
Nadvoitsy 502 B3 Respublika Kareliya, NW Russian Federation
Nadym 506 C3 Yamalo-Nenetskiy Avtonomnyy Okrug, N Russian Federation
Náfpaktos 497 B5 var. Návpaktos. Dytikí Ellás, C Greece
Náfplio 497 B6 prev. Návplion. Pelopónnisos, S Greece
Naga 531 E2 off. Naga City; prev. Nueva Caceres. Luzon, N Philippines
Nagano 523 C5 Nagano, Honshū, S Japan
Nagaoka 523 D5 Niigata, Honshū, C Japan
Nagara Pathom see Nakhon Pathom
Nagara Sridharmaraj see Nakhon Si Thammarat
Nagara Svarga see Nakhon Sawan
Nagasaki 523 A7 Nagasaki, Kyūshū, SW Japan
Nagato 523 A7 Yamaguchi, Honshū, SW Japan
Nāgercoil 524 C3 Tamil Nādu, SE India
Nagorno-Karabakhskaya Avtonomnaya Oblast see Nagornyy Karabakh
Nagornyy Karabakh 509 G3 var. Nagorno-Karabakhskaya Avtonomnaya Oblast, Arm. Lerrnayin Gharabakh, Az. Dağliq Qarabağ. former autonomous region SW Azerbaijan

Nagoya 523 C6 Aichi, Honshū, SW Japan
Nāgpur 526 D4 Mahārāshtra, C India
Nagqu 518 C5 Chin. Na-ch'ü; prev. Hei-ho. Xizang Zizhiqu, W China
Nagykálló 491 E6 Szabolcs-Szatmár-Bereg, E Hungary
Nagykanizsa 491 C7 Ger. Grosskanizsa. Zala, SW Hungary
Nagykőrös 491 D7 Pest, C Hungary
Nagyszentmiklós see Sânnicolau Mare
Naha 522 A3 Okinawa, Okinawa, SW Japan
Nahariya see Nahariyya
Nahariyya 511 A5 var. Nahariya. Northern, N Israel
Nahr al 'Āṣī see Orantes
Nahr al Līṭānī see Līṭānī, Nahr el
Nahr an Nīl see Nile
Nahr el Aassi see Orantes
Nahuel Huapi, Lago 457 B5 lake W Argentina
Nā'īn 512 D3 Eşfahān, C Iran
Nain 431 F2 Newfoundland, NE Canada
Nairobi 461 E5 country capital (Kenya) Nairobi Area, S Kenya
Nairobi 465 C6 international airport Nairobi Area, S Kenya
Najaf see An Najaf
Najima see Fukuoka
Najin 521 E3 NE North Korea
Najrān 513 B6 var. Abā as Su'ūd. Najrān, S Saudi Arabia
Nakambé see White Volta
Nakamura 523 B7 Kōchi, Shikoku, SW Japan
Nakatsugawa 523 C6 var. Nakatugawa. Gifu, Honshū, SW Japan
Nakatugawa see Nakatsugawa
Nakhodka 507 G5 Primorskiy Kray, SE Russian Federation
Nakhon Pathom 529 C5 var. Nagara Pathom, Nakorn Pathom. Nakhon Pathom, W Thailand
Nakhon Ratchasima 529 C5 var. Khorat, Korat. Nakhon Ratchasima, E Thailand
Nakhon Sawan 529 C5 var. Muang Nakhon Sawan, Nagara Svarga. Nakhon Sawan, W Thailand
Nakhon Si Thammarat 529 C7 var. Nagara Sridharmaraj, Nakhon Sithammaraj. Nakhon Si Thammarat, SW Thailand
Nakhon Sithammaraj see Nakhon Si Thammarat
Nakorn Pathom see Nakhon Pathom
Nakuru 465 C6 Rift Valley, SW Kenya
Nal'chik 503 B8 Kabardino-Balkarskaya Respublika, SW Russian Federation
Nālūt 463 F2 NW Libya
Namakan Lake 432 A1 lake Canada/USA
Namangan 515 F2 Namangan Wiloyati, E Uzbekistan
Nambala 470 D2 Central, C Zambia
Nam Co 518 C5 lake W China
Nam Định 528 D3 Nam Ha, N Vietnam
Namib Desert 470 B3 desert W Namibia
Namibe 470 A2 Port. Moçâmedes, Mossâmedes. Namibe, SW Angola
Namibia 470 B3 off. Republic of Namibia, var. South West Africa, Afr. Suidwes-Afrika, Ger. Deutsch-Südwestafrika; prev. German Southwest Africa, South-West Africa. country S Africa
Namo see Namu Atoll
Nam Ou 528 C3 river N Laos
Nampa 438 D3 Idaho, NW USA
Nampula 471 E2 Nampula, NE Mozambique
Namsos 476 B4 Nord-Trøndelag, C Norway
Nam Tha 528 C4 river N Laos
Namu Atoll 536 D2 var. Namo. atoll Ralik Chain, C Marshall Islands
Namur 479 C6 Dut. Namen. Namur, SE Belgium
Namyit Island 520 C8 island S Spratly Islands
Nan 528 C4 var. Muang Nan. Nan, NW Thailand
Nanaimo 428 D5 Vancouver Island, British Columbia, SW Canada
Nanchang 520 C5 var. Nan-ch'ang, Nanch'ang-hsien. Jiangxi, S China
Nanch'ang-hsien see Nanchang
Nan-ching see Nanjing
Nancy 482 D3 Meurthe-et-Moselle, NE France
Nandaime 444 D3 Granada, SW Nicaragua
Nānded 526 D5 Mahārāshtra, C India
Nandyāl 524 C1 Andhra Pradesh, E India

Nanjing – Norden

Nanjing *520 D5 var.* Nan-ching, Nanking; *prev.* Chianning, Chian-ning, Kiang-ning. Jiangsu, E China
Nanking *see* Nanjing
Nanning *520 B6 var.* Nan-ning; *prev.* Yung-ning. Guangxi Zhuangzu Zizhiqu, S China
Nan-ning *see* Nanning
Nanortalik *474 C5* S Greenland
Nanpan Jiang *528 D2 river* S China
Nanping *520 D6 var.* Nan-p'ing; *prev.* Yenping. Fujian, SE China
Nansei-Shotō *522 A2 var.* Ryukyu Islands. *island group* SW Japan
Nansei Syotō Trench *see* Ryukyu Trench
Nansen Basin *548 C4 undersea feature* Arctic Ocean
Nansen Cordillera *548 B3 var.* Arctic-Mid Oceanic Ridge, Nansen Ridge. *undersea feature* Arctic Ocean
Nansen Ridge *see* Nansen Cordillera
Nanterre *482 D1* Hauts-de-Seine, N France
Nantes *482 B4 Bret.* Naoned; *anc.* Condivincum, Namnetes. Loire-Atlantique, NW France
Nantucket Island *433 G3 island* Massachusetts, NE USA
Nanumaga *537 E3 var.* Nanumanga. *atoll* NW Tuvalu
Nanumanga *see* Nanumaga
Nanumea Atoll *537 E3 atoll* NW Tuvalu
Nanyang *520 C5 var.* Nan-yang. Henan, C China
Napa *439 B6* California, W USA
Napier *542 E4* Hawke's Bay, North Island, NZ
Naples *472 D5 anc.* Neapolis. Campania, S Italy
Naples *435 E5* Florida, SE USA
Napo *448 A3 province* NE Ecuador
Napo, Río *452 C1 river* Ecuador/Peru
Naracoorte *541 B7* South Australia
Naradhivas *see* Narathiwat
Narathiwat *529 C7 var.* Naradhivas. Narathiwat, SW Thailand
Narbada *see* Narmada
Narbonne *483 C6 anc.* Narbo Martius. Aude, S France
Narborough Island *see* Fernandina, Isla
Nares Abyssal Plain *see* Nares Plain
Nares Plain *427 E6 var.* Nares Abyssal Plain. *undersea feature* NW Atlantic Ocean
Nares Strait *474 D1 Dan.* Nares Stræde. *strait* Canada/Greenland
Narew *490 E3 river* E Poland
Narmada *516 B3 var.* Narbada. *river* C India
Narowlya *499 C8 Rus.* Narovlya. Homyel'skaya Voblasts', SE Belorussia
Närpes *477 D5 Fin.* Närpiö. Vaasa, W Finland
Narrabri *541 D6* New South Wales, SE Australia
Narrogin *539 B6* Western Australia
Narva *498 E2 prev.* Narova. *river* Estonia/Russian Federation
Narva *498 E2* Ida-Virumaa, NE Estonia
Narva Bay *498 E2 Est.* Narva Laht, *Ger.* Narwa-Bucht, *Rus.* Narvskiy Zaliv. *bay* Estonia/Russian Federation
Narva Reservoir *498 E2 Est.* Narva Veehoidla, *Rus.* Narvskoye Vodokhranilishche. *reservoir* Estonia/Russian Federation
Narvik *476 C3* Nordland, C Norway
Nar'yan-Mar *502 D3 prev.* Beloshchel'ye, Dzerzhinskiy. Nenetskiy Avtonomnyy Okrug, NW Russian Federation
Naryn *515 G2* Narynskaya Oblast', C Kyrgyzstan
Năsăud *500 B3 Ger.* Nussdorf, *Hung.* Naszód. Bistriţa-Năsăud, N Romania
Nase *see* Naze
Nāshik *526 C5 prev.* Nāsik. Mahārāshtra, W India
Nashua *433 G3* New Hampshire, NE USA
Nashville *434 C1 state capital* Tennessee, S USA
Näsijärvi *477 D5 lake* SW Finland
Nāsiri *see* Ahvāz
Nasiriya *see* An Nāşirīyah
Nassau *446 C1 country capital* (Bahamas) New Providence, N Bahamas
Nasser, Lake *464 B3 var.* Buhayrat Nasir, Buḩayrat Nāşir, Buḩeiret Nâşir. *lake* Egypt/Sudan
Nata *470 C3* Central, NE Botswana
Natal *455 G2* Rio Grande do Norte, E Brazil
Natal Basin *533 A6 var.* Mozambique Basin. *undersea feature* W Indian Ocean
Natanya *see* Netanya
Natchez *434 B3* Mississippi, S USA
Natchitoches *434 A2* Louisiana, S USA
Nathanya *see* Netanya
Natitingou *467 F4* NW Benin
Natuna Islands *516 D4 island group* W Indonesia
Naturaliste Plateau *533 E6 undersea feature* E Indian Ocean
Naugard *see* Nowogard
Naujamiestis *498 C4* Panevėžys, C Lithuania
Nauru *536 D2 off.* Republic of Nauru; *prev.* Pleasant Island. *country* W Pacific Ocean
Nauta *452 C2* Loreto, N Peru
Navahrudak *499 C6 Pol.* Nowogródek, *Rus.* Novogrudok. Hrodzyenskaya Voblasts', W Belorussia
Navapolatsk *499 D5 Rus.* Novopolotsk. Vitsyebskaya Voblasts', N Belorussia
Navarra *485 E2 cultural region* N Spain
Navassa Island *446 C3 US unincorporated territory* C West Indies
Navojoa *442 C2* Sonora, NW Mexico
Navolat *442 C3 var.* Navolato. Sinaloa, C Mexico
Navolato *see* Navolat
Návpaktos *see* Náfpaktos
Nawabashah *see* Nawābshāh
Nawābshāh *526 B3 var.* Nawabashah. Sind, S Pakistan
Nawoiy *515 E2 Rus.* Navoi. Nawoiy Wiloyati, C Uzbekistan
Naxçıvan *509 G3 Rus.* Nakhichevan'. SW Azerbaijan
Náxos *497 D6 var.* Naxos. Náxos, Kykládes, Greece, Aegean Sea
Náxos *497 D6 island* Kykládes, Greece, Aegean Sea
Nayoro *522 D2* Hokkaidō, NE Japan
Nazca *452 D4* Ica, S Peru
Nazca Ridge *449 A5 undersea feature* E Pacific Ocean
Naze *522 B3 var.* Nase. Kagoshima, Amami-ōshima, SW Japan
Naẕerat *511 A5 Ar.* En Nazira, *Eng.* Nazareth. Northern, N Israel
Nazilli *508 A4* Aydın, SW Turkey
Nazrēt *465 C5 var.* Adama, Hadama. C Ethiopia
N'Dalatando *470 B1 Port.* Salazar, Vila Salazar. Cuanza Norte, NW Angola
Ndélé *468 C4* Bamingui-Bangoran, N Central African Republic
Ndendé *469 B6* Ngounié, S Gabon
Ndindi *469 A6* Nyanga, S Gabon
Ndjamena *468 B3 var.* N'Djamena; *prev.* Fort-Lamy. *country capital* (Chad) Chari-Baguirmi, W Chad
Ndjolé *469 A5* Moyen-Ogooué, W Gabon
Ndola *470 D2* Copperbelt, C Zambia
Neagh, Lough *481 B5 lake* E Northern Ireland, UK
Néa Moudanía *496 C4 var.* Néa Moudhaniá. Kentrikí Makedonía, N Greece
Néa Moudhaniá *see* Néa Moudanía
Neápoli *496 B4 prev.* Neápolis. Dytikí Makedonía, N Greece
Neápoli *497 D8* Kríti, Greece, E Mediterranean Sea
Neápoli *497 C7* Pelopónnisos, S Greece
Neapolis *see* Nablus
Near Islands *428 A2 island group* Aleutian Islands, Alaska, USA
Néa Zíchni *496 C3 var.* Néa Zíkhni; *prev.* Néa Zíkhna. Kentrikí Makedonía, NE Greece
Néa Zíkhna *see* Néa Zíchni
Néa Zíkhni *see* Néa Zíchni
Nebaj *444 B2* Quiché, W Guatemala
Nebitdag *514 B2* Balkanskiy Velayat, W Turkmenistan
Neblina, Pico da *454 C1 mountain* NW Brazil
Nebraska *436 D4 off.* State of Nebraska; also known as Blackwater State, Cornhusker State, Tree Planters State. *state* C USA
Nebraska City *437 F4* Nebraska, C USA
Neches River *441 H3 river* Texas, SW USA
Neckar *487 B6 river* SW Germany
Necochea *457 D5* Buenos Aires, E Argentina
Neder Rijn *478 D4 Eng.* Lower Rhine. *river* C Netherlands
Nederweert *479 D5* Limburg, SE Netherlands
Neede *478 E3* Gelderland, E Netherlands
Neerpelt *479 D5* Limburg, NE Belgium
Neftekamsk *503 D5* Respublika Bashkortostan, W Russian Federation
Negēlē *465 D5 var.* Negelli, *It.* Neghelli. S Ethiopia
Negelli *see* Negēlē
Neghelli *see* Negēlē
Negomane *471 E2 var.* Negomano. Cabo Delgado, N Mozambique
Negomano *see* Negomane
Negombo *524 C3* Western Province, SW Sri Lanka
Negotin *492 E4* Serbia, E Yugoslavia
Negra, Punta *452 A3 headland* NW Peru
Negreşti-Oaş *500 B3 Hung.* Avasfelsőfalu; *prev.* Negreşti. Satu Mare, NE Romania
Negro, Río *457 C5 river* E Argentina
Negro, Río *454 D1 river* N South America
Negro, Río *456 D4 river* Brazil/Uruguay
Negros *531 E2 island* C Philippines
Nehbandān *512 E3* Khorāsān, E Iran
Neijiang *520 B5* Sichuan, C China
Nei Monggol Zizhiqu *see* Inner Mongolia
Nei Mongol *see* Inner Mongolia
Neiva *450 B3* Huila, S Colombia
Nellore *524 D2* Andhra Pradesh, E India
Nelson *429 G4 river* Manitoba, C Canada
Nelson *543 C5* Nelson, South Island, NZ
Néma *466 D3* Hodh ech Chargui, SE Mauritania
Neman *498 A4 Bel.* Nyoman, *Ger.* Memel, *Lith.* Nemunas, *Pol.* Niemen, *Rus.* Neman. *river* NE Europe
Neman *498 B4 Ger.* Ragnit. Kaliningradskaya Oblast', W Russian Federation
Neméa *497 B6* Pelopónnisos, S Greece
Nemours *482 C3* Seine-et-Marne, N France
Nemuro *522 E2* Hokkaidō, NE Japan
Neochóri *497 B5* Dytikí Ellás, C Greece
Nepal *527 E3 off.* Kingdom of Nepal. *country* S Asia
Nereta *498 C4* Aizkraukle, S Latvia
Neretva *492 C4 river* Bosnia and Herzegovina/Croatia
Neringa *498 A3 Ger.* Nidden; *prev.* Nida. Neringa, SW Lithuania
Neris *499 C5 Bel.* Viliya, *Pol.* Wilia; *prev. Pol.* Wilja. *river* Belorussia/Lithuania
Nerva *484 C4* Andalucía, S Spain
Neryungri *507 F4* Respublika Sakha (Yakutiya), NE Russian Federation
Neskaupstadhur *475 E5* Austurland, E Iceland
Ness, Loch *480 C3 lake* N Scotland, UK
Néstos *496 C3 Bul.* Mesta, *Turk.* Kara Su. *river* Bulgaria/Greece *see also* Mesta
Netanya *511 A6 var.* Natanya, Nathanya. Central, C Israel
Netherlands *478 C3 off.* Kingdom of the Netherlands, *var.* Holland, *Dut.* Koninkrijk der Nederlanden, Nederland. *country* NW Europe
Netherlands Antilles *447 E5 prev.* Dutch West Indies. *Dutch autonomous region* S Caribbean Sea
Netherlands New Guinea *see* Irian Jaya
Nettilling Lake *429 G3 lake* Baffin Island, Nunavut, N Canada
Neubrandenburg *486 D3* Mecklenburg-Vorpommern, NE Germany
Neuchâtel *487 A7 Ger.* Neuenburg. Neuchâtel, W Switzerland
Neuchâtel, Lac de *487 A7 Ger.* Neuenburger See. *lake* W Switzerland
Neufchâteau *479 D8* Luxembourg, SE Belgium
Neumünster *486 B2* Schleswig-Holstein, N Germany
Neunkirchen *487 A5* Saarland, SW Germany
Neuquén *457 B5* Neuquén, SE Argentina
Neuruppin *486 C3* Brandenburg, NE Germany
Neusiedler See *487 E6 Hung.* Fertő. *lake* Austria/Hungary
Neustadt an der Weinstrasse *487 B5 prev.* Neustadt an der Haardt, *hist.* Niewenstat, *anc.* Nova Civitas. Rheinland-Pfalz, SW Germany
Neustrelitz *486 D3* Mecklenburg-Vorpommern, NE Germany
Neu-Ulm *487 B6* Bayern, S Germany
Neuwied *487 A5* Rheinland-Pfalz, W Germany
Neuzen *see* Terneuzen
Nevada *439 C5 off.* State of Nevada; also known as Battle Born State, Sagebrush State, Silver State. *state* W USA
Nevada, Sierra *484 D5 mountain range* S Spain
Nevers *482 C4 anc.* Noviodunum. Nièvre, C France
Neves *468 E2* São Tomé, S Sao Tome and Principe
Nevinnomyssk *503 B7* Stavropol'skiy Kray, SW Russian Federation
Nevşehir *508 C3 var.* Nevshehr. Nevşehir, C Turkey
Nevshehr *see* Nevşehir
Newala *465 C8* Mtwara, SE Tanzania
New Albany *432 C5* Indiana, N USA
New Amsterdam *451 G3* E Guyana
Newark *433 F4* New Jersey, NE USA
New Bedford *433 G3* Massachusetts, NE USA
Newberg *438 B3* Oregon, NW USA
New Bern *435 F1* North Carolina, SE USA
New Braunfels *441 G4* Texas, SW USA
Newbridge *481 B6 Ir.* An Droichead Nua. C Ireland
New Britain *536 B3 island* E PNG
New Brunswick *431 E4 Fr.* Nouveau-Brunswick. *province* SE Canada
New Caledonia *536 D4 var.* Kanaky, *Fr.* Nouvelle-Calédonie. *French overseas territory* SW Pacific Ocean
New Caledonia *536 C5 island* SW Pacific Ocean
New Caledonia Basin *534 C4 undersea feature* W Pacific Ocean
Newcastle *see* Newcastle upon Tyne
Newcastle *541 D6* New South Wales, SE Australia
Newcastle upon Tyne *480 D4 var.* Newcastle; *hist.* Monkchester, *Lat.* Pons Aelii. NE England, UK
New Delhi *526 D3 country capital* (India) Delhi, N India
Newfoundland *431 G3 Fr.* Terre-Neuve. *island* Newfoundland, SW Canada
Newfoundland *431 F2 Fr.* Terre Neuve. *province* E Canada
Newfoundland Basin *458 B3 undersea feature* NW Atlantic Ocean
New Georgia Islands *536 C3 island group* NW Solomon Islands
New Glasgow *431 F4* Nova Scotia, SE Canada
New Goa *see* Panaji
New Guinea *536 A3 Dut.* Nieuw Guinea, *Ind.* Irian. *island* Indonesia/PNG
New Hampshire *433 F2 off.* State of New Hampshire; also known as The Granite State. *state* NE USA
New Haven *433 G3* Connecticut, NE USA
New Iberia *434 B3* Louisiana, S USA
New Ireland *536 C3 island* NE PNG
New Jersey *433 F4 off.* State of New Jersey; also known as The Garden State. *state* NE USA
Newman *538 B4* Western Australia
Newmarket *481 E6* E England, UK
New Mexico *440 C2 off.* State of New Mexico; also known as Land of Enchantment, Sunshine State. *state* SW USA
New Orleans *434 B3* Louisiana, S USA
New Plymouth *542 C4* Taranaki, North Island, NZ
Newport *432 C4* Kentucky, S USA
Newport *481 D7* S England, UK
Newport *481 C7* SE Wales, UK
Newport *433 G2* Vermont, NE USA
Newport News *433 F5* Virginia, NE USA
New Providence *446 C1 island* N Bahamas
Newquay *481 C7* SW England, UK
Newry *481 B5 Ir.* An tIúr. SE Northern Ireland, UK
New Sarum *see* Salisbury
New Siberian Islands *505 see* Novosibirskiye Ostrova
New South Wales *541 C6 state* SE Australia
Newton *437 G3* Iowa, C USA
Newtownabbey *481 B5 Ir.* Baile na Mainistreach. E Northern Ireland, UK
New Ulm *437 F2* Minnesota, N USA
New York *433 F4* New York, NE USA
New York *433 F3 state* NE USA
New Zealand *542 A4 abbrev.* NZ. *country* SW Pacific Ocean
Neyveli *524 C2* Tamil Nādu, SE India
Ngangzê Co *518 B5 lake* W China
Ngaoundéré *468 B4 var.* N'Gaoundéré. Adamaoua, N Cameroon
N'Giva *470 B3 var.* Ondjiva, *Port.* Vila Pereira de Eça. Cunene, S Angola
Ngo *469 B6* Plateaux, SE Congo
Ngoko *469 B5 river* Cameroon/Congo
Ngourti *467 H3* Diffa, E Niger
Nguigmi *467 H3 var.* N'Guigmi. Diffa, SE Niger
Nguru *467 G3* Yobe, NE Nigeria
Nha Trang *529 E6* Khanh Hoa, S Vietnam
Niagara Falls *432 D3 waterfall* Canada/USA
Niagara Falls *433 E3* New York, NE USA
Niagara Falls *430 D5* Ontario, S Canada
Niamey *467 F3 country capital* (Niger) Niamey, SW Niger
Niangay, Lac *467 E3 lake* E Mali
Nia-Nia *469 E5* Haut-Zaïre, NE Congo (Zaire)
Nias, Pulau *530 A3 island* W Indonesia
Nicaragua *444 D3 off.* Republic of Nicaragua. *country* Central America
Nicaragua, Lago de *444 D4 var.* Cocibolca, Gran Lago, *Eng.* Lake Nicaragua. *lake* S Nicaragua
Nicaragua, Lake *see* Nicaragua, Lago de
Nicaria *see* Ikaría
Nice *483 D6 It.* Nizza; *anc.* Nicaea. Alpes-Maritimes, SE France
Nicephorium *see* Ar Raqqah
Nicholas II Land *see* Severnaya Zemlya
Nicholls Town *446 C1* Andros Island, NW Bahamas
Nicobar Islands *516 B4 island group* India, E Indian Ocean
Nicosia *494 C5 Gk.* Lefkosia, *Turk.* Lefkoşa. *country capital* (Cyprus) C Cyprus
Nicoya *444 D4* Guanacaste, W Costa Rica
Nicoya, Golfo de *444 D5 gulf* W Costa Rica
Nicoya, Península de *444 D4 peninsula* NW Costa Rica
Nidzica *490 D3 Ger.* Niedenburg. Olsztyn, N Poland
Niedere Tauern *491 A6 mountain range* C Austria
Nieuw Amsterdam *451 G3* Commewijne, NE Surinam
Nieuw-Bergen *478 D4* Limburg, SE Netherlands
Nieuwegein *478 C4* Utrecht, C Netherlands
Nieuw Nickerie *451 G3* Nickerie, NW Surinam
Niğde *508 C4* Niğde, C Turkey
Niger *467 F3 off.* Republic of Niger. *country* W Africa
Niger *467 F4 river* W Africa
Nigeria *467 F4 off.* Federal Republic of Nigeria. *country* W Africa
Niger, Mouths of the *467 F5 delta* S Nigeria
Nihon *see* Japan
Niigata *523 D5* Niigata, Honshū, C Japan
Niihama *523 B7* Ehime, Shikoku, SW Japan
Niihau *439 A7 island* Hawaii, USA, C Pacific Ocean
Nii-jima *523 D6 island* E Japan
Nijkerk *478 D3* Gelderland, C Netherlands
Nijlen *479 C5* Antwerpen, N Belgium
Nijmegen *478 D4 Ger.* Nimwegen; *anc.* Noviomagus. Gelderland, SE Netherlands
Nikaria *see* Ikaría
Nikel' *502 C2* Murmanskaya Oblast', NW Russian Federation
Nikiniki *531 E5* Timor, S Indonesia
Nikopol' *501 F3* Dnipropetrovs'ka Oblast', SE Ukraine
Nikšić *493 C5* Montenegro, SW Yugoslavia
Nikumaroro *537 E3 prev.* Gardner Island, Kemins Island. *atoll* Phoenix Islands, C Kiribati
Nikunau *537 E3 var.* Nukunau; *prev.* Byron Island. *atoll* Tungaru, W Kiribati
Nile *460 D3 Ar.* Nahr an Nil. *river* N Africa
Nile *464 B2 former province* NW Uganda
Nile Delta *464 B1 delta* N Egypt
Nîmes *483 C6 anc.* Nemausus, Nismes. Gard, S France
Nine Degree Channel *524 B* *channel* India/Maldives
Ninetyeast Ridge *533 D5 un* *feature* E Indian Ocean
Ninety Mile Beach *542 C1 b* North Island, NZ
Ningbo *520 D5 var.* Ning-po, hsien; *prev.* Ninghsien. Zhej SE China
Ninghsien *see* Ningbo
Ning-po *see* Ningbo
Ningxia *520 B4 off.* Ningxia H Zizhiqu, *var.* Ning-hsia, Nin *Eng.* Ningsia Hui, Ningsia H Autonomous Region. Admi region *autonomous region* N
Ningxia Huizu Zizhiqu *see* Ningxia
Nio *see* Íos
Niobrara River *437 E3 river* Nebraska/Wyoming, C USA
Nioro *466 D3 var.* Nioro du S Kayes, W Mali
Nioro du Sahel *see* Nioro
Niort *482 B4* Deux-Sèvres, W France
Nipigon *430 B4* Ontario, S C
Nipigon, Lake *430 B3 lake* C S Canada
Nippon *see* Japan
Niš *493 E5 Eng.* Nish, *Ger.* Nis *anc.* Naissus. Serbia, SE Yug
Nişab *512 B4* Al Ḩudūd ash Shamālīyah, N Saudi Arabia
Nisibin *see* Nusaybin
Nisiros *see* Nísyros
Nisko *490 E4* Tarnobrzeg, SE Poland
Nísyros *497 E7 var.* Nisiros. Dodekánisos, Greece, Aege
Nitra *491 C6 Ger.* Neutra, *Hu* Nyitra. *river* W Slovakia
Nitra *491 C6 Ger.* Neutra, *Hu* Nyitra. Západné Slovensko, SW Slovakia
Niuatobutabu *see* Niuatoput
Niuatoputapu *537 E4 var.* Niuatobutabu; *prev.* Keppel *island* N Tonga
Niue *537 F4 self-governing ter in free association with NZ* S Ocean
Niulakita *537 E3 var.* Nuraki S Tuvalu
Niutao *537 E3 atoll* NW Tuva
Nivernais *482 C4 cultural reg* C France
Nizāmābād *526 D5* Andhra Pradesh, C India
Nizhnekamsk *503 C5* Respu Tatarstan, W Russian Feder
Nizhnevartovsk *506 D3* Kha Mansiyskiy Avtonomnyy O C Russian Federation
Nizhniy Novgorod *503 C5 p* Gor'kiy. Nizhegorodskaya C W Russian Federation
Nizhniy Odes *502 D4* Respu Komi, NW Russian Federat
Nizhnyaya Tunguska *507 E* Lower Tunguska. *river* N Ru Federation
Nizhyn *501 E1 Rus.* Nezhin. Chernihivs'ka Oblast', NE U
Njazidja *see* Grande Comore
Njombe *465 C8* Iringa, S Tan
Nkayi *469 B6 prev.* Jacob. La Bouenza, S Congo
Nkongsamba *468 A4 var.* N'Kongsamba. Littoral, W Cameroon
Nmai Hka *528 B2 var.* Me H *river* N Burma
Nobeoka *523 B7* Miyazaki, K SW Japan
Noboribetsu *522 D3 var.* Noboribetu. Hokkaidō, NE
Noboribetu *see* Noboribetsu
Nogales *440 B3* Arizona, SW
Nogales *442 B1* Sonora, NW Mexico
Nogal Valley *see* Dooxo Nug
Nokia *477 D5* Häme, SW Fin
Nokou *468 B3* Kanem, W Ch
Nola *469 B5* Sangha-Mbaéré SW Central African Republ
Nolinsk *503 C5* Kirovskaya (NW Russian Federation
Nongkaya *see* Nong Khai
Nong Khai *528 C4 var.* Mi C Nongkaya. Nong Khai, E Th
Nonouti *536 D2 prev.* Sydenh Island. *atoll* Tungaru, W Ki
Noord-Beveland *478 B4 var.* Beveland. *island* SW Nethe
Noordwijk aan Zee *478 C3* Holland, W Netherlands
Nora *477 C6* Örebro, C Swed
Norak *515 E3 Rus.* Nurek. W Tajikistan
Nord *475 F1* N Greenland
Nordaustlandet *475 G1 islan* NE Svalbard
Norden *486 A3* Niedersachse NW Germany

Norderstedt – Opatija

erstedt 486 B3 Schleswig-stein, N Germany
riesische Inseln see North an Islands
hausen 486 C4 Thüringen, ermany
horn 486 A3 Niedersachsen, Germany
kapp 476 D1 Eng. North Cape. lland N Norway
lk 437 E3 Nebraska, C USA
lk 433 F5 Virginia, NE USA
lk Island 534 D4 Australian nal territory SW Pacific Ocean
lk Ridge 534 D4 undersea ure W Pacific Ocean
s 441 G5 Texas, SW USA
sk 506 D3 Taymyrskiy lgano-Nenetskiy) Avtonomnyy ug, N Russian Federation
an 441 G1 Oklahoma, C USA
andie 482 B3 Eng. Normandy. ural region N France
andy see Normandie
anton 540 C3 Queensland, Australia
öping 477 C6 Östergötland, eden
älje 477 C6 Stockholm, eden
man 539 B6 Western ralia
Albanian Alps 493 C5 Alb. kët e Namuna, SCr. letije. mountain range nia/Yugoslavia
allerton 481 D5 N England,
am 539 A6 Western Australia
America 426 continent
ampton 481 D6 C England,
Andaman 525 F2 island aman Islands, India, ndian Ocean
Australian Basin 533 E5 Fr. in Nord de l' Australie. ersea feature E Indian Ocean
Bay 430 D4 Ontario, nada
Beveland see Noord-land
Cape 458 D1 headland New nd, NE PNG
Cape 542 C1 headland North d, NZ
Cape 548 see Nordkapp
Carolina 435 E1 off. State of h Carolina; also known as Old h State, Tar Heel State, entine State. state SE USA
Channel 432 D2 lake channel ada/USA
Charleston 435 F2 South lina, SE USA
Dakota 436 D2 off. State of h Dakota; also known as ertail State, Peace Garden , Sioux State. state N USA
eim 486 B4 Niedersachsen, rmany
ern Cook Islands 537 F4 d group N Cook Islands
ern Cyprus, Turkish ublic of 494 D5 disputed n N Cyprus
ern Dvina see Severnaya a
ern Ireland 480 B4 var. The ounties. political division UK
ern Mariana Islands 534 B1 ommonwealth territory acific Ocean
ern Sporades see Vóreioi ides
ern Territory 536 A5 ory N Australia
European Plain 473 E3 N Europe
field 437 F2 Minnesota, A
Fiji Basin 534 D3 undersea re N Coral Sea
Frisian Islands 486 B2 var. friesische Inseln. island group rmany
Huvadhu Atoll 524 B5 var. Alifu Atoll. atoll S Maldives
Island 542 B2 island N NZ
Korea 521 E3 off. ocratic People's Republic of , Kor. Chosŏn-minjujuŭi-n-kanghwaguk. country
Little Rock 434 B1 nsas, C USA
Minch see Minch, The
Mole 485 G4 harbour wall Gibraltar
Platte 437 E4 Nebraska, A
Platte River 436 D4 river A
Pole 548 B3 pole Arctic n
Saskatchewan 429 F5 river ta/Saskatchewan, S Canada
North Sea 472 C3 Dan. Nordsøen, Dut. Noordzee, Fr. Mer du Nord, Ger. Nordsee, Nor. Nordsjøen; prev. German Ocean, Lat. Mare Germanicum. sea NW Europe
North Siberian Lowland 504 see Severo-Sibirskaya Nizmennost'
North Siberian Plain see Severo-Sibirskaya Nizmennost'
North Taranaki Bight 542 C3 gulf North Island, NZ
North Uist 480 B3 island NW Scotland, UK
Northwest Atlantic Mid-Ocean Canyon 426 E4 undersea feature N Atlantic Ocean
North West Highlands 480 C3 mountain range N Scotland, UK
Northwest Pacific Basin 505 G4 undersea feature NW Pacific Ocean
Northwest Providence Channel 446 C1 channel N Bahamas
Northwest Territories 429 E3 Fr. Territoires du Nord-Ouest. territory NW Canada
Northwind Plain 548 B2 undersea feature Arctic Ocean
Norton Sound 428 C2 inlet Alaska, USA
Norway 477 A5 off. Kingdom of Norway, Nor. Norge. country N Europe
Norwegian Basin 475 F4 undersea feature NW Norwegian Sea
Norwegian Sea 475 F4 Nor. Norske Havet. sea NE Atlantic Ocean
Norwich 481 E6 E England, UK
Noshiro 522 D4 var. Nosiro; prev. Noshirominato. Akita, Honshū, C Japan
Noshirominato see Noshiro
Nosiro see Noshiro
Nosivka 501 E1 Rus. Nosovka. Chernihivs'ka Oblast', NE Ukraine
Noṣratābād 512 E3 Sīstān va Balūchestān, E Iran
Nossob 470 C4 river E Namibia
Noteć 490 C3 Ger. Netze. river NW Poland
Nóties Sporádes see Dodekánisos
Nottingham 481 D6 C England, UK
Nouâdhibou 466 B2 prev. Port-Étienne. Dakhlet Nouâdhibou, W Mauritania
Nouakchott 466 B2 country capital (Mauritania) Nouakchott District, SW Mauritania
Nouméa 536 C5 dependent territory capital (New Caledonia) Province Sud, S New Caledonia
Nouvelle-Calédonie see New Caledonia
Nova Gorica 487 D8 W Slovenia
Nova Gradiška 492 C3 Ger. Neugradisk, Hung. Újgradiska. Brod-Posavina, NE Croatia
Nova Iguaçu 455 F4 Rio de Janeiro, SE Brazil
Novara 488 B2 anc. Novaria. Piemonte, NW Italy
Nova Scotia 431 F4 Fr. Nouvelle Écosse. province SE Canada
Nova Scotia 427 E5 physical region SE Canada
Novaya Sibir', Ostrov 507 F1 island Novosibirskiye Ostrova, NE Russian Federation
Novaya Zemlya 502 D1 island group N Russian Federation
Novaya Zemlya Trench see East Novaya Zemlya Trench
Novgorod 502 B4 Novgorodskaya Oblast', W Russian Federation
Novi Iskŭr 496 C2 Grad Sofiya, W Bulgaria
Novi Pazar 493 D5 Turk. Yenipazar. Serbia, S Yugoslavia
Novi Sad 492 D3 Ger. Neusatz, Hung. Újvidék. Serbia, N Yugoslavia
Novoazovs'k 501 G4 Rus. Novoazovsk. Donets'ka Oblast', E Ukraine
Novocheboksarsk 503 C5 Chuvashskaya Respublika, W Russian Federation
Novocherkassk 503 B7 Rostovskaya Oblast', SW Russian Federation
Novodvinsk 502 C3 Arkhangel'skaya Oblast', NW Russian Federation
Novohrad-Volyns'kyy 500 D2 Rus. Novograd-Volynskiy. Zhytomyrs'ka Oblast', N Ukraine
Novokazalinsk 506 B4 Kaz. Zhangaqazaly. Kzyl-Orda, SW Kazakhstan
Novokuznetsk 506 D4 prev. Stalinsk. Kemerovskaya Oblast', S Russian Federation
Novolazarevskaya 546 C2 Russian research station Antarctica
Novo Mesto 487 E8 Ger. Rudolfswert; prev. Ger. Neustadtl. SE Slovenia
Novomoskovs'k 501 F3 Rus. Novomoskovsk. Dnipropetrovs'ka Oblast', E Ukraine
Novomoskovsk 503 B5 Tul'skaya Oblast', W Russian Federation
Novorossiysk 503 A7 Krasnodarskiy Kray, SW Russian Federation
Novoshakhtinsk 503 B6 Rostovskaya Oblast', SW Russian Federation
Novosibirsk 506 D4 Novosibirskaya Oblast', C Russian Federation
Novosibirskiye Ostrova 507 F1 Eng. New Siberian Islands. island group N Russian Federation
Novotroitsk 503 D6 Orenburgskaya Oblast', W Russian Federation
Novotroyits'ke 501 F4 Rus. Novotroitskoye. Khersons'ka Oblast', S Ukraine
Novovolyns'k 500 C1 Rus. Novovolynsk. Volyns'ka Oblast', NW Ukraine
Novy Dvor 499 B6 Rus. Novyy Dvor. Hrodzyenskaya Voblasts', W Belorussia
Novyy Buh 501 E3 Rus. Novyy Bug. Mykolayivs'ka Oblast', S Ukraine
Novyy Uzen' 506 A4 Kaz. Zhangaözen. Mangistau, W Kazakhstan
Nowogard 490 B2 var. Nowógard, Ger. Naugard. Szczecin, NW Poland
Nowógard see Nowogard
Nowy Dwór Mazowiecki 490 D3 Warszawa, C Poland
Nowy Sącz 491 D5 Ger. Neu Sandec. Nowy Sącz, S Poland
Nowy Tomyśl 490 B3 var. Nowy Tomysl. Poznań, W Poland
Noyon 482 C3 Oise, N France
Nsanje 471 E3 Southern, S Malawi
Nsawam 467 E5 SE Ghana
Ntomba, Lac 469 C6 var. Lac Tumba. lake NW Congo (Zaire)
Nubian Desert 464 B3 desert NE Sudan
Nueva Gerona 446 B2 Isla de la Juventud, S Cuba
Nueva Rosita 442 D2 Coahuila de Zaragoza, NE Mexico
Nuevitas 446 C2 Camagüey, E Cuba
Nuevo, Bajo 445 G1 island NW Colombia
Nuevo Casas Grandes 442 C1 Chihuahua, N Mexico
Nuevo, Golfo 457 C6 gulf S Argentina
Nuevo Laredo 443 E2 Tamaulipas, NE Mexico
Nui Atoll 537 E3 atoll W Tuvalu
Nûk see Nuuk
Nuku'alofa 537 E5 country capital (Tonga) Tongatapu, S Tonga
Nukufetau Atoll 537 E3 atoll C Tuvalu
Nukulaelae Atoll 537 E3 var. Nukulailai. atoll E Tuvalu
Nukulailai see Nukulaelae Atoll
Nukunau see Nikunau
Nukunonu Atoll 537 E3 island C Tokelau
Nukus 514 C2 Qoraqalpoghiston Respublikasi, W Uzbekistan
Nullarbor Plain 539 C6 plateau South Australia/Western Australia
Nunap Isua see Uummannarsuaq
Nunavut 429 F3 territory N Canada
Nuneaton 481 D6 C England, UK
Nunivak Island 428 B2 island Alaska, USA
Nunspeet 478 D3 Gelderland, E Netherlands
Nuoro 489 A5 Sardegna, Italy, C Mediterranean Sea
Nuquí 450 A3 Chocó, W Colombia
Nurakita see Niulakita
Nuremberg see Nürnberg
Nurmes 476 E4 Pohjois-Karjala, E Finland
Nürnberg 487 C5 Eng. Nuremberg. Bayern, S Germany
Nurota 515 E2 Rus. Nurata. Nawoiy Wiloyati, C Uzbekistan
Nusa Tenggara 531 E5 Eng. Lesser Sunda Islands. island group C Indonesia
Nusaybin 509 F4 var. Nisibin. Manisa, SE Turkey
Nuuk 474 C4 var. Nûk, Dan. Godthaab, Godthåb. dependent territory capital (Greenland) SW Greenland
Nyagan' 506 C3 Khanty-Mansiyskiy Avtonomnyy Okrug, N Russian Federation
Nyainqêntanglha Shan 518 C5 mountain range W China
Nyala 464 A4 Southern Darfur, W Sudan
Nyamapanda 470 D3 Mashonaland East, NE Zimbabwe
Nyamtumbo 465 C8 Ruvuma, S Tanzania
Nyandoma 502 C4 Arkhangel'skaya Oblast', NW Russian Federation
Nyantakara 465 B7 Kagera, NW Tanzania
Nyasa, Lake 471 E2 var. Lake Malawi; prev. Lago Nyassa. lake E Africa
Nyasvizh 499 C6 Pol. Nieśwież, Rus. Nesvizh. Minskaya Voblasts', C Belorussia
Nyaunglebin 528 B4 Pegu, SW Burma
Nyeri 465 C6 Central, C Kenya
Nyima 518 C5 Xizang Zizhiqu, W China
Nyíregyháza 491 D6 Szabolcs-Szatmár-Bereg, NE Hungary
Nykøbing 477 B8 Storstrøm, SE Denmark
Nyköping 477 C6 Södermanland, S Sweden
Nylstroom 470 D4 Northern, NE South Africa
Nyngan 541 D6 New South Wales, SE Australia
Nyurba 507 F3 Respublika Sakha (Yakutiya), NE Russian Federation
Nyzhn'ohirs'kyy 501 F4 Rus. Nizhnegorskiy. Respublika Krym, S Ukraine
Nzega 465 C7 Tabora, C Tanzania
Nzérékoré 466 D4 Guinée-Forestière, SE Guinea
Nzwani see Anjouan

O

Oahu 439 A7 Haw. O'ahu. island Hawaii, USA, C Pacific Ocean
Oak Harbor 438 B1 Washington, NW USA
Oakland 439 B6 California, W USA
Oamaru 543 B7 Otago, South Island, NZ
Oaxaca 443 F5 var. Oaxaca de Juárez; prev. Antequera. Oaxaca, SE Mexico
Oaxaca de Juárez see Oaxaca
Ob' 504 C2 river C Russian Federation
Obal' 499 D5 Rus. Obol'. Vitsyebskaya Voblasts', N Belorussia
Oban see Halfmoon Bay
Oban 480 C4 W Scotland, UK
Obando see Puerto Inírida
Obeliai 498 C4 Rokiškis, NE Lithuania
Oberhollabrunn see Tulln
Ob, Gulf of 504 see Obskaya Guba
Obihiro 522 D2 Hokkaidō, NE Japan
Obo 468 D4 Haut-Mbomou, E Central African Republic
Obock 464 D4 E Djibouti
Oborniki 490 C3 Poznań, W Poland
Obskaya Guba 506 D3 Eng. Gulf of Ob'. gulf N Russian Federation
Ob' Tablemount 533 B7 undersea feature S Indian Ocean
Ocala 435 E4 Florida, SE USA
Ocaña 484 D3 Castilla-La Mancha, C Spain
Ocaña 450 B2 Norte de Santander, N Colombia
Occidental, Cordillera 453 E4 mountain range Bolivia/Chile
Occidental, Cordillera 450 B2 mountain range W Colombia
Occidental, Cordillera 452 D4 mountain range W Peru
Ocean Falls 428 D5 British Columbia, SW Canada
Ocean Island see Banaba
Oceanside 439 C8 California, W USA
Ochakiv 501 E4 Rus. Ochakov. Mykolayivs'ka Oblast', S Ukraine
Och'amch'ire 509 E2 Rus. Ochamchira. W Georgia
Ocho Rios 446 B4 C Jamaica
Ochrida, Lake see Ohrid, Lake
Ocotal 444 D3 Nueva Segovia, NW Nicaragua
Ocozocuautla 443 G5 Chiapas, SE Mexico
Ocú 445 F5 Herrera, S Panama
Ōdate 522 D3 Akita, Honshū, C Japan
Oddur see Xuddur
Ödemiş 508 A4 İzmir, SW Turkey
Odense 477 B7 Fyn, C Denmark
Oder 490 B3 Cz./Pol. Odra. river C Europe
Oderhaff see Szczeciński, Zalew
Odesa 501 E4 Rus. Odessa. Odes'ka Oblast', SW Ukraine
Odessa 441 E3 Texas, SW USA
Odienné 466 D4 NW Ivory Coast
Ôdôngk 529 D6 Kâmpóng Spoe, S Cambodia
Odoorn 478 E2 Drenthe, NE Netherlands
Of 509 E2 Trabzon, NE Turkey
Ofanto 489 D5 river S Italy
Offenbach 487 B5 var. Offenbach am Main. Hessen, W Germany
Offenbach am Main see Offenbach
Offenburg 487 B6 Baden-Württemberg, SW Germany
Ogaden 465 D5 Som. Ogaadeen. plateau Ethiopia/Somalia
Ōgaki 523 C6 Gifu, Honshū, SW Japan
Ogallala 436 D4 Nebraska, C USA
Ogbomosho 467 F4 Oyo, W Nigeria
Ogden 436 B4 Utah, W USA
Ogdensburg 433 F2 New York, NE USA
Ogulin 492 A3 Karlovac, NW Croatia
Ohio 432 C4 off. State of Ohio; also known as The Buckeye State. state N USA
Ohio River 432 C4 river N USA
Ohrid 493 D6 Turk. Ochrida, Ohri. SW FYR Macedonia
Ohrid, Lake 493 D6 var. Lake Ochrida, Alb. Liqeni i Ohrit, Mac. Ohridsko Ezero. lake Albania/FYR Macedonia
Ohridsko Ezero see Ohrid, Lake
Ohura 542 D3 Manawatu-Wanganui, North Island, NZ
Oirschot 479 C5 Noord-Brabant, S Netherlands
Oise 482 C3 river N France
Oistins 447 G2 S Barbados
Ōita 523 B7 Ōita, Kyūshū, SW Japan
Ojinaga 442 D2 Chihuahua, N Mexico
Ojos del Salado, Cerro 456 B3 mountain W Argentina
Okaihau 542 C2 Northland, North Island, NZ
Okāra 526 C2 Punjab, E Pakistan
Okavanggo see Cubango
Okavango see Cubango
Okavango 470 C3 district NW Namibia
Okavango Delta 470 C3 wetland N Botswana
Okayama 523 B6 Okayama, Honshū, SW Japan
Okazaki 523 C6 Aichi, Honshū, C Japan
Okeechobee, Lake 435 E4 lake Florida, SE USA
Okefenokee Swamp 435 E3 wetland Georgia, SE USA
Okhotsk 507 G3 Khabarovskiy Kray, E Russian Federation
Okhotskoye More 507 G3 sea NW Pacific Ocean
Okhotsk, Sea of 505 F3 sea NW Pacific Ocean
Okhtyrka 501 F2 Rus. Akhtyrka. Sums'ka Oblast', NE Ukraine
Oki-guntō see Oki-shotō
Okinawa 522 A3 island SW Japan
Okinawa-shotō 522 A3 island group SW Japan
Oki-shotō 523 B6 var. Oki-guntō. island group SW Japan
Oklahoma 441 F2 off. State of Oklahoma; also known as The Sooner State. state C USA
Oklahoma City 441 G1 state capital Oklahoma, C USA
Okmulgee 441 G1 Oklahoma, C USA
Oko, Wadi 464 C3 river NE Sudan
Oktyabr'skiy 503 D6 Volgogradskaya Oblast', SW Russian Federation
Oktyabr'skoy Revolyutsii, Ostrov 507 E2 Eng. October Revolution Island. island Severnaya Zemlya, N Russian Federation
Okulovka see Uglovka
Okushiri-tō 522 C3 var. Okusiri Tô. island NE Japan
Okusiri Tô see Okushiri-tō
Öland 477 C7 island S Sweden
Olavarría 457 D5 Buenos Aires, E Argentina
Oława 490 C4 Ger. Ohlau. Wrocław, SW Poland
Olbia 489 A5 prev. Terranova Pausania. Sardegna, Italy, C Mediterranean Sea
Oldebroek 478 D3 Gelderland, E Netherlands
Oldenburg 486 B3 Niedersachsen, NW Germany
Oldenburg 486 C2 Schleswig-Holstein, N Germany
Oldenzaal 478 E3 Overijssel, E Netherlands
Old Harbour 446 B5 C Jamaica
Olëkma 507 F4 river C Russian Federation
Olëkminsk 507 F3 Respublika Sakha (Yakutiya), NE Russian Federation
Oleksandrivka 501 E3 Rus. Aleksandrovka. Kirovohrads'ka Oblast', C Ukraine
Oleksandriya 501 F3 Rus. Aleksandriya. Kirovohrads'ka Oblast', C Ukraine
Olenegorsk 502 C2 Murmanskaya Oblast', NW Russian Federation
Olenëk 507 E3 river NE Russian Federation
Oléron, Île d' 483 A5 island W France
Olevs'k 500 D1 Rus. Olevsk. Zhytomyrs'ka Oblast', N Ukraine
Ölgiy 518 C2 Bayan-Ölgiy, W Mongolia
Olhão 484 B5 Faro, S Portugal
Olifa 470 B3 Kunene, NW Namibia
Ólimbos see Ólympos
Olimpo see Fuerte Olimpo
Oliva 485 F4 País Valenciano, E Spain
Olivet 482 C4 Loiret, C France
Olmaliq 515 E2 Rus. Almalyk. Toshkent Wiloyati, E Uzbekistan
Olomouc 491 C5 Ger. Olmütz, Pol. Ołomuniec. Severní Morava, E Czech Republic
Olonets 502 B3 Respublika Kareliya, NW Russian Federation
Olovyannaya 507 F4 Chitinskaya Oblast', S Russian Federation
Olpe 486 B4 Nordrhein-Westfalen, W Germany
Olsztyn 490 D2 Ger. Allenstein. Olsztyn, N Poland
Olt 500 B5 var. Oltul, Ger. Alt. river S Romania
Oltenița 500 C5 prev. Eng. Oltenitsa, anc. Constantiola. Călărași, SE Romania
Oltul see Olt
Olvera 484 D5 Andalucía, S Spain
Olympia 438 B2 state capital Washington, NW USA
Olympic Mountains 438 A2 mountain range Washington, NW USA
Ólympos 496 B4 var. Ólimbos, Eng. Mount Olympus. mountain N Greece
Olympus, Mount see Ólympos
Omagh 481 B5 Ir. An Ómaigh. W Northern Ireland, UK
Omaha 437 F4 Nebraska, C USA
Oman 513 D6 off. Sultanate of Oman, Ar. Salṭanat 'Umān; prev. Muscat and Oman. country SW Asia
Oman, Gulf of 512 E4 Ar. Khalīj 'Umān. gulf N Arabian Sea
Omboué 469 A6 Ogooué-Maritime, W Gabon
Omdurman 464 B4 var. Umm Durmān. Khartoum, C Sudan
Ometepe, Isla de 444 D4 island S Nicaragua
Ommen 478 E3 Overijssel, E Netherlands
Omsk 506 C4 Omskaya Oblast', C Russian Federation
Ōmuta 523 A7 Fukuoka, Kyūshū, SW Japan
Onda 485 F3 País Valenciano, E Spain
Ondjiva see N'Giva
Öndörhaan 519 E2 Hentiy, E Mongolia
Onega 502 B4 river NW Russian Federation
Onega 502 C3 Arkhangel'skaya Oblast', NW Russian Federation
Onega, Lake 504 see Onezhskoye Ozero
Onex 487 A7 Genève, SW Switzerland
Onezhskoye Ozero 502 B4 Eng. Lake Onega. lake NW Russian Federation
Ongole 524 D1 Andhra Pradesh, E India
Onitsha 467 G5 Anambra, S Nigeria
Onon Gol 519 E2 river N Mongolia
Ononte see Orantes
Onslow 538 A4 Western Australia
Onslow Bay 435 F1 bay North Carolina, E USA
Ontario 430 B3 province S Canada
Ontario, Lake 433 E3 lake Canada/USA
Onteniente see Ontinyent
Ontinyent 485 F4 var. Onteniente. País Valenciano, E Spain
Ontong Java Rise 517 H4 undersea feature W Pacific Ocean
Oostakker 479 B5 Oost-Vlaanderen, NW Belgium
Oostburg 479 B5 Zeeland, SW Netherlands
Oostende 479 A5 Eng. Ostend, Fr. Ostende. West-Vlaanderen, NW Belgium
Oosterbeek 478 D4 Gelderland, SE Netherlands
Oosterhout 478 C4 Noord-Brabant, S Netherlands
Opatija 492 A2 It. Abbazia. Primorje-Gorski Kotar, NW Croatia

Opava – Parnaíba

Opava 491 C5 Ger. Troppau. Severní Morava, E Czech Republic
Opelika 434 D2 Alabama, S USA
Opelousas 434 B3 Louisiana, S USA
Opmeer 478 C2 Noord-Holland, NW Netherlands
Opochka 502 A4 Pskovskaya Oblast', W Russian Federation
Opole 490 C4 Ger. Oppeln. Opole, SW Poland
Opotiki 542 E3 Bay of Plenty, North Island, NZ
Oppidum Ubiorum see Köln
Oqtosh 515 E2 Rus. Aktash. Samarqand Wiloyati, C Uzbekistan
Oradea 500 B3 prev. Oradea Mare, Ger. Grosswardein, Hung. Nagyvárad. Bihor, NW Romania
Orahovac 493 D5 Alb. Rahovec. Serbia, S Yugoslavia
Oran 462 D2 var. Ouahran, Wahran. NW Algeria
Orange 483 D6 anc. Arausio. Vaucluse, SE France
Orange 541 D6 New South Wales, SE Australia
Orangeburg 435 E2 South Carolina, SE USA
Orange Cone see Orange Fan
Orange Fan 461 C7 var. Orange Cone. undersea feature SW Indian Ocean
Orange Mouth see Oranjemund
Orangemund see Oranjemund
Orange River 470 B4 Afr. Oranjerivier. river S Africa
Orange Walk 444 C1 Orange Walk, N Belize
Oranienburg 486 D3 Brandenburg, NE Germany
Oranjemund 470 B4 var. Orangemund; prev. Orange Mouth. Karas, SW Namibia
Oranjestad 447 E5 dependent territory capital (Aruba) W Aruba
Orantes 510 B3 var. Ononte, Ar. Nahr el Aassi, Nahr al 'Aṣī. river SW Asia
Oravița 500 A4 Ger. Orawitza, Hung. Oravicabánya. Caraș-Severin, SW Romania
Orbetello 488 B4 Toscana, C Italy
Orcadas 546 A1 Argentinian research station South Orkney Islands, Antarctica
Orchard Homes 436 B1 Montana, NW USA
Ordino 483 A8 NW Andorra
Ordos Desert see Mu Us Shamo
Ordu 508 D2 anc. Cotyora. Ordu, N Turkey
Ordzhonikidze 501 F3 Dnipropetrovs'ka Oblast', E Ukraine
Orealla 451 G3 E Guyana
Örebro 477 C6 Örebro, C Sweden
Oregon 438 B3 off. State of Oregon; also known as Beaver State, Sunset State, Valentine State, Webfoot State. state NW USA
Oregon City 438 B3 Oregon, NW USA
Orël 503 B5 Orlovskaya Oblast', W Russian Federation
Orem 436 B4 Utah, W USA
Orenburg 503 D6 prev. Chkalov. Orenburgskaya Oblast', W Russian Federation
Oreor 536 A2 var. Koror. country capital (Palau) Oreor, N Palau
Orestiáda 496 D3 prev. Orestiás. Anatolikí Makedonía kai Thráki, NE Greece
Organ Peak 440 D3 mountain New Mexico, SW USA
Orgeyev see Orhei
Orhei 500 D3 var. Orheiu, Rus. Orgeyev. N Moldavia
Orheiu see Orhei
Oriental, Cordillera 452 D3 mountain range Bolivia/Peru
Oriental, Cordillera 453 F4 mountain range C Bolivia
Oriental, Cordillera 450 B3 mountain range C Colombia
Orihuela 485 F4 País Valenciano, E Spain
Orikhiv 501 G3 Rus. Orekhov. Zaporiz'ka Oblast', SE Ukraine
Orinoco, Río 451 E2 river Colombia/Venezuela
Orissa 527 F4 state NE India
Orissaare 498 C2 Ger. Orissaar. Saaremaa, W Estonia
Oristano 489 A5 Sardegna, Italy, C Mediterranean Sea
Orito 450 A4 Putumayo, SW Colombia
Orizaba, Volcán Pico de 427 C7 var. Citlaltépetl. mountain S Mexico
Orkney see Orkney Islands
Orkney Islands 480 C2 var. Orkney, Orkneys. island group N Scotland, UK
Orkneys see Orkney Islands
Orlando 435 E4 Florida, SE USA
Orléanais 482 C4 cultural region C France
Orléans 482 C4 anc. Aurelianum. Loiret, C France
Orléansville see Chlef
Orly 482 E2 international airport (Paris) Essonne, N France
Orlya 499 B6 Rus. Orlya. Hrodzyenskaya Voblasts', W Belorussia
Ormuz, Strait of see Hormuz, Strait of
Örnsköldsvik 477 C5 Västernorrland, C Sweden
Oromocto 431 F4 New Brunswick, SE Canada
Orona 537 F3 prev. Hull Island. atoll Phoenix Islands, C Kiribati
Orosirá Rodhópis see Rhodope Mountains
Orpington 481 B8 SE England, UK
Orsha 499 E6 Rus. Orsha. Vitsyebskaya Voblasts', NE Belorussia
Orsk 506 B4 Orenburgskaya Oblast', W Russian Federation
Orșova 500 A4 Ger. Orschowa, Hung. Orsova. Mehedinți, SW Romania
Orthez 483 B6 Pyrénées-Atlantiques, SW France
Ortona 488 D4 Abruzzi, C Italy
Oruba see Aruba
Oruro 453 F4 Oruro, W Bolivia
Ōsaka 523 C6 hist. Naniwa. Ōsaka, Honshū, SW Japan
Osa, Península de 445 E5 peninsula S Costa Rica
Osborn Plateau 533 D5 undersea feature E Indian Ocean
Osh 515 F2 Oshskaya Oblast', SW Kyrgyzstan
Oshawa 430 D5 Ontario, SE Canada
Oshikango 470 B3 Ohangwena, N Namibia
Ō-shima 523 D6 island S Japan
Oshkosh 432 B2 Wisconsin, N USA
Osijek 492 C3 prev. Osiek, Osjek, Ger. Esseg, Hung. Eszék. Osijek-Baranja, E Croatia
Oskaloosa 437 G4 Iowa, C USA
Oskarshamn 477 C7 Kalmar, S Sweden
Oskil 501 G2 Rus. Oskol. river Russian Federation/Ukraine
Oslo 477 B6 prev. Christiania, Kristiania. country capital (Norway) Oslo, S Norway
Osmaniye 508 D4 Adana, S Turkey
Osnabrück 486 A3 Niedersachsen, NW Germany
Osogovske Planine see Osogovski Planina
Osogovski Planina 496 B3 var. Osogovske Planine, Mac. Osogovski Planini. mountain range Bulgaria/FYR Macedonia
Osogovski Planini see Osogovski Planina
Osorno 457 B5 Los Lagos, C Chile
Oss 478 D4 Noord-Brabant, S Netherlands
Ossa, Serra d' 484 C4 mountain range SE Portugal
Ossora 507 H2 Koryakskiy Avtonomnyy Okrug, E Russian Federation
Ostend see Oostende
Ostende see Oostende
Oster 501 E1 Chernihivs'ka Oblast', N Ukraine
Östersund 477 C5 Jämtland, C Sweden
Ostfriesische Inseln 486 A3 Eng. East Frisian Islands. island group NW Germany
Ostiglia 488 C2 Lombardia, N Italy
Ostrava 491 C5 Severní Morava, E Czech Republic
Ostróda 490 D3 Ger. Osterode, Osterode in Ostpreussen. Olsztyn, N Poland
Ostrołęka 490 D3 Ger. Wiesenhof, Rus. Ostrolenka. Ostrołęka, NE Poland
Ostrov 502 A4 Latv. Austrava. Pskovskaya Oblast', W Russian Federation
Ostrovets see Ostrowiec Świętokrzyski
Ostrów see Ostrów Wielkopolski
Ostrowiec see Ostrowiec Świętokrzyski
Ostrowiec Świętokrzyski 490 D4 var. Ostrowiec, Rus. Ostrovets. Kielce, SE Poland
Ostrów Mazowiecka 490 D3 var. Ostrów Mazowiecki. Ostrołęka, NE Poland
Ostrów Mazowiecki see Ostrów Mazowiecka
Ostrowo see Ostrów Wielkopolski
Ostrów Wielkopolski 490 C4 var. Ostrów, Ger. Ostrowo. Kalisz, C Poland
Osum see Osumit, Lumi i
Ōsumi-shotō 523 A8 island group SW Japan
Osumit, Lumi i 493 D7 var. Osum. river SE Albania
Osuna 484 D4 Andalucía, S Spain
Oswego 433 F2 New York, NE USA
Otago Peninsula 543 B7 peninsula South Island, NZ
Otaki 542 D4 Wellington, North Island, NZ
Otaru 522 C2 Hokkaidō, NE Japan
Otavalo 452 B1 Imbabura, N Ecuador
Otavi 470 B3 Otjozondjupa, N Namibia
Oțelu Roșu 500 B4 Ger. Ferdinandsberg, Hung. Nándorhgy. Caras-Severin, SW Romania
Otepää 498 D3 Ger. Odenpäh. Valgamaa, SE Estonia
Oti 467 E4 river W Africa
Otira 543 C6 West Coast, South Island, NZ
Otjiwarongo 470 B3 Otjozondjupa, N Namibia
Otorohanga 542 D3 Waikato, North Island, NZ
Otranto, Strait of 493 C6 It. Canale d'Otranto. strait Albania/Italy
Otrokovice 491 C5 Ger. Otrokowitz. Jižní Morava, SE Czech Republic
Ōtsu 523 C6 var. Ōtu. Shiga, Honshū, SW Japan
Ottawa 433 E2 Fr. Outaouais. Admin. region river Ontario/Québec, SE Canada
Ottawa 430 D5 country capital (Canada) Ontario, SE Canada
Ottawa 432 B3 Illinois, N USA
Ottawa 437 F5 Kansas, C USA
Ottawa Islands 430 C1 island group Nunavut, C Canada
Ottignies 479 C6 Walloon Brabant, C Belgium
Ottumwa 437 G4 Iowa, C USA
Ōtu see Ōtsu
Ouachita Mountains 434 A1 mountain range Arkansas/Oklahoma, C USA
Ouachita River 434 B2 river Arkansas/Louisiana, C USA
Ouadi Howa see Howar, Wādi
Ouagadougou 467 E4 var. Wagadugu. country capital (Burkina) C Burkina
Ouahigouya 467 E3 NW Burkina
Ouahran see Oran
Oualata see Oualâta
Oualâta 466 D3 var. Oualata. Hodh ech Chargui, SE Mauritania
Ouanary 451 H3 E French Guiana
Ouanda Djallé 468 D4 Vakaga, NE Central African Republic
Ouarâne 466 D2 desert C Mauritania
Ouargla 463 E2 var. Wargla. NE Algeria
Ouarzazate 462 C3 S Morocco
Oubangui see Ubangi
Oubangui-Chari see Central African Republic
Ouessant, Île d' 482 A3 Eng. Ushant. island NW France
Ouésso 469 B5 La Sangha, NW Congo
Oujda 462 D2 Ar. Oudjda, Ujda. NE Morocco
Oujeft 466 C2 Adrar, C Mauritania
Oulu 476 D4 Swe. Uleåborg. Oulu, C Finland
Oulujärvi 476 D4 Swe. Uleträsk. lake C Finland
Oulujoki 476 D4 Swe. Uleälv. river C Finland
Ounasjoki 476 D3 river N Finland
Ounianga Kébir 468 C2 Borkou-Ennedi-Tibesti, N Chad
Oup see Auob
Oupeye 479 D6 Liège, E Belgium
Our 479 D6 river NW Europe
Ourense 484 C1 Cast. Orense; Lat. Aurium. Galicia, NW Spain
Ourique 484 B4 Beja, S Portugal
Ourthe 479 D7 river E Belgium
Ouse 481 D5 river N England, UK
Outer Hebrides 480 B3 var. Western Isles. island group NW Scotland, UK
Outer Islands 471 G1 island group SW Seychelles
Outes 484 B1 Galicia, NW Spain
Ouvéa 536 D5 island Îles Loyauté, NE New Caledonia
Ouyen 541 C6 Victoria, SE Australia
Ovalle 456 B3 Coquimbo, N Chile
Ovar 484 B2 Aveiro, N Portugal
Overflakkee 478 B4 island SW Netherlands
Overijse 479 C6 Vlaams Brabant, C Belgium
Oviedo 484 C1 anc. Asturias. Asturias, NW Spain
Ovruch 500 D1 Zhytomyrs'ka Oblast', N Ukraine
Owando 469 B5 prev. Fort-Rousset. Cuvette, C Congo
Owase 523 C6 Mie, Honshū, SW Japan
Owatonna 437 F3 Minnesota, N USA
Owen Fracture Zone 532 B4 tectonic feature W Arabian Sea
Owen, Mount 543 C5 mountain South Island, NZ
Owensboro 432 B5 Kentucky, S USA
Owen Stanley Range 536 B3 mountain range S PNG
Owerri 467 G5 Imo, S Nigeria
Owo 467 F5 Ondo, SW Nigeria
Owyhee River 438 C4 river Idaho/Oregon, NW USA
Oxford 481 D6 Lat. Oxonia. S England, UK
Oxford 543 C6 Canterbury, South Island, NZ
Oxkutzcab 443 H4 Yucatán, SE Mexico
Oxnard 439 B7 California, W USA
Oyama 523 D5 Tochigi, Honshū, S Japan
Oyem 469 B5 Woleu-Ntem, N Gabon
Oyo 469 B6 Cuvette, C Congo
Oyo 467 F4 Oyo, W Nigeria
Ozark 434 D3 Alabama, S USA
Ozark Plateau 437 G5 plain Arkansas/Missouri, C USA
Ozarks, Lake of the 437 F5 reservoir Missouri, C USA
Ozbourn Seamount 544 D4 undersea feature W Pacific Ocean
Ózd 491 D6 Borsod-Abaúj-Zemplén, NE Hungary
Ozero Khanka see Khanka, Lake
Ozero Ubsu-Nur see Uvs Nuur
Ozieri 489 A5 Sardegna, Italy, C Mediterranean Sea

P

Paamiut 474 B4 var. Pâmiut, Dan. Frederikshåb. S Greenland
Pa-an 528 B4 Karen State, S Burma
Pabna 527 G4 Rajshahi, W Bangladesh
Pachuca 443 E4 var. Pachuca de Soto. Hidalgo, C Mexico
Pachuca de Soto see Pachuca
Pacific-Antarctic Ridge 546 B5 undersea feature S Pacific Ocean
Pacific Ocean 544 D3 ocean
Padalung see Phatthalung
Padang 530 B4 Sumatera, W Indonesia
Paderborn 486 B4 Nordrhein-Westfalen, NW Germany
Padma see Brahmaputra
Padova 488 C2 Eng. Padua; anc. Patavium. Veneto, NE Italy
Padre Island 441 G5 island Texas, SW USA
Padua see Padova
Paducah 432 B5 Kentucky, S USA
Paeroa 542 D3 Waikato, North Island, NZ
Páfos 494 C5 var. Paphos. W Cyprus
Pag 492 A3 It. Pago. island C Croatia
Page 440 B1 Arizona, SW USA
Pago Pago 537 F4 dependent territory capital (American Samoa) Tutuila, W American Samoa
Pahiatua 542 D4 Manawatu-Wanganui, North Island, NZ
Pahsien see Chongqing
Paide 498 D2 Ger. Weissenstein. Järvamaa, N Estonia
Paihia 542 D2 Northland, North Island, NZ
Päijänne 477 D5 lake S Finland
Paine, Cerro 457 A7 mountain S Chile
Painted Desert 440 B1 desert Arizona, SW USA
Paisley 480 C4 W Scotland, UK
País Valenciano 485 F3 cultural region NE Spain
País Vasco 485 E1 cultural region N Spain
Paita 452 B3 Piura, NW Peru
Pakanbaru see Pekanbaru
Pakaraima Mountains 451 E3 var. Serra Pacaraim, Sierra Pacaraima. mountain range N South America
Pakistan 526 A2 off. Islamic Republic of Pakistan, var. Islami Jamhuriya e Pakistan. country S Asia
Paknam see Samut Prakan
Pakokku 528 A3 Magwe, C Burma
Pak Phanang 529 C7 var. Ban Pak Phanang. Nakhon Si Thammarat, SW Thailand
Pakruojis 498 C4 Pakruojis, N Lithuania
Paks 491 C7 Tolna, S Hungary
Pakxé see Pakxé
Pakxé 529 D5 var. Paksé. Champasak, S Laos
Palafrugell 485 G2 Cataluña, NE Spain
Palagruža 493 B5 It. Pelagosa. island SW Croatia
Palaiá Epídavros 497 C6 Pelopónnisos, S Greece
Palaiseau 482 D2 Essonne, N France
Palamós 485 G2 Cataluña, NE Spain
Palamuse 498 E2 Ger. Sankt-Bartholomäi. Jõgevamaa, E Estonia
Pālanpur 526 C4 Gujarāt, W India
Palapye 470 D3 Central, SE Botswana
Palau 536 A2 var. Belau. country W Pacific Ocean
Palawan 531 E2 island W Philippines
Palawan Passage 530 D2 passage W Philippines
Paldiski 498 D2 prev. Baltiski, Eng. Baltic Port, Ger. Baltischport. Harjumaa, NW Estonia
Palembang 530 B4 Sumatera, W Indonesia
Palencia 484 D2 anc. Palantia, Pallantia. Castilla-León, NW Spain
Palermo 489 C7 Fr. Palerme; anc. Panhormus, Panormus. Sicilia, Italy, C Mediterranean Sea
Pāli 526 C3 Rājasthān, N India
Palikir 536 C2 country capital (Micronesia) Pohnpei, E Micronesia
Palimé see Kpalimé
Palioúri, Ákra 496 C4 var. Akra Kanestron. headland N Greece
Palk Strait 524 C3 strait India/Sri Lanka
Palliser, Cape 543 D5 headland North Island, NZ
Palma 485 G3 var. Palma de Mallorca. Mallorca, Spain, W Mediterranean Sea
Palma del Río 484 D4 Andalucía, S Spain
Palma de Mallorca see Palma
Palmar Sur 445 E5 Puntarenas, SE Costa Rica
Palma Soriano 446 C3 Santiago de Cuba, E Cuba
Palm Beach 540 E1 New South Wales, SE Australia
Palmer 546 A2 US research station Antarctica
Palmer Land 546 A3 physical region Antarctica
Palmerston 537 F4 island S Cook Islands
Palmerston North 542 D4 Manawatu-Wanganui, North Island, NZ
Palmi 489 D7 Calabria, SW Italy
Palmira 450 B3 Valle del Cauca, W Colombia
Palm Springs 439 D7 California, W USA
Palmyra see Tudmur
Palmyra Atoll 537 G2 US privately owned unincorporated territory C Pacific Ocean
Palo Alto 439 B6 California, W USA
Palu 531 E4 prev. Paloe. Sulawesi, C Indonesia
Pamiers 483 B6 Ariège, S France
Pamir 515 var. Daryā-ye Pāmīr, Taj. Dar"yoi Pomir. river Afghanistan/Tajikistan see also Pāmīr, Daryā-ye
Pamirs 515 F3 Pash. Daryā-ye Pāmīr, Rus. Pamir. mountain range C Asia
Pâmiut see Paamiut
Pamlico Sound 435 G1 sound North Carolina, SE USA
Pampa 441 E1 Texas, SW USA
Pampas 456 C4 plain C Argentina
Pamplona 485 E1 Basq. Iruñea; prev. Pampeluna, anc. Pompaelo. Navarra, N Spain
Pamplona 450 C2 Norte de Santander, N Colombia
Panaji 524 B1 var. Pangim, Panjim, New Goa. Goa, W India
Panama 445 G5 off. Republic of Panama. country Central America
Panamá 445 G4 var. Ciudad de Panamá, Eng. Panama City. country capital (Panama) Panamá, C Panama
Panama Basin 427 C8 undersea feature E Pacific Ocean
Panama Canal 445 F4 canal E Panama
Panama City see Panamá
Panama City 434 D3 Florida, SE USA
Panamá, Golfo de 445 G5 var. Gulf of Panama. gulf S Panama
Panama, Gulf of see Panamá, Golfo de
Panamá, Isthmus of see Panamá, Istmo de
Panamá, Istmo de 445 G4 Eng. Isthmus of Panama; prev. Isthmus of Darien. isthmus E Panama
Panay Island 531 E2 island C Philippines
Pančevo 492 D3 Ger. Pantsch[…] Hung. Pancsova. Serbia, N Yugoslavia
Paneas see Bāniyās
Panevėžys 498 C4 Panevėžys, C Lithuania
Pangim see Panaji
Pangkalpinang 530 C4 Pulau Bangka, W Indonesia
Pang-Nga see Phang-Nga
Panjim see Panaji
Pánormos 497 C7 Kríti, Gree[…] E Mediterranean Sea
Pantanal 455 E3 var. Pantana[…] Grossense. swamp SW Brazil
Pantanalmato-Grossense se[…] Pantanal
Pantelleria, Isola di 489 B7 is[…] SW Italy
Pánuco 443 E3 Veracruz-Llav[…] E Mexico
Pao-chi see Baoji
Paoki see Baoji
Paola 494 B5 E Malta
Pao-shan see Baoshan
Pao-t'ou see Baotou
Paotow see Baotou
Papagayo, Golfo de 444 C4 g[…] NW Costa Rica
Papakura 542 D3 Auckland, […] Island, NZ
Papantla 443 F4 var. Papantla[…] Olarte. Veracruz-Llave, E Me[…]
Papantla de Olarte see Papan[…]
Papeete 537 H4 dependent ter[…] capital (French Polynesia) Ta[…] W French Polynesia
Paphos see Páfos
Papilė 498 B3 Akmenė, NW Lithuania
Papillion 437 F4 Nebraska, C[…]
Papua, Gulf of 536 B3 gulf S […]
Papua New Guinea 536 B3 o[…] Independent State of Papua […] Guinea; prev. Territory of Pa[…] and New Guinea, abbrev. PN[…] country NW Melanesia
Papuk 492 C3 mountain range NE Croatia
Pará 455 E2 off. Estado do Par[…] state NE Brazil
Pará see Belém
Paracel Islands 517 E3 dispu[…] territory SE Asia
Paraćin 492 D4 Serbia, C Yug[…]
Paragua, Río 451 E3 river SE Venezuela
Paraguay 456 D2 var. Río Par[…] river C South America
Paraguay 456 C2 country C S[…] America
Paraguay, Río see Paraguay
Paraíba 455 G2 off. Estado da[…] Paraíba; prev. Parahiba, Para[…] state E Brazil
Parakou 467 F4 C Benin
Paramaribo 451 G3 country […] (Surinam) Paramaribo, N Su[…]
Paramushir, Ostrov 507 H3 SE Russian Federation
Paraná 455 E5 off. Estado do Paraná. state S Brazil
Paraná 449 C5 var. Alto Paran[…] river C South America
Paraná 455 E4 Entre Ríos, E Argentina
Paranéstio 496 C3 Anatolikí Makedonía kai Thráki, NE […]
Paraparaumu 543 D5 Wellin[…] North Island, NZ
Parchim 486 C3 Mecklenburg[…] Vorpommern, N Germany
Parczew 490 E4 Biała Podlask[…] E Poland
Pardubice 491 B5 Ger. Pardu[…] Východní Čechy, C Czech Republic
Parechcha 499 B5 Rus. Porec[…] Hrodzyenskaya Voblasts', NE Belorussia
Parecis, Chapada dos 454 D[…] Serra dos Parecis. mountain […] W Brazil
Parepare 531 E4 Sulawesi, C Indonesia
Párga 497 A5 Ípeiros, W Gre[…]
Paria, Gulf of 451 E1 var. Go[…] Paria. gulf Trinidad and Tobago/Venezuela
Parika 451 F2 NE Guyana
Paris 482 D1 anc. Lutetia, Lut[…] Parisiorum, Parisii. country […] (France) Paris, N France
Paris 441 G2 Texas, SW USA
Parkersburg 432 D4 West Vi[…] NE USA
Parkes 541 D6 New South W[…] SE Australia
Parma 488 B2 Emilia-Romag[…] N Italy
Parnahyba see Parnaíba
Parnaíba 455 F2 var. Parnahy[…] Piauí, E Brazil

Pärnu – Pólis

498 D2 Ger. Pernau, Latv.
ava; prev. Rus. Pernov.
umaa, SW Estonia
498 D2 var. Parnu Jõgi, Ger.
au. river SW Estonia
-Jaagupi 498 D2 Ger. Sankt-
i. Pärnumaa, SW Estonia
Jõgi see Pärnu
Laht 498 D2 Ger. Pernauer
t. bay SW Estonia
497 C6 island Kykládes,
ce, Aegean Sea
497 D6 Páros, Kykládes,
ce, Aegean Sea
see Hidalgo del Parral
456 B4 Maule, C Chile
matta 540 D1 New South
s, SE Australia
442 D3 var. Parras de la
te. Coahuila de Zaragoza,
lexico
de la Fuente see Parras
s 437 F5 Kansas, C USA
na 439 C7 California,
SA
na 441 H4 Texas, SW USA
i 500 C3 Hung. Páskán. Iaşi,
omania
438 C2 Washington,
USA
Calais see Dover, Strait of
alk 486 D3 Mecklenburg-
ommern, NE Germany
er 509 F3 Erzurum,
urkey
490 D2 Ger. Preußisch
nd. Elbląg, N Poland
526 A3 Baluchistān,
akistan
e Indios 457 B6 Chubut,
entina
487 D6 Bayern, SE Germany
del Brennero see Brenner
Fundo 455 E5 Rio Grande do
Brazil
y 499 C5 Pol. Postawy, Rus.
vy. Vitsyebskaya Voblasts',
Belorussia
a, Río 452 B2 river
dor/Peru
450 A4 Nariño, SW Colombia
s 498 C4 Pasvalys,
huania
nia 449 B7 physical region
ntina/Chile
ng see Phatthalung
see Pattani
m see Padova
42 D4 Taranaki, North
d, NZ
n 433 F3 New Jersey,
SA
n see Bassein
s 497 D6 island Dodekánisos,
e, Aegean Sea
527 F3 var. Azimabad. Bihār,
lia
509 F3 Ağrı, E Turkey
Lagoa dos 455 E5 lagoon
zil
97 B5 Eng. Patras; prev.
. Dytikí Ellás, S Greece
529 C7 var. Patani. Pattani,
hailand
529 C5 Chon Buri,
iland
, Río 444 D2 river
nduras
B6 Pyrénées-Atlantiques,
rance
k 429 E3 Northwest
ories, NW Canada
le 528 B4 Pegu, C Burma
88 B2 anc. Ticinum.
ardia, N Italy
ta 498 B3 Liepāja, W Latvia
ni 496 D2 Loveshka Oblast,
garia
r 506 C4 Pavlodar,
zakhstan
rad 501 G3 Rus. Pavlograd.
opetrovs'ka Oblast',
aine
28 B3 river C Burma
97 A5 island Iónioi Nísoi,
, C Mediterranean Sea
bispo see Chetumal
dú 456 D4 Paysandú,
uguay
09 E2 Rize, NE Turkey
zhik 496 C3 prev. Tatar
dzhik. Plovdivska Oblast,
lgaria
iver 434 B3 river
ana/Mississippi, S USA
441 F4 Texas, SW USA
D5 Alb. Pejë, Turk. Ipek.
, S Yugoslavia
a 502 D3 river NW Russian
ation
a 502 D3 Respublika Komi,
ussian Federation
skoye More 502 D2 Eng.
a Sea. sea NW Russian
ation

Pecos 441 E3 Texas, SW USA
Pecos River 441 E3 river New Mexico/Texas, SW USA
Pécs 491 C7 Ger. Fünfkirchen; Lat. Sopianae. Baranya, SW Hungary
Pedra Lume 466 A3 Sal, NE Cape Verde
Pedro Cays 446 C3 island group S Jamaica
Pedro Juan Caballero 456 D2 Amambay, E Paraguay
Peer 479 D5 Limburg, NE Belgium
Pegasus Bay 543 C6 bay South Island, NZ
Pegu 528 B4 var. Bago. Pegu, SW Burma
Pehuajó 456 C4 Buenos Aires, E Argentina
Pei-ching see Beijing
Peine 486 B3 Niedersachsen, C Germany
Pei-p'ing see Beijing
Peipus, Lake 498 E3 Est. Peipsi Järv, Ger. Peipus-See, Rus. Chudskoye Ozero. lake Estonia/Russian Federation
Peiraías 497 C6 prev. Piraiévs, Eng. Piraeus. Attikí, C Greece
Pèk 528 D4 var. Xieng Khouang; prev. Xiangkhoang. Xiangkhoang, N Laos
Pekalongan 530 C4 Jawa, C Indonesia
Pekanbaru 530 B3 var. Pakanbaru. Sumatera, W Indonesia
Pekin 432 B4 Illinois, N USA
Peking see Beijing
Pelagie, Isole 489 B8 island group SW Italy
Pelly Bay 429 G3 Nunavut, N Canada
Peloponnese see Pelopónnisos
Peloponnesus see Pelopónnisos
Pelopónnisos 497 B6 var. Morea, Eng. Peloponnese; anc. Peloponnesus. peninsula S Greece
Pematangsiantar 530 B3 Sumatera, W Indonesia
Pemba 471 F2 prev. Port Amelia, Porto Amélia. Cabo Delgado, NE Mozambique
Pemba 465 D7 island E Tanzania
Pembroke 430 D4 Ontario, SE Canada
Penang see George Town
Penang see Pinang, Pulau
Penas, Golfo de 457 A7 gulf S Chile
Penderma see Bandırma
Pendleton 438 C3 Oregon, NW USA
Pend Oreille, Lake 438 D2 lake Idaho, NW USA
Peneius see Pineiós
Peng-pu see Bengbu
Peniche 484 B3 Leiria, W Portugal
Péninsule de la Gaspésie see Gaspé, Péninsule de
Pennine Alps 487 A8 Fr. Alpes Pennines, It. Alpi Pennine; Lat. Alpes Penninae. mountain range Italy/Switzerland
Pennine Chain see Pennines
Pennines 481 D5 var. Pennine Chain. mountain range N England, UK
Pennsylvania 432 D3 off. Commonwealth of Pennsylvania; also known as The Keystone State. state NE USA
Penobscot River 433 G2 river Maine, NE USA
Penong 541 A6 South Australia
Penonomé 445 F5 Coclé, C Panama
Penrhyn 537 G3 atoll N Cook Islands
Penrhyn Basin 535 F3 undersea feature C Pacific Ocean
Penrith 540 D1 New South Wales, SE Australia
Penrith 481 D5 NW England, UK
Pensacola 434 C3 Florida, SE USA
Pentecost 538 D4 Fr. Pentecôte. island C Vanuatu
Penza 503 C6 Penzenskaya Oblast', W Russian Federation
Penzance 481 C7 SW England, UK
Peoria 432 B4 Illinois, N USA
Perchtoldsdorf 487 E6 Niederösterreich, NE Austria
Percival Lakes 538 C4 lakes Western Australia
Perdido, Monte 485 F1 mountain NE Spain
Perece Vela Basin see West Mariana Basin
Pereira 450 B3 Risaralda, W Colombia
Pergamino 456 C4 Buenos Aires, E Argentina
Périgueux 483 C5 anc. Vesuna. Dordogne, SW France
Perito Moreno 457 B6 Santa Cruz, S Argentina
Perlas, Archipiélago de las 445 G5 Eng. Pearl Islands. island group SE Panama
Perlas, Laguna de 445 E3 Eng. Pearl Lagoon. lagoon E Nicaragua
Perleberg 486 C3 Brandenburg, N Germany
Perm' 506 C3 prev. Molotov. Permskaya Oblast', NW Russian Federation
Pernambuco 455 G2 off. Estado de Pernambuco. state E Brazil
Pernambuco Abyssal Plain see Pernambuco Plain
Pernambuco Plain 459 C5 var. Pernambuco Abyssal Plain. undersea feature E Atlantic Ocean
Pernau see Pärnu
Pernik 496 B2 prev. Dimitrovo. Sofiyska Oblast, W Bulgaria
Perote 443 F4 Veracruz-Llave, E Mexico
Perovsk see Kzyl-Orda
Perpignan 483 C6 Pyrénées-Orientales, S France
Perryton 441 F1 Texas, SW USA
Perryville 437 H5 Missouri, C USA
Persian Gulf see Gulf, The
Perth 539 A6 state capital Western Australia
Perth 480 C4 C Scotland, UK
Perth Basin 533 E6 undersea feature SE Indian Ocean
Peru 452 C3 off. Republic of Peru. country W South America
Peru see Beru
Peru Basin 459 A5 undersea feature E Pacific Ocean
Peru-Chile Trench 448 A4 undersea feature E Pacific Ocean
Perugia 488 C4 Fr. Pérouse; anc. Perusia. Umbria, C Italy
Péruwelz 479 B6 Hainaut, SW Belgium
Pervomays'k 501 E3 prev. Ol'viopol'. Mykolayivs'ka Oblast', S Ukraine
Pervyy Kuril'skiy Proliv 507 H3 strait E Russian Federation
Pesaro 488 C3 anc. Pisaurum. Marche, C Italy
Pescara 488 D4 anc. Aternum, Ostia Aterni. Abruzzi, C Italy
Peshāwar 526 C1 North-West Frontier Province, N Pakistan
Peshkopi 493 C6 var. Peshkopia, Peshkopija. Dibër, NE Albania
Peshkopia see Peshkopi
Peshkopija see Peshkopi
Peski Karakumy see Garagumy
Pessac 483 B5 Gironde, SW France
Petach-Tikva see Petah Tiqwa
Petah Tiqva see Petah Tiqwa
Petah Tiqwa 511 A6 var. Petach-Tikva, Petah Tiqva. Tel Aviv, C Israel
Pétange 479 D8 Luxembourg, SW Luxembourg
Petchaburi see Phetchaburi
Peterborough 481 E6 prev. Medeshamstede. E England, UK
Peterborough 430 D5 Ontario, SE Canada
Peterborough 541 B6 South Australia
Peterhead 480 D3 NE Scotland, UK
Peter I Island 546 A3 Norwegian dependency Antarctica
Petermann Bjerg 475 E3 mountain C Greenland
Petersburg 433 E5 Virginia, NE USA
Peters Mine 451 F3 var. Peter's Mine. N Guyana
Peto 443 H4 Yucatán, SE Mexico
Petoskey 432 C2 Michigan, N USA
Petra see Wādī Mūsā
Petrich 496 C3 Sofiyska Oblast, SW Bulgaria
Petrinja 492 B3 Sisak-Moslavina, C Croatia
Petrodvorets 502 A4 Fin. Pietarhovi. Leningradskaya Oblast', NW Russian Federation
Petrograd see Sankt-Peterburg
Petropavlovsk 506 C4 Kaz. Petropavl. Severnyy Kazakhstan, N Kazakhstan
Petropavlovsk-Kamchatskiy 507 H3 Kamchatskaya Oblast', E Russian Federation
Petroşani 500 B4 var. Petroşeni, Ger. Petroschen, Hung. Petrozsény. Hunedoara, W Romania
Petroschen see Petroşani
Petroşeni see Petroşani
Petrozavodsk 506 B2 Fin. Petroskoi. Respublika Kareliya, NW Russian Federation
Petrozsény see Petroşani
Pevek 507 G1 Chukotskiy Avtonomnyy Okrug, NE Russian Federation
Pezinok 491 C6 Ger. Bösing, Hung. Bazin. Západné Slovensko, SW Slovakia
Pforzheim 487 B6 Baden-Württemberg, SW Germany
Pfungstadt 487 B5 Hessen, W Germany
Phangan, Ko 529 C6 island SW Thailand
Phang-Nga 529 B7 var. Pang-Nga, Phangnga. Phangnga, SW Thailand
Phangnga see Phang-Nga
Phanom Dang Raek see Dângrêk, Chuŏr Phnum
Phanom Dong Rak see Dângrêk, Chuŏr Phnum
Phan Rang see Phan Rang-Thap Cham
Phan Rang-Thap Cham 529 E6 var. Phanrang, Phan Rang, Phan Rang Thap Cham. Ninh Thuân, S Vietnam
Phan Thiêt 529 E6 Binh Thuân, S Vietnam
Pharnacia see Giresun
Phatthalung 529 C7 var. Padalung, Patalung. Phatthalung, SW Thailand
Phayao 528 C4 var. Muang Phayao. Phayao, NW Thailand
Phenix City 434 D2 Alabama, S USA
Phet Buri see Phetchaburi
Phetchaburi 529 C5 var. Bejraburi, Petchaburi, Phet Buri. Phetchaburi, SW Thailand
Philadelphia see 'Ammān
Philadelphia 433 F4 Pennsylvania, NE USA
Philippine Basin 517 F3 undersea feature W Pacific Ocean
Philippines 531 E1 off. Republic of the Philippines. country SE Asia
Philippines 531 E1 island group W Pacific Ocean
Philippine Sea 517 F3 sea W Pacific Ocean
Philippine Trench 534 A1 undersea feature W Philippine Sea
Phitsanulok 528 C4 var. Bisnulok, Muang Phitsanulok, Pitsanulok. Phitsanulok, C Thailand
Phlórina see Flórina
Phnom Penh see Phnum Penh
Phnum Penh 529 D6 var. Phnom Penh. country capital (Cambodia) Phnum Penh, S Cambodia
Phoenix 440 B2 state capital Arizona, SW USA
Phoenix Islands 537 E3 island group C Kiribati
Phôngsali 528 C3 var. Phong Saly. Phôngsali, N Laos
Phong Saly see Phôngsali
Phrae 528 C4 var. Muang Phrae, Prae. Phrae, NW Thailand
Phra Nakhon Si Ayutthaya see Ayutthaya
Phra Thong, Ko 529 B6 island SW Thailand
Phuket 529 B7 var. Bhuket, Puket, Mal. Ujung Salang; prev. Junkseylon, Salang. Phuket, SW Thailand
Phuket, Ko 529 B7 island SW Thailand
Phumĭ Kâmpóng Trâbêk 529 D5 Kâmpóng Chhnăng, N Cambodia
Phumĭ Sâmraông 529 D5 Poŭthĭsăt, NW Cambodia
Phu Vinh see Tra Vinh
Piacenza 488 B2 Fr. Paisance; anc. Placentia. Emilia-Romagna, N Italy
Piatra-Neamţ 500 C4 Hung. Karácsonkő. Neamţ, NE Romania
Piauí 455 F2 off. Estado do Piauí; prev. Piauhy. state E Brazil
Picardie 482 C3 Eng. Picardy. cultural region N France
Pichilemu 456 B4 Libertador, C Chile
Pico 484 A5 var. Ilha do Pico. island Azores, Portugal, NE Atlantic Ocean
Picos 455 F2 Piauí, E Brazil
Picton 543 C5 Marlborough, South Island, NZ
Piedras Negras 443 E2 var. Ciudad Porfirio Díaz. Coahuila de Zaragoza, NE Mexico
Pielinen 476 E4 var. Pielisjärvi. lake E Finland
Pielisjärvi see Pielinen
Piemonte 488 A2 Eng. Piedmont. cultural region NW Italy
Pierre 437 E3 state capital South Dakota, N USA
Piešt'any 491 C6 Ger. Pistyan, Hung. Pöstyén. Západné Slovensko, W Slovakia
Pietermaritzburg 470 C5 var. Maritzburg. KwaZulu/Natal, E South Africa
Pietersburg 470 D4 Northern, NE South Africa
Pigs, Bay of see Cochinos, Bahía de
Pijijiapán 443 G5 Chiapas, SE Mexico
Pikes Peak 436 C5 mountain Colorado, C USA
Pikeville 432 D5 Kentucky, S USA
Pikinni see Bikini Atoll
Piła 490 B3 Ger. Schneidemühl. Piła, NW Poland
Pilar 456 D3 var. Villa del Pilar. Ñeembucú, S Paraguay
Pilcomayo 449 C5 river C South America
Pilos see Pýlos
Pinang see George Town
Pinang, Pulau 530 B3 var. Penang, Pinang; prev. Prince of Wales Island. island Peninsular Malaysia
Pinar del Río 446 A2 Pinar del Río, W Cuba
Píndhos see Píndos
Píndhos Óros see Píndos
Píndos 496 A4 var. Píndhos Óros, Eng. Pindus Mountains; prev. Píndhos. mountain range C Greece
Pindus Mountains see Píndos
Pine Bluff 434 B2 Arkansas, C USA
Pine Creek 538 D2 Northern Territory, N Australia
Pinega 502 C3 river NW Russian Federation
Pineiós 496 B4 var. Piniós; anc. Peneius. river C Greece
Pineland 441 H3 Texas, SW USA
Pingdingshan 520 C4 Henan, C China
Pingkiang see Harbin
Ping, Mae Nam 528 B4 river W Thailand
Piniós see Pineiós
Pinkiang see Harbin
Pínnes, Ákra 496 C4 headland N Greece
Pinos, Isla de see Juventud, Isla de la
Pinotepa Nacional 443 F5 var. Santiago Pinotepa Nacional. Oaxaca, SE Mexico
Pinsk 499 B7 Pol. Pińsk. Brestskaya Voblasts', SW Belorussia
Pinta, Isla 452 A4 var. Abingdon. island Galapagos Islands, Ecuador, E Pacific Ocean
Piombino 488 B3 Toscana, C Italy
Pioneer Mountains 438 D3 mountain range Montana, N USA
Pionerskiy 498 A4 Ger. Neukuhren. Kaliningradskaya Oblast', W Russian Federation
Piotrków Trybunalski 490 D4 Ger. Petrikau, Rus. Petrokov. Piotrków, C Poland
Piraeus see Peiraías
Pirgos see Pýrgos
Piripiri 455 F2 Piauí, E Brazil
Pirna 486 D4 Sachsen, E Germany
Pirot 493 E5 Serbia, SE Yugoslavia
Pisa 488 B3 var. Pisae. Toscana, C Italy
Pisae see Pisa
Pisco 452 D4 Ica, SW Peru
Písek 491 A5 Jižní Čechy, SW Czech Republic
Pishan 518 A3 var. Guma. Xinjiang Uygur Zizhiqu, NW China
Pishpek see Bishkek
Pistoia 488 B3 anc. Pistoria, Pistoriæ. Toscana, C Italy
Pisz 490 D3 Ger. Johannisburg. Suwałki, NE Poland
Pita 466 C4 Moyenne-Guinée, NW Guinea
Pitalito 450 B4 Huila, S Colombia
Pitcairn Island 535 G4 island S Pitcairn Islands
Pitcairn Islands 535 G4 UK dependent territory C Pacific Ocean
Piteå 476 D4 Norrbotten, N Sweden
Piteşti 500 B5 Argeş, S Romania
Pitsanulok see Phitsanulok
Pittsburg 437 F5 Kansas, C USA
Pittsburgh 433 E4 Pennsylvania, NE USA
Pittsfield 433 F3 Massachusetts, NE USA
Piura 452 B2 Piura, NW Peru
Pivdennyy Buh 501 E3 Rus. Yuzhnyy Bug. river S Ukraine
Placetas 446 B2 Villa Clara, C Cuba
Plainview 441 E2 Texas, SW USA
Planeta Rica 450 B2 Córdoba, NW Colombia
Planken 486 E1 C Liechtenstein
Plano 441 G2 Texas, SW USA
Plasencia 484 C3 Extremadura, W Spain
Plata, Río de la 456 D4 var. River Plate. estuary Argentina/Uruguay
Plateau du Bemaraha see Bemaraha
Platinum 428 C3 Alaska, USA
Plattensee see Balaton
Platte River 437 E4 river Nebraska, C USA
Plattsburgh 433 F2 New York, NE USA
Plauen 487 C5 var. Plauen im Vogtland. Sachsen, E Germany
Plauen im Vogtland see Plauen
Pļaviņas 498 D4 Ger. Stockmannshof. Aizkraukle, S Latvia
Plây Cu 529 E5 var. Pleiku. Gia Lai, C Vietnam
Pleiku see Plây Cu
Plenty, Bay of 542 E3 bay North Island, NZ
Plérin 482 A3 Côtes d'Armor, NW France
Plesetsk 502 C3 Arkhangel'skaya Oblast', NW Russian Federation
Pleszew 490 C4 Kalisz, C Poland
Pleven 496 C2 prev. Plevna. Loveshka Oblast, N Bulgaria
Pljevlja 492 C4 prev. Plevlja, Plevlje. Montenegro, N Yugoslavia
Ploče 492 B4 It. Plocce; prev. Kardeljevo. Dubrovnik-Neretva, SE Croatia
Płock 490 D3 Ger. Plozk. Płock, C Poland
Plöcken Pass 487 C7 Ger. Plöckenpass, It. Passo di Monte Croce Carnico. pass SW Austria
Ploieşti 500 C5 prev. Ploeşti. Prahova, SE Romania
Plomári 497 D5 prev. Plomárion. Lésvos, E Greece
Płońsk 490 D3 Ciechanów, C Poland
Plovdiv 496 C3 prev. Eumolpias, anc. Evmolpia, Philippopolis, Lat. Trimontium. Plovdivska Oblast, C Bulgaria
Plungė 498 B3 Plungė, W Lithuania
Plyeshchanitsy 499 D5 Rus. Pleshchenitsy. Minskaya Voblasts', N Belorussia
Plymouth 447 G3 dependent territory capital (Montserrat) SW Montserrat
Plymouth 481 C7 SW England, UK
Plzeň 491 A5 Ger. Pilsen, Pol. Pilzno. Západní Čechy, W Czech Republic
Po 472 D4 river N Italy
Pobeda Peak see Pobedy, Pik
Pobedy, Pik 518 B3 var. Pobeda Peak, Chin. Tomur Feng. mountain China/Kyrgyzstan see also Tomur Feng
Pocahontas 434 B1 Arkansas, C USA
Pocatello 438 E4 Idaho, NW USA
Pochinok 503 A5 Smolenskaya Oblast', W Russian Federation
Pocking 487 D6 Bayern, SE Germany
Poděbrady 491 B5 Ger. Podiebrad. Střední Čechy, C Czech Republic
Podgorica 493 C5 prev. Titograd. Montenegro, SW Yugoslavia
Podil's'ka Vysochyna 500 D3 Rus. Podol'skaya Vozvyshennost'. mountain range SW Ukraine
Podol'sk 503 B5 Moskovskaya Oblast', W Russian Federation
Podravska Slatina 492 C3 Hung. Szlatina; prev. Slatina. Virovitica-Podravina, NE Croatia
Podujevo 493 D5 Serbia, S Yugoslavia
Po, Foci del 488 C2 var. Bocche del Po. river NE Italy
Pogradec 493 D6 var. Pogradeci. Korçë, SE Albania
Pogradeci see Pogradec
Pohnpei 536 C2 prev. Ponape Ascension Island. island E Micronesia
Poinsett, Cape 546 D4 headland Antarctica
Pointe-à-Pitre 447 G3 Grande Terre, C Guadeloupe
Pointe-Noire 469 B6 Le Kouilou, S Congo
Point Lay 428 C2 Alaska, USA
Poitiers 482 B4 prev. Poictiers, anc. Limonum. Vienne, W France
Poitou 482 B4 cultural region W France
Pokhara 527 E3 Western, C Nepal
Pokrovs'ke 501 G3 Rus. Pokrovskoye. Dnipropetrovs'ka Oblast', E Ukraine
Pola de Lena 484 D1 Asturias, N Spain
Poland 490 B4 off. Republic of Poland, var. Polish Republic, Pol. Polska, Rzeczpospolita Polska; prev. Pol. Polska Rzeczpospolita Ludowa, Polish People's Republic. country C Europe
Poland 473 E3 Kiritimati, E Kiribati
Polatlı 508 C3 Ankara, C Turkey
Polatsk 499 D5 Rus. Polotsk. Vitsyebskaya Voblasts', N Belorussia
Pol-e Khomrī 515 E4 var. Pul-i-Khumri. Baghlān, NE Afghanistan
Poli see Pólis
Polikastro see Polýkastro
Políkastron see Polýkastro
Polikrayshte 496 D2 Loveshka Oblast, N Bulgaria
Pólis 494 C5 var. Poli. W Cyprus

Pollença – Qeqertarssuaq

Pollença *485 G3 var.* Pollensa. Mallorca, Spain, W Mediterranean Sea
Pollensa *see* Pollença
Polohy *501 G3 Rus.* Pologi. Zaporiz'ka Oblast', SE Ukraine
Polonne *500 D2 Rus.* Polonnoye. Khmel'nyts'ka Oblast', NW Ukraine
Polsko Kosovo *496 D2* Loveshka Oblast, N Bulgaria
Poltava *501 F2* Poltavs'ka Oblast', NE Ukraine
Põlva *498 E3 Ger.* Pölwe. Põlvamaa, SE Estonia
Polyarnyy *502 C2* Murmanskaya Oblast', NW Russian Federation
Polýkastro *496 B3 var.* Polikastro; *prev.* Políkastron. Kentrikí Makedonía, N Greece
Polynesia *535 F4 island group* C Pacific Ocean
Pomeranian Bay *486 D2 Ger.* Pommersche Bucht, *Pol.* Zatoka Pomorska. *bay* Germany/Poland
Pomorskiy Proliv *502 D2 strait* NW Russian Federation
Pompano Beach *435 F5* Florida, SE USA
Ponca City *441 G1* Oklahoma, C USA
Ponce *447 F3* C Puerto Rico
Pondicherry *524 C2 var.* Puduchcheri, *Fr.* Pondichéry. Pondicherry, SE India
Pondichéry *see* Pondicherry
Ponferrada *484 C1* Castilla-León, NW Spain
Poniatowa *490 E4* Lublin, E Poland
Pons Aelii *see* Newcastle upon Tyne
Ponta Delgada *484 B5* São Miguel, Azores, Portugal, NE Atlantic Ocean
Ponta Grossa *455 E4* Paraná, S Brazil
Pontarlier *482 D4* Doubs, E France
Ponteareas *484 B2* Galicia, NW Spain
Ponte da Barca *484 B2* Viana do Castelo, N Portugal
Pontevedra *484 B1 anc.* Pons Vetus. Galicia, NW Spain
Pontiac *432 D3* Michigan, N USA
Pontianak *530 C4* Borneo, C Indonesia
Pontivy *482 A3* Morbihan, NW France
Pontoise *482 C3 anc.* Briva Isarae, Cergy-Pontoise, Pontisarae. Val-d'Oise, N France
Ponziane, Isole *489 C5 island* C Italy
Poole *481 D7* S England, UK
Poopó, Lago *453 F4 var.* Lago Pampa Aullagas. *lake* W Bolivia
Popayán *450 B4* Cauca, SW Colombia
Poperinge *479 A6* West-Vlaanderen, W Belgium
Poplar Bluff *437 G5* Missouri, C USA
Popocatépetl *443 E4 volcano* S Mexico
Poprad *491 D5 Ger.* Deutschendorf, *Hung.* Poprád. Východné Slovensko, NE Slovakia
Poprad *491 D5 Ger.* Popper, *Hung.* Poprád. *river* Poland/Slovakia
Porbandar *526 B4* Gujarāt, W India
Porcupine Plain *472 B3 undersea feature* E Atlantic Ocean
Pordenone *488 C2 anc.* Portenau. Friuli-Venezia Giulia, NE Italy
Poreč *492 A2 It.* Parenzo. Istra, NW Croatia
Pori *477 D5 Swe.* Björneborg. Turku-Pori, SW Finland
Porirua *543 D5* Wellington, North Island, NZ
Porkhov *502 A4* Pskovskaya Oblast', W Russian Federation
Porlamar *451 E1* Nueva Esparta, NE Venezuela
Póros *497 A5* Kefallinía, Iónioi Nísoi, Greece, C Mediterranean Sea
Póros *497 C6* Póros, S Greece
Porsangen *476 D2 fjord* N Norway
Porsgrunn *477 B6* Telemark, S Norway
Portachuelo *453 G4* Santa Cruz, C Bolivia
Portadown *481 B5 Ir.* Port An Dúnáin. S Northern Ireland, UK
Portalegre *484 C3 anc.* Ammaia, Amoea. Portalegre, E Portugal
Port Alexander *428 D4* Baranof Island, Alaska, USA
Port Alfred *470 D5* Eastern Cape, S South Africa
Port An Dúnáin *see* Portadown
Port Angeles *438 B1* Washington, NW USA
Port Antonio *446 B5* NE Jamaica
Port Arthur *441 H4* Texas, SW USA
Port Augusta *541 B6* South Australia
Port-au-Prince *446 D3 country capital* (Haiti) C Haiti
Port-au-Prince *427 D7 international airport* E Haiti
Port Blair *525 F2* Andaman and Nicobar Islands, SE India
Port Charlotte *435 E4* Florida, SE USA
Port d'Envalira *483 B8* E Andorra
Port Douglas *540 D3* Queensland, NE Australia
Port Elizabeth *470 C5* Eastern Cape, S South Africa
Porterville *439 C7* California, W USA
Port-Gentil *469 A6* Ogooué-Maritime, W Gabon
Port Harcourt *467 G5* Rivers, S Nigeria
Port Hardy *428 D5* Vancouver Island, British Columbia, SW Canada
Port Harrison *see* Inukjuak
Port Hedland *538 B4* Western Australia
Port Huron *432 D3* Michigan, N USA
Portimão *484 B4 var.* Vila Nova de Portimão. Faro, S Portugal
Port Jackson *540 E1 harbour* New South Wales, SE Australia
Port Láirge *see* Waterford
Portland *433 G2* Maine, NE USA
Portland *438 B3* Oregon, NW USA
Portland *441 G4* Texas, SW USA
Portland *541 B7* Victoria, SE Australia
Portland Bight *446 B5 bay* S Jamaica
Portlaoighise *see* Portlaoise
Portlaoise *481 B6 Ir.* Portlaoighise; *prev.* Maryborough. C Ireland
Port Lavaca *441 G4* Texas, SW USA
Port Lincoln *541 A6* South Australia
Port Louis *471 H3 country capital* (Mauritius) NW Mauritius
Port Macquarie *541 E6* New South Wales, SE Australia
Portmore *446 B5* C Jamaica
Port Moresby *536 B3 country capital* (PNG) Central/National Capital District, SW PNG
Port Musgrave *541 B9 bay* Queensland, N Australia
Port Natal *see* Durban
Porto *484 B2 Eng.* Oporto; *anc.* Portus Cale. Porto, NW Portugal
Porto Alegre *455 E5 var.* Pôrto Alegre. *state capital* Rio Grande do Sul, S Brazil
Porto Alegre *468 E2* São Tomé, S Sao Tome and Principe
Porto Bello *see* Portobelo
Portobelo *445 G4 var.* Porto Bello, Puerto Bello. Colón, N Panama
Port O'Connor *441 G4* Texas, SW USA
Porto Edda *see* Sarandë
Portoferraio *488 B4* Toscana, C Italy
Port-of-Spain *447 H5 country capital* (Trinidad and Tobago) Trinidad, Trinidad and Tobago
Porto Grande *see* Mindelo
Portogruaro *488 C2* Veneto, NE Italy
Porto-Novo *467 F5 country capital* (Benin) S Benin
Porto Santo *462 A2 var.* Ilha do Porto Santo. *island* Madeira, Portugal, NE Atlantic Ocean
Porto Torres *489 A5* Sardegna, Italy, C Mediterranean Sea
Porto Velho *454 D2 var.* Velho. *state capital* Rondônia, W Brazil
Portoviejo *452 A2 var.* Puertoviejo. Manabí, W Ecuador
Port Pirie *541 B6* South Australia
Port Said *464 B1 Ar.* Būr Saʿīd. N Egypt
Portsmouth *433 G3* New Hampshire, NE USA
Portsmouth *432 D4* Ohio, N USA
Portsmouth *481 D7* S England, UK
Portsmouth *433 F5* Virginia, NE USA
Port Stanley *see* Stanley
Port Sudan *464 C3* Red Sea, NE Sudan
Port Swettenham *see* Klang
Port Talbot *481 C7* S Wales, UK
Portugal *484 B3 off.* Republic of Portugal. *country* SW Europe
Port-Vila *536 D4 var.* Vila. *country capital* (Vanuatu) Éfaté, C Vanuatu
Porvenir *457 B8* Magallanes, S Chile
Porvenir *453 E3* Pando, NW Bolivia
Porvoo *477 E6 Swe.* Borgå. Uusimaa, S Finland
Posadas *456 D3* Misiones, NE Argentina
Posterholt *479 D5* Limburg, SE Netherlands
Postojna *487 D8 Ger.* Adelsberg, *It.* Postumia. SW Slovenia
Potamós *497 C7* Antikýthira, S Greece
Potenza *489 D5 anc.* Potentia. Basilicata, S Italy
P'ot'i *509 F2* W Georgia
Potiskum *467 G4* Yobe, NE Nigeria
Potomac River *433 E5 river* NE USA
Potosí *453 F4* Potosí, S Bolivia
Potsdam *486 D3* Brandenburg, NE Germany
Potwar Plateau *526 C2 plateau* NE Pakistan
Poŭthĭsăt *529 D6 prev.* Pursat. Poŭthĭsăt, W Cambodia
Po Valley *488 C2 It.* Valle del Po. *valley* N Italy
Považská Bystrica *491 C5 Ger.* Waagbistritz, *Hung.* Vágbeszterce. Stredné Slovensko, NW Slovakia
Poverty Bay *542 E4 inlet* North Island, NZ
Póvoa de Varzim *484 B2* Porto, NW Portugal
Powder River *436 D2 river* Montana/Wyoming, NW USA
Powell *436 C2* Wyoming, C USA
Powell, Lake *436 B5 lake* Utah, W USA
Požarevac *492 D4 Ger.* Passarowitz. Serbia, NE Yugoslavia
Poza Rica *443 F4 var.* Poza Rica de Hidalgo. Veracruz-Llave, E Mexico
Poza Rica de Hidalgo *see* Poza Rica
Požega *492 D4* Serbia, W Yugoslavia
Poznań *490 C3 Ger.* Posen, Posnania. Poznań, W Poland
Pozoblanco *484 D4* Andalucía, S Spain
Pozzallo *489 C8* Sicilia, Italy, C Mediterranean Sea
Prachatice *491 A5 Ger.* Prachatitz. Jižní Čechy, SW Czech Republic
Prae *see* Phrae
Prague *472 D3* Oklahoma, C USA
Praha *491 A5 Eng.* Prague, *Ger.* Prag, *Pol.* Praga. *country capital* (Czech Republic) Střední Čechy, NW Czech Republic
Praia *466 A3 country capital* (Cape Verde) Santiago, S Cape Verde
Prato *488 B3* Toscana, C Italy
Pratt *437 E5* Kansas, C USA
Prattville *434 D2* Alabama, S USA
Pravda *496 D1 prev.* Dogrular. Razgradska Oblast, NE Bulgaria
Pravia *484 C1* Asturias, N Spain
Prenzlau *486 D3* Brandenburg, NE Germany
Přerov *491 C5 Ger.* Prerau. Severní Morava, E Czech Republic
Presa de la Amistad *see* Amistad Reservoir
Preschau *see* Prešov
Prescott *440 B2* Arizona, SW USA
Preševo *493 D5* Serbia, SE Yugoslavia
Presidente Epitácio *455 E4* São Paulo, S Brazil
Prešov *491 D5 var.* Preschau, *Ger.* Eperies, *Hung.* Eperjes. Východné Slovensko, NE Slovakia
Prespa, Lake *493 D6 Alb.* Liqen i Prespës, *Gk.* Límni Megáli Préspa, Limni Prespa, *Mac.* Prespansko Ezero, *Serb.* Prespansko Jezero. *lake* SE Europe
Presque Isle *433 H1* Maine, NE USA
Preston *481 D5* NW England, UK
Prestwick *480 C4* W Scotland, UK
Pretoria *470 D4 var.* Epitoli, Tshwane. *country capital* (South Africa-administrative capital) Gauteng, NE South Africa
Préveza *497 A5* Ípeiros, W Greece
Pribilof Islands *428 A3 island group* Alaska, USA
Priboj *492 C4* Serbia, W Yugoslavia
Price *436 B4* Utah, W USA
Prichard *434 C3* Alabama, S USA
Priekulė *498 B3 Ger.* Prökuls. Gargždai, W Lithuania
Prienai *499 B5 Pol.* Preny. Prienai, S Lithuania
Prieska *470 C4* Northern Cape, C South Africa
Prijedor *492 B3* NW Bosnia and Herzegovina
Prijepolje *492 D4* Serbia, W Yugoslavia
Prilep *493 D6 Turk.* Perlepe. S FYR Macedonia
Primorsk *498 A4 Ger.* Fischhausen. Kaliningradskaya Oblast', W Russian Federation
Primorsko *496 E2 prev.* Keupriya. Burgaska Oblast, SE Bulgaria
Prince Albert *429 F5* Saskatchewan, S Canada
Prince Edward Island *431 F4 Fr.* Île-du Prince-Édouard. *province* SE Canada
Prince Edward Islands *461 E8 island group* S South Africa
Prince George *429 E5* British Columbia, SW Canada
Prince of Wales Island *429 F2 island* Queen Elizabeth Islands, Nunavut, NW Canada
Prince of Wales Island *540 B1 island* Queensland, E Australia
Prince Patrick Island *429 E2 island* Parry Islands, Northwest Territories, NW Canada
Prince Rupert *428 D4* British Columbia, SW Canada
Prince's Island *see* Príncipe
Princess Charlotte Bay *540 C2 bay* Queensland, NE Australia
Princess Elizabeth Land *546 C3 physical region* Antarctica
Príncipe *469 A5 var.* Príncipe Island, *Eng.* Prince's Island. *island* N Sao Tome and Principe
Príncipe Island *see* Príncipe
Prinzapolka *445 E3* Región Autónoma Atlántico Norte, NE Nicaragua
Pripet *499 C7 Bel.* Prypyats', *Ukr.* Pryp"yat'. *river* Belorussia/Ukraine
Pripet Marshes *499 B7 wetland* Belorussia/Ukraine
Priština *493 D5 Alb.* Prishtinë. Serbia, S Yugoslavia
Privas *483 D5* Ardèche, E France
Prizren *493 D5 Alb.* Prizreni. Serbia, S Yugoslavia
Probolinggo *530 D5* Jawa, C Indonesia
Progreso *443 H3* Yucatán, SE Mexico
Prokhladnyy *503 B8* Kabardino-Balkarskaya Respublika, SW Russian Federation
Prokuplje *493 D5* Serbia, SE Yugoslavia
Prome *528 B4 var.* Pyè. Pegu, C Burma
Promyshlennyy *502 E3* Respublika Komi, NW Russian Federation
Prostějov *491 C5 Ger.* Prossnitz, *Pol.* Prościejów. Jižní Morava, SE Czech Republic
Provence *483 D6 cultural region* SE France
Providence *see* Fort Providence
Providence *433 G3 state capital* Rhode Island, NE USA
Providencia, Isla de *445 F3 island* NW Colombia
Provideniya *548 B1* Chukotskiy Avtonomnyy Okrug, NE Russian Federation
Provo *436 B4* Utah, W USA
Prudhoe Bay *428 D2* Alaska, USA
Prusa *see* Bursa
Pruszków *490 D3 Ger.* Kaltdorf. Warszawa, C Poland
Prut *500 D4 Ger.* Pruth. *river* E Europe
Pruzhany *499 B6 Pol.* Prużana. Brestskaya Voblasts', SW Belorussia
Prydniprovs'ka Vysochyna *501 G3 Rus.* Pridneprovskaya Vozvyshennost'. *mountain range* NW Ukraine
Prydz Bay *546 D3 bay* Antarctica
Pryluky *501 E2 Rus.* Priluki. Chernihivs'ka Oblast', NE Ukraine
Prymors'k *501 G4 Rus.* Primorsk; *prev.* Primorskoye. Zaporiz'ka Oblast', SE Ukraine
Przemyśl *491 E5 Rus.* Peremyshl. Przemyśl, SE Poland
Psará *497 D5 island* E Greece
Psël *501 F2 river* Russian Federation/Ukraine
Pskov *506 B2 Ger.* Pleskau, *Latv.* Pleskava. Pskovskaya Oblast', W Russian Federation
Pskov, Lake *498 E3 Est.* Pihkva Järv, *Ger.* Pleskauer See, *Rus.* Pskovskoye Ozero. *lake* Estonia/Russian Federation
Ptsich *499 C7 Rus.* Ptich'. *river* SE Belorussia
Ptsich *499 C7 Rus.* Ptich'. Homyel'skaya Voblasts', SE Belorussia
Ptuj *487 E7 Ger.* Pettau; *anc.* Poetovio. NE Slovenia
Pucallpa *452 C3* Ucayali, C Peru
Puck *490 C2* Gdańsk, N Poland
Pudasjärvi *476 D4* Oulu, C Finland
Puduchcheri *see* Pondicherry
Puebla *443 F4 var.* Puebla de Zaragoza. Puebla, S Mexico
Puebla de Zaragoza *see* Puebla
Pueblo *436 D5* Colorado, C USA
Puerto Acosta *453 E4* La Paz, W Bolivia
Puerto Aisén *457 B6* Aisén, S Chile
Puerto Ángel *443 F5* Oaxaca, SE Mexico
Puerto Ayacucho *450 D3* Amazonas, SW Venezuela
Puerto Baquerizo Moreno *452 B4 var.* Baquerizo Moreno. Galapagos Islands, Ecuador, E Pacific Ocean
Puerto Barrios *444 C2* Izabal, E Guatemala
Puerto Bello *see* Portobelo
Puerto Berrío *450 B2* Antioquia, C Colombia
Puerto Cabello *450 D1* Carabobo, N Venezuela
Puerto Cabezas *445 E2 var.* Bilwi. Región Autónoma Atlántico Norte, NE Nicaragua
Puerto Carreño *450 D3* Vichada, E Colombia
Puerto Cortés *444 C2* Cortés, NW Honduras
Puerto Cumarebo *450 C1* Falcón, N Venezuela
Puerto Deseado *457 C7* Santa Cruz, SE Argentina
Puerto Escondido *443 F5* Oaxaca, SE Mexico
Puerto Francisco de Orellana *452 B1 var.* Coca. Napo, N Ecuador
Puerto Gallegos *see* Río Gallegos
Puerto Inírida *450 D3 var.* Obando. Guainía, E Colombia
Puerto La Cruz *451 E1* Anzoátegui, NE Venezuela
Puerto Lempira *445 E2* Gracias a Dios, E Honduras
Puerto Limón *see* Limón
Puertollano *484 D4* Castilla-La Mancha, C Spain
Puerto López *450 C1* La Guajira, N Colombia
Puerto Maldonado *453 E3* Madre de Dios, E Peru
Puerto México *see* Coatzacoalcos
Puerto Montt *457 B5* Los Lagos, C Chile
Puerto Natales *457 B7* Magallanes, S Chile
Puerto Obaldía *445 H5* San Blas, NE Panama
Puerto Plata *447 E3 var.* San Felipe de Puerto Plata. N Dominican Republic
Puerto Princesa *531 E2 off.* Puerto Princesa City. Palawan, W Philippines
Puerto Rico *447 F3 off.* Commonwealth of Puerto Rico; *prev.* Porto Rico. *US commonwealth territory* C West Indies
Puerto Rico *448 B1 island* C West Indies
Puerto Rico Trench *448 B1 undersea feature* NE Caribbean Sea
Puerto San José *see* San José
Puerto San Julián *457 B7 var.* San Julián. Santa Cruz, SE Argentina
Puerto Suárez *453 H4* Santa Cruz, E Bolivia
Puerto Vallarta *442 D4* Jalisco, SW Mexico
Puerto Varas *457 B5* Los Lagos, C Chile
Puerto Viejo *445 E4* Heredia, NE Costa Rica
Puertoviejo *see* Portoviejo
Puget Sound *438 B1 sound* Washington, NW USA
Puglia *489 E5 Eng.* Apulia. *cultural region* SE Italy
Pukaki, Lake *543 B6 lake* South Island, NZ
Pukekohe *542 D3* Auckland, North Island, NZ
Puket *see* Phuket
Pukhavichy *499 C6 Rus.* Pukhovichi. Minskaya Voblasts', C Belorussia
Pula *492 A3 It.* Pola; *prev.* Pulj. Istra, NW Croatia
Pulaski *432 D5* Virginia, NE USA
Pulau Butung *see* Buton, Pulau
Puławy *490 D4 Ger.* Neu Amerika. Lublin, E Poland
Pul-i-Khumri *see* Pol-e Khomrī
Pullman *438 C2* Washington, NW USA
Pułtusk *490 D3* Ciechanów, C Poland
Puná, Isla *452 A2 island* SW Ecuador
Pune *526 C5 prev.* Poona. Mahārāshtra, W India
Punjab *526 C2 prev.* West Punjab, Western Punjab. *province* E Pakistan
Puno *453 E4* Puno, SE Peru
Punta Alta *457 C5* Buenos Aires, E Argentina
Punta Arenas *457 B8 prev.* Magallanes. Magallanes, S Chile
Punta Gorda *445 E4* Región Autónoma Atlántico Sur, SE Nicaragua
Punta Gorda *444 C2* Toledo, SE Belize
Puntarenas *444 D4* Puntarenas, W Costa Rica
Punto Fijo *450 C1* Falcón, N Venezuela
Pupuya, Nevado *453 E4 mou*… W Bolivia
Puri *527 F5 var.* Jagannath. Or… E India
Puriramya *see* Buriram
Purmerend *478 C3* Noord-H… C Netherlands
Purus, Rio *454 C2 Sp.* Río Pu… *river* Brazil/Peru
Pusan *521 E4 off.* Pusan-gwangyŏksi, *var.* Busan, *Jap.* Fusan. SE South Korea
Püspökladány *491 D6* Hajdú-Bihar, E Hungary
Putorana Mountains *see* Put… Plato
Putorana, Plato *506 D3 var.* … Putorana, *Eng.* Putorana Mountains. *mountain range* N Russian Federation
Puttalam *524 C3* North West… Province, W Sri Lanka
Puttgarden *486 C2* Schleswig-Holstein, N Germany
Putumayo, Río *450 B5 var.* R… *river* NW South America *see* Içá, Rio
Putumayo, Río *see* Içá, Rio
Puurmani *498 D2 Ger.* Talkh… Jõgevamaa, E Estonia
Pyatigorsk *503 B7* Stavropol' Kray, SW Russian Federatio…
P"yatykhatky *501 F3 Rus.* Pyatikhatki. Dnipropetrovs'… Oblast', E Ukraine
Pyè *see* Prome
Pyetrykaw *499 C7 Rus.* Petrik… Homyel'skaya Voblasts', SE Belorussia
Pyinmana *528 B4* Mandalay, C Burma
Pýlos *497 B6 var.* Pilos. Pelopónnisos, S Greece
P'yŏngyang *521 E3 var.* P'yŏngyang-si, *Eng.* Pyongy… *country capital* (North Kore… SW North Korea
P'yŏngyang-si *see* P'yŏngyan…
Pyramid Lake *439 C5 lake* N… W USA
Pyrenees *494 B2 Fr.* Pyrénée… Pirineos; *anc.* Pyrenaei Mo… *mountain range* SW Europe
Pýrgos *497 B6 var.* Pírgos. Dy… Ellás, S Greece
Pyryatyn *501 E2 Rus.* Piryati… Poltavs'ka Oblast', NE Ukra…
Pyrzyce *490 B3 Ger.* Pyritz. Szczecin, NW Poland
Pyu *528 B4* Pegu, C Burma
Pyuntaza *528 B4* Pegu, SW …

Q

Qā' al Jafr *511 C7 lake* S Jord…
Qaanaaq *474 D1 var.* Qânâq… Thule. N Greenland
Qābis *see* Gabès
Qacentina *see* Constantine
Qafṣah *see* Gafsa
Qagan Us *see* Dulan
Qaidam Pendi *518 C4 basin* C China
Qal'aikhum *515 F3 Rus.* Kalaikhum. S Tajikistan
Qal'at Bīshah *513 B5* 'Asīr, SW Saudi Arabia
Qamdo *518 D5* Xizang Zizh… W China
Qamishly *see* Al Qāmishlī
Qânâq *see* Qaanaaq
Qaqortoq *474 C4 Dan.* Julia… S Greenland
Qara Qum *see* Garagumy
Qarkilik *see* Ruoqiang
Qarokŭl *515 F3 Rus.* Karak… E Tajikistan
Qars *see* Kars
Qarshi *515 E3 Rus.* Karshi; … Bek-Budi. Qashqadaryo W… S Uzbekistan
Qasigianguit *see* Qasigiann…
Qasigiannguit *474 C3 var.* Qasigianguit, *Dan.* Christi… C Greenland
Qasr Farâfra *464 B2* W Eg…
Qaṭanā *511 B5 var.* Katana. Dimashq, S Syria
Qatar *512 C4 off.* State of Q… Dawlat Qaṭar. *country* SW…
Qattara Depression *see* Qa… Monkhafad el
Qaṭṭâra, Monkhafad el *46*… Munkhafaḍ al Qaṭṭārah, *E*… Qattara Depression. *desert* NW Egypt
Qazimämmäd *509 H3 Rus.* Magomed. SE Azerbaijan
Qazvīn *512 C2 var.* Kazvin. NW Iran
Qena *464 B2 var.* Qinā; *anc.* Caenepolis. E Egypt
Qeqertarssuaq *see* Qeqerta…

Qeqertarsuaq – Road Town

tarsuaq 474 C3 var.
rtarssuaq, Dan. Godhavn.
enland
tarsuaq 474 C3 island
eenland
tarsuup Tunua 474 C3 Dan.
Bugt. inlet W Greenland
n see Qorveh
512 D4 var. Jazīreh-ye
m, Qeshm Island. island
n
Island see Qeshm
e Guizhou
Shan 518 D3 var. Kilien
tains. mountain range
ina
seriarsuaq 474 C2 Dan.
lle Bugt, Eng. Melville Bay.
W Greenland
e Qena
e Qinghai
o 520 D4 var. Ching-Tao,
g-tao, Tsingtao, Tsintao, Ger.
tau. Shandong, E China
ai 518 C4 var. Chinghai, Koko
Qing, Qinghai Sheng,
hai. Admin. region province
na
ai Hu 518 D4 var. Ch'ing Hai,
Hai, Mong. Koko Nor. lake
na
ai Sheng see Qinghai
ang Gaoyuan 518 B4 var.
g Gaoyuan, Eng. Plateau of
plateau W China
angdao 520 D3 Hebei,
na
ou 520 B6 Guangxi Zhuangzu
qu, S China
see Hainan
ar 520 D2 var. Ch'i-ch'i-ha-
sitsihar; prev. Lungkiang.
ngjiang, NE China
8 B4 Xinjiang Uygur
qu, NW China
18 C3 Xinjiang Uygur
qu, NW China
see Jīzān
rda see Kzyl-Orda
um see Kyzyl Kum
bot 515 G3 Rus. Kyzylrabot.
ikistan
12 C3 var. Kum, Qum.
azī, N Iran
see Hami
z see Kunduz
512 C3 var. Qerveh,
h. Kordestān, W Iran
iyât 510 B4 var. Al Qubayyāt.
anon
ntina see Constantine
Ngai 529 E5 var. Quangngai,
g Nghia. Quang Ngai,
tnam
ngai see Quang Ngai
Nghia see Quang Ngai
hou 520 D6 var. Ch'uan-
Tsinkiang; prev. Chin-
g. Fujian, SE China
hou 520 C6 Guangxi
ngzu Zizhiqu, S China
pelle 429 F5 river
tchewan, S Canada
s, Pegunungan 531 E4
tain range Sulawesi,
onesia
ero see Kvarner
Sant' Elena 489 A6
gna, Italy, C Mediterranean
09 H2 Rus. Kuba.
rbaijan
see Ba'qūbah
431 E4 var. Quebec.
ec, SE Canada
430 D3 var. Quebec.
n. region province SE Canada
Charlotte Islands 428 C5
s de la Reine-Charlotte.
group British Columbia,
anada
Charlotte Sound 428 C5
ea British Columbia,
nada
Elizabeth Islands 429 F2
s de la Reine-Élisabeth.
group Nunavut, N Canada
sland 540 B4 state
tralia
stown 470 D5 Eastern Cape,
h Africa
stown 543 B7 Otago, South
, NZ
ane 471 E3 var. Kilimane,
in, Quilimane. Zambézia,
ozambique
s 445 E4 Puntarenas, S Costa
aro 443 E4 Querétaro de
ga, C Mexico
a 445 E4 var. Ciudad
da, San Carlos. Alajuela,
sta Rica
526 B2 Baluchistān,
akistan
lcoalco see Coatzacoalcos
ltenango see Quezaltenango

Quezaltenango 444 A2 *var.* Quetzaltenango. Quezaltenango, W Guatemala
Quibdó 450 A3 Chocó, W Colombia
Quilimane *see* Quelimane
Quillabamba 452 D3 Cusco, C Peru
Quilon 524 C3 *var.* Kolam, Kollam. Kerala, SW India
Quimper 482 A3 *anc.* Quimper Corentin. Finistère, NW France
Quimperlé 482 A3 Finistère, NW France
Quincy 432 A4 Illinois, N USA
Qui Nhon *see* Quy Nhơn
Quissico 471 E4 Inhambane, S Mozambique
Quito 452 B1 *country capital* (Ecuador) Pichincha, N Ecuador
Qullai Garmo *see* Kommunizm, Qullai
Qum *see* Qom
Qunaytra *see* Al Qunayṭirah
Qŭqon 515 F2 *var.* Khokand, *Rus.* Kokand. Farghona Wiloyati, E Uzbekistan
Qurein *see* Al Kuwayt
Qŭrghonteppa 515 E3 *Rus.* Kurgan-Tyube. SW Tajikistan
Qurlurtuuq *see* Coppermine
Qurveh *see* Qorveh
Quṣayr *see* Al Quṣayr
Quy Nhơn 529 E5 *var.* Quinhon, Qui Nhon. Binh Đinh, C Vietnam
Qyteti Stalin *see* Kuçovë
Qyzylorda *see* Kzyl-Orda

R

Raab 492 B1 *Hung.* Rába. *river* Austria/Hungary *see also* Rába
Raahe 476 D4 *Swe.* Brahestad. Oulu, W Finland
Raalte 478 D3 Overijssel, E Netherlands
Raamsdonksveer 478 C4 Noord-Brabant, S Netherlands
Raasiku 498 D2 *Ger.* Rasik. Harjumaa, NW Estonia
Rába 491 B7 *Ger.* Raab. *river* Austria/Hungary *see also* Raab
Rabat 462 C2 *var.* al Dar al Baida. *country capital* (Morocco) NW Morocco
Rabat *see* Victoria
Rabat 494 B5 W Malta
Rabbah Ammon *see* 'Ammān
Rabbath Ammon *see* 'Ammān
Rabinal 444 B2 Baja Verapaz, C Guatemala
Rabka 491 D5 Nowy Sącz, S Poland
Răbniṭa *see* Rîbniṭa
Rabyanāh, Ramlat 463 G4 *var.* Rebiana Sand Sea, *ṣaḥrā'* Rabyanāh. *desert* SE Libya
Race, Cape 431 H3 *headland* Newfoundland, E Canada
Rach Gia 529 D6 Kiên Giang, S Vietnam
Rach Gia, Vinh 529 D6 *bay* S Vietnam
Racine 432 B3 Wisconsin, N USA
Rădăuṭi 500 C3 *Ger.* Radautz, *Hung.* Rádóc. Suceava, N Romania
Radom 490 D4 Radom, C Poland
Radomsko 490 D4 *Rus.* Novoradomsk. Piotrków, C Poland
Radomyshl' 500 D2 Zhytomyrs'ka Oblast', N Ukraine
Radoviš 493 E6 *prev.* Radovište. E FYR Macedonia
Radviliškis 498 B4 Radviliškis, N Lithuania
Radzyń Podlaski 490 E4 Biała Podlaska, E Poland
Rae-Edzo 429 E4 Nunavut, NW Canada
Raetihi 542 D4 Manawatu-Wanganui, North Island, NZ
Rafa *see* Rafah
Rafaela 456 C3 Santa Fe, E Argentina
Rafah 511 A7 *var.* Rafa, Rafaḥ, *Heb.* Rafiaḥ, Raphiah. SW Gaza Strip
Rafaḥ *see* Rafah
Rafḥah 512 B4 Al Ḥudūd ash Shamālīyah, N Saudi Arabia
Rafiaḥ *see* Rafah
Raga 465 A5 Western Bahr el Ghazal, SW Sudan
Ragged Island Range 446 C2 *island group* S Bahamas
Ragusa 489 C7 Sicilia, Italy, C Mediterranean Sea
Rahachow 499 D7 *Rus.* Rogachëv. Homyel'skaya Voblasts', SE Belorussia
Rahaeng *see* Tak
Rahaṭ, Ḥarrat 513 B5 *lavaflow* W Saudi Arabia
Rahīmyār Khān 526 C3 Punjab, SE Pakistan
Raiatea 537 G4 *island* Îles Sous le Vent, W French Polynesia
Rāichūr 524 C1 Karnātaka, C India
Rainier, Mount 426 A4 *volcano* Washington, NW USA
Rainy Lake 430 A4 *lake* Canada/USA
Raipur 527 E4 Madhya Pradesh, C India
Rājahmundry 527 E5 Andhra Pradesh, E India
Rajang *see* Rajang, Batang
Rajang, Batang 530 D3 *var.* Rajang. *river* East Malaysia
Rājapālaiyam 524 C3 Tamil Nādu, SE India
Rājasthān 526 C3 *state* NW India
Rājkot 526 C4 Gujarāt, W India
Rāj Nāndgaon 527 E4 Madhya Pradesh, C India
Rajshahi 527 G3 *prev.* Rampur Boalia. Rajshahi, W Bangladesh
Rakahanga 537 F3 *atoll* N Cook Islands
Rakaia 543 B6 *river* South Island, NZ
Rakka *see* Ar Raqqah
Rakke 498 E2 Lääne-Virumaa, NE Estonia
Rakvere 498 E2 *Ger.* Wesenberg. Lääne-Virumaa, N Estonia
Ralik Chain 536 D1 *island group* Ralik Chain, W Marshall Islands
Ramadi *see* Ar Ramādī
Ramlat Ahl Wahībah *see* Wahībah, Ramlat Āl
Ramlat Al Wahaybah *see* Wahībah, Ramlat Āl
Râmnicu Sărat 500 C4 *prev.* Rîmnicul-Sărat, Rîmnicu-Sărat. Buzău, E Romania
Râmnicu Vâlcea 500 B4 *prev.* Rîmnicu Vîlcea. Vâlcea, C Romania
Ramree Island 528 A4 *island* W Burma
Ramtha *see* Ar Ramthā
Rancagua 456 B4 Libertador, C Chile
Rānchi 527 F4 Bihār, N India
Randers 477 B7 Århus, C Denmark
Rangiora 543 C6 Canterbury, South Island, NZ
Rangitaiki 542 D4 *river* North Island, NZ
Rangoon 516 *see* Yangon
Rangpur 527 G3 Rajshahi, N Bangladesh
Rankin Inlet 429 G3 Nunavut, C Canada
Ranong 529 B6 Ranong, SW Thailand
Rapa Nui *see* Easter Island
Raphiah *see* Rafah
Rapid City 436 D3 South Dakota, N USA
Räpina 498 E3 *Ger.* Rappin. Põlvamaa, SE Estonia
Rapla 498 D2 *Ger.* Rappel. Raplamaa, NW Estonia
Rarotonga 537 G5 *island* S Cook Islands, C Pacific Ocean
Ras al 'Ain *see* Ra's al 'Ayn
Ra's al 'Ayn 510 D1 *var.* Ras al 'Ain. Al Ḥasakah, N Syria
Ra's an Naqb 511 B7 Ma'ān, S Jordan
Raseiniai 498 B4 Raseiniai, C Lithuania
Ras Hafun *see* Xaafuun, Raas
Rasht 512 C2 *var.* Resht. Gīlān, NW Iran
Râşnov 500 C4 *prev.* Rîşno, Rozsnyó, *Hung.* Barcarozsnyó. Braşov, C Romania
Ratak Chain 536 D1 *island group* Ratak Chain, E Marshall Islands
Ratan 477 C5 Jämtland, C Sweden
Rat Buri *see* Ratchaburi
Ratchaburi 529 C5 *var.* Rat Buri. Ratchaburi, W Thailand
Rat Islands 428 A2 *island group* Aleutian Islands, Alaska, USA
Ratlām 526 D4 *prev.* Rutlam. Madhya Pradesh, C India
Ratnapura 524 D4 Sabaragamuwa Province, S Sri Lanka
Raton 440 D1 New Mexico, SW USA
Rättvik 477 C5 Kopparberg, C Sweden
Raudhatain *see* Ar Rawḍatayn
Raufarhöfn 475 E4 Nordhurland Eystra, NE Iceland
Raukawa *see* Cook Strait
Raukumara Range 542 E3 *mountain range* North Island, NZ
Rauma 477 D5 *Swe.* Raumo. Turku-Pori, SW Finland
Raurkela 527 F4 *prev.* Rourkela. Orissa, E India
Ravenna 488 C3 Emilia-Romagna, N Italy
Rāvi 526 C2 *river* India/Pakistan
Rāwalpindi 526 C1 Punjab, NE Pakistan
Rawa Mazowiecka 490 D4 Skierniewice, C Poland
Rawicz 490 C4 *Ger.* Rawitsch. Leszno, W Poland
Rawlins 436 C3 Wyoming, C USA
Rawson 457 C6 Chubut, SE Argentina
Rayak 510 B4 *var.* Rayaq, Riyāq. E Lebanon
Rayaq *see* Rayak
Rayleigh 435 F1 *state capital* North Carolina, SE USA
Rayong 529 C5 Rayong, S Thailand
Razāzah, Buḥayrat ar 512 B3 *var.* Baḥr al Milḥ. *lake* C Iraq
Razgrad 496 D2 Razgradska Oblast, NE Bulgaria
Razim, Lacul 500 D5 *prev.* Lacul Razelm. *lagoon* NW Black Sea
Reading 433 F4 Pennsylvania, NE USA
Reading 481 D7 S England, UK
Realicó 456 C4 La Pampa, C Argentina
Reăng Kesei 529 D5 Bătdâmbâng, W Cambodia
Rebecca, Lake 539 C6 *lake* Western Australia
Rebiana Sand Sea *see* Rabyanāh, Ramlat
Rebun-tō 522 C2 *island* NE Japan
Rechytsa 499 D7 *Rus.* Rechitsa. Brestskaya Voblasts', SW Belorussia
Recife 455 G2 *prev.* Pernambuco. *state capital* Pernambuco, E Brazil
Recklinghausen 486 A4 Nordrhein-Westfalen, W Germany
Recogne 479 C7 Luxembourg, SE Belgium
Reconquista 456 D3 Santa Fe, C Argentina
Red Deer 429 E5 Alberta, SW Canada
Redding 439 B5 California, W USA
Redon 482 B4 Ille-et-Vilaine, NW France
Red River 528 C2 *var.* Yuan, *Chin.* Yuan Jiang, *Vtn.* Sông Hông Hà. *river* China/Vietnam
Red River 437 E1 *river* Canada/USA
Red River 434 B3 *river* Louisiana, S USA
Red River 427 C6 *river* S USA
Red Sea 464 C3 *anc.* Sinus Arabicus. *sea* Africa/Asia
Red Wing 437 G2 Minnesota, N USA
Reefton 543 C5 West Coast, South Island, NZ
Reese River 439 C5 *river* Nevada, W USA
Refahiye 509 E3 Erzincan, C Turkey
Regensburg 487 C6 *Eng.* Ratisbon, *Fr.* Ratisbonne; *hist.* Ratisbona, *anc.* Castra Regina, Reginum. Bayern, SE Germany
Regenstauf 487 C6 Bayern, SE Germany
Reggane 462 D3 C Algeria
Reggio *see* Reggio nell' Emilia
Reggio Calabria *see* Reggio di Calabria
Reggio di Calabria 489 D7 *var.* Reggio Calabria, *Gk.* Rhegion; *anc.* Regium, Rhegium. Calabria, SW Italy
Reggio Emilia *see* Reggio nell' Emilia
Reggio nell' Emilia 488 B2 *var.* Reggio Emilia, *abbrev.* Reggio; *anc.* Regium Lepidum. Emilia-Romagna, N Italy
Reghin 500 C4 *Ger.* Sächsisch-Reen, *Hung.* Szászrégen; *prev.* Reghinul Săsesc, *Ger.* Sächsisch-Regen. Mureş, C Romania
Regina 429 F5 Saskatchewan, S Canada
Registan *see* Rīgestān
Regium *see* Reggio di Calabria
Regium Lepidum *see* Reggio nell' Emilia
Rehoboth *see* Reḥovot
Rehoboth 470 B3 Hardap, C Namibia
Reḥovot 511 A6 *var.* Rehoboth, Rehovoth. Central, C Israel
Rehovoth *see* Reḥovot
Reid 539 D6 Western Australia
Reikjavik *see* Reykjavík
Ré, Île de 482 A4 *island* W France
Reims 482 D3 *Eng.* Rheims; *anc.* Durocortorum, Remi. Marne, N France
Reindeer Lake 429 F4 *lake* Manitoba/Saskatchewan, C Canada
Reinga, Cape 542 C1 *headland* North Island, NZ
Reinosa 484 D1 Cantabria, N Spain
Reliance 429 F4 Nunavut, C Canada
Rendina *see* Rentína
Rendsburg 486 B2 Schleswig-Holstein, N Germany
Rengat 530 B4 Sumatera, W Indonesia
Reni 500 D4 Odes'ka Oblast', SW Ukraine
Rennell 536 C4 *var.* Mu Nggava. *island* S Solomon Islands
Rennes 482 B3 *Bret.* Roazon; *anc.* Condate. Ille-et-Vilaine, NW France
Reno 439 C5 Nevada, W USA
Renqiu 520 C4 Hebei, E China
Rentína 497 B5 *var.* Rendina. Thessalía, C Greece
République Centrafricaine *see* Central African Republic
Repulse Bay 429 G3 Nunavut, N Canada
Resht *see* Rasht
Resistencia 456 D3 Chaco, NE Argentina
Reşiṭa 500 A4 *Ger.* Reschitza, *Hung.* Resicabánya. Caraş-Severin, W Romania
Resolute 429 F2 Cornwallis Island, Nunavut, N Canada
Resolution Island 431 E1 *island* Nunavut, NE Canada
Resolution Island 543 A7 *island* SW NZ
Réunion 471 H4 *off.* La Réunion. *French overseas department* W Indian Ocean
Réunion 533 B5 *island* W Indian Ocean
Reus 485 F2 Cataluña, E Spain
Reutlingen 487 B6 Baden-Württemberg, S Germany
Reuver 479 D5 Limburg, SE Netherlands
Revillagigedo Islands *see* Revillagigedo, Islas
Revillagigedo, Islas 442 B5 *Eng.* Revillagigedo Islands. *island group* W Mexico
Rexburg 438 E3 Idaho, NW USA
Reyes 453 F3 Beni, NW Bolivia
Rey, Isla del 445 G5 *island* Archipiélago de las Perlas, SE Panama
Reykjanes Basin 474 C5 *var.* Irminger Basin. *undersea feature* N Atlantic Ocean
Reykjanes Ridge 472 A1 *undersea feature* N Atlantic Ocean
Reykjavík 475 E5 *var.* Reikjavik. *country capital* (Iceland) Höfudhborgarsvaedhi, W Iceland
Reynosa 443 E2 Tamaulipas, C Mexico
Rezé 482 A4 Loire-Atlantique, NW France
Rēzekne 498 D4 *Ger.* Rositten; *prev.* Rus. Rezhitsa. Rēzekne, SE Latvia
Rezovo 496 E3 *Turk.* Rezve. Burgaska Oblast, SE Bulgaria
Rhegion *see* Reggio di Calabria
Rhegium *see* Reggio di Calabria
Rhein *see* Rhine
Rheine 486 A3 *var.* Rheine in Westfalen. Nordrhein-Westfalen, NW Germany
Rheine in Westfalen *see* Rheine
Rheinisches Schiefergebirge 487 A5 *var.* Rhine State Uplands, *Eng.* Rhenish Slate Mountains. *mountain range* W Germany
Rhenish Slate Mountains *see* Rheinisches Schiefergebirge
Rhine 472 D4 *Dut.* Rijn, *Fr.* Rhin, *Ger.* Rhein. *river* W Europe
Rhinelander 432 B2 Wisconsin, N USA
Rhine State Uplands *see* Rheinisches Schiefergebirge
Rho 488 B2 Lombardia, N Italy
Rhode Island 433 G3 *off.* State of Rhode Island and Providence Plantations; also known as Little Rhody, Ocean State. *state* NE USA
Rhodes *see* Ródos
Rhodope Mountains 496 C3 *var.* Rodhópi Óri, *Bul.* Rhodope Planina, Rodopi, *Gk.* Orosirá Rodhópis, *Turk.* Dospad Dagh. *mountain range* Bulgaria/Greece
Rhodope Planina *see* Rhodope Mountains
Rhodos *see* Ródos
Rhône 472 C4 *river* France/Switzerland
Rhône 483 D6 *department* E France
Rhum 480 B3 *var.* Rum. *island* W Scotland, UK
Ribble 481 D5 *river* NW England, UK
Ribeira 484 B1 Galicia, NW Spain
Ribeirão Preto 455 F4 São Paulo, S Brazil
Riberalta 453 F2 Beni, N Bolivia
Rîbniṭa 500 D3 *var.* Râbniṭa, *Rus.* Rybnitsa. NE Moldavia
Rice Lake 432 A2 Wisconsin, N USA
Richard Toll 466 B3 N Senegal
Richfield 436 B4 Utah, W USA
Richland 438 C2 Washington, NW USA
Richmond 433 E5 *state capital* Virginia, NE USA
Richmond 432 C5 Kentucky, S USA
Richmond 543 C5 Tasman, South Island, NZ
Richmond Range 543 C5 *mountain range* South Island, NZ
Ricobayo, Embalse de 484 C2 *reservoir* NW Spain
Ridgecrest 439 C7 California, W USA
Ried *see* Ried im Innkreis
Ried im Innkreis 487 D6 *var.* Ried. Oberösterreich, NW Austria
Riemst 479 D6 Limburg, NE Belgium
Riesa 486 D4 Sachsen, E Germany
Rift Valley *see* Great Rift Valley
Riga 498 C3 *Eng.* Riga. *country capital* (Latvia) Rīga, C Latvia
Riga, Gulf of 498 C3 *Est.* Liivi Laht, *Ger.* Rigaer Bucht, *Latv.* Rīgas Jūras Līcis, *Rus.* Rizhskiy Zaliv; *prev. Est.* Riia Laht. *gulf* Estonia/Latvia
Rīgān 512 E4 Kermān, SE Iran
Rīgestān 514 D5 *var.* Registan. *desert region* S Afghanistan
Riihimäki 477 D5 Häme, S Finland
Rijeka 492 A2 *Ger.* Sankt Veit am Flaum, *It.* Fiume, *Slvn.* Reka; *anc.* Tarsatica. Primorje-Gorski Kotar, NW Croatia
Rijssel *see* Lille
Rijssen 478 E3 Overijssel, E Netherlands
Rimah, Wādī ar 512 B4 *var.* Wādī ar Rummah. *dry watercourse* C Saudi Arabia
Rimini 488 C3 *anc.* Ariminum. Emilia-Romagna, N Italy
Rimouski 431 E4 Quebec, SE Canada
Ringebu 477 B5 Oppland, S Norway
Ringkøbing Fjord 477 A7 *fjord* W Denmark
Ringvassøy 476 C2 *island* N Norway
Rio *see* Rio de Janeiro
Riobamba 452 B1 Chimborazo, C Ecuador
Rio Branco 448 B3 *state capital* Acre, W Brazil
Río Bravo 443 E2 Tamaulipas, C Mexico
Río Cuarto 456 C4 Córdoba, C Argentina
Rio de Janeiro 455 F4 *var.* Rio. *state capital* Rio de Janeiro, SE Brazil
Río Gallegos 457 B7 *var.* Gallegos, Puerto Gallegos. Santa Cruz, S Argentina
Rio Grande 455 E5 *var.* São Pedro do Rio Grande do Sul. Rio Grande do Sul, S Brazil
Río Grande 442 D3 Zacatecas, C Mexico
Rio Grande do Norte 455 G2 *off.* Estado do Rio Grande do Norte. *state* E Brazil
Rio Grande do Sul 455 E5 *off.* Estado do Rio Grande do Sul. *state* S Brazil
Rio Grande Plateau *see* Rio Grande Rise
Rio Grande Rise 449 E6 *var.* Rio Grande Plateau. *undersea feature* SW Atlantic Ocean
Ríohacha 450 B1 La Guajira, N Colombia
Río Lagartos 443 H3 Yucatán, SE Mexico
Riom 483 C5 *anc.* Ricomagus. Puy-de-Dôme, C France
Río San Juan 445 E4 *department* S Nicaragua
Rioverde *see* Río Verde
Río Verde 443 E4 *var.* Rioverde. San Luis Potosí, C Mexico
Ripoll 485 G2 Cataluña, NE Spain
Rishiri-tō 522 C2 *var.* Risiri Tô. *island* NE Japan
Risiri Tô *see* Rishiri-tō
Risti 498 D2 *Ger.* Kreuz. Läänemaa, W Estonia
Rivas 444 D4 Rivas, SW Nicaragua
Rivera 456 D3 Rivera, NE Uruguay
River Falls 432 A2 Wisconsin, N USA
River Plate *see* Plata, Río de la
Riverside 439 C7 California, W USA
Riverton 543 A7 Southland, South Island, NZ
Riverton 436 C3 Wyoming, C USA
Rivière-du-Loup 431 E4 Quebec, SE Canada
Rivne 500 C2 *Pol.* Równe, *Rus.* Rovno. Rivnens'ka Oblast', NW Ukraine
Rivoli 488 A2 Piemonte, NW Italy
Riyadh 504 *see* Ar Riyāḍ
Riyāq *see* Rayak
Rize 509 E2 Rize, NE Turkey
Rizhao 520 D4 Shandong, E China
Rkîz 466 C3 Trarza, W Mauritania
Road Town 447 F3 *dependent territory capital* (British Virgin Islands) Tortola, C British Virgin Islands

Roanne – Sale

Roanne *483 C5 anc.* Rodunma. Loire, E France
Roanoke *433 E5* Virginia, NE USA
Roanoke River *435 F1 river* North Carolina/Virginia, SE USA
Roatán *444 C2 var.* Coxen Hole, Coxin Hole. Islas de la Bahía, N Honduras
Robbie Ridge *535 E3 undersea feature* W Pacific Ocean
Robert Williams *see* Caála
Robinson Range *539 B5 mountain range* Western Australia
Robson, Mount *429 E5 mountain* British Columbia, SW Canada
Robstown *441 G4* Texas, SW USA
Roca Partida, Isla *442 B5 island* W Mexico
Rocas, Atol das *455 G2 island* E Brazil
Rochefort *482 B4 var.* Rochefort sur Mer. Charente-Maritime, W France
Rochefort *479 C7* Namur, SE Belgium
Rochefort sur Mer *see* Rochefort
Rochester *437 G3* Minnesota, N USA
Rochester *433 G2* New Hampshire, NE USA
Rochester *433 E3* New York, NE USA
Rockall Bank *472 B2 undersea feature* N Atlantic Ocean
Rockall Trough *472 B2 undersea feature* N Atlantic Ocean
Rockdale *540 E2* New South Wales, SE Australia
Rockford *432 B3* Illinois, N USA
Rockhampton *540 D4* Queensland, E Australia
Rock Hill *435 E1* South Carolina, SE USA
Rockies *see* Rocky Mountains
Rockingham *539 A6* Western Australia
Rock Island *432 B3* Illinois, N USA
Rock Sound *446 C1* Eleuthera Island, C Bahamas
Rock Springs *436 C3* Wyoming, C USA
Rockstone *451 F3* C Guyana
Rocky Mount *435 F1* North Carolina, SE USA
Rocky Mountains *426 B4 var.* Rockies, *Fr.* Montagnes Rocheuses. *mountain range* Canada/USA
Roden *478 E2* Drenthe, NE Netherlands
Rodez *483 C5 anc.* Segodunum. Aveyron, S France
Rodhópi Óri *see* Rhodope Mountains
Ródhos *see* Ródos
Rodi *see* Ródos
Rodopi *see* Rhodope Mountains
Ródos *497 E7 var.* Ródhos, *Eng.* Rhodes, *It.* Rodi; *anc.* Rhodos. *island* Dodekánisos, Greece, Aegean Sea
Roermond *479 D5* Limburg, SE Netherlands
Roeselare *479 A6 Fr.* Roulers; *prev.* Rousselaere. West-Vlaanderen, W Belgium
Rogatica *492 C4* SE Bosnia and Herzegovina
Rogers *434 A1* Arkansas, C USA
Roger Simpson Island *see* Abemama
Roi Ed *see* Roi Et
Roi Et *529 D5 var.* Muang Roi Et, Roi Ed. Roi Et, E Thailand
Roja *498 C2* Talsi, NW Latvia
Rokiškis *498 C4* Rokiškis, NE Lithuania
Rokycany *491 A5 Ger.* Rokytzan. Západní Čechy, W Czech Republic
Rôlas, Ilha das *468 E2 island* S Sao Tome and Principe
Rolla *437 G5* Missouri, C USA
Roma *488 C4 Eng.* Rome. *country capital* (Italy) Lazio, C Italy
Roma *541 D5* Queensland, E Australia
Roman *500 C4 Hung.* Románvásár. Neamț, NE Romania
Roman *496 C2* Oblast Montana, NW Bulgaria
Romania *500 B4 Bul.* Rumŭniya, *Ger.* Rumänien, *Hung.* Románia, *Rom.* România, *SCr.* Rumunjska, *Ukr.* Rumuniya; *prev.* Republica Socialistă România, Roumania, Rumania, Socialist Republic of Romania, *Rom.* Romînia. *country* SE Europe
Rome *see* Roma
Rome *434 D2* Georgia, SE USA
Romny *501 F2* Sums'ka Oblast', NE Ukraine
Rømø *477 A7 Ger.* Röm. *island* SW Denmark
Roncador, Serra do *448 D4 mountain range* C Brazil
Ronda *484 D5* Andalucía, S Spain
Rondônia *454 D3 off.* Estado de Rondônia; *prev.* Território de Rondônia. *state* W Brazil
Rondonópolis *455 E3* Mato Grosso, W Brazil
Rongelap Atoll *536 D1 var.* Rōņļap. *atoll* Ralik Chain, NW Marshall Islands
Rõngu *498 D3 Ger.* Ringen. Tartumaa, SE Estonia
Rōņļap *see* Rongelap Atoll
Rønne *477 B8* Bornholm, E Denmark
Ronne Ice Shelf *546 A3 ice shelf* Antarctica
Roosendaal *479 C5* Noord-Brabant, S Netherlands
Roosevelt Island *546 B4 island* Antarctica
Roraima *454 D1 off.* Estado de Roraima; *prev.* Território de Rio Branco, Território de Roraima. *state* N Brazil
Roraima, Mount *451 E3 mountain* N South America
Røros *477 B5* Sør-Trøndelag, S Norway
Rosa, Lake *446 D2 lake* Great Inagua, S Bahamas
Rosario *456 D2* San Pedro, C Paraguay
Rosario *456 D4* Santa Fe, C Argentina
Rosarito *442 A1* Baja California, NW Mexico
Roscommon *432 C2* Michigan, N USA
Roseau *447 G4 prev.* Charlotte Town. *country capital* (Dominica) SW Dominica
Roseburg *438 B4* Oregon, NW USA
Rosenberg *441 G4* Texas, SW USA
Rosengarten *486 B3* Niedersachsen, N Germany
Rosenheim *487 C6* Bayern, S Germany
Rosia *485 H5* W Gibraltar
Rosia Bay *485 H5 bay* SW Gibraltar
Roșiori de Vede *500 B5* Teleorman, S Romania
Roslavl' *503 A5* Smolenskaya Oblast', W Russian Federation
Rosmalen *478 C4* Noord-Brabant, S Netherlands
Ross *543 B6* West Coast, South Island, NZ
Rossano *489 E6 anc.* Roscianum. Calabria, SW Italy
Ross Ice Shelf *546 B4 ice shelf* Antarctica
Rosso *466 B3* Trarza, SW Mauritania
Rossosh' *503 B6* Voronezhskaya Oblast', W Russian Federation
Ross Sea *546 B4 sea* Antarctica
Rostak *see* Ar Rustāq
Rostock *486 C2* Mecklenburg-Vorpommern, NE Germany
Rostov *see* Rostov-na-Donu
Rostov-na-Donu *503 B7 var.* Rostov, *Eng.* Rostov-on-Don. Rostovskaya Oblast', SW Russian Federation
Rostov-on-Don *see* Rostov-na-Donu
Roswell *440 D2* New Mexico, SW USA
Rota *536 B1 island* S Northern Mariana Islands
Rothera *546 A2 UK research station* Antarctica
Rotorua *542 D3* Bay of Plenty, North Island, NZ
Rotorua, Lake *542 D3 lake* North Island, NZ
Rotterdam *478 C4* Zuid-Holland, SW Netherlands
Rottweil *487 B6* Baden-Württemberg, S Germany
Rotuma *537 E4 island* NW Fiji
Roubaix *482 C2* Nord, N France
Rouen *482 C3 anc.* Rotomagus. Seine-Maritime, N France
Round Rock *441 G3* Texas, SW USA
Roussillon *483 C6 cultural region* S France
Rouyn-Noranda *430 D4* Quebec, SE Canada
Rovaniemi *476 D3* Lappi, N Finland
Rovigo *488 C2* Veneto, NE Italy
Rovinj *492 A3 It.* Rovigno. Istra, NW Croatia
Rovuma, Rio *471 F2 var.* Ruvuma. *river* Mozambique/Tanzania *see also* Ruvuma
Rovuma, Rio *see* Ruvuma
Roxas City *531 E2* Panay Island, C Philippines
Royale, Isle *432 B1 island* Michigan, N USA
Royan *483 B5* Charente-Maritime, W France
Rozdol'ne *501 F4 Rus.* Razdolnoye. Respublika Krym, S Ukraine
Rožňava *491 D6 Ger.* Rosenau, *Hung.* Rozsnyó. Východné Slovensko, E Slovakia
Ruapehu, Mount *542 D4 mountain* North Island, NZ
Ruapuke Island *543 B8 island* SW NZ
Ruatoria *542 E3* Gisborne, North Island, NZ
Ruawai *542 D2* Northland, North Island, NZ
Rubizhne *501 H3 Rus.* Rubezhnoye. Luhans'ka Oblast', E Ukraine
Ruby Mountains *439 D5 mountain range* Nevada, W USA
Rucava *498 B3* Liepāja, SW Latvia
Rūd-e Hīrmand *see* Helmand, Daryā-ye
Rūdiškės *499 B5* Trakai, S Lithuania
Rudnik *496 E2* Varnenska Oblast, E Bulgaria
Rudny *see* Rudnyy
Rudnyy *506 C4 var.* Rudny. Kustanay, N Kazakhstan
Rudolf, Lake *465 C6 var.* Lake Turkana. *lake* N Kenya
Rudzyensk *499 C6 Rus.* Rudensk. Minskaya Voblasts', C Belorussia
Rufiji *465 C7 river* E Tanzania
Rufino *456 C4* Santa Fe, C Argentina
Rugāji *498 D4* Balvi, E Latvia
Rügen *486 D2 headland* NE Germany
Ruggell *486 E1* N Liechtenstein
Ruhnu *498 C2 var.* Ruhnu Saar, *Swe.* Runö. *island* SW Estonia
Ruhnu Saar *see* Ruhnu
Rūjiena *498 D3 Est.* Ruhja, *Ger.* Rujen. Valmiera, N Latvia
Rukwa, Lake *465 B7 lake* SE Tanzania
Rum *see* Rhum
Ruma *492 D3* Serbia, N Yugoslavia
Rumadiya *see* Ar Ramādī
Rumbek *465 B5* El Buhayrat, S Sudan
Rum Cay *446 D2 island* C Bahamas
Rumia *490 C2* Gdańsk, N Poland
Rummah, Wādī ar *see* Rimah, Wādī ar
Runanga *543 B5* West Coast, South Island, NZ
Runaway Bay *446 B4* C Jamaica
Rundu *470 C3 var.* Runtu. Okavango, NE Namibia
Runö *see* Ruhnu
Runtu *see* Rundu
Ruoqiang *518 C3 var.* Jo-ch'iang, *Uigh.* Charkhlik, Charkhliq, Qarkilik. Xinjiang Uygur Zizhiqu, NW China
Rupea *500 C4 Ger.* Reps, *Hung.* Kőhalom; *prev.* Cohalm. Brașov, C Romania
Rupel *479 B5 river* N Belgium
Rupert, Rivière de *430 D3 river* Quebec, C Canada
Ruschuk *see* Ruse
Rusçuk *see* Ruse
Ruse *496 D1 var.* Ruschuk, Rustchuk, *Turk.* Rusçuk. Razgradska Oblast, N Bulgaria
Rus Krymskaya ASSR *see* Crimea
Russellville *434 A1* Arkansas, C USA
Russian Federation *504 D2 off.* Russian Federation, *var.* Russia, *Latv.* Krievija, *Rus.* Rossiyskaya Federatsiya. *country* Asia/Europe
Rustaq *see* Ar Rustāq
Rust'avi *509 G2* SE Georgia
Rustchuk *see* Ruse
Ruston *434 B2* Louisiana, S USA
Rutanzige |M, Lake *see* Edward, Lake
Rutba *see* Ar Ruṭbah
Rutland *433 F2* Vermont, NE USA
Rutog *518 A4 var.* Rutok. Xizang Zizhiqu, W China
Rutok *see* Rutog
Ruvuma *461 E5 var.* Rio Rovuma. *river* Mozambique/Tanzania *see also* Rovuma, Rio
Ruvuma *see* Rovuma, Rio
Ruwenzori *469 E5 mountain range* Uganda/Congo (Zaire)
Ruzhany *499 B6 Rus.* Ruzhany. Brestskaya Voblasts', SW Belorussia
Ružomberok *491 C5 Ger.* Rosenberg, *Hung.* Rózsahegy. Stredné Slovensko, N Slovakia
Rwanda *465 B6 off.* Rwandese Republic; *prev.* Ruanda. *country* C Africa
Ryazan' *503 B5* Ryazanskaya Oblast', W Russian Federation
Rybinsk *502 B4 prev.* Andropov. Yaroslavskaya Oblast', W Russian Federation
Rybnik *491 C5* Katowice, S Poland
Rybnitsa *see* Rîbnița
Ryde *540 E1* New South Wales, SE Australia
Ryki *490 D4* Lublin, E Poland
Rypin *490 C3* Włocławek, C Poland
Ryssel *see* Lille
Rysy *491 C5 mountain* S Poland
Ryukyu Islands *517 E3 island group* SW Japan
Ryukyu Trench *517 F3 var.* Nansei Syotō Trench. *undersea feature* S East China Sea
Rzeszów *491 E5* Rzeszów, SE Poland
Rzhev *502 B4* Tverskaya Oblast', W Russian Federation

S

Saale *486 C4 river* C Germany
Saalfeld *487 C5 var.* Saalfeld an der Saale. Thüringen, C Germany
Saalfeld an der Saale *see* Saalfeld
Saarbrücken *487 A6 Fr.* Sarrebruck. Saarland, SW Germany
Sääre *498 C2 var.* Sjar. Saaremaa, W Estonia
Saaremaa *498 C2 Ger.* Oesel, Ösel; *prev.* Saare. *island* W Estonia
Saariselkä *476 D2 Lapp.* Suoločielgi. Lappi, N Finland
Sab' Ābār *510 C4 var.* Sab'a Biyar, Sa'b Bi'ār. Ḥimṣ, C Syria
Sab'a Biyar *see* Sab' Ābār
Šabac *492 D3* Serbia, W Yugoslavia
Sabadell *485 G2* Cataluña, E Spain
Sabah *530 D3 cultural region* Borneo, SE Asia
Sabanalarga *450 B1* Atlántico, N Colombia
Sabaneta *450 C1* Falcón, N Venezuela
Sab'atayn, Ramlat as *513 C6 desert* C Yemen
Sabaya *453 F4* Oruro, S Bolivia
Sa'b Bi'ār *see* Sab' Ābār
Şāberī, Hāmūn-e *514 var.* Daryācheh-ye Hāmūn, Daryācheh-ye Sīstān. *lake* Afghanistan/Iran *see also* Sīstān, Daryācheh-ye
Sabhā *463 F3* C Libya
Sabi, Rio *see* Save, Rio
Sabinas *443 E2* Coahuila de Zaragoza, NE Mexico
Sabinas Hidalgo *443 E2* Nuevo León, NE Mexico
Sabine River *441 H3 river* Louisiana/Texas, SW USA
Sabkha *see* As Sabkhah
Sable, Cape *435 E5 headland* Florida, SE USA
Sable Island *431 G4 island* Nova Scotia, SE Canada
Şabyā *513 B6* Jīzān, SW Saudi Arabia
Sabzawar *see* Sabzevār
Sabzevār *512 D2 var.* Sabzawar. Khorāsān, NE Iran
Sachsen *486 D4 Eng.* Saxony, *Fr.* Saxe. *state* E Germany
Sachs Harbour *429 E2* Banks Island, Northwest Territories, N Canada
Sacramento *439 B5 state capital* California, W USA
Sacramento Mountains *440 D2 mountain range* New Mexico, SW USA
Sacramento River *439 B5 river* California, W USA
Sacramento Valley *439 B5 valley* California, W USA
Şa'dah *513 B6* NW Yemen
Sado *523 C5 var.* Sadoga-shima. *island* C Japan
Sadoga-shima *see* Sado
Safad *see* Ẕefat
Safed *see* Ẕefat
Säffle *477 B6* Värmland, C Sweden
Safford *440 C3* Arizona, SW USA
Safi *462 B2* W Morocco
Safīd Kūh, Selseleh-ye *514 D4 Eng.* Paropamisus Range. *mountain range* W Afghanistan
Sagaing *528 B3* Sagaing, C Burma
Sagami-nada *523 D6 inlet* SW Japan
Sāgar *526 D4 prev.* Saugor. Madhya Pradesh, C India
Saghez *see* Saqqez
Saginaw *432 C3* Michigan, N USA
Saginaw Bay *432 D2 lake bay* Michigan, N USA
Sagua la Grande *446 B2* Villa Clara, C Cuba
Sagunt *see* Sagunto
Sagunto *485 F3 var.* Sagunt, *Ar.* Murviedro; *anc.* Saguntum. País Valenciano, E Spain
Saguntum *see* Sagunto
Sahara *462 B3 desert* Libya/Algeria
Sahara el Gharbîya *464 B2 var.* Aş Şaḥrā' al Gharbīyah, *Eng.* Western Desert. *desert* C Egypt
Saharan Atlas *see* Atlas Saharien
Sahel *466 D3 physical region* C Africa
Sāḩilīyah, Jibāl as *510 B3 mountain range* NW Syria
Sāhīwāl *526 C2 prev.* Montgomery. Punjab, E Pakistan
şaḥrā' Rabyanāh *see* Rabyanāh, Ramlat
Saïda *511 A5 var.* Şaydā, Sayida; *anc.* Sidon. W Lebanon
Saidpur *527 G3 var.* Syedpur. Rajshahi, NW Bangladesh
Saigon *see* Hô Chi Minh
Sai Hun *see* Syr Darya
Saimaa *477 E5 lake* SE Finland
St Albans *481 E6 anc.* Verulamium. E England, UK
Saint Albans *432 D5* West Virginia, NE USA
St Andrews *480 C4* E Scotland, UK
Saint Anna Trough *see* Svyataya Anna Trough
St.Ann's Bay *446 B4* C Jamaica
St.Anthony *431 G3* Newfoundland, SE Canada
Saint Augustine *435 E3* Florida, SE USA
St Austell *481 C7* SW England, UK
St-Brieuc *482 A3* Côtes d'Armor, NW France
St. Catharines *430 D5* Ontario, S Canada
St-Chamond *483 D5* Loire, E France
St.Clair, Lake *432 D3 Fr.* Lac à L'Eau Claire. *lake* Canada/USA
St-Claude *483 D5 anc.* Condate. Jura, E France
Saint Cloud *437 F2* Minnesota, N USA
St Croix *447 F3 island* S Virgin Islands (US)
Saint Croix River *432 A2 river* Minnesota/Wisconsin, N USA
St David's Island *434 B5 island* E Bermuda
St-Denis *471 G4 dependent territory capital* (Réunion) NW Réunion
St-Dié *482 E4* Vosges, NE France
St-Egrève *483 D5* Isère, E France
Saintes *483 B5 anc.* Mediolanum. Charente-Maritime, W France
St-Étienne *483 D5* Loire, E France
St-Flour *483 C5* Cantal, C France
Saint Gall *see* Sankt Gallen
St-Gaudens *483 B6* Haute-Garonne, S France
St George *434 B4* N Bermuda
Saint George *541 D5* Queensland, E Australia
Saint George *436 A5* Utah, W USA
St.George's *447 G5 country capital* (Grenada) SW Grenada
St-Georges *451 H3* E French Guiana
St-Georges *431 E4* Quebec, SE Canada
St George's Channel *481 B6 channel* Ireland/Wales, UK
St George's Island *434 B4 island* E Bermuda
Saint Helena *461 B6 UK dependent territory* C Atlantic Ocean
St.Helena Bay *470 B5 bay* SW South Africa
St Helier *481 D8 dependent territory capital* (Jersey) S Jersey, Channel Islands
Saint Ignace *432 C2* Michigan, N USA
St-Jean, Lac *431 E4 lake* Quebec, SE Canada
Saint Joe River *438 D2 river* Idaho, NW USA
Saint John *433 H1 river* Canada/USA
St.John *431 F4* New Brunswick, SE Canada
St John's *447 G3 country capital* (Antigua and Barbuda) Antigua, Antigua and Barbuda
St.John's *431 H3* Newfoundland, E Canada
Saint Joseph *437 F4* Missouri, C USA
St Julian's *494 B5* N Malta
St Kilda *480 A3 island* NW Scotland, UK
Saint Kitts and Nevis *447 F3 off.* Federation of Saint Christopher and Nevis, *var.* Saint Christopher-Nevis. *country* E West Indies
St-Laurent-du-Maroni *451 H3 var.* St-Laurent. NW French Guiana
St.Lawrence *431 E4 Fr.* Fleuve St-Laurent. *river* Canada/USA
St.Lawrence, Gulf of *431 F3 gulf* NW Atlantic Ocean
Saint Lawrence Island *428 B2 island* Alaska, USA
St-Lô *482 B3 anc.* Briovera, Laudus. Manche, N France
St-Louis *482 E4* Haut-Rhin, NE France
Saint Louis *437 G4* Missouri, C USA
Saint Louis *466 B3* NW Senegal
Saint Lucia *447 E1 country* SE West Indies
Saint Lucia Channel *447 H4 channel* Martinique/Saint Luc
St-Malo *482 B3* Ille-et-Vilaine, NW France
St-Malo, Golfe de *482 A3 gulf* NW France
St Matthew's Island *see* Zadet Kyun
St.Matthias Group *536 B3 isl group* NE PNG
St-Maur-des-Fossés *482 E2* V Marne, N France
St.Moritz *487 B7 Ger.* Sankt M *Rmsch.* San Murezzan. Graubünden, SE Switzerland
St-Nazaire *482 A4* Loire-Atlan NW France
St-Omer *482 C2* Pas-de-Calais N France
Saint Paul *437 F2 state capital* Minnesota, N USA
St-Paul, Île *533 C6 var.* St.Paul Island. *island* NE French Sou and Antarctic Territories
St Peter Port *481 D8 depender territory capital* (Guernsey) C Guernsey, Channel Islands
Saint Petersburg *see* Sankt-Peterburg
Saint Petersburg *435 E4* Flori SE USA
St-Pierre and Miquelon *427* Îles St-Pierre et Miquelon. *Fr territorial collectivity* NE Nor America
St-Quentin *482 C3* Aisne, N F
Saint Vincent *447 G4 island* N Vincent and the Grenadines
Saint Vincent and the Grena *427 D7 country* SE West Indi
Saint Vincent Passage *447 H passage* Saint Lucia/Saint Vin and the Grenadines
Saipan *534 B1 island country c* (Northern Mariana Islands) S Northern Mariana Islands
Sajama, Nevado *453 F4 moun* W Bolivia
Sajószentpéter *491 D6* Borsoc Abaúj-Zemplén, NE Hungar
Sakākah *512 B4* Al Jawf, NW S Arabia
Sakakawea, Lake *436 D1 rese* North Dakota, N USA
Sakata *522 D4* Yamagata, Hon C Japan
Sakhalin *517 see* Sakhalin, Os
Sakhalin, Ostrov *507 G4 var.* Sakhalin. *island* SE Russian Federation
Sakhon Nakhon *see* Sakon Na
Şäki *509 G2 Rus.* Sheki; *prev.* N NW Azerbaijan
Sakishima-shotō *522 A3 var.* Sakisima Syotō. *island group* SW Japan
Sakisima Syotô *see* Sakishima shotō
Sakiz *see* Saqqez
Sakiz-Adasi *see* Chíos
Sakon Nakhon *528 D4 var.* M Sakon Nakhon, Sakhon Nakh Sakon Nakhon, E Thailand
Saky *501 F5 Rus.* Saki. Respub Krym, S Ukraine
Sal *466 A3 island* Ilhas de Barlavento, NE Cape Verde
Sala *477 C6* Västmanland, C Sweden
Salacgrīva *498 C3 Est.* Salatsi. Limbaži, N Latvia
Sala Consilina *489 D5* Campa S Italy
Salado, Río *456 C3 river* C Argentina
Salado, Río *454 D5 river* E Argentina
Şalālah *513 D6* SW Oman
Salamá *444 B2* Baja Verapaz, C Guatemala
Salamanca *484 D2 anc.* Helma Salmantica. Castilla-León, NW Spain
Salamanca *456 B4* Coquimbo C Chile
Salamīyah *510 B3 var.* As Salamīyah. Ḥamāh, W Syria
Salang *see* Phuket
Salantai *498 B3* Kretinga, NW Lithuania
Salavan *529 D5 var.* Saravan, Saravane. Salavan, S Laos
Salavat *503 D6* Respublika Bashkortostan, W Russian Federation
Sala y Gomez *545 F4 island* C E Pacific Ocean
Sala y Gomez Fracture Zone Sala y Gomez Ridge
Sala y Gomez Ridge *545 G4* Sala y Gomez Fracture Zone. *tectonic feature* SE Pacific Oc
Šalčininkai *499 C5* Šalčininka SE Lithuania
Saldus *498 B3 Ger.* Frauenbur Saldus, W Latvia
Sale *541 C7* Victoria, SE Austr

Sarpsborg – Sibut

Sarpsborg 477 B6 Østfold, S Norway
Sartène 483 E7 Corse, France, C Mediterranean Sea
Sarthe 482 B4 cultural region N France
Sárti 496 C4 Kentrikí Makedonía, N Greece
Saruhan see Manisa
Saryesik-Atyrau, Peski 515 G1 desert E Kazakhstan
Sary-Tash 515 F2 Oshskaya Oblast', SW Kyrgyzstan
Sasebo 523 A7 Nagasaki, Kyūshū, SW Japan
Saskatchewan 429 F5 river Manitoba/Saskatchewan, C Canada
Saskatchewan 429 F5 province SW Canada
Saskatoon 429 F5 Saskatchewan, S Canada
Sasovo 503 B5 Ryazanskaya Oblast', W Russian Federation
Sassandra 466 D5 var. Ibo, Sassandra Fleuve. river S Ivory Coast
Sassandra 466 D5 S Ivory Coast
Sassandra Fleuve see Sassandra
Sassari 489 A5 Sardegna, Italy, C Mediterranean Sea
Sassenheim 478 C3 Zuid-Holland, W Netherlands
Sassnitz 486 D2 Mecklenburg-Vorpommern, NE Germany
Sátoraljaújhely 491 D6 Borsod-Abaúj-Zemplén, NE Hungary
Sātpura Range 526 D4 mountain range C India
Satsunan-shotō 522 A3 var. Satunan Syotô. island group SW Japan
Sattanen 476 D3 Lappi, NE Finland
Satu Mare 500 B3 Ger. Sathmar, Hung. Szatmárnémeti. Satu Mare, NW Romania
Satunan Syotô see Satsunan-shotō
Saudi Arabia 513 B5 off. Kingdom of Saudi Arabia, Ar. Al 'Arabīyah as Su'ūdīyah, Al Mamlakah al 'Arabīyah as Su'ūdīyah. country SW Asia
Sauer see Sûre
Saulkrasti 498 C3 Rīga, C Latvia
Sault Sainte Marie 432 C1 Michigan, N USA
Sault Ste.Marie 430 C4 Ontario, S Canada
Saumur 482 B4 Maine-et-Loire, NW France
Saurimo 470 C1 Port. Henrique de Carvalho, Vila Henrique de Carvalho. Lunda Sul, NE Angola
Sava 492 B3 Eng. Save, Ger. Sau, Hung. Száva. river SE Europe
Sava 499 E6 Rus. Sava. Mahilyowskaya Voblasts', E Belorussia
Savá 444 D2 Colón, N Honduras
Savai'i 537 E4 island NW Samoa
Savannah 435 E2 Georgia, SE USA
Savannah River 435 E2 river Georgia/South Carolina, SE USA
Savanna-La-Mar 446 A5 W Jamaica
Save, Rio 471 E3 var. Rio Sabi. river Mozambique/Zimbabwe
Saverne 482 E3 var. Zabern; anc. Tres Tabernae. Bas-Rhin, NE France
Savigliano 488 A2 Piemonte, NW Italy
Savigsivik see Savissivik
Savinski see Savinskiy
Savinskiy 502 C3 var. Savinski. Arkhangel'skaya Oblast', NW Russian Federation
Savissivik 474 D1 var. Savigsivik. N Greenland
Savoie 483 D5 cultural region E France
Savona 488 A2 Liguria, NW Italy
Savu Sea 531 E5 Ind. Laut Sawu. sea S Indonesia
Sawakin see Suakin
Sawdirī see Sodiri
Sawhāj see Sohâg
Şawqirah 513 D6 var. Suqrah. S Oman
Sayanskiy Khrebet 504 D3 mountain range S Russian Federation
Sayat 514 D3 Lebapskiy Velayat, E Turkmenistan
Sayaxché 444 B2 Petén, N Guatemala
Şaydā see Saïda
Sayḩūt 513 D6 E Yemen
Sayida see Saïda
Saynshand 519 E2 Dornogovĭ, SE Mongolia
Sayre 433 E3 Pennsylvania, NE USA
Say'ūn 513 C6 var. Saywūn. C Yemen
Saywūn see Say'ūn
Scandinavia 458 D2 geophysical region NW Europe
Scarborough 481 D5 N England, UK
Schaan 486 E1 W Liechtenstein
Schaerbeek 479 C6 Brussels, C Belgium
Schaffhausen 487 B7 Fr. Schaffhouse. Schaffhausen, N Switzerland
Schagen 478 C2 Noord-Holland, NW Netherlands
Schebschi Mountains see Shebshi Mountains
Scheessel 486 B3 Niedersachsen, NW Germany
Schefferville 431 E2 Quebec, E Canada
Scheldt 479 B5 Dut. Schelde, Fr. Escaut. river W Europe
Schell Creek Range 439 D5 mountain range Nevada, W USA
Schenectady 433 F3 New York, NE USA
Schertz 441 G4 Texas, SW USA
Schiermonnikoog 478 D1 Fris. Skiermûntseach. island Waddeneilanden, N Netherlands
Schijndel 478 D4 Noord-Brabant, S Netherlands
Schiltigheim 482 E3 Bas-Rhin, NE France
Schleswig 486 B2 Schleswig-Holstein, N Germany
Schleswig-Holstein 486 B2 cultural region N Germany
Schönebeck 486 C4 Sachsen-Anhalt, C Germany
Schooten see Schoten
Schoten 479 C5 var. Schooten. Antwerpen, N Belgium
Schouwen 478 B4 island SW Netherlands
Schwabenalb see Schwäbische Alb
Schwäbische Alb 487 B6 var. Schwabenalb, Eng. Swabian Jura. mountain range S Germany
Schwandorf 487 C5 Bayern, SE Germany
Schwarzwald 487 B6 Eng. Black Forest. mountain range SW Germany
Schwaz 487 C7 Tirol, W Austria
Schweinfurt 487 B5 Bayern, SE Germany
Schwerin 486 C3 Mecklenburg-Vorpommern, N Germany
Schwiz see Schwyz
Schwyz 487 B7 var. Schwiz. Schwyz, C Switzerland
Scilly, Isles of 481 B8 island group SW England, UK
Scio see Chíos
Scoresby Sound see Ittoqqortoormiit
Scoresbysund see Ittoqqortoormiit
Scotia Sea 449 C8 sea SW Atlantic Ocean
Scotland 480 C3 national region UK
Scott Base 546 B4 NZ research station Antarctica
Scott Island 546 B5 island Antarctica
Scottsbluff 436 D3 Nebraska, C USA
Scottsboro 434 D1 Alabama, S USA
Scottsdale 440 B2 Arizona, SW USA
Scranton 433 F3 Pennsylvania, NE USA
Scupi see Skopje
Scutari see Shkodër
Scutari, Lake 493 C5 Alb. Liqeni i Shkodrës, SCr. Skadarsko Jezero. lake Albania/Yugoslavia
Scyros see Skýros
Searcy 434 B1 Arkansas, C USA
Seattle 438 B2 Washington, NW USA
Sébaco 444 D3 Matagalpa, W Nicaragua
Sebastían Vizcaíno, Bahía 442 A2 bay NW Mexico
Sechura, Bahía de 452 A3 bay NW Peru
Secunderābād 526 D5 var. Sikandarabad. Andhra Pradesh, C India
Sedan 482 D3 Ardennes, N France
Seddon 543 D5 Marlborough, South Island, NZ
Seddonville 543 C5 West Coast, South Island, NZ
Sédhiou 466 B3 SW Senegal
Sedona 440 B2 Arizona, SW USA
Seesen 486 B4 Niedersachsen, C Germany
Segestica see Sisak
Segezha 502 B3 Respublika Kareliya, NW Russian Federation
Ségou 466 D3 var. Segu. Ségou, C Mali
Segovia 484 D2 Castilla-León, C Spain
Segoviao Wangkí see Coco, Río
Segu see Ségou
Séguédine 467 H2 Agadez, NE Niger
Seguin 441 G4 Texas, SW USA
Segura 485 E4 river S Spain
Seinäjoki 477 D5 Swe. Östermyra. Vaasa, W Finland
Seine 482 D1 river N France
Seine, Baie de la 482 B3 bay N France
Sekondi see Sekondi-Takoradi
Sekondi-Takoradi 467 E5 var. Sekondi. S Ghana
Selat Balabac see Balabac Strait
Selenga 519 E1 Mong. Selenge Mörön. river Mongolia/Russian Federation
Sélestat 482 E4 Ger. Schlettstadt. Bas-Rhin, NE France
Selfoss 475 E5 Sudhurland, SW Iceland
Sélibabi 466 C3 var. Sélibaby. Guidimaka, S Mauritania
Sélibaby see Sélibabi
Selma 439 C6 California, W USA
Selway River 438 D2 river Idaho, NW USA
Selwyn Range 540 B3 mountain range Queensland, C Australia
Selzaete see Zelzate
Semarang 530 C5 var. Samarang. Jawa, C Indonesia
Sembé 469 B5 La Sangha, NW Congo
Seminole 441 E3 Texas, SW USA
Seminole, Lake 434 D3 reservoir Florida/Georgia, SE USA
Semipalatinsk 506 D4 Kaz. Semey. Semipalatinsk, E Kazakhstan
Semnān 512 D3 var. Samnān. Semnān, N Iran
Semois 479 C8 river SE Belgium
Sendai 523 A8 Kagoshima, Kyūshū, SW Japan
Sendai 522 D4 Miyagi, Honshū, C Japan
Sendai-wan 522 D4 bay E Japan
Senec 491 C6 Ger. Wartberg, Hung. Szenc; prev. Szempcz. Západné Slovensko, W Slovakia
Senegal 466 C3 Fr. Sénégal. river W Africa
Senegal 466 B3 off. Republic of Senegal, Fr. Sénégal. country W Africa
Senftenberg 486 D4 Brandenburg, E Germany
Senica 491 C6 Ger. Senitz, Hung. Szenice. Západné Slovensko, W Slovakia
Senj 492 A3 Ger. Zengg, It. Segna; anc. Senia. Lika-Senj, NW Croatia
Senja 476 C2 prev. Senjen. island N Norway
Senkaku-shotō 522 A3 island group SW Japan
Senlis 482 C3 Oise, N France
Sennar 464 C4 var. Sannār. Sinnar, C Sudan
Sens 482 C3 anc. Agendicum, Senones. Yonne, C France
Sên, Stœng 529 D5 river C Cambodia
Senta 492 D3 Hung. Zenta. Serbia, N Yugoslavia
Seo de Urgel see La See d'Urgel
Seoul 517 see Sŏul
Sept-Îles 431 E3 Quebec, SE Canada
Seraing 479 D6 Liège, E Belgium
Serakhs 514 D3 var. Saragt. Akhalskiy Velayat, S Turkmenistan
Seram, Pulau 531 F4 var. Serang, Eng. Ceram. island Maluku, E Indonesia
Serang see Seram, Pulau
Serang 530 C5 Jawa, C Indonesia
Serasan, Selat 530 C3 strait Indonesia/Malaysia
Serbia 492 D4 Ger. Serbien, Serb. Srbija. Admin. region republic Yugoslavia
Serdica see Sofiya
Seremban 530 B3 Negeri Sembilan, Peninsular Malaysia
Serenje 470 D2 Central, E Zambia
Seres see Sérres
Seret see Siret
Sereth see Siret
Sérifos 497 C6 anc. Seriphos. island Kykládes, Greece, Aegean Sea
Serov 506 C3 Sverdlovskaya Oblast', C Russian Federation
Serowe 470 D3 Central, SE Botswana
Serpa Pinto see Menongue
Serpent's Mouth, The 451 F2 Sp. Boca de la Serpiente. strait Trinidad and Tobago/Venezuela
Serpukhov 503 B5 Moskovskaya Oblast', W Russian Federation
Serra dos Parecis see Parecis, Chapada dos
Sérrai see Sérres
Serrana, Cayo de 445 F2 island group NW Colombia
Serranilla, Cayo de 445 F2 island group NW Colombia
Serra Pacaraim see Pakaraima Mountains
Serra Tumucumaque see Tumuc Humac Mountains
Serravalle 488 E1 N San Marino
Sérres 496 C3 var. Seres; prev. Sérrai. Kentrikí Makedonía, NE Greece
Sert see Siirt
Sesto San Giovanni 488 B2 Lombardia, N Italy
Sesvete 492 B2 Grad Zagreb, N Croatia
Setabis see Xátiva
Sète 483 C6 prev. Cette. Hérault, S France
Setesdal 477 A6 valley S Norway
Sétif 463 E2 var. Stif. N Algeria
Setté Cama 469 A6 Ogooué-Maritime, SW Gabon
Setúbal 484 B4 Eng. Saint Ubes, Saint Yves. Setúbal, W Portugal
Setúbal, Baía de 484 B4 bay W Portugal
Seul, Lac 430 B3 lake Ontario, S Canada
Sevan 509 G2 C Armenia
Sevana Lich 509 G3 Eng. Lake Sevan, Rus. Ozero Sevan. lake E Armenia
Sevastopol' 501 F5 Eng. Sebastopol. Respublika Krym, S Ukraine
Severn 481 D6 Wel. Hafren. river England/Wales, UK
Severn 430 B2 river Ontario, S Canada
Severnaya Dvina 502 C4 var. Northern Dvina. river NW Russian Federation
Severnaya Zemlya 507 E2 var. Nicholas II Land. island group N Russian Federation
Severnyy 502 E3 Respublika Komi, NW Russian Federation
Severodvinsk 502 C3 prev. Molotov, Sudostroy. Arkhangel'skaya Oblast', NW Russian Federation
Severomorsk 502 C2 Murmanskaya Oblast', NW Russian Federation
Severo-Sibirskaya Nizmennost' 507 E2 var. North Siberian Plain, Eng. North Siberian Lowland. lowlands N Russian Federation
Sevier Lake 436 A4 lake Utah, W USA
Sevilla 484 C4 Eng. Seville; anc. Hispalis. Andalucía, SW Spain
Seville see Sevilla
Sevlievo 496 D2 Loveshka Oblast, C Bulgaria
Seychelles 471 G1 off. Republic of Seychelles. country W Indian Ocean
Seydhisfjördhur 475 E5 Austurland, E Iceland
Seydi 514 D2 prev. Neftezavodsk. Lebapskiy Velayat, E Turkmenistan
Seyhan see Adana
Sfákia 497 C8 Kríti, Greece, E Mediterranean Sea
Sfântu Gheorghe 500 C4 Ger. Sankt-Georgen, Hung. Sepsiszentgyőrgy; prev. Şepşi-Sângeorz, Sfîntu Gheorghe. Covasna, C Romania
Sfax 463 F2 Ar. Şafāqis. E Tunisia
's-Gravenhage 478 B4 var. Den Haag, Eng. The Hague, Fr. La Haye. country capital (Netherlands-seat of government) Zuid-Holland, W Netherlands
's-Gravenzande 478 B4 Zuid-Holland, W Netherlands
Shaan see Shaanxi
Shaanxi 520 B5 var. Shaan, Shaanxi Sheng, Shan-hsi, Shenshi, Shensi. Admin. region province C China
Shaanxi Sheng see Shaanxi
Shache 518 A3 var. Yarkant. Xinjiang Uygur Zizhiqu, NW China
Shackleton Ice Shelf 546 D3 ice shelf Antarctica
Shaddādī see Ash Shadādah
Shāhābād see Eslāmābād
Shahjahanabad see Delhi
Shahr-e Kord 512 C3 var. Shahr Kord. Chahār Maḩall va Bakhtīārī, C Iran
Shahr Kord see Shahr-e Kord
Shāhrūd 512 D2 prev. Emāmrūd, Emāmshahr. Semnān, N Iran
Shandī see Shendi
Shandong 520 D4 var. Lu, Shandong Sheng, Shantung. Admin. region province E China
Shandong Sheng see Shandong
Shanghai 520 D5 var. Shang-hai. Shanghai Shi, E China
Shang-hai see Shanghai
Shangrao 520 D5 Jiangxi, S China
Shan-hsi see Shaanxi
Shan-hsi see Shanxi
Shannon 481 A6 Ir. An tSionainn. river W Ireland
Shan Plateau 528 B3 plateau E Burma
Shansi see Shanxi
Shantarskiye Ostrova 507 G3 Eng. Shantar Islands. island group E Russian Federation
Shantou 520 D6 var. Shan-t'ou, Swatow. Guangdong, S China
Shantung see Shandong
Shanxi 520 C4 var. Jin, Shan-hsi, Shansi, Shanxi Sheng. Admin. region province C China
Shan Xian see Sanmenxia
Shanxi Sheng see Shanxi
Shaoguan 520 C6 var. Shao-kuan, Cant. Kukong; prev. Ch'u-chiang. Guangdong, S China
Shao-kuan see Shaoguan
Shaqrā see Shuqrah
Shaqrā' 512 B4 Ar Riyāḑ, C Saudi Arabia
Shari see Chari
Shari 522 D2 Hokkaidō, NE Japan
Shark Bay 539 A5 bay Western Australia
Shashe 470 D3 var. Shashi. river Botswana/Zimbabwe
Shashi see Shashe
Shatskiy Rise 517 G1 undersea feature N Pacific Ocean
Shatt al-Hodna see Hodna, Chott El
Shaţţ al Jarīd see Jerid, Chott el
Shawnee 441 G1 Oklahoma, C USA
Shchadryn 499 D7 Rus. Shchedrin. Homyel'skaya Voblasts', SE Belorussia
Shchëkino 503 B5 Tul'skaya Oblast', W Russian Federation
Shchors 501 E1 Chernihivs'ka Oblast', N Ukraine
Shchuchinsk 506 C4 prev. Shchuchye. Kokshetau, N Kazakhstan
Shchuchyn 499 B5 Pol. Szczuczyn Nowogródzki, Rus. Shchuchin. Hrodzyenskaya Voblasts', W Belorussia
Shebekino 503 A6 Belgorodskaya Oblast', W Russian Federation
Shebeli 465 D5 Amh. Wabē Shebelē Wenz, It. Scebeli, Som. Webi Shabeelle. river Ethiopia/Somalia
Sheberghān 515 E3 var. Shibarghān, Shiberghan, Shiberghān. Jowzjān, N Afghanistan
Sheboygan 432 B2 Wisconsin, N USA
Shebshi Mountains 468 A4 var. Schebschi Mountains. mountain range E Nigeria
Shechem see Nablus
Shedadi see Ash Shadādah
Sheffield 481 D5 N England, UK
Shekhem see Nablus
Shelby 436 B1 Montana, NW USA
Sheldon 437 F3 Iowa, C USA
Shelekhov Gulf 505 see Shelikhova, Zaliv
Shelikhova, Zaliv 507 G2 Eng. Shelekhov Gulf. gulf E Russian Federation
Shendi 464 C4 var. Shandī. River Nile, NE Sudan
Shengking see Liaoning
Shenking see Liaoning
Shenshi see Shaanxi
Shensi see Shaanxi
Shenyang 520 D3 Chin. Shen-yang, Eng. Moukden, Mukden; prev. Fengtien. Liaoning, NE China
Shepetivka 500 D2 Rus. Shepetovka. Khmel'nyts'ka Oblast', NW Ukraine
Shepparton 541 C7 Victoria, SE Australia
Sherbrooke 431 E4 Quebec, SE Canada
Shereik 464 C3 River Nile, N Sudan
Sheridan 436 C2 Wyoming, C USA
Sherman 441 G2 Texas, SW USA
's-Hertogenbosch 478 C4 Fr. Bois-le-Duc, Ger. Herzogenbusch. Noord-Brabant, S Netherlands
Shetland Islands 480 D1 island group NE Scotland, UK
Shibarghān see Sheberghān
Shiberghān see Sheberghān
Shibetsu 522 D2 var. Sibetu. Hokkaidō, NE Japan
Shibh Jazīrat Sīnā' see Sinai
Shibushi-wan 523 B8 bay SW Japan
Shigatse see Xigazê
Shih-chia-chuang see Shijiazhuang
Shihezi 518 C2 Xinjiang Uygur Zizhiqu, NW China
Shihmen see Shijiazhuang
Shijiazhuang 520 C4 var. Shih-chia-chuang; prev. Shihmen. Hebei, E China
Shikārpur 526 B3 Sind, S Pakistan
Shikoku 523 C7 var. Sikoku. island SW Japan
Shikoku Basin 517 F2 var. Sik Basin. undersea feature N Philippine Sea
Shikotan, Ostrov 522 E2 Jap. Shikotan-tō. island NE Russ Federation
Shilabo 465 D5 SE Ethiopia
Shiliguri 527 F3 prev. Siliguri Bengal, NE India
Shilka 507 F4 river S Russian Federation
Shimbir Berris see Shimbiris
Shimbiris 464 E4 var. Shimbi Berris. mountain N Somalia
Shimoga 524 C2 Karnātaka, W India
Shimonoseki 523 A7 var. Simonoseki; hist. Akamagas Bakan. Yamaguchi, Honshū, SW Japan
Shinano-gawa 523 C5 var. Sir Gawa. river Honshū, C Japan
Shīndand 514 D4 Farāh, W Afghanistan
Shingū 523 C6 var. Singû. Wakayama, Honshū, SW Jap
Shinjō 522 D4 var. Sinzyô. Yamagata, Honshū, C Japan
Shinyanga 465 C7 Shinyanga NW Tanzania
Shiprock 440 C1 New Mexico SW USA
Shīrāz 512 D4 var. Shīrāz. Fār S Iran
Shivpuri 526 D3 Madhya Pra C India
Shizugawa 522 D4 Miyagi, H NE Japan
Shizuoka 523 D6 var. Sizuok Shizuoka, Honshū, S Japan
Shklow 499 D6 Rus. Shklov. Mahilyowskaya Voblasts', E Belorussia
Shkodër 493 C5 var. Shkodra Scutari, SCr. Skadar. Shkodë NW Albania
Shkodra see Shkodër
Shkubinit, Lumi i 493 C6 va Shkumbî, Shkumbin. river C Albania
Shkumbî see Shkubinit, Lum
Shkumbin see Shkubinit, Lur
Sholāpur see Solāpur
Shostka 501 F1 Sums'ka Obla NE Ukraine
Show Low 440 B2 Arizona, SW USA
Shpola 501 E3 Cherkas'ka Ob N Ukraine
Shreveport 434 A2 Louisian S USA
Shrewsbury 481 D6 hist. Scrobesbyrig'. W England,
Shu 506 C5 Kaz. Shū. Zhamb SE Kazakhstan
Shuang-liao see Liaoyuan
Shumagin Islands 428 B3 is group Alaska, USA
Shumen 496 D2 Varnenska C NE Bulgaria
Shumilina 499 E5 Rus. Shum Vitsyebskaya Voblasts', NE Belorussia
Shuqrah 513 B7 var. Shaqrā. SW Yemen
Shwebo 528 B3 Sagaing, C B
Shyichy 499 C7 Rus. Shiichi. Homyel'skaya Voblasts', SE Belorussia
Shymkent 506 B5 prev. Chim Yuzhnyy Kazakhstan, S Kazakhstan
Shyshchytsy 499 C6 Rus. Shishchitsy. Minskaya Vobl C Belorussia
Si see Syr Darya
Siam, Gulf of see Thailand,
Sian see Xi'an
Siang see Brahmaputra
Siangtan see Xiangtan
Šiauliai 498 B4 Ger. Schauler Šiauliai, N Lithuania
Sibay 503 D6 Respublika Bashkortostan, W Russian Federation
Šibenik 492 B4 It. Sebenico. Šibenik, S Croatia
Siberia 504 see Sibir'
Siberut, Pulau 530 A4 prev. Siberoet. island Kepulauan Mentawai, W Indonesia
Sibetu see Shibetsu
Sibi 526 B2 Baluchistān, SW Pakistan
Sibir' 507 E3 var. Siberia. phy region NE Russian Federati
Sibiti 469 B6 La Lékoumou, S Congo
Sibiu 500 B4 Ger. Hermanns Hung. Nagyszeben. Sibiu, C Romania
Sibolga 530 B3 Sumatera, W Indonesia
Sibu 530 D3 Sarawak, East M
Sibut 468 C4 prev. Fort-Sibut Kémo, S Central African R

Sibuyan Sea – South Pole

n Sea 531 E2 sea
lippines
529 C6 var. Ban Sichon, Si
. Nakhon Si Thammarat,
hailand
n 520 B5 var. Chuan, Sichuan
, Ssu-ch'uan, Szechuan,
wan. Admin. region province
ina
n Pendi 520 B5 depression
ina
n Sheng see Sichuan
489 C7 Eng. Sicily; anc.
cria. island Italy,
diterranean Sea
n Channel see Sicily, Strait of
ee Sicilia
Strait of 489 B7 var. Sicilian
nel. strait C Mediterranean

i 453 E4 Cusco, S Peru
496 A4 Kérkyra, Iónioi Nísoi,
e, C Mediterranean Sea
30 C4 Borneo, C Indonesia
o 489 D7 Calabria, SW Italy
rrâni 464 A1 NW Egypt
l Abbès 462 D2 var. Sidi bel
s, Sidi-Bel-Abbès.
Algeria
kastro 496 C3 prev.
rókastron. Kentrikí
donía, NE Greece
Mount 546 B4 mountain
ctica
436 D1 Montana, NW USA
436 D4 Nebraska, C USA
432 C4 Ohio, N USA
see Saïda
ee Surt
490 E3 Ger. Sedlez, Rus.
ets. Siedlce, E Poland
486 B4 Nordrhein-Westfalen,
rmany
tycze 490 E3 Białystok,
and
488 B3 Fr. Sienne; anc. Saena
Toscana, C Italy
z 490 C4 Sieradz, C Poland
490 D3 Płock, C Poland
de Soconusco see Sierra
e
Leone 466 C4 off. Republic of
Leone. country W Africa
Leone Basin 458 C4
sea feature E Atlantic Ocean
Leone Ridge see Sierra
e Rise
Leone Rise 458 C4 var.
a Leone Ridge, Sierra Leone
elle. undersea feature
antic Ocean
Leone Schwelle see Sierra
e Rise
Madre 444 B2 var. Sierra de
nusco. mountain range
emala/Mexico
Madre see Madre Occidental,
a
Nevada 439 C6 mountain
W USA
Pacaraima see Pakaraima
tains
Vieja 440 D3 mountain range
, SW USA
Vista 440 B3 Arizona,
JSA
497 C6 anc. Siphnos. island
ides, Greece, Aegean Sea
30 A3 Sumatera, W Indonesia
ördhur 475 E4 Nordhurland
a, N Iceland
Peak 440 A2 mountain
na, SW USA
n see Xi'an
546 A2 UK research station
Orkney Islands, Antarctica
epeque 444 C2 Comayagua,
onduras
466 D4 Haute-Guinée,
uinea
ärvi 476 E4 Kuopio,
nland
09 F4 var. Sert; anc.
ncerta. Siirt, SE Turkey
larabad see Secunderābād
o 466 D4 Sikasso, S Mali
on 437 H5 Missouri, C USA
e-Alin', Khrebet 507 G4
ntain range SE Russian
ration
see Xi'an
491 C7 Baranya,
Hungary
u see Shikoku
u Basin see Shikoku Basin
498 B4 Šilalė, W Lithuania
r 527 G3 Assam, NE India
490 B4 Montana, NW USA
508 C4 anc. Seleucia. İçel,
key
Co 518 C5 lake W China
ot see Xilinhot
a 496 E1 var. Silistria; anc.
storum. Razgradska Oblast,
Bulgaria
ia see Silistra

Sillamäe 498 E2 Ger. Sillamäggi. Ida-Virumaa, NE Estonia
Šilutė 498 B4 Ger. Heydekrug. Šilutė, W Lithuania
Silvan 509 E4 Dıyarbakır, SE Turkey
Silverek 509 E4 Şanlıurfa, SE Turkey
Simanggang see Sri Aman
Simanichy 499 C7 Rus. Simonichi. Homyel'skaya Voblasts', SE Belorussia
Simav 508 B3 Kütahya, W Turkey
Simav Çayı 508 A3 river NW Turkey
Simeto 489 C7 river Sicilia, Italy, C Mediterranean Sea
Simeulue, Pulau 530 A3 island NW Indonesia
Simferopol' 501 F5 Respublika Krym, S Ukraine
Simitli 496 C3 Sofiyska Oblast, SW Bulgaria
Şimleu Silvaniei 500 B3 Hung. Szilágsomlyó; prev. Şimlăul Silvaniei, Şimleul Silvaniei. Sălaj, NW Romania
Simonoseki see Shimonoseki
Simpelveld 479 D6 Limburg, SE Netherlands
Simplon Pass 487 B8 pass S Switzerland
Simpson see Fort Simpson
Simpson Desert 540 B4 desert Northern Territory/South Australia
Sīnā' see Sinai
Sinai 464 C2 var. Sinai Peninsula, Ar. Shibh Jazīrat Sīnā', Sīnā'. physical region NE Egypt
Sinaia 500 C4 Prahova, SE Romania
Sinai Peninsula see Sinai
Sinano Gawa see Shinano-gawa
Sincelejo 450 B2 Sucre, NW Colombia
Sind 526 B3 var. Sindh. Admin. region province SE Pakistan
Sindelfingen 487 B6 Baden-Württemberg, SW Germany
Sindh see Sind
Sindi 498 D2 Ger. Zintenhof. Pärnumaa, SW Estonia
Sines 484 B4 Setúbal, S Portugal
Singan see Xi'an
Singapore 530 A1 off. Republic of Singapore. country SE Asia
Singapore 530 B3 country capital (Singapore) S Singapore
Singen 487 B6 Baden-Württemberg, S Germany
Singida 465 C7 Singida, C Tanzania
Singkang 531 E4 Sulawesi, C Indonesia
Singkawang 530 C3 Borneo, C Indonesia
Singora see Songkhla
Singû see Shingū
Sining see Xining
Siniscola 489 A5 Sardegna, Italy, C Mediterranean Sea
Sinj 492 B4 Split-Dalmacija, SE Croatia
Sinkiang see Xinjiang Uygur Zizhiqu
Sinkiang Uighur Autonomous Region see Xinjiang Uygur Zizhiqu
Sinnamarie see Sinnamary
Sinnamary 451 H3 var. Sinnamarie. N French Guiana
Sinnicolau Mare see Sânnicolau Mare
Sinoie, Lacul 500 D5 prev. Lacul Sinoe. lagoon SE Romania
Sinop 508 D2 anc. Sinope. Sinop, N Turkey
Sinsheim 487 B6 Baden-Württemberg, SW Germany
Sint Maarten 447 G3 Eng. Saint Martin. island N Netherlands Antilles
Sint-Michielsgestel 478 C4 Noord-Brabant, S Netherlands
Sint-Niklaas 479 B5 Fr. Saint-Nicolas. Oost-Vlaanderen, N Belgium
Sint-Pieters-Leeuw 479 B6 Vlaams Brabant, C Belgium
Sintra 484 B3 prev. Cintra. Lisboa, W Portugal
Sinujiif 465 E5 Nugaal, NE Somalia
Sinus Aelaniticus see Aqaba, Gulf of
Sinyang see Xinyang
Sinzyô see Shinjō
Sion 487 A7 Ger. Sitten; anc. Sedunum. Valais, SW Switzerland
Sioux City 437 F3 Iowa, C USA
Sioux Falls 437 F3 South Dakota, N USA
Siping 520 D3 var. Ssu-p'ing, Szeping; prev. Ssu-p'ing-chieh. Jilin, NE China
Siple, Mount 546 A4 mountain Siple Island, Antarctica
Siquirres 445 E4 Limón, E Costa Rica
Siracusa 489 D7 Eng. Syracuse. Sicilia, Italy, C Mediterranean Sea
Sir Darya see Syr Darya
Sir Edward Pellew Group 540 B2 island group Northern Territory, NE Australia
Siret 500 C3 var. Siretul, Ger. Sereth, Rus. Seret, Ukr. Siret. river Romania/Ukraine
Siret see Siret
Siretul see Siret
Sirikit Reservoir 528 C4 lake N Thailand
Sīrjān 512 D4 prev. Sa'īdābād. Kermān, S Iran
Sirna see Sýrna
Şırnak 509 F4 Şırnak, SE Turkey
Síros see Sýros
Sirte see Surt
Sirte, Gulf of see Surt, Khalij
Sisak 492 B3 var. Siscia, Ger. Sissek, Hung. Sziszek; anc. Segestica. Sisak-Moslavina, C Croatia
Siscia see Sisak
Sisimiut 474 C3 var. Holsteinborg, Holsteinsborg, Holstenborg, Holstensborg. S Greenland
Sissek see Sisak
Sistema Penibético see Béticos, Sistemas
Siteía 497 D8 var. Sitía. Kríti, Greece, E Mediterranean Sea
Sitges 485 G2 Cataluña, NE Spain
Sitía see Siteía
Sittang 528 B4 var. Sittoung. river S Burma
Sittard 479 D5 Limburg, SE Netherlands
Sittoung see Sittang
Sittwe 528 A3 var. Akyab. Arakan State, W Burma
Siuna 444 D3 Región Autónoma Atlántico Norte, NE Nicaragua
Siut see Asyût
Sivas 508 D3 anc. Sebastia, Sebaste. Sivas, C Turkey
Sivers'kyy Donets' 501 G2 Rus. Severskiy Donets. river Russian Federation/Ukraine see also Severskiy Donets
Siwa 464 A2 var. Sīwah. NW Egypt
Sīwah see Siwa
Six-Fours-les-Plages 483 D6 Var, SE France
Siyäzän 509 H2 Rus. Siazan'. NE Azerbaijan
Sizuoka see Shizuoka
Sjar see Sääre
Sjælland 477 B8 Eng. Zealand, Ger. Seeland. island E Denmark
Sjenica 493 D5 Turk. Seniça. Serbia, SW Yugoslavia
Skadar see Shkodër
Skagerak see Skagerrak
Skagerrak 477 A6 var. Skagerak. channel N Europe
Skagit River 438 B1 river Washington, NW USA
Skalka 476 C3 lake N Sweden
Skaudvilė 498 B4 Tauragė, SW Lithuania
Skegness 481 E6 E England, UK
Skellefteå 476 D4 Västerbotten, N Sweden
Skellefteälven 476 C4 river N Sweden
Ski 477 B6 Akershus, S Norway
Skíathos 497 C5 Skíathos, Vóreioi Sporádes, Greece, Aegean Sea
Skidal' 499 B5 Rus. Skidel'. Hrodzyenskaya Voblasts', W Belorussia
Skiftet 498 C1 Fin. Kihti. strait Gulf of Bothnia/Gulf of Finland
Skíros see Skýros
Skópelos 497 C5 Skópelos, Vóreioi Sporádes, Greece, Aegean Sea
Skopje 493 D6 var. Üsküb, Turk. Üsküp; prev. Skoplje, anc. Scupi. country capital (FYR Macedonia) N FYR Macedonia
Skoplje see Skopje
Skovorodino 507 F4 Amurskaya Oblast', SE Russian Federation
Skuodas 498 B3 Ger. Schoden, Pol. Szkudy. Skuodas, NW Lithuania
Skye, Isle of 480 B3 island NW Scotland, UK
Skýros 497 C5 var. Skíros. Skýros, Vóreioi Sporádes, Greece, Aegean Sea
Skýros 497 C5 var. Skíros; anc. Scyros. island Vóreioi Sporádes, Greece, Aegean Sea
Slagelse 477 B7 Vestsjælland, E Denmark
Slatina 500 B5 Olt, S Romania
Slavonska Požega 492 C3 prev. Požega, Ger. Poschega, Hung. Pozsega. Požega-Slavonija, NE Croatia
Slavonski Brod 492 C3 Ger. Brod, Hung. Bród; prev. Brod, Brod na Savi. Brod-Posavina, NE Croatia
Slavuta 500 C2 Khmel'nyts'ka Oblast', NW Ukraine
Slawharad 499 E7 Rus. Slavgorod. Mahilyowskaya Voblasts', E Belorussia
Sławno 490 C2 Słupsk, NW Poland
Sléibhte Chill Mhantáin see Wicklow Mountains
Slēmānī see As Sulaymānīyah
Sliema 494 B5 N Malta
Sligeach see Sligo
Sligo 481 A5 Ir. Sligeach. NW Ireland
Sliven 496 D2 var. Slivno. Burgaska Oblast, E Bulgaria
Slivnitsa 496 B2 Sofiyska Oblast, W Bulgaria
Slivno see Sliven
Slobozia 500 C5 Ialomiţa, SE Romania
Slonim 499 B6 Pol. Słonim, Rus. Slonim. Hrodzyenskaya Voblasts', W Belorussia
Slovakia 491 C6 off. Slovenská Republika, Ger. Slowakei, Hung. Szlovákia, Slvk. Slovensko. country C Europe
Slovenia 487 D8 off. Republic of Slovenia, Ger. Slowenien, Slvn. Slovenija. country SE Europe
Slovenské Rudohorie 491 D6 Eng. Slovak Ore Mountains, Ger. Slowakisches Erzgebirge, Ungarisches Erzgebirge. mountain range C Slovakia
Slov''yans'k 501 G3 Rus. Slavyansk. Donets'ka Oblast', E Ukraine
Słubice 490 B3 Ger. Frankfurt. Gorzów, W Poland
Sluch 500 D1 river NW Ukraine
Słupsk 490 C2 Ger. Stolp. Słupsk, NW Poland
Slutsk 499 C6 Rus. Slutsk. Minskaya Voblasts', S Belorussia
Smallwood Reservoir 431 F2 lake Newfoundland, S Canada
Smara 462 B3 var. Es Semara. N Western Sahara
Smarhon' 499 C5 Pol. Smorgonie, Rus. Smorgon'. Hrodzyenskaya Voblasts', W Belorussia
Smederevo 492 D4 Ger. Semendria. Serbia, N Yugoslavia
Smederevska Palanka 492 D4 Serbia, C Yugoslavia
Smila 501 E2 Rus. Smela. Cherkas'ka Oblast', C Ukraine
Smiltene 498 D3 Ger. Smilten. Valka, N Latvia
Smøla 476 A4 island W Norway
Smolensk 503 A5 Smolenskaya Oblast', W Russian Federation
Snake 426 B4 river Yukon Territory, NW Canada
Snake River 438 C3 river NW USA
Snake River Plain 438 D4 plain Idaho, NW USA
Sneek 478 D2 Friesland, N Netherlands
Sněžka 490 B4 Ger. Schneekoppe. mountain N Czech Republic
Śniardwy, Jezioro 490 D3 Ger. Spirdingsee. lake NE Poland
Snina 491 E5 Hung. Szinna. Východné Slovensko, E Slovakia
Snowdonia 481 C6 mountain range NW Wales, UK
Snyder 441 F3 Texas, SW USA
Sobradinho, Represa de 455 F2 var. Barragem de Sobradinho. reservoir E Brazil
Sochi 503 A7 Krasnodarskiy Kray, SW Russian Federation
Société, Archipel de la 537 G4 var. Archipel de Tahiti, Îles de la Société, Eng. Society Islands. island group W French Polynesia
Society Islands 535 see Société, Archipel de la
Socorro 440 D2 New Mexico, SW USA
Socorro, Isla 442 B5 island W Mexico
Socotra 504 see Suquṭrā
Soc Trăng 529 D6 var. Khanh. Soc Trăng, S Vietnam
Socuéllamos 485 E3 Castilla-La Mancha, C Spain
Sodankylä 476 D3 Lappi, N Finland
Sodari see Sodiri
Söderhamn 477 C5 Gävleborg, C Sweden
Södertälje 477 C6 Stockholm, C Sweden
Sodiri 464 B4 var. Sawdirī, Sodari. Northern Kordofan, C Sudan
Sofia see Sofiya
Sofiya 496 C2 var. Sophia, Eng. Sofia; Lat. Serdica. country capital (Bulgaria) Grad Sofiya, W Bulgaria
Sogamoso 450 B3 Boyacá, C Colombia
Sognefjorden 477 A5 fjord NE North Sea
Sohâg 464 B2 var. Sawhāj, Suliag. C Egypt
Sohar see Şuḩār
Sohm Plain 458 B3 undersea feature NW Atlantic Ocean
Sohrau see Żory
Sokal' 500 C2 Rus. Sokal. L'vivs'ka Oblast', NW Ukraine
Söke 508 A4 Aydın, SW Turkey
Sokhumi 509 E1 Rus. Sukhumi. NW Georgia
Sokodé 467 F4 C Togo
Sokol 502 C4 Vologodskaya Oblast', NW Russian Federation
Sokółka 490 E3 Białystok, NE Poland
Sokolov 491 A5 Ger. Falkenau an der Eger; prev. Falknov nad Ohří. Západní Čechy, W Czech Republic
Sokone 466 B3 W Senegal
Sokoto 467 F4 river NW Nigeria
Sokoto 467 F3 Sokoto, NW Nigeria
Sokotra see Suquṭrā
Solāpur 516 B3 var. Sholāpur. Mahārāshtra, W India
Solca 500 C3 Ger. Solka. Suceava, N Romania
Sol, Costa del 484 D5 coastal region S Spain
Soldeu 483 B7 NE Andorra
Solec Kujawski 490 C3 Bydgoszcz, W Poland
Soledad see East Falkland
Soledad 450 B1 Anzoátegui, NE Venezuela
Solikamsk 506 C3 Permskaya Oblast', NW Russian Federation
Sol'-Iletsk 503 D6 Orenburgskaya Oblast', W Russian Federation
Solingen 486 A4 Nordrhein-Westfalen, W Germany
Sollentuna 477 C6 Stockholm, C Sweden
Solok 530 B4 Sumatera, W Indonesia
Solomon Islands 536 C3 prev. British Solomon Islands Protectorate. country W Pacific Ocean
Solomon Islands 536 C3 island group PNG/Solomon Islands
Solomon Sea 536 B3 sea W Pacific Ocean
Soltau 486 B3 Niedersachsen, NW Germany
Sol'tsy 502 A4 Novgorodskaya Oblast', W Russian Federation
Solwezi 470 D2 North Western, NW Zambia
Sōma 522 D4 Fukushima, Honshū, C Japan
Somalia 465 D5 off. Somali Democratic Republic, Som. Jamuuriyada Demuqraadiga Soomaaliyeed, Soomaaliya; prev. Italian Somaliland, Somaliland Protectorate. country E Africa
Somali Basin 461 E5 undersea feature W Indian Ocean
Sombor 492 C3 Hung. Zombor. Serbia, NW Yugoslavia
Someren 479 D5 Noord-Brabant, SE Netherlands
Somerset 434 A5 var. Somerset Village. W Bermuda
Somerset 432 C5 Kentucky, S USA
Somerset Island 429 F2 island Queen Elizabeth Islands, Nunavut, NW Canada
Somerset Island 434 A5 island W Bermuda
Somerset Village see Somerset
Somers Islands see Bermuda
Somerton 440 A2 Arizona, SW USA
Someş 500 B3 var. Somesch, Someşul, Szamos, Ger. Samosch. river Hungary/Romania
Somesch see Someş
Someşul see Someş
Somme 482 C2 river N France
Somotillo 444 C3 Chinandega, NW Nicaragua
Somoto 444 D3 Madriz, NW Nicaragua
Songea 465 C8 Ruvuma, S Tanzania
Sông Hông Hà see Red River
Songkhla 529 C7 var. Songkla, Mal. Singora. Songkhla, SW Thailand
Songkla see Songkhla
Sông Srepok see Srêpôk, Tônle
Sông Tiên Giang see Mekong
Sonoran Desert 440 A3 var. Desierto de Altar. desert Mexico/USA see also Altar, Desierto de
Sonsonate 444 B3 Sonsonate, W El Salvador
Soochow see Suzhou
Sop Hao 528 D3 Houaphan, N Laos
Sophia see Sofiya
Sopot 490 C2 Ger. Zoppot. Gdańsk, N Poland
Sopron 491 B6 Ger. Ödenburg. Győr-Moson-Sopron, NW Hungary
Sorgues 483 D6 Vaucluse, SE France
Sorgun 508 D3 Yozgat, C Turkey
Soria 485 E2 Castilla-León, N Spain
Soroca 500 D3 Rus. Soroki. N Moldavia
Sorong 531 F4 Irian Jaya, E Indonesia
Sørøy see Sørøya
Sørøya 476 C2 var. Sørøy. island N Norway
Sortavala 502 B3 Respublika Kareliya, NW Russian Federation
Sotavento, Ilhas de 466 A3 var. Leeward Islands. island group S Cape Verde
Sotkamo 476 E4 Oulu, C Finland
Souanké 469 B5 La Sangha, NW Congo
Soueida see As Suwaydā'
Souflí 496 D3 prev. Souflíon. Anatolikí Makedonía kai Thráki, NE Greece
Soufrière 447 F2 S Dominica
Soukhné see As Sukhnah
Sŏul 521 E4 off. Sŏul-t'ŭkpyŏlsi, Eng. Seoul, Jap. Keijō; prev. Kyŏngsŏng. country capital (South Korea) NW South Korea
Soûr 511 A5 var. Şūr; anc. Tyre. SW Lebanon
Souris River 437 E1 var. Mouse River. river Canada/USA
Sourpi 497 B5 Thessalía, C Greece
Sousse 463 F2 var. Sūsah. NE Tunisia
South Africa 470 C4 off. Republic of South Africa, Afr. Suid-Afrika. country S Africa
South America 448 continent
Southampton 481 D7 hist. Hamwih, Lat. Clausentum. S England, UK
Southampton Island 429 G3 island Nunavut, NE Canada
South Andaman 525 F2 island Andaman Islands, India, NE Indian Ocean
South Australia 541 A5 state S Australia
South Australian Basin 534 B5 undersea feature SW Indian Ocean
South Bend 432 C3 Indiana, N USA
South Beveland see Zuid-Beveland
South Bruny Island 541 C8 island Tasmania, SE Australia
South Carolina 435 E2 off. State of South Carolina; also known as The Palmetto State. state SE USA
South Carpathians see Carpaţii Meridionali
South China Basin 517 E4 undersea feature SE South China Sea
South China Sea 516 D4 Chin. Nan Hai, Ind. Laut Cina Selatan, Vtn. Biên Đông. sea SE Asia
South Dakota 436 D2 off. State of South Dakota; also known as The Coyote State, Sunshine State. state N USA
Southeast Indian Ridge 533 D7 undersea feature Indian Ocean/Pacific Ocean
Southeast Pacific Basin 545 E5 var. Belling Hausen Mulde. undersea feature SE Pacific Ocean
South East Point 541 C7 headland Victoria, S Australia
Southend-on-Sea 481 E6 E England, UK
Southern Alps 543 B6 mountain range South Island, NZ
Southern Cook Islands 537 F4 island group S Cook Islands
Southern Cross 539 B6 Western Australia
Southern Indian Lake 429 F4 lake Manitoba, C Canada
Southern Ocean 459 B7 ocean
Southern Uplands 480 C4 mountain range S Scotland, UK
South Fiji Basin 534 D4 undersea feature S Pacific Ocean
South Geomagnetic Pole 546 B3 pole Antarctica
South Georgia 449 D8 island South Georgia and the South Sandwich Islands, SW Atlantic Ocean
South Goulburn Island 538 E2 island Northern Territory, N Australia
South Huvadhu Atoll 524 A5 var. Gaafu Dhaalu Atoll. atoll S Maldives
South Indian Basin 533 D7 undersea feature Indian Ocean/Pacific Ocean
South Island 543 C6 island S NZ
South Korea 521 E4 off. Republic of Korea, Kor. Taehan Min'guk. country E Asia
South Lake Tahoe 439 C5 California, W USA
South Orkney Islands 546 A2 island group Antarctica
South Ossetia 509 F2 former autonomous region SW Georgia
South Pacific Basin see Southwest Pacific Basin
South Platte River 436 D4 river Colorado/Nebraska, C USA
South Pole 546 B3 pole Antarctica

Tafassâsset, Ténéré du – Thunder Bay

ìsset, Ténéré du 467 G2 : N Niger
see Aṭ Ṭafilah
rog 503 A7 Rostovskaya st', SW Russian Federation
rog, Gulf of 501 G4 Rus. nrogskiy Zaliv, Ukr. nroz'ka Zatoka. gulf Russian ration/Ukraine
inga 455 F3 Tocantins, zil
484 C3 Port. Rio Tejo, Sp. Río river Portugal/Spain
Plain 472 A4 undersea feature intic Ocean
463 E4 mountain SE Algeria
537 H4 island Îles du Vent, ench Polynesia
uah 441 G1 Oklahoma, A
, Lake 439 B5 lake rnia/Nevada, W USA
a 467 F3 Tahoua, W Niger
ung 520 D6 Jap. Taichū; prev. in. C Taiwan
543 B7 river South Island, NZ
e 542 D4 Manawatu-ganui, North Island, NZ
Bend 541 B7 South alia
n 520 D6 Jap. Tainan; prev. an. S Taiwan
520 D6 Jap. Taihoku; prev. oku. country capital (Taiwan) wan
g 530 B3 Perak, Peninsular ysia
n 520 D6 off. Republic of na, var. Formosa, Formo'sa. ry E Asia
n Haihsia see Taiwan Strait
n Haixia see Taiwan Strait
n Strait 520 D6 var. Formosa , Chin. T'aiwan Haihsia, n Haixia. strait China/Taiwan
n 520 C4 prev. T'ai-yuan, yüan, Yangku. Shanxi, ina
513 B7 SW Yemen
stan 515 E3 off. Republic of istan, Rus. Tadzhikistan, Taj. urii Tojikiston; prev. Tajik . country C Asia
8 C4 var. Rahaeng. Tak, hailand
see Kaohsiung
ka 523 C5 Toyama, Honshū, apan
una 542 D2 Auckland, North d, NZ
atosh 514 C2 Rus. Takhiatash. qalpoghiston Respublikasi, zbekistan
akŭpir 514 D1 Rus. takupyr. Qoraqalpoghiston ublikasi, NW Uzbekistan
wa 522 D2 Hokkaidō, apan
Makan Desert 516 see makan Shamo
nakan Shamo 518 B3 Eng. Makan Desert. desert China
see Kaohsiung
ea 537 G4 island S Cook ds
yn 499 D6 Rus. Tolochin. ebskaya Voblasts', elorussia
anca, Cordillera de 445 E5 ntain range S Costa Rica
452 B2 Piura, NW Peru
515 F2 Talasskaya Oblast', Kyrgyzstan
, Kepulauan 531 F3 island E Indonesia
ra de la Reina 484 D3 anc. arobriga, Talabriga. Castilla-ancha, C Spain
456 B4 Maule, C Chile
uano 457 B5 Bío Bío, C Chile
korgan 506 C5 Kaz. yqorghan; prev. Taldy-Kurgan. ykorgan, SE Kazakhstan
n see Dalian
an see Tāloqān
499 C6 Rus. Tal'ka. Minskaya asts', C Belorussia
assee 434 D3 prev. kogean. state capital Florida, SA
Abyaḍ see At Tall al Abyaḍ
n 498 D2 Ger. Reval, Rus. ; prev. Revel. country capital onia) Harjumaa, NW Estonia
alakh 510 B4 var. Tell Kalakh. s, C Syria
ah 434 B2 Louisiana, S USA
kh 506 D3 Taymyrskiy gano-Nenetskiy) Avtonomnyy g, N Russian Federation
501 E3 Rus. Tal'noye. kas'ka Oblast', C Ukraine
441 F1 Oklahoma, C USA
ān 515 E3 var. Taliq-an. ār, NE Afghanistan

Talsi 498 C3 Ger. Talsen. Talsi, NW Latvia
Taltal 456 B2 Antofagasta, N Chile
Talvik 476 D2 Finnmark, N Norway
Tamabo, Banjaran 530 D3 mountain range East Malaysia
Tamale 467 E4 C Ghana
Tamana 537 E3 prev. Rotcher Island. atoll Tungaru, W Kiribati
Tamanrasset 463 E4 var. Tamenghest. S Algeria
Tamar 481 C7 river SW England, UK
Tamar see Tudmur
Tamatave see Toamasina
Tamazunchale 443 E4 San Luis Potosí, C Mexico
Tambacounda 466 C3 SE Senegal
Tambov 503 B6 Tambovskaya Oblast', W Russian Federation
Tambura 465 B5 Western Equatoria, SW Sudan
Tamchaket see Tâmchekkeṭ
Tâmchekkeṭ 466 C3 var. Tamchaket. Hodh el Gharbi, S Mauritania
Tamenghest see Tamanrasset
Tamiahua, Laguna de 443 F4 lagoon E Mexico
Tamil Nādu 524 C3 prev. Madras. state SE India
Tam Ky 529 E5 Quang Nam-Đa Năng, C Vietnam
Tampa 435 E4 Florida, SE USA
Tampa Bay 435 E4 bay Florida, SE USA
Tampere 477 D5 Swe. Tammerfors. Häme, SW Finland
Tampico 443 E3 Tamaulipas, C Mexico
Tamworth 541 D6 New South Wales, SE Australia
Tana 476 D2 var. Tenojoki, Fin. Teno, Lapp. Dealnu. river Finland/Norway see also Teno
Tana 476 D2 Finnmark, N Norway
Tanabe 523 C7 Wakayama, Honshū, SW Japan
T'ana Hāyk' 464 C4 Eng. Lake Tana. lake NW Ethiopia
Tanais see Don
Tanami Desert 538 D3 desert Northern Territory, N Australia
Ṭăndărei 500 D5 Ialomiṭa, SE Romania
Tandil 457 D5 Buenos Aires, E Argentina
Tanega-shima 523 B8 island Nansei-shotō, SW Japan
Tane Range 528 B4 Bur. Tanen Taunggyi. mountain range W Thailand
Tanezrouft 462 D4 desert Algeria/Mali
Ṭanf, Jabal aṭ 510 D4 mountain SE Syria
Tanga 461 E5 Tanga, E Tanzania
Tanga 465 C7 region E Tanzania
Tanganyika, Lake 465 B7 lake E Africa
Tangeh-ye Hormoz see Hormuz, Strait of
Tanger 462 C2 var. Tangiers, Tangier, Fr./Ger. Tangerk, Sp. Tánger; anc. Tingis. NW Morocco
Tangerk see Tanger
Tanggula Shan 518 C4 var. Dangla, Tangla Range. mountain range W China
Tangier see Tanger
Tangiers see Tanger
Tangla Range see Tanggula Shan
Tangra Yumco 518 B5 var. Tangro Tso. lake W China
Tangro Tso see Tangra Yumco
Tangshan 520 D3 var. T'ang-shan. Hebei, E China
T'ang-shan see Tangshan
Tanimbar, Kepulauan 531 F5 island group Maluku, E Indonesia
Tanna 536 D4 island S Vanuatu
Tan-Tan 462 B3 SW Morocco
Tan-tung see Dandong
Tanzania 465 C7 off. United Republic of Tanzania, Swa. Jamhuri ya Muungano wa Tanzania; prev. German East Africa, Tanganyika and Zanzibar. country E Africa
Taoudenit see Taoudenni
Taoudenni 467 E2 var. Taoudenit. Tombouctou, N Mali
Tapa 498 E2 Ger. Taps. Lääne-Virumaa, NE Estonia
Tapachula 443 G5 Chiapas, SE Mexico
Tapajós, Rio 455 E2 var. Tapajóz. river NW Brazil
Tapajóz see Tapajós, Rio
Ṭarābulus 463 F2 var. Ṭarābulus al Gharb, Eng. Tripoli. country capital (Libya) NW Libya
Ṭarābulus see Tripoli
Ṭarābulus al Gharb see Ṭarābulus
Ṭarābulus ash Shām see Tripoli
Taraclia 500 D4 Rus. Tarakilya. S Moldavia
Taranaki, Mount 542 C4 var. Egmont. mountain North Island, NZ
Tarancón 485 E3 Castilla-La Mancha, C Spain
Taranto 489 E5 var. Tarentum. Puglia, SE Italy
Taranto, Golfo di 489 E6 Eng. Gulf of Taranto. gulf S Italy
Tarapoto 452 C2 San Martín, N Peru
Tarare 483 D5 Rhône, E France
Tarascon 483 D6 Bouches-du-Rhône, SE France
Tarawa 536 D2 atoll Tungaru, W Kiribati
Tarazona 485 E2 Aragón, NE Spain
Tarbes 483 B6 anc. Bigorra. Hautes-Pyrénées, S France
Tarcoola 541 A6 South Australia
Taree 541 D6 New South Wales, SE Australia
Tarentum see Taranto
Târgovişte 500 C5 prev. Tîrgovişte. Dâmboviṭa, S Romania
Târgu Jiu 500 B4 prev. Tîrgu Jiu. Gorj, W Romania
Târgul-Neamṭ see Târgu-Neamṭ
Târgu Mureş 500 B4 prev. Oşorhei, Tîrgu Mures, Ger. Neumarkt, Hung. Marosvásárhely. Mureş, C Romania
Târgu-Neamṭ 500 C3 var. Târgul-Neamṭ; prev. Tîrgu-Neamṭ. Neamṭ, NE Romania
Târgu Ocna 500 C4 Hung. Aknavásár; prev. Tîrgu Ocna. Bacău, E Romania
Târgu Secuiesc 500 C4 Ger. Neumarkt, Szekler Neumarkt, Hung. Kezdivásárhely; prev. Chezdi-Oşorheiu, Târgul-Săcuiesc, Tîrgu Secuiesc. Covasna, E Romania
Tarija 453 G5 Tarija, S Bolivia
Tarīm 513 C6 C Yemen
Tarim Basin 516 C2 basin NW China
Tarim He 518 B3 river NW China
Tarma 452 C3 Junín, C Peru
Tarn 483 C6 cultural region S France
Tarn 483 C6 river S France
Tarnobrzeg 490 D4 Tarnobrzeg, SE Poland
Tarnów 491 D5 Tarnów, SE Poland
Tarragona 485 G2 anc. Tarraco. Cataluña, E Spain
Tàrrega 485 F2 var. Tarrega. Cataluña, NE Spain
Tarsus 508 C4 İçel, S Turkey
Tartu 498 D3 Ger. Dorpat; prev. Rus. Yurev, Yur'yev. Tartumaa, SE Estonia
Ṭarṭūs 510 A3 Fr. Tartouss; anc. Tortosa. Ṭarṭūs, W Syria
Ta Ru Tao, Ko 529 B7 island S Thailand
Tarvisio 488 D2 Friuli-Venezia Giulia, NE Italy
Tashi Chho Dzong see Thimphu
Tashkent 504 see Toshkent
Tash-Kumyr 515 F2 Kir. Tash-Kömür. Dzhalal-Abadskaya Oblast', W Kyrgyzstan
Tashqurghan see Kholm
Tasikmalaya 530 C5 prev. Tasikmalaja. Jawa, C Indonesia
Tasman Basin 534 C5 var. East Australian Basin. undersea feature S Tasman Sea
Tasman Bay 543 C5 inlet South Island, NZ
Tasmania 541 B8 prev. Van Diemen's Land. state SE Australia
Tasmania 544 B4 island SE Australia
Tasman Plateau 534 C5 var. South Tasmania Plateau. undersea feature SW Tasman Sea
Tasman Sea 534 C5 sea SW Pacific Ocean
Tassili-n-Ajjer 463 E4 plateau E Algeria
Tatabánya 491 C6 Komárom-Esztergom, NW Hungary
Tathlīth 513 B5 'Asīr, S Saudi Arabia
Tatra Mountains 491 D5 Ger. Tatra, Hung. Tátra, Pol./Slvk. Tatry. mountain range Poland/Slovakia
Ta-t'ung see Datong
Tatvan 509 F3 Bitlis, SE Turkey
Ta'ū 537 F4 var. Tau. island Manua Islands, E American Samoa
Tau see Ta'ū
Taukum, Peski 515 G1 desert SE Kazakhstan
Taumarunui 542 D4 Manawatu-Wanganui, North Island, NZ
Taungdwingyi 528 B3 Magwe, C Burma
Taunggyi 528 B3 Shan State, C Burma
Taunton 481 C7 SW England, UK
Taupo 542 D3 Waikato, North Island, NZ
Taupo, Lake 542 D3 lake North Island, NZ
Tauragė 496 B4 Ger. Tauroggen. Tauragė, SW Lithuania
Tauranga 542 D3 Bay of Plenty, North Island, NZ
Tauris see Tabrīz
Tavas 508 B4 Denizli, SW Turkey
Tavira 484 C5 Faro, S Portugal
Tavoy 529 B5 var. Dawei. Tenasserim, S Burma
Tavoy Island see Mali Kyun
Tawakoni, Lake 441 G2 reservoir Texas, SW USA
Tawau 530 D3 Sabah, East Malaysia
Ṭawkar see Tokar
Tawzar see Tozeur
Taxco 443 E4 var. Taxco de Alarcón. Guerrero, S Mexico
Taxco de Alarcón see Taxco
Tay 480 C3 river C Scotland, UK
Taylor 441 G3 Texas, SW USA
Taymā' 512 A4 Tabūk, NW Saudi Arabia
Taymyr, Ozero 507 E2 lake N Russian Federation
Taymyr, Poluostrov 507 E2 peninsula N Russian Federation
Taz 506 D3 river N Russian Federation
T'bilisi 509 G2 Eng. Tiflis. country capital (Georgia) SE Georgia
T'bilisi 504 B4 international airport S Georgia
Tchien see Zwedru
Tchongking see Chongqing
Tczew 490 C2 Ger. Dirschau. Gdańsk, N Poland
Te Anau 543 A7 Southland, South Island, NZ
Te Anau, Lake 543 A7 lake South Island, NZ
Teapa 443 G4 Tabasco, SE Mexico
Teate see Chieti
Tebingtinggi 530 B3 Sumatera, N Indonesia
Tebriz see Tabrīz
Techirghiol 500 D5 Constanṭa, SE Romania
Tecomán 442 D4 Colima, SW Mexico
Tecpan 443 E5 var. Tecpan de Galeana. Guerrero, S Mexico
Tecpan de Galeana see Tecpan
Tecuci 500 C4 Galaṭi, E Romania
Tedzhen 514 C3 Turkm. Tejen. Akhalskiy Velayat, S Turkmenistan
Tedzhen see Harīrūd
Tees 481 D5 river N England, UK
Tefé 454 D2 Amazonas, N Brazil
Tegal 530 C4 Jawa, C Indonesia
Tegelen 479 D5 Limburg, SE Netherlands
Tegucigalpa 444 C3 country capital (Honduras) Francisco Morazán, SW Honduras
Teheran see Tehrān
Tehrān 512 C3 var. Teheran. country capital (Iran) Tehrān, N Iran
Tehuacán 443 F4 Puebla, S Mexico
Tehuantepec 443 F5 var. Santo Domingo Tehuantepec. Oaxaca, SE Mexico
Tehuantepec, Golfo de 443 F5 var. Gulf of Tehuantepec. gulf S Mexico
Tehuantepec, Gulf of see Tehuantepec, Golfo de
Tehuantepec, Isthmus of see Tehuantepec, Istmo de
Tehuantepec, Istmo de 443 F5 var. Isthmus of Tehuantepec. isthmus SE Mexico
Tejen see Harīrūd
Te Kao 542 C1 Northland, North Island, NZ
Tekax 443 H4 var. Tekax de Álvaro Obregón. Yucatán, SE Mexico
Tekax de Álvaro Obregón see Tekax
Tekeli 506 C5 Taldykorgan, SE Kazakhstan
Tekirdağ 508 A2 It. Rodosto; anc. Bisanthe, Raidestos, Rhaedestus. Tekirdağ, NW Turkey
Te Kuiti 542 D3 Waikato, North Island, NZ
Tela 444 C2 Atlántida, NW Honduras
Telanaipura see Jambi
Tel Aviv-Jaffa see Tel Aviv-Yafo
Tel Aviv-Yafo 511 A6 var. Tel Aviv-Jaffa. Tel Aviv, C Israel
Teles Pirés see São Manuel, Rio
Telish 496 C2 prev. Azizie. Loveshka Oblast, NW Bulgaria
Tell Abiad see At Tall al Abyaḍ
Tell Abyad see At Tall al Abyaḍ
Tell Kalakh see Tall Kalakh
Tell Shedadi see Ash Shadādah
Telšiai 498 B3 Ger. Telschen. Telšiai, NW Lithuania
Temerin 492 D3 Serbia, N Yugoslavia
Temirtau 506 C4 prev. Samarkandski, Samarkandskoye. Karaganda, C Kazakhstan
Tempio Pausania 489 A5 Sardegna, Italy, C Mediterranean Sea
Temple 441 G3 Texas, SW USA
Temuco 457 B5 Araucanía, C Chile
Temuka 543 B6 Canterbury, South Island, NZ
Tenasserim 529 B6 Tenasserim, S Burma
Ténenkou 466 D3 Mopti, C Mali
Ténéré 467 G3 physical region C Niger
Tenerife 462 A3 island Islas Canarias, Spain, NE Atlantic Ocean
Tengger Shamo 519 E3 desert N China
Tengréla 466 D4 var. Tingréla. N Ivory Coast
Tenkodogo 467 E4 S Burkina
Tennant Creek 540 A3 Northern Territory, C Australia
Tennessee 434 C1 off. State of Tennessee; also known as The Volunteer State. state SE USA
Tennessee River 434 C1 river S USA
Teno see Tana
Tenojoki see Tana
Tepelena see Tepelenë
Tepelenë 493 C7 var. Tepelena, It. Tepeleni. Gjirokastër, S Albania
Tepeleni see Tepelenë
Tepic 442 D4 Nayarit, C Mexico
Teplice 490 A4 Ger. Teplitz; prev. Teplice-Šanov, Teplitz-Schönau. Severní Čechy, NW Czech Republic
Tequila 442 D4 Jalisco, SW Mexico
Teraina 537 G2 prev. Washington Island. atoll Line Islands, E Kiribati
Teramo 488 C4 anc. Interamna. Abruzzi, C Italy
Tercan 509 E3 Erzincan, NE Turkey
Terceira 484 A5 var. Ilha Terceira. island Azores, Portugal, NE Atlantic Ocean
Teresina 455 F2 var. Therezina. state capital Piauí, NE Brazil
Termia see Kýthnos
Términos, Laguna de 443 G4 lagoon SE Mexico
Termiz 515 E3 Rus. Termez. Surkhondaryo Wiloyati, S Uzbekistan
Termoli 488 D4 Molise, C Italy
Terneuzen 479 B5 var. Neuzen. Zeeland, SW Netherlands
Terni 488 C4 anc. Interamna Nahars. Umbria, C Italy
Ternopil' 500 C2 Pol. Tarnopol, Rus. Ternopol'. Ternopil's'ka Oblast', W Ukraine
Terracina 489 C5 Lazio, C Italy
Terrassa 485 G2 Cast. Tarrasa. Cataluña, E Spain
Terre Adélie 546 C4 disputed region SE Antarctica
Terre Haute 432 B4 Indiana, N USA
Territoire du Yukon see Yukon Territory
Terschelling 478 C1 Fris. Skylge. island Waddeneilanden, N Netherlands
Teruel 485 F3 anc. Turba. Aragón, E Spain
Tervel 496 E1 prev. Kurtbunar, Rom. Curtbunar. Varnenska Oblast, NE Bulgaria
Tervueren see Tervuren
Tervuren 479 C6 var. Tervueren. Vlaams Brabant, C Belgium
Teseney 464 C4 var. Tessenei. W Eritrea
Tessalit 467 E2 Kidal, NE Mali
Tessaoua 467 G3 Maradi, S Niger
Tessenderlo 479 C5 Limburg, NE Belgium
Tessenei see Teseney
Testigos, Islas los 451 E1 island group N Venezuela
Tete 471 E2 Tete, NW Mozambique
Teterow 486 C3 Mecklenburg-Vorpommern, NE Germany
Tétouan 462 C2 var. Tetouan, Tetuán. N Morocco
Tetovo 493 D5 Alb. Tetova, Tetovë, Turk. Kalkandelen. NW FYR Macedonia
Tetuán see Tétouan
Tevere 488 C4 Eng. Tiber. river C Italy
Teverya 511 B5 var. Tiberias. Northern, N Israel
Te Waewae Bay 543 A7 bay South Island, NZ
Texarkana 434 A2 Arkansas, C USA
Texarkana 441 H2 Texas, SW USA
Texas 441 F3 off. State of Texas; also known as The Lone Star State. state S USA
Texas City 441 H4 Texas, SW USA
Texel 478 C2 island Waddeneilanden, NW Netherlands
Texoma, Lake 441 G2 reservoir Oklahoma/Texas, C USA
Teziutlán 443 F4 Puebla, S Mexico
Thaa Atoll see Kolhumadulu Atoll
Thai Binh 528 D3 Thai Binh, N Vietnam
Thailand 529 C5 off. Kingdom of Thailand, Th. Prathet Thai; prev. Siam. country SE Asia
Thailand, Gulf of 529 C6 var. Gulf of Siam, Th. Ao Thai, Vtn. Vinh Thai Lan. gulf SE Asia
Thai Nguyên 528 D3 Băc Thai, N Vietnam
Thakhèk 528 D4 prev. Muang Khammouan. Khammouan, C Laos
Thamarīd see Thamarīt
Thamarīt 513 D6 var. Thamarīd, Thumrayt. SW Oman
Thames 481 B8 river S England, UK
Thames 542 D3 Waikato, North Island, NZ
Thanh Hoa 528 D3 Vinh Phu, N Vietnam
Thanintari Taungdan see Bilauktaung Range
Thar Desert 526 C3 var. Great Indian Desert, Indian Desert. desert India/Pakistan
Tharthār, Buḥayrat ath 512 B3 lake C Iraq
Thásos 496 C4 island E Greece
Thásos 496 C4 Thásos, E Greece
Thaton 528 B4 Mon State, S Burma
Thayetmyo 528 A4 Magwe, C Burma
The Crane 447 H2 var. Crane. S Barbados
The Dalles 438 B3 Oregon, NW USA
The Flatts Village see Flatts Village
The Hague see 's-Gravenhage
Theodosia see Feodosiya
The Pas 429 F5 Manitoba, C Canada
the Pines, The Isle of see Juventud, Isla de la
Therezina see Teresina
Thérma 497 D6 Ikaría, Dodekánisos, Greece, Aegean Sea
Thermaïkós Kólpos 496 B4 Eng. Thermaic Gulf; anc. Thermaicus Sinus. gulf N Greece
Thermiá see Kýthnos
Thérmo 497 B5 Dytikí Ellás, C Greece
The Rock 485 H4 E Gibraltar
The Six Counties see Northern Ireland
Thessaloníki 496 C3 Eng. Salonica, Salonika, SCr. Solun, Turk. Selânik. Kentrikí Makedonía, N Greece
The Valley 447 G3 dependent territory capital (Anguilla) E Anguilla
The Village 441 G1 Oklahoma, C USA
Thiamis see Thýamis
Thibet see Xizang Zizhiqu
Thief River Falls 437 F1 Minnesota, N USA
Thienen see Tienen
Thiers 483 C5 Puy-de-Dôme, C France
Thiès 466 B3 W Senegal
Thimbu see Thimphu
Thimphu 527 G3 var. Thimbu; prev. Tashi Chho Dzong. country capital (Bhutan) W Bhutan
Thionville 482 D3 Ger. Diedenhofen. Moselle, NE France
Thíra 497 D7 prev. Santorin, Santoríni, anc. Thera. island Kykládes, Greece, Aegean Sea
Thíra 497 D7 Thíra, Kykládes, Greece, Aegean Sea
Thiruvanathapuram see Trivandrum
Thitu Island 520 C8 island NW Spratly Islands
Tholen 478 B4 island SW Netherlands
Thomasville 434 D3 Georgia, SE USA
Thompson 429 F4 Manitoba, C Canada
Thonon-les-Bains 483 D5 Haute-Savoie, E France
Thorlákshöfn 475 E5 Sudhurland, SW Iceland
Thouars 482 B4 Deux-Sèvres, W France
Thracian Sea 496 D4 Gk. Thrakikó Pélagos; anc. Thracium Mare. sea Greece/Turkey
Three Kings Islands 542 C1 island group N NZ
Thrissur see Trichūr
Thuin 479 B7 Hainaut, S Belgium
Thule see Qaanaaq
Thumrayt see Thamarīt
Thun 487 A7 Fr. Thoune. Bern, W Switzerland
Thunder Bay 430 B4 Ontario, S Canada

Tulare Lake Bed – Växjö

: Lake Bed 439 C7 salt flat 'ornia, W USA
ı 452 B1 Carchi, N Ecuador
ı 500 D5 Tulcea, E Romania
yn 500 D3 Rus. Tul'chin. 'yts'ka Oblast', C Ukraine
r see Toliara
441 E2 Texas, SW USA
483 C5 anc. Tutela. Corrèze, ance
487 E6 var. Oberhollabrunn. erösterreich, NE Austria
540 D3 Queensland, Australia
441 G1 Oklahoma, C USA
450 B3 Valle del Cauca, olombia
507 E4 Irkutskaya Oblast', ssian Federation
co 450 A4 Nariño, Colombia
a, Lac see Ntomba, Lac
es 452 A2 Tumbes, NW Peru
ūr 524 C2 Karnātaka, W India
c Humac Mountains 455 E1 Serra Tumucumaque. ntain range N South America
uru 465 C8 Ruvuma, nzania
zha 496 D3 Turk. Tunca Nehri. Bulgaria/Turkey see also a Nehri
abhadra Reservoir 524 C2 S India
aru 537 E2 prev. Gilbert nds. island group W Kiribati
-shan see Xuzhou
sten 428 D4 Northwest itories, W Canada
t'ing Hu see Dongting Hu
463 E1 var. Tūnis. country tal (Tunisia) NE Tunisia
s see Tunis
, Golfe de 494 D3 Ar. Khalīj is. gulf NE Tunisia
ia 463 F2 off. Republic of isia, Ar. Al Jumhūrīyah at isīyah, Fr. République isienne. country N Africa
450 B3 Boyacá, C Colombia
g Buong see T,ơng Đ,ơng
o 434 C2 Mississippi, S USA
a 453 G5 Potosí, S Bolivia
ah 513 B5 Makkah, W Saudi bia
igi 542 D4 Waikato, North nd, NZ
ı Lowland 514 C2 var. Turan n, Kaz. Turan Oypaty, Rus. nskaya Nizmennost', Turk. an Pesligi, Uzb. Turon tekisligi. plain C Asia
ı Oypaty see Turan Lowland
ı Pesligi see Turan Lowland
ı Plain see Turan Lowland
nskaya Nizmennost' see an Lowland
yf 512 A3 Al Ḥudūd ash māliyah, NW Saudi Arabia
at 526 A3 Baluchistān, Pakistan
a 500 B4 Ger. Thorenburg, g. Torda. Cluj, NW Romania
n see Turpan
n see Torino
ana, Lake see Rudolf, Lake
estan 506 B5 Kaz. Türkistan. hnyy Kazakhstan, azakhstan
ey 508 B3 off. Republic of key, Turk. Türkiye mhuriyeti. country SW Asia
menbashi 514 B2 prev. snovodsk. Balkanskiy Velayat, Turkmenistan
menistan 514 B2 off. kmenistan; prev. Turkmenskaya iet Socialist Republic. country sia
menskiy Zaliv 514 B2 Turkm. kmen Aylagy. lake gulf Turkmenistan
s and Caicos Islands 447 E2 dependent territory N West ies
ock 439 B6 California, W USA
again, Cape 542 D4 headland rth Island, NZ
hout 479 C5 Antwerpen, elgium
ov 490 B4 Ger. Turnau. chodní Čechy, N Czech ublic
u Măgurele 500 B5 var. nu-Măgurele. Teleorman, omania
n Pasttekisligi see Turan wland
an 518 C3 var. Turfan. Xinjiang gur Zizhiqu, NW China
an Pendi 518 C3 Eng. Turpan pression. depression NW China
kŭl 514 D2 Rus. Turtkul'; prev. roaleksandrovsk. raqalpoghiston Respublikasi, Uzbekistan
Turuga see Tsuruga
Turuoka see Tsuruoka
Tuscaloosa 434 C2 Alabama, S USA
Tusima see Tsushima
Tuticorin 524 C3 Tamil Nādu, SE India
Tutrakan 496 D1 Razgradska Oblast, NE Bulgaria
Tutuila 537 F4 island W American Samoa
Tuvalu 537 E3 prev. Ellice Islands. country SW Pacific Ocean
Ţuwayq, Jabal 513 C5 mountain range C Saudi Arabia
Tuxpán 443 F4 var. Tuxpán de Rodríguez Cano. Veracruz-Llave, E Mexico
Tuxpan 442 D4 Jalisco, C Mexico
Tuxpan 442 D4 Nayarit, C Mexico
Tuxpán de Rodríguez Cano see Tuxpán
Tuxtepec 443 F4 var. San Juan Bautista Tuxtepec. Oaxaca, S Mexico
Tuxtla 443 G5 var. Tuxtla Gutiérrez. Chiapas, SE Mexico
Tuxtla see San Andrés Tuxtla
Tuxtla Gutiérrez see Tuxtla
Tuy Hoa 529 E5 Phu Yên, S Vietnam
Tuz Gölü 508 C3 lake C Turkey
Tuzla 492 C3 NE Bosnia and Herzegovina
Tver' 502 B4 prev. Kalinin. Tverskaya Oblast', W Russian Federation
Twin Falls 438 D4 Idaho, NW USA
Tychy 491 D5 Ger. Tichau. Katowice, S Poland
Tyler 441 G3 Texas, SW USA
Tympáki 497 C8 var. Timbaki; prev. Timbákion. Kríti, Greece, E Mediterranean Sea
Tynda 507 F4 Amurskaya Oblast', SE Russian Federation
Tyne 480 D4 river N England, UK
Tyôsi see Chōshi
Tyre see Soûr
Týrnavos 496 B4 var. Tírnavos. Thessalía, C Greece
Tyrrhenian Sea 489 B6 It. Mare Tirreno. sea N Mediterranean Sea
Tyumen' 506 C3 Tyumenskaya Oblast', C Russian Federation
Tyup 515 G2 Kir. Tüp. Issyk-Kul'skaya Oblast', NE Kyrgyzstan
Tywyn 481 C6 W Wales, UK
Tzekung see Zigong
T,ơng Đ,ơng 528 D4 var. Tuong Buong. Nghê An, N Vietnam

U

Uanle Uen see Wanlaweyn
Uaupés, Rio see Vaupés, Río
Ubangi 469 C5 Fr. Oubangui. river C Africa
Ubangi-Shari see Central African Republic
Ube 523 B7 Yamaguchi, Honshū, SW Japan
Ubeda 485 E4 Andalucía, S Spain
Uberaba 455 F4 Minas Gerais, SE Brazil
Uberlândia 455 F4 Minas Gerais, SE Brazil
Ubol Rajadhani see Ubon Ratchathani
Ubol Ratchathani see Ubon Ratchathani
Ubon Ratchathani 529 D5 var. Muang Ubon, Ubol Rajadhani, Ubol Ratchathani, Udon Ratchathani. Ubon Ratchathani, E Thailand
Ubrique 484 D5 Andalucía, S Spain
Ucayali, Río 452 D3 river C Peru
Uchiura-wan 522 D3 bay NW Pacific Ocean
Uchquduq 514 D2 Rus. Uchkuduk. Nawoiy Wiloyati, N Uzbekistan
Uchtagan, Peski 514 C2 Turkm. Uchtagan Gumy. desert NW Turkmenistan
Udaipur 526 C3 prev. Oodeypore. Rājasthān, N India
Uddevalla 477 B6 Göteborg och Bohus, S Sweden
Udine 488 D2 anc. Utina. Friuli-Venezia Giulia, NE Italy
Udintsev Fracture Zone 546 A5 tectonic feature S Pacific Ocean
Udipi see Udupi
Udon Ratchathani see Ubon Ratchathani
Udon Thani 528 C4 var. Ban Mak Khaeng, Udorndhani. Udon Thani, N Thailand
Udorndhani see Udon Thani
Udupi 524 B2 var. Udipi. Karnātaka, SW India
Uele 469 D5 var. Welle. river NE Congo (Zaire)
Uelzen 486 C3 Niedersachsen, N Germany
Ufa 503 D6 Respublika Bashkortostan, W Russian Federation
Ugāle 498 C2 Ventspils, NW Latvia
Uganda 465 B6 off. Republic of Uganda. country E Africa
Uglovka 502 B4 var. Okulovka. Novgorodskaya Oblast', W Russian Federation
Uhuru Peak see Kilimanjaro
Uíge 470 B1 Port. Carmona, Vila Marechal Carmona. Uíge, NW Angola
Uinta Mountains 436 B4 mountain range Utah, W USA
Uitenhage 470 C5 Eastern Cape, S South Africa
Uithoorn 478 C3 Noord-Holland, C Netherlands
Ujelang Atoll 536 C1 var. Wujlān. atoll Ralik Chain, W Marshall Islands
Ujungpandang 531 E4 var. Macassar, Makassar; prev. Makasar. Sulawesi, C Indonesia
Ujung Salang see Phuket
Ukhta 506 C3 Respublika Komi, NW Russian Federation
Ukiah 439 B5 California, W USA
Ukmergė 498 C4 Pol. Wiłkomierz. Ukmergė, C Lithuania
Ukraine 500 C2 off. Ukraine, Rus. Ukraina, Ukr. Ukrayina; prev. Ukrainian Soviet Socialist Republic, Ukrainskaya S.S.R. country SE Europe
Ulaanbaatar 519 E2 Eng. Ulan Bator. country capital (Mongolia) Töv, C Mongolia
Ulaangom 518 C2 Uvs, NW Mongolia
Ulan Bator 516 see Ulaanbaatar
Ulanhad see Chifeng
Ulan-Ude 507 E4 prev. Verkhneudinsk. Respublika Buryatiya, S Russian Federation
Ulft 478 E4 Gelderland, E Netherlands
Ullapool 480 C3 N Scotland, UK
Ulm 487 B6 Baden-Württemberg, S Germany
Ulsan 521 E4 Jap. Urusan. SE South Korea
Ulster 481 B5 cultural region N Ireland
Ulungur Hu 518 B2 lake NW China
Uluru 539 D5 var. Ayers Rock. rocky outcrop Northern Territory, C Australia
Ulyanivka 501 E3 Rus. Ul'yanovka. Kirovohrads'ka Oblast', C Ukraine
Ul'yanovsk 503 C5 prev. Simbirsk. Ul'yanovskaya Oblast', W Russian Federation
Uman' 501 E3 Rus. Uman. Cherkas'ka Oblast', C Ukraine
Umán 443 H3 Yucatán, SE Mexico
Umanak see Uummannaq
Umanaq see Uummannaq
Umbro-Marchigiano, Appennino 488 C3 Eng. Umbrian-Machigian Mountains. mountain range C Italy
Umeå 476 C4 Västerbotten, N Sweden
Umeälven 476 C4 river N Sweden
Umiat 428 D2 Alaska, USA
Umm Buru 464 A4 Western Darfur, W Sudan
Umm Durmān see Omdurman
Umm Ruwaba 464 C4 var. Umm Ruwābah, Um Ruwāba. Northern Kordofan, C Sudan
Umm Ruwābah see Umm Ruwaba
Umnak Island 428 A3 island Aleutian Islands, Alaska, USA
Um Ruwāba see Umm Ruwaba
Umtali see Mutare
Umtata 470 D5 Eastern Cape, SE South Africa
Una 492 B3 river Bosnia and Herzegovina/Croatia
Unac 492 B3 river W Bosnia and Herzegovina
Unalaska Island 428 A3 island Aleutian Islands, Alaska, USA
'Unayzah 512 B4 var. Anaiza. Al Qaşīm, C Saudi Arabia
Uncía 453 F4 Potosí, C Bolivia
Uncompahgre Peak 436 B5 mountain Colorado, C USA
Ungava Bay 431 E1 bay Quebec, E Canada
Ungava, Péninsule d' 430 D1 peninsula Quebec, SE Canada
Ungheni 500 D3 Rus. Ungeny. W Moldavia
Unimak Island 428 B3 island Aleutian Islands, Alaska, USA
Union 435 E1 South Carolina, SE USA
Union City 434 Tennessee, S USA
United Arab Emirates 513 C5 Ar. Al Imārāt al 'Arabīyah al Muttaḩidah, abbrev. UAE; prev. Trucial States. country SW Asia
United Kingdom 481 B5 off. UK of Great Britain and Northern Ireland, abbrev. UK. country NW Europe
United States of America 427 B5 off. United States of America, var. America, The States, abbrev. U.S., USA. country
Unst 480 D1 island NE Scotland, UK
Ünye 508 D2 Ordu, W Turkey
Upala 444 D4 Alajuela, NW Costa Rica
Upata 451 E2 Bolívar, E Venezuela
Upemba, Lac 469 D7 lake SE Congo (Zaire)
Upernavik 474 C2 var. Upernivik. C Greenland
Upernivik see Upernavik
Upington 470 C4 Northern Cape, W South Africa
Upolu 537 F4 island SE Samoa
Upper Klamath Lake 438 A4 lake Oregon, NW USA
Upper Lough Erne 481 A5 lake SW Northern Ireland, UK
Upper Red Lake 437 F1 lake Minnesota, N USA
Uppsala 477 C6 Uppsala, C Sweden
Ural 504 B3 Kaz. Zayyq. river Kazakhstan/Russian Federation
Ural Mountains 504 see Ural'skiye Gory
Ural'sk 506 B3 Kaz. Oral. Zapadnyy Kazakhstan, NW Kazakhstan
Ural'skiye Gory 506 C3 var. Ural'skiy Khrebet, Eng. Ural Mountains. mountain range Kazakhstan/Russian Federation
Ural'skiy Khrebet see Ural'skiye Gory
Uraricoera 454 D1 Roraima, N Brazil
Urbandale 437 F3 Iowa, C USA
Uren' 503 C5 Nizhegorodskaya Oblast', W Russian Federation
Urganch 514 D2 Rus. Urgench; prev. Novo-Urgench. Khorazm Wiloyati, W Uzbekistan
Urgut 515 E3 Samarqand Wiloyati, C Uzbekistan
Uroševac 493 D5 Alb. Ferizaj. Serbia, S Yugoslavia
Ŭroteppa 515 E2 Rus. Ura-Tyube. NW Tajikistan
Uruapan 443 E4 var. Uruapan del Progreso. Michoacán de Ocampo, SW Mexico
Uruapan del Progreso see Uruapan
Uruguai, Rio see Uruguay
Uruguay 456 D4 off. Oriental Republic of Uruguay; prev. La Banda Oriental. country E South America
Uruguay 456 D3 var. Rio Uruguai, Río Uruguay. river E South America
Uruguay, Río see Uruguay
Urumchi see Ürümqi
Urumqi see Ürümqi
Ürümqi 518 C3 var. Tihwa, Urumchi, Urumqi, Urumtsi, Wu-lu-k'o-mu-shi, Wu-lu-mu-ch'i; prev. Ti-hua. autonomous region capital Xinjiang Uygur Zizhiqu, NW China
Urumtsi see Ürümqi
Urup, Ostrov 507 H4 island Kuril'skiye Ostrova, SE Russian Federation
Urziceni 500 C5 Ialomiţa, SE Romania
Usa 502 E3 river NW Russian Federation
Uşak 508 B3 prev. Ushak. Uşak, W Turkey
Ushuaia 457 B8 Tierra del Fuego, S Argentina
Usinsk 502 E3 Respublika Komi, NW Russian Federation
Üsküb see Skopje
Üsküp see Skopje
Usmas Ezers 498 B3 lake NW Latvia
Usol'ye-Sibirskoye 507 E4 Irkutskaya Oblast', C Russian Federation
Ussel 483 C5 Corrèze, C France
Ussuriysk 507 G5 prev. Nikol'sk, Nikol'sk-Ussuriyskiy, Voroshilov. Primorskiy Kray, SE Russian Federation
Ustica, Isola d' 489 B6 island S Italy
Ust'-Ilimsk 507 E4 Irkutskaya Oblast', C Russian Federation
Ústí nad Labem 490 A4 Ger. Aussig. Severní Čechy, N Czech Republic
Ustka 490 C2 Ger. Stolpmünde. Słupsk, NW Poland
Ust'-Kamchatsk 507 H2 Kamchatskaya Oblast', E Russian Federation
Ust'-Kamenogorsk 506 D5 Kaz. Öskemen. Vostochnyy Kazakhstan, E Kazakhstan
Ust'-Kut 507 E4 Irkutskaya Oblast', C Russian Federation
Ust'-Olenëk 507 E3 Respublika Sakha (Yakutiya), NE Russian Federation
Ust Urt see Ustyurt Plateau
Ustyurt Plateau 514 B1 var. Ust Urt, Uzb. Ustyurt Platosi. plateau Kazakhstan/Uzbekistan
Ustyurt Platosi see Ustyurt Plateau
Usulután 444 C3 Usulután, SE El Salvador
Usumacinta, Río 444 B1 river Guatemala/Mexico
Utah 440 A1 off. State of Utah; also known as Beehive State, Mormon State. state W USA
Utah Lake 436 B4 lake Utah, W USA
Utena 498 C4 Utena, E Lithuania
Utica 433 F3 New York, NE USA
Utrecht 478 C4 Lat. Trajectum ad Rhenum. Utrecht, C Netherlands
Utsunomiya 523 D5 var. Utunomiya. Tochigi, Honshū, S Japan
Uttar Pradesh 527 E3 prev. United Provinces, United Provinces of Agra and Oudh. state N India
Utunomiya see Utsunomiya
Uulu 498 D2 Pärnumaa, SW Estonia
Uummannaq 474 C3 var. Umanak, Umanaq. C Greenland
Uummannarsuaq 474 B5 var. Nunap Isua, Dan. Kap Farvel, Eng. Cape Farewell. headland S Greenland
Uvalde 441 F4 Texas, SW USA
Uvaravichy 499 D7 Rus. Uvarovichi. Homyel'skaya Voblasts', SE Belorussia
Uvea, Île 537 E4 island N Wallis and Futuna
Uvs Nuur 518 C1 var. Ozero Ubsu-Nur. lake Mongolia/Russian Federation
'Uwaynāt, Jabal al 464 A3 var. Jebel Uweinat. mountain Libya/Sudan
Uyo 467 G5 Akwa Ibom, S Nigeria
Uyuni 453 F5 Potosí, W Bolivia
Uzbekistan 514 D2 off. Republic of Uzbekistan. country C Asia
Uzhhorod 500 B2 Rus. Uzhgorod; prev. Ungvár. Zakarpats'ka Oblast', W Ukraine
Užice 492 D4 prev. Titovo Užice. Serbia, W Yugoslavia

V

Vaal 470 D4 river C South Africa
Vaals 479 D6 Limburg, SE Netherlands
Vaasa 477 D5 Swe. Vasa; prev. Nikolainkaupunki. Vaasa, W Finland
Vaassen 478 D3 Gelderland, E Netherlands
Vác 491 C6 Ger. Waitzen. Pest, N Hungary
Vadodara 526 C4 prev. Baroda. Gujarāt, W India
Vaduz 486 E2 country capital (Liechtenstein) W Liechtenstein
Váh 491 C5 Ger. Waag, Hung. Vág. river W Slovakia
Väinameri 498 C2 prev. Muhu Väin, Ger. Moon-Sund. sea E Baltic Sea
Valachia see Wallachia
Valday 502 B4 Novgorodskaya Oblast', W Russian Federation
Valdecañas, Embalse de 484 D3 reservoir W Spain
Valdepeñas 485 E4 Castilla-La Mancha, C Spain
Valdés, Península 457 C6 peninsula SE Argentina
Valdez 428 C3 Alaska, USA
Valdia see Weldiya
Valdivia 457 B5 Los Lagos, C Chile
Val-d'Or 430 D4 Quebec, SE Canada
Valdosta 435 E3 Georgia, SE USA
Valence 483 D5 anc. Valentia, Valentia Julia, Ventia. Drôme, E France
Valencia 438 D1 California, W USA
Valencia 450 D1 Carabobo, N Venezuela
Valencia 485 F3 País Valenciano, E Spain
Valencia, Golfo de 485 F3 var. Gulf of Valencia. gulf E Spain
Valencia, Gulf of see Valencia, Golfo de
Valenciennes 482 D2 Nord, N France
Valera 450 C2 Trujillo, NW Venezuela
Valga 498 D3 Ger. Walk, Latv. Valka. Valgamaa, S Estonia
Valira 483 A8 river Andorra/Spain
Valjevo 492 C4 Serbia, W Yugoslavia
Valjok 476 D2 Finnmark, N Norway
Valka 498 D3 Ger. Walk. Valka, N Latvia
Valkenswaard 479 D5 Noord-Brabant, S Netherlands
Valladolid 484 D2 Castilla-León, NW Spain
Valladolid 443 H3 Yucatán, SE Mexico
Vall d'Uxó 485 F3 País Valenciano, E Spain
Valle de La Pascua 450 D2 Guárico, N Venezuela
Valledupar 450 B1 Cesar, N Colombia
Vallejo 439 B6 California, W USA
Vallenar 456 B3 Atacama, N Chile
Valletta 489 C8 prev. Valetta. country capital (Malta) E Malta
Valley City 437 E2 North Dakota, N USA
Valls 485 G2 Cataluña, NE Spain
Valmiera 498 D3 Est. Volmari, Ger. Wolmar. Valmiera, N Latvia
Valozhyn 499 C5 Pol. Wołożyn, Rus. Volozhin. Minskaya Voblasts', C Belorussia
Valparaiso 432 C3 Indiana, N USA
Valparaíso 456 B4 Valparaíso, C Chile
Valverde del Camino 484 C4 Andalucía, S Spain
Van 509 F3 Van, E Turkey
Vanadzor 509 F2 prev. Kirovakan. N Armenia
Vancouver 428 D5 British Columbia, SW Canada
Vancouver 438 B3 Washington, NW USA
Vancouver Island 428 D5 island British Columbia, SW Canada
Van Diemen Gulf 538 D2 gulf Northern Territory, N Australia
Vänern 477 B6 Eng. Lake Vaner; prev. Lake Vener. lake S Sweden
Vangaindrano 471 G4 Fianarantsoa, SE Madagascar
Van Gölü 509 F3 Eng. Lake Van; anc. Thospitis. salt lake E Turkey
Van Horn 440 D3 Texas, SW USA
Van, Lake 504 see Van Gölü
Vannes 482 A3 anc. Dariorigum. Morbihan, NW France
Vantaa 477 D6 Swe. Vanda. Uusimaa, S Finland
Vanua Levu 537 E4 island N Fiji
Vanuatu 536 C4 off. Republic of Vanuatu; prev. New Hebrides. country SW Pacific Ocean
Van Wert 432 C4 Ohio, N USA
Varakļani 498 D4 Madona, C Latvia
Vārānasi 527 E3 prev. Banaras, Benares, hist. Kasi. Uttar Pradesh, N India
Varangerfjorden 476 E2 fjord N Norway
Varangerhalvøya 476 D2 peninsula N Norway
Varannó see Vranov nad Topl'ou
Varaždin 492 B2 Ger. Warasdin, Hung. Varasd. Varaždin, N Croatia
Varberg 477 B7 Halland, S Sweden
Vardar 493 E6 Gk. Axiós. river FYR Macedonia/Greece see also Axiós
Varde 477 A7 Ribe, W Denmark
Varėna 499 B5 Pol. Orany. Varėna, S Lithuania
Varese 488 B2 Lombardia, N Italy
Vârful Moldoveanu 500 B4 var. Moldoveanul; prev. Vîrful Moldoveanu. mountain C Romania
Varkaus 477 E5 Kuopio, C Finland
Varna 496 E2 prev. Stalin, anc. Odessus. Varnenska Oblast, NE Bulgaria
Varnenski Zaliv 496 E2 prev. Stalinski Zaliv. bay E Bulgaria
Vasilikí 497 A5 Lefkáda, Iónioi Nísoi, Greece, C Mediterranean Sea
Vasilishki 499 B5 Pol. Wasiliszki, Rus. Vasilishki. Hrodzyenskaya Voblasts', W Belorussia
Vaslui 500 D4 Vaslui, C Romania
Västerås 477 C6 Västmanland, C Sweden
Vasyl'kiv 501 E2 Rus. Vasil'kov. Kyyivs'ka Oblast', N Ukraine
Vatican City 489 A7 off. Vatican City State. country S Europe
Vatnajökull 475 E5 glacier SE Iceland
Vättern 477 B6 Eng. Lake Vatter; prev. Lake Vetter. lake S Sweden
Vaughn 440 D2 New Mexico, SW USA
Vaupés, Río 450 C4 var. Rio Uaupés. river Brazil/Colombia see also Uaupés, Rio
Vava'u Group 537 E4 island group N Tonga
Vavuniya 524 D3 Northern Province, N Sri Lanka
Vawkavysk 499 B6 Pol. Wołkowysk, Rus. Volkovysk. Hrodzyenskaya Voblasts', W Belorussia
Växjö 477 C7 var. Vexiö. Kronoberg, S Sweden

Vaygach, Ostrov – Wanganui

Vaygach, Ostrov *502 E2 island* NW Russian Federation
Veendam *478 E2* Groningen, NE Netherlands
Veenendaal *478 D4* Utrecht, C Netherlands
Vega *476 B4 island* C Norway
Veisiejai *499 B5* Lazdijai, S Lithuania
Vejer de la Frontera *484 C5* Andalucía, S Spain
Veldhoven *479 D5* Noord-Brabant, S Netherlands
Velebit *492 A3 mountain range* C Croatia
Velenje *487 E7 Ger.* Wöllan. N Slovenia
Veles *493 E6 Turk.* Köprülü. C FYR Macedonia
Velho *see* Porto Velho
Velika Morava *492 D4 var.* Glavn'a Morava, Morava, *Ger.* Grosse Morava. *river* C Yugoslavia
Velikaya *505 G2 river* NE Russian Federation
Velikiye Luki *502 A4* Pskovskaya Oblast', W Russian Federation
Veliko Tŭrnovo *496 D2 prev.* Tirnovo, Trnovo, Tŭrnovo. Loveshka Oblast, N Bulgaria
Velingrad *496 C3* Plovdivska Oblast, SW Bulgaria
Vel'ký Krtíš *491 D6* Stredné Slovensko, S Slovakia
Vellore *524 C2* Tamil Nādu, SE India
Velobriga *see* Viana do Castelo
Velsen *see* Velsen-Noord
Velsen-Noord *478 C3 var.* Velsen. Noord-Holland, W Netherlands
Vel'sk *502 C4 var.* Velsk. Arkhangel'skaya Oblast', NW Russian Federation
Velsk *see* Vel'sk
Velvendos *see* Velvendós
Velvendós *496 B4 var.* Velvendos. Dytikí Makedonía, N Greece
Velykyy Tokmak *see* Tokmak
Vendôme *482 C4* Loir-et-Cher, C France
Venezia *488 C2 Eng.* Venice, *Fr.* Venise, *Ger.* Venedig; anc.Venetia. Veneto, NE Italy
Venezuela *450 D2 off.* Republic of Venezuela; *prev.* Estados Unidos de Venezuela, United States of Venezuela. *country* N South America
Venezuela, Golfo de *450 C1 Eng.* Gulf of Maracaibo, Gulf of Venezuela. *gulf* NW Venezuela
Venezuelan Basin *448 B1 undersea feature* E Caribbean Sea
Venice *see* Venezia
Venice *434 C4* Louisiana, S USA
Venice, Gulf of *488 C2 It.* Golfo di Venezia, *Slvn.* Beneški Zaliv. *gulf* N Adriatic Sea
Venlo *479 D5 prev.* Venloo. Limburg, SE Netherlands
Venta *498 B3 Ger.* Windau. *river* Latvia/Lithuania
Ventimiglia *488 A3* Liguria, NW Italy
Ventspils *498 B2 Ger.* Windau. Ventspils, NW Latvia
Vera *456 D3* Santa Fe, C Argentina
Veracruz *443 F4 var.* Veracruz Llave. Veracruz-Llave, E Mexico
Veracruz Llave *see* Veracruz
Vercelli *488 A2 anc.* Vercellae. Piemonte, NW Italy
Verdalsøra *476 B4* Nord-Trøndelag, C Norway
Verde, Costa *484 D1 coastal region* N Spain
Verden *486 B3* Niedersachsen, NW Germany
Veria *see* Véroia
Verkhoyanskiy Khrebet *507 F3 mountain range* NE Russian Federation
Vermillion *437 F3* South Dakota, N USA
Vermont *433 F2 off.* State of Vermont; also known as The Green Mountain State. *state* NE USA
Vernal *436 B4* Utah, W USA
Vernon *441 F2* Texas, SW USA
Véroia *496 B4 var.* Veria, Vérroia, *Turk.* Karaferiye. Kentrikí Makedonía, N Greece
Verona *488 C2* Veneto, NE Italy
Vérroia *see* Véroia
Versailles *482 D1* Yvelines, N France
Verviers *479 D6* Liège, E Belgium
Vesdre *479 D6 river* E Belgium
Veselinovo *496 D2* Varnenska Oblast, E Bulgaria
Vesoul *482 D4 anc.* Vesulium, Vesulum. Haute-Saône, E France
Vesterålen *476 B2 island group* N Norway
Vestfjorden *476 C3 fjord* C Norway
Vestmannaeyjar *475 E5* Sudhurland, S Iceland
Vesuvio *489 D5 Eng.* Vesuvius. *volcano* S Italy
Veszprém *491 C7 Ger.* Veszprim. Veszprém, W Hungary
Vetrino *496 E2* Varnenska Oblast, NE Bulgaria
Veurne *479 A5 var.* Furnes. West-Vlaanderen, W Belgium
Vexiö *see* Växjö
Viacha *453 F4* La Paz, W Bolivia
Viana de Castelo *see* Viana do Castelo
Viana do Castelo *484 B2 var.* Viana de Castelo; *anc.* Velobriga. Viana do Castelo, NW Portugal
Vianen *478 C4* Zuid-Holland, C Netherlands
Viangchan *528 C4 Eng./Fr.* Vientiane. *country capital* (Laos) C Laos
Viangphoukha *528 C3 var.* Vieng Pou Kha. Louang Namtha, N Laos
Viareggio *488 B3* Toscana, C Italy
Viborg *477 A7* Viborg, NW Denmark
Vic *485 G2 var.* Vich; *anc.* Ausa, Vicus Ausonensis. Cataluña, NE Spain
Vicenza *488 C2 anc.* Vicentia. Veneto, NE Italy
Vich *see* Vic
Vichy *483 C5* Allier, C France
Vicksburg *434 B2* Mississippi, S USA
Victoria *494 A5 var.* Rabat. Gozo, NW Malta
Victoria *471 H1 country capital* (Seychelles) Mahé, SW Seychelles
Victoria *441 G4* Texas, SW USA
Victoria *428 D5* Vancouver Island, British Columbia, SW Canada
Victoria *541 C7 state* SE Australia
Victoria Bank *see* Vitória Seamount
Victoria de Durango *see* Durango
Victoria de las Tunas *see* Las Tunas
Victoria Falls *470 C2 waterfall* Zambia/Zimbabwe
Victoria Falls *470 C3* Matabeleland North, W Zimbabwe
Victoria Island *429 F3 island* Nunavut, NW Canada
Victoria, Lake *465 B6 var.* Victoria Nyanza. *lake* E Africa
Victoria Land *546 C4 physical region* Antarctica
Victoria Nyanza *see* Victoria, Lake
Victoria River *538 D3 river* Northern Territory, N Australia
Victorville *439 C7* California, W USA
Vicus Ausonensis *see* Vic
Vidalia *435 E2* Georgia, SE USA
Vidin *496 B1 anc.* Bononia. Oblast Montana, NW Bulgaria
Vidzy *499 C5 Rus.* Vidzy. Vitsyebskaya Voblasts', NW Belorussia
Viedma *457 C5* Río Negro, E Argentina
Vieng Pou Kha *see* Viangphoukha
Vienna *see* Wien
Vienne *483 D5 anc.* Vienna. Isère, E France
Vienne *482 B4 river* W France
Vientiane *516 see* Viangchan
Vierzon *482 C4* Cher, C France
Viesīte *498 C4 Ger.* Eckengraf. Jēkabpils, S Latvia
Vietnam *528 D4 off.* Socialist Republic of Vietnam, *Vtn.* Công Hoa Xa Hôi Chu Nghia Viêt Nam. *country* SE Asia
Vietri *see* Viêt Tri
Viêt Tri *528 D3 var.* Vietri. Vinh Phu, N Vietnam
Vieux Fort *447 F2* S Saint Lucia
Vigo *484 B2* Galicia, NW Spain
Vijayawāda *524 D1 prev.* Bezwada. Andhra Pradesh, SE India
Vijosa *see* Vjosës, Lumi i
Vijosë *see* Vjosës, Lumi i
Vila *see* Port-Vila
Vila Artur de Paiva *see* Cubango
Vila da Ponte *see* Cubango
Vila de Mocímboa da Praia *see* Mocímboa da Praia
Vila do Conde *484 B2* Porto, NW Portugal
Vila do Zumbo *470 D2 prev.* Vila do Zumbu, Zumbo. Tete, NW Mozambique
Vilafranca del Penedès *485 G2 var.* Villafranca del Panadés. Cataluña, NE Spain
Vila General Machado *see* Camacupa
Viļaka *498 D4 Ger.* Marienhausen. Balvi, NE Latvia
Vilalba *484 C1* Galicia, NW Spain
Vila Nova de Gaia *484 B2* Porto, NW Portugal
Vila Nova de Portimão *see* Portimão
Vila Pereira de Eça *see* N'Giva
Vila Real *484 C2 var.* Vila Rial. Vila Real, N Portugal
Vila Rial *see* Vila Real
Vila Robert Williams *see* Caála
Vila Serpa Pinto *see* Menongue
Vilhelmina *476 C4* Västerbotten, N Sweden
Vilhena *454 D3* Rondônia, W Brazil
Vília *497 C5* Attikí, C Greece
Viliya *499 C5 Lith.* Neris, *Rus.* Viliya. *river* W Belorussia
Viljandi *498 D2 Ger.* Fellin. Viljandimaa, S Estonia
Vilkaviškis *498 B4 Pol.* Wyłkowyszki. Vilkaviškis, SW Lithuania
Villa Acuña *see* Acuña
Villa Bella *453 F2* Beni, N Bolivia
Villacarrillo *485 E4* Andalucía, S Spain
Villa Cecilia *see* Ciudad Madero
Villach *487 D7 Slvn.* Beljak. Kärnten, S Austria
Villacidro *489 A5* Sardegna, Italy, C Mediterranean Sea
Villa Concepción *see* Concepción
Villa del Pilar *see* Pilar
Villafranca de los Barros *484 C4* Extremadura, W Spain
Villafranca del Panadés *see* Vilafranca del Penedès
Villahermosa *443 G4 prev.* San Juan Bautista. Tabasco, SE Mexico
Villajoyosa *485 F4 var.* La Vila Jojosa. País Valenciano, E Spain
Villa María *456 C4* Córdoba, C Argentina
Villa Martín *453 F5* Potosí, SW Bolivia
Villanueva *442 D3* Zacatecas, C Mexico
Villanueva de la Serena *484 C3* Extremadura, W Spain
Villanueva de los Infantes *485 E4* Castilla-La Mancha, C Spain
Villarrica *456 D2* Guairá, SE Paraguay
Villavicencio *450 B3* Meta, C Colombia
Villaviciosa *484 D1* Asturias, N Spain
Villazón *453 G5* Potosí, S Bolivia
Villena *485 F4* País Valenciano, E Spain
Villeurbanne *483 D5* Rhône, E France
Villingen-Schwenningen *487 B6* Baden-Württemberg, S Germany
Vilnius *499 C5 Pol.* Wilno, *Ger.* Wilna; *prev. Rus.* Vilna. *country capital* (Lithuania) Vilnius, SE Lithuania
Vil'shanka *501 E3 Rus.* Olshanka. Kirovohrads'ka Oblast', C Ukraine
Vilvoorde *479 C6 Fr.* Vilvorde. Vlaams Brabant, C Belgium
Vilyeyka *499 C5 Pol.* Wilejka, *Rus.* Vileyka. Minskaya Voblasts', NW Belorussia
Vilyuy *507 F3 river* NE Russian Federation
Viña del Mar *456 B4* Valparaíso, C Chile
Vinaròs *485 F3* País Valenciano, E Spain
Vincennes *432 B4* Indiana, N USA
Vindhya Mountains *see* Vindhya Range
Vindhya Range *526 D4 var.* Vindhya Mountains. *mountain range* N India
Vineland *433 F4* New Jersey, NE USA
Vinh *528 D4* Nghê An, N Vietnam
Vinh Loi *see* Bac Liêu
Vinh Thai Lan *see* Thailand, Gulf of
Vinishte *496 C2* Oblast Montana, NW Bulgaria
Vinita *441 G1* Oklahoma, C USA
Vinkovci *492 C3 Ger.* Winkowitz, *Hung.* Vinkovcze. Vukovar-Srijem, E Croatia
Vinnytsya *500 D2 Rus.* Vinnitsa. Vinnyts'ka Oblast', C Ukraine
Vinson Massif *546 A3 mountain* Antarctica
Viranşehir *509 E4* Şanlıurfa, SE Turkey
Vîrful Moldoveanu *see* Vârful Moldoveanu
Virginia *433 E5 off.* Commonwealth of Virginia; also known as Mother of Presidents, Mother of States, Old Dominion. *state* NE USA
Virginia *437 G1* Minnesota, N USA
Virginia Beach *433 F5* Virginia, NE USA
Virgin Islands *see* British Virgin Islands
Virgin Islands (US) *447 F3 var.* Virgin Islands of the United States; *prev.* Danish West Indies. *US unincorporated territory* E West Indies
Virgin Islands of the United States *see* Virgin Islands (US)
Virôchey *529 E5* Rôtânôkiri, NE Cambodia
Virovitica *492 C2 Ger.* Virovititz, *Hung.* Verőcze; *prev. Ger.* Werowitz. Virovitica-Podravina, NE Croatia
Virton *479 D8* Luxembourg, SE Belgium
Virtsu *498 D2 Ger.* Werder. Läänemaa, W Estonia
Vis *492 B4 It.* Lissa; *anc.* Issa. *island* S Croatia
Vis *see* Fish
Visaginas *498 C4 prev.* Sniečkus. Ignalina, E Lithuania
Visākhapatnam *527 E5* Andhra Pradesh, SE India
Visalia *439 C6* California, W USA
Visby *477 C7 Ger.* Wisby. Gotland, SE Sweden
Viscount Melville Sound *429 F2 prev.* Melville Sound. *sound* Nunavut, N Canada
Visé *479 D6* Liège, E Belgium
Viseu *484 C2 prev.* Vizeu. Viseu, N Portugal
Visoko *492 C4* C Bosnia and Herzegovina
Vistula *see* Wisła
Vistula Lagoon *490 C2 Ger.* Frisches Haff, *Pol.* Zalew Wiślany, *Rus.* Vislinskiy Zaliv. *lagoon* Poland/Russian Federation
Viterbo *488 C4 anc.* Vicus Elbii. Lazio, C Italy
Viti Levu *537 E4 island* W Fiji
Vitim *507 F4 river* C Russian Federation
Vitoria *see* Vitoria-Gasteiz
Vitória *455 F4* Espírito Santo, SE Brazil
Vitoria Bank *see* Vitória Seamount
Vitória da Conquista *455 F3* Bahia, E Brazil
Vitoria-Gasteiz *485 E1 var.* Vitoria, *Eng.* Vittoria. País Vasco, N Spain
Vitória Seamount *459 B5 var.* Victoria Bank, Vitoria Bank. *undersea feature* C Atlantic Ocean
Vitré *482 B3* Ille-et-Vilaine, NW France
Vitsyebsk *499 E5 Rus.* Vitebsk. Vitsyebskaya Voblasts', NE Belorussia
Vittoria *see* Vitoria-Gasteiz
Vittoria *489 C7* Sicilia, Italy, C Mediterranean Sea
Vizianagaram *527 E5 var.* Vizianagram. Andhra Pradesh, E India
Vizianagram *see* Vizianagaram
Vjosës, Lumi i *493 C7 var.* Vijosa, Vijosë, *Gk.* Aóos. *river* Albania/Greece *see also* Aóos
Vlaardingen *478 B4* Zuid-Holland, SW Netherlands
Vladikavkaz *503 B8 prev.* Dzaudzhikau, Ordzhonikidze. Respublika Severnaya Osetiya, SW Russian Federation
Vladimir *503 B5* Vladimirskaya Oblast', W Russian Federation
Vladivostok *507 G5* Primorskiy Kray, SE Russian Federation
Vlagtwedde *478 E2* Groningen, NE Netherlands
Vlasotince *493 E5* Serbia, SE Yugoslavia
Vlieland *478 C1 Fris.* Flylân. *island* Waddeneilanden, N Netherlands
Vlijmen *478 C4* Noord-Brabant, S Netherlands
Vlissingen *479 B5 Eng.* Flushing, *Fr.* Flessingue. Zeeland, SW Netherlands
Vlorë *493 C7 prev.* Vlonë, *It.* Valona, Vlora. Vlorë, SW Albania
Vöcklabruck *487 D6* Oberösterreich, NW Austria
Vohimena, Tanjona *471 F4 Fr.* Cap Sainte Marie. *headland* S Madagascar
Voiron *483 D5* Isère, E France
Vojvodina *492 D3 Ger.* Wojwodina. *cultural region* N Yugoslavia
Volcán de Chiriquí *see* Barú, Volcán
Volga *503 B7 river* NW Russian Federation
Volga Uplands *473 G3 Russ.* Privolzhskaya Vozvyshennost'. *mountain range* W Russian Federation
Volgodonsk *503 B7* Rostovskaya Oblast', SW Russian Federation
Volgograd *503 B7 prev.* Stalingrad, Tsaritsyn. Volgogradskaya Oblast', SW Russian Federation
Volkhov *502 B4* Leningradskaya Oblast', NW Russian Federation
Volnovakha *501 G3* Donets'ka Oblast', SE Ukraine
Volodymyr-Volyns'kyy *500 C1 Pol.* Włodzimierz, *Rus.* Vladimir-Volynskiy. Volyns'ka Oblast', NW Ukraine
Vologda *502 B4* Vologodskaya Oblast', W Russian Federation
Vólos *497 B5* Thessalía, C Greece
Vol'sk *503 C6* Saratovskaya Oblast', W Russian Federation
Volta *467 E5 river* SE Ghana
Volta Blanche *see* White Volta
Volta, Lake *467 E5 reservoir* SE Ghana
Volta Noire *see* Black Volta
Volturno *489 D5 river* S Italy
Volzhskiy *503 B6* Volgogradskaya Oblast', SW Russian Federation
Võnnu *498 E3 Ger.* Wendau. Tartumaa, SE Estonia
Voorst *478 D3* Gelderland, E Netherlands
Voranava *499 C5 Pol.* Werenów, *Rus.* Voronovo. Hrodzyenskaya Voblasts', W Belorussia
Vorderrhein *487 B7 river* SE Switzerland
Vóreioi Sporádes *497 C5 var.* Vórioi Sporádhes, *Eng.* Northern Sporades. *island group* E Greece
Vórioi Sporádhes *see* Vóreioi Sporádes
Vorkuta *506 C2* Respublika Komi, NW Russian Federation
Vormsi *498 C2 var.* Vormsi Saar, *Ger.* Worms, Swed. Ormsö. *island* W Estonia
Vormsi Saar *see* Vormsi
Voronezh *503 B6* Voronezhskaya Oblast', W Russian Federation
Võru *498 D3 Ger.* Werro. Võrumaa, SE Estonia
Vosges *482 E4 mountain range* NE France
Vostochno-Sibirskoye More *507 F1 Eng.* East Siberian Sea. *sea* Arctic Ocean
Vostock Island *see* Vostok Island
Vostok *546 C3 Russian research station* Antarctica
Vostok Island *537 G3 var.* Vostock Island; *prev.* Stavers Island. *island* Line Islands, SE Kiribati
Voznesens'k *501 E3 Rus.* Voznesensk. Mykolayivs'ka Oblast', S Ukraine
Vrangelya, Ostrov *507 F1 Eng.* Wrangel Island. *island* NE Russian Federation
Vranje *493 E5* Serbia, SE Yugoslavia
Vranov *see* Vranov nad Topl'ou
Vranov nad Topl'ou *491 D5 var.* Vranov, *Hung.* Varannó. Východné Slovensko, E Slovakia
Vratsa *496 C2* Oblast Montana, NW Bulgaria
Vrbas *492 C3 river* N Bosnia and Herzegovina
Vrbas *492 C3* Serbia, NW Yugoslavia
Vsetín *491 C5 Ger.* Wsetin. Severní Morava, E Czech Republic
Vučitrn *493 D5* Serbia, S Yugoslavia
Vukovar *492 C3 Hung.* Vukovár. Vukovar-Srijem, E Croatia
Vulcano, Isola *489 C7 island* Isole Eolie, S Italy
Vung Tau *529 E6 prev. Fr.* Cape Saint Jacques, Cap Saint-Jacques. Ba Ria-Vung Tau, S Vietnam
Vyatka *503 C5 river* NW Russian Federation
Vyborg *502 B3 Fin.* Viipuri. Leningradskaya Oblast', NW Russian Federation
Vyerkhnyadzvinsk *499 D5 Rus.* Verkhnedvinsk. Vitsyebskaya Voblasts', N Belorussia
Vyetryna *499 D5 Rus.* Vetrino. Vitsyebskaya Voblasts', N Belorussia
Vynohradiv *500 B3 Cz.* Sevluš, *Hung.* Nagyszöllös, *Rus.* Vinogradov; *prev.* Sevlyush. Zakarpats'ka Oblast', W Ukraine

W

Wa *467 E4* NW Ghana
Waal *478 C4 river* S Netherlands
Wabash *432 C4* Indiana, N USA
Wabash River *432 B5 river* N USA
Waco *441 G3* Texas, SW USA
Waddān *463 F3* NW Libya
Waddeneilanden *478 C1 Eng.* West Frisian Islands. *island group* N Netherlands
Waddenzee *478 C1 var.* Wadden Zee. *sea* SE North Sea
Waddington, Mount *428 D5 mountain* British Columbia, SW Canada
Wādī as Sīr *511 B6 var.* Wadi es Sir. 'Ammān, NW Jordan
Wadi es Sir *see* Wādī as Sīr
Wadi Halfa *464 B3 var.* Wādī Ḥalfā'. Northern, N Sudan
Wādī Mūsā *511 B7 var.* Petra. Ma'ān, S Jordan
Wad Madanī *see* Wad Medan
Wad Medani *464 C4 var.* Wac Madanī. Gezira, C Sudan
Waflia *531 F4* Pulau Buru, E Indonesia
Wagadugu *see* Ouagadougou
Wagga Wagga *541 C7* New S Wales, SE Australia
Wagin *539 B7* Western Austra
Wāh *526 C1* Punjab, NE Pakis
Wahai *531 F4* Pulau Seram, E Indonesia
Wahiawa *439 A8 Haw.* Wahia Oahu, Hawaii, USA, C Pacif Ocean
Wahībah, Ramlat Āl *513 E5* Ramlat Ahl Wahibah, Raml Al Wahaybah, *Eng.* Wahibah Sands. *desert* N Oman
Wahibah Sands *see* Wahībah, Ramlat Āl
Wahpeton *437 F2* North Dak N USA
Wahran *see* Oran
Waiau *543 A7 river* South Isla NZ
Waigeo, Pulau *531 G4 island* Maluku, E Indonesia
Waikaremoana, Lake *542 E4* North Island, NZ
Wailuku *439 B8* Maui, Hawai USA, C Pacific Ocean
Waimate *543 B6* Canterbury, Island, NZ
Waiouru *542 D4* Manawatu-Wanganui, North Island, NZ
Waipara *543 C6* Canterbury, Island, NZ
Waipawa *542 E4* Hawke's Bay North Island, NZ
Waipukurau *542 D4* Hawke's North Island, NZ
Wairau *543 C5 river* South Isl NZ
Wairoa *542 D2 river* North Isl NZ
Wairoa *542 E4* Hawke's Bay, N Island, NZ
Waitaki *543 B6 river* South Isl NZ
Waitara *542 D4* Taranaki, No Island, NZ
Waiuku *542 D3* Auckland, No Island, NZ
Wakasa-wan *523 C6 bay* C Ja
Wakatipu, Lake *543 A7 lake* S Island, NZ
Wakayama *523 C6* Wakayam Honshū, SW Japan
Wake Island *534 D1 atoll* NW Pacific Ocean
Wake Island *544 C2 US unincorporated territory* NW Pacific Ocean
Wakkanai *522 C1* Hokkaidō, NE Japan
Walachei *see* Wallachia
Walachia *see* Wallachia
Wałbrzych *490 B4 Ger.* Waldenburg, Waldenburg in Schlesien. Wałbrzych, SW Po
Walcourt *479 C7* Namur, S Be
Wałcz *490 B3 Ger.* Deutsch Kr Piła, NW Poland
Waldia *see* Weldiya
Wales *481 C6 Wel.* Cymru. *na region* UK
Wales *428 C2* Alaska, USA
Wales Island, Prince of *see* P Pulau
Walgett *541 D5* New South W SE Australia
Walker Lake *439 C5 lake* Nev W USA
Wallachia *500 B5 var.* Walach *Ger.* Walachei, *Rom.* Valachia *cultural region* S Romania
Walla Walla *438 C2* Washingt NW USA
Wallis and Futuna *537 E4 Fr.* Territoire de Wallis et Futuna *French overseas territory* C Pa Ocean
Walnut Ridge *434 B1* Arkansa C USA
Walthamstow *481 B7* SE Engl UK
Walvis Bay *470 A4 Afr.* Walvis Erongo, NW Namibia
Walvish Ridge *see* Walvis Rid
Walvis Ridge *461 B7 var.* Walv Ridge. *undersea feature* E Atla Ocean
Wan *see* Anhui
Wanaka *543 B6* Otago, South Island, NZ
Wanaka, Lake *543 A6 lake* So Island, NZ
Wanchuan *see* Zhangjiakou
Wandel Sea *475 E1 sea* Arctic Ocean
Wandsworth *481 A8* SE Engla UK
Wanganui *542 D4* Manawatu-Wanganui, North Island, NZ

Wangaratta – Yaransk

aratta 541 C7 Victoria, ustralia
, Río see Coco, Río
weyn 465 D6 var. Wanle , It. Uanle Uen. Shabeellaha e, SW Somalia
Weyn see Wanlaweyn
ian 520 B5 Sichuan, C China
gal 527 E5 Andhra Pradesh, lia
rg 486 B4 Nordrhein- falen, W Germany
429 E4 British Columbia, anada
me 479 C6 Liège, E Belgium
486 C3 Mecklenburg- ommern, NE Germany
a see Ouargla
vorth 542 D2 Auckland, h Island, NZ
münde 486 C2 lenburg-Vorpommern, Germany
r 441 G1 Oklahoma, C USA
s 453 G4 Santa Cruz, livia
go River 541 C5 seasonal New South s/Queensland, E Australia
n 432 D3 Michigan, N USA
n 432 D3 Ohio, N USA
n 433 E3 Pennsylvania, JSA
467 F5 Delta, S Nigeria
ambool 541 B7 Victoria, ustralia
w see Warszawa
awa 490 D3 Eng. Warsaw, Ger. schau, Rus. Varshava. country al (Poland) Warszawa, land
490 B3 Ger. Warthe. river land
ick 541 E5 Queensland, stralia
ngton 436 A2 off. State of ington; also known as ook State, Evergreen State. NW USA
ngton DC 433 E4 country al (USA) District of mbia, NE USA
ngton, Mount 433 G2 tain New Hampshire, SA
The 481 E6 inlet E England,
m 445 E2 var. Waspán. ón Autónoma Atlántico Norte, Nicaragua
n see Waspam
pone 531 E4 var. Bone. wesi, C Indonesia
bury 433 F3 Connecticut, JSA
ford 481 B6 Ir. Port Láirge. and
loo 437 G3 Iowa, C USA
town 433 F2 New York, JSA
town 437 F2 South Dakota, A
ville 433 G2 Maine, NE USA
rd 481 A7 SE England, UK
469 E5 Haut-Zaïre, Congo (Zaire)
Bar Lake 434 reservoir essee, S USA
65 B5 var. Wâw. Western Bahr azal, S Sudan
gan 432 B3 Illinois, N USA
esha 432 B3 Wisconsin, A
u 432 B2 Wisconsin, N USA
ly 437 G3 Iowa, C USA
479 C6 Walloon Brabant, lgium
ee Wau
430 C4 Ontario, S Canada
oss 435 E3 Georgia, SE USA
nouth see Sunderland
er City 437 F3 Iowa, C USA
ll Plain 546 A2 undersea re SW Atlantic Ocean
ll Sea 546 A2 sea Atlantic Ocean
r 486 A3 Niedersachsen, Germany
479 D5 Limburg, etherlands
478 C3 Noord-Holland, therlands
rzewo 490 D2 Ger. rburg. Suwałki, NE Poland
ar 486 C4 Thüringen, rmany
enburg 487 C6 Bayern, ermany
ampach 479 D7 Diekirch, xembourg
rowo 490 C2 Gdańsk, Poland
man Hall 447 G1 C Barbados
ya 464 C4 var. Waldia, It. a. N Ethiopia

Welkom 470 D4 Free State, C South Africa
Welle see Uele
Wellesley Islands 540 B2 island group Queensland, N Australia
Wellington 543 D5 country capital (NZ) Wellington, North Island, NZ
Wellington see Wellington, Isla
Wellington 437 F5 Kansas, C USA
Wellington, Isla 457 A7 var. Wellington. island S Chile
Wells 438 D4 Nevada, W USA
Wellsford 542 D2 Auckland, North Island, NZ
Wells, Lake 539 C5 lake Western Australia
Wels 487 D6 anc. Ovilava. Oberösterreich, N Austria
Wembley 481 A8 SE England, UK
Wemmel 479 B6 Vlaams Brabant, C Belgium
Wenatchee 438 B2 Washington, NW USA
Wenchi 467 E4 W Ghana
Wen-chou see Wenzhou
Wenchow see Wenzhou
Wenmen Island see Wolf, Isla
Wenzhou 520 D5 var. Wen-chou, Wenchow. Zhejiang, SE China
Werda 470 C4 Kgalagadi, S Botswana
Werkendam 478 C4 Noord-Brabant, S Netherlands
Weser 486 B3 river NW Germany
Wessel Islands 540 B1 island group Northern Territory, N Australia
West Antarctica see Lesser Antarctica
West Bank 511 A6 disputed region SW Asia
West Bend 432 B3 Wisconsin, N USA
West Bengal 527 F4 state NE India
West Cape 543 A7 headland South Island, NZ
West Des Moines 437 F3 Iowa, C USA
Westerland 486 B2 Schleswig-Holstein, N Germany
Western Australia 538 B4 state W Australia
Western Desert see Sahara el Gharbiya
Western Dvina 477 E7 Bel. Dzvina, Ger. Düna, Latv. Daugava, Rus. Zapadnaya Dvina. river W Europe
Western Ghats 526 C5 mountain range SW India
Western Isles see Outer Hebrides
Western Sahara 462 B3 UK disputed territory N Africa
Westerschelde 479 B5 Eng. Western Scheldt; prev. Honte. inlet S North Sea
West Falkland 457 C7 var. Gran Malvina. island W Falkland Islands
West Fargo 437 F2 North Dakota, N USA
West Irian see Irian Jaya
West Mariana Basin 534 B1 var. Perece Vela Basin. undersea feature W Pacific Ocean
West Memphis 434 B1 Arkansas, C USA
West New Guinea see Irian Jaya
Weston-super-Mare 481 D7 SW England, UK
West Palm Beach 435 F4 Florida, SE USA
Westport 543 C5 West Coast, South Island, NZ
West River see Xi Jiang
West Siberian Plain 504 see Zapadno-Sibirskaya Ravnina
West Virginia 432 D4 off. State of West Virginia; also known as The Mountain State. state NE USA
Wetar, Pulau 531 F5 island Kepulauan Damar, E Indonesia
Wetzlar 487 B5 Hessen, W Germany
Wevok 428 C2 var. Wewuk. Alaska, USA
Wewuk see Wevok
Wexford 481 B6 Ir. Loch Garman. SE Ireland
Weyburn 429 F5 Saskatchewan, S Canada
Weymouth 481 D7 S England, UK
Wezep 478 D3 Gelderland, E Netherlands
Whakatane 542 E3 Bay of Plenty, North Island, NZ
Whale Cove 429 G3 Nunavut, C Canada
Whangarei 542 D2 Northland, North Island, NZ
Wharton Basin 533 D5 var. West Australian Basin. undersea feature E Indian Ocean
Whataroa 543 B6 West Coast, South Island, NZ
Wheatland 436 D3 Wyoming, C USA

Wheeler Peak 440 D1 mountain New Mexico, SW USA
Wheeling 432 D4 West Virginia, NE USA
Whitby 481 D5 N England, UK
Whitefish 436 B1 Montana, NW USA
Whitehaven 481 C5 NW England, UK
Whitehorse 428 D4 territory capital Yukon Territory, W Canada
White Nile 464 B4 Ar. Al Baḩr al Abyaḑ, An Nīl al Abyaḑ, Bahr el Jebel. river SE Sudan
White Nile 464 B4 var. Bahr el Jebel. river S Sudan
White River 436 D3 river South Dakota, N USA
White Sea 548 see Beloye More
White Volta 467 E4 var. Nakambé, Fr. Volta Blanche. river Burkina/Ghana
Whitianga 542 D2 Waikato, North Island, NZ
Whitney, Mount 439 C6 mountain California, W USA
Whitsunday Group 540 D3 island group Queensland, E Australia
Whyalla 541 B6 South Australia
Wichita 437 F5 Kansas, C USA
Wichita Falls 441 F2 Texas, SW USA
Wichita River 441 F2 river Texas, SW USA
Wickenburg 440 B2 Arizona, SW USA
Wicklow 481 B6 Ir. Cill Mhantáin. cultural region E Ireland
Wicklow Mountains 481 B6 Ir. Sléibhte Chill Mhantáin. mountain range E Ireland
Wieliczka 491 D5 Kraków, S Poland
Wieluń 490 C4 Sieradz, C Poland
Wien 487 E6 Eng. Vienna, Hung. Bécs, Slvk. Vídeň, Slvn. Dunaj; anc. Vindobona. country capital (Austria) Wien, NE Austria
Wiener Neustadt 487 E6 Niederösterreich, E Austria
Wierden 478 E3 Overijssel, E Netherlands
Wiesbaden 487 B5 Hessen, W Germany
Wight, Isle of 481 D7 island S England, UK
Wijchen 478 D4 Gelderland, SE Netherlands
Wijk bij Duurstede 478 D4 Utrecht, C Netherlands
Wilcannia 541 C6 New South Wales, SE Australia
Wilhelm, Mount 536 B3 mountain C PNG
Wilhelm-Pieck-Stadt see Guben
Wilhelmshaven 486 B3 Niedersachsen, NW Germany
Wilkes Barre 433 F3 Pennsylvania, NE USA
Wilkes Land 546 C4 physical region Antarctica
Willard 440 D2 New Mexico, SW USA
Willcox 440 C3 Arizona, SW USA
Willebroek 479 B5 Antwerpen, C Belgium
Willemstad 447 E5 dependent territory capital (Netherlands Antilles) Curaçao, Netherlands Antilles
Williston 436 D1 North Dakota, N USA
Wilmington 433 F4 Delaware, NE USA
Wilmington 435 F2 North Carolina, SE USA
Wilmington 432 C4 Ohio, N USA
Wilrijk 479 C5 Antwerpen, N Belgium
Winchester 481 D7 hist. Wintanceaster, Lat. Venta Belgarum. S England, UK
Winchester 433 E4 Virginia, NE USA
Windhoek 470 B3 Ger. Windhuk. country capital (Namibia) Khomas, C Namibia
Windorah 540 C4 Queensland, C Australia
Windsor 433 G3 Connecticut, NE USA
Windsor 540 D1 New South Wales, SE Australia
Windsor 430 C5 Ontario, S Canada
Windsor 481 D7 S England, UK
Windward Islands 447 H4 island group E West Indies
Windward Islands see Barlavento, Ilhas de
Windward Passage 446 D3 Sp. Paso de los Vientos. channel Cuba/Haiti
Winisk 430 C2 river Ontario, S Canada
Winisk 430 C2 Ontario, C Canada
Winnebago, Lake 432 B2 lake Wisconsin, N USA

Winnemucca 439 C5 Nevada, W USA
Winnipeg 429 G5 Manitoba, S Canada
Winnipeg, Lake 429 G5 lake Manitoba, C Canada
Winnipegosis, Lake 430 A3 lake Manitoba, C Canada
Winona 437 G3 Minnesota, N USA
Winschoten 478 E2 Groningen, NE Netherlands
Winsen 486 B3 Niedersachsen, N Germany
Winston Salem 435 E1 North Carolina, SE USA
Winsum 478 D1 Groningen, NE Netherlands
Winterswijk 478 E4 Gelderland, E Netherlands
Winterthur 487 B7 Zürich, NE Switzerland
Winton 540 C4 Queensland, E Australia
Winton 543 A7 Southland, South Island, NZ
Wisconsin 432 A2 off. State of Wisconsin; also known as The Badger State. state N USA
Wisconsin Rapids 432 B2 Wisconsin, N USA
Wisconsin River 432 B3 river Wisconsin, N USA
Wisła 490 C2 Eng. Vistula, Ger. Weichsel. river C Poland
Wismar 486 C2 Mecklenburg-Vorpommern, N Germany
Wittenberge 486 C3 Brandenburg, N Germany
Wittlich 487 A5 Rheinland-Pfalz, SW Germany
Wittstock 486 C3 Brandenburg, NE Germany
W.J. van Blommesteinmeer 451 G3 reservoir E Surinam
Władysławowo 490 C2 Gdańsk, N Poland
Włocławek 490 C3 Ger./Rus. Vlotslavsk. Włocławek, C Poland
Włodawa 490 E4 Rus. Vlodava. Chełm, SE Poland
Wlotzkasbaken 470 B3 Erongo, W Namibia
Wodonga 541 C7 Victoria, SE Australia
Wodzisław Śląski 491 C5 Ger. Loslau. Katowice, S Poland
Wōjjā see Wotje Atoll
Woking 481 D7 SE England, UK
Wolf, Isla 452 A4 var. Wenmen Island. island W Ecuador
Wolfsberg 487 D7 Kärnten, SE Austria
Wolfsburg 486 C3 Niedersachsen, N Germany
Wolgast 486 D2 Mecklenburg-Vorpommern, NE Germany
Wollaston Lake 429 F4 Saskatchewan, C Canada
Wollongong 541 D6 New South Wales, SE Australia
Wolvega 478 D2 Fris. Wolvegea. Friesland, N Netherlands
Wolverhampton 481 D6 C England, UK
Wŏnsan 521 E3 SE North Korea
Woodburn 438 B3 Oregon, NW USA
Woodland 439 B5 California, W USA
Woodruff 432 B2 Wisconsin, N USA
Woods, Lake of the 430 A3 Fr. Lac des Bois. lake Canada/USA
Woodville 542 D4 Manawatu-Wanganui, North Island, NZ
Woodward 441 F1 Oklahoma, C USA
Worcester 481 D6 hist. Wigorna Ceaster. W England, UK
Worcester 433 G3 Massachusetts, NE USA
Worcester 470 C5 Western Cape, SW South Africa
Workington 481 C5 NW England, UK
Worland 436 C3 Wyoming, C USA
Worms 487 B5 anc. Augusta Vangionum, Borbetomagus, Wormatia. Rheinland-Pfalz, SW Germany
Worms see Vormsi
Worthington 437 F3 Minnesota, N USA
Wotje Atoll 536 D1 var. Wōjjā. atoll Ratak Chain, E Marshall Islands
Woudrichem 478 C4 Noord-Brabant, S Netherlands
Wrangel Island 505 see Vrangelya, Ostrov
Wrangel Plain 548 B2 undersea feature Arctic Ocean
Wrocław 490 C4 Eng./Ger. Breslau. Wrocław, SW Poland
Września 490 C3 Poznań, C Poland
Wuchang see Wuhan

Wuday 'ah 513 C6 Najrān, S Saudi Arabia
Wuhai 519 E3 Nei Mongol Zizhiqu, N China
Wuhan 520 C5 var. Han-kou, Han-k'ou, Hanyang, Wuchang, Wu-han; prev. Hankow. Hubei, C China
Wuhsi see Wuxi
Wuhsien see Suzhou
Wuhu 520 D5 var. Wu-na-mu. Anhui, E China
Wujlān see Ujelang Atoll
Wukari 467 G4 Taraba, E Nigeria
Wuliang Shan 520 A6 mountain range SW China
Wu-lu-k'o-mu-shi see Ürümqi
Wu-lu-mu-ch'i see Ürümqi
Wu-na-mu see Wuhu
Wuppertal 486 A4 prev. Barmen-Elberfeld. Nordrhein-Westfalen, W Germany
Würzburg 487 B5 Bayern, SW Germany
Wusih see Wuxi
Wuxi 520 D5 var. Wuhsi, Wu-hsi, Wusih. Jiangsu, E China
Wuyi Shan 517 E3 mountain range SE China
Wye 481 C6 Wel. Gwy. river England/Wales, UK
Wyndham 538 D3 Western Australia
Wyoming 436 B3 off. State of Wyoming; also known as The Equality State. state C USA
Wyoming 432 C3 Michigan, N USA
Wyszków 490 D3 Ger. Probstberg. Ostrołęka, NE Poland

X

Xaafuun, Raas 464 E4 var. Ras Hafun. headland NE Somalia
Xaçmaz 509 H2 Rus. Khachmas. N Azerbaijan
Xaignabouli 528 C4 prev. Muang Xaignabouri, Fr. Sayaboury. Xaignabouli, N Laos
Xai-Xai 471 E4 prev. João Belo, Vila de João Belo. Gaza, S Mozambique
Xalapa 443 F4 var. Jalapa, Jalapa Enríquez. Veracruz-Llave, SE Mexico
Xam Nua 528 D3 var. Sam Neua. Houaphan, N Laos
Xankändi 509 G3 Rus. Khankendi; prev. Stepanakert. SW Azerbaijan
Xánthi 496 C3 Anatolikí Makedonía kai Thráki, NE Greece
Xátiva 485 F3 var. Jativa; anc. Setabis. País Valenciano, E Spain
Xauen see Chefchaouen
Xeres see Jeréz de la Frontera
Xiaguan see Dali
Xiamen 520 D6 var. Hsia-men; prev. Amoy. Fujian, SE China
Xi'an 520 C4 var. Changan, Sian, Signan, Siking, Singan, Xian. Shaanxi, C China
Xian see Xi'an
Xiangkhoang see Pèk
Xiangtan 520 C5 var. Hsiang-t'an, Siangtan. Hunan, S China
Xiao Hinggan Ling 520 D2 Eng. Lesser Khingan Range. mountain range NE China
Xichang 520 B5 Sichuan, C China
Xieng Khouang see Pèk
Xieng Ngeun see Muong Xiang Ngeun
Xigaze see Xigazê
Xigazê 518 C5 var. Jih-k'a-tse, Shigatse, Xigaze. Xizang Zizhiqu, W China
Xi Jiang 516 D3 var. Hsi Chiang, Eng. West River. river S China
Xilinhot 519 F2 var. Silinhot. Nei Mongol Zizhiqu, N China
Xilokastro see Xylókastro
Xin see Xinjiang Uygur Zizhiqu
Xingkai Hu see Khanka, Lake
Xingu, Rio 455 E2 river C Brazil
Xingxingxia 518 D3 Xinjiang Uygur Zizhiqu, NW China
Xining 519 E4 var. Hsining, Hsi-ning, Sining. province capital Qinghai, C China
Xinjiang see Xinjiang Uygur Zizhiqu
Xinjiang Uygur Zizhiqu 518 B3 var. Sinkiang, Sinkiang Uighur Autonomous Region, Xin, Xinjiang. Admin. region autonomous region NW China
Xinpu see Lianyungang
Xinxiang 520 C4 Henan, C China
Xinyang 520 C5 var. Hsin-yang, Sinyang. Henan, C China
Xinzo de Limia 484 C2 Galicia, NW Spain
Xiqing Shan 516 D2 mountain range C China
Xizang see Xizang Zizhiqu
Xizang Gaoyuan see Qingzang Gaoyuan

Xizang Zizhiqu 518 B4 var. Thibet, Tibetan Autonomous Region, Xizang, Eng. Tibet. Admin. region autonomous region W China
Xolotlán see Managua, Lago de
Xuddur 465 D5 var. Hudur, It. Oddur. Bakool, SW Somalia
Xuwen 520 C7 Guangdong, S China
Xuzhou 520 D4 var. Hsu-chou, Suchow, Tongshan; prev. T'ung-shan. Jiangsu, E China
Xylókastro 497 B5 var. Xilokastro. Pelopónnisos, S Greece

Y

Ya'an 520 B5 var. Yaan. Sichuan, C China
Yabēlo 465 C5 S Ethiopia
Yablis 445 E2 Región Autónoma Atlántico Norte, NE Nicaragua
Yablonovyy Khrebet 507 F4 mountain range S Russian Federation
Yabrai Shan 519 E3 mountain range NE China
Yafran 463 F2 NW Libya
Yaghan Basin 459 B7 undersea feature SE Pacific Ocean
Yahotyn 501 E2 Rus. Yagotin. Kyyivs'ka Oblast', N Ukraine
Yahualica 442 D4 Jalisco, SW Mexico
Yakima 438 B2 Washington, NW USA
Yakima River 438 B2 river Washington, NW USA
Yakoruda 496 C3 Sofiyska Oblast, SW Bulgaria
Yaku-shima 523 B8 island Nansei-shotō, SW Japan
Yakutat 428 D4 Alaska, USA
Yakutsk 507 F3 Respublika Sakha (Yakutiya), NE Russian Federation
Yala 529 C7 Yala, SW Thailand
Yalizava 499 D6 Rus. Yelizovo. Mahilyowskaya Voblasts', E Belorussia
Yalong Jiang 520 A5 river C China
Yalova 508 B3 İstanbul, NW Turkey
Yalpuh, Ozero 500 D4 Rus. Ozero Yalpug. lake SW Ukraine
Yalta 501 F5 Respublika Krym, S Ukraine
Yalu 517 E2 Chin. Yalu Jiang, Jap. Oryokko, Kor. Amnok-kang. river China/North Korea
Yamaguchi 523 B7 var. Yamaguti. Yamaguchi, Honshū, SW Japan
Yamaguti see Yamaguchi
Yamal, Poluostrov 506 D2 peninsula N Russian Federation
Yambio 465 B5 var. Yambiyo. Western Equatoria, S Sudan
Yambiyo see Yambio
Yambol 496 D2 Turk. Yanboli. Burgaska Oblast, E Bulgaria
Yamdena, Pulau 531 G5 prev. Jamdena. island Kepulauan Tanimbar, E Indonesia
Yam HaMelaḥ see Dead Sea
Yam Kinneret see Tiberias, Lake
Yamoussoukro 466 D5 country capital (Ivory Coast) C Ivory Coast
Yamuna 526 D3 prev. Jumna. river N India
Yana 507 F2 river NE Russian Federation
Yanbu 'al Baḩr 513 A5 Al Madīnah, W Saudi Arabia
Yangambi 469 D5 Haut-Zaïre, N Congo (Zaire)
Yangchow see Yangzhou
Yangiyūl 515 E2 Rus. Yangiyul'. Toshkent Wiloyati, E Uzbekistan
Yangon 528 B4 Eng. Rangoon. country capital (Burma) Yangon, S Burma
Yangtze 544 see Chang Jiang
Yangtze Kiang see Chang Jiang
Yangzhou 520 D5 var. Yangchow. Jiangsu, E China
Yankton 437 E3 South Dakota, N USA
Yannina see Ioánnina
Yanskiy Zaliv 505 F2 bay N Russian Federation
Yantai 520 D4 var. Yan-t'ai; prev. Chefoo, Chih-fu. Shandong, E China
Yan-t'ai see Yantai
Yaoundé 469 B5 var. Yaunde. country capital (Cameroon) Centre, S Cameroon
Yap 536 A1 island Caroline Islands, W Micronesia
Yapanskoye More see Japan, Sea of
Yapen, Pulau 531 G4 prev. Japen. island E Indonesia
Yap Trench 534 B2 var. Yap Trough. undersea feature SE Philippine Sea
Yap Trough see Yap Trench
Yapurá see Caquetá, Río
Yapurá see Japurá, Rio
Yaqui, Río 442 C2 river NW Mexico
Yaransk 503 C5 Kirovskaya Oblast', NW Russian Federation

Yarega – Zyryanovsk

Yarega *502 D4* Respublika Komi, NW Russian Federation
Yarkant *see* Shache
Yarlung Zangbo Jiang *see* Brahmaputra
Yarmouth *see* Great Yarmouth
Yarmouth *431 F5* Nova Scotia, SE Canada
Yaroslavl' *502 B4* Yaroslavskaya Oblast', W Russian Federation
Yarumal *450 B2* Antioquia, NW Colombia
Yasyel'da *499 B7 river* SW Belorussia
Yatsushiro *523 A7 var.* Yatusiro. Kumamoto, Kyūshū, SW Japan
Yatusiro *see* Yatsushiro
Yaunde *see* Yaoundé
Yavarí *see* Javari, Rio
Yaviza *445 H5* Darién, SE Panama
Yavoriv *500 B2 Pol.* Jaworów, *Rus.* Yavorov. L'vivs'ka Oblast', NW Ukraine
Yazd *512 D3 var.* Yezd. Yazd, C Iran
Yazoo City *434 B2* Mississippi, S USA
Yding Skovhøj *477 A7 hill* C Denmark
Ýdra *497 C6 var.* Ídhra. *island* S Greece
Ye *529 B5* Mon State, S Burma
Yecheng *518 A3 var.* Kargilik. Xinjiang Uygur Zizhiqu, NW China
Yefremov *503 B5* Tul'skaya Oblast', W Russian Federation
Yekaterinburg *506 C3 prev.* Sverdlovsk. Sverdlovskaya Oblast', C Russian Federation
Yelets *503 B5* Lipetskaya Oblast', W Russian Federation
Yell *480 D1 island* NE Scotland, UK
Yellowknife *429 E4 territory capital* Northwest Territories, W Canada
Yellow River *544 see* Huang He
Yellow Sea *520 D4 Chin.* Huang Hai, *Kor.* Hwang-Hae. *sea* E Asia
Yellowstone River *436 C2 river* Montana/Wyoming, NW USA
Yel'sk *499 C7 Rus.* Yel'sk. Homyel'skaya Voblasts', SE Belorussia
Yelwa *467 F4* Kebbi, W Nigeria
Yemen *513 C7 off.* Republic of Yemen, *Ar.* Al Jumhūrīyah al Yamanīyah, Al Yaman. *country* SW Asia
Yemva *502 D4 prev.* Zheleznodorozhnyy. Respublika Komi, NW Russian Federation
Yenakiyeve *501 G3 Rus.* Yenakiyevo; *prev.* Ordzhonikidze, Rykovo. Donets'ka Oblast', E Ukraine
Yenangyaung *528 A3* Magwe, W Burma
Yendi *467 E4* NE Ghana
Yengisar *518 A3* Xinjiang Uygur Zizhiqu, NW China
Yenierenköy *see* Agialoúsa
Yenisey *506 D3 river* Mongolia/Russian Federation
Yenping *see* Nanping
Yeovil *481 D7* SW England, UK
Yeppoon *540 D4* Queensland, E Australia
Yerevan *509 F3 var.* Erevan, *Eng.* Erivan. *country capital* (Armenia) C Armenia
Yeu, Île d' *482 A4 island* NW France
Yevlax *509 G2 Rus.* Yevlakh. C Azerbaijan
Yevpatoriya *501 F5* Respublika Krym, S Ukraine
Yeya *501 H4 river* SW Russian Federation
Yezd *see* Yazd
Yezyaryshcha *499 E5 Rus.* Yezerishche. Vitsyebskaya Voblasts', NE Belorussia
Yiannitsá *see* Giannitsá
Yichang *520 C5* Hubei, C China
Yıldızeli *508 D3* Sivas, N Turkey
Yinchuan *520 B4 var.* Yinch'uan, Yin-ch'uan, Yinchwan. Ningxia, N China
Yinchwan *see* Yinchuan
Yin-hsien *see* Ningbo
Yining *518 B2 var.* I-ning, *Uigh.* Gulja, Kuldja. Xinjiang Uygur Zizhiqu, NW China
Yíthion *see* Gýtheio
Yogyakarta *530 C5 prev.* Djokjakarta, Jogjakarta, Jokyakarta. Jawa, C Indonesia
Yokohama *523 D5* Aomori, Honshū, C Japan
Yokohama *522 A2* Kanagawa, Honshū, S Japan
Yokote *522 D4* Akita, Honshū, C Japan
Yola *467 H4* Adamawa, E Nigeria
Yonago *523 B6* Tottori, Honshū, SW Japan
Yong'an *520 D6 var.* Yongan. Fujian, SE China
Yonkers *433 F3* New York, NE USA
Yonne *482 C4 river* C France
Yopal *450 C3 var.* El Yopal. Casanare, C Colombia
York *481 D5 anc.* Eboracum, Eburacum. N England, UK
York *437 E4* Nebraska, C USA
York, Cape *540 C1 headland* Queensland, NE Australia
Yorkton *429 F5* Saskatchewan, S Canada
Yoro *444 C2* Yoro, C Honduras
Yoshkar-Ola *503 C5* Respublika Mariy El, W Russian Federation
Youngstown *432 D4* Ohio, N USA
Youth, Isle of *see* Juventud, Isla de la
Yreka *438 B4* California, W USA
Yssel *see* IJssel
Ysyk-Köl *see* Issyk-Kul', Ozero
Yu *see* Henan
Yuan *see* Red River
Yuan Jiang *see* Red River
Yuba City *439 B5* California, W USA
Yucatan Channel *443 H3 Sp.* Canal de Yucatán. *channel* Cuba/Mexico
Yucatan Peninsula *427 C7 peninsula* Guatemala/Mexico
Yuci *520 C4* Shanxi, C China
Yue *see* Guangdong
Yueyang *520 C5* Hunan, S China
Yugoslavia *492 D4 off.* Federal Republic of Yugoslavia, *SCr.* Jugoslavija, Savezna Republika Jugoslavija. *country* SE Europe
Yukhavichy *499 D5 Rus.* Yukhovichi. Vitsyebskaya Voblasts', N Belorussia
Yukon *428 C2 river* Canada/USA
Yukon *see* Yukon Territory
Yukon Territory *428 D3 var.* Yukon, *Fr.* Territoire du Yukon. *Admin. region territory* NW Canada
Yulin *520 C6* Guangxi Zhuangzu Zizhiqu, S China
Yuma *440 A2* Arizona, SW USA
Yumen *520 A3 var.* Laojunmiao, Yümen. Gansu, N China
Yun *see* Yunnan
Yungki *see* Jilin
Yung-ning *see* Nanning
Yunjinghong *see* Jinghong
Yunki *see* Jilin
Yunnan *520 A6 var.* Yun, Yunnan Sheng, Yünnan, Yun-nan. *Admin. region province* SW China
Yunnan *see* Kunming
Yunnan Sheng *see* Yunnan
Yuruá, Río *see* Juruá, Rio
Yushu *518 D4* Qinghai, C China
Yuty *456 D3* Caazapá, S Paraguay
Yuzhno-Sakhalinsk *507 H4 Jap.* Toyohara; *prev.* Vladimirovka. Ostrov Sakhalin, Sakhalinskaya Oblast', SE Russian Federation
Yuzhou *see* Chongqing
Yylanly *see* Il'yaly

Z

Zaanstad *478 C3 prev.* Zaandam. Noord-Holland, C Netherlands
Zabaykal'sk *507 F5* Chitinskaya Oblast', S Russian Federation
Zabern *see* Saverne
Zabīd *513 B7* W Yemen
Ząbkowice *see* Ząbkowice Śląskie
Ząbkowice Śląskie *490 B4 var.* Ząbkowice, *Ger.* Frankenstein, Frankenstein in Schlesien. Wałbrzych, SW Poland
Zábřeh *491 C5 Ger.* Hohenstadt. Severní Morava, E Czech Republic
Zacapa *444 B2* Zacapa, E Guatemala
Zacatecas *442 D3* Zacatecas, C Mexico
Zacatepec *443 E4* Morelos, S Mexico
Zacháro *497 B6 var.* Zaharo, Zakháro. Dytikí Ellás, S Greece
Zadar *492 A3 It.* Zara; *anc.* Iader. Zadar-Knin, W Croatia
Zadetkyi Kyun *529 B6 var.* St. Matthew's Island. *island* Mergui Archipelago, S Burma
Zafra *484 C4* Extremadura, W Spain
Zagazig *464 B1 var.* Az Zaqāzīq. N Egypt
Zagreb *492 B2 Ger.* Agram, *Hung.* Zágráb. *country capital* (Croatia) Grad Zagreb, N Croatia
Zāgros, Kūhhā-ye *512 C3 Eng.* Zagros Mountains. *mountain range* W Iran
Zāgros Mountains *see* Zāgros, Kūhhā-ye
Zaharo *see* Zacháro
Zāhedān *512 E4 var.* Zahidan; *prev.* Duzdab. Sīstān va Balūchestān, SE Iran
Zahidan *see* Zāhedān
Zaḩlah *see* Zahlé
Zahlé *510 B4 var.* Zaḩlah. C Lebanon
Záhony *491 E6* Szabolcs-Szatmár-Bereg, NE Hungary
Zaire *see* Congo
Zaječar *492 E4* Serbia, E Yugoslavia
Zakháro *see* Zacháro
Zākhō *512 B2 var.* Zākhū. N Iraq
Zākhū *see* Zākhō
Zákinthos *see* Zákynthos
Zakota Gdańska *see* Danzig, Gulf of
Zákynthos *497 A6 var.* Zákinthos, *It.* Zante. *island* Iónioi Nísoi, Greece, C Mediterranean Sea
Zalaegerszeg *491 B7* Zala, W Hungary
Zalău *500 B3 Ger.* Waltenberg, *Hung.* Zilah; *prev. Ger.* Zillenmarkt. Sălaj, NW Romania
Ẕalim *513 B5* Makkah, W Saudi Arabia
Zambesi *see* Zambezi
Zambeze *see* Zambezi
Zambezi *470 D2 var.* Zambesi, *Port.* Zambeze. *river* S Africa
Zambezi *470 C2* North Western, W Zambia
Zambia *470 C2 off.* Republic of Zambia; *prev.* Northern Rhodesia. *country* S Africa
Zamboanga *531 E3 off.* Zamboanga City. Mindanao, S Philippines
Zambrów *490 E3* Łomża, E Poland
Zamora *484 D2* Castilla-León, NW Spain
Zamora de Hidalgo *442 D4* Michoacán de Ocampo, SW Mexico
Zamość *490 E4 Rus.* Zamoste. Zamość, SE Poland
Zancle *see* Messina
Zanda *518 A4* Xizang Zizhiqu, W China
Zanesville *432 D4* Ohio, N USA
Zanjān *512 C2 var.* Zenjan, Zinjan. Zanjān, NW Iran
Zante *see* Zákynthos
Zanthus *539 C6* Western Australia
Zanzibar *465 C7 Swa.* Unguja. *island* E Tanzania
Zanzibar *465 D7* Zanzibar, E Tanzania
Zaozhuang *520 D4* Shandong, E China
Zapadna Morava *492 D4 Ger.* Westliche Morava. *river* C Yugoslavia
Zapadnaya Dvina *502 A4* Tverskaya Oblast', W Russian Federation
Zapadno-Sibirskaya Ravnina *506 C3 Eng.* West Siberian Plain. *plain* C Russian Federation
Zapadnyy Sayan *506 D4 Eng.* Western Sayans. *mountain range* S Russian Federation
Zapala *457 B5* Neuquén, W Argentina
Zapiola Ridge *459 B6 undersea feature* SW Atlantic Ocean
Zapolyarnyy *502 C2* Murmanskaya Oblast', NW Russian Federation
Zaporizhzhya *501 F3 Rus.* Zaporozh'ye; *prev.* Aleksandrovsk. Zaporiz'ka Oblast', SE Ukraine
Zapotiltic *442 D4* Jalisco, SW Mexico
Zaqatala *509 G2 Rus.* Zakataly. NW Azerbaijan
Zara *508 D3* Sivas, C Turkey
Zarafshan *514 D2 Rus.* Zarafshan. Nawoiy Wiloyati, N Uzbekistan
Zaragoza *485 F2 Eng.* Saragossa; *anc.* Caesaraugusta, Salduba. Aragón, NE Spain
Zarand *512 D3* Kermān, C Iran
Zaranj *514 D5* Nīmrūz, SW Afghanistan
Zarasai *498 C4* Zarasai, E Lithuania
Zárate *456 D4 prev.* General José F.Uriburu. Buenos Aires, E Argentina
Zarautz *485 E1 var.* Zarauz. País Vasco, N Spain
Zarauz *see* Zarautz
Zaraza *451 E2* Guárico, N Venezuela
Zarghūn Shahr *515 E4 var.* Katawaz. Paktīkā, SE Afghanistan
Zaria *467 G4* Kaduna, C Nigeria
Zarós *497 D8* Kríti, Greece, E Mediterranean Sea
Zarqa *see* Az Zarqā'
Żary *490 B4 Ger.* Sorau, Sorau in der Niederlausitz. Zielona Góra, W Poland
Zaunguzskiye Garagumy *514 C2 Turkm.* Üngüz Angyrsyndaky Garagum. *desert* N Turkmenistan
Zavet *496 D1* Razgradska Oblast, NE Bulgaria
Zavidovići *492 C3* N Bosnia and Herzegovina
Zawia *see* Az Zāwiyah
Zawiercie *490 D4 Rus.* Zavertse. Katowice, S Poland
Zawīlah *463 F3 var.* Zuwaylah, *It.* Zueila. C Libya
Zaysan, Ozero *506 D5 Kaz.* Zaysan Köl. *lake* E Kazakhstan
Zbarazh *500 C2* Ternopil's'ka Oblast', W Ukraine
Zduńska Wola *490 C4* Sieradz, C Poland
Zeebrugge *479 A5* West-Vlaanderen, NW Belgium
Zeewolde *478 D3* Flevoland, C Netherlands
Ẕefat *511 B5 var.* Safed, *Ar.* Safad. Northern, N Israel
Zeist *478 C4* Utrecht, C Netherlands
Zele *479 B5* Oost-Vlaanderen, NW Belgium
Zelenoborskiy *502 B2* Murmanskaya Oblast', NW Russian Federation
Zelenograd *503 B5* Moskovskaya Oblast', W Russian Federation
Zelenogradsk *498 A4 Ger.* Cranz, Kranz. Kaliningradskaya Oblast', W Russian Federation
Zelle *see* Celle
Zel'va *499 B6 Pol.* Zelwa. Hrodzyenskaya Voblasts', W Belorussia
Zelzate *479 B5 var.* Selzaete. Oost-Vlaanderen, NW Belgium
Žemaičių Aukštumas *498 B4 physical region* W Lithuania
Zemst *479 C5* Vlaams Brabant, C Belgium
Zemun *492 D3* Serbia, N Yugoslavia
Zenica *492 C4* C Bosnia and Herzegovina
Zenjan *see* Zanjān
Zeravshan *515 E3 Taj./Uzb.* Zarafshon. *river* Tajikistan/Uzbekistan
Zevenaar *478 D4* Gelderland, SE Netherlands
Zevenbergen *478 C4* Noord-Brabant, S Netherlands
Zeya *505 E3 river* SE Russian Federation
Zgierz *490 C4 Ger.* Neuhof, *Rus.* Zgerzh. Łódź, C Poland
Zgorzelec *490 B4 Ger.* Görlitz. Jelenia Góra, SW Poland
Zhabinka *499 A6 Pol.* Żabinka, *Rus.* Zhabinka. Brestskaya Voblasts', SW Belorussia
Zhambyl *506 C5 prev.* Aulie Ata, Auliye-Ata, Dzhambul. Zhambyl, S Kazakhstan
Zhang-chia-k'ou *see* Zhangjiakou
Zhangdian *see* Zibo
Zhangjiakou *520 C3 var.* Changkiakow, Zhang-chia-k'ou, *Eng.* Kalgan; *prev.* Wanchuan. Hebei, E China
Zhangzhou *520 D6* Fujian, SE China
Zhanjiang *520 C7 var.* Chanchiang, Chan-chiang, *Cant.* Tsamkong, *Fr.* Fort-Bayard. Guangdong, S China
Zhaoqing *520 C6* Guangdong, S China
Zhe *see* Zhejiang
Zhejiang *520 D5 var.* Che-chiang, Chekiang, Zhe, Zhejiang Sheng. *Admin. region province* SE China
Zhejiang Sheng *see* Zhejiang
Zheleznodoroznyy *498 A4 Ger.* Gerdauen. Kaliningradskaya Oblast', W Russian Federation
Zheleznogorsk *503 A5* Kurskaya Oblast', W Russian Federation
Zhengzhou *520 C4 var.* Ch'eng-chou, Chengchow; *prev.* Chenghsien. Henan, C China
Zhezkazgan *506 C4 Kaz.* Zhezqazghan; *prev.* Dzhezkazgan. Zhezkazgan, C Kazakhstan
Zhlobin *499 D7* Homyel'skaya Voblasts', SE Belorussia
Zhmerynka *500 D2 Rus.* Zhmerinka. Vinnyts'ka Oblast', C Ukraine
Zhodzina *499 D6 Rus.* Zhodino. Minskaya Voblasts', C Belorussia
Zhovkva *500 B2 Pol.* Żółkiew, *Rus.* Zholkev, Zholkva; *prev.* Nesterov. L'vivs'ka Oblast', NW Ukraine
Zhovti Vody *501 F3 Rus.* Zhëltyye Vody. Dnipropetrovs'ka Oblast', E Ukraine
Zhovtneve *501 E4 Rus.* Zhovtnevoye. Mykolayivs'ka Oblast', S Ukraine
Zhydachiv *500 B2 Pol.* Żydaczów, *Rus.* Zhidachov. L'vivs'ka Oblast', NW Ukraine
Zhytkavichy *499 C7 Rus.* Zhitkovichi. Homyel'skaya Voblasts', SE Belorussia
Zhytomyr *500 D2 Rus.* Zhitomir. Zhytomyrs'ka Oblast', NW Ukraine
Zibo *520 D4 var.* Zhangdian. Shandong, E China
Zielona Góra *490 B4 Ger.* Grünberg, Grünberg in Schlesien, Grüneberg. Zielona Góra, W Poland
Zierikzee *478 B4* Zeeland, SW Netherlands
Zigong *520 B5 var.* Tzekung. Sichuan, C China
Ziguinchor *466 B3* SW Senegal
Žilina *491 C5 Ger.* Sillein, *Hung.* Zsolna. Stredné Slovensko, NW Slovakia
Zimbabwe *470 D3 off.* Republic of Zimbabwe; *prev.* Rhodesia. *country* S Africa
Zimnicea *500 C5* Teleorman, S Romania
Zimovniki *503 B7* Rostovskaya Oblast', SW Russian Federation
Zinder *467 G3* Zinder, S Niger
Zinjan *see* Zanjān
Zipaquirá *450 B3* Cundinamarca, C Colombia
Zittau *486 D4* Sachsen, E Germany
Zlatni Pyasŭtsi *496 E2* Varnenska Oblast, NE Bulgaria
Zlín *491 C5 prev.* Gottwaldov. Jižr Morava, SE Czech Republic
Złotów *490 C3* Piła, NW Poland
Znam"yanka *501 F3 Rus.* Znamenka. Kirovohrads'ka Oblast', C Ukraine
Żnin *490 C3* Bydgoszcz, W Polan
Znojmo *491 B5 Ger.* Znaim. Jižni Morava, S Czech Republic
Zoetermeer *478 C4* Zuid-Hollan W Netherlands
Zolochiv *500 C2 Pol.* Złoczów, *R* Zolochev. L'vivs'ka Oblast', W Ukraine
Zolochiv *501 G2 Rus.* Zolochev. Kharkivs'ka Oblast', E Ukraine
Zolote *501 H3 Rus.* Zolotoye. Luhans'ka Oblast', E Ukraine
Zolotonosha *501 E2* Cherkas'ka Oblast', C Ukraine
Zomba *471 E2* Southern, S Malav
Zongo *469 C5* Equateur, N Cong (Zaire)
Zonguldak *508 C2* Zonguldak, NW Turkey
Zonhoven *479 D6* Limburg, NE Belgium
Żory *491 C5 var.* Zory, *Ger.* Sohra Katowice, S Poland
Zouar *468 C2* Borkou-Ennedi-Tibesti, N Chad
Zouérat *466 C2 var.* Zouérate, Zouîrât. Tiris Zemmour, N Mauritania
Zouérate *see* Zouérat
Zouîrât *see* Zouérat
Zrenjanin *492 D3 prev.* Petrovgra Veliki Bečkerek, *Ger.* Grossbetschkerek, *Hung.* Nagybecskerek. Serbia, N Yugoslavia
Zubov Seamount *459 D5 unders feature* E Atlantic Ocean
Zueila *see* Zawīlah
Zug *487 B7 Fr.* Zoug. Zug, C Switzerland
Zugspitze *487 C7 mountain* S Germany
Zuid-Beveland *479 B5 var.* Sout Beveland. *island* SW Netherlan
Zuidhorn *478 E1* Groningen, NE Netherlands
Zuidlaren *478 E2* Drenthe, NE Netherlands
Zula *464 C4* E Eritrea
Zundert *479 C5* Noord-Brabant, S Netherlands
Zunyi *520 B5* Guizhou, S China
Županja *492 C3 Hung.* Zsupanya Vukovar-Srijem, E Croatia
Zürich *487 B7 Eng./Fr.* Zurich, *It.* Zurigo. Zürich, N Switzerland
Zürichsee *487 B7 Eng.* Lake Zuri *lake* NE Switzerland
Zutphen *478 D3* Gelderland, E Netherlands
Zuwārah *463 F2* NW Libya
Zuwaylah *see* Zawīlah
Zuyevka *503 D5* Kirovskaya Obla NW Russian Federation
Zvenyhorodka *501 E2 Rus.* Zvenigorodka. Cherkas'ka Obla C Ukraine
Zvishavane *470 D3 prev.* Shaban Matabeleland South, S Zimbabw
Zvolen *491 C6 Ger.* Altsohl, *Hung* Zólyom. Stredné Slovensko, C Slovakia
Zvornik *492 C4* E Bosnia and Herzegovina
Zwedru *466 D5 var.* Tchien. E Liberia
Zwettl *487 E6* Wien, NE Austria
Zwevegem *479 A6* West-Vlaanderen, W Belgium
Zwickau *487 C5* Sachsen, E Germany
Zwolle *478 D3* Overijssel, E Netherlands
Zyôetu *see* Jōetsu
Zyryanovsk *506 D5* Vostochnyy Kazakhstan, E Kazakhstan

GENERAL INDEX
AND CREDITS

591

INDEX

Page numbers in **bold** type refer to main entries

A

G

O

PICTURE SOURCES

The publisher would like to thank the following for their kind permission to reproduce the photographs:

ABBREVIATIONS

t-top	cra-center right above	c-center
b-bottom	cl-center left	ca-center above
l-left	cr-center right	cb-center below
r-right	clb-center left below	bc-bottom center
tl-top left	crb-center right below	tc-top center
tr-top right	bl-bottom left	
cla-center left above	br-bottom right	

A

©Aardman Animations 186c.
Action-Plus 196t, 199clb/Chris Barry 213c; R.Francis 197cb, 199bl; Tony Henshaw 193c, 199c, 215cr; Mike Hewitt 212br; Glyn Kirk 212crb, 215tc; Robert Lewis 190br. Lorna Ainger 162b, 178tc. AKG, London 132cb, 133crb, 144cb, 145c, 172bl, 188tr, l, 242crb. Allsport/David Klutho 201bc. Alton Telegraph Photo/Robert Graul 129car. Ampex 187bl. Ancient Art and Architecture Collection 32cl, 135bc, 142cr, 166tl, cal, 250 tc, 382cl, 384tl, 385cl/Ronald Sheridan 373br. Animals Unlimited 105cl. Directed and Produced by Animation City/ AC Live 184bc. Archiv fur Kunst und Geschicte, Berlin 182tc, 184tr, 380c, 381c, bl, 390bl. Ardea/ Liz Bomford 97tc. Art Directors/ Carl Young 152c. Aviation Photographers International 265cb.

B

B&U International Picture Service 279c. BFI Stills, Posters & Designs 164cra, 186tr. Barnaby's Picture Library/Georg Sturm 142c. Michael Barrett Levy 182bl, 187cr. Norman Barratt 190. Basketball Hall of Fame, Springfield, Massachusetts 190crb. ©Bayreuther Festspiele GmbH/ Wilhelm Rauh 314bc. Bibliotheque de L'Assemblée Nationale,Paris 190cra. Biofotos/Heather Angel 92crb. ©1993 Boeing Commercial Airplane Group 265br. Bridgeman Art Library/ Bodleian Library, Oxford 386tl; British Museum, London 160cr; Christie's, London 162cr; City of Bristol Museum & Art Gallery 393cr; British Library, London 350ca, 392bl; Department of the Environment, London 385tc; Egyptian National Museum, Cairo 374ca; Fervers Gallery, London 169cr; Giraudon 69cr, 161cl; Greater London Council 132cl; Hermitage, St.Petersburg 160cl; Historiches Museum Der Stadt,Vienna 169cr; Institute of Directors, London 397; Sir Godfrey Kneller 145cra; Louvre, Paris 374bc; Musée de L'Armée, Paris/Giraudon 395cr; Museum of Mankind 138tc;
Nationalgalerie, Berlin, *Hornform*, 1924, Wassily Kandinsky © ADAGP, Paris & DACS, London, 1995 161cb; Prado, Madrid 390cl; Private Collection 133clb, 190ca, 390tl, 397tl; Salvator Rosa 145tl; Royal College of Physicians, London 133cra; Tretyakov Gallery, Moscow 324c; Trinity College, Dublin 310br; by courtesy of the Board of Trustees of the V&A, London 391cl, 169c. British Library 141cra. British Red Cross 132crb. Brothers Quay 186cl. Bureau International des Poids et Mesure Sevres 240clb.

C

Camera Press/Curtis/RBO 409bcl; Karsh of Ottawa 409bl; Herbie Knott 410c; Ian Stone 409br; Eli Weinberg 408tl. California Institute of Technology 44bl. J.Allan Cash Ltd. 140bc, 340br, 342cl, 348cb, 379bl, 390br. Casio Electronics Co.Ltd. 182cb, bc. Jean-Loup Charmet 166cbr, 173br, 239br. Lester Cheeseman 143cl. Chicago Historical Institute 157cl. Christies Colour Library 47br. Bruce Coleman Ltd. 66c/Fred Bruemmer 291cr; Jane Burton 86cr, 93cbr; Alain Compost 95cb; Gerald Cubitt 336cl, 354bl; Peter Davey 101cb; Andrew Davies 272bl; Jack Dermid 93crb; Keith Gunnar 43ct; David C.Houston 288clb; Stephen J.Krasemann 63br, 106bl; S.Nielsen 23cr; Dieter & Mary Plage 335cr; Dr.Eckart Pott 108bc, 101bc, 291tr; Andy Price 354br; Mr.Jens Rydell 235c; John Shaw 50clb; Austin James Steven 93tr, 95tl; Kim Taylor 95tr, 236crb; Barrie Wilkins 106c; Gunter Ziesler 112cl; Christian Zuber 329c. Colorsport 194bc, 196cr, 197c, cr, 199bc, 200cl, 210bl, bc, 213cr, 214c, cr, 215bl/ © duomo-David Madison 191cra, William R.Sallaz 214cl/Olympia, Roberto Bettini 217cb/Sipa Sport, Pascal Huit 216cb, Lacombe 217c, R,Martin 215bc. Comstock 379br, 381tr.Michael Copsey 46cb, 53tr & cra, 56cla, cl, 75tl, 138c, 141cl, 242c, 326br, 344cl, 352c.

D

Daihatsu 253cr. James Davis Travel Photography 142bl, 143cr, 171bl, 303ca, 350bc. Dessau/Peter Kuhn 156cb. ©The Walt Disney Company 186tl, cl, cb. C.M. Dixon 161tc, tr, 373cra, 377tc, 378bc. Courtesy Anthony d'Offay Gallery, London 161bl. Dominic Photography/Catherine Ashmore 174c. Dr. Peter Dorrell 373tl. Dulciana/J.D. Sharp 184cl.

E

E.T.Archive 139cb, 169tr, 172bc, 374br, 377cl, 395bc, 398br, 401bl, 402tl/
Biblioteca Marciana, Venice 190cla; Metropolitan Museum of Art 176br; Plymouth City Art Gallery 176bc. Mary Evans Picture Library 18cla, 18cra, 32tr, tl, cla, c, cra & clb, 68cr, 69cl, 71tr, cla, 132cra, 133tr, 140cra, 143tr, bl, 144cr, cra, crb, 145ca, cra, 152tc, cr, 167cl, cr, 169cla, 176cb, 178ca, cl, clb, 190c, cr, 239cr, cb, 247tr, cra, cl, clb, 248tc, 249tl, cr, cb, 264ca, 265cra, cl, cr, 357crb, 380cl, 386c, 388tc, 389br, 393cl, 394cra, 396clb, c, 397ca, 398bl, 399tr, cr, 402tr, 415cr, 416, 417tl, cl, c, Elenore Plaisted Abbott 178cr; Carrey, Le Petit Parisien 264cra; A.W. Diggelmann in La Conquete du Ciel 264cr; Explorer 133cla, 169ca; G.W. Lambert 419c; Alexander Meledin Collection 402bl, 420br; J.K. Stieler 395crb; Steve Rumney 169cl; N.C. Wyeth 138tr.

F

Werner Forman Archive 161cra/ Anthropology Museum, Veracruz University, Jalapa 377tl; British Museum, London 190tr; J. Paul Getty Museum, Malibu, USA 190cal; Private Collection, Prague 354cl; Tanzania National Museum, Dar es Salaam 169tc. Fotomas Index 395bl. John Frost Historical Newspaper Service 188cla, cl, c, cb. Fuji 164bc.

G

Genesis 34bl. Geoscience Features 51clb. courtesy of Andy Goldsworthy 161bc. Ronald Grant Archive 169crb, 184ca, clb, 185bl. Greenpeace/Gleizes 153tc; Morgan 357bl.

H

Sonia Halliday Photographs 135tc, 157ca, 160tc, 161c, 188tc, 381tl, l, Laura Lushington 381bc; James Wellard 331tr. Robert Harding Picture Library 42cl, 66ca, tr, 71tl, 171tr, 290bl, 309br, 330tr, 331bl, 340crb, 345tr, 366bc, 371tl, 374c, cra, cb, crb, 377clb, 385bl, 392tr, Mohamed Amin 31bc; Bildagentur Schuster/
Kim Hart 309bl/Layda 348cra; C.Bowman 293bl; Cordier/Explorer 336bc; K.Gillham 317cr; Ian Griffiths 334c; Kosel 51cl; J.Desmarteau 394tc; FPG International 398clb, 400bl; Robert Francis 46c; Robert Frerck/ Odyssey/Chicago 278bc; David Hughes 157cla; F.Jackson 342cr, 343bl; Krafft 43tc; Robert McLeod 62bl, 410br; Geoff Renner 55bl; Christopher Rennie 383bl; Rolf Richardson 320cl, 379bc; Paul van Riel 411cl; Sackim 315cr; Andy Williams 279tl; JHC Wilson 184cra; Adam Woolfitt 319br, 342cla; Earl Young 152tr, 293tc; John Hedgecoe 165cl, c. The Hindu Newspaper 188clb. Michael Holford 89clb, 154tl, 160tl, 374cr, 375c, cra, 376cb, cb, cl, cbr, crb, 377bl, 380cb, 394cl, 378cr. Rebecca Hossack Gallery 146tr. Hulton-Deutsch Collection 18ca, 34tr, 45c, 132br, 144clb, 145clb, 151cr, 153c, 156crb, 160crb, bl, 165c, 166bar, 169bl, 170clb, crb, 174cra, cr, 176bl, 178br, bc, 181tc, tr, tl, ca, 182tl, 188cr, 190c, bl, 193crb, 194crb, 245cla, 261bl, 264cl, c, clb, crb, 396tl, 398cra, 400crb, 401br, 406tc, cl, br, 407tr, 408tc, 416c, 417tr, bc, 422crb/ Bettmann Archive 182cra; Terry Fincher 407tl. Robert Hunt Library 404tc. Henry E. Huntington Library & Art Gallery 18clb. Hutchison Library 171c, 337br/ H.R.Dorig 377cla; Sarah Errington 148ca, 363tl; Melanie Friend 141bl; Julia Highet 171cra; Michael McIntyre 139cr, 146cb, 171lc, 347c; Christine Pemberton 141tr; Pern 146bc; Bernard Regent 143tl; John Ryle 148tl; Liba Taylor 142cra; Anna Tully 171tl.

I

The Image Bank/Charles S.Allen 272cl; Alan Becker 314c; A.Boccaccio 274tl; Lionel F.Brown 276tr; Gary Cralle 53crb; Fotoworld 308bc; Chris Hackett 294cr; G.Heisler 276tr; Lionel Isy-Schwart 171t, 354cra; Ronald Johnson 272clb; Tadao Kimura 379cra; Kim Keitt/Stockphotos,Inc. 169bc; Romilly Lockyer 310bl; Michael Melford 109clb; Arthur Meyerson 363tr; Alfred Pasieka 268tr; Co.Rentmeester 274cla; Guido Alberto Rossi 53br, 320br, 346cr, 363crb; Steve Satushek 321c; Michael Skott 367bl; Harold Sund 293tl, 324ca; A.T.Willett 245br; Trevor Wood 43cl. Image Select 129tr, 132clb, 172bc, br, bl, 178cb, crb, 392cl. ©Imax Corporation 184br. Impact Photos 250cr/Steve Benbow 297tc; John Cole 293cr. A.J.Deane 319clb; Paul Forster 354cl; Alan

ILLUSTRATORS

Evi Antoniou: 61r, cb, 71cra, 85cr, 98cl, c, cr, 102cl, c, acrb, 103cb, 107br, 301cr, c

David Ashby: 140tl, cl, 141tl, cl, **142tl, cl, 143cla, cr, bl, br,** 158r, 191cb, 287l, 291cb, 302bc, 305cb, 310c, cr, 311tc, cb, c, 312cr, 313tc, 315, 316cl, 320c, 329tl, 340l, 343cl, 344c, 347cr, 349c, 370-1t, 372-3t, 374-5t, 376-7t, 378-9t, 380-1t, 382-3t, 384-5t, 385-7t, 388-9t, al, 390-91t, 392-3t, 394-5t, 396-7 t, 398-9t, 400-1t, 402-3t, 404-5t, 406t, cr, 407t, 408-9t, 410-1t, 412-3t, 414-5t, 416cl, 417br, 420-1, 422-3

Rick Blakeley: 21br, 26-7t, c, 30bl, 31cla, 183bl, 222cl, tr, 223tl, 224c, cr, bc, br, 225cla, c, crb, b, 226bl, 227b, 228tr, 230t, cl, c, b, 233t, bl, br

Cathy Brear: 263cla

Peter Bull Art Studio: **41tr, clb,** 46ca, cr, 52c, bl, 54ca, cr, 55trb, brb, 56cr, 82cr, 221cb, br, 222br, 231cl, 258l, b, 259t, b, 260c, b, 261t, b, 262l, br, 264cla, clb, b, 265t, tr, cr, cl, 266c

Mike Courtney: 122cl, br, 124tl, cr, 125tl, tr, c, cr, 126tl, c, 127cr, 128tc, 129tc, c, 130tc, br, cl

Jane Craddock-Watson: 81b

William Donohoe: 42b, 43b, 53tc, 54c, cr, bl, 55tl, c, br, 56t, 77bl, 82bc, 147c, 149c, 370bc, br, 372bl, 373c, cl, cr, 374c, acl, cl, 375c, acl, 376b, 377c, 381c, 382c, 383br, 384c, 385tr, bc, 386bcr, crb, 387tl, bc, 388tc, cl, 391tr, cr, crb, 393bc, 395tl, 396bl, 405c, 407br, 408cr, 410b, 424cr

Angelika Elsebach: 63b, 85cra, 86tc, 88tc, 90tc, 91tc, 92tc, 94tc, 96ca, 98tr, 102tc, 110tr, cr, 111cl, cr, 112t, cra

Simone End: 74tl, ca, cb, 78tl, 80crb, 82cra, 86c, 88c, cr, 90c, 91c, 92c, 94ca, 96c, cr, 99tl

John Crawford Fraser: 148c, 149cr, 166t, cl, 168tl, c, l, 305b, 317b, 318clb, 322cra, 320ca, 321tc, bc, 341cl

Eugene Fleury: 40c, crb, b, 42t, 44t, 48tr, 50tr, 52t, 56 t, 78b, 107tc, 139t, 140t, cra, clb, c, 141tc, c, cr, br, 142tl, c, br, 143tc

Shirley Gwillym: 78tr, tl, 138bc, 178tr, cla, 243cl, 332cla

Mike Grey: 20cl, 21cra, 28c, 29tl, tr, 300c, cr, 306cb, br, 326c, cr, 338c, cr, 352b, br

Nicholas Hall: 38t, bl, 39t, 48cl, 52b

Nick Hewetson: 18-9b, 33tc, 142tl, 174t, 191cr, b, 196c, b, 197tr, 201t, cr, 202br, 203tr, cl, cr, b, 204tl, 205t, cl, 206t, 207tl, 208tl, 210t, tl, cl, 214bl, 215tr, cl, 220br, 221cl, 32 crb

Bruce Hogarth: 252b

Christian Hook: 173cl

Richard Hook/Linden Artists: 370c, bl, 371bl, crb, 372cr, 374bl, 377br, 378tl, br, 380tr, 381cr, 383tr, 384c, 387cl, 388bl, 389tl, bc, crb, 391bc,

393c, 394br, 395cl, 396crb, 397tr, br

Aziz Khan: 268c, 269t, 370ac, 371tc, c, 372cl, 374tc, 375tl, 376cla, tl, tc, tr, 377tr, 378tr, bl, 379ca, 380br, 381tc, 382c, 384ca, 385c, 386c, 387ca, 389c, 391tc, 392tl, 393tc, 395tc, 396tc, 397tc, 398cl, 399bc, 400c, 402tc, 403tc, 404l, 40cr, 406c, 407tc, cl, 412-3

David Lewis Agency

Jason Lewis: 135tc, abr, 136br, 154**c, b, l,** 179l, 188cra, 324cl, br, 290cl, 291tc, cr, 29c, cr, b, 293c, br, 296c, 297c, 300tr, bl, 305c, 306tr, c, cr, 310clb, tc, cr, c, 316cr, 318cr, 319cl, bl, 326tr, 327clb, c, bl, br, 328ca, cb, cr, 329cr, 330tl, tc, cl, 331tr, 332bc, 333tr, 335clb, cb, 336cl, c, cra, 337cl, bc, 338tr, ca, br, 343cl, bl, c, 346cl, 347tr, c, 347cr, tr, 348cl, c, cr, 350cl, cr, 351cl, 352tr, c, bc, 354cr, 356bl, cla, 357cl

Richard Lewis: 50ca, 51bl

Angus McBride/Linden Artists: 373bl, br, 376cl, c, cr, 379tc, cl, c, cr, 380bl, 383tl, cl, 384bl, br, tl, 385cb, crb, 388tl, tr, 391tl, 392c, 394bl, 397bl, cra, 398tc, 404cr, 405cl

Ruth Lindsay: 76tl, 77tl, 111t, 298cl, 349cr, 348bc, 349tr

Sean Milne: 82tc, 86bl, 87bl, 90bl

Tony Morris/Linda Ragcas: 404br

Gilly Newman: 160tr, 161tr

Alex Pang: 191tc, b

Roger Payne/Linden Artists: 114br, 382tl, 383crb, 388bc, 389tr, 394c, crb, 395cra

Pond and Giles: 22br, 23b, 31cra, 46b, 49cl, 62c, 86cl, 88cl, 90l, 91tl, 92cl, 96cl, 290cla, 291bl, 296cl, 302c, clb, 303tc, c, 305tc, 308tc, bl, br, 309tc, 310cl, 311c, cb, 312tc, bc, 313tc, 314tc, 315tc, c, 316tc, 317tr, 318tc, 320tr, bl, 324tc, 328tc, 329br, 330cl, 332tc, 336ca, 340tc, 342tc, 344tc, 345bc, br, 349tc, 350bl, 354tc

Daniel Pyne: 18l, 19tl, cr, 23crb, 33tl, b, 83tc, tr, clb, br

Sebastian Quigley/Linden Artists: 41tr, b, 191ca, 192cl, cr, 193, cr, crb, 194t, 198tc, cl, 199cl, clb, 200tr, 201tl, ca, 202tr, crb, 203l, 204tr, 205l, b, cl, 206c, crb, 207tc, 208tc, br, 209tr, c, 210tr, clb, 211cr, 212tr, bl, 213tr, 214c, 215tr, c, 216tl, cl, cr, 217bl, 218cra, bl, br, 242tr, cr, 268cb, 269cl

Mike Saunders: 115al, cl, 116ar, 117tl, 118acl, c, br, 121t, cr

Pete Serjeant: 18t, 25t, c, bl, bc, br, 170cr

Rodney Shackell: 36tl, 44br, 45tl, tr, cra, 56bl, 75cra, bc, 79cra, bc, 79b, 107cl, cr, 110c, 122bl, 123bl, 124bl, 125bl, 126tr, bl, 127tr, 128bl, 129cr, 130bl, 132t, tr, bc, 133br, 138c, cl, 144br, 145r, 152bl, 153br, 157cr, 163tr, 169cla, 179tr, 188br, 190cl, 193bl, 196br, 199br, 209br, 211br, 214br, 220bl, b, bc, 221tr, 222bl, 223br, 225ar,

226cb, 227cr, 228cl, 229c, 230cl, bl, 233tr, 234bl, 235cl, 236c, 237br, 238bc, 240br, 241br, 242crb, 243t, 245c, 246cl, 250br, 254c, 255cl, 256cb, 257ab, 258cr, 262cb, 265bl, 266cra, 268cl, crb, 269cr, 273bl, 274b, 279bl, 371cr, bc, 361tr, 368br, 372bc, 373tr, 375cl, br, 377bc, 378br, 380bc, 381br, 383cra, 384cr, cla, 385cr, 386tr, cl, 387cr, bl, 388cr, 389c, 390tr, cr, 391c, 392cr, 393tr, cra, bl, 394bc, 395br, 396tr, 397cl, 398c, 399bl, 400tr, 401cl, bc, 402br, 403bc, 405br, 406bl, bc, 407cr, 408tr, 416cl, 418cl

Rob Shone: 41br, 147tr, bl, 181br

Clive Spong/Linden Artists: 192b, 193b, 194cr, crb, cb, 195b, cra, clb, b, 197cl, c, b, 198cr, r, br, 199, 201crb, 203br, 205c, 206cr, cb, b, 207c, cl, 208, 209cla, 210c, c, 211c, bl, bc, br, 212c, 213cl, 215cbl, 216c, bl, 218tl, c, clb, b, 252cl, crb, c, ac

Roger Stewart: 226t, c, 232t, cl, cb

Eric Thomas: 162t, 171bc, 256l, b, 257l, b

George Thomson: 101tr

Gill Tomblin: 86 br, bc, 87ca, 91b, 298cl

Raymond Turvey: 30 t

Peter Visscher: 52cl

Richard Ward: 22cl, crb, 23clb, 28bl, 33c, 38br, 40t, 44cl, 47bl, 49c, 50cl, br, 51tl, tc, 74bc, crb, 75cr, 76cl, 79tc, c, 159br, 183c, 185t, 187cr, 234c, crb, 237bl, bc, 255t, 290tr, 299cl, 302tr, 308tr, 311tc, tr, cb, 313tc, 324tr, 390tr, 340tr, 354tr

Steve Western

Paul Williams: 399tr, br, 402c, 403br, 405tr, cl, c

John Woodcock: 19ctb, 20bl, 24bl, 25clb, 26ca, 27bc, 30cb, 31br, 39c, bc, 43tr, 47bl, 49crb, 51tr, 53bl, bc, 55bc, 56bl, l, 59c, 60bl, 61bl, 63cl, 64crb, 65crb, 71c, cb, 75bl, 76crb, br, 77tc, 80bl, 81br, 82br, bl, 85c, 86crb, 87bc, 89bl, 90cl, clb, 91abr, br, 92cb, br, 93ca, 94br, 96crb, 100tc, bl, 101 cl, 102tl, 103crb, 104br, 105br, 107cb, 111cl, 112bl, 115cr, 116bl, 117br, 118bcl, 119bl, 120cr, 121bl, 150bl, 151tr, 157bc, br, abr, 170br, 171cr, 174cr, 176cr, 182br, 183br, 261cr, 273cla, 298c, b, crb, 299t, cr, b, 300bc, br, b, 301br, 302tc, tl, cl, cr, 303l, tr, b, 304tc, c, l, 307br, 308c, ca, cb, 309c, cb, 311cr, clb, bcr, br, 312cl, bc, clb, 313tl, ca, 314cr, 315crb, c, bc, 320cr, 321bl, br, 323tc, bl, b, 322tr, 327c, cl, br, 328cr, 335cl, cb, 339bl, cb, 340ca, br 341, 344br, c, cr, 345c, bc, cl, 350br, 353br, 357c, 364br, 366br, 367br

Martin Woodward: 58br, 167t, b, 325b

Dan Wright: 48-9b, 49tl, 56r, 64bl, 66t, c, b, 83tl, c, cl, cr, 88tl, 97br, c, cbr, 114t, cr, bl, cb, 116c, bc, br, 117bl, c,

119cb, br, 120cl, 170tr, cra, 226cl, 230br, 231cr, 233c, 244bl

Additional artwork

Russell Barnet: Steven Biesty: Kyokan G. Chen, Stephen Conlin: Luciano Corbella: Julia Cobbold: Brian Delf: Gill Elsbury: Giuliano Fornari: Andrew Green: Jerry Gower: Ann George Marsh: Mark Iley: Kenneth Lily: Mick Loates: Chris Lyon: Kevin Marks: Stuart Mackay: Andrew McDonald: David More: Peter Morter: Gordon Munro: Richard Orr: Sergio: Guy Smith, Kevin Toy: Phil Weare: Anne Winterbotham

ACKNOWLEDGEMENTS

Additional editorial and research assistance
Céline Carez, Christiane Gunzi, Robin Griffiths, Kitty Hauser, Francesca Stich

Additional design assistance
Chetan Joshi, Duncan Brown, Diane Clouting, Sharon Grant, Jill Plank

Indexer Hilary Bird

Proofreader Jill Somerscales

In addition, Dorling Kindersley would like to thank the following people and organizations for their assistance in the production of this book:

All embassies, consulates, and high commissions for supplying information; Alpine Club Library; American Society of Plastic and Reconstructive Surgeons; Amstrad; ; Anglo-American Corporation; Dr. Louis Arrington, University of Wisconsin; *Automotive News*; Baha'i Faith National Centre; BBC Engineering Department; BBC Radio; BBC TV; Bernafron UK Ltd; Ian Blatchford; Blockbuster Entertainment; British Film Institute; British Geological Survey; British Humanities Library; British Library Environmental Information Service; British Meteorological Office; British Olympic Association; British Olympic Federation; British Paralympic Association; British Science Library; British Telecom; British Trust for Ornithology; Broadcasters' Audience Research Board Ltd; Buddhist Society; Carluccio's; Centre for Global Energy Studies; Dr. Gerry Cherry, University of Georgia; Christie's International Fine Art Auctioneers; Church of Scientology; Confederation of European Paper Industries; Cousins' Properties; Mick Czaky, Antelope Films; Far East Trading Service Inc; First Interstate World Center; Food and Agriculture Organization; Stephanie Giordano; Great British China

Centre; Greenpeace; Linda Hoyt, Maguire Thomas Partners; Independent Television Library; Institute for African Alternatives; International Coffee Organisation; International Olympic Committee; John Oliver Jones; Kenya Wildlife Service; Julie Kusminska, London Video Access; Language of Dance Centre; Bernard Lavery; London Contemporary Dance Theatre; Mac Warehouse; Magnetic Trading Company; Margarita Publications Ltd; Sir Robert Menzies Centre for Australian Studies; Ministry of Agriculture, Fisheries and Food; *Motor Trend* Magazine; MTV International; Museum of Mankind; National Agricultural Centre; National Earthquake Information Center, US Geological Survey; National Motor Museum, Beaulieu; National Society's Religious Education Centre; Natural History Museum; OPEC; Overseas Development Administration; OXFAM; Oxford Museum of the History of Science; Philips Corporation; Pilkington Research Laboratories; Population Concern, Fiona Barr; Refugee Council, Jill Rutter; Andy Roor, US Department of Agriculture; Royal Air Force Museum; Royal Botanic Gardens, Kew; Royal Institute of the Blind; Royal National Institute for the Deaf; Scout Association; *Screen Digest*; Dr Kanwaljit Singh; Smithsonian Institution; Sony; STC Submarine Systems Ltd; Survival International, London; Swiss Bank Corporation, Leslie Prescott; Tea

Board of India; Theatre Museum; UNESCO; UNICEF, Anne Luzeekyi; United Airlines; United Nations; Virtual Vision; Voluntary Services Overseas, Tom Crick; Wales Green Party; Professor David A. Warrell, John Radcliffe Hospital, Oxford University; Water Aid; Wellcome Foundation Ltd; Dr. Andrew Wilkins, MRC, The Gambia; Andrew Wilson, Department of Anthropology Oxford University; Woodlands Heritage Museum; World Bank; World Conservation Monitoring Centre; World Health Organization

Logos and Insignias
The Major League Baseball Club insignias depicted in this book are reproduced with the permission of Major League Baseball Properties and are the exclusive property of the respective Major League Clubs and may not be reproduced without their written consent.

The helmet logos on page 205 are registered trademarks of the Teams indicated.

The Silver Fern Device and the New Zealand Rugby Union logo on page 203 are trademarked and owned by the New Zealand Rugby Football Union and used with their permission.

Model of dinosaur page 70, Roby Braun